BOOKS FOR COLLEGE LIBRARIES

BOOKS FOR COLLEGE LIBRARIES

A CORE COLLECTION OF 50,000 TITLES

Third edition

A project of the Association of College and Research Libraries

Volume 2
Language and Literature

American Library Association
Chicago and London 1988

Preliminary pages composed by Impressions, Inc.,
   in Times Roman on a Penta-driven
   Autologic APS-μ5
   Phototypesetting system

Text pages composed by Logidec, Inc., in Times Roman on an
   APS-5 digital typesetter

Printed on 50 lb. Glatfelter B-16, a pH neutral stock,
   and bound in Roxite B-grade cloth by
   Edwards Brothers.

The paper used in this publication meets the minimum
requirements of American National Standard for Information
Sciences—Permanence of Paper for Printed Library Materials,
ANSI Z39.48-1984.

Library of Congress Cataloging-in-Publication Data

   Books for college libraries.

      "A project of the Association of College and Research
   Libraries."

      Contents: v. 1.   Humanities—v. 2.   Language
   and literature—v. 3.   History—[etc.]
      1.   Libraries, University and college—Book
   lists.   2.   Bibliography—Best books.   I.   Association of
   College and Research Libraries.
   Z1039.C65B67   1988   025.2′1877   88-16714
   ISBN 0-8389-3357-2 (v. 1)
   ISBN 0-8389-3356-4 (v. 2)
   ISBN 0-8389-3355-6 (v. 3)
   ISBN 0-8389-3354-8 (v. 4)
   ISBN 0-8389-3358-0 (v. 5)
   ISBN 0-8389-3359-9 (v. 6)

BOOKS FOR COLLEGE LIBRARIES

Volumes 1–6   Contents

Volume 2   Contents

Contents

Introduction

Books for College Libraries (BCL3) presents a third recommended core collection for undergraduate libraries in full awareness of the tensions and paradoxes implicit in such list making. There is the pull between ideals of excellence and sufficient coverage of all subjects. There is the balance to be weighed among subjects. There are the rival temptations to identify the basic with the time tested and to equate the important with the new. There is the risk of ranking with the obsolete the merely temporary victims of scholarly fashion. There is the certainty that new definitive works will be published just as the selection closes.

That BCL3 exists supposes some resolution of these problems. A final paradox remains: BCL3 can fully succeed only by failing. It would be disastrous should the collection it suggests serve perfectly to ratify the finished work of the book selection in any library. Some inclusions and some omissions should displease everyone; for on-going professional questioning and the search for individual library answers remain as basic to collection development as basic book lists.

In overall plan and appearance, BCL3 is much the same as BCL2 (1975). The division into five volumes takes the same liberties with Library of Congress classification to provide coherent subject groups and volumes similar in size. Individual entries contain the same elements of full cataloging and classification information; and within volumes, entries are arranged in exact call number order.

BCL3 also exists as a database to allow further development of formats alternative to print. An electronic tape version will be made available. Since BCL2, online catalogs and reference databases have become familiar library tools. The provision of BCL3 in searchable form is thus important; and it may add possible uses of the list within larger libraries—easy identification of key titles in very large online catalogs, for instance.

HISTORY

The first bibliography to bear this title was published in 1967 as a replacement for Charles B. Shaw's *List of Books for College Libraries* (1931). The origin of BCL1 was in the University of California's New Campuses Program (1961–1964), which also made use of other compilations such as the published catalog of Harvard's Lamont Library (1953) and the shelflist of the undergraduate library of the University of Michigan. The 1963 cut-off date for BCL1 titles deliberately coincided with the 1964 beginning of *Choice*, whose current reviews for academic libraries were foreseen as a complementary, on-going revision and supplement. Such a role proved impossible, however, even for so comprehensive a journal as *Choice* with its 6,600 reviews a year and its retrospective evaluation of perhaps another 1,000 titles in topical monthly bibliographic essays. Periodic reassessments that could include categories of material not usually reviewed by *Choice* (revisions, fiction, works published abroad, for instance) seemed still an essential aid in college library collection development. BCL2 appeared in 1975; work on BCL3 began in late 1985.

SIZE AND SCOPE: STANDARDS, LIBRARIES AND BOOK LISTS

The number of books of which college libraries need potentially to be aware continues its relentless growth. In the years from the Shaw list to BCL1, total annual United States book output averaged slightly more than 11,500 volumes. Between the cut-off dates for BCL1 and BCL2, that figure (revised to show titles, a lesser number) was just under 32,000. Since the 1973 BCL2 cut-off, the annual average has been 41,000.[1] Given such increase, the task of book selectors would be challenging enough, even had the growth of buildings and book budgets characteristic of the late 1960s and early 1970s continued. By the time BCL2 was published, however, the rate of academic library book acquisitions had begun to fall. This downward trend continues, and it makes careful title selection ever more vital, especially for the small library.[2]

When BCL1 was published, the already outdated 1959 standards for college libraries called for a minimum undergraduate collection of only 50,000 titles; BCL1 recommended 53,400. BCL2 and the 1975 revision of those standards appeared in the same year. The new standards set out a formula whose add-on stipulations plus a starting figure of 85,000 raised basic requirements for even very small institutions to 100,000. The 1970 proposal for BCL2 called for a list of 40,000 titles. The thinking behind this lower figure may be explained by a published study of 1977 library

[1]*Bowker Annual of Library & Book Trade Information.* New York: Bowker. 26th ed., 1981; 32nd ed., 1987.

[2]"Three Years of Change in College and University Libraries, Prepared by the National Center for Education Statistics, Washington, D.C." *College & Research Libraries News* 45 (July/August 1984): 359–361.

statistics against the 1975 standards. This analysis found that 52 percent of all undergraduate libraries still reported fewer than 100,000 volumes and that 55 percent of private undergraduate libraries held even fewer than the "starter" figure of 85,000.[3] A very brief basic list might thus serve rather than intimidate the many libraries still far below standard.

The college library standards were revised again in 1985, just as work on BCL3 began.[4] The same formula (Standard 2.2, Formula A) was recommended. Applying it to a very small hypothetical college of 100 faculty and 1,000 students pursuing majors in only 10 fields of study yields a basic book requirement of 104,000 volumes. BCL3 suggests about half that number, hoping again to pause somewhere between usefulness and utopia. Very recent figures show that the average book expenditures for academic libraries in 26 U.S. states fall below the figure that would be necessary to meet the median annual growth rate of our hypothetical library, also set by the 1985 standards.[5]

In scope, the focus of BCL3 remains the traditionally book-using disciplines. Contributors were asked to keep in mind an imaginary college or small university that concentrates on the customary liberal arts and sciences curriculum but also offers work at the undergraduate level in business, computer science, engineering, and the health sciences. The proportions of the broad subject groupings by volume have remained roughly constant through the three BCL editions. (See Table 1.) There have been steady decreases in the humanities and literature allocations, however, very slightly offset by increased use of single-entry "complete works" citations that include large numbers of titles.

These changes have come about despite editorial quotas candidly designed to minimize them. Sharp

[3]Ray L. Carpenter, "College Libraries: A Comparative Analysis in Terms of the ACRL Standards," *College and Research Libraries* 42 (January 1981): 7–18.

[4]"Standards for College Libraries, 1986, Prepared by the College Library Standards Committee, Jacquelyn M. Morris, chair," *College & Research Libraries News* 47 (March 1986): 189–200.

[5]*Bowker Annual of Library & Book Trade Information.* 32nd ed. New York: Bowker, 1987. The preceding calculation by the BCL editor is based on figures given in the *Bowker Annual* using the formula in the standards cited in note 4.

difficulties confront both BCL editors and librarians juggling hopes for lasting value, necessities for current coverage, and the certainties of obsolescence. Some of the growth in Volume 5 is attributable to a marked increase in its bibliography component, which serves all subjects; but it may be well to repeat, with reference both to Volume 4 and to Volume 5, a statement from my BCL2 introduction that "Perhaps only those works already sufficiently outdated to be ranked as history may safely be included in a 'basic' collection." Despite their increases, both volumes remain brief in comparison with the volume of publication.

As to those titles constituting the rest of the minimal 104,000 requirement but not named in BCL3, much of any collection must respond uniquely to the demands of individual and current curricula. But some, it is to be hoped, will continue to consist of those works, especially belles lettres, not subject to cumulation and replacement by current scholarship. These are often difficult to continue to justify in lists which though "basic" cannot remain immune to shifts in academic enthusiasms.

Across these proportionate subject representations, the focus remains the undergraduate user of the undergraduate library. Both are protean concepts, but they permit some limitation, for instance almost wholly to works in English except for dictionaries and editions chosen to support foreign-language study. With the exception of some of the more basic surveys among "annual reviews" and some serial reference works, the limitation is not only to print but, further, to monographs. There is a need for college-level model collections of periodicals and of nonprint material, but this project does not address it. Still further to define the print universe, BCL3 contributors were asked not to recommend classroom texts unless exceptional, especially for their bibliographies. Volumes of previously published works are seldom listed except for literary anthologies which, together with their indexes, received special consideration in this edition. In-print availability was not considered an important factor.

CONTRIBUTORS AND WORKING MATERIALS

BCL3 was from the beginning designed as a two-stage selection process and there were two distinct sets

Table 1. Distribution of Titles by Volume. (In percentages.)

Volumes & Subjects	BCL1	BCL2	BCL3
v. 1 (Humanities)	16.4	15.1	13.6
v. 2 (Language & Literature)	32.2	30.0	28.4
v. 3 (History)	18.7	19.7	18.8
v. 4 (Social Sciences)	20.8	21.2	22.2
v. 5 (Psychology, Science, Technology, Bibliography)	11.9	14.0	17.0

of contributors. The first-round team numbered more than 400 college faculty members and about 50 academic reference librarians who made the reference selections. The second group consisted of 64 academic librarian referees, picked for their combination of subject specialization and collection development skills. The librarian referees were asked to review broader subject areas than their faculty counterparts with the intent of adding a wider perspective to help assure the overall coverage and balance to the collection.

Virtually all of the first-round contributors and about half of the second-round referees are *Choice* reviewers. They were selected for excellence, needed subject coverage, altruism (all served unpaid), and availability at the crucial time. (A few sabbaticals were much regretted in the BCL office.) Contributors were not selected with statistical games in mind, but it is an interesting if incidental function of the nature of the *Choice* reviewer pool that they prove a nationally representative lot. They come from 265 institutions in 44 states. The 10 states with the most academic institutions provide 8 of the 10 largest contributor groups. Institutions are divided between public, including federal (145) and private (120), with a mix of small and large from each sector. There are 10 representatives of 2-year campuses. There are 134 women. There are 15 Canadian and 2 British contributors.

As working materials, the round-one contributors received pages from BCL2 (latest titles 1973) and selected *Choice* review cards (1972 through 1985). Approximately 60,000 of some 85,000 reviews published in those years were distributed. Contributors were asked to assign one of four rankings to each title; they were also urged to recommend any other titles they felt essential to undergraduate work in their fields. Many did so. Assignments, some of which overlapped, ranged from 25 to 600 titles.

Preparation of 450 packets of working lists involved the fascinating task of reconciling various assumptions about the organization of knowledge. It was necessary to "deconstruct" and rearrange the LC-classed BCL2 and the subject organization of *Choice* to match the convictions of academics as to just what constituted the definitions and boundaries of their subjects.

COMPILATION AND REVIEW

Working list packets came back displaying varying neatness, erudition, zeal, and attention to editorial instructions and deadlines. A very few were reassigned; most were extremely well done and miraculously on time. All titles rated "essential" (and some lesser ratings, depending on subject coverage and the rigor of contributor selectivity) were requested, by LC card number if possible, from the Utlas database. (Utlas, the Canadian bibliographic utility, had previously been

selected as the vendor to house the BCL3 database while the collection was being compiled.)

As lists came in and major blocks of LC classification were judged to be reasonably complete, Utlas was asked to produce provisional catalogs in LC class order, showing complete catalog records. These catalogs, after review by the editor, were divided among the second-round referees, whose assignments typically included the work of several first-round contributors. Referees were asked to assess overall quality and suitability of the selections, coverage of the various aspects of a field, and compliance with numerical quotas. The editor's review included the making and insertion of page headings and further observations of (and occasional interventions in) rival views of knowledge as the academic visions of round one were once more refracted through the prism, the worldview of LC classification. A second set of provisional catalogs, reviewed by the editor's assistant, incorporated referee suggestions and the page headings for a final check before typesetting.

PRESENTATION: HEADINGS, ENTRIES, AND ARRANGEMENT

Page headings are phrased to outline LC classification, to gloss the sometimes very miscellaneous contents of the sections they head, and to indicate the method of arrangement of some special sequences. The printed BCL3 entries contain conventionally complete cataloging and classification information, but not every element of a full LC MARC record. Among notes, only the general (MARC tag 500) are printed; cross-reference and authority information tagged in the 800s is omitted. Those entries for items retained from BCL2 in exactly the same version carry a special symbol, a heavy dot (.) preceding the item number. Entries are sequentially numbered within each volume. The cataloging in some of the entries made by contributors to the Utlas database is less full than the original LC cataloging; some entries vary in other ways.

Database response to titles requested for the collection displayed significant changes since the compilation of BCL2. During that project, both LC MARC and electronic cataloging and bibliographic utilities were new. Nearly two-thirds of BCL2 entries had to be converted especially for that project. BCL3 is in some ways the victim of the success of such cataloging enterprises. There are now many versions of catalog records, especially for pre-1968 titles. These offer varying degrees of adoption of AACR2 and equally various and often unsignalled states of adherence to LC classification, to say nothing of the range of simple cataloging and typing skills. It is therefore impossible to repeat here the certainties of the BCL2 Introduction about the use of LC cataloging and classification, although preference was certainly for LC records. Call numbers completed or assigned by BCL are identified with "x" as the final character, but there are numbers not so flagged that are not LC assignments. BCL3 is designed as a book selection guide, however, not as an exemplar of either cataloging or classification.

Arrangement has been stated to be by LC call number; but some catalog records carry more than one number, some sections of LC classification are being redeveloped, and some allow alternate treatments. BCL3's editor, therefore, had decisions to make. In all volumes, the existence of new LC sequences is signposted with cross-references. Individual subject classification of titles published in series was preferred to numerical gatherings within series. For Volume 2, alternate national literature numbers were selected or created in preference to PZ3 and PZ4 for fiction. Works by and about individual Canadian, Caribbean, African, South Asian, and Australasian authors writing in English have been pulled from the PR4000–6076 sequence and united with the general historical and critical material on those literatures in the PR9000s. Volume 5 displays the decision to keep most subject bibliography in class Z.

INDEXES

The computer-made Author Index lists personal and institutional names of writers, editors, compilers, translators, sponsoring bodies, and others identified in the numbered "tracings" that bear roman numerals at the ends of entries. The Title Index, also machine generated, lists both uniform and title page titles from the printed entries, including nondistinctive titles and adding variant titles if traced. Because of the use of many "complete works" entries, many famous and highly recommended titles, especially novels, are absent from this index though present by implication in the list. References in the Author and Title indexes are to the sequential numbers, within volume, as-

signed to each entry. The Subject Index is a handmade guide to classification. It has its own brief explanatory introduction.

LACUNAE, ERRORS AND REVISIONS

The virtual absence of serials and the exclusion of formats other than print have been noted under Size and Scope. Additionally, although undergraduate study ranges ever wider, student information needs outside fairly "academic" disciplines and some traditional sporting activities are not fulfilled here; users are referred to college bookstores and recommended lists for public libraries for titles in many craft, technical, and recreational subjects.

Errors of cataloging and questionable classifications will, as it has been stated, be noted. They are present in the database used and though many were corrected, others as surely remain. Reports of errors, expressions of opinion about favorite titles missing and abhorrences present, and general suggestions for future revisions are sincerely sought. They may be addressed to: Editor, Books for College Libraries, c/o *Choice*, 100 Riverview Center, Middletown, CT 06457–3467.

With the breakup of BCL1 into the individual volumes of BCL2, separate revision in an on-going project was predicted. That did not happen, and it would offer some difficulties in indexing and the handling of subjects split among volumes. It is a challenge to assemble the mix of organization to command the seemingly more and more specialized contributors required, the technology to facilitate presentation, and the finance to enable the whole. But it is to be hoped that the even greater challenges college libraries face in collection development will continue to find *Choice* and its reviewers, ACRL, and ALA ready with the help future circumstances require.

VIRGINIA CLARK, *Editor*

Acknowledgments

Without the contributors and referees of the many subject lists, BCL3 would not exist. They are named in the appropriate volumes and identified by academic or other professional institution and by subject field. To enable the calling together of this team, however, and the presentation of its work took vision, planning, determination, and much help from many groups and individuals.

Both the users and the editorial staff of BCL3 owe thanks to the staff and two successive Executive Directors of the Association of College and Research Libraries (ACRL). Julie Virgo and JoAn S. Segal convened a preliminary investigative committee and commissioned a request for proposal (RFP) that established the first outline of the project for the revised edition. Patricia Sabosik, newly appointed Editor and Publisher of *Choice*, encompassed in her initial plans for the magazine the BCL project. Her response to ACRL's RFP involved the *Choice* staff in the editorial work and the Canadian bibliographic utility Utlas in the technical construction of the database. The staffs of *Choice* and BCL3 are grateful to ACRL for accepting this proposal and to Publishing Services of the American Library Association for co-funding the project with ACRL. Patricia Sabosik served as Project Manager. Liaison with ALA Books was Managing Editor Helen Cline.

An editorial advisory committee, chaired by Richard D. Johnson, SUNY College at Oneonta, was selected to allow the BCL3 Editor to draw advice from representatives of academic libraries of different types, sizes, and locales. Stephen L. Gerhardt, Cerritos College; Michael Haeuser, Gustavus Adolphus College; Barbara M. Hirsh, formerly Marist College; Thomas Kirk, Berea College; Craig S. Likness, Trinity University; and Mary K. Sellen, Spring Valley College, served the project well. Special thanks are due Richard D. Johnson and Craig S. Likness, each of whom also contributed subject lists, and Michael Haeuser, who spent several days as a volunteer in the BCL office and served as committee secretary.

The BCL project was housed in space in the *Choice* office and enjoyed a unique member/guest relationship that involved virtually every member of the *Choice* staff in some work for BCL. The subject editors—Robert Balay, Claire C. Dudley, Ronald H. Epp, Francine Graf, Helen MacLam, and Kenneth McLintock—suggested from their reviewer lists most of the BCL contributors and several referees. Claire C. Dudley and Helen MacLam served as referees; Claire C. Dudley and Francine Graf gave much other valuable help. Library Technical Assistant Nancy Sbona, Systems Manager Lisa Gross, Office Assistant Mary Brooks, and Administrative Assistant Lucille Calarco deserve special mention for extraordinary assistance.

In addition to using the bibliographic and personnel resources of *Choice*, the Editor of BCL relied for vital support on the collections, equipment, and staffs of five very gracious institutions. Particular thanks go to the libraries of Kenyon College, Wesleyan University, and the Library Association, London, for use of behind-the-scenes cataloging and classification tools in addition to reference sources publicly available; to Trinity University, San Antonio, for tapes of BCL2; and to Trinity College, Hartford, for outstanding help from George R. Graf on preliminary aspects of the project in addition to those for which he is named in the contributor lists.

For work without regard for office hours or job description the Editor would particularly like to thank Judith Douville. She edited the science sections of Volume 5 in addition to assisting the Editor with some parts of Volume 4. She coordinated the corrections to the BCL3 computer file and reviewed the final page proofs. Her enthusiasm and dedication were vital in bringing the project to completion.

BCL3 secretary Anna Barron worked throughout the project. Special thanks are also owed to short-term staff members Alison Johnson and Virginia Carrington.

CONTRIBUTORS

Title selection for BCL3 reflects three types of expert opinion: from scholars teaching in the field, from reference librarians, and from special referees chosen for their combination of subject and collection-development knowledge. Names appear in the approximate order of contributions in the volume, but Library of Congress classification will have scattered many titles selected by those named here into other sections of the list. The topical labels try to suggest both the depth of specialization required of some contributors and the broad knowledge and responsibility demanded of others; but no list such as this can do more than hint at the nature and amount of work for which these contributors are most gratefully thanked.

LANGUAGE & LINGUISTICS: Michael D. Linn, University of Minnesota.

COMMUNICATION: Christopher Sterling, George Washington University.

CLASSICAL LANGUAGES & LITERATURES: Z. Philip Ambrose, University of Vermont; John E. Rexine, Colgate University; Robert B. Lloyd, Randolph-Macon Woman's College. *Reference & Referee*: William S. Moran, Dartmouth College.

ROMANCE LANGUAGES & LITERATURES: *French*: Mary H. Nachtsheim, College of St. Catherine; Robert A. Picken, Queens College, CUNY; Lois Ann Russell, Rosemont College; Jean-Charles Seigneuret, University of Cincinnati; Allen Thiher, University of Missouri–Columbia. *Italian*: Charles Fantazzi, University of Windsor. *Spanish*: M. S. Arrington Jr., University of Mississippi; Rosa Levin, University of Colorado at Boulder; Douglas R. McKay, University of Colorado at Colorado Springs. *Portuguese*: Joseph Snow, University of Georgia. *Reference*: W. Daviess Menefee, Jr., Ohio State University. *Referees*: Nadine George, Kenyon College; Norma Kobzina, University of California, Berkeley; Eva Sartori, University of Nebraska–Lincoln.

GERMANIC LANGUAGES & LITERATURES: *German*: Henrich Brockhaus, Western Washington University; Esther N. Elstun, George Mason University; Peter D. Hertz-Ohmes, SUNY College at Oswego. *Dutch*: Martha L. Brogan, University of Minnesota. *Scandinavian*: Francis G. Gentry, University of Wisconsin–Madison; Faith Ingwersen, University of Wisconsin–Madison; Torborg Lundell, University of California, Santa Barbara. *Reference*: Stephen Lehmann, University of Pennsylvania. *Referees*: James H. Spohrer, University of California, Berkeley; Mariann E. Tiblin, University of Minnesota.

SLAVIC LANGUAGES & LITERATURES: *Russian*: Donald Barton Johnson, University of California, Santa Barbara; Anne Tyler Netick, College of William and Mary. *Czech*: Harlan E. Marquess, University of Wisconsin–Madison; *Serbo-Croatian, Yugoslav*: Cynthia Simmons, University of Wisconsin–Madison; *Polish*: Halina Filipowicz, University of Wisconsin–Madison. *Reference & Referee*: Dennis Kimmage, SUNY College at Plattsburgh.

ORIENTAL LANGUAGES & LITERATURES: *Hebrew & Yiddish*: Emanuel S. Goldsmith, Queens College, CUNY. *Arabic & Persian*: Paul Sprachman, University of Chicago. *Indic*: Peter Gaeffke, University of Pennsylvania. *Japanese*: Seiko Mieczkowski, SUNY at Binghamton. *Chinese*: Howard Goldblatt, San Francisco State University. *Southeast Asian*: Lee S. Dutton, Northern Illinois University. *Reference & Referees*: M. Keith Ewing, St. Cloud State University; Hide Ikehara, Eastern Michigan University; Karen Wei, University of Illinois at Urbana-Champaign.

AFRICAN LANGUAGES & LITERATURES: John Povey, University of California, Los Angeles. *Reference &*

Referee: David L. Easterbrook, University of Illinois at Chicago.

ENGLISH LANGUAGE & LITERATURE: *Language*: Michael D. Linn, University of Minnesota. *Reference*: John B. Ladley, Bowdoin College. *Anglo-Saxon Language & Literature*: Norma J. Engberg, University of Nevada–Las Vegas. *English Literature—Medieval*: Louis B. Hall, University of Colorado at Denver; Beth Robertson, University of Colorado at Boulder. *Renaissance*: Jean R. Buchert, University of North Carolina at Greensboro; Robert P. Griffin, Southern Illinois University; David C. Redding, SUNY at Albany. *18th Century*: Donna Landry, University of Southern California; David J. Littlefield, Middlebury College; B. Eugene McCarthy, College of the Holy Cross. *19th Century*: John W. Bicknell, Drew University, emeritus; George A. Cevasco, St. John's University; Sandra Ann Parker, Hiram College; Michael Timko, Queens College, CUNY; Rosemary T. Van Arsdel, University of Puget Sound. *20th Century*: Paul A. Doyle, Nassau Community College; Paul Schlueter, Warren County Community College; Joan E. Steiner, Drew University. *Regional, Irish, & Commonwealth Literatures*: Robert D. Thornton, SUNY College at New Paltz, emeritus (Scottish); Edward F. Callahan, College of the Holy Cross (Irish); R. Islwyn Pritchard, Cardiff (Welsh); Alan L. McLeod, Rider College (Australian, Canadian, New Zealand, Caribbean). *Reference*: Eric J. Carpenter, Oberlin College. *Referees*: James K. Bracken, Purdue University; William S. Brockman, Drew University; Sharon Propas, University of Cincinnati.

AMERICAN LITERATURE: Jane J. Benardete, Hunter College, CUNY; Vincent Freimarck, SUNY at Binghamton, emeritus; Edward Guereschi, St. John's University; William White, Oakland University. *Special Literatures*: M. Thomas Inge, Randolph-Macon College (Southern Literature); Robert G. O'Meally, Wesleyan University (Afro-American Literature); Andrew O. Wiget, New Mexico State University (Native American Literature). *Reference*: Eric J. Carpenter, Oberlin College; John C. Phillips, University of Toledo; Agnes Haigh Widder, Michigan State University. *Referees*: Judith Adams, Auburn University; Janell Rudolph, Memphis State University.

SPECIAL FIELDS: Doris H. Banks, Whitworth College (Children's Literature); David A. Barton, University of Southern California (Poetry); Jeanine Basinger, Wesleyan University (Film); Robert E. Blackmon, California State University, Los Angeles (Journalism); Robert S. Bravard, Lock Haven University (Literary Censorship, Comics); Larry L. Bronson, Central Michigan University (Medieval Literature); Joe R. Christopher, Tarleton State University (Popular Literature); John Miles Foley, University of Missouri–Columbia (Folk Literature: see v. 4); Richard D. Johnson, SUNY College at Oneonta (Musical Theatre); Peter E. Kane, SUNY College at Brockport

(Speech, Freedom of Expression); Craig Likness, Trinity University (Anthologies, Analytical Indexes); June Schlueter, Lafayette College (Drama, Theatre); Patrocinio Schweickart, University of New Hampshire (Criticism); Christopher Sterling, George Washington University (Mass Media, Communications); Don Burton Wilmeth, Brown University (Drama, Theatre). *Reference*: William Miller, Florida Atlantic University. *Referees*: Cynthia Alcorn, Emerson College; Marcia Pankake, University of Minnesota.

P Language and Literature

P11–93 GENERAL WORKS

P21–29.5 Collections. Dictionaries

Hill, Archibald A. • **2.1**
Linguistics today / edited by Archibald A. Hill. — New York: Basic Books [1969] xii, 291 p.; 22 cm. Based on material prepared for the Forum series of the Voice of America. 1. Linguistics — Addresses, essays, lectures. 2. Language and languages — Addresses, essays, lectures. I. Voice of America (Organization). II. T.
P25.H5   410   *LC* 68-54149

Readings in applied English linguistics / [edited by] Harold B. **2.2**
Allen, Michael D. Linn.
3rd ed. — New York: Knopf, c1982. ix, 592 p.: ill.; 24 cm. 1. Linguistics — Addresses, essays, lectures. 2. English language — Addresses, essays, lectures. 3. English language — Study and teaching — Addresses, essays, lectures. I. Allen, Harold Byron, 1902- II. Linn, Michael D.
P25.R38 1982   410 19   *LC* 81-18663   *ISBN* 0394327500

Sebeok, Thomas Albert, 1920- ed. • **2.3**
Current trends in linguistics / edited by Thomas A. Sebeok. — The Hague: Mouton, 1963-. v. in 22; 27 cm. — 1. Language and languages — Collections. I. T.
P25.S4   *LC* 64-3663

Ferguson, Charles Albert, 1921-. • **2.4**
Language structure and language use; essays, by Charles A. Ferguson. Selected and introduced by Anwar S. Dil. — Stanford, Calif.: Stanford University Press, 1971. xiv, 327 p.; 24 cm. — (Language science and national development) 'The eighteen articles selected for this volume cover the period from 1959 to 1970.' 1. Language and languages — Addresses, essays, lectures. I. T.
P27.F4   410   *LC* 79-150322   *ISBN* 0804707804

Firth, J. R. (John Rupert), 1890-1960. • **2.5**
Selected papers, 1952–59. Edited by F.R. Palmer. — Bloomington: Indiana University Press, [1968] ix, 209 p.; 23 cm. (Indiana University studies in the history and theory of linguistics) 1. Linguistics — Addresses, essays, lectures 2. Comparative linguistics — Addresses, essays, lectures I. Palmer, Frank Robert, ed. II. T.
P27.F52x

Greenberg, Joseph Harold, 1915-. • **2.6**
Essays in linguistics / by Joseph H. Greenberg. — Chicago: University of Chicago Press; Toronto: University of Toronto Press, 1957. vii, 108 p.; 26 cm. 1. Language and languages — Addresses, essays, lectures. I. T.
P27.G7 1957   *LC* 57-6273

Hockett, Charles Francis. **2.7**
The view from language: selected essays, 1948–1974 / by C. F. Hockett. — Athens: University of Georgia Press, c1977. 338 p.; 24 cm. 1. Language and languages — Collected works. 2. Linguistics — Collected works. I. T.
P27.H45   301.2/1   *LC* 75-3818   *ISBN* 082030381X

Nida, Eugene Albert, 1914-. **2.8**
Language structure and translation: essays / by Eugene A. Nida; selected and introduced by Anwar S. Dil. — Stanford, Calif.: Stanford University Press, 1975. xiv, 283 p.: ill.; 24 cm. (Language science and national development.) 1. Nida, Eugene Albert, 1914- 2. Language and languages — Addresses, essays, lectures. 3. Translating and interpreting — Addresses, essays, lectures. 4. Linguistics — Addresses, essays, lectures. I. T. II. Series.
P27.N5   410   *LC* 75-183   *ISBN* 0804708851

Sapir, Edward, 1884-1939. • **2.9**
Selected writings in language, culture and personality / edited by David G. Mandelbaum. — Berkeley: University of California Press, 1963. xv, 617 p.; 24 cm. 1. Culture 2. Language and languages 3. Personality and culture I. Mandelbaum, David Goodman, 1911- II. T.
P27.S33 1963   408.1

Whorf, Benjamin Lee, 1897-1941. • **2.10**
Language, thought, and reality; selected writings. Edited and with an introd. by John B. Carroll. Foreword by Stuart Chase. — [Cambridge]: Technology Press of Massachusetts Institute of Technology, [1956] xi, 278 p.: illus., port.; 24 cm. — (Technology Press books in the social sciences) 1. Language and languages — Addresses, essays, lectures. 2. Sapir-Whorf hypothesis I. T.
P27.W53   404   *LC* 56-5367

Ducrot, Oswald. **2.11**
[Dictionnaire encyclopédique des sciences du langage. English] Encyclopedic dictionary of the sciences of language / by Oswald Ducrot and Tzvetan Todorov; translated by Catherine Porter. — Baltimore: Johns Hopkins University Press, c1979. xiii, 380 p.; 24 cm. Translation of Dictionnaire encyclopédique des sciences du langage. 1. Linguistics — Dictionaries — French. I. Todorov, Tsvetan, joint author. II. T.
P29.D813   410/.3   *LC* 78-23901   *ISBN* 080182155X

Hartmann, R. R. K. **2.12**
Dictionary of language and linguistics / [by] R. R. K. Hartmann and F. C. Stork. — New York: Wiley, [1972] xviii, 302 p.: ill.; 23 cm. 'A Halsted Press book.' 1. Language and languages — Dictionaries 2. Linguistics — Dictionaries. I. Stork, F. C. joint author. II. T.
P29.H34   410/.3   *LC* 72-6251   *ISBN* 0470356677

Pei, Mario, 1901-. • **2.13**
Glossary of linguistic terminology / Mario Pei. — Garden City, N.Y.: Anchor Books, 1966. xvi, 299 p.; 18 cm. — 1. Language and languages — Dictionaries 2. Grammer, Comparative and general — Terminology. I. T.
P29.P39 1966   410.3   *LC* 66-21013

Urdang, Laurence. **2.14**
Literary, rhetorical, and linguistics terms index / Laurence Urdang, editor in chief; Frank R. Abate, managing editor. — 1st ed. — Detroit, Mich.: Gale Research Co., c1983. 305 p.; 24 cm. 'An alphabetically arranged list of words and phrases used in the English-speaking world in the analysis of language and literature, selected from authoritative and widely consulted sources, presented in a format designed for quick reference, and including a descriptive bibliography of the sources.' Includes index. 1. Philology — Terminology — Indexes. I. Abate, Frank R. II. T.
P29.5.U72 1983   410/.14 19   *LC* 83-1636   *ISBN* 0810311984

P31–85 Theory. History of Philology

Henson, Hilary. **2.15**
British social anthropologists and language: a history of separate development. — Oxford: Clarendon Press, 1974. viii, 147 p.; 22 cm. — (Oxford monographs on social anthropology) 1. Linguistics 2. Ethnology I. T.
P35.H4   301.2/1   *LC* 74-164647   *ISBN* 0198231849

Ong, Walter J. **2.16**
Orality and literacy: the technologizing of the word / Walter J. Ong. — London; New York: Methuen, 1982. x, 201 p.; 21 cm. — (New accents) Includes index. 1. Language and culture 2. Oral tradition 3. Writing 4. Oral-formulaic analysis I. T.
P35.O5 1982   001.54 19   *LC* 82-6305   *ISBN* 041671370X

Handbook of applied psycholinguistics: major thrusts of research **2.17**
and theory / edited by Sheldon Rosenberg.
Hillsdale, N.J.: L. Erlbaum Associates, c1982. xiii, 615 p.; 24 cm. 1. Psycholinguistics — Handbooks, manuals, etc. 2. Applied linguistics — Handbooks, manuals, etc. I. Rosenberg, Sheldon.
P37.H3 1982   401/.9 19   *LC* 81-9891   *ISBN* 0898591732

Hatch, Evelyn Marcussen. **2.18**
Psycholinguistics: a second language perspective / Evelyn Marcussen Hatch. — Rowley, Mass.: Newbury House, 1983. ix, 266 p.: ill.; 23 cm. Includes indexes. 1. Psycholinguistics 2. Language acquisition I. T.
P37.H34 1983   401/.9 19   *LC* 82-8275   *ISBN* 0883772507

Innate ideas / edited by Stephen P. Stich. **2.19**
Berkeley: University of California Press, [1975] x, 222 p.: ill.; 24 cm. 1. Cartesian linguistics — Addresses, essays, lectures. 2. Languages —

Philosophy — Addresses, essays, lectures. 3. Psycholinguistics — Addresses, essays, lectures. I. Stich, Stephen P.
P37.I5   121   *LC* 74-81441   *ISBN* 0520028228

Advances in the social psychology of language / edited by Colin Fraser and Klaus R. Scherer.   2.20
Cambridge; New York: Cambridge University Press; Paris: Editions de la Maison des Sciences de l'Homme, 1982. vii, 264 p.: ill.; 24 cm. — (European studies in social psychology.) 1. Sociolinguistics 2. Psycholinguistics I. Fraser, Colin. II. Scherer, Klaus Rainer. III. Series.
P40.A33 1982   401/.9 19   *LC* 81-15551   *ISBN* 0521231922

Halliday, M. A. K. (Michael Alexander Kirkwood), 1925-.   2.21
Language as social semiotic: the social interpretation of language and meaning / M.A.K. Halliday. — Baltimore: University Park Press, 1978. 256 p.; 24 cm. Includes indexes. 1. Sociolinguistics — Addresses, essays, lectures. 2. Semiotics — Addresses, essays, lectures. 3. Education — Addresses, essays, lectures. I. T.
P40.H34 1978   301.2/1   *LC* 77-21227   *ISBN* 0839111835

Hymes, Dell H.   2.22
Foundations in sociolinguistics; an ethnographic approach [by] Dell Hymes. — Philadelphia: University of Pennsylvania Press, [1974] x, 245 p.; 24 cm. 1. Sociolinguistics I. T.
P40.H9   301.2/1   *LC* 73-89288   *ISBN* 0812276752

Language and social identity / edited by John J. Gumperz.   2.23
Cambridge [Cambridgeshire]; New York: Cambridge University Press, 1983 (c1982). x, 272 p.; 22 cm. — (Studies in interactional sociolinguistics. 2) Includes indexes. 1. Sociolinguistics — Addresses, essays, lectures. 2. Interpersonal communication — Addresses, essays, lectures. 3. Intercultural communication — Addresses, essays, lectures. 4. Discourse analysis — Addresses, essays, lectures. I. Gumperz, John Joseph, 1922- II. Series.
P40.L289 1982   401/.9 19   *LC* 82-4331   *ISBN* 052124692X

Bernstein, Basil B.   2.24
Class, codes and control [by] Basil Bernstein. — London: Routledge and K. Paul, 1971-75. 3 v.: illus.; 23 cm. — (Primary socialization, language and education, 4) 1. Sociolinguistics — Addresses, essays, lectures. 2. Children — Language — Addresses, essays, lectures. 3. Educational sociology — Addresses, essays, lectures. I. T. II. Series.
P40.P68 vol. 4, 1971   301.2/1 s 301.2/1   *LC* 72-185544   *ISBN* 0710070608

Can language be planned?: Sociolinguistic theory and practice for developing nations / Edited by Joan Rubin and Björn H. Jernudd.   • 2.25
[1st ed. — Honolulu]: University Press of Hawaii, [c1971] xxiv, 343 p.; 24 cm. 'An East-West Center book.' Revised papers from a meeting held Apr. 7-10, 1969, in Hawaii. 1. Sociolinguistics — Addresses, essays, lectures. I. Rubin, Joan, 1932- ed. II. Jernudd, Björn H. ed.
P41.C3   301.2/1   *LC* 70-129618   *ISBN* 0824801008

Farb, Peter.   2.26
Word play; what happens when people talk. — [1st ed.]. — New York: Knopf; [distributed by Random House], 1974 [c1973] x, 350, xiv p.; 22 cm. 1. Language and languages 2. Psycholinguistics I. T.
P41.F3   301.2/1   *LC* 73-7298   *ISBN* 0394486757

Gumperz, John Joseph, 1922-.   2.27
Directions in sociolinguistics; the ethnography of communication. Edited by John J. Gumperz [and] Dell Hymes. — New York: Holt, Rinehart and Winston, [1972] x, 598 p.; 24 cm. 1. Sociolinguistics — Addresses, essays, lectures. I. Hymes, Dell H. joint author. II. T.
P41.G79   301.2/1   *LC* 77-168981   *ISBN* 0030777453

Haugen, Einar Ingvald, 1906-.   2.28
The ecology of language; essays by Einar Haugen. Selected and introduced by Anwar S. Dil. — Stanford, Calif.: Stanford University Press, 1972. xiv, 366 p.; 24 cm. — (Language science and national development) 1. Sociolinguistics — Addresses, essays, lectures. I. T.
P41.H34   301.2/1   *LC* 73-183888   *ISBN* 0804708029

Labov, William.   2.29
Sociolinguistic patterns. — Philadelphia: University of Pennsylvania Press, [1973, c1972] xviii, 344 p.: illus.; 24 cm. 1. Sociolinguistics I. T.
P41.L26 1973   301.2/1   *LC* 72-80375   *ISBN* 0812276574

Linguistics and the teacher / edited by Ronald Carter.   2.30
London; Boston: Routledge & K. Paul, 1982. xiii, 197 p.; 22 cm. — (Language, education, and society.) Includes index. 1. Language and education 2. Teachers — Training of 3. Sociolinguistics I. Carter, Ronald. II. Series.
P41.L54 1982   400 19   *LC* 82-12209   *ISBN* 0710091931

McGann, Jerome J.   2.31
A critique of modern textual criticism / Jerome J. McGann. — Chicago: University of Chicago Press, 1983. 146 p.; 21 cm. 1. Criticism, Textual I. T.
P47.M34 1983   801/.959 19   *LC* 82-20151   *ISBN* 0226558517

Henle, Paul, ed.   • 2.32
Language, thought and culture, by Roger W. Brown. Ann Arbor: U. of Michigan P., 1958. 273 p. "This collection of essays (is the result of a) study at the University of Michigan during the academic year 1951-52." 'Ann Arbor paperback' 1. Language and languages — Addresses, essays, lectures. 2. Communication — Addresses, essays, lectures I. Brown, Roger William. II. T.
P49.H43 1965   *LC* 58-5908

Jakobson, Roman, 1896-.   2.33
Verbal art, verbal sign, verbal time / Roman Jakobson; Krystyna Pomorska and Stephen Rudy, editors; with the assistance of Brent Vine. — Minneapolis: University of Minnesota Press, c1985. xiv, 208 p.: ill.; 24 cm. 'Based on a special issue of Poetics today ... Autumn 1980'—Verso t.p. 1. Philology — Addresses, essays, lectures. 2. Semiotics — Addresses, essays, lectures. 3. Space and time in language — Addresses, essays, lectures. 4. Space and time in literature — Addresses, essays, lectures. I. Pomorska, Krystyna. II. Rudy, Stephen. III. Poetics today. IV. T.
P49.J35 1985   808/.00141 19   *LC* 84-7268   *ISBN* 0816613583

Language: introductory readings / Virginia P. Clark, Paul A. Eschholz, Alfred F. Rosa, editors.   2.34
4th ed. — New York: St. Martin's Press, c1985. xii, 740 p.: ill.; 24 cm. 1. Language and languages — Addresses, essays, lectures. 2. Linguistics — Addresses, essays, lectures. I. Clark, Virginia P. II. Eschholz, Paul A. III. Rosa, Alfred F.
P49.L23 1985   400 19   *LC* 84-51144   *ISBN* 0312467974

Bleich, David.   2.35
Subjective criticism / David Bleich. — Baltimore: The Johns Hopkins University Press, c1978. 309 p.; 24 cm. 1. Philology — Study and teaching. 2. English philology — Study and teaching 3. Criticism I. T.
P51.B55   410/.7   *LC* 77-12968   *ISBN* 0801820324

Rivers, Wilga M.   2.36
Communicating naturally in a second language: theory and practice in language teaching / Wilga M. Rivers. — Cambridge [Cambridgeshire]; New York: Cambridge University Press, c1983. ix, 243 p. 23 cm. Includes index. 1. Language and languages — Study and teaching I. T.
P51.R5 1983   418/.007 19   *LC* 82-23620   *ISBN* 0521254019

Wilkins, D. A. (David Arthur).   2.37
Linguistics in language teaching [by] D. A. Wilkins. — Cambridge: MIT Press, [1972] viii, 243 p.; 23 cm. 1. Language and languages — Study and teaching 2. Linguistics I. T.
P53.W45 1972b   418   *LC* 72-3671   *ISBN* 0262230607

P61–85 HISTORY. BIOGRAPHY

Robins, R. H. (Robert Henry)   • 2.38
A short history of linguistics, by R. H. Robins. Bloomington, Indiana University Press [1968, c1967] vi, 248 p. illus. 22 cm. (Indiana University studies in the history and theory of linguistics) 1. Linguistics — History I. T.
P61.R6 1968   410/.9   *LC* 68-10276

Hovdhaugen, Even.   2.39
Foundations of Western linguistics: from the beginning to the end of the first millenium A.D. / Even Hovdhaugen. — Oslo: Universitetsforlaget: Irvington-on-Hudson, N.Y.: Distribution office in the U.S.A. and Canada, Columbia University Press, c1982. 156 p.; 23 cm. Includes index. 1. Linguistics — History I. T.
P63.H68 1982   410/.9 19   *LC* 83-103564   *ISBN* 8200060551

Pedersen, Holger, 1867-1953.   • 2.40
The discovery of language: linguistic science in the nineteenth century / translated by John Webster Spargo. — Bloomington: Indiana University Press, [1962, c1959] 360 p.: ill.; 21 cm. (Midland books) 'MB-40.' Translation of Sprogvidenskaben i det nittende aarhundrede. 1. Philology — History. 2. Comparative linguistics — History. 3. Philologists — Portraits. I. T.
P75.P4x   409   *LC* 63-6784

Sampson, Geoffrey.   2.41
Schools of linguistics / Geoffrey Sampson. — Stanford, Calif.: Stanford University Press, 1980. 283 p.: ill.; 23 cm. Includes index. 1. Linguistics — History — 20th century. I. T.
P77.S35   410/.9 19   *LC* 80-81140   *ISBN* 0804710848

Sebeok, Thomas Albert, 1920- ed.   • **2.42**
Portraits of linguists; a biographical source book for the history of western linguistics, 1746–1963. Edited by Thomas A. Sebeok. Bloomington, Indiana University Press [1966] 2 v. 24 cm. (Indiana University studies in the history and theory of linguistics) English, French, or German. 1. Linguists I. T.
P83.S4   410.922   *LC* 64-64663

Culler, Jonathan D.   **2.43**
Roland Barthes / Jonathan Culler. — New York: Oxford University Press, 1983. 130 p.; 22 cm. Includes index. 1. Barthes, Roland. I. T.
P85.B33 C84 1983   410/.92/4 19   *LC* 83-2384   *ISBN* 0195204204

Lavers, Annette.   **2.44**
Roland Barthes, structuralism and after / Annette Lavers. — Cambridge, Mass.: Harvard University Press, 1982. 300 p.; 24 cm. Includes index. 1. Barthes, Roland. 2. Structuralism 3. Semiotics 4. Languages — Philosophy 5. Literature — Philosophy I. T.
P85.B33 L3 1982   410/.92/4 19   *LC* 81-13447   *ISBN* 0674777212

Wasserman, George Russell, 1927-.   **2.45**
Roland Barthes / by George R. Wasserman. — Boston: Twayne Publishers, 1981. 135 p.; 21 cm. — (Twayne's world authors series; TWAS 614. France) Includes index. 1. Barthes, Roland. 2. Criticism 3. Semiotics 4. Discourse analysis I. T.
P85.B33 W3   808/.00141 19   *LC* 81-4118   *ISBN* 0805764569

Harman, Gilbert. comp.   **2.46**
On Noam Chomsky; critical essays. — [1st ed.]. — Garden City, N.Y.: Anchor Press, 1974. xii, 348 p.: illus.; 21 cm. — (Modern studies in philosophy) 1. Chomsky, Noam — Addresses, essays, lectures. 2. Linguistics — Research — United States — Addresses, essays, lectures. I. T.
P85.C47 H3   410/.92/4   *LC* 74-3558   *ISBN* 0385037651

Leiber, Justin.   **2.47**
Noam Chomsky; a philosophic overview. — Boston: Twayne Publishers, [1975] 192 p.: port.; 22 cm. — (Twayne's world leaders series) Based on lectures given at Lehman College of the City University of New York in the 1973 spring term. 1. Chomsky, Noam. I. T.
P85.C47 L4   410/.92/4   *LC* 74-10583   *ISBN* 0805736611

Culler, Jonathan D.   **2.48**
Ferdinand de Saussure / Jonathan Culler. New York: Penguin Books, 1977, c1976. xix, 140 p.; 18 cm. (Penguin modern masters) Includes index. 1. Saussure, Ferdinand de, 1857-1913. 2. Structural linguistics 3. Semiotics I. T.
P85.S18 C8 1977   410/.92/4   *LC* 76-25161   *ISBN* 0140043691

P87–99.5 Communication. Mass Media

Cherry, Colin.   **2.49**
On human communication: a review, a survey, and a criticism / Colin Cherry. — 3d ed. — Cambridge, Mass.: MIT Press, c1978. xv, 374 p.: ill.; 22 cm. — (Studies in communication) Includes index. 1. Communication 2. Language and languages I. T.
P90.C55 1978   P90 C55 1978.   001.5   *LC* 77-12574   *ISBN* 0262030659

Hovland, Carl Iver, 1912-.   • **2.50**
Communication and persuasion; psychological studies of opinion change, by Carl I. Hovland, Irving L. Janis, and Harold H. Kelley. — New Haven: Yale University Press, 1953. xii, 315 p.: illus.; 24 cm. 1. Communication 2. Persuasion (Rhetoric) 3. Psychology, Applied I. Janis, Irving Lester, 1918- II. Kelley, Harold H. III. T.
P90.H69   808   *LC* 53-7776   *ISBN* 0300005733

McLuhan, Marshall, 1911-.   • **2.51**
Understanding media: the extensions of man / by Marshall McLuhan. — [1st ed.] New York: McGraw-Hill [1964] vii, 359 p.; 22 cm. 1. Communication 2. Communication and traffic 3. Technology and civilization I. T. II. Title: The extensions of man.
P90.M26   301.2   *LC* 64-16296

Miller, George Armitage, 1920- comp.   **2.52**
Communication, language, and meaning: psychological perspectives / edited by George A. Miller. — New York: Basic Books [1973] xi, 304 p.; 22 cm. 1. Communication — Addresses, essays, lectures. 2. Language and languages — Addresses, essays, lectures. I. T.
P90.M48   401/.9   *LC* 70-174815   *ISBN* 0465012833

Schramm, Wilbur Lang, 1907-.   **2.53**
Men, women, messages, and media: understanding human communication / Wilbur Schramm, William E. Porter. — 2nd ed. — New York: Harper & Row, c1982. ix, 278 p.: ill.; 25 cm. Rev. ed. of: Men, messages, and media. 1973. 1. Communication 2. Mass media I. Porter, William Earl. II. T.
P90.S375 1982   001.51 19   *LC* 81-20123   *ISBN* 0060457988

Howkins, John, 1945-.   **2.54**
Mass communication in China / John Howkins. — New York: Longman, c1982. xvii, 160 p.: 1 map; 24 cm. — (Annenberg/Longman communication books.) Includes index. 1. Mass media — China. 2. Mass media policy — China. I. T. II. Series.
P92.C5 H58   302.2/3 19   *LC* 81-8375   *ISBN* 0582282640

Tunstall, Jeremy.   **2.55**
The media in Britain / Jeremy Tunstall. — New York: Columbia University Press, 1983. xiv, 304 p.; 23 cm. 'Communication & society series'. Includes index. 1. Mass media — Great Britain. I. T. II. Title: Communication & society series. III. Title: Communication and society series.
P92.G7 T86 1983   001.51/0941 19   *LC* 83-14482   *ISBN* 0231058160

Communication arts in the ancient world / edited by Eric A.   **2.56**
Havelock and Jackson P. Hershbell.
New York: Hastings House, [1978] xiv, 162 p.: ill. — (Humanistic studies in the communication arts) (Communication arts books) 1. Communication — Greece — History — Addresses, essays, lectures. 2. Communication — Rome — History — Addresses, essays, lectures. I. Havelock, Eric Alfred. II. Hershbell, Jackson P., 1935-
P92.G75 C65   P92G75 C65.   301.14/0937   *LC* 78-17482   *ISBN* 0803812523

Bagdikian, Ben H.   **2.57**
The information machines; their impact on men and the media [by] Ben H. Bagdikian. — [1st ed.]. — New York: Harper & Row, [1971] xxxvi, 359 p.: illus.; 22 cm. 1. Mass media — United States 2. Communication — Social aspects I. T.
P92.U5 B3   301.161/0973   *LC* 71-123913   *ISBN* 0060101989

Rucker, Bryce W.   **2.58**
The first freedom [by] Bryce W. Rucker. Foreword by Howard Rusk Long. Introd. by Morris L. Ernst. — Carbondale: Southern Illinois University Press, [1968] xvii, 322 p.; 24 cm. — (New horizons in journalism) 1. Mass media — United States I. T.
P92.U5 R8   301.16/0973   *LC* 68-11651

Schiller, Herbert I., 1919-.   **2.59**
Who knows: information in the age of the Fortune 500 / by Herbert I. Schiller. — Norwood, N.J.: ABLEX Pub. Corp., c1981. xviii, 187 p.; 24 cm. — (Communication and information science.) 1. Communication — United States. 2. Communication, International 3. Communication — Economic aspects. I. T. II. Series.
P92.U5 S3   001.5 19   *LC* 81-3572   *ISBN* 0893910694

Sterling, Christopher H., 1943-.   **2.60**
The mass media: Aspen Institute guide to communication industry trends / Christopher H. Sterling, Timothy R. Haight. — New York: Praeger, 1978. xl, 457 p.; 26 cm. — (Praeger special studies in U.S. economic, social, and political issues) 'Published with the Aspen Institute for Humanistic Studies.' 1. Mass media — United States I. Haight, Timothy R. joint author. II. Aspen Institute for Humanistic Studies. III. T.
P92.U5 S68   301.16/1/0973   *LC* 76-24370   *ISBN* 0275240207

Tebbel, John William, 1912-.   **2.61**
The media in America [by] John Tebbel. Crowell [c1974] ix, 422 p. 1. Mass media — United States I. T.
P92.U5 T4   *LC* 74-9891   *ISBN* 0690005008

Tunstall, Jeremy.   **2.62**
The media are American / Jeremy Tunstall. — New York: Columbia University Press, 1977. 352 p., [7] leaves of plates: ill.; 23 cm. Includes index. 1. Mass media — United States — History. 2. Mass media — History. 3. Mass media — Economic aspects. I. T.
P92.U5 T77 1977   301.16/1/0973   *LC* 77-2581   *ISBN* 0231042922

P95–95.6 ORAL COMMUNICATION. SPEECH

Goffman, Erving.   **2.63**
Forms of talk / Erving Goffman. — Philadelphia: University of Pennsylvania Press, 1981. 335 p.; 24 cm. (University of Pennsylvania publications in conduct and communication) Includes index. 1. Oral communication I. T.
P95.G58 1981   001.54/2 19   *LC* 80-52806   *ISBN* 0812277902

Speech communication in the 20th century / edited by Thomas   **2.64**
W. Benson.
Carbondale: Southern Illinois University Press, c1985. xii, 475 p.: ill.; 24 cm.
Includes index. 1. Oral communication — History — 20th century. I. Benson,
Thomas W. II. Title: Speech communication in the twentieth century.
P95.S63 1985   302.2 19   *LC* 84-20247   *ISBN* 0809311968

Gumperz, John Joseph, 1922-.   **2.65**
Discourse strategies / John J. Gumperz. — Cambridge [Cambridgeshire]; New
York: Cambridge University Press, 1982. xii, 225 p.; 22 cm. — (Studies in
interactional sociolinguistics. 1) Includes indexes. 1. Conversation
2. Sociolinguistics 3. Intercultural communication 4. Nonverbal
communication I. T. II. Series.
P95.45.G8 1982   401/.9 19   ·   *LC* 81-20627   *ISBN* 0521246911

Searle, John R.   **2.66**
Expression and meaning: studies in the theory of speech acts / John R. Searle.
— Cambridge, Eng.; New York: Cambridge University Press, 1979. xiv, 187 p.;
23 cm. Includes index. 1. Speech acts (Linguistics) I. T.
P95.55.S4   401   *LC* 79-12271   *ISBN* 0521229014

Bach, Kent.   **2.67**
Linguistic communication and speech acts / Kent Bach, Robert M. Harnish. —
Cambridge, Mass.: MIT Press, c1979. xvii, 327 p.: ill.; 24 cm. Includes index.
1. Speech acts (Linguistics) 2. Languages — Philosophy 3. Oral
communication I. Harnish, Robert M. joint author. II. T.
P95.55.B3   410   *LC* 79-15892   *ISBN* 0262021366

Holdcroft, David.   **2.68**
Words and deeds: problems in the theory of speech acts / David Holdcroft. —
Oxford [Eng.]: Clarendon Press, 1978. xi, 178 p.; 23 cm. Includes index.
1. Speech acts (Linguistics) 2. Meaning (Philosophy) I. T.
P95.55.H6   410   *LC* 77-30411   *ISBN* 0198245815

P95.8–96 POLITICAL AND OTHER SPECIAL ASPECTS

Alisky, Marvin.   **2.69**
Latin American media: guidance and censorship / Marvin Alisky. — 1st ed. —
Ames: Iowa State University Press, 1981. ix, 265 p.; 24 cm. ix, 265 p. 1. Mass
media — Political aspects — Latin America. 2. Mass media — Censorship —
Latin America. I. T.
P95.82.L29 A4   P95.82L29 A4.   302.2/3 19   *LC* 81-5084
     ISBN 0813815258

Gitlin, Todd.   **2.70**
The whole world is watching: mass media in the making & unmaking of the
New Left / Todd Gitlin. — Berkeley: University of California Press, c1980. xiii,
327 p.; 24 cm. Includes index. 1. Students for a Democratic Society (U.S.).
2. Mass media — Political aspects — United States. 3. College students —
United States — Political activity. I. T.
P95.82.U6 G57   302.2/3   *LC* 78-68835   *ISBN* 0520038894

Encyclopedia of mystery and detection / Chris Steinbrunner and   **2.71**
Otto Penzler, editors–in–chief; Marvin Lachman and Charles
Shibuk, senior editors.
New York: McGraw-Hill, c1976. [11], 436 p.: ill.; 24 cm. 1. Detectives in mass
media — Dictionaries. I. Steinbrunner, Chris. II. Penzler, Otto.
P96.D4 E5 1976   808.83/872/0321 19   *LC* 75-31645   *ISBN*
0070611211

Stott, William, 1940-.   **2.72**
Documentary expression and thirties America / William Stott. — Chicago:
University of Chicago Press, 1986. xv, 369 p., [64] p. of plates: ill., ports.; 21
cm. Reprint. Originally published: New York: Oxford University Press, 1973.
With new afterword. Includes index. 1. Documentary mass media — United
States. 2. United States — Popular culture I. T.
P96.D622 U67 1986   302.2/34/0973 19   *LC* 85-31819   *ISBN*
0226775593

Who owns the media?: concentration of ownership in the mass   **2.73**
communications industry / by Benjamin M. Compaine ... [et
al.].
2nd ed., completely rev. and expanded. — White Plains, NY: Knowledge
Industry Publications, c1982. xv, 529 p.; 24 cm. — (Communications library.)
Rev. ed. of: Who owns the media? / Benjamin M. Compaine. c1979. Includes
index. 1. Mass media — Economic aspects — United States. 2. Mass media —
Political aspects — United States. I. Compaine, Benjamin M. Who owns the
media? II. Series.
P96.E252 U68 1982   380.3/0973 19   *LC* 82-13039   *ISBN*
0867290072

Rovin, Jeff.   **2.74**
The encyclopedia of superheroes / Jeff Rovin. — New York, NY: Facts on file,
c1985. xi, 443 p. [32] p. of leaves: ill. (some col.); 29 cm. Includes index.
1. Heroes in mass media — Dictionaries. I. T.
P96.H46 R68 1985   001.51 19   *LC* 85-10329   *ISBN* 0816011680

King, Stephen, 1947-.   **2.75**
[Danse macabre] Stephen King's Danse macabre. — 1st ed. — New York:
Everest House, c1981. 400 p.: ill.; 25 cm. Includes index. 1. Horror in mass
media I. T. II. Title: Danse macabre.
P96.H65 K5 1981   302.2/3   *LC* 79-28056   *ISBN* 0896960765

P99–99.5 SEMIOTICS. SIGNS. NONVERBAL COMMUNICATION

Barthes, Roland.   **2.76**
[S/Z. English] S/Z. Translated by Richard Miller. Pref. by Richard Howard.
[1st American ed.] New York, Hill and Wang [1974] xi, 271 p. 22 cm. Includes
text of Balzac's Sarrasine (p. 221-254) 1. Balzac, Honoré de, 1799-1850.
Sarrasine. 2. Semiotics I. Balzac, Honoré de, 1799-1850. Sarrasine. English.
1974. II. T.
P99.B313 1974   301.2/1   *LC* 72-95045   *ISBN* 0809083752

Berger, Arthur Asa, 1933-.   **2.77**
Signs in contemporary culture: an introduction to semiotics / Arthur Asa
Berger; illustrations by the author. — New York: Longman, c1984. xi, 196 p.:
ill.; 24 cm. — (Annenberg/Longman communication books.) Includes index.
1. Signs and symbols 2. Semiotics I. T. II. Series.
P99.B437 1984   001.51 19   *LC* 83-17529   *ISBN* 0582284872

Deely, John N.   **2.78**
Introducing semiotic: its history and doctrine / by John Deely; with a foreword
by Thomas A. Sebeok. — Bloomington: Indiana University Press, 1982. xvi,
246 p.; 25 cm. — (Advances in semiotics.) Includes indexes. 1. Semiotics I. T.
II. Series.
P99.D4 1982   149/.946 19   *LC* 82-47782   *ISBN* 0253330807

Eco, Umberto.   **2.79**
The role of the reader: explorations in the semiotics of texts / Umberto Eco. —
Bloomington: Indiana University Press, 1979 (c1978). viii, 273 p.; 24 cm. —
(Advances in semiotics.) 1. Semiotics — Addresses, essays, lectures.
2. Discourse analysis — Addresses, essays, lectures. I. T. II. Series.
P99.E28   801/.95   *LC* 78-18299   *ISBN* 0253111390

Eco, Umberto.   **2.80**
A theory of semiotics / Umberto Eco. — Bloomington: Indiana University
Press, c1976. ix, 354 p.: ill. (Advances in semiotics.) Includes index.
1. Semiotics I. T. II. Series.
P99.E3   P99 E3.   301.2/1   *LC* 74-22833   *ISBN* 0253359554

Greimas, Algirdas Julien.   **2.81**
[Sémiotique. English] Semiotics and language: an analytical dictionary / A.J.
Greimas and J. Courtés; translation by Larry Crist ... [et al.]. — Bloomington:
Indiana University Press, 1983 (c1982). xvi, 409 p.; 24 cm. — (Advances in
semiotics.) Translation of: Sémiotique. 1. Semiotics — Dictionaries.
I. Courtés, Joseph, 1936- II. T. III. Series.
P99.G6913 1982   401/.41 19   *LC* 81-47828   *ISBN* 0253351693

Peirce, Charles S. (Charles Sanders), 1839-1914.   **2.82**
Semiotic and significs: the correspondence between Charles S. Peirce and Lady
Victoria Welby / edited by Charles S. Hardwick, with the assistance of James
Cook. — Bloomington: Indiana University Press, c1977. xxxiv, 201 p.: ill.; 25
cm. 1. Peirce, Charles S. (Charles Sanders), 1839-1914. 2. Welby, Victoria,
Lady, 1837-1912. 3. Semiotics — Addresses, essays, lectures. I. Welby,
Victoria, Lady, 1837-1912. II. T.
P99.P4 1977   412   *LC* 76-12369   *ISBN* 0253351634

Silverman, Kaja.   **2.83**
The subject of semiotics / by Kaja Silverman. — New York: Oxford University
Press, 1983. xii, 304 p.; 22 cm. Includes index. 1. Semiotics 2. Discourse
analysis 3. Psychoanalysis 4. Communication — Sex differences I. T.
P99.S52 1983   001.51 19   *LC* 82-6306   *ISBN* 0195031776

Todorov, Tzvetan, 1939-.   **2.84**
[Theories du symbole. English] Theories of the symbol / Tzvetan Todorov;
translated by Catherine Porter. — Ithaca, N.Y.: Cornell University Press, 1982.
302 p.; 24 cm. Translation of: Théories du symbole. Includes index.
1. Semiotics — Addresses, essays, lectures. 2. Rhetoric — Addresses, essays,
lectures. I. T.
P99.T613 1982   001.51 19   *LC* 81-17420   *ISBN* 0801411920

Key, Mary Ritchie.   2.85
Nonverbal communication: a research guide & bibliography / by Mary Ritchie
Key. Metuchen, N.J.: Scarecrow Press, 1977. x, 439 p.; 23 cm. Includes index.
1. Nonverbal communication I. T.
P99.5.K4   001.56   LC 76-53024   ISBN 081081014X

P101–1099 LANGUAGE. COMPARATIVE PHILOLOGY

P101–120 Philosophy. Psychology. Origin

Crosby, Donald A.   2.86
Horace Bushnell's theory of language: in the context of other nineteenth-
century philosophies of language / by Donald A. Crosby. — The Hague:
Mouton, 1975. 300 p.; 22 cm. (Studies in philosophy; 22) Includes indexes.
1. Bushnell, Horace, 1802-1876. 2. Languages — Philosophy 3. Languages —
Religious aspects — Christianity — History. I. T.
P103.C78   401   LC 76-356428   ISBN 9027930449

Brown, Roger William, 1925-.   • 2.87
Words and things. — Glencoe, Ill.: The Free Press, [1958] 398 p.; 22 cm.
1. Language and languages I. T.
P105.B77   400   LC 58-9395

Cassirer, Ernst, 1874-1945.   • 2.88
[Sprache und Mythos. English] Language and myth. Translated by Susanne K.
Langer. [1st Dover ed. New York] Dover Publications [c1946] 103 p. 21 cm.
'Originally published in German as number VI of the 'Studien der Bibliothek
Warburg." 1. Language and languages 2. Mythology 3. Religion, Primitive
4. Ethnopsychology I. T.
P105.C32 1946a   401   LC 53-9352

Derrida, Jacques.   2.89
[La grammatologie. English] Of grammatology / by Jacques Derrida;
translated by Gayatri Chakravorty Spivak. — 1st American ed. — Baltimore:
Johns Hopkins University Press, 1977 (c1976). xc, 354 p.; 24 cm. Translation of
De la grammatologie. 1. Languages — Philosophy I. T.
P105.D5313   410   LC 76-17226   ISBN 0801818419. ISBN
0801818796 pbk

Firth, J. R. (John Rupert), 1890-1960.   • 2.90
The tongues of men, and Speech [by] J. R. Firth. — London, Oxford University
Press, 1964. x, 211 p. illus. 20 cm. — (Language and language learning, 2)
Reprint of the works first published in 1937 and 1930, respectively.
1. Language and languages 2. Speech I. Firth, J. R. (John Rupert), 1890-1960.
Speech. II. T. III. Title: Speech.
P105.F5 1964   401   LC 65-4007

Hjelmslev, Louis, 1899-1965.   • 2.91
Prolegomena to a theory of language. Translated by Francis J. Whitfield. [Rev.
English ed.] Madison, University of Wisconsin Press, 1961. 144 p. 23 cm.
Translation of Omkring sprogteoriens grundlæggelse. 1. Language and
languages I. T.
P105.H514 1961   LC 62-7095

Hoijer, Harry, 1904- ed.   • 2.92
Language in culture: conference on the interrelations of language and other
aspects of culture / with papers by Franklin Fearing [and others. — Chicago]:
University of Chicago Press [1954] xi, 286 p.; 25 cm. — (Comparative studies of
cultures and civilizations) 'The conference was held in Chicago from March 23
to 27, 1953, inclusive, under the sponsorship of the Department of
Anthropology, University of Chicago.' 'Also published as Memoir no. 79 of the
American Anthropological Association.' Includes bibliographies. 1. Language
and languages 2. Meaning (Psychology) I. University of Chicago. Dept. of
Anthropology. II. T.
P105.H63 1954   401   LC 54-11977

Jespersen, Otto, 1860-1943.   • 2.93
Language, its nature, development and origin. — London: Allen and Unwin,
1949. 448 p.; 22 cm. 1. Language and languages I. T.
P105.J45 1949   410   LC 49-8298

Sapir, Edward, 1884-1939.   • 2.94
Language, an introduction to the study of speech, by Edward Sapir. — New
York: Harcourt, Brace and company, 1921. vii, 258 p.; 20 cm. 1. Language and
languages I. T.
P105.S2   LC 21-20134

Schlauch, Margaret, 1898-.   • 2.95
[Gift of tongues] The gift of language. New York, Dover Publications [1955]
342 p. illus. 22 cm. First published in 1942 under title: The gift of tongues.
1. Language and languages I. T.
P105.S27 1955   400   LC 56-13531

Urban, Wilbur Marshall, 1873-.   • 2.96
Language and reality; the philosophy of language and the principles of
symbolism. London, Allen & Unwin; New York, Macmillan [1951] 755 p. 23
cm. (Muirhead library of philosophy) 1. Language and languages
2. Symbolism 3. Meaning (Psychology) I. T.
P105.U7 1951   401   LC 52-7828

Vygotskiĭ, L. S. (Lev Semenovich), 1896-1934.   • 2.97
[Myshlenie i rech'. English] Thought and language / Edited and translated by
Eugenia Hanfmann and Gertrude Vakar. Cambridge: M.I.T. Press,
Massachusetts Institute of Technology, 1962. xxi, 168 p.; 24 cm. (Studies in
communication) 'Comments on Vygotsky's critical remarks concerning The
language and thought of the child, and Judgment and reasoning in the child, by
Jean Piaget': 14 p. in pocket. 1. Psycholinguistics 2. Children — Language
3. Child study. I. T.
P105.V913   153.65   LC 61-15594

Wheelwright, Philip Ellis, 1901-.   • 2.98
The burning fountain; a study in the language of symbolism. — Bloomington,
Indiana University Press, 1954. ix, 406 p. illus. 25 cm. Bibliographical references
included in 'Notes' (p. 365-396) 1. Language and languages 2. Symbolism
3. Meaning (Psychology) I. T.
P105.W57   401   LC 54-6206

Approaches to language / edited by Roy Harris.   2.99
1st ed. — Oxford; New York: Pergamon Press, 1983. viii, 181 p.; 24 cm. —
(Language & communication library. v. 4) 1. Language and languages —
Addresses, essays, lectures. I. Harris, Roy, 1931- II. Series.
P106.A64 1983   400 19   LC 82-12390   ISBN 008028910X

Blackburn, Simon.   2.100
Spreading the word: groundings in the philosophy of language / by Simon
Blackburn. — Oxford [Oxfordshire]: Clarendon Press; New York: Oxford
University Press, c1984. xi, 368 p.; 22 cm. Includes index. 1. Languages —
Philosophy I. T.
P106.B47 1984   401 19   LC 83-17253   ISBN 0198246501

Bolinger, Dwight Le Merton, 1907-.   2.101
Language, the loaded weapon: the use and abuse of language today / Dwight
Bolinger. — London; New York: Longman, 1980. ix, 214 p.; 23 cm. Includes
index. 1. Language and languages 2. Language and culture 3. Thought and
thinking I. T.
P106.B594   401/.9   LC 80-40301   ISBN 0582291070

Chomsky, Noam.   • 2.102
Language and mind. — Enl. ed. — New York: Harcourt Brace Jovanovich,
[1972] xii, 194 p.; 24 cm. 1. Psycholinguistics 2. Thought and thinking I. T.
P106.C52 1972   401/.9   LC 70-187121   ISBN 0151478104

Chomsky, Noam.   2.103
Rules and representations / Noam Chomsky. — New York: Columbia
University Press, 1980. viii, 299 p.; 22 cm. — (Woodbridge lectures delivered at
Columbia University; no. 11, 1978) 1. Languages — Philosophy
2. Psycholinguistics I. T.
P106.C544   301.2/1 19   LC 79-26145   ISBN 0231048262

Davidson, Donald, 1917-.   2.104
Inquiries into truth and interpretation / Donald Davidson. — Oxford
[Oxfordshire]: Clarendon Press; New York: Oxford University Press, 1984. xx,
292 p.; 22 cm. Companion v. to: Essays on actions and events. Includes index.
1. Languages — Philosophy — Addresses, essays, lectures. I. T.
P106.D27 1984   401 19   LC 83-15136   ISBN 019824617X

Hacking, Ian.   2.105
Why does language matter to philosophy? / Ian Hacking. — Cambridge; New
York: Cambridge University Press, 1975. 200 p.: diagrs.; 20 cm. Includes index.
1. Languages — Philosophy I. T.
P106.H284   P106 H284.   401   LC 75-19432   ISBN 0521209234

Heidegger, Martin, 1889-1976.   • 2.106
[Unterwegs zur Sprache. English] On the way to language. Translated by Peter
D. Hertz. [1st ed.] New York, Harper & Row [1971] 200 p. 22 cm. Translation
of Unterwegs zur Sprache. 1. Languages — Philosophy I. T.
P106.H3613   401   LC 77-124708

Lakoff, George.   **2.107**
Metaphors we live by / George Lakoff and Mark Johnson. — Chicago: University of Chicago Press, 1980. xiii, 242 p.; 22 cm. 1. Languages — Philosophy 2. Metaphor 3. Concepts 4. Truth I. Johnson, Mark, 1949- joint author. II. T.
P106.L235   401   *LC* 80-10783   *ISBN* 0226468011

Landesman, Charles.   **2.108**
Discourse and its presuppositions. — New Haven, Yale University Press, 1972. ix, 161 p. 22 cm. 1. Languages — Philosophy I. T.
P106.L27 1972   401   *LC* 72-75201   *ISBN* 0300015267

Languages and their status / [edited by] Timothy Shopen.   **2.109**
Cambridge, Mass.: Winthrop Publishers, c1979. xii, 335 p.; ill.; 24 cm. 1. Language and languages 2. Language and culture I. Shopen, Timothy.
P106.L319   301.2/1   *LC* 78-10973   *ISBN* 0876264852

Lyons, John, 1932-.   • **2.110**
Introduction to theoretical linguistics. — London: Cambridge U.P., 1968. x, 519 p.; 23 cm. 1. Linguistics 2. Grammar, Comparative and general I. T.
P106.L9   410   *LC* 68-31743   *ISBN* 0521056179

Sefler, George F.   **2.111**
Language and the world; a methodological synthesis within the writings of Martin Heidegger and Ludwig Wittgenstein, by George F. Sefler. — New York: Humanities Press, 1974. xxxiii, 228 p.; 23 cm. 1. Heidegger, Martin, 1889-1976. 2. Wittgenstein, Ludwig, 1889-1951. 3. Languages — Philosophy I. T.
P106.S35   111   *LC* 73-18045   *ISBN* 0391002287

P115–119 BILINGUALISM. LANGUAGE ACQUISITION

Bilingualism, social issues and policy implications / Andrew W.   **2.112**
Miracle, Jr., editor.
Athens, Ga.: University of Georgia Press, c1983. x, 188 p.: ill., maps; 23 cm. — (Southern Anthropological Society proceedings. no. 16) Includes papers presented in a symposium of the 16th Annual Meeting of the Southern Anthropological Society, Fort Worth, Tex., Apr. 1981. Includes index. 1. Bilingualism — Congresses. 2. Language policy — Congresses. 3. Education, Bilingual — Congresses. I. Miracle, Andrew W. II. Southern Anthropological Society. Meeting. (16th: 1981: Fort Worth, Tex.) III. Series.
P115.B5x   301 s 306/.4 19   *LC* 82-13447   *ISBN* 0820306460

Lewis, E. Glyn.   **2.113**
Bilingualism and bilingual education: a comparative study / E. Glyn Lewis; foreword by Bernard Spolsky. — 1st ed. — Albuquerque: University of New Mexico Press, c1980. xv, 455 p.: ill.; 24 cm. Includes index. 1. Bilingualism 2. Education, Bilingual I. T.
P115.L4   404/.2   *LC* 79-55982   *ISBN* 0826305326

Gal, Susan.   **2.114**
Language shift: social determinants of linguistic change in bilingual Austria / Susan Gal. — New York: Academic Press, 1979 [c1978] xii, 201 p.: ill.; 24 cm. — (Language, thought, and culture) Includes index. 1. Bilingualism — Austria — Oberwart. 2. Language and languages — Variation 3. German language — Social aspects. 4. Hungarian language — Social aspects. 5. Oberwart (Austria) — Languages. I. T.
P115.5.O2 G3   301.2/1

Anisfeld, Moshe.   **2.115**
Language development from birth to three / Moshe Anisfeld. — Hillsdale, N.J.: Lawrence Erlbaum Associates, 1984. xii, 293 p.: ill.; 24 cm. Includes indexes. 1. Children — Language 2. Language acquisition I. T.
P118.A5x   *ISBN* 0898592844

Bickerton, Derek, 1926-.   **2.116**
Roots of language / Derek Bickerton. — Ann Arbor, Mich.: Karoma Publishers, 1981. xiii, 351 p. 1. Language acquisition I. T.
P118.B52   P118 B42.   *ISBN* 0897200446

Bruner, Jerome S. (Jerome Seymour)   **2.117**
Child's talk: learning to use language / Jerome Bruner, with the assistance of Rita Watson. — 1st ed. — New York: W.W. Norton, c1983. 144 p.: ill.; 22 cm. 1. Language acquisition 2. Children — Language I. Watson, Rita. II. T.
P118.B695 1983   401/.9 19   *LC* 83-2215   *ISBN* 0393017532

The Child's conception of language / editors, A. Sinclair, R. J.   **2.118**
Jarvella, W. J. M. Levelt.
Berlin; New York: Springer-Verlag, 1978. viii, 268 p.; 24 cm. (Springer series in language and communication. 2) 1. Language acquisition — Addresses, essays, lectures. 2. Language awareness in children — Addresses, essays, lectures.

I. Sinclair, A. (Anne) II. Jarvella, R. J. III. Levelt, W. J. M. (Willem J. M.), 1938- IV. Series.
P118.C48   401/.9 19   *LC* 80-512674   *ISBN* 038709153X

Halliday, M. A. K. (Michael Alexander Kirkwood), 1925-.   **2.119**
Learning how to mean: explorations in the development of language / M. A. K. Halliday. — New York: Elsevier, 1977, c1975. xii, 164 p.; 23 cm. 1. Children — Language 2. Semiotics I. T.
P118.H3 1977   401/.9   *LC* 76-51756   *ISBN* 0444002006

Language acquisition: the state of the art / edited by Eric   **2.120**
Wanner and Lila R. Gleitman.
Cambridge; New York: Cambridge University Press, 1982. x, 532 p.: ill.; 25 cm. Includes index. 1. Language acquisition — Addresses, essays, lectures. I. Wanner, Eric. II. Gleitman, Lila R.
P118.L255 1982   401/.9 19   *LC* 82-4407   *ISBN* 052123817X

Language development / editor, Stan A. Kuczaj II.   **2.121**
Hillsdale, N.J.: L. Erlbaum Associates, 1982. — 501 p.: ill.; 23 cm. — (Child psychology.) Includes index. 1. Language acquistion — Addresses, essays, lectures. 2. Grammar, Comparative and general — Syntax — Addresses, essays, lectures. 3. Semantics — Addresses, essays, lectures. I. Kuczaj, Stan A. II. Series.
P118.L36 1982   401/.9 19   *LC* 80-29090   *ISBN* 0898591007

Lightfoot, David.   **2.122**
The language lottery: toward a biology of grammars / David Lightfoot. — Cambridge, Mass.: MIT Press, c1982. xii, 224 p.: ill.; 24 cm. Includes index. 1. Language acquisition 2. Biolinguistics 3. Generative grammar I. T.
P118.L47 1982   401/.9 19   *LC* 82-13082   *ISBN* 0262120968

Reich, Peter A., 1940-.   **2.123**
Language development / Peter A. Reich. — Englewood Cliffs, N.J.: Prentice-Hall, c1986. xii, 387 p.: ill.; 23 cm. Includes indexes. 1. Language acquisition 2. Language disorders in children 3. Language and languages — Study and teaching I. T.
P118.R42 1986   401/.9 19   *LC* 85-24453   *ISBN* 0135230691

Talking to children: language input and acquisition: papers from   **2.124**
a conference sponsored by the Committee on Sociolinguistics of the Social Science Research Council (USA) / edited by Catherine E. Snow, Charles A. Ferguson.
Cambridge; New York: Cambridge University Press, 1977. x, 369 p.: ill.; 24 cm. 1. Language acquisition — Congresses. 2. Mother and child — Congresses. 3. Sociolinguistics — Congresses. 4. Psycholinguistics — Congresses. I. Snow, Catherine E. II. Ferguson, Charles Albert, 1921- III. Social Science Research Council. Committee on Sociolinguistics.
P118.T3   401/.9   *LC* 76-11094   *ISBN* 0521213185

Linguistic minorities, policies, and pluralism / edited by John   **2.125**
Edwards.
London; Orlando: Academic Press, 1984. xii, 320 p.: ill.; 24 cm. (Applied language studies.) 1. Linguistic minorities — Addresses, essays, lectures. 2. Language policy — Addresses, essays, lectures. 3. Language and culture — Addresses, essays, lectures. 4. Pluralism (Social sciences) — Addresses, essays, lectures. 5. Ethnicity — Addresses, essays, lectures. I. Edwards, John, 1947- II. Series.
P119.315.L567 1984   305.7 19   *LC* 83-73316   *ISBN* 0122327608

P120 SEXISM IN LANGUAGE. LANGUAGE CHANGE

Cameron, Deborah, 1958-.   **2.126**
Feminism and linguistic theory / Deborah Cameron. — New York: St. Martin's Press, c1985. ix, 195 p.; 23 cm. Includes index. 1. Language and languages — Sex differences 2. Sexism in language 3. Women — Language 4. Feminism I. T.
P120.S48 C35 1985   401/.9 19   *LC* 84-15150   *ISBN* 0312287461

Kramarae, Cheris.   **2.127**
Women and men speaking: frameworks for analysis / Cheris Kramarae. — Rowley, MA: Newbury House Publishers, 1981. xviii, 194 p.; 23 cm. Includes index. 1. Language and languages — Sex differences 2. Sexism in language I. T.
P120.S48 K7   401/.9   *LC* 80-16802   *ISBN* 0883771799

Language, gender, and society / edited by Barrie Thorne, Cheris   **2.128**
Kramarae, Nancy Henley.
Rowley, Mass.: Newbury House, 1983. x, 342 p.; 23 cm. Includes index. 1. Language and languages — Sex differences — Addresses, essays, lectures. 2. Communication — Sex differences — Addresses, essays, lectures. I. Thorne, Barrie. II. Kramarae, Cheris. III. Henley, Nancy.
P120.S48 L36 1983   401/.9 19   *LC* 82-22537   *ISBN* 088377268X

Sexist language: a modern philosophical analysis / edited by   **2.129**
Mary Vetterling–Braggin.
Totowa, N.J.: Rowman and Littlefield, 1981. 329 p.; 22 cm. 1. Sexism in language 2. Feminism 3. Racism in language 4. Truth I. Vetterling-Braggin, Mary.
P120.S48 S48 1981   401/.9 19   *LC* 80-26263   *ISBN* 0847662934

Bright, William, 1928-.   **2.130**
Variation and change in language: essays / by William Bright; selected and introduced by Anwar S. Dil. — Stanford, Calif.: Stanford University Press, 1976. xiv, 283 p.: ill.; 24 cm. (Language science and national development.) 1. Language and languages — Variation — Addresses, essays, lectures. 2. Linguistic change — Addresses, essays, lectures. 3. Sociolinguistics — Addresses, essays, lectures. 4. Anthropological linguistics — Addresses, essays, lectures. 5. Indic languages — Addresses, essays, lectures. 6. Indians of North America — Languages — Addresses, essays, lectures. I. T. II. Series.
P120.V37.B75 1976   410   *LC* 76-23370   *ISBN* 0804709262

P121–149 Linguistics

Bloomfield, Leonard, 1887-1949.   • **2.131**
Language. New York: Holt, Rinehart and Winston, c1933. 564 p. 1. Language and languages 2. English language — Pronunciation I. T.
P121.B46   *LC* 33-7406

Chomsky, Noam.   • **2.132**
Current issues in linguistic theory. The Hague, Mouton, 1964. 119 p. 23 cm. (Janua linguarum. Series minor. nr. 38) 'A revised and expanded version of a report presented to the session: 'The logical basis of linguistic theory,' Ninth International Congress of Linguists, Cambridge, Mass., 1962.' 1. Linguistics — Research I. T. II. Series.
P121.C47 1964   *LC* 65-4375

Fodor, Jerry A. ed.   • **2.133**
The structure of language; readings in the philosophy of language [by] Jerry A. Fodor [and] Jerrold J. Katz. — Englewood Cliffs, N.J.: Prentice-Hall, [1964] xii, 612 p.: illus.; 25 cm. 1. Language and languages 2. Languages — Philosophy I. Katz, Jerrold J. joint ed. II. T.
P121.F6   410.82   *LC* 63-13288

Harris, Zellig Sabbettai, 1909-.   • **2.134**
Structural linguistics. — [Chicago] University of Chicago Press [1960, c1951] 384 p. illus. 21 cm. — (Phoenix books, P52) Published in 1951 under title: Methods in structural linguistics. 1. Language and languages I. T.
P121.H37   *LC* A 62-5118

Hockett, Charles Francis.   • **2.135**
A course in modern linguistics. New York: Macmillan, [1958] 621 p.: illus.; 22 cm. 1. Linguistics 2. English language — Pronunciation 3. English language — Grammar — 1950- I. T.
P121.H63   400   *LC* 58-5007

Langacker, Ronald W.   • **2.136**
Language and its structure; some fundamental linguistic concepts [by] Ronald W. Langacker. — 2d ed. — New York: Harcourt Brace Jovanovich, [1973] ix, 275 p.: illus.; 23 cm. 1. Linguistics 2. Language and languages I. T.
P121.L38 1973   410   *LC* 73-2180   *ISBN* 015549192X

Lehmann, Winfred Philipp, 1916-.   • **2.137**
Historical linguistics: an introduction. — New York: Holt, Rinehart and Winston, [1962] 297 p.: illus.; 22 cm. 1. Historical linguistics I. T.
P121.L45   409   *LC* 62-12987

Martinet, André.   • **2.138**
Elements of general linguistics. With a foreword by L. R. Palmer. Translated by Elisabeth Palmer. [Chicago] University of Chicago Press [1964] 205 p. 22 cm. Bibliography: p. 199-201. 1. Language and languages I. T.
P121.M3133   410   *LC* 64-19845

Pei, Mario, 1901-.   • **2.139**
The story of language / by Mario Pei. — Rev. ed. — Philadelphia: Lippincott, c1965. 491 p. 1. Language and languages I. T.
P121.P37   *LC* 65-12599

Quirk, Randolph.   • **2.140**
Investigating linguistic acceptability / by Randolph Quirk and Jan Svartvik. — The Hague: Mouton, 1966. 117 p.: ill. — (Janua linguarum. Series minor. no. 54) 1. Linguistics — Research I. Svartvik, Jan. joint author. II. T. III. Series.
P121.Q5   410.072   *LC* 66-6743

Saussure, Ferdinand de, 1857-1913.   • **2.141**
Course in general linguistics / edited by Charles Bally and Albert Sechehaye in collaboration with Albert Reidlinger; translated from the French by Wade Baskin. New York, Philosophical Library, 1959. 240 p. illus. 22 cm. 1. Language and languages 2. Comparative linguistics I. T.
P121.S363   *LC* 59-16472   *ISBN* 0070165246

Sturtevant, Edgar Howard, 1875-1952.   • **2.142**
An introduction to linguistic science. New Haven, Yale Univ. Press, 1947. 173 p. 25 cm. 'Published on the Louis Stern Memorial Fund.' Bibliographical footnotes. 1. Language and languages I. T.
P121.S815   400   *LC* 47-5586 *

Sturtevant, Edgar Howard, 1875-1952.   • **2.143**
Linguistic change; an introduction to the historical study of language. With a new introd. by Eric P. Hamp. — [Chicago] University of Chicago Press [1961, c1917] 185 p. illus. 21 cm. — (Phoenix books, P60) 1. Language and languages I. T.
P121.S82 1961   409   *LC* 61-1441

Trager, George Leonard, 1906-.   • **2.144**
Language and languages / [by] George L. Trager. — San Francisco: Chandler Pub. Co., [1972] xvi, 378 p.: ill.; 24 cm. — (Chandler publications in anthropology and sociology) 1. Language and languages I. T.
P121.T67   400   *LC* 68-21787   *ISBN* 0810200163

Anderson, James Maxwell, 1933-.   **2.145**
Structural aspects of language change. [London] Longman [c1973.] 250 p. illus. 23 cm. (Longman linguistics library, 13) 1. Linguistic change 2. Structural linguistics I. T.
P 123 A543 1973   *LC* 73-181191   *ISBN* 0582550327

Barthes, Roland.   **2.146**
[Eléments de sémiologie. English] Elements of semiology. Translated from the French by Annette Lavers and Colin Smith. [1st American ed.] New York, Hill and Wang [1968] 111 p. illus. 20 cm. Translation of Éléments de sémiologie. 1. Semantics I. T.
P123.B3813 1968   412   *LC* 68-30769

Chomsky, Noam.   • **2.147**
Cartesian linguistics: a chapter in the history of rationalist thought. [1st ed.] New York, Harper & Row [1966] xi, 119 p. 21 cm. (Studies in language) 1. Cartesian linguistics 2. Creativity (Linguistics) 3. Generative grammar I. T. II. Title: Linguistics.
P123.C53   401   *LC* 66-15670

Directions for historical linguistics; a symposium. Edited by W.   • **2.148**
P. Lehmann and Yakov Malkiel.
Austin: University of Texas Press, [1968] ix, 199 p.: illus.; 24 cm. 1. Historical linguistics — Congresses. I. Lehmann, Winfred Philipp, 1916- ed. II. Malkiel, Yakov, 1914- ed.
P123.D5   417/.7   *LC* 68-8399

Exceptional language and linguistics / edited by Loraine K.   **2.149**
Obler and Lise Menn.
New York: Academic Press, 1982. xviii, 372 p.: ill.; 24 cm. — (Perspectives in neurolinguistics, neuropsychology, and psycholinguistics.) 1. Linguistics 2. Psycholinguistics I. Obler, Loraine K. II. Menn, Lise. III. Series.
P123.E95 1982   401 19   *LC* 82-6815   *ISBN* 0125236808

Hoenigswald, Henry M., 1915-.   • **2.150**
Language change and linguistic reconstruction. — [Chicago]: University of Chicago Press, [1960] 168 p.: illus.; 24 cm. 1. Linguistic change 2. Grammar, Comparative and general — Phonology 3. Comparative linguistics I. T.
P123.H55   410   *LC* 59-12287

Jameson, Frederic.   **2.151**
The prison–house of language; a critical account of structuralism and Russian formalism. — Princeton, N.J.: Princeton University Press, [1972] x, 230 p.; 23 cm. — (Princeton essays in European and comparative literature) 1. Structural linguistics I. T.
P123.J34   415   *LC* 78-173757   *ISBN* 069106220X

Lamb, Sydney M.   • **2.152**
Outline of stratificational grammar / by Sydney M. Lamb; with an appendix by Leonard E. Newell. — Washington: Georgetown University Press [1966] 109 p. ill.; 23 cm. — Includes index. 1. Structural linguistics I. Newell, Leonard E. II. T.
P123.L3x   410   *LC* 66-28562

Samuels, M. L. (Michael Louis)   • **2.153**
Linguistic evolution: with special reference to English / [by] M. L. Samuels. — Cambridge [Eng.]: University Press, 1972. 203 p.; 24 cm. (Cambridge studies in linguistics. 5) 1. Historical linguistics 2. Linguistic change I. T. II. Series.
P123.S26   417/.7   *LC* 72-176255   *ISBN* 0521083850

Révész, Géza, 1878-1955.   • **2.154**
[Ursprung und Vorgeschichte der Sprache. English] The origins and prehistory of language. Translated from the German by J. Butler. Westport, Conn., Greenwood Press [1970, c1956] viii, 240 p. 23 cm. Translation of Ursprung und Vorgeschichte der Sprache. 1. Language and languages — Origin I. T.
P131.R4513 1970   401   *LC* 78-138128   *ISBN* 0837141672

Lenneberg, Eric H.   • **2.155**
Biological foundations of language / [by] Eric H. Lenneberg; with appendices by Noam Chomsky and Otto Marx. — New York: Wiley, [1967] xvi, 489 p.: ill.; 24 cm. 1. Biolinguistics I. T.
P132.L4   410   *LC* 66-28746

Hopper, Robert.   **2.156**
Children's speech: a practical introduction to communication development [by] Robert Hopper [and] Rita C. Naremore. — New York: Harper & Row, [1973] x, 140 p.; 21 cm. 1. Language acquisition I. Naremore, Rita C. joint author. II. T.
P136.H6   401/.9   *LC* 72-86372   *ISBN* 0060447222

Bynon, Theodora.   **2.157**
Historical linguistics / Theodora Bynon. — Cambridge; New York: Cambridge University Press, 1977. x, 301 p.: ill.; 24 cm. — (Cambridge textbooks in linguistics) Includes index. 1. Historical linguistics 2. Languages in contact I. T.
P140.B95   410   *LC* 76-62588   *ISBN* 052121582X

Hawkes, Terence.   **2.158**
Structuralism & semiotics / Terence Hawkes. — Berkeley: University of California Press, c1977. 192 p.; 19 cm. — (Campus; 189) Includes index. 1. Structural linguistics 2. Structuralism (Literary analysis) 3. Semiotics I. T.
P146.H3 1977c   808   *LC* 77-153914   *ISBN* 0520034228

Halliday, M. A. K. (Michael Alexander Kirkwood), 1925-.   **2.159**
Halliday: system and function in language: selected papers / edited by G. R. Kress. — London: Oxford University Press, 1976. xxi, 250 p.; 23 cm. Includes index. 1. Halliday, M. A. K. (Michael Alexander Kirkwood), 1925- 2. Functionalism (Linguistics) — Collected works. 3. Systemic grammar — Collected works. I. Kress, Gunther R. II. T. III. Title: System and function in language.
P149.H34   415   *LC* 77-359080   *ISBN* 0194371271

P151–297 Grammar

Moore, Terence.   **2.160**
Language understanding: towards a post–Chomskyan linguistics / Terence Moore and Christine Carling. — New York: St. Martin's Press, 1982. x, 225 p.; 22 cm. Includes index. 1. Chomsky, Noam. 2. Linguistics 3. Grammar, Comparative and general I. Carling, Christine. II. T.
P151.M64 1982   415 19   *LC* 82-10568   *ISBN* 0312469225

Robins, R. H. (Robert Henry)   • **2.161**
Ancient & mediaeval grammatical theory in Europe: with particular reference to modern linguistic doctrine / [by] R. H. Robins. — Port Washington, N.Y.: Kennikat Press [1971] vii, 104 p.; 21 cm. (Kennikat classics series) Reprint of the 1951 ed. 1. Grammar, Comparative and general 2. Linguistics — Research — Europe — History. I. T.
P151.R68 1971   415/.09   *LC* 71-113296   *ISBN* 0804612021

Pike, Kenneth Lee, 1912-.   • **2.162**
Language in relation to a unified theory of the structure of human behavior, by Kenneth L. Pike. 2d, rev. ed. The Hague, Mouton, 1967. 762 p. illus., port. 27 cm. (Janua linguarum. Series maior. 24) 1. Psycholinguistics 2. Human behavior I. T. II. Series.
P153.P5 1967   401.9   *LC* 67-6371

Newmeyer, Frederick J.   **2.163**
Linguistic theory in America: the first quarter–century of transformational generative grammar / Frederick J. Newmeyer. — New York: Academic Press, c1980. xiii, 290 p.: ill.; 24 cm. Includes indexes. 1. Generative grammar — History. 2. Linguistics — United States — History. I. T.
P158.N4   415   *LC* 79-27195   *ISBN* 0125171501

Radford, Andrew.   **2.164**
Transformational syntax: a student's guide to Chomsky's extended standard theory / Andrew Radford. — Cambridge; New York: Cambridge University Press, 1982 (c1981). ix, 402 p.: ill.; 24 cm. — (Cambridge textbooks in linguistics.) Includes index. 1. Chomsky, Noam. 2. Generative grammar I. T. II. Series.
P158.R3 1981   415 19   *LC* 81-10025   *ISBN* 0521242746

Jespersen, Otto, 1860-1943.   • **2.165**
The Philosophy of grammar / by Otto Jespersen. — New York: Norton, 1965. 347 p.: ill.; 20 cm. — (Norton library. N307) 1. Grammar, Comparative and general 2. Languages — Philosophy I. T. II. Series.
P201.J55 1965   415   *LC* 65-3607   *ISBN* 0393003078

Muller, Siegfried Hermann, 1902-.   • **2.166**
The world's living languages: basic facts of their structure, kinship, location, and number of speakers. New York, Ungar [1964] xii, 212 p. 21 cm. Bibliography: p. 191-194. 1. Language and languages I. T.
P201.M84   410   *LC* 64-15694

Weinreich, Uriel.   • **2.167**
Languages in contact: Findings and problems / With a pref. by André Martinet. — New York: Linguistic Circle of New York, 1953. xii, 148 p.; 24 cm. (Publications of the Linguistic Circle of New York; no. 1) I. T.
P202.W4   371.98   *LC* 53-3034

P211–214 WRITING. ALPHABET

Chappell, Warren, 1904-.   **2.168**
The living alphabet / Warren Chappell. — Charlottesville: University Press of Virginia, 1975. 49 p.: ill.; 15 x 22 cm. 1. Alphabet I. T.
P211.C47   471/.1   *LC* 75-5884

Diringer, David, 1900-.   • **2.169**
The alphabet; a key to the history of mankind. — 3d ed. completely revised with the assistance of Reinhold Regensburger. — New York: Funk & Wagnalls, [1968] 2 v.: illus.; 26 cm. Vol. 2 consists of 452 p. of illus. 1. Alphabet 2. Writing — History I. Regensburger, Reinhold. II. T.
P211.D53 1968b   411   *LC* 68-22369

Diringer, David, 1900-.   • **2.170**
Writing. New York, Praeger [1962] 261 p. illus., plates, 3 maps, facsims., tables. 21 cm. (Ancient peoples and places, v. 25) (Books that matter) 1. Writing — History I. T.
P211.D55   411   *LC* 62-8211

Gelb, Ignace J., 1907-.   • **2.171**
A study of writing. — Rev. [i.e. 2d] ed. — [Chicago]: University of Chicago Press, [1963] xix, 319 p.: illus.; 21 cm. 1. Writing — History I. T.
P211.G37 1963   411   *LC* 63-18845

Jensen, Hans, 1884-.   • **2.172**
[Geschichte der Schrift. English] Sign, symbol, and script: an account of man's efforts to write / by Hans Jensen; translated from the German by George Unwin. — 3d rev. and enl. ed. New York: Putnam [1969] 613 p.: ill. 26 cm. Translation of Geschichte der Schrift. 1. Writing — History 2. Alphabet I. T.
P211.J413 1969   411/.09   *LC* 69-13545

Staples Press, ltd., London.   **2.173**
[Staples alphabet exhibition] A history of the alphabet / [by] David Diringer, assisted by H. Freeman. — Old Woking: Unwin Bros. Ltd., 1977. 78 p.: ill.; maps; 27 cm. Originally published in 1953 under title: Staples alphabet exhibition. 1. Alphabet — History. 2. Writing — History I. Diringer, David, 1900- II. T.
P211.S67 1977   411/.09   *LC* 79-307206   *ISBN* 0905418123

Stock, Brian.   **2.174**
The implications of literacy: written language and models of interpretation in the eleventh and twelfth centuries / Brian Stock. — Princeton, N.J.: Princeton University Press, c1983. x, 604 p.; 25 cm. Includes index. 1. Written communication — Europe — History. 2. Civilization, Medieval I. T.
P211.S69 1983   001.54/3/094 19   *LC* 82-47616   *ISBN* 0691053685

P215–240 PHONETICS

Hyman, Larry M.   **2.175**
Phonology: theory and analysis / Larry M. Hyman. — New York: Holt, Rinehart and Winston, [1975] xiii, 268 p.; 24 cm. Includes indexes. 1. Grammar, Comparative and general — Phonology I. T.
P217.H9   415   *LC* 74-32172   *ISBN* 0030121418

Jakobson, Roman, 1896-.   **2.176**
The sound shape of language / by Roman Jakobson & Linda Waugh; assisted by Martha Taylor. — Bloomington: Indiana University Press, c1979. xii, 308 p.: ill.; 25 cm. Includes indexes. 1. Grammar, Comparative and general — Phonology I. Waugh, Linda R. joint author. II. T.
P217.J33   414   *LC* 78-19552   *ISBN* 0253164176

Linell, Per, 1944-.   **2.177**
Psychological reality in phonology: a theoretical study / Per Linell. — Cambridge; New York: Cambridge University Press, 1979. xvi, 295 p.: ill.; 24 cm. — (Cambridge studies in linguistics. 25 0068-676X) 1. Grammar, Comparative and general — Phonology 2. Psycholinguistics 3. Generative grammar 4. Morphophonemics I. T. II. Series.
P217.L53   414   *LC* 78-67429   *ISBN* 0521222346

Trubetskoĭ, Nikolaĭ Sergeevich, kniaz', 1890-1938.   ● **2.178**
Principles of phonology [by] N. S. Trubetzkoy. Translated by Christiane A. M. Baltaxe. — Berkeley: University of California Press, 1969. xvi, 344 p.; 24 cm. Translation of Grundzüge der Phonologie. 1. Grammar, Comparative and general — Phonology I. T.
P217.T72   414   *LC* 68-16112   *ISBN* 0520015355

Catford, John Cunnison, 1917-.   **2.179**
Fundamental problems in phonetics / by J. C. Catford. Bloomington: Indiana University Press, 1977, c1976. 278 p.: ill.; 23 cm. Includes index. 1. Phonetics 2. Speech I. T.
P221.C3 1977   414   *LC* 76-47168   *ISBN* 025332520X

Heffner, Roe-Merrill Secrist, 1892-.   ● **2.180**
General phonetics. With a foreword by W. F. Twaddell. Madison: University of Wisconsin Press, 1949 i.e. 1950. xvii, 253 p.: ill.; 24 cm. 1. Phonetics I. T.
P221.H4   *LC* 50-14864

Jakobson, Roman, 1896-.   ● **2.181**
Fundamentals of language, by Roman Jakobson and Morris Halle. 's-Gravenhage: Mouton, 1956. 87 p.; 23 cm. — (Janua linguarum, nr. 1) 1. Grammar, Comparative and general — Phonology 2. Phonetics 3. Aphasia I. Halle, Morris. II. T.
P221.J3   414   *LC* 57-888

Ladefoged, Peter.   ● **2.182**
Preliminaries to linguistic phonetics. — Chicago: University of Chicago Press, [1971] ix, 122 p.; 24 cm. Published in 1967 under title: Linguistic phonetics. 1. Phonetics I. T.
P221.L23 1971   414   *LC* 75-179318   *ISBN* 0226467864

O'Connor, J. D. (Joseph Desmond)   **2.183**
Phonetics [by] J. D. O'Connor. — Harmondsworth: Penguin, 1973. 320, [8] p.: illus.; 19 cm. Includes index. 1. Phonetics I. T.
P221.O25   414   *LC* 74-161212   *ISBN* 0140215603

Pike, Kenneth Lee, 1912-.   ● **2.184**
Phonemics: a technique for reducing languages to writing. Ann Arbor: University of Michigan P., c1947. xx, 254 p.: ill. (University of Michigan. University of Michigan publications. Linguistics; v.3.) 1. Phonetics 2. Language and languages — Phonetic transcriptions I. T. II. Series.
P221 P5   411   *LC* 48-1648   *ISBN* 0472087320

Pike, Kenneth Lee, 1912-.   ● **2.185**
Phonetics: a critical analysis of phonetic theory and a technic for the practical description of sounds / by Kenneth L. Pike. Ann Arbor: University of Michigan Press, [c1943] 3 p. l., v-ix, [1], 182, ii p.: ill.; 24 cm. (University of Michigan publications. Language and literature; Vol. xxi) 1. Phonetics I. T.
P221.P54 PN35.M5

International Phonetic Association.   ● **2.186**
The principles of the International Phonetic Association: being a description of the International phonetic alphabet and the manner of using it / illustrated by texts in 51 languages. — London, 1949. 53 p.: ill.; 22 cm. Cover title. 1. Phonetic alphabet I. T.
P227.I5   421.4   *LC* 52-17468

P241 MORPHOLOGY. SYNTAX

Elson, Benjamin Franklin, 1921-.   ● **2.187**
An introduction to morphology and syntax by Benjamin Elson and Velma Pickett. 1st edition. Santa Ana, California: Summer Institute of Linguistics, 1962. 167 p.: ill.; 28 cm. 1. Grammar, Comparative and general — Word formation 2. Grammar, Comparative and general — Syntax I. Pickett, Velma Bernice. II. T. III. Title: Morphology and syntax.
P241.E4   *LC* 65-2583

Matthews, P. H. (Peter Hugoe)   **2.188**
Morphology: an introduction to the theory of word-structure / P. H. Matthews. — London; New York: Cambridge University Press, 1974. x, 242 p.; 24 cm. (Cambridge textbooks in linguistics) 1. Grammar, Comparative and general — Morphology I. T.
P241.M3   415   *LC* 73-91817   *ISBN* 0521204488. *ISBN* 0521098564 pbk

Nida, Eugene Albert, 1914-.   ● **2.189**
Morphology, the descriptive analysis of words / Eugene A. Nida. — 2d ed. — Ann Arbor: University of Michigan Press; Rexdale, Ont.: J. Wiley & Sons Canada, 1949. xvi, 28 p.; 28 cm. 1. Grammar, Comparative and general — Word formation 2. Grammar, Comparative and general — Inflection I. T.
P241.N53 1949b   *ISBN* 0472086847

Chomsky, Noam.   ● **2.190**
Aspects of the theory of syntax. Cambridge: M.I.T. Press [1965] x, 251 p.: ill.; 21 cm. (Massachusetts Institute of Technology. Research Laboratory of Electronics. Special technical report no. 11) 1. Grammar, Comparative and general — Syntax I. T. II. Title: Theory of syntax.
P291.C4   415   *LC* 65-19080

Chomsky, Noam.   ● **2.191**
Syntactic structures. — The Hague: Mouton, 1968. 120 p.; 23 cm. — (Janua linguarum. Series minor. 4) 1. Grammar, Comparative and general — Syntax 2. Generative grammar I. T. II. Series.
P291.C5 1968   *LC* 76-490810   8.00

P301-310 Style. Translating. Interpreting

Linguistics and style / volume edited by John Spencer.   ● **2.192**
London: Oxford University Press, 1964. xii, 109 p.: ill. — (Language and language learning. 6) 1. Language and languages — Style 2. Style, Literary I. Spencer, John Walter II. Enkvist, Nils Erik. III. Gregory, Michael J. IV. Series.
P301.L55

Congrat-Butlar, Stefan.   **2.193**
Translation & translators: an international directory and guide / compiled and edited by Stefan Congrat-Butlar. — New York: R. R. Bowker Co., 1979. xi, 241 p.; 29 cm. Includes index. 1. Translating and interpreting — Handbooks, manuals, etc. 2. Translators — Directories. I. T.
P306.A2 C6   418/.02   *LC* 79-6965   *ISBN* 0835211584

Larson, Mildred L.   **2.194**
Meaning-based translation: a guide to cross-language equivalence / Mildred L. Larson. — Lanham, MD: University Press of America, c1984. x, 537 p.: ill.; 24 cm. Includes index. 1. Translating and interpreting I. T.
P306.L34 1984   418/.02 19   *LC* 84-17385   *ISBN* 0819143006

Meaning and translation: philosophical and linguistic approaches   **2.195**
/ edited by F. Guenthner and M. Guenthner-Reutter.
New York: New York University Press, 1978. 364 p.: ill.; 25 cm. Includes index. 1. Translating and interpreting 2. Semantics (Philosophy) 3. Reference (Philosophy) 4. Languages — Philosophy I. Guenthner, Franz. II. Guenthner-Reutter, M.
P306.2.M4 1978b   418/.02   *LC* 78-57003   *ISBN* 0814729746

P321-325 Etymology. Semantics

Jacobs, Noah Jonathan, 1907-.   ● **2.196**
Naming-day in Eden: the creation and recreation of language. — New York: Macmillan, 1958. 159 p.; 22 cm. 1. Language and languages — Anecdotes, facetiae, etc. 2. Names — Anecdotes, facetiae, satire, etc. I. T.
P323.J3   408.8   *LC* 58-10198

Names and their varieties: a collection of essays in onomastics /   **2.197**
compiled, with a preface, by Kelsie B. Harder; American Name Society.
Lanham, MD: University Press of America: The Society, c1986. v, 317 p.; 23 cm. 1. Onomastics — Addresses, essays, lectures. I. Harder, Kelsie B. II. American Name Society.
P323.N36 1986   412 19   *LC* 85-29628   *ISBN* 0819152323

Caton, Charles Edwin, 1928- ed.   ● **2.198**
Philosophy and ordinary language. — Urbana: University of Illinois Press, 1963. xii, 246 p.; 21 cm. 1. Semantics 2. Ordinary-language philosophy I. T.
P325.C35   401   *LC* 63-7250

Leech, Geoffrey N. 2.199
Semantics [by] Geoffrey Leech. — Harmondsworth: Penguin, 1974. xii, 386 p.: illus.; 19 cm. Includes index. 1. Semantics I. T.
P325.L36   412   *LC* 74-173945   *ISBN* 0140216944

Ullmann, Stephen, 1914-. • 2.200
The principles of semantics / by Stephen Ullmann. [2d ed. with additional material] Glasgow, Jackson [1959, c1957] xii, 348 p. diagrs. 23 cm. (Glasgow University publications, 84) Imprint covered by label: New York, Barnes & Noble. 1. Semantics I. T.
P325.U5 1959   *LC* 63-1709

Ullmann, Stephen. • 2.201
Semantics: an introduction to the science of meaning. 1st ed. New York: Barnes & Noble, 1962. 278 p.; 23 cm. 1. Semantics I. T.
P325.U52   *LC* 62-5829

Ziff, Paul. • 2.202
Semantic analysis. — Ithaca, N. Y., Cornell University Press [1960] xi, 255 p. 24 cm. 1. Semantics 2. English language — Semantics I. T.
P325.Z5   422   *LC* 60-50079

P327–365 Lexicography. General Dictionaries

Landau, Sidney I. 2.203
Dictionaries: the art and craft of lexicography / Sidney I. Landau. — New York: Scribner, c1984. xiii, 370 p.: ill.; 24 cm. 1. Lexicography I. T.
P327.L3 1984   413/.028 19   *LC* 83-27112   *ISBN* 0684180960

Britannica world language dictionary. • 2.204
[Chicago, 1958] 1483-2015 p. illus. 29 cm. 1. Dictionaries, Polyglot 2. English language — Dictionaries — Polyglot I. Encyclopædia Britannica.
P361.B7 1958   *LC* 58-4491

Acronyms, initialisms & abbreviations dictionary. 2.205
5th ed. (1976)-   . — Detroit, Mich.: Gale Research Co., 1976-. v.; 29 cm. Each volume separately titled: v. 1, Acronyms, initialisms & abbreviations dictionary; v. 2, New acronyms, initialisms & abbreviations; v. 3, Reverse acronyms, initialisms & abbreviations dictionary. Issued in 3 volumes. Vol. 1 of each ed. kept up to date by periodic supplement, designated as v. 2, with title: New acronyms, initialisms & abbreviations. 1. Acronyms 2. Abbreviations I. Gale Research Company. II. Reverse acronyms, initialisms & abbreviations dictionary. III. New acronyms, initialisms & abbreviations.
P365.A28   423/.1 19   *LC* 84-643188

P367–381 Dialectology. Linguistic Geography

Dialect and language variation / edited by Harold B. Allen, Michael D. Linn. 2.206
Orlando, Fla.: Academic Press, 1986. x, 616 p.: ill.; 23 cm. 1. Dialectology — Addresses, essays, lectures. 2. Language and languages — Variation — Addresses, essays, lectures. 3. English language — United States — Addresses, essays, lectures. I. Allen, Harold Byron, 1902- II. Linn, Michael D.
P367.D48 1986   417/.2 19   *LC* 85-48209   *ISBN* 0120511304

Francis, W. Nelson (Winthrop Nelson), 1910-. 2.207
Dialectology: an introduction / W.N. Francis. — London; New York: Longman, 1983. ix, 240 p.: ill.; 22 cm. — (Longman linguistics library. title no. 29) Includes index. 1. Dialectology I. T. II. Series.
P367.F7 1983   417/.2 19   *LC* 82-20856   *ISBN* 0582291178

Petyt, K. M. 2.208
The study of dialect: an introduction to dialectology / K.M. Petyt. — Boulder, Colo.: Westview Press, 1980. 235 p.: ill.; 23 cm. Published simultaneously in London by A. Deutsch in series: The Language library. Includes indexes. 1. Dialectology I. T.
P367.P4 1980b   417/.2 19   *LC* 80-51350   *ISBN* 0865310602

Language in the USA / edited by Charles A. Ferguson, Shirley Brice Heath, with the assistance of David Hwang; foreword by Dell H. Hymes. 2.209
Cambridge [Eng.]; New York: Cambridge University Press, 1981. xxxviii, 592: ill., maps. Includes index. 1. United States — Languages I. Ferguson, Charles Albert, 1921- II. Heath, Shirley Brice. III. Hwang, David.
P377.L3   P377 L3.   409/.73 19   *LC* 80-49985   *ISBN* 052123140X

Allen, C. G. (Charles Geoffry) 2.210
A manual of European languages for librarians / C. G. Allen. — London; New York: Bowker [for] the London School of Economics, 1976 (c1975). xiii, 803 p.; 25 cm. 1. Europe — Languages — Handbooks, manuals, etc. I. T.
P380.A4   409/.4   *LC* 73-6062   *ISBN* 0859350282

Skendi, Stavro. 2.211
Balkan cultural studies / Stavro Skendi. — Boulder, [Colo.]: East European Monographs; New York: distributed by Columbia University Press, 1980. x, 278 p.; 23 cm. — (East European monographs. no. 72) Includes index. 1. Folk literature — Balkan Peninsula — History and criticism — Addresses, essays, lectures. 2. Balkan Peninsula — Languages — Addresses, essays, lectures. 3. Balkan Peninsula — History — Addresses, essays, lectures. I. T. II. Series.
P381.B3 S55   949.6 19   *LC* 80-66058   *ISBN* 0914710664

Language in the British Isles / edited by Peter Trudgill. 2.212
Cambridge; New York: Cambridge University Press, 1984. xii, 587 p.: ill.; 24 cm. 1. Sociolinguistics — British Isles. 2. British Isles — Languages. I. Trudgill, Peter.
P381.G7 L36 1984   409/.41 19   *LC* 83-7616   *ISBN* 0521240573

Lockwood, W. B. (William Burley) 2.213
Languages of the British Isles past and present / W. B. Lockwood. — London: A. Deutsch, 1975. 262 p.; 23 cm. — (Language library.) 1. British Isles — Languages. I. T. II. Series.
P381.G7 L6   409/.41   *LC* 76-351262   *ISBN* 0233966668

Price, Glanville. 2.214
The languages of Britain / Glanville Price. — London; New York: E. Arnold, 1984. 245 p.: ill.; 24 cm. 1. Great Britain — Languages. I. T.
P381.G7 P75 1984   409/.41 19   *LC* 85-118456   *ISBN* 0713163968

Reinecke, John E. • 2.215
Language and dialect in Hawaii; a sociolinguistic history to 1935, by John E. Reinecke. Edited by Stanley M. Tsuzaki. — Honolulu: University of Hawaii Press, 1969. 254 p.: maps; 24 cm. A revision of the author's thesis, University of Hawaii, 1935. 1. Ethnology — Hawaii 2. Sociolinguistics 3. Hawaii — Languages. I. Tsuzaki, Stanley M., ed. II. T.
P381.H3 R4   427/.9/969   *LC* 70-89651   *ISBN* 0870226940

Lewis, E. Glyn. 2.216
Multilingualism in the Soviet Union. Aspects of language policy and its implementation. [By] E. Glyn Lewis. The Hague, Mouton, 1972 [1973]. xx, 332 p. fold. map. 24 cm. (Contributions to the sociology of language. 3) 1. Sociolinguistics 2. Languages — Political aspects 3. Multilingualism — Soviet Union. 4. Soviet Union — Languages I. T. II. Series.
P381.R8 L4 1973   301.2/1   *LC* 72-88222

Matthews, William Kleesmann, 1901-1958. • 2.217
Languages of the U.S.S.R. / by W. K. Matthews. New York: Russell & Russell [1968] ix, 178 p.: ill., maps.; 23 cm. Reprint of the 1951 ed. 1. Soviet Union — Languages I. T.
P381.R8 M3 1968   409.47   *LC* 68-11328

P501–769 Comparative Indo–European Philology

Lehmann, Winfred Philipp, 1916- comp. • 2.218
A reader in nineteenth century historical Indo–European linguistics. Edited and translated by Winfred P. Lehmann. Bloomington, Indiana University Press [1967] vi, 266 p. illus. 25 cm. (Indiana University studies in the history and theory of linguistics) 1. Indo-European languages — Addresses, essays and lectures. I. T.
P511.L4   *LC* 67-63012

Sommerfelt, Alf, 1892-. • 2.219
Diachronic and synchronic aspects of language; selected articles. 's-Gravenhage, Mouton, 1962. 421 p. (Janua linguarum. Series maior, 7) French or English. 1. Language and languages — Addresses, essays, lectures. I. T.
P513.S6   408   *LC* 63-3733

Baldi, Philip.   **2.220**
An introduction to the Indo–European languages / by Philip Baldi. — Carbondale: Southern Illinois University Press, c1983. xiv, 214 p.; 24 cm. Includes indexes. 1. Indo-European languages I. T.
P561.B3 1983   410 19   *LC* 82-19218   *ISBN* 0809310902

Hudson-Williams, Thomas, 1873-.   • **2.221**
A Short introduction to the study of comparative grammar (Indo–European) / by T. Hudson–Williams. — Cardiff: University of Wales Press Board, 1935. x, 78 p.; 19 cm. 1. Indo-European languages — Grammar, Comparative I. T.
P575.H8   *LC* 36-11697

Lehmann, Winfred Philipp, 1916-.   **2.222**
Proto–Indo–European syntax / by Winfred P. Lehmann. — Austin: University of Texas Press, [1974] x, 278 p.; 23 cm. 1. Proto-Indo-European language — Syntax. I. T.
P671.L4   417/.7   *LC* 74-10526   *ISBN* 0292764197

Bréal, Michel, 1832-1915.   • **2.223**
[Essai de sémantique. English] Semantics: studies in the science of meaning, by Michel Bréal. Translated by Mrs. Henry Cust. With a new introd. by Joshua Whatmough. New York, Dover Publications [1964] lxxviii, 341 p. 22 cm. Translation of Essai de sémantique. 'Unabridged and unaltered republication of the work first published by Henry Holt & Company in 1900.' 1. Indo-European languages — Semantics. 2. Language and languages I. T.
P741.B8 1964   412   *LC* 64-18841

Buck, Carl Darling, 1866-1955.   • **2.224**
A dictionary of selected synonyms in the principal Indo–European languages; a contribution to the history of ideas, by Carl Darling Buck. With the co-operation of colleagues and assistants. — Chicago: University of Chicago Press, [1949] xix, 1515 p.; 25 cm. 1. Indo-European languages — Glossaries, vocabularies, etc. 2. Indo-European languages — Semantics. 3. Indo-European languages — Etymology. I. T.
P765.B8   413 19   *LC* 49-11769

P901–1099 Extinct Languages

Doblhofer, Ernst.   • **2.225**
[Zeichen und Wunder. English] Voices in stone: the decipherment of ancient scripts and writings / translated by Mervyn Savill. — Clifton [N.J.] A. M. Kelley, 1973 [c1961] 327 p.: ill.; 22 cm. (Viking reprint editions) Translation of Zeichen und Wunder. Reprint of the ed. published by Viking Press, New York. 1. Extinct languages 2. Alphabet 3. Writing — History I. T.
P901.D613 1973   417/.7   *LC* 71-122076   *ISBN* 0678031525

Friedrich, Johannes, 1893-1972.   • **2.226**
[Entzifferung verschollener Schriften und Sprachen. English] Extinct languages. Westport, Conn., Greenwood Press [1971, c1957] x, 182 p. illus. 23 cm. Translation of Entzifferung verschollener Schriften und Sprachen. 1. Extinct languages 2. Inscriptions — History. 3. Writing — History I. T.
P901.F713 1971   417/.7   *LC* 74-139132   *ISBN* 083715748X

Chadwick, John, 1920-.   • **2.227**
The decipherment of linear B. — 2nd ed. — London: Cambridge U.P., 1967 [i.e. 1968]. x, 164 p.: 3 plates (1 fold.), illus., map, port.; 22 cm. 1. Ventris, Michael. 2. Inscriptions, Linear B I. T.
P1035.C5 1968   481/.7   *LC* 67-26066   30/-

Bonfante, Giuliano.   **2.228**
The Etruscan language: an introduction / Giuliano Bonfante and Larissa Bonfante. — New York: New York University Press, 1983. ix, 174 p.; 22 cm. Includes index. 1. Etruscan language I. Bonfante, Larissa. II. T.
P1078.B58 1983   499/.94 19   *LC* 83-13219   *ISBN* 0814710476

PA Classical Languages and Literatures

PA1–999 CLASSICAL LANGUAGES (GENERAL)

Feder, Lillian. • 2.229
Crowell's handbook of classical literature / by Lillian Feder. — New York: Crowell, 1964. viii, 448 p.: maps; 23 cm. — (A Crowell reference book) 1. Classical literature — Dictionaries. I. T. II. Title: Handbook of classical literature.
PA31.F4   880.3   *LC* 64-18162   *ISBN* 0690225377

Grant, Michael, 1914-. 2.230
Greek and Latin authors, 800 B.C.–A.D. 1000 / by Michael Grant. — New York: H. W. Wilson Co., 1980. xiv, 490 p.: ports.; 27 cm. — (The Wilson authors series) 1. Classical literature — Dictionaries. I. T.
PA31.G7   880/.9 920   *LC* 79-27446   *ISBN* 0824206401

Sandys, John Edwin, Sir, 1844-1922. • 2.231
A history of classical scholarship. — New York: Hafner Pub. Co., 1958. 3 v.: illus., ports.; 22 cm. 1. Classical philology — History. 2. Learning and scholarship I. T.
PA51.S3 1958   880.9   *LC* 58-11720

Rademaker, C. S. M. 2.232
[Gerardus Joannes Vossius (1577–1649). English] Life and work of Gerardus Joannes Vossius (1577–1649) / C.S.M. Rademaker. — Assen: Van Gorcum, 1981. xxvii, 462 p.: port.; 25 cm. — (Respublica literaria Neerlandica. 5) Translation of: Gerardus Joannes Vossius (1577-1649) 1. Vossius, Gerardus Joannes, 1577-1649. 2. Humanists — Netherlands — Biography. I. T. II. Series.
PA85.V6 R313   480/.092/4 B 19   *LC* 81-174574   *ISBN* 9023217853

Halporn, James W. • 2.233
The meters of Greek and Latin poetry by James W. Halporn, Martin Ostwald and Thomas G. Rosenmeyer. Indianapolis, Bobbs-Merrill, 1963. vii, 2, 137 p. 21 cm. (Library of liberal arts.) 1. Greek language — Metrics and rhythmics 2. Latin language — Metrics and rhythmics I. T. II. Series.
PA186.H25   *LC* 62-21264

PA201–1179 GREEK

Smyth, Herbert Weir, 1857-1937. • 2.234
Greek grammar. Rev. by Gordon M. Messing. Cambridge, Harvard University Press, 1956. 784 p. 21 cm. First published in 1916 under title: A Greek grammar for schools and colleges. 1. Greek language — Grammar. I. Messing, Gordon M. II. T.
PA 254 S66   *LC* 57-2203

Stanford, William Bedell. • 2.235
The sound of Greek; studies in the Greek theory and practice of euphony, by W. B. Stanford. — Berkeley: University of California Press, 1967. vi, 177 p. and phonodisc (2 s. 7 in. 33 1/3 rpm. microgroove) in pocket; 27 cm. — (Sather classical lectures. v. 38) 1. Greek language — Phonology. I. T. II. Series.
PA265.S7   481/.5   *LC* 67-12491

Allen, W. Sidney (William Sidney), 1918-. • 2.236
Vox Graeca: a guide to the pronunciation of classical Greek, by W. Sidney Allen. — London: Cambridge U.P., 1968. xvi, 157 p.: plate, 2 illus.; 23 cm. 1. Greek language — Pronunciation. I. T.
PA267.A4   481/.5   *LC* 68-10327   *ISBN* 0521040213

Sturtevant, Edgar Howard, 1875-1952. • 2.237
The pronunciation of Greek and Latin. 2d ed. Philadelphia Linguistic Society of America, University of Pennsylvania 1940. 192p. (William Dwight Whitney Linguistic series, v. 7) 1. Greek language — Pronunciation 2. Latin language — Pronunciation I. T.
PA267 S8 1940

Havelock, Eric Alfred. 2.238
The literate revolution in Greece and its cultural consequences / Eric A. Havelock. — Princeton, N.J.: Princeton University Press, c1982. viii, 362 p.: ill.; 22 cm. — (Princeton series of collected essays.) 1. Greek language — Alphabet 2. Oral tradition 3. Greek literature — History and criticism. 4. Oral-formulaic analysis I. T. II. Series.
PA273.H27 1982   481 19   *LC* 81-47133   *ISBN* 0691093962

Denniston, J. D. (John Dewar), 1887-1949. • 2.239
The Greek particles / by J. D. Denniston. — 2d ed. Oxford: Clarendon Press, 1954. lxxxii, 658 p. 1. Greek language — Particles. I. T.
PA351.D4 1954   485.9   *LC* 54-11585

Dover, Kenneth James. • 2.240
Greek word order / by K.J. Dover. Cambridge [Eng.] University Press, 1960. xiii, 72 p. Based on the J. H. Grey lectures, Cambridge University, 1959. 1. Greek language — Word order. I. T.
PA 373 D6   485.3   *LC* 61-16008

Denniston, J. D. (John Dewar), 1887-1949. • 2.241
Greek prose style / by J. D. Denniston. — Oxford: Clarendon Press, 1952. x, 139 p.; 23 cm. 1. Greek language — Style. I. T.
PA401.D4   880/.9   *LC* 53-2343

Stanford, William Bedell. • 2.242
Ambiguity in Greek literature; studies in theory and practice. Oxford Blackwell 1939. 185p. 1. Greek language — Style I. T.
PA401 S8   *LC* 41-13798

Stanford, William Bedell. • 2.243
Greek metaphor, studies in theory and practice. Oxford B. Blackwell 1936. 156p. 1. Greek language — Figures of speech 2. Metaphor I. T.
PA404 M4 S8   *LC* 37-11815

Maas, Paul, 1880-. • 2.244
Greek metre / by Paul Maas; translated by Hugh Lloyd–Jones. — Oxford: Clarendon Press, 1962. 116 p.; 19 cm. 1. Greek language — Metrics and rhythmics I. T.
PA411.M33 1962   486   *LC* 62-51368

Raven, D. S. • 2.245
Greek metre; an introduction. London Faber and Faber [1962] 125p. 1. Greek language — Metrics and rhythmics I. T.
PA415 L9 R3   *LC* 66-4924

Ostwald, Martin, 1922-. • 2.246
Nomos and the beginnings of the Athenian democracy. — Oxford: Clarendon P., 1969. xiv, 228 p.; 23 cm. 1. Nomos (The word) 2. Greek language — Semantics. 3. Greece — Politics and government — To 146 B.C. I. T.
PA430.N6 O8   482   *LC* 70-415889   *ISBN* 0198142773

Liddell, Henry George, 1811-1898. 2.247
A Greek–English lexicon, compiled by Henry George Liddell and Robert Scott. — Rev. and augm. throughout by Sir Henry Stuart Jones, with the assistance of Roderick McKenzie and with the co-operation of many scholars. With a supplement, 1968. — Oxford: Clarendon Press, [1968] xlv, 2042, xi, 153 p.; 30 cm. Reprint of the 9th ed. (1925-1940) with a new supplement edited by E. A. Barber and others. 1. Greek language — Dictionaries — English. I. Scott, Robert, 1811-1887, joint author. II. Jones, Henry Stuart, 1867-1939, ed. III. McKenzie, Roderick, 1887-1937, ed. IV. Barber, Eric Arthur, 1888- ed. V. T.
PA445.E5 L6 1968   483/.2   *LC* 71-2271

Blass, Friedrich Wilhelm, 1843-1907. • 2.248
[Grammatik des neutestamentlichen Griechisch. English] A Greek grammar of the New Testament and other early Christian literature [by] F. Blass and A. Debrunner. A translation and revision of the 9th–10th German ed., incorporating supplementary notes of A. Debrunner, by Robert W. Funk. [Chicago] University of Chicago Press [1961] xxxvii, 325 p. 27 cm. 1. Greek language, Biblical — Grammar. I. Debrunner, Albert, 1884- joint author. II. Funk, Robert Walter, 1926- ed. and tr. III. T.
PA813.B513 1961   487.3   *LC* 61-8077

Kittel, Gerhard, 1888-1948. ed. • 2.249
[Theologisches Wörterbuch zum Neuen Testament. English] Theological dictionary of the New Testament / translator and editor: Geoffrey W. Bromiley. — Grand Rapids, Mich.: Eerdmans [1964-. v. 25 cm. Vol. 5- edited by Gerhard Friedrich. 1. Bible. N.T — Dictionaries. 2. Greek language,

Biblical — Dictionaries I. Bromiley, Geoffrey William. ed. and tr. II. Friedrich, Gerhard, 1908- ed. III. T.
PA881.K513   487.3   LC 64-15136   *ISBN* 0802822509

Pring, J. T. (Julian Talbot)   • 2.250
The Oxford dictionary of modern Greek (Greek–English) / compiled by J.T. Pring. — Oxford: Clarendon Press, 1965. xiv, 219 p.; 20 cm. 1. Greek language, Modern — Dictionaries — English I. T.
PA1139.E5 P76   LC 65-9620

PA2001–2995 LATIN

Hammond, Mason.   2.251
Latin: a historical and linguistic handbook / [by] Mason Hammond. Cambridge, Mass.; London: Harvard University Press, 1976. xi, 292 p.; 24 cm. Index. 1. Latin language I. T.
PA2057.H3   470   LC 75-33359   *ISBN* 0674512901

Palmer, Leonard Robert.   • 2.252
The Latin language / by L.R. Palmer. — London: Faber and Faber, 1954. viii, 372 p.: map; 23 cm. — (The Great languages) Includes indexes. 1. Latin language — History. 2. Latin language — Grammar — 1870- I. T.
PA2071.P26 1954   470   LC 54-3075   *ISBN* 0571068138

Allen, Joseph Henry, 1820-1898.   2.253
[New Latin grammar] Allen and Greenough's New Latin grammar for schools and colleges, founded on comparative grammar / edited by J. B. Greenough ... [et. al.]. — New Rochelle, N.Y.: Caratzas Bros., 1979. x, 490 p.; 22 cm. (College classical series.) Reprint of the 1903 ed. published by Ginn, Boston. 1. Latin language — Grammar — 1870-1975 I. Greenough, J. B. (James Bradstreet), 1833-1901. II. T. III. Title: New Latin grammar for schools and colleges, founded on comparative grammar. IV. Series.
PA2087.A525 1979   478.2/421 19   LC 80-19039   *ISBN* 0892410019

Woodcock, Eric Charles.   • 2.254
A new Latin syntax. — Cambridge: Harvard University Press, [1959] 267 p.; 23 cm. 1. Latin language — Syntax I. T.
PA2285.W6   LC 60-1729

Lindsay, W. M. (Wallace Martin), 1858-1937.   • 2.255
Early Latin verse. Oxford Clarendon Press 1922. 372p. 1. Plautus, Titus Maccius. 2. Menander, of Athens. 3. Latin language — Metrics and rhythmics 4. Latin language, Preclassical to ca. 100 B.C. I. T.
PA2329 L5   LC 23-8438

Raven, D. S.   • 2.256
Latin metre, an introduction. London Faber and Faber [1965] 182p. 1. Latin language — Metrics and rhythmics I. T.
PA2329 R3   LC 65-84643

Platnauer, Maurice.   • 2.257
Latin elegiac verse; a study of the metrical usages of Tibullus, Propertius & Ovid. Hamden, Conn., Archon Books, 1971. viii, 121, [1] p. 20 cm. Reprint of the 1951 ed. 1. Tibullus. 2. Propertius, Sextus. 3. Ovid, 43 B.C.-17 or 18 A.D — Versification. 4. Latin language — Metrics and rhythmics 5. Elegiac poetry, Latin — History and criticism. I. T.
PA2335.E5 P6 1971   476   LC 79-143886   *ISBN* 0208011161

Andrews, E. A. (Ethan Allen), 1787-1858.   • 2.258
A Latin dictionary founded on Andrews' edition of Freund's Latin dictionary. Rev. Oxford, Clarendon Press [1955] xiv, 2019 p. 26 cm. 1. Latin language — Dictionaries — English. I. Freund, William, 1806-1894. II. Lewis, Charlton Thomas, 1834-1904. III. Short, Charles, 1821-1886. IV. T.
PA2365.E5 A7 1955   LC 56-58003

Oxford Latin dictionary / edited by P.G.W. Glare.   2.259
Oxford [Oxfordshire]: Clarendon Press; New York: Oxford University Press, 1982, c1968-c1982. xxiii, 2126 p.; 32 cm. 1. Latin language — Dictionaries — English. I. Glare, P. G. W.
PA2365.E5 O9 1982   473/.21 19   LC 82-8162   *ISBN* 0198642245

Cassell's new Latin dictionary. Latin–English, English–Latin by D. P. Simpson.   • 2.260
New York: Funk & Wagnalls, [1960, c1959] xviii, 883 p.; 24 cm. Originally published under title: Cassell's new Latin-English, English-Latin dictionary. 1. Latin language — Dictionaries — English. 2. English language — Dictionaries — Latin. I. Simpson, D. P. ed.
PA2365.L3 C3 1960   473.2   LC 60-7805

PA3000–3049 CLASSICAL LITERATURES (GENERAL)

Fifty years (and twelve) of classical scholarship; being Fifty years of classical scholarship, revised with appendices.   • 2.261
[2d ed.]. — New York: Barnes & Noble, 1968. xiv, 523 p.: illus.; 23 cm. First ed., 1954, edited by Maurice Platnauer, has title: Fifty years of classical scholarship. 1. Classical literature — History and criticism. 2. Authors, Greek 3. Authors, Latin I. Platnauer, Maurice. Fifty years of classical scholarship.
PA3001.F5 1968   LC 68-5952

Hadas, Moses, 1900-1966.   • 2.262
Ancilla to classical reading. — New York: Columbia University Press, 1954. 397 p.; 24 cm. — (Columbia bicentennial editions and studies) 1. Classical literature — History and criticism. 2. Authors, Greek 3. Authors, Latin 4. Authorship 5. Classical philology — History. I. T.
PA3001.H3   880.9   LC 54-6132

Grube, G. M. A. (George Maximilian Anthony)   2.263
The Greek and Roman critics [by] G. M. A. Grube. Toronto, University of Toronto Press [1965] xi, 372 p. 23 cm. Bibliography: p. [357]-364. 1. Criticism — Greece. 2. Criticism — Rome. I. T.
PA3013.G7   801.950938   LC 65-5311

Russell, D. A. (Donald Andrew) comp.   2.264
Ancient literary criticism: the principal texts in new translations; edited by D. A. Russell and M. Winterbottom. Oxford, Clarendon Press, 1972. xvi, 607 p. 22 cm. 1. Criticism — Greece. 2. Criticism — Rome. I. Winterbottom, Michael. joint comp. II. T.
PA3013.R8   801/.95/0938   LC 72-179197   *ISBN* 0198143591

Walsh, George B., 1946-.   2.265
The varieties of enchantment: early Greek views of the nature and function of poetry / George B. Walsh. — Chapel Hill: University of North Carolina Press, c1984. ix, 170 p.; 21 cm. 1. Greek literature — History and criticism. 2. Poetics I. T.
PA3015.P62 W36 1984   881/.01/09 19   LC 83-6467   *ISBN* 0807815764

Romilly, Jacqueline de.   • 2.266
Time in Greek tragedy. — Ithaca, N.Y.: Cornell University Press, [1968] viii, 180 p.; 23 cm. — (Messenger lectures on the evolution of civilization, 1967) Revised version published in French (Paris, 1971) under title: Le temps dans la tragédie grecque. 1. Greek drama (Tragedy) — History and criticism. 2. Time in literature I. T.
PA3015.T6 R6   882/.0093   LC 68-16380

Bowra, C. M. (Cecil Maurice), 1898-1971.   • 2.267
Greek lyric poetry from Aleman to Simonides. — 2d rev. ed. — Oxford, Clarendon Press, 1961. 444 p. 22 cm. 1. Greek poetry — Hist. & crit. 2. Poets, Greek I. T.
PA3019.B6 1961   884.09   LC 61-1937

Hathorn, Richmond Yancey, 1917-.   • 2.268
Crowell's handbook of classical drama, by Richmond Y. Hathorn. — New York: Crowell, [1967] 350 p.: maps.; 24 cm. — (A Crowell reference book) 1. Classical drama — History and criticism. I. T. II. Title: Handbook of classical drama.
PA3024.H35   882/.003   LC 67-12403

Anderson, Graham.   2.269
Ancient fiction: the novel in the Graeco–Roman world / Graham Anderson. — Totowa, N.J.: Barnes & Noble, 1984. vii, 248 p.; 23 cm. Includes index. 1. Classical fiction — History and criticism. 2. Fiction — Technique I. T.
PA3040.A47 1984   883/.01/09 19   LC 84-12319   *ISBN* 0389205168

Hägg, Tomas.   2.270
[Antika romanen. English] The novel in antiquity / Tomas Hägg. — English ed. / revised by the author for the English edition. — Berkeley: University of California Press, c1983. xii, 264 p.: ill.; 24 cm. Translation of: Den antika romanen. Maps on lining papers. Includes index. 1. Classical fiction — History and criticism. I. T.
PA3040.H2813 1983   883/.01/09 19   LC 82-45906   *ISBN* 0520049233

Perry, B. E. (Ben Edwin), 1892-1968.   • 2.271
The ancient romances: a literary–historical account of their origins. Berkeley, University of California Press, 1967. xii, 407 p. 24 cm. (Sather classical lectures. v. 37) 1. Classical fiction — History and criticism. I. T. II. Series.
PA3040.P4   880/.09   LC 67-63003

Momigliano, Arnaldo.   2.272
The development of Greek biography; four lectures. — Cambridge, Mass.: Harvard University Press, 1971. 127 p.; 22 cm. 'Lectures are substantially published as they were delivered at Harvard University as the Carl Newell Jackson classical lectures in April 1968.' 1. Biography (as a literary form) 2. Greek literature — History and criticism. I. T.
PA3043.M6   888/.01/09   LC 73-139716   ISBN 0674200403

Stuart, Duane Reed, 1873-1941.   • 2.273
Epochs of Greek and Roman biography. — New York: Biblo and Tannen, 1967. vii, 270 p.; 23 cm. Reprint of the 1928 ed. 1. Biography (as a literary form) 2. Greek literature — History and criticism. 3. Latin literature — History and criticism. I. T.
PA3043.S8 1967   880/.09   LC 67-19532

PA3050–4500 GREEK (ANCIENT, TO 600 A.D.)

PA3051–3281 Literary History

Beye, Charles Rowan.   2.274
Ancient Greek literature and society / Charles Rowan Beye. — 1st ed. — Garden City, N.Y.: Anchor Press, 1975. 469 p.; 18 cm. Includes index. 1. Greek literature — History and criticism. I. T.
PA3052.B4   PA3052 B4.   880/.9   LC 74-21235   ISBN 0385064438

Greek literature / edited by P.E. Easterling and B.M.W. Knox.   2.275
Cambridge [Cambridgeshire]; New York: Cambridge University Press, 1985. xv, 936 p., [8] p. of plates: ill.; 24 cm. (Cambridge history of classical literature. 1) 1. Greek literature — History and criticism. I. Easterling, P. E. II. Knox, Bernard MacGregor Walker. III. Series.
PA3052.G73 1985   880/.9 19   LC 82-22048   ISBN 0521210429

Hadas, Moses, 1900-1966.   • 2.276
A history of Greek literature. — New York: Columbia University Press, 1950. vi, 327 p.; 24 cm. 1. Greek literature — History and criticism. I. T.
PA3052.H3 1950   880.9   LC 50-7015

Rose, H. J. (Herbert Jennings), 1883-1961.   • 2.277
A handbook of Greek literature, from Homer to the age of Lucian. [4th ed. rev.] London Methuen [1950] 454p. 1. Greek literature — History and criticism I. T.
PA3052 R6 1950   LC 52-188

Trypanis, C. A. (Constantine Athanasius), 1909-.   2.278
Greek poetry: from Homer to Seferis / by C.A. Trypanis. — Chicago: University of Chicago Press, 1981. 896 p.; 26 cm. Includes index. 1. Greek poetry — History and criticism. 2. Byzantine poetry — History and criticism. 3. Greek poetry, Modern — History and criticism. I. T.
PA3052.T7 1981b   881/.009 19   LC 81-1160   ISBN 0226813169

Kitto, Humphrey Davy Findley.   • 2.279
Poiesis: structure and thought / by H. D. F. Kitto. — Berkeley: University of California Press, 1966. x, 407 p.; 24 cm. — (Sather classical lectures. v. 36) 1. Shakespeare, William, 1564-1616. Coriolanus 2. Greek literature — History and criticism. I. T. II. Series.
PA3054.K5   880.9   LC 66-15665

Romilly, Jacqueline de.   2.280
[Précis de littérature grecque. English] A short history of Greek literature / Jacqueline de Romilly; translated by Lillian Doherty. — Chicago: University of Chicago Press, 1985. xii, 293 p.: map; 24 cm. Translation of: Précis de littérature grecque. Includes index. 1. Greek literature — History and criticism. I. T.
PA3055.R6513 1985   880/.9 19   LC 84-16457   ISBN 0226143112

Lesky, Albin, 1896-.   • 2.281
History of Greek literature / Albin Lesky; translated by James Willes and Cornelis de Heer. — New York: Crowell, 1966. xviii, 921 p. 1. Greek literature — History and criticism. I. T.
PA3057.L413 1966   880.9001   LC 65-25033   ISBN 069038372X

Lefkowitz, Mary R., 1935-.   2.282
The lives of the Greek poets / Mary R. Lefkowitz. — Baltimore, Md.: Johns Hopkins University Press, 1981. xi, 187 p.; 23 cm. Includes index. 1. Poets, Greek — Biography. I. T.
PA3064.L44 1981   881/.01/9 B 19   LC 81-83450   ISBN 0801827485

Webster, T. B. L. (Thomas Bertram Lonsdale), 1905-1974.   • 2.283
Greek art and literature, 700–530 B.C.; the beginnings of modern civilization [by] T. B. L. Webster. — London: Methuen, [1959] xviii, 125 p.: illus.; 22 cm. — (De Carle lectures, 1959) 1. Greek literature — History and criticism. 2. Art, Greek 3. Art and literature I. T.
PA3079.W4x   709.38   LC 79-1355   22/6

Courcelle, Pierre Paul, 1912-.   • 2.284
[Lettres grecques en Occident. English] Late Latin writers and their Greek sources [by] Pierre Courcelle. Translated by Harry E. Wedeck. Cambridge, Mass., Harvard University Press, 1969. x, 467 p. 25 cm. Translation of Les lettres grecques en Occident, de Macrobe à Cassiodore. 1. Greek literature, Hellenistic — History and criticism. 2. Christian literature, Early — History and criticism. I. T.
PA3081.C753 1969   870.9/001   LC 69-12721

PA3092–3129 POETRY

Symonds, John Addington, 1840-1893.   2.285
Studies of the Greek poets. 3d ed. London, A. and C. Black, 1920. 593 p. 23 cm. 1. Greek poetry — History and criticism. I. T.
PA3092.S8 1920   881.09   LC 63-6780 rev

Burnett, Anne Pippin, 1925-.   2.286
Three archaic poets: Archilochus, Alcaeus, Sappho / Anne Pippin Burnett. — Cambridge, Mass.: Harvard University Press, 1983. 320 p.; 25 cm. 1. Archilochus — Criticism and interpretation. 2. Alcaeus — Criticism and interpretation. 3. Sappho — Criticism and interpretation. 4. Greek poetry — History and criticism. I. T.
PA3105.B87 1983   884/.01/09 19   LC 83-157   ISBN 0674888200

Murray, Gilbert, 1866-1957.   • 2.287
The rise of the Greek epic. — [4th ed.]. — New York, Oxford University Press, 1960. 356 p. 21 cm. — (A Galaxy book GB41) 1. Homer — Criticism and interpretation. 2. Epic poetry, Greek — Hist. & crit. I. T.
PA3105.M85 1960   883.09   LC 60-13910

Campbell, David A.   2.288
The golden lyre: the themes of the Greek lyric poets / David A. Campbell. — London: Duckworth, 1983. 312 p.; 24 cm. Includes indexes. 1. Greek poetry — History and criticism. 2. Greek poetry 3. Greek poetry — Translations into English. 4. English prose literature — Translations from Greek. 5. Lyric poetry — Themes, motives. I. T.
PA3110.C25 1983   884/.01/09 19   LC 83-211575   ISBN 0715615637

PA3131–3251 DRAMA. THEATER

Ferguson, John, 1921-.   2.289
A companion to Greek tragedy. — Austin: University of Texas Press, [1972] xi, 623 p.: illus.; 23 cm. 1. Greek drama (Tragedy) — History and criticism. 2. Greek drama (Satyr play) — History and criticism. I. T.
PA3131.F4   882/.01/09   LC 74-38380   ISBN 0292710003

Kitto, Humphrey Davy Findley.   • 2.290
Form and meaning in drama; a study of six Greek plays and of Hamlet. — London, Methuen; New York, Barnes & Noble [1960] 341 p. 21 cm. — (University paperbacks, UP-2) 1. Shakespeare, William, 1564-1616. Hamlet 2. Greek drama (Tragedy) — History and criticism. I. T.
PA3131.K48 1960   882.09   LC 60-51546

Kitto, Humphrey Davy Findley.   • 2.291
Greek tragedy, a literary study. — [3d ed.]. — New York: Barnes & Noble, [1961] 399 p.; 23 cm. 1. Greek drama (Tragedy) — History and criticism. I. T.
PA3131.K5 1961   882.09   LC 61-66643

Lesky, Albin, 1896-. • **2.292**
Greek tragedy / Albin Lesky; translated by H.A. Frankfort; with foreword by E.G. Turner. — [1st English ed.] — London: E. Benn; New York: Barnes & Noble, [1965]. xiii, 229 p.; 22 cm. 1. Greek drama (Tragedy) — History and criticism. I. T.
PA3131.L3913 1965   882   *LC* 65-9616

Pickard-Cambridge, Arthur Wallace, Sir, 1873-1952. • **2.293**
Dithyramb, tragedy and comedy / by the late Sir Arthur Pickard–Cambridge. — 2d ed. rev. by T. B. L. Webster. — Oxford: Clarendon Press, 1962. 334 p.: ill. Greek texts: p. [291]-299. 1. Dithyramb. 2. Greek drama (Tragedy) — History and criticism. 3. Greek drama (Comedy) — History and criticism. I. T.
PA3131.P5 1962   882   *LC* 62-6351

Vickers, Brian. **2.294**
Towards Greek tragedy: drama, myth, society / Brian Vickers. — London: Longman, 1973. xv, 658 p., [4] leaves of plates: ill.; 23 cm. (His Comparative tragedy; 1) Includes index. 1. Greek drama (Tragedy) — History and criticism. 2. Drama I. T. II. Series.
PN1892.V45 vol. 1 PA3131   PA3131 V5.   809.2/51 s 882/.01/09   *LC* 75-309385   *ISBN* 0582504473

Greek tragedy / edited for the Department of Classics by T. F. **2.295**
Gould and C. J. Herington.
Cambridge; New York: Cambridge University Press, 1977. ix, 350 p.: 24 cm. (Yale classical studies. v. 25) 1. Greek drama (Tragedy) — History and criticism — Addresses, essays, lectures. I. Gould, Thomas. II. Herington, C. J. III. Series.
PA25.Y3 vol. 25 PA3133.G7x   870/.9 s 882/.01   *LC* 76-8156
   ISBN 0521211123

Lattimore, Richmond Alexander, 1906-. • **2.296**
Story patterns in Greek tragedy [by] Richmond Lattimore. — Ann Arbor: University of Michigan Press, [1964] 106 p.; 21 cm. 1. Greek drama (Tragedy) — History and criticism. I. T.
PA3133.L3   882.09   *LC* 64-10298

Herington, C. J. **2.297**
Poetry into drama: early tragedy and the Greek poetic tradition / by John Herington. — Berkeley: University of California Press, c1985. xiv, 292 p.; 24 cm. (Sather classical lectures. v. 49) Includes index. 1. Greek drama (Tragedy) — History and criticism. 2. Greek poetry — History and criticism. 3. Performing arts — Greece — History. 4. Tragic, The I. T. II. Series.
PA3135.H47 1985   882/.01/09 19   *LC* 83-9146   *ISBN* 0520051009

Walcot, Peter. **2.298**
Greek drama in its theatrical and social context / Peter Walcot. — Cardiff: University of Wales Press, 1976. 112 p. 1. Greek drama I. T.
PA3136.W34   PA3136 W34.   *ISBN* 0708306020 pa

Sandbach, F. H. **2.299**
The comic theatre of Greece and Rome / F. H. Sandbach. — New York: Norton, c1977. 168 p.; 20 cm. — (Ancient culture and society) Includes index. 1. Classical drama (Comedy) — History and criticism. I. T.
PA3161.S2   882/.009   *LC* 77-3141   *ISBN* 0393044831

Henderson, Jeffrey. **2.300**
The maculate muse: obscene language in Attic comedy / Jeffrey Henderson. — New Haven: Yale University Press, 1975. xii, 251 p.; 25 cm. Includes indexes. 1. Greek drama (Comedy) — History and criticism. 2. Greek language — Semantics. 3. Sex — Terminology. I. T.
PA3166.H4   882/.01/0935   *LC* 74-82746   *ISBN* 0300017863

Arnott, Peter D. • **2.301**
Greek scenic conventions in the fifth century B.C. / by Peter Arnott. — Oxford: Clarendon Press, 1962. ix, 147 p.; 23 cm. 1. Theater — Greece I. T.
PA3201.A75 1978   792/.0938

Arnott, Peter D. • **2.302**
An introduction to the Greek theatre. With a foreword by H. D. F. Kitto. — London: Macmillan; New York: St. Martin's Press, 1959. 239 p.: illus.; 23 cm. 1. Theater — Greece I. T.
PA3201.A76   792.0938   *LC* 59-1584

Bieber, Margarete, 1879-. • **2.303**
The history of the Greek and Roman theater. — [2d ed., rev. and enl.]. — Princeton, N.J.: Princeton University Press, 1961. xiv, 343 p.: illus., plans.; 29 cm. 1. Theater — Greece 2. Theater — Rome. 3. Theaters — Greece 4. Theaters — Rome. 5. Art, Classical 6. Art, Roman I. T.
PA3201.B52 1961   882.09   *LC* 60-9367

Pickard-Cambridge, Arthur Wallace, Sir, 1873-1952. • **2.304**
The dramatic festivals of Athens, by the late Sir Arthur Pickard–Cambridge. — 2nd ed. Revised by John Gould and D. M. Lewis. — London: Oxford U.P., 1968. iii-xxiv, 358 p.: 72 plates, illus.; 24 cm. 1. Theater — Greece 2. Greek

drama — History and criticism. I. Gould, John, 1927- II. Lewis, David Malcolm. III. T.
PA3201.P5 1968   792/.0938   *LC* 68-106615   *ISBN* 0198142587

Taplin, Oliver Paul. **2.305**
Greek tragedy in action / by Oliver Taplin. — Berkeley: University of California Press, c1978. x, 203 p., [4] leaves of plates: ill.; 23 cm. Includes indexes. 1. Theater — Greece 2. Greek drama (Tragedy) — History and criticism. I. T.
PA3201.T3   PA3201 T3.   882/.051   *LC* 77-76184   *ISBN* 0520037049

Walton, J. Michael, 1939-. **2.306**
Greek theatre practice / J. Michael Walton. — Westport, Conn.: Greenwood Press, c1980. viii, 237 p.: ill.; 22 cm. — (Contributions in drama and theatre studies. no. 3 0163-3821) Includes index. 1. Theater — Greece 2. Greek drama (Tragedy) — History and criticism. 3. Electra (Greek mythology) in literature. I. T. II. Series.
PA3201.W35   792/.0938   *LC* 79-8580   *ISBN* 0313220433

Webster, T. B. L. (Thomas Bertram Lonsdale), 1905-1974. • **2.307**
Greek theatre production [by] T. B. L. Webster. [2d ed.] London, Methuen [c1970] xvii, 214 p. illus. 23 cm. 'Distributed in the U.S.A. by Barnes & Noble, inc.' 1. Theater — Greece I. T.
PA3201.W4 1970   792.0938   *LC* 79-467351

PA3255–3281 PROSE

Jebb, Richard Claverhouse, Sir, 1841-1905. • **2.308**
The Attic orators from Antiphon to Isaeos. New York: Russell & Russell, 1962. 2 v. 1. Speeches, addresses, etc., Greek — History and criticism. 2. Orators, Greek. I. T.
PA3263.J4 1962   *LC* 62-8230

Kennedy, George Alexander, 1928-. • **2.309**
The art of persuasion in Greece / by George Kennedy. — Princeton, N.J.: Princeton University Press, 1963. xi, 350 p. (A History of rhetoric; v.1) 1. Rhetoric, Ancient I. T.
PA3265.K4   *LC* 63-7070   *ISBN* 0691060088

PA3300–3516 Collections. Series (except Loeb)

Bowra, C. M. (Cecil Maurice), 1898-1971. • **2.310**
Early Greek elegists, by C. M. Bowra. New York, Cooper Square, 1969. 208 p. 23 cm. (Martin classical lectures. v. 7) Reprint of the 1938 ed. 1. Elegiac poetry, Greek — History and criticism. I. T. II. Series.
PA25.M3 vol. 7, 1969 PA3313.B6x   884/.01/09   *LC* 77-85209
   ISBN 0815400306

Hesiod. • **2.311**
Theogonia. Opera et dies. Scvtvm / Hesiodi; edidit Friedrich Solmsen; fragmenta selecta edidervnt R. Merkelbach et M.L. West. — Oxonii: Clarendoniano, 1970. xxv, 246 p. — (Scriptorvm classicorvm bibliotheca Oxoniensis) Text in Greek; introductory material in Latin. I. Solmsen, Friedrich, 1904- II. Merkelbach, Reinhold, 1918- III. West, M.L. (Martin Litchfield)) IV. T. V. Title: Opera et dies. VI. Title: Scutum. VII. Series.
PA3405.S8 H44   PA4009.T5 1970.   *LC* 72-580610   *ISBN* 0108145683

Menander, of Athens. • **2.312**
Dyscolus. Recensuit H. Lloyd–Jones. — Oxonii, E Typographeo Clarendoniano, 1960. xi, 84 p. — (Scriptorum classicorum bibliotheca Oxoniensis.) Errata slip inserted. Text in Greek. I. Lloyd–Jones, H., ed. II. T. III. Series.
PA3405.S8M4 1960   *LC* 61-961

Pindar. • **2.313**
[Selected works. English] The Olympian and Pythian odes; with an introductory essay, notes, and indexes, by Basil L. Gildersleeve. New York, American Book Co. St. Clair Shores, Mich., Scholarly Press, 1970 [c1885] cxv, 395 p. illus. 21 cm. (Harper's classical series for schools and colleges) Text in Greek. I. Gildersleeve, Basil L. (Basil Lanneau), 1831-1924. ed. II. T.
PA3411.H3 P5 1970   881/.01   *LC* 71-107187   *ISBN* 0403003318

Ehrenberg, Victor, 1891-. • **2.314**
Documents illustrating the reigns of Augustus & Tiberius / collected by Victor Ehrenberg and A. H. M. Jones. — 2d ed. — Oxford: Clarendon Press, 1955. xii,

171 p. Chiefly in Latin or Greek; part in Latin and Greek. 1. Inscriptions, Classical 2. Classical literature 3. Rome — History — Empire, 30 B. C.-284 A.D. — Sources I. Augustus, Emperor of Rome, 63 B.C.-14 A.D. II. Tiberius, Emperor of Rome, 42 B.C.-37 A.D. III. T.
PA3427.Z5 E5 1955   *LC* 55-14697

Lobel, Edgar, 1888- ed.   • **2.315**
Poetarum Lesbiorum fragmenta ediderunt Edgar Lobel et Denys Page. — Oxford, Clarendon Press, 1955. xxxviii, 337 p. 23 cm. 'Catalogus manuscriptorum': p. ix—xi. 1. Greek poetry (Collections) I. Sappho. II. Alcaeus. III. Page, Denys Lionel, joint ed. IV. T.
PA3432.L6   *LC* 55-2058

Campbell, David A.   • **2.316**
Greek lyric poetry: a selection of early Greek lyric, elegiac and iambic poetry / by David A. Campbell. — London: Macmillan, c1967. xxxiv, 460 p. Poems in Greek, introd. and notes in English. 1. Greek poetry I. T.
PA3433.C3 1967   *LC* 67-17137

The Oxford book of Greek verse, chosen by Gilbert Murray, Cyril Bailey, E. A. Barber, T. F. Higham and C. M. Bowra, with an introduction by C. M. Bowra,   • **2.317**
Oxford, The Clarendon press, 1930. xiviii, 607, [1] p. 17 cm. 1. Greek poetry (Collections) I. Murray, Gilbert, i.e. George Gilbert Aimé, 1866-1957, comp. II. Bailey, Cyril, 1871-1957. joint comp. III. Barber, Eric Arthur, joint comp. IV. Higham, Thomas Farrant, 1890- joint comp. V. Bowra, C. M. (Cecil Maurice), 1898-1971. joint comp.
PA3433.O88   881.08   *LC* 30-23410

Page, Denys Lionel, comp.   • **2.318**
Lyrica Graeca selecta; edidit breviqve adnotatione critica instrvxit D. L. Page. — Oxonii (Oxford), E Typographeo Clarendoniano (Clarendon P.), 1968. vii, 268 p. 19 cm. — (Scriptorum classicorum bibliotheca Oxoniensis.) Text in Greek. 1. Greek poetry (Collections) I. T. II. Series.
PA3443.P28   *LC* 68-108815

Page, Denys Lionel, ed.   • **2.319**
Poetae melici Graeci; Alcmanis, Stesichori, Ibyci, Anacreontis, Simonidis, Corinnae, poetarum minorum reliquiae, carmina popularia et convivialia quaeque adespota feruntur. — Oxford, Clarendon Press, 1962. xi, 623 p. 23 cm. 1. Greek poetry (Collections) 2. Lyric poetry I. T.
PA3443.P3   *LC* 62-51367

The Greek anthology: Hellenistic epigrams / Ed. by A.S.F. Gow and D.L. Page.   • **2.320**
Cambridge, Eng.: University Press, 1965. 2 v. Text in Greek. 1. Epigrams, Greek I. Gow, Andrew Sydenham Farrar, 1886- ed. II. Page, Denys Lionel, ed. III. Title: Hellenistic epigrams.
PA3458.A3 1965   *LC* 65-14352

Edmonds, John Maxwell, ed.   • **2.321**
Fragments of Attic comedy after Meineke, Bergk, and Kock. Augm., newly edited with their contexts, annotated, and completely translated into English verse. — Leiden, E.J. Brill, 1957-61. 3 v. in 4.; 25 cm. Greek and English. Errata slips inserted. Bibliographical footnotes. I. Meineke, August, 1790-1870 II. Bergk, Theodor, 1812-1881 III. Kock, Theodor, 1820-1901 IV. T.
PA3465.A2x

Diels, Hermann, 1848-1922.   • **2.322**
Doxographi graeci / collegit recensuit prolegomenis indicibusque instruxit Hermannus Diels. — Editio iterata. — Berolini et Lipsiae: apud W. de Gruyter et socios, 1929. x, 854 p.; 25 cm. First published 1879. 'Opus Academiae litterarum regiae borussicae praemio ornatum.' 1. Philosophy, Ancient 2. Greek literature (Collections) I. T.
PA3502.D5   180.8   *LC* 31-21047

PA3517–3564 Criticism (General)

Lattimore, Richmond Alexander, 1906-.   • **2.323**
The poetry of Greek tragedy. — Baltimore: Johns Hopkins Press, [1958] 157 p.; 22 cm. 'Six lectures ... given at the Johns Hopkins University in January, 1957, on the Percy Turnbull Memorial Lectureship of Poetry.' 1. Greek drama (Tragedy) — History and criticism. 2. Greek language — Metrics and rhythmics I. T.
PA3545.L3   882.09   *LC* 57-13289

Webster, T. B. L. (Thomas Bertram Lonsdale), 1905-1974.   • **2.324**
Studies in later Greek comedy, by T. B. L. Webster. [2d ed. Manchester, Eng.] Manchester University Press; New York, Barnes & Noble [1970] xiv, 282 p.

illus. 23 cm. (Barnes and Noble) 1. Greek drama (Comedy) — History and criticism. I. T.
PA3553.W43 1970   882/.01/09   *LC* 79-18890   *ISBN* 0389039896

PA3611–3612 Loeb Library (Greek)

Greek anthology.   • **2.325**
The Greek anthology, with an English translation by W. R. Paton. London, W. Heinemann; New York, G. P. Putnam's sons, 1925-1927. 5 v. illus. 17 cm. (Loeb classical library.) Greek and English on opposite pages. 1. Greek poetry — Translations into English. 2. English poetry — Translations from Greek. I. Paton, William R., tr. II. T. III. Series.
PA3611.A2 1925d   881/.008

Page, Denys Lionel, Sir. tr.   • **2.326**
Greek literary papyri / Texts, translations, and notes by D. L. Page. — Cambridge: Harvard University Press, 1942-. v. — (Loeb classical library.) 'The first edition was destroyed by enemy action, and the translator has revised this reprint.' No more published. A volume of prose papyri was planned to accompany this volume of poetic papyri. Forms a continuation of A. S. Hunt's collection of non-literary papyri published 1932-34 under title: Select papyri. Greek and English on opposite pages. 1. Greek literature 2. Greek literature — Translations into English. 3. English literature — Translations from Greek. 4. Manuscripts, Greek (Papyri) I. T. II. Series.
PA3611.A22 1942   *LC* a 42-4500

Apostolic fathers. English & Greek.   • **2.327**
The Apostolic fathers; with an English translation by Kirsopp Lake. London, W. Heinemann; New York, G. P. Putnam's sons, 1930. 2 v. 17 cm. (Loeb classical library.) Vol. 1, "first published September 1912; reprinted July 1914 and December 1919, 1925, 1930." Vol. 2, "first printed, 1913; Reprinted, 1917, 1924, 1930." 1. Fathers of the church (Collections) I. Ignatius, Saint, Bishop of Antioch, d. ca. 110. Epistolae. II. Polycarp, Saint, Bishop of Smyrna. Epistola ad Philippenses. III. Clement I, Pope. Epistola ad Corinthios. I. IV. Clement I, Pope. supposed author. Epistola ad Corinthios. II. V. Lake, Kirsopp, 1872- ed. and tr. VI. Martyrdom of Polycarp. VII. Epistle to Diognetus. VIII. Teaching of the twelve apostles. IX. Bible. N.T. Apocryphal books. Epistle of Barnabas. X. Hermas. XI. T. XII. Series.
PA3611.A7 1930d

Aristotle.   **2.328**
Historia animalium / with an English translation by A. L. Peck. — London: Heinemann, 1965-70. 2 v.: ill. — (Loeb classical library.) Greek and English. 1. Zoology — Pre-Linnean works I. Peck, Arthur Leslie, 1902- II. T. III. Series.
PA3611.A76   591.09014   *LC* 66-903

Bulmer-Thomas, Ivor, 1905-.   • **2.329**
Selections illustrating the history of Greek mathematics / [selected] with an English translation by Ivor Thomas. — Cambridge, Mass.: Harvard University Press, 1939-1941. 2 v.: ill.; 17 cm. — (The Loeb classical library: Greek authors) On spine: Greek mathematical works. Greek and English. 1. Mathematics, Greek I. T. II. Title: Greek mathematical works. III. Series.
PA3611.A95 1939

Elegy and iambus: being the remains of all the Greek elegiac and iambic poets from Callinus to Crates, excepting the choliambic writers, with the Anacreontea, in two volumes / newly edited and translated by J. M. Edmonds.   • **2.330**
London: W. Heinemann, 1931. 2 v. — (The Loeb classical library. [Greek authors]) Greek and English on opposite pages. 1. Greek poetry 2. Greek poetry — Translations into English. 3. English poetry — Translations from Greek. 4. Greek poetry — History and criticism. 5. Lyric poetry I. Edmonds, John Maxwell. II. Anacreon. III. Series.
PA3611.E6 E4   *LC* 32-3143

PA3612 Individual Authors, A–Z

PA3612 A–Ar

Achilles Tatius.   • **2.331**
Achilles Tatius, with an English translation by S. Gaselee ... — London: W. Heinemann; New York: G.P. Putnam's, 1917. xvi, 461, [1] p. 17 cm. — (Half-title: The Loeb classical library) Greek and English on opposite pages. Bibliography: p. XV-XVI. 1. Gaselee, Stephen, Sir, 1882- tr. I. T.
PA3612.A16 1917a   *LC* 17-13968

Aeschylus.   • **2.332**
Aeschylus, with an English translation by Herbert Weir Smyth ... — London, W. Heinemann; New York, G. P. Putnam's sons 1922-26. 2 v. 17 cm. — (Half-title: The Loeb classical library. [Greek authors]) Greek and English on opposite pages. I. Smyth, Herbert Weir, 1857- tr. II. T.
PA3612.A4 1922   *LC* 23-2840

Apollodorus.   • **2.333**
[Bibliothēkē. English & Greek] The library, with an English translation by Sir James George Frazer ... London, W. Heinemann; New York, G. P. Putnam's sons, 1921. 2 v. 17 cm. (The Loeb classical library. [Greek authors]) Greek text of Bibliothēkē and English translation on opposite pages. Until modern times the author was often wrongly identified with the grammarian Apollodorus, of Athens. 1. Frazer, James George, Sir, 1854-1941. ed. and tr. I. Apollodorus, of Athens. Bibliothēkē. II. T. III. Series.
PA3612.A5 1921   *LC* 21-15885

Apollonius, Rhodius.   • **2.334**
Apollonius Rhodius, the Argonautica / with an English translation by R.C. Seaton. — London: W. Heinemann; New York: The Macmillan, 1912. xvi, 431 p.; 17 cm. — (Loeb classical library.) Greek and English on opposite pages. 1. Greek poetry 2. Greek poetry — Translations into English. I. Seaton, Robert Cooper, 1853-1915. II. T. III. Title: Argonautica. IV. Series.
PA3612.A6 1912   *ISBN* 0674990013

Appianus, of Alexandria.   • **2.335**
Appian's Roman history; with an English translation, by Horace White ... — Cambridge, Mass., Harvard University press; London, W. Heinemann [1912-13] 4 v. 17 cm. — (Half-title: The Loeb classical library) 1. Rome — Hist. I. White, Horace, 1834-1916. tr. II. Dennison, John Dewar, ed. III. Robson, Edgar Iliff, ed. IV. T.
PA3612.A64 1912a   *LC* 13-5584

Aristophanes.   • **2.336**
Aristophanes with the English translation of Benjamin Bickley Rogers. London, W. Heinemann; Cambridge, Mass., Harvard Univ. Press 1930-37. 3 v. 17 cm. (Half Title: The Loeb classical library [Greek authors]) I. Rogers, Benjamin Bickley, 1828-1919. tr. II. T.
PA3612 A7 1930d

PA3612 Aristotle

Aristotle.   • **2.337**
[Selected works. Greek and English] On the soul. Parva naturalia. On breath. With an English translation by W.S. Hett. [Rev.] Cambridge Harvard University Press 1957. 527p. (The Loeb classical library. Greek authors) 1. Psychology — Early works to 1850 I. Hett, Walter Stanley, tr. II. T.
PA3612.A8   *LC* 58-17

Aristotle.   • **2.338**
The Athenian constitution; the Eudemian ethics; On virtues and vices; with an English translation by H. Rackham ... — Cambridge, Mass., Harvard university press; London, W. Heinemann, ltd., 1935. vii, 505, [1] p. 17 cm. — (Half-title: The Loeb classical library. [Greek authors]) At head of title: Aristotle. Greek and English on opposite pages. 1. Athens. Constitution. 2. Ethics I. Rackham, Harris, 1868- tr. II. T.
PA3612.A8A13 1935   838.5   *LC* 35-10031

Aristotle.   • **2.339**
[Selections. English. 1982 English. 1936] Minor works ... with an English translation by W.S. Hett. — Cambridge, Mass: Harvard University Press, 1936-. v.: diagrs.;17 cm. — (The Loeb classical library. [Greek authors]) AT head of title: Aristotle. Greek and English on opposite pages. I. Hett, Walter Stanley, tr. II. T.
PA3612.A8 A13 1936   *LC* 36-12210

Aristotle.   • **2.340**
On sophistical refutations [and] On coming-to-be and passing away [translated] by E. S. Forster. On the cosmos [translated] by D. J. Furley. — Cambridge, Harvard University Press, 1955. vii, 429 p. 17 cm. — (Loeb classical library, Greek authors [no. 400]) Greek and English. I. Forster, Edward Seymour, 1879- ed. and tr. II. Furley, D. J., ed. and tr. III. T. IV. Series.
PA3612.A8A13 1955   888.5   *LC* A 56-8604

Aristotle.   • **2.341**
[On the generation of animals English & Greek] Generation of animals, with an English translation by A.L. Peck. Cambridge Harvard University Press 1943. 607;1p. (The Loeb classical library) 1. Reproduction 2. Zoology — Pre-Linnean works I. Peck, Arthur Leslie, 1902- II. T.
PA3612.A8 D28 1943

Aristotle.   • **2.342**
Parts of animals, with an English translation by A. I. Peck. Movement of animals, Progression of animals, with an English translation by E. S. Forster.

Cambridge, Mass., Harvard University Press [1937] 555p. (The Loeb classical library.) Greek and English on opposite pages. The De animalium motu ('Movement of animals') has been generally considered a spurious work, though recent opinion has favoured its genuineness. cf. Introd. 1. Zoology — Pre-Linnean works 2. Animal locomotion I. Aristotle, Spurious and doubtful works. Movement of animals. II. Aristotle. Progression of animals. III. T. IV. Title: Movement of animals. V. Title: Progression of animals.
PA3612.A8 D3 1937   *LC* 38-4213

Aristotle.   • **2.343**
On the heavens, with an English translation by W. K. C. Guthrie. Cambridge, Mass., Harvard University Press; London, W. Heinemann, 1939. 378 p. diagrs. 17 cm. (The Loeb classical library [Greek authors]) Greek and English on opposite pages. 1. Astronomy, Greek I. Guthrie, W. K. C. (William Keith Chambers), 1906- tr. II. T. III. Series.
PA3612.A8D4 1939d

Aristoteles.   • **2.344**
Nicomachean ethics. With an English translation by H. Rackham. — Cambridge: Harvard University Press; London: H. Heineman, 1934. xxxiii, 649 p.; 17 cm. (Loeb classical library) Greek and English on opposite pages. Bibliography: p. xxxi-xxxiii. I. Rackham, Harris, 1868- tr. II. T.
PA3612.A8 E6 1934d

Aristotle.   • **2.345**
Meteorologica. With an English translation by H. D. P. Lee. — Cambridge, Harvard University Press, 1952. xxx, 432 p. fold. map, diagrs. 17 cm. — (The Loeb classical library. [Greek authors]) Bibliography: p. xxviii—xxx. 1. Meteorology — Early works to 1800. I. T. II. Series.
PA3612.A8M47   888.5   *LC* 52-14795

Aristotle.   • **2.346**
The Metaphysics ... with an English translation by Hugh Tredennick ... — London, W. Heinemann, ltd.; New York, G. P. Putnam's sons, 1933-35. 2v. 17 cm. — (Half-title: The Loeb classical library. [Greek authors]) At head of title: Aristotle. Greek and English on opposite pages. Bibliography: v. 1, p. xxxv-xxxvi. 1. Metaphysics I. Tredennick, Hugh, tr. II. T.
PA3612.A8M5 1933 PA3803.M5 1933   110   *LC* 33-17911

Aristotle.   • **2.347**
The Organon. — Cambridge, Harvard University Press, 1938-. v. diagrs. 17 cm. — (Loeb classical library. 325) Vol. 2, with title on spine only, has special t. p. Greek and English. Includes bibliographies. 1. Logic I. Cooke, Harold Percy, 1882- tr. II. Tredennick, Hugh, tr. III. Forster, Edward Seymour, 1879-1950, tr. IV. Aristoteles. Posterior analytics. V. T. VI. Series.
PA3612.A8O7 1938   160   *LC* 38-12666 rev*

Aristotle.   • **2.348**
Aristotle, the Physics, with an English translation by Philip H. Wicksteed ... and Francis M. Cornford ... in two volumes. — London, W. Heinemann, ltd; New York, G. P. Putnam's sons, 1929-34. 2 v. diagrs. 17 cm. — (Half-title: The Loeb classical library ... [Greek authors]) Greek and English on opposite pages. Vol. 2 has imprint: London, W. Heinemann, ltd.; Cambridge, Mass., Harvard university press. I. Wicksteed, Philip Henry, 1844-1927. ed. and tr. II. Cornford, Francis Macdonald, 1874-1943. ed. and tr. III. T.
PA3612.A8P3 1929   888.5   *LC* 30-5834

Aristotle.   • **2.349**
Aristotle: The poetics. "Longinus": On the sublime. Demetrius: On style. London, W. Heinemann, New York, G. P. Putnam's sons, 1932. xx, 500 p. 17 cm. (The Loeb classical library. [Greek authors]) The Poetics and On the sublime translated by W. H. Fyfe; On style, by W. R. Roberts. First published 1927. Revised and reprinted 1932. Greek and English on opposite pages. 1. Poetry — Early works to 1800. 2. Aesthetics — Early works to 1800. I. Demetrius, of Phaleron, b. 350 B.C. Spurious and doubtful works. De elocutione. Eng. 1932. II. Roberts, W. Rhys (William Rhys), 1858-1929. tr. III. Longinus, Cassius, ca. 213-273. Spurious and doubtful works. De sublimitate. Eng. 1932. IV. Fyfe, William Hamilton, 1878- tr. V. T. VI. Series.
PA3612.A8P5 1932d   808.1

Aristotle.   • **2.350**
Politics / Aristotle; with an English translation by H. Rackham. — London: Heinemann, 1932. xxiii, 683 p. — (The Loeb classical library[Greek authors]) 1. Political science — Early works to 1800 I. Rackham, Harris, 1868- II. T. III. Series.
PA3612.A8P6x   320.1

Aristotle.   • **2.351**
Problems. With an English translation by W. S. Hett. — Cambridge, Harvard University Press; London, Heinemann, 1936-37. 2 v. diagrs. 17 cm. — (Half-title: The Loeb classical library. [Greek authors]) At head of title: Aristotle. Greek and English on opposite pages. Not genuine works of Aristotle. Vol. II has title: ... Problems ... with an English translation by W. S. Hett ... Rhetorica

ad Alexandrum, with an English translation by H. Rackham. I. Hett, Walter Stanley, tr. II. Rackham, Harris, 1868- tr. III. T.
PA3612.A8P9   888.5   LC 37-4525 Rev

Aristotle. • 2.352
Aristotle: with an English translation: the 'Art' of rhetoric / by John Henry Freese. — London: W. Heinemann; New York: G.P. Putnam, 1926. xlvii, 491 p.; 17 cm. — (The Loeb classical library. [Greek authors]) Greek and English on opposite pages. 1. Rhetoric, Ancient I. Freese, John Henry. II. T. III. Series.
PA3612.A8 R4   LC 27-2022

PA3612 Arr–E

Arrian. 2.353
[Selected works. English and Greek] Arrian / with an English translation by P. A. Brunt. — Rev. text and translation / with new introd., notes, and appendixes by P. A. Brunt. — Cambridge, Mass.: Harvard University Press, 1976-1983. 2 v.: fold. col. map; 17 cm. — (Loeb classical library. 236, 269) On spine: History of Alexander and Indica. Vol. 2 has imprint: Cambridge, Mass.: Harvard University Press; London: W. Heineman. In Greek and English, with introd. and editorial matter in English. 1. Alexander, the Great, 356-323 B.C. 2. Iran — History — To 640 3. India — Description and travel — To 1000 I. Brunt, P. A. II. T. III. Title: History of Alexander and Indica. IV. Series.
PA3612.A85x 1976   938/.07/0924 B   LC 76-367911   ISBN 0674992601

Marcus Aurelius, Emperor of Rome, 121-180. • 2.354
The communings with himself of Marcus Aurelius Antoninus, Emperor of Rome, together with his speeches and sayings; a rev. text and a translation into English by C.R. Haines. [Rev. ed.] London Heinemann 1930. 415p. (The Loeb classical library) I. Haines, Charles Reginald, tr. II. T.
PA3612.A98 1930d

Barlaam and Joasaph. English. • 2.355
St. John Damascene Barlaam and Ioasaph, with an English translation, by the Rev. G.R. Woodward...and H. Mattingly. London, William Heinemann, 1914. 640 p. ill. (Loeb classical library.) Some useful books of reference, p. xvi. Greek and English on opposite pages. I. John, of Damascus, Saint. II. Mattingly, Harold, 1884-1964. III. Woodward, George Ratcliffe, 1848- IV. T. V. Series.
PA3612 B4 1914   294   LC 14-9138

Basil, Saint, Bishop of Caesarea, ca. 329-379. • 2.356
Saint Basil: the letters / with an English translation by Roy J. Deferrari ... — London: W. Heinemann; New York: G. P. Putnam's sons, [1926-34] 4 v.: map; 17 cm. — (The Loeb classical library [Greek authors]) Vol. 4 has imprint: London, W. Heinemann, ltd.; Cambridge, Mass., Harvard university press. Greek and English on opposite pages. 'Address to young men on reading Greek literature,' with an English translation by R. J. Deferrari and M. R. P. McGuire: v. 4, p. [363]-435. I. Deferrari, Roy Joseph, 1890- II. McGuire, Martin Rawson Patrick, 1897- III. T.
PA3612.B45 1926   922.1   LC 27-2019 Rev

Callimachus. 2.357
[Works. English & Greek] Aetia, Iambi, lyric poems, Hecale, minor epic and elegiac poems, and other fragments / Callimachus; text, translation, and notes by C. A. Trypanis. Hero and Leander / Musaeus; introd., text, and notes by Thomas Gelzer; with an English translation by Cedric Whitman. — Cambridge: Harvard University Press, 1975. xvi, 421 p.; 17 cm. (Loeb classical library. 421) 1. Greek poetry 2. Greek poetry — Translations into English. 3. English literature — Translations from Greek. I. Musaeus, Grammaticus. Hero et Leander. English & Greek. 1975. II. T. III. Series.
PA3612.C18Ax 1975   881/.01   LC 76-351822   ISBN 0674994639

Cassius Dio Cocceianus. • 2.358
Dio's Roman history / with an English translation by Earnest Cary; on the basis of the version of Herbert Baldwin Foster. — London: W. Heinemann, 1914-1927. 9 v.; 17 cm. — (Loeb classical library. no. 53) Vols. 4-9 have imprint: London, W. Heinemann; New York, G.P. Putnam's Sons. Vol. 3 has imprint: London, W. Heinemann; Cambridge, Mass., Harvard University Press. Greek and English on opposite pages. 1. Rome — History I. Cary, Earnest, 1879- II. Foster, Herbert Baldwin, 1874-1906. III. T. IV. Series.
PA3612.C3 1914   LC 14-4947

Demosthenes. • 2.359
[Selected works Greek and English. 1935] Demosthenes against Meidias, Androtion, Aristocrates, Timocrates, Aristogeiton; with an English translation by J.H. Vince. Cambridge Harvard University Press 1935. 596;2p. (The Loeb classical library. [Greek authors]) I. Vince, James Herbert, 1865-, tr. II. T.
PA3612.D37 1935

Demosthenes. • 2.360
Private orations / Demosthenes; with an English translation by A.T. Murray. London: W. Heinemann, 1936-1939. 3 v. (The Loeb classical library. Greek authors.) I. Murray, Augustus Taber, 1866-, ed. II. T.
PA3612.D38 1936d

Demosthenes. • 2.361
De corona and De falsa legatione, with an English translation by C. A. Vince and J. H. Vince. London, W. Heinemann; New York, G. P. Putnam's sons, 1926. [479] p. front. 17 cm. (The Loeb classical library. [Greek authors]) Greek and English on opposite pages. I. Vince, Charles Anthony, 1855- tr. II. Vince, James Herbert, 1865- joint tr. III. T. IV. Series.
PA3612.D4 1926d   855/.01

Demosthenes. • 2.362
Olynthiacs: Philippics; Minor public speeches; Speech against Leptines / Demosthenes; with an English translation by J. H. Vince ... Cambridge: harvard Univ. Press, [c1954]. 607 p. (The Loeb classical library. [Greek authors]) I. Vince, James Herbert, 1865- II. T.
PA3612.D43 1954   885.6   LC 63-24144

Diogenes Laertius. • 2.363
Lives of eminent philosphers, with an English translation by R. D. Hicks. London, W. Heinemann; Cambridge, Mass., Harvard University Press, 1938-1931. 2 v. 17 cm. (The Loeb classical library. [Greek authors]) Greek and English on opposite pages. Vol. 1, London, Cambridge, Mass., 1938. First pub. 1925. Revised & reprinted 1938. Vol. 2, London, New York, G. P. Putnam's Sons, 1931. First pub. 1925. Revised and reprinted 1931. 1. Philosophers, Ancient 2. Philosophy, Ancient I. Hicks, Robert Drew, 1850-1929, tr. II. T. III. Series.
PA3612.D5 1931d

Dionysius, of Halicarnassus. • 2.364
The Roman antiquities of Dionysius of Halicarnassus / with an English translation by Earnest Cary on the basis of the version of Edward Spelman. — London: Heinemann, 1937-1950. 7 v.; 18 cm. — (The Loeb classical library. 319, 347, 357, 364, 372, 378, 388: Greek authors) Greek and English on opposite pages. 1. Rome — History 2. Rome — Antiquities 3. Rome — Politics and goverment. I. Cary, Earnest, 1879- II. Spelman, Edward, d. 1767. III. T.
PA3612.D53 1937   LC 38-42

Dionysius, of Halicarnassus. 2.365
The critical essays / Dionysius of Halicarnassus; with an English translation by Stephen Usher. — Cambridge, Mass.: Harvard University Press, 1974-1985. 2 v.; 17 cm. (Loeb classical library. 465) English and Greek. I. T. II. Series.
PA3612.D53 1974 PA3966.A6   080 s 885/.01/09   LC 75-305450   ISBN 0674995120

Epictetus. • 2.366
Epictetus: the discourses as reported by Arrian, the manual, and fragments / with an English translation by W.A. Oldfather. — London: Heinemann, 1926-28. 2 v.; 17 cm. — (Loeb classical library.) Greek and English on opposite pages. I. Oldfather, William Abbott, 1880-1945. II. T. III. Series.
PA3612.E6 1925   LC 26-15260

Eusebius, of Caesarea, Bishop of Caesarea, ca. 260-ca. 340. • 2.367
The ecclesiastical history / with an English translation by Kirsopp Lake. — London: W. Heinemann; New York: G.P. Putnam's sons, 1926-32. 2 v. — (Loeb classical library. [Greek authors]) Greek and English on opposite pages. Vol. 2 'with an English translation of J.E.L. Oulton ... taken from the edition published in conjunction with H.J. Lawlor'. 1. Church history — Primitive and early church, ca. 30-600 I. Lake, Kirsopp, 1872- II. Oulton, John Ernest Leonard, 1886- III. Lawlor, Hugh Jackson, 1860-1938. IV. T.
BR160.E4 L3   PA3612.E85.   LC 27-2020

PA3612 G–M

Galen. • 2.368
Galen On the natural faculties, with an English translation by Arthur John Brock ... — London, W. Heinemann; New York, G. P. Putnam's sons, 1916. lv, 339, [1] p. 17 cm. — (Half-title: The Loeb classical library. [Greek authors]) Greek and English on opposite pages. Bibliography: p. xii. I. Brock, Arthur John. tr. II. T.
PA3612.G3 1916   LC 17-16

Herodian. • 2.369
Herodian. With an English translation by C. R. Whittaker. Cambridge, Mass., Harvard University Press, 1969-70. 2 v. 17 cm. (Loeb classical library.) English and Greek. 1. Rome — History — Empire, 30 B.C.-284 A.D. I. Whittaker, C. R. tr. II. T. III. Series.
PA3612.H49 1969   937/.06   LC 74-7907   ISBN 0674995015

Herodotus. • 2.370
Herodotus / with an English translation by A. D. Godley. London: W. Heinemann; New York: Putnam, 1921-1924. 4 v.: fold. maps; 17 cm. (The Loeb classical library. Greek authors) Greek and English on opposite pages. Includes indexes. 1. History, Ancient 2. Greece — History I. Godley, A. D. (Alfred Denis), 1856-1925. II. T. III. Series.
PA3612.H5 1921   *LC* 21-6980

Hesiod. 2.371
Hesiod: the Homeric hymns, and Homerica / with an English translation by Hugh G. Evelyn–White. — Cambridge, Mass.: Harvard University Press; London: Heinemann, 1977. xlviii, 657 p.; 17 cm. — (The Loeb classical library. Greek authors) Greek and English on opposite pages. 1. Epic poetry, Greek 2. Greek poetry — Translations into English. 3. English poetry — Translations from Greek. I. Evelyn-White, Hugh Gerard, 1924- II. Homer. Hymns. English. 1914. III. T. IV. Series.
PA3612.H6 1914   *ISBN* 0674990633

Hippocrates. • 2.372
[Works. English and Greek. 1923] Hippocrates, with an English translation by W. H. S. Jones. London, Heinemann; New York, Putnam, 1923-31. 4 v. illus., diagr., facism. 17 cm. (Loeb classical library.) 'On the universe [by] Heraclitus, with an English translation by W. H. S. Jones.': v. 4, [449]-509. 1. Medicine — Collected works. 2. Medicine, Greek and Roman I. Heraclitus, of Ephesus. II. Jones, W. H. S. (William Henry Samuel), 1876-1963. tr. III. T. IV. Series.
PA3612.H65 1923   *LC* 23-12030

Homer. 2.373
The Iliad / with an English translation by A.T. Murray. — Cambridge, Mass.: Harvard University Press, 1934-37. 2 v.; 17 cm. — (The Loeb classical library) At head of title: Homer. I. Murray, Augustus Taber, 1866- II. T.
PA3612.H79 1934

Homer. 2.374
The Odyssey, with an English translation by A. T. Murray ... — London, W. Heinemann; New York, G. P. Putnam's sons, 1919. 2 v. front. (port.) 17 cm. — (Half-title: The Loeb classical library) Bibliography: v. 1, p. xiii—xiv. I. Murray, Augustus Taber, 1866- tr. II. T.
PA3612.H8 1919   *LC* 19-16044

Isocrates. • 2.375
Isocrates / with an English translation by George Norlin. — London: Heinemann; Cambridge, Mass.: Harvard University Press, 1928-45. 3 v. — (Loeb classical library.) Vol.3, translated by Larue Van Hook. Greek and English on opposite pages. I. Norlin, George, 1871-1942. II. T. III. Series.
PA3612.I9 1928   885.4   *LC* 28-16429

Josephus, Flavius. • 2.376
[Works. English & Greek. 1926] Josephus / with an English translation by H.St.J. Thackeray. — London: W. Heinemann; New York: Putnam, 1926-1965. 9 v.: genealogical tables, maps; 17 cm. — (Loeb classical library. [Greek authors]) Greek and English on opposite pages. Vols. 5-9 have imprint: Cambridge: Harvard University Press. Vols. 1-4 translated by H.St.J. Thackeray; v. 5 by H.St.J. Thackeray and R. Marcus; v. 6-8 by R. Marcus (v. 8 completed and edited by A. Wikgren); v. 9 by L.H. Feldman. 1. Jews — Biography 2. Jews — History I. Thackeray, Henry St. John, 1869?-1930. II. Marcus, Ralph, 1900-1956. III. Wikgren, Allen Paul, 1906- IV. Feldman, Louis H. V. T. VI. Series.
PA3612.J6 1926   *LC* 26-15261/r2

Julian, Emperor of Rome, 331-363. • 2.377
The works of the Emperor Julian / with an English translation by Wilmer Cave Wright. — London: Heinemann; New York: Macmillan, 1913-1923. 3 v.; 17 cm. — (Loeb classical library.) I. Wright, Wilmer Cave France. II. T. III. Series.
PA3612.J9 1913   PA4225.J4 1913.   *LC* w 13-70

Longus. • 2.378
Daphnis & Chloe / by Longus; with the English translation of George Thornly. The love romances of Parthenius, and other fragments; with an English translation by S. Gaselee. — Rev. and augm. by J. M. Edmonds. — London: W. Heinemann, 1916. xxiii, 423, [1] p.; 17 cm. — (Loeb classical library: Greek authors; 69) Greek and English on opposite pages. I. Thornley, George, b. 1614. II. Edmonds, John Maxwell. III. Parthenius, of Nicaea. IV. Gaselee, Stephen, 1882-1943. V. T.
PA3612.L6 1916   *LC* 17-14

Lysias. • 2.379
Lysias, with an English translation by W.R.M. Lamb. Cambridge Harvard University Press 1943. 706;2p. (The Loeb classical library [Greek authors]) I. Lamb, Walter Rangeley Maitland, Sir 1882-, tr. II. T.
PA3612.L8 1943

Lucian, of Samosata. 2.380
Lucian / with an English translation by A. M. Harmon ... In eight volumes. — London: W. Heinemann; New York, Macmillan, 1913-1967. — 8 v.; 17 cm. —

(The Loeb classical library. Greek authors) Vols. 3-4 have imprint: London, Heinemann; New York, Putnam; v. 5-7, London, Heinemann; Cambridge, Harvard University Press; v. 8. Cambridge, Harvard University Press; London, Heinemann. Vol. 6 translated by K. Kilburn; v. 7-8 by M.D. Macleod. I. Harmon, Austin Morris. ed. and tr. II. Kilburn, K. III. Macleod, M. D. IV. T.
PA3612.L7 1913   *LC* 13-5615

Menander, of Athens. • 2.381
Menander, the principal fragments, with an English translation by Francis G. Allinson. London, W. Heinemann; New York, G. P. Putnam's sons, 1930. 539 p. front. (port.) 17 cm. (Loeb classical library.) Greek and English on opposite pages. First printed 1921; reprinted and revised 1930. I. T. II. Series.
PA3612.M4 1930d

PA3612 P–Z

Pausanias. • 2.382
Pausanias Description of Greece, with an English translation by W.H.S. Jones. London, W. Heinemann; New York, G.P. Putnam's sons, 1918-35. 5 v. ill. 17 cm. (The Loeb classical library) Greek and English on opposite pages. Vol. II translated by W.H.S. Jones and H.A. Ormerod. 1. Greece — Antiquities 2. Greece — Description and travel I. Jones, W. H. S. (William Henry Samuel), 1876-1963. II. Ormerod, Henry Arderne, 1886-1964. III. T.
PA3612.P3 1918   *LC* 19-6903

Philo, of Alexandria. • 2.383
Philo / with an English translation by F. H. Colson and G. H. Whitaker. — London: Heinemann, 1929-1962. 10 v. — (Loeb classical library.) Greek and English. Vols. 6-10 translated by F. H. Colson. I. Colson, Francis Henry, 1857-1943. II. Whitaker, George Herbert, 1846 or 7-1930. III. T. IV. Scries.
PA3612.P35 1929   PA4268.A2 1929.   *LC* 29-21681

Philostratus, the Athenian, 2nd/3rd cent. • 2.384
Philostratus, Imagines; Callistratus, Descriptions; with an English translation by Arthur Fairbanks... London, W. Heinemann, ltd., 1931. 429 p. ill. (The Loeb classical library. [Greek authors]) Greek and English on opposite pages. The later series of Imagines is called 'Posteriores' to distinguish it from the first. In the preface of the present edition, the earlier 'Imagines' are ascribed to Philostratus the Lemnian, son of Nervianus. 1. Painting — Early works to 1800. 2. Painting, Greco-Roman I. Philostratus, the Younger, 3rd cent. II. Philostratus, the Lemnian, 3rd cent. III. Callistratus, Sophista. Statuae. IV. T. V. Series.
PA3612.P38 1931   888.9   *LC* 32-3145

Philostratus, the Athenian, 2nd/3rd cent. • 2.385
The life of Apollonius of Tyana / Philostratus; with an English translation by F.C. Conybeare. — London: Wm. Heinemann, 1912. 2 v.: ill. — (Loeb classical library.) 'The treatise of Eusebius, the son of Pamphilus, against the Life of Apollonius of Tyana, written by Philostratus, occasioned by the parallel drawn by Hierocles between him and Christ' (Greek and English, vol. II, p.484-605) Greek and English on opposite pages. 1. Apollonius, of Tyana. 2. Hierocles, Sossianus, Proconsul of Bithynia, fl. A.D. 293-303. I. Eusebius, of Caesarea, Bishop of Caesarea, ca. 260-ca. 340. Adversus Hieroclem. II. Conybeare, F. C. (Frederick Cornwallis), 1856-1924. III. T. IV. Series.
PA3612 P4 1912   *LC* 13-5590

Philostratus, the Athenian, 2nd/3rd cent. • 2.386
The lives of the Sophists / Philostratus and Eunapius with an English translation by Wilmer Cave Wright. — London: Heinemann, 1922. xliii, 595 p.; 17 cm. — (Loeb classical library. no. 134) Greek and English on opposite pages. 1. Sophists (Greek philosophy) I. Eunapius. II. Wright, Wilmer Cave France. III. T. IV. Series.
PA3612.P42 1922   *LC* 22-12854

Pindar. • 2.387
The odes of Pindar, including the principal fragments. With an introduction and an English translation by Sir John Sandys. London, W. Heinemann; Cambridge, Mass., Harvard University Press, 1937. 635 p. front. 17 cm. (Loeb classical library.) Greek and English on opposite pages. First edition 1915; second & revised edition 1919; revised and reprinted 1937. I. Sandys, John Edwin, Sir, 1844-1922. tr. II. T. III. Series.
PA3612.P5 1937d

Plato. • 2.388
Plato: with an English translation. — Cambridge: Harvard University Press; London: Heinemann, 1914-1937, t.p. 1960-1977. 12 v.; 17 cm. — (The Loeb classical library) Translators: v.1, 4, 7, 10. H. N. Fowler.—v.2, 3, 8, 12. W.R.M. Lamb.—v.5, 6. P. Shorey.—v.9-11. R. G. Bury. Greek and English on opposite pages. I. T.
PA3612.P6 1925d   *ISBN* 0674990404

Plotinus. • 2.389
[Enneads Greek and English] Plotinus, with an English translation by A. H. Armstrong. London, Heinemann; Cambridge (Mass.), Harvard U.P., 1966-. v.

17 cm. (Loeb classical library.) I. Armstrong, A. H. (Arthur Hilary). tr. II. T. III. Series.
PA3612.P683   186/.4   *LC* 67-76101

Plutarch.   • **2.390**
Plutarch's Moralia / with an English translation by Frank Cole Babbitt. — London: W. Heinemann, 1927-. v.: facsim. — (The Loeb classical library. [Greek authors]) Greek and English on opposite pages. Translators: v. 1-5, F. C. Babbitt; v. 6, W. C. Helmbold; v. 7, P. H. DeLacy and B. Einarson; v. 8. P. A. Clement and H. B. Hoffleit; v. 9, E. L. Minar, F. H. Sandbach and W. C. Helmbold; v. 10, H. N. Fowler; v. 11, L. Pearson and F. H. Sandbach; v. 12, H. Cherniss and W. C. Helmbold; v. 13, pt. 1-2, H. Cherniss; v. 14, B. Einarson and P. H. DeLacy. I. Babbitt, Frank Cole, 1867-1935. II. T. III. Title: Moralia. IV. Series.
PA3612.P69 1927   PA4368.A2 1927.   *LC* 27-26689

Polybius.   • **2.391**
The histories / with an English translation by W. R. Paton. — London: W. Heinemann; New York: G.P. Putnam's sons, 1922-27. 6 v.; 17 cm. (The Loeb classical library. [Greek Authors]) Includes indexes. Greek and English on opposite pages. 1. History, Ancient 2. Greece — History 3. Rome — History — Republic, B.C. 510-30. I. Paton, William Roger, 1921- II. T. III. Series.
PA3612.P8 1922   PA4391.A2 1922.   *LC* 23-2839

Procopius.   • **2.392**
Procopius / with an English translation by H. B. Dewing. — London: W. Heinemann; Cambridge, Mass.: Harvard University Press, 1953-62. 7 v.: ill., maps; 17 cm. (Loeb classical library. Greek authors) Includes indexes. Greek and English on opposite pages. 1. Justinian I, Emperor of the East, 483?-565. 2. Byzantine Empire — History — Justinian I, 527-565 I. Dewing, H. B. (Henry Bronson), 1882- II. T. III. Series.
PA3612.P85   *LC* 64-3759   *ISBN* 0674990544

Strabo.   • **2.393**
The geography of Strabo, with an English translation by Horace Leonard Jones ... Based in part upon the unfinished version of John Robert Sitlington Sterrett ... — London, W. Heinemann; New York, G. P. Putnam's sons, 1917-33. 8 v. front. (map) 17 cm. — (Half-title: The Loeb classical library. [Greek authors]) Greek and English on opposite pages. Bibliography: v. 1, p. xxix-xliii. I. Jones, Horace Leonard, 1879- tr. II. Sterrett, John Robert Sitlington, 1851-1914. III. T.
PA3612.S8 1917 G87.S9J6 1917   *LC* 17-13967

Theophrastus.   • **2.394**
The characters of Theophrastus / newly edited and translated by J.M. Edmonds. — London: W. Heinemann, 1929. vii, 132 p., [1] folded leaf of plates: diagr. — (Loeb classical library.) Greek and English on opposite pages. Also included in the vol.: Herodes, Cercidas and the Greek choliambic poets (except Callimachus and Babrius) edited and translated by A.D. Knox. 1. Characters and characteristics I. Edmonds, J.M. (John Maxwell) II. T. III. Series.
PA3612 T35 1929 PA4448 A4 1929   *LC* 29-26911

Theophrastus.   • **2.395**
Enquiry into plants and minor works on odours and weather signs, with an English translation by Sir Arthur Hort, bart. ... London, W. Heinemann; New York, G. P. Putnam's sons, 1916. 2 v. front. 17 cm. (Half-title: The Loeb classical library. [Greek authors]) Greek and English on opposite pages. Bibliography: v. 1, p. ix-xvi. 1. Botany — Pre-Linnean works I. Hort, Arthur, Sir, 1864-1935. ed. II. T.
PA3612.T4 1916   *LC* 17-2706

Theophrastus.   **2.396**
De causis plantarum, 1 / [by] Theophrastus; with an English translation by Benedict Einarson and George K.K. Link. London: Harvard, 1976. lxvii, 361 p.; 17 cm. (Loeb classical library. 471) In 3 vols. Parallel Greek text and English translation, English introduction and notes. 1. Plants — Early works to 1800. I. Einarson, Benedict. II. Link, George Konrad Karl. III. T. IV. Series.
PA3612.T4 1927   581   *ISBN* 0434994715

Thucydides.   **2.397**
Thucydides, with an English translation by C. Forster Smith ... in four volumes ... History of the Peloponnesian War. Books I [–VIII] London, W. Heinemann; New York, G.P. Putnam's Sons, 1919-23. 4 v. fronts. (ports., v. 1, 3, 4) maps (part fold.) 17 cm. (The Loeb classical library ...) On t.-p. of vol. I name of translator appears as C. Foster [!] Smith. 1. Greece — History — Peloponnesian War, 431-404 B.C. I. Smith, Charles Forster, 1852- II. T.
PA3612.T5 1919   *LC* 20-3182

Xenophon.   **2.398**
Xenophon, with an English tranlation. London, W. Heinemann; New York, G. P. Putnam's sons, 1918-23. 4 v. fold. map. 17 cm. (Loeb classical library.) Greek and English on opposite pages. The translations of the Hellenica and Anabasis are by C. L. Brownson; of the Symposium and Apology by O. J. Todd; of the Memorabilia and Oeconomicus by E. C. Marchant. I. Brownson, Carleton

Lewis, 1866- tr. II. Todd, Otis Johnson, tr. III. Marchant, Edgar Cardew, tr. IV. T. V. Series.
PA3612.X3 1918   *LC* 18-22449

Xenophon.   • **2.399**
Scripta minora, with an English translation by E.C. Marchant. London:4bW. Heinemann, 1925. 463;1p. (The Loeb classical library. [Greek authors]) I. Marchant, Edgar Cardew. tr. II. T.
PA3612.X35 1925   *LC* 25-14729

Xenophon.   • **2.400**
Cyropaedia / Xenophon; with an English translation by Walter Miller. — London: W. Heinemann; New York: G. P. Putnam's, 1925-1932. 2 v.; 17 cm. — (Loeb classical library.) Greek and English on opposite pages. 1. Cyrus, King of Persia, d. 529 B.C. I. Miller, Walter, 1864-1949. II. T. III. Series.
PA3612.X4 1925d   *LC* 46-39509

PA3621–3623 Translations (Collections)

White, K. D.   **2.401**
Country life in classical times / K. D. White. — Ithaca, N.Y.: Cornell University Press, 1977. xix, 138 p., [12] leaves of plates: ill.; 25 cm. Includes indexes. 1. Classical literature — Translations into English. 2. English literature — Translations from classical literature. 3. Country life — Literary collection. I. T.
PA3621.W55   880/.08/032   *LC* 77-74923   *ISBN* 0801411149

Godolphin, Francis Richard Borroum, ed.   • **2.402**
Great classical myths. — New York: Modern Library, [1964] xxxi, 469 p.; 21 cm. — (The Modern library of the world's best books) 1. Classical poetry — Translations into English. 2. English poetry — Translations from classical literature. 3. Mythology, Classical I. T.
PA3622.A2 G6   881.082   *LC* 64-10293

The Oxford book of Greek verse in translation, edited by T. F.   • **2.403**
Higham and C. M. Bowra.
Oxford: The Clarendon press, 1938. cxii, 781, [1] p.; 17 cm. 'Every piece in the Oxford book of Greek verse is here translated, and the same arrangement of authors and numerations is followed ... Wherever possible, we have used existing translations.'—Pref. 1. Greek poetry — Translations into English. 2. English poetry — Translations from Greek. I. Higham, Thomas Farrant, 1890- ed. II. Bowra, Cecil Maurice, 1898- joint ed.
PA3622.A2 H5   881.0822   *LC* 38-27322

Lattimore, Richmond Alexander, 1906- ed. and tr.   • **2.404**
Greek lyrics. — 2d ed., rev. and enl. — [Chicago] University of Chicago Press [1960] 81 p. illus. 21 cm. 1. Greek poetry — Translations into English. 2. English poetry — Translations from Greek. I. T.
PA3622.L3 1960   884.082   *LC* 60-50177

To you, Simonides: epigrams & fragments from the Greek /   **2.405**
translated by William J. Philbin; drawings by Joachim Boske.
Dublin, Ireland: Dolmen Press; New York: distributed in the United States of America and in Canada by Humanities Press, 1973. 116 p.: ill.; 23 cm. — (Dolmen editions; 19) Includes index. 1. Epigrams, Greek 2. Greek poetry — Translations into English. 3. English poetry — Translations from Greek. I. Mac Philibín, Liam.
PA3623.A5 M34   888/.002   *LC* 77-379781   *ISBN* 0851052312

PA3818–4500 Authors, A–Z

PA3825–3849 Aeschylus

Aeschylus.   **2.406**
[Septem quae supersunt tragoedias. Page] Septem quae supersunt tragoedias [sic]: edidit Denys Page. Oxonii, Clarendon Press, 1972. 335 p. 20 cm. (Scriptorum classicorum bibliotheca Oxoniensis.) Text in Greek: pref. in Latin. I. Page, Denys Lionel, Sir, 1908- II. T. III. Series.
PA 3825 A2 1972   *LC* 73-157634   *ISBN* 0198145705

Aeschylus.   • **2.407**
The Oresteia of Aeschylus / edited with introduction, translation, and a commentary in which is included the work of Walter G. Headlam by George Thomson. — Cambridge: At the University Press, 1938. 2 v. Volume 1: Text in

Greek and English on opposite pages. I. Headlam, Walter George, 1866-1908. II. Thomson, George Derwent. III. T.
PA3825 A6 1938

Lebeck, Anne.   • **2.408**
The Oresteia; a study in language and structure. — Washington: Center for Hellenic Studies; distributed by Harvard University Press, Cambridge, Mass., 1971. x, 222 p.; 22 cm. — (Publications of the Center for Hellenic Studies) 1. Aeschylus. Oresteia. I. T.
PA3825.A6 1971   882/.01   LC 73-139724   ISBN 0674642201

Vellacott, Philip.   **2.409**
The logic of tragedy: morals and integrity in Aeschylus' Oresteia / Philip Vellacott. — Durham, N.C.: Duke University Press, 1984. ix, 190 p.; 25 cm. Includes indexes. 1. Aeschylus. Oresteia. 2. Aeschylus — Ethics. 3. Ethics in literature. 4. Integrity in literature. 5. Moral conditions in literature. I. T.
PA3825.A6 V37 1984   882/.01 19   LC 84-4057   ISBN 0822305976

Aeschylus.   • **2.410**
Agamemnon / Aeschylus; edited with a commentary by Eduard Fraenkel. — Oxford: Clarendon Press, [1950] 3 v. I. Fraenkel, Eduard, 1888-1970. II. T.
PA3825.A8 1950   882.1   LC 51-3273

Conacher, D. J.   **2.411**
Aeschylus' Prometheus bound: a literary commentary / D.J. Conacher. — Toronto; Buffalo: University of Toronto Press, 1980. xii, 198 p.; 24 cm. 1. Aeschylus. Prometheus bound I. T.
PA3825.P8 C6   882/.01 19   LC 81-116850   ISBN 0802023916

Thalmann, William G., 1947-.   **2.412**
Dramatic art in Aeschylus's Seven against Thebes / William G. Thalmann. — New Haven: Yale University Press, 1978. viii, 193 p.; 24 cm. — (Yale classical monographs. 1) A revision of the author's thesis, Yale University, 1975. 'Index of Aeschylean passages': 189-193. 1. Aeschylus. Seven against Thebes 2. Aeschylus — Criticism and interpretation. I. T. II. Series.
PA3825.S4 T5 1978   882/.01   LC 78-6585   ISBN 0300022190

Aeschylus.   • **2.413**
[Plays. English. 1953] Aeschylus. [Chicago] University of Chicago Press [1953-56] 2 v. 22 cm. (The Complete Greek tragedies) I. Lattimore, Richmond Alexander, 1906- ed. and tr. II. T.
PA3827.A47   882.1   LC 53-9655

Hogan, James C.   **2.414**
A commentary on the Complete Greek tragedies—Aeschylus / James C. Hogan. — Chicago: University of Chicago Press, 1985, [c1984] 332 p.: ill.; 21 cm. 1. Aeschylus — History and criticism. I. Aeschylus. Plays. English. 1956. II. T. III. Title: Complete Greek tragedies.
PA3829.H62 1984   882/.01 19   LC 84-2688   ISBN 0226348423

Otis, Brooks.   **2.415**
Cosmos & tragedy: an essay on the meaning of Aeschylus / Brooks Otis; edited with notes and a pref. by E. Christian Kopff. — Chapel Hill: University of North Carolina Press, c1981. xii, 119 p.; 23 cm. 1. Aeschylus — Criticism and interpretation. I. Kopff, E. Christian. II. T.
PA3829.O8   882/.01 19   LC 80-25320   ISBN 0807814652

Podlecki, Anthony J.   • **2.416**
The political background of Aeschylean tragedy / Anthony J. Podlecki. — Ann Arbor: University of Michigan Press, 1966. x, 188 p. 1. Aeschylus. 2. Greece — Politics and government I. T.
PA3829.P57   LC 66-11085

Taplin, Oliver Paul.   **2.417**
The stagecraft of Aeschylus: the dramatic use of exits and entrances in Greek tragedy / by Oliver Taplin. — Oxford [Eng.]: Clarendon Press, 1977. vi, 508 p.; 23 cm. Originally presented as the author's thesis, Oxford. Includes indexes. 1. Aeschylus — Technique. 2. Greek drama (Tragedy) — History and criticism. I. T.
PA3829.T36 1977   882/.01   LC 77-5920   ISBN 0198140061

Stanford, William Bedell.   • **2.418**
Aeschylus in his style; a study in language and personality. Dublin, The University press;[etc.,etc.] 1942. 2 p. l., 147 p. 22 cm. 1. Aeschylus — Style. I. T.
PA 3849 S78 1972   LC 43-7642

PA3870 Apollodorus

Apollodorus.   **2.419**
[Bibliothēkē. English] Gods and heroes of the Greeks: The library of Apollodorus / translated with introd. and notes by Michael Simpson; drawings by Leonard Baskin. — Amherst: University of Massachusetts Press, 1976. vi, 311 p.: ill.; 24 cm. Translation of Vivliothēkē, often formerly believed to be the work of Apollodorus, the Athenian grammarian, but now generally ascribed to

a later Apollodorus. Includes index. 1. Mythology, Greek I. Apollodorus, of Athens. Vivliothēkē. II. Simpson, Michael, 1934- III. Baskin, Leonard, 1922- IV. T.
PA3870.A55 A28   292/.2/11   LC 75-32489   ISBN 0870232053

Apollodorus, of Athens.   **2.420**
The library of Greek mythology / by Apollodorus; translated, with notes and indices by Keith Aldrich; drawings by Voula Tsouvelli. — Lawrence, Kan.: Colorado Press, 1975. x, 297 p., 9 leaves of plates: ill. Includes index. 1. Mythology, Greek I. Aldrich, Keith. II. Tsouvelli, Voula. III. T.
PA3870.A8 1975   PA3870 A8 1975.   ISBN 0872910725

Beye, Charles Rowan.   **2.421**
Epic and romance in the Argonautica of Apollonius / Charles Rowan Beye; foreword by John Gardner. — Carbondale: Southern Illinois University Press, c1982. xiv, 191 p.; 24 cm. — (Literary structures.) Includes index. 1. Apollonius, Rhodius. Argonautica 2. Argonauts (Greek mythology) in literature. I. T. II. Series.
PA3872.Z4 B4 1982   883/.01 19   LC 81-21402   ISBN 0809310201

PA3873 Archilochus

Rankin, H. D.   **2.422**
Archilochus of Paros / by H. D. Rankin. — Park Ridge, N.J.: Noyes Press, c1977. ix, 142 p. — (Noyes classical studies) Includes indexes. 1. Archilochus. 2. Poets, Greek — Biography. I. T.
PA3873.A77 R3   PA3873A77 R3.   884/.01   LC 77-6157   ISBN 0815550537

PA3875–3888 Aristophanes

Aristophanes.   **2.423**
Ecclesiazusae; edited with introduction and commentary by R. G. Ussher. Oxford, Clarendon Press, 1973. xlviii, 259 p. 20 cm. Greek text, English introduction and notes. I. Ussher, Robert Glenn, 1927- ed. II. T.
PA3875.E3 1973   882/.01   LC 73-153855   ISBN 0198141912

Aristophanes.   **2.424**
Clouds / edited with translation and notes by Alan H. Sommerstein. — Warminster, Wiltshire, England: Aris & Phillips, c1982. x, 232 p.; 22 cm. — (The Comedies of Aristophanes; v. 2 [i.e. 3]) Greek and English on opposite pages. I. Sommerstein, Alan H. II. T.
PA3875.N8x 1982   ISBN 0856682098

Aristophanes.   • **2.425**
The frogs. Edited, with introd., rev. text, commentary and index, by W.B. Stanford. 2d ed. London, Macmillan; New York, St. Martin's Press, 1963 [c1958] 211 p. 17 cm. Text in Greek. I. Stanford, William Bedell. II. T.
PA3875.R3

Aristophanes.   **2.426**
[Acharnians. English & Greek. 1980] Acharnians / edited with translation and notes by Alan H. Sommerstein. — Warminster, Wilts., England: Aris & Phillips, 1980. viii, 215 p.; 22 cm. — (The comedies of Aristophanes; v. 1) I. Sommerstein, Alan H. II. T.
PA3877.A6 1980   882/.01 19   LC 81-114153   ISBN 0856681679

Aristophanes.   **2.427**
[Knights. English & Greek] Knights / edited with translation and notes by Alan H. Sommerstein. — Warminster, Wilts, England: Aris & Phillips, 1981. ix, 220 p.; 22 cm. (The Comedies of Aristophanes; v. 2) Translation of: Equites. English and Greek. I. Sommerstein, Alan H. II. T.
PA3877.E7 1981   882/.01 19   LC 81-193617   ISBN 0856681776

Aristophanes.   **2.428**
[Lysistrata English.] Lysistrata / Aristophanes; translated by Douglass Parker;with sketches by Ellen Raskin. Ann Arbor: University of Michigan P., 1964. 98p.: ill.; 24cm. (Complete Greek comedy.) I. Parker, Douglass. II. T. III. Series.
PA3877.L8 1964   882   LC 63-9899

Aristophanes.   **2.429**
[Peace English & Greek] Peace / edited with translation and notes by Alan H. Sommerstein. — Chicago, Il.: Bolchazy-Carducci Publishers; Warminster, Wiltshire: Aris & Phillips, c1985. xxv, 196 p.: ill.; 22 cm. (The Comedies of Aristophanes; vol. 5) English and Greek. 1. Greece — History — Peloponnesian War, 431-404 B.C. — Drama. I. Sommerstein, Alan H. II. T.
PA3877.P2 1985   882/.01 19   LC 85-209233   ISBN 0865160902

Aristophanes.   **2.430**
[Wasps. English & Greek] Wasps / edited with translation and notes by Alan H. Sommerstein. — Warminster, Wilts, England: Aris & Phillips, c1983. xxii,

248 p.; 22 cm. (The Comedies of Aristophanes; v. 4) English and Greek. Translation of: Vespae. I. Sommerstein, Alan H. II. T.
PA3877.V5 1983   882/.01 19   *LC* 83-162649   *ISBN* 0856682128

Dearden, C. W.   **2.431**
The stage of Aristophanes / C. W. Dearden. — London: University of London, Athlone Press; [Atlantic Highlands] N.J.: [distributed by] Humanities Press, 1976. xiii, 203 p.: ill.; 23 cm. — (University of London classical studies; 7) 1. Aristophanes — Dramatic production. 2. Theater — Greece I. T.
PA3879.D38 1976   792/.0938/5   *LC* 77-374513   *ISBN* 0485137070

Dover, Kenneth James.   **2.432**
Aristophanic comedy [by] K. J. Dover. — Berkeley: University of California Press, 1972. xiv, 253 p.: illus.; 23 cm. 1. Aristophanes. I. T.
PA3879.D6   882/.01   *LC* 70-182681   *ISBN* 0520019768

Ehrenberg, Victor, 1891-.   **• 2.433**
The people of Aristophanes; a sociology of old Attic comedy. [3d rev. ed.] New York, Schocken Books [1962] xii, 384 p. illus. 21 cm. (Schocken paperbacks) 1. Aristophanes. 2. Athens (Greece) — Social conditions. 3. Athens (Greece) — Economic conditions. I. T. II. Title: A sociology of old Attic comedy.
PA3879.E5 1962   *LC* 62-13137

McLeish, Kenneth, 1940-.   **2.434**
The theatre of Aristophanes / Kenneth McLeish. — New York: Taplinger Pub. Co., 1980. 192 p.: ill.; 25 cm. Includes indexes. 1. Aristophanes — Criticism and interpretation. I. T.
PA3879.M3 1980   882/.01 19   *LC* 79-3142   180087630X

Whitman, Cedric Hubbell.   **• 2.435**
Aristophanes and the comic hero / by Cedric H. Whitman. — Cambridge, Mass.: Published for Oberlin College by Harvard University Press, 1964. ix, 333 p. — (Martin classical lectures. v.19) 1. Aristophanes. I. Oberlin College. II. T. III. Series.
PA25.M3 vol.19 PA3879.W5x   *LC* 64-22724

PA3890–3933 Aristotle

Aristotle.   **• 2.436**
[Organon Greek. 1949] Prior and posterior analytics; a revised text with introd. and commentary by W.D. Ross. Oxford Clarendon Press 1949. 690p. I. T.
PA3891 A2 1949

Aristotle.   **• 2.437**
De anima / Aristotle; edited, with introduction and commentary, by Sir David Ross. — Oxford: Clarendon Press, 1961. 338 p. Text in Greek. 1. Psychology — Early works to 1850 I. Ross, W. D. (William David), 1877- II. T.
PA3892.A2 1961   128   *LC* 61-3335

Aristotle.   **• 2.438**
[Metaphysics] Aristotle's Metaphysics / a revised text with introduction and commentary by W.D. Ross. — Oxford: Clarendon Press, 1924 (1981 printing). 2 v.; 23 cm. — Title in Greek at head of title. 1. Metaphysics — Early works to 1800 I. Ross, W. D. (William David), 1877- II. T.
B434.R77   PA3893 M5 1924.   *LC* 26-3482   *ISBN* 0198141076

Aristotle.   **• 2.439**
Parva naturalia / Aristotle. — Oxford: Clarendon Press, 1955. 354 p. I. Ross, W. D. (William David), 1877- II. T.
PA3893.P2 1955   *LC* 55-14546

Bonitz, Hermann, 1814-1888.   **• 2.440**
Index Aristotelicus / H. Bonitz. — 2. ed. — Graz: Akademische Druck- u. Verlagsanstalt, 1955. viii, 878 p. Part of the index, comprising the sociological terms, was begun by J. B. Meyer (letter a) and completed by B. A. Langkavel. 1. Aristotle — Dictionaries, indexes, etc. I. Meyer, Jürgen Bona, 1839-1897. II. Langkavel, Bernhard August, 1825-1902. III. T.
PA3926.Z8 B6 1955   *LC* 57-30166

PA3943–3970 B–E

Bacchylides.   **• 2.441**
Bacchylides. The poems and fragments. Cambridge, University press, 1905. xviii, 524 p. III facsim. 23 cm. 1. Manuscripts, Greek (Papyri) — Facsimiles. I. Jebb, Richard Claverhouse, Sir, 1841-1905. ed. II. British Museum. Manuscript. Papyrus DCCXXIII. III. T.
PA3943.A2 1905   *LC* 05-36113

Bacchylides.   **• 2.442**
Complete poems. Translated by Robert Fagles. With a foreword by Maurice Bowra. Introd. and notes by Adam M. Parry. New Haven Yale University Press 1961. 123p. I. Fagles, Robert. tr. II. T.
PA3943 E5 1961

Burnett, Anne Pippin, 1925-.   **2.443**
The art of Bacchylides / Anne Pippin Burnett. — Cambridge, Mass.: Published for Oberlin College by Harvard University Press, 1985. 207 p.; 25 cm. (Martin classical lectures. v. 29) Odes in English and Greek with commentary in English. Includes indexes. 1. Bacchylides — Criticism and interpretation. 2. Bacchylides — Translations, English. 3. Odes — History and criticism. I. T. II. Series.
PA25.M3 vol. 29 PA3943.Z5   937 s 884/.01 19   *LC* 84-10764   *ISBN* 0674046668

Millar, Fergus.   **• 2.444**
A study of Cassius Dio / by Fergus Millar. — Oxford [Eng.]: Clarendon Press, 1964. 239 p. 1. Cassius Dio Cocceianus. Historia romana. I. T.
PA3947.Z5 M5   *LC* 64-7145

Schmeling, Gareth L.   **2.445**
Chariton, by Gareth L. Schmeling. — New York: Twayne Publishers, [1974] 179 p.; 21 cm. — (Twayne's world authors series, TWAS 295. Greece) 1. Chariton. I. T.
PA3948.C32 S3   883/.01   *LC* 73-14672   *ISBN* 0805722076

Demetrius, of Phaleron, b. 350 B.C. Spurious and doubtful works.   **• 2.446**
A Greek critic: Demetrius on style, by G. M. A. Grube. — [Toronto] University of Toronto Press, 1961. ix, 171 p. 24 cm. — (The Phoenix; journal of the Classical Association of Canada. Supplementary volume, 4) Traditionally ascribed to Demetrius, of Phaleron; real author unknown. Translation of De elocutione. Bibliographical footnotes. I. Grube, Georges Maximilien Antoine, ed. and tr. II. T.
PA3948.D5E5   808   *LC* 61-2073

Demosthenes.   **• 2.447**
[Selected works Greek and English. 1949] Funeral speech, Erotic essay 60, 61, Exordia and Letters, with an English translation by Norman W. DeWitt and Norman J. DeWitt. London Heinemann 1949. 387p. I. De Witt, Norman Wentworth, 1876-, tr. II. T.
PA3949 A3 D4   *LC* 51-33843

Jones, Christopher Prestige.   **2.448**
The Roman world of Dio Chrysostom / C. P. Jones. — Cambridge, Mass.: Harvard University Press, 1978. vi, 208 p.: map; 24 cm. — (Loeb classical monographs) Includes index. 1. Dio, Chrysostom — Contemporary Greece. 2. Greece — History I. T. II. Series.
PA3965.D22 J6   938/.09   *LC* 78-5869   *ISBN* 0674779150

Dionysius, of Halicarnassus.   **• 2.449**
Dionysius of Halicarnassus On literary composition, being the Greek text of the De compositione verborvm, edited with introduction, translation, notes, glossary, and appendices, by W. Rhys Roberts. London Macmillan 1910. 358p. 1. Rhetoric, Ancient I. Roberts, W. Rhys (William Rhys), 1858-1929. tr. II. T.
PA3966 D3 1910   *LC* 10-9539

Dionysius, of Halicarnassus.   **2.450**
[De Thucydide. English] On Thucydides / Dionysius of Halicarnassus; English translation, based on the Greek text of Usener–Radermacher, with commentary by W. Kendrick Pritchett. — Berkeley: University of California Press, [1975] xxxvi, 164 p.; 24 cm. 1. Thucydides. I. Pritchett, W. Kendrick (William Kendrick), 1909- II. T.
PA3966.D6 E5   938/.007/2024   *LC* 74-27296   *ISBN* 0520029224

Epicurus.   **• 2.451**
Epicurus, the extant remains, with short critical apparatus, translation and notes by Cyril Bailey. Oxford Clarendon Press 1926. 432p. I. Bailey, Cyril, 1871-1957. ed. and tr. II. T.
PA3970 E2 1926

PA3973–3992 Euripides

Euripides.   **• 2.452**
Bacchae / Euripides; edited with introd. and commentary by E. R. Dodds. — 2d ed. — Oxford: Clarendon Press, 1960. lix, 253 p.; 19 cm. I. Dodds, Eric Robertson, 1893- II. T.
PA3973.B2 1960   882   *LC* 60-2664

Segal, Charles, 1936-.   **2.453**
Dionysiac poetics and Euripides' Bacchae / Charles Segal. — Princeton, N.J.: Princeton University Press, c1982. xiv, 364 p.; 24 cm. Includes index. 1. Euripides. Bacchae. I. T.
PA3973.B2 S56 1982   882/.01 19   *LC* 82-47612   *ISBN* 0691065284

Euripides.   **• 2.454**
Electra / Euripides; edited with introduction and commentary by J.D. Denniston. — Oxford: The Clarendon press, 1939. xliv, 225 p. — (The plays of

Euripides) 1. Euripides Electra — Criticism and interpretation. I. Denniston, J. D. (John Dewar), 1887-1949. II. T.
PA3973.E5 1939   882.3   LC 39-30574

Euripides.   ● 2.455
Helen / Euripides; edited with introduction and commentary by A.M. Dale. — Oxford: Clarendon Press, 1967. xxxiv, 179 p.; 20 cm. Text in Greek, introduction and notes in English. I. Dale, Amy Marjorie. II. T.
PA3973.H4 1967   LC 67-75839

Zuntz, Günther, 1902-.   ● 2.456
The political plays of Euripides, by G. Zuntz. — [Corr. reprint. — Manchester]: Manchester University Press, [1963] xi, 157 p.; 23 cm. 1. Euripides. Heraclidae. 2. Euripides. Supplices. I. T.
PA3973.H6 Z8 1963   LC 68-38415

Euripides.   ● 2.457
Hippolytos / Euripides; edited with introd. and commentary by W. S. Barrett. — Oxford: Clarendon Press, 1964. xvi, 453 p.: map.; 23 cm. Text in Greek; commentary in English. Errata slip inserted. I. Barrett, William Spencer. II. T.
PA3973.H7 1964   882   LC 64-5188

Euripides.   ● 2.458
Ion: edited with introduction and commentary, by A. S. Owen ... — Oxford, The Clarendon press, 1939. xliii, [1], 196 p. 19 cm. I. Owen, Arthur Synge, ed. II. T.
PA3973.I6 1939   882.3   LC 40-3210

Euripides.   ● 2.459
Iphigenia in Tauris / Euripides; edited with introduction and commentary by M. Platnauer. — Oxford: The Clarendon press, 1938. xix, 186 p. — (The plays of Euripides) 'The text and critical apparatus...are those of Professor Murray as published in the series of Oxford classical texts, second edition, 1913'-Pref. 1. Euripides Iphigenia in Tauris — Criticism and interpretation. I. Platnauer, Maurice. II. T.
PA3973.I8   882.3   LC a 38-567

Euripides.   ● 2.460
[Medea. Greek. 1938] Medea; the text edited with introd. and commentary by Denys L. Page. Oxford Clarendon Press 1938. 190p. I. Page, Denys Lionel, ed. II. T.
PA3973 M4 1938   LC 39-13850

Pucci, Pietro.   2.461
The violence of pity in Euripides' Medea / Pietro Pucci. — Ithaca, N.Y.: Cornell University Press, c1980. 238 p.: ill.; 24 cm. (Cornell studies in classical philology; v. 41) 1. Euripides. Medea. 2. Sympathy in literature. I. T.
PA3973.M4 P8   882/.01   LC 79-52501   ISBN 0801411904

Euripides.   2.462
Troades / Euripides; edited with introduction and commentary by K.H. Lee. — Basingstoke [England]: Macmillan; [New York]: St. Martin's Press, c1976. xxxiv, 299 p.; 17 cm. Greek text; English introd. and commentary. Includes indexes. I. Lee, K. H. II. T.
PA3973.T8 1976   882/.01   LC 77-366282   ISBN 0333178912

Euripides.   ● 2.463
Alcestis / Euripides; edited with introd. and commentary by A. M. Dale. — Oxford: Clarendon Press, 1954. xl, 130 p.; 19 cm. 'The text ... is that of Professor Gilbert Murray ... published in 1902 in the series of Oxford classical texts.' Text in Greek; introductory matter in English. I. Dale, Amy Marjorie. ed. II. T.
PA3975.A5 1954x   LC A 55-6291

Euripides.   ● 2.464
Euripides. With an introd. by Richmond Lattimore. — [Chicago]: University of Chicago Press, [1955-59] 5 v.; 22 cm. — (The Complete Greek tragedies) I. Lattimore, Richmond Alexander, 1906- ed. II. T.
PA3975.A1 1955   882   LC 55-5787

Burnett, Anne Pippin, 1925-.   2.465
Catastrophe survived: Euripides' plays of mixed reversal. — Oxford, Clarendon Press, 1971. ix, 234 p. 23 cm. 1. Euripides. I. T.
PA3978.B8   882/.01   LC 70-29942   ISBN 0198141866

Conacher, D. J.   ● 2.466
Euripidean drama; myth, theme and structure [by] D. J. Conacher. — [Toronto]: University of Toronto Press, [1967] xiii, 354 p.; 24 cm. 1. Euripides. I. T.
PA3978.C74   882/.01   LC 68-76826

Foley, Helene P., 1942-.   2.467
Ritual irony: poetry and sacrifice in Euripides / Helene P. Foley. — Ithaca, N.Y.: Cornell University Press, 1985. 285 p.; 24 cm. Includes index.

1. Euripides — Criticism and interpretation. 2. Ritual in literature 3. Sacrifice in literature. 4. Irony in literature I. T.
PA3978.F6 1985   882/.01 19   LC 84-17470   ISBN 0801416922

Grube, G. M. A. (George Maximilian Anthony)   ● 2.468
The drama of Euripides. New York, Barnes & Noble [1961] 456 p. 23 cm. 'First published in 1941; reprinted with minor corrections 1961.' 1. Euripides. I. T.
PA3978.G7 1961   882   LC 61-3808

Halleran, Michael R.   2.469
The stagecraft in Euripides / Michael R. Halleran. — Totowa, N.J.: Barnes & Noble, 1984, c1985. 127 p.; 23 cm. Includes index. 1. Euripides — Technique. 2. Euripides — Dramatic production. I. T.
PA3978.H28 1985   882/.01 19   LC 84-12314   ISBN 0389205133

Lucas, F. L. (Frank Laurence), 1894-1967.   ● 2.470
Euripides and his influence. Introd. by R. W. Livingstone. New York, Cooper Square Publishers, 1963. xv, 188 p. 19 cm. (Our debt to Greece and Rome.) 1. Euripides — Influence. I. T. II. Series.
PA3978.L8 1963   882   LC 63-10275

Murray, Gilbert, 1866-1957.   ● 2.471
Euripides and his age / Gilbert Murray; with a new introduction by H. D. F. Kitto. — London: Oxford University Press, 1965. xii, 132 p.; 20 cm. — (Oxford paperbacks; no. 99) 1. Euripides. I. T.
PA3978.M8 1965b   PA3978.M8 1965.   882.01   LC 65-29787

Vellacott, Philip.   2.472
Ironic drama: a study of Euripides' method and meaning / [by] Philip H. Vellacott. — London; New York: Cambridge University Press, 1975. x, 266 p.; 24 cm. 1. Euripides — Criticism and interpretation. I. T.
PA3978.V38   PA3978 V38.   882/.01   LC 74-19522   ISBN 0521205905

Barlow, Shirley Ann.   2.473
The imagery of Euripides: a study in the dramatic use of pictorial language [by] Shirley A. Barlow. — London: Methuen, 1971. xii, 169 p.; 23 cm. 'Distributed in the U.S.A. by Barnes & Noble Inc.' Based on the author's thesis, University of London, 1963. 1. Euripides — Style. I. T.
PA3992.B3 1971   882/.01   LC 78-596134   ISBN 0416081304

PA3998–4017 H

Heliodorus, of Emesa.   ● 2.474
An Ethiopian romance / Heliodorus; translated with an introd. by Moses Hadas. — Ann Arbor,: Univ. of Michigan Press, [1957]. 277 p.; 23 cm. Translation of Aethiopica historia. I. T.
PA3998.H2 E5 1976   883/.01   LC 57-7744

Fornara, Charles W.   ● 2.475
Herodotus: an interpretative essay, [by] Charles W. Fornara. — Oxford: Clarendon Press, 1971. [10], 98 p.; 21 cm. 1. Herodotus. I. T.
PA4004.F6   938/.0072/024   LC 71-577168   ISBN 0198142933

How, Walter Wybergh, 1861-.   ● 2.476
A commentary on Herodotus, with introd. and appendixes, by W.W. How and J. Wells. Oxford Clarendon Press [1928] 2 v. 1. Herodotus. I. Wells, Joseph, 1855-1929, jt. author II. T.
PA4004 H6 1928

Immerwahr, Henry R.   ● 2.477
Form and thought in Herodotus, by Henry R. Immerwahr. — Cleveland: Published for the American Philological Association [Chapel Hill, N.C.] by the Press of Western Reserve University, 1966. xv, 374 p.; 25 cm. — (Philological monographs. no. 23) 1. Herodotus. I. American Philological Association. II. T. III. Series.
PA4004.I4   888/.01/08   LC 66-25319

Hesiod.   2.478
Theogony / edited with prolegomena and commentary by M. L. West. — Oxford: Clarendon, 1966. xiii, 459 p.: ill. Greek text, English prolegomena and commentary. I. West, M. L. (Martin Litchfield), 1937- II. T.
PA4009.T5 1966   LC 67-70100

Hesiod.   ● 2.479
[Works and days. English] The works and days. Theogony. The shield of Herakles. Translated by Richmond Lattimore. Illustrated by Richard Wilt. Ann Arbor, University of Michigan Press [1959] 241 p. illus. 21 cm. In verse. I. Lattimore, Richmond Alexander, 1906- ed. and tr. II. T. III. Title: Theogony. IV. Title: Shield of Herakles.
PA4010.E5 O6 1959   883   LC 59-6027

Hesiod.   2.480
[Works and days. English] Works & days / Hesiod; edited with prolegomena and commentary by M. L. West. — Oxford [Eng.]: Clarendon Press, 1978. xiii,

399 p.; 23 cm. Greek text with English commentary. I. West, M. L. (Martin Litchfield), 1937- II. T.
PA4010.E5 O7 1978   881/.01   *LC* 77-6326   *ISBN* 0198140053

PA4018–4209 Homer

Homer.   • **2.481**
[Iliad. German & Greek] Homērou Ilias: the Iliad of Homer / edited with general and grammatical introds., notes and appendices by Walter Leaf and M. A. Bayfield. — [2nd ed.]. — London: Macmillan, 1965. 2 v.: ill. I. Leaf, Walter, 1852-1927, ed. II. Bayfield, Matthew Albert, 1852-1922. ed. III. T.
PA4019 A2   *LC* 65-7160

Homer.   • **2.482**
The Odyssey of Homer, edited with general and grammatical introd., commentary, and indexes, by W. B. Stanford. — 2d ed. — London, Macmillan; New York, St Martin's Press, 1962-64 [v. 1, 1964] 2 v. illus. 18 cm. — (Classical series) I. Stanford, William Bedell. ed. II. T.
PA4021.A2   883   *LC* 65-7161

Homer.   • **2.483**
[Hymns. Greek. 1936] The Homeric hymns, edited by T.W. Allen, W.R. Halliday and E.E. Sikes. 2d ed. Oxford Clarendon Press 1936. I. Allen, Thomas William, 1862-, ed. II. T.
PA4023 H8 1936

Homer.   • **2.484**
Chapman's Homer: the Iliad, the Odyssey, and the lesser Homerica / edited, with introductions, textual notes, commentaries, and glossaries, by Allardyce Nicoll. — 2nd ed. — Princeton, N.J.: Princeton University Press, 1967. 2 v.: facsims.; 25 cm. — (Bollingen series. 41) I. Chapman, George, 1559?-1634. II. T. III. Series.
PA4025.A1C5 1967   883.1

Homer.   **2.485**
[Iliad. German & Greek English] The Iliad [by] Homer. Translated by Robert Fitzgerald, with drawings by Hans Erni. [1st ed.] Garden City, N.Y., Anchor Press, 1974. 594 p. 24 cm. I. Fitzgerald, Robert, 1910- tr. II. T.
PA4025.A2 F5   883/.01   *LC* 74-3528   *ISBN* 038505940X

Homer.   • **2.486**
[Iliad. German & Greek English] The Iliad. Translated with an introd. by Richmond Lattimore. Drawings by Leonard Baskin. [Chicago] University of Chicago Press [1962] 526 p. plates. 29 cm. I. Lattimore, Richmond Alexander, 1906- ed. and tr. II. T.
PA4025.A2 L35 1962   883   *LC* 62-19604

Mason, H. A. (Harold Andrew)   **2.487**
To Homer through Pope; an introduction to Homer's Iliad and Pope's translation, by H. A. Mason. New York, Barnes & Noble Books [1972] vi, 216 p. 23 cm. 1. Homer. Iliad. 2. Pope, Alexander, 1688-1744. I. T.
PA4025.A2 P654   883/.01   *LC* 73-156597   *ISBN* 0064946347

Logue, Christopher, 1926-.   **2.488**
War music: an account of books 16 to 19 of Homer's Iliad / Christopher Logue. — London: J. Cape, 1981. 83 p.; 23 cm. I. Homer. Iliad. Book 16-19. English. II. T.
PA4025.A3 L6 1981   821/.914 19   *LC* 81-157081   *ISBN* 0224015346

Homer.   • **2.489**
[Odyssea. English. 1967] The Odyssey of Homer. Translated with an introd. by Richmond Lattimore. New York, Harper & Row [1967] x, 374 p. 24 cm. I. Lattimore, Richmond Alexander, 1906- tr. II. T.
PA4025.A5 E6 1967   883/.01   *LC* 66-20740

Homer.   • **2.490**
The Odyssey. Translated by Robert Fitzgerald. With drawings by Hans Erni. Garden City, N.Y., Anchor Press/Doubleday, 1961. 474 p. illus. 25 cm. I. Fitzgerald, Robert, 1910- tr. II. T.
PA4025.A5 F5   883   *LC* 61-8886

Homer.   **2.491**
[Hymni. English] The Homeric hymns / translation, introd., and notes [by] Apostolos N. Athanassakis. — Baltimore: Johns Hopkins University Press, c1976. xiii, 107 p.; 26 cm. I. Athanassakis, Apostolos N. II. T.
PA4025.H8 A8 1976   883/.01   *LC* 75-40305   *ISBN* 0801817919.
ISBN 0801817927 pbk

PA4035 Criticism

Bassett, Samuel Eliot, 1873-1936.   • **2.492**
The poetry of Homer, by Samuel Eliot Bassett. Berkeley, Calif., University of California Press, 1938. 273 p. (Sather classical lectures, v. 15, 1938) 1. Homer — Criticism and interpretation. I. T.
PA4037.B35   *LC* 39-28064

Beye, Charles Rowan.   • **2.493**
The Iliad, the Odyssey, and the epic tradition. [1st ed.] Garden City, N.Y., Anchor Books, 1966. ix, 263 p. 19 cm. 1. Homer. Iliad. 2. Homer. Odyssea. I. T.
PA4037.B503   883.01   *LC* 66-26857

Finley, M. I. (Moses I.), 1912-.   **2.494**
The world of Odysseus / by M. I. Finley. — Rev. ed. — New York: Viking Press, 1978, c1977. 192 p.: map; 22 cm. Includes indexes. 1. Civilization, Homeric I. T.
PA4037.F48 1978   883/.01   *LC* 77-28903   *ISBN* 0670737647

Kirk, G. S. (Geoffrey Stephen), 1921-.   **2.495**
The Iliad, a commentary / G.S. Kirk. — Cambridge [Cambridgeshire]; New York: Cambridge University Press, 1985-. v. <1 >: map; 24 cm. Includes index. 1. Homer. Iliad. I. Homer. Iliad. II. T.
PA4037.K458 1985   883/.01 19   *LC* 84-11330   *ISBN* 0521237092

Kirk, G. S. (Geoffrey Stephen), 1921-.   • **2.496**
The songs of Homer / by G.S. Kirk. — Cambridge: University Press, 1962. xiii, 423 p.: ill., maps. 1. Homer. I. T.
PA4037.K46   883   *LC* 62-52685

Knight, W. F. Jackson (William Francis Jackson), 1895-1964.   • **2.497**
Many–minded Homer; an introduction. Edited by John D. Christie. New York, Barnes & Noble [1968, i.e. 1969] 224 p. 23 cm. 1. Homer. I. Christie, John D., ed. II. T.
PA4037.K57 1969   881/.01   *LC* 71-3559

Luce, John Victor, 1920-.   **2.498**
Homer and the heroic age / J. V. Luce. — 1st U.S. ed. — New York: Harper & Row, c1975. 200 p.: ill. (some col.); 25 cm. 1. Homer. 2. Civilization, Homeric I. T.
PA4037.L68 1975b   883/.01   *LC* 74-29422   *ISBN* 0060127228

Mueller, Martin, 1939-.   **2.499**
The Iliad / Martin Mueller. — London; Boston: G. Allen & Unwin, 1984. 210 p.; 23 cm. — (Unwin critical library.) Includes index. 1. Homer. Iliad. I. T. II. Series.
PA4037.M78 1984   883/.01 19   *LC* 84-354   *ISBN* 0048000272

Nilsson, Martin Persson, 1874-1967.   • **2.500**
Homer and Mycenae, by Martin P. Nilsson. New York, Cooper Square Publishers, 1968. xii, 283 p. illus., maps, plans. 24 cm. (Methuen's handbooks of archaeology) 'A Marandell book.' Reprint of the 1933 ed. 1. Homer. 2. Civilization, Homeric 3. Civilization, Mycenaean I. T.
PA4037.N57 1968   881/.01   *LC* 68-54548

Owen, Eric Trevor, 1882-.   • **2.501**
The story of the Iliad: as told in the Iliad / E.T. Owen. — New York: Oxford University Press, 1947 [c1946] viii, 248 p.; 21 cm. — 1. Homer. Iliad. I. T.
PA4037.O68 1946   883.1   *LC* 47-30648 *

Page, Denys Lionel.   • **2.502**
History and the Homeric Iliad. Berkeley, University of California Press, 1959. vi, 350 p. illus., maps (part fold.) 24 cm. (Sather classical lectures. v. 31) 1. Homer. Iliad. 2. Oral-formulaic analysis 3. Troy (Ancient city) I. T. II. Series.
PA4037.P27   883   *LC* 59-5243

Redfield, James M., 1935-.   **2.503**
Nature and culture in the Iliad: the tragedy of Hector / James M. Redfield. — Chicago: University of Chicago Press, 1975. xvi, 287 p.; 24 cm. Includes index. 1. Homer. Iliad. I. T.
PA4037.R38   883/.01   *LC* 74-33511   *ISBN* 0226706516

Scott, John Adams, 1867-1947.   • **2.504**
The unity of Homer / J. A. Scott. — New York: Biblo and Tannen, 1965. 275 p.; 24 cm. 1. Homer. I. T.
PA4037.S42   *LC* 65-15246

Vivante, Paolo.   • **2.505**
The Homeric imagination; a study of Homer's poetic perception of reality. Bloomington, Indiana University Press [1970] viii, 215 p. 22 cm. 1. Homer. I. T.
PA4037.V5   883/.01   *LC* 77-126221   *ISBN* 0253138558

Wace, A. J. B. (Alan John Bayard), 1879-1957. ed.   • **2.506**
A companion to Homer. Edited by Alan J. B. Wace and Frank H. Stubbings. — London, Macmillan; New York, St. Martin's Press, 1962. xxix, 595 p. illus., maps, facsims. 25 cm. 'References to the poems [etc.]' (card) inserted. Includes bibliographical references. 1. Homer. 2. Civilization, Homeric I. Stubbings, Frank H. joint ed. II. T.
PA4037.W15 1962   883   LC 62-6433

Whitman, Cedric Hubbell.   • **2.507**
Homer and the heroic tradition. Cambridge, Harvard University Press, 1958. xii, 365 p. 24 cm. 1. Homer. 2. Oral-formulaic analysis I. T.
PA4037.W66   883.1   LC 58-7252

Bowra, C. M. (Cecil Maurice), 1898-1971.   • **2.508**
Tradition and design in the Iliad, by C. M. Bowra ... — Oxford: The Clarendon press, 1930. 278 p.; 23 cm. 1. Homer. Iliad — Criticism and interpretation. I. T.
PA4067.B63 1930   883.1   LC 31-14543

Lord, George de Forest, 1919-.   **2.509**
Homeric renaissance; the Odyssey of George Chapman, by George deF. Lord. — [Hamden, Conn.]: Archon Books, 1972. 224 p.: facsim.; 22 cm. Reprint of the 1956 ed. Originally published as Yale studies in English, v. 131. 1. Homer — Translations, English. 2. Chapman, George, 1559?-1634. I. T.
PA4152.E5 L6 1972   883/.01   LC 70-179566   ISBN 0208011307

Arnold, Matthew, 1822-1888.   • **2.510**
On translating Homer. New ed. with introd. & notes by W. H. D. Rouse. [1st AMS ed.] London, J. Murray, 1905. [New York, AMS Press, 1971] 200 p. 19 cm. 1. Homer. 2. Translating and interpreting I. Rouse, W. H. D. (William Henry Denham), 1863-1950. ed. II. T.
PA4153.A7 1971   883/.01   LC 78-136411   ISBN 0404003885

Austin, Norman.   **2.511**
Archery at the dark of the moon: poetic problems in Homer's Odyssey / Norman Austin. — Berkeley: University of California Press, 1975. xiii, 297 p.; 24 cm. Includes index. 1. Homer. Odyssea. 2. Homer — Criticism and interpretation. 3. Oral-formulaic analysis I. T.
PA4167.A9   883/.01   LC 73-94442   ISBN 0520027132

Page, Denys Lionel.   • **2.512**
The Homeric Odyssey / by Denys Page. — Oxford: Clarendon Press, 1955. vi, 186 p.; 23 cm. — (The Mary Flexner lectures; 1954) 1. Homer. Odyssey I. T.
PA4167.P3   883.1   LC 55-14743

Kirk, G. S. (Geoffrey Stephen), 1921- ed.   • **2.513**
The language and background of Homer; some recent studies and controversies, selected and introduced by G. S. Kirk. — Cambridge [Eng.] W. Heffer [1964] xvi, 159 p. map. 22 cm. — (Views and controversies about classical antiquity) Bibliographical footnotes. 1. Homer — Language. I. T. II. Series.
PA4175.K5   883.01   LC 65-8542

Parry, Milman.   **2.514**
The making of Homeric verse: the collected papers of Milman Parry; edited by Adam Parry. Oxford, Clarendon Press, 1971. lxii, 483 p., 2 plates. 2 ports. 24 cm. Includes English translations of dissertations originally written in French. 1. Homer — Versification. 2. Oral-formulaic analysis I. Parry, Adam. ed. II. T.
PA4205.P3   883/.01   LC 79-28426   ISBN 0198141815

Cunliffe, Richard John.   • **2.515**
A lexicon of the Homeric dialect. [New ed.] Norman, University of Oklahoma Press [1963] ix, 445 p. 23 cm. 1. Homer — Dictionaries. I. T.
PA4209.C8 1963   LC 63-17165

Dunbar, Henry, d. 1883, comp.   • **2.516**
A complete concordance to the Odyssey of Homer. New ed. completely rev. and enl. Hildesheim G. Olm 1962. 398p. 1. Homer — Concordances I. Marzullo, Benedetto, 1923-, ed. II. T.
PA4209 D7 1962

Prendergast, Guy Lushington.   • **2.517**
A complete concordance to the Iliad of Homer / Guy Lushington Prendergast; completely rev. and enl. by Benedetto Marzullo. — 3rd ed. — Hildesheim: G. Olms, 1983. 427 p.; 28 cm. 1. Homer Iliad — Concordances. I. Marzullo, Benedetto, 1923- II. T.
PA4209.P7   883.01   ISBN 3487041618

PA4229–4278 L–P

Longinus, Cassius, ca. 213-273. Spurious and doubtful works.   • **2.518**
[Sublimate. English] 'Longinus' On the sublime / edited with introduction and commentary by D.A. Russell. — Oxford: Clarendon Press, 1964. lv, 208 p.

1. Sublime, The. 2. Rhetoric, Ancient I. Russell, D. A. (Donald Andrew) II. T. III. Title: On the sublime.
PA4229.L4 1964   808   LC 64-4514

McCulloh, William E.   • **2.519**
Longus, by William E. McCulloh. New York, Twayne [1970] 143 p. 22 cm. (Twayne's world authors series, TWAS 96. Greece) 1. Longus. Daphnis and Chloe. Classical Greek & Modern Greek. 2. Daphnis (Greek mythology) — Fiction. I. T.
PA4229.L9 M3   883/.01   LC 77-99541

Allinson, Francis Greeleaf, 1856-.   • **2.520**
Lucian, satirist and artist / by Francis G. Allinson. — New York: Cooper Square Publishers, 1963. ix, 204 p.; 19 cm. — (Our debt to Greece and Rome.) 1. Lucian, of Samosata. I. T. II. Series.
PA4236 A7 1963   887   LC 63-10286

Robinson, Christopher.   **2.521**
Lucian and his influence in Europe / Christopher Robinson. — Chapel Hill: University of North Carolina Press, c1979. 248 p., [1] leaf of plates: ill.; 23 cm. Includes index. 1. Lucian, of Samosata. 2. Lucian, of Samosata — Influence. 3. European literature — History and criticism. I. T.
PA4236.R6   887/.01   LC 79-16580   ISBN 0807814040

Dover, Kenneth James.   • **2.522**
Lysias and the corpus Lysiacum, by K. J. Dover. — Berkeley: University of California Press, 1968. viii, 200 p.; 24 cm. — (Sather classical lectures. v. 39) 1. Lysias. I. T. II. Series.
PA4243.D6   885/.01   LC 68-63337

Menander, of Athens.   • **2.523**
Dyskolos. Edited by E.W. Handley. Cambridge, Harvard University Press, 1965. x, 323 p. 23 cm. Text in Greek. I. Handley, Eric Walter, ed. II. T.
PA4245.D9 1965   LC 66-45447

Menander, of Athens.   **2.524**
[Dyscolus. English] The dyskolos / by Menander; translated with an introd. and notes by Carroll Moulton. — New York: New American Library, 1977. xxiii, 72 p.; 18 cm. — (A Mentor book) I. T.
PA4246.E5 D9 1977   882/.01   LC 76-41983   ISBN 0451615409

Gerber, Douglas E.   **2.525**
Pindar's Olympian one: a commentary / Douglas E. Gerber. — Toronto; Buffalo: University of Toronto Press, c1982. 202 p.; 24 cm. — (Phoenix. Supplementary volume. 0079-1784; 15) Text in Greek, commentary in English. Includes indexes. 1. Pindar. Olympia. 1. Pindar. Olympia. 1982. II. T. III. Series.
PA4274.O5 G47 1982   884/.01 19   LC 82-177008   ISBN 0802055079

Pindar.   • **2.526**
[Works. English] The odes of Pindar, translated by Richmond Lattimore. Chicago, Ill., The University of Chicago press [1947] xii, 169, [1] p. 20 cm. 'Of the translations in this collection, the first, third, fourth, eighth, and tenth Pythians have been previously published under the title Some odes of Pindar.' I. Lattimore, Richmond Alexander, 1906- tr. II. T.
PA4275.E5 L24   884.5   LC 47-3185

Pindar.   **2.527**
Pindar's Victory songs / translation, introd., prefaces, Frank J. Nisetich. — Baltimore: Johns Hopkins University Press, c1980. xiii, 367 p.: ill.; 26 cm. Includes index. I. Nisetich, Frank J. II. T.
PA4275.E5 N57   884/.01   LC 79-3739   ISBN 0801823501

Pindar.   • **2.528**
Selected odes. Translated with interpretative essays, by Carl A. P. Ruck and William H. Matheson. Ann Arbor, University of Michigan Press [1968] 269 p. 21 cm. I. Ruck, Carl A. P. tr. II. Matheson, William H., tr. III. T.
PA4275.E5 R8   881/.01   LC 68-16442

Pindar.   **2.529**
[Works. English. 1974] Pindar's odes. Translated, with pref., introd., and notes, by Roy Arthur Swanson. Foreword by Kimon Friar. [Indianapolis, Bobbs-Merrill, 1974] lvii, 358 p. illus. 21 cm. (The Library of liberal arts) I. Swanson, Roy Arthur, 1925- tr. II. T.
PA4275.E5 S8   884/.01   LC 72-90908   ISBN 0672515431 ISBN 0672612453

Crotty, Kevin, 1948-.   **2.530**
Song and action: the victory odes of Pindar / Kevin Crotty. — Baltimore, Md.: Johns Hopkins University Press, c1982. xii, 173 p.; 24 cm. Originally presented as the author's thesis (Ph.D.—Yale University, 1975) Includes indexes. 1. Pindar — Criticism and interpretation. I. T.
PA4276.C7 1982   884/.01 19   LC 81-48180   ISBN 0801827469

Norwood, Gilbert, 1880-1954.   • **2.531**
Pindar / by Gilbert Norwood. — Berkeley: University of California Press, c1945. 302 p., [2] leaves of plates: ill.; 24 cm. — (Sather classical lectures. v. 19) 1. Pindar. 2. Symbolism in literature I. T. II. Series.
PA4276.N6   *LC* a46-1980

PA4279 Plato

Plato.   • **2.532**
Plato's Euthyphro, Apology of Socrates and Crito / edited with notes by John Burnet. — Oxford: The Clarendon Press, 1924, 1974 printing. vii, 219 p. Text in Greek; notes in English. I. Burnet, John, 1863-1928. II. T.
PA4279 A3 1924   PA4279 A3 1924b.   *LC* 25-4241   *ISBN* 0198141432

Plato.   • **2.533**
Gorgias / Plato; a rev. text with introd. and commentary by E.R. Dodds. — Oxford: Clarendon Press, 1959. 406 p. I. T.
PA4279.G7 1959   *LC* 59-65168   *ISBN* 019814153X

Plato.   • **2.534**
Meno. Edited with introd. and commentary by R. S. Bluck. — Cambridge [Eng.] University Press, 1961. viii, 473 p. illus. 23 cm. Bibliography: p. 462-466. I. Bluck, Richard Stanley Harold, ed. II. T.
PA4279.M4 1961   888   *LC* 61-16257

Plato.   • **2.535**
The Republic. Edited, with critical notes, commentary, and appendixes, by James Adam. 2d ed., with an introd. by D.A. Rees. Cambridge [Eng.] University Press, 1963. 2v.: diagrs.; 23 cm. In Greek. Erratum slip inserted in v.2. 1. Utopias I. Adam, James, 1860-1907. II. T.
PA4279.R4 1963   321.07   *LC* 64-168

PA4362–4412 P–S

Barrow, Reginald Haynes, 1893-.   • **2.536**
Plutarch and his times, by R. H. Barrow. Bloomington, Indiana University Press, 1967. xv, 202 p. geneal. table, map. 23 cm. 1. Plutarch. I. T.
PA4382.B3   938/.007/2024 B   *LC* 67-10109

Jones, Christopher Prestige.   **2.537**
Plutarch and Rome, [by] C. P. Jones. Oxford, Clarendon Press, 1971. xiii, 158 p. 23 cm. 1. Plutarch. 2. Rome — History I. T.
PA4382.J6   938/.0072/024 B   *LC* 72-873625   *ISBN* 019814363X

Wardman, Alan.   **2.538**
Plutarch's Lives. Berkeley, University of California Press, 1974. xiii, 274 p. 23 cm. 1. Plutarch. Vitae parallelae. I. T.
PA4385.W3   329/.0092/2 B   *LC* 73-89369   *ISBN* 0520026632

Walbank, F. W. (Frank William), 1909-.   • **2.539**
A historical commentary on Polybius. Oxford, Clarendon Press, 1957-79. 3 v. port., maps, plans. 23 cm. 1. Polybius. Historiae 2. History, Ancient 3. Rome — History — Republic, 510-30 B.C. 4. Greece — History — 146 B.C.-323 A.D. I. T.
PA4393.W3   937/.04   *LC* 57-1830

Page, Denys Lionel.   • **2.540**
Sappho and Alcaeus; an introduction to the study of ancient Lesbian poetry. — Oxford, Clarendon Press, 1955. viii, 340 p. 23 cm. Bibliographical footnotes. 1. Sappho. 2. Alcaeus. I. T.
PA4409.P2   884.2   *LC* 55-14565

PA4413–4434 Sophocles

Sophocles.   • **2.541**
Sophoclis Fabvlae, recognovit breviqve adnotatione critica instrvxit A. C. Pearson ... — Oxonii, e Typographeo Clarendoniano, 1924. 1 V. l., iii-xxiv, [404] p. 19 cm. — (Added t.-p.: Scriptorum classicorum bibliotheca oxoniensis [Scriptores graeci]) I. Pearson, Alfred Chilton, 1861- ed. II. T.
PA4413.A2 1924   *LC* 25-4005

Sophocles.   • **2.542**
Sophocles; the plays and fragments with critical notes, commentary, and translation in English prose, by R. C. Jebb. Cambridge, University Press, 1889-1908. — St. Clair Shores, Mich.: Scholarly Press, 1972. 7 v.; 21 cm. No more published. I. Jebb, Richard Claverhouse, Sir, 1841-1905. ed. II. T.
PA4413.A2 1972   882/.01   *LC* 72-115277   *ISBN* 0403002893

Sophocles.   • **2.543**
Ajax / Sophocles; with introduction, revised text, commentary, appendixes, indexes and bibliography by W.B. Stanford. — London: Macmillan, 1963. lxiv, 311 p. I. T.
PA4413.A5   882/.01   *LC* 64-57951

Knox, Bernard MacGregor Walker.   • **2.544**
Oedipus at Thebes. New Haven, Yale University Press, 1957. 280 p. illus. 22 cm. 1. Sophocles. Oedipus Rex I. T.
PA4413.O7 K55   882.2   *LC* 57-6340

Sophocles.   • **2.545**
Sophocles. With an introd. by David Grene. [Chicago] University of Chicago Press [1954-57] 2 v. 22 cm. (The Complete Greek tragedies) I. Grene, David. ed. II. T.
PA4414.A1 G7   882.2   *LC* 54-10731

Kirkwood, Gordon MacDonald, 1916-.   • **2.546**
A study of Sophoclean drama. Ithaca, N.Y., Cornell University Press [1958] xiii, 304 p. 24 cm. (Cornell studies in classical philology, v. 31) 1. Sophocles. I. T.
PA25.C7 vol. 31 PA4417.K48   882.2   *LC* 58-2546

Kitto, Humphrey Davy Findley.   • **2.547**
Sophocles, dramatist & philosopher: three lectures delivered at King's College, Newcastle–upon–Tyne. — London, New York, Oxford University Press, 1958. 64 p., 19 cm. 1. Sophocles. I. T.
PA4417.K5   *LC* 58-1587

Knox, Bernard MacGregor Walker.   • **2.548**
The heroic temper: studies in Sophoclean tragedy / by Bernard M. W. Knox. — Berkeley: University of California Press, 1964. 209 p.; 24 cm. — (Sather classical lectures. v.35) 1. Sophocles — Criticism and interpretation. I. T. II. Series.
PA4417.K55   882   *LC* 64-21684

Seale, David.   **2.549**
Vision and stagecraft in Sophocles / David Seale. — Chicago: University of Chicago Press, 1982. 269 p.; 23 cm. Revision of thesis (Ph.D.)—University of London, 1973. Includes index. 1. Sophocles — Criticism and interpretation. I. T.
PA4417.S45 1982   882/.01 19   *LC* 82-50459   *ISBN* 0226744043

Segal, Charles, 1936-.   **2.550**
Tragedy and civilization: an interpretation of Sophocles / Charles Segal. — Cambridge, Mass.: Published for Oberlin College by Harvard University Press, 1981. xii, 506 p.; 24 cm. — (Martin classical lectures. v. 26) Includes indexes. 1. Sophocles — Criticism and interpretation. I. T. II. Series.
PA25.M3 vol. 26 PA4417.S5x   937 s 882/.01 19   *LC* 80-19765   *ISBN* 0674902068

Whitman, Cedric Hubbell.   • **2.551**
Sophocles: a study of heroic humanism / Cedric H. Whitman. — Cambridge, Mass.: Harvard University Press, 1951. 292 p. 1. Sophocles. I. T.
PA4417.W5   882.2   *LC* 51-10794   *ISBN* 0674821408

PA4435–4500 T–Z

Theocritus.   • **2.552**
Bucolici Graeci, recensuit A. S. F. Gow. — Oxonii, E Typographeo Clarendoniano [1962] xv, 188 p. 19 cm. — (Scriptorum classicorum bibliotheca Oxoniensis.) Greek text. 'First published 1952. Reprinted ... from corrected sheets of the first edition, 1958 [and] 1962.' 1. Pastoral poetry, Greek I. Gow, Andrew Sydenham Farrar, 1886- ed. II. T. III. Series.
PA4442.A2   *LC* 65-7256

Theocritus.   • **2.553**
Theocritus / edited with a translation and commentary by A.S.F. Gow. — Cambridge: University Press, 1950. 2 v., 15 leaves of plates: ill., map, plan. I. Gow, Andrew Sydenham Farrar, 1886- II. T.
PA4442 A2 1950   *LC* 52-1185

Theocritus.   • **2.554**
[Works. Greek and English. 1953] The Greek Bucolic poets, translated with brief notes by A.S.F. Gow. Cambridge University Press 1953. 156p. 1. Pastoral poetry, Greek 2. Greek poetry — Translations into English 3. English poetry — Translations from Greek I. T.
PA4443 E5 G613   *LC* 53-8679

Greek pastoral poetry; Theocritus, Bion, Moschus, the pattern poems, translated with an introduction and notes by Anthony Holden.   **2.555**
Harmondsworth, Penguin, 1974. 250 p. 19 cm. (Penguin classics) 1. Greek poetry — Translations into English. 2. English poetry — Translations from

Greek. 3. Pastoral poetry, Greek I. Theocritus. II. Bion, of Phlossa near Smyrna. III. Moschus, of Syracuse. IV. Holden, Anthony, 1947- tr.
PA4443.E5 H6   884/.01/08   *LC* 74-168342   *ISBN* 0140442944

Walker, Steven F.   **2.556**
Theocritus / by Steven F. Walker. — Boston: Twayne Publishers, 1980. 167 p.; 21 cm. — (Twayne's world authors series; TWAS 609: Greece) Includes index. 1. Theocritus — Criticism and interpretation. I. T.
PA4444.W3   884/.01   *LC* 80-15705   *ISBN* 0805764518

Theophrastus.   • **2.557**
The Characters of Theophrastus. Edited with introd., commentary and index by R.G. Ussher. London Macmillan 1960. 296p. 1. Characters and characteristics I. Ussher, Robert Glenn, 1927-, ed. II. T.
PA4448 A4 E45

Theophrastus.   • **2.558**
The characters [by] Theophrastus. Plays and fragments [by] Menander. Translated by Philip Vellacott. — Baltimore: Penguin Books, [1967] 246 p.; 19 cm. — (The Penguin classics) I. Menander, of Athens. Plays and fragments. Works. English. 1967. II. Vellacott, Philip. tr. III. T.
PA4449.E5 C5 1967b   882/.01   *LC* 67-9756

Thucydides.   • **2.559**
Thucydides, Book VI. Edited by K. J. Dover. — Oxford, Clarendon Press, 1965. xxix, 104, 111 p. map. 1. Greece — Hist. — Peloponnesian War, 431-404, B.C. I. Dover, Kenneth James. ed. II. T.
PA4452.A36 1965   488.642   *LC* 65-6993

Thucydides.   • **2.560**
Thucydides, Book VII / with an introduction and commentary by K.J. Dover. — Oxford: Clarendon Press, 1965. 1 v. (various pagings); 19 cm. 1. Greece — History — Peloponnesian War, 431-404 B.C. I. Dover, Kenneth James. II. T.
PA4452.A37 1965   *LC* 65-6992

Connor, W. Robert (Walter Robert), 1934-.   **2.561**
Thucydides / W. Robert Connor. — Princeton, N.J.: Princeton University Press, c1984. xii, 266 p.; 25 cm. 1. Thucydides. History of the Peloponnesian War 2. Greece — History — Peloponnesian War, 431-404 B.C. I. T.
PA4461.C58 1984   938/.05 19   *LC* 83-43066   *ISBN* 0691035695

Gomme, Arnold Wycombe, 1886-1959.   • **2.562**
A historical commentary on Thucydides / by A. W. Gomme. — Oxford: The Clarendon Press, 1945-1981. 5 v.: maps (1 fold.); 23 cm. Vols. 4-5 edited by A.W. Gomme, A. Andrewes and K.J. Dover. 1. Thucydides. I. Andrewes, Antony, 1910-. II. Dover, Kenneth James, 1920-. III. T.
PA4461.G6   *LC* a 45-4190/rev   *ISBN* 019814198X

Romilly, Jacqueline de.   • **2.563**
Thucydides and Athenian imperialism. Translated by Philip Thody. New York, Barnes and Noble, 1963 [i.e. 1964] xi, 400 p. 23 cm. 1. Thucydides. 2. Athens (Greece) — History 3. Greece — History — Peloponnesian War, 431-404 B.C. I. T.
PA4461.R733   *LC* 64-655

Woodhead, A. G. (Arthur Geoffrey)   • **2.564**
Thucydides on the nature of power [by] A. Geoffrey Woodhead. Cambridge, Published for Oberlin College by Harvard University Press, 1970. xii, 222 p. 22 cm. (Martin classical lectures. v. 24) 1. Thucydides. 2. Power (Social sciences) I. T. II. Series.
PA25.M3 vol. 24 PA4461.W6x   938/.0072/0924   *LC* 77-89973   *ISBN* 0674891368

Anderson, J. K. (John Kinloch)   **2.565**
Xenophon [by] J. K. Anderson. New York, Scribner [1974] 206 p. illus. 23 cm. (Classical life and letters) 1. Xenophon. I. T.
PA4497.A5 1974b   913/.38/0350924 B   *LC* 73-14392   *ISBN* 068413666X

PA5000–5665 GREEK (BYZANTINE AND MODERN)

Politēs, Linos, 1906-.   **2.566**
A history of modern Greek literature. — Oxford: Clarendon Press, 1973. xiii, 338 p.; 23 cm. 1. Greek literature, Modern — History and criticism. I. T.
PA5210.P6   889/.09   *LC* 73-154139   *ISBN* 0198157215

Lorentzatos, Zēsimos.   **2.567**
'The lost center' and other essays on Greek poetry / by Zissimos Lorenzatos; translated by Kay Cicellis. — Princeton, N.J.: Princeton University Press, c1980. vi, 200 p.; 23 cm. (Princeton essays in literature) Includes index. 1. Greek literature, Modern — 20th century — History and criticism — Collected works. I. T.
PA5225.L67   889/.13/09   *LC* 79-3221   *ISBN* 0691062463

Modern Greek writers: Solomos, Calvos, Matesis, Palamas, Cavafy, Kazantzakis, Seferis, Elytis. Edited by Edmund Keeley and Peter Bien.   • **2.568**
[Princeton, N.J.]: Princeton University Press, [1972] 261 p.; 23 cm. — (Princeton essays in European and comparative literature, 7) Papers presented at a Modern Greek Studies Association symposium, held at Princeton University, Oct. 30-Nov. 1, 1969. 1. Greek literature, Modern — Addresses, essays, lectures. I. Keeley, Edmund. ed. II. Bien, Peter. ed. III. Modern Greek Studies Association.
PA5225.M6   889/.09   *LC* 78-166379   *ISBN* 0691062153

Doulis, Thomas.   **2.569**
Disaster and fiction: modern Greek fiction and the Asia Minor disaster of 1922 / Thomas Doulis. — Berkeley: University of California Press, c1977. x, 313 p.; 23 cm. Includes index. 1. Greek fiction, Modern — 20th century — History and criticism. 2. Greco-Turkish War, 1921-1922 — Literature and the war. I. T.
PA5230.G74 D6   889/.3/03   *LC* 75-22654   *ISBN* 0520031121

Keeley, Edmund.   **2.570**
Modern Greek poetry: voice and myth / Edmund Keeley. — Princeton, N.J.: Princeton University Press, c1983. xvi, 232 p.; 22 cm. Includes indexes. 1. Greek poetry, Modern — 20th century — History and criticism — Addresses, essays, lectures. I. T.
PA5250.K44 1983   889/.13/09 19   *LC* 83-11041   *ISBN* 0691065861

Sherrard, Philip.   • **2.571**
The marble threshing floor; studies in modern Greek poetry. — London: Vallentine, Mitchell, [1956] vii, 258 p.; 24 cm. 1. Greek poetry, Modern — History and criticism. I. T.
PA5250.S5   889/.1/209   *LC* 56-2868

Beaton, Roderick.   **2.572**
Folk poetry of modern Greece / Roderick Beaton. — Cambridge [Eng.]; New York: Cambridge University Press, 1980. xii, 229 p. Includes index. 1. Folk poetry, Greek (Modern) — History and criticism. I. T.
PA5255.B4   PA5255 B4.   398.2/09495   *LC* 79-7644   *ISBN* 0521228530

Friar, Kimon. comp.   **2.573**
Modern Greek poetry / Translation, introd., an essay on translation, and notes by Kimon Friar. — New York: Simon and Schuster, [1973] xx, 780 p.; 23 cm. 1. Greek poetry, Modern — Translations into English. 2. English poetry — Translations from Greek (Modern) I. T.
PA5289.E6 F7   889/.1/3208   *LC* 70-171604   *ISBN* 0671210254

Keeley, Edmund.   • **2.574**
Six poets of modern Greece. Chosen, translated, and introduced by Edmund Keeley and Philip Sherrard. [1st American ed.] New York, Knopf, 1961 [c1960] 183 p. 25 cm. (Unesco collection of contemporary works. European series) 1. Greek poetry, Modern — Translations into English. 2. English poetry — Translations from Greek, Modern. I. Sherrard, Philip. II. T.
PA5289.E6 K4   *LC* 61-11505

Eighteen texts; writings by contemporary Greek authors. Edited by Willis Barnstone.   • **2.575**
Cambridge, Mass.: Harvard University Press, 1972. xxii, 187 p.; 24 cm. Translation of Dekaochtō keimena. 1. Short stories, Greek (Modern) I. Barnstone, Willis, 1927- ed.
PA5295.D413   889/.08/0034   *LC* 74-188347   *ISBN* 0674241754

Timarion. English.   **2.576**
Timarion / translated with introduction and commentary by Barry Baldwin. — Detroit: Wayne State University Press, 1984. ix, 161 p.; 24 cm. — (Byzantine texts in translation.) Includes index. I. Baldwin, Barry. II. T. III. Series.
PA5385.T54 E5 1984   883/.02 19   *LC* 84-10426   *ISBN* 0814317715

PA5610–5630 Modern Authors, A–Z

PA5610 A–K

Elytēs, Odysseas, 1911-. 2.577
The sovereign sun: selected poems / Odysseus Elytis; translated with an introd. and notes by Kimon Friar. — Philadelphia: Temple University Press, 1974. vii, 200 p.; 22 cm. I. Friar, Kimon. tr. II. T.
PA5610.E43 A23　889/.1/32　LC 74-77777　ISBN 0877220190

Elytēs, Odysseas, 1911-. 2.578
[Selections. English] Odysseus Elytis, selected poems / chosen and introduced by Edmund Keeley and Philip Sherrard; translated by Edmund Keeley ... [et al.]. — New York: Viking Press, c1981. xiv, 114 p.; 24 cm. I. Keeley, Edmund. II. Sherrard, Philip. III. T.
PA5610.E43 A25 1981　889/.132 19　LC 81-65282　ISBN 067029246X

Elytēs, Odysseas, 1911-. 2.579
[Axion esti. English & Greek] [Tō axion esti] The axion esti [by] Odysseus Elytis. Translated and annotated by Edmund Keeley and George Savidis. [Pittsburgh] University of Pittsburgh Press [1974] 159 p. 23 cm. (Pitt poetry series) 'An international Poetry Forum selection.' I. Keeley, Edmund. tr. II. Savvídēs, Geõrgios P. III. T.
PA5610.E43 A96 1974　889/.1/32　LC 74-4521　ISBN 0822932830 ISBN 0822952521

Elytēs, Odysseas, 1911-. 2.580
[Maria Nephelē. English] Maria Nephele: a poem in two voices / Odysseus Elytis; translated from the Greek by Athan Anagnostopoulos. — Boston: Houghton Mifflin Co., 1981. xiv, 74 p.; 24 cm. I. Anagnostopoulos, Athan. II. T.
PA5610.E43 M313　889/.132 19　LC 81-2691　ISBN 0395294657

Cavafy, Constantine, 1863-1933. 2.581
Collected poems / C. P. Cavafy [i.e. K. P. Kabaphēs]; translated by Edmund Keeley and Philip Sherrard; edited by George Savidis. — Princeton, N.J.: Princeton University Press, [1975] xvii, 451 p.; 25 cm. English and Greek. Includes index. I. Keeley, Edmund. tr. II. Sherrard, Philip. tr. III. Savvídēs, Geõrgios P. IV. T.
PA5610.K2 1975　889/.1/32　LC 74-2977　ISBN 069106279X

Cavafy, Constantine, 1863-1933. • 2.582
The complete poems of Cavafy / Konstantinos Petrov Kabaphes; translated by Rae Dalven; with an introd. by W. H. Auden. [1st ed.] New York: Harcourt, Brace & World, [1961] 234 p. 22 cm. Includes bibliography. I. T.
PA5610.K2A23　879.1　889.1　LC 60-10936

Cavafy, Constantine, 1863-1933. 2.583
[Poems. English] Selected poems / [by] C. P. Cavafy; translated by Edmund Keeley and Philip Sherrard. — Princeton, N.J.: Princeton University Press [1972] ix, 97, [1] p. 23 cm. I. T.
PA5610.K2 A24 1972　889/.1/32　LC 70-39789　ISBN 0691062285 ISBN 0691013041

Keeley, Edmund. 2.584
Cavafy's Alexandria: study of a myth in progress / Edmund Keeley. — Cambridge, Mass.: Harvard University Press, 1976. viii, 196 p.; 24 cm. Includes indexes. 1. Cavafy, Constantine, 1863-1933. 2. Greeks in Egypt. I. T.
PA5610.K2 Z73　889/.1/32　LC 76-6997　ISBN 0674104307

Liddell, Robert, 1908-. 2.585
Cavafy: a biography / Robert Liddell. — New York: Schocken Books, 1976, c1974. 220 p., [4] leaves of plates: ill.; 23 cm. Includes index. 1. Cavafy, Constantine, 1863-1933. I. T.
PA5610.K2 Z74 1976　889/.1/32 B　LC 76-9135　ISBN 0805236341

Karkavitsas, Andreas, 1866-1923. 2.586
[Zētianos. English] The beggar: a novel / by Andreas Karkavitsas; translated by William F. Wyatt, Jr.; with an appendix on Andreas Karkavitsas and nineteenth century Greek literature by P.D. Mastrodemetres. — New Rochelle, N.Y.: Caratzas Bros., 1982. 191 p.; 23 cm. — (UNESCO collection of representative works. European series.) Translation of: Ho zētianos. Includes index. I. T. II. Series.
PA5610.K3 Z313 1982　889/.332 19　LC 82-71510　ISBN 0892413727

Kazantzakis, Nikos, 1883-1957. 2.587
[Sodoma kai Gomora. English] Two plays / by Nikos Kazantzakis; translated from the Greek and with an introduction by Kimon Friar; with an introduction to Comedy, a tragedy in one act, by Karl Kerényi, translated by Peter Bien. — St. Paul, Minn.: North Central Pub. Co., 1982. 120 p.: port.; 22 cm. — (Nostos book. no. 8) 1. Kazantzakis, Nikos, 1883-1957 — Translations, English. I. Kazantzakis, Nikos, 1883-1957. Kōmōdia. English. 1982. II. T. III. Series.
PA5610.K39 A24 1982　889/.232 19　LC 82-62510　ISBN 0935476121

Kazantzakis, Nikos, 1883-1957. • 2.588
[Bios kai politeia tou Alexē zorma. English] Zorba the Greek; translated by Carl Wildman. New York, Simon and Schuster, 1953 [c1952] 311 p. 22 cm. I. T.
PA5610.K39 B5x　889.3　LC 53-7756

Kazantzakēs, Nikos, 1885-1957. • 2.589
The Greek passion; translated by Jonathan Griffin. — New York, Simon and Schuster, 1954 [c1953] 432 p. 22 cm. I. T.
PA5610.K39 C5x　LC 53-10810

Kazantzakis, Nikos, 1885-1957. • 2.590
The Rock Garden: a novel / by Nikos Kazantzakis; translated from the French by Richard Howard; passages from The saviors of God translated by Kimon Friar. New York: Simon and Schuster, 1963. 251 p.; 21 cm. I. T.
PA5610.K39 J313 1963　LC 63-9270

Kazantzakēs, Nikos, 1885-1957. • 2.591
Freedom or death, a novel. Translated by Jonathan Griffin. Pref. by A. Den Doolaard. — New York, Simon and Schuster, 1956. viii, 433 p. 22 cm. 1. Crete — Hist. — Fiction. I. T.
PA5610.K39 K3x　889.3　LC 55-8809

Kazantzakis, Nikos, 1883-1957. • 2.592
[Odyseia English] The Odyssey; a modern sequel. Translation into English verse, introd., synopsis, and notes by Kimon Friar. Illus. by Ghika. New York, Simon and Schuster, 1958. xxxviii, 824 p. illus. 25 cm. I. Friar, Kimon. tr. II. Homer. Odyssea. III. T.
PA5610.K39 O33　883.1　LC 58-9048

Kazantzakis, Nikos, 1883-1957. 2.593
[Ophis kai krino. English.] Serpent and lily: a novella, with a manifesto, The sickness of the age / Nikos Kazantzakis; translated, with introd. and notes, by Theodora Vasils. — Berkeley: University of California Press, c1980. vii, 117 p.; 23 cm. Translation of Ophis kai krinos. 1. Kazantzakis, Nikos, 1883-1957. Arrōstia tou aiōnos. English. 1980. II. Vasils, Theodora. III. T.
PA5610.K39 O613 1980 PA5610.K39　889/.332 19　LC 78-68832　ISBN 0520038851

Kazantzakis, Nikos, 1883-1957. • 2.594
[Ho phtochoules tou Theou. English] Saint Francis, a novel. Translated from the Greek by P. A. Bien. New York, Simon and Schuster, 1962. 379 p. 22 cm. 1. Francis, of Assisi, Saint, 1182-1226 — Fiction. I. T.
PA5610.K39 P5x　LC 62-9606

Kazantzakis, Nikos, 1883-1957. 2.595
[Symposion. English] Symposium [by] Nikos Kazantzakis. Translated by Theodora Vasils and Themi Vasils. New York, Crowell [1975, c1974] 96 p. 21 cm. I. T.
PA5610.K39 S913 1975　889/.3/32　LC 74-18393　ISBN 0690005814 ISBN 0308101332

Kazantzakis, Nikos, 1883-1957. • 2.596
[Teleutaios peirasmos. English] The last temptation of Christ. Translated from the Greek by P. A. Bien. New York, Simon and Schuster, 1960. 506 p. 22 cm. 1. Jesus Christ — Fiction I. T.
PA5610.K39 T4x　889.3　LC 60-10985

Kazantzakis, Nikos, 1883-1957. 2.597
[Voudas. English] Buddha / Nikos Kazantzakis; translated from the Greek by Kimon Friar and Athena Dallis–Damis. — 1st English language ed. — San Diego, Calif.: Avant Books, 1983, c1982. xx, 172 p.; 24 cm. Translation of: Voudas. I. T.
PA5610.K39 V613 1983　889/.232 19　LC 83-2642　ISBN 0932238149

Kazantzakis, Nikos, 1883-1957. 2.598
The suffering god: selected letters to Galatea and to Papastephanou / Nikos Kazantzakis; translated by Philip Ramp and Katerina Anghelaki Rooke; introduction by Katerina Anghelaki Rooke. — New Rochelle, N.Y.: Caratzas Brothers, 1979. 114 p.; 23 cm. 1. Kazantzakis, Nikos, 1883-1957 — Correspondence. 2. Papastephanou, Emmanuel. 3. Kazantzakē, Galateia — Correspondence. 4. Authors, Greek (Modern) — 20th century — Correspondence. I. Kazantzakē, Galateia. II. Papastephanou, Emmanuel. III. T.
PA5610.K39 Z48 1979　889/.83209 B 19　LC 78-75133　ISBN 0892410884

Kazantzakis, Nikos, 1883-1957. ● **2.599**
[Anaphora ston Greko. English] Report to Greco [by] Nikos Kazantzakis. Translated from the Greek by P. A. Bien. New York, Simon and Schuster [1965] 512 p. 22 cm. I. T.
PA5610.K39 Z513 1965　　889.8/32/09 B　　LC 65-22535

Bien, Peter. **2.600**
Nikos Kazantzakis. New York, Columbia University Press, 1972. 48 p. 20 cm. (Columbia essays on modern writers, 62) 1. Kazantzakis, Nikos, 1883-1957. I. T. II. Series.
PA5610.K39 Z59　　889/.8/3209　　LC 79-186642　　ISBN 0231035322

Lea, James F. **2.601**
Kazantzakis: the politics of salvation / James F. Lea; with a foreword by Helen Kazantzakis. — University, Ala.: University of Alabama Press, c1979. xiii, 207 p.; 22 cm. Includes index. 1. Kazantzakis, Nikos, 1883-1957 — Political and social views. I. T.
PA5610.K39 Z775　　889/.8/3209　　LC 78-8644　　ISBN 0817370021

Levitt, Morton. **2.602**
The Cretan glance: the world and art of Nikos Kazantzakis / Morton P. Levitt. — Columbus: Ohio State University Press, c1980. xvi, 187 p.; 24 cm. 1. Kazantzakis, Nikos, 1883-1957 — Criticism and interpretation. I. T.
PA5610.K39 Z777　　889/.3/32　　LC 79-23990　　ISBN 0814203043

Myrivēlēs, Stratēs, 1892-. ● **2.603**
The mermaid Madonna / by Stratis Myrivilis; translated from the Greek by Abbott Rick. — New York: T.Y. Crowell, c1959. vi, 310 p. Translation of Hē panaghia hē gorgona. I. T.
PZ3M996 Me　　PA5610M9 P313.　　889/.3　　889/.3　　LC 59-7759

Myrivēlēs, Stratēs, 1892-. **2.604**
[Zōē en taphō. English] Life in the tomb / by Stratis Myrivilis; translated from the modern Greek original by Peter Bien. — Hanover, N.H.: Published for Dartmouth College by the University Press of New England, 1977. xix, 325 p., [2] leaves of plates: maps; 24 cm. Translation of Hē zōē en taphō. 1. World War, 1914-1918 — Fiction. I. T.
PZ3.M996 Li PA5610.M9Z6x　　889/.3/32　　LC 76-50678　　ISBN 0874511348

Palamas, Kōstēs, 1859-1943. **2.605**
[Ho dōdekalogos tou gyphtou. English] The twelve words of the Gypsy / Kostes Palamas; translated by Theodore Ph. Stephanides and George C. Katsimbalis. — [Memphis]: Memphis State University Press, [1975] xl, 314 p.; 22 cm. Epic poem. Translation of Ho dōdekalogos tou gyphtou. English and Greek. I. Stephanides, Theodore Ph. II. Katsimpalēs, Geōrgios Kōnstantinou, 1899- III. T.
PA5610.P3 D63 1975　　889/.1/32　　LC 75-12894　　ISBN 0878700250. ISBN 0878700293 pbk

Maskaleris, Thanasis. **2.606**
Kostis Palamas. — New York: Twayne Publishers, [1972] 156 p.; 21 cm. — (Twayne's world authors series, TWAS 197. Greece) 1. Palamos, Kostēs, 1859-1943 — Criticism and interpretation. I. T.
PA5610.P3 Z78　　889/.1/32　　LC 75-161804

Sachtourēs, Miltos, 1919-. **2.607**
[Poems. English. Selections. 1982] Selected poems / Miltos Sahtouris; translated from the Greek, and with an introduction by Kimon Friar. — Old Chatham, N.Y.: Sachem Press, c1982. 127 p.; 23 cm. I. Friar, Kimon. II. T.
PA5610.S18 A24 1982　　889/.134 19　　LC 81-21374　　ISBN 0937584037

Seferis, George, 1900-1971. ● **2.608**
George Seferis: collected poems, 1924–1955. Translated, edited, and introd. by Edmund Keeley and Philip Sherrard. Princeton, N.J., Princeton University Press, 1967. xxi, 490 p. front. 24 cm. English and Greek. 1. Seferis, George, 1900-1971 — Translations, English. I. Sherrard, Philip. ed. II. Keeley, Edmund. ed. III. T.
PA5610.S36 A27　　889/.1/34　　LC 65-17142

Seferis, George, 1900-1971. **2.609**
[Meres tou chilia enneakosia saranta pente-chilia enneakosia penēnta hena. English] Days of 1945–1951: a poet's journal / [by] George Seferis; translated by Athan Anagnostopoulos. — Cambridge, Mass.: Belknap Press of Harvard University Press, 1974. xviii, 206 p.; 21 cm. Translation of Meres tou chilia enneakosia saranta pente-chilia enneakosia penēnta hena. 1. Seferis, George, 1900-1971. I. T.
PA5610.S36 Z5213 1974　　889/.1/34 B　　LC 73-92634　　ISBN 0674680405

Sikelianos, Angelos, 1884-1951. **2.610**
Selected poems / Angelos Sikelianos; translated and introduced by Edmund Keeley and Philip Sherrard. — Princeton, N.J.: Princeton University Press,

c1979. xx, 150 p.; 23 cm. — (The Lockert library of poetry in translation) English and Greek. I. Keeley, Edmund. II. Sherrard, Philip. III. T.
PA5610.S5 A24　　889/.1/32　　LC 79-84017　　ISBN 0691064059

Taktsis, Costas, 1927-. ● **2.611**
The third wedding; translated from the Greek by Leslie Finer. — Harmondsworth: Penguin, 1969. 256 p.; 18 cm. Translation of To trito stephani (romanized form) I. T.
PZ4.T1376 Th3 PA5610.T26　　889/.3/34　　LC 76-409421

Taktsis, Costas, 1927-. **2.612**
[Trito stephano. English] The third wedding / translated from the Greek by Leslie Finer. — New York: Red Dust, [1971, c1967] 303 p.; 22 cm. Translation of To trito stephani. I. T.
PZ4.T1376 Th5 PA5610.T26　　889/.1/34　　LC 79-155440　　ISBN 0873760182

Doulis, Thomas. **2.613**
George Theotokas. — New York: Twayne Publishers, [1974] 185 p.: illus.; 21 cm. — (Twayne's world authors series, TWAS 339. Greece) 1. Theotokas, Giōrgos. I. T.
PA5610.T5 Z6　　889/.8/3409　　LC 74-14564　　ISBN 0805728813

PA5612–5637 Authors, 1960–

Anagnōstakēs, Manolēs. **2.614**
The target: selected poems / Manolis Anagnostakis; translated from the modern Greek with an introduction by Kimon Friar. — New York, N.Y.: Pella Pub. Co., 1981 (c1980). xxx, 135 p.; 22 cm. — (Modern Greek poetry series. no. 5) English and Greek. I. Friar, Kimon. II. T. III. Series.
PA5612.N28 A24　　889/.134 19　　LC 80-81164　　ISBN 0918618177

Decavalles, Andonis. **2.615**
Ransoms to time: selected poems / Andónis Decaválles; translated from the modern Greek with an introduction and notes by Kimon Friar. — Rutherford [N.J.]: Fairleigh Dickinson University Press, c1984. 142 p.; 22 cm. 1. Decavalles, Andonis — Translations, English. I. Friar, Kimon. II. T.
PA5615.E25 A24 1984　　889/.134 19　　LC 82-49314　　ISBN 0838631800

Ritsos, Giannēs, 1909-. **2.616**
Scripture of the blind / Yannis Ritsos; translated from the Greek, with an introd. by Kimon Friar and Kostas Myrsiades. — Columbus: Ohio State University Press, c1979. xxvi, 251 p.; 24 cm. English and Greek. I. T.
PA5629.I7 A23　　889/.1/32　　LC 78-14319　　ISBN 0814202985

Ritsos, Giannēs, 1909-. **2.617**
[Selections. English. 1977] The fourth dimension: selected poems of Yannis Ritsos / translated by Rae Dalven. — Boston: D. R. Godine, 1977. xxiv, 156 p.; 23 cm. I. Dalven, Rae. II. T.
PA5629.I7 A2x 1977　　889/.1/32　　LC 75-11463　　ISBN 0879231815

Ritsos, Giannēs, 1909-. **2.618**
Ritsos in parentheses / translations and introd. by Edmund Keeley. — Princeton, N.J.: Princeton University Press, c1979. xxvi, 175 p.; 24 cm. — (The Lockert library of poetry in translation) Poems in English and Greek. I. Keeley, Edmund. II. T.
PA5629.I7 A24　　889/.1/32　　LC 78-70317　　ISBN 0691063974

Ritsos, Giannēs, 1909-. **2.619**
[Dekaochtō lianotragouda tēs pikrēs patridas. English] Eighteen short songs of the bitter motherland / Yannis Ritsos; translated from the Greek by Amy Mims; with ill. by the poet; edited and with an introd. by Theophanis G. Stavrou. — St. Paul, Minn.: North Central Pub. Co., 1974. 59 p.: ill.; 22 cm. Added t.p.: Dekaochtō lianotragouda tēs pikrēs patridas. English and Greek. I. Mims, Amy, tr. II. T. III. Title: Dekaochtō lianotragouda tēs pikrēs patridas.
PA5629.I7 D4x　　889/.1/32　　LC 74-15984

Ritsos, Giannēs, 1909-. **2.620**
Erotica / Yánnis Rítsos; translated from the Greek by Kimon Friar. — Old Chatham, N.Y.: Sachem Press, c1982. 96 p.; 24 cm. 1. Erotic poetry, Greek (Modern) — Translations into English. 2. Erotic poetry, English — Translations from modern Greek. I. Friar, Kimon. II. T.
PA5629.I7 E7 1982　　889/.132 19　　LC 82-17018　　ISBN 0937584053

Ritsos, Giannēs, 1909-. **2.621**
[Kyra tōn ampeliōn. English & Greek] The lady of the vineyards / Yannis Ritsos; translated by Apostolos N. Athanassakis. — New York: Pella, 1981 (c1978) 77 p.; 22 cm. — (Modern Greek poetry series. no. 4) English and Greek. Translation of: Kyra tōn ampeliōn. I. T. II. Series.
PA5629.I7 K913　　889/.132 19　　LC 80-84407　　ISBN 091861810X

Sinopoulos, Takēs.   2.622
Landscape of death: the selected poems of Tákis Sinópoulos / translated from the Greek, with an introd. by Kimon Friar. — Columbus: Ohio State University Press, c1979. xlvii, 288 p.: ill.; 24 cm. English and Greek. I. T.
PA5630.I5 A23 1979   889/.1/34   *LC* 78-15020   *ISBN* 0814202993

Vasilikos, Vasilēs, 1934-.   2.623
[Psarontoupheko. English] The harpoon gun / translated by Barbara Bray. — [1st ed.] New York: Harcourt Brace Jovanovich, [1973] viii, 246 p.; 21 cm. Translation of To psarontoupheko. I. T.
PZ4.V325 Har3 PA5633.V3   889/.3/34   *LC* 72-79925   *ISBN* 0151388008

PA6000–6961 LATIN (ANCIENT)

PA6001–6098 Literary History

Copley, Frank Olin.   • 2.624
Latin literature; from the beginnings to the close of the second century A.D., by Frank O. Copley. Ann Arbor, University of Michigan Press [1969] 372 p. 24 cm. 1. Latin literature — History and criticism. I. T.
PA6003.C6   870.9/001   *LC* 76-90760

Duff, J. Wight (John Wight), 1866-1944.   • 2.625
A literary history of Rome, from the origins to the close of the Golden Age. Edited by A. M. Duff. [3d ed.] New York, Barnes & Noble [1960] 543 p. 23 cm. 1. Latin literature — History and criticism. I. T.
PA6003.D8 1960   870.9   *LC* 60-1962

Grant, Michael, 1914-.   • 2.626
Roman literature. [New ed.] [Harmondsworth, Mddx.] Penguin Books [1958] 287p. (Pelican books, A 427) 1. Latin literature — History and criticism I. T.
PA6003 G7 1958

Latin literature / edited by E.J. Kenney; advisory editor, W.V. Clausen.   2.627
Cambridge [Eng.]; New York: Cambridge University Press, 1982. xviii, 973 p., [2] leaves of plates; 24 cm. — (Cambridge history of classical literature. 2) Includes index. 1. Latin literature — History and criticism. I. Kenney, E. J. II. Series.
PA6003.L3   870/.9   *LC* 79-121   *ISBN* 0521210437

Rose, H. J. (Herbert Jennings), 1883-1961.   • 2.628
A handbook of Latin literature: from the earliest times to the death of St. Augustine [by] H. J. Rose. — New York, Dutton [1960] 557 p. — (A Dutton paperback) I. T.
PA6003.R6 1966   870.9   *LC* 67-76490

Hadas, Moses, 1900-1966.   • 2.629
A history of Latin literature. — New York, Columbia University Press, 1952. viii, 474 p. 24 cm. 'Bibliographical notes': p. [447]-459. 1. Latin literature — Hist. & crit. I. T.
PA6004.H3   870.9   *LC* 52-7637

Frank, Tenney, 1876-1939.   • 2.630
Life and literature in the Roman republic / by Tenney Frank. — Cambridge: University Press, 1930. vi, 256 p. — (Sather classical lectures. v. 7) 1. Latin literature — History and criticism. I. T. II. Series.
PA6011.F7   870.9   *LC* 30-30200

Lyne, R. O. A. M.   2.631
The Latin love poets: from Catullus to Horace / by R.O.A.M. Lyne. — Oxford: Clarendon Press; New York: Oxford University Press, 1980. xiv, 316 p.; 21 cm. Includes indexes. 1. Love poetry, Latin — History and criticism. I. T.
PA6029.L6 L96 1980   871/.01/09354 19   *LC* 80-41356   *ISBN* 0198144539

Sullivan, J. P. (John Patrick)   2.632
Literature and politics in the age of Nero / J.P. Sullivan. — Ithaca: Cornell University Press, 1985. 218 p.; 24 cm. 'Based on the Charles Beebe Martin Lectures delivered at Oberlin College in March 1976'—Pref. Includes index. 1. Latin literature — History and criticism. 2. Politics and literature — Rome. 3. Politics in literature 4. Rome — History — Nero, 54-68 I. T.
PA6029.P64 S85 1985   870/.9/001 19   *LC* 84-14278   *ISBN* 0801417406

Duff, J. Wight (John Wight), 1866-1944.   • 2.633
A literary history of Rome in the silver age: from Tiberius to Hadrian / by J. Wight Duff; edited by A. M. Duff. — 3d ed. — London: Benn; New York: Barnes & Noble, 1964. xvi, 599 p.; 21 cm. 1. Latin literature — History and criticism. I. Duff, A. M. (Arnold Mackay), 1900- II. T.
PA6042.D8 1964   870.9   *LC* 65-775

Binns, J. W.   2.634
Latin literature of the fourth century, edited by J. W. Binns. — London: Routledge & K. Paul, 1974. x, 189 p.; 23 cm. — (Greek and Latin studies; classical literature and its influences) 1. Latin literature — History and criticism. I. T.
PA6043.B5   870/.9/001   *LC* 73-91031   *ISBN* 0710077963

PA6047–6098 SPECIAL FORMS

Sellar, William Young, 1825-1890.   • 2.635
The Roman poets of the republic / by W.Y. Sellar. — 3rd ed., rev. and enl. — New York: Biblo and Tannen, 1965. xix, 474 p. 1. Latin poetry — History and criticism I. T.
PA6047.S4 1965   *LC* 65-23490

Sellar, William Young, 1825-1890.   • 2.636
The Roman poets of the Augustan age; Horace and the elegiac poets. With a memoir of the author by Andrew Lang. New York Biblo and Tannen 1965. 362p. 1. Horace. 2. Latin poetry — History and criticism 3. Elegiac poetry I. Lang, Andrew, 1844-1912. II. T.
PA6047 S54 1965

Williams, Gordon Willis.   2.637
Tradition and originality in Roman poetry [by] Gordon Williams. — Oxford: Clarendon P., 1968. ix, 810 p.; 24 cm. 1. Latin poetry — History and criticism. I. T.
PA6047.W45   871/.01/09   *LC* 72-368081

Coffey, Michael.   2.638
Roman satire / Michael Coffey. London: Methuen; New York: Barnes & Noble, 1977. xvi, 289 p.; 23 cm. Includes index. 1. Satire, Latin — History and criticism. I. T.
PA6056.C6 1976   877   *LC* 77-360003   *ISBN* 0064712516

Knoche, Ulrich, 1902-1968.   2.639
[Römische Satire. English] Roman satire / Ulrich Knoche; translated by Edwin S. Ramage. — Bloomington: Indiana University Press, [1975] xi, 243 p.; 25 cm. Translation of Die römische Satire. Includes indexes. 1. Satire, Latin — History and criticism. I. T.
PA6056.K613 1975   877/.01/09   *LC* 74-25014   *ISBN* 0253350204

Luck, Georg, 1926-.   • 2.640
The Latin love elegy. — 2nd ed. — London: Methuen, 1969. 192 p.; 22 cm. 'Distributed in the U.S.A. by Barnes & Noble.' 1. Elegiac poetry, Latin — History and criticism. I. T.
PA6059.E6 L8 1969   874/.009   *LC* 73-453406   *ISBN* 0416142303

Beare, William.   • 2.641
The Roman stage; a short history of Latin drama in the time of the Republic [by] W. Beare. [3d ed.] New York, Barnes & Noble [1965] xiii, 397 p. illus. 23 cm. 1. Latin drama — History and criticism. 2. Theater — Italy — Rome. I. T.
PA6067.B4 1965   *LC* 65-3282

Duckworth, George Eckel, 1903-.   • 2.642
The nature of Roman comedy, a study in popular entertainment. — Princeton, Princeton University Press, 1952. xiii, 501 p. illus. 25 cm. Bibliography: p. [445]-464. 1. Latin drama (Comedy) — Hist. & crit. I. T.
PA6069.D8   872.09   *LC* 52-7321

Kennedy, George Alexander, 1928-.   2.643
The art of rhetoric in the Roman world, 300 B.C.–A.D. 300, by George Kennedy. Princeton, N.J., Princeton University Press, 1972. xvi, 658 p. 23 cm. (His A history of rhetoric v. 2) 1. Rhetoric, Ancient I. T.
PA6085.K4   808/.047/1   *LC* 72-166380   *ISBN* 0691035059

Duff, J. Wight (John Wight), 1866-1944.   • 2.644
Roman satire: its outlook on social life / by J. Wight Duff. — Hamden, Conn.: Archon Books, 1964. 205 p. — (Sather classical lectures. v. 12) 1. Satire, Latin — History and criticism I. T. II. Series.
PA6095.D8 1964   *LC* 64-18540

PA6100–6140 Series (except Loeb)

Catullus, Gaius Valerius.   • **2.645**
Carmina. Recognovit breviqve adnotatione critica instrvxit R. A. B. Mynors. — Oxonii, E Typographeo Clarendoniano 1960, c1958. xvi, 113 p. — (Scriptorum classicorum bibliotheca Oxoniensis.) I. Mynors, Roger Aubrey Baskerville, ed. II. T. III. Series.
PA6105.S8C26 1958

Persius.   • **2.646**
A. Persi Flacci et D. Iuni Iuvenalis saturae. Edidit brevique adnotatione critica instruxit W. V. Clausen. — Oxonii, E Typographeo Clarendoniano, 1959. xiv, 198 p. 19 cm. — (Scriptorum classicorum bibliotheca Oxoniensis.) I. Clausen, Wendell Vernon, 1923- ed. II. Juvenalis, Decimus Junius. Satirae. III. T. IV. Series.
PA6105.S8P3 1959   877   LC 59-4906

Tibullus.   • **2.647**
Tibulli aliorumque carminum libri tres; recognovit brevique adnotatione critica instruxit Iohannes Percival Postgate. Editio altera. Oxonii, E Typographeo Clarendoniano [1959] xiv, [82] p. 19 cm. (Scriptorum classicorum bibliotheca Oxoniensis) This edition first published 1915. I. Postgate, John Percival, 1853-1926, ed. II. T.
PA6787.A33x PA6105.S8 T5x

PA6141–6144 Criticism (General)

Wilkinson, L. P.   • **2.648**
Golden Latin artistry. — Cambridge [Eng.] University Press, 1963. 282 p. 24 cm. Includes bibliography. 1. Latin literature — Hist. & crit. 2. Latin language — Metrics and rhythmics 3. Latin language — Style. I. T.
PA6141.Z5W5   870.9   LC 63-3404

PA6156 Loeb Library (Latin)

PA6156.A–C

Apuleius.   • **2.649**
The golden ass; being the metamorphoses of Lucius Apuleius. With an English translation by W. Adlington, 1566, rev. by S. Gaselee. London Heinemann 1935. 607p. (The Loeb classical library) I. Adlington, William, fl. 1566. tr. II. T.
PA6156.A7 1935

Augustine, Saint, Bishop of Hippo.   • **2.650**
St. Augustine's Confessions / with an English translation by William Watts, 1631. — London: W. Heinemann; New York: Macmillan Co, 1912. 2 v.; 17 cm. — (Loeb classical library.) 'This is a reprint of William Watts' translation (with Scripture references) corrected according to Knöll's text, with the help of the translations of Pusey (1838) and C. Biggs (Books I. to IX.; Methuen, 1897-1909) and the annotated text of J. Gibb and W. Montgomery (Cambridge Patristic texts, 1908)'—Pref. Preface signed: W.H.D. Rouse. I. Watts, William, 1590?-1649. II. Rouse, W. H. D. (William Henry Denham), 1863-1950. III. T. IV. Series.
PA6156.A8 1912   BR65.A6 1912.   LC 13-5585

Bede, the Venerable, Saint, 673-735.   • **2.651**
Baedae Opera historica, with an English translation by J. E. King ... — London, W. Heinemann, New York, G. P. Putnam's Sons, 1930. 2 v. fronts., fold. map. 17 cm. — (Half-title: The Loeb classical library. [Latin authors]) 1. Gt. Brit. — Church history — Anglo-Saxon period. 2. Abbots I. Stapleton, Thomas, 1535-1598. II. King, John Edward, 1858-1939, tr. III. T.
PA6156.B4 1930   274.2   LC 31-26352

Caesar, Julius.   • **2.652**
Caesar. The civil wars, with an English translation by A. G. Peskett. London, W. Heinemann; New York, G. P. Putnam's sons, 1928. 369 p. front. (port.) 6 maps. 17 cm. (Loeb classical library.) Latin and English on opposite pages. 1. Rome — History — Civil War, 49-48 B.C. I. Peskett, Arthur George, tr. II. T. III. Title: The civil wars. IV. Series.
PA6156.C18 1928d

Caesar, Julius.   **2.653**
The Gallic war / Caesar; with and English translation / by H. Edwards. — Cambridge, Mass.: Harvard University Press, [1970, 1917] xxii, 619, [1] p. front. 17 cm. — (Loeb classical library. 72) At head of title: Caesar. Latin and English on opposite pages. I. Edwards, Henry John, 1869-1923, tr. II. T. III. Series.
PA6156.C2 1917   878.1   LC 17-28110

Cato, Marcus Porcius, 234-149 B.C.   • **2.654**
Marcus Porcius Cato, On agriculture; Marcus Terentius Varro, On agriculture; with an English translation by William Davis Hooper ... revised by Harrison Boyd Ash ... Cambridge, Mass., Harvard university press; London, W. Heinemann, ltd., 1934. xxv, 542, [2] p. [5-5] 17 cm. (Half-title: The Loeb classical library. [Latin authors]) 'Printed in Great Britain.' Latin and English on opposite pages. Bibliography: p. xxiii-xxv. 1. Agriculture — Early works to 1800. I. Varro, Marcus Terentius. Rerum rusticarum libri tres II. Hooper, William Davis, 1868-1945, tr. III. Ash, Harrison Boyd, tr. IV. T.
PA6156.C3D4 1934   630.945   LC 35-177

Catullus, Gaius Valerius.   • **2.655**
[Works. English & Latin. 1966] Catullus, Tibullus, and Pervigilium Veneris. London, W. Heinemann; Cambridge, Harvard University Press, 1966 [c1962] xiv, 379 p. 17 cm. (Loeb classical library.) Latin and English on opposite pages. The poems of Gaius Valerius Catullus, translated by F. W. Cornish; Tibullus, by J. P. Postgate; and Pervigilium Veneris, by J. W. Mackail. I. Tibullus. II. Warre Cornish, Francis, 1839-1916. tr. III. Postgate, John Percival, 1853-1926, tr. IV. Mackail, J. W. (John William), 1859-1945. tr. V. Vigil of Venus. VI. T. VII. Series.
PA6156.C34 1966   871/.01/08   LC 76-15298

PA6156.C5 Cicero

Cicero, Marcus Tullius.   • **2.656**
De natura deorum; Academica; with an English translation by H. Rackham. London, W. Heinemann; New York, G. P. Putnam's Sons, 1933. xix, 663 p. 17 cm. (The Loeb classical library. [Latin authors]) Latin and English on opposite pages. I. Rackham, Harris, 1868- tr. II. T. III. Series.
PA6156.C5 A2 1933d

Cicero, Marcus Tullius.   • **2.657**
De senectute, De amicitia, De divinatione, with an English translation by William Armistead Falconer. Cambridge, Mass., Harvard University Press; London, W. Heinemann, 1938. vii, 567 p. 17 cm. (Loeb classical library.) 'First printed 1923. Reprinted 1927, 1930, 1938.' 1. Divination 2. Old age 3. Friendship I. Falconer, William Armistead, tr. II. T. III. Series.
PA6156.C5 A2 1938d

Cicero, Marcus Tullius.   • **2.658**
De inventione; De optimo genere oratorum; Topica / Cicero; with an English translation by H. M. Hubell. — London: W. Heinemann; Cambridge, Mass.: Harvard University Press, 1949. xviii, 466 p.; 17 cm. (Loeb classical library. Latin authors. no. 385) (Cicero in twenty-eight volumes; 2.) Includes index. Latin text, parallel English translation. I. Cicero, Marcus Tullius. De optimo genere oratorum. II. Cicero, Marcus Tullius. Topica. III. Hubbell, Harry Mortimer, 1881- IV. T. V. Series.
PA6156.C5 A2 1949   LC 49-49645   ISBN 0434993867

Cicero, Marcus Tullius.   **2.659**
In Catilinam I–IV; Pro Murena; Pro Sulla; Pro Flacco / Cicero; with an English translation by C. Macdonald. — Cambridge, Mass.: Harvard University Press; London: Heinemann, 1977. 595 p. — (Loeb classical library. 324) (Cicero in twenty-eight volumes; 10) 'Replaces the edition by Louis E. Lord, first published in 1937.' Latin and English on opposite pages. I. Macdonald, C. II. Cicero, Marcus Tullius. Pro Flacco III. Cicero, Marcus Tullius. Pro Sulla. IV. Cicero, Marcus Tullius. Pro Murena. V. T. VI. Title: Pro Murena. VII. Title: Pro Sulla. VIII. Title: Pro Flacco. IX. Series.
PA6156.C5 A2 1977x   937/.05/0924   ISBN 0674993586

Cicero, Marcus Tullius.   • **2.660**
The speeches, with an English translation. Pro Archia poeta—Post reditum in senatu—Post reditum ad quirites—De domo sua—De haruspicum responsis—Pro Plancio. By N. H. Watts ... London, W. Heinemann; New York, G. P. Putnam's sons, 1923. vii, 550 p., 1 l. 17 cm. (Half-title: The Loeb classical library) At head of title: Cicero. I. Watts, Nevile, 1884- tr. II. T.
PA6156.C5A3 1923 PA6279.A4W3   LC 24-2281

Cicero, Marcus Tullius.   • **2.661**
Speeches. With an English translation by R. Gardner. — London, Heinemann; Cambridge, Harvard University Press, 1958. 2 v. (xx, 758 p.) 17 cm. — (The Loeb classical library. Latin authors) Bibliography: v. 2, p. 737-742. I. Gardner, Robert, 1890- tr. II. T. III. Series.
PA6156.C5A4 1958   875.1   LC 58-4351

Cicero, Marcus Tullius. • **2.662**
Philippics, with an English translation by Walter C.A. Ker. London, W. Heinemann; New York, G.P. Putnam's Sons, 1926. xii, 655 p. 17 cm. (The Loeb classical library. Latin authors) Latin and English on opposite pages. I. Ker, Walter Charles Alan, 1853-1929. II. T. III. Series.
PA6156.C5 P4 1926   *LC 27-2023*

Cicero, Marcus Tullius. • **2.663**
The Verrine orations, with an English translation by L. H. G. Greenwood. — London, Heinemann; New York, Putnam, 1928-35. 2 v. 17 cm. — (Loeb classical library; 221,293) Vol. 2 has imprint: London, Heinemann; Cambridge, Harvard University Press. I. T.
PA6156.C5 V4 1928   875.2   *LC 29-2709* *

Cicero, Marcus Tullius. • **2.664**
De finibus bonorum et malorum, with an English translation by H. Rackham. [2d ed.] London, W. Heinemann; New York, G. P. Putnam's sons, 1931. 511 p. 17 cm. (Loeb classical library.) Latin and English on opposite pages. "The text of this edition is founded on that of Madvig ... dated 1876."—Introd. I. Rackham, Harris, 1868- tr. II. T. III. Series.
PA6156.C6 D2 1931d

Cicero, Marcus Tullius. • **2.665**
De officiis / Cicero; with an English translation by Walter Miller. — London: W. Heinemann; New York: Macmillan Co., 1913. xvi, 424 p.: ill.; 17 cm. — (Loeb classical library. Latin authors. no. 30.) (Cicero in twenty-eight volumes; 21.) Includes index. Latin text, parallel English translation. I. Miller, Walter, 1864- II. T. III. Series.
PA6156.C6 D5 1913   *LC 14-5345*   *ISBN* 0434991546

Cicero, Marcus Tullius. • **2.666**
De oratore. — Cambridge, Mass., Harvard university press; London, W. Heinemann ltd., 1942. 2 v. 17 cm. — (Loeb classical library. 348-349) Imprint on vol. II: London, Heinemann; Cambridge, Mass., Harvard University. Latin and English on opposite pages. Printed in Great Britain. 1. Oratory 2. Rhetoric, Ancient I. Sutton, Edward William, 1871- ed. and tr. II. Rackham, Harris, 1868- ed. and tr. III. T. IV. Series.
PA6156.C6D6 1942   PA6296.D6 1942.   875.3   *LC A 42-4498* Revised

Cicero, Marcus Tullius. • **2.667**
[De republica. Latin and English. 1970] De republica, De Legibus, with an English translation by Clinton Walker Keyes. London W. Heinemann 1970. 533p. (The Loeb classical library. [Latin authors]) I. Keyes, Clinton Walker, 1888- II. T.
PA6156.C6 D8 1970

Cicero, Marcus Tullius. **2.668**
The letters to his friends, with an English translation by W. Glynn Williams ... London, W. Heinemann, ltd.; New York, G.P. Putnam's sons, 1927-1929. 3 v. 17 cm. (Loeb classical library. [Latin authors]) At head of title: Cicero. Latin and English on opposite pages. I. Williams, William Glynn, tr, II. T.
PA6156.C6 E3 1927   *LC 28-4491*

Cicero, Marcus Tullius. • **2.669**
Cicero. Letters to Atticus; with an English translation by E. O. Winstedt. London, W. Heinemann; New York, G. P. Putnam's sons, 1925-1928. 3 v. front. (port.) 17 cm. (Loeb classical library.) 1. Atticus, Titus Pomponius. I. Winstedt, Eric Otto, ed. and tr. II. T. III. Series.
PA6156.C6 E6 1925d

Cicero, Marcus Tullius. • **2.670**
... Tusculan disputations, with an English translation by J. E. King, LITT. D. London, W. Heinemann; New York, G. P. Putnam's sons, 1927. xxxvii, 577, [1] p. 17 cm. (The Loeb classical library. [Latin authors]) At head of title: Cicero. Appendix: Cicero's translations from the Greek': p. [549]-569. I. T.
PA6156.C6 T6 1927   *LC 27-11854*

PA6156. H–O

Horace. • **2.671**
The odes and epodes, with an English translation by C. E. Bennett. Cambridge, Mass. Harvard University Press; London, W. Heinemann, 1934. xix, 430 p. 17 cm. (The Loeb classical library. [Latin authors]) "First printed 1914. Reprinted and revised 1927, 1929, 1930, 1934." Latin and English on opposite pages. I. Bennett, Charles Edwin, 1858- tr. II. T. III. Series.
PA6156.H6 A3 1934d

Horace. • **2.672**
[Selected works. Latin and English. 1932] Satires, Epistles and Ars poetica, with an English translation by H. Rushton Fairclough. London Heinemann 1932. 508p. (The Loeb classical library) I. T.

Juvenal. • **2.673**
Juvenal and Persius; with an English translation by G.G. Ramsay ... London, W. Heinemann; New York, G.P. Putnam's Sons, 1918. lxxxii, 415 p. 17 cm. (The Loeb classical library. Latin authors) Latin and English on opposite pages. I. Persius. II. Ramsay, George Gilbert, 1839-1921. III. T. IV. Series.
PA6156.J8 1918   *LC 18-21762*

Livy. • **2.674**
[Works. English & Latin. 1919] Livy, with an English translation by B.O. Foster. London, Heinemann; New York, Putnam, 1919-59. 14 v. fold. col. maps. (Loeb classical library. [Latin authors]) Latin and English. Vols. 6-8 translated by F.G. Moore; v.9-11 by E.T. Sage; v.12 by E.T. Sage and A.C. Schlesinger; v.13 by A.C. Schlesinger; v.14 by A.C. Schlesinger, with a general index to Livy by R.M. Geer. I. T.
PA6156.L5 1919   937   *LC 20-2836//r*

Lucan, 39-65. • **2.675**
Lucan, with an English translation by J. D. Duff. The Civil war, books I–X. London, W. Heinemann; New York, G. P. Putnam's sons, 1928. 637 p. 17 cm. (The Loeb classical library. [Latin authors]) Latin and English on opposite pages. 1. Pharsalus, Battle of, 48 B.C. 2. Rome — History — Civil War, 49-48 B.C. I. Duff, J. D. (James Duff), 1860-1940. ed. II. T. III. Series.
PA6156.L7 1928d

Lucretius Carus, Titus. **2.676**
[De rerum natura English & Latin] De rerum natura / Lucretius; with an English translation by W. H. D. Rouse; rev. and new text, introd., notes, and index by Martin Ferguson Smith. — Cambridge, Mass.: Harvard University Press, 1975. lxii, 601 p.; 18 cm. (Loeb classical library) Latin and English on opposite pages. Includes index. I. Rouse, W. H. D. (William Henry Denham), 1863-1950. II. Smith, Martin Ferguson. III. T. IV. Series.
PA6156.L83D47   *LC 76-351626*   *ISBN* 0674992008

Martial. • **2.677**
Epigrams, with an English translation by Walter C. A. Ker. London, W. Heinemann; New York, G. P. Putnam's sons, 1930. 2 v. 17 cm. (The Loeb classical library. [Latin authors]) Latin and English on opposite pages. 1. Epigrams I. Ker, Walter Charles Alan, 1853-1929, tr. II. T. III. Series.
PA6156.M3 1930d

Ovid, 43 B.C.-17 or 18 A.D. **2.678**
The art of love: and other poems / with an English translation by J.H. Mozley. — 2d ed. / rev. by G.P. Goold. — Cambridge, Mass.: Harvard University Press, 1979. xiii, 381 p.; 17 cm. — (The Loeb classical library : Latin authors; 232.) (Ovid in six volumes; 2) Latin and English on opposite pages. I. Mozley, J.H. II. Goold, G. P. III. T. IV. Title: Ars amatoria. V. Series.
PA6156.O82 1979   *ISBN* 0674992555

Ovid, 43 B.C.-17 or 18 A.D. • **2.679**
Ovid's Fasti, with an English translation by Sir James George Frazer ... — London, W. Heinemann; New York, G. P. Putnam's sons, 1931. xxxii, 460 p., 1 l. 16.5 cm. — (Half-title: The Loeb classical library. [Latin authors]) Latin and English on opposite pages. I. Frazer, James George, Sir, 1854-1941. ed. and tr. II. T.
PA6156.O85 1931   871.2   *LC 32-3144*

Ovid, 43 B.C.-17 or 18 A.D. **2.680**
Heroides and Amores / Ovid; with an English translation by Grant Showerman. — 2d ed. / rev. by G. P. Goold. — Cambridge, Mass.: Harvard University Press, 1977. viii, 527 p.; 18 cm. — (Loeb classical library: Latin authors; no. 41) 'Ovid in six volumes, 1.' Latin and English on opposite pages; commentaries in English. I. Showerman, Grant, 1870-1935. II. Ovid, 43 B.C.-17 or 18 A.D. Amores. III. T. IV. Title: Amores.
PA6156.O86 1977   *ISBN* 0674990455(American)

Ovid, 43 B.C.-17 or 18 A.D. **2.681**
Metamorphoses / Ovid; with an English translation by Frank Justus Miller. — Cambridge, Mass.: Harvard University Press, 1916, 1976-1977 printing. 2 v.; 17 cm. — (The Loeb classical library: Latin authors; no. 42, 43) Vol. 1, 3rd ed., 1977, revised by G. P. Goold. I. Miller, Frank Justus, 1858- II. T.
PA6156.087M2x   *ISBN* 0674990463

Ovid, 43 B.C.-17 or 18 A.D. • **2.682**
Ovid with an English translation: Tristia, Ex Ponto, by Arthur Leslie Wheeler ... — London, Heinemann; New York, Putnam's sons, 1924. xliv, 510 p., 1 l. 17 cm. — (Half-title: The Loeb classical library. [Latin authors]) Latin and English on opposite pages. 'Selected bibliography': p. xlii—xliv. Reprint of 1924 edition. I. Wheeler, Arthur Leslie, 1871-1932, tr. II. T. III. Title: Tristia.
PA6156.O89 1965   871.2   *LC 24-16056*

PA6156.P–Z

Petronius Arbiter. **2.683**
Petronius; with an English translation by Michael Heseltine. — [1st ed.] revised by E. H. Warmington; and, Apocolocyntosis [of] Seneca; with an English

translation by W. H. D. Rouse. — Cambridge, Mass.: Harvard University Press, 1969. xlvi, 497 p. 17 cm. — (Loeb classical library. 15) English and Latin. First editions of these translations originally published 1912. I. Heseltine, Michael, tr. II. Warmington, E. H. (Eric Herbert), 1898- III. Seneca, Lucius Annaeus, ca. 4 B.C.-65 A.D. Apocolocyntosis. 1969. IV. Rouse, William Henry Denham, tr. V. T. VI. Series.
PA6156.P4 1969 PA6558.A2   873/.01   *LC* 70-597933

Plautus, Titus Maccius.   **2.684**
Plautus, with an English translation by Paul Nixon ... — London, W. Heinemann; New York, G. P. Putnam's sons, 1916-. 5 v.; 17 cm. — (Half-title: The Loeb classical library. [Latin authors]) Latin and English on opposite pages. Includes bibliographies. I. Nixon, Paul, 1882- tr. II. T.
PA6156.P5 1916   *LC* 16-14367

Pliny, the Younger.   • **2.685**
[Epistulae. English and Latin] Letters, and Panegyricus [by] Pliny. With an English translation by Betty Radice. Cambridge, Harvard University Press, 1969. 2 v. col. maps. 17 cm. (Loeb classical library. 55, 59) Translation of Epistulae and Panegyricus. Latin and English. I. Pliny, the Younger. Panegyricus. English and Latin. 1969. II. Radice, Betty. tr. III. T. IV. Title: Panegyricus. V. Series.
PA6156.P6 1969   876/.01   *LC* 72-7735

Pliny, the Elder.   **2.686**
[Naturalis historia English & Latin] Natural history. With an English translation by H. Rackham. Cambridge, Harvard University Press, 1961-. v. 17 cm. (Loeb classical library.) Latin and English on opposite pages. Vols. 6-8 translated by W. H. S. Jones. In v. 4, London, W. Heinemann precedes the Cambridge imprint. 1. Natural history — Pre-Linnean works I. Rackham, Harris, 1868-1944, tr. II. Jones, W. H. S. (William Henry Samuel), 1876-1963. tr. III. T. IV. Series.
PA6156.P65 1961   500   *LC* 74-15292

Pliny, the Elder.   **2.687**
Natural history / Pliny; with an English translation in ten volumes by H. Rackham. — Cambridge, Mass.: Harvard University Press; London: Heinemann, 1938-1963. 10 v.; 17 cm. — (Loeb classical library.) Latin and English on opposite pages. V.6-8 translated by W.H.S. Jones; v. 10 by D.E. Eichholz. 1. Natural history — Pre-Linnean works I. Rackham, Harris, 1968- II. T. III. Series.
PA6156.P6x   QH41.P773   878.9   937

Propertius, Sextus.   • **2.688**
Propertius; with an English translation, by H. E. Butler ... — London, W. Heinemann; New York, G. P. Putnam's sons, 1916. xvi, 362, [1] p. 17 cm. — (Loeb classical library. 18) Latin and English on opposite pages. 'First published, 1912; reprinted, October 1916.' 'Bibliographical note': p. xv—xvi. I. Butler, Harold Edgeworth, ed. and tr. II. T. III. Series.
PA6156.P8 1916   874.4   *LC* 19-6667

Prudentius, b. 348.   • **2.689**
Prudentius / with an English translation by H. J. Thomson. — London: W. Heinemann; Cambridge, Mass.: Harvard University Press, 1949-1953. 2 v.; 17 cm. (Loeb classical library. Latin authors. no. 387, 398.) Includes index. Latin text, parallel English translation. I. Thomson, H. J. II. T. III. Series.
PA6156.P85 1949   *LC* 49-49735

Quintilian.   • **2.690**
The Instituto oratoria of Quintilian, with an English translation by H.E. Butler. London: W. Heinemann; New York: G.P. Putnam's Sons, 1921-1922. 4 v. 17 cm. (The Loeb classical library. Latin authors) I. Butler, Harold Edgeworth, 1878- II. T. III. Series.
PA6156.Q5 1921   *LC* 21-6981

Sallust, 86-34 B.C.   • **2.691**
Sallust, with an English translation by J. C. Rolfe ... London, W. Heinemann; New York, G. P. Putnam's sons, 1931. xxvi, 535, [1] p. 17 cm. (Half-title: The Loeb classical library, ed. by T. E. Page, E. Capps [and] W. H. D. Rouse) 'Bibliographical note': p. xxiv-xxv. I. Rolfe, John Carew, 1859-1943. tr. II. T.
PA6156.S3 1931   878.2   *LC* 42-50642

Seneca, Lucius Annaeus, ca. 4 B.C.-65 A.D.   • **2.692**
Moral essays, with an English translation by John W. Basore. London, W. Heinemann, New York, G. P. Putnam's Sons; Cambridge, Mass. Harvard University Press, 1928-1935. 3 v. 17 cm. (The Loeb classical library. [Latin authors]) Latin and English on opposite pages. I. Basore, John William, 1870- tr. II. T. III. Series.
PA6156.S4 A7 1928d

Seneca, Lucius Annaeus, ca. 4 B.C.-65 A.D.   • **2.693**
Ad Lucilium epistulae morales / Seneca; with an English translation by Richard M. Gummere. — London: Heinemann; New York: G.P. Putnam, 1917-1925. 3 v. — (The Loeb classical library) V.1 is 1925 reprint of 1918 ed. Latin and English on opposite pages. I. T.
PA6156.S4 E6 1917   PA6661.E6 1917.   *LC* 17-28199

Seneca, Lucius Annaeus, ca. 4 B.C.-65 A.D.   • **2.694**
Seneca's tragedies, with an English translation by Frank Justus Miller. London, W. Heinemann; New York, G. P. Putnam's Sons, 1927. 2 v. 17 cm. (Loeb classical library) Latin and English on opposite pages. "First printed 1917." I. Miller, Frank Justus, 1858- tr. II. T. III. Series.
PA6156.S5 1927d

Statius, P. Papinius (Publius Papinius)   • **2.695**
Statius, with an English translation by J. H. Mozley ... in two volumes ... — London, W. Heinemann, ltd.; New York, G. P. Putnam's sons, 1928. 2 v. front. (fold. map) 16.5 cm. — (Half-title: The Loeb classical library. [Latin authors]) Latin and English on opposite pages. Bibliography: v. 1, p. xxxii. I. Mozley, John Henry, tr. II. T.
PA6156.S8 1928   *LC* 28-16431

Suetonius, ca. 69-ca. 122.   • **2.696**
Suetonius, with an English translation by J. C. Rolfe. Cambridge, Mass., Harvard University Press; London, W. Heinemann, 1930-1935. 2 v. front. (port.) 17 cm. (Loeb classical library.) Latin and English on opposite pages. 1. Roman emperors I. Rolfe, John Carew, 1859-1943. tr. II. T. III. Series.
PA6156.S9 1930d

Tacitus, Cornelius.   • **2.697**
The Histories / Tacitus; with an English translation by Clifford H. Moore. The annals / Tacitus; with an English translation by John Jackson. — London: W. Heinemann; New York: G. P. Putnam's, 1925-1937. 4 v.: col. maps (fold.); 17 cm. (Loeb classical library. Latin authors. no. 111, 249.) Includes index. Latin text, parallel English translation. 1. Rome — History — Flavians, 69-96 I. Tacitus, Cornelius. Annales II. Moore, Clifford H. (Clifford Herschel), 1866-1931. III. Jackson, John, 1881- IV. T. V. Series.
PA6156.T25 1925   *LC* 26-7877

Terence.   • **2.698**
Terence; with an English translation by John Sargeaunt. London, W. Heinemann, New York, G. P. Putnam's Sons, 1931. 2 v. front. 17 cm. (Loeb classical library.) "First printed 1912. Reprinted ... 1931." I. Sargeaunt, John, 1857- ed. and tr. II. T. III. Series.
PA6156.T4 1931d

Vitruvius Pollio.   • **2.699**
On architecture, edited from the Harleian manuscript 2767 and translated into English by Frank Granger. London, W. Heinemann; New York, G. P. Putnam's Sons, 1931-1934. 2 v. front., plates, plans. diagrs. 17 cm. (The Loeb classical library. [Latin authors]) Latin and English on opposite pages. 1. Architecture — Early works to 1800. I. Granger, Frank Stephen, 1864- tr. II. T. III. Series.
PA6156.V5 1931d

Virgil.   **2.700**
[Selections. Latin and English. 1960] Virgil. With an English translation by H. Rushton Fairclough. Rev. ed. London Heinemann 1960. 2 v. (Loeb classical library.) I. Fairclough, Henry Rushton, 1862-1936, tr. II. T. III. Series.
PA6156.V5 F3 1960

PA6164–6165 Translations (Collections)

Allen, Michael J. B. comp.   **2.701**
Sources and analogues of Old English poetry: the major Latin texts in translation / translated by Michael J. B. Allen and Daniel G. Calder. — Cambridge Eng.: D. S. Brewer; Totowa, N.J.: Rowman and Littlefield, 1976. xviii, 235 p.; 23 cm. 1. Christian poetry, Latin — Translations into English. 2. English prose literature — Translation from Latin. 3. English poetry — Old English, ca. 450-1100 — History and criticism. I. Calder, Daniel Gillmore. joint comp. II. T.
PA6164.A5   871/.01   *LC* 75-2240   *ISBN* 087471687X

Horace.   **2.702**
The satires of Horace and Persius; a verse translation with an introduction and notes by Niall Rudd. London, Penguin, 1973. [7], 193 p. 19 cm. (The Penguin classics) Includes index. 1. Satire, Latin 2. Latin literature — Translations into English. 3. English literature — Translations from Latin. I. Persius. Satirae. English. 1973. II. Rudd, Niall. tr. III. T.
PA6164.H713   871/.01/08   *LC* 74-162411   *ISBN* 0140442790

Duckworth, George Eckel, 1903- ed.   • **2.703**
The complete Roman drama; all the extant comedies of Plautus and Terence, and the tragedies of Seneca, in a variety of translations, edited, and with an introduction, by George E. Duckworth. New York, Random house [1942] 2 v. 24 cm. 'First printing.' 'A companion volume to The complete Greek drama, edited by Whitney J. Oates and Eugene O'Neill, jr.'—Pref. 1. Latin drama —

Translations into English. 2. English drama — Translations from Latin. I. Plautus, Titus Maccius. II. Terence. III. Seneca, Lucius Annaeus, ca. 4 B.C.-65 A.D. IV. T.
PA6165.D8   872   *LC* 42-36335

PA6202–6961 Authors, A–Z

PA6209–6217 Apuleius

Apuleius.   **2.704**
[Psyche et Cupido. English] Amor and Psyche: the psychic development of the feminine: a commentary on the tale by Apuleius / by Erich Neumann; translated from the German by Ralph Manheim. — [Princeton, N.J.]: Princeton University Press, 1971, c1956. 181 p.; 21 cm. — (Bollingen series. 54) (Princeton/Bollingen paperbacks; 239) Original title: Psyche et Cupido. Includes index. I. Neumann, Erich. II. T. III. Series.
PA6209.M5 N4 1971   873/.01   *LC* 75-510731   *ISBN* 0691097011.
ISBN 0691017727 pbk

Tatum, James.   **2.705**
Apuleius and The golden ass / James Tatum. — Ithaca: Cornell University Press, 1979. 199 p.: ill.; 23 cm. Includes indexes. 1. Apuleius. Metamorphoses. I. T.
PA6217.T3   873/.01   *LC* 78-74220   *ISBN* 0801411637

PA6274–6276 Catullus

Catullus, Gaius Valerius.   **• 2.706**
[Works. Latin. 1893] Catullus; edited by Elmer Truesdell Merrill. Boston Ginn 1893. 273p. (College series of Latin authors) I. Merrill, Elmer Truesdell, 1860-1936, ed. II. T.
PA6274 A2 1893

Catullus, Gaius Valerius.   **• 2.707**
Catullus. A commentary by C. J. Fordyce. — Oxford, Clarendon Press, 1961. xxviii, 419 p. 19 cm. Poems in Latin, with commentary in English. Bibliography: p. [411] Includes bibliographical references. I. Fordyce, C. J. (Christian James), 1901- II. T.
PA6274.A2 1961   874   *LC* 62-216

Havelock, Eric Alfred.   **• 2.708**
The lyric genius of Catullus, by E. A. Havelock. New York Russell & Russell [1967] 1. Catullus, Gaius Valerius. I. Catullus, Gaius Valerius. II. T.
PA6274.A25 1967   *LC* 67-15472

Catullus, Gaius Valerius.   **2.709**
[Works. English & Latin. 1983] Catullus / edited with introduction, translation, and notes by G.P. Goold. — London: Duckworth, 1983. 266 p.; 23 cm. — (Duckworth classical, medieval, and renaissance editions.) Latin text and parallel English translation. 1. Catullus, Gaius Valerius — Translations, English. I. Goold, G. P. II. T. III. Series.
PA6275.E5 G66 1983   874/.01 19   *LC* 82-128237   *ISBN* 0715614355

Frank, Tenney, 1876-1939.   **• 2.710**
Catullus and Horace; two poets in their environment. — New York, Russell & Russell, 1965 [c1928] 291 p. plan. 22 cm. Bibliographical references included in 'Notes' (p. 279-286) 1. Catullus C. Valerius. 2. Horatius Flaccus, Quintus. I. T.
PA6276.F6 1965   874   *LC* 65-13941

Quinn, Kenneth.   **• 2.711**
The Catullan revolution / Kenneth Quinn. — [Carlton]: Melbourne University Press, 1959. 119 p. 1. Catullus, Gaius Valerius. 2. Latin poetry — History and criticism I. T.
PA6276.Q5   *LC* 60-491

Quinn, Kenneth.   **2.712**
Catullus; an interpretation. New York, Barnes & Noble [1973] xi, 305 p. 23 cm. 1. Catullus, Gaius Valerius. I. T.
PA6276.Q52 1973   874/.01   *LC* 73-157934   *ISBN* 0064957578

Ross, David O.   **• 2.713**
Style and tradition in Catullus [by] David O. Ross, Jr. Cambridge, Harvard University Press, 1969. viii, 188 p. 22 cm. (Loeb classical monographs) 1. Catullus, Gaius Valerius. I. T. II. Series.
PA6276.R57   871/.01   *LC* 69-18043   *ISBN* 0674853407

PA6278–6370 Cicero

Cicero, Marcus Tullius.   **• 2.714**
[Correspondence English] The correspondence. Arranged according to its chronological order; with a revision of the text, a commentary, and introductory essays by Robert Yelverton Tyrrell and Louis Claude Purser. Hildesheim, G. Olms, 1969. 7 v. 21 cm. Reprinted from volumes previously published, Dublin and London: v. 1, 3d ed., 1904; v. 2-6, 2d ed., 1906-1933; v. 7, 1st ed., 1901. Vol. 7: Index. I. Tyrrell, Robert Yelverton, 1844-1914. ed. II. Purser, Louis Claude, 1854-1932, ed. III. T.
PA6297.A1 1969   937/.05/0924 B 19   *LC* 75-437862

Cicero, Marcus Tullius.   **• 2.715**
Cicero's letters to Atticus / edited by D.R. Shackleton Bailey. — Cambridge, Eng.: At the University Press, 1965-70. 7 v.: cartes (certaines pliées); 23 cm. — (Cambridge classical texts and commentaries; 3-9) Traduction anglaise en regard du texte latin. I. Atticus, Titus Pomponius. II. Bailey, David Roy Shackleton. III. T. IV. Title: Letters to Atticus. V. Series.
PA6297 A5 1965   876/.1   *LC* 65-18929

PA6382 Ennius

Ennius, Quintus.   **• 2.716**
The tragedies of Ennius: the fragments / edited with an introduction and commentary, by H. D. Jocelyn. — London: Cambridge University Press, 1967. viii, 472 p.; 23 cm. — (Cambridge classical texts and commentaries; 10) I. Jocelyn, H.D. II. T.
PA6382.A2   *LC* 67-11525

Ennius, Quintus.   **2.717**
[Annales. English] The Annals of Q. Ennius / edited with introduction and commentary by Otto Skutsch. — Oxford [Oxfordshire]: Clarendon Press; New York: Oxford University Press, 1985. xviii, 848 p.; 22 cm. Includes indexes. I. Skutsch, Otto. II. T.
PA6382.A3 E5 1985   873.01 19   *LC* 83-8048   *ISBN* 0198144482

PA6393–6444 Horace

Horace.   **• 2.718**
[Carmina. English and Latin. Liber III] The third book of Horace's 'Odes'; edited with translation and running commentary, by Gordon Williams. Oxford, Clarendon P., 1969. vii, 165 p. 21 cm. English and Latin. I. Williams, Gordon Willis. ed. II. T.
PA6393.C43 1969   874/.01   *LC* 71-421855   *ISBN* 0199120013

Brink, C. O. (Charles Oscar), 1907-.   **2.719**
Horace on poetry / by C. O. Brink. — Cambridge [Eng.] University Press, 1963-1982. 3 v.; 25 cm. 1. Horace. Ars poetica. 2. Horace. Epistulae 3. Horace. Satirae I. T.
PA6393.E7B7   808.1   *LC* 63-4908   *ISBN* 0521200695

Rudd, Niall.   **• 2.720**
The 'Satires' of Horace: a study. — London, Cambridge U. P., 1966. xi, 318 p. 22.5 cm. I. T.
PA6393.S8R8   877.01   *LC* 66-11031

Horace.   **2.721**
[Carmina. English] The complete Odes and Epodes: with the Centennial hymn / Horace; translated with notes by W.G. Shepherd; with an introduction by Betty Radice. — Harmondsworth, Middlesex, England; New York, N.Y., U.S.A.: Penguin, 1983. 253 p.; 19 cm. (Penguin classics.) Includes index. 1. Horace — Translations, English. I. Shepherd, W. G. (William Guy), 1935- II. Horace. Epodi. English III. T. IV. Series.
PA6394.S48 1983   874/.01 19   *LC* 83-209608   *ISBN* 014044422X

Bailey, D. R. Shackleton (David Roy Shackleton), 1917-.   **2.722**
Profile of Horace / D.R. Shackleton Bailey. — Cambridge, Mass.: Harvard University Press, 1982. x, 142 p.; 22 cm. 1. Horace — Criticism and interpretation. I. T.
PA6411.B28 1982   PA6411 B28 1982.   874/.01 19   *LC* 82-1010
    ISBN 0674713257

Commager, Henry Steele, 1902-.   **• 2.723**
The Odes of Horace; a critical study. — New Haven, Yale University Press, [1966, c1962] xiv, 365 p. 24 cm. Bibliographical footnotes. 1. Horace. Carmina. I. T.
PA6411.C59   874   *LC* 62-8241

Fraenkel, Eduard, 1888-1970.   **• 2.724**
Horace. — Oxford, Clarendon Press, 1957. xiv, 463 p. 24 cm. — (Oxford paperbacks, 105) Bibliographical footnotes. 1. Horatius Flaccus, Quintus. I. T.
PA6411.F67   874.5   *LC* 58-37

Nisbet, R. G. M. (Robin George Murdoch)   **2.725**
A commentary on Horace: Odes, book 1, by R. G. M. Nisbet and Margaret Hubbard. Oxford: Clarendon P., 1970. lviii, 440 p. 23 cm. I. Horace. Carmina. Liber I. I. Hubbard, Margaret, 1924- joint author. II. T.
PA6411.N55   874/.01   *LC* 72-489364   *ISBN* 0198144393

Nisbet, R. G. M. (Robin George Murdoch)   **2.726**
A commentary on Horace: Odes, book II / by R. G. M. Nisbet and Margaret Hubbard. — Oxford [Eng.]: Clarendon Press, 1978. xvi, 355 p.; 23 cm. Includes indexes. 1. Horace. Carmina. Liber II. I. Hubbard, Margaret, 1924- joint author. II. T.
PA6411.N56   874/.01   *LC* 77-30366   *ISBN* 0198144520

Wilkinson, L. P.   • **2.727**
Horace & his lyric poetry, by L. P. Wilkinson. 2nd ed. [revised]. London, Cambridge U.P., 1968. vi, 185 p. 20 cm. 1. Horace. I. T.
PA6411.W5 1968   874/.01   *LC* 76-356974   *ISBN* 0521095530

PA6445–6518 J–M

Juvenal.   **2.728**
[Selections. 1970] D. Ivnii Ivvenalis satvrae XIV. Fourteen satires of Juvenal, edited by J.D. Duff. [1st ed.] reset and reprinted, with a new introduction by Michael Coffey. London, Cambridge University Press, 1970. [4], xc, 473 p. 17 cm. (Pitt Press series) Latin text, English introduction and notes. Originally published in 1898. I. Duff, J. D. (James Duff), 1860-1940. ed. II. T.
PA6446.A5 1970   871/.01   *LC* 76-126036   *ISBN* 0521073707

Juvenal.   • **2.729**
The sixteen satires [by] Juvenal. Translated with an introd. and notes by Peter Green. — Harmondsworth: Penguin Books, [1967] 317 p.; 18 cm. — (The Penguin classics, L194) Translation of Satirae. I. Green, Peter, 1924- ed. II. T.
PA6447.E5 G7   877/.01   *LC* 67-109119

Courtney, E. (Edward), 1932-.   **2.730**
A commentary on the satires of Juvenal / by E. Courtney. — London: Athlone Press, 1980. x, 650 p.: ill.; 23 cm. Includes indexes. 1. Juvenal — Criticism and interpretation. I. T.
PA6448.C68   871/.01 19   *LC* 80-146655   *ISBN* 048511190X

Highet, Gilbert, 1906-1978.   • **2.731**
Juvenal the satirist, a study. — Oxford, Clarendon Press, 1954. xviii, 373 p. 23 cm. Bibliography: p. [339]-346. 1. Juvenal. I. T.
PA6448.H5   *LC* A 54-7469

Briscoe, John, 1938-.   **2.732**
A commentary on Livy, books XXXI–XXXIII. Oxford, Clarendon Press, 1973. xviii, 370 p. 23 cm. Includes indexes. 1. Livy. Ab urbe condita. Books 31-33. I. T.
PA6459.B7   937/.04 19   *LC* 73-175676   *ISBN* 0198144423

Briscoe, John, 1938-.   **2.733**
A commentary on Livy, books XXXIV–XXXVII / by John Briscoe. — Oxford: Clarendon Press, c1981. xx, 442 p.: maps; 22 cm. Includes indexes. 1. Livy. Ab urbe condita. Books 34-37. I. T.
PA6459.B72   937/.0072024 19   *LC* 80-41210   *ISBN* 0198144555

Ogilvie, R. M. (Robert Maxwell), 1932-.   **2.734**
A commentary on Livy, books 1–5, by R. M. Ogilvie. — Oxford, Clarendon Press, 1965. xi, 774 p. 2 fold. maps. 23 cm. Bibliography: p. 22. Includes bibliographical references. 1. Livy. Ab urbe condita libri I-V. I. T.
PA6459.O4   937   *LC* 65-3228

Walsh, P. G. (Patrick Gerard)   • **2.735**
Livy: his historical aims and methods. — Cambridge [Eng.] University Press, 1961. 300 p. 23 cm. Includes bibliography. 1. Livius, Titus. I. T.
PA6459.W37 1961   907.2   *LC* 61-474

Ahl, Frederick M.   **2.736**
Lucan: an introduction / Frederick M. Ahl. — Ithaca, N.Y.: Cornell University Press, 1976. 379 p.; 24 cm. (Cornell studies in classical philology; v. 39) Includes indexes. 1. Lucan, 39-65. Pharsalia 2. Pharsalus, Battle of, 48 B.C — Literature and the war. 3. Rome — History — Civil War, 49-48 B.C. — Literature and the war. I. T.
PA6480.A4   873/.01   *LC* 75-16926   *ISBN* 0801408377

Morford, Mark P. O., 1929-.   • **2.737**
The poet Lucan; studies in rhetorical epic, by M. P. O. Morford. New York, Barnes & Noble, 1967. xi, 93 p. 23 cm. 'Substantially a revision of a doctoral thesis presented in 1963 at the University of London under the title: Some aspects of Lucan's rhetoric.' 1. Lucan, 39-65. I. T.
PA6480.M6 1967a   873/.01   *LC* 67-6696

Lucretius Carus, Titus.   **2.738**
De rerum natura. Ed. [and tr.] by Cyril Bailey. — Oxford, Clarendon Press, 1947. 3 v. (1785 p.) 23 cm. I. Bailey, Cyril, 1871-1957. ed. and tr. II. T.
PA6482.A2 1947   871.1   *LC* 48-3624 *

Lucretius Carus, Titus.   **2.739**
[De rerum natura. English] The nature of things / Lucretius; translated by Frank O. Copley. — 1st ed. — New York: Norton, c1977. xxi, 177 p.; 22 cm. Translation of De rerum natura. I. Copley, Frank Olin. II. T.
PA6483.E5 C6 1977   871/.01   *LC* 77-14335   *ISBN* 0393064263. *ISBN* 0393090949 pbk

West, David Alexander.   • **2.740**
The imagery and poetry of Lucretius / [by] David West. — Edinburgh: Edinburgh U.P., 1969. viii, 142 p.; 21 cm. 1. Lucretius Carus, Titus. I. T.
PA6484.W4 1969   871/.01   *LC* 68-58944   *ISBN* 0852240635

Martial.   • **2.741**
[Epigrammata. English and Latin. Selections] Sixty poems of Martial, in translation [by] Dudley Fitts. [1st ed.] New York, Harcourt, Brace & World [1967] xiii, 127 p. 21 cm. Selections, in Latin and English, from the Epigrammata of Martial. I. Fitts, Dudley, 1903- tr. II. T.
PA6501.A3 F5   *LC* 67-19196

Howell, Peter, M. Phil.   **2.742**
A commentary on book one of the Epigrams of Martial / Peter Howell. — London: Athlone Press, 1980. vi, 369 p., [8] p. of plates: ill.; 23 cm. Includes parallel text in English and Latin of book one of the Epigrams. Includes indexes. 1. Martial. Epigrammata. Book 1. I. Martial. Epigrammata. Book 1. English & Latin. 1980. II. T.
PA6501.B1 H68 1980   878/.0102 19   *LC* 82-195642   0485111818

PA6519–6553 Ovid

Ovid, 43 B.C.-17 or 18 A.D.   **2.743**
[Amores. Book I. Latin and English. 1973] Ovid's Amores, Book 1; edited with translation and running commentary by John A. Barsby. Oxford Clarendon Press 1973. 180p. I. Barsby, John A. II. T. III. Title: Amores
PA6519 A7 1973

Ovid, 43 B.C.-17 or 18 A.D.   **2.744**
Ars amatoria, book I / Ovid; edited with an introd. and commentary by A. S. Hollis. — Oxford: Clarendon Press, 1977. xxii, 171 p.: ill.; 20 cm. Text in Latin with English introd. and notes. Includes index. I. Hollis, A. S. (Adrian Swayne) II. T.
PA6519.A83 A1 1977   *LC* 77-571514   *ISBN* 0198144415

Jacobson, Howard, 1940-.   **2.745**
Ovid's Heroides. Princeton, N.J., Princeton University Press [1974] xiv, 437 p. 25 cm. 1. Ovid, 43 B.C.-17 or 18 A.D. Heroides I. Ovid, 43 B.C.-17 or 18 A.D. Heroides. 1974. II. T.
PA6519.H7 J3   871/.01   *LC* 73-16754   *ISBN* 0691062714

Galinsky, Karl, 1942-.   **2.746**
Ovid's Metamorphoses: an introduction to the basic aspects / G. Karl Galinsky. — Berkeley: University of California Press, 1975. xi, 285 p., [1] leaf of plates: ill.; 24 cm. 1. Ovid, 43 B.C.-17 or 18 A.D. Metamorphoses. I. T.
PA6519.M9 G3   873/.01   *LC* 74-84146   *ISBN* 0520028481

Ovid, 43 B.C.-17 or 18 A.D.   **2.747**
The erotic poems / Ovid; translated with an introduction and notes by Peter Green. — Harmondsworth, Middlesex, England; New York, N.Y.: Penguin Books, 1982. 449 p.; 18 cm. (Penguin classics.) Includes index. 1. Ovid, 43 B.C.-17 or 18 A.D — Translations, English. 2. Erotic poetry, Latin — Translations into English. 3. Erotic poetry, English — Translations from Latin. I. Green, Peter, 1924- II. T. III. Series.
PA6522.A2 1982   871/.01 19   *LC* 83-166458   *ISBN* 0140443606

Ovid, 43 B.C.-17 or 18 A.D.   **2.748**
[Metamorphoses. English] Metamorphoses of Ovid / Translated and with an introd. by Mary M. Innes. Harmondsworth: Penguin, 1955. 363p. (Penguin classics. L58.) I. Innes, Mary M. II. T. III. Series.
PA6522.M2 I5 1955   *ISBN* 0140440585

Binns, J. W.   **2.749**
Ovid, edited by J. W. Binns. London, Boston, Routledge & K. Paul [1973] viii, 250 p. 22 cm. (Greek and Latin studies; classical literature and its influence) 1. Ovid, 43 B.C.-17 or 18 A.D — Criticism and interpretation. I. T.
PA6537.B48   871/.01   *LC* 73-83118   *ISBN* 0710076398

Fränkel, Hermann Ferdinand, 1888-.   • **2.750**
Ovid; a poet between two worlds, by Hermann Fränkel. Berkeley and Los Angeles, University of California press, 1945. viii p., 1 l., 282 p., 24 cm. (Sather classical lectures. v.18, 1945.) I. T. II. Series.
PA6537.F7   *LC* A 45-3905

Otis, Brooks.   • **2.751**
Ovid as an epic poet. 2d ed. Cambridge [Eng.] University Press, 1970. xviii, 441 p. 23 cm. 1. Ovid, 43 B.C.-17 or 18 A.D — Criticism and interpretation. I. T.
PA6537.O8 1970   873/.01   *LC* 75-96098

Rand, Edward Kennard, 1871-1945.   • **2.752**
Ovid and his influence. — New York, Cooper Square Publishers, 1963. xi, 184 p. illus. 19 cm. — (Our debt to Greece and Rome) Bibliography: p. 180-184. 1. Ovidius Naso, Publius. I. T.
PA6537.R3 1963   871   *LC* 63-10269

Wilkinson, L. P.   • **2.753**
Ovid recalled. — Cambridge [Eng.] University Press, 1955. 483 p. illus. 23 cm. Includes bibliographies. 1. Ovidius Naso, Publius. I. T.
PA6537.W5   871.2   *LC* 55-13646

PA6554–6651 P–Q

Bramble, J. C.   **2.754**
Persius and the programmatic satire; a study in form and imagery, by J. C. Bramble. Cambridge [Eng.], University Press, 1974. xiv, 224 p. 23 cm. (Cambridge classical studies.) 1. Persius — Style. 2. Persius — Language. I. T. II. Series.
PA6556.B7   877/.01   *LC* 72-83579   *ISBN* 0521087031

Dessen, Cynthia S.   • **2.755**
Iunctura callidus acri: a study of Persius' Satires [by] Cynthia S. Dessen. Urbana, University of Illinois Press, 1968. viii, 117 p. 24 cm. (Illinois studies in language and literature. 59) 1. Persius. Works I. T. II. Series.
PA6556.D4   877/.01   *LC* 68-64010   *ISBN* 0252784022

Morford, Mark P. O., 1929-.   **2.756**
Persius / by Mark Morford. — Boston: Twayne Publishers, c1984. 136 p.: ill.; 23 cm. — (Twayne's world authors series; TWAS 713. Latin literature) Includes index. 1. Persius — Criticism and interpretation. I. T.
PA6556.M67 1984   871/.01 19   *LC* 84-537   *ISBN* 0805765603

Petronius Arbiter.   • **2.757**
The Satyricon. Translated, with an introd., by William Arrowsmith. — Ann Arbor, University of Michigan Press [1959] xxiii, 218 p. 21 cm. I. Arrowsmith, William, 1924- tr. II. T.
PA6558.E5A7   877   *LC* 59-6026

Sullivan, J. P. (John Patrick)   • **2.758**
The Satyricon of Petronius; a literary study [by] J. P. Sullivan. [1st American ed.] Bloomington, Indiana University Press [1968] 302 p. 23 cm. 1. Petronius Arbiter. Satyricon I. T.
PA6559.S8 1968   877/.01   *LC* 68-14596

Walsh, P. G. (Patrick Gerard)   • **2.759**
The Roman novel. The 'Satyricon' of Petronius and the 'Metamorphoses' of Apuleius, by P. G. Walsh. Cambridge [Eng,] University Press, 1970. xiv, 272 p. 22 cm. 1. Petronius Arbiter. Satyricon 2. Apuleius. Metamorphoses. I. T.
PA6559.W3   873/.01/09   *LC* 70-98700   *ISBN* 0521076587

Plautus, Titus Maccius.   **2.760**
[Selections. English. 1983] Plautus, the darker comedies / translated from the Latin, with introduction and notes, by James Tatum. — Baltimore: Johns Hopkins University Press, c1983. x, 213 p.; 24 cm. I. Tatum, James. II. T.
PA6570.A3 1983   872/.01 19   *LC* 82-21160   *ISBN* 0801829003

Norwood, Gilbert, 1880-.   • **2.761**
Plautus and Terence. New York, Cooper Square Publishers, 1963. vii, 212 p. 19 cm. (Our debt to Greece and Rome.) 1. Plautus, Titus Maccius — Criticism and interpretation. 2. Terence — Criticism and interpretation. 3. Latin drama (Comedy) — History and criticism. I. T. II. Series.
PA6585.N6 1963   872   *LC* 63-10276

Segal, Erich, 1937-.   • **2.762**
Roman laughter; the comedy of Plautus [by] Erich Segal. Cambridge, Harvard University Press, 1968. ix, 229 p. 22 cm. (Harvard studies in comparative literature, v. 29) 1. Plautus, Titus Maccius. I. T.
PA6585.S4   872/.01   *LC* 68-25618

Slater, Niall W., 1954-.   **2.763**
Plautus in performance: the theatre of the mind / Niall W. Slater. — Princeton, N.J.: Princeton University Press, c1985. x, 190 p.; 22 cm. Includes indexes. 1. Plautus, Titus Maccius — Criticism and interpretation. 2. Plautus, Titus Maccius — Dramatic production. I. T.
PA6585.S55 1985   872/.01 19   *LC* 84-15958   *ISBN* 0691066248

Propertius, Sextus.   **2.764**
[Elegiae] Elegies, I–IV / Propertius; edited, with introd. and commentary by L. Richardson, Jr. — Norman: University of Oklahoma Press, c1977. xi, 489 p.; 25

cm. (American Philological Association series of classical texts) Includes index. I. Richardson, Lawrence. II. T.
PA6644.A2 1977   874/.01   *LC* 76-26153

Propertius, Sextus.   • **2.765**
Elegies: book IV / Propertius; edited by W. A. Camps. — Cambridge[Eng.], University Press, 1965. ix, 167 p. cm. — (Latin texts and commentaries) I. Camps, William Anthony. II. T. III. Series.
PA6644.B4 1979   874/.01   *LC* 78-67126   *ISBN* 0405115970

Hubbard, Margaret, 1924-.   **2.766**
Propertius / Margaret Hubbard. — New York: Scribner, c1975. viii, 182 p., [1] leaf of plates: ill.; 23 cm. (Classical life and letters) Includes indexes. 1. Propertius, Sextus. I. T.
PA6646.H78 1975   874/.01   *LC* 75-11481   *ISBN* 0684144646

Kennedy, George Alexander, 1928-.   • **2.767**
Quintilian, by George Kennedy. New York, Twayne Publishers [1969] 155 p. 22 cm. (Twayne's world authors series, 66. Latin literature) 1. Quintilian. I. T.
PA6651.K4   875/.01   *LC* 68-57477

PA6656–6799 S–T

Earl, Donald C.   • **2.768**
The political thought of Sallust / by D.C. Earl. — Cambridge: University Press, 1961. 132 p.; 23 cm. — (Cambridge classical studies) 1. Sallust, 86-34 B.C. I. T.
PA6656.E2   878   *LC* 61-66646

Syme, Ronald, Sir, 1903-.   • **2.769**
Sallust. — Berkeley, University of California Press [c1964] vi, 381 p. 24 cm. — (Sather classical lectures. v. 33) Bibliography: p. 355-363. 1. Sallustius Crispus, C. I. T. II. Series.
PA6656.S9   *LC* 64-17069

Seneca, Lucius Annaeus, ca. 4 B.C.-65 A.D.   **2.770**
L. Annaei Senecae Dialogorum libri duodecim / recognovit brevique adnotatione critica instruxit L. D. Reynolds. — Oxonii: E typographeo Clarendoniano, 1977. xx, 327 p. — (Scriptorum classicorum bibliotheca Oxoniensis.) I. Reynolds, Leighton Durham. II. T. III. Title: Dialogorum libri duodecim. IV. Series.
PA6105.S8 S46   PA6661.D8 1977.   *LC* 78-373163   *ISBN* 0198146590

Seneca, Lucius Annaeus, ca. 4 B.C.-65 A.D.   • **2.771**
Four tragedies, and Octavia / Seneca; translated with an introduction by E.F. Watling. — Harmondsworth: Penguin, 1966. 318 p. — (Penguin classics) Translated from the Latin. I. T.
PA6666.A1 W3 1966a   *LC* 66-67336

Costa, Charles Desmond Nuttall.   **2.772**
Seneca / edited by C. D. N. Costa. — London; Boston: Routledge & K. Paul, 1974. viii, 246 p.; 22 cm. (Greek and Latin studies: classical literature and its influence) 1. Seneca, Lucius Annaeus, ca. 4 B.C.-65 A.D. I. T.
PA6675.Z9 C67   188   *LC* 74-79358   *ISBN* 0710079001

Pratt, Norman T. (Norman Twombly), 1911-.   **2.773**
Seneca's drama / Norman T. Pratt. — Chapel Hill: University of North Carolina Press, c1983. 229 p.; 24 cm. 1. Seneca, Lucius Annaeus, ca. 4 B.C.-65 A.D — Dramatic works. I. T.
PA6685.P7 1983   872/.01 19   *LC* 82-23791   *ISBN* 0080781551

Tacitus, Cornelius.   • **2.774**
Cornelii Taciti Annalium libri I–IV. Edited with introduction and notes for the use of schools and junior students by H. Furneaux ... — 2d ed. — Oxford, Clarendon press, 1897. 4 p. l., 400 p. 17.5 cm. — (Clarendon press series) I. Furneaux, Henry, 1829-1900, ed. II. T.
PA6705.A6 1897   *LC* 01-21822

Tacitus, Cornelius.   • **2.775**
[Agricola Ogilvie] De vita Agricolae; edited by R. M. Ogilvie and the late Sir Ian Richmond. Oxford, Clarendon, Press, 1967. xii, 344 p., [4] leaves of plates: ill., maps, plans: 19 cm. I. Ogilvie, R. M. (Robert Maxwell), 1932- II. Richmond, Ian Archibald, Sir, 1902-1965. III. T.
PA 6706 A3 1967   *LC* 68-75099   *ISBN* 0198144385

Martin, Ronald H.   **2.776**
Tacitus / Ronald Martin. — Berkeley, CA: University of California Press, c1981. 288 p.; 23 cm. Includes indexes. 1. Tacitus, Cornelius — Criticism and interpretation. 2. Historiography I. T.
PA6716.M37   937/.0072024 19   *LC* 80-28910   *ISBN* 0520044274

Syme, Ronald, Sir, 1903-.   • **2.777**
Tacitus. — Oxford, Clarendon Press, 1958. 2 v. (xii, 856 p.) 24 cm. Bibliography: v. 2, p. [809]-823. 1. Tacitus, Cornelius. I. T.
PA6716.S9   878.6   *LC* A 58-4608

Terence.   **2.778**
Adelphoe / Terence; edited by R. H. Martin. — Cambridge; New York: Cambridge University Press, 1976. viii, 259 p.; 20 cm. (Cambridge Greek and Latin classics) Includes index. I. Martin, Ronald H. II. T.
PA6755.A5 1976   872/.01   *LC* 75-36173   *ISBN* 0521209366

Forehand, Walter.   **2.779**
Terence / by Walter E. Forehand. — Boston: Twayne Publishers, c1985. 145 p.: ill.; 23 cm. (Twayne's world authors series; TWAS 745. Latin literature) Includes index. 1. Terence — Criticism and interpretation. I. T.
PA6768.F6 1985   872/.01 19   *LC* 85-743   *ISBN* 080576593X

Tibullus.   **2.780**
[Elegiae] The Elegies of Albius Tibullus: the Corpus Tibullianum / edited with introd. and notes on Books I, II, and IV, 2–14 by Kirby Flower Smith. — New York: Ayer, 1979, [1913]. 542 p.; 21 cm. (Latin texts and commentaries) Reprint of the ed. published by American Book Co., New York, in series: Morris and Morgan's Latin series. I. Smith, Kirby Flower, 1862-1918. II. T. III. Series.
PA6787.A2 1979   874/.01   *LC* 78-67151   *ISBN* 0405116195

Cairns, Francis.   **2.781**
Tibullus, a Hellenistic poet at Rome / Francis Cairns. — Cambridge [Eng.]; New York: Cambridge University Press, 1979. xii, 250 p.; 24 cm. 1. Tibullus — Criticism and interpretation. I. T.
PA6789.C26   874/.01   *LC* 79-50231   *ISBN* 0521224136

Putnam, Michael C. J.   **2.782**
Tibullus: a commentary [by] Michael C. J. Putnam. Norman, University of Oklahoma Press, in co-operation with the American Philological Association [1973] xi, 210 p. 19 cm. (The American Philological Association series of classical texts) 'Commentary is limited to the sixteen poems which comprise the first two books of the Corpus Tibullianum'; with the Latin text of books 1-2. 1. Tibullus. I. T.
PA6789.P8   478/.6/421   *LC* 72-9255   *ISBN* 0806110619

PA6801–6961 Virgil

Virgil.   **2.783**
The Aeneid of Virgil, edited with introduction and notes by R. D. Williams. — [London]: Macmillan; [New York]: St. Martin's Press, 1972-1973. 2 v.; 18 cm. Latin text; English introd. and notes. I. Williams, R. D. (Robert Deryck), 1917- II. T.
PA6801.A5   873/.01   *LC* 70-188875   *ISBN* 0333118731

Virgil.   **2.784**
Aeneidos liber primvs. With a commentary by R. G. Austin. — Oxford [Eng.] Clarendon Press, 1971. xxi, 239 p. 19 cm. Latin text with English commentary. I. Austin, R. G. (Roland Gregory), 1901-1974. II. T.
PA6803.B21 A9   873/.01   *LC* 72-200255

Vergilius Maro, Publius.   **2.785**
Aeneidos. Liber secundus. With a commentary by R. G. Austin. — Oxford, Clarendon Press, 1966. xxviii, 311 p. plates. 20 cm. Bibliography: p. [xxv]-xxvii. I. Austin, R. G. (Roland Gregory), 1901-1974. II. T.
PA6803.B22A8   873   *LC* 64-2001

Virgil.   • **2.786**
Aeneidos: liber tertius / P. Vergili Maronis; edited with a commentary by R.D. Williams. — Oxford: Clarendon Press, 1962. vi, 220 p. I. Williams, R. D. (Robert Deryck), 1917- II. T.
PA6803.B23 W5   *LC* 62-4131

Virgil.   • **2.787**
Aeneidos, liber quartus / P. Vergili Maronis; edited with a commentary by R.G. Austin. — Oxford: Clarendon Press, 1955. xix, 212 p. I. Austin, R. G. (Roland Gregory), 1901-1974. II. T.
PA6803.B24 A8   *LC* 55-4075

Virgil.   • **2.788**
P. Vergili Maronis Aeneidos, liber quintus / edited with a commentary by R.D. Williams. — Oxford: Clarendon Press, 1960. xxx, 219 p.; 19 cm. Text in Latin, notes and introd. in English. I. Williams, R. D. (Robert Deryck), 1917- II. T. III. Title: Aeneidos, liber quintus.
PA6803.B25 W5   *LC* 60-2294

Virgil.   **2.789**
P. Vergili Maronis Aeneidos, liber sextus: with a commentary / by R. G. Austin. Oxford: Clarendon Press, 1977. x, 303 p.; 19 cm. Latin text with English commentary. I. Austin, R. G. (Roland Gregory), 1901-1974. II. T.
PA6803.B26 A9   873/.01   *LC* 77-570804   *ISBN* 0198720777

Berg, William J.   **2.790**
Early Virgil. London, Athlone Press; [Distributed by Humanities Press, New York] 1974. x, 222 p. plate. 22 cm. Includes the text of Virgil's Bucolics in English and Latin. 1. Virgil. Bucolica I. Virgil. Bucolica. 1974. II. T.
PA6804.B7 B4 1974   871/.01   *LC* 74-160364   *ISBN* 0485111454

Putnam, Michael C. J.   • **2.791**
Virgil's pastoral art; studies in the Eclogues [by] Michael C. J. Putnam. Princeton, N.J., Princeton University Press, 1970. xi, 398 p. 23 cm. 1. Virgil. Bucolica I.
PA6804.B7 P8   871/.01   *LC* 77-90956   *ISBN* 0691061785

Van Sickle, John.   **2.792**
The design of Virgil's Bucolics / John Van Sickle. — Roma: Edizioni dell'Ateneo & Bizzarri, 1978. 258 p.; 23 cm. (Filologia e critica. 24) Includes index. 1. Virgil. Bucolica I. T. II. Series.
PA6804.B7 V3   871/.01   *LC* 79-308194   L10000

Miles, Gary B.   **2.793**
Virgil's Georgics: a new interpretation / Gary B. Miles. — Berkeley: University of California Press, c1980. xiv, 297 p.; 24 cm. 1. Vergilius Maro, Publicus. Georgica. I. T.
PA6804.G4 M5   871/.01   *LC* 78-64460   *ISBN* 0520037898

Putnam, Michael C. J.   **2.794**
Virgil's poem of the earth: studies in the Georgics / Michael C. J. Putnam. — Princeton, N.J.: Princeton University Press, 1979. xiii, 336 p.; 23 cm. Includes index. 1. Virgil. Georgica I. T.
PA6804.G4 P8   871/.01   *LC* 78-70315   *ISBN* 0691063915

Wilkinson, L. P.   **2.795**
The Georgics of Virgil: a critical survey [by] L. P. Wilkinson. London, Cambridge U.P., 1969. xii, 364 p. 23 cm. 1. Virgil. Georgica I. T.
PA6804.G4 W5   871/.01   *LC* 75-79058   *ISBN* 0521074509

Virgil.   **2.796**
[Aeneis. English] The Aeneid / Virgil; translated by Robert Fitzgerald. — 1st ed. — New York: Random House, c1983. 402 p.; 24 cm. Translation of the Aeneis. I. Fitzgerald, Robert, 1910- II. T.
PA6807.A5 F53 1983   873/.01 19   *LC* 83-3101   *ISBN* 0394528271

Virgil.   • **2.797**
[Aeneis. English] The Aeneid of Virgil. Translated by C. Day Lewis. With an introd. by C. Day Lewis and an appreciation by John Pollard. Original illus. by David Whitfield. [London] Distributed by Heron Books [1969] xv, 311 p. 21 cm. (Books that have changed man's thinking) I. Day Lewis, C. (Cecil), 1904-1972. II. T.
PA6807.A5 L4   873/.01   *LC* 71-24571

Virgil.   **2.798**
The Aeneid of Virgil. A verse translation by Allen Mandelbaum. Drawings by Guy Davenport. — Berkeley, University of California Press, 1971. xii, 401 p. illus. 23 cm. I. Mandelbaum, Allen, 1926- tr. II. T.
PA6807.A5 M23 1971   873/.01   *LC* 70-99487   *ISBN* 0520016203

PA6823–6961 *Criticism*

Anderson, William Scovil, 1927-.   • **2.799**
The art of the Aeneid [by] William S. Anderson. Englewood Cliffs, N.J., Prentice-Hall [1969] v, 121 p. map. 22 cm. (Landmarks in literature) 1. Virgil. Aeneis I. T.
PA6825.A72   873/.01   *LC* 73-90971   *ISBN* 0130471593

Camps, William Anthony.   • **2.800**
An introduction to Virgil's 'Aeneid' [by] W. A. Camps. London, Oxford U.P., 1969. ix, 164 p. map. 22 cm. 1. Virgil. Aeneis I. T.
PA6825.C36   873/.01   *LC* 76-424692   *ISBN* 0198720238

Highet, Gilbert, 1906-1978.   **2.801**
The speeches in Vergil's Aeneid. Princeton, N.J., Princeton University Press [1972] vii, 380 p. 23 cm. 1. Virgil. Aeneis I. T.
PA6825.H53   873/.01   *LC* 73-39787   *ISBN* 069106234X

Otis, Brooks.   **2.802**
Virgil, a study in civilized poetry. Oxford, Clarendon Press, 1963 [i.e. 1964] ix, 436 p. 22 cm. 1. Virgil. I. T.
PA6825.O8   871   *LC* 64-4257

Pöschl, Viktor.   • **2.803**
[Dichtkunst Virgils. English] The art of Vergil; image and symbol in the Aeneid. Translated by Gerda Seligson. Ann Arbor, University of Michigan Press [1962] 216 p. 22 cm. Translation of Die Dichtkunst Virgils. 1. Virgil. Aeneis I. T.
PA6825.P613   873   *LC* 62-12160

Putnam, Michael C. J.   • **2.804**
The poetry of the Aeneid; four studies in imaginative unity and design [by] Michael C. J. Putnam. — Cambridge, Mass., Harvard University Press, 1965. xv, 238 p. 22 cm. Bibliographical references included in 'Notes' (p. 205-228) 1. Virgil. Aeneis. I. T.
PA6825.P8   873   *LC* 65-12787

Quinn, Kenneth.   • **2.805**
Virgil's Aeneid; a critical description. Ann Arbor, University of Michigan Press [1968] xii, 448 p. 23 cm. I. Virgil. Aeneis II. T.
PA6825.Q5   873/.01   *LC* 68-12248

Williams, Gordon Willis.   **2.806**
Technique and ideas in the Aeneid / Gordon Williams. — New Haven: Yale University Press, c1983. x, 301 p.; 25 cm. Includes indexes. 1. Virgil. Aeneis I. T.
PA6825.W535 1983   873/.01 19   *LC* 82-7008   *ISBN* 0300028520

Comparetti, Domenico Pietro Antonio, 1835-1927.   • **2.807**
[Virgilio nel medio evo. English] Vergil in the Middle Ages. Translated by E. F. M. Benecke, with an introd. by Robinson Ellis. Hamden, Conn., Archon Books, 1966. xvi, 376 p. 23 cm. Reprint of 2d ed., 1908. 1. Virgil. 2. Literature, Medieval — History and criticism I. T.
PA6961.C63 1966a   873.01   *LC* 66-23443

PA8001–8595 Latin (Medieval and Modern)

Wright, Frederick Adam, 1869-1946.   **2.808**
A history of later Latin literature from the middle of the fourth to the end of the seventeenth century, by F.A. Wright and T.A. Sinclair. London Dawsons of Pall Mall 1969. 417p. 1. Latin literature — History and criticism 2. Latin literature, Medieval and modern — History and criticism I. Sinclair, T. A. (Thomas Alan), 1899-1961. jt. author II. T.
PA8015 W7 1969

Haskins, Charles Homer, 1870-1937.   • **2.809**
The Renaissance of the twelfth century. New York: Meridian Books, 1957 [c1955] 437 p.; 19 cm. (Meridian books, M49) 1. Civilization, Medieval — 12th century 2. Latin literature, Medieval and modern — History and criticism. 3. Civilization, Medieval I. T.
PA8035.H3 1957   879.09   *LC* 57-10835

Hélin, Maurice.   • **2.810**
[Littérature d'Occident. English] A history of medieval Latin literature / by Maurice Hélin;translated by Jean Chapman Snow. — Rev. ed. — New York: W. Salloch, 1949. v, 130 p.; 23 cm. Spine title: Medieval Latin literature. Translation of: Littérature d'Occident: histoire des lettres latines du Moyen Age. 1. Latin literature, Medieval and modern — History and criticism. I. T.
PA 8035 H47 E5 1949   *LC* 49-11654

Raby, Frederic James Edward, 1888-.   **2.811**
A history of secular Latin poetry in the Middle Ages. — 2d ed. — Oxford, Clarendon Press, 1957. 2 v. 24 cm. 'In some measure complementary to ... [the author's] History of Christian-Latin poetry.' Bibliography: v. 2, p. 361-399. 1. Latin poetry, Medieval and modern — History and criticism. I. T. II. Title: Secular Latin poetry in the Middle Ages.
PA8051.R3 1957   879.109   *LC* 57-59358

Raby, Frederic James Edward, 1888-.   **2.812**
A history of Christian-Latin poetry from the beginnings to the close of the Middle Ages. 2d ed. Oxford Clarendon Press 1953. 494p. 1. Religious poetry — History and criticism 2. Latin poetry, Medieval and modern — History and criticism I. T. II. Title: Christian-Latin poetry
PA8056 R3 1953

The Oxford book of medieval Latin verse. Newly selected and   • **2.813**
edited by F. J. E. Raby.
Oxford, Clarendon Press, 1959. 512 p. 18 cm. 1. Latin poetry, Medieval and modern I. Raby, Frederic James Edward, 1888- ed.
PA8122.O9 1959   *LC* 59-1256

Waddell, Helen, 1889-1965.   • **2.814**
Mediaeval Latin lyrics. — 5th ed. London: Constable; New York: Barnes & Noble, [1966]. 342 p. Latin and English. 1. Latin poetry, Medieval and modern — Translations into English. 2. English poetry — Translations from Latin. I. T.
PA8122.W3 1948   874.0308   *LC* 67-2460

Renaissance Latin verse: an anthology / compiled and edited by   **2.815**
Alessandro Perosa and John Sparrow.
Chapel Hill: University of North Carolina Press, 1979. xxix, 560 p.; 24 cm. Text in Latin; introductory material in English. 1. Latin poetry, Medieval and modern I. Perosa, Alessandro, 1910- II. Sparrow, John Hanbury Angus, 1906-
PA8123.R4 1979   871/.04/08   *LC* 78-10969   *ISBN* 0807813508

An Anthology of neo–Latin poetry / edited and translated by   **2.816**
Fred J. Nichols.
New Haven: Yale University Press, 1979. xi, 734 p.; 24 cm. Texts of poems in English and Latin. 1. Latin poetry, Medieval and modern 2. Latin poetry, Medieval and modern — Translations into English. 3. English literature — Translations from Latin. I. Nichols, Fred J., 1939-
PA8164.A5   871/.04/08   *LC* 78-9944   *ISBN* 0300020171

The Goliard poets: medieval Latin songs and satires / with verse   **2.817**
translation by George F. Whicher.
Westport, Conn.: Greenwood Press, 1979, c1949. 303 p.: ill.; 23 cm. English and Latin. Reprint of the ed. published by New Directions, Norfolk, Conn. Includes index. 1. Students' songs — Texts. 2. Goliards — Songs and music. I. Whicher, George Frisbie, 1889-1954.
PA8164.G6 1979   871/.03   *LC* 78-23583   *ISBN* 0313211922

Bernard Silvestris, fl. 1136.   **2.818**
[Cosmographia. English] The Cosmographia of Bernardus Silvestris. A translation with introd. and notes by Winthrop Wetherbee. New York, Columbia University Press, 1973. viii, 180 p. 24 cm. I. Wetherbee, Winthrop, 1938- ed. II. T.
PA8275.B25 C613   128   *LC* 73-479   *ISBN* 0231036766

Colonne, Guido delle, 13th century.   **2.819**
[Historia Trojana. English] Historia destructionis Troiae / Translated with an introd. and notes, by Mary Elizabeth Meek. — Bloomington: Indiana University Press, 1974. xxxiv, 324 p.; 24 cm. (Indiana University humanities series, no. 71) 1. Troy (Ancient city) — Romances. I. T.
PA8310.C6 H5 1974   873/.03   *LC* 72-85603   *ISBN* 0253327407

Hrotsvitha, ca. 935-ca. 975.   **2.820**
[Plays. English.] The plays of Hrotsvitha of Gandersheim / translated by Larissa Bonfante, with the collaboration of Alexandra Bonfante–Warren. — New York: New York University Press, 1979. 182 p.: ill.; 24 cm. — (Monograph publishing: Imprint series) I. Bonfante, Larissa. II. T.
PA8340.A225   872/.03   *LC* 79-90053   *ISBN* 081471028X

Guy, Bp. of Amiens, d. 1075?   **2.821**
The Carmen de Hastingae proelio: text in English and Latin / ed. by Catherine Morton and Hope Muntz. — Oxford: Clarendon Press, 1972. lxxv, 149, iv, p. [2] leaves.: illus., facsim., geneal. tables, maps.; 23 cm. — (Oxford medieval texts) Latin poem with English translation and text. 1. Hastings, Battle of, 1066 — Poetry. I. Morton, Catherine, ed. II. Muntz, Hope. ed. III. T.
PA8445.W48 C3 1972   873/.03   *LC* 72-194967   *ISBN* 0198222166

Contemporaries of Erasmus: a biographical register of the   **2.822**
Renaissance and Reformation / Peter G. Bietenholz, editor;
Thomas B. Deutscher, associate editor.
Toronto; Buffalo: University of Toronto Press, c1985- <c1986 >. v. <1-2 >: ill., ports.; 26 cm. Intended to accompany: Collected Works of Erasmus. 1974. 1. Erasmus, Desiderius, d. 1536 — Contemporaries. 2. Erasmus, Desiderius, d. 1536 — Dictionaries, indexes, etc, 3. Renaissance — Biography — Dictionaries. 4. Reformation — Biography — Dictionaries. I. Bietenholz, Peter G. II. Deutscher, Thomas Brian, 1949- III. Erasmus, Desiderius, d. 1536. Works. English. 1974
PA8500 1974 Suppl   920/.04 19   *LC* 85-672492   *ISBN* 0802025072

Erasmus, Desiderius, d. 1536.   **2.823**
Literary and educational writings / edited by Craig R. Thompson. — Toronto; Buffalo: University of Toronto Press, c1978. 2 v. (lxix, 774 p.): ill., port.; 26 cm. — (Collected works of Erasmus; v. 23-24) Includes indexes. I. Thompson, Craig R. (Craig Ringwalt), 1911- II. T.
PA8502.E5 T5 1978   089/.71   *LC* 78-6904   *ISBN* 0802053955

Kaiser, Walter Jacob.   **2.824**
Praisers of folly: Erasmus, Rabelais, Shakespeare. — Cambridge: Harvard University Press, 1963. viii, 318 p.; 25 cm. (Harvard studies in comparative literature. 25) Bibliographical footnotes. Bibliography: p. [299]-311. 1. Erasmus, Desiderius, d. 1536. Moriae encomium 2. Rabelais, François, ca.

1490-1553? Pantagruel 3. Shakespeare, William, 1564-1616. King Henry IV. 4. Fools and jesters in literature I. T. II. Series.
PA8515.K3   809.93   *LC* 63-17202

Essays on the works of Erasmus / edited by Richard L. DeMolen.   **2.825**
New Haven: Yale University Press, 1978. vii, 282 p.; 25 cm. 'Publications of Craig R. Thompson on sixteenth-century subjects': p. 267-269. 1. Erasmus, Desiderius, d. 1536 — Criticism and interpretation — Addresses, essays, lectures. 2. Thompson, Craig R. (Craig Ringwalt), 1911- 3. Theology — Addresses, essays, lectures. I. DeMolen, Richard L.
PA8518.A1 E8   199/.492   *LC* 78-3481   *ISBN* 0300021771

PB1–431 GENERAL WORKS

Teaching modern languages / edited by G. Richardson.   **2.826**
London: Croom Helm; New York: Nichols Pub. Co., 1983. 240 p.: ill.; 22 cm.
English and French. 1. Languages, Modern — Study and teaching
I. Richardson, Geoffrey.
PB35.T43 1983   418/.007 19   *LC* 83-4205   *ISBN* 0893971588

PB1001–3029 CELTIC LITERATURES

Jackson, Kenneth Hurlstone, 1909- ed. and tr.   **2.827**
A Celtic miscellany; translations from the Celtic literatures [selected and translated by] Kenneth Hurlstone Jackson. Rev. ed. Harmondsworth, Penguin, 1971. 343 p. 19 cm. (The Penguin classics, 247) 1. Celtic literature — Translations into English. 2. English literature — Translations from Celtic. I. T.
PB1100.J3 1971   891.6   *LC* 72-176066   *ISBN* 0140442472

Nagy, Joseph Falaky.   **2.828**
The wisdom of the outlaw: the boyhood deeds of Finn in Gaelic narrative tradition / Joseph Falaky Nagy. — Berkeley: University of California Press, c1985. ix, 338 p.; 24 cm. Based on the author's thesis (Ph.D.—Harvard, 1978) under title: The boyhood deeds of Finn in the Fenian tradition. Includes index. 1. Finn MacCumhaill, 3rd cent — Legends — History and criticism. 2. Tales — Ireland — History and criticism. I. T.
PB1397.F5 N33 1985   398.2/2/09415 19   *LC* 84-8826   *ISBN* 0520052846

Chapman, Malcolm (Malcolm Kenneth)   **2.829**
The Gaelic vision in Scottish culture / Malcolm Chapman. — London: Croom Helm, c1978. 264 p.; 23 cm. Based on the author's B.Litt. thesis, Oxford. Includes index. 1. Gaelic poetry — History and criticism. 2. Folklore — Scotland. 3. Scotland — Civilization I. T.
PB1607.C4   941.11   *LC* 79-303360   *ISBN* 0856647527

Thomson, Derick S.   **2.830**
An introduction to Gaelic poetry [by] Derick Thomson. — [New York]: St. Martin's Press, [1974] 335 p.; 23 cm. 1. Gaelic poetry — History and criticism. I. T.
PB1607.T5   891.6/3/1009   *LC* 73-86601

PB2202–2369 Welsh

The Oxford companion to the literature of Wales / compiled   **2.831**
and edited by Meic Stephens.
Oxford [Oxfordshire]; New York: Oxford University Press; 1986. xvi, 682 p.; 25 cm. 'This book was commissioned by Yr Academi Gymreig (The Welsh Academy)'—T.p. verso. 1. Welsh literature — Dictionaries and encyclopedias. I. Stephens, Meic. II. Welsh Academy.
PB2202.O94 1986   891.6/6/03 19   *LC* 85-7095   *ISBN* 0192115863

A guide to Welsh literature / edited by A. O. H. Jarman and   **2.832**
Gwilym Rees Hughes.
Swansea: C. Davies, 1976-. 2 v.: ill., facsims., map; 23 cm. 1. Welsh literature — History and criticism. I. Jarman, A. O. H. (Alfred Owen Hughes) II. Hughes, Gwilym Rees.
PB2206.G8   891/.6/6/09   *LC* 76-370995   *ISBN* 0715401246

Parry, Thomas, 1904-.   • **2.833**
A history of Welsh literature / translated from the Welsh by H. Idris Bell. — Oxford: Clarendon Press, 1955. xii, 534 p.; 23 cm. 1. Welsh literature — History and criticism I. T.
PB2206 P33

Williams, Gwyn.   **2.834**
An introduction to Welsh literature / Gwyn Williams. — [Cardiff]: University of Wales Press on behalf of the Welsh Arts Council, 1978. 123 p.; 25 cm. — (Writers of Wales 0141-5050) 1. Welsh literature — History and criticism. I. T.
PB2206.W64   891.6/6/09   *LC* 79-303826   *ISBN* 0708306977

Williams, Ifor, Sir 1881-.   **2.835**
Lectures on early Welsh poetry / by Sir Ifor Williams. — Dublin: Dublin Institute for Advanced Studies, 1944, t.p. 1970. 76p. 1. Welsh poetry — Addresses, essays, lectures I. Dublin Institute for Advanced Studies. II. T.
PB2231.W5

Dafydd ap Gwilym, 14th cent.   **2.836**
[Poems. English] Dafydd ap Gwilym: the poems / translation and commentary by Richard Morgan Loomis; illustrations by Mary Guerriere Loomis. — Binghamton, N.Y.: Center for Medieval & Early Renaissance Studies, 1982. 346 p.: ill., maps; 23 cm. — (Medieval & Renaissance texts & studies. v. 9) I. Loomis, Richard Morgan, 1926- II. T. III. Series.
PB2273.D3 A27 1982   891.6/611 19   *LC* 81-16968   *ISBN* 0866980156

Bromwich, Rachel.   **2.837**
Dafydd ap Gwilym / Rachel Bromwich. — [Cardiff]: University of Wales Press [for] the Welsh Arts Council, 1974. [3], 94 p., plate: 1 ill.; 25 cm. (Writers of Wales) 1. Dafydd ap Gwilym, 14th cent. I. T.
PB2273.D3 B69   891.6/6/11   *LC* 75-310684   *ISBN* 0708305725

Morgan, Prys.   **2.838**
Iolo Morganwg / [by] Prys Morgan. — [Cardiff]: University of Wales Press [for] the Welsh Arts Council, 1975. [3], 98 p., plate: port.; 25 cm. — (Writers of Wales) 1. Iolo, Morganwg, 1746-1826. I. T.
PB2273.I5 M6x   891.6/6/12   *LC* 76-367703   *ISBN* 0708306098

Hughes, Glyn Tegai.   **2.839**
Williams Pantycelyn / Glyn Tegai Hughes. — [Cardiff]: University of Wales Press on behalf of the Welsh Arts Council, 1983. 139 p., [1] leaf of plates: ill.; 25 cm. (Writers of Wales. 0141-5050) 1. Williams, William, 1717-1791 — Criticism and interpretation. I. T. II. Series.
PB2297.W5 Z68 1983   891.6/612 19   *LC* 83-133874   *ISBN* 0708308406

Thomas, Gwyn, 1913-.   **2.840**
Ellis Wynne / Gwyn Thomas. — [Cardiff]: University of Wales Press on behalf of Welsh Arts Council, 1984. 69 p.: ill.; 25 cm. (Writers of Wales. 0141-5050) 1. Wynne, Ellis, 1671-1734. 2. Authors, Welsh — 18th century — Biography. I. T. II. Series.
PB2297.W8 Z89 1984   891.6/68208 19   *LC* 84-195629   *ISBN* 0708308635

Lloyd, David Myrddin.   **2.841**
Emrys ap Iwan / D. Myrddin Lloyd. — [Cardiff]: University of Wales Press on behalf of the Welsh Arts Council, 1979. 61 p., [1] leaf of plates: port.; 23 cm. — (Writers of Wales 0141-5050) 1. Ap Iwan, Emrys, 1851-1906. 2. Authors, Welsh — 19th century — Biography. 3. Critics — Wales — Biography. I. T.
PB2298.A57 Z77   891.6/68209 B 19   *LC* 80-497620   *ISBN* 0708307396

Lewis, Saunders, 1893-.   **2.842**
Presenting Saunders Lewis; edited by Alun R. Jones and Gwyn Thomas. Cardiff, University of Wales Press, 1973. iii, xix, 361 p., 2 leaves. 2 ports. 24 cm. Includes biographical and critical essays about S. Lewis. I. Jones, Alun R. (Alun Richard) ed. II. Thomas, Gwyn, 1913- ed. III. T.
PB2298.L49 P7   891.6/6/8209   *LC* 73-164337   *ISBN* 0708304524

Griffiths, Bruce, 1938-.   **2.843**
Saunders Lewis / Bruce Griffiths. — [Cardiff]: University of Wales Press on behalf of the Welsh Arts Council, 1979. 139 p., [1] leaf of plates: port.; 25 cm. — (Writers of Wales 0141-5050) 1. Lewis, Saunders, 1893- 2. Authors, Welsh — 20th century — Biography. I. T.
PB2298.L49 Z68   891.6/6/8209   *LC* 79-306789   *ISBN* 0708307000

Morgan, Derec Llwyd.   **2.844**
Kate Roberts / Derec Llwyd Morgan. — [Cardiff]: University of Wales Press on behalf of the Welsh Arts Council, 1974. 97 p., [1] leaf of plates: port.; 25 cm. (Writers of Wales) 1. Roberts, Kate, 1891- I. T.
PB2298.R63 Z77   891.6/6/32   LC 75-325440

Jenkins, Dafydd.   **2.845**
D. J. Williams. — [Cardiff]: University of Wales Press [for] the Welsh Arts Council, 1973. 3, 96 p., leaf.: ports.; 25 cm. — (Writers of Wales) Limited edition of 1000 numbered copies. This is no. 270. 1. Williams, David John, 1885-1970 — Criticism and interpretation. I. T.
PB2298.W44 Z7   891.6/6/32   LC 74-167111   ISBN 0708304613

Nicholas, James.   **2.846**
Waldo Williams / James Nicholas. — [Cardiff]: University of Wales Press [for] the Welsh Arts Council, 1975. [3], 92 p., plate: port.; 25 cm. (Writers of Wales) 1. Williams, Waldo, 1904-1971. I. T.
PB2298.W54 Z8   891.6/6/12   LC 75-322592   ISBN 0708305857

Mabinogion.   • **2.847**
The Mabinogion, translated by Gwyn Jones and Thomas Jones. — London: J. M. Dent; New York: E. P. Dutton, [1949] xxxiii, [1], 282 p.; 18 cm. — (Everyman's library, no. 97) 'Based upon the White book of Rhydderch ... Its omissions ... have been supplied from the Red book of Hergest.' I. Jones, Gwyn, 1907- tr. II. Jones, Thomas, 1870- tr. III. T.
PB2363.M2J6x   LC a 51-8904

Welsh verse / [translations by] Tony Conran.   **2.848**
[2nd rev. ed.]. — [S.l.]: Penguin, 1987. [300] p.; 21 cm. 1. Welsh poetry — Translations into English. 2. English poetry — Translations from Welsh. I. Conran, Anthony, 1931- II. Title: The Penguin book of Welsh verse.
PB2369.W45 1987   891.6/61/008 19   LC 86-63544

Williams, Gwyn. comp.   **2.849**
Welsh poems, sixth century to 1600. Translated with an introd. and notes by Gwyn Williams. — Berkeley: University of California Press, 1974 [c1973] 128 p.; 21 cm. 1. Welsh poetry — Translations into English. 2. English poetry — Translations from Welsh. I. T.
PB2369.W54 1974   891.6/6/1108   LC 73-86661   ISBN 0520026039

PC ROMANCE LANGUAGES

PC601–872 Romanian Language

Levițchi, Leon.   **2.850**
Dicționar român–englez. editia a 3–a Revăzută și adăugită de autor și de Andrei Bantaș. — București Editura Științifică 1973. 600p. 1. Romanian language — Dictionaries — English I. T.
PC779 L4 1965   LC 74-323988

PC1001–1977 Italian Language

Devoto, Giacomo.   **2.851**
[Linguaggio d'Italia. English] The languages of Italy / Giacomo Devoto; translated by V. Louise Katainen. — Chicago: University of Chicago Press, 1978. xvi, 357 p.: maps; 24 cm. — (The History and structure of languages) Translation of Il linguaggio d'Italia. 1. Italian language — History. 2. Latin language — History. 3. Italic languages and dialects I. T.
PC1075.D3913   450   LC 78-3391   ISBN 0226143686

Migliorini, Bruno.   **2.852**
[Storia della lingua italiana. English] The Italian language / by Bruno Migliorini; abridged, recast and revised by T. Gwynfor Griffiths. — London: Faber, 1984. 553 p.; 23 cm. (The Great languages) Translation of: Storia della lingua italiana. 1. Italian language — History. I. Griffith, T. Gwynfor (Thomas Gwynfor), 1926- II. T. III. Title: Storia della lingua italiana. English IV. Series.
PC1075.M513x 1984   450/.9 19   LC 87-673380

Momigliano Lepschy, Anna Laura.   **2.853**
The Italian language today / [by] Anna Laura Lepschy, Giulio Lepschy. — London: [s.n.], 1978. 248 p.; 23 cm. English or Italian. Includes index.
1. Italian language — 20th century. 2. Italian language — Grammar — 1950- 3. Italy — Languages I. Lepschy, Giulio C. joint author. II. T.
PC1087.M6   458/.2/421   LC 78-320142   ISBN 0091280206

Hall, Robert Anderson, 1911-.   • **2.854**
Descriptive Italian grammar. Ithaca, Cornell University Press, 1948. xi, 228 p. (Cornell Romance Studies, 2) 1. Italian language — Grammar I. T.
PC1105.H3

The Cambridge Italian dictionary / general editor, Barbara Reynolds.   **2.855**
Cambridge: Cambridge University Press, 1981. 2 v. 1. Italian language — Dictionaries — English 2. English language — Dictionaries — Italian I. Reynolds, Barbara, 1914-
PC1640 C3 1981   LC 80-41234

Cassell's Italian–English, English–Italian dictionary; prepared by Piero Rebora with the assistance of Francis M. Guercio and Arthur L. Hayward.   • **2.856**
7th ed. — London: Cassell, 1967. xxi, 1096 p.; 22 cm. 1. Italian language — Dictionaries — English. 2. English language — Dictionaries — Italian. I. Rébora, Piero, 1889- II. Guercio, Francis Michael. III. Hayward, Arthur Lawrence, 1885-1967.
PC1640.C33 1967   453/.2   LC 70-392670

Dizionario inglese italiano, italiano inglese: adattamento e ristrutturazione dell'originale 'Advanced learner's dictionary of current English' della Oxford University Press.   **2.857**
4a ed. — Torino: Società editrice internazionale, 1981. lxv, 1894 p.; 25 cm. 1. Italian language — Dictionaries — English. 2. English language — Dictionaries — Italian. I. Advanced learner's dictionary of current English.
PC1640.D54 1981   453/.21 19   LC 82-188974   ISBN 8805049298

I dizionari Sansoni: inglese–italiano, italiano–inglese = The Sansoni dictionaries: English–Italian, Italian–English / realizzato dal Centro Lessicografico Sansoni sotto la direzione di Vladimiro Macchi.   **2.858**
Firenze: Sansoni Editore, 1981. 2 v. in 1. 1. Italian language — Dictionaries — English. 2. English language — Dictionaries — Italian. I. Macchi, Vladimiro. II. Title: The Sansoni dictionaries: English-Italian, Italian-English.
PC1640. D55

Hazon, Mario, 1885-.   • **2.859**
[Dizionario inglese-italiano, italiano-inglese. English] Garzanti comprehensive Italian–English, English–Italian dictionary. New York, McGraw-Hill [1963, c1961] ix, 2099 p. 25 cm. Published in 1961 under title: Dizionario inglese-italiano, italiano-inglese. 1. Italian language — Dictionaries — English. 2. English language — Dictionaries — Italian. I. T. II. Title: Comprehensive Italian-English, English-Italian dictionary.
PC1640.H35 1963   453.2   LC 62-20508

PC2001–3761 French Language

Ewert, Alfred, 1891-.   • **2.860**
The French language. [2d ed.] London, Faber & Faber [1961] xii, 440 p. 23 cm. (The Great languages) Imprint covered by label: New York, Barnes & Noble. 1. French language — Grammar, Historical. 2. French language — History. I. T.
PC2073.E8 1961   LC 63-24009

Wagner, Robert Léon.   • **2.861**
Introduction à la linguistique française / R.-L. Wagner. — 3e. tirage. — Genève: Droz, 1965. 88, 71 p. — (Société de publications romanes et françaises. [Publication] 27) 'Supplément bibliographique, 1947-1953' (71 p. at end) was published in 1955 as no. 47 in the series Publications romanes et françaises. 1. French language 2. French language — Bibliography. I. T. II. Series.
PC2073.W3

Cohen, Marcel Samuel Raphaël, 1884-.   • **2.862**
Histoire d'une langue: le français, des lointaines origines à nos jours. Paris Éditions Hier et aujourd'hui 1947. 384p. (Collection Civilisation française) 1. French language — History I. T.
PC2075 C58

Pope, Mildred Katharine, 1872-.   • **2.863**
From Latin to modern French, with especial consideration of Anglo-Norman; phonology and morphology. [2d, rev. ed. Manchester] Manchester University Press [1966,c1952] xxxii, 571 p. illus. 22 cm. (Publications of the University of Manchester, no. 229. French series, no. 6) 1. French language — History. 2. Anglo-Norman dialect I. T.
PC2075.P6 1966   440.9   LC 52-4373

Rohlfs, Gerhard, 1892-.   ● **2.864**
From Vulgar Latin to Old French; an introduction to the study of the Old French language. Translated from the German by Vincent Almazan & Lillian McCarthy. — Detroit: Wayne State University Press, 1970. 289 p.; 24 cm. Translation of Vom Vulgärlatein zum Altfranzösischen. 1. French language — Old French — History. 2. Romance languages — History. I. T.
PC2077.R613   447/.01   *LC* 76-98131   *ISBN* 0814314090

PC2101–2559 GRAMMAR. STYLE. PROSODY

Judge, Anne.   **2.865**
A reference grammar of modern French / Anne Judge, F.G. Healey. — London; Baltimore, Md.: E. Arnold, 1983. xxxviii, 486 p.: ill.; 24 cm. Includes index. 1. French language — Grammar — 1950- 2. French language — Textbooks for foreign speakers — English I. Healey, F. G. II. T.
PC2105.J83 1983   448.2/421 19   *LC* 85-122001   *ISBN* 0713162856

Grevisse, Maurice.   **2.866**
Le bon usage: grammaire française, avec des remarques sur la langue française d'aujourd'hui / Maurice Grevisse. — 11e éd. rev. — Paris: Duculot, 1980. xiii, 1519 p.; 24 cm. Includes index. 1. French language — Grammar — 1950- 2. French language — Usage. I. T.
PC2112.G84 1980   448.2 19   *LC* 84-123036   *ISBN* 2801102423

Harper's grammar of French / Samuel N. Rosenberg ... [et al.].   **2.867**
New York: Harper & Row, c1983. x, 373 p.; 24 cm. Includes index. 1. French language — Grammar — 1950- I. Rosenberg, Samuel N.
PC2112.H32 1983   448.2/421 19   *LC* 82-21281   *ISBN* 0060455810

Mansion, J. E. (Jean Edmond), 1870-1942.   ● **2.868**
French reference grammar for schools and colleges. Westport, Conn., Greenwood Press [1971] 247 p. 23 cm. 'Originally published in 1928?' 1. French language — Grammar — 1950- I. T.
PC2112.M313 1971   448/.2/421   *LC* 72-98855   *ISBN* 0837131251

Martinet, André.   ● **2.869**
La prononciation du français contemporain / André Martinet. — Paris: Droz, 1945. 249 p.: ill., maps. — (Société de publications romanes et françaises. [Publications]; 23) 1. French language — Pronunciation. I. T. II. Series.
PC2137.M448   *LC* 47-2358

Sayce, Richard Anthony.   **2.870**
Style in French prose: a method of analysis / by R.A. Sayce. — London: Oxford University Press, 1970. 166 p.: ill., facsims. 1. French prose literature — Style. 2. French language — Style. I. T.
PC2410.S3 1965

Vinay, Jean Paul.   ● **2.871**
Stylistique comparée du français et de l'anglais; méthode de traduction [par] J.-P. Vinay [et] J. Darbelnet. Paris Didier [1958] 331p. (Bibliothèque de stylistique comparée, 1) 1. French language — Translating 2. English language — Translating I. Darbelnet, Jean, 1904- jt. author II. T. III. Series.
PC2498 V5

Holyoake, Sydney John.   **2.872**
An introduction to French sixteenth century poetic theory: texts and commentary [by] S. John Holyoake. — Manchester: Manchester University Press; New York: Barnes & Noble, 1973. xiii, 226 p.; 20 cm. 1. French language — Versification. 2. French poetry — 16th century — History and criticism. I. T.
PC2501.H6   841/.3/09   *LC* 73-161710

Lewis, Roy, 1922-.   **2.873**
On reading French verse: a study of poetic form / Roy Lewis. — [S.l.]: Oxford, 1982. xvi, 255 p.; 22 cm. Includes indexes. 1. French language — Versification. 2. French poetry — History and criticism. I. T.
PC2511.L4 1982   841/.009 19   *LC* 82-217012   *ISBN* 0198157835

PC2571–2693 DICTIONARIES

Hope, T. E.   **2.874**
Lexical borrowing in the Romance languages; a critical study of Italianisms in French and Gallicisms in Italian from 1100 to 1900 [by] T. E. Hope. — New York: New York University Press, 1971. 2 v. (xiv, 782 p.): illus.; 24 cm. 1. French language — Foreign elements — Italian. 2. Italian language — Foreign elements — French. I. T.
PC2582.I8 H6 1971b   442/.4/51   *LC* 79-151224   *ISBN* 0814733603

Littré, Emile, 1801-1881.   **2.875**
Dictionnaire de la langue française / Emile Littré. – . Éd. intégrale. — [Paris: Pauvert, 1956-58]. 7 v. Vol.s 5-7 have imprint: [Paris] Gallimard. 1. French language — Dictionaries I. T.
PC2625.L6 1956

Robert, Paul, 1910-.   **2.876**
Dictionnaire alphabétique et analogique de la langue française / par Paul Robert; rédaction dirigée par A. Rey et J. Rey–Debove. — Nouvelle éd. — Paris: Société du Nouveau Littré, 1977. xxxi, 2171 p.; 25 cm. On cover: Petit Robert 1. 1. French language — Dictionaries I. Rey, Alain. II. Rey-Debove, Josette. III. T. IV. Title: Petit Robert un.
PC2625.R553 1977   443   *LC* 77-569782   *ISBN* 2850360309

Le Robert méthodique: dictionnaire méthodique du français actuel / rédaction dirigée par Josette Rey–Debove.   **2.877**
Paris: Le Robert, c1982. xxiii, 1617 p.; 25 cm. 1. French language — Dictionaries I. Robert, Paul, 1910- II. Rey-Debove, Josette. III. Robert (Firm) IV. Title: Dictionnaire méthodique du français actuel.
PC2625.R555 1982   443 19   *LC* 82-243037   *ISBN* 2850360899

Cotgrave, Randle, d. 1634?   ● **2.878**
A dictionarie of the French and English tongues. Reproduced from the 1st ed., London, 1611. With introd. by William S. Woods. Columbia, University of South Carolina Press, 1950. [7] p., reprint: [966], 10 p.; 29 cm. 1. French language — Dictionaries — English. I. T.
PC 2640 A2 C8   *LC* 51-4027

The New Cassell's French dictionary; French–English, English–French. Completely rev. by Denis Girard. With the assistance of Gaston Dulong, Oliver Van Oss, and Charles Guinness.   ● **2.879**
New York: Funk & Wagnalls, [c1967] xvi, 762, 655 p.; 24 cm. First ed. published in 1920 under title: Cassell's French-English, English-French dictionary. 1. French language — Dictionaries — English. 2. English language — Dictionaries — French. I. Girard, Denis. ed. II. Title: Cassell's French dictionary. III. Title: Cassell's French-English, English-French dictionary.
PC2640.C3 1967   443/.2   *LC* 73-3999

The Concise Oxford French dictionary: French–English / compiled by A. Chevalley and M. Chevalley; English–French, compiled by G. W. F. R. Goodridge.   ● **2.880**
Oxford: the Clarendon Press, 1940. xx, 895, v, 295 p.: ill., map, plan; 19 cm. Each part also published separately: pt.2 published under title: A practical English-French dictionary for English-speaking countries. 1. French language — Dictionaries — English. 2. English language — Dictionaries — French. I. Chevalley, Marguerite, 1880- II. Goodridge, Gerald William Frank Radcliffe. III. Chevalley, Abel, 1868-1934.
PC2640.C54 1940   443.2   *LC* 42-24458

Harrap's new standard French and English dictionary [edited] by J. E. Mansion. Pt. 1: French–English.   **2.881**
[Completely rev. and enl. ed.] Rev. and edited by R. P. L. Ledésert and Margaret Ledésert. New York, Scribner [1973] 2 v. 29 cm. A revision of pt. 1 of Harrap's standard French and English dictionary, pt. 2 of which completes the present ed. 1. French language — Dictionaries — English. I. Mansion, J. E. (Jean Edmond), 1870-1942. ed. II. Ledésert, R. P. L. (René Pierre Louis) ed. III. Ledésert, Margaret. ed. IV. Harrap's standard French and English dictionary.
PC2640.H32 1972b   443/.21   *LC* 72-2297   *ISBN* 0684130068

Dubois, Jean, grammarian.   **2.882**
Dictionnaire du français classique, par Jean Dubois, René Lagane [et] Alain Lerond. Paris Larousse [1971] 564p. 1. French language — Early modern (to 1700) — Dictionaries I. Lagane, René. jt. author II. Lerond, Alain, jt. author III. T.
PC2650 D83   *LC* 71-884265

PC2700–3761 DIALECTS. PROVENÇAL. SLANG

Briffault, Robert, 1876-1948.   ● **2.883**
[Troubadours et le sentiment romanesque. English] The troubadours. Translated from the French by the author. Edited by Lawrence F. Koons. Bloomington, Indiana University Press, 1965. xvi, 296 p. illus., maps, ports. 21 cm. Includes troubadour songs (unacc.) Translation of Les troubadours et le sentiment romanesque. 1. Troubadours 2. Romances — History and criticism. I. T.
PC3304.B683 1965   809.1   *LC* 65-12281

Bogin, Meg.   **2.884**
The women troubadours / Meg Bogin. — New York: Paddington Press, c1976. 190 p.: ill.; 22 cm. Includes index. 1. Provençal poetry — Women authors 2. Provençal poetry — Women authors — Translations into English.

3. English poetry — Translations from Provençal. 4. Troubadours 5. Women poets — France — Provence — Biography. 6. Poets, Provençal — Biography. I. T.
PC3308.B64   849/.1/04   LC 75-22960   ISBN 0846701138

Wilhelm, James J.   **2.885**
Seven troubadours: the creators of modern verse, by James J. Wilhelm. — University Park, Pennsylvania State University Press [1970] 235 p. illus., map. 24 cm. 1. Provençal poetry — History and criticism. 2. Troubadours I. T.
PC3315.W5   841/.1/09   LC 79-84668   ISBN 0271000996

PC4001–4977 Spanish Language

Entwistle, William J. (William James), 1895-1952.   • **2.886**
The Spanish language, together with Portuguese, Catalan and Basque. — London, Faber & Faber [1962] 367 p. 1. Spanish language — Hist. 2. Portuguese language — Hist. 3. Catalan language 4. Basque language 5. Spain — Languages I. T.
PC4075.E5 1965   460   LC 63-6431

Lapesa, Rafael.   **2.887**
Historia de la lengua española / Rafael Lapesa; prólogo de Ramón Menéndez Pidal. — 9a ed. corr. y aum. — Madrid: Gredos, 1981. 690 p., [4] folded leaves of plates: 4 maps (some col.); 20 cm. — (Biblioteca románica hispánica. Manuales. 45) 1. Spanish language — History. I. T. II. Series.
PC4075.L3 1981   460/.9 19   LC 81-154525   ISBN 8424900723

Spaulding, Robert Kilburn, 1898-.   • **2.888**
How Spanish grew, by Robert K. Spaulding. Berkeley and Los Angeles, University of California press, 1943. xii p., 3 l., 259 p. illus. (map) 22.5 cm. Includes bibliographies. 1. Spanish language — History. I. T.
PC4075.S6   860.9   LC 43-52698

Menéndez Pidal, Ramón, 1869-1968.   **2.889**
[Manual elemental de gramática histórica española] Manual de gramática histórica española / [por] R. Menéndez Pidal. — 15. ed. — Madrid: Espasa-Calpe, 1977. vii, 367 p., [2] leaves of plates: map; 23 cm. 1. Spanish language — Grammar, Historical. I. T.
PC4101.M4 1977   465   LC 78-370944   ISBN 8423947556

Bello, Andrés, 1781-1865.   • **2.890**
Gramática de la lengua castellana [por] Andrés Bello [y] Rufino J. Cuervo. Nueva ed. hecha sobre la última del autor con extensas notas y copiosos índices alfabéticos. Buenos Aires, Ediciones Anaconda [c1941] 366, 160 p. 'Notas á la Gramática de la lengua castellana,' with special t.p.: 160 p. at end. 1. Spanish language — Grammar. I. Cuervo, Rufino José, 1844-1911. ed. II. T.
PC4105.B5 1941   465 BEL   LC 42-5624

Navarro Tomás, Tomás, 1884-.   **2.891**
Manual de pronunciación española / T. Navarro Tomás. — 20 ed. — Madrid: Consejo Superior de Investigaciones Científicas, Instituto 'Miguel de Cervantes' 1980. 326 p.: ill.; 21 cm. — (Publicaciones de la Revista de filología española; no. 3) 1. Spanish language — Pronunciation. I. T.
PC4137.N4 1968

Gili Gaya, Samuel.   **2.892**
Curso superior de sintaxis española / Samuel Gili Gaya. — 13. edición. — Barcelona: Bibliograf, 1981, c1961. 347 p. 1. Spanish language — Syntax I. T.
PC4361.G5 1973   LC 74-310020   ISBN 8471533073

PC4571–4822 Dictionaries

Corominas, Joan.   • **2.893**
Diccionario critico etimológico de la lengua castellana. Madrid Gredos [1954] 4 v.; 25 cm. (Biblioteca románica hispánica. Diccionarios.) 1. Spanish language — Etymology — Dictionaries I. T. II. Series.
PC4580 C6

García de Diego, Vicente, 1878-.   **2.894**
Diccionario etimológico español e hispánico / por Vicente García de Diego; una introducción de Rafael Lapesa. — 2a ed. considerablemente aum. — Madrid: Editorial Espasa-Calpe, 1985. xvi, 1091 p. 'Con materiales inéditos del autor ... a cargo de Carmen García de Diego.' 1. Spanish language — Dictionaries 2. Spanish language — Etymology I. García de Diego, Carmen. II. T.
PC4580 G33 1954

Diccionario de sinónimos: ideas afines y contrarios / [han   **2.895**
colaborado en la elaboración de esta obra Santiago Pey y Juan
Ruiz Calonja].
Barcelona: Editorial Teide, 1966. 527 p.; 22 cm. 1. Spanish language — Synonyms and antonyms. I. Pey, Santiago. II. Ruiz i Calonja, Juan.
PC4591.D48   LC 67-52587

Diccionaro de la lengua española (Real Academia Española)   **2.896**
Diccionario de la lengua española. — 20a ed. — Madrid: Real Academia Española, 1984. 2 v.; 31 cm. 1. Spanish language — Dictionaries I. Real Academia Española. II. T.
PC4625.A3 1984   463 19   LC 85-127969   ISBN 8423947777

Moliner, María.   **2.897**
Diccionario de uso del español / Maria Moliner. — Madrid: Editorial Gredos, [1966-1967] 2 v. — (Biblioteca románica hispánica. Diccionarios. [5]) 1. Spanish language — Dictionaries 2. Spanish language — Idioms, corrections, errors I. T. II. Series.
PC4625.M6   463   LC 67-58643

Vox: Diccionario general ilustrado de la lengua española /   **2.898**
prólogo de Ramón Menéndez Pidal.
2. ed. corr. y notablemente ampliada por Samuel Gili Gaya. — Barcelona: Spes, 1964, c1961. 1815p.: ill., diagrs.; 25cm. 1. Spanish language — Dictionaries I. Gili Gaya, Samuel. II. Title: Diccionario general ilustrado de la langua española.
PC4625.V6 1961

Cassell's Spanish–English, English–Spanish dictionary; edited by   • **2.899**
Edgar Allison Peers [and others].
6th ed. London, Cassell, 1968. xv, 1477 p. 22 cm. 1. Spanish language — Dictionaries — English. 2. English language — Dictionaries — Spanish. I. Peers, E. Allison (Edgar Allison), 1891-1952. ed.
PC4640.C35 1968   463/.2   LC 71-396569   ISBN 0304928119

Cuyás, Arturo, 1845-1925.   **2.900**
[Appleton's new English-Spanish and Spanish-English dictionary] Appleton's new Cuyás English–Spanish and Spanish–English dictionary. Rev. and enl. by Lewis E. Brett (part 1) and Helen S. Eaton (part 2) with the assistance of Walter Beveraggi–Allende. Revision editor, 5th ed., Catherine B. Avery. 5th ed., rev. New York, Appleton-Century-Crofts, 1972. 2 v. in 1. 25 cm. Added t.p., in Spanish. First published in 1928 under title: Appleton's new English-Spanish and Spanish-English dictionary. 1. English language — Dictionaries — Spanish. 2. Spanish language — Dictionaries — English. I. T.
PC4640.C8 1972   463/.21   LC 75-182137   ISBN 0390252220

Simon and Schuster's international dictionary. Diccionario   **2.901**
internacional Simon and Schuster. English/Spanish, Spanish/
English. Tana de Gámez, editor in chief.
New York: Simon and Schuster, [1973] xviii, 1605 p.; 29 cm. Published in 1975 under title: Simon and Schuster's concise international dictionary. 1. Spanish language — Dictionaries — English. 2. English language — Dictionaries — Spanish. I. De Gamez, Tana, 1920- ed. II. Title: Diccionario internacional Simon and Schuster.
PC4640.S48   463/.21   LC 71-180718   ISBN 0671215078

The University of Chicago Spanish dictionary; a new concise   **2.902**
Spanish–English and English–Spanish dictionary of words and
phrases basic to the written and spoken languages of today.
Comp. by Carlos Castillo & Otto F. Bond, with the assistance
of Barbara M. Garcia. Rev. by D. Lincoln Canfield.
[Rev. ed.] Chicago, University of Chicago Press [1972] xlvi, 202, xiii, 233 p. 24 cm. Added t.p. in Spanish. 1. Spanish language — Dictionaries — English. 2. English language — Dictionaries — Spanish. I. Castillo, Carlos, 1890- ed. II. Bond, Otto Ferdinand, 1885- ed. III. Canfield, D. Lincoln (Delos Lincoln), 1903- ed.
PC4640.U5 1972   463/.21   LC 78-177425   ISBN 0226096718

Velázquez de la Cadena, Mariano, 1778-1860.   • **2.903**
A new pronouncing dictionary of the Spanish and English languages, compiled by Mariano Velázquez de la Cadena with Edward Gray and Juan L. Iribas. — Rev. ed. — New York: Appleton-Century-Crofts, 1967. 2 v. in 1.; 27 cm. At head of title: Velázquez. Part 2 has t.p. in Spanish. Published in 1852 under title: A pronouncing dictionary of the Spanish and English languages. 1. Spanish language — Dictionaries — English. 2. English language — Dictionaries — Spanish. I. Gray, Edward, 1849-1920. II. Iribas, Juan L. III. T.
PC4640.V5 1967   463.2   LC 67-14911

Vox new college Spanish and English dictionary: English–   **2.904**
Spanish/Spanish–English / preface by Theodore V. Higgs;
dictionary compiled by Carlos F. MacHale and the editors of
Biblograf, S.A.; North American edition prepared by the editors
of National Textbook Company.
Lincolnwood, Ill., U.S.A.: National Textbook Co., c1984. xix, 1456, 60 p.: ill.; 25 cm. (National Textbook language dictionaries.) 1. Spanish language — Dictionaries — English. 2. English language — Dictionaries — Spanish.

I. MacHale, Carlos F. II. Biblograf, S.A. III. National Textbook Company. IV. Series.
PC4640.V696 1984   463/.21 19   *LC* 84-61106   *ISBN* 0844279986

Williams, Edwin Bucher, 1891-1975.   • **2.905**
[Holt Spanish and English dictionary] Dictionary Spanish and English. Expanded ed. Diccionario inglés y español. Ed. aumentada. New York, Holt, Rinehart and Winston [c1963] xvi, 623, lxv, 620 p. 25 cm. Published in 1955 under title: Holt Spanish and English dictionary. 1. Spanish language — Dictionaries — English. 2. English language — Dictionaries — Spanish. I. T. II. Title: Diccionario inglés y español.
PC4640.W55 1963   *LC* 63-11903

Armistead, Samuel G., 1927-.   **2.906**
The Judeo–Spanish ballad chapbooks of Yacob Abraham Yoná, by Samuel G. Armistead [and] Joseph H. Silverman. Berkeley, University of California Press, 1971. xiii, 640 p. illus. 25 cm. (Folk literature of the Sephardic Jews. 1) 'The ballads [in Spanish and English]': p. 37-365. 'The chapbooks [in Hebrew characters]': p. 367-530. 1. Yoná, Yacob Abraham, 1847-1922. 2. Ballads, Ladino — Texts. 3. Chap-books, Ladino. I. Silverman, Joseph H. joint author. II. T. III. Series.
PC4813.7.A76   860   *LC* 71-78565   *ISBN* 0520016483

Kany, Charles Emil, 1895-.   • **2.907**
American–Spanish euphemisms. Berkeley, University of California Press, 1960. x, 249 p. illus. 24 cm. 1. Spanish language — Euphemism. 2. Spanish language — Provincialisms — Latin America. 3. Spanish language — Slang. I. T.
PC4822.K3   467.98   *LC* 60-11847

Santamaría, Francisco Javier, 1889-.   • **2.908**
Diccionario general de Americanismos ... / Francisco J. Santamaria. — 1. ed. — Méjico, D. F.: Editorial Pedro Roberedo, 1942 [i.e. 1943] 3 v. Colophon, v.3, dated 1943. At head of title: Francisco J. Santamaria. 1. Spanish language — Provincialisms — Latin America. 2. Spanish language — Dictionaries I. T.
PC4822 S3   *LC* a 43-2977

PC5001–5498 Portuguese Language

Cunha, Celso Ferreira da.   **2.909**
Gramática do português contemporâneo: de acordo com a Nomenclatura gramatical brasileira / Celso Cunha. — 6a. ed. rev. — Belo Horizonte: B. Alvares, 1976, c1972. 509 p.: ill; 22 cm. 1. Portuguese language — Grammar — 1950- I. T.
PC5067.3.C8x 1976   *LC* 84-672335

Dicionário brasileiro da lingua portuguesa.   **2.910**
7 ed. — São Paulo: Encyclopaedia Britannica do Brasil, 1982. 2 v. (1881 p.); 30 cm. 1. Portuguese language — Dictionaries.
PC5327.D513   469/.3   *LC* 76-453869

Houaiss, Antônio. ed.   • **2.911**
The new Appleton dictionary of the English and Portuguese languages. Editors: Antônio Houaiss and Catherine B. Avery. Associate editor: José E. A. do Prado. Assistant editors: Edna Jansen de Mello Clarke [and] Fernando Antônio de Mello Vianna. — New York: Appleton-Century-Crofts, 1967. xx, 636, xx, 666 p.; 26 cm. Added t.p. in Portuguese. 1. Portuguese language — Dictionaries — English. 2. English language — Dictionaries — Portuguese. I. Avery, Catherine B. joint ed. II. T.
PC5333.H6 1967   469.32   *LC* 68-2398

Nôvo Michaelis, dicionário ilustrado ... / Seção Lexicográfica   **2.912**
das Edições Melhoramentos; orientação de Franz Wimmer e Fritz Pietzschke; illustrações redesenhadas por Wilson Mariotti.
São Paulo: Melhoramentos, 1983. 2 v.: ill.; 24 cm. Added t.p.: The New Michaelis, illustrated dictionary. 1. Portuguese language — Dictionaries — English. 2. English language — Dictionaries — Portuguese. I. Michaelis, H. (Henriette), b. 1849. Nôvo dicionário da língua portuguêsa e linglêsa. II. Pietzschke, Fritz. III. Wimmer, Franz. IV. Edições Melhoramentos. Seção Lexicográfica. V. Title: The New Michaelis, illustrated dictionary.
PC5333.N6 1983   469/.3/21

Taylor, James L. (James Lumpkin), 1892-.   • **2.913**
A Portuguese–English dictionary [by] James L. Taylor. — Rev., with corrections and additions by the author and Priscilla Clark Martin. — Stanford, Calif.: Stanford University Press, 1970 [c1958] xx, 655 p.; 26 cm. 1. Portuguese language — Dictionaries — English. I. Martin, Priscilla Clark. II. T.
PC5333.T3 1970   469/.3/21   *LC* 72-26595   *ISBN* 0804704805

PD Germanic and Scandinavian Languages

Lehmann, Winfred Philipp, 1916-.   **2.914**
The development of Germanic verse form [by] Winfred P. Lehmann. — New York: Gordian Press, 1971 [c1956] xix, 217 p.; 22 cm. 1. Germanic languages — Metrics and rhythmics. I. T.
PD505.L4 1971   436   *LC* 70-131252   *ISBN* 0877520143

Arngrímur Sigurðsson, 1933-.   **2.915**
Íslenzk–ensk orðabók. Reykjavík, Prentsmiðjan Leiftur [1970] 925 p. 22 cm. 1. Icelandic language — Dictionaries — English. I. T.
PD2437.A7   *LC* 73-263432

Sören Sörenson.   **2.916**
Ensk–íslensk orðabök: með alfraeðilegu ívafi. — Rijkavijk: Örn og Örlygur, 1984. 1 v. I. T.
PD2437.S6x

Haugen, Einar Ingvald, 1906-.   • **2.917**
The Norwegian language in America; a study in bilingual behavior [by] Einar Haugen. [2d ed.] Bloomington, Indiana University Press [1969] 2 v. in 1 (xxiv, 699 p.) 25 cm. (Publications of the American Institute, University of Oslo, in coöperation with the Department of American Civilization, Graduate School of Arts and Sciences, University of Pennsylvania) (Indiana University studies in the history and theory of linguistics.) 1. Norwegian language — History. 2. Norwegian language — Dialects — United States. 3. Norwegian Americans 4. Bilingualism I. T.
PD2615.H3 1969   439.8/2/7973   *LC* 70-85187   *ISBN* 0253341159

Bjerke, Lucie.   **2.918**
[Engelsk-norsk ordbok] English–Norwegian dictionary [by] Lucie Bjerke and Haakon Søraas. London, G. G. Harrap [1964] x, 562 p. 21 cm. First published in 1963 under title: Engelsk-norsk ordbok. 1. English language — Dictionaries — Norwegian. I. Søraas, Haakon, 1887- joint author. II. T.
PD2691.B48 1964   439.8/3/32   *LC* 71-6944

Norwegian English dictionary: a pronouncing and translating   **2.919**
dictionary of modern Norwegian [Bokmål and Nynorsk]: with a historical and grammatical introduction / Einar Haugen, editor-in-chief, Kenneth G. Chapman, Dag Gundersen, Jørgen Rischel, associate editors.
New and enl. American print. — Oslo: Universitetsforlaget; Madison: University of Wisconsin Press, 1974, printing 1980. 504 p.; 25 cm. Added t.p.: Norsk engelsk ordbok. 1. Norwegian language — Dictionaries — English. I. Haugen, Einar Ingvald, 1906- ed.
PD2691.N6 1974   439.8/2/321   *LC* 75-304876   *ISBN* 029903870X

Kjaerulff Nielsen, Bernhard, 1901-.   **2.920**
Engelsk–dansk ordbog / B. Kjærulff Nielsen, medred., Jens Axelsen; konsulent, C. A. Bodelsen. — 2. udg. [København]: Gyldendal, 1981. 1273 p.; 25 cm. 1. English language — Dictionaries — Danish. I. Axelsen, Jens. joint author. II. T.
PD3640.K4 1974   *ISBN* 8701449710

Vinterberg, Hermann, 1881-.   **2.921**
Dansk–engelsk ordbog / Hermann Vinterberg og C. A. Bodelsen. 2. rev. og udvidede udg. ved C. A. Bodelsen, medred., Jens Axelsen, B. Kjærulff Nielsen og Edith Frey, 3. opl. med tillæg. — [København]: Gyldendal, [1976] 2 v.; 25 cm. 1. Danish language — Dictionaries — English. 1. Bodelsen, Carl Adolf Gottlieb, 1894- joint author. II. T.
PD3640.V5 1976   *LC* 76-474943   *ISBN* 8700671614

Bergman, Nils Gösta, 1894-.   • **2.922**
[Kortfattad svensk språkhistoria. English] A short history of the Swedish language, tr. and adapted by Francis P. Magoun, Jr. [and] Helge Kökeritz. Stockholm, Swedish Institute for Cultural Relations, 1947. 106 p. illus., maps, 21 cm. Translation of Kortfattad svensk språkhistoria. 1. Swedish language — History. I. Magoun, Francis Peabody, 1895- tr. II. T.
PD5075.B413   439.7/09   *LC* a 48-3460

Modern engelsk svensk och svensk engelsk ordbok.   • **2.923**
Prisma's Modern Swedish–English and English–Swedish dictionary. — 1st American ed. — Minneapolis: University of Minnesota Press; Stockholm: Bokförlaget Prisma, 1984. 542, 394 p.; 21 cm. Originally published: Modern engelsk svensk och svensk engelsk ordbok. 1. Swedish language — Dictionaries — English. 2. English language — Dictionaries — Swedish. I. Modern svensk-

engelsk ordbok. 1984. II. Modern engelsk-svensk ordbok. 1984. III. T. IV. Title: Modern Swedish-English and English-Swedish dictionary.
PD5640.M558 1984   439.7/321 19   *LC* 83-23375   *ISBN* 0816613141

PE ENGLISH LANGUAGE

Partridge, Eric, 1894-.   2.924
Eric Partridge in his own words / edited by David Crystal; with appreciations by Anthony Burgess, Ralph Elliott, Winston Graham, and Randolph Quirk. — New York: Macmillan, c1980. 251 p.; 25 cm. Includes indexes. 1. Partridge, Eric, 1894- — Bibliography. 2. English language — Collected works. I. Crystal, David, 1941- II. T.
PE27.P3 1980   420 19   *LC* 80-24366   *ISBN* 0025289608

Murray, Katharine Maud Elisabeth.   2.925
Caught in the web of words: James A.H. Murray and the Oxford English dictionary / K.M. Elisabeth Murray; with a pref. by R.W. Burchfield. — New Haven: Yale University Press, 1977. 386 p.: ill.; 24 cm. 1. Murray, James Augustus Henry, Sir, 1837-1915. 2. New English dictionary on historical principles. 3. Lexicographers — Great Britain — Biography. I. T.
PE64.M8 M78   423/.092/4 B   *LC* 77-76309   *ISBN* 0300021313

Moss, Richard J.   2.926
Noah Webster / by Richard J. Moss. — Boston: Twayne Publishers, c1984. 131 p.: port.; 22 cm. — (Twayne's United States authors series. TUSAS 465) Includes index. 1. Webster, Noah, 1758-1843. I. T. II. Series.
PE64.W5 M68 1984   423/.092/4 B 19   *LC* 83-18558   *ISBN* 0805774068

Morse, Josiah Mitchell, 1912-.   2.927
The irrelevant English teacher [by] J. Mitchell Morse. — Philadelphia: Temple University Press, [1972] ix, 142 p.; 21 cm. 1. English philology — Study and teaching (Higher) — Addresses, essays, lectures. I. T.
PE65.M65   428/.007/1173   *LC* 72-80762   *ISBN* 0877220166

Lefevre, Carl A.   2.928
Linguistics, English, and the Language arts [by] Carl A. Lefevre. — New York: Teachers College Press, [1973, c1970] xxii, 371 p.: illus.; 21 cm. Reprint of the ed. published by Allyn and Bacon, Boston. 1. English language — Study and teaching (Higher) I. T.
PE66.L4 1973   420/.7   *LC* 73-15655

The English curriculum under fire: what are the real basics? /   2.929
George Hillocks, Jr., editor.
Urbana, Ill.: National Council of Teachers of English, c1982. vii, 88 p.; 23 cm. Papers presented at a conference held in 1978 and sponsored by the University of Chicago's Dept. of Education and the Illinois Humanities Council. 1. English philology — Study and teaching — United States — Congresses. I. Hillocks, George. II. University of Chicago. Dept. of Education. III. Illinois Humanities Council.
PE68.U5 E56 1982   428/.007/1073 19   *LC* 82-12440   *ISBN* 0814113982

PE100–408 Anglo–Saxon Language

Marckwardt, Albert Henry, 1903-1975.   • 2.930
Old English language and literature [by] Albert H. Marckwardt [and] James L. Rosier. — [1st ed.]. — New York: Norton, [1972] xviii, 394 p.; 22 cm. 1. English philology — Old English, ca. 450-1100 I. Rosier, James L. joint author. II. T.
PE123.M3 1972   429   *LC* 70-166086   *ISBN* 0393099911

Mitchell, Bruce, 1920-.   2.931
A guide to Old English / Bruce Mitchell and Fred C. Robinson. — Rev. ed. with texts and glossary. — Toronto; Buffalo: University of Toronto Press, 1982. xiv, 271 p.; 23 cm. Includes indexes. 1. English language — Old English, ca. 450-1100 — Grammar. 2. English language — Old English, ca. 450-1100 — Texts. 3. Anglo-Saxons I. Robinson, Fred C. II. T.
PE131.M5 1982   429/.82421 19   *LC* 83-101023   *ISBN* 0802024890

Quirk, Randolph.   • 2.932
An Old English grammar, by Randolph Quirk and C. L. Wrenn. New York: Holt, Rinehart & Winston, 195-? 166 p.; 19 cm. (Methuen's Old English library:

Studies.) 1. English language — Old English, ca. 450-1100 — Grammar. I. Wrenn, Charles Leslie, 1895- II. T. III. Series.
PE131.Q5

Wright, Joseph, 1855-1930.   • 2.933
Old English grammar, by Joseph Wright and Elizabeth Mary Wright. London: H. Frowde, 1908. xiv, 351 p.; 20 cm. (The students' series of historical and comparative grammars) Bibliography: p. [xiii]-xiv. I. Wright, Elizabeth Mary (Lea) 1863- jt. author II. T.
PE131.W8

Alston, R. C.   • 2.934
An introduction to Old English / by R. C. Alston. Leeds: University [1967] [1], 59 p.; 20 1/2 cm. Maps on endpapers. 1. English language — Old English, ca. 450-1100 — Grammar. I. T.
PE135.A46

Brook, G. L. (George Leslie), 1910-.   • 2.935
An introduction to Old English. — Manchester [Eng.] University Press [1955] 138 p. illus. 19 cm. 1. English language — Old English, ca. 450-1100 — Grammar. I. T.
PE135.B8   429.5   *LC* 56-17375

Diamond, Robert E.   • 2.936
Old English grammar & reader, by Robert E. Diamond. — Detroit: Wayne State University Press, 1970? 304 p.; 21 cm. — (A Savoyard book) 1. English language — Old English, ca. 450-1100 — Grammar. 2. English language — Old English, ca. 450-1100 — Versification. 3. English language — Old English, ca. 450-1100 — Readers. I. T.
PE135.D5 1970   429   *LC* 79-79477   *ISBN* 0814313906

Kispert, Robert J.   • 2.937
Old English; an introduction [by] Robert J. Kispert. — New York: Holt, Rinehart and Winston, [1971] x, 275 p.: illus., map.; 24 cm. 1. English language — Old English, ca. 450-1100 — Grammar. I. T.
PE135.K45   429/.8/2421   *LC* 76-130648   *ISBN* 003083256X

Moore, Samuel, 1877-1934.   • 2.938
The elements of Old English; elementary grammar, reference grammar and reading selections, by Samuel Moore and Thomas A. Knott. 8th ed., rev. and enl. Ann Arbor G. Wahr 1940. 337p. 1. English language — Old English, ca. 450-1100 — Grammar I. Knott, Thomas Albert, 1880-1945. jt. author II. T.
PE135 M6 1940

Bright, James Wilson, 1852-1926.   2.939
[Old English grammar & reader] Bright's Old English grammar & reader. Edited by Frederic G. Cassidy and Richard N. Ringler. 3d ed. New York, Holt, Rinehart and Winston [c1971] xiv, 494 p. illus., col. plate. 24 cm. Earlier ed. published under title: An Anglo-Saxon reader. 1. English language — Old English, ca. 450-1100 — Readers. 2. English language — Old English, ca. 450-1100 — Grammar. I. Cassidy, Frederic Gomes, 1907- ed. II. Ringler, Richard N., ed. III. T.
PE137.B7 1971   429/.8/2421   *LC* 76-179921   *ISBN* 0030847133

Sweet, Henry, 1845-1912.   • 2.940
Sweet's Anglo-Saxon reader in prose and verse. 15th ed., revised throughout by Dorothy Whitelock. — London: Oxford U.P., 1967. xiii, 404 p.; 20 cm. 1. English language — Old English, ca. 450-1100 — Readers. I. Whitelock, Dorothy. ed. II. T. III. Title: Anglo-Saxon reader in prose and verse.
PE137.S8 1967   429.6   *LC* 67-103589

Wyatt, Alfred John, 1858-.   • 2.941
The threshold of Anglo-Saxon. Cambridge University Press 1926. 126p. 1. English language — Old English, ca. 450-1100 — Chrestomathies and readers I. T.
PE137 W83

Partridge, A. C. (Astley Cooper)   • 2.942
Tudor to Augustan English: a study in syntax and style from Caxton to Johnson [by] A. C. Partridge. London, Deutsch, 1969. 242 p. 23 cm. (Language library.) 1. English language — Syntax 2. English language — Style 3. English literature — History and criticism I. T. II. Series.
PE225.P3   420/.9   *LC* 74-478719   *ISBN* 0233960929

Barney, Stephen A.   2.943
Word-hoard: an introduction to Old English vocabulary / Stephen A. Barney, with the assistance of Ellen Wertheimer and David Stevens. — New Haven: Yale University Press, 1977. xv, 108 p.; 24 cm. Includes indexes. 1. English language — Old English, ca. 450-1100 — Glossaries, vocabularies, etc. I. T.
PE274.B3   429/.81 19   *LC* 76-47003   *ISBN* 0300020260

Meritt, Herbert Dean, 1904-.   • 2.944
Fact and lore about Old English words. — Stanford, Calif.: Stanford University Press, 1954. 226 p. (Stanford University publications. University series.

Language and literature, v.13) 1. English language — Old English, ca. 450-1100 — Glossaries, vocabularies, etc. I. T.
PE274.M37

Bosworth, Joseph, 1789-1876.   • 2.945
An Anglo–Saxon dictionary, based on the manuscript collections of the late Joseph Bosworth. Edited and enlarged by T. Northcote Toller. London, H. Milford, Oxford University Press [19—] 1302p. Originally issued in 4 parts, 1882-1898. — Supplement, by T. Northcote Toller. [London] Oxford University Press [1921] 16.25. Originally issued in 3 parts, 1908-1921. Library has: suppl. 1. English language — Old English, ca. 450-1100 — Dictionaries — English. I. Toller, Thomas Northcote, 1844- ed. II. T.
PE279.B52   LC 39-13893

Hall, John Richard Clark, 1855-.   • 2.946
A concise Anglo–Saxon dictionary. 4th ed., with a supplement by Herbert D. Meritt. Cambridge [Eng.] University Press, 1960 [i.e. 1961] xv, 432, [20] p. 23 cm. 1. English language — Old English, ca. 450-1100 — Dictionaries — English. I. Meritt, Herbert Dean, 1904- II. T.
PE279.H3 1961   429.32   LC 61-1911

Jember, Gregory K.   2.947
English–Old English, Old English–English dictionary / edited by Gregory K. Jember, with John C. Carrell ... [et al.]. — Boulder, Colo.: Westview Press, 1975. xxxiii, 178 p.; 24 cm. 1. English language — Old English, ca. 450-1100 — Dictionaries — English. 2. English language — Dictionaries — Anglo-Saxon. I. T.
PE279.J4   429/.3/21   LC 75-30928   ISBN 0891580069

Sweet, Henry, 1845-1912.   • 2.948
The student's dictionary of Anglo–Saxon. New York; Londone: Macmillan Company, 1897. 217p. 1. English language — Old English, ca. 450-1100 — Dictionaries — English 2. English language — Dictionaries — Anglo-Saxon I. T.
PE279 S8   LC 04-13141

PE451–693 Middle English

Wardale, Edith Elizabeth.   • 2.949
An introduction to Middle English, by E. E. Wardale ... — London, K. Paul, Trench, Trubner & co., ltd., 1937. x, 130 p. illus. (map) 19 cm. 1. English language — Middle English — (1100-1500) — Hist. 2. English language — Middle English (1100-1500) — Grammar, Historical. I. T.
PE525.W3   427.02   LC 38-3394

Brunner, Karl, 1887-.   • 2.950
An outline of Middle English grammar / Translated by Grahame Johnston. Cambridge: Harvard University Press, 1963. 111 p.; 22 cm. 1. English language — Middle English, 1100-1500 — Grammar I. T.
PE531.B713   427/.02   LC 63-5505

Jones, Charles, 1939-.   • 2.951
An introduction to Middle English. — New York: Holt, Rinehart and Winston, [1972] xi, 228 p.: illus.; 24 cm. 1. English language — Middle English, 1100-1500 — Grammar, Historical. 2. English language — Middle English, 1100-1500 — Dialects. I. T.
PE531.J56   427/.02   LC 77-155295   ISBN 0030844797

Wright, Joseph, 1855-1930.   • 2.952
An elementary middle English grammar / by Joseph Wright and Elizabeth Mary Wright. — Oxford; New York: H. Milford, Oxford University Press, 1923. xi, 214 p.; 19 cm. Includes index. 1. English language — Middle English, 1100-1500 — Grammar 2. English language — Middle English, 1100-1500 — Phonology. I. Wright, Elizabeth Mary, 1863- joint author. II. T.
PE531.W74 1979   427/.02   LC 24-15713

Mossé, Fernand.   • 2.953
A handbook of Middle English; translated by James A. Walker. — Baltimore, Johns Hopkins Press, 1952. xxiv, 495 p. maps, facsims. 24 cm. 'Translation of the second part of ... Manuel [de l'anglais du Moyen Age]' Bibliography: p. xxi-xxiv. 1. English language — Middle English, 1100-1500 — Grammar 2. English literature — Middle English, 1100-1500 I. T.
PE535.M62   425   LC 52-13031

Świeczkowski, Walerian.   • 2.954
Word order patterning in Middle English; a quantitative study based on Piers Plowman and Middle English sermons. 'S-Gravenhage Mouton 1962. 114p. (Janua linguarum, studia memoriae Nicolai van Wijk dedicata, nr. 19) 1. Langland, William, 1330?-1400? 2. English language — Middle English (1100-1500) — Word order 3. Sermons, English (Middle) I. T. II. Series.
PE631 S95   LC 64-2697

Turville-Petre, Thorlac.   2.955
The alliterative revival / Thorlac Turville–Petre. — Ipswich, Eng.: D. S. Brewer; Totowa, N.J.: Rowman & Littlefield, c1977. 152 p.; 24 cm. 1. English language — Middle English, 1100-1500 — Versification. 2. Alliteration 3. English poetry — Middle English, 1100-1500 — History and criticism. I. T.
PE659.A6 T8   426   LC 77-658   ISBN 0874719550

Björkman, Erik, 1872-1919.   • 2.956
Scandinavian loan–words in Middle English. — New York: Greenwood Press, [1969] iv, 360 p.; 23 cm. Reprint of the work first issued in 2 pts., 1900-1902. Pt. 1 forms author's thesis, Uppsala. 1. English language — Middle English, 1100-1500 — Foreign words and phrases — Scandinavian. I. T.
PE664.S3 B4 1969   427/.02   LC 69-13829   ISBN 0837118034

Middle English dictionary / Hans Kurath, editor, Sherman M.   • 2.957
Kuhn, associate editor.
Ann Arbor, Mich.: University of Michigan Press, 1952-. v.; 28 cm. Issued in parts. Editors vary. Editors vary. 1. English language — Middle English, 1100-1500 — Dictionaries I. Kurath, Hans, 1891- II. Kuhn, Sherman M. (Sherman McAllister), 1907-
PE679.M54   LC 53-62158   ISBN 0472011421

PE1001–3729 Modern English (1500–)

Frye, Northrop.   • 2.958
Sound and poetry / edited with an introd. by Northrop Frye. — New York: Columbia University Press, 1957. xxvii, 156 p. — (English Institute essays; 1956) (English Institute essays; 1956) 1. Poetry — Addresses, essays, lectures. 2. Music and literature I. T. II. Series.
PE1010.E5 1956   LC 57-11003

Ellmann, Richard, 1918- ed.   • 2.959
Edwardians and late Victorians. — New York: Columbia University Press, 1960. x, 245 p.; 21 cm. — (English Institute. Essays, 1959) 1. English literature — 20th century. — Addresses, essays, lectures. 2. English literature — 19th century. — Addresses, essays, lectures. I. T. II. Series.
PE1010.E5 1959   820.903   LC 60-13103

Bagnall, Nicholas.   2.960
New movements in the study and teaching of English. Edited by Nicholas Bagnall. — [S.l.]: Transatlantic Arts, 1976, c1973. 255 p.; 23 cm. 1. English language — Study and teaching I. T.
PE1065.B22   420/.7   ISBN 0851170447

Pooley, Robert Cecil, 1898-.   2.961
The teaching of English usage [by] Robert C. Pooley. — Urbana, Ill.: National Council of Teachers of English, [1974] xiii, 241 p.; 23 cm. Edition for 1946 published under title: Teaching English usage. 1. English language — Study and teaching I. T.
PE1065.P55   428/.007/12   LC 73-91939   ISBN 0814127786

Bryant, Margaret M., 1900-.   • 2.962
Modern English and its heritage. — 2d ed. — New York: Macmillan, [1962] 492 p.: illus.; 22 cm. 1. English language — History 2. English language — Phonetics 3. English language — Grammar — 1950- 4. English language — Word formation I. T.
PE1072.B75 1962   420.9   LC 62-7796

Burchfield, R. W.   2.963
The English language / Robert Burchfield. — Oxford [Oxfordshire]; New York: Oxford University Press, 1985. viii, 194 p.: ill.; 22 cm. (An OPUS book) Includes index. 1. English language I. T.
PE1072.B79 1985   420 19   LC 84-9677   ISBN 019219173X

James B. McMillan: essays in linguistics by his friends and   2.964
colleagues / edited by James C. Raymond and I. Willis Russell.
University: University of Alabama Press, c1977. xvii, 184 p.: ill.; 22 cm. 1. McMillan, James B., 1907- 2. English language — Addresses, essays, lectures. I. McMillan, James B., 1907- II. Raymond, James C., 1940- III. Russell, I. Willis, 1903-
PE1072.J35   410   LC 77-7169   ISBN 0817305033

Nash, Walter.   2.965
Our experience of language. — New York: St. Martin's Press, [c1971] 222 p.: ill.; 23 cm. 1. English language I. T.
PE1072.N3 1971b   420   LC 76-165542

Jones, Richard Foster, 1886-.   • **2.966**
The triumph of the English language; a survey of opinions concerning the vernacular from the introduction of printing to the Restoration. — Stanford, Stanford University Press [1953] xii, 340 p. 24 cm. Bibliographical footnotes. 1. English language I. T.
PE1073.J6   420   LC 52-6350

PE1075–1400 HISTORY

Baugh, Albert Croll, 1891-.   • **2.967**
A history of the English language. — 2d ed. — New York: Appleton-Century-Crofts, [1957] 506 p.: illus.; 22 cm. 1. English language — History I. T.
PE1075.B3 1957   420.9   LC 57-9806

Jesperson, Otto, 1860-1943.   • **2.968**
Growth and structure of the English language. 9th ed. Oxford [Eng.] B. Blackwell, 1948. iv, 244 p. 19 cm. 1. English language — History I. T.
PE1075.J4 1948   LC 48-8493

Leith, Dick, 1947-.   **2.969**
A social history of English / Dick Leith. — London; Boston: Routledge & K. Paul, 1983. ix, 224 p.: ill.; 23 cm. (Language and society series) 1. English language — History 2. English language — Social aspects I. T. II. Series.
PE1075.L44 1983   420/.9 19   LC 82-13181   ISBN 0710092601

Nist, John A.   • **2.970**
A structural history of English / John Nist. — New York: St. Martin's Press, c1966. xvii, 426 p.: maps; 24 cm. 1. English language — History I. T.
PE1075 N5   420.09   LC 66-12685

Peters, Robert Anthony, 1926-.   • **2.971**
A linguistic history of English [by] Robert A. Peters. — Boston: Houghton Mifflin, [1968] xvi, 352 p.: illus.; 21 cm. 1. English language — History I. T.
PE1075.P47   420   LC 68-7302

Pyles, Thomas, 1905-.   • **2.972**
The origins and development of the English language. — New York: Harcourt, Brace & World, [1964] viii, 388 p.; 22 cm. 1. English language — History I. T.
PE1075.P9   420.9   LC 64-15846

Robertson, Stuart, 1892-1940.   • **2.973**
The development of modern English. — 2d ed., rev. by Frederic G. Cassidy. — New York: Prentice-Hall, 1954. 469 p.: illus.; 22 cm. 1. English language — History I. Cassidy, Frederic Gomes, 1907- II. T.
PE1075.R57 1954   420.9   LC 53-13011

Schlauch, Margaret, 1898-.   • **2.974**
English language in modern times, since 1400 / by Margaret Schlauch. Warszawa: Państwowe Wydawnictwo Naukowe, 1959. vii, 316 p.: maps. 1. English language — History 2. English language — Dialects I. T.
PE1075.S37   420.7   LC 61-29993

Strang, Barbara M. H.   • **2.975**
A history of English [by] Barbara M. H. Strang. — [London]: Methuen, [1970] xxiv, 453 p.: illus., map.; 23 cm. 1. English language — History I. T.
PE1075.S85   420/.9   LC 70-17104   ISBN 0416168205

Williams, Joseph M.   **2.976**
Origins of the English language, a social and linguistic history / Joseph M. Williams. — New York: Free Press, [1975] ix, 422 p.: ill.; 24 cm. Includes indexes. 1. English language — History 2. Sociolinguistics I. T.
PE1075.W55   420/.9   LC 74-12596   ISBN 0029352800

Wrenn, Charles Leslie, 1895-.   • **2.977**
The English language / by C. L. Wrenn. — London: Methuen, 1949. vi, 236 p. — (Home study books) 1. English language — History I. T.
PE1075.W7 1949b   420.9

Wyld, Henry Cecil Kennedy, 1870-1945.   • **2.978**
The historical study of the mother tongue; an introduction to philological method. — New York: Greenwood Press, [1969] xi, 412 p.; 23 cm. Reprint of the 1906 ed. 1. English language — History I. T.
PE1075.W8 1969   420/.9   LC 69-14160   ISBN 0837118735

Wyld, Henry Cecil Kennedy, 1870-1945.   • **2.979**
A history of modern colloquial English. 3d ed., with additions. New York: Barnes & Noble, 1953. xviii, 433 p.; 23 cm. Bibliography: p. [xi]—xv. 1. English language — Spoken English — History. I. T.
PE1075.W9 1953   420.9   LC 53-3567

Barber, Charles Laurence.   **2.980**
Early modern English / [by] Charles Barber. — London: Deutsch, 1977. 360 p.: ill.; 23 cm. (Language library.) Includes index. 1. English language — Early modern, 1500-1700 — History. I. T. II. Series.
PE1081.B3   420/.9/031   LC 76-382522

Leonard, Sterling Andrus, 1888-1931.   • **2.981**
The doctrine of correctness in English usage, 1700–1800. — New York, Russell & Russell, 1962. 361 p. 23 cm. Issued also in 1929 as thesis, Columbia University. 1. English language — 18th cent. 2. English language — Grammar, Historical 3. English language — Hist. I. T. II. Title: Correctness in English usage.
PE1083.L4 1962   420.9   LC 62-13838 rev

PE1097–1400 GRAMMAR

Finegan, Edward, 1940-.   **2.982**
Attitudes toward English usage: the history of a war of words / Edward Finegan. New York: Teachers College Press, Teachers College, Columbia University, 1980. xi, 196 p.; 23 cm. Includes index. 1. English language — Usage 2. English language in the United States. 3. Linguistics — History 4. Lexicography — History. I. T.
PE1098.F5   420/.973   LC 79-28462   ISBN 0807725811

Michael, Ian, 1915-.   • **2.983**
English grammatical categories and the tradition to 1800 [by] Ian Michael. London, Cambridge U.P., 1970. xvi, 622 p. 24 cm. 1. English language — Grammatical categories I. T.
PE1098.M5   425   LC 77-111133   ISBN 052107634X

Morton, Jacqueline.   **2.984**
English grammar for students of French / Jacqueline Morton. — Ann Arbor, Mich.: Olivia and Hill Press, c1979. 145 p.; 23 cm. 1. English language — Grammar, Comparative — French. 2. French language — Grammar, Comparative — English. 3. English language — Grammar — 1950- 4. French language — Grammar — 1950- I. T.
PE1099.M67   428/.2   LC 79-87578   ISBN 0934034001

Zorach, Cecile.   **2.985**
English grammar for students of German / Cecile Zorach. — Ann Arbor, Mich.: Olivia and Hill Press, 1980. vi, 167 p. (English grammar series) Includes index. 1. English language — Grammar, Comparative — German. 2. German language — Grammar, Comparative — English. I. T.
PE1099.Z67   438.2421   LC 80-82773   ISBN 0934034028

Jespersen, Otto, 1860-1943.   • **2.986**
A modern English grammar on historical principles / by Otto Jespersen. — London: Allen & Unwin, 1928-. v.; 20 cm. 1. English language — Grammar, Historical 2. English language — Syntax I. T.
PE1101.J5 1928   LC 32-34028

Sweet, Henry, 1845-1912.   • **2.987**
A short historical English grammar, by Henry Sweet ... Oxford, Clarendon Press, 1892. xii, 264 p. 18 cm. (Clarendon press series) An abridgement of the historical portions of the author's New English grammar. cf. Pref. 1. English language — Grammar, Historical 2. English language I. T.
PE1101.S85   LC 04-13133

Wright, Joseph, 1855-1930.   • **2.988**
An elementary historical new English grammar / by Joseph Wright and Elizabeth Mary Wright. — London: Oxford University Press, 1924. xi, 224 p.; 19 cm. 1. English language — Grammar, Historical I. Wright, Elizabeth Mary, 1863- II. T.
PE1101.W7   LC 26-14865

Wyld, Henry Cecil Kennedy, 1870-1945.   • **2.989**
A short history of English: with a bibliography [of recent books on the subject] and lists of texts and editions / [by] Henry Cecil Wyld. — [3d ed., rev. and enl.]. — New York: E. P. Dutton, [1927] vii, [1], 294 p., 1 l. 23 cm. 'First published 1914.' Bibliography: p. 1-13. 1. English language — Grammar, Historical I. T.
PE1101.W8   LC 29-17907

Curme, George Oliver, 1860-1948.   • **2.990**
Principles and practice of English grammar, by George O. Curme ... — New York, Barnes & Noble, inc. [1947] x, 308 p. 21 cm. — (College outline series) 'Based in part upon College English grammar published 1925.' 1. English language — Grammar — 1870- I. Curme, George Oliver, 1880- College English grammar. II. T.
PE1105.C77   425   LC 47-2452

Curme, George Oliver, 1860-1948.   • **2.991**
Parts of speech and accidence, by George O. Curme ... — Boston, New York [etc.] D.C. Heath and company [c1935] xiii p., 1 l., 370 p. 22 cm. — (Added t.-

p.: A grammar of the English language ... vol. II) 1. English language — Grammar, Historical 2. English language — Inflection I. T.
PE1105.G7 vol. 2　　425.1　　*LC* 35-17513

Hill, Archibald A.　　• **2.992**
Introduction to linguistic structures; from sound to sentence in English. — New York: Harcourt, Brace, [1958] 496 p.; 22 cm. 1. English language — Grammar — 1950- I. T. II. Title: Linguistic structures.
PE1105.H5　　425　　*LC* 58-5918

Jespersen, Otto, 1860-1943.　　• **2.993**
Essentials of English grammar. — University, Ala.: University of Alabama Press, [1964] 387 p.; 21 cm. — ([Alabama linguistic and philological series, 1]) 'A one-volume grammar embodying the principles explained in 'The philosophy of grammar' and partly carried out in the four volumes of my 'Modern English grammar."—Pref. 1. English language — Grammar — 1870-1949 I. T. II. Series.
PE1105.J4 1964　　425　　*LC* 64-21942

Long, Ralph Bernard, 1906- .　　• **2.994**
The sentence and its parts: a grammar of contemporary English / Ralph B. Long. — Chicago: University of Chicago Press, 1961. 528 p.; 21 cm. Includes index. 1. English language — Grammar — 1950- I. T.
PE1105.L66 1961　　425　　*LC* 61-11895　　*ISBN* 0226492583

A Comprehensive grammar of the English language / Randolph　　**2.995**
Quirk ... [et. al.]; index by David Crystal.
London; New York: Longman, 1985. x, 1779 p.; 26 cm. Includes index. 1. English language — Grammar — 1950- I. Quirk, Randolph.
PE1106.C65 1985　　428.2 19　　*LC* 84-27848　　*ISBN* 0582517346

A Grammar of contemporary English [by] Randolph Quirk ...　　• **2.996**
[and others].
[London]: Longman, 1972. xii, 1120 p.: illus.; 24 cm. Includes index. 1. English language — Grammar — 1950- I. Quirk, Randolph.
PE1106.G67　　425　　*LC* 74-155578　　*ISBN* 058252444X

Lamberts, J. J. (Jacob Justin), 1910-.　　• **2.997**
A short introduction to English usage [by] J. J. Lamberts. New York, McGraw-Hill [1971, c1972] xiv, 385 p. 23 cm. 1. English language — Usage I. T.
PE1106.L28　　428　　*LC* 78-159309　　*ISBN* 0070360839

PE1109–1131 Textbooks

Kruisinga, Etsko, 1875-1944.　　• **2.998**
An English grammar, by E. Kruisinga and P.A. Erades. 6th ed., rev. with the assistance of P. A. Erades. — Groningen Djakarta, P. Noordhoff 1941-. v.; 24 cm. First published, 1911 under title: A grammar of present day English. Second-fifth editions have title: An English grammar for Dutch students. 'Texts and addenda' (cover-title, 24, [8] p.) inserted in v.1, pt. 1; 'Addenda' (cover-title, [16] p.) inserted in v.1, pt. 2. 1. English language — Grammar — 1870- 2. English language — Phonetics I. Erades, P. A, jt. author II. T.
PE1111.K85　　*LC* 46-42669

Sledd, James H.　　• **2.999**
A short introduction to English grammar. — Chicago: Scott, Foresman, [1959] 346 p.; 22 cm. 1. English language — Grammar — 1950- 2. English language — Rhetoric I. T.
PE1111.S487　　425　　*LC* 59-10796

Long, Ralph Bernard, 1906-.　　• **2.1000**
The system of English grammar [by] Ralph B. Long & Dorothy R. Long. — Glenview, Ill.: Scott, Foresman, [1971] ix, 531 p.; 24 cm. 1. English language — Grammar — 1950- I. Long, Dorothy R., joint author. II. T. III. Title: English grammar.
PE1112.L6　　428/.2　　*LC* 75-159449

Partridge, Eric, 1894-.　　• **2.1001**
English: a course for human beings. — London: Macdonald, [1962] xv, 192, 174, 173 p.; 23 cm. 1. English language — Grammar — 1870- I. T.
PE1112.P3 1962　　428.2　　808　　*LC* 65-7574

Strang, Barbara M. H.　　• **2.1002**
Modern English structure [by] Barbara M. H. Strang. — 2nd ed. — London: Edward Arnold, 1968. xiii, 264 p.: 4 plates, illus.; 22 cm. 1. English language — Grammar — 1950- I. T.
PE1112.S77 1968　　428.2　　*LC* 68-143307　　*ISBN* 0713154144

Zandvoort, R. W. (Reinard Willem), 1894-.　　• **2.1003**
A handbook of English grammar, by R. W. Zandvoort. 3d ed. Englewood Cliffs, N. J., Prentice-Hall, 1966, c1965. xiii, 349 p. 21 cm. 1. English language — Grammar — 1950- I. T.
PE1112.Z3 1965　　482/.2　　*LC* 66-3064

Bremner, John B., 1920-.　　**2.1004**
Words on words: a dictionary for writers and others who care about words / John B. Bremner. — New York: Columbia University Press, 1980. xi, 405 p.; 24 cm. 1. English language — Usage — Dictionaries 2. Journalism — Handbooks, manuals, etc. I. T.
PE1116.J6 B7　　428.1　　*LC* 80-256　　*ISBN* 0231044925

Mosier, Richard David, 1917-.　　**2.1005**
Making the American mind; social and moral ideas in the McGuffey readers. New York, King's Crown Press, 1947. vi, 207 p. 24 cm. Issued also as thesis, Columbia Univ. 1. McGuffey, William Holmes, 1800-1873. 2. United States — Civilization I. T.
PE1117.M23 M6 1947a　　*LC* 47-5812

Paulston, Christina Bratt, 1932-.　　**2.1006**
Teaching English as a second language: techniques and procedures / Christina Bratt Paulston, Mary Newton Bruder. — Cambridge, Mass.: Winthrop Publishers, c1976. xii, 255 p.: ill.; 23 cm. 1. English language — Study and teaching — Foreign speakers I. Bruder, Mary Newton, 1939- joint author. II. T.
PE1128.A2 P34　　428/.2/4　　*LC* 75-38835　　*ISBN* 087626967X

Leech, Geoffrey N.　　**2.1007**
A communicative grammar of English / Geoffrey Leech, Jan Svartvik. — London: Longman, 1975. 324 p.: diagrs.; 24 cm. 'Based on A Grammar of contemporary English, by Randolph Quirk ... [et al.]' Errata slip inserted. Includes index. 1. English language — Text-books for foreigners. 2. English language — Grammar — 1950- I. Svartvik, Jan. joint author. II. A Grammar of contemporary English. III. T.
PE1128.L45　　428/.2/4　　*LC* 77-376321　　*ISBN* 0582552389

PE1133–1168 Phonology. Phonetics

Balmuth, Miriam.　　**2.1008**
The roots of phonics: a historical introduction / by Miriam Balmuth; foreword by Jeanne S. Chall. — New York: McGraw-Hill, c1982. xiii, 251 p.; 24 cm. Includes index. 1. English language — Phonology, Historical 2. English language — Pronunciation 3. English language — Orthography and spelling I. T.
PE1133.B26　　421/.5/09 19　　*LC* 81-6041　　*ISBN* 0070034907

Chomsky, Noam.　　• **2.1009**
The sound pattern of English [by] Noam Chomsky [and] Morris Halle. — New York: Harper & Row, [1968] xiv, 470 p.; 27 cm. — (Studies in language) 1. English language — Phonology 2. English language — Grammar, Generative 3. Distinctive features (Linguistics) I. Halle, Morris. joint author. II. T.
PE1133.C5　　421/.5　　*LC* 67-23446

Ellis, Alexander John, 1814-1890.　　• **2.1010**
On early English pronunciation, with especial reference to Shakspere and Chaucer: containing an investigation of the correspondence of writing with speech in England from the Anglosaxon period to the present day, preceded by a systematic notation of all spoken sounds by means of the ordinary printing types; including a re-arrangement of F. J. Child's memoirs on the language of Chaucer and Gower, and reprints of the rare tracts by Salesbury on English, 1547, and Welch, 1567, and by Barcley on French, 1521. New York: Greenwood Press [1968] 5 v. (2267 p.): fold maps.; 23 cm. On spine: The Early English Text Society. Reprint of the 1869 ed. 1. English language — Phonology 2. English language — Pronunciation 3. English language — Middle English, 1100-1500 4. English language — Early modern, 1500-1700 5. Phonetic alphabet 6. English language — Dialects — Phonology I. Child, Francis James, 1825-1896. Observations on the language of Chaucer and Gower. II. Salesbury, William, 1520?-1600? III. Schmeller, Johann Andreas, 1785-1852. IV. Barcley, Alexander, 1475?-1552. V. Bonaparte, Louis-Lucien, prince, 1813-1891. VI. Winkler, Johan, 1840-1916. VII. Early English Text Society. VIII. T.
PE1133.E45 1968　　421/.52　　*LC* 68-30998

Moore, Samuel, 1877-.　　• **2.1011**
Historical outlines of English sounds and inflections; rev. by Albert H. Marckwardt. Ann Arbor, G. Wahr Pub. Co., 1951. 179 p. ill. 24 cm. 1. Chaucer, Geoffrey — Language. 2. English language — Phonology 3. English language — Middle English, 1100-1500 — Phonology. I. T. II. Title: English sounds and inflections.
PE1133.M7 1951　　*LC* 52-9195

Ross, Alan Strode Campbell.　　• **2.1012**
Etymology, with especial reference to English. New Jersey: Essential Books, 1958. 169p. (The Language library) 1. English language — Phonology 2. Language and languages 3. Language and languages — Etymology I. T.
PE1133 R6　　*LC* 58-3714

Wolfram, Walt, 1941-.   **2.1013**
Phonological analysis: focus on American English / by Walt Wolfram and
Richard Johnson. — Washington, D.C.: Center for Applied Linguistics, 1982.
v, 217 p.: ill. Tables on end papers. 1. English language — Phonology
I. Johnson, Richard. II. T.
PE1133.W65   PE1133 W65.   *ISBN* 0872811662

Gleason, Henry Allan, 1917-.   • **2.1014**
An introduction to descriptive linguistics. — Rev. ed. — New York: Holt,
Rinehart and Winston, [1961] 503 p.: illus.; 22 cm. 1. English language —
Phonetics 2. Language and languages I. T. II. Title: Descriptive linguistics.
PE1135.G59 1961   421.5   *LC* 61-8588

Jones, Daniel, 1881-1967.   • **2.1015**
An outline of English phonetics. 8th ed. Cambridge, Heffer, 1956. 378 p. ill. 22
cm. 1. English language — Pronunciation 2. English language — Phonetics
I. T. II. Title: English phonetics.
PE 1135 J77 1957

Kenyon, John Samuel, 1874-.   • **2.1016**
American pronunciation / by John Samuel Kenyon. — 10th ed. — Ann Arbor:
Wahr Pub., 1950, t.p. 1977. 265 p.: ill. 1. English language — Phonetics
2. English language — Pronunciation I. T.
PE1135.K4 1950   PE1135 K46 1950.   421.5   *LC* 51-5688

West, Robert W. (Robert William), 1892-.   • **2.1017**
Phonetics: an introduction to the principles of phonetic science from the point
of view of English speech [by] Claude E. Kantner and Robert West.
Cartographer: Harry S. Wise. — Rev. ed. — New York: Harper [1960] xxii,
433 p.: ill.; 21 cm. Author's names in reverse order in first ed. published in 1933
under title: Kinesiologic phonetics. 1. English language — Phonetics
2. Speech I. Kantner, Claude Edgar, joint author. II. T.
PE1135. W4 1960   421.5   *LC* 60-7010

PE1137–1139 PRONUNCIATION

Bronstein, Arthur J.   • **2.1018**
The pronunciation of American English; an introduction to phonetics. — New
York: Appleton-Century-Crofts, [1960] 320 p.: illus.; 22 cm. 1. English
language — Pronunciation I. T.
PE1137.B77   421.5   *LC* 60-6750

Bullock-Davies, Constance.   • **2.1019**
English pronunciation from the fifteenth to the eighteenth century: a handbook
to the study of historical grammar / selected and edited by Constance Davies.
— London: Dent, 1934. xiii, 167 p.; 23 cm. 1. English language —
Pronunciation 2. English language — Grammar, Historical I. T.
PE1137.B79   421/.52   *LC* 35-9277

Dobson, E. J. (Eric John)   • **2.1020**
English pronunciation 1500–1700, by E. J. Dobson. 2nd ed. Oxford, Clarendon
P., 1968. 2 v. facsims. 25 cm. 1. English language — Pronunciation 2. English
language — Phonology, Historical I. T.
PE1137.D58 1968   421/.55/09031   *LC* 70-351301   *ISBN*
0198119313

Ehrlich, Eugene H.   **2.1021**
NBC handbook of pronunciation. — 4th ed. / revised and updated by Eugene
Ehrlich and Raymond Hand, Jr. — New York: Harper & Row, c1984. 539 p.;
22 cm. Compiled originally by James F. Bender. 1. English language —
Pronunciation — Handbooks, manuals, etc. 2. Television broadcasting —
Handbooks, manuals, etc. 3. Americanisms — Handbooks, manuals, etc.
I. Hand, Raymond. II. Bender, James F. (James Frederick), 1905- NBC
handbook of pronunciation. III. National Broadcasting Company, inc. IV. T.
V. Title: N.B.C. handbook of pronunciation.
PE1137.E52 1984   421/.52/0202 19   *LC* 84-47592   *ISBN*
0061811424

Jones, Daniel, 1881-1967.   • **2.1022**
The pronunciation of English / by Daniel Jones. — 4th ed., rev. & enl. —
Cambridge [Eng.]: University Pr., 1956. xxiv, 223 p.: ill.; 19 cm. 1. English
language — Pronunciation 2. English language — Phonetics 3. Phonetics
I. T.
PE1137.J56 1956   421.5   *LC* 57-129   *ISBN* 0521054486

Kenyon, John Samuel, 1874-.   **2.1023**
Pronouncing dictionary of American English / by John Samuel Kenyon and
Thomas Albert Knott. — 4th ed. Springfield, Mass.: G.&C. Merriam, 1953.
484 p. 1. English language — Pronunciation 2. Americanisms I. Knott,
Thomas Albert, 1880-1945. II. T.
PE1137.K37 1953   421.5   *LC* 53-1416   *ISBN* 0877790477

Lass, Abraham Harold, 1907-.   **2.1024**
Dictionary of pronunciation / Abraham and Betty Lass. New York:
Quadrangle/The New York Times Book Co., c1976. 334 p.; 24 cm. 1. English

language — Pronunciation 2. English language — Dictionaries I. Lass, Betty,
joint author. II. T.
PE1137.L38   428/.1   *LC* 75-36252   *ISBN* 0812906144

PE1141–1153 SPELLING

Scragg, D. G.   **2.1025**
A history of English spelling / D. G. Scragg. — Manchester, [Eng.]:
Manchester University Press; New York: Barnes & Noble Books, 1974. x,
130 p., [3] leaves of plates: ill.; 23 cm. (Mont Follick series. v. 3) Includes
indexes. 1. English language — Orthography and spelling — History. I. T.
II. Series.
PE1141.S3   421/.52   *LC* 75-301767   *ISBN* 0064961389

Hart, John, d. 1574.   • **2.1026**
Works on English orthography and pronunciation; 1551, 1569, 1570. By Bror
Danielsson. Stockholm Almqvist & Wiksell 1955-. (Acta Universitatis
Stockholmiensis. Stockholm studies in English. 5) 1. English language — Early
modern, 1500-1700 — Orthography and spelling 2. English language — Early
modern, 1500-1700 — Pronunciation I. Danielsson, Bror, 1905- ed. II. T.
III. Series.
PE1142 H37   *LC* A 56-4471

Lounsbury, Thomas Raynesford, 1838-1915.   • **2.1027**
English spelling and spelling reform. — Westport, Conn.: Greenwood Press,
[1970] xiii, 356 p.; 23 cm. 'Originally published in 1909.' 1. English language —
Orthography and spelling 2. Spelling reform I. T.
PE1143.L6 1970   421/.52   *LC* 74-109774   *ISBN* 0837142644

Leslie, Louis A., 1900-.   **2.1028**
20,000+ words: spelled and divided for quick reference. — 8th ed. / Charles E.
Zoubek, Gregg A. Condon, Louis A. Leslie. — New York: Gregg Division,
McGraw-Hill, c1986. vi, 281 p.; 15 cm. Rev. ed. of 20,000 words. 7th ed.,
c1977. 1. Spellers I. Zoubek, Charles E., 1913- II. Condon, Gregg A., 1947- III. T.
IV. Title: Twenty thousand plus words.
PE1146.L4 1986   428.1 19   *LC* 85-7802   *ISBN* 0070374627

PE1171–1395 Morphology. Syntax

Joos, Martin.   • **2.1029**
The English verb: form and meanings. — [2d ed.]. — Madison: University of
Wisconsin Press, 1968. x, 251 p.: ill.; 22 cm. 1. English language — Verb I. T.
PE1271.J6 1968   425   *LC* 75-3813

Bolinger, Dwight Le Merton, 1907-.   • **2.1030**
The phrasal verb in English [by] Dwight Bolinger. — Cambridge, Mass.:
Harvard University Press, 1971. xviii, 187 p.; 22 cm. 1. English language —
Verb phrase 2. English language — Syntax I. T.
PE1319.B6   425   *LC* 73-150011   *ISBN* 0674666259

Traugott, Elizabeth Closs.   • **2.1031**
A history of English syntax: a transformational approach to the history of
English sentence structure. — New York: Holt, Rinehart and Winston, [1972]
vii, 216 p.; 24 cm. — (The Transatlantic series in linguistics) 1. English
language — Syntax 2. English language — Grammar, Historical 3. English
language — Grammar, Generative I. T.
PE1361.T7   425   *LC* 73-172650   *ISBN* 0030796008

Fries, Charles Carpenter, 1887-.   • **2.1032**
The structure of English; an introduction to the construction of English
sentences. — New York: Harcourt, Brace, 1952. 304 p.; 22 cm. 1. English
language — Sentences 2. English language — Composition and exercises I. T.
PE1375.F7   425.2   *LC* 52-6440

PE1402–1497 RHETORIC. STYLE.
COMPOSITION

The Rhetorical tradition and modern writing / edited by James   **2.1033**
J. Murphy.
New York: Modern Language Association of America, 1982. vii, 149 p.; 24 cm.
1. English language — Rhetoric — Study and teaching (Higher) — Addresses,
essays, lectures. 2. Rhetoric — History — Addresses, essays, lectures.
I. Murphy, James Jerome.
PE1404.R5 1982   808/.042/07073 19   *LC* 82-2103   *ISBN*
0873520971

Shaughnessy, Mina P.   2.1034
Errors and expectations: a guide for the teacher of basic writing / Mina P. Shaughnessy. New York: Oxford University Press, 1977. viii, 311 p.; 24 cm. Includes index. 1. English language — Rhetoric — Study and teaching I. T.
PE1404.S5   808/.042/0711   LC 76-53701   ISBN 0195021576

Smith, Adam, 1723-1790.   • 2.1035
Lectures on rhetoric and belles lettres, delivered in the University of Glasgow by Adam Smith, reported by a student in 1762–63. Edited with an introd. and notes by John M. Lothian. Foreword by David Potter. — Carbondale: Southern Illinois University Press, [1971] xl, 205 p.: port.; 23 cm. — (Landmarks in rhetoric and public address.) 1. English language — Rhetoric 2. English language — Style 3. Rhetoric, Ancient I. T. II. Series.
PE1407.S47 1971   808   LC 72-145447   ISBN 080930502X

Strunk, William, 1869-1946.   2.1036
The elements of style / by William Strunk, Jr.; with revisions, an introd., and a chapter on writing by E. B. White. — 3d ed. — New York: Macmillan, c1979. xvii, 85 p.; 21 cm. 1. English language — Rhetoric I. White, E. B. (Elwyn Brooks), 1899- II. T.
PE1408.S772 1979   808   LC 78-18444   ISBN 0024182303. ISBN 0024182206 pbk

Gibson, W. Walker.   • 2.1037
Tough, sweet & stuffy: an essay on modern American prose styles. — Bloomington: Indiana University Press, [1966] xii, 179 p.; 21 cm. 1. English language — Style 2. American prose literature — 20th century — History and criticism. I. T.
PE1421.G5   808.0427   LC 66-22449

Joos, Martin.   • 2.1038
The five clocks. With an introd. by Albert H. Marckwardt. — New York: Harcourt, Brace & World, [1967] xiv, 108 p.; 19 cm. — (A Harbinger book) 'HO58.' 1. English language — Style I. T.
PE1421.J65 1967   808.04/2   LC 67-5160

Read, Herbert Edward, Sir, 1893-1968.   • 2.1039
English prose style. [New ed.] New York, Pantheon Books [c1952] 216 p. 22 cm. 1. English language — Style I. T.
PE1421.R35 1952a   808   LC 52-9671

Copperud, Roy H., 1915-.   2.1040
American usage and style, the consensus / Roy H. Copperud. — New York: Van Nostrand Reinhold, c1980. vi, 433 p.; 24 cm. 'This book revises, brings up to date, and consolidates [the author's] two earlier ones: A dictionary of usage and style and American usage.' Includes index. 1. English language — Rhetoric 2. English language in the United States. 3. English language — Dictionaries I. T.
PE1460.C648   428   LC 79-11055   ISBN 0442216300

Gibaldi, Joseph, 1942-.   2.1041
MLA handbook for writers of research papers / Joseph Gibaldi, Walter S. Achtert. — 2nd ed. — New York: Modern Language Association of America, 1984. vii, 221 p.; 22 cm. Rev. ed. of: MLA handbook for writers of research papers, theses, and dissertations. 1st ed. 1977. Includes index. 1. English language — Rhetoric — Handbooks, manuals, etc. 2. Report writing — Handbooks, manuals, etc. 3. Bibliography — Methodology — Handbooks, manuals, etc. 4. Bibliographical citations — Handbooks, manuals, etc. I. Achtert, Walter S. II. Modern Language Association of America. III. Modern Language Association of America. MLA handbook for writers of research papers, theses, and dissertations. IV. T. V. Title: M.L.A. handbook for writers of research papers.
PE1478.M57 1984   808/.02 19   LC 84-10819   ISBN 0873521323

PE1501–1561 Prosody. Versification

Omond, Thomas Stewart, 1846-1923.   • 2.1042
English metrists: being a sketch of English prosodical criticism from Elizabethan times to the present day. — New York: Phaeton Press, 1968. viii, 336 p.; 22 cm. Reprint of the 1921 ed. 1. English language — Versification 2. Criticism — Great Britain. I. T.
PE1501.O53 1968   426   LC 68-15694

Attridge, Derek.   2.1043
The rhythms of English poetry / Derek Attridge. — London; New York: Longman, 1982. xii, 395 p.; 22 cm. — (English language series. 14) Includes index. 1. English language — Versification 2. English language — Rhythm I. T. II. Series.
PE1505.A87 1982   821/009 19   LC 80-42114   ISBN 0582551056

Fussell, Paul, 1924-.   • 2.1044
Theory of prosody in eighteenth–century England. — [Hamden, Conn.] Archon Books, 1966 [c1954. x, 170 p. 23 cm. Bibliographical footnotes. 1. English language — Versification I. T.
PE1505.F8 1966   426   LC 66-23444

Saintsbury, George, 1845-1933.   • 2.1045
A history of English prosody, from the twelfth century to the present day. — [2d ed.]. — New York, Russell & Russell, 1961 [c1923] 3 v. 23 cm. 1. English language — Versification I. T.
PE1505.S163   426.09   LC 60-10708

Stillman, Frances.   2.1046
The poet's manual and rhyming dictionary. Based on The improved rhyming dictionary, by Jane Shaw Whitfield. New York, Crowell [1965] xviii, 387 p. 24 cm. 1. English language — Versification 2. English language — Rhyme — Dictionaries I. Whitfield, Jane Shaw. The improved rhyming dictionary. II. T.
PE1505.S8   426   LC 65-11650

Abrahams, Roger D.   • 2.1047
Jump–rope rhymes: a dictionary / edited by Roger D. Abrahams. — Austin: Published for the American Folklore Society by the University of Texas Press [1969] xxiv, 228 p.; 24 cm. (Publications of the American Folklore Society. Bibliographical and special series, v. 20) 1. Jump rope rhymes 2. English language — Rhyme — Dictionaries I. T.
PE1519.A2   398.8   LC 75-88607   ISBN 0292784007

Lees, Gene.   2.1048
The modern rhyming dictionary: how to write lyrics: including a practical guide to lyric writing for songwriters and poets / Gene Lees. — 1st ed. — Greenwich, CT.: Cherry Lane Books, c1981. 360 p.; 25 cm. 1. English language — Rhyme — Dictionaries I. T.
PE1519.L37   423/.1 19   LC 81-4832   0895241307

Walker, John, 1732-1807.   • 2.1049
The rhyming dictionary of the English language: in which the whole language is arranged according to its terminations with an index of allowable rhymes / by J. Walker. — Rev. and enl. /by Lawrence H. Dawson. London: Routledge & Kegan Paul, 1924. vii, [1], 549 p. Cover title: Walker's rhyming dictionary of the English language. 'With an index of allowable rhymes.' —t.p. 1. English language — Rime — Dictionaries. I. Dawson, Lawrence Hawkins. ed. II. T. III. Title: Walker's rhyming dictionary of the English language.
PE1519.W3 1924   ISBN 0710022476

Wood, Clement, 1888-1950.   • 2.1050
[Unabridged rhyming dictionary] Wood's Unabridged rhyming dictionary, by Clement Wood. Introduction by Ted Robinson. Cleveland, New York, The World publishing company [1943] xv, 1040 p. 25 cm. 1. English language — Rhyme — Dictionaries 2. English language — Versification 3. Poetics I. T. II. Title: Unabridged rhyming dictionary. III. Title: Rhyming dictionary.
PE1519.W62   426.603   LC 43-51188

Saintsbury, George, 1845-1933.   • 2.1051
A History of English prose rhythm / by George Saintsbury. — Bloomington: Indiana University Press, [1965]. xiv, 489 p.; 22 cm. Reprint of the 1912 ed. Includes index. 1. English language — Rhythm 2. English prose literature — History and criticism 3. English language — Style I. T.
PE1561 S3 1965   828.08   LC 65-28662

PE1571–1585 Etymology

Shipley, Joseph Twadell, 1893-.   2.1052
The origins of English words: a discursive dictionary of Indo–European roots / Joseph T. Shipley. — Baltimore: Johns Hopkins University Press, c1984. xxxii, 636 p.; 24 cm. Includes index. 1. English language — Etymology 2. English language — Word formation 3. English language — Roots 4. Indo-European languages — Etymology. I. T.
PE1571.S46 1984   422 19   LC 83-8415   ISBN 0801830044

Davies, Peter, 1940-.   2.1053
Roots, family histories of familiar words / by Peter Davies. — New York: McGraw-Hill, c1981. vii, 216 p.; 24 cm. Includes index. 1. English language — Etymology I. T.
PE1574.D3   422 19   LC 80-24118   ISBN 007015449X

Funk, Charles Earle, 1881-1957.   • 2.1054
Thereby hangs a tale: stories of curious word origins / Charles Earle Funk. — New York: Harper, 1950. xii, 303 p. –. Includes index. 1. English language — Etymology I. T.
PE1574.F78   LC 50-6750

Greenough, J. B. (James Bradstreet), 1833-1901.   • **2.1055**
Words and their ways in English speech / James Bradstreet Greenough and George Lyman Kittredge; [with a new introd. by Simeon Potter] — Boston: Beacon Press [1962] xv, 431 p.; 21 cm. (Beacon paperbacks. BP136) 1. English language — Etymology 2. English language — History I. Kittredge, George Lyman, 1860-1941. joint author. II. T. III. Series.
PE1574.G8 1962   LC 62-5068

Partridge, Eric, 1894-.   • **2.1056**
A charm of words; essays and papers on language. — New York, Macmillan [1961, c1960] 190 p. 22 cm. 1. English language — Etymology 2. English language — Style 3. English language — Addresses, essays, lectures. I. T.
PE1574.P26 1961   422   LC 61-4951

Klein, Ernest.   • **2.1057**
A comprehensive etymological dictionary of the English language; dealing with the origin of words and their sense development thus illustrating the history of civilization and culture. — Unabridged, one vol. ed. — Amsterdam; New York: Elsevier Pub. Co., 1971. xxv, 845 p.; 30 cm. 1. English language — Etymology — Dictionaries I. T.
PE1580.K47 1971   422/.03   LC 73-172090   ISBN 0444409300

Morris, William, 1913-.   **2.1058**
Morris Dictionary of word and phrase origins / William and Mary Morris; foreword by Edwin Newman. — 1st ed. — New York: Harper & Row, c1977. x, 654 p.; 25 cm. 'Four-in-one volume of Dictionary of word and phrase origins' which includes vols. 1-3 previously published 1962-1972. Includes index. 1. English language — Etymology — Dictionaries 2. English language — Terms and phrases I. Morris, Mary, 1913- joint author. II. T. III. Title: Dictionary of word and phrase origins.
PE1580.M6 1977   422/.03   LC 77-3763   ISBN 006013058X

Onions, C. T. (Charles Talbut), 1873-1965. ed.   • **2.1059**
The Oxford dictionary of English etymology / edited by C. T. Onions with the assistance of G. W. S. Friedrichsen and R. W. Burchfield. Oxford: Clarendon P., 1966. xvi, 1025 p. 1. English language — Etymology — Dictionaries I. Friedrichen, George Washington Salisbury II. Burchfield, R. W. III. T.
PE1580.O5   422.03   LC 66-71621

Partridge, Eric, 1894-.   • **2.1060**
Origins; a short etymological dictionary of modern English. [3d ed.] New York, Macmillan, 1963 [c1961] xix, 972 p. 26 cm. 1. English language — Etymology — Dictionaries I. T.
PE1580.P3 1963   LC 64-2188

Skeat, Walter W. (Walter William), 1835-1912.   • **2.1061**
A concise etymological dictionary of the English language. Oxford, The Clarendon press, 1911. xv, [1], 663, [1] p. 20 cm. 1. English language — Etymology — Dictionaries I. T.
PE1580.S52 1911   LC 11-35890

Weekley, Ernest, 1865-1954.   • **2.1062**
A concise etymological dictionary of modern English. Rev. ed. New York: Dutton, 1952. xv, 480 p.; 21 cm. 1. English language — Etymology — Dictionaries I. T.
PE 1580 W39   LC 52-4616

Geipel, John, 1937-.   **2.1063**
The Viking legacy: the Scandinavian influence on the English and Gaelic languages. — [S.l.]: Rowman and Littlefield, 1972 (c1971). 225 p.,: ill.; maps.; 23 cm. 1. English language — Foreign elements — Scandinavian. 2. Gaelic language — Foreign elements — Scandinavian. I. T.
PE1582.S3 G4   422/.4/395   LC 75-863444   ISBN 0715349600

Partridge, Eric, 1894-.   • **2.1064**
Name into word; proper names that have become common property; a discursive dictionary; with a foreword. [2d ed.] New York, Macmillan, 1950. xv, 648 p. 22 cm. 1. English language — Etymology — Dictionaries 2. Names, English I. T.
PE1583.P35 1950a   LC 53-31511

Empson, William, 1906-.   • **2.1065**
The structure of complex words. [New York] New Directions [1951] 449 p. 23 cm. 1. English language — Semantics 2. English literature — History and criticism I. T.
PE1585.E6   422   LC 51-12406

Hayakawa, S. I. (Samuel Ichiyé), 1906-.   • **2.1066**
Language in thought and action / [by] S. I. Hayakawa; in consultation with Leo Hamalian and Geoffrey Wagner. — 2d ed. New York: Harcourt, Brace & World [c1964] xvii, 350 p.; 22 cm. 1. English language — Semantics I. T.
PE1585.H36 1964   425   LC 64-10333

Ullmann, Stephen.   • **2.1067**
Words and their use. New York Philosophical Library [1951] 108;2p. (Man and society series) 1. Semantics 2. English language — Semantics I. T.
PE1585.U44   LC 51-3031

PE1591–1596 Synonyms. Antonyms. Eponyms

The Random House thesaurus / edited by Jess Stein and Stuart Berg Flexner.   **2.1068**
College ed. — New York: Random House, c1984. 812 p.; 25 cm. 'Based upon the Reader's digest Family word finder, c1975'—T.p. verso. 1. English language — Synonyms and antonyms I. Stein, Jess M. II. Flexner, Stuart Berg. III. Random House (Firm) IV. Family word finder.
PE1591.R28 1984   423/.1 19   LC 84-4914   ISBN 0394529499

Roget, Peter Mark, 1779-1869.   • **2.1069**
Thesaurus of English words and phrases. — New ed., completely rev. and modernized by Robert A. Dutch. — New York: St. Martin's Press, [1964, c1962] lii, 1309 p.; 23 cm. 1. English language — Synonyms and antonyms I. Dutch, Robert A., ed. II. T.
PE1591.R7 1964   423/.1   LC 64-23442

Roget, Peter Mark, 1779-1869.   **2.1070**
[Thesaurus of English words and phrases] Roget's Thesaurus of English words and phrases. — New ed. / prepared by Susan M. Lloyd. — Harlow, Essex: Longman, 1982. xxxxxii, 1247 p.; 23 cm. Includes index. 1. English language — Synonyms and antonyms I. Lloyd, Susan M. II. T. III. Title: Thesaurus of English words and phrases.
PE1591.R7 1982   423/.1 19   LC 82-201294   ISBN 058255635X

Roget's international thesaurus.   • **2.1071**
[1st] - ed. New York, Crowell. [1911 -. v.; 24-28 cm. Title varies: 1911 The Standard thesaurus of English words and phrases. Editor: 1911-39, C.O.S. Mawson
PE1591.R73   LC 62-12806   ISBN 0690708904

Webster's collegiate thesaurus.   **2.1072**
1st ed. — Springfield, Mass.: G. & C. Merriam Co., 1976. 32, 944 p.; 26 cm. 1. English language — Synonyms and antonyms
PE1591.W38   423/.1   LC 75-45167   ISBN 0877790698

Webster's new dictionary of synonyms; a dictionary of discriminated synonyms with antonyms and analogous and contrasted words.   • **2.1073**
Springfield, Mass.: Merriam, [1968] 31a, 909 p.; 26 cm. Based on the unabridged Webster's Third New International Dictionary. Previously published under title: Webster's dictionary of synonyms. 1. English language — Synonyms and antonyms
PE1591.W4 1968   LC 68-5579

Eponyms dictionaries index / edited by James A. Ruffner, associate editors, Jennifer Berger, Georgia Schoenung.   **2.1074**
Detroit: Gale Research Co., c1977. xxviii, 730 p.; 29 cm. 1. English language — Eponyms — Dictionaries. 2. Biography I. Ruffner, James A. II. Berger, Jennifer. III. Schoenung, Georgia.
PE1596.E6   423/.1   LC 76-20341   ISBN 0810306883

PE1601–1693 Lexicography. Dictionaries

Friend, Joseph H.   • **2.1075**
The development of American lexicography 1798–1864. The Hague, Paris, Mouton, 1967. 132 p. photos. (Janua linguarum. Series practica, 37) 1. English language — Lexicography I. T.
PE1611.F7   423   LC 67-27205

Partridge, Eric, 1894-.   • **2.1076**
The gentle art of lexicography as pursued and experienced by an addict. New York: Macmillan [1963] 119 p.; 23 cm. 1. English language — Lexicography I. T.
PE1611.P3 1963a   LC 63-12833

Starnes, De Witt Talmage, 1888-1967.   • **2.1077**
The English dictionary from Cawdrey to Johnson, 1604–1755, by De Witt T. Starnes ... and Gertrude E. Noyes ... — Chapel Hill, The University of North Carolina press, 1946. x p., 1 l., 299 p. facsims. 23.5 cm. 'Bibliography and

census of dictionaries in American libraries': p. 228-241. 1. English language — Lexicography I. Noyes, Gertrude Elizabeth, 1905- joint author. II. T.
PE1611.S68   423   *LC* 46-5776

Sledd, James H.   • **2.1078**
Dr. Johnson's Dictionary; essays in the biography of a book, by James H. Sleed and Gwin J. Kolb. — [Chicago] University of Chicago Press [1955] 255 p. illus. 22 cm. 1. Johnson, Samuel, 1709-1784. A dictionary of the English language. I. Kolb, Gwin J. II. T.
PE1617.J7S7   423   *LC* 55-5145

Johnson, Samuel, 1709-1784.   **2.1079**
Dictionary of the English language / Samuel Johnson. — New York: Arno Press, 1979. ca. 1350 p. in various pagings; 40 cm. Reprint of the 1755 ed. printed by W. Strahan, London. 1. English language — Dictionaries. I. T.
PE1620.J6 1979   423   *LC* 79-14941   *ISBN* 0405124147

PE1625–1691 Dictionaries

The American Heritage dictionary of the English language /   • **2.1080**
William Morris, editor.
[New York]: American Heritage Pub. Co. [1969] l, 1550 p.: ill., maps, ports. 29 cm. 1. English language — Dictionaries I. Morris, William, 1913- ed.
PE1625.A54   423   *LC* 76-86995   *ISBN* 0395090660

The New Century cyclopedia of names, edited by Clarence L.   • **2.1081**
Barnhart with the assistance of William D. Halsey and a staff of more than 350 consulting scholars, special editors, and other contributors.
New York: Appleton-Century-Crofts, [1954] 3 v. (xxviii, 4342 p.); 28 cm. 1. Geography — Dictionaries 2. Biography — Dictionaries. 3. Names — Dictionaries. I. Barnhart, Clarence Lewis, 1900- ed.
PE1625.C43 1954   929.4   *LC* 52-13879

The Concise Oxford dictionary of current English: based on the   **2.1082**
Oxford English dictionary and its supplements / first edited by
H.W. Fowler and F.G. Fowler.
7th ed. / edited by J.B. Sykes. — Oxford: Clarendon Press, c1982, 1984. xx, 1258 p.; 23 cm. 1. English language — Dictionaries I. Sykes, J. B. (John Bradbury) II. Fowler, Henry Watson, 1858-1933. III. Title: Oxford English dictionary.
PE1625.C65 1982   PE1628.F6 1982.   423

Little, William, 1848-1922.   **2.1083**
The shorter Oxford English dictionary on historical principles / prepared by William Little, H. W. Fowler and Jessie Coulson; revised and edited by C. T. Onions. — 3rd. ed.; completely reset with etymologies revised by G. W. S. Friedrichsen and with revised addenda. Oxford: Clarendon Press, 1973. xxix, 2672 p.; 28 cm. 'An abridgement officially authorized by the Delegates of the Oxford University Press of A new English dictionary on historical principles, later known as The Oxford English dictionary.' 1. English language — Dictionaries I. Fowler, H. W. (Henry Watson), 1858-1933, joint author. II. Coulson, Jessie Senior, 1903- joint author. III. Onions, C. T. (Charles Talbut), 1873-1965. ed. IV. Friedrichsen, George Washington Salisbury. V. T. VI. Title: Oxford English dictionary.
PE1625.L53 1973   423   *LC* 74-174806   *ISBN* 0198611161

The Oxford English dictionary; being a corrected reissue with   • **2.1084**
an introduction, supplement, and bibliography of A new English dictionary on historical principles, founded mainly on the materials collected by the Philogical society and edited by James A. H. Murray [and others]
Oxford, At the Clarendon press, 1933. 13 v. 32 cm. Vol. 13 ('Supplement and bibliography') unnumbered. 'A list of books quoted in the Oxford English dictionary': [v. 13], 91 p. at end. 1. English language — Dictionaries I. Murray, James Augustus Henry, Sir, 1837-1915. ed. II. Philological Society (Great Britain)
PE1625.N53 1933   423   *LC* A 33-3399 Rev 2

A Supplement to the Oxford English dictionary / edited by   **2.1085**
R.W. Burchfield.
Oxford [Oxfordshire]: Clarendon Press, 1972- < 1986 >. v. < 1-4 >; 31 cm. 1. English language — Dictionaries I. Burchfield, R. W. II. Title: Oxford English dictionary.
PE1625.N53 1933 Suppl   423 19   *LC* 82-6411   *ISBN* 0198611153

The Random House dictionary of the English language / Jess   **2.1086**
Stein, editor in chief, Laurence Urdang, managing editor.
Unabridged ed. — New York: Random House, c1981. xxxii, 2059 p., 64 p. of plates: ill. (some col.); 32 cm. — (Random House dictionaries.) 1. English language — Dictionaries I. Stein, Jess M. II. Urdang, Laurence. III. Series.
PE1625.R3 1981   423 19   *LC* 82-143767   *ISBN* 0394471768

The Random House college dictionary.   **2.1087**
Rev. ed. — New York: Random House, 1975. xxxii, 1568 p.: ill.; 26 cm. Based on the Random House dictionary of the English language, unabridged ed. Published in 1968 under title: The Random House dictionary of the English language, college ed. 1. English language — Dictionaries
PE1625.R34 1975   423   *LC* 75-4858   *ISBN* 0394435001

Webster's third new international dictionary of the English   • **2.1088**
language, unabridged: A Merriam–Webster / editor in chief:
Philip Babcock Gove and the Merriam–Webster editorial staff.
Springfield, Mass.: G. & C. Merriam Co., [1961] 56a, 2662 p.: ill. (part col.) col. port.; 34 cm. 1. English language — Dictionaries I. Gove, Philip Babcock, 1902-1972. ed.
PE1625.W36 1961   423   *LC* 61-65336

The American college dictionary / C.L. Barnhart, editor in   • **2.1089**
chief; Jess Stein, managing editor; assisted and advised by 355 authorities and specialists.
New York: Random House, [c1963] xxviii, 1444 p.: ill.; 26 cm. 'Newly revised.'- Dust jacket. 1. English language — Dictionaries I. Barnhart, Clarence Lewis, 1900- ed.
PE1628A55 1963   *LC* 63-12822

Fowler, Henry Watson, 1858-1933.   • **2.1090**
A dictionary of modern English usage / by H. W. Fowler. — 2d ed. rev. by Sir Ernest Gowers. — Oxford: Clarendon Press, 1965. xx, 725 p. 'Reprinted with corrections.' 1. English language 2. English language — Idioms, corrections, errors. I. Gowers, Ernest, Sir, 1880-1966. ed. II. T. III. Title: Modern English usage.
PE1628.F65 1965   *LC* 65-2840/r

Webster's New World dictionary of the American language /   **2.1091**
David B. Guralnik, editor in chief.
2nd college ed. — New York: Prentice Hall Press, c1986. xxxvi, 1692 p.: ill.; 25 cm. 1. English language — Dictionaries 2. Americanisms — Dictionaries. I. Guralnik, David Bernard, 1920-
PE1628.W5633 1986   423 19   *LC* 85-26216   *ISBN* 0671418092

Webster's ninth new collegiate dictionary.   **2.1092**
Springfield, Mass.: Merriam-Webster, c1983. 1563 p.: ill.; 26 cm. Based on Webster's third new international dictionary. Rev. ed. of: Webster's new collegiate dictionary. c1981. Includes index. 1. English language — Dictionaries I. Merriam-Webster, Inc. II. Webster's new collegiate dictionary. III. Title: Ninth new collegiate dictionary.
PE1628.W5638 1983   423 19   *LC* 82-20801   *ISBN* 0877795088

12,000 words: a supplement to Webster's third new international   **2.1093**
dictionary.
Springfield, Mass.: Merriam-Webster, c1986. 24, 212 p.; 25 cm. 1. Words, New — English — Dictionaries. 2. English language — Dictionaries I. Webster's third new international dictionary of the English language, unabridged. II. Title: Twelve thousand words.
PE1630.A17 1986   423 19   *LC* 86-12598   *ISBN* 0877792070

The Barnhart dictionary of new English since 1963. [Edited by]   • **2.1094**
Clarence L. Barnhart, Sol Steinmetz [and] Robert K. Barnhart.
[1st ed.]. — Bronxville, N.Y.: Barnhart/Harper & Row, [1973] 512 p.; 25 cm. 1. Words, New — English — Dictionaries. I. Barnhart, Clarence Lewis, 1900- ed. II. Steinmetz, Sol. ed. III. Barnhart, Robert K. ed.
PE1630.B3   423   *LC* 73-712   *ISBN* 0060102233

The Second Barnhart dictionary of new English / [edited by]   **2.1095**
Clarence L. Barnhart, Sol Steinmetz, Robert K. Barnhart.
1st ed. — Bronxville, N.Y.: Barnhart Books, c1980. xv, 520 p.; 25 cm. Published in 1973 under title: The Barnhart dictionary of new English since 1963. 1. Words, New — English — Dictionaries. I. Barnhart, Clarence Lewis, 1900- II. Steinmetz, Sol. III. Barnhart, Robert K. IV. Title: Barnhart dictionary of new English since 1963.
PE1630.B3 1980   423 19   *LC* 80-65573   *ISBN* 0060101547

BBC pronouncing dictionary of British names / edited and   **2.1096**
transcribed by G.E. Pointon.
2nd ed. — Oxford; New York: Oxford University Press, 1983. xxvii, 274 p.; 18 cm. 1. Names, English — Pronunciation — Dictionaries. 2. Names — Great Britain — Pronunciation — Dictionaries. I. Pointon, G. E. (Graham E.) II. British Broadcasting Corporation. III. Title: B.B.C. pronouncing dictionary of British names.
PE1660.B3 1983   423/.1 19   *LC* 83-4097   *ISBN* 0192129767

Bliss, Alan Joseph.   • **2.1097**
A dictionary of foreign words and phrases in current English [by] A. J. Bliss. — New York: Dutton, [1966] ix, 389 p.; 23 cm. 1. English language — Foreign words and phrases — Dictionaries I. T.
PE1670.B55 1966a   423.1   *LC* 66-8411

Carroll, David, 1942-.	2.1098
The dictionary of foreign terms in the English language. — New York: Hawthorn Books, [1973] ix, 212 p.; 25 cm. 1. English language — Foreign words and phrases — Dictionaries I. T.
PE1670.C3 1973	422/.4	LC 70-39281

Guinagh, Kevin, 1897-.	2.1099
Dictionary of foreign phrases and abbreviations / translated and compiled by Kevin Guinagh. — 3rd ed. — New York: H.W. Wilson Co., 1983. xix, 261 p.; 24 cm. 1. English language — Foreign words and phrases — Dictionaries I. T.
PE1670.G8 1983	422/.4/03 19	LC 82-8486	ISBN 0824206754

Mawson, C. O. Sylvester (Christopher Orlando Sylvester), 1870-1938.	2.1100
Dictionary of foreign terms. Rev. and updated by Charles Berlitz. — 2d ed. — New York: Crowell, [1975] x, 368 p.; 22 cm. Previously published under title: Dictionary of foreign terms found in English and American writings of yesterday and today. 1. English language — Foreign words and phrases — Dictionaries I. Berlitz, Charles Frambach, 1913- II. T.
PE1670.M3 1975	422/.4	LC 74-12492	ISBN 0690001711

Morris, William, 1913-.	2.1101
Harper dictionary of contemporary usage / William and Mary Morris; with the assistance of a panel of 166 distinguished consultants on usage. — 2nd ed. — New York: Harper & Row, c1985. xxx, 641 p.; 24 cm. 1. English language — Terms and phrases 2. English language — Errors of usage — Dictionaries. I. Morris, Mary, 1913- II. Harper & Row, Publishers. III. T. IV. Title: Dictionary of contemporary usage.
PE1680.M59 1985	423/.1 19	LC 83-48797	ISBN 006181606X

–ologies & –isms / Laurence Urdang, editor in chief; Anne Ryle and Tanya H. Lee, editors; Frank R. Abate, associate editor.	2.1102
3rd ed. — Detroit, Mich.: Gale Research Co., c1986. 795 p.; 24 cm. 'A Laurence Urdang reference book.' Includes index. 1. English language — Reverse indexes 2. Learning and scholarship — Dictionaries. I. Urdang, Laurence. II. Ryle, Anne. III. Lee, Tanya H. IV. Title: -ologies and -isms.
PE1680.O4 1986	423/.1 19	LC 85-31217	ISBN 0810311968

Idioms and phrases index / Laurence Urdang, editor in chief; foreword by Richard W. Bailey.	2.1103
1st ed. — Detroit, Mich.: Gale Research Co., c1983. 3 v. (xix, 1691 p.); 29 cm. 'An unrivaled collection of idioms, phrases, expressions, and collocutions of two or more words which are part of the English lexicon and for which the meaning of the whole is not transparent from the sum of the meanings of the constituent parts, also including nominal, verbal, and other phrases which exhibit syntactic and semantic character peculiar to the English language, the entries gathered from more than thirty sources, each described in the bibliography provided, with all items arranged alphabetically both by first word and any significant words.' 1. English language — Terms and phrases 2. English language — Idioms — Dictionaries I. Urdang, Laurence.
PE1689.I3 1983	423/.1 19	LC 83-17192	ISBN 0810315475

Longman dictionary of English idioms / [editorial director, Thomas Hill Long].	2.1104
Harlow [Eng.]: Longman, 1979. xx, 387 p.; 23 cm. Text on lining papers. 1. English language — Idioms I. Long, T. H.
PE1689.L66	423/.1 19	LC 80-512672	ISBN 0582555248

Oxford dictionary of current idiomatic English.	2.1105
London: Oxford University Press, 1975-1983. 2 v.; 23 cm. Includes indexes. 1. English language — Idioms — Dictionaries I. Cowie, Anthony Paul. II. Mackin, Ronald. III. McCaig, I. R. (Isabel R.)
PE1689.O94	423/.1	LC 77-351530	ISBN 0194311457

Picturesque expressions: a thematic dictionary / Laurence Urdang, editorial director; Nancy LaRoche, editor in chief.	2.1106
Detroit, Mich.: Gale Research Co., c1980. 408 p.; 24 cm. Includes index. 1. English language — Terms and phrases 2. Figures of speech 3. English language — Etymology I. Urdang, Laurence. II. LaRoche, Nancy.
PE1689.P5	428.3 19	LC 80-22705	ISBN 0810311224

Wall, C. Edward.	• 2.1107
Words and phrases index: a guide to antedatings, new words, new compounds, new meanings, and other published scholarship supplementing the Oxford English dictionary, Dictionary of Americanisms, Dictionary of American English, and other major dictionaries of the English language / compiled by C. Edward Wall and Edward Przebienda. — Ann Arbor, Mich.: Pierian Press, 1969-. v.	; 29 cm. 1. English language — Terms and phrases — Indexes. 2. English language — Dictionaries I. Przebienda, Edward, joint author. II. T.
PE1689.W3	016.423	LC 68-58894

PE1693 Abbreviations

De Sola, Ralph, 1908-.	2.1108
Abbreviations dictionary / Ralph De Sola. — Augm. international 7th ed. — New York: Elsevier, c1986. xviii, 1240 p.; 24 cm. Subtitle: Abbreviations, acronyms, airlines, appelations, astronomical terminology, bafflegab divulged (euphemisms explained), birthstones, British and Irish county abbreviations, Canadian Provinces, chemical elements, Citizens-band call signs, computer jargon, contractions, criminalistic terms, data processing, diacritical marks, Dysphemistic place-names, earthquake data, eponyms, fishing ports, geographical equivalents, government agencies, Greek alphabet, historical, musical, and mythological data, international conversions, international vehicle license letters, medical terms, nations, nicknames, numbered abbreviations, numeration, ports of the world, prisons of the world, railroads, Roman numerals, Russian alphabet, short forms, short cuts, signs & symbols, slang, steamship lines, superlatives, weather symbols (Beaufort scale), wedding anniversaries, winds of the world, zip coding, zodiac. 1. Abbreviations, English — Dictionaries. 2. Acronyms — Dictionaries. 3. Signs and symbols — Dictionaries. I. T.
PE1693.D4 1986	423/.1 19	LC 85-1595	ISBN 0444008071

PE1700–3601 DIALECTS. AMERICANISMS

English as a world language / edited by Richard W. Bailey and Manfred Görlach.	2.1109
Ann Arbor: University of Michigan Press, c1982. viii, 496 p.: maps; 26 cm. Includes index. 1. English language — Variation 2. English language — Dialects 3. English language — Foreign countries 4. Communication, International I. Bailey, Richard W. II. Görlach, Manfred.
PE1700.E5 1982	420/.9 19	LC 81-21904	ISBN 0472100165

Wakelin, Martyn Francis.	2.1110
English dialects: an introduction [by] Martyn F. Wakelin. — London: Athlone Press, 1972. xvi, 207 p.: maps.; 23 cm. Distributed by Humanities Press, New York. 1. English language — Dialects I. T.
PE1702.W3	427	LC 73-151515	ISBN 0485111365

The Linguistic atlas of England / edited by Harold Orton, Stewart Sanderson, and John Widdowson.	2.1111
London: Croom Helm; Atlantic Highlands, N.J.: Humanities Press, c1978. ca. 450 p.: maps; 36 cm. Includes index. 1. English language — Dialects — England — Maps. I. Orton, Harold, 1898-1975. II. Sanderson, Stewart. III. Widdowson, J. D. A. (John David Allison)
PE1705.L56	912/.1/427	LC 79-304375	ISBN 0391007599

Wells, J. C. (John Christopher)	2.1112
Accents of English / J.C. Wells. — Cambridge [Cambridgeshire]; New York: Cambridge University Press, 1982. 3 v.: ill.; 23 cm. Includes index. 1. English language — Dialects 2. English language — Variation 3. English language — Phonology I. T.
PE1711.W4	427 19	LC 81-10127	ISBN 0521229197

Wright, Joseph, 1855-1930. ed.	• 2.1113
The English dialect dictionary. London, H. Frowde [1898-1905] 6 v. 32 cm. 1. English language — Dialects 2. English language — Dictionaries I. T.
PE1766.W8 1962	LC 65-5677

Survey of English dialects / [edited] by Harold Orton and Eugen Dieth.	• 2.1114
[Leeds: Published for the University of Leeds by E. J. Arnold, 1962-. v.: maps.; 24 cm. Results of a survey carried out from the Dept. of English Language and Medieval English Literature in 1960-61. 1. English language — Dialects — England, North. I. Orton, Harold, 1898-1975. ed. II. Dieth, Eugen, 1893-1956, ed. III. Leeds, Eng. University. Dept. of English Language and Medieval English Literature.
PE1771.S8	LC 67-6774

Chambers, R. W. (Raymond Wilson), 1874-1942. ed.	• 2.1115
A book of London English, 1384–1425, edited by R. W. Chambers & Marjorie Daunt; with an appendix on English documents in the Record office by M. M. Weale. Oxford, The Clarendon press, 1931. 395, [1] p. 20 cm. 1. English language — Dialects — London. 2. English language — Middle English, 1100-1500 — Readers. 3. London (England) — History — Sources. I. Daunt, Marjorie, joint ed. II. Weale, Magdalene Marie. III. T. IV. Title: London English, 1384-1425.
PE1963.C5	427.1	LC 32-2701

The Concise Scots dictionary / editor-in-chief, Mairi Robinson.	2.1116
Aberdeen: Aberdeen University Press, 1985. xli, 819 p.: ill.; 24 cm. 1. Scots language — Dictionaries. I. Robinson, Mairi.
PE2106.C66 1985	427/.9411 19	LC 85-212232	ISBN 0080284914

Craigie, William A. (William Alexander), Sir, 1867-1957.   • 2.1117
A dictionary of the older Scottish tongue: from the twelfth century to the end of
the seventeenth / by Sir William A. Craigie. — Chicago, Ill.: The University of
Chicago Press; London: H. Milford, Oxford University Press [1937-. v.; 30 cm.
1. English language — Dialects — Scottish — Dictionaries. I. T.
PE2116.C7   427/.9411 19   LC 38-21689

Platt, John Talbot.   2.1118
The new Englishes: what are they? / John Platt, Heidi Weber, Ho Mian Lian.
— London; Boston: Routledge & Kegan Paul, 1984. viii, 225 p.: ill.; 23 cm.
Includes index. 1. English language — Foreign countries 2. English language
— Study and teaching — Foreign speakers 3. Bilingualism 4. English language
— Variation 5. Languages in contact I. Weber, Heidi. II. Ho, Mian Lian.
III. T.
PE2751.P57 1984   427 19   LC 83-26888   ISBN 0710099509

PE2801–3102 United States

Atwood, Elmer Bagby, 1906-.   • 2.1119
A survey of verb forms in the eastern United States / E. Bagby Atwood. — Ann
Arbor, Mich.: University of Michigan Press, c1953. viii, 53 p.: maps; 29 cm. —
(Studies in American English; 2) 1. English language — Verb I. T.
PE2802.M53 v.2   LC 53-7458

Kurath, Hans, 1891-.   • 2.1120
A word geography of the eastern United states. [Ann Arbor] University of
Michigan Press, 1949. x, 88 p. 163 (i.e. 164) maps. 29 cm. 1. English language
— Maps 2. Americanisms 3. English language — Provincialisms — Atlantic
States I. T.
PE2802.M53 vol. 1   LC 49-50233

Kurath, Hans, 1891-.   • 2.1121
The pronunciation of English in the Atlantic States; based upon the collections
of the linguistic atlas of the Eastern United States. By Hans Kurath [and] Raven
I. McDavid, Jr. Ann Arbor, University of Michigan Press [1961] xi, 182 p. 180
maps, tables. 29 cm. (Studies in American English; 3) 1. English language —
Dialects — Atlantic States. 2. English language — Pronunciation I. McDavid,
Raven Ioor. joint author. II. T. III. Series.
PE2802.M53 vol. 3   427.973   LC 60-5671

Craigie, William A. (William Alexander), Sir, 1867-1957.   • 2.1122
The growth of American English. Westport, Conn., Greenwood Press [1971]
200-264 p. 23 cm. 'Originally published in 1940 as S.P.E. Tracts LVI and LVII
of the Society for Pure English.' 1. English language in the United States. I. T.
PE2808.C7 1971   422   LC 74-109967   ISBN 0837144698

Daniels, Harvey A.   2.1123
Famous last words: the American language crisis reconsidered / Harvey A.
Daniels. — Carbondale: Southern Illinois University Press, c1983. vii, 295 p.;
24 cm. Includes index. 1. English language — United States 2. English
language — Usage 3. English language — Variation I. T.
PE2808.D3 1983   427/.973 19   LC 82-10281   ISBN 0809310554

Krapp, George Philip, 1872-1934.   • 2.1124
The English language in America. — New York, F. Ungar Pub. Co. [1960] 2 v.
24 cm. 1. English language — History 2. Americanisms I. T.
PE2808.K7 1960   427.97   LC 60-9103

Laird, Charlton Grant, 1901-.   • 2.1125
Language in America [by] Charlton Laird. — New York: World Pub. Co.,
[1970] x, 543 p.: illus., maps.; 24 cm. 1. English language in the United States.
2. America — Languages I. T.
PE2808.L3   420/.973   LC 68-29790

Marckwardt, Albert Henry, 1903-1975.   2.1126
American English / Albert H. Marckwardt; revised by J.L. Dillard. — 2d ed.
— New York: Oxford University Press, 1980. xi, 192 p.; 22 cm. Includes index.
1. English language in the United States. 2. English language — History
I. Dillard, J. L. (Joey Lee), 1924- II. T.
PE2808.M3 1980   420/.973   LC 79-27599   ISBN 0195026004

Mencken, H. L. (Henry Louis), 1880-1956.   • 2.1127
The American language; an inquiry into the development of English in the
United States. 4th ed. corr., enl. and rewritten. New York: Knopf, 1936. 769,
xxix p. bibl. 1. English language 2. Americanisms 3. Names — United States.
4. Names, Personal — United States. I. T.
PE2808.M43 1936   420.9   LC 36-27236

Wolfram, Walt, 1941-.   2.1128
The study of social dialects in American English [by] Walt Wolfram [and]
Ralph W. Fasold. Englewood Cliffs, N.J., Prentice-Hall [1974] xv, 239 p. illus.
24 cm. 1. English language in the United States. 2. English language —

Dialects 3. Speech and social status — United States. 4. Linguistics —
Research — United States. I. Fasold, Ralph W. joint author. II. T.
PE2808.W6   301.2/1   LC 74-782   ISBN 0138587876

Dillard, J. L. (Joey Lee), 1924-.   2.1129
All-American English / J. L. Dillard. — 1st ed. — New York: Random House,
[1975] xiii, 369 p.; 24 cm. Includes index. 1. English language in the United
States — History. I. T.
PE2809.D54   420/.9   LC 74-26995   ISBN 0394489659

Dillard, J. L. (Joey Lee), 1924-.   2.1130
Toward a social history of American English / by J.L. Dillard; with a chapter
on Appalachian English by Linda L. Blanton. — Berlin; New York: Mouton,
c1985. vii, 301 p.; 24 cm. (Contributions to the sociology of language. 39)
1. English language — United States — History. 2. English language —
United States — Social aspects. 3. English language — Dialects —
Appalachian Region. I. T. II. Series.
PE2809.D544 1985   420/.973 19   LC 84-20644   ISBN 3110105845

Francis, W. Nelson (Winthrop Nelson), 1910-.   • 2.1131
The structure of American English. With a chapter on American English
dialects by Raven I. McDavid, Jr. New York, Ronald Press Co. [1958] vii,
614 p. illus. 22 cm. 1. English language in the United States — Grammar —
1950- 2. Language and languages I. T.
PE2811.F67   425   LC 58-5647

Fries, Charles Carpenter, 1887-.   • 2.1132
American English grammar: the grammatical structure of present-day
American English with especial reference to social differences or class dialects /
by Charles Carpenter Fries. — New York; London: D. Appleton-Century Co.,
[c1940] viii p., 2 l., 313 p.: diagrs.; 24 cm. — (Half-title: National council of
teachers of English. English monograph. no. 10) The report of an investigation
financed by the National Council of teachers of English and supported by the
Modern language association and the Linguistic society of America. 1. English
language — Grammar 2. Americanisms I. T.
PE2811.F7   425   LC 41-347

Krapp, George Philip, 1872-1934.   • 2.1133
The pronunciation of standard English in America. New York: AMS Press,
[1969] xv, 235 p.; 23 cm. Reprint of the 1919 ed. 1. English language in the
United States. 2. English language — Pronunciation I. T.
PE2815.K7 1969   421/.54   LC 76-97891

Pike, Kenneth Lee, 1912-.   • 2.1134
The intonation of American English / by Kenneth L. Pike. Ann Arbor:
University of Michigan press, [1963, c1945] xi, 200 p.: ill. (diagrs.); 27x21 cm.
(Half-title: University of Michigan publications. Linguistics. Vol. I)
'Lithoprinted.' 'Largely an expansion and revision of materials which were
published in the author's Pronunciation, vol. I of An intensive course in English
for Latin-American students by the English language institute of the University
of Michigan.' Bibliography: p. 191-200. 1. English language — Intonation
I. T.
PE2815.P5x   421.6   LC A 45-4529

Craigie, William A. (William Alexander), Sir, 1867-1957. ed.   • 2.1135
A dictionary of American English on historical principles, compiled at the
University of Chicago under the editorship of Sir William A. Craigie ... and
James R. Hulbert. Chicago, Ill., University of Chicago Press [1938-44] 4 v. 31
cm. Paged continuously. 1. English language in the United States —
Dictionaries. 2. Americanisms I. Hulbert, James Root, 1884- joint ed. II. T.
PE2835.C72   427.9   LC 39-8203

A Dictionary of Americanisms on historical principles, edited by   • 2.1136
Mitford M. Mathews.
Chicago: University of Chicago Press, [1956, c1951] xvi, 1946 p.: illus.; 29 cm.
1. Americanisms I. Mathews, Mitford McLeod, 1891- ed.
PE2835.D5 1956   427.9   LC 56-2254

Evans, Bergen, 1904-.   • 2.1137
A dictionary of contemporary American usage / by Bergen Evans and Cornelia
Evans. — New York: Random House, [1957] viii, 567 p.; 26 cm.
1. Americanisms 2. English language — Usage — Dictionaries 3. English
language — Usage I. Evans, Cornelia, joint author. II. T. III. Title:
Contemporary American usage.
PE2835.E84   427.09 427.9*   LC 57-5379

Follett, Wilson, 1887-1963.   • 2.1138
Modern American usage; a guide. Edited and completed by Jacques Barzun in
collaboration with Carlos Baker [and others. 1st ed.] New York, Hill & Wang
[1966] [xi], 436 p. 22 cm. Bibliography: p. [xi] 1. English language in the
United States — Dictionaries. I. Barzun, Jacques, 1907- ed. II. Baker, Carlos,
1909-1987. ed. III. T.
PE2835.F6   423.1   LC 66-18993

Nicholson, Margaret.   • **2.1139**
A dictionary of American–English usage, based on Fowler's Modern English usage. — New York: Oxford University Press, 1957. xii, 671 p.; 20 cm. 1. Americanisms I. T. II. Title: American-English usage.
PE2835.N5   423   *LC* 57-5560

Oxford American dictionary / [compiled by] Eugene Ehrlich ...   **2.1140**
[et al.].
New York: Oxford University Press, 1980. xvi, 816 p.; 24 cm. 1. English language — Dictionaries 2. English language in the United States. I. Ehrlich, Eugene H.
PE2835.O9   423   *LC* 80-16510   *ISBN* 0195027957

Kučera, Henry.   • **2.1141**
Computational analysis of present–day American English / by Henry Kučera and W. Nelson Francis; with a foreword by W. F. Twaddell; a study by Mary Lois Marckworth and Laura M. Bell; and an analytical essay by John B. Carroll. — Providence: Brown University Press, 1967. xxv, 424 p.: ill.; 27 cm. 1. English language in the United States — Word frequency. I. Francis, W. Nelson (Winthrop Nelson), 1910- II. T.
PE2839.K8   427/.9/73   *LC* 67-10213

Herman, Lewis Helmar, 1905-.   • **2.1142**
[Manual of American dialects, for radio, stage, screen, and television] American dialects; a manual for actors, directors, and writers, by Lewis Herman and Marguerite Shalett Herman. New York, Theatre Arts Books [1959] 328 p. illus. 24 cm. First published in 1947 under title: Manual of American dialects, for radio, stage, screen, and television. 1. English language in the United States — Dialects. I. Herman, Marguerite Shalett, joint author. II. T.
PE2841.H4 1959   427.9   *LC* 59-13238

Kurath, Hans, 1891-.   **2.1143**
Studies in area linguistics. Bloomington: Indiana University Press, [1972] xii, 202 p.: maps.; 25 cm. — (Indiana University studies in the history and theory of linguistics) 1. English language — Dialects — United States 2. English language — Foreign elements 3. Dialectology 4. Linguistic change I. T.
PE2841.K8   427/.9/73   *LC* 72-75391   *ISBN* 0253355303

Dictionary of American regional English / Frederic G. Cassidy,   **2.1144**
chief editor.
Cambridge, Mass.: Belknap Press of Harvard University Press, 1985. 1 v.: ill.; 29 cm. 1. English language — Provincialisms — United States — Dictionaries. 2. English language — Dialects — United States — Dictionaries. 3. English language — United States — Dictionaries. I. Cassidy, Frederic Gomes, 1907-
PE2843.D52 1985   427/.973 19   *LC* 84-29025   *ISBN* 0674205111

PE2846 Slang

Allen, Irving L., 1931-.   **2.1145**
The language of ethnic conflict: social organization and lexical culture / Irving Lewis Allen. — New York: Columbia University Press, 1983. 162 p.; 23 cm. Includes index. 1. English language — United States — Slang. 2. Epithets 3. English language — Etymology 4. English language — Social aspects — United States. 5. Nicknames — United States. 6. United States — Ethnic relations I. T.
PE2846.A44 1983   306/.4 19   *LC* 82-9610   *ISBN* 0231055560

Chapman, Robert L.   **2.1146**
New dictionary of American slang / edited by Robert L. Chapman. — New York: Harper & Row, c1986. xxxvi, 485 p.; 25 cm. Rev. ed. of: Dictionary of American slang / compiled and edited by Harold Wentworth and Stuart Berg Flexner. 2nd supplemented ed. 1975. 1. English language — United States — Slang — Dictionaries. 2. English language — Slang — Dictionaries 3. Americanisms — Dictionaries. I. Wentworth, Harold, 1904- Dictionary of American slang. II. T.
PE2846.C46 1986   427/.973 19   *LC* 86-45086   *ISBN* 0061811572

Pearl, Anita May.   **2.1147**
The Jonathan David dictionary of popular slang / by Anita Pearl. — Middle Village, N.Y.: Jonathan David Publishers, c1980. viii, 191 p.; 24 cm. 1. English language — Slang — Dictionaries 2. Americanisms I. T. II. Title: Dictionary of popular slang.
PE2846.P4   427/.9/73   *LC* 79-21062   0284602463

Wentworth, Harold, 1904-.   **2.1148**
Dictionary of American slang / compiled and edited by Harold Wentworth and Stuart Berg Flexner. 2d supplemented ed. — New York: Crowell, [1975] xviii, 766 p.; 24 cm. 1. English language — Slang — Dictionaries 2. Americanisms I. Flexner, Stuart Berg. joint author. II. T.
PE2846.W4 1975   427/.09   *LC* 75-8644   *ISBN* 0690006705

PE2901–3101 Regions. States

Randolph, Vance, 1892-.   • **2.1149**
Down in the holler: a gallery of Ozark folk speech / [by] Vance Randolph & George P. Wilson. — [1st ed.] Norman: University of Oklahoma Press [1953] ix, 320 p.; 25 cm. 1. English language — Dialects — Ozark Mountains. I. Wilson, George Pickett, 1888- II. T.
PE2970.O9R3   427.9   *LC* 53-5480   *ISBN* 0806102675

Watts, Peter Christopher.   **2.1150**
A dictionary of the Old West, 1850–1900 / by Peter Watts. — 1st ed. — New York: Knopf, 1977. xii, 399 p.: ill.; 24 cm. 1. Americanisms 2. English language — Provincialisms — West (U.S.) 3. English language — 19th century 4. West (U.S.) — Social life and customs. I. T.
PE2970.W4 W3 1977   427/.9/78   *LC* 76-13724

Labov, William.   **2.1151**
The social stratification of English in New York City / by William Labov. — [Washington]: Center for Applied Linguistics, 1966. 655 p.: ill.; 23 cm. (Urban language series) 1. English language — Dialects — New York (N.Y.) I. T. II. Series.
PE3101 N7 L3 1966   *LC* 66-24073

Atwood, Elmer Bagby, 1906-.   • **2.1152**
The regional vocabulary of Texas. — Austin: University of Texas Press, [1962] xiii, 273 p.: maps, tables.; 24 cm. 1. English language — Provincialisms — Texas. 2. English language — Maps I. T.
PE3101.T4 A85   427.9764   *LC* 62-9784

PE3102.N4 Black English

Dillard, J. L. (Joey Lee), 1924-.   • **2.1153**
Black English; its history and usage in the United States [by] J. L. Dillard. [1st ed.] New York, Random House [1972] xiv, 361 p. illus. 25 cm. 1. Afro-Americans — Language. I. T.
PE3102.N4 D5   427/.9/73   *LC* 71-102330   *ISBN* 0394467604

Labov, William.   **2.1154**
Language in the inner city: studies in the Black English vernacular. — Philadelphia: University of Pennsylvania Press, 1973 (c1972) xxiv, 412 p.: ill.; 24 cm. 1. Black English 2. Intercultural education — United States. I. T.
PE3102.N4 L3   427/.9/73   *LC* 72-80377   *ISBN* 0812276582

Perspectives on black English / ed. J. Dillard.   **2.1155**
The Hague: Mouton, [1975] 391 p.; 24 cm. — (Contributions to the sociology of language. 4) English or German. 1. Black English — Addresses, essays, lectures. I. Dillard, J. L. (Joey Lee), 1924- II. Series.
PE3102.N4 P4   427/.9/73   *LC* 75-331633   *ISBN* 9027978115

Baugh, John, 1949-.   **2.1156**
Black street speech: its history, structure, and survival / by John Baugh. — 1st ed. — Austin: University of Texas Press, 1983. x, 149 p.: ill.; 23 cm. (Texas linguistics series.) Includes index. 1. Black English 2. English language — Social aspects — United States. 3. English language — Spoken English — United States. 4. Afro-Americans — Social conditions 5. Afro-Americans — Education — Language arts. I. T. II. Series.
PE3102.N42 B38 1983   427/.973 19   *LC* 83-10578   *ISBN* 0292707452

Black English: a seminar / edited by Deborah Sears Harrison,   **2.1157**
Tom Trabasso.
Hillsdale, N.J.: Lawrence Erlbaum Associates; New York: distributed by Halsted Press Division of Wiley, 1976. 301 p.; 24 cm. 1. Black English — Addresses, essays, lectures. I. Harrison, Deborah Sears. II. Trabasso, Tom.
PE3102.N42 B6   301.2/1   *LC* 75-38897   *ISBN* 0470013958

Folb, Edith A.   **2.1158**
Runnin' down some lines: the language and culture of Black teenagers / Edith A. Folb. — Cambridge, Mass.: Harvard University Press, 1980. xxii, 260 p.; 24 cm. 1. Black English 2. Afro-American youth — California — Los Angeles. 3. Sociolinguistics I. T.
PE3102.N42 F6   427/.9794/94   *LC* 79-26708   *ISBN* 0674780396

Haskins, James, 1941-.   **2.1159**
The psychology of Black language / [by] Jim Haskins and Hugh F. Butts. — New York: Barnes & Noble Books, [1973] ix, 95 p.; 21 cm. — (College outline series) 1. Black English 2. Psycholinguistics I. Butts, Hugh F., joint author. II. T.
PE3102.N42 H3   301.2/1   *LC* 72-6313   *ISBN* 0064601420

Dillard, J. L. (Joey Lee), 1924-.   **2.1160**
Lexicon of Black English / J. L. Dillard. — New York: Seabury Press, 1977.
xiv, 199 p.; 24 cm. — (A Continuum book) 1. Black English I. T.
PE3102.N46 D5   427/.9/73   LC 76-30389   ISBN 081649309X

PE3201-3501 Canada. India

A Dictionary of Canadianisms on historical principles;   • **2.1161**
dictionary of Canadian English. Produced for W. J. Gage
Limited by the Lexicographical Centre for Canadian English,
University of Victoria, Victoria, British Columbia, Canada.
Editorial board: Walter S. Avis, editor-in-chief [and others].
Toronto: W. J. Gage, ltd., 1967. xxiii, 926, [1] p.: illus.; 25 cm. 1. English
language — Provincialisms — Canada. 2. English language — Dictionaries
I. Avis, Walter Spencer, 1919- ed. II. Lexicographical Centre for Canadian
English. III. Title: Dictionary of Canadian English.
PE3243.D5   427/.9/71   LC 78-5962

Yule, Henry, Sir, 1820-1889.   • **2.1162**
Hobson-jobson: a glossary of colloquial Anglo-Indian words and phrases, and
of kindred terms, etymological, historical, geographical and discursive / by
Henry Yule and A. C Burnell. — New [2d] ed., edited by William Crooke. New
York: Humanities Press, [1968] xlviii, 1021 p.; 23 cm. This ed. first published in
1903. 1. Hobson-jobson 2. English language — Etymology —
Glossaries, vocabularies, etc. 3. English language — Provincialisms — India —
Glossaries, vocabularies, etc. 4. English language — Foreign words and
phrases — Indic — Glossaries, vocabularies, etc. 5. Indic languages —
Influence on English — Glossaries, vocabularies, etc. 6. India — Languages —
Glossaries, vocabularies, etc. I. Burnell, A. C. (Arthur Coke), 1840-1882. joint
author. II. Crooke, William, 1848-1923. ed. III. T.
PE3501.Y78 1968c   422/.4/91   LC 72-4603   ISBN 0710028865

PE3701-3729 Slang

Partridge, Eric, 1894-.   • **2.1163**
Slang to-day and yesterday: with a short historical sketch and vocabularies of
English, American, and Australian slang. — 4th ed., rev. and brought up to
date. — New York: Barnes & Noble, [1970] ix, 476 p.; 24 cm. 1. English
language — Slang I. T.
PE3711.P3 1970   427.09   LC 72-16925   ISBN 0389039772

Partridge, Eric, 1894-.   • **2.1164**
A dictionary of slang and unconventional English; colloquialisms and catch-
phrases, solecisms and catachreses, nicknames, vulgarisms, and such
Americanisms as have been naturalized. — 6th ed. — New York: Macmillan,
[1967] xiv, 1474 p.; 25 cm. 1. English language — Slang — Dictionaries
2. Americanisms I. T.
PE3721.P3 1967   427.09   LC 67-30122

Spears, Richard A.   **2.1165**
Slang and euphemism: a dictionary of oaths, curses, insults, sexual slang and
metaphor, racial slurs, drug talk, homosexual lingo, and related matters / by
Richard A. Spears. — Middle Village, N.Y.: David Publishers, c1981. xxviii,
448 p.; 24 cm. 1. English language — Slang — Dictionaries I. T.
PE3721.S67 1981   427   LC 80-18714   ISBN 0824602595

Partridge, Eric, 1894-.   • **2.1166**
A dictionary of the underworld, British & American. New York, Macmillan,
1950. xv, 804 p. 26 cm. 1. Cant — Dictionaries. 2. English language — Slang
— Dictionaries I. T.
PE3726.P3   LC 50-8598

Major, Clarence.   • **2.1167**
Dictionary of Afro-American slang. [1st ed.] New York: International
Publishers [1970] 127 p.; 21 cm. 1. Afro-Americans — Language (New words,
slang, etc.) 2. English language in the United States — Slang — Dictionaries.
I. T.
PE3727.N4 M3   427.09   LC 79-130863   ISBN 071780268X

PF West Germanic Languages

PF1-979 Dutch

Brachin, Pierre.   **2.1168**
[La langue néerlandaise. English] The Dutch language: a survey / Pierre
Brachin; translated from the French by Paul Vincent. — Cheltenham: Thornes,
1985. viii, 150 p.: 1 map; 24 cm. Translation of: La langue néerlandaise.
1. Dutch language I. T.
PF73.B7313 1985   PF73 B7313 1985.   439.3/1 19   ISBN
0859502465

Vandeputte, Omer.   **2.1169**
Dutch, the language of twenty million Dutch and Flemish people. — [Flanders,
Belgium]: Stichting Ons Erfdeel vzw, 1981. 64 p.: ill.; 20 cm. Written by Omer
Vandeputte; English translation and adaptation by P. Vincent and T. Hermans.
1. Dutch language I. Stichting Ons Erfdeel. II. T.
PF95.V3 1981   439.3/1 19   LC 81-201818

Shetter, William Z.   **2.1170**
Introduction to Dutch: a practical grammar / by William Z. Shetter. — 5th ed.,
thoroughly rev. — Leiden: M. Nijhoff, 1984. 245 p.: ill.; 24 cm. Dutch and
English. 'English translations of the practice sentences': p. [213]-226. 1. Dutch
language — Grammar — 1950- 2. Dutch language — Text-books for foreign
speakers — English. I. T.
PF112.S53 1984   439.3/182421 19   LC 85-122009   ISBN
9024799783

Cassell's New English-Dutch, Dutch-English dictionary /   **2.1171**
compiled by J.A. Jockin-La Bastide and G. van Kooten.
1st McMillan ed. — London: Cassell; New York McMillan, 1981. xiv, 682 p.,
vii, 729 p.; 19 cm. English ed. of: Kramers' Engels woordenboek / J. Kramers.
— 36. geheel herziene en vermeerderde druk. 1. English language —
Dictionaries — Dutch. 2. Dutch language — Dictionaries — English.
I. Jockin-La Bastide, J. A. II. Kooten, G. van. III. Kramers, Jacob,
1802-1869. Kramers' Engels woordenboek IV. Title: New English-Dutch,
Dutch-English dictionary.
PF640.C375 1981   439.3/1321 19   LC 81-11766

Martin, W.   **2.1172**
Groot woordenboek Engels-Nederlands / door W. Martin en G.A.J. Tops, in
samenwerking met J.L. Bol ... [et al.]. — Utrecht: Van Dale Lexicografie,
c1984. 1594 p.; 25 cm. (Van Dale woordenboeken voor hedendaags taalgebruik)
At head of title: Van Dale. 1. English language — Dictionaries — Dutch.
I. Tops, Guy A. J. II. T. III. Title: Van Dale groot woordenboek Engels-
Nederlands. IV. Series.
PF640.M37 1984   423/.3931 19   LC 84-198721   ISBN
906648103X

Martin, W.   **2.1173**
Groot woordenboek Nederlands-Engels / door W. Martin en G.A.J. Tops, in
samenwerking met A.P.A. Broeders ... [et al.]. — Utrecht: Van Dale
Lexicografie, c1986. 1560 p.; 25 cm. — (Van Dale woordenboeken voor
hedendaags taalgebruik) At head of title: Van Dale. 1. Dutch language —
Dictionaries — English. I. Tops, Guy A. J. II. T. III. Title: Van Dale groot
woordenboek Nederlands-Engels.
PF640.M38 1986   439.3/1321 19   LC 86-221171   ISBN
9066481072

PF3001-5999 German

Bach, Adolf, 1890-.   • **2.1174**
Geschichte der deutschen Sprache. 8., stark erw. Aufl. — Heidelberg, Quelle u.
Meyer, 1965. 495 p. with maps. 23 cm. — ([Hochschulwissen in
Einzeldarstellungen]) I. T.
PF3075.B25 1965   430/.9   LC 67-110506

Waterman, John T.   • **2.1175**
A history of the German language, with special reference to the cultural and
social forces that shaped the standard literary language, by John T. Waterman.
— Seattle: University of Washington Press, 1966. xiii, 266 p.: illus., facsims.,
maps.; 25 cm. 1. German language — History. I. T.
PF3075.W3   430.09   LC 66-13542

Blackwall, Eric Albert.   • 2.1176
The emergence of German as a literary language, 1700–1775. — Cambridge,
Eng.: University Press, 1959. 538 p.; 23 cm. 1. German language — History.
2. German language — Style. 3. German literature — 18th century — History
and criticism I. T.
PF3083.B6   LC 59-802

PF3097–3561 Grammar. Style.
Prosody

Priebsch, Robert, 1866-1935.   • 2.1177
The German language / by R. Priebsch and W.E. Collinson. — 6th ed., rev. —
London: Faber & Faber, 1966. xx, 496 p.: ill., maps.; 23 cm. — (The great
languages) 1. German language — Grammar, Historical. 2. German language
— History. I. Collinson, William Edward, 1889- joint author. II. T.
PF3101.P67 1966   430.9   LC 66-73164

Lederer, Herbert, 1921-.   • 2.1178
Reference grammar of the German language. Based on Grammatik der
deutschen Sprache, by Dora Schulz and Heinz Griesbach. — American ed. by
Herbert Lederer. — New York: Scribner, [1969] xx, 709 p.; 23 cm. 1. German
language — Grammar — 1950- I. Griesbach, Heinz. Grammatik der
deutschen Sprache. II. T.
PF3105.L43   438/.2/42   LC 69-17352

Bithell, Jethro, 1878-1962.   • 2.1179
German pronunciation and phonology. London Methuen [1952] 514p.
1. German language — Phonology 2. German language — Pronunciation
I. T.
PF3131 B57

Russ, Charles V. J.   2.1180
Historical German phonology and morphology / Charles V. J. Russ. —
Oxford: Clarendon Press; [New York: Oxford University Press], 1978. xv,
181 p.; 23 cm. — (Oxford history of the German language) 1. German
language — Phonology. 2. German language — Morphology. 3. German
language — History. I. T.
PF3131.R8   PF3131 R8.   431/.5   LC 78-40248   ISBN
0198157274

Fox, Anthony.   2.1181
German intonation: an outline / Anthony Fox. — Oxford [Oxfordshire]:
Clarendon Press; Oxford [Oxfordshire]; New York: Oxford University Press,
1984. vi, 120 p.: ill.; 23 cm. Includes index. 1. German language — Intonation.
I. T.
PF3139.5.F6 1984   431/.6 19   LC 83-24399   ISBN 0198157940

Taylor, Ronald, 1924-.   2.1182
A German–English dictionary of idioms: idiomatic and figurative German
expressions with Engl. translations / Ronald Taylor, Walter Gottschalk. — 4.
Aufl. — München: Hueber, 1973, c1960. 597 p.; 22 cm. (Sprachen der Welt)
1. German language — Idioms. 2. English language — Idioms 3. German
language — Dictionaries — English. I. Gottschalk, Walter, 1894- joint author.
II. T.
PF3460.T3 1973   433/.2/1   LC 75-551593

PF3571–3693 Etymology.
Dictionaries

Kluge, Friedrich, 1856-1926.   2.1183
Etymologisches Wörterbuch der deutschen Sprache / Friedrich Kluge. — 21.
unveränderte Aufl. / bearb. von Walther Mitzka. — Berlin: W. de Gruyter,
1975. xvi, 915 p.; 25 cm. Abbreviations: p. [viii]-ix. 1. German language —
Etymology — Dictionaries. I. Mitzka, Walther. II. T.
PF3580.K5 1975   432/K71/1975   ISBN 3110057093

Farrell, R. B. (Ralph Barstow), 1908-.   2.1184
Dictionary of German synonyms / R. B. Farrell. 3d ed. — Cambridge; New
York: Cambridge University Press, 1977. ix, 412 p.; 23 cm. English and
German. 1. German language — Synonyms and antonyms. 2. English
language — Dictionaries — German. I. T.
PF3591.F37 1977   433/.21   LC 75-36175   ISBN 0521211891

Grimm, Jacob, 1785-1863.   2.1185
Deutsches Wörterbuch / von Jacob und Wilhelm Grimm. — [München]:
Deutscher Taschenbuch Verlag, [1984]. 33 v.: ill., port.; 24 cm. Title vignettes.
On cover: Grimm. 1. German language — Dictionaries I. Grimm, Wilhelm,
1786-1859. II. T. III. Title: Grimm.
PF3625.G7 1984   ISBN 3423059451

Küpper, Heinz.   • 2.1186
Wörterbuch der deutschen Umgangssprache. 3., neubearb. und erweiterte Aufl.
— [Hamburg]: Claassen, [c1963-. v.; 26 cm. 1. German language —
Dictionaries 2. German language — Slang — Dictionaries. I. T.
PF3625.K8 1963   LC 64-49309

Wahrig, Gerhard.   2.1187
Deutsches Wörterbuch mit einem 'Lexikon der deutschen Sprachlehre' /
Gerhard Wahrig; hrsg. in Zusammenarbeit mit zahlreichen Wissenschaftlern
und anderen Fachleuten. — Völlig überarbeitete Neuausgabe. — [München]:
Mosaik Verlag, 1980. 4358 columns. 'Lexikon der deutschen Sprachlehre' by
W. Ludewig: column 49-230. Includes index. 1. German language —
Dictionaries I. Ludewig, Walter. II. T.
PF3625.W2 1980   ISBN 3570007715

Oxford–Duden Bildwörterbuch: Dt. u. Engl. / hrsg. von d.   2.1188
Dudenred. u.d. German Sect. of the Oxford Univ. Press,
Dictionary Dep.; [red. Leitung d. zweisprach. Ausg., John
Pheby, Werner Scholze].
Mannheim; Wien; Zürich: Bibliographisches Institut, 1979. 677, 87, 96 p.; 23
cm. Includes indexes. Based on the 3rd rev. ed. of the Duden Bildwörterbuch.
Simultaneously published as Oxford-Duden pictorial German-English
dictionary. 1. Picture dictionaries, German 2. Picture dictionaries, English
3. German language — Dictionaries — English. 4. English language —
Dictionaries — German. I. Dudenredaktion (Bibliographisches Institut)
II. Oxford University Press. Dictionary Dept. German Section.
PF3629.O915 1979   433/.21 19   LC 80-498735   ISBN 3411017651

Betteridge, Harold T. ed.   2.1189
Cassell's German dictionary: German–English, English–German: based on the
editions by Karl Breul / completely rev. and re–edited by Harold T. Betteridge;
with a foreword by Gerhard Cordes. — New York: Macmillan, 1977, c1971. xx,
632 p.; 24 cm. 1. German language — Dictionaries — English. 2. English
language — Dictionaries — German. I. Breul, Karl, 1860-1932. II. T.
III. Title: Cassell's German dictionary.
PF3640.B45 1977   433/.21   LC 77-7386   ISBN 0025225502. ISBN
002522560X

Langenscheidt's new Muret–Sanders encyclopedic dictionary of   2.1190
the English and German languages / ed. by Otto Springer.
Rev. ed. New York, Barnes & Noble 1974-75. 4 v. Added t. p.: Der neue
Muret—Sanders, Langenscheidts enzyklopädisches Wörterbuch der englischen
und deutschen Sprache. German ed. has title: Langenscheidts enzyklopädisches
Wörterbuch der englischen und deutschen Sprache. 1. English language —
Dictionaries — German. 2. German language — Dictionaries — English.
I. Springer, Otto, 1905- ed. II. Muret, Eduard, 1833-1904. Enzyklopädisches
englisch-deutsches und deutsch-englisches Wörterbuch.
PF3640.L257   LC 62-6984 rev

Wildhagen, Karl, 1873-1945.   • 2.1191
The new Wildhagen German dictionary; German–English, English–German;
an encyclopedic and strictly scientific representation of the vocabulary of the
modern and present–day languages, with special regard to syntax, style, and
idiomatic usage [by] Karl Wildhagen [and] Will Héraucourt. [Editors: Eva
Ruetz and Richard Wiezell]. — Chicago: Follett Pub. Co., 1965. xxi, 1061 p.;
25 cm. 1. German language — Dictionaries — English. 2. English language —
Dictionaries — German. I. Héraucourt, Will. joint author. II. T.
PF3640.W546   433.2   LC 65-24302

PF4043–4345 Middle High German

Lexer, Matthias, 1830-1892.   2.1192
[Mittelhochdeutsches Taschenwörterbuch] Matthias Lexers
mittelhochdeutsches Taschenwörterbuch. — 36. Aufl., mit neuarbeiten und
erw. Nachträgen. — Stuttgart: S. Hirzel, 1981. viii, 504 p.; 21 cm. Contains
Nachträge zum Mittelhochdeutschen Taschenwörterbuch / unter Mithilfe von
Dorothea Hannover und Rena Lippin neuarbeitet und aus den Quellen ergänzt
von Ulrich Pretzel. Errata slip laid in. 1. German language — Middle High
German, 1050-1500 — Dictionaries. I. Pretzel, Ulrich. Nachträge zum
mittelhochdeutschen Taschenwörterbuch. II. T.
PF4327.L42x 1981   LC 86-672397   ISBN 3777603597

PG Slavic Languages and Literatures

√ **Entwistle, William J. (William James), 1895-1952.**   • **2.1193**
Russian and the Slavonic languages / by W. J. Entwistle and W. A. Morison. —
2d ed. — London: Faber and Faber, 1964. 407 p.: fold. col. maps.; 23 cm. (The
Great languages) 1. Russian language — History. 2. Slavic languages —
History I. Morison, Walker Angus, joint author. II. T. III. Series.
PG45.E6   491.8   *ISBN* 0571061095

Trubetskoĭ, Nikolaĭ Sergeevich, kniaz', 1890-1938.   • **2.1194**
The common Slavic element in Russian culture / Nikolaĭ Trubetzkoy, ed. by
Leon Stilman. — 2nd rev. ed. — New York: Columbia University, Dept. of
Slavic Studies, c1949. 49 p.; 22 cm. (Columbia University. Department of Slavic
Studies. Slavic studies: Slavic philology series) Various translators. 1. Slavic
languages — History 2. Church Slavic language — History I. Stilman, Leon.
II. T. III. Series.
PG45.E6 1964

√ **De Bray, R. G. A. (Reginald George Arthur)**   **2.1195**
Guide to the Slavonic languages / by R.G.A. de Bray. — 3rd. ed., rev. and
expanded. — Columbus, Ohio: Slavica Publishers, 1980. 3 v.; 24 cm. 1. Slavic
languages I. T.
PG53.D4 1980   491.8 19   *LC* 80-154015   *ISBN* 0893570605

Tschiževskij, Dmitrij, 1894-.   **2.1196**
[Vergleichende Geschichte der slavischen Literaturen. English] Comparative
history of Slavic literatures, by Dmitrij Čiževskij. Translated by Richard Noel
Porter and Martin P. Rice. Edited, with a foreword, by Serge A. Zenkovsky.
[Nashville, Tenn.] Vanderbilt University Press, 1971. ix, 225 p. 24 cm.
Translation of Vergleichende Geschichte der slavischen Literaturen. 1. Slavic
literature — History and criticism. 2. Literature, Comparative I. T.
PG501.C513   891.8   *LC* 74-124115   *ISBN* 0826511597

√ **Modern Slavic literatures. Compiled and edited by Vasa D.**   **2.1197**
Mihailovich.
New York: F. Ungar Pub. Co., [c1972-1976] 2 v.; 25 cm. — (Library of literary
criticism.) 'Vol. 2 Compiled and edited by V. D. Mihailovich [et al.]' 1. Slavic
literature — 20th century — History and criticism. 2. Russian literature —
20th century — History and criticism I. Mihailovich, Vasa D. ed. II. Series.
PG501.M518   891.7/09/004   *LC* 72-170319   *ISBN* 0804431760

PG551–584 Yugoslav Literature

Barac, Antun, 1894-1955.   **2.1198**
A history of Yugoslav literature / Antun Barac; [translated by Petar
Mijušković]. Ann Arbor: Michigan Slavic Publications, Dept. of Slavic
Languages and Literatures, University of Michigan, 1973. 266 p.; 24 cm.
([Publication series - Joint Committee on Eastern Europe; no. 1]) Translation of
Jugoslavenska književnost. Includes index. 1. Yugoslav literature — History
and criticism. I. T.
PG561.B313   891.8   *LC* 76-623278

Eekman, Thomas.   **2.1199**
Thirty years of Yugoslav literature, 1945–1975 / Thomas Eekman. — Ann
Arbor: Published under the auspices of the Joint Committee on Eastern Europe,
American Council of Learned Societies, and the Social Science Research
Council by Michigan Slavic Publications, 1978. 328 p.: map (on lining papers);
24 cm. (The Joint Committee on Eastern Europe publication series; no. 5)
Cover title: Yugoslav literature, 1945-1975. 1. Yugoslav literature — 20th
century — History and criticism. I. T. II. Title: Yugoslav literature,
1945-1975.
PG567.E34   891.8/2/09005 19   *LC* 78-53535

Johnson, Bernard. comp.   • **2.1200**
New writing in Yugoslavia. — Harmondsworth: Penguin, 1970. 342 p.; 20 cm.
— (Writing today) Translated from the Macedonian, Serbo-Croatian and
Slovenian. 1. Yugoslav literature — Translations into English. 2. English
literature — Translations from Yugoslav literature. I. T.
PG584.E1 J6   891.8/2/08005   *LC* 72-21722   *ISBN* 0140031146

Mikasinovich, Branko. comp.   **2.1201**
Introduction to Yugoslav literature; an anthology of fiction and poetry. Edited
by Branko Mikasinovich, Dragan Milivojević and Vasa D. Mihailovich. —
New York: Twayne Publishers, [c1973] xiii, 647 p.; 22 cm. — (World literature

series) 1. Yugoslav literature — Translations into English. 2. English
literature — Translations from Yugoslav literature. 3. Yugoslav literature —
History and criticism. I. Milivojević, Dragan Dennis. joint comp.
II. Mihailovich, Vasa D. joint comp. III. T.
PG584.E1 M5   891.8   *LC* 71-188558

Lenski, Branko, 1928-.   • **2.1202**
Death of a simple giant, and other modern Yugoslav stories / edited by Branko
Lenski. — New York: Vanguard Press 1965. — 306 p.; 22 cm. 1. Short stories,
Yugoslav — Translations into English. 2. Short stories, English —
Translations from Serbo-Croatian. 3. Short stories, English — Translations
from Slovenian. I. T.
PG584.E8 L36   Fic   *LC* 64-23319

PG801–1158 Bulgarian Literature

Moser, Charles A.   **2.1203**
A history of Bulgarian literature 865–1944. By Charles A. Moser. — The
Hague: Mouton, 1972. 282 p.; 25 cm. — (Slavistic printings and reprintings.
112) 1. Bulgarian literature — History and criticism. I. T. II. Series.
PG1001.M67   891.8/1/09   *LC* 76-170000

Vazov, Ivan Minchov, 1850-1921.   **2.1204**
[Pod igoto. English] Under the yoke. Translated by Marguerite Alexieva and
Theodora Atanassova. Edited by Lilla Lyon Zabriskie. New York, Twayne
Publishers [1971] 400 p. 22 cm. Translation of Pod igoto. 1. Bulgaria —
History — 1762-1878 — Fiction. I. T.
PZ3.V48 U7 PG1037.V3   891.8/1/32   *LC* 70-146052

√ **Kirilov, Nikolaĭ, 1922- comp.**   • **2.1205**
Introduction to modern Bulgarian literature; an anthology of short stories.
Edited by Nikolai Kirilov and Frank Kirk. — New York, Twayne Publishers
[1969] 480 p. 22 cm. — (Twayne's introductions to world literature series)
1. Short stories, Bulgarian — Translations into English. 2. Short stories,
English — Translations from Bulgarian. I. Kirk, Frank, joint comp. II. T.
PZ1.K583 In PG1145.E8x   891.8/1/3008   *LC* 72-91322

PG1201–1798 Serbo–Croatian Language and Literature

Magner, Thomas F.   **2.1206**
Introduction to the Croatian and Serbian language, by Thomas F. Magner. —
[State College, Pa.: Singidunum Press], 1972. vii, 351 p.; 24 cm. First-2d ed.
published under title: Introduction to the Serbo-Croatian language. 1. Serbo-
Croatian language — Grammar. I. T.
PG1231.M26 1972   491.8/2/82421   *LC* 72-179490

√ **Andrić, Ivo, 1892-1975.**   • **2.1207**
The woman from Sarajevo / translated from the Serbo–Croatian by Joseph
Hitrec. — 1st American ed. — New York: Knopf, 1965. 245 p.; 22 cm.
Translation of Gospodjica. I. T.
PG1418.A6 Gx   *LC* 64-19100

√ **Andrić, Ivo, 1892-1975.**   **2.1208**
Bosnian chronicle. New York: Knopf, 1963. 429p. I. T.
PG1418 A6 T73 1963

Hawkesworth, Celia, 1942-.   **2.1209**
Ivo Andrić: bridge between East and West / Celia Hawkesworth. — London;
Dover, N.H.: Athlone Press, 1984. 270 p., [1] leaf of plates: port.; 22 cm.
Includes index. 1. Andrić, Ivo, 1892-1975 — Criticism and interpretation.
I. T.
PG1418.A6 Z69 1984   891.8/235 19   *LC* 84-9186   *ISBN*
0485112558

√ **Andrić, Ivo, 1892-1975.**   • **2.1210**
The bridge on the Drina / translated from the Serbo–Croat by Lovett F.
Edwards. — New York: Macmillan, 1959. 314 p.; 22 cm. I. T.
PG1418.A6x   Fic   *LC* 59-9676

√ **Bulatović, Miodrag, 1930-.**   • **2.1211**
[Heroj na magarcu. English] A hero on a donkey. New York, World Pub. Co.
[1969] 261 p. 22 cm. (An NAL book.) Translation of Heroj na magarcu. I. T.
PZ4.B934 He5 PG1418.B78 H4x   891.8/2/35   *LC* 69-18520

Ćosić, Dobrica, 1921-.   **2.1212**
[Vreme smrti. English] A time of death / Dobrica Ćosić; translated by Muriel Heppell. — 1st ed. — New York: Harcourt Brace Jovanovich, c1978. 437 p.; 25 cm. Translation of Vreme smrti. 1. World War, 1914-1918 — Fiction. I. T.
PZ4.C835 Ti3 PG1418.C63 V7x   891.8/2/35   LC 77-73047   ISBN 0151904480

Kiš, Danilo, 1935-.   **2.1213**
[Grobnica za Borisa Davidoviča. English] A tomb for Boris Davidovich: a novel / by Danilo Kiš; translated by Duška Mikić–Mitchell. — 1st ed. — New York: Harcourt Brace Jovanovich, [1978] 135 p.; 22 cm. Translation of Grobnica za Borisa Davidoviča. I. T.
PZ4.K6132 To 1978 PG1419.21.I8 G7x   891.8/235   LC 77-15004
   ISBN 0151904863

Šćepanović, Branimir, 1937-.   **2.1214**
[Usta puna zemlje. English] Mouth full of earth / Branimir Šćepanović; translated from the Serbo–Croat by Lovett Fielding Edwards. — 1st U.S. ed. — Nantucket: Longship Press, 1980, c1975. 83 p.; 22 cm. Translation of Usta puna zemlje. I. T.
PZ4.S296 Mo 1980 PG1419.29.C4 U8x   891.8/2/35 19   LC 78-72283
   ISBN 0917712072

Koljević, Svetozar.   **2.1215**
The epic in the making / Svetozar Koljević. — Oxford: Clarendon Press; New York: Oxford University Press, 1980. xii, 376 p., [4] leaves of plates: ill.; 23 cm. Rewritten and expanded translation of the author's Naš junački ep. Includes index. 1. Epic poetry, Serbian — History and criticism. 2. Epic poetry, Croatian — History and criticism. 3. Oral-formulaic analysis I. T.
PG1451.K6313   891.8/2/103   LC 79-41149   ISBN 0198157592

Marko the Prince: Serbo–Croat heroic songs / translated by   **2.1216**
Anne Pennington and Peter Levi; with introduction and notes by
Svetozar Koljević.
New York: St. Martin's Press, 1984. xvii, 173 p.; 24 cm. Translated from the Serbo-Croatian (Cyrillic) 1. Marko, Prince of Serbia, 1335?-1394 — Poetry. 2. English poetry — Translations from Serbo-Croatian. 3. Epic poetry, Serbian — Translations into English. 4. Kosovo, Battle of, 1389 — Poetry. I. Pennington, Anne Elizabeth. II. Levi, Peter. III. Koljević, Svetozar.
PG1465.M3 1984   891.8/2103 19   LC 83-40589   ISBN 0312515375

Monumenta Serbocroatica: a bilingual anthology of Serbian and   **2.1217**
Croatian texts from the 12th to the 19th century / Thomas
Butler.
Ann Arbor: Michigan Slavic Publications, 1980. xxii, 482 p.: ill.; 24 cm. (Publications series - Joint Committee on Eastern Europe; no. 6) 1. Serbian literature 2. Croatian literature 3. Serbian literature — Translations into English. 4. Croatian literature — Translations into English. 5. English literature — Translations from Serbo-Croatian. 6. Church Slavic literature — Yugoslavia. I. Butler, Thomas, 1929-
PG1595.E1 M66   891.8/2/08   LC 80-10409   ISBN 0930042328

Anthology of Serbian poetry: the golden age / [compiled] by   **2.1218**
Mihailo Đorđević.
New York, N.Y.: Philosophical Library, 1984. xvi, 206 p.; 22 cm. English and Serbo-Croatian (Cyrillic) in parallel columns. 1. Serbian poetry — 19th century. 2. Serbian poetry — 20th century 3. Serbian poetry — Translations into English. 4. English poetry — Translations from Serbo-Croatian. I. Đorđević, Mihailo.
PG1595.E3 A5 1984   891.8/214/08 19   LC 84-7672   ISBN 0802224679

Krleža, Miroslav, 1893-.   **2.1219**
[Cvrčak pod vodopadom. English] The cricket beneath the waterfall, and other stories. Edited by Branko Lenski. New York, Vanguard Press [1972] 269 p. 22 cm. Translation of Cvrčak pod vodopadom. I. T.
PZ3.K925 Cr PG1618.K69 C9x   891.8/2/35   LC 72-83354   ISBN 0814906990

Krleža, Miroslav, 1893-.   **2.1220**
[Na rubu pameti. English] On the edge of reason: a novel / by Miroslav Krleža; translated by Zora Depolo. — New York: Vanguard Press, c1976. 182 p.; 22 cm. Translation of Na rubu pameti. I. T.
PZ3.K925 On3 PG1618.K69 N3x   891.8/2/35   LC 74-81810
   ISBN 0814907474

Krleža, Miroslav, 1893-.   **● 2.1221**
[Povratak Filipa Latinovicza. English] The return of Philip Latinovicz, by Miroslav Krleža. New York, Vanguard Press [c1969] 222 p. 22 cm. A novel. Translation of Povratak Filipa Latinovicza. I. T.
PZ3.K925 Re4 PG1618.K69 P6x   891.8/2/35   LC 67-29443
   ISBN 0814901360

PG2001–2850 RUSSIAN LANGUAGE

An introduction to Russian language and literature / edited by **2.1222**
Robert Auty and Dimitri Obolensky; with the editorial
assistance of Anthony Kingsford.
Cambridge: Cambridge University Press, 1977. xiii, 300 p.; 24 cm. —
(Companion to Russian studies, 2) 1. Russian philology — History. I. Auty,
Robert. II. Obolensky, Dimitri, 1918- III. Series.
PG2051.I5   891.7   *LC* 75-10689   *ISBN* 0521208947

Comrie, Bernard, 1947-. **2.1223**
The Russian language since the revolution / Bernard Comrie and Gerald Stone.
— Oxford [Eng.]: Clarendon Press, 1978. x, 258 p.; 23 cm. Includes indexes.
1. Russian language — Social aspects. 2. Russian language — History —
1917- 3. Russian language — Usage. I. Stone, Gerald. joint author. II. T.
PG2074.C6   491.7   *LC* 77-30204   *ISBN* 0198156480

Matthews, William Kleesmann, 1901-1958. • **2.1224**
Russian historical grammar. London, University of London, Athlone Press,
1960. 362 p. illus. 23 cm. (London East European series. Group II: Historical
grammars) 1. Russian language — Grammar, Historical. I. T.
PG2101.M25 1960   491.75   *LC* 60-52141

Perry, James W. (James Whitney), 1907-. • **2.1225**
Scientific Russian: a textbook for classes and self–study / James W. Perry. —
2d. ed. — New York: Interscience Publishers, 1961. xxvi, 565 p.; 24 cm.
1. Russian language — Technical Russian I. T.
PG2111.P45 1961   491.78242   *LC* 61-9139

Unbegaun, Boris Ottokar, 1898-1973. • **2.1226**
[Grammaire russe. English] Russian grammar. Oxford, Clarendon Press, 1957.
315 p. 19 cm. 1. Russian language — Grammar — 1950- I. T.
PG2111.U453   491.75   *LC* 57-1762

Jones, Daniel, 1881-1967. • **2.1227**
The phonetics of Russian [by] the late Daniel Jones and Dennis Ward. London
Cambridge University Press 1969. [308] p.: ill.; 22 cm. 1. Russian language —
Phonetics 2. Russian language — Consonants. 3. Russian language — Vowels.
I. Ward, Dennis. II. T.
PG2135 J6 1969   *LC* 69-10430   *ISBN* 521067367

Boyanus, Semen Karlovich, 1871-1952. • **2.1228**
Russian pronunciation; the Russian system of speech habits in sounds, stress,
rhythm and intonation, together with a Russian phonetic reader, by S.C.
Boyanus. Cambridge, Mass., Harvard University Press, 1955. 2 v. in 1 (xi, 122,
vii, 200) illus. Also paged continuously. 1. Russian language — Phonetics I. T.
PG2137.B62

Powers, D. B. • **2.1229**
A dictionary of irregular Russian verb forms [by] D. B. Powers. New York,
Wiley [1968] xiv, 353 p. 23 cm. 1. Russian language — Verb — Tables.
2. Russian language — Dictionaries — English. I. T.
PG2197.P6   491.75   *LC* 68-31648   *ISBN* 0471695955

Daum, E. (Edmund) **2.1230**
[Russischen Verben. English] A dictionary of Russian verbs: bases of inflection,
aspects, regimen, stressing, meanings / E. Daum, W. Schenk; with an essay on
the syntax and semantics of the verb in present–day Russian by Rudolf
Ružička. — New York: Hippocrene Books, c1974. 750 p.; 23 cm. Translation of
Die russischen Verben. 1. Russian language — Verb. I. Schenk, Werner. joint
author. II. T.
PG2271.D313 1974b   491.7/5   *LC* 76-17455   *ISBN* 0882544209

Unbegaun, Boris Ottokar, 1898-1973. • **2.1231**
Russian versification. Oxford Clarendon Press 1956. 164p. 1. Russian language
— Versification I. T.
PG2509 U5 1956

Preobrazhenskiĭ, Aleksandr Grigor'evich, d. 1918. • **2.1232**
Etymological dictionary of the Russian language. Columbia University Press,
1951. 2 v. in 1. (Columbia Slavic studies) 1. Russian language — Etymology —
Dictionaries. I. T.
PG2580.P7   *LC* a 52-3699

Katzner, Kenneth. **2.1233**
English–Russian, Russian–English dictionary / Kenneth Katzner. — New
York: Wiley, c1984. xiii, 904 p.; 24 cm. 'A Wiley-Interscience publication.'
1. English language — Dictionaries — Russian. 2. Russian language —
Dictionaries — English. I. T.
PG2640.K34 1984   491.73/21 19   *LC* 82-24747   *ISBN* 0471867632

Miuller, V. K. (Vladimir Karlovich), 1880-. **2.1234**
English–Russian dictionary: 70,000 entries / compiled by V. K. Müller. — 14th
ed., newly rev. — New York: Dutton, c1973. 912 p.; 24 cm. Originally
published under title: Anglo-russkiĭ slovar'. Added t.p. in Russian. 1. English
language — Dictionaries — Russian. 2. Russian language — Dictionaries —
English. I. T. II. Title: Anglo-russkiĭ slovar'
PG2640.M8 1973b   491.7/3/21   *LC* 58-9590   *ISBN* 0525195203

The Oxford English–Russian dictionary / edited by P.S. Falla. **2.1235**
Oxford [Oxfordshire]: Clarendon Press, 1984. xvi, 1052 p.; 24 cm. 1. English
language — Dictionaries — Russian. I. Falla, P. S. (Paul Stephen), 1913-
PG2640.O9 1984   423/.9171 19   *LC* 83-17344   *ISBN* 0198641176

Vitek, Alexander. **2.1236**
Russian–English idiom dictionary, by Alexander J. Vitek. Edited by Harry H.
Josselson. Detroit, Wayne State University Press, 1973. x, 327 p. 32 cm.
1. Russian language — Idioms. 2. English language — Idioms — Dictionaries
3. Russian language — Dictionaries — English. I. T.
PG2640.V5   491.7/3/21   *LC* 72-14076   *ISBN* 081431497X

Wheeler, Marcus. **2.1237**
The Oxford Russian–English dictionary / by Marcus Wheeler; general editor
B.O. Unbegaun, with the assistance of D.P. Costello and W.F. Ryan. — 2nd ed.
— Oxford; New York: Oxford University Press, 1984. xiv, 930 p.; 24 cm.
1. Russian language — Dictionaries — English. I. Unbegaun, Boris Ottokar,
1898-1973. II. T.
PG2640.W5 1984   491.73/21 19   *LC* 83-13447   *ISBN* 0198641540

Wilson, Elizabeth A. M. **2.1238**
The modern Russian dictionary for English speakers: English–Russian / by
Elizabeth A.M. Wilson; Russian editor, Popova, L.P., assistant Russian editors,
Litvinova, M.D., Semyonova, N.; assistant compilers, E. Wilson, A. Lee, J.
McNair. — 1st ed. — Oxford; New York: Pergamon Press, 1982. 715 p.; 25 cm.
1. English language — Dictionaries — Russian. I. Popova, L. P. (Lucy P.)
II. T.
PG2640.W54 1982   423/.9171 19   *LC* 81-12141   *ISBN*
0080205542

Crowe, Barry. • **2.1239**
Concise dictionary of Soviet terminology, institutions, and abbreviations / by
Barry Crowe. — [1st ed.]. — Oxford; New York: Pergamon Press, [1969] viii,
182 p.; 20 cm. — (Pergamon Oxford Russian series.) (The Commonwealth and
international library of science, technology, engineering and liberal studies)
1. Abbreviations, Russian 2. Russian language — Terms and phrases —
Dictionaries. 3. Words, New — Russian. I. T. II. Series. III. Series: The
Commonwealth and international library of science, technology, engineering
and liberal studies
PG2693.C7 1969   491/.70138/C88c/1969   *LC* 69-10545   *ISBN*
0080129889

Library of Congress. Aerospace Technology Division. **2.1240**
Glossary of Russian abbreviations and acronyms. — Washington: Library of
Congress; [for sale by the Supt. of Docs., U.S. Govt. Print. Off.], 1967. x, 806 p.;
27 cm. 1. Abbreviations, Russian 2. Russian language — Acronyms I. T.
PG2693.U47   491.731   *LC* 68-60006

PG2900–3698 RUSSIAN LITERATURE

PG2900–2998 Literary History and Criticism

Konovalov, Serge, comp.   • 2.1241
Russian critical essays: XXth century, edited by S. Konovalov and D. J. Richards. Oxford, Clarendon Press, 1971. x, 246 p. 19 cm. (Oxford Russian readers) Russian text; English introd. and notes. 1. Russian literature — History and criticism — Addresses, essays, lectures. I. Richards, David, 1933- joint comp. II. T.
PG2932.K6   491.7/8/6421   LC 77-31408   ISBN 0198720300

Matejka, Ladislav, 1919- comp.   2.1242
Readings in Russian poetics: formalist and structuralist views. Edited by Ladislav Matejka and Krystyna Pomorska. Cambridge, MIT Press [1971] x, 306 p. 24 cm. 1. Literature — History and criticism — Theory, etc. — Addresses, essays, lectures. 2. Formalism (Literary analysis) — Addresses, essays, lectures. 3. Poetics — Addresses, essays, lectures. I. Pomorska, Krystyna. joint comp. II. T.
PG2932.M3x PN441.M34   801/.95/0947   LC 76-137472   ISBN 0262130696

Twentieth–century Russian literary criticism / edited by Victor Erlich.   2.1243
New Haven: Yale University Press, 1975. ix, 317 p.; 24 cm. 1. Russian literature — History and criticism — Addresses, essays, lectures. 2. Criticism — Russia — Addresses, essays, lectures. I. Erlich, Victor, 1914-
PG2932.T9   891.7/09/004   LC 74-29720   ISBN 0300018630

Handbook of Russian literature / edited by Victor Terras.   2.1244
New Haven: Yale University Press, c1985. xix, 558 p.; 29 cm. Includes index. 1. Russian literature — Dictionaries. I. Terras, Victor.
PG2940.H29 1985   891.7/03/21 19   LC 84-11871   ISBN 0300031556

The Literary appreciation of Russian writers / [edited by] Tom Stableford.   2.1245
Cambridge [Cambridgeshire]; New York: Cambridge University Press, 1981. x, 227 p.; 23 cm. English and Russian. Includes index. 1. Russian literature — Explication. 2. Russian language — Readers. 3. Russian language — Textbooks for English speakers. I. Stableford, Tom.
PG2945.L58 1981   891.7/09 19   LC 81-6192   ISBN 0521234980

Ermolaev, Herman.   • 2.1246
Soviet literary theories, 1917–1934; the genesis of socialist realism. Berkeley, University of California Press, 1963. 261 p. 24 cm. (University of California publications in modern philology, v.69) 1. Russian literature — 20th century — History and criticism 2. Literature — Philosophy I. T.
PG2948.E7   LC 63-63188

Tschižewskij, Dmitrij, 1894-.   • 2.1247
History of Russian literature; from the eleventh century to the end of the Baroque. 'S-Gravenhage Mouton 1960. 451p. (Slavistic printings and reprintings. 12) 1. Russian literature — History and criticism I. T. II. Series.
PG2951 C4

Lavrin, Janko, 1887-.   2.1248
A panorama of Russian literature. — New York: Barnes & Noble, [1973]. – 325 p.; 24 cm. — 1. Russian literature — History and criticism. I. T.
PG2951.L3   891.709   ISBN 0064940799

Mirsky, D. S., Prince, 1890-1939.   • 2.1249
A history of Russian literature, comprising A history of Russian literature and Contemporary Russian literature; edited and abridged by Francis J. Whitfield. New York, A. A. Knopf, 1949. xi, 518, xxiv p. 22 cm. 1. Russian literature — History and criticism. I. Whitfield, Francis J. (Francis James), 1916- ed. II. T.
PG2951.M49 1949   891.709   LC 49-10390

Slonim, Marc, 1894-1976.   • 2.1250
The epic of Russian literature from its origins through Tolstoy. — New York: Oxford University Press, 1950. vi, 367 p.; 25 cm. — 1. Russian literature — History and criticism. I. T.
PG2951.S5 1964   891.7/09   LC 49-11763

Tertz, Abram, pseud.   2.1251
On socialist realism. Introd. by Czeslaw Milosz. [Translated by George Dennis. — New York] Pantheon Books [c1960] 95 p. 22 cm. 1. Realism in literature 2. Russian literature — Hist. & crit. I. T. II. Title: Socialist realism.
PG2975.T413   891.7091   LC 61-10028

Mathewson, Rufus W.   2.1252
The positive hero in Russian literature / Rufus W. Mathewson, Jr. — 2d ed. — Stanford, Calif.: Stanford University Press, 1975. xix, 369 p.; 23 cm. 1. Heroes in literature 2. Russian literature — History and criticism. I. T.
PG2989.H4 M3 1975   891.7/09/352   LC 72-97207   ISBN 0804708363

PG3001–3026 History, by Period

Gudziĭ, N. K. (Nikolaĭ Kallinikovich), 1887-1965.   • 2.1253
[Istoriia drevneĭ russkoĭ literatury. English] History of early Russian literature, by N. K. Gudzy. Translated from the 2d Russian ed. by Susan Wilbur Jones. Introd. by Gleb Struve. New York, Octagon Books, 1970 [c1949] xix, 545 p. 25 cm. Added t.p. in Russian. Translation of Istoriia drevneĭ russkoĭ literatury (romanized form) 1. Russian literature — To 1700 — History and criticism. I. T.
PG3001.G762 1970   891.7/09001   LC 70-120620

Brown, William Edward, 1904-.   2.1254
A history of seventeenth-century Russian literature / William Edward Brown. — Ann Arbor: Ardis, c1980. 182 p.: ill.; 24 cm. Includes index. 1. Russian literature — To 1700 — History and criticism. I. T.
PG3002.B7   891.7/09/001   LC 79-21979   ISBN 0882333437

Brown, William Edward, 1904-.   2.1255
A history of 18th century Russian literature / William Edward Brown. — Ann Arbor, Mich.: Ardis, c1980. 659 p.: ill.; 24 cm. Includes index. 1. Russian literature — 18th century — History and criticism. I. T.
PG3007.B7   891.7/09/002   LC 79-21986   ISBN 0882333410

Fennell, John Lister Illingworth.   2.1256
Nineteenth century Russian literature; studies of ten Russian writers. Edited by John Fennell. — Berkeley, University of California Press, 1973. 356 p. 23 cm. 1. Russian literature — 19th century — Addresses, essays, lectures. I. T.
PG3011.F4 1973b   891.7/09/003   LC 72-89800   ISBN 0520023501

Tschižewskij, Dmitrij, 1894-.   2.1257
[Russische Literaturgeschichte des 19. Jahrhunderts. English] History of nineteenth–century Russian literature, by Dmitrij Cizevskij. Translated by Richard Noel Porter. Edited, with a foreword, by Serge A. Zenkovsky. Nashville, Vanderbilt University Press, 1974-. v. 22 cm. Translation of Russische Literaturgeschichte des 19. Jahrhunderts. 1. Russian literature — 19th century — History and criticism I. T.
PG3012.C513   891.7/09/003   LC 72-2878   ISBN 0826511872

Hingley, Ronald.   • 2.1258
Russian writers and society, 1825-1904. — New York: McGraw-Hill, [1967] 253 p.: illus. (part col.), maps (part col.), ports.; 19 cm. — (World University library) 1. Authors, Russian — Political and social views. 2. Literature and society I. T.
PG3012.H5   891.7/09003   LC 66-16480

Jackson, Robert Louis.   • 2.1259
Dostoevsky's underground man in Russian literature. 'S-Gravenhage Mouton 1958. 223p. (Slavistic printings and reprintings. 15) 1. Dostoyevsky, Fyodor, 1821-1881. 2. Russian literature — 19th century — History and criticism 3. Russian literature — 20th century — History and criticism I. T. II. Series.
PG3012 J3

Poggioli, Renato, 1907-1963.   • 2.1260
The phoenix and the spider; a book of essays about some Russian writers and their view of the self. Cambridge, Harvard University Press, 1957. 238 p. 25 cm. 1. Russian literature — History and criticism. 2. Literature — Psychology 3. Self-knowledge in literature I. T.
PG3012.P6   891.709   LC 57-11659

Roberts, Spencer E. comp.   • 2.1261
Essays in Russian literature; the conservative view: Leontiev, Rozanov, Shestov. Selected, edited, translated and with an introd. by Spencer E. Roberts. Athens, Ohio University Press, 1968. xxiii, 392 p. 22 cm. 1. Russian literature — 19th century — Addresses, essays, lectures. I. Leont'ev, Konstantin Nikolaevich, 1831-1891. II. Rozanov, V. V. (Vasiliĭ Vasil'evich), 1856-1919. III. Shestov, Lev, 1866-1938. IV. T.
PG3012.R6   891.7/09003   LC 68-19641

Slonim, Marc, 1894-1976.   **2.1262**
From Chekhov to the revolution; Russian literature, 1900–1917. New York Oxford University Press 1962. 253p. (Galaxy books, GB92) 1. Russian literature — 19th century — History and criticism 2. Russian literature — 20th century — History and criticism I. T.
PG3012 S57

Wilson, Edmund, 1895-1972.   **2.1263**
A window on Russia, for the use of foreign readers. — New York: Farrar, Straus and Giroux, [1972] 280 p.; 20 cm. 1. Russian literature — 19th century — Addresses, essays, lectures. 2. Russian literature — 20th century — Addresses, essays, lectures. 3. Russian language — Addresses, essays, lectures. I. T.
PG3012.W5   891.7/09   *LC* 70-183236   *ISBN* 0374290946

Literature and society in imperial Russia, 1800–1914 / edited by   **2.1264**
William Mills Todd, III; contributors, Robert L. Belknap ... [et al.].
Stanford, Calif.: Stanford University Press, 1978. x, 306 p.; 24 cm. Essays presented at a conference held at Stanford University on October 23 and 24, 1975. 1. Russian literature — 19th century — History and criticism — Congresses. 2. Literature and society — Congresses. I. Todd, William Mills, 1944- II. Belknap, Robert L. III. Stanford University.
PG3015.5.S6 L5   PG3015.5S6 L5.   891.7/09/003   *LC* 77-76153
  ISBN 0804709610

PG3016–3026 20TH CENTURY

Russian Modernism: culture and the avant–garde, 1900–1930 /   **2.1265**
edited by George Gibian and H. W. Tjalsma.
Ithaca, N.Y.: Cornell University Press, 1976. 239 p.: ill.; 23 cm. Outgrowth of a 1971 conference sponsored by the Dept. of Russian Literature, Cornell University. Appendices (p. [209]-231): 1. Russian text of poems by Mayakovsky.—2. Russian text of Kuzmin, The trout breaking through the ice. 1. Russian literature — 20th century — History and criticism 2. Modernism (Literature) — Soviet Union. 3. Art, Russian 4. Modernism (Art) — Soviet Union. 5. Literature, Experimental — Soviet Union. I. Gibian, George. II. Tjalsma, H. W.
PG3020.5.M6 R8   891.7/09/38   *LC* 75-36523   *ISBN* 0801408423

Gorky, Maksim, 1868-1936.   **2.1266**
[Selected works. English. 1973] On literature [by] Maxim Gorky. Seattle, University of Washington Press [1973] 396 p. 20 cm. (Soviet literary criticism) 1. Gorky, Maksim, 1868-1936. 2. Russian literature — 20th century — Addresses, essays, lectures. I. T.
PG3021.G643 1973   891.7/09   *LC* 72-11682

Terts, Abram, 1925-.   • **2.1267**
For freedom of imagination, by Andrei Sinyavsky. Translated and with an introd. by Laszlo Tikos and Murray Peppard. — [1st ed.]. — New York, Holt, Rinehart, and Winston [c1971] xxiii, 212 p. 22 cm. Essays. 1. Russian literature — 20th century — Addresses, essays, lectures. I. T.
PG3021.S5 1971   891.7/09/004   *LC* 79-122252   *ISBN* 0030852684

Brown, Deming, 1919-.   **2.1268**
Soviet Russian literature since Stalin / Deming Brown. — Cambridge; New York: Cambridge University Press, 1978. vi, 394 p.; 24 cm. Includes index. 1. Russian literature — 20th century — History and criticism I. T.
PG3022.B68   891.7/09/0044   *LC* 77-73275   *ISBN* 052121694X

Brown, Edward James, 1909-.   **2.1269**
Russian literature since the Revolution / Edward J. Brown. — Rev. and enl. ed. — Cambridge, Mass.: Harvard University Press, 1982. viii, 413 p.; 24 cm. Includes index. 1. Russian literature — 20th century — History and criticism I. T.
PG3022.B7 1982   891.7/09/004 19   *LC* 82-6064   *ISBN* 0674782038

Hayward, Max.   • **2.1270**
Literature and revolution in Soviet Russia, 1917–1962: a symposium / edited by Max Hayward and Leopold Labedz. — London; New York: Oxford University Press, 1963. xx, 235 p.; 23 cm. 1. Russian literature — 20th century — Addresses, essays, lectures. I. Labedz, Leopold. II. T.
PG3022.H3   *LC* 64-164

Hingley, Ronald.   **2.1271**
Russian writers and Soviet society, 1917–1978 / Ronald Hingley. — 1st American ed. — New York: Random House, c1979. xxi, 296 p.; 22 cm. Includes index. 1. Russian literature — 20th century — History and criticism I. T.
PG3022.H5 1979   891.7/09/0042   *LC* 78-21814   *ISBN* 0394427327

Maguire, Robert A., 1930-.   • **2.1272**
Red virgin soil; Soviet literature in the 1920's [by] Robert A. Maguire. — Princeton, N. J., Princeton University Press, 1968. xiv, 482 p. 23 cm. — (Studies of the Russian Institute, Columbia University) Bibliography: p. [447]-456. 1. Krasnaia nov'. 2. Russian literature — 20th cent. — Hist. & crit. I. T.
PG3022.M3   *LC* 67-12347

Muchnic, Helen.   **2.1273**
From Gorky to Pasternak: six writers in Soviet Russia / Helen Muchnic. — New York: Hippocrene Books, 1979, c1961. 438 p.; 24 cm. Reprint of the ed. published by Random House, New York. Includes index. 1. Russian literature — 20th century — History and criticism 2. Russian literature — 19th century — History and criticism I. T.
PG3022.M8 1979   891.7/09   *LC* 78-26018   *ISBN* 0374959862

Slonim, Marc, 1894-1976.   **2.1274**
Soviet Russian literature: writers and problems, 1917–1977 / Marc Slonim. 2d rev. ed. — New York: Oxford University Press, 1977. viii, 437 p.; 22 cm. Includes index. 1. Russian literature — 20th century — History and criticism I. T.
PG3022.S54 1977   891.7/09/0042   *LC* 76-426661   *ISBN* 0195021517

Struve, Gleb.   • **2.1275**
[Soviet Russian literature] Russian literature under Lenin and Stalin, 1917–1953. [1st ed.] Norman, University of Oklahoma Press [1971] xvi, 454 p. 24 cm. Revision of the 1951 ed. of Soviet Russian literature. 1. Russian literature — 20th century — History and criticism I. T.
PG3022.S82 1971   891.7/09/004   *LC* 68-31370   *ISBN* 0806109319

Erlich, Victor, 1914-.   • **2.1276**
Russian formalism. History–doctrine. 3d ed. The Hague, Mouton, 1969. 311 p. 24 1/2 cm. (Slavistic printings and reprintings, 4) 1. Formalism (Literary analysis) 2. Russian literature — History and criticism. I. T.
PG3026.F6 E7 1969   891.7/09   *LC* 70-468634

Trotsky, Leon, 1879-1940.   • **2.1277**
Literature and revolution. — New York, Russell & Russell, 1957. 255 p. 21 cm. 1. Russian literature — 20th cent. — Hist. & crit. 2. Socialism in literature I. T.
PG3026.P6T715 1957   891.70904   *LC* 57-11985

PG3041–3155 Special Literary Forms

PG3041–3089 POETRY. DRAMA

Hingley, Ronald.   **2.1278**
Nightingale fever: Russian poets in revolution / Ronald Hingley. — 1st ed. — New York: Knopf, 1981. xiii, 269 p.: ports.; 25 cm. Includes index. 1. Mandel'shtam, Osip, 1891-1938 — Criticism and interpretation. 2. Akhmatova, Anna Andreevna, 1889-1966 — Criticism and interpretation. 3. Pasternak, Boris Leonidovich, 1890-1960 — Criticism and interpretation. 4. TSvetaeva, Marina, 1892-1941 — Criticism and interpretation. 5. Russian poetry — 20th century — History and criticism I. T.
PG3056.H5   891.71/42/09 19   *LC* 81-47498   *ISBN* 0394504518

Poggioli, Renato, 1907-1963.   • **2.1279**
The poets of Russia, 1890–1930. Cambridge, Mass., Harvard University Press, 1960. xix, 383 p. 24 cm. Bibliography: p. 345-367. 1. Poets, Russian I. T.
PG3056.P6   891.71309   *LC* 60-8000

Markov, Vladimir.   • **2.1280**
Russian futurism; a history. — Berkeley, University of California Press, 1968. xi, 467 p. illus., facsims., ports. 24 cm. 1. Futurism. 2. Russian poetry — 20th century — History and criticism I. T.
PG3065.F8 M33   891.7/1/3091   *LC* 68-14975

Segel, Harold B., 1930-.   **2.1281**
Twentieth–century Russian drama: from Gorky to the present / Harold B. Segel. — New York: Columbia University Press, 1979. xvi, 502 p.: ill.; 24 cm. Includes index. 1. Russian drama — 20th century — History and criticism. I. T.
PG3086.S44   891.7/2/509   *LC* 79-11673   *ISBN* 023104576X

Yershov, Peter, 1895-.   • **2.1282**
Comedy in the Soviet theater. New York: Published for the Research Program
on the U.S.S.R. by Praeger, 1957, c1956. 280 p. (Research monographs of the
Research Program on the U.S.S.R.; no.2) (Praeger publications in Russian
history and world communism; no. 26) 1. Russian drama (Comedy) — History
& criticism. I. T.
PG3089.C6 Y4   *LC* 56-13219

PG3095–3140 FICTION. FOLK LORE

Dunham, Vera Sadomirsky, 1912-.   **2.1283**
In Stalin's time: middleclass values in Soviet fiction / Vera S. Dunham; introd.
by Jerry F. Hough. — Cambridge [Eng.]; New York: Cambridge University
Press, 1976. xiv, 283 p.; 24 cm. Includes index. 1. Russian fiction — 20th
century — History and criticism. 2. Literature and state — Russia.
3. Communism and literature 4. Middle classes — Russia. 5. Russia —
Politics and government — 1936-1953. I. T.
PG3095.D8   891.7/3/03   *LC* 75-10238   *ISBN* 0521209498

Freeborn, Richard.   **2.1284**
The rise of the Russian novel; studies in the Russian novel from Eugene Onegin
to War and Peace. — Cambridge [Eng.]: Cambridge University Press, 1973.
289 p.; 23 cm. 1. Russian fiction — 19th century — History and criticism. I. T.
PG3095.F7   891.7/3/03   *LC* 75-190417   *ISBN* 0521085888

Reeve, F. D. (Franklin D.), 1928-.   • **2.1285**
The Russian novel, by F. D. Reeve. [1st ed.] New York, McGraw-Hill [1966] vi,
397 p. 21 cm. Bibliography: p. 379-386. 1. Russian fiction — History and
criticism. I. T.
PG3095.R4   891.7303   *LC* 65-24895

O'Toole, L. M. (Lawrence Michael), 1934-.   **2.1286**
Structure, style, and interpretation in the Russian short story / L. Michael
O'Toole. — New Haven: Yale University Press, 1982. viii, 272 p.; 25 cm.
Includes index. 1. Short stories, Russian — History and criticism. 2. Russian
fiction — 19th century — History and criticism. I. T. II. Title: Russian short
story.
PG3097.O85 1982   891.73/01/09 19   *LC* 81-11650   *ISBN*
0300027303

Calder, Angus.   **2.1287**
Russia discovered: nineteenth–century fiction from Pushkin to Chekhov /
Angus Calder. — London: Heinemann; New York: Barnes and Noble, 1976.
xiii, 302 p.; 23 cm. Includes index. 1. Russian fiction — 19th century —
History and criticism. I. T.
PG3098.3.C3 1976   PG3098.3 C3 1976.   891.7/3/309   *LC*
76-380652   *ISBN* 0064909247

Mersereau, John, 1925-.   **2.1288**
Russian romantic fiction / John Mersereau, Jr. — Ann Arbor: Ardis, c1983.
336 p.: ill.; 24 cm. 1. Russian fiction — 19th century — History and criticism.
2. Romanticism I. T.
PG3098.3.M47 1983   891.73/3/09 19   *LC* 82-20758   *ISBN*
0882337394

The Russian novel from Pushkin to Pasternak / edited by John   **2.1289**
Garrard.
New Haven: Yale University Press, c1983. xii, 300 p.; 24 cm. Includes index.
1. Russian fiction — 19th century — History and criticism — Addresses,
essays, lectures. 2. Russian fiction — 20th century — History and criticism —
Addresses, essays, lectures. I. Garrard, John Gordon.
PG3098.3.R87 1983   891.73/009 19   *LC* 83-1070   *ISBN*
0300029357

Clark, Katerina.   **2.1290**
The Soviet novel: history as ritual / Katerina Clark. — Chicago: University of
Chicago Press, c1981. xv, 293 p.; 22 cm. Includes index. 1. Russian fiction —
20th century — History and criticism. 2. Socialist realism in literature I. T.
PG3098.4.C4   891.73/409   *LC* 80-18758   *ISBN* 0226107663

Hosking, Geoffrey A.   **2.1291**
Beyond socialist realism: Soviet fiction since Ivan Denisovich / Geoffrey
Hosking. — New York: Holmes & Meier Publishers, 1980. x, 260 p.; 23 cm.
Includes index. 1. Russian fiction — 20th century — History and criticism.
I. T.
PG3098.4.H67 1980   891.7/3/4409   *LC* 78-31891   *ISBN*
0841904847

Afanas'ev, A. N. (Aleksandr Nikolaevich), 1826-1871.   **2.1292**
Russian fairy tales / translated by Norbert Guterman from the collections of
Aleksandr Afanas'ev; ill. by Alexander Alexeieff; folkloristic commentary by
Roman Jakobson. — New York: Pantheon Books, c1973. 661 p.: ill.; 25 cm.
Translation of selections from Narodnyia russkiia skazki. 1. Fairy tales,

Russian. 2. Folklore — Russia. I. Guterman, Norbert, 1900- II. Alexeieff,
Alexandre, 1901- III. Jakobson, Roman, 1896- IV. T.
PG3115.A3713 1975   398.2/0947   *LC* 45-37884   *ISBN*
0394730909

Down along the Mother Volga: an anthology of Russian folk   **2.1293**
lyrics / translated and edited by Roberta Reeder; with an
introductory essay by V. Ja. Propp.
Philadelphia: University of Pennsylvania Press, [1975] xvii, 246 p.: ill.; 21 cm.
— (University of Pennsylvania publications in folklore and folklife) The
introductory essay by Propp is a translation of O russkoĭ narodnoĭ liricheskoĭ
pesne which was originally published in Narodnye liricheskie pesni, 1961.
Includes index. 1. Folk-songs, Russian — Soviet Union — Texts. I. Reeder,
Roberta. II. Propp, V. IA. (Vladimir IAkovlevich), 1895-1970. O russkoĭ
narodnoĭ liricheskoi pesne. English. 1975.
PG3140.D6 1975   784.4/947   *LC* 74-84293   *ISBN* 0812276688

PG3200–3299 Collections

The Ardis anthology of recent Russian literature / edited by   **2.1294**
Carl Proffer & Ellendea Proffer.
Ann Arbor [Mich.]: Ardis, [1975] xvi, 420 p.: ill.; 24 cm. 1. Russian literature
— 20th century — Translations into English. 2. English literature —
Translations from Russian. I. Proffer, Carl R. II. Proffer, Ellendea.
PG3213.A7   891.7/1/4408   *LC* 75-330592

The Ardis anthology of Russian romanticism / edited by   **2.1295**
Christine Rydel.
Ann Arbor: Ardis, c1984. 536 p.: ill.; 25 cm. Translated from Russian.
1. Russian literature — 19th century — Translations into English. 2. English
literature — Translations from Russian. 3. Russian literature — 19th century
— History and criticism — Addresses, essays, lectures. I. Rydel, Christine.
II. Title: Russian romanticism.
PG3213.A74 1984   891.7/08/03 19   *LC* 83-15494   *ISBN*
0882337416

The Bitter air of exile: Russian writers in the West, 1922–1972   **2.1296**
/ edited by Simon Karlinsky and Alfred Appel, Jr.
Rev. — Berkeley: University of California Press, c1977. 473 p.: ill.; 22 cm.
'Originally published as Russian literature and culture in the West: 1922-1972,
volumes 27 (spring 1973) and 28 (fall 1973) of TriQuarterly.' 1. Russian
literature — 20th century — Translations into English. 2. English literature —
Translations from Russian. 3. Russian literature — Foreign countries
I. Karlinsky, Simon. II. Appel, Alfred. III. Tri-quarterly.
PG3213.B5 1977   891.7/4/208   *LC* 74-84147   *ISBN* 0520028465.
ISBN 0520028953 pbk

Blake, Patricia. ed.   • **2.1297**
Dissonant voices in Soviet literature, edited by Patricia Blake and Max
Hayward. — [New York]: Pantheon Books, [1962] 308 p.; 22 cm. 1. Russian
literature — 20th century — Translation into English. 2. English literature —
Translations from Russian. I. Hayward, Max. joint ed. II. T.
PG3213.B55 1962   891.7083   *LC* 62-11083

Gibian, George. comp.   • **2.1298**
Russia's lost literature of the absurd: a literary discovery. Selected works of
Daniil Kharms and Alexander Vvedensky. Edited and translated by George
Gibian. — Ithaca, Cornell University Press [1971] ix, 208 p. 20 cm. 1. Russian
literature — Translations into English. 2. English literature — Translations
from Russian. 3. Russian literature — 20th century I. Kharms, Daniil,
1905-1942. II. Vvedenskiĭ, Aleksandr Ivanovich, 1904-1941. III. T.
PG3213.G5   891.7/08/0044   *LC* 74-160847   *ISBN* 0801406536

Guerney, Bernard Guilbert, 1894- ed.   • **2.1299**
A treasury of Russian literature; being a comprehensive selection of many of the
best things by numerous authors in practically every field of the rich literature
of Russia from its beginnings to the present, with much material now first made
available in English, and all of the accepted favorites newly translated or their
current translations thoroughly revised. Selected and edited, with a foreword
and biographical and critical notes, by Bernard Guilbert Guerney. New York,
The Vanguard press [1943] xx p., 1 l., 1048 p., 1 l. 23 cm. 1. Russian literature
— Translations into English. 2. English literature — Translations from
Russian. I. T.
PG3213.G8 1943   PG3213.G8.   891.7082   *LC* 43-17369

McLean, Hugh, 1925- ed.   **2.1300**
The year of protest, 1956; an anthology of soviet literary materials. Translated
and edited, with an introd., by Hugh McLean and Walter N. Vickery. —
Westport, Conn.: Greenwood Press, [1974, c1961] 269 p.; 22 cm. Reprint of the
ed. published by Vintage Books, New York, which was issued as no. V-730 of
Vintage Russian library. 1. Russian literature — 20th century — Translations

into English. 2. English literature — Translations from Russian. I. Vickery, Walter N., 1921- joint ed. and tr. II. T.
PG3213.M3 1974   891.7/08/0044   *LC* 74-8359   *ISBN* 0837175755

Metropol', 1979 g. English.   **2.1301**
Metropol: literary almanac / edited by Vasily Aksyonov ... [et al.]; foreword by Kevin Klose. — 1st ed. — New York, N.Y.: W.W. Norton, c1982. xx, 636 p.: ill.; 22 cm. Translation of: Metropol', 1979 g. 1. Russian literature — 20th century — Translations into English. 2. English literature — Translations from Russian. I. Aksenov, Vasiliĭ Pavlovich, 1932- II. T.
PG3213.M47 1982   891.7/08/0044 19   *LC* 81-9540   *ISBN* 039301438X

Pachmuss, Temira, 1927-.   **2.1302**
A Russian cultural revival: a critical anthology of émigré literature before 1939 / Temira Pachmuss, editor and translator. — 1st ed. — Knoxville: The University of Tennessee Press, c1981. xxii, 454 p.; 24 cm. 1. Russian literature — 20th century — Translations into English. 2. Russian literature — Foreign countries 3. Russian literature — France. 4. English literature — Translations from Russian. I. T.
PG3213.P3   891.7 19   *LC* 80-20670   *ISBN* 0870492969

The Portable twentieth century Russian reader / edited, with an   **2.1303**
introduction and notes, by Clarence Brown.
New York: Viking, 1985. xviii, 599 p.; 19 cm. (Viking portable library.) 1. Russian literature — 20th century — Translations into English. 2. English literature — Translations from Russian. I. Brown, Clarence, 1929- II. Title: Portable 20th century Russian reader. III. Series.
PG3213.P67 1985   891.7/008/004 19   *LC* 84-17354   *ISBN* 0670805319

Kunitz, Joshua, 1896-.   **2.1304**
Russian literature since the Revolution / edited by Joshua Kunitz. — New York: Boni and Gaer, c1948. x, 932 p. 1. Russian literature — Translations into English. 2. English literature — Translations from Russian. I. T.
PG3213.R88   891.7   *LC* 48-8087

Segel, Harold B., 1930- comp.   **2.1305**
The literature of eighteenth–century Russia; an anthology of Russian literary materials of the age of classicism and the Enlightenment from the reign of Peter the Great, 1689–1725, to the reign of Alexander I, 1801–1825. Edited and translated, and with an introd. and notes, by Harold B. Segel. [1st ed.] New York, Dutton, 1967. 2 v. illus., facsims., ports. 20 cm. 1. Russian literature — Translations into English. 2. English literature — Translations from Russian. 3. Russian literature — 18th century — History and criticism. I. T.
PG3213.S4   891.7/08/002   *LC* 67-21985

The Silver age of Russian culture: an anthology / edited by Carl   **2.1306**
Proffer & Ellendea Proffer.
Ann Arbor: Ardis, c1975. xii, 432, [22] p.: ill.; 24 cm. Appendix (p. [433]-[454]): Russian texts. 1. Russian literature — Translations into English. 2. English literature — Translations from Russian. 3. Russian literature — History and criticism — Addresses, essays, lectures. I. Proffer, Carl R. II. Proffer, Ellendea. III. Russian literature triquarterly.
PG3213.S5   891.7/08/003   *LC* 75-331080   *ISBN* 088233171X

Women writers in Russian modernism: an anthology / translated   **2.1307**
and edited by Temira Pachmuss.
Urbana: University of Illinois Press, c1978. xvi, 340 p.: ill.; 23 cm. 1. Russian literature — 20th century — Translations into English. 2. English literature — Translations from Russian. 3. Russian literature — Women authors. 4. Modernism (Literature) — Soviet Union. I. Pachmuss, Temira, 1927-
PG3213.W6   891.7/08/09287 19   *LC* 78-8957   *ISBN* 0252002245

Medieval Russia's epics, chronicles, and tales / edited,   • **2.1308**
translated, and with an introd. by Serge A. Zenkovsky.
New York: Dutton, 1963. xi, 436 p.: ill. 1. Epic literature, Russian — Translations into English. I. Zenkovsky, Serge A.
PG3213.Z4   PG3130.M4.   891.7/08/001   *LC* 63-8606

PG3230–3238 Poetry

The Oxford book of Russian verse, chosen by the Hon. Maurice   • **2.1309**
Baring.
2d ed. supplemented by D.P. Costello. Oxford The Clarendon press 1948. xliv, 3ll p. 'Notes [by Prince D.S. Mirsky]': p. 277-304. 1. Russian poetry (Collections) I. Baring, , Maurice, Hon. 1874-1945, comp. II. Costello, D.P.
PG3233.O8 1948   PG3230.5 O8 1948.   *LC* 49-8794

The Ardis anthology of Russian futurism / edited by Ellendea   **2.1310**
Proffer, Carl R. Proffer.
Ann Arbor, Mich.: Ardis, c1980. 392 p., [18] leaves of plates: ill.; 24 cm. 1. Russian poetry — 20th century — Translations into English. 2. English

poetry — Translations from Russian. I. Proffer, Ellendea. II. Proffer, Carl R. III. Title: Russian futurism. IV. Title: Futurism.
PG3237.E5 A7   891.71/42/08 19   *LC* 80-131708   *ISBN* 0882334697

Chadwick, Nora K. (Nora Kershaw), 1891-1972. tr.   • **2.1311**
Russian heroic poetry, by N. Kershaw Chadwick. New York, Russell & Russell, 1964. xv, 294 p. illus., plans, port. 22 cm. 'First published in 1932. Reisssued, 1964.' 1. Byliny 2. Russian poetry — Translations into English. 3. English poetry — Translations from Russian. I. T.
PG3237.E5 C5 1964   *LC* 64-10386

Markov, Vladimir. comp.   • **2.1312**
Modern Russian poetry; an anthology with verse translations, edited, and with an introd. by Vladimir Markov and Merrill Sparks. [1st American ed.] Indianapolis, Bobbs-Merrill [1967] lxxx, 842 p. 21 cm. Text in English and Russian. Bibliographical references included in 'Notes' (p. 827-842) 1. Russian poetry — 20th century 2. Russian poetry — Translations into English. 3. English poetry — Translations from Russian. I. Sparks, Merrill, joint comp. II. T.
PG3237.E5M28 1967   891.7/1/408   *LC* 66-29900

Obolensky, Dimitri, 1918- ed.   **2.1313**
[Penguin book of Russian verse] The heritage of Russian verse / introduced and edited by Dimitri Obolensky, with plain prose translations of each poem. — Bloomington: Indiana University Press, 1976. lx, 472 p.; 22 cm. Reprint of the rev. ed. published in 1965 by Penguin Books, Harmondsworth, Eng., under title: The Penguin book of Russian verse. Includes indexes. 1. Russian poetry — Translations into English. 2. English literature — Translations from Russian. 3. Russian poetry I. T.
PG3237.E5 O2 1976   891.7/1/008   *LC* 75-23893   *ISBN* 0253327350. *ISBN* 0253327369 pbk

Reavey, George, 1907- ed.   • **2.1314**
The new Russian poets, 1953–1966; an anthology. [1st ed.] New York, October House [1966] xxvii, 292 p. 23 cm. 'Bilingual edition.' Bibliography: p. 270-282. 1. Russian poetry — 20th century 2. Russian poetry — Translations into English. 3. English poetry — Translations from Russian. I. T.
PG3237.E5R4   891.7108   *LC* 66-15272

Russian poetry, the modern period / edited by John Glad and   **2.1315**
Daniel Weissbort.
Iowa City: University of Iowa Press, c1978. lxii, 356 p.; 23 cm. (Iowa translations.) 1. Russian poetry — 20th century — Translations into English. 2. Russian poetry — Foreign countries — Translations into English. 3. English poetry — Translations from Russian. I. Glad, John. II. Weissbort, Daniel. III. Series.
PG3237.E5 R8   891.7/1/408   *LC* 78-8650   *ISBN* 0877450838

Yarmolinsky, Avrahm, 1890- ed.   • **2.1316**
Two centuries of Russian verse; an anthology from Lomonosov to Voznesensky. Translations from the Russsian by Babette Deutsch. New York, Random House [1966] xxvi, 322 p. 22 cm. ' A thoroughly revised and much expanded edition of An anthology of Russian verse, 1812-1960, published in 1962 [which] ... is a revised and augmented edition of a treasury of Russian verse, published in 1949.' 1. Russian poetry — Translations into English. 2. English poetry — Translations from Russian. I. Deutsch, Babette, 1895- tr. II. T.
PG3237.E5 Y3 1966   *LC* 66-10992

PG3240–3255 Drama

Four Russian plays. Fonvízin: The infant; Griboyédov: Chatsky;   **2.1317**
Gógol: The inspector; Ostróvsky: Thunder; translated from the
Russian with an introduction and notes by Joshua Cooper.
Harmondsworth: Penguin, 1972. 394 p.; 19 cm. — (The Penguin classics) 1. Russian drama — Translations into English. 2. English drama — Translations from Russian. I. Cooper, Joshua, tr.
PG3245.F59   891.7/2/208   *LC* 72-187965   *ISBN* 0140442588

Reeve, F. D. (Franklin D.), 1928- ed. and tr.   • **2.1318**
An anthology of Russian plays; edited, translated, and introduced, by F. D. Reeve. New York, Vintage Books [1961-63] 2 v. 19 cm. (Vintage Russian library, V-731-V732) 1. Russian drama — Translations into English. 2. English drama — Translations from Russian. I. T.
PG3245.R4   891.72082   *LC* 61-14896

Reeve, F. D. (Franklin D.), 1928- comp.   • **2.1319**
Contemporary Russian drama, selected and translated by Franklin D. Reeve. With a pref. by Victor Rozov. New York, Pegasus [1968] 303 p. 22 cm. 1. Russian drama — 20th century. 2. Russian drama — Translations into English. 3. English drama — Translations from Russian. I. T.
PG3245.R42   891.72/4/408   *LC* 68-21038

Russian satiric comedy: six plays / edited and translated, with   **• 2.1320**
an introduction, by Laurence Senelick.
New York : Performing Arts Journal Publications, 1983. 198 p. (PAJ playscript
series) 1. Russian drama (Comedy) 2. Satire, Russian I. Senelick, Laurence.
PG3245.R87 1983   *LC* 83-61195   *ISBN* 0933826524

PG3260–3299 PROSE

Yarmolinsky, Avrahm, 1890-.   **• 2.1321**
Soviet short stories. — 1st ed. — Garden City, N.Y.: Anchor books, 1960.
301 p.; 18 cm. — (A Doubleday Anchor original; A218) 1. Short stories,
Russian — Translations into English I. T.
PG3270.5.Y25   *LC* 60-13565

Contemporary Russian prose / edited by Carl & Ellendea   **2.1322**
Proffer.
Ann Arbor, MI: Ardis, c1982. xxxii, 430 p.: ports.; 24 cm. 1. Russian fiction —
20th century — Translations into English. 2. English fiction — Translations
from Russian. I. Proffer, Carl R. II. Proffer, Ellendea.
PG3276.C6   891.73/44/08 19   *LC* 81-14903   *ISBN* 0882335960

Rahv, Philip, 1908-1973.   **• 2.1323**
Great Russian short novels / edited with an introduction by Philip Rahv. —
New York: Dial Press, c1951. xix, 774 p.; 22 cm. — (A Permanent library book)
1. Russian fiction — Translations into English. 2. English fiction —
Translations from Russian. I. T.
PG3276.R3   *LC* 51-13886

Russian and Polish women's fiction / translated and edited by   **2.1324**
Helena Goscilo.
Knoxville: University of Tennessee Press, c1985. xii, 343 p.: ill.; 23 cm.
1. Russian fiction — Women authors — Translations into English. 2. Polish
fiction — Women authors — Translations into English. 3. English fiction —
Translations from Russian. 4. English fiction — Translations from Polish.
I. Goscilo, Helena, 1945-
PG3276.R87 1985   891.73/008/09287 19   *LC* 84-20915   *ISBN*
0870494562

An anthology of Russian neo–realism: the 'Znanie' School of   **2.1325**
Maxim Gorky / Nicholas Luker, edited & translated.
Ann Arbor, Mich.: Ardis, c1982. 283 p.: ill.; 24 cm. 1. Short stories, Russian —
Translations into English. 2. Short stories, English — Translations from
Russian. I. Luker, Nicholas J. L. II. Title: 'Znanie' School of Maxim Gorky.
PG3286.A57 1982   891.73/01/08 19   *LC* 81-12758   *ISBN*
0882334212

The Barsukov triangle, The two–toned blonde & other stories /   **2.1326**
edited by Carl R. Proffer & Ellendea Proffer.
Ann Arbor, Mich.: Ardis, c1984. xxxiv, 370 p.; 22 cm. Translation from
Russian. 1. Short stories, Russian — Translations into English. 2. Short
stories, English — Translations from Russian. I. Proffer, Carl R. II. Proffer,
Ellendea.
PG3286.B3 1984   891.73/01/08 19   *LC* 84-387   *ISBN* 0882338056

Fifty years of Russian prose; from Pasternak to Solzhenitsyn.   **2.1327**
Edited by Krystyna Pomorska.
Cambridge, Mass.: MIT Press, [c1971] 2 v.: port.; 24 cm. 1. Short stories,
Russian — Translations into English. 2. Short stories, English — Translations
from Russian. I. Pomorska, Krystyna. ed.
PG3286.F5x   891.7/3/408   *LC* 70-122263   *ISBN* 0262160374

Scammell, Michael. comp.   **• 2.1328**
Russia's other writers; selections from Samizdat literature. Selected and
introduced by Michael Scammell. Foreword by Max Hayward. — New York:
Praeger, [1971, c1970] viii, 216 p.; 23 cm. 1. Russian fiction — Translations
into English. 2. English fiction — Translations from Russian. 3. Underground
literature — Russia. I. T.
PG3286.S3x   891.7/3/4408   Fic   *LC* 74-83344

Yarmolinsky, Avrahm, 1890-.   **• 2.1329**
A treasury of great Russian short stories, Pushkin to Gorky, edited by Avrahm
Yarmolinsky. New York, The Macmillan company, 1944. xxi p., 1 l., 1018 p. 24
cm. 'First printing.' 1. Short stories, Russian 2. Russian fiction — Translations
into English. 3. English fiction — Translations from Russian. I. T.
PG3286.Y3x   *LC* 44-1281

PG3300–3698 Individual Authors (by Period)

PG3300–3319 To 1800

Slovo o polku Igoreve. English.   **2.1330**
The song of Igor's campaign: an epic of the twefth century / Slovo o polku
Igoreve; translated from Old Russian by Vladimir Nabokov. — New York:
Vintage Books, c1960. 135 p.: map. 1. Soviet Union — History — To 1533
I. Nabokov, Vladimir Vladimirovich, 1899-1977. II. T.
PG3300.S6 E57   *LC* 60-7688

Karamzin, Nikolaĭ Mikhaĭlovich, 1766-1826.   **• 2.1331**
[Short stories. Selections. English] Selected prose. Translated and with an
introd. by Henry M. Nebel, Jr. Evanston, Northwestern University Press, 1969.
xv, 214 p. 23 cm. (Publications of eighteenth-century Russian literature) I. T.
PG3314.A25   891.73/2   *LC* 68-54886

Cross, Anthony Glenn.   **• 2.1332**
N. M. Karamzin: a study of his literary career, 1783–1803 [by] A. G. Cross. —
Carbondale: Southern Illinois University Press, [1971] xxi, 306 p.: illus., ports.;
24 cm. 1. Karamzin, Nikolaĭ Mikhaĭlovich, 1766-1826. I. T.
PG3314.Z7 C7   891.7/8/209   *LC* 78-112385   *ISBN* 080930452X

Nebel, Henry M.   **• 2.1333**
N. M. Karamzin, a Russian sentimentalist, by Henry M. Nebel, Jr. — The
Hague: Mouton, 1967. 190 p.; 25 cm. — (Slavistic printings and reprintings. 60)
1. Karamzin, Nikolaĭ Mikhaĭlovich, 1766-1826 — Criticism and
interpretation. I. T. II. Series.
PG3314.Z7 N4   *LC* 67-5596

Kochetkova, N. D.   **2.1334**
Nikolay Karamzin / by Natalya Kochetkova. — New York: Twayne
Publishers, [1975] 154 p.: port.; 21 cm. (Twayne's world authors series; TWAS
250: Russia) Includes index. 1. Karamzin, Nikolaĭ Mikhaĭlovich, 1766-1826 —
Criticism and interpretation. I. T.
PG3314.Z8 K6   891.7/8/209   *LC* 70-188827   *ISBN* 0805724885

Jones, W. Gareth, 1936-.   **2.1335**
Nikolay Novikov, enlightener of Russia / W. Gareth Jones. — Cambridge
[Cambridgeshire]; New York: Cambridge University Press, 1984. ix, 273 p.; 23
cm. — (Cambridge studies in Russian literature.) Includes index. 1. Novikov,
Nikolaĭ Ivanovich, 1744-1818. 2. Novikov, Nikolaĭ Ivanovich, 1744-1818 —
Contemporary Russia. 3. Authors, Russian — 18th century — Biography.
4. Enlightenment 5. Soviet Union — Intellectual life — 18th century. I. T.
II. Series.
PG3317.N6 Z67 1984   070.5/092/4 B 19   *LC* 83-19040   *ISBN*
0521258227

McConnell, Allen, 1923-.   **• 2.1336**
A Russian philosopher, Alexander Radishchev, 1749–1802 / by Allen
McConnell — The Hague: M. Nijhoff, 1964. ix, 228 p. 1. Radishchev,
Aleksandr Nikolaevich, 1749-1802. I. T.
PG3317.R3 Z74   *LC* 65-6449

PG3320–3347 1800-1870

PG3320–3321 A–C

Serman, Il'ia Zakharovich.   **2.1337**
Konstantin Batyushkov / by Ilya Z. Serman. — New York: Twayne Publishers,
[1974] 187 p.: port.; 22 cm. — (Twayne's world authors series; TWAS 287)
Includes index. 1. Batiushkov, Konstantin Nikolaevich, 1787-1855 —
Criticism and interpretation. I. T.
PG3321.B4 Z85   891.7/1/3   *LC* 70-169624   *ISBN* 0805721185

Chernyshevsky, Nikolay Gavrilovich, 1828-1889.   **• 2.1338**
What is to be done? Tales about new people. Introd. by E. H. Carr. The
Benjamin R. Tucker translation, rev. and abridged by Ludmila B. Turkevich.
New York, Vintage Books [1961] 354 p. 19 cm. (Vintage Russian library,
V-723) I. T.
PG3321.C6A28 1961   *LC* 61-2225

PG3325–3328 Dostoevsky

Dostoyevsky, Fyodor, 1821-1881.   • **2.1339**
The notebooks for The possessed. Edited and with an introd. by Edward Wasiolek. Translated by Victor Terras. Chicago, University of Chicago Press [1968] 431 p. facsims. 24 cm. Translation of Zapisnye tetradi rearranged in approximate chronological order with some omissions (romanized form) I. Wasiolek, Edward. ed. II. T. III. Title: The possessed.
PG3325.A16 Z313 1968   891.7/3/3   LC 68-26763

Terras, Victor.   **2.1340**
A Karamazov companion: commentary on the genesis, language, and style of Dostoevsky's novel / Victor Terras. — Madison: University of Wisconsin Press, 1981. xiv, 482 p.; 22 cm. Includes index. 1. Dostoyevsky, Fyodor, 1821-1881. Brat'ia Karamazovy. I. T.
PG3325.B73 T47   891.73/3 19   LC 80-5117   ISBN 0299083101

Dostoyevsky, Fyodor, 1821-1881.   • **2.1341**
[F.M. Dostoevskiĭ; materialy i issledovaniia. English. Selections] The notebooks for the Brothers Karamazov [by] Fyodor Dostoevsky. Edited and translated by Edward Wasiolek. Chicago, University of Chicago Press [1971] 279 p. facsims., port. 25 cm. Translation of selections from F. M. Dostoevskiĭ; materialy i issledovaniia (romanized form) 1. Dostoyevsky, Fyodor, 1821-1881. Brat'ia Karamazovy. I. Dostoyevsky, Fyodor, 1821-1881. Brat'ia Karamazovy. II. T.
PG3325.B73 W3313   891.7/3/3   LC 74-126073   ISBN 0226159671

Dostoyevsky, Fyodor, 1821-1881.   • **2.1342**
The notebooks for The idiot [by] Fyodor Dostoevsky. Edited and with an introd. by Edward Wasiolek. Translated by Katharine Strelsky. — Chicago, University of Chicago Press [1967] 254 p. facsims. 24 cm. Translation of Iz arkhiva F. M. Dostoevskogo: Idiot; neizdannye materialy (romanized form) I. Wasiolek, Edward. ed. II. Dostoyevsky, Fyodor, 1821-1881. Idiot. III. T.
PG3325.I33 W313   891.7/3/3   LC 67-25513

Dostoyevsky, Fyodor, 1821-1881.   • **2.1343**
The notebooks for A raw youth [by] Fyodor Dostoevsky. Edited and with an introd. by Edward Wasiolek. Translated by Victor Terras. Chicago, University of Chicago Press [1969] 570 p. facsims., port. 25 cm. I. Dostoyevsky, Fyodor, 1821-1881. Podrostok. II. T.
PG3325.P53 W313   891.7/3/3   LC 75-84588   ISBN 0226159655

Dostoyevsky, Fyodor, 1821-1881.   • **2.1344**
[Prestuplenie i nakazanie; neizdannye materialy. English] The notebooks for Crime and punishment [by] Fyodor Dostoevsky. Edited and translated by Edward Wasiolek. Chicago, University of Chicago Press [1967] vi, 246 p. illus. 24 cm. Translation of Prestuplenie i nakazanie; neizdannye materialy (romanized form) I. T.
PG3325.P73 A53   891.73/3   LC 66-23702

Jackson, Robert Louis. comp.   **2.1345**
Twentieth century interpretations of Crime and punishment; a collection of critical essays. Englewood Cliffs, N.J., Prentice-Hall [1973, c1974] iv, 122 p. 21 cm. (A Spectrum book) 1. Dostoyevsky, Fyodor, 1821-1881 Prestuplenie i nakazanie — Addresses, essays, lectures. I. T.
PG3325.P73 J3 1974   891.7/3/3   LC 73-15716   ISBN 0131930869
ISBN 0131930788

Dostoyevsky, Fyodor, 1821-1881.   • **2.1346**
[Selected works. English] The short novels of Dosetoevsky, with an introduction by Thomas Mann. New York, Dial Press [1945] xx, 811 p. 22 cm. (A permanent library book) 'Translated ... by Constance Garnett.' I. Mann, Thomas, 1875-1955. II. Garnett, Constance Black, 1862-1946. tr. III. T.
PG3326.A15 1945   LC 46-555

Dostoyevsky, Fyodor, 1821-1881.   • **2.1347**
The short stories of Dostoevsky, edited, with an introduction, by William Phillips. — New York, The Dial press [1946] xx, 614 p. 22 cm. — ([Permanent library books]) 'Translated by Constance Garnett.' I. Phillips, William, 1907 Nov. 14- ed. II. Garnett, Constance Black, 1862-1946. tr. III. T.
PZ3.D742Si PG3326.A15P5   891.73   LC 46-8667 rev

Dostoyevsky, Fyodor, 1821-1881.   • **2.1348**
The diary of a writer; tr. and annotated by Boris Brasol. New York C. Scribner's Sons 1949. I. T.
PG3326 A16 B7

Dostoyevsky, Fyodor, 1821-1881.   **2.1349**
[Selections. English. 1972] The gambler, with Polina Suslova's diary / Fyodor Dostoevsky; translated by Victor Terras; edited by Edward Wasiolek. — Chicago: University of Chicago Press, 1972. xxxix, 366 p.; 21 cm. Includes additional selections by P. Suslova, all translated from Gody blizosti s Dostoevskim, plus portions of letters by Dostoevsky. I. Suslova, Apollinariia Prokof'evna, 1840-1918. Gody blizosti s Dostoevskim. English. Selections. 1972. II. Terras, Victor. III. Wasiolek, Edward. IV. T.
PG3326.A2 T4   891.7/3/3   LC 72-80227   ISBN 0226159701

Dostoyevsky, Fyodor, 1821-1881.   **2.1350**
[Bednye liudi. English] Poor folk / Dostoevsky; translated and with an introduction by Robert Dessaix. — Ann Arbor, Mich.: Ardis, c1982. 143 p.; 21 cm. Translation of: Bednye liudi. I. T.
PG3326.B4 1982   891.73/3 19   LC 82-16286   ISBN 0882337556

Dostoyevsky, Fyodor, 1821-1881.   • **2.1351**
The possessed, a novel in three parts, by Fyodor Dostoevsky; from the Russian by Constance Garnett. New York: Macmillan, 1948. 617 p.; 19 cm. I. Garnett, Constance Black, 1862-1946. tr. II. T.
PG3326.B6G3 1923   LC 49-786

Dostoyevsky, Fyodor, 1821-1881.   **2.1352**
[Brat'ia Karamazovy. English] The Brothers Karamazov: the Constance Garnett translation revised by Ralph E. Matlaw: backgrounds and sources, essays in criticism / edited by Ralph E. Matlaw. — New York: Norton, c1976. xviii, 887 p.; 22 cm. — (A Norton critical edition) Translation of Brat'ia Karamazovy. I. Garnett, Constance Black, 1862-1946. II. Matlaw, Ralph E. III. T.
PZ3.D742 Br53 PG3326.B7x 1976   891.7/3/3   LC 75-37792
   ISBN 0393044262. ISBN 0393092143 pbk

Dostoyevsky, Fyodor, 1821-1881.   **2.1353**
[Dvoĭnik. English] The double: two versions / Fyodor Dostoevsky; translated by Evelyn Harden. — Ann Arbor, Mich.: Ardis, c1985. xxxvi, 294 p.; 23 cm. Translation of the original 1846 version of Dvoĭnik and a later revision. I. Harden, Evelyn J. II. T.
PG3326.D8 1985   891.73/3 19   LC 84-20385   ISBN 0882337564

Dostoyevsky, Fyodor, 1821-1881.   • **2.1354**
[Idiot. English] The idiot / Fyodor Dostoyevsky; translated by Constance Garnett; with illustrations by Boardman Robinson. — 2nd Modern Library ed. — New York: Modern Library, 1983, c1962. 586 p., [9] leaves of plates: ill.; 22 cm. Translation of: Idiot. I. Garnett, Constance Black, 1862-1946. II. T.
PG3326.I3 1983   891.73/3 19   LC 82-42864   ISBN 0394604342

Dostoyevsky, Fyodor, 1821-1881.   **2.1355**
[Krokodil. English] The crocodile: an extraordinary event, or a show in the arcade ... / Fyodor Dostoevsky; translated by S.D. Cioran. — Ann Arbor, Mich.: Ardis, c1985. 94 p.; 20 cm. Translation of: Krokodil. I. Cioran, Samuel D. (Samuel David), 1941- II. T.
PG3326.K6 1985   891.73/3 19   LC 84-20383   ISBN 0882335901

Dostoyevsky, Fyodor, 1821-1881.   • **2.1356**
[Netochka Nezvanova. English] Netochka Nezvanova, by Fyodor Dostoyevsky. Translated by Ann Dunnigan. Englewood Cliffs, N.J., Prentice-Hall [c1970] vi, 201 p. 24 cm. Translation of Netochka Nezvanova. I. T.
PZ3.D742 Ne PG3326.N4   891.7/3/3   LC 76-113048

Dostoyevsky, Fyodor, 1821-1881.   **2.1357**
[Podrostok. English] The adolescent [by] Fyodor Dostoyevsky. A new translation by Andrew R. MacAndrew. [1st ed.] Garden City, N.Y., Doubleday, 1971. xxxiii, 585 p. 25 cm. Translation of Podrostok. I. T.
PZ3.D742 Ad PG3326.P5   891.7/3/3   LC 74-144260

Dostoyevsky, Fyodor, 1821-1881.   • **2.1358**
[Prestuplenie i nakazanie. English] Crime and punishment, by Fyodor Dostoevsky: the Coulson translation; backgrounds and sources, essays in criticism. Edited by George Gibian. [1st ed.] New York, W. W. Norton [1964] viii, 688 p. 21 cm. (Norton critical editions, N310) I. T.
PG3326.P7x   LC 64-10893

Dostoyevsky, Fyodor, 1821-1881.   • **2.1359**
The insulted and injured. Translated from the Russian by Constance Garnett. [Evergreen ed.] New York Grove Press [1955] 333p. (An Evergreen book, E-22) I. T.
PG3326 U5 G3 1955

Dostoyevsky, Fyodor, 1821-1881.   • **2.1360**
Memoirs from the House of the Dead. Translated by Jessie Coulson. London, New York, Oxford University Press, 1956. xii, 294 p. 19 cm. I. T. II. Title: House of the Dead.
PG3326.Z3x   LC 56-58405

Dostoyevsky, Fyodor, 1821-1881.   • **2.1361**
[Zapiski iz podpol'ia. English] Notes from underground / Fyodor Dostoevsky; edited by Robert G. Durgy; translated by Serge Shishkoff. — Washington, D.C.: University Press of America, [1982] c1969. xxvi, 262 p.; 21 cm. Translation of: Zapiski iz podpol'ia. Reprint. Originally published: New York: Crowell, [c1969] 1. Dostoyevsky, Fyodor, 1821-1881. Zapiski iz podpol'ia. I. Durgy, Robert G. II. T.
PG3326.Z4 1982   891.73/3 19   LC 82-45080   ISBN 081912415X

PG3328 Biography and Criticism

Chapple, Richard L., 1944-.   2.1362
A Dostoevsky dictionary / Richard Chapple. — Ann Arbor, Mich.: Ardis, c1983. 511 p.; 24 cm. Includes index. 1. Dostoyevsky, Fyodor, 1821-1881 — Dictionaries, indexes, etc. I. T.
PG3328.A09 C5 1983   891.73/3 19   LC 82-18514   ISBN 0882336169

Dostoyevsky, Fyodor, 1821-1881.   • 2.1363
Letters of Fyodor Michailovitch Dostoevsky to his family and friends. Translated by Ethel Colburn Mayne. With an introd. by Avrahm Yarmolinsky. New York, Horizon Press [1961] xxiv, 344 p. illus., ports. 24 cm. I. T.
PG3328.A3M3 1961   928.917   LC 61-8505

Frank, Joseph, 1918-.   2.1364
Dostoevsky: the seeds of revolt, 1821–1849 / Joseph Frank. — Princeton, N.J.: Princeton University Press, c1976. xvi, 401 p.: ill.; 24 cm. 1. Dostoyevsky, Fyodor, 1821-1881. I. T.
PG3328.F7   891.7/3/3 B   LC 76-3704   ISBN 0691062609

Frank, Joseph, 1918-.   2.1365
Dostoevsky: the stir of liberation, 1860–1865 / Joseph Frank. — Princeton, N.J.: Princeton University Press, c1986. xv, 395 p.: ill., ports.; 25 cm. Includes index. 1. Dostoyevsky, Fyodor, 1821-1881 — Biography. 2. Dostoyevsky, Fyodor, 1821-1881 — Political and social views. 3. Novelists, Russian — 19th century — Biography. 4. Soviet Union — Intellectual life — 1801-1917 I. T.
PG3328.F73 1986   891.73/3 B 19   LC 85-43280   ISBN 0691066523

Frank, Joseph, 1918-.   2.1366
Dostoevsky: the years of ordeal, 1850–1859 / Joseph Frank. — Princeton, N.J.: Princeton University Press, c1983. xv, 320 p.: ill., ports.; 24 cm. 1. Dostoyevsky, Fyodor, 1821-1881 — Biography. 2. Authors, Russian — 19th century — Biography. 3. Soviet Union — Intellectual life — 1801-1917 I. T.
PG3328.F74 1983   891.73/3 B 19   LC 83-11216   ISBN 0691065764

Gide, André, 1869-1951.   • 2.1367
Dostoevsky / introductory note to the 1st English ed., 1925, by Arnold Bennett; new introd. by Albert J. Guerard. — New York: New Directions, 1961. 181 p.; 19 cm. — (A New Directions paperback; 100) 1. Dostoyevsky, Fyodor, 1821-1881. I. T. II. Series.
PG3328.G52 1961   LC 61-14898

Hingley, Ronald.   2.1368
Dostoyevsky, his life and work / Ronald Hingley. — New York: Charles Scribner's Sons, c1978. 222p.: ill.; 24 cm. Includes indexes. 1. Dostoyevsky, Fyodor, 1821-1881. 2. Novelists, Russian — 19th century — Biography. I. T.
PG3328.H54 1978b   891.7/3/3 B   LC 78-7162   ISBN 0684159163

Mochul'skiĭ, K. (Konstantin), 1892-1948.   • 2.1369
Dostoevsky: his life and work. Translated, with an introd., by Michael A. Minihan. — [Princeton, N. J.] Princeton University Press, 1967. xxii, 687 p. port. 25 cm. Translated from the Russian. (romanized: Dostoevskiĭ; zhizn' i tvorchestvo) Bibliographical footnotes. 1. Dostoevsky, Fyodor, 1821-1881. I. T.
PG3328.M613   891.7/3/3   LC 65-10833

Wellek, René. ed.   • 2.1370
Dostoevsky; a collection of critical essays. Englewood Cliffs, N.J., Prentice-Hall [1962] 180 p. 21 cm. (A Spectrum book: Twentieth century views, STC-16) 1. Dostoyevsky, Fyodor, 1821-1881. I. T.
PG3328.W4   891.733   LC 62-16963

Yarmolinsky, Avrahm, 1890-.   • 2.1371
Dostoevsky; works and days. New York, Funk & Wagnalls [1971] 438 p. ports. 24 cm. 1. Dostoyevsky, Fyodor, 1821-1881. I. T.
PG3328.Y34   891.7/3/3 B   LC 73-142910

Dostoevsky & Gogol: texts and criticism / edited [and   2.1372
translated] by Priscilla Meyer & Stephen Rudy.
Ann Arbor: Ardis, c1979. xxxix, 295 p.; 24 cm. Includes index. 1. Dostoyevsky, Fyodor, 1821-1881 — Criticism and interpretation — Addresses, essays, lectures. 2. Gogol', Nikolaĭ Vasil'evich, 1809-1852 — Criticism and interpretation — Addresses, essays, lectures. 3. Gogol', Nikolaĭ Vasil'evich, 1809-1852 — Influence — Dostoevskiĭ — Addresses, essays, lectures. I. Meyer, Priscilla. II. Rudy, Stephen.
PG3328.Z6 D628   891.73/3   LC 79-51642   ISBN 0882333151

Fanger, Donald.   • 2.1373
Dostoevsky and romantic realism: a study of Dostoevsky in relation to Balzac, Dickens, and Gogol. Cambridge, Harvard University Press, 1965. x, 307 p. 25 cm. (Harvard studies in comparative literature. 27) 1. Dostoyevsky, Fyodor, 1821-1881 — Criticism and interpretation. 2. Balzac, Honoré de, 1799-1850.

3. Dickens, Charles, 1812-1870. 4. Gogol', Nikolaĭ Vasil'evich, 1809-1852. I. T. II. Series.
PG3328.Z6 F25   809.3   LC 65-13841

Ivanov, V. I. (Viacheslav Ivanovich), 1866-1949.   • 2.1374
Freedom and the tragic life; a study in Dostoevsky. Foreword by Sir Maurice Bowra. [Translated by Norman Cameron; edited by S. Konovalov]. — New York, Noonday Press [1952] 166 p. 22 cm. 1. Dostoyevsky, Fyodor, 1821-1881. I. T.
PG3328.Z6I8 1952   *891.733   LC A 53-9868

Leatherbarrow, William J.   2.1375
Fedor Dostoevsky / by William J. Leatherbarrow. — Boston: Twayne Publishers, 1981. 185 p.: port.; 21 cm. — (Twayne's world authors series; TWAS 636: Russia) Includes index. 1. Dostoyevsky, Fyodor, 1821-1881 — Criticism and interpretation. I. T.
PG3328.Z6 L36   891.73/3 19   LC 80-28318   ISBN 0805764801

New essays on Dostoyevsky / edited by Malcolm V. Jones and   2.1376
Garth M. Terry.
Cambridge; New York: Cambridge University Press, 1983. ix, 252 p.; 23 cm. 1. Dostoyevsky, Fyodor, 1821-1881 — Criticism and interpretation — Addresses, essays, lectures. I. Jones, Malcolm V. II. Terry, Garth M.
PG3328.Z6 N43 1983   891.73/3 19   LC 82-14566   ISBN 0521248906

Wasiolek, Edward.   • 2.1377
Dostoevsky: the major fiction. Cambridge, Mass., M.I.T. Press [1964] xiv, 255 p. 21 cm. 1. Dostoyevsky, Fyodor, 1821-1881 — Criticism and interpretation. I. T.
PG3328.Z6 W3   891.733   LC 64-8089

Gibson, A. Boyce (Alexander Boyce), 1900-1972.   2.1378
The religion of Dostoevsky. Philadelphia, Westminster Press [1974, c1973] x, 216 p. 23 cm. 1. Dostoyevsky, Fyodor, 1821-1881 — Religion. I. T.
PG3328.Z7 R424   891.7/3/3   LC 73-9956   ISBN 0664209890

PG3332–3335 Gogol

Gogol', Nikolaĭ Vasil'evich, 1809-1852.   • 2.1379
Collected tales and plays / edited, with an introd. and notes, by Leonard J. Kent. — New York: Pantheon Books, [1964] xxxix, 768 p.; 22 cm. 'Constance Garnett translation ... revised throughout by the editor.' Partial contents:-The inspector general. I. Kent, Leonard J., 1927- II. Garnett, Constance Black, 1862-1946. III. T.
PG3333.A1 1964   891.733   LC 64-10980

Gogol', Nikolaĭ Vasil'evich, 1809-1852.   2.1380
[Short stories. English] The complete tales of Nikolai Gogol / edited, with an introduction and notes, by Leonard J. Kent. — Chicago: University of Chicago Press, 1985. 2 v.; 21 cm. 'The Constance Garnett translation has been revised throughout by the editor.' I. Kent, Leonard J., 1927- II. T.
PG3333.A15 1985   891.73/3 19   LC 84-16221   ISBN 0226300684

Gogol', Nikolaĭ Vasil'evich, 1809-1852.   2.1381
The theater of Nikolay Gogol: plays and selected writings / edited with an introd. and notes by Milton Ehre; translated by Milton Ehre and Fruma Gottschalk. — Chicago: University of Chicago Press, 1980. xxvi, 205 p.; 22 cm. I. Ehre, Milton, 1933- II. T.
PG3333.A19 1980   891.7/2/3   LC 79-23745   ISBN 0226300641

Gogol', Nikolaĭ Vasil'evich, 1809-1852.   2.1382
[Mertvye dushi. English] Dead souls: the Reavey translation, backgrounds and sources, essays in criticism / Nikolai Gogol; edited by George Gibian. — New York: W.W. Norton, c1985. viii, 585 p.; 22 cm. (A Norton critical edition) Translation of: Mertvye dushi. 1. Gogol', Nikolaĭ Vasil'evich, 1809-1852 — Translations, English. 2. Gogol', Nikolaĭ Vasil'evich, 1809-1852 Mertvye dushi — Addresses, essays, lectures. 3. Gogol', Nikolaĭ Vasil'evich, 1809-1852 — Criticism and interpretation — Addresses, essays, lectures. I. Gibian, George. II. T.
PG3333.M4 1985   891.73/3 19   LC 84-8027   ISBN 0393952924

Gogol', Nikolaĭ Vasil'evich, 1809-1852.   • 2.1383
Letters of Nikolai Gogol / selected and edited by Carl R. Proffer; translated by Carl R. Proffer in collaboration with Vera Krivoshein. — Ann Arbor: University of Michigan Press, c1967. vii, 247 p. port. 1. Gogol', Nikolaĭ Vasil'evich, 1809-1852. 2. Authors — Russia — Correspondence, reminiscences, etc. I. Proffer, Carl R. II. T.
PG3335.A4 P7   891.7/6/3   LC 67-25343   ISBN 0472375008

Gippius, Vasiliĭ Vasil'evich, 1890-.   2.1384
[Gogol'. English] Gogol / V.V. Gippius; edited and translated by Robert A. Maguire. — Ann Arbor: Ardis, c1981. 216 p.; 24 cm. (Sources and translation series of the Russian Institute Columbia University) Translation of Gogol'.

1. Gogol', Nikolaĭ Vasil'evich, 1809-1852. 2. Authors, Russian — 19th century — Biography. I. T.
PG3335.G4913　　891.78/309 B 19　　*LC* 80-21888　　*ISBN* 0882336126

Lindstrom, Thaïs S.　　　　　　　　　　　**2.1385**
Nikolay Gogol. New York, Twayne Publishers [1974] 216 p. 21 cm. (Twayne's world authors series, TWAS 299. Russia) 1. Gogol', Nikolaĭ Vasil'evich, 1809-1852. I. T.
PG3335.L52　　891.7/8/309　　*LC* 73-17457　　*ISBN* 0805723773

Nabokov, Vladimir Vladimirovich, 1899-1977.　　● **2.1386**
Nikolai Gogol, by Vladimir Nabokov. — Norfolk, Conn., New Directions, [1944] 172 p.; 19 cm. — (The Makers of modern literature) Includes bibliographical references. Includes index. 1. Gogol', Nikolaĭ Vasil'evich, 1809-1852. I. T.
PG3335.N3 1961　　891.73　　*LC* 44-8135　　*ISBN* 0811201201

Erlich, Victor, 1914-.　　　　　　　　　　● **2.1387**
Gogol. — New Haven, Yale University Press, 1969. xi, 230 p. 22 cm. — (Yale Russian and East European studies, 8) 1. Gogol', Nikolaĭ Vasil'evich, 1809-1852. I. T. II. Series.
PG3335.Z8 E68　　891.7/8/309　　*LC* 76-81416　　*ISBN* 300011202

Fanger, Donald.　　　　　　　　　　　　**2.1388**
The creation of Nikolai Gogol / Donald Fanger. — Cambridge, Mass.: Belknap Press of Harvard University Press, 1979. xi, 300 p.: ill.; 24 cm. 1. Gogol', Nikolaĭ Vasil'evich, 1809-1852 — Criticism and interpretation. I. T.
PG3335.Z8 F3　　891.7/8/309　　*LC* 79-14135　　*ISBN* 0674175654

Maguire, Robert A.　　　　　　　　　　　**2.1389**
Gogol from the twentieth century; eleven essays. Selected, edited, translated, and introduced by Robert A. Maguire. — Princeton, N.J.: Princeton University Press, [1974] xi, 415 p.; port.; 25 cm. 1. Gogol', Nikolaĭ Vasil'evich, 1809-1852 — Criticism and interpretation — Addresses, essays, lectures. I. T.
PG3335.Z8 M18　　PG3335 Z8 M18.　　891.7/8/309　　*LC* 73-16750　　*ISBN* 0691062684

PG3337 G–P

Goncharov, Ivan Aleksandrovich, 1812-1891.　　● **2.1390**
Oblomov / by Ivan Goncharov; translated by Natalie Duddington; introduction by Renato Poggioli. — New York: E.P. Dutton, 1960. xxiii, 517 p. (A Dutton Everyman paperback; D56) I. T.
PZ3.G5875 Ob 1979 PG3337.G6　　891.7/3/3　　*LC* 61-19147

Goncharov, Ivan Aleksandrovich, 1812-1891.　　● **2.1391**
[Obyknovennaia istoriia. English] The same old story. [Translated from the Russian by Ivy Litvinova] Moscow, Foreign Languages Pub. House [1957] 438 p. port. 21 cm. (Classics of Russian literature) Added t.p. in Russian. Translation of Obyknovennaia istoriia (romanized form) I. T.
PZ3.G5875 Sam PG3337.G6　　891.7/3/3　　*LC* 75-213888

Ehre, Milton, 1933-.　　　　　　　　　　**2.1392**
Oblomov and his creator; the life and art of Ivan Goncharov. Princeton, N.J., Princeton University Press [1974, c1973] ix, 295 p. 23 cm. (Studies of the Russian Institute, Columbia University) 1. Goncharov, Ivan Aleksandrovich, 1812-1891. I. T.
PG3337.G6 Z633　　891.7/3/3　　*LC* 72-5378　　*ISBN* 0691062455

Lavrin, Janko, 1887-.　　　　　　　　　　● **2.1393**
Goncharov. — New York: Russell & Russell, [1969] 62 p.; 23 cm. Reprint of the 1954 ed. 1. Goncharov, Ivan Aleksandrovich, 1812-1891. I. T.
PG3337.G6 Z64 1969　　891.7/3/3　　*LC* 68-27070

Krylov, Ivan Andreevich, 1768-1844.　　　● **2.1394**
Krylov's fables / translated into English verse with a pref. by Bernard Pares. — New York: Harcourt, Brace, [1927] 271 p.; 21 cm. Translation of Basni. 1. Fables, Russian. I. Pares, Bernard, Sir, 1867-1949. II. T.
PG3337.K7 B34　　891.7/8/207

Stepanov, Nikolaĭ Leonidovich, 1902-.　　　**2.1395**
Ivan Krylov, by Nikolay Stepanov. — New York: Twayne Publishers, [c1973] 174 p.; 21 cm. — (Twayne's world authors series, TWAS 247: Russia) 1. Krylov, Ivan Andreevich, 1768-1844. I. Krylov, Ivan Andreevich, 1768-1844. II. T.
PG3337.K7 Z9324　　891.7/8/207　　*LC* 76-187633

Lermontov, Mikhail IUr'evich, 1814-1841.　　**2.1396**
A hero of our time; a novel. Translated from the Russian by Vladimir Nabokov in collaboration with Dmitri Nabokov. — [1st ed.]. — Garden City, N. Y., Doubleday, 1958. 210 p. 18 cm. — (Doubleday anchor books, A133) I. T.
PZ3.L562Her11 PG3337.L4G413　　*LC* 58-6583

Garrard, John Gordon.　　　　　　　　　**2.1397**
Mikhail Lermontov / by John Garrard. — Boston: Twayne Publishers, c1982. 173 p.: port.; 21 cm. — (Twayne's world authors series. TWAS 667) Includes index. 1. Lermontov, Mikhail IUr'evich, 1814-1841 — Criticism and interpretation. I. T. II. Series.
PG3337.L46 G3 1982　　891.71/3 19　　*LC* 82-6194　　*ISBN* 080576514X

Leskov, N. S. (Nikolaĭ Semenovich), 1831-1895.　● **2.1398**
[Soboriane. English] The cathedral folk. Translated from the Russian of Nicolai Lyeskov (Leskov) by Isabel F. Hapgood. Westport, Conn., Greenwood Press [1971] 439 p. 23 cm. Translation of Soboriane (romanized form) I. T.
PZ3.L5647 Cat5 PG3337.L5　　891.7/3/3　　*LC* 75-110855　　*ISBN* 0837145228

Leskov, N. S. (Nikolaĭ Semenovich), 1831-1895.　● **2.1399**
Satirical stories. Translated and edited by William B. Edgerton. New York, Pegasus [1969] 411 p. 21 cm. I. Edgerton, William Benbow, 1914- ed. II. T.
PG3337.L5A24　　891.7/3/3　　*LC* 68-27987

Leskov, N. S. (Nikolaĭ Semenovich), 1831-1895.　　**2.1400**
'The sealed angel' and other stories / by Nikolay Leskov; K.A. Lantz, editor and translator. — Knoxville: University of Tennessee Press, c1984. xiii, 251 p.; 23 cm. Translated from the Russian. I. Lantz, K. A. II. T.
PG3337.L5 A24 1984　　891.73/3 19　　*LC* 83-14547　　*ISBN* 0870494112

Leskov, N. S. (Nikolaĭ Semenovich), 1831-1895.　● **2.1401**
Selected tales / Nikolai Leskov; trans. by David Magarshack; with an introd. by V.S. Prittchett. — New York: Farrar, [c1961] xviii, 300 p. I. T.
PG3337.L5 A6 1961　　Fic　　*LC* 61-10959

Lantz, K. A.　　　　　　　　　　　　　**2.1402**
Nikolay Leskov / by K.A. Lantz. — Boston: Twayne Publishers, 1979. 165 p.: port.; 21 cm. (Twayne's world authors series; TWAS 523: Russia) Includes index. 1. Leskov, N. S. (Nikolaĭ Semenovich), 1831-1895 — Criticism and interpretation. I. T.
PG3337.L5 Z7495　　891.7/3/3　　*LC* 78-14757　　*ISBN* 0805763643

Nekrasov, Nikolaĭ Alekseevich, 1821-1877.　　● **2.1403**
[Komu na Rusi zhit' khorosho. English] Who can be happy and free in Russia, by Nicholas Nekrassov. Translated by Juliet M. Soskice. With an introd. by David Soskice. New York, AMS Press [1970] xxi, 339 p. port. 23 cm. Translation of Komu na Rusi zhit' khorosho (romanized form) I. Soskice, Juliet M. (Hueffer) tr. II. T.
PG3337.N4 K62 1970　　891.7/1/3　　*LC* 72-120571　　*ISBN* 0404046770

Ostrovsky, Aleksandr Nikolaevich, 1823-1886.　● **2.1404**
Five plays. Translated and edited by Eugene K. Bristow. — New York, Pegasus [1969] 480 p. 21 cm. — (A Pegasus original, P1070) I. Bristow, Eugene Kerr, 1927- ed. II. T.
PG3337.O8 A23　　891.7/2/3　　*LC* 68-27985

Ostrovsky, Aleksandr Nikolaevich, 1823-1886.　● **2.1405**
[Selected works. English] Plays by Alexander Ostrovsky ... a translation from the Russian, edited by George Rapall Noyes. New York, AMS Press [1969] 305 p. 23 cm. I. Noyes, George Rapall, 1873-1952. ed. II. T.
PG3337.O8 A25 1969　　891.7/2/3　　*LC* 70-98632

Pisemskiĭ, Alekseĭ Feofilaktovich, 1820-1881.　● **2.1406**
[Tysiacha dush. English] One thousand souls, by Alexei Pisemsky. Translated from the Russian by Ivy Litvinov. New York, Greenwood Press [1969] 472 p. 23 cm. Translation of Tysiacha dush (romanized form) I. T.
PZ3.P676 On5 PG3337.P5　　891.7/3/3　　*LC* 69-14035　　*ISBN* 0837122397

PG3340–3359 Pushkin

Pushkin, Aleksandr Sergeevich, 1799-1837.　　● **2.1407**
[Poems. English & Russian] Pushkin threefold; narrative, lyric, polemic, and ribald verse. The originals with linear and metric translations by Walter Arndt. [1st ed.] New York, Dutton, 1972. xlix, 455 p. illus. 21 cm. English and Russian. I. Arndt, Walter W., 1916- tr. II. T.
PG3341.A7 1972　　891.7/1/3　　*LC* 69-17218　　*ISBN* 0525186522
ISBN 0525472606

Pushkin, Aleksandr Sergeevich, 1799-1837.　　**2.1408**
[Short stories. English] Alexander Pushkin, complete prose fiction / translated, with an introduction and notes, by Paul Debreczeny; verse passages translated by Walter Arndt. — Stanford, Calif.: Stanford University Press, 1983. x, 545 p.: ill.; 24 cm. I. Arndt, Walter W., 1916- II. T.
PG3347.A15 1983　　891.73/3 19　　*LC* 81-85450　　*ISBN* 0804711429

Pushkin, Aleksandr Sergeevich, 1799-1837.   2.1409
[Poems. English. Selections] Aleksandr Pushkin, epigrams and satirical verse / edited and translated by Cynthia H. Whittaker. — Ann Arbor, Mich.: Ardis Publishers, c1984. xiii, 126 p.: ill. 1. Pushkin, Aleksandr Sergeevich, 1799-1837 — Translations, English. I. Whittaker, Cynthia H., 1941- II. T.
PG3347.A17 1984   891.71/3 19   LC 84-253   ISBN 0882338862

Pushkin, Aleksandr Sergeevich, 1799-1837.   2.1410
[Poems. English. Selections] Three comic poems / Alexander Pushkin; translated and edited by William E. Harkins. — Ann Arbor: Ardis, c1977. 85 p.; 23 cm. — (Sources and translation series of the Russian Institute, Columbia University) I. Harkins, William Edward. II. T.
PG3347.A2 H3 1977   891.7/1/3   LC 77-150109   ISBN 088233221X

Pushkin, Aleksandr Sergeevich, 1799-1837.   • 2.1411
The poems, prose and plays by Alexander Pushkin; selected and edited, with an introduction, by Avrahm Yarmolinsky. — New York: The Modern library, [1943] viii, [2], 11-896 p.; 21 cm. — (The Modern library of the world's best books. [Modern library giants] [G62]) 'First Modern library giant edition, 1943.' I. Yarmolinsky, Avrahm, 1890- ed. II. T.
PG3347.A2 Y3   891.7081   LC 43-51102

Pushkin, Aleksandr Sergeevich, 1799-1837.   • 2.1412
Eugene Onegin, a novel in verse. A new translation in the Onegin stanza with an introd. and notes by Walter Arndt. [1st ed.] New York, Dutton [1963] xix, 224 p. 19 cm. 'D132.' I. Arndt, Walter, 1916- ed. and tr. II. T.
PG3347.E8A7   891.713   LC 63-24729

Pushkin, Aleksandr Sergeevich, 1799-1837.   2.1413
[Evgeniĭ Onegin. English & Russian] Eugene Onegin: a novel in verse / by Aleksandr Pushkin; translated from the Russian, with a commentary by Vladimir Nabokov. — Rev. ed. — [Princeton, N.J.]: Princeton University Press, c1975. 4 v.: port.; 22 cm. — (Bollingen series. 72) I. Nabokov, Vladimir Vladimirovich, 1899-1977. II. T. III. Series.
PG3347.E8 N3 1975   891.7/1/3   LC 70-38781   ISBN 0691097445

Pushkin, Aleksandr Sergeevich, 1799-1837.   2.1414
[Ruslan i Liudmila. English] Ruslan and Liudmila / Alexander Pushkin; translated by Walter Arndt. — 1st ed. — Ann Arbor, Mich.: Ardis, 1974. xxi, 105 p.; 23 cm. Translation of Ruslan i Liudmila. I. T.
PG3347.R85 A7   891.7/1/3   LC 74-14072   ISBN 0882330691

Pushkin, Aleksandr Sergeevich, 1799-1837.   • 2.1415
Letters. Translated, with pref., introd., and notes by J. Thomas Shaw. Bloomington Indiana University Press [1964] I. T.
PG3347 Z5 S5

PG3350–3359 Biography and Criticism

Simmons, Ernest Joseph, 1903-1972.   • 2.1416
Pushkin. Cambridge, Mass. Harvard University Press 1937. 8;3-485p. 1. Pushkin, Aleksandr Sergieevich, 1799-1837 I. T.
PG3350 S52

Troyat, Henri, 1911-.   • 2.1417
[Pouchkine. English] Pushkin. Translated from the French by Nancy Amphoux. Garden City, N.Y., Doubleday, 1970. xiii, 655 p. illus., ports. 25 cm. Translation of Pouchkine. 1. Pushkin, Aleksandr Sergeevich, 1799-1837 — Biography. 2. Poets, Russian — 19th century — Biography. I. T.
PG3350.T714 1970   891.7/1/3 B   LC 70-116181

Vickery, Walter N., 1921-.   • 2.1418
Alexander Pushkin, by Walter N. Vickery. New York, Twayne Publishers [1970] 211 p. 21 cm. (Twayne's world authors series, TWAS 82. Russia) 1. Pushkin, Aleksandr Sergeevich, 1799-1837. I. T.
PG3350.V5   891.7/1/3   LC 79-99547

Bayley, John, 1925-.   • 2.1419
Pushkin; a comparative commentary. Cambridge [Eng.] University Press, 1971. vii, 368 p. 23 cm. (Companion studies) 1. Pushkin, Aleksandr Sergeevich, 1799-1837 — Criticism and interpretation. I. T.
PG3356.B3   891.7/1/3 B   LC 75-139711   ISBN 0521079543

Briggs, A. D. P.   2.1420
Alexander Pushkin: a critical study / A.D.P. Briggs. — London: Croom Helm; Totowa, N.J.: Barnes & Noble Books, 1983. 257 p.; 22 cm. 1. Pushkin, Aleksandr Sergeevich, 1799-1837 — Criticism and interpretation. I. T.
PG3356.B74 1983   891.71/3 19   LC 82-16242   ISBN 0389203408

Debreczeny, Paul.   2.1421
The other Pushkin: a study of Alexander Pushkin's prose fiction / Paul Debreczeny. — Stanford, Calif.: Stanford University Press, 1983. ix, 386 p.: ill.; 23 cm. Includes index. 1. Pushkin, Aleksandr Sergeevich, 1799-1837 — Fictional works. I. T.
PG3358.F5 D4 1983   891.73/3 19   LC 81-85449   ISBN 0804711437

PG3360–3363 S–T

Saltykov, Mikhail Evgrafovich, 1826-1889.   2.1422
[Gospoda Golovlevy. English] The Golovlyov family / Saltykov; translated by Samuel D. Cioran; [introd. by Carl R. Proffer]. — Ann Arbor, Mich.: Ardis, c1977. xxxiv, 251 p.: ill.; 24 cm. Translation of Gospoda Golovlevy. I. Cioran, Samuel D. (Samuel David), 1941- II. T.
PZ3.S182 Go 1977b PG3361.S3   891.7/3/3   LC 76-57547   ISBN 0882332090

Saltykov, Mikhail Evgrafovich, 1826-1889.   • 2.1423
The Golovlyov family, by Nikolai Evgrafovich Shchedrin [pseud.] (M. E. Saltykov) London & Toronto, J. M. Dent & sons, ltd.; New York, E. P. Dutton & co., inc. [1934] x p., 1 l., 324 p. 18 cm. (Half-title: Everyman's library, ed. by Ernest Rhys. Fiction. [no. 908]) Title-page and page facing it (with quotation) within ornamental border; illustrated lining-papers. Translated by Natalie Duddington. Introduction by Edward Garnett. 'Bibliographical note': p. x. I. Duddington, Natalia Aleksandrovna (Ertel'), Mrs. tr. II. Garnett, Edward, 1868-1937. ed. III. T.
PZ3.S18Go PG3361.S3G613 1962   LC A 35-156

Lotman, L. M. (Lidiia Mikhaĭlovna), 1917-.   2.1424
Afanasy Fet / by Lydia M. Lotman; translated from the Russian by Margaret Wettlin. — Boston: Twayne Publishers, c1976. 180 p.: port.; 21 cm. (Twayne's world authors series; TWAS 279. Russia) 'Prepared for publication in cooperation with Novosti Press Agency (APN) Publishing House, USSR.' Includes index. 1. Fet, A. A. (Afanasiĭ Afanas'evich), 1820-1892. I. T.
PG3361.S4 Z7   891.7/1/3   LC 75-37834   ISBN 0805723099

Tiutchev, F. I. (Fedor Ivanovich), 1803-1873.   • 2.1425
Versions from Fyodor Tyutchev, 1803–1873, by Charles Tomlinson. With an introd. by Henry Gifford. London, New York, Oxford University Press, 1960. 45 p. 23 cm. Poems. I. Tomlinson, Charles, 1927- tr. II. T.
PG3361.T5A27   891.713   LC 60-51883 rev

Tiutchev, F. I. (Fedor Ivanovich), 1803-1873.   2.1426
[Selected works. 1973] Poems & political letters of F. I. Tyutchev. Translated with introd. and notes by Jesse Zeldin. [1st ed.] Knoxville, University of Tennessee Press [1973] ix, 236 p. 22 cm. I. Zeldin, Jesse, 1923- tr. II. T.
PG3361.T5 A29 1973   891.7/1/3   LC 73-4397   ISBN 0870491466

Dalton, Margaret.   2.1427
A. K. Tolstoy / Margaret Dalton. — New York: Twayne Publishers, 1972. 181 p.; 21 cm. — (Twayne's world authors series; TWAS 168. Russia) 1. Tolstoy, Aleksey Konstantinovich, graf, 1817-1875. 2. Tolstoy, A.K. 3. Authors, Russian — Biography. I. T.
PG3363.Z8 D3   891.7/8/309   LC 72-120512

PG3365–3417 Tolstoy

Christian, Reginald Frank.   • 2.1428
Tolstoy's 'War and peace'; a study. Oxford [Eng.] Clarendon Press, 1962. 184 p. 23 cm. 1. Tolstoy, Leo, graf, 1828-1910. Voĭna i mir. I. T.
PG3365.V65C47   891.733   LC 62-53246

Tolstoy, Leo, graf, 1828-1910.   • 2.1429
The works of Leo Tolstoy ... Oxford [For the Tolstoy society, Oxford university press, H. Milford, 1928-37] 21 v. fronts. (incl. ports.) Title from cover. Each volume has special t.-p. 'Tolstóy centenary edition.' Vol. 20 wanting in L.C. I. Maude, Aylmer, 1858-1938. II. Maude, Louise Shanks, 1855-1939. III. Duff, J. D. (James Duff), 1860-1940. IV. T.
PG3366 A1x   LC 29-29751

Tolstoy, Leo, graf, 1828-1910.   • 2.1430
[Anna Karenina. English] Anna Karenina [by] Leo Tolstoy. The Maude translation, backgrounds and sources, essays in criticism. Edited by George Gibian. [1st ed.] New York, W. W. Norton [c1970] xvi, 920 p. 21 cm. (Norton critical edition) I. T.
PZ3.T588 A51 PG3366A6 Mx   891.7/3/3   LC 68-24263   ISBN 0393042774

PG3370–3417 Biography and Criticism

Tolstoy, Leo, graf, 1828-1910.   • 2.1431
Last diaries / translated by Lydia Weston–Kesich; edited and with an introduction by Leon Stiman. — New York: Capricorn Books, 1960. 285 p., 19 cm. — (A Putnam Capricorn book; CAP21) Translation of Diaries and note

books of 1910, (transliterated: Dnevniki i zapisnye knizhki tysiacha deviat'sot desiatogo goda). I. T.
PG3377.E5 W4   *LC* 60-6121

Tolstoy, Leo, graf, 1828-1910.   **2.1432**
[Correspondence. English. 1978] Tolstoy's letters / selected, edited, and translated by R. F. Christian. — New York: Scribner, c1978. 2 v. (xiii, 737 p., [4] leaves of plates): ill.; 24 cm. 1. Tolstoy, Leo, graf, 1828-1910 — Correspondence. 2. Authors, Russian — 19th century — Correspondence. I. Christian, Reginald Frank. II. T.
PG3379.A2 E5 1978b   *891.7/3/3*   *LC* 77-90494   *ISBN* 0684155966

Gifford, Henry.   **2.1433**
Tolstoy / Henry Gifford. — Oxford; New York: Oxford University Press, (1983 printing), c1982. 88 p.; 23 cm. — (Past masters.) Includes index. 1. Tolstoy, Leo, graf, 1828-1910 — Addresses, essays, lectures. 2. Novelists, Russian — 19th century — Biography — Addresses, essays, lectures. I. T. II. Series.
PG3385.G53 1983   *891.73/3 B 19*   *LC* 83-158030   *ISBN* 0192875450

Maude, Aylmer, 1858-1938.   **2.1434**
The life of Tolstoy / by Aylmer Maude. — London: Oxford University Press, [1930] 2 v.: ports. (The world's classics) 1. Tolstoy, Leo, graf, 1828-1910 — Biography. 2. Authors, Russian — 19th century — Biography. I. T.
PG3385.M[3 1910]

Simmons, Ernest Joseph, 1903-1972.   • **2.1435**
Leo Tolstoy, by Ernest J. Simmons ... Boston, Little, Brown and company, 1946. 790 p. front., illus. (map) plates, ports., facsims., double geneal. tab. 22.5 cm. 'An Atlantic monthly press book.' 1. Tolstoy, Leo, graf, 1828-1910. I. T.
PG3385.S5 1946   *928.917*   *LC* 47-1423

Simmons, Ernest Joseph, 1903-1972.   **2.1436**
Tolstoy, by Ernest J. Simmons. London, Boston, Routledge and K. Paul, 1973. xi, 260 p. 22 cm. (Routledge author guides) 1. Tolstoy, Leo, graf, 1828-1910. I. T.
PG3385.S54 1973   *891.7/3/3*   *LC* 72-95126   *ISBN* 0710073941   *ISBN* 071007395X

Tolstoĭ, Il'ia L'vovich, graf, 1866-1933.   **2.1437**
[Moi vospominaniia. English] Tolstoy, my father; reminiscences, by Ilya Tolstoy. Translated from the Russian, by Ann Dunnigan. Chicago, Cowles Book Co. [c1971] vi, 322 p. ports. 24 cm. Translation of Moi vospominaniia. 1. Tolstoy, Leo, graf, 1828-1910. I. T.
PG3385.T743   *891.7/3/3 B*   *LC* 74-163246

Troyat, Henri, 1911-.   • **2.1438**
[Tolstoĭ. English] Tolstoy. Translated from the French by Nancy Amphoux. [1st ed.] Garden City, N.Y., Doubleday, 1967. vi, 762 p. illus., ports. 24 cm. 1. Tolstoy, Leo, graf, 1828-1910. I. T.
PG3385.T8713   *891.7/8/309*   *LC* 67-22472

Matlaw, Ralph E. comp.   • **2.1439**
Tolstoy; a collection of critical essays, edited by Ralph E. Matlaw. Englewood Cliffs, N.J., Prentice-Hall [1967] 178 p. 21 cm. (Twentieth century views) (A Spectrum book.) 1. Tolstoy, Leo, graf, 1828-1910. I. T.
PG3386.M36   *891.73/3*   *LC* 67-18700

Cain, T. G. S. (Thomas Grant Steven)   **2.1440**
Tolstoy / T. G. S. Cain. — New York: Barnes & Noble Books, 1977. xiii, 210 p.; 23 cm. Includes index. 1. Tolstoy, Leo, graf, 1828-1910 — Criticism and interpretation. I. T.
PG3410.C27 1977b   *891.7/3/3*   *LC* 76-53287   *ISBN* 0064908909

Christian, Reginald Frank.   • **2.1441**
Tolstoy: a critical introduction [by] R. F. Christian. London, Cambridge U.P., 1969. vii, 291 p. 23 cm. 1. Tolstoy, Leo, graf, 1828-1910 — Criticism and interpretation. I. T.
PG3410.C55   *891.7/3/3*   *LC* 69-19373   *ISBN* 0521074932

Eĭkhenbaum, Boris Mikhaĭlovich, 1886-1959.   **2.1442**
[Lev Tolstoĭ, semidesiatye gody. English] Tolstoi in the Seventies / Boris Eikhenbaum; translated by Albert Kaspin. — Ann Arbor, Mich.: Ardis, c1982. 174 p.; 24 cm. Translation of: Lev Tolstoĭ, semidesiatye gody / B.M. Eĭkhenbaum. 1. Tolstoy, Leo, graf, 1828-1910 — Criticism and interpretation. I. T.
PG3410.E4913 1982   *891.73/3 19*   *LC* 81-10984   *ISBN* 0882334727

Eĭkhenbaum, Boris Mikhaĭlovich, 1886-1959.   **2.1443**
[Molodoĭ Tolstoĭ. English] The young Tolstoi. Translation edited by Gary Kern. Ann Arbor [Mich.] Ardis [1972] xviii, 152 p. ports. 22 cm. Translation of Molodoĭ Tolstoĭ. 1. Tolstoy, Leo, graf, 1828-1910 — Criticism and interpretation. I. T.
PG3410.E513   *891.7/3/3*   *LC* 72-178327

Eĭkhenbaum, Boris Mikhaĭlovich, 1886-1959.   **2.1444**
Tolstoi in the sixties / Boris Eikhenbaum; translated by Duffield White. — Ann Arbor: Ardis, c1982. xxv, 255 p.; 24 cm. Translated from the Russian. 1. Tolstoy, Leo, graf, 1828-1910 — Criticism and interpretation. 2. Tolstoy, Leo, graf, 1828-1910. Voina i mir. I. T. II. Title: Tolstoi in the 60s.
PG3410.E53 1982   *891.73/3 19*   *LC* 81-14942   *ISBN* 0882334700

Berlin, Isaiah, Sir.   **2.1445**
The hedgehog and the fox: an essay on Tolstoy's view of history / by Isaiah Berlin; with an introduction by Michael Walzer. — New York: Simon & Schuster, 1986, c1953. 86 p.; 22 cm. (A Touchstone book) 1. Tolstoy, Leo, graf, 1828-1910 — Knowledge — History. 2. Tolstoy, Leo, graf, 1828-1910 — Social and political views. 3. Tolstoy, Leo, graf, 1828-1910 — Philosophy. 4. History — Philosophy I. T.
PG3415.H5 B4 1986   *891.73/3 19*   *LC* 86-1057   *ISBN* 0671606018

Greenwood, Edward Baker, 1933-.   **2.1446**
Tolstoy: the comprehensive vision / E. B. Greenwood. — New York: St. Martin's Press, 1975. v, 184 p.; 23 cm. Includes index. 1. Tolstoy, Leo, graf, 1828-1910 — Philosophy. 2. Tolstoy, Leo, graf, 1828-1910 — Religion. I. T.
PG3415.P5 G7   *891.7/3/3*   *LC* 74-23030

PG3420–3445 Turgenev

Turgenev, Ivan Sergeevich, 1818-1883.   • **2.1447**
Three famous plays: A month in the country, A provincial lady, A poor gentleman / Ivan Turgenev; translated from the Russian by Constance Garnett; with an introd. by David Garnett. London: Duckworth, [c1951]. 235 p. (A Mermaid dramabook, MD15) I. T. II. Title: A month in the country. III. Title: A provincial lady. IV. Title: A poor gentleman.
PG3421.A19 G3   *891.72*

Turgenev, Ivan Sergeevich, 1818-1883.   • **2.1448**
[Selections. English. 1970] The plays of Ivan S. Turgenev. Translated from the Russian by M. S. Mandell. With an introd. by William Lyon Phelps. New York, Russell & Russell [1970] xiii, 583 p. 20 cm. I. T.
PG3421.A19 M3 1970   *891.7/2/3*   *LC* 70-102552

Turgenev, Ivan Sergeevich, 1818-1883.   • **2.1449**
[Selections. English. 1970] A desperate character, and other stories. Translated from the Russian by Constance Garnett. London, W. Heinemann, 1899. New York, AMS Press [1970] xiii, 317 p. 23 cm. (His Novels, v. 14) I. T.
PZ3.T844 AG3 vol. 14 PG3421.Ax   *891.7/3/3*   *LC* 78-10270   *ISBN* 0404019005

Turgenev, Ivan Sergeevich, 1818-1883.   • **2.1450**
[Selections. English. 1970] The diary of a superfluous man, and other stories, Translated from the Russian by Constance Garnett. London, W. Heinemann, 1899. New York, AMS Press [1970] 325 p. 23 cm. (His Novels, v. 13) I. T.
PZ3.T844 AG3 vol. 13 PG3421.Ax   *891.7/3/3*   *LC* 70-10268   *ISBN* 0404019137

Turgenev, Ivan Sergeevich, 1818-1883.   • **2.1451**
[Selections. English. 1970] Dream tales and prose poems. Translated from the Russian by Constance Garnett. London, W. Heinemann, 1897. New York, AMS Press [1970] 323 p. 23 cm. (His Novels, v. 10) I. T.
PZ3.T844 AG3 vol. 10 PG3421.Ax   *891.7/3/3*   *LC* 76-10267   *ISBN* 0404019102

Turgenev, Ivan Sergeevich, 1818-1883.   • **2.1452**
[Selections. English. 1970] The Jew, and other stories. Translated from the Russian by Constance Garnett. London, W. Heinemann, 1899. New York, AMS Press [1970] xiv, 321 p. 23 cm. (His Novels, v. 15) I. T.
PZ3.T844 AG3 vol. 15 PG3421.Ax   *891.7/3/3*   *LC* 75-10272   *ISBN* 0404019005

Turgenev, Ivan Sergeevich, 1818-1883.   • **2.1453**
[Selections. English. 1970] A Lear of the steppes, and other stories. Translated from the Russian by Constance Garnett. London, W. Heinemann, 1898. New York, AMS Press [1970] xv, 318 p. 23 cm. (His Novels, v. 12) I. T. II. Title: Faust. III. Title: Acia.
PZ3.T844 AG3 vol. 12 PG3421.Ax   *891.7/3/3*   *LC* 76-10303   *ISBN* 0404019129

Turgenev, Ivan Sergeevich, 1818-1883.   • **2.1454**
[Selections. English. 1970] The torrents of spring. Translated from the Russian by Constance Garnett. London, W. Heinemann, 1897. New York, AMS Press [1970] 405 p. 23 cm. (His Novels, v. 11) I. T. II. Title: First love. III. Title: Mumu.
PZ3.T844 AG3 vol. 11 PG3421.Ax   *891.7/3/3*   *LC* 75-10351   *ISBN* 0404019110

Turgenev, Ivan Sergeevich, 1818-1883.   • **2.1455**
[Dym. English] Smoke; a novel. Translated from the Russian by Constance
Garnett. London, W. Heinemann, 1896. New York, AMS Press [1970] xv,
315 p. 23 cm. (His Novels, v. 5) Translation of Dym. I. T.
PZ3.T844 AG3 vol. 5 PG3421.Dx   891.7/3/3   LC 75-10319
ISBN 0404019056

Turgenev, Ivan Sergeevich, 1818-1883.   • **2.1456**
A house of gentlefolk; a novel. Translated from the Russian by Constance
Garnett. London, W. Heinemann, 1894;. — New York: AMS Press, [1970] xix,
311 p.; 23 cm. — (His Novels, v. 2) Translation of Dvorianskoe gnezdo
(romanized form) I. T.
PZ3.T844 AG3 vol. 2 PG3421.Dx   891.7/3/3   LC 71-10350
ISBN 0404019021

Turgenev, Ivan Sergeevich, 1818-1883.   • **2.1457**
[Nov' English] Virgin soil; a novel. Translated from the Russian by Constance
Garnett. London, W. Heinemann, 1896. New York, AMS Press [1970] 2 v. 23
cm. (His Novels, v. 6-7) Translation of Nov'. I. T.
PZ3.T844 AG3 vol. 6-7 PG3421.Nx   891.7/3/3   LC 71-10271
ISBN 0404019005

Turgenev, Ivan Sergeevich, 1818-1883.   • **2.1458**
[Ottsy i deti. English] Fathers and children; a novel. Translated from the
Russian by Constance Garnett. London, W. Heinemann, 1895. New York,
AMS Press [1970] xxiii, 358 p. 23 cm. (His Novels, v. 4) Translation of Ottsy i
deti (romanized form) I. T.
PZ3.T844 AG3 vol. 4 PG3421.Ox   891.7/3/3   LC 70-10320
ISBN 0404019048

Turgenev, Ivan Sergeevich, 1818-1883.   **2.1459**
[Rudin. English] Rudin / Ivan Turgenev; translated by Richard Freeborn. —
Baltimore, Md.: Penguin Books, 1975, c1974. 185 p.; 18 cm. — (Penguin
classics) Translation of Rudin. I. T.
PZ3.T844 Rq5 PG3421.Rx   891.7/3/3   LC 75-323307   *ISBN*
0140443045

Turgenev, Ivan Sergeevich, 1818-1883.   • **2.1460**
[Rudin. English] Rudin; a novel, by Ivan Turgenev. Translated from the
Russian by Constance Garnett. London, W. Heinemann, 1894. New York,
AMS Press [1970] xxxi, 259 p. 23 cm. (His Novels, v. 1) Translation of Rudin.
I. T.
PZ3.T844 AG3 vol. 1 PG3421.Rx   891.7/3/3   LC 78-10317
ISBN 0404019013

Turgenev, Ivan Sergeevich, 1818-1883.   • **2.1461**
A sportsman's sketches. Translated from the Russian by Constance Garnett.
London, W. Heinemann, 1902;. — New York: AMS Press, [1970] 2 v.; 23 cm.
— (His Novels, v. 8-9) Translation of Zapiski okhotnika (romanized form) I. T.
PZ3.T844 AG3 vol. 8-9 PG3421.Zx   891.7/3/3   LC 73-10269
ISBN 0404019080

Moser, Charles A.   **2.1462**
Ivan Turgenev, by Charles A. Moser. — New York: Columbia University
Press, 1972. 48 p.; 20 cm. — (Columbia essays on modern writers, 60)
1. Turgenev, Ivan Sergeevich, 1818-1883. 2. Turgenev, Ivan Sergeevich. I. T.
II. Series.
PG3435.M6   891.7/3/3   LC 71-186640   *ISBN* 0231034121

Schapiro, Leonard Bertram, 1908-.   **2.1463**
Turgenev, his life and times / Leonard Schapiro. — 1st American ed. — New
York: Random House, c1978. xiii, 382 p., [8] leaves of plates: ill.; 24 cm.
Includes indexes. 1. Turgenev, Ivan Sergeevich, 1818-1883 — Biography.
2. Authors, Russian — 19th century — Biography. I. T.
PG3435.S3 1978   891.7/3/3 B   LC 78-5190   *ISBN* 039449640X

Yarmolinsky, Avrahm, 1890-.   • **2.1464**
Turgenev, the man, his art and his age. New York, Orion Press [1959] 406 p.
illus. 22 cm. 1. Turgenev, Ivan Sergeevich, 1818-1883. I. T.
PG3435.Y3 1959   928.917   LC 59-7894

Freeborn, Richard.   • **2.1465**
Turgenev: the novelist's novelist, a study. [London] Oxford University Press,
1960. 201 p. 23 cm. 1. Turgenev, Ivan Sergeevich, 1818-1883. I. T.
PG3443.F7   891.733   LC 60-50639

PG3447 U–Z

Semenko, Irina Mikhailovna.   **2.1466**
Vasily Zhukovsky / by Irina M. Semenko. — Boston: Twayne Publishers,
c1976. 167 p.; port.; 21 cm. — (Twayne's world authors series; TWAS 271:
Russia) Includes index. 1. Zhukovskiĭ, Vasiliĭ Andreevich, 1783-1852 —
Criticism and interpretation. I. T.
PG3447.Z5 Z874 PG3447Z5 Z878.   891.7/1/3   LC 75-23419
ISBN 080572995X

PG3450–3470 1870–1917

PG3450–3453 A–B

Andreyev, Leonid, 1871-1919.   • **2.1467**
Plays / by Leonid Andreyeff; translated from the Russian by Clarence L.
Meader and Fred Newton Scott;with an introductory essay by V.V. Brusyanin.
— Authorised ed. — New York: C. Scribner's Sons, 1915. xxvi, 214 p., [1] leaf
of plates: ill., port.; 20 cm. 'The present versions of 'The life of man' and 'The
black maskers' are based respectively on the texts printed in the seventh and
tenth volume of the 'Collected works' of Andreyeff, published by the
Prosveshchenie Company, of Petrograd; the version of 'The Sabine women' is
based the Russian text published by J. Ladyschnikow, in Berlin.' I. Meader,
Clarence Linton, 1868- II. Scott, Fred Newton, 1860-1931. III. Brusianin,
Vasiliĭ Vasil'evich, 1867- IV. T. V. Title: The black maskers. VI. Title: The
life of man. VII. Title: The Sabine women.
PG3452.A25   LC 15-5036

Andreyev, Leonid, 1871-1919.   **2.1468**
The seven that were hanged, and other stories / Leonid Andreyev. — New
York: Random House, [1958] 249 p.; 19 cm. — (Modern library paperbacks;
P40) I. T.
PG3452.S43   LC 58-6369

Blok, Aleksandr Aleksandrovich, 1880-1921.   **2.1469**
Selected poems. Introduced and edited by Avril Pyman. Illustrated by Kirill
Sokolov. — [1st ed.]. — Oxford; New York: Pergamon Press, [1972] xix, 366 p.:
illus., ports.; 24 cm. — (The Commonwealth and international library)
(Pergamon Oxford Russian series) At head of title: Alexander Blok. Poems in
Russian. I. Pyman, Avril. ed. II. T.
PG3453.B6 A6 1972   LC 67-31506

Mochul'skiĭ, K. (Konstantin), 1892-1948.   **2.1470**
[Aleksandr Blok. English] Aleksandr Blok / by Konstantin Mochulsky;
translated by Doris V. Johnson. — Detroit: Wayne State Univ. Press, 1983.
451 p.; 27 cm. Translation of: Aleksandr Blok. 1. Blok, Aleksandr
Aleksandrovich, 1880-1921. 2. Poets, Russian — 20th century — Biography.
I. T.
PG3453.B6 Z6813 1983   891.71/3 19   LC 82-20212   *ISBN*
081431726X

Pyman, Avril.   **2.1471**
The life of Aleksandr Blok / Avril Pyman. — Oxford [Eng.]; New York:
Oxford University Press, 1979-1980. 2 v.: ill., geneal. tables, ports. 1. Blok,
Aleksandr Aleksandrovich, 1880-1921 — Biography. 2. Poets, Russian — 20th
century — Biography. I. T.
PG3453.B6 Z6958   891.7/1/3 B   LC 78-40201   *ISBN* 0192117149

Reeve, F. D. (Franklin D.), 1928-.   • **2.1472**
Aleksandr Blok: between image and idea. New York, Columbia University
Press, 1962. vi, 268 p. ports., facsims. 25 cm. (Columbia studies in the
humanities, no.1) 1. Blok, Aleksandr Aleksandrovich, 1880-1921. I. T.
PG3453.B6 Z696 1962   LC 61-15468

Bryusov, Valery Yakovlevich, 1873-1924.   • **2.1473**
The fiery angel, a sixteenth century romance. Translated by Ivor Montagu and
Sergei Nalbandov. London H. Toulmin [1930] 392p. I. T. II. Title: Ognennyĭ
angel
PG3453 B7 O313

Bely, Andrey, 1880-1934.   **2.1474**
[Peterburg. English] Petersburg / Andrei Bely [i.e. B. N. Bugaev]; translated,
annotated, and introduced by Robert A. Maguire and John E. Malmstad. —
Bloomington: Indiana University Press, c1978. xxvii, 356 p.; 24 cm. — (Sources
and translation series of the Russian Institute, Columbia University) I. T.
PZ3.B8647 Pe 1978 PG3453.B84   891.73/3 19   LC 77-74442
ISBN 0253344107

Bely, Andrey, 1880-1934.   **2.1475**
[Serebrianyĭ golub'. English] The silver dove / Andrey Biely [i.e. B. N. Bugaev];
translated from the Russian and with an introd. by George Reavey; pref. by
Harrison E. Salisbury. — New York: Grove Press: distributed by Random
House, [1974] xlii, 419 p.; 22 cm. Translation of Serebrianyĭ golub'. I. T.
PZ3.B8647 Si4 PG3453.B84   891.73/3 19   LC 73-21040   *ISBN*
0802100449

Elsworth, J. D. (John David)   **2.1476**
Andrey Bely, a critical study of the novels / J.D. Elsworth — Cambridge
[Cambridgeshire]; New York: Cambridge University Press, 1983. viii, 263 p.;
23 cm. — (Cambridge studies in Russian literature.) Includes index. 1. Bely,
Andrey, 1880-1934 — Criticism and interpretation. I. T. II. Series.
PG3453.B84 Z634 1983   891.73/42 19   LC 83-1793   *ISBN*
0521247241

Bunin, Ivan Alekseevich, 1870-1953.   • **2.1477**
The Gentleman from San Francisco, and other stories / authorized translation from the Russian by Bernard Guilbert Guerney. — New York: Vintage Books, 1964, c1951. 813 p.; 19 cm. — (Vintage Russian library; V-743.) I. T. II. Series.
PG3453.B9 A15 1963   *LC* 64-55376

Bunin, Ivan Alekseevich, 1870-1953.   • **2.1478**
The village, by Ivan Bunin ... authorized translation from the Russian by Isabel F. Hapgood. New York, A. A. Knopf, 1923. 291 p. 20 cm. I. Hapgood, Isabel Florence, 1850-1928. tr. II. T.
PG3453.B9 Dx   *LC* 23-9538

Bunin, Ivan Alekseevich, 1870-1953.   • **2.1479**
The well of days / Ivan Bunin. — New York: Knopf, 1934. 305 p.; 21 cm. Translation of Zhizn' Arsen'eva: Istoki dnei. I. T.
PG3453.B9 Z1   891.7/3/3   *LC* 34-27024

Bunin, Ivan Alekseevich, 1870-1953.   • **2.1480**
[Vospominaniia. English] Memories and portraits, by Ivan Bunin. Translated by Vera Traill and Robin Chancellor. New York, Greenwood Press, 1968 [c1951] 217 p. group port. 21 cm. Translation of Vospominaniia (romanized form) I. T.
PG3453.B9 Z52 1968   891.7/8/303 B   *LC* 68-8053

Connolly, Julian W.   **2.1481**
Ivan Bunin / by Julian W. Connolly. — Boston: Twayne Publishers, c1982. 159 p.; 21 cm. — (Twayne's world authors series. TWAS 666) Includes index. 1. Bunin, Ivan Alekseevich, 1870-1953 — Criticism and interpretation. I. T. II. Series.
PG3453.B9 Z594 1982   891.78/309 19   *LC* 82-3108   *ISBN* 0805765131

Woodward, James B.   **2.1482**
Ivan Bunin: a study of his fiction / by James B. Woodward. — Chapel Hill: University of North Carolina Press, c1980. xii, 275 p.; 23 cm. Includes index. 1. Bunin, Ivan Alekseevich, 1870-1953 — Fictional works. I. T.
PG3453.B9 Z93   891.7/8/309 19   *LC* 79-12790   *ISBN* 080781394X

PG3455–3458 Chekhov

Chekhov, Anton Pavlovich, 1860-1904.   • **2.1483**
[Works. English. 1964] The Oxford Chekhov. Translated and edited by Ronald Hingley. London, New York, Oxford University Press, 1964 [i.e. 1965]- <1980 >. v. <1-5, 7, 9 > 23 cm. I. Hingley, Ronald. ed. and tr. II. T.
PG3456.A1 1965   891.783   *LC* 65-436

Chekhov, Anton Pavlovich, 1860-1904.   **2.1484**
[Short stories. English. Selections] Chekhov, the early stories, 1883–1888 / chosen and translated by Patrick Miles and Harvey Pitcher. — New York: Macmillan, [1983], c1982. 203 p.; 22 cm. I. Miles, Patrick. II. Pitcher, Harvey J. III. T.
PG3456.A15 M5 1983   891.73/3 19   *LC* 82-24893   *ISBN* 0025246208

Chekhov, Anton Pavlovich, 1860-1904.   **2.1485**
Anton Chekhov's plays / translated and edited by Eugene K. Bristow. — 1st ed. — New York: Norton, c1977. xxxii, 412 p.: maps. — (A Norton critical edition) I. Bristow, Eugene Kerr, 1927- II. T.
PG3456.A19 B7 1977   PG3456A19 B7 1977.   891.7/2/3   *LC* 77-21521   *ISBN* 0393044327

Jackson, Robert Louis. comp.   • **2.1486**
Chekhov; a collection of critical essays. Englewood Cliffs, N.J., Prentice-Hall [1967] viii, 213 p. 21 cm. (Twentieth century views) (A Spectrum book.) A Spectrum book, S-TC-71. 1. Chekhov, Anton Pavlovich, 1860-1904. I. T.
PG3458.A1 J3 1967   891.7/8/309   *LC* 67-23501

Chekhov, Anton Pavlovich, 1860-1904.   **2.1487**
[Correspondence. English. Selections] Letters of Anton Chekhov. Translated from the Russian by Michael Henry Heim in collaboration with Simon Karlinsky. Selection, commentary and introd. by Simon Karlinsky. [1st ed.]. New York, Harper & Row [c1973] xiv, 494 p. 25 cm. 1. Chekhov, Anton Pavlovich, 1860-1904. Correspondence I. Karlinsky, Simon. comp. II. T.
PG3458.A3 K3 1973   891.7/2/3 B   *LC* 72-9098   *ISBN* 0060122633

Chekhov, Anton Pavlovich, 1860-1904.   **2.1488**
[Correspondence English. 1975] Anton Chekhov's life and thought: selected letters and commentary / translated from the Russian by Michael Henry Heim, in collaboration with Simon Karlinsky; selection, commentary and introd. by Simon Karlinsky. — Berkeley: University of California Press, 1975, c1973. xiv, 494 p.; 23 cm. Published in 1973 under title: Letters of Anton Chekhov.

Includes index. 1. Chekhov, Anton Pavlovich, 1860-1904. Correspondence I. Karlinsky, Simon. II. T.
PG3458.A3 K3 1975   891.7/2/3 B   *LC* 76-357949   *ISBN* 0520026845

Eekman, Thomas, comp.   • **2.1489**
Anton Čechov, 1860–1960; some essays. — Leiden: E.J. Brill, 1960. viii, 335 p.: diagrs.; 25 cm. Twenty essays written in commemoration of Chekhov's 100th birthday. 1. Chekhov, Anton Pavlovich, 1860-1904 — Addresses, essays, lectures. 2. Authors, Russian — 19th century — Biography — Addresses, essays, lectures. I. T.
PG3458.E315   891.72/3 19   *LC* 61-4736

Hingley, Ronald.   **2.1490**
A new life of Anton Chekhov / Ronald Hingley. — 1st American ed. — New York: Knopf, 1976. xx, 352, vi p., [9] leaves of plates: ill.; 25 cm. Includes indexes. 1. Chekhov, Anton Pavlovich, 1860-1904 — Biography. I. T.
PG3458.H475 1976   PG3458 H475 1976.   891.7/2/3 B   *LC* 75-36818   *ISBN* 0394490584

Simmons, Ernest Joseph, 1903-1972.   • **2.1491**
Chekhov; a biography. — Boston, Little, Brown [1962] 669 p. illus. 22 cm. — (An Atlantic monthly press book.) 1. Chekhov, Anton Pavlovich, 1860-1904. I. T.
PG3458.S5   928.917   *LC* 62-16958

Chekhov's great plays: a critical anthology / edited, and with an   **2.1492**
introduction, by Jean–Pierre Barricelli.
New York: New York University Press, 1981. xvii, 268 p.: ill.; 24 cm. (The Gotham library of the New York University Press) 1. Chekhov, Anton Pavlovich, 1860-1904 — Dramatic works — Addresses, essays, lectures. I. Barricelli, Jean Pierre.
PG3458.Z9 D723   891.72/3 19   *LC* 81-3968   *ISBN* 0814710360

Peace, Richard Arthur.   **2.1493**
Chekhov, a study of the four major plays / Richard Peace. — New Haven: Yale University Press, 1983. 186 p.; 23 cm. 1. Chekhov, Anton Pavlovich, 1860-1904 — Dramatic works. I. T.
PG3458.Z9 D755 1983   891.72/3 19   *LC* 83-40001   *ISBN* 0300029616

Pitcher, Harvey J.   **2.1494**
The Chekhov play: a new interpretation / by Harvey Pitcher. — New York: Barnes & Noble, [1973] viii, 224 p.; 23 cm. 1. Chekhov, Anton Pavlovich, 1860-1904 — Dramaturgy. I. T.
PG3458.Z9 D76   891.7/2/3   *LC* 73-171115   *ISBN* 0064955850

Styan, J. L.   • **2.1495**
Chekhov in performance; a commentary on the major plays [by] J. L. Styan. — Cambridge [Eng.]: University Press, 1971. vii, 341 p.; 22 cm. 1. Chekhov, Anton Pavlovich, 1860-1904 — Dramaturgy. I. T.
PG3458.Z9 D77   891.7/2/3   *LC* 73-134614   *ISBN* 0521079756

PG3460 G

Garshin, V. M. (Vsevolod Mikhaĭlovich), 1855-1888.   • **2.1496**
[Selected works. English] The signal, and other stories. Translated from the Russian of Wsewolod Mikhailovich Garshin by Rowland Smith. Freeport, N.Y., Books for Libraries Press [1971] xi, 356 p. 21 cm. (Short story index reprint series) I. T.
PZ3.G1975 Si4 PG3460.G3   891.7/3/3   *LC* 77-163027   *ISBN* 0836939417

Yarwood, Edmund.   **2.1497**
Vsevolod Garshin / by Edmund Yarwood. — Boston: Twayne, 1981. 147 p.: port.; 21 cm. — (Twayne's world authors series; TWAS 627: Russia) Includes index. 1. Garshin, V. M. (Vsevolod Mikhaĭlovich), 1855-1888 — Criticism and interpretation. I. T.
PG3460.G3 Z94   891.73/3 19   *LC* 80-23865   *ISBN* 0805764690

Gippius, Z. N. (Zinaida Nikolaevna), 1869-1945.   **2.1498**
[Selected works. English] Selected works of Zinaida Hippius. Translated and edited by Temira Pachmuss. Urbana, University of Illinois Press [1972] ix, 315 p. 21 cm. I. T.
PZ3.G4409 Se6 PG3460.G5A1x   891.7/1/3   *LC* 72-188447   *ISBN* 0252002601

Pachmuss, Temira, 1927-.   • **2.1499**
Zinaida Hippius; an intellectual profile, by Temira Pachmuss. — Carbondale: Southern Illinois University Press, [c1971] xiii, 491 p.: illus., facsims., ports.; 22 cm. 1. Hippius, Zinaida Nikolaevna, 1869-1945. I. T.
PG3460.G5 Z8 1971   891.7/1/3 B   *LC* 70-86187   *ISBN* 0809304090

Zlobin, Vladimir. 2.1500
[Tiazhelaia dusha. English] A difficult soul: Zinaida Gippius / Vladimir Zlobin; edited, annotated, and with an introductory essay by Simon Karlinsky. — Berkeley: University of California Press, c1980. 197 p., [2] leaves of plates: ill.; 22 cm. — (Documentary studies in modern Russian poetry) Translation of Tiazhelaia dusha. 1. Gippius, Z. N. (Zinaida Nikolaevna), 1869-1945. 2. Poets, Russian — 20th century — Biography. I. Karlinsky, Simon. II. T. III. Series.
PG3460.G5 Z9813   891.71/3 B   *LC* 78-66043   *ISBN* 0520038673

PG3462–3465 Gorkii

Gorky, Maksim, 1868-1936. 2.1501
Mother / Maxim Gorky; with an introduction by Howard Fast; [translated by Isidore Schneider]. — Secaucus, N. J.: Citadel Press, c1947. vii, 406 p.; 21 cm. Translation of: Mat'. I. T.
PG3462.M3513 1947   891.7/3/3

Gorky, Maksim, 1868-1936. • 2.1502
[Selected works. English] Selected short stories. With an introductory essay by Stefan Zweig. New York, F. Ungar Pub. Co. [1959] 348 p. 22 cm. I. T.
PG3463.A15 1959x   *LC* 58-8959

Gorky, Maksim, 1868-1936. • 2.1503
The lower depths and other plays / translated by Alexander Bakshy in collaboration with Paul S. Nathan. — New Haven: Yale University Press, [1959, c1945] 220 p.; 21 cm. — (A Yale paperbound; Y-4) I. T.
PG3463.A19 1959   *LC* 59-13678

Gorky, Maksim, 1868-1936. • 2.1504
[Delo Artamonovykh. English] The Artamonov business / by Maxim Gorki; translated from the Russian by Alec Brown. — New York: Pantheon Books [1948] viii, 344 p.; 18 cm. — (The Novel library) I. T.
PG3463.D4B7 1948

Gorky, Maksim, 1868-1936. • 2.1505
[Detstvo. English] Childhood Translated by Margaret Wettlin; translation revised by Jessie Coulson. With an introduction by C. P. Snow. London, Oxford University Press, 1961. 330 p. 16 cm. (The World's classics, 581) I. T.
PG3465.A32 W4 1961

Gorky, Maksim, 1868-1936. 2.1506
The autobiography of Maxim Gorky / Maxim Gorky; with an introd. by Abrahm Yarmolinsky. — New York: Collier Books, c1962. 639 p. — (Collier Books. Russian classics; BS68V) I. T.
PG3465.A33   928/.917   *LC* 62-13161

Gorky, Maksim, 1868-1936. 2.1507
[Zametki iz dnevnika. English] Fragments from my diary [by] Maxim Gorki. Translated by Moura Budberg. New York, Praeger [1972, c1940] xvii, 265 p. 23 cm. Translation of Zametki iz dnevnika. 1. Gorky, Maksim, 1868-1936. I. T.
PG3465.A35 1972b   891.7/8/303 B   *LC* 77-185595

Gorky, Maksim, 1868-1936. • 2.1508
Letters of Gorky and Andreev, 1899–1912. Edited with an introd. by Peter Yershov. Letters, introd., and notes translated by Lydia Weston. New York, Columbia University Press, 1958. vii, 200 p. 22 cm. 1. Soviet Union — Intellectual life I. Andreyev, Leonid, 1871-1919. II. Yershov, Peter, 1895- III. T.
PG3465.A39 A6   928.917   *LC* 57-9948

Hare, Richard. • 2.1509
Maxim Gorky, romantic realist and conservative revolutionary. London, New York, Oxford University Press, 1962. 156 p. illus. 23 cm. 1. Gor'kĭ, Maksim, 1868-1936. I. T.
PG3465.H3 1962   891.7842   *LC* 62-4685

Levin, Dan. 2.1510
Stormy petrel: the life and work of Maxim Gorky / by Dan Levin. — East Norwalk, Conn.: Appleton, 1986. 348 p.; 21 cm. Originally published: New York: Appleton-Century, 1965. With original notes. 1. Gorky, Maksim, 1868-1936. 2. Authors, Russian — 19th century — Biography. 3. Authors, Russian — 20th century — Biography. I. T.
PG3465.L38 1986   891.78/309 B 19   *LC* 85-2485   *ISBN* 0805207880

Weil, Irwin. • 2.1511
Gorky: his literary development and influence on Soviet intellectual life. — New York: Random House, [1966]. — ix, 238 p.; 19 cm. — (Studies in language and literature; SLL5) 'English translations of Gorky's works': p. [221]-223. 1. Gorky, Maksim, 1868-1936 — Criticism and interpretation. I. T. II. Series.
PG3465.Z8 W4   *LC* 66-19855

Wolfe, Bertram David, 1896-1977. • 2.1512
The bridge and the abyss; the troubled friendship of Maxim Gorky and V. I. Lenin, by Bertram D. Wolfe. New York, Published for the Hoover Institution on War, Revolution and Peace, Stanford University, Stanford, Calif. [by] F. A. Praeger [1967] x, 180 p. illus., facsims., ports. 21 cm. 1. Gorky, Maksim, 1868-1936 — Friends and associates. 2. Lenin, Vladimir Il'ich, 1870-1924 — Friends and associates. I. Hoover Institution on War, Revolution, and Peace. II. T.
PG3465.Z9 L48   891.7/8/309   *LC* 67-27953

PG3467–3470 K–Z

Korolenko, Vladimir Galaktionovich, 1853-1921. • 2.1513
Makar's dream, and other stories. Translated from the Russian, with an introd., by Marian Fell. — Freeport, N.Y.: Books for Libraries Press, [1971] xiii, 297 p.: port.; 21 cm. — (Short story index reprint series) I. T.
PZ3.K843 M5 PG3467.K6   891.7/3/3   *LC* 74-163037   *ISBN* 0836939514

Korolenko, Vladimir Galaktionovich, 1853-1921. • 2.1514
[Slepoĭ muzykant. English] The blind musician. (From the Russian of Korolenko) by Sergius Stepniak and William Westall. Westport, Conn., Greenwood Press, [1970] viii, 187 p. 23 cm. Translation of Slepoĭ muzykant (romanized form) I. T.
PZ3.K843 Bl8 PG3467.K6   891.7/3/3   *LC* 69-13961   *ISBN* 0837140935

Kuprin, A. I. (Aleksandr Ivanovich), 1870-1938. • 2.1515
Yama: < The pit > a novel in three parts, translated from the original Russian by Bernard Guilbert Guerney, foreword by Arthur Garfield Hays ... New York City, B. G. Guerney [c1929] xviii p., 1 l., 21-447 p. front. (port.) 23 cm. Author's postscript: p. 443-447. At head of title: Alexandre Kuprin. I. Guerney, Bernard Guilbert. tr. II. T. III. Title: The pit.
PG3467.K8Y313   *LC* 30-1954

Kuzmin, Mikhail Alekseevich, 1875-1936. 2.1516
[Selections. English.] Selected prose & poetry / Mikhail Kuzmin; edited & translated by Michael Green. — Ann Arbor, Mich.: Ardis, c1980. xxviii, 416 p., [1] leaf of plates: port.; 22 cm. — I. T.
PG3467.K93 A244 1980   891.73/3 19   *LC* 79-55038   *ISBN* 0882331779

Leont'ev, Konstantin Nikolaevich, 1831-1891. • 2.1517
[Selections. English. 1969] Against the current; selections from the novels, essays, notes, and letters of Konstantin Leontiev. Edited, with an introd. and notes, by George Ivask. Translated from the Russian by George Reavey. New York, Weybright and Talley [1969] xxv, 286 p. 22 cm. 1. Leont'ev, Konstantin Nikolaevich, 1831-1891. I. Ivask, George, 1910- ed. II. T.
PG3467.L4 A27   891.7/3/3   *LC* 68-31243

Merezhkovsky, Dmitry Sergeyevich, 1865-. • 2.1518
Peter and Alexis. New York, The Modern library [c1931] 3 p.l., v-vi p., 1 l., 591 p. 17 cm. 1. Pctcr I, Emperor of Russia, 1672-1725 — Fiction. 2. Alexis, Czarevitch, son of Peter I, Emperor of Russia, 1690-1718 — Fiction. I. Guerney, Bernard Guilbert, tr. II. T.
PG3467.M4 K2x

Merezhkovsky, Dmitry Sergeyevich, 1865-1941. • 2.1519
The death of the gods / translated from the original Russian of Dmitri Merejkowski by Bernard Guilbert Guerney. — New York: Modern Library, 1929. x, 473 p. At head of title-page: Julian the Apostate. 1. Julian, Emperor of Rome, 331-363 — Fiction. I. T. II. Title: Julian the Apostate.
PG3467.M4 K33

Merezhkovsky, Dmitry Sergeyevich, 1865-. • 2.1520
The romance of Leonardo da Vinci, translated from the original Russian of Dimitri Merejkovski, by Bernard Guilbert Guerney ... New York, The Modern library [1928] xii p., 1 l., 637 p. 17 cm. (Half-title: The modern library of the world's best books) 1. Leonardo da Vinci — Fiction. I. Guerney, Bernard Guilbert. tr. II. T.
PG3467.M4K42 1928   *LC* 29-18338

Serafimovich, A., 1863-1949. 2.1521
[Zheleznyĭ potok. English] The iron flood [by] A. Serafimovich. 3d ed. Westport, Conn., Hyperion Press [1973] 209 p. illus. 23 cm. (Library of selected Soviet literature) Translation of Zheleznyĭ potok. Reprint of the 1957 ed. 1. Soviet Union — History — Revolution, 1917-1921 — Fiction. I. T.
PZ3.P818 Irl0 PG3470.P6   891.7/3/3   *LC* 72-90311   *ISBN* 0883550210

Serafimovich, A., 1863-1949. 2.1522
[Zheleznyĭ potok. English] The iron flood: a novel / Alexander Serafimovich; [translated from the Russian; illustrated by M. Grekov and A. Kokorin]. — 4th rev. ed. — Moscow: Progress Publishers, 1974. 175 p.: ill.; 21 cm. Translation of

Zheleznyĭ potok. 1. Russia — History — Revolution, 1917-1921 — Fiction. I. T.
PZ3.P818 Ir13 PG3470.P6   891.7/3/3   LC 75-331229

Prishvin, Mikhail Mikhaĭlovich, 1873-1954.   **2.1523**
[Kalendar' prirody. English. 1952] The lake and the woods; or, Nature's calendar. Translated by W. L. Goodman; with wood–engravings by Brian Hope–Taylor. London: Routledge & Paul, [1951] vii, 258 p. illus. 25 cm. Translation of Kalendar' prirody. I. T.
PG3470.P7 K3 1952   891.78   LC 51-8939

Remizov, Alekseĭ, 1877-1957.   **2.1524**
[Selections. English. 1985] Selected prose / Alexei Remizov; edited by Sona Aronian. — Ann Arbor, Mich.: Ardis, c1985. 218 p.: ill., ports.; 24 cm. 1. Remizov, Alekseĭ, 1877-1957 — Translations, English. 2. Remizov, Alekseĭ, 1877-1957 — Bibliography. I. Aronian, Sona. II. T.
PG3470.R4 A2 1985   891.73/44 19   LC 84-24577   ISBN 0882335081

Remizov, Alekseĭ, 1877-1957.   • **2.1525**
The clock. London, Chatto & Windus, 1924. xi, 212 p. 20 cm. I. Cournes, John, 1881- tr. II. T.
PG3470.R4 C35x   LC 25-6932

Remizov, Alekseĭ, 1877-1957.   • **2.1526**
The fifth pestilence: together with The history of the tinkling cymbal and sounding brass, Ivan Semyonovitch Stratilatov / By Alexei Remizov, translated from the Russian with a preface by Alec Brown. — London: Wishart, 1927. xxv, 235, [1] p. Translation of Piataia iazva. I. Brown, Alec, 1900-1962. II. T.
PG3470.R4 P513   LC 27-28084

Remizov, Alekseĭ, 1877-1957.   • **2.1527**
On a field azure. London, L. Drummond, 1946. 125 p. illus. 19 cm. I. Scott, Beatrice, tr. II. T.
PG3470.R4 V3x   LC 47-5365

Rozanov, V. V. (Vasiliĭ Vasil'evich), 1856-1919.   • **2.1528**
[Uedinennoe. English] Solitaria / V. V. Rozanov; with an abridged account of the author's life by E. Gollerbach; other biographical material, and matter from The apocalypse of our times; translated by S. S. Koteliansky. — Westport, Conn.: Greenwood Press, 1979. viii, 188 p.: port.; 22 cm. Translation of Uedinennoe. Reprint of the 1927 ed. published by Wishart, London. I. Gollerbakh, Ė. F. (Ėrikh Fedorovich), 1895- II. T.
PG3470.R77 U313 1979   891.7/8/307   LC 79-13120   ISBN 0313220042

Sologub, Fyodor, 1863-1927.   **2.1529**
The kiss of the unborn, and other stories / by Fedor Sologub [i.e. F. K. Teternikov].; translated, and with an introd., by Murl G. Barker. — 1st ed. — Knoxville: University of Tennessee Press, c1977. xxxvi, 214 p. I. T.
PZ3.T292 Ki5 PG3470.T4   PG3470T4 A3.   891.7/3/3   LC 76-27836   ISBN 0870492020

Sologub, Fyodor, 1863-1927.   • **2.1530**
The created legend; authorized translation from the Russian by John Cournos. New York: Stokes, [1916] 318 p. I. Cournos, John, 1881-1966. II. T.
PG3470.T4 Cx   LC 17-24700

Sologub, Fyodor, 1863-1927.   **2.1531**
[Melkiĭ bes. English] The petty demon / Fyodor Sologub; translated and introduced by S.D. Cioran, with an appendix and critical articles; edited by Murl Barker. — Ann Arbor, Mich.: Ardis, c1983. 355 p.; 24 cm. Translation of: Melkiĭ bes. I. Cioran, Samuel D. (Samuel David), 1941- II. Barker, Murl. III. T.
PG3470.T4 M413 1983   891.73/3 19   LC 83-2723   ISBN 0882338072

Sologub, Fyodor, 1863-1927.   • **2.1532**
The petty demon / Fyodor Sologub; translated from the Russian, with a preface and notes, by Andrew Field; introduction by Ernest J. Simmons. — New York: Random House, 1962. 355 p.; 24 cm. Translation of: Melkiĭ bes. I. T.
PG3470.T4 M43 1962   891.73/3 19   LC 62-12736

Sologub, Fyodor, 1863-1927.   **2.1533**
Bad dreams / Fyodor Sologub; translated by Vassar W. Smith. — Ann Arbor, Mich.: Ardis, 1978. 298 p. At head of title: Fyodor Sologub. I. T.
PG3470T4 T513   ISBN 0882331280

Teternikov, Fedor Kuz'mich, 1863-1927.   **2.1534**
The created legend / Fyodor Sologub [i.e. F.K. Teternikov]; translated and with an introd. by Samuel D. Cioran. — Ann Arbor, Mich.: Ardis, 1979. 3 v.; 21 cm. Complete translation of Tvorimaia legenda in 3 volumes. I. T. II. Title: Drops of blood. III. Title: Queen Ortruda. IV. Title: Smoke and ashes.
PG3470.T4 T823 1979   LC 78-74208   ISBN 0882331302

PG3475–3476 1917–1960

PG3476 A–D

Abramov, Fyodor.   • **2.1535**
One day in the 'New Life' / Fyodor Abramov; translated by David Floyd. — New York: Praeger, 1963. 174 p.; 21 cm. I. T. II. Title: The dodgers.
PZ4.A15On   PG3476.A22 Vx.   LC 63-18177

Akhmatova, Anna Andreevna, 1889-1966.   **2.1536**
[Selected works English. 1976] Selected poems / Anna Akhmatova; edited and translated by Walter Arndt; also with Requiem, translated by Robin Kemball, and A poem without a hero, translated and annotated by Carl R. Proffer. — Ann Arbor, Mich.: Ardis, c1976. xxxvi, 202 p.: ports.; 24 cm. I. Arndt, Walter W., 1916- II. Kemball, Robin. III. Proffer, Carl R. IV. T.
PG3476.A324 A22 1976   891.7/1/42   LC 76-150538   ISBN 0882331795

Akhmatova, Anna Andreevna, 1889-1966.   **2.1537**
Way of all the Earth / Anna Akhmatova; translated by D. M. Thomas. — Athens, Ohio: Ohio University Press, c1979. 95 p.; 23 cm. I. Thomas, D. M. II. T.
PG3476.A324 W3 1979b   891.71/42   LC 79-1953   ISBN 0821404296

Driver, Sam N., 1929-.   **2.1538**
Anna Akhmatova [by] Sam N. Driver. New York, Twayne Publishers [c1972] 162 p. 21 cm. (Twayne's world authors series, 198. Soviet Union) 1. Akhmatova, Anna Andreevna, 1889-1966. I. T.
PG3476.A324 Z63   891.7/1/42   LC 70-169621

Haight, Amanda.   **2.1539**
Anna Akhmatova: a poetic pilgrimage / Amanda Haight. New York: Oxford University Press, 1976. x, 213 p.: ill.; 24 cm. Based on the author's thesis, University of London, 1971. Includes index. 1. Akhmatova, Anna Andreevna, 1889-1966. 2. Poets, Russian — 20th century — Biography. I. T.
PG3476.A324 Z7 1976   891.7/1/42 B   LC 76-22841   ISBN 0192117319

Babel', I. (Isaak), 1894-1941.   **2.1540**
The collected stories. Edited and translated by Walter Morison. With an introd. by Lionel Trilling. New York, Criterion Books [1955] 381 p. At head of title: Isaac Babel. 'The text of this volume follows that of the 1934 Russian edition of Babel's stories, which included Red Cavalry, Tales of Odessa, and all but the last five of the group called Stories.' (Rasskazy) I. Morison, Walter Angus II. T.
PG3476.B2 Ax   LC 55-7842

Carden, Patricia.   **2.1541**
The art of Isaac Babel. Ithaca, Cornell University Press [1972] xii, 223 p. 22 cm. 1. Babel', I. (Isaak), 1894-1941. I. T.
PG3476.B2 Z6   891.7/3/42   LC 72-2359   ISBN 0801407206

Bulgakov, Mikhail Afanas'evich, 1891-1940.   • **2.1542**
[Belaia gvardiia. English] The white guard [by] Mikhail Bulgakov. Translated from the Russian by Michael Glenny, with an epilogue by Viktor Nekrasov. New York, McGraw-Hill Book Co. [c1971] 319 p. 23 cm. Translation of Belaia gvardiia. 1. Ukraine — History — Revolution, 1917-1921 — Fiction. I. T.
PZ3.B869 Wh3 PG3476.B78   891.7/3/42   LC 70-140252

Bulgakov, Mikhail Afanas'evich, 1891-1940.   • **2.1543**
The master and Margarita; translated from the Russian by Michael Glenny. — 1st U.S. ed. — New York: Harper & Row, 1967. 394 p. I. T.
PG3476.B78 M3x   LC 67-22898

Proffer, Ellendea.   **2.1544**
Bulgakov: life and work / by Ellendea Proffer. — Ann Arbor, MI: Ardis, c1984. xiv, 670 p.: ill.; 24 cm. Includes index. 1. Bulgakov, Mikhail Afanas'evich, 1891-1940. 2. Authors, Russian — 20th century — Biography. I. T.
PG3476.B78 Z8 1984   891.7/84209 B 19   LC 83-16199   ISBN 0882331981

Chukovskaia, Lidiia Korneevna.   • **2.1545**
[Opustelyĭ dom. English] The deserted house, by Lydia Chukovskaya. Translated by Aline B. Werth. [1st ed.] New York, Dutton, 1967. 144 p. 22 cm. 'Russian edition published in France under title Opustelyĭ dom.' 1. Soviet Union — History — 1925-1953 — Fiction. I. T.
PZ4.C5593 De   PG3476.C485 Ox.   LC 67-26599

Dombrovskiĭ, IUriĭ Osipovich.   • **2.1546**
The keeper of antiquities, a novel [by] Yury Dombrovsky. Translated from the Russian by Michael Glenny. — [1st ed.] — New York: McGraw-Hill, [1969] 273 p.; 21 cm. — I. T.
PZ3.D6977 Ke PG3476.D613   PG3476.D613.   891.7/3/44   LC 69-16252

Dudintsev, Vladimir Dmitrievich, 1918-.   • **2.1547**
Not by bread alone by Vladimir Dudintsev. Translated from the Russian by Edith Bone. — [1st ed.]. — New York: Dutton, 1957. 512 p.; 21 cm. — I. T.
PZ4.D835 No   PG3476.D83 Nx.   LC 57-11252

PG3476 E–I

Ėrenburg, Il'ia, 1891-1967.   • **2.1548**
Julio Jurenito. Translated by Anna Bostock in collaboration with Yvonne Kapp. London MacGibbon & Kee 1958. 317p. I. T.
PG3476 E5 N42

Ėrenburg, Il'ia, 1891-1967.   **2.1549**
A change of season. [Translated from the Russian by Manya Harari and Humphrey Higgins.] [1st American ed.] New York Knopf [c1961] 299p. (Borzoi books) I. T. II. Title: The thaw III. Title: The spring
PG3476 E5 O713 1962

Ėrenburg, Il'ia, 1891-1967.   • **2.1550**
The war, 1941–45 / Ilya Ehrenburg; translated by Tatiana Shebunina, in collaboration with Yvonne Kapp. — London: MacGibbon & Kee, 1964. 198 p.: ports.; 23 cm. 1. World War, 1939-1945 — Soviet Union I. T.
PG3476.E5 Z526   LC 65-87534

Ėrenburg, Il'ia, 1891-1967.   **2.1551**
People and life, 1891–1921. Translated from the Russian by Anna Bostock and Yvonne Kapp. — [1st American ed.]. — New York, Knopf, 1962. 453 p. 22 cm. I. T.
PG3476 E5Z53 1962   891.7842   LC 62-8671

Ėrenburg, Il'ia, 1891-1967.   **2.1552**
Post–war years, 1945–1954 [by] Ilya Ehrenburg. Translated by Tatiana Shebunina, in collaboration with Yvonne Kapp. Cleveland, World Pub. Co. [1967] 349 p. ports. 22 cm. '[Volume 6] of Men, years—life.' 1. World Peace Council. I. T.
PG3476.E5 Z533   891.7/8/4203   LC 67-13851

Ėrenburg, Il'ia, 1891-1967.   **2.1553**
Memoirs: 1921–1941 / Ilya Ehrenburg; translated by Tatania Shebunina in collaboration with Yvonne Kapp. — [1st ed.]. — Cleveland: World Pub. Co., 1964. 543 p. 1. Ėrenburg, Il'ia, 1891-1967. 2. Authors — Correspondence I. T.
PG3476.E5 Z55   LC 64-12061

Goldberg, Anatol, d. 1982.   **2.1554**
Ilya Ehrenburg: revolutionary, novelist, poet, war correspondent, propagandist: the extraordinary epic of a Russian survivor / Anatol Goldberg; with an introduction, postscript, and additional material by Erik de Mauny.. — 1st American ed. — New York: Viking, 1984. 312 p.: ill.; 22 cm. Includes index. 1. Ėrenburg, Il'ia, 1891-1967. 2. Authors, Russian — 20th century — Biography. I. T.
PG3476.E5 Z687 1984   891.73/42 B 19   LC 84-40264   ISBN 0670393541

Esenin, Sergeĭ Aleksandrovich, 1895-1925.   **2.1555**
[Poems. English. 1973] Confessions of a hooligan; fifty poems. Translated from the Russian and introduced by Geoffrey Thurley. [Cheadle Hulme, Eng.] Carcanet Press [1973] 107 p. port. 23 cm. (Translations) I. Thurley, Geoffrey. tr. II. T.
PG3476.E8 A28 1973   891.7/1/42   LC 73-179183   ISBN 0902145487 ISBN 085635001X

McVay, Gordon.   **2.1556**
Esenin: a life / by Gordon McVay. Ann Arbor, Mich.: Ardis, c1976. 352 p., [31] leaves of plates: ill.; 24 cm. Includes indexes. 1. Esenin, Sergeĭ Aleksandrovich, 1895-1925 — Biography. 2. Poets, Russian — 20th century — Biography. I. T.
PG3476.E8 Z774   891.7/1/42 B   LC 76-361860   ISBN 0882331825

Yevtushenko, Yevgeny Aleksandrovich, 1933-.   **2.1557**
[IAgodnye mesta. English] Wild berries / Yevgeny Yevtushenko; translated by Antonina W. Bouis. — 1st U.S. ed. — New York: W. Morrow, 1984. 296 p.; 25 cm. Translation of: IAgodnye mesta. I. T.
PG3476.E96 I2513 1984   891.73/44 19   LC 84-60445   ISBN 0688032591

Yevtushenko, Yevgeny Aleksandrovich, 1933-.   • **2.1558**
A precocious autobiography. Translated from the Russian by Andrew R. MacAndrew. [1st ed.] New York: Dutton, 1963. 124 p.; ill.; 22 cm. Translation of primechaniia k avtobiografii (romanized form) I. T.
PG3476 E96 Z523   LC 63-19740

Yevtushenko, Yevgeny Aleksandrovich, 1933-.   **2.1559**
Yevtushenko's reader, by Yevgeny Yevtushenko. English translations: Robin Milner–Gulland [and others. 1st ed.] New York, E. P. Dutton, 1972. 158 p. 22 cm. 1. Yevtushenko, Yevgeny Aleksandrovich, 1933- I. Yevtushenko, Yevgeny Aleksandrovich, 1933- Primechaniia k avtobiografii. English. 1972. II. T.
PG3476.E96 Z529   891.7/3/44   LC 72-77171   ISBN 0525239103 ISBN 0525048804

Fadeev, Aleksandr, 1901-1956.   **2.1560**
[Razgrom. English] The nineteen, by A. Fadeyev. Translated from the Russian by R. D. Charques. Westport, Conn., Hyperion Press [1973] vi, 293 p. 23 cm. Translation of Razgrom. Reprint of the 1929 ed. 1. Soviet Union — History — Revolution, 1917-1921 — Fiction. I. T.
PZ3.F12 Ni8 PG3476.F2   891.7/3/42   LC 72-90293   ISBN 0883550032

Fedin, Konstantin, 1892-.   • **2.1561**
Cities and years: a novel / by Konstantin Fedin; translated by Michael Scammell. — New York: Dell Pub. Co., 1962. 415 p.; 17 cm. — (A Laurel edition; LY113) Translation of Goroda i gody. I. T.
PZ3.F318 Ci   PG3476.F4 G6513 1962.   LC 62-5751

Furmanov, Dm. (Dmitriĭ), 1891-1926.   **2.1562**
[Chapaev. English] Chapayev [by] Dmitri Furmanov. Westport, Conn., Hyperion Press [1973] 423 p. 23 cm. Translation of Chapaev. Reprint of the 1935 ed. 1. Chapaev, Vasiliĭ Ivanovich, 1887-1919 — Fiction. I. T.
PZ3.F9807 Ch10 PG3476.F79   891.7/3/42   LC 72-90294   ISBN 0883550040

Gladkov, Fedor, 1883-1958.   • **2.1563**
Cement, a novel. [Translated from the Russian by A. S. Arthur and C. Ashleigh]. — New York, F. Ungar Pub. Co. [1960] 311 p. 24 cm. I. T.
PZ3.G4535Ce2 PG3476.G53T83   891.7342   LC 60-13978

Grossman, Vasiliĭ Semenovich.   **2.1564**
[Vse techet. English] Forever flowing [by] Vasily Grossman. Translated from the Russian by Thomas P. Whitney. [1st ed.] New York, Harper & Row [1972] 247 p. 22 cm. Translation of Vse techet. I. T.
PZ4.G8812 Fo PG3476.G7   891.7/3/42   LC 72-181655   ISBN 0060116137

Il'f, Il'ia, 1897-1937.   • **2.1565**
The twelve chairs, by Ilf & Petrov. Translated from the Russian by John H. C. Richardson. Introd. by Maurice Friedberg. [1st Vintage ed.] New York, Vintage Books [1961] 395 p. 19 cm. (Vintage Russian library, V-727) I. Petrov, Evgeniĭ, 1903-1942. joint author. II. T.
PZ3.I25 Tw   PG3476.I44 Dx.   LC 61-2146

PG3476 K–M

Kataev, Valentin, 1897-.   **2.1566**
[Rastrachiki. English] Embezzlers / Valentin Kataev; translated by Charles Rougle. Envy / Yury Olesha; translated by T. S. Berczynski. — Ann Arbor: Ardis, [1975]. ix, 257 p.; 24 cm. Translation of Rastrachiki by V. Kataev and of Zavist' by Y. Olesha. I. Olesha, IUriĭ Karlovich, 1899-1960. Zavist'. English. 1975. II. T.
PZ3.K153 Em13 PG3476.K4   891.7/3/42   LC 75-309700

Kataev, Valentin, 1897-.   • **2.1567**
The holy well [by] Valentin Katayev. Translated from the Russian by Max Hayward and Harold Shukman. New York: Walker [1967] 160 p.; 22 cm. Translation of Sviatoi Kolodets (romanized form) I. T.
PZ3.K153Ho PG3476.K4S913 1967a   LC 67-13226

Kataev, Valentin, 1897-.   • **2.1568**
Time, forward. Authorized translation from the Russian by Charles Malamuth. New York Farrar & Rinehart [c1933] 345 p.; 21 cm. Translation of: Vremia, vpered. I. T. II. Title: Vremia, vpered.
PG3476 K4 V713   LC 33-32417

Kaverin, V. (Veniamin), 1902-.   **2.1569**
[Dva kapitana. English] Two captains [by] Veniamin Kaverin [translated from the Russian by Bernard Isaacs] Moscow, Progress Publishers [1972] 670 p. 18 cm. (Soviet novels series) Translation of Dva kapitana. I. T.
PZ3.K177 Tw5 PG3476.K43   891.7/3/42   LC 73-155385

Leonov, Leonid, 1899-.   • **2.1570**
The badgers: a novel / by Leonid Leonov; translated from the Russian by Hilda Kazanina. — London: Hutchinson International Authors, 1947. 336 p.; 23 cm. Translation of Barsuki. I. T.
PZ3.L555 Bad4 PG3476.L5   891.7/3/42   LC 47-5673

Leonov, Leonid, 1899-.   • **2.1571**
The thief / by Leonid Leonov; translated by Hubert Butler. — New York:
Vintage Books, 1960. 519 p.; 19 cm. (Vintage Russian library; R-1005) I. T.
PG3476.L5 V613 1960   891.73   *LC* 60-3195

Mayakovsky, Vladimir, 1893-1930.   **2.1572**
[Selected works. English. 1975] The bedbug [a play] and selected poetry /
Vladimir Mayakovsky; edited with an introd. by Patricia Blake; translated by
Max Hayward and George Reavey. — Bloomington: Indiana University Press,
1975, c1960. 317 p.; 21 cm. Poems in English and Russian. Reprint of the ed.
published by Meridian Books, New York. I. T.
PG3476.M3 A24 1975   891.7/1/42   *LC* 75-10805   *ISBN*
0253311306. *ISBN* 0253201896 pbk

Brown, Edward James, 1909-.   **2.1573**
Mayakovsky; a poet in the revolution, by Edward J. Brown. Princeton, N.J.,
Princeton University Press [c1973] ix, 386 p. illus. 25 cm. (Columbia
University. Studies of the Russian Institute) 1. Mayakovsky, Vladimir,
1893-1930. I. T.
PG3476.M312 B7   891.7/1/42 B   *LC* 72-14022   *ISBN* 0691062552

Mandel'shtam, Osip, 1891-1938.   • **2.1574**
Prose of Osip Mandelstam: Noise of time. Theodosia, The Egyptian stamp.
Translated with a criticial essay, by Clarence Brown. Princeton, N.J.: Princeton
U.P., 1965. viii, 209 p.: ill., map, ports.; 22 cm. I. Brown, Clarence Fleetwood,
ed. and tr. II. T.
PG3476.M355 A22   891.78308   *LC* 65-17133

Mandel'shtam, Osip, 1891-1938.   **2.1575**
[Selections. English. 1979] The complete critical prose and letters /
Mandelstam; edited by Jane Gary Harris; translated by Jane Gary Harris and
Constance Link. — Ann Arbor, Mich.: Ardis, c1979. 725 p., [2] leaves of plates:
ports.; 24 cm. 1. Mandel'shtam, Osip, 1891-1938 — Correspondence. 2. Poets,
Russian — 20th century — Correspondence. 3. Books — Reviews I. Harris,
Jane Gary. II. T.
PG3476.M355 A243 1979   891.7/8/308   *LC* 78-64999   *ISBN*
0882331639

Mandel'shtam, Osip, 1891-1938.   **2.1576**
[Selections. English. 1973] Complete poetry of Osip Emilevich Mandelstam.
Translated by Burton Raffel and Alla Burago. With an introd. and notes by
Sidney Monas. [1st ed.] Albany, State University of New York Press, 1973. x,
353 p. port. 26 cm. (Russian literature in translation, 2) I. Raffel, Burton. tr.
II. Burago, Alla, tr. III. Monas, Sidney. IV. T. V. Series.
PG3476.M355 A27   891.7/1/3   *LC* 76-38004   *ISBN* 0873952103
ISBN 0873952111

Brown, Clarence, 1929-.   **2.1577**
Mandelstam [by] Clarence Brown. Cambridge [Eng.] University Press, 1973.
viii, 320 p. 22 cm. 1. Mandel'shtam, Osip, 1891-1938. I. T.
PG3476.M355 Z575   891.7/1/3 B   *LC* 72-90491   *ISBN*
052120142X

Mandel'shtam, Nadezhda, 1899-.   • **2.1578**
[Vospominaniia. English] Hope against hope; a memoir [by] Nadezhda
Mandelstam. Translated from the Russian by Max Hayward, with an introd. by
Clarence Brown. [1st ed.] New York, Atheneum, 1970. xvi, 431 p. ports. 25 cm.
Translation of Vospominaniia (romanized form) 1. Mandel'shtam, Osip,
1891-1938. 2. Mandel'shtam, Nadezhda, 1899- 3. Russia — Politics and
government — 1917-1936. 4. Russia — Intellectual life — 1917- I. T.
PG3476.M355 Z813 1970   891.7/1/3 B   *LC* 77-124984

Mandel'shtam, Nadezhda, 1899-.   **2.1579**
Hope abandoned [by] Nadezhda Mandelstam. Translated from the Russian by
Max Hayward. — [1st ed.]. — New York: Atheneum, 1974. xii, 687 p.; 25 cm.
Translation of Vtoraia kniga. 1. Mandel'shtam, Osip, 1891-1938.
2. Mandel'shtam, Nadezhda, 1899- 3. Soviet Union — Politics and
government — 1917- 4. Soviet Union — Intellectual life — 1917- I. T.
II. Title: Vtoraia kniga.
PG3476.M355 Z8313   891.7/1/3 B   *LC* 76-871412   *ISBN*
0689105495

PG3476 Nabokov
(see also: PS3527)

Nabokov, Vladimir Vladimirovich, 1899-1977.   • **2.1580**
Laughter in the dark. — New York: New Directions Books, 1960, c1938. 292 p.
I. T.
PG3476.N3   891.7/3/42   *LC* 60-16644

Nabokov, Vladimir Vladimirovich, 1899-1977.   • **2.1581**
The Gift; a novel. Translated from the Russian by Michael Scammell with the
collaboration of the author. New York, Putnam [1963] 378 p. 22 cm. I. T.
PZ3.N121Gi PG3476.N3D313   *LC* 63-9667

Nabokov, Vladimir Vladimirovich, 1899-1977.   • **2.1582**
Despair; a novel, by Vladimir Nabokov. New York: Putnam, [1966] 222 p.; 22
cm. I. T.
PG3476.N3O813 1966   *LC* 65-20683

Nabokov, Vladimir.   • **2.1583**
Invitation to a beheading / Vladimir Nabokov; translated by Dimitri Nabokov
in collaboration with the author. — New York: G.P. Putnam's, 1959. 223 p.
Translation of Priglashenie na Kazń. I. T.
PZ3.N121In   PG3476.N3 Px.   891.7342   *LC* 59-11024

Nabokov, Vladimir Vladimirovich, 1899-1977.   • **2.1584**
The defense: a novel / by Vladimir Nabokov; translated by Michael Scammell
in collaboration with the author. — New York: Putnam, 1964. 256 p.
Translation of Zashchita Luzhina. I. T.
PZ3N121 Dc   PG3476N3 Z2413.   *LC* 64-13017

Field, Andrew, 1938-.   **2.1585**
VN, the life and art of Vladimir Nabokov / Andrew Field. — New York:
Crown, c1986. p. cm. Includes index. 1. Nabokov, Vladimir Vladimirovich,
1899-1977. 2. Authors, Russian — 20th century — Biography. 3. Authors,
American — 20th century — Biography. I. T. II. Title: Life and art of
Vladimir Nabokov.
PG3476.N3 Z66 1986   813/.54 B 19   *LC* 86-2254   *ISBN*
0517561131

Hyde, G. M. (George M.), 1941-.   **2.1586**
Vladimir Nabokov: America's Russian novelist / G. M. Hyde. — London: M.
Boyars, 1977. 230 p.; 23 cm. — (Critical appraisals series) Label mounted on
t.p.: Distributed in the U.S.A. by Humanities Press, Atlantic Highlands, N.J.
Includes index. 1. Nabokov, Vladimir Vladimirovich, 1899-1977 — Criticism
and interpretation. I. T.
PG3476.N3 Z68 1977b   813/.5/4   *LC* 78-307708   *ISBN*
0714525731

Johnson, Donald B. (Donald Barton), 1933-.   • **2.1587**
Worlds in regression: some novels of Vladimir Nabokov / D. Barton Johnson.
— Ann Arbor: Ardis, c1985. x, 223 p.: ill.; 24 cm. 1. Nabokov, Vladimir
Vladimirovich, 1899-1977 — Criticism and interpretation. I. T.
PG3476.N3 Z696 1985   813/.54 19   *LC* 84-28359   *ISBN*
0882339087

PG3476 Ne–R

Nekrasov, Viktor, 1911-.   • **2.1588**
Kira Georgievna. Translated from the Russian by Walter N. Vickery. New
York: Pantheon Books, [1962, c1961] 183 p.; 22 cm. I. T.
PG3476 N47 K513

Olesha, IUriĭ Karlovich, 1899-1960.   **2.1589**
Complete short stories & Three fat men / Yury Olesha; translated by Aimee
Anderson. — Ann Arbor, Mich.: Ardis, c1979. 261 p.: port.; 24 cm. I. Olesha,
IUriĭ Karlovich, 1899-1960. Tri tolstiaka. English. 1979. II. T.
PZ3.O4557 Co 1979 PG3476.O37   891.7/3/42   *LC* 78-74197
ISBN 0882332139

Ostrovsky, Nikolay, 1904-1936.   **2.1590**
The making of a hero. Translated from the Russian by Alec Brown. New York:
E.P. Dutton, 1937. 440 p. 21 cm. Translation of Kak zakalialas' stal'. Other
English translation, published Moscow, 1952 has title: How the steel was
tempered. I. T. II. Title: Kak zakalialas' stal'. III. Title: How the steel was
tempered.
PG 3476 O85 K1 E5 1937   *LC* 37-16535

Panova, Vera Fedorovna, 1905-1973.   **2.1591**
The train / Vera Papova; translated from the Russian by Marie Budberg. — 1st
American ed. — New York: A. A. Knopf, 1949. 281 p. Translation of Sputniki.
I. T.
PG3476.P255 S613   *LC* 49-8213

PG3476 Pasternak

Pasternak, Boris Leonidovich, 1890-1960.   **2.1592**
[Selected works. English. 1977] Collected short prose / Boris Pasternak; edited
with an introd. by Christopher Barnes. — New York: Praeger, 1977. ix, 283 p.;
24 cm. I. Barnes, Christopher J. II. T.
PG3476.P27 A22 1977   891.7/8/4208   *LC* 73-189901   *ISBN*
0275503909

Pasternak, Boris Leonidovich, 1890-1960.   • **2.1593**
[Poems. English] The poetry of Boris Pasternak, 1917–1959. Selected, edited,
and translated by George Reavey. With an essay on the life and the writings of
Pasternak, and a bibliography, by George Reavey. Also containing three

important prose pieces of Boris Pasternak. New York, Putnam [1959] 256 p. 22 cm. I. Reavey, George, 1907- ed. and tr. II. T.
PG3476.P27 A26   891.7142   LC 59-13787

Pasternak, Boris Leonidovich, 1890-1960.   • **2.1594**
Doctor Zhivago. [Translated from the Russian by Max Hayward and Manya Harari.] [New York] Pantheon [1958] 558p. I. T.
PG3476 P27 D62 1958A

Pasternak, Boris Leonidovich, 1890-1960.   • **2.1595**
I remember: sketch for an autobiography / translated with a preface and notes by David Magarshack; with an essay on translating Shakespeare, translated by Manya Harari. — New York: Pantheon, 1959. 191 p.: ill.; 21 cm. I. T.
PG3476.P27.Z523   LC 59-8586

Hughes, Olga Raevsky.   **2.1596**
The Poetic world of Boris Pasternak [by] Olga R. Hughes. — [Princeton, N.J.]: Princeton University Press, [1974] xv, 192 p.; 23 cm. — (Princeton essays in European and comparative literature) 1. Pasternak, Boris Leonidovich, 1890-1960. I. T.
PG3476.P27 Z69   891.7/1/42   LC 73-2467   ISBN 0691062625

Mallac, Guy de, 1936-.   **2.1597**
Boris Pasternak, his life and art / by Guy de Mallac; foreword by Rimvydas Šilbajoris. — 1st ed. — Norman: University of Oklahoma Press, c1981. xxv, 449 p.: ill.; 26 cm. Includes index. 1. Pasternak, Boris Leonidovich, 1890-1960. 2. Authors, Russian — 20th century — Biography. I. T.
PG3476.P27 Z736   891.71/42 B 19   LC 81-2616   ISBN 0806116609

Pasternak: a collection of critical essays / edited by Victor Erlich.   **2.1598**
Englewood Cliffs, N.J.: Prentice-Hall, c1978. x, 192 p.; 21 cm. — (Twentieth century views) (A Spectrum book) 1. Pasternak, Boris Leonidovich, 1890-1960 — Addresses, essays, lectures. I. Erlich, Victor, 1914-
PG3476.P27 Z747   891.7/1/42   LC 77-21223   ISBN 0136528341

Paustovsky, Konstantin, 1893-1968.   **2.1599**
Story of a life / [by] Konstantin Paustovsky; Translated [from the Russian] by Manya Harari and Michael Duncan. — London: Harvill P., [c1964-1974) 6 v. Translation of Povest' o zhizni. 1. Paustovsky, Konstantin, 1893-1968. I. T.
PG3476.P29 Z513 1967   891.73   LC 67-96914

Platonov, Andreĭ Platonovich, 1899-1951.   **2.1600**
[Kotlovan. English and Russian] The foundation pit. Kotlovan (romanized form) [By] Andreĭ Platonov. English translation by Thomas P. Whitney. Pref. by Joseph Brodsky. Bi-lingual ed. [Ann Arbor, Mich., Ardis, c1973] xii, 284 p. 24 cm. English and Russian. I. T.
PZ3.P6953 Fo4 PG3476.P543   891.7/3/42   LC 74-166468   ISBN 0882330446 ISBN 0882330454

Platonov, Andreĭ Platonovich, 1899-1951.   **2.1601**
[Selections. English. 1978] Collected works / Andrei Platonov; pref. by Joseph Brodsky; translations by Thomas P. Whitney ... [et al.]. — Ann Arbor, Mich.: Ardis, 1978. xii, 438 p.; 24 cm. I. T.
PG3476.P543 A28   891.7/3/42   LC 78-110678   ISBN 0882331345. ISBN 0882331353 pbk

Platonov, Andreĭ Platonovich, 1899-1951.   **2.1602**
Chevengur / Andrei Platonov; translated by Anthony Olcott. — Ann Arbor, Mich.: Ardis, c1978. xvii, 333 p.; 24 cm. — I. T.
PG3476.P543 C513 1978   891.7/3/42   LC 78-57177   ISBN 0882333097

PG3476 S–Z

Sholokhov, Mikhail Aleksandrovich, 1905-.   • **2.1603**
The silent Don / by Mikhail Sholokhov; translated from the Russian by Stephen Garry. — New York: Knopf, 1942. 777 p. 'Reissued in one volume June 1942.' 1. World War, 1914-1918 — Fiction. 2. Russia — History — Revolution,1917-1921. — Fiction. I. Garry, Stephen. II. T. III. Title: And quiet flows the Don. IV. Title: Don flows home to the sea.
PG3476.S52 T418 1942   LC 42-36259

Ermolaev, Herman.   **2.1604**
Mikhail Sholokhov and his art / Herman Ermolaev. — Princeton, N.J.: Princeton University Press, c1982. xvi, 375 p., [6] p. of plates: ill.; 25 cm. Includes index. 1. Sholokhov, Mikhail Aleksandrovich, 1905- Tikhiĭ Don. I. T.
PG3476.S52 T57   891.73/42 19   LC 81-47123   ISBN 0691076340

Simonov, Konstantin Mikhaĭlovich, 1915-.   • **2.1605**
The living and the dead [by] Konstantin Simonov. Translated from the Russian by R. Ainsztein. — [1st ed.]. — New York: Greenwood Press, 1968 [c1962]

552 p.; 24 cm. Translation of Zhivye i mertvye (romanized form) 1. World War, 1939-1945 — Fiction. I. T.
PZ3.S59636 Li4 PG3476.S53   891.7/3/42   LC 68-54438

Sinjavskij, Andrej Donat'evič, 1925-.   • **2.1606**
The trial begins / by Abram Tertz; translated by Max Hayward. — 1st American ed. — New York: Pantheon Books, c1960. 128 p. I. T.
PZ 4.T332.Tr2   PG3476.S5414x.   LC 60-11760

Tendriakov, Vladimir Fedorovich, 1923-.   **2.1607**
[Selected works. English] Three, seven, ace & other stories [by] Vladimir Tendryakov. Translated from the Russian by David Alger, Olive Stevens, [and] Paul Falla. With a foreword by Max Hayward. [1st ed.] New York, Harper & Row [c1973] 252 p. 22 cm. Translation of Troĭka, semerka, tuz. I. T.
PZ4.T28727 Th3 PG3476.T42   891.7/3/44   LC 72-8319

Tolstoy, Aleksey Nikolayevich, 1883-1945.   • **2.1608**
Road to Calvary [by] Alexei Tolstoy; translated by Edith Bone. New York, A. A. Knopf, 1946. 4 p. l., 885, [1] p. 22 cm. 'First American edition.' 'Stalin prize novel.' Translation of (transliterated): Khozhdenie po mukam. I. Bone, Edith, tr. II. T.
PG3476.T6 Kx   LC 46-3966

Tolstoy, Aleksey Nikolayevich, graf, 1883-1945.   • **2.1609**
Peter the First / by Alexey Tolstoy; translated by Tatiana Shebunina. — New York: Macmillan, 1959. 768 p.; 22 cm. Fictionized biography. 1. Peter I, Emperor of Russia, 1672-1725 — Fiction. I. T.
PG3476.T6 P3713 1959   LC 59-11459

TSvetaeva, Marina, 1892-1941.   **2.1610**
Selected poems [of] Marina Tsvetayeva; translated by Elaine Feinstein with a foreword by Max Hayward. London, New York, Oxford University Press, 1971. xix, 103 p. 23 cm. I. Feinstein, Elaine. tr. II. T.
PG3476.T75 A23 1971   891.7/1/42   LC 75-877318   ISBN 019211803X

TSvetaeva, Marina, 1892-1941.   **2.1611**
[Selections. English. 1980] A captive spirit: selected prose / Marina Tsvetaeva; edited and translated by J. Marin King. — Ann Arbor: Ardis, c1980. iv, 479 p.: ill.; 24 cm. Translated from the Russian. 1. TSvetaeva, Marina, 1892-1941 — Biography — Addresses, essays, lectures. 2. Voloshin, Maksimilian Aleksandrovich, 1877-1932 — Addresses, essays, lectures. 3. Pushkin, Aleksandr Sergeevich, 1799-1837 — Appreciation — Addresses, essays, lectures. 4. Poets, Russian — 20th century — Biography — Addresses, essays, lectures. 5. Poets, Russian — 19th century — Biography — Addresses, essays, lectures. I. King, J. Marin. II. T.
PG3476.T75 A25 1980   891.78/4209   LC 80-11664   ISBN 0882333526

Pil'niak, Boris, 1894-1937.   • **2.1612**
Mother earth, and other stories [by] Boris Pilnyak. Translated from the Russian and edited by Vera T. Reck and Michael Green. — New York: Praeger, [1968] xviii, 291 p. 22 cm. I. T.
PZ3.V86Mo PG3476.V6A27   LC 68-26787

Pil'niak, Boris, 1894-1937.   **2.1613**
[Golyĭ god. English] The naked year, by Boris Pilnyak. Translated, and with an afterword by Alexander R. Tulloch. — Ann Arbor: Ardis, c1975. 203, [4] p. Translation of Golyĭ god. I. T.
PZ3.V86 Nak6 PG3476.V6   PG3476V6 G63 1975.   891.7/3/42   ISBN 0404067786

Zamiatin, Evgeniĭ Ivanovich, 1884-1937.   **2.1614**
[My English] We [by] Yevgeny Zamyatin. Translated by Mirra Ginsburg. New York, Viking Press [1972] xix, 204 p. 22 cm. Translation of My. I. T.
PZ3.Z158 We17 PG3476.Z34   891.7/3/42   LC 73-183514   ISBN 0670753181

Zamiatin, Evgeniĭ Ivanovich, 1884-1937.   **2.1615**
The islanders / Ergeny Zamyatin; [translated by T.S. Berczynski]. Armored-train 14-69 / [by] Vsevolod Ivanov; [translated by Frank Miller]. — Ann Arbor: Trilogy Publishers, c1978. 109 p.: ill. I. Ivanov, Vsevolod Viacheslavovich, 1895-1963. Bronepoezd 14-69. English. 1978 II. T. III. Title: Armored train 14-69
PG3476Z34 O813   LC 78-58278   ISBN 0931558018

Shane, Alex M.   **2.1616**
The life and works of Evgenij Zamjatin [by] Alex M. Shane. — Berkeley: University of California Press, 1968. 302 p.: port.; 23 cm. — (Russian and East European studies.) 1. Zamiatin, Evgeniĭ Ivanovich, 1884-1937. I. T. II. Series.
PG3476.Z34 Z84   891.7/3/42 B   LC 68-19643

Zoshchenko, Mikhail, 1895-1958.   • **2.1617**
Nervous people, and other satires / Mikhail Zoshchenko; edited, with an introd., by Hugh McLean; translated from the Russian by Maria Gordon and Hugh McLean. — New York: Pantheon Books, [1963] 449 p.; 21 cm. I. T.
PZ3.Z79 Ne4 PG3476.Z7   891.7/3/42   *LC* 63-7648

Zoshchenko, Mikhail, 1895-1958.   • **2.1618**
Scenes from the bathhouse, and other stories of Communist Russia. Translated, with an introd., by Sidney Monas. Stories selected by Marc Slonim. Ann Arbor: University of Michigan Press, 1961. xvii, 248 p.; 24 cm. I. T.
PZ3.Z79 Sc   PG3476.Z7 Ax.   *LC* 61-13499

PG3477–3490 1961-

Aĭtmatov, Chingiz.   **2.1619**
[Dol'she veka dlitsia den'. English] The day lasts more than a hundred years / Chingiz Aitmatov; translated by John French; foreword by Katerina Clark. — Bloomington: Indiana University Press, c1983. xix, 352 p.; 22 cm. Translation of: Dol'she veka dlitsia den'. I. T.
PG3478.I8 D613 1983   891.73/44 19   *LC* 83-48135   *ISBN* 0253115957

Aĭtmatov, Chingiz.   **2.1620**
[Voskhozhdenie na Fudzhiamu. English & Russian] The ascent of mount Fuji: a play / by Chingiz Aitmatov and Kaltai Mukhamedzhanov; translated by Nicholas Bethell. — 1st ed. — New York: Farrar, Straus and Giroux, 1975. 211 p.; 21 cm. Translation of Voskhozhdenie na Fudzhiamu. English and Russian. I. Mukhamedzhanov, Kaltaĭ, joint author. II. T.
PG3478.I8Vx   894/.3   *LC* 75-15525   *ISBN* 0374106290

Aksenov, Vasiliĭ Pavlovich, 1932-.   **2.1621**
[Ostrov Krym. English] The island of Crimea: a novel / by Vassily Aksyonov; translated from the Russian by Michael W. Heim. — 1st ed. — New York: Random House, 1983. 369 p.; 22 cm. Translation of: Ostrov Krym. I. T.
PG3478.K7 O813 1983   891.73/44 19   *LC* 83-42756   *ISBN* 0394524314

Aksenov, Vasiliĭ Pavlovich, 1932-.   **2.1622**
[Ozhog. English] The burn: a novel in three books: (late sixties–early seventies) / Vassily Aksyonov; translated from the Russian by Michael Glenny. — New York: Random House; Boston: Houghton Mifflin, c1984. 528 p.; 25 cm. Translation of: Ozhog. I. T.
PG3478.K7 O913 1984   891.73/44 19   *LC* 84-42521   *ISBN* 0394524926

Aksenov, Vasiliĭ Pavlovich, 1932-.   • **2.1623**
A ticket to the stars. Translated by Andrew R. MacAndrew. [New York] New American Library [1963] 176 p. 18 cm. (Signet books, P2315) Translation of: Zvezdnyĭ bilet (romanized form). I. T.
PG3478.K7 Z813   *LC* 63-24949

Anatoliĭ, A., 1929-1979.   • **2.1624**
[Babiĭ IAr. English] Babi Yar; a document in the form of a novel [by] A. Anatoli (Kuznetsov). Translated by David Floyd. New York, Farrar, Straus and Giroux [1970] 477 p. 21 cm. Translation of Babiĭ IAr. 1. Babiy Yar Massacre, 1941 — Fiction. I. T.
PZ4.A5375 Bab 1970b PG3478.N34   891.7/3/44   *LC* 70-125154   *ISBN* 0374107610

Brodsky, Joseph, 1940-.   **2.1625**
[Chast' rechi. English] A part of speech / Joseph Brodsky. — 1st ed. — New York: Farrar, Straus, Giroux, 1980. 151 p.; 24 cm. Translation of Chast' rechi. I. T.
PG3479.4.R64 C4513 1980   891.71/44   *LC* 80-613   *ISBN* 0374229872

Bykaŭ, Vasil', 1924-.   **2.1626**
[Sotnikov. English] The ordeal [by] Vasily Bykov. Translated from the Russian by Gordon Clough. [1st ed.]. New York, E. P. Dutton, 1972. 170 p. 22 cm. Translation of Sotnikov. 1. World War, 1939-1945 — Underground movements — White Russia — Fiction. I. T.
PG3479.4.Y47S6x   891.7/3/44   *LC* 77-179837   *ISBN* 0525171959

Demin, Mikhail.   **2.1627**
[Blatnoĭ. English] The day is born of darkness / by Mikhail Dyomin; translated from the Russian by Tony Kahn. — 1st American ed. — New York: Knopf: distributed by Random House, 1976. 368 p.; 22 cm. Translation of Blatnoĭ; abridged. 'Originally published in Germany as Die Tätowierten by S. Fischer Verlag, Frankfurt.' 1. Demin, Mikhail. in fiction, drama, poetry, etc. 2. Crime and criminals — Russia — Correspondence, reminiscences, etc. I. T.
PZ4.D3794 Day 1976 PG3479.6.E478   891.7/3/44   *LC* 75-36783   *ISBN* 0394491661

Iskander, Fazil'.   **2.1628**
[Sozvezdie kozlotura. English] The goatibex constellation / Fazil Iskander; translated by Helen Burlingame. — Ann Arbor, Mich.: Ardis Publishers, [1975] 132 p.: port.; 24 cm. Translation of Sozvezdie kozlotura. I. T.
PZ4.I79 Go PG3482.S5   891.7/3/44   *LC* 75-307543   *ISBN* 0882330713

Rasputin, Valentin Grigor'evich.   **2.1629**
[Zhivi i pomni. English] Live and remember / Valentin Rasputin; translated from the Russian by Antonina W. Bouis. — New York: Macmillan, 1978. 216 p.; 25 cm. Translation of Zhivi i pomni. I. T.
PZ4.R229 Li PG3485.5.A85   891.7/3/44   *LC* 77-18884   *ISBN* 0026011301

Rasputin, Valentin Grigor'evich.   **2.1630**
[Vek zhivi—vek liubi. English] You live and love and other stories / by Valentin Rasputin; translated by Alan Myers; foreword by Richard Lourie. — New York: Vanguard Press, [1986?], c1985. xxii, 180 p.; 22 cm. Translation of: Vek zhivi—vek liubi. 1. Rasputin, Valentin Grigor'evich — Translations, English. I. T.
PG3485.5.A85 A25 1986   891.73/44 19   *LC* 85-26575   *ISBN* 0814909167

Shalamov, Varlam Tikhonovich.   **2.1631**
[Kolymskie rasskazy. English] Kolyma Tales / by Varlam Shalamov; translated from the Russian by John Glad. — 1st ed. — New York: W. W. Norton, c1980. 222 p.; 22 cm. Translation of Kolymskie rasskazy. I. T.
PZ4.S52697 Ko 1980 PG3487.A592   891.7/3/42   *LC* 79-20245   *ISBN* 0393013243

Shukshin, Vasiliĭ Makarovich.   **2.1632**
Snowball berry red & other stories / Vasily Shukshin; edited by Donald M. Fiene; with translations by Donald M. Fiene ... [et al.]. — Ann Arbor, Mich.: Ardis, c1979. x, 253 p.: port.; 24 cm. Includes indexes. I. T.
PZ4.S5627 Sn PG3487.U5   891.7/3/44   *LC* 79-103566   *ISBN* 088233283X

Shukshin, Vasiliĭ Makarovich.   **2.1633**
[Selections. English. 1985] Roubles in words, kopeks in figures, and other stories / Vasily Shukshin; translated from the Russian by Natasha Ward and David Iliffe; introduction by Yevgeny Yevtushenko. — London; New York: Marion Boyars, 1985. 207 p.; 23 cm. 1. Shukshin, Vasiliĭ Makarovich — Translations, English. I. T.
PG3487.U5 A27 1985   *LC* 84-14675   *ISBN* 0714528137

Sokolov, Sasha, 1943-.   **2.1634**
[Shkola dlia durakov. English] A school for fools / Sasha Sokolov; translated by Carl R. Proffer. — Ann Arbor, Mich.: Ardis, c1977. 228 p.; 23 cm. Translation of Shkola dlia durakov. I. T.
PZ4.S68435 Sc PG3488.O356   891.7/3/44   *LC* 76-57545   *ISBN* 0882332481

Solzhenitsyn, Aleksandr Isaevich, 1918-.   **2.1635**
[Avgust chetyrnadtsatogo. English] August 1914 [by] Alexander Solzhenitsyn. Translated by Michael Glenny. New York, Farrar, Straus and Giroux [1972-. v. 25 cm. Translation of Avgust chetyrnadtsatogo. 1. Tannenberg, Battle of, 1914 — Fiction. I. T.
PZ4.S69 Au PG3488.O4   891.7/3/44   *LC* 78-178883   *ISBN* 0374106843

Solzhenitsyn, Aleksandr Isaevich, 1918-.   • **2.1636**
Cancer ward [by] Alexander Solzhenitsyn. Translated from the Russian by Nicholas Bethell and David Burg. — New York: Farrar, Straus and Giroux, [1969] xiv, 560 p.; 22 cm. Translation of Rakovyĭ korpus (romanized form) I. T.
PZ4.S69 Can3 PG3488.O4   891.7/3/44   *LC* 68-8813

✓ **Dunlop, John B. comp.**   **2.1637**
Aleksandr Solzhenitsyn: critical essays and documentary materials, edited by: John B. Dunlop, Richard Haugh [and] Alexis Klimoff. Belmont, Mass., Nordland Pub. Co. [c1973] 569 p. 23 cm. 1. Solzhenitsyn, Aleksandr Isaevich, 1918- — Addresses, essays, lectures. I. Haugh, Richard S. (Richard Stanley), 1942- joint comp. II. Klimoff, Alexis, joint comp. III. T.
PG3488.O4 A23   891.7/8/4409   *LC* 73-88869   *ISBN* 0913124036

Solzhenitsyn, Aleksandr Isaevich, 1918-.   • **2.1638**
One day in the life of Ivan Denisovich / by Alexander Solzhenitsyn; translated by Max Hayward and Ronald Hingley; introduction by Max Hayward and Leopold Labedz. — New York: Praeger, 1963. xxiv, 210 p.; 22 cm. — (Books that matter) First published in Novy mir, November 20, 1962. 1. Russian fiction — Translations into English. I. T.
PG3488.O4 O33 1963   *LC* 63-12769

Solzhenitsyn, Aleksandr Isaevich, 1918-.   • **2.1639**
[V kruge pervom. English] The first circle [by] Aleksandr I. Solzhenitsyn. Translated from the Russian by Thomas P. Whitney. [1st ed.] New York,

Harper & Row [1968] xiii, 580 p. 25 cm. Translation of V kruge pervom (romanized form) I. T.
PZ4.S69 Fi   PG3488.O4 V2x.   LC 68-54547

Scammell, Michael.   **2.1640**
Solzhenitsyn: a biography / Michael Scammell. — 1st ed. — New York: Norton, c1984. 1051 p., 16 p. of plates: ill., map, ports.; 24 cm. Map on lining papers. Includes index. 1. Solzhenitsyn, Aleksandr Isaevich, 1918- — Biography. 2. Authors, Russian — 20th century — Biography. I. T.
PG3488.O4 Z873 1984   891.73/44 B 19   LC 83-42647   ISBN 0393018024

Solzhenitsyn in exile: critical essays and documentary materials   **2.1641**
/ edited by John B. Dunlop, Richard S. Haugh, Michael Nicholson.
Stanford, Calif.: Hoover Institution, c1985. [414] p.; 24 cm. Includes index. 1. Solzhenitsyn, Aleksandr Isaevich, 1918- — Criticism and interpretation — Addresses, essays, lectures. I. Dunlop, John B. II. Haugh, Richard S. (Richard Stanley), 1942- III. Nicholson, Michael (Michael A.)
PG3488.O4 Z8865 1985   891.73/44 19   LC 84-10821   ISBN 0817980512

Trifonov, IUriĭ Valentinovich, 1925-.   **2.1642**
[Drugaia zhizn'. English] Another life; and, The House on the embankment / by Yuri Trifonov; translated from the Russian by Michael Glenny. — New York: Simon and Schuster, c1983. 350 p.; 22 cm. Translation of: Drugaia zhizn' and Dom na naberezhnoĭ. English. 1983. II. T. III. Title: Another life. IV. Title: House on the embankment.
PG3489.R5 D713 1983   891.73/44 19   LC 83-17576   ISBN 0671242660

Trifonov, IUriĭ Valentinovich, 1925-.   **2.1643**
[Starik. English] The old man / Yuri Trifonov; translated from the Russian by Jacqueline Edwards and Mitchell Schneider. — New York: Simon and Schuster, c1984. 267 p.; 23 cm. Translation of: Starik. I. T.
PG3489.R5 S713 1984   891.73/44 19   LC 84-14067   ISBN 0671252836

Vampilov, Aleksandr Valentinovich.   **2.1644**
[Proshchanie v iiune. English] Farewell in June: four Russian plays / A. Vampilov; translated by Kevin Windle and Amanda Metcalf. — St. Lucia; New York: University of Queensland Press; Hamel Hempstead, Herts., England: Distributed by Prentice-Hall International, 1983. xiii, 273 p.; 23 cm. — (Contemporary Russian writing.) Translation of: Proshchanie v iiune. I. T. II. Series.
PG3489.3.A45 A28 1983   891.72/44 19   LC 82-11161   ISBN 0702218626

Voĭnovich, Vladimir, 1932-.   **2.1645**
[Zhizn' i neobychaĭnye prikliucheniia soldata Ivana Chonkina. English] The life and extraordinary adventures of Private Ivan Chonkin / Vladimir Voinovich; translated by Richard Louric. — 1st ed. — New York: Farrar, Straus and Giroux, 1977. 315 p.; 21 cm. Translation of Zhizn' i neobychaĭnye prikliucheniia soldata Ivana Chonkina. I. T.
PZ4.V8955 Li PG3489.4.I53   891.7/3/44   LC 76-47579   ISBN 0374186219

Voĭnovich, Vladimir, 1932-.   **2.1646**
[Antisovetskiĭ Sovetskiĭ Soiuz. English] The anti–Soviet Soviet Union / Vladimir Voinovich; translated from the Russian by Richard Lourie. — 1st ed. — San Diego: Harcourt Brace Jovanovich, 1986. xxv, 325 p.; 22 cm. Translation of: Antisovetskiĭ Sovetskiĭ Soiuz. I. T.
PG3489.4.I53 A25 1986   891.74/44 19   LC 86-327   ISBN 0151078408

Voĭnovich, Vladimir, 1932-.   **2.1647**
[Moskorep. English] Moscow 2042 / Vladimir Voinovich; translated from the Russian by Richard Lourie. — 1st ed. — San Diego: Harcourt Brace Jovanovich, c1987. viii, 424 p.; 24 cm. Translation of: Moskorep. I. T. II. Title: Moscow two thousand forty two.
PG3489.4.I53 M6513 1987   891.73/44 19   LC 86-31796   ISBN 0151624445

Voznesenskiĭ, Andreĭ, 1933-.   **2.1648**
[Selections. English & Russian. 1987] An arrow in the wall: selected poetry and prose / Andrei Voznesensky; edited by William Jay Smith and F.D. Reeve; poems translated by W.H. Auden ... [et al.]; prose translated by Antonina W. Bouis. — 1st ed. — New York: H. Holt, c1987. xxiii, 344 p.; 24 cm. Text of poetry in Russian, parallel English translation. 1. Voznesenskiĭ, Andreĭ, 1933- — Translations, English. I. Smith, William Jay, 1918- II. Reeve, F. D. (Franklin D.), 1928- III. T.
PG3489.4.Z6 A2234 1987   891.71/44 19   LC 86-10301   ISBN 080500100X

Zinoviev, Aleksandr, 1922-.   **2.1649**
[Ziiaiushchie vysoty. English] The yawning heights / Alexander Zinoviev; translated from the Russian by Gordon Clough. — 1st ed. — New York: Random House, 1979. 828 p.; 24 cm. Translation of Ziiaiushchie vysoty. I. T.
PZ4.Z79 Yaw 1979 PG3490.I498   891.7/3/44   LC 78-21802   ISBN 0394427106

Zinoviev, Aleksandr, 1922-.   **2.1650**
[Svetloe budushchee. English] The radiant future / Alexander Zinoviev; translated from the Russian by Gordon Clough. — 1st Trade ed. — New York: Random House, 1980. 287 p.; 24 cm. Translation of Svetloe budushchee. I. T.
PG3490.I498 S913   891.73/44   LC 80-5305   ISBN 039451257X

PG3801–3987 UKRAINIAN LITERATURE

Tschiżewskij, Dmitrij, 1894-.   **2.1651**
[Istoriia ukraïns'koï literatury vid pochatkiv do doby realizmu. English] A history of Ukrainian literature, from the 11th to the end of the 19th century / Dmytro Čyževs'kyj; translated by Dolly Ferguson, Doreen Gorsline, and Ulana Petyk; edited and with a foreword by George S. N. Luckyj. — Littleton, Colo.: Ukrainian Academic Press, 1975. xii, 681 p.; 24 cm. Translation of Istoriia ukraïns'koï literatury vid pochatkiv do doby realizmu. Includes index. 1. Ukrainian literature — History and criticism. I. T.
PG3905.C513   891.7/9/09   LC 73-94029   ISBN 0872870936

Grabowicz, George G.   **2.1652**
Toward a history of Ukrainian literature / George G. Grabowicz. — Cambridge, Mass.: Harvard Ukrainian Research Institute, c1981. 101 p.; 24 cm. — (Monograph series / Harvard Ukrainian Research Institute) 1. Tschiżewskij, Dmitrij, 1894- History of Ukrainian literature. 2. Ukrainian literature — History and criticism. I. T.
PG3905.C52   LC 80-53801   ISBN 0674896769

PG5001–5146 CZECH LITERATURE

Novák, Arne, 1880-1939.   **2.1653**
Czech literature / Arne Novák; translated from the Czech by Peter Kussi; edited with a suppl. by William E. Harkins. — Ann Arbor: Michigan Slavic Publications, 1976. ix, 375 p.; 24 cm. (The Joint Committee on Eastern Europe publication series; no. 4) Translation of Stručné dějiny literatury české. 'Supplement: 1945-1974': p. 333-355. 1. Czech literature — History and criticism. I. Harkins, William Edward. II. T.
PG5001.N6313   891.8/6/09   LC 76-374418

Wellek, René.   **●2.1654**
Essays on Czech literature / René Wellek; introduced by Peter Demetz. — The Hague: Mouton, 1963. 214 p.: port.; 25 cm. — (Slavistic printings and reprintings. 43) 1. Czech literature — Addresses, essays, lectures. I. T. II. Series.
PG5003.W4   LC 64-3517

Součková, Milada, 1901-.   **●2.1655**
The Czech romantics. 's-Gravenhage, Mouton, 1958. 168 p.; 25 cm. (Slavistische Drukken en Herdrukken, 17) 1. Czech literature — History and criticism 2. Romanticism I. T. II. Series.
PG5006.S6x

Czech literature since 1956: a symposium / edited by William   **2.1656**
E. Harkins, Paul I. Trensky.
New York: Bohemica, 1980. iv, 161 p.; 24 cm. — (Columbia Slavic studies) 1. Czech literature — 20th century — History and criticism — Addresses, essays, lectures. I. Harkins, William Edward. II. Trensky, Paul I. III. Series.
PG5007.C9   891.8/6/09005 19   LC 80-120127   ISBN 0935504001

French, A. (Alfred), 1916-.   **2.1657**
Czech writers and politics, 1945–1969 / A. French. — Boulder: East European monographs; New York: Distributed by Columbia University Press, 1982. 435 p.: ill.; 23 cm. — (East European monographs. no. 94) Includes index. 1. Czech literature — 20th century — History and criticism. 2. Politics and

literature — Czechoslovakia. 3. Czechoslovakia — Politics and government — 1945- I. T. II. Series.
PG5007.F73 1982   891.8/6/09005 19   *LC* 81-65947   *ISBN* 0914710885

French, A. (Alfred), 1916-.   • **2.1658**
The poets of Prague: Czech poetry between the wars. London, New York, Oxford U.P., 1969. ix, 129 p., plates. illus. 23 cm. 1. Czech poetry — 20th century — History and criticism. I. T.
PG5008.F7   891.8/6/1509   *LC* 71-458344   *ISBN* 0192112864

Goetz-Stankiewicz, Marketa.   **2.1659**
The silenced theatre: Czech playwrights without a stage / Marketa Goetz-Stankiewicz. — Toronto; Buffalo: University of Toronto Press, c1979. xii, 319 p., [6] leaves of plates: ill.; 24 cm. Includes index. 1. Czech drama — 20th century — History and criticism. 2. Dramatists, Czech — 20th century — Biography. I. T.
PG5009.G6   792/.09437   *LC* 79-13423   *ISBN* 0802054269

Trensky, Paul I.   **2.1660**
Czech drama since World War II / by Paul I. Trensky; with an introd. by William E. Harkins. — White Plains, N.Y.: M. E. Sharpe, 1978. viii, 250 p.; 24 cm. — (Columbia Slavic studies) Includes index. 1. Czech drama — 20th century — History and criticism. I. T. II. Series.
PG5009.T7   891.8/6/2509   *LC* 78-64936   *ISBN* 0873321294

French, A. (Alfred), 1916- comp.   **2.1661**
Anthology of Czech poetry: a bilingual anthology / introduced by Renée Wellek. — Ann Arbor, Mich.: Michigan Slavic Translations, 1973. v. illus. 23 cm. (Michigan Slavic translations. no. 2) On cover: Czech poetry. English and Czech. 1. Czech poetry 2. Czech poetry — Translations into English. 3. English poetry — Translations from Czech. I. T. II. Series.
PG5025.F68   891.8/6/1008   *LC* 73-171082

PG5038–5039 Individual Authors, by Period

PG5038 1800–1960, A–Z

Čapek, Karel, 1890-1938.   • **2.1662**
[Krakatit. English] An atomic phantasy, Krakatit: a novel / by Karel Čapek; translated by Lawrence Hyde. — New York: Arts [1951] 294 p.; 19 cm. (Science fiction) Reprint of the 1925 ed. published by G. Bles, London. I. T. II. Title: Krakatit. English III. Series.
PZ3.C1695 Kr6 PG5038.C3   891.8/6/35

Čapek, Karel, 1890-1938.   • **2.1663**
In praise of newspapers, and other essays on the margin of literature. Translated [from the original Czech 'Marsyas'] by M. and R. Weatherall. London: G. Allen [1951] 138 p.; 19 cm. I. T.
PG5038.C3M36 1951   891.864   *LC* 52-421

Čapek, Karel, 1890-1938.   • **2.1664**
R.U.R. and The insect play, by the Brothers Čapek. [Translated from the Czech by P. Selver]. — London, Oxford University Press, 1961. 179 p. 20 cm. — (Oxford paperbacks, no. 34) I. Čapek, Josef, 1887-1945. II. T. III. Title: The insect play.
PG5038.C3R6 1961   891.862   *LC* 61-66137

Čapek, Karel, 1890-1938.   • **2.1665**
War with the newts / translated by M. & R. Weatherall. — New York: Putnam, [c1937] 348 p.: ill.; 21 cm. I. Weatherall, Marie, 1897- II. Weatherall, Robert, 1899- III. T.
PG5038.C3 V33   *LC* 37-17329

Čapek, Karel, 1890-1938.   **2.1666**
Apocryphal stories. Tr. by Dora Round. London, G. Allen & Unwin; New York, Macmillan Co. [1949] 155 p. 21 cm. I. T.
PG5038.C3x   891.863   *LC* 49-5662 *

Čapek, Karel, 1890-1938.   • **2.1667**
Three novels: Hordubal, An ordinary life [and] Meteor. Translated by M. and R. Weatherall. [Omnibus ed.] New York, A.A. Wyn [1948] 469 p.; 20 cm. I. T. II. Title: Hordubal. III. Title: Meteor. IV. Title: An ordinary life.
PG5038.F85x   891.8635   *LC* 49-7788

Frýd, Norbert.   • **2.1668**
A box of lives / Norbert Frýd; [translated by Iris Urwin. — Prague]: Artia [c1962] 446 p.; 20 cm. — (Artia pocket books.) I. T.
PG5038.F85x   *LC* 63-50138

Hašek, Jaroslav, 1883-1923.   **2.1669**
[Osudy dobrého vojáka Švejka za světové války. English] The good soldier Švejk and his fortunes in the World War. In a new and unabridged translation by Cecil Parrott, with the original illus. by Josef Lada. New York, Crowell [1974, c1973] xxii, 752 p. illus. 21 cm. Translation of Osudy dobrého vojaka Švejka za světové války. I. Lada, Josef, 1887-1957. illus. II. T.
PZ3.H2693 Go20 PG5038.H28   891.8/6/35   *LC* 73-13703   *ISBN* 0690001231 *ISBN* 0690004664

Hašek, Jaroslav, 1883-1923.   **2.1670**
[Short stories. English. Selections] The red commissar: including further adventures of the good soldier Švejk and other stories / Jaroslav Hašek; translated [from the Czech] by Cecil Parrott; original illustrations by Josef Lada. — New York: The Dial Press, c1981. xvi, 283 p.: ill.; 23 cm. I. Lada, Josef, 1887-1957. II. T.
PG5038.H28 A26   891.8/635 19   *LC* 81-179427   *ISBN* 0385272375

Parrott, Cecil, Sir, 1909-.   **2.1671**
Jaroslav Hašek: a study of Švejk and the short stories / Cecil Parrott. — Cambridge; New York: Cambridge University Press, 1982. xi, 219 p., [9] p. of plates: ill., ports.; 23 cm. — (Major European authors.) Includes index. 1. Hašek, Jaroslav, 1883-1923 — Criticism and interpretation. I. T. II. Series.
PG5038.H28 Z8134 1982   891.8/635 19   *LC* 81-12227   *ISBN* 0521243521

Holub, Miroslav, 1923-.   **2.1672**
Interferon, or on theater / Miroslav Holub, translated by Dana Hábová and David Young, introduction by David Young. — Oberlin: Oberlin College, c1982. 158 p. — (Field translation series. 7) I. T. II. Title: On theater III. Series.
PG5038H64 I5 1982   *LC* 82-82128   *ISBN* 0932440126

Jirásek, Alois, 1851-1930.   • **2.1673**
[Filosofská historie. English] Gaudeamus igitur / Alois Jirásek; [translated by Erika Vilímová. — 1st ed. — Prague]: Artia [1964? c1961] 164 p.; 21 cm. (Artia pocket books.) Translation of Filosofská historie. I. T.
PZ3.J568 Gau4 PG5038.J5   891.8/6/35   *LC* 76-58010   *ISBN* 0837194695

Kohout, Pavel.   **2.1674**
[Ubohý vrah. English] Poor murderer: a play / by Pavel Kohout; translated by Herbert Berghof and Laurence Luckinbill. — New York: Viking Press, 1977. ix, 100 p.: ill.; 21 cm. 'A Richard Seaver book.' Translation of Ubohý vrah. I. T.
PG5038.K64 U213   891.7/2/44   *LC* 76-51259   *ISBN* 0670564451

Lustig, Arnošt.   **2.1675**
Darkness casts no shadow / by Arnost Lustig; translated by Jeanne Nemcova. — Washington: Inscape, c1976. 144 p., [4] leaves of plates: ill.; 22 cm. — (His Children of the Holocaust; v. [2]) 1. Holocaust, Jewish (1939-1945) — Fiction. 2. World War, 1939-1945 — Children — Fiction. I. T.
PZ4.L97 Ch vol. 2 PG5038.L85   891.8/6/35 s 891.8/6/35   *LC* 76-41232   *ISBN* 0879534060

Lustig, Arnošt.   **2.1676**
Diamonds of the night / by Arnost Lustig; translated by Jeanne Němcová. Washington: Inscape, c1977. (His Children of the Holocaust; v. 3) Translation of Démanty noci. 1. Holocaust, Jewish (1939-1945) — Fiction. 2. World War, 1939-1945 — Fiction. I. T. II. Series.
PZ4.L97 Ch vol. 3 PG5038.L85   891.8/6/35 s 891.8/6/35   *LC* 77-10807   *ISBN* 0879534079

Lustig, Arnošt.   • **2.1677**
Night and hope / by Arnost Lustig; [translated by George Theiner]. — New York: Dutton, [1962]. 206 p. 206 p.; 21 cm. Short stories. I. T.
PZ4.L97 Ch vol. 1 PG5038.L85   891.8/635   *LC* 62-4574

Němcová, Božena, 1820-1862.   • **2.1678**
[Babička. English] Granny: scenes from country life / Božena Němcová; translated by Edith Pargeter. — [Prague: Artia, c1962] 349 p.; 19 cm. (Artia pocket books.) Translation of Babička. I. T.
PZ3.N341 Gr5 PG5038.N4   891.86/3/5   *LC* 76-48902   *ISBN* 0837193559

Neruda, Jan, 1834-1891.   • **2.1679**
Tales of the Little Quarter / Jan Neruda; translated from the original Czech by Edith Pargeter. — Melbourne; Toronto: Heinemann, 1957. viii, 296 p.; 23 cm. Translation of Povídky malostranské. I. T.
PZ3.N36 Tal   PG5038.N45x   891.8/6/34   *LC* 57-38557

Seifert, Jaroslav, 1901-.   **2.1680**
[Poems. English. Selections. 1986] The selected poetry of Jaroslav Seifert / translated from the Czech by Ewald Osers; edited and with additional translations by George Gibian. — New York: Macmillan Pub. Co., [c1986.] 194 p.; 24 cm. I. Osers, Ewald, 1917- II. Gibian, George. III. T.
PG5038.S45 A6 1986   891.8/615 19   *LC* 85-23685   *ISBN* 002609150X

Škvorecký, Josef.   **2.1681**
[Bassaxofon. English] The bass saxophone / by Josef Škvorecký; translated from the Czech by Kača Poláčková–Henley. — 1st American ed. — New York: Knopf, 1979, c1977. 208 p.; 21 cm. Translation of the author's Bassaxofon and Legenda Emöke. I. Poláčková-Henley, Káča. II. Škvorecký, Josef. Legenda Emöke. English. 1979. III. T.
PZ4.S619734 Bas 1979 PG5038.S527   891.8/6/35   *LC* 78-7270   *ISBN* 0394502671

Škvorecký, Josef.   **2.1682**
[Lvíče. English] Miss Silver's past / Josef Skvorecky; translated from the Czech by Peter Kussi; foreword by Graham Greene. — New York: Ecco Press, 1985. 251 p.; 21 cm. Translation of Lvíče. I. T.
PG5038.S527 L913 1985   891.8/635 19   *LC* 84-13691   *ISBN* 0880010746

Škvorecký, Josef.   **2.1683**
[Příběh inženýra lidských duší. English] The engineer of human souls: an entertainment on the old themes of life, women, fate, dreams, the working class, secret agents, love, and death / Josef Skvorecky; translated from the Czech by Paul Wilson. — 1st American ed. — New York: A.A. Knopf, 1984. 571 p.; 24 cm. Translation of: Příběh inženýra lidských duší. I. T.
PG5038.S527 P6813 1984   891.8/635 19   *LC* 83-48888   *ISBN* 039450500X

Škvorecký, Josef.   **2.1684**
[Zbabělci. English] The cowards / Josef Škvorecký; translated by Jeanne Němcova. — New York: Ecco Press, 1980, c1970. 416 p.; 21 cm. — (Neglected books of the twentieth century.) Translation of Zbabělci. I. T. II. Series.
PG5038.S527 Z213 1980   891.8/635   *LC* 80-13087   *ISBN* 091294675X

PG5039 1961-

Gruša, Jiří.   **2.1685**
[Dotazník. English] The questionnaire, or, Prayer for a town & a friend / Jiří Gruša; translated from the Czech by Peter Kussi. — New York, N.Y.: Farrar, Straus & Giroux, c1982. 278 p.: ill., geneal. table; 22 cm. Translation of: Dotazník. 'Published simultaneously in Canada by McGraw-Hill Ryerson Ltd., Toronto'—T.p. verso. I. T. II. Title: Prayer for a town & a friend.
PG5039.17.R87 D613 1982   891.8/635 19   *LC* 82-5042   *ISBN* 0374240108

Hrabal, Bohumil, 1914-.   **2.1686**
The death of Mr. Baltisberger, by Bohumil Hrabal. Translated from the Czech by Michael Heim. Introd. translated from the Czech by Kaca Polackova. — [1st ed.]. — Garden City, N.Y.: Doubleday, 1975. xx, 193 p.; 22 cm. Translation of Automat svět. I. T.
PZ1.H8428 De PG5039.18.R2   891.8/6/35   *LC* 74-4737   *ISBN* 0385006926

Hrabal, Bohumil, 1914-.   **2.1687**
[Ostře sledované vlaky. English] Closely watched trains / Bohumil Hrabal; translated from the Czech by Edith Pargeter; introd. by Josef Škvorecký; translated from the Czech by Paul Wilson. — New York: Penguin Books, 1981. 107 p.; 20 cm. — (Writers from the other Europe.) Originally published in 1968 by Grove Press, New York. Translation of Ostře sledované vlaky. I. T. II. Series.
PG5039.18.R2 O813 1981   891.8/635 19   *LC* 80-28160   *ISBN* 0140058087

Kundera, Milan.   **2.1688**
[Směšné lásky. English] Laughable loves. Translated from the Czech by Suzanne Rappaport. 1st American ed. New York, Knopf; [distributed by Random House] 1974. xvi, 242 p. 22 cm. Translation of Směšné lásky. I. T.
PZ4.K96475 Lau3 PG5039.21.U6   891.8/6/35   *LC* 73-16156   *ISBN* 0394474120

Kundera, Milan.   **2.1689**
[Valčík na rozloučenou. English] The farewell party / by Milan Kundera; translated from the Czech by Peter Kussi. — 1st American ed. — New York: Knopf distributed by Random House, 1976. 209 p.; 22 cm. Translation of Valčík na vozloučenou. I. T.
PZ4.K96475 Far3 PG5039.21.U6   891.8/6/35   *LC* 76-13675   *ISBN* 0394496604

Kundera, Milan.   **2.1690**
[Kniha smíchu a zapomnění. English] The book of laughter and forgetting / Milan Kundera; translated from the Czech by Michael Henry Heim. — 1st American ed. — New York: A. A. Knopf, 1980. 228 p.; 22 cm. Translation of Kniha smíchu a zapomnění. I. T.
PG5039.21.U6 K613 1980   891.8/635   *LC* 80-7657   *ISBN* 0394508963

Kundera, Milan.   **2.1691**
[Nesnesitelná lehkost bytí. English] The unbearable lightness of being / Milan Kundera; translated from the Czech by Michael Henry Heim. — 1st ed. — New York: Harper & Row, c1984. 314 p.; 22 cm. Translation of: Nesnesitelná lehkost bytí. I. T.
PG5039.21.U6 N413 1984   891.8/635 19   *LC* 83-48363   *ISBN* 0060152583

Kundera, Milan.   **2.1692**
[Žert. English] The joke / Milan Kundera; translated from the Czech by Michael Henry Heim. — 1st U.S. ed. of a complete translation. — New York: Harper & Row, c1982. xii, 267 p.; 22 cm. Translation of: Žert. I. Heim, Michael Henry. II. T.
PG5039.21.U6 Z313 1982   891.8/635 19   *LC* 81-48055   *ISBN* 0060149876

Vaculík, Ludvík.   **2.1693**
[Sekyra. English] The axe. Translated from the Czech by Marian Sling. [1st U.S. ed.] New York, Harper & Row [1973] 222 p. 21 cm. Translation of Sekyra. I. T.
PZ4.V117 Ax3 PG5039.32.A2   891.8/6/35   *LC* 73-4163   *ISBN* 0060144866

Drvota, Mojmir.   **2.1694**
Triptych / by Mojmir Drvota; translated from the Czech by Jarmila Veltrusky; pref. by Howard Schwartz; [cover ill. by Yitzhak Greenfield]. — St. Louis: Cauldron Press, 1980. 167 p.; 22 cm. — I. T.
PZ4.D7953 Tr PG5069.D75   891.8/635   *LC* 80-112294

PG5145–5146 TRANSLATIONS (COLLECTIONS)

The Writing on the wall: an anthology of contemporary Czech literature / edited by Peter Kussi and Antonin Liehm.   **2.1695**
Princeton: Karz-Cohl Pub., c1983. xviii, 252 p.; 22 cm. 1. Short stories, Czech — Translations into English. 2. Short stories, English — Translations from Czech. 3. Czech fiction — 20th century — Translations into English. 4. English fiction — Translations from Czech. I. Kussi, Peter. II. Liehm, Antonín J., 1924-
PG5145.E8 W74 1983   891.8/6301/08 19   *LC* 83-4375   *ISBN* 0943828538

PG6001–7446 POLISH LANGUAGE AND LITERATURE

Miłosz, Czesław.   • **2.1696**
The history of Polish literature / by Czesław Miłosz. — 2nd ed. — Berkeley: University of California Press, 1983. xix, 583 p., [16] p. of plates: ill.; 24 cm. 'First California edition'—Verso of t.p. Includes index. 1. Polish literature — History and criticism I. T.
PG7012.M48 1983   891.8/5/09 19   *LC* 82-20227   *ISBN* 0520044657

Levine, Madeline G.   **2.1697**
Contemporary Polish poetry, 1925–1975 / by Madeline G. Levine. — Boston: Twayne Publishers, 1981. 195 p.; 21 cm. — (Twayne's world authors series; TWAS 586: Poland) Includes index. 1. Polish poetry — 20th century — History and criticism I. T.
PG7070.L4   891.8/57/09 19   *LC* 81-429   *ISBN* 0805764283

PG7158 Individual Authors, 1801–1960

PG7158 A–M

Andrzejewski, Jerzy.   **2.1698**
[Popiół i diament. English] Ashes and diamonds / by Jerzy Andrzejewski; translated from the Polish by D. J. Welsh; introd. by Heinrich Böll. — Harmondsworth, Eng.; New York: Penguin Books, 1980. xiii, 238 p.; 20 cm. — (Writers from the other Europe.) Translation of Popiół i diament. I. T. II. Series.
PZ3.A576 As 1980 PG7158.A7   891.8/537   *LC* 80-466593   *ISBN* 0140052771

Borowski, Tadeusz.   **2.1699**
This way for the gas, ladies and gentlemen; and other stories. Selected and translated by Barbara Vedder. — New York: Viking Press, [1967] 159 p.; 21 cm. 1. Concentration camps — Fiction. I. T.
PG7158.B613x   *LC* 67-21889

Brandys, Kazimierz.   **2.1700**
[Miesiace. English] A Warsaw diary: 1978–1981 / Kazimierz Brandys; translated from the Polish by Richard Lourie. — 1st American ed. — New York: Random House, c1983. 260 p.; 22 cm. Translation of: Miesiace. 1. Brandys, Kazimierz — Biography. 2. Authors, Polish — 20th century — Biography. 3. Poland — History — 1980- I. T.
PG7158.B632 A3513 1983   891.8/58703 B 19   *LC* 83-42782 *ISBN* 0394528565

Fredro, Aleksander, hrabia, 1793-1876.   • **2.1701**
The major comedies of Alexander Fredro. Translated, with an introd. & commentaries, by Harold B. Segel. — Princeton, N.J.: Princeton University Press, 1969. xiv, 405 p.; 23 cm. — (Columbia Slavic studies) I. Segel, Harold B., 1930- tr. II. T. III. Series.
PG7158.F7 A6 1969   891.8/5/26   *LC* 68-20879

Prus, Bolesław, 1847-1912.   **2.1702**
[Lalka. English] The doll. Translated by David Welsh. New York, Twayne Publishers [1972] 702 p. 21 cm. Translation of Lalka. I. T.
PZ3.G519 Do PG7158.G6   891.8/5/36   *LC* 75-125261

Gombrowicz, Witold.   **2.1703**
[Ślub. English] The marriage. Translated from the Polish by Louis Iribarne. New York, Grove Press [c1969] 158 p. 21 cm. Translation of Ślub. I. T.
PG7158.G669 S53   891.852/7   *LC* 68-58135

Thompson, Ewa Majewska, 1937-.   **2.1704**
Witold Gombrowicz / by Ewa M. Thompson. — Boston: Twayne Publishers, 1979. 171 p.: port.; 21 cm. — (Twayne's world authors series; TWAS 510: Poland) Includes index. 1. Gombrowicz, Witold — Criticism and interpretation. I. T.
PG7158.G6692 T48   891.8/5/37   *LC* 78-15571   *ISBN* 0805763511

Hłasko, Marek.   • **2.1705**
The eighth day of the week / Marek Hlasko; translated from the Polish by Norbert Guterman; with an introd. by Harrison E. Salisbury. — New York: Dutton, 1958. 128 p.; 19 cm. Translation of Ósmy dzień tygodnia. I. T.
PZ4.H678 Ei4 PG7158.H55   891.8/5/37   *LC* 58-9585

Kochanowski, Jan, 1530-1584.   • **2.1706**
Poems / by Jan Kochanowski; translated from the Polish by Dorothea Prall Radin ... [et al.]. — Berkeley, Calif.: University of California Press, 1928. 156 p. — (University of California syllabus series; no. 214) Part of the poems were turned into English verse on the basis of the literal prose versions of the editor, G.R. Noyes. cf. Pref. I. Noyes, George Rapall, 1873-1952. II. Radin, Dorothea Prall III. T.
PG7158K55 P6   PG7157K6 P6 1928a.   *LC* 29-3513

Konwicki, Tadeusz.   **2.1707**
[Kompleks polski. English] The Polish complex / Tadeusz Konwicki; translated by Richard Lourie. — New York: Farrar Straus Giroux, c1982. vii, 211 p.; 22 cm. Translation of: Kompleks polski. I. T.
PG7158.K6513 K613 1982   891.8/537 19   *LC* 81-5385   *ISBN* 0374235481

Lem, Stanisław.   **2.1708**
[Cyberiada. English] The cyberiad; fables for the cybernetic age. Translated from the Polish by Michael Kandel. Illustrated by Daniel Mróz. New York, Seabury Press [1974] 295 p. illus. 22 cm. (A Continuum book) I. T.
PZ4.L537 Cy3 PG7158.L39   891.8/5/37   *LC* 73-6420   *ISBN* 081649164X

Lem, Stanisław.   **2.1709**
[Solaris. English] Solaris. Translated from the French by Joanna Kilmartin and Steve Cox. Afterword by Darko Suvin. New York, Walker [1970] 216 p. 22 cm. I. T.
PZ4.L537 So PG7158.L39   891.8/5/37   *LC* 75-123267   *ISBN* 0802755267

Lem, Stanisław.   **2.1710**
[Dzienniki gwiazdowe. English. Selections] Memoirs of a space traveler: further reminiscences of Ijon Tichy / Stanisław Lem; translated by Joel Stern and Maria Swiecicka–Ziemianek. — 1st ed. — New York: Harcourt Brace Jovanovich, c1983. 153 p.: ill.; 22 cm. Translation of: Dzienniki gwiazdowe. 1971. 'A Helen and Kurt Wolff book.' I. T.
PG7158.L39 D9132 1983   891.8/537 19   *LC* 81-47310   *ISBN* 0151588562

Lem, Stanisław.   **2.1711**
[Dzienniki gwiazdowe. English. Selections] The star diaries / by Stanisław Lem; translated from the Polish by Michael Kandel; with line drawings by Lem. — 1st Harvest/HBJ ed. — San Diego: Harcourt Brace Jovanovich, 1985, c1976. x, 275 p.: ill.; 18 cm. Translation of: Dzienniki gwiazdowe. I. T.
PG7158.L39 D9213 1985   891.8/537 19   *LC* 84-25133   *ISBN* 0156849054

Lem, Stanisław.   **2.1712**
[Fiasko. English] Fiasco / Stanisław Lem; translated from the Polish by Michael Kandel. — 1st ed. — San Diego: Harcourt Brace Jovanovich, c1987. viii, 322 p.; 24 cm. Translation of: Fiasko. 'A Helen and Kurt Wolff book.' I. T.
PG7158.L39 F5313 1987   891.8/537 19   *LC* 86-31816   *ISBN* 0151306400

Lem, Stanisław.   **2.1713**
[Głos pana. English] His master's voice / Stanislaw Lem; translated from the Polish by Michael Kandel. — 1st Havrest/HBJ ed. — San Diego: Harcourt Brace Jovanovich, 1984, c1983. 199 p.; 18 cm. Translation of: Głos pana. 'A Helen and Kurt Wolff Book.' I. T.
PG7158.L39 G613 1984   891.8/537 19   *LC* 83-18467   *ISBN* 0156403005

Mickiewicz, Adam, 1798-1855.   **2.1714**
[Selected works. English. 1975] Konrad Wallenrod and other writings of Adam Mickiewicz / translated from the Polish by Jewell Parish ... [et al.]. — Westport, Conn.: Greenwood Press, 1975. ix, 209 p.; 22 cm. Reprint of the 1925 ed. published by the University of California Press, Berkeley, which was issued as no. 170 of the University of California syllabus series. I. Parish, Jewell. II. T.
PG7158.M5 A26 1975   891.8/5/16   *LC* 74-12764   *ISBN* 083717743X

Mickiewicz, Adam, 1798-1855.   • **2.1715**
New selected poems. [Translated by Louise Bogan and others] Introd. by George N. Shuster. Edited by Clark Mills. Front. by Eugène Delacroix. New York, Voyage Press [c1957] 84 p. illus. I. Mills, Clark, 1913- II. T.
PG7158.M5Ax   891.851

Mickiewicz, Adam, 1798-1855.   • **2.1716**
Pan Tadeusz, or, The last foray in Lithuania. Translated by Watson Kirkconnell; with an introductory essay by William J. Rose and notes by Harold B. Segel. New York, Polish Institute of Arts and Sciences in America, c1962. 388 p. Translated from the Polish. I. T. II. Title: The last foray in Lithuania.
PG7158.M5 P312 1962a   *LC* 63-5072

Weintraub, Wiktor.   • **2.1717**
The poetry of Adam Mickiewicz. 'S-Gravenhage: Mouton, 1954. 302p. (Slavistic printings and reprintings. 2) 1. Mickiewicz, Adam, 1798-1855. I. T. II. Series.
PG7158 M5 Z94   *LC* 55-59147

Miłosz, Czesław.   **2.1718**
Bells in winter / Czeslaw Milosz; translated by the author and Lillian Vallee. — New York: Ecco Press, 1978. 71 p.; 23 cm. — I. T.
PG7158.M553 B4   891.8/5/17   *LC* 78-5617   *ISBN* 0912946563

Miłosz, Czesław.   **2.1719**
[Dolina Issy. English] The Issa Valley / Czeslaw Milosz; translated from the
Polish by Louis Iribarne. — New York: Farrar, Straus, Giroux, c1981. 288 p.;
23 cm. Translation of: Dolina Issy. I. T.
PG7158.M553 D613 1981   891.8/537 19   LC 81-5087   *ISBN*
0374177988

Miłosz, Czesław.   **2.1720**
[Rodzinna Europa. English] Native realm: a search for self–definition.
Translated from the Polish by Catherine S. Leach. [1st ed.] Garden City, N.Y.,
Doubleday, 1968. 300 p. 22 cm. Translation of Rodzinna Europa. 1. Miłosz,
Czesław. I. T.
PG7158.M553 R612   891.8/5/8703 B   LC 68-17807

PG7158 N–Z

Gömöri, George, 1934-.   **2.1721**
Cyprian Norwid. — New York: Twayne Publishers, [1974] 162 p. : port. —
(Twayne's world authors series, TWAS 305. Poland) 1. Norwid, Cyprian,
1821-1883. I. T.
PG7158.N57 Z64   891.8/5/16   LC 73-17341   *ISBN* 080572656X

Orzeszkowa, Eliza, 1842-1910.   **2.1722**
[Meir Ezofowicz. English] The forsaken, or, Meir Ezofowich / by Eliza
Orzeszkowa; translated from the Polish by Edward Königsberger. —
Bournemouth, England: Delamare Pub., c1980. 248 p.; 21 cm. Translation of:
Meir Ezofowicz. I. T. II. Title: Forsaken.
PG7158.O7 M413 1980   891.8/536 19   LC 83-208737   *ISBN*
095082030X

Reymont, Władysław Stanisław, 1867-1925.   • **2.1723**
The peasants ... from the Polish of Ladislas St. Reymont. New York, A. A.
Knopf, 1924-25. 4 v. 20 cm. Translated by Michael H. Dziewicki. cf.
Publisher's note. Vol. 4 wanting in L. C. I. Dziewicki, Michael Henry II. T.
PG7158.R4 C513   LC 24-28889

Krzyżanowski, Jerzy Ryszard.   **2.1724**
Władyslaw Stanislaw Reymont, by Jerzy R. Krzyzanowski. — New York:
Twayne Publishers, [c1972] 169 p.; 21 cm. — (Twayne's world authors series,
TWAS 248. Poland) 1. Reymont, Władysław Stanisław, 1867-1925. I. T.
PG7158.R4 Z75   891.8/5/37   LC 72-187632

Różewicz, Tadeusz.   **2.1725**
The card index, and other plays, by Tadeusz Rozewicz. Translated by Adam
Czerniawski. — New York: Grove Press, [1970, c1969] viii, 136 p.; 23 cm. I. T.
PG7158.R63 A22 1970   891.8/5/27   LC 74-101390

Różewicz, Tadeusz.   **2.1726**
The survivor and other poems / Tradeusz Różeqicz: translated and introduced
by Magnus J. Krynski and Robert A. Maguire. — Princeton, N.J.: Princeton
University Press, c1976. xix, 160 p. (The Lockert library of poetry in
translation) I. Krynski, Magnus J., 1922- II. Maguire, Robert A. III. T.
PG7158.R63 A26   PG7158R63 A26.   891.8517   LC 76-3034
     ISBN 069106315X

Schulz, Bruno, 1892-1942.   **2.1727**
Sanatorium under the sign of the hourglass / Bruno Schulz; translated from the
Polish by Celina Wieniewska. — 1st ed. — New York: Walker, 1978. xi, 178 p.:
ill.; 24 cm. I. T.
PG7158S33 S313   LC 77-90486   *ISBN* 0802705928

Sienkiewicz, Henryk, 1846-1916.   • **2.1728**
[Pan Wołodyjowski. English] Pan Michael; an historical novel of Poland, the
Ukraine, and Turkey. Authorized and unabridged translation from the Polish
by Jeremiah Curtin. [Popular ed.] New York, Greenwood Press, 1968. xvi,
527 p. 22 cm. Reprint of the 1898 ed. Third vol. of the author's trilogy, the 1st of
which is With fire and sword, and the 2d, Deluge. Translation of Pan
Wołodyjowski. 1. Poland — History — Michael Wisniowiecki, 1669-1673 —
Fiction. I. Curtin, Jeremiah, 1835-1906. tr. II. T.
PZ3.S57 P12 PG7158.S4   891.8/5/36   LC 69-10155

Sienkiewicz, Henryk, 1846-1916.   • **2.1729**
[Potop. English] The deluge: an historical novel of Poland, Sweden and Russia;
a sequel to With fire and sword, by Henryk Sienkiewicz. Translated from the
Polish by Jeremiah Curtin. Boston, Little, Brown, 1891. St. Clair Shores, Mich.,
Scholarly Press, 1970 [c1891] 2 v. port. 23 cm. Translation of Potop. 1. Poland
— History — John II Casimir, 1648-1668 — Fiction. I. Curtin, Jeremiah,
1835-1906. tr. II. T.
PZ3.S57 D6 PG7158.S4   891.85/3/6   LC 76-108539

Sienkiewicz, Henryk, 1846-1916.   • **2.1730**
[Quo vadis. English] Quo vadis: a narrative of the time of Nero / by Henryk
Sienkiewicz; translated from the Polish by Jeremiah Curtin. — New ed. —
Boston: Little, Brown, 1943. 422 p. 1. Church history — Primitive and early

church, ca. 30-600 — Fiction 2. Rome — History — Nero, 54-68 — Fiction
I. T.
PG7158.54 Q413 1943

Słowacki, Juliusz, 1809-1849.   • **2.1731**
Anhelli [by] Juljusz Słowacki. Translated from the Polish by Dorothea Prall
Radin. Edited with an introd. by George Rapall Noyes. London Allen & Unwin
[1930] 118p. I. T.
PG7158 S62 A713 1930   LC 30-8816

Staff, Leopold, 1878-1957.   **2.1732**
An empty room / Leopold Staff; translated by Adam Czerniawski. —
Newcastle upon Tyne: Bloodaxe Books, 1983. 60 p.: port. I. Czerniawski,
Adam, 1934- II. T.
PG7158.S7 A24   891.8517   *ISBN* 0906427525

Tuwim, Julian, 1894-1953.   • **2.1733**
[Poems. English] The dancing Socrates, and other poems. Selected and
translated by Adam Gillon. [1st ed.] New York, Twayne Publishers [c1968]
63 p. 22 cm. I. Gillon, Adam, 1921- tr. II. T.
PG7158.T8 A38   891.8/51/6   LC 68-57476

Wat, Aleksander.   **2.1734**
Mediterranean poems / Aleksander Wat; edited & translated by Czeslaw
Milosz. Ann Arbor: Ardis, c1977. x, 58 p.; 24 cm. (Ardis world poets in
translation series; no. 1) I. Miłosz, Czesław. II. T.
PG7158.W28 A25   891.8/5/17   LC 77-150075   *ISBN* 0882332058

Wierzyński, Kazimierz, 1894-1969.   • **2.1735**
Selected poems [by] Kazimierz Wierzynski. Edited by Clark Mills and Ludwik
Krzyzanowski. Introd. by Donald Davie. — New York: Voyages Press, 1959.
45 p.: port.; 21 cm. I. Mills, Clark, 1913- ed. II. Krzyżanowski, Ludwik, 1906-
ed. III. T.
PG7158.W42 A6 1959   891.8/51/7   LC 77-555763

Witkiewicz, Stanisław Ignacy, 1885-1939.   **2.1736**
Beelzebub sonata: plays, essays, and documents / Stanisław I. Witkiewicz;
edited and translated by Daniel Gerould and Jadwiga Kosicka. — 1st ed. —
New York: Performing Arts Journal Publications, c1980. 183 p.: ill. —
(Performing Arts Journal playscript) I. Gerould, Daniel Charles, 1928-
II. Kosicka, Jadwiga. III. T. IV. Series.
PG7158W5 B4 1980   891.8527   LC 80-81998   *ISBN* 0933826095

Witkiewicz, Stanisław Ignacy, 1885-1939.   **2.1737**
[Nienasycenie. English] Insatiability: a novel in two parts / by Stanisław Ignacy
Witkiewicz; translated, with an introd. and commentary by Louis Iribarne. —
Urbana: University of Illinois Press, c1977. xlv, 447 p.; 24 cm. Translation of
Nienasycenie. 'Russian and East European Center, published in conjunction
with the Office of International Programs and Studies.' I. Illinois. University at
Urbana-Champaign. Russian and East European Center. II. University of
Illinois at Urbana-Champaign. Office of International Programs and Studies.
III. T.
PZ3.W7813 In5 PG7158.W52   891.8/5/37   LC 76-10760   *ISBN*
0252005724

Witkiewicz, Stanisław Ignacy, 1885-1939.   • **2.1738**
[Wariat i zakonnica. English] The madman and the nun, and other plays.
Translated & edited by Daniel C. Gerould and C. S. Durer. With a foreword by
Jan Kott. Seattle, University of Washington Press [1968] liii, 303 p. illus., ports.
24 cm. Translation of Wariat i zakonnica. I. T.
PG7158.W52 W313 1968   891.8/5/27   LC 68-11036

Gerould, Daniel Charles, 1928-.   **2.1739**
Witkacy: Stanisław Ignacy Witkiewicz as an imaginative writer / by Daniel
Gerould. — Seattle: University of Washington Press, c1981. xviii, 362 p., [12]
leaves of plates: ill.; 25 cm. Includes index. 1. Witkiewicz, Stanisław Ignacy,
1885-1939 — Criticism and interpretation. I. T.
PG7158.W522 G4   891.8/58709 19   LC 79-3872   *ISBN*
029595714X

PG7159–7185 1961–

Herbert, Zbigniew.   • **2.1740**
[Selections. English. 1968] Selected poems; translated by Czesław Miłosz and
Peter Dale Scott, with an introduction by A. Alvarez. Harmondsworth,
Penguin, 1968. 140 p. 19 cm. (Penguin modern European poets, D104)
I. Miłosz, Czesław. tr. II. Scott, Peter Dale. tr. III. T.
PG7167.E64 A25   891.8/5/17   LC 68-93642

Mrożek, Sławomir.   • **2.1741**
The elephant. Translated from the Polish by Konrad Syrop. Illustrated by Daniel Mroz. New York, Grove Press [1963, c1962] 176 p. illus. 21 cm. I. T.
PG7172.R65x   LC 63-12838

Nowakowski, Marek.   **2.1742**
[Raport o stanie wojennym. English] The canary and other tales of martial law / Marek Nowakowski; translated by Krystyna Bronkowska; with a preface by Leszek Kolakowski. — Garden City, N.Y.: Dial Press, 1984. 144 p.; 22 cm. 'First published in Polish as Raport o stanie wojennym by Institut Litteraire, Paris 1982 and 1983.'—T.p. verso. 1. Poland — History — 1980- — Fiction. I. T. II. Title: Canary.
PG7173.O83 R3613 1984   891.8/537 19   LC 83-45562   ISBN 0385279884

Szymborska, Wisława.   **2.1743**
[Poems. English. Selections] Sounds, feelings, thoughts: seventy poems / by Wisława Szymborska; translated and introduced by Magnus J. Krynski and Robert A. Maguire. — Princeton, N.J.: Princeton University Press, c1981. xi, 215 p.: ill.; 23 cm. — (Lockert library of poetry in translation.) Selected poems, translated from the Polish. I. Krynski, Magnus J., 1922- II. Maguire, Robert A., 1930- III. T. IV. Series.
PG7178.Z9 A24   891.8/517 19   LC 80-8579   ISBN 0691064695

PG7445 Translations (Collections)

Introduction to modern Polish literature: an anthology of fiction   • **2.1744**
and poetry / edited by Adam Gillon and Ludwik Krzyzanowski.
2nd ed. / with a new poetry section edited by Adam Gillon and Krystyna Olszer. — New York: Hippocrene, c1982; London: Distributed by Orbis Books. 513 p.; 23 cm. 1. Polish literature — 20th century — Translations into English. 2. English literature — Translations from Polish. I. Gillon, Adam. II. Krzyżanowski, Ludwik. III. Olszer, Krystyna.
PG7445.E1   891.8/5/08007 19   LC 81-86230   ISBN 0882545167

Peterkiewicz, Jerzy, 1916-.   • **2.1745**
Five centuries of Polish poetry, 1450–1970, by Jerzy Peterkiewicz and Burns Singer. 2nd ed.; with new poems translated in collaboration with Jon Stallworthy. London, New York, Oxford U.P., 1970. xxx, 137 p. 22 cm. 1. Polish poetry — Translations into English. 2. English poetry — Translations from Polish. I. Singer, Burns. joint comp. II. Stallworthy, Jon. III. T.
PG7445.E3 P53 1970   891.8/5/108   LC 74-541903   ISBN 0192112988

Postwar Polish poetry: an anthology / selected and edited by   • **2.1746**
Czesław Miłosz.
3rd, expanded ed. — Berkeley: University of California Press, 1983. xiv, 191 p.; 22 cm. 1. Polish poetry — 20th century — Translations into English. 2. English poetry — Translations from Polish. I. Miłosz, Czesław.
PG7445.E3 P67 1983   891.8/517/08 19   LC 82-16084   ISBN 0520044754

Polish romantic drama: three plays in English translation /   **2.1747**
selected and edited, with an introd., by Harold B. Segel.
Ithaca, N.Y.: Cornell University Press, 1977. 320 p.: ill.; 22 cm. 1. Polish drama — 19th century — Translations into English. 2. English drama — Translations from Polish. I. Segel, Harold B., 1930- II. Mickiewicz, Adam, 1798-1855. Dziady. Part 3. English. 1977. III. Krasiński, Zygmunt, hrabia, 1812-1859. Nie-Boska komedia. English. 1977. IV. Słowacki, Juliusz, 1809-1849. Fantazy. English. 1977.
PG7445.E5 P6   891.8/5/2608   LC 76-50264   ISBN 0801408717

Twentieth–century Polish avant–garde drama: plays, scenarios,   **2.1748**
critical documents / by Stanisław Ignacy Witkiewicz ... et al.;
edited, with an introd., by Daniel Gerould; translated by Daniel
Gerould, in collaboration with Eleanor Gerould.
Ithaca: Cornell University Press, 1977. 287 p.: ill.; 23 cm. 1. Polish drama — 20th century — Translations into English. 2. English drama — Translations

from Polish. 3. Experimental theater — Addresses, essays, lectures. I. Witkiewicz, Stanisław Ignacy, 1885-1939. II. Gerould, Daniel Charles, 1928-
PG7445.E5 T9   PG7445E5 T9.   891.8/5/2708   LC 76-13659   ISBN 0801409527

PH BALTIC. FINNISH. HUNGARIAN LITERATURES

Rubulis, Aleksis, 1922-.   • **2.1749**
Baltic literature; a survey of Finnish, Estonian, Latvian, and Lithuanian literatures. — Notre Dame: University of Notre Dame Press, [1970] xv, 215 p.; 24 cm. Includes texts in translation. 1. Finnish literature — History and criticism. 2. Estonian literature — History and criticism. 3. Baltic literature — History and criticism. I. T.
PH302.R8   891.9   LC 79-105728   ISBN 0268003939

Finnish folk poetry, epic: an anthology in Finnish and English /   **2.1750**
edited and translated by Matti Kuusi, Keith Bosley, Michael
Branch.
Helsinki: Finnish Literature Society; London: C. Hurst; Montreal: McGill-Queen's University Press, 1977. 607 p., [12] leaves of plates: ill., maps, ports.; 24 cm. — (Publications of the Finnish Literature Society; 329) Text in English and Finnish in parallel columns. Includes index. 1. Folk poetry, Finnish 2. Epic poetry, Finnish I. Kuusi, Matti, 1914-. II. Branch, Michael, 1940-. III. Bosley, Keith. IV. Suomalaisen Kirjallisuuden Seura, Helsinki V. Series.
PH319 F54 1977   894/.541/1008

Kalevala.   • **2.1751**
Kalevala, the land of heroes / translated from the orginal Finnish by W.F. Kirby. — London: Dent; New York: Dutton, 1923-25. 2 v.; 19 cm. — (Everyman's library; 259-260.) 1. Finnish poetry — Translations into English. 2. English poetry — Translations from Finnish. I. Kirby, W. F. (William Forsell), 1844-1912. II. T.
PH324.E5 Kx   LC 36-37675

Kalevala.   • **2.1752**
The Kalevala; or, Poems of the Kaleva District. Compiled by Elias Lönnrot. A prose translation with foreword and appendices by Francis Peabody Magoun, Jr. Cambridge, Mass., Harvard University Press, 1963. xxiv, 410 p. illus., ports., map (on lining paper) 26 cm. Bibliographical references included in 'Appendices' (p. [339]-382) I. Lönnrot, Elias, 1802-1884. II. Magoun, Francis Peabody, 1895- tr. III. T.
PH324.E5M3   LC 63-19142

Snow in May: an anthology of Finnish writing, 1945–1972 /   **2.1753**
edited by Richard Dauenhauer and Philip Binham.
Rutherford, N.J.: Fairleigh Dickinson University Press, c1978. 389 p.: ill.; 24 cm. 1. Finnish literature — 20th century — Translations into English. 2. English literature — Translations from Finnish. 3. Swedish literature — Finland — Translations into English. 4. English literature — Translations from Swedish. I. Dauenhauer, Richard. II. Binham, Philip.
PH401.E1 S6   894/.541/08003   LC 77-24549   ISBN 083861583X

Czigány, Lóránt.   **2.1754**
The Oxford history of Hungarian literature from the earliest times to the present / Lóránt Czigány. — Oxford [Oxfordshire]: Clarendon Press; New York: Oxford University Press, c1984. x, 582 p.; 25 cm. Includes index. 1. Hungarian literature — History and criticism. I. T.
PH3012.C94 1984   894/.511/09 19   LC 83-3997   ISBN 0198157819

Modern Hungarian poetry / edited, and with an introd. by   **2.1755**
Miklós Vajda; foreword by William Jay Smith.
New York: Columbia University Press, 1977. xxxiv, 286 p., [6] leaves of plates: ports.; 24 cm. Includes indexes. 1. Hungarian poetry — 20th century — Translations into English. 2. English poetry — Translations from Hungarian. I. Vajda, Miklós, 1931-
PH3441.E3 M6   894/.511/1308   LC 76-2453   ISBN 0231040229

Hungarian short stories: with an introduction.   • **2.1756**
New York: Oxford University Press, 1967. 432p. (World's classics. 609.) 1. Short stories, Hungarian — Translations into English. 2. Short stories, English — translations from Hungarian. I. Series.
PH3441.E8 H8   894.511301   LC 67-101523

PJ1–995 General Works

Dictionary of Oriental literatures / general editor, Jaroslav   2.1757
Průšek.
New York: Basic Books, 1975 (c1974). 3 v.; 24 cm. Volume editors: v. 1, Z. Słupski; v. 2. D. Zbavitel; v. 3, J. Bečka. 1. Oriental literature — Dictionaries. I. Průšek, Jaroslav.
PJ31.D5   808.8   *LC* 73-82742   *ISBN* 0465016499

Conference on Oriental Classics in General Education,   • 2.1758
Columbia University, 1958.
Approaches to the Oriental classics: Asian literature and thought in general education / edited by Wm. Theodore De Bary. — New York: Columbia University Press, 1959. p. 'Proceedings of a conference held at Columbia University, September 12 and 13, 1958.' 1. Oriental literature — Congresses. I. De Bary, William Theodore, 1918- ed. II. T.
PJ309.C6 1958   890.631   *LC* 59-9905

K'uei hsing: a repository of Asian literature in translation /   2.1759
edited by Liu Wu-chi ... [et al.].
Bloomington: [Published] for the International Affairs Center [by] Indiana University Press, [1974] xii, 176 p.: ill.; 25 cm. (Indiana University East Asian series) 1. Oriental literature — Translations into English. 2. English literature — Translations from Oriental literature. I. Liu, Wu-chi, 1907- ed. II. Indiana University. International Affairs Center.
PJ409.K77 1974   PJ409 K77 1974.   895.1/08   *LC* 74-149799
ISBN 0253391016

New writing from the Middle East / edited with an introd. and   2.1760
commentary by Leo Hamalian and John D. Yohannan.
New York: F. Ungar, c1978. xxii, 506 p.; 22 cm. 1. Middle Eastern literature — 20th century — Translations into English. 2. English literature — Translations from foreign languages I. Hamalian, Leo. II. Yohannan, John D.
PJ409.N4 1978b   808.8/9956   *LC* 78-4411   *ISBN* 0804423385

Schimmel, Annemarie.   2.1761
[Und Muhammad ist sein Prophet. English] And Muhammad is his messenger: the veneration of the Prophet in Islamic piety / by Annemarie Schimmel. — Chapel Hill: University of North Carolina Press, c1985. xii, 377 p.: ill.; 24 cm. (Studies in religion) Translation of: Und Muhammad ist sein Prophet. Includes indexes. 1. Moehammad. in literature. 2. Moehammad — Cult. 3. Islamic poetry — History and criticism. I. T.
PJ827.S3313 1985   809.1/9351 19   *LC* 84-17374   *ISBN* 0807816396

Marzubān-nāmah. English.   • 2.1762
The tales of Marzuban. Translated from the Persian by Reuben Levy. — New York: Greenwood Press, 1968. 254 p.; 23 cm. Reprint of the 1959 ed. Attributed to Marzubān ibn Rustam. 1. Fables, Persian I. Marzubān ibn Rustam, 11th cent. II. Levy, Reuben. tr. III. T.
PJ939.M3 1968   398.21/0935   *LC* 68-8337

PJ1001–1989 Egyptology

Erman, Adolf, 1854-1937.   2.1763
[Literatur der Aegypter. English] The literature of the ancient Egyptians; poems, narratives, and manuals of instruction, from the third and second millennia B.C. Translated into English by Aylward M. Blackman. [New York] B. Blom [1971] xliv, 318 p. illus. 21 cm. Reprint of the 1927 ed. Translation of Die literatur der Aegypter. 1. Egyptian literature — Translations into English. 2. English literature — Translations from Egyptian. I. Blackman, Aylward M. (Aylward Manley), 1883-1956. tr. II. T.
PJ1481.E7 1971   893.1   *LC* 68-56522

Book of the dead.   2.1764
The Book of the dead; an English translation of the chapters, hymns, etc., of the Theban recension / with introd., notes, etc. by Sir E.A. Wallis Budge. — 2d ed.,

rev. and enl. — London: Routledge & K. Paul, 1974. 3 v. in 1 (ccvi, 698 p.): ill. I. Budge, E. A. Wallis (Ernest Alfred Wallis), Sir, 1857-1934. II. T.
PJ1555.E5 B7x   299.31   *ISBN* 0710011288

Erman, Adolf, 1854-1937. ed. and tr.   • 2.1765
The ancient Egyptians; a sourcebook of their writings. Translated [from the German] by Aylward M. Blackman. — Introd. to the Torchbook ed. by William Kelly Simpson. — New York, Harper & Row [1966] lxxii, 318 p. illus. 21 cm. — (Harper torchbooks. The Academy library, TB1233P) Translation of Die Literatur der Aegypter. Bibliography: p. xxxix—xl. 1. Egyptian literature — Translations into English. 2. English literature — Translations from Egyptian. I. T.
PJ1943.E72 1966   893.108   *LC* 66-875

Simpson, William Kelly. comp.   • 2.1766
The literature of ancient Egypt; an anthology of stories, instructions, and poetry. Edited with an introd. by William Kelly Simpson. With translations by R. O. Faulkner, Edward F. Wente, Jr. [and] William Kelly Simpson. — New Haven: Yale University Press, 1972. vi, 328 p.: illus.; 21 cm. 1. Egyptian literature — Translations into English. 2. English literature — Translations from Egyptian. I. T.
PJ1943.S5   893/.1   *LC* 75-151589   *ISBN* 0300014821

PJ3001–8518 Semitic Languages and Literatures

PJ3101–4091 Assyrian. Sumerian

Gilgamesh. English.   2.1767
Gilgamesh: translated from the Sîn-leqi-unninnî version / John Gardner, John Maier, with the assistance of Richard A. Henshaw. — 1st ed. — New York: Knopf, 1984. ix, 304 p., [1] leaf of plates: ill.; 24 cm. Translation of: Gilgamesh. I. Gardner, John, 1933- II. Maier, John R. III. Henshaw, Richard A. (Richard Aurel), 1921- IV. T.
PJ3771.G5 E5 1984   892/.1 19   *LC* 84-4442   *ISBN* 0394537718

Heidel, Alexander, 1907-.   • 2.1768
The Gilgamesh epic and Old Testament parallels. 2d ed. Chicago, Univ. of Chicago Press [1949] ix, 269 p. 25 cm. 'A companion to ... [the author's] monograph The Babylonian Genesis.' 1. Gilgamesh. 2. Bible. O.T. — Criticism, interpretation, etc. 3. Death 4. Deluge I. T.
PJ3771.G6 H4 1949   892.191   *LC* 49-5734

Kramer, Samuel Noah, 1897-.   • 2.1769
Sumerian mythology; a study of spiritual and literary achievement in the third millennium B.C. Rev. ed. New York, Harper [1961] 130 p. illus. 21 cm. (Harper torchbooks. The Academy library, TB1055) 1. Mythology, Sumerian I. T.
PJ4047.K7 1961   299.2   *LC* 61-66533

Gordon, Edmund I., ed.   • 2.1770
Sumerian proverbs; glimpses of everyday life in ancient Mesopotamia, by Edmund I. Gordon. With a chapter by Thorkild Jacobsen. — New York: Greenwood Press, 1968. xxvi, 555, 79 p.: illus.; 28 cm. Reprint of the 1959 ed. 1. Proverbs, Sumerian. I. T.
PJ4075.G6 1968   398.9/99/95   *LC* 69-10100

PJ4501–5060 Hebrew

Sivan, Reuven.   2.1771
The new Bantam-Megiddo Hebrew & English dictionary / Reuven Sivan and Edward A. Levenston. — New York: Schocken Books, 1977, c1975. 732 p. in various pagings; 24 cm. Added t.p.: Bantam-Megido milon 'Ivri ve-Angli hadash. Based on The Megiddo modern dictionary, English-Hebrew, by E. A. Levenston and R. Sivan. 1. English language — Dictionaries — Hebrew. 2. Hebrew language — Dictionaries — English. I. Levenston, Edward A. joint

author. II. Levenston, Edward A. Megiddo modern dictionary, English-Hebrew. III. T. IV. Title: Bantam-Megido milon 'Ivri ve-Angli hadash.
PJ4833.S56 1977   492.4/3/21   *LC* 77-75289   *ISBN* 080523666X

Waxman, Meyer, 1884-.   • **2.1772**
A history of Jewish literature. — New York, T. Yoseloff [c1960] 5 v. in 6. illus. 22 cm. Includes bibliography. First published in 1930 under title: A history of Jewish literature from the close of the Bible to our own days. 1. Jewish literature — Hist. & crit. 2. Hebrew literature — Hist. & crit. I. T.
PJ5008.W323   892.409   *LC* 61-1793

Zinberg, Israel, 1873-1938.   • **2.1773**
[Geshikhte fun der literatur bay Yidn. English] A history of Jewish literature. Translated and edited by Bernard Martin. Cleveland, Press of Case Western Reserve University, 1972-78. 12 v. 26 cm. Translation of Di geshikhte fun der literatur bay Yidn. Vols. 4-12 published by Hebrew Union College Press, Cincinnati. 1. Jewish literature — History and criticism. I. T.
PJ5008.Z5313   809/.889/24   *LC* 72-183310   *ISBN* 0829502289

Halkin, Simon, 1898-.   • **2.1774**
Modern Hebrew literature, from the Enlightenment to the birth of the State of Israel; trends and values. [New ed.] New York, Schocken Books [1970] 238 p. 22 cm. 1. Hebrew literature, Modern — History and criticism. I. T.
PJ5017.H3 1970   892.4/09   *LC* 71-110610

Klausner, Joseph, 1874-1958.   **2.1775**
[Novo-evreĭskaia literatura. English] A history of modern Hebrew literature (1785–1930) Authorized translation from the Hebrew by Herbert Danby. Edited by Leon Simon. Westport, Conn., Greenwood Press [1972] v, 204 p. 22 cm. 'This translation [of Novo-evreĭskaia literatura] ... has been made from the Hebrew version published in 1920.' 1. Hebrew literature, Modern — History and criticism. I. T.
PJ5017.K513 1972   892.4/09   *LC* 79-97289   *ISBN* 0837126126

Silberschlag, Eisig, 1903-.   **2.1776**
From renaissance to renaissance. New York, Ktav Pub. House [1973]-77. 2 v. 24 cm. 1. Hebrew literature, Modern — History and criticism. 2. Israeli literature — History and criticism. I. T.
PJ5017.S39   892.4/09   *LC* 72-5817   *ISBN* 0870681842

Wallenrod, Reuben.   • **2.1777**
The literature of modern Israel. New York, Abelard-Schuman [1957, c1956] 253 p. 22 cm. (Ram's horn books) 1. Israeli literature — History and criticism. I. T.
PJ5020.W3   892.409   *LC* 56-12168

PJ5050–5054 INDIVIDUAL AUTHORS

Mendele Mokher Sefarim, 1835-1917.   **2.1778**
Fishke the lame. New York, T. Yoseloff [1960] 221 p. illus. 22 cm. I. T.
PZ3.A158 Fi PJ5053.A2 F5x   *LC* 60-6836

Agnon, Shmuel Yosef, 1888-1970.   • **2.1779**
The bridal canopy / S. Y. Agnon. Translated by I. M. Lask. New York, Schocken Books [1967] vi, 389 p. 22 cm. Translation of (romanized: Hakhnasat kalah) I. T.
PJ5053.A4 Hx   *LC* 67-14955

Agnon, Shmuel Yosef, 1888-1970.   • **2.1780**
[Oreah natah la-lun. English] A guest for the night [by] S. Y. Agnon. New York, Schocken Books [1968] 485 p. 22 cm. Translation of Oreah natah la-lun. 'The basic translation into English is the work of Misha Louvish. For the rendition in its present form the publisher had the cooperation of Professors Naftali C. Brandwein, Allen Mandelbaum, and Oscar Shaftel.' —Publisher's note. I. T.
PJ5053.A4 Ox   *LC* 68-13723

Agnon, Shmuel Yosef, 1888-1970.   • **2.1781**
[Selections. English] Twenty–one stories. Edited by Nahum N. Glatzer. New York, Schocken Books [1970] 287 p. 23 cm. Translated from the Hebrew. I. Glatzer, Nahum Norbert, 1903- ed. II. T.
PZ3.A2733 Tu PJ5053.A4x   892.4/3/5   *LC* 71-108902

Bialik, Hayyim Nahman, 1873-1934.   **2.1782**
[Poems. English & Hebrew. Selections] [Mi–shire Byalik] Selected poems [by] Chaim Nachman Bialik, with English translation by Maurice Samuel. Illustrated by Maida Silverman. [New York] Union of American Hebrew Congregations [1972] xii, 132 p. col. illus. 29 cm. Hebrew text vocalized. I. Samuel, Maurice, 1895-1972. tr. II. Silverman, Maida. illus. III. T.
PJ5053.B5 A6 1972   892.4/1/5   *LC* 67-21071

PJ5059–5060 TRANSLATIONS
(COLLECTIONS)

Contemporary Israeli literature: an anthology = Sifrut yisraelit   **2.1783**
bat zemanenu / edited by Elliot Anderson; poetry edited by Robert Friend; introd. by Shimon Sandbank; afterword by Robert Alter.
1st ed. — Philadelphia: Jewish Publication Society of America, 1977. 342 p.: ill.; 25 cm. 1. Hebrew literature, Modern — Translations into English. 2. Hebrew literature, Modern — History and criticism. I. Anderson, Elliot. II. Friend, Robert. III. Title: Sifrut yisraelit bat zemanenu.
PJ5059.E1 C6x   839.093   *LC* 76-45285   *ISBN* 0827600887

New writing in Israel / edited by Ezra Spicehandler, co-edited   **2.1784**
by Curtis Arnson.
New York: Schocken Books, c1976. 224 p.; 21 cm. 1. Israeli literature — Translations into English. 2. English literature — Translations from Hebrew. I. Spicehandler, Ezra. II. Arnson, Curtis.
PJ5059.E1 N4   892.4/08/006   *LC* 75-36497   *ISBN* 0805236252

Eight great Hebrew short novels / edited and introduced by   **2.1785**
Alan Lelchuk and Gershon Shaked.
New York: New American Library, c1983. xxii, 392 p.; 21 cm. 'A Meridan book.' 1. Hebrew fiction — Translations into English. 2. English fiction — Translations from Hebrew. I. Lelchuk, Alan. II. Shaked, Gershon.
PJ5059.E8 E33 1983   892.4/35/08 19   *LC* 82-14496   *ISBN* 0452006058

Modern Hebrew literature / edited, with introductions and   **2.1786**
notes, by Robert Alter.
New York: Behrman House, c1975. xi, 398 p.; 24 cm. (Library of Jewish studies) 1. Short stories, Hebrew — Translations into English. 2. Short stories, English — Translations from Hebrew. I. Alter, Robert.
PZ1.M7193 PJ5059.E8 Mx   892.4/3/01   *LC* 75-9928   *ISBN* 0874412188

PJ5111–5192 Yiddish

Never say die!: a thousand years of Yiddish in Jewish life and   **2.1787**
letters / edited by Joshua A. Fishman.
The Hague; New York: Mouton, c1981. xv, 763 p.: ill.; 29 cm. — (Contributions to the sociology of language. 30) English and Yiddish. Added t.p.: Lo amut, ki ehyeh. 1. Yiddish language — Social aspects — Addresses, essays, lectures. 2. Jews — Languages — Addresses, essays, lectures. I. Fishman, Joshua A. II. Title: Lo amut, ki ehyeh. III. Series.
PJ5111.N4   437/.947 19   *LC* 81-3957   *ISBN* 9027979782

Goldsmith, Emanuel S., 1935-.   **2.1788**
Architects of Yiddishism at the beginning of the twentieth century: a study in Jewish cultural history / Emanuel S. Goldsmith. — Rutherford [N.J.]: Fairleigh Dickinson University Press, c1976. 309 p.: ill.; 22 cm. Includes index. 1. Yiddish language — History. 2. Jews — Languages — History. I. T.
PJ5113.G66   437/.9/47   *LC* 73-2894   *ISBN* 0838613845

Goldsmith, Emanuel S., 1935-.   **2.1789**
Modern Yiddish culture: the story of the Yiddish language movement. — New York: Shapolsky Publishers, 1987. 309 p. I. T.
PJ5113.Gx

Katz, Dovid.   **2.1790**
Grammar of the Yiddish language / by Dovid Katz. — London: Duckworth, 1987. xxv, 290 p. 1. Yiddish language — Grammar. I. T.
PJ5115.K3x   437/.947 19   *ISBN* 0715621629

Liptzin, Solomon, 1901-.   **2.1791**
A history of Yiddish literature [by] Sol Liptzin. — Middle Village, N.Y.: J. David, [1972] x, 521 p.; 24 cm. 1. Yiddish literature — History and criticism. I. T.
PJ5120.L55   839/.09/09   *LC* 79-164519   *ISBN* 0824601246

Madison, Charles Allan.   • **2.1792**
Yiddish literature; its scope and major writers [by] Charles A. Madison. — New York: F. Ungar Pub. Co., [1968] xii, 540 p.; 21 cm. 1. Yiddish literature — History and criticism. I. T.
PJ5120.M2   *LC* 68-18597

Wiener, Leo, 1862-1939.   **2.1793**
The history of Yiddish literature in the nineteenth century. With a new introd. by Elias Schulman. — 2d ed. — New York: Hermon Press, 1973 [c1972] xxxvii, 402 p.; 24 cm. Reprint of the 1899 ed. published by Scribner, New York; with

new introd. 1. Wiener, Leo, 1862-1939. 2. Yiddish literature — History and criticism. I. T.
PJ5120.W5 1972   839/.09/09   LC 73-136773   ISBN 0872030326

PJ5129 Individual Authors

PJ5129 A–M

Mendele Mokher Sefarim, 1835-1917.   2.1794
The nag, by Mendele Mocher Seforim [pseud.] Translated from the Yiddish by Moshe Spiegel. Illus. by Kurt Werth. New York, Beechhurst Press [1955] 223 p. illus. 21 cm. I. T.
PJ5129.A2 K56 E6   LC 54-10690

Mendele Mokher Sefarim, 1835-1917.   2.1795
The parasite. New York, T. Yoseloff [1956] 174 p. illus. 22 cm. I. T.
PJ5129.A2 P3   LC 56-8958

Mendele Mokher Sefarim, 1835-1917.   2.1796
The travels and adventures of Benjamin the Third / Mendele Mocher Seforim [i.e. S. H. Jacob]; translated from the Yiddish by Moshe Spiegel. — New York: Schocken Books, 1949. 124 p. — (Schocken paperback edition) I. T.
PJ5129.A2 T73   LC 49-9256

Asch, Sholem, 1880-1957.   2.1797
From many countries; the collected short stories of Sholem Asch. London, Macdonald [1958] 376 p. I. T.
PJ5129.A8 A1x   839.0933

Asch, Sholem, 1880-1957.   • 2.1798
Tales of my people [by] Sholem Asch. Translated by Meyer Levin. Freeport, N.Y., Books for Libraries Press [1970, c1948] x, 272 p. 23 cm. (Short story index reprint series) I. T.
PZ3.A798 Tal5 PJ5129.A8Ax   892.49/3/3   LC 75-128752   ISBN 0836936094

Asch, Sholem, 1880-1957.   2.1799
East river, a novel. Translation by A. H. Gross. New York, G. P. Putnam's sons [1946] 3 p.l., 3-438 p. 22 cm. I. Gross, A. H., tr. II. T.
PZ3.A798 Eas PJ5129.A8 E3x   LC 46-7365

Asch, Sholem, 1880-1957.   2.1800
[Tehilim-Yid. English] Salvation [by] Sholem Asch. Translated by Willa and Edwin Muir. [2d ed.] New York, Schocken Books [1968, c1962] vii, 343 p. 22 cm. Translation of Der Tehilim-Yid. I. T.
PZ3.A798 Sal6 PJ5129.A8 T4x   LC 68-25867

Siegel, Ben, 1925-.   2.1801
The controversial Sholem Asch: an introduction to his fiction / Ben Siegel. — Bowling Green, Ohio: Bowling Green University Popular Press, c1976. xi, 313 p.; 24 cm. Includes index. 1. Asch, Sholem, 1880-1957. 2. Authors, Yiddish — Biography. I. T.
PJ5129.A8 Z926   839/.09/33   LC 76-43446   ISBN 087972076X

Glatstein, Jacob, 1896-1971.   2.1802
The selected poems of Jacob Glatstein. Translated from the Yiddish and with an introd. by Ruth Whitman. New York: October House, [1972] 185 p.: illus.; 23 cm. I. Whitman, Ruth, 1922- tr. II. T.
PJ5129.G535 A28   839/.09/13   LC 72-157663   ISBN 080790173X

Glatstein, Jacob, 1896-1971.   2.1803
[Ven Yash iz geforn. English] Homeward bound. Translated from the Yiddish by Abraham Goldstein. New York, T. Yoseloff [1969] 142 p. 22 cm. Translation of Ven Yash iz geforn. I. T.
PJ5129.G535 V413 1969   839/.09/33   LC 68-10640   ISBN 0498066568

Glatstein, Jacob, 1896-1971.   2.1804
Homecoming at twilight / Jacob Glatstein; foreword by Maurice Samuel; translated from the Yiddish by Norbert Guterman. — New York; Toronto: T. Yoseloff, 1962. 271 p.; 21 cm. Translation of Ven Yash iz gekumen. I. T. II. Title: Ven Yash iz gekumen.
PJ 5129 G54 V44 E5 1962   839.0933   LC 62-14963

Grade, Chaim, 1910-.   2.1805
[Tsemah Atlas. English] The Yeshiva / by Chaim Grade; translated from the Yiddish, with an introd., by Curt Leviant. — Indianapolis: Bobbs-Merrill, c1976-1977. 2 v.; 24 cm. Translation of Tsemah Atlas. Vol. 2 also has title: Masters and disciples. I. T. II. Title: Masters and disciples.
PZ4.G73 Ye PJ5129.G68 Yx   839/.09/33   LC 76-11608   ISBN 0672522640

Der Nister, 1884-1950.   2.1806
[Mishpokhe Mashber. English] The family Mashber: a novel / by Der Nister ('the Hidden One'); translated from the Yiddish by Leonard Wolf. — New York: Summit Books, c1987. 688 p.; 25 cm. Translation of: Di mishpokhe Mashber. I. T.
PJ5129.K27 M513 1987   839/.0933 19   LC 87-6470   ISBN 0671527681

Manger, Itzik, 1900-1969.   2.1807
The book of paradise: the wonderful adventures of Shmuel–Aba Abervo / by Itzik Manger; illustrated by Mendel Reif; translated from the Yiddish by Leonard Wolf. — 1st ed. — New York: Hill and Wang, 1965. 236 p.: ill. I. T.
PJ5129M26 B63 1965   LC 65-12944

PJ5129 N–Z

Opatoshu, Joseph, 1886-1954.   2.1808
In Polish woods. Philadelphia, The Jewish publication society of America, 1938. 3 p.l., 3-392 p., 1 l. 22 cm. I. Goldberg, Isaac, 1887-1938. tr. II. T.
PZ3.O612 In PJ5129.O6 I5x   LC 39-2386

Peretz, Isaac Leib, 1851 or 2-1915.   • 2.1809
In this world and the next: selected writings / by I.L. Peretz; translated from the Yiddish by Moshe Spiegel. New York: T. Yoseloff, c1958. 377 p. — I. T.
PJ5129.P4 Ax   839.0933   LC 57-13111

Peretz, Isaac Leib, 1851 or 2-1915.   • 2.1810
The book of fire, stories. New York, T. Yoseloff [1960] 448 p. 24 cm. I. T.
PZ3.P4145 Bo PJ5129.P4 Bx   LC 60-9881

Sholem Aleichem, 1859-1916.   2.1811
Tevye's daughters / Sholom Aleichem; translated by Frances Butwin, with illustrations by Ben Shahn. — Deluxe ill. ed. — New York: Crown Pub. Inc., 1949. — xvii, 302 p.: ill.; 22 cm. (Collected stories of Sholom Aleichem.) I. Butwin, Frances. II. T.
PJ5129.R2 A23   LC 49-7020

Sholem Aleichem, 1859-1916.   2.1812
[Oyf vos badarfn Yidn a land. English] Why do the Jews need a land of their own? / Sholom–Aleichem; translated from the Yiddish and Hebrew by Joseph Leftwich and Mordecai S. Chertoff. — New York: Cornwall Books, c1984. 242 p.; 24 cm. Translation of: Oyf vos badarfn Yidn a land. 'A Herzl Press publication.' 1. Zionism — Literary collections. 2. Zionism — Addresses, essays, lectures. I. T.
PJ5129.R2 A26 1984   839/.0933 19   LC 83-45297   ISBN 0845347748

Sholem Aleichem, 1859-1916.   • 2.1813
The old country, by Sholom Aleichem [pseud.] translated by Julius and Frances Butwin. New York, Crown publishers [1946] xii p., 1 l., 434 p. 22 cm. Short stories. I. T.
PJ5129.R2 Ax   LC 46-5235

Butwin, Joseph, 1943-.   2.1814
Sholom Aleichem / by Joseph Butwin and Frances Butwin. — Boston: Twayne Publishers, c1977. 173 p.; 21 cm. (Twayne's world authors series; TWAS 460: Yiddish literature) Includes index. 1. Sholem Aleichem, 1859-1916. 2. Authors, Yiddish — Biography. I. Butwin, Frances. joint author. II. T.
PJ5129.R2 Z565   839/.09/33 B   LC 77-3495   ISBN 0805762973

Rabon, Israel, b. 1900.   2.1815
[Gas. English] The street: a novel / by Israel Rabon; translated from the Yiddish by Leonard Wolf. — New York: Schocken, 1985. 192 p.; 22 cm. Translation of: Di gas. I. T.
PJ5129.R217 G313 1985   839/.0933 19   LC 84-23601   ISBN 0805239812

Raboy, Isaac.   2.1816
Nine brothers: a novel / by Isaac Raboy; translated from the Yiddish by Max Rosenfeld with a foreword by Itche Goldberg. — New York: Yiddisher Kultur Farband, [1968]. 1 v. I. T.
PJ5129.R22 N4x

Rosenfeld, Morris, 1862-1923.   2.1817
Morris Rosenfeld: selections from his poetry and prose / edited by Itche Goldberg and Max Rosenfeld. — New York: Yiddisher Kultur Farbaud, c1964. 144 p., [1] leaf of plates: ill., port. I. T.
PJ5129R6 A29 1964   892.498   LC 65-2885

Shapiro, Lamed, 1878-1948.   2.1818
The Jewish government and other stories. Edited and translated, with an introd., by Curt Leviant. — New York: Twayne Publishers, [1971] xvii, 186 p.; 22 cm. I. T.
PZ4.S5292 Je PJ5129.S43   839/.09/33   LC 77-120532

PJ5129.S49 Singer

Singer, Isaac Bashevis, 1904-.   • **2.1819**
[Gimpl tam un andere destseylungen. English] Gimpel the fool, and other stories. New York, Noonday Press [c1957] 205 p. 21 cm. Translated by Saul Bellow and others. I. T.
PZ3.S61657 Gi PJ5129.S49 Gx   *LC* 58-1234

Singer, Isaac Bashevis, 1904-.   • **2.1820**
Satan in Goray. — New York, Noonday Press, 1955. 239 p. 22 cm. I. T.
PZ3.S61657Sat PJ5129.S49S63   *LC* 55-10731 rev

Singer, Israel Joshua, 1893-1944.   **2.1821**
[Brider Ashkenazi. English] The brothers Ashkenazi / I.J. Singer; a new translation from the Yiddish by Joseph Singer. — 1st ed. — New York: Atheneum, 1980. xvi, 426 p.; 25 cm. Translation of Di brider Ashkenazi. I. T.
PJ5129.S5 B713 1980   839/.0933   *LC* 80-66017   *ISBN* 0689111029

Singer, Israel Joshua, 1893-1944.   **2.1822**
[Mishpohe Karnovski. English] The family Carnovsky. Translated by Joseph Singer. New York, Vanguard Press [1969] 405 p. 22 cm. Translation of Di mishpohe Karnovski. I. T.
PZ3.S6166 Fam PJ5129.S5 Fx   892.49/3/3   *LC* 68-8089   *ISBN* 0814900038

Singer, Israel Joshua, 1893-1944.   **2.1823**
Yoshe Kalb / Introd. by Isaac Bashevis Singer; translated from the Yiddish by Maurice Samuel. — New York: Harper & Row, [1965]. 246 p. I. T. II. Title: The sinner.
PJ5129.S5 Yx   839.0933   *LC* 65-20988

PJ5181-5192 Translations

Howe, Irving, 1920- ed.   • **2.1824**
A treasury of Yiddish stories, edited by Irving Howe & Eliezer Greenberg. With drawings by Ben Shahn. New York, Viking Press, 1954. 630 p. illus. 22 cm. 1. Short stories, Yiddish 2. Short stories, English 3. Yiddish literature I. T.
PZ1.H837 Tr PJ5181.E8 Hx   *LC* 54-9599

Leftwich, Joseph, 1892- comp.   **2.1825**
An anthology of modern Yiddish literature / compiled and edited by Joseph Leftwich. — The Hague: Mouton, 1974. 346 p.; 24 cm. (International P.E.N. books: Anthologies; 1) Stories, plays, essays and poems translated from the Yiddish. 'Under the auspices of International PEN.' 1. Yiddish literature — Translations into English. 2. English literature — Translations from Yiddish. I. P.E.N. II. T.
PJ5191.E1 L43   839/.09/08003   *LC* 74-82386

Howe, Irving. comp.   • **2.1826**
A treasury of Yiddish poetry. Edited by Irving Howe and Eliezer Greenberg. — [1st ed.]. — New York: Holt, Rinehart and Winston, [1969] xx, 378 p.; 24 cm. 1. Yiddish poetry — Translations into English. 2. English poetry — Translations from Yiddish. I. Greenberg, Eliezer, 1896- joint comp. II. T.
PJ5191.E3 H6   892.49/1/308   *LC* 74-80350   *ISBN* 003066425X

Landis, Joseph C. ed. and tr.   **2.1827**
[Dybbuk, and other great Yiddish plays] The great Jewish plays, translated and edited by Joseph C. Landis. New York, Horizon Press [1973] ix, 356 p. 24 cm. First published in 1966 under title: The dybbuk, and other great Yiddish plays. 1. Yiddish drama — Translations into English. 2. English drama — Translations from Yiddish. I. T.
PJ5191.E5 L3 1972   839/.09/2308   *LC* 72-86741   *ISBN* 0818004051

Ashes out of hope: fiction by Soviet–Yiddish writers / edited by   **2.1828**
Irving Howe and Eliezer Greenberg.
New York: Schocken Books, 1977. 218 p.; 21 cm. 1. Yiddish fiction — Translations into English. 2. English fiction — Translations from Yiddish. 3. Yiddish fiction — Russia. I. Howe, Irving. II. Greenberg, Eliezer, 1896-
PZ1.A79974 PJ5191.E8 Ax   839/.09/3008   *LC* 76-49731   *ISBN* 0805236473

The Shtetl / translated and edited by Joachim Neugroschel.   **2.1829**
New York: Richard Marek Publishers, c1979. 572 p.; 24 cm. Collection of Yiddish tales depicting Jewish life in the shtetls in Eastern Europe. 1. Yiddish fiction — Europe — Translations into English. 2. English fiction — Translations from Yiddish. I. Neugroschel, Joachim.
PJ5191.E8 S5   839/.09/301   *LC* 79-13624   *ISBN* 0399900330

PJ6001-8518 Arabic

Stetkevych, Jaroslav.   • **2.1830**
The modern Arabic literary language; lexical and stylistic developments. Chicago, University of Chicago Press [1970] xxi, 135 p. 23 cm. (Publications of the Center for Middle Eastern Studies, no. 6) 1. Arabic language — History. I. T.
PJ6075.S7   492.7/09   *LC* 79-123749   *ISBN* 0226773388

Caspari, Carl Paul, 1819-1892.   • **2.1831**
A grammar of the Arabic language; translated from the German of Caspari and edited with numerous additions and corrections by W. Wright; 3rd ed. revised by W. Robertson Smith and M. J. de Goeje. — London: Cambridge U.P., 1933. 2 v. Translation of Grammatica Arabica. 1. Arabic language — Grammar I. Wright, William, 1830-1889. tr. II. Smith, W. Robertson (William Robertson), 1846-1894. III. Goeje, M. J. de (Michael Jan de), 1836-1909. IV. T.
PJ6305.C5 1933   492.7/5

Wehr, Hans, 1909-.   • **2.1832**
A dictionary of modern written Arabic. Edited by J. Milton Cowan. — Ithaca, N.Y.: Cornell University Press, 1961. xvii, 1110 p.; 25 cm. 1. Arabic language — Dictionaries — English. I. Cowan, J. Milton. II. T.
PJ6640.W43 1971   492/.7/321   *LC* 61-3227

Arabic literature to the end of the Umayyad period / edited by   **2.1833**
A.F.L. Beeston ... [et al.].
Cambridge [Cambridgeshire]; New York: Cambridge University Press, 1984 (c1983). xvi, 547 p.: ill., maps; 24 cm. — (Cambridge history of Arabic literature.) Includes index. 1. Arabic literature — To 622 — History and criticism. 2. Arabic literature — 622-750 — History and criticism. 3. Islamic Empire — Intellectual life. I. Beeston, A. F. L. (Alfred Felix Landon) II. Series.
PJ7510.A8   892/.7/09 19   *LC* 82-23528   *ISBN* 0521240158

Brockelmann, Carl, 1868-1956.   • **2.1834**
Geschichte der arabischen Litteratur. 2. den Supplementbänden angepasste Aufl. 2. Aufl. Leiden E.J. Brill 1943-49. 1. Arabic literature — History and criticism I. T.
PJ7510 B7 1943

Goldziher, Ignác, 1850-1921.   **2.1835**
[Arab irodalom rövid története. English] A short history of classical Arabic literature. Translated, rev. and enl. by Joseph Desomogyi. Hildesheim, G. Olms, 1966. x, 172 p. 21 cm. Translation of Az arab irodalom rövid története. 1. Arabic literature — History and criticism. I. Desomogyi, Joseph, ed. and tr. II. T.
PJ7510.G6313   892.7/09   *LC* 68-76129

Nicholson, Reynold Alleyne, 1868-1945.   **2.1836**
A literary history of the Arabs by Reynold A. Nicholson. — London: Cambridge U.P., 1969. xxxi, 506 p.: front.; 22 cm. First published 1907. 1. Arabic literature — History and criticism. I. T.
PJ7510.N5 1969   892.7/09   *LC* 72-401710   *ISBN* 0521095727

Sulaiman, Khalid A.   **2.1837**
Palestine and modern Arab poetry / Khalid A. Sulaiman. — London: Zed; Totowa, N.J.: U.S. distributor, Biblio Distribution Centre, 1985 (c1984). 240 p.; 22 cm. (Middle East, culture and revolution.) 1. Palestine in literature. 2. Arabic poetry — 20th century — History and criticism. 3. Jewish-Arab relations in literature I. T. II. Series.
PJ7542.P35 S85   892/.7/09325694 19   *LC* 84-200295   *ISBN* 0862322383

al-Mu'allaqāt.   • **2.1838**
The seven odes; the first chapter in Arabic literature [by A. J. Arberry. London, G. Allen & Unwin; New York, Macmillan [1957] 258p. I. Arberry, A. J. (Arthur John), 1905-1969. II. T.
PJ7642.E5 A7   *LC* 57-13803

Classical Arabic poetry: 162 poems from Imrulkais to Macarri /   **2.1839**
translated with an introduction by Charles Greville Tuetey.
London: Routledge & Kegan Paul, 1985. 300 p. Includes index. 1. Arabic poetry — History and criticism. 2. Arabic poetry — Translations into English. 3. English poetry — Translations from Arabic. I. Tuetey, Charles Greville, 1930-
PJ7650.C53   *ISBN* 0710301103

Darwīsh, Maḥmūd.   **2.1840**
Victims of a map / Mahmud Darwish, Samih al–Qasim, Adonis; translated by Abdullah al–Udhari. — London: Al Saqi Books: Distributed by Zed Press, 1984. 165 p.; 21 cm. Cover title: Dahāyā al-kharītah. 1. Arabic poetry — Translations into English. 2. English poetry — Translations — from Arabic.

3. Arabic poetry — 20th century I. Qāsim, Samīḥ. II. Adūnīs, 1930- III. T. IV. Title: Dahāyā al-kharītah.
PJ7694.E3 D37 1984   892/.716/08 19   LC 85-165710   ISBN 0863560229

Khouri, Mounah Abdallah. comp.   **2.1841**
An anthology of modern Arabic poetry. Selected, edited, and translated by Mounah A. Khouri and Hamid Algar. Berkeley: University of California Press, [1974] xii, 252 p.; 24 cm. English and Arabic. 1. Arabic poetry — 20th century — Translations into English. 2. English poetry — Translations from Arabic. 3. Arabic poetry — 20th century I. Algar, Hamid. joint comp. II. T.
PJ7695.E3 K48   892/.7/1608   LC 77-189220   ISBN 0520022343

PJ7696–7876 Individual Authors or Works

Arabian nights. English. Selections.   • **2.1842**
The Arabian nights' entertainments; or, The book of a thousand nights and a night; a selection of the most famous and representative of these tales from the plain and literal translations by Richard F. Burton; the stories have been chosen and arranged by Bennett A. Cerf and are printed complete and unabridged with many of Burton's notes; introductory essay by Ben Ray Redman. New York, The Modern library [c1932] 2 p. l., iii-xiv, 823 p. 17 cm. (The Modern library of the world's best books) 'First Modern library edition, 1932.' I. Burton, Richard Francis, Sir, 1821-1890. tr. II. Cerf, Bennett, 1898-1971. III. Redman, Ben Ray, 1896-1961. IV. T.
PJ7715.B8 1932b   892.73 398.21   LC 32-28027

Jāhiz, d. 868 or 9.   **2.1843**
[Selections. English] The life and works of Jāhiz; translations of selected texts [by] Charles Pellat. Translated from the French by D. M. Hawke. Berkeley, University of California Press, 1985. xiv, 286 p. 23 cm. (The Islamic world series) I. Pellat, Charles, 1914- tr. II. T. III. Series.
PJ7745.J3 A26   892.7/8/3408   LC 69-12475

Darwīsh, Mahmūd.   **2.1844**
[Selections. English] Selected poems, introduced and translated by Ian Wedde and Fawwaz Tuqan. [Cheadle Hulme: Carcanet Press, 1974 (c1973)] 88 p. 23 cm. I. Wedde, Ian. tr. II. Tūqān, Fawwāz. tr. III. T.
PJ7820.A7 A27   892/.7/16   LC 74-167709   ISBN 0856350640 ISBN 0856350656

Hakīm, Tawfīq.   **2.1845**
[Selected works. English] Fate of a cockroach; four plays of freedom [by] Tewfik al Hakim. Selected and translated from the Arabic by Denys Johnson-Davies. London, Heinemann [1973] viii, 184 p. 19 cm. (African writers series, no. 117) Imprint covered by label: Distributed in the U.S.A. by Humanities Press, New York. I. T.
PJ7828.K52 A25 1973   892/.7/25   LC 73-164698   ISBN 0435901176

Al-Hakim, Tawfiq.   • **2.1846**
The tree climber: a play in two acts / [by] Tewfik al-Hakim; translated from the Arabic by Denys Johnson-Davies. — London, [etc.] Oxford University Press 1966. [7], 87 p.; 18 1/2 cm. (A Three crowns book) I. T.
PJ7828K52 Y313

Mahfūz, Najīb, 1912-.   **2.1847**
God's world; an anthology of short stories [by] Nagib Mahfuz. Translated with an introd. by Akef Abadir and Roger Allen. Minneapolis, Bibliotheca Islamica, 1973. xvi, 240 p. illus. 23 cm. (Studies in Middle Eastern literatures, no. 2) I. T.
PZ4.M2134 Go PJ7846.A46   892/.7/36   LC 73-79201   ISBN 0882970062

Rifaat, Alifa.   **2.1848**
[Short stories. English. Selections] Distant view of a minaret and other stories / Alifa Rifaat; translated by Denys Johnson-Davies. — London; New York: Quartet Books, 1984 (c1983). ix, 116 p.; 23 cm. I. Johnson-Davies, Denys. II. T.
PJ7860.I35 A24   892/.736 19   LC 84-672074   ISBN 0704324016

PK Indo-Iranian Languages and Literatures

Cannon, Garland Hampton, 1924-.   • **2.1849**
Oriental Jones, a biography of Sir William Jones, 1746–1794. Bombay, New York, Asia Pub. House [for] Indian Council for Cultural Relations [1964] x, 215 p. port. 25 cm. 1. Jones, William, Sir, 1746-1794. I. T.
PK109.J6 C3   LC sa 63-600

Macdonell, Arthur Anthony, 1854-1930.   • **2.1850**
A Vedic reader for students, by Arthur Anthony Macdonell ... Containing thirty hymns of the Rigveda in the original samhita and pada texts, with transliteration, translation, explanatory notes, introduction, vocabulary. Oxford: Clarendon Press, [1928] xxxi, 263 p.; 19 cm. 'Impression of 1928. First edition 1917.' 1. Vedic language — Chrestomathies and readers I. T.
PK237 M3 1960   LC 43-29499

Banerji, Sures Chandra, 1917-.   **2.1851**
A companion to Sanskrit literature; spanning a period of over three thousand years, containing brief accounts of authors, works, characters, technical terms, geographical names, myths, legends, and twelve appendices. — [1st ed.]. — Delhi: Motilal Banarsidass, [1971] xvi, 729 p.; 23 cm. 1. Sanskrit literature — Dictionaries. I. T.
PK414.B3   891/.2/09   LC 70-923517

De, Sushil Kumar.   • **2.1852**
History of Sanskrit poetics. — 2d rev. ed. — Calcutta: Firma K. L. Mukhopadhyay, 1960. 2 v. in 1.; 22 cm. First edition published in 1923-25 under the title: Studies in the history of Sanskrit poetics.' 1. Sanskrit poetry — History and criticism. 2. Sanskrit language — Metrics and rhythmics I. T.
PK871.D42   LC 74-239313

PK1501–2899 Modern Indo-Aryan: (Special Languages and Dialects)

Chatterji, Suniti Kumar, 1890-1977.   • **2.1853**
Languages and literatures of modern India. With a foreword by C. P. Ramaswami Aiyar. Calcutta, Bengal Publishers [1963] xxviii, 380, xxxi p. ports. fold. maps (part col.) facsims. 26 cm. 1. Indic philology I. T.
PK1508.C45   LC sa 63-3748

PK1651–1799 Bengali

Ghosh, Jyotish Chandra.   • **2.1854**
Bengali literature. — London, Oxford Univ. Press, 1948. 198 p. 23 cm. 1. Bengali literature — History and criticism. I. T.
PK1701.G5   891.4409   LC 49-3150 *

Sen, Sukumar.   **2.1855**
History of Bengali literature. Foreword by Jawaharlal Nehru. — Rev. ed. — New Delhi: Sahitya Akademi, [1971] xii, 394 p.; 22 cm. 1. Bengali literature — History and criticism. I. T.
PK1701.S483 1971   891/.44/09   LC 75-921882

Zbavitel, Dušan.   **2.1856**
Bengali literature / Dusan Zbavitel. — Wiesbaden: Harassowitz, 1976. p. 120-307; 24 cm. — (A History of Indian literature; v.9: Modern Indo-Aryan literatures, pt.2; fasc. 3) 1. Bengali literature — History and criticism. I. T.
PK1701.Z2   PK1701 Z2.   891/.44/09   LC 77-361725   ISBN 3447016736

Dasgupta, Shashi Bhushan, 1912-1964.   **2.1857**
Obscure religious cults. [3d ed.] Calcutta Firma K.L. Mukhopadhyay 1969. 436p. 1. Bengali literature — History and criticism 2. Buddhist sects I. T.
PK1706 D3 1969

PK1718–1729 Individual Authors, A–Z

Bandyopadhyay, Manik, 1908-1956.   **2.1858**
[Padma nadir majhi. English] Boatman of the Padma / Manik Bandyopadhyay; translated from the Bengali by Hirendranath Mukerjee. — 2d ed. — New Delhi: National Book Trust, India, 1977, c1975. vi, 144 p.; 22 cm. — (Outstanding books of the world) A novel. I. Mukerjee, Hirendranath, 1907- II. National Book Trust. III. T. IV. Series.
PZ4.B2145 Bo 1977 PK1718.B28 Ex   891/.44/37   *LC* 78-900101

Bandyopadhyay, Manik, 1908-1956.   **2.1859**
[Putula nācera itikathā. English] The puppets' tale; a novel, by Manik Bandopadhyaya. Translated from the Bengali by Sachindralal Ghosh. Edited by Arthur Isenberg. New Delhi, Sahitya Akademi [1968] xi, 268 p. 23 cm. (UNESCO collection of representative works. Indian series) 'This work has been accepted in the Indian Translation Series of the United Nations Educational Scientific and Cultural Organisation (UNESCO)' I. Ghosh, Sachindralal. tr. II. Isenberg, Artur, ed. III. T.
PZ4.B2145 Pu3 PK1718.B28 Px   *LC* 70-900011

Bandyopadhyay, Bibhutibhushan, 1894-.   **2.1860**
A strange attachment and other stories / Bibhutibhushan Bandyopadhyay; translated by Phyllis Granoff. — Oakville, Ont.: Mosaic Press, 1984. 277 p. I. T.
PK1718.B28 Sx   891/.4437 19   *ISBN* 0889622213

Bandyopādhyāya, Bibhūtibhūshana, 1896?-1950.   **2.1861**
Pather panchali. Song of the road; a Bengali novel by Bibhutibhushan Banerji. Translated into English by T. W. Clark and Tarapada Mukherji. Bloomington, Indiana University Press [1968] 326 p. 23 cm. (UNESCO collection of representative works. Indian series.) I. T. II. Title: Song of the road. III. Series.
PK1718.B298 P313 1968   891.4/4/36   *LC* 68-11277

Bandyopādhyāya, Tārāśankara, 1898-1971.   **2.1862**
[Gana-debatā. English] Ganadevata (The temple pavilion). Translated by Lila Ray. Bombay, Pearl Publications; [sole distributors: India Book House, 1969] 260 p. 22 cm. I. Ray, Lila. tr. II. T.
PZ4.B2147 Gan PK1718.B2985   *LC* 73-902282

Bandyopādhyāya, Tārāśankara, 1898-1971.   **2.1863**
[Ganadebatā. English] Panchagram (Five villages). Translated by Marcus F. Franda & Suhrid K. Chatterjee. [Delhi] Manohar Book Service, 1973. 352 p. 23 cm. Translation of the 2d pt. of the author's Ganadebatā. A novel. I. Franda, Marcus F. tr. II. Chatterjee, Suhrid K., tr. III. T. IV. Title: Pañcagrama.
PZ4.B2147 Pan5 PK1718.B2985   891/.443/7   *LC* 73-900909

Basu, Manoje.   **2.1864**
The Forest Goddess. — New York: [s.n.], 1961. 1 v. I. T.
PK1718.B3x   *LC* 61-18220

Ray, Dvijendra Lala, 1863-1913.   **2.1865**
Mevar patan, or Fall of Mevar: a play in five acts / translated from Bengali by Dilip Kumar Roy, Bryan Rhys and Joyce Chadwick. — 1st ed. — Bombay: Bharatiya Vidya Bhavan, 1958. xvi, 135 p. — (Bhavan's book university,; 51) 1. Udaipur (India) — History — Drama. I. T. II. Title: Fall of Mevar.
PK1718.R6x

Sen, Samar Ranjan, 1916-.   **2.1866**
The complete poems of Samar Sen. Transcreated from the Bengali by Pritish Nandy. — [Calcutta: Writers Workshop, 1970] xxxiii, 192 p.; 23 cm. 'A Writers Workshop saffronbird book.' I. Nandy, Pritish. tr. II. T.
PK1718.S418 A26   *LC* 76-916146

PK1719–1727 Tagore

Tagore, Rabindranath, 1861-1941.   **2.1867**
Collected poems and plays of Rabindranath Tagore. London, Macmillan and co., limited, 1948 [c1942]. v, 577, [1] p. 21 cm. I. T.
PK1722.A2 1936   *LC* 36-32600

Tagore, Rabindranath, 1861-1941.   **2.1868**
Later poems of Rabindranath Tagore / translated from the Bengali by Aurobindo Bose; foreword by Yehudi Menuhin. — New York: Funk & Wagnalls, 1976, c1974. 142 p.; 22 cm. I. Bose, Aurobindo. II. T.
PK1722.A2 B6 1976   891/.44/14   *LC* 75-34824   *ISBN* 0308102398

Tagore, Rabindranath, 1861-1941.   • **2.1869**
The herald of spring; poems from Mohua. Translated from the Bengali by Aurobindo Bose; with a life of Tagore by the translator. London J. Murray [1957] 83p. (Wisdom of the East series) I. Bose, Aurobindo. tr. II. T. III. Series.
PK1722.A2 B6x

Tagore, Rabindranath, 1861-1941.   • **2.1870**
A Tagore reader / edited by Amiya Chakravarty. — New York: Macmillan, 1961. xiii, 401 p.: facsim., front. — (UNESCO collection of representative works. Indian series.) Includes three plays: Sacrifice, The post office, and Chandalika. I. Chakravarty, Amiya Chandra. II. T. III. Title: Sacrifice. IV. Title: Post office. V. Title: Chandalika. VI. Series.
PK1722.A2C4   891.448   *LC* 61-7056

Tagore, Rabindranath, 1861-1941.   • **2.1871**
Gora / by Rabindranath Tagore.— London, Macmillan and co., limited, 1924. v, 408 p. 20 cm. 'Translated into English by the author.'—Second supplementary catalogue of Bengali books in the ... Brit Mus. ... London, 1939. 'Surendranath Tagore ... made the final corrections and revisions for this translation.' —p.v. I. Tagore, Surendranath. II. T.
PK1722.G6x   *LC* 25-10221//r442

Kripalani, Krishna.   • **2.1872**
Rabindranath Tagore: a biography / Krishna Kripalani. — New York: Grove Press, 1962. 417 p., [8] leaves of plates: ill., ports. 1. Tagore, Rabindranath, 1861-1941. 2. Poets, Indian — Biography. I. T.
PK1725.K7x   928.9144   *LC* 61-11776

Sarkar, Badal.   **2.1873**
Three plays / Badal Sircar. — Calcutta: Seagull Books, 1983 (1985 printing) xi, 138 p., [4] p. of plates; ill.; 22 cm. I. T.
PK1730.39 R3 T4   *ISBN* 086132045X

PK1771–1772 Translations (Collections)

Humayun Kabir, 1906-1969. comp.   • **2.1874**
Green and gold; stories and poems from Bengal. Edited by Humayun Kabir. Associate editors Tarasankar Banerjee [and] Premendra Mitra. — New York: New Directions, [1959] xi, 288 p.; 23 cm. 1. Bengali literature — Translations into English. 2. English literature — Translations from Bengali. I. T.
PK1771.E1 H8 1970   891.4/4/3708   *LC* 58-12636

Dimock, Edward C.   • **2.1875**
In praise of Krishna: songs from the Bengali / translations by Edward C. Dimock, Jr. and Denise Levertov; with an introd. and notes by Edward C. Dimock, Jr; illus. by Anju Chandhuri. — [1st ed.]. — Garden City, N.Y.: Doubleday, 1967. xxii, 95 p.: ill.; 18 cm. — (UNESCO collection of representative works. Indian series.) (A Doubleday Anchor original; A545) Bibliography: p. xxi-xxii. 1. Krishna — Poetry. 2. Bengali poetry — Translations into English. 3. English poetry — Translations from Bengali. I. T. II. Series.
PK1771.E3 D5   491.4/4/1   *LC* 66-24319

Ghose, Sukumar, 1935- comp.   **2.1876**
Contemporary Bengali literature: fiction. Selected and edited by Sukumar Ghose. Calcutta, Academic Publishers [1972] 162 p. port. 23 cm. On cover: Three novels by Tarasankar, Premendra Mitra, Manik Bandyopadhyay: contemporary Bengali literature; fiction. 1. Bengali fiction — 20th century — Translations into English. 2. English fiction — Translations from Bengali. I. Bandyopādhyāya, Tārāśankara, 1898-1971. The eternal lotus. 1972. II. Mitra, Premendra. The twelfth manu. 1972. III. Bandyopadhyay, Manik, 1908-1956. Reptile ways. 1972. IV. T.
PZ1.G34 Co PK1771.E8   *LC* 72-901969

PK1801–1831 Bihari

Vidyāpati Thākura, 15th cent.   • **2.1877**
Love songs of Vidyāpati. Translated by Deben Bhattacharya. Edited with an introd., notes, and comments by W. G. Archer. New York, Grove Press [1970, c1969] 148 p. illus. 21 cm. (UNESCO collection of representative works. Indian series) (Evergreen original.) I. Bhattacharya, Deben. tr. II. T.
PK1818.9.V5 A22 1970   891.4/5   *LC* 76-110334

PK1931–2142 Hindi

At play with Krishna: pilgrimage dramas from Brindavan / John   **2.1878**
Stratton Hawley in association with Shrivatsa Goswami.
Princeton, N.J.: Princeton University Press, c1981. xvi, 339 p.: ill.; 23 cm. Translated from Braj. Includes index. 1. Folk-drama, Braj — India — Vrindāban — Translations into English. 2. English drama — Translations from Braj. 3. Krishna (Hindu deity) — Drama. I. Hawley, John Stratton, 1941- II. Goswami, Shrivatsa.
PK1967.7.A85   398.2/1/09542 19   *LC* 80-8552   *ISBN* 0691064709

Bryant, Kenneth E.   **2.1879**
Poems to the child–god: structures and strategies in the poetry of Sūrdās / Kenneth E. Bryant. — Berkeley: University of California Press, 1978. xvi, 247 p.; 23 cm. Includes index. 1. Sūradāsa, 1483?-1563? I. T.
PK2095.S8 Z63   PK1967.9S87 Z677.   *LC* 77-80467   *ISBN* 0520035402

Hawley, John Stratton, 1941-.   **2.1880**
Sūr Dās: poet, singer, saint / John Stratton Hawley. — Seattle: University of Washington Press, c1984. xx, 233 p.: ill.; 24 cm. (Publications on Asia of the Henry M. Jackson School of International Studies; v. 40) Includes English translations of selected poems from Sūradāsa's Sūrasāgara. Includes indexes. 1. Sūradāsa, 1483?-1563? Criticism and interpretation. I. Sūradāsa, 1483?-1563? Sūrasāgara. English. Selections. 1984. II. T.
PK1967.9.S9 Z68 1984   891/.4312 19   *LC* 84-40327   *ISBN* 0295961023

Platts, John Thompson, 1830-1904.   • **2.1881**
A dictionary of Urdū, classical Hindī, and English. [London] Oxford University Press [1960] viii, 1259 p. 26 cm. 1. Urdu language — Dictionaries — English. 2. English language — Dictionaries — Urdu. 3. Hindi language — Dictionaries — English. 4. English language — Dictionaries — Hindi. I. T.
PK1986.P4 1960   *LC* 61-1139

Dwivedi, Ram Awadh.   **2.1882**
A critical survey of Hindi literature. Delhi, Motilal Banarsidass [1966] ii, 3, 304 p. 23 cm. 1. Hindi literature — History and criticism. I. T.
PK2031.D88   *LC* sa 67-4285

McGregor, Ronald Stuart.   **2.1883**
Hindi Literature from its beginnings to the Nineteenth century / Ronald Stuart McGregor. — Wiesbaden: O. Harrassowitz, 1984. viii, 239 p. — (History of Indian literature. V. 8, Fasc. 6) I. T. II. Series.
PK2031 M212 1984

Gaeffke, Peter, 1927-.   **2.1884**
Hindi literature in the twentieth century / Peter Gaeffke. — Wiesbaden: Harrassowitz, 1978. 118 p.; 24 cm. — (History of Indian literature. v. 8: Modern Indo-Aryan literatures; fasc. 5) 1. Hindi literature — 20th century — History and criticism. I. T. II. Series.
PK2038.G28   891/.43/09   *LC* 78-325070   *ISBN* 3447016140

PK2095–2098 Individual Authors

Kabir, 15th cent.   **2.1885**
[Bijaka. English] The Bījak of Kabir / translated by Linda Hess and Shukdev Singh; essays and notes by Linda Hess. — San Francisco: North Point Press, 1983. xiii, 200 p.; 24 cm. I. Hess, Linda. II. Singh, Shuk Deo, 1933- III. T.
PK2095.K3 B4913 1983   891/.4312 19   *LC* 82-73716   *ISBN* 0865471142

Tulasīdāsa, 1532-1623.   **2.1886**
The Ramayana of Goswami Tulsidas, by S. P. Bahadur. Bombay, Jaico Pub. House, 1972. xiv, 414 p. 22 cm. 1. Rāma (Hindu deity) — Poetry. I. Bahadur, Satya Prakash, ed. and tr. II. T.
PK2095.T8 R312 1972   891/.43/12   *LC* 72-906707

Ashk, Upendra Nath, 1910-.   **2.1887**
[Barpha kā darda. English] Sorrow of the snows [by] Upendranath Ashk. Translated from Hindi by Jai Ratan. Calcutta, Writers Workshop, 1971. 112 p. 23 cm. Translation of Barpha kā darda. I. T.
PZ3.A825 So PK2098.A8   891/.43/37   *LC* 70-921862

Pant, Sumitra Nandan, 1900-.   **2.1888**
[Cidambarā. Selections. English] Fifty poems from Chidambara [by] Sumitranandan Pant. Translated by Debabrata Mukhopadhyaya [and others] Edited by Alokeranjan Dasgupta [and] Lakshmichandra Jain. [1st ed. Calcutta] Bharatiya Jnanpith Publication [1969] 127 p. 22 cm. (Jnanpith lokoday series, no. 300) Title on jacket: Chidambara sanchayan. I. Mukerjea, Devavrata, tr. II. Dasgupta, Alokeranjan. ed. III. Jain, Lakshmi Chandra, 1909- IV. T. V. Title: Chidambara sanchayan.
PK2098.P32 C513 1969   891/.2/15   *LC* 73-927576

Rākeśa, Mohana, 1925-1972.   **2.1889**
[Andhere banda kamare. English] Lingering shadow. [Translated by Jai Ratan. Delhi] Hind Pocket Books [1970] 214 p. 18 cm. Translation of Andhere banda kamare. 'An Orient paperback.' I. Jai Ratan, 1920- II. T.
PZ4.R16 Li PK2098.R36   *LC* 78-913095

Premacanda, 1881-1936.   • **2.1890**
The gift of a cow: a translation of the Hindu novel Godaan, by Premchand; translated by Gordon C. Roadarmel. — London: Allen & Unwin, 1968. 442 p.; 23 cm. — (UNESCO collection of representative works. Indian series.) I. T. II. Series.
PZ3.S7737 Gi3 PK2098.S7   891.4/3/36   *LC* 78-366600

Naravane, Vishwanath S.   **2.1891**
Premchand, his life and work / V.S. Naravane. — New Delhi: Vikas, c1980. viii, 291 p., [1] leaf of plates: port.; 23 cm. 1. Srivasta, Dhanpat Rai, 1881-1936. 2. Authors, Hindi — 20th century — Biography. I. T.
PK2098.P767 Z79   PK2098.S7 Z6.   891/.4335 B 19   *LC* 80-904341   *ISBN* 0706910915

Swan, Robert O.   • **2.1892**
Munshi Premchand of Lamhi village, by Robert O. Swan. Durham, N.C., Duke University Press, 1969. ix, 149 p. 25 cm. (Publication series of the Program in Comparative Studies on Southern Asia, no. 3) 1. Premacanda, 1881-1936. I. T.
PK2098.S7 Z93   891.4/3/36 B   *LC* 77-80813

Tripathi, Surya Kant, 1896-1961.   **2.1893**
A season on the earth: selected poems of Nirala / translated by David Rubin. Columbia University Press, c1977. 152 p. (Unesco collection of representative works: Indian series) 'Sponsored by the Asian Literature Program of the Asia Society, New York.' I. Rubin, David, 1924- II. Asia Society. Asian Literature Program. III. T.
PK2098.T7 A27 1977   *LC* 76-40026   *ISBN* 0231041608

Vatsyayan, Sachchidanand Hiranand, 1911-.   **2.1894**
Selected poems of Agyeya; The unmastered lute and other poems. Translated from Hindi by Sachchidananda Vatsyayan in collaboration with Leonard Nathan. [Calcutta, Rina Nandy; distributors: Stechert-Hafner, New York, 1969] [16] p. 23 cm. (Dialogue Calcutta, anthology 9) I. Nathan, Leonard, 1924- II. T. III. Title: Unmastered lute.
PK2098.V34 A25   *LC* 79-909184

Yashpal.   **2.1895**
Short stories of Yashpal. Translated and introduced by Corinne Friend. — Philadelphia: University of Pennsylvania Press, [c1969] xii, 143 p.; 23 cm. I. T.
PZ3.Y23 Sh PK2098.Y3   891.4/3/37   *LC* 78-87939   *ISBN* 0812276019

PK2141–2142 Translations (Collections)

Roadarmel, Gordon C., 1932- comp.   **2.1896**
A death in Delhi; modern Hindi short stories. Translated and edited by Gordon C. Roadarmel. Berkeley, University of California Press [1972] 211 p. 23 cm. (UNESCO collection of representative works. Indian series) 1. Short stories, English — Translations from Hindi. 2. Short stories, Hindi — Translations into English. I. T.
PK2141.E8 R6x   891/.43/301   *LC* 74-187871   *ISBN* 0520022203

PK2151–2200 Urdu

Sadiq, Muhammad.   • **2.1897**
A history of Urdu literature. London, Oxford University Press, 1964. ix, 429 p. 23 cm. 'References and notes': p. [409]-420. 1. Urdu literature — History and criticism. I. T.
PK2155.S25   891.43   *LC* 65-3696

Schimmel, Annemarie.   **2.1898**
Classical Urdu literature from the beginning to Iqbāl / Annemarie Schimmel. — Wiesbaden: Harrassowitz, 1975. p. 126-261; 24 cm. (A history of Indian literature; v. 8: Modern Indo-Aryan literatures; fasc. 3) 1. Urdu literature — History and criticism. I. T.
PK2155.S38   891/.439/09   *LC* 76-354483   *ISBN* 344701671X

Ghalib, Mirza Asadullah Khan, 1797-1869.   • **2.1899**
Ghazals of Ghalib; versions from the Urdu, by Aijaz Ahmad [and others] Edited by Aijaz Ahmad. New York, Columbia University Press, 1971. xxx, 174 p. 23 cm. English and Urdu. I. Aijaz Ahmad, ed. II. T.
PK2198.G4 A6 1971   891/.439/13   *LC* 76-173987   *ISBN* 0231034784

Faiz, Faiz Ahmad, 1911-.   • **2.1900**
Poems by Faiz; translated [from the Urdu MS], with an introduction and notes by V. G. Kiernan. London, Allen and Unwin, 1971. 288 p. 23 cm. (UNESCO collection of representative works. Pakistan series) Urdu text with parallel English translation, with English introduction and notes. I. Kiernan, V. G. (Victor Gordon), 1913- II. T. III. Series.
PK2199.F255 A24 1971   891/.439/17   *LC* 75-869421   *ISBN* 0048910406

Iqbal, Muhammad, Sir, 1877-1938.   • **2.1901**
Poems from Iqbal, translated by V.G. Kiernan. [1st ed.] London Murray [1955] 112p. (The Wisdom of the East series) I. T. II. Series.
PK2199.I65Ax

Ruswa, Mirza Mohammad Hadi, 1857-1931.   **2.1902**
[Umrā'o Jān Adā. English] The courtesan of Lucknow (Umrao Jan Ada), by Mirza Ruswa. Translated by Khushwant Singh [and] M. A. Husaini. [Delhi] Hind Pocket Books [1970] 240 p. 19 cm. (UNESCO collection of representative works. Indian series) 'An Orient paperback.' Translation of Umrā'o Jān Adā. I. Singh, Khushwant, tr. II. Husaini, M. A., tr. III. T.
PZ4.R97 Co4 PK2199.R8   *LC* 70-913093

Chandar, Krishan.   **2.1903**
[Ek gadhe kī sarguzasht. English] Mr. Ass comes to town / Krishan Chander; translated from the Urdu by Helen H. Bouman. — Delhi: Hind Pocket Books, c1968. 167 p.; 18 cm. Translation of Ek gadhe kī sarguzasht. 'Orient paperbacks, E-36.' I. T.
PZ4.C455 Mi PK2200.C5   891/.439/37   *LC* 74-901558

Rahbar, Daud, 1927-.   **2.1904**
The cup of Jamshid: a collection of original Ghazal poetry / by Muhammad Daud Rahbar; translated from the Urdū by the author. — Cape Cod, Mass.: C. Stark, [1974] xiv, 199 p.; 24 cm. I. T.
PK2200.R219 C8   PK2200R2312 C8.   891/.439/17   *LC* 74-76004

Ali, Ahmed, 1908- comp.   **2.1905**
The golden tradition; an anthology of Urdu poetry. Selected, translated, and with an introd. by Ahmed Ali. New York, Columbia University Press, 1973. 286 p. 23 cm. (Studies in Oriental culture. 8) 1. Urdu poetry — Translations into English. I. T. II. Series.
PK 2211 E3 A39 1973   *LC* 72-10181   *ISBN* 0231036876

Ali, Ahmed, 1908-.   • **2.1906**
Twilight in Delhi: a novel. — 2nd ed. — Bombay; London, [etc.]: Oxford U.P., 1966 [i.e.1967]. ix, 290 p.; 19 1/2 cm. — (Champak library) I. T.
PK2211.E3 Ax   *LC* 67-89219

PK2351-2458 Marathi

Tulpule, Shankar Gopal, 1914-.   **2.1907**
Classical Marāthī literature: from the beginning to A.D. 1818 / Shankar Gopal Tulpule. — Wiesbaden: Harrassowitz, 1979. p. 312-471; 24 cm. — (History of Indian literature. v. 9, fasc. 4) Includes index. 1. Marathi literature — History and criticism. I. T. II. Series.
PK2401.T84   891/.46/09 19   *LC* 80-485720   *ISBN* 3447020474

Pendse, Shripad Narayan, 1913-.   **2.1908**
[Gārambīcā Bāpū. English] Wild Bapu of Garambi. Garambica Bapu, by Shripad Narayan Pendse. Translated from the Marathi by Ian Raeside. New Delhi, Sahitya Akademi [1969] viii, 256 p. 22 cm. (UNESCO collection of representative works. Indian series) Translation of Gārambīcā Bāpū. I. Raeside, Ian. tr. II. T.
PZ4.P3974 Wi PK2418.P4   *LC* 79-911515

Phadke, Narayan Sitaram.   **2.1909**
Where angels sell eggs and other stories / by N.S. Phadke. — Bombay: Jaico Pub. House, 1957. 255 p.; 18 cm. — I. T.
PK2418.P5   PR9499.3.P45 W5   823 19   *LC* 80-915720

PK2595-2599 Nepali

Devkota, Laxmi Prasad, 1908-1959.   **2.1910**
Nepali visions, Nepali dreams: the poetry of Laxmiprasad Devkota / with translations of selected poems by David Rubin. — New York: Columbia University Press, 1980. xiii, 170 p.; 22 cm. — (Modern Asian literature series.) (UNESCO collection of representative works: Nepalese series) I. Rubin, David, 1924- II. T. III. Series. IV. Series: UNESCO collection of representative works: Nepalese series
PK2598.D37 A27   891/.49   *LC* 80-106   *ISBN* 0231050143

Vaidya, Karuna Kar, 1917- comp.   **2.1911**
Nepalese short stories / translated by Karuna Kar Vaidya. — 1st U.S. ed. — Essex, Conn.: Gallery Press, c1976. 127 p.; 22 cm. 1. Short stories, Nepali — Translations into English. 2. Short stories, English — Translations from Nepali. I. T.
PZ1.V25 Ne5 PK2598.Z95E   PK2598Z95 E5 1976.   891/.49   *LC* 75-12436   *ISBN* 0913622036

PK2630-2659 Panjabi

Amrita Pritam, 1919-.   **2.1912**
Two faces of Eve. — [Delhi]: Hind Pocket Books, [1971] 160 p.; 18 cm. I. Suri, G. S. P., tr. II. Machwe, Prabhakar Balvant, 1917- tr. III. T.
PZ4.A5275 Tw PK2659.A44   891/.42/37   *LC* 73-925338

Amrita Pritam, 1919-.   **2.1913**
Selected poems. Edited by Pritish Nandy and translated from the original Panjabi by Khushwant Singh [and others. — Calcutta]: Dialogue Calcutta Publications, [1970] [23] p.; 22 cm. I. Nandy, Pritish. ed. II. Singh, Khushwant, tr. III. T.
PK2659.A44 A27   *LC* 75-915032

Amrita Pritam, 1919-.   **2.1914**
Black rose. English versions of the Punjabi by Charles Brasch in collaboration with the poetess. [New Delhi, Nagmani, c1967] 31, [1] p. I. Brasch, Charles. II. T.
PK2659.A44 B5   *LC* 68-2058

Amrita Pritam, 1919-.   **2.1915**
Doctor Dev / translated by K. Gujrat. — Delhi: [s.n.], 1968. 1 v. I. T.
PK2659.A44Dx   *LC* 68-17020

Amrita Pritam, 1919-.   **2.1916**
Existence and other poems / translated by M. Kulashresta. — New Delhi: [s.n.], 1968. 1 v. I. T.
PK2659.A44Ex   *LC* 68-19037

Duggal, Kartar Singh, 1917-.   **2.1917**
Death of a song and other stories / K.S. Duggal. — New Delhi: Arnold-Heinemann India 1973. 186 p. I. T.
PK2659D8   PK2659D8 D3.   891'.42'37   *LC* 73-901177

PK2781-2789 Sindhi

Schimmel, Annemarie.   **2.1918**
Sindhi literature [by] Annemarie Schimmel. — Wiesbaden: Harrassowitz, 1974. 41 p.; 24 cm. — (A History of Indian literature, v. 8: Modern Indo-Aryan literatures; pt. 2) 1. Sindhi literature — History and criticism. I. T. II. Series.
PK2788.S34   891/.41/09 19   *LC* 74-181871   *ISBN* 3447015608

PK2901-4485 Modern Indo-Aryan: (General. Vedic. Sanskrit)

Dasgupta, Surendranath, 1885-1952. ed.   • **2.1919**
A history of Sanskrit literature, classical period. 2d ed. [Calcutta] University of Calcutta 1962-. v. 1. Sanskrit literature — History and criticism I. T.
PK2903.D32   *LC* sa 63-3762

Keith, Arthur Berriedale, 1879-1944.   • **2.1920**
A history of Sanskrit literature, by A. Berriedale Keith ... — Oxford: Clarendon Press, 1928. xxxvi, 575, [1] p. 23 cm. 1. Sanskrit literature — Hist. & crit. I. T.
PK2903.K45 1920   *LC* 29-9436

The Literatures of India: an introduction / Edward C. Dimock, Jr. ... [et. al.].   **2.1921**
Chicago: University of Chicago Press, 1974. xiii, 265 p. 1. Indic literature — History and criticism. 2. India — Literatures I. Dimock, Edward C.
PK2903.L58   PK2903 L58.   891.4   *LC* 73-87300   *ISBN* 0266152324

Macdonell, Arthur Anthony, 1854-1930.   • **2.1922**
A history of Sanskrit literature. — New York: Haskell House, 1968. ix, 472 p.; 23 cm. Reprint of the 1900 ed. 1. Sanskrit literature — History and criticism. I. T.
PK2903.M3 1968   891.2/09   *LC* 68-24966

Macdonell, Arthur Anthony, 1854-1930.   • **2.1923**
India's past; a survey of her literatures, religions, languages and antiquities, by A. A. Macdonell. Oxford, The Clarendon press, 1927. xii, 293 p. illus. 20 cm. 1. Sanskrit literature — History and criticism 2. Indic literature — History and criticism 3. Inscriptions — India. 4. Numismatics — India. 5. India — Religion I. T.
PK2903.M35   *LC* 28-5526

Sahitya Akademi.   • **2.1924**
Who's who of Indian writers. Honolulu, East-West Center Press [1964, c1961] 410 p. 24 cm. 1. Authors, Indic I. T.
PK2903.S3 1964   928.914   *LC* 64-7590

Schimmel, Annemarie.   **2.1925**
Islamic literatures of India / Annemarie Schimmel. — Wiesbaden: Harrassowitz, 1973. 60 p.; 24 cm. (A History of Indian literature; v. 7: Modern

Indo-Iranian literatures, pt. 1) 1. Indic literature — Muslim authors — History and criticism. I. T.
PK2905.S36　　809/.8954　　*LC* 75-332048　　*ISBN* 3447015098

Who's who of Indian writers, 1983 / compiled and edited by S. 　**2.1926**
Balu Rao; with a foreword by V.K. Gokak.
New Delhi: Sahitya Akademi, 1983. xix, 731 p.; 25 cm. 'Contains biographical and bibliographical information about nearly 6,000 living writers in 22 Indian languages including English'—Half t.p. verso. 1. Indic literature — Bio-bibliography. 2. Authors, Indic — Directories. I. Bālurāv, S.
PK2908.W49 1983　　891/.4/0922 B 19　　*LC* 83-905615

Keith, Arthur Berriedale, 1879-1944. 　• **2.1927**
The Sanskrit drama in its origin, development, theory and practice / by A. Berriedale Keith. — Oxford: The Clarendon Press, 1924. 405 p. 1. Sanskrit drama — History and criticism I. T.
PK2931.K4　　*LC* 24-24835

Alphonso-Karkala, John B., 1923- comp. 　**2.1928**
An anthology of Indian literature, edited by John B. Alphonso-Karkala. — Harmondsworth: Penguin, 1971. 630 p.; 19 cm. — (Pelican books) 1. Indic literature I. T.
PK2975.A4　　891/.1　　*LC* 72-175866　　*ISBN* 0140212485

Lin, Yutang, 1895-1976. ed. 　• **2.1929**
The wisdom of China and India, edited by Lin Yutang. New York, Random House [1942] xiii, 1104 p. 24 cm. 1. Indic literature — Translations into English. 2. Chinese literature — Translations into English. I. T.
PK 2978 E5 L7　　*LC* 42-50902

PK3001–3581 Vedic Literature
(see also: BL1112-1115)

Vedas. Rgveda. English. Selections. 　• **2.1930**
Vedic hymns / translated by F. Max Müller. — Delhi: M. Banarsidass, [1964] 2v. (The Sacred books of the East (New York); v.32, 46) (UNESCO collection of representative works. Indian series.) Vol. 2 translated by Hermann Oldenberg. 1. Brahmanism — Sacred books I. Müller, F. Max (Friedrich Max), 1823-1900. II. Oldenberg, Hermann, 1854-1920. III. T. IV. Series. V. Series: UNESCO collection of representative works. Indian series.
PK3016.A2 E5 1964　　*LC* 65-4279

Vedas. Atharvaveda. English. 　• **2.1931**
Hymns of the Atharva-Veda, together with extracts from the ritual books and the commentaries. Translated by Maurice Bloomfield. — New York: Greenwood Press, [1969] lxxiv, 716 p.; 23 cm. — (The Sacred books of the East [v. 42]) I. Bloomfield, Maurice, 1855-1928. ed. II. T. III. Series.
PK3406.E5 1969　　294/.15　　*LC* 69-14131　　*ISBN* 0837118794

Upanishads. English. 　• **2.1932**
The Upanishads. New York, Christian Literature Co., 1897. 2 v. in 1. port., tables. 23 cm. I. Müller, F. Max (Friedrich Max), 1823-1900. ed. and tr. II. T.
PK3505.A1 E5x　　BL1010.S34 vol. 1　　*LC* 32-5219

PK3591–4485 Sanskrit (Post–Vedic) Literature

Puranas. Bhāgavatapurāna. English. 　**2.1933**
The Bhāgavata purāna: pt. 1–2 / translated and annotated by Ganesh Vasudeo Tagare. — Delhi: Motilal Bánarsidass, 1976. 419 p. — (Ancient Indian tradition & myth series; 7-8) I. Tagare, Ganesh Vasudeo. II. T. III. Series.
PK3621.B5 E5　　*ISBN* 0842608559

Bhagavadgītā. Sanskrit and English. 　• **2.1934**
The Bhagavad gītā. Translated and interpreted by Franklin Edgerton. Cambridge, Mass., Harvard University Press, 1944. 2 v. (Harvard Oriental series; v.38-39) Sanskrit transliteration and English translation on opposite pages of v.1. I. Edgerton, Franklin, 1885-1963. II. Arnold, Edwin, Sir, 1832-1904. III. T. IV. Series.
PK3631.B5 1944　　294.5924　　*LC* a 44-5744

Mahābhārata. English. 　**2.1935**
The Mahābhārata. Translated and edited by J. A. B. van Buitenen. Chicago, University of Chicago Press [1973-. v. illus. 25 cm. I. Buitenen, J. A. B. van (Johannes Adrianus Bernardus van) tr. II. T.
PK3633.A2 B8　　294.5/923　　*LC* 72-97802　　*ISBN* 0226846482

Mahābhārata. English. Selections. 　• **2.1936**
Mahābhārata: an English version based on selected verses / Chakravarthi V. Narasimhan. — New York: Columbia U.P., 1965. — xxv, 254 p.; 21 cm. — (Records of civilization, sources & studies; no.71.) Prepared for the Columbia

College program of translations from the Oriental classics. I. Narasimhan, Chakravarthi V. II. Columbia College (Columbia University) III. T. IV. Series.
PK3633.A2 N3 1965　　891.21　　*LC* 64-10347　　*ISBN* 0231083211

Vālmīki. 　• **2.1937**
The Ramayana and the Mahabharata, condensed into English verse by Romesh C. Dutt. London & Toronto, Dent; New York, Dutton [1929] xiv, 335 p. 18 cm. (Everyman's library. Philosophy and theology. [no. 403]) "First issue of this edition 1910 ... Reset 1929." "A note on the late Romesh C. Dutt," by S. K. Ratcliffe: p. ix-x. I. Dutt, Romesh Chunder, 1848-1909. tr. II. Mahābhārata. III. T.
PK3653.A2D8x　　891.21　　*LC* 36-37622

Vālmīki. 　• **2.1938**
The Ramayan of Valmiki / translated into English verse by Ralph T. H. Griffith; with a memoir by M. N. Venkataswami. — [3d ed.]. — Varanasi: Chowkhamba Sanskrit Series Office, 1963. ix, 576 p. — (The Chowkhamba Sanskrit studies; v. 29) I. Griffith, Ralph T. H. (Ralph Thomas Hotchkin), 1826-1906. II. T. III. Series.
PK3653.A2 G75 1963　　*LC* sa 63-4749

Vālmīki. 　**2.1939**
The Ramayana of Valmiki. Translated by Hari Prasad Shastri. — 3rd ed. — London: Shantisadan, 1976. 3 v. I. Shastri, Hari Prasad, 1882-1956. tr. II. T.
PK3653.A2 S5 1962

Hitopadeśa. English. 　• **2.1940**
The book of good counsels: from the Sanskrit of the 'Hitopadeśa,' by Edwin Arnold. With illus. by Harrison Weir. London, Smith, Elder, 1861. — [New York: AMS Press, 1971] xii, 167 p.: illus.; 19 cm. I. Arnold, Edwin, Sir, 1832-1904. ed. II. T.
PK3741.H6 E5 1971　　398.24/52　　*LC* 75-149688　　*ISBN* 040403277X

Panchatantra. English. 　• **2.1941**
The Panchatantra / translated from the Sanskrit by Arthur W. Ryder. — Chicago: University of Chicago Press, 1925. — vii, 470 p. I. Ryder, Arthur William, 1877-1938. II. T.
PK3741.P3 E5 1972　　891.23　　*LC* 25-21523　　*ISBN* 0226732487

Panchatantra. English. 　• **2.1942**
The Panchatantra. Translated from the Sanskrit by Franklin Edgerton. –. South Brunswick, N.J.: A.S. Barnes, [1966, c1965] 151 p. (UNESCO collection of representative works: Indian series.) Reprints of the author's translation, first published in volume 2 of his Panchatantra reconstructed, 1924, with some minor alterations. I. Edgerton, Franklin, 1885-1963. tr. II. T.
PK3741.P3 E5 1972　　398.2/452/0934　　*LC* 66-24653

Bhartrhari. 　• **2.1943**
[Śatakatrya. English and Sanskrit] Bhartrihari: poems. Translated by Barbara Stoler Miller. With the transliterated Sanskrit text of the Śatakatrayam: Nīti, Sriṅgāra, Vairāgya. New York, Columbia University Press, 1967. xxviii, 156 p. 22 cm. (UNESCO collection of representative works. Indian series) I. Miller, Barbara Stoler. II. T.
PK3791.B28 S213 1967　　891/.2/1　　*LC* 66-26001

Dandin, 7th cent. 　• **2.1944**
Dasha-kumara-charita. The ten princes. Translated from the Sanskrit by Arthur W. Ryder. Chicago University Press [1966, c1927] 240p. I. Ryder, Arthur William, 1877-1938. tr. II. T. III. Title: The ten princes
PK3794 D4 D313 1927　　*LC* 61-1496

Jayadeva, 12th cent. 　**2.1945**
[Gītagovinda. English and Sanskrit] Love song of the dark lord: Jayadeva's Gitagovinda / edited and translated by Barbara Stoler Miller. — New York: Columbia University Press, 1977. xx, 225 p.; 24 cm. (UNESCO collection of representative works. Indian series) 'Translations from the Oriental classics.' English and Sanskrit. 1. Krishna — Poetry. I. Miller, Barbara Stoler. II. T.
PK3794.J3 G53 1977b　　891/.2/1　　*LC* 76-13165　　*ISBN* 0231040288

Kālidāsa. 　**2.1946**
[Plays. English. Selections] Theater of memory: the plays of Kālidāsa / edited by Barbara Stoler Miller; translated by Edwin Gerow, David Gitomer, Barbara Stoler Miller. — New York: Columbia University Press, 1984. xiv, 387 p.; 24 cm. — (Translations from the Oriental classics.) (UNESCO collection of representative works. Indian series.) I. Miller, Barbara Stoler. II. T. III. Series. IV. Series: UNESCO collection of representative works. Indian series.
PK3795.E5 1984　　891.21 19　　*LC* 83-26362　　*ISBN* 0231058381

Kālidāsa. 　• **2.1947**
Shakuntala and other writings / by Kalidasa; translated with an introd. by Arthur W. Ryder; pref. by G.L. Anderson. — New York: Dutton, 1959. 216 p.; 19 cm. — (A Dutton everyman paperback; D40) 1. Indic literature —

Translations into English. I. Ryder, Arthur William, 1877-1938. II. T. III. Series.
PK3795.E6 R9   PK3795.E5 1959.   *LC* 60-1496   *ISBN* 0525470409

Kālidāsa.   **2.1948**
[Meghadūta. English & Sanskrit] The transport of love = The Meghadūta of Kālidāsa / translation and introd. by Leonard Nathan. — Berkeley: University of California Press, c1976. viii, 116 p.; 21 cm. 'Sponsored by the Center for South and Southeast Asia Studies, University of California, Berkeley.' English and Sanskrit. I. Nathan, Leonard, 1924- II. T.
PK3796.M6 N3   891/.2/1   *LC* 75-13157   *ISBN* 0520030311

Kālidāsa.   • **2.1949**
Kālidāsa's Abhijñāna–Śakuntala; translated from the Bengali recension by M. B. Emeneau. — Berkeley: University of California Press, 1962. 115 p. I. Emeneau, M. B. (Murray Barnson), 1904- tr. II. T. III. Title: Abhijñāna-Śakuntalā IV. Title: Śakuntalā
PK3796.S4 E5 1962   *LC* 62-15247

Krsnalīlāśukamuni, 1193-1293.   **2.1950**
[Krsnakarnāmrta English & Sanskrit] The love of Krishna: the Krsnakarnāmrta of Līlāśuka Bilvamañgala / edited with an introd. by Frances Wilson. — Philadelphia: University of Pennsylvania Press, [1975] ix, 463 p.; 24 cm. — (Haney Foundation series; 14) Sanskrit transcription with parallel English translation. Includes indexes. 1. Krishna — Poetry. I. Wilson, Frances. II. T.
PK3798.K59 K63 1975   891/.2/1   *LC* 74-153426   *ISBN* 0812276558

Sūdraka.   • **2.1951**
[Mrcchakatika English] Mrcchakatikā = The little clay cart: a drama in ten acts / attributed to King Sūdraka; now newly translated from the Sanskrit with introd. and notes by Revilo Pendleton Oliver. — Urbana: University of Illinois Press, 1938. 250 p.; 23 cm. (Illinois studies in language and literature. v. 23, no. 1-2) I. Oliver, Revilo P. (Revilo Pendleton), 1910- ed. II. T. III. Title: Little clay cart. IV. Series.
PK3798.S91 M73 1975   891/.2/2   *LC* 74-14116   *ISBN* 0837177898

Two plays of ancient India: The little clay cart: The minister's   • **2.1952**
seal / translated from Sanskrit and Prakit, with an introduction
by J.A.B. Buitenen.
New York: Columbia University Press, 1968. viii, 278 p.; 20 cm. Prepared for the Columbia College Program of translations from the Oriental classics and sponsored by the Committee on Oriental Studies, Columbia University. Translation of Mrcchakatika and Mudrārāksasa, respectively. I. Buitenen, J. A. B. van (Johannes Adrianus Bernardus van) II. Śūdraka. The little clay cart. III. Viśākhadatta. The minister's seal. IV. Title: The little clay cart. V. Title: The minister's seal.
PK3798.S91 M73 1968   *LC* 67-25441

PK4471–4485 Translations (Collections)

The Hermit & The love thief: Sanskrit poems of Bharitrihari   **2.1953**
and Bilhana / translated by Barbara Stoler Miller.
New York: Columbia University Press, 1978. 127 p. (p. 123-127 publisher's list); 22 cm. (UNESCO collection of representative works. Indian series) Poems from Bhartrhari's Śatakatrayam, and from Bilhana's Caurapañcāśikā. 'Translations from the Oriental classics.' 1. Sanskrit poetry — Translations into English. 2. English poetry — Translations from Sanskrit. I. Miller, Barbara Stoler. II. Bhartrhari. Śatakatraya. English. Selections. 1978. III. Bilhana, 11th cent. Caurapañcāśikā. English. Selections. 1978.
PK4474.A3 H47   891/.2/1   *LC* 78-14513   *ISBN* 0231046448.
ISBN 0231046456 pbk

Vidyākara. comp.   • **2.1954**
Anthology of Sanskrit court poetry: Vidyākara's "Subhāsitaratnakosa." Cambridge, Mass.: Harvard U.P., 1965. 611p. (UNESCO collection of representative works. Indian series.) (Harvard oriental series; v.44.) 1. Sanskrit poetry — Translations into English. 2. English poetry — Translations from Sanskrit. I. T. II. Series. III. Series: Harvard oriental series; v.44.
PK4474.A3 V5   891.2108   *LC* 64-19581

Three Sanskrit plays / translated with an introduction by   **2.1955**
Michael Coulson.
Harmondsworth, Middlesex, England; New York, N.Y.: Penguin Books, 1981. 429 p.; 20 cm. — (Penguin classics.) 1. Sanskrit drama — Translations into English. 2. English drama — Translations from Sanskrit. I. Kālidāsa. Śakuntalā. English. 1981. II. Viśākhadatta. Mudrārāksasa. English. 1981. III. Bhavabhūti, 8th cent. Mālatīmādhava. English. 1981. IV. Series.
PK4474.T5 1981   891/.22 19   *LC* 82-126455   *ISBN* 0140443746

Natwar-Singh, K. ed.   • **2.1956**
Tales from modern India, edited, with an introd. and notes, by K. Natwar-Singh. — New York: Macmillan, [1966] xii, 274 p.; 21 cm. 1. Short stories,

Indic — Translations into English. 2. Short stories, English — Translations from Indic. 3. Short stories, English I. T.
PK5440.E5 Nx   *LC* 66-23791

Indian poetry today. Edited by Swadesh Bharati.   **2.1957**
Calcutta: Rupambara Prakashan, [1969-. v. in; 23 cm. — (New Writers, 6-8) Vol. 4, pt. 1 issued without series statement. 1. Indic poetry — Translations into English. 2. English poetry — Translations from Indic literature. I. Swadesh Bharati, 1941- ed.
PK5461.A3 I54   891/.4/1   *LC* 70-913531

Nandy, Pritish. comp.   **2.1958**
Modern Indian poetry. Edited by Pritish Nandy. — New Delhi: Arnold-Heinemann Publishers (India), [1974] 231 p.; 23 cm. 1. Indic poetry — Translations into English. 2. English poetry — Translations from Indic literature. 3. Indic poetry (English) I. T.
PK5461.A3 N34   891/.4   *LC* 74-900588

Modern Indian short stories / editor, K.S. Duggal.   **2.1959**
New Delhi: Indian Council for Cultural Relations, 1975- < 1983 > . v. < 1, 4 >; 25 cm. Vol. 4. edited by Kishori Charan Das. 1. Short stories, Indo-Aryan — Translations into English. 2. Short stories, English — Translations from Indo-Aryan languages. I. Duggal, Kartar Singh, 1917-
PZ1.M71938 PK5461.A6D8x   808.83/1   *LC* 75-906745

Modern Indian short stories / editor Suresh Kohli.   **2.1960**
London: Heinemann Educational, 1975. 164 p.; 23 cm. Some stories translated from various Indian languages. 1. Short stories, Indic — Translations into English. 2. Short stories, English — Translations from Indic literature. I. Kohli, Suresh.
PK5461.A6K6x   891/.4   *ISBN* 0435990209

Indian poetry today / general editor, Keshav Malik.   **2.1961**
Rev. ed. — New Delhi: Indian Council for Cultural Relations, 1985-. v. < 1-2 >; 22 cm. Vol. 2: enl. rev. ed. 1. Indic poetry — 20th century — Translations into English. 2. English poetry — Translations from Indic languages. I. Malik, Keshav.
PK5461.I55 1985   891/.4 19   *LC* 85-903755

PK6001–6996 Iranian (Persian) Language and Literature

Browne, Edward Granville, 1862-1926.   **2.1962**
A literary history of Persia / by Edward G. Browne. — Cambridge [Eng.]: University Press, 1929. 4 v.: ill., facsims., ports. 1. Persian literature — History and criticism 2. Persian literature — Translations into English 3. English literature — Translations from Persian 4. Manuscripts, Persian — Facsimiles 5. Illumination of books and manuscripts — Specimens, reproductions, etc. I. T.
PK6097.B7 1929   *LC* 30-15417   *ISBN* 0521043441

Rypka, Jan, 1886-1968.   **2.1963**
[Dějiny jerské A tadžické literatury. English] History of Iranian literature. Written in collaboration with Otakar Klíma [and others] Edited by Karl Jahn. Dordrecht, D. Reidel [1968] xxvii, 929 p. col. plate. fold. map. 25 cm. Translation of Dějiny jerské A tadžické literatury. 1. Persian literature — History and criticism. I. Jahn, Karl, 1906- ed. II. T.
PK6097.R913   891.5   *LC* 68-95715

Steingass, Francis Joseph, 1825-1903.   **2.1964**
A comprehensive Persian–English dictionary: including the Arabic words and phrases to be met with in Persian literature: being Johnson and Richardson's Persian, Arabic & English dictionary, revised, enlarged and entirely reconstructed / by F. Steingass. — 7th impression. London: Routledge, 1984. viii, 1539 p. Titre au dos: Persian-English dictionary. 1. Persian language — Dictionaries — English. I. Johnson, Francis, 1796?-1876. Dictionary, Persian, Arabic and English. II. T. III. Title: A dictionary, Persian, Arabic and English. IV. Title: Persian-English dictionary.
PK6379 S82 1981

Ta'ziyeh, ritual and drama in Iran / edited by Peter J.   **2.1965**
Chelkowski.
New York: New York University Press, 1979. xxi, 288 p.: ill.; 24 cm. (New York University studies in Near Eastern civilization; no. 7) Proceedings of an international symposium on Ta'ziyeh held in Aug. 1976 at the Shiraz Festival of Arts, Shiraz, Iran. 1. Ta'ziyah — Congresses. 2. Shī'ah — Iran — Congresses. I. Chelkowski, Peter J.
PK6422.T3   891/.55/22   *LC* 78-20543   *ISBN* 0814713750

'Attār, Farīd al-Dīn, d. ca. 1230.   **2.1966**
[Mantiq al-tayr English] The conference of the birds / Farid ud–Din Attar; translated with an introduction by Afkham Darbandi and Dick Davis. — Harmondsworth, Middlesex, England; New York, N.Y., U.S.A.: Penguin Books, 1984. 233 p.; 20 cm. (Penguin classics.) Translation of: Mantiq al-tayr. 'Biographical index': p. [230]-234. 1. Sufi poetry 2. Sufi poetry, Persian 3. Sufism — Early works to 1800. I. Davis, Dick, 1945- II. Darbandi, Afkham, 1948- III. T. IV. Series.
PK6451.F4 M2813 1984   891/.5511 19   LC 84-211777   ISBN 0140444343

Firdawsī.   **2.1967**
The Shánámá of Firdausi / done into English by Arthur George Warner and Edmond Warner. — London: K. Paul, Trench, Trübner & Co., 1905-1925. 9 v. I. Warner, Arthur George II. Warner, Edmond III. T.
PK6456.A1 R7   891/.55/11   LC 73-906254

Hāfiz, 14th cent.   **2.1968**
Fifty poems of Hafiz. Texts and translations collected and made, introduced and annotated by Arthur J. Arberry. Cambridge: University Press, 1962. 187p. I. Arberry, A. J. (Arthur John), 1905-1969. ed. and tr. II. T.
PK6465 Z31 A7 1962

Jalāl al-Dīmī, Mawlānā, 1207-1283.   • **2.1969**
Rūmī, poet and mystic, 1207-1273: selections from his writings / translated from the Persian with introd. and notes by Reynold A. Nicholson. — London: Allen and Unwin, 1950. 190 p. — (Ethical and religious classics of the East and West; no.1) I. Nicholson, Reynold Alleyne, 1868-1945. II. T.
PK6480.E5 N5 1950   LC 51-32475

Jalāl al-Dīn Rūmī, Maulana, 1207-1273.   **2.1970**
[Selections. English] Rūmī, poet and mystic / translations, introd. and notes by Reynold A. Nicholson. — [s.l.]: Samuel Weiser Inc, 1974. 191 p.; 20 cm. 'Mandala books.' 1. Sufi poetry 2. Sufi poetry, Persian I. Nicholson, Reynold Alleyne, 1868-1945. II. T.
PK6480.E5 N5 1978   891/.55/11   LC 78-40217   ISBN 0048910473

Omar Khayyam.   • **2.1971**
Fitzgerald's Rubáiyát. Edited with an introd. and notes by Carl J. Weber and with A check–list of the Rubáiyát collection in the Colby College Library, compiled by James Humphry III. Centennial ed. Waterville, Me., Colby College Press, 1959. 158 p. illus. 23 cm. I. FitzGerald, Edward, 1809-1883. II. Colby College. Library. A check-list of the Rubáiyát collection in the Colby College Library. III. T. IV. Title: Rubáiyát.
PK6513.A1 1959   LC 59-2192

Omar Khayyam.   • **2.1972**
Rubáiyát of Omar Khayyám / The 1st and 4th editions in English verse by Edward FitzGerald; with ill. by Eugene Karlin; introd. by T. Cuyler Young. — New York: Crowell, 1964. ix, 80 p.: ill. 1. Persian poetry — Translations into English. 2. English poetry — Translations from Persian. I. FitzGerald, Edward. II. T.
PK6513.A1 1964   891.551   LC 64-20696   ISBN 0690713886

Dashtī, 'Alī, 1895-.   • **2.1973**
[Damī bā Khayyām. English] In search of Omar Khayyam. Translated from the Persian by L. P. Elwell–Sutton. [New York] Columbia University Press [c1971] 276 p. front. 23 cm. (Persian studies monographs, no. 1) Translation of Damī bā Khayyām. 1. Omar Khayyam. I. T. II. Series.
PK6525.D313 1971b   891/.55/11   LC 77-168669   ISBN 0231031882

Sa'dī.   **2.1974**
[Būstān. English] Morals pointed and tales adorned: the Būstān of Sa'dī / translated by G. M. Wickens; [ill. by Yüksel Hassan]. — Toronto; Buffalo: University of Toronto Press, c1974. xxviii, 316 p.; 22 cm. (Persian heritage series; no. 17) I. Wickens, G. M. II. T.
PK6541.B2 W5   891/.55/11   LC 70-185746   ISBN 0802018408

Sa'di, 1184-1292.   **2.1975**
The Gulistan, or Rose garden of Sa'di. Translated by Edward Rehatsek. Edited with a pref. by W.G. Archer. Introd. by G.M. Wickens. New York: Putnam, 1965. 265p. I. Archer, W. G. (William George), 1907- ed. II. T. III. Title: Rose garden
PK6541 G2 A7

Āl Ahmad, Jalāl.   **2.1976**
[Mudīr-i madrasah. English] The school principal: a novel / Jalal Al–e Ahmad; translated from the Persian by John K. Newton; introd. and notes by Michael C. Hillmann. — Minneapolis: Bibliotheca Islamica, 1974. 144 p.; 23 cm. (Studies in Middle Eastern literatures; no. 4) Translation of Mudīr-i madrasah. I. T.
PZ4.A284 Sc PK6561.A38   891/.55/33   LC 75-300709   ISBN 0882970089

Farrukhzād, Furūgh.   **2.1977**
Bride of Acacias: selected poems of Forugh Farrokhzad / translated by Jascha Kessler with Amin Banani; introduction by Amin Banani; afterword by Farzaneh Milani. — Delmar, N.Y.: Caravan Books, 1982. 158 p.; 24 cm. — (Modern Persian literature series. no. 5) I. Kessler, Jascha Frederick, 1929- II. Banani, Amin. III. T. IV. Series.
PK6561.F264 A24 1982   891/.5513 19   LC 82-1156   ISBN 0882060503

Jamālzādah, Muhammad 'Alī.   **2.1978**
[Yakī būd, yakī nabūd English] Once upon a time = (Yeki bud, yeki nabud) / Mohammad Ali Jamalzada; translated from the Persian by Heshmat Moayyad and Paul Sprachman. — New York: Bibliotheca Persica, 1985. 112 p. (Modern Persian literature series. no. 6) Translation of: Yakī būd, yakī nabūd. I. Moayyad, Heshmat. II. Sprachman, Paul. III. T. IV. Title: Yeki bud, yeki nabud. V. Series.
PK6561.J3 Y413 1985   891/.5533 19   LC 85-9148   ISBN 0933273002

PL55–248 Turkish Language and Literature

Yūsuf, khāss-hājib, 11th cent.   **2.1979**
[Ḳutadğu biliğ. English] Wisdom of royal glory: a Turko–Islamic mirror for princes / Yūsuf Khāss Hājib; translated, with an introduction and notes, by Robert Dankoff. — Chicago: University of Chicago Press, 1983. viii, 281 p.; 24 cm. — (Publications of the Center for Middle Eastern Studies. no. 16) Translation of: Ḳutadğu biliğ. I. Dankoff, Robert. II. T. III. Series.
PL55.U539 Y8713 1983   894/.3 19   LC 82-20159   ISBN 0226971791

Lewis, Geoffrey L.   **2.1980**
Turkish grammar [by] G. L. Lewis. — Oxford: Clarendon Press, 1967. xxiv, 303 p.; 22 1/2 cm. 1. Turkish language — Grammar. I. T.
PL123.L4   494/.35/5   LC 68-75910

Lewis, Geoffrey L.   **2.1981**
Teach yourself Turkish. New York: McKay, for English Universities Press [1953] 175 p.; 18 cm. (Teach yourself books.) 1. Turkish language — Self-instruction. I. T. II. Series.
PL123.L49

Gibb, Hamilton Alexander Rosskeen, 1895-.   **2.1982**
A history of Ottoman poetry / by Hamilton Gibb. — London: Luzac & Co., 1958-1967. 6 v. 1. Turkish poetry — History and criticism. I. T.
PL217.G5

Contemporary Turkish literature: fiction and poetry / edited, with an introd., by Talat Sait Halman.   **2.1983**
Rutherford [N.J.]: Fairleigh Dickinson University Press, c1982. 454 p.; 24 cm. 1. Turkish literature — 20th century I. Halman, Talât Sait.
PL232.C6 1982   894/.3508003   LC 77-74391   ISBN 0838613608

Kitab-i Dede Korkut. English.   **2.1984**
The book of Dede Korkut, translated with an introduction and notes by Geoffrey Lewis. — Harmondsworth: Penguin, 1974. 213 p.: map.; 18 cm. — (Penguin classics) I. Lewis, Geoffrey L. ed. II. T.
PL248.K54 E5 1974   398.2/2/0958   LC 74-172789   ISBN 0140442987

PL490–4961 East Asian Languages and Literatures

PL501–888 Japanese

PL501–699 Japanese Language

Miller, Roy Andrew.   • **2.1985**
The Japanese language / Roy Andrew Miller. — Chicago: University of Chicago Press, 1967. xix, 428, [47] p.: ill.; 23 cm. — (History and structure of languages) 1. Japanese language I. T.
PL523.M493   495.6   *LC* 67-16777   *ISBN* 0226527174

Miller, Roy Andrew.   **2.1986**
Origins of the Japanese language: lectures in Japan during the academic year, 1977–78 / Roy Andrew Miller. — Seattle : University of Washington Press, 1981 (c1980). xiii, 217 p.: maps; 24 cm. (Publications on Asia of the School of International Studies; no. 34) Includes indexes. 1. Japanese language — History. 2. Japanese language — Grammar, Comparative — Altaic. 3. Altaic languages — Grammar, Comparative — Japanese. I. T.
PL525.M49   495.6/09 19   *LC* 80-50871   *ISBN* 0295957662

Miller, Roy Andrew.   **2.1987**
Japanese and the other Altaic languages. — Chicago: University of Chicago Press, [1971] xviii, 331 p.; 24 cm. — (History and structure of languages) 1. Japanese language — Grammar, Comparative — Altaic. 2. Altaic languages — Grammar, Comparative — Japanese. I. T.
PL529.M46   490   *LC* 79-151129   *ISBN* 0226527190

Bloch, Bernard, 1907-1965.   **2.1988**
Bernard Bloch on Japanese. Edited with an introd. and analytic index by Roy Andrew Miller. New Haven, Yale University Press, 1970. xli, 190 p. 25 cm. (Yale linguistic series.) 1. Japanese language — Grammar — 1950- Addresses, essays, lectures. 2. Japanese language — Phonetics — Addresses, essays, lectures. I. Miller, Roy Andrew. ed. II. T. III. Series.
PL533.B55 1970   495.6/5   *LC* 72-99834

Martin, Samuel Elmo, 1924-.   **2.1989**
Essential Japanese: an introduction to the standard colloquial language / by Samuel E. Martin. — 3d rev. ed. — Rutland, Vt.: C.E. Tuttle, 1954. viii, 462 p.; 20 cm. 1. Japanese language — Spoken Japanese I. T.
PL539.M3 1954   *LC* 59-5072

Kenkyusha's new English–Japanese dictionary / Yoshio Koine,   **2.1990**
editor in chief.
5th ed. — Tokyo, Japan: Kenkyusha, 1980. xxi, 2477 p.: ill.; 27 cm. Title in colophon (inserted): Kenkyūsha shin Ei-Wa daijiten. 1. English language — Dictionaries — Japanese. I. Koine, Yoshio. II. Title: New English-Japanese dictionary. III. Title: Kenkyūsha shin Ei-Wa daijiten. IV. Title: Shin Ei-Wa daijiten.
PL679.K388 1980   423/.956 19   *LC* 81-101348

Kenkyusha's new Japanese–English dictionary. Koh Masuda,   **2.1991**
general editor.
4th ed. — Tokyo: Kenkyusha, [1974] xiii, 2110 p.; 26 cm. Japanese title in colophon: Kenkyūsha shin Wa-Ei daijiten. 1. Japanese language — Dictionaries — English. I. Masuda, Kō, 1890- ed. II. Title: New Japanese-English dictionary.
PL679.K4 1974   495.6/3/21   *LC* 74-173947

Miura, Akira, 1927-.   **2.1992**
Japanese words and their uses / by Akira Miura. — Rutland, Vt.: C.E. Tuttle, c1983. 240 p.; 19 cm. Includes index. 1. Japanese language — Usage — Dictionaries — English. I. T.
PL679.M58 1983   495.6/321 19   *LC* 82-51099   *ISBN* 0804813868

Nelson, Andrew Nathaniel.   **2.1993**
The modern reader's Japanese–English character dictionary. [Saishin Kan–Ei jiten (romanized form)] Rev. ed. Rutland, Vt.: C. E. Tuttle Co. [1966, c1962] 1109 p.; 24 cm. 1. Chinese characters — Dictionaries — Japanese. 2. Japanese characters — Dictionaries — Chinese. I. T. II. Title: Japanese-English character dictionary. III. Title: Saishin Kan-Ei jiten.
PL679.N4 1966   495.6/3/21   *LC* 70-24036   *ISBN* 0804804087

PL700–888 Japanese Literature

Ueda, Makoto, 1931-.   **2.1994**
Literary and art theories in Japan. Cleveland, Press of Western Reserve University [c1967] xiii, 274 p. illus., ports. 24 cm. 1. Japanese literature — History and criticism. 2. Aesthetics, Japanese I. T.
PL708.U33   700/.1/0952   *LC* 67-14521

Keene, Donald.   • **2.1995**
Japanese literature; an introduction for Western readers. [1st ed.] London J. Murray [1953] 114p. (The Wisdom of the East series) 1. Japanese literature — History and criticism I. T. II. Series.
PL717.K4x

Kokusai Bunka Shinkōkai.   • **2.1996**
Introduction to contemporary Japanese literature / edited by Kokusai Bunka Shinkokai. — Tokyo: Kokusai Bunka Shinkokai, 1939. xiii, 485 p.; 27 cm. — (K.B.S. publication series A, no. 12) Includes index. 1. Japanese literature — Translations into English. 2. English literature — Translations from Japanese. 3. Authors, Japanese 4. Japanese literature — History and criticism. I. T.
PL717.K619

Hisamatsu, Sen'ichi, 1894-1976.   **2.1997**
Biographical dictionary of Japanese literature / Sen'ichi Hisamatsu. 1st ed. New York: Kodansha International; Tokyo: in collaboration with International Society for Educational Information; New York: distributed through Harper & Row, 1976. 437 p.: diagrs.; 22 cm. 1. Authors, Japanese — Biography — Dictionaries. 2. Japanese literature I. T.
PL723.B63   *LC* 75-14730   *ISBN* 0870112538

Miner, Earl Roy.   **2.1998**
The Princeton companion to classical Japanese literature / by Earl Miner, Hiroko Odagiri, and Robert E. Morrell. — Princeton, N.J.: Princeton University Press, c1985. xxi, 570 p.: ill.; 25 cm. Includes index. 1. Japanese literature — To 1868 — Handbooks, manuals, etc. I. Odagiri, Hiroko. II. Morrell, Robert E. III. T.
PL726.1.M495 1985   895.6/09 19   *LC* 83-24475   *ISBN* 0691065993

LaFleur, William R.   **2.1999**
The karma of words: Buddhism and the literary arts in medieval Japan / William R. LaFleur. — Berkeley: University of California Press, 1983. xvi, 204 p.; 24 cm. Includes index. 1. Japanese literature — 1185-1600 — History and criticism. 2. Buddhism in literature 3. Japan — Civilization — Buddhist influences I. T.
PL726.33.B8 L34 1983   895.6/2/09382 19   *LC* 82-45909   *ISBN* 0520046005

Keene, Donald.   **2.2000**
World within walls: Japanese literature of the pre–modern era, 1600–1867 / Donald Keene. — 1st ed. — New York: Holt, Rinehart and Winston, c1976. xiii, 606 p. 1. Japanese literature — Edo period, 1600-1868 — History and criticism. I. T.
PL726.35.K4   PL726.35 K4.   895.6/09   *LC* 75-21484   *ISBN* 0030136261

Keene, Donald.   **2.2001**
Dawn to the West: Japanese literature of the modern era / Donald Keene. — 1st ed. — New York: Holt, Rinehart, and Winston, c1984. 2 v.; 24 cm. 1. Japanese literature — 1868- — History and criticism. I. T.
PL726.55.K39 1984   895.6/09 19   *LC* 82-15445   *ISBN* 0030628148

Ueda, Makoto, 1931-.   **2.2002**
Modern Japanese writers and the nature of literature / Makoto Ueda. — Stanford, Calif.: Stanford University Press, 1976. vii, 292 p.: ports. (on lining papers); 23 cm. Includes index. 1. Japanese literature — 1868- — History and criticism. 2. Japanese literature — Themes, motives. 3. Literature — Philosophy I. T.
PL726.55.U28   895.6/34   *LC* 75-39336   *ISBN* 0804709041

Yamanouchi, Hisaaki, 1934-.   **2.2003**
The search for authenticity in modern Japanese literature / Hisaaki Yamanouchi. — Cambridge [Eng.]; New York: Cambridge University Press, 1978. x, 214 p.; 23 cm. Includes index. 1. Japanese literature — 1868- — History and criticism. 2. Japanese literature — European influences. 3. Japanese literature — American influences. 4. Authors, Japanese — Psychology. I. T.
PL726.55.Y32   895.6/09/004   *LC* 77-84815   *ISBN* 052121856X

Rubin, Jay, 1941-.   **2.2004**
Injurious to public morals: writers and the Meiji state / Jay Rubin. — Seattle: University of Washington Press, c1984. xvi, 331 p.: ill.; 24 cm. Includes index. 1. Japanese literature — Meiji period, 1868-1912 — History and criticism.

2. Japanese literature — 20th century — History and criticism. 3. Censorship — Japan — History. 4. Literature and state — Japan — History. I. T.
PL726.63.C37 R8 1984   895.6/4/09 19   *LC* 83-47976   *ISBN* 0295960434

PL727–751 Special Forms

Keene, Donald.   2.2005
Landscapes and portraits, appreciations of Japanese culture. — Tokyo; Palo Alto [Calif.]: Kodansha International Ltd., [1971] 343 p.: illus.; 22 cm. 1. Japanese literature — Addresses, essays, lectures. 2. Japan — Civilization — Addresses, essays, lectures. I. T.
PL727.5.K38   895.6/009   *LC* 75-135144   *ISBN* 0870111469

Blyth, Reginald Horace.   2.2006
A history of haiku. [By] R. H. Blyth. [Tokyo] Hokuseido Press [c1963-64] 2v. illus. Label mounted on end leaf at back: Imported and distributed by Japan Publications Trading Co., Rutland, Vt. Includes poems in Japanese. 1. Haiku — History and criticism. I. T.
PL729.B55   *LC* 63-23741

Miner, Earl Roy.   2.2007
Japanese linked poetry: an account with translations of renga and haikai sequences / by Earl Miner. — Princeton, N.J.: Princeton University Press, 1979. xix, 376 p.; 22 cm. Includes index. 1. Renga — History and criticism. 2. Haikai — History and criticism. 3. Japanese poetry — To 1868 — History and criticism. 4. Renga — Translations into English. 5. Haikai — Translations into English. 6. English poetry — Translations from Japanese. I. T.
PL732.R4 M5   895.6/009   *LC* 78-51182   *ISBN* 0691063729

Brower, Robert Hopkins, 1923-.   • 2.2008
Japanese court poetry, by Robert H. Brower and Earl Miner. Stanford, Calif., Stanford University Press, 1961. xvi, 527 p. illus., ports. 24 cm. (Stanford studies in the civilizations of eastern Asia) 'Imperial anthologies': p. [481]-487. 'Bibliographical note': p. [489]-502. 1. Japanese poetry — History and criticism. I. Miner, Earl Roy. joint author. II. T. III. Series.
PL733.2.B7x   895.6109   *LC* 61-10925

Ueda, Makoto, 1931-.   2.2009
Modern Japanese poets and the nature of literature / Makoto Ueda. — Stanford, Calif.: Stanford University Press, 1983. viii, 451 p.: ill.; 23 cm. Includes index. 1. Japanese poetry — 1868- — History and criticism. I. T.
PL733.55.U38 1983   895.6/14/09 19   *LC* 82-60487   *ISBN* 0804711666

Hibbett, Howard.   • 2.2010
The floating world in Japanese fiction. — Freeport, N.Y.: Books for Libraries Press, [1970, c1959] xiii, 232 p.: illus.; 23 cm. 1. Japanese fiction — Edo period, 1600-1868 — History and criticism. 2. Japanese fiction — Translations into English. 3. English fiction — Translations from Japanese. I. T.
PL740.H5 1970   895.6/3/08   *LC* 70-126238   *ISBN* 0836954653

Miyoshi, Masao.   2.2011
Accomplices of silence; the modern Japanese novel. — Berkeley: University of California Press, [1974] xviii, 194 p.; 25 cm. 1. Japanese fiction — 1868- — History and criticism. I. T.
PL747.55.M5   895.6/3/03   *LC* 73-83062   *ISBN* 0520025407

Rimer, J. Thomas.   2.2012
Modern Japanese fiction and its traditions: an introduction / J. Thomas Rimer. — Princeton, N.J.: Princeton University Press, c1978. ix, 313 p.; 23 cm. Includes index. 1. Japanese fiction — 1868- — History and criticism. 2. Japanese literature — History and criticism. I. T.
PL747.55.R55   895.6/3/009   *LC* 78-51188   *ISBN* 0691063621

Nakamura, Mitsuo, pseud.   2.2013
Modern Japanese fiction 1868–1926. — [Revised ed.]. — Tokyo: Kokusai Bunka Shinkokai, [1968] 119, 61 p.: illus.; 24 cm. — (Japanese life and culture series) 'Originally published in two separate volumes entitled Japanese fiction in the Meiji era and Japanese fiction in the Taishô era.' 1. Japanese fiction — History and criticism. I. Kokusai Bunka Shinkôkai. II. T.
PL747.6.N28 1968   895.6/3/409   *LC* 68-58248

Walker, Janet A., 1942-.   2.2014
The Japanese novel of the Meiji period and the ideal of individualism / Janet A. Walker. — Princeton, N.J.: Princeton University Press, c1979. xiii, 315 p.; 23 cm. Includes index. 1. Shimazaki, Tôson, 1872-1943 — Criticism and interpretation. 2. Japanese fiction — Meiji period, 1868-1912 — History and criticism. 3. Individualism in literature. I. T.
PL747.6.W34   895.6/303   *LC* 79-4501   *ISBN* 0691064008

Kimball, Arthur G.   2.2015
Crisis in identity and contemporary Japanese novels, by Arthur G. Kimball. — Rutland, Vt.: C. E. Tuttle Co., [1973] 190 p.; 19 cm. 'Syllabus: a suggested

reading course': p. 167-187. 1. Japanese fiction — 20th century — Addresses, essays, lectures. I. T.
PL747.65.K5   895.6/3/03   *LC* 72-91549   *ISBN* 0804810907

Nakamura, Mitsuo, pseud.   2.2016
[Nihon no gendai shōsetsu. English] Contemporary Japanese fiction, 1926–1968. [1st ed.] Tokyo, Kokusai Bunka Shinkokai [Distributed by Japan Publications Trading Co., San Francisco] 1969. 185 p. illus., ports. 25 cm. (Japanese life and culture series) Translation of Nihon no gendai shōsetsu. 1. Japanese fiction — 20th century — History and criticism. I. Kokusai Bunka Shinkōkai. II. T.
PL747.7.N313   895.6/3/509   *LC* 70-80077

PL752–783 Collections

Keene, Donald. ed.   • 2.2017
Anthology of Japanese literature, from the earliest era to the mid–nineteenth century. — New York: Grove Press, [1955] 442 p.: illus.; 22 cm. — (UNESCO collection of representative works. Japanese series) 1. Japanese literature — Translations into English. 2. English literature — Translations from Japanese. I. T.
PL753.K4 A6x   895.6082   *LC* 55-5110

Keene, Donald.   • 2.2018
Modern Japanese literature, an anthology. — New York: Grove Press, [1956] 440 p.: illus.; 22 cm. 1. Japanese literature — Translation into English. 2. English literature — Translations from Japanese. I. T.
PL753.K4 M6x   895.6082   *LC* 56-8439

Mishima, Yukio, 1925-1970. comp.   2.2019
New writing in Japan; edited by Yukio Mishima and Geoffrey Bownas. Harmondsworth, Penguin, 1972. 249 p. 19 cm. (Writing today) 1. Japanese literature — 20th century I. Bownas, Geoffrey. joint comp. II. T.
PL755.65.M5   895.6/08/005   *LC* 73-157181   *ISBN* 0140034269

Waley, Arthur. tr.   • 2.2020
Japanese poetry, the 'uta.' London: P. Lund, Humphries, 1959[c1956] 110 p.; 19 cm. 1. Japanese poetry — Translations into English 2. English poetry — Translations from Japanese 3. Japanese poetry (Collections) I. T. II. Title: The 'uta.'
PL757.W3x

Man'yōshū.   • 2.2021
The Manyōshū, the Nippon Gakujutsu Shinkōkai translation of One thousand poems, with the texts im Romaji. With a new forword by Donald Keene. New York, Columbia University Press, 1965. lxxxii, 502 p. ill., maps (part fold.) 24 cm. (UNESCO collection of representative works. Japanese series.) (Records of civilization: sources & studies, 70) 'Reissued for the Columbia College Program of Translations from the Oriental classics.' Translation prepared by the Special Manyoshu Committee, Japanese Classic Translation Committee, Nippon Gakujutsu Shinkōkai. 1. Man'yōshū. I. Nippon Gakujutsu Shinkōkai. Dai 17 Shō (Nihon Koten Hon'yaku) Iinkai II. T. III. Series.
PL 758.15 E5 1965a   *LC* 65-15376   *ISBN* 0231028180

Kokin wakashū. English.   2.2022
Kokinshū: a collection of poems ancient and modern / translated and annotated by Laurel Rasplica Rodd with Mary Catherine Henkenius. — Princeton, N.J.: Princeton University Press, c1984. ix, 442 p.; 25 cm. — (Princeton library of Asian translations.) 'Including a study of Chinese influences on the Kokinshū prefaces by John Timothy Wixted and an annotated translation of the Chinese preface by Leonard Grzanka.' Translation of: Kokin wakashū / compiled by Ki no Tsurayuki. Includes indexes. 1. Waka — Translations into English. 2. Japanese poetry — 794-1185 — Translations into English. 3. Waka, English — Translations from Japanese. I. Rodd, Laurel Rasplica. II. Henkenius, Mary Catherine. III. Ki, Tsurayuki, d. 945 or 6. IV. T. V. Series.
PL758.22.A3 1984   895.6/11/08 19   *LC* 83-43090   *ISBN* 0691065934

Mishima, Yukio, 1925-1970.   • 2.2023
Five modern nō plays. Translated from the Japanese by Donald Keene. [1st American ed.] New York, Knopf, 1957. xvii, 198 p. illus. 21 cm. I. T.
PL765.M5x   895.62   *LC* 57-8684 rev

Nippon Gakujustu Shink1-okai. Dai 17 Sh1-o (Nihon Koten   • 2.2024
Hon'yaku) Iinkai.
The Noh drama: ten plays from the Japanese / selected and translated by the Special Noh Committee, Japanese Classics Translation Committee, Nippon Gakujutsu Shinkokai. — Tokyo, Rutland, Vt., C. E. Tuttle Co. [1960] xvi, 192 p. illus., col. map. 27 cm. 1. Nō (Japanese drama and theater) I. T.
PL765.N5x   *LC* 60-11007

Waley, Arthur.   • 2.2025
The nō plays of Japan. With letters by Oswald Sickert. — New York: Grove Press, [1957] 319 p.: plans.; 21 cm. — (Evergreen books, E62) 1. Nō plays —

Translations into English. 2. English drama — Translations from Japanese.
I. Sickert, Oswald. II. T.
PL765.W3x   895.62   *LC* 57-7376

Sakanishi, Shio, 1896- tr.   • **2.2026**
Japanese folk–plays: The ink–smeared lady, and other Kyogen. Tokyo,
Rutland, Vt., C. E. Tuttle Co. [1960] 150 p. illus. 20 cm. 1. Kyōgen (Japanese
drama and theater) 2. Japanese drama — Translations into English. 3. English
drama — Translations from Japanese. I. T. II. Title: The ink-smeared lady.
PL766.S3x   *LC* 60-1954

Henderson, Harold Gould. ed. and tr.   • **2.2027**
An introduction to haiku; an anthology of poems and poets from Bashō to
Shiki. Garden City, N.Y., Doubleday, 1958. 179 p. illus. 22 cm. (Doubleday
anchor books) Original Japanese words are given in footnotes to the English
verse translations. 1. Haiku — Translations into English. 2. Haiku, English —
Translations from Japanese. I. T.
PL768.H3 H4   895.61082   *LC* 58-11314

Ernst, Earle. ed.   • **2.2028**
Three Japanese plays from the traditional theatre. — London, New York,
Oxford University Press, 1959. xv, 200 p. 23 cm. I. T.
PL772.E7   895.62082   *LC* 59-1489 rev

Contemporary Japanese literature: an anthology of fiction, film,   **2.2029**
and other writing since 1945 / edited by Howard Hibbett.
1st ed. — New York: Knopf, 1977. p. cm. 1. Japanese literature — 20th
century — Translations into English. 2. English literature — Translations
from Japanese. I. Hibbett, Howard.
PL782.E1 C6   895.6/08/005   *LC* 77-4762   *ISBN* 0394491416

Reischauer, Edwin O. (Edwin Oldfather), 1910-.   • **2.2030**
Translations from early Japanese literature, by Edwin O. Reischauer and
Joseph K. Yamagiwa. Cambridge Published for the Harvard-Yenching
Institute [by] Harvard University Press 1951. 467 p.; 26 cm. 1. Japanese
literature — Translations into English. 2. English literature — Translations
from Japanese. I. Yamagiwa, Joseph K. (Joseph Koshimi), 1906- II. Harvard-
Yenching Institute. III. T.
PL782 E1 R4   *LC* 51-10360

Guest, Harry. comp.   **2.2031**
Post–war Japanese poetry; edited and translated by Harry and Lynn Guest and
Kajima Shôzô. Harmondsworth, Penguin, 1972. 167 p. illus. 18 cm. (The
Penguin poets) 1. Japanese poetry — 20th century — Translations into
English. 2. English poetry — Translations from Japanese. I. Guest, Lynn,
1939- joint comp. II. Kajima, Shōzō, 1923- joint comp. III. T.
PL782.E3 G8   895.6/1/508   *LC* 73-158152   *ISBN* 0140421459

Modern Japanese poetry / translated by James Kirkup; edited   **2.2032**
and introduced by A. R. Davis.
St. Lucia, Q.: University of Queensland Press, 1978. lxii, 323 p.; 22 cm. —
(Asian and Pacific writing. 9) 1. Japanese poetry — Translations into English.
2. English poetry — Translations from Japanese. 3. Japanese poetry — 1868-
4. Authors, Japanese — Biography. I. Kirkup, James, 1918- II. Davis, A. R.
(Albert Richard), 1924- III. Series.
PL782.E3 M64   895.6/1/408   *LC* 79-300530   *ISBN* 0702211486

One hundred more poems from the Japanese / [compiled and   **2.2033**
translated] by Kenneth Rexroth.
New York: New Directions Pub. Corp., 1976. v, 120 p.; 21 cm. — (A New
Directions book) 1. Japanese poetry — Translations into English. 2. English
poetry — Translations from Japanese. I. Rexroth, Kenneth, 1905-
PL782.E3 O5   895.6/1/008   *LC* 76-7486   *ISBN* 0811206181

Brandon, James R.   **2.2034**
Kabuki: five classic plays / translated by James R. Brandon. — Cambridge:
Harvard University Press, 1975. x, 378 p.: ill.; 24 cm. Includes index.
1. Kabuki plays — Translations into English. 2. English drama —
Translations from Japanese. I. T.
PL782.E5 K3   895.6/2/308   *LC* 74-82192   *ISBN* 0674304853

Akutagawa, Ryūnosuke, 1892-1927.   **2.2035**
Japanese short stories. New York, Liveright Pub. Corp. [1961] 234 p. illus. 21
cm. I. T.
PL782.E8 A5x   *LC* 61-18087

Keene, Donald.   • **2.2036**
The Old woman, the wife, and the archer: three modern Japanese short novels /
translated, and with an introduction, by Donald Keene. — New York: Viking
Press, 1961. 172 p.; 21 cm. 1. Japanese fiction — Translations into English.
2. English fiction — Translations from Japanese. I. T.
PL 782 E8 K26   [Fic]   *LC* 61-16603

Morris, Ivan I. ed.   • **2.2037**
Modern Japanese stories, an anthology. With translations by Edward
Seidensticker [and others] and woodcuts by Masakazu Kuwata. — [1st ed.]. —

Tokyo; Rutland, Vt.: C. E. Tuttle Co., [1961, c1962] 512 p.: illus.; 23 cm. —
(UNESCO collection of representative works: Japanese series) 1. Short stories,
Japanese — Translations into English. 2. Short stories, English — Translations
from Japanese. I. T.
PL782.E8 M6x   *LC* 61-11971

Stories by contemporary Japanese women writers / translators   **2.2038**
and editors, Noriko Mizuta Lippit, Kyoko Iriye Selden.
Armonk, New York: M.E. Sharpe, c1982. xxiii, 221 p.; 24 cm. 1. Short stories,
Japanese — Women authors — Translations into English. 2. Japanese fiction
— 20th century — Translations into English. 3. Short stories, English —
Translation from Japanese. I. Lippit, Noriko Mizuta. II. Selden, Kyoko.
PL782.E8 S8 1982   895.6/301/089287 19   *LC* 82-10270   *ISBN*
0873321936

This kind of woman: ten stories by Japanese women writers,   **2.2039**
1960–1976 / edited by Yukiko Tanaka and Elizabeth Hanson;
with translations by Mona Nagai ... [et al.].
Stanford, Calif.: Stanford University Press, 1982. xxv, 287 p.; 24 cm. 1. Short
stories, Japanese — Women authors — Translations into English. 2. Japanese
fiction — 20th century — Translations into English. 3. Short stories, English
— Translations from Japanese. I. Tanaka, Yukiko. II. Hanson, Elizabeth.
PL782.E8 T44 1982   895.6/301/089287 19   *LC* 81-51332   *ISBN*
0804711305

PL784–866 Individual Authors (by Period)

PL784–799 To 1185

Doe, Paula.   **2.2040**
A warbler's song in the dusk: the life and work of Ōtomo Yakamochi (718–785)
/ Paula Doe. — Berkeley: University of California Press, c1982. ix, 260 p.: ill.;
24 cm. Includes index. 1. Ōtomo, Yakamochi, 718?-785. 2. Poets, Japanese —
To 794 — Biography. I. Ōtomo, Yakamochi, 718?-785. Selections. English.
1982. II. T.
PL785.4.Z5 D6 1982   895.6/11 B 19   *LC* 80-29236   *ISBN*
0520043464

Ise monogatari. English.   • **2.2041**
Tales of Ise; lyrical episodes from tenth–century Japan. Translated, with an
introd. and notes, by Helen Craig McCullough. — Stanford, Calif.: Stanford
University Press, 1968. 277 p.; 23 cm. I. McCullough, Helen Craig. tr. II. T.
PL787.I813   895.6/1/1   *LC* 68-17135

Konjaku monogatari. English. Selections.   **2.2042**
Tales of times now past: sixty–two stories from a medieval Japanese collection /
Marian Ury. — Berkeley: University of California Press, 1980 (c1979). xi,
199 p.: ill.; 23 cm. Partial translation of: Konjaku monogatari. 1. Folk
literature, Japanese — Translations into English. 2. Folk literature, English —
Translations from Japanese. 3. Japanese literature — Heian period, 794-1185
— Translations into English. 4. English literature — Translations from
Japanese. I. Ury, Marian. II. T.
PL787.K62 E5   895.6/31/08 19   *LC* 78-66019   *ISBN* 0520038649

Kelsey, W. Michael, 1945-.   **2.2043**
Konjaku monogatari–shū / by W. Michael Kelsey. — Boston: Twayne
Publishers, c1982. 174 p.: ill.; 21 cm. — (Twayne's world authors series. TWAS
621) Includes index. 1. Konjaku monogatari. 2. Folk literature, Japanese —
History and criticism. 3. Japanese literature — Heian period, 794-1185 —
History and criticism. 4. Legends, Buddhist — Japan — History and criticism.
I. T. II. Series.
PL787.K63 K4 1982   895.6/31/08 19   *LC* 82-2914   *ISBN*
0805764631

Tales of Yamato: a tenth century poem–tale / translated by   **2.2044**
Mildred M. Tahara; foreword by Donald Keene.
Honolulu: University Press of Hawaii, c1980. xvi, 318 p.; 22 cm. Translation of
Yamato monogatari. A revision of the translator's thesis, Columbia University,
1969. Includes indexes. I. Tahara, Mildred M., 1941-
PL787.Y3 E5 1980   895.6/1108   *LC* 79-28535   *ISBN* 0824806174

Ochikubo monogatari. English.   **2.2045**
Ochikubo monogatari: the tale of Lady Ochikubo: a tenth century Japanese
novel / translated by Wilfrid Whitehouse and Eizo Yanagisawa. Garden City,
N.Y.: Anchor Books, 1971,c1965. vi, 271 p.; 18 cm. (UNESCO collection of
representative works. Japanese series.) (A Doubleday Anchor original) Original
English translation: Tokyo: Hokuseido Press,c1965 1. Ochikubo monogatari.
English I. Whitehouse, Wilfrid. II. Yanagisawa, Eizo, 1902- III. T. IV. Title:
The tale of the Lady Ochikubo V. Series.
PL787.O2513 1971

Ki, Tsurayuki, d. 945 or 6.   • **2.2046**
[Tosa nikki. English] The Tosa diary / translated from the Japanese by William N. Porter. — London: H. Frowde, 1912. 148 p.; 18 cm. Text in Romaji with English translation. 'Written in the year A.D. 935 by Ki no Tsurayuki, a court nobleman of high rank.' Reprint of the 1912 ed. published by H. Frowde, London. 1. Ki, Tsurayuki, d. 945 or 6 — Diaries. I. T.
PL788.3.Z5 A313   952/.01/0924 B   *LC* 75-41164   *ISBN* 0404146775

Murasaki Shikibu, b. 978?   **2.2047**
[Genji monogatari English] The tale of Genji / Murasaki Shikibu; translated with an introd. by Edward Seidensticker. — 1st ed. — New York: Knopf, 1976. 2 v. (xix, 1090 p.): ill.; 25 cm. Translation of Genji monogatari. I. T.
PL788.4.G4 E5 1976   895.6/3/1   *LC* 76-13680   *ISBN* 0394483286

Puette, William J.   **2.2048**
Guide to The tale of Genji by Murasaki Shakibu / William J. Puette. — Rutland, Vt.: C.E. Tuttle, c1983. 196 p. 1. Murasaki Shikibu, b. 978? Genji monogatari I. T. II. Title: The tale of Genji.
PL788.4.G413 Z858   895.631   *LC* 82-74088   *ISBN* 0804814546

Murasaki Shikibu, b. 978?   • **2.2049**
[Genji monogatori. English] The tale of Genji; a novel in six parts, by Lady Murasaki. Translated from the Japanese by Arthur Waley. New York, Modern Library [1960] 1135 p. 21 cm. (The Modern library of the world's best books. [A Modern library giant, G-38]) I. T.
PL788.4.T3x   PZ3.M9317 Tal5   *LC* 60-52014

Murasaki Shikibu, b. 978?   **2.2050**
[Murasaki Shikibu nikki. English] Murasaki Shikibu, her diary and poetic memoirs: a translation and study / by Richard Bowring. — Princeton, N.J.: Princeton University Press, c1982. ix, 290 p., [8] p. of plates: ill.; 24 cm. — (Princeton library of Asian translations.) Translation of Murasaki Shikibu nikki and Murasaki Shikibu shū. Includes indexes. 1. Murasaki Shikibu, b. 978? — Diaries. 2. Murasaki Shikibu, b. 978? — Translations, English. 3. Authors, Japanese — Biography. I. Bowring, Richard John, 1947- II. Murasaki Shikibu, b. 978? Murasaki Shikibu shū. English. 1982. III. T. IV. Series.
PL788.4.Z5 A3513 1982   895.6/8103 B 19   *LC* 81-47908   *ISBN* 0691065071

Saigyō, 1118-1190.   **2.2051**
[Sankashū English. Selections] Mirror for the moon: a selection of poems / by Saigyō; translated with an introd. by William R. LaFleur; foreword by Gary Snyder. — New York: New Directions Pub. Corp., c1978. xxvi, 100 p.; 20 cm. Translation of selections from Sankashū. Includes index. I. LaFleur, William R. II. T.
PL788.5.S22 E5 1978   895.6/1/1   *LC* 78-5952   *ISBN* 081120698X. *ISBN* 0811206998 pbk

Sei Shōnagon, b. ca. 967.   • **2.2052**
[Makura no sōchi. English] The pillow book of Sei Shōnagon. Translated and edited by Ivan Morris. New York, Columbia University Press, 1967. 2 v. illus., geneal. tables, maps, plans. 24 cm. (Records of civilization, sources and studies. no. 77) (UNESCO collection of representative works. Japanese series.) 'Prepared for the Columbia College Program of Translations from the Oriental classics.' Translation of Makura no soshi (romanized form) I. Morris, Ivan I. ed. II. T. III. Series. IV. Series: UNESCO collection of representative works. Japanese series.
PL788.6.M3 E56 1967b   895.6/8/107   *LC* 67-24962

Michitsuna no Haha, ca. 935-995.   • **2.2053**
The gossamer years; the diary of a noblewomen of Heian, Japan. Tokyo, Rutland, Vt., C. E. Tuttle Co. [1964] 201 p. illus., map. 23 cm. 1. Japan — Court and courtiers I. Siedensticker, Edward, tr. II. T.
PL789.F8 K313   *LC* 64-22750

Sugawara no Takasue no Musume, b. 1008.   **2.2054**
[Hamamatsu Chūnagon monogatari English] A tale of eleventh century Japan: Hamamatsu Chūnagon monogatari / introduction and translation by Thomas H. Rohlich. — Princeton, N.J.: Princeton University Press, 1983. 247 p.; 23 cm. (Princeton library of Asian translations.) Translation of: Hamamatsu Chūnagon monogatari / Sugawara no Takasue no Musume. I. Rohlich, Thomas H., 1946- II. T. III. Title: Hamamatsu chūnagon monogatari. IV. Series.
PL789.S8 H313 1983   895.6/31 19   *LC* 82-61380   *ISBN* 0691053774

Sugawara no Takasue no Musume, b. 1008.   2.2055
[Sarashina nikki. English] As I crossed a bridge of dreams; recollections of a woman in eleventh-century Japan. Translated from the Japanese by Ivan Morris. London, Oxford University Press; [New York, Dial Press] 1971. 159 p. illus., maps (on lining papers) 24 cm. Translation of Sarashina nikki. I. T.
PL789.S8 S2513   895.6/8/109   *LC* 79-144386   *ISBN* 0192125532

PL790-792 1185-1600

Heike monogatari. English.   **2.2056**
The tale of the Heike = Heike monogatari / translated by Hiroshi Kitagawa, Bruce T. Tsuchida; with a foreword by Edward Seidensticker. — [Tokyo]: University of Tokyo Press, c1975. xli, 807 p.: ill.; 24 cm. Includes index. 1. Taira family — Fiction. 2. Japan — History — Gempei Wars, 1180-1185 — Fiction. I. T.
PZ3.H3632 1975 PL790.H4   895.6/3/2   *LC* 75-325691   *ISBN* 0860081281

Mills, D. E.   • **2.2057**
A collection of tales from Uji; a study and translation of Uji shūi monogatari [by] D. E. Mills. Cambridge [Eng.] University Press, 1970. xii, 459 p. illus. 24 cm. (University of Cambridge Oriental publications, no. 15) A revision of the author's thesis, London. 'The text used for this translation is that in the edition of Watanabe and Nishio, in the Nihon koten bungaku taikei series.' 1. Uji shūi monogatari. 2. Short stories, Japanese — Translations into English. 3. Short stories, English — Translations from Japanese. I. Uji shūi monogatari. English. 1970. II. T.
PL790.U4 M5   895.6/3/208   *LC* 72-114604   *ISBN* 0521077540

Yoshida, Kenkō, 1282?-1350.   • **2.2058**
[Tsurezuregusa English] Essays in idleness; the Tsurezuregusa of Kenkō. Translated by Donald Keene. New York, Columbia University Press, 1967. xxii, 213 p. illus. 23 cm. (Records of civilization, sources and studies. no. 78) UNESCO collection of representative works: Japanese series. I. T. II. Series.
PL791.6.T7 E48   895.6/4/2   *LC* 67-23566

Nakanoin Masatada no Musume, b. 1258.   **2.2059**
[Towazugatari. English] The confessions of Lady Nijō. Translated from the Japanese by Karen Brazell. [1st ed.] Garden City, N.Y., Anchor Books [1973] xxxi, 288 p. 19 cm. Translation of Towazugatari. 1. Nakanoin Masatada no Musume, b. 1258 — Biography. 2. Authors, Japanese — 1185-1600 — Biography. 3. Japan — Court and courtiers I. T.
PL792.N3 T613 1973   895.6/3/2   *LC* 72-96272   *ISBN* 0385036795

PL793-795 1601-1788

Chikamatsu, Monzaemon, 1653-1725.   • **2.2060**
Major plays of Chikamatsu / translated by Donald Keene. — New York: Columbia University Press, 1961. xiv, 485 p.: ill., ports. — (Records of civilization, sources and studies. no. 66) 1. Japanese drama — Translations into English 2. English drama — Translations from Japanese I. Keene, Donald. tr. II. T. III. Series. IV. Series: Records of civilization, sources and studies. no. 66
PL793.4.A25   *LC* 61-15106

Chikamatsu, Monzaemon, 1653-1725.   • **2.2061**
The battles of Coxinga, Chikamatsu's puppet play, its background and importance, by Donald Keene. With a pref. by Mark Van Doren. London, Taylor's Foreign Press, 1951. x, 205 p. 3 plates. 26 cm. (Cambridge oriental series, no.4) Editor statement covered by label: By Donald Lawrence Keene. Thesis statement from label mounted on t.p. I. Keene, Donald. ed. II. T. III. Series.
PL793.4.K6 E5   *LC* 54-34551

Ihara, Saikaku, 1642-1693.   • **2.2062**
Five women who loved love. [1st ed.] Tokyo, Rutland, Vt., C. E. Tuttle Co. [1955] 264 p. illus. 20 cm. I. T.
PZ3.I235 Fi   PL794.F5x.   *LC* 55-10619

Ihara, Saikaku, 1642-1693.   • **2.2063**
The Japanese family storehouse. Cambridge, University Press, 1959. xlix, 281 p. illus., maps (1 fold.) 24 cm. I. T. II. Title: The millionaire's gospel modernised.
PL794.J3x   PZ3.I235 Jap   *LC* 59-1893

Matsuo, Bashō, 1644-1694.   • **2.2064**
The narrow road to the Deep North, and other travel sketches; translated from the Japanese with an introduction by Nobuyuki Yuasa. Harmondsworth: Penguin, 1966. 167 p.: ill., maps, facsim., diagr.; 18 cm. (Penguin classics, L185) I. T.
PL794.4.A29   *LC* 67-71320

Matsuo, Bashō, 1644-1694.   **2.2065**
[Oku no hosomichi English] A haiku journey: Bashō's The narrow road to the far north and selected haiku / photos. by Dennis Stock; translated and introduced by Dorothy Britton. — 1st ed. — Tokyo; New York: Kodansha International; New York: distributor, Harper & Row, 1974. 111 p.: col. ill.; 30 cm. Translation of Oku no hosomichi. 1. Matsuo, Bashō, 1644-1694 — Journeys. 2. Japan — Description and travel — Poetry. I. Britton, D. Guyver (Dorothy Guyver), 1922- II. Stock, Dennis. III. T.
PL794.4.O5 E52 1974   895.6/1/3   *LC* 74-24903   *ISBN* 0870112392

Ueda, Akinari, 1734-1809.   **2.2066**
[Harusame monogatari English] Tales of the spring rain = Harusame monogatari / by Ueda Akinari; translated and with an introd. by Barry Jackman. — Tokyo: University of Tokyo Press, c1975. xxiii, 249 p.; 24 cm. — (Japan Foundation translation series) I. Jackman, Barry. II. T.
PZ3.U25 Tan PL794.8.U4 H3x   895.6/3/3   LC 75-330677   ISBN 0860081138

Ueda, Akinari, 1734-1809.   **2.2067**
[Ugetsu monogatari. English] Tales of moonlight and rain; Japanese Gothic tales, by Uyeda Akinari. Translated by Kengi Hamada. New York, Columbia University Press, 1972 [c1971] xxix, 150 p. illus. 24 cm. Translation of Ugetsu monogatari. I. T.
PZ3.U25 Tal3 PL794.8.U4 U5 1972x   895.6/3/3   LC 79-175064   ISBN 0231036310

Ueda, Akinari, 1734-1809.   **2.2068**
[Ugetsu monogatari. English] Ugetsu monogatari: tales of moonlight and rain: a complete English version of the eighteenth–century Japanese collection of tales of the supernatural / by Ueda Akinari; based on the first woodblock edition of 1776 with illustrations and an introduction for Western readers; translated and edited by Leon M. Zolbrod. — Vancouver: University of British Columbia Press, 1974. 280 p.: ill.; 23 cm. — (UNESCO collection of representative work: Japanese series) I. T. II. Title: Tales of moonlight and rain. III. Series.
PL794.8.U4 U5 1974x PZ3.U25Ug5   895.6/3/3   LC 73-93888   ISBN 0774800267

PL796–799 1789–1867

Jippensha, Ikku, 1765-1831.   • **2.2069**
Shanks' mare, being a translation of the Tokaido volumes of Hizakurige, Japan's great comic novel of travel & ribaldry. Illustrated with full–color reproductions of a rare version of the famed series of woodblock prints 'The fifty–three stages of the Tokaido' by Hiroshige Ando & faithfully rendered into English by Thomas Satchell. Tokyo, Rutland, Vt., C. E. Tuttle Co. [1960] 414 p. illus. (part mounted col.) 24 cm. 1. Tōkaidō. 2. Japan — Social life and customs I. Andō, Hiroshige, 1797-1858. Tōkaidō gojūsantsugi tsuzukie. II. T.
PL797.H59x   895.63   LC 60-14370

Ryōkan, 1758-1831.   **2.2070**
Ryōkan, Zen monk–poet of Japan / translated by Burton Watson. — New York: Columbia University Press, 1977. 126 p.; 22 cm. Consists chiefly of translations of selected Japanese and Chinese poems, the former with romanized Japanese text in parallel columns. 'Translations from the Oriental classics.' I. Watson, Burton, 1925- II. T.
PL797.6.A29 1977   895.6/1/3   LC 77-11140   ISBN 0231044143

PL800–820 1868–1926

Akutagawa, Ryūnosuke, 1892-1927.   **2.2071**
Rashomon, and other stories; translated by Takashi Kojima. Introd. by Howard Hibbett. Illus. by M. Kuwata. New York, Liveright [1952] 119 p. ill. 21 cm. I. T.
PL 801 K8 R2 E5 1952   LC 52-9665

Arishima, Takeo, 1878-1923.   **2.2072**
[Aru onna. English] A certain woman / Arishima Takeo; translated, and with an introd. by Kenneth Strong. — Tokyo: University of Tokyo Press; Forest Grove, Or.: [distributed by] ISBS, c1978. 382 p.; 24 cm. — (UNESCO collection of representative works. Japanese series.) Translation of Aru onna. Distributor stamped on t.p. I. T. II. Series.
PZ3.A698 Ce PL801.R5 A7x   895.6/3/4   LC 79-670025   ISBN 0680082377

Ryan, Marleigh Grayer.   • **2.2073**
Japan's first modern novel: Ukigumo of Futabatei Shimei. Translation and critical commentary by Marleigh Grayer Ryan. New York: Columbia University Press, 1967. xvi, 381 p. 24 cm. (Studies of the East Asian Institute) I. Futabatei, Shimei, 1864-1909. Ukigumo. II. T.
PZ3.R95714 Jap   PL806.T3 Ux.   LC 67-15896

Danly, Robert Lyons, 1947-.   **2.2074**
In the shade of spring leaves: the life and writings of Higuchi Ichiyō, a woman of letters in Meiji Japan / Robert Lyons Danly. — New Haven: Yale University Press, c1981. ix, 355 p., [8] leaves of plates: ill.; 24 cm. Includes index. 1. Higuchi, Ichiyō, 1872-1896. 2. Higuchi, Ichiyō, 1872-1896 — Translations, English. 3. Authors, Japanese — Biography. I. Higuchi, Ichiyō, 1872-1896. Selections. English. 1981. II. T.
PL808.I4 Z63   895.6/34 B 19   LC 81-50434   ISBN 0300026145

Ishikawa, Takuboku, 1885-1912.   **2.2075**
[Kanashiki gangu. English & Japanese] Sad toys = Kanashiki gangu / by Takuboku Ishikawa; translated from the Japanese with an introd. and notes by Sanford Goldstein and Seishi Shinoda. — West Lafayette, Ind.: Purdue

University Press, 1977. vii, 198 p.; 22 cm. English and Japanese. I. Goldstein, Sanford. II. Shinoda, Seishi, 1906- III. T.
PL809.S5 K313 1977   895.6/1/4   LC 76-42864   ISBN 0911198474

Beichman, Janine.   **2.2076**
Masaoka Shiki / by Janine Beichman. — Boston: Twayne Publishers, c1982. 174 p.: port.; 21 cm. — (Twayne's world authors series. TWAS 661) Includes index. 1. Masaoka, Shiki, 1867-1902 — Criticism and interpretation. I. T. II. Series.
PL811.A83 Z57 1982   895.6/14 19   LC 82-3116   ISBN 0805765042

Mori, Ōgai, 1862-1922.   • **2.2077**
The wild geese. Translated by Kingo Ochiai and Sanford Goldstein. [1st ed.] Rutland, Vt., C. E. Tuttle Co. [1959] 119 p. 22 cm. (Library of Japanese literature) I. T.
PZ3.M82387Wi PL811.O7G313   895.63   LC 59-14087

Mori, Ōgai, 1862-1922.   **2.2078**
[Ita sekusuarisu English] Vita sexualis. Translated from the Japanese by Kazuji Ninomiya & Sanford Goldstein. Rutland, Vt., C. E. Tuttle Co. [1972] 153 p. 20 cm. Translation of Ita sekusuarisu. I. T.
PZ3.M82387 Vi PL811.O7 I7x   895.6/3/4   LC 72-79020   ISBN 0804810486

Bowring, Richard John, 1947-.   **2.2079**
Mori Ōgai and the modernization of Japanese culture / Richard John Bowring. — Cambridge [Eng.]; New York: Cambridge University Press, c1979. xii, 297 p.: ports.; 23 cm. (University of Cambridge oriental publications. no. 28) Includes index. 1. Mori, Ōgai, 1862-1922. 2. Authors, Japanese — Biography. I. T. II. Series.
PL811.O7 Z58   895.6/3/4 B   LC 76-11074   ISBN 0521213193

Rimer, J. Thomas.   **2.2080**
Mori Ōgai / by J. Thomas Rimer. — New York: Twayne Publishers, [1975] 135 p.: port.; 21 cm. (Twayne's world leaders authors [i.e.. authors] series; TWAS 355 Japan) Includes index. 1. Mori, Ōgai, 1862-1922 — Criticism and interpretation. I. T.
PL811.O7 Z83   895.6/3/4   LC 74-28163   ISBN 0805726365

Seidensticker, Edward, 1921-.   • **2.2081**
Kafū the Scribbler; the life and writings of Nagai Kafū, 1879–1959 [by] Edward Seidensticker. — Stanford, Calif. Stanford University Press, 1965. vi, 360 p. illus., map (on lining papers) port. 24 cm. 'Bibliographical note': p. [350]-352. 1. Nagal, Kafū, 1879-1959. I. T.
PL812.A4Z88   895.634   LC 65-21492

Natsume, Sōseki, 1867-1916.   **2.2082**
The wayfarer / translated from the Japanese by Beongcheon Yu. — Detroit: Wayne State University Press, c1967. 326 p. I. T.
PL812.A8 K58x   LC 66-26974

Natsume, Sōseki, 1867-1916.   • **2.2083**
Kokoro, a novel; translated from the Japanese, and with a foreword by Edwin McClellan. Chicago, H. Regnery [c1957] vi, 248 p. 19 cm. A Gateway edition. I. T.
PL812.A8K613 1957   895.63   LC 57-10097

Natsume, Sōseki, 1867-1916.   **2.2084**
[Meian. English] Light and darkness; an unfinished novel. Translated from the Japanese, with a critical essay by V. H. Viglielmo. [1st American ed.] Honolulu, University of Hawaii Press, 1970. 397 p. 23 cm. (UNESCO collection of representative works. Japanese series.) Translation of Meian (romanized form) I. T. II. Series.
PZ3.N216 Li3 PL812.A8 M4x   895.6/3/4   LC 73-122552   ISBN 087022770X

Natsume, Sōseki, 1867-1916.   **2.2085**
Grass on the wayside (Michikusa); a novel. Translated from the Japanese, and with an introd., by Edwin McClellan. Chicago, University of Chicago Press [1969] xi, 169 p. 24 cm. (UNESCO collection of representative works. Japanese series.) Translation of Michikusa (romanized form) I. T. II. Series.
PZ3.N216Gr PL812.A8M513   895.6/3/4   LC 70-81224

Natsume, Sōseki, 1867-1916.   **2.2086**
[Sorekara. English] And then = Sorekara / Natsume Sōseki as novel; translated from the Japanese with an afterword and selected bibliography by Norma Moore Field. — Baton Rouge: Louisiana State University Press, c1978. 277, [3] p. — (UNESCO collection of representative works. Japanese series.) I. T. II. Title: Sorekara. III. Series.
PZ3.N216 An PL812.A8   PL812A8 S613.   895.6/3/4   LC 77-13175   ISBN 080710387X

Doi, Takeo, 1920-.   **2.2087**
[Soseki no shinteki sekai. English] The psychological world of Natsume Sōseki = Sōseki no shinteki sekai / by Doi Takeo; translated from the Japanese with

an introd. and synopses by William Jefferson Tyler. — Cambridge, Mass.: East Asian Research Center, Harvard University: distributed by Harvard University Press, 1976. xii, 160 p.; 24 cm. — (Harvard East Asian monographs. 68) 1. Natsume, Sōseki, 1867-1916 — Characters. 2. Natsume, Sōseki, 1867-1916 — Knowledge — Psychology. I. T. II. Series.
PL812.A8 Z613   895.6/3/4   LC 76-6889   ISBN 0674721160

McClellan, Edwin, 1925-.   **2.2088**
Two Japanese novelists; Sōseki and Tōson. — Chicago: University of Chicago Press, [1969] xii, 168 p.; 24 cm. 1. Natsume, Sōseki, 1867-1916. 2. Shimazaki, Tōson, 1872-1943. I. T.
PL812.A8 Z78   895.6/3/409   LC 76-81223

Shiga, Naoya, 1883-1971.   **2.2089**
[An'ya kōro. English] A dark night's passing / Naoya Shiga; translated by Edwin McClellan. — 1st ed. — Tokyo; New York: Kodansha International, 1976. 408 p.; 22 cm. — (UNESCO collection of representative works. Japanese series.) Translation of An'ya kōro. I. T. II. Series.
PZ3.S55594 Dar3 PL816.H5 A6x   895.6/3/4   LC 76-9351   ISBN 0870112791

Sibley, William F.   **2.2090**
The Shiga hero / William F. Sibley. — Chicago: University of Chicago Press, c1979. viii, 221 p.; 23 cm. Includes (p. 129-210) translations of ten short stories by Shiga. Includes index. 1. Shiga, Naoya, 1883-1971 — Criticism and interpretation. I. Shiga, Naoya, 1883-1971. II. T.
PL816.H5 Z846   895.6/3/4   LC 79-14120   ISBN 0226756203

Shimazaki, Tōson, 1872-1943.   **2.2091**
[Hakai. English] The broken commandment / by Shimazaki Toson; translated [from the Japanese] by Kenneth Strong. — [Tokyo]: University of Tokyo Press, [1974.] 249 p.; 24 cm. — (UNESCO collection of representative works. Japanese series.) (Japan Foundation translation series) Translation of Hakai. I. T. II. Series.
PZ3.S557 Br5 PL816.H55 H3x   895.6/3/4   LC 75-309384   ISBN 0860081109

Ryan, Marleigh Grayer.   **2.2092**
The development of realism in the fiction of Tsubouchi Shōyō / Marleigh Grayer Ryan. — Seattle: University of Washington Press, [1975] 133 p.; 23 cm. (Publications on Asia of the Institute for Comparative and Foreign Area Studies; no. 26) Includes index. 1. Tsubouchi, Shōyō, 1859-1935 — Criticism and interpretation. 2. Realism in literature I. T.
PL817.S8 Z86   895.6/3/4   LC 75-1451   ISBN 0295953829

PL821–866 1926–1945

Dazai, Osamu.   • **2.2093**
No longer human / translated by Donald Keene. — [Norfolk, Conn.] New Directions [1958] 177 p. Translation of Ningen shikkaku. I. T.
PL825.A8 N513   895.635   LC 58-9509

Dazai, Osamu, 1909-1948.   • **2.2094**
The setting sun. Translated by Donald Keene. [Norfolk, Conn., J. Laughlin, 1956] 189 p. 21 cm. (A New Directions book) I. T.
PZ3.D338Se PL825.A8S513   LC 56-13350 rev

Lyons, Phyllis I., 1942-.   **2.2095**
The saga of Dazai Osamu: a critical study with translations / Phyllis I. Lyons. — Stanford, Calif.: Stanford University Press, 1985. xi, 410 p.: ill.; 24 cm. Includes index. 1. Dazai, Osamu, 1909-1948. 2. Dazai, Osamu, 1909-1948 — Translations, English. 3. Authors, Japanese — 20th century — Biography. I. Dazai, Osamu, 1909-1948. Selections. English. 1985. II. T.
PL825.A8 Z74117 1985   895.6/34 19   LC 83-42542   ISBN 0804711976

Enchi, Fumiko, 1905-.   **2.2096**
[Onnazaka. English] The waiting years [by] Fumiko Enchi. Translated by John Bester. [1st ed.] Tokyo, Palo Alto, Calif., Kodansha International [1981] 203 p. 22 cm. Translation of Onnazaka. I. T.
PZ3.E562 Wai PL826.N3 O6x   895.6/3/5   LC 72-158644   ISBN 0870111590

Ibuse, Masuji, 1898-.   **2.2097**
Black rain / Masuji Ibuse: translated by John Bester. — Tokyo: Kodansha International, 1982, c1969. 300 p. Translation of Kuroi ame. I. T.
PL830.B8 K813   895.6/3/4   ISBN 087011364X

Itaya, Kikuo, 1898-.   **2.2098**
[Tengu dōji. English] Tengu child: stories / by Kikuo Itaya; translated by John Gardner & Nobuko Tsukui. — Carbondale [Ill.]: Southern Illinois University Press, c1983. xxv, 214 p.; ill.; 24 cm. Short stories. Translation of: Tengu dōji. I. T.
PL830.T35 T413 1983   895.6/35 19   LC 82-5876   ISBN 0809310813

Kawabata, Yasunari, 1899-1972.   **2.2099**
[Meijin. English] The master of go. Translated from the Japanese by Edward G. Seidensticker. [1st American ed.] New York, Knopf, [distributed by Random House] 1972. viii, 187 p. illus. 22 cm. Translation of Meijin. I. T.
PZ3.K1775 Mas3 PL832.A9 M4x   895.6/3/4   LC 72-2228   ISBN 0394475410

Kawabata, Yasunari, 1899-1972.   **2.2100**
[Mizuumi. English] The lake. Translated by Reiko Tsukimura. [1st ed. New York] Kodansha International; [distributed by Harper & Row, 1974] 160 p. 23 cm. Translation of Mizuumi. I. T.
PZ3.K1775 Lak3 PL832.A9 M5x   895.6/3/4   LC 73-89699   ISBN 0870112163

Kawabata, Yasunari, 1899-1972.   **2.2101**
Beauty and sadness / Yasunari Kawabata; translated from the Japanese by Howard Hibbett. — 1st American ed. — New York: Knopf: distributed by Random House, [1975] 206 p.; 22 cm. Translation of Utsukushisa to kanashimi to. I. T.
PZ3.K1775 Be3 PL832.A9 U8x   895.6/3/4   LC 74-21281   ISBN 0394460553

Kawabata, Yasunari, 1899-1972.   **2.2102**
The sound of the mountain. Translated from the Japanese by Edward M. [i.e. G.] Seidensticker. — New York: Knopf, 1970. 276 p.; 22 cm. Translation of Yama no oto (romanized form) I. T.
PZ3.K1775 So PL832.A9 Y3x   895.6/3/4   LC 77-98666

Kawabata, Yasunari, 1899-1972.   • **2.2103**
Snow country, and Thousand cranes: the Nobel Prize edition of two novels / translated from the Japanese by Edward G. Seidensticker. — New York: Knopf, 1969 [c1956, 1958] x, 175, vi, 147 p.: ill; 20 cm. (Borzoi book) Translation of Yukiguni and Sembazuru. I. Kawabata, Yasunari, 1899-1972. Sembazuru. English II. T. III. Title: Thousand cranes. IV. Title: Yukiguni. V. Title: Sembazuru.
PL832.A9 Y9x   LC 69-17239

Kinoshita, Junji, 1914-.   **2.2104**
[Kami to hito to no aida. English] Between God and man: a judgment on war crimes: a play in two parts / by Kinoshita Junji; translated, and with an introd. by Eric J. Gangloff. — Tokyo: University of Tokyo Press; Seattle: University of Washington Press, c1979. ix, 171 p., [1] leaf of plates: ill.; 24 cm. Translation of Kami to hito to no aida. Play. 1. War crime trials — Japan — Drama. I. T.
PL832.I5 K313   895/.6/2/5   LC 79-84890   ISBN 0295956704

Rimer, J. Thomas.   **2.2105**
Toward a modern Japanese theatre: Kishida Kunio [by] J. Thomas Rimer. — [Princeton, N.J.]: Princeton University Press, [1974] viii, 306 p.: illus.; 23 cm. 1. Kishida, Kunio, 1890-1954. 2. Theater — Japan — History. I. T.
PL832.I8 Z85   895.6/2/4   LC 73-16747   ISBN 0691062498

Mishima, Yukio, 1925-1970.   **2.2106**
[Akatsuki no tera. English] The temple of dawn. Translated from the Japanese by E. Dale Saunders and Cecilia Segawa Seigle. [1st American ed.] New York, Knopf; [distributed by Random House] 1973. 334 p. 22 cm. (His The sea of fertility [3]) Translation of Akatsuki no tera. I. T.
PZ3.M6878 Se vol. 3 PL833.I7 A5x   895.6/3/5   LC 73-7277   ISBN 0394466144

Mishima, Yukio, 1925-1970.   **2.2107**
Spring snow / Yukio Mishima; translated from the Japanese by Michael Gallagher. — New York: Knopf, 1972. 389 p. — (His The Sea of fertility; 1) (UNESCO collection of representative works. Japanese series.) Translation of Haru no yuki. I. T. II. Series.
PL833I7   PL833I7 H3713 1972.   895.6'3'5s   895.6'3'5   LC 74-154940   ISBN 0394442393

Mishima, Yukio, 1925-1970.   **2.2108**
[Homma. English] Runaway horses. Translated from the Japanese by Michael Gallagher. [1st American ed.] New York, Knopf; [distributed by Random House] 1973. 421 p. 22 cm. (His The sea of fertility [2]) Translation of Homma. I. T.
PZ3.M6878 Se vol. 2 PL833.I7 H6x   895.6/3/5   LC 72-11039   ISBN 0394466187

Mishima, Yukio, 1925-1970.   • **2.2109**
Confessions of a mask / translated by Meredith Weatherby. — Norfolk, Conn.: New Directions, 1958. 255 p. 21 cm. — Translation of Kamen no Kokuhaku. I. T.
PL833.I7 K15E5 1958   PL833.I7 K313 1958.   LC 58-12637   ISBN 081120118X

Mishima, Yukio, 1925-1970. • 2.2110
[Kinkakuji. English.] The temple of the golden pavilion / translated by Ivan Morris; introd. by Nancy Wilson Ross; drawings by Fumi Komatsu. — [1st American ed.] New York: Knopf, 1959. 262 p. illus. 22 cm. I. T.
PZ3.M6878 Te   PL833.I7 K5x.   895.63   LC 59-7222

Mishima, Yukio, 1925-1970. 2.2111
[Shiosai. English] The sound of waves, by Yukio Mishima [pseud.] Translated by Meredith Weatherby, drawings by Yoshinori Kinoshita. [1st ed.] New York, A. A. Knopf, 1956. 182 p. illus. 21 cm. I. T.
PL833.I7 S5x   895.63   LC 56-8911

Mishima, Yukio, 1925-1970. 2.2112
[Taiyō to tetsu. English] Sun & steel. Translated by John Bester. [1st ed. Tokyo] Kodansha International [1970] 104 p. 25 cm. Translation of Taiyō to tetsu. I. T.
PL833.I7 T313   895.6/3/5 B   LC 76-100628   ISBN 0870111175

Mishima, Yukio, 1925-1970. 2.2113
[Tennin gosui. English] The decay of the angel. Translated from the Japanese by Edward G. Seidensticker. [1st American ed.] New York, Knopf; [distributed by Random House] 1974. 236 p. 22 cm. (His The sea of fertility [4]) Translation of Tennin gosui. I. T.
PZ3.M6878 Se vol. 4 PL833.I7 T4x   895.6/3/5   LC 73-21525
   ISBN 0394466136

Mishima, Yukio, 1925-1970. 2.2114
After the banquet. Translated from the Japanese by Donald Keene. New York, Knopf, 1963, t.p. 1974. 270 p. 22 cm. Translation of Utage no Ato. I. T. II. Title: Utage no Ato.
PL833.I7 U8x   LC 62-15564

Noma, Hiroshi, 1915-. 2.2115
Zone of emptiness. [Translated from the French by Bernard Frechtman. [1st ed.] Cleveland World Pub. Co. [1956] 317p. 1. World War, 1939-1945 — Fiction I.
PL834 O6 S513

Ōoka, Shōhei, 1909-. • 2.2116
Fires on the plain. Translated from the Japanese by Ivan Morris. [1st ed.] New York, A. A. Knopf, 1957. 246 p. 22 cm. 1. World War, 1939-1945 — Fiction. I. T.
PZ4.O575Fi2 PL835.O5H613 1957   895.63   LC 57-5651

Osaragi, Jirō, 1897-1973. • 2.2117
Homecoming / translated from the Japanese by Brewster Horwitz, with an introd. by Harold Strauss. — [1st ed.] New York: Knopf, 1955 [c1954] 303 p.; 22 cm. I. T.
PZ3.O807Ho PL835.S3 K5x   LC 54-12040/R

Tanizaki, Jun'ichirō, 1886-1965. • 2.2118
Ashikari and The story of Shunkin: modern Japanese novels / by Jun–ichiro Tanizaki; translated from the Japanese by Roy Humpherson and Hajime Okita. — Westport, Conn.: Greenwood Press, 1970, c1936. iv, 172 p.: ill.; 23 cm. I. Humpherson, Roy. II. Okita, Hajime. III. T. IV. Title: The story of Shunkin.
PL839.A7 A83 1970   LC 71-98879   ISBN 0837131502

Tanizaki, Jun'ichirō, 1886-1965. 2.2119
The key. Translated from the Japanese by Howard Hibbett. New York, Knopf, 1961. 183 p. 21 cm. Translation of Kagi. I. T. II. Title: Kagi.
PL 839 A7 K12 E5 1961   LC 60-53232

Tanizaki, Jun'ichirō, 1886-1965. • 2.2120
[Sasameyuki. English] The Makioka sisters. Translated from the Japanese by Edward G. Seidensticker. [1st American ed.] New York, A. A. Knopf, 1957. 530 p. 22 cm. I. T.
PL839.A7 M3x   PZ3.T1626 Mak   895.63   LC 57-10311

Tanizaki, Junichiro. • 2.2121
Seven Japanese tales / by Junichiro Tanizaki; translated from the Japanese by Howard Hibbett. — 1st American ed. — New York: Knopf, 1963. ix, 298 p.: ill. I. T.
PL839.A7 S4x   PZ3.T1626 Se   LC 62-15574

Tanizaki, Jun'ichirō, 1886-1965. • 2.2122
[Tade kuu mushi. English] Some prefer nettles / translated from the Japanese by Edward G. Seidensticker. — [1st ed.] New York: Knopf, 1955. 202 p. illus. 21 cm. I. T.
PZ3.T1626 So   PL839.A7 T3x.   LC 55-5616

Yokomitsu, Riichi, 1898-1947. 2.2123
Love and other stories of Yokomitsu Riichi / translated and with an introd. by Dennis Keene. — [Tokyo]: University of Tokyo Press, [1974] xxii, 266 p.: port. (on lining papers); 23 cm. — (The Japan Foundation translation series) I. T.
PZ3.Y75 Lo5 PL842.O5 L6x   895.6/3/4   LC 74-81987   ISBN 0860081168

PL844–866 1945–

Abe, Kōbō, 1924-. 2.2124
[Hakootoko. English] The box man / by Kobo Abe; translated from the Japanese by E. Dale Saunders. — New York: Perigee Books, [1980] c1974. 178 p.: ill.; 20 cm. Translation of Hakootoko. Reprint of the ed. published by Knopf, New York. I. T.
PL845.B4 H313 1980   895.6/35   LC 80-14709   ISBN 0399504850

Abe, Kōbō, 1924-. 2.2125
[Suna no onna. English] The woman in the dunes. Translated from the Japanese by E. Dale Saunders. With drawings by Machi Abé. [1st American ed.] New York, Knopf, 1964. 239 p. illus. 22 cm. I. T.
PL845.B4 S8x   LC 64-15853

Abe, Kōbō, 1924-. 2.2126
[Tomodachi. English] Friends; [play] Translated from the Japanese by Donald Keene. New York, Grove Press [1969] 94 p. 21 cm. Translation of Tomodachi (romanized form) I. T.
PL845.B4 T613   895.6/2/5   LC 68-58139

Ariyoshi, Sawako, 1931-. 2.2127
The doctor's wife / Sawako Ariyoshi; translated by Wakako Hironaka and Ann Siller Kostant. — 1st ed. — Tokyo: Kodansha International, 1978. viii, 174 p.; 22 cm. I. T.
PL845.R5 H3x   LC 78-55080   ISBN 0870113372

Ariyoshi, Sawako, 1931-. 2.2128
[Kōkotsu no hito. English] The twilight years / Sawako Ariyoshi; translated by Mildred Tahara. — 1st ed. — Tokyo; New York: Kodansha International; New York, N.Y.: Distributed in the U.S. by Kodansha International/USA, through Harper & Row, 1984. 216 p.; 22 cm. (UNESCO collection of representative works. Japanese series.) Translation of: Kōkotsu no hito. I. T. II. Series.
PL845.R5 K613 1984   895/.635 19   LC 84-47687   ISBN 4770011776

Endō, Shūsaku, 1923-. 2.2129
Silence / by Shūsaku Endō:translated by William Johnston. — New York: Taplinger Pub. Co., 1980, c1969. 294 p.; 22 cm. Translation of Chimmoku. 'A Pivot book.' I. T.
PL849.N4 C5x PZ4.E563 Si 1979   895.6/3/5   LC 78-27168   ISBN 0800871863

Endō, Shūsaku, 1923-. 2.2130
[Obakasan. English] Wonderful fool [by] Shusaku Endo; a novel, translated from the Japanese by Francis Mathy. London, Owen [1974] 237 p. 19 cm. Translation of Obakasan. I. T.
PL849.N4 O2x PZ4.E563 Wo   895.6/3/5   LC 74-162335   ISBN 0720604923

Endō, Shūsaku, 1923-. 2.2131
[Samurai. English] The samurai: a novel / Shusaku Endo; translated from the Japanese by Van C. Gessel. — 1st U.S. ed. — New York, N.Y.: Harper & Row: Kodansha International, c1982. 272 p.; 22 cm. Translation of: Samurai. Reprint. Originally published: London: Peter Owen, 1982. 1. Hasekura, Tsunenaga, 1571-1622 — Fiction. I. T.
PL849.N4 S2413 1982   895.6/35 19   LC 82-47851   0068598526

Kaikō, Takeshi, 1930-. 2.2132
[Natsu no yami. English] Darkness in summer. Translated by Cecilia Segawa Seigle. [1st American ed.] New York, Knopf; [distributed by Random House] 1973. 210 p. 22 cm. Translation of Natsu no yami. I. T.
PZ4.K1432 Dar3 PL855.A32 N3x   895.6/3/5   LC 73-7299   ISBN 039448441X

Ōe, Kenzaburō, 1935-. 2.2133
[Kojinteki na taiken. English] A personal matter. New York, Grove Press [1968] ix, 214 p. 21 cm. Translation of Kojinteki na taiken (romanized form) I. T.
PL858.E14 K6x   LC 68-22007

Ōe, Kenzaburō, 1935-. 2.2134
Teach us to outgrow our madness: four short novels / by Kenzaburō Ōe; translated and with an introd. by John Nathan. 1st ed. — New York: Grove Press: distributed by Random House, 1977. xxv, 261 p.; 22 cm. I. T.
PZ4.O287 Te 1977 PL858.E14 T4x   895.6/3/5   LC 76-54582
   ISBN 080210133X

Tsushima, Yūko.   **2.2135**
[Chōji. English] Child of fortune / Yūko Tsushima; translated by Geraldine
Harcourt. — 1st English ed. — Tokyo; New York: Kodansha International,
1983. x, 161 p.; 22 cm. Translation of: Chōji. I. T.
PL862.S76 C413 1983   895.6/35 19   *LC* 82-48168   *ISBN*
0870115324

Yamazaki, Masakazu, 1934-.   **2.2136**
[Zeami. English] Mask and sword: two plays for the contemporary Japanese
theater / by Yamazaki Masakazu; translated by J. Thomas Rimer. — New
York: Columbia University Press, 1980. 221 p., [4] leaves of plates: ill.; 24 cm.
(Modern Asian literature series.) Translation of Zeami and Sanetomo shuppan.
1. Zeami, 1363-1443 — Drama. 2. Minamoto, Sanetomo, 1192-1219 —
Drama. I. Yamazaki, Masakazu, 1934- Sanetomo shuppan. English. 1980.
II. T. III. Series.
PL865.A57 Z2813   895.6/25 19   *LC* 79-26162   *ISBN* 0231049323

Yasuoka, Shōtarō, 1920-.   **2.2137**
[Selections. English. 1984] A view by the sea / Yasuoka Shōtarō; translated by
Kären Wigen Lewis. — New York: Columbia University Press, 1984. xviii,
196 p.; 22 cm. — (Modern Asian literature series) A novella plus five short
stories translated from Japanese. 1. Yasuoka, Shōtarō, 1920- — Translations,
English. I. T.
PL865.A7 A24 1984   895.6/35 19   *LC* 83-21081   *ISBN*
0231058721

PL901–988 Korean

Lee, Peter H., 1929-.   **2.2138**
Songs of flying dragons: a critical reading / Peter H. Lee. — Cambridge, Mass.:
Harvard University Press, 1975. xvi, 314 p.: geneal. table; 24 cm. (UNESCO
collection of representative works. Korean series.) (Harvard-Yenching Institute
monograph series; v. 22) Includes index. 1. Yongbi ŏch'ŏn'ga. I. Yongbi
ŏch'ŏn'ga. English. 1975. II. T. III. Series.
PL961.23.Y63 L4   895.7/1/2   *LC* 73-92866   *ISBN* 0674820754

Lee, Peter H., 1929- comp.   **2.2139**
Flowers of fire: twentieth–century Korean stories / edited by Peter H. Lee. —
Honolulu: University Press of Hawaii, [1974] xxv, 486 p.; 23 cm. 'An East-West
Center book.' 1. Short stories, English — Translations from Korean. 2. Short
stories, Korean — Translations into English. I. T.
PZ1.L52 Fl PL980.6   PL980.6 L4.   895.7/3/01   *LC* 73-90853
    ISBN 0824803027

Lee, Peter H., 1929- comp.   **2.2140**
Poems from Korea; a historical anthology. Compiled and translated by Peter H.
Lee. Foreword by Norman Holmes Pearson. [Rev. ed.] Honolulu, University
Press of Hawaii [1974] 196 p. 23 cm. (UNESCO collection of representative
works. Korean series.) First published in 1964 under title: Anthology of Korean
poetry from the earliest era to the present. 1. Korean poetry — Translations
into English. 2. English poetry — Translations from Korean. I. T. II. Series.
PL984.E3 L4 1974   895.7/1/008   *LC* 73-80209   *ISBN* 0824802632

PL1001–3208 Chinese

PL1001–2245 Chinese Language

Chao, Yuen Ren, 1892-.   **2.2141**
Aspects of Chinese sociolinguistics: essays / by Yuen Ren Chao; selected and
introduced by Anwar S. Dil. — Stanford, Calif.: Stanford University Press,
1976. xiv, 415 p.; 24 cm. — (Language science and national development)
1. Chinese language — Addresses, essays, lectures. I. T.
PL1071.C476   PL1071 C437.   301.2/1   *LC* 75-44900   *ISBN*
0804709092

Karlgren, Bernhard, 1889-.   • **2.2142**
Sound and symbol in Chinese. Rev. ed. [Hong Kong] University Press 1962.
99p. (Chinese companion series, 1) 1. Chinese language I. T. II. Series.
PL1073 K373 1962

Karlgren, Bernhard, 1889-.   • **2.2143**
The Chinese language: an essay on its nature and history / By Bernhard
Karlgren. — New York: Ronald press, 1949. vi, 122 p.; 22 cm. Translation of

Fran Kinas Sprakvarld by the author with assistance of A. F. P. Hulsewé.
1. Chinese language I. T.
PL1091.K32   *LC* 49-11524 *

DeFrancis, John, 1911-.   **2.2144**
The Chinese language: fact and fantasy / John DeFrancis. — Honolulu:
University of Hawaii Press, c1984. x, 330 p.: ill.; 24 cm. Includes index.
1. Chinese language — Writing 2. Chinese language — Reform 3. Chinese
language — Social aspects. 4. Chinese language — Psychological aspects. I. T.
PL1171.D38 1984   495.1 19   *LC* 84-8546   *ISBN* 0824808665

Hsia, Tao-tai, 1921-.   • **2.2145**
China's language reforms. New Haven, Institute of Far Eastern Publications,
Yale University, c1956. 200 p. 24 cm. (Mirror series A, 21) 1. Chinese language
— History. 2. Chinese language — Transliteration I. T. II. Series.
PL 1171 H87 1956   *LC* 57-871

Language reform in China: documents and commentary / edited   **2.2146**
with an introd. by Peter J. Seybolt and Gregory Kuei–Ke
Chiang.
White Plains, N.Y.: M. E. Sharpe, 1979. xiii, 410 p.; 24 cm. 1. Chinese
language — Reform — Addresses, essays, lectures. I. Seybolt, Peter J.
II. Chiang, Gregory Kuei-Ke.
PL1175.L36   495.1/1   *LC* 76-4302   *ISBN* 0873320816

Cheng, I-li.   **2.2147**
[Ying Hua ta tz'u tien] = A new English–Chinese dictionary / first edited by
Zheng Yi Li and Cao Cheng Xiu; second revised edition edited by Zheng Yi Li
... [et al.]. — 2nd rev. ed. — Beijing: Commerical Press; New York: Wiley,
c1984. vii, 1613 p.; 27 cm. Title in Chinese characters. 1. English language —
Dictionaries — Chinese. I. Ts'ao, Che'eng-hsiu. II. T. III. Title: New
English-Chinese dictionary.
PL1455.C584 1984b   423/.951 19   *LC* 85-211292   *ISBN*
0471808962

Chi, Wen-shun.   **2.2148**
Chinese–English dictionary of contemporary usage / compiled by Wen–shun
Chi; with the assistance of John S. Service, Mei–hsia Huang, Chi–ping Chen. —
Berkeley: University of California Press, c1977. xix, 484 p.; 23 cm. Includes
index. 1. Chinese language — Dictionaries — English. 2. Chinese language —
Government jargon. I. T.
PL1455.C59   495.1/3/21   *LC* 73-90663   *ISBN* 0520026551

Mathews, R. H. (Robert Henry).   • **2.2149**
Mathews' Chinese–English dictionary. Rev. American ed. Cambridge, Mass.
Harvard University Press 1966. 1226p. 1. Chinese language — Dictionaries —
English I. T.
PL1455 M34 1966

Shih yung Han Ying tz'u tien.   **2.2150**
[Hsin Han Ying tz'u tien / Ting Kuang–hsün chu pien] = A New Chinese–
English dictionary / editor in chief, Ding Guang–xun. — Seattle: University of
Washington Press, 1985. 44, 1401 p.; 20 cm. Originally published: Shih yung
Han Ying tz'u tien. Parallel title in Chinese characters with author statement.
Includes index. 1. Chinese language — Dictionaries — English. I. Ting, K. H.
II. T. III. Title: New Chinese-English dictionary.
PL1455.S463 1985   495.1/321 19   *LC* 85-40978   *ISBN* 0295963360

PL2250–3208 Chinese Literature

Modern Chinese literature in the May Fourth Era / edited by   **2.2151**
Merle Goldman; sponsored by the Social Science Research
Council.
Cambridge: Harvard University Press, 1977. viii, 464 p.; 25 cm. (Harvard East
Asian series. 89) The chapters are drawn from the conference which was held at
Endicott House in Dedham, Mass., Aug. 26-30, 1974 and from a workshop that
preceded it at the Harvard East Asian Research Center. 1. Chinese literature
— 20th century — Congresses. I. Goldman, Merle. II. Social Science
Research Council (U.S.) III. Harvard University. East Asian Research Center.
IV. Series.
PL2253.M6   895.1/09/005   *LC* 76-47652   *ISBN* 0674579100

Studies in Chinese literary genres / edited by Cyril Birch.   **2.2152**
Berkeley: University of California Press, [1974] x, 398 p.; 24 cm. Papers
presented at a research conference held in Bermuda in Jan. 1967 and sponsored
by the Committee on Studies of Chinese Civilization of the American Council of
Learned Societies. Includes index. 1. Chinese literature — History and
criticism — Congresses. 2. Literary form — Congresses. I. Birch, Cyril, 1925-
ed. II. American Council of Learned Societies. Committee on Studies of
Chinese Civilization.
PL2253.S8   895.1/09   *LC* 77-157825   *ISBN* 0520020375

Gálik, Marián.   **2.2153**
The genesis of modern Chinese literary criticism (1917–1930) / Marián Gálik; [translation, Peter Tkáč]. — London: Curzon Press; Totowa, N.J.: Rowman and Littlefield, 1980. 349 p.; 25 cm. — ([Asian and African studies]; v. 16) Includes index. 1. Chinese literature — 20th century — History and criticism. I. T. II. Series.
PL2262.G3x   895.1/09/005 19   *LC* 80-505544   *ISBN* 0847660818

Hawkes, David.   **2.2154**
Classical, modern, and humane: essays in Chinese literature / [by] David Hawkes. — Hong Kong: Chinese University, 1986. Collected essays since 1961. I. T.
PL2263.H3x

Liu, Hsieh, ca. 465-ca. 522.   • **2.2155**
The literary mind and the carving of dragons: a study of thought and pattern in Chinese literature; translated with an introd. and notes by Vincent Yu–chung Shih. New York: Columbia University Press, 1959. xlvi, 298 p.; 24 cm. (Records of civilization, sources and studies. no. 58) Includes index. 1. Chinese literature — History and criticism. I. Shih, Yu-chung, 1902- II. T. III. Series.
PL2263.L5x   895.109   *LC* 58-13768

Liu, Wu-chi, 1907-.   • **2.2156**
An introduction to Chinese literature /Liu Wu–Chi. — Bloomington: Indiana University Press, 1966. vii, 321 p.: ill.; 24 cm. Includes bibliographical references. 1. Chinese literature — History and criticism. I. T.
PL2265.L5   895.109   *LC* 66-12729

Lee, Leo Ou-fan.   **2.2157**
The romantic generation of modern Chinese writers. — Cambridge, Mass.: Harvard University Press, 1973. xiv, 365 p.: illus.; 25 cm. — (Harvard East Asian series. 71) 'Revised version of ... [the author's] dissertation at Harvard University.' 1. Authors, Chinese 2. Chinese literature — 20th century — History and criticism. I. T. II. Series.
PL2277.L4 1973   895.1/0/914   *LC* 73-75058   *ISBN* 0674779304

✓ **Watson, Burton, 1925-.**   • **2.2158**
Early Chinese literature / by Burton Watson. — New York: Columbia University Press, 1962. 304 p.; 23 cm. 1. Chinese literature — History and criticism. I. T.
PL2280.W3   *LC* 62-17552   *ISBN* 0231086717 pbk

Hsia, Tsi-an, 1916-1965.   **2.2159**
The gate of darkness; studies on the leftist literary movement in China. — Seattle: University of Washington Press, [1968] xxix, 266 p.; 25 cm. — (Far Eastern and Russian Institute. Publications on Asia, no. 17) 1. Chinese literature — 20th century — History and criticism. I. T.
PL2302.H72   895.1/09005   *LC* 68-8510

Průšek, Jaroslav.   **2.2160**
The lyrical and the epic: studies of modern Chinese literature / by Jaroslav Průšek; edited by Leo Ou–fan Lee. — Bloomington: Indiana University Press, c1980. xiii, 268 p.; 24 cm. — (Studies in Chinese literature and society.) 1. Chinese literature — 20th century — History and criticism — Addresses, essays, lectures. I. Lee, Leo Ou-fan. II. T. III. Series.
PL2302.P7   895.1/5/09   *LC* 80-7491   *ISBN* 0253102839

After Mao: Chinese literature and society, 1978–1981 / edited   **2.2161**
by Jeffrey C. Kinkley.
Cambridge, Mass.: Council on East Asian Studies, Harvard University: Distributed by Harvard University Press, 1985. xiv, 345 p.; 23 cm. (Harvard East Asian monographs. 115) (Harvard contemporary China series. 1) 'Essays originally presented at St. John's University, New York City, during an international research conference convened under the auspices of the National Endowment for the Humanities, 28-31 May 1982'—Pref. Includes index. 1. Chinese literature — 20th century — History and criticism — Congresses. I. Kinkley, Jeffrey C., 1948- II. National Endowment for the Humanities. III. Series. IV. Series: Harvard contemporary China series. 1
PL2303.A28 1985   895.1/5/09 19   *LC* 84-23185   *ISBN* 0674008855

Literature of the Hundred Flowers / edited by Hualing Nieh.   **2.2162**
New York: Columbia University Press, 1981-. v. <2 >; 24 cm. — (Modern Asian literature series.) 1. Chinese literature — 20th century — History and criticism — Addresses, essays, lectures. 2. Communism and literature — Addresses, essays, lectures. 3. Chinese literature — 20th century 4. China — Intellectual life — Addresses, essays, lectures. I. Nieh, Hua-ling, 1926- II. Series.
PL2303.L55   895.1/5/09   *LC* 80-36748

PL2307–2357 Poetry. Drama

Liu, James J. Y.   • **2.2163**
The art of Chinese poetry / by James J. Y. Liu. — Chicago: University of Chicago Press, 1962. xii, 164 p. 1. Chinese poetry — History and criticism I. T.
PL2307.L57 1962a   *LC* 62-7475   *ISBN* 0226486869

Liu, James J. Y.   **2.2164**
The interlingual critic: interpreting Chinese poetry / James J.Y. Liu. — Bloomington: Indiana University Press, c1982. xix, 132 p.; 24 cm. Includes index. 1. Chinese poetry — History and criticism. 2. Criticism I. T.
PL2307.L572 1982   895.1/1/009 19   *LC* 81-47010   *ISBN* 0253330300

Owen, Stephen, 1946-.   **2.2165**
The great age of Chinese poetry: the High T'ang / Stephen Owen. — New Haven [Conn.]: Yale University Press, c1981. xv, 440 p.; 26 cm. Includes index. 1. Chinese poetry — T'ang dynasty, 618-907 — History and criticism. I. T.
PL2321.O94   895/.1/13   *LC* 80-141   *ISBN* 0300023677

Owen, Stephen.   **2.2166**
The poetry of the early T'ang / Stephen Owen. — New Haven: Yale University Press, 1977. xv, 455 p. 1. Chinese poetry — T'ang dynasty, 618-907 — History and criticism. I. T.
PL2321.O95   PL2321 O95.   895.1/1/209   *LC* 77-3884   *ISBN* 0300021038

Liu, James J. Y.   **2.2167**
Major lyricists of the Northern Sung, A.D. 960–1126, by James J. Y. Liu. — [Princeton, N.J.]: Princeton University Press, [1974] 215 p.; 23 cm. Includes lyrics in English and Chinese. 1. Tz'u — History and criticism. I. T.
PL2343.L5   895.1/1/04   *LC* 73-10290   *ISBN* 0691062595

Shih, Chung-wen.   **2.2168**
The golden age of Chinese drama, Yüan 'tsa-chü' / [by] Chung–wen Shih. Princeton; Guildford: Princeton University Press, 1976. xvi, 312 p., 8 plates: ill., facsims., music; 23 cm. Index. 1. Chinese drama — History and criticism. I. T.
PL2357   895.1/2/409   *LC* 74-2979   *ISBN* 0691062706

Dolby, William.   **2.2169**
A history of Chinese drama / William Dolby. — New York: Barnes & Noble, 1976. x, 327 p., [4] leaves of plates: ill., map; 24 cm . — 1. Chinese drama — History and criticism. 2. Theater — China I. T.
PL2357.D65 1976   895.1209   *ISBN* 0064917363

PL2415–2442 Fiction

Chinese narrative: critical and theoretical essays; Andrew H.   **2.2170**
Plaks, editor; contributors, Kenneth J. DeWoskin ... [et al.].
Princeton, N.J.: Princeton University Press, c1977. xii, 365 p. 'Revisions or rewritings of papers originally presented at the Princeton Conference on Chinese Narrative Theory held at Princeton University on January 21 and 22, 1974.' 1. Chinese fiction — History and criticism — Congresses. 2. Narration (Rhetoric) — Congresses. I. Plaks, Andrew Henry, 1945- II. Dewoskin, Kenneth Joel III. Princeton Conference on Chinese Narrative Theory, Princeton University, 1974.
PL2415.C48   PL2415 C48.   895.1/3/009   *LC* 76-45907   *ISBN* 0691063281

Lu, Hsün, 1881-1936.   **2.2171**
[Chung-kuo hsiao shuo shih lüeh. English] A brief history of Chinese fiction [by] Lu Hsun. [Translated by Yang Hsien–Yi and Gladys Yang] Hazelwood, Mo.: Great Wall Press, 1973. 462 p. illus. 23 cm. Translation of Chung-kuo hsiao shuo shih lüeh. Reprint of the 1959 ed. published by Foreign Languages Press, Peking, which was issued as no. 7 of China knowledge series. 1. Chinese fiction — History and criticism. I. T.
PL2415.C513 1973   895.1/3/009   *LC* 73-870   *ISBN* 0913466077

✓ **Hsia, Chih-tsing, 1921-.**   • **2.2172**
The classic Chinese novel; a critical introduction, by C. T. Hsia. — New York: Columbia University Press, 1968. xi, 413 p.; 23 cm. — (Companions to Asian studies.) 1. Chinese fiction — History and criticism. I. T. II. Series.
PL2415.H8   895.1/3/009   *LC* 68-18997

Hanan, Patrick.   **2.2173**
The Chinese vernacular story / Patrick Hanan. — Cambridge, Mass.: Harvard University Press, 1981. viii, 276 p.; 24 cm. — (Harvard East Asian series. 94) Includes index. 1. Short stories, Chinese — History and criticism. 2. Chinese fiction — History and criticism. 3. Folk literature, Chinese — History and criticism. I. T. II. Series.
PL2417.H3   895.1/30109   *LC* 80-17840   *ISBN* 0674125657

Hegel, Robert E., 1943-.   2.2174
The novel in seventeenth–century China / Robert E. Hegel. — New York: Columbia University Press, 1981. xx, 336 p.: ill.; 23 cm. Includes index. 1. Chinese fiction — Ming dynasty, 1368-1644 — History and criticism. 2. Chinese fiction — Ch'ing dynasty, 1644-1912 — History and criticism. I. T.
PL2436.H4   895.1/3409 19   LC 80-24105   ISBN 0231049285

The Chinese novel at the turn of the century / edited by Milena   2.2175
Doleželová–Velingerová.
Toronto; Buffalo: University of Toronto Press, c1980. viii, 240 p., [6] leaves of plates: ill.; 24 cm. — (Modern East Asian studies; 1) Includes index. 1. Chinese fiction — Ch'ing dynasty, 1644-1912 — History and criticism — Addresses, essays, lectures. I. Doleželová-Velingerová, Milena, 1932- II. Series.
PL2437.C54   895/.1/3/03   LC 79-22783   ISBN 0802054730

Hsia, Chih-tsing, 1921-.   • 2.2176
A history of modern Chinese fiction / by C. T. Hsia. — 2d ed. — New Haven: Yale University Press, 1971. xvi, 701 p.; 21 cm. First ed. published in 1961 under title: A history of modern Chinese fiction, 1917-1957. Includes index. 1. Chinese fiction — 20th century — History and criticism. I. T.
PL2442.H8 1971   895.1/3/509   LC 79-108225   ISBN 0300014627

Link, E. Perry (Eugene Perry), 1944-.   2.2177
Mandarin ducks and butterflies: popular fiction in early twentieth–century Chinese cities / E. Perry Link, Jr. — Berkeley: University of California Press, c1981. x, 313 p.: ill.; 24 cm. Includes index. 1. Chinese fiction — 20th century — History and criticism. I. T.
PL2442.L5   895.1/35/09   LC 80-15149   ISBN 0520041119

PL2450–2659 Collections

Legge, James, 1815-1897. ed. and tr.   • 2.2178
The Chinese classics; with a translation, critical and exegetical notes, prolegomena, and copious indexes. — Hong Kong: Hong Kong University Press, [1970, c1960] 5 v.: fold. col. maps, port.; 28 cm. Texts in Chinese and English. The text reprinted here is that of the last Oxford editions (v. 1-2 of the 2d ed. and v. 3-5 of the original ed.), with added concordances and corrections. The work was originally planned for 7 v. The I ching and Li chi, which were intended to complete it, were published in Sacred books of the East, v. 16 and 27-28 respectively. 1. Chinese literature 2. Chinese literature — Translations into English. 3. English literature — Translations from Chinese. 4. China — Maps. 5. China — History I. T.
PL2461.R43 1970   LC 76-15551

Shchutskiĭ, IUlian Konstantinovich, 1897-.   2.2179
[Kitaĭskaia klassicheskaia Kniga peremen. English] Researches on the I Ching / by Iulian K. Shchutskii; translated by William L. MacDonald and Tsuyoshi Hasegawa with Hellmut Wilhelm; with an introduction by Gerald W. Swanson. — Princeton, N.J.: Princeton University Press, c1979. lxvi, 255 p.; 21 cm. (Bollingen series. 62.2) Translation of Kitaĭskaia klassicheskiia Kniga peremen. Includes index. 1. I ching. I. T. II. Series.
PL2464.Z7 S4713 1979   299/.5128/2   LC 78-63600   ISBN 0691099391

Wilhelm, Hellmut, 1905-.   2.2180
Heaven, earth, and man in The book of changes: seven Eranos lectures / Hellmut Wilhelm. Seattle: University of Washington Press, c1977. xi, 230 p.; 24 cm. (Publications on Asia of the Institute for Comparative and Foreign Area Studies; no. 28) 1. I ching. I. I ching. II. T.
PL2464.Z7 W55   299/.5128/2   LC 76-7801   ISBN 0295955163

I ching. English.   • 2.2181
The I ching; or, Book of changes. The Richard Wilhelm translation rendered into English by Cary F. Baynes. Foreword by C. G. Jung. Pref. to the 3d ed. by Hellmut Wilhelm. [3d ed.] [Princeton, N.J.] Princeton University Press [1967] lxii, 740 p. 21 cm. (Bollingen series, 19) I. Wilhelm, Richard, 1873-1930. tr. II. Baynes, Cary F. tr. III. T. IV. Title: Book of changes.
PL2478.D8 1967   299/.514/82   LC 67-24740

Shih ching. English.   • 2.2182
The book of songs / translated from the Chinese by Arthur Waley. — New York: Grove Press, 1960. 358 p.;20 cm. — (An Evergreen book; E-209) 1. Chinese poetry — Translations into English. 2. English poetry — Translations from Chinese. I. Waley, Arthur. tr. II. T.
PL2478.F85 1960   LC 60-6341

Trees on the mountain: an anthology of new Chinese writing /   2.2183
edited by Stephen C. Soong and John Minford.
Hong Kong: Chinese University Press, c1984. 396 p.: ill.; 27 cm. — (Renditions books) Poems in English and Chinese. Translated from the Chinese. 1. Chinese literature — 20th century 2. Chinese poetry — 20th century — Translations into English. 3. English poetry — 20th century — Translations from Chinese. I. Sung, Ch'i. II. Minford, John. III. Series.
PL2513.T74   ISBN 962201335X

Ch'u tz'u. English.   2.2184
The songs of the south: an ancient Chinese anthology of poems by Qu Yuan and other poets / translated, annotated, and introduced by David Hawkes. — Harmondsworth, Middlesex, England; New York, N.Y., U.S.A.: Penguin Books, 1985. 352 p.: maps; 20 cm. (Penguin classics) Translation of: Ch'u tz'u. I. Hawkes, David. II. T.
PL2521.C524 1985   895.1/11 19   LC 86-110526   ISBN 0140443754

Birch, Cyril, 1925- ed.   • 2.2185
Anthology of Chinese literature, compiled and edited by Cyril Birch. Associate editor, Donald Keene. New York, Grove Press [1965-. v. 24 cm. (UNESCO collection of representative works. Chinese series.) 1. Chinese literature — Translations into English. 2. English literature — Translations from Chinese. I. Keene, Donald. joint ed. II. T. III. Series.
PL2658.E1 B5   895.108   LC 65-14202

Literature of the People's Republic of China / edited by Kai–yu   2.2186
Hsu, co-editor, Ting Wang, with the special assistance of
Howard Goldblatt, Donald Gibbs, and George Cheng.
Bloomington: Indiana University Press, c1980. xiv, 976 p.; 24 cm. — (Chinese literature in translation.) Includes indexes. 1. Chinese literature — 20th century — Translations into English. 2. English literature — Translations from Chinese. I. Hsu, Kai-yu, 1922- II. Series.
PL2658.E1 L55   895.1/08/005   LC 78-24807   ISBN 0253160154

Revolutionary literature in China: an anthology / selected and   2.2187
introd. by John Berninghausen and Ted Huters.
White Plains [N. Y.]: M. E. Sharpe, 1976. 103 p.: ill., music, ports. 1. Chinese literature — Translations into English 2. English literature — Translations from Chinese I. Huters, Ted II. Pai, Chih-ang
PL2658.E1 R496   PL2658El R496.   LC 76-51581   ISBN 0873321030

Stubborn weeds: popular and controversial Chinese literature   2.2188
after the Cultural Revolution / edited by Perry Link.
Bloomington: Indiana University Press, c1983. 292 p.; 24 cm. — (Chinese literature in translation.) Ser. statement from jacket. 1. Chinese literature — 20th century — Translations into English. 2. English literature — Translations from Chinese. I. Link, E. Perry (Eugene Perry), 1944- II. Series.
PL2658.E1 S78 1983   895.1/08/005 19   LC 82-48268   ISBN 0253355125

PL2658.E3 Poetry

The Columbia book of Chinese poetry: from early times to the   2.2189
thirteenth century / translated and edited by Burton Watson.
New York: Columbia University Press, 1984. 385 p.: ill.; 25 cm. (Translations from the Oriental classics.) Includes index. 1. Chinese poetry — Translations into English. 2. English poetry — Translations from Chinese. I. Watson, Burton, 1925- II. Series.
PL2658.E3 C66 1984   895.1/1/008 19   LC 83-26182   ISBN 0231056826

Graham, A. C. (Angus Charles) ed. and tr.   • 2.2190
Poems of the late T'ang / translated [from the Chinese] with an introduction by A. C. Graham. — [1st ed.] reprinted. — Harmondsworth; New York [etc.]: Penguin, 1977. 175 p.; 19 cm. — (UNESCO collection of representative works. Chinese series.) (The Penguin classics) Reprint (with additional pref.) of the 1965 ed. published by Penguin, Baltimore. 1. Chinese poetry — T'ang dynasty, 618-907 — Translations into English. 2. English poetry — Translations from Chinese. I. T. II. Series.
PL2658.E3 G7 1977   895.1/1/308   LC 78-317993   ISBN 0140441573

Hsu, Kai-yu, 1922-.   • 2.2191
Twentieth century Chinese poetry, an anthology. Translated and edited by Kai-yu Hsu. [1st ed.] Garden City, N.Y., Doubleday, 1963. 434 p. 22 cm. 1. Chinese poetry — Translations into English. 2. English poetry — Translations into Chinese. I. T.
PL2658.E3 H8   895.11082   LC 63-7725

The jade mountain; a Chinese anthology, being Three hundred   • 2.2192
poems of the T'ang dynasty, 618–906. Translated by Witter
Bynner from the texts of Kiang Kang-hu.
New York, Knopf, 1929. xxxvii, 279 p. ill. 22 cm. 1. Chinese poetry — Translations into English. I. Kiang, Kang-hu, 1883- II. Title: Three hundred poems of the T'ang dynasty.
PL 2658 E3 J22 1929   LC 29-25006 rev.2

Payne, Robert, 1911-.   • 2.2193
The white pony; an anthology of Chinese poetry from the earliest times to the present day, newly translated. London G. Allen & Unwin [1949] 356p.

1. Chinese poetry — Translations into English 2. English poetry — Translations from Chinese I. T.
PL2658 E3 P3

Sunflower splendor: three thousand years of Chinese poetry /   2.2194
co–edited by Wu–chi Liu and Irving Yucheng Lo.
1st ed. — Garden City, N.Y.: Anchor Books, 1975. lxiv, 630 p.; 22 cm. Includes index. 1. Chinese poetry — Translations into English. 2. English poetry — Translations from Chinese. I. Liu, Wu-chi, 1907- II. Lo, Irving Yucheng, 1922-
PL2658.E3 S84 1975   PL2658E3 S84 1975.   895.1/1/008   LC
74-25136   ISBN 0385097166

Watson, Burton, 1925- comp.   2.2195
Chinese rhyme–prose; poems in the fu form from the Han and Six Dynasties periods. Translated and with an introd. by Burton Watson. — New York: Columbia University Press, 1971. 128 p.; 23 cm. — (UNESCO collection of representative works. Chinese series.) 1. Chinese poetry — Translations into English. 2. English poetry — Translations from Chinese. 3. Fu I. T. II. Series.
PL2658.E3 W34   895.1/1/2   LC 75-159674   ISBN 0231035535

✓ **Waley, Arthur. tr.**   • 2.2196
Translations from the Chinese, by Arthur Waley, illustrated by Cyrus LeRoy Baldridge. — New York: A. A. Knopf, 1941. 10 p., l., 3-325 p., 1 l.: illus., col. plates.; 28 cm. Issued in case. 'The translations ... were made over twenty years ago ... In arranging the poems for this illustrated edition I have corrected a certain number of mistakes. But on the whole I have reprinted the poems as they stood in 1918 and 1919 [under titles] A hundred and seventy Chinese poems, and More translations from the Chinese.'—Pref. 1. Chinese poetry — Translations into English. 2. English poetry — Translations from Chinese. I. T.
PL2658.E3 W3x   895.110822   LC 41-4061

PL2658.E5–.E8 Drama. Fiction

Eight Chinese plays from the thirteenth century to the present /   2.2197
translated with an introd. by William Dolby.
New York: Columbia University Press, 1978. 164 p.; 23 cm. 1. Chinese drama — Translations into English. 2. English drama — Translations from Chinese. I. Dolby, A. W. E.
PL2658.E5 E37 1978   PL2658E5 E37 1978.   895.1/2/008   LC
77-15601   ISBN 0231044887

Twentieth–century Chinese drama: an anthology / edited by   2.2198
Edward M. Gunn.
1st Midland book ed. — Bloomington: Indiana University Press, 1983. xxiii, 517 p.; 25 cm. — (Chinese literature in translation.) 1. Chinese drama — 20th century — Translations into English. 2. English drama — Translations from Chinese. I. Gunn, Edward M. II. Title: 20th century Chinese drama. III. Series.
PL2658.E5 T88 1983   895.1/25/08 19   LC 82-47923   ISBN
0253361095

Classical Chinese tales of the supernatural and the fantastic: 2.2199
**selections from the third to the tenth century / edited by Karl
S.Y. Kao.**
Bloomington: Indiana University Press, c1985. x, 406 p.: maps; 25 cm. (Chinese literature in translation.) 1. Fantastic fiction, Chinese — Translations into English. 2. Fantastic fiction, English — Translations from Chinese. I. Kao, Karl S. Y. II. Series.
PL2658.E8 C56 1985   895.1/30876/08 19   LC 84-47966   ISBN
0253313759

Feng, Meng–lung, 1574-1646. comp.   • 2.2200
[Ku chin hsiao shuo English] Stories from a Ming collection. Translations of Chinese short stories published in the seventeenth century, by Cyril Birch. New York, Grove Press [196-? c1958] 205 p. illus. 21 cm. (UNESCO collection of representative works. Chinese series.) (An Evergreen book, E-473.) Translation of selections from Ku chin hsiao shuo (romanized form) 1. Short stories, Chinese — Translations into English. 2. Short stories, English — Translations from Chinese. I. Birch, Cyril, 1925- tr. II. T. III. Series.
PL2658.E8 F4x   LC 68-44187

The Golden casket: Chinese novellas of two milennia /   • 2.2201
**translated by Christopher Levenson from Wolfgang Bauer's and
Herbert Franke's German version of the original Chinese with
an introduction by Herbert Franke.**
1st ed. — New York: Harcourt, Brace & World, c1964. 391 p.: ill. 'A Helen and Kurt Wolff book.' I. Franke, Herbert, 1914- II. Bauer, Wolfgang.
PL2658.E8 G6x   LC 64-18278

✓ **Hsia, Chih-tsing, 1921- comp.**   2.2202
Twentieth–century Chinese stories. Edited by C. T. Hsia, with the assistance of Joseph S. M. Lau. New York, Columbia University Press, 1971. xiv, 239 p. 23

cm. (Companions to Asian studies.) 1. Short stories, Chinese — Translations into English. 2. Short stories, English — Translations from Chinese. I. T. II. Series.
PL2658.E8 H8x   895.1/3/01   LC 72-173986   ISBN 0231035896
ISBN 023103590X

Isaacs, Harold Robert, 1910- comp.   2.2203
Straw sandals; Chinese short stories, 1918–1933. Edited by Harold R. Isaacs. Foreword by Lu Hsün. — Cambridge: MIT Press, [1974] lxxiii, 444 p.: port.; 21 cm. 1. Short stories, English — Translations from Chinese. 2. Short stories, Chinese — Translations into English. I. T.
PL2658.E8 I8x   895.1/3/01   LC 73-12853   ISBN 0262090147

Modern Chinese stories and novellas, 1919–1949 / edited by   2.2204
Joseph S. M. Lau, C. T. Hsia, and Leo Ou–Fan Lee.
New York: Columbia University Press, 1981. xxvii, 578 p., [3] leaves of plates: ill.; 26 cm. — (Modern Asian literature series.) Includes index. 1. Chinese fiction — 20th century — Translations into English. 2. English fiction — Translations from Chinese. I. Lau, Joseph S. M., 1934- II. Hsia, Chih-tsing, 1921- III. Lee, Leo Ou-fan. IV. Series.
PL2658.E8 M6   895.1/301/08 19   LC 80-27572   ISBN
0231042027

Roses and thorns: the second blooming of the Hundred Flowers   2.2205
in Chinese fiction, 1979–80 / Perry Link, editor.
Berkeley: University of California Press, c1984. x, 346 p.; 24 cm. 1. Chinese fiction — 20th century — Translations into English. 2. English fiction — Translations from Chinese. I. Link, E. Perry (Eugene Perry), 1944-
PL2658.E8 R6 1984   895.1/35 19   LC 83-9147   ISBN 0520049799

Snow, Edgar, 1905-1972. ed.   • 2.2206
Living China; modern Chinese short stories, compiled and edited by Edgar Snow. With an introd. by the editor and an essay on modern Chinese literature by Nym Wales. — New York: Reynal & Hitchcock, [1937] 360 p.: port.; 23 cm. 1. Short stories, Chinese — Translation into English. 2. Short stories, English — Translation from Chinese. I. T.
PZ1.S664 Li5 PL2658.E8   PL2658.E8 S5x.   895.1/3/01   LC
37-27319

Traditional Chinese stories: themes and variations / edited by Y.   2.2207
W. Ma and Joseph S. M. Lau, editor.
New York: Columbia University Press, 1978. xxvi, 603 p.; 26 cm. Includes index. 1. Chinese fiction — Translations into English. 2. English fiction — Translations from Chinese. I. Ma, Y. W. (Yau-Woon), 1940- II. Lau, Joseph S. M., 1934-
PL2658.E8 T7   895.1/3/01   LC 77-21133   ISBN 023104058X.
ISBN 0231040598 pbk

The Unbroken chain: an anthology of Taiwan fiction since 1926   2.2208
/ edited by Joseph S.M. Lau.
Bloomington: Indiana University Press, c1983. xvi, 279 p.; 25 cm. — (Chinese literature in translation.) 1. Chinese fiction — Taiwan — Translations into English. 2. Chinese fiction — 20th century — Translations into English. 3. English fiction — Translations from Chinese. I. Lau, Joseph S. M., 1934- II. Series.
PL2658.E8 U52 1983   895.1/35/080951249 19   LC 83-47904
ISBN 0253361621

Wang, Chi-chên, 1899- comp.   • 2.2209
Contemporary Chinese stories. Translated by Chi–chên Wang. — New York: Greenwood Press, [1968, c1944] ix, 242 p.; 23 cm. 1. Short stories, Chinese — Translations into English. 2. Short stories, English — Translations from Chinese. I. T.
PL2658.E8 W28 1968   895.1/3/01   LC 69-14137

Wang, Chi-chên, 1899- tr.   • 2.2210
Traditional Chinese tales, translated by Chi–chen Wang. New York, Greenwood Press [1968, c1944] 225 p. 23 cm. 1. Tales — China 2. Chinese literature — Translations into English. 3. English literature — Translations from Chinese. I. T.
PL2658.E8 W3 1968   398.2/0951   LC 69-14138

Yang, Hsien-i.   • 2.2211
The courtesan's jewel box: Chinese stories of the Xth–XVIIth centuries / [Translated by Yang Hsien–yi and Gladys Yang]. — Peking: Foreign Languages Press, 1957. 553 p. 1. Short stories, Chinese — Translations into English. 2. Short stories, English — Translations from Chinese. I. Yang, Gladys. II. T.
PL2658.E8 Y3   LC 57-41973

PL2661–3208 Individual Authors, by Period

PL2661–2678 To 960

Cooper, Arthur D., comp.   2.2212
Li Po and Tu Fu; poems selected and translated with an introd. and notes by Arthur Cooper. Chinese Calligraphy by Shui Chien–Tung. [Harmondsworth, Eng.] Penguin Books [1973] 249 p. 19 cm. (Penguin Classics) 1. Li, Po, 701-762. 2. Tu, Fu, 712-770. I. Li, Po, 701-762. II. Tu, Fu, 712-770. III. T.
PL2671.C6   895.1/1/308   *LC* 73-175444

Waley, Arthur.   • 2.2213
The life and times of Po Chü-i, 772–846 A. D. — London, G. Allen & Unwin [1949] 238 p. port., fold. map, geneal. table. 25 cm. 1. Pai, 772-846. I. T.
PL2674.W3x   928.951   *LC* 50-13630

Hung, William, 1893-.   • 2.2214
Tu Fu, China's greatest poet / by William Hung. — New York: Russell & Russell, [1969, c1952] x, 300 p.: map; 25 cm. The text includes selections from Tu Fu's poems translated by the author into English free verse. 1. Tu, Fu, 712-770. I. T.
PL2675.H87 1969   *LC* 75-77672   *ISBN* 0846213451

Wang, Wei, 701-761.   2.2215
The poetry of Wang Wei: new translations and commentary / Pauline Yu. — Bloomington: Indiana University Press, c1980. xiii, 274 p.; 25 cm. — (Chinese literature in translation.) English and Chinese. Includes indexes. I. Yu, Pauline, 1949- II. T. III. Series.
PL2676.A285   895.1/13   *LC* 79-3623   *ISBN* 0253177723

PL2679–2698 960–1644

Li, Ch'ing-chao, 1081-ca. 1141.   2.2216
Li Ch'ing-chao, complete poems / translated and edited by Kenneth Rexroth and Ling Chung. — New York: New Directions, c1979. 118 p.; 21 cm. 1. Li, Ch'ing-chao, 1081-ca. 1141. 2. Poets, Chinese — Biography. I. Rexroth, Kenneth, 1905- II. Chung, Ling, 1945- III. T.
PL2682.A27 1979   895.1/14 19   *LC* 79-15596   *ISBN* 0811207447

Egan, Ronald C., 1948-.   2.2217
The literary works of Ou-yang Hsiu (1007–72) / Ronald C. Egan. — Cambridge [Cambridgeshire]; New York: Cambridge University Press, 1984. 269 p.; 24 cm. (Cambridge studies in Chinese history, literature, and institutions.) Includes translations from the Chinese. Includes index. 1. Ou-yang, Hsiu, 1007-1072 — Criticism and interpretation. I. T. II. Series.
PL2683.Z5 E3 1984   895.1/14 19   *LC* 84-1740   *ISBN* 052125888X

Su, Shih, 1036-1101.   • 2.2218
Su Tung-p'o: selections from a Sung dynasty poet. Translated and with an introd. by Burton Watson. New York, Columbia University Press, 1965. x, 139 p. 21 cm. (UNESCO collection of representative works. Chinese series.) I. Watson, Burton, 1925- ed. and tr. II. T. III. Series.
PL2685.A28   895.11   *LC* 65-13619

Tung, Chieh-yüan, fl. 1189-1208.   2.2219
[Hsi hsiang chi. English] Master Tung's Western chamber romance = Tung Hsi–hsiang chu–kung–tiao: a Chinese chantefable / translated from the Chinese and with an introd. by Li-li Ch'en. — Cambridge [Eng.]; New York: Cambridge University Press, 1976. xxviii, 238 p.; 24 cm. — (Cambridge studies in Chinese history, literature and institutions) Translation of Tung Chieh-yüan Hsi hsiang chi. Includes index. I. Ch'en, Li-li. II. T. III. Title: Western chamber romance.
PL2687.T9 H813 1976   895.1/1/4   *LC* 75-12469   *ISBN* 0521208718

Kuan, Han-ch'ing, ca. 1210-ca. 1298.   • 2.2220
Selected plays of Kuan Han–ching / translated by Yang Hsien–yi and Gladys Yang; [with a foreword by Wang Chi–ssu]. — Shanghai: New Art and Literature Publishing House, 1958. 227 p., [8] leaves of plates: ill.; 22 cm. I. T.
PL2689.A27   *LC* 61-39292

Lo, Kuan-chung, ca. 1330-ca. 1400.   • 2.2221
[San Kuo chih Yen-i. English.] Romance of the three kingdoms: San Kuo chih yen–i / Lo Kuan–Chung; translated by C. H. Brewitt–Taylor. — Rutland, Vt.; Tokyo: C.E. Tuttle, 1959. 2 v.: map (on lining papers), 23 cm. I. Lo, Kuan-chung, ca. 1330-ca. 1400. San Kuo Chih Yen-i. English. 1959. II. Brewitt-Taylor, C. H. III. T.
PL 2690 S19   *LC* 59-10407

Lo, Kuan-chung, ca. 1330-ca. 1400.   2.2222
[San kuo chih yen i English] Three kingdoms: China's epic drama / by Lo Kuan–chung; translated from the Chinese and edited by Moss Roberts. — 1st ed. — New York: Pantheon Books, c1976. xxv, 318 p.: ill.; 25 cm. Abridged translation of San kuo chih yen i. Includes index. 1. China — History — Three kingdoms, 220-265 — Fiction. I. Roberts, Moss, 1937- II. T.
PL2690.S3 E53 1976   895.1/3/4   *LC* 76-9607   *ISBN* 0394407229

Wang, Shih-fu, fl. 1295-1307.   • 2.2223
[Hsi hsiang chi English] The romance of the western chamber. Translated by S.I. Hsiung. New York, Columbia University Press, 1968. xliv, 280 p. illus. 19 cm. (UNESCO collection of representative works. Chinese series.) Generally ascribed to Wang. Earlier it was believed that Wang wrote the first four parts and Kwang Han-ch'ing wrote the Continuation. The theme is based on the short story by Yuan Cheng, a poet of the eighth century. Cf. p. xxii and xxxviii. Half title: (Hsi hsiang chi) Hsiung Shih-i i (romanized form) A reprint of the 1936 ed., with a new introd. by C.T. Hsia. 'Reissued for the Columbia College program of translations from the oriental classics.' Appendix (p. 271-[281]):— The story of Ts'ui Ying-ying, by Yüan Chên (779-831 A.D.) I. Kuan, Han-ch'ing, ca. 1210-ca. 1298. Hsü Hsi hsiang chi. II. Yüan, Chen, 779-831. Hui chen chi III. Hsiung, Shih-i, 1902- tr. IV. T. V. Title: Western chamber. VI. Series.
PL2693.H75E5 1968   895.1/2/4   *LC* 68-22412

Shui hu chuan. English.   2.2224
Outlaws of the marsh / by Shi Nai'an and Luo Guanzhong; translated by Sidney Shapiro. — Beijing: Foreign Languages Press; Bloomington: Indiana University Press, c1981. 2 v.: ill.; 22 cm. Translation of Shui hu chuan. I. Shih, Nai-an, ca. 1290-ca. 1365. II. Lo, Kuan-chung, ca. 1330-ca. 1400. III. Shapiro, Sidney. IV. T.
PL2694.S5 E5 1981   895.1/34 19   *LC* 80-8665   *ISBN* 025312574X

T'ang, Hsien-tsu, 1550-1616.   2.2225
[Mu tan t'ing. English] The peony pavilion = Mudan ting / Tang Xianzu; translated by Cyril Birch. — Bloomington: Indiana University Press, c1980. xv, 343 p.; 24 cm. — (Chinese literature in translation.) Play. Includes index. I. T. II. Title: Mudan ting. III. Series.
PL2695.M8 E5 1980   895.1/24   *LC* 79-9631   *ISBN* 0253357233

Wu, Ch'eng-en, ca. 1500-ca. 1582.   • 2.2226
Monkey. Translated from the Chinese by Arthur Waley. — London: Allen & Unwin, [1942] 305, [1] p.; 21 cm. 1. Hsüan-tsang, ca. 596-664 — Fiction. I. T.
PL2697.H75 E59 1942   895.13   *LC* a 43-273

Wu, Ch'eng-en, ca. 1500-ca. 1582.   2.2227
The journey to the west / translated and edited by Anthony C. Yu. — Chicago: University of Chicago Press, 1977-1980. 4 v. I. Yu, Anthony C., 1938- II. T.
PL2697.H75 E596 1977   895.1/3/4   *LC* 75-27896   *ISBN* 0226971457 vol. 1

Hsiao-hsiao-shêng.   2.2228
[Chin P'ing Mei tz'ŭ hua. English] The Golden Lotus; a translation, from the Chinese original, of the novel Chin P'ing Mei, by Clement Egerton. London, Routledge & K. Paul [1972] 4 v. 23 cm. I. Egerton, Clement, tr. II. T.
PZ3.H85923 Go3 PL2698.H73   895.1/3/4   *LC* 73-154469   *ISBN* 0710073496

PL2699–2832 1644–1949

Wu tse t'ien ssu ta ch'i an. English. Selections.   2.2229
Celebrated cases of Judge Dee = Dee goong an: an authentic eighteenth-century Chinese detective novel / translated and with an introd. and notes by Robert van Gulik. Unabridged, slightly corr. version. — New York: Dover Publications, 1976. xxiii, 237 p., [9] leaves of plates: ill.; 22 cm. 1. Ti, Jen-chieh, 629-700— Fiction. I. Gulik, Robert Hans van, 1910-1967. II. T. III. Title: Dee goong an.
PZ3.W953 Ce4 PL2699.W8x   895.1/3/4   *LC* 76-5059   *ISBN* 0486233375

K'ung, Shang-jen, 1648-1718.   2.2230
[T'ao hua shan. English] The peach blossom fan = T'ao–hua–shan / by K'ung Shang–jên; translated by Chen Shih–hsiang and Harold Acton, with the collaboration of Cyril Birch. — Berkeley: University of California Press, c1976. xxi, 312 p.: ill.; 24 cm. I. T.
PL2717.U47 T313 1976   895.1/2/4   *LC* 74-27294   *ISBN* 0520029283

Li, Ju-chen, ca. 1763-ca. 1830.   • 2.2231
Flowers in the mirror / by Li Ju–chen; translated and edited by Lin Tai–yi. — Berkeley: University of California Press, 1965. 310 p.; 24 cm. Translation of Ching hua yüan. I. Lin, Tai-yi, 1926- II. T.
PL2718.I15C513 1965   *LC* 65-28004

P'u, Sung-ling, 1640-1715.   • 2.2232
[Liao chai chih i English] Strange stories from a Chinese studio. Translated and annotated by Herbert A. Giles. New York, Dover Publications [1969] xxiii,

488 p. 22 cm. Translation of Liao chai chih i. I. Giles, Herbert Allen, 1845-1935. tr. II. T.
PZ3.P9603 St7 PL2722.U2   895.1/3/4   *LC* 73-94319   *ISBN* 0486223957

Ts'ao, Hsüeh-ch'in, ca. 1717-1763.   **2.2233**
The story of the stone: a novel in five volumes / by Cao Xueqin; translated by David Hawkes. — Bloomington: Indiana University Press, [1979-. v.; 24 cm. — (Chinese literature in translation.) Translation of Hung lou meng. I. Hawkes, David. II. T. III. Series.
PZ3.T783 St 1979 PL2727.S2   895.1/3/4   *LC* 78-20279   *ISBN* 0253192668

Wu, Ching-tzu, 1701-1754.   **2.2234**
[Ju lin wai shih English] The scholars. Translated by Yang Hsien–yi and Gladys Yang. With a foreword by C.T. Hsia. Illus. by Cheng Shih–fa. New York, Grosset and Dunlap [1972] 692 p. illus. 21 cm. (Grosset's universal library, UL 263) Translation of Ju lin wai shih. I. T.
PZ3.W95 Sc4 PL2732.U22   895.1/3/4   *LC* 73-151941   *ISBN* 0448002639

Ting, Ling, 1904-.   **2.2235**
[T'ai yang chao tsai Sang-kan ho shang. English] The sun shines over the Sanggan River / Ding Ling; [translated by Yang Xianyi and Gladys Yang]. — 1st ed. — Beijing, China: Foreign Languages Press: Distributed by China Publications Centre, 1984. 379 p.; 19 cm. (Modern Chinese literature library.) Translation of: T'ai yang chao tsai Sang-kan ho shang. I. Yang, Hsien-i. II. Yang, Gladys. III. T. IV. Series.
PL2747.P5 T313 1984   *LC* 84-183690   *ISBN* 0835110087

Feuerwerker, Yi-tsi Mei, 1928-.   **2.2236**
Ding Ling's fiction: ideology and narrative in modern Chinese literature / Yi-tsi Mei Feuerwerker. — Cambridge, Mass.: Harvard University Press, 1982. xii, 196 p.: port.; 25 cm. — (Harvard East Asian series. 98) Includes index. 1. Ting, Ling, 1904- — Criticism and interpretation. I. T. II. Series.
PL2747.P5 Z65 1982   895.1/35 19   *LC* 82-3022   *ISBN* 0674207653

Ch'ien, Chung-shu, 1911-.   **2.2237**
[Wei ch'eng. English] Fortress besieged / by Ch'ien Chung–shu; translated by Jeanne Kelly and Nathan K. Mao. — Bloomington: Indiana University Press, c1979. xxix, 377 p.; 24 cm. — (Chinese literature in translation.) Translation of Wei ch'eng. I. T. II. Series.
PZ3.C435 Fo 1979 PL2749.C8 W4x   895.1/3/5   *LC* 78-24846   *ISBN* 0253165180

Huters, Theodore.   **2.2238**
Qian Zhongshu / by Theodore Huters. — Boston: Twayne Publishers, c1982. 187 p.; 21 cm. — (Twayne's world authors series. TWAS 660) Includes index. 1. Ch'ien, Chung-shu, 1911- — Criticism and interpretation. I. T. II. Series.
PL2749.C8 Z69 1982   895.1/8509 19   *LC* 82-888   *ISBN* 0805765034

Lu, Hsün, 1881-1936.   **2.2239**
Silent China; selected writings of Lu Xun. Edited and translated by Gladys Yang. — London, New York, Oxford University Press, 1973. xii, 196 p. 21 cm. — (A Galaxy book, GB 405) I. Yang, Gladys. ed. II. T.
PL2754.S5 A29 1973   895.1/8/509   *LC* 74-159806   *ISBN* 0192811509

Lu, Hsün, 1881-1936.   **2.2240**
[Na han. English] The complete stories of Lu Xun / translated by Yang Xianyi and Gladys Yang. — Bloomington: Indiana University Press; Beijing: Foreign Languages Press, c1981. x, 295 p.; 22 cm. Translation of: Na han and P'ang huang. 1. Lu, Hsün, 1881-1936 — Translations, English. I. Lu, Hsün, 1881-1936. P'ang huang. English. 1981. II. T.
PL2754.S5 A294 1981   895.1/35 19   *LC* 81-47585   *ISBN* 0253313961

Lu Xun and his legacy / edited with an introduction by Leo Ou–fan Lee.   **2.2241**
Berkeley: University of California Press, c1985. xix, 324 p.; 24 cm. Papers from a conference held at the Asilomar Conference Center, Pacific Grove, Calif., on Aug. 23-28, 1981. 1. Lu, Hsün, 1881-1936 — Criticism and interpretation — Congresses. I. Lee, Leo Ou-fan.
PL2754.S5 Z7567 1985   895.1/8509 19   *LC* 83-18048   *ISBN* 0520051580

Lyell, William A.   **2.2242**
Lu Hsün's vision of reality / William A. Lyell, Jr. — Berkeley: University of California Press, c1976. x, 355 p.: ill.; 25 cm. Includes index. 1. Lu, Hsün, 1881-1936. 2. Authors, Chinese — Biography. I. T.
PL2754.S5 Z759   895.1/8509 B 19   *LC* 74-30527   *ISBN* 0520029402

Pollard, David E.   **2.2243**
A Chinese look at literature; the literary values of Chou Tso–jên in relation to the tradition, by David E. Pollard. Berkeley, University of California Press [c1973] xi, 183 p. 23 cm. 1. Chou, Tso-jen, 1885-1967. 2. Chinese literature — History and criticism. I. T.
PL2754.T75 Z8   895.1/09   *LC* 72-97732   *ISBN* 0520024095

Pa, Chin, 1905-.   **2.2244**
[Chia. English] The family / by Pa Chin [i.e. F. Li]; [translated by Sidney Shapiro; ill. by Liu Tan–Chai]. — 3d ed. — Peking: Foreign Languages Press, [1985?]. 284 p., [7] leaves of plates: ill.; 22 cm. Translation of Chia. The 1st vol. of the trilogy, Turbulent stream; the 2d vol. is Spring; the 3d, Autumn. I. T.
PZ3.L612 Fam 1978 PL2780.F4 C5 1985x   895.1/3/5   *LC* 79-105565

Pa, Chin, 1905-.   **2.2245**
Family [by] Pa Chin. Introd. by Olga Lang. — Garden City, N.Y., Anchor Books, 1972. xxvi, 329 p. 18 cm. Translation of Chia. The 1st vol. of the trilogy, Turbulent stream; the 2d vol. is Spring; the 3d, Autumn. I. T.
PZ3.L612 Fam4 PL2780.F4 C5x   895.1/3/5   *LC* 72-79433   *ISBN* 0385057873

Lang, Olga.   • **2.2246**
Pa Chin and his writings: Chinese youth between the two revolutions / by Olga Lang. — Cambridge, Mass.: Harvard University Press, 1967. x, 402 p.: ill.; 25 cm. — (Harvard East Asian series. 28) I. T. II. Series.
PL2780.F4 Z82   895./1/35   *LC* 67-17314

Nieh, Hua-ling, 1926-.   **2.2247**
Shen Ts'ung-wen, by Hua–ling Nieh. New York, Twayne Publishers [c1972] 139 p. 21 cm. (Twayne's world authors series, TWAS 237, China) 1. Shen, Ts'ung-wen, 1902- I. T.
PL2801.N18 Z64   895.1/3/5   *LC* 70-187637

Mao, Tun, 1896-.   **2.2248**
[Tzu yeh. English] Midnight [by] Mao Tun. Peking, Foreign Languages Press, 1957. [Washington, Center for Chinese Research Materials, Association of Research Libraries, 1970] 524 p. on [265] l. illus. 28 cm. Translation of Tzu yeh. I. T.
PZ3.S54723 Mi4 PL2801.N2 T9x   895.1/3/5   *LC* 72-5088

Lao, She, 1899-1966.   **2.2249**
[Lo t'o Hsiang-tzu. English] Rickshaw = the novel Lo–t'o Hsiang Tzu / by Lao She [i.e. Shu Ch'ing–ch'un]; translated by Jean M. James; [maps by William C. Stanley]. — Honolulu: University Press of Hawaii, c1979. xi, 249 p.: maps; 22 cm. I. T. II. Title: Lo-to Hsiang Tzu.
PZ3.S5619 Rh PL2804.C5 L6x   895.1/3/5   *LC* 79-10658   *ISBN* 0824806166

Two writers and the cultural revolution: Lao She and Chen Jo– hsi / edited by George Kao.   **2.2250**
Hong Kong: Chinese University Press; Seattle: distributed by University of Washington Press, c1980. 212 p.: ill.; 28 cm. (A Renditions book) Includes Lao She's pre-1949 output and Chen's writings in English and/or Chinese, together with essays about the two writers. 1. Lao, She, 1899-1966 — Criticism and interpretation. 2. Ch'en, Jo-hsi — Criticism and interpretation. 3. China — Politics and government — 1949-1976 I. Kao, George, 1912- II. Lao, She, 1899-1966. III. Ch'en, Jo-hsi.
PL2804.C5 Z92   895.1/35 19   *LC* 80-116596   *ISBN* 9622012027

PL2832.5– 1949–

Hsiao, Chün, 1908-.   • **2.2251**
Village in August, by T'ein Chün [pseud.] Introd. by Edgar Snow. New York, Smith & Durrell [1942] 313 p. (China's great war novel.) 1. China — History — 1937-1945 — Fiction. I. T.
PL2862.I3x   895.135   *LC* 42-11707

Bishop, John Lyman.   • **2.2252**
The colloquial short story in China; a study of the Sanyen collections. Cambridge, Harvard University Press, 1956. xi, 144 p. 26 cm. (Harvard-Yenching Institute studies, v. 14) Includes bibliographies. 1. Short stories, Chinese — History and criticism. I. T. II. Title: Sanyen collections. III. Series.
PL2937.B5   895.1309   *LC* 56-7211

PL3030–3032 Provincial, Local Literature

Symposium on Taiwan Fiction (1979: University of Texas at Austin)   **2.2253**
Chinese fiction from Taiwan: critical perspectives / edited by Jeannette L. Faurot. — Bloomington: Indiana University Press, c1980. 272 p.; 25 cm.

(Studies in Chinese literature and society.) Includes index. 1. Chinese fiction — Taiwan — History and criticism — Congresses. 2. Chinese fiction — 20th century — History and criticism — Congresses. I. Faurot, Jeannette L. II. T. III. Series.
PL3031.T3 S97 1979　　895.1/35/09951249　　LC 80-7490　　ISBN 0253124093

Gunn, Edward M. 2.2254
Unwelcome muse: Chinese literature in Shanghai and Peking, 1937–1945 / Edward M. Gunn, Jr. — New York: Columbia University Press, 1980. x, 330 p.: ill.; 24 cm. (Studies of the East Asian Institute, Columbia University) Includes index. 1. Chinese literature — China — Shanghai — History and criticism. 2. Chinese literature — China — Peking — History and criticism. 3. Chinese literature — 20th century — History and criticism. I. T.
PL3032.S48 G8　　895.1/09/005　　LC 79-19754　　ISBN 0231047304

PL3301–4961 Other Asian Languages and Literatures

Essays on literature and society in Southeast Asia: political and 2.2255
sociological perspectives / edited by Tham Seong Chee.
[S.l.]: Ohio University, 1981. xii, 360 p.; 24 cm. Title on spine: Literature and society in Southeast Asia. 1. Literature and society — Asia, Southeastern. 2. Asia, Southeastern — Literatures — History and criticism. I. Tham, Seong Chee. II. Title: Literature and society in Southeast Asia.
PL3508.05.E87x 1981　　LC 81-941975

Mi-la-ras-pa, 1040-1123. • 2.2256
The hundred thousand songs of Milarepa; the life–story and teaching of the greatest poet–saint ever to appear in the history of Buddhism. Translated and annotated by Garma C. C. Chang. — New Hyde Park, N.Y.: University Books, [1962] 2 v. (xvii, 730 p.): front.; 25 cm. Title also in Tibetan. I. Chang, Ch'eng-ch'i. ed. and tr. II. T.
PL3748.M5 M413 1962　　895.41　　LC 62-8255

Htin Aung, U, 1909-. • 2.2257
Burmese drama: a study, with translations, of Burmese plays / Maung Htin Aung. — London: Oxford University Press, 1937. xx, 266 p. 1. Burmese drama I. T.
PL3971.H7　　LC 38-10511 rev

Mosel, James Norman, 1918-. • 2.2258
Trends and structure in contemporary Thai poetry: with translation and bibliography. — Ithaca, N.Y.: Southeast Asia Program, Dept. of Far Eastern Studies, Cornell University, 1961. 53 p.; 28 cm. — (Data paper (Cornell University. Southeast Asia Program) no. 43) I. T. II. Series.
PL4202M63　　LC 62-4684

Interpretative translations of Thai poets / by M.R. Seni 2.2259
Pramoj.
4th ed. — [S.l.]: Thai Watana Panich, 1978. 48 p.; 26 cm. Text in Thai and English. 1. Thai poetry 2. Thai poetry — Translations into English. I. Seni Pramoj, M. R., 1905-
PL 4206 I62 1965

PL4371–4383 Vietnamese

Durand, Maurice M. 2.2260
[Introduction à la littérature vietnamienne. English] An introduction to Vietnamese literature / Maurice M. Durand and Nguyen Tran Huan; translated from the French by D.M. Hawke. — New York: Columbia University Press, 1985. xiii, 213 p.; 22 cm. Translation of: Introduction à la littérature vietnamienne. Includes index. 1. Vietnamese literature — History and criticism. I. Nguyễn, Trần Huân. II. T.
PL4378.D813 1985　　895.9/22/09 19　　LC 84-12754

Vienamese literature / translated and edited by Khac Vien 2.2261
Nguyen and Ngoc Huu.
Hanoi: Foreign Language Publishing House, 1983. 1 v. I. Nguyễn, Khac Viên. II. Ngoc Huu.
PL4378.V5x

The Heritage of Vietnamese poetry / edited and translated by 2.2262
Huỳnh Sanh Thông.
New Haven: Yale University Press, 1969. xlv, 303 p.; 24 cm. Includes index. 1. Vietnamese poetry — Translations into English. 2. English poetry — Translations from Vietnamese. I. Huỳnh, Sanh Thông, 1926-
PL4382.E3 H47　　895.9/2/21008　　LC 78-17092　　ISBN 0300022646

Nguyễn, Ngoc Bích. comp. 2.2263
A thousand years of Vietnamese poetry / edited by Nguyễn Ngoc Bích; translated by Nguyễn Ngoc Bích, with Burton Raffel and W. S. Merwin. — 1st ed. — New York: Knopf, 1975, c1974. xx, 210, iii, p. 1. Vietnamese poetry — Translations into English. 2. English poetry — Translations from Vietnamese. I. T.
PL4382.E3 N4 1975　　895.9/22/1008　　LC 74-7752　　ISBN 0394494225

PL4641–4664 Kannada

Ramanujan, A. K., 1929- comp. 2.2264
Speaking of Śiva; translated with an introduction by A. K. Ramanujan. — Harmondsworth: Penguin, 1973. 199 p.; 19 cm. — (The Penguin classics) 1. Kannada poetry — Translations into English. 2. English poetry — Translations from Kannada. I. T.
PL4663.E3 R32　　894/.814/1108　　LC 73-165848　　ISBN 0140442707

PL4711–4723 Malayalam

George, K. M. 2.2265
A survey of Malayalam literature [by] K. M. George. — London: [s.n.], 1968. xii, 354 p.; 22 cm. 1. Malayalam literature — History and criticism. I. T.
PL4718.G37 1968　　894/.812/09　　LC 76-902552

Krishna Chaitanya, 1918-. 2.2266
A history of Malayalam literature. [New Delhi] Orient Longman [1971] 596p. 1. Malayalam literature — History and criticism I. T.
PL4718 N32

Basheer, Vaikom Muhammad, 1910-. 2.2267
'Me grandad 'ad an elephant!': three stories of Muslim life in South India / by Vaikom Muhammad Basheer; translated from the Malayalam by R.E. Asher and Achamma Coilparampil Chandersekaran. — Edinburgh: Edinburgh University Press, 1980. xviii, 204 p.; 19 cm. I. T.
PL4718.9.B33 A23　　894/.81236 19　　LC 81-100415　　ISBN 0852243863

Śaṅkarakkuruppá, Ji., 1901-1978. 2.2268
Selected poems of G. Sankara Kurup. Translated from the original Malayalam by A. K. Ramanujan [and others. Calcutta, Dialogue Calcutta; distributors: Stechert-Hafner, New York, c1969] [16] p. 23 cm. (Dialogue Calcutta, anthology 11) I. Ramanujan, A. K., 1929- tr. II. T.
PL4718.9.S315 A6 1969　　LC 72-911898

Sivaśaṅkarapilla, Takali, 1914-. • 2.2269
Chemmeen; a novel. Translated by Narayana Menon. Introd. by Santha Rama Rau. London: V. Gollancz, 1962. 228 p. 22 cm. (UNESCO collection of representative works. Indian series.) Translation of Cemmīn. I. T. II. Title: Cemmīn. III. Series.
PL4718.9.S57 C5x　　LC 62-9921

Sivaśaṅkarapilla, Takali, 1914-. 2.2270
[Paramārthaṅṅal. English] The unchaste [by] T. Sivasankara Pillai. [Translated by M. K. Bhaskaran. Delhi] Hind Pocket Books [1971] 112 p. 19 cm. Translation of Paramārthaṅṅal. 'Orient paperbacks, E-79.' I. Bhaskaran, M. K., tr. II. T.
PZ4.S6193 Un PL4718.9.S57 P3x　　LC 71-925340

PL4751–4763 Tamil

Zvelebil, Kamil. 2.2271
The smile of Murugan on Tamil literature of South India. — Leiden: Brill, 1973. xvi, 378 p., 3 p. of photos., fold. l.; 25 cm. 1. Tamil literature — History and criticism. I. T.
PL4758.Z9　　894/.811/09　　LC 73-163643　　ISBN 9004035915

Zvelebil, Kamil. 2.2272
Tamil literature / Kamil Veith Zvelebil. — Wiesbaden: Harrassowitz, 1974. viii, 316 p.: ill.; 24 cm. (A History of Indian literature; v. 10: Dravidian literatures; fasc. 1) 1. Tamil literature — History and criticism. I. T.
PL4758.Z93 1974　　894/.811/09　　LC 75-331957　　ISBN 3447015829

Beck, Brenda E. F. 2.2273
The three twins: the telling of a South Indian folk epic / Brenda E.F. Beck. — Bloomington: Indiana University Press, c1982. 248 p.: ill.; 24 cm. Includes index. 1. Epic poetry, Tamil — History and criticism. 2. Oral tradition — India — Tamil Nadu. I. T.
PL4758.2.B4 1982　　894/.811103 19　　LC 80-8841　　ISBN 0253360145

Jeyakāntan, 1934-.   2.2274
Game of cards and other stories [by] Jayakanthan. English rendering: K. Diraviam. [1st ed.] Madras, Asian Book Co. [1972] 148 p. 19 cm. I. Diraviam, K. II. T.
PZ4.J4255 Gam3 PL4758.9.J3 G3x   *LC* 72-907503

Kampar, 9th cent.   • 2.2275
The Ayodhya canto of the Ramayana, as told by Kamban. Translated from the Tamil by C. Rajagopalachari. London: Allen & Unwin, [1961] 127 p. 23 cm. (UNESCO collection of representative works. Indian series.) I. Rajagopalachari, C. (Chakravarti), 1878-1972. II. T. III. Title: The Ramayana. IV. Series.
PL4758.9.K27 R353   *LC* 63-5069

Nammālvār.   2.2276
[Tiruvāymoli English. Selections] Hymns for the drowning: poems for Visnu / by Nammālvār; translated from Tamil by A.K. Ramanujan. — Princeton, N.J.: Princeton University Press, c1981. xviii, 176 p.; 23 cm. — (Princeton library of Asian translations.) Translation from: Tiruvāymoli and Tiruviruttam. Includes index. 1. Vishnu (Hindu deity) — Poetry. I. Ramanujan, A. K., 1929- II. Nammālvār. Tiruviruttam. English. Selections. III. T. IV. Series.
PL4758.9.N3155 A27   294.5/95 19   *LC* 81-47151   *ISBN* 069106492X

Patmanāpan, Nīla, 1938-.   2.2277
The generations [by] Neela Padmanabhan. Translated by Ka Naa Subramanyam. — Delhi: Hind Pocket Books, [1972] 192 p.; 23 cm. 'Orient paperbacks, E-98.' Translation of Talaimuraikal. I. Subramanyam, K. N., 1912- tr. II. T.
PZ4.P1235 Ge PL4758.9.P218 T3x   891/.43/37   *LC* 72-907504

Pāratiyār, 1882-1921.   2.2278
The voice of Bharati: being English renderings from the Tamil originals of poems by Subramanya Bharati. — 4th ed. — Calcutta: Bharathi Tamil Sangham, 1982. xiii, 159 p.; 23 cm. — (Bharati centenary series; 4) Revised version of the voice of a poet, 3rd ed., 1975. I. T.
PL4758.9.P29x 1982

PSaratiÿsar, 1882-1921.   2.2279
[Kannan pāttu. English] Songs to Krishna / Subramania Bharati; transcreated from the Tamil by David Bunce. — Calcutta: A Writers Workshop publication, c1973. 40 p.; 22 cm. 'A Writers Workshop saffronbird book.' 1. Krishna (Hindu deity) — Poetry. I. Bunce, David, 1948- tr. II. T.
PL4758.9.S8437 K3313   894/.811/15   *LC* 74-901125

Kuruntokai. English. Selections.   • 2.2280
The interior landscape; love poems from a classical Tamil anthology. Translated by A. K. Ramanujan. Bloomington, Indiana University Press [1967] 125 p. 22 cm. (UNESCO collection of representative works. Indian series) 1. Tamil poetry — Translations into English. 2. English poetry — Translations from Tamil. I. Ramanujan, A. K., 1929- tr. II. T.
PL4760.E3 K8   894/.8/11110803   *LC* 67-25136

Poets of the Tamil anthologies: ancient poems of love and war /   2.2281
[translated by] George L. Hart III.
Princeton, N.J.: Princeton University Press, c1979. 212 p.; 25 cm. — (Princeton library of Asian translations.) 1. Tamil poetry — To 1500 — Translation into English. 2. English poetry — Translations from Tamil. I. Hart, George L. II. Series.
PL4762.E3 P6   894/.811/11   *LC* 79-83993   *ISBN* 0691064067

Swaminathan, K.   2.2282
The plough and the stars; stories from Tamilnad. Editors: K. Swaminathan, Periaswami Thooran [and] M. R. Perumal Mudaliar. [s.l.]: Madras, 1963. xxxii, 205 p. 22 cm. (Modern Indian literature) 1. Short stories, Tamil — Translations into English. I. T.
PL 4762 E8 S97 1963

PL4771–4784 Telugu

Venkata Sitapati, Gidugu, 1885-1969.   2.2283
History of Telugu literature / G.V. Sitapati. — New Delhi: Sahitya Akademi, 1968. xii, 314 p.; 22 cm. 1. Telugu literature — History and criticism. I. T.
PL4780.V423   894/.827/09 19   *LC* 70-903289

PL5001–7101 Oceanic Languages and Literatures

PL5071–5139 Indonesian. Malay

Teeuw, A.   2.2284
Modern Indonesian literature, by A. Teeuw. — 's-Gravenhage: Martinus Nijhoff, 1967. xv, 309 p.: 14 p. of photos.; 24 cm. — (Koninklijk Instituut voor Taal-, Land-en Volkenkunde. Translation series, no. 10) 1. Indonesian literature — History and criticism. I. T.
PL5080.T4   *LC* 68-87766

Johns, Anthony H. (Anthony Hearle)   2.2285
Cultural options and the role of tradition: a collection of essays on modern Indonesian and Malaysian literature / Anthony H. Johns. — Canberra: Faculty of Asian Studies in association with the Australian National University Press, 1979. vi, 241 p.; 25 cm. 1. Indonesian literature — History and criticism — Addresses, essays, lectures. 2. Malay literature — 20th century — History and criticism — Addresses, essays, lectures. I. T.
PL5080.5.J64   899/.221/209   *LC* 78-74666   *ISBN* 0708103413

Contemporary Indonesian poetry: poems in bahasa Indonesia   2.2286
and English / by W.S. Rendra ... [et al.]; edited and translated
by Harry Aveling.
St. Lucia, Q.: University of Queensland Press, 1975. xxiii, 261 p.; 22 cm. (Asian and Pacific writing. 5) 1. Indonesian poetry — Translations into English. 2. English poetry — Translations from Indonesian. 3. Indonesian poetry I. Rendra, W. S. II. Aveling, Harry. III. Series.
PL5086.5.E5 C66 1975   899/.221/1208   *LC* 75-322821   *ISBN* 0702209317. *ISBN* 0702209325 pbk

Anwar, Chairil, 1922-1949.   2.2287
The complete poetry and prose of Chairil Anwar. Edited and translated by Burton Raffel. Albany, State University of New York Press [1970] xxii, 208 p. port. 19 cm. Parallel texts in English and Indonesian. I. Raffel, Burton. II. T.
PL5089.A56 1970   *LC* 76-91201   *ISBN* 873950615

Mohd. Taib Osman, 1934-.   2.2288
An introduction to the development of modern Malay language & literature [by] Mohd. Taib Osman. Singapore, Published by D. Moore for Eastern Universities Press [1961] 57 p. 19 cm. 1. Malay literature — History and criticism. I. T.
PL5130.M58   899/.2   *LC* 75-261748

Winstedt, Richard Olof, Sir, 1878-.   2.2289
A history of classical Malay literature [by] Sir Richard Winstedt. — Kuala Lumpur; New York: Oxford Univeristy Press, 1969. x, 323 p.; 23 cm. — (Oxford in Asia. Historical reprints) Reprint of the 1961 ed. 1. Malay literature — History and criticism. I. T.
PL5130.W5 1969   899/.2   *LC* 75-11340

PL5501–5348 Philippine

Brown heritage: essays on Philippine cultural tradition and   2.2290
literature.
Quezon City, Ateneo de Manila University Press, 1967. xv, 885 p. illus. 24 cm. 1. Philippine literature — Addresses, essays, lectures. I. Manuud, Antonio G., ed. II. Quezon, Philippines. Ateneo de Manila. Institute of Philippine Literature.
PL5533.B7   *LC* 67-29955

Mojares, Resil B.   2.2291
Origins and rise of the Filipino novel: a generic study of the novel until 1940 / Resil B. Mojares. — Quezon City, Philippines: University of the Philippines Press; [Honolulu]: Distributed outside the Philippines by University of Hawaii Press, 1983. ix, 389 p.; 24 cm. 'A U.P. diamond jubilee publication.' Includes index. 1. Philippine fiction — History and criticism. I. T.
PL5542.M64 1983   809.3/99599 19   *LC* 83-232361   *ISBN* 9711050005

Maramba, Asuncion David. comp.   2.2292
Early Philippine literature from ancient times to 1940. With an introd. by Alejandro R. Roces. Manila, Distributed by National Book Store [1971] xxv, 388 p. 23 cm. English, Spanish, or Tagalog. 1. Tagalog literature — Translations into English. 2. English literature — Translations from Tagalog. 3. Philippine literature (Spanish) — Translations into English. 4. English

literature — Translations from Spanish. 5. Tagalog literature 6. Philippine literature (English) 7. Philippine literature (Spanish) I. T.
PL5543.D38   809/.89599   LC 79-309443

Epics of the Philippines / editors, Jovita Ventura Castro ... [et al.].   **2.2293**
[S.l.]: ASEAN Committee on Culture and Information, 1983. 492 p.: maps; 24 cm. — (Anthology of ASEAN literatures. v. 1a) On spine: ASEAN literatures. Texts in original languages with English translations and introductions. 1. Epic poetry, Philippine. 2. Epic poetry, Philippine — Translations into English. 3. English poetry — Translations from Philippine. I. Ventura Castro, Jovita II. Series.
PL5544.5.E5 E6   ISBN 9711029006

PL8000–8844 African Languages and Literatures

(see also: PQ3980-3989; PQ9900-9948; PR9340-9405)

Greenberg, Joseph Harold, 1915-.   ● **2.2294**
[Studies in African linguistics classification] The languages of Africa, by Joseph H. Greenberg. [2d ed. with additions and corrections] Bloomington, Indiana University, 1966. vi, 180 p. maps. 25 cm. (Indiana University. Research Center in Anthropology, Folklore, and Linguistics. Publication 25) 'Expanded and extensively revised version of the author's Studies in African Linguistic classification ... 1955.' 1. African languages I. T.
PL8005.G7 1966   496   LC 68-64685

Awoonor, Kofi, 1935-.   **2.2295**
The breast of the Earth: a survey of the history, culture, and literature of Africa south of the Sahara / Kofi Awoonor. — 1st ed. — Garden City, N.Y.: Anchor Press, 1975. 387p. cm. Includes index. 1. African literature — History and criticism. 2. Africa — Civilization — History. I. T.
PL8010.A9   PL8010 A9.   896   LC 72-79371   ISBN 0385070535

Dathorne, O. R., 1934-.   **2.2296**
The Black mind: a history of African literature / O. R. Dathorne. — Minneapolis: University of Minnesota Press, [1974] ix, 527 p.; 24 cm. Includes index. 1. African literature — History and criticism. I. T.
PL8010.D37   PL8010 D37.   809/.896   LC 74-76744   ISBN 0816607192

Finnegan, Ruth H.   ● **2.2297**
Oral literature in Africa [by] Ruth Finnegan. London, Clarendon P., 1970. xix, 558 p., fold. plate. map. 23 cm. (Oxford library of African literature) 1. Folk literature — Africa — History and criticism. 2. Oral tradition — Africa. I. T.
PL8010.F5   398/.0967   LC 70-596309   ISBN 0198151314

Gérard, Albert S.   **2.2298**
African language literatures: an introduction to the literary history of Sub-Saharan Africa / Albert S. Gérard. — 1st American ed. — Washington, D.C.: Three Continents, c1981. xv, 398 p.: ill.; 24 cm. 1. African literature — History and criticism. I. T.
PL8010.G39 1981   809/.889/6 19   LC 79-3103   ISBN 0914478656

Gérard, Albert S.   **2.2299**
Four African literatures: Xhosa, Sotho, Zulu, Amharic [by] Albert S. Gérard. — Berkeley, University of California Press [1971] 458 p. maps. 24 cm. 1. African literature — History and criticism. I. T.
PL8010.G4   809.8/96   LC 74-126763   ISBN 0520017889

Herdeck, Donald E., 1924-.   **2.2300**
African authors; a companion to Black African writing, 1300–1973, by Donald E. Herdeck. Washington, Black Orpheus Press, 1973. ix, 605 p. 24 cm. (Dimensions of the Black intellectual experience) 1. African literature — Bio-bibliography. I. T. II. Series.
PL8010.H38   809/.89/6 B   LC 73-172338   ISBN 0879530081

Killam, G. D. comp.   **2.2301**
African writers on African writing, edited by G. D. Killam. — Evanston, Northwestern University Press, 1973. xiii, 172 p. 23 cm. — (Studies in African literature.) 1. African literature — Addresses, essays, lectures. I. T. II. Series.

PL8010.K5   820/.9   LC 72-97110   ISBN 0810104113 ISBN 0810104202

Moore, Gerald, 1924-.   ● **2.2302**
Twelve African writers / Gerald Moore. — Bloomington: Indiana University Press, c1980. 327 p.; 22 cm. Includes index. 1. African literature — History and criticism — Addresses, essays, lectures. I. T.
PL8010.M63 1980b   809/.896   LC 80-7988   ISBN 0253196191

Mphahlele, Ezekiel.   **2.2303**
The African image. Rev. ed. New York, Praeger [1974] 316 p. 21 cm. 1. African literature — History and criticism. 2. Africans in literature 3. Black race I. T.
PL8010.M7 1974   809/.933/52   LC 72-86431

Nkosi, Lewis.   **2.2304**
Tasks and masks: themes and styles of African literature / Lewis Nkosi. — Harlow, Essex: Longman, 1981. 202 p.; 24 cm. 1. African literature — History and criticism. I. T.
PL8010.N55   809/.896 19   LC 82-107343   ISBN 0582641454

Soyinka, Wole.   **2.2305**
Myth, literature, and the African world / Wole Soyinka. — Cambridge; New York: Cambridge University Press, c1976. xii, 168 p. Includes bibliographical references and index. 1. African literature — History and criticism — Addresses, essays, lectures. 2. Literature and society — Addresses, essays, lectures. 3. Africa — Civilization — Addresses, essays, lectures. I. T.
PL8010.S64   PL8010 S64.   896   LC 75-38184   ISBN 0521211905

Poems of Black Africa / edited and with an introd. by Wole Soyinka.   **2.2306**
1st American ed. — New York: Hill and Wang, 1975. 378 p.; 21 cm. 1. African poetry I. Soyinka, Wole.
PL8011.P6 1975   896   LC 75-5796   ISBN 0809077477

Kgositsile, Keorapetse. comp.   **2.2307**
The word is here; poetry from modern Africa. — [1st ed.]. — Garden City, N.Y., Anchor Books, 1973. xvii, 173 p. 21 cm. 1. African poetry I. T.
PL8013.E5 K4   821   LC 70-186034   ISBN 038501516X

Modern poetry from Africa / edited by Gerald Moore and Ulli Beier.   ● **2.2308**
Harmondsworth [Middlesex]: Penguin Books, 1963. 192 p. — (Penguin African library; AP7) 1. African poetry — Translations into English 2. English poetry — Translations from African languages I. Moore, Gerald, 1924- II. Beier, Ulli.
PL8013.E5 M6   808.81   LC 63-24143

Mphahlele, Ezekiel. ed.   ● **2.2309**
African writing today. — Harmondsworth: Penguin, 1967. 347 p.; 20 cm. Includes African Portuguese literature. 1. African literature — Translations into English. 2. English literature — Translations from African. I. T.
PL8013.E5 M64   896   LC 67-76486

p'Bitek, Okot.   **2.2310**
Song of Lawino; &, Song of Ocol / Okot p'Bitek; introduction by G.A. Heron; illustrations by Frank Horley. — London: Heinemann, 1984. 151 p.: ill.; 19 cm. — (African writers series. 266) I. T. II. Title: Song of Ocol. III. Series.
PL8041.9.P3 S6x   896/.5 19   ISBN 0435902660

p'Bitek, Okot, 1931-.   **2.2311**
[Wer pa Lawino. English] Song of Lawino; an African lament. New York, Meridian books [1969, c1966] 216 p. illus. 21 cm. Poems. Translation of Wer pa Lawino. 'Translated from the Acoli by the author.' I. T.
PL8041.9.P3 W413 1969   896.5   LC 71-92536

Zimbabwe: prose and poetry.   **2.2312**
[1st English ed.]. — Washington: Three Continents Press, [1974] 276 p.: illus.; 19 cm. 1. Shona literature — Translations into English. 2. English literature — Translations from Shona. 3. Shona poetry I. Mutswairo, Solomon M. Feso. English. 1974.
PL8681.6.Z5 1974   896/.39   LC 74-7822   ISBN 0914478028

Kunene, Daniel P.   **2.2313**
Heroic poetry of the Basotho [by] Daniel P. Kunene. — Oxford [Eng.] Clarendon Press, 1971. xxiii, 203 p. 23 cm. — (Oxford library of African literature) 1. Epic poetry, Sotho — History and criticism. I. T.
PL8689.5.K8   398.22/0968   LC 70-30759   ISBN 0198151322

Rasmussen, Knud, 1879-1933. 2.2314
[Snehyttens sange. English] Eskimo poems from Canada and Greenland. Translated by Tom Lowenstein, from material originally collected by Knud Rasmussen. [Pittsburgh] University of Pittsburgh Press [1973] xxiii, 149 p. 23 cm. (Pitt poetry series) Translation of Snehyttens sange. 'An International Poetry Forum selection.' 1. Eskimo poetry — Canada — Translations into English. 2. Canadian poetry — Translations from Eskimo. 3. Eskimo poetry — Greenland — Translations into English. I. Lowenstein, Tom. tr. II. T.
PM64.Z95 E5 1973b   897/.1   LC 73-7606   ISBN 0822911108

Ramsey, Jarold, 1937-. 2.2315
Reading the fire: essays in the traditional Indian literatures of the Far West / Jarold Ramsey. — Lincoln: University of Nebraska Press, c1983. xxi, 250 p.; 23 cm. Includes index. 1. Indian literature — West (U.S.) — History and criticism — Addresses, essays, lectures. I. T.
PM155.R35 1983   897 19   LC 82-21775   ISBN 0803238649

Traditional literatures of the American Indian: texts and 2.2316
interpretations / compiled and edited by Karl Kroeber.
Lincoln: University of Nebraska Press, c1981. 162 p.; 21 cm. 1. Indian literature — North America — History and criticism — Addresses, essays, lectures. 2. Indians of North America — Legends — Addresses, essays, lectures. I. Kroeber, Karl, 1926-
PM155.T7   897   LC 80-18338   ISBN 0803227043

Wiget, Andrew. 2.2317
Native American literature / by Andrew Wiget. — Boston: Twayne Publishers, c1985. 147 p.: ill.; 23 cm. (Twayne's United States authors series. TUSAS 467) Includes index. 1. Indian literature — North America — History and criticism. 2. American literature — Indian authors — History and criticism. I. T. II. Series.
PM155.W54 1985   810/.9/897 19   LC 84-19809   ISBN 0805774084

Critical essays on Native American literature / [edited by] 2.2318
Andrew Wiget.
Boston, Mass.: G.K. Hall, c1985. viii, 266 p. — (Critical essays on American literature.) 1. Indian literature — North America — History and criticism — Addresses, essays, lectures. 2. American literature — Indian authors — History and criticism — Addresses, essays, lectures. I. Wiget, Andrew. II. Series.
PM156.C75 1985   897 19   LC 84-19210   ISBN 0816186871

Smoothing the ground: essays on native American oral literature 2.2319
/ edited by Brian Swann.
Berkeley: University of California Press, c1983. xix, 364 p.: ill.; 26 cm. 1. Indian literature — History and criticism — Addresses, essays, lectures. I. Swann, Brian.
PM156.S6 1983   810/.9/897 19   LC 82-16155   ISBN 0520049020

Levitas, Gloria B. comp. 2.2320
American Indian prose and poetry: we wait in the darkness / edited and introduced by Gloria Levitas, Frank Robert Vivelo, Jacqueline J. Vivelo. — New York: Putnam, [1974] xlii, 325 p.; 22 cm. 1. Indian literature — Translations into English. 2. American literature — Translations from Indian languages. 3. American literature — Indian authors I. Vivelo, Frank Robert, joint comp. II. Vivelo, Jackie. joint comp. III. T.
PM197.E1 L4   897   LC 72-97301   ISBN 0399111158

Milton, John R. comp. 2.2321
The American Indian speaks. Edited by John R. Milton. — Vermillion: Dakota Press, University of South Dakota, 1969. 194 p.: illus. (part col.), ports.; 23 cm. A collection of Indian writing and painting reprinted exactly as published in the South Dakota review, v. 7, no. 2. 1. Indian literature — Translations into English. 2. American literature — Translations from Indian languages. 3. Indians of North America — Art I. T.
PM197.E1 M5   897   LC 71-106810

Sanders, Thomas Edward, 1926- comp. 2.2322
Literature of the American Indian / [compiled by] Thomas E. Sanders [and] Walter W. Peek. — New York: Glencoe Press, [1973] xviii, 534 p.: port.; 27 cm. 1. Indian literature — Translations into English. 2. American literature — Translations from Indian languages. 3. American literature — Indian authors I. Peek, Walter W., joint comp. II. T.
PM197.E1 S2   897   LC 72-89050

Witt, Shirley Hill, comp. 2.2323
The way; an anthology of American Indian literature, edited by Shirley Hill Witt and Stan Steiner. [1st ed.] New York, Knopf, 1972. xxix, 261 p. 22 cm. (A

MARC Corporation book) 1. Indian literature — Translations into English. I. Steiner, Stan. joint comp. II. T.
PM197.E1 W5 1972b   897   LC 73-171156   ISBN 0394473701

Bierhorst, John. comp. 2.2324
Four masterworks of American Indian literature: Quetzalcoatl/The ritual of condolence/Cuceb/The night chant, edited, and with commentaries and new translations, by John Bierhorst. New York, Farrar, Straus and Giroux [1974] xxiv, 371 p. illus. 22 cm. 1. Indian literature — Translations into English. 2. American literature — Translations from Indian languages. 3. Indians — Religion and mythology I. T.
PM197.E3 B48   897   LC 74-2084   ISBN 0374157928

Rothenberg, Jerome, 1931- comp. 2.2325
Shaking the pumpkin; traditional poetry of the Indian North Americas. [1st ed.] Garden City, N.Y., Doubleday, 1972. xxvi, 475 p. illus. 22 cm. 1. Indian poetry — North America — Translations into English. 2. American poetry — Translations from Indian languages. I. T.
PM197.E3 R6   897 19   LC 74-171317

American Indian literature: an anthology / edited and with an 2.2326
introd. by Alan R. Velie; illustrated by Danny Timmons.
1st ed. — Norman: University of Oklahoma Press, c1979. xii, 356 p.: ill.; 24 cm. 1. Indian literature — United States — Translations into English. 2. English literature — Translations from Indian languages. 3. American literature — Indian authors I. Velie, Alan R., 1937-
PM198.E1 A4   897   LC 78-21387   ISBN 0806115300

First fire: Central and South American Indian poetry / edited 2.2327
with an introduction by Hugh Fox.
1st ed. — Garden City, N.Y.: Anchor Books, 1978. xxvi, 454 p.; 21 cm. 1. Indian literature — Translations into English. 2. American literature — Translations from Indian languages. 3. Indians — Religion and mythology I. Fox, Hugh, 1932-
PM198.E3 F5   897   LC 77-11528   ISBN 0385038151

The South corner of time: Hopi, Navajo, Papago, Yaqui tribal 2.2328
literature / edited by Larry Evers ... [et al.].
Tucson, Ariz.: Sun Tracks, 1980. x, 240 p.: ill., ports.; 22 x 28 cm. (Sun tracks. 0300-788X; v. 6) 1. Indian literature — Southwest, New. 2. American literature — Indian authors I. Evers, Larry. II. Series.
PM464.S6x   810/.8 s 810/.8/0897 19   LC 76-617570   ISBN 0936350008

Hymes, Dell H. 2.2329
'In vain I tried to tell you': essays in Native American ethnopoetics / Dell Hymes. — Philadelphia: University of Pennsylvania Press, 1981. 402 p.: maps; 24 cm. — (Studies in Native American literature. 1) (University of Pennsylvania publications in conduct and communication.) Includes indexes. 1. Indians of North America — Northwest, Pacific — Poetry — History and criticism. 2. Indians of North America — Northwest, Pacific — Legends. I. T. II. Series. III. Series: University of Pennsylvania publications in conduct and communication.
PM483.5.H9 1981   897 19   LC 81-51138   ISBN 0812278062

PM549–2711 By Language, United States and Canada

Spirit mountain: an anthology of Yuman story and song / 2.2330
Leanne Hinton and Lucille J. Watahomigie, editors.
Tucson, Ariz.: Sun Tracks and the University of Arizona Press, c1984. xii, 344 p.: ill.; 23 x 26 cm. — (Sun tracks. v. 10) Stories and songs in Yuman languages and English. 1. Yuman literature 2. Yuman Indians — Legends. 3. Indians of North America — Southwest, New — Legends. 4. Yuman languages — Texts. I. Hinton, Leanne. II. Watahomigie, Lucille J. III. Series.
PM2701.Z77   810/.8 s 897/.5 19   LC 84-112   ISBN 0816508437

Tedlock, Dennis, 1939-. 2.2331
Finding the center; narrative poetry of the Zuñi Indians. Translated by Dennis Tedlock. From performances in the Zuñi by Andrew Peynetsa and Walter Sanchez. — New York: Dial Press, 1972. xxxv, 298 p.: illus.; 21 cm. 1. Zuñi

poetry — Translations into English. 2. American poetry — Translations from Zuñi. I. T.
PM2711.Z95 E5 1972   897.4   *LC* 79-163589

PM3001–7356 By Language, Latin America

Burns, Allan F. (Allan Frank), 1945-.   **2.2332**
An epoch of miracles: oral literature of the Yucatec Maya / translated with commentaries by Allan F. Burns; foreword by Dennis Tedlock. — 1st ed. — Austin: University of Texas Press, 1983. xiv, 266 p.: ill.; 24 cm. — (Texas Pan American series.) 1. Maya literature — Translations into English. 2. Mayas — Folklore 3. Indians of Mexico — Folklore. I. T. II. Series.
PM3968.55.E5 B87 1983   398.2/08997 19   *LC* 82-8508   *ISBN* 0292720378

León Portilla, Miguel.   **2.2333**
[Las literaturas precolombinas de México. English] Pre–Columbian literatures of Mexico. Translated from the Spanish by Grace Lobanov and the author. — Norman: University of Oklahoma Press, [1969] xiii, 191 p., [4] leaves of plates: ill., facsims.; 24 cm. — (Civilization of the American Indian series. [92]) 1. Aztec literature — History and criticism. 2. Maya literature — History and criticism. 3. Mixtec literature — History and criticism. I. T. II. Series.
PM4068.L413   PM4068 L413.   897/.4   *LC* 68-15688   5.95

Cantares en idioma mexicano. English & Aztec.   **2.2334**
Cantares mexicanos = Songs of the Aztecs / translated from the Nahuatl, with an introduction and commentary, by John Bierhorst. — Stanford, Calif.: Stanford University Press, 1985. xiii, 559 p.; 24 cm. Aztec and English. Includes index. 1. Aztec poetry 2. Aztec poetry — Translations into English. 3. English poetry — Translations from Aztec. I. Bierhorst, John. II. T. III. Title: Songs of the Aztecs.
PM4068.6.C3 1985   897/.4 19   *LC* 82-61071   *ISBN* 0804711828

Yaqui deer songs, Maso Bwikam: a native American poetry /   **2.2335**
Larry Evers and Felipe S. Molina.
Tucson: Sun Tracks: University of Arizona Press, c1987. 239 p.: ill.; 23 cm. — (Sun tracks. v. 14) English and Yaqui. Includes index. 1. Yaqui poetry 2. Yaqui Indians — Rites and ceremonies. 3. Indians of North America — Arizona — Rites and ceremonies. 4. Yaqui poetry — Translations into English. 5. American poetry — Translations from Yaqui. 6. Indians of Mexico — Rites and ceremonies I. Evers, Larry. II. Molina, Felipe S. III. Series.
PM4526.Z77   810/.8 s 897/.4 19   *LC* 86-19313   *ISBN* 0816509913

PM7801–7895 Mixed Languages. Creole and Pidgin Languages

Pidgin and creole linguistics / edited by Albert Valdman.   **2.2336**
Bloomington: Indiana University Press, c1977. xvi, 399 p.: ill.; 24 cm. Includes index. 1. Pidgin languages — Addresses, essays, lectures. 2. Creole dialects — Addresses, essays, lectures. 3. Sociolinguistics — Addresses, essays, lectures. I. Valdman, Albert.
PM7802.P48   301.2/1   *LC* 76-48496   *ISBN* 0253344956

Bickerton, Derek, 1926-.   **2.2337**
Dynamics of a creole system / Derek Bickerton. London; New York: Cambridge University Press, 1975. viii, 224 p.; 23 cm. Includes index. 1. Creole dialects, English — Guyana. I. T.
PM7874.G8 B5   427/.9/881   *LC* 74-12971   *ISBN* 052120514X

Todd, Loreto.   **2.2338**
Modern Englishes: pidgins and creoles / Loreto Todd. — Oxford, England: B. Blackwell in association with A. Deutsch, 1984. xii, 286 p.: ill.; 23 cm. (Language library.) 1. Pidgin English 2. Creole dialects, English I. T. II. Series.
PM7891.T63 1984   427/.9 19   *LC* 84-129929   *ISBN* 063113655X

PN37 COLLECTED WORKS

Barthes, Roland.   **2.2339**
Image, music, text / Roland Barthes; essays selected and translated by Stephen Heath. — New York: Hill and Wang, c1977. 220 p., [4] leaves of plates: ill.; 21 cm. 1. Literature — Collected works. 2. Performing arts — Collected works. I. Heath, Stephen. II. T.
PN37.B29   809   *LC* 77-16702   *ISBN* 0809057409

Blanchot, Maurice.   **2.2340**
The sirens' song: selected essays / by Maurice Blanchot; edited and with an introduction by Gabriel Josipovici; translated by Sacha Rabinovitch. — Bloomington: Indiana University Press, c1982. vi, 255 p.; 23 cm. 1. Literature — Addresses, essays, lectures. I. Josipovici, Gabriel, 1940- II. T.
PN37.B56 1982   809 19   *LC* 81-48510   *ISBN* 025335255X

Emerson, Ralph Waldo, 1803-1882.   **2.2341**
Emerson's literary criticism / edited by Eric W. Carlson. — Lincoln: University of Nebraska Press, c1979. xlix, 251 p.; 21 cm. (Regents critics series) Includes index. 1. Literature — Collected works. I. Carlson, Eric W. II. T.
PN37.E45 1979   809   *LC* 75-38053   *ISBN* 0803214030

Hughes, Richard Arthur Warren, 1900-1976.   **2.2342**
Fiction as truth: selected literary writings / by Richard Hughes; edited and introduced by Richard Poole. — Bridgend, Mid Glamorgan: Poetry Wales Press; Chester Springs, PA: Dufour Editions, 1984, c1983. 174 p.: ill.; 23 cm. U.S. publisher from label on t.p. verso. 1. Literature — Addresses, essays, lectures. I. Poole, Richard, 1945- II. T.
PN37.H84 1984   809 19   *LC* 84-71578   *ISBN* 090747618X

Mukařovský, Jan.   **2.2343**
The word and verbal art: selected essays by Jan Mukařovský / translated and edited by John Burbank and Peter Steiner; foreword by René Wellek. New Haven: Yale University Press, 1977. xvii, 238 p.; 24 cm. (Yale Russian and East European studies; 13) 1. Literature — Collected works. 2. Structuralism (Literary analysis) — Collected works. I. T. II. Series.
PN37.M79   809   *LC* 76-49733   *ISBN* 0300015739

Tate, Allen, 1899-.   • **2.2344**
Collected essays / Allen Tate. — Denver: A. Swallow, [1959] 578 p.; 23 cm. 1. Literature — Addresses, essays, lectures 2. American literature — Addresses, essays, lectures 3. English literature — Addresses, essays, lectures I. T.
PN37.T26   *LC* 59-15664

PN41–44.5 DICTIONARIES. ENCYCLOPEDIAS

Benét, William Rose, 1886-1950. ed.   • **2.2345**
The reader's encyclopedia. — 2d ed. — New York: Crowell, [1965] viii, 1118 p.: illus.; 26 cm. 1. Literature — Dictionaries. 2. Art — Dictionaries. 3. Music — Dictionaries I. T.
PN41.B4 1965   803   *LC* 65-12510

Cassell's encyclopaedia of world literature / General editor: J. Buchanan–Brown.   **2.2346**
Rev. and enl. — New York: Morrow, [1973] 3 v.; 25 cm. First published in 1953 under title: Cassell's encyclopaedia of literature, edited by S. H. Steinberg. 1. Literature — Dictionaries. 2. Literature — Bio-bibliography. I. Buchanan-Brown, John. ed.
PN41.C3 1973   803   *LC* 73-10405   *ISBN* 0688002285

Cuddon, John A.   **2.2347**
A dictionary of literary terms / J. A. Cuddon. — Rev. ed. — London: Deutsch, 1979. 761 p.; 23 cm. 1. Literature — Dictionaries. I. T.
PN41.C83 1979   803   *LC* 79-320298   *ISBN* 0385127138

Holman, C. Hugh (Clarence Hugh), 1914-.   **2.2348**
A handbook to literature. — 5th ed. / C. Hugh Holman, William Harmon. — New York: Macmillan; London: Collier Macmillan, c1986. vii, 647 p.; 24 cm. 'Based on the original edition by William Flint Thrall and Addison Hibbard.' Includes index. 1. Literature — Dictionaries. 2. English literature — Outlines, syllabi, etc. 3. American literature — Outlines, syllabi, etc. I. Harmon, William, 1938- II. Thrall, William Flint, 1880- Handbook to literature. III. T.
PN41.H6 1986   803 19   *LC* 85-24133   *ISBN* 0023564105

Shipley, Joseph Twadell, 1893-.   • **2.2349**
Dictionary of world literary terms, forms, technique, criticism. Edited by Joseph T. Shipley. — Completely rev. and enl. ed. — Boston: Writer, [1970] xiii, 466 p.; 24 cm. Earlier editions published under title: Dictionary of world literature. 1. Literature — Dictionaries. I. T.
PN41.S5 1970   803   *LC* 75-91879   *ISBN* 0871160129

Brewer, Ebenezer Cobham, 1810-1897.   • **2.2350**
[Dictionary of phrase and fable] Brewer's Dictionary of phrase and fable. Rev. by Ivor H. Evans. Centenary ed. New York, Harper & Row [c1970] xvi, 1175 p. port. 22 cm. 1. Literature — Dictionaries. 2. Allusions I. Evans, Ivor H. ed. II. T. III. Title: Dictionary of phrase and fable.
PN43.B65 1970b   803   *LC* 79-107024   *ISBN* 006010466X

Brewer, Ebenezer Cobham, 1810-1897.   **2.2351**
The dictionary of phrase and fable, giving the derivation, source, or origin of common phrases, allusions, and words that have a tale to tell / by E. Cobham Brewer; with an introd. by Alix Gudefin. — Classic ed. — New York: Avenel Books: distributed by Crown Publishers, 1978. ix, 1324 p.; 24 cm. 1. Literature — Dictionaries. 2. Allusions I. T.
PN43.B65 1978   803   *LC* 78-56842   *ISBN* 0517259214

Kindlers Literatur Lexikon / Chefredakteure, Gert Woerner, Rolf Geisler und Rudolf Radler.   **2.2352**
Zürich: Kindler, 1965-1972. 12 v.; 27 cm. 'Dieses Werklexikon ... entstand auf der Grundlage des 'Dizionario delle opere di tutti i tempi e di tutte le letterature,' herausgegeben von Valentino Bompiani.' 'Die deutsche Ausgabe wurde begründet von Wolfgang von Einsiedel unter Mitarbeit zahlreicher Fachberater.' Vol. 12: Supplement und index, edited by J. Zeitler. Each vol. accompanied by index inserted at end. 1. Literature — Stories, plots, etc. I. Woerner, Gert. II. Geisler, Rolf. III. Radler, Rudolf, 1934-
PN44.K54 1965

Magill, Frank Northen, 1907- ed.   • **2.2353**
Cyclopedia of literary characters. — New York: Harper & Row, [1963] viii, 1280, xiv, 50 p.; 24 cm. 'Also appears under the title of Masterplots cyclopedia of literary characters.' 1. Literature — Stories, plots, etc. 2. Literature — Dictionaries. 3. Characters and characteristics in literature I. T.
PN44.M3 1963   803   *LC* 62-14570

Magill, Frank Northen, 1907- ed.   **2.2354**
Masterplots: 2010 plot stories & essay reviews from the world's fine literature / edited by Frank N. Magill; story editor, Dayton Kohler. — Rev. ed., including the four series and further critical evaluations. — Englewood Cliffs, N.J.: Salem Press, c1976. 12 v.; 24 cm. Includes index. 1. Literature — Stories, plots, etc. 2. Literature — History and criticism — Addresses, essays, lectures. I. Kohler, Dayton, 1907-1972, ed. II. T.
PN44.M33 1976   809   *LC* 76-5606

Magill, Frank Northen, 1907- comp.   **2.2355**
Survey of contemporary literature: updated reprints of 2,300 essay–reviews from Masterplots annuals, 1954–1976, and survey of contemporary literature supplement: with 3,300 bibliographical reference sources / edited by Frank N. Magill. Rev. ed. — Englewood Cliffs, N.J.: Salem Press, c1977. 12 v. (xii, 8507, xxv p.); 24 cm. Includes index. 1. Literature — Stories, plots, etc. I. Masterplots annual. II. T.
PN44.M34 1977   809/.04   *LC* 77-79874   *ISBN* 0893560502

Abrams, M. H. (Meyer Howard), 1912-.   **2.2356**
A glossary of literary terms / M. H. Abrams. — 4th ed. — New York: Holt, Rinehart and Winston, 1981. vii, 220 p.; 24 cm. 1. Literature — Terminology I. T.
PN44.5.A2 1981   803/.21 19   *LC* 80-26095   *ISBN* 0030541662

Beckson, Karl E., 1926-.   **2.2357**
Literary terms: a dictionary / by Karl Beckson and Arthur Ganz. — Rev. and enl. ed. — New York: Farrar, Straus and Giroux, 1975. 280 p.; 21 cm. Edition for 1961 published under title: A reader's guide to literary terms. 1. Literature — Terminology I. Ganz, Arthur F., 1928- joint author. II. T.
PN44.5.B334 1975   803   *LC* 75-4507   *ISBN* 0374188009

Ruttkowski, W. V. (Wolfgang Victor), 1935-.   **2.2358**
Nomenclator litterarius / edidit W.V. Ruttkowski. — Bern: Francke, 1980. 548 p. German, English, Dutch, French, Spanish, Italian and Russian. 1. Literature — Dictionaries — Polyglot. 2. Dictionaries, Polyglot I. T.
PN44.5.R82 1980   *ISBN* 3772015018

Scott, Arthur Finley, 1907-.   • **2.2359**
Current literary terms: a concise dictionary of their origin and use / by A. F. Scott. — London: Macmillan; New York: St. Martin's Press, 1965. vii, 324 p.; 23 cm. Includes index. 1. Literature — Terminology I. T.
PN44.5.S3   803

PN45–58 THEORY. PHILOSOPHY. AESTHETICS

Babbitt, Irving, 1865-1933.   • **2.2360**
On being creative: and other essays. — New York: Biblo and Tannen, 1968 [c1960] xliii, 265 p.; 21 cm. 1. Literature — Philosophy 2. Humanism — 20th century 3. Imagination I. T.
PN45.B2 1968   809   *LC* 68-13152

Blanchot, Maurice.   **2.2361**
[Espace littéraire. English] The space of literature / by Maurice Blanchot; translated, with an introduction, by Ann Smock. — Lincoln: University of Nebraska Press, 1982. 276 p.; 24 cm. 1. Literature — Philosophy 2. Creation (Literary, artistic, etc.) I. T.
PN45.B42413 1982   801 19   *LC* 82-2062   *ISBN* 080321166X

Ingarden, Roman, 1893-.   **2.2362**
[Vom Erkennen des literarischen Kunstwerks. English] The cognition of the literary work of art. Translated by Ruth Ann Crowley and Kenneth R. Olson. Evanston [Ill.] Northwestern University Press, 1973. xxx, 436 p. 24 cm. (Northwestern University Studies in phenomenology & existential philosophy) Translation of Vom Erkennen des literarischen Kunstwerks. 1. Literature — Philosophy 2. Literature — Aesthetics I. T. II. Series.
PN45.I513   801/.9   *LC* 73-80117   *ISBN* 0810104245

Kermode, Frank, 1919-.   • **2.2363**
The sense of an ending: studies in the theory of fiction [by] Frank Kermode. — New York, Oxford University Press, 1967. xi, 187 p. 21 cm. — (Mary Flexner lectures, 1965) Lectures delivered at Bryn Mawr College under the title The long perspectives. Bibliographical references included in 'Notes' (p. 181-187) 1. Literature — Philosophy I. T.
PN45.K44 1967   801   *LC* 67-15128

Macherey, Pierre.   **2.2364**
[Pour une théorie de la production littéraire. English] A theory of literary production / Pierre Macherey; translated from the French by Geoffrey Wall. — London; Boston: Routledge & Kegan Paul, 1978. ix, 326 p.; 23 cm. Translation of Pour une théorie de la production littéraire. Includes index. 1. Literature — Philosophy I. T.
PN45.M31713   801/.95   *LC* 78-40559   *ISBN* 0710089783

Relations of literary study; essays on interdisciplinary   • **2.2365**
contributions. Edited by James Thorpe.
New York: Modern Language Association of America, [1967] xiv, 151 p.: music.; 24 cm. 'Sponsored by members of the Committee on Research Activities in the Modern Language Association of America.' 1. Literature — Addresses, essays, lectures. I. Thorpe, James Ernest, 1915- ed. II. Modern Language Association of America. Committee on Research Activities.
PN45.R39   809   *LC* 75-261981

Rosenblatt, Louise M. (Louise Michelle)   **2.2366**
The reader, the text, the poem: the transactional theory of the literary work / Louise M. Rosenblatt. — Carbondale: Southern Illinois University Press, c1978. xv, 196 p.; 24 cm. 1. Reader-response criticism I. T.
PN45.R587   801/.95   *LC* 78-16335   *ISBN* 0809308835

Schlegel, Friedrich von, 1772-1829.   • **2.2367**
Literary notebooks, 1797–1801 / Friedrich Schlegel; edited with introd. and commentary by Hans Eichner. — [Toronto]: University of Toronto Press, 1957. 342 p.: facsim. 1. Literature I. Eichner, Hans. II. T.
PN45.S247 1957b

Vivas, Eliseo.   • **2.2368**
Creation and discovery; essays in criticism and aesthetics. — Freeport, N.Y.: Books for Libraries Press, [1972, c1955] xiv, 306 p.; 22 cm. — (Essay index reprint series) 1. Literature — Aesthetics 2. Literature — History and criticism 3. Criticism I. T.
PN45.V55 1972   801/.93   *LC* 72-3365   *ISBN* 0836929314

Wellek, René.   • **2.2369**
Theory of literature [by] René Wellek & Austin Warren. — 3rd (revised) ed. — New York: Harcourt Brace Jovanovich, 1956. 374 p.; 23 cm. 1. Literature — Philosophy I. Warren, Austin, 1899- joint author. II. T.
PN45.W36 1956   801   *LC* 78-379213   *ISBN* 0156890844

West, Rebecca, Dame, 1892-.   • **2.2370**
The court and the castle: some treatments of a recurrent theme / Rebecca West. — New Haven: Yale University Press, 1957. 319 p. — (Terry lectures.) 1. Literature, Modern — History and criticism. I. T. II. Series.
PN45.W45   *LC* 57-11922

Interrelations of literature / edited by Jean–Pierre Barricelli   **2.2371**
and Joseph Gibaldi.
New York: Modern Language Association of America, 1982. vi, 329 p.; 24 cm. 1. Literature — Addresses, essays, lectures. I. Barricelli, Jean Pierre. II. Gibaldi, Joseph, 1942-
PN45.8.I56 1982   809 19   *LC* 82-7956   *ISBN* 0873520904

Boyd, John D.   • **2.2372**
The function of mimesis and its decline [by] John D. Boyd. — Cambridge, Mass.: Harvard University Press, 1968. xiv, 317 p.; 22 cm. A revision of the author's thesis, Harvard University. 1. Literature — Philosophy 2. Poetry 3. Criticism I. T.
PN47.B63 1968   801/.951   *LC* 68-28691

Girard, René, 1923-.   **2.2373**
'To double business bound': essays on literature, mimesis, and anthropology / René Girard. — Baltimore: Johns Hopkins University Press, c1978. xvi, 229 p.; 24 cm. 1. Mimesis in literature — Addresses, essays, lectures. 2. Rites and ceremonies — Addresses, essays, lectures. 3. Structural anthropology — Addresses, essays, lectures. I. T.
PN47.G5   809   *LC* 78-8418   *ISBN* 0801821142

Olson, Glending.   **2.2374**
Literature as recreation in the later Middle Ages / Glending Olson. — Ithaca: Cornell University Press, 1982. 245 p.; 23 cm. 1. Literature and society — Europe. 2. Amusements — History. 3. Civilization, Medieval 4. Books and reading I. T.
PN47.O58 1982   809/.02 19   *LC* 82-2462   *ISBN* 0801414946

PN49–55 Relation to Special Subjects

Hoffman, Frederick John.   • **2.2375**
Freudianism and the literary mind. — 2d ed. — Baton Rouge: Louisiana State University Press, 1957. xi, 350 p.; 24 cm. 1. Freud, Sigmund, 1856-1939. 2. Psychoanalysis and literature 3. Literature, Modern — 20th century — History and criticism I. T.
PN49.H6 1957   809.04   *LC* 57-11542

Holland, Norman Norwood, 1927-.   **2.2376**
5 readers reading / Norman N. Holland. — New Haven: Yale University Press, 1975. xvi, 418 p., [1] leaf of plates: diagr.; 25 cm. 1. Literature — Psychology I. T.
PN49.H65   150/.8   *LC* 74-26004   *ISBN* 0300018541

Jewish Theological Seminary of America. Institute for Religious   • **2.2377**
and Social Studies.
Spiritual problems in contemporary literature / edited by Stanley Romaine Hopper. — [1st Harper torchbook ed.]. — New York: Harper [1957] 298 p.; 21 cm. — (The Library of religion and culture) Harper torchbooks, TB21. 1. Religion in literature I. Hopper, Stanley Romaine, 1907- ed. II. T.
PN49.I64 1957   804   *LC* 57-10118 rev

Knight, George Wilson, 1897-.   **2.2378**
The Christian renaissance, with interpretations of Dante, Shakespeare and Goethe and new discussions of Oscar Wilde and the Gospel of Thomas. — New York, W. W. Norton [1962] 356 p. 22 cm. 1. Wilde, Oscar, 1854-1900. 2. Bible as literature. 3. Religion in poetry 4. Dante — Criticism and interpretation. 5. Shakespeare, William — Criticism and interpretation. 6. Goethe, Johann Wolfgang von — Criticism and interpretation. I. T.
PN49.K6 1962   801   *LC* 62-10099

Weitz, Morris.   • **2.2379**
Philosophy in literature: Shakespeare, Voltaire, Tolstoy & Proust. — Detroit: Wayne State University Press, 1963. 116 p.; 21 cm. (A Waynebook original) 1. Shakespeare, William, 1564-1616. Hamlet 2. Voltaire, 1694-1778. Candide

3. Tolstoy, Leo, graf, 1828-1910. Anna Karenina. 4. Proust, Marcel, 1871-1922. A la recherche du temps perdu. 5. Philosophy in literature I. T.
PN49.W38   809.93   LC 63-7173

Green, Martin Burgess, 1927-.   2.2380
Cities of light and sons of the morning; a cultural psychology for an age of revolution, by Martin Green. — [1st ed.]. — Boston: Little, Brown, [1972] xi, 465 p.: illus.; 22 cm. 1. Literature and society 2. Creation (Literary, artistic, etc.) 3. Revolutions I. T.
PN51.G7   801/.92   LC 76-161858

Lowenthal, Leo.   • 2.2381
Literature and the image of man; sociological studies of the European drama and novel, 1600–1900. — Freeport, N.Y.: Books for Libraries Press, [1970, c1957] 242 p.; 23 cm. — (Essay index reprint series) 1. Literature and society — Europe. 2. European literature — History and criticism. I. T.
PN51.L58 1970   809/.03   LC 78-134110   ISBN 0836919823

Mohl, Ruth, 1891-.   • 2.2382
The three estates in medieval and Renaissance literature. — New York: F. Ungar Pub. Co., 1962 (c1961). 425 p.: ill.; 21 cm. 1. Social problems in literature 2. Estates (Social orders) 3. Literature, Comparative — Themes, motives 4. Literature, Medieval — History and criticism 5. Literature, Modern — History and criticism. 6. English literature — History and criticism I. T.
PN51.M6 1961   LC 62-10897

The Sociology of literature: applied studies / issue editor, Diana   2.2383
Laurenson.
[Keele] Eng.: University of Keele, 1979 (c1978). 284 p.; 22 cm. — (Sociological review monograph. 26) 1. Literature and society — Addresses, essays, lectures. I. Laurenson, Diana T. II. Series.
PN51.S61x   301.08 s 301.5   LC 79-313008   ISBN 0904425053

The Sociology of literature: theoretical approaches / issue   2.2384
editors, Jane Routh and Janet Wolff.
Keele: University of Keele, 1979 (c1977). [6], 180 p.; 22 cm. — (Sociological review monograph. 25) 1. Literature and society — Addresses, essays, lectures. I. Routh, Jane. II. Wolff, Janet. III. Series.
PN51.S62x   301 s 801/.3   LC 79-300643   ISBN 0904425045

Marx, Karl, 1818-1883.   • 2.2385
Literature and art: selections from their writings / by Karl Marx and Frederick Engels. — New York: International Publishers, 1947-. v. 1. Art and society — Addresses, essays, lectures. 2. Literature — History and criticism — Addresses, essays, lectures. I. Engels, Friedrich, 1820-1895. II. T.
PN53.M32   LC 47-4102

Praz, Mario, 1896-.   2.2386
Mnemosyne: the parallel between literature and the visual arts. — [Princeton, N.J.]: Princeton University Press, [1970] xv, 261 p.: 121 illus.; 27 cm. — (Bollingen series, 35. The A. W. Mellon lectures in the fine arts, 16) 1. Art and literature I. T.
PN53.P7   700   LC 68-20876

Smith, Barbara Herrnstein.   2.2387
On the margins of discourse: the relation of literature to language / Barbara Herrnstein Smith. — Chicago: University of Chicago Press, 1979 (c1978). xvii, 225 p.; 23 cm. 1. Literature — Philosophy 2. Style, Literary 3. Language and languages — Style I. T.
PN54.S6   809   LC 78-18274   ISBN 0226764524

Huxley, Aldous, 1894-1963.   • 2.2388
Literature and science. [1st ed.] New York, Harper & Row [1963] 118 p. 22 cm. 1. Literature and science I. T.
PN55.H8   809.93   LC 63-16511

PN56 Special Topics, A–Z

PN56 A–L

Fletcher, Angus John Stewart, 1930-.   2.2389
Allegory: the theory of a symbolic mode / Angus John Stewart Fletcher. — Ithaca, N.Y. Cornell University Press [1964] xii, 418 p.: ill. 1. Allegory I. T.
PN56.A5 F5   LC 64-11415   ISBN 0801401313

Honig, Edwin.   • 2.2390
Dark conceit: the making of allegory. — Evanston [Ill.]: Northwestern University Press, [1959] 210 p.; 23 cm. 1. Allegory 2. Literature — History and criticism I. T.
PN56.A5 H6   809.93   LC 59-6734

Frye, Northrop.   2.2391
The great code: the Bible and literature / Northrop Frye. — 1st ed. — New York: Harcourt Brace Jovanovich, c1982. xxiii, 261 p.: ill.; 24 cm. 1. Bible and literature I. T.
PN56.B5 F7   809/.93522 19   LC 81-47303   ISBN 015136902X

Heroic epic and saga: an introduction and handbook to the   2.2392
world's great folk epics / edited by Felix J. Oinas.
Bloomington: Indiana University Press, c1978. viii, 373 p.; 24 cm. 1. Epic literature — History and criticism. 2. Folk literature — History and criticism I. Oinas, Felix J.
PN56.E65 H4   809.1/3   LC 77-9637   ISBN 0253327385

Rabkin, Eric S.   2.2393
The fantastic in literature / by Eric S. Rabkin. — Princeton, N.J.: Princeton University Press, c1976. xi, 234 p.: ill.; 23 cm. 1. Fantastic literature — History and criticism. I. T.
PN56.F34 R3   809/.91/5   LC 75-30201   ISBN 069106301X

Survey of modern fantasy literature / edited by Frank N.   2.2394
Magill.
Englewood Cliffs, N.J.: Salem Press, c1983. 5. v. (xviii, 2538, li p.); 24 cm. 1. Fantastic literature — History and criticism — Addresses, essays, lectures. I. Magill, Frank Northen, 1907-
PN56.F34 S97 1983   808.8/015 19   LC 83-15189   ISBN 0893564508

Timmerman, John H.   2.2395
Other worlds: the fantasy genre / John H. Timmerman. — Bowling Green, Ohio: Bowling Green University Popular Press, c1983. 124 p.; 24 cm. 1. Fantastic literature — History and criticism. I. T.
PN56.F34 T55 1983   809.3/876 19   LC 83-72015   ISBN 087972241X

Concepts of the hero in the Middle Ages and the Renaissance: 2.2396
papers of the fourth and fifth annual conferences of the Center for Medieval and Early Renaissance Studies, State University of New York at Binghamton, 2–3 May 1970, 1–2 May 1971 / edited by Norman T. Burns & Christopher J. Reagan.
1st ed. — Albany: State University of New York Press, 1975. xiii, 293 p., [11] leaves of plates: ill.; 24 cm. 1. Heroes in literature — Congresses. I. Burns, Norman T., ed. II. Reagan, Christopher J., ed. III. State University of New York at Binghamton. Center for Medieval and Early Renaissance Studies.
PN56.H45 C65   809/.933/51   LC 74-34081   ISBN 0873952766.
ISBN 0873952774 microfiche

Murray, Albert.   2.2397
The hero and the blues. — [Columbia]: University of Missouri Press, [1973]. -. 107 p.; 23 cm. — (The Paul Anthony Brick lectures; 9th ser.) 'Originally presented at the University of Missouri, Columbia, in the form of three public lectures on October 7, 8, and 9, 1972'. - 1. Heroes in literature I. T. II. Series.
PN56.H45 M8   PN56H47 M8.   809/.933/52   LC 72-97763   ISBN 0826201474

Owen, Douglas David Roy.   2.2398
Noble lovers / by D. D. R. Owen. — New York: New York University Press, 1975. 191 p., [15] leaves of plates: ill. (some col.); 26 cm. — Includes index. 1. Love in literature 2. Literature — History and criticism 3. Love stories I. T.
PN56.L6 O85 1975   LC 75-4303   ISBN 0814773656

PN56 M–Z

Crews, Frederick C.   2.2399
Out of my system: psychoanalysis, ideology, and critical method / Frederick Crews. — New York: Oxford University Press, 1975. xv, 214 p.; 22 cm. 1. Psychoanalysis and literature I. T.
PN56.P92 C7   809/.933/5   LC 75-7361   ISBN 0195019474

Holland, Norman Norwood, 1927-.   2.2400
Poems in persons; an introduction to the psychoanalysis of literature [by] Norman N. Holland. — [1st ed.]. — New York: Norton, [1973] xi, 183 p.; 21 cm. 1. Psychoanalysis and literature 2. Poetry I. T.
PN56.P92 H6   801/.92   LC 73-4691   ISBN 0393010996

Auerbach, Erich, 1892-1957.   • **2.2401**
[Mimesis. English] Mimesis; the representation of reality in Western literature. Translated from the German by Willard R. Trask. Princeton, Princeton University Press, 1953. 563 p. 25 cm. 1. Literature — History and criticism 2. Reality in literature I. T.
PN56.R3 A83   809   *LC* 52-13152

Becker, George Joseph. ed.   • **2.2402**
Documents of modern literary realism. — Princeton, N.J.: Princeton University Press, 1963. 609 p.; 25 cm. 1. Realism in literature 2. Criticism — History. I. T. II. Title: Modern literary realism.
PN56.R3 B4   809.91   *LC* 63-7064

Lukács, György, 1885-1971.   • **2.2403**
The meaning of contemporary realism [by] Georg Lukács. Translated from the German by John and Necke Mander. — London, Merlin Press [1962] 137 p. 23 cm. 1. Realism in literature 2. Socialism in literature I. T.
PN56.R3L793 1963   *LC* 64-6860

Frye, Northrop.   **2.2404**
The secular scripture: a study of the structure of Romance / Northrop Frye. — Cambridge, Mass.: Harvard University Press, 1976. viii, 199 p.; 22 cm. — (Charles Eliot Norton lectures. 1974-1975) 1. Romanticism 2. Literature, Comparative — Themes, motives I. T. II. Series.
PN56.R6 F7   809/.91/4   *LC* 75-37627   *ISBN* 0674796756

Auden, W. H. (Wystan Hugh), 1907-1973.   • **2.2405**
The enchafèd flood; or, The romantic iconography of the sea. — London: Faber and Faber, 1951. 126 p. 1. Sea in literature 2. Romanticism 3. Literature, Modern — 19th century — History and criticism I. T. II. Title: The romantic iconography of the sea.
PN56.S4 A8 1951   809.03   *LC* 52-2449

Ellmann, Mary.   • **2.2406**
Thinking about women. — [1st ed.]. — New York: Harcourt, Brace & World, [1968] xvi, 240 p.; 22 cm. 1. Sex in literature 2. Women in literature I. T.
PN56.S5 E4   809.9/33   *LC* 67-20309

Heilbrun, Carolyn G., 1926-.   **2.2407**
Toward a recognition of androgyny, by Carolyn G. Heilbrun. — [1st ed.]. — New York: Knopf, 1973. xxi, 189, v p.; 22 cm. 1. Sex differences (Psychology) in literature I. T.
PN56.S52 H4   809/.933/53   *LC* 77-171149   *ISBN* 0394461754

Bleiler, Everett Franklin, 1920-.   **2.2408**
The guide to supernatural fiction / by Everett F. Bleiler. — Kent, Ohio: Kent State University Press, c1983. ix, 723 p.; 29 cm. Subtitle: A full description of 1,775 books from 1750 to 1960, including ghost stories, weird fiction, stories of supernatural horror, fantasy, Gothic novels, occult fiction, and similar literature. Includes indexes. 1. Supernatural in literature 2. English fiction — Stories, plots, etc. 3. American fiction — Stories, plots, etc. I. T.
PN56.S8 B57 1983   809.3/937 19   *LC* 82-25477   0873382289

Tindall, William York, 1903-.   • **2.2409**
The literary symbol. — Bloomington: Indiana University Press, [c1955] 278 p.; 20 cm. — (A Midland book, MB-7) 1. Symbolism in literature I. T.
PN56.S9 T5 1955a   809   *LC* 58-6957

Meyerhoff, Hans.   • **2.2410**
Time in literature / Hans Meyerhoff. — Berkeley: University of California Press, 1955. 160 p. 1. Time in literature 2. Time 3. Literature — History and criticism I. T.
PN56.T5 M4   *LC* 55-5450

Rogers, Katharine M.   • **2.2411**
The troublesome helpmate; a history of misogyny in literature, by Katharine M. Rogers. Seattle, University of Washington Press [1966] xvi, 288 p. 24 cm. 1. Women in literature 2. Sexism in literature. 3. Misogyny I. T.
PN56.W6 R6   809.933   *LC* 66-19565

PN56.3–57 Characters and Themes in Literature

Johnson, Lemuel A.   **2.2412**
The devil, the gargoyle, and the buffoon: the Negro as metaphor in Western literature / [by] Lemuel A. Johnson. — Port Washington, N.Y.: Kennikat Press [1971] x, 185 p.; 24 cm. (Kennikat Press national university publications. Series on literary criticism) A revision of the author's thesis, University of Michigan.

1. Blacks in literature. 2. Poetry — Black authors — History and criticism. I. T.
PN56.3.N4 J6 1971   809.9/33/52   *LC* 76-139355   *ISBN* 0804690065

Amos, William.   **2.2413**
The originals: who's really who in fiction / William Amos. — London: J. Cape, 1985. xx, 614 p., [24] p. of plates: ports.; 23 cm. Includes index. 1. Characters and characteristics in literature 2. Biography I. T.
PN56.4.A4 1985b   809/.927 19   *LC* 86-191609   *ISBN* 0224023195

The Lost tradition: mothers and daughters in literature / edited   **2.2414**
by Cathy N. Davidson and E.M. Broner.
New York: F. Ungar Pub. Co., c1980. xiii, 327 p.; 24 cm. Includes index. 1. Mothers and daughters in literature — Addresses, essays, lectures. I. Davidson, Cathy N., 1949- II. Broner, E. M.
PN56.5.M67 L6   809/.933/54   *LC* 79-4832   *ISBN* 0804420831

The Image of the prostitute in modern literature / edited by   **2.2415**
Pierre L. Horn and Mary Beth Pringle.
New York: F. Ungar, c1984. 147 p.; 22 cm. 1. Literature, Modern — 19th century — History and criticism — Addresses, essays, lectures. 2. Literature, Modern — 20th century — History and criticism — Addresses, essays, lectures. 3. Prostitutes in literature — Addresses, essays, lectures. I. Horn, Pierre L. II. Pringle, Mary Beth, 1943-
PN56.5.P74 I45 1984   809/.933520692 19   *LC* 83-18256   *ISBN* 080442702X

Dudley, Edward J.   **2.2416**
The wild man within; an image in Western thought from the Renaissance to romanticism, edited by Edward Dudley and Maximillian E. Novak. — [Pittsburgh]: University of Pittsburgh Press, [1973, c1972] xi, 333 p.: illus.; 24 cm. 1. Wild men in literature I. Novak, Maximillian E. joint author. II. T.
PN56.5.W5 D8 1973   809/.933/52   *LC* 72-77191   *ISBN* 0822932466

Knight, Stephen Thomas.   **2.2417**
Arthurian literature and society / Stephen Knight. — New York: St. Martin's Press, 1983. xvi, 229 p., [16] p. of plates: ill.; 23 cm. 1. Arthurian romances — History and criticism. 2. Literature and society I. T.
PN57.A6 K64 1983   809/.93351 19   *LC* 83-15947   *ISBN* 0312054726

Loomis, Roger Sherman, 1887-1966. ed.   • **2.2418**
Arthurian literature in the Middle Ages: a collaborative history. — Oxford: Clarendon Press, 1959. xvi, 574 p.: 8 plates.; 25 cm. 1. Arthurian romances — History and criticism. 2. Literature, Comparative — Themes, motives I. T.
PN57.A6 L6   809.93   *LC* 60-110

Stanford, William Bedell.   • **2.2419**
The Ulysses theme: a study in the adaptability of a traditional hero. — 2d ed. New York: Barnes and Noble, 1964. x, 340 p.; 23 cm. 1. Odysseus (Greek mythology) 2. Literature, Comparative — Themes, motives I. T.
PN57.O3 S8 1964   809.93   *LC* 64-1681

PN59–73 STUDY. TEACHING. LITERARY RESEARCH

Pound, Ezra, 1885-1972.   • **2.2420**
ABC of reading / by Ezra Pound. — New York: J. Laughlin, 1960. 206 p.; 19 cm. (New Directions paperbook; no.89) Prose and poems. 1. Poetry 2. Literature — Study and teaching 3. English poetry — History and criticism I. T.
PN83.P57 1951   PN59.P6 1960.   *LC* 60-3034   *ISBN* 081120151

Bayley, John, 1925-.   • **2.2421**
The characters of love: a study in the literature of personality. — New York: Basic Books, c1960. 295 p. 1. Chaucer, Geoffrey, d. 1400. Troilus and Criseyde 2. Shakespeare, William, 1564-1616. Othello 3. James, Henry, 1843-1916. Golden bowl 4. Love in literature I. T.
PN65L6 B3   *LC* 61-5551

Burton, Dwight L.   • **2.2422**
Literature study in the high schools, [by] Dwight L. Burton. — 3d ed. — New York: Holt, Rinehart and Winston, [1970] viii, 357 p.; 22 cm. 1. Literature — Study and teaching (Secondary) — United States. I. T.
PN70.B8 1970   807   *LC* 74-94346   *ISBN* 0030811198

Oakman, Robert L., 1941-.　　　　　　　　　　2.2423
Computer methods for literary research / Robert L. Oakman. — Rev. ed. — Athens: University of Georgia Press, 1984. xxv, 235 p.: ill.; 24 cm. Includes index. 1. Literature — Research — Data processing. I. T.
PN73.O24 1984　　802/.8/5 19　　*LC* 83-9273　　*ISBN* 082030686X

PN75–99 CRITICISM

English Institute, Columbia University.　　　　● 2.2424
Northrop Frye in modern criticism: selected papers from the English Institute / Edited with an introductory essay by Murray Krieger. — New York: Columbia University Press, 1966. x, 203 p. 1. Frye, Northrop, 1912- 2. Criticism — History I. Frye, Nothrop, 1912- II. Krieger, Murray, 1923- III. T.
PN75.F7 K7　　801　　*LC* 66-23968

Sweezy, Paul Marlor, 1910-.　　　　　　　　● 2.2425
F.O. Matthiessen, 1902–1950; a collective portrait. Edited by Paul M. Sweezy and Leo Huberman. New York, Schuman [1950] xii, 154 p. ports. 22 cm. 'Originally published as the October, 1950, issue of ... Monthly review.' 1. Matthiessen, F. O. (Francis Otto), 1902-1950. I. Huberman, Leo, 1903-1968. II. T.
PN75.M3 S9　　928.1　　*LC* 50-58262

English Institute.　　　　　　　　　　　　● 2.2426
Literary criticism and historical understanding; selected papers from the English Institute. Edited with a foreward by Phillip Damon. — New York: Columbia University Press, 1967. vii, 190 p.; 21 cm. Essays from the four conferences held at the twenty-fifth session of the English Institute, Sept. 6-Sept. 9, 1966. 1. Criticism — Congresses. I. Damon, Phillip, ed. II. T.
PN80.5.E5　　801/.95　　*LC* 67-24335

Austin, Timothy R., 1952-.　　　　　　　　　2.2427
Language crafted: a linguistic theory of poetic syntax / Timothy R. Austin. — Bloomington: Indiana University Press, c1984. x, 170 p.: ill.; 25 cm. Includes indexes. 1. Criticism 2. Style, Literary I. T.
PN81.A86 1984　　801/.95 19　　*LC* 83-48933　　*ISBN* 0253331978

Belsey, Catherine.　　　　　　　　　　　　2.2428
Critical practice / Catherine Belsey. — London; New York: Methuen, 1980. 168 p.: ill.; 20 cm. — (New accents) Includes index. 1. Criticism I. T.
PN81.B395　　801/.95 19　　*LC* 79-41685　　*ISBN* 0416729401

Booth, Wayne C.　　　　　　　　　　　　2.2429
Critical understanding: the powers and limits of pluralism / Wayne C. Booth. — Chicago: University of Chicago Press, 1979 (c1978). xiii, 408 p.; 24 cm. 1. Criticism I. T.
PN81.B58　　801/.95　　*LC* 78-15107　　*ISBN* 0226065545

Crane, Ronald Salmon, 1886- ed.　　　　　　● 2.2430
Critics and criticism, ancient and modern / by R. S. Crane [et al.]. — [Chicago]: University Press, [1952] 647 p. 1. Criticism 2. Literature — History and criticism I. T.
PN81.C8　　*LC* 52-7330

Kaplan, Charles, 1919-.　　　　　　　　　　2.2431
Criticism: the major statements / selected and edited by Charles Kaplan. — 2nd ed. — New York: St. Martin's Press, c1986. ix, 661 p.; 23 cm. Includes index. 1. Criticism 2. Poetry I. T.
PN81.C85 1986　　801/.95 19　　*LC* 85-61246　　*ISBN* 0312175272

Daiches, David, 1912-.　　　　　　　　　　● 2.2432
Critical approaches to literature. — Englewood Cliffs, N.J.: Prentice-Hall, 1956. 404 p.; 24 cm. 1. Criticism 2. Poetry I. T.
PN81.D3　　801　　*LC* 56-5702

Daiches, David, 1912- ed.　　　　　　　　　● 2.2433
Century of the essay: British and American. — New York: Harcourt,Brace, 1951. v, 500 p.; 21 cm. 1. English essays 2. American essays I. T.
PN81.D3 1951　　*LC* 52-148

Fischer, Michael, 1949-.　　　　　　　　　　2.2434
Does deconstruction make any difference?: poststructuralism and the defense of poetry in modern criticism / Michael Fischer. — Bloomington: Indiana University Press, c1985. xiv, 142 p.; 25 cm. Includes index. 1. Criticism 2. Deconstruction I. T.
PN81.F545 1985　　801/.95 19　　*LC* 84-48044　　*ISBN* 0253318106

Fish, Stanley Eugene.　　　　　　　　　　　2.2435
Is there a text in this class?: The authority of interpretive communities / Stanley Fish. — Cambridge, Mass.: Harvard University Press, 1980. viii, 394 p.; 24 cm. 1. Criticism I. T.
PN81.F56　　801/.95 19　　*LC* 80-19438　　*ISBN* 0674467256

Frye, Northrop.　　　　　　　　　　　　　● 2.2436
Anatomy of criticism: four essays / Northrop Frye. — Princeton: Princeton University Press, 1957. x, 383 p.; 25 cm. 1. Criticism I. T.
PN81.F75　　801　　*LC* 56-8380　　*ISBN* 0691060045

Guerin, Wilfred L.　　　　　　　　　　　　2.2437
A handbook of critical approaches to literature / Wilfred L. Guerin ... [et al.]. — 2d ed. — New York: Harper & Row, c1979. xviii, 350 p.; 21 cm. Includes index. 1. Criticism I. T.
PN81.G8 1979　　801.95　　*LC* 78-12477　　*ISBN* 0060425547

Hirsch, E. D. (Eric Donald), 1928-.　　　　　2.2438
The aims of interpretation / E. D. Hirsch, Jr. Chicago: University of Chicago Press, c1976. vi, 177 p.; 24 cm. 1. Hermeneutics I. T.
PN81.H49　　220.6/3　　*LC* 75-21269　　*ISBN* 0226342409

Johnson, Barbara, 1947-.　　　　　　　　　2.2439
The critical difference: essays in the contemporary rhetoric of reading / Barbara Johnson. — Baltimore: Johns Hopkins University Press, 1981, c1980. xii, 156 p.; 24 cm. 1. Criticism 2. Literature I. T.
PN81.J56 1981　　801/.95 19　　*LC* 80-21533　　*ISBN* 0801824583

Leavis, F. R. (Frank Raymond), 1895-.　　　● 2.2440
Towards standards of criticism: selections from the Calendar of modern letters, 1925-7 / chosen and with an introduction by F.R. Leavis. — London: Wishart, 1933. 200 p. 1. Criticism 2. Books — Reviews I. Calendar: a quarterly review. II. T.
PN81.L36　　*LC* 34-2682

Richards, I. A. (Ivor Armstrong), 1893-.　　　● 2.2441
Principles of literary criticism / Ivor A. Richards. — New York: Harcourt, Brace and World, 1925. 299 p. (Harvest Book, HB43.) 1. Criticism I. T.
PN81.R5 1925　　*LC* 25-120

Said, Edward W.　　　　　　　　　　　　2.2442
The world, the text, and the critic / Edward W. Said. — Cambridge, Mass.: Harvard University Press, 1983. vi, 327 p.; 24 cm. 1. Criticism 2. Literature — History and criticism I. T.
PN81.S223 1983　　801/.95 19　　*LC* 82-11969　　*ISBN* 0674961862

Schorer, Mark, 1908- ed.　　　　　　　　　● 2.2443
Criticism; the foundations of modern literary judgment, edited by Mark Schorer, Josephine Miles [and] Gordon McKenzie. — Rev. ed. — New York: Harcourt, Brace, [1958] 553 p.; 25 cm. 1. Criticism I. T.
PN81.S23 1958　　801　　*LC* 59-5509

Stallman, R. W. (Robert Wooster), 1911- ed.　● 2.2444
Critiques and essays in criticism, 1920–1948: representing the achievement of modern British and American critics / with a foreword by Cleanth Brooks. — New York: Ronald Press Co. [1949] xxii, 571 p.; 24 cm. 'Much of this material has not received previous book publication, is available only in books and journals which are now out of print, or appears here for the first time.' 'A selected bibliography of modern criticism: 1920-1948': p. 519-571. 1. Criticism 2. Poetics 3. English literature — Hist. & crit. I. T.
PN81.S67　　801　　*LC* 49-7475 *

Sutton, Walter. ed.　　　　　　　　　　　● 2.2445
Modern criticism, theory and practice. Edited by Walter Sutton and Richard Foster. — New York, Odyssey Press [1963] 643 p. 24 cm. 1. Criticism 2. English literature — History and criticism 3. American literature — History and criticism I. Foster, Richard Jackson, 1928- joint ed. II. T.
PN81.S8　　801.9　　*LC* 63-8234

Wimsatt, William K. (William Kurtz), 1907-1975. ed.　● 2.2446
Explication as criticism: selected papers from the English Institute, 1941–1952 / edited with a foreword by W. K. Wimsatt, Jr. — New York Columbia University Press 1963. xv, 202 p. 1. Criticism 2. English poetry — Addresses, essays, lectures. 3. Music and literature I. English Institute. II. T.
PN81.W482　　801.9　　*LC* 63-18436

PN83 Reading

Adler, Mortimer Jerome, 1902-.   • **2.2447**
How to read a book / by Mortimer J. Adler and Charles van Doren. — Rev. and updated ed. — New York: Simon and Schuster, [1972] xiii, 426 p.; 22 cm. 1. Reading I. Van Doren, Charles Lincoln, 1926- joint author. II. T.
PN83.A43 1972   028   *LC* 72-81451   *ISBN* 067121280X

Iser, Wolfgang.   **2.2448**
[Akt des Lesens. English] The act of reading: a theory of aesthetic response / by Wolfgang Iser. — Baltimore: Johns Hopkins University Press, 1979 (c1978). xii, 239 p.; 24 cm. Translation of Der Akt des Lesens. 1. Reader-response criticism I. T.
PN83.I813   001.54/3   *LC* 78-58296   *ISBN* 0801821010

Pound, Ezra, 1885-1972.   • **2.2449**
How to read, by Ezra Pound. New York, Haskell House, 1971. 55 p. 23 cm. Reprint of the 1931 ed. 1. Books and reading I. T.
PN83.P6 1971   028   *LC* 79-169105   *ISBN* 0838313159

Suleiman, Susan.   **2.2450**
The reader in the text: essays on audience and interpretation / edited by Susan Suleiman and Inge Crosman. — Princeton, N.J.: Princeton University Press, 1982. viii, 441 p.: diagrs.; 23 cm. Includes index. 1. Reading — Addresses, essays, lectures. I. Crosman, Inge Karalus. II. T.
PN83.R4   801/.95   *LC* 79-27619   *ISBN* 0691064369

Richards, I. A.   • **2.2451**
How to read a page: a course in efficient reading with an introd. to a hundred great words / J. A. Richards. — Boston: Beacon Press, 1959, c1942. 246 p. — (Beacon paperback; no.78) 1. Reading 2. Meaning (Psychology) 3. Semantics I. T.
PN83R51959   153.66   *LC* 59-6393

PN85–94 History

Eliot, T. S. (Thomas Stearns), 1888-1965.   • **2.2452**
The frontiers of criticism: a lecture delivered at the University of Minnesota Williams Arena on April 30, 1956. — [Minneapolis: University of Minnesota, 1956] 20 p.; 22 cm. — (The Gideon D. Seymour memorial lecture series) 1. Criticism — Addresses, essays, lectures. I. T. II. Series.
PN85.E48   *LC* 56-63614

Gardner, Helen.   • **2.2453**
The business of criticism. Oxford, Clarendon Press, 1959. 157 p. 19 cm. 1. Criticism — Addresses, essays, lectures. I. T.
PN85.G33   801.9   *LC* 59-3455

Lewes, George Henry, 1817-1878.   **2.2454**
Literary criticism of George Henry Lewes / edited by Alice R. Kaminsky. — Lincoln: University of Nebraska Press, [1964] xxiii, 159 p.; 21 cm. — (Regents critics series) 1. Criticism — Addresses, essays, lectures 2. Literature — History and criticism — Addresses, essays, lectures I. Kaminsky, Alice R. II. T. III. Series.
PN85.L47 1964   *LC* 64-17230

Read, Herbert Edward, Sir, 1893-1968.   • **2.2455**
The tenth muse: essays in criticism. — Freeport, N.Y.: Books for Libraries Press [1969, c1957] ix, 330 p.: 8 ill.; 23 cm. (Essay index reprint series) 1. Criticism — Addresses, essays, lectures. 2. Arts — Addresses, essays, lectures. I. T.
PN85.R4 1969   701   *LC* 73-99646   *ISBN* 0836914279

Wellek, René.   • **2.2456**
Concepts of criticism; [essays] Edited and with an introd. by Stephen G. Nichols, Jr. — New Haven: Yale University Press, 1963. 403 p.; 21 cm. 1. Criticism 2. Literature — History and criticism I. T.
PN85.W38   801.9   *LC* 63-7953

West, Ray Benedict, 1908- ed.   • **2.2457**
Essays in modern literary criticism. New York, Rinehart [1952] 611 p. 24 cm. 1. Criticism 2. Literature, Modern — History and criticism. I. T.
PN85.W4   801   *LC* 52-5602

Wimsatt, William K. (William Kurtz), 1907-1975.   • **2.2458**
Hateful contraries: studies in literature and criticism / by W. K. Wimsatt; with an essay on English meter written in collaboration with Monroe C. Beardsley.

— [Lexington]: University of Kentucky Press [1965] xix, 260 p.: ill.; 23 cm. 1. Criticism — Addresses, essays, lectures. 2. Literature — Addresses, essays, lectures. I. T.
PN85.W49   809   *LC* 65-11823

Winters, Yvor, 1900-1968.   • **2.2459**
The function of criticism; problems and exercises. [1st ed.] Denver, A. Swallow [1957] 200 p. 23 cm. 1. Criticism 2. Literature — History and criticism I. T.
PN85.W5   801   *LC* 57-1652

Bate, Walter Jackson, 1918- ed.   • **2.2460**
Criticism: the major texts. Enl. ed. New York, Harcourt Brace Jovanovich [c1970] xv, 719 p. 25 cm. 1. Criticism — Addresses, essays, lectures. I. T.
PN86.B3 1970   809   *LC* 70-136968   *ISBN* 0155161482

Eagleton, Terry, 1943-.   **2.2461**
The function of criticism: from the Spectator to post–structuralism / Terry Eagleton. — London: Verso, 1984. 133 p.; 21 cm. Includes index. 1. Criticism — History. I. T.
PN86.E34 1984   801/.95/0942 19   *LC* 84-201613   *ISBN* 0860910911

Hyman, Stanley Edgar, 1919-1970.   • **2.2462**
Poetry and criticism: four revolutions in literary taste. — [1st ed.]. — New York: Atheneum, 1961. 178 p.; 21 cm. 1. Criticism — History. 2. Greek drama (Tragedy) — History and criticism. 3. English poetry — History and criticism I. T.
PN86.H9   *LC* 61-6741

Saintsbury, George, 1845-1933.   • **2.2463**
A history of criticism and literary taste in Europe from the earliest texts to the present day. — Edinburgh, Blackwood, 1949. 3 v. 1. Criticism — Hist. 2. Literature — Hist. & crit. 3. Literature, Medieval I. T.
PN86.S32   801   *LC* 50-12723

Wellek, René.   **2.2464**
A history of modern criticism: 1750–1950. — New Haven, Yale University Press, 1955-1986. 7 v.; 24 cm. Includes bibliographical references. 1. Criticism — History 2. Literature, Modern — history and criticism I. T. II. Title: Modern criticism.
PN86.W4   801   *LC* 85-12005

Wimsatt, William K. (William Kurtz), 1907-1975.   • **2.2465**
Literary criticism; a short history [by] William K. Wimsatt, Jr. & Cleanth Brooks. [1st ed.] New York, Knopf, 1957. 755 p. illus. 24 cm. 1. Criticism — History. 2. Literature — History and criticism I. Brooks, Cleanth, 1906- joint author. II. T.
PN86.W5   801   *LC* 57-5286

Lanham, Richard A.   **2.2466**
The motives of eloquence: literary rhetoric in the Renaissance / Richard A. Lanham. — New Haven: Yale University Press, 1976. xi, 234 p.; 22 cm. Includes index. 1. Rhetoric — 1500-1800 — History. 2. Literature, Modern — 15th and 16th centuries — History and criticism I. T.
PN88.L3   808/.009/024   *LC* 75-43323   *ISBN* 0300020023

Spingarn, Joel Elias, 1875-1939.   • **2.2467**
A history of literary criticism in the Renaissance / by J. E. Spingarn. — 2d ed., rev. and augmented. — New York: The Columbia University Press, 1908. xi, 350 p.; 19 cm. (Half-title: Columbia university studies in comparative literature) Bibliography: p. 337-343. 1. Criticism 2. Renaissance I. T.
PN88.S6 1908   *LC* 08-14513

Eagleton, Terry, 1943-.   **2.2468**
Literary theory: an introduction / Terry Eagleton. — Minneapolis: University of Minnesota Press, c1983. viii, 244 p.; 23 cm. Includes index. 1. Criticism — History — 20th century. 2. Literature — History and criticism — Theory, etc. I. T.
PN94.E2 1983   801/.95/0904 19   *LC* 83-184242   *ISBN* 0816612382

Goldberg, Gerald Jay.   • **2.2469**
The modern critical spectrum / edited by Gerald Jay Goldberg, Nancy Marmer Goldberg. — Englewood Cliffs, N. J.: Prentice-Hall, 1962. xvii, 344 p. — (Prentice-Hall English literature series) 1. Criticism 2. Literature — History and criticism I. Goldberg, Nancy Marmer. II. T.
PN94.G6   *LC* 62-12665

Hartman, Geoffrey H.   **2.2470**
Criticism in the wilderness: the study of literature today / Geoffrey H. Hartman. — New Haven: Yale University Press, 1980. 323 p. Includes index. 1. Criticism — 20th century. I. T.
PN94.H34   801/.95/0904   *LC* 80-13491   *ISBN* 0300020856

Hyman, Stanley Edgar, 1919-1970.   • 2.2471
The armed vision: a study in the methods of modern literary criticism / Stanley Edgar Hyman. — New York: Knopf, c1948, t.p. 1952. xv, 417, xxii p.; 22 cm. Includes index. 1. Criticism — History — 20th century. I. T.
PN94.H9   801/.95/0904   LC 48-6970

Lentricchia, Frank.   2.2472
After the new criticism / Frank Lentricchia. — Chicago: University of Chicago Press, 1980. xiv, 384 p.; 24 cm. 1. Criticism — History — 20th century. 2. Criticism — United States — History — 20th century. I. T.
PN94.L43   801/.95   LC 79-23715   ISBN 0226471977

Lipking, Lawrence I., 1934- comp.   • 2.2473
Modern literary criticism, 1900–1970 / edited by Lawrence I. Lipking and A. Walton Litz. — [1st ed.]. — New York: Atheneum, 1972. xv, 554 p.; 26 cm. 1. Criticism 2. Literature — Addresses, essays, lectures. I. Litz, A. Walton. joint comp. II. T.
PN94.L48   801/.95/0904   LC 71-152045

Scholes, Robert E.   2.2474
Textual power: literary theory and the teaching of English / Robert Scholes. — New Haven: Yale University Press, c1985. xii, 176 p.; 22 cm. 1. Criticism 2. Literature — Study and teaching (Higher) I. T.
PN94.S25 1985   808/.042/071173 19   LC 84-19628   ISBN 0300033508

Textual strategies: perspectives in post–structuralist criticism /   2.2475
edited and with an introd. by Josué V. Harari.
Ithaca, N.Y.: Cornell University Press, 1979. 475 p.; 21 cm. Includes indexes. 1. Criticism — Addresses, essays, lectures. I. Harari, Josué V.
PN94.T4   801/.95   LC 79-7617   ISBN 0801412188

Tynan, Kenneth, 1927-.   • 2.2476
Tynan right & left; plays, films, people, places and events. — [1st American ed.]. — New York: Atheneum, 1967. ix, 479 p.; 25 cm. 1. Criticism I. T.
PN94.T9 1967   801/.95   LC 67-25489

PN98 Special Topics, A–Z

Drewry, John Eldridge, 1902-.   2.2477
Writing book reviews / by John E. Drewry. — Boston: The Writer, c1966. — xv, 230 p.; 21 cm. 1. Book reviewing I. T.
PN98.B7 D7 1966   808.066   LC 66-21115

Eagleton, Terry, 1943-.   2.2478
Criticism and ideology: a study in Marxist literary theory / Terry Eagleton. — London: NLB: Atlantic Highlands: Humanities Press, c1976. 191 p.; 22 cm. 1. Marxist criticism I. T.
PN98.C6 E2   801/.95   LC 76-40251   ISBN 0391006649

Eagleton, Terry, 1943-.   2.2479
Marxism and literary criticism / Terry Eagleton. — Berkeley: University of California Press, 1976. viii, 87 p.; 21 cm. Includes index. 1. Marxist criticism I. T.
PN98.C6 E23 1976b   801/.95   LC 76-6707

Jameson, Fredric.   2.2480
Marxism and form; twentieth–century dialectical theories of literature. Princeton, N.J., Princeton University Press [1972, c1971] xix, 432 p. 23 cm. 1. Marxist criticism 2. Dialectical materialism I. T.
PN98.C6 J3 1972   801/.95   LC 71-155962   ISBN 0691062048

Culler, Jonathan D.   2.2481
On deconstruction: theory and criticism after structuralism / Jonathan Culler. — Ithaca, N.Y.: Cornell University Press, 1982. 307 p.; 23 cm. Includes index. 1. Deconstruction I. T.
PN98.D43 C8 1982   801/.95 19   LC 82-7414   ISBN 0801413222

Leitch, Vincent B., 1944-.   2.2482
Deconstructive criticism: an advanced introduction / Vincent B. Leitch. — New York: Columbia University Press, 1983. xii, 290 p.; 24 cm. 1. Deconstruction I. T.
PN98.D43 L4 1983   808/.00141 19   LC 82-4269   ISBN 0231054726

Norris, Christopher.   2.2483
Deconstruction, theory and practice / Christopher Norris. — London; New York: Methuen, 1982. xiii, 157 p.; 21 cm. — (New accents) Includes index. 1. Deconstruction I. T.
PN98.D43 N6 1982   801/.95 19   LC 81-22422   ISBN 0416320600

Skura, Meredith Anne, 1944-.   2.2484
The literary use of the psychoanalytic process / Meredith Anne Skura. — New Haven: Yale University Press, c1981. viii, 280 p.; 22 cm. 1. Psychoanalysis and literature 2. Criticism I. T.
PN98.P75 S58   801/.92 19   LC 80-23990   ISBN 0300023804

Jauss, Hans Robert.   2.2485
Toward an aesthetic of reception / Hans Robert Jauss; translation from German by Timothy Bahti; introduction by Paul de Man. — Minneapolis: University of Minnesota Press, c1982. xxix, 231 p.; 24 cm. — (Theory and history of literature. v. 2) Includes index. 1. Reader-response criticism — Addresses, essays, lectures. I. T. II. Series.
PN98.R38 J38 1982   801/.95 19   LC 81-16260   ISBN 0816610347

Mailloux, Steven.   2.2486
Interpretive conventions: the reader in the study of American fiction / Steven Mailloux. — Ithaca, N.Y.: Cornell University Press, 1982. 228 p.; 23 cm. Includes index. 1. Reader-response criticism 2. Criticism — United States. 3. American fiction — History and criticism. I. T.
PN98.R38 M3 1982   801/.95/0973 19   LC 81-70712   ISBN 0801414768

Reader–response criticism: from formalism to post–structuralism   2.2487
/ edited by Jane P. Tompkins.
Baltimore: Johns Hopkins University Press, 1981 (c1980). xxvi, 275 p.; 24 cm. Includes index. 1. Reader-response criticism — Addresses, essays, lectures. I. Tompkins, Jane P.
PN98.R38 R4   801/.95 19   LC 80-7996   ISBN 0801824001

Culler, Jonathan D.   2.2488
The pursuit of signs—semiotics, literature, deconstruction / Jonathan Culler. — Ithaca, N.Y.: Cornell University Press, 1981. xiii, 242 p.; 22 cm. 1. Criticism 2. Semiotics and literature 3. Deconstruction I. T.
PN98.S46 C84   808/.00141 19   LC 80-70539   ISBN 0801414172

Scholes, Robert E.   2.2489
Semiotics and interpretation / Robert Scholes. — New Haven: Yale University Press, c1982. xiv, 161 p.; 22 cm. Includes index. 1. Criticism 2. Semiotics and literature I. T.
PN98.S46 S3 1982   808/.00141 19   LC 81-15971   ISBN 0300027982

Sammons, Jeffrey L.   2.2490
Literary sociology and practical criticism: an inquiry / Jeffrey L. Sammons. — Bloomington: Indiana University Press, 1978 (c1977). xiii, 235 p.; 24 cm. Includes index. 1. Criticism 2. Literature and society I. T.
PN98.S6 S3   801/.95/0943   LC 77-74445   ISBN 0253335647

Culler, Jonathan D.   2.2491
Structuralist poetics: structuralism, linguistics, and the study of literature / Jonathan Culler. — Ithaca, N.Y.: Cornell University Press, 1975. xi, 301 p.; 23 cm. Includes index. 1. Structuralism (Literary analysis) 2. Criticism I. T.
PN98.S7 C8   801/.95   LC 74-11608   ISBN 0801409284

Scholes, Robert E.   2.2492
Structuralism in literature; an introduction [by] Robert Scholes. — New Haven: Yale University Press, 1974. xii, 221 p.; 22 cm. 1. Structuralism (Literary analysis) I. T.
PN98.S7 S3   801/.9   LC 73-90578   ISBN 0300017502

Donovan, Josephine, 1941-.   2.2493
Feminist literary criticism: explorations in theory / Josephine Donovan, editor. — Lexington: University Press of Kentucky, c1975. 81 p.; 22 cm. 1. Feminist literary criticism 2. Women and literature I. T.
PN98.W64 F4   809/.933/52   LC 75-12081

The New feminist criticism: essays on women, literature, and   2.2494
theory / edited by Elaine Showalter.
1st ed. — New York: Pantheon, c1985. ix, 403 p.; 25 cm. 1. Feminist literary criticism — Addresses, essays, lectures. I. Showalter, Elaine.
PN98.W64 N48 1985   809/.89287 19   LC 84-22625   ISBN 0394539133

Theory and practice of feminist literary criticism / edited by   2.2495
Gabriela Mora and Karen S. Van Hooft.
Ypsilanti, Mich.: Bilingual Press/Editorial Bilingüe, c1982. ix, 291 p.; 22 cm. (Studies in literary analysis.) 1. Feminist literary criticism — Addresses, essays, lectures. I. Mora, Gabriela. II. Van Hooft, Karen S. III. Series.
PN98.W64 T47   809.8/99287 19   LC 81-67051   ISBN 0916950239

PN99 Criticism in Special Countries, A–Z

Liu, James J. Y.   **2.2496**
Chinese theories of literature / James J. Y. Liu. — Chicago: University of Chicago Press, [1975] x, 197 p.; 23 cm. Includes index. 1. Chinese literature — History and criticism — Theories, etc. I. T.
PN99.C5 L58   801   *LC* 74-11631   *ISBN* 0226486923

Fowlie, Wallace, 1908-.   • **2.2497**
The French critic, 1549–1967. With a pref., by Harry T. Moore. — Carbondale: Southern Illinois University Press, [1968] vi, 184 p.; 22 cm. — (Crosscurrents: modern critiques) 1. Criticism — France — History. I. T.
PN99.F8 F6   840.9   *LC* 68-21415

Le Sage, Laurent, 1913-.   • **2.2498**
The French new criticism: an introduction and a sampler. — University Park: Pennsylvania State University Press, 1967. x, 219 p.; 23 cm. 1. New Criticism — France. I. T.
PN99.F8 L4   801/.950944   *LC* 66-26270

Elledge, Scott. ed.   • **2.2499**
The continental model; selected French critical essays of the seventeenth century, in English translation. Edited by Scott Elledge and Donald Schier. — Rev. ed. — Ithaca, [N.Y.]: Cornell University Press, [1970] xviii, 412 p.; 22 cm. — (Cornell paperbacks) Includes L'Art poétique by N. Boileau-Despréaux in French and English on opposite pages. 1. Criticism — France. I. Schier, Donald Stephen, 1914- joint ed. II. T.
PN99.F82 E55 1970   801/.95/0944   *LC* 79-130315   *ISBN* 0801491118

Simon, John K.   **2.2500**
Modern French criticism; from Proust and Valéry to structuralism. Edited by John K. Simon. — Chicago: University of Chicago Press, [1972] xvi, 405 p.; 22 cm. 1. Criticism — France — Addresses, essays, lectures. I. T.
PN99.F82 S55   801/.95/0944   *LC* 79-160840   *ISBN* 0226758540

German romantic criticism / edited by A. Leslie Willson;   **2.2501**
foreword by Ernst Behler.
New York: Continuum, 1982. xix, 292 p.; 22 cm. — (German library. v. 21) 1. Criticism — Germany — Addresses, essays, lectures. 2. Literature — Addresses, essays, lectures. I. Willson, A. Leslie (Amos Leslie), 1923- II. Series.
PN99.G4 G4 1982   801/.95/0943 19   *LC* 82-5016   *ISBN* 0826402326

Atkins, John William Hey, 1874-1951.   • **2.2502**
English literary criticism: 17th and 18th centuries. — London, Methuen [1951] xi, 383 p. 23 cm. 1. Criticism — Great Britain — Hist. I. T.
PN99.G7A78   801   *LC* 52-1387

Atkins, John William Hey, 1874- .   • **2.2503**
English literary criticism: the medieval phase. — Gloucester, Mass.: P. Smith, 1961. 211 p.; 21 cm. 1. Criticism — Great Britain — History. I. T.
PN99.G7 A8 1961   *LC* 61-30549

Atkins, John William Hey, 1874-1951.   • **2.2504**
English literary criticism: the Renascence. — New York: Barnes & Noble, [1968] xi, 371 p.; 23 cm. Reprint of the 1947 ed. 1. Criticism — Great Britain — History. 2. Renaissance — England. I. T.
PN99.G7 A83 1968   801/.9509/42   *LC* 68-6918

Enright, D. J. (Dennis Joseph), 1920- ed.   • **2.2505**
English critical texts, 16th century to 20th century, edited with notes and an appendix of classical extracts, by D. J. Enright and Ernst de Chickera. — London, Oxford University Press, 1962. 398 p. 23 cm. 1. Criticism — Gt. Brit. I. De Chickera, Ernst, joint ed. II. T.
PN99.G7E5   801.9   *LC* 62-5117

Hudson, Derek. ed.   • **2.2506**
English critical essays, twentieth century; second series. London: Oxford University Press, 1958. xv, 363 p.; 16 cm. (The World's classics, 567) 'Consists of work written or published since 1933 and is a sequel to the collection of English critical essays: twentieth century, selected and introduced by Phyllis M. Jones.' 1. Criticism — Great Britain 2. English literature — History and criticism 3. English essays I. T.
PN99 G7 H8   *LC* a 61-1398

Hyman, Stanley Edgar, 1919-1970.   • **2.2507**
The critical performance: an anthology of American and British literary criticism of our century / Stanley Edgar Hyman. — 1st ed. — New York:

Vintage Books, 1956. x, 337 p. — (Vintage books; K-38) 1. Criticism — Great Britain 2. Criticism — United States 3. English literature — History and criticism — Addresses, essays, lectures 4. Literature — Addresses, essays, lectures I. T.
PN99G7 H9   PN99G7 H9.   *LC* 56-58000

Watson, George, 1927-.   • **2.2508**
The literary critics; a study of English descriptive criticism. — London, Chatto & Windus, 1964 [c1962] 222 p. 23 cm. 'Select bibliography of modern editions and studies': p. [206]-214. 1. Criticism — Gt. Brit. — Hist. I. T.
PN99.G7W3 1964b   801.9   *LC* 64-3464

Stacy, R. H. (Robert H.), 1919-.   **2.2509**
Russian literary criticism, a short history [by] R. H. Stacy. [1st ed.] [Syracuse] Syracuse University Press, 1974. ix, 267 p. 23 cm. 1. Criticism — Soviet Union — History. I. T.
PN99.R9 S8   801/.95/0947   *LC* 74-10434   *ISBN* 0815601077

Norris, Frank, 1870-1902.   • **2.2510**
Literary criticism. Edited by Donald Pizer. — Austin, University of Texas Press [1964] xxiv, 247 p. 24 cm. 'Bibliographical note and Checklist of Norris' literary criticism': p. [233]-240. 1. Criticism — U.S. 2. American fiction — Hist. & crit. I. Pizer, Donald. ed. II. T.
PN99.U5N6   818.4   *LC* 63-17618 rev

Rathbun, John Wilbert, 1924-.   **2.2511**
American literary criticism / John W. Rathbun. — Boston: G. K. Hall, 1980 (c1979). 3 v.; 21 cm. — (Twayne's United States authors series; TUSAS 339-341) Vol. 2 by J. W. Rathbun and H. H. Clark; v. 3 by A. L. Goldsmith. 1. Criticism — United States — History. I. Clark, Harry Hayden, 1901-1971. joint author. II. Goldsmith, Arnold L. joint author. III. T.
PN99.U5 R37   801/.95/0973   *LC* 79-9903   0805772642

Stovall, Floyd, 1896- ed.   • **2.2512**
The development of American literary criticism, by Harry H. Clark [and others]. — Chapel Hill, University of North Carolina Press, 1955. ix, 262 p. 24 cm. Bibliography: p. 247-253. 1. Criticism — U.S. — Hist. 2. American literature — Hist. & crit. I. Clark, Harry Hayden, 1901-1971. II. T.
PN99.U5S75   801   *LC* 55-1459

Sutton, Walter.   • **2.2513**
Modern American criticism. Englewood Cliffs, N.J.: Prentice-Hall, 1963. 298 p.; 22 cm. (The Princeton studies, humanistic scholarship in America) 1. Criticism — United States — History. I. T. II. Series.
PN99.U5 S8   810.904   *LC* 63-8462

Winters, Yvor, 1900-1968.   • **2.2514**
The anatomy of nonsense [by] Yvor Winters. Norfolk, Conn., New directions [1943] 255 p. 22 cm. 1. Criticism 2. American literature — History and criticism I. T.
PN99.U5W5   810.4   *LC* 43-11973

Daiches, David, 1912-.   • **2.2515**
English literature. Englewood Cliffs, N.J.: Prentice-Hall, [1964] xv, 174 p.; 22 cm. (The Princeton studies: humanistic scholarship in America) Erratum slip inserted. 1. Criticism — United States. 2. Literature — Research 3. English literature — History and criticism I. T. II. Series.
PN99.U52 D3   820.9   *LC* 64-16034

O'Connor, William Van, 1915-1966.   • **2.2516**
An age of criticism: 1900–1950. — Chicago: H. Regnery Co., 1952. 182 p.; 22 cm. — (Twentieth-century literature in America) 1. Criticism — United States. I. T.
PN99.U52 O3   801   *LC* 52-12476

PN101–249 AUTHORSHIP

Allen, Walter Ernest, 1911- ed.   • **2.2517**
Writers on writing. London: Phoenix House, [1958, c1948; label: Boston: The Writer, inc.] 258 p.; 23 cm. 1. Authorship I. T.
PN137.A4   *LC* 59-16830

Achtert, Walter S.   • **2.2518**
The MLA style manual / by Walter S. Achtert and Joseph Gibaldi. — New York: Modern Language Association of America, 1985. p. cm. Includes index. 1. Authorship — Style manuals I. Gibaldi, Joseph, 1942- II. Modern Language Association of America. III. T.
PN147.A28 1985   808/.02 19   *LC* 85-4972   *ISBN* 0873521366

Commins, Dorothy.   2.2519
What is an editor?: Saxe Commins at work / Dorothy Commins. — Chicago: University of Chicago Press, 1978. xv, 243 p.: ill.; 23 cm. Includes index. 1. Commins, Saxe. 2. Editors — United States — Biography. 3. American literature — 20th century — History and criticism. I. T.
PN149.9.C6 C6   070.5/092/4 B   *LC* 77-81716   *ISBN* 0226114279

Berg, A. Scott (Andrew Scott)   2.2520
Max Perkins, editor of genius / A. Scott Berg. — 1st ed. — New York: Dutton, c1978. viii, 498 p., [8] leaves of plates: ill.; 24 cm. 'Thomas Congdon books.' 1. Perkins, Maxwell E. (Maxwell Evarts), 1884-1947. 2. Editors — United States — Biography. I. T.
PN149.9.P4 B4   070.4/092/4 B   *LC* 77-25944   *ISBN* 0525154272

Bentley, Gerald Eades, 1901-.   • 2.2521
The profession of dramatist in Shakespeare's time, 1590–1642. — [Princeton, N.J.]: Princeton University Press, 1971. ix, 329 p.; 23 cm. 1. Playwriting 2. Dramatists, English — Early modern, 1500-1700 3. Theater — England — History. 4. English drama — Early modern and Elizabethan, 1500-1600 — History and criticism. I. T.
PN151.B54   822/.3/09   *LC* 75-154990   *ISBN* 0691062056

Lewis, Wyndham, 1882-1957.   • 2.2522
The writer and the absolute / by Wyndham Lewis. — London: Methuen, [1952] vi, 202 p. 1. Authorship I. T.
PN151.L45   PR6023.E97 W7 1952.   *LC* 62-3008

Balkin, Richard.   2.2523
A writer's guide to book publishing / by Richard Balkin, with two chapters by Jared Carter. New York: Hawthorn Books, c1977. xiv, 236 p.; 25 cm. Includes index. 1. Authors and publishers 2. Publishers and publishing I. Carter, Jared. II. T.
PN155.B3   808/.025   *LC* 76-24230   *ISBN* 0801589355

Skillin, Marjorie E.   2.2524
Words into type / based on studies by Marjorie E. Skillin, Robert M. Gay, and other authorities. — 3d ed., completely rev. — Englewood Cliffs, N.J.: Prentice-Hall, [1974] xx, 585 p.: ill.; 24 cm. 1. Authorship — Handbooks, manuals, etc. 2. Printing, Practical — Style manuals I. Gay, Robert M. (Robert Malcolm), 1879-1961. joint author. II. T.
PN160.S52 1974   808/.02   *LC* 73-21726   *ISBN* 0139642625

Literary market place: the directory of American book publishing.   • 2.2525
1940-. New York: Bowker, 1940-. v. Annual. None published for 1941. Subtitle varies. 1972/73-   Includes Names and numbers (previously published separately) 1. Publishers and publishing — United States — Directories.
PN161.L5   655.473   *LC* 41-51571   *ISBN* 0835210421

Brookes, B. C. (Bertram Claude) ed.   • 2.2526
Editorial practice in libraries. London Aslib 1961. 204p. 1. Editing 2. Printing, Practical 3. Technical writing I. T.
PN162 B7   *LC* 61-65491

Gaskell, Philip.   2.2527
From writer to reader: studies in editorial method / by Philip Gaskell. Oxford [Eng.]: Clarendon Press, 1978. p. cm. Includes index. 1. Editing — Case studies. I. T.
PN162.G3   808/.02   *LC* 77-30111   *ISBN* 019818171X

Plotnik, Arthur.   2.2528
The elements of editing: a modern guide for editors and journalists / by Arthur Plotnik. — New York: Macmillan; London: Collier Macmillan, c1982. xiii, 156 p.: ill.; 22 cm. 1. Journalism — Editing I. T.
PN162.P55 1982   070.4/1 19   *LC* 82-4672   *ISBN* 0025977008

Spence, Joseph, 1699-1768.   2.2529
Observations, anecdotes, and characters of books and men, collected from conversation; edited by James M. Osborn. — [New ed.]. — [S.l.]: Oxford University Press, 1966. 2 v.; 22 1/2 cm. 1. Pope, Alexander, 1688-1744. 2. Authors, English 3. Literature — Anecdotes, facetiae, satire, etc. I. Osborn, James Marshall. ed. II. T.
PN165.S63 1966   820.9005   *LC* 67-70335

PN173–185 Rhetoric

Aristotle.   2.2530
The Rhetoric of Aristotle: an expanded translation with supplementary examples for students of composition and public speaking / by Lane Cooper. —

New York; London: D. Appleton and company, 1932. xiviii p., 1 l., 259 p.; 22 cm. 1. Rhetoric, Ancient I. Cooper, Lane, 1875-1959. tr. II. T.
PN173.A7 C6   888.5 808   *LC* 32-1678

Murphy, James Jerome.   2.2531
Rhetoric in the Middle Ages: a history of rhetorical theory from Saint Augustine to the Renaissance / James J. Murphy. — Berkeley: University of California Press, [1974] xiv, 395 p.; 24 cm. 1. Rhetoric, Medieval 2. Rhetoric, Ancient I. T.
PN173.M8   808/.009   *LC* 73-76102   *ISBN* 0520024397

Richards, I. A. (Ivor Armstrong), 1893-.   • 2.2532
The philosophy of rhetoric / by I. A. Richards. — New York; London: Oxford University Press, 1936. ix, 138 p.; 23 cm. — (Half-title: The Mary Flexner lectures on the humanities, III) 'First edition.' 1. Rhetoric I. T.
PN175.R45   808   *LC* 36-35023

IJsseling, Samuel, 1932-.   2.2533
[Retoriek en filosofie. English] Rhetoric and philosophy in conflict: an historical survey / by Samuel IJsseling. — The Hague: M. Nijhoff, 1976. 142 p.; 24 cm. Translation of Retoriek en filosofie. 1. Rhetoric — Philosophy 2. Rhetoric — History. I. T.
PN179.I513   PN179 I513.   808/.009   *LC* 77-460072   *ISBN* 9024719011

Golden, James L.   2.2534
The rhetoric of Western thought / James L. Golden, Goodwin F. Berquist, William E. Coleman. — 3rd ed. — Dubuque, Iowa: Kendall/Hunt Pub. Co., c1983. xi, 476 p.: ill.; 23 cm. 1. Rhetoric — History. I. Berquist, Goodwin F. (Goodwin Fauntleroy), 1930- II. Coleman, William E. III. T.
PN183.G6 1983   808 19   *LC* 82-84271   *ISBN* 0840329164

Murphy, James Jerome. comp.   • 2.2535
Three medieval rhetorical arts / Edited by James J. Murphy. — Berkeley: University of California Press, [1971] xxiii, 235 p.; 24 cm. 1. Rhetoric, Medieval I. Vinsauf, Geoffrey de, fl. 1200. Poetria nova. English. 1971. II. Robert de Basevorn, fl. 1322. Forma praedicandi. English. 1971. III. Rationes dictandi. English. 1971. IV. T.
PN185.M8   808.04/71/75   *LC* 72-132416   *ISBN* 0520018206

PN203 Literary Style

Barthes, Roland.   2.2536
[Degré zéro de l'écriture. English] Writing degree zero. Pref. by Susan Sontag. Translated from the French by Annette Lavers and Colin Smith. [1st American ed.] New York, Hill and Wang [1968] xxi, 88 p. 20 cm. Translation of Le degré zéro de l'écriture. 1. Style, Literary 2. French literature — History and criticism. I. T.
PN203.B313 1968   808.02   *LC* 68-14789

Chapman, Raymond.   2.2537
Linguistics and literature: an introduction to literary stylistics. [London]: E. Arnold, [c1973] 119 p.; 21 cm. 1. Style, Literary I. T.
PN 203 C46 1973   *ISBN* 0713156856

Frye, Northrop.   • 2.2538
The well–tempered critic. — Bloomington, Indiana University Press [1963] 160 p. 21 cm. 'Consists of lectures delivered at the University of Virginia in March 1961 for the Page-Barbour Foundation, with some expansion and revision.' 1. Style, Literary 2. Criticism I. T.
PN203.F7   801.9   *LC* 63-9716

Lucas, F. L. (Frank Laurence), 1894-1967.   • 2.2539
Style. New York: Collier Books, [1962] 284p. 1. Style, Literary I. T.
PN203 L8 1962

Murry, John Middleton, 1889-1957.   • 2.2540
The problem of style / by J. Middleton Murry. — London: Oxford U.P., 1960. x, 133 p.; 20 cm. (Oxford paperbacks; no. 11) 1. Style, Literary 2. Criticism I. T.
PN203.M8 1960   *LC* 60-50596   *ISBN* 0192810049 pa

Symposium on Literary Style, Bellagio, Italy, 1969.   • 2.2541
Literary style; a symposium; edited and (in part) translated by Seymour Chatman. — London; New York: Oxford University Press, 1971. xv, 427 p.; 24 cm. 1. Style, Literary — Congresses. I. Chatman, Seymour Benjamin, 1928- ed. II. T.
PN203.S9 1969   418   *LC* 71-146949   *ISBN* 019501345X

Walcutt, Charles Child, 1908-.   **2.2542**
Man's changing mask; modes and methods of characterization in fiction. — Minneapolis: University of Minnesota Press, [1966] viii, 368 p.; 24 cm. 1. Characters and characteristics in literature 2. Fiction — Technique I. T.
PN218.W3   808.3   *LC* 66-24088

PN241 Translating

Arrowsmith, William, 1924- ed.   **• 2.2543**
The craft and context of translation: a symposium / edited by William Arrowsmith and Roger Shattuck. — Austin: University of Texas Press, 1961. 206 p.; 24 cm. The first 10 essays ... were delivered at a Symposium on Translation held at the University of Texas in November, 1959. 1. Translating and interpreting I. Shattuck, Roger. joint ed. II. Symposium on Translation, University of Texas, 1959. III. T.
PN241.A74 1971   *LC* 61-15827   *ISBN* 0292732023

Brower, Reuben Arthur, 1908- ed.   **• 2.2544**
On translation. Cambridge, Harvard University Press, 1959. xi, 297 p. illus. 24 cm. 1. Translating and interpreting 2. Translating and interpreting — Bibliography. I. T.
PN241.B7   *LC* a 58-8641

Lefevere, André.   **2.2545**
Translating literature: the German tradition from Luther to Rosenzweig / André Lefevere. — Assen: Van Gorcum, 1977. vii, 116 p.; 24 cm. — (Approaches to translation studies. no. 4) Includes index. 1. Translating and interpreting — Germany — Addresses, essays, lectures. I. T. II. Series.
PN241.L35   418/.02/0943   *LC* 78-309364   *ISBN* 9023215133

PN451–1008 LITERARY HISTORY. BIOGRAPHY

Index to the Wilson authors series.   **2.2546**
Rev. 1986 ed. — New York: H.W. Wilson Co., c1986. 104 p.; 27 cm. 'Biographical dictionaries in the Wilson authors series: American authors, 1600-1900, British authors before 1800, British authors of the nineteenth century, European authors, 1000-1900, Greek and Latin authors, 800 B.C.-A-D. 1000, Twentieth century authors, Twentieth century authors: First supplement, World authors, 1950-1970, World authors, 1970-1975, World authors, 1975-1980.' 1. H.W. Wilson Company. 2. Wilson authors series — Indexes. 3. Authors — Biography — Indexes.
PN451.I5 1986   016.809 B 19   *LC* 86-5486   *ISBN* 0824207319

Kunitz, Stanley, 1905-.   **• 2.2547**
European authors, 1000–1900: a biographical dictionary of European literature / edited by Stanley J. Kunitz and Vineta Colby. — New York: H.W. Wilson, 1967. ix, 1016 p.; ports.; 26 cm. (The Authors series) 'Complete in one volume with 967 biographies and 309 portraits.' Includes Continental European writers born after the year 1000 and dead before 1925. Nearly a thousand major and minor contributors to thirty-one different literatures are discussed. 1. Literature, Modern — Bio-bibliography. 2. Authors, European I. Colby, Vineta. II. T.
PN451.K8   809.03   *LC* 67-13870

Magill, Frank Northen, 1907- ed.   **2.2548**
Cyclopedia of world authors. Edited by Frank N. Magill. Associate editors: Dayton Kohler [and] Tench Francis Tilghman. — Rev. ed. — Englewood Cliffs, N.J.: Salem Press, [1974] 3 v. (vii, 1973, xi p.); 24 cm. 'An earlier edition ... appears under the title of Masterplots cyclopedia of world authors.' 1. Literature — Bio-bibliography. I. Kohler, Dayton, 1907-1972, joint ed. II. Tilghman, Tench Francis. joint ed. III. T.
PN451.M36 1974   803   *LC* 74-174980

Commire, Anne.   **2.2549**
Something about the author. v. 1- 1971-. Detroit, Gale Research c1971-. v. ill., ports. 29 cm. 'Facts and pictures about contemporary authors and illustrators of books for young people.' 1. Children's literature — Bio-bibliography — Periodicals. I. Gale Research Company. II. T.
PN451.S6   028.52/0922 920 B   *LC* 72-27107

Wakeman, John.   **2.2550**
World authors, 1950–1970: a companion volume to Twentieth century authors / edited by John Wakeman; editorial consultant: Stanley J. Kunitz. — New York: Wilson, 1975. 1594 p.: ill.; 27 cm. (The Authors series) 'Continues the

work done by Stanley J. Kunitz and Howard Haycraft in Twentieth century authors [and its first suppl.]' 1. Literature, Modern — 20th century — Bio-bibliography. I. Kunitz, Stanley, 1905- Twentieth century authors. II. T. III. Series.
PN451.W3   809/.04 B   *LC* 75-172140   *ISBN* 0824204190

Dronke, Peter.   **2.2551**
Women writers of the Middle Ages: a critical study of texts from Perpetua (203) to Marguerite Porete (1310) / Peter Dronke. — Cambridge: Cambridge University Press, 1984. xi, 338 p. 1. Women authors I. T.
PN471   PN471 D76 1984.   809/.89287 19   *LC* 83-7456   *ISBN* 0521255805

Hardwick, Elizabeth.   **2.2552**
Seduction and betrayal; women and literature. — [1st ed.]. — New York: Random House, [1974] 208 p.; 22 cm. 1. Women authors 2. Women in literature I. T.
PN471.H3   809/.933/52   *LC* 73-3982   *ISBN* 039449069X

Moers, Ellen, 1928-.   **2.2553**
Literary women / Ellen Moers. — 1st ed. — Garden City, N.Y.: Doubleday, 1976. xvi, 336 p., [12] leaves of plates: ill.; 24 cm. Includes index. 1. Women authors I. T.
PN471.M63   809/.89287   *LC* 74-33686   *ISBN* 0385074271

Russ, Joanna, 1937-.   **2.2554**
How to suppress women's writing / by Joanna Russ. — 1st ed. — Austin: University of Texas Press, 1983. 159 p.; 22 cm. 1. Women authors 2. Authorship I. T.
PN471.R87 1983   809/.89287 19   *LC* 83-5910   *ISBN* 0292724446

Woolf, Virginia, 1882-1941.   **• 2.2555**
A room of one's own / Virginia Woolf. — New York: Fountain Press, 1929. 4p., l, 3-199 p.; 20 cm. 1. Women authors 2. Women — History and women — Social conditions. 3. Women — Great Britain 4. English fiction — History and criticism. 5. Women in literature 6. Women in art I. T.
PN471.W6 1929   *LC* 30-1

Writing and sexual difference / edited by Elizabeth Abel.   **2.2556**
Chicago: University of Chicago Press, 1982. 315 p.; 23 cm. 'The articles in this volume originally appeared in Critical inquiry'—Verso t.p. 1. Women and literature — Addresses, essays, lectures. I. Abel, Elizabeth.
PN481.W75 1982   809/.89287 19   *LC* 82-11131   *ISBN* 0226000761

PN500–509 Collections

European writers: the Middle Ages and the Renaissance / William T.H. Jackson, editor, George Stade, editor in chief.   **2.2557**
New York: Scribner, [1983] 2 v.; 29 cm. 1. European literature — History and criticism — Addresses, essays, lectures. I. Jackson, W. T. H. (William Thomas Hobdell), 1915- II. Stade, George.
PN501.E9 1983   809/.894 19   *LC* 83-16333   *ISBN* 0684165945

Hardison, O. B. comp.   **• 2.2558**
Modern continental literary criticism / O. B. Hardison, Jr., editor. — New York: Appleton-Century-Crofts, 1962. xix, 352 p.; 21 cm. — (Goldentree books) 1. Literature — History and criticism 2. Criticism — History. 3. Aesthetics I. T.
PN501.H27   *LC* 62-9415   *ISBN* 0390410586

Howe, Irving.   **• 2.2559**
Modern literary criticism, an anthology. — Boston, Beacon Press [1958] 438 p. 21 cm. 1. Literature — Hist. & crit. 2. Criticism I. T.
PN501.H65   809   *LC* 59-6165

Phillips, William, Nov. 14, 1907- ed.   **• 2.2560**
Art and psychoanalysis. — Cleveland: World Pub. Co. [1963] xxiv, 533 p.; 21 cm. — (Meridian books, M161) Includes bibliographies. 1. Literature — Hist. & crit. 2. Psychoanalysis 3. Creation (Literary, artistic, etc.) I. T.
PN501.P5 1963   801   *LC* 63-19729

Slote, Bernice. ed.   **• 2.2561**
Myth and symbol: critical approaches and applications, by Northrop Frye, C. Knights, and others. A selection of papers delivered at the joint meeting of the Midwest Modern Language Association and the Central Renaissance Conference, 1962. Lincoln: University of Nebraska, [1963] viii, 196 p.; 21 cm. — (A Bison book) 'BB141.' 1. Literature — Addresses, essays, lectures. 2. Symbolism in literature 3. Criticism — Addresses, essays, lectures. I. Frye,

Northrop. II. Midwest Modern Language Association. III. Central Renaissance Conference. University of Nebraska, 1962. IV. T.
PN501.S55   809.91   *LC* 63-9960

PN510–519 Collected Essays of Individual Critics

PN511 AMERICAN AND ENGLISH CRITICS, 1801–

PN511 A–G

Auden, W. H. (Wystan Hugh), 1907-1973.   2.2562
Forewords and afterwords, by W. H. Auden. Selected by Edward Mendelson. [1st ed.] New York, Random House [1973] x, 529 p. 25 cm. 1. Literature — Addresses, essays, lectures. I. T.
PN511.A78   809   *LC* 72-10230   *ISBN* 0394483596

Barzun, Jacques, 1907-.   • 2.2563
The energies of art: studies of authors classic and modern. — [1st ed.] New York: Harper [1956] 355 p. 1. Literature — History and criticism I. T.
PN511.B35   *LC* 56-6020

Bogan, Louise, 1897-1970.   • 2.2564
Selected criticism, prose, poetry. — [New York: Noonday Press], 1955. 404 p.; 22 cm. 1. Literature — History and criticism — Addresses, essays, lectures. 2. Poetry — History and criticism — Addresses, essays, lectures. 3. Books — Reviews — Addresses, essays, lectures. I. T.
PN511.B54   *LC* 55-8230

Burke, Kenneth, 1897-.   • 2.2565
Counter–statement. — [2d ed.]. — Los Altos, Calif.: Hermes Publications, [1953] xvii, 219 p.; 22 cm. 1. Literature — History and criticism — Addresses, essays, lectures. 2. Criticism — Addresses, essays, lectures. I. T.
PN511.B79 1953   *LC* 52-11629

Burke, Kenneth, 1897-.   • 2.2566
Language as symbolic action; essays on life, literature, and method. — Berkeley: University of California Press, 1966. xiv, 514 p.; 24 cm. 1. Literature — Addresses, essays, lectures. I. T.
PN511.B793   801.95   *LC* 66-27655

Burke, Kenneth, 1897-.   • 2.2567
The philosophy of literary form; studies in symbolic action. — 2d ed. — Baton Rouge: Louisiana State University Press, [1967] xxvi, 455 p.; 24 cm. 1. Literature — Addresses, essays, lectures. 2. Literature — Philosophy 3. Criticism I. T. II. Title: Studies in symbolic action.
PN511.B795 1967   801   *LC* 67-12214

Chesterton, G. K. (Gilbert Keith), 1874-1936.   • 2.2568
A handful of authors: essays on books & writers / edited by Dorothy Collins. — New York: Sheed and Ward, 1953. 214 p.; 21 cm. 1. Literature, Modern — Hist. & crit. I. T.
PN511.C42   824.91   *LC* 53-9800

De la Mare, Walter, 1873-1956.   • 2.2569
Private view / by Walter de la Mare; with an introd. by Lord David Cecil. — London: Faber & Faber, 1953. xvi, 256 p. 1. Literature — Addresses, essays, lectures I. T.
PN511 D34   PN511 D34.   *LC* 53-3025

Enright, D. J. (Dennis Joseph), 1920-.   • 2.2570
The apothecary's shop: essays on literature / by D. J. Enright. — Philadelphia: Dufour Editions, [c1957] 236 p.; 21 cm. 1. Literature — History and criticism — Addresses, essays, lectures. I. T.
PN511.E58 1957a   809   *LC* 75-15663   *ISBN* 0837182220

Fiedler, Leslie A.   • 2.2571
No! in thunder: essays on myth and literature. — Boston: Beacon Press, [1960] 336 p.; 21 cm. 1. Literature, Modern — Addresses, essays, lectures. 2. American literature — Addresses, essays, lectures. I. T.
PN511.F5   809   *LC* 60-14676

Garrod, Heathcote William, 1878-1960.   • 2.2572
The study of good letters / edited by John Jones. — Oxford: Clarendon Press 1963. vi, 211 p.: port.; 19 cm. 1. Literature — Addresses, essays, lectures I. T.
PN511 G3

PN511 H–O

Highet, Gilbert, 1906-1978.   • 2.2573
A clerk of Oxenford: essays on literature and life. — New York: Oxford University Press [c1954] xii, 272 p.; 21 cm. Includes bibliographies. 1. Literature — Addresses, essays, lectures. I. T.
PN511.H48   804   *LC* 54-10897

Highet, Gilbert, 1906-1978.   • 2.2574
Talents and geniuses: the pleasures of appreciation. — New York: Oxford U.P.; 1957. 347 p. 1. Literature — Addresses, essays, lectures. 2. Art — Addresses, essays, lectures. I. T.
PN511.H485   *LC* 57-11635

Huxley, Aldous, 1894-1963.   • 2.2575
Texts & pretexts, an anthology with commentaries, by Aldous Huxley. London, Chatto & Windus, 1932. viii, 311, [1] p. 20 cm. 1. Poetry — History and criticism 2. Poetry — Collections I. T.
PN511.H85 1932   *LC* 33-1352

Hyman, Stanley Edgar, 1919-1970.   • 2.2576
The promised end: essays and reviews, 1942–1962. — Freeport, N.Y.: Books for Libraries Press, [1972, c1963] 380 p.; 23 cm.— (Essay index reprint series) Reprint of the 1963 ed. 1. Literature — Addresses, essays, lectures. I. T.
PN511.H9 1972   809   *LC* 78-156662   *ISBN* 0836925971

Kazin, Alfred, 1915-.   • 2.2577
The inmost leaf: a selection of essays. [1st ed.]. — New York: Harcourt, Brace, [c1955]. 273 p.; 21 cm. 1. Literature — History and criticism — Addresses, essays, lectures. I. T.
PN511.K25   814   *LC* 55-10810

Lesser, Simon O.   2.2578
The whispered meanings: selected essays of Simon O. Lesser / edited by Robert Sprich and Richard W. Noland. — Amherst: University of Massachusetts Press, 1977. 237 p.; 24 cm. 1. Literature — History and criticism — Addresses, essays, lectures. 2. Psychoanalysis and literature — Addresses, essays, lectures. I. T.
PN511.L358   809   *LC* 77-73480   *ISBN* 0870232436

Levin, Harry, 1912-.   • 2.2579
Contexts of criticism. — Cambridge, Harvard University Press, 1957. 294 p. 22 cm. — (Harvard studies in comparative literature, 22) English or French. 1. Literature — Hist. & crit. I. T.
PN511.L36   804   *LC* 57-7613

Maugham, W. Somerset (William Somerset), 1874-1965.   • 2.2580
Points of view; five essays. New York, Greenwood Press, 1968 [c1958] 284 p. 23 cm. 1. Literature — Addresses, essays, lectures. 2. Fiction — History and criticism I. T.
PN511.M346 1968   809   *LC* 69-10132

More, Paul Elmer, 1864-1937.   • 2.2581
The demon of the absolute / by Paul Elmer More. — Princeton: Princeton University Press, 1928. xiii p., 1 l., 183 p.; 19 cm. 1. Literature — Addresses, essays, lectures. 2. Literature — Philosophy I. Mahābhārata. Sāvitryupākhyāna. II. T.
PN511.M48   *LC* 28-24755

Murry, John Middleton, 1889-1957.   • 2.2582
Selected criticism, 1916–1957 / chosen and introduced by Richard Rees. — London: Oxford University Press, 1960. 306 p.: ill.; 23 cm. 1. Literature — History and criticism I. T.
PN511.M838   *LC* 60-3219

Ong, Walter J.   • 2.2583
The barbarian within, and other fugitive essays and studies. — New York, Macmillan, 1962. 292 p. 22 cm. 1. Literature — Addresses, essays, lectures. 2. Education — Addresses, essays, lectures. I. T.
PN511.O55   814.54   *LC* 62-12425

PN511 P–S

Pound, Ezra, 1885-1972.   • 2.2584
Literary essays. Edited with an introd. by T. S. Eliot. [Norfolk, Conn.] New Directions [1954] xv, 464 p. 23 cm. 1. Literature — Addresses, essays, lectures. 2. Poetry — Addresses, essays, lectures. 3. Poetics I. T.
PN511.P625 1954   804   *LC* 54-7905

Pound, Ezra, 1885-1972.   • **2.2585**
Make it new; essays by Ezra Pound. New Haven, Yale University Press, 1935. St. Clair Shores, Mich., Scholarly Press, 1971. vii, 407 p. 21 cm. 'Published on the Mary Cady Tew memorial fund.' 1. Literature — Addresses, essays, lectures. I. T.
PN511.P63 1971   809   LC 71-145243   ISBN 0403011582

Pound, Ezra, 1885-1972.   • **2.2586**
Polite essays [by] Ezra Pound. Freeport, N.Y., Books for Libraries Press [1966] vii, 207 p. 19 cm. (Essay index reprint series) Reprint of the 1937 ed. 1. Literature — Addresses, essays, lectures. I. T.
PN511.P633 1966   814/.5/2   LC 67-22111

Quiller-Couch, Arthur Thomas, Sir, 1863-1944.   • **2.2587**
The poet as citizen, and other papers / by Sir Arthur Guiller-Couch. — New York: The Macmillan company; Cambridge, Eng.: The University Press, 1935. viii, 230 p.; 23 cm. 1. Literature — Addresses, essays, lectures. 2. Poetry — Hist. & crit. 3. English literature — Addresses, essays, lectures. I. T.
PN511.Q5 1935   804   LC 35-1600

Rahv, Philip, 1908-1973.   • **2.2588**
Image and idea; fourteen essays on literary themes. New York, New Directions, 1949. 164 p. 22 cm. 1. Literature — History and criticism I. T.
PN511.R27   LC 49-8967

Read, Herbert Edward, Sir, 1893-1968.   • **2.2589**
[Collected essays in literary criticism] The nature of literature. Freeport, N.Y., Books for Libraries Press [1970, c1956] 381 p. 23 cm. (Essay index reprint series) First published under title: Collected essays in literary criticism. 1. Literature — Addresses, essays, lectures. 2. Criticism I. T.
PN511.R335 1970   809   LC 74-105034   ISBN 0836914783

Read, Herbert Edward, Sir, 1893-1968.   • **2.2590**
Reason and romanticism: essays in literary criticism. — New York: Russell & Russell, 1963. 229 p.; 23 cm. 1. Literature — Addresses, essays, lectures. 2. English literature — Hist. & crit. 3. Criticism I. T.
PN511.R35 1963   809   LC 63-15175

Read, Herbert Edward, Sir, 1893-1968.   • **2.2591**
Collected essays in literary criticism. — [2d ed.]. — London, Faber and Faber [1951] 381 p. 22 cm. 1. Literature — Addresses, essays, lectures. 2. Criticism I. T.
PN511.R4   LC A 52-2558

Santayana, George, 1863-1952.   • **2.2592**
Essays in literary criticism. New York, Scribner [1956] xxviii, 414 p. 25 cm. 1. Literature — History and criticism I. T.
PN511.S28   LC 56-9884

Sherman, Stuart Pratt, 1881-1926.   • **2.2593**
Shaping men and women; essays on literature and life. Edited by Jacob Zeitlin. — [1st ed.]. — New York: Greenwood Press, 1968 [c1928] xlv, 277 p.; 19 cm. 1. Literature — Addresses, essays, lectures. 2. English literature — History and criticism — Addresses, essays, lectures. 3. Teaching I. T.
PN511.S48 1968   814/.5/2   LC 69-10153

Steiner, George, 1929-.   • **2.2594**
Language and silence: essays on language, literature, and the inhuman. — [1st ed.]. — New York: Atheneum, 1967. xiv, 426 p.; 25 cm. 1. Literature — Addresses, essays, lectures. 2. Literature — Philosophy I. T.
PN511.S687   801/.08   LC 67-14332

Stoll, Elmer Edgar, 1874-1959.   • **2.2595**
Poets and playwrights: Shakespeare, Jonson, Spenser, Milton, by Elmer Edgar Stoll. Minneapolis, The University of Minnesota press, 1930. viii, 304 p. 23 cm. Essays. 1. Shakespeare, William, 1564-1616 — Criticism and interpretation 2. Jonson, Ben, 1573?-1637. 3. Spenser, Edmund, 1552?-1599. 4. Milton, John, 1608-1674 — Criticism and interpretation. 5. Literature — Addresses, essays, lectures. 6. English drama — Early modern and Elizabethan, 1500-1600 — History and criticism. I. T.
PN511.S69   LC 30-8126

Strachey, Lytton, 1880-1932.   • **2.2596**
Literary essays. — London, Chatto and Windus, 1961. 295 p. 19 cm. 'First published 1948.' Companion volume to the author's Biographical essays. 1. English literature — Hist. & crit. 2. French literature — Hist. & crit. I. T.
PN511.S72   820.4   LC 49-11685 *

PN511 T–Z

Thompson, Francis, 1859-1907.   • **2.2597**
Literary criticisms. Newly discovered and collected by Terence L. Connolly. — [1st ed.]. — New York, E. P. Dutton, 1948. xiv, 617 p. port. 25 cm. 'A bibliography of Francis Thompson's uncollected book reviews and literary criticism contributed to periodicals': p.563-596. 1. Books — Reviews 2. Literature — Hist. & crit. 3. English literature — Hist. & crit. I. Connolly, Terence Leo, 1888- ed. II. T.
PN511.T53   804   LC 48-1442 *

Trilling, Lionel, 1905-1975.   • **2.2598**
The opposing self: nine essays in criticism. — New York: Viking Press, 1955. 232 p.; 22 cm. 1. Literature, Modern — Addresses, essays, lectures. I. T.
PN511.T76   804   LC 55-5871

Van Doren, Mark, 1894-1972.   • **2.2599**
The private reader: selected articles & reviews / Mark Van Doren. — [New York]: H. Holt, [1942] xvi, 416 p.; 22 cm. 1. Literature — History and criticism — Addresses, essays, lectures. 2. Books — Reviews 3. Moving-picture play — History and criticism — Addresses, essays, lectures. I. T.
PN511.V273   LC 42-6988

Vivas, Eliseo.   • **2.2600**
The artistic transaction and essays on theory of literature / by Eliseo Vivas. — Columbus: Ohio State University Press, 1963. ix, 267 p.; 23 cm. 1. Literature — Addresses, essays, lectures. 2. Criticism — Addresses, essays, lectures. 3. Aesthetics — Addresses, essays, lectures. I. T.
PN511 V55   LC 63-15650

Warren, Austin, 1899-.   • **2.2601**
Rage for order: essays in criticism. — Chicago: Univ. of Chicago Press [1948] ix, 164 p.; 20 cm. 1. Literature, Modern — Addresses, essays, lectures. I. T.
PN511.W32   820.4   LC 48-5447 *

Weigand, Hermann John, 1892-.   • **2.2602**
Surveys and soundings in European literature, by Hermann J. Weigand. Edited by A. Leslie Willson. — Princeton, N.J.: Princeton University Press, 1966. viii, 360 p.; 24 cm. 1. European literature — History and criticism — Addresses, essays, lectures. I. T.
PN511.W42   809   LC 66-10931

West, Anthony, 1914-.   • **2.2603**
Principles and persuasions; the literary essays of Anthony West. [1st ed.] New York, Harcourt, Brace [1957] 245 p. 21 cm. 1. Books — Reviews 2. Literature, Modern — Addresses, essays, lectures. I. T.
PN511.W44   LC 57-5539

Wilson, Edmund, 1895-1972.   • **2.2604**
The wound and the bow: seven studies in literature. New York: Oxford University Press, 1965. 242 p. (A Galaxy book) 1. Literature — Addresses, essays, lectures. 2. Authors I. T.
PN511.W6x   LC 48-8265

Woolf, Virginia, 1882-1941.   • **2.2605**
The common reader, first series / Virginia Woolf. — New York: Harcourt, Brace & World, c1953. x, 246 p.; 19 cm. — (Harvest books; 10) Analyzed in Essay and general literature index. 1. English literature I. T.
PN511.W7 1953

Woolf, Virginia, 1882-1941.   • **2.2606**
The second Common reader, by Virginia Woolf ... New York, Harcourt, Brace and Company [c1932] viii, 295 p. 23 cm. London edition (L. & Virginia Woolf) has title: The common reader. Second series. 'First printing.' 1. English literature — History and criticism I. T.
PN511.W72   820.4   LC 32-31590

PN513 French Critics

Sartre, Jean Paul, 1905-.   • **2.2607**
What is literature? / translated from the French by Bernard Frechtman; introd. by Wallace Fowlie. — New York: Harper & Row, [1965] xviii, 299 p. — (Colophon books (New York, N.Y.) 1. Literature — Addresses, essays, lectures. I. T. II. Series.
PN513.S2413   LC 66-377

Sartre, Jean Paul, 1905-.   • **2.2608**
Literary and philosophical essays. Translated from the French by Annette Michelson. New York, Criterion Books [1955] 239 p. 22 cm. 'Translated from the author's Situations I and III.' 1. Literature — Addresses, essays, lectures. I. T.
PN513.S26 1955a   804   LC 55-11158

Benjamin, Walter, 1892-1940.   **2.2609**
[Illuminationen. English] Illuminations. Edited and with an introd. by Hannah Arendt. Translated by Harry Zohn. [1st ed.] New York, Harcourt, Brace & World [1968] 280 p. 22 cm. 'A Helen and Kurt Wolff book.' Selected and translated from the author's Schriften. 1. Literature — History and criticism I. T.
PN514.B3623   809   LC 68-24382

PN521–595 World Histories

Ford, Ford Madox, 1873-1939.   • **2.2610**
The march of literature, from Conficius to modern times / by Ford Madox Ford. — London: G. Allen and Unwin, ltd, 1939. vii, 878 p.; 23 cm. 'First published in the U.S.A. in 1938. First published in Great Britain in 1939.' 1. Literature — History and criticism I. T.
PN523.F6 1939   LC 40-8268

Brett-James, Antony, 1920-.   • **2.2611**
The triple stream: four centuries of English, French, and German literature, 1531–1930. — [Cambridge, Eng.]: Bowes & Bowes, [1953] x, 178 p.; 23 cm. Includes indexes. 1. Literature, Modern — Outlines, syllabi, etc. I. T.
PN524.B8   LC 54-2465

Great foreign language writers / edited by James Vinson and   **2.2612**
Daniel Kirkpatrick.
New York: St. Martin's Press, 1984. x, 714 p.; 24 cm. Includes index. 1. Literature — History and criticism 2. Literature — Bio-bibliography. 3. Authors — Biography I. Vinson, James, 1933- II. Kirkpatrick, D. L.
PN524.G74 1984   809 19   LC 83-40552   ISBN 0312345852

Staël, Madame de (Anne-Louise-Germaine), 1766-1817.   **2.2613**
De la littérature considérée dans ses rapports avec les institutions sociales / Madame de Staël. — Éd. critique / par Paul van Tieghem. — Genève: Droz; Paris: Minard, 1959. 2 v. (lxvi, 444 p.); 19 cm. — (Textes littéraires français. 82) Volume 1 has reproduction of t.p. of earlier ed.: 2. éd., rev. corr. et augm. Paris, Impr. de Crapelet, 1801. 1. Literature — History and criticism I. Van Tieghem, Paul, 1871-1948. II. T. III. Series.
PN542.S83 1959   LC a 59-6813

PN597–605 Special Movements

Abrams, M. H. (Meyer Howard), 1912-.   **2.2614**
Natural supernaturalism; tradition and revolution in romantic literature [by] M. H. Abrams. [1st ed.] New York, Norton [1971] 550 p. facsims. 25 cm. 1. Romanticism I. T.
PN603.A3   809.9/1/4   LC 71-80021   ISBN 0393043053

Babbitt, Irving, 1865-1933.   • **2.2615**
Rousseau and romanticism, by Irving Babbitt ... Boston and New York, Houghton Mifflin company [1935] xxiii, 426 p. 21 cm. 'Published May, 1919; seventh impression, June, 1935.' Bibliography: p. [399]-419. 1. Rousseau, Jean Jacques — Influence. 2. Romanticism I. T.
PN603.B3 1935   809.08   LC 35-19544

Barzun, Jacques, 1907-.   • **2.2616**
[Romanticism and the modern ego] Classic, romantic, and modern. [2d rev. ed.] Boston: Little, Brown [1961] 255 p.; 21 cm. First ed. published in 1943 under title: Romanticism and the modern ego. 1. Romanticism I. T.
PN603.B35 1961   809.91   LC 61-14543

English Institute.   • **2.2617**
Romanticism reconsidered; selected papers from the English Institute. Edited with a foreword by Northrop Frye. — New York: Columbia University Press, 1963. ix, 144 p.; 21 cm. 'Four papers read at the English Institute, September 1962.' 1. Romanticism — Congresses. I. Frye, Northrop. ed. II. T.
PN603.E5   809/.9/14   LC 63-18020

Furst, Lilian R.   • **2.2618**
Romanticism in perspective: a comparative study of aspects of the Romantic movements in England, France and Germany, [by] Lilian R. Furst. — London; Melbourne [etc.]: Macmillan; New York: St. Martin's P., 1969. 366 p.; 23 cm. 1. Romanticism I. T.
PN603.F8 1969   809/.033   LC 72-389175   ISBN 0333088859

Hocke, Gustav René, 1908-.   **2.2619**
Manierismus in der Literatur: Sprach–Alchimie und esoterische Kombinationskunst: Beiträge zur vergleidenden europäischen Literaturgeschichte. — [Reinbek b. Hamburg]: Rowohlt, [c1959] 341 p. — (Rowohlts deutsche Enzyklopädie. 82-83) 1. Literature, Modern — History and criticism. 2. Style, Literary I. T. II. Series.
PN605.M3 H6   LC a 61-408

Mirollo, James V.   **2.2620**
Mannerism and Renaissance poetry: concept, mode, inner design / James V. Mirollo. — New Haven: Yale University Press, 1985 (c1984). xv, 225 p.: ill.; 25 cm. Includes index. 1. Mannerism (Literature) 2. Petrarchism 3. European poetry — Renaissance, 1450-1600 — History and criticism. 4. Mannerism (Art) I. T.
PN605.M3 M57 1984   809/.91 19   LC 84-40199   ISBN 0300032277

PN611–779 Literary History: Special Periods

PN665–694 MEDIEVAL

Jones, Charles Williams, 1905- ed.   • **2.2621**
Medieval literature in translation. [1st ed.] New York: Longmans, Green, 1950. xx, 1004 p.: maps; 24 cm. 1. Literature, Medieval — Translations into English. 2. English literature — Translations from foreign languages I. T.
PN667.J6   LC 50-5084

Medieval women writers / edited by Katharina M. Wilson.   **2.2622**
Athens, Ga.: University of Georgia Press, c1984. xxix, 366 p.; 24 cm. 1. Literature, Medieval 2. European literature — Women authors. I. Wilson, Katharina M.
PN667.M43 1984   808.8/99287 19   LC 82-13380   ISBN 082030641X

O'Donoghue, Bernard.   **2.2623**
The courtly love tradition / Bernard O'Donoghue. — Manchester: Manchester University Press; Totowa, N.J.: Barnes & Noble, 1982. vi, 314 p.; 21 cm. (Literature in context) 1. Literature, Medieval — Translations into English. 2. English literature — Translations from foreign languages 3. Courtly love I. T.
PN667.O3 1982   808.81/9354 19   LC 82-18180   ISBN 0389203475

Ker, W. P. (William Paton), 1855-1923.   • **2.2624**
Epic and romance: essays on medieval literature. — New York: Dover Publications [1957] 398 p.; 21 cm. 'An unaltered and unabridged republication of the last edition.' 1. Literature, Medieval — Hist. & crit. 2. Epic poetry — Hist. & crit. 3. Romances — Hist. & crit. I. T.
PN671.K4x   809.02   LC 57-3853

Lewis, C. S. (Clive Staples), 1898-1963.   • **2.2625**
The discarded image; an introduction to medieval and Renaissance literature, by C. S. Lewis. — Cambridge [Eng.] University Press, 1964. ix, 231 p. 21 cm. Bibliographical footnotes. 1. Literature, Medieval — Hist. & crit. 2. Latin literature — Hist. & crit. I. T. II. Title: An introduction to medieval and Renaissance literature.
PN671.L4   809.02   LC 64-21555

Curtius, Ernst Robert, 1886-1956.   • **2.2626**
European literature and the Latin Middle Ages; translated from the German by Willard R. Trask. — Princeton, Princeton University Press [c1953] xv, 662 p. 24 cm. — (Bollingen series. 36) 'Bibliographical note': p. 599-600. 1. Latin literature, Medieval and modern — Hist. & crit. 2. Literature, Medieval — Hist. & crit. 3. Literature — Philosophy I. T. II. Series.
PN674.C82 1953   879.09   LC 52-10619

English Institute.   • **2.2627**
Critical approaches to medieval literature; selected papers from the English Institute, 1958–1959. Edited with a foreword by Dorothy Bethurum. — New York: Columbia University Press, 1960. ix, 171 p.; 21 cm. 1. Literature, Medieval — Congresses. 2. Criticism — Congresses. I. Bethurum, Dorothy, ed. II. T.
PN681.E5   809/.02   LC 60-13104

Lewis, C. S. (Clive Staples), 1898-1963.   • **2.2628**
Studies in medieval and Renaissance literature / collected by Walter Hooper. — Cambridge [Eng.]: University Press, 1966. x, 195 p.; 24 cm. 1. Literature, Medieval — Addresses, essays, lectures. 2. Literature, Modern — 15th and 16th century — Addresses, essays, lectures. I. Hooper, Walter. ed. II. T.
PN681.L4   809.02   LC 66-12749

Robertson, D. W. (Durant Waite), 1914-.   **2.2629**
Essays in medieval culture / D. W. Robertson, Jr. — Princeton, N.J.: Princeton University Press, c1980. xx, 404 p.: ill.; 24 cm. Includes index. 1. Literature, Medieval — History and criticism — Addresses, essays, lectures. I. T.
PN681.R55   809/.02   LC 80-13130   ISBN 0691064490

Murdoch, Brian, 1944-.   2.2630
The recapitulated fall: a comparative study in mediaeval literature / [by] Brian O. Murdoch. — Amsterdam: Rodopi, 1974. 207 p.; 22 cm. (Amsterdamer Publikationen zur Sprache und Literatur. Bd. 11) Includes index. 1. Literature, Medieval — History and criticism 2. Literature, Comparative — Themes, motives 3. Fall of man in literature 4. Temptation in literature 5. Jesus Christ in fiction, drama, poetry, etc. I. T. II. Series.
PN682.F3 M8   809/.02   LC 73-91188   ISBN 9062030211

Hanning, Robert W.   2.2631
The individual in twelfth-century romance / Robert W. Hanning. — New Haven: Yale University Press, 1977. xi, 303 p.; 22 cm. 1. Romances — History and criticism. 2. Individuality in literature. I. T.
PN682.I5 H3 1977   809.1/9/14   LC 77-75378   ISBN 0300021011

Ferrante, Joan M., 1936-.   2.2632
Woman as image in medieval literature from the twelfth century to Dante / Joan M. Ferrante. — Durham, N.C.: Labyrinth Press, c1985. 166 p.; 23 cm. Reprint. Originally published: Columbia University Press, 1975. 1. Literature, Medieval — History and criticism 2. Women in literature I. T.
PN682.W6 F4 1985   809/.93352042 19   LC 84-29689   ISBN 0939464438

Loomis, Roger Sherman, 1887-1966. ed.   • 2.2633
Medieval romances, edited by Roger Sherman Loomis and Laura Hibbard Loomis. — [1st Modern library ed.]. — New York: [Random House, 1957] 426 p.; 19 cm. — (The Modern library of the world's best books [133]) 1. Romances 2. Literature, Medieval I. Loomis, Laura Alandis (Hibbard), 1883- joint author. II. T.
PN683.L6   398.22   LC 57-11169

Loomis, Roger Sherman, 1887-1966.   • 2.2634
The development of Arthurian romance. — London: [Hutchinson, 1963] 199 p.; 20 cm. — (Hutchinson university library: Modern languages and literature) 1. Arthurian romances — History and criticism. I. T.
PN685.L62   809.93   LC 64-2756

Moorman, Charles.   2.2635
An Arthurian dictionary / Charles & Ruth Moorman; with a pref. by Geoffrey Ashe. — [Jackson]: University Press of Mississippi, 1978. xxvi, 117 p.; 21 cm. 1. Arthurian romances — Dictionaries. I. Moorman, Ruth. joint author. II. T.
PN685.M6   809/.933/51   LC 78-16694   ISBN 0878050833

Chambers, E. K. (Edmund Kerchever), 1866-1954.   • 2.2636
Arthur of Britain. Cambridge, Speculum Historiale; New York, Barnes & Noble [1964] vii, 320 p. 19 cm. 'Originally published 1927. Reprinted with supplementary bibliography.' Includes bibliographies. 1. Arthur, King. I. T.
PN686.A7C5 1964   809.92   LC 65-4054

Morris, Rosemary.   2.2637
The character of King Arthur in medieval literature / Rosemary Morris. — Cambridge [Cambridgeshire]: D.S. Brewer; Totowa, N.J.: Rowman & Littlefield, 1982. 175 p.; 25 cm. — (Arthurian studies. 0261-9814; 4) Includes index. 1. Arthurian romances — History and criticism. I. T. II. Series.
PN686.A7 M67 1982   809/.93351 19   LC 82-3712   ISBN 0847671186

Loomis, Roger Sherman, 1887-1966.   • 2.2638
The Grail: from Celtic myth to Christian symbol. — Cardiff: University of Wales Press; New York: Columbia University Press, 1963. xi, 287 p.: ill.; 22 cm. Bibliographical footnotes. 'Bibliography of critical works and of major texts of the Grail legend': p. [278]-279. 1. Grail. I. T.
PN686.G7L6 1963   809.93   LC 63-12947

Weston, Jessie Laidlay, 1850-1928.   2.2639
From ritual to romance, by Jessie L. Weston. Cambridge [Eng.] University Press 1920. 202p. 1. Grail. I. T.
PN686 G7 W45

Lewis, C. S. (Clive Staples), 1898-1963.   • 2.2640
The allegory of love: a study in medieval tradition / by C. S. Lewis. — Oxford: The Clarendon press, 1936. viii p., 1 l., 378 p., 1 l.; 22 1/2 cm. 1. Courtly love 2. Allegory 3. Literature, Comparative — Themes, motives 4. English poetry — Middle English, 1100-1500 — History and criticism. I. T.
PN688.L4   809   LC 36-34602

Stevens, John E., 1921-.   2.2641
Medieval romance: themes and approaches / [by] John Stevens. — New York: Norton [1974, c1973] 255 p.; 19 cm. (The Norton library, N715) 1. Romances — History and criticism. I. T.
PN688.S75 1974   809.1/9/35   LC 73-22200   ISBN 0393007154

Dronke, Peter.   2.2642
The medieval lyric. — London: Hutchinson, 1968. 266 p.: music.; 22 cm. — (Modern languages and literature) 1. Poetry, Medieval — History and criticism. 2. Lyric poetry — History and criticism. I. T.
PN691.D7   809.1/4   LC 68-141559   ISBN 0090864506

PN695–779 MODERN

Weapons of criticism: Marxism in America and the literary tradition / edited by Norman Rudich.   2.2643
Palo Alto, Calif.: Ramparts Press, c1976. 389 p.: ill.; 21 cm. 1. Literature, Modern — History and criticism — Addresses, essays, lectures. 2. Marxist criticism — United States — Addresses, essays, lectures. I. Rudich, Norman.
PN701.W4   809/.04   LC 74-9178   ISBN 0878670564

Bogan, Louise, 1897-1970.   • 2.2644
A poet's alphabet; reflections on the literary art and vocation. Edited by Robert Phelps and Ruth Limmer. — [1st ed.]. — New York: McGraw-Hill, [1970] xvi, 474 p.; 24 cm. Includes the author's Selected criticism, published in 1955; most of her articles, reviews, and miscellaneous critical pieces published since that date; and a few earlier pieces. 1. Literature, Modern — Addresses, essays, lectures. I. T.
PN710.B59 1970   809/.04   LC 71-121655

Gosse, Edmund, 1849-1928.   • 2.2645
Aspects and impressions. Freeport, N.Y., Books for Libraries Press [1970] 299 p. 23 cm. (Essay index reprint series) Reprint of the 1922 ed. 1. Literature, Modern — Collected works. I. T.
PN710.G63 1970   809   LC 77-105016   ISBN 0836914694

Hartman, Geoffrey H.   2.2646
Beyond formalism: literary essays, 1958–1970 / by Geoffrey H. Hartman. — New Haven: Yale University Press, 1970. xvi, 396 p.; 21 cm. 1. Literature, Modern — Addresses, essays, lectures. I. T.
PN710.H32   809   LC 79-115371   ISBN 0300013272

James, Henry, 1843-1916.   • 2.2647
Selected literary criticism. Edited by Morris Shapira. Prefaced with a note on 'James as critic' by F. R. Leavis. New York, Horizon Press [1964] xiii, 349 p. 23 cm. Bibliographical references included in 'Editors note' (p. ix—xi) 1. Literature, Modern — Addresses, essays, lectures. I. Shapira, Morris. ed. II. T.
PN710.J3 1964   809.03   LC 64-15187

Levin, Harry, 1912-.   2.2648
Memories of the moderns / Harry Levin. — London: Faber and Faber, c1980. 257 p.; 24 cm. 1. Literature, Modern — History and criticism — Addresses, essays, lectures. I. T.
PN710.L438 1980   PN710 L438.   809/.04   ISBN 0571117058

Lewis, Wyndham, 1882-1957.   2.2649
Enemy salvoes: selected literary criticism / by Wyndham Lewis; edited with sectional introductions and notes by C. J. Fox; general introd. by C. H. Sisson. — New York: Barnes & Noble Books, 1976. 272 p.; 23 cm. 1. Literature, Modern — History and criticism — Collected works. I. T.
PN710.L44 1976   809   LC 75-39325   ISBN 0064942589

Lewis, Wyndham, 1882-1957.   • 2.2650
Men without art. — New York: Russell & Russell, 1964. 303 p.; 23 cm. 1. Literature, Modern — Addresses, essays, lectures. I. T.
PN710.L45 1964   809   LC 64-13930

Pritchett, V. S. (Victor Sawdon), 1900-.   • 2.2651
Books in general [by] V. S. Pritchett. Westport, Conn., Greenwood Press [1970] viii, 258 p. 23 cm. Reprint of the 1953 ed. 1. Literature, Modern — Addresses, essays, lectures. I. T.
PN710.P68 1970   809/.03   LC 70-110378   ISBN 0837145821

Quiller-Couch, Arthur Thomas, Sir, 1863-1944.   • 2.2652
Adventures in criticism. New York, Scribner, 1896. — Grosse Pointe, Mich.: Scholarly Press, 1968. viii, 408 p.; 20 cm. 1. Literature, Modern — Addresses, essays, lectures. I. T.
PN710.Q5 1969   809/.03   LC 73-8569

Rahv, Philip, 1908-1973.   2.2653
Essays on literature and politics, 1932–1972 / Philip Rahv; edited by Arabel J. Porter and Andrew J. Dvosin; with a memoir by Mary McCarthy. — Boston: Houghton Mifflin, 1978. xvi, 366 p.; 24 cm. 1. Literature, Modern — History and criticism — Addresses, essays, lectures. 2. Politics and literature — Addresses, essays, lectures. I. Porter, Arabel J. II. Dvosin, Andrew J. III. T.
PN710.R327 1978   809   LC 78-13373   ISBN 039527270X

Rosenfeld, Isaac, 1918-1956.   • 2.2654
Age of enormity: life and writing in the forties and fifties. / Edited and introduced by Theodore Solotaroff. Foreword by Saul Bellow. [1st ed.] Cleveland: World Pub. Co., c1962. 347 p.; 21 cm. 1. Literature, Modern — 20th century — History and criticism — Addresses, essays, lectures. I. Solotaroff, Theodore. II. T.
PN710 R6   818.54   *LC* 62-10622

Saintsbury, George, 1845-1933.   • 2.2655
Prefaces and essays. Westport, Conn., Greenwood Press [1970] xvi, 446 p. port. 23 cm. Reprint of the 1933 ed. 1. Longfellow, Henry Wadsworth, 1807-1882. 2. Poe, Edgar Allan, 1809-1849. 3. English literature — History and criticism 4. French literature — History and criticism. I. T.
PN710.S25 1970   809   *LC* 77-100202   *ISBN* 0837140110

Tate, Allen, 1899-.   • 2.2656
On the limits of poetry, selected essays: 1928–1948. — Freeport, N.Y.: Books for Libraries Press, [1970, c1969] xviii, 379 p.; 23 cm. — (Essay index reprint series) Reprint of the 1948 ed. 1. Literature, Modern — Addresses, essays, lectures. I. T.
PN710.T33 1970   809.1   *LC* 74-105042   *ISBN* 0836914848

Tuve, Rosemond, 1903-1964.   • 2.2657
Allegorical imagery; some mediaeval books and their posterity. — Princeton, N.J.: Princeton University Press, 1966. 461 p.: illus.; 25 cm. 1. Literature, Modern — 15th and 16th century — History and criticism. 2. Allegory I. T.
PN731.T8   809.031   *LC* 65-14312

Fish, Stanley Eugene.   2.2658
Self–consuming artifacts; the experience of seventeenth–century literature, by Stanley E. Fish. — Berkeley: University of California Press, [c1972] xiv, 432 p.; 24 cm. 1. Literature, Modern — 17th century — History and criticism. 2. Style, Literary I. T.
PN741.F5   820/.9/003   *LC* 76-187747   *ISBN* 0520022300

Warnke, Frank J.   2.2659
Versions of baroque: European literature in the seventeenth century / by Frank J. Warnke. — New Haven: Yale University Press, 1972. xi, 229 p.; 23 cm. 1. European literature — 17th century — History and criticism. 2. Baroque literature — History and criticism. I. T.
PN741.W3   809.89/4   *LC* 70-151593   *ISBN* 0300014856

PN750–769 18th–19th Centuries

Praz, Mario, 1896-.   • 2.2660
[Carne, la morte e il diavolo nella letteratura romantica. English] The romantic agony; translated from the Italian by Angus Davidson. 2nd ed. [reissued with corrections]; with a new foreword by Frank Kermode. London, New York, Oxford U.P., 1970. xxv, 479 p. 21 cm. Translation of La carne, la morte e il diavolo nella letteratura romantica. 1. Romanticism 2. Literature, Modern — 19th century — History and criticism 3. Sex in literature 4. Devil in literature I. T.
PN755.P713 1970   809/.034   *LC* 72-555865   *ISBN* 0192125117

Becker, George Joseph.   2.2661
Master European realists of the nineteenth century / George J. Becker. — New York: F. Ungar Pub. Co., 1983 (c1982). 294 p.; 22 cm. Includes index. 1. European literature — 19th century — History and criticism. 2. Realism in literature I. T.
PN761.B35   809/.912 19   *LC* 81-70124   *ISBN* 0804420467

Hartman, Geoffrey H., 1929-.   • 2.2662
The unmediated vision: an interpretation of Wordsworth, Hopkins, Rilke, and Valéry. — New Haven: Yale University Press, [1954] xii, 206 p.; 24 cm. 1. Wordsworth, William, 1770-1850. 2. Rilke, Rainer Maria, 1875-1926. 3. Valéry, Paul Ambroise, 1871-1945. 4. Hopkins, Gerard Manley, 1844-1889. 5. Literature, Modern — 19th century — History and criticism 6. Literature, Modern — 20th century — History and criticism I. T.
PN761.H26   *LC* 54-5084

James, Henry, 1843-1916.   • 2.2663
Partial portraits. — Westport, Conn.: Greenwood Press, [1970] 408 p.; 23 cm. Reprint of the 1888 ed. 1. Literature, Modern — 19th century — Addresses, essays, lectures. I. T.
PN761.J3 1970   809   *LC* 74-98842   *ISBN* 0837127971

Nineteenth–century literature criticism.   2.2664
Vol. 1-   . — Detroit: Gale Research Co., 1981-. v.; 29 cm. 1. Literature, Modern — 19th century — History and criticism — Addresses, essays, lectures. 2. Literature, Modern — 19th century — Bio-bibliography. I. Harris, Laurie Lanzen. II. Gale Research Company.
PN761.N56   809/.034 19   *LC* 84-643008

Pritchett, V. S. (Victor Sawdon), 1900-.   2.2665
The myth makers: literary essays / Victor Sawdon Pritchett. — New York: Random House, c1979. 190 p.; 22 cm. 1. Literature, Modern — 19th century — History and criticism — Addresses, essays, lectures. 2. Literature, Modern — 20th century — History and criticism — Addresses, essays, lectures. I. T.
PN761.P7 1979   809 19   *LC* 78-21801   *ISBN* 0394504720

Rahv, Philip, 1908-1973.   • 2.2666
Literature and the sixth sense. — Boston: Houghton Mifflin, 1969. xi, 445 p.; 22 cm. 1. Literature, Modern — 19th century — Addresses, essays, lectures. 2. Literature, Modern — 20th century — Addresses, essays, lectures. I. T.
PN761.R26   809   *LC* 70-79390

Croce, Benedetto, 1866-1952.   • 2.2667
[Poesia e non poesia. English] European literature in the nineteenth century. Translated from the Italian with an introd. by Douglas Ainslie. New York, Haskell House, 1967. ix, 373 p. 24 cm. Translation of Poesia e non poesia. Reprint of the 1924 ed. 1. European literature — 19th century — History and criticism. I. T.
PN765.C72 1967   *LC* 67-30822

Abrams, M. H. (Meyer Howard), 1912-.   • 2.2668
The mirror and the lamp: romantic theory and the critical tradition. New York, Oxford University Press, 1953. xii, 406 p. 25 cm. 1. Romanticism I. T.
PN769.R7 A2   801   *LC* 53-7616

PN771–779 20th Century

The Avant–garde tradition in literature / edited with an introduction by Richard Kostelanetz.   2.2669
Buffalo, N.Y.: Prometheus Books, 1982. xii, 424 p.: ill.; 24 cm. 1. Literature, Modern — 20th century — History and criticism — Addresses, essays, lectures. 2. Avant-garde (Aesthetics) — Addresses, essays, lectures. I. Kostelanetz, Richard.
PN771.A92 1982   809/.91 19   *LC* 81-86334   *ISBN* 0879751738

Columbia dictionary of modern European literature / Jean– Albert Bédé and William B. Edgerton, general editors.   2.2670
2d ed., fully rev. and enl. — New York: Columbia University Press, 1980. xxi, 895 p.; 27 cm. 1. European literature — 20th century — Dictionaries. 2. European literature — 20th century — Bio-bibliography. 3. Authors, European — 20th century — Biography. I. Bédé, Jean Albert. II. Edgerton, William Benbow, 1914-
PN771.C575 1980   803   *LC* 80-17082   *ISBN* 0231037171

Contemporary literary criticism: excerpts from criticism of the works of today's novelists, poets, playwrights, and other creative writers / ed. by Carolyn Riley.   2.2671
CLC 1- 1973-. Detroit: Gale Research Co. v.; 27 cm. One issue each year called: Contemporary literary criticism yearbook, 1984- 1. Literature, Modern — 20th century — History and criticism — Periodicals. I. Riley, Carolyn, ed. II. Contemporary literary criticism yearbook.
PN771.C59   809/.04   *LC* 76-38938

Cook, Albert Spalding.   • 2.2672
Prisms; studies in modern literature, by Albert Cook. Bloomington, Indiana University Press, 1967. xii, 196 p. 22 cm. 1. Literature, Modern — 20th century — History and criticism — Addresses, essays, lectures. I. T.
PN771.C6   809/.04   *LC* 67-13020

Eastman, Max, 1883-1969.   • 2.2673
The literary mind; its place in an age of science. — New York: Octagon Books, 1969 [c1931] ix, 343 p.; 21 cm. Essays. 1. Literature, Modern — 20th century — History and criticism 2. Literature and science I. T.
PN771.E3 1969   801/.9   *LC* 72-75992

Encyclopedia of world literature in the 20th century: based on the first edition edited by Wolfgang Bernard Fleischmann / Leonard S. Klein, general editor.   2.2674
Rev. ed. — New York: Ungar, c1981-c1984. 4 v. in 5: ports.; 29 cm. Includes separate vol. for index. 1. Literature, Modern — 20th century — Bio-bibliography. 2. Literature, Modern — 20th century — Dictionaries. I. Klein, Leonard S.
PN771.E5 1981   803 19   *LC* 81-3357   *ISBN* 0804431353

Frank, Joseph, 1916-.   • 2.2675
The widening gyre: crisis and mastery in modern literature / J. Frank. — New Brunswick, N.J.: Rutgers University Press, 1963. xiii, 278 p.; 22 cm. 1. Literature, Modern — 20th century — History and criticism — Addresses, essays, lectures. I. T.
PN771.F7   809.93   *LC* 63-16300

Gale Research Company.   **2.2676**
Twentieth–century literary criticism. v. 1- 1978-. Detroit, Mich., Gale Research Co. v. 29 cm. Annual. 1. Literature, Modern — 20th Century — History and criticism — Periodicals. 2. Literature, Modern — 19th century — History and criticism — Periodicals. I. T.
PN771.G27   809/.04   *LC* 76-46132

Hassan, Ihab Habib, 1925-.   **2.2677**
The dismemberment of Orpheus: toward a postmodern literature / Ihab Hassan. — 2nd ed. — Madison, Wis.: University of Wisconsin Press, 1982. xix, 315 p.; 22 cm. 1. Literature, Modern — 20th century — History and criticism 2. Postmodernism I. T.
PN771.H33 1982   809/.04 19   *LC* 81-69821   *ISBN* 0299091201

Howe, Irving.   • **2.2678**
A world more attractive; a view of modern literature and politics. — Freeport, N.Y.: Books for Libraries Press, [1970, c1963] xii, 307 p.; 23 cm. — (Essay index reprint series) 1. Literature, Modern — 20th century — Addresses, essays, lectures. I. T.
PN771.H6 1970   809/.04   *LC* 70-134096   *ISBN* 0836919580

Hyman, Stanley Edgar, 1919-1970.   • **2.2679**
Standards; a chronicle of books for our time. — New York: Horizon Press, [1966] 286 p.; 22 cm. 1. Literature, Modern — 20th century — Addresses, essays, lectures. I. T.
PN771.H9   809.04   *LC* 66-16306

Kenyon review.   • **2.2680**
Kenyon critics; studies in modern literature from the Kenyon review, edited by John Crowe Ransom. [1st ed.] Cleveland World, 1951. x, 342 p.; 22 cm. 1. Literature, Modern — 20th century — History and criticism I. Ransom, John Crowe, ed. II. T.
PN771.K4   809.04   *LC* 51-4381

Kunitz, Stanley Jasspon, ed.   • **2.2681**
Twentieth century authors, a biographical dictionary of modern literature, edited by Stanley J. Kunitz and Howard Haycraft. New York: H.W. Wilson company, 1942 [i.e. 1966, c1942] vii, 1577 p.: ill. (ports., 2 mounted); 26 cm. — (The Authors series.) 1. Literature, Modern — 20th century — Bio-bibliography. I. Haycraft, Howard. ed. II. T. III. Series.
PN771.K86   *LC* 43-51003

Pound, Ezra, 1885-1972.   • **2.2682**
Instigations of Ezra Pound. Together with, An essay on the Chinese written character / by Ernest Fenollosa. — New York: Boni and Liveright, 1920. viii, 388 p. 1. French poetry — 19th century — History and criticism 2. English literature — 20th century — History and criticism 3. Greek literature — Translations 4. Chinese language — Writing I. Fenollosa, Ernest Francisco, 1853-1908. II. T.
PN771 P7

Sontag, Susan, 1933-.   • **2.2683**
Against interpretation, and other essays. — New York: Farrar, Straus & Giroux, [1966] ix, 304 p.; 22 cm. 1. Literature, Modern — 20th century — Addresses, essays, lectures. 2. Criticism I. T.
PN771.S62   809.04   *LC* 65-20916

Spender, Stephen, 1909-.   • **2.2684**
The struggle of the modern. — Berkeley, University of California Press, 1963. 266 p. 23 cm. — (CAL, 109) 1. Literature, Modern — 20th cent. — Hist. & crit. 2. Art, Modern — 20th cent. I. T.
PN771.S625   809.04   *LC* 63-4035

Spender, Stephen, 1909-.   • **2.2685**
The creative element; a study of vision, despair and orthodoxy among some modern writers. — Freeport, N.Y.: Books for Libraries Press, [1971, c1953] 199 p.; 23 cm. 1. Literature, Modern — 20th century — History and criticism 2. Literature, Modern — 19th century — History and criticism 3. Creation (Literary, artistic, etc.) I. T.
PN771.S63 1971   809/.034   *LC* 70-164628   *ISBN* 0836959116

Sypher, Wylie, 1905-.   • **2.2686**
Loss of the self in modern literature and art. New York: Random House, 1962. 179 p.; 21 cm. 1. Literature, Modern — 20th century — History and criticism 2. Art, Modern — 20th century 3. Art and science 4. Self I. T.
PN771.S95 1962   809.04   *LC* 62-8461

Wilson, Edmund, 1895-1972.   • **2.2687**
Axel's castle; a study in the imaginative literature of 1870–1930, by Edmund Wilson. New York: Scribner, 1931. 5 p. l., 319 p. 21 cm. 1. Literature, Modern — 20th century — History and criticism 2. Literature, Modern — 19th century — History and criticism 3. Symbolism in literature I. T.
PN771.W55   809   *LC* 31-26550

Zabel, Morton Dauwen, 1901-1964. ed.   • **2.2688**
Literary opinion in America; essays illustrating the status, methods, and problems of criticism in the United States in the twentieth century. — 3d ed., rev. — New York, Harper & Row [1962] 2 v. 21 cm. — (Harper torchbooks, TB3013-3014. The University library) 1. Criticism — U.S. 2. Literature — Hist. & crit. 3. American essays I. T.
PN771.Z2 1962   820.82   *LC* 62-52885

PN801–1008 Comparative Literature. Folk Literature

Andersson, Theodore Murdock, 1934-.   **2.2689**
The legend of Brynhild / Theodore M. Andersson. — Ithaca, N.Y.: Cornell University Press, 1980. 270 p.; 23 cm. — (Islandica. 43) Includes indexes. 1. Germanic literature — Themes, motives. 2. Brunhild. 3. Heldensage I. T. II. Series.
PN831.A5   830/.09   *LC* 80-16008   *ISBN* 0801413028

Ethnic perspectives in American literature: selected essays on   **2.2690**
the European contribution: a source book / edited by Robert J. Di Pietro and Edward Ifkovic.
New York: Modern Language Association of America, 1983. 333 p.; 22 cm. 1. United States — Literatures — History and criticism — Addresses, essays, lectures. I. Di Pietro, Robert J. II. Ifkovic, Edward, 1943-
PN843.E8 1983   810/.9 19   *LC* 82-14265   *ISBN* 0873521269

Zell, Hans M.   **2.2691**
A new reader's guide to African literature. — 2nd, completely rev. and expanded ed. / edited by Hans M. Zell, Carol Bundy, and Virginia Coulon; associate editors, Donald Burness ... [et al.]. — New York: Africana Pub. Co., 1983. xvi, 553 p.: map, ports.; 23 cm. Previous ed. published as: A reader's guide to African literature. 1972. Includes index. 1. Africa — Literatures — Bio-bibliography. 2. Africa — Literatures — History and criticism — Bibliography. I. Zell, Hans M. Reader's guide to African literature. II. Bundy, Carol. III. Coulon, Virginia. IV. T.
PN849.A35 Z44 1983   809/.8896 19   *LC* 83-15472   *ISBN* 0841906394

The New Oxford book of Australian verse / chosen by Les A. Murray.   **2.2692**
Melbourne; New York: Oxford University Press, 1986. xxv, 399 p.; 23 cm. Includes indexes. 1. Australian poetry 2. Australian aboriginal poetry — Translations into English. 3. English poetry — Translations from Australian languages. 4. Australia — Literatures. I. Murray, Les A., 1938-
PN849.A952 N49 1986   821/.008/0994 19   *LC* 85-243897   *ISBN* 0195546180

Caribbean writers: a bio–bibliographical–critical encyclopedia /   **2.2693**
editor, Donald E. Herdeck, associate editors, Maurice A. Lubin ... [et al.], Margaret Laniak–Herdeck; [drawings by Tom Gladden, drawings of Dominican writers by Nick Clapp].
Washington: Three Continents Press, c1979. xiv, 943 p.: ports.; 24 cm. 1. Caribbean literature — Bio-bibliography. 2. Caribbean literature — History and criticism — Bibliography. I. Herdeck, Donald E., 1924- II. Lubin, Maurice Alcibiade, 1917- III. Herdeck, Margaret, 1949-
PN849.C3 C3   809/.89729   *LC* 77-3841   *ISBN* 0914478745

Coulthard, G.R.   **2.2694**
Caribbean literature: an anthology / selected and edited by G.R. Coulthard. — London: University of London Press, 1966. 128 p.; 22 cm. 1. Caribbean literature I. T.
PN849.C3 C57   *LC* 66-70518

Coulthard, G.R.   **2.2695**
Race and colour in Caribbean literature / issued under the auspices of the Institute of Race Relations. — London; New York: Oxford University Press, 1962. 152 p.; 23 cm. Translation of Raza y color en la literatura antillana. 1. Race problems in literature. 2. Caribbean literature — History and criticism. I. T.
PN849.C3 C63 1962   *LC* 62-52572

Dathorne, O. R., 1934-.   **2.2696**
Dark ancestor: the literature of the Black man in the Caribbean / O. R. Dathorne. — Baton Rouge: Louisiana State University Press, c1981. x, 288 p.; 24 cm. Includes index. 1. Caribbean literature — Black authors — History and criticism. 2. American literature — Afro-American authors — History and criticism. 3. Caribbean Area — Civilization — African influences I. T.
PN849.C3 D37   809/.896 19   *LC* 80-22581   *ISBN* 080710759X

Yearbook of comparative and general literature. • **2.2697**
1- 1952-. [Bloomington] Indiana University [etc.] v. ports. 26 cm. Annual. No. 1-9 issued as University of North Carolina studies in comparative literature no. 6-7, 9, 14, 16, 18, 21, 25, 27. 1. Literature, Comparative — Yearbooks. I. Indiana University. II. National Council of Teachers of English. Comparative Literature Committee. III. Modern Language Association of America. Comparative Literature Section. IV. American Comparative Literature Association.
PN851.Y4   LC 53-62589

Friederich, Werner P. (Werner Paul), 1905-. • **2.2698**
Outline of comparative literature from Dante Alighieri to Eugene O'Neill / by Werner P. Friederich with the collaboration of David Henry Malone. — Chapel Hill: University of North Carolina Press, 1954. 451 p.; 23 cm. — (University of North Carolina studies in comparative literature; 11) 1. Literature, Comparative 2. Literature — History and criticism I. T.
PN871.F7   LC 55-477

Peyre, Henri, 1901-. • **2.2699**
Literature and sincerity. New Haven, Yale University Press, 1963. 362 p. 23 cm. (Yale Romanic studies, 2d ser., 9) 1. Literature, Comparative 2. Authors 3. Sincerity and literature I. T.
PN871.P4   809.93   LC 63-7945

Highet, Gilbert, 1906-1978. • **2.2700**
The classical tradition; Greek and Roman influences on western literature. — New York: Oxford University Press, 1949. xxxviii, 763 p.; 23 cm. 1. Literature, Comparative — Classical and modern 2. Literature, Comparative — Modern and classical I. T.
PN883.H5   809   LC 49-11655

Thompson, Stith, 1885-. • **2.2701**
The folktale, by Stith Thompson. — New York: The Dryden press, 1946. x, 510 p.; 25 cm. 1. Tales — History and criticism. I. T.
PN1001.T5   398.21   LC 47-30175

PN1008.5–1009 Children's Literature

Carpenter, Humphrey.   **2.2702**
The Oxford companion to children's literature / Humphrey Carpenter and Mari Prichard. — Oxford [Oxfordshire]; New York: Oxford University Press, 1984. x, 586 p.: ill., facsims., ports.; 24 cm. 1. Children's literature — Dictionaries. I. Prichard, Mari. II. T.
PN1008.5.C37 1984   809/.89282 19   LC 83-15130   ISBN 0192115820

Egoff, Sheila A.   **2.2703**
Only connect: readings on children's literature / edited by Sheila Egoff, G.T. Stubbs, and L.F. Ashley. — 2d ed. — Toronto; New York: Oxford University Press, 1980. xix, 457 p.; 21 cm. Includes index. 1. Children's literature — History and criticism — Addresses, essays, lectures. I. Stubbs, G. T. (Gordon Thomas), 1928- joint author. II. Ashley, L. F. joint author. III. T.
PN1009.A1 E28 1980   809/.89282 19   LC 81-452868   ISBN 0195403096

Meigs, Cornelia Lynde, 1884- ed. • **2.2704**
A critical history of children's literature; a survey of children's books in English. Prepared in four parts by Cornelia Meigs [and others] Decorations by Vera Bock. — Rev. ed. — [New York]: Macmillan, [1969] xxviii, 708 p.; 24 cm. 1. Children's literature — History and criticism. I. T.
PN1009.A1 M4 1969   028.5/09   LC 73-7659

White, Dorothy Neal.   **2.2705**
Books before five. New York, Oxford University Press, 1954. xii, 196 p. illus. 23 cm. 1. Children's literature — History and criticism. I. T.
PN1009.A1 W48   LC 54-10840

PN1010–5650 SPECIAL FORMS OF LITERATURE

PN1010–1551 Poetry

PN1021–1025 DICTIONARIES. INDEXES

Princeton encyclopedia of poetry and poetics / Alex Preminger,   **2.2706**
editor; Frank J. Warnke and O. B. Hardison, Jr., associate editors.
Enl. ed. — Princeton, N.J.: Princeton University Press, 1975 [c1974] xxiv, 992 p.; 25 cm. Published in 1965 under title: Encyclopedia of poetry and poetics. 1. Poetry — Dictionaries. 2. Poetics — Dictionaries. 3. Poetry — History and criticism I. Preminger, Alex. II. Warnke, Frank J. III. Hardison, O. B.
PN1021.E5 1974   808.1/03   LC 75-310165   ISBN 0691062803

Granger, Edith. • **2.2707**
[Index to poetry and recitations] Granger's index to poetry. 5th ed., completely rev. and enl., indexing anthologies published through June 30, 1960. Edited by William F. Bernhardt. New York, Columbia University Press, 1962. xxxix, 2123 p. 26 cm. Previous editions published under title: Index to poetry and recitations. Supplemented by 'Supplement. Indexing anthologies published from July 1, 1960, to December 31, 1965. Edited by William F. Bernhardt and Kathryn W. Sewny' (xvi, 416 p. 25 cm.) published: New York, Columbia University Press, 1967. PN1022.G7 1962 Suppl. 1. Poetry — Indexes. 2. English poetry — Indexes. I. Bernhardt, William F. II. Sewny, Kathryn W. III. T. IV. Title: Index to poetry.
PN1022.G7 1962   808.81/0016 19   LC 62-3885

Granger, Edith.   **2.2708**
[Index to poetry] Granger's Index to poetry. 6th ed., completely rev. and enl., indexing anthologies published through December 31, 1970. Edited by William James Smith. New York, Columbia University Press, 1973. xxxvii, 2223 p. 26 cm. 1. Poetry — Indexes. 2. English poetry — Indexes. I. Smith, William James, 1918- ed. II. T. III. Title: Index to poetry.
PN1022.G7 1973   016.80881 19   LC 73-4186   ISBN 0231036418

Granger, Edith.   **2.2709**
[Index to poetry] Granger's Index to poetry. — 7th ed., indexing anthologies published from 1970 through 1981 / edited by William James Smith and William F. Bernhardt. — New York: Columbia University Press, 1982. xxvi, 1329 p.; 25 cm. 1. Poetry — Indexes. 2. English poetry — Indexes. I. Smith, William James, 1918- II. Bernhardt, William F. III. T. IV. Title: Index to poetry.
PN1022.G7 1982   016.80881 19   LC 81-18155   ISBN 023105002X

Granger, Edith.   **2.2710**
[Index to poetry] Granger's Index to poetry. — 8th ed., completely rev. and enl., indexing anthologies published through June 30, 1985 / edited by William F. Bernhardt. — New York: Columbia University Press, 1986. xxxiii, 2014 p.; 25 cm. Accompanied by 'Librarians' key to symbols' (p. [xiii]-xxxiii). 1. Poetry — Indexes. 2. English poetry — Indexes. I. Bernhardt, William F. II. T. III. Title: Index to poetry.
PN1022.G7 1986   016.80881 19   LC 85-32571   ISBN 0231062761

Brewton, John Edmund, 1898-.   **2.2711**
Index to children's poetry; a title, subject, author, and first line index to poetry in collections for children and youth, compiled by John E. and Sara W. Brewton. — New York: Wilson, 1942. xxxii, 965 p.; 26 cm. First supplement, compiled by John E. and Sara W. Brewton. New York, Wilson, 1954. Second supplement. Compiled by John E. and Sara W. Brewton. New York, Wilson, 1965. 1. Children's poetry — Indexes. 2. American poetry — Indexes. 3. English poetry — Indexes. I. Brewton, Sara Westbrook. II. T.
PN1023.B7   821.0016   LC 42-20148

Guy, Patricia A.   **2.2712**
Women's poetry index / by Patricia A. Guy. — Phoenix, Ariz.: Oryx Press, 1985. xv, 174 p.; 29 cm. 1. Poetry — Women authors — Indexes. I. T.
PN1024.G89 1985   016.8081 19   LC 84-42816   ISBN 0897741730

PN1031 THEORY

Barfield, Owen, 1898-.   • 2.2713
Poetic diction, a study in meaning. Introd. by Howard Nemerov. New York, McGraw-Hill [1964] 216 p. 22 cm. Bibliographical footnotes. 1. Poetry 2. Diction 3. English language — Diction I. T.
PN1031.B3 1964   808.1   *LC* 64-21250

Buchler, Justus, 1914-.   2.2714
The main of light; on the concept of poetry. — New York: Oxford University Press, 1974. 183 p.; 22 cm. 1. Poetry I. T.
PN1031.B85   808.1   *LC* 73-87621   *ISBN* 019501748X

Empson, William, 1906-.   • 2.2715
Seven types of ambiguity / William Empson. — 2d ed. New York: New Directions, 1947. xv, 258 p.; 21 cm. (New Directions paperbook, NDP 204) 1. Poetry 2. English poetry — History. I. T.
PN1031.E5   *LC* 48-78

Graves, Robert, 1895-.   • 2.2716
Poetic unreason, and other studies. — New York: Biblo and Tannen, 1968. 276 p.; 21 cm. Reprint of the 1925 ed. 1. Poetry I. T.
PN1031.G7 1968   808.1   *LC* 68-59244

Heidegger, Martin, 1889-1976.   2.2717
Poetry, language, thought. Translations and introd. by Albert Hofstadter. — [1st ed.]. — New York: Harper & Row, [1971] xxv, 229 p.; 22 cm. — (His Works) 1. Poetry 2. Languages — Philosophy I. T.
PN1031.H38   801   *LC* 79-161639   *ISBN* 0060638486

Hungerland, Isabel Payson Creed, 1907-.   • 2.2718
Poetic discourse / by Isabel C. Hungerland. — Berkeley: University of California Press, 1958. iv, 177 p.; 24 cm. 1. Poetry I. T.
PN1031.H74   801/.951

Puttenham, Richard, 1520?-1601? supposed author.   • 2.2719
The arte of English poesie, by George Puttenham; edited by Gladys Doidge Willcock and Alice Walker. Cambridge, Eng. . The University Press, 1936. cx, 2, 358, 1 p. illus. (port.) 22 cm. With facsimile of original t.-p.. The arte of English poesie. Contriued into three bookes: the first of poets and poesie, the second of proportion, the third of ornament. Printer's mark. At London, Printed by Richard Field ... 1589. Ascribed both to Richard and George Puttenham; the present editors favor the ascription to the latter. 1. Poetry — Early works to 1800. I. Puttenham, George, d. 1590. supposed author. II. Willcock, Gladys Doidge, ed. III. Walker, Alice, joint ed. IV. T.
PN1031.P8 1936   *LC* 36-7861

Ransom, John Crowe, 1888-1974.   • 2.2720
The new criticism, by John Crowe Ransom. Norfolk, Conn., New Directions [c1941] xiii, 339 p. diagrs. 21 cm. 1. Criticism 2. Poetry — History and criticism I. T.
PN1031.R3   801   *LC* 41-16905

Read, Herbert Edward, Sir, 1893-1968.   • 2.2721
Form in modern poetry. — [London]: Vision, [1948] 85 p.; 20 cm. 1. Poetry 2. English poetry — History and criticism I. T.
PN1031.R38 1948

Richards, I. A. (Ivor Armstrong), 1893-.   • 2.2722
Poetries and sciences, a reissue of Science and poetry (1926, 1935) with commentary [by] I. A. Richards. New York, Norton [1970] 121 p. illus. 21 cm. 1. Poetry 2. English poetry — 20th century — History and criticism. I. T.
PN1031.R5 1970   821/.009   *LC* 68-22852   *ISBN* 0393043088

Skelton, Robin, 1925-.   • 2.2723
Poetry / Robin Skelton. — London: English Universities Press, 1963. 179 p.; 19 cm. — (Teach yourself books.) 1. Poetry 2. Poetry — Study and teaching I. T. II. Series.
PN1031.S552   *LC* 64-55209   *ISBN* 0340056908

Warren, Alba Houghton, 1915-.   2.2724
English poetic theory, 1825-1865, by Alba H. Warren. — Princeton: Princeton University Press, 1950. vii, 243 p.; 24 cm. — (Princeton studies in English; no. 29) 1. Poetry — History and criticism 2. Criticism — Great Britain. I. T. II. Series.
PN1031.W27 1950   801.951   *LC* 51-92

Wimsatt, William K. (William Kurtz), 1907-1975.   • 2.2725
The verbal icon; studies in the meaning of poetry, by W. K. Wimsatt, Jr., and two preliminary essays written in collaboration with Monroe C. Beardsley. — Lexington, University of Kentucky Press [1954] xviii, 299 p. 24 cm. 'Notes and references': p. [281]-293. 1. Poetry 2. Criticism I. T.
PN1031.W517   808.1   *LC* 54-7479

Croce, Benedetto, 1866-1952.   2.2726
[Poesia. English] Benedetto Croce's Poetry and literature: an introduction to its criticism and history / translated, with an introd. and notes, by Giovanni Gullace. — Carbondale: Southern Illinois University Press , c1981. lxxiv, 210 p.: port.; 29 cm. Translation of La poesia. Includes index. 1. Poetry 2. Literature I. Gullace, Giovanni. II. T.
PN1035.C713 1981   801/.951 19   *LC* 80-19511   *ISBN* 0809309823

PN1040-1059 POETICS

Aristotle.   • 2.2727
Aristotle's Art of poetry: a Greek view of poetry and drama / with an introduction and explanations by W. Hamilton Fyfe. — Oxford: The Clarendon Press, 1940. xxxii, 82 p.; 20 cm. 'Translation here used is that of Ingram Bywater, which the editor ... has ventured to alter slightly in a few places.' - p. [v] 1. Poetry — Early works to 1800. 2. Aesthetics — Early works to 1800. I. Fyfe, William Hamilton, 1878- II. Bywater, Ingram, 1840-1914. III. T. IV. Title: Art of poetry.
PN1040.A5 F9   *LC* 41-1024

Hardison, O. B.   • 2.2728
Aristotle's Poetics; a translation and commentary for students of literature. Translation by Leon Golden. Commentary by O. B. Hardison, Jr. Englewood Cliffs, N.J., Prentice-Hall [1968] ix, 307 p. illus. 21 cm. 1. Aristotle. Poetics I. Aristotle. Poetics. English. 1968. II. T.
PN1040.A5 H3   808.2 19   *LC* 68-19424

Allen, Donald Merriam, 1912- comp.   2.2729
Poetics of the new American poetry / edited by Donald Allen & Warren Tallman. — 1. Evergreen ed. — New York: Grove Press: distributed by Random House, 1974 (c1973). –. xv, 463 p.; 21 cm. — 1. Poetics — Addresses, essays, lectures. I. Tallman, Warren E., 1921- joint comp. II. T.
PN1042.A54   PN1042 A54 1973.   808.1   *LC* 73-6222   *ISBN* 0394178017

Gross, Harvey Seymour, 1922- ed.   • 2.2730
The structure of verse; modern essays on prosody, edited with an introd. and commentary by Harvey Gross. Greenwich, Conn., Fawcett Publications [1966] 272 p. 18 cm. (Literature and ideas series, 4) A Fawcett premier book, M304. 1. Versification I. T.
PN1042.G7   808.1   *LC* 66-4396

Hope, A. D. (Alec Derwent), 1907-.   2.2731
The new cratylus: notes on the craft of poetry / A. D. Hope. — Melbourne; New York: Oxford University Press, 1979. xi, 179 p.; 23 cm. 1. Poetics I. T.
PN1042.H58   808.1   *LC* 79-322552   *ISBN* 019550576X

Koch, Kenneth, 1925-.   2.2732
Sleeping on the wing: an anthology of modern poetry, with essays on reading and writing / Kenneth Koch and Kate Farrell. — New York: Random House, c1981. xvii, 313 p.; 22 cm. 1. Poetics 2. Poetry, Modern I. Farrell, Kate. joint author. II. T.
PN1042.K55   808.81 19   *LC* 80-5277   *ISBN* 0394509749

Nemerov, Howard.   2.2733
Figures of thought: speculations on the meaning of poetry & other essays / Howard Nemerov. — Boston: D. R. Godine, c1978. 198 p.: ill.; 24 cm. 1. Poetry — Addresses, essays, lectures. I. T.
PN1042.N44   801/.95   *LC* 77-78361   *ISBN* 0879232129

Perrine, Laurence.   2.2734
Sound and sense: an introduction to poetry / Laurence Perrine, with the assistance of Thomas R. Arp. — 6th ed. — New York: Harcourt Brace Jovanovich, c1982. xx, 345 p.; 22 cm. Includes index. 1. Poetics 2. Poetry — Collection. I. Arp, Thomas R. II. T.
PN1042.P4 1982   808.1 19   *LC* 81-82425   *ISBN* 0155826069

Smith, Barbara Herrnstein.   • 2.2735
Poetic closure; a study of how poems end. — Chicago: University of Chicago Press, [1968] xvi, 289 p.; 23 cm. 1. Poetics 2. Closure (Rhetoric) I. T.
PN1042.S65   801/.951   *LC* 68-15034

Wimsatt, William K. (William Kurtz), 1907-1975.   • 2.2736
Versification: major language types; sixteen essays. Edited with a foreword by W. K. Wimsatt. — New York, Modern Language Association, 1972. xxvii, 252 p. 24 cm. 1. Versification — Addresses, essays, lectures. I. T.
PN1042.W52   416   *LC* 72-89366   *ISBN* 0814791557

Poetik des Barock / hrsg. von Marian Szyrocki.   2.2737
[Reinbek b. Hamburg]: Rowohlt, [1968] 266 p. — (Rowohlts Klassiker der Literatur und der Wissenschaft. 508/509) (Deutsche Literatur; Bd. 23) (Texte deutscher Literatur 1500-1800) 1. Poetics I. Szyrocki, Marian. II. Series.

III. Series: Deutsche Literatur; Bd. 23 IV. Series: Texte deutscher Literatur 1500-1800
PN1044.S94   *LC* 72-399571

Blackmur, R. P. (Richard P.), 1904-1965.   • **2.2738**
Language as gesture; essays in poetry. [1st ed.] New York, Harcourt, Brace [1952] 440 p. 21 cm. 1. Poetry — Addresses, essays, lectures. 2. English poetry — History and criticism 3. American poetry — History and criticism. I. T.
PN1055.B55   808.1   *LC* 52-6451

Pottle, Frederick Albert, 1897-.   • **2.2739**
The idiom of poetry. — Rev. [i.e. 2d] ed., with other essays. — Bloomington: Indiana University Press, 1963. xiii, 234 p.; 20 cm. 'A Midland book: poetry & criticism, MB54.' 1. Poetry — Addresses, essays, lectures. I. T.
PN1055.P6 1963   808.1   *LC* 63-16577

Stevens, Wallace, 1879-1955.   • **2.2740**
The necessary angel; essays on reality and the imagination. — [1st ed.]. — New York: Knopf, 1951. x, 176 p.; 22 cm. 1. Poetry — History and criticism — Addresses, essays, lectures. I. T.
PN1055.S68   808.1   *LC* 51-12072

Tate, Allen, 1899- ed.   • **2.2741**
The language of poetry, by Philip Wheelwright [and others] Edited by Allen Tate. — New York: Russell & Russell, 1960. 125 p.: illus.; 21 cm. 'Essays ... read ... at Princeton University in the spring of 1941 under the auspices of the creative arts program.' 1. Poetry — Addresses, essays, lectures. I. Wheelwright, Philip Ellis, 1901- II. T.
PN1055.T35 1960   808.1   *LC* 60-6037

Day Lewis, C. (Cecil), 1904-1972.   • **2.2742**
The poetic image / by C. Day Lewis. — New York: Oxford University Press, 1947. 157 p.; 21 cm. (The Clark lectures given at Cambridge in 1946) 1. Poetry — Addresses, essays, lectures. 2. Symbolism in literature I. T.
PN1059.I4 D299

PN1064 POETS ON POETRY

Allen, Don Cameron, 1904- ed.   • **2.2743**
The moment of poetry. — Baltimore, Johns Hopkins Press [1962] 135 p. 22 cm. — (The Percy Graeme Turnbull memorial lectures on poetry, 1961) 1. Poetry — Addresses, essays, lectures. I. T. II. Series.
PN1064.A5 1962   808.1   *LC* 62-12569

Ciardi, John, 1916-.   • **2.2744**
Dialogue with an audience. — [1st ed.]. — Philadelphia: J. B. Lippincott, 1963. 316 p.; 22cm. 1. Poetry — History and criticism — Addresses, essays, lectures. I. T.
PN1064.C5   *LC* 63-15440

Eliot, T. S. (Thomas Stearns), 1888-1965.   • **2.2745**
The Three voices of poetry. — New York: Cambridge University Press, 1954. 39 p.; 20 cm. 1. Poetry — History and criticism I. T. II. Title: The 3 voices of poetry.
PN1064.E6 1954   PR6009.L7 T4 1954.   *LC* 54-3180

MacNeice, Louis, 1907-1963.   • **2.2746**
Modern poetry: a personal essay; with an introduction by Walter Allen. — 2nd ed. — Oxford: Clarendon P., 1968. xxiii, 205 p.; 19 cm. 1. Poetry 2. Imagist poetry — History and criticism. I. T.
PN1064.M3 1968   808.1   *LC* 79-376072   *ISBN* 0198116748

Roethke, Theodore, 1908-1963.   • **2.2747**
On the poet and his craft: selected prose / edited with an introd. by Ralph J. Mills, Jr. — Seattle: University of Washington Press, 1965. xvi, 154 p.; 21 cm. 1. Poetics — Addresses, essays, lectures. I. Mills, Ralph J. II. T.
PN1064.R6   *LC* 65-22387

Stafford, William, 1914-.   **2.2748**
Writing the Australian crawl: views on the writer's vocation / William Stafford. — Ann Arbor: University of Michigan Press, 1978 (c1977). x, 161 p.; 21 cm. — (Poets on poetry.) 1. Poetry — Addresses, essays, lectures. I. T. II. Series.
PN1064.S77 1978   808.1   *LC* 77-5711   *ISBN* 0472873008

PN1065–1083 POETRY AND SPECIAL SUBJECTS

Santayana, George, 1863-1952.   • **2.2749**
Interpretations of poetry and religion. New York: Harper, 1957. xi, 290 p.; 21 cm. — (Library of religion and culture.) (Harper torchbooks. TB9.) 1. Poetry — History and criticism 2. Religion 3. Aesthetics I. T. II. Series. III. Series: Harper torchbooks. TB9.
PN1077.S3   808.1   *LC* 57-13624

Santayana, George, 1863-1952.   • **2.2750**
Three philosophical poets: Lucretius, Dante, and Goethe. New York, Cooper Square Publishers, 1970 [c1910] viii, 215 p. 22 cm. (Harvard studies in comparative literature, v. 1) 1. Lucretius Carus, Titus. 2. Dante Alighieri, 1265-1321. 3. Goethe, Johann Wolfgang von, 1749-1832. I. T.
PN1077.S3 1970   809.1   *LC* 74-134467   *ISBN* 0815403615

Weatherby, Harold L., 1934-.   **2.2751**
The keen delight: the Christian poet in the modern world / Harold L. Weatherby. — Athens: University of Georgia Press, c1975. 167 p.; 23 cm. Includes index. 1. Thomas, Aquinas, Saint, 1225?-1274. 2. Newman, John Henry, 1801-1890. 3. Religion in poetry I. T.
PN1077.W4   809/.933/1   *LC* 74-80043   *ISBN* 0820303674

Rosenthal, Marilyn, 1934-.   **2.2752**
Poetry of the Spanish Civil War / Marilyn Rosenthal. — New York: New York University Press, 1975. xxii, 321 p.; 24 cm. 1. Poetry, Modern — 20th century — History and criticism. 2. Spain — History — Civil War, 1936-1939 — Literature and the war I. T.
PN1080.R65   809.1   *LC* 74-18952   *ISBN* 0814773567

Toliver, Harold E.   **2.2753**
The past that poets make / Harold Toliver. — Cambridge, Mass.: Harvard University Press, 1981. 256 p.: ill.; 24 cm. 1. Poetry — History and criticism 2. Literature and history I. T.
PN1080.T6   821/.009/358   *LC* 80-18825   *ISBN* 0674656768

Miłosz, Czesław.   **2.2754**
The witness of poetry / Czeslaw Milosz. — Cambridge, Mass.: Harvard University Press, 1983. 121 p.; 24 cm. — (Charles Eliot Norton lectures. 1981-1982) Includes index. 1. Poetry — Addresses, essays, lectures. 2. Literature and society — Addresses, essays, lectures. I. T. II. Series.
PN1081.M5 1983   809.1 19   *LC* 82-15471   *ISBN* 0674953827

PN1105–1279 HISTORY. CRITICISM

Bowra, C. M. (Cecil Maurice), 1898-1971.   • **2.2755**
Inspiration and poetry. — London, Macmillan; New York, St. Martin's Press, 1955. vii, 265 p. 23 cm. 1. Poetry — Hist. & crit. I. T.
PN1111.B53   809.1   *LC* 55-14774

Kermode, Frank, 1919-.   • **2.2756**
Romantic image. — London, Routledge and Paul [1957] 171 p. illus. 23 cm. 1. Yeats, W. B. (William Butler), 1865-1939. 2. Poetry, Modern — Hist. & crit. 3. Criticism I. T.
PN1111.K4 1957   808.1   *LC* 57-3302 rev

Neff, Emery Edward, 1892-.   **2.2757**
A revolution in European poetry, 1660–1900 [by] Emery Neff. — New York: Columbia Univ. Press, 1940. xi, 279 p.; 23 cm. 1. Poetry — History and criticism 2. Literature, Comparative I. T.
PN1111.N4 1974   809/.1

Van Doren, Mark, 1894-1972.   • **2.2758**
The noble voice, a study of ten great poems, by Mark Van Doren. 1st ed. [New York] H. Holt and company [1946] xviii, 328 p.; 22 cm. 'First printing.' 1. Poetry — History and criticism I. T.
PN1111.V3   809.1   *LC* 46-7823

Sansom, Clive, 1910-.   • **2.2759**
The World of poetry: poets and critics on the art and functions of poetry / extracts selected and arranged by Clive Sansom. — London: Phoenix House, 1959. xiv, 224 p.; 22 cm. 1. Poetry — History and criticism I. T.
PN1111.W6   *LC* a 60-423

Fehrman, Carl Abraham Daniel, 1915-.   **2.2760**
[Diktaren och de skapande ögonblicken. English] Poetic creation: inspiration or craft / by Carl Fehrman; translated by Karin Petherick. — Minneapolis: University of Minnesota Press, c1980. vii, 229 p.; 24 cm. Translation of Diktaren och de skapande ögonblicken. 1. Poetry, Modern — History and criticism. 2. Creation (Literary, artistic, etc.) I. T.
PN1116.F413   808.1   *LC* 79-17901   *ISBN* 0816608997

Murray, Gilbert, 1866-1957.   • **2.2761**
The classical tradition in poetry. — New York: Russell & Russell, [1968, c1927]
xi, 274 p.; 20 cm. — (The Charles Eliot Norton lectures) 1. Literature,
Comparative — Classical and modern 2. Literature, Comparative — Modern
and classical I. T. II. Series.
PN1126.M8 1968   809.1   LC 68-27075

Brooks, Cleanth, 1906-.   • **2.2762**
Modern poetry and the tradition. Chapel Hill: University of North Carolina
Press, 1939. xi, 253 p.; 22 cm. 1. Poetry — History & criticism. I. T.
PN1136.B75   LC 39-22007

Ransom, John Crowe, 1888-1974.   • **2.2763**
The world's body. — Baton Rouge: Louisiana State University Press, [1968]
xiv, 390 p.; 22 cm. — (Louisiana paperbacks, L-28) 1. Poetry — Addresses,
essays, lectures. 2. Criticism I. T.
PN1136.R3 1968   809.1   LC 68-7658

Tate, Allen, 1899-.   • **2.2764**
Reactionary essays on poetry and ideas. — Freeport, N.Y.: Books for Libraries
Press, [1968] xii, 240 p.; 22 cm. — (Essay index reprint series) Reprint of 1936
ed. 1. Poetry — Addresses, essays, lectures. 2. American literature —
Addresses, essays, lectures. I. T.
PN1136.T3 1968   809.1   LC 68-24856

Segel, Harold B., 1930-.   **2.2765**
The baroque poem; a comparative survey, together with 150 illustrative texts
from English, American, Dutch, German, French, Italian, Spanish, Mexican,
Portuguese, Polish, Modern Latin, Czech, Croatian, and Russian poetry, in the
original languages and accompanying English translations [by] Harold B. Segel.
— [1st ed.]. — New York: Dutton, 1974. xx, 328 p.; 22 cm. 1. Poetry, Modern
— 17th century — History and criticism. 2. Baroque literature 3. Poetry,
Modern — 17th century I. T.
PN1221.S4   808.81   LC 74-95501   ISBN 0525061185

Bowra, Cecil Maurice, Sir.   • **2.2766**
Heritage of symbolism. New York: Schocken Books, 1961, 1943. 231p.; 21 cm.
1. Poetry, Modern — History and criticism. — 20th century 2. Symbolism in
literature I. T.
PN1271.B6 1943   LC 61-14921

Hass, Robert.   **2.2767**
Twentieth century pleasures: prose on poetry / Robert Hass. — 1st ed. — New
York: Ecco Press, 1984. 308 p. 1. Poetry, Modern — 20th century — History
and criticism — Addresses, essays, lectures. I. T. II. Title: 20th century
pleasures.
PN1271.H35 1984   809.1/04 19   LC 83-16394   ISBN 0880010452

Jackson, Laura (Riding), 1901-.   • **2.2768**
A survey of modernist poetry, by Laura Riding and Robert Graves. New York,
Haskell House, 1969. 295 p. 23 cm. Reprint of the 1928 ed. 1. Poetry, Modern
— 20th century — History and criticism. 2. Free verse 3. Modernism
(Literature) I. Graves, Robert, 1895- joint author. II. T.
PN1271.J25 1969   821/.9/1209   LC 76-95444   ISBN 0838312004

Jarrell, Randall, 1914-1965.   • **2.2769**
Poetry and the age. — [1st Octagon ed.]. — New York: Octagon Books, 1972
[c1953] x, 271 p.; 22 cm. 1. Poetry, Modern — 20th century — History and
criticism — Addresses, essays, lectures. I. T.
PN1271.J3 1972   809.1/04   LC 70-184415   ISBN 0374942013

PN1301–1551 SPECIAL TYPES OF POETRY

Bowra, C. M. (Cecil Maurice), 1898-1971.   • **2.2770**
From Virgil to Milton / by C. M. Bowra. — London: Macmillan; New York:
St. Martin's Press, 1961. 246 p.; 23 cm. First published 1945. 1. Camões, Luís
de, 1524?-1580. 2. Tasso, Torquato, 1544-1595. 3. Milton, John, 1608-1674.
4. Virgil. 5. Epic poetry — History and criticism I. T.
PN1303.B65   808.13   LC 45-6069

Greene, Thomas McLernon, 1926-.   • **2.2771**
The descent from heaven: a study in epic continuity. New Haven: Yale
University Press, 1963. 434 p.; 24 cm. 1. Epic poetry — History and criticism.
2. Literature, Comparative — Themes, motives 3. Divine messengers in
literature I. T.
PN1303 G7   809.13   LC 63-7934   ISBN 0300014570

Poggioli, Renato, 1907-1963.   **2.2772**
The oaten flute: essays on pastoral poetry and the pastoral ideal / Renato
Poggioli. Cambridge: Harvard University Press, 1975. vi, 340 p.: ill.; 24 cm.
1. Pastoral poetry — History and criticism. I. T.
PN1421.P6 1975   809.1   LC 74-16540   ISBN 0674629507

Fuller, John.   **2.2773**
The sonnet. [London] Methuen & Co. [1972] 58 p. 20 cm. (The critical idiom,
26) Distributed in the U.S.A. by Harper & Row Publishers, Barnes & Noble
Import Division. 1. Sonnet I. T.
PN1514.F8   809.1   LC 73-152332   ISBN 0416656803 ISBN
0416656900

PN1560–1590 Performing Arts. Show Business

Sharp, Harold S. comp.   **2.2774**
Index to characters in the performing arts, compiled by Harold S. Sharp and
Marjorie Z. Sharp. — New York: Scarecrow Press, 1966-73. 4 v. in 6; 22 cm.
Parts 2-4 have imprint: Metuchen, N. J., Scarecrow Press. 1. Performing arts
— Dictionaries. 2. Characters and characteristics in literature — Dictionaries.
I. Sharp, Marjorie Z., joint comp. II. T.
PN1579.S45   808.8292703   LC 66-13744   ISBN 0810804867

Variety international showbusiness reference / Mike Kaplan,   **2.2775**
editor.
New York: Garland Pub., 1981. 1135 p.; 29 cm. — (Garland reference library
of the humanities. v. 292) 1. Performing arts — Dictionaries. I. Kaplan, Mike,
1918- II. Daily variety. III. Series.
PN1579.V3 1981   790.2/03/21 19   LC 81-2329   ISBN 0824093410

Wilmeth, Don B.   **2.2776**
The language of American popular entertainment: a glossary of argot, slang,
and terminology / Don B. Wilmeth. — Westport, Conn.: Greenwood Press,
c1981. xxi, 305 p.; 25 cm. 1. Performing arts — United States — Dictionaries.
2. English language — Slang — Dictionaries 3. United States — Popular
culture — Dictionaries. I. T.
PN1579.W5   790.2/03   LC 80-14795   ISBN 0313224978

The New York Times theater reviews, 1920–1970.   **2.2777**
New York: New York Times, 1971-. v. : illus.; 32 cm. Vols. 1-8: reviews; 9-10:
index. 1. Performing arts — Reviews. I. New York Times
PN1581.N4   792/.09747/1   LC 72-166218

The London stage, 1660–1800; a calendar of plays,   • **2.2778**
entertainments & afterpieces, together with casts, box–receipts
and contemporary comment. Compiled from the playbills,
newspapers and theatrical diaries of the period.
[1st ed.]. — Carbondale: Southern Illinois University Press, 1960-68 [v. 1, 1965]
5 v. in 11.: illus., ports., facsims.; 25 cm. 1. Performing arts — England —
London — History. 2. London (England) — History.
PN1582.G72 L65   792/.09421   LC 60-6539

Archer, Leonard Courtney, 1911-.   **2.2779**
Black images in the American theatre; NAACP protest campaigns—stage,
screen, radio & television, by Leonard C. Archer. [1st ed.] Brooklyn, N.Y.,
Pageant-Poseidon [1973] xi, 351 p. illus. 22 cm. 1. National Association for the
Advancement of Colored People. 2. Afro-Americans in the performing arts
I. T.
PN1590.N4 A7   791/.0973   LC 79-175230   ISBN 0818102969

PN1600–3299 Drama. Theater

Dukore, Bernard Frank, 1931-.   **2.2780**
Dramatic theory and criticism: Greeks to Grotowski / [compiled by] Bernard
F. Dukore. — New York: Holt, Rinehart and Winston, [1974] xiv, 1003 p.; 25
cm. 1. Drama — History and criticism I. T.
PN1621.D8   PN1621 D8.   808.2   LC 73-9778   ISBN
0030911524

Ellis-Fermor, Una Mary, 1894-1958.   • **2.2781**
The frontiers of drama [by] Una Ellis–Fermor. With an introd. by Allardyce
Nicoll and a bibliography by Harold Brooks. — [2d ed. — London]: Methuen,
[1964] xiii, 162 p.; 22 cm. 1. Drama — History and criticism I. T.
PN1623.E6 1964   809.2   LC 64-56584

Gassner, John, 1903-1967. • 2.2782
Dramatic soundings; evaluations and retractions culled from 30 years of dramatic criticism. Introd. and posthumous editing by Glenn Loney. — New York: Crown Publishers, [1968] xx, 716 p.: port.; 22 cm. 1. Drama — Addresses, essays, lectures. 2. Theater — United States — Addresses, essays, lectures. I. Loney, Glenn Meredith, 1928- ed. II. T.
PN1623.G3   792/.0973   LC 66-15119

Enciclopedia dello spettacolo. • 2.2783
Roma Casa editrice La Maschere [1954-] 1. Theater — Dictionaries 2. Opera — Dictionaries 3. Motion pictures — Dictionaries
PN1625 E7

Gassner, John, 1903-1967. • 2.2784
The reader's encyclopedia of world drama, edited by John Gassner & Edward Quinn. — New York: Crowell, [1969] xi, 1030 p.: illus.; 26 cm. — (A Crowell reference book) 1. Drama — Dictionaries. I. Quinn, Edward G., 1932- joint author. II. T.
PN1625.G3 1969   809.2   LC 69-11830

McGraw–Hill encyclopedia of world drama: an international reference work in 5 volumes / Stanley Hochman, editor in chief. 2.2785
2nd ed. — New York, N.Y.: McGraw-Hill, c1984. 5 v.: ill.; 28 cm. 1. Drama — Dictionaries. 2. Theater — Dictionaries. 3. Drama — Bio-bibliography. I. Hochman, Stanley. II. McGraw-Hill, inc. III. Title: World drama.
PN1625.M3 1984   809.2 19   LC 83-9919   ISBN 0070791694

Vaughn, Jack A., 1935-. 2.2786
Drama A to Z: a handbook / Jack A. Vaughn. — New York: Ungar, 1979 (c1978). 239 p.; 22 cm. 1. Drama — Dictionaries. I. T.
PN1625.V3   809.2   LC 78-4298   ISBN 0804429375

Trefny, Beverly Robin, 1945-. 2.2787
Index to children's plays in collections, 1975–1984 / by Beverly Robin Trefny and Eileen C. Palmer. — Metuchen, N.J.: Scarecrow Press, 1986. xvi, 108 p.; 23 cm. Rev. ed. of: Index to children's plays in collections / by Barbara A. Kreider. 2nd ed. 1977. 1. Children's plays — Indexes. I. Palmer, Eileen C. II. Kreider, Barbara A. Index to children's plays in collections. III. T. IV. Title: Children's plays in collections, 1975-1984.
PN1627.T73 1986   016.80882 19   LC 86-6418   ISBN 0810818930

Boughner, Daniel Cliness, 1909-. 2.2788
The braggart in Renaissance comedy; a study in comparative drama from Aristophanes to Shakespeare, by Daniel C. Boughner. — Westport, Conn.: Greenwood Press, [1970, c1954] ix, 328 p.; 23 cm. 1. Boastfulness in literature 2. European drama (Comedy) — History and criticism. I. T.
PN1633.B6 B69 1970   809.2/9/3   LC 75-100223   ISBN 0837130069

Daniels, Barry V. 2.2789
Revolution in the theatre: French romantic theories of drama / [selected by] Barry V. Daniels. — Westport, Conn.: Greenwood Press, 1983. xii, 249 p.: ill.; 25 cm. (Contributions in drama and theatre studies. 0163-3821; no. 7) Includes index. 1. Drama — Addresses, essays, lectures. 2. Romanticism — France — Addresses, essays, lectures. 3. Theater — France — History — 19th century — Addresses, essays, lectures. 4. Dramatic criticism — France. 5. French prose literature — 19th century. I. T. II. Series.
PN1633.R65 R48 1983   842/.7/09145 19   LC 83-1705   ISBN 0313224765

Brook, Peter. • 2.2790
The empty space. — [1st American ed.]. — New York: Atheneum, 1968. 141 p.; 22 cm. 1. Theater 2. Drama I. T.
PN1655.B74 1968   792/.01   LC 68-12531

Styan, J. L. 2.2791
Drama, stage, and audience / J. L. Styan. — London: Cambridge University Press, [1975] viii, 256 p.; 22 cm. Includes index. 1. Drama 2. Theater 3. Theater audiences I. T.
PN1655.S74   PN1655 S74.   792   LC 74-76948   ISBN 0521205042

Styan, J. L. • 2.2792
The elements of drama. — Cambridge [Eng.]: University Press, 1960. 306 p.; 23 cm. 1. Drama — History and criticism 2. Theater I. T.
PN1655.S75   792.01   LC 60-3899

Young, Stark, 1881-1963. • 2.2793
The theatre. New York, Hill and Wang [1958, c1954] 124 p. 19 cm. (Dramabooks, D12) 1. Theater
PN1655.Y6 1959   792   LC 58-6067   ISBN 0809005123

PN1660–1861 TECHNIQUE OF DRAMATIC COMPOSITION

Archer, William, 1856-1924. • 2.2794
Play–making; a manual of craftsmanship. With a new introd. to the Dover ed. by John Gassner. — New York: Dover Publications, [1960] 277 p.; 21 cm. 'An unabridged and unaltered republication of the first edition.' 1. Drama — Technique I. T.
PN1661.A8 1960   808.2   LC 60-50046

Baker, George Pierce, 1866-1935. • 2.2795
Dramatic technique. — Westport, Conn.: Greenwood Press, [1970, c1919] vi, 531 p.: illus.; 23 cm. 1. Drama — Technique I. T.
PN1661.B3 1970   808.2   LC 74-100220   ISBN 0837130050

Clark, Barrett Harper, 1890-1953. • 2.2796
European theories of the drama, with a supplement on the American drama; an anthology of dramatic theory and criticism from Aristotle to the present day, in a series of selected texts, with commentaries, biographies, and bibliographies. — Newly rev. by Henry Popkin. — New York: Crown Publishers, [1965] xiv, 628 p.; 24 cm. 1. Drama — History & criticism. I. T.
PN1661.C55 1955   809.2   LC 63-12071

Cole, Toby, 1916- ed. • 2.2797
Playwrights on playwriting; the meaning and making of modern drama from Ibsen to Ionesco. Introd. by John Gassner. — New York: Hill and Wang, [1960] 299 p.; 20 cm. 1. Drama — Technique I. T.
PN1661.C56   808.2   LC 60-7642

Matthews, Brander, 1852-1929. ed. • 2.2798
Papers on playmaking. Edited by Brander Matthews. With a pref. by Henry W. Wells. — Freeport, N.Y.: Books for Libraries Press, [1970, c1957] viii, 312 p.; 23 cm. — (Essay index reprint series) 1. Drama — Technique 2. Drama — History and criticism 3. Playwriting 4. Theater — Addresses, essays, lectures. I. T.
PN1661.M29 1970   809.2   LC 75-111852   ISBN 0836918908

Rowell, George. 2.2799
Victorian dramatic criticism; selected and introduced by George Rowell. — London, Methuen, 1971. xxv, 372 p. 25 cm. 1. Dramatic criticism — Great Britain. I. T.
PN1707.R6   792/.0942   LC 76-597310   ISBN 0416123201

Russian dramatic theory from Pushkin to the Symbolists: an anthology / translated and edited by Laurence Senelick. 2.2800
1st ed. — Austin: University of Texas Press, 1981. lv, 336 p.; 23 cm. — (University of Texas Press Slavic series. no. 5) (Dan Danciger publication series.) Includes indexes. 1. Dramatic criticism — Soviet Union — Addresses, essays, lectures. 2. Theater — Soviet Union — History — 19th century — Sources. I. Senelick, Laurence. II. Series. III. Series: Dan Danciger publication series.
PN1707.R8   891.72/009 19   LC 81-1718   ISBN 0292770251

Ward, A. C. (Alfred Charles), 1891- ed. • 2.2801
Specimens of English dramatic criticism, XVII–XX centuries. Selected and introduced by A. C. Ward. Westport, Conn., Greenwood Press [1970] x, 355 p. 16 cm. Reprint of the 1945 ed. 1. Dramatic criticism — Great Britain. 2. Theater — Great Britain — Reviews. I. T.
PN1707.W34 1970   792/.0942   LC 73-138605   ISBN 0837155452

PN1720–1861 History

Gassner, John, 1903-1967. • 2.2802
Masters of the drama. 3d rev. and enl. ed. [New York] Dover Publications [1954] xxi, 890 p. illus., ports. 22 cm. 1. Drama — History and criticism 2. Dramatists I. T.
PN1721.G3 1954   809.2   LC 54-12577

Nicoll, Allardyce, 1894-. • 2.2803
Masks, mimes and miracles; studies in the popular theatre. New York, Cooper Square Publishers, 1963. 407 p. ill. 29 cm. 1. Mime 2. Theater — History 3. Commedia dell' arte. I. T.
PN 1721 N64 1963   LC 63-17895

Hunningher, Benjamin. • 2.2804
The origin of the theater, an essay. [1st American ed.] New York, Hill and Wang [1961] 114 p. illus. 19 cm. (A Dramabook, D28) 1. Drama — History and criticism 2. Theater — History 3. Theater — Moral and ethical aspects. I. T.
PN1737.H8 1961   792.0902   LC 61-6945

Young, Karl, 1879-.   • **2.2805**
The drama of the medieval church, by Karl Young. — Oxford, The Clarendon press, 1933. 2 v. (incl. fronts., facsims.) 25.5 cm. Collection of extant examples of church drama employed by the medieval church in western Europe as a part of public worship; text interspersed with commentary. 1. Catholic Church — Liturgy 2. Drama, Medieval 3. Drama, Medieval — History and criticism. 4. Mysteries and miracle-plays, Latin. 5. Latin drama, Medieval and modern I. T.
PN1751.Y6   792.1   *LC* 33-17914

Bentley, Eric, 1916-.   • **2.2806**
The playwright as thinker: a study of drama in modern times. New York, Meridian Books, 1955 [c1946] 314 p. 18 cm. (Meridian books, M6) 1. Drama — 19th century — History and criticism. 2. Drama — 20th century — History and criticism I. T.
PN1851.B4 1955   808.2   *LC* 55-5157

Lucas, F. L. (Frank Laurence), 1894-1967.   • **2.2807**
The drama of Chekhov, Synge, Yeats, and Pirandello [by] F. L. Lucas. [2d ed.] London, Cassell [1965, c1963] xii, 452 p. ports. 23 cm. 1. Drama — 19th century — History and criticism — Addresses, essays, lectures. 2. Drama — 20th century — History and criticism — Addresses, essays, lectures. I. T.
PN1851.L8 1965   809.2   *LC* 66-9552

Matlaw, Myron, 1924-.   • **2.2808**
Modern world drama; an encyclopedia. — [1st ed.]. — New York: Dutton, 1972. xxi, 960 p.: illus.; 25 cm. 1. Drama — 19th century — Dictionaries. 2. Drama — 20th century — Dictionaries. I. T.
PN1851.M36   809.2/34   *LC* 71-185032   *ISBN* 0525159029

PN1861 20TH CENTURY

Clark, Barrett Harper, 1890-1953. ed.   • **2.2809**
A history of modern drama, ed. by Barrett H. Clark and George Freedley. New York, D. Appleton-Century Co. [1947] xii, 832 p. 25 cm. 1. Drama — 20th century — History and criticism I. Freedley, George, 1904- joint ed.
PN1861.C55   809.2   *LC* 47-11445

Crowell's handbook of contemporary drama, by Michael Anderson ... and others.   • **2.2810**
New York: Crowell, [1971] vi, 505 p.; 24 cm. — (A Crowell reference book) 1. Drama — 20th century — Dictionaries. I. Anderson, Michael John, 1937-
PN1861.C7   809.2/04   *LC* 79-158714   *ISBN* 0690226438

Esslin, Martin.   **2.2811**
The theatre of the absurd / Martin Esslin. — 3rd ed., rev. and enl. ed. — Harmondsworth, Middlesex, England; New York, N.Y.: Penguin; [London]: Eyre & Spottiswoode, 1980. 480 p.; 18 cm. Includes index. 1. Drama — 20th century — History and criticism 2. Theater of the absurd I. T.
PN1861.E8 1980   809.2/04 19   *LC* 81-169374   *ISBN* 0140209298

Grossvogel, David I., 1925-.   • **2.2812**
Four playwrights and a postscript: Brecht, Ionesco, Beckett, Genet. — Ithaca, N.Y.: Cornell University Press, [1962] 209 p.; 23 cm. 1. Drama — 20th century — History and criticism I. T.
PN1861.G7 1962   809.2   *LC* 62-17817

Styan, J. L.   • **2.2813**
The dark comedy: the development of modern comic tragedy [by] J. L. Styan. — 2nd ed. — London: Cambridge U.P., 1968. viii, 311 p.; 23 cm. 1. Drama — 20th century — History and criticism 2. Tragicomedy — History and criticism. I. T.
PN1861.S75 1968   *LC* 68-23185   *ISBN* 0521065720

Styan, J. L.   **2.2814**
Modern drama in theory and practice / J. L. Styan. — Cambridge; New York: Cambridge University Press, 1981. 3 v.: ill.; 23 cm. 1. Drama — 20th century — History and criticism 2. Theater — History — 20th century I. T.
PN1861.S76   809.2   *LC* 79-15947

Wellwarth, George E., 1932-.   • **2.2815**
The theater of protest and paradox: developments in the avant-garde dramma, by George Wellwarth. — [New York]: New York University Press, 1964. xv, 315 p.; 22 cm. 1. Drama — 20th century — History and criticism I. T. II. Title: Developments in the avant-garde drama.
PN1861.W4   809.2   *LC* 64-16901

PN1865–1998 SPECIAL TYPES OF DRAMA

PN1880–1919 Tragedy. Tragicomedy. Melodrama

Lucas, F. L. (Frank Laurence), 1894-1967.   • **2.2816**
Tragedy; serious drama in relation to Aristotle's Poetics. Rev. ed. New York, Collier Books [1962] 160 p. 18 cm. (Collier books, AS442V) First published in 1927 under title: Tragedy in relation to Aristotle's Poetics. 1. Aristotle. Poetics 2. Tragedy I. T.
PN1892.L8 1962   808.2   *LC* 62-19121

Tragedy, modern essays in criticism / edited by Laurence   • **2.2817**
Michel, Richard B. Sewall.
Englewood Cliffs, N.J.: Prentice-Hall, [1963] 340 p.; 22 cm. — (Prentice-Hall English literature series) 1. Tragedy — History and criticism — Addresses, essays, lectures. I. Michel, Laurence Anthony. II. Sewall, Richard Benson.
PN1892.M5   *LC* 63-14305

Steiner, George, 1929-.   • **2.2818**
The death of tragedy. — [1st ed.]. — New York: Knopf, 1961. 354 p.; 21 cm. 1. Tragedy I. T.
PN1892.S7   809.2   *LC* 60-53442

Herrick, Marvin Theodore, 1899-.   • **2.2819**
Tragicomedy, its origin and development in Italy, France and England. — Urbana: University of Illinois Press, 1955. vii, 331 p.; 26 cm. (Illinois studies in language and literature. v.39) 1. Tragicomedy — History and criticism. I. T. II. Series.
PN1902 H4   809.2   *LC* 55-6942

Rahill, Frank.   • **2.2820**
The world of melodrama. — University Park: Pennsylvania State University Press, 1967. xviii, 334 p.; 24 cm. 1. Melodrama — History and criticism. I. T.
PN1912.R3   809.52   *LC* 66-25466

Disher, Maurice Willson, 1893-.   • **2.2821**
Melodrama, plots that thrilled: illustrated from the Raymond Mander and Joe Mitchenson Theatre Collection. — London: Rockliff, [1954] 210 p.: ill. 1. Melodrama — History and criticism. I. T.
PN1917.D5 1954   *LC* 54-3051

Grimsted, David.   **2.2822**
Melodrama unveiled: American theater and culture, 1800–1850 / David Grimsted. — Chicago: University of Chicago Press, [1968] xii, 285 p.: ill. (on lining papers); 24 cm. 1. Melodrama — History and criticism. 2. Theater — United States — History. I. T.
PN1918.U5 G7   792.2/0973   *LC* 68-15575

PN1920–1969 Comedy. Burlesque. Vaudeville

Grawe, Paul H.   **2.2823**
Comedy in space, time, and the imagination / Paul H. Grawe. — Chicago: Nelson-Hall, c1983. vi, 362 p.; 23 cm. Includes index. 1. Comedy I. T.
PN1922.G7 1983   809/.917 19   *LC* 82-10603   *ISBN* 0882296310

Meredith, George, 1828-1909.   • **2.2824**
An essay on comedy, and the uses of the comic spirit. Edited, with an introd. and notes, by Lane Cooper. — Port Washington, N.Y.: Kennikat Press, [1972] ix, 326 p.; 18 cm. 'First published in 1897.' 1. Comedy I. T.
PN1922.M4 1972   809.9/1/7   *LC* 73-153230   *ISBN* 0804615403

Cooper, Lane, 1875-1959.   • **2.2825**
An Aristotelian theory of comedy: with an adaptation of the Poetics, and a translation of the 'Tractatus Coislinianus' / by Lane Cooper. — New York: Harcourt, Brace, 1922. xxi, 323 p. 1. Comedy 2. Greek drama (Comedy) — History and criticism I. T. II. Title: Tractatus Coislinianus.
PN1924 C8   *LC* 24-5701

Janko, Richard, 1955-.   **2.2826**
Aristotle on comedy: towards a reconstruction of Poetics II / Richard Janko. — Berkeley: University of California Press, 1984. viii, 294 p., [4] p. of plates: ill.; 23 cm. Includes indexes. 1. Aristotle — Authorship. 2. Tractatus Coislinianus. 3. Comedy I. Aristotle. Poetics II. T.
PN1924.J36 1984   808.2/523 19   *LC* 84-2460   *ISBN* 0520053036

Bermel, Albert. 2.2827
Farce: a history from Aristophanes to Woody Allen / Albert Bermel. — New York: Simon and Schuster, c1982. 464 p.; 25 cm. 1. Farce I. T.
PN1942.B4 1982 809.2/52 19 *LC* 81-16672 *ISBN* 0671251481

Clinton-Baddeley, V. C. (Victor Clinton), 1900-1970. • 2.2828
The burlesque tradition in the English theatre after 1660, by V. C. Clinton-Baddeley. New York, B. Blom, 1971. xvi, 152 p. illus., ports. 22 cm. Reprint of the 1952 ed. 1. English drama — History and criticism. 2. Burlesque (Literature) I. T.
PN1947.C55 1971 792.7 *LC* 70-93160

Felner, Mira, 1947-. 2.2829
Apostles of silence: the modern French mimes / Mira Felner. — Rutherford [N.J.]: Fairleigh Dickinson University Press; London: Associated University Presses, c1985. 212 p.: ill.; 25 cm. Includes index. 1. Mimes — France. 2. Mime I. T.
PN1948.F7 F44 1985 792.3/092/2 19 *LC* 83-48682 *ISBN* 0838631967

Gilbert, Douglas, 1889-1948. 2.2830
American vaudeville, its life and times. New York Whittlesey House, McGraw-Hill [c1940] 428p. 1. Vaudeville — U.S. I. T.
PN1967 G55

Sobel, Bernard. • 2.2831
A pictorial history of vaudeville / Bernard Sobel; foreword by George Jessel. — New York: Citadel, 1961. 224 p.: ill. 1. Vaudeville — United States — Pictorial works 2. Theater I. T.
PN1967.S63 792.209

Scott, Harold. 2.2832
The early doors: origins of the music hall / [by] Harold Scott. Wakefield: EP Publishing, 1977. [4], 3-259 p., leaf of plate, [12] p. of plates: ill., facsims.; 22 cm. Index. 1. Music-halls (Variety-theaters, cabarets, etc.) — Great Britain — History. I. T.
PN1968.G7 792.7/0941 `ISBN 071581219X

Cheshire, David F. 2.2833
Music hall in Britain / D. F. Cheshire. — 1st American ed. — Rutherford [N.J.]: Fairleigh Dickinson University Press, 1974. 112 p.: ill.; 26 cm. (Illustrated sources in history) 1. Music-halls (Variety-theaters, cabarets, etc.) — Great Britain. I. T.
PN1968.G7 C5 1974b 792.7/0942 *LC* 74-2581 *ISBN* 0838615635

DiMeglio, John E. 2.2834
Vaudeville U.S.A. / by John E. DiMeglio. — Bowling Green, Ohio: Bowling Green University Popular Press, [1973]. –. 259 p.: ill.; 23 cm. — 1. Vaudeville — United States — History. I. T.
PN1968.U5 D5 792.7 *LC* 73-78161 *ISBN* 0879720530

PN1970–1981 Marionettes. Puppets

Speaight, George. • 2.2835
The history of the English toy theatre. — [Rev. ed.]. — Boston: Plays, inc., [1969] 224 p.: illus. (part col.); 26 cm. 1946 ed. published under title: Juvenile drama: the history of the English toy theatre. 1. Toy theaters I. T. II. Title: English toy theatre.
PN1972.S6 1969b 791.5 *LC* 69-13124

Keene, Donald. • 2.2836
Bunraku; the art of the Japanese puppet theatre. Text by Donald Keene. Photos. by Kaneko Hiroshi. With an introd. by Tanizaki Junichirō. [1st ed.] Tokyo, Kodansha International, ltd.; [distributed by Japan Publications Trading Co., Rutland, Vt., 1965] 287 p. 360 illus. (part mounted col.) music, ports. and phonodisc in pocket. 38 cm. 'List of plays':p. 269-271. 1. Bunraku I. Kaneko, Hiroshi, 1933- illus. II. T. III. Title: The art of the Japanese puppet theatre.
PN1978.J3 K4 791.530952 *LC* 65-19187

McPharlin, Paul, 1903-1948. • 2.2837
The puppet theatre in America: a history, 1524–1948. With a supplement: Puppets in America since 1948, by Marjorie Batchelder McPharlin. — Boston: Plays, inc., [1969] xi, 734 p.: illus., ports.; 24 cm. Based on the author's thesis, University of Michigan. 1. Puppets and puppet-plays — U.S. — History. I. Batchelder, Marjorie Hope, 1903- II. T. III. Title: Puppets in America since 1948.
PN1978.U6 M22 1969 791.5/3/0973 *LC* 79-97944

Brandon, James R. comp. 2.2838
On thrones of gold; three Javanese shadow plays, edited with an introd. by James R. Brandon. — Cambridge: Harvard University Press, 1970. xvi, 407 p.: illus. (part col.); 25 cm. 'English versions ... from the standard Javanese wajang kulit repertory.' 1. Wayang plays I. T.
PN1980.B63 899/.222/2 *LC* 73-88802 *ISBN* 0674637755

PN1985–1988 Pantomimes

Broadbent, R. J. • 2.2839
A history of pantomime. — New York: B. Blom, [1964] 226 p.; 21 cm. 1. Pantomime I. T.
PN1985.B7 1964 792.309 *LC* 64-14694

Mander, Raymond. 2.2840
Pantomime; a story in pictures [by] Raymond Mander & Joe Mitchenson. Foreword by Danny La Rue. New York, Taplinger Pub. Co. [c1973] 56 p., [112] p. of illus. 26 cm. 'The story of pantomime', by G. B. Shaw, p. 1-47. 1. Pantomime — Great Britain — Pictorial works. I. Mitchenson, Joe. joint author. II. Shaw, Bernard, 1856-1950. The story of pantomime. 1973. III. T.
PN1985.M25 1973 792.3/0942 *LC* 73-6176 *ISBN* 0800862333

Mayer, David. 2.2841
Harlequin in his element; the English pantomime, 1806–1836. — Cambridge, Mass.: Harvard University Press, 1969. xvii, 400 p.: illus., facsims.; 25 cm. 'Appendix B: Pantomime music': p. [337]-377. 1. Grimaldi, Joseph, 1779-1837. 2. Pantomime — Great Britain. 3. Harlequin I. T.
PN1985.M3 792.3/0942 *LC* 79-88809 *ISBN* 0674372751

Wilson, A. E. (Albert Edward), 1885-1949. 2.2842
The story of pantomime, by A. E. Wilson. With a new introd. by Roy Hudd. [Wakefield, Eng.] EP Pub. [Totowa, N.J.] Rowman and Littlefield, 1974. 142 p. illus. 23 cm. 1. Pantomime (Christmas entertainment) I. T.
PN1985.W54 1974 792.3/0942 *LC* 74-168189 *ISBN* 0874714853

PN1990–1992.95 Radio. Television Broadcasts
(see also: HE7601-8700.8, TK6630-6720)

Boyd, Douglas A. 2.2843
Broadcasting in the Arab world: a survey of radio and television in the Middle East / Douglas A. Boyd. — Philadelphia: Temple University Press, c1982. xv, 306 p.: map; 24 cm. — (International and comparative broadcasting.) Includes index. 1. Broadcasting — Arab countries. I. T. II. Series.
PN1990.6.A65 B69 1982 384.54/0917/4927 19 *LC* 81-23309 *ISBN* 0877222371

Terkel, Studs, 1912-. 2.2844
Talking to myself: a memoir of my times / Studs Terkel. — 1st ed. — New York: Pantheon Books, c1977. xiv, 316 p.; 24 cm. 1. Terkel, Studs, 1912- 2. Broadcasters — United States — Biography. 3. Authors, American — 20th century — Biography. I. T.
PN1990.72.T4 A37 070/.92/4 B *LC* 76-54308 *ISBN* 0394411021

Dunning, John, 1942-. 2.2845
Tune in yesterday: the ultimate encyclopedia of old–time radio, 1925–1976 / John Dunning. — Englewood Cliffs, N.J.: Prentice-Hall, c1976. xiii, 703 p., [16] leaves of plates: ill.; 24 cm. Includes index. 1. Radio programs — United States — Dictionaries. I. T.
PN1991.3.U6 D8 PN1991.3U6 D8. 791.44/5 *LC* 76-28369 *ISBN* 0139326162

MacDonald, J. Fred. 2.2846
Don't touch that dial!: Radio programming in American life, 1920–1960 / J. Fred MacDonald. — Chicago: Nelson-Hall, c1979. xii, 412 p., [10] leaves of plates: ill.; 23 cm. Includes indexes. 1. Radio broadcasting — United States — History. 2. United States — Popular culture I. T.
PN1991.3.U6 M3 791.44/0973 *LC* 79-87700 *ISBN* 0882295284

Brooks, Tim. 2.2847
The complete directory to prime time network TV shows, 1946–present / Tim Brooks and Earle Marsh. — 3rd ed. — New York: Ballantine Books, 1985. xxi, 1123 p.: ill.; 23 cm. Includes index. 1. Television broadcasting — United States — Dictionaries. 2. Television programs — United States — Plots, themes, etc. I. Marsh, Earle. II. T. III. Title: Prime time network TV shows, 1946-present.
PN1992.18.B68 1985 791.45/75/0973 19 *LC* 84-45671 *ISBN* 0345318641

Brown, Les, 1928-. 2.2848
[Encyclopedia of television] Les Brown's Encyclopedia of television. — New York: New York Zoetrope, 1982. 496 p.: ill.; 25 cm. Expanded ed. of: New

York times encyclopedia of television. 1977. 1. Television broadcasting — Dictionaries. I. T. II. Title: Encyclopedia of television.
PN1992.18.B7 1982   791.45/03 19   *LC* 82-7867   *ISBN* 0918432286

Steinberg, Cobbett.   **2.2849**
TV facts / by Cobbett Steinberg. — Rev. and updated. — New York, N.Y.: Facts on File, c1985. xi, 478 p.; 29 cm. Includes index. 1. Television broadcasting — United States — Dictionaries. 2. Television industry — United States — Statistics. I. T.
PN1992.18.S75 1985   384.55/0973 19   *LC* 82-15528   *ISBN* 0871967332

Arlen, Michael J.   **• 2.2850**
Living–room war [by] Michael J. Arlen. — New York: Viking Press, [1969] xiv, 242 p.; 23 cm. 1. Television broadcasting — United States. I. T.
PN1992.3.U5 A9 1969   791.45/0973 19   *LC* 69-12255

Gianakos, Larry James.   **2.2851**
Television drama series programming: a comprehensive chronicle, 1959–1975 / by Larry James Gianakos. — Metuchen, N.J.: Scarecrow Press, 1978. xi, 794 p.; 23 cm. Includes index. 1. Television programs — United States — Handbooks, manuals, etc. 2. Television plays — United States — Handbooks, manuals, etc. I. T.
PN1992.3.U5 G5   791.45/7/0202   *LC* 78-650   *ISBN* 0810811162

Marc, David.   **2.2852**
Demographic vistas: television in American culture / David Marc. — Philadelphia: University of Pennsylvania Press, c1984. xviii, 214 p.; 22 cm. Includes indexes. 1. Television broadcasting — United States. 2. Comedy programs — United States — History and criticism. 3. United States — Popular culture I. T.
PN1992.3.U5 M26 1984   302.2/345/0973 19   *LC* 83-12329   *ISBN* 0812279077

Terrace, Vincent, 1948-.   **2.2853**
The complete encyclopedia of television programs, 1947–1976. — South Brunswick: A. S. Barnes, c1976. 2 v.: ill.; 27 cm. 1. Television programs — United States — Catalogs. I. T.
PN1992.3.U5 T46   791.45/7   *LC* 74-10022   *ISBN* 0498015610

TV genres: a handbook and reference guide / edited by Brian G.   **2.2854**
Rose; Robert S. Alley, advisory editor.
Westport, Conn.: Greenwood Press, 1985. ix, 453 p.; 24 cm. 1. Television programs — United States — Addresses, essays, lectures. 2. Television plays — History and criticism — Addresses, essays, lectures. I. Rose, Brian Geoffrey. II. Alley, Robert S., 1932- III. Title: T.V. genres.
PN1992.3.U5 T88 1985   791.45/75/0973 19   *LC* 84-22460   *ISBN* 0313237247

Parish, James Robert.   **2.2855**
Actors' television credits, 1950–1972. Editing associates: Paige Lucas, Florence Solomon [and] T. Allan Taylor. — Metuchen, N.J.: Scarecrow Press, 1973. x, 869 p.; 22 cm. 1. Television programs — United States. 2. Actors — United States. I. T.
PN1992.4.A2 P3   791.45/028/0922   *LC* 73-9914   *ISBN* 0810806738

Broadcasting research methods / [edited] by Joseph R.   **2.2856**
Dominick and James E. Fletcher.
Boston: Allyn and Bacon, c1985. viii, 330 p.: ill.; 25 cm. 1. Television broadcasting — Research — Addresses, essays, lectures. I. Dominick, Joseph R. II. Fletcher, James E.
PN1992.45.B76 1985   384.55/4072 19   *LC* 84-18404   *ISBN* 0205083072

Eastman, Susan Tyler.   **2.2857**
Broadcast/cable programming: strategies and practices / Susan Tyler Eastman, Sydney W. Head, Lewis Klein. — 2nd ed. — Belmont, Calif.: Wadsworth Pub. Co., c1985. 529 p.: ill.; 25 cm. — (Wadsworth series in mass communication.) Rev. ed. of: Broadcast programming, strategies for winning television and radio audiences. c1981. Includes indexes. 1. Television programs — Planning. 2. Radio programs — Planning. I. Head, Sydney W. II. Klein, Lewis, 1927- III. Eastman, Susan Tyler. Broadcast programming, strategies for winning television and radio audiences. IV. T. V. Series.
PN1992.55.E18 1985   791.44/0973 19   *LC* 84-13172   *ISBN* 0534033539

Rowland, Willard D.   **2.2858**
The politics of TV violence: policy uses of communication research / by Willard D. Rowland, Jr.; foreword by Horace Newcomb. — Beverly Hills, Calif.: Sage, c1983. 320 p.; 23 cm. — (People and communication. v. 16) 1. Television broadcasting — Social aspects — United States. 2. Violence in television —

United States. I. T. II. Title: Politics of T.V. violence. III. Title: Politics of television violence. IV. Series.
PN1992.6.R68 1983   302.2/435/0973 19   *LC* 82-23009   *ISBN* 0803919522

Millerson, Gerald.   **2.2859**
The technique of television production / Gerald Millerson. — 11th ed. — London; Boston: Focal Press, 1985. 445 p.: ill.; 25 cm. (Library of communication techniques.) Includes index. 1. Television — Production and direction I. T. II. Series.
PN1992.75.M5 1985   791.45/0232 19   *LC* 85-4391   *ISBN* 0240512529

Zettl, Herbert.   **• 2.2860**
Television production handbook / Herbert Zettl. — 4th ed. — Belmont, Calif.: Wadsworth Pub. Co., c1984. xxi, 614 p.: ill.; 24 cm. 1. Television — Production and direction — Handbooks, manuals, etc. I. T.
PN1992.75.Z4 1984   791.45/0232 19   *LC* 83-6850   *ISBN* 053401464X

Woolery, George W., 1937-.   **2.2861**
Children's television, the first thirty–five years, 1946–1981 / by George W. Woolery. — Metuchen, N.J.: Scarecrow Press, 1983. 386 p.; 23 cm. Includes indexes. 1. Television programs for children — United States — Plots, themes, etc. I. T.
PN1992.8.C46 W6 1983   791.45/75 19   *LC* 82-5841   *ISBN* 0810815575

Eisner, Joel, 1959-.   **2.2862**
Television comedy series: an episode guide to 153 TV sitcoms in syndication / by Joel Eisner & David Krinsky. — Jefferson, N.C.: McFarland, c1984. xlv, 866 p.: ports.; 24 cm. Includes index. 1. Comedy programs — United States — Plots, themes, etc. I. Krinsky, David, 1959- II. T.
PN1992.8.C66 E37 1984   791.45/09/0917 19   *LC* 83-42901   *ISBN* 0899500889

The Video source book.   **2.2863**
1st. ed.-   . — Syosset, N.Y.: National Video Clearinghouse, 1979-. v.: ill.; 28 cm. Annual. Title from cover. 1. Video recordings — Catalogs — Periodicals. I. National Video Clearinghouse.
PN1992.95.V52   011/.37 19   *LC* 84-643226

PN1993–1999 Motion Pictures

Film. 1967/68- .   **• 2.2864**
New York: Simon and Schuster, 1967/68-   . v.; annual. 'An anthology by the National Society of Film Critics.' 1. Motion pictures — Yearbooks. 2. Motion pictures — Reviews — Yearbooks. I. National Society of Film Critics.
PN1993.3F38   791.4305   *LC* 68-19946

International motion picture almanac.   **2.2865**
1929-. New York [etc.]: Quigley Pub. Co. [etc.] v.: ill.; 24-32 cm. Annual. 1. Motion pictures — Yearbooks. 2. Television broadcasting — Yearbooks.
PN1993.3.I55   791.43/05   *LC* 29-8663

Magill's cinema annual.   **2.2866**
1982-   . — Englewood Cliffs, N.J.: Salem Press, c1982-. v.; 24 cm. Annual. Each issue covers films released the previous year as well as some films of the past. 1. Motion pictures — Yearbooks. I. Magill, Frank Northen, 1907-
PN1993.3.M34   791.43/75/05 19   *LC* 83-644357

Screen world.   **• 2.2867**
Vol.1 (1949)-. New York: Crown, 1949-. v.: ill.; 22-24 cm. Annual. Title varies. 1. Motion pictures — United States — Yearbooks. 2. Motion pictures — Yearbooks. I. Blum, Daniel C. II. Willis, John.
PN 1993.3 S43   791.43   *LC* 50-3023

Armour, Robert A.   **2.2868**
Film, a reference guide / Robert A. Armour. — Westport, Conn.: Greenwood Press, 1980. xxiv, 251 p.; 24 cm. — (American popular culture. 0193-6859) 1. Motion pictures — Dictionaries. 2. Motion pictures — Bibliography I. T. II. Series.
PN1993.45.A75   791.43/029   *LC* 79-6566   *ISBN* 031322241X

Halliwell, Leslie.   **2.2869**
[Film guide] Halliwell's film guide / Leslie Halliwell. — 5th ed. — New York: Scribner, 1986. xxvi, 1124 p.; 22 cm. Includes index. 1. Motion pictures — Dictionaries. I. T. II. Title: Film guide.
PN1993.45.H27 1986   791.43/03/21 19   *LC* 85-62558   *ISBN* 0684186349

Halliwell, Leslie.   **2.2870**
[Filmgoer's companion] Halliwell's Filmgoer's companion / Leslie Halliwell. — 8th ed. — New York: C. Scribner's Sons, c1984. xvi, 704 p.: ill.; 25 cm. 1. Motion pictures — Dictionaries. I. T. II. Title: Filmgoer's companion.
PN1993.45.H3 1984   791.43/03 19   *LC* 84-51624   *ISBN* 0684181835

Katz, Ephraim.   **2.2871**
The film encyclopedia / by Ephraim Katz. — 1st ed. — New York: Crowell, c1979. viii, 1266 p.; 25 cm. 1. Motion pictures — Dictionaries. I. T.
PN1993.45.K34 1979   791.43/03   *LC* 79-7089   *ISBN* 0690012047

Magill's survey of cinema—English language films, first series /   **2.2872**
edited by Frank N. Magill; associate editors, Patricia King
Hanson, Stephen L. Hanson.
Englewood Cliffs, N.J.: Salem Press, c1980. 4 v.; 24 cm. Includes indexes. 1. Motion pictures — Plots, themes, etc. — Dictionaries. I. Magill, Frank Northen, 1907- II. Hanson, Patricia King. III. Hanson, Stephen L.
PN1993.45.M3   791.43/75 19   *LC* 80-52131   *ISBN* 0893562254

The Oxford companion to film / edited by Liz–Anne Bawden.   **2.2873**
New York: Oxford University Press, 1976. ix, 767 p., [4] leaves of plates: ill.; 25 cm. 1. Motion pictures — Dictionaries. I. Bawden, Liz-Anne.
PN1993.45.O9   791.43/03   *LC* 76-1463   *ISBN* 0192115413

Steinberg, Cobbett.   **2.2874**
Film facts / by Cobbett S. Steinberg. — New York: Facts on File, c1980. xi, 476 p.; 26 cm. Includes index. 1. Motion pictures — Dictionaries. I. T.
PN1993.45.S75   791.43   *LC* 79-27427   *ISBN* 0871963132

PN1993.5 History

Agee, James, 1909-1955.   **• 2.2875**
Agee on film. Drawings by Tomi Ungerer. — [New York]: McDowell, Obolensky, [1958-60] 2 v.: illus.; 24 cm. 1. Motion pictures — History. I. T.
PN1993.5.A1 A35   791.409 792.93*   *LC* 58-12581

Armes, Roy.   **2.2876**
Film and reality; an historical survey. — Harmondsworth: Penguin, 1974. 3-254 p.; 18 cm. — (Pelican books; A1701) Includes index. 1. Motion pictures — History and criticism. I. T.
PN1993.5.A1 A74   791.43/09/04   *LC* 74-166369   *ISBN* 0140217010

Cook, David A.   **2.2877**
A history of narrative film / David A. Cook. — 1st ed. — New York: Norton, c1981. xxiii, 721 p.: ill. Includes index. 1. Motion pictures — History. I. T.
PN1993.5.A1 C65 1981   791.43/09   *LC* 79-25862   *ISBN* 0393013707

Fell, John L., 1927-.   **2.2878**
A history of films / John Fell. — New York: Holt, Rinehart, and Winston, c1979. xv, 588 p.: ill.; 24 cm. 1. Motion pictures — History. I. T.
PN1993.5.A1 F38   791.43/09   *LC* 78-16203   *ISBN* 0030363160

Film before Griffith / edited by John Fell.   **2.2879**
Berkeley: University of California Press, c1983. xii, 395 p.: ill.; 22 cm. Includes indexes. 1. Motion pictures — History — Addresses, essays, lectures. 2. Motion picture industry — History — Addresses, essays, lectures. 3. Motion picture plays — History and criticism — Addresses, essays, lectures. I. Fell, John L., 1927-
PN1993.5.A1 F48 1983   384/.8/09 19   *LC* 82-8540   *ISBN* 0520047389

Macgowan, Kenneth, 1888-1963.   **• 2.2880**
Behind the screen: the history and techniques of the motion picture. — New York: [Delacorte Press, 1965] xv, 528 p.: ill., facsims.; 24 cm. 1. Motion pictures — History. I. T.
PN1993.5.A1 M28   791.4309   *LC* 63-17220

Ceram, C. W., 1915-1972.   **• 2.2881**
Archaeology of the cinema [by] C. W. Ceram. [Translated by Richard Winston]. — 1st American ed. — New York: Harcourt, Brace & World, [1965] 264 p.: illus., ports.; 24 cm. 1. Motion pictures — History. I. T.
PN1993.5.A1 M383   778.509   *LC* 65-19106

Mast, Gerald, 1940-.   **2.2882**
A short history of the movies / Gerald Mast. — 4th ed. — New York: Macmillan; London: Collier Macmillan, c1986. xi, 562 p., [16] p. of plates: ill. (some col.); 23 cm. Includes index. 1. Motion pictures — History. I. T.
PN1993.5.A1 M39 1986b   791.43/09 19   *LC* 85-24013   *ISBN* 0023770600

Pratt, George C.   **2.2883**
Spellbound in darkness; a history of the silent film [by] George C. Pratt. — [Rev. ed.]. — Greenwich, Conn.: New York Graphic Society, [1973] xi, 548 p.: illus.; 28 cm. 1. Silent films — History. I. T.
PN1993.5.A1 P7 1973   791.43/7   *LC* 72-80412   *ISBN* 0821204866

Rhode, Eric, 1934-.   **2.2884**
A history of the cinema from its origins to 1970 / Eric Rhode. — New York: Hill and Wang, c1976. 674 p.: ill.; 24 cm. Includes index. 1. Motion pictures — History. I. T.
PN1993.5.A1 R46   791.43/09   *LC* 75-23154   *ISBN* 0809054809

PN1993.5.A3–.Z By Country, A–Z

Brazilian cinema / [edited by] Randal Johnson and Robert   **2.2885**
Stam.
Rutherford: Fairleigh Dickinson University Press; London: Associated University Presses, c1982. 373 p.: ill.; 25 cm. 1. Motion pictures — Brazil — Collected works. I. Johnson, Randal, 1948- II. Stam, Robert, 1941-
PN1993.5.B6 B7   791.43/0981 19   *LC* 80-66323   *ISBN* 0838630782

Leyda, Jay, 1910-.   **2.2886**
Dianying: an account of films and the film audience in China. — Cambridge, Mass.: MIT Press, [1972] xvii, 515 p.: ill.; 23 cm. 1. Motion pictures — China — History. I. T.
PN1993.5.C4 L4   791.43/0951   *LC* 78-175719   *ISBN* 0262120461

Liehm, Antonín J., 1924-.   **2.2887**
Closely watched films; the Czechoslovak experience [by] Antonín J. Liehm. White Plains, N.Y., International Arts and Sciences Press [1974] 485 p. illus. 24 cm. 1. Motion pictures — Czechoslovakia. 2. Motion picture producers and directors — Interviews. I. T.
PN1993.5.C9 L48   791.43/09437   *LC* 72-94987   *ISBN* 0873320360

Armes, Roy.   **2.2888**
The ambiguous image: narrative style in modern European cinema / Roy Armes. Bloomington: Indiana University Press, c1976. 255 p.: ill.; 24 cm. Includes index. 1. Motion pictures — Europe — History. I. T.
PN1993.5.E8 A7   791.43/094   *LC* 75-37266   *ISBN* 0253305608

Liehm, Mira.   **2.2889**
The most important art: Eastern European film after 1945 / Mira Liehm, Antonín J. Liehm. Berkeley: University of California Press, c1977. 467 p.: ill.; 25 cm. Includes index. 1. Motion pictures — Europe, Eastern — History. I. Liehm, Antonín J., 1924- joint author. II. T.
PN1993.5.E8 L5   791.43/0947   *LC* 75-40663   *ISBN* 0520031571

Stoil, Michael Jon, 1950-.   **2.2890**
Cinema beyond the Danube: the camera and politics. — Metuchen, N.J.: Scarecrow Press, 1974. x, 198 p.: illus.; 22 cm. 1. Motion pictures — Europe, Eastern — History. 2. Motion pictures — Political aspects. I. T.
PN1993.5.E82 S8   791.43/0947   *LC* 74-5274   *ISBN* 081080722X

Abel, Richard, 1941-.   **2.2891**
French cinema: the first wave, 1915–1929 / Richard Abel. — Princeton, NJ: Princeton University Press, c1984. xxi, 672 p.: ill.; 26 cm. Includes index. 1. Motion pictures — France — History. 2. Motion picture industry — France — History. 3. Motion picture plays — History and criticism 4. Experimental films — France — History. 5. Motion pictures — Societies, etc. — France — History. I. T.
PN1993.5.F7 A64 1984   384/.8/0944 19   *LC* 83-43057   *ISBN* 0691054088

Armes, Roy.   **2.2892**
French cinema / by Roy Armes. — New York: Oxford University Press, 1985. 310 p., [32] p. of plates: ill.; 24 cm. Includes index. 1. Motion pictures — France — History. I. T.
PN1993.5.F7 A77 1985   791.43/0944 19   *LC* 85-117656   *ISBN* 0195204719

Bazin, André, 1918-1958.   **2.2893**
French cinema of the occupation and resistance: the birth of a critical esthetic / André Bazin; collected and with an introd. by Francois Truffaut; translated by Stanley Hochman. — New York, N.Y.: F. Ungar Pub. Co., c1981. viii, 166 p.: ill.; 22 cm. Translation of Le cinéma de l'occupation et de la résistance. Includes index. 1. Motion pictures — France — Collected works. 2. Motion pictures — Reviews I. Truffaut, François. II. T.
PN1993.5.F7 B313   791.43/0944 19   *LC* 80-5343   *ISBN* 080442022X

Monaco, James.   **2.2894**
The new wave: Truffaut, Godard, Chabrol, Rohmer, Rivette / James Monaco. New York: Oxford University Press, 1976. xii, 372 p.: ill.; 25 cm. 1. Motion

pictures — France. 2. Motion picture producers and directors — France — Biography. I. T.
PN1993.5.F7 M6   791.43/0233/0922   *LC* 75-38099   *ISBN* 019501992X

Corrigan, Timothy.   **2.2895**
New German film: the displaced image / by Timothy Corrigan. — 1st ed. — Austin: University of Texas Press, 1983. xiv, 213 p.: ill.; 24 cm. Includes index. 1. Motion pictures — Germany (West) 2. Motion picture plays — History and criticism I. T.
PN1993.5.G3 C67 1983   791.43/75/0943 19   *LC* 83-10210   *ISBN* 0292710860

Low, Rachael.   **2.2896**
The history of the British film: 1918–1929 / by Rachael Low. — [New York]: Distributed in the United States by Bowker, 1973 (c1971). 544 p.: ill. 1. Motion pictures — Great Britain. I. Manvell, Roger, 1909- joint author. II. T. III. Title: The British film.
PN1993.5.G7 L6 1973   *LC* 74-162852   *ISBN* 0047910024

Low, Rachael.   **2.2897**
The history of the British film 1929–1939: documentary and educational films of the 1930s / by Rachael Low. — London: George Allen & Unwin, 1979. 244 p.: ill. 1. Motion pictures — Great Britain — History I. T. II. Title: Documentary and educational films of the 1930s
PN1993.5G7 L63   *LC* 78-41277   *ISBN* 0047910364

Low, Rachael.   **2.2898**
The history of the British film, 1929–1939: films of comment and persuasion of the 1930s / by Rachael Low. — London: Allen & Unwin; New York: distributed by Bowker, 1979. xii, 256 p.: ill.; 22 cm. Includes index. 1. Motion pictures — Great Britain — History. I. T. II. Title: Films of comment and persuasion of the 1930s.
PN1993.5.G7 L64   PN1993.5G7 L64.   791.43/0941   *LC* 78-41296   *ISBN* 0047910372

Schuster, Mel.   **2.2899**
The contemporary Greek cinema / by Mel Schuster. — Metuchen, N.J.: Scarecrow Press, 1979. vii, 360 p.: ill.; 23 cm. Includes index. 1. Motion pictures — Greece. I. T.
PN1993.5.G75 S38 1979   791.43/09495   *LC* 78-20969   *ISBN* 0810811960

Barnouw, Erik, 1908-.   **• 2.2900**
Indian film / [by] Erik Barnouw and S. Krishnaswamy. — New York: Columbia University Press, 1963. 301 p.: ill.; 24 cm. 1. Motion pictures — India. I. Krishnaswamy, Subrahmanyam. joint author. II. T.
PN1993.5.I8 B3   791.430954   *LC* 63-14112

Bondanella, Peter E., 1943-.   **2.2901**
Italian cinema: from neorealism to the present / Peter Bondanella. — New York: F. Ungar Pub. Co., c1983. viii, 440 p.: ill.; 22 cm. — (Ungar film library.) Includes index. 1. Motion pictures — Italy. I. T. II. Series.
PN1993.5.I88 B58 1983   791.43/0945 19   *LC* 82-40255   *ISBN* 0804420645

Leprohon, Pierre.   **2.2902**
The Italian cinema. Translated from the French by Roger Greaves and Oliver Stallybrass. — New York: Praeger, [1972] 256 p.: illus.; 22 cm. Rev. and expanded translation of the author's Le cinéma italien, published in 1966. 1. Motion pictures — Italy. I. T.
PN1993.5.I88 L413   791.43/0945   *LC* 70-99314

Richie, Donald, 1924-.   **• 2.2903**
Japanese cinema; film style and national character. — Garden City: Doubleday, 1971. xxvi, 261 p.: illus.; 21 cm. 1961 ed. published under title: Japanese movies. 1. Motion pictures — Japan — History. I. T.
PN1993.5.J3 R5 1971   791.43/0952   *LC* 77-163122

Mora, Carl J.   **2.2904**
Mexican cinema: reflections of a society, 1896–1980 / Carl J. Mora. — Berkeley: University of California Press, c1982. xv, 287 p.: ill.; 25 cm. 1. Motion pictures — Mexico — History. I. T.
PN1993.5.M4 M6 1982   791.43/0972 19   *LC* 81-7507   *ISBN* 0520042875

Leyda, Jay, 1910-.   **• 2.2905**
Kino, a history of the Russian and Soviet film. New York: Macmillan, 1960. 493 p.: ill.; 25 cm. 1. Motion pictures — Soviet Union — History. I. T.
PN1993.5.R9 L47   791.430947 19   *LC* 60-3292

PN1993.5.U6 United States

The American film industry / edited by Tino Balio.   **2.2906**
Rev. ed. — Madison, Wis.: University of Wisconsin Press, c1985. xi, 664 p.: ill.; 23 cm. Includes indexes. 1. Motion picture industry — United States — History — Addresses, essays, lectures. I. Balio, Tino.
PN1993.5.U6 A87 1985   384/.8/0973 19   *LC* 84-40143   *ISBN* 0299098745

Behlmer, Rudy.   **2.2907**
America's favorite movies: behind the scenes / Rudy Behlmer. — New York: F. Ungar Pub. Co., c1982. xix, 324 p.: ill.; 24 cm. 1. Motion pictures — United States — History. I. T.
PN1993.5.U6 B36 1982   791.43/0973 19   *LC* 81-70117   *ISBN* 080442036X

Bergman, Andrew.   **2.2908**
We're in the money: Depression America and its films. — New York: New York University Press, 1971. xxiii, 200 p.: illus.; 24 cm. Originally presented as the author's thesis, University of Wisconsin. 1. Motion pictures — U.S. — History. 2. Depressions — 1929 — U.S. I. T.
PN1993.5.U6 B38 1971   791.43/0973   *LC* 74-159533   *ISBN* 0814709648

Bordwell, David.   **2.2909**
The classical Hollywood cinema: film style & mode of production to 1960 / David Bordwell, Kristin Thompson, and Janet Staiger. — New York: Columbia University Press, 1985. xv, 506 p., 64 leaves of plates: ill.; 26 cm. Includes index. 1. Motion pictures — United States — History. 2. Motion picture industry — United States — History. 3. Motion pictures — Aesthetics I. Thompson, Kristin, 1950- II. Staiger, Janet. III. T.
PN1993.5.U6 B655 1985   791.43/0973 19   *LC* 85-372   *ISBN* 0231060548

Brownlow, Kevin.   **• 2.2910**
The parade's gone by. — [1st ed.]. — New York: Knopf, 1968. 577, xiii p.: illus., ports.; 26 cm. 1. Motion pictures — United States — History. I. T.
PN1993.5.U6 B7   791.43/0973   *LC* 68-23955

Brownlow, Kevin.   **2.2911**
The war, the West, and the wilderness / Kevin Brownlow. — 1st ed. — New York: Knopf; distributed by Random House, 1979, c1978. xvi, 602 p.: ill.; 26 cm. 1. Motion pictures — United States — History. 2. Silent films — History and criticism. 3. World War, 1914-1918 — Motion pictures and the war. 4. Western films — History and criticism. 5. Documentary films — United States — History. I. T.
PN1993.5.U6 B76 1979   791.43/0973   *LC* 78-54934   *ISBN* 0394489217

Ceplair, Larry.   **2.2912**
The inquisition in Hollywood: politics in the film community, 1930–1960 / Larry Ceplair & Steven Englund. — 1st ed. — Garden City, N.Y.: Anchor Press/Doubleday, 1980. xiv, 536 p., [8] leaves of plates: ill.; 25 cm. Includes index. 1. Motion picture industry — United States 2. Blacklisting of entertainers — United States. 3. Communism — United States — 1917- I. Englund, Steven. joint author. II. T.
PN1993.5.U6 C4   791.43/09794/94   *LC* 77-25587   *ISBN* 0385129009

Crowther, Bosley.   **• 2.2913**
The lion's share: the story of an entertainment empire. — [1st ed.] New York: Dutton, 1957. 320 p.: ill.; 23 cm. 1. Metro-Goldwyn-Mayer. 2. Motion pictures — History. I. T.
PN1993.5.U6 C7   *LC* 57-5325

Everson, William K.   **2.2914**
American silent film / William K. Everson. — New York: Oxford University Press, 1978. vii, 387 p., [38] leaves of plates: ill.; 24 cm. — (A History of the American film; 1) Includes index. 1. Motion pictures — United States — History. 2. Silent films — History and criticism. I. T. II. Series.
PN1993.5.U6 E9   791.43/0973   *LC* 77-25188   *ISBN* 019502348X

Fell, John L., 1927-.   **2.2915**
Film and the narrative tradition [by] John L. Fell. — [1st ed.]. — [Norman]: University of Oklahoma Press, [1974] xx, 284 p.: illus.; 23 cm. 1. Motion pictures — United States — History. I. T.
PN1993.5.U6 F4 1974   791.43/0973   *LC* 73-7428   *ISBN* 0806111275

Film noir: an encyclopedic reference to the American style /   **2.2916**
edited by Alain Silver and Elizabeth Ward, co–editors, Carl Macek and Robert Porfirio.
Woodstock, N.Y.: Overlook Press, 1980 (c1979). 393 p.: ill.; 29 cm. Includes index. 1. Motion pictures — United States 2. Motion picture plays — History

and criticism 3. Motion pictures — Plots, themes, etc. I. Silver, Alain, 1947- II. Ward, Elizabeth, 1952-
PN1993.5.U6 F5   791.43/0909/12   *LC* 76-47092   *ISBN* 0879510552

Gomery, Douglas.   2.2917
The Hollywood studio system / Douglas Gomery. — New York: St. Martin's Press, 1986. xii, 213 p.: ill., ports.; 23 cm. Includes index. 1. Motion picture industry — United States — History. I. T.
PN1993.5.U6 G58 1986   384/.8/0979494 19   *LC* 85-14595   *ISBN* 0312388454

Jacobs, Lewis.   • 2.2918
The rise of the American film, a critical history. With an essay: Experimental cinema in America, 1921–1947. — New York: Teachers College Press, [1968] xxxii, 631 p.: illus.; 24 cm. — (Studies in culture & communication) 1. Motion pictures — United States — History. I. T. II. Title: Experimental cinema in America, 1921-1947. III. Series.
PN1993.5.U6 J2 1968   791.43/0973   *LC* 68-25845

Jowett, Garth.   2.2919
Film: the democratic art / Garth Jowett; for the American Film Institute. 1st ed. — Boston: Little, Brown, c1976. xx, 518 p.; 24 cm. ([The American Film Institute series]) Includes index. 1. Motion pictures — United States 2. Motion pictures — Social aspects I. T.
PN1993.5.U6 J67   791.43/0973   *LC* 75-32411   *ISBN* 0316473707

Kings of the Bs: working within the Hollywood system: an   2.2920
anthology of film history and criticism / edited by Todd McCarthy and Charles Flynn.
1st ed. — New York: E. P. Dutton, 1975. xiii, 561 p.: ill.; 22 cm. 1. Motion pictures — United States I. McCarthy. Todd. II. Flynn, Charles.
PN1993.5.U6 K48   791.43/0233/0922   *LC* 74-10478   *ISBN* 0525140905

Maltin, Leonard.   2.2921
The great movie shorts / foreword by Peter Smith. — New York: Crown Publishers, [1972] x, 236 p.: ill.; 29 cm. 1. Motion pictures — U.S. I. T.
PN1993.5.U6 M23   791.43/0973   *LC* 72-168318

Mamber, Stephen.   2.2922
Cinema verite in America: studies in uncontrolled documentary. Cambridge, Mass., MIT Press [1974] vi, 288 p. illus. 23 cm. 1. Motion pictures — United States I. T.
PN1993.5.U6 M24   791.43/53   *LC* 73-13706   *ISBN* 0262130920

Mekas, Jonas.   2.2923
Movie journal: the rise of the new American cinema, 1959–1971 / Jonas Mekas. — New York: Collier Books, c1972. xi, 434 p.: ill. 1. Motion pictures — United States 2. Experimental films — Addresses, essays, lectures. I. T.
PN1993.5.U6 M35 1972   *LC* 74-171569

Miller, Don, 1927-.   2.2924
'B' movies; an informal survey of the American low–budget film, 1933–1945. — New York: Curtis Books, [c1973] 350 p.: illus.; 18 cm. — (The Curtis film series) 1. Motion pictures — United States — History. I. T.
PN1993.5.U6 M57   791.43/0973   *LC* 74-168300

Navasky, Victor S.   2.2925
Naming names / Victor S. Navasky. — New York: Viking Press, 1980. xxvi, 482 p.; 24 cm. 1. Motion picture industry — United States 2. Blacklisting of entertainers — United States. 3. Communism — United States — 1917- I. T.
PN1993.5.U6 N4 1980   791.43/09794/94   *LC* 80-15044   *ISBN* 0670503932

Osborne, Robert A.   2.2926
50 golden years of Oscar: the official history of the Academy of Motion Picture Arts & Sciences / by Robert Osborne; designed by Ernest E. Schworck. — [La Habra, Calif.: ESE California; Beverly Hills, CA: Academy of Motion Picture Arts and Sciences, c1979] ca. 300 p.: ill. (some col.); 30 cm. Includes index. 1. Academy of Motion Picture Arts and Sciences. 2. Academy Awards (Motion pictures) 3. Motion pictures — United States — History. I. T.
PN1993.5.U6 O87   791.43/079 19   *LC* 80-117365   *ISBN* 0912076305

Ramsaye, Terry, 1885-1954.   • 2.2927
A million and one nights; a history of the motion picture. — New York: Simon and Schuster, [1964, c1926] lxx, 868 p.: illus., ports., facsims.; 21 cm. 1. Motion pictures — United States — History. 2. Silent films — History and criticism. 3. Cinematography — History. I. T.
PN1993.5.U6 R35 1964b   791.43/0973   *LC* 64-12078

Sarris, Andrew.   • 2.2928
The American cinema: directors and directions, 1929–1968. — [1st ed.]. — New York: Dutton, 1968. 383 p.; 22 cm. 1. Motion pictures — United States 2. Motion pictures — United States — Biography. I. T.
PN1993.5.U6 S3   791.43/0233/0922 19   *LC* 69-12602

Shale, Richard, 1947-.   2.2929
Academy awards: an Ungar reference index / compiled and introduced by Richard Shale; foreword by Fay Kanin. — 2nd ed., updated. — New York: Ungar, c1982. 691 p.: ill.; 25 cm. — (Ungar film library.) Includes index. 1. Academy Awards (Motion pictures) I. T. II. Series.
PN1993.5.U6 S47 1982   791.43/079 19   *LC* 82-40254

The Whole film sourcebook / edited by Leonard Maltin.   2.2930
New York: Universe Books, 1983. x, 454 p.; 21 cm. 1. Motion picture industry — United States — Addresses, essays, lectures. 2. Motion pictures — History — Bibliography. 3. Motion pictures — Study and teaching — United States — Addresses, essays, lectures. 4. Motion picture film collections — United States — Addresses, essays, lectures. 5. Film festivals — Addresses, essays, lectures. 6. Fund raising — Addresses, essays, lectures. I. Maltin, Leonard.
PN1993.5.U6 W47 1983b   384/.8/0973 19   *LC* 82-84314   *ISBN* 0876634161

Powdermaker, Hortense, 1903-1970.   • 2.2931
Hollywood, the dream factory: an anthropologist looks at the movie–makers / by Hortense Powdermaker. — Boston: Little, Brown, 1950, t.p. 1951. 342 p.; 22 cm. — Includes index. 1. Motion pictures I. T.
PN1993.5.U65 P6   791.4   *LC* 50-10280

Spehr, Paul C.   2.2932
The movies begin: making movies in New Jersey, 1887–1920 / Paul C. Spehr. — Newark: Newark Museum, c1977. 191 p.: ill.; 26 cm. Includes indexes. 1. Motion picture industry — New Jersey — History. I. Newark Museum. II. T.
PN1993.5.U696 S6   791.43/09749   *LC* 77-73649   *ISBN* 0871001217

PN1993.8 STUDY. TEACHING

American Film Institute.   2.2933
The American Film Institute guide to college courses in film and television / editor, Sam L. Grogg, Jr., associate editor, Victoria A. Venker, editorial supervisor, Mel Konecoff. Princeton, N.J.: Peterson's Guides, 19— xii, 286 p.; 22 cm. 'An American Film Institute book.' Includes index. 1. Motion pictures — Study and teaching — United States — Directories. 2. Television broadcasting — Study and teaching — United States — Directories. I. Grogg, Sam L. II. T. III. Title: Guide to college courses in film and television.
PN1993.8.U5 A45   791.43/07/1173   *LC* 75-15345

PN1994 GENERAL WORKS

Arnheim, Rudolf.   • 2.2934
Film as art. — Berkeley: University of California Press, 1957. 230 p.: illus.; 19 cm. 'The greater part ... is an adaptation of [the author's] Film, published ... in 1933.' 1. Motion pictures I. T.
PN1994.A672   791.4 792.93*   *LC* 57-10496

Balázs, Béla, 1884-1949.   2.2935
[Filmkultúra. English] Theory of the film; character and growth of a new art. Translated from the Hungarian by Edith Bone. New York, Dover Publications [1970] 291 p. illus., ports. 22 cm. Translation of Filmkultúra. 1. Motion pictures I. T.
PN1994.B266 1970   791.43   *LC* 77-130963   *ISBN* 0486226859

Bazin, André.   • 2.2936
What is cinema? / essays selected and translated by Hugh Gray. — Berkeley: University of California Press, [1967] vi, 183 p.; 23 cm. Translation of: selections from Qu'est-ce que le cinéma? 1. Motion pictures I. Gray,Hugh, 1900- II. T.
PN1994.B3513   791.43/01   *LC* 67-18899   *ISBN* 0520000919

Geduld, Harry M. comp.   2.2937
Authors on film. Edited by Harry M. Geduld. — Bloomington: Indiana University Press, [1972] xiii, 303 p.; 21 cm. 1. Motion pictures — Addresses, essays, lectures. 2. Motion pictures and literature I. T.
PN1994.G365   791.43   *LC* 72-75390   *ISBN* 0253310806

Gessner, Robert, 1907-.   • 2.2938
The moving image; a guide to cinematic literacy. — [1st ed.]. — New York: Dutton, 1968. 444 p.: illus.; 24 cm. 1. Motion picture plays — History and criticism I. T.
PN1994.G43   791.43/09/04   *LC* 68-17287

Kracauer, Siegfried, 1889-1966.   **2.2939**
Theory of film: the redemption of physical reality. — New York: Oxford University Press, 1960. 364 p.: ill.; 24 cm. 1. Motion pictures I. T. II. Title: Film.
PN1994.K7   791.43   *LC* 60-13209

Kuleshov, L. V. (Lev Vladimirovich)   **2.2940**
Kuleshov on film: writings / by Lev Kuleshov; selected, translated and edited, with an introd. by Ronald Levaco. — Berkeley: University of California Press, c1974. xi, 226 p.; 22 cm. Includes index. 1. Motion pictures — Addresses, essays, lectures. I. T.
PN1994.K78   791.43   *LC* 73-90666   *ISBN* 0520026594

Mast, Gerald, 1940-.   **2.2941**
Film theory and criticism: introductory readings / Gerald Mast, Marshall Cohen. — 3rd ed. — New York: Oxford University Press, 1985. xxi, 852 p.: ill.; 22 cm. 1. Motion pictures — Addresses, essays, lectures. I. Cohen, Marshall. II. T.
PN1994.M364 1985   791.43 19   *LC* 84-27243   *ISBN* 0195035739

Monaco, James.   **2.2942**
How to read a film: the art, technology, language, history, and theory of film and media / James Monaco; with diagrs. by David Lindroth. — Rev. ed. — New York: Oxford University Press, 1981. xv, 533 p.: ill.; 24 cm. Includes index. 1. Motion pictures I. T.
PN1994.M59 1981   791.43/01/5   *LC* 80-16848   *ISBN* 0195028023

Movies and methods: an anthology / edited by Bill Nichols.   **2.2943**
Berkeley: University of California Press, c1976-c1985. 2 v.: ill.; 25 cm. Includes index. 1. Motion pictures I. Nichols, Bill.
PN1994.M7   791.43   *LC* 74-22968   *ISBN* 0520028902

Spottiswoode, Raymond, 1913-1970.   • **2.2944**
A grammar of the film; an analysis of film technique. — Berkeley: University of California Press, 1950. 328 p.: illus.; 20 cm. 1. Motion pictures I. T.
PN1994.S65 1950   791.4   *LC* 50-7096

PN1995 CRITICISM. AESTHETICS. PSYCHOLOGY

Affron, Charles.   **2.2945**
Star acting: Gish, Garbo, Davis / Charles Affron. New York: Dutton, c1977. x, 354 p.: ill.; 27 cm. Includes index. 1. Gish, Lillian, 1896- 2. Garbo, Greta, 1905- 3. Davis, Bette, 1908- 4. Motion picture acting I. T.
PN1995.A27   791.43/028/0922   *LC* 76-8039   *ISBN* 0525209689

Andrew, James Dudley, 1945-.   **2.2946**
Concepts in film theory / Dudley Andrew. — Oxford; New York: Oxford University Press, 1984. xiv, 239 p.; 22 cm. — Includes index. 1. Motion pictures — Philosophy. I. T.
PN1995.A49 1984   791.43/01 19   *LC* 83-17365   *ISBN* 0195034287

Andrew, James Dudley, 1945-.   **2.2947**
Film in the aura of art / Dudley Andrew. — Princeton, N.J.: Princeton University Press, c1984. xiv, 207 p., [17] p. of plates: ill. (some col.); 23 cm. 1. Motion picture plays — History and criticism — Addresses, essays, lectures. 2. Motion pictures — Aesthetics — Addresses, essays, lectures. I. T.
PN1995.A494 1984   791.43/75 19   *LC* 84-1788   *ISBN* 0691065853

Battcock, Gregory, 1937- comp.   • **2.2948**
The new American cinema: a critical anthology / edited by Gregory Battcock. — [1st ed.]. — New York: Dutton, 1967. 256 p.: ill.; 19 cm. 1. Motion picture plays — History and criticism 2. Motion pictures — Aesthetics I. T.
PN1995.B315   791.43/09   *LC* 67-9569

Cahiers du cinéma, the 1950s: neo-realism, Hollywood, new wave / edited by Jim Hillier.   **2.2949**
Cambridge, Mass.: Harvard University Press, 1985. xiii, 312 p.; 25 cm. 1. Motion pictures — Philosophy — Addresses, essays, lectures. 2. Motion pictures — Aesthetics — Addresses, essays, lectures. 3. Motion pictures — France — History — Addresses, essays, lectures. 4. Motion pictures — Italy — History — Addresses, essays, lectures. 5. Motion pictures — United States — History — Addresses, essays, lectures. I. Hillier, Jim. II. Cahiers du cinéma.
PN1995.C29 1985   791.43/01 19   *LC* 84-25215   *ISBN* 0674090608

Clifton, N. Roy, 1909-.   **2.2950**
The figure in film / N. Roy Clifton. — Newark: University of Delaware Press; London: Associated University Presses, c1983. 394, [30] p. of plates: ill.; 25 cm. 'An Ontario Film Institute book.' Includes indexes. 1. Motion picture plays — History and criticism I. T.
PN1995.C54 1983   791.43/01/5 19   *LC* 80-54539   *ISBN* 0874131898

Eberwein, Robert T., 1940-.   **2.2951**
A viewer's guide to film theory and criticism / by Robert T. Eberwein. — Metuchen, N.J.: Scarecrow Press, 1979. 235 p.; 22 cm. Includes indexes.

1. Motion pictures — Philosophy. 2. Motion picture plays — History and criticism I. T.
PN1995.E33   791.43/01/5   *LC* 79-9380   *ISBN* 0810812371

Eidsvik, Charles, 1943-.   **2.2952**
Cineliteracy: film among the arts / Charles Eidsvik. — 1st ed. — New York: Horizon Press, 1979. xii, 303 p.: ill.; 24 cm. Includes index. 1. Motion pictures — Aesthetics. I. T.
PN1995.E44   PN1995 E44.   791.43/01   *LC* 77-94015   *ISBN* 0818007087

Eisenstein, Sergei, 1898-1948.   • **2.2953**
Film form; essays in film theory, ed. and tr. by Jay Leyda. — [1st ed.]. — New York, Harcourt, Brace [1949] xi, 279 p. illus. 21 cm. 'Sources': p. 268-272. 1. Motion pictures I. Leyda, Jay, 1910- ed. and tr. II. T.
PN1995.E5   791.4   *LC* 49-8349 *

Eisenstein, Sergei, 1898-1948.   • **2.2954**
The film sense. [New ed.] Faber and Faber [1948] 228 p. 1. Motion pictures I. Leyda, Jay, 1910- ed. and tr. II. T.
PN1995.E52 1948   *LC* 48-11715

Film review annual.   **2.2955**
1981- . — Englewood, NJ: J.S. Ozer, c1982-. v.; 25 cm. Annual. 1. Motion pictures — United States — Reviews — Yearbooks.
PN1995.F465   791.43/75/0973 19   *LC* 85-644173

Greene, Graham, 1904-.   **2.2956**
Graham Greene on film; collected film criticism, 1935–1940. Edited by John Russell Taylor. — New York: Simon and Schuster, [1972] 284 p.: illus.; 26 cm. British ed. published under title: The pleasure-dome. 1. Motion pictures — Reviews I. T.
PN1995.G68 1972   791.43/7   *LC* 72-83894   *ISBN* 0671214128

Hoberman, J.   **2.2957**
Midnight movies / J. Hoberman and Jonathan Rosenbaum. — 1st ed. — New York: Harper & Row, c1983. ix, 338 p.: ill.; 25 cm. Includes index. 1. Motion picture plays — History and criticism 2. Motion pictures — United States I. Rosenbaum, Jonathan. II. T.
PN1995.H58 1983   791.43/0973 19   *LC* 82-47526   *ISBN* 0060150521

Lindgren, Ernest.   • **2.2958**
The art of the film. — [2d ed.]. — New York: Macmillan, 1963. 258 p.: plates.; 23 cm. 1. Motion pictures I. T.
PN1995.L47 1963   791.4   *LC* 63-6007

Luhr, William.   **2.2959**
Authorship and narrative in the cinema: issues in contemporary aesthetics and criticism / William Luhr, Peter Lehman; illustrations by Stuart Auld. — New York: Putnam, c1977. 320 p.: ill.; 22 cm. 1. Motion pictures — Aesthetics 2. Motion pictures — United States I. Lehman, Peter. joint author. II. T.
PN1995.L83   791.43/01   *LC* 76-13887   *ISBN* 0399117857

McCreadie, Marsha, 1943-.   **2.2960**
Women on film: the critical eye / Marsha McCreadie. — New York, N.Y.: Praeger, 1983. xvii, 156 p.; 24 cm. Errata slip inserted. Includes index. 1. Women film critics 2. Film criticism I. T.
PN1995.M377 1983   791.43/01/50922 19   *LC* 82-13221   *ISBN* 0030627680

Metz, Christian.   **2.2961**
[Langage et cinéma. English] Language and cinema. Translated by Donna Jean Umiker-Sebeok. The Hague, Mouton, 1974. 303 p. 25 cm. (Approaches to semiotics. 26) Translation of Langage et cinéma. 1. Motion pictures — Philosophy. 2. Languages — Philosophy I. T. II. Series.
PN1995.M45213   791.43/01   *LC* 73-81079

Münsterberg, Hugo, 1863-1916.   **2.2962**
[Photoplay] The film: a psychological study; the silent photoplay in 1916. New York, Dover Publications [1970] xv, 100 p. 22 cm. Reprint of the 1916 ed., published under title: The photoplay, and with a new foreword by Richard Griffith. 1. Motion pictures — Psychological aspects. 2. Motion pictures — Aesthetics I. T.
PN1995.M75 1970   791.43/01/9   *LC* 76-94325   *ISBN* 0486224767

The New York Times directory of the film.   • **2.2963**
1971-. [New York] Arno Press. v. ill. 32 cm. Annual. 1. Motion pictures — Reviews — Indexes. 2. Motion pictures — Biography — Periodicals. I. New York Times
PN1995.N39   *LC* 72-622071

The New York Times film reviews.   **2.2964**
1913/68- . — New York: New York Times, 1970- . — ill. 32 cm.
Biennial. Reviews for 1913/68 published in 6 vols.: v.1-5, reviews, v.6, index.
1. Moving-pictures — Reviews — Periodicals. I. New York Times.
PN1995.N4   791.43/7   *LC* 70-112777

Pate, Michael.   • **2.2965**
The film actor; acting for motion pictures and television. South Brunswick,
[N.J.] A.S. Barnes [1970] 245 p. illus. 25 cm. 1. Motion picture acting
2. Acting for television I. T.
PN1995.P3   791.43/028   *LC* 69-15782

Perkins, V. F., 1936-.   **2.2966**
Film as film: understanding and judging movies. — [Harmondsworth]: Penguin
Books, [1972] 198p. 1. Film criticism I. T.
PN1995 P47

Pudovkin, Vsevolod Illarionovich, 1893-1953.   • **2.2967**
Film technique, and Film acting. Translated and edited by Ivor Montagu. —
Memorial ed. [rev. and enl.] with portrait, memoir and a rev. and completed
record of the author's film work. — New York: Grove Press, [1960] 388 p.:
illus.; 21 cm. — (Evergreen original, E-248) 1. Motion pictures 2. Motion
picture acting I. T. II. Title: Film acting.
PN1995.P832 1960   791.4302   *LC* 60-11104

Sarris, Andrew.   **2.2968**
The primal screen; essays on film and related subjects. — New York: Simon and
Schuster, [1973] 337 p.; 22 cm. 1. Motion pictures — Addresses, essays,
lectures. I. T.
PN1995.S354   791.43/08   *LC* 72-90401   *ISBN* 0671213415

Selected film criticism / edited by Anthony Slide.   **2.2969**
Metuchen, N.J.: Scarecrow Press, 1982-1985. 7 v.: port.; 23 cm. Includes
indexes. 1. Motion pictures — Reviews I. Slide, Anthony.
PN1995.S426 1982   791.43/75 19   *LC* 81-23344   *ISBN*
0810815753

Tudor, Andrew, 1942-.   **2.2970**
Theories of film. — New York: Viking Press, [1974, c1973] 168 p.: illus.; 20 cm.
— (Cinema one, 23) 1. Motion pictures I. T.
PN1995.T78 1974   791.43/01   *LC* 73-8380   *ISBN* 0670698113

Variety film reviews, 1907–1980 / ed. by Mike Kaplan.   **2.2971**
New York: Garland Pub., 1984 (c1983) 15 v.; 31 cm. Vols. 1-16 have title:
Variety film reviews, 1907-1980. 1. Motion pictures — Reviews I. Daily
variety. II. Title: Variety film reviews, 1907-1980.
PN1995.V34 1983   791.43/75 19   *LC* 82-15691   *ISBN* 0824052005

Vogel, Amos.   **2.2972**
Film as a subversive art / Amos Vogel. — New York: Random House, [1974]
336 p.: ill.; 26 cm. Includes index. 1. Motion pictures I. T.
PN1995.V6 1974b   791.43/0909/35   *LC* 73-16720   *ISBN*
0394490789

Wollen, Peter.   **2.2973**
Signs and meaning in the cinema [by] Peter Wollen. — New and enl. [3d ed.]. —
Bloomington: Indiana University Press, [1972] 175 p.: illus.; 19 cm. — (Cinema
one, 9) 1. Motion pictures — Aesthetics I. T.
PN1995.W64 1972   791.43/01   *LC* 72-82722   *ISBN* 0253181429

PN1995.3 FILM AND LITERATURE

Beja, Morris.   **2.2974**
Film & literature, an introduction / Morris Beja. — New York: Longman,
c1979. xv, 335 p.: ill.; 24 cm. Includes index. 1. Motion pictures and literature
2. Film adaptations 3. Motion pictures — History. I. T.
PN1995.3.B4   791.43/0909/23   *LC* 78-26167   *ISBN* 058228094X

McConnell, Frank D., 1942-.   **2.2975**
Storytelling and mythmaking: images from film and literature / Frank
McConnell. — New York: Oxford University Press, 1979. viii, 303 p.: ill.; 22
cm. Includes index. 1. Motion pictures and literature 2. Motion pictures —
Plots, themes, etc. I. T.
PN1995.3.M26   791.43/7   *LC* 78-27538   *ISBN* 0195025725

PN1995.7 FILM AND SOUND

Geduld, Harry M.   **2.2976**
The birth of the talkies: from Edison to Jolson / Harry M. Geduld. —
Bloomington: Indiana University Press, [1975] xiii, 337 p.; ill.; 25 cm. 1. Sound
motion pictures — History. I. T.
PN1995.7.G36 1975   791.43/0973   *LC* 74-11887   *ISBN*
0253107431

Gomery, J. Douglas.   **2.2977**
The coming of sound to the American cinema: a history of the transformation of
an industry / by J. Douglas Gomery. — 1975. 511 p. 1. Sound motion pictures
— History. 2. Motion pictures — United States I. T.
PN1995.7 G5

Magill's survey of cinema—silent films / edited by Frank N.   **2.2978**
Magill; associate editors, Patricia King Hanson, Stephen L.
Hanson.
Englewood Cliffs, N.J.: Salem Press, c1982. 3 v. (xxvii, 1280, lviii p.); 23 cm.
Includes indexes. 1. Silent films — Reviews. I. Magill, Frank Northen, 1907-
II. Hanson, Patricia King. III. Hanson, Stephen L. IV. Title: Survey of
cinema—silent films.
PN1995.75.M33 1982   791.43/75 19   *LC* 82-60577   *ISBN*
0893562394

PN1995.9 SPECIAL TOPICS, A–Z

PN1995.9 A–G

Kerr, Walter, 1913-.   **2.2979**
The silent clowns / by Walter Kerr. — 1st ed. — New York: Knopf, 1975.
372 p.: ill.; 31 cm. Includes index. 1. Comedy films — History and criticism.
2. Silent films — History and criticism. I. T.
PN1995.9.C55 K4   791.43/0909/17   *LC* 75-8231   *ISBN*
0394469070

Mast, Gerald, 1940-.   **2.2980**
The comic mind: comedy and the movies / Gerald Mast. — 2d ed. — Chicago:
University of Chicago Press, 1979. x, 369 p. [20] leaves of plates: ill; 24 cm.
Includes index. 1. Comedy films — History and criticism. I. T.
PN1995.9.C55 M38 1979   791.43/02907   *LC* 78-68546   *ISBN*
0226509761

Tuska, Jon.   **2.2981**
Dark cinema: American film noir in cultural perspective / Jon Tuska. —
Westport, Conn.: Greenwood Press, 1984. xxiv, 305 p., [18] p. of plates: ill.; 24
cm. (Contributions to the study of popular culture. 0198-9871; no. 9) Includes
index. 1. Detective and mystery films — United States — History and
criticism. I. T. II. Title: Film noir in cultural perspective. III. Series.
PN1995.9.D4 T79 1984   791.43/09/09355 19   *LC* 84-710   *ISBN*
0313230455

Alexander, William, 1938-.   **2.2982**
Film on the left: American documentary film from 1931 to 1942 / William
Alexander. — Princeton, N.J.: Princeton University Press, c1981. xviii, 355 p.,
[6] leaves of plates: ill.; 34 cm. Includes index. 1. Documentary films — United
States — History and criticism. I. T.
PN1995.9.D6 A38   791.43/53 19   *LC* 80-8534   *ISBN* 0691046786

Barsam, Richard Meran.   **2.2983**
Nonfiction film; a critical history. Foreword by Richard Dyer MacCann. [1st
ed.] New York, Dutton, 1973. xviii, 332 p. illus. 21 cm. 1. Documentary films
— History and criticism. I. T.
PN1995.9.D6 B38   791.43/7   *LC* 72-82161   *ISBN* 0525168273
ISBN 0525473319

Grierson, John, 1898-1972.   • **2.2984**
Grierson on documentary / edited by Forsyth Hardy. — Rev. ed. — Berkeley:
University of California Press, 1966. 411 p.: ill., ports.; 23 cm. Bibliography: p.
399-402. 1. Documentary films I. Hardy, Forsyth. ed. II. T.
PN1995.9.D6G75 1966a   791.43022   *LC* 66-14091

Jacobs, Lewis. comp.   **2.2985**
The documentary tradition / selected arranged, and introduced by Lewis
Jacobs. — 2d ed. — New York: W. W. Norton, c1979. 594 p.: ill.; 24 cm.
Includes index. 1. Documentary films — History and criticism — Addresses,
essays, lectures. I. T.
PN1995.9.D6 J3 1979   791.43/53   *LC* 79-14953   *ISBN*
0393950425

Rotha, Paul, 1907-.   • **2.2986**
Documentary film; the use of the film medium to interpret creatively and in
social terms the life of the people as it exists in reality, by Paul Rotha in
collaboration with Sinclair Road [and] Richard Griffith. — [3d ed., rev. and
enl.]. — New York: Hastings House, [1963] 412 p.: illus.; 23 cm. —
(Communication arts books) 1. Documentary films 2. Motion pictures —
Bibliography I. T.
PN1995.9.D6 R68 1963   791.435   *LC* 64-57386

Renan, Sheldon, 1941-.   • 2.2987
An introduction to the American underground film. [1st ed.] New York: Dutton, 1967. 318 p.: ill.; 19 cm. 1. Motion pictures — United States 2. Experimental films — United States — History and criticism. I. T.
PN1995.9.E96 R4   791.43/0973   LC 68-1070

Tyler, Parker.   • 2.2988
Underground film; a critical history. New York, Grove Press [1970, c1969] 249 p. illus. 24 cm. 1. Experimental films — History and criticism. I. T.
PN1995.9.E96 T9   791.43   LC 77-103054

Walsh, Martin, d. 1977.   2.2989
The Brechtian aspect of radical cinema / Martin Walsh; edited by Keith M. Griffiths. — London: BFI Pub., c1981. 136 p.: ill.; 21 cm. 1. Brecht, Bertolt, 1898-1956. 2. Radicalism 3. Motion pictures I. Griffiths, Keith M. II. T.
PN1995.9.E96 W34   791.43/75 19   LC 81-151542   ISBN 0851701124

Lee, Walt.   2.2990
Reference guide to fantastic films; science fiction, fantasy, & horror, compiled by Walt Lee, assisted by Bill Warren. — Los Angeles: Chelsea-Lee Books, 1972-74. 3 v.: illus.; 28 cm. 1. Fantastic films — Catalogs. I. T. II. Title: Fantastic films.
PN1995.9.F36 L4   016.79143   LC 72-88775   ISBN 0913974048

PN1995.9 H–R

Russo, Vito.   2.2991
The celluloid closet: homosexuality in the movies / Vito Russo. — 1st ed. — New York: Harper & Row, c1981. xii, 276 p.: ill.; 25 cm. Includes index. 1. Homosexuality in motion pictures I. T.
PN1995.9.H55 R8 1981   791.43/09/09353 19   LC 79-1682   ISBN 0060137045

Clarens, Carlos.   • 2.2992
An illustrated history of the horror films. — New York: Putnam, [1967] xv, 256 p.: illus., ports.; 24 cm. Revised ed. published in 1967 under title: Horror movies. 1. Horror films — History and criticism. I. T.
PN1995.9.H6 C5   791.43/090916   LC 67-10951

The Kaleidoscopic lens: how Hollywood views ethnic groups /   2.2993
edited by Randall M. Miller.
Englewood, N.J.: Ozer, 1981 (c1980). xiii, 222 p.: ill.; 25 cm. Includes index. 1. Minorities in motion picture — United States. 2. Motion pictures — United States — History. I. Miller, Randall M.
PN1995.9.M56 K3 1980   791.43/09/0935203   LC 80-16797   ISBN 0891981209

Sennett, Ted.   2.2994
Hollywood musicals / Ted Sennett. — New York: H. N. Abrams, 1981. 384 p.: ill.; 35 cm. Includes index. 1. Musical films — United States — History and criticism. I. T.
PN1995.9.M86 S4   782.81/0973 19   LC 80-25896   ISBN 0810910756

Welch, David.   2.2995
Propaganda and the German cinema, 1933–1945 / David Welch. — Oxford: Clarendon Press; New York: Oxford University Press, 1983. xiv, 352 p., [8] p. of plates: ill.; 23 cm. Includes index. 1. National socialism in motion pictures 2. Motion pictures — Germany — History. 3. Motion pictures in propaganda — Germany. I. T.
PN1995.9.N36 W45 1983   791.43/09/09358 19   LC 83-165099   ISBN 0198225989

Bogle, Donald.   2.2996
Toms, coons, mulattoes, mammies, and bucks; an interpretive history of Blacks in American films. New York, Viking Press [1973] xviii, 260 p. illus. 24 cm. 1. Afro-Americans in motion pictures 2. Motion pictures — United States — History. I. T.
PN1995.9.N4 B6   791.43/0909/352   LC 72-76776   ISBN 0670719358

Cripps, Thomas.   2.2997
Black film as genre / Thomas Cripps. — Bloomington: Indiana University Press, c1978. viii, 184 p.: ill.; 22 cm. Includes index. 1. Afro-Americans in motion pictures I. T.
PN1995.9.N4 C68   791.43/0909/352   LC 77-23630   ISBN 0253375029

Cripps, Thomas.   2.2998
Slow fade to Black: the Negro in American film, 1900–1942 / Thomas Cripps. New York: Oxford University Press, 1977. xi, 447 p.: ill.; 24 cm. Cover title:

The Negro in American film, 1900-1942. 1. Afro-Americans in the motion picture industry I. T. II. Title: The Negro in American film, 1900-1942.
PN1995.9.N4 C7   791.43/028/0922   LC 74-21818   ISBN 0195018648

Klotman, Phyllis Rauch.   2.2999
Frame by frame: a Black filmography / Phyllis Rauch Klotman. — Bloomington: Indiana University Press, c1979. xviii, 700 p.; 25 cm. Includes indexes. 1. Afro-Americans in the motion picture industry — Dictionaries. 2. Afro-American motion picture actors and actresses — Dictionaries. 3. Motion pictures — United States — Catalogs. I. T.
PN1995.9.N4 K57   791.43/0909/352   LC 78-20403   ISBN 0253164230

Goodell, Gregory.   2.3000
Independent feature film production: a complete guide from concept through distribution / by Gregory Goodell. — 1st ed. — New York, N.Y.: St Martin's Press, 1983 (c1982). xxv, 323 p.; 22 cm. Includes index. 1. Motion pictures — Production and direction — Handbooks, manuals, etc. I. T.
PN1995.9.P7 G64 1982   791.43/068 19   LC 82-5746   ISBN 0312413076

Hollywood directors, 1914–1940 / [compiled by] Richard   2.3001
Koszarski.
New York: Oxford University Press, 1976. xx, 364 p.: ill.; 22 cm. Includes index. 1. Motion pictures — Production and direction — Addresses, essays, lectures. 2. Motion picture producers and directors — United States — Biography. I. Koszarski, Richard.
PN1995.9.P7 H64   792/.023/0922   LC 76-9262   ISBN 0195020855

Stephenson, Ralph.   2.3002
The cinema as art / [by] Ralph Stephenson, Jean R. Debrix. — Rev. ed. — Harmondsworth; Baltimore, Md.: Penguin, 1969, 1974 printing. 270 p., [16] leaves of plates: ill.; 18 cm. (A Pelican book; A677) Includes index. 1. Motion pictures — Production and direction I. Debrix, Jean R., 1906- joint author. II. T.
PN1995.9.P7 S7 1974   791.43/01   LC 76-363047   ISBN 0140206779

Wiese, Michael.   2.3003
The independent filmmaker's guide / by Michael Wiese. — 2nd printing, rev. — Sausalito, Calif.: Michael Wiese Film Productions, c1981. 229 p.: ill. 1. Motion pictures — Production and direction 2. Motion picture industry — Finance 3. Motion pictures — Distribution I. T.
PN1995.9.P7 W43 1981   791.43023   ISBN 0941188019

PN1995.9 S–Z

Desser, David.   2.3004
The samurai films of Akira Kurosawa / by David Desser. — Ann Arbor, Mich.: UMI Research Press, c1983. vi, 164 p.: ill.; 24 cm. — (Studies in cinema. no. 23) Includes indexes. 1. Kurosawa, Akira, 1910- 2. Samurai films — History and criticism. I. T. II. Series.
PN1995.9.S24 D47 1983   791.43/0233/0924 19   LC 83-15563   ISBN 0835714950

Baxter, John.   2.3005
Science fiction in the cinema. — New York: A. S. Barnes, [1970] 240 p.: illus.; 16 cm. — (International film guide series) 1. Science fiction films — History and criticism. I. T.
PN1995.9.S26 B3   791.43/09/093   LC 69-14896   ISBN 049807416X

Brosnan, John.   2.3006
Future tense: the cinema of science fiction / John Brosnan. — New York: St. Martin's Press, c1978. 320 p.: ill.; 24 cm. Includes indexes. 1. Science fiction films — History and criticism. I. T.
PN1995.9.S26 B7 1979   791.43/7   LC 78-4003   ISBN 0312314884

Barsacq, Léon, 1906-1969.   2.3007
Caligari's cabinet and other grand illusions: a history of film design / Léon Barsacq; [translated by Michael Bullock]; foreword by René Clair. — 1st English language ed. / rev. and edited by Elliott Stein. — Boston: New York Graphic Society, c1976. vii, 264 p.: ill.; 29 cm. Includes index. 1. Motion pictures — Setting and scenery — Histor. I. T.
PN1995.9.S4 B3413 1976   791.43/025/09   LC 75-27222   ISBN 0821206206

Monaco, Paul.   2.3008
Cinema and society: France and Germany during the Twenties / Paul Monaco. — New York: Elsevier, c1976. 194 p.; 22 cm. Based on the author's thesis, Brandeis University, 1973, presented under title: Cinema and society in France and Germany, 1919-29. Includes index. 1. Motion pictures — Social aspects

2. Motion pictures — France — History. 3. Motion pictures — Germany — History. I. T.
PN1995.9.S6 M6   791.43/013   *LC* 75-40650   *ISBN* 0444990194

Campbell, Edward D. C., 1946-.   **2.3009**
The celluloid South: Hollywood and the southern myth / by Edward D.C. Campbell, Jr. — 1st ed. — Knoxville: University of Tennessee Press, c1981. xvii, 212 p.: ill.; 23 cm. Includes index. 1. Southern States in motion pictures I. T.
PN1995.9.S66 C3   791.43/09/093275 19   *LC* 81-7457   *ISBN* 0870493272

Baxter, John, 1939-.   **2.3010**
Stunt; the story of the great movie stunt men. — [1st ed. in U.S.A.]. — Garden City, N.Y.: Doubleday, 1974 [c1973] 316 p.: illus.; 25 cm. 1. Stunt men and women I. T.
PN1995.9.S7 B3 1974   791.43/028/0922   *LC* 73-83614   *ISBN* 0385065205

Smith, Julian, 1937-.   **2.3011**
Looking away: Hollywood and Vietnam. — New York: Scribner, [1975] xvii, 236 p.: ill.; 24 cm. 1. War films — History and criticism. 2. Vietnamese Conflict, 1961-1975 — United States 3. Motion pictures — United States I. T.
PN1995.9.W3 S6   PN1995.9W3 S6.   791.43/0909/3   *LC* 74-13520   *ISBN* 0684139545

Fenin, George N.   • **2.3012**
The Western, from silents to cinerama [by] George N. Fenin and William K. Everson. New York, Orion Press [c1962] 362 p. illus. 23 cm. Edition for 1973 published under title: The Western, from silents to the seventies. 1. Western films — History and criticism. I. Everson, William K. joint author. II. T.
PN1995.9.W4 F4   791.435   *LC* 62-15016

Wright, Will.   **2.3013**
Six guns and society: a structural study of the Western / by Will Wright. — Berkeley: University of California Press, c1975. 217 p.; 25 cm. Includes index. 1. Western films — History and criticism. I. T.
PN1995.9.W4 W7   791.43/0909/32   *LC* 74-77735   *ISBN* 0520027531

Haskell, Molly.   **2.3014**
From reverence to rape: the treatment of women in the movies. — [1st ed.]. — New York: Holt, Rinehart and Winston, [1974] xii, 388 p.: illus.; 22 cm. 1. Women in motion pictures I. T.
PN1995.9.W6 H3   791.43/0909/352   *LC* 72-91580   *ISBN* 0030076064

Kaplan, E. Ann.   **2.3015**
Women and film: both sides of the camera / E. Ann Kaplan. — New York: Methuen, 1983. xii, 259 p.: ill.; 24 cm. Includes index. 1. Women in motion pictures 2. Women in the motion picture industry 3. Feminist motion pictures — History and criticism. I. T.
PN1995.9.W6 K3 1983   791.43/09/09352042 19   *LC* 83-8198   *ISBN* 0416317502

Women and the cinema: a critical anthology / edited by Karyn   **2.3016**
Kay and Gerald Peary.
1st ed. — New York: Dutton, c1977. xvi, 464 p.: ill.; 21 cm. Includes index. 'A Dutton paperback.' 1. Women in motion pictures — Addresses, essays, lectures. 2. Women in the motion picture industry — Addresses, essays, lectures. I. Kay, Karyn. II. Peary, Gerald.
PN1995.9.W6 W65   PN1995.9W6 W65.   791.43/028/0922   *LC* 77-71301   *ISBN* 0525474595

PN1996–1997.85 Editing. Writing

Reisz, Karel.   • **2.3017**
The technique of film editing. Written and compiled by Karel Reisz and Gavin Millar, with the guidance of the following committee appointed by the British Film Academy: Thorold Dickinson, chairman [and others] Introduced by Thorold Dickinson. — [2d enl. ed.]. — New York: Hastings House, [1968] 411 p.: illus., ports.; 23 cm. — (Communication arts books) (The Library of communication techniques.) 1. Motion pictures — Editing I. Millar, Gavin, joint author. II. British Film Academy. III. T.
PN1996.R43 1968   791.43/023   *LC* 68-17119

Rilla, Wolf Peter.   **2.3018**
The writer and the screen; on writing for film and television, by Wolf Rilla. Foreword by Carl Foreman. — New York: Morrow, 1974 [c1973] xii, 191 p.; 22 cm. 1. Motion picture authorship 2. Television authorship I. T.
PN1996.R5 1974   808.2/3   *LC* 74-159830   *ISBN* 068800234X

Tromberg, Sheldon.   **2.3019**
Making money, making movies: the independent movie–makers' handbook / Sheldon Tromberg. — New York: New Viewpoints/Vision Books, c1980.

204 p.; 24 cm. Includes index. 1. Motion picture authorship 2. Motion pictures — Production and direction 3. Motion pictures — Distribution 4. Motion picture industry I. T.
PN1996.T7   791.43   *LC* 79-18245   *ISBN* 0531063704

Vale, Eugene.   **2.3020**
The technique of screenplay writing: an analysis of the dramatic structure of motion pictures. — Rev. and enl. ed. — New York: Grosset & Dunlap, [1972] 306 p.; 22 cm. 1. Motion picture plays — Technique I. T.
PN1996.V28 1972   808.2/3   *LC* 78-158770   *ISBN* 0448011409

Masterworks of the German cinema: the Golem, Nosferatu, M,   **2.3021**
the Threepenny opera. Introd. by Roger Manvell.
[1st U.S. ed.]. — New York: Harper & Row, [c1973] 300 p.: illus.; 21 cm. — (Icon editions) 1. Motion picture plays
PN1997.A1 M27 1973b   832/.03   *LC* 73-13005   *ISBN* 0064353303

Knox, Donald, 1936-.   **2.3022**
The magic factory; how MGM made An American in Paris. Foreword by Andrew Sarris. New York, Praeger [1973] xix, 217 p. 24 cm. 1. Metro-Goldwyn-Mayer. 2. American in Paris. [Motion picture] I. T.
PN1997.A343 K5   791.43/7   *LC* 72-89638

Silva, Fred, comp.   • **2.3023**
Focus on The birth of a nation. Englewood Cliffs, N.J.: Prentice-Hall [1971] viii, 184 p.: ill.; 21 cm. (Film focus) (A Spectrum book) 1. Birth of a nation (Motion picture) I. T.
PN1997.B567   791.43/7   *LC* 71-163859   *ISBN* 0130772305 *ISBN* 0130772224

Koch, Howard. comp.   **2.3024**
Casablanca: script and legend / preface by Howard Koch; introductory note by Ralph J. Gleason; essays by Howard Koch and Richard Corliss; reviews by Bosley Crowther and Howard Barnes; the script by Julius J. Epstein, Phillip [sic] G. Epstein and Howard Koch. — Woodstock, N.Y.: Overlook Press, [1973] 223 p.: ill.; 25 cm. 'The script': p. 31-182. 1. Casablanca (Motion picture) I. Epstein, Julius J., 1909- Casablanca. 1973. II. Casablanca (Motion picture) III. T.
PN1997.C352 K6 1973   812/.5/2   *LC* 72-94412   *ISBN* 0879510064

The Citizen Kane book: Raising Kane, by Pauline Kael. The   **2.3025**
shooting script, by Herman J. Mankiewicz and Orson Welles,
and the cutting continuity of the completed film.
[1st ed.] Boston, Little, Brown [1971] 440 p. illus. 29 cm. 'An Atlantic Monthly Press book.' 1. Citizen Kane (Motion picture) I. Kael, Pauline. Raising Kane. 1971. II. Mankiewicz, Herman J. (Herman Jacob), 1897-1953. III. Welles, Orson, 1915- IV. Citizen Kane (Motion picture)
PN1997.C5117   791.43/7   *LC* 72-149462

Carringer, Robert L.   **2.3026**
The making of Citizen Kane / Robert L. Carringer. — Berkeley: University of California Press, c1985. xiv, 180 p.: ill.; 24 cm. Includes index. 1. Citizen Kane (Motion picture) I. T.
PN1997.C51173 C374 1985   791.43/72 19   *LC* 84-8777   *ISBN* 0520053672

Flamini, Roland.   **2.3027**
Scarlett, Rhett, and a cast of thousands: the filming of Gone with the wind / Roland Flamini. — New York: Macmillan, c1975. 355 p.: ill.; 23 cm. Includes index. 1. Gone with the wind (Motion picture) I. T.
PN1997.G59 F55   791.43/7   *LC* 75-29463   *ISBN* 0025386700

Syberberg, Hans Jürgen, 1935-.   **2.3028**
[Hitler, ein Film aus Deutschland. English] Hitler, a film from Germany / Hans–Jürgen Syberberg; preface by Susan Sontag; translated by Joachim Neugroschel. — New York: Farrar Straus & Giroux, c1982. xvi, 267 p.: ill.; 23 cm. Translation of: Hitler, ein Film aus Deutschland. 1. Hitler, ein Film aus Deutschland (Motion picture) — Addresses, essays, lectures. I. Hitler, ein Film aus Deutschland (Motion picture) II. T.
PN1997.H5513 1982   791.43/72 19   *LC* 81-17500   *ISBN* 0374515654

Kozintsev, Grigoriĭ Mikhaĭlovich.   **2.3029**
[Prostranstvo tragedii. English] King Lear, the space of tragedy: the diary of a film director / Grigori Kozintsev; translated by Mary Mackintosh; with a foreword by Peter Brook. — Berkeley: University of California Press, 1977. xii, 260 p., [4] leaves of plates: ill.; 25 cm. Translation of Prostranstvo tragedii. 1. Kozintsev, Grigoriĭ Mikhaĭlovich 2. Shakespeare, William, 1564-1616. King Lear 3. Shakespeare, William, 1564-1616 — Film and video adaptations 4. Korol' Lir. [Motion picture] I. T.
PN1997.K67653 K613 1977b   791.43/7   *LC* 76-50248   *ISBN* 0520033922

Wisconsin / Warner Bros. screenplay series. 2.3030
Madison, WI: published for the Wisconsin Center for Film and Theater Research by the University of Wisconsin Press, 1979-. v.: ill.; 23 cm. 1. Motion picture plays — Collections I. Wisconsin Center for Film and Theater Research.
PN1997.W5x

Maltin, Leonard. 2.3031
Of mice and magic: a history of American animated cartoons / Leonard Maltin; research associate, Jerry Beck. — New York: McGraw-Hill, c1980. ix, 470 p., [4] leaves of plates: ill.; 25 cm. Includes index. 1. Animated films — United States — History and criticism. I. T.
PN1997.5.M3 1980b　　791.43/3　　LC 79-21923　　ISBN 0070398356

The International dictionary of films and filmmakers / editor, 2.3032
Christopher Lyon; assistant editor Susan Doll.
Chicago: St. James Press, 1984- < 1986 >. v. < 1-3 >; 24 cm. Vol. 3- edited by James Vinson and others. 1. Motion pictures — Plots, themes, etc. 2. Motion picture producers and directors — Biography. I. Lyon, Christopher, 1949- II. Doll, Susan, 1954- III. Vinson, James, 1933-
PN1997.8.I58 1984　　791.43/03 19　　LC 83-24616　　ISBN 091228904X

PN1998 BIOGRAPHY. CRITICISM

Corliss, Richard. 2.3033
Talking pictures: screenwriters in the American cinema, 1927–1973 / Richard Corliss; pref. by Andrew Sarris. — Woodstock, N.Y.: Overlook Press, 1974. xxviii, 398 p.; 24 cm. 1. Screenwriters 2. Motion pictures — United States I. T.
PN1998.A2 C644　　812/.03　　LC 72-94413　　ISBN 0879510072

Fine, Richard. 2.3034
Hollywood and the profession of authorship, 1928–1940 / by Richard Fine. — Ann Arbor, Mich.: UMI Research Press, c1985. viii, 206 p.: ill. — (Studies in cinema. no. 29) Revision of thesis (Ph.D.)—University of Pennsylvania, 1979. 1. Screenwriters — United States — Biography. 2. Motion picture industry — United States — History. I. T. II. Series.
PN1998.A2 F536 1985　　384/.8/0973 19　　LC 84-28129　　ISBN 0835716023

PN1998.A3 Individuals, A–H

Bergman, Ingmar, 1918-. 2.3035
[Bergman om Bergman. English] Bergman on Bergman; interviews with Ingmar Bergman by Stig Björkman, Torsten Manns [and] Jonas Sima. Translated from the Swedish by Paul Britten Austin. New York, Simon and Schuster [c1973] 288 p. illus. 25 cm. I. Björkman, Stig, 1938- II. Manns, Torsten, 1923- III. Sima, Jonas, 1937- IV. T.
PN1998.A3 B461313 1973b　　791.43/0233/0924　　LC 73-13391　　ISBN 0671217194

Buñuel, Luis, 1900-. 2.3036
[Mon dernier soupir. English] My last sigh / Luis Buñuel; translated by Abigail Israel. — 1st American ed. — New York: Knopf, 1983. 256 p., [16] p. of plates: ill.; 22 cm. Translation of: Mon dernier soupir. Includes list of author's films. 1. Buñuel, Luis, 1900- 2. Motion picture producers and directors — Spain — Biography. I. T.
PN1998.A3 B7413 1983　　791.43/0233/0924 B 19　　LC 83-48105　　ISBN 0394528549

Glatzer, Richard. 2.3037
Frank Capra: the man and his films / edited by Richard Glatzer and John Raeburn. — Ann Arbor, Mich.: University of Michigan Press; Don Mills, Ont.: Longman Canada, 1975. xiv, 190 p., 12 leaves of plates: ill.; 21 cm. — (Ann Arbor paperbacks; 195) 1. Capra, Frank, 1897- 2. Motion picture producers and directors I. Raeburn, John. II. T.
PN1998.A3 C264　　PN1998A3 C264.　　ISBN 047206195X

Bordwell, David. 2.3038
The films of Carl–Theodor Dreyer / David Bordwell. — Berkeley: University of California Press, 1981. 251 p.: ill., ports. Includes index. 1. Dreyer, Carl Theodor, 1889-1968. I. T.
PN1998.A3 D7　　PN1998A3 D7.　　791.43/0233/0924 19　　LC 79-65769　　ISBN 0520039874

Eisenstein, Sergei, 1898-1948. 2.3039
Immoral memories: an autobiography / by Sergei M. Eisenstein; translated by Herbert Marshall. — Boston: Houghton Mifflin, 1983. xxv, 292 p., [48] p. of plates: ill.; 24 cm. 1. Eisenstein, Sergei, 1898-1948. 2. Motion picture producers and directors — Soviet Union — Biography. I. Marshall, Herbert, 1912- II. T.
PN1998.A3 E519 1983　　791.43/0233/0924 B 19　　LC 83-8417　　ISBN 0395331013

Barna, Ion. 2.3040
[Serghei Eisenstein. English] Eisenstein, by Yon Barna. With a foreword by Jay Leyda. Bloomington, Indiana University Press [1973] 287 p. illus. 23 cm. (Cinema two) Translation of Serghei Eisenstein. 1. Eisenstein, Sergei, 1898-1948. 2. Motion picture producers and directors — Soviet Union — Biography. I. T.
PN1998.A3 E53413　　791.43/0233/0924 B　　LC 73-81159　　ISBN 0253121353

Fellini, Federico. 2.3041
Fellini on Fellini / Federico Fellini; translated from the Italian by Isabel Quigley. — [New York]: Delacorte Press/S. Lawrence, c1976. 180 p.: ill.; 21 cm. German translation has title: Aufsätze und Notizen. Includes index. 1. Fellini, Federico. I. T.
PN1998.A3 F337　　791.43/0233/0924 B　　LC 76-363747　　ISBN 0440025281

Rosenthal, Stuart. 2.3042
The cinema of Federico Fellini / Stuart Rosenthal. South Brunswick: A. S. Barnes, c1976. 190 p.; ill.; 26 cm. 1. Fellini, Federico. I. T.
PN1998.A3 F355 1976　　791.43/0233/0924　　LC 73-13193　　ISBN 0498014509

Calder-Marshall, Arthur, 1908-. • 2.3043
The innocent eye: the life of Robert J. Flaherty / based on research material by Paul Rotha and Basil Wright. — [1st American ed.]. — New York: Harcourt, Brace & World, [1966, c1963] 303 p.: ill., ports.; 22 cm. 1. Flaherty, Robert Joseph, 1884-1951. I. Rotha, Paul, 1907- II. Wright, Basil. III. T.
PN1998.A3 F47 1966　　791.430230924 (B)　　LC 66-12357

Rotha, Paul, 1907-. 2.3044
Robert J. Flaherty, a biography / Paul Rotha; edited by Jay Ruby. — Philadelphia: University of Pennsylvania Press, 1983. xiii, 359 p., [30] p. of plates: ill., ports.; 24 cm. 'The films of Robert J. Flaherty:' p. 295-299. Includes index. 1. Flaherty, Robert Joseph, 1884-1951. 2. Motion picture producers and directors — United States — Biography. I. Ruby, Jay. II. T.
PN1998.A3 F5535 1983　　791.43/0233/0924 B 19　　LC 83-6986　　ISBN 0812278879

Place, Janey Ann, 1946-. 2.3045
The Western films of John Ford / by J. A. Place. — 1st ed. — Secaucus, N.J.: Citadel Press, [1974] 246 p.: ill.; 29 cm. 1. Ford, John, 1894-1973. 2. Western films — History and criticism. I. T.
PN1998.A3 F62　　791.43/0233/0924　　LC 74-80827　　ISBN 0806504455

Godard, Jean Luc, 1930-. 2.3046
[Jean-Luc Godard. English] Godard on Godard; critical writings. Edited by Jean Narboni and Tom Milne. With an introd. by Richard Roud. New York, Viking Press [1972] 292 p. illus. 22 cm. Translation of Jean-Luc Godard, a collection of essays selected from La gazette du cinéma and Les cahiers du cinéma. 1. Motion pictures — Addresses, essays, lectures. I. T.
PN1998.A3 G5613　　791.43/0233/0924　　LC 70-83245　　ISBN 0670342777 ISBN 0670019356

Brown, Karl. 2.3047
Adventures with D. W. Griffith. New York, Farrar, Straus and Giroux [1973] xi, 251 p. illus. 24 cm. 1. Griffith, D. W. (David Wark), 1875-1948. 2. Brown, Karl. 3. Cinematographers — Biography. I. T.
PN1998.A3 G7216　　791.43/0233/0924 B　　LC 72-97001　　ISBN 0374100934

Henderson, Robert M. • 2.3048
D. W. Griffith: his life and work [by] Robert M. Henderson. New York: Oxford University Press, 1972. ix, 326 p.: ill.; 24 cm. 1. Griffith, D. W. (David Wark), 1875-1948. I. T.
PN1998.A3 G748　　791.43/0233/0924 B　　LC 75-182425

Wagenknecht, Edward, 1900-. 2.3049
The films of D. W. Griffith / by Edward Wagenknecht and Anthony Slide; with a foreword by Lillian Gish. — New York: Crown Publishers, [1975] xi, 276 p.: ill.; 28 cm. Includes index. 1. Griffith, D. W. (David Wark), 1875-1948. I. Slide, Anthony. joint author. II. T.
PN1998.A3 G785　　791.43/0233/0924　　LC 75-19196　　ISBN 0517523264

Poague, Leland A., 1948-. 2.3050
Howard Hawks / Leland A. Poague. — Boston: Twayne Publishers, 1982. 195 p.: ill.; 21 cm. — (Twayne's filmmakers series.) Includes index. 1. Hawks, Howard, 1896- I. T. II. Series.
PN1998.A3 H353 1982　　791.43/0233/0924 19　　LC 82-961　　ISBN 0805792856

Wood, Robin, 1931-.   **2.3051**
Howard Hawks / Robin Wood. — Rev. ed. — [s.l]: BFI publishing, 1981. 216 p.: ill., port. 1. Hawks, Howard, 1896- I. T.
PN1998.A3H355   PN1998A3 H45 1981.   791.43/0233/0924
    ISBN 0851701116

Durgnat, Raymond.   **2.3052**
The strange case of Alfred Hitchcock: or, The plain man's Hitchcock / Raymond Durgnat. — Cambridge, Mass.: MIT Press, 1974. 419 p., [12] leaves of plates: 49 ill.; 21 cm. Includes index. 1. Hitchcock, Alfred, 1899- I. T.
PN1998.A3 H5464 1974b   791.43/0233/0924   *LC* 74-7239   *ISBN*
0262040417

Rohmer, Eric, 1920-.   **2.3053**
[Hitchcock. English] Hitchcock, the first forty-four films / Eric Rohmer, Claude Chabrol; translated by Stanley Hochman. — New York: F. Ungar, c1979. x, 178 p.: ill.; 22 cm. — (Ungar film library) Includes index. 1. Hitchcock, Alfred, 1899- I. Chabrol, Claude, 1930- joint author. II. T.
PN1998.A3 H5513 1979   791.43/0233/0924   *LC* 78-20538   *ISBN*
0804427437

Spoto, Donald, 1941-.   **2.3054**
The art of Alfred Hitchcock: fifty years of his motion pictures / Donald Spoto. — New York: Hopkinson and Blake, [1976] xv, 523 p.: ill.; 25 cm. Includes index. 1. Hitchcock, Alfred, 1899- I. T.
PN1998.A3 H564   791.43/0233/0924   *LC* 75-38208   *ISBN*
0911974210. *ISBN* 0911974229 pbk

Taylor, John Russell.   **2.3055**
Hitch: the life and times of Alfred Hitchcock / by John Russell Taylor. — 1st American ed. — New York: Pantheon Books, c1978. 320 p., [8] leaves of plates: ill.; 22 cm. Includes index. 1. Hitchcock, Alfred, 1899- 2. Motion picture producers and directors — Great Britain — Biography. I. T.
PN1998.A3 H567 1978   791.43/0233/0924 B   *LC* 78-53501   *ISBN*
0394499964

Truffaut, François.   **2.3056**
[Cinéma selon Hitchcock. English] Hitchcock / by Franc̦ois Truffaut; with the collaboration of Helen G. Scott. — Rev. ed. — New York: Simon and Schuster, c1984. 367 p.: ill.; 29 cm. Dialogue between Truffaut and Hitchcock. Translation of Le cinéma selon Hitchcock. Includes indexes. 1. Hitchcock, Alfred, 1899- I. Hitchcock, Alfred, 1899- II. Scott, Helen G. III. T.
PN1998.A3 H573 1984   791.43/0233/0924 19   *LC* 84-10686
    ISBN 0671526014

Weis, Elisabeth, 1944-.   **2.3057**
The silent scream: Alfred Hitchcock's sound track / Elisabeth Weis. — Rutherford [N.J.]: Fairleigh Dickinson University Press, c1982. 188 p.: ill.; 22 cm. Includes index. 1. Hitchcock, Alfred, 1899- I. T.
PN1998.A3 H578 1982   791.43/0233/0924 19   *LC* 80-71093
    ISBN 0838630790

Wood, Robin, 1931-.   **2.3058**
Hitchcock's films / Robin Wood. — South Brunswick, N.J.: A. S. Barnes, c1977. 174 p.: ill.; 25 cm. 1. Hitchcock, Alfred, 1899- I. T.
PN1998.A3 H58 1977   791.43/0233/0924   *LC* 75-20615   *ISBN*
0498017494

PN1998.A3 Individuals, K–Z

Kazan, Elia.   **2.3059**
Kazan on Kazan / [by] Michel Ciment. — Viking Press [c1974] 199 p.: ill. (Cinema one, 26) A series of taped interviews conducted by M. Ciment, chiefly in Aug. 1971. 'Biofilmography, by Michel Ciment and Olivier Eyquem': p. 180-199. I. Ciment, Michel, 1938- II. T.
PN1998.A3 K345 1974   *LC* 73-11978   *ISBN* 0670411876

Richie, Donald, 1924-.   **2.3060**
The films of Akira Kurosawa / by Donald Richie with additional material by Joan Mellen. — Rev. ed. — Berkeley: University of California Press, 1984. 255 p.: ill.; 26 cm. Includes index. 1. Kurosawa, Akira, 1910- I. Mellen, Joan. II. T.
PN1998.A3 K795 1984   791.43/0924 19   *LC* 83-5078   *ISBN*
0520051912

Eisner, Lotte H.   **2.3061**
Fritz Lang / Lotte H. Eisner; [translated by Gertrud Mander and edited by David Robinson]. — New York: Oxford University Press, 1977, c1976. 416 p.: ill.; 25 cm. 1. Lang, Fritz, 1890-1976 — Criticism and interpretation. I. T.
PN1998.A3 L357713 1977   791.43/0233/0924   *LC* 76-41081
    ISBN 019519912X

Eisner, Lotte H.   **2.3062**
Murnau, by Lotte H. Eisner. [Rev. and enl.] Berkeley, University of California Press [1973, c1964] 287 p. illus. 22 cm. (A Shadows book) A rev. translation of

the French work published in 1964 under title: F. W. Murnau. 1. Murnau, F. W. (Friedrich Wilhelm), 1889-1931. I. T.
PN1998.A3 M843 1973   791.43/0233/0924   *LC* 72-82222   *ISBN*
0520022858 *ISBN* 0520024257

Bazin, André, 1918-1958.   **2.3063**
Jean Renoir / André Bazin; edited with an introduction by François Truffaut; translated from the French by W. W. Halsey II and William H. Simon. — New York: Simon and Schuster, c1973. 320 p.: ill. 1. Renoir, Jean, 1894- I. Truffaut, François. ed. II. T.
PN1998.A3 R3913 1973   791.43/0233/0924   *LC* 72-88943   *ISBN*
0671214640

Durgnat, Raymond.   **2.3064**
Jean Renoir / Raymond Durgnat. — Berkeley: University of California Press, 1975 (c1974). xiii, 429 p.: ill.; 24 cm. Includes index. 1. Renoir, Jean, 1894- I. T.
PN1998.A3 R42   791.43/0233/0924   *LC* 72-82221   *ISBN*
0520022831

Renoir, Jean, 1894-.   **2.3065**
[Ma vie et mes films. English] My life and my films / by Jean Renoir; translated by Norman Denny. — 1st American ed. — New York: Atheneum, 1974. 287 p., [16] leaves of plates: ill.; 24 cm. Translation of Ma vie et mes films. Includes index. 1. Renoir, Jean, 1894- 2. Motion picture producers and directors — Biography. I. T.
PN1998.A3 R45713   791.43/023/0924 B   *LC* 74-77856   *ISBN*
0689106297

Selznick, David O., 1902-1965.   **2.3066**
Memo from David O. Selznick / selected and edited by Rudy Behlmer; with an introd. by S. N. Behrman. — New York: Viking Press, [1972] 518 p.: ill.; 24 cm. 'Memorandums, letters, teletypes, and telegrams.' 1. Selznick, David O., 1902-1965. I. T.
PN1998.A3 S38 1972b   791.43/0232/0924   *LC* 72-75743   *ISBN*
0670467669

Haver, Ronald.   **2.3067**
David O. Selznick's Hollywood / written & produced by Ronald Haver; designed by Thomas Ingalls. — 1st ed. — New York: Knopf, 1980. ix, 425 p.: ill. (some col.); 37 cm. Includes index. 1. Selznick, David O., 1902-1965. I. T.
PN1998.A3 S397 1980   791.43/0232/0924   *LC* 79-2224   *ISBN*
0394425952

Pfaff, Françoise.   **2.3068**
The cinema of Ousmane Sembene, a pioneer of African film / Françoise Pfaff; foreword by Thomas Cripps. — Westport, Conn.: Greenwood Press, 1984. xx, 207 p.: ill.; 22 cm. (Contributions in Afro-American and African studies. 0069-9624; no. 79) Includes index. 1. Sembène, Ousmane, 1923- 2. Motion picture producers and directors — Senegal — Biography. I. T. II. Series.
PN1998.A3 S4256 1984   791.43/0233/0924 19   *LC* 84-3842   *ISBN*
0313244006

Insdorf, Annette.   **2.3069**
François Truffaut / Annette Insdorf. — Boston: Twayne Publishers, 1978. 250 p.: ill.; 21 cm. — (Twayne's theatrical arts series) Includes index. 1. Truffaut, François. I. T.
PN1998.A3 T745   791.43/0233/0924   *LC* 77-20810   *ISBN*
0805792538

Vidor, King, 1895-1982.   **2.3070**
King Vidor on film making. New York, McKay [1972] xi, 239 p. illus. 22 cm. 1. Vidor, King, 1895-1982. 2. Motion pictures — Production and direction I. T.
PN1998.A3 V48 1972   791.43/0233/0924   *LC* 72-86969

Nowell-Smith, Geoffrey.   **2.3071**
Luchino Visconti. New York, Viking Press [1973] 220 p. illus. 20 cm. (Cinema one, 3) 1. Visconti, Luchino, 1906-1976. I. T.
PN1998.A3 V5855 1973   791.43/0233/0924   *LC* 73-17729   *ISBN*
067044426X *ISBN* 0670019798

Weinberg, Herman G.   **2.3072**
Stroheim: a pictorial record of his nine films / by Herman G. Weinberg. — New York: Dover Publications, [1975] xvii, 259 p.: ill.; 24 cm. 1. Von Stroheim, Erich, 1885-1957. I. T.
PN1998.A3 V6537   791.43/0233/0924   *LC* 74-15006   *ISBN*
0486227235

Koch, Stephen.   **2.3073**
Stargazer: Andy Warhol's world and his films. — New York: Praeger, [1973] 155 p.: ill.; 24 cm. 1. Warhol, Andy, 1928- I. T.
PN1998.A3 W277   791.43/0233/0924   *LC* 72-93433

PN1998.A4–Z Miscellany

Academy of Motion Picture Arts and Sciences.   • **2.3074**
Who wrote the movie and what else did he write? An index of screen writers and
their film works, 1936–1969. [By] the Academy of Motion Picture Arts &
Sciences and the Writers Guild of America, West. — Los Angeles, 1970. xix,
491 p.; 29 cm. 1. Motion picture plays — Indexes. 2. Screenwriters I. Writers
Guild of America, West. II. T.
PN1998.A53   016.812/5/209   LC 78-27347

**Feature films on 8mm, 16mm, and videotape: a directory of   2.3075
feature films available for rental, sale, and lease in the United
States and Canada.**
6th ed.-7th ed. — New York: R.R. Bowker Co., 1979-. v.; 29 cm. 1. Motion
pictures — Catalogs — Periodicals. I. Limbacher, James L.
PN1998.F39   011/.37   LC 82-643104

Film notes. Edited by Eileen Bowser.   • **2.3076**
[New York: Museum of Modern Art, c1969] v, 128 p.: ill.; 21 x 22 cm.
Chronological annotated list of American fiction films produced between
1894-1950, presently distributed to colleges and universities by the Dept. of
Film of the New York Museum of Modern Art. 1. Motion pictures — United
States — Catalogs. I. Bowser, Eileen. ed. II. Museum of Modern Art (New
York, N.Y.)
PN1998.F55   791.43/8   LC 68-54926

Maltin, Leonard.   **2.3077**
Leonard Maltin's TV movies and video guide / edited by Leonard Maltin;
associate editors, Mike Clark ... [et al.]. — 1987 ed. — New York, N.Y.: New
American Library, c1986. xiv, 1121 p.; 18 cm. 'A Signet book.' Previously
published as: Leonard Maltin's TV movies. 1984. 1. Motion pictures —
Catalogs 2. Video recordings — Catalogs. 3. Motion pictures — Reviews
4. Video recordings — Reviews. 5. Television broadcasting of films — Plots,
themes, etc. I. Maltin, Leonard. TV movies II. T. III. Title: TV movies and
video guide.
PN1998.M277 1986   016.79143/75 19   LC 87-124448   ISBN
0451145313

PN1999 Film Corporations, A–Z

Eames, John Douglas.   **2.3078**
The MGM story: the complete history of fifty roaring years / by John Douglas
Eames. — New York: Crown Publishers, c1975. 400 p.: ill. (some col.); 33 cm.
Includes index. 1. Metro-Goldwyn-Mayer. I. T.
PN1999.M4 E2 1975   791.43/0973   LC 75-328523   ISBN
0517523892

Balio, Tino.   **2.3079**
United Artists: the company built by the stars / Tino Balio. — Madison:
University of Wisconsin Press, 1976. xviii, 323 p.: ill.; 24 cm. 1. United Artists
Corporation. I. T.
PN1999.U5 B3   791.43/06/579494   LC 75-12208   ISBN
0299069400

Silke, James R.   **2.3080**
Here's looking at you, kid: 50 years of fighting, working, and dreaming at
Warner Bros. / by James R. Silke. 1st ed. — Boston: Little, Brown, c1976.
317 p.: ill.; 31 cm. 1. Warner Bros. Pictures. I. T.
PN1999.W3 S5   791.43/0973   LC 75-22747   ISBN 0316791318

PN2000–2219 Dramatic
Representation. The Theater

Theatre (International Theatre Institute of the United States)   • **2.3081**
Theatre / International Theatre Institute of the United States. Vol. 1 (1969)-
. — New York: The Institute, 1969?-. v.: ill., ports.; 26 cm. Annual.
Subtitle varies. 1. Theater — United States — Periodicals. I. International
Theatre Institute of the United States. II. T.
PN2000.T33   792/.0973   LC 79-76179

Artaud, Antonin, 1896-1948.   • **2.3082**
The theater and its double. Translated from the French by Mary Caroline
Richards. — New York, Grove Press [1958] 159 p. illus. 21 cm. — (Evergreen
books, E-127) 1. Theater — Addresses, essays, lectures. I. T.
PN2021.A713   792.04   LC 58-59840 rev

Brecht, Bertolt, 1898-1956.   • **2.3083**
Brecht on theatre; the development of an aesthetic. Edited and translated by
John Willett. — [1st ed.]. — New York: Hill and Wang, [1964] 294 p.: illus.,
ports.; 21 cm. 1. Theater — Addresses, essays, lectures. I. Willett, John. ed.
and tr. II. T. III. Title: On theatre.
PN2021.B68   792.082   LC 63-18479

James, Henry, 1843-1916.   • **2.3084**
The scenic art: notes on acting & the drama, 1872–1901 / Henry James; edited,
with an introd. and notes, by Allan Wade. — New Brunswick: Rutgers
University Press, 1948. xxv, 384 p.: ill. 1. Theater — Addresses, essays,
lectures. 2. Drama — History and criticism 3. Drama — 19th century —
History and criticism. I. Wade, Allan, 1881-1955. II. T.
PN2021.J27 1948   LC 48-3626

Nathan, George Jean, 1882-1958.   • **2.3085**
The magic mirror: selected writings on the theatre / by George Jean Nathan.
Edited, together with an introd. by Thomas Quinn Curtiss. — 1st ed. — New
York: Knopf, 1960. xviii, 262 p., xiii: ill., port. 1. Theater — Addresses, essays,
lectures. 2. Drama — Addresses, essays, lectures. I. T.
PN2021.N3   792.04   LC 60-11316

Shaw, Bernard, 1856-1950.   • **2.3086**
[Prose works. 1958] Shaw on theatre. Edited by E. J. West. New York, Hill and
Wang [1958] 306 p. 20 cm. Essays, lectures, and reviews. 1. Theater —
Addresses, essays, lectures. 2. Drama — Addresses, essays, lectures. I. T.
PN2021.S5   792.04   LC 58-8406

**The Encyclopedia of world theater: with 420 illustrations and an   2.3087
index of play titles / introd. by Martin Esslin.**
New York: Scribner, c1977. 320 p.: ill.; 30 cm. Based on Friedrichs
Theaterlexikon, by K. Gröning and W. Kliess; translated by Estella Schmid,
adapted and amplified under the general editorship of Martin Esslin. 1. Theater
— Dictionaries. I. Esslin, Martin. II. Gröning, Karl. Friedrichs
Theaterlexikon.
PN2035.E52 1977   792/.03   LC 76-19741   ISBN 068414834X

**The Oxford companion to the theatre / edited by Phyllis   2.3088
Hartnoll.**
4th ed. — Oxford [Oxfordshire]; New York: Oxford University Press, 1983. vii,
934 p., 96 p. of plates: ill.; 24 cm. 1. Theater — Dictionaries. I. Hartnoll,
Phyllis.
PN2035.O9 1983   792/.03/21 19   LC 83-235664   ISBN
0192115464

Rae, Kenneth, ed.   • **2.3089**
An international vocabulary of technical theatre terms, in eight languages:
American, Dutch, English, French, German, Italian, Spanish, Swedish. Edited
by Kenneth Rae and Richard Southern for the International Theatre Institute.
— New York: Theatre Arts Books, [1960, c1959] 139 p.; 18 cm. Introductory
matter in English and French. 1. Theater — Dictionaries — Polyglot.
2. Theater — Terminology. I. Southern, Richard. joint ed. II. International
Theatre Institute. III. T.
PN2035.R28 1960   792.03   LC 60-4780

Craig, Edward Gordon, 1872-1966.   • **2.3090**
On the art of the theatre. — New York: Theatre Arts Books, [c1956] 295 p.:
illus.; 21 cm. 1. Theater I. T.
PN2037.C6 1956   792   LC 56-9610

Craig, Edward Gordon, 1872-1966.   • **2.3091**
The theatre advancing / by E. Gordon Craig. — New York: B. Blom, 1963.
289 p. 1. Theater — Addresses, essays, lectures. I. T.
PN2037.C7 1963   792.04   LC 63-23182

Gassner, John, 1903-1967.   • **2.3092**
Producing the play, by John Gassner, with the New scene technician's
handbook, by Philip Barber. — Rev. ed. — New York: Dryden Press, [1953]
915 p.: illus.; 22 cm. 1. Theater — Production and direction 2. Theaters —
Stage-setting and scenery I. Barber, Philip Willson, 1903- New scene
technician's handbook. II. T.
PN2037.G3 1953   792.02   LC 52-14799

Simonson, Lee, 1888-.   • **2.3093**
The stage is set. [Rev. and amended] New York, Theatre Arts Books [1964,
c1963] xxv, 581 p. illus., plans. 21 cm. (TAB paperbook, no. 8) 1. Theater
2. Theaters — Stage-setting and scenery I. T.
PN2037.S5 1964   792.025   LC 62-12338

Hopkins, Arthur.   • **2.3094**
Reference point; reflections on creative ways in general with special reference to
creative ways in the theatre. New York S. French [c1948] 135p. 1. Theater —
Addresses, essays, lectures I. Summer Theatre Seminar, Fordham University,
1947 II. T.
PN2038 H6

Jones, Robert Edmond, 1887-1954.   • **2.3095**
The dramatic imagination: reflections and speculations on the art of the theatre / Robert Edmond Jones. — New York: Theatre Arts Books, 1941. 157 p. 1. Theater — Addresses, essays, lectures. I. T.
PN2038.J6   *LC* 56-9607   *ISBN* 087830035X

Appia, Adolphe, 1862-1928.   • **2.3096**
[Oeuvre d'art vivant. English] The work of living art; a theory of the theatre, translated by H. D. Albright; and, Man is the measure of all things, translated by Barnard Hewitt, edited by Barnard Hewitt. Coral Gables, Fla., University of Miami Press [1960] 131 p. illus. 24 cm. (Books of the theatre series, no. 2) 1. Theater I. T. II. Title: Man is the measure of all things.
PN2039.A613   792   *LC* 60-13830

Carlson, Marvin A., 1935-.   **2.3097**
Theories of the theatre: a historical and critical survey from the Greeks to the present / Marvin Carlson. — Ithaca: Cornell University Press, 1984. 529 p.; 25 cm. 1. Theater — History 2. Dramatic criticism — History. I. T.
PN2039.C26 1984   792/.01 19   *LC* 84-7658   *ISBN* 0801416787

Cole, David, 1941-.   **2.3098**
The theatrical event: a mythos, a vocabulary, a perspective / David Cole. — 1st ed. — Middletown, Conn.: Wesleyan University Press, [1975] xii, 177 p.: ill.; 22 cm. 1. Theater I. T.
PN2039.C64   PN2039 C64.   792   *LC* 74-21922   *ISBN* 0819540781

Schechner, Richard, 1934-.   **2.3099**
Essays on performance theory, 1970–1976 / Richard Schechner. — 1st ed. — New York: Drama Book Specialists, c1977. 212 p.; 23 cm. 1. Theater — Addresses, essays, lectures. I. T.
PN2039.S37   PN2039 S37.   792   *LC* 77-23197   *ISBN* 0910482810

Conolly, L. W. (Leonard W.)   **2.3100**
The censorship of English drama, 1737–1824 / by L. W. Conolly. — San Marino, [Calif.]: Huntington Library, c1976. x, 223 p.: ill.; 24 cm. 1. Theater — Censorship — Great Britain — History. 2. English drama — 18th century — History and criticism. 3. English drama — 19th century — History and criticism. I. T.
PN2044.G6 C6   792/.0942   *LC* 75-32840   *ISBN* 0873280687

Baker, Michael, 1948-.   **2.3101**
The rise of the Victorian actor / Michael Baker. — London: C. Helm; Totowa, N.J.: Rowman and Littlefield, 1978. 249 p.: geneal. tables; 23 cm. (Croom Helm social history series) Includes index. 1. Theater — England — History — 19th century. 2. Theater and society — England — History. 3. Actors — England. I. T.
PN2049.B34 1978   792/.028/0941   *LC* 77-25403   *ISBN* 0847660338

Barish, Jonas A.   **2.3102**
The antitheatrical prejudice / Jonas Barish. — Berkeley: University of California Press, c1981. x, 499 p., [8] p. of plates: ill.; 25 cm. 1. Theater — Moral and ethical aspects. I. T.
PN2049.B37   809.2/9353 19   *LC* 78-59445   *ISBN* 0520037359

Ritual, play, and performance: readings in the social sciences/ theatre / edited by Richard Schechner and Mady Schuman.   **2.3103**
New York: Seabury Press, c1976. xviii, 230 p.: ill. — (A Continuum book) 1. Theater and society 2. Rites and ceremonies 3. Human behavior I. Schechner, Richard, 1934- II. Schuman, Mady, 1950-
PN2049.R5   PN2049 R5.   301.5/7   *LC* 76-6910   *ISBN* 0816492859

Rousseau, Jean-Jacques, 1712-1778.   **2.3104**
Politics and the arts, letter to M. d'Alembert on the theatre. Glencoe, Ill. Free Press [1960] 153p. (Agora editions) 1. Theater — Moral and religious aspects I. Alembert, Jean Le Rond d', 1717-1783. II. T.
PN2051 R713

PN2053 Management. Production

Benedetti, Robert L.   **2.3105**
The director at work / Robert L. Benedetti; with a foreword by John Houseman. — Englewood Cliffs, N.J.: Prentice-Hall, c1985. xiv, 240 p.: ill.; 24 cm. Includes index. 1. Shakespeare, William, 1564-1616. Hamlet 2. Shakespeare, William, 1564-1616 — Stage history — Oregon. 3. Theater — Production and direction. I. T.
PN2053.B37 1985   792/.0233 19   *LC* 84-15047   *ISBN* 0132149095

Chekhov, Michael, 1891-1955.   • **2.3106**
To the director and playwright / compiled and written by Charles Leonard [i.e. C. L. Appleton]. — [pseud. 1st ed.] New York: Harper & Row, [1963]. 329 p.: ill., ports.; 21 cm. Includes the play Revisor by Nikolai Gogol, with rehearsal notes. 1. Theater — Production and direction 2. Playwriting I. Appleton, Charles Leonard, 1900- II. Gogol', Nikolai Vasil'evich, 1809-1852. Revizor. English III. T. IV. Title: Revisor V. Title: To the director and playwright
PN2053.C4   *LC* 62-14537

Clurman, Harold, 1901-.   • **2.3107**
On directing. — New York, Macmillan [1972] xii, 308 p. 21 cm. 1. Theater — Production and direction I. T.
PN2053.C54   792/.0233   *LC* 72-77648

Cohen, Robert, 1938-.   **2.3108**
Creative play direction / Robert Cohen, John Harrop. — 2nd ed. — Englewood Cliffs, N.J.: Prentice-Hall, c1984. ix, 339 p.: ill.; 24 cm. Includes index. 1. Theater — Production and direction I. Harrop, John, 1932- II. T.
PN2053.C58 1984   792/.0233 19   *LC* 83-2417   *ISBN* 0131909266

Cole, Toby, 1916-.   **2.3109**
Directors on directing; a source book of the modern theater / edited by Toby Cole and Helen Krich Chinoy; with an illustrated history of directing by Helen Krich Chinoy. — 2d [Rev. ed.]. — Indianapolis: Bobbs-Merrill, [1976] 464 p.: illus.; 22 cm. First ed. published in 1953 under title: Directing the play. 1. Theater — Production and direction I. Chinoy, Helen Krich. II. T. III. Title: Directing the play.
PN2053.C6 [1976]   792.02

Hodge, Francis.   **2.3110**
Play directing: analysis, communication, and style / Francis Hodge. — 2nd ed. — Englewood Cliffs, N.J.: Prentice-Hall, c1982. xiv, 385 p.: ill.; 24 cm. Includes index. 1. Theater — Production and direction I. T.
PN2053.H6 1982   792/.0233 19   *LC* 81-15388   *ISBN* 013682823X

Plummer, Gail.   **2.3111**
The business of show business. 1st ed. New York: Harper, 1961. 238 p.: ill.; 25 cm. 1. Theater — Production and direction 2. Amateur theater I. T.
PN2053.P55   792.022   *LC* 61-7923

PN2055–2071 Acting

Benedetti, Robert L.   **2.3112**
The actor at work / Robert L. Benedetti; foreword by Ted Danson. — 4th ed. — Englewood Cliffs, N.J.: Prentice-Hall, c1986. xv, 288 p.: ill.; 24 cm. Includes index. 1. Acting I. T.
PN2061.B39 1986   792/.028 19   *LC* 85-19091   *ISBN* 013003732X

Boleslavsky, Richard, 1889-1937.   • **2.3113**
Acting; the first six lessons, by Richard Boleslavsky, for National theatre conference. New York, Theatre arts inc. [c1933] 122 p. 19 1/2 cm. 1. Acting I. National theatre conference. I. T.
PN2061.B55   792   *LC* 33-27079

Chekhov, Michael, 1891-1955.   • **2.3114**
To the actor; on the technique of acting. Drawings by Nicolai Remisoff. — [1st ed.]. — New York: Harper, [c1953] 201 p.: illus.; 22 cm. 1. Acting I. T.
PN2061.C54   792.9   *LC* 52-11680

Diderot, Denis, 1713-1784.   • **2.3115**
The paradox of acting, by Denis Diderot [translated by Walter Herries Pollock] and Masks or faces? By William Archer. Introd. by Lee Strasberg. — New York: Hill and Wang, 1957. xiv, 240 p.; 19 cm. — (Dramabooks, D4) 1. Acting 2. Actors I. Archer, William, 1856-1924. Masks or faces? II. T. III. Title: Masks or faces?
PN2061.D5 1957   792.028   *LC* 57-5838

Duerr, Edwin, 1906-.   • **2.3116**
The length and depth of acting. With a foreword by A. M. Nagler. New York, Holt, Rinehart and Winston [1962] 590 p. illus. 24 cm. Includes index. 1. Acting — History. 2. Theater — History I. T.
PN2061.D8   792.028   *LC* 62-9517

Grotowski, Jerzy, 1933-.   • **2.3117**
Towards a poor theatre. Pref. by Peter Brook. New York, Simon and Schuster [c1968, c1970] 262 p. illus. 22 cm. At head of title: Jerzy Grotowski. Articles by Jerzy Grotowski, interviews with him and other supplementary material presenting his method and training. 1. Acting I. T.
PN2061.G75 1970   792/.028   *LC* 73-92200   *ISBN* 0671203924

Hagen, Uta, 1919-.   **2.3118**
Respect for acting/ [by] Uta Hagen, with Haskel Frankel. — New York: Macmillan, c1973. 227 p.; 22 cm. 1. Acting I. Frankel, Haskel. joint author. II. T.
PN2061.H28   792/.028   *LC* 73-2328

Joseph, Bertram Leon. • 2.3119
Elizabethan acting, by B. L. Joseph. — 2d ed. — [London] Oxford University Press, 1964. vii, 114 p. illus. 23 cm. Bibliographical footnotes. 1. Acting — Hist. 2. Theater — England — Hist. I. T.
PN2061.J6 1964   792.028   *LC* 64-3768

Matthews, Brander, 1852-1929. ed. • 2.3120
Papers on acting. With a pref. by Henry W. Wells. — New York, Hill and Wang [1958] 303 p. 20 cm. — (A Dramabook, D 11) 1. Acting 2. Actors I. T.
PN2061.M26   792.082   *LC* 58-6066

Redgrave, Michael. • 2.3121
The actor's ways and means. — New York: Theatre Arts Books, [1953] 90 p.: illus.; 23 cm. — (The Rockefeller Foundation lectures, Dept. of Drama, University of Bristol, 1952-53) 1. Acting I. T.
PN2061.R4   792.9   *LC* 54-38459

Cole, Toby, 1916- ed. • 2.3122
Actors on acting; the theories, techniques, and practices of the great actors of all times as told in their own words. Edited with introductions & biographical notes by Toby Cole and Helen Krich Chinoy. — New rev. ed. — New York: Crown Publishers, [1970] xvii, 715 p.; 24 cm. 1. Acting 2. Actors I. Chinoy, Helen Krich. joint ed. II. T.
PN2065.C55 1970   792/.028   *LC* 76-93395

Stanislavsky, Konstantin, 1863-1938. • 2.3123
Building a character / Constantin Stanislavski; translated by Elizabeth Reynolds Hapgood; introd. by Joshua Logan. — New York: Theatre Arts Books, 1949. xx, 292 p.; 22 cm. Translation of v.2 of Rabota aktera nad soboĭ (romanized form). 1. Acting I. T.
PN2065.S672   *LC* 49-5265

Stanislavsky, Konstantin, 1863-1938. • 2.3124
[Rabota aktera nad soboĭ. Pt. 2. English] An actor prepares; translated by Elizabeth Reynolds Hapgood. Introd. by John Gielgud. Anniversary ed. New York, Theatre Arts Books, 1948. xx, 295 p. 21 cm. Explains the art of acting in semi-fiction form. Translation of pt. 2 of Rabota aktera nad soboĭ. 1. Acting I. T.
PN2065.S713 1948   792   *LC* 48-7880

Stanislavsky, Konstantin, 1863-1938. • 2.3125
Creating a role. Translated by Elizabeth Reynolds Hapgood. Edited by Hermine I. Popper. Foreword by Robert Lewis. New York, Theatre Arts Books [1961] 271 p. 21 cm. Translated from a Russian manuscript; published in Russia under title: Rabota aktera nad roliu. 1. Acting I. T. II. Title: Rabota aktera nad roliu.
PN 2065 S784   *LC* 61-10494

PN2067–2071 COSTUME. MAKE-UP. SPECIAL TOPICS

Barton, Lucy, 1891-. • 2.3126
Historic costume for the stage. Boston W.H. Baker [c1935] 605p. 1. Costume 2. Costume — History I. T.
PN2067 B3

Prisk, Berneice. • 2.3127
Stage costume handbook. — New York: Harper & Row, [1966] x, 198 p.: illus., forms.; 26 cm. 1. Costume I. T.
PN2067.P7   792.026   *LC* 66-10606

Shaw, William Harlan. 2.3128
Basic pattern drafting for the theatrical costume designer. — [1st ed.]. — New York: Drama Book Specialists/Publishers, [1974] vii, 40 p.: illus.; 28 cm. 1. Costume design 2. Dressmaking — Pattern design 3. Tailoring — Pattern design I. T.
PN2067.S5   646.4/7   *LC* 73-16405   *ISBN* 0910482497

Corson, Richard. 2.3129
Stage makeup / Richard Corson. — 7th ed. — Englewood Cliffs, N.J.: Prentice-Hall, c1986. xxii, 389 p.: ill. (some col.); 29 cm. Includes index. 1. Make-up, Theatrical I. T.
PN2068.C65 1986   792/.027 19   *LC* 85-3578   *ISBN* 0138405212

Herman, Lewis Helmar, 1905-. • 2.3130
[Manual of foreign dialects for radio, stage, screen] Foreign dialects; a manual for actors, directors, and writers, by Lewis Herman and Marguerite Shalett Herman. New York, Theatre Arts Books [1958? c1943] 415 p. illus. 24 cm. First published in 1943 under title: Manual of foreign dialects for radio, stage, and screen. 1. Acting 2. English language — Pronunciation by foreign speakers 3. English language — Dialects 4. English language — Phonetics 5. National characteristics I. Herman, Marguerite Shalett, joint author. II. T.
PN2071.F6 H4 1958   792.028   *LC* 58-10332

Kipnis, Claude. 2.3131
The mime book. Edited and coordinated by Neil Kleinman. Photos. by Edith Chustka. — [1st ed.]. — New York: Harper & Row, [1974] 226 p.: illus.; 24 x 26 cm. — (An Umbrella book) 1. Mime I. T.
PN2071.G4 K5   PN2071 G4 K5.   792.3   *LC* 73-14266   *ISBN* 0060124040

Spolin, Viola. • 2.3132
Improvisation for the theater; a handbook of teaching and directing techniques. [Evanston, Ill.] Northwestern University Press [1963] 395 p. 24 cm. 1. Improvisation (Acting) 2. Amateur theater I. T.
PN2071.I5 S6   792.028   *LC* 63-7579

Laban, Rudolf von, 1879-1958. 2.3133
The mastery of movement / [by] Rudolf Laban. — 4th ed., revised and enlarged / by Lisa Ullmann. — Plymouth: Macdonald and Evans, 1980. xii, 196 p.: ill.; 25 cm. 1. Movement (Acting) I. Ullmann, Lisa. II. T.
PN2071.M6 L3 1980   792/.028 19   *LC* 80-147265   *ISBN* 0712112871

Fisher, Seymour. 2.3134
Pretend the world is funny and forever: a psychological analysis of comedians, clowns, and actors / Seymour Fisher, Rhoda L. Fisher. — Hillsdale, N.J.: L. Erlbaum Associates, 1981. xiv, 252 p.; 24 cm. Includes indexes. 1. Actors — Psychology 2. Comedians — Psychology. 3. Wit and humor — Psychological aspects. I. Fisher, Rhoda L. (Rhoda Lee), 1924- joint author. II. T.
PN2071.P78 F5   791/.092/2   *LC* 80-17777   *ISBN* 0898590736

PN2074–2078 Careers. Study

Saint-Denis, Michel, 1897-. 2.3135
Training for the theatre: premises & promises / Michel Saint-Denis; edited by Suria Saint-Denis. — New York: Theatre Arts Books; London: Heinemann, c1982. 243 p., [8] p. of plates: ill.; 21 cm. Includes index. 1. Saint-Denis, Michel, 1897- 2. Acting — Study and teaching I. Saint-Denis, Suria. II. T.
PN2075.S24 1982   792/.028 19   *LC* 81-86083   *ISBN* 0878305769

Wickham, Glynne William Gladstone. • 2.3136
Drama in a world of science, and three other lectures. — Toronto, University of Toronto Press, 1962. 92 p. illus. 22 cm. 1. Bristol, Eng. University. Dept. of Drama. 2. Theater — Study and teaching. 3. English drama — 20th cent. — Hist. & crit. I. T.
PN2075.W5 1962a   792.0942   *LC* 63-1012 rev

Directory of American college theatre. • 2.3137
1st- ed.; 1960-. East Lansing, Mich. American Educational Theatre Association. v. Irregular. 1. College theatre — Directories 2. Theater — Study and teaching — Directories. I. American Educational Theatre Association.
PN2078 U6 D5x   *LC* 60-4683

Hirsch, Foster. 2.3138
A method to their madness: the history of the Actors Studio / Foster Hirsch. — 1st ed. — New York: W.W. Norton, c1984. 367 p.: ill.; 24 cm. Includes index. 1. Actors Studio (New York, N.Y.) 2. Method (Acting) I. T.
PN2078.U62 N384 1984   792/.028/0607471 19   *LC* 83-25515   *ISBN* 0393017834

PN2081–2096 The Stage. Lighting. Sets. Scenery

Jones, Margo. • 2.3139
Theatre-in-the-round. — Westport, Conn.: Greenwood Press, [1970, c1951] 244 p.: illus.; 23 cm. 1. Dallas. Theatre '50. 2. Arena theater I. T.
PN2081.A7 J6 1970   792/.0228/0976428   *LC* 76-100250   *ISBN* 0837129834

Aronson, Arnold. 2.3140
The history and theory of environmental scenography / by Arnold Aronson. — Ann Arbor, Mich.: UMI research Press, c1981. xiv, 282 p.: ill.; 24 cm. — (Theater and dramatic studies. no. 3) Includes index. 1. Theater, Environmental I. T. II. Title: Environmental scenography. III. Series.
PN2081.E58 A7 1981   792/.025/09 19   *LC* 81-11677   *ISBN* 0835712249

Bentham, Frederick. 2.3141
The art of stage lighting / Frederick Bentham. 2d ed., rev. and expanded. — New York: Theatre Arts Books, 1976. 361 p.: ill.; 26 cm. (Theatre and stage series) 1. Stage lighting I. T.
PN2091.E4 B398 1976   792/.025   *LC* 77-351421   *ISBN* 0878300090

Bergman, Gösta Mauritz, 1905-1975.   **2.3142**
Lighting in the theatre / by Gösta M. Bergman. — Stockholm: Almqvist & Wiksell International; Totowa, N.J.: Rowman and Littlefield, 1977. 426 p.: ill.; 24 cm. Includes index. 1. Stage lighting — History. I. T.
PN2091.E4 B45 1977 792/.025 *LC* 77-372895 *ISBN* 0874716020

McCandless, Stanley Russell.   **• 2.3143**
A method of lighting the stage. — 4th ed. amended and rev. — New York: Theatre Arts Books, [1958] 143 p.: illus.; 21 cm. 1. Stage lighting I. T.
PN2091.E4 M3 1958 792.025 *LC* 58-10331

Pilbrow, Richard.   **2.3144**
Stage lighting / Richard Pilbrow; foreword by Lord Olivier. — Rev. ed. / with contributions by William Bundy and John B. Read. — New York: Drama Book Specialists, 1979. 176 p.: ill.; 26 cm. Includes index. 1. Stage lighting I. T.
PN2091.E4 P5 1979 792/.025 *LC* 78-10184 *ISBN* 0896760057

Rees, Terence.   **2.3145**
Theatre lighting in the age of gas / [by] Terence Rees. — London: Society for Theatre Research, 1978. x, 238 p.: ill., facsims., plans; 25 cm. 1. Stage lighting — History. 2. Gas-lighting — History. 3. Theater — History — 19th century I. T.
PN2091.E4 R38 792/.025 *LC* 79-314824 *ISBN* 0854300252

Burris-Meyer, Harold, 1902-.   **• 2.3146**
Scenery for the theatre; the organization, processes, materials, and techniques used to set the stage [by] Harold Burris–Meyer and Edward C. Cole. Contributing authors: Nicholas L. Bryson [and others]. — Rev. ed. — Boston: Little, Brown, [1971] xix, 518 p.: illus.; 27 cm. 1. Theaters — Stage-setting and scenery I. Cole, Edward Cyrus. joint author. II. T.
PN2091.S8 B8 1971 694 *LC* 72-154968

Gillette, A. S. (Arnold S.), 1904-.   **2.3147**
Stage scenery, its construction and rigging / A. S. Gillette, J. Michael Gillette. — 3rd ed. — New York: Harper & Row, c1981. xv, 448 p.: ill.; 27 cm. Includes index. 1. Theaters — Stage-setting and scenery I. Gillette, J. Michael. II. T.
PN2091.S8 G5 1981 792/.025 19 *LC* 81-568 *ISBN* 0060423323

Hainaux, René.   **2.3148**
Stage design throughout the world, 1970–75 / René Hainaux. — New York: Theatre Arts Books, 1976. 158 p.: ill. (some col.); 31 cm. Captions in English and French. Includes indexes. 1. Theaters — Stage-setting and scenery 2. Theater — Pictorial works. I. T.
PN2091.S8 H22 792/.025/09047 *LC* 75-7879 *ISBN* 087830133X

Hainaux, René. comp.   **2.3149**
Stage design throughout the world since 1960. Text and illus. collected by the national centres of the International Theatre Institute. Chosen and presented by René Hainaux, with the collaboration of Yves–Bonnat. Foreword by Paul–Louis Mignon. — New York, Theatre Arts Books [1973, c1972] 239 p. (chiefly illus. (part col.)) 31 cm. 1. Theaters — Stage-setting and scenery 2. Theater — Pictorial works. I. Bonnat, Yves. joint comp. II. International Theatre Institute. III. T.
PN2091.S8 H23 1973 792/.025 *LC* 72-87117 *ISBN* 0878301291

International Theatre Institute.   **2.3150**
Stage design throughout the world since 1935. Texts and illus. collected by the national centres of the International Theatre Institute; chosen and presented by René Hainaux with the technical advice of Yves–Bonnat. A sketch to serve as foreword by Jean Cocteau. Pref. by Kenneth Rae. — New York: Theater Arts Books, 1956. 219 p. (chiefly plates (part col.)); 31 cm. — (Its Publications) 1. Theaters — Stage-setting and scenery 2. Theater — Pictorial works. I. Hainaux, René. ed. II. T.
PN2091.S8 I49 792.92* *LC* 58-26357

International Theatre Institute.   **• 2.3151**
Stage design throughout the world since 1950. Texts and illus. collected by the national centres of the International Theatre Institute, chosen and presented by René Hainaux, with the technical advice of Yves–Bonnat. Foreword by Paul–Louis Mignon. — New York: Theatre Arts Books, [1964] 276 p. (chiefly illus. (part col.)); 31 cm. — (Its Publications) 1. Theaters — Stage-setting and scenery 2. Theater — Pictorial works. I. Hainaux, René. ed. II. T.
PN2091.S8 I53 792.025 *LC* 63-20345

The Italian baroque stage: documents / by Giulio Troili ... [et   **2.3152**
al.]; translated and with commentary by Dunbar H. Ogden.
Berkeley: University of California Press, c1978. xi, 187 p.: facsims.; 29 cm. 1. Theaters — Italy — Stage-setting and scenery — History — Sources. 2. Architecture, Baroque — Italy — History — Sources. 3. Scene painting — Italy — History — Sources. 4. Perspective — Early works to 1800. I. Troili, Giulio, 1613-1685. II. Ogden, Dunbar H.
PN2091.S8 I75 PN2091S8 I75. 792/.025/0945 *LC* 75-7197
ISBN 0520030060

McNamara, Brooks.   **2.3153**
Theatres, spaces, environments: 18 projects / Brooks McNamara, Jerry Rojo, Richard Schechner. — New York: Drama Book Specialists, [1975] [viii], 181 p.: ill., plans. 1. Theaters — United States — Stage-setting and scenery. 2. Theaters — United States — Construction. I. Rojo, Jerry. II. Schechner, Richard, 1934- III. T.
PN2091.S8 M24 PN2091S8 M24. 792 *LC* 75-29018 *ISBN* 0910482632

Moussinac, Léon, 1890-1964.   **• 2.3154**
The new movement in the theatre; a survey of recent developments in Europe and America. With an introd. by R. H. Packman and a foreword by Gordon Craig. — New York: B. Blom, [1967] xi, 23 p.: illus. (part col.), 128 plates (part col.); 39 cm. First published in 1931. 1. Theaters — Stage-setting and scenery 2. Costume I. T.
PN2091.S8 M76 1967 792/.02 *LC* 65-19619

Parker, W. Oren (Wilford Oren)   **2.3155**
Scene design and stage lighting / W. Oren Parker, Harvey K. Smith, R. Craig Wolf. — 5th ed. — New York: Holt, Rinehart, and Winston, 1985. ix, 596 p., [16] p. of plates: ill. (some col.); 26 cm. Includes index. 1. Theaters — Stage-setting and scenery 2. Stage lighting I. Smith, Harvey K. (Harvey Kennedy) II. Wolf, R. Craig. III. T.
PN2091.S8 P3 1985 792/.025 19 *LC* 84-10927 *ISBN* 0030642485

Rosenfeld, Sybil Marion, 1903-.   **2.3156**
Georgian scene painters and scene painting / Sybil Rosenfeld. — Cambridge [Eng.]; New York: Cambridge University Press, 1981. xiv, 206 p., [40] p. of plates: ill.; 26 cm. 1. Theaters — Great Britain — Stage-setting and scenery. 2. Scene painting — Great Britain — History. 3. Scene painters — Great Britain. I. T.
PN2091.S8 R587 792/.025/0941 19 *LC* 80-41549 *ISBN* 0521233399

Rosenfeld, Sybil, 1903-.   **2.3157**
A short history of scene design in Great Britain [by] Sybil Rosenfeld. — Totowa, N.J.: Rowman and Littlefield, [1973] xviii, 214 p.: illus.; 22 cm. — (Drama and theatre studies.) 1. Theaters — Great Britain — Stagesetting and scenery — History. I. T. II. Series.
PN2091.S8 R59 1973 792/.025/0942 *LC* 73-1621 *ISBN* 0874711789

Serlio, Sebastiano, 1475-1554.   **• 2.3158**
The renaissance stage: documents of Serlio, Sabbattini and Furtenbach. Translated by Allardyce Nicoll, John H. McDowell [and] George R. Kernodle. Edited by Barnard Hewitt. — Coral Gables [Fla.]: University of Miami Press, 1958. ix, 256 p.: ill., plans. — (Books of the theatre series; no. 1) 1. Theaters — Stage-setting and scenery 2. Theater — Italy — History I. Furttenbach, Joseph, 1591-1667. II. Sabbattini, Nicola, ca. 1575-1654. III. Hewitt, Barnard Wolcott, 1906- ed. IV. T.
PN2091.S8 S48 *LC* 58-14141

Southern, Richard.   **• 2.3159**
Changeable scenery, its origin and development in the British theatre. — London, Faber and Faber [1952] 411 p. illus. 26 cm. 1. Theaters — Stage-settings and scenery. I. T.
PN2091.S8S627 792 *LC* 52-2462

Oenslager, Donald, 1902-1975.   **2.3160**
The theatre of Donald Oenslager / Donald M. Oenslager. — 1st ed. — Middletown, Conn.: Wesleyan University Press, c1978. xv, 176 p., [8] leaves of plates: ill.; 23 x 29 cm. 'Productions designed by Donald Oenslager': p. 147-167. Includes index. 1. Oenslager, Donald, 1902-1975. 2. Set designers — United States — Biography. 3. Theater — New York (N.Y.) — History. 4. Theaters — United States — Stage-setting and scenery. I. T.
PN2096.O4 A37 1978 792/.025/0924 B *LC* 77-16026 *ISBN* 0819550256

PN2100–2193 History: General

Brockett, Oscar Gross, 1923-.   **2.3161**
History of the theatre / Oscar G. Brockett. — 5th ed. — Boston: Allyn and Bacon, c1987. xii, 779 p.: ill.; 25 cm. Includes index. 1. Theater — History 2. Drama — History and criticism I. T.
PN2101.B68 1987 792/.09 19 *LC* 86-26535 *ISBN* 0205104878

Cheney, Sheldon.   **2.3162**
The theatre: three thousand years of drama, acting, and stagecraft. — Rev. and reset illustrated ed., with a new bibliography. — New York: McKay, 1972. xv, 710 p.: ill. 1. Theater — History 2. Drama — History and criticism I. T.
PN2101.C5 1972 *LC* 74-155254

Kernodle, George Riley, 1907-.   • **2.3163**
From art to theatre; form and convention in the renaissance [by] George R. Kernodle. — Chicago: University of Chicago press, [1944] ix, 255 p.: illus.; 29 cm. Without thesis note. 1. Theater — History 2. Theaters — Stage-setting and scenery I. T.
PN2101 K4   LC a 44-3462

Nagler, A. M. (Alois Maria), 1907- ed.   **2.3164**
[Sources of theatrical history] A source book in theatrical history = Sources of theatrical history / by A. M. Nagler. — New York: Dover Publications, 1959, c1952. xxiii, 611 p., [1] leaf of plates: ill.; 21 cm. 'This Dover edition ... is an unabridged, unaltered republication of the first edition.' 1. Theater — History — Sources. I. T.
PN2101.N3 1959   792/.09   LC 77-375275   ISBN 0486205150

Nicoll, Allardyce, 1894-.   • **2.3165**
The Development of the theatre: a study of theatrical art from the beginnings to the present day. — 5th ed., rev. — New York: Harcourt, Brace & World, 1967, c1966. xix, 292 p.: illus, plans.; 27 cm. 1. Theater — History 2. Drama — History and criticism I. T.
PN2101.N5 1967   LC 67-10645

Nicoll, Allardyce, 1894-.   • **2.3166**
World drama from Æschylus to Anouilh. — New York: Harcourt, Brace, [1950?] 1000 p.: plates, port.; 23 cm. 1. Drama — History and criticism I. T.
PN2101.N55 1950   809.2   LC 50-6848

Berthold, Margot, 1922-.   **2.3167**
[Weltgeschichte des Theaters. English] A history of world theater. [Translated by Edith Simmons from the original German] New York, Ungar [1972] x, 733 p. illus. 24 cm. Translation of Weltgeschichte des Theaters. 1. Theater — History I. T.
PN2104.B413   792/.09   LC 70-127203   ISBN 0804420378

Molinari, Cesare, 1935-.   **2.3168**
[Teatro. English] Theatre through the ages. Translated by Colin Hamer. New York, McGraw-Hill [1975] 324 p. illus. 30 cm. Translation of Teatro. 1. Theater — History I. T.
PN2105.M613   792/.09   LC 74-1165   ISBN 0070426651

Ridgeway, William, Sir, 1853-1926.   • **2.3169**
The dramas and dramatic dances of non–European races in special reference to the origin of Greek tragedy, with an appendix on the origin of Greek comedy. New York, B. Blom [1964] xv, 448 p. illus. 26 cm. 'First published by Cambridge University Press, 1915.' 'A sequel to ... [the author's] Origin of tragedy, published in 1910, or rather ... an expansion of a short chapter in that work.' 1. Drama — History and criticism 2. Greek drama — History and criticism. 3. Drama — Origin 4. Dancing — History. I. T.
PN2122.R5 1964   792.09   LC 63-23187

PN2131–2193 By Period

Chambers, E. K. (Edmund Kerchever), 1866-1954.   • **2.3170**
The mediaeval stage / by E. K. Chambers. — Oxford, Clarendon Press, 1903. 2 v.: ill. 1. Theater — History 2. Drama, Medieval — History and criticism. I. T.
PN2152.C4   LC 04-1915

Tydeman, William.   **2.3171**
The theatre in the Middle Ages: Western European stage conditions, c. 800–1576 / William Tydeman. — Cambridge; New York: Cambridge University Press, 1978. xii, 298 p.: ill., maps, plans; 22 cm. Includes index. 1. Theater — History — Medieval, 500-1500 I. T.
PN2152.T9   PN2152 T9.   792/.09/02   LC 77-85683   ISBN 0521218918

Wickham, Glynne William Gladstone.   **2.3172**
The medieval theatre / Glynne Wickham. — 3rd ed. — Cambridge [Cambridgeshire]; New York: Cambridge University Press, 1987, c1974. xv, 260 p., [24] p. of plates: ill.; 24 cm. Includes index. 1. Theater — History — Medieval, 500-1500 I. T.
PN2152.W5 1987   809.2/02 19   LC 86-20742   ISBN 0521320690

Baur-Heinhold, Margarete.   • **2.3173**
[Theater des Barock. English] The baroque theatre; a cultural history of the 17th and 18th centuries. Photos. by Helga Schmidt–Glassner. New York, McGraw-Hill [1967] 292 p. illus. (part col.) 29 cm. Translation of Theater des Barock. 1. Theater — History — 17th century. 2. Theater — History — 18th century I. T.
PN2174.B313 1967b   792/.094   LC 67-24946

Lewes, George Henry, 1817-1878.   • **2.3174**
On actors and the art of acting. — New York: Greenwood Press, 1968. 237 p.; 23 cm. Reprint of the 1957 ed. 1. Actors 2. Acting 3. Theater — History — 19th century I. T.
PN2185.L5 1968   792/.028   LC 68-56038

Bentley, Eric, 1916-.   • **2.3175**
In search of theater. New York, Vintage Books, 1954 [c1953] 385 p. 19 cm. (A Vintage book, K6) 1. Theater — History — 20th century 2. Drama — 20th century — History & criticism. I. T.
PN2189.B4 1954   792.0904   LC 54-12046

Brockett, Oscar Gross, 1923-.   • **2.3176**
Century of innovation: a history of European and American theatre and drama since 1870, [by] Oscar G. Brockett [and] Robert R. Findlay. — Englewood Cliffs, N.J.: Prentice-Hall, [1973] xiv, 826 p.: illus.; 24 cm. — (Prentice-Hall series in theatre and drama) 1. Theater — History — 20th century 2. Drama — 20th century — History and criticism I. Findlay, Robert R., 1932- joint author. II. T.
PN2189.B64   792/.09   LC 72-5425   ISBN 0131227475

Brustein, Robert Sanford, 1927-.   • **2.3177**
The theatre of revolt; an approach to the modern drama [by] Robert Brustein. — [1st ed.]. — Boston: Little, Brown, [1964] ix, 435 p.; 22 cm. 1. Drama — 20th century — History and criticism I. T.
PN2189.B7   809.2   LC 64-17473

Cheney, Sheldon, 1886-.   • **2.3178**
The new movement in the theatre. — Westport, Conn.: Greenwood Press, [1971] 303 p.: illus.; 23 cm. Reprint of the 1914 ed. 1. Theater 2. Drama — 20th century — History and criticism 3. Theaters — Stage-setting and scenery I. T.
PN2189.C5 1971b   792/.08   LC 70-95089   ISBN 0837130816

Croyden, Margaret.   **2.3179**
Lunatics, lovers, and poets: the contemporary experimental theatre / Margaret Croyden. — New York: McGraw-Hill, 1974. xxvi, 320 p.: ill.; 23 cm. 1. Experimental theater 2. Drama — 20th century — History and criticism I. T.
PN2189.C7   792/.09/04   LC 73-9904   ISBN 0070147809

Downer, Alan Seymour, 1912-.   • **2.3180**
The American theater today, edited by Alan S. Downer. — New York: Basic Books, [1967] ix, 212 p.; 22 cm. 1. Theater — United States 2. American drama — 20th century — History and criticism. I. T.
PN2189.D6   792.0973   LC 67-17389

Gassner, John, 1903-1967.   • **2.3181**
[Form and ideas in modern theatre] Directions in modern theatre and drama, an expanded ed. of Form and idea in modern theatre. New York, Holt, Rinehart and Winston [1965] xvi, 457 p. illus. 22 cm. 1. Theater 2. Drama — History and criticism I. T.
PN2189.G3 1965   792.015   LC 65-14551

Hayman, Ronald, 1932-.   **2.3182**
Theatre and anti–theatre: new movements since Beckett / Ronald Hayman. — New York: Oxford University Press, 1979. xiii, 272 p.; 22 cm. Includes index. 1. Theater — History — 20th century 2. Drama — 20th century — History and criticism I. T.
PN2189.H34   792/.09/04   LC 78-73778   ISBN 0195200896

Roose-Evans, James.   **2.3183**
Experimental theatre from Stanislavsky to Peter Brook / James Roose–Evans. — New York: Universe Books, c1984. x, 210 p., [20] p. of plates: ill.; 22 cm. Rev. ed. of: Experimental theatre from Stanislavsky to today. New rev. ed. 1973. Includes index. 1. Experimental theater I. Roose-Evans, James. Experimental theatre from Stanislavsky to today. II. T. III. Title: Experimental theater from Stanislavsky to Peter Brook. IV. Title: Experimental theatre.
PN2189.R6 1984   792/.09/04 19   LC 84-2602   ISBN 0876635648

PN2205–2219 Biography: International

Wagenknecht, Edward, 1900-.   • **2.3184**
Merely players [by] Edward Wagenknecht. [1st ed.] Norman, University of Oklahoma Press [1966] xiv, 270 p. illus., ports. 23 cm. 1. Actors — Great Britain. 2. Actors — United States. I. T.
PN2205.W28   792.0280922   LC 66-22715

Appignanesi, Lisa.   **2.3185**
The cabaret / Lisa Appignanesi. New York: Universe Books, 1976. 192 p.: ill.; 29 cm. Includes index. 1. Music-halls (Variety-theaters, cabarets, etc.) I. T.
PN2219.C2 A6 1976   792.7   LC 75-39866   ISBN 0876632355

PN2220–3030 The Theater: Particular Countries

PN2220–2298 United States

Bordman, Gerald Martin.   **2.3186**
The Oxford companion to American theatre / Gerald Bordman. — New York: Oxford University Press, 1984. vi, 734 p.; 25 cm. 1. Theater — United States — Handbooks, manuals, etc. 2. Drama — Handbooks, manuals, etc. I. T.
PN2220.B6 1984   792/.0973 19   *LC* 83-26812   *ISBN* 0195034430

Coad, Oral Sumner, 1887-1976.   • **2.3187**
The American stage, by Oral Sumner Coad [and] Edwin Mims, jr. New Haven, Yale University Press; [etc., etc.] 1929. 3 p. l., 362 p. col. front., illus. (incl. ports., facsims.) 26 1/2 cm. (The Pageant of America. [Vol. XIV]) 1. Theater — United States — History. 2. Actors 3. Actresses I. Mims, Edwin, 1900-joint author. II. T.
PN2221.C6x E178.5.P2 vol. 14   *LC* 29-22306

Dunlap, William, 1766-1839.   • **2.3188**
History of the American theatre, and anecdotes of the principal actors. 2d ed., improved, incorporating a list of early plays and A narrative of his connection with the Old American Company, 1792-1797, by John Hodgkinson. 3 v. in 1. New York, Burt Franklin, 1963. 412, 387, 23 p. illus. 22 cm. (Burt Franklin research & source works series no. 36) 1. Old American Company. 2. Theater — United States — History. 3. American drama — Bibliography. I. Hodgkinson, John, ca. 1767-1805. A narrative of his connection with the Old American Company. II. T.
PN2221.D8 1963   792.0973   *LC* 63-12663

Hewitt, Barnard Wolcott, 1906-.   • **2.3189**
Theatre U.S.A., 1668 to 1957. — New York: McGraw-Hill, 1959. 528 p.: illus.; 24 cm. 1. Theater — United States — History. 2. Drama — History and criticism I. T.
PN2221.H4   792.0973   *LC* 58-11982

Hornblow, Arthur, 1865-.   • **2.3190**
A history of the theatre in America from its beginnings to the present time / by Arthur Hornblow. — Philadelphia: J.B. Lippincott, 1919. 2 v. : ill. 1. Theater — United States — History. I. T.
PN2221.H6   *LC* 20-683

Hughes, Glenn, 1894-1964.   • **2.3191**
A history of the American theatre, 1700–1950. — New York: S. French, [1951] ix, 562 p.: illus., ports.; 22 cm. 1. Theater — United States — History. I. T.
PN2221.H76   792   *LC* 51-7975

Moses, Montrose Jonas, 1878-1934. ed.   • **2.3192**
The American theatre as seen by its critics, 1752–1934, edited by Montrose J. Moses and John Mason Brown. New York, Cooper Square Publishers, 1967 [c1934] 391 p. 24 cm. 1. Theater — United States 2. American drama — History and criticism. I. Brown, John Mason, 1900-1969. joint ed. II. T.
PN2221.M7 1967   792/.0973   *LC* 66-30782

Seilhamer, George Overcash, 1839-1916.   • **2.3193**
History of the American theatre. — [New York: B. Blom, 1968] 3 v.; 25 cm. Reprint of the 1888-91 ed. with a new introd. by Norman Philbrick. 1. Theater — United States — History. I. T. II. Title: The American theatre.
PN2221.S4 1968   792/.0973   *LC* 68-58198

Seldes, Gilbert Vivian, 1893-.   • **2.3194**
The 7 lively arts. — New York: Sagamore Press, [1957] 306 p.; 22 cm. 1. Journalism. 2. Theater — United States 3. Motion pictures 4. Music — History and criticism 5. American wit and humor 6. American wit and humor, Pictorial 7. Dancing 8. Circus I. T.
PN2221.S43 1957   792.0973   *LC* 57-12434

Wilson, Garff B.   • **2.3195**
Three hundred years of American drama and theatre: from Ye bare and ye cubb to Chorus line / Garff B. Wilson. — 2nd ed. — Englewood Cliffs, N.J.: Prentice-Hall, c1982. xii, 350 p.: ill.; 24 cm. Includes index. 1. Theater — United States — History. 2. American drama — History and criticism. I. T.
PN2221.W5 1982   792/.0973 19   *LC* 81-5838   *ISBN* 0139203303

Ethnic theatre in the United States / edited by Maxine   **2.3196**
Schwartz Seller.
Westport, Conn.: Greenwood Press, 1983. viii, 606 p.: ill.; 25 cm. 1. Ethnic theater — United States — Addresses, essays, lectures. I. Seller, Maxine, 1935-.
PN2226.E85 1983   792/.0973 19   *LC* 81-13494   *ISBN* 0313212309

Moody, Richard, 1911-.   • **2.3197**
America takes the stage: romanticism in American drama and theatre, 1750–1900. — Bloomington: Indiana University Press, 1955. viii, 322 p.: ill., facsims., music.; 25 cm. 1. Theater — United States — History. 2. American drama — History and criticism. I. T.
PN2226.M6 1969   792   *LC* 55-6271

Poggi, Jack, 1928-.   • **2.3198**
Theater in America; the impact of economic forces, 1870–1967. — Ithaca, N.Y.: Cornell University Press, [1968] xx, 328 p.: illus.; 22 cm. 1. Theater — United States 2. Theater — Economic aspects. I. T.
PN2226.P6   792/.0973   *LC* 68-28805

Wilson, Garff B.   • **2.3199**
A history of American acting, by Garff B. Wilson. — Bloomington: Indiana University Press, [1966] x, 310 p.: illus., ports.; 24 cm. 1. Actors — United States. 2. Acting I. T.
PN2226.W5   792.0922   *LC* 66-12736

Women in American theatre: careers, images, movements: an   **2.3200**
illustrated anthology and sourcebook / edited by Helen Krich
Chinoy and Linda Walsh Jenkins.
1st ed. — New York: Crown Publishers, c1981. xi, 370 p., [16] leaves of plates: ill.; 24 cm. 'A Herbert Michelman book.' Includes index. 1. Women in the theater — United States. I. Chinoy, Helen Krich. II. Jenkins, Linda Walsh.
PN2226.W6 1981   792/.088042   *LC* 80-16786   *ISBN* 051753729X

PN2237–2269 Special Periods

Toll, Robert C.   **2.3201**
On with the show!: The first century of show business in America / Robert C. Toll. — New York: Oxford University Press, 1976. 361 p.: ill., ports.; 29 cm. Includes index. 1. Performing arts — United States — History. I. T.
PN2245.T58   PN2245 T58.   790.2/0973   *LC* 75-46355

Hodge, Francis.   • **2.3202**
Yankee theatre: the image of America on the stage, 1825–1850 / Francis Hodge. — Austin: University of Texas Press, c1964. 320 p.: ill., facsims. — 1. Theater — United States 2. American drama (Comedy) — History and criticism. 3. Comedians, American. I. T.
PN2248.H6   *LC* 64-19417

Frick, John W.   **2.3203**
New York's first theatrical center: the Rialto at Union Square / by John W. Frick. — Ann Arbor, Mich.: UMI Research Press, c1985. x, 209 p.: ill.; 24 cm. (Theater and dramatic studies. no. 26) 'A revision of the author's thesis, New York University, 1983'—T.p. verso. 1. Theater — New York (N.Y.) — History — 19th century. 2. Theaters — New York (N.Y.) — History — 19th century. 3. Amusements — New York (N.Y.) — History — 19th century. 4. New York (N.Y.) — Popular culture — History — 19th century. I. T. II. Title: Union Square. III. Series.
PN2256.F68 1985   792/.09747/1 19   *LC* 84-16255   *ISBN* 0835716120

McArthur, Benjamin.   **2.3204**
Actors and American culture, 1880–1920 / Benjamin McArthur. — Philadelphia: Temple University Press, 1984. xiv, 289 p.: ill.; 24 cm. — (American civilization.) Includes index. 1. Theater — United States — History. 2. Actors — United States. 3. Theater and society — United States. 4. United States — Popular culture I. T. II. Series.
PN2256.M39 1984   792/.028/0973 19   *LC* 83-24091   *ISBN* 0877223335

Bentley, Eric, 1916-.   • **2.3205**
The dramatic event, an American chronicle. — New York, Horizon Press, 1954. 278 p. 22 cm. 1. Theater — United States 2. Drama — Hist. & crit. I. T.
PN2266.B45   792.0973   *LC* 54-12279

Blum, Daniel C.   **2.3206**
A pictorial history of the American theatre, 1860–1985 / by Daniel Blum; enlarged by John Willis. — New 6th ed. — New York: Crown Publishers, c1986. 496 p.: ill.; 32 cm. Includes index. 1. Theater — United States — History — Pictorial works. I. Willis, John (John A.) II. T. III. Title: American theatre, 1860-1985.
PN2266.B585 1986   792/.0973 19   *LC* 87-117298   *ISBN* 0517562588

Brown, John Mason, 1900-1969.   • **2.3207**
Dramatis personae; a retrospective show. New York, Viking Press [1963] 563 p. 22 cm. 1. Theater — United States 2. Drama — 20th century — History and criticism I. T.
PN2266.B687   818.52   *LC* 63-12359

Flanagan, Hallie, 1890-1969.   • **2.3208**
Arena; the history of the Federal Theatre, by Hallie Flanagan. [New York] B. Blom [1965, c1940] ix, 475 p. illus. 24 cm. 1. Federal Theatre Project (U.S.) 2. American drama — 20th century — History and criticism. I. T.
PN2266.D37 1965   792.0973   *LC* 65-23693

De Hart-Mathews, Jane. • **2.3209**
The Federal Theatre, 1935–1939; plays, relief, and politics. Princeton, N.J., Princeton University Press, 1967. xii, 342 p. illus., ports. 23 cm. 1. Federal Theatre Project (U.S.) I. T.
PN2266.M33   792/.0973   LC 67-14412

The Theatre book of the year... a record and an interpretation. • **2.3210**
1942/43.
New York, A.A. Knopf, 1943-. v. 22 cm. 1942/43-   by G.J. Nathan. 1. Theater — Yearbooks. 2. Theater — United States I. Nathan, George Jean, 1882-1958.
PN2266.N373   LC 43-51298

Novick, Julius, 1939-. • **2.3211**
Beyond Broadway; the quest for permanent theatres. — [1st ed.]. — New York: Hill and Wang, [1968] xiv, 393 p.: illus., ports.; 22 cm. 1. Theater — United States 2. Theater — Canada. I. T.
PN2266.N6   792/.0973   LC 68-18847

Zeigler, Joseph Wesley. **2.3212**
Regional theatre: the revolutionary stage. — Minneapolis, University of Minnesota Press [1973] xv, 277 p. illus. 24 cm. 1. Theater — United States I. T.
PN2266.Z4   792/.0973   LC 73-75795   ISBN 0816606757

Cheney, Sheldon, 1886-. • **2.3213**
The art theater; its character as differentiated from the commercial theater; its ideals and organization; and a record of certain European and American examples. Rev. and enl. ed. New York, B. Blom, 1972. vii, 281 p. illus. 22 cm. 'First published in 1917.' 1. Little theater movement I. T.
PN2267.C5 1972   792/.0223   LC 72-160616

PN2270.A35 Afro–American Theater

Fabre, Geneviève. **2.3214**
[Théâtre noir aux Etats-Unis. English] Drumbeats, masks, and metaphor: contemporary Afro–American theatre / Geneviève Fabre; translated by Melvin Dixon. — Cambridge, Mass.: Harvard University Press, 1983. 274, [12] p. of plates: ill.; 24 cm. Translation of: Le théâtre noir aux Etats-Unis. 1. Afro-American theater I. T.
PN2270.A35 F3213 1983   792/.08996073 19   LC 83-4344   ISBN 0674216784

The Theater of Black Americans: a collection of critical essays **2.3215**
/ edited by Errol Hill.
Englewood Cliffs, N.J.: Prentice-Hall, c1980. 2 v.; 21 cm. — (Twentieth century views). (A Spectrum book) 1. Afro-American theater — Addresses, essays, lectures. 2. American drama — Afro-American authors — History and criticism — Addresses, essays, lectures. I. Hill, Errol. II. Series.
PN2270.A35 T48 1980   792/.0973 19   LC 79-16658   ISBN 013912733X

Woll, Allen L. **2.3216**
Dictionary of the Black theatre: Broadway, off–Broadway, and selected Harlem theatre / Allen Woll. — Westport, Conn.: Greenwood Press, 1983. xvi, 359 p.; 25 cm. Includes index. 1. Afro-American theater — New York (N.Y.) — Dictionaries. I. T.
PN2270.A35 W64 1983   792/.08996073   LC 82-21090   ISBN 0313225613

PN2273–2277 Local History

Clapp, William Warland, 1826-1891. • **2.3217**
A record of the Boston stage. — New York: Greenwood Press, [1969] xiii, 479 p.; 18 cm. Reprint of the 1853 ed. I. T.
PN2277.B6 C5 1969   792/.09744/61   LC 69-13861

Tompkins, Eugene. • **2.3218**
The history of the Boston Theatre, 1854–1901. Compiled with the assistance of Quincy Kilby. Boston, Houghton Mifflin, 1908. 550 p. illus. 1. Boston Theatre — History. I. Kilby, Quincy. II. T.
PN2277.B7 B7   792.09744

Guthrie, Tyrone, Sir, 1900-1971. • **2.3219**
A new theatre. — [1st ed.]. — New York: McGraw-Hill, [1964] 188 p.: illus., plan.; 21 cm. 1. Tyrone Guthrie Theatre, Minneapolis. I. T.
PN2277.M55 T94   792.09776579   LC 64-22458

Theatre world. • **2.3220**
1944/45-. [New York, D. C. Blum, 1945-. 1. Theater — New York (City). 2. Theater — Year-books.
PN2277.N5 A17   LC 46-13321

Atkinson, Brooks, 1894-. **2.3221**
Broadway [by] Brooks Atkinson. Rev. ed. New York, Macmillan [1974] ix, 564 p. illus. 24 cm. 1. Theater — New York (City) — History. I. T.
PN2277.N5 A78 1974   792/.09747/1   LC 74-12077   ISBN 0025041800

Greenberger, Howard. **2.3222**
The off–Broadway experience. — Englewood Cliffs, N.J.: Prentice-Hall, [1971] 207 p.: illus.; 22 cm. 1. Off-Broadway theater I. T.
PN2277.N5 G7   792/.097471   LC 75-156167   ISBN 0136306160

Henderson, Mary C., 1928-. **2.3223**
The city and the theatre; New York playhouses from Bowling Green to Times Square [by] Mary C. Henderson. Clifton, N.J., J. T. White [1973] xiv, 323 p. illus. 27 cm. 1. Theaters — New York (N.Y.) — History. 2. Theater — New York (N.Y.) — History. I. T.
PN2277.N5 H4   792/.09747/1   LC 73-9970   ISBN 088371003X

Himelstein, Morgan Yale. • **2.3224**
Drama was a weapon: the left–wing theatre in New York, 1929–1941. With a foreword by John Gassner. New Brunswick, N.J., Rutgers University Press [1963] 300 p. illus. 22 cm. 1. Theater — New York (City) — History. 2. Theater — Political aspects 3. Communism — United States — 1917-4. Socialism and theater I. T.
PN2277.N5 H5   792.097471   LC 62-21161

Leiter, Samuel L. **2.3225**
The encyclopedia of the New York stage, 1920–1930 / Samuel L. Leiter, editor-in-chief; Holly Hill, associate editor. — Westport, Conn.: Greenwood Press, 1985. 2 v. (xxxiii, 1331 p.); 24 cm. Includes indexes. 1. Theater — New York (N.Y.) — Dictionaries. I. Hill, Holly. II. T.
PN2277.N5 L36 1985   792.9/5/097471 19   LC 84-6558   ISBN 0313236151

Little, Stuart W. • **2.3226**
Off–Broadway: the prophetic theater, by Stuart W. Little. — New York: Coward, McCann & Geoghegan, [1972] 323 p.: illus.; 22 cm. 1. Off-Broadway theater I. T.
PN2277.N5 L47   792   LC 76-187144

Little, Stuart W. • **2.3227**
The playmakers [by] Stuart W. Little & Arthur Cantor. — [1st ed.]. — New York: Norton, [1970] 320 p.: illus., map (on lining papers), ports.; 22 cm. 1. Theater — New York (City) I. Cantor, Arthur, 1920- joint author. II. T.
PN2277.N5 L5   792/.097471   LC 72-90987   ISBN 0393043150

McCarthy, Mary, 1912-. • **2.3228**
Theatre chronicles, 1937–1962 / by Mary McCarthy. — New York: Farrar, Straus, [1963]. -. xxi, 248 p.; 21 cm. — 1. Theater — New York (N.Y.) 2. Drama — History and criticism I. T. II. Title: Sights and spectacles.
PN2277.N5 M22 1963b   792.0973   LC 63-18449

Morehouse, Ward, 1898-. • **2.3229**
Matinee tomorrow: fifty years of our theater / by Ward Morehouse. — New York: Whittlesey House, c1949. xii, 340 p.: ill. 1. Theater — New York (City) — History. I. T.
PN2277.N5 M55   LC 49-11261

Odell, George Clinton Densmore, 1866-1949. • **2.3230**
Annals of the New York stage. New York, AMS Press [1970, c1927-49] 15 v. illus., map, ports. 27 cm. 1. Theater — New York (N.Y.) — History. I. T.
PN2277.N5 O4 1970   792/.097471   LC 77-116018   ISBN 0404078303

Pollock, Thomas Clark, 1902-. • **2.3231**
The Philadelphia theatre in the eighteenth century, together with the Day book of the same period. — New York: Greenwood Press, 1968 [c1933] xviii, 445 p.: facsim.; 24 cm. 1. Theater — Pennsylvania — Philadelphia. I. T.
PN2277.P5 P6 1968   792/.09748/11   LC 69-10147

Wood, William Burke, 1779-1861. • **2.3232**
Old Drury of Philadelphia; a history of the Philadelphia stage, 1800–1835 [edited by Reese D. James. — New York: Greenwood Press, 1968 [c1932] xv, 694 p.: illus.; 24 cm. Consists chiefly of the diary or daily account book of W. B. Wood, co-manager with W. Warren of the Chesnut Street Theatre, during the theatre company's annual appearances in Philadelphia, Baltimore, Washington, and Alexandria from June 18, 1810, to Feb. 21, 1835. 1. Chestnut Street Theatre (Philadelphia, Pa.) 2. Theater — Pennsylvania — Philadelphia. I. James, Reese Davis, 1889- ed. II. Chestnut Street Theatre (Philadelphia, Pa.) III. T.
PN2277.P52 C5 1968   792/.09748/11   LC 69-10108

PN2285–2286 COLLECTIVE BIOGRAPHY

Alpert, Hollis.   • 2.3233
The Barrymores. — New York: Dial Press, 1964. xviii, 397 p.: ill. 1. Barrymore family I. T.
PN2285.A45   LC 64-20278

Contemporary theatre, film, and television.   2.3234
Vol. 1-   . — Detroit, MI: Gale Research Co., c1984-. v.: ill.; 29 cm. V. 1 ed. by Monica M. O'Donnell. 1. Performing arts — United States — Biography — Dictionaries. 2. Performing arts — Great Britain — Biography — Dictionaries. I. Gale Research Company.
PN2285.C58   791/.092/2 B 19   LC 84-649371

Kotsilibas-Davis, James.   2.3235
The Barrymores: the royal family in Hollywood / by James Kotsilibas-Davis. — 1st ed. — New York: Crown Publishers, c1980. 376 p.: ill.; 25 cm. Includes index. 1. Barrymore family. 2. Motion picture actors and actresses — United States — Biography. I. T.
PN2285.K74   791.43/028/0922 B   LC 80-18597   ISBN 0517528967

Producers on producing / Stephen Langley, ed.   2.3236
1st ed. — New York: Drama Book Specialist, c1976. 341 p.: ports.; 24 cm. A series of interviews with theatrical producers. 1. Theatrical producers and directors — United States — Interviews. I. Langley, Stephen.
PN2285.P7   792/.0232/0922   LC 75-26817   ISBN 0910482683

Rigdon, Walter, ed.   • 2.3237
The biographical encyclopaedia & who's who of the American theatre. Introd. by George Freedley. — [1st ed.]. — New York: J. H. Heineman, [1966, c1965] xiv, 1101 p.; 29 cm. 1. Theater — United States — Biography — Dictionaries. I. T.
PN2285.R5   792.0922 B   LC 65-19390

Mitchell, Loften.   2.3238
Voices of the Black theatre / by Loften Mitchell. — Clifton, N.J.: J. T. White, [1975] ix, 238 p.: ill.; 24 cm. Contains taped individual recollections of Black theatrical figures with introductory essays and comments by L. Mitchell. Includes index. 1. Theater — United States 2. Afro-American actors 3. American drama — Afro-American authors — History and criticism. I. T.
PN2286.M5   792/.028/0922   LC 74-30081   ISBN 0883710064

PN2287 INDIVIDUAL BIOGRAPHY

Kinne, Wisner Payne.   • 2.3239
George Pierce Baker and the American theatre. — New York: Greenwood Press, 1968 [c1954] xiv, 348 p.: illus., ports.; 24 cm. 1. Baker, George Pierce, 1866-1935. 2. Drama — Study and teaching 3. American drama — 20th century — History and criticism. 4. Theater — United States. I. T.
PN2287.B15 K5 1968   792/.0924   LC 68-8741

Barrymore, Ethel, 1879-1959.   • 2.3240
Memories, an autobiography. — [1st ed.]. — New York: Harper, [1955] 310 p.: illus.; 22 cm. 1. Barrymore, Ethel, 1879-1959. 2. Actors — Correspondence, reminiscences, etc. I. T.
PN2287.B3 A3   927.92   LC 55-6565

Fowler, Gene, 1890-1960.   • 2.3241
Good night, sweet prince, by Gene Fowler. — New York: The Viking press, 1944. xvi, 477 p.: plates, port.; 22 cm. At head of title: The life & times of John Barrymore. 'First published ... January, 1944 ... Sixth printing February, 1944.' 1. Barrymore, John, 1882-1942. I. T.
PN2287.B35 F6 1944a   927.92   LC 44-4430

Barrymore, Lionel, 1878-1954.   • 2.3242
We Barrymores, by Lionel Barrymore, as told to Cameron Shipp. New York, Appleton-Century-Crofts [1951] vii, 311 p. illus., ports., geneal. table (on lining papers) 21 cm. 1. Actors — Correspondence, reminiscences, etc. I. Shipp, Cameron. II. T.
PN2287.B37 A3   LC 51-10470

Kotsilibas-Davis, James.   2.3243
Great times, good times: the odyssey of Maurice Barrymore / James Kotsilibas-Davis. — 1st ed. — Garden City, N.Y.: Doubleday, 1977. 538 p.: ill., ports. Includes index. 1. Barrymore, Maurice, 1849-1905. 2. Actors — United States — Biography. I. T.
PN2287.B35 K6   PN2287B38 K6.   792/.028/0924 B   LC 72-76182   ISBN 0385049536

Marker, Lise-Lone, 1934-.   2.3244
David Belasco; naturalism in the American theatre. — [Princeton, N.J.]: Princeton University press, [1974, c1975] xiv, 248 p.: illus.; 23 cm. 1. Belasco, David, 1853-1931. I. T.
PN2287.B4 M37   PN2287B4 M37.   792/.0233/0924   LC 74-2970   ISBN 0691046263

Timberlake, Craig.   • 2.3245
The Bishop of Broadway: the life & work of David Belasco / by Craig Timberlake. — New York: Library Publishers, c1954. 491 p.: ill., ports. 1. Belasco, David, 1853-1931. 2. Theater — United States I. T.
PN2287.B4 T5   927.92   LC 54-11646

Ruggles, Eleanor, 1916-.   • 2.3246
Prince of players: Edwin Booth. — [1st ed.]. — New York: Norton, [c1953] xii, 401 p.: illus., ports.; 22 cm. 1. Booth, Edwin, 1833-1893. I. T.
PN2287.B5 R9   927.92   LC 53-5986

Chaplin, Charlie, 1889-1977.   2.3247
My life in pictures / by Charles Chaplin; designed by David King; introd. by Francis Wyndham. — New York: Grosset & Dunlap, 1975, 1978 printing, c1974. 310, [10] p.: chiefly ill. (some col.); 29 cm. 1. Chaplin, Charlie, 1889-1977 — Portraits. 2. Motion picture actors and actresses — United States — Portraits. I. T.
PN2287.C5 A35 1975   791.43/028/0924   LC 75-18583   ISBN 0448120372. ISBN 0448148382 pbk

McCabe, John, 1920-.   2.3248
Charlie Chaplin / John McCabe. — 1st ed. — Garden City, N.Y.: Doubleday, 1978. xii, 297 p., [8] leaves of plates: ill.; 22 cm. Includes index. 1. Chaplin, Charlie, 1889-1977. 2. Motion picture actors and actresses — United States — Biography. 3. Comedians — United States — Biography. I. T.
PN2287.C5 M2   791.43/028/0924 B   LC 77-11771   ISBN 0385114451

Manvell, Roger, 1909-.   2.3249
Chaplin. — [1st ed.]. — Boston: Little Brown, [1974] ix, 240 p.: ill.; 21 cm. — (The Library of world biography) 1. Chaplin, Charlie, 1889-1977. I. T.
PN2287.C5 M28   791.43/028/0924 B   LC 74-13119   ISBN 0316545503

Sobel, Raoul.   2.3250
Chaplin: genesis of a clown / Raoul Sobel and David Francis. — London: Quartet Books, 1978 (c1977). 253 p.: ill., ports.; 23 cm. 1. Motion picture actors and actresses — United States — Biography. I. Francis, David. II. T.
PN2287.C5 S7   791.43028   ISBN 070432150X

Morehouse, Ward, 1898-1966.   2.3251
George M. Cohan, prince of the American theater. Westport, Conn., Greenwood Press [1972, c1943] 240 p. illus. 22 cm. 1. Cohan, George M. (George Michael), 1878-1942. I. T.
PN2287.C56 M6 1972   792/.092/4 B   LC 79-165445   ISBN 0837162254

Leach, Joseph.   • 2.3252
Bright particular star; the life & times of Charlotte Cushman. New Haven, Yale University Press, 1970. xvi, 453 p. illus., facsim., ports. 24 cm. 1. Cushman, Charlotte, 1816-1876. I. T.
PN2287.C8 L4   792/.028/0924 B   LC 76-99829   ISBN 0300012055

Felheim, Marvin, 1914-.   • 2.3253
The theater of Augustin Daly; an account of the late nineteenth century American stage. — New York: Greenwood Press, [1969, c1956] ix, 329 p.: illus., ports.; 23 cm. 1. Daly, Augustin, 1838-1899. 2. Theater — U.S. — History. I. T.
PN2287.D254 F4 1969   792/.0924 B   LC 77-90503   ISBN 0837122090

Binns, Archie, 1899-.   • 2.3254
Mrs. Fiske and the American theatre, by Archie Binns, in collaboration with Olive Kooken. New York, Crown Publishers [1955] x, 436 p. illus., ports., facsim. 22 cm. 1. Fiske, Minnie Maddern, 1865-1932. 2. Theater — United States — History. I. T.
PN2287.F5 B5   927.92   LC 55-10173

Moody, Richard, 1911-.   • 2.3255
Edwin Forrest: first star of the American stage / by Richard Moody. — 1st ed. — New York: A.A. Knopf, 1960. xi, 415, [1], xi p.: ill., ports. 1. Forrest, Edwin, 1806-1872. 2. Actors — United States — Biography. I. T.
PN2287.F6 M57   LC 60-6648

Gregory, Dick.   2.3256
Up from Nigger / Dick Gregory with James R. McGraw. — New York: Stein and Day, 1976. 256 p.: ill.; 24 cm. Includes index. 1. Gregory, Dick. 2. Afro-Americans — Civil rights I. McGraw, James R. joint author. II. T.
PN2287.G68 A37   818/.5/409 B   LC 75-12817   *ISBN* 0812818326

Houseman, John.   2.3257
Final dress / John Houseman. — New York: Simon and Schuster, c1983. 559 p., [32] p. of plates: ill., ports.; 22 cm. Continues: Front and center. Includes index. 1. Houseman, John. 2. Theatrical producers and directors — United States — Biography. I. T.
PN2287.H7 A26 1983   792/.023/0924 B 19   LC 83-423   *ISBN* 0671420313

Houseman, John.   2.3258
Front and center / John Houseman. — New York: Simon and Schuster, c1979. 512 p., [24] leaves of plates: ill.; 22 cm. Continued by: Final dress. 1. Houseman, John. 2. Theatrical producers and directors — United States — Biography. I. T.
PN2287.H7 A295   792/.023/0924 B   LC 79-17482   *ISBN* 0671243284

Houseman, John.   2.3259
Run–through: a memoir / by John Houseman. — New York: Simon and Schuster, 1972. 507 p.: ill.; 23 cm. 'Portions of this work have appeared in Audience.' 1. Houseman, John. 2. Theatrical producers and directors — United States — Biography. I. T.
PN2287.H7 A3   792/.0232/0924 B   LC 70-179582   *ISBN* 0671413902

Lahr, John, 1941–.   • 2.3260
Notes on a cowardly lion; the biography of Bert Lahr. [1st ed.] New York, Knopf, 1969. x, 394 p. illus., ports. 25 cm. 1. Lahr, Bert, 1895-1967. 2. Entertainers — United States — Biography. I. T.
PN2287.L15 L3 1969   791/.0924 B   LC 78-79344

Schickel, Richard.   2.3261
Harold Lloyd: the shape of laughter / Richard Schickel. — Boston: New York Graphic Society, 1974. 218 p.: ill.; 29 cm. 'Filmography, by Eileen Bowser': p. [216]-[217] 1. Lloyd, Harold, 1894-1971. I. T.
PN2287.L5 S3   791.43/028/0924 B   LC 73-89958   *ISBN* 0821205951

Prince, Hal.   2.3262
Contradictions: notes on twenty–six years in the theatre / Hal Prince. — New York: Dodd, Mead, [1974] x, 242 p., [4] leaves of plates: ill.; 22 cm. Includes index. 1. Prince, Hal. I. T.
PN2287.P73 A33   PN2287P73 A33.   792/.023/0924   LC 74-10399   *ISBN* 0396070191

Rogers, Will, 1879-1935.   • 2.3263
Autobiography: selected and edited by Donald Day, with a foreword by Bill and Jim Rogers. Boston, Houghton Mifflin Co., 1949. xvii, 410 p. port. 21 cm. 1. Rogers, Will, 1879-1935. 2. Humorists, American — Biography. I. Day, Donald, 1899- ed. II. T.
PN2287.R74 A3   928.1   LC 49-11206

Seldes, Marian.   2.3264
The bright lights: a theatre life / Marian Seldes. — Boston: Houghton Mifflin, 1978. vii, 280 p.: ill., ports. 1. Seldes, Marian. 2. Actresses — United States — Biography. I. T.
PN2287.S346 A32   PN2287S346 A32.   792/.028/0924 B   LC 78-17221   *ISBN* 0395264812

PN2289 DIRECTORIES. GUIDEBOOKS

The Lively arts information directory / Steven R. Wasserman and Jacqueline Wasserman O'Brien, editors.   2.3265
2nd ed. — Detroit, Mich.: Gale Research Co., c1985. xi, 1040 p.; 29 cm. 'A guide to the fields of music, dance, theater, film, radio, and television in the United States and Canada, covering professional and trade organizations, arts agencies, government grant sources, foundations, educational programs, journals and periodicals, consultants, special libraries, research and information centers, festivals, awards, and book and media publishers.' Includes indexes. 1. Performing arts — United States — Directories. 2. Performing arts — Canada — Directories. I. Wasserman, Steven R. II. O'Brien, Jacqueline Wasserman.
PN2289.L55 1985   790.2/025/73 19   LC 85-6949   *ISBN* 0810303213

PN2291–2297 MANAGEMENT. PRODUCTION

Bernheim, Alfred L., 1893–.   • 2.3266
The business of the theatre; an economic history of the American theatre, 1750–1932. Prepared on behalf of the Actors' Equity Association by Alfred L. Bernheim, assisted by Sara Harding and the staff of the Labor Bureau, inc. — New York: B. Blom, [1964] xii, 217 p.; 33 cm. First published in Equity magazine, July 1930-Feb. 1932. 1. Theater 2. Theater — United States I. Actors' Equity Association. II. T.
PN2291.B4 1964   792.0973   LC 64-14693

Farber, Donald C.   2.3267
From option to opening / Donald C. Farber. — 3d rev. ed. — New York: Drama Book Specialists, [1977] 144 p. 1. Theater — Production and direction 2. Off-Broadway theater I. T.
PN2291.F3 1977   PN2291 F3 1977.   792/.02   LC 76-58845   *ISBN* 0910482802

Langley, Stephen.   2.3268
Theatre management in America: principle and practice: producing for the commercial, stock, resident, college, and community theatre / Stephen Langley. — Rev. ed. — New York: Drama Book Specialists, c1980. xv, 490 p.: ill.; 25 cm. Edition statement also appears as: Second edition. Includes index. 1. Theater management — United States. I. T.
PN2291.L3 1980   658/.91/7920973   LC 79-26028

Moore, Thomas Gale.   • 2.3269
The economics of the American theater. — Durham, N.C.: Duke University Press, 1968. xv, 192 p.: illus.; 24 cm. 1. Theater — United States — Economic aspects. I. T.
PN2291.M6   338.4/7/7920973   LC 68-28521

Graham, Philip, 1898–.   • 2.3270
Showboats; the history of an American institution. — Austin: University of Texas Press, 1951. x, 224 p.: illus., ports.; 24 cm. 1. Showboats I. T.
PN2293.S4 G7   792   LC 51-14160

Eaton, Walter Prichard, 1878-1957.   • 2.3271
The Theatre Guild; the first ten years, by Walter Prichard Eaton. With articles by the directors. — Freeport, N.Y.: Books for Libraries Press, [1970] 299 p.: illus.; 23 cm. Reprint of the 1929 ed. 1. Theatre Guild. I. T.
PN2295.T5 E3 1970   792/.0973   LC 75-107799   *ISBN* 0836951808

Waldau, Roy S.   2.3272
Vintage years of the Theatre Guild, 1928–1939 [by] Roy S. Waldau. — Cleveland: Press of Case Western Reserve University, 1972. xiv, 519 p.: illus.; 24 cm. 1. Theatre Guild. I. T.
PN2295.T5 W3   792/.0973   LC 79-141463   *ISBN* 0829502033

Clurman, Harold, 1901–.   • 2.3273
The fervent years; the story of the Group Theatre and the thirties. — New York: Hill and Wang, [1957] 302 p.; 19 cm. — (A Dramabook, D8) 1. Group Theatre. 2. Theater — United States I. T.
PN2297.G7 C5 1957   LC 57-7910

Deutsch, Helen.   • 2.3274
The Provincetown; a story of the theatre, by Helen Deutsch and Stella Hanau. — New York: Russell & Russell, [1972, c1931] xvi, 313 p.: illus.; 23 cm. 1. Provincetown Players. I. Hanau, Stella, joint author. II. T.
PN2297.P7 D4 1972   792/.09744/92   LC 79-173532

Sarlós, Robert Károly, 1931–.   2.3275
Jig Cook and the Provincetown Players: theatre in ferment / Robert Károly Sarlós. — Amherst: University of Massachusetts Press, c1982. xii, 265 p.: ill.; 25 cm. Includes index. 1. Cook, George Cram, 1873-1924. 2. Provincetown Players. 3. Theater — Massachusetts — Provincetown — History — 20th century. 4. Theater — New York (N.Y.) — History — 20th century. 5. American drama — 20th century — History and criticism. I. T.
PN2297.P7 S27 1982   792/.09744/92 19   LC 81-16104   *ISBN* 0870233491

Davis, R. G.   2.3276
The San Francisco mime troupe: the first ten years / R. G. Davis; introd. by Robert Scheer. — 1st ed. — Palo Alto, Calif.: Ramparts Press, c1975. 220 p.: ill.; 21 cm. Includes index. 1. San Francisco Mime Troupe. 2. Mime I. T.
PN2297.S25 D3   LC 74-19934   *ISBN* 0878670580

PN2300–2309 Canada. Latin America

Evans, Chad, 1951–.   2.3277
Frontier theatre: a history of nineteenth century theatrical entertainment in the Canadian Far West and Alaska / Chad Evans. — Victoria, B.C.: Sono Nis, 1983. 326 p., 20 p. of plates: ill. 1. Theater — British Columbia — History —

19th century. 2. Theater — Yukon Territory — History — 19th century. 3. Theater — Alaska — History — 19th century. I. T.
PN2305B7 E8   792/.09711 19   *ISBN* 0919203248

Jones, Willis Knapp, 1895-.   **2.3278**
Behind Spanish American footlights. — Austin: University of Texas Press, [1966] xvi, 609 p.; 24 cm. 1. Theater — Latin America — History. I. T.
PN2309.J59   792.098   *LC* 65-11145

PN2570 Europe: General

Macgowan, Kenneth, 1888-1963.   • **2.3279**
Continental stagecraft [by] Kenneth Macgowan [and] Robert Edmond Jones. — New York: B. Blom, [1964] xvi, 233 p.: plates.; 24 cm. 1. Theaters — Stage-setting and scenery 2. Theater — Europe. 3. Theaters — Europe. I. Jones, Robert Edmond, 1887-1954. joint author. II. T.
PN2570.M3 1964   792.094   *LC* 64-14711

Quigley, Austin E., 1942-.   **2.3280**
The modern stage and other worlds / Austin E. Quigley. — New York: Methuen, 1985. xvi, 294 p.; 24 cm. Includes index. 1. European drama — 19th century — History and criticism. 2. European drama — 20th century — History and criticism. 3. Theater I. T.
PN2570.Q54 1985   809.2 19   *LC* 84-20759   *ISBN* 0416393101

PN2575-2609 Britain

Nicoll, Allardyce, 1894-.   • **2.3281**
The English theatre; a short history. — Westport, Conn.: Greenwood Press, [1970] xi, 252 p.: illus.; 23 cm. Reprint of the 1936 ed. Based on the author's The English stage. 1. Theater — England — History. I. T.
PN2581.N5 1970   792/.09421   *LC* 75-98861   *ISBN* 0837131332

PN2585-2595 SPECIAL PERIODS

Bridges-Adams, William, 1889-1965.   • **2.3282**
The irresistible theatre / W. Bridges-Adams. — Cleveland: World Pub. Co., [1957] xiv, 446 p.: illus., ports., facsims., plans.; 23 cm. 1. Theater — England — History. 2. English drama — History and criticism. I. T.
PN2585.B7   792.0942   *LC* 57-9279

Thaler, Alwin, 1891-.   • **2.3283**
Shakspere to Sheridan: a book about the theatre of yesterday and to-day / by Alwin Thaler; with ill. from the Harvard Theatre Collection. — New York: B. Blom, 1963. xviii, 339 p.: ill., facsims., ports. 1. Theater — England — History 2. English drama — History and criticism 3. Actors — England 4. London (England) — Theaters I. T.
PN2585.T5 1963   *LC* 63-23190

Southern, Richard.   **2.3284**
The medieval theatre in the round: a study of the staging of The castle of perseverance and related matters / by Richard Southern. — Rev. and expanded ed. — New York: Theatre Arts Books, 1975. xxi, 264 p., fold. leaf, leaf of plate, 4 p. of plates. : ill. 1. Theater — Great Britain — History. 2. Theaters — Great Britain — Stage-setting and scenery. 3. Castle of perseverance (Morality play). 4. Arena theater I. T.
PN2587.S6 1975   *ISBN* 0878300856

Wickham, Glynne William Gladstone.   • **2.3285**
Early English stages, 1300 to 1660. London, Routledge and Paul; New York, Columbia University Press, 1959-<1981 >. <v. 1-3 in 4 > illus., plates, map, plans. 26 cm. 1. Theater — England — History. 2. Theaters — Stage-setting and scenery I. T.
PN2587.W53   792/.0941   *LC* 59-2245   *ISBN* 0231089376

Adams, Joseph Quincy, 1881-1946.   • **2.3286**
Shakespearean playhouses: a history of English theatres from the beginnings to the Restoration / by Joseph Quincy Adams. — Gloucester, Mass.: P. Smith, 1960, [c1917]. 473 p.: ill.; 21 cm. 1. Shakespeare, William, 1564-1616 — Stage history — To 1625 2. Theater — England — History. 3. London (England) — Theaters. I. T.
PN2589.A3 1960   PN2596.L6 A55 1960.   *LC* 61-908

Bentley, Gerald Eades, 1901-.   **2.3287**
The profession of player in Shakespeare's time, 1590-1642 / Gerald Eades Bentley. — Princeton, N.J.: Princeton University Press, c1984. xiv, 315 p.; 23 cm. 1. Theater — England — History. 2. Actors — England. I. T.
PN2589.B46 1984   792/.028/0942 19   *LC* 83-43059   *ISBN* 0691065969

Chambers, E. K. (Edmund Kerchever), 1866-1954.   • **2.3288**
The Elizabethan stage, by E. K. Chambers ... Oxford, The Clarendon press, 1923. 4 v. fronts., illus (incl. plans) 23 cm. 1. Shakespeare, William, 1564-1616 — Stage history — To 1625 2. Theater — England — History. 3. Theaters — England — London. 4. English drama — Early modern and Elizabethan, 1500-1600 — History and criticism. 5. Actors, English. I. T.
PN2589.C4   792.0942   *LC* 24-4078

Craik, T. W. (Thomas Wallace)   • **2.3289**
The Tudor interlude: stage, costume, and acting. — Leicester: University Press, 1958. 158 p., [6] leaves of plates.; 22 cm. Includes index. 1. Theater — England — History. 2. English drama — Early modern and Elizabethan, 1500-1600 — History and criticism. I. T.
PN2589.C7   822.309   *LC* 59-398

Foakes, R. A.   **2.3290**
Illustrations of the English stage, 1580–1642 / R.A. Foakes. — Stanford, Calif.: Stanford University Press, 1985. xviii, 180 p.: ill.; 31 cm. 1. Shakespeare, William, 1564-1616 — Stage history — To 1625 2. Theater — Great Britain — History — 16th century — Sources. 3. Theater — Great Britain — History — 17th century — Sources. 4. Theaters — England — Pictorial works. 5. English drama — Early modern and Elizabethan, 1500-1600 — Illustrations. 6. English drama — 17th century — Illustrations. 7. Drawing, Renaissance — England. 8. London (England) — Description — Views. I. T.
PN2589.F6 1985   792/.0941 19   *LC* 83-40517   *ISBN* 0804712360

Lawrence, William John, 1862-1940.   • **2.3291**
The physical conditions of the Elizabethan public playhouse. — New York: Cooper Square Publishers, 1968. viii, 129 p.: illus.; 23 cm. Reprint of the 1927 ed. 1. Shakespeare, William, 1564-1616 — Stage history — To 1625 2. Theaters — Great Britain. 3. Theater — London — History. I. T.
PN2589.L35 1968   792.09   *LC* 68-31297

Murray, John Tucker.   • **2.3292**
English dramatic companies, 1558–1642. — New York: Russell & Russell, 1963. 2 v.: map, tables.; 22 cm. 1. Theater — Great Britain — History. I. T.
PN2589.M8 1963   792.0942   *LC* 63-15174

Southern, Richard.   **2.3293**
The staging of plays before Shakespeare. — New York: Theatre Arts Books, 1973. 603 p.: ill.; 26 cm. 1. Theater — England — History. 2. Interludes, English — History and criticism. I. T.
PN2589.S6 1973b   PN2589 S6 1973.   792/.0942   *LC* 73-76707   *ISBN* 0878301305

Campbell, Lily Bess, 1883-1967.   • **2.3294**
Scenes and machines on the English stage during the renaissance, a classical revival. Cambridge: University Press, 1923. 302p. 1. Theaters — Stage-setting and scenery 2. Theater — Great Britain — History 3. Theaters — Great Britain. I. T.
PN2590 S7 C3   *LC* 23-18967

King, Thomas James, 1925-.   **2.3295**
Shakespearean staging, 1599–1642 [by] T. J. King. — Cambridge, Mass., Harvard University Press, 1971. xii, 163 p. illus., facsim., plans. 24 cm. 1. Theater — England — History. 2. Stage directions 3. Theaters — Stage-setting and scenery — History. I. T.
PN2590.S7 K5   792/.025   *LC* 77-127880   *ISBN* 0674804902

Great Britain. Office of the Revels.   • **2.3296**
The dramatic records of Sir Henry Herbert, master of Revels, 1623–1673 / edited by Joseph Quincy Adams. — New York: B. Blom, [1964?] xiii, 155 p.: facsim., port.; 24 cm. Includes index. 1. Theater — Great Britain — History. I. Herbert, Henry, Sir, 1595-1673. II. Adams, Joseph Quincy, 1881-1946. III. T.
PN2592.A5 1964   *LC* 63-23180

Bentley, Gerald Eades, 1901-.   • **2.3297**
The Jacobean and Caroline stage. — Oxford: Clarendon Press, 1941-68. 7 v.; 23 cm. 1. Theater — England — History. 2. Theater — London — History. 3. English drama — Early modern and Elizabethan — History and criticism. 4. Actors, English. I. T.
PN2592.B4   792.0942   *LC* a 41-3671

Gurr, Andrew.   **2.3298**
The Shakespearean stage, 1574–1642. — Cambridge [Eng.] University Press, 1970. ix, 192 p. illus., plans, ports. 22 cm. 1. Theater — England — History. I. T.
PN2592.G8   792/.0942   *LC* 72-116747   *ISBN* 521078164

Hotson, Leslie, 1897-.   • **2.3299**
The Commonwealth and Restoration stage. New York, Russell & Russell, 1962 [c1928] 424 p. illus. 23 cm. 1. Theater — England — London — History. 2. Theaters — England — London. 3. Actors — England — London. I. T. II. Title: Restoration stage.
PN2592.H6 1962   792.094212   *LC* 62-10686

Schneider, Ben Ross, 1920-. 2.3300
Index to The London stage, 1660–1800 / compiled, with an introd. by Ben Ross Schneider, Jr.; foreword by George Winchester Stone, Jr. — Carbondale: Southern Illinois University Press, c1979. xx, 939 p.; 28 cm. 1. The London stage, 1660-1800 — Indexes. 2. Performing arts — England — London — History — Indexes. 3. London (England) — History — Indexes. I. T.
PN2592.L63 S3   792/.09421   *LC* 79-102595   *ISBN* 0809309076

The London theatre world, 1660–1800 / edited by Robert D. 2.3301
Hume.
Carbondale: Southern Illinois University Press, c1980. xix, 394 p.: ill.; 24 cm. 'Dedicated to A. H. Scouten on the occasion of his seventieth birthday.' Includes index. 1. Scouten, Arthur Hawley, 1910- 2. Theater — England — London — History. 3. English drama — Restoration, 1660-1700 — History and criticism. 4. English drama — 18th century — History and criticism. I. Hume, Robert D. II. Scouten, Arthur Hawley, 1910-
PN2592.L64   792/.09421   *LC* 79-20410   *ISBN* 0809309262

McCollum, John I. • 2.3302
The Restoration stage. — Boston: Houghton Mifflin, 1961. 236 p. , 25 cm. — (Houghton Mifflin Research series; 8) 1. Theater — England — History. 2. English drama — Restoration, 1660-1700 — History and criticism. I. T.
PN2592.M25   *LC* 61-2469

Orgel, Stephen. 2.3303
The illusion of power: political theater in the English Renaissance / [by] Stephen Orgel. Berkeley [etc.]; London: University of California Press, 1975. [1], xi, 95 p.: ill., plans; 21 cm. (Quantum books.) ISBN 0-520-02741-8 Pbk: £1.75. 1. Theater — England — History. I. T. II. Series.
PN2592.O7x   792/.0942   *LC* 73-80827   *ISBN* 0520025059

Summers, Montague, 1880-1948. • 2.3304
The restoration theatre. — New York, Humanities Press, 1964. xxi, 352 p. 24 plates (incl. facsims., plan, ports) 24 cm. 'First published 1934 ... Reprinted 1964.' Appendices (p. 297-329): I. A reprint of Robert Gould's The play-house, a satyr.—II. A reprint of chapter v of Vincent's Young gallant's academy, 1674: Instructions for a young gallant how to behave himself in the play-house.—III. The Phoenix Society for the Production of Old Plays. 1. Theater — England — Hist. 2. English drama — Restoration — Hist. & crit. I. Gould, Robert, d. 1709? II. T.
PN2592.S86 1964   792.0942   *LC* 64-14679

Wilson, John Harold, 1900-. • 2.3305
A preface to Restoration drama. — Boston: Houghton Mifflin, 1965. vii, 208 p.; 21 cm. — (Riverside studies in literature; L6) 1. Theater — England — History. 2. English drama — Restoration — History and criticism. I. T.
PN2592.W52   792.0942   *LC* 65-29523

PN2593–2595 18th, 19th, 20th Centuries

Manchester Symposium on Theatre, 2d, 1971. 2.3306
Essays on the eighteenth–century English stage: the proceedings of a symposium sponsored by the Manchester University Department of Drama; edited by Kenneth Richards and Peter Thomson. London, Methuen, 1972. 195, [8] p. illus., map, music. 23 cm. 'Distributed in the U.S.A. by Harper & Row Publishers, Inc., Barnes and Noble Import Division.' 1. Theater — England — History — Congresses. I. Richards, Kenneth Roland, ed. II. Thomson, Peter, 1938- ed. III. Victoria University of Manchester. Dept. of Drama. IV. T. V. Title: The eighteenth-century English stage.
PN2593.M3 1971   792/.0942   *LC* 73-155446   *ISBN* 0416756409

Nicoll, Allardyce, 1894-. 2.3307
The Garrick stage: theatres and audience in the eighteenth century / Allardyce Nicoll; edited by Sybil Rosenfeld. — Athens: University of Georgia Press, c1980. viii, 184 p.: ill.; 25 cm. 1. Garrick, David, 1717-1779. 2. Theater — England — History. I. Rosenfeld, Sybil Marion, 1903- II. T.
PN2593.N5 1980b   792/.0942 19   *LC* 80-145062   *ISBN* 0820305103

Booth, Michael R. 2.3308
Victorian spectacular theatre, 1850–1910 / Michael R. Booth. — Boston: Routledge & Kegan Paul, c1981. ix, 190 p., [16] p. of plates: ill.; 24 cm. (Theatre production studies.) Includes index. 1. Theater — Great Britain — History — 19th century. I. T. II. Title: Spectacular theatre. III. Series.
PN2594.B6 1981   792/.0941 19   *LC* 80-41729   *ISBN* 0710007396

Rowell, George. 2.3309
Theatre in the age of Irving / George Rowell. — Totowa, N.J.: Rowman and Littlefield, 1981. x, 189 p.: ill.; 25 cm. — (Drama and theatre studies.) Includes index. 1. Irving, Henry, Sir, 1838-1905. 2. Theater — England — History — 19th century. I. T. II. Series.
PN2594.R648   792/.0942 19   *LC* 81-149744   *ISBN* 0847670465

Rowell, George. • 2.3310
The Victorian theatre, 1792–1914: a survey / by George Rowell. — 2d ed. — Cambridge [Eng.]; New York: Cambridge University Press, 1978. xiii, 239 p., [8] leaves of plates: ill.; 23 cm. Includes index. 1. Theater — England — History — 19th century. 2. English drama — 19th century — History and criticism. 3. Theater — England — Bibliography. I. T.
PN2594.R65 1978   792/.0941   *LC* 78-2900   *ISBN* 052122070X

Southern, Richard. • 2.3311
The Victorian theatre; a pictorial survey. — New York: Theatre Arts Books, [1970] 112 p.: illus. (part col.), ports.; 26 cm. 1. Theater — Gt. Brit. — History. I. T.
PN2594.S6   792/.0942   *LC* 70-129989

Stokes, J. (John) 2.3312
Resistible theatres: enterprise and experiment in the late nineteenth century. New York: Barnes and Noble, 1972. 203p.,illus.,bibl. 1. Theater — England — History. I. T.
PN2594.S7 1972   *ISBN* 0064965686

Trewin, J. C. (John Courtenay), 1908-. 2.3313
The Edwardian theatre / J. C. Trewin. — Totowa, N.J.: Rowman and Littlefield, 1976. xiv, 193 p., [8] leaves of plates: ill.; 22 cm. (Drama and theatre studies) 1. Theater — Great Britain — History. 2. English drama — 20th century — History and criticism. I. T.
PN2595.T694   792/.0941   *LC* 76-13878   *ISBN* 0874718473

PN2596 SPECIAL CITIES

Agate, James, 1877-1947. comp. • 2.3314
Those were the nights. New York, B. Blom [1969] ix, 145 p. ports. 24 cm. 'First published 1947.' 1. Theater — England — London. 2. Actors, English — London. I. T.
PN2596.L6 A63 1969   792/.09421   *LC* 77-91890

Beerbohm, Max, Sir, 1872-1956. • 2.3315
Around theatres. — New York: Greenwood Press, [1968, c1930] xvi, 583 p.; 24 cm. 1. Theater — London — Reviews. I. T.
PN2596.L6 B4 1968   792/.09421   *LC* 69-13814

Hughes, Leo, 1908-. 2.3316
The drama's patrons; a study of the eighteenth–century London audience. — Austin: University of Texas Press, [1971] viii, 209 p.; 24 cm. 1. Theater — London — History. 2. Theater audiences — London. I. T.
PN2596.L6 H8   792   *LC* 74-146971   *ISBN* 0292700911

Mander, Raymond. • 2.3317
The theatres of London / by Raymond Mander and Joe Mitchenson; foreword by Ian Albery. — New ed. revised and enlarged. — London: New English Library, 1975. xv, 344 p.: ill., map; 22 cm. 1. Theaters — England — London. 2. Theater — England — London. I. Mitchenson, Joe. joint author. II. T.
PN2596.L6 M35 1975   792/.09421   *LC* 76-366416   *ISBN* 0450021238

Studies in the Elizabethan theatre / edited by Charles T. • 2.3318
Prouty.
[Hamden, Conn.]: Shoe String Press, 1961. xi, 198 p.: ill., plans.; 23 cm. Includes index. 1. Great Britain. Office of the Revels. 2. Theater — England — History 3. London (England) — Theaters. I. Prouty, Charles Tyler, 1909-
PN2596.L6 P7   *LC* 61-9877

Rosenfeld, Sybil Marion, 1903-. • 2.3319
The theatre of the London fairs in the 18th century. — Cambridge [Eng.] University Press, 1960. 194 p. illus. 22 cm. Includes bibliography. 1. Theater — London — Hist. 2. London — Fairs. I. T.
PN2596.L6R6   792.09421   *LC* 60-50866

Shaw, Bernard, 1856-1950. • 2.3320
Plays & players: essays on the theatre / Bernard Shaw; sected, with an introd. by A.C. Ward. — London: Oxford University Press, 1952. xv, 350 p. (The World's classics; 535) 1. Theater — London — History. 2. Drama — History and criticism I. T.
PN2596.L6 S49   *LC* 54-12926

Shaw, Bernard, 1856-1950. • 2.3321
[Prose works. 1971] Shaw's dramatic criticism (1895–98); a selection by John F. Matthews. Westport, Conn., Greenwood Press [1971, c1959] viii, 306 p. 23 cm. 'The present selection ... has been made from contributions to the Saturday review from January 1895 to May 1898.' 1. Theater — England — London — Reviews. I. T.
PN2596.L6 S493 1971   792/.09421   *LC* 77-136084   *ISBN* 0837152348

Vice Chamberlain Coke's theatrical papers, 1706–1715 / edited   **2.3322**
from the manuscripts in the Harvard Theatre Collection and
elsewhere by Judith Milhous and Robert D. Hume.
Carbondale: Southern Illinois University Press, c1982. xlii, 274 p.; 24 cm.
Includes index. 1. Theater — England — London — History — 18th century
— Sources. 2. Opera — England — London — Sources. I. Coke, Thomas,
1674-1727. II. Milhous, Judith. III. Hume, Robert D.
PN2596.L6 V5   792/.09421/2 19   LC 81-5616   ISBN 0809310244

Watson, Ernest Bradlee, 1879-.   • **2.3323**
Sheridan to Robertson; a study of the nineteenth–century London stage. —
New York, B. Blom [1963] xix, 485 p. plates, ports., fold. map, facsims. 24 cm.
Bibliography: p. [449]-455. 1. Theater — London. 2. Actors, English.
3. English drama — 19th cent. — Hist. & crit. 4. London — Theaters. I. T.
PN2596.L6W3 1963   792.09421   LC 63-23191

Wearing, J. P.   **2.3324**
The London stage, 1890–1899: a calendar of plays and players / by J. P.
Wearing. — Metuchen, N.J.: Scarecrow Press, 1976. 2 v. (xiii, 1229 p.); 23 cm.
1. Theater — England — London — Calendars. I. T.
PN2596.L6 W37   792/.09421/2   LC 76-1825   ISBN 0810809109

Wearing, J. P.   **2.3325**
The London stage, 1900–1909: a calendar of plays and players / by J.P.
Wearing. — Metuchen, N.J.: Scarecrow Press, 1981. 2 v.; 23 cm. Includes
index. 1. Theater — England — London — Calendars. I. T.
PN2596.L6 W38   792/.09421/2 19   LC 80-28353   ISBN
081081403X

Wearing, J. P.   **2.3326**
The London stage, 1910–1919: a calendar of plays and players / by J.P.
Wearing. — Metuchen, N.J.: Scarecrow Press, 1982. 2 v. (xvi, 1369 p.); 23 cm.
Includes indexes. 1. Theater — England — London — Calendars. I. T.
PN2596.L6 W383 1982   792/.09421/2 19   LC 82-19190   ISBN
0810815966

Wearing, J. P.   **2.3327**
The London stage, 1920–1929: a calendar of plays and players / by J.P.
Wearing. — Metuchen, N.J.: Scarecrow Press, 1984. 3 v.; 23 cm. 1. Theater —
England — Calendars. 2. Theater — England — London —
History — 20th century — Sources. I. T.
PN2596.L6 W384 1984   792/.09421 19   LC 84-10665   ISBN
0810817152

Smith, Irwin, 1892-.   • **2.3328**
Shakespeare's Blackfriars Playhouse: its history and its design / foreword by
James G. McManaway. — [New York]: New York University Press, [1964] xx,
577 p.: ill., maps, plans.; 26 cm. 1. Shakespeare, William, 1564-1616 — Stage
history 2. London. Blackfriars Theatre. I. T.
PN2596.L7 B57   LC 64-16902

At the Royal Court: 25 years of the English Stage Company /   **2.3329**
edited by Richard Findlater.
1st ed. — New York: Grove Press: Distributed by Random House, 1981. 201,
[56] p.: ill.; 25 cm. Includes indexes. 1. Royal Court Theatre. 2. English Stage
Company. I. Findlater, Richard, 1921-
PN2596.L7 R515 1981b   792/.09421/34 19   LC 80-85375   ISBN
0802102115

Arundell, Dennis Drew.   • **2.3330**
The story of Sadler's Wells, 1683–1977 / Dennis Arundell. — 2d extended ed.
— Newton Abbot [Eng.]; North Pomfret, Vt.: David & Charles, 1978. xvi,
352 p., [11] leaves of plates: ill.; 22 cm. 1. Sadler's Wells Theatre, London. I. T.
PN2596.L7 S312   792/.09421/43   LC 78-316129   ISBN
0715376209

Beauman, Sally.   **2.3331**
The Royal Shakespeare Company: a history of ten decades / Sally Beauman. —
Oxford; New York: Oxford University Press, 1982. xii, 388 p., [32] p. of plates:
ill.; 24 cm. Includes index. 1. Shakespeare, William, 1564-1616 — Stage history
2. Royal Shakespeare Company. I. T.
PN2596.S82 R683 1982   792/.09424/89 19   LC 81-16969   ISBN
0192122096

PN2597 Collective Biography

Donaldson, Frances Lonsdale, Lady.   • **2.3332**
The actor–managers [by] Frances Donaldson. — Chicago: Regnery, [c1970]
195 p.: ports.; 23 cm. 1. Actors — Great Britain. I. T.
PN2597.D55 1970   792/.0922   LC 73-124399

Highfill, Philip H.   **2.3333**
A biographical dictionary of actors, actresses, musicians, dancers, managers &
other stage personnel in London, 1660–1800, by Philip H. Highfill, Jr., Kalman
A. Burnim, and Edward A. Langhans. Carbondale, Southern Illinois

University Press [1973-<c1984 >. v. <1-10 > illus. 26 cm. 1. Performing
arts — England — London — Biography. I. Burnim, Kalman A. joint author.
II. Langhans, Edward A. joint author. III. T.
PN2597.H5   790.2/092/2 B   LC 71-157068   ISBN 0809305186

Joseph, Bertram Leon.   • **2.3334**
The tragic actor / by Bertram Joseph. — London: Routledge and Kegan Paul,
1959. xv, 415 p.: ill. 1. Actors, English. 2. Theaters — England — History.
I. T.
PN2597.J6 1959   LC 59-2950

Pearson, Hesketh, 1887-1964.   • **2.3335**
The last actor–managers. With illus. from the Raymond Mander and Joe
Mitchenson Theatre Collection. — Freeport, N.Y.: Books for Libraries Press,
[1971, c1950] xii, 83 p.: illus., ports.; 23 cm. — (Biography index reprint series)
1. Actors — Great Britain. I. T.
PN2597.P4 1971   792/.028/0922 B   LC 77-148225   ISBN
0836980727

PN2598 Individual Biography

Marshall, Herbert, 1906-.   • **2.3336**
Ira Aldridge, the Negro tragedian, by Herbert Marshall and Mildred Stock.
London, Rockliff [c1958] 355 p. illus. 1. Aldridge, Ira Frederick, d. 1867.
I. Stock, Mildred. II. T.
PN2598.A52 M3   792.0942   LC 59-22897

Peters, Margot.   **2.3337**
Mrs. Pat: the life of Mrs. Patrick Campbell / by Margot Peters. — 1st ed. —
New York: Knopf: Distributed by Random House, 1984. 531 p., [44] p. of
plates: ill. (some col.); 24 cm. Includes index. 1. Campbell, Patrick, Mrs.,
1865-1940. 2. Actors — Great Britain — Biography. I. T. II. Title: Mistress
Pat.
PN2598.C23 P47 1984   792/.028/0924 19   LC 83-48860   ISBN
0394521897

Nash, Mary, 1925-.   **2.3338**
The provoked wife: the life and times of Susanna Cibber / Mary Nash. 1st ed.
— Boston: Little, Brown, c1977. xii, 369 p.: ill.; 24 cm. Includes index.
1. Cibber, Susannah Maria Arne, 1714-1766. 2. Actors — Great Britain —
Biography. I. T.
PN2598.C4 N3   792/.028/0924 B   LC 76-30336   ISBN
0316598313

Innes, C. D.   **2.3339**
Edward Gordon Craig / Christopher Innes. — Cambridge [Cambridgeshire];
New York: Cambridge University Press, 1983. xiv, 240 p.: ill.; 24 cm. —
(Directors in perspective.) Includes index. 1. Craig, Edward Gordon,
1872-1966. I. T. II. Series.
PN2598.C85 I56 1983   792/.0233/0924 19   LC 83-1829   ISBN
0521253713

Barton, Margaret, 1897-.   • **2.3340**
Garrick. New York, Macmillan Co., 1949 [c1948] 312 p. illus., ports. 22 cm.
1. Garrick, David, 1717-1779. I. T.
PN2598.G3 B3 1949   927.92   LC 49-8036

Burnim, Kalman A.   • **2.3341**
David Garrick, director. With a foreword by Geo. Winchester Stone, Jr.
[Pittsburgh] University of Pittsburgh Press [1961] 234 p. ill. 24 cm. 1. Garrick,
David, 1717-1779. 2. Shakespeare, William, 1564-1616 — Stage history
3. Drury Lane Theatre. I. T.
PN 2598 G3 B96 1961   LC 61-9392

Price, Cecil John Layton.   **2.3342**
Theatre in the age of Garrick [by] Cecil Price. — Totowa, N.J.: Rowman and
Littlefield, [1973] 212 p.: illus.; 22 cm. — (Drama and theatre studies)
1. Garrick, David, 1717-1779. 2. Performing arts — England — History. I. T.
PN2598.G3 P7   792/.028/0924   LC 73-160784   ISBN 0874711517

Stone, George Winchester, 1907-.   **2.3343**
David Garrick, a critical biography / by George Winchester Stone, Jr. and
George M. Kahrl. — Carbondale: Southern Illinois University Press, c1979. xx,
771 p.: ill.; 24 cm. Includes indexes. 1. Garrick, David, 1717-1779. 2. Actors
— England — Biography. 3. Dramatists, English — 18th century —
Biography. I. Kahrl, George Morrow, 1904- joint author. II. T.
PN2598.G3 S67   792/.028/0924 B   LC 79-9476   ISBN
0809309319

Gielgud, John, Sir, 1904-.   • **2.3344**
Stage directions. New York, Random House [1964, c1963] xiv, 146 p. illus.,
port. 22 cm. 1. Gielgud, John, Sir, 1904- 2. Actors — Great Britain —
Biography. I. T.
PN2598.G45 A33   792   LC 64-1042

Guthrie, Tyrone, Sir, 1900-1971. • **2.3345**
A life in the theatre. — [1st ed.]. — New York: McGraw-Hill, [1959] 357 p.; 22 cm. Autobiography. 1. Guthrie, Tyrone, Sir, 1900-1971. 2. Actors — Correspondence, reminiscences, etc. I. T.
PN2598.G85 A3   927.92   *LC* 59-14450

Irving, Laurence, 1897-. • **2.3346**
Henry Irving: the actor and his world / by his grandson, Laurence Irving. — London: Faber, 1951. 734 p.: ill., ports.; 24 cm. 1. Irving, Henry, Sir, 1838-1905. 2. Actors — England — Biography I. T.
PN2598.I7 I74 1951   *LC* 52-851

Hillebrand, Harold Newcomb, 1887-. • **2.3347**
Edmund Kean, by Harold Newcomb Hillebrand ... New York, Columbia university press, 1933. viii p., 1 l., 387 p., 1 l. 1. Kean, Edmund, 1787-1833. I. T.
PN2598.K3 H5

Williamson, Jane. • **2.3348**
Charles Kemble, man of the theatre. — Lincoln: University of Nebraska Press, [1970] x, 267 p.: port.; 23 cm. 1. Kemble, Charles, 1775-1854. I. T.
PN2598.K375 W5 1970   792/.0924 B   *LC* 69-19105   *ISBN* 0803207271

Furnas, J. C. (Joseph Chamberlain), 1905-. **2.3349**
Fanny Kemble: leading lady of the nineteenth–century stage: a biography / by J.C. Furnas. — New York: Dial Press, c1982. xiv, 494 p., 8 p. of plates: ill.; 24 cm. Includes index. 1. Kemble, Fanny, 1809-1893. 2. Actors — Great Britain — Biography. I. T.
PN2598.K4 F87   792/.028/0924 B 19   *LC* 81-9849   *ISBN* 0385272081

Baker, Herschel Clay, 1914-. • **2.3350**
John Philip Kemble; the actor in his theatre, by Herschel Baker. — New York: Greenwood Press, [1969, c1942] viii, 414 p.; 23 cm. 1. Kemble, John Philip, 1757-1823. I. T.
PN2598.K5 B3 1969   792/.028/0924 B   *LC* 76-90701   *ISBN* 0837122791

Appleton, William Worthen. • **2.3351**
Charles Macklin; an actor's life. — Cambridge, Harvard University Press, 1960. 280 p. illus. 22 cm. Includes bibliography. 1. Macklin, Charles, 1697?-1797. I. T.
PN2598.M2A6   927.92   *LC* 60-13296

Downer, Alan Seymour, 1912-. • **2.3352**
The eminent tragedian: William Charles Macready / Alan S. Downer. — Cambridge: Harvard University Press, 1966. xiv, 392 p., [5] leaves of plates: ill., ports.; 25 cm. 1. Macready, William Charles, 1793-1873. 2. Theater — Great Britain — History. I. T.
PN2598.M3 D6   792.0924   *LC* 66-14441

Redgrave, Michael, Sir. • **2.3353**
Mask or face: reflections in an actor's mirror / Michael Redgrave — New York: Theatre Arts Books, [1959, c1958] 188 p.: ill. 1. Actors — Biography 2. Acting I. T.
PN2598.R42 A3 1959

Manvell, Roger, 1909-. • **2.3354**
Sarah Siddons: portrait of an actress. [1st American ed.] New York, Putnam [1971, c1970] xii, 385 p. illus., facsims., geneal. table, ports. 22 cm. 1. Siddons, Sarah, 1755-1831. I. T.
PN2598.S5 M28 1971   792/.028/0924 B   *LC* 76-105596

Terry, Ellen, Dame, 1848-1928. • **2.3355**
Ellen Terry and Bernard Shaw: a correspondence / edited by Christopher St. John. — New York: Theatre Arts Books, 1952. xxxviii, 433 p.: ill. 1. Actors — Correspondence 2. Authors — Correspondence I. Shaw, Bernard, 1856-1950. II. St. John, Christopher Marie. III. T.
PN2598T4 A4 1949   *LC* 78-76887

Manvell, Roger, 1909-. • **2.3356**
Ellen Terry / Roger Manvell. — 1st American ed. — New York: Putnam, 1968. x, 390 p.: ill., ports. 1. Actresses — Biography. I. T.
PN2598.T4M33   792.024   *LC* 68-12102

Bingham, Madeleine, Baroness Clanmorris. **2.3357**
The great lover: the life and art of Herbert Beerbohm Tree / Madeleine Bingham. — 1st American ed. — New York: Atheneum, 1979. viii, 293 p., [8] leaves of plates: ill.; 23 cm. Includes index. 1. Tree, Herbert Beerbohm, Sir, 1853-1917. 2. Actors — Great Britain — Biography. I. T.
PN2598.T7 B5 1979   792/.028/0924 B   *LC* 78-65197   *ISBN* 0689109504

Appleton, William Worthen. **2.3358**
Madame Vestris and the London stage [by] William W. Appleton. — New York: Columbia University Press, 1974. ix, 230 p.: illus.; 24 cm. 1. Vestris, Lucia Elizabeth Bartolozzi, 1797-1856. I. T.
PN2598.V5 A7   792/.092/4 B   *LC* 73-10259   *ISBN* 0231037945

PN2600–2798 Other European Countries

Clark, William Smith, 1900-. • **2.3359**
The early Irish stage, the beginnings to 1720. — Oxford, Clarendon Press, 1955. x, 227 p. illus., ports. 23 cm. Bibliography: p. [210]-217. 1. Theater — Ireland — Hist. I. T.
PN2601.C6   792.09415   *LC* 55-14157

Gregory, Lady, 1852-1932. **2.3360**
Our Irish theatre; a chapter of autobiography. With a foreword by Roger McHugh. [New enl. ed.] New York, Oxford University Press, 1972. 279 p. illus. 23 cm. (The Coole edition, of Lady Gregory's work, v. 4) 1. Theater — Ireland. I. T.
PN2601.G7 1972   792/.09415   *LC* 73-158930

Kavanagh, Peter. • **2.3361**
The story of the Abbey Theatre, from its origins in 1899 to the present. New York, Devin-Adair, 1950. xi, 243 p. ill., ports. 24 cm. Bibliographical references included in 'Notes' (p. 225-228) 1. Abbey Theatre. I. T.
PN 2602 D82 A345 K22 1950   *LC* 50-8644

Hawkins, Frederick William, 1849-1900. • **2.3362**
Annals of the French stage, from its origin to the death of Racine. New York, Greenwood Press [1969] 2 v. ports. 23 cm. Reprint of the 1884 ed. 1. Comédie-Française. 2. Theater — France — History. 3. French drama — History and criticism. I. T.
PN2621.H35 1969   792/.0944   *LC* 68-57607   *ISBN* 0837121728—837121736

Wiley, William Leon. • **2.3363**
The early public theatre in France. — Cambridge: Harvard University Press, 1960. 326 p.: illus.; 22 cm. 1. Theater — France — History. I. T.
PN2625.W5   792.0944   *LC* 60-11561

Arnott, Peter D. **2.3364**
An introduction to the French theatre / Peter D. Arnott. — Totowa, N.J.: Rowman and Littlefield, 1977. xii, 164 p.; 23 cm. 1. Theater — France — History. 2. French drama — 17th century — History and criticism. I. T.
PN2632.A7 1977b   792/.0944   *LC* 77-150984   *ISBN* 0874719496

Lough, John. **2.3365**
Seventeenth–century French drama: the background / John Lough. — Oxford: Clarendon Press; New York: Oxford University Press, 1979. vi, 127 p. Includes index. 1. Theater — France — History. 2. French drama — 17th century — History and criticism. I. T.
PN2632.L6   PN2632 L6.   792/.0944   *LC* 79-40294   *ISBN* 0198157568

Carlson, Marvin A., 1935-. **2.3366**
The French stage in the nineteenth century, by Marvin Carlson. — Metuchen, N.J.: Scarecrow Press, 1972. 326 p.; 22 cm. 1. Theater — France — History. I. T.
PN2634.C35   792/.0944   *LC* 72-3981   *ISBN* 0810805162

Barrault, Jean Louis, 1910-. • **2.3367**
The theatre of Jean–Louis Barrault / translated by Joseph Chiari; with a pref. by Armand Salacrou. — New York: Hill and Wang, [1961] 244 p.: ill.; 22 cm. Translation of Nouvelles réflexions sur le théâtre. 1. Barrault, Jean Louis, 1910- 2. Actors — France — Biography. 3. Theater — France. 4. Drama — History and criticism 5. Actresses — France — Biography. I. T.
PN2635.B273 1961   *LC* 61-9965

Hawkins, Frederick William, 1849-1900. • **2.3368**
The French stage in the eighteenth century. New York, Greenwood Press [1969] 2 v. port. 23 cm. Reprint of the 1888 ed. 'Chronology of the French stage, 1699-1799': v. 2, p. 423-441. 1. Comédie-Française. 2. Theater — Paris — History. 3. French drama — History and criticism. I. T.
PN2636.P3 H3 1969b   792/.09443/6   *LC* 68-57608   *ISBN* 0837127467

Waxman, Samuel Montefiore, b. 1885. • **2.3369**
Antoine and the théâtre–libre. New York, B. Blom, [1964] viii, 247 p. plans 24 cm. 1. Antoine, André, 1858-1943. 2. Paris. Théâtre Libre. 3. French drama — 19th century — History and criticism. I. T.
PN2636.P4 T75 1964   *LC* 63-23192

Barrault, Jean Louis.   • 2.3370
Reflections on the theatre / Jean Louis Barrault; with illustrations by Christian Bérard ... [et al.]; translated by Barbara Wall. — London: Rockliff, 1951. xi, 185 p., 4 leaves of plates: ill. Translation of Réflexions sur le théâtre. Includes index. 1. Actors — Biography I. T.
PN2638.B27 A32   LC 51-8629

Bernhardt, Sarah, 1844-1923.   • 2.3371
[Ma double vie. English] Memories of my life, being my personal, professional, and social recollections as woman and artist. New York, B. Blom, 1968. xvi, 456 p. illus., ports. 24 cm. Reprint of the 1908 ed. Translation of Ma double vie. 1. Bernhardt, Sarah, 1844-1923. I. T.
PN2638.B5 A3 1968   792.0924 B   LC 68-56475

Bernhardt, Sarah, 1844-1923.   • 2.3372
[Art du théâtre. English] The art of the theatre. Translated by H. J. Stenning. With a pref. by James Agate. New York, B. Blom [1969] 224 p. 20 cm. Reprint of the 1924 ed. 1. Bernhardt, Sarah, 1844-1923. 2. Acting 3. Actors — Correspondence I. T.
PN2638.B5 A37 1969   792/.028/0924   LC 70-82819

Knapp, Bettina Liebowitz, 1926-.   • 2.3373
Louis Jouvet, man of the theatre. With a foreword by Michael Redgrave. — New York: Columbia University Press, 1957. 345 p.: illus.; 23 cm. 1. Jouvet, Louis, 1887-1951. I. T.
PN2638.J6 K5 1957   927.92   LC 56-8264

Saint-Denis, Michel, 1897-.   • 2.3374
Theatre, the rediscovery of style / Michel Saint–Denis; introduction by Sir Laurence Olivier. — New York: Theatre Arts Books, 1960. 110 p.: ill. 1. Theater — Addresses, essays, lectures. 2. Drama — Addresses, essays, lectures. I. T.
PN2638.S27 A5   LC 60-10492

Patterson, Michael.   2.3375
German theatre today: post–war theatre in West and East Germany, Austria and Northern Switzerland / [by] Michael Patterson. London: Pitman, 1976. ix, 129 p.; 24 cm. (Theatre today) Includes index. 1. Theater — Germany. 2. Theater — Austria. 3. Theater — Switzerland. 4. German drama — 20th century — History and criticism. I. T.
PN2654.P33   792/.0943   LC 76-378015   ISBN 027300350X

Patterson, Michael.   2.3376
The revolution in German theatre, 1900–1933 / Michael Patterson. — Boston: Routledge & K. Paul, c1981. xiii, 232 p., [16] p. of plates: ill.; 24 cm. — (Theatre production studies.) Includes index. 1. Theater — Germany — History — 20th century. I. T. II. Series.
PN2654.P34   792/.0943 19   LC 80-41730   ISBN 0710006594

Willett, John.   2.3377
The theatre of Erwin Piscator / by John Willett. — New York: Holmes & Meier, 1979. 224 p.: ill., maps. Maps on lining papers. 1. Theatrical producers and directors — Germany — Biography. 2. Theater — Political aspects I. T.
PN2658.P5 W55 1979   792/.0233/0924 B   LC 79-11941   ISBN 0841905010

Styan, J. L.   2.3378
Max Reinhardt / J.L. Styan. — Cambridge [Cambridgeshire]; New York: Cambridge University Press, 1982. xvi, 171 p.: ill.; 24 cm. — (Directors in perspective.) Includes index. 1. Reinhardt, Max, 1873-1943. I. T. II. Series.
PN2658.R4 S8 1982   792/.0233/0924 19   LC 81-18172   ISBN 0521224446

Weaver, William, 1923-.   2.3379
Duse, a biography / William Weaver. — 1st American ed. — San Diego: Harcourt Brace Jovanovich, c1984. 383 p.: ill.; 24 cm. Includes index. 1. Duse, Eleonora, 1858-1924. 2. Actors — Italy — Biography. I. T.
PN2688.D8 W4 1984   792/.028/0924 B 19   LC 84-4600   ISBN 0151266905

Marshall, Herbert, 1906-.   2.3380
The pictorial history of the Russian theatre / by Herbert Marshall; introd. by Harold Clurman. — New York: Crown Publishers, c1977. xv, 208 p.: ill.; 29 cm. Includes index. 1. Theater — Russia — History. I. T.
PN2721.M3   792/.0947   LC 76-12822   ISBN 0517520206

Slonim, Marc, 1894-1976.   2.3381
Russian theater, from the Empire to the Soviets. [1st ed.] Cleveland, World Pub. Co. [1961] 354 p. illus. 24 cm. 1. Theater — Soviet Union — History. 2. Drama — History and criticism 3. Opera — Soviet Union — History and criticism. I. T.
PN2721.S55   792.0947   LC 61-15304

Golub, Spencer.   2.3382
Evreinov, the theatre of paradox and transformation / by Spencer Golub. — Ann Arbor, Mich.: UMI Research Press, c1984. xx, 307 p.: ill.; 23 cm. —

(Theater and dramatic studies. no. 19) Revision of thesis (Ph. D.)—University of Kansas, 1977. Includes index. 1. Evreinov, N. N. (Nikolaĭ Nikolaevich), 1879-1953. 2. Theater — Soviet Union — 20th century — History. I. T. II. Series.
PN2728.E8 G6 1984   891.72/3 19   LC 84-80   ISBN 083571540X

Rennert, Hugo Albert, 1858-1927.   • 2.3383
The Spanish stage in the time of Lope de Vega. New York: Dover Publications, [1963] xv, 403 p. 22 cm. 'Unabridged and unaltered republication of ... the work first published by the Hispanic Society of America in 1909. The 'List of Spanish actors and actresses, 1560-1680' ... has been omitted.' Includes bibliographical references. 1. Theater — Spain — History. I. T.
PN2782.R4 1963   792.0946   LC 63-19513

Shergold, N. D.   • 2.3384
A history of the Spanish stage: from medieval times until the end of the seventeenth century [by] N. D. Shergold. — Oxford: Clarendon P., 1967. xxx, 624 p.: 20 plates (incl. plans, facsims.); 22 1/2 cm. 1. Theater — Spain — History. I. T.
PN2782.S45 1967   PN2782 S45 1967.   792/.0946   LC 67-77654

Osiński, Zbigniew.   2.3385
Grotowski and his laboratory / by Zbigniew Osiński; translated and abridged by Lillian Vallee and Robert Findlay. — 1st ed. — New York: PAJ Publications, c1986. 185 p.: ill., ports. 1. Grotowski, Jerzy, 1933- 2. Experimental theater — Poland. I. Vallee, Lillian. II. Findlay, Robert R., 1932- III. T.
PN2859.P66G78213   LC 85-63863   ISBN 0933826893

PN2860–2960 Asia

Brandon, James R.   2.3386
Theatre in Southeast Asia [by] James R. Brandon. — Cambridge, Mass.: Harvard University Press, 1967. xiii, 370 p.: illus., maps.; 24 cm. 1. Theater — Asia, Southeastern. I. T.
PN2860.B7   792.095   LC 67-14338

Scott, A. C. (Adolphe Clarence), 1909-.   2.3387
The theatre in Asia [by] A. C. Scott. [1st American ed.] New York, Macmillan [1973, c1972] 289 p. illus. 21 cm. 1. Performing arts — Asia. I. T.
PN2860.S2 1973   792/.095   LC 72-94010

Chinese theater: from its origins to the present day / edited by Colin Mackerras.   2.3388
Honolulu: University of Hawaii Press, c1983. viii, 220 p., [16] p. of plates: ill.; 24 cm. 1. Theater — China 2. Chinese drama — History and criticism. I. Mackerras, Colin.
PN2871.C534 1983   792/.0951 19   LC 83-6687   ISBN 0824808134

Mackerras, Colin.   2.3389
The Chinese theatre in modern times, from 1840 to the present day / Colin Mackerras. — Amherst: University of Massachusetts Press, c1975. 256 p.: ill.; 23 cm. 1. Theater — China — History. I. T.
PN2871.M3 1975b   792/.0951   LC 75-13827   ISBN 0870231960

Crump, J. I. (James Irving), 1921-.   2.3390
Chinese theater in the days of Kublai Khan / J. I. Crump. — Tucson: University of Arizona Press, c1980. ix, 429 p.: ill.; 24 cm. Includes index. 1. Theater — China — History. 2. Chinese drama — Yüan dynasty, 1260-1368 — Translation into English. 3. English drama — Translations from Chinese. I. T.
PN2872.C7   792/.0951   LC 79-20046   ISBN 0816506973

Mackerras, Colin.   2.3391
The performing arts in contemporary China / Colin Mackerras. — London; Boston: Routledge & Kegan Paul, 1981. x, 243 p., [16] p. of leaves: ill.; 23 cm. 1. Performing arts — China — History — 20th century. I. T.
PN2874.M3   790.2/0951 19   LC 80-42215   ISBN 0710007787

Gārgī, Balawanta, 1916-.   • 2.3392
Theatre in India. New York, Theatre Arts Books [1962] 245 p. illus. 22 cm. 1. Theater — India 2. Indic drama — History and criticism. I. T.
PN2881.G3   792.0954   LC 62-13887

Sanskrit drama in performance / edited by Rachel Van M. Baumer and James R. Brandon.   2.3393
Honolulu: University Press of Hawaii, c1981. xvi, 318 p., [16] p. of plates: ill.; 25 cm. Based on a conference held at the University of Hawaii in 1972. 1. Theater — India — Congresses. 2. Sanskrit drama — History and criticism — Congresses. I. Baumer, Rachel Van M., 1928- II. Brandon, James R.
PN2881.S26   792/.0954 9   LC 80-26900   ISBN 0824806883

Yājñika, Ramanalāla Ke., 1895-1960. • 2.3394
The Indian theatre, its origins and its later developments under European influence, with special reference to western India, by R. K. Yajnik. New York, Haskell House, 1970. 284 p. 23 cm. 1. Shakespeare, William, 1564-1616 — Appreciation — India. 2. Theater — India I. T.
PN2881.Y3 1970   792/.0954   LC 74-92995   ISBN 0838312144

Mukhopādhyāya, Susīla, 1911-. 2.3395
The story of Calcutta theatres, 1753-1980 / Sushil Kumar Mukherjee. — Calcutta, New Delhi: K. P. Bagchi & Co., 1982. xvi, 806 p., 10 leaves of plates: ill. Includes index. 1. Calcutta (India) — Theaters — History. I. T.
PN2886.C3 M8 1982

Bowers, Faubion, 1917-. • 2.3396
Japanese theatre. Foreword by Joshua Logan. — New York: Hill and Wang, [1959, c1952] 294 p.: illus.; 21 cm. — (A Dramabook, D16) 1. Theater — Japan — History. 2. Japanese drama — History and criticism. I. T.
PN2921.B6 1959   792.0952   LC 59-8782

Ernst, Earle. • 2.3397
The kabuki theatre. New York, Oxford University Press, 1956. xxiii, 296 p. illus., plans. 26 cm. Bibliography: p. 288-290. 1. Theater — Japan 2. Japanese drama — History and criticism. I. T.
PN2921.E7   792.0952   LC 56-14007

Inoura, Yoshinobu, 1914-. 2.3398
The traditional theater of Japan / by Yoshinobu Inoura and Toshio Kawatake. — 1st one-volume ed. — New York: Weatherhill in collaboration with the Japan Foundation, 1981. viii, 259 p., [24] leaves of plates: ill.; 24 cm. Originally published in 1971 in 2 separate volumes: A history of Japanese theater 1: Noh and KYōgen and A history of Japanese theater 2: Bunraku and Kabuki. Includes index. 1. Theater — Japan — History. I. Kawatake, Toshio, 1924- joint author. II. T.
PN2921.I67 1981   792/.0952 19   LC 80-29635   ISBN 0834801612

The Art of Kabuki: famous plays in performance / translated, 2.3399
with commentary, by Samuel L. Leiter.
Berkeley: University of California Press, c1979. xxi, 298 p.: ill.; 23 cm. Includes index. 1. Kabuki 2. Kabuki plays — Translations into English. 3. English drama — Translations from Japanese. I. Leiter, Samuel L.
PN2924.5.K3 A7   895.6/2/008   LC 77-83107   ISBN 0520035550

Chūshingura: studies in kabuki and the puppet theater / edited 2.3400
by James R. Brandon.
Honolulu: University Press of Hawaii, c1982. xii, 231 p., [8] p. of plates: ill. (some col.); 25 cm. Includes text of: The Forty-seven samurai. 1. Takeda, Izumo, 1691-1756 Kanadehon Chūshingura — Addresses, essays, lectures. 2. Puppets and puppet-plays — Japan — History and criticism — Addresses, essays, lectures. 3. Kabuki — Addresses, essays, lectures. I. Brandon, James R. II. Takeda, Izumo, 1691-1756. Kanadehon Chūshingura. English.
PN2924.5.K3 C48 1982   895.6/23 19   LC 82-1921   ISBN 0824807936

Scott, A. C. (Adolphe Clarence), 1909-. • 2.3401
The kabuki theatre of Japan / by A. C. Scott; with illustrations by the author. — London: George Allen and Unwin, 1955. 317 p.: ill. 1. Kabuki 2. Japanese drama — History and criticism. 3. Theater — Japan I. T.
PN2924.5.K3 S38

Konparu, Kunio, 1926-. 2.3402
[Nō e no izanai. English] The noh theater: principles and perspectives / Kunio Komparu. — 1st ed. — New York: Weatherhill/Tankosha, 1983. xxiv, 376 p.: ill.; 23 cm. Rev. and expanded translation of: Nō e no izanai. Includes indexes. 1. Nō I. T.
PN2924.5.N6 K54213 1983   895.6/2/009 19   LC 83-5860   ISBN 083481529X

PN3035 JEWISH THEATER

Lifson, David S. • 2.3403
The Yiddish theatre in America [by] David S. Lifson. New York, T. Yoseloff [1965] 659 p. illus. 22 cm. 1. Theater, Yiddish — New York (City) 2. Theater — New York (City) I. T.
PN3035.L46 1965   792.0973   LC 64-17112

Sandrow, Nahma. 2.3404
Vagabond stars: a world history of Yiddish theater / Nahma Sandrow. — 1st ed. — New York: Harper & Row, c1977. xi, 435 p.: ill.; 25 cm. Includes index. 1. Gordin, Jacob, 1853-1909. 2. Theater, Yiddish — History. I. T.
PN3035.S25   792/.09   LC 75-25065   ISBN 0060137568

PN3171 DRAMA IN EDUCATION

Duke, Charles R. 2.3405
Creative dramatics and English teaching / Charles R. Duke. — Urbana, Ill.: National Council of Teachers of English, [1974] x, 180 p.; 23 cm. 1. Drama in education 2. English philology — Study and teaching I. T.
PN3171.D77 1974   792/.07/1   LC 74-81362

Siks, Geraldine Brain. 2.3406
Drama with children / Geraldine Brain Siks. — 2nd ed. — New York: Harper & Row, c1983. xx, 332 p.: ill.; 25 cm. 1. Drama in education I. T.
PN3171.S535 1983   371.3/32 19   LC 82-21291   ISBN 0060461527

PN3195 MINSTREL SHOWS

Wittke, Carl Frederick, 1892-1971. • 2.3407
Tambo and bones; a history of the American minstrel stage, by Carl Wittke. — New York: Greenwood Press, 1968 [c1930] ix, 269 p.; 18 cm. 1. Minstrel shows I. T.
PN3195.W5 1968   791.1/2/0973   LC 69-10174

PN3311–3503 Prose. Prose Fiction

Allott, Miriam Farris. ed. • 2.3408
Novelists on the novel. — New York: Columbia University Press, 1959. xv, 336 p.; 22 cm. 1. Fiction I. T.
PN3321.A4   808.3   LC 59-8290

English Institute. • 2.3409
Aspects of narrative; selected papers from the English Institute. Edited with a foreword by J. Hillis Miller. New York, Columbia University Press, 1971. x, 210 p. 20 cm. Seven essays presented at three conferences of the English Institute during 1969-70. 1. Prose literature — History and criticism — Addresses, essays, lectures. 2. Narration (Rhetoric) — Addresses, essays, lectures. I. Miller, J. Hillis (Joseph Hillis), 1928- ed. II. T.
PN3321.E5   809.9/2/3   LC 70-160843   ISBN 0231035799

Norris, Frank, 1870-1902. • 2.3410
The responsibilities of the novelist: and other literary essays. — New York: Greenwood Press, [1968, c1903] 311 p.: port.; 23 cm. 1. Fiction — Addresses, essays, lectures. I. T.
PN3324.N6 1968   808.3/3   LC 69-10143

Woolf, Virginia, 1882-1941. • 2.3411
Granite and rainbow; essays. — [1st American ed.]. — New York, Harcourt, Brace [1958] 239 p. 21 cm. 1. Fiction — Addresses, essays, lectures. 2. American fiction — Hist. & crit. 3. English fiction — Hist. & crit. 4. Biography — Addresses, essays, lectures. I. T.
PN3324.W6   808.3   LC 58-10898

De Voto, Bernard Augustine, 1897-1955. • 2.3412
World of fiction / by Bernard De Voto. — Boston: Houghton Mifflin, 1950. xii, 299 p. 1. Literature — Psychology 2. Fiction — Technique 3. Authors and readers I. T.
PN3331.D4   808.3   LC 50-6694

James, Henry, 1843-1916. • 2.3413
Theory of fiction: Henry James. Edited with an introd. by James E. Miller, Jr. — Lincoln: University of Nebraska Press, [1972] xviii, 366 p.; 24 cm. 1. Fiction I. Miller, James Edwin, 1920- ed. II. T.
PN3331.J3 1972   808.3   LC 78-147168   ISBN 0803207999

Miller, James Edwin, 1920- ed. • 2.3414
Myth and method; modern theories of fiction. — [Lincoln]: University of Nebraska Press, 1960. 165 p.; 21 cm. — (A Bison book, BB105) 1. Fiction 2. Literature — Addresses, essays, lectures. I. T.
PN3331.M5   808.3   LC 60-12941

Liddell, Robert, 1908-. • 2.3415
A treatise on the novel / Robert Liddell. — London: Cape, 1947. 168 p.; 21 cm. 1. Compton-Burnett, Ivy, 1892- 2. James, Henry, 1843-1916. Turn of the screw. 3. Fiction — Technique 4. Fiction — History and criticism I. T.
PN3335.L5

Alter, Robert. 2.3416
Partial magic: the novel as a self-conscious genre / Robert Alter. — Berkeley: University of California Press, c1975. xvi, 248 p.; 23 cm. Errata slip inserted.

1. Fiction — History and criticism 2. Fiction — Technique 3. Realism in literature I. T.
PN3340.A4　　809.3　　*LC* 74-77725　　*ISBN* 0520027558

Goldmann, Lucien.　　　　　　　　　　　　　　　**2.3417**
[Pour une sociologie du roman. English] Towards a sociology of the novel / Lucien Goldmann; translated from the French by Alan Sheridan. — London: Tavistock Publications, 1975. ix, 181 p.; 22 cm. Translation of Pour une sociologie du roman. 1. Fiction — Social aspects. 2. Fiction — 20th century — History and criticism I. T.
PN3344.G613 1975　　843/.9/12　　*LC* 75-316769　　*ISBN* 0422742406

Swingewood, Alan.　　　　　　　　　　　　　**2.3418**
The novel and revolution / Alan Swingewood. — New York: Barnes & Noble Books, 1976 (c1975). ix, 288 p.; 23 cm. 1. Fiction — History and criticism 2. Fiction — Social aspects. I. T.
PN3344.S9　　809.3/3　　*LC* 75-21103　　*ISBN* 0064966828

Tanner, Tony.　　　　　　　　　　　　　　　**2.3419**
Adultery in the novel: contract and transgression / Tony Tanner. — Baltimore: Johns Hopkins University Press, 1980 (c1979). xii, 383 p.: ill.; 24 cm. Includes index. 1. Fiction — 18th century — History and criticism. 2. Fiction — 19th century — History and criticism. 3. Adultery in literature. I. T.
PN3352.A38 T3　　809.3/3　　*LC* 79-4948　　*ISBN* 0801821789

Blair, John G.　　　　　　　　　　　　　　　**2.3420**
The confidence man in modern fiction: a rogue's gallery with six portraits / John G. Blair. — New York: Barnes & Noble Books, 1979. 142 p.: ill.; 23 cm. — (Barnes & Noble critical studies) 1. Fiction — History and criticism 2. Swindlers and swindling in literature I. T.
PN3352.S94 B5　　809.3/93520692　　*LC* 79-50928　　*ISBN* 0064904490

Forster, E. M. (Edward Morgan), 1879-1970.　　　　• **2.3421**
Aspects of the novel. New York, Harcourt, Brace [1956, c1954] 176 p. 19 cm. (Harvest books, 19) 1. Fiction 2. English fiction — History and criticism. I. T.
PN3353.F6x　　808.3　　*LC* 56-14186

Liddell, Robert, 1908-.　　　　　　　　　　　• **2.3422**
Some principles of fiction. — Bloominton: Indiana University Press, 1954. 162 p.; 21 cm. 1. Fiction I. T.
PN3353.L53　　*LC* 54-11280

Muir, Edwin, 1887-1959.　　　　　　　　　　• **2.3423**
The structure of the novel. — London: Hogarth Press, 1957. 151 p.; 20 cm. 1. Fiction 2. English fiction — History and criticism. I. T.
PN3353.M8x　　*LC* 79-4574

James, Henry, 1843-1916.　　　　　　　　　• **2.3424**
The future of the novel; essays on the art of fiction. Edited with an introd. by Leon Edel. — [1st ed.]. — New York: Vintage Books, 1956. xviii, 286, [1], v p.; 19 cm. — (Vintage books, K-41) 1. Fiction — History and criticism I. T.
PN3354.J3　　808.3　　*LC* 56-58001

PN3355–3385 Technique. Study. Teaching

Aldridge, John W. ed.　　　　　　　　　　　• **2.3425**
Critiques and essays on modern fiction, 1920–1951, representing the achievement of modern American and British critics; with a foreword by Mark Schorer. — New York: Ronald Press Co., [1952] xx, 610 p.; 24 cm. 1. Fiction — Technique 2. American fiction — 20th century — History & criticism. 3. English fiction — 20th century — History & criticism. 4. American fiction — 20th century — History & criticism — Bibliography. 5. English fiction — 20th century — History & criticism — Bibliography. I. T.
PN3355.A8　　808.3　　*LC* 52-6180

Brooks, Cleanth, 1906- ed.　　　　　　　　　**2.3426**
Understanding fiction / [edited by] Cleanth Brooks, Robert Penn Warren. — 3d ed. — Englewood Cliffs, N.J.: Prentice-Hall, c1979. xvi, 515 p.; 23 cm. 1. Fiction — History and criticism 2. Short stories I. Warren, Robert Penn, 1905- joint ed. II. T.
PN3355.B74 1979　　808.3　　*LC* 78-27116　　*ISBN* 0139366903

Cawelti, John G.　　　　　　　　　　　　　　**2.3427**
Adventure, mystery, and romance: formula stories as art and popular culture / John G. Cawelti. — Chicago: University of Chicago Press, 1976. viii, 336 p.; 24 cm. Includes index. 1. Fiction — Technique 2. Fiction — History and criticism I. T.
PN3355.C36　　808.3　　*LC* 75-5077　　*ISBN* 0226098664

Lubbock, Percy, 1879-.　　　　　　　　　　　• **2.3428**
The craft of fiction. — [Compass books ed.]. — New York: Viking Press, [1957] 274 p.; 21 cm. 1. Fiction — History and criticism 2. Fiction — Technique I. T.
PN3355.L8 1957　　808.3　　*LC* 57-3468

Macauley, Robie.　　　　　　　　　　　　　• **2.3429**
Technique in fiction [by] Robie Macauley [and] George Lanning. — New York, Harper & Row [1964] xi, 227 p. 22 cm. Bibliography: p. 219-220. 1. Fiction — Technique I. Lanning, George, 1925- joint author. II. T.
PN3355.M2 1964　　808.3　　*LC* 64-12803

University of Minnesota.　　　　　　　　　　• **2.3430**
Forms of modern fiction; essays collected in honor of Joseph Warren Beach, ed. by William Van O'Connor. Minneapolis, Univ. of Minnesota Press [1948] 305 p. 23 cm. 1. Beach, Joseph Warren, 1880-1957. 2. Fiction — Technique I. O'Connor, William Van, 1915-1966. ed. II. T.
PN3355.M5　　808.3　　*LC* 48-7160

Somerlott, Robert.　　　　　　　　　　　　• **2.3431**
The writing of modern fiction. — Boston: The Writer, [1972] x, 147 p.; 22 cm. 1. Fiction — Technique I. T.
PN3355.S58　　808.3　　*LC* 71-188590　　*ISBN* 0871160684

Wharton, Edith Newbold Jones, 1862-1937.　　　• **2.3432**
The writing of fiction. New York, Octagon Books, 1966 [c1953] 178 p. 21 cm. 1. Fiction — Technique I. T.
PN3355.W5 1966　　808.3　　*LC* 66-28379

West, Ray Benedict, 1908- ed.　　　　　　　• **2.3433**
The art of modern fiction [by] Ray B. West, Jr. [and] Robert Wooster Stallman. New York, Rinehart, 1949. x, 652 p. 24 cm. 1. Short stories 2. Fiction — Technique I. Stallman, R. W. (Robert Wooster), 1911- joint ed. II. T.
PN3358.W4　　808.3　　*LC* 49-10213

Wright, Austin McGiffert, 1922-.　　　　　　**2.3434**
The formal principle in the novel / Austin M. Wright. — Ithaca, N.Y.: Cornell University Press, 1982. 317 p.; 23 cm. Includes index. 1. Fiction — Technique I. T.
PN3365.W7 1982　　808.3 19　　*LC* 81-70711　　*ISBN* 0801414628

Lohafer, Susan.　　　　　　　　　　　　　　**2.3435**
Coming to terms with the short story / Susan Lohafer. — Baton Rouge: Louisiana State University Press, c1983. ix, 171 p.; 24 cm. Includes index. 1. Short story I. T.
PN3373.L56 1983　　808.3/1 19　　*LC* 82-20366　　*ISBN* 0807110868

O'Connor, Frank, 1903-1966.　　　　　　　　• **2.3436**
The lonely voice, a study of the short story [by] Frank O'Connor [pseud. 1st ed.] Cleveland, World Pub. Co. [1963] 220 p. 21 cm. 1. Short story I. T.
PN3373.O36　　808.31　　*LC* 63-8782

O'Faoláin, Seán, 1900-.　　　　　　　　　　• **2.3437**
The short story / by Sean O'Faolain. — New York: Devin-Adair, 1951. 370 p.; 22 cm. 1. Short story 2. Short stories I. T.
PN3373.O37 1951　　*LC* 51-9370

Shaw, Valerie, 1941-.　　　　　　　　　　　**2.3438**
The short story, a critical introduction / Valerie Shaw. — London; New York: Longman, 1983. ix, 294 p.; 22 cm. Includes index. 1. Short story I. T.
PN3373.S384 1983　　808.3/1 19　　*LC* 83-986　　*ISBN* 0582486874

May, Charles Edward, 1941-.　　　　　　　　**2.3439**
Short story theories / edited by Charles E. May. [Athens]: Ohio University Press, c1976. xiv, 251 p.; 24 cm. 1. Short story — Addresses, essays, lectures. I. T.
PN3373.S39　　809.3/1　　*LC* 75-36982　　*ISBN* 0821401890

Summers, Hollis Spurgeon, 1916- ed.　　　　• **2.3440**
Discussions of the short story / edited with an introd. by Hollis Summers. — Boston: Heath, [1963] ix, 118 p.; 24 cm. — (Discussions of literature) 1. Short story I. T.
PN3373.S78　　808.31　　*LC* 63-24007

Canby, Henry Seidel, 1878-1961.　　　　　　• **2.3441**
A study of the short story. By Henry Seidel Canby ... and Alfred Dashiell ... Rev. New York, H. Holt, c1935. 375 p. 22 cm. 1. Short story 2. Short stories I. Dashiell, Alfred, 1901- joint author. II. T.
PN 3375 C22 1935　　*LC* 35-11314

Humphrey, Robert, fl. 1954-.　　　　　　　　• **2.3442**
Stream of consciousness in the modern novel. — Berkeley: University of California Press, 1954. 127 p.; 22 cm. — (Perspectives in criticism, 3) 1. Stream of consciousness fiction 2. Fiction — Technique I. T.
PN3377.5.S77 H8　808.3/83　　*LC* 54-6673

Brooks, Peter. 2.3443
Reading for the plot: design and intention in narrative / Peter Brooks. — 1st ed. — New York: A.A. Knopf, 1984. xviii, 363 p.; 22 cm. Includes index. 1. Fiction — Technique 2. Plots (Drama, novel, etc.) 3. Narration (Rhetoric) I. T.
PN3378.B76 1984   808.3 19   LC 83-48929   ISBN 0394505972

Gilbert, Michael Francis, 1912-. 2.3444
Crime in good company: essays on criminals and crime–writing / [by] Josephine Bell [pseud.] and others. — London: Constable, 1959. 242 p. 1. Detective and mystery stories — Technique 2. Crime and criminals I. T.
PN3383.D4 G5   808.06   808.3   LC 59-3427

Clews, Hetty, 1929-. 2.3445
The only teller: readings in the monologue novel / Hetty Clews. — Victoria, B.C.: Sono Nis Press, 1985. 217 p.; 24 cm. Includes index. 1. First person narrative I. T.
PN3383.N35 C54 1985   809.3/923 19   ISBN 0919203507

Spatial form in narrative / edited by Jeffrey R. Smitten and 2.3446
Ann Daghistany; with a foreword by Joseph Frank.
Ithaca: Cornell University Press, 1981. 275 p.; 22 cm. Includes index. 1. Fiction — Technique — Addresses, essays, lectures. 2. Narration (Rhetoric) — Addresses, essays, lectures. 3. Fiction — 20th century — History and criticism — Addresses, essays, lectures. I. Smitten, Jeffrey R. II. Daghistany, Ann, 1942-
PN3383.N35 S64   808.3 19   LC 81-3244   ISBN 0801413753

Brown, E. K. (Edward Killoran), 1905-1951. • 2.3447
Rhythm in the novel. — [Toronto]: University of Toronto Press, 1950. xiii, 118 p.; 23 cm. — (The Alexander lectures, 1949-50) 1. Forster, E. M. (Edward Morgan), 1879-1970. A passage to India. 2. Fiction — Hist. & crit. I. T.
PN3383.R5B7   808.3   LC 51-5069

PN3401–3448 Special Topics and Types of Fiction

The Representation of women in fiction / edited, with an 2.3448
introduction, by Carolyn G. Heilbrun and Margaret R.
Higonnet.
Baltimore: Johns Hopkins University Press, c1983. xxii, 190 p.; 21 cm. — (Selected papers from the English Institute; 1981, new ser., no. 7) 1. Fiction — History and criticism 2. Women in literature I. Heilbrun, Carolyn G., 1926- II. Higonnet, Margaret R.
PN3401.R46 1983   809/.93352042 19   LC 82-12685   ISBN 0801829283

Parker, Alexander Augustine. • 2.3449
Literature and the delinquent: the picaresque novel in Spain and Europe, 1599–1753 [by] Alexander A. Parker. Edinburgh, Edinburgh U.P., 1967. xiii, 195 p. 11 plates (incl. facsims.) 21 cm. (Norman Maccoll lectures 1965) 1. Picaresque literature, European — History and criticism. I. T. II. Series.
PN3428.P3   LC 67-90731

Chandler, Frank Wadleigh, 1873-1947. • 2.3450
The literature of roguery. New York, B. Franklin, 1958 [c1907] 2 v. (viii, 584 p.); 25 cm. (The Types of English literature) Burt Franklin bibliographical series, 9. 1. Picaresque literature — History and criticism 2. Rogues and vagabonds I. T.
PN3430.G6 C5 1958   820.9   LC 61-30806

Adams, Percy G. 2.3451
Travel literature and the evolution of the novel / Percy G. Adams. — Lexington, Ky.: University Press of Kentucky, c1983. xi, 368 p.; 24 cm. 1. European fiction — Renaissance, 1450-1600 — History and criticism. 2. European fiction — 17th century — History and criticism. 3. European fiction — 18th century — History and criticism. 4. Travel in literature 5. Voyages, Imaginary — History and criticism. 6. Voyages and travels I. T.
PN3432.A32 1983   809.3 19   LC 83-19683   ISBN 0813114926

Gove, Philip Babcock, 1902-1972. • 2.3452
The imaginary voyage in prose fiction; a history of its criticism and a guide for its study, with an annotated check list of 215 imaginary voyages from 1700 to 1800. New York Columbia University Press 1941. xi, 445 p.; 22 cm. (Columbia University studies in English and comparative literature, no. 152) 1. Voyages, Imaginary — History and criticism 2. Fiction — History and criticism 3. Voyages, Imaginary — Bibliography I. T. II. Series.
PN3432 G68

The Science fiction reference book: a comprehensive handbook 2.3453
and guide to the history, literature, scholarship, and related
activities of the science fiction and fantasy fields / edited by
Marshall B. Tymn.
Mercer Island, Wash.: Starmont House, c1981. ix, 536 p.: ill.; 23 cm. Includes bibliographies and index. 1. Science fiction — Handbooks, manuals, etc. 2. Fantastic literature — Handbooks, manuals, etc. I. Tymn, Marshall B., 1937-
PN3433.5.S33   809.3/876 19   LC 80-28888   ISBN 0916732495

Anatomy of wonder: a critical guide to science fiction / edited 2.3454
by Neil Barron.
3rd ed. — New York: Bowker, 1987. xvii, 874 p. 1. Science fiction — Bibliography. 2. Science fiction — History and criticism I. Barron, Neil, 1934-
Z5917.S36 A52 1987 PN3433.8Ax   016.80883/876 19   LC 87-9305   ISBN 0835223124

Lem, Stanisław. 2.3455
Microworlds: writings on science fiction and fantasy / Stanisław Lem; edited by Franz Rottensteiner. — [1st ed.]. — San Diego: Harcourt Brace Jovanovich, c1984. xviii, 285 p.; 22 cm. 'A Helen and Kurt Wolff book.' 1. Science fiction — History and criticism — Addresses, essays, lectures. 2. Fantastic fiction — History and criticism — Addresses, essays, lectures. I. Rottensteiner, Franz. II. T.
PN3433.8.L4 1984   809.3/876 19   LC 84-12837   ISBN 0151594805

Birkhead, Edith. • 2.3456
The tale of terror; a study of the Gothic romance. — New York: Russell & Russell, 1963. xi, 241 p.; 23 cm. 1. English fiction — History and criticism. 2. Supernatural in literature 3. Gothic revival (Literature) I. T. II. Title: The Gothic romance.
PN3435.B5 1963   823.093   LC 63-15149

Frank, Frederick S. 2.3457
Guide to the Gothic: an annotated bibliography of criticism / by Frederick S. Frank. — Metuchen, N.J.: Scarecrow Press, 1984. xvi, 421 p.; 23 cm. Includes indexes. 1. Gothic revival (Literature) — Bibliography. 2. Fiction — History and criticism — Bibliography. I. T.
Z5917.G66 F7 1984 PN3435.F7x   016.8093/872 19   LC 83-24507   ISBN 0810816695

Jackson, Rosemary. 2.3458
Fantasy, the literature of subversion / Rosemary Jackson. — London; New York: Methuen, 1981. viii, 211 p.; 20 cm. — (New accents) Includes indexes. 1. Fantastic fiction — History and criticism. I. T.
PN3435.J3 1981   809.3/915 19   LC 80-41387   ISBN 0416711804

Le Guin, Ursula K., 1929-. 2.3459
The language of the night: essays on fantasy and science fiction / by Ursula K. Le Guin; edited and with introductions by Susan Wood. — New York: Putnam, c1979. 270 p.; 23 cm. 1. Fantastic fiction — History and criticism — Addresses, essays, lectures. 2. Science fiction — History and criticism — Addresses, essays, lectures. I. Wood, Susan, 1948-1980. II. T.
PN3435.L4   809.3/876   LC 78-24350   ISBN 0399123253

Lovecraft, H. P. (Howard Phillips), 1890-1937. 2.3460
Supernatural horror in literature. With a new introd. by E. F. Bleiler. New York, Dover Publications [1973] 106 p. 22 cm. Reprint of the 1945 ed. published by B. Abramson, New York. 1. Horror tales — History and criticism. 2. Supernatural in literature I. T.
PN3435.L64 1973   809.3/872   LC 73-75869   ISBN 0486201058

MacAndrew, Elizabeth, 1924-. 2.3461
The Gothic tradition in fiction / by Elizabeth MacAndrew. — New York: Columbia University Press, 1979. xi, 289 p.; 24 cm. Includes index. 1. Gothic revival (Literature) 2. English fiction — History and criticism. I. T.
PN3435.M3   823/.0872   LC 79-9447   ISBN 023104674X

Supernatural fiction writers: fantasy and horror / E.F. Bleiler, 2.3462
editor.
New York: Scribner, c1985. 2 v. (xix, 1169 p.); 29 cm. 1. Fantastic fiction — History and criticism. 2. Horror tales — History and criticism. 3. Supernatural in literature 4. Authors — Biography I. Bleiler, Everett Franklin, 1920-
PN3435.S96 1985   809.3/876 19   LC 84-27588   ISBN 0684178087

Todorov, Tzvetan, 1939-. 2.3463
[Introduction à la littérature fantastique. English] The fantastic; a structural approach to a literary genre [by] Tzvetan Todorov. Translated from the French by Richard Howard. Cleveland, Press of Case Western Reserve University, 1973. 179 p. 24 cm. (A Volume in the CWRU Press translations) Translation of Introduction à la littérature fantastique. 1. Fantastic fiction — History and criticism. I. T.
PN3435.T613   809/.91/5   LC 72-87175   ISBN 0829502459

Waggoner, Diana.   **2.3464**
The hills of faraway: a guide to fantasy / Diana Waggoner. — New York:
Atheneum, 1978. x, 326 p.: ill.; 24 cm. Includes indexes. 1. Fantastic fiction —
Bibliography. 2. Fantastic fiction — History and criticism. I. T.
Z5917.F3 W33 PN3435.W3x   809.3/876   *LC* 76-900   *ISBN*
068910846X

Lüthi, Max, 1909-.   **2.3465**
[Volksmärchen als Dichtung. English] The fairytale as art form and portrait of
man / Max Lüthi; translated by Jon Erickson. — Bloomington: Indiana
University Press, 1984. xi, 207 p.; 25 cm. Translation of: Das Volksmärchen als
Dichtung. Includes indexes. 1. Fairy tales — History and criticism. I. T.
PN3437.L79813 1984   398.2 19   *LC* 83-48897   *ISBN* 0253320992

Feuchtwanger, Lion, 1884-1958.   • **2.3466**
The house of Desdemona: or, The laurels and limitations of historical fiction /
by Lion Feuchtwanger; translated from the German with a foreword by Harold
A. Basilius. — Detroit: Wayne State University Press, 1963. 236 p.; 21 cm. —
(A Waynebook original; no. 12) Translation of Das Haus der Desdemona: oder,
Grösse und Grenzen der historischen Dichtung. 1. Historical fiction I. T.
II. Title: The laurels and limitations of historical fiction. III. Series.
PN3441.F413   *LC* 63-8063

Lukács, György, 1885-1971.   • **2.3467**
The historical novel / Georg Lukács;translated from the German by Hannah
and Stanley Mitchell; pref. to the American ed. by Irving Howe. — Boston:
Beacon Press [1963, c1962] 363 p.; 21 cm. — (Beacon BP159.) 1. Historical
fiction 2. Historical drama 3. Fiction — History and criticism I. T.
PN3441.L813   *LC* 62-52468

PN3448 By Topic or Type, A–Z

PN3448.A–C

Armstrong, Judith.   **2.3468**
The novel of adultery / Judith Armstrong. — New York: Barnes & Noble,
1976. 182 p. 1. Adultery 2. Sex in literature I. T.
PN3448.A28 A7 1976   *ISBN* 006490203X

PN3448.D4 Detective Fiction

Adey, Robert C.S.   **2.3469**
Locked rooms and other impossible crimes. — London: Ferret Fantasy, 1979.
190 p. 1. Detective and mystery stories — Bibliography. I. T.
PN3448.D4 A4x

Breen, Jon L., 1943-.   **2.3470**
What about murder?: a guide to books about mystery and detective fiction / by
Jon L. Breen. — Metuchen, N.J.: Scarecrow Press, 1981. xviii, 157 p.; 23 cm.
Includes index. 1. Detective and mystery stories — History and criticism —
Bibliography. 2. Detective and mystery stories — Technique — Bibliography.
I. T.
Z5917.D5 B73 PN3448.D4 B7x   016.823/0872 19   *LC* 81-645
ISBN 0810814137

Harper, Ralph, 1915-.   **2.3471**
The world of the thriller. — Cleveland: Press of Case Western Reserve
University, 1969. xii, 139 p.; 22 cm. 1. Detective and mystery stories — History
and criticism. I. T.
PN3448.D4 H25   809/.3/872   *LC* 69-17681   *ISBN* 0829501487

Lambert, Gavin.   **2.3472**
The dangerous edge / Gavin Lambert. New York: Grossman Publishers, 1976,
c1975. xiii, 271, [1] p.; 22 cm. 1. Detective and mystery stories — History and
criticism. 2. Detective and mystery films — History and criticism. I. T.
PN3448.D4 L33 1976   823/.0872   *LC* 76-2377   *ISBN* 0670255815

The murder mystique: crime writers on their art / edited by   **2.3473**
Lucy Freeman.
New York: Ungar, c1982. ix, 140 p.; 22 cm. — (Recognitions.) 1. Detective and
mystery stories — History and criticism — Addresses, essays, lectures.
2. Detective and mystery stories — Technique — Addresses, essays, lectures.
I. Freeman, Lucy. II. Series.
PN3448.D4 M83 1982   809.3/872 19   *LC* 82-40259   *ISBN*
0804422125

The Mystery story / John Ball, editor ... [et al.].   **2.3474**
San Diego: University Extension, University of California, c1976. xii, 390 p.:
ports.; 24 cm. (The Mystery library) 1. Detective and mystery stories —
History and criticism — Addresses, essays, lectures. I. Ball, John Dudley,
1911- II. Series.
PN3448.D4 M98   813/.0872   *LC* 76-7110   *ISBN* 0891630198

Symons, Julian, 1912-.   **2.3475**
Bloody murder: from the detective story to the crime novel: a history / Julian
Symons. — New York: Viking, c1985. 261 p.; 23 cm. First U.S. ed. published
under title: Mortal consequences. 'Revised and updated edition ...'—T.p. verso.
Includes index. 1. Detective and mystery stories — History and criticism.
I. Symons, Julian, 1912- Mortal consequences. II. T.
PN3448.D4 S87 1985   809.3/872 19   *LC* 84-51885   *ISBN*
0670800961

Boucher, Anthony, 1911-1968.   **2.3476**
Multiplying villanies; selected mystery criticism, 1942–1968, by Anthony
Boucher. Edited by Robert E. Briney and Francis M. Nevins, Jr. Foreword by
Helen McCloy. Boston; Bouchercon; 1973. 136 p. 23 cm. 'A Bouchercon book.'
'Limited edition of 500 copies.' 1. Detective and mystery stories — History and
criticism. I. T.
PN3448.D4 W48 1973   809.3/872   *LC* 74-170882

PN3448.E–P

Altman, Janet Gurkin, 1945-.   **2.3477**
Epistolarity: approaches to a form / Janet Gurkin Altman. — Columbus: Ohio
State University Press, c1982. 235 p.; 24 cm. Includes index. 1. Epistolary
fiction — History and criticism. I. T.
PN3448.E6 A4 1982   809.3 19   *LC* 81-16866   *ISBN* 0814203132

Singer, Godfrey Frank, 1905-.   • **2.3478**
The epistolary novel: its origin, development, decline, and residuary influence.
New York: Russell & Russell, 1963. ix, 266 p.; 23 cm. 1. Epistolary fiction —
History and criticism. 2. English fiction — History and criticism. 3. English
letters — History and criticism. I. T.
PN3448.E6 S5 1963   *LC* 63-9508

Blotner, Joseph Leo, 1923-.   • **2.3479**
The political novel. — Garden City, N.Y.: Doubleday, 1955. 100 p.; 24 cm. —
(Doubleday short studies in political science 18) 1. Politics in literature
2. Fiction — History and criticism I. T.
PN3448.P6 B6   808.3   *LC* 55-6672

Howe, Irving.   • **2.3480**
Politics and the novel. — Freeport, N.Y.: Books for Libraries Press, [1970,
c1957] 251 p.; 23 cm. — (Essay index reprint series) 1. Politics in literature
2. Fiction — History and criticism I. T.
PN3448.P6 H5 1970   809.3   *LC* 74-117810   *ISBN* 0836917103

Cohn, Dorrit Claire.   **2.3481**
Transparent minds: narrative modes for presenting consciousness in fiction /
Dorrit Cohn. — Princeton, N.J.: Princeton University Press, c1978. x, 331 p.;
22 cm. Includes index. 1. Psychological fiction I. T.
PN3448.P8 C6   809.3/83   *LC* 78-51161   *ISBN* 0691063699

Friedman, Melvin J.   • **2.3482**
Stream of consciousness: a study in literary method / by Melvin Friedman. —
New Haven: Yale University Press, 1955. -. xi, 279 p.; 24 cm. — Includes
index. 1. Psychological fiction 2. Fiction — 20th century — History and
criticism 3. Stream of consciousness fiction I. T.
PN3448.P8 F7   809.3   *LC* 55-8701

Kumar, Shiv Kumar, 1921-.   • **2.3483**
Bergson and the stream of consciousness novel. — New York: New York
University Press, 1963, c1962. ix, 174 p., 22 cm. 1. Bergson, Henri, 1859-1941.
2. Stream of consciousness fiction 3. English fiction — 20th century — History
and criticism. I. T.
PN3448.P8 K8 1963   *LC* 63-14035

PN3448.S45 Science Fiction

Reginald, R.   **2.3484**
Science fiction and fantasy literature: a checklist, 1700–1974: with
Contemporary science fiction authors II / R. Reginald. — Detroit: Gale
Research Co., c1979. 2 v. (xi, 1141 p., [16] leaves of plates): ill.; 29 cm. The 1st
ed. of v.2 was published separately under title: Contemporary science fiction
authors. Includes indexes. 1. Science fiction — Biobibliography. 2. Fantastic
fiction — Bibliography. 3. Authors — 20th century — Biography. I. Reginald,
R. Contemporary science fiction authors. 1979. II. T.
Z5917.S36 R42 PN3448.S45   016.823/0876   *LC* 76-46130   *ISBN*
0810310511

Tymn, Marshall B., 1937-.   **2.3485**
A research guide to science fiction studies: an annotated checklist of primary
and secondary sources for on fantasy and science fiction / compiled and edited
by Marshall B. Tymn, Roger C. Schlobin, L.W. Currey; with a bibliography of
doctoral dissertations by Douglas R. Justus. — New York: Garland Pub., 1977.
ix, 165 p.; 23 cm. (Garland reference library of the humanities. v. 87) Includes
indexes. 1. Reference books — Science fiction. 2. Bibliography —

Bibliography — Science fiction. 3. Science fiction — History and criticism — Bibliography. I. Schlobin, Roger C. joint author. II. Currey, L. W. joint author. III. T. IV. Series.
Z5917.S36 T93 PN3448.S45   016.823/0876   LC 76-52682   ISBN 0824098862

Bailey, James Osler, 1903-.   • 2.3486
Pilgrims through space and time: trends and patterns in scientific and utopian fiction / by J. O. Bailey; foreword to the reprint ed. by Thomas D. Clareson. — Westport, Conn.: Greenwood Press, [1972, c1947] ix, 341 p.: ill.; 22 cm. 1. Science fiction — History and criticism 2. Science fiction — Bibliography. I. T.
PN3448.S45 B27 1972   809.3/876   LC 76-38126   ISBN 083715605X

Bretnor, Reginald.   2.3487
Science fiction, today and tomorrow; a discursive symposium, by Ben Bova [and others] Edited by Reginald Bretnor. [1st ed.] New York, Harper & Row [1974] ix, 342 p. 22 cm. 1. Science fiction — Addresses, essays, lectures. I. Bova, Ben, 1932- II. T.
PN3448.S45 B7   809.3/876   LC 73-4142   ISBN 0060104678

Gunn, James E., 1923-.   2.3488
Alternate worlds: the illustrated history of science fiction / by James Gunn. — Englewood Cliffs, N.J.: Prentice-Hall, [1975] 256 p.: ill.; 32 cm. Includes index. 1. Science fiction — History and criticism I. T.
PN3448.S45 G8   809.3/876   LC 75-8561   ISBN 013023267X

Lundwall, Sam J., 1941-.   2.3489
Science fiction, an illustrated history / Sam J. Lundwall. — 1st American ed. — New York: Grosset & Dunlap, 1978, c1977. 208 p.: ill. (some col.); 28 cm. Includes index. 1. Science fiction — History and criticism 2. Science fiction films — History and criticism. 3. Science fiction — Illustrations. I. T.
PN3448.S45 L79 1978   809.3/876   LC 77-75997   ISBN 0448144131

Meyers, Walter Earl, 1939-.   2.3490
Aliens and linguists: language study and science fiction / Walter E. Meyers. — Athens: University of Georgia Press, c1980. 257 p.; 24 cm. (South Atlantic Modern Language Association award study.) Includes index. 1. Science fiction — History and criticism 2. Linguistics in literature. 3. Communication in literature. I. T. II. Series.
PN3448.S45 M46   809.3/0876   LC 79-23574   ISBN 0820304875

Scholes, Robert E.   2.3491
Science fiction: history, science, vision / Robert Scholes, Eric S. Rabkin. New York: Oxford University Press, 1977. viii, 258 p.; 22 cm. Includes index. 1. Science fiction — History and criticism I. Rabkin, Eric S. joint author. II. T.
PN3448.S45 S26   809.3/876   LC 76-42615   ISBN 0195021738

Science fiction: a collection of critical essays / edited by Mark   2.3492
Rose.
Englewood Cliffs, N.J.: Prentice-Hall, c1976. x, 174 p.; 21 cm. (Twentieth century views) (A Spectrum book) 1. Science fiction — History and criticism — Addresses, essays, lectures. I. Rose, Mark.
PN3448.S45 S27   809.3/8/76   LC 76-19008   ISBN 0137949669

Science fiction: a critical guide / edited by Patrick Parrinder.   2.3493
London; New York: Longman, 1979. 238 p.; 23 cm. 1. Science fiction — History and criticism — Addresses, essays, lectures. I. Parrinder, Patrick.
PN3448.S45 S274   809.3/876   LC 78-40686   ISBN 0582489288

The science fiction encyclopedia / general editor, Peter   2.3494
Nicholls, associate editor, John Clute, technical editor, Carolyn
Eardley, contributing editors, Malcolm Edwards, Brian
Stableford.
1st ed. — Garden City, N.Y.: Doubleday, 1979. 672 p.: ill.; 27 cm. 1. Science fiction — Dictionaries. I. Nicholls, Peter, 1939-
PN3448.S45 S29   809.3/876   LC 77-15167   ISBN 0385130007

The Science fiction novel: imagination and social criticism /   • 2.3495
Basil Davenport...[et al.].
[1st ed.] — Chicago: Advent, 1959. 160 p.; 23 cm. 1. Science fiction — History and criticism 2. Social problems in literature I. Davenport, Basil, 1905-
PN3448.S45 S35   809.3876   LC 58-7492

Suvin, Darko, 1930-.   2.3496
Metamorphoses of science fiction: on the poetics and history of a literary genre / Darko Suvin. — New Haven: Yale University Press, 1979. xviii, 317 p.; 24 cm. Includes index. 1. Science fiction — History and criticism I. T.
PN3448.S45 S897   809.3/876   LC 78-6265   ISBN 0300022506

Voices for the future: essays on major science fiction writers /   2.3497
Thomas D. Clareson, editor.
Bowling Green, Ohio: Bowling Green University Popular Press, c1976-. 2 v.; 24 cm. 1. Science fiction — History and criticism — Addresses, essays, lectures. I. Clareson, Thomas D.
PN3448.S45 V6   813/.0876   LC 76-10939   ISBN 0879721197

PN3448.T–Z

Mendilow, Adam Abraham, 1909-.   • 2.3498
Time and the novel, by A. A. Mendilow. Introd. by J. Isaacs. — New York: Humanities Press, 1972 [c1952] viii, 245 p.; 23 cm. 1. Fiction — History and criticism 2. Time in literature I. T.
PN3448.T5 M4 1972   809.3   LC 77-189133   ISBN 0391000201

The First World War in fiction: a collection of critical essays /   2.3499
edited by Holger Klein.
New York: Barnes & Noble, 1977. x, 246 p.; 23 cm. Includes index. 1. Fiction — 20th century — History and criticism — Addresses, essays, lectures. 2. World War, 1914-1918 — Literature and the war — Addresses, essays, lectures. I. Klein, Holger Michael, 1938-
PN3448.W3 F5 1977   809.3/9/3   LC 76-28822   ISBN 0064937925

The Second World War in fiction / edited by Holger Klein with   2.3500
John Flower and Eric Homberger.
London: Macmillan, 1984. ix, 249 p.; 23 cm. (Macmillan studies in twentieth-century literature.) Includes indexes. 1. War stories — History and criticism. 2. World War, 1939-1945 — Literature and the war 3. Fiction — 20th century — History and criticism I. Klein, Holger Michael, 1938- II. Flower, J. E. (John Ernest) III. Homberger, Eric. IV. Series.
PN3448.W3 S43 1984   809.3/9358 19   LC 85-115698   ISBN 0333259645

PN3451–3503 HISTORY

Booth, Wayne C.   2.3501
The rhetoric of fiction. 2nd ed. [Chicago] University of Chicago Press [1983] 522 p.; 21 cm. 1. Fiction — Technique I. T.
PN3451.B597 1983   808.3   LC 82-13592

Howells, William Dean, 1837-1920.   • 2.3502
Criticism and fiction, and other essays. Edited with introds. and notes by Clara Marburg Kirk and Rudolf Kirk. — [New York]: New York University Press, 1959. xix, 413 p.; 22 cm. 1. Fiction — History and criticism 2. American fiction — History and criticism. 3. Criticism I. T.
PN3451.H6   809.3   LC 59-6248

Krutch, Joseph Wood, 1893-1970.   • 2.3503
Five masters; a study in the mutations of the novel. — Bloomington: Indiana University Press, [1959] 328 p.; 20 cm. — (Midland books, MB17) 1. Fiction — Addresses, essays, lectures. 2. Authors I. T.
PN3451.K7 1959   809.3   LC 59-8983

Scholes, Robert E.   • 2.3504
The nature of narrative [by] Robert Scholes [and] Robert Kellogg. — New York: Oxford University Press, 1966. 326 p.; 24 cm. 1. Fiction — History and criticism I. Kellogg, Robert. joint author. II. T.
PN3451.S3 1966   809.3923   LC 66-14481

Auchincloss, Louis, 1917-.   • 2.3505
Reflections of a Jacobite. Boston: Houghton Mifflin, 1961. 220 p.; 21 cm. 1. James, Henry, 1843-1916. 2. Fiction — Addresses,essays,lectures. I. T.
PN3463.A8   809.3   LC 61-8700

Girard, René, 1923-.   2.3506
Deceit, desire, and the novel; self and other in literary structure. Translated by Yvonne Freccero. — Baltimore, Johns Hopkins Press [1965] 318 p. 22 cm. Translation of Mensonge romantique et vérité romanesque. 1. Fiction — Hist. & crit. 2. Example I. T. II. Title: Desire, and the novel.
PN3463.G513   809.33   LC 65-28582

Blackmur, R. P. (Richard P.), 1904-1965.   • 2.3507
Eleven essays in the European novel [by] R. P. Blackmur. New York, Harcourt, Brace & World [1964] ix, 243 p. 22 cm. 1. Dostoyevsky, Fyodor, 1821-1881. 2. European fiction — History and criticism — Addresses, essays, lectures. I. T.
PN3491.B55   809.3   LC 64-19367

Guérard, Albert J. (Albert Joseph), 1914-.   2.3508
The triumph of the novel: Dickens, Dostoevsky, Faulkner / Albert J. Guérard. — New York: Oxford University Press, 1976. 365 p.; 24 cm. 1. Dickens, Charles, 1812-1870 — Criticism and interpretation. 2. Dostoyevsky, Fyodor,

1821-1881 — Criticism and interpretation. 3. Faulkner, William, 1897-1962 — Criticism and interpretation. 4. Fiction — History and criticism I. T.
PN3491.G8   809.3/3   *LC* 75-46357   *ISBN* 0195020669

Iser, Wolfgang.   **2.3509**
[Implizite Leser. English] The implied reader; patterns of communication in prose fiction from Bunyan to Beckett. Baltimore, Johns Hopkins University Press [1974] xiv, 303 p. 23 cm. Translation of Der implizite Leser. 1. Fiction — History and criticism I. T.
PN3491.I813   809.3/3   *LC* 73-20075   *ISBN* 080181569X

Levin, Harry, 1912-.   • **2.3510**
Symbolism and fiction. — Charlottesville: University of Virginia Press, 1956. 43 p.; 20 cm. — (Peters Rushton seminars in contemporary prose and poetry; May 1956) 1. Fiction — History and criticism 2. Symbolism I. T. II. Series.
PN3491.L4   *LC* 56-63657

Maugham, W. Somerset (William Somerset), 1874-1965.   • **2.3511**
[Great novelists and their novels] The art of fiction: an introduction to ten novels and their authors. — New York: Greenwood Press, 1968 [c1954] 318 p.; 23 cm. Originally published under title: Great novelists and their novels. 1. Fiction — History and criticism — Addresses, essays, lectures. I. T.
PN3491.M3 1968   809.3/3   *LC* 69-10131

O'Connor, Frank, 1903-1966.   • **2.3512**
The mirror in the roadway: a study of the modern novel / by Frank O'Connor [i.e. M. O'Donovan]. — 1st ed. New York: Knopf, 1956. 316 p.; 22 cm. — (Borzoi book.) 1. Fiction — History and criticism I. T. II. Series.
PN3491.O3   *LC* 56-8926

Reed, Walter L.   **2.3513**
An exemplary history of the novel: the Quixotic versus the picaresque / Walter L. Reed. — Chicago: University of Chicago Press, 1981. viii, 334 p.; 24 cm. 1. Fiction — History and criticism 2. English fiction — 18th century — History and criticism. 3. English fiction — 19th century — History and criticism. 4. American fiction — 19th century — History and criticism. I. T.
PN3491.R43   809.3/1   *LC* 80-17908   *ISBN* 0226706834

Spiegel, Alan.   **2.3514**
Fiction and the camera eye: visual consciousness in film and the modern novel / Alan Spiegel. Charlottesville: University Press of Virginia, 1976. xvi, 203 p.; 23 cm. 1. Fiction — History and criticism 2. Motion pictures and literature I. T.
PN3491.S65   809.3/3   *LC* 75-22353   *ISBN* 0813905982

Weinstein, Arnold L.   **2.3515**
Fictions of the self, 1550–1800 / Arnold Weinstein. — Princeton, N.J.: Princeton University Press, c1981. x, 302 p.; 23 cm. Includes index. 1. European fiction — History and criticism. 2. Characters and characteristics in literature I. T.
PN3491.W4   809.3/927 19   *LC* 80-7558   *ISBN* 0691064482

Wilson, Angus.   **2.3516**
Diversity and depth in fiction: selected critical writings of Angus Wilson / edited by Kerry McSweeney. — New York: Viking Press, 1984, c1983. xvi, 303 p.; 22 cm. 1. Fiction — History and criticism — Addresses, essays, lectures. 2. English fiction — History and criticism — Addresses, essays, lectures. I. McSweeney, Kerry, 1941- II. T.
PN3491.W47 1984   809.3 19   *LC* 84-140736   *ISBN* 0670770760

Williams, Ioan M.   **2.3517**
The idea of the novel in Europe, 1600–1800 / Ioan Williams. — New York: New York University Press, 1979. xiii, 253 p.; 23 cm. — (The Gotham library of the New York University Press) Includes indexes. 1. European fiction — 17th century — History and criticism. 2. European fiction — 18th century — History and criticism. I. T.
PN3491.W48 1979b   809.3/3   *LC* 78-78112   *ISBN* 0814791875

Fletcher, John, 1937-.   **2.3518**
Novel and reader / John Fletcher. — London; Boston: M. Boyars, 1981 (c1980). 192 p.; 23 cm. Includes index. 1. Fiction — 19th century — History and criticism. 2. Fiction — 20th century — History and criticism I. T.
PN3499.F53   809.3 19   *LC* 79-56842   *ISBN* 0714526207

James, Henry, 1843-1916.   • **2.3519**
The art of fiction, and other essays; with an introd. by Morris Roberts. New York, Oxford Univ. Press, 1948. xxiv, 240 p. 23 cm. 1. Emerson, Ralph Waldo, 1803-1882. 2. Fiction — History and criticism 3. Criticism — Addresses, essays, lectures. I. T.
PN3499.J25   808.3   *LC* 48-6136

James, Henry, 1843-1916.   • **2.3520**
The house of fiction: essays on the novel / by Henry James, edited with an introd. by Leon Edel. — London: Hart-Davis, 1957. 286 p.; 21 cm. 1. Fiction — 19th century — History and criticism — Addresses, essays, lectures. I. Edel, Leon, 1907- II. T.
PN3499.J28   808.3   *LC* 58-1584

James, Henry, 1843-1916.   • **2.3521**
Notes on novelists, with some other notes. — New York: Biblo and Tannen, 1969 [c1914] vi, 455 p.; 22 cm. 1. Fiction — History and criticism 2. Novelists I. T.
PN3499.J3 1969   809.3/3   *LC* 68-56451

Maurois, André, 1885-1967.   • **2.3522**
The art of writing. Translated by Gerard Hopkins. [1st ed.] New York, Dutton, 1960. 320 p. 21 cm. Essays, chiefly translations from Lecture mon doux plaisir. 1. Fiction — 19th century — History and criticism. I. T.
PN3499.M33 1960a   *LC* 60-52314

PN3503 20th Century

Beach, Joseph Warren, 1880-1957.   • **2.3523**
The twentieth century novel: studies in technique. New York: Appleton-Century-Crofts, 1932. viii, 569 p.; 21 cm. 1. Fiction — 20th century — History and criticism I. T.
PN3503 B4   808.3   *LC* 32-32792

Bruffee, Kenneth A.   **2.3524**
Elegiac romance: cultural change and loss of the hero in modern fiction / Kenneth A. Bruffee. — Ithaca: Cornell University Press, 1983. 230 p.; 23 cm. 1. Fiction — 20th century — History and criticism I. T.
PN3503.B765 1983   809.3/9353 19   *LC* 83-45140   *ISBN* 0801415799

Dillard, Annie.   **2.3525**
Living by fiction / by Annie Dillard. — 1st ed. — New York: Harper & Row, c1982. 192 p. cm. 1. Fiction — 20th century — History and criticism 2. Fiction I. T.
PN3503.D5 1982   PN3503 D5.   809.3/04 19   *LC* 81-47882   *ISBN* 0060149604

Hirsch, Marianne.   **2.3526**
Beyond the single vision: Henry James, Michel Butor, Uwe Johnson / by Marianne Hirsch. — York, S.C.: French Literature Publications Co., 1981. 205 p.; 24 cm. Includes index. 1. James, Henry, 1843-1916 — Criticism and interpretation. 2. Butor, Michel — Criticism and interpretation. 3. Johnson, Uwe, 1934- — Criticism and interpretation. 4. Fiction — 20th century — History and criticism 5. Culture conflict in literature. 6. Travel in literature I. T.
PN3503.H5 1981   809.3 19   *LC* 81-68414   *ISBN* 0917786211

Morris, Wright, 1910-.   **2.3527**
About fiction; reverent reflections on the nature of fiction with irreverent observations on writers, readers & other abuses. — [1st ed.]. — New York: Harper & Row, [1975] vi, 182 p.; 21 cm. 1. Fiction — 20th century — History and criticism I. T.
PN3503.M62   809.3/3   *LC* 74-6771   *ISBN* 0060130822

Robbe-Grillet, Alain, 1922-.   • **2.3528**
[Pour un nouveau roman. English] For a new novel: essays on fiction. Translated by Richard Howard. New York, Grove Press [1966, c1965] 175 p. 19 cm. 1. Fiction — 20th century — Addresses, essays, lectures. I. T.
PN3503.R583 1966   809.33   *LC* 66-14094

Sarraute, Nathalie.   • **2.3529**
[Ere du soupçon. English] The age of suspicion; essays on the novel. Translated by Maria Jolas. New York, G. Braziller, 1963. 147 p. 22 cm. 1. Fiction — 20th century — History & criticism. I. T.
PN3503.S313   809.3   *LC* 63-10739

Scholes, Robert E.   **2.3530**
Fabulation and metafiction / Robert Scholes. — Urbana: University of Illinois Press, c1979. 222 p.; 24 cm. Includes index. 1. Fiction — 20th century — History and criticism 2. Fiction I. T.
PN3503.S32   813/.5/09   *LC* 78-10776   *ISBN* 0252007042

Weinstein, Arnold L.   **2.3531**
Vision and response in modern fiction [by] Arnold L. Weinstein. — Ithaca [N.Y.]: Cornell University Press, [1974] 282 p.; 23 cm. 1. Fiction — 20th century — History and criticism 2. Fiction — 19th century — History and criticism. I. T.
PN3503.W39 1974   809.3   *LC* 73-20793   *ISBN* 0801408334

PN4001–4321 Oratory. Speech. Debate

Baskerville, Barnet.   **2.3532**
The people's voice: the orator in American society / Barnet Baskerville. — Lexington: University Press of Kentucky, c1979. 259 p.; 23 cm. 1. Oratory — United States — History. I. T.
PN4055.U5 B33   PN4055U5 B33.   815/.01   *LC* 79-4001   *ISBN* 0813113857

Methods of rhetorical criticism: a twentieth–century perspective.   **2.3533**
2d ed., rev. / edited by Bernard L. Brock and Robert L. Scott. — Detroit: Wayne State University Press, 1980. 503 p.; 24 cm. Edition for 1972 entered under R. L. Scott. Includes index. 1. Oratory — Addresses, essays, lectures. 2. Criticism — Addresses, essays, lectures. I. Brock, Bernard L. II. Scott, Robert Lee, 1928- comp. Methods of rhetorical criticism.
PN4061.S37 1980   801/.955 19   *LC* 80-11422   *ISBN* 0814316484

Wallace, Karl Richards, 1905-1973. ed.   ● **2.3534**
History of speech education in America; background studies. Prepared under the auspices of the Speech Association of America; Karl R. Wallace, editor, Warren Guthrie [and others] editorial board. New York, Appleton-Century-Crofts [1954] x, 687 p. illus., map. 25 cm. 1. Rhetoric — Study and teaching — History. 2. Speech — Study and teaching — History. 3. Amateur theater I. Speech Association of America. II. T. III. Title: Speech education in America.
PN4091.W3   *LC* 54-6203

Thonssen, Lester, 1904-.   **2.3535**
Speech criticism [by] Lester Thonssen, A. Craig Baird [and] Waldo W. Braden. — 2d ed. — New York, Ronald Press Co. [1970] x, 580 p. 24 cm. 1. Public speaking 2. Elocution 3. Speech I. Baird, Albert Craig, 1883- joint author. II. Braden, Waldo Warder, 1911- joint author. III. T.
PN4121.T528 1970   808.5   *LC* 70-123054

Linklater, Kristin.   **2.3536**
Freeing the natural voice / Kristin Linklater; drawings by Douglas Florian. — 1st ed. — New York: Drama Book Specialists, c1976. 210 p.: ill.; 25 cm. 1. Voice culture I. T.
PN4162.L55   808.5   *LC* 75-28172   *ISBN* 0910482675

Ehninger, Douglas.   **2.3537**
Decision by debate / Douglas Ehninger, Wayne Brockriede. — 2d ed. — New York: Harper & Row, c1978. xiii, 238 p.; 25 cm. 1. Debates and debating I. Brockriede, Wayne. joint autho. II. T.
PN4181.E48 1978   808.53   *LC* 77-9490   *ISBN* 0060418672

Freeley, Austin J.   **2.3538**
Argumentation and debate: critical thinking for reasoned decision making / Austin J. Freeley. — 6th ed. — Belmont, Calif.: Wadsworth Pub. Co., c1986. xvi, 427 p.: ill.; 25 cm. 1. Debates and debating 2. Decision-making I. T.
PN4181.F68 1986   808.53 19   *LC* 85-20392   *ISBN* 0534055265

Berry, Cicely.   **2.3539**
Voice and the actor / Cicely Berry. — 1st American ed. — New York: Macmillan, 1974, c1973. 149 p.: ill.; 22 cm. Includes index. 1. Voice culture — Exercises I. T.
PN4197.B46 1974   808.5   *LC* 74-2646

PN4700–5650 Journalism. The Press

Snyder, Louis Leo, 1907- ed.   ● **2.3540**
A treasury of great reporting; 'literature under pressure' from the sixteenth century to our own time. Edited by Louis L. Snyder and Richard B. Morris. 2d ed., rev. and enl. New York, Simon and Schuster [c1962] 795 p. 21 cm. An Essandess paperback. 1. Reporters and reporting I. Morris, Richard Brandon, 1904- joint ed. II. T.
PN4726.S6 1962   808.8   *LC* 62-8901

Hughes, Helen MacGill, 1903-.   ● **2.3541**
News and the human interest story. — New York: Greenwood Press, [1968, c1940] xxiii, 313 p.; 23 cm. 1. Journalism 2. Newspapers I. T.
PN4731.H815 1968   070.4/3   *LC* 68-57790

Merrill, John Calhoun, 1924-.   **2.3542**
The imperative of freedom; a philosophy of journalistic autonomy. — New York: Hastings House, [1974] xviii, 228 p.: illus.; 23 cm. — (Studies in public communication) (Communication arts books) 1. Journalism — Philosophy. I. T.
PN4731.M44   070/.01   *LC* 74-2064   *ISBN* 0803833911

Merrill, John Calhoun, 1924-.   **2.3543**
Philosophy and journalism / John C. Merrill, S. Jack Odell. — New York: Longman, c1983. xiii, 190 p.; 24 cm. — (Longman series in public communication.) 1. Journalism — Philosophy. I. Odell, S. Jack, 1933- II. T. III. Series.
PN4731.M444 1983   070/.01 19   *LC* 82-7770   *ISBN* 0582281571

Merrill, John Calhoun, 1924-.   **2.3544**
The world's great dailies: profiles of fifty newspapers / by John C. Merrill and Harold A. Fisher. — New York: Hastings House, c1980. xiv, 399 p.: ill.; 25 cm. — (Communication arts books) Includes index. 1. Newspapers I. Fisher, Harold A. joint author. II. T.
PN4731.M446 1980   070   *LC* 79-19075   *ISBN* 0803880952

Salmon, Lucy Maynard, 1853-1927.   ● **2.3545**
The newspaper and the historian. New York, Oxford university press, 1923. 566 p. ill. Biographical notes, p. [495]-516. 1. Newspapers 2. History 3. Journalism I. T.
PN4731.S2   070   *LC* 23-10928

Siebert, Fredrick Seaton, 1902-.   ● **2.3546**
Four theories of the press: the authoritarian, libertarian, social responsibility, and Soviet concepts of what the press should be and do / Fred S. Siebert, Theodore Peterson, Wilbur Schramm. — Urbana: University of Illinois Press, 1956. 153 p.: 24 cm. 'Essays ... prepared in connection with a study of the social responsibility of mass communications ... [being conducted] for the Department of the Church and Economic Life of the National Council of Churches.' 1. Press 2. Journalism 3. Communication I. Peterson, Theodore Bernard, 1918- II. Schramm, Wilbur Lang, 1907- III. T.
PN4731.S49   *LC* 56-11881/rev   *ISBN* 02527224216

Smith, Anthony, 1938-.   **2.3547**
The newspaper: an international history / Anthony Smith. — London: Thames and Hudson, c1979. 192 p.: ill., ports; 24 cm. — Includes index. 1. Newspapers — History. 2. Newspaper publishing — History. I. T.
PN4734.S55   070.17209   *LC* 78-55193   *ISBN* 0500012040

PN4735–4749 RELATION TO THE STATE. REGULATION

Commission on Freedom of the Press.   ● **2.3548**
A free and responsible press; a general report on mass communication: newspapers, radio, motion pictures, magazines, and books. — Chicago, Ill., The University of Chicago press [1947] xii, 138, [1] p. 20 cm. 1. Press — United States. 2. Radio — United States. 3. Motion pictures 4. Freedom of the press — United States. I. T.
PN4735.C6   070.973   *LC* 47-1785

Hohenberg, John.   ● **2.3549**
Free press/free people; the best cause. New York, Columbia University Press, 1971. xvii, 514 p. 24 cm. 1. Freedom of the press I. T.
PN4735.H6   323.44/5   *LC* 70-133912   *ISBN* 023103315X

Kurian, George.   **2.3550**
World press encyclopedia / edited by George Thomas Kurian; indexed by Marjorie B. Bank and James Johnson. — New York: Facts on File, 1982. 2 v. 1. Freedom of the press 2. Government and the press I. T.
PN4735.K87   PN4735 K87.   070 19   *LC* 80-25120   *ISBN* 0871963922

Press control around the world / edited by Jane Leftwich Curry and Joan R. Dassin.   **2.3551**
New York, N.Y.: Praeger Publishers, 1982. xvi, 283 p.; 24 cm. 1. Freedom of the press — Addresses, essays, lectures. I. Curry, Jane Leftwich, 1948- II. Dassin, Joan.
PN4735.P68 1982   323.44/5 19   *LC* 82-9837   *ISBN* 0030598699

The Third World and press freedom / edited by Philip C. Horton; foreword by John Chancellor.   **2.3552**
New York: Praeger, 1978. xv, 253 p.; 24 cm. 1. Journalism — Developing countries 2. Freedom of the press — Developing countries. 3. News agencies I. Horton, Philip C.
PN4736.T48   323.44/5   *LC* 78-17072   *ISBN* 0030455510

Cater, Douglass, 1923-.   • **2.3553**
The fourth branch of Government. — Boston, Houghton Mifflin, 1959. 194 p. 22 cm. 1. Government and the press — U.S. 2. Government publicity — U.S. I. T.
PN4738.C3   070.1   *LC* 59-7616

Rivers, William L.   **2.3554**
The other government: power & the Washington media / William L. Rivers. — New York: Universe Books, 1982. 240 p.; 22 cm. Includes index. 1. Government and the press — United States. 2. United States — Politics and government — 1945- I. T.
PN4738.R53 1982   071/.53 19   *LC* 81-40694   *ISBN* 0876633653

Small, William J.   • **2.3555**
Political power and the press [by] William J. Small. — [1st ed.]. — New York: W. W. Norton, [1972] 423 p.; 22 cm. 1. Government and the press — United States. 2. Press and politics I. T.
PN4738.S6   323.44/5   *LC* 72-3102   *ISBN* 0393053393

Smith, Culver H.   **2.3556**
The press, politics, and patronage: the American government's use of newspapers, 1789–1875 / Culver H. Smith. Athens: University of Georgia Press, c1977. xv, 351 p., [4] leaves of plates: ill.; 24 cm. Includes index. 1. Government and the press — United States — History. I. T.
PN4738.S65   070.4/12   *LC* 75-26051   *ISBN* 0820304042

Cohen, Bernard Cecil, 1926-.   • **2.3557**
The press and foreign policy. — Princeton, N.J.: Princeton University Press, 1963. ix, 288 p.; 23 cm. 1. Government and the press — United States. 2. United States — Foreign relations — 1945- I. T.
PN4745.C6   070.1   *LC* 63-12668

Reston, James, 1909-.   • **2.3558**
The artillery of the press; its influence on American foreign policy, by James Reston. — [1st ed.]. — New York: Published for the Council on Foreign Relations by Harper & Row, [1967] x, 116 p.; 21 cm. — (Elihu Root lectures. 1965-66) 1. Government and the press — United States. 2. United States — Foreign relations I. Council on Foreign Relations. II. T. III. Series.
PN4745.R4 1967   071.3   *LC* 67-11330

Sarkar, Ranadhir Sarma, 1908-.   **2.3559**
The press in India / R.C.S. Sarkar. — New Delhi: S. Chand, 1984. xvi, 320 p.; 22 cm. Includes index. 1. Freedom of the press — India. I. T.
PN4748.I6S3x   342.54/0853 345.402853 19   *LC* 84-901202

Pollak, Richard.   **2.3560**
Up against apartheid: the role and the plight of the press in South Africa / Richard Pollak. — Carbondale, IL: Southern Illinois University Press, c1981. 157 p.; 22 cm. — (Science and international affairs.) 1. Government and the press — South Africa. 2. South African newspapers 3. English newspapers — South Africa. I. T. II. Series.
PN4748.S58 P6   079/.68 19   *LC* 80-22363   *ISBN* 0809310139

PN4756–4784 Ethics. Editing. Reporting

Goodwin, H. Eugene, 1922-.   **2.3561**
Groping for ethics in journalism / H. Eugene Goodwin. — 1st ed. — Ames: Iowa State University Press, 1983. x, 335 p.: ill.; 24 cm. 1. Journalistic ethics I. T.
PN4756.G66 1983   174/.9097 19   *LC* 83-8566   *ISBN* 0813808162

Hulteng, John L., 1921-.   **2.3562**
The messenger's motives: ethical problems of the news media / John L. Hulteng. — 2nd ed. — Englewood Cliffs, N.J.: Prentice-Hall, c1985. xii, 239 p.; 23 cm. Includes index. 1. Journalistic ethics I. T.
PN4756.H8 1985   174/.9097 19   *LC* 84-6878   *ISBN* 013577487X

Baskette, Floyd K.   **2.3563**
The art of editing / Floyd K. Baskette, Jack Z. Sissors, Brian S. Brooks. — 4th ed. — New York: Macmillan; London: Collier Macmillan, c1986. ix, 534 p.: ill.; 27 cm. Includes index. 1. Journalism — Editing 2. Copy-reading I. Sissors, Jack Zanville, 1919- II. Brooks, Brian S. III. T.
PN4778.B3 1986   070.4/1 19   *LC* 85-13746   *ISBN* 0023062908

Krieghbaum, Hillier.   • **2.3564**
Facts in perspective; the editorial page and news interpretation. — Englewood Cliffs, N.J.: Prentice-Hall, 1956. 518 p.: illus.; 22 cm. — (Prentice-Hall journalism series) 1. Editorials I. T.
PN4778.K7   070.432   *LC* 56-5109

Charnley, Mitchell Vaughn, 1898-.   • **2.3565**
Reporting / Mitchell V. Charnley, Blair Charnley. — 4th ed. — New York: Holt, Rinehart, and Winston, c1979. xii, 432 p.: ill.; 24 cm. 1. Reporters and reporting I. Charnley, Blair. joint author. II. T.
PN4781.C43 1979   070.4   *LC* 78-16594   *ISBN* 0030188717

MacDougall, Curtis Daniel, 1903-.   **2.3566**
Interpretative reporting / Curtis D. MacDougall, Robert D. Reid. — 9th ed. — New York: Macmillan; London: Collier Macmillan, c1987. x, 527 p.; 26 cm. Includes index. 1. Reporters and reporting I. Reid, Robert D. (Robert Delaware), 1940- II. T.
PN4781.M153 1987   070.4/3 19   *LC* 86-17984   *ISBN* 0023731400

The Reporter's handbook: an investigator's guide to documents   **2.3567**
and techniques / Investigative Reporters and Editors, Inc. under the editorship of John Ullmann and Stephen Honeyman.
New York: St. Martin's Press, c1983. xxxviii, 504 p. 1. Reporters and reporting — Handbooks, manuals, etc. 2. Public records — United States — Handbooks, manuals, etc. I. Honeyman, Steve. II. Ullmann, John. III. Investigative Reporters and Editors, Inc.
PN4781.U56 1983   070.4/3 19   *LC* 83-10970   *ISBN* 0312673949

PN4784 Special Topics, A–Z

Feiffer, Jules. ed.   **2.3568**
The great comic book heroes. — [1st ed.]. — New York, Dial Press, 1965. 189 p. illus. (part col.) 31 cm. 1. Comic books, strips, etc — Hist. & crit. 2. Newspapers — Sections, columns, etc. — Comics I. T.
PN4784.C68F4   813.5   *LC* 65-23962

Janowitz, Morris.   • **2.3569**
The community press in an urban setting: the social elements of urbanism / by Morris Janowitz; with a postscript by Scott Greer. — 2d ed. — Chicago: University of Chicago Press, 1967. xxiii, 275 p.; 21 cm. 1. Community newspapers 2. American newspapers — Chicago I. T.
PN4784.C73 J3   071.73   *LC* 67-21391

Desmond, Robert William, 1900-.   **2.3570**
Crisis and conflict: world news reporting between two wars, 1920–1940 / Robert W. Desmond. — Iowa City: University of Iowa Press, c1982. xii, 518 p.; 24 cm. Continues: Windows on the world. c1980. Includes index. 1. Foreign news — History — 20th century. 2. News agencies — History — 20th century. 3. Journalism — History — 20th century. I. T.
PN4784.F6 D47 1982   070.4/33 19   *LC* 82-8584   *ISBN* 0877451117

Desmond, Robert William, 1900-.   **2.3571**
Tides of war: world news reporting, 1931–1945 / Robert W. Desmond. — Iowa City: University of Iowa Press, c1984. xi, 544 p.; 24 cm. Continues: Crisis and conflict. c1982. Includes index. 1. Foreign news — History — 20th century. 2. Reporters and reporting — History — 20th century. 3. War correspondents 4. World War, 1939-1945 — Journalists I. T.
PN4784.F6 D474 1984   070.4/33 19   *LC* 84-2504   *ISBN* 0877451257

International Press Institute.   • **2.3572**
The flow of the news: a study by the International Press Institute, in cooperation with editors, agency executives, and foreign correspondents in ten countries. — Zurich, 1953. 266 p. 1. Foreign news I. T.
PN4784.F6 I64

Kronick, David A. (David Abraham), 1917-.   **2.3573**
A history of scientific & technical periodicals: the origins and development of the scientific and technical press, 1665–1790 / by David A. Kronick. — 2d ed. — Metuchen, N.J.: Scarecrow Press, 1976. xvi, 336 p.; 23 cm. Includes indexes. 1. Journalism, Scientific — History. 2. Journalism, Technical — History. 3. Periodicals — History. I. T.
PN4784.T3 K7 1976   505   *LC* 75-41487   *ISBN* 0810808447

PN4801–4836 History: General

Desmond, Robert William, 1900-.   **2.3574**
The information process: world news reporting to the twentieth century / Robert W. Desmond. — Iowa City: University of Iowa Press, 1978. xiv, 495 p.; 24 cm. Includes index. 1. Newspapers — History. 2. News agencies — History. 3. Foreign news — History. I. T.
PN4801.D45   070/.9 19   *LC* 77-9491   *ISBN* 0877450706

Smith, Anthony, 1938-. 2.3575
Goodbye, Gutenberg: the newspaper revolution of the 1980s / Anthony Smith. — New York: Oxford University Press, 1980. xiii, 367 p.: ill.; 24 cm. 1. Newspapers — History. 2. Communication — History. I. T.
PN4801.S535　　070　　LC 79-24263　　ISBN 0195027094

Desmond, Robert William, 1900-. 2.3576
Windows on the world: the information process in a changing society, 1900–1920 / Robert W. Desmond. — Iowa City: University of Iowa Press, c1980. xii, 608 p.; 24 cm. Continues the author's The information process. Includes index. 1. Journalism — History — 20th century. 2. News agencies — History — 20th century. 3. World War, 1914-1918 — Journalists. I. T.
PN4815.D4　　070/.9 19　　LC 80-19397　　ISBN 0877451044

Innis, Harold Adams, 1894-1952. • 2.3577
The press: a neglected factor in the economic history of the twentieth century / by H.A. Innis. — London; Toronto: Oxford University Press, 1949. 48 p. — (Stamp memorial lecture; 1949) 1. Newspapers 2. American newspapers I. T. II. Series.
PN4815.I5　　LC 49-4076

Knightley, Phillip. 2.3578
The first casualty: from the Crimea to Vietnam: the war correspondent as hero, propagandist, and myth maker / Phillip Knightly. — 1st ed. — New York: Harcourt Brace Jovanovich, [1975] 465 p., [16] leaves of plates: ill.; 25 cm. Includes index. 1. War correspondents I. T.
PN4823.K5　　070.4/092/2　　LC 75-11684　　ISBN 0151312648

Mathews, Joseph James, 1908-. • 2.3579
Reporting the wars / by Joseph J. Mathews. — Minneapolis: University of Minnesota Press, 1957. 322 p. 1. War correspondents 2. Reporters and reporting I. T.
PN4823.M3 1957　　070.42　　LC 57-13144

Hoffman, Frederick John. • 2.3580
The little magazine: a history and a bibliography / by Frederick J. Hoffman, Charles Allen, Carolyn F. Ulrich. — Princeton, N.J.: Princeton University Press, 1946. 440 p.: ill. 'List of references': p. [399]-403. 1. American periodicals — History. 2. American periodicals — Bibliography. 3. English periodicals — History. 4. English periodicals — Bibliography 5. Literature — Periodicals — History. I. Allen, Charles Albert, 1913- II. Ulrich, Carolyn Farquhar, 1881- III. T.
PN4836.H6　　052　　LC 46-17

PN4840–5650 Journalism, by Country

PN4840–4900 United States

Gramling, Oliver. • 2.3581
AP; the story of news. — Port Washington, N.Y.: Kennikat Press, [1969, c1940] x, 506 p.; 23 cm. 1. Associated Press. 2. Journalism — United States 3. Press — United States. I. T.
PN4841.G7 1969　　070.4/3　　LC 77-94561　　ISBN 0804606900

Morris, Joe Alex, 1904- • 2.3582
Deadline every minute: the story of the United Press. — Garden City, N.Y.: Doubleday, 1957. 356p. 1. United Press Associations. I. T.
PN4841.U65M6　　LC 57-12472

Bleyer, Willard Grosvenor, 1873-1935. • 2.3583
Main currents in the history of American journalism, by Willard Grosvenor Bleyer ... Boston, New York [etc.] Houghton Mifflin Company [c1927] x, 464 p. front., illus. (incl. facsims.) ports. 21 cm. 1. Journalism — United States 2. Press — United States. I. T.
PN4855.B6　　LC 27-1938

Emery, Edwin. 2.3584
The press and America: an interpretive history of the mass media / Edwin Emery, Michael Emery. — 5th ed. — Englewood Cliffs, N.J.: Prentice-Hall, c1984. viii, 773 p.: ill.; 25 cm. 1. Press — United States. 2. American newspapers I. Emery, Michael C. II. T.
PN4855.E6 1984　　071/.3 19　　LC 83-26852　　ISBN 0136979882

Lee, Alfred McClung, 1906-. • 2.3585
The daily newspaper in America: the evolution of a social instrument / by Alfred McClung Lee. — New York: Macmillan, 1937. xiv, 797 p.: diagrs., maps (1 fold.); 22 cm. 'A part of this study [was prepared] for submission as a dissertation for the degree of doctor of philosophy to the Yale graduate school [1933]'—Pref. 1. American newspapers — History. 2. Press — United States. 3. Journalism — United States I. T.
PN4855.L38

Mott, Frank Luther, 1886-1964. • 2.3586
American journalism; a history, 1690–1960. — 3d ed. — New York, Macmillan [1962] 901 p. illus. 25 cm. 1. Journalism — U.S. 2. American newspapers 3. Press — U.S. I. T.
PN4855.M63 1962　　071.3　　LC 62-7157

Mott, Frank Luther, 1886-1964. • 2.3587
The news in America. — Cambridge, Harvard University Press, 1952. 236 p. 22 cm. — (The Library of Congress series in American civilization) 1. Journalism — U.S. 2. Press — U.S. 3. News agencies 4. Radio journalism I. T. II. Series.
PN4855.M65　　071　　LC 52-8218

Rosewater, Victor, 1871-1940. • 2.3588
History of coöperative news–gathering in the United States. New York, D. Appleton, 1930. — New York Johnson Reprint Corp., [1970] xiv, 430 p.: facsim., ports.; 20 cm. — (Series in American studies) Cover title: Coöperative news gathering. 1. Journalism — U.S. — History. 2. News agencies I. T. II. Title: Coöperative news gathering. III. Series.
PN4855.R6 1970　　070.4/3/0973　　LC 77-18556

Rutland, Robert Allen, 1922-. 2.3589
The newsmongers; journalism in the life of the Nation, 1690–1972 [by] Robert A. Rutland. — New York: Dial Press, 1973. xv, 430 p.; 22 cm. — (Two centuries of American life) 1. Journalism — United States — History. I. T.
PN4855.R8 1973　　071/.3　　LC 72-10757

Schudson, Michael. 2.3590
Discovering the news: a social history of American newspapers / Michael Schudson. — New York: Basic Books, c1978. xi, 228 p.; 22 cm. 1. Journalism — United States — History. 2. Journalism — Objectivity I. T.
PN4855.S3　　071/.3　　LC 78-54997　　ISBN 0465016693

Weisberger, Bernard A., 1922-. • 2.3591
The American newspaperman. — Chicago: University of Chicago Press, [1961] 226 p.: illus.; 21 cm. — (The Chicago history of American civilization) 1. Journalism — United States I. T.
PN4855.W4　　071.3　　LC 61-8647

PN4858–4867 Special Periods

Brigham, Clarence Saunders, 1877-1963. • 2.3592
Journals and journeymen; a contribution to the history of early American newspapers. Westport, Conn., Greenwood Press [1971, c1950] xiv, 114 p. facsims. 23 cm. 'The A. S. W. Rosenbach fellowship in bibliography.' 'The present lectures are an outgrowth of ... [the author's] Bibliography of American newspapers.' 1. American newspapers — History. I. A. S. W. Rosenbach Fellowship in Bibliography Fund. II. T.
PN4858.B7 1971　　071/.3　　LC 72-147216　　ISBN 0837159814

Cook, Elizabeth Christine, 1876-. • 2.3593
Literary influences in colonial newspapers, 1704–1750. New ed. with an introd. by Donald W. Stewart. Port Washington, N.Y., Kennikat Press [1966, c1912] 279 p. 21 cm. Reprint of a work issued also as thesis, Columbia University. 1. American newspapers I. T.
PN4861.C7 1966　　LC 65-27119

The Press & the American Revolution / edited by Bernard 2.3594
Bailyn and John B. Hench; with a foreword by Marcus A.
McCorison; and an afterword by James Russell Wiggins.
Worcester, [Mass.]: American Antiquarian Society, 1980. 383 p.; 27 cm. 1. Press — United States — History — 18th century. 2. Printing — United States — History — 18th century. 3. United States — History — Revolution, 1775-1783 I. Bailyn, Bernard. II. Hench, John B.
PN4861.P7　　071.3 19　　LC 79-89434　　ISBN 0912296186

Schlesinger, Arthur Meier, 1888-1965. • 2.3595
Prelude to independence; the newspaper war on Britain, 1764–1776. — [1st ed.]. — New York: Knopf, 1958 [c1957] ix, 318, xvi p.; 25 cm. 1. Press — United States. 2. United States — History — Revolution, 1775-1783 — Causes I. T.
PN4861.S3　　071　　LC 57-12068

Benjaminson, Peter, 1945-. 2.3596
Death in the afternoon: America's newspaper giants struggle for survival / Peter Benjaminson. — Kansas City: Andrews, McMeel & Parker, c1984. xiii, 202 p.; 24 cm. Includes index. 1. American newspapers — History — 20th century. I. T.
PN4867.B38 1984　　071/.3/0904 19　　LC 84-14499　　ISBN 0836279557

Hohenberg, John. 2.3597
A crisis for the American press / John Hohenberg. — New York: Columbia University Press, 1978. xii, 316 p.; 23 cm. 1. American newspapers 2. Government and the press — United States. I. T.
PN4867.H58　　071/.3　　LC 78-9631　　ISBN 0231045786

Isaacs, Norman E., 1908-.   2.3598
Untended gates: the mismanaged press / Norman E. Isaacs. — New York:
Columbia University Press, 1986. 258 p.; 24 cm. Includes index. 1. Press —
United States. I. T.
PN4867.I8 1986   071/.3 19   *LC* 85-13296   *ISBN* 0231058764

Liebling, A. J. (Abbott Joseph), 1904-1963.   • 2.3599
The wayward pressman. Westport, Conn., Greenwood Press [1972, c1947]
284 p. 22 cm. 1. Press — United States. I. T.
PN4867.L5 1972   071/.3   *LC* 71-157959   *ISBN* 0837161738

PN4871–4874 Biography. Reminiscences

Stewart, Kenneth Norman.   • 2.3600
Makers of modern journalism [by] Kenneth Stewart [and] John Tebbel. New
York, Prentice-Hall, 1952. 514 p. illus. 22 cm. (Prentice-Hall journalism series)
1. Journalists, American. I. T.
PN4871.S7   071   *LC* 52-8617

Marzolf, Marion.   2.3601
Up from the footnote: a history of women journalists / by Marion Marzolf. —
New York: Hastings House, c1977. x, 310 p.; 22 cm. — (Communication arts
books) 1. Women journalists — United States. 2. Women journalists —
Europe. I. T.
PN4872.M37   070.4/092/2 B   *LC* 77-5398   *ISBN* 0803875029

PN4874 Individuals, A–Z

PN4874 A–C

Cooney, John.   2.3602
The Annenbergs / by John Cooney. — New York: Simon and Schuster, c1982.
428 p., [16] p. of plates: ill.; 24 cm. Includes index. 1. Annenberg, Walter H.,
1908- 2. Annenberg, Moses Louis, 1878- 3. Journalists — United States —
Biography. 4. Publishers and publishing — United States — Biography.
5. Ambassadors — United States — Biography. I. T.
PN4874.A56 C66 1982   070.5/092/2 B 19   *LC* 81-21258   *ISBN*
0671421050

Baillie, Hugh, 1890-1966.   • 2.3603
High tension; the recollections of Hugh Baillie. — Freeport, N.Y.: Books for
Libraries Press, [1970, c1959] x, 300 p.: illus., ports.; 23 cm. — (Essay index
reprint series) 1. Baillie, Hugh, 1890-1966. 2. Journalists — Correspondence,
reminiscences, etc. 3. World politics — 20th cent. I. T.
PN4874.B24 A3 1970   070/.924   *LC* 79-90604   *ISBN* 0836915437

Baker, Ray Stannard, 1870-1946.   • 2.3604
American chronicle, the autobiography of Ray Stannard Baker < David
Grayson >. New York, C. Scribner's Sons, 1945. vii p., 2 β., 531 p. 22 cm.
1. Journalists — Correspondence, reminiscences, etc. I. T.
PN4874.B25 A3   928.1   *LC* 45-2441

Bok, Edward William, 1863-1930.   • 2.3605
The Americanization of Edward Bok; the autobiography of a Dutch boy fifty
years after. — New York: Scribner, 1921. xxiii, 461 p.: illus.; 22 cm. — 'First
edition, September, 1920. Eighth edition, August, 1921.' 1. Bok, Edward
William, 1863-1930. I. T.
PN4874.B62 A4 1921   070/.92/4 B   *LC* 21-18540

Markham, James Walter, 1910-.   • 2.3606
Bovard of the Post–dispatch. Baton Rouge: Louisiana State University Press,
1954. 226 p.: ill. (Journalism monographs; no. 5) 1. Bovard, Oliver Kirby,
1872-1945. 2. St. Louis post-dispatch. 3. Journalists — Biography I. T.
II. Series.
PN4874.B628 M3   920.5   *LC* 54-11614

De Armond, Anna Janney, 1910-.   • 2.3607
Andrew Bradford, colonial journalist. — New York: Greenwood Press, [1969]
ix, 272 p.: facsims.; 23 cm. Reprint of 1949 ed. 1. Bradford, Andrew,
1686-1742. 2. The American weekly mercury. 3. The American magazine.
4. Pennsylvania — History — Colonial period, ca. 1600-1775 I. T.
PN4874.B66 D4 1969   070.9/24   *LC* 79-91758   *ISBN* 0837124298

Carter, Hodding, 1907-1972.   • 2.3608
First person rural. — 1st ed. — Garden City, N.Y.: Doubleday, 1963. viii,
249 p. , 22 cm. Autobiographical. 1. Journalists — Correspondence,
reminiscences, etc. I. T.
PN4874.C27 A32   *LC* 63-18226

Catledge, Turner, 1901-.   • 2.3609
My life and The Times. — [1st ed.]. — New York: Harper & Row, [1971] xiii,
319 p.: illus., ports.; 25 cm. 1. Catledge, Turner, 1901- I. New York times
II. T.
PN4874.C32 A3 1971   070.4/0924 B   *LC* 73-123919

King, Homer W.   • 2.3610
Pulitzer's prize editor; a biography of John A. Cockerill, 1845–1896 / by
Homer W. King. — Durham, N.C.: Duke University Press, 1965. xx, 336 p.:
ill., ports.; 23 cm. 1. Cockerill, John Albert, 1845-1896 2. Journalists —
Biography I. T.
PN4874.C6 Z7   920.5   *LC* 64-7798

Cooper, Kent, 1880-.   • 2.3611
Kent Cooper and the Associated Press; an autobiography. New York, Random
House [1959] 334 p. illus. 24 cm. 1. Associated Press. 2. Journalists —
Correspondence, reminiscences, etc. I. T.
PN4874.C685A3   920.5   *LC* 59-6640

PN4874 D–O

Burlingame, Roger, 1889-1967.   • 2.3612
Don't let them scare you; the life and times of Elmer Davis. [1st ed.]
Philadelphia, Lippincott [1961] 352 p. illus. 22 cm. 1. Davis, Elmer Holmes,
1890-1958. I. T.
PN4874.D36B8   928.1   *LC* 61-8669

Thornbrough, Emma Lou.   2.3613
T. Thomas Fortune; militant journalist. — Chicago: University of Chicago
Press, [1972] xi, 388 p.; 23 cm. — (Negro American biographies and
autobiographies) 1. Fortune, Timothy Thomas, 1856-1928. I. T. II. Series.
PN4874.F574 T5   070.4/092/4 B   *LC* 73-175305   *ISBN*
0226798321

Gauvreau, Emile Henry, 1891-.   • 2.3614
My last million readers, by Emile Gauvreau. New York, E.P. Dutton & Co.,
inc., 1941. 488 p. 23 cm. Autobiography. 'First edition.' 1. Journalists —
Correspondence, reminiscences, etc. I. T.
PN4874.G33 A3   920.5   *LC* 41-17181

Swanberg, W. A., 1907-.   • 2.3615
Citizen Hearst, a biography of William Randolph Hearst. — New York:
Scribner, [1961] 555 p.: illus.; 24 cm. 1. Hearst, William Randolph, 1863-1951.
I. T.
PN4874.H4 S83   920.5   *LC* 61-7220

Tebbel, John William, 1912-.   • 2.3616
The life and good times of William Randolph Hearst / by John Tebbel. — [1st
ed.]. — New York: E.P. Dutton, 1952. 386 p. Includes index. 1. Hearst,
William Randolph, 1863-1951. 2. Journalists — United States — Biography
I. T.
PN4874.H4 T4   *LC* 52-8258

Steel, Ronald.   2.3617
Walter Lippmann and the American century / by Ronald Steel. — 1st ed. —
Boston: Little, Brown, c1980. xvii, 669 p., [8] leaves of plates: ill.; 24 cm. 'An
Atlantic Monthly Press book.' Includes index. 1. Lippmann, Walter,
1889-1974. 2. Journalists — United States — Biography. I. T.
PN4874.L45 S8   070/.92/4 B   *LC* 80-11691   *ISBN* 0316811904

Swanberg, W. A., 1907-.   • 2.3618
Luce and his empire [by] W. A. Swanberg. — New York: Scribner, [1972] xiii,
529 p.: illus.; 24 cm. 1. Luce, Henry Robinson, 1898-1967. I. T.
PN4874.L76 S9   070.5/092/4 B   *LC* 73-162778   *ISBN* 0684125927

McClure, Samuel Sidney, 1857-1949.   • 2.3619
My autobiography / introd. by Louis Filler. — New York: F. Ungar Pub. Co.,
[1963] 266 p.: ill.; 21 cm. — (American classics) 1. McClure, Samuel Sidney,
1857-1949. 2. Journalists — Biography I. T. II. Series.
PN4874.M35 A3 1963   *LC* 63-11334

Lyon, Peter, 1915-.   • 2.3620
Success story; the life and times of S. S. McClure. Deland, Fla., Everett/
Edwards [1967] xv, 433 p. illus., ports. 24 cm. 'Author's note and
bibliography': p. 413-422. 1. McClure, Samuel Sidney, 1857-1949.
2. McClure's magazine. I. T.
PN4874.M35 L9 1967   051./0924   *LC* 67-18243

Britt, George, 1895-.   • 2.3621
Forty years—forty millions; the career of Frank A. Munsey. — Port
Washington, N.Y.: Kennikat Press, [1972, c1935] vi, 309 p.: port.; 23 cm.
1. Munsey, Frank Andrew, 1854-1925. I. T.
PN4874.M8 B7 1972   070.5/0924 B   *LC* 72-153203   *ISBN*
0804615136

Kendrick, Alexander.   • 2.3622
Prime time; the life of Edward R. Murrow. — [1st ed.]. — Boston: Little, Brown, [1969] viii, 548 p.: illus., ports.; 24 cm. 1. Murrow, Edward R. I. T. PN4874.M89 K4   070/.924   LC 72-83740

Mydans, Carl.   • 2.3623
More than meets the eye. [1st ed.] New York, Harper [1959] 310 p. 23 cm. 1. Journalists — Correspondence, reminiscences, etc. 2. War correspondents, American — Correspondence, reminiscences, etc. I. T. PN4874.M9A3   920.5   LC 59-10589

Johnson, Gerald White, 1890-.   • 2.3624
An honorable Titan, a biographical study of Adolph S. Ochs, by Gerald W. Johnson. — Westport, Conn.: Greenwood Press, [1970, c1946] ix, 313 p.; 23 cm. 1. Ochs, Adolph Simon, 1858-1935. I. T. PN4874.O4 J6 1970   070.4/0924 B   LC 74-109293   ISBN 0837138361

PN4874 P–Z

Farr, Finis.   2.3625
Fair enough: the life of Westbrook Pegler / Finis Farr. — New Rochelle, N.Y.: Arlington House Publishers, [1975] 236 p.: ill.; 24 cm. Includes index. 1. Pegler, Westbrook, 1894-1969. I. T. PN4874.P43 F3   070.4/092/4 B   LC 74-32276   ISBN 0870002341

Ireland, Alleyne, 1871-.   • 2.3626
An adventure with a genius: recollections of Joseph Pulitzer / by Alleyne Ireland. — New ed. — New York: E.P. Dutton, 1937. 236 p. 1. Pulitzer, Joseph, 1847-1911. I. Ireland, Alleyne, 1871- Joseph Pulitzer, reminiscences of a secretary. II. T. III. Title: Joseph Pulitzer, reminiscences of a secretary. PN4874.P8 I7 1937   LC 38-14818

Juergens, George.   • 2.3627
Joseph Pulitzer and the New York World. Princeton, N.J., Princeton University Press, 1966. xv, 392 p. illus., facsims., ports. 24 cm. 1. Pulitzer, Joseph, 1847-1911. 2. The World (New York, N.Y.: 1860-1931) I. T. PN4874.P8 J8   070.924   LC 66-11974

Swanberg, W. A., 1907-.   • 2.3628
Pulitzer, by W. A. Swanberg. — New York: Scribner, [1967] xiv, 462 p.: illus.; 24 cm. 1. Pulitzer, Joseph, 1847-1911. I. T. PN4874.P8 S9   071/.3/0924 B   LC 67-23695

Miller, Lee Graham, 1902-1961.   • 2.3629
The story of Ernie Pyle. Westport, Conn., Greenwood Press [1970, c1950] viii, 439 p. ports. 23 cm. 1. Pyle, Ernie, 1900-1945. I. T. PN4874.P86 M53 1970   070.9/24 B   LC 78-100169   ISBN 0837137438

Brown, Francis, 1903-.   • 2.3630
Raymond of the Times [by] Francis Brown. Westport, Conn., Greenwood Press [1970, c1951] viii, 345 p. illus., ports. 23 cm. 1. Raymond, Henry Jarvis, 1820-1869. I. T. PN4874.R3 B7 1970   070.4/0924 B   LC 79-100216   ISBN 0837132568

Thurber, James, 1894-1961.   • 2.3631
The years with Ross. With drawings by the author. [1st ed.] Boston, Little, Brown [1959] 310 p. illus. 22 cm. 1. Ross, Harold Wallace, 1892-1951. 2. New Yorker (New York, 1925-) I. T. PN4874.R65 T5   920.5   LC 58-11443

Schuyler, George Samuel, 1895-.   2.3632
Black and conservative: the autobiography of George S. Schuyler. New Rochelle, N.Y.: Arlington House, 1966. 362 p. 1. Schuyler, George Samuel, 1895- 2. Journalists — Biography I. T. PN4874.S35 A3   LC 66-23140

Scripps, Edward Wyllis, 1854-1926.   • 2.3633
I protest; selected disquisitions of E. W. Scripps, edited and with a biographical introd. by Oliver Knight. Madison, University of Wisconsin Press, 1966. xv, 799 p. ports. 25 cm. 1. Scripps, Edward Wyllis, 1854-1926. I. Knight, Oliver. II. T. PN4874.S37 A5   LC 66-11806

Stearns, Harold, 1891-1943.   2.3634
The confessions of a Harvard man: the street I know revisited a journey through literary Bohemia: Paris & New York in the 1920s & 30s / Harold Stearns; edited and introduced by Hugh Ford; with a preface by Kay Boyle. — Sutton West, Ont.: Paget Press, 1984. xxv, 423 p., [32] p. of plates: ill., ports. — (Paget modernist series) Includes index. 1. Journalists — United States — Biography. 2. Journalists — France — Biography. 3. Authors, American — 20th century — Biography. I. T. II. Title: The street I know. III. Series. PN4874 S67 A3 1984   070/.92/4 19   ISBN 0920348335

Steffens, Lincoln, 1866-1936.   • 2.3635
The autobiography of Lincoln Steffens. — New York: Harcourt, Brace & World, [1968, c1958] 2 v. (x, 884 p.): illus., facsims.; 21 cm. 'A Harvest book.' 1. Steffens, Lincoln, 1866-1936. 2. Journalists — United States — Biography. I. T. PN4874.S68 A3 1968   LC 68-5917

Horton, Homer L. Russell M.   2.3636
Lincoln Steffens. — New York: Twayne Publishers, [1974] 169 p.; 21 cm. — (Twayne's world leaders series) 1. Steffens, Lincoln, 1866-1936. I. T. PN4874.S68 H6   070.4/092/4 B   LC 74-3089   ISBN 0805737219

Weeks, Edward, 1898-.   2.3637
Writers and friends / by Edward Weeks. — 1st ed. — Boston: Little, Brown, c1981. xii, 323 p., [16] p. of plates: ports.; 24 cm. 'An Atlantic Monthly Press book.' Includes index. 1. Weeks, Edward, 1898- 2. Atlantic (Boston, Mass.: 1932) 3. Journalists — United States — Biography. 4. Editors — United States — Biography. 5. Authors, American — 20th century — Biography. I. T. PN4874.W369 A33   070.4/1/0924 B 19   LC 81-19383   ISBN 0316927910

White, William Allen, 1868-1944.   • 2.3638
The autobiography of William Allen White. — New York: The Macmillan company, 1946. 7 p. l., 3-669 p.: ports.; 22 cm. 'First printing.' 1. White, William Allen, 1868-1944. I. T. PN4874.W52 A3   920.5   LC 46-1656

PN4877–4900 NEWSPAPERS. MAGAZINES

Mott, Frank Luther, 1886-1964.   • 2.3639
A history of American magazines. — Cambridge, Mass.: Harvard University Press, 1938-1968. 5 v.: ill., facsims., ports; 23 cm. 1. American periodicals — History I. T. II. Title: American magazines PN4877.M63 1938   LC 39-2823

Peterson, Theodore Bernard, 1918-.   • 2.3640
Magazines in the twentieth century / by Theodore Peterson. — 2d ed. — Urbana: University of Illinois Press, 1964. x, 484 p.: ill.; 24 cm. 'This book...grew out of a doctoral dissertation at the University of Illinois' 1. American periodicals — History. I. T. PN4877.P4 1964   051.09   LC 64-18668

Richardson, Lyon Norman, 1898-.   • 2.3641
A history of early American magazines, 1741–1789, by Lyon N. Richardson. — New York: Octagon Books, 1966 [c1931] xi, 414 p.; 21 cm. 1. American periodicals — History. 2. American periodicals — Bibliography. I. T. II. Title: Early American magazines, 1741-1789. PN4877.R5 1966   051/.09   LC 66-28376

Daniel, Walter C.   2.3642
Black journals of the United States / Walter C. Daniel. — Westport, Conn.: Greenwood Press, 1982. x, 432 p.; 24 cm. — (Historical guides to the world's periodicals and newspapers.) 1. Afro-American periodicals — History. I. T. II. Series. PN4882.5.D36 1982   051 19   LC 81-13440   ISBN 0313207046

Park, Robert Ezra, 1864-1944.   • 2.3643
The immigrant press and its control. With a new introd. by Read Lewis. — Montclair, N.J.: Patterson Smith, 1971 [c1922] xxxiii, 487 p.: illus.; 22 cm. — (Americanization studies: the acculturation of immigrant groups into American society, 7) (Patterson Smith reprint series in criminology, law enforcement, and social problems. Publication no. 125) 1. American newspapers — Foreign language press 2. U.S. — Foreign population. I. T. PN4884.P3x   070.4/84/0973   LC 70-37241

Wittke, Carl Frederick, 1892-1971.   • 2.3644
The German-language press in America. [Lexington] University of Kentucky Press [1957] 311 p. 24 cm. 1. German-American newspapers I. T. PN4885.G3W5   071   LC 57-5832

Fisher, Charles.   • 2.3645
The columnists, by Charles Fisher. — New York, Howell, Soskin [1944] 4 p. l., 317 p. 20 cm. 1. Journalists, American. I. T. PN4888.C58F5   920.5   LC 44-40077

Fielding, Raymond.   2.3646
The American newsreel, 1911–1967. [1st ed.] Norman: University of Oklahoma Press [1972] xv, 392 p.: ill.; 23 cm. 1. Newsreels — History. 2. Motion picture journalism — United States — History. I. T. PN4888.M6 F5   791.43/53   LC 73-177334   ISBN 080611004X

Fielding, Raymond.   2.3647
The March of time, 1935–1951 / Raymond Fielding. — New York: Oxford University Press, 1978. viii, 359 p.: ill.; 24 cm. Filmography: p. [335]-347.

Includes index. 1. March of time (Motion picture) 2. Motion picture journalism — United States — History. I. T.
PN4888.M6 F53   791.43/53   *LC* 76-51711   *ISBN* 0195022122

Detweiler, Frederick German, 1881-1960.   • **2.3648**
The Negro press in the United States. — College Park, Md.: McGrath Pub. Co., 1968 [c1922] x, 274 p.; 23 cm. 1. Afro-American press I. T.
PN4888.N4 D4 1968   071/.3   *LC* 68-7818

**Perspectives of the Black press, 1974 / edited by Henry G. La   2.3649
Brie III.**
Kennebunkport, Me.: Mercer House Press, c1974. xi, 231 p.: ill.; 24 cm. 1. Afro-American press — Addresses, essays, lectures. I. La Brie, Henry G.
PN4888.N4 P45   071/.3   *LC* 74-20050   *ISBN* 0890800006

Wolseley, Roland Edgar, 1904-.   • **2.3650**
The Black press, U.S.A. [by] Roland E. Wolseley. With an introd. by Robert E. Johnson. [1st ed.] Ames, Iowa State University Press [1971] xiii, 362 p. illus., ports. 24 cm. 1. Afro-American press I. T.
PN4888.N4 W6   070.4/84   *LC* 74-126160   *ISBN* 0813801850

Halberstam, David.   **2.3651**
The powers that be / David Halberstam. — 1st ed. — New York: Knopf, 1979. 771 p.; 25 cm. Includes index. 1. Press and politics — United States. I. T.
PN4888.P6 H3 1979   070.4/0973   *LC* 78-20605   *ISBN* 0394503813

Matusow, Barbara.   **2.3652**
The evening stars: the making of the network news anchor / Barbara Matusow. — Boston: Houghton Mifflin, 1983. xi, 302 p., [32] p. of plates: ill.; 24 cm. Includes index. 1. Television broadcasting of news — United States. I. T.
PN4888.T4 M37 1983   070/.92/2 19   *LC* 83-321   *ISBN* 0395339685

Small, William J.   • **2.3653**
To kill a messenger; television news and the real world, by William Small. — [1st ed.]. — New York: Hastings House, [1970] xv, 302 p.; 25 cm. — (Studies in public communication) (Communication arts books.) 1. Television broadcasting of news 2. Television broadcasting — U.S. I. T.
PN4888.T4 S6   070/.1   *LC* 76-110070   *ISBN* 0803870949

Glessing, Robert J.   • **2.3654**
The underground press in America, by Robert J. Glessing. — Bloomington, Indiana: University Press, [1970] xvi, 207 p.: 12 facsims.; 22 cm. 1. Underground press — U.S. I. T.
PN4888.U5 G5   071/.3   *LC* 71-126209   *ISBN* 0253190088

Kessler, Lauren.   **2.3655**
The dissident press: alternative journalism in American history / Lauren Kessler. — Beverly Hills, Calif.: Sage Publications, c1984. 160 p.; 23 cm. — (Sage commtext series. v. 13) 1. Underground press — United States — History. 2. Ethnic press — United States — History. 3. Press and politics — United States — History. 4. Radicalism — United States — History. 5. Dissenters — United States. I. T. II. Series.
PN4888.U5 K47 1984   071/.3 19   *LC* 83-21112   *ISBN* 0803920865

Karolevitz, Robert F.   • **2.3656**
Newspapering in the Old West; a pictorial history of journalism and printing on the frontier, by Robert F. Karolevitz. [1st ed.] Seattle, Superior Pub. Co. [1965] 191 p. illus., facsims., ports. 28 cm. 1. American newspapers — West (U.S.) — History. I. T.
PN4894.K36   071.8   *LC* 65-23450

PN4899 Special Newspapers, by City, A–Z

Lyons, Louis Martin, 1897-.   • **2.3657**
Newspaper story; one hundred years of the Boston globe [by] Louis M. Lyons. — Cambridge: Belknap Press of Harvard University Press, 1971. xv, 482 p.: illus.; 28 cm. 1. The Boston globe. I. T.
PN4899.B65B65   071/.44/61   *LC* 74-152697   *ISBN* 0674622251

Canham, Erwin D.   • **2.3658**
Commitment to freedom: the story of the Christian Science monitor / Erwin D. Canham; ill. with photos. — Boston: Houghton Mifflin, 1958. 454 p.: ill. 1. Christian Science monitor, The. I. T.
PN4899.B65C53   *LC* 58-9055

Gottlieb, Robert.   **2.3659**
Thinking big: the story of the Los Angeles times, its publishers, and their influence on Southern California / Robert Gottlieb and Irene Wolt. — New York: Putnam, c1977. 603 p., [16] p. of plates: ill.; 24 cm. Includes index. 1. Los Angeles times. I. Wolt, Irene. joint author. II. T.
PN4899.L64 L6625 1977   071/.94/94   *LC* 76-51847   *ISBN* 0399117660

Churchill, Allen, 1911-.   • **2.3660**
Park Row. — New York, Rinehart [1958] 344 p. 22 cm. Includes bibliography. 1. American newspapers — New York (City) 2. Journalists — New York (City) I. T.
PN4899.N4C5   071.47   *LC* 58-5137

Laney, Al, 1896-.   • **2.3661**
Paris herald; the incredible newspaper. New York, Greenwood Press [1968, c1947] x, 334 p. 23 cm. 1. New York herald tribune (European edition) I. T.
PN4899.N42 H44 1968   074/.436   *LC* 69-13963

Nevins, Allan, 1890-1971.   • **2.3662**
The Evening post; a century of journalism. — New York: Russell & Russell, [1968, c1922] 590 p.: ports.; 23 cm. 1. New York Post. I. T.
PN4899.N42 P7 1968   071/.471   *LC* 68-25047

Berger, Meyer, 1898-1959.   **2.3663**
The story of the New York times, 1851–1951. — New York, Simon and Schuster [1951] xiv, 589 p. illus., port., facsims. 24 cm. 1. New York times. I. T.
PN4899.N42T53   071.47   *LC* 51-6775

Salisbury, Harrison Evans, 1908-.   **2.3664**
Without fear or favor: the New York times and its times / Harrison E. Salisbury. — New York: Ballantine, 1981, c1980. x, 630 p.; 25 cm. Includes index. 1. New York times I. T.
PN4899.N42 T567 1981   071/.47/1 19

Talese, Gay.   • **2.3665**
The kingdom and the power. — New York: World Pub. Co., [1969] 555 p.: ports.; 24 cm. 'An NAL book.' 1. New York times I. T.
PN4899.N42 T574   071/.471   *LC* 73-81757

McAuliffe, Kevin.   **2.3666**
The great American newspaper: the rise and fall of the Village voice / Kevin Michael McAuliffe. — New York: Scribner, c1978. 486 p., [8] leaves of plates: ill.; 24 cm. Includes index. 1. The Village voice. I. T.
PN4899.N42 V535   071/.3   *LC* 78-17217   *ISBN* 0684156024

Barrett, James Wyman, 1885- ed.   • **2.3667**
The end of the World; a post–mortem by its intangible assets. Freeport, N.Y., Books for Libraries Press [1970, c1931] ix, 273 p. illus., facsims., port. 23 cm. 1. The World (New York, N.Y.: 1860-1931) I. T.
PN4899.N42W62 1970   071/.471   *LC* 72-117866   *ISBN* 0836953193

Andrews, J. Cutler, 1908-.   • **2.3668**
Pittsburgh's Post–gazette: 'The first newspaper west of the Alleghenies' [by] J. Cutler Andrews. — Westport, Conn.: Greenwood Press, [c1936, 1970] vii, 324 p.: illus., facsims., ports.; 23 cm. 1. Pittsburgh post-gazette. I. T.
PN4899.P56P64 1970   071/.48/86   *LC* 76-98805   *ISBN* 0837129567

Rammelkamp, Julian S.   • **2.3669**
Pulitzer's Post–dispatch, 1878–1883, by Julian S. Rammelkamp. — Princeton, N.J.: Princeton University Press, 1967. xiii, 326 p.: illus., ports.; 25 cm. 1. Pulitzer, Joseph, 1847-1911. 2. St. Louis post-dispatch. I. T.
PN4899.S27 P75   071.78/66   *LC* 66-21839

Rosten, Leo Calvin, 1908-.   • **2.3670**
The Washington correspondents, by Leo C. Rosten. New York, Harcourt, Brace and Company [1937] xx, 436 p. incl. facsims. 23 cm. Plan on lining-papers. 'First edition.' 1. Journalists — Washington, D.C. 2. Reporters and reporting 3. Press — Washington, D.C. 4. Washington (D.C.) — Public life. I. T.
PN4899.W3 C68   071   *LC* 37-37583

Roberts, Chalmers McGeagh, 1910-.   **2.3671**
The Washington post: the first 100 years / Chalmers M. Roberts. — Boston: Houghton Mifflin, 1977. xiii, 495 p., [8] leaves of plates: ill.; 25 cm. Includes index. 1. Washington post (1877) I. T.
PN4899.W31 W35   071/.53   *LC* 77-21907   *ISBN* 0395258545

Ames, William E.   • **2.3672**
A history of the National intelligencer, by William E. Ames. — Chapel Hill: University of North Carolina Press, [1972] xi, 376 p.; 24 cm. 1. Gales, Joseph, 1786-1860. 2. Seaton, William Winston, 1785-1866. 3. Smith, Samuel Harrison, 1772-1845. 4. National intelligencer, Washington, D.C. I. T.
PN4899.W35 N32   071/.53   *LC* 75-109462   *ISBN* 0807811785

PN4900 Special Magazines, A–Z

Singleton, Marvin Kenneth.   • 2.3673
H.L. Mencken and the American mercury adventure / M.K. Singleton. — Durham, N.C.: Duke University Press, 1962. vii, 269 p.: facsims.; 23 cm. 1. Mencken, H. L. (Henry Louis), 1880-1956. 2. American mercury. I. T.
PN4900.A55 S5 1962   051

Hamblin, Dora Jane, 1920-.   2.3674
That was the Life / by Dora Jane Hamblin. — 1st ed. — New York: Norton, c1977. 320 p.: ill.; 24 cm. Includes index. 1. Life (Chicago) I. T.
PN4900.L55 H28 1977   051   LC 76-30804   ISBN 0393087646

Kramer, Dale.   • 2.3675
Ross and the New Yorker. [1st ed.] Garden City, N.Y., Doubleday, 1951. 306 p. illus. 22 cm. 1. Ross, Harold Wallace, 1892-1951. 2. The New Yorker. I. T.
PN4900.N35 K7   LC 51-14118

Busch, Noel Fairchild, 1906-.   • 2.3676
Briton Hadden, a biography of the co–founder of Time. New York, Farrar, Straus [1949] 236 p. 21 cm. 1. Hadden, Briton, 1898-1929. 2. Time, the weekly news-magazine. I. T.
PN4900.T5B8   051   LC 49-3106 *

PN4901–4920 Canada

Kesterton, Wilfred H.   2.3677
A history of journalism in Canada [by] W. H. Kesterton. With a foreword by Wilfrid Eggleston. [Toronto] McClelland and Stewart [c1967] ix, 304, [3] p. 19 cm. (The Carleton library, no. 36) 1. Press — Canada — History. 2. Journalism — Canada — History. I. T.
PN4904.K4   LC 67-98869

Canada. Royal Commission on Newspapers.   2.3678
Royal Commission on Newspapers. — Hull, Que.: Available from Canadian Govt. Pub. Centre, Supply and Services Canada, c1981. xiii, 296 p.: ill.; 25 cm. 'Chairman Tom Kent'—p. ii. 1. Newspaper publishing — Canada. I. T.
PN4908.C28 1981   071/.1 19   LC 81-198688   ISBN 0660109549

The News: inside the Canadian media / edited by Barrie   2.3679
Zwicker, Dick MacDonald.
Ottawa: Deneau Publishers, [1982] xi, 356 p.; 23 cm. 1. Journalism — Canada — Addresses, essays, lectures. I. Zwicker, Barrie. II. MacDonald, Dick, 1943- III. Content
PN4908.N48   071/.1 19   ISBN 0888790538

PN5111–5140 Britain

Storey, Graham, 1920-.   • 2.3680
Reuters; the story of a century of news–gathering. Foreword by Lord Layton. New York, Greenwood Press [1969] xii, 276 p. illus., ports. 23 cm. Reprint of the 1951 ed. 1. Reuters ltd. I. T.
PN5111.R4 S8 1969   070.4/3   LC 78-94619   ISBN 0837125715

Herd, Harold, 1893-.   2.3681
The march of journalism; the story of the British press from 1622 to the present day. — Westport, Conn.: Greenwood Press, [1973] 352 p.: facsims.; 23 cm. Reprint of the 1952 ed. published by Allen & Unwin, London. 1. Journalism — Great Britain — History. I. T.
PN5112.H4 1973   072   LC 73-722   ISBN 0837167884

Andrews, Alexander, 1824?-1873.   • 2.3682
The history of British journalism, from the foundation of the newspaper press in England, to the repeal of the Stamp act in 1855; with sketches of press celebrities. London, R. Bentley, 1859. — Grosse Point, Mich.: Scholarly Press, 1968. 2 v.; 22 cm. 1. Journalism — Great Britain — History. I. T.
PN5114.A6 1968b   072   LC 73-1900

Curran, James.   2.3683
Power without responsibility: the press and broadcasting in Britain / James Curran and Jean Seaton. — [London]: Fontana, 1981. 395 p.; 18 cm. — (Fontana paperbacks; 4638) Includes index. 1. Press — Great Britain. 2. Broadcasting — Great Britain. I. Seaton, Jean. II. T.
PN5114.C84   072 19   LC 81-148374   ISBN 0006346383

Morison, Stanley, 1889-1967.   2.3684
The English newspaper; some account of the physical development of journals printed in London between 1622 & the present day, by Stanley Morison ... — Cambridge [Eng.] The University press, 1932. xii, 335 p. illus. 33 cm.

Bibliographical footnotes. 1. English newspapers — London. 2. English newspapers — Hist. I. T.
PN5114.M7   072   LC 32-16201

Frank, Joseph, 1916-.   • 2.3685
The beginnings of the English newspaper: 1620–1660. — Cambridge, Harvard University Press, 1961. x, 384 p. facsims. 24 cm. Bibliography: p. [285]-295. Bibliographical references included in 'Notes' (p. [297]-362) 1. Journalism — Gt. Brit. I. T.
PN5115.F7 1961   072   LC 61-13735

Shaaber, M. A. (Matthias Adam), 1897-.   • 2.3686
Some forerunners of the newspaper in England, 1476–1622 / by M. A. Shaaber. — New York: Octagon Books, 1966. xi, 368 p.: ill., facsim.; 24 cm. Reprint of the 1929 ed. which was also issued as thesis, University of Pennsylvania. 1. English newspaper — History. 2. English literature — Early modern, 1500-1700 — History and criticism. 3. Press — Great Britain. 4. Journalism — Great Britain. 5. Broadsides I. T.
PN5115.S5 1966   072   LC 66-17494

Lee, Alan J.   2.3687
The origins of the popular press in England, 1855–1914 / Alan J. Lee. London: Croom Helm; Totowa, N.J.: Rowman and Littlefield, 1976. 310 p.: ill.; 23 cm. Includes index. 1. Press — England — History. I. T.
PN5117.L4 1976   072   LC 76-17808   ISBN 0874718562

British literary magazines / edited by Alvin Sullivan.   2.3688
Westport, Conn.: Greenwood Press, 1983-. v.; 25 cm. — (Historical guides to the world's periodicals and newspapers.) 1. English periodicals — History. 2. Literature — Periodicals — History. 3. English literature — Periodicals — History I. Sullivan, Alvin. II. Series.
PN5124.L6 B74 1983   820/.8 19   LC 82-21136   ISBN 031322871X

The Victorian periodical press: samplings and soundings / edited   2.3689
by Joanne Shattock and Michael Wolff.
[Leicester]: Leicester University Press; Toronto; Buffalo: University of Toronto Press, 1982. xix, 400 p., [12] p. of plates: ill.; 24 cm. 1. English periodicals — History — 19th century — Addresses, essays, lectures. I. Shattock, Joanne. II. Wolff, Michael, 1927-
PN5124.P4 V49 1982   052/.09/034 19   LC 82-184551   ISBN 0718511905

Victorian periodicals: a guide to research / Scott Bennett ... [et   2.3690
al.]; edited by J. Don Vann and Rosemary T. VanArsdel.
New York: Modern Language Association of America, 1978. xi, 188 p.; 24 cm. Includes index. 1. English periodicals — History — 19th century. 2. Great Britain — History — Victoria, 1837-1901 — Sources. I. Bennett, Scott. II. Vann, J. Don (Jerry Don), 1938- III. VanArsdel, Rosemary T. IV. Modern Language Association of America.
PN5124.P4 V5   052   LC 77-94918   ISBN 0873522567. ISBN 0873522575 pbk

Adburgham, Alison.   2.3691
Women in print: writing women and women's magazines from the Restoration to the accession of Victoria. London, Allen and Unwin, 1972. 3-302, (15) p. illus., facsims., music, ports. 24 cm. 1. Women's periodicals, English — History. 2. Women authors, English 3. English literature — History and criticism I. T.
PN5124.W6 A3   052   LC 72-197099   ISBN 0040700054

Werkmeister, Lucyle (Thomas).   • 2.3692
The London daily press, 1772–1792 / by Lucyle Werkmeister. — Lincoln: University of Nebraska, 1963. ix, 470 p., [2] leaves of plates: ill. 1. English newspapers — London. 2. Press — London. I. T.
PN5129.L6 W45   LC 63-7228

Carlson, Carl Lennart.   • 2.3693
The first magazine; a history of the Gentleman's magazine, with an account of Dr. Johnson's editorial activity and of the notice given America in the magazine. Providence, R.I. Brown University 1938. 3;3-281p. (Brown university studies. vol. 4) 1. Cave, Edward, 1691-1754 2. Johnson, Samuel, 1709-1784. 3. The Gentleman's magazine I. T.
PN5130 G5 C3   LC 39-5252

PN5160–5645 Other Countries

Freiberg, J. W.   2.3694
The French press: class, state, and ideology / J.W. Freiberg; foreword by Ernest Mandel. — New York: Praeger, 1981. xxvii, 320 p.; 24 cm. Includes index. 1. Press — France. 2. Industrial relations — France. 3. Government and the press — France. 4. Journalism — Political aspects — France. I. T.
PN5178.F75   074 19   LC 80-25581   ISBN 0030583098

Kruglak, Theodore Eduard.   • **2.3695**
The two faces of TASS. — Minneapolis, University of Minnesota Press [1962] 263 p. 23 cm. Includes bibliography. 1. Telegrafnoe agentstvo SSSR. I. T.
PN5271.T454   070.431   *LC* 62-16631

Kumar, R. P. (Ramesh Pal), 1948-.   **2.3696**
Research periodicals of colonial India, 1780–1947 / R.P. Kumar. — Delhi, India: Academic Publications, c1985. viii, 230 p.; 25 cm. (Academic series in library and information science. v. 2) Includes index. 'Indian periodicals, 1780-1947: a bibliographical census': p. [30]-136. 1. Indic periodicals — History. 2. Indic periodicals — Bibliography. 3. Scholarly periodicals — India — History. 4. Scholarly periodicals — India — Bibliography. I. T. II. Series.
PN5377.P4 K86 1985   059/.911 19   *LC* 84-903286

Whittemore, Edward P.   • **2.3697**
The press in Japan today: a case study. — Columbia: University of South Carolina Press, 1961. vii, 91 p.: ill.; 24 cm. — (Studies in international affairs - Institute of International Studies, University of South Carolina; no. 1) 1. Japanese newspapers 2. Japan — Politics and government — 1945- I. T.
PN5404.W45   *LC* 61-64390

Barton, Frank.   **2.3698**
The press of Africa: persecution and perseverance / Frank Barton. — New York: Africana Pub. Co., 1979. xi, 304 p.; 22 cm. Includes index. 1. Press — Africa — History. I. T.
PN5450.B38 1979   079/.6   *LC* 78-7363   *ISBN* 084190393X

Omu, Fred I. A.   **2.3699**
Press and politics in Nigeria, 1880–1937 / Fred I. A. Omu. — Atlantic Highlands, N.J.: Humanities Press, 1978. xi, 290 p.; 23 cm. — (Ibadan history series) Includes index. 1. Press and politics — Nigeria — History. 2. Nigeria — Politics and government I. T. II. Series.
PN5499.N5 O4 1978   079/.669   *LC* 77-25099   *ISBN* 0391005618

Holden, Willis Sprague, 1909-.   • **2.3700**
Australia goes to press. Detroit, Wayne State University Press, 1961. xv, 297 p. map, facsims., tables. 24 cm. 1. Journalism — Australia. I. T.
PN5510.H6   079.94   *LC* 61-15295

PN6010–6525 COLLECTIONS OF LITERATURE

Seymour, A. J. (Arthur J.)   **2.3701**
New writing in the Caribbean. Edited by A. J. Seymour. — [Georgetown]: Printed by Guyana Lithographic Co., 1972. 324 p.; 22 cm. 1. Caribbean literature I. T.
PN6010.S45   808.8/99729   *LC* 73-163497

Giant talk; an anthology of Third World writings / compiled   **2.3702**
and edited by Quincy Troup and Rainer Schulte.
1st ed. — New York: Random House, [1975] xliv, 546 p.; 24 cm. 1. Literature, Modern — 20th century 2. Developing countries — Literatures. I. Troupe, Quincy. II. Schulte, Rainer, 1937-
PN6014.G38   808.88   *LC* 75-11549   *ISBN* 0394488008

Kostelanetz, Richard. comp.   **2.3703**
Breakthrough fictioneers; an anthology. Edited and with an introd. by Richard Kostelanetz. — Barton: Something Else Press, 1973. xxiv, 359 p.: illus.; 25 cm. 1. Literature, Modern — 20th century I. T.
PN6014.K74   808.8/004   *LC* 72-75710   *ISBN* 0871100878

The Norton anthology of world masterpieces / Maynard Mack,   **2.3704**
general editor ... [et al.].
5th ed. — New York: Norton, c1985. 2 v.; 22 cm. 1. Literature — Collections I. Mack, Maynard, 1909-
PN6014.N66 1985   808.8 19   *LC* 84-18882   *ISBN* 0393954285

Partisan review.   • **2.3705**
The Partisan reader: ten years of Partisan review, 1934–1944, an anthology / edited by William Phillips and Philip Rahv; introd. by Lionel Trilling. — New York: Dial Press, 1946. xvi, 688 p. 1. American literature — 20th century 2. Literature, Modern — 20th century I. Phillips, William, Nov. 14, 1907- II. Rahv, Philip, 1908-1973. III. T.
PN6014.P25   *LC* 46-7220

Partisan review (Periodical).   • **2.3706**
The New Partisan reader, 1945–1953 / edited by William Philips and Philip Rahv. — [1st ed.]. — New York: Harcourt Brace, 1953. 621 p.; 22 cm.

1. American literature — 20th century 2. Literature, Modern — 20th century I. Phillips, William, 1907 Nov. 14- II. Rahv, Philip, 1908-1973. III. T.
PN6014.P366   808.8   *LC* 53-7841

The Paris review.   • **2.3707**
Best short stories / introd. by William Styron. — [1st ed.] New York: Dutton, 1959. 245 p.; 21 cm. 1. Short stories I. T.
PN6014.P3x   *LC* 59-10771

Rutherford, Peggy. ed.   • **2.3708**
[Darkness and light] African voices: an anthology of native African writing. — New York: Vanguard Press [1960, c1958] 208 p.; 22 cm. First published in 1958 under title: Darkness and light. 1. African literature — Translations into English. 2. English literature — Translations from foreign literature. I. T.
PN6014.R79 1960   808.89   *LC* 60-9719

The Short story, 25 masterpieces.   **2.3709**
New York: St. Martin's Press, c1979. ix, 428 p.; 21 cm. Edited by Ellen Wynn. 1. Short stories, American 2. Short stories, English I. Wynn, Ellen.
PN6014.S5x   823/.01   *LC* 78-71722   *ISBN* 0312722184

Hemingway, Ernest, 1890-1961, ed.   • **2.3710**
Men at war: the best war stories of all time based on a plan by William Kozlenko. — New complete ed. New York: Crown Publishers [1955, c1942] 1072 p.; 22 cm. 1. War stories 2. Military history 3. Short stories I. T.
PN6017.W35 H4x   808.83   *LC* 56-3676

Prose and poetry of the continental Renaissance in translation /   **2.3711**
selected and edited by Harold Hooper Blanchard.
2d ed. New York: Longmans, Green, 1955. 1084 p.; 25 cm. 1. Literature — Collections 2. English literature — Translations from foreign literature. 3. Literature, Modern — 15th and 16th centuries I. Blanchard, Harold Hooper, 1891-
PN6019.B5 1955   808.8   *LC* 55-14853

Haydn, Hiram Collins, 1907-1973. ed.   • **2.3712**
A Renaissance treasury: a collection of representative writings of the Renaissance on the continent of Europe, edited by Hiram Haydn and John Charles Nelson. — [1st ed.]. — New York: Greenwood Press, 1968 [c1953] xvi, 432 p.; 24 cm. 1. Renaissance 2. European literature — Renaissance, 1450-1600 — Translations into English. 3. English literature — Translations from foreign literature. I. Nelson, John Charles, joint ed. II. T.
PN6019.H2 1968   808.89/94   *LC* 69-10105

Pound, Ezra, 1885-1972.   **2.3713**
Translations / with an introd. by Hugh Kenner. — Enl.ed. Norfolk,Conn.: New Directions 1963. 448 p. (New Directions Paperbook; 145) Includes some original poems, with translations on opposite pages. 1. English literature — Translations from foreign literature 2. Literature — Collections 3. Nō plays — Translations into English. I. Pound, Ezra, 1885-1972. Translations of Ezra Pound. II. T. III. Title: Translations of Ezra Pound. IV. Series.
PN6020.P6 1963   808.8   *LC* 64-1552

Kesteloot, Lilyan.   **2.3714**
Anthologie négro-africaine. Panorama critique des prosateurs, poètes et dramaturges noirs du XXe siècle. — (Verviers, Gèrard & Co., 1967) 430 p. port., illus. 18 cm. — (Marabout-Université, v. 129) 1. Negro literature. 2. Negro literature — History and criticism. I. T.
PN6068.K4   *LC* 70-448789

The Oxford book of death / chosen and edited by D.J. Enright.   **2.3715**
Oxford [Oxfordshire]; New York: Oxford University Press, 1983. xiii, 351 p.; 23 cm. Includes indexes. 1. Death — Literary collections. I. Enright, D. J. (Dennis Joseph), 1920-
PN6071.D4 O95 1983   082 19   *LC* 82-14341   *ISBN* 0192141295

Queen, Ellery. ed.   **2.3716**
101 years' entertainment: the great detective stories, 1841–1941 / edited by Ellery Queen. New York: The Modern Library, 1946. 999 p. illus.; 21 cm. 1. Detective and mystery stories I. T. II. Title: The great detective stories, 1841-1941.
PN6071.D45 Qx

Magical realist fiction: an anthology / edited by David Young   **2.3717**
and Keith Hollaman.
New York: Longman, c1984. vii, 519 p.; 23 cm. 1. Fantastic fiction I. Young, David, 1930- II. Hollaman, Keith. III. Title: Realist fiction.
PN6071.F25 M24 1984   808.83/876 19   *LC* 83-19974   *ISBN* 058228452X

The Other persuasion: an anthology of short fiction about gay men and women / edited and with an introd. by Seymour Kleinberg.   2.3718
1st ed. — New York: Vintage Books, 1977. xxi, 349 p.; 21 cm. I. Kleinberg, Seymour, 1933-
PZ1.O77 PN6071.H724   808.83/9/352   LC 76-62492   ISBN 039472237X

Calamus: male homosexuality in twentieth–century literature: an international anthology / edited by David Galloway and Christian Sabisch.   2.3719
1st U.S. ed. — New York: Morrow, 1982. 503 p.; 25 cm. 1. Homosexuality, Male — Literary collections. 2. Literature, Modern — 20th century I. Galloway, David D. II. Sabisch, Christian.
PN6071.H724 C3 1982   808.8/0353 19   LC 81-13836   ISBN 068800797X

London, Ephraim, ed.   • 2.3720
The world of law; a treasury of great writing about and in the law, short stories, plays, essays, accounts, letters, opinions, pleas, transcripts of testimony; from Biblical times to the present. New York, Simon and Schuster [1960] 2 v. 25 cm. 1. Law in literature 2. Law — Collected works. 3. Literature — Collections I. T.
PN6071.L33 L6   LC 60-12587

Middle age, old age: short stories, poems, plays, and essays on aging / edited by Ruth Granetz Lyell.   2.3721
New York: Harcourt Brace Janovich, c1980. x, 390 p.; 24 cm. 1. Old age — Literary collections. 2. Middle age — Literary collections. 3. Literature — Collections I. Lyell, Ruth Granetz.
PN6071.O5 M5   808.8/0352056   LC 79-91423   ISBN 0155586602

Rottensteiner, Franz. comp.   2.3722
View from another shore; European science fiction. Edited and with an introd. by Franz Rottensteiner. — New York: Seabury Press, [1973] xvi, 234 p.; 22 cm. — (A Continuum book) Translations from various languages by different translators. 1. Science fiction, English — Translations from foreign literature. 2. Science fiction I. T.
PZ1.R74 Vi PN6071.S33   808.83/876   LC 73-78082   ISBN 0816491518

Healy, Raymond J., ed.   2.3723
Adventures in time and space, an anthology of modern science–fiction stories, edited by Raymond J. Healy and J. Francis McComas. — New York: Random house, [1946] xv, 997 p.; 22 cm. 1. Science fiction I. McComas, J. Francis, joint ed. II. T.
PN6071.S33 H4x   LC 46-7121

Dulles, Allen Welsh, 1893-1969. comp.   2.3724
Great spy stories from fiction. — [1st ed.] — New York: Harper & Row, [1969] xiv, 433 p.; 22 cm. 'A Giniger book.' 1. Spy stories I. T.
PZ1.D655 Gr PN6071.S64   808.83/872   LC 69-15272

Images of women in literature / Mary Anne Ferguson.   2.3725
4th ed. — Boston: Houghton Mifflin Co., c1986. xi, 606 p.; 24 cm. 1. Women — Literary collections I. Ferguson, Mary Anne.
PN6071.W7 I43 1986   808.8/0352042 19   LC 85-80772   ISBN 0395369088

PN6080–6095 Quotations

King, William Francis Henry, 1843-1909. ed. and tr.   2.3726
Classical and foreign quotations: a polyglot dictionary of historical and literary quoatations, proverbs and popular sayings, compiled and edited, with translations and indexes . — New York: Ungar, [1958?] ixviii, 412 p.; 24 cm. 1. Quotations I. T.
PN6080.K5 1958   808.882   LC 58-8962

The Oxford dictionary of quotations.   2.3727
3d ed. — Oxford; New York: Oxford University Press, 1979. xx, 907 p.; 24 cm. Includes indexes. 1. Quotations 2. Quotations, English
PN6080.O95 1979   808.88/2   LC 79-40699   ISBN 019211560X

Bartlett, John, 1820-1905. comp.   2.3728
Familiar quotations: a collection of passages, phrases, and proverbs traced to their sources in ancient and modern literature / John Bartlett; edited by Emily Morison Beck, and the editorial staff of Little, Brown and Company. — 15th and 125th anniversary ed., rev. and enl. — Boston: Little Brown, 1980. lviii, 1540 p.; 26 cm. Includes indexes. 1. Quotations, English I. Beck, Emily Morison. II. T.
PN6081.B27 1980   808.88/2   LC 80-17076   ISBN 0316082759

Evans, Bergen, 1904-.   2.3729
Dictionary of quotations, collected and arranged and with comments by Bergen Evans. — New York: Delacorte Press, [1968] lxxxix, 2029 p.; 24 cm. 1. Quotations, English I. T.
PN6081.E9   808.88/2   LC 68-14825

Stevenson, Burton Egbert, 1872-1962. comp.   • 2.3730
The home book of quotations, classical and modern. — 10th ed. — New York: Dodd, Mead, 1967. xlii, 2816 p.; 25 cm. 1. Quotations I. T.
PN6081.S73 1967   808.88/2   LC 67-13583

Tripp, Rhoda Thomas.   2.3731
The international thesaurus of quotations. — New York: Crowell, [1970] 1088 p.; 24 cm. — (A Crowell reference book) 1. Quotations, English I. T.
PN6081.T77   808.88/2   LC 73-106587   ISBN 0690445849

Quotations in black / compiled and edited by Anita King.   2.3732
Westport, Conn.: Greenwood Press, 1981. xviii, 344 p.; 25 cm. Includes indexes. 1. Blacks — Quotations 2. Proverbs, Black I. King, Anita, 1931-
PN6081.3.Q67   081 19   LC 80-1794   ISBN 0313221286

The Quotable woman, 1800–1975 / compiled and edited by Elaine Partnow.   2.3733
Los Angeles: Corwin Books, c1977. xxxiii, 539 p.; 25 cm. Includes indexes. 1. Women — Quotations 2. Quotations, English I. Partnow, Elaine.
PN6081.5.Q6   082/.088042 19   LC 77-76016   ISBN 0894740067

The Quotable woman, from Eve to 1799 / compiled and edited by Elaine Partnow, assistant editor, Claudia B. Alexander.   2.3734
New York, N.Y.: Facts on File Publications, c1985. xv, 533 p.; 26 cm. Includes indexes. 1. Women — Quotations 2. Quotations, English I. Partnow, Elaine. II. Alexander, Claudia B.
PN6081.5.Q64 1985   082/.088042 19   LC 85-116211

Rosten, Leo Calvin, 1908-.   2.3735
[Treasury of Jewish quotations] Leo Rosten's treasury of Jewish quotations. New York, McGraw-Hill [1972] xi, 716 p. 25 cm. 1. Jews — Quotations I. T. II. Title: Treasury of Jewish quotations.
PN6095.J4 R6   808.88/2   LC 72-298   ISBN 0070539782

PN6099–6110 Poetry

Leaping poetry: an idea with poems and translations / [selected by] Robert Bly.   2.3736
Boston: Beacon Press, [1975] 93 p.; 21 cm. 'A Seventies Press book.' English, or English and Spanish. 1. Poetry, Modern — 20th century 2. Poetry I. Bly, Robert.
PN6099.L4   808.81   LC 73-6243   ISBN 0807063924

Anthology of magazine verse and yearbook of American poetry.   2.3737
1980-. Beverly Hills, Calif., Monitor Book Co. [etc.] v. 26 cm. Annual. 1. Poetry, Modern — 20th century — Periodicals. 2. American poetry — 20th century — Periodicals. 3. Canadian poetry — 20th century — Periodicals. I. Pater, Alan Frederick.
PN6099.6.A57   811/.008 19   LC 80-645223

Priest, Harold Martin, ed.   • 2.3738
Renaissance and Baroque lyrics: an anthology of translations from the Italian, French, and Spanish. — [n.p.]: Northwestern University Press, [c1962] 288 p.; 23 cm. 1. English poetry — Translations from foreign literature. 2. Lyric poetry I. T.
PN6100.P7   808.814   LC 62-16249

Auden, W. H. (Wystan Hugh), 1907-1973.   2.3739
Poets of the English language / edited by W.H.Auden and Norman Holmes Pearson. — [New York, Viking Press, 1950] 5 v.; 17 cm. — (The Viking portable library; [49-53]) 1. English poetry 2. American poetry 3. English poetry — Bio-bibliography. 4. American poetry — Bio-bibliography. I. Pearson, Norman Holmes, 1909-1975. II. T.
PN 6101 A89   LC 50-9508   ISBN 0670562505

The Contemporary world poets / edited by Donald Junkins.   2.3740
New York: Harcourt Brace Jovanovich, c1976. xxxi, 415 p.; 22 cm. 'Most of the poems are translations.' 1. Poetry, Modern — 20th century I. Junkins, Donald, 1931-
PN6101.C654   821/.008   LC 75-36286   ISBN 0155138170

Gross, Ronald. comp.   2.3741
Open poetry; four anthologies of expanded poems. Edited by Ronald Gross and George Quasha, with Emmett Williams, John Robert Colombo and Walter

Lowenfels. — New York: Simon and Schuster, [1973] xix, 614 p.: illus.; 25 cm.
1. Poetry, Modern — 20th century I. Quasha, George. joint comp. II. T.
PN6101.G77   808.81/04   *LC* 72-83078   *ISBN* 0671211390

Merwin, W. S. (William Stanley), 1927- comp.   • 2.3742
Selected translations, 1948–1968 [by] W. S. Merwin. New York, Atheneum,
1968. xiv, 176 p. 24 cm. Poems. 1. Poetry — Translations into English.
2. English poetry — Translations from foreign literature. I. T.
PN6101.M45   808.81   *LC* 68-9727

Miles, Josephine, 1911- ed.   • 2.3743
[Poem] The ways of the poem. [Rev. ed.] Englewood Cliffs, N.J., Prentice-Hall
[1972] xvii, 404 p. 22 cm. (Prentice-Hall English literature series) A slightly
revised, shorter version of The poem. 1. Poetry, Modern I. T.
PN6101.M5 1972   821/.008   *LC* 78-146676

The Norton introduction to poetry / [edited by] J. Paul Hunter.   2.3744
3rd ed. — New York: Norton, c1986. xxiii, 576 p.; 22 cm. Includes indexes.
1. Poetry — Collections I. Hunter, J. Paul, 1934-
PN6101.N6 1986   821/.008 19   *LC* 86-880   *ISBN* 0393954870

The Oxford book of verse in English translation / chosen and   2.3745
edited by Charles Tomlinson.
Oxford; New York: Oxford University Press, 1980. xlviii, 608 p.; 23 cm.
1. Poetry — Translations into English. 2. English poetry — Translations from
foreign languages I. Tomlinson, Charles, 1927-
PN6101.O89   808.81 19   *LC* 79-42643   *ISBN* 0192141031

Pilling, John.   2.3746
A reader's guide to fifty modern European poets / by John Pilling. — London:
Heinemann; Totowa, N.J.: Barnes & Noble Books, 1982. 479 p.; 21 cm. —
(Reader's guide series) 1. European poetry — 19th century — Translations
into English. 2. European poetry — 20th century — Translations into English.
3. English poetry — Translations from foreign languages I. T.
PN6101.P454 1982   808.81/034 19   *LC* 82-11363   *ISBN*
038920241X

Hughes, Langston, 1902-1967. ed.   • 2.3747
The poetry of the Negro, 1746–1970: an anthology / edited by Langston
Hughes and Arna Bontemps. — [Rev. and updated ed.] Garden City, N.Y.:
Doubleday, 1970. xxiv, 645 p.; 22 cm. 1. Poetry — Black authors 2. American
poetry — Afro-American authors 3. Black race — Poetry. I. Bontemps, Arna
Wendell, 1902-1973. joint ed. II. T.
PN6109.7.H8 1970   811/.008   *LC* 68-10584

A Book of women poets from antiquity to now / edited by Aliki   2.3748
Barnstone & Willis Barnstone.
New York: Schocken Books, 1980. xx, 612 p.; 24 cm. Includes indexes.
1. Poetry — Women authors I. Barnstone, Aliki. II. Barnstone, Willis, 1927-
PN6109.9.B6   808.81   *LC* 78-54391   *ISBN* 0805236937

The Penguin book of women poets / edited by Carol Cosman,   2.3749
Joan Keefe, Kathleen Weaver; consulting editors, Joanna
Banker, Doris Earnshaw, Deirdre Lashgari.
New York: Penguin Books, 1979, c1978. 399 p.; 28 cm. Includes index.
1. Poetry — Women authors I. Cosman, Carol. II. Keefe, Joan. III. Weaver,
Kathleen.
PN6109.9.P4 1979b   808.81   *LC* 78-26699   *ISBN* 0140422250

Women poets of the world / edited by Joanna Bankier and   2.3750
Deirdre Lashgari; associate editor, Doris Earnshaw.
New York: Macmillan; London: Collier Macmillan, c1983. xxxviii, 442 p.; 21
cm. Includes indexes. 1. Poetry — Women authors I. Bankier, Joanna.
II. Lashgari, Deirdre. III. Earnshaw, Doris.
PN6109.9.W66 1983   808.81 19   *LC* 82-7794   *ISBN* 0023057203

A Green place: modern poems / compiled by William Jay   2.3751
Smith; illustrated by Jacques Hnizdovsky.
New York, N.Y.: Delacorte Press/Seymour Lawrence, c1982. xiii, 225 p.: ill.; 23
cm. 'A Merloyd Lawrence book.' Includes indexes. 1. Children's poetry
I. Smith, William Jay, 1918- II. Hnizdovsky, Jacques, 1915- ill.
PN6109.97.G7 1982   808.81/024054 19   *LC* 82-2363   *ISBN*
0440029201

Talking to the sun: an illustrated anthology of poems for young   2.3752
people / selected and introduced by Kenneth Koch and Kate
Farrell.
New York: Metropolitan Museum of Art: Holt, Rinehart, and Winston, c1985.
112 p.: col. ill.; 25 cm. Includes indexes. 1. Children's poetry 2. Art — Juvenile
literature. 3. Metropolitan Museum of Art (New York, N.Y.) I. Koch,
Kenneth, 1925- II. Farrell, Kate. III. Metropolitan Museum of Art (New
York, N.Y.)
PN6109.97.T35 1985   808.81/0088054 19   *LC* 85-15428   *ISBN*
0870994360

Harrison, Thomas Perrin, 1897-.   2.3753
The pastoral elegy, an anthology. Austin, The University of Texas [c1939] xi,
312 p. illus. (facsim.) 24 cm. 1. Pastoral poetry 2. Elegiac poetry I. Leon,
Harry Joshua II. T.
PN6110.C8 H3   *LC* 39-32751

Medieval epics.   • 2.3754
New York, Modern Library [1963] 590 p. 21 cm. (The Modern library of the
world's best books) Modern library giants, G87. 1. Epic poetry, European
2. Poetry, Medieval
PN6110.E6 M4   808.813   *LC* 63-7651

The Penguin book of homosexual verse / edited by Stephen   2.3755
Coote.
Harmondsworth, Middlesex, England; New York, N.Y., U.S.A.: Penguin,
1983. 410 p.; 20 cm. — (Penguin poets) Includes indexes. 1. Homosexuality —
Poetry. I. Coote, Stephen.
PN6110.H65 P46 1983   808.81/9353 19   *LC* 83-204864   *ISBN*
0140422935

The Faber book of nonsense verse: with a sprinkling of nonsense   2.3756
prose / chosen, with an introd. by Geoffrey Grigson.
London; Boston: Faber & Faber, 1979. 352 p.; 21 cm. 1. Nonsense-verses
I. Grigson, Geoffrey, 1905-
PN6110.N6 F3   808.81/8   *LC* 79-670146   *ISBN* 0571113567

The Oxford book of war poetry / chosen and edited by Jon   2.3757
Stallworthy.
Oxford [Oxfordshire]; New York: Oxford University Press, 1984. xxxi, 358 p.;
23 cm. Includes indexes. 1. War poetry I. Stallworthy, Jon.
PN6110.W28 O93 1984   808.81/9358 19   *LC* 83-19303   *ISBN*
0192141252

PN6111–6120 Drama

The Best short plays.   • 2.3758
Philadelphia: Chilton Book Co, [19—]-. v. Annual. Continues: Best one-act
plays. ISSN 0731-5570. Suspended 1961-1967. 1. One-act plays — Collected
works. I. Best one-act plays.
PN6111.B47   *LC* 38-8006

Our dramatic heritage / edited by Philip G. Hill.   2.3759
Rutherford [N.J.]: Fairleigh Dickinson University Press; London; Cranbury,
N.J.: Associated University Presses, c1983-<c1985 >. v. <1-2 >; 24 cm.
1. European drama I. Hill, Philip G. (Philip George), 1934-
PN6111.O87 1983   808.82 19   *LC* 81-65294   *ISBN* 0838631061

Bentley, Eric, 1916- ed.   • 2.3760
From the modern repertoire. [Denver] University of Denver Press [1949-56] 3
v. illus. 23 cm. Series 3 published by Indiana University Press, Bloomington.
1. Drama — Collections I. T.
PN6112.B4   808.82   *LC* 49-11785

Bentley, Eric, 1916- ed.   • 2.3761
The play, a critical anthology. New York: Prentice-Hall, 1951. xii, 774 p.; 20
cm. (Prentice-Hall English composition and introduction to literature series)
1. Drama — Collections I. T.
PN6112.B43   808.82   *LC* 51-9662

The Best plays of....   • 2.3762
New York: Dodd, Mead, 1919-. v.: ill. Annual. 'The Burns Mantle yearbook.'
1. American drama 2. Theater — United States — Yearbooks.
PN6112.B45   *LC* 20-21432

Guernsey, Otis L., 1918-.   • 2.3763
Directory of the American theater, 1894–1971; indexed to the complete series of
Best plays theater yearbooks; titles, authors, and composers of Broadway, off-
Broadway, and off-off Broadway shows and their sources. Compiled and edited
by Otis L. Guernsey, Jr. New York, Dodd, Mead [1971] vi, 343 p. 25 cm.
1. Best plays — Indexes. 2. Drama — 20th century — Indexes. 3. Theater —
United States — Indexes. I. Best plays. II. T.
PN6112.B4524   812/.5/08   *LC* 71-180734   *ISBN* 0396064280

Block, Haskell M. ed.   • 2.3764
Masters of modern drama. Edited, with introductions and notes, by Haskell M.
Block and Robert G. Shedd. — New York: Random House, [1962] 1198 p.:
illus.; 28 cm. 1. English drama — Translations from foreign languages
I. Shedd, Robert Gordon, 1921- joint ed. II. T.
PN6112.B48   808.82   *LC* 62-10776

Cerf, Bennett, 1898-1971. comp.   2.3765
Sixteen famous European plays. Garden City, N.Y., Garden City publishing co., inc. [1943] xxv, 1052 p. 24 cm. 1. Drama — Collections 2. English drama — Translations from foreign literature. I. Cartmell, Van H., joint comp. II. T.
PN6112.C4   LC 43-51094

Cerf, Bennett, 1898-1971. ed.   2.3766
Thirty famous one act plays, edited by Bennett Cerf and Van H. Cartmell, with an introduction by Richard Watts, jr. Garden City, N.Y., Garden City publishing co., inc. [1943] xxii, 617 p. 24 cm. 1. One-act plays 2. One-act plays, English 3. English drama — Translations from foreign literature. I. Cartmell, Van Henry, 1896- joint ed. II. T.
PN6112.C42   808.82   LC 43-18980

Dickinson, Thomas Herbert, 1877- ed.   • 2.3767
Chief contemporary dramatists; twenty plays from the recent drama of England, Ireland, America, Germany, France, Belgium, Norway, Sweden, and Russia, selected and ed. by Thomas H. Dickinson ... — Boston, New York [etc.] Houghton Mifflin company [c1915] lx, 676 p. 22 cm. 1. Drama — Collections I. T.
PN6112.D5   LC 15-5813

Dickinson, Thomas Herbert, 1877- ed.   • 2.3768
Chief contemporary dramatists, second series; eighteen plays from the recent drama of England, Ireland, America, France, Germany, Austria, Italy, Spain, Russia, and Scandinavia, selected and ed. by Thomas H. Dickinson ... Boston, New York [etc.] Houghton Mifflin company [c1921] vi, 734 p. 21 cm. 1. Drama — 19th century 2. Drama — 20th century I. T.
PN6112.D52 1921   LC 21-7435

Dickinson, Thomas Herbert, 1877- ed.   • 2.3769
Chief contemporary dramatists, third series: twenty plays from the recent drama of the United States, Great Britain, Germany, Austria, France, Italy, Spain, Russia, Hungary, Czechoslovakia, the Yiddish theatre, and Scandinavia, selected and edited by Thomas H. Dickinson. Boston, New York [etc.] Houghton Mifflin company [c1930] ix, 698 p. 21 cm. 1. Drama — 19th century 2. Drama — 20th century I. T.
PN6112.D53 1930   808.82   LC 30-13765

Gassner, John, 1903-1967. comp.   • 2.3770
A treasury of the theatre; from Aeschylus to Ostrovsky. — 3d ed. — New York: Simon and Schuster; distributed by Holt, Rinehart and Winston, [1967] xv, 1037 p.: illus.; 26 cm. First ed. published in 1935, edited by B. Mantle and J. Gassner. Pages 1034-1037 blank for 'Notes.' 1. Drama — Collections I. Mantle, Robert Burns, 1873-1948, comp. A treasury of the theatre. II. T.
PN6112.G38 1967   LC 67-11743

Gassner, John, 1903-1967. ed.   • 2.3771
Twenty best European plays on the American stage. — New York: Crown Publishers, [1957] 733 p.; 25 cm. 1. Drama — Collections I. T. II. Title: European plays on the American stage.
PN6112.G39   808.82   LC 56-7195

Moon, Samuel, ed.   • 2.3772
One act; short plays of the modern theatre. — New York: Grove Press, [1961] 370 p.; 21 cm. — (Evergreen original, E-271) 1. One-act plays I. T.
PN6112.M54   808.82   LC 60-11101

Seven plays of the modern theatre / with an introd. by Harold   • 2.3773
Clurman.
New York: Grove Press, [1962] xii, 548 p.; 24 cm. 1. Drama — 20th century
PN6112.S45   808.82/04   LC 62-9779

Shank, Theodore J. ed.   • 2.3774
A digest of 500 plays; plot outlines and production notes / edited by Theodore J. Shank. — New York: Collier Books, [1966, c1963]. 475 p.; 18 cm. 1. Drama — Stories, plots, etc. I. T.
PN6112.5.S42   808.82   LC 67-9505

Shipley, Joseph Twadell, 1893-.   2.3775
The Crown guide to the world's great plays, from ancient Greece to modern times / by Joseph T. Shipley. — Rev., updated ed. — New York: Crown Publishers, c1984. xiii, 866 p.; 25 cm. Rev. ed. of: Guide to great plays, 1956. Includes index. 1. Drama — Stories, plots, etc. 2. Drama — History and criticism 3. Theater — History I. Shipley, Joseph Twadell, 1893- Guide to great plays. II. T.
PN6112.5.S45 1984   809.2 19   LC 83-27211   ISBN 0517553929

PN6120.15–.95 Fiction

The Norton anthology of short fiction / [compiled by] R.V.   2.3776
Cassill.
2nd ed., shorter. — New York: Norton, c1981. xxix, 720 p.; 23 cm. Includes index. 1. Short stories I. Cassill, R. V. (Ronald Verlin), 1919-
PN6120.2.N59 1981   808.83/1 19   LC 81-18792   ISBN 0393951820

Short shorts: an anthology of the shortest stories / edited by   2.3777
Irving Howe and Ilana Wiener Howe; with an introduction by
Irving Howe.
1st ed. — Boston, Mass.: D.R. Godine, 1982. xvii, 262 p.; 20 cm. 1. Short stories I. Howe, Irving. II. Howe, Ilana Wiener.
PN6120.2.S47 1982   808.83/1 19   LC 81-85128   ISBN 0879234318

Sixteen short novels: an anthology / selected and with an   2.3778
introduction by Wilfrid Sheed.
1st ed. — New York: E.P. Dutton, c1985. xx, 1067 p.; 25 cm. 1. Fiction — 19th century 2. Fiction — 20th century I. Sheed, Wilfrid.
PN6120.2.S59 1985   808.83 19   LC 85-72562   ISBN 0525243704

PN6121–6140 Orations. Letters

Copeland, Lewis.   2.3779
The world's great speeches / edited by Lewis Copeland and Lawrence W. Lamm. — 3rd ed., rev. and enl. — New York: Dover Publications, 1973. xxi, 842 p.; 22 cm. 1. Speeches, addresses, etc. 2. Speeches, addresses, etc. I. Lamm, Lawrence W. II. T.
PN6121.C   808.5   LC 74-139518   ISBN 0486204685

An Historical anthology of select British speeches. Edited by   • 2.3780
Donald C. Bryant [and others]
New York, Ronald Press [1967] xii, 542 p. 24 cm. 1. Speeches, addresses, etc., English I. Bryant, Donald Cross, 1905- ed. II. Title: Select British speeches.
PN6122.H54   825/.008   LC 67-21676

Parrish, Wayland Maxfield, 1887- ed.   • 2.3781
American speeches. [1st ed.] New York, Longmans, Green, 1954. 518 p.; 22 cm. 1. Speeches, addresses, etc. 2. Speeches, addresses, etc. I. Hochmuth, Marie, joint ed. II. T.
PN6122.P3   LC 54-10208

Brockway, Wallace, 1905- ed.   • 2.3782
A second treasury of the world's great letters: a mixed mailbag including intimate exchanges and cycles of correspondence by famed men and women of history and the acts / selected, edited, integrated, with historical settings and biographical backgrounds and consequences, by Wallace Brockway & Bart Keith Winer; together with a prefatory note by M. Lincoln Schuster. — New York: Simon and Schuster, 1941. xxxix, 636 p.: ports., facsim.; 24 cm. 1. Letters I. Winer, Bart Keith, joint ed. II. T. III. Title: Treasury of the world's great letters.
PN6131.B7   LC 41-25720

Schuster, Max Lincoln, 1897- ed.   • 2.3783
A treasury of the world's great letters from ancient days to our own time, containing the characteristic and crucial communications, and intimate exchanges and cycles of correspondence, of many of the outstanding figures of world history, and some notable contemporaries, selected, edited, and integrated with biographical backgrounds and historical settings and consequences, by M. Lincoln Schuster. — New York: Simon and Schuster, 1940. xlviii, 563 p.: facsims.; 24 cm. 'Third printing.' 1. Letters I. T.
PN6131.S35 1940c   808.86   LC 40-27773

PN6147-6231 Wit and Humor. Satire

PN6147-6153 HISTORY. GENERAL WORKS

Eastman, Max, 1883-1969.   • 2.3784
Enjoyment of laughter. New York, Simon and Schuster, 1936. — New York: Johnson Reprint Corp., [1970] xviii, 367 p.: illus.; 24 cm. — (Belles lettres in English) 1. Laughter 2. Comic, The 3. Wit and humor I. T.
PN6147.E27 1970   809.7   LC 70-135897

Schaeffer, Neil, 1940-.   2.3785
The art of laughter / Neil Schaeffer. — New York: Columbia University Press, 1981. 166 p.; 23 cm. 1. Wit and humor — History and criticism 2. Wit and humor — Philosophy. I. T.
PN6147.S3   809.7/009 19   LC 81-3807   ISBN 0231052243

Bergson, Henri, 1859-1941.   • 2.3786
Laughter, an essay on the meaning of the comic / by Henri Bergson; authorised translation, by Cloudesley Brereton, and Fred Rothwell. — New York: Macmillan, 1911. vii, 200 p.; 20 cm. 1. Laughter — Addresses, essays, lectures. 2. Comedy — Addresses, essays, lectures. I. T.
PN6149.P5 B5   LC 11-28319

Freud, Sigmund, 1856-1939.   2.3787
[Witz und seine Beziehung zum Unbewussten. English] Wit and its relation to the unconscious / by Sigmund Freud. — New York: Harper, 1916. vii, 388 p.; 22 cm. Translation of: Der Witz und seine Beziehung zum Unbewussten. Includes index. 1. Wit and humor — Psychological aspects. 2. Subconsciousness I. T.
PN6149.P5 F6813 1916   809.7/01/9 19   LC 82-466833

Freud, Sigmund, 1856-1939.   2.3788
Jokes and their relation to the unconscious. Newly translated from the German and edited by James Strachey. New York, Norton [1960] 258 p. 22 cm. 1. Wit and humor — Psychological aspects. 2. Subconsciousness I. T.
PN6149.P5 F7 1960   LC 60-15727

Highet, Gilbert, 1906-1978.   • 2.3789
The anatomy of satire. — Princeton, N.J.: Princeton University Press, 1962. 301 p.: illus.; 23 cm. 1. Satire — History and criticism I. T.
PN6149.S2 H5 1962   809.7   LC 61-12099

Worcester, David.   • 2.3790
The art of satire. — New York: Russell & Russell, 1960 [c1940] 191 p.; 22 cm. 1. Satire — History and criticism I. T.
PN6149.S2 W6 1960   808.7   LC 60-6038

PN6157-6162 UNITED STATES

Blair, Walter, 1900- ed.   • 2.3791
Native American humor. — San Francisco: Chandler Pub. Co., [1960] 565 p.: illus.; 21 cm. 1. American wit and humor 2. National characteristics, American 3. American wit and humor — History and criticism. 4. American literature — 19th century — History and criticism. 5. American wit and humor — Bibliography. I. T.
PN6161.B633 1960   817.3082   LC 60-15796

Dunne, Finley Peter, 1867-1936.   • 2.3792
Mr. Dooley: now and forever / created by Finley Peter Dunne; selected, with commentary and introd., by Louis Filler. — Stanford, Calif.: Academic Reprints 1954. xv, 298 p.: ill., port.; 20 cm. (American culture and economics series, no. 4) I. T.
PN6161 D8

Lardner, Ring, 1885-1933.   • 2.3793
The story of a wonder man: being the autobiography of Ring Lardner; illustrated by Margaret Freeman. — New York: C. Scribner's sons, 1927. x, 151 p.: ill. 1. Lardner, Ring, 1885-1933. I. T.
PN6161L35753   PS3523A7 Z52.   LC 27-6560

Nye, Bill, 1850-1896.   • 2.3794
The best of Bill Nye's humor: selections from the nineteenth-century American humorist / edited for the modern reader by Louis Hasley. — New Haven, Conn.: College & University Press, [1972] 249 p.; 21 cm. — (The Masterworks of literature series) I. T.
PN6161.N815 1972   818/.4/07   LC 73-168388

Perelman, S. J. (Sidney Joseph), 1904-.   • 2.3795
The best of S.J. Perelman / with a critical introd. by Sidney Namlerep. — New York: Modern Library, c1947. xiv, 300 p. — (The Modern library of the world's best books; 247) I. T.
PN6161.P458   LC 47-30316

Thurber, James, 1894-1961.   2.3796
My life and hard times, by James Thurber. New York, London, Harper & brothers [c1933] xviii p., 1 l., 153 p. incl. front., illus., plates. 22 cm. I. T.
PN6161.T562 1933a   817.5   LC 36-13237

White, E. B. (Elwyn Brooks), 1899- ed.   • 2.3797
A subtreasury of American humor. [1st Modern Library giant ed.] New York, Modern Library [1948, c1941] xxxii, 814 p. illus. 21 cm. 1. American wit and humor I. White, Katharine Angell, Sergeant, joint ed. II. T.
PN6161.W5223 1948   LC 48-7290

PN6173-6222 OTHER COUNTRIES

Mikasinovich, Branko.   2.3798
Modern Yugoslav satire / edited with an introd. by Branko Mikasinovich. — 1st ed. — Merrick, N.Y.: Cross-Cultural Communications, 1979. xix, 204 p.; 22 cm. Includes index. 1. Satire, Yugoslav I. T.
PN6222.Y8 M6   891.8   LC 79-83730   ISBN 0893040290

PN6231 SPECIAL TOPICS, A-Z

The New limerick: 2750 unpublished examples, American and British / edited by G. Legman.   2.3799
New York: Crown Publishers, 1977. xxxiii, 729 p.; 24 cm. Includes index. 1. Limericks I. Legman, G. (Gershon), 1917-
PN6231.L5 N44 1977   821/.08   LC 77-2130   ISBN 0517530910

Macdonald, Dwight. ed.   • 2.3800
Parodies: an anthology from Chaucer to Beerbohm-and after. — New York: Random House [c1960] xxiii, 574 p.; 21 cm. — (The Random House lifetime library) 1. Parodies 2. English literature (Collections) 3. American literature (Collections) I. T.
PN6231.P3M3 1960b   827.082   LC 60-12147

Legman, G. (Gershon), 1917-.   2.3801
Rationale of the dirty joke: an analysis of sexual humor / by G. Legman. — 2. series. — New York: Breaking Point, c1975. 992 p. 1. Sex — Anecdotes, facetiae, satire, etc. I. T.
PN6231S54 L4 1975   LC 68-29924

PN6269-6525 Aphorisms. Proverbs

Auden, W. H. (Wystan Hugh), 1907-1973. ed.   • 2.3802
The Viking book of aphorisms: a personal selection / by W. H. Auden and Louis Kronenberger. — New York: Viking Press [1966] x, 431 p.; 20 cm. 1. Aphorisms and apothegms I. Kronenberger, Louis, 1904- joint ed. II. T.
PN6271.A85 1966   LC 66-3191

The Oxford book of aphorisms / chosen by John Gross.   2.3803
Oxford [Oxfordshire]; New York: Oxford University Press, 1983. x, 383 p.; 23 cm. Includes index. 1. Aphorisms and apothegms 2. Quotations, English I. Gross, John J.
PN6271.O9 1983   082 19   LC 82-14263   ISBN 0192141112

Mottoes: a compilation of more than 9,000 mottoes from around   **2.3804**
the world and throughout history ... / Laurence Urdang,
editorial director; Ceila Dame Robbins, editor; Frank R. Abate,
associate editor.
1st ed. — Detroit, Mich.: Gale Research Co., c1986. 1162 p.; 24 cm. Includes
indexes. 1. Mottoes I. Urdang, Laurence. II. Robbins, Ceila Dame.
III. Abate, Frank R.
PN6309.M68 1986   080 19   *LC* 86-12122   *ISBN* 0810320762

Great treasury of Western thought: a compendium of important   **2.3805**
statements on man and his institutions by the great thinkers in
Western history / edited by Mortimer J. Adler & Charles Van
Doren.
New York: Bowker, 1977. xxv, 1771 p.; 25 cm. Includes indexes. 1. Quotations,
English I. Adler, Mortimer Jerome, 1902- II. Van Doren, Charles Lincoln,
1926-
PN6331.G675   080   *LC* 77-154   *ISBN* 0835208338

The Wisdom of many: essays on the proverb / edited by   **2.3806**
Wolfgang Mieder, Alan Dundes.
New York: Garland Pub., 1981. xiv, 326 p.: ill.; 23 cm. — (Garland folklore
casebooks. v. 1) 1. Proverbs — History and criticism — Addresses, essays,
lectures. I. Mieder, Wolfgang. II. Dundes, Alan. III. Series.
PN6401.W57 1981   398.9 19   *LC* 80-8512   *ISBN* 0824094727

Gluski, Jerzy.   **2.3807**
Proverbs. Proverbes. Sprichwörter. Proverbi. Proverbios. Poslovitsy
(romanized form): A comparative book of English, French, German, Italian,
Spanish and Russian proverbs with a Latin appendix. Compiled and edited by
Jerzy Gluski. — Amsterdam; New York: Elsevier Pub. Co., 1971. xxxviii,
448 p.; 20 cm. 1. Proverbs I. T.
PN6404.G6   398.9   *LC* 75-135483   *ISBN* 0444409041

Stevenson, Burton Egbert, 1872-1962. ed.   • **2.3808**
[Home book of proverbs, maxims, and familiar phrases] The Macmillan book of
proverbs, maxims, and famous phrases. New York, Macmillan [1965, c1948]
viii, 2957 p. 25 cm. First published in 1948 under title: The home book of
proverbs, maxims and familiar phrases. 1. Proverbs 2. Maxims I. T.
PN6405.S8 1965   808.88   *LC* 65-3787

The Oxford dictionary of English proverbs.   • **2.3809**
3rd ed.; revised by F. P. Wilson with an introduction by Joanna Wilson. Oxford:
Clarendon P., 1970. xix, 930 p.; 24 cm. First-2d editions by W. G. Smith.
1. Proverbs, English I. Wilson, F. P. (Frank Percy), 1889-1963. II. Smith,
William George. The Oxford dictionary of English proverbs.
PN6421.O9 1970   398.9/2/03   *LC* 75-18203   *ISBN* 0198691181

Taylor, Archer, 1890-1973. comp.   • **2.3810**
A dictionary of American proverbs and proverbial phrases, 1820–1880 / by
Archer Taylor and Bartlett Jere Whiting. — Cambridge: Belknap Press of
Harvard University Press, 1958. xxii, 418 p.; 24 cm. Bibliography: p. xiii—xxii.
1. Proverbs, English 2. Quotations, American I. Whiting, Bartlett Jere, 1904-
joint comp. II. T. III. Title: American proverbs and proverbial phrases.
PN6426.T28   398.903   *LC* 58-10406

PN6700–6790 Comic Books, Strips, etc

Kunzle, David.   **2.3811**
History of the comic strip. — Berkeley: University of California Press, [c1973-.
v. : illus. (part col.); 36 cm. Based on the author's thesis, University of London.
1. Comic books, strips, etc — History and criticism. I. T.
PN6710.K85   741.5/909 s 741.5/909   *LC* 70-136026   *ISBN*
0520018656

The World encyclopedia of comics / edited by Maurice Horn.   **2.3812**
New York: Chelsea House Publishers, 1976. 2 v. (898 p.): ill.; 31 cm. Includes
indexes. 1. Comic books, strips, etc — Dictionaries. I. Horn, Maurice.
PN6710.W6 1976b   741.5/03   *LC* 76-7322   *ISBN* 087754042X

Robbins, Trina.   **2.3813**
Women and the comics / by Trina Robbins and Catherine Yronwode. —
Guerneville, CA.: Eclipse Books, c1985. 127 p.: ill.; 28 cm. Includes index.
1. Women cartoonists 2. Cartoonists 3. Comic books, strips, etc.
I. Yronwode, Catherine, 1947- II. T.
PN6719.R6x 1985   741.0922   *ISBN* 0913035025

Estren, Mark James.   **2.3814**
A history of underground comics / by Mark James Estren. — San Francisco:
Straight Arrow Books; New York: distributed by Quick Fox Inc., c1974. 319 p.:
ill.; 29 cm. 1. Comic books, strips, etc — United States — History and
criticism. 2. Comic books, strips, etc — Moral and religious aspects. I. T.
PN6725.E8   741.5/973   *LC* 73-90732   *ISBN* 0879320753

Lee, Stan.   **2.3815**
Origins of Marvel Comics. — New York: Simon and Schuster, [1974] 254 p.:
illus.; 26 cm. 1. Marvel Comics Group. 2. Comic books, strips, etc — United
States. I. T.
PN6725.L4   741.5/973   *LC* 74-11141   *ISBN* 0671218646

Robinson, Jerry.   **2.3816**
The comics: an illustrated history of comic strip art / by Jerry Robinson. —
New York: Putnam, [1974] 256 p., [16] leaves of plates: ill. (some col.); 31 cm.
Includes indexes. 1. Comic books, strips, etc — United States — History and
criticism. I. T.
PN6725.R6 1974   741.5/973   *LC* 72-94257   *ISBN* 0399109374

Smithsonian Institution.   **2.3817**
The Smithsonian collection of newspaper comics / edited by Bill Blackbeard
and Martin Williams; foreword by John Canaday. — Washington: Smithsonian
Institution Press, [1977] 336 p.: chiefly ill.; 36 cm. Includes index. 1. Comic
books, strips, etc — United States. I. Blackbeard, Bill. II. Williams, Martin T.
III. T.
PN6726.S6 1977   741.5/973   *LC* 77-608090   *ISBN* 0874741726

PQ1–841 History. Criticism

Balzac, Honoré de, 1799-1850.   **2.3818**
[Short stories. English. Selections] Selected short stories [of] Honore de Balzac / selected and translated with an introduction by Sylvia Raphael. — Harmondsworth; New York: Penguin, 1977. 270 p.; 18 cm. — (Penguin classics) I. Raphael, Sylvia. II. T.
PZ3.B22 Sc 1977 PQ21.A1x   843/.7   *LC* 77-366318   *ISBN* 0140443258

Beaumarchais, Jean-Pierre de.   **2.3819**
Dictionnaire des littératures de langue française / J.–P. de Beaumarchais, Daniel Couty, Alain Rey. — Paris: Bordas, c1984-. 3 v.: ill. (some col.) 1. French literature — Dictionaries. 2. French literature — Foreign countries — Dictionaries. I. Couty, Daniel. II. Rey, Alain. III. T.
PQ41.B4 1984   840/.3 19   *LC* 84-213743   *ISBN* 2040153330

Braun, Sidney David, 1912- ed.   **• 2.3820**
Dictionary of French literature, edited by Sidney D. Braun. — Westport, Conn.: Greenwood Press, [1971, c1958] xiii, 362 p.: ports.; 23 cm. 1. French literature — Dictionaries. I. T.
PQ41.B7 1971   840/.9   *LC* 70-138576   *ISBN* 0837157757

The Concise Oxford dictionary of French literature / edited by   **2.3821**
Joyce M. H. Reid.
Oxford: Clarendon Press, 1976. 669 p.: map. 1. French literature — Dictionaries. I. Reid, Joyce M. H.
PQ41.C66   PQ41 C66.   *ISBN* 0198661185

Dictionnaire des lettres françaises / publié sous la direction de   **• 2.3822**
Georges Grente...[et al.].
Paris: A. Fayard, 1951-. v.; 28 cm. 1. French literature — Dictionaries. 2. French literature — Bio-bibliography. I. Grente, Georges, 1872-
PQ41.D53   *LC* 52-2304

Harvey, Paul, Sir, 1869-1948. ed.   **• 2.3823**
The Oxford companion to French literature / comp. and ed. by Sir Paul Harvey and J.E. Heseltine. Oxford: Clarendon Press, 1966, c1959. 771 p.: maps. 1. French literature — Dictionaries, indexes, etc. 2. French literature — Bio-bibliography. I. Heseltine, Janet E., ed. II. T.
PQ41.H3   *LC* 59-2367

PQ100–150 History: General

Littérature française, publiée sous la direction de Joseph Bédier   **• 2.3824**
[et] Paul Hazard.
Nouv. éd. refondue et augm. sous la direction de Pierre Martino. — Paris: Larousse, [1948-49] 2 v.: illus. (part col.) ports.; 30 cm. Previously published under title: Histoire de la littérature française illustrée. 1. French literature — History and criticism. I. Bédier, Joseph, 1864-1938. ed.
PQ101.II52   840.9   *LC* 50-24609

Lanson, Gustave, 1857-1934.   **• 2.3825**
Historie de la littérature française. Remaniée et complétée pour la période 1850–1950 par Paul Tuffrau. [Paris] Hachette [1952] 1441 p. 1. French literature — History and criticism. I. Tuffrau, Paul, 1887- II. T.
PQ101.L3x   840.9   *LC* 55-7139

Castex, Pierre-Georges, 1915-.   **• 2.3826**
Manuel des études littéraires françaises / Pierre–Georges Castex, Paul Surer; avec la collaboration de Georges Becker. — Paris: Hachette, 1946-1953. 6 v.: ill. 1. French literature — History and criticism. I. Surer, Paul, 1905- II. Becker, Georges, 1916- III. T.
PQ116 C34   *LC* 48-409

Lanson, Gustave, 1857-1934.   **• 2.3827**
Manuel illustré d'histoire de la littérature française [par] G. Lanson [et] P. Tuffrau. Éd. complétée pour la période 1919-1950. [Paris] Hachette [1957,c1953] 984 p. illus. 20 cm. (Classiques Hachette) Adapted for school use

from Lanson's Histoire de la littérature française. 1. French literature — History and criticism. I. Tuffrau, Paul, 1887- II. T.
PQ116.L3 1957   *LC* 55-2310

Van Tieghem, Philippe, 1898-.   **• 2.3828**
Histoire de la littérature française. Paris A. Fayard [1949] 724p. (Les Grandes études historiques) 1. French literature — History and criticism I. T.
PQ116 V3

Brereton, Geoffrey.   **2.3829**
A short history of French literature / Geoffrey Brereton. — 2nd ed. — Harmondsworth; Baltimore: Penguin, 1976. 368 p.; 19 cm. — (Pelican books) Includes index. 1. French literature — History and criticism. I. T.
PQ119.B7 1976   PQ119 B7 1976.   840/.9   *LC* 76-366424   *ISBN* 0140202978

Moore, Will Grayburn.   **• 2.3830**
French achievement in literature [by] Will G.Moore. — New York: Barnes & Noble, 1969. v, 132, [3] p.; 20 cm. 1. French literature — History and criticism. I. T.
PQ119.M6 1969   840.9   *LC* 71-3969

Strachey, Lytton, 1880-1932.   **• 2.3831**
Landmarks in French literature [by] Lytton Strachey. London, New York [etc.] 1969. 150 p. 21 cm. (Oxford paperbacks university series, opus 42) 1. French literature — History and criticism. I. T.
PQ119.S8 1969   840.9   *LC* 70-430624   *ISBN* 0198880421

France, Anatole, 1844-1924.   **• 2.3832**
La vie littéraire / Anatole France. — Paris: Calmann Lévy, [19—]. 4 v.; 19 cm. — (Bibliothèque comtemporaine.) 1. French literature — History and criticism I. T.
PQ139.F8   *LC* 01-17877

Jones, Percy Mansell.   **• 2.3833**
French introspectives, from Montaigne to André Gide, by P. Mansell Jones. — Westport, Conn.: Greenwood Press, [1970] xii, 115 p.; 23 cm. Reprint of the 1937 ed. 1. Autobiography 2. Biography (as a literary form) 3. French literature — History and criticism. I. T.
PQ145.J6 1970b   840.9   *LC* 73-95107   *ISBN* 0837131138

Brombert, Victor H.   **2.3834**
[Prison romantique. English] The romantic prison: the French tradition / Victor Brombert. — Princeton, N.J.: Princeton University Press, c1978. 241 p.: port.; 23 cm. Translation of La prison romantique. Includes index. 1. French literature — History and criticism. 2. Prisons in literature I. T.
PQ145.4.P7 B713   840/.9/32   *LC* 77-85532   *ISBN* 0691063524

Poulet, Georges.   **• 2.3835**
Studies in human time. Translated by Elliott Coleman. — Baltimore, Johns Hopkins Press [1956] 363 p. 22 cm. 'The Appendix, Time and American writers [p. 323-360] was written especially for this translated edition.' 1. Time in literature 2. French literature — Hist. & crit. 3. American literature — Hist. & crit. I. T.
PQ145.6.T5P6   840.9   *LC* 56-7715

Lough, John.   **2.3836**
Writer and public in France: from the Middle Ages to the present day / by John Lough. — Oxford [Eng.]: Clarendon Press, 1978. vi, 435 p.: 23 cm. Includes index. 1. Authors, French 2. Books and reading — France. 3. French literature — Social aspects. I. T.
PQ146.L66   840/.9   *LC* 77-30365   *ISBN* 0198157495

Brée, Germaine.   **2.3837**
Women writers in France: variations on a theme. New Brunswick, N.J.: Rutgers University Press, [1973] xii, 90 p.; 22 cm. — (Brown and Haley lectures. 1973) 1. Women authors — France. I. T. II. Series.
PQ149.B7   840/.9/9287   *LC* 73-13700   *ISBN* 0813507715

Crosland, Margaret, 1920-.   **2.3838**
Women of iron and velvet: French women writers after George Sand / Margaret Crosland. — New York: Taplinger Pub. Co., 1976. 255 p., [5] leaves of plates: ill.; 23 cm. Includes index. 1. Women authors, French — Biography. I. T.
PQ149.C7   840/.9/9287 B   *LC* 75-8202   *ISBN* 0800884361

PQ151–307 Special Periods

PQ151–221 MEDIEVAL TO 1500

Fox, John Howard.   **2.3839**
The Middle Ages / John Fox. — London: Benn; New York: Barnes & Noble Books, 1974. xx, 380 p.; 23 cm. (A literary history of France) Distributed in Canada by the General Pub. Co., Toronto. Includes index. 1. French literature — To 1500 — History and criticism. I. T. II. Series.
PQ103.L5 vol. 1 PQ151   PQ151 F687.   840/.9 s 840/.9/001   LC 75-308674   ISBN 0064922189

Payen, Jean Charles.   **2.3840**
Le Moyen âge. — Paris: Arthaud, 1970-1971. 2 v.: ill. — 1. French literature — To 1500 — History and criticism. I. Poirion, Daniel. II. T.
PQ 151.P39 1970   PQ101.P56 v.1-2.

Kelly, Douglas.   **2.3841**
Medieval imagination: rhetoric and the poetry of courtly love / Douglas Kelly. — Madison: University of Wisconsin Press, 1978. xvi, 330 p. Includes index. 1. French poetry — To 1500 — History and criticism. 2. Love poetry, French — History and criticism. 3. Courtly love I. T.
PQ155.L7 K44 1978   PQ155L7 K44 1978.   841/.1   LC 78-3522   ISBN 0299076105

Calin, William, 1936-.   **2.3842**
A muse for heroes: nine centuries of the epic in France / William Calin. — Toronto: University of Toronto Press, 1983. 513 p. — (University of Toronto romance series. 0082-5336; 46) 1. Epic poetry, French — History and criticism. I. T. II. Series.
PQ201 C356 1983   841/.0309 19   ISBN 0802055990

Ferrier, Janet Mackay.   **2.3843**
Forerunners of the French novel; an essay on the development of the nouvelle in the late Middle Ages. Manchester Manchester University Press`1954. 124p. 1. French fiction — Old French — History and criticism I. T.
PQ221 F4

PQ226–307 MODERN

Van Tieghem, Philippe, 1898-.   • **2.3844**
Les grandes doctrines littéraires en France de la Pléiade au surréalisme / Philippe Van Tieghem. — 8e éd. — Paris: Presses Universitaires de France, 1968. viii, 302 p. 1. French literature — History and criticism. I. T.
PQ226.V3 1968   LC 78-407256

McFarlane, I. D. (Ian Dalrymple)   **2.3845**
Renaissance France, 1470–1589 [by] I. D. McFarlane. London, E. Benn; New York, Barnes & Noble Books, 1974. xxiv, 557 p. 23 cm. (A literary history of France [v. 2]) Includes index. 1. French literature — 16th century — History and criticism. I. T. II. Series.
PQ103.L5 vol. 2 1974 PQ231.M2x   840/.9 s 840/.9/003   LC 74-180343   ISBN 0064947009

PQ241–299 17th–19th Centuries

Adam, Antoine.   • **2.3846**
Histoire de la littérature française au XVIIe siècle. — Paris, Del Duca [1962] 5 v. — 19 cm. — (Editions mondiales.) 'Note bibliographique': v. 1, p. 597. Bibliographical footnotes. 1. French literature — 17th cent. — Hist. & crit. I. T.
PQ241.A3 1962   LC 65-515

Moore, Will Grayburn.   • **2.3847**
French classical literature: an essay / by Will G. Moore. — London: Oxford University Press, 1961. 174 p.; 19 cm. 1. French literature — 17th century — History and criticism I. T.
PQ241.M64   840.903   LC 61-66246   ISBN

Nurse, Peter H.   **2.3848**
Classical voices; studies of Corneille, Racine, Molière, Mme de Lafayette [by] Peter H. Nurse. — Totowa, N.J.: Rowman and Littlefield, [1971] 230 p.: ports.; 21 cm. 1. French literature — 17th century — History and criticism. I. T.
PQ241.N8 1971b   842/.4/09   LC 72-192661   ISBN 0874710758

Yarrow, Philip John.   • **2.3849**
The seventeenth century, 1600–1715 [by] P. J. Yarrow. — London: Benn; New York: Barnes & Noble, 1967. xvi, 432 p.; 22 1/2 cm. — (A Literary history of France v. 2) 1. French literature — 17th century — History and criticism. I. T. II. Series.
PQ103.L5 vol. 2 PQ241.Y3x   840.9/004   LC 67-87141

Adam, Antoine.   **2.3850**
Grandeur and illusion: French literature and society, 1600–1715 / Antoine Adam; translated by Herbert Tint. — New York: Basic Books, [1972] ix, 311 p.; 22 cm. — (Literature and society) Includes index. 1. French literature — 17th century — History and criticism. 2. Literature and society I. T.
PQ245.A313 1972b   840/.9/004   LC 74-187000   ISBN 0465026974

Borgerhoff, E. B. O. (Elbert Benton Op'tEynde), 1908-1968.   • **2.3851**
The freedom of French classicism. New York, Russell & Russell [1968, c1950] xi, 266 p. front. 23 cm. (Princeton publications in modern languages, no. 9) 1. Classicism 2. French literature — 17th century — History and criticism. I. T.
PQ245.B6 1968   840.9/004   LC 68-27051

Krailsheimer, A. J.   • **2.3852**
Studies in self–interest: from Descartes to La Bruyère. — Oxford, Clarendon Press, 1962. 222 p. 23 cm. Includes bibliography. 1. French literature — 17th cent. — Hist. & crit. 2. Self-interest 3. France — Intellectual life I. T.
PQ245.K7   840.9   LC 63-73

Mornet, Daniel, 1878-1954.   • **2.3853**
La Pensée française au XVIIIe siècle / Daniel Mornet. — Paris: A. Colin, 1969. 220 p. — (Collection U2; 57) 1. France — Intellectual life 2. Enlightenment 3. French literature — 18th century — History and criticism. I. T.
PQ261.M6 1969   LC 70-423822

Saulnier, Verdun Louis.   • **2.3854**
La littérature française du siècle philosophique (1715–1802) Paris Presses universitaires de France 1948. 134p. ('Que sais-je?' Le point des connaissances actuelles [128]) 1. French literature — 18th century — History and criticism I. T.
PQ261 S3

Mason, Haydn Trevor.   **2.3855**
French writers and their society, 1715–1800 / Haydn Mason. — London: Macmillan, 1982. vi, 261 p.; 23 cm. Includes index. 1. Authors, French — 18th century. 2. French literature — 18th century — History and criticism. 3. France — Social conditions — 18th century I. T.
PQ265.M3   PQ265 M36.   ISBN 0333264657

Thibaudet, Albert, 1874-1936.   • **2.3856**
[Histoire de la littérature française de 1789 à nos jours English] French literature from 1795 to our era. Translated by Charles Lam Markmann. New York, Funk & Wagnalls [1968, c1967] xviii, 510 p. 24 cm. Translation of Histoire de la littérature française de 1789 à nos jours. 1. French literature — 19th century — History and criticism. 2. French literature — 20th century — History and criticism. I. T.
PQ281.T513 1968   840.903   LC 67-29536

Fairlie, Alison.   **2.3857**
Imagination and language: collected essays on Constant, Baudelaire, Nerval, and Flaubert / Alison Fairlie; edited by Malcolm Bowie. — Cambridge [Eng.]; New York: Cambridge University Press, 1981. xiv, 479 p.: ill.; 23 cm. Includes index. 1. French literature — 19th century — History and criticism — Addresses, essays, lectures. I. Bowie, Malcolm. II. T.
PQ282.F3   840/.9/007 19   LC 80-40307   ISBN 0521232910

Poulet, Georges.   • **2.3858**
The interior distance. Translated by Elliott Coleman. Baltimore, Johns Hopkins Press [1959] 302 p. 22 cm. (His Studies in human time, 2) 1. French literature — 19th century — History and criticism 2. French literature — 18th century — History and criticism. 3. Literature — Philosophy 4. Philosophy, French I. T.
PQ282.P843   840.9   LC 59-10766

Baudelaire, Charles, 1821-1867.   **2.3859**
L'art romantique: suivi de La fanfarlo / par Charles Baudelaire; introduction, éclaircissements et notes de Blaise Allan. — Lausanne: Guilde du livre [1950] 462 p.; 22 cm. 1. French literature — 19th century — History and criticism. 2. Painting, French 3. Painting, Modern — 19th century — France 4. Arts, Modern — 19th century — France. 5. Romanticism — France. 6. Romanticism in art — France. 7. Romanticism in music I. T.
PQ286.B35

James, Henry, 1843-1916.   **2.3860**
French poets and novelists. — London: Macmillan, 1878. 439 p.; 23 cm. — 1. French literature — 19th century — History and criticism. 2. Authors, French — 19th century — Biography. I. T.
PQ286.J3 1878   840.9   LC 13-5185

Bishop, Lloyd, 1933-. 2.3861
The romantic hero and his heirs in French literature / Lloyd Bishop. — New York: P. Lang, c1984. 287 p.; 23 cm. (American university studies. Romance languages and literature. 0740-9257; vol. 10) Includes index. 1. French literature — 19th century — History and criticism. 2. Romanticism — France. 3. Heroes in literature 4. French literature — 20th century — History and criticism. I. T. II. Series.
PQ287.B57 1984   840/.9/145 19   *LC* 83-49351   *ISBN* 0820400963

Giraud, Jean, Agrégé des lettres. • 2.3862
L'école romantique française; les doctrines et les hommes. Paris A. Colin 1927. 203p. (Collection Armand Colin (Section de langues et littératures) 1. Romanticism — France 2. French literature — 19th century — History and criticism I. T.
PQ287 G5

Michaud, Guy, ed. • 2.3863
Le romantisme; l'histoire, la doctrine, les oeuvres. Présenté par Guy Michaud et Ph. Van Tieghem. — Paris, Hachette [1963, c1952] 188 p. illus., ports. 19 cm. — (Les Documents France. Mouvements littéraires) Classiques. Bibliography: p. [186] 1. French literature — 19th cent. — Hist. & crit. 2. Romanticism 3. French literature (Selections: Extracts, etc.) I. Van Tieghem, Philippe 1898- joint ed. II. T.
PQ287.Mx   840.91   *LC* 65-7497

Martino, Pierre, 1880-1953. • 2.3864
Parnasse et symbolisme. — Paris: Colin, 1967. 192 p.; 18 cm. — (Collection U2; 11.) 1. Symbolism in literature 2. French poetry — 19th century — History and criticism. 3. Parnassianism I. T.
PQ295.N2 M3 1967   *LC* 68-79194

Symons, Arthur, 1865-1945. • 2.3865
The symbolist movement in literature. — Rev. and enl. ed. — New York: Haskell House, 1971. v, 429 p.; 23 cm. Reprint of the 1919 ed. 1. French literature — 19th century — History and criticism. 2. Symbolism (Literary movement) I. T.
PQ295.S9 S8 1971   840.9/15   *LC* 79-166209   *ISBN* 0838313167

Clouard, Henri. • 2.3866
Histoire de la litterature francaise, du symbolisme a nos jours. — Nouv. ed., rev. et corr. — Paris: A. Michel, 1960- c1947-. v. ; 21 cm. 1. French literature — 19th century — History and criticism. 2. French literature — 20th century — History and criticism. I. T.
PQ296.C48   *LC* 63-5248

PQ305–307 20th Century

Boisdeffre, Pierre de. • 2.3867
Dictionnaire de litterature contemporaine / par R.M. Alberes et al.; sous la direction de Pierre de Boisdeffre. 3. ed., revue et mise a jour. Paris: Editions universitaires, 1963. 700 p. I. Albères, René-Marill, 1920- II. T.
PQ305.B54 1963   840.9   *LC* 67-115530

Boisdeffre, Pierre de. • 2.3868
Une Histoire vivante de la littérature d'aujourd'hui / Pierre de Boisdeffre; avec la collaboration d'André Alter ... [et al.]. — 7. éd., entièrement refondue et mise à jour. — Paris: Librairie Académique Perrin, 1968. 1103 p.; 21 cm. 1. French literature — 20th century — History and criticism I. T.
PQ305.B56 1968   840.9/009/1   *LC* 68-107002

Brée, Germaine. 2.3869
Twentieth–century French literature / Germaine Brée; translated by Louise Guiney. — Chicago: University of Chicago Press, c1983. viii, 390 p.; 24 cm. Translation of: Le XXe siècle. Volume 2 / Pierre-Olivier Walzer, Germaine Brée. Includes index. 1. French literature — 20th century — History and criticism. I. Walzer, Pierre Olivier. XXe siècle. English. Volume 2. II. T. III. Title: 20th-century French literature.
PQ305.B64 1983   840/.9/0091 19   *LC* 82-15980   *ISBN* 0226071952

Lemaître, Georges Édouard. • 2.3870
From cubism to surrealism in French literature. [Rev. ed.] Cambridge, Mass. Harvard university press, 1947. 256 p. plates. 23 cm. Bibliography: p. 219-240. 1. French literature — 20th century — History and criticism. 2. Cubism 3. Surrealism I. T.
PQ305.L4 1947   840.904   *LC* 47-12095

Picon, Gaëtan. 2.3871
Contemporary French literature, 1945 and after. [Translated from the French manuscript by Kelvin W. Scott and Graham D. Martin]. — New York: F. Ungar Pub. Co., [1974] xii, 227 p.; 21 cm. 1. French literature — 20th century — History and criticism. I. T.
PQ305.P4813   840/.9/00914   *LC* 72-89056   *ISBN* 0804432554

Simon, Pierre Henri, 1903-1972. • 2.3872
Histoire de la littérature française au XXe siècle. Paris, A. Colin, 1967. 2 v. 16 cm. (Collection U2, 18-19) 1. French literature — 20th century — History and criticism. I. T.
PQ305.S5 1967   840.90091   *LC* 68-116290

Nadeau, Maurice. • 2.3873
Littérature présente. — Paris, Corrêa, 1952. 357 p. 20 cm. 1. French literature — 20th cent. — Hist. & crit. I. T.
PQ306.N3   840.904   *LC* 53-880

PQ400–841 Special Forms

PQ400–491 POETRY

Brereton, Geoffrey. 2.3874
An introduction to the French poets: Villon to the present day. — 2nd ed. — London: Methuen, 1973. xii, 320 p.; 23 cm. Distributed in the USA by Harper & Row Publishers, Barnes & Noble Import Division. 1. Poets, French 2. French poetry — History and criticism. I. T.
PQ401.B7 1973   841/.009   *LC* 73-162190   *ISBN* 041676620X

Poulet, Georges. 2.3875
[Poésie éclatée. English] Exploding poetry: Baudelaire/Rimbaud / Georges Poulet; translated and with an introduction by Françoise Meltzer. — Chicago: University of Chicago Press, 1984. xviii, 141 p.; 23 cm. Translation of: La poésie éclatée. 1. Baudelaire, Charles, 1821-1867 — Criticism and interpretation. 2. Rimbaud, Arthur, 1854-1891 — Criticism and interpretation. 3. French poetry — 19th century — History and criticism. I. T.
PQ431.P6813 1984   841/.8/09 19   *LC* 83-18062   *ISBN* 0226676501

Raymond, Marcel, 1897-. • 2.3876
[De Baudelaire au surréalisme. English] From Baudelaire to surrealism. Translated from the French. London, Methuen [1970] 356 p. facsims., ports. 21 cm. (University paperbacks, UP355) 'First published as De Baudelaire au surréalisme 1933.' 'Distributed in USA by Barnes & Noble Inc.' 1. French poetry — 20th century — History and criticism. 2. French poetry — 19th century — History and criticism. 3. Symbolism (Literary movement) 4. Surrealism (Literature) — France. I. T.
PQ437.R314 1970   841/.09   *LC* 76-18474

Balakian, Anna Elizabeth, 1915-. • 2.3877
Literary origins of surrealism; a new mysticism in French poetry [by] Anna Balakian. [New ed. New York] New York University Press [1966, c1947] ix, 159 p. 22 cm. Bibliography: p. [148]-156. 1. Surrealism 2. French poetry — 19th century — History and criticism. 3. French poetry — 20th century — History and criticism. I. T.
PQ439.B3 1966   841.8091   *LC* 66-5217

Cornell, William Kenneth. • 2.3878
The symbolist movement / by Kenneth Cornell. — New Haven: Yale University Press, 1951. viii, 217 p. — (Yale Romanic studies. 2d ser.; 2) 1. Symbolism in literature 2. French poetry — 19th century — History and criticism. I. T. II. Series.
PQ439.C65   841/.8/09   *LC* 51-13940   *ISBN* 0208009477

Michaud, Guy. • 2.3879
Message poétique du symbolisme. Paris Nizet 1947. 3 v.; 24 cm. 1. Symbolism in literature 2. French poetry — 19th century — History and criticism 3. French poetry — 20th century — History and criticism I. T.
PQ439 M55

Peyre, Henri, 1901-. 2.3880
[Qu'est-ce que le symbolisme? English] What is symbolism? / Henri Peyre; translated by Emmett Parker. — University: University of Alabama Press, c1980. 176 p.; 25 cm. Translation of Qu'est-ce que le symbolisme? Includes index. 1. French poetry — 19th century — History and criticism. 2. Symbolism in literature I. T.
PQ439.P413   841/.8/0915   *LC* 79-4686   *ISBN* 0817370048

Balakian, Anna Elizabeth, 1915-. • 2.3881
Surrealism; the road to the absolute [by] Anna Balakian. Rev. and enl. New York, Dutton, 1970. 256 p. illus., ports. 22 cm. 1. French poetry — 20th century — History and criticism. 2. Surrealism (Literature) — France. I. T.
PQ443.B3 1970   841/.91/091 19   *LC* 76-87200   *ISBN* 0525051031

Caws, Mary Ann. 2.3882
About French poetry from Dada to 'Tel quel'; text and theory. Edited by Mary Ann Caws. — Detroit: Wayne State University Press, 1974. 298 p.; 24 cm. 1. French poetry — 20th century — Addresses, essays, lectures. 2. Surrealism (Literature) — France. I. T.
PQ443.C28   841/.9/1209   LC 74-10962   ISBN 0814315208

Caws, Mary Ann. • 2.3883
The poetry of Dada and sur–realism: Aragon, Breton, Tzara, Eluard & Desnos. — Princeton, N.J.: Princeton University Press, 1970. x, 226 p.; 23 cm. 1. French poetry — 20th century — History and criticism. 2. Dadaism 3. Surrealism (Literature) — France. I. T.
PQ443.C3   841/.9/1209   LC 68-56304   ISBN 0691061645

PQ500–591 DRAMA

Knight, Alan E. 2.3884
Aspects of genre in late medieval French drama / Alan E. Knight. — [Manchester]: Manchester University Press, c1983. viii, 190 p.; 23 cm. Includes index. 1. French drama — To 1500 — History and criticism. 2. French drama — 16th century — History and criticism. 3. Drama, Medieval — History and criticism. I. T.
PQ511.K64 1983   842/.2/09 19   LC 82-62255   ISBN 071900862X

Lazard, Madeleine. 2.3885
Le théâtre en France au XVIe siècle / Madeleine Lazard. — 1ère éd. — Paris: Presses universitaires de France, 1980. 253 p.; 21 cm. — (Littératures modernes. 25) 1. French drama — 16th century — History and criticism. 2. Theater — France — History — 16th century. I. T. II. Series.
PQ521.L3   842/.3 19   LC 80-150497   ISBN 2130365485

Moore, Will Grayburn. 2.3886
The classical drama of France [by] Will G. Moore. — London, New York, Oxford University Press, 1971. xi, 138 p. 21 cm. index. Bibliography: p. [134]-135. 1. French drama — 17th century — History and criticism. I. T.
PQ526.M6   842/.4/09   LC 74-850453   ISBN 0198850557

Turnell, Martin. • 2.3887
The classical moment; studies of Corneille, Molière, and Racine. Westport, Conn., Greenwood Press [1971] xv, 261 p. ports. 23 cm. 'Originally published in 1948.' 1. Corneille, Pierre, 1606-1684. 2. Molière, 1622-1673. 3. Racine, Jean, 1639-1699. I. T.
PQ527.T8 1971   842/.4/09   LC 79-138601   ISBN 0837158036

Fowlie, Wallace, 1908-. • 2.3888
Dionysus in Paris; a guide to contemporary French theater. — New York, Meridian Books [1960] 314 p. illus. 18 cm. — (Meridian books, M92) Includes bibliographies. 1. French drama — 20th cent. — Hist. & crit. 2. Theater — France. I. T.
PQ556.F6   842.91082   LC 60-6740

Guicharnaud, Jacques, 1924-. • 2.3889
Modern French theatre; from Giraudoux to Genet, by Jacques Guicharnaud in collaboration with June Guicharnaud. [Rev. ed.] New Haven, Yale University Press, 1967. ix, 383 p. 21 cm. (Yale Romanic studies, 2d ser., 7) 1. French drama — 20th century — History and criticism. I. Guicharnaud, June, joint author. II. T. III. Series.
PQ556.G8 1967   842/.9/109   LC 67-26198

Grossvogel, David I., 1925-. • 2.3890
20th century French drama / by David I. Grossvogel. — Columbia paperback ed. — New York: Columbia University Press, 1961. 378 p.; 21 cm. 1. French drama — 20th century — History and criticism. I. T.
PQ558.G7 1961   LC 65-7487

Pronko, Leonard Cabell. • 2.3891
Avant–garde: the experimental theater in France. — Berkeley: University of California Press, 1962. ix, 225 p.: illus., ports.; 23 cm. 1. French drama — 20th century — History and criticism. 2. Avant-garde (Aesthetics) I. T.
PQ558.P7 1962   842.914   LC 62-16920

Brereton, Geoffrey. 2.3892
French tragic drama in the sixteenth and seventeenth centuries. — London: Methuen [Distributed in the USA by Harper & Row Publishers, Barnes & Noble Import Division, 1973] viii, 312 p.; 23 cm. 1. French drama (Tragedy) — History and criticism. I. T.
PQ561.B67   PQ561 B67.   842/.051   LC 74-157940   ISBN 0416076300

Brereton, Geoffrey. 2.3893
French comic drama, from the sixteenth to the eighteenth century / Geoffrey Brereton. — London: Methuen; [New York]: Harper&Row, 1977. x, 290 p. 1. French drama (Comedy) — History and criticism I. T.
PQ566.B47   PQ566 B47.   ISBN 0416807100 pbk

PQ601–771 PROSE. PROSE FICTION

Étiemble, René, 1909- ed. • 2.3894
Romanciers du XVIIIe siècle / textes établis, présentés et annotés par Étiemble. — Paris: Gallimard, 1960-. v.; 18 cm. — (Bibliothèque de la Pléiade; 144) 1. French fiction — 18th century I. T. II. Series.
PQ618.E8 1960   LC a 61-1189

Turnell, Martin. • 2.3895
The novel in France: Mme, De La Fayette, Laclos, Constant, Stendhal, Balzac, Flaubert, Proust. — New York: New Directions, [1951] xv, 432 p.: ports.; 23 cm. 1. French fiction — History and criticism. I. T.
PQ631.T8   843.0903   LC 51-9687

Turnell, Martin. 2.3896
The rise of the French novel: Marivaux, Crébillon fils, Rousseau, Stendhal, Flaubert, Alain–Fournier, Raymond Radiguet / by Martin Turnell. — New York: New Directions, c1978. 309 p.; 20 cm. Includes index. 1. French fiction — History and criticism. I. T.
PQ631.T83   843/.03   LC 77-26792   0811206862

Turnell, Martin. • 2.3897
The art of French fiction: Prévost, Standahl, Zola, Maupassant, Gide, Mauriac, Proust. — [New York: New Directions, 1959] 394 p.: illus.; 23 cm. 1. French fiction — History and criticism. I. T.
PQ635.T8   843.809   LC 59-9491

Ullmann, Stephen. • 2.3898
Style in the French novel. Cambridge [Eng.] University Press, 1957. vii, 272 p. 22 cm. 1. French fiction — history and criticism. 2. Style, Literary I. T.
PQ635.U4   LC a 58-1105

Brombert, Victor H. • 2.3899
Intellectual hero: studies in the French novel, 1880–1955 / V.H. Brombert. — Philadelphia : Lippincott, 1961. 255p.bibl. 1. French literature — History and criticism. 2. Intellectuals in literature I. T.
PQ637.I5 B7   843.9109   LC 61-8673

Levin, Harry, 1912-. • 2.3900
The gates of horn; a study of five French realists. — New York: Oxford University Press, 1963. 554 p.; 22 cm. 1. French fiction — History and criticism. 2. Realism in literature I. T.
PQ637.R4 L4   843.091   LC 63-12552

Romanciers du XVIIe siècle: Sorel, Scarron, Furetière, Madame • 2.3901
de La Fayette / textes présentés et annotés par Antoine Adam. [Paris]: Gallimard, 1958. 1508 p.; 18 cm. — (Bibliothèque de la Pléiade; 131) 1. French fiction — 17th century — History and criticism. 2. Authors, French I. Adam, Antoine.
PQ645 A3   LC 58-39481

Kamuf, Peggy, 1947-. 2.3902
Fictions of feminine desire: disclosures of Heloise / by Peggy Kamuf. — Lincoln: University of Nebraska Press, c1982. xix, 170 p.; 23 cm. Includes index. 1. Héloïse, 1101-1164. 2. French fiction — 17th century — History and criticism. 3. French fiction — 18th century — History and criticism. 4. Desire in literature. I. T.
PQ645.K3   843/.4/09353 19   LC 81-10290   ISBN 0803227051

Showalter, English. 2.3903
The evolution of the French novel, 1641–1782. — [Princeton, N.J.] Princeton University Press [1972] vi, 372 p. 22 cm. 1. French fiction — 17th century — History and criticism. 2. French fiction — 18th century — History and criticism. I. T.
PQ645.S5   843/.03   LC 78-37577   ISBN 0691062293

Brooks, Peter. 2.3904
The novel of worldliness; Crébillon, Marivaux, Laclos, Stendhal. — Princeton, N.J.: Princeton University Press, 1969. ix, 295 p.; 23 cm. 1. French fiction — 18th century — History and criticism. I. T.
PQ648.B7   843/.5/09   LC 68-56303

Mylne, Vivienne. • 2.3905
The eighteenth–century French novel: techniques of illusion / by Vivienne Mylne. — New York: Barnes & Noble, 1965. viii, 280 p. Includes index. 1. French fiction — 18th century — History and criticism. I. T.
PQ648.M9 1981   843/.5/09 19

Houston, John Porter.   **2.3906**
Fictional technique in France, 1802–1927; an introduction. — Baton Rouge: Louisiana State University Press, [1972] ix, 159 p.; 23 cm. 1. French fiction — 19th century — History and criticism. 2. French fiction — 20th century — History and criticism. I. T.
PQ651.H6   843/.03   LC 72-181568   ISBN 0807100412

Castex, Pierre Georges, 1915-.   • **2.3907**
Le conte fantastique en France de Nodier à Maupassant. Paris, J. Corti [1951] 466 p. 23 cm. 1. Fantastic fiction — History and criticism. 2. French fiction — 19th century — History and criticism. 3. Short stories, French — History and criticism. I. T.
PQ653.C3   LC 51-8789

Gershman, Herbert S.   • **2.3908**
Anthology of critical prefaces to the nineteenth–century French novel [by] Herbert S. Gershman and Kernan B. Whitworth, Jr. Columbia, University of Missouri Press [c1962] 233p. (University of Missouri studies, v.37) In French; introd. in English. 1. French fiction — 19th century — History and criticism. 2. Prefaces I. Whitworth, Kernan B., joint author. II. T.
PQ661.G4   LC 62-7960

PQ671 20th Century

Brée, Germaine.   • **2.3909**
An age of fiction; the French novel from Gide to Camus, by Germaine Brée and Margaret Guiton. — New Brunswick, N.J., Rutgers University Press, 1957. 242 p. 22 cm. 1. French fiction — 20th century — History and criticism. I. Guiton, Margaret, joint author. II. T.
PQ671.B7   843.9109   LC 57-7303

Cruickshank, John. ed.   • **2.3910**
The novelist as philosopher; studies in French fiction, 1935–1960, by John Cruickshank [and others]. — London, New York, Oxford University Press, 1962. 257 p. 23 cm. Includes bibliographies. 1. French fiction — 20th cent. — Addresses, essays, lectures. 2. Authors, French I. T.
PQ671.C7 1962   843.91082   LC 62-6484

Frohock, W. M. (Wilbur Merrill), 1908-.   • **2.3911**
Style and temper: studies in French fiction, 1925–1960 / W. M. Frohock. — Cambridge, Mass.: Harvard University Press, 1967. xxii, 153 p.; 23 cm. — 1. French fiction — 20th century — Addresses, essays, lectures. I. T.
PQ671.F7   843/.9/109   LC 67-3155

Magny, Claude Edmonde.   • **2.3912**
Histoire du roman français depuis 1918. — [Paris] Éditions du Seuil [c1950] 349 [1] p. 21 cm. — (Collection 'Pierres vives') No more published. 1. French fiction — 20th century — History and criticism. I. T.
PQ671.M3   843.9109   LC 51-182

Marill, René.   • **2.3913**
Bilan littéraire du XXe siècle / R.–M. Albérès [i.e. R. Marill]. — 3. éd., revue et augm. — Paris: A.-G. Nizet, 1971, c1970. 222 p.; 22 cm. 1. French literature — 20th century — History and criticism. I. T.
PQ671.M34 1971   LC 76-580106

Nadeau, Maurice.   **2.3914**
[Roman français depuis la guerre. English] The French novel since the War. Translated by A. M. Sheridan Smith. New York, Grove Press [1969] 193, [15] p. 21 cm. (Evergreen original, E-511) Translation of Le roman français depuis la guerre. 1. French fiction — 20th century — History and criticism. I. T.
PQ671.N313 1969   843/.9/1409   LC 75-75958

Roudiez, Leon Samuel, 1917-.   **2.3915**
French fiction today: a new direction, by Leon S. Roudiez. — New Brunswick, N.J., Rutgers University Press [1972] 413 p. 24 cm. 1. French fiction — 20th century — History and criticism. I. T.
PQ671.R64   843/.03   LC 70-185392   ISBN 0813507243

Sturrock, John.   • **2.3916**
The French new novel: Claude Simon, Michel Butor, Alain Robbe–Grillet. — London; New York [etc.]: Oxford U.P., 1969. [7], 244 p.; 23 cm. 1. Simon, Claude. 2. Butor, Michel. 3. Robbe-Grillet, Alain, 1922- — Criticism and interpretation. I. T.
PQ671.S76 1969   843/.9/1409   LC 77-102633   ISBN 0192121782

PQ1101–1297 COLLECTIONS OF FRENCH LITERATURE

Lagarde, André.   **2.3917**
Les grands auteurs français du programme / André Lagarde, Laurent Michard. — Paris: Bordas, 1966. 6 v.: ill. (some col.); 21 cm. — (Collection littéraire) 1. French literature 2. French literature — History and criticism. I. Michard, Laurent. joint author. II. T.
PQ1109.L24   840.8   ISBN 2040000100

Sullerot, Evelyne.   **2.3918**
[Histoire et mythologie de l'amour. English] Women on love: eight centuries of feminine writing / Evelyne Sullerot; translated by Helen R. Lane. — 1st ed. — Garden City, N.Y.: Doubleday, 1979. xi, 334 p.: ill.; 24 cm. Translation of Histoire et mythologie de l'amour. 1. French literature — Women authors — Translations into English. 2. English literature — Translations from French. 3. Love — Literary collections. 4. Women — Literary collections 5. French literature — Women authors — History and criticism. I. T.
PQ1113.S9   840/.9/9287   LC 76-51985   ISBN 0385112475

Fellows, Otis Edward, 1908- ed.   • **2.3919**
The age of enlightenment; an anthology of eighteenth–century French literature. Edited by Otis E. Fellows and Norman L. Torrey. — 2d ed. — New York, Appleton-Century-Crofts [1971] xiii, 678 p. ports. 25 cm. In French; editorial matter in English. Includes bibliographical references. 1. French literature — 18th century 2. Enlightenment I. Torrey, Norman L. (Norman Lewis), 1894- joint ed. II. T.
PQ1131.F4 1971   840.8/005   LC 73-147121   ISBN 0390306169

Lagarde, André.   • **2.3920**
XXe siècle [par] André Lagarde [et] Laurent Michard. Avec la collaboration de Raoul Audibert, Henri Lemaitre [et] Thérèse van der Elst. [Paris] Bordas [c1962] 640p. illus., ports. (Collection Textes et littérature, 6) 1. French literature — 20th century 2. French literature — 20th century — History and criticism. I. Michard, Laurent. joint author. II. T.
PQ1141.L3   LC 64-3763

PQ1161–1193 Poetry

Boase, Alan Martin.   **2.3921**
The poetry of France; an anthology. With introd. and notes by Alan M. Boase. London, Methuen; [distributed in the U.S.A. by Barnes & Noble] [1964-1973] 4 v.; 21 cm. (University paperbacks, U.P. 89) 1. French poetry 2. French poetry — Collected works. I. T.
PQ1165.B58   841/.008   LC 67-9386

The Oxford book of French verse, XIIIth century–XXth century, chosen by St. John Lucas.   • **2.3922**
2d ed., edited by P. Mansell Jones. — Oxford, Clarendon Press, 1957. xliii, 641 p. 18 cm. 1. French poetry (Collections) I. Lucas, St. John Welles Lucas, 1879-
PQ1165.O84 1957   LC 57-13844

Contemporary French women poets: a bilingual critical anthology / edited and translated by Carl Hermey.   **2.3923**
Van Nuys, Calif.: Perivale Press; San Rafael, Calif.: distributed by B & H Books, 1977. viii, 207 p.; 22 cm. 1. French poetry — Women authors 2. French poetry — 20th century 3. French poetry — Translations into English. 4. English poetry — Translations from French. I. Hermey, Carl.
PQ1167.C6   841/.9/14   LC 76-3065   ISBN 0912288086

Four French Symbolist poets: Baudelaire, Rimbaud, Verlaine, Mallarmé: translation and introduction / by Enid Rhodes Peschel; pref. by Germaine Brée.   **2.3924**
Athens, Ohio: Ohio University Press, c1981. 359 p.: ill.; 24 cm. The poems are in French and English. 1. French poetry — 19th century 2. French poetry — 19th century — Translations into English. 3. English poetry — Translations from French. 4. Symbolism (Literary movement) — France. I. Peschel, Enid Rhodes.
PQ1170.E6 F6   841/.8/08 19   LC 80-29625   ISBN 0821405578

French feminist poems from the Middle Ages to the present: a   **2.3925**
bilingual anthology / edited and with an introduction by Domna
C. Stanton.
[New York]: Feminist Press, 1986. xxix, 207 p.; 24 cm. — (Defiant muse.)
English and French. 1. Feminism — Poetry. 2. French poetry — Women
authors — Translations into English. 3. French poetry — Women authors
4. English poetry — Translations from French. I. Stanton, Domna C.
II. Series.
PQ1170.E6 F68 1986   841/.009/9287 19   *LC* 85-16270   *ISBN*
0935312463

Modern French poetry: a bilingual anthology / edited and   **2.3926**
translated by Patricia Terry and Serge Gavronsky.
New York: Columbia University Press, 1975. xii, 241 p.; 22 cm. English and
French on opposite pages. 1. French poetry — Translations into English.
2. English poetry — Translations from French. 3. French poetry — 19th
century 4. French poetry — 20th century I. Terry, Patricia Ann, 1929-
II. Gavronsky, Serge.
PQ1170.E6 M57   841/.008   *LC* 75-17893   *ISBN* 0231039573

The Random House book of twentieth–century French poetry: **2.3927**
with translations by American and British poets / edited by
Paul Auster.
1st ed. — New York: Random House, c1982. xlix, 635 p.: 25 cm. English and
French. 1. French poetry — 20th century 2. French poetry —
Translations into English. 3. English poetry — Translations from French.
I. Auster, Paul, 1947- II. Title: Twentieth-century French poetry.
PQ1170.E6 R36 1982   841/.91/08 19   *LC* 82-280   *ISBN*
0394521978

Labé, Louise, 1526?-1566.   **2.3928**
Œuvres poétiques / Louise Labé. Précédées des Rymes de Pernette Du Guillet.
Avec un choix de Blasons du corps féminin / édition présentée, établie et
annotée par Françoise Charpentier. — [Paris]: Gallimard, c1983. 188 p.; 18 cm.
(Collection Poésie; 173) 1. French poetry — 16th century 2. French poetry —
Women authors 3. Love poetry, French 4. Women — Poetry. I. Charpentier,
Françoise. II. Du Guillet, Pernette, 1520?-1545. Rymes. 1983. III. Blasons
anatomiques du corps féminin. Selections. 1983. IV. T.
PQ1173.L3 1983   841/.3 19   *LC* 84-109049   *ISBN* 2070322386

Schmidt, Albert-Marie. comp.   • **2.3929**
Poètes du XVIe siècle / texte établi et présenté par Albert–Marie Schmidt. —
Paris: Gallimard, 1953. 1102 p.; 18 cm. — (Bibliothèque de la Pléiade; v. 96)
I. T. 1. French Poetry — 16th century. 2. Pléiade.
PQ1173.S37   *LC* 53-40493

Allemand, Maurice, 1872- ed.   **2.3930**
Anthologie poétique française, XVIIe siècle. II. Choix, introduction et notices
par Maurice Allem. Paris, Garnier-Flammarion, 1966. 446 p. 18 cm. (Garnier-
Flammarion. Texte intégral; 84) 1. French poetry — 17th century 2. French
poetry — Bio-bibliography. I. T.
PQ1175.A5 1966

Allemand, Maurice, 1872- ed.   **2.3931**
Anthologie poétique française, XVIIIe siècle. Choix, introduction et notices par
Maurice Allem. — Paris, Garnier-Flammarion, 1919?. xlv, 512 p. 18 cm. —
(Collection des classiques Garnier.) Cover illustrated in color. 1. French poetry
— 18th cent. 2. French poetry — Bio-bibl. I. T.
PQ1177.A5 1966   *LC* 67-88966

Gavronsky, Serge. comp.   • **2.3932**
Poems & texts; an anthology of French poems, translations, and interviews with
Ponge, Follain, Guillevic, Frénaud, Bonnefoy, DuBouchet, Roche, and
Pleynet. Selected and translated, with interviews and an introd., by Serge
Gavronsky. — New York: October House, [1969] xii, 211 p.: ports.; 22 cm.
English and French. 1. French poetry — 20th century I. T.
PQ1184.G3   841/.9/109   *LC* 68-29818

PQ1211–1279 Drama. Fiction

Théâtre du XVIIe [i.e. dix–septième] siècle: textes / choisis,   **2.3933**
établis, présentés et annotés par Jacques Scherer.
[Paris]: Gallimard, [1975-. v.   ; 18 cm. (Bibliothèque de la Pléiade; 257)
Includes index. 1. French drama   — 17th century I. Schérer, Jacques.
PQ1220.T5   842/.4/08   *LC* 75-505186

Truchet, Jacques. comp.   **2.3934**
Théâtre du XVIIIe siècle. Textes choisis, établis, présentés et annotés par
Jacques Truchet. — [Paris]: Gallimard, [1972-. v.   ; 18 cm. — (Bibliothèque
de la Pléiade, 241, 251) 1. French drama — 18th century I. T.
PQ1221.T7   *LC* 73-344233

Benay, Jacques G., comp.   **2.3935**
Panorama du théâtre nouveau. Edited by Jacques G. Benay [and] Reinhard
Kuhn. New York, Appleton-Century-Crofts, [1967-68] 4 v. illus. 21 cm. Text in
English. 1. French drama — 20th century 2. French language — Readers
I. Kuhn, Reinhard Clifford. joint comp. II. T.
PQ1223.B4   448.6/4/2   *LC* 67-12385

Bishop, Thomas, 1929-.   **2.3936**
L'avant–garde théâtrale; French theatre since 1950. Edited by Tom Bishop.
Lexington, Mass., D. C. Heath [1970] xi, 435 p. 24 cm. 1. French drama —
20th century I. T.
PQ1223.B5   *LC* 70-96852

Brée, Germaine. comp.   **2.3937**
Twentieth century French drama. Edited by Germaine Brée [and] Alexander Y.
Kroff. — [New York]: Macmillan, [1969] vii, 732 p.; 24 cm. Text in French.
1. French drama — 20th century I. Kroff, Alexander Yale, 1912- joint comp.
II. T.
PQ1223.B68   842/.9/108   *LC* 69-12947

Stone, Donald. ed.   • **2.3938**
Four Renaissance tragedies. With an introd. and glossary by Donald Stone, Jr.
Cambridge, Distributed for the Dept. of Romance Languages and Literatures
of Harvard University by Harvard University Press, 1966. 1 v. (various pagings)
21 cm. 1. French drama (Tragedy) I. Buchanan, George, 1506-1582. Jephté ou
le voeu. II. Bèze, Théodore de, 1519-1605. Abraham sacrifiant. III. Jodelle,
Etienne, 1532-1573. Didon se sacrifiant. IV. La Taille, Jean de, 1533?-1611 or
12. Saul le furieux. V. Harvard University. Dept. of Romance Languages
andLiteratures. VI. T.
PQ1227.S8   842/.3   *LC* 66-4592

Benedikt, Michael, 1935- ed. and tr.   **2.3939**
Modern French theatre: the avant–garde, Dada, and surrealism; an anthology
of plays. Edited and translated by Michael Benedikt and George E. Wellwarth.
— [1st ed.]. — New York: Dutton, 1964. xxxv, 406 p.; 22 cm. 1. French drama
— Translations into English. 2. English drama — Translations from French.
I. Wellwarth, George E., 1932- ed. and tr. II. T.
PQ1240.E5 B4   842.91082   *LC* 64-18407

Four French Renaissance plays: in translation with introductions   **2.3940**
and notes, preceded by an essay on French Renaissance drama /
Arthur P. Stabler, general editor.
[Pullman]: Washington State University Press, 1978. 368 p.; 23 cm. 1. French
drama — 16th century — Translations into English. 2. English drama —
Translations from French. I. Stabler, Arthur Phillips.
PQ1240.E5 F58   842/.3/08   *LC* 79-101203

Jourda, Pierre, 1898- ed.   • **2.3942**
Conteurs français du XVIe siècle; textes présentés et annotés par Pierre Jourda.
— [Paris, Gallimard, 1956] xlviii, 1470 p. 18 cm. — (Bibliothèque de la Pléiade,
v. 177) Bibliography: p. [1449]-1454. 1. Short stories, French 2. French fiction
— 16th cent. I. T.
PQ1275.J68   *LC* 65-80844

PQ1300–1595 Old French
Literature

PQ1300–1393 Collections

Pauphilet, Albert.   • **2.3943**
Jeux et sapience du moyen âge ... texte établi et annoté par Albert Pauphilet.
Paris, Éditions de la Nouvelle revue française, 1943. x p., 1 l., 925 p., 1 l.; 18 cm.
(Bibliothèque de la Pléiade 61) On cover: Jeux et sagesse du moyen âge.
Signature title: Moyen âge III. The editor's Poètes et romanciers du moyen âge,
Paris, 1939, bears signature title: Moyen âge II. 1. French drama — To 1500
2. French literature — To 1500 I. T.
PQ 1301 P33   *LC* 47-3062

Pauphilet, Albert, 1884-1948.   • **2.3944**
Poètes et romanciers du moyen âge / Texte établi et annoté par Albert
Pauphilet. Paris: Nouvelle Revue Française, 1939. 929 p.; 18 cm. (Bibliothèque
de la Pléiade; 52) A companion vol. to no. 48 of the same series, the editor's
Historiens et chroniqueurs du moyen âge, Paris, 1938. 1. French literature —
To 1500 I. T.
PQ1305.Px

PQ1411–1545 Individual Authors and Works to 1400

Chrétien, de Troyes, 12th cent.   • 2.3945
Érec et Énide; roman traduit de l'ancien français d'après l'édition de Mario Roques par René Louis. — Paris, H. Champion, 1967. ix, 193 p. 19 cm. At head of title: Chrétien de Troyes. First published in 1953. I. Louis, René. ed. I. Louis, René, ed. II. T.
PQ1445.E6A36   LC 78-435247

Chrétien, de Troyes, 12th cent.   2.3946
[Chevalier de la charrette. English & Old French] Lancelot, or, The knight of the cart = Le chevalier de la charrete / Chrétien de Troyes; edited and translated by William W. Kibler. — New York: Garland Pub., 1981. xxxvi, 312 p.: ill.; 23 cm. (Garland library of medieval literature; v. 1. Series A) Old French text and English translation of: Le chevalier de la charrette. Includes index. 1. Lancelot (Legendary character) — Romances. I. T.
PQ1445.L3 1981   841/.1 19   LC 80-8960   ISBN 0824094425

Chrétien, de Troyes, 12th cent.   • 2.3947
Le roman de Perceval; ou, Le conte du Graal / publié d'après le Ms. Fr. 12576 de la Bibliothèque nationale par William Roach. — Genève: E. Droz, 1956. xiv, 313 p. — (Textes littéraires français) I. Roach, William, 1907- II. France. Bibliothèque nationale. Mss. (Fr. 12576) III. Perceval (Romances, etc.) IV. Grail. Legend. V. T.
PQ1445 P4 1956   LC 57-921

Chrétien, de Troyes, 12th cent.   • 2.3948
Cligès: roman / Chréstien de Troyes; traduit de l'ancien français par Alexandre Micha. — Paris: H. Champion, 1976. 187 p. I. T.
PQ1446.M5 1976

Chrétien, de Troyes, 12th cent.   • 2.3949
Ywain, the knight of the lion. Translated, with an introd., by Robert W. Ackerman and Frederick W. Locke. — New York, Ungar [1957] vii, 64 p. 21 cm. — (Milestones of thought in the history of ideas) Bibliography: p. vi. I. Arthur, King. (Romances, etc.) II. T. III. Series.
PQ1447.E5A2   841.14   LC 57-9410

Frappier, Jean.   2.3950
Chrétien de Troyes, the man and his work / Jean Frappier; translated by Raymond J. Cormier. — Athens, Ohio: Ohio University Press, c1982. xix, 241 p.: ill.; 23 cm. Translation of: Chrétien de Troyes, l'homme et l'oeuvre. Includes index. 1. Chrétien, de Troyes, 12th cent — Criticism and interpretation. I. Cormier, Raymond J., 1938- II. T.
PQ1448.F713   841/.1 19   LC 81-9475   ISBN 0821406035

Holmes, Urban Tigner, 1900-.   • 2.3951
Chrétien de Troyes. New York, Twayne Publishers [1970] 195 p. 21 cm. (Twayne's world authors series. TWAS94. France) 1. Chrétien, de Troyes, 12th cent. I. T.
PQ1448.H74   841/.1   LC 77-79392

Topsfield, L. T.   2.3952
Chrétien de Troyes: a study of the Arthurian romances / L. T. Topsfield. — Cambridge [Eng.]; New York: Cambridge University Press, 1981. 367 p.; 23 cm. Includes selections of the romances in English and Old French. Includes indexes. Includes index. 1. Chrétien, de Troyes, 12th cent — Criticism and interpretation. I. Chrétien, de Troyes, 12th cent. Selections. English and Old French. 1981. II. T.
PQ1448.T66   841/.1 19   LC 80-49938   ISBN 0521233615

Goldmann, Lucien.   2.3953
Le dieu caché; étude sur la vision tragique dans les Pensées de Pascal et dans le théâtre de Racine. Paris, Gallimard, 1955 [i.e. 1956] 451 p. 23 cm. (Bibliothèque des idées) Errata slip inserted. 1. Pascal, Blaise, 1623-1662. Pensées 2. Racine, Jean, 1639-1699. 3. God in literature I. T.
PQ1451.G6 G6   LC 56-4477

Marie, de France, 12th cent.   2.3954
The fables of Marie de France: an English translation by Mary Lou Martin; with a foreword by Norris J. Lacy. — Birmingham, Ala: Summa Publications, 1984. 259 p.: ill. Text in Old French, foreword, introduction and translation in English. 1. Fables, French — Translations into English 2. Fables, English — Translations from French I. Martin, Mary Lou. II. T.
PQ1494F3 E55 1984   ISBN 0917786343

Marie, de France, 12th cent.   2.3955
[Lais. English] The lais of Marie de France / translated, with an introd. and notes, by Robert Hanning & Joan Ferrante; foreword by John Fowles. — 1st ed.

— New York: Dutton, c1978. xiii, 237, [1] p.; 22 cm. I. Hanning, Robert W. II. Ferrante, Joan M., 1936- III. T.
PQ1494.L3 E5 1978   841/.1   LC 78-8378   ISBN 0525143408

Mickel, Emanuel J., 1937-.   2.3956
Marie de France, by Emanuel J. Mickel, Jr. New York, Twayne Publishers [1974] 189 p. facsim. 22 cm. (Twayne's world authors series, TWAS 306. France) 1. Marie, de France, 12th cent. I. T.
PQ1495.M5   841/.1   LC 73-17350   ISBN 0805725911

Roman de Renart. English.   2.3957
Renard the Fox / translated from the Old French by Patricia Terry. — Boston: Northeastern University Press, 1983. 179 p.: ill.; 24 cm. Translation of a medieval French poem. 1. Foxes — Poetry. 2. Animals — Poetry I. Terry, Patricia Ann, 1929- II. Reynard the Fox. English. III. T.
PQ1508.E5 T47 1983   841/.1 19   LC 83-8128   ISBN 0930350472

Chanson de Roland.   • 2.3958
La Chanson de Roland; publiée d'après le manuscrit d'Oxford et traduite par Joseph Bédier. [26 ed.] — Paris, L'Edition d'art, H. Piazza [1922?] xvii, 322 p.; 19 cm. Text and translation in modern French prose on opposite pages. I. Bédier, Joseph, 1864-1938. II. T.
PQ1517.B4

Jenkins, Thomas Atkinson, 1868-1935, ed.   2.3959
La chanson de Roland: Oxford version / edition, notes and glossary by T. Atkinson Jenkins. — Boston [etc.]: D.C. Heath [c1924] 378p. (Heath's modern language series) I. T.
PQ1517 J4

Chanson de Roland. English & Old French.   2.3960
The Song of Roland. — Analytical ed. / Gerard J. Brault. — University Park: Pennsylvania State University Press, c1978. 2 v.: ill. Includes index. 1. Roland — Romances. I. Brault, Gerard Joseph II. T.
PQ1521.E5 B7 1978   PQ1521E5 B7 1978.   841/.1   LC 77-22946
   ISBN 0271005165

Chanson de Roland. English.   • 2.3961
The song of Roland / translated by C.K. Scott Moncrieff; with an introd. by G.K. Chesterton, and a note on technique by George Saintsbury. — [1st ed.] Ann Arbor: University of Michigan Press [1959] x, 139 p.; 21 cm. (Ann Arbor paperbacks, AA32) 1. Roland (Legendary character) — Romances. I. Scott-Moncrieff, C. K. (Charles Kenneth), 1889-1930. tr. II. T.
PQ1521.E5 S42   841.1   LC 59-16354

Vance, Eugene.   • 2.3962
Reading the Song of Roland. — Englewood Cliffs, N.J.: Prentice-Hall, [1970] ix, 118 p.: front.; 22 cm. — (Landmarks in literature) 1. Chanson de Roland. I. T.
PQ1522.V35   841/.1   LC 74-97924   ISBN 0137535333

Roman de la Rose.   • 2.3963
Le Roman de la Rose [par] Guillaume de Lorris & Jean de Meun; mis en français moderne par André Mary. [Nouv. éd. Paris]. — Gallimard [1949] 383 p. 19 cm. 'Ouvrage couronné par l'Académie française.' I. Guillaume, de Lorris, fl. 1230. II. Jean, de Meun, d. 1305? III. Mary, André, 1880- IV. T.
PQ1528.A25 1949   841.18   LC 49-27605 *

Guillaume, de Lorris, fl. 1230.   • 2.3964
[Roman de la Rose English] The Romance of the rose, by Guillaume de Lorris and Jean de Meun. Translated by Charles Dahlberg. Princeton, N.J., Princeton University Press, 1971. xv, 450 p. 64 illus. 25 cm. Translation of: Roman de la Rose. I. Jean, de Meun, d. 1305? II. Dahlberg, Charles, 1919- tr. III. T.
PQ1528.A43   841/.1   LC 75-120754   ISBN 0691061971

Béroul, 12th cent.   2.3965
The romance of Tristan; a poem of the twelfth century, edited by A. Ewert. [New Jersey]: Barnes & Noble, 1971. 2 v. 19 cm. 1. Tristan — Romances. I. Bernard, Antoine, 1890-1969 II. Ewert, Alfred, 1891-1969. III. T.
PQ 1537 A1 1939

Vàrvaro, Alberto.   2.3966
[Roman de Tristran di Béroul. English] Beroul's Rõmance of Tristran; translated [from the Italian] by John C. Barnes. Manchester, Manchester University Press; New York, Barnes & Noble, 1972. viii, 219 p. 23 cm. Translation of Il roman de Tristran di Béroul. 1. Béroul, 12th cent. Le roman de Tristran. I. T.
PQ1537.V313   LC 72-197276   ISBN 0389046493

Tristan.   • 2.3967
Le roman de Tristan et Iseut, renouvelé par Joseph Bédier ... — L'Édition d'art. — Paris, Art H. Piazza [c1946] xii, 248 p.; 19 cm. 'Ouvrage couronné par l'Académie française.' I. Bédier, Joseph, 1864-1938. II. T.
PQ1542.A2B5   398.22   LC 47-20349

PQ1551–1595 Individual Authors and Works, 1400–1500

Cent nouvelles nouvelles. English.   • **2.3968**
The hundred tales (Les cent nouvelles nouvelles) Translated by Rossell Hope Robbins. Illustrated by Alexander Dobkin. — New York: [Crown Publishers, 1960] xxvi, 390 p.: illus.; 24 cm. 'Authors and selected analogues': p. 381-386. I. Robbins, Rossell Hope, 1912- tr. II. T.
PQ1553.C3 A25   843.2   *LC* 60-15389

Charles, d'Orléans, 1394-1465.   **2.3969**
The poems of Charles of Orleans; selected and introduced by Sally Purcell. Cheadle, Carcanet Press, 1973. 112 p. geneal. table. 19 cm. (Fyfield books) 'Several of the English poems are followed by the French and a translation into modern English.' I. Purcell, Sally, 1944- ed. II. T.
PQ1553.C5 1973   841/.2   *LC* 73-169450   *ISBN* 0902145681 *ISBN* 090214569X

Fein, David A.   **2.3970**
Charles d'Orléans / by David A. Fein. — Boston: Twayne Publishers, c1983. 166 p.: ill.; 23 cm. (Twayne's world authors series. TWAS 699) Includes index. 1. Charles, d'Orléans, 1394-1465 — Criticism and interpretation. I. T. II. Series.
PQ1553.C5 F44 1983   841/.2 19   *LC* 83-5838   *ISBN* 0805765468

Chartier, Alain, 15th cent.   **2.3971**
The poetical works of Alain Chartier / edited by J. C. Laidlaw. — London; New York: Cambridge University Press, 1974. v, 526 p., [1] leaf of plates: ill.; 24 cm. English and Old French. Includes indexes. I. Laidlaw, J. C., ed. II. T.
PQ1557.A14   PQ1557 A14.   841/.2   *LC* 73-77177   *ISBN* 0521079403

Pathelin.   • **2.3972**
Maistre Pierre Pathelin, reproduction en fac–similé de l'édition imprimée en 1489 par Pierre Levet. — Genève, Librairie E. Droz, 1953. x p., facsim.: [42] l. illus. 19 cm. — (Textes littéraires français.) Introduction signed: Richard T. Holbrook. I. T. II. Series.
PQ1573.A1 1489e   *LC* 54-42323

Christine, de Pisan, ca. 1364-ca. 1431.   **2.3973**
[Epistles. English. Selections] The epistle of the prison of human life; with, An epistle to the Queen of France; and, Lament on the evils of the civil war / Christine de Pizan; edited and translated by Josette A. Wisman. — New York: Garland, 1984. xlv, 99 p.: ill.; 23 cm. — (Garland library of medieval literature; v. 21. Series A) French text, parallel English translation. Includes index. 1. Christine, de Pisan, ca. 1364-ca. 1431 — Translations, English. 2. Consolation 3. War — Moral aspects. 4. France — History — Charles VI, 1380-1422 — Sources. I. Wisman, Josette A. II. T.
PQ1575.A28 1984   846/.2 19   *LC* 83-49393   *ISBN* 0824094123

Willard, Charity Cannon.   **2.3974**
Christine de Pizan: her life and works / Charity Cannon Willard. — New York, N.Y.: Persea Books, c1984. 266 p.: ill.; 24 cm. Includes index. 1. Christine, de Pisan, ca. 1364-ca. 1431. 2. Authors, French — To 1500 — Biography. I. T.
PQ1575.Z5 W55 1984   841/.2 B 19   *LC* 84-1081   *ISBN* 0892550848

Villon, François, b. 1431.   • **2.3975**
[Poems. English and French] Complete works. Translated with a biography and notes by Anthony Bonner, with an introd. by William Carlos Williams. New York, D. McKay Co. [1960] xxvi, 228 p. 22 cm. English and French. Includes the rondeau for voice and 2 instruments, MOrt, j'appelle, by an anonymous composer. I. T.
PQ1590.A2 1960a   841.2   *LC* 60-14600

Villon, François, b. 1431.   • **2.3976**
Oeuvres / editées par Auguste Longnon. — 4. éd. / rev. par Lucien Foulet. — Paris: H. Champion, 1967. xxiv, 170 p. — (Les Classiques français du moyen âge; [2]) I. Longnon, Auguste, 1844-1911. II. Foulet, Lucien. III. T.
PQ1590 A2 1967

PQ1600–2699 MODERN FRENCH LITERATURE: INDIVIDUAL AUTHORS

PQ1600–1709 16th Century

PQ1601–1637 A–M

Aubigné, Agrippa d', 1552-1630.   • **2.3977**
[Works] Œuvres. Introduction, tableau chronologique et historique par Henri Weber. Texte établi par Henri Weber et annoté par Henri Weber, Jacques Bailbé et Marguerite Soulié. [Paris,] Gallimard, 1969. lxvi, 1595 p. 18 cm. (Bibliothèque de la Pléiade, v. 206) At head of title: Agrippa d'Aubigné. I. Weber, Henri, professeur. ed. II. Bailbé, Jacques, ed. III. Soulié, Marguerite. ed. IV. T.
PQ1603.A18   *LC* 75-412587

Buffum, Imbrie, 1915-.   • **2.3978**
Agrippa d'Aubigné's Les Tragiques: a study of the baroque style in poetry / by Imbrie Buffum. — New Haven: Yale University Press, 1951. 151 p. — (Yale Romanic studies: second series; 1) 1. Aubigné, Agrippa d', 1552-1630. Tragiques. 2. Baroque literature — History and criticism. I. T. II. Series.
PQ1603.A73 B8   *LC* 51-13034

Cameron, Keith.   **2.3979**
Agrippa d'Aubigné / by Keith Cameron. — Boston: Twayne Publishers, c1977. 169 p.: port.; 21 cm. — (Twayne's world authors series; TWAS 443: France) Includes index. 1. Aubigné, Agrippa d', 1552-1630. 2. Authors, French — 16th century — Biography. I. T.
PQ1603.C3   841/.3   *LC* 77-540   *ISBN* 0805762809

Des Périers, Bonaventure, 1500?-1544?   **2.3980**
Nouvelles récréations et joyeux devis: I–XC / Bonaventure Des Périers; éd. critique avec introd. et notes par Krystyna Kasprzyk. — Paris: H. Champion, 1980. lii, 376 p.: ill.; 19 cm. At head of title: Société des textes français modernes. Includes index. I. Kasprzyk, Krystyna. II. Société des textes français modernes (Paris, France) III. T.
PQ1609.D3 N6 1980   843/.3 19   *LC* 80-122559   *ISBN* 2865031713

Labé, Louise, 1526?-1566.   • **2.3981**
Œuvres poétiques de Louise Labé, suivies d'un commentaire de Maurice Fombeure. Paris, le Club français du livre, 1967. 130 p. port. 13 cm. (Privilège, 26) I. T.
PQ1628.L2 A17 1967

Labé, Louise, 1526?-1566.   **2.3982**
[Sonnets. English & French] Sonnets [by] Louise Labé. Introd. and commentaries by Peter Sharratt. Translations by Graham Dunstan Martin. Austin, University of Texas [c1972] x, 107 p. 21 cm. (Edinburgh bilingual library, 7) Sonnets in French and English. I. Sharratt, Peter. II. Martin, Graham Dunstan. tr. III. T. IV. Series.
PQ1628.L2 A17 1972   841/.3   *LC* 72-2042   *ISBN* 0292746032

La Taille, Jean de, 1533?-1611 or 12.   • **2.3983**
Dramatic works; edited by Kathleen M. Hall and C. N. Smith. London, Athlone Press; distributed by Tiptree Book Services ltd., 1972. [7], 212 p. 21 cm. (Athlone Renaissance library) Distributed in U.S.A. by Oxford University Press, New York. Text in French; introd. and notes in English. I. T.
PQ1628.L35 A6 1972   842/.3   *LC* 72-181388   *ISBN* 0485138042 *ISBN* 0485128047

La Taille, Jean de, 1533?-1611 or 12.   **2.3984**
[Corrivaus. English] The rivals / Jean de La Taille; translated with an introduction and notes by H.P. Clive. — Waterloo, Ont., Canada: Wilfrid Laurier University Press; Atlantic Highlands, N.J.: Distributed by Humanities Press, 1981. xxxiii, 58 p.; 18 cm. — (Carleton Renaissance plays in translation. 0704-4569; 4) Translation of: Les Corrivaus. I. Clive, H. P. II. T. III. Series.
PQ1628.L35 A6413 1981   842/.3 19   *LC* 82-187795   *ISBN* 088920120X

Lemaire de Belges, Jean, b. 1473.   • 2.3985
La concorde des deux langages. Éd. critique pub. par Jean Frappier. — Paris, Droz, 1947. lxviii, 112 p. 19 cm. — (Textes littéraires français) 'Bibliographie sommaire': p. [82]-84. I. Frappier, Jean. ed. II. T.
PQ1628.L5A65   *LC* 49-23751 *

Marguerite, Queen, consort of Henry II, King of Navarre, 1492-1549.   2.3986
[Heptaméron. English] The Heptameron / Marguerite de Navarre; translated with an introduction by P.A. Chilton. — Harmondsworth, Middlesex, England; New York, N.Y., U.S.A.: Penguin Books, 1984. 542 p.; 20 cm. (Penguin classics.) Translation of: Heptaméron. I. Chilton, Paul A. (Paul Anthony) II. T. III. Series.
PQ1631.H3 E5 1984   843/.3 19   *LC* 84-186955   *ISBN* 014044355X

Marguerite, Queen, consort of Henry II, King of Navarre, 1492-1549.   • 2.3987
L'Heptaméron / Marguerite de Navarre; [texte étalbi sur les manuscrits avec une introd. des notes et un index des noms propres par Michel François]. — Éd. illustrée. — Paris: Garnier, 1960. xxix, 516 p.: ports.; 19 cm. — (Classiques Garnier) I. François, Michel. II. T.
PQ1631.H3x   *LC* a 61-426

Tetel, Marcel.   2.3988
Marguerite de Navarre's Heptameron: themes, language, and structure. Durham, N.C., Duke University Press, 1973. 217 p. 25 cm. 1. Marguerite, Queen, consort of Henry II, King of Navarre, 1492-1549. L'Heptaméron. I. T.
PQ1631.H4 T4   843/.3   *LC* 72-88735   *ISBN* 0822302799

Marot, Clément, 1495?-1544.   2.3989
Oeuvres complètes / Clément Marot; édition critique par C.A. Mayer. — Genève: Slatkine, 1980?-. v. I. Mayer, Claude Albert. II. T.
PQ1635 A1 1980   *ISBN* 2051001790

PQ1641–1653 Montaigne

Montaigne, Michel de, 1533-1592.   • 2.3990
Oeuvres complètes / Montaigne; préface d'André Maurois; texte établi et annoté par Robert Barral en collaboration avec Pierre Michel. — Paris: Editions du Seuil, 1967. 621 p. — (L'Intégrale) I. Barral, Robert. II. T.
PQ1641.A1 1967   *LC* 67-102713

Montaigne, Michel de, 1533-1592.   2.3991
[Journal de voyage en Italie. English] Montaigne's Travel journal / translated and with an introduction by Donald M. Frame; foreword by Guy Davenport. — San Francisco: North Point Press, 1983. xxxvii, 175 p.; 22 cm. Translation of: Journal de voyage en Italie. 1. Montaigne, Michel de, 1533-1592 — Diaries. 2. Montaigne, Michel de, 1533-1592 — Journeys — Italy. 3. Authors, French — 16th century — Diaries. 4. Italy — Description and travel — 1501-1800 5. Germany — Description and travel 6. Switzerland — Description and travel I. Frame, Donald Murdoch, 1911- II. T. III. Title: Travel journal.
PQ1641.J6813 1983   914.5/047 19   *LC* 83-61397   *ISBN* 0865471231

Montaigne, Michel de, 1533-1592.   • 2.3992
The complete works of Montaigne: essays, travel journal, letters / newly translated by Donald M. Frame. — Stanford, Calif.: Stanford University Press, 1957. xxvi, 1093 p. 25 cm. I. T.
PQ1642.E5 F7 1957   844.3   *LC* 57-11676

Frame, Donald Murdoch, 1911-.   • 2.3993
Montaigne: a biography, by Donald M. Frame. [1st ed.] New York, Harcourt, Brace & World [1965] viii, 408 p. illus., facsims., geneal. table, map (on lining papers) ports. 25 cm. 'Table of contents of Montaigne's essays': p. 324-326. Bibliographical references included in 'Notes' (p. 329-393) 1. Montaigne, Michel de, 1533-1592. I. T.
PQ1643.F69   844.3   *LC* 65-19055

Frame, Donald Murdoch, 1911-.   • 2.3994
Montaigne's discovery of man; the humanization of a humanist. — New York, Columbia University Press, 1955. viii, 202 p. 23 cm. Bibliographical references included in 'Notes' (p. [171]-202) 1. Montaigne, Michel Eyquem de, 1533-1592. I. T.
PQ1643.F72   844.31   *LC* 55-7926 rev

Starobinski, Jean.   2.3995
Montaigne en mouvement / Jean Starobinski. — [Paris]: Gallimard, c1982. 379 p.; 23 cm. — (Bibliothèque des idées) 1. Montaigne, Michel de, 1533-1592 — Criticism and interpretation. I. T.
PQ1643.S733x 1982   *LC* 83-672441   *ISBN* 2070224791

Tetel, Marcel.   2.3996
Montaigne. New York, Twayne Publishers [1974] 138 p. port. 22 cm. (Twayne's world authors series, TWAS 317. France) 1. Montaigne, Michel de,

1533-1592 — Criticism and interpretation. 2. Montaigne, Michel de, 1533-1592. Essais. I. T.
PQ1643.T4   844/.3   *LC* 74-2250   *ISBN* 0805726233

PQ1661–1679 The Pléiade

Belleau, Remy, 1527?-1577.   • 2.3997
La bergerie. Texte de l'édition de 1565, publié avec une introd., des notes et un glossaire par Doris Delacourcelle. Genève Droz 1954. 152p. (Textes littéraires français) I. Delacourcelle, Doris Winifred (Hill) II. T.
PQ1666 B4 1954

Du Bellay, Joachim, 1525 (ca.)-1560.   • 2.3998
Les regrets, suivis des Antiquités de Rome. Texte établi et présenté par Pierre Grimal. — Paris, A. Colin [1958] 292 p. 18 cm. — (Bibliothèque de Cluny) Bibliography: p. 292. I. Grimal, Pierre, ed. II. T. III. Title: Antiquités de Rome.
PQ1668.R4 1958   841.3   *LC* 66-31805

Ronsard, Pierre de, 1524-1585.   • 2.3999
Oeuvres complètes. Paris: Gallimard, [c1958]. 2v. (Bibliothèque de la Pléiade. 45-46) I. Cohen, Gustave, 1879-1958. II. T. III. Series.
PQ1674.Ax

Bishop, Morris, 1893-1973.   • 2.4000
Ronsard; prince of poets, by Morris Bishop. London, New York [etc.] Oxford University Press, 1940. 5 p. β., 3-253 p. 22 cm. 'Printed in the United States of America.' 1. Ronsard, Pierre de, 1524-1585. I. T.
PQ1677.B5   928.4   *LC* 40-8281

Cave, Terence.   2.4001
Ronsard the poet, edited by Terence Cave. London, Methuen, 1973. [6], 360 p. facsim. 21 cm. Distributed in the USA by Harper & Row, Barnes & Noble Import Division. Includes index. 1. Ronsard, Pierre de, 1524-1585. I. T.
PQ1677.C3   841/.3   *LC* 73-177851   *ISBN* 041608060X *ISBN* 0416080707

Cohen, Gustave, 1879-.   • 2.4002
Ronsard, sa vie et son oeuvre [par] Gustave Cohen. Nouv. éd., refondue, corr. et augm. — [Paris] Gallimard [1956] 301 p. 21 cm. Bibliography: p. [289]-301. 1. Ronsard, Pierre de, 1524-1585. I. T.
PQ1677.C6 1956   *LC* 56-36290

PQ1681–1696 Rabelais

Rabelais, François, ca. 1490-1553?   • 2.4003
[Works] Œuvres complètes / Rabelais; texte établi et annoté par Jacques Boulenger. — Éd. revue et commentée par Lucien Scheler. — [Paris]: Gallimard, 1978. xxiii, 1033 p.; 18 cm. (Bibliothèque de la Pléiade; 15) Middle French, French, Latin or Greek. I. Boulenger, Jacques. II. Scheler, Lucien. III. T.
PQ1682.B68   843/.3   *LC* 79-382305

Rabelais, François, ca. 1490-1553?   • 2.4004
The five books of Gargantua and Pantagruel in the modern translation of Jacques Le Clercq. — New York: The Modern library, c1944. xxxii, 841 p. — (The Modern library of the world's best books.) At head of title: The complete works of Rabelais. I. T. II. Title: Gargantua and Pantagruel.
PQ1685.E5 L4 1936   *LC* 44-40127

Screech, M. A. (Michael Andrew)   2.4005
Rabelais / M. A. Screech. — Ithaca, N.Y.: Cornell University Press, 1979. xviii, 494 p.; 24 cm. Includes indexes. 1. Rabelais, François, ca. 1490-1553? — Criticism and interpretation. I. T.
PQ1694.S36   843/.3   *LC* 79-2448   *ISBN* 0801412684

Tetel, Marcel.   • 2.4006
Rabelais. New York, Twayne Publishers [1967] 153 p. 21 cm. (Twayne's world authors series, 11. France) 1. Rabelais, François, ca. 1490-1553? I. T.
PQ1694.T4   *LC* 66-29179

Febvre, Lucien Paul Victor, 1878-1956.   2.4007
[Problème de l'incroyance au XVIe siècle, la religion de Rabelais. English] The problem of unbelief in the sixteenth century, the religion of Rabelais / by Lucien Febvre; translated by Beatrice Gottlieb. — Cambridge, Mass.: Harvard University Press, 1982. xxxii, 516 p.: ill.; 24 cm. Translation of: Le problème de l'incroyance au XVIe siècle, la religion de Rabelais. Includes index. 1. Rabelais, François, ca. 1490-1553? — Religion. I. T.
PQ1697.R4 E3 1982   843/.3 19   *LC* 82-1009   *ISBN* 0674708253

PQ1703–1709 S–Z

Scève, Maurice, 16th cent.   • **2.4008**
The 'Délie' of Maurice Scève / edited with an introduction and notes by I.D.
McFarlane. — London: Cambridge University Press, 1966. xii, 507 p.: facsims.
Text of poem in French. I. McFarlane, I. D. (Ian Dalrymple) II. T.
PQ1705.S5 D4 1966   *LC* 65-15306

Mulhauser, Ruth E., 1913-.   **2.4009**
Maurice Scève / by Ruth Mulhauser. — New York: Twayne Publishers, c1977.
138 p.: front port. (Twayne's world authors series; TWAS 424: France)
Includes index. 1. Scève, Maurice, 16th cent. I. T.
PQ1705.S5 Z8   PQ1705S5 Z77.   841/.3 B   *LC* 76-28722   *ISBN*
0805762647

Sponde, Jean de, 1557-1595.   • **2.4010**
Sonnets on love and death / by Jean de Sponde; translation and commentary by
Robert Nugent. — Painesville, Ohio: [Lake Erie College Press], 1962. vi, 77 p.;
23 cm. — (Lake Erie College studies; v. 2) 1. Sonnets, French — Translations
into English. 2. Sonnets, English — Translations from French. 3. Sonnets,
French I. Nugent, Robert. II. T. III. Series.
PQ1705.S7 A26 1979   841/.3

Sponde, Jean de, 1557-1595.   **2.4011**
Œuvres littéraires, suivies d'Écrits apologétiques avec des Juvénilia / Jean de
Sponde; édités avec une introduction et des notes par Alan Boase; avant–propos
de Marcel Raymond. — Genève: Droz, 1978. 364 p.: ill.; 18 cm. (Textes
littéraires français; 256) I. Boase, Alan Martin. II. T.
PQ1705.S7 A6 1978   841/.3   *LC* 79-338303

PQ1710–1935 17th Century

PQ1710–1737 A–C

Boileau Despréaux, Nicolas, 1636-1711.   • **2.4012**
Œuvres complètes. Introduction par Antoine Adam. Textes établis et annotés
par Françoise Escal. [Paris, Gallimard, c1966] 1315p. (Bibliothèque de la
Pléiade, 188) I. Escal, François. II. T.
PQ1719.A2 1966   *LC* 67-77705

Pocock, Gordon.   **2.4013**
Boileau and the nature of neo–classicism / Gordon Pocock. — Cambridge
[Eng.]; New York: Cambridge University Press, 1980. 215 p.; 23 cm. (Major
European authors) Includes index. 1. Boileau Despréaux, Nicolas, 1636-1711.
2. Neoclassicism (Literature) 3. Authors, French — 17th century —
Biography. I. T.
PQ1723.P6   841/.4   *LC* 79-50885   *ISBN* 0521227720

Bossuet, Jacques Bénigne, 1627-1704.   • **2.4014**
Oeuvres. Textes établis et annotés par l'Abbé Velat et Yvonne Champailler.
[Paris, Gallimard, 1961] 1573 p. 18 cm. (Bibliothèque de la Pléiade, 33) Cover
title: Oraisons funèbres. Panégyriques. I. T.
PQ1725.Ax

PQ1741–1789 Corneille

Corneille, Pierre, 1606-1684.   **2.4015**
[Works. 1980] Œuvres complètes / Corneille; textes établis, présentés et
annotés par Georges Couton. — Nouv. éd. — [Paris]: Gallimard,
c1980- < c1984 >. v. < 1-2 >; 18 cm. (Bibliothèque de la Pléiade; no 19- < 20
>) I. Couton, Georges. II. T.
PQ1741 1980   842/.4 19   *LC* 80-150470   *ISBN* 2070110834

Corneille, Pierre, 1606-1684.   **2.4016**
[Plays English. 1975] The Cid; Cinna; The theatrical illusion / [by] Pierre
Corneille; translated and introduced by John Cairncross. — Harmondsworth:
Penguin, 1975. 281 p.; 18 cm. (The Penguin classics) 1. Cid, ca. 1043-1099 —
Romances. 2. Cinna, Gnaeus Cornelius — Drama. I. Cairncross, John. II. T.
III. Title: Cid.
PQ1745.E5 C3 1975   842/.4   *LC* 76-453793   *ISBN* 0140443126

Corneille, Pierre, 1606-1684.   • **2.4017**
Chief plays / translated into English blank verse with an introductory study of
Corneille, by Lacy Lockert. — [2d ed.]. — Princeton: Princeton University
Press, 1957. xiv, 386 p.; 23 cm. I. Lockert, Lacy, ed. and tr. II. T.
PQ1745.E5 L6 1957   842.41   *LC* 57-9718

Abraham, Claude.   **2.4018**
Pierre Corneille / by Claude Abraham. — New York: Twayne Publishers,
1972. 169 p. (Twayne's world authors series, TWAS 214: France.) 1. Corneille,
Pierre, 1606-1684 — Criticism and interpretation. I. T.
PQ1772.A54   842/.4   *LC* 76-186715

Nelson, Robert James, 1925-.   • **2.4019**
Corneille, his heroes and their worlds. — Philadelphia: University of
Pennsylvania Press, 1963. 322 p.; 22 cm. 1. Corneille, Pierre, 1606-1684.
2. Heroes in literature I. T.
PQ1782.N4   *LC* 63-7859   *ISBN* 0812273842

PQ1791–1805 C–L

Cyrano de Bergerac, 1619-1655.   • **2.4020**
Other worlds: the comical history of the states and empires of the moon and the
sun / Cyrano de Bergerac; translated and introduced by Geoffrey Strachan. —
London: Oxford University Press, 1965. xvi, 232 p. — (The Oxford library of
French classics) Translation of Histoire comique. I. T. II. Title: Histoire
comique.
PQ1793.A2 E5   847.4   *LC* 66-3414

Desjardins, Marie Catherine Hortense, known as Mme de   **2.4021**
Villedieu, d.1683.
Les Désordres de l'amour / Madame de Villedieu. — Éd. critique / par
Micheline Cuénin; préf. de Pierre Moreau. — Genève: Droz, 1970. lxiv, 257 p.:
facsim., geneal. table.; 18 cm. — (Textes littéraires français; 174) I. Cuénin,
Micheline II. T.
PQ1794.D5 A65 1970   *LC* 73-563143

Fénelon, François de Salignac de La Mothe-, 1651-1715.   **2.4022**
[Selections. 1983] Œuvres / Fénelon; édition établie par Jacques Le Brun. —
[Paris]: Gallimard, c1983-. v. < 1 >; 18 cm. — (Bibliothèque de la Pléiade; 307)
I. Le Brun, Jacques. II. T.
PQ1795.A16 1983   848/.409 19   *LC* 83-191310   *ISBN* 2070110176

Davis, James Herbert.   **2.4023**
Fénelon / by James Herbert Davis, Jr. — Boston: Twayne Publishers, 1979.
186 p.: port.; 21 cm. — (Twayne's world authors series; TWAS 542: France)
Includes index. 1. Fénelon, François de Salignac de La Mothe-, 1651-1715 —
Criticism and interpretation. I. T.
PQ1796.D3   848/.4/09   *LC* 78-31470   *ISBN* 0805763848

La Bruyère, Jean de, 1645-1696.   **2.4024**
Oeuvres complètes / La Bruyère; édition établie et annotée par Julien Benda. —
[Paris]: Gallimard, 1984, c1951. 739 p.; 18 cm. — (Bibliothèque de la Pléiade;
23) I. Benda, Julien, 1867-1956. II. T.
PQ1803.A1 [1978]   *ISBN* 2070102947

La Bruyère, Jean de, 1645-1696.   • **2.4025**
Characters / La Bruyère; translated by Henri van Laun; introduced by Denys
C. Potts. — London: Oxford University Press, 1963. — xi, 321 p.; 19 cm. (The
Oxford library of French classics.) 1. Characters and characteristics I. Van
Laun, Henri, 1820-1896. II. T.
PQ1803 A63 1963   848.4   *LC* 63-24731

Knox, Edward C.   **2.4026**
Jean de la Bruyère, by Edward C. Knox. — New York: Twayne Publishers,
c1973. 140 p.; 20 cm. — (Twayne's world authors series, TWAS 298. France)
1. La Bruyère, Jean de, 1645-1696. I. T.
PQ1803.K5 1974   848/.4/07   *LC* 73-15836   *ISBN* 0805725075

La Fayette, Madame de (Marie-Madeleine Pioche de La   • **2.4027**
Vergne), 1634-1693.
The Princess of Cleves; translated by Nancy Mitford. [New York, New
Directions, 1951] xxviii, 210 p. 19 cm. (The New classics series [31]) Supposed
to have been written with the assistance of Segrais and La Rochefoucauld.
I. Segrais, Jean Regnauld de, 1624-1701. II. La Rochefoucauld, François, duc
de, 1613-1680. III. T. IV. Series.
PQ1805.L5 A71 1951   *LC* 51-10612

Haig, Stirling.   **2.4028**
Madame de Lafayette. New York, Twayne Publishers [1970] 164 p. 21 cm.
(Twayne's world authors series. TWAS 90. France) 1. La Fayette, Madame de
(Marie-Madeleine Pioche de La Vergne), 1634-1693. I. T.
PQ1805.L5 A756   843/.4   *LC* 71-79207

PQ1806–1812 La Fontaine

La Fontaine, Jean de, 1621-1695.   • **2.4029**
Oeuvres completes. Paris: Gallimard, 1958-63, v.1, 1963, c1954. 2 v.
(Bibliothèque de la Pléiade. 10, 62) I. Groos, Rene, 1898- II. Schiffrin,
Jacques. III. Clarac, Pierre, 1894- IV. T. V. Series.
PQ1806.1963

Lapp, John C., 1917-. 　　　　　　　　　**2.4030**
The esthetics of negligence: La Fontaine's Contes [by] John C. Lapp. —
Cambridge [Eng.] University Press, 1971. ix, 180 p. 23 cm. 1. La Fontaine,
Jean de, 1621-1695. Contes et nouvelles en vers 2. Sex in literature I. T.
PQ1809.L3　　　841/.4　　　*LC* 72-142130　　　*ISBN* 0521080673

La Fontaine, Jean de, 1621-1695. 　　　　　　• **2.4031**
[Fables. English] The fables of La Fontaine. Translated by Marianne Moore.
New York, Viking Press [1964] x, 338 p. 20 cm. (Compass books, C146)
'Marianne Moore has revised her translations of a number of the fables ... for
this new edition.' Translator's presentation copy to the Bollingen Foundation.
Translated into English verse. I. Moore, Marianne, 1887-1972. tr. II. T.
PQ1811.E3 M6 1964　　　841/.4　　　*LC* 74-158172

Wadsworth, Philip Adrian, 1913-. 　　　　　　• **2.4032**
Young La Fontaine; a study of his artistic growth in his early poetry and first
fables, by Philip A. Wadsworth. — New York: AMS Press, [1970, c1952] ix,
236 p.; 24 cm. — (Northwestern University humanities series, v. 29) 1. La
Fontaine, Jean de, 1621-1695. I. T.
PQ1812.W3 1970　　　841/.4　　　*LC* 78-128943　　　*ISBN* 0404507298

PQ1814–1820 L–M

La Rochefoucauld, François, duc de, 1613-1680. 　　　• **2.4033**
Oeuvres complètes. Édition établie par L. Martin–Chauffier, revue et
augmentée par Jean Marchand. Introd. par Robert Kanters, chronologie et
index par Jean Marchand. [Paris, Gallimard, c1964] 996 p. (Bibliothèque de la
Pléiade) Includes "table de concordance de la suite complète des maximes".
I. Marchand, Jean. ed. II. Martin-Chauffier, Louis, 1894- ed. III. T.
PQ1815.A1x

La Rochefoucauld, François, duc de, 1613-1680. 　　　• **2.4034**
Maxims / [by] La Rochefoucauld; translated by Louis Kronenberger. — New
York: Random House, 1959. 158 p. 1. Maxims I. T.
PQ1815.A72 1967　　　848　　　*LC* 59-10837

Moore, Will Grayburn. 　　　　　　　　　• **2.4035**
La Rochefoucauld: his mind and art [by] W. G. Moore. — Oxford: Clarendon
P., 1969. [9], 134 p.; 23 cm. 1. La Rochefoucauld, François, duc de, 1613-1680.
I. T.
PQ1815.M59　　　848/.4/02　　　*LC* 78-410844　　　*ISBN* 0198153848

Mourgues, Odette de. 　　　　　　　　　**2.4036**
Two French moralists: La Rochefoucauld & La Bruyère / Odette de Mourgues.
— Cambridge [Eng.]; New York: Cambridge University Press, 1978. x, 180 p.;
22 cm. — (Major European authors) Includes index. 1. La Rochefoucauld,
François, duc de, 1613-1680 — Criticism and interpretation. 2. La Bruyère,
Jean de, 1645-1696 — Criticism and interpretation. I. T.
PQ1815.M68　　　PQ1815 M68.　　　848/.4　　　*LC* 77-82506　　　*ISBN*
0521218233

Malherbe, François de, 1555-1628. 　　　　　• **2.4037**
Œuvres poétiques [par] Malherbe. Texte établi et présenté par René
Fromilhauge et Raymond Lebègue. Paris, les Belles lettres [c1968] 2v. (Les
Textes français. Collection des universités de France) I. T.
PQ1819.A6 1968　　　*LC* 68-120746

Abraham, Claude Kurt, 1931-. 　　　　　　**2.4038**
Enfin Malherbe; the influence of Malherbe on French lyric prosody, 1605–1674
[by] Claude K. Abraham. — [Lexington]: University Press of Kentucky, [1971]
354 p.; 24 cm. 1. Malherbe, François de, 1555-1628 — Influence. 2. French
poetry — 17th century — History and criticism. I. T.
PQ1819.A83　　　841/.04　　　*LC* 70-160042　　　*ISBN* 0813112540

PQ1821–1869 Molière

Molière, 1622-1673. 　　　　　　　　　**2.4039**
Oeuvres complètes. Textes établis, présentés, et annotés par Georges Couton. —
[Paris] Gallimard [1971] 2 v. 18 cm. — (Bibliothèque de la Pléiade)
Bibliography: v. 1, p. [ixi]-ixviii. I. Couton, Georges. ed. II. T.
PQ1821 1971　　　*LC* 72-327150

Molière, 1622-1673. 　　　　　　　　　• **2.4040**
Tartuffe, and other plays. Translated with an introd. by Donald M. Frame.
[New York] New American Library [1967] iv, 384 p. 22 cm. I. Frame, Donald
Murdoch, 1911- tr. II. T.
PQ1825.E5F68　　　842/.4　　　*LC* 67-16940

Molière, 1622-1673. 　　　　　　　　　• **2.4041**
Comedies; in two volumes. Introd. by F. C. Green. London, Dent; New York,
Dutton [1962-65] 2 v. (Everyman's library, nos. 830, 831) I. Green, Frederick
Charles, 1891-1964. II. T.
PQ1825.E5 Gx

Howarth, W. D. (William Driver). 　　　　　**2.4042**
Molière, a playwright and his audience / W.D. Howarth. — Cambridge
[Cambridgeshire]; New York: Cambridge University Press, 1982. xiii, 325 p.;
23 cm. — (Major European authors.) Includes index. 1. Molière, 1622-1673 —
Criticism and interpretation. I. T. II. Series.
PQ1860.H68 1982　　　842/.4 19　　　*LC* 81-18173　　　*ISBN* 0521244250

Molière: stage and study; essays in honour of W. G. Moore. 　**2.4043**
Edited by W. D. Howarth and Merlin Thomas.
Oxford, Clarendon Press, 1973. xvi, 293 p. illus. 22 cm. 1. Molière, 1622-1673
— Addresses, essays, lectures. 2. Moore, Will Grayburn. I. Moore, Will
Grayburn. II. Howarth, W. D. (William Driver). ed. III. Thomas, Merlin. ed.
PQ1860.M57　　　842/.4　　　*LC* 73-175955　　　*ISBN* 0198157126

Moore, Will Grayburn. 　　　　　　　　• **2.4044**
Molière: a new criticism, by W. G. Moore. Oxford, Clarendon P., 1968. 147 p. 1
illus. 19 cm. 1. Molière, 1622-1673. I. T.
PQ1860.M6 1968　　　842/.4　　　*LC* 68-120218　　　*ISBN* 0198153813

PQ1877 Perrault

Barchilon, Jacques. 　　　　　　　　　**2.4045**
Charles Perrault / by Jacques Barchilon and Peter Flinders. — Boston: Twayne
Publishers, 1981. 192 p.: port.; 21 cm. — (Twayne's world authors series;
TWAS 639. France) Includes index. 1. Perrault, Charles, 1628-1703.
2. Authors, French — 17th century — Biography. I. Flinders, Peter. II. T.
PQ1877.B3　　　841/.4 B 19　　　*LC* 81-4189　　　*ISBN* 0805764836

PQ1885–1909 Racine

Racine, Jean, 1639-1699. 　　　　　　　**2.4046**
Oeuvres complètes. Présentation, notes et commentaires par Rene Groos,
Edmond Pilon et Raymond Picard. [Paris: Gallimard, 1966-] 2 v.; 18 cm. —
(Bibliothèque de la Pléiade, 5, 90) v.1: Théâtre-Poésies. v.2. Prose. I. T.
PQ1885 1966

Racine, Jean, 1639-1699. 　　　　　　　• **2.4047**
Three plays of Racine: Andromache, Britannicus [and] Phaedra / translated by
George Dillon. — Chicago: University of Chicago Press, 1961, 1970 printing.
xxiii, 184 p. I. Dillon, George, 1906- II. T. III. Title: Andromache IV. Title:
Britannicus V. Title: Phaedra
PQ1888E5 D5　　　PQ1888E5 D5 1961.　　　842.4　　　*LC* 61-15938
　　ISBN 0226150771

Racine, Jean, 1639-1699. 　　　　　　　**2.4048**
Phèdre. Phaedra. Edited and translated by R. C. Knight. Austin, University of
Texas Press [c1971] 144 p. 21 cm. (Edinburgh bilingual library, 2) English and
French. 1. Phaedra (Greek mythology) — Drama. I. Knight, R. C. (Roy
Clement), 1907- tr. II. T. III. Title: Phaedra. IV. Series.
PQ1898.A2 K55 1971　　　842/.4　　　*LC* 79-38577　　　*ISBN* 0292764030

Racine, Jean, 1639-1699. 　　　　　　　• **2.4049**
[Phèdre. English] Phaedra and Figaro: Racine's Phèdre [translated by] Robert
Lowell [and] Beaumarchais's Figaro's marriage [translated by] Jacques Barzun.
New York, Farrar, Straus and Cudahy [1961] 213 p. illus. 22 cm. 1. Phaedra
(Greek mythology) — Drama. I. Beaumarchais, Pierre Augustin Caron de,
1732-1799. Figaro's marriage. Le mariage de Figaro. English. 1961. II. Lowell,
Robert, 1917-1977. tr. III. T.
PQ1898.A44　　　842.4　　　*LC* 61-8664

Abraham, Claude Kurt, 1931-. 　　　　　　**2.4050**
Jean Racine / by Claude Abraham. — Boston: Twayne Publishers, c1977.
179 p.: port. — (Twayne's world authors series; TWAS 458: France) Includes
index. 1. Racine, Jean, 1639-1699. 2. Dramatists, French — 17th century —
Biography. I. T.
PQ1904.A66　　　PQ1904 A66.　　　842/.4 B　　　*LC* 77-2377　　　*ISBN*
0805762957

Pommier, Jean, 1893-1973. 　　　　　　　• **2.4051**
Aspects de Racine, suivi de L'histoire littéraire d'un couple tragique. Paris
Nizet 1954. 465p. 1. Racine, Jean, 1639-1699. I. T. II. Title: L'Histoire
littéraire d'un couple tragique
PQ1904 P65

Barthes, Roland. 　　　　　　　　　　• **2.4052**
On Racine. Translated from the French by Richard Howard. New York, Hill
and Wang, 1964, c1960. xii, 172 p. 19 cm. 1. Racine, Jean, 1639-1699. I. T.
PQ1905.B313 1964b　　　*LC* 64-25351

Stendhal, 1783-1842. 　　　　　　　　　• **2.4053**
Racine and Shakespeare [by] Stendhal [pseud.] Translated by Guy Daniels.
With a foreword by André Maurois. [New York] Crowell-Collier Press [1962]

220 p. 22 cm. 1. Racine, Jean, 1639-1699. 2. Shakespeare, William, 1564-1616. 3. Romanticism — France. I. T.
PQ1905.B4523 1962   842.4   *LC 62-17488*

Lapp, John C., 1917-.   ● **2.4054**
Aspects of Racinian tragedy. Toronto: University of Toronto Press, [1964, c1955]. 195 p. (University of Toronto romance series, 2) I. T.
PQ1905.L3

Mourgues, Odette de.   **2.4055**
Racine, or, The triumph of relevance. London, Cambridge U.P., 1967. iv, 171 p. 22 1/2 cm. 1. Racine, Jean, 1639-1699. I. T. II. Title: The triumph of relevance.
PQ1905.M64   *LC 67-11520*

PQ1922–1935 S–Z

Scudéry, Madeleine de, 1607-1701.   **2.4056**
Le Grand Cyrus; Clélie, hystoire romaine. Episodes choisis avec le résumé des deux romans et une introduction par Rita Santa Celoria. Présentation de Mario Bonfantini. — Torino: Giappichelli, 1973. lxxxiii, 432 p.; 22 cm. — (Collana di classici stranieri. Sezione francese) (Her Romans) I. Santa Celoria, Rita, ed. II. Scudéry, Madeleine de, 1607-1701. Clélie. 1973. III. T. IV. Title: Clélie.
PQ1922.A8 1973   *LC 74-162062*

Sévigné, Marie de Rabutin-Chantal, marquise de, 1626-1696.   ● **2.4057**
Letters of Madame de Sévigné to her daughter and her friends, selected, with an introductory essay, by Richard Aldington; with an appendix of biographical and historical information, and an index. London, G. Routledge & sons, ltd., 1927. 2 v. fronts., plates, ports. 22 cm. I. Aldington, Richard, 1892-1962. ed. II. T.
PQ1925.A213   *LC 28-10208*

Sévigné, Marie de Rabutin-Chantal, marquise de, 1626-1696.   ● **2.4058**
Lettres. Texte établi et annoté par Gérard–Gailly. [Paris, Gallimard, 1953-57] 3 v. 18 cm. (Bibliothèque de la Pléiade, 97, 112, 124) I. Gérard-Gailly, Émile. II. T.
PQ1925.A6 G4   846.4   *LC 54-17962*

Williams, Charles G. S.   **2.4059**
Madame de Sévigné / by Charles G.S. Williams. — Boston: Twayne Publishers, 1981. 167 p.: port.; 22 cm. — (Twayne's world authors series; TWAS 596. France) Includes index. 1. Sévigné, Marie de Rabutin-Chantal, marquise de, 1626-1696. 2. Authors, French — 17th century — Biography. I. T.
PQ1925.W5   846/.4 B 19   *LC 81-4104*   *ISBN* 0805764380

Viau, Théophile de, 1590-1626.   ● **2.4060**
OEuvres poétiques. Éd. critique avec introd. et commentaire par Jeanne Streicher. Genève Droz 1951-. (Textes littéraires français) I. Streicher, Jeanne, ed. II. T.
PQ1933 A1 1951

PQ1947–2147 18th Century

PQ1947–1977 A–D

Beaumarchais, Pierre Augustin Caron de, 1732-1799.   ● **2.4061**
Théâtre. Lettres relatives a son théâtre. Texte établi et annoté par Maurice Allem et Paul–Courant. [Paris Gallimard] [1957] 855p. (Bibliothèque de la Pléiade, 22) I. T.
PQ1956 A1 1957

Schérer, Jacques.   ● **2.4062**
La dramaturgie de Beaumarchais. — Paris, Nizet, 1954. 258 p. 19 cm. 1. Beaumarchais, Pierre Augustin Caron de, 1732-1799. I. T.
PQ1956.S3x   *LC A 54-5482*

Sungolowsky, Joseph.   **2.4063**
Beaumarchais. — New York: Twayne Publishers, [1974] 116 p.: port.; 21 cm. — (Twayne's world authors series, TWAS 334. France) 1. Beaumarchais, Pierre Augustin Caron de, 1732-1799. I. T.
PQ1956.S8   PQ1956 S8.   842/.5   *LC 74-10580*   *ISBN* 0805721223

Charrière, Isabelle de, 1740-1805.   **2.4064**
Four tales, by Isabella A. (van Tuyll) de Charrière (Zelide, pseud.) Translated by S. M. S. Freeport, N.Y., Books for Libraries Press [1970] xxix, 263 p. illus., ports. 21 cm. (Short story index reprint series) I. T.
PZ3.C3839 Fo5 PQ1963.C55   843/.5   *LC 75-140327*   *ISBN* 0836937198

Chénier, André, 1762-1794.   **2.4065**
[Selections. English and French. 1978] Elegies and Camille / André Chénier; translated by L. R. Lind. — Washington: University Press of America, c1978. 134 p.; 22 cm. Poems in English and French, with introd. and notes in English. I. Lind, Levi Robert, 1906- II. T.
PQ1965.A195 1978   841/.5   *LC 77-18578*   *ISBN* 0819104124

Chénier, André, 1762-1794.   ● **2.4066**
Oeuvres complètes. Texte établi et commenté par Gérard Walter. [Paris, Gallimard, 1958] 1073 p. (Bibliothèque de la Pléiade. v.57) I. Walter, Gérard, 1896-1974. ed. II. T.
PQ1965.A1x

Smernoff, Richard A.   **2.4067**
André Chénier / by Richard A. Smernoff. — Boston: Twayne Publishers, 1977. 168 p.: port.; 21 cm. — (Twayne's world author series; TWAS 418: France) 1. Chénier, André, 1762-1794. 2. Authors, French — 18th century — Biography. I. T.
PQ1965.S6   PQ1965 S6.   841/.5   *LC 76-50038*   *ISBN* 0805762582

PQ1979 Diderot

Diderot, Denis, 1713-1784.   **2.4068**
Oeuvres. Texte établi et annoté par André Billy. [Paris Gallimard] [1982] 1474p. (Bibliothèque de la Pléiade.) I. T.
PQ1979 A1 1982

Diderot, Denis, 1713-1784.   ● **2.4069**
[Selected works. 1967] Œuvres romanesques. [Texte établi, avec présentation et notes, par Henri Bénac]. Paris, Éditions Garnier frères [1967, c1962] xxx, 906 p. illus. 19 cm. (Classiques Garnier.) I. Bénac, Henri, 1913- ed. II. T.
PQ1979.A6 B4 1967   843/.5 19   *LC 78-216120*

Diderot, Denis, 1713-1784.   ● **2.4070**
Lettres à Sophie Volland / D. Diderot; textes publiés d'après les manuscrits originaux avec une introduction, des variantes et des notes par André Babelon. — 8. éd. — Paris: Gallimard, 1938. 2 v. en 1. I. Babelon, André. II. T.
PQ1979.A82 V6 1938   *LC 38-25315*

Diderot, Denis, 1713-1784.   **2.4071**
[Correspondence. English. 1972] Diderot's letters to Sophie Volland: a selection; translated [from the French] by Peter France. London, Oxford University Press, 1972. [5], 218 p., leaf. port. 23 cm. A selection from the original Letters ed. published in 1938: Lettres à Sophie Volland. I. Volland, Louise Henriette, known as Sophie, 1716-1784. II. T.
PQ1979.A82 V613 1972   194   *LC 73-151601*   *ISBN* 0192125516

Fellows, Otis Edward, 1908-.   **2.4072**
Diderot / by Otis Fellows. — Boston: Twayne Publishers, c1977. 193 p.: port. — (Twayne's world authors series; TWAS 425: France) Includes index. 1. Diderot, Denis, 1713-1784. I. T.
PQ1979.F44   PQ1979 F44.   848/.5/09   *LC 76-43041*   *ISBN* 0805762655

Wilson, Arthur McCandless, 1902-.   ● **2.4073**
Diderot, by Arthur M. Wilson. — New York, Oxford University Press, 1972. 917 p. illus. 24 cm. 'Part I of this book was published in 1957 under title of Diderot: the testing years, 1713-1759.' 1. Diderot, Denis, 1713-1784. I. T.
PQ1979.W52   194 B   *LC 73-151716*

PQ1981–2029 D–R

Laclos, Pierre Ambroise François Choderlos de, 1741-1803.   ● **2.4074**
Œuvres complètes. Texte établi et annoté par Maurice Allem. [Paris, Gallimard, 1959, c1951] xxv, 917 p. facisms. 18 cm. (Bibliothèque de la Pléiade, 6) I. Allemand, Maurice, 1872- ed. II. T.
PQ1993.L22 1959

Laclos, Pierre Ambroise François Choderlos de, 1741-1803.   ● **2.4075**
Dangerous acquaintances / translated by Richard Aldington. — Norfolk, Conn.: J. Laughlin, 1952. 370 p.; 21 cm. — (A New Directions book) I. T.
PQ1993.L22 L53 1952   *LC 52-12138*

Malraux, André, 1901-1976. 2.4076
Le triangle noir. [Paris] Gallimard [1970] 135 p. 21 cm. 1. Laclos, Pierre Ambroise François Choderlos de, 1741-1803. Les liaisons dangereuses. 2. Goya, Francisco, 1746-1828. 3. Saint-Just, 1767-1794. I. T.
PQ1993.L22 L65 LC 70-508204

Rosbottom, Ronald C., 1942-. 2.4077
Choderlos de Laclos / by Ronald C. Rosbottom. — Boston: Twayne Publishers, 1978. 166 p.: port.; 21 cm. — (Twayne's world authors series; TWAS 502: France) Includes index. 1. Laclos, Pierre Ambroise François Choderlos de, 1741-1803. Liaisons dangereuses. I. T.
PQ1993.L22 L68 843/.6 LC 78-18722 ISBN 0805763430

Marivaux, Pierre Carlet de Chamblain de, 1688-1763. • 2.4078
Romans, suivis de Récits, contes & nouvelles, extraits des essais et des journaux. Teste présenté et préf. par Marcel Arland. — [Paris, Gallimard, 1949] liv, 1138 p. 18 cm. — (Bibliothèque de la Pléiade, 68) 'Principaux ouvrages publiés sur Marivaux': p. [1138] I. T.
PQ2003.A1 1949 LC 50-1399

Marivaux, Pierre Carlet de Chamblain de, 1688-1763. • 2.4079
Théâtre complet. Texte préfacé et annoté par Marcel Arland. [Paris, Gallimard, 1961] lxii, 1570 p. 18 cm. (Bibliothèque de la Pléiade, v.79) I. Arland, Marcel, 1899- ed. II. T.
PQ2003.A1x

Haac, Oscar A. 2.4080
Marivaux, by Oscar A. Haac. — New York: Twayne Publishers, [1974, c1973] 166 p.; 22 cm. — (Twayne's world authors series; TWAS 294. France) 1. Marivaux, Pierre Carlet de Chamblain de, 1688-1763. I. T.
PQ2003.Z5 H3 842/.5 LC 73-17338 ISBN 0805725938

Montesquieu, Charles de Secondat, baron de, 1689-1755. 2.4081
Oeuvres complètes; texte présenté et annoté par Roger Caillois. [Paris, Gallimard, 1949-51] 2 v. 18 cm. (Bibliothèque de la Pléiade, v. 81, 86) I. Caillois, Roger, 1913- II. T.
PQ2011.A1 1949 840.81 [844.52] LC 50-28249

Montesquieu, Charles de Secondat, baron de, 1689-1755. 2.4082
[Lettres persanes. English] Persian letters. Translated with an introd. and notes, by C. J. Betts. [Harmondsworth, Eng., Baltimore] Penguin Books [1973] 341 p. 18 cm. (The Penguin classics L281) Translation of Lettres persanes. I. T.
PQ2011.L5 E37 843/.5 LC 73-163802 ISBN 0140442812

Prévost, abbé, 1697-1763. 2.4083
Histoire du chevalier Des Grieux et de Manon Lescaut / abbé Prévost; texte présenté et commenté par Robert Mauzi; illustrations d'Alain Bonnefoit. — Paris: Imprimerie nationale, 1980. 315 p.: ill. — (Lettres françaises, 0222-6502) I. Mauzi, Robert. II. T. III. Title: Manon Lescaut.
PQ2021 M3 1980 ISBN 2110807393

Prévost, Antoine François, called Prévost d'Exiles, 1697-1763. • 2.4084
Manon Lescaut / Abbé Prévost; [translated by D.C. Moylan]. Carmen / Prosper Mérimée; [translated by Edmund H. Garrett. Introd. by Philip Henderson. Memoir of Mérimée by Imogen Guiney] — London: Dent; New York: Dutton [1951] viii, 216 p.: 18 cm. — (Everyman's library, no. 834.) I. T.
PQ2021.M3 E5 1951

Smernoff, Richard A. 2.4085
L'Abbé Prévost / by Richard A. Smernoff. — Boston: Twayne Publishers, c1985. 137 p.: 1 port.; 23 cm. (Twayne's world authors series; TWAS 746. French literature) Includes index. 1. Prévost, abbé, 1697-1763 — Criticism and interpretation. I. T.
PQ2021.Z5 S65 1985 843/.5 19 LC 84-22522 ISBN 0805765948

Restif de La Bretonne, 1734-1806. • 2.4086
Les nuits de Paris. [Paris] Hachette [1960] 296 p.; 19 cm. (Collection du flambeau) I. Chadourne, Marc, 1895- II. T.
PQ2025 N8 1960

PQ2030–2058 Rousseau

Rousseau, Jean-Jacques, 1712-1778. • 2.4087
Oeuvres complètes. Éd. publiée sous la direction de Bernard Gagnebin et Marcel Raymond. — [Paris, Gallimard, 1959-69. 4 v. 18 cm. — (Bibliothèque de la Pléiade, 11) I. Gagnebin, Bernard. ed. II. Raymond, Marcel, 1897- ed. III. T.
PQ2030 1959 LC A 59-6809

Rousseau, Jean-Jacques, 1712-1778. • 2.4088
The confessions of Jean Jacques Rousseau. New York, Modern Library [1945] xviii, 683 p. 19 cm. (The Modern library of the world's best books) I. T.
PQ2036.A5 1945 928.4 LC 46-25064 *

Rousseau, Jean-Jacques, 1712-1778. • 2.4089
La nouvelle Héloïse. Julie; or, The new Eloise: letters of two lovers, inhabitants of a small town at the foot of the Alps. Translated and abridged by Judith H. McDowell. — University Park, Pennsylvania State University Press, 1968. 421 p. 24 cm. Bibliographical footnotes. I. McDowell, Judith H., ed. II. T. III. Title: Julie. IV. Title: The new Eloise.
PQ2039.A46 843/.5 LC 67-27114

Rousseau, Jean-Jacques, 1712-1778. 2.4090
[Discours sur les sciences et les arts. English] The first and second discourses. Edited, with introd. and notes, by Roger D. Masters. Translated by Roger D. and Judith R. Masters. New York, St. Martin's Press [1964] 248 p. illus. 19 cm. Contains the author's Discourse on the sciences and arts and his Discourse on the origin and foundations of inequality. 1. Civilization 2. Equality 3. Natural law 4. Political science I. Rousseau, Jean-Jacques, 1712-1778. Discours sur l'origine et les fondements de l'inégalité parmi les hommes. English. 1964. II. Masters, Roger D. ed. and tr. III. Masters, Judith R., tr. IV. T.
PQ2040.D63 E54 194 LC 64-16357

Rousseau, Jean-Jacques, 1712-1778. 2.4091
[Rêveries du promeneur solitaire. English] The reveries of the solitary walker / Jean-Jacques Rousseau; translated, with pref., notes, and an interpretative essay by Charles E. Butterworth. — New York: New York University Press, 1979. xxi, 268 p.; 22 cm. Translation of Les rêveries du promeneur solitaire. I. Butterworth, Charles E. II. T.
PQ2040.R5 E5 1979 848/.5/09 B LC 78-24806 ISBN 0814710190

Cranston, Maurice William, 1920-. 2.4092
Jean-Jacques: the early life and work of Jean-Jacques Rousseau, 1712–1754 / Maurice Cranston. — 1st American ed. — [New York]: W.W. Norton, 1983. 382 p., [8] p. of plates: ill., map. 1. Rousseau, Jean-Jacques, 1712-1778 — Biography I. T.
PQ2043.C7 ISBN 0393017443

Crocker, Lester G. • 2.4093
Jean-Jacques Rousseau, by Lester G. Crocker. New York, Macmillan [1968-73] 2 v. 24 cm. 1. Rousseau, Jean-Jacques, 1712-1778. I. T.
PQ2043.C76 848/.5/09 B LC 68-22818

Guéhenno, Jean, 1890-. • 2.4094
Jean-Jacques Rousseau; translated from the French by John and Doreen Weightman. London, Routledge & K. Paul; New York, Columbia U. P., 1966. 2 v. 22 1/2 cm. Originally published as Jean-Jacques. Paris, Gallimard, 1962. 1. Rousseau, Jean-Jacques, 1712-1778. I. T.
PQ2043.G813 1966 194.0924 (B) LC 66-12112

PQ2063 Sade

Sade, marquis de, 1740-1814. 2.4095
[Works. 1972] Œuvres complètes [de] Sade. Saint-Michel-sur-Orge, Frontières éditions [1972-. v. 21 cm. I. T.
PQ2063.S3 1972 843/.6 LC 75-514043

Sade, marquis de, 1740-1814. • 2.4096
The complete Justine, Philosophy in the bedroom, and other writings. Compiled and translated by Richard Seaver & Austryn Wainhouse. With introductions by Jean Paulhan & Maurice Blanchot. New York, Grove Press [1965] xvi, 752 p. illus., facsims. 18 cm. I. Sade, marquis de, 1740-1814. Philosophy in the bedroom. II. T. III. Title: Philosophy in the bedroom.
PQ2063.S3 A275 848.5 LC 66-1538

Sade, marquis de, 1740-1814. • 2.4097
Justine: ou, Les malheurs de la vertu / par le marquis de Sade; préf. de Georges Bataille. — [Paris?]: J. J. Pauvert, 1955. 417 p.; 16 cm. (10/18; 444-445) I. T. II. Title: Les malheurs de la vertu.
PQ2063.S3 A69 1969 LC 76-493287

Sade, marquis de, 1740-1814. • 2.4098
La philosophie dans le boudoir. [Paris]: J.-J. Pauvert, 1953. 306 p.; 17 cm. (His Œuvres complètes, t. 1) I. T. II. Series.
PQ2063.S3 Ax 843/.6 s 843/.6 LC 75-514042

Lély, Gilbert. • 2.4099
The Marquis de Sade, a biography. Translated by Alec Brown. New York, Grove Press [1962, c1961] 464 p. 21 cm. Translation of Vie du marquis de Sade. 1. Sade, marquis de, 1740-1814. I. T.
PQ2063.S3 L413 1962 928.4 LC 62-17529

Lynch, Lawrence W. 2.4100
The Marquis de Sade / by Lawrence W. Lynch. — Boston: Twayne Publishers, c1984. 150 p.: ill.; 23 cm. — (Twayne's world authors series; TWAS 724. French literature) Includes index. 1. Sade, marquis de, 1740-1814 — Criticism and interpretation. I. T.
PQ2063.S3 L9 1984 843/.6 19 LC 83-22748 ISBN 0805765719

PQ2070–2144 Voltaire

Voltaire, 1694-1778.   • **2.4101**
Mélanges / Voltaire; préface par Emmanuel Berl; texte établi et annoté par Jacques van den Heuvel. — Paris: Gallimard, 1961. xxxii, 1553 p. — (Bibliothèque de la Pléiade; 152) I. Heuvel, Jacques van den. ed. II. T.
PQ2073.H4   LC 67-95897

Voltaire, 1694-1778.   • **2.4102**
[Selected works. English. 1949] The portable Voltaire, ed., and with an introd., by Ben Ray Redman. New York, Viking Press, 1949. v, 569 p. 17 cm. (The Viking portable library [41]) I. Redman, Ben Ray, 1896-1961. ed. II. T.
PQ2075 1949   840.81   LC 49-7412

Voltaire, 1694-1778.   **2.4103**
Romans et contes / Voltaire; édition établie par Frédéric Deloffre et Jacques van den Heuvel. — [Paris]: Gallimard, c1979. lxxiv, 1316 p.: ill.; 18 cm. (Bibliothèque de la Pléiade; 3) I. Deloffre, Frédéric. II. Heuvel, Jacques van den. III. T.
PQ2081.A235   843/.5   LC 80-465304

Voltaire, 1694-1778.   • **2.4104**
[Candide. English] Candide; or, Optimism: a new translation, backgrounds, criticism. Translated and edited by Robert M. Adams. [1st ed.] New York, Norton [1966] viii, 194 p. 21 cm. (A Norton critical edition) I. Adams, Robert Martin, 1915- ed. II. T. III. Title: Optimism.
PQ2082.C3 E5 1966   843.5   LC 65-27469

Wade, Ira Owen, 1896-.   • **2.4105**
Voltaire and Candide; a study in the fusion of history, art, and philosophy, by Ira O. Wade. Port Washington, N.Y., Kennikat Press [1972, c1959] xvi, 369 p. illus. 23 cm. Issued without facsim. of text of the La Vallière ms. of Candide. 1. Voltaire, 1694-1778. Candide. I. T.
PQ2082.C4W3 1972   843/.4   LC 74-168068   ISBN 0804616884

Voltaire, 1694-1778.   • **2.4106**
Select letters. Translated and edited by Theodore Besterman. — London, New York, T. Nelson [1963] xii, 180 p. 25 cm. I. Besterman, Theodore, 1904-1976. ed. and tr. II. T.
PQ2084.Z4B4   846.5   LC 63-25741

Bottiglia, William F., comp.   • **2.4107**
Voltaire; a collection of critical essays, edited by William F. Bottiglia. Englewood Cliffs, N.J., Prentice-Hall [c1968] xi, 177 p. 21 cm. (Twentieth century views) (A Spectrum book.) 1. Voltaire, 1694-1778 — Addresses, essays, lectures. I. T.
PQ2099.B6   848/.5/08   LC 68-17823

Mason, Haydn Trevor.   **2.4108**
Voltaire: a biography / Haydn Mason. — Baltimore, Md.: Johns Hopkins University Press, 1981. xiii, 194 p., [8] p. of plates: ill.; 24 cm. Includes index. 1. Voltaire, 1694-1778 — Biography. 2. Authors, French — 18th century — Biography. I. T.
PQ2099.M26 1981   848/.509 B 19   LC 80-8868   ISBN 080182611X

Mason, Haydn Trevor.   **2.4109**
Voltaire / Haydn Mason. — New York: St. Martin's Press, 1975. 204 p.; 22 cm. Includes index. 1. Voltaire, 1694-1778 — Criticism and interpretation. I. T.
PQ2122.M3 1975b   848/.5/09   LC 74-24741

PQ2149–2551 19th Century

PQ2157–2185 Balzac

Balzac, Honoré de, 1799-1850.   **2.4110**
La comédie humaine / Balzac; éd. publiée sous la direction de Pierre–Georges Castex; avec la collaboration de Pierre Citron ... [et al.]. — [Paris]: Gallimard, c1976-c1981. 12 v.; 18 cm. — (Bibliothèque de la Pléiade; 26-27, 30-32, 35, 38-40, 42, 141, 292) I. Castex, Pierre Georges, 1915- II. T.
PQ2159.C7 1976   843/.7   LC 76-478711

Canfield, Arthur Graves, 1859-1947.   • **2.4111**
The reappearing characters in Balzac's Comédie humaine. Edited by Edward B. Ham. — Chapel Hill, University of North Carolina Press [1961] xiii, 61 p.; 23 cm. (North Carolina. University. Studies in the Romance languages and literatures, no. 37) Bibliographical footnotes. I. T.
PQ2159.C72 C3x

Hunt, Herbert James.   • **2.4112**
Balzac's Comédie humaine / Herbert James Hunt. — [London]: University of London, Athlone Press, 1959. 508 p.: ill.; 23 cm. 1. Balzac, Honoré de. La comédie humaine I. T.
PQ2159.C72 H8 1964   LC 59-3610

Lotte, Fernand.   • **2.4113**
Dictionnaire biographique des personnages fictifs de La comédie humaine / Fernand Lotte; avec un avant–propos de Marcel Bouteron. — Paris: J. Corti, c1952. xxxii, 763 p.; 23 cm. 1. Balzac, Honoré de, 1790-1850. Comédie humaine — Dictionaries, indexes, etc. I. T.
PQ2159.C72 L6 1952   LC a 53-506

Balzac, Honoré de, 1799-1850.   **2.4114**
[Ténébreuse affaire. English] A murky business. (Une ténébreuse affaire) Translated and introduced by Herbert J. Hunt. [Harmondsworth, Eng., Baltimore] Penguin Books [1972] 222 p. 19 cm. (Penguin classics) I. T.
PZ3.B22 Mr8 PQ2161.A2x   843/.7   LC 72-171388   ISBN 0140442715

Balzac, Honoré de.   • **2.4115**
The short novels of Balzac / Honoré de Balzac; with an introd. by Jules Romains. — New York: Dial Press, 1948. 503 p. — (The Permanent library series) 'Gobseck, Juana and the vicar of Tours...translated by Katherine Prescott Wormeley.' I. Wormeley, Katherine Prescott, 1830-1908 II. T.
PQ2161.W6x   PZ3.B22Sg   LC 48-5594

Balzac, Honoré de, 1799-1850.   **2.4116**
The Chouans; translated with an introduction by Marion Ayton Crawford. — Harmondsworth: Penguin, 1972. 389 p.: map.; 19 cm. — (The Penguin classics, L260) Translation of Les Chouans. 1. Chouans — Fiction. I. T.
PZ3.B22 Cho9 PQ2163.C5   843/.7   LC 72-187000   ISBN 014044260X

Balzac, Honoré de, 1799-1850.   • **2.4117**
Droll stories, by Honoré de Balzac ... — New York, The Modern library [1931] xi, 553 p. 17 cm. — (Half-title: The modern library of the world's best books) 'First Modern library edition 1931.' I. T.
PZ3.B22Dr   PQ2164.A45x.   843.73   LC 31-28422

Balzac, Honoré de, 1799-1850.   • **2.4118**
Cousin Bette. Translated from the French by Kathleen Raine. — New York, Modern Library [1958] xi, 432 p. 19 cm. — (The Modern library of the world's best books [299]) I. T.
PQ2165.C5 E5x   PZ3.B22Cub12   843.73   LC 58-11475

Balzac, Honoré de, 1799-1850.   • **2.4119**
Père Goriot, and Eugénie Grandet; translated from the French by E. K. Brown, Dorothea Walter and John Watkins. With an introd. by E. K. Brown. — New York, Modern Library [1950] xvi, 496 p. 19 cm. — (Modern Library college editions, T2) Bibliography: p. xv–xvi. I. T. II. Title: Eugénie Grandet.
PZ3.B22Per31   PQ2168.E5x.   843.73   LC 50-12197

Balzac, Honoré de, 1799-1850.   • **2.4120**
The Country doctor / by Honore de Balzac; [translated by Ellen Marriage] — London: Dent; New York: Dutton, [1923]. xv, 287 p.; 18 cm. (Everyman's library; 530) 'Introduction by Marcel Gerard.' I. Marriage, Ellen. II. T.
PQ2170.S31   LC 36-37337

Bertault, Philippe.   • **2.4121**
Balzac and The human comedy / by Philippe Bertault; English version by Richard Monges. — [New York]: New York University Press, 1963. xvi, 212 p.; 22 cm. 1. Balzac, Honoré de, 1799-1850. La comédie humaine. 2. Balzac, Honoré de, 1799-1850. I. T.
PQ2178 B3753   843.7   LC 63-19362

Billy, André, 1882-1971.   • **2.4122**
Vie de Balzac ... — Paris, Flammarion [1944] 2 v. plates, ports., facsim. 21.5 cm. 1. Balzac, Honoré de, 1799-1850. I. T.
PQ2178.B5   928.4   LC 46-14699

Hunt, Herbert James.   • **2.4123**
Honoré de Balzac, a biography. [London] University of London, Athlone press, 1957. xii, 198 p. port. 24 cm. 1. Balzac, Honoré de, 1799-1850. I. T.
PQ2178.H8   LC a 57-5737

Levin, Harry.   • **2.4124**
Toward Balzac. — [New York, New Directions, 1948, c1947] 74 p. 24 cm. — (Direction, 3) 1. Balzac, Honoré de, 1799-1850. I. T. II. Series.
PQ2178.L4x   843.73   LC 48-3434 *

Maurois, André, 1885-1967.   • **2.4125**
[Prométhée. English] Prometheus; the life of Balzac. Translated by Norman Denny. [1st ed.] New York, Harper & Row [1966, c1965] 573 p. illus., ports. 25 cm. 1. Balzac, Honoré de, 1799-1850 — Biography. I. T.
PQ2178.M333 1966   843.7   LC 66-13912

Pritchett, V. S. (Victor Sawdon), 1900-. **2.4126**
Balzac [by] V. S. Pritchett. [1st American ed.] New York, Knopf; [distributed by Random House] 1973. 272 p. illus. (part col.) 27 cm. 1. Balzac, Honoré de, 1799-1850. I. T.
PQ2178.P74 1973   843/.7 B   *LC* 72-8681   *ISBN* 039448357X

Prendergast, Christopher. **2.4127**
Balzac: fiction and melodrama / Christopher Prendergast. — New York: Holmes and Meier Publishers, 1979 (c1978). 205 p.; 24 cm. Includes index. 1. Balzac, Honoré de, 1799-1850 — Criticism and interpretation. 2. Melodrama I. T.
PQ2181.P68   843/.7   *LC* 78-11267   *ISBN* 084190457X

Butler, Ronnie, 1931-. **2.4128**
Balzac and the French Revolution / Ronnie Butler. — London: Croom Helm; Totowa, N.J.: Barnes & Noble Books, 1983. 279 p.; 23 cm. Includes index. 1. Balzac, Honoré de, 1799-1850 — Knowledge — History. 2. Balzac, Honoré de, 1799-1850. Comédie humaine 3. Revolutions in literature. 4. Social history in literature. 5. France — History — Revolution, 1789-1799 — Literature and the revolution. 6. France — History — Revolution, 1789-1799 — Influence I. T.
PQ2184.H55 B87 1983   843/.7 19   *LC* 83-9926   *ISBN* 0389204064

Kanes, Martin. **2.4129**
Balzac's comedy of words / by Martin Kanes. — Princeton, N.J.: Princeton University Press, 1976 (c1975). x, 299 p.: port.; 23 cm. Includes index. 1. Balzac, Honoré de, 1799-1850 — Language. I. T.
PQ2185.K3   843/.7   *LC* 75-2993   *ISBN* 069106282X

PQ2187 Ban–Bar

Banville, Théodore Faullain de, 1823-1891. • **2.4130**
Poésies de Théodore de Banville: Les cariatides (1839–1842). Paris: A. Lemerre, 1877. ii, 296 p.: front. (port.); 16 cm. I. T. II. Title: Les cariatides.
PQ2187.C3   841/.8   *LC* 75-41015   *ISBN* 0404145043

Banville, Théodore Faullain de, 1823-1891. • **2.4131**
[Odes funambulesques] Poésies de Théodore de Banville: Odes funambulesques, suivies d'un commentaire. — Paris,: A. Lemerre [1873] 392 p.; 18 cm. First published anonymously, 1857. I. T. II. Title: Odes funambulesques.
PQ2187.O4   841/.8   *LC* 75-41016   *ISBN* 0404145051

Chartier, Armand B. **2.4132**
Barbey d'Aurevilly / by Armand B. Chartier. — Boston: Twayne, c1977. 182 p.: port.; 21 cm. — (Twayne's world authors series; TWAS 468: France) Includes index. 1. Barbey d'Aurevilly, J. (Jules), 1808-1889 — Criticism and interpretation. I. T.
PQ2189.B32 Z656   848/.8/09   *LC* 77-8024   *ISBN* 0805763058

PQ2191 Baudelaire

Baudelaire, Charles, 1821-1867. • **2.4133**
Œuvres complètes [de] Baudelaire ... Texte établi et annoté par Y.–G. Le Dantec. Édition révisée, complétée et présentée par Claude Pichois. [Paris,] Gallimard, 1968. xxx, 1874 p. 18 cm. (Bibliothèque de la Pléiade, v. 1, 7) I. Le Dantec, Y.-G. (Yves-Gérard), 1898-1958. ed. II. Pichois, Claude. ed. III. T.
PQ2191.A1 1968b   *LC* 75-394829

Baudelaire, Charles, 1821-1867. **2.4134**
Les fleurs du mal. Ed. du centenaire. Texte établi par Marcel A. Ruff. Suivi d'une postface. Portrait en couleurs de l'auteur par lui–même. Ed. du centenaire. Paris J.J. Pauvert 1957. 465p. I. Ruff, Marcel A, 1896-, ed. II. T.
PQ2191 F6 1957

Baudelaire, Charles, 1821-1867. • **2.4135**
Flowers of evil, from the French of Charles Baudelaire by George Dillon [and] Edna St. Vincent Millay; with the original texts and with a preface by Miss Millay. — New York, London, Harper & brothers, 1936. xxxix, 282 p., 1 l. 22.5 cm. French and English on opposite pages. 'First edition.' I. Dillon, George, 1906- tr. II. Millay, Edna St. Vincent, 1892-1950. tr. III. T.
PQ2191.F6 E4 1936   841.8   *LC* 36-8362

Baudelaire, Charles, 1821-1867. **2.4136**
Les fleurs du mal: the complete text of The flowers of evil / Charles Baudelaire; in a new translation by Richard Howard; illustrated with nine original monotypes by Michael Mazur. — Boston: D.R. Godine, 1982. xxxii, 365 p.: ill.; 24 cm. English & French. Includes index. I. Howard, Richard, 1929- II. T. III. Title: Flowers of evil.
PQ2191.F6 E4 1982   841/.8 19   *LC* 81-13283   *ISBN* 0879234253

Baudelaire, Charles, 1821-1867. • **2.4137**
Les paradis artificiels. Précédé de La pipe d'opium, Le hachich, Le club des hachichins, par Théophile Gautier. Édition établie et présentée par Claude

Pichois. [Paris Club du meilleur livre] [1961] 232p. (Le Club du meilleur livre. Astrée 39) I. Gautier, Théophile, 1811-1872. II. Pichois, Claude. ed. III. T.
PQ2191 P3 1961

Baudelaire, Charles, 1821-1867. • **2.4138**
Journaux intimes. Fusées. Mon coeur mis à nu. Carnet. Éd. critique établie par Jacque Crépet et Georges Blin. — Paris, J. Corti [1949] 475 p. 23 cm. 'Bibliographie': p. [445]-456. I. T.
PQ2191Z5.A24x   *LC* A 50-3707

Baudelaire, Charles, 1821-1867. • **2.4139**
Intimate journals / Charles Baudelaire; translated by Christopher Isherwood; introd. by W. H. Auden. — Boston: Beacon Press, 1957. 71 p.: ill. I. Auden, W. H. (Wystan Hugh), 1907-1973. II. T.
PQ2191.Z5 A2613 1947   846.8

Bertocci, Angelo Philip, 1907-. • **2.4140**
From symbolism to Baudelaire. With a pref. by Harry T. Moore. — Carbondale, Southern Illinois University Press [1964] vii, 223 p. 22 cm. — (Crosscurrents: modern critiques) Bibliography: p. [215]-218. 1. Baudelaire, Charles, 1821-1867. 2. Symbolism in literature I. T.
PQ2191.Z5B43   841.8   *LC* 64-19801

Hemmings, F. W. J. (Frederick William John), 1920-. **2.4141**
Baudelaire the damned: a biography / F.W.J. Hemmings. — New York: Scribner, c1982. xi, 251 p., [8] p. of plates: ill.; 24 cm. 1. Baudelaire, Charles, 1821-1867 — Biography. 2. Authors, French — 19th century — Biography. I. T.
PQ2191.Z5 H4 1982   841/.8 19   *LC* 82-10298   *ISBN* 0684177749

Hyslop, Lois Boe, 1908-. **2.4142**
Baudelaire, man of his time / Lois Boe Hyslop. — New Haven: Yale University Press, c1980. xviii, 207 p.; 22 cm. 1. Baudelaire, Charles, 1821-1867 — Contemporaries. 2. Poets, French — 19th century — Biography. I. T.
PQ2191.Z5 H9   841/.8 B   *LC* 80-145   *ISBN* 0300025130

Peyre, Henri, 1901- ed. • **2.4143**
Baudelaire, a collection of critical essays. Englewood Cliffs, N.J., Prentice-Hall [1962] vi, 184 p. 21 cm. (A Spectrum book: Twentieth century views S-TC-18) 1. Baudelaire, Charles, 1821-1867. I. T.
PQ2191.Z5 P39   841.8   *LC* 62-18082

Sartre, Jean Paul, 1905-. • **2.4144**
Baudelaire. Translated from the French by Martin Turnell. [Norfolk, Conn., New Directions, 1950] 192p. (Direction, 17) 1. Baudelaire, Charles, 1821-1867. I. T.
PQ2191.Z5 S32   *LC* 50-6845

Starkie, Enid Mary. • **2.4145**
Baudelaire / by Enid Starkie. — Norfold, Ct.: New Directions, c1958. 622p.: ill.; 21 cm. 1. Baudelaire, Charles, 1821-1867 — Criticism and interpretation. I. T.
PQ2191. Z5S8   928.4   *LC* 57-13080

Turnell, Martin. • **2.4146**
Baudelaire: a study of his poetry. — Norfold: New Directions, 1954. 328 p.: ill.; 22 cm. 1. Baudelaire, Charles, 1821-1867. I. T.
PQ2191.Z5 T79   *LC* 54-602

PQ2193–2211 B–C

Bloy, Léon, 1846-1917. • **2.4147**
Pages. Choisies par Raïssa Maritain et présentées par Jacques Maritain. Paris: Mercure de France, 1951. 414 p.; 19 cm. I. Maritain, Raïssa. comp. II. Maritain, Jacques, 1882-1973. ed. III. T.
PQ2198 B18 A6 1951

Bourget, Paul, 1852-1935. • **2.4148**
Le disciple. Introd. de Émile Henriot. Lithographie originale de Maurice Mourlot. Paris Impr. nationale [1953] 358p. (Grand prix des meilleurs romans du 19e siècle, 13) I. T.
PQ2199 D5 1953

Chateaubriand, François-René, vicomte de, 1768-1848. • **2.4149**
Œuvres romanesques et voyages ... Texte établi, présenté et annoté par Maurice Regard. [Paris] Gallimard, 1969. 2 v. ill. (Bibliothèque de la Pléiade, 209-210) At head of title: Chateaubriand. I. Regard, Maurice. II. T.
PQ2205.A6 1969   848.7   *LC* 71-412003

Chateaubriand, François-René, vicomte de, 1768-1848. • **2.4150**
[Atala. English] Atala and René / François–René de Chateaubriand; translated by Rayner Heppenstall; introduced by Robert Baldick. — London: Oxford University Press, c1963. xv, 96 p. — (Oxford Library of French classics)

I. Chateaubriand, François-René, vicomte de, 1768-1848. René. II. T. III. Title: René.
PQ2205.A813 1963   PZ3.C391 At6   *LC* 63-24894

Chateaubriand, François-René, vicomte de, 1768-1848.   2.4151
Mémoires d'outre–tombe. Éd. nouv. établie d'après l'édition originale et les deux dernières copies du texte, avec une introd. des variantes, des notes, un appendice et des index par Maurice Levaillant et Georges Moulinier. [Paris, Gallimard, 1958, c1951] 2 v. (Bibliothèque de la Pléiade, v.67, 71) Tome 2 published in 1952. I. Levaillant, Maurice, 1883- ed. II. T.
PQ2205.Z5 Ax

Maurois, André, 1885-1967.   • 2.4152
[Chateaubriand. English] Chateaubriand; poet, statesman, lover. Translated from the French by Vera Fraser. New York, Greenwood Press [1969] x, 352 p. ports. 23 cm. 'Originally published in 1938.' 1. Chateaubriand, François-René, vicomte de, 1768-1848. I. T.
PQ2205.Z5M32 1969   848/.6/09 B   *LC* 72-88905   *ISBN* 083712705X

Painter, George Duncan, 1914-.   2.4153
Chateaubriand: a biography/ George D. Painter. — 1st American ed. — New York: Knopf; distributed by Random House, 1978, c1977-. 327 p.: ill. Includes index. 1. Chateaubriand, François-René, vicomte de, 1768-1848 — Biography. 2. Authors, French — 19th century — Biography. I. T.
PQ2205.Z5 P34 1978   848/.6/09 s   *LC* 77-27522   *ISBN* 0394426584

Constant, Benjamin, 1767-1830.   • 2.4154
Œuvres. Texte présenté et annoté par Alfred Roulin. [Paris, Gallimard, 1957] 1681 p. 18 cm. (Bibliothèque de la Pléiade, 123) I. T.
PQ2211.C24 1957   *LC* 57-43294

Constant, Benjamin, 1767-1830.   • 2.4155
Adolphe [by] Benjamin Constant. Translated with an introd. by L. W. Tancock. Baltimore, Penguin Books [1964] 125 p. 19 cm. (Penguin classics, L134) I. T.
PQ2211.C24 Ax   *LC* 64-4933

Corbière, Tristan, 1845-1875.   • 2.4156
Selections from Les amours jaunes / Tristan Corbière; translated with an introduction and notes by C.F. MacIntyre. — Berkeley: University of California Press, 1954. 242 p. I. MacIntyre, Carlyle Ferren, 1890-1967. II. T. III. Title: Les amours jaunes.
PQ2211.C32 A814   841.8   *LC* 54-6472

Coster, Charles de, 1827-1879.   2.4157
La legende et les aventures héroïques, joyeuses et glorieuses d'Ulenspiegel et de Lamme Goedzak au pays de Flandres et ailleurs. Éd. définitive. Bruxelles Renaissance du livre [1959] 521p. I. Hanse, Joseph. ed. II. Eulenspiegel (Satire). III. T.
PQ2211 C4 L3 1959

Cros, Charles, 1842-1888.   • 2.4158
[Works. 1970] Œuvres complètes [de] Charles Cros [et] Tristan Corbière. Charles Cros: éd. établie par Louis Forestier et Pierre–Olivier Walzer. Tristan Corbière: éd. établie par Pierre–Olivier Walzer avec la collaboration de Francis F. Burch pour la correspondance. [Paris] Gallimard [1970] 1503 p. 18 cm. (Bibliothèque de la Pléiade. 221) I. Corbière, Tristan, 1845-1875. [Works. 1970] II. T. III. Series.
PQ2211.C65   *LC* 71-561458

PQ2216 Daudet

Daudet, Alphonse, 1840-1897.   • 2.4159
Contes du lundi. — Paris: A. Lemerre, 1873. 258 p.; 18 cm. I. T.
PQ2216.C7

Daudet, Alphonse, 1840-1897.   • 2.4160
Lettres de mon moulin / Alphonse Daudet; illustrations de A. Chazelle. — [Paris]: Hachette, [c1952] 186 p.: ill.; 21 cm. (Idéal-Bibliothèque) I. T.
PQ2216.L5

Daudet, Alphonse, 1840-1897.   • 2.4161
[Lettres de mon moulin. English] Letters from my mill. Translated by John P. Macgregor. Illustrated by Barbosa. New York, Taplinger Pub. Co. [1967, c1962] 204 p. illus. 21 cm. I. T.
PQ2216.L5x   PZ3.D263 Le5   *LC* 66-20235

Daudet, Alphonse, 1840-1897.   • 2.4162
Numa Roumestan: moeurs parisiennes, par Alphonse Daudet. — Paris, New-York [etc.] Nelson [1915] 379, [1] p., 1 l., 16 cm. — (Collection Nelson) 'Printed in Great Britain.' 'Première édition ... 1880.' I. T.
PQ2216.N8 1915   843.88   *LC* 42-12264

Daudet, Alphonse, 1840-1897.   • 2.4163
Le Petit chose ... — Paris, Fasquelle [1960] 355 p. 19 cm. I. T.
PQ2216.P4   843.88   *LC* 39-3809

Daudet, Alphonse, 1840-1897.   • 2.4164
Sapho; moeurs parisiennes. — Paris: E. Fasquelle, 1928. 337 p.; 19 cm. (Bibliotheque Charpentier) I. T.
PQ2216.S3   843.88   *LC* 39-4131

Daudet, Alphonse, 1840-1897.   • 2.4165
[Tartarin. Flammarion] Tartarin de Tarascon. Illustré par J. Girardet, Montégut, de Myrbach, Picard, Rossi. Paris, E. Flammarion [1911] 233 p. illus. 19 cm. (Collection Guillaume) I. T.
PQ 2216 T4 1911   *LC* 20-23713

Daudet, Alphonse, 1840-1897.   • 2.4166
Tartarin sur les Alpes; nouveaux exploits du héros tarasconnais. — Paris, Flammarion [1912] 365 p.: ill.; 19 cm. Sequel to 'Tartarin de Tarascon'. I. T.
PQ2216.T5 1942   *LC* 18-16834

Daudet, Alphonse, 1840-1897.   • 2.4167
Tartarin of Tarascon; Tartarin on the Alps [by] Alphonse Daudet. — London: J. M. Dent; New York: E. P. Dutton [1930] xiv, 230 p.; 18 cm. (Half-title: Everyman's library. [no. 423]) Bibliography: p. viii-ix. 'First published in this edition, 1910; reprinted ... 1930.' I. T. II. Title: Tartarin on the Alps.
PQ2216.T5x   *LC* 36-37192

Sachs, Murray, 1924-.   • 2.4168
The career of Alphonse Daudet, a critical study. Cambridge, Mass., Harvard University Press, 1965. x, 227 p. 22 cm. 1. Daudet, Alphonse, 1840-1897. I. T.
PQ2216.Z5 S26   *LC* 65-24451

PQ2217–2220 Ducasse (Lautréamont)

Lautréamont, comte de, 1846-1870.   • 2.4169
Œuvres complètes: Les chants de Maldoror. Paris, J. Corti, 1956. 425 p. ports., facsims. 19 cm. I. T. II. Title: Chants de Maldoror.
PQ2220.D723 1956   *LC* a 57-1747

Lautréamont, comte de, 1846-1870.   • 2.4170
Maldoror (Les chants de Maldoror) [New York] New Directions [c1965] x, 342 p. 21 cm. I. Lautréamont, comte de, 1846-1870. Poésies. II. Wernham, Guy, tr. III. T.
PQ2220.D723 C53 1965   *LC* 66-12289

Fowlie, Wallace, 1908-.   2.4171
Lautréamont. New York, Twayne Publishers 1974 (c1973) 135 p. 22 cm. (Twayne's world authors series, TWAS 284. France) 1. Lautréamont, comte de, 1846-1870. I. T.
PQ2220.D723 Z654   841/.8   *LC* 73-14588   *ISBN* 0805725113

PQ2221–2231 Dumas (père et fils)

Dumas, Alexandre, 1802-1870.   • 2.4172
Le comte de Monte–Cristo / [introd., bibliographie, notes et relevé des variantes, par J.–H. Bornecque.— Ed. illustrée.— Paris: Éditions Garnier frères [1963, c1962] 2 v.: ill., facsims., ports.; 19 cm. — (Selecta) Bibliography: v. 1, p. [lxv]–lxvi. I. Bornecque, Jacques Henry II. T.
PQ2226.A1 1963   PQ2226.   *LC* 65-7021

Dumas, Alexandre, 1802-1870.   • 2.4173
The count of Monte Cristo / Alexandre Dumas. — New York: Grosset & Dunlap, 1946. x, 1365 p.: ill. I. T.
PQ2226.E5 G7x

Dumas, Alexandre, 1802-1870.   • 2.4174
Les trois mousquetaires. Vingt ans après. Édition présentée et annotée par Gilbert Sigaux. [Paris Gallimard] [c1962] 1733p. (Bibliothèque de la Pléiade, 159) I. Sigaux, Gilbert, 1918- ed. II. T. III. Title: Vingt ans après
PQ2228 A1 1962

Dumas, Alexandre, 1802-1870.   • 2.4175
The three musketeers, in a new translation by Jacques Le Clercq. New York, Modern Library [1950] xvii, 712 p. 19 cm. (The Modern library of the world's best books) 1. France — History — Louis XIII, 1610-1643 — Fiction. I. T.
PQ2228.E5 L4x   *LC* 50-5390

Dumas, Alexandre, 1802-1870.   • 2.4176
The man in the iron mask / Alexandre Dumas; illus. by Edy Legrand, and an introd. by André Maurois. — New York: Printed for the members of the Limited Editions Club, 1965 [c1964] xiv, 430 p.: col. ill.; 25 cm. 1. France — History — Louis XIV, 1643-1715 — Fiction I. T.
PZ3.D89 Man13 1970   PQ2229.V42 L4.

Dumas, Alexandre, 1802-1870. • 2.4177
Twenty years after / Alexandre Dumas; with an introd. by R. Brimley Johnson. — London: Collins, 1962. 543 p.: ports. I. T.
PQ2229.V6x

Dumas, Alexandre, 1802-1870. • 2.4178
My memoirs ... — Radnor: Chilton, [c1961]. 256 p.: ill. 1. Dumas, Alexandre, 1802-1870. I. T.
PQ2230.A27 1961 B

Maurois, André, 1885-1967. • 2.4179
[Trois Dumas. English] The Titans; a three–generation biography of the Dumas. Translated from the French by Gerard Hopkins. Westport, Conn., Greenwood Press [1971, c1957] 508 p. illus. 24 cm. Translation of Les trois Dumas. 1. Dumas, Thomas Alexandre, 1762-1806. 2. Dumas, Alexandre, 1802-1870. 3. Dumas, Alexandre, 1824-1895. I. T.
PQ2230.M3313 1971 840.9/007 B LC 78-156201 ISBN 0837161517

Stowe, Richard S. 2.4180
Alexandre Dumas (père) / by Richard S. Stowe. Boston: Twayne Publishers, c1976. 164 p.: port.; 22 cm. (Twayne's world authors series; TWAS 388: France) Includes index. 1. Dumas, Alexandre, 1802-1870. I. T.
PQ2230.S84 843/.7 LC 75-43919 ISBN 0805762302

Dumas, Alexandre, 1824-1895. • 2.4181
Camille, by Alexandre Dumas, fils; introduction by Edmund Gosse. — New York, The Modern library [1925] xv p., 1 l., 270 p. 17 cm. — (Half-title: The Modern library of the world's best books) 'First modern library edition, 1925.' I. T.
PQ2231.D22x PZ3.D891C14 LC 26-8619

Dumas, Alexandre, 1824-1895. • 2.4182
La dame aux camélias / par Alexandre Dumas fils; préface de Jules Janin. — Nouv. éd. Paris: Calman Lévy, 1899. xx, 299 p.; 19 cm. I. T.
PQ2231 D3

PQ2246–2250 Flaubert

Flaubert, Gustave, 1821-1880. 2.4183
Œuvres complètes / Gustave Flaubert; préf. de Jean Bruneau, présentation et notes de Bernard Masson. — Paris: Éditions du Seuil, 1964. 2 v.: port. — (L'Intégrale) I. Masson, Bernard. II. T.
PQ2246A1 1964b PQ2246 A1 1964b. LC 71-406635

Flaubert, Gustave. • 2.4184
Bouvard and Pecuchet / Gustave Flaubert; translated by T. W. Earp and G. W. Stonier; with an introd. by Lionel Trilling. — Norfolk, Conn.: J. Laughlin, 1954. xxxvii, 347 p.; 21 cm. 'A New Directions book'. I. T.
PQ2246.B682x PZ3.F618B 18 843.84 LC 54-8413

Flaubert, Gustave, 1821-1880. • 2.4185
Dictionnaire des idées reçues: suivi du catalogue des idées chic / G. Flaubert. — Paris: J. Aubier, 1951. 156 p.: port. 1. French wit and humor I. T.
PN6183.F53 LC a51-5828

Flaubert, Gustave, 1821-1880. • 2.4186
Sentimental education [by] Gustave Flaubert. London, J. M. Dent & son ltd; New York, E. P. Dutton & co., inc. [1941] xiv, 401, [1] p. 17 cm. (Everyman's library, [No. 969]) 'Translated, with introduction and notes, by Anthony Goldsmith.' 'First published in the edition 1941.' I. Goldsmith, Anthony, tr. II. T.
PQ2246.E4x 843.84 LC 42-36001

Flaubert, Gustave, 1821-1880. • 2.4187
Madame Bovary; patterns of provincial life. A new translation by Francis Steegmuller. New York, Modern Library [c1957] 396 p. 19 cm. (Modern library books, 28) I. T.
PQ2246.M2x LC 58-1892

Bart, Benjamin F. ed. • 2.4188
Madame Bovary and the critics; a collection of essays, edited by B. F. Bart. — [New York]: New York University Press, 1966. vii, 197 p.; 22 cm. 1. Flaubert, Gustave, 1821-1880. Madame Bovary. I. T.
PQ2246.M3 B3 843.8 LC 66-12596

Flaubert, Gustave, 1821-1880. 2.4189
[Première éducation sentimentale. English] The first sentimental education. Translated by Douglas Garman. With an introd. by Gerhard Gerhardi. Berkeley, University of California Press, 1972. xviii, 291 p. 22 cm. Translation of La première éducation sentimentale. I. T.
PZ3.F618 Fi6 PQ2246.P7x 843/.8 LC 77-149947 ISBN 0520019679

Flaubert, Gustave, 1821-1880. • 2.4190
Salammbo. — London & Toronto: J. M. Dent; New York: E. P. Dutton [1931] xvi, 319 p.; 18 cm. — (Everyman's library; no.869) 1. Carthage — History — Fiction. I. T.
PQ2246.S3 E43 LC 37-5593

Flaubert, Gustave, 1821-1880. • 2.4191
La tentation de saint Antoine. Avec introd., notes et variantes par Édouard Maynial. — Paris, Éditions Garnier frères [1954] xxii, 313 p. illus., ports. 19 cm. 1. Antonius, the Great, Saint — Fiction. I. Maynial, Édouard, 1879- ed. II. T.
PQ2246.T4 1954 LC 67-115692

Flaubert, Gustave, 1821-1880. 2.4192
[Tentation de saint Antoine. English] The temptation of Saint Antony / Gustave Flaubert; translated with an introduction and notes by Kitty Mrosovsky. — Ithaca, N.Y.: Cornell University Press, 1981, c1980. 293 p., [8] p. of plates: ill.; 23 cm. Translation of: La Tentation de saint Antoine. 1. Anthony, of Egypt, Saint, ca. 250-355 or 6 — Fiction. I. Mrosovsky, Kitty. II. T.
PQ2246.T4 E5 1981 843/.8 19 LC 80-70452 ISBN 0801412390

Flaubert, Gustave, 1821-1880. • 2.4193
Trois contes. Un Coeur simple. La Légende de saint Julien l'Hospitalier. Hérodias. Édition augmentée d'une chronologie par Jacques Suffel. [Introduction, notes et relevé de variantes par Édouard Maynial] Paris, Garnier frères, 1969. xxxiv, 237 p. plates. 18 cm. (Classiques Garnier) Illustrated cover. I. Maynial, Édouard, 1879- ed. II. T. III. Title: Un coeur simple. IV. Title: La légende de Saint Julien l'Hospitalier. V. Title: Hérodias.
PQ2246.T7 1969 LC 70-425563

Flaubert, Gustave, 1821-1880. • 2.4194
Three tales. Translated with an introd. by Robert Baldick. Baltimore, Penguin Books [1961] 124 p. 18 cm. (The Penguin classics, L106) I. T. II. Title: A simple heart. III. Title: The legend of St. Julian Hospitator. IV. Title: Herodias.
PQ2246.T7x LC 61-2729

Flaubert, Gustave, 1821-1880. • 2.4195
[Correspondence. English. 1971] The selected letters of Gustave Flaubert. Translated and edited with an introd. by Francis Steegmuller. Freeport, N.Y., Books for Libraries Press [1971, c1953] xxx, 281 p. 23 cm. (Biography index reprint series) 1. Flaubert, Gustave, 1821-1880. I. Steegmuller, Francis, ed. II. T.
PQ2247.A23 E57 1971 843/.8 B LC 78-160919 ISBN 0836980824

Flaubert, Gustave, 1821-1880. 2.4196
The letters of Gustave Flaubert, 1830–1857 / selected, edited, and translated by Francis Steegmuller. — Cambridge, Mass.: Harvard University Press, 1980 (c1979). xvii, 250 p. Includes index. 1. Flaubert, Gustave, 1821-1880 — Correspondence. 2. Novelists, French — 19th century — Correspondence. I. Steegmuller, Francis, 1906- II. T.
PQ2247.A23 E57 1980 843/.8 B LC 79-13505 ISBN 0674526368

Bart, Benjamin F. • 2.4197
Flaubert [by] Benjamin F. Bart. — [1st ed. — Syracuse, N.Y.] Syracuse University Press [1967] xiii, 791 p. illus., ports. 24 cm. 1. Flaubert, Gustave, 1821-1880. I. T.
PQ2247.B3 843/.8 B LC 67-27410

Nadeau, Maurice. 2.4198
[Gustave Flaubert. English] The greatness of Flaubert. Translated by Barbara Bray. New York, Library Press, 1972. 307 p. 23 cm. Translation of Gustave Flaubert, écrivain, essai. 1. Flaubert, Gustave, 1821-1880. 2. Novelists, French — 19th century — Biography. I. T.
PQ2247.N313 843/.8 LC 77-161408 ISBN 0912050098

Sartre, Jean Paul, 1905-. 2.4199
[Idiot de la famille. English] The family idiot: Gustave Flaubert, 1821–1857 / Jean–Paul Sartre; translated by Carol Cosman. — Chicago: University of Chicago Press, 1981-. x, 627 p. Translation of: L'Idiot de la famille. 1. Flaubert, Gustave. 2. Novelists, French — 19th century — Biography. I. T. II. Title: Idiot de la famille. English
PQ2247.S313 843/.8 B 19 LC 81-1694 ISBN 0226735095

Starkie, Enid. • 2.4200
Flaubert: the making of the master. — [1st American ed.]. — New York: Atheneum, 1967. xvii, 403 p.: illus., facsim., ports.; 25 cm. Sequel: Flaubert: the master. 1. Flaubert, Gustave, 1821-1880. I. T.
PQ2247.S77 1967b 843/.8 LC 67-28968

Starkie, Enid.   **2.4201**
Flaubert: the master; a critical and biographical study (1856–1880). — [1st American ed.]. — New York: Atheneum, 1971. 390 p.: illus.; 25 cm. Sequel to Flaubert: the making of the master. 1. Flaubert, Gustave, 1821-1880. I. T.
PQ2247.S78 1971b   843/.8 B   *LC* 75-139328

Giraud, Raymond Dorner, ed.   • **2.4202**
Flaubert; a collection of critical essays, edited by Raymond Giraud. Englewood Cliffs, N.J., Prentice-Hall [1964] 180 p. 21 cm. (Twentieth century views, S-TC-42) (A Spectrum book.) 1. Flaubert, Gustave, 1821-1880. I. T.
PQ2249.G5   843.8   *LC* 64-23564

PQ2254 France

France, Anatole, 1844-1924.   **2.4203**
[Works. 1984] Oeuvres / Anatole France; édition établie, présentée et annotée par Marie–Claire Bancquart. — Paris: Gallimard, 1984-. v. — (Bibliothèque de la Pléiade) I. Bancquart, Marie Claire. II. T.
PQ2254 A1 1984

France, Anatole, 1844-1924.   • **2.4204**
Crainquebille, Putois, Riquet et plusieurs autres récits profitables / Anatole France. — Paris: Calmann-Levy, [1907?] 315 p. I. T. II. Title: Putois. III. Title: Riquet.
PQ2254.C6 1907   *LC* 90-12257

France, Anatole, 1844-1924.   • **2.4205**
Le Crime de Sylvestre Bonnard: suivi de Le livre de mon ami. — [Paris,] Calmann-Lévy, [1958] 475 p.: ill., facsims., ports.; 21 cm. I. T.
PQ2254.C7   *LC* 68-116288

France, Anatole, 1844-1924.   • **2.4206**
The crime of Sylvestre Bonnard. London, John Lane; [1931] viii p., 3 l., [3]-310 p. front., illus., plates. 25 cm. I. Hearn, Lafcadio, 1850-1904. tr. II. Gay, Zhenya, illus. III. T.
PQ2254.C7x   PZ3.F844 Cri13   *LC* 33-7855

France, Anatole, 1844-1924.   • **2.4207**
Les dieux ont soif. — Paris: Calmann-Lévy, [1912?]. 360 p.; 19 cm. I. T.
PQ2254 D4 1912   *LC* 12-15480 revised

France, Anatole, 1844-1924.   • **2.4208**
L'île des pingouins / Anatole France. — Paris: Calmann-Lévy, [1908]. xv, 419 p.; 19 cm. I. T.
PQ2254 I27 1908

France, Anatole, 1844-1924.   **2.4209**
Penguin island. New York, The Modern library [1933] xvi, 295 p. 17 cm. I. T.
PQ2254.I2x   *LC* 33-2521

France, Anatole, 1844-1924.   • **2.4210**
Le livre de mon ami / par Anatole France. — Paris, Calmann-Lévy [1902] 330 p.; 19 cm. I. T.
PQ 2254 L78   *LC* 17-14325

France, Anatole, 1844-1924.   • **2.4211**
Le Lys rouge. — [Paris]: Calmann-Lévy, [1918] 411 p.; 19 cm. I. T.
PQ2254.L9x   *LC* 76-534

France, Anatole, 1844-1924.   • **2.4212**
La rôtisserie de la reine Pédauque / par Anatole France. — 32. éd. Paris: Calmann-Lévy, 1899. 388 p.; 19 cm. I. T.
PQ2254 R7

France, Anatole, 1844-1924.   • **2.4213**
At the sign of the Reine Pédauque, and The revolt of the angels. London, J. M. Dent & sons ltd. [1941] xiii, 416 p., 1 l. 18 cm. I. Jackson, Emilie, tr. II. T. III. Title: The revolt of the angels.
PQ2254.R7x   *LC* 41-51845

France, Anatole, 1844-1924.   • **2.4214**
Thaïs. Paris: Calmann Lévy [1906] 2;350p. I. T.
PQ2254 T4 1906

France, Anatole, 1844-1924.   **2.4215**
[Thaïs. English] Thaïs / Anatole France; translated by Basia Gulati; with an introd. by Wayne C. Booth. — Chicago: University of Chicago Press, c1976. 183 p.; 22 cm. I. Gulati, Basia. II. T.
PZ3.F844 Th26 PQ2254.T4x   843/.8   *LC* 75-20893   *ISBN* 0226259889

PQ2257–2277 G–H

Gaboriau, Emile, 1832-1873.   **2.4216**
The mystery of Orcival / Émile Gaboriau. — New York: Scribner, 1900. 288 p. 'Translated from the French.' Originally Le crime d'Orcival (1867). I. T.
PZ3 G133My 8   PQ2257G2 C713 1900.

Gautier, Théophile, 1811-1872.   • **2.4217**
Le capitaine Fracasse, texte complet (1863) [Introd. et notes par Adolphe Boschot] Paris, Éditions Garnier frères [1964, c1961] xxxii, 504 p. illus., facsim. 19 cm. (Selecta) I. Boschot, Adolphe, 1871-1955. ed. II. T.
PQ2258.C2   *LC* 65-7042

Gautier, Théophile, 1811-1872.   • **2.4218**
Émaux et camées. — Éd. critique. — Paris: Hachette, 1927. xvi, 166 p.; 19 cm. With a reprint of the title page of the first 7 editions, 1852-1884. At head of title: Société des textes français modernes. I. Société des textes français modernes (Paris, France) II. T.
PQ2258.E41927   *LC* 28-12584

Gautier, Théophile, 1811-1872.   • **2.4219**
Mademoiselle de Maupin. (Texte complet,1835) Introduction et notes par Adolphe Boschot ... Paris, Librairie Garnier frères, 1930. xxxvi, 449 p. 11. (Classiques Garnier.) I. Boschot, Adolphe, 1871-1955. II. T. III. Series.
PQ2258.M3 1930   848/.77   *LC* a 40-202

Richardson, Joanna.   • **2.4220**
Théophile Gautier, his life & times. [1st American ed.] New York, Coward-McCann [1959, c1958] 335 p. 22 cm. 1. Gautier, Théophile, 1811-1872. I. T.
PQ2258.Z5 R49 1959   *LC* 59-8739

Nerval, Gérard de, 1808-1855.   • **2.4221**
Oeuvres / Gérard de Nerval; texte établi, annoté et présenté par Albert Béguin et Jean Richer. [Paris, Gallimard, 1952-. v. 18 cm. (Bibliothèque de la Pléiade. v. 89) (Bibliothèque de la Pléiade. 117) I. Béguin, Albert, 1898-1957 ed. II. Richer, Jean, 1915- III. T. IV. Series. V. Series: Bibliothèque de la Pléiade. 117
PQ2260.G36

Nerval, Gérard de, 1808-1855.   • **2.4222**
Selected writings: translated with a critical introduction and notes by Geoffrey Wagner. — Limited ed. New York: Grove Press [1957] 257 p.:21 cm. I. T.
PQ2260.G36 A27 1957   *LC* 57-5158   *ISBN* 0472061631

Nerval, Gérard de, 1808-1855.   **2.4223**
Les chimères. Edited by Norma Rinsler. London, Athlone Press [distributed in the U.S.A. by Humanities Press, New York] 1973. 144 p. 21 cm. (Athlone French poets) Poems. I. Rinsler, Norma, ed. II. T.
PQ2260.G36 C5 1973   841/.7   *LC* 73-177864   *ISBN* 0485147025 *ISBN* 0485147024

Jones, Robert Emmet, 1928-.   **2.4224**
Gérard de Nerval. New York, Twayne Publishers [1974] 188 p. port. 21 cm. (Twayne's world authors series, TWAS 326. France) 1. Nerval, Gérard de, 1808-1855. I. T.
PQ2260.G36 Z66   848/.7/09   *LC* 74-4085   *ISBN* 0805726527

Knapp, Bettina Liebowitz, 1926-.   **2.4225**
Gérard de Nerval, the mystic's dilemma / Bettina L. Knapp. — University: University of Alabama Press, c1980. viii, 372 p.; 24 cm. Includes index. 1. Nerval, Gérard de, 1808-1855 — Criticism and interpretation. I. T.
PQ2260.G36 Z666   848/.7/09   *LC* 75-40296   *ISBN* 0817376089

Rinsler, Norma.   **2.4226**
Gérard de Nerval. London, Athlone Press, 1973. ix, 162 p. 21 cm. (Athlone French poets) Includes index. 1. Nerval, Gérard de, 1808-1855. I. T.
PQ2260.G36 Z78   848/.7/09   *LC* 73-177675   *ISBN* 0485146010 *ISBN* 0485122014

Goncourt, Edmond de, 1822-1896.   • **2.4227**
Journal; mémoires de la vie littéraire [par] Edmond et Jules de Goncourt. Avant–propos de l'Académie Goncourt. Texte intégral établi et annoté par Robert Ricatte. Paris, Fasquelle [c1956] 4 v. I. Goncourt, Jules de, 1830-1870. II. Ricatte, Robert. III. T.
PQ2261.Z5 A2 1959   848.8   *LC* 61-41813

Goncourt, Edmond de, 1822-1896.   • **2.4228**
[Journal des Goncourt. English] The Goncourt journals, 1851–1870. Edited and translated from the Journal of Edmond and Jules de Goncourt. With an introd., notes and a biographical repertory by Lewis Galantiere. New York, Greenwood Press, 1968 [c1937] xv, 377 p. 21 cm. 1. Goncourt, Edmond de, 1822-1896. I. Goncourt, Jules de, 1830-1870. joint author. II. T.
PQ2261.Z5 A225 1968   848/.8/03   *LC* 69-10099

Grant, Richard B.　　　　　　　　　　　　　　　　　　**2.4229**
The Goncourt brothers, by Richard B. Grant. New York, Twayne Publishers [1972] 163 p. 21 cm. (Twayne's world authors series, TWAS183. France) 1. Goncourt, Edmond de, 1822-1896. 2. Goncourt, Jules de, 1830-1870. I. T.
PQ2261.Z5 G7　　843/.8/08　　*LC* 75-147186

Goncourt, Edmond de, 1822-1896.　　　　　　　　　　**2.4230**
[Fille Élisa. English] Elisa. Translated by Margaret Crosland. New York, H. Fertig, 1975. 190 p. 21 cm. Translation of La fille Élisa. Reprint of the 1959 ed. published by N. Spearman, London. I. T.
PZ3.G588 El 4 PQ2263.F4　　843/.8　　*LC* 74-5136

Goncourt, Edmond de, 1822-1896.　　　　　　　　　• **2.4231**
La fille Élise; roman. Éd. définitive. Paris, Flammarion [1956] 217 p. I. T.
PQ2263.F4x

Heredia, José-Maria de, 1842-1905.　　　　　　　　• **2.4232**
Les trophées. Paris A. Lemerre 1893. 218p. I. T.
PQ2275 H3 T7

PQ2279–2307 Hugo

Hugo, Victor, 1802-1885.　　　　　　　　　　　　　• **2.4233**
[Selected works] Romans. Présentation d'Henri Guillemin. Paris, Éditions du Seuil [1965] c1963-. v. port. 23 cm. (L'Intégrale) I. Guillemin, Henri, 1903- ed. II. T.
PQ2281.A27 1965　　*LC* 76-238370

Hugo, Victor, 1802-1885.　　　　　　　　　　　　　• **2.4234**
Théâtre complet / Victor Hugo; préf. par Roland Purnal; notices et notes par J. J. Thierry et Josette Mélèze. — [Paris]: Gallimard, 1963-1964. 2 v. — (Bibliothèque de la Pléiade; 66, 170) I. Purnal, Roland. II. Thierry, Jean Jacques. III. T.
PQ2281.D6　　*LC* 64-47509

Hugo, Victor, 1802-1885.　　　　　　　　　　　　　• **2.4235**
Poésie. Préf. de Jean Gaulmier. Présentation et notes de Bernard Leuilliot. Paris, Éditions du Seuil [1972] 3 v. illus. (L'Intégrale) I. Leuilliot, Bernard. II. T.
PQ2281.P59 1972　　841.7　　*LC* 72-367662

Hugo, Victor, 1802-1885.　　　　　　　　　　　　　• **2.4236**
Les misérables, by Victor Hugo; translated from the French by Charles E. Wilbour. — New York, The Modern library [1931] viii p., 2 l., 3-1222 p. 21 cm. — (Half-title: The Modern library of the world's best books) 'First Modern library edition 1931.' I. Wilbour, Charles E. (Charles Edwin), 1833-1896. tr. II. T.
PQ2286.Ax　　PZ3.H875Mi37　　843.78　　*LC* 32-17680

Hugo, Victor, 1802-1885.　　　　　　　　　　　　　• **2.4237**
[Notre Dame de Paris. English] The hunchback of Notre Dame / by Victor Hugo.— New York: Dodd, Mead, c1947. 424 p., [10] leaves of plates: ill., ports. (Great illustrated classics) Translation of Notre Dame de Paris. I. T. II. Title: Notre Dame de Paris. English
PQ2286.E5x　　PZ3.H875 Hu22　　*LC* 47-12434　　*ISBN* 0396019684

Hugo, Victor, 1802-1885.　　　　　　　　　　　　　• **2.4238**
Toilers of the sea, by Victor Hugo. London, J. M. Dent & sons, ltd.; New York, E. P. Dutton & co. [1911] xvi, 368 p. 17 cm. (Everyman's library. ed. by Ernest Rhys. Fiction. [no. 509]) Translated by W. Moy Thomas. Introduction by Ernest Rhys. I. Thomas, William Moy, 1828-1910, tr. II. T.
PQ2289.T7 E5x　　*LC* a 13-980

Houston, John Porter.　　　　　　　　　　　　　　**2.4239**
Victor Hugo. New York, Twayne Publishing, 1974. 165 p. port. 22 cm. (Twayne's world authors series, TWAS 312. France) 1. Hugo, Victor, 1802-1885. I. T.
PQ2293.H66　　848/.7/09　　*LC* 74-8729　　*ISBN* 0805724435

Maurois, André, 1885-1967.　　　　　　　　　　　• **2.4240**
Olympio: the life of Victor Hugo / by André Maurois; translated from the French by Gerard Hopkins. — 1st ed. — New York: Harper, 1956. xii, 498 p.: ill.; 24 cm. 1. Hugo, Victor, 1802-1885. 2. Authors, French — Biography. I. T.
PQ2293.M353 1956a　　PQ2293 M353 1956.　　928.4

Richardson, Joanna.　　　　　　　　　　　　　　　**2.4241**
Victor Hugo / Joanna Richardson. — New York: St. Martin's Press, 1977 (c1976). x, 334 p., [4] leaves of plates: ill.; 24 cm. Includes index. 1. Hugo, Victor, 1802-1885. 2. Authors, French — 19th century — Biography. I. T.
PQ2293.R5　　848/.7/09 B　　*LC* 76-10564　　*ISBN* 0312840357

Affron, Charles.　　　　　　　　　　　　　　　　　**2.4242**
A stage for poets; studies in the theatre of Hugo & Musset. Princeton, N.J., Princeton University Press, 1971. xii, 254 p. illus. 23 cm. (Princeton essays in

European and comparative literature) 1. Hugo, Victor, 1802-1885 — Dramatic works. 2. Musset, Alfred de, 1810-1857. 3. French drama — 19th century — History and criticism. I. T.
PQ2301.A3　　842/.7/09　　*LC* 75-153847　　*ISBN* 0691062013

Brombert, Victor H.　　　　　　　　　　　　　　　**2.4243**
Victor Hugo and the visionary novel / Victor Brombert. — Cambridge, Mass.: Harvard University Press, 1984. xii, 286 p., [16] p. of plates: ill.; 25 cm. Includes index. 1. Hugo, Victor, 1802-1885 — Fictional works. 2. Myth in literature I. T.
PQ2304.M88 B76 1984　　843/.7 19　　*LC* 83-26584　　*ISBN* 0674935500

PQ2309.H4 Huysmans

Huysmans, J.-K. (Joris-Karl), 1848-1907.　　　　　• **2.4244**
Against the grain (A rebours). With an introd. by Havelock Ellis. New York, Dover Publications [1969] xlix, 206 p. port. 22 cm. Translation of A rebours. 'An unabridged republication of the English Translation published ... in 1931. The introduction by Havelock Ellis ... has been slightly abridged for this edition.' I. T.
PZ3.H987 Ah PQ2309.H4　　843/.8　　*LC* 77-81802　　*ISBN* 0486221903

Huysmans, J.-K. (Joris-Karl), 1848-1907.　　　　　• **2.4245**
A Rebours / par J.K. Huysmans; avec une preface de l'auteur ecrite vingt ans apres le roman. — Paris: Fasquelle, 1968. 269 p.; 21 cm. I. T.
PQ2309.H4 A62 1968　　*LC* 73-438367

Huysmans, J.-K. (Joris-Karl), 1848-1907.　　　　　• **2.4246**
La cathédrale / [par] J.-K. Huysmans. — Paris, Plon [1961] 378 p.; 18 cm. I. T.
PQ2309.H4C3

Huysmans, J.-K. (Joris-Karl), 1848-1907.　　　　　• **2.4247**
Là–bas. — Paris: Plon, [c1938] 307 p.; 19 cm. I. T.
PQ2309.H4 L3

Huysmans, J.-K. (Joris-Karl), 1848-1907.　　　　　• **2.4248**
Down there (La bas): a study in satanism / by J. K. Huysmans; translated by Keene Wallis; introd. by Robert Baldick. — New Hyde Park, N.Y.: University Books, c1958. xxxviii, 317 p. I. Baldick, Robert. II. T.
PQ2309.H4 L313 1958　　*LC* 56-13015

PQ2323–2342 L

Laforgue, Jules, 1860-1887.　　　　　　　　　　　• **2.4249**
Poesies. 16. ed. Paris: Mercure de France, 19— 2 v. I. T.
PQ2323.L8 A17

Laforgue, Jules, 1860-1887.　　　　　　　　　　　• **2.4250**
Poems / translated by Patricia Terry; foreword by Henri Peyre. — Berkeley: University of California Press, 1958. 208 p.; 19 cm. French and English.
PQ2323.L8 Ax　　*ISBN* 0631159401

Laforgue, Jules, 1860-1887.　　　　　　　　　　　**2.4251**
Les complaintes / [par] Jules Laforgue; edited by Michael Collie. — London: Athlone Press, 1977. viii, 184 p.; 21 cm. — (Athlone French poets) French text, English introd. and commentaries. Poems. I. Collie, Michael. II. T.
PQ2323.L8 C6 1977　　841/.8　　*LC* 77-378474　　*ISBN* 0485147130

Laforgue, Jules, 1860-1887.　　　　　　　　　　　• **2.4252**
Derniers vers / Jules Laforgue; edited with an introduction and notes by Michael Collie and J.–M. L'Heureux. — Toronto: University of Toronto Press, 1965. vii, 111p.; 24cm. I. Collie, Michael. II. L'Heureux, J.M. III. T.
PQ2323.L8 D4x　　841.8　　*LC* 65-29506

Collie, Michael.　　　　　　　　　　　　　　　　　**2.4253**
Jules Laforgue / by Michael Collie. — London: Athlone Press, 1977. [10], 134 p.; 21 cm. (Athlone French poets) Distributed in the U.S.A. and Canada by Humanities Press, New Jersey. Includes index. 1. Laforgue, Jules, 1860-1887. 2. Poets, French — 19th century — Biography. I. T.
PQ2323.L8 Z59　　848/.8/09 B　　*LC* 77-378629　　*ISBN* 0485146061

Lamartine, Alphonse Marie Louis de, 1790-1869.　• **2.4254**
Œuvres poétiques / Lamartine; édition présentée, établie et annotée par Marius–François Guyard. — [Paris]: Gallimard, 1963. xxxviii, 2030 p.; 18 cm. — (Bibliotèque de la Pléiade; 165) 1. French poetry I. Guyard, Marius François, 1921- . II. Guyard, Marius François. III. T.
PQ2325.A17 G8 1963　　*LC* 64-9894

Lamartine, Alphonse de, 1790-1869. ● **2.4255**
Graziella. Raphaël. [Textes établis et présentés par Jean des Cognets.]. — [Ed. illustre]. — Paris, Garnier [1960] 322 p. illus. — (Classiques Garnier) I. T. II. Title: Raphaël.
PQ2325.G7 1960

Lamartine, Alphonse de, 1790-1869. ● **2.4256**
Jocelyn / Alphonse de Lamartine; chronologie et introd. par Marius–François Guyard. Paris: Garnier-Flammarion, c1967. 250 p.; 18 cm. (Texte integral; 138) I. T.
PQ2325.J6 1967 LC 68-94968

Fortescue, William, 1945-. **2.4257**
Alphonse de Lamartine: a political biography / William Fortescue. — New York: St. Martin's Press, c1983. 296 p.; 23 cm. 1. Lamartine, Alphonse de, 1790-1869 — Biography. 2. Poets, French — 19th century — Biography. 3. Politicians — France — Biography. I. T.
PQ2326.F58 1983 841/.7 B 19 LC 82-42927 ISBN 0312021380

Guillemin, Henri, 1903-. ● **2.4258**
Lamartine; l'homme et l'oeuvre. Paris Boivin [1940] 165, [1] p.; 17 cm. (Le Livre de l'étudiant) 1. Lamartine, Alphonse de, 1790-1869. I. T.
PQ2326 G82

Leconte de Lisle, 1818-1894. ● **2.4259**
Choix de poèmes [de] Leconte de Lisle, avec une notice biographique ... des notes ... par Pierre Gallissaires ... Paris, Larousse, 1969. 146 p. illus. (part col.) 17 cm. (Nouveaux classiques Larousse) I. Gallissaires, Pierre, ed. II. T.
PQ2332.A6 1969

Lemaître, Jules, 1853-1914. ● **2.4260**
En marge des vieux livres; contes. Paris Société française d'imprimerie et de librairie [1905-07] 2 v.; 19 cm. I. Cavaignac, Jacques Marie Eug8ene Godefroy, 1853-1905, jt. author II. T.
PQ2337 L3 E57

PQ2344 Mallarmé

Mallarmé, Stéphane. ● **2.4261**
Oeuvres complètes / Stéphane Mallarmé; texte établi et annoté par Henri Mondor et G. Jean-Aubry. — [Paris: Editions Gallimard], c1945. xxvii, 1659 p.; 18 cm. — (Bibliothèque de la Pléiade; 65) 1. French literature — 19th century I. T.
PQ2344.A1 1945a LC 49-43847

Mallarmé, Stéphane, 1842-1898. ● **2.4262**
Poems, translated by Roger Fry, with commentaries by Charles Mauron. [New York, New Directions, c1951] viii, 312 p. 19 cm. (The New classics series [28]) Original poems and English translations on opposite pages. I. Fry, Roger Eliot, 1866-1934. tr. II. Mauron, Charles. ed. III. T.
PQ2344.A13 1951 LC 51-14119

Mallarmé, Stéphane, 1842-1898. **2.4263**
Mallarmé: the poems: a bilingual edition / translated with an introd. by Keith Bosley. — Harmondsworth [Eng.]; New York: Penguin, 1977. 303 p.; 18 cm. — (The Penguin poets) English and French. Includes index. I. Bosley, Keith. II. T.
PQ2344.A213 841/.8 LC 77-374844 ISBN 014042203X

Bowie, Malcolm. **2.4264**
Mallarmé and the art of being difficult / Malcolm Bowie. — Cambridge; New York: Cambridge University Press, 1978. x, 197 p.; 23 cm. Includes index. 1. Mallarmé, Stéphane, 1842-1898 — Criticism and interpretation. I. T.
PQ2344.Z5 B6 841/.8 LC 77-82488 ISBN 0521218136

Fowlie, Wallace, 1908-. ● **2.4265**
Mallarmé / Wallace Fowlie; with ten line drawings by Henri Matisse. — Chicago: University of Chicago Press, 1953. 299 p.: ill. 1. Mallarmé, Stéphane, 1842-1898. I. T.
PQ2344.Z5 F58 LC a 53-9931 ISBN 0226258807

Mondor, Henri, 1885-1962. ● **2.4266**
Vie de Mallarmé. Édition complète en un volume. — 8. éd. [Paris] Gallimard [c1943] [7]-827 p. 21 cm. — (Leurs Figures) 'L'édition originale de cet ouvrage [est] en deux volumes.' 1. Mallarmé, Stéphane, 1842-1898. I. T.
PQ2344.Z5M6 928.4 LC 47-36848

PQ2349–2358 Maupassant

Maupassant, Guy de, 1850-1893. ● **2.4267**
Boule de suif / Guy de Maupassant. — Paris: Flammarion, [1933?] 284 p.; 19 cm. Short stories. I. T.
PQ2349.A2 1933 LC 40-6382

Maupassant, Guy de, 1850-1893. ● **2.4268**
Contes et nouvelles. Textes présentés, corrigés, classés et augmentés de pages inédites, par Albert–Marie Schmidt avec la collaboration de Gérard Delaisement. — Paris, A. Michel, 1956-. v. 20 cm. I. T.
PQ2349.A2 1956a LC 57-21351

Maupassant, Guy de, 1850-1893. ● **2.4269**
[Selected works. English. 945] The best stories of Guy de Maupassant, selected, and with an introduction, by Saxe Commins. New York [Random House, 1945] xiv, 551 p. 17 cm. (The Modern library of the world's best books) I. Commins, Saxe. comp. II. T.
PQ2349.A4 E5x PZ3.M445 Bg LC 45-9767

Maupassant, Guy de, 1850-1893. ● **2.4270**
Bel–ami. [Texte établi, avec introd., notes at relevé de variantes, par Gérard Delaisement. — Éd. illustrée]. — Paris, Éditions Garnier frères [1959] ixxxiii, 412 p. facsims., port. 19 cm. — (Classiques Garnier) Bibliography: p. [405]-409. I. Delaisement, Gérard, ed. II. T.
PQ2349.B3 1959 LC 65-7299

Steegmuller, Francis, 1906-. **2.4271**
Maupassant, a lion in the path. New York, Random House [1949] ix, 430 p. illus., ports. 24 cm. 'Note on bibliography, etc.': p. 393-415. 1. Maupassant, Guy de, 1850-1893. I. T.
PQ2353.S8 928.4 LC 49-11109 *

PQ2359–2387 M–R

Mérimée, Prosper, 1803-1870. **2.4272**
Romans et nouvelles. Texte établi et annoté par Henri Martineau. [Paris, Gallimard, 1962] xl, 843 p. 18 cm. (Bibliothèque de la Pléiade. 21) I. Martineau, Henri, 1882-1958. ed. II. T. III. Series.
PQ2362.A1x

Smith, Maxwell Austin, 1894-. **2.4273**
Prosper Mérimée, by Maxwell A. Smith. — New York: Twayne Publishers, 1973 (c1972) 199 p.; 21 cm. — (Twayne's world authors series, TWAS 249. France) 1. Mérimée, Prosper, 1803-1870. I. T.
PQ2362.Z5 S6 848/.7/09 LC 72-1485

Musset, Alfred de, 1810-1857. **2.4274**
Oeuvres complètes. Texte établi et présenté par Philippe Van Tieghem. Paris, Éditions du Seuil [c1963] 941 p. 23 cm. (L'Intégrale) I. Van Tieghem, Philippe 1898- ed. II. T.
PQ2369.A1x

Nodier, Charles, 1780-1844. ● **2.4275**
Contes et nouvelles de Charles Nodièr / publiés avec une introduction d'Edmond Jaloux. — Paris: Payot [1927] xxi, 297 p.: front. (port.) ill.; 19 cm. (Collection Prose et vers.) I. T.
PQ2376.N6 C82

Renan, Ernest, 1823-1892. ● **2.4276**
Pages choisies. Paris, Calmann-Lévy [1938] ii, 345 p. 19 cm. I. T.
PQ2386.R37 A19 1938 LC 39-3808

PQ2387.R5 Rimbaud

Rimbaud, Arthur, 1854-1891. ● **2.4277**
Oeuvres complètes. Texte établi et annoté par Rolland de Renéville et Jules Mouquet. [Paris Gallimard] [1946] xxviii, 825 p.: fold. facsim.; 18 cm. (Bibliothèque de la Pléiade, v. 68) I. T.
PQ2387 R5 A1 1946

Rimbaud, Arthur, 1854-1891. ● **2.4278**
Complete works, selected letters/ Rimbaud; translation, introd. and notes by Wallace Fowlie. — Chicago: University of Chicago Press, 1966. xi, 370 p.; 21 cm. French and English. Includes indexes. I. Fowlie, Wallace, 1908- II. T.
PQ2387.R5 A245 848.809 LC 66-13885 ISBN 0226719731 pbk

Rimbaud, Arthur, 1854-1891. **2.4279**
Illuminations: coloured plates / [by] Arthur Rimbaud; edited by Nick Osmond. — London: Athlone Press, 1976. viii, 183 p.; 21 cm. (Athlone French poets) French text; English introduction and commentaries. Distributed in the U.S. and Canada by Humanities Press, Atlantic Highlands, N.J. I. Osmond, Nick. II. T.
PQ2387.R5 I4 1976 841/.8 LC 77 351570 ISBN 0485147106

Fowlie, Wallace, 1908-. ● **2.4280**
Rimbaud. — [Chicago] University of Chicago Press [1966] viii, 280 p. port. 21 cm. 'A rewriting of two earlier books ... Rimbaud, the myth of childhood ... [and] Rimbaud's Illuminations.' Bibliography: p. 269-273. 1. Rimbaud, Jean

Nicolas Arthur, 1954-1891. I. Fowlie, Wallace, 1908- Rimbaud, the myth of childhood. II. Rimbaud, Arthur, 1854-1891. Rimbaud's Illuminations. III. T.
PQ2387.R5Z6743   841.8   LC 65-20963

Frohock, W. M. (Wilbur Merrill), 1908-.   • **2.4281**
Rimbaud's poetic practice: image and theme in the major poems. Cambridge, Harvard University Press, 1963. 250 p. 22 cm. 1. Rimbaud, Arthur, 1854-1891. I. T.
PQ2387.R5 Z675   841.8   LC 63-13810

Starkie, Enid Mary.   • **2.4282**
Arthur Rimbaud / by Enid Starkie. — New ed. — New York: New Directions, c1961. 491p.; 22 cm. 1. Rimbaud, Arthur, 1854-1891 — Criticism and interpretation. I. T.
PQ2387. R5Z89   841.8   LC 61-18468

PQ2391 Sainte–Beuve

Sainte-Beuve, Charles Augustin, 1804-1869.   • **2.4283**
Oeuvres. Texte présenté et annoté par Maxime Leroy. [Paris Gallimard] [1949-. v.; 18 cm. (Bibliothèque de la Pléiade, v. 80.) I. Leroy, Macime, 1873- II. T.
PQ2391 A1 1949

Chadbourne, Richard McClain.   **2.4284**
Charles–Augustin Sainte-Beuve / by Richard M. Chadbourne. — Boston: Twayne Publishers, 1978 (c1977). 193 p.: port.; 21 cm. — (Twayne's world authors series; TWAS 453: France) Includes index. 1. Sainte-Beuve, Charles Augustin, 1804-1869 — Criticism and interpretation. I. T.
PQ2391.Z5 C48   848/.7/09   LC 77-25321   ISBN 0805762906

PQ2393–2433 Sand. Sénancour. Staël

Sand, George, 1804-1876.   • **2.4285**
Elle et lui / par George Sand. — 4. éd. Paris: Michel-Lévy, 1864. 310 p.; 18 cm. — (Oeuvres de George Sand) I. T.
PQ2401.E3

Sand, George, 1804-1876.   **2.4286**
[François le Champi. English] The country waif = François le Champi / George Sand; translated by Eirene Collis; introduction by Dorothy Wynne Zimmerman. — Lincoln: University of Nebraska Press, c1977. xxviii, 181 p.; 21 cm. 'A Bison book.' Text of this edition reprinted from a volume published in 1930 by Scholartis Press, London, which also included George Sand's The castle of Pictordu. I. T.
PZ3.S21 Cut5 PQ2402.C6x   843/.8   LC 76-14125   ISBN 080320888X. ISBN 080325850X pbk

Sand, George, 1804-1876.   **2.4287**
[Lucrezia Floriani. English] Lucrezia Floriani / by George Sand; translated by Julius Eker; preface and foreword translated by Betsy Wing. — Chicago: Academy Chicago Publishers, 1985. xxiii, 230 p.; 23 cm. I. T.
PQ2407.L913 1985   843/.7 19   LC 85-3876   ISBN 0897331435

Sand, George, 1804-1876.   • **2.4288**
Les maîtres sonneurs. [Texte établi avec introd., notes et choix de variantes par Pierre Salomon et Jean Mallion] Paris, Garnier [1958] xxviii, 548 p. illus.; 19 cm. Bibliography: p. [xxv]-xxviii. I. T.
PQ2407.M6x

Sand, George, 1804-1876.   • **2.4289**
La mare au diable: François le Champi / George Sand. — Paris: Editions Garnier Frères, 1960. xxviii, 443 p.: ill., facsims. I. T. II. Title: François le Champi.
PQ2408.A2 R4

Sand, George, 1804-1876.   • **2.4290**
La petite Fadette. [Texte présenté, établi, et annoté, par Pierre Salomon et Jean Mallion] Paris, Garnier frères [1967, c1958] L, 316 p. illus., facsim., map. 19 cm. (Selecta) I. Salomon, Pierre. ed. II. Mallion, Jean. ed. III. T.
PQ2411.P4 1967x   LC 76-1637

Sand, George, 1804-1876.   • **2.4291**
Histoire de ma vie. Adaptation de Noelle Roubaud. Préf. de Jérome et Jean Tharaud. [Paris] Stock [c1945] 346p. I. Roubaud, Noelle II. T.
PQ2412 A2 1945

Sand, George, 1804-1876.   • **2.4292**
George Sand et Alfred de Musset: correspondance; journal intime de George Sand, 1834; nombreux documents, annexes et lettres inédites. Texte établi, annoté et présenté par Louis Evrard. — Monaco, Éditions du Rocher [1956] 328 p. port., facsims. 20 cm. Bibliography: p. [287]-291. I. Musset, Alfred de, 1810-1857. II. Evrard, Louis, 1926- III. T.
PQ2412.A4M8 1834   LC 56-45408

Maurois, André, 1885-1967.   • **2.4293**
Lélia, the life of George Sand; translated from the French by Gerard Hopkins. New York, Harper [1953] 482 p. illus., ports. facsim. 25 cm. 1. Sand, George, 1804-1876 — Biography. 2. Authors, French — Biography. I. T.
PQ2412.M313 1953a   928.4   LC 53-7740

Maurras, Charles, 1868-1952.   • **2.4294**
Les amants de Venise: George Sand et Musset / Charles Maurras. — Nouv. ed. — Paris: Flammarion, [1926] xii, 368 p. 1. Sand, George, 1804-1876 — Relations with men — Musset, Alfred de, 1810-1857 2. Musset, Alfred de, 1810-1857 — Relations with women — Sand, George, 1804-1876 I. T.
PQ2414 M3 1926   PQ2414 M38 1926.   LC 28-25196

Manifold, Gay, 1943-.   **2.4295**
George Sand's theatre career / by Gay Manifold. — Ann Arbor, Mich.: UMI Research Press, c1985. xvi, 188 p.: ill.; 24 cm. (Theater and dramatic studies. no. 28) Revision of thesis (doctoral)—University of California, Los Angeles, 1983. Includes index. 1. Sand, George, 1804-1876 — Dramatic works. 2. Sand, George, 1804-1876 — Knowledge — Performing arts. 3. Theater — France — History — 19th century. 4. Dramatists, French — 19th century — Biography. 5. Little theater movement — France. I. T. II. Series.
PQ2419.M3 1985   842/.7 19   LC 84-28098   ISBN 0835716538

Senancour, Etienne Pivert de, 1770-1846.   • **2.4296**
Oberman; texte original de 1804, précédé du Journal intime d'Oberman par Andre Monglond. [Grenoble, B. Arthaud, 1947] 3 v. illus., facsims., ports.; 20 cm. Each vol. has special t.p. Errata slip inserted in v. 3. I. Monglond, André. Journal intime d'Oberman II. T.
PQ2427.S7 O26 1947

Staël, Madame de (Anne-Louise-Germaine), 1766-1817.   **2.4297**
Madame de Staël on politics, literature, and national character. Translated, edited, and with an introd. by Morroe Berger. [1st ed.] Garden City, N. Y., Doubleday, 1964. viii, 371 p. 22 cm. I. Berger, Morroe. II. T.
PQ2431.A23   LC 64-11288

Staël, Madame de (Anne-Louise-Germaine), 1766-1817.   **2.4298**
Delphine / Madame de Staël; [édition féministe de Claudine Herrmann]. — Paris: Des Femmes, c1981. 2 v.; 18 cm. (Des femmes du M.L.F. éditent—) I. Herrmann, Claudine, 1926- II. T. III. Series.
PQ2431.D43 1981   843/.6 19   LC 83-234343   ISBN 2721002155

Gutwirth, Madelyn.   **2.4299**
Madame de Staël, novelist: the emergence of the artist as woman / Madelyn Gutwirth. — Urbana: University of Illinois Press, c1978. xiii, 324 p.: ill.; 24 cm. Includes index. 1. Staël, Madame de (Anne-Louise-Germaine), 1766-1817 — Fictional works. 2. Women — France — History — 18th century. I. T.
PQ2431.Z5 G87   843/.6   LC 78-5836   ISBN 0252006763

PQ2435–2444 Stendhal

Stendhal, 1783-1842.   • **2.4300**
Oeuvres intimes de Stendhal [pseud.] / texte etabli et annote par Henri Martineau. Paris: Gallimard, c1955, 1960 printing. 1742 p. (Bibliothèque de la Pléiade, 109) I. T. II. Series.
PQ2435.A2 M33   LC 55-4590

Stendhal, 1783-1842.   • **2.4301**
Romans et nouvelles [de] Stendhal [pseud.] Texte établi et annoté par Henri Martineau. [Paris, Gallimard, 1956, c1952] 2 v. (His [Oeuvres] 1-2) (Bibliothèque de la Pléiade, 4, 13.) I. Martineau, Henri, 1882-1958. ed. II. T.
PQ2435.A2 Mx

Stendhal, 1783-1842.   • **2.4302**
The shorter novels of Stendhal ... translated from the French by C. K. Scott–Moncrieff. New York, Liveright Pub. Corp. [1946] 11-269 p. 23 cm. At head of title: Marie-Henri Beyle (de Stendhal) I. Scott-Moncrieff, C. K. (Charles Kenneth), 1889-1930. tr. II. T.
PQ2435.A3S35   LC 46-7901

Stendhal, 1783-1842.   • **2.4303**
The Charterhouse of Parma. Translated from the French by C.K. Scott Moncrieff. New York Boni & Liveright 1925. (The Works of Stendhal, 1) I. T.
PQ2435 C413 1925

Stendhal, 1783-1842.   • **2.4304**
Memoirs of a tourist [by] Stendhal [pseud.] Translated by Allan Seager. With illus. by Roger Barr. [Evanston, Ill.] Northwestern University Press [1962] 304p. 1. France — Description and travel I. T.
PQ2435 M4 E5

Stendhal, 1783-1842.   • **2.4305**
Red and black: a new translation, backgrounds and sources, criticism / Translated and edited by Robert M. Adams. — [1st ed.]. — New York: Norton,

[1969] xii, 572 p.; 22 cm. — (A Norton critical edition) Translation of Le rouge et le noir. I. Adams, Robert Martin, 1915- ed. II. T.
PZ3.B468 R22 PQ2435.R7x 843/.7 LC 67-16619

Stendhal, 1783-1842. • 2.4306
The private diaries of Stendhal (Marie–Henri Beyle) [1st ed.] Garden City, N.Y., Doubleday, 1954. xiv, 570 p. illus., ports., facsims. 24 cm. I. T.
PQ2436.A2 J63 LC 54-11160

Stendhal, 1783-1842. • 2.4307
The life of Henry Brulard [by] Stendhal [pseud.] Translated by Jean Stewart and B.C.J.G. Knight. New York, Noonday Press [1958] viii, 347 p. illus. 22 cm. I. T.
PQ2436.A2 V43 1958 LC 58-13192

Alter, Robert. 2.4308
A lion for love: a critical biography of Stendhal / by Robert Alter, in collaboration with Carol Cosman. — New York: Basic Books, c1979. xiii, 285 p., [7] leaves of plates: ill.; 24 cm. 1. Stendhal, 1783-1842. 2. Novelists, French — 19th century — Biography. I. Cosman, Carol. joint author. II. T.
PQ2436.A5 848/.3/09 B LC 79-7335 ISBN 0465041248

Fowlie, Wallace, 1908-. • 2.4309
Stendhal. [New York] Macmillan [1969] xii, 240 p. 22 cm. (Masters of world literature series) 1. Stendhal, 1783-1842. I. T.
PQ2436.F6 843/.7 LC 70-75903

Richardson, Joanna. 2.4310
Stendhal / Joanna Richardson. — New York: Coward, McCann & Geoghegan, [1974] 344 p., [4] leaves of plates: ports.; 24 cm. Includes index. 1. Stendhal, 1783-1842. I. T.
PQ2436.R5 848/.7/09 B LC 73-93760 ISBN 0698105974

Brombert, Victor H. ed. • 2.4311
Stendhal; a collection of critical essays. Englewood Cliffs, N.J., Prentice-Hall [1962] 171 p. 21 cm. (Twentieth century views) (A Spectrum book, S-TC-7.) 1. Stendhal, 1783-1842. I. T.
PQ2441.B7 843.7 LC 62-9306

Martineau, Henri, 1882-1958. • 2.4312
L'oeuvre de Stendhal: histoire de ses livres te de sa pensée. — Paris, Michel [1951] 638 p. illus., ports. 21 cm. Bibliographical footnotes. 1. Stendhal, 1783-1842. I. T.
PQ2441.M19 1951 840.81 LC 51-6593

PQ2459–2467 Verhaeren. Verlaine

Verhaeren, Emile, 1855-1916. 2.4313
Choix de poèmes. 23. éd. Paris, Mercvre de France [1917] 248 p. front. (port.) 19 cm. I. T.
PQ2459.V8 C45 1917 LC 34-25327

Verhaeren, Emile, 1855-1916. 2.4314
Afternoon, by Emile Verhaeren ... tr. by Charles R. Murphy. New York, John Lane Company, 1917. 77 p. 20 cm. I. Murphy, Charles Royier, 1884- II. T.
PQ2459.V8 H613 LC 17-7037

Verlaine, Paul, 1844-1896. • 2.4315
Oeuvres en prose complètes / Verlaine; texte établi, présenté et annoté par Jacques Borel. — Paris: Gallimard, 1972. 1541 p. –. (Bibliothèque de la Pléiade; 239) 1. Borel, Jacques, 1925- ed. I. T.
PQ2463.A13 1972 LC 73-309605

Verlaine, Paul, 1844-1896. • 2.4316
Selected poems / Paul Verlaine; translated by C.F. MacIntyre. — Berkeley: University of California Press, 1948. — xx, 228 p.; 19 cm. — French and English on opposite pages. I. MacIntyre, Carlyle Ferren, 1890-1967. tr. II. T.
PQ2463.A6 1948 841 LC 48-9157 ISBN 0520012984

Verlaine, Paul, 1844-1896. 2.4317
Oeuvres poétiques complètes [par] Verlaine. Texte établi et annoté par Y.–G. Le Dantec. Éd. rév., complétée et présentée par Jacques Borel. [Paris, Gallimard, 1962] xliv, 1491 p. 18 cm. (Bibliothèque de la Pléiade [47]) I. Le Dantec, Y.-G. (Yves-Gérard), 1898-1958. ed. II. Borel, Jacques, ed. III. T.
PQ2463.Ax

Verlaine, Paul, 1844-1896. 2.4318
Romances sans paroles / Paul Verlaine; edited by D. Hillery. — London: Athlone Press, 1976. [6], 106 p.; 21 cm. (Athlone French poets) French text, English introduction and commentaries. Distributed in U.S.A. and Canada by Humanities Press, New Jersey. I. Hillery, D. II. T.
PQ2463.R6 1976 841/.8 LC 76-375316 ISBN 0485147122

Adam, Antoine. • 2.4319
[Verlaine. English] The art of Paul Verlaine. Translated by Carl Morse. [New York] New York University Press, 1963. 180 p. 22 cm. Translation of Verlaine. 1. Verlaine, Paul, 1844-1896. I. T.
PQ2464.A453 LC 63-19361

PQ2468–2471 Verne

Verne, Jules, 1828-1905. • 2.4320
De la terre à la lune: trajet direct en 97 heures 20 minutes / 41 dessins et une carte par De Montaut. — Paris: Librarie générale française, 1966. ill. (Verne, Jules, 1828-1905. Les voyages extraordinaires) (Bibliothèque d'éducation et de récréation) Le Livre de poche Jules Verne. I. T. II. Series.
PQ2469.D3 1966 LC 67-87867

Miller, Walter James, 1918-. 2.4321
The annotated Jules Verne, From the earth to the moon, direct in ninety–seven hours and twenty minutes / Walter James Miller. — 1st ed. — New York: Crowell, c1978. xix, 171 p.: ill.; 28 cm. 'The only completely rendered and annotated edition.' 1. Verne, Jules, 1828-1905. De la terre à la lune. I. Verne, Jules, 1828-1905. De la terre à la lune. II. T.
PQ2469.D33 M5 1978 843/.8 LC 78-3327 ISBN 0690017014

Verne, Jules, 1828-1905. • 2.4322
[Tour du monde en quatre-vingts jours. English] Around the world in eighty days. With illus. by Edward A. Wilson and an introd. by Ray Bradbury. New York: Heritage Press [1962] xiv, 268 p. col. illus. 27 cm. Translation of Le tour du monde en quatre-vingts jours. I. Wilson, Edward Arthur, 1886-1970. illus. II. T.
PQ2469.T7 E56 843/.8 LC 74-20475

Verne, Jules, 1828-1905. 2.4323
Le tour du monde en 80 jours. Une fantaisie du Docteur Ox et autres nouvelles. Paris, Lidis [1964] 1 v. 1. French fiction I. T. II. Title: Une fantaisie du Docteur Ox.
PQ2469.Tx

Verne, Jules, 1828-1905. • 2.4324
20000 lieues sous les mers. Ill. de Jean Reschofsky. [Paris] Hachette [c1954] 2 v. ill. (part. en coul.) 21 cm. (Idéal-bibliothèque, 75-76) I. T. II. Title: Vingt mille lieues sous les mers
PQ2469.V4 1954 848.7 V531v A5 843.8 V531 A5

Verne, Jules, 1828-1905. • 2.4325
Twenty thousand leagues under the sea. A definitive modern translation by Walter James Miller, assisted by Judith Ann Tirsch. Afterword by Damon Knight. Illustrated by Walter Brooks. New York, Washington Square Press, 1965. xxii, 389 p. illus. 22 cm. I. T.
PQ2469.V4x LC 65-25245

Costello, Peter. 2.4326
Jules Verne, inventor of science fiction / Peter Costello. — New York: Scribner, c1978. 239 p., [4] leaves of plates: ill.; 22 cm. Includes index. 1. Verne, Jules, 1828-1905 — Biography. 2. Novelists, French — 19th century — Biography. I. T.
PQ2469.Z5 C66 1978 843/.8 B LC 78-57528 ISBN 0684158248

PQ2472 Viaud (Pierre Loti)

Loti, Pierre, 1850-1923. • 2.4327
Mon frère Yves / [par] Pierre Loti. — Paris: Calmann Lévy, 1893. 395 p.; 18 cm. Author's pseud., Pierre Loti, at head of title. I. T.
PQ2472.M7 LC 13-4047

Loti, Pierre, 1850-1923. • 2.4328
Pêcheur d'Islande, par Pierre Loti [pseud.] ... — Paris, Calmann-Lévy , [1905]. 344 p.; 19 cm. I. T.
PQ2472.P4 843.89 LC 35-30816

Loti, Pierre, 1850-1923. • 2.4329
Iceland fisherman [by] Pierre Loti [pseud.]. — London, J. M. Dent & sons, ltd. [1935] ix, 242 p., 1 l. 17.5 cm. — (Half-title: Everyman's library, ed. by Ernest Rhys. Fiction. [no. 920]) Translated by W. P. Baines. Bibliography: p. viii. I. Baines, William Peter, 1878- tr. II. T.
PQ2472.P4x 843.89 LC 37-31213

Loti, Pierre, 1850-1923. • 2.4330
Ramuntcho / par Pierre Loti. Paris: Calmann-Lévy, [191-?]. 351 p.; 19 cm. (Bibliothèque contemporaine.) I. T.
PQ 2472 R18

Lerner, Michael G.   **2.4331**
Pierre Loti, by Michael G. Lerner. New York, Twayne Publishers [1974] 172 p. port. 22 cm. (Twayne's world authors series, TWAS 285. France) 1. Loti, Pierre, 1850-1923. I. T.
PQ2472.Z8 L44   843/.8 B   *LC* 73-2368   *ISBN* 0805725466

PQ2474-2484 V

Vigny, Alfred de, 1797-1863.   **2.4332**
Oeuvres complètes. Préface, présentation et notes de Paul Viallaneix. — Paris, Éditions du Seuil [1965] 661 p. illus. 22 cm. — (L'integrale) I. Viallaneix, Paul. ed. II. T.
PQ2474.A1 1965   *LC* 14-11939

Castex, Pierre Georges, 1915-.   ● **2.4333**
Vigny, l'homme et l'oeuvre / par Pierre-Georges Castex. — Paris: Boivin, c1952. 176 p. — (Connaissance des lettres; 34) 1. Vigny, Alfred de, 1797-1863 — Criticism and interpretation. I. T.
PQ2474.Z5 C3   848   *LC* 52-35356

Doolittle, James.   ● **2.4334**
Alfred de Vigny. New York, Twayne Publishers [1967] 154 p. 21 cm. (Twayne's world authors series, TWAS 18) 1. Vigny, Alfred de, 1797-1863. I. T.
PQ2474.Z5 D67   841/.7   *LC* 67-19339

Villiers de L'Isle-Adam, comte de, 1838-1889.   ● **2.4335**
[Axel. English] Axel. Translated by Marilyn Gaddis Rose. [Dublin] Dolmen Press; [distributed by Dufour Editions, Chester Springs, Pa., 1970] xv, 175 p. 23 cm. I. T.
PQ2476.V4 A93 1970b   842/.8   *LC* 70-19500   *ISBN* 019647518X

Villiers de L'Isle-Adam, Auguste, comte de, 1838-1889.   ● **2.4336**
Contes cruels. Paris: J. Corti [1954]-56. 2 v.; 19 cm. Vol.2: 'Étude historique et litéraire par Pierre-Georges Castex et Joseph Bollery d'après des documents inédits.' I. Castex, Pierre, 1915- II. Bollery, Joseph, 1890- III. T.
PQ2476.V4C6x

Villiers de L'Isle-Adam, Auguste, comte de, 1838-1889.   ● **2.4337**
Cruel tales. Translated by Robert Baldick. Introduced by A. W. Raitt. London, New York, Oxford University Press, 1963. xiv, 257 p. 20 cm. (Oxford library of French classics) I. T.
PQ2476.V4 C6x   PZ3.V718Cr   *LC* 63-24947

Villiers de L'Isle-Adam, Auguste, comte de, 1838-1889.   **2.4338**
[Eve future. English] Tomorrow's Eve / Villiers de L'Isle-Adam; translated by Robert Martin Adams. — Urbana: University of Illinois Press, c1982. 222 p.; 24 cm. Translation of: L'Eve future. I. T.
PQ2476.V4 E9213 1982   843/.8 19   *LC* 82-13411   *ISBN* 0252009428

Raitt, A. W. (Alan William)   **2.4339**
The life of Villiers de l'Isle-Adam / A.W. Raitt. — Oxford: Clarendon Press; New York: Oxford University Press, 1981. xviii, 452 p., [8] p. of plates: ports.; 22 cm. Includes index. 1. Villiers de L'Isle-Adam, comte de, 1838-1889 — Biography. 2. Authors, French — 19th century — Biography. I. T.
PQ2476.V4 Z768 1981   848/.809 B 19   *LC* 80-41596   *ISBN* 0198157711

PQ2489-2548 Zola

Zola, Emile, 1840-1902.   **2.4340**
[Débâcle. English] The debacle (1870-71) / translated with an introd. by L. W. Tancock. — [Harmondsworth, Eng.,; Baltimore]: Penguin Books [1972] 509 p. 18 cm. (The Penguin classics) 1. Franco-German War, 1870-1871 — Fiction I. T.
PQ2500.A3 W4x 1972   843/.8   *LC* 73-156279   *ISBN* 0140442804

Zola, Emile, 1840-1902.   ● **2.4341**
Germinal. Translated from the French by Havelock Ellis, with an introd. by Henri de Montherlant and illus. by Berthold Mahn. New York, Heritage Press [1956, c1942] viii, 374 p. illus. 26 cm. I. T.
PQ2504.A3x   *LC* 56-14039

Grant, Elliott Mansfield, 1895-1969.   ● **2.4342**
Zola's Germinal: a critical and historical study [by] Elliott M. Grant. . — [1st ed.] 2nd impression with corrections. — Leicester: Leicester U.P., 1970. 244 p.; 22 cm. Contains French text of Zola's 'Ebaundre' and Personnages' (MSS. 10307/8) 1. Zola, Emile, 1840-1902. Germinal. I. T.
PQ2504.G733   843/.8   *LC* 72-518818   *ISBN* 0718510917

Zola, Emile, 1840-1902.   ● **2.4343**
Nana, by Emile Zola, introduction by Ernest Boyd. New York, The Modern library [c1928] xii, 517 p. 17 cm. (Half-title: The modern library of the world's best books) 'First Modern library edition.' I. Boyd, Ernest Augustus, 1887-1946. II. T.
PZ3.Z74N17 PQ2510.A42   *LC* 28-10872

Zola, Emile, 1840-1902.   ● **2.4344**
Les Rougon-Macquart, histoire naturelle et sociale d'une famille sous le Second Empire. Texte intégral établi, annoté et présenté par Armand Lanoux et Henri Mitterand. [Paris] Gallimard [1960-. v. 18 cm. (Bibliothèque de la Pléiade, 146) I. Lanoux, Armand. II. Mitterand, Henri. III. T.
PQ2518.Ax   *LC* a 61-436

Grant, Richard B.   ● **2.4345**
Zola's Son Excellence Eugène Rougon: an historical and critical study. — Durham, N.C.: Duke University Press, 1960. 146 p.; 23 cm. 1. Zola, Emile, 1840-1902. Son Excellence Eugène Rougon. I. T.
PQ2519.S73 G7   *LC* 60-6649

Zola, Emile, 1840-1902.   ● **2.4346**
Therese Raquin / Émile Zola; translated and wth an introd. by Leonard Tancock. — Harmondsworth: Penguin, 1962. 255 p. I. T.
PQ2521.T3 E5x   *ISBN* 0140441204

Hemmings, F. W. J. (Frederick William John), 1920-.   ● **2.4347**
Émile Zola [by] F. W. J. Hemmings. — 2nd ed. — Oxford, Clarendon P. 1966. [7], 330 p. 22.5 cm. I. T.
PQ2528.H4 1966   843.8   *LC* 66-72002

Hemmings, F. W. J. (Frederick William John), 1920-.   **2.4348**
The life and times of Emile Zola / F. W. J. Hemmings. — New York: Scribner, c1977. 192 p.: ill.; 25 cm. 1. Zola, Emile, 1840-1902 — Biography. 2. Authors, French — 19th century — Biography. I. T.
PQ2528.H44 1977b   843/.8   *LC* 77-73899   *ISBN* 0684152274

Wilson, Angus.   ● **2.4349**
Émile Zola, an introductory study of his novels. — New York, Morrow [1952] 148 p. 19 cm. 1. Zola, Emile, 1840-1902. I. T.
PQ2528.W5 1952a   843.89   *LC* 52-9802

Knapp, Bettina Liebowitz, 1926-.   **2.4350**
Émile Zola / Bettina L. Knapp. — New York: Ungar, c1980. xii, 174 p.; 21 cm. — (Modern literature monographs) 'Latest translations of Emile Zola's works': p. 163-165. Includes index. 1. Zola, Emile, 1840-1902 — Criticism and interpretation. I. T.
PQ2538.K64   843/.8   *LC* 79-48079   *ISBN* 0804424829

Robert, Guy.   ● **2.4351**
Émile Zola; principes et caractères généraux de son oeuvre. — Paris, Société d'édition les belles lettres [1952] 205 p. 21 cm. 1. Zola, Emile, 1840-1902. I. T.
PQ2538.R6   *LC* 52-34199

PQ2600-2651 Individual Authors, 20th Century, to 1960

PQ2601 A

Adamov, Arthur.   ● **2.4352**
Théâtre. — Paris, Gallimard [1953-. v. 19 cm. I. T.
PQ2601.D323A19 1953   842.91   *LC* 54-17346

PQ2601 Anouilh

Anouilh, Jean, 1910-.   ● **2.4353**
... Plays. — New York: Hill and Wang, [1958-67] 3 v.; 19 cm. — (A Mermaid dramabook, MD 10, 13, 39) I. T.
PQ2601.N67 A2 1958   *LC* 58-6064

Anouilh, Jean, 1910-.   ● **2.4354**
[Alouette. English] The lark; [play] Translated by Christopher Fry. New York, Oxford University Press, 1956 [c1955] 103 p. 20 cm. 1. Joan, of Arc, Saint, 1412-1431 — Drama. I. T.
PQ2601.N67 A692 1956   842.91   *LC* 56-5472

Anouilh, Jean, 1910-.   ● **2.4355**
Ring around the moon: a charade with music / Jean Anouilh; translated by Christopher Fry; with a pref. by Peter Brook. — New York: Oxford University Press, 1950. 104 p.; 20 cm. Translation of L'invitation au château. Without music. I. Fry, Christopher, 1907- II. T.
PQ2601.N67 I53 1950   *LC* 50-10868

Anouilh, Jean, 1910-.   • 2.4356
Nouvelles pièces noires: Jézabel, Antigone, Roméo et Jeanette, Médée. Paris,
La Table ronde [1947, c1946] 403 p. 19 cm. I. T.
PQ2601.N67 N6   LC 49-16137

Anouilh, Jean, 1910-.   • 2.4357
Pièces roses. — Paris, La Table ronde, 1958. 374 p. 21 cm. I. T.
PQ2601.N67P   LC A 59-4700

Anouilh, Jean, 1910-.   • 2.4358
Pièces brillantes: L'invitation au château, Colombe, La répétition ou L'amour
puni [et] Cécile, ou L'école des pères. — Paris, La Table ronde [c1951] 537 p. 19
cm. I. T.
PQ2601.N67P46   LC 52-22312

Anouilh, Jean, 1910-.   • 2.4359
Pièces costumés / Jean Anouilh. — Paris: La Table ronde, c1960. 371 p.; 21 cm.
I. T. II. Title: L'alouette. III. Title: Becket. IV. Title: La foire d'empoigne.
V. Title: L'honneur de Dieu.
PQ2601.N67 P463 1960   LC 61-3333

Anouilh, Jean, 1910-.   • 2.4360
Pièces noires / Jean Anouilh. — Paris: La Table Ronde, 1966. 541 p.; 21 cm.
I. T.
PQ2601.N67P48 1966   LC 74-407046

Anouilh, Jean, 1910-.   • 2.4361
The waltz of the toreadors / by Jean Anouilh; translated by Lucienne Hill. —
1st American ed. — New York: Coward-McCann, 1957, c1953. 126 p., [1] leaf
of plates: ill.; 20 cm. Translation of: La valse des toréadors. A play. I. Anouilh,
Jean, 1910- Valse des toréadors. English. 1957. II. T.
PQ2601.N67 V313 1957   PQ2601.N67 V33.   LC 57-7128

Pronko, Leonard Cabell.   • 2.4362
The world of Jean Anouilh. — Berkeley: University of California Press, 1961.
264 p.: illus.; 23 cm. — (Perspectives in criticism, 7) 1. Anouilh, Jean, 1910-
I. T.
PQ2601.N67 Z73   842.914   LC 61-6778

PQ2601 Apollinaire

Apollinaire, Guillaume, 1880-1918.   • 2.4363
Oeuvres poétiques. Texte établi et annoté par Marcel Adéma et Michel
Décaudin. Préf. d'André Billy. [Paris: Gallimard, 1959, c1956] 1283p.
(Bibliothèque de la Pléiade, 121) I. T.
PQ2601 P6 A17

Apollinaire, Guillaume, 1880-1918.   • 2.4364
[Selected works. English] Selected writings of Guillaume Apollinaire.
Translated, with a critical introd., by Roger Shattuck. [New York New
Directions Pub. Corp., 1971] 273 p. illus., ports. 21 cm. (A New Directions
book. A New Directions paperbook, NDP310) The verse selections (p. [55]-
[225]) are also in the original French. I. Shattuck, Roger. ed. II. T.
PQ2601.P6 A28 1971   841/.9/12   LC 72-145928

Apollinaire, Guillaume, 1880-1918.   • 2.4365
Alcools / translated by Anne Hyde Greet; with a foreword by Warren Ramsey.
— Berkeley: University of California Press, 1965. xxx, 289 p.: ports.; 21 cm.
Poems. I. Greet, Anne Hyde. II. T.
PQ2601.P6 A713 1965   LC 65-20148

Apollinaire, Guillaume, 1880-1918.   2.4366
Calligrammes: poems of peace and war (1913–1916) / Guillaume Apollinaire;
translated by Anne Hyde Greet; with an introd. by S. I. Lockerbie and
commentary by Anne Hyde Greet and S. I. Lockerbie. — Berkeley: University
of California Press, c1980. xii, 513 p.; 24 cm. 1. World War, 1914-1918 —
Poetry. I. Greet, Anne Hyde. II. T.
PQ2601.P6 C313 1980   841/.912   LC 73-149946   ISBN
0520019687

Mackworth, Cecily.   • 2.4367
Guillaume Apollinaire and the cubist life. [1st American ed.] New York,
Horizon Press, 1963 [c1961] 244 p. illus. 23 cm. 1. Apollinaire, Guillaume,
1880-1918. 2. Cubism I. T.
PQ2601.P6 Z698 1963   LC 63-11181

Steegmuller, Francis, 1906-.   • 2.4368
Apollinaire, poet among the painters. New York, Farrar, Straus [1963] xiii,
365 p. illus., ports. 22 cm. 1. Apollinaire, Guillaume, 1880-1918. 2. Poets,
French — 20th century — Biography. I. T.
PQ2601.P6 Z83   841.912   LC 63-17063

PQ2601 Aragon

Aragon, 1897-.   • 2.4369
Aragon, une etude par Claude Roy; choix de poemes, inedits manuscrits,
lithographie, portraits. Paris: P. Seghers, 1945. 155 p.; ill.; 16 cm. (Poètes
d'aujourd'hui. 2.) I. Roy, Claude, 1915- II. T. III. Series.
PQ2601.R2 A6 1945

Aragon, 1897-.   • 2.4370
Aurélien / Aragon. — [Paris]: Gallimard, 1944. 519 p.; 21 cm. I. T.
PQ2601.R2 A9

Aragon, 1897-.   • 2.4371
Les beaux quartiers, roman. Paris, Denoël et Steele [1936] 503 p. 22 cm. At
head of title: Aragon. I. T.
PQ2601.R2 B4   843.91   LC 37-2828

Aragon, 1897-.   • 2.4372
Les cloches de Bâle; roman / Aragon. — Paris: Denoël, c1934. 441 p.; 19 cm.
I. T.
PQ2601.R2 C5 1934   LC 35-8791

Aragon, 1897-.   • 2.4373
Le libertinage. Paris, Nouvelle revue français [c1924.] 254 p. 19 cm. I. T.
PQ 2601 R2 L6 1924   LC 24-22310

Aragon, 1897-.   • 2.4374
Le paysan de Paris. Paris, Gallimard, c1926. 252 p.: ill.; 19 cm. I. T.
PQ2601.R2 P3 1926   LC 27-2606

Aragon, 1897-.   • 2.4375
La semaine sainte; roman. Paris Gallimard [1958] 598 p.; 21 cm. I. T.
PQ2601 R2 S38

Aragon, 1897-.   • 2.4376
Holy Week, a novel. Translated by Haakon Chevalier. New York, Putnam
[1961] 541 p. 22 cm. I. T.
PZ3.A662Ho PQ2601.R2S413   LC 61-5679

Aragon, 1897-.   • 2.4377
Les voyageurs de l'Impériale: roman. — Paris: Gallimard, 1947. 630 p.; 21 cm.
I. T.
PQ2601.R2 V635 1947a

Aragon, 1897-.   • 2.4378
Les Yeux d'Elsa / Aragon. — Paris: Seghers, c1945. 157 p.; 19 cm. Poems. I. T.
PQ2601.R2 Y4

PQ2601 Arrabal. Artaud

Arrabal, Fernando.   • 2.4379
[Plays English. Selections] Guernica, and other plays, by Arrabal. Translated
from the French by Barbara Wright. New York, Grove Press [1969, c1967]
126 p. 21 cm. (Evergreen original, E-521) Translation of four plays originally
published in v. 2 of Théâtre. I. T.
PQ2601.R65 A283   842/.9/14   LC 79-84570

Arrabal, Fernando, 1932-.   2.4380
Viva la muerte / Arrabal. — Paris: Avant-scène du cinéma, c1971. 50 p.: ill.; 27
cm. (L'Avant-scène cinéma; no. 116 (juillet 1971).) I. L'Avant-scène, cinéma.
II. T.
PQ2601 R65.B3 1971

Artaud, Antonin, 1896-1948.   2.4381
[Selections. English. 1975] Selected writings / Antonin Artaud; edited, and
with an introd. by Susan Sontag; translated from the French by Helen Weaver;
notes by Susan Sontag and Don Eric Levine. — New York: Farrar, Straus and
Giroux, c1976. lix, 661 p., [7] leaves of plates: ill.; 22 cm. 'Translated from the
French, Œuvres complètes.' I. T.
PQ2601.R677 A28 1976   841/.9/12   LC 79-143303   ISBN
0374260486

Costich, Julia F.   2.4382
Antonin Artaud / by Julia F. Costich. — Boston: Twayne Publishers, 1978.
132 p.: port.; 21 cm. — (Twayne's world authors series; TWAS 492. France)
Includes index. 1. Artaud, Antonin, 1896-1948 — Criticism and
interpretation. I. T.
PQ2601.R677 Z632 1978   842/.9/12   LC 78-4641   ISBN
0805763333

Esslin, Martin.   **2.4383**
Antonin Artaud / Martin Esslin. New York: Penguin Books, 1977, c1976. 148 p.; 18 cm. (Penguin modern masters) Includes index. 1. Artaud, Antonin, 1896-1948. 2. Authors, French — 20th century — Biography. I. T.
PQ2601.R677 Z636 1977   841/.9/12   *LC* 77-1269   *ISBN* 0140043683

Hayman, Ronald, 1932-.   **2.4384**
Artaud and after / Ronald Hayman. — Oxford [Eng.]; New York: Oxford University Press, 1977. xv, 189 p., [8] leaves of plates: ill.; 21 cm. Includes index. 1. Artaud, Antonin, 1896-1948 — Biography. 2. Authors, French — 20th century — Biography. I. T.
PQ2601.R677 Z674   841/.9/12 B   *LC* 77-30070   *ISBN* 0192117440

Sellin, Eric, 1933-.   • **2.4385**
The dramatic concepts of Antonin Artaud. — Chicago: University of Chicago Press, [1968] xiii, 190 p.: illus.; 23 cm. 1. Artaud, Antonin, 1896-1948 — Technique. I. T.
PQ2601.R677 Z8   842/.9/12   *LC* 68-15932

Aymé, Marcel, 1902-1967.   • **2.4386**
Les contes bleus du chat perché. Paris] Gallimard [1963] 157 p. col. illus. 25 cm. I. T.
PQ2601.Y5Cx PZ26.3.A89   *LC* 65-46592

PQ2603.A52 Barrès

Soucy, Robert, 1933-.   **2.4387**
Fascism in France; the case of Maurice Barrès. — Berkeley: University of California Press, 1972. x, 350 p.; 24 cm. 1. Barrès, Maurice, 1862-1923 — Political and social views. 2. Fascism — France. I. T.
PQ2603.A52 Z88   843/.9/12   *LC* 77-153554   *ISBN* 0520020286

PQ2603 Beauvoir

Beauvoir, Simone de, 1908-.   • **2.4388**
L'invitee. — Paris: Gallimard, 1943. 418 p.; 18 cm. I. T.
PQ2603.E362 I5   *LC* 46-45228

Beauvoir, Simone de, 1908-.   • **2.4389**
The Mandarins: a novel / by Simone de Beauvoir; translated by Leonard M. Friedman. — 1st ed. — Cleveland: World Pub. Co., 1956. 610 p.; 24 cm. Translation of Les Mandarins: roman. I. T.
PZ.B3852 Man   PQ/2603.E362 M2713 1956.   *LC* 56-5315

Beauvoir, Simone de, 1908-.   • **2.4390**
Les mandarins, roman. — Paris, Gallimard [1954] 579 p. 21 cm. I. T.
PQ2603.E362M3   *LC* 54-43551

Beauvoir, Simone de, 1908-.   • **2.4391**
Une mort très douce; [récit. — Paris] Gallimard [1964] 163 p. 19 cm. I. T.
PQ2603.E362M6   *LC* 65-37009

Beauvoir, Simone de, 1908-.   • **2.4392**
Le sang des autres: roman. [Paris] Gallimard [1947, c1945] 224 p.; 21 cm. I. T.
PQ2603 E362 S3 1947

Beauvoir, Simone de, 1908-.   • **2.4393**
Tous les hommes sont mortels: roman / Simone de Beauvoir. — [Paris]: Gallimard, 1946. 359 p.; 21 cm. I. T.
PQ2603E362 T6   *LC* 47-20441

Beauvoir, Simone de, 1908-.   • **2.4394**
Force de l'âge / Simone de Beauvoir. — Paris: Gallimard, c1960. 622 p.; 21 cm. 1. Beauvoir, Simone de, 1908- I. T.
PQ2603.E362 Z515   *LC* 61-22358

Beauvoir, Simone de, 1908-.   • **2.4395**
The prime of life / Simone de Beauvoir; translated by Peter Green. — [1st American ed.]. — Cleveland: World, 1962. 479 p.; 25 cm. Translation of La Force de l'Age. 1. Beauvoir, Simone de. 2. Authors, French — Biography. I. T.
PQ2603.E362 Z5153 1962   553

Beauvoir, Simone de, 1908-.   • **2.4396**
Mémoires d'une jeune fille rangée. — Paris, Gallimard [1958] 359 p. 21 cm. I. T.
PQ2603.E362Z52   *LC* 58-47716

Beauvoir, Simone de, 1908-.   • **2.4397**
Memoirs of a dutiful daughter / translated by James Kirkup. 1st ed. Cleveland: World Pub. Co.; 1959. 382 p.; 24 cm. Translation of Memoires d'une jeune fille rangee. I. T.
PQ2603.E362 Z523   *LC* 59-7748

Beauvoir, Simone de, 1908-.   • **2.4398**
La force des choses. [Paris] Gallimard [1963] 686 p.; 21 cm. 1. Beauvoir, Simone de, 1908- — Biography 2. Authors, French — 20th century — Biography I. T.
PQ2603.E362 Z524   848.914   *LC* 64-28600

Beauvoir, Simone de, 1908-.   • **2.4399**
Force of circumstance / Simone de Beauvoir; translated from the French by Richard Howard. — New York: Putnam, 1965. vii, 658 p.; 24 cm. 1. Authors — Biography I. T.
PQ2603.E362Z5243 1965   *LC* 65-13290   *ISBN*

Beauvoir, Simone de, 1908-.   **2.4400**
Tout compte fait. [Paris] Gallimard [1972] 512 p. 20 cm. I. T.
PQ2603.E362 Z525   *LC* 72-367284

Beauvoir, Simone de, 1908-.   • **2.4401**
All said and done / Simone de Beauvoir; translated by Patrick O'Brian. — 1st American ed. — New York: Putnam, 1974. 463 p.; 24 cm. Translation of Toute compte fait. 1. Beauvoir, Simone de, 1908- — Biography. I. T.
PQ2603.E362 Z52513 1974b   848/.9/1409   *LC* 73-93722   *ISBN* 0399112510

Keefe, Terry.   **2.4402**
Simone de Beauvoir: a study of her writings / Terry Keefe. — Totowa, N.J.: Barnes & Noble, 1983. 247 p.: ill.; 23 cm. Includes index. 1. Beauvoir, Simone de, 1908- — Criticism and interpretation. I. T.
PQ2603.E362 Z75 1983   848/.91409 19   *LC* 83-6024   *ISBN* 0389203653

PQ2603 Beckett
(see also PR6003)

Beckett, Samuel, 1906-.   **2.4403**
Comment c'est; [roman. — Paris]: Éditions de Minuit, [1961] 117 p.; 19 cm. — I. T.
PQ2603.E378 C6 1961   843/.9/14   *LC* a 61-5183

Beckett, Samuel, 1906-.   • **2.4404**
[Comment c'est. English] How it is. Translated from the French by the author. New York, Grove Press [1964] 147 p. 21 cm. I. T.
PZ3.B38868 Ho   PQ2603.E378 C6x.   *LC* 63-16998

Beckett, Samuel, 1906-.   • **2.4405**
[En attendant Godot. English] Waiting for Godot; tragicomedy in 2 acts, by Samuel Beckett. [Translated from his original French text by the author] New York, Grove Press [1954] 60 p. illus. 22 cm. I. T.
PQ2603.E378 E53   842.91   *LC* 54-6803

Beckett, Samuel, 1906-.   • **2.4406**
[Fin de partie. English] Endgame, a play in one act, followed by Act without words, a mime for one player. Translated from the French by the author. New York, Grove Press [1958] 91 p. 21 cm. (Evergreen books, E-96) Translation of Fin de partie; suivi de Acte sans paroles. I. T. II. Title: Act without words.
PQ2603.E378 F53   842.91   *LC* 58-5532

Beckett, Samuel, 1906-.   **2.4407**
L'innommable. Paris Ed. de Minuit`1953. 262p. I. T.
PQ2603 E378 I6

Beckett, Samuel, 1906-.   **2.4408**
Malone meurt. [Paris] Éditions de Minuit [1951] 217 p. 19 cm. I. T.
PQ2603.E378 M3   *LC* 52-29711

Beckett, Samuel, 1906-.   **2.4409**
Molloy. Paris: Éditions de Minuit, 1951. 271 p. I. T.
PQ2603.E378 M64   PR6003.E282 M59.   843.91   *LC* 51-29578

Beckett, Samuel, 1906-.   • **2.4410**
Molloy, Malone dies and The unnamable; three novels. [Translated from the French]. — New York, Grove Press [1959] 577 p. 21 cm. I. T. II. Title: Malone dies. III. Title: The unnamable.
PZ3.B38868Mq   PQ2603.E378 M6x.   843.914   *LC* 59-13886

Beckett, Samuel, 1906-.   • **2.4411**
Théâtre / Samuel Beckett. — Paris: Éditions de Minuit, c1971-. v. I. T.
PQ2603.E378 T5   *LC* 72-354137

PQ2603 Bernanos

Bernanos, Georges, 1888-1948.   • **2.4412**
Oeuvres romanesques, suivies de Dialogues des carmélites. Préf. par Gaetan Picon. Texte établi et annoté par Michel Esteve. — [Paris, Gallimard, 1961] liv, 1898 p. 18 cm. — (Bibliothèque de la Pléiade, 155) Bibliography: p. [1889]-1893. I. Estève, Michel. ed. II. T. III. Title: Dialogues des carmélites. PQ2603.E5875A6 1961   *LC* 67-96113

Bernanos, Georges, 1888-1948.   • **2.4413**
The diary of a country priest; translated from the French by Pamela Morris. — New York, The Macmillan company, 1937. 3 p. l., 298 p. 22 cm. I. Morris, Pamela. tr. II. T.
PZ3.B45593Di PQ2603.E5875J713 1937a   843.91   *LC* 37-24111

Bernanos, Georges, 1888-1948.   • **2.4414**
Under the sun of Satan: a novel / by Georges Bernanos; translated by Harry L. Binsse. — New York: Pantheon, c1949. 252 p.; 21 cm. Translation of Sous le soleil de Satan. I. T.
PZ3.B45593 Un   PQ2603.E589 S613 1949.   PQ2603.E5875 Sx.   843/.91   *LC* 49-10776

Bernanos, Georges, 1888-1948.   • **2.4415**
Bernanos par lui–même. [Images et textes inédits présentés par] Albert Béguin. [Paris] Éditions du Seuil [1954] 191p. (Écrivains de toujours, 21) I. Béguin, Albert, 1898- II. T.
PQ2603 E5875 Z55

PQ2603 Bl–Br

Blanchot, Maurice.   **2.4416**
[Thomas l'obscur. English] Thomas the obscure. New version translated by Robert Lamberton. New York, D. Lewis, 1973. 117 p. 25 cm. I. T.
PZ3.B5938 Th PQ2603.L3343   843/.9/12   *LC* 73-85970

Bonnefoy, Yves.   **2.4417**
Poèmes / Yves Bonnefoy; préface de Jean Starobinski. — [Paris]: Gallimard, 1982. 345 p. — (Collection Poésie; 158) I. Bonnefoy, Yves. Du mouvement et de l'immobilité de Douve. II. Bonnefoy, Yves. Hier régnant désert. III. Bonnefoy, Yves. Pierre écrite. IV. Bonnefoy, Yves. Dans le leurre du seuil. V. T. VI. Title: Du mouvement et de l'immobilité de Douve. VII. Title: Hier régnant désert. VIII. Title: Pierre écrite. IX. Title: Dans le leurre du seuil.
PQ2603.O533 A17 1982   841/.9/14   *ISBN* 2070322211

Bonnefoy, Yves.   **2.4418**
[Pierre écrite. English & French] Words in stone = Pierre écrite / Yves Bonnefoy; translated by Susanna Lang. — Amherst: University of Massachusetts Press, 1976. xxii, 134 p. 1. Lang, Susanna, 1956- I. T. II. Title: Pierre écrite.
PQ2603.O533 P513   PQ2603O533 P513.   841/.9/14   *LC* 75-32481   *ISBN* 0870232037

Caws, Mary Ann.   **2.4419**
Yves Bonnefoy / by Mary Ann Caws. — Boston: Twayne Publishers, c1984. xviii, 114 p.; 23 cm. — (Twayne's world authors series; TWAS 702. French literature) Includes index. 1. Bonnefoy, Yves — Criticism and interpretation. I. T.
PQ2603.O533 Z6 1984   841/.914 19   *LC* 83-22833   *ISBN* 0805765492

Naughton, John T.   **2.4420**
The poetics of Yves Bonnefoy / John T. Naughton. — Chicago: University of Chicago Press, c1984. xi, 209 p.: ill.; 24 cm. Includes index. 1. Bonnefoy, Yves — Criticism and interpretation. I. T.
PQ2603.O533 Z8 1984   841/.914 19   *LC* 83-18075   *ISBN* 0226569470

Breton, André, 1896-1966.   **2.4421**
[Poems. Selections. English & French] Poems of André Breton: a bilingual anthology / translated and edited by Jean–Pierre Cauvin and Mary Ann Caws. — 1st ed. — Austin: University of Texas Press, 1982. xxxviii, 260 p., [1] leaf of plates: ill., ports.; 24 cm. I. Cauvin, Jean Pierre. II. Caws, Mary Ann. III. T.
PQ2603.R35 A23 1982   841/.912 19   *LC* 82-4846   *ISBN* 0292764766

Breton, André, 1896-1966.   • **2.4422**
Oeuvres choisies; une étude par Jean–Louis Bedouin. [Paris] P. Seghers [1950] 226 p.; 16 cm. (Poetes d'aujourd'hui, no. 18) I. Bedouin, Jean Louis, ed. II. T.
PQ2603 R35 A6 1950

Breton, André,1896-1966.   • **2.4423**
Nadja / by André Breton; translated by Richard Howard. New York: Grove, 1960. 160 p.: ill.; 21 cm. (Evergreen original; E-253.) I. T. II. Series.
PQ2603.R35 N3 1960   843.912   *LC* 60-7639

Breton, André, 1896-1966.   • **2.4424**
Les pas perdus. — 7e éd. — [Paris]: Gallimard, [1949] 217 p.; 19 cm. I. T.
PQ2603.R35 P3   *LC* 76-480012

Breton, André, 1896-1966.   • **2.4425**
Poèmes. Paris: Gallimard, 1948. 271 p.; 21 cm. I. T.
PQ2603.R35 P55   *LC* 49-24274

Breton, André, 1896-1966.   • **2.4426**
Le revolver à cheveux blancs. — [Paris] Éditions des Cahiers libres, 1932. 173 p. 20 cm. — I. T.
PQ2603.R35R4

Breton, André, 1896-1966.   • **2.4427**
Les vases communicants. — Paris, Gallimard [1955] 207 p. illus. 19 cm. I. T.
PQ2603.R35V3 1955   *LC* 55-36671

Balakian, Anna Elizabeth, 1915-.   • **2.4428**
André Breton, magus of surrealism [by] Anna Balakian. — New York: Oxford University Press, 1971. xii, 289 p.: illus., ports.; 24 cm. 1. Breton, André, 1896-1966. I. T.
PQ2603.R35 Z59   841/.9/12 B   *LC* 78-83006

Matthews, J. H.   • **2.4429**
André Breton, by J. H. Matthews. — New York, Columbia University Press, 1967. 48 p. 21 cm. — (Columbia essays on modern writers, no. 26) Bibliography: p. 46-48. 1. Breton, André, 1896-1966. I. T. II. Series.
PQ2603.R35Z75   848/.91/209   *LC* 67-16892

Mauriac, Claude, 1914-.   • **2.4430**
André Breton; essai. Paris Éditions de Flore [1949] 358 p.; 19 cm. 1. Breton, André, 1896-1966. 2. Surrealism I. T.
PQ2603 R35 Z76

Vercors, 1902-.   • **2.4431**
Le silence de la mer: et autres récits / [par] Vercors [pseud.] — Éd. définitive. — Paris, Michel [1951] 189 p. 19 cm. 1. World War, 1939-1945 — Fiction. I. T.
PQ2603.R924S5 1951   843.91   *LC* 51-33178

Vercors, 1902-.   • **2.4432**
The silence of the sea / by Vercors; translated by Cyril Connolly. — New York: Macmillan, 1944. xiv, 47 p. Traduction de: Le silence de la mer. 1. World War, 1939-1945 — Fiction I. T. II. Title: Put out the light.
PQ2603.R924 S513x   843.914   *LC* 44-1668 rev.

PQ2603 Butor

Butor, Michel.   • **2.4433**
Degrés; roman. Paris Gallimard [1960] 389 p.; 21 cm. I. T.
PQ2603.U73 D4

Butor, Michel.   • **2.4434**
[Emploi du temps. English] Passing time & A change of heart; two novels. Translated from the French by Jean Stewart. New York, Simon and Schuster [1969] 561 p. map. 22 cm. Translation of L'emploi du temps and La modification. I. Butor, Michel. Modification. English. 1969. II. T. III. Title: Change of heart.
PZ4.B988 Pas4 PQ2603.U73 Ex   843/.9/14   *LC* 71-5021

Butor, Michel.   • **2.4435**
La Modification. Paris: Éditions de minuit, 1957. 236 p.,; 23 cm. I. T.
PQ2603.U73 M64   *LC* 58-3925

Butor, Michel.   • **2.4436**
Mobile, study for a representation of the United States. Translated from the French by Richard Howard. New York, Simon and Schuster, 1963. 319 p. 24 cm. Translation of Mobile; étude pour une representation des Etats-Unis. 1. United States. I. T.
PQ2603.U73 M6x   *LC* 63-9275

Lydon, Mary.   **2.4437**
Perpetuum mobile: a study of the novels and aesthetics of Michel Butor / Mary Lydon. — Edmonton: University of Alberta Press, 1980. xv, 295 p.; 24 cm. 1. Butor, Michel, 1926- — Criticism and interpretation. I. T.
PQ2603.U73 Z68   848/.914   *ISBN* 0888640552

Spencer, M. C. (Michael Clifford).   **2.4438**
Michel Butor, by Michael Spencer. New York, Twayne Publishers [1974] 187 p. 22 cm. (Twayne's world authors series, TWAS 275. France) 1. Butor, Michel — Criticism and interpretation. I. T.
PQ2603.U73 Z89   848/.9/1409 B   *LC* 73-8071   *ISBN* 080572186X

PQ2605 Camus

Camus, Albert, 1913-1960.   2.4439
Œuvres complètes d'Albert Camus / notices de Roger Grenier. — Paris: Éditons du Club de l'honnête homme, 1983. 9 v.: ill, facsims., ports.; 24 cm. I. Grenier, Roger, 1919- II. T.
PQ2605.A1x

Camus, Albert, 1913-1960.   • 2.4440
Essais. Introd. par R. Quilliot. Textes établie et annotée par R. Quilliot et L. Faucon. Paris: Gallimard, c1965. xiv, 1975 p.; 18 cm. (Bibliothèque de la Pléiade. 83) 1. Good and evil 2. Reconstruction (1939-1951) — France. 3. Europe — Politics and government 4. France — Politics and government — 1945- I. Quilliot, Roger, 1925- II. Faucon, Louis, 1913- ed. III. T. IV. Series.
PQ2605.A3734 A16 1965   LC 67-371

Camus, Albert, 1913-1960.   • 2.4441
Resistance, rebellion, and death. Translated from the French and with an introd. by Justin O'Brien. — [1st American ed.]. — New York: Knopf, 1961 [c1960] 271 p.; 22 cm. Twenty-three essays selected by the author from his Actuelles. 1. Good and evil 2. Europe — Politics and government — Addresses, essays, lectures. I. T.
PQ2605.A3734 A25   844.914   LC 60-16703

Camus, Albert, 1913-1960.   • 2.4442
Théâtre, récits, nouvelles / préf. par Jean Grenier; textes établis et annotés par Roger Quilliot. — Paris: Gallimard, 1962. xxxvii, 2090 p.; 18 cm. (Bibliothèque de la Pléiade. 161) I. Quilliot, Roger. II. T. III. Series.
PQ2605.A3734 A6 1962

Camus, Albert, 1913-1960.   • 2.4443
[Caligula. English] Caligula & three other plays. Translated from the French by Stuart Gilbert. With a pref. written specially for this ed., and translated by Justin O'Brien. [1st American ed.] New York, Knopf, 1958. x, 302 p. 21 cm. 1. Caligula, Emperor of Rome, 12-41 — Drama. I. T. II. Title: Misunderstanding. III. Title: State of siege. IV. Title: Just assassins.
PQ2605.A3734 C33 1958   842.91   LC 58-11227

Camus, Albert, 1913-1960.   • 2.4444
[Chute. English] The fall. Translated from the French by Justin O'Brien. [1st American ed.] New York, Knopf, 1957 [c1956] 147 p. 20 cm. I. O'Brien, Justin, 1906-1968. II. T.
PZ3.C1574 Fal   PQ2605.A3734 C5x.   843/.914 19   LC 57-5652

Camus, Albert, 1913-1960.   • 2.4445
L'été. — Paris, Gallimard [1954] 184 p. 19 cm. — (Les Essais, 68) I. T.
PQ2605.A3734E79   LC 54-25937

Camus, Albert, 1913-1960.   • 2.4446
[Etranger. English] The stranger, by Albert Camus, translated from the French by Stuart Gilbert. New York, A. A. Knopf, 1946. 4 p. l., 154 p., 1 l. 19 cm. 'Originally published as L'étranger ... 1942.' 'First American edition.' I. Gilbert, Stuart. tr. II. T.
PZ3.C1574 St   PQ2605.A3734 E8x.   843.91   LC 46-3068

Camus, Albert, 1913-1960.   • 2.4447
[Exil et le royaume. English] Exile and the kingdom. Translated from the French by Justin O'Brien. [1st American ed.] New York, Knopf, 1958. 213 p. 20 cm. Short stories. I. T.
PZ3.C1574 Ex   PQ2605.A3734 E9x.   843.91   LC 58-6531

Camus, Albert, 1913-1960.   • 2.4448
Le malentendu: suivi de Caligula. Nouvelles versions. Paris: Gallimard, [1963, c1958] 250 p.; 18 cm. 1. Caligula, Emperor of Rome, 12-41 — Drama. I. T. II. Title: Caligula.
PQ2605.A3734 M3   LC 66-93960

Camus, Albert, 1913-1960.   2.4449
[Mort heureuse. English] A happy death. Translated from the French by Richard Howard. Afterword and notes by Jean Sarocchi. [1st American ed.] New York, Knopf; [distributed by Random House] 1972. 192 p. 22 cm. (His Cahier 1) Translation of La mort heureuse. I. T.
PQ2605.A3734 M6x   843/.9/14   LC 78-171141   ISBN 0394472624

Camus, Albert, 1913-1960.   • 2.4450
Le mythe de Sisyphe. Paris: Gallimard, 1942. 168 p.; 19 cm. (Les Essais, 12.) I. T. II. Series.
PQ2605.A3734 M9 1942   LC 49-56466

Camus, Albert, 1913-1960.   • 2.4451
[Mythe de Sisyphe. English] The myth of Sisyphus, and other essays. Translated from the French by Justin O'Brien. [1st American ed.] New York, Knopf, 1955. 212 p. 22 cm. I. T.
PQ2605.A3734 M93   844.91   LC 55-9276

Camus, Albert, 1913-1960.   • 2.4452
Noces. Nouv. ed. [Paris] Charlot [1947] 102 p.; 18 cm. I. T.
PQ2605 A3734 N6

Camus, Albert, 1913-1960.   • 2.4453
[Peste. English] The plague. Translated from the French by Stuart Gilbert. New York, Modern Library [c1948] 278 p. 19 cm. (The Modern library of the world's best books [169]) I. T.
PZ3.C1574 Pl2   PQ2605.A3734 P4x.   LC 61-16144

Camus, Albert, 1913-1960.   • 2.4454
[Possédés. English] The possessed, a play in three parts. Translated from the French by Justin O'Brien. [1st American ed.] New York, Knopf, 1960. 182 p. 21 cm. I. T.
PQ2605.A3734 P63   842.914   LC 60-7296

Camus, Albert, 1913-1960.   • 2.4455
[Carnets English] Notebooks. [1st American ed.] New York, Knopf, 1963-. v. 22 cm. I. T.
PQ2605.A3734 Z52 1963   848.914   LC 63-9127

Brée, Germaine. ed.   • 2.4456
Camus; a collection of critical essays. Englewood Cliffs, N.J., Prentice-Hall [1962] viii, 182 p. 21 cm. (A Spectrum book: Twentieth century views, S-TC-1) 1. Camus, Albert, 1913-1960 — Criticism and interpretation. I. T.
PQ2605.A3734 Z62   848.914   LC 62-9305

Cruickshank, John.   • 2.4457
Albert Camus and the literature of revolt. London, New York, Oxford University Press, 1959. 248 p. illus. 23 cm. Includes bibliography. 1. Camus, Albert, 1913-1960. I. T.
PQ2605.A3734Z63   840.81   LC 59-3952

Lottman, Herbert R.   2.4458
Albert Camus: a biography / Herbert R. Lottman. — 1st ed. — Garden City, N.Y.: Doubleday, 1979. xii, 753 p., [8] leaves of plates: ill.; 24 cm. 1. Camus, Albert, 1913-1960 — Biography. 2. Authors, French — 20th century — Biography.
PQ2605.A3734 Z698   848/.9/1409 B   LC 78-8199   ISBN 0385116640

Quilliot, Roger, 1925-.   • 2.4459
[Mer et les prisons. English] The sea and prisons; a commentary on the life and thought of Albert Camus. Translated by Emmett Parker. University, Ala., University of Alabama Press [1970] xxv, 280 p. 24 cm. Translation of La mer et les prisons. 'The original French edition ... was extensively revised and augmented by the author for this, the first English language edition.' 1. Camus, Albert, 1913-1960. I. T.
PQ2605.A3734 Z7313   843/.9/12   LC 76-104931   ISBN 0817376615

PQ2605 Ce–Ch

Cendrars, Blaise, 1887-1961.   2.4460
Complete postcards from the Americas: poems of road and sea / Blaise Cendrars; translated, with an introd., by Monique Chefdor. Berkeley: University of California Press, 1976. viii, 251 p., [4] leaves of plates: ill.; 23 cm. Selections from the author's Du monde entier au coeur du monde. English and French. I. T.
PQ2605.E55 A24 1976   841/.9/12   LC 73-94445   ISBN 0520027167

Cendrars, Blaise, 1887-1961.   • 2.4461
[Selected works. English and French] Selected writings. Edited, with a critical introd., by Walter Albert, and with a pref. by Henry Miller. [New York, New Directions Pub. Corp., 1966] x, 273 p. 21 cm. (A New Directions book) In French and in English; prose in English verse. I. Albert, Walter. ed. II. T.
PQ2605.E55 A6 1966   848/.9/1209   LC 65-27557

Cendrars, Blaise, 1887-1961.   • 2.4462
Moravagine, roman. Paris B. Grasset 1926. 362p. 362 p.; 19 cm. I. T.
PQ2605 E55 M6

Bochner, Jay, 1940-.   2.4463
Blaise Cendrars: discovery and re–creation / Jay Bochner. — Toronto; Buffalo: University of Toronto Press, c1978. 311 p., [5] leaves of plates: ill.; 24 cm. (University of Toronto romance series. 32) Includes index. 1. Cendrars, Blaise, 1887-1961. 2. Authors, Swiss — 20th century — Biography. I. T. II. Series.
PQ2605.E55 Z563   841/.9/12 B   LC 77-2580   ISBN 0802053521

Char, René, 1907-.　　　　　　　　　　　　　　　　　　2.4464
[Works. 1983] Œuvres complètes / René Char; introduction de Jean Roudaut.
— [Paris]: Gallimard, c1983. lxxxv, 1364 p.; 18 cm. — (Bibliothèque de la
Pléiade; v. 308) I. Roudaut, Jean. II. T.
PQ2605.H3345 1983　　　841/.912 19　　　LC 83-195974　　　ISBN
2070110656

Char, René, 1907-.　　　　　　　　　　　　　　　　　　2.4465
Poems of René Char / translated and annotated by Mary Ann Caws and
Jonathan Griffin. Princeton, N.J.: Princeton University Press, c1976. xxx,
292 p., [2] leaves of plates: ill.; 22 cm. (The Lockert library of poetry in
translation) English and French. I. Caws, Mary Ann. II. Griffin, Jonathan.
III. T.
PQ2605.H3345 A23　　　841/.9/12　　　LC 75-30189　　　ISBN 0691062978

Char, René, 1907-.　　　　　　　　　　　　　　　　• 2.4466
Hypnos walking: poems and prose / selected and translated by Jackson
Mathews, with the collaboration of William Carlos Williams ... et. al. — New
York: Random House, 1956. 279 p.; 20cm. English and French. I. T.
PQ2605.H3345 A6 1956　　　LC 55-8157

Caws, Mary Ann.　　　　　　　　　　　　　　　　　　2.4467
The presence of René Char / Mary Ann Caws. — Princeton, N.J.: Princeton
University Press, c1976. xii, 336 p., [2] leaves of plates: facsims., port.; 22 cm.
1. Char, René, 1907- — Criticism and interpretation. I. T.
PQ2605.H3345 Z63　　　848/.9/1209　　　LC 75-30188　　　ISBN
0691063052

Caws, Mary Ann.　　　　　　　　　　　　　　　　　　2.4468
René Char / by Mary Ann Caws. — Boston: Twayne Publishers, c1977. 174 p.:
ill.; 21 cm. — (Twayne's world authors series; TWAS 428: France) Includes
index. 1. Char, René, 1907- 2. Char, René. 3. Authors, French — 20th
century — Biography. I. T.
PQ2605.H3345 Z633　　　848/.9/1209　　　LC 76-50031　　　ISBN
080576268X

Chedid, Andrée, 1920-.　　　　　　　　　　　　　　　2.4469
Théâtre / Andrée Chedid. — Paris: Flammarion, c1981-. v. < 1 >; 19 cm. I. T.
PQ2605.H4245 A19 1981　　　842/.914 19　　　LC 81-153647　　　ISBN
2080643797

Chedid, Andrée, 1920-.　　　　　　　　　　　　　　　2.4470
Visage premier; Suivi de, Terre et poésie / Andrée Chedid. — [Paris]:
Flammarion, [1972] 98 p.; 19 cm. (Poésie) Poems. I. Chedid, Andrée, 1920-
Terre et poésie. 1972. II. T. III. Title: Visage premier. IV. Title: Terre et
poésie
PQ2605.H4245 V5　　　LC 72-327794

PQ2605 Claudel

Claudel, Paul, 1868-1955.　　　　　　　　　　　　• 2.4471
Cinq grandes odes; suivies d'un Processionnal pour saluer le siècle nouveau; La
cantate à trois vois / Paul Claude; préface de Jean Grosjean. — Paris:
Gallimard, 1966. 192 p.; 16 cm. — (Collection Poésie) I. T. II. Title:
Processional pour saluer le siècle nouveau. III. Title: La Cantate à trois voix.
PQ2605.L2 C5 1966　　　LC 67-94124

Claudel, Paul, 1868-1955.　　　　　　　　　　　　• 2.4472
Two dramas: Break of noon (Partage de midi) The tidings brought to Mary.
(L'annonce faite à Marie) Translations and introductions [by] Wallace Fowlie.
Chicago, H. Regnery Co. [c1960] 295p. illus. 295 p.: illus.; 19 cm. I. T.
II. Title: Break of noon. III. Title: The tidings brought to Mary.
PQ2605.L2P353　　　LC 60-14057

Claudel, Paul, 1868-1955.　　　　　　　　　　　　• 2.4473
The satin slipper; or, The worst is not the surest, by Paul Claudel. Translated by
the Rev. Fr. John O'Connor, with the collaboration of the author. New York,
Sheed & Ward, 1945. xxvi, 310 p. 22 1/2 cm. 'Spanish play in four days.'
I. O'Connor, John, 1870- tr. II. T.
PQ2605.L2S62 1945　　　LC 46-3559

Claudel, Paul, 1868-1955.　　　　　　　　　　　　• 2.4474
Théâtre. Introduction et chronologie de la vie et de l'œuvre par Jacques
Madaule. [Paris, Gallimard, 1947-48] 2 v. 18 cm. (Bibliothèque de la Pléiade,
72-73) I. Madaule, Jacques, 1895- II. T.
PQ2605.L2 T54　　　842.91　　　LC 49-17890

Claudel, Paul, 1868-1955.　　　　　　　　　　　　• 2.4475
Mémoires improvisés. [Entretiens avec Paul Claudel] recueillis par Jean
Amrouche. — Paris, Gallimard [1954] 349 p. 21 cm. I. Amrouche, Jean, 1906-
II. T.
PQ2605.L2Z52　　　LC 54-27010

PQ2605 Cocteau

Cocteau, Jean, 1889-1963.　　　　　　　　　　　　• 2.4476
Poèmes, 1916–1955 / Jean Cocteau. — 4e éd. — Paris: Gallimard, 1956. 231 p.;
19 cm. T.
PQ2605 .O15 A17 1956　　　LC 56-58718

Cocteau, Jean, 1889-1963.　　　　　　　　　　　　• 2.4477
Théâtre. [Paris] Gallimard [1948-. v. 19 cm. I. T.
PQ2605.O15 A19 1948　　　842.91　　　LC 49-26047

Cocteau, Jean, 1889-1963.　　　　　　　　　　　　• 2.4478
Five plays. — New York: Hill and Wang, [1961] 310 p.; 19 cm. — (A Mermaid
dramabook, MD22) I. T.
PQ2605.O15 A24　　　842.912　　　LC 61-14473

Cocteau, Jean, 1889-1963.　　　　　　　　　　　　• 2.4479
The infernal machine, and other plays. — [Norfolk, Conn.]: New Directions,
[1964, c1963] 409 p.; 21 cm. I. T.
PQ2605.O15 A26　　　842.912　　　LC 63-18631

Cocteau, Jean, 1889-1963.　　　　　　　　　　　　• 2.4480
Les enfants terribles / Jean Cocteau. — Paris: B. Grasset, 1930. 228 p.; 19 cm.
I. T.
PQ2605O15 E6 1930

Cocteau, Jean, 1889-1963.　　　　　　　　　　　　• 2.4481
Les parents terribles; pièce en trois actes. Paris Gallimard [1939] 251 p.; 19 cm.
I. T.
PQ2605 O15 P35 1939

Cocteau, Jean, 1889-1963.　　　　　　　　　　　　• 2.4482
Thomas l'imposteur, histoire. Paris Nouvelle revue française [c1923] 184 p.; 19
cm. I. T.
PQ2605 O15 T5

Cocteau, Jean, 1889-1963.　　　　　　　　　　　　• 2.4483
Professional secrets; an autobiography of Jean Cocteau, drawn from his lifetime
writings by Robert Phelps. Translated from the French by Richard Howard. —
New York: Farrar, Straus & Giroux, 1970. xiii, 331 p.: illus., facsim., ports.; 22
cm. I. Phelps, Robert, 1922- ed. II. T.
PQ2605.O15 Z5　　　838/.9/1209 B　　　LC 70-82626

Cocteau, Jean, 1889-1963.　　　　　　　　　　　　• 2.4484
The journals of Jean Cocteau / Jean Cocteau; edited and translated with an
introd. by Wallace Fowlie; illustrated with 16 drawings by the author. — New
York: Criterion, [c1956]. 250 p.: ill.; 25 cm. 1. Cocteau, Jean, 1889-1963 —
Biography. 2. Authors, French — 20th century — Biography. I. T.
PQ2605.O15 Z515 1957　　　844

Steegmuller, Francis, 1906-.　　　　　　　　　　　• 2.4485
Cocteau, a biography. [1st ed.] Boston, Little, Brown [1970] xiv, 583 p. illus.,
ports. 25 cm. 'An Atlantic Monthly Press book.' 1. Cocteau, Jean, 1889-1963
— Biography. 2. Authors, French — 20th century — Biography. 3. Artists —
France — Biography. 4. Motion picture producers and directors — France —
Biography. I. T.
PQ2605.O15 Z86　　　848/.9/1209 B　　　LC 76-117039

PQ2605 Colette

Colette, 1873-1954.　　　　　　　　　　　　　　　　2.4486
[Works. 1984] Œuvres / Colette; édition publiée sous la direction de Claude
Pichois. — [Paris]: Gallimard, c1984-. v. < 1 >: plans; 18 cm. (Bibliothèque de
la Pléiade; v. 314-) I. Pichois, Claude. II. T.
PQ2605.O28 1984　　　848/.91209 19　　　LC 84-232777　　　ISBN
2070110796

Colette, 1873-1954.　　　　　　　　　　　　　　　• 2.4487
Short novels; with an introd. by Glenway Wescott. New York, Dial Press, 1951.
733 p. 22 cm. (A Permanent library book) I. T.
PQ2605.O28 A27　　　LC 51-13864

Colette, 1873-1954.　　　　　　　　　　　　　　　　2.4488
[Selections. English. 1983] The collected stories of Colette / edited, and with an
introduction, by Robert Phelps; translated by Matthew Ward ... [et al.]. — New
York: Farrar, Straus, Giroux, c1983. xvi, 605 p.; 24 cm. 1. Colette, 1873-1954
— Translations, English. I. Phelps, Robert, 1922- II. T.
PQ2605.O28 A285 1983　　　843/.912 19　　　LC 83-16449　　　ISBN
0374126291

Colette, 1873-1954.　　　　　　　　　　　　　　　• 2.4489
[Blé en herbe. English] Ripening seed. Translated by Roger Senhouse.
Westport, Conn., Greenwood Press [1972, c1955] 152 p. 19 cm. Original ed.

issued as no. 7 of Uniform edition of works by Colette. Translation of Le blé en herbe. I. T.
PZ3.C67984 Rj8 PQ2605.O28 B5x   843/.9/12   *LC* 73-178784
ISBN 0837162920

Colette, 1873-1954.   **2.4490**
The cat. Translated from the French by Morris Bentinck. Decorations by Susanne Suba. New York, Farrar & Rinehart [c1936] 164 p. I. Bentinck, Morris. II. T.
PQ2605.O28 C4x   843.91

Colette, 1873-1954.   **2.4491**
Chéri and The last of Chéri [by] Colette. — New York: Farrar, Straus & Giroux, c1951. 296 p.; 21 cm. — I. T. II. Title: The last of Chéri.
PZ3.C67984 Ch10 PQ2605.O28 C5x   843/.9/12   *ISBN* 0374121028

Colette, 1873-1954.   **2.4492**
The complete Claudine / Colette; translated by Antonia White. — New York: Farrar, Straus, and Giroux, c1976. 632 p.; 22 cm. I. T.
PZ3.C67984 Cr5 PQ2605.O28 C6x   843/.9/12   *LC* 76-21070

Colette, 1873-1954.   **• 2.4493**
[Fanal bleu. English] The blue lantern. Translated by Roger Senhouse. Westport, Conn., Greenwood Press [1972, c1963] 161 p. 22 cm. Translation of Le fanal bleu. I. T.
PZ3.C67984 Bl5 PQ2605.O28 F3x   843/.9/12   *LC* 72-178781
ISBN 0837162912

Colette, 1873-1954.   **• 2.4494**
Gigi. Julie de Carneilhan. Chance acquaintances. New York, Farrar, Straus and Young [1952] 315 p. illus. 22 cm. I. T. II. Title: Julie de Carneilhan. III. Title: Chance acquaintances.
PZ3.C67984 Gi   PQ2605.O28 G3x.   843.91   *LC* 52-13845

Colette, 1873-1954.   **2.4495**
My mother's house, and Sido [by] Colette. Westport, Conn., Greenwood Press [1972, c1953] xviii, 217 p. 22 cm. Translations of La maison de Claudine and Sido. 1. Colette, 1873-1954. I. Colette, 1873-1954. Sido. English. 1972. II. T. III. Title: Sido.
PQ2605.O28 M32 1972   848/.9/1203 B   *LC* 76-178782   *ISBN* 0837162947

Colette, 1873-1954.   **2.4496**
Mitsou [translated by Raymond Postgate] and Music–Hall side lights [translated by Anne–Marie Callimachi] New York, Farrar, Straus and Cudahy [1958] 260 p. 20 cm. I. Colette, Sidonie Gabrielle, 1873-1954. Music-Hall sidelights. II. T. III. Title: Music-Hall sidelights.
PQ2605.O28 M5x   *LC* 58-8498

Colette, 1873-1954.   **• 2.4497**
[Seconde. English] The other one. Translated by Elizabeth Tait and Roger Senhouse. Westport, Conn., Greenwood Press [1972, c1960] 160 p. 22 cm. Translation of La seconde. I. T.
PZ3.C67984 Ot7 PQ2605.O28 S4x   843/.9/12   *LC* 70-178783
ISBN 0837162955

Colette, 1873-1954.   **• 2.4498**
[Vagabonde. English] The vagabond. Translated by Enid McLeod. Westport, Conn., Greenwood Press [1973, c1955] 223 p. 20 cm. I. T.
PZ3.C67984 Vag6 PQ2605.O28 V3x   843/.9/12   *LC* 77-178785
ISBN 0837162939

Colette, 1873-1954.   **2.4499**
[Autobiographie tirée des œuvres de Colette. English] Earthly paradise; an autobiography, drawn from her lifetime writings by Robert Phelps. Translated by Herma Briffault, Derek Coltman, and others. New York, Farrar, Straus & Giroux, 1966. xxxiv, 505 p. 22 cm. 1. Colette, 1873-1954. I. Phelps, Robert, 1922- ed. II. T.
PQ2605.O28 Z5   848.91203   *LC* 65-23837

Colette, 1873-1954.   **• 2.4500**
My apprenticeships, and Music–hall sidelights. London, Secker and Warburg, 1957. 260 p. 19 cm. (Uniform edition of works by Colette, 9) Translation of Mes apprentissages, by Helen Beauclerk, and L'envers du music-hall, by Anne-Marie Callimachi. 1. Authors — Correspondence, reminiscences, etc. I. T. II. Title: Music-hall sidelights.
PQ2605.O28 Z552 1957   928.4   *LC* 58-254

Cottrell, Robert D.   **2.4501**
Colette [by] Robert D. Cottrell. New York, F. Ungar Pub. Co. [1974] ix, 150 p. 21 cm. (Modern literature monographs) 1. Colette, 1873-1954. I. T.
PQ2605.O28 Z638   848/.9/1209   *LC* 73-84598   *ISBN* 0804421307

Goudeket, Maurice, 1889-1977.   **• 2.4502**
[Près de Colette. English] Close to Colette; an intimate portrait of a woman of genius. With an introd. by Harold Nicolson. Westport, Conn., Greenwood Press [1972, c1957] vii, 245 p. illus. 22 cm. Translation of Près de Colette. Uniform title: Près de Colette. English 1. Colette, 1873-1954. I. T.
PQ2605.O28 Z673 1972   848/.9/1209 B   *LC* 70-178786   *ISBN* 0837162904

Le Hardouin, Maria.   **• 2.4503**
Colette / Maria le Hardouin. — Paris: Éditions Universitaires, [1956]. 129, [7] p.; 18 cm. (Classiques du XXe siècle; no 24) 1. Colette, 1873-1954. I. T.
PQ2605 O28Z68

Marks, Elaine.   **• 2.4504**
Colette / Elaine Marks. — New Brunswick, N.J.: Rutgers University Press, 1960. 265 p.; 22 cm. 1. Colette, 1873-1954. I. T.
PQ2605.O28 Z719   843.912   *LC* 60-9694

Stewart, Joan Hinde.   **2.4505**
Colette / by Joan Hinde Stewart. — Boston: Twayne Publishers, c1983. 158 p., [1] leaf of plates: port.; 21 cm. — (Twayne's world authors series. TWAS 679) Includes index. 1. Colette, 1873-1954 — Criticism and interpretation. I. T. II. Series.
PQ2605.O28 Z834 1983   848/.91209 19   *LC* 82-17475   *ISBN* 0805765271

PQ2607 Desnos. Destouches (Céline)

Caws, Mary Ann.   **2.4506**
The surrealist voice of Robert Desnos / Mary Ann Caws. — Amherst: University of Massachusetts Press, 1977. vi, 222 p.: ill.; 24 cm. Includes index. 1. Desnos, Robert, 1900-1945 — Criticism and interpretation. I. T.
PQ2607.E75 Z6   841/.9/12   *LC* 76-25145   *ISBN* 0870232231

Poulet, Robert, 1893-.   **• 2.4507**
Entretiens familiers avec L.–F. Céline. Suivis d'un chapitre inédit de Casse-pipe. [Paris] Plon [1958] 113 p. 21 cm. (Tribune libre, 14) 1. Céline, Louis-Ferdinand, 1894-1961. I. Céline, Louis-Ferdinand, 1894-1961. Casse pipe. II. T. III. Title: Casse-pipe.
PQ 2607 E81 Z7 P86 1958   *LC* A 05-84961

Céline, Louis-Ferdinand, 1894-1961.   **• 2.4508**
Mort à crédit / Louis–Ferdinand Céline. — Paris: Gallimard, 1969,c1952. 693 p.; 20 cm. — (Collection Soleil; 260) I. T.
PQ2607.E834 M6 1969   *LC* 74-535888

Céline, Louis-Ferdinand, 1894-1961.   **• 2.4509**
[Mort à crédit. English] Death on the installment plan, by Louis–Ferdinand Céline. Translated from the French by Ralph Manheim. [New York, New Directions Pub. Corp., 1966] xi, 592 p. 21 cm. (A New Directions book) Translation of Mort à crédit. I. T.
PZ3.D475 De4   PQ2607.E834 Mx.   *LC* 66-18692

Céline, Louis-Ferdinand, 1894-1961.   **2.4510**
[Nord. English] North [by] Louis–Ferdinand Céline. Translated by Ralph Manheim. New York, Delacorte Press [1972] v, 454 p. 22 cm. The first of a trilogy, the title of the second being Castle to castle, and that of the third being Rigadoon. I. T.
PZ3.D475 No5 PQ2607.E834 Nx   843/.9/12   *LC* 75-164849

Céline, Louis-Ferdinand, 1894-1961.   **• 2.4511**
Voyage au bout de la nuit, suivi de Mort à crédit [par] Céline. [Paris, Gallimard, 1962] xxviii, 1088 p. 18 cm. I. Céline, Louis-Ferdinand, 1894-1961. Mort à crédit. II. T. III. Title: Mort à crédit.
PQ2607.E834 V6 1962   *LC* 67-118685

Céline, Louis-Ferdinand, 1894-1961.   **2.4512**
[Voyage au bout de la nuit. English] Journey to the end of the night / by Louis–Ferdinand Céline; translated from the French by Ralph Manheim. — New York: New Directions, 1983. 446 p.; 21 cm. Translation of: Voyage au bout de la nuit. I. Manheim, Ralph, 1907- II. T.
PQ2607.E834 V613 1983   843/.912 19   *LC* 82-7970   *ISBN* 081120846X

O'Connell, David.   **2.4513**
Louis–Ferdinand Céline / by David O'Connell. — Boston: Twayne Publishers, c1976. 175 p.: port.; 21 cm. — (Twayne's world authors series; TWAS 416: France) Includes index. 1. Céline, Louis-Ferdinand, 1894-1961. I. T.
PQ2607.E834 Z795   843/.9/12 B   *LC* 76-26059   *ISBN* 0805762566

Ostrovsky, Erika.   **• 2.4514**
Céline and his vision. New York, New York University Press, 1967. xiii, 225 p. 22 cm. 1. Céline, Louis-Ferdinand, 1894-1961. I. T.
PQ2607.E834 Z8   843/.9/12   *LC* 66-22221

Thiher, Allen, 1941-.   **2.4515**
Céline: the novel as delirium. New Brunswick, N.J., Rutgers University Press [1972] 275 p. 21 cm. 1. Céline, Louis-Ferdinand, 1894-1961. 2. Mental illness in literature I. T.
PQ2607.E834 Z9   843/.9/12   *LC* 77-185394   *ISBN* 0813507170

PQ2607.R–2611 Dr–F

Soucy, Robert, 1933-.   **2.4516**
Fascist intellectual, Drieu La Rochelle / Robert Soucy. — Berkeley: University of California Press, c1979. x, 451 p., [4] leaves of plates; 25 cm. Includes index. 1. Drieu La Rochelle, Pierre, 1893-1945. 2. Authors, French — 20th century — Biography. 3. Intellectuals — France — Biography. 4. Fascism — France. I. T.
PQ2607.R5 Z88   843/.9/12 B   *LC* 77-73504   *ISBN* 0520034635

Duhamel, Georges, 1884-1966.   ● **2.4517**
Chronique des Pasquier. — [Paris] Mercure de France [1964] 2 v. I. T.
PQ2607.U53C43x

Duras, Marguerite.   **2.4518**
L'amant / Marguerite Duras. — Paris: Editions de minuit, c1984. 142 p.; 19 cm. I. T.
PQ2607.U8245 A626 1984   843/.912 19   *LC* 84-239371   *ISBN* 2707306959

Duras, Marguerite.   ● **2.4519**
Amante anglaise. Paris: Gillimard, 1967. 198 p.; 18 cm. I. T.
PQ2607.U8245 A63   *LC* 67-89700

Duras, Marguerite.   **2.4520**
[Des journées entières dans les arbres. English] Whole days in the trees / by Marguerite Duras; translated from the French by Anita Barrows. — London: J. Calder; New York: Riverrun Press, 1984. 157 p.; 20 cm. — (A Calderbook; CB 406) ([Riverrun writers]) Translation of: Des journées entières dans les arbres. 1. Duras, Marguerite — Translations, English. I. T.
PQ2607.U8245 D413 1984   843/.912 19   *LC* 84-181895   *ISBN* 071453854X

Duras, Marguerite.   **2.4521**
Moderato cantabile / Marguerite Duras. — Paris: Éditions de minuit, 1958. 155 p. I. T.
PQ2607.U8245 M63   *LC* a 58-5260

Duras, Marguerite.   **2.4522**
Moderato cantabile. Translated by Richard Seaver. New York, Grove Press [1960] 120 p. 21 cm. (An evergreen original, E-257) I. T.
PQ2607.U8245 Mx   *LC* 60-11093

Cismaru, Alfred, 1929-.   **2.4523**
Marguerite Duras. — New York: Twayne Publishers, [1971] 171 p.; 21 cm. — (Twayne's world authors series, TWAS 147. France) 1. Duras, Marguerite. I. T.
PQ2607.U8245 Z6   843/.9/12   *LC* 70-125249

Eluard, Paul, 1895-1952.   ● **2.4524**
Oeuvres complètes ... Préface et chronologie de Lucien Scheler. Textes établis et annotés par Marcelle Dumas et Lucien Scheler. — [Paris,] Gallimard, 1968. 2 v. illus. 18 cm. — (Bibliothèque de la Pléiade) Bibliography: v. 2, p. [1317]-1446. I. Dumas, Marcelle, ed. II. Scheler, Lucien. ed. III. T.
PQ2609.L75 1968   848/.9/1209   *LC* 68-116324

Eluard, Paul, 1895-1952.   ● **2.4525**
Selected writings / Paul Eluard; with English translations by Lloyd Alexander, and introductory notes by Aragon, Louis Parrot and Claude Roy. — [New York: New Directions, 1951] xxxvi, 218 p.; 22 cm. — (New Directions series of selected writings.) I. Alexander, Lloyd. tr. II. T.
PQ2609.L75 A6 1951   *LC* 51-12202

Nugent, Robert.   **2.4526**
Paul Eluard. New York, Twayne Publishers [1974] 153 p. port. 22 cm. (Twayne's world authors series, TWAS 322. France) 1. Eluard, Paul, 1895-1952 — Criticism and interpretation. I. T.
PQ2609.L75 Z78   841/.9/12   *LC* 74-4132   *ISBN* 0805722998

Feydeau, Georges, 1862-1921.   ● **2.4527**
Théâtre complet. — Paris, Éditions du Bélier [1948-1956] 9 v. ports. 25 cm. — (Les Documents littéraires) I. T. II. Series.
PQ2611.E86 1948   842.91   *LC* 49-27665 *

Feydeau, Georges, 1862-1921.   ● **2.4528**
Four farces. Translated and with an introd. by Norman R. Shapiro. Chicago, University of Chicago Press [1970] liv, 346 p. illus. 23 cm. I. T.
PQ2611.E86 A28   842.8   *LC* 78-125164   *ISBN* 0226244768

Follain, Jean, 1903-1971.   **2.4529**
[D'après tout. English] D'après tout: poems / by Jean Follain; translated by Heather McHugh. — Princeton, N.J.: Princeton University Press, c1981. xiv, 184 p.; 23 cm. — (Lockert library of poetry in translation.) I. McHugh, Heather, 1948- II. T. III. Series.
PQ2611.O612 D313 1981   841/.912 19   *LC* 81-47126   *ISBN* 0691064768

Alain-Fournier, 1886-1914.   ● **2.4530**
Le Grand Meaulnes / Alain–Fournier. Paris: Émile-Paul, c1913, [1963 printing]. — 317 p.; 19 cm. I. T.
PQ2611.O85 G7 1963

Alain-Fournier, 1886-1914.   ● **2.4531**
[Grand Meaulnes. English] The wanderer (Le grand Meaulnes) Translated from the French by Françoise Delisle. Clifton [N.J.] A.M. Kelley, 1973 [c1928] xxxii, 306 p. 22 cm. (Houghton Mifflin reprint editions) Reprint of the ed. published by Houghton Mifflin, Boston. I. Delisle, Françoise Roussel. tr. II. T.
PZ3.F8263 Wan8 PQ2611.O85 G7x   843/.9/12   *LC* 74-128078   *ISBN* 0678035520

PQ2613 Genêt

Genet, Jean, 1910-.   ● **2.4532**
Oeuvres complètes / de Jean Genet. — [Paris]: Gallimard, c1951-. v.; 21 cm. 1. Genet, Jean, 1910- I. Sartre, Jean Paul, 1905- Saint Genet. II. T. III. Title: Saint Genet, comédien et martyr.
PQ2613.E53 1951   *LC* 51-28693

Genet, Jean, 1910-.   ● **2.4533**
[Balcon. English] The balcony (Le balcon) a play in nine scenes. Translated by Bernard Frechtman. New York, Grove Press [1958] 118 p. 21 cm. I. T.
PQ2613.E53 B313 1958a   842.91   *LC* 58-9490

Genet, Jean, 1910-.   ● **2.4534**
[Bonnes. English] The maids. Death watch. Two plays, translated from the French by Bernard Frechtman. With an introd. by Jean–Paul Sartre. New York, Grove Press [1954] 166 p. 20 cm. Translation of Les bonnes and Haute surveillance. I. T. II. Title: Deathwatch.
PQ2613.E53 B613   842.91   *LC* 53-7149

Genet, Jean, 1910-.   ● **2.4535**
The thief's journal / by Jean Genet; foreword by Jean–Paul Sartre; translated from the French by Bernard Frechtman. — New York: Grove Press, 1964. 268 p.; 21 cm. Translation of: Journal du Voleur. I. T. II. Title: Journal du Voleur.
PQ2613.E53 J613 1964   *LC* 64-24077

Genet, Jean, 1910-.   ● **2.4536**
Miracle of the rose / Translated from the French by Bernard Frechtman. — London: Blond, [c1965] 291 p. — I. T.
PZ3.G2866 Mi   PQ2613.E53M53.   848   *LC* 66-72583

Genet, Jean, 1910-.   ● **2.4537**
[Nègres, clownerie. English] The blacks, a clown show. Translated from the French by Bernard Frechtman. [1st ed.] New York, Grove Press [1960] 128 p. 21 cm. I. T.
PQ2613.E53 N43   842.912   *LC* 60-6340

Genet, Jean, 1910-.   ● **2.4538**
[Notre-Dame des Fleurs. English] Our Lady of the Flowers. Translated by Bernard Frechtman. Introd. by Jean–Paul Sarte. New York, Grove Press [1963] 318 p. 21 cm. I. T.
PZ3.G2866 Ou3   PQ2613.E53 Nx.   *LC* 61-6715

Genet, Jean, 1910-.   ● **2.4539**
The screens; a play in seventeen scenes. Translated from the French by Bernard Frechtman. — New York, Grove Press [1962] 201 p. 21 cm. I. T.
PQ2613.E53P33 1962   842.912   *LC* 62-13055

Genet, Jean, 1910-.   **2.4540**
[Querelle de Brest. English] Querelle / Jean Genet; translated from the original French by Anselm Hollo. — New York: Grove Press: distributed by Random House, 1974. 276 p.; 21 cm. Translation of Querelle de Brest. I. T.
PZ3.G2866 Qd3 PQ2613.E53 Q8x   843/.9/12   *LC* 73-17693   *ISBN* 0802100104

McMahon, Joseph H.   ● **2.4541**
The imagination of Jean Genet. — New Haven, Yale University Press, 1963. viii, 273 p. 21 cm. — (Yale Romanic studies, 2d ser., 10) Bibliography: p. 265-267. 1. Genet, Jean, 1910- I. T. II. Series.
PQ2613.E53Z77   842.912   *LC* 63-13969

Sartre, Jean Paul, 1905-. • 2.4542
Saint Genet, actor and martyr / J.P. Sartre; translated from the French by Bernard Frechtman. — New York: G. Baziller, 1963. 625 p.; 25 cm. 1. Genet, Jean, 1910- I. T.
PQ2613.E53 Z883   928.4   LC 63-15828

PQ2613 Ghelderode

Ghelderode, Michel de, 1898-1962. • 2.4543
Théâtre. — [Paris] Gallimard [1950-. v. 19 cm. I. T.
PQ2613.H17A19 1950   842.91   LC 51-20201

Ghelderode, Michel de, 1898-1962. • 2.4544
[Selected works. English. 1960] Seven plays. With an introd. by George Hauger. New York, Hill and Wang [1960-64] 2 v. 19 cm. (A Mermaid dramabook, MD19, MD30) I. T.
PQ2613.H17 A24   842.912   LC 60-14169

PQ2613 Gide

Gide, André, 1869-1951. • 2.4545
Théâtre. [Paris] Gallimard [1942] 364 p. 19 cm. At head of title: André Gide. On p. [4] of cover: 2. éd. I. T.
PQ2613.I2 A19 1942   LC 46-32092

Gide, André, 1869-1951. • 2.4546
My theater; five plays and an essay. Translated from the French by Jackson Mathews. [1st American ed. New York, Knopf, 1952, c1951] 274 p. 20 cm. I. T.
PQ2613I2 A26   LC 51-11098

Gide, André, 1869-1951. • 2.4547
[Selections. English. 1971] Pretexts; reflections on literature and morality. Selected, edited, and introduced by Justin O'Brien. [Translated by Angelo P. Bertocci and others] Freeport, N.Y., Books for Libraries Press [1971, c1959] 352 p. 23 cm. (Essay index reprint series) Essays from Prétextes, Nouveaux prétextes, Divers, and Incidences. 1. French literature — History and criticism. I. O'Brien, Justin, 1906-1968. ed. II. T.
PQ2613.I2 A27 1971   844/.9/12   LC 75-156648   ISBN 0836923960

Gide, André, 1869-1951. • 2.4548
Romans, récits et soties; œuvres lyriques. Introd. par Maurice Nadeau. Notices et bibliographie par Yvonne Davet et Jean–Jacques Thierry. [Paris, Gallimard, 1958] 1614 p. 18 cm. (Bibliothèque de la Pléiade, 135) I. T.
PQ2613.I2 A6 1958   LC 59-31061

Gide, André, 1869-1951. • 2.4549
So be it; or, The chips are down (Ainsi soit–il; ou, Les jeux sont faits) Translated from the French, with an introd. and notes by Justin O'Brien. 1st American ed. New York, Knopf, 1959. 165 p. 20 cm. I. T.
PQ2613.I2 A743   848.912   LC 59-8003

Gide, André, 1869-1951. 2.4550
Lafcadio's adventures / by André Gide; translated from the French by Dorothy Bussy. — New York: Knopf, 1928. 1v. I. T.
PQ2613.I2 C413 1980   843/.9/12   LC A29-362

Gide, André, 1869-1951. • 2.4551
[Faux-monnayeurs. English] The counterfeiters; with Journal of The counterfeiters. The novel translated from the French by Dorothy Bussy; the Journal translated from the French and annotated by Justin O'Brien. New York, Vintage Books [1973, c1951] ix, 467 p. 19 cm. I. Gide, André, 1869-1951. Journal des Faux-monnayeurs. English. 1973. II. T. III. Title: Journal of The Counterfeiters.
PZ3.G3613 Co18 PQ2613.I2 F3x   843/.9/12   LC 72-8064   ISBN 0394718429

Gide, André, 1869-1951. • 2.4552
Imaginary interviews / Translated from the French by Malcolm Cowley. New York: A.A. Knopf, 1944. xvii, 3-172 p., 1 l. 19 cm. The translation is based on the French text of Interviews imaginaires. At head of title: André Gide. First American edition in English. 1. French literature — History and criticism. I. Cowley, Malcolm, 1898- II. T.
PQ2613.I2 I47   848.91   LC 44-8537

Gide, André, 1869-1951. • 2.4553
The immoralist / André Gide; tr. from the French by Dorothy Bussy. — New York: Knopf, 1948. xi, 205 p.; 20 cm. Originally published as L'immoraliste. I. T.
PZ3.G3613 Im7 PQ2613.I2 I6x   843/.9/12

Gide, André, 1869-1951. • 2.4554
The fruits of the earth. Les nourritures terrestres & Les nouvelles nourritures; tr. from the French by Dorothy Bussy. [1st American ed.] New York, A. A. Knopf, 1949. 292 p. 20 cm. Translation of: Les nourritures terrestres. The author's Later fruits of the earth [les nouvelles nourritures] included: p. [165]-255. I. Gide, André, 1869-1951. Later fruits of the earth. 1949. II. T.
PQ2613.I2 N72   848.91   LC 49-10557

Gide, André, 1869-1951. • 2.4555
Oedipus and Theseus / André Gide; translated from the French by John Russell. — Standard ed. — London: Secker & Warburg, 1950. v, 116 p.; 19 cm. Translation of Oedipe, 1930 and Thesée, 1946. I. T. II. Title: Theseus.
PQ2613.I2 O42 1950a   LC 52-18674

Gide, André, 1869-1951. • 2.4556
Two symphonies: [Isabelle and The pastoral symphony] Translated from the French by Dorothy Bussy. New York: Knopf 1949[c1931] 233 p.; 20 cm. I. T. II. Title: Isabelle III. Title: The pastoral symphony
PQ2613.I2 Tx

Gide, André, 1869-1951. 2.4557
[Correspondence. English. Selections] Selected letters of André Gide and Dorothy Bussy / edited by Richard Tedeschi; with an introduction by Jean Lambert. — Oxford; New York: Oxford University Press, 1983. xxiii, 316 p.; 23 cm. Translation of selections from: Correspondance André Gide-Dorothy Bussy. 1. Gide, André, 1869-1951. Correspondence 2. Bussy, Dorothy — Correspondence. 3. Authors, French — 20th century — Correspondence. 4. Authors, English — 20th century — Correspondence. I. Bussy, Dorothy. Correspondence. English. Selections. 1983. II. Tedeschi, Richard. III. T.
PQ2613.I2 Z48513 1983   848/.91209 B 19   LC 82-14317   ISBN 019212224X

Gide, André, 1869-1951. 2.4558
Madeleine (Et nunc manet in te) [by] André Gide, tr. from the French, with an introduction and notes by Justin O'Brien. New York, Alfred A. Knopf, 1952. 98 p.: ill.; 20 cm. 1. Gide, Madeleine Louise Mathilde Rondeaux, 1867 (ca.)-1938 I. O'Brien, Justin, 1906-1968. II. T.
PQ2613.I2 Z523   848

Gide, André, 1869-1951. • 2.4559
The journals of André Gide, tr. from the French, with an introd. and notes, by Justin O'Brien. [1st American ed.] New York, A.A. Knopf, 1947-51. 4 v. port. 25 cm. 1. Authors — Correspondence, reminiscences, etc. I. O'Brien, Justin, 1906-1968. II. T.
PQ2613.I2 Z526   928.4   LC 47-30956

Gide, André, 1869-1951. • 2.4560
Journal, 1939–1942. — Paris: Gallimard, 1946. 230 p. 1. World War, 1939-1945 — Personal narratives, French. I. T.
PQ2613.I2 Z5282   LC 47-21162

Gide, André, 1869-1951. • 2.4561
If it die; an autobiography. Translated by Dorothy Bussy. New York: Random House [1957] 310 p.; 19 cm. (Modern library paperbacks) Translation of Si le grain ne meurt. I. T.
PQ2613.I2 Z52x   LC 57-11766

Gide, André, 1869-1951. • 2.4562
Self-portraits, the Gide/Valéry letters, 1890–1942. Edited by Robert Mallet. Abridged and translated by June Guicharnaud. Chicago, University of Chicago Press [c1966] 340 p.; 25 cm. Translation of André Gide - Paul Valéry: correspondance, 1890-1942. I. Valéry, Paul, 1871-1945. II. T.
PQ2613.I2 Z5693   LC 65-25125

Brée, Germaine. • 2.4563
[André Gide, l'insaisissable Protée. English] Gide. New Brunswick, N.J., Rutgers University Press [1963] vii, 302 p. 22 cm. Translation of André Gide, l'insaisissable protée. 1. Gide, André, 1869-1951 — Criticism and interpretation. I. T.
PQ2613.I2 Z61243   848.912   LC 62-18946

Hytier, Jean. • 2.4564
André Gide. Translated by Richard Howard. [1st ed.] Garden City, N. Y., Doubleday, 1962. 239 p. 19 cm. (Anchor books, A307) 1. Gide, André, 1869-1951. I. T.
PQ2613.I2Z6433   848.912   LC 62-10462

Martin, Claude, 1933-. • 2.4565
André Gide par lui même. [Paris] Éditions du Seuil [1963] 191 p. illus., ports., facsims. 18 cm. (Écrivains de toujours, 62) 1. Gide, André, 1869-1951. I. T.
PQ2613.I2 Z654615   LC 63-53350

PQ2613 Giono. Giraudoux. Gracq. Green

Giono, Jean, 1895-1970. • **2.4566**
Œuvres romanesques complètes. Éd. établie par Robert Ricatte avec la collaboration de Pierre Citron [et al.] [Paris] Gallimard [1971]-c1983. 6 v. illus. 18 cm. (Bibliothèque de la Pléiade, 230, 237, 256, 268, 285, 312) Includes index. I. Ricatte, Robert. II. T.
PQ2613.I57 1971   843/.912 19   *LC* 72-301762   *ISBN* 2070110710

Giono, Jean, 1895-1970. • **2.4567**
Giono par lui-même. Images et textes présentés par Claudine Chonez. Paris: Éditions du Seuil, 1956. 191 p.: ill.; 18 cm. (Écrivains de toujours. 32.) I. Chonez, Claudine, 1912- II. T. III. Series.
PQ2613.I57 A6 1956   *LC* 56-6108

Giraudoux, Jean, 1882-1944. • **2.4568**
Plays. Translated by Christopher Fry. With an introd. by Harold Clurman. New York, Oxford University Press, 1963-. v. 22 cm. Vol. 2 translated by Roger Gellert. I. T.
PQ2613.I74 A24   842.912   *LC* 63-6000

Giraudoux, Jean, 1882-1944. • **2.4569**
Théâtre. [Paris] B. Grasset, 1958-. v. 22 cm. I. T.
PQ2613.I74 Ax

Giraudoux, Jean, 1882-1944. **2.4570**
Siegfried et le Limousin / Jean Giraudoux. — Paris: Grasset, c1959. 244 p.; 17 cm. — (Le Livre de poche; 175) I. T.
PQ2613.I74 S5x

Giraudoux, Jean, 1882-1944. • **2.4571**
Three plays / Jean Giraudoux; translated by Phyllis la Farge with Peter H. Judd. — 1st ed. — New York: Hill and Wang, [1966,c1964]. 247p.; 20 cm. (Mermaid dramabook. MD31.) 'Volume 2' I. T. II. Series.
PQ2613.I74T43   *LC* 64-57870   *ISBN* 0809049600

Cohen, Robert, 1938-. • **2.4572**
Giraudoux; three faces of destiny [by] Robert Cohen. — Chicago: University of Chicago Press, [1968] viii, 164 p.; 23 cm. 1. Giraudoux, Jean, 1882-1944. I. T.
PQ2613.I74 Z564   842/.9/12   *LC* 68-29058

Le Sage, Laurent, 1913-. • **2.4573**
Jean Giraudoux; his life and works. [University Park] Pennsylvania State University, 1959. 238 p. 24 cm. Bibliographical references included in 'Notes' (p. 211-234) 1. Giraudoux, Jean, 1882-1944. I. T.
PQ2613.I74Z68   840.81   *LC* 59-12342

Gracq, Julien, 1910-. • **2.4574**
Le rivage des Syrtes / Julien Gracq. — Paris: J. Corti, c1951. 353 p.; 19 cm. I. T.
PQ2613.R124 R56

Green, Julien, 1900-. **2.4575**
[Autre. English] The other one [by] Julien Green. Translated from the French by Bernard Wall. [1st American ed.] New York, Harcourt Brace Jovanovich [1973] 282 p. 21 cm. 'A Helen and Kurt Wolff book.' Translation of L'Autre. I. T.
PZ3.G8237 Ot3 PQ2613.R3   843/.9/12   *LC* 72-91843   *ISBN* 0151704457

Green, Julien, 1900-. **2.4576**
Moïra / Julien Green. — Paris: Gallimard, 1982. 221 p. — (Collection 1000 soleils) I. T.
PQ2613.R3 M5x   *ISBN* 207050168X

Burne, Glenn S. (Glenn Stephen), 1921-. **2.4577**
Julian Green, by Glenn S. Burne. — New York, Twayne Publishers [1972] 159 p. 21 cm. — (Twayne's world authors series, TWAS 195. France) 1. Green, Julien, 1900- I. T.
PQ2613.R3 Z598   843/.9/12   *LC* 70-161816

PQ2617 Ionesco

Ionesco, Eugène. • **2.4578**
[Plays. 1954] Théâtre / Eugène Ionesco; préface de Jacques Lemarchand. — Paris: Gallimard, c1954-<c1981 >. v. <1-5, 7 >; 19-21 cm. I. T.
PQ2617.O6 A19 1954   842/.914 19   *LC* 55-17223

Ionesco, Eugène. • **2.4579**
Four plays: The bald soprano, The lesson, Jack; or, The submission, The chairs. Translated by Donald M. Allen. — New York, Grove Press [1958] 160 p. 21 cm. I. T. II. Title: The bald soprano. III. Title: The lesson. IV. Title: Jack; or, The submission. V. Title: The chairs.
PQ2617.O6A23 1958a   842.91   *LC* 58-1484

Ionesco, Eugène. • **2.4580**
[Journal en miettes. English] Fragments of a journal. Translated by Jean Stewart. New York, Grove Press [1968] 149 p. 21 cm. Translation of Journal en miettes. 1. Ionesco, Eugène — Biography. I. T.
PQ2617.O6 J613 1968b   848/.9/1403   *LC* 68-22009

Ionesco, Eugène. • **2.4581**
[Notes et contre-notes. English] Notes and counter notes; writings on the theatre. Translated from the French by Donald Watson. New York, Grove Press [1964] 271 p. 21 cm. 1. Ionesco, Eugène — Aesthetics — Addresses, essays, lectures. 2. Drama — Addresses, essays, lectures. I. T.
PQ2617.O6 N613   848.914   *LC* 64-13774

Ionesco, Eugène. • **2.4582**
[Plays. English] Rhinoceros, and other plays. Translated by Derek Prouse. New York, Grove Press [1960] 141 p. illus. 21 cm. (Evergreen original, E-259) I. T.
PQ2617.O6 R5 1960   842.914   *LC* 60-11090

Ionesco, Eugène. **2.4583**
[Présent passé, passé présent. English] Present past, past present; a personal memoir. Translated from the French by Helen R. Lane. New York, Grove Press [1971] 192 p. 22 cm. I. T.
PQ2617.O6 Z513   848/.9/1403 B   *LC* 70-139253

Coe, Richard N. • **2.4584**
Ionesco. — New York: Barnes & Noble, [1965, c1961] 120 p.; 19 cm. — (Writers and critics) 1. Ionesco, Eugène. I. T. II. Series.
PQ2617.O6 Z64   *LC* 65-8223

PQ2619 J

Jabès, Edmond. **2.4585**
[El. English] The book of questions: El, or, The last book / Edmond Jabès; translated from the French by Rosemarie Waldrop. — 1st ed. — Middletown, Conn.: Wesleyan University Press; Scranton, Pa.: Distributed by Harper & Row, c1984. 105 p.: ill. Translation of: El, ou, Le dernier livre. I. T. II. Title: El, or, The last book.
PQ2619.A112 E3813 1984   848/.91407 19   *LC* 83-27369   *ISBN* 0819551090

Jabès, Edmond. **2.4586**
Le livre des questions. [Paris] Gallimard [1963-65] 3 v.; 21 cm. I. T.
PQ2619.A112. L5   *LC* 66-33033

The Sin of the book, Edmond Jabès / edited by Eric Gould. **2.4587**
Lincoln: University of Nebraska Press, c1985. xxv, 252 p.; 23 cm. Includes index. 1. Jabès, Edmond — Criticism and interpretation — Addresses, essays, lectures. 2. Books and reading in literature — Addresses, essays, lectures. 3. Judaism in literature — Addresses, essays, lectures. 4. Jews in literature — Addresses, essays, lectures. I. Gould, Eric, 1943-
PQ2619.A112 Z88 1985   848/.91407 19   *LC* 84-5270   *ISBN* 0803221150

Jacob, Max, 1876-1944. • **2.4588**
Le cornet à dés. [Paris] Gallimard [1945] 248 p.; 19 cm. I. T.
PQ2619 A17 C6

Jacob, Max, 1876-1944. • **2.4589**
Le cornet à dés, II. Note liminaire d'André Salmon. Paris Gallimard [1955] 195 p.; 19 cm. I. T.
PQ2619 A17 C62

Jarry, Alfred, 1873-1907. **2.4590**
[Works. 1972.] Oeuvres complètes / Alfred Jarry;textes établis, présentés, et annotés par Michel Arrivé. — Paris: Gallimard, 1972. v.: ill. — (Bibliothèque de la Pléiade; 236) I. Arrivé, Michel. ed. II. T.
PQ2619.A65 1972   *LC* 72-361320

Jarry, Alfred, 1873-1907. • **2.4591**
Selected works. Edited by Roger Shattuck and Simon Watson Taylor. New York, Grove Press [1965] 280 p. illus., facsims., ports. 22 cm. The poems are in French and English, the prose selections in English translation. I. Shattuck, Roger. II. Taylor, Simon Watson. III. T.
PQ2619.A65 A26   848.8   *LC* 63-17002

Jarry, Alfred, 1873-1907. • **2.4592**
The Ubu plays. Edited, with an introd., by Simon Watson Taylor. — New York: Grove Press, [1969, c1968] 148 p.; 20 cm. — (An Evergreen original, E-496) I. T.
PQ2619.A65 A28 1969   842/.8   *LC* 69-19439

Jarry, Alfred, 1873-1907. • **2.4593**
Alfred Jarry, une étude par Jacques–Henry Levesque; oeuvres choisies. — [Paris] P. Seghers [1951] 219 p. illus., ports., facsims. 16 cm. — (Poètes

d'aujourd'hui, 24) 'Bibliographie des oeuvres d'Alfred Jarry': p. 207-215.
I. Levesque, Jacques Henry, ed. II. T.
PQ2619.A65A6 1951   *LC* A 52-6550

Beaumont, Keith, 1944-.   **2.4594**
Alfred Jarry: a critical and biographical study / Keith Beaumont. — New York: St. Martin's Press, 1984. 364 p., [16] p. of plates: ill., ports.; 24 cm. Includes index. 1. Jarry, Alfred, 1873-1907. 2. Authors, French — 19th century — Biography. I. T.
PQ2619.A65 Z58 1984   842/.8 B 19   *LC* 84-40443   *ISBN* 031201712X

LaBelle, Maurice Marc, 1939-.   **2.4595**
Alfred Jarry, nihilism and the theater of the absurd / Maurice Marc LaBelle. — New York: New York University Press, c1980. ix, 194 p.; 24 cm. — (The Gotham library of the New York University Press) Includes index. 1. Jarry, Alfred, 1873-1907 — Criticism and interpretation. 2. Nihilism in literature I. T.
PQ2619.A65 Z72   842/.8   *LC* 79-3009   *ISBN* 081474995X

PQ2621–2623 K–L

Kessel, Joseph, 1898-.   • **2.4596**
Le Lion: roman. — Paris: Gallimard, 1958. 316 p.; 19 cm. I. T.
PQ2621.E77 L5   *LC* a 59-2284

Klossowski, Pierre.   **2.4597**
La revocation de l'edit de Nantes: [Recit. — Paris]: Editions de minuit, 1959. 186 p. I. T.
PQ2621.L6 R4   *LC* A 59-7825

Larbaud, Valéry, 1881-1957.   **2.4598**
Œuvres. [Paris, Gallimard, c1957] 1310 p. 18 cm. I. T.
PQ2623.A65 1957   *LC* 58-23588

Leblanc, Maurice, 1864-1941.   **2.4599**
The exploits of Arsène Lupin / by Maurice Leblanc; translated by Alexander Teixeira de Mattos. — New York: Harper, 1907. 313 p. Translation of Aventures extraordinaires d'Arsène Lupin; 1st American publication. I. Teixeira de Mattos, Alexander, 1865-1921. II. T.
PQ2623.E24   843.91   *LC* 07-31976

Leduc, Violette, 1907-1972.   **2.4600**
La Bâtarde. With a foreword by Simone de Beauvoir. Translated from the French by Derek Coltman. New York, Farrar, Straus and Giroux [1965] xviii, 488 p. 25 cm. I. T.
PQ2623.E3657 B33   848.91403   *LC* 65-20104

Perse, Saint-John, 1889-1975.   **2.4601**
Song for an equinox / St.-John Perse; translated from the French by Richard Howard. Princeton, N.J.: Princeton University Press, c1977. 31 p.; 21 cm. — (Bollingen series. 69, 2) English and French. I. T. II. Series.
PQ2623.E386 C3813   841/.9/12   *LC* 76-45920   *ISBN* 0691099383

Perse, Saint-John, 1889-1975.   • **2.4602**
Éloges and other poems / St.-John Perse; translation by Louise Varèse. — Bilingual ed. — New York: Pantheon Books, c1956. viii, 103 p.; 24 cm. — (Bollingen series. 55) French and English on opposite pages. I. Varèse, Louise McCutcheon, 1890- II. T. III. Series.
PQ2623.E386 E4 1956   841.91   *LC* 56-10427

Léger, Alexis Saint-Léger, 1889-.   **2.4603**
Exil [by] Saint-John Perse; edited by Roger Little. — London: Athlone Press, 1973. xi, 119 p.; 21 cm. — (Athlone French poets.) French text, English introd. and notes. I. Little, Roger, ed. II. T. III. Series.
PQ2623.E386 E9 1973   841/.9/12   *LC* 73-177762   *ISBN* 0485147068

Leiris, Michel, 1901-.   **2.4604**
L'Age d'homme: précédé de De la Littérature considérée comme une tauromachie / Michel Leiris. — [Paris]: Gallimard, 1973. 215 p.; 18 cm. (Collection Folio; 435) 1. Leiris, Michel, 1901- I. Leiris, Michel, 1901- De la littérature considérée comme une tauromachie. 1973. II. T.
PQ2623.E424 Z5 1973   848/.9/1209 B   *LC* 74-196584

PQ2625.A3–A7 Maeterlinck. Mallet–Jorris

Maeterlinck, Maurice, 1862-1949.   **2.4605**
[Blue bird] The blue bird; and, The betrothal / by Maurice Maeterlinck; annotated by Paul P. Ricchio; illustrated by Michael Goscinsky. — Quakertown, Pa.: Philosophical Pub. Co., c1984. xxv, 271 p., [4] leaves of plates: ill. (some col.); 23 cm. 1. Maeterlinck, Maurice, 1862-1949 —

Translations, English. 2. Fairy tales — France. I. Ricchio, Paul P. II. Maeterlinck, Maurice, 1862-1949. Betrothal. c1984. III. T.
PQ2625.A33 1984   843/.8 19   *LC* 84-62200

Mallet-Joris, Françoise, 1930-.   **2.4606**
Le rempart des béguines: roman / Françoise Mallet–Joris. — Paris: R. Julliard, [1951] 190 p. I. T.
PQ2625.A711 R4   *LC* A51-8492

Mallet-Joris, Françoise, 1930-.   **2.4607**
The illusionist / Françoise Mallet–Joris; translated from the French by Herma Briffault. — New York: Farrar, Straus and Cudahy, [c1952] 250 p. Translation of Le rempart des béguines. I. T.
PQ2625.A711 R413   *LC* 52-12277

Mallet-Joris, Françoise, 1930-.   **2.4608**
The Red room / translated from the French by Herma Briffault. — New York: Farrar, Straus & Cudahy, 1956. 247 p. Translated of La Chambre rouge. I. T.
PQ2625.A7124 C313   *LC* 56-6154

Mallet-Joris, Françoise, 1930-.   **2.4609**
Le jeu du souterrain. — Paris: B. Grasset, [1973] 286 p.; 21 cm. — I. T.
PQ2625.A7124 J4   843/.9/14   *LC* 73-168840

Mallet-Joris, Françoise, 1930-.   **2.4610**
La maison de papier. — Paris, B. Grasset [1970] 272 p. 21 cm. I. T.
PQ2625.A7124M3   *LC* 72-475971

PQ2625 Malraux

Malraux, André, 1901-1976.   • **2.4611**
Malraux par lui–même / Gaëtan Picon. — Paris: Éditions du Seuil, 1959. 190 p.: ill., ports.; 19 cm. — (Écrivains de toujours; 12) 1. Malraux, André, 1901-1976. I. Picon, Gaëtan. II. T.
PQ2625A716 A16

Malraux, André, 1901-1976.   • **2.4612**
Romans. [Paris Gallimard] [1969] 863 p.; 18 cm. (Bibliothèque de la Pléiade, 70) I. T.
PQ2625 A716 A6

Malraux, André, 1901-1976.   • **2.4613**
Anti–memoirs. Translated by Terence Kilmartin. — [1st American ed.]. — New York: Holt, Rinehart, and Winston, [1968] 420 p.; 24 cm. I. T.
PQ2625.A716 A73 1968   848/.9/1203   *LC* 68-24751

Malraux, André, 1901-1976.   • **2.4614**
[Condition humaine. English] Man's fate (La condition humaine) Translated by Haakon M. Chevalier. New York, Random House [1968, c1934] 283 p. 22 cm.
PZ3.M2989 Man8 PQ2625.A716 C6x   843/.9/12   *LC* 68-7701

Malraux, André, 1901-1976.   • **2.4615**
[Conquérants. English] The conquerors / André Malraux; translated by Winifred Stephens Whale. — New York: Harcourt, Brace and Company, [1929] 4 p. l., 3-270 p.; 20 cm. Translation of Les conquérants. 1. China — History — 1912-1928 — Fiction. 2. China — History — 1928-1937 — Fiction. I. T.
PZ3.M2989 Co12 PQ2625.A716 C7x   843/.9/12   *LC* 72-91594   *ISBN* 0030077168

Malraux, André, 1901-1976.   **2.4616**
Man's hope / by André Malraux; translated from the French by Stuart Gilbert and Alastair Macdonald. New York, Random House [c1938] 4 p.l., 3-511 p. 22 cm. 'First printing.' London edition (G. Routledge and Sons, ltd.) has title: Days of hope. 1. Spain — History — Civil war, 1936-1939 — Fiction. I. T.
PQ2625.A716 E7x   843.91   *LC* 38-28904

Malraux, André, 1901-1976.   • **2.4617**
Les noyers de l'Altenburg / André Malraux. — [Paris]: Gallimard, 1948. 291 p.; 22 cm. 'Le texte suit celui de l'édition originale, après les coupures de la censure suisse.' I. T.
PQ2625A716 N6   *LC* 50-5882

Malraux, André, 1901-1976.   **2.4618**
[Noyers de l'Altenbourg. English.] The walnut trees of Altenburg / André Malraux; translated from the French by A.W. Fielding. — London [England]: J. Lehmann, 1952. 224 p.; 21 cm. Translation of: Les noyers de l'Altenbourg I. T.
PQ2625.A716 N613 1952   *LC* 52-30355

Malraux, André, 1901-1976. • **2.4619**
La voie royale. — Paris, B. Grasset [1930] 3 p. l., [11]-269, [1] p., 2 l. 19 cm. — (His Les puissances du desert. [1]) 'Cet ouvrage a paru précédemment dans les 'Cahiers verts'.' I. T.
PQ2625.A716V6 1930   843.91   *LC* 31-8720

Malraux, André, 1901-1976. • **2.4620**
The royal way. Translated by Stuart Gilbert. — New York, Random House [1955, c1935] 250 p. 19 cm. — (A Vintage book, V-136) (Modern library paperbacks, P15) I. T.
PZ3   PQ2625.A716 V6x.   *LC* 55-5730

Malraux, André, 1901-1976. **2.4621**
[Lazare. English] Lazarus / André Malraux; translated by Terence Kilmartin. — New York: Holt, Rinehart and Winston, 1977. 149 p.; 22 cm. — (His The mirror of limbo) Translation of Lazare. 1. Malraux, André, 1901-1976 — Biography. 2. Authors, French — 20th century — Biography. I. T.
PQ2625.A716 Z51713   843/.9/12 B   *LC* 76-58426   *ISBN* 0030153514

Boak, Denis. • **2.4622**
André Malraux. — Oxford: Clarendon P., 1968. xiv, 268 p.: plate, port.; 23 cm. 1. Malraux, André, 1901-1976. I. T.
PQ2625.A716 Z63   848/.9/1208   *LC* 68-103250   *ISBN* 0198153791

Lacouture, Jean. **2.4623**
[André Malraux. English] André Malraux / Jean Lacouture; translated from the French by Alan Sheridan. — 1st American ed. — New York: Pantheon Books, 1976. 510 p., [4] leaves of plates: ill.; 25 cm. 1. Malraux, André, 1901-1976 — Biography. I. T.
PQ2625.A716 Z686813 1975   843/.9/12   *LC* 75-10361   *ISBN* 0394483677

Lewis, R. W. B. (Richard Warrington Baldwin). ed. • **2.4624**
Malraux; a collection of critical essays. Englewood Cliffs, N.J., Prentice-Hall [1964] 181 p. 21 cm. (A Spectrum book: Twentieth century views, S-TC-37) 1. Malraux, André, 1901-1976. I. T.
PQ2625.A716 Z69   843.912   *LC* 64-14537

PQ2625 Martin du Gard. Mauriac

Martin du Gard, Roger, 1881-. • **2.4625**
Jean Barois / translated by Stuart Gilbert. — New York: Viking Press, 1949. 365 p.; 22 cm. A novel I. T.
PQ2625.A823 J413   *LC* 49-8550

Martin Du Gard, Roger, 1881-1958. • **2.4626**
The Thibaults / Roger Martin du Gard; translated by Stuart Gilbert. — New York: Viking Press, 1939. 371 p.; 22 cm. I. T.
PQ2625.A823 Tx

Mauriac, Claude, 1914-. • **2.4627**
La marquise sortit à cinq heures: roman / Claude Mauriac. —. Paris: Michel, 1961. 313 p. I. T.
PQ2625.A929 M3   *LC* a 62-1069

Mauriac, François, 1885-1970. **2.4628**
[Selected works. 1978] Œuvres romanesques et théâtrales complètes / Mauriac; ed. établie, présentée et annotée par Jacques Petit. — [Paris]: Gallimard, c1978-c1985. 4 v.: maps; 18 cm. (Bibliothèque de la Pléiade; 271, 279, 288, 323) I. Petit, Jacques, 1928- II. T.
PQ2625.A93 A6 1978   843/.9/12   *LC* 78-374821

Mauriac, François, 1885-1970. • **2.4629**
The desert of love. Translated by Gerard Hopkins. New York, Pellegrini & Cudahy [1951] 214 p. 21 cm. I. T.
PZ3.M4463De2 PQ2625.A93D413 1951   843.91   *LC* 51-12060

Mauriac, François, 1885-1970. • **2.4630**
The Frontenacs. Translated by Gerard Hopkins. New York, Farrar, Straus and Cudahy [1961] 185 p. 21 cm. Translation of Le mystère Frontenac. I. T.
PQ2625.A93 Mx   *LC* 61-12297

Mauriac, François, 1885-1970. • **2.4631**
Vipers' tangle / trans. by Warre B. Wells. Garden City, N.Y.: Image Books 1957. 199 p.; 19 cm. (Doubleday image books; D51.) I. T.
PQ2625.A93 N6x   843.91   *LC* 57-3389

Mauriac, François, 1885-1970. • **2.4632**
Thérèse: a portrait in four parts, [by] François Mauriac; translated by Gerald Hopkins. Garden City, N.Y.: Doubleday, 1956. 308 p.; 18 cm. (Doubleday anchor book; A79.) I. T.
PQ2625A93 T5x   *LC* 47-31392   *ISBN* 0374503338

PQ2625.E–2629 Me–O

Michaux, Henri, 1899-. • **2.4633**
Henri Michaux, une étude, un choix de poèmes, et une bibliographie par René Bertelé, un manuscrit, des inédits, des dessins et des peintures. — Nouv. ed. — [Paris] P. Seghers [1949] 219 p. illus., facsim. 16 cm. — (Poètes d'aujourd'hui, 5) 'Bibliographie des oeuvres d'Henri Michaux': p. 211-215. I. Bertelé, René. ed. II. T.
PQ2625.I2A17

Michaux, Henri, 1899-. • **2.4634**
[Espace du dedans. English and French] Selected writings: The space within. Translated with an introd. by Richard Ellman. [New York, New Directions Pub. Corp., 1968] xxiii, 2-297 p. 21 cm. (A New Directions paperbook, 269) French text and English translation of L'espace du dedans. I. T. II. Title: Space within.
PQ2625.I2 A6 1968   841/.9/12   *LC* 68-25547

Michaux, Henri, 1899-. **2.4635**
[Grandes épreuves de l'esprit. English] The major ordeals of the mind, and the countless minor ones. Translated by Richard Howard. [1st ed.] New York, Harcourt Brace Jovanovich [1974] 170 p. 21 cm. 'A Helen and Kurt Wolff book.' Translation of Les grandes épreuves de l'esprit et les innombrables petites. Autobiographical. 1. Michaux, Henri, 1899- 2. Drug abuse I. T.
PQ2625.I2 Z5213   848/.9/1207 B   *LC* 73-16237   *ISBN* 0151557209 *ISBN* 0156552507

Broome, Peter, 1937-. **2.4636**
Henri Michaux / by Peter Broome. — London: Athlone Press, 1977. [6], 153 p.; 21 cm. — (Athlone French poets) Distributed by Humanities Press, Atlantic Highlands, N.J. Includes index. 1. Michaux, Henri, 1899- — Criticism and interpretation. I. T.
PQ2625.I2 Z585 1977   841/.9/12   *LC* 78-300411   *ISBN* 0485146053

La Charité, Virginia A. **2.4637**
Henri Michaux / by Virginia A. La Charité. — Boston: Twayne Publishers, c1977. 148 p.: port.; 21 cm. — (Twayne's world authors series; TWAS 465: France) Includes index. 1. Michaux, Henri, 1899- — Criticism and interpretation. I. T.
PQ2625.I2 Z68   848/.9/1209   *LC* 77-5325   *ISBN* 0805763023

Montherlant, Henry de, 1896-1972. • **2.4638**
Romans et oeuvres de fiction non théâtrales / Montherlant; préface de Roger Secrétain. — [Paris]: Gallimard, 1959. xxxiv, 1564 p. — (Bibliothèque de la Pléiade; 136) I. T.
PQ2625.O45 A1 1959

Montherlant, Henry de, 1896-1972. • **2.4639**
Théâtre. Préf. de J. de Laprade. [Paris: Gallimard, 1955, c1954] xl, 1089 p.; 17 cm. (Bibliothèque de la Pléiade. 106.) I. Laprade, Jacques de. II. T. III. Series.
PQ2625.O45 A19 1955   *LC* 55-6575

Montherlant, Henry de, 1896-1972. • **2.4640**
[Jeunes filles. English] The girls; a tetralogy of novels. Translated from the French by Terence Kilmartin. Introd. by Peter Quennell. [1st U.S. ed.] New York, Harper & Row [1968]. 639 p. 22 cm. Translation of Les jeunes filles. I. T.
PZ3.M7683 Gi3 PQ2625.O45 J4x   843/.9/12   *LC* 68-28224

Obaldia, René de. **2.4641**
La passion d'Émile / René de Obaldia. — Paris: Balland, c1979. 138 p.; 20 cm. — (L'Instant romanesque) I. T.
PQ2629.B3 P3   843/.914   *LC* 80-455679   *ISBN* 2715801769

Oyono, Ferdinand, 1929-. **2.4642**
The old man and the medal; translated from the French by John Reed. London Heinemann 1967. 5,167p. I. T.
PQ2629 Y65 V553

PQ2631 P

Pagnol, Marcel, 1895-1974. **2.4643**
Oeuvres complètes de Marcel Pagnol. — Paris: Club de l'Honnête Homme, 1977-. v.: ill. I. T.
PQ2631.A3

Péguy, Charles, 1873-1914. • **2.4644**
Oeuvres poétiques complètes / Charles Péguy; introduction de François Porché, chronologie de la vie de l'oeuvre par Pierre Péguy . — [Paris]: Gallimard, 1948. xl, 1404 p.; 18 cm. (Bibliothèque de la Pléiade. 60) I. T. II. Series.
PQ2631.E25 A17

Péguy, Charles, 1873-1914. • **2.4645**
Basic verities, prose and poetry; rendered into English by Ann and Julian Green. — New York, Pantheon books inc. [1943] 282 p. 24 cm. At head of title: Charles Péguy. 'First edition.' French and English on opposite pages. 'Sources': p. 281-282. I. Green, Anne, 1899- tr. II. Green, Julien, 1900- joint tr. III. T.
PQ2631.E25A6 1943   348.91   *LC* 43-1662

Péret, Benjamin, 1899-1959. **2.4646**
[Poems. English & French. Selections] A marvelous world: poems / by Benjamin Péret; translated, with an introduction, by Elizabeth R. Jackson. — A Bilingual ed. — Baton Rouge: Louisiana State University Press, c1985. xxi, 97 p.; 24 cm. I. T.
PQ2631.E348 A24 1985   841/.912   *LC* 80-13631   *ISBN* 080710664X

Matthews, J. H. **2.4647**
Benjamin Péret / by J. H. Matthews. — Boston: Twayne Publishers, [1975] 176 p.: port.; 22 cm. (Twayne's world authors series; TWAS 359: France) Includes index. 1. Péret, Benjamin, 1899-1959 — Criticism and interpretation. I. T.
PQ2631.E348 Z7   PQ2631E348 Z7.   841/.912   *LC* 74-30229   *ISBN* 0805726918

Pieyre de Mandiargues, André, 1909-. • **2.4648**
La motocyclette / André Pieyre de Mandiargues. — Paris: Gallimard, 1963. 223 p. I. T.
PQ2631.I49 M6   *LC* 66-48449

Pieyre de Mandiargues, André, 1909-. • **2.4649**
The motorcycle / by André Pieyre de Mandiargues; translated from the French by Richard Howard. — New York: Grove Press, c1965. 187 p.; 21 cm. Translation of La motocyclette. I. T.
PZ4.P619 Mo7   PQ2631.I49 M613.   843/.9/14   *LC* 65-14199

Bond, David J. **2.4650**
The fiction of André Pieyre de Mandiargues / David J. Bond. — 1st ed. — [Syracuse]: Syracuse University Press, 1982. xvii, 133 p.; 24 cm. Includes index. 1. Pieyre de Mandiargues, André, 1909- — Criticism and interpretation. I. Pieyre de Mandiargues, André, 1909- II. T.
PQ2631.I49 Z56 1982   843/.914 19   *LC* 82-5894   *ISBN* 0815622651

Pinget, Robert. • **2.4651**
... Plays. — [1st American ed.]. — New York: Hill and Wang, [1966]-. v.   ; 21 cm. Translated from the French by Barbara Bray. I. T.
PQ2631.I638 A23 1966   842.914   *LC* 66-15897

Pinget, Robert. **2.4652**
Fable / Robert Pinget; translated by Barbara Wright. — New York: Red Dust, 1980. 63 p.; 22 cm. I. T.
PQ2631.I638 F33   *LC* 80-50203   *ISBN* 0873760360

Pinget, Robert. **2.4653**
The Libera me Domine / translated by Barbara Wright. — New York: Red Dust, 1978. 239 p.; 21 cm. I. T.
PZ4.P653 Li PQ2631.I638Lx   843/.9/14   *LC* 78-53831   *ISBN* 0873760255

Pinget, Robert. **2.4654**
Passacaglia: a novel / Robert Pinget; translated by Barbara Wright. — New York: Red Dust, 1978, c1975. 96 p.; 22 cm. Translation of Passacaille. I. T.
PQ2631I638 P3513 1978   843.91   *LC* 78-53832   *ISBN* 0873760336

Pinget, Robert. **2.4655**
[Quelqu'un. English] Someone / Robert Pinget; translated by Barbara Wright. — New York: Red Dust, 1984. 168 p.; 22 cm. 'Originally published as Quelqu'un by Les Editions de Minuit, Paris, 1965.' I. T. II. Title: Quelqu'un. English
PQ2631.I638 Q3 E5 1984   [Fic]   *LC* 83-63101   *ISBN* 0873760433

Ponge, Francis. **2.4656**
The voice of things. Edited and translated with an introd. by Beth Archer. — [1st ed.]. — New York, McGraw-Hill Book Co. [1972] ix, 190 p. 22 cm. Includes a selection of poems from the author's Le parti pris des choses and other works. I. Brombert, Beth Archer. tr. II. T.
PQ2631.O643 A23   848/.9/1407   *LC* 72-3185   *ISBN* 0070737533

Ponge, Francis. **2.4657**
Le parti pris des choses / Francis Ponge; edited by Ian Higgins. — London: Athlone Press; [Atlantic Highlands], N.J.: distributed by Humanities Press, 1979. x, 116 p.; 21 cm. — (Athlone French poets) Text in French with introduction and commentary in English. I. Higgins, Ian. II. T.
PQ2631.O643 P3 1979   841/.914   *LC* 80-465301   *ISBN* 0485147149

Sorrell, Martin. **2.4658**
Francis Ponge / by Martin Sorrell. — Boston: Twayne Publishers, 1981. 155 p.; 21 cm. — (Twayne's world authors series; TWAS 577: France) Includes index. 1. Ponge, Francis. 2. Authors, French — 20th century — Biography. I. T.
PQ2631.O643 Z815   841/.914 19   *LC* 80-19178   *ISBN* 0805764194

Prévert, Jacques, 1900-. **2.4659**
Histoires et d'autres histoires. — [Paris, Gallimard, 1963] 246 p.; 19 cm. — (Le point du jour) Poems. I. T.
PQ2631.R387 P3

Prévert, Jacques, 1900-. • **2.4660**
Paroles / Jacque Prévert. — [Paris: Éditions du Point du jour] 1945 [c1946] 224 p.; 22 cm. (Le point du jour) I. T.
PQ2631.R387 P3

PQ2631 Proust

Proust, Marcel, 1871-1922. • **2.4661**
A la recherche du temps perdu. Texte établi et présenté par Pierre Clarac et André Ferré. — [Paris, Gallimard, 1954] 3 v. 18 cm. — (Bibliothèque de la Piéiade, 100-102) 'Errata de l'index des noms propres': 7 p. inserted in v. 3. I. T.
PQ2631.R63A7 1954   *LC* 55-35954

Proust, Marcel, 1871-1922. **2.4662**
[A la recherche du temps perdu. English] Remembrance of things past / [Marcel Proust]; translated by C.K. Scott Moncrieff and Terence Kilmartin. — New York: Random House, c1981. 3 v.; 21 cm. Vol. 3's Time regained, translated by Andreas Mayor. Translation of A la recherche du temps perdu. I. T.
PQ2631.R63 A72 1981   843/.912 19   *LC* 79-5542   *ISBN* 0394506448

Brée, Germaine. • **2.4663**
[Du temps perdu au temps retrouvé. English] Marcel Proust and deliverance from time. Translated from the French by C. J. Richards and A. D. Truitt. [2d ed.] New Brunswick, N.J., Rutgers University Press [1969] viii, 252 p. 22 cm. Translation of Du Temps perdu au Temps retrouvé. 1. Proust, Marcel, 1871-1922. A la recherche du temps perdu. I. T.
PQ2631.R63 A782 1969   843/.9/12   *LC* 75-4549   *ISBN* 0813505925

Genette, Gérard, 1930-. **2.4664**
[Discours du récit. English.] Narrative discourse: an essay in method / Gérard Genette; translated by Jane E. Lewin; foreword by Jonathan Culler. — Ithaca, N.Y.: Cornell University Press, 1980. 285 p.; 23 cm. Translation of Discours du récit, a portion of the 3d vol. of the author's Figures, essais. Includes index. 1. Proust, Marcel, 1871-1922. A la recherche du temps perdu. 2. Discourse analysis, Narrative I. T.
PQ2631.R63 A791713   808.3/3   *LC* 79-13499   *ISBN* 0801410991

Hewitt, James Robert. **2.4665**
Marcel Proust / James Robert Hewitt. — New York: F. Ungar Pub. Co., [1975] x, 124 p.; 21 cm. (Modern literature monographs) Includes index. 1. Proust, Marcel, 1871-1922. A la recherche du temps perdu. I. T.
PQ2631.R63 A818   843/.9/12   *LC* 74-76127   *ISBN* 0804423822

Proust, Marcel, 1871-1922. • **2.4666**
Contre Sainte–Beuve; suivi de Nouveaux mélanges. Préf. de Bernard de Fallois. — Paris, Gallimard [1954] 446 p. 19 cm. I. T. II. Title: Nouveaux mélanges.
PQ2631.R63C62   *LC* 55-199

Proust, Marcel, 1871-1922. • **2.4667**
On art and literature, 1896–1919. Translated by Sylvia Townsend Warner. — [New York]: Meridian Books, [1958] 416 p.; 21 cm. — (Greenwich editions) Translation of Contre Sainte-Beuve; suivi de Nouveax melanges. I. T.
PQ2631.R63 C72   801   *LC* 57-6687

Proust, Marcel, 1871-1922. • **2.4668**
Jean Santeuil. Préf. d'André Maurois. [Paris] Gallimard [1952] 3 v.; 19 cm. I. T.
PQ2631.R63 J4

Proust, Marcel, 1871-1922. • **2.4669**
Jean Santeuil. Translated by Gerard Hopkins. With a pref. by André Maurois. New York, Simon and Schuster, 1956 [c1955] xxiv, 744 p. 22 cm. I. T.
PQ2631.R63J413 1956   *LC* 55-12297

Proust, Marcel, 1871-1922. **2.4670**
[Correspondence. Selections. English] Marcel Proust, selected letters, 1880–1903 / edited by Philip Kolb; translated by Ralph Manheim; introductions by J.M. Cocking. — 1st ed. — Garden City, N.Y.: Doubleday, 1983. xxv, 376 p.: ports.; 24 cm. Translation of selections from Marcel Proust's Correspondance. Includes index. 1. Proust, Marcel, 1871-1922.

Correspondence 2. Novelists, French — 20th century — Correspondence. I. Kolb, Philip. II. T.
PQ2631.R63 Z48 1983   843/.912 B 19   *LC* 81-43567   *ISBN* 038514394X

Fernandez, Ramon, 1894-1944.   • **2.4671**
Proust / par Ramon Fernandez. — Paris: Nouvelle Revue critique, [1944]. 207 p.: ports., fac-sim.; 25 cm. — (A la gloire de...) I. T.
PQ2631.R63 Z586   *LC* 50-53035

Girard, René, 1923- ed.   • **2.4672**
Proust: a collection of critical essays. — Englewood Cliffs, N.J.: Prentice-Hall, [1962] 182 p.; 21 cm. — (Twentieth century views) (A Spectrum book, S-TC-4.) 1. Proust, Marcel, 1871-1922 — Criticism and interpretation — Addresses, essays, lectures. I. T.
PQ2631.R63 Z6135   843.912   *LC* 62-9308

Hindus, Milton.   • **2.4673**
A reader's guide to Marcel Proust. — [New York]: Farrar, Straus and Cudahy, [1962] 275 p.; 21 cm. 1. Proust, Marcel, 1871-1922. I. T.
PQ2631.R63 Z626   843.912   *LC* 62-11524

Painter, George Duncan, 1914-.   • **2.4674**
Proust, by George D. Painter. Maps drawn by Samuel H. Bryant. — [1st ed.]. — Boston: Little, Brown, [1959-1965] 2 v.: illus., maps, ports.; 22 cm. 'An Atlantic Monthly Press Book.' 1. Proust, Marcel, 1871-1922 — Biography. I. T.
PQ2631.R63 Z7896   928.4   *LC* 59-7629

Poulet, Georges.   **2.4675**
[Espace proustien. English] Proustian space / by Georges Poulet; translated by Elliott Coleman. — Baltimore: Johns Hopkins University Press, c1977. 113 p.; 21 cm. Translation of L'espace proustien. 1. Proust, Marcel, 1871-1922 — Criticism and interpretation. I. T.
PQ2631.R63 Z82713   843/.9/12   *LC* 76-47390   *ISBN* 0801819210

PQ2633 Q

Queneau, Raymond, 1903-1976.   **2.4676**
[Poems. Selections. English & French] Pounding the pavements; Beating the bushes; and other pataphysical poems / Raymond Queneau; translated by Teo Savory. — Greensboro, N.C.: Unicorn Press, c1985. vii, 207 p.; 23 cm. English and French. Half title: Pataphysical poems. Title on added t.p.: Courir les rues; Battre la campagne; et d'autres poèmes pataphysiques. 1. Queneau, Raymond, 1903-1976 — Translations, English. I. Savory, Teo. II. T. III. Title: Pounding the pavements. IV. Title: Beating the bushes. V. Title: Pataphysical poems. VI. Title: Courir les rues. VII. Title: Battre la campagne.
PQ2633.U43 A27 1985   841/.912 19   *LC* 84-28012   *ISBN* 0877751722

Queneau, Raymond, 1903-1976.   **2.4677**
[Dimanche de la vie. English] The Sunday of life: a novel / by Raymond Queneau; translated from the French by Barbara Wright. — New York: New Directions, 1977. xi, 180 p.; 21 cm. Translation of Le Dimanche de la vie. I. T.
PQ2633.U43 D513 1977   843/.9/12   *LC* 76-49628   *ISBN* 0811206459

Queneau, Raymond, 1903-1976.   • **2.4678**
Exercices de style. — Paris: Gallimard, 1947. 199 p.; 19 cm. I. T.
PQ2633.U43 E9   848.91   *LC* 47-7229

Queneau, Raymond, 1903-1976.   **2.4679**
[On est toujours trop bon avec les femmes. English] We always treat women too well: a novel / by Raymond Queneau; translated from the French by Barbara Wright. — New York: New Directions, 1981. 174 p.: maps; 21 cm. Translation of On est toujours trop bon avec les femmes. 'Originally published under the pseudonym Sally Mara.' I. T.
PQ2633.U43 O513 1981   843/.912 19   *LC* 80-26462   *ISBN* 0811207927

Queneau, Raymond, 1903-1976.   **2.4680**
[Vol d'Icare. English] The flight of Icarus. Translated by Barbara Wright. [New York, New Directions Pub. Corp., 1973] 191 p. 21 cm. (A New Directions book) Translation of Le vol d'Icare. I. T.
PQ2633.U43 V613 1973   843/.9/12   *LC* 73-76900   *ISBN* 0811204820 *ISBN* 0811204839

Queneau, Raymond, 1903-1976.   • **2.4681**
Zazie dans le metro. — Paris: Gallimard, 1959. 253 p.; 17 cm. (Collection Folio) I. T.
PQ2633.U43 Z25   *LC* 60-417

Sagan, Françoise, 1935-.   • **2.4682**
Bonjour tristesse, roman [par] Françoise Sagan [pseud.]. — Paris, Julliard [1954] 188 p. 19 cm. I. T.
PQ2633.U74B6   *LC* 54-26075 rev

PQ2635 R

Radiguet, Raymond, 1903-1923.   • **2.4683**
Le Diable au corps: roman. — Paris: B. Grasset, 1925. 240 p.; 20 cm. I. T.
PQ2635.A25 D5   *LC* 44-50663

Radiguet, Raymond, 1903-1923.   • **2.4684**
[Diable au corps. English] The devil in the flesh: a novel; translated from the French by A. M. Sheridan Smith. London, Calder & Boyars, 1968. 127 p. 21 cm. Translation of Le diable au corps. I. T.
PZ3.R118 De7   PQ2635.A25 D5x.   *LC* 68-100457

Renard, Jules, 1864-1910.   • **2.4685**
Oeuvres / Jules Renard; textes établis, presentés, et annotés par Léon Guichard. — [Paris]: Gallimard, 1970-. v. (Bibliothèque de la Pléiade, 222..) I. Guichard, Léon, 1899- II. T.
PQ2635.E48 1970   843   *LC* 72-558449

Reverdy, Pierre, 1889-1960.   **2.4686**
Roof slates and other poems of Pierre Reverdy / translated, with prefaces by Mary Ann Caws and Patricia Terry. — Boston: Northeastern University Press, 1981. xx, 273 p.; 24 cm. Includes index. I. Caws, Mary Ann. II. Terry, Patricia Ann, 1929- III. T.
PQ2635.E85 A17 1981   841/.912 19   *LC* 80-26806   *ISBN* 093035009X

Robbe-Grillet, Alain, 1922-.   **2.4687**
Dans le Labyrinthe / Alain Robbe–Grillet. — Paris: Éditions de minuit, 1959. 221 p.; 20 cm. I. T.
PQ2635.O117 D3   *LC* 60-2764   *ISBN* 2707300829

Robbe-Grillet, Alain, 1922-.   **2.4688**
[Djinn. English] Djinn / Alain Robbe–Grillet; translated from the French by Yvone Lenard and Walter Wells. — 1st ed. — New York: Grove Press, 1982. 128 p.; 22 cm. — I. T.
PQ2635.O117 D5413 1982   843/.914 19   *LC* 81-86393   *ISBN* 0394525698

Robbe-Grillet, Alain, 1922-.   • **2.4689**
Les gommes. [Paris] Éditions de Minuit [1953] 257 p. 22 cm. I. T.
PQ2635.O117 G6   *LC* 53-33111

Robbe-Grillet, Alain, 1922-.   • **2.4690**
The erasers. Translated by Richard Howard. New York, Grove Press, c1964. 256 p. 21 cm. Translation of Les gommes. I. T.
PQ2635.O117.G6x   *LC* 61-11766

Robbe-Grillet, Alain, 1922-.   • **2.4691**
La jalousie: roman. Paris: Editions de minuit, c1957. 218 p.; 19 cm. I. T.
PQ2635.O117 J3   *LC* 57-6825

Robbe-Grillet, Alain, 1922-.   • **2.4692**
Jealousy, a novel. Translated by Richard Howard. New York, Grove Press [1959] 149 p. illus. 21 cm. I. T.
PQ2635.O117 Jx   *LC* 59-13890

Robbe-Grillet, Alain, 1922-.   • **2.4693**
Le voyeur: roman. Paris: Editions de Minuit, c1955. 255 p.; 20 cm. I. T.
PQ2635.O117 V6   *LC* 55-10483

Leki, Ilona.   **2.4694**
Alain Robbe–Grillet / by Ilona Leki. — Boston: Twayne Publishers, c1983. 187 p.: port.; 21 cm. — (Twayne's world authors series. TWAS 682) Includes index. 1. Robbe-Grillet, Alain, 1922- — Criticism and interpretation. I. T. II. Series.
PQ2635.O117 Z72 1983   843/.914 19   *LC* 82-15654   *ISBN* 0805765298

Morrissette, Bruce, 1911-.   **2.4695**
[Romans de Robbe-Grillet. English] The novels of Robbe–Grillet / by Bruce Morrissette; translated from the French, rev., updated, and expanded by the author; with a foreword by Roland Barthes. — Ithaca: Cornell University Press, 1975. 318 p.; 23 cm. Translation of Les romans de Robbe-Grillet. 1. Robbe-Grillet, Alain, 1922- — Criticism and interpretation. I. T.
PQ2635.O117 Z7613   843/.9/14   *LC* 74-29089   *ISBN* 0801408520

Roblès, Emmanuel.   **2.4696**
Three plays / by Emmanuel Roblès; translated, with an introd. by James A. Kilker; foreword by Emmanuel Roblès; with a bibliography of the theatre of

Roblès by Marie J. Kilker. — Carbondale: Southern Illinois University Press, c1977. xxiii, 200 p.: ill.; 24 cm. In English. I. T.
PQ2635.O1845 A25   842/.9/12   *LC* 77-24662   *ISBN* 0809308223

Rochefort, Christiane.   **2.4697**
Le repos du guerrier. — [Paris] B. Grasset [1958] 245 p. I. T.
PQ2635.O2122R4 1958

Rolland, Romain, 1866-1944.   **2.4698**
Jean–Christophe. Éd. définitive. Paris, Editions Albin Michel, 1948, i.e. [1949] xviii, 1593, [12] p.; 20 cm. I. T.
PQ2635.O5 J2 1949

Rolland, Romain, 1866-1944.   **2.4699**
Jean–Christophe in Paris: The market–place, Antoinette, The house, by Romian Rolland, translated by Gilbert Cannan. New York, H. Holt and company, 1911. 3 p.l., 3-473 p. 20 cm. Second series of the whole work; in the original in three separate vols. Preceded by Jean-Christophe (the first series, in the original in four vols.) and followed by Jean-Christophe - Journey's end (the third series, in the original in three vols.) I. Cannan, Gilbert, 1884-1955. tr. II. T.
PQ2635.O5 Jx   *LC* 11-27915

Rostand, Edmond, 1868-1918.   • **2.4700**
Cyrano de Bergerac: comédie heroïque en cinq actes et vers. — Paris, E. Fasquelle, 1898. 5 p. l., [13]-225 p. 20 cm. I. T.
PQ2635.O7 C9 1898c   *LC* 13-4520

Roy, Claude, 1915-.   **2.4701**
La traversée du pont des Arts: roman / Claude Roy. — [Paris]: Gallimard, c1979. 244 p.; 21 cm. — I. T.
PQ2635.O9644 T7   843/.914   *LC* 80-455673

PQ2637–2643 S

Saint-Exupéry, Antoine de, 1900-1944.   • **2.4702**
Wind, sand, and stars / Antoine de Saint–Exupéry; translated from the French by Lewis Galantière; illustrated by John O'H. Cosgrave, II. — Illustrated ed. — New York: Harcourt, Brace, 1940. 306 p.: ill. — (Harbrace modern classics; [18]) 1. Saint-Exupéry, Antoine de, 1900-1944. I. T.
PQ2637.A274T43 1949   843.91   *LC* 51-51161

Saint-Exupéry, Antoine de, 1900-1944.   **2.4703**
Oeuvres. Préf. de Roger Caillois. [Paris, Gallimard, c1959] xxx, 1008 p. illus. 18 cm. (Bibliothèque de la Pléiade, v.98) I. T.
PQ2637.A274 Ax

PQ2637 Sarraute

Sarraute, Nathalie.   **2.4704**
[Plays. English] Collected plays / Nathalie Sarraute; translated from the French by Maria Jolas and Barbara Wright. — New York: G. Braziller, 1981. 107 p.; 21 cm. I. T.
PQ2637.A783 A24   842/.9/14   *LC* 78-7111

Sarraute, Nathalie.   **2.4705**
[Disent les imbéciles. English] 'Fools say': a novel / by Nathalie Sarraute; translated by Maria Jolas. — New York: G. Braziller, c1977. 152 p.; 21 cm. Translation of Disent les imbéciles. I. T.
PZ4.S2488 Fo PQ2637.A783 D5x   843/.9/14   *LC* 76-16696   *ISBN* 0807608378

Sarraute, Nathalie.   • **2.4706**
Les fruits d'or / Nathalie Sarraute. — [Paris]: Gallimard, 1963. 226 p.; 19 cm. I. T.
PQ2637.A783 F7   *LC* 65-46754

Sarraute, Nathalie.   **2.4707**
The golden fruits; translated by Maria Jolas. — New York: G. Braziller, 1964. 177 p.; 21 cm. I. T.
PQ2637.A783 F7x   *LC* 64-12394

Sarraute, Nathalie.   • **2.4708**
Martereau, roman. — [Paris] Gallimard [1953] 291 p. 19 cm. I. T.
PQ2637.A783M3   *LC* 53-33104

Sarraute, Nathalie.   • **2.4709**
Martereau: a novel / translated by Maria Jolas. — New York: G. Braziller, 1959, c1953. 250 p.; 22 cm. I. T.
PQ2637.A783 M313 1959   *LC* 59-12067

Sarraute, Nathalie.   • **2.4710**
Le planétarium: roman / Nathalie Sarraute. — Paris: Gallimard, 1959. 310 p.; 19 cm. I. T.
PQ2637 A783P54   *LC* 59-7385

Sarraute, Nathalie.   **2.4711**
The Planetarium: a novel / translated by Maria Jolas. — New York: G. Braziller, 1960. 296 p.;c22cm. I. T.
PQ2637.A783 P5513 1960   *LC* 60-6952

Sarraute, Nathalie.   • **2.4712**
Tropismes. Paris: Editions de Minuit, 1957. 140 p. , 19 cm. Prose sketches. I. T.
PQ2637.A783 T7   *LC* 58-1595

Sarraute, Nathalie.   **2.4713**
[Tropismes. English] Tropisms, and The age of suspicion; translated from the French by Maria Jolas. London, Calder & Boyars, 1963 [i.e.1967] 136 p. 20 1/2 cm. (A Calderbook, CB126) Translation of Tropismes and L'ère du soupçon. 1. Fiction — 20th century — History and criticism I. Sarraute, Nathalie. Ere du soupçon. English. 1967. II. T. III. Title: Age of suspicion.
PQ2637.A783 T7x   *LC* 67-93185

Sarraute, Nathalie.   **2.4714**
[Vous les entendez? English] Do you hear them? A novel. Translated by Maria Jolas. New York, G. Braziller [1973] 147 p. 21 cm. Translation of Vous les entendez? I. T.
PZ3.S247 Do PQ2637.A783 V6x   843/.9/14   *LC* 72-86680   *ISBN* 0807606634

Besser, Gretchen R.   **2.4715**
Nathalie Sarraute / by Gretchen Rous Besser. — Boston: Twayne Publishers, 1979. 192 p.: port.; 21 cm. — (Twayne's world authors series; TWAS 534: France) Includes index. 1. Sarraute, Nathalie — Criticism and interpretation. I. T.
PQ2637.A783 Z58   848/.9/1409   *LC* 78-27319   *ISBN* 0805763767

Minogue, Valerie.   **2.4716**
Nathalie Sarraute and the war of the words: a study of five novels / Valerie Minogue. — Edinburgh: Edinburgh University Press, 1981. vi, 230 p.; 23 cm. Includes index. 1. Sarraute, Nathalie — Criticism and interpretation. I. T.
PQ2637.A783 Z766 1981   843/.914 19   *LC* 81-144274   *ISBN* 0852244053

Watson-Williams, Helen.   **2.4717**
The novels of Nathalie Sarraute, towards an aesthetic / Helen Watson-Williams. — Amsterdam: Rodopi, 1981. iv, 155, xviii p.; 23 cm. — (Degré second; 5) Includes index. 1. Sarraute, Nathalie — Aesthetics. 2. Sarraute, Nathalie — Criticism and interpretation. 3. Aesthetics in literature. 4. Art in literature 5. Artists in literature I. T.
PQ2637.A783 Z936 1981   843/.914 19   *LC* 81-192646   *ISBN* 9062037038

PQ2637 Sartre

Sartre, Jean Paul, 1905-.   **2.4718**
Œuvres romanesques / Jean–Paul Sartre; édition établie par Michel Contat et Michel Rybalka, avec la collaboration de Geneviève Idt et de George H. Bauer. — [Paris]: Gallimard, c1981. cxii, 2174 p.; 18 cm. (Bibliothèque de la Pléiade. 295) I. Contat, Michel. II. Rybalka, Michel. III. T. IV. Series.
PQ2637.A82 A15 1981   843/.914 19   *LC* 82-144638   *ISBN* 2070110028

Sartre, Jean Paul, 1905-.   • **2.4719**
Théâtre. — [Paris] Gallimard [1947-. v. 19 cm. I. T.
PQ2637.A82A19 1947   *LC* 47-7837 *

Sartre, Jean Paul, 1905-.   • **2.4720**
Three plays; tr. from the French by Lionel Abel. [1st American ed.] New York A.A. Knopf 1949. 272 p.; 20 cm. I. T. II. Title: Dirty hands III. Title: The respectful prostitute IV. Title: The victors
PQ2637 A82 A214

Sartre, Jean Paul, 1905-.   • **2.4721**
The age of reason / Jean–Paul Sartre; trnslated from the French by Eric Sutton. — New York: Knopf, 1947. 397 p.; 20 cm. 'Originally published in France as Les chemins de la liberté. I: L'âge de raison ... 1945.' I. T.
PZ3.S2494S2 PQ2637.A82C53   843.91   *LC* 47-4526 *

Sartre, Jean Paul, 1905-.   • **2.4722**
Le diable et le bon Dieu: trois actes et onze tableaux. — Paris: Gallimard, 1951. 282 p.; 19 cm. I. T.
PQ2637.A82 D5   *LC* 52-17030

Sartre, Jean Paul, 1905-. • **2.4723**
[Diable et le bon Dieu. English] The Devil & the Good Lord, and two other plays [Kean, based on the play by Alexandre Dumas, and Nekrassov. 1st American ed.] New York, Knopf, 1960. 438 p. 21 cm. I. Dumas, Alexandre, 1802-1870. Kean. II. T. III. Title: Nekrassov.
PQ2637.A82 D513 1960   842.914   *LC* 59-15317

Sartre, Jean Paul, 1905-. • **2.4724**
[Huis clos. English] No exit (Huis clos) a play in one act, & The flies (Les mouches) a play in three acts, by Jean-Paul Sartre. English versions by Stuart Gilbert. New York: A. A. Knopf, 1947 [c1946] 4 p.l., 3-166 p., 1 l. 19 cm. 'Copyright 1946.' 'First American edition.' 'Published in Great Britain under the title The flies and In camera ... in 1946.' I. Gilbert, Stuart. tr. II. T.
PQ2637.A82 H82 1947   842.91   *LC* 47-1619

Sartre, Jean Paul, 1905-. • **2.4725**
Les jeux sont faits. — Paris, Nagel [c1947] 194 p.; 29 cm. I. T.
PQ2637.A82J4   *LC* A 49-6 *

Sartre, Jean Paul, 1905-. • **2.4726**
Mains sales: pièce en sept tableaux / Edited by Geoffrey Brereton. London: Methuen, 1963. 191 p.; 19 cm. (Methuen's twentieth century texts.) I. Brereton, Geoffrey. ed. II. T.
PQ2637.A82 M3 1963   *LC* 65-32687

Sartre, Jean Paul, 1905-. • **2.4727**
The Wall: and other stories / Jean-Paul Sartre; translated by Lloyd Alexander. — New York: New Directions, c1948. 270 p.; 24 cm. I. T.
PQ2637 A82 M813 1948   *LC* 48-9642

Sartre, Jean Paul, 1905-. • **2.4728**
[Nausée English] Nausea. Tr. from the French by Lloyd Alexander. [Norfolk, Conn.] New Directions [1949] 238 p. 20 cm. I. T.
PZ3.S2494 Nau   PQ2637.A82 N3x.   832.91   *LC* 49-8942

Sartre, Jean Paul, 1905-. • **2.4729**
Nekrassov: pièce en huit tableaux / Jean-Paul Sartre. — Paris: Gallimard, 1956. 214 p.; 19 cm. I. T.
PQ2637.A82 N4   *LC* 56-33780

Sartre, Jean Paul, 1905-. • **2.4730**
Nekrassov: a farce / translated from the French by Sylvia and George Leeson. — London: H. Hamilton, 1956. 157 p.; 20 cm. I. T.
PQ2637.A82 N4x   *LC* 57-3009

Sartre, Jean Paul, 1905-. • **2.4731**
La putain, respectueuse; pièce en un acte et deux tableaux. — Paris, Nagel [1946] 163, [1] p., 2 l. 19 cm. On cover: 12. éd. I. T.
PQ2637.A82P8

Sartre, Jean Paul, 1905-. • **2.4732**
[Séquestrés d'Altona. English] The condemned of Altona; a play in five acts. Translated from the French by Sylvia and George Leeson. [1st American ed.] New York, Knopf, 1961. 178 p. 21 cm. I. T.
PQ2637.A82 S43 1961   842.914   *LC* 61-9231

Sartre, Jean Paul, 1905-. • **2.4733**
The reprieve; tr. from the French by Eric Sutton. [1st American ed.] New York, A.A. Knopf, 1947. 445 p. 20 cm. (His The roads to freedom, 2) I. Sutton, Eric II. T.
PZ3.S2494 Re   PQ2637.A82 S8x.   843.91   *LC* 47-11584

Sartre, Jean Paul, 1905-. **2.4734**
[Théâtre de situations. English] Sartre on theater / Jean-Paul Sartre; documents assembled, edited, introduced, and annotated by Michel Contat and Michel Rybalka; translated from the French by Frank Jellinek. — 1st American ed. — New York: Pantheon Books, c1976. xiii, 352 p.; 22 cm. Translation of Un théâtre de situations. 1. Sartre, Jean Paul, 1905- — Criticism and interpretation. 2. Drama — Collected works. I. T.
PQ2637.A82 T513 1976   848/.9/1409   *LC* 75-38121   *ISBN* 0394492471

Sartre, Jean Paul, 1905-. • **2.4735**
Troubled sleep. — [1st American ed.] Translated from the French by Gerard Hopkins. — New York: Knopf, 1951 [i.e. 1950] 421 p.; 20 cm. — (Sartre, Jean Paul, 1905- Roads to freedom; 3) Translation of La mort dans l'âme. London ed. (Hamilton) has title: Iron in the soul. I. T. II. Series.
PQ2637.A82 T8   *LC* 50-58029

Sartre, Jean Paul, 1905-. • **2.4736**
Les mots. — [Paris] Gallimard [1964] 213 p. 19 cm. I. T.
PQ2637.A82Z5   *LC* 65-34191

Sartre, Jean Paul, 1905-. • **2.4737**
[Mots. English] The words. Translated from the French by Bernard Frechtman. New York, G. Braziller [1964] 255 p. 21 cm. Autobiographical. 1. Sartre, Jean Paul, 1905- I. T.
PQ2637.A82 Z513   848.914   *LC* 64-21764

Collins, Douglas, 1945-. **2.4738**
Sartre as biographer / Douglas Collins. — Cambridge, Mass.: Harvard University Press, 1980. 220 p.; 24 cm. 1. Sartre, Jean Paul, 1905- Criticism and interpretation. 2. Biography (as a literary form) 3. Authors, French — Biography. I. T.
PQ2637.A82 Z597   840/.9 19   *LC* 79-25863   *ISBN* 0674789504

Contat, Michel. **2.4739**
The writings of Jean-Paul Sartre / compiled by Michel Contat and Michel Rybalka; translated by Richard C. McCleary. — Evanston: Northwestern University Press, 1974. 2 v.; 24 cm. (Northwestern University studies in phenomenology & existential philosophy) Translation, with revisions and additions, of Les écrits de Sartre. Includes index. 1. Sartre, Jean Paul, 1905- I. Rybalka, Michel. joint author. II. Sartre, Jean Paul, 1905- Selected prose. 1974. III. T. IV. Series.
PQ2637.A82 Z598   848/.9/1409   *LC* 74-196813   *ISBN* 0810104393

Halpern, Joseph. **2.4740**
Critical fictions: the literary criticism of Jean-Paul Sartre / Joseph Halpern. — New Haven: Yale University Press, 1976. 176 p.; 22 cm. (Yale Romanic studies; 2d ser., 26) Includes index. 1. Sartre, Jean Paul, 1905- — Knowledge — Literature. 2. Criticism I. T. II. Series.
PQ2637.A82 Z725   840/.9   *LC* 75-18172   *ISBN* 0300019432

Sartre, Jean Paul, 1905-. • **2.4741**
Sartre par lui-même / [Images et textes présentés par Francis Jeanson]. — Paris: Éditions du Seuil, 1955. 191 p.: ill.,ports,facsims,; 18 cm. (Écrivains de toujours. 29.) I. Jeanson, Francis, 1922- ed. II. T. III. Series.
PQ2637.A82 Z75   *LC* 56-935

Kern, Edith, 1912- ed. • **2.4742**
Sartre, a collection of critical essays. — Englewood Cliffs, N.J.: Prentice-Hall, [1962] 179 p.; 21 cm. — (Twentieth century views) (A Spectrum book, S-TC-21.) 1. Sartre, Jean Paul, 1905- 2. Existentialism I. T.
PQ2637.A82 Z76   848.914   *LC* 62-17794

Suhl, Benjamin. • **2.4743**
Jean-Paul Sartre: the philosopher as a literary critic. — New York: Columbia University Press, 1970. xi, 311 p.; 24 cm. 1. Sartre, Jean Paul, 1905- I. T.
PQ2637.A82 Z84   840.9   *LC* 71-116377   *ISBN* 0231033389

Thody, Philip Malcolm Waller, 1928-. • **2.4744**
Jean-Paul Sartre: a literary and political study / by Philip Thody. — New York: Macmillan [1961, c1960] 269 p.; 23 cm. 1. Sartre, Jean Paul, 1905- I. T.
PQ2637 .A82 Z85   *LC* 61-754

PQ2637.C–U Sc–Su

Schwarz-Bart, André, 1928-. • **2.4745**
[Dernier des justes. English] The last of the just. Translated from the French by Stephen Becker. [1st American ed.] New York, Atheneum Publishers, 1960. 374 p. 22 cm. I. T.
PQ2637.C736 D4x   PZ4.S415 Las   *LC* 60-11947

Schwarz-Bart, André, 1928-. • **2.4746**
Le dernier des Justes, roman. Paris, Éditions du Seuil [1959] 345 p. 21 cm. I. T.
PQ2637.C736 L4x   *LC* a 60-2795

Simenon, Georges, 1903-. **2.4747**
[Maigret et l'homme du banc. English] Maigret and the man on the bench / Georges Simenon; translated from the French by Eileen Ellenbogen. — 1st ed. — New York: Harcourt Brace Jovanovich, [1975] 180 p.; 21 cm. Translation of Maigret et l'homme du banc. 'A Helen and Kurt Wolff book.' I. T.
PZ3.S5892 Maegr PQ2637.I53 Mx   843/.9/12   *LC* 75-8566   *ISBN* 0151551456

Simenon, Georges, 1903-. **2.4748**
The patience of Maigret / Translated from the French by Geoffrey Sainsbury. — [S.l.]: Harcourt, Brace, 1940. 1 v. Originally published as La patience de Maigret. I. T.
PQ2637.I53 P3213   843.91

Fallois, Bernard de. **2.4749**
Simenon. [N.p.] Gallimard [1961] 305p. (La Bibliothèque idéale) 1. Simenon, Georges, 1903- I. T.
PQ2637 I53 Z63

Simon, Claude. 2.4750
La route des Flandres / Claude Simon. Suivi de Le tissu de mémoire / par Lucien Dällenbach. — Paris: Minuit, 1985. 316 p.; 18 cm. — I. Dällenbach, Lucien. Le tissu de mémoire. II. T.
PQ2637.I547 R6 *ISBN* 2707306290

Gould, Karen L. 2.4751
Claude Simon's mythic muse / by Karen L. Gould. — Columbia, S. C.: French Literature Publications Co., 1979. 152 p.; 24 cm. Includes index. 1. Simon, Claude — Criticism and interpretation. 2. Myth in literature I. T.
PQ2637.I547 Z74 843/.9/14 *LC* 79-110372 *ISBN* 0917786106

Jiménez Fajardo, Salvador. 2.4752
Claude Simon / by Salvador Jiménez–Fajardo. — Boston: Twayne Publishers, [1975] 203 p.: port.; 21 cm. — (Twayne's world authors series; TWAS 346. France) Includes index. 1. Simon, Claude — Criticism and interpretation. I. T.
PQ2637.I547 Z76 843/.9/14 *LC* 74-30154 *ISBN* 0805628287

Loubère, J. A. E. 2.4753
The novels of Claude Simon / by J. A. E. Loubère. — Ithaca, N.Y.: Cornell University Press, 1975. 267 p.; 21 cm. Includes index. 1. Simon, Claude — Criticism and interpretation. I. T.
PQ2637.I547 Z79 PQ2637I547 Z79. 843/.9/14 *LC* 74-25372 *ISBN* 0801408490

Stil, André. 2.4754
Soixante–quatre coquelicots / André Stil. — [Paris]: Balland, c1984. 89 p.; 20 cm. — (Instant romanesque.) I. T.
PQ2637.T56 S65 1984 *ISBN* 2715804741

Supervielle, Jules, 1884-1960. • 2.4755
Choix de poèmes. [Paris] Gallimard [1947] 318 p. 21 cm. I. T.
PQ2637.U6 A17 1947 *LC* 48-13224

PQ2639 T

Tardieu, Jean, 1903-. 2.4756
Théâtre de chambre. Paris, Gallimard [1955-60] 2 v. 18 cm. I. T.
PQ2639.A72 A19 1955 *LC* 55-42066

Tardieu, Jean, 1903-. 2.4757
[Formeries. English] Formeries / Jean Tardieu; translated by Gail Graham and Sylvie Mathé. — Ann Arbor: Translation Press/Ardis Book, c1983. 84 p.; 24 cm. Translation of: Formeries. I. T.
PQ2639.A72 F613 1983 841/.912 19 *LC* 82-16112 *ISBN* 0931556104

Thirion, André, 1907-. 2.4758
[Révolutionnaires sans révolution. English] Revolutionaries without revolution. Translated by Joachim Neugroschel. [1st American ed.] New York, Macmillan [1975] viii, 499 p. illus. 24 cm. 1. Thirion, André, 1907- — Biography. I. T.
PQ2639.H368 Z513 1975 322.4/2/0924 B *LC* 74-9859 *ISBN* 0026174006

Tzara, Tristan, 1896-1963. 2.4759
Approximate man, and other writings. Translated with an introd. and notes by Mary Ann Caws / Tristan Tzara. — Detroit: Wayne State University Press, 1973. 267 p.; 24 cm. Poems. 1. French poetry I. T.
PQ2639.Z3 A23 1973 841/.9/12 *LC* 72-3390 *ISBN* 0814314821

Tzara, Tristan, 1896-1963. • 2.4760
La fuite: poème dramatique en quatre actes et un épilogue / Tristan Tzara. — [Paris]: Gallimard, 1947. 97 p. I. T.
PQ2639.Z3 F8 *LC* 48-12616

PQ2643 Valéry

Valéry, Paul, 1871-1945. • 2.4761
Oeuvres. Ed. établie et annotée par Jean Hytier. — [Paris, Gallimard, 1957-1960] 2 v. — (Bibliothaeque de la Pléiade, 127, 148.) Includes bibliography. I. Hytier, Jean, ed. II. T.
PQ2643.A26 1957

Valéry, Paul, 1871-1945. • 2.4762
[Works. English. 1956] The collected works of Paul Valéry, edited by Jackson Mathews. [Princeton, N.J., Princeton University Press, 1956-[75] [v. 1, 1971] 15 v. 21 cm. (Bollingen series. 45) Vols. 3-4, 7 and 12 published by Pantheon Books, New York; v. 5, 10, and 13 published by the Bollingen Foundation, New York; distributed by Pantheon Books. I. T. II. Series.
PQ2643.A26 A23 848/.9/1209 *LC* 56-9337 *ISBN* 069109859X

Valéry, Paul, 1871-1945. 2.4763
[Selected works. English. 1977] Paul Valéry, an anthology: selected, with an introd., by James R. Lawler from The collected works of Paul Valéry, edited by Jackson Mathews. — Princeton, N.J.: Princeton University Press, c1977. xxiii, 355 p.; 21 cm. — (Bollingen series. 45-A) I. T. II. Series.
PQ2643.A26 A23 1977 848/.9/1209 *LC* 76-3026 *ISBN* 0691099286

Valéry, Paul, 1871-1945. • 2.4764
[Selections. English. 1950] Selected writings. [New York, New Directions, 1950] 256 p. 22 cm. 'With the exception of the poetry section, the selection is identical with ... [the author's] Morceaux choisis [Paris, 1930]' I. T.
PQ2643.A26 A25 848.91 *LC* 50-7546

Cohen, Gustave, 1879-1958. • 2.4765
Essai d'explication du Cimetière marin, précédé d'un avant–propos de Paul Valéry au sujet du Cimetière marin. — [Paris] Gallimard [1933] 111 p., 2 l. incl. front. 17 cm. 'Appendice bibliographique': p. [103]-111. 1. Valéry, Paul, 1871-1945. Le cimetière marin. I. T.
PQ2643.A26C65 841.91 *LC* 33-20259

Crow, Christine M. 2.4766
Paul Valéry and the poetry of voice / Christine M. Crow. — Cambridge [Cambridgeshire]; New York: Cambridge University Press, 1982. xviii, 302 p.: ill.; 23 cm. — (Major European authors.) Includes index. 1. Valéry, Paul, 1871-1945 — Criticism and interpretation. I. T. II. Series.
PQ2643.A26 Z57734 1982 841/.912 19 *LC* 81-10069 *ISBN* 0521241820

Grubbs, Henry Alexander, 1904-. • 2.4767
Paul Valéry, by Henry A. Grubbs. — New York: Twayne Publishers, [1968] 153 p.; 22 cm. — (Twayne's world authors series, TWAS43. France) 1. Valéry, Paul, 1871-1945. I. T.
PQ2643.A26 Z637 848/.9/1209 *LC* 67-25204

Hytier, Jean. • 2.4768
The poetics of Paul Valéry / Translated from the French by Richard Howard. [1st ed. in English] Garden City, N.Y. Anchor Books [1966] vi, 353 p.; 18 cm. 1. Valéry, Paul, 1871-1945. I. T.
PQ2643.A26 Z6513 841.912 *LC* 66-21975

Mackay, Agnes Ethel. • 2.4769
The universal self; a study of Paul Valéry. Toronto, University of Toronto Press [1961] 263 p. illus. 23 cm. 1. Valéry, Paul, 1871-1945. I. T.
PQ2643.A26 Z715 841.912 *LC* 61-65142

PQ2643.A34–2651 V–Z

Vandercammen, Edmond, 1901-. 2.4770
Poèmes choisis, 1931–1959 / préf. de J. Cassou. — Paris: Editions universitaires, c1961. 362 p.; 22 cm. I. T.
PQ2643.A349 A6 1961 *LC* 66-44746

Vian, Boris, 1920-1959. 2.4771
L'ecume des jours; suive de Un langage–univers par Jacques Bens. Paris, Union Generale d'editions, 1963. 184 p. (Le monde en 10/18.) I. T. II. Title: Un Langage-univers. Jacques Bens.
PQ2643.I152 E3

Yourcenar, Marguerite. 2.4772
[Œuvre au noir. English] The abyss / Marguerite Yourcenar; translated from the French by Grace Frick in collaboration with the author. — New York: Farrar, Straus and Giroux, c1976. 374 p.; 22 cm. Translation of L'Œuvre au noir. I. T.
PZ3.Y897 Ab PQ2649.O8 843/.9/12 *LC* 76-72 *ISBN* 0374100403

Yourcenar, Marguerite. 2.4773
Plays / Marguerite Yourcenar; translated from the French by Dori Katz; in collaboration with the author. — New York: Performing Arts Journal Publications, c1984. 164 p.; 23 cm. I. T.
PQ2649.O8 A19 1984 *LC* 83-62616 *ISBN* 093382663X(cloth)

Yourcenar, Marguerite. • 2.4774
Mémoires d'Hadrien. Paris Plon [1951] 321 p.; 21 cm. 1. Hadrian, Emperor of Rome, 76-138 — Fiction I. T.
PQ2649 O8 M4

Yourcenar, Marguerite. • 2.4775
[Mémoires d'Hadrien English] Memoirs of Hadrian, and reflections on the composition of memoirs of Hadrian. Translated from the French by Grace Frick, in collaboration with the author. New York, Farrar, Straus, 1963. 347 p. illus. 24 cm. 1. Hadrian, Emperor of Rome, 76-138 — Fiction. I. T.
PZ3.Y897 Me4 PQ2649.O8 Mx. *LC* 62-18317

PQ2660–2686 Individual Authors, 1961–

PQ2661–2672 A–L

Chawaf, Chantal.   **2.4776**
Blé de semences / Chantal Chawaf. [Paris]: Mercure de France, 1976. 121 p.; 21 cm. I. T.
PQ2663.H379 B55   843/.9/14   *LC* 77-463916

Chawaf, Chantal.   **2.4777**
Retable; [La rêverie] / Chantal Chawaf. — Paris: Éditions des Femmes, [1974] 165 p.: ill. (some col.); 18 cm. I. Chawaf, Chantal. Rêverie. 1974. II. T.
PQ2663.H379 R4   843/.9/14   *LC* 75-504277   *ISBN* 2721000101

Cixous, Hélène, 1937-.   **2.4778**
Le Prénom de Dieu. Paris, B. Grasset, 1967. 208 p. 19 cm. I. T.
PQ2663.I9 P7   *LC* 67-98614

Cixous, Hélène, 1937-.   **2.4779**
Vivre l'orange = To live the orange / Hélène Cixous. — [Paris]: Des femmes, 1979. 113 p.; 19 cm. English text by Hélène Cixous from the translation of Ann Liddle and Sarah Cornell. English and French on opposite pages. I. T. II. Title: To live the orange.
PQ2663.I9 V53 1979   *ISBN* 2721001582

Conley, Verena Andermatt, 1943-.   **2.4780**
Hélène Cixous: writing the feminine / Verena Andermatt Conley. — Lincoln: University of Nebraska Press, c1984. 181 p., [1] leaf of plates: port.; 23 cm. Includes index. 1. Cixous, Hélène, 1937- — Criticism and interpretation. 2. Feminism in literature. I. T.
PQ2663.I9 Z6 1984   848/.91409 19   *LC* 83-23600   *ISBN* 0803214243

Deguy, Michel.   **2.4781**
Given giving: selected poems of Michel Deguy / translated by Clayton Eshleman; with an introduction by Kenneth Koch. — Berkeley: University of California Press, c1984. xxiii, 189 p.; 22 cm. English and French. 1. Deguy, Michel — Translations, English. I. Eshleman, Clayton. II. T.
PQ2664.E45 A23 1984   841/.914 19   *LC* 84-40332   *ISBN* 0520047281

Jaccottet, Philippe.   **2.4782**
Breathings; the poems of Philippe Jaccottet. Translated by Cid Corman. Illustrated by Anne–Marie Jaccottet. — [1st ed. — New York]: Grossman Publishers, [1974] 131 p.: illus.; 24 cm. 'A Mushinska book.' I. T.
PQ2670.A225 B7   841/.9/14   *LC* 73-89804   *ISBN* 0670188689

Jaccottet, Philippe.   **2.4783**
[Semaison. English. Selections] Seedtime = (La semaison): extracts from the notebooks, 1954–1967 / prose selections translated by André Lefevere; verse translated by Michael Hamburger. — New York: New Directions, 1977. 60 p.; 21 cm. I. Hamburger, Michael. II. T.
PQ2670.A225 S413 1977   848/.9/1409   *LC* 76-45640   *ISBN* 081120636X. *ISBN* 0811206378 pbk

Le Clézio, J.-M. G. (Jean-Marie Gustave), 1940-.   **2.4784**
[Guerre. English] War [by] J. M. G. Le Clézio. Translated from the French by Simon Watson Taylor. [1st American ed.] New York, Atheneum, 1973. 288 p. 21 cm. Translation of La guerre. I. T.
PZ4.L4535 War3 PQ2672.E25   843/.9/14   *LC* 72-94243   *ISBN* 0689105479

PQ2673–2686 M–Z

Modiano, Patrick, 1945-.   **2.4785**
Rue des boutiques obscures / Patrick Modiano. — [Paris]: Gallimard, c1978. 213 p.; 21 cm. — I. T.
PQ2673.O3 R8   843/.9/14   *LC* 79-353581

Navarre, Yves, 1940-.   **2.4786**
Le jardin d'acclimatation: roman. Paris: Flammarion, 1980. 392 p.; 20 cm. I. T.
PQ 2674.A9   PQ2674A88 J3.   *ISBN* 208064291X

Perec, Georges, 1936-1982.   **2.4787**
La vie, mode d'emploi: romans / Georges Perec. — [Paris]: Hachette, 1978. 699 p.: ill.; 21 cm. — (POL 0181-6071) (Hachette littérature) Includes index. I. T.
PQ2676.E67 V5   843/.9/14   *LC* 79-344124   *ISBN* 2010054903

Perec, Georges, 1936-1982.   **2.4788**
W: ou, Le souvenir d'enfance / Georges Perec. — Paris: Denoël, [1975] 220 p.; 20 cm. (Les Lettres nouvelles) I. T.
PQ2676.E67 W2   *LC* 75-512030

Roche, Maurice.   **2.4789**
Compact, roman. Paris, Éditions du Seuil, 1966. 166p. 18cm. (Collection Tel quel) Illustrated cover. I. T.
PQ2678.O29 C6   *LC* 67-94645

Roubaud, Jacques, 1932-.   **2.4790**
La belle Hortense: roman / Jacques Roubaud. — Paris: Éditions Ramsay, 1985. 269 p. — (Collection 'Mots') I. T.
PQ2678.O77 B4x   *ISBN* 2859564071

Sarrazin, Albertine.   **2.4791**
L'astragale: roman / par Albertine Sarrazin. — [Paris]: J.J. Pauvert, c1965. 246 p.; 19 cm. I. T.
PQ2679.A7 A8   *LC* 66-37221

Sollers, Philippe, 1936-.   **2.4792**
Portrait du joueur: roman / Philippe Sollers. — Paris: Gallimard, c1984. 312 p.; 21 cm. I. T.
PQ 2679 O49 P85 1984   *ISBN* 2070703177

Tournier, Michel.   **2.4793**
[Roi des Aulnes. English] The ogre. Translated from the French by Barbara Bray. Garden City, N.Y., Doubleday, 1972. 373 p. 22 cm. Translation of Le roi des Aulnes. I. T.
PZ4.T729 Og PQ2680.O83   843/.9/14   *LC* 75-186310

Cloonan, William J.   **2.4794**
Michel Tournier / by William Cloonan. — Boston: Twayne Publishers, c1985. 110 p.: 1 port.; 23 cm. (Twayne's world authors series; TWAS 747. French literature) Includes index. 1. Tournier, Michel — Criticism and interpretation. I. T.
PQ2680.O83 Z65 1985   843/.914 19   *LC* 84-22403   *ISBN* 0805765956

Wittig, Monique.   **2.4795**
Les Guérillères. — Paris: Éditions de Minuit, 1969. 209 p.; 18 cm. — I. T.
PQ2683.I8 G8   *LC* 75-457628

Wittig, Monique.   **2.4796**
Les guérillères. Translated from the French by David Le Vay. — New York: Viking Press, [1971] 144 p.; 21 cm. — I. T.
PZ4.W832 Gu3 PQ2683.I8G8   843/.9/14   *LC* 70-158421   *ISBN* 0670424633

Wouters, Liliane.   **2.4797**
Le Gel. — Paris: Seghers, 1966. 96p. I. T.
PQ2683 O8 G4

Littératures de langue française hors de France: anthologie   2.4798
didactique / [publiée par la] Fédération internationale des
professeurs de français.
Sèvres (1, Av. Léon-Journault, 92310): F.I.P.F., 1976. 704 p.: ill. (some col.); 22
cm. 'Diffuseur général: Éditions J. Duculot, Gembloux, Belgique.' 1. French
literature — Foreign countries I. International Federation of Teachers of
French.
PQ3809.L57   840/.8   LC 77-452850   ISBN 2901106013

PQ3810–3858 BELGIUM
(Individual authors interfiled, PQ2149-2686)

Lettres vivantes: deux générations d'écrivains français en   2.4799
Belgique, 1945–1975 / publié sous la direction de Adrien Jans;
[avec la collaboration de Albert Ayguesparse et al.].
[Bruxelles]: La Renaissance du livre, [c1975] 421 p.: ill.; 24 cm. Includes index.
1. French literature — Belgian authors — History and criticism. 2. French
literature — 20th century — History and criticism. I. Jans, Adrien.
PQ3814.L4   LC 76-450749

Mallinson, Vernon.   • 2.4800
Modern Belgian literature, 1830–1960. New York, Barnes & Noble [1966]
205 p. 23 cm. 1. Belgian literature — History and criticism I. T.
PQ3814.M25   809.89493   LC 66-31528

Guiette, Robert, 1895-.   2.4801
Écrivains français de Belgique au XIXe siécle. Paris, Bordas; Bruxelles, Asedi,
[1968?] 64 p. plates. 21 cm. 1. French literature — Belgian authors I. T.
PQ3840.G8   LC 68-131456

PQ3897 FRENCH LITERATURE BY BLACK AUTHORS (GENERAL)
(see also: PQ3940-3949; PQ3980-3989)

Kesteloot, Lilyan.   2.4802
[Ecrivains noirs de langue française. English] Black writers in French: a literary
history of negritude / Lilyan Kesteloot; translated by Ellen Conroy Kennedy.
Philadelphia: Temple University Press, 1974. xxix, 401 p.: ill.; 24 cm.
Translation of Les écrivains noirs de langue française. Originally presented as
the author's thesis, Brussels, 1961. Includes index. 1. Etudiant noir. 2. Egitime
défense. 3. Tropiques; revue culturelle. 4. French literature — Black authors
— History and criticism. I. T.
PQ3897.K3913 1974   840/.9/896   LC 73-79479   ISBN 0877220565

Kesteloot, Lilyan.   2.4803
Les écrivains noirs de langue française: naissance d'une littérature / Lilyan
Kesteloot. — 3e éd. — Bruxelles: Université libre de Bruxelles: Institut de
sociologie, 1967. –. 343 p.: tables.; 24 cm. — (Études africaines) 1. L'Étudiant
noir. 2. Legitime défense. 3. Tropiques; revue culturelle. 4. French literature
— Black authors and criticism. I. T.
PQ3897.L3 1967   840   LC 68-78527

PQ3900–3919 CANADA
(Canadian Literature in English: see PR9100–9199.3)

Dictionnaire des œuvres littéraires du Québec / sous la   2.4804
direction de Maurice Lemire.
Montréal: Fides, <c1980-c1984 >. v. <2-4 >: ill. (some col.), facsims., ports.;
25 cm. 1. French-Canadian literature — Dictionaries. 2. French-Canadian

literature — Bio-bibliography. 3. Authors, French-Canadian — Biography.
4. Québec (Province) in literature — Dictionaries. I. Lemire, Maurice.
PQ3901.D5   840/.9 19   LC 80-117300   ISBN 2762109981

Hamel, Réginald.   2.4805
Dictionnaire pratique des auteurs québécois / Réginald Hamel, John Hare,
Paul Wyczynski. — Montréal: Fides, c1976. xxv, 723 p.: ports.; 20 cm. Includes
index. 1. French-Canadian literature — Bio-bibliography. I. Hare, John Ellis,
1933- joint author. II. Wyczynski, Paul, 1921- joint author. III. T.
PQ3904.H3   840/.9   LC 77-453346   ISBN 0775505978

Bosquet, Alain, 1919- ed.   • 2.4806
Poésie du Québec. Anthologie composée par Alain Bosquet: Alain Grandbois,
Simone Routier, François Hertel, Saint–Denys Garneau ... [etc.]. — Paris:
Seghers; Montréal: HMH, 1968. 276 p.; 21 cm. First published in 1962 under
title: La poésie canadienne. 1. French-Canadian poetry I. Grandbois, Alain,
1900-1975. II. T.
PQ3914.B6 1968   LC 75-365246

Cotnam, Jacques. comp.   2.4807
Poètes du Québec, 1860–1968; anthologie présentée par Jacques Cotnam et
précédée d'une bibliographie. Montréal, Fides [1969] 222 p. 17 cm.
(Bibliothèque canadienne-française) Bibliography: p. 12-19. 1. French-
Canadian poetry I. T.
PS9292.C6   PQ3914.C6.   LC 77-463590

Twelve modern French Canadian poets / translated by G.R.   • 2.4808
Roy, with French text.
Toronto: Ryerson Press, 1958. xi, 99 p. Added t.p. in French with title: Douze
poètes modernes du Canada français. French and English on opposite pages.
1. French-Canadian poetry — 20th century. 2. French-Canadian poetry —
Translations into English. 3. Canadian poetry — Translations from French.
I. Roy, G. Ross (George Ross), 1924- II. Title: 12 modern French Canadian
poets. III. Title: Douze poètes modernes du Canada français.
PQ3914.R65   LC 63-28261

PQ3919 Individual Authors, to 1960

Blais, Marie Claire.   2.4809
[Pays voilés. English] Veiled countries; Lives / Marie–Claire Blais; translated
by Michael Harris. — Montréal: Véhicule Press, c1984. 181 p. — (Signal
editions) Poems. Translation of: Pays voilés and Existences. I. Blais, Marie
Claire. Existences. English II. T.
PQ3919.B6 A24 1984   C841/.54 19   ISBN 0919890547

Blais, Marie Claire.   2.4810
[Insoumise. English] The fugitive / Marie–Claire Blais; translated by David
Lobdell. — [Ottawa]: Oberon Press, c1978. 96 p.; 21 cm. Translation of
L'Insoumise. I. T.
PZ4.B637 Fu PQ3919.B6 I6x   843   LC 79-305492   ISBN
0887502830

Blais, Marie Claire, 1939-.   2.4811
L'insoumise: roman. — Montreal: Editions du jour, 1974. 119 p. — (Collection
Les Romanciers du jour;$VR-17) I. T. II. Series.
PQ3919.B6 I6x   ISBN 077600123X

Blais, Marie Claire.   2.4812
[Joualonais, sa Joualonie. English] St. Lawrence blues; a novel. Translated from
the French by Ralph Manheim. New York, Farrar, Straus and Giroux [1974]
229 p. 21 cm. Translation of Un Joualonais, sa Joualonie. I. T.
PZ4.B637 Sai PQ3919.B6 J6x   843   LC 74-4318   ISBN
0374269459

Blais, Marie Claire.   • 2.4813
Une saison dans la vie d'Emmanuel; roman. Montréal, Les Éditions du jour
[1965] 128 p.; 21 cm. (Collection: Les Romanciers du jour) I. T.
PQ3919.B6 S2x

Gélinas, Gratien, 1909-.   • **2.4814**
Tit–Coq, pièce en trois actes. — [Montréal]: Beauchemin, [1950] 196 p.: ill.; 21 cm. I. T.
PQ3919.G35 T5   PS8513.E45 T5 1950.   *LC* 50-27832

Hébert, Anne, 1916-.   **2.4815**
Le torrent: suivi de deux nouvelles inédites / Anne Hébert. — Nouv. éd. — Montréal: Editions HMH, 1974, c1963. 248 p. — (Collection l'arbre; v. 1) I. T.
PQ3919.H37 T69   *ISBN* 0775800252

Hébert, Anne.   **2.4816**
The torrent; novellas and short stories. Translated by Gwendolyn Moore. — Montreal: Harvest House, [1973] 141 p.; 19 cm. — (French writers of Canada series) I. T.
PZ4.H444 To PQ3919.H37T6x   843   *LC* 73-83340   *ISBN* 0887721400

Russell, Delbert W.   **2.4817**
Anne Hébert / by Delbert W. Russell. — Boston: Twayne, c1983. 155 p.: port.; 21 cm. — (Twayne's world authors series. TWAS 684) Includes index. 1. Hébert, Anne — Criticism and interpretation. I. T. II. Series.
PQ3919.H37 Z86 1983   848 19   *LC* 82-15798   *ISBN* 080576531X

Laroque, Robert.   **2.4818**
Testament of my childhood / by Robert de Roquebrune; translated by Felix Walter. — Toronto: University of Toronto Press, 1964. 160 p.; 22 cm. — (Canadian university paperbacks; 20) Translation of Testament de mon enfance; recit 1. La Roque de Roquebrune, Robert, 1889- — Biography. I. T. II. Series.
PS9523.A7Z53e   PQ3919.L315 Z523.   PS8523.A72 Z523.   848/.912   *LC* 64-4160   *ISBN* 0802060226

Panneton, Phillippe, 1895-.   **2.4819**
Thirty acres / by Ringuet. Introd. by Albert LeGrand. — Toronto: McClelland and Stewart, 1970. 249 p. — (New Canadian library, no.12) I. T. II. Series.
PQ3919.P27Tx   *ISBN* 0771091125

Roy, Gabrielle, 1909-.   **2.4820**
Bonheur d'occasion; roman [par] Gabrielle Roy. Nouv. éd. Montréal, Beauchemin, 1973 [c1965] 345 p. 20 cm. I. T.
PQ3919.R74 B6 1973   843   *LC* 74-169008   *ISBN* 0775000795

Roy, Gabrielle, 1909-.   **2.4821**
[Bonheur d'occasion. English] The tin flute / Gabrielle Roy; translated by Alan Brown. — Toronto: McClelland and Stewart, c1980. 384 p.: port.; 25 cm. Translation of: Bonheur d'occasion. In slipcase. I. Brown, Alan. II. T. III. Title: Bonheur d'occasion. English.
PQ3919.R74B6x   C843/.54 19   *ISBN* 0771078412

Roy, Gabrielle, 1909-.   **2.4822**
La Petite Poule d'Eau. Éd. rev. Montréal, Beauchemin, 1970. 272 p. 20 cm. I. T.
PQ3919.R74 P4 1970   843   *LC* 74-168433

Roy, Gabrielle, 1909-.   **2.4823**
Street of riches; translated by Harry Binsse. — New York, Harcourt, Brace [1957] 246 p. 22 cm. Translation of Rue Deschambault. I. T.
PQ3919.R74 R8x   843.91   *LC* 57-10065

Roy, Gabrielle, 1909-.   **2.4824**
Where nests the water hen / Gabrielle Roy; introd. by Gordon Roper; trans. from the French by Harry L. Binsse, general editor Malcolm Ross. — Toronto: McClelland & Stewart, 1970. x, 160 p. — (New Canadian library; 25) Translation of: La petite poule d'eau. I. T. II. Series.
PQ3919.R74W5x   *ISBN* 0771091257

Hesse, M. G. (Marta Gudrun)   **2.4825**
Gabrielle Roy / by M.G. Hesse. — Boston: Twayne Publishers, c1984. 113 p.: ill.; 23 cm. (Twayne's world authors series. TWAS 726) Includes index. 1. Roy, Gabrielle, 1909- — Criticism and interpretation. I. T. II. Series.
PQ3919.R74 Z659 1984   843 19   *LC* 83-22663   *ISBN* 0805765735

Lewis, Paula Gilbert.   **2.4826**
The literary vision of Gabrielle Roy: an analysis of her works / Paula Gilbert Lewis. — Birmingham, Ala.: Summa Publications, 1984. 319 p.; 24 cm. 1. Roy, Gabrielle, 1909- — Criticism and interpretation. I. T.
PQ3919.R74 Z76 1984   843 19   *LC* 84-50323   *ISBN* 091778605X

PQ3919.2 Individual Authors, 1961–

Dubé, Marcel, 1930-.   • **2.4827**
Les beaux dimanches: pièce en trois actes et deux tableaux / de Marcel Dubé. — [Montréal?]: Leméac, 1968. 185 p.: ill. — (Collection Théâtre canadien; v.3) I. T. II. Series.
PQ3919.2.D76 B4 PS9507.U2 B4   PR9265.U16 B3 1968.   PS8507.U22 B4.   *LC* 68-141753

Dubé, Marcel, 1930-.   **2.4828**
Zone, pièce en trois actes. — [Ottawa] Leméac [1968] 190 p. illus. 20 cm. — (Collection Théâtre canadien, 1) I. T.
PQ3919.2.D76Z3   842   *LC* 68-122744

Laroche, Maximilien.   **2.4829**
Marcel Dubé. — Montreal, Fides, [c1970] 189 p. illus., ports. 18 cm. — (Ecrivains canadiens d'aujourd'hui, 9) Bibliography: p. 187-189. 1. Dubé, Marcel, 1930- Criticism and interpretation. I. Dubé, Marcel, 1930- II. T. III. Series.
PQ3919.2.D76Z76   *LC* 79-598872

Ferron, Jacques.   **2.4830**
[Cotnoir. English] Dr. Cotnoir; a novel. Translated by Pierre Cloutier. Montreal, Harvest House [1973] 86 p. 19 cm. (French writers of Canada series) Translation of Cotnoir. I. T.
PZ4.F39 Do PQ3919.2.F4   843   *LC* 73-83339   *ISBN* 0887720400

Langevin, André, 1927-.   **2.4831**
[Chaîne dans le parc. English] Orphan Street / André Langevin; translated by Alan Brown. — 1st American ed. — Philadelphia: Lippincott, c1976. 287 p.; 25 cm. Translation of Une chaîne dans le parc. I. T.
PZ4.L278 Or8 PQ3919.2.L238   843   *LC* 76-151467   *ISBN* 0397012047

Tremblay, Michel, 1943-.   **2.4832**
Les belles–soeurs / Michel Tremblay; introd. de Alain Pontaut. — [Montréal]: Leméac, [c1972] 156 p., [8] leaves of plates: ports.; 20 cm. — (Théâtre canadien; 26) Play. Includes text in English. Includes biography of the author and reviews of the play. I. Pontaut, Alain, 1925- II. T. III. Series.
PQ3919.2.T73B4   C842/.5/4   *LC* 73-351360   *ISBN* 0776100254

PQ3940–3949 WEST INDIES

Ormerod, Beverley, 1937-.   **2.4833**
An introduction to the French Caribbean novel / Beverley Ormerod. — London; Portsmouth, N.H., USA: Heinemann, 1985. 152 p.; 22 cm. (Studies in Caribbean literature.) Includes index. 1. West Indian fiction (French) — History and criticism. 2. French fiction — 20th century — History and criticism. I. T. II. Series.
PQ3944.O76 1985   843 19   *LC* 85-150162   *ISBN* 0435918397

Hoffmann, Léon-François.   **2.4834**
Essays on Haitian literature / Léon–François Hoffmann. — 1st ed. — Washington, D.C.: Three Continents Press, c1984. 184 p.; 23 cm. Includes index. 1. Haitian literature — History and criticism — Addresses, essays, lectures. I. T.
PQ3948.5.H2 H64 1984   840/.9/97294 19   *LC* 82-50882   *ISBN* 0894103458

Césaire, Aimé.   **2.4835**
[Poems. English & French. Selections] Aimé Césaire, the collected poetry / translated, with an introduction and notes by Clayton Eshleman and Annette Smith. — Berkeley: University of California Press, c1983. xv, 408 p.: ill.; 26 cm. Text in English and French. 1. Césaire, Aimé — Translations, English. I. Eshleman, Clayton. II. Smith, Annette (Annette J.) III. T.
PQ3949.C44 A24 1983   841 19   *LC* 82-17394   *ISBN* 0520043472

Césaire, Aimé.   **2.4836**
Aimé Césaire, une étude de Lilyan Kesteloot; avec un choix de poèmes, une bibliography, vingt illus. — Nouv. éd. — [Paris] P. Seghers [1970, c1962] 190 p. ports. 16 cm. — (Poètes d'aujourd'hui, 85) 'Bibliographie': p. 185. I. Kesteloot, Lilyan. ed. II. T.
PQ3949.C44 A6x   *LC* 64-48361

Césaire, Aimé. **2.4837**
La tragédie du roi Christophe / Aimé Césaire. — Paris: Présence africaine, 1963. 161 p. 1. Henri Christophe, King of Haiti, 1767-1820 — Drama I. T.
PQ3949.C44 T7x   LC 65-57030

Frutkin, Susan. **2.4838**
Aimé Césaire; Black between worlds. — [Coral Gables, Fla.]: Center for Advanced International Studies, University of Miami, 1973. xi, 66 p.; 23 cm. — (Monographs in international affairs) 'Outgrowth of a master's thesis ... University of Miami in 1968.' 1. Césaire, Aimé. I. T. II. Series.
PQ3949.C44 Z67 1973   841 B   LC 73-85305

Dépestre, René. **2.4839**
[Arc-en-ciel pour l'occident chrétien. English] A rainbow for the Christian West / René Depestre; translated, with an introd., by Joan Dayan. — Amherst, Ma.: University of Massachusetts Press, 1977. xi, 258 p.; 24 cm. Translation of Un arc-en-ciel pour l'occident chrétien. Includes indexes. I. Dayan, Joan, 1949- II. T.
PQ3949.D46 A813 1977   841   LC 76-45047   ISBN 0870232290

Roumain, Jacques, 1907-1944. **2.4840**
[Gouverneurs de la rosée. English] Masters of the dew. Translated by Langston Hughes and Mercer Cook. With an introd. by Mercer Cook. New York, Collier Books [1971, c1941] 192 p. 18 cm. (African/American library) Translation of Gouverneurs de la rosée. I. T. II. Series.
PZ3.R759 Mas5 PQ3949.R73 G6x   843   LC 70-144148

Desportes, Georges, 1921-. **2.4841**
Cette île qui est la nôtre. — [Montreal]: Leméac, [1973] 242 p.; 20 cm. — (Collection Francophonie vivante) I. T.
PQ3949.2.D44 C4   LC 74-178852

PQ3980-3989 AFRICA

Blair, Dorothy S. **2.4842**
African literature in French: a history of creative writing in French from west and equatorial Africa / Dorothy S. Blair. — Cambridge [Eng.]; New York: Cambridge University Press, 1976. xix, 348 p.: 1 port., map. 1. African literature (French) — History and criticism. I. T.
PQ3980.B5   PQ3980 B5.   840/.9   LC 75-39374   ISBN 0521211956

Erickson, John D. **2.4843**
Nommo: African fiction in French south of the Sahara / by John D. Erickson. — York, S.C.: French Literature Publications Co., 1979. 285 p.: ill.; 24 cm. Includes index. 1. African fiction (French) — History and criticism. I. T.
PQ3984.E27   843/.009   LC 78-73310   ISBN 0917786076

✓ **The Negritude poets: an anthology of translations from the** **2.4844**
French / edited and with an introd. by Ellen Conroy Kennedy.
New York: Viking Press, [1975] xxxiii, 284 p.; 25 cm. 'A Richard Seaver book.' 1. French poetry — Negro authors — Translations into English. 2. English poetry — Translations from French. 3. French poetry — 20th century — Translations into English. I. Kennedy, Ellen Conroy.
PQ3986.Z5 E55   PQ3986Z5 E55.   841   LC 72-78987   ISBN 067050579X

French African verse / with English translations by John Reed **2.4845**
& Clive Wake.
London: Heinemann, [1972] xvi, 213 p.; 19 cm. — (African writers series; 106) English and French. 'An H.E.B. paperback.' 1. African poetry (French) I. Wake, Clive. joint comp. II. Reed, John, professor.
PQ3986.R4   PQ3986.Z5 F7.   841/.008   LC 73-156424   ISBN 0435901060

Anthologie de la nouvelle poésie algérienne: un essai et un choix **2.4846**
/ de Jean Sénac.
Paris: Librairie Saint-Germain-des-Prés, 1971. 126 p.: ill.; 18 cm. — (Poésie I; no 14) 1. Algerian poetry (French) I. Sénac, Jean.
PQ3988.A6 A5   LC 72-344193

Anthologie des écrivains français du Maghreb / sous la **2.4847**
direction de [sic] Albert Memmi; choix et présentation de
Jacqueline Arnaud, Jean Déjeux, Arlette Roth.
Paris: Présence africaine, 1969. 365 p. — (Anthologie des littératures maghrébines; t. 2) 1. African literature (French) — Africa, North I. Memmi, Albert. ed. II. Arnaud, Jacqueline. comp. III. Déjeux, Jean. joint comp. IV. Roth-Loly, Arlette, joint comp. V. Series.
PQ3988.N6 A58   LC 71-485129

Blair, Dorothy S. **2.4848**
Senegalese literature: a critical history / Dorothy S. Blair. — Boston: Twayne, c1984. 176 p.; 23 cm. — (Twayne's world authors series. TWAS 696) Includes index. 1. Senegalese literature (French) — History and criticism. I. T. II. Series.
PQ3988.5.S38 B55 1984   840/.9/9663 19   LC 83-16619   ISBN 0805765433

PQ3989 Individual Authors, to 1960

Camara, Laye. **2.4849**
L'enfant noir, roman. — Paris: Plon, [1953] 256 p.; 19 cm. 1. Camara, Laye — Biography. 2. Authors, Guinean — Biography. I. T.
PQ3989.C27 Z465   843 B   LC a 54-2532

Lee, Sonia. **2.4850**
Camara Laye / by Sonia Lee. — Boston: Twayne Publishers, c1984. 126 p.; 26 cm. — (Twayne's world authors series; TWAS 695. French literature) Includes index. 1. Camara, Laye — Criticism and interpretation. I. T.
PQ3989.C27 Z75 1984   843 19   LC 83-12780   ISBN 0805765425

Dadié, Bernard Binlin, 1916-. **2.4851**
Îles de tempête; pièce en sept tableaux [par] Bernard B. Dadié. — Paris: Présence africaine, [1973] 141 p.; 21 cm. — (Théâtre) I. T.
PQ3989.D28 I4   842   LC 74-168801

Dadié, Bernard Binlin, 1916-. **2.4852**
Légendes et poèmes / Bernard B. Dadié. — Paris: Seghers, c1966. 257 p. I. T.
PQ3989.D28 L4   LC 66-78007

Dadié, Bernard Binlin, 1916-. **2.4853**
Un nègre à Paris / Bernard B. Dadié. — Paris: Présence africaine, [c1959]. 229 p. I. T.
PQ3989.D28 N4   LC a 60-2999

Oyono, Ferdinand, 1929-. **2.4854**
Une vie de boy / Ferdinand Oyono. — [Paris]: Julliard, c1956. 185 p.; 18 cm. — I. T.
PQ3989.O9 V5   ISBN 2266004697

Oyono, Ferdinand, 1929-. **2.4855**
Le vieux nègre et la médaille: roman / Ferdinand Oyono. — Paris: Julliard, 1972, c1956. 191 p.; 18 cm. — (Collection 10/18; 695) I. T.
PQ3989.O9 V5 1972

Oyono, Ferdinand, 1929-. **2.4856**
Houseboy; translated from the French by John Reed. — London, Heinemann [1966] 140 p. 21 cm. — (African writers series, 29) Originally published as Une vie de boy. Paris, Julliard, 1958. I. T.
PZ4.O988Ho PQ3989.O9V53   LC 66-70765

Rabearivelo, Jean Joseph, 1901-1937. **2.4857**
Translations from the night: selected poems of Jean-Joseph Rabearivelo / edited with English translations by John Reed and Clive Wake. — London: Heinemann Educational, 1975. xxii, 73 p.; 19 cm. (African writers series; 167) English and French or Malagasy parallel text. I. T.
PQ3989.R23 A26 1975   PQ3989R23 A26 1975.   841   LC 75-326551   ISBN 0435901672

Sembène, Ousmane, 1923-. **2.4858**
Les bouts de bois de Dieu: Banty Mam Yall. — Paris, Le livre contemporain, [1960] 381 p.; 22 cm. A novel. I. T.
PQ3989.S46.B6   LC a 61-766

Sembène, Ousmane, 1923-. **2.4859**
[Bouts de bois de Dieu. English] God's bits of wood. Translated by Francis Price. Introd. by A. Adu Boahen. — Garden City, N.Y.: Anchor Books, 1970. 360 p.; 18 cm. Translation of Les bouts de bois de Dieu. I. T.
PQ3989.S46 B613 1970   843 19   LC 75-133620

Sembène, Ousmane, 1923-. **2.4860**
[Mandat. English] The money-order; with, White genesis; translated by Clive Wake. London, Heinemann, 1972. [5], 138 p. 19 cm. (African writers series, 92) Translation of Vehi-Ciosane ou Blanche-Genèse suivi du Mandat. I. Sembène, Ousmane, 1923- Vehi-Ciosane. English. 1972. II. T.
PQ3989.S46 M313   843 19   LC 72-197852   ISBN 0435900927

Sembène, Ousmane, 1923-.   **2.4861**
[Xala. English] Xala / Sembene Ousmane; translated by Clive Wake. — 1st U.S. ed. — Westport, Conn.: L. Hill & Co., 1976, c1974. 114 p.: ill.; 22 cm. I. T.
PQ3989.S46 X313 1976   843 19   *LC* 75-41811   *ISBN* 0882080679

Senghor, Léopold Sédar, 1906-.   **2.4862**
Selected poems of Léopold Sédar Senghor / edited by Abiola Irele. — Cambridge; New York: Cambridge University Press, 1977. 134 p.: map; 24 cm. I. Irele, Abiola. II. T.
PQ3989.S47 A17 1977   PQ3989S47 A17 1977.   841   *LC* 76-16919
ISBN 0521213398

Senghor, Léopold Sédar, 1906-.   **2.4863**
Poèmes. — [4. éd. — Paris] Éditions du Seuil [1969, c1964] 253 p. 20 cm. I. T.
PQ3989.S47A6 1969c   *LC* 79-30690

Leusse, Hubert de.   **2.4864**
Léopold Sédar Senghor: l'africain / Hubert de Leusse. — [Paris]: Hatier, c1967. 253 p.: ill., portr.; 19 cm. 1. Senghor, Lépold Sédar, 1906- I. T.
PQ3989.S47 Z76   841   *LC* 67-111786

Mezu, Sebastian Okechukwu.   **2.4865**
The poetry of Léopold Sédar Senghor [by] S. Okechukwu Mezu. — [1st American ed.]. — Rutherford [N.J.]: Fairleigh Dickinson University Press, [1973] 101 p.; 22 cm. 1. Senghor, Léopold Sédar, 1906- I. T.
PQ3989.S47 Z79 1973b   841   *LC* 73-5107   *ISBN* 0838613918

PQ3989.2 Individual Authors, 1961–

Bâ, Mariama.   **2.4866**
Une si longue lettre / Mariama Bâ. — Dakar: Nouvelles éditions africaines, [1980] 131 p.; 21 cm. — I. T.
PQ3989.2.B23 S5   843 19   *LC* 81-151322   *ISBN* 2723604306

Bâ, Mariama.   **2.4867**
[Si longue lettre. English] So long a letter / Mariama Bâ; translated from the French by Modupé Bodé–Thomas. — London: Heinemann, 1981. 90 p.; 19 cm. — (African writers series. 248) Translation of: Une si longue lettre. I. T. II. Series.
PQ3989.2.B23 S513 1981   843 19   *LC* 82-106728   *ISBN* 0435902482

Beti, Mongo, 1932-.   **2.4868**
[Le pauvre Christ de Bomba. English] The poor Christ of Bomba; translated by Gerald Moore. London, Heinemann, 1971. [4], 219 p. 21 cm. Translation of Le pauvre Christ de Bomba. I. T.
PZ4.B564 Po PQ3989.2.B45   843   *LC* 72-177858   *ISBN* 0435906321

Beti, Mongo, 1932-.   **2.4869**
Mission to Kala / Mongo Beti; translated from the French by Peter Green. — London: Heinemann Educational Books, 1964. 182 p. — (African writers series; 13.) Translation of Mission terminée. I. T.
PQ3989.2.B45 M5 1964   *LC* 58-12436   *ISBN* 0435900137

Diop, David.   **2.4870**
Hammer blows and other writings [by] David Mandessi Diop. Translated and edited by Simon Mpondo and Frank Jones. — Bloomington: Indiana University Press, [1973] vi, 88 p.: port.; 21 cm. In English, with poems also in original French. I. Mpondo, Simon, tr. II. Jones, Frank, 1915- tr. III. T.
PQ3989.2.D56 H3   841   *LC* 73-75398   *ISBN* 0253327032

Kane, Hamidou.   **2.4871**
L'aventure ambigüe: récit / par Cheikh Hamidou Kane; préf. de Vincent Monteil. — Paris: Julliard, 1961. 191 p. I. T.
PQ3989.2.K3 A98 1961   *LC* 64-311

Fall, Aminata Sow.   **2.4872**
La grève des Bàttu: ou Les déchets humains / Aminata Sow Fall. — Dakar: Nouveles Éditions Africaines, 1979. 131 p.; 21 cm. I. T. II. Title: Les déchets humains.
PQ3989.2S731 G837 1979   PQ3989.F34 G7.   *ISBN* 2723604373

PQ4001–4199 HISTORY. CRITICISM

**Questioni e correnti di storia letteraria, a cura di U. Bosco [et. • 2.4873
al.]**
Milano C. Marzorati [1949] 965p. (Problemi ed orientamenti critici di lingus e di letteratura italiana, v. 3) 1. Italian literature — Addresses, essays, lectures I. Bosco, Umberto, 1900- II. Series.
PQ4003 Q4

**Dictionary of Italian literature / Peter Bondanella, Julia   2.4874
Conaway Bondanella, co–editors.**
Westport, Conn.: Greenwood Press, 1979. xxvii, 621 p.; 24 cm. Includes index. 1. Italian literature — Dictionaries. I. Bondanella, Peter E., 1943- II. Bondanella, Julia Conaway.
PQ4006.D45   850/.3   *LC* 78-4022   *ISBN* 0313204217

Weinberg, Bernard, 1909-1973.   • 2.4875
A history of literary criticism in the Italian Renaissance. — [Chicago] University of Chicago Press [1961] 2 v. (x, 1184 p.) 24 cm. Bibliography: v. 2, p. 1113-1158. 1. Italian literature — 16th cent. — Hist. & crit. 2. Criticism — Hist. I. T. II. Title: Literary criticism in the Italian Renaissance.
PQ4027.W4   850.903   *LC* 60-5470

Binni, Walter, 1913-.   • 2.4876
Storia letteraria delle regioni d'Italia. [Di] Walter Binni [e] Natalino Sapegno. Firenze, Sansoni, 1968. 885 p. illus., plates. 22 1/2 cm. "Scritti apparsi su Tuttitalia, enciclopedia articolata in monografie dell'Italia antica e moderna." 1. Italian literature — History and criticism I. Sapegno, Natalino, 1901- II. T.
PQ4037.B5

**Storia della letteratura italiana / direttori, Emilio Cecchi e   • 2.4877
Nataliano Sapegno.**
1. ed. — Milano: Garzanti, 1965-1969, 1976 printing. 9 v.: ill. — (Collezione maggiore Garzanti) 1. Italian literature — History and criticism I. Cecchi, Emilio, 1884-1966. II. Sapegno, Natalino, 1901-
PQ4037 C4   850.9   *LC* 68-117229

De Sanctis, Francesco, 1817-1883.   • 2.4878
[Storia della letteratura italiana. English] History of Italian literature. Translated by Joan Redfern. New York, Barnes & Noble [1968, c1931] 2 v. (viii, 972 p.) 23 cm. Translation of Storia della letteratura italiana. 1. Italian literature — History and criticism I. T.
PQ4037.D413 1968   850.9   *LC* 68-20699

Donadoni, Eugenio, 1870-1924.   2.4879
[Breve storia della letteratura italiana. English] A history of Italian literature. With additional materials on twentieth–century literature by Ettore Mazzali and Robert J. Clements. Translated by Richard Monges. New York, New York University Press, 1969. 2 v. (xiii, 685 p.) 21 cm. (The Gotham library) Translation of Breve storia della letteratura italiana. 1. Italian literature — History and criticism I. Mazzali, Ettore. II. Clements, Robert John, 1912- III. T.
PQ4037.D613 1969   850.9   *LC* 68-13026

Wilkins, Ernest Hatch, 1880-1966.   2.4880
A history of Italian literature / by Ernest Hatch Wilkins. — Rev. / by Thomas G. Bergin. — Cambridge: Harvard University Press, 1974. xi, 570 p.; 25 cm. Includes index. 1. Italian literature — History and criticism I. Bergin, Thomas Goddard, 1904- II. T.
PQ4038.W5 1974   PQ4038 W5 1974.   850/.9   *LC* 74-80444
       ISBN 0674397010

PQ4064–4185 Special Periods. Special Forms

Croce, Benedetto, 1866-1952.   • 2.4881
Storia della età barocca in Italia; pensiero–poesia e letteratura–vita morale. 5. Ed. Bari G. Laterza 1967. 518p. (His Scritti di storia letteraria e politica, 23)
1. Italian literature — 17th century — History and criticism 2. Baroque literature I. T.
PQ4082 C7 1967

Pacifici, Sergio.   • 2.4882
A guide to contemporary Italian literature, from futurism to neorealism. Pref. by Thomas G. Bergin. — Cleveland: World Pub. Co., [1962] 352 p.; 18 cm. — (Meridian books, M122) 1. Italian literature — 20th century — History and criticism. I. T. II. Title: Contemporary Italian literature.
PQ4087.P23   850.904   *LC* 61-15743

**Writers & society in contemporary Italy: a collection of essays   2.4883
/ edited by Michael Caesar and Peter Hainsworth.**
New York: St. Martin's Press, 1984. xii, 289 p.; 23 cm. 1. Italian literature — 20th century — History and criticism — Addresses, essays, lectures. 2. Italy — Civilization — 1945- — Addresses, essays, lectures. I. Caesar, Michael. II. Hainsworth, Peter. III. Title: Writers and society in contemporary Italy.
PQ4088.W75 1984   850/.9/00914 19   *LC* 83-40503   *ISBN* 0312893507

Herrick, Marvin Theodore, 1899-.   • 2.4884
Italian comedy in the Renaissance [by] Marvin T. Herrick. — Freeport, N.Y.: Books for Libraries Press, [1970, c1960] vi, 238 p.; 23 cm. — (Essay index reprint series) 1. Italian drama (Comedy) — History and criticism. I. T.
PQ4149.H4 1970   852/.052   *LC* 70-128259   *ISBN* 0836918827

Lea, Kathleen Marguerite.   • 2.4885
Italian popular comedy; a study in the Commedia dell'arte, 1560–1620, with special reference to the English stage. — New York, Russell & Russell, 1962. 2 v. illus. 23 cm. 'First published in 1934. Reissued, 1962.' Includes bibliography. 1. Commedia dell'arte 2. English drama — Early modern and Elizabethan — Hist. & crit. 3. Literature, Comparative — English and Italian. I. T.
PQ4155.L4 1962   852.409   *LC* 62-10692

Nicoll, Allardyce, 1894-.   • 2.4886
The world of Harlequin: a critical study of the commedia dell'arte / by Allardyce Nicoll. — Cambridge [Eng.]: University Press, 1963. xiv, 242 p.: ill. 1. Commedia dell'arte I. T.
PQ4155.N5   *LC* 63-5661   *ISBN* 0521058341

PQ4201–4263 COLLECTIONS OF ITALIAN LITERATURE

Letteratura dell'Italia unita, 1861–1968 / Gianfranco Contini.   • 2.4887
Firenze: Sansoni, c1968. vii, 1118 p.; 24 cm. — 1. Italian literature — 19th century 2. Italian literature — 20th century I. Contini, Gianfranco. comp.
PQ4204.A9C6   850.9   *LC* 68-117555

**The Oxford book of Italian verse: XIIIth century–XIXth   • 2.4888
century / chosen by St. John Lucas.**
2d ed. rev. with XXth century Suppl. by C. Dionisotti. — Oxford: Clarendon Press, 1952. xxxvi, 615 p.; 17 cm. 1. Italian poetry I. Lucas, St. John Welles Lucas, 1879-1934.
PQ4208.O8 1952   *LC* 52-14934

**Poeti del Duecento: poesia cortese toscana e settentrionale / a   • 2.4889
cura di Gianfranco Contini.**
Torino: G. Einaudi, c1976. 2 v. (ix, 362 p.); 20 cm. (Classici Ricciardi; 4) 'Questa edizione riproduce esattamente parte del vol. 2, tomi I e II ... La Letteratura italiana; storia e testi ... pubblicato nell'anno 1960.' 1. Italian poetry — To 1400 I. Contini, Gianfranco.
PQ4213.A2 P69   *LC* 76-474482

**Poeti del Duecento: poesia didattica del Nord / a cura di   • 2.4890
Gianfranco Contini.**
Torino: G. Einaudi, 1978. vi, 282 p.; 20 cm. — (Classici Ricciardi; 80) Reprint of the 1960 ed. published by R. Ricciardi, Milan, which was issued as part of v. 2, t. 1-2 of La Letteratura italiana: Storia e testi. 1. Italian poetry — To 1400 2. Didactic poetry, Italian. 3. Italian poetry — Italy, Northern. I. Contini, Gianfranco.
PQ4213.A2 P69 1978   *LC* 79-390070

**Poeti del Duecento: poesia popolare e giullaresca / a cura di • 2.4891
Gianfranco Contini.**
Torino: G. Einaudi, 1978. 192 p.; 20 cm. — (Classici Ricciardi; 76) Reprint of the 1960 ed. published by R. Ricciardi, Milan-Naples, which was issued as part of v. 2, t. 1-2 of La Letteratura italiana: Storia e testi. 1. Italian poetry — To 1400 I. Contini, Gianfranco.
PQ4213.A2 P693 1978   851/.1/08   LC 78-391438

**Poeti del Duecento: poesia realistica toscana / a cura di • 2.4892
Gianfranco Contini.**
Torino: G. Einaudi, 1977. vi, 120 p.; 20 cm. (Classici Ricciardi; 34) 'Questa edizione riproduce esattamente parte del vol. 2, tomi I e II ... La Letteratura italiana; storia e testi ... pubblicato nell'anno 1960.' 1. Italian poetry — To 1400 I. Contini, Gianfranco.
PQ4213.A2 P694   LC 77-464085

Lind, Levi Robert, 1906- comp. 2.4893
Twentieth–century Italian poetry; a bilingual anthology, edited by L. R. Lind, with an introd. and biographical notes by Edward Williamson. — [Indianapolis: Bobbs-Merrill, 1974] xxxi, 400 p.; 21 cm. — (The Library of liberal arts) 1. Italian poetry — 20th century 2. Italian poetry — 20th century — Translations into English. 3. English poetry — Translations from Italian. I. T.
PQ4214.L5 1974   PQ4214 L5 1974.   851/.9/108   LC 73-11343
ISBN 0672514095

The New Italian poetry, 1945 to the present: a bilingual 2.4894
anthology / edited and translated by Lawrence R. Smith.
Berkeley: University of California Press, c1981. xvii, 483 p.; 24 cm. 1. Italian poetry — Translations into English. 2. English poetry — Translations from Italian. 3. Italian poetry — 20th century I. Smith, Lawrence R., 1945-
PQ4214.N4   851/.914/08 19   LC 78-66014   ISBN 0520038592

Sanguineti, Edoardo. • 2.4895
Poesia del Novecento. A cura di Edoardo Sanguineti. [Torino] G. Einaudi [1969] lxii, 1146 p. plates. 22 cm. (Parnaso italiano, 11) Millenni, 27. 1. Italian poetry — 20th century I. T. II. Series.
PQ 4214 S22 1969   LC 70-462741

Kay, George R. • 2.4896
The Penguin book of Italian verse / with plain prose translations of each poem. Harmondsworth, Middlesex: Penguin Books, 1958. 424 p. (Penguin poets. D37.) 1. Italian poetry (Collections) 2. Italian poetry — Translations into English. 3. English literature — Translations from Italian. I. T. II. Series.
PQ4225.E8 K3   LC 59-2301

Five Italian Renaissance comedies / edited by Bruce Penman. 2.4897
Harmondsworth; New York: Penguin, 1978. 444 p.; 18 cm. — (Penguin classics) 1. Italian drama (Comedy) 2. Italian drama — To 1700 3. Italian drama — Translations into English. 4. English drama — Translations from Italian. I. Penman, Bruce.
PQ4233.F58   852/.052   LC 79-304949   ISBN 014044338X

Bentley, Eric, 1916- ed. 2.4898
The classic theatre. [1st ed.] Garden City, N.Y., Doubleday, 1958-61. 4 v. 19 cm. (Doubleday anchor books, A155) 1. English drama — Translations from foreign literature. I. T.
PQ4244.E5 B4   852.082   LC 58-12033

Bentley, Eric, 1916-. • 2.4899
Genius of the Italian theater. — [New York]: New American Library, 1964. 584 p. (Mentor book, MQ599.) Seven plays, and five essays on the Italian theater and playwrights. 1. Italian drama — Translations into English 2. English drama — Translations from Spanish. 3. Italian drama — Addresses, essays, lectures. I. T.
PQ4244.E6 B4   852.082   LC 64-25082

Corrigan, Robert Willoughby, 1927- comp. • 2.4900
Masterpieces of the modern Italian theatre; six plays, edited by Robert W. Corrigan. — New York: Collier Books, [1967] 352 p.; 19 cm. 1. Italian drama — Translations into English. 2. English drama — Translations from Italian. I. T.
PQ4244.E6 C6   852/.008   LC 66-18765

PQ4265–4886 Individual Authors and Works

PQ4265–4556 To 1400

PQ4266–4297 Boccaccio

Boccaccio, Giovanni, 1313-1375. • 2.4901
[Works. 1980] Opere / [di] Giovanni Boccaccio; a cura di Cesare Segre; commento di Maria Segre Consigli e Antonia Benvenuti. — Milano: U. Mursia, [1980?] xxix, 1398 p.; 21 cm. — (Grandi scrittori di ogni paese. Serie italiana.) I. Segre, Cesare. II. Segre Consigli, Maria. III. Benvenuti, Antonia. IV. T. V. Series.
PQ4266.A1 1980   858/.109 19   LC 81-117191

Boccaccio, Giovanni, 1313-1375. • 2.4902
Antologia delle opere minori volgari. A cura di Giuseppe Gigli. Nuova presentazione di Vittore Branca. Firenze Sansoni [1961] 335p. (Biblioteca carducciana. 2. ser., 1) I. Gigli, Giuseppe, 1863-1921 II. T.
PQ4266 A3 G5 1961

Boccaccio, Giovanni, 1313-1375. • 2.4903
Il Decameron / Giovanni Boccaccio; nuova ed. a cura di Charles S. Singleton. — Bari: Laterza, 1955. 2 v. — (Scrittori d'Italia; n. 97-98) (His Opere; 7-8) I. Singleton, Charles Southward, 1909- II. T.
PQ4267.A2 1955   LC 56-1498

Boccaccio, Giovanni, 1313-1375. 2.4904
[Decamerone. English] The Decameron; translated with an introduction by G. H. McWilliam. Harmondsworth, Penguin, 1972. 833 p. 19 cm. (Penguin classics) I. McWilliam, George Henry, tr. II. T.
PQ4272.E5 A355 1972   853/.1   LC 73-150738   ISBN 0140442693

Boccaccio, Giovanni, 1313-1375. 2.4905
[Decamerone. English] The Decameron: a new translation: 21 novelle, contemporary reactions, modern criticism / Giovanni Boccaccio; selected, translated, and edited by Mark Musa and Peter E. Bondanella. — 1st ed. — New York: Norton, c1977. xvi, 334 p.; 22 cm. — (A Norton critical edition) Translation of Decamerone. I. Musa, Mark. II. Bondanella, Peter E., 1943- III. T.
PQ4272.E5 A357 1977   853/.1   LC 77-5664   ISBN 0393044580.
ISBN 0393091325 pbk

Boccaccio, Giovanni, 1313-1375. 2.4906
[Decamerone. English] Decameron / Giovanni Boccaccio; the John Payne translation, revised and annotated by Charles S. Singleton. — Berkeley: University of California Press, c1982. 3 v. (xx, 948 p.): ill.; 25 cm. Translation of: Decamerone. 'This revision of the John Payne translation is based on the newly identified holograph manuscript of the Decameron known as Hamilton 90'—T.p. verso. Includes index. I. Payne, John, 1842-1916. II. Singleton, Charles Southward, 1909- III. T.
PQ4272.E5 A36 1982   853/.1 19   LC 77-83112   ISBN 0520035577

Boccaccio, Giovanni, 1313-1375. 2.4907
[Decamerone. English] The Decameron / Giovanni Boccaccio; translated by Mark Musa and Peter Bondanella. — New York: Norton, c1982. ix, 689 p. Translation of: Decamerone. I. Musa, Mark. II. Bondanella, Peter E., 1943- III. T.
PQ4272.E5 A357 1983   PQ4272E5 A363 1983.   853/.1 19   LC 82-24674   ISBN 0393017540

Boccaccio, Giovanni, 1313-1375. 2.4908
[Decamerone. English] The Decameron; translated from the Italian by Frances Winwar [pseud. 1st Modern Library ed.] New York, Modern Library [1955] xxxviii, 666 p. 19 cm. (The Modern library of the world's best books [71]) I. Winwar, Frances, pseud. tr. II. T.
PQ4272.E5 A39 1955   853.15   LC 55-5731

Boccaccio, Giovanni, 1313-1375. 2.4909
[Ameto. English] L'Ameto / Giovanni Boccaccio; translated by Judith Serafini-Sauli. — New York: Garland, 1985. xxix, 171 p.: ill.; 23 cm. (Garland library of medieval literature; v. 33. Series B) I. Serafini-Sauli, Judith Powers. II. T.
PQ4272.E5 A95 1985   853/.1 19   LC 84-48066   ISBN 0824089189

Boccaccio, Giovanni, 1313-1375.   **2.4910**
[Corbaccio. English] The corbaccio / Giovanni Boccaccio; translated and edited by Anthony K. Cassell. — Urbana: University of Illinois Press, [1975] xxvii, 194 p.; 24 cm. I. T.
PQ4272.E5 C6 1975   853/.1   *LC* 75-9844   *ISBN* 0252004795

Boccaccio, Giovanni, 1313-1375.   **• 2.4911**
[Il ninfale Fiesolano. English] The nymph of Fiesole: (Il ninfale fiesolano) / by Giovanni Boccaccio; a translation by Daniel J. Donno; illus. by Angela Conner. — New York: Columbia University press, 1960. — xvii, 149 p.; 22 cm. Translation based on the Italian text of Vincenzo Pernicone. I. Donno, Daniel J. II. Boccaccio, Giovanni, 1313-1375. Nymph of Fiesole 1960. III. T.
PQ4272.E5 N23   *LC* 60-5817

Bergin, Thomas Goddard, 1904-.   **2.4912**
Boccaccio / Thomas G. Bergin. — New York: Viking Press, 1981. viii, 392 p.; 24 cm. Includes index. 1. Boccaccio, Giovanni, 1313-1375 — Criticism and interpretation. I. T.
PQ4286.B4   858/.109 19   *LC* 81-65281   *ISBN* 0670177350

PQ4299 Cavalcanti

Cavalcanti, Guido, d. 1300.   **• 2.4913**
Le rime, a cura di Guido Favati. — Milano: R. Ricciardi, 1957. xvii, 426 p. — (Documenti di filologia; 1) I. Favati, Guido. II. T.
PQ4299 C2 1957   *LC* 58-22657

PQ4300–4464 Dante

Dante Alighieri, 1265-1321.   **• 2.4914**
Tutte le opere; a cura di Luigi Blasucci. — [Firenze] Sansoni [1965] xxii, 941 p.; 22 cm. 'Glossario italiano': p. [827]-872. I. Blasucci, Luigi, ed. II. T.
PQ4300.A1x

Dante Alighieri, 1265-1321.   **2.4915**
[Divina commedia English & Italian] The Divine comedy. — [1st American ed.] New York, Oxford University Press, 1948. 3 v. 21 cm. 1. Inferno. 2. Purgatorio. 3. Paradiso. I. T.
PQ4302.F48   *LC* 49-8778

Dante Alighieri, 1265-1321.   **2.4916**
[Divina commedia English & Italian] The divine comedy. Translated, with a commentary, by Charles S. Singleton. [Princeton, N.J.] Princeton University Press [1970-75] 3 v. in 6. illus., maps. 21 cm. (Bollingen series. 80) Each of the three parts consists of a volume of text and a volume of commentary. I. Singleton, Charles Southward, 1909- II. T. III. Series.
PQ4302.F70   851/.1   *LC* 74-169252

Dante Alighieri, 1265-1321.   **2.4917**
La divina commedia. Edited and annotated by C. H. Grandgent. Rev. by Charles S. Singleton. Cambridge, Mass., Harvard University Press, 1972. xxxvii, 950 p. illus. 23 cm. Italian text with English annotation. I. Grandgent, C. H. (Charles Hall), 1862-1939. ed. II. Singleton, Charles Southward, 1909- ed. III. T.
PQ4302.F72   851/.1   *LC* 72-78429

Dante Alighieri, 1265-1321.   **• 2.4918**
[Rime. English and Italian] Dante's lyric poetry [edited and translated from the Italian by] K. Foster and P. Boyde. Oxford, Clarendon P., 1967. 2 v. 22 1/2 cm. 1. Dante Alighieri, 1265-1321. Rime. I. Foster, Kenelm. ed. II. Boyde, Patrick. ed. III. T.
PQ4309.A1 1967   851/.1   *LC* 67-84064

Dante Alighieri, 1265-1321.   **• 2.4919**
[Poems. Italian. 1946] Rime; a cura di Gianfranco Contini. 2. Ed., rev. e accresciuta. Torino G. Einaudi 1946. 295p. (Nuova raccolta di classici italiani annotati, 1) I. Contini, Gianfranco. ed. II. T.
PQ4309 A1 1946

Dante Alighieri, 1265-1321.   **• 2.4920**
[Vita nuova. English & Italian] Vita nuova. A translation and an essay by Mark Musa. A new ed. Bloomington, Indiana University Press [1973] xiv, 210 p. 20 cm. (A Midland book, MB-162) Prose in English; sonnets in English and Italian. 'An essay on the Vita nuova': p. [87]-174. I. Musa, Mark. tr. II. T.
PQ4310.V2 1973   851/.1   *LC* 72-79905   *ISBN* 0253201624

Mazzaro, Jerome.   **2.4921**
The figure of Dante: an essay on the Vita nuova / by Jerome Mazzaro. — Princeton, N.J.: Princeton University Press, c1981. xix, 150 p.; 22 cm. — (Princeton essays in literature.) Includes index. 1. Dante Alighieri, 1265-1321. Vita nuova. I. T. II. Series.
PQ4310.V4 M3   851/.1 19   *LC* 81-47146   *ISBN* 0691064741

Singleton, Charles Southward, 1909-.   **• 2.4922**
An essay on the Vita nuova. Cambridge Pub. for the Dante Society by the Harvard University Press 1958. 168p. 1. Dante Alighieri, 1265-1321. Vita nuova I. T.
PQ4310 V4 S5

Dante Alighieri, 1265-1321.   **2.4923**
The divine comedy of Dante Alighieri: a verse translation / with introductions & commentary by Allen Mandelbaum; drawings by Barry Moser. — Berkeley; London: University of California Press, c1982. xxviii, 303 p.: ill.; 29 cm. Spine title: Purgatorio. I. Mandelbaum, Allen, 1926- II. T. III. Title: Purgatorio.
PQ4315. M3x   851/.1 18   851/.1 19   *LC* 73-94441   *ISBN* 0520045165

Dante Alighieri, 1265-1321.   **2.4924**
[Divina commedia. English] The divine comedy / Dante; a new verse translation by C.H. Sisson. — American ed. / foreword to the American edition by Thomas G. Bergin; introduction, commentary, notes, and bibliography by David H. Higgins. — Chicago: Regnery Gateway, c1981. iii, 688 p.; 21 cm. Translation of: Divina commedia. I. Sisson, C. H. (Charles Hubert), 1914- II. Higgins, David H. III. T.
PQ4315.S57 1981   851/.1 19   *LC* 81-52140   *ISBN* 0895266652

Dante Alighieri, 1265-1321.   **• 2.4925**
[Inferno. English] The Inferno; translated in verse by John Ciardi. Historical introd. by A.T. McAllister. New Brunswick, N.J., Rutgers University Press, 1954. 288 p. illus. 22 cm. 1. Hell — Poetry. I. Ciardi, John, 1916- tr. II. T.
PQ4315.2.C5   851.15   *LC* 54-9668

Dante Alighieri, 1265-1321.   **• 2.4926**
The Purgatorio / Dante Alighieri; a verse translation for the modern reader by John Ciardi; introd. by Archibald T. MacAllister. New York: New American Library, 1961. xxix, 350 p. (A Mentor book; ME1567) I. MacAllister, Archibald T. II. Ciardi, John, 1916- III. T.
PQ4315.3 C5   *LC* 61-18103   *ISBN* 0451615670

Dante Alighieri, 1265-1321.   **• 2.4927**
[Paradiso. English] The Paradiso. A verse rendering for the modern reader [by] John Ciardi. Introd. by John Freccero. New York, New American Library [1970] xxi, 367 p. 18 cm. (A Mentor book, MY 1036) 1. Heaven — Poetry. I. Ciardi, John, 1916- tr. II. T.
PQ4315.4.C5   851/.1   *LC* 72-130872

Dante Alighieri, 1265-1321.   **2.4928**
[Paradiso. English] Dante's Paradise / translated with notes and commentary by Mark Musa. — Bloomington: Indiana University Press, c1984. vii, 405 p.: ill.; 22 cm. Translation of: Paradiso. 1. Heaven — Poetry. I. Musa, Mark. II. T. III. Title: Paradise.
PQ4315.4.M8 1984   851/.1 19   *LC* 83-48828   *ISBN* 0253316197

PQ4330–4464 Biography. Criticism

Dante commentaries: eight studies of the Divine Comedy /   **2.4929**
edited by David Nolan.
Dublin: Published for University College and the Italian Cultural Institute [by] Irish Academic Press; Totowa, N.J.: Rowman and Littlefield, 1977. 184 p.; 22 cm. 1. Dante Alighieri, 1265-1321. Divina commedia I. Nolan, David.
PQ4332.D28   851/.1   *LC* 77-379363   *ISBN* 0874719666

Freccero, John. ed.   **• 2.4930**
Dante; a collection of critical essays. — Englewood Cliffs, N.J.: Prentice-Hall, [1965] 182 p.; 21 cm. — (A Spectrum book: Twentieth century views, S-TC-46) 1. Dante Alighieri, 1265-1321. I. T.
PQ4332.F7   851.1   *LC* 65-13596

Enciclopedia dantesca.   **• 2.4931**
Roma: Istituto della Enciclopedia italiana, c1970-1978. 6 v.: ill. 'Direttore Umberto Bosco.' Vol. 6: Appendice. 1. Dante Alighieri, 1265-1321 — Dictionaries, indexes, etc. I. Bosco, Umberto, 1900-
PQ4333.E5   *LC* 79-854728

Toynbee, Paget Jackson, 1855-1932.   **2.4932**
Concise dictionary of proper names and notable matters in the works of Dante. — New York: Phaeton Press, 1968. viii, 568 p.: geneal. tables.; 22 cm. Reprint of the 1914 ed. 1. Dante Alighieri, 1265-1321 — Dictionaries, indexes, etc. I. T.
PQ4333.T72 1968   851/.1   *LC* 68-15695

Barbi, Michele, 1867-1941.   **• 2.4933**
Life of Dante; translated and edited by Paul Ruggiers. — Berkeley, University of California Press, 1966 [c1954] 132 p. 19 cm. — (Paperback, Cal. 36) Translation of Dante: vita, opere e fortuna. 1. Dante Alighieri, 1265-1321. 2. Dante Alighieri, 1265-1321. Divina commedia I. T.
PQ4339.B453 1966   851.15   *LC* 54-6466

Anderson, William.   **2.4934**
Dante the maker / William Anderson. — London; Boston: Routledge & Kegan Paul, 1980. xii, 497 p.; 24 cm. Includes index. 1. Dante Alighieri, 1265-1321 — Criticism and interpretation. I. T.
PQ4390.A62   851/.1   *LC* 79-41311   *ISBN* 0710003226

Auerbach, Erich, 1892-1957.   • **2.4935**
Dante, poet of the secular world. Translated by Ralph Manheim. — [Chicago] University of Chicago Press [1961] viii, 194 p. 21 cm. Translation of Dante als Dichter der irdischen Welt. Bibliographical references included in 'Notes' (p. 181-191) 1. Dante Alighieri, 1265-1321. I. T.
PQ4390.A853   851.1   *LC* 61-11893

Bergin, Thomas Goddard, 1904-.   • **2.4936**
Dante's Divine comedy. — Englewood Cliffs, N.J.: Prentice-Hall, [1971] xi, 116 p.; 21 cm. — (Landmarks in literature) 1. Dante Alighieri, 1265-1321. Divina commedia I. T.
PQ4390.B573   851/.1   *LC* 73-151516   *ISBN* 0131974343

Croce, Benedetto, 1866-1952.   **2.4937**
[Poesia di Dante. English] The poetry of Dante. Translated by Douglas Ainslie. Mamaroneck, N.Y., P. P. Appel, 1971 [c1922] vi, 313 p. port. 22 cm. 1. Dante Alighieri, 1265-1321 — Criticism and interpretation. I. T.
PQ4390.C8 1971   851/.1   *LC* 74-162490   *ISBN* 0911858121

Mazzotta, Giuseppe, 1942-.   **2.4938**
Dante, poet of the desert: history and allegory in the Divine comedy / Giuseppe Mazzotta. — Princeton, N.J.: Princeton University Press, c1979. x, 343 p.; 23 cm. 1. Dante Alighieri, 1265-1321. Divina commedia 2. Dante Alighieri, 1265-1321 — Symbolism. 3. Allegory I. T.
PQ4390.M54   851/.1   *LC* 78-27468   *ISBN* 0691063990

Vossler, Karl, 1872-1949.   • **2.4939**
Mediaeval culture; an introduction to Dante and his times. New York, Ungar [1958] 2 v. 24 cm. Translation of Die göttliche Komödie. 1. Dante Aligihiere, 1265-1321 — Criticism and interpretation. 2. Civilization, Medieval I. T. II. Title: Die göttliche Komödie.
PQ 4390 V97 E5 1958   *LC* 58-10378   *ISBN* 0804419574

Williams, Charles, 1886-1945.   • **2.4940**
The figure of Beatrice; a study in Dante. — New York: Noonday Press, [1961] 236 p.; 21 cm. — (Noonday, 208) 1. Dante Alighieri, 1265-1321 — Characters — Beatrice. I. T.
PQ4410.B3 W5 1961   851.1   *LC* 61-8474

Gilson, Etienne, 1884-1978.   • **2.4941**
[Dante et la philosophie. English] Dante and philosophy, by Étienne Gilson. Translated by David Moore. Gloucester, Mass., P. Smith, 1968. xii, 338 p. 21 cm. Reprint of the 1949 ed. published under title Dante, the philosopher. 1. Dante Alighieri, 1265-1321 — Philosophy. I. T.
PQ4412.G55 1968   851/.1   *LC* 78-2368

Fergusson, Francis.   **2.4942**
Dante's drama of the mind, a modern reading of the Purgatorio, by Francis Fergusson. Princeton, Princeton University Press, 1953. x, 232 p. 23 cm. 1. Dante Alighieri, 1265-1321. Purgatorio. 2. Purgatory in literature. I. T.
PQ4447.F4   851.15   *LC* 52-13147

Boyde, Patrick.   • **2.4943**
Dante's style in his lyric poetry. — Cambridge [Eng.]: University Press, 1971. xii, 359 p.; 24 cm. A revision of the author's thesis, Cambridge, 1963. 1. Dante Alighieri, 1265-1321 — Style. I. T.
PQ4456.B6 1971   851/.1   *LC* 74-130906   *ISBN* 0521079187

Grandgent, C. H. (Charles Hall), 1862-1939.   **2.4944**
Companion to the Divine comedy / commentary by C. H. Grandgent as edited by Charles S. Singleton. — Cambridge, Mass.: Harvard University Press, 1975. xii, 316 p.: ill.; 22 cm. Includes index. 1. Dante Alighieri, 1265-1321 Divina commedia — Concordances. I. Singleton, Charles Southward, 1909- II. Dante Alighieri, 1265-1321. La divina commedia. III. T.
PQ4464.G7 1975   851/.1   *LC* 73-92714   *ISBN* 0674151755

Wilkins, Ernest Hatch, 1880-1966.   • **2.4945**
A concordance to the Divine comedy of Dante Alighieri / edited for the Dante Society of America by Ernest Hatch Wilkins and Thomas Goddard Bergin; associate editor: Anthony J. De Vito. — Cambridge, Mass.: Belknap Press of Harvard University Press, 1965. ix, 636 p.; 25 cm. Text in Italian. 1. Dante Alighieri, 1265-1321. 2. Dante Alighieri, 1265-1321 — Concordances. I. Bergin, Thomas Goddard, 1904- II. Dante Society of America. III. T.
PQ4464.W5 1966   *LC* 65-11195

PQ4475–4550 Petrarca

Petrarca, Francesco, 1304-1374.   • **2.4946**
Rime, trionfi, e poesie latine / a cura di F. Neri [et al.]. — Milano,: R. Ricciardi, [1951] xviii, 900 p.; 23 cm. — (Letteratura italiana. Storia e testi. v. 6) I. Neri, Ferdinando, 1880-1954. ed. II. T. III. Series.
PQ4475.A2 1951   *LC* 52-39807

Petrarca, Francesco, 1304-1374.   • **2.4947**
Prose. A cura di G. Martellotti [et al.] Milano R. Ricciardi [1955] 1205p. (Letteratura italiana. Storia e testi. v. 7) I. Martellotti, Guido, 1905- ed. II. T. III. Series.
PQ4489 A5 1955

Petrarca, Francesco, 1304-1374.   **2.4948**
[Rime English & Italian. 1976] Petrarch's lyric poems: the Rime sparse and other lyrics / translated and edited by Robert M. Durling. — Cambridge, Mass.: Harvard University Press, 1976. xii, 657 p.; 24 cm. English and Italian. Includes index. I. Durling, Robert M. II. T.
PQ4496.E23 D8   851/.1   *LC* 76-3716   *ISBN* 0674663454

Petrarca, Francesco, 1304-1374.   • **2.4949**
The triumphs of Petrarch / translated by Ernest Hatch Wilkins; drawings by Virgil Burnett. — Chicago: University of Chicago Press, 1962. ix, 112 p.: ill.; 23 cm. Poems. I. Petrarca, Francesco, 1304-1374. Trionfi. English. 1962. II. Wilkins, Ernest Hatch, 1880-1966. III. T.
PQ4496.E25 1962   *LC* 62-19622

Petrarca, Francesco, 1304-1374.   **2.4950**
Rerum familiarium libri, XVII–XXIV: v. 3: Letters on Familiar / tr. by Aldo S. Bernardo. — Baltimore: Johns Hopkins University Press, 1985. 352 p. 1. Petrarca, Francesco, 1304-1374 — Correspondence 2. Authors, Italian — To 1500 — Correspondence I. Petrarca, Francesco, 1304-1374. Rerum familiarium libri, XVII-XXIV II. T.
PQ4496.E29 E23 1982   *LC* 75-2418   *ISBN* 0801827507

Bishop, Morris, 1893-1973.   • **2.4951**
Petrarch and his world. Drawings by Alison Mason Kingsbury. Bloomington, Indiana University Press, 1963. 399 p. illus., map. 24 cm. 'Bibliography and notes': p. [376]-391. 1. Petrarca, Francesco, 1304-1374. I. T.
PQ4505.B5   831.1   *LC* 63-16611 rev

Wilkins, Ernest Hatch, 1880-1966.   • **2.4952**
Studies in the life and works of Petrarch. — Cambridge, Mass., Mediaeval Academy of America, 1955. xiv, 324 p. 24 cm. — (Publication (Mediaeval Academy of America) no. 63) Includes bibliographies. 1. Petrarca, Francesco, 1304-1374. I. T. II. Series.
PQ4505.Z5W5   928.5   *LC* 55-8492

Mann, Nicholas.   **2.4953**
Petrarch / Nicholas Mann. — Oxford [Oxfordshire]; New York: Oxford University Press, 1984. 121 p.; 23 cm. (Past masters.) Includes index. 1. Petrarca, Francesco, 1304-1374 — Criticism and interpretation. I. T. II. Series.
PQ4540.M3 1984   851/.1 19   *LC* 84-4404   *ISBN* 0192876104

Foster, Kenelm.   **2.4954**
Petrarch: poet and humanist / Kenelm Foster. — [Edinburgh]: Edinburgh University Press, c1984. xii, 214 p.; 22 cm. — (Writers of Italy series. 9) Includes indexes. 1. Petrarca, Francesco, 1304-1374 — Philosophy. 2. Petrarca, Francesco, 1304-1374 — Criticism and interpretation. I. T. II. Series.
PQ4542.F67 1984   851/.1 19   *LC* 84-231563   *ISBN* 0852244851

PQ4561–4664 Individual Authors, 1400–1700

PQ4563 Aretino

Aretino, Pietro, 1492-1556.   **2.4955**
[Works. 1976] Opere / di Pietro Aretino e di Anton Francesco Doni; a cura di Carlo Cordié. — Milano; Napoli: R. Ricciardi, 1976. viii, 1035 p.; 23 cm. — (Folengo, Aretino, Doni; t. 2) (Letteratura italiana: Storia e testi; 26, t. 2) Includes index. I. Doni, Anton Francesco, 1513-1574. Selections 1976. II. Cordié, Carlo. III. T. IV. Series. V. Series: Letteratura italiana: Storia e testi; 26, t. 2
PQ4204.A5 F64 t. 2 PQ4563.A1   *LC* 78-339928

Aretino, Pietro, 1492-1556.   • **2.4956**
Tutte le commedie / Pietro Aretino; A cura di G.B. De Sanctis. — Milano: Mursia, [1968]. –. 542 p.; 18 cm. — (Grande universale Mursia. Letteratura,; 13) Classici antiche e moderni, 30. Nota bio-bibliografica: p.[22]-26. I. De Sanctis, G.B. II. T.
PQ4563.A19 1972   LC 78-424604

Aretino, Pietro, 1492-1556.   **2.4957**
[Correspondence. 1976] Selected letters [of] Aretino / translated with an introduction by George Bull. — Harmondsworth; New York: Penguin, 1976. 252 p.; 19 cm. — (The Penguin classics) I. T.
PQ4564.A4 E5 1976   856/.3   LC 76-380093   ISBN 0140443177

PQ4566–4603 Ariosto

Ariosto, Lodovico, 1474-1533.   • **2.4958**
Orlando furioso. A cura di Lanfranco Caretti. — Milano, R. Ricciardi [1954] 1248 p. 23 cm. — (Letteratura italiana. Storia e testi. v. 19) Comments and critical notes included in the author's Opere minori. Milano, 1954. I. T. II. Series.
PQ4567.A2 1954   LC 55-4540

Ariosto, Lodovico, 1474-1533.   • **2.4959**
Opere minori. A cura di Cesare Segre. — Milano, R. Ricciardi [1954] xxv, 1253 p.; 23 cm. (Letteratura italiana, storia e testi, v. 20) Bibliography: p. xxii-xxv. I. Segre, Cesare, ed. II. T.
PQ4578 A1 1954

Ariosto, Lodovico, 1474-1533.   **2.4960**
[Orlando furioso. English] Orlando furioso. Translated into English heroical verse by Sir John Harington (1591). Edited with an introd. by Robert McNulty. Oxford, Clarendon Press, 1972. liv, 588 p. plates. 28 cm. 1. Roland — Romances. I. Harington, John, Sir, 1560-1612. tr. II. T.
PQ4582.E5 A35 1972   851/.3   LC 72-187149

Ariosto, Lodovico, 1474-1533.   **2.4961**
[Orlando furioso. English] Orlando furioso = The frenzy of Orlando: a romantic epic / by Ludovico Ariosto; translated with an introduction by Barbara Reynolds. — Harmondsworth; Baltimore: Penguin, 1975-. v.   : ill., geneal. tables; 19 cm. — (The Penguin classics) Translation of Orlando furioso. 1. Roland (Legendary character) — Romances. I. Reynolds, Barbara. II. T. III. Title: Frenzy of Orlando.
PQ4582.E5 A368 1975   851/.3   LC 75-327748   ISBN 0140443118

Ariosto, Lodovico, 1474-1533.   **2.4962**
[Orlando furioso. English] Orlando Furioso [by] Ludovico Ariosto; an English prose translation by Guido Waldman. London, New York, Oxford University Press, 1974. xvii, 630 p. 21 cm. 1. Roland — Romances. I. Waldman, Guido. tr. II. T.
PQ4582.E5 A38 1974   851/.3   LC 74-174554   ISBN 0192125761 ISBN 0192811614

PQ4608–4634 B–T

Bembo, Pietro, 1470-1547.   • **2.4963**
Prose e rime; a cura di Carlo Dionisotti. [2d ed. accresciuta. Torino] Unione tipografico-editrice torinese [1966] 731 p. illus. I. Dionisotti, Carlo. II. T.
PQ4608.A1x

Bembo, Pietro, 1470-1547.   • **2.4964**
[Asolani. English] Gli Asolani. Translated by Rudolf B. Gottfried. Freeport, N.Y., Books for Libraries Press [1971, c1954] xx, 200 p. 23 cm. (Indiana University publications. Humanities series, no. 31) I. T.
PQ4608.A6 1971   858/.3/07   LC 76-168501   ISBN 0836959418

Boiardo, Matteo Maria, 1440 or 41-1494.   **2.4965**
Tutte le opere di Matteo M. Boiardo: a cura di Angelandrea Zottoli. — Milano: A. Mondadori, [1936-37] 2 v.; 18 cm. — (I classici Mondadori, fondazione Borletti) I. Zottoli, Angelandrea, ed. II. T.
PQ4612.A1   LC 37-2643

Michelangelo Buonarroti, 1475-1564.   **2.4966**
Complete poems and selected letters of Michelangelo / translated, with foreword and notes, by Creighton Gilbert; edited, with biographical introd., by Robert N. Linscott. — Princeton, N.J.: Princeton University Press, c1980. lvii, 317 p.; 22 cm. 'Third edition.' I. Gilbert, Creighton. II. Linscott, Robert Newton, 1886- III. T.
PQ4615.B6 A23 1980   851/.4 19   LC 79-87767   ISBN 0691072345

Michelangelo Buonarroti, 1475-1564.   • **2.4967**
[Rime. English] The sonnets of Michelangelo. Translated by Elizabeth Jennings, with a selection of Michelangelo drawings and an introd. by Michael

Ayrton. [1st ed. in the U.S.] Garden City, N.Y., Doubleday, 1970 [c1961] 119 p. illus. 24 cm. Translation of Rime. I. Jennings, Elizabeth, tr. II. T.
PQ4615.B6 A27 1970   851/.4   LC 71-89122

Cambon, Glauco.   **2.4968**
Michelangelo's poetry: fury of form / Glauco Cambon. — Princeton, N.J.: Princeton University Press, c1985. xvi, 220 p.: ill.; 23 cm. Includes index. 1. Michelangelo Buonarroti, 1475-1564 — Criticism and interpretation. I. T.
PQ4615.B6 C3 1985   851/.4 19   LC 85-42679   ISBN 0691066485

Clements, Robert John, 1912-.   • **2.4969**
The poetry of Michelangelo, by Robert J. Clements. New York: New York University Press, 1965. xiii, 368 p. illus., facsims. 24 cm. 1. Michelangelo Buonarroti, 1475-1564. I. T.
PQ4615.B6 C55   851/.4   LC 65-19514   ISBN

Guarini, Battista, 1538-1612.   **2.4970**
[Pastor fido. English & Italian] Il pastor fido = The faithfull shepherd / Battista Guarini; translated (1647) by Richard Fanshawe; edited, with introd., by J.H. Whitfield. — Austin: University of Texas Press, c1976. x, 413 p.; 21 cm. (Edinburgh bilingual library; 11) English and Italian. I. Fanshawe, Richard, Sir, 1608-1666. II. Whitfield, John Humphreys. III. T. IV. Title: Faithful shepherd. V. Series.
PQ4626.Z3 1976   852/.4   LC 76-11575   ISBN 0292764316

Machiavelli, Niccolò, 1469-1527.   **2.4971**
[Plays. English & Italian] The comedies of Machiavelli / edited and translated by David Sices and James B. Atkinson. — Bilingual ed. — Hanover: Published for Dartmouth College by University Press of New England, 1985. 408 p.; 23 cm. English and Italian. I. Sices, David. II. Atkinson, James B., 1934- III. T.
PQ4627.M2 A25 1985   852/.3 19   LC 84-40595   ISBN 0874513294

Medici, Lorenzo de', 1449-1492.   • **2.4972**
Opere, a cura di Attilio Simioni. — Bari, G. Laterza, 1939. 2 v.; 22 cm. (Scrittori d'Italia) Bibliography: v. 2, p. 366-375. I. Simioni, Attilio, ed. II. T.
PQ4630.M3 1939

Poliziano, Angelo, 1454-1494.   • **2.4973**
Stanze per la giostra, Orfeo–Rime [con un'appendice di prose volgari] / Agnolo Poliziano; edited by Bruno Maier. — Novara: Istituto geografico de Agostini, 1969. 303 p., [6] leaves of plates: ill.; 21 cm. I. Maier, Bruno. II. T.
PQ4630.P5 A6 1969   LC 73-434577

Poliziano, Angelo, 1454-1494.   **2.4974**
[Stanze cominciate per la giostra del Magnifico Giuliano de Medici. English] The stanze of Angelo Poliziano / translated by David Quint. — Amherst: University of Massachusetts Press, 1979. xxiv, 103 p.; 24 cm. Translation of Stanze cominciate per la giostra del Magnifico Giuliano de Medici. I. T.
PQ4630.P5 A713 1979   851/.2   LC 78-53180   ISBN 0870231456

Poliziano, Angelo, 1454-1494.   • **2.4975**
Rime. Testo e note a cura di Natalino Sapegno. 2d ed. — [Roma] Ateneo [1967] xii, 284 p. 22 cm. (Testi di letteratura italiana) I. Sapegno, Natalino, 1901- ed. II. T.
PQ4630.P5 Ax

Porta, Giambattista della, 1535?-1615.   **2.4976**
[Duoi fratelli rivali. English & Italian] Gli duoi fratelli rivali = The two rival brothers / Giambattista della Porta; edited and translated by Louise George Clubb. — Berkeley: University of California Press, c1980. 329 p.; 21 cm. (Biblioteca italiana) Italian text, parellel English translation, commentary in English. I. Clubb, Louise George. II. T. III. Title: The two rival brothers.
PQ4630.P6 G5713   852/.4   LC 78-64458   ISBN 0520037863

Pulci, Luigi, 1432-1484.   • **2.4977**
Morgante, a cura di Franca Ageno. — Milano, R. Ricciardi [1955] xxx, 1179 p. 23 cm. — (La Letteratura italiana; storia e testi, v. 17) 'Bibliografia': p. xxiii-xxx. I. Ageno, Franca, ed. II. T. III. Series.
PQ4631.M3 1955   LC A 57-6806

PQ4636–4661 Tasso

Tasso, Torquato, 1544-1595.   • **2.4978**
Poesie / Torquato Tasso; a cura di Francesco Flora. — Milano: R. Ricciardi, 1952. xvi, 1027 p. — (La Letteratura italiana, storia e testi; v.21) I. Flora, Francesco, 1891- II. T.
PQ4637.A1 1952   LC 53-32535

Tasso, Torquato, 1544-1595.   • **2.4979**
Gerusalemme liberata di Torquato Tasso raccontata da Alfredo Giuliani. Con una scelta del poema. Torino Einaudi 1970. 243p. (Gli struzzi, 12) I. Giuliani, Alfredo II. T.
PQ4638 E70   LC 73-577782

Tasso, Torquato, 1544-1595.   • **2.4980**
Prose. A cura di Ettore Mazzali, con una premessa di Francesco Flora. Milano R. Ricciardi [1959] 1163p. (Letteratura italiana. Storia e testi. v. 22) I. Mazzali, Ettore. ed. II. T. III. Series.
PQ4640 A1 1959

Tasso, Torquato, 1544-1595.   **2.4981**
[Selections. English. 1982] Tasso's dialogues: a selection with the Discourse on the art of the dialogue / translated with introduction and notes by Carnes Lord and Dain A. Trafton. — Berkeley: University of California Press, c1983. 264 p.; 21 cm. — (Biblioteca italiana.) I. Lord, Carnes. II. Trafton, Dain A. III. T. IV. Series.
PQ4642.E2 1982   195 19   *LC* 81-12937   *ISBN* 0520044649

Tasso, Torquato, 1544-1595.   • **2.4982**
[Gerusalemme liberata. English] Jerusalem delivered: the Edward Fairfax translation / Torquato Tasso; newly introduced by Roberto Weiss. — Carbondale, Southern Illinois University Press [1962] xxi, 545 p. facsim., port.; 23 cm. — (Centaur classics) I. Fairfax, Edward, d. 1635. II. T.
PQ4642.E21 F3 1962   *LC* 62-7386

Tasso, Torquato, 1544-1595.   **2.4983**
[Gerusalemme liberata. English] Jerusalem delivered. Translated into verse and with an introd. by Joseph Tusiani. Rutherford [N.J.] Fairleigh Dickinson University Press [1970] 469 p. 25 cm. Translation of Gerusalemme liberata. I. Tusiani, Joseph, 1924- tr. II. T.
PQ4642.E21 T8 1970   851/.4   *LC* 75-85928   *ISBN* 0838675328

Caretti, Lanfranco.   • **2.4984**
Ariosto e Tasso. — [2. ed.] [2. ed., riv. — Torino] G. Einaudi [1967] 124 p.; 22 cm. (Saggi, 292) Bibliographical footnotes. I. T.
PQ4654.A2 C3x   *LC* 68-136423

PQ4675-4734 Individual Authors, 1701-1900

PQ4676-4692 A–G

Alfieri, Vittorio, 1749-1803.   • **2.4985**
Opere. Introduzione e scelta a cura di Vittore Branca. [1. ed. Milano] U. Mursia Editore [1965] 1275 p. 21 cm. (I classici italiani, 9) I. T.
PQ4677.A1x

Alfieri, Vittorio, 1749-1803.   • **2.4986**
Memoirs; the anonymous translation of 1810, revised by E. R. Vincent. — London, New York, Oxford University Press, 1961. xix, 310 p. 19 cm. — (Oxford library of Italian classics) 1. Alfieri, Vittorio, 1749-1803 — Biography. 2. Authors, Italian — 19th century — Biography I. T. II. Series.
PQ4681.A3E63 1961   928.5   *LC* 61-65513

Belli, Giuseppe Gioachino, 1791-1863.   **2.4987**
Sonnets of Giuseppe Belli / translated, with an introduction, by Miller Williams. — Bilingual ed. — Baton Rouge: Louisiana State University Press, c1981. xxiii, 159 p.: ports; 22 cm. Includes indexes. I. Williams, Miller. II. T.
PQ4683.B43 A28   851/.7 19   *LC* 80-24331   *ISBN* 080710762X

Fogazzaro, Antonio, 1842-1911.   • **2.4988**
The little world of the past. Translated by W.J. Strachan. With an introd. by Tommaso Gallarati Scotti. London, Oxford University Press, 1962. 358 p. (The Oxford library of Italian classics) I. T.
PQ4688.F6 P6x   853.8   *LC* 62-51293

Foscolo, Ugo, 1778-1827.   • **2.4989**
Opere; con un saggio critico e note di Enzo Noè Girardi. Milano, Le Stelle [1966-. v. front. I. Girardi, Enzo Noè. ed. II. T.
PQ4689.Ax

Foscolo, Ugo, 1778-1827.   • **2.4990**
[Ultime lettere di Jacopo Ortis. English] Ultime lettere di Jacopo Ortis; a translation by Douglas Radcliff-Umstead. Chapel Hill, University of North Carolina Press [1970] 167 p. 24 cm. (University of North Carolina. Studies in the Romance languages and literatures, no. 89) Text in English. I. T.
PQ4690.E5 U8 1970   853/.6   *LC* 74-635127

PQ4693-4701 Goldoni

Goldoni, Carlo, 1707-1793.   • **2.4991**
Tutte le opere di Carlo Goldoni / a cura di Giuseppe Ortolani. — 4. éd. — Milano: A. Mondadori, 1935-1960. 14 v.: facsim.; 18 cm. — (I Classici Mondadori) I. T.
PQ4693.A1 1935   *LC* 37-36164

Goldoni, Carlo, 1707-1793.   • **2.4992**
Three comedies / Carlo Goldoni. — London: Oxford University Press, 1961. xxvii, 293 p. 19 cm. — (The Oxford library of Italian classics) I. T. II. Series.
PQ4695.E5 1961   PQ4695 E5 1961.   852.6   *LC* 61-65489

Goldoni, Carlo, 1707-1793.   • **2.4993**
[Selected works. English. 1968] Four comedies [by] Goldoni; translated and introduced by Frederick Davies. Harmondsworth, Penguin, 1968. 332 p. 19 cm. (The Penguin classics, L 204) I. T.
PQ4695.E5 1968   852/.6   *LC* 78-402268

Goldoni, Carlo, 1707-1793.   • **2.4994**
Memoirs of Carlo Goldoni, written by himself, translated from the original French by John Black; edited, with an introd. by William A. Drake. New York Knopf 1926. 484p. (Blue jade library) I. Black, John, 1783-1855. tr. II. Drake, William A, 1899-. ed. III. T.
PQ4698 A6 E5 1926   *LC* 26-17257

Riedt, Heinz, 1919-.   **2.4995**
[Carlo Goldoni. English] Carlo Goldoni. Translated by Ursule Molinaro. New York, F. Ungar [1974] 146 p. illus. 20 cm. (World dramatists) 1. Goldoni, Carlo, 1707-1793 — Criticism and interpretation. I. T.
PQ4699.R513   852/.6   *LC* 73-85411   *ISBN* 0804427291

PQ4703 Gozzi

Gozzi, Carlo, conte, 1722-1806.   • **2.4996**
Opere: teatro e polemiche teatrali. A cura di Giuseppe Petronio. [1. ed.] Milano, Rizzoli [1962] 1202 p. plates, ports. 20 cm. (I Classici Rizzoli) I. Petronio, Giuseppe. ed. II. T.
PQ4703.A1x

PQ4708-4710 Leopardi

Leopardi, Giacomo, 1798-1837.   • **2.4997**
Opere de Giacomo Leopardi; a cura di Giovanni Getto. Commento di Edoardo Sanguineti. [1. ed. Milano] Mursia [1966] cv, 1178 p. 21 cm. (I classici italiani, 11) I. Sanguineti, Edoardo. ed. II. Getto, Giovanni. ed. III. T.
PQ4708.A1x

Leopardi, Giacomo, 1798-1837.   **2.4998**
[Pensieri. English & Italian] Pensieri / Giacomo Leopardi; translated by W.S. Di Piero. — A bilingual ed. — Baton Rouge: Louisiana State University Press, c1981. 172 p.; 23 cm. I. Di Piero, W. S. II. T.
PQ4708.P6 E5 1981   851/.7 19   *LC* 81-11745   *ISBN* 0807108855

Leopardi, Giacomo, 1798-1837.   **2.4999**
A Leopardi reader / editing and translations by Ottavio M. Casale. — Urbana: University of Illinois Press, c1981. xv, 271 p.; 23 cm. I. Casale, Ottavio M. II. T.
PQ4709.E5 A1 1981   851/.7 19   *LC* 80-29068   *ISBN* 0252008243

Leopardi, Giacomo, 1798-1837.   **2.5000**
Operette morali: essays and dialogues / Giacomo Leopardi; translated with introduction and notes by Giovanni Cecchetti. — Berkeley: University of California Press, c1983. x, 544 p.; 21 cm. — (Biblioteca italiana.) English and Italian. I. Cecchetti, Giovanni, 1922- II. T. III. Series.
PQ4709.E5 A13 1982   854/.7 19   *LC* 82-2627   *ISBN* 0520047044

PQ4713-4715 Manzoni

Manzoni, Alessandro, 1785-1873.   • **2.5001**
Opere, a cura di Riccardo Bacchelli. — Milano, R. Ricciardi [1953] xxx, 1190 p. 23 cm. — (Letteratura italiana. Storia e testi. v. 53) Includes bibliographical references. I. Bacchelli, Riccardo, 1891- ed. II. T. III. Series.
PQ4713.A1 1953   *LC* 54-1628

Manzoni, Alessandro, 1785-1873.   • **2.5002**
I promessi sposi / Alessandro Manzoni; a cura di Natalino Sapegno, Gorizio Viti. — Firenze: Le Monnier, 1971. xii, 728 p.; 24 cm. (Le Monnier per la scuola) I. Sapegno, Natalino, 1901- II. Viti, Gorizio. III. T. IV. Series.
PQ4713.P3 1971   *LC* 72-334329

Manzoni, Alessandro, 1785-1873. • 2.5003
The betrothed 'I promessi sposi'; a tale of XVII century Milan. Translated with
a pref. by Archibald Colquhoun. — London, Dent; New York, Dutton [1962]
xxvi, 535 p. 19 cm. — (Everyman's library, 999. Fiction) I. T.
PQ4713.P3E5 1956 853.72 LC 56-2556

Manzoni, Alessandro, 1785-1873. 2.5004
The betrothed; translated with an introduction by Bruce Penman. —
Harmondsworth: Penguin, 1983. 720 p.; 19 cm. — (The Penguin classics)
Translation of I promessi sposi. I. Penman, Bruce, tr. II. T.
PZ3.M326 B48 PQ4714.A2 853/.7 LC 73-165908 ISBN
014044274X

PQ4716–4734 Me–V

Metastasio, Pietro, 1698-1782. 2.5005
Opere / di Pietro Metastasio. — Milan: Rizzoli, 1965. 732 p. 'Volume unico.'
1. Operatic scenes — To 1800 — Librettos I. T.
PQ4717 A1 1859

Monti, Vincenzo, 1754-1828. • 2.5006
Opere, a cura di Manara Valgimigli e Carlo Muscetta. — Milano, R. Ricciardi
[1953] lvii, 1260 p. 23 cm. — (Letteratura italiana. Storia e testi. v. 54) I. T.
II. Series.
PQ4720.M5 1953 LC 54-2683

Nievo, Ippolito, 1831-1861. • 2.5007
[Confessioni di un ottuagenario. English] The Castle of Fratta. Translated by
Lovett F. Edwards. Westport, Conn., Greenwood Press [1974, c1957] xv, 589 p.
22 cm. Reprint of the 1958 ed. published by Houghton Mifflin, Boston.
Translation of Le confessioni di un ottuagenario. I. T.
PZ3.N559 Cas6 PQ4720.N7 853/.7 LC 74-10017 ISBN
0837176603

Nievo, Ippolito, 1831-1861. • 2.5008
Opere, a cura di Sergio Romagnoli. — Milano, R. Ricciardi [1952] xxx, 1196 p.
23 cm. — (La Letteratura italiana; storia a testi, v. 57) Bibliography: p. xxviii-
xxx. I. T. II. Series.
PQ4720.N7A6 1952 LC 53-39161

Parini, Giuseppe, 1729-1799. • 2.5009
Opere ... A cura di Ettore Bonora. Milano, U. Mursia, 1967. xxxix, 1125 p. 20
cm. (I Classici italiani, 8) 'Nota bio-bibliografica': p. [xxxi]-xxxix. I. Bonora,
Ettore. II. T.
PQ4721.A1 1967 LC 68-137269

Pellico, Silvio, 1789-1854. • 2.5010
[Mie prigioni. English] My prisons = Le mie prigioni / Silvio Pellico;
translation, introd., and notes by I. G. Capaldi; foreword by Archibald
Colquhoun. — Westport, Conn.: Greenwood Press, 1978, c1963. xxiv, 199 p.;
23 cm. Reprint of the ed. published by Oxford University Press, New York,
issued in series: The Oxford library of Italian classics. 1. Pellico, Silvio,
1789-1854 — Biography — Imprisonment — Czechoslovakia — Brno.
2. Carbonari — History — Sources. 3. Authors, Italian — 19th century —
Biography. 4. Political prisoners — Italy — Biography. 5. Political prisoners
— Czechoslovakia — Biography. 6. Spielberg (Castle) 7. Milan (Italy) —
History — 1535-1859 — Sources. I. T.
PQ4728.A2 C3 1978 858/.7/09 B LC 78-12351 ISBN
0313210535

Porta, Carlo Antonio Melchiore Filippo, 1775-1821. • 2.5011
Poesie / ed. critica integrale, a cura di Dante Isella. — 1. ed. — Firenze: Nuova
Italia, [1954] 2 v.: ill.; 23 cm. I. Isella, Dante. II. T.
PQ4730.P7 A125 1975 LC 55-15111

PQ4734 Verga

Verga, Giovanni, 1840-1922. • 2.5012
Opere, a cura di Luigi Russo. — Milano, R. Ricciardi [1968] xxxiii, 980 p.; 23
cm. (Letteratura italiana; storia e testi, v. 63) Bibliography and notes: p. [xxix]-
xxxiii. I. Russo, Luigi, 1892-1961. II. T.
PQ4734.V5 A1x

Verga, Giovanni, 1840-1922. • 2.5013
The she-wolf: and other stories / Giovanni Verga; translated with an introd. by
Giovanni Cecchetti. — Berkeley: University of California Press, 1958. xxii,
197 p.: ill. I. T.
PQ4734.V5 A23 PZ3V587 Sh 853.84 LC 58-6524 rev.

Verga, Giovanni, 1840-1922. • 2.5014
Cavalleria rusticana: and other stories / by Giovanni Verga; translated by D.H.
Lawrence. — New York: L. MacVeagh, the Dial Press; Toronto: Longmans,
Green, 1928. 301 p. I. Lawrence, D. H. (David Herbert), 1885-1930. II. T.
PQ4734.V5 C4313 LC 28-20569

Verga, Giovanni, 1840-1922. • 2.5015
The house by the Medlar–tree / Giovanni Verga; translated from the Italian by
Eric Mosbacher. — New York: Grove Press, c1953. 247 p. I. T.
PQ4734.V5 H8 1953 LC 53-8070

Verga, Giovanni, 1840-1922. 2.5016
[Mastro-don Gesualdo. English] Mastro–don Gesualdo: a novel / Giovanni
Verga; translated, with an introd., by Giovanni Cecchetti. — Berkeley:
University of California Press, c1979. xix, 329 p.; 24 cm. I. T.
PQ4734.V5 M513 1979 853/.8 LC 77-20331 ISBN 0520035984

Cecchetti, Giovanni, 1922-. 2.5017
Giovanni Verga / by Giovanni Cecchetti. — Boston: Twayne Publishers,
c1978. 172 p.: port.; 21 cm. — (Twayne's world authors series; TWAS 489:
Italy) Includes index. 1. Verga, Giovanni, 1840-1922 — Criticism and
interpretation. I. T.
PQ4734.V5 Z6527 853/.8 LC 77-19342 ISBN 0805763309

PQ4800–4851 Individual Authors, 1901–1960

PQ4801–4829 A–L

D'Annunzio, Gabriele, 1863-1938. • 2.5018
Poesie, teatro, prose. A cura di Mario Praz e Ferdinando Gerra. — Milano, R.
Ricciardi [1966] xlvii, 1236 p. 23 cm. — (La Letteratura italiana; storia e testi,
v. 62) Bibliography: p. [ixl]-xiv. I. Praz, Mario, 1896- ed. II. Gerra,
Ferdinando. ed. III. T. IV. Series.
PQ4803.A1 1966 LC 68-4803

Jullian, Philippe. 2.5019
[D'Annunzio. English] D'Annunzio. Translated from the French by Stephen
Hardman. New York, Viking Press [1973, c1972] xviii, 366 p. illus. 22 cm.
1. D'Annunzio, Gabriele, 1863-1938. I. T.
PQ4804.J813 1973 858/.8/09 B LC 72-78981 ISBN 067025603X

Bacchelli, Riccardo, 1891-. • 2.5020
The mill on the Po, translated by Frances Frenaye. [New York] Pantheon
[1950] 590 p. maps (on lining papers) 24 cm. Combines, in translation, the first
two volumes of the author's trilogy Il mulino del Po. I. T.
PQ4807.A23 M8x LC 50-9509

Bassani, Giorgio. • 2.5021
[Cinque storie ferraresi. English] Five stories of Ferrara. Translated from the
Italian by William Weaver. [1st ed.] New York, Harcourt Brace Jovanovich
[1971] 203 p. 21 cm. 'A Helen and Kurt Wolff book.' Translation of Cinque
storie ferraresi. I. T.
PZ4.B3176 Fi PQ4807.A79 853/.9/14 LC 76-153681 ISBN
0151314004

Bassani, Giorgio. 2.5022
[Odore del fieno. English] The smell of hay / Giorgio Bassani; translated by
William Weaver. — 1st ed. — New York: Harcourt Brace Jovanovich, [1975]
193 p.; 22 cm. 'A Helen and Kurt Wolff book.' Translation of L'odore del fieno.
I. T.
PZ4.B3176 Sm PQ4807.A79 853/.9/14 LC 75-16222 ISBN
0151831467

Bassani, Giorgio. • 2.5023
[Giardino dei Finzi-Contini. English] The garden of the Finzi–Continis /
Giorgio Bassani; translated from the Italian by William Weaver. — San Diego:
Harcourt Brace Jovanovich, [1983], c1977. 200 p.; 21 cm. (A Harvest/HBJ
book) Translation of: Giardino dei Finzi-Contini. 'A Helen and Kurt Wolff
book.' I. T.
PQ4807.A79 G513 1983 853/.914 19 LC 83-6751 ISBN
0156345706

Betti, Ugo, 1892-1953. • 2.5024
Three plays / by Ugo Betti; translated and with a foreword by Henry Reed. —
New York: Grove Press, [1958], c1956. 283 p. — (Evergreen books; E-90) I. T.
II. Title: The Queen and the rebels. III. Title: The burnt flower-bed. IV. Title:
Summertime.
PQ4807.E85 A27 1958 LC 58-5442

Calvino, Italo. • 2.5025
The baron in the trees / Italo Calvino; translated by Archibald Colquhoun.
New York: Random House, 1959. 217 p. Translation of Il barone rampante.
I. T.
PZ3.C13956 Bar8 PQ4809.A45 853/.9/14 LC 59-10800

Calvino, Italo.   **2.5026**
[Castello dei destini incrociati. English] The castle of crossed destinies / Italo Calvino; translated from the Italian by William Weaver. — 1st ed. — New York: Harcourt Brace Jovanovich, c1977. 129 p., [4] leaves of plates: ill.; 24 cm. Translation of Il castello dei destini incrociati. 'A Helen and Kurt Wolff book.' I. T.
PZ3.C13956 Cas PQ4809.A45   853/.9/14   *LC* 76-27423   *ISBN* 015115998X

Calvino, Italo.   **2.5027**
[Città invisibili. English] Invisible cities. Translated from the Italian by William Weaver. [1st ed.] New York, Harcourt Brace Jovanovich [1974] 165 p. 21 cm. 'A Helen and Kurt Wolff book.' Translation of Le città invisibili. 1. Polo, Marco, 1254-1323? — Fiction. 2. Kublai Khan, 1216-1294 — Fiction. I. T.
PZ3.C13956 In PQ4809.A45   853/.9/14   *LC* 74-8836   *ISBN* 0151452903

Calvino, Italo.   • **2.5028**
[Cosmicomiche. English] Cosmicomics / by Italo Calvino; translated from the Italian by William Weaver. — New York: Harcourt Brace Jovanovich, 1976, c1968. 153 p.; 19 cm. — (Harbrace paperbound library; HPL 69) Translation of Le cosmicomiche. 'A Helen and Kurt Wolff book.' I. T.
PZ3.C13956 Co8 PQ4809.A45   853/.9/14   *LC* 76-14795   *ISBN* 0156226006

Calvino, Italo.   **2.5029**
[Se una notte d'inverno un viaggiatore. English] If on a winter's night a traveler / Italo Calvino; translated from the Italian by William Weaver. — 1st ed. — New York: Harcourt Brace Jovanovich, c1981. 260 p.; 22 cm. Translation of Se una notte d'inverno un viaggiatore. 'A Helen and Kurt Wolff book.' I. T.
PQ4809.A45 S3713   853/.914 19   *LC* 80-8741   *ISBN* 0151436894

Calvino, Italo.   • **2.5030**
The nonexistent knight & The cloven viscount; two short novels. Translated from the Italian by Archibald Colquhoun. New York, Random House [1962] 246 p. 21 cm. Translation of Il Cavaliere Inesistente and Il Visconte Dimezzato. I. Calvino, Italo. Cloven viscount. II. T. III. Title: The cloven viscount. IV. Title: Il Cavaliere Inesistente. V. Title: Il Visconte Dimezzato.
PQ 4809 A47 C37 E5 1962   *LC* 62-8445

Campana, Dino, 1885-1932.   **2.5031**
[Canti orfici. English] Orphic songs / Dino Campana; translated by Charles Wright; introduction by Jonathan Galassi. — [Oberlin, Ohio]: Oberlin College, c1984. 130 p.; 20 cm. — (Field translation series. 9) Translation of: Canti orfici. I. Wright, Charles, 1935- II. T. III. Series.
PQ4809.A52 C313 1984   851/.912 19   *LC* 83-63448   *ISBN* 0932440169

Cassola, Carlo, 1917-.   • **2.5032**
Fausto and Anna / Carlo Cassola; [translated by Isabel Quigly]. — New York: Pantheon Books, c1960. 318 p.; 22 cm. Translation of Fausto e Anna. 1. World War, 1939-1945 — Fiction I. T.
PQ4809.A679 F3x   *LC* 60-6793

Gadda, Carlo Emilio, 1893-1973.   • **2.5033**
That awful mess on Via Merulana; a novel. Translated from the Italian and with an introd. by William Weaver. New York, G. Braziller [1965] 388 p. I. T.
PQ4817.A33 Q4x   853.91   *LC* 65-19320

Ginzburg, Natalia.   • **2.5034**
[Lessico famigliare. English] Family sayings. Translated from the Italian and with an introd. by D. M. Low. New York, Dutton, 1967. 222 p. 21 cm. 1. Ginzburg, Natalia — Biography. 2. Authors, Italian — 20th century — Biography. I. T.
PQ4817.I5 L43   858.91203   *LC* 67-11942

Gozzano, Guido, 1883-1916.   **2.5035**
[Selections. English] The man I pretend to be: the Colloquies and selected poems of Guido Gozzano / translated and edited by Michael Palma; with an introductory essay by Eugenio Montale. — Princeton, N.J.: Princeton University Press, c1981. xxv, 254 p.; 22 cm. — (Lockert library of poetry in translation) I. Palma, Michael, 1945- II. T.
PQ4817.O9 A26 1981   851/.912 19   *LC* 80-8551   *ISBN* 0691064679

Luzi, Mario.   **2.5036**
In the dark body of metamorphosis & other poems. Translated by I. L. Salomon. — [1st ed.]. — New York: Norton, [1975] 110 p.; 22 cm. I. Salomon, Isidore Lawrence, 1899- tr. II. T.
PQ4827.U9 I5   PQ4827 U9 I5.   851/.9/12   *LC* 74-11122   *ISBN* 0393043916

PQ4829 Montale

Montale, Eugenio, 1896-.   • **2.5037**
[Poesie. English] Selected poems of Eugenio Montale; translated and with an introduction by George Kay. Harmondsworth, Penguin, 1969. 126 p. 19 cm. (Penguin modern European poets) Originally published as 'Poésie. Poems'. Edinburgh, Edinburgh University P., 1964. I. Kay, George R., tr. II. T.
PQ4829.O565 A24   *LC* 75-454634   *ISBN* 0140420991

Montale, Eugenio, 1896-.   **2.5038**
[Satura. English. Selections] New poems: a selection from Satura and Diario del '71 e del '72 / Eugenio Montale; translated and introduced by G. Singh; with an essay on Xenia by F. R. Leavis. — New York: New Directions Pub. Corp., 1976. xxxiii, 124 p.; 21 cm. — (A New Directions book) Includes index. I. Montale, Eugenio, 1896- Diario del '71 e del '72. English. Selections. 1976. II. T.
PQ4829.O565 A28 1976   851/.9/12   *LC* 75-31600   *ISBN* 0811205983. *ISBN* 0811205991 pbk

Montale, Eugenio, 1896-.   **2.5039**
[Altri versi e poesie disperse. English] Otherwise: last and first poems of Eugenio Montale / translated from the Italian by Jonathan Galassi. — 1st American ed. — New York: Random House, c1984. xiii, 159 p.; 25 cm. Translation of: Altri versi e poesie disperse. English and Italian. I. Galassi, Jonathan. II. T.
PQ4829.O565 A7813 1984   851/.912 19   *LC* 84-42533   *ISBN* 0394529634

Almansi, Guido, 1931-.   **2.5040**
Eugenio Montale: the private language of poetry / [by] Guido Almansi and Bruce Merry. — Edinburgh: Edinburgh University Press, 1977. xii, 167 p.: port.; 22 cm. — (Writers of Italy series; 4) Spine title: Montale. Includes index. 1. Montale, Eugenio, 1896- — Criticism and interpretation. I. Merry, Bruce. joint author. II. T. III. Title: Montale.
PQ4829.O565 Z556   851/.9/12   *LC* 78-308179   *ISBN* 0852242980

Cambon, Glauco.   **2.5041**
Eugenio Montale's poetry: a dream in reason's presence / Glauco Cambon. — Princeton, N.J.: Princeton University Press, c1982. xi, 274 p.; 23 cm. 1. Montale, Eugenio, 1896- — Criticism and interpretation. I. T.
PQ4829.O565 Z573 1982   851/.912 19   *LC* 82-47584   *ISBN* 0691065209

Singh, G.   **2.5042**
Eugenio Montale: a critical study of his poetry, prose, and criticism, by G. Singh. New Haven, Yale University Press, 1973. xi, 297 p. 24 cm. 1. Montale, Eugenio, 1896- — Criticism and interpretation. I. T.
PQ4829.O565 Z88   851/.9/12   *LC* 72-75209   *ISBN* 0300014422

PQ4829 Morante. Moravia

Morante, Elsa, 1916-.   **2.5043**
[Storia. English] History: a novel / Elsa Morante; translated from the Italian by William Weaver. — 1st American ed. — New York: Knopf: distributed by Random House, 1977. ix, 561 p.; 25 cm. Translation of La storia. 1. World War, 1939-1945 — Fiction. I. T.
PQ4829.O615 S813 1977   853/.9/12   *LC* 76-45755   *ISBN* 039449802X

Moravia, Alberto, 1907-.   • **2.5044**
[Agostino. English] Two adolescents; the stories of Agostino and Luca. New York, Farrar, Straus [1950] 268 p. 21 cm. Translation of Agostino and La disubbidienza. I. Moravia, Alberto, 1907- La disubbidienza. English. 1950. II. T.
PQ4829.O62 Ax   *LC* 50-8597

Moravia, Alberto, 1907-.   • **2.5045**
The time of indifference [by] Alberto Moravia. Translated by Angus Davidson. New York, Farrar, Straus and Young [1953] 303 p. 22 cm. Translation of Gli indifferenti. I. T. II. Title: Gli indifferenti.
PQ4829.O62 G5x   *LC* 53-7082

Moravia, Alberto, 1907-.   • **2.5046**
Roman tales / Selected and translated by Angus Davidson. New York: Farrar, Straus and Cudahy, 1957. 229 p. I. T.
PZ3.M7962 Mo   PQ4829.O62 N83 1957.   *LC* 57-8717

PQ4835 Pa

Pascoli, Giovanni, 1855-1912.   • **2.5047**
Poesie ... [Milano], A. Mondadori, 1969. 4 v. illus. 18 1/2 cm. (Gil Oscar) I. Contini, Gianfranco. II. T.
PQ4835.A3 A17 1969   *LC* 74-426072

Pasolini, Pier Paolo, 1922-1975.   **2.5048**
[Poems. English. Selections] Poems / Pier Paolo Pasolini; selected and translated by Norman MacAfee with Luciano Martinengo; foreword by Enzo Siciliano. — 1st ed. — New York: Random House, c1982. xiii, 231 p.; 24 cm. + 3 microfiches (10 x 15 cm.) I. MacAfee, Norman. II. Martinengo, Luciano. III. T.
PQ4835.A48 A25 1982   851/.914 19   *LC* 81-48293   *ISBN* 0394522982

Siciliano, Enzo, 1934-.   **2.5049**
[Vita di Pasolini. English] Pasolini: a biography / by Enzo Siciliano; translated from the Italian by John Shepley. — 1st American ed. — New York: Random House, c1982. 435 p., [16] p. of plates: ill.; 24 cm. 1. Pasolini, Pier Paolo, 1922-1975 — Biography. 2. Authors, Italian — 20th century — Biography. 3. Motion picture producers and directors — Italy — Biography. I. T.
PQ4835.A48 Z8813 1982   858/.91409 B 19   *LC* 81-48294   *ISBN* 0394522990

Pavese, Cesare.   • **2.5050**
Selected works. Translated from the Italian and with an introd. by R. W. Flint. — New York: Farrar, Straus and Giroux, [1968] xxiii, 390 p.; 22 cm. I. T.
PQ4835.A846 Ax   *LC* 68-14914

Pavese, Cesare.   • **2.5051**
Dialogues with Leucò / Cesare Pavese; translated by William Arrowsmith and D. S. Carne–Ross. — Ann Arbor: University of Michigan Press, 1965. 116 p. Translation of Dialoghi con Leucò. I. T.
PQ4835.A846 D513   *LC* 63-14009

Pavese, Cesare.   **2.5052**
[Lavorare stanca. English] Hard labor: [poems] / Cesare Pavese; translated by William Arrowsmith. — New York: Grossman Publishers, 1976. xlii, 123 p.; 23 cm. Translation of Lavorare stanca. I. Arrowsmith, William, 1924- II. T.
PQ4835.A846 L313 1976   851/.9/12   *LC* 76-10727   *ISBN* 0670361380

Pavese, Cesare.   • **2.5053**
The moon and the bonfires / Cesare Pavese; translated from the Italian by Marianne Ceconi; with a foreword by Paolo Milano. New York: Farrar, Straus and Young, c1953. 206 p.; 21 cm. Translation of La luna e i falò. I. T.
PQ4835.A846 L8x   *LC* 53-7083

Pavese, Cesare.   • **2.5054**
This business of living: diary, 1935–1950 / edited and translated by A.C. Murch. — London: Owen, [c1961]. 278 p. 1. Authors — Correspondence, reminiscences, etc. I. T. II. Title: The burning brand: diaries, 1935-1950.
PQ4835.A846 Z533 1961a   858

PQ4835 Pirandello

Pirandello, Luigi, 1867-1936.   • **2.5055**
Naked masks, five plays; edited by Eric Bentley. — [1st ed.]. — New York: Dutton, 1952. xxvii, 386 p.; 19 cm. — (Everyman's library, 647A. Drama) I. T.
PQ4835.I7 A27   852.91   *LC* 52-5310

Pirandello, Luigi, 1867-1936.   • **2.5056**
Short stories. Selected, translated, and introduced by Frederick May. — London, New York, Oxford University Press, 1965. xxxvi, 260 p. 19 cm. — (Oxford library of Italian classics) Bibliography: p. 231-260. I. May, Frederick, tr. II. T.
PQ4835.I7 Ax   *LC* 65-2087

Pirandello, Luigi, 1867-1936.   • **2.5057**
Right you are = Cosí è (se vi pare) / by Luigi Pirandello; a stage version with an introduction and notes by Eric Bentley. — New York: Columbia University Press, 1954. xxvi, 165 p.: ill. — (Columbia bicentennial editions and studies) I. T.
PQ4835.I7 C62   *LC* 54-6484

Oliver, Roger W., 1945-.   **2.5058**
Dreams of passion: the theater of Luigi Pirandello / Roger W. Oliver. — New York: New York University Press, c1979. xv, 167 p.; 24 cm. (The Gotham library of the New York University Press) 1. Pirandello, Luigi, 1867-1936 — Criticism and interpretation. I. T.
PQ4835.I7 Z719   852/.9/12   *LC* 79-2179   *ISBN* 0814761577

Ragusa, Olga.   **2.5059**
Luigi Pirandello: an approach to his theatre / Olga Ragusa. — Edinburgh: Edinburgh University Press, c1980. x, 198 p.: port.; 22 cm. — (Writers of Italy series. 8) Includes index. 1. Pirandello, Luigi, 1867-1936 — Criticism and interpretation. I. T. II. Series.
PQ4835.I7 Z756   852/.912 19   *LC* 81-111458   *ISBN* 0852243731

PQ4835.R–4841.A Pr–Sa

Pratolini, Vasco, 1913-.   **2.5060**
Cronache di poveri amanti, romanzo. [Firenze] Vallecchi [1947] 557 p. I. T.
PQ4835.R37 C7

Quasimodo, Salvatore, 1901-1968.   **2.5061**
To give and to have, and other poems / Translated by Edith Farnsworth. — Chicago: H. Regnery Co., [1969] 185 p.; 24 cm. English and Italian. I. Farnsworth, Edith, tr. II. T.
PQ4837.U3 A6 1969b   851/.9/12   *LC* 72-88850   7.95

Quasimodo, Salvatore, 1901-1968.   • **2.5062**
Tutte le poesie. Con prefazioni di Sergio Solmi e Carlo Bo. [4. ed. Milano] A. Mondadori [1962] 389 p. 20 cm. (Lo specchio; i poeti del nostro tempo) "Il Discorso sulla poesia [p. 373-379] apparve per la prima volta in volume como appendice a Il falso e vero verde (Mondadori, 1956)"-cf. p. [371] I. T. II. Series.
PQ4837.U3 Ax

De Roberto, Federico, 1861-1927.   • **2.5063**
The viceroys / tr. from the Italian by Archibald Colquhoun; with an intro. by the translator. — New York: Harcourt, Brace & World, 1962. 627p. I. T.
PQ4839.O3 V5x   *LC* 62-10497   457

Saba, Umberto, 1883-1957.   • **2.5064**
Il canzoniere (1900–1954) / Umberto Saba. — 4. ed. — [Torino]: Einaudi, 1974, c1961. viii, 633 p.; 23 cm. — I. T.
PQ4841.A18 C3 1974   *LC* 77-565936   L8000

PQ4841 Schmitz (Italo Svevo)

Svevo, Italo, 1861-1928.   • **2.5065**
Further confessions of Zeno [by] Italo Svevo. — Berkeley, University of California Press [1969] 302 p. 21 cm. — (The Uniform edition of Svevo's works, v. 5) I. T.
PQ4841.C482 A24   858/.8/08   *LC* 69-19076   5.95

Svevo, Italo, 1861-1928.   • **2.5066**
[Coscienza di Zeno. English] Confessions of Zeno [by] Italo Svevo. Translated by Beryl de Zoete. Westport, Conn., Greenwood Press [1973] 412 p. 22 cm. Translation of La coscienza di Zeno. Reprint of the 1930 ed. published by Putnam, London, New York. I. T.
PZ3.S357 Co10 PQ4841.C482 Cx   853/.8   *LC* 70-137074   *ISBN* 0837155371

Svevo, Italo, 1861-1928.   • **2.5067**
As a man grows older [by] Italo Svevo [pseud.] Translated by Beryl de Zoete. With an introd. by Stanislaus Joyce, and an essay on Svevo by Edouard Roditi. [New York, New Directions, 1949?] xxii, 245 p. 22 cm. (The Modern readers series) I. T. II. Series.
PZ3.S357As PQ4841.C482 Sx   853.91   *LC* 49-11089

Svevo, Italo, 1861-1928.   • **2.5068**
A life, by Italo Svevo [pseud.] Translated from the Italian by Archibald Colquhoun. [1st American ed.] New York, Knopf, 1973, c1963. 398 p. 21 cm. I. T.
PQ4841.C482Vx   *LC* 62-15565

Furbank, Philip Nicholas.   • **2.5069**
Italo Svevo; the man and the writer [by] P. N. Furbank. Berkeley, University of California Press [c1966] xi, 232 p. illus., ports. 23 cm. 1. Svevo, Italo, 1861-1928. I. T.
PQ4841.C482 Z65 1966a   853.8   *LC* 66-29426

PQ4841.I–4851 Si–Z

Silone, Ignazio, 1900-1978.   **2.5070**
[Fontamara. English] Fontamara / Ignazio Silone; translated from the Italian by Eric Mosbacher; introduction by Michael Foot. — London: Dent, 1985. — xii, 180 p.; 23 cm. Translation of: Fontamara. I. Mosbacher, Eric, 1903- II. Silone, Ignazio, 1900-1978. Fontamara. 1985. III. T.
PQ4841.I4   853/.912 19   *ISBN* 0460046640

Silone, Ignazio, 1900-1978.   • **2.5071**
[Pane e vino. English] Bread and wine. A new version translated from the Italian by Harvey Fergusson II, with a new pref. by the author. New York, Atheneum, 1962. 331 p. 21 cm. I. T.
PQ4841.I4 Px   *LC* 62-17288

Tomasi di Lampedusa, Giuseppe, 1896-1957.   • **2.5072**
[Gattopardo. English] The leopard [by] Giuseppe di Lampedusa. Translated from the Italian by Archibald Colquhoun. [New York] Pantheon [1960] 319 p. 22 cm. I. T.
PQ4843.O53 Gx   853.912   LC 60-6794

Ungaretti, Giuseppe, 1888-1970.   • **2.5073**
Vita d'un uomo. Tutte le poesie. A cura di Leone Piccioni. [Milano] Mondadori [1970, c1969] xcv, 905 p. 18 cm. (I Meridiani) I. Piccioni, Leon, ed. II. T.
PQ4845.N4 1970

Ungaretti, Giuseppe, 1888-1970.   • **2.5074**
Life of a man / Giuseppe Ungaretti; a version with introd. by Allen Mandelbaum. — London: Hamish Hamilton; New York, N.Y.: New Directions, c1958. xiv, 160 p. Italian and English. I. T.
PQ4845N4 A24   851.91   LC 58-14981

Ungaretti, Giuseppe, 1888-1970.   **2.5075**
Selected poems of Giuseppe Ungaretti / translated and edited by Allen Mandelbaum. — Ithaca: Cornell University Press, 1975. xx, 228 p.; 23 cm. English and Italian. I. Mandelbaum, Allen, 1926- II. T.
PQ4845.N4 A24 1975   PQ4845N4 A24 1975.   851/.9/12   LC 74-31761   ISBN 0801408504

Ungaretti, Giuseppe, 1880-1970.   **2.5076**
Selected poems; edited and translated, with an introduction and notes, by Patrick Creagh. Harmondsworth, Penguin, 1971. 110 p. 18 cm. (Penguin modern European poets) I. Creagh, Patrick. ed. II. T.
PQ4845.N4 A6 1971b   851/.9/12   ISBN 0140421394

Jones, Frederic Joseph.   **2.5077**
Giuseppe Ungaretti: poet and critic / [by] Frederic J. Jones. — Edinburgh: Edinburgh University Press, 1977. xi, 229 p.: port.; 22 cm. (Writers of Italy series; 5) Includes index. 1. Ungaretti, Giuseppe, 1888-1970 — Criticism and interpretation. I. T.
PQ4845.N4 Z68   851/.9/12   LC 78-309363   ISBN 0852242999

Vittorini, Elio, 1908-1966.   • **2.5078**
In Sicily / Elio Vittorini; translated by Wilfred David; introd. by Ernest Hemingway. — — New York: New Directions, [1949] 163 p.; 21 cm. 'A New Directions book.' Translation of Conversazione in Sicilia. I. T.
PQ4847.I77 C6213 1949   Fic

PQ4860–4886 Individual Authors, 1961–

Eco, Umberto.   **2.5079**
[Nome della rosa. English] The name of the rose / Umberto Eco; translated from the Italian by William Weaver. — 1st ed. — San Diego: Harcourt Brace Jovanovich, c1983. 502 p.; 25 cm. Translation of: Il nome della rosa. 'A Helen and Kurt Wolff book.' I. T.
PQ4865.C6 N613 1983   853/.914 19   LC 82-21286   ISBN 0151446474

Eco, Umberto.   **2.5080**
[Postille a Il nome della rosa. English] Postscript to The name of the rose / Umberto Eco; translated from the Italian by William Weaver. — 1st ed. — San Diego: Harcourt Brace Jovanovich, c1984. ix, 84 p.: ill.; 20 cm. Translation of: Postille a Il nome della rosa. 'A Helen and Kurt Wolff book.' I. Eco, Umberto. Nome della rosa. II. T.
PQ4865.C6 P613 1984   853/.914 19   LC 84-15652   ISBN 015173156X

Fallaci, Oriana.   **2.5081**
[Uomo. English] A man / Oriana Fallaci; translated from the Italian by William Weaver. — New York: Simon and Schuster, c1980. 463 p.; 25 cm. Translation of Un uomo. I. T.
PQ4866.A4 U513 1980   853/.914   LC 80-17838   ISBN 0671252410

Sciascia, Leonardo.   **2.5082**
[Giorno della civette. English] The day of the owl; Equal danger / Leonard Sciascia; with an afterword by Frank Kermode. — Boston: D.R. Godine, 1984. 122, 119, xiii p.; 21 cm. (Godine double detective. no. 4) Translations of: Il giorno della civetta and Il contesto. Reprint (1st work). Originally published: Mafia vendetta. New York: Knopf, 1964. Reprint (2nd work). Originally published: New York: Harper, 1973. I. Sciascia, Leonardo. Contesto. English II. T. III. Series.
PQ4879.C54 G413 1984   853/.914 19   LC 83-48890   ISBN 0879235160

PQ6001–6167 History. Criticism

✓ **The Oxford companion to Spanish literature / edited by Philip**   **2.5083**
Ward.
Oxford, [Eng.]: Clarendon Press, c1978. viii, 629 p.; 24 cm. 1. Spanish literature — Dictionaries. 2. Spanish literature — Bio-bibliography. I. Ward, Philip.
PQ6006.O93   PQ6006 O93.   860.03   ISBN 0198661142

Alborg, Juan Luis.   **2.5084**
✓ Historia de la literatura española / Juan Luis Alborg. — 2. ed. ampliada. — Madrid: Editorial Gredos, 1970-. v.; 25 cm. Editions vary. 1. Spanish literature — History and criticism I. T.
PQ6032.A45 1970   ISBN 8424931246

Díaz-Plaja, Guillermo, 1909-.   **2.5085**
[Historia de la literatura española. English] A history of Spanish literature. Translated, edited, and with a pref., introductory chapter, selective bibliography, and addendum on contemporary literature, by Hugh A. Harter. New York, New York University Press, 1971. xxii, 374 p. 24 cm. Translation of Historia de la literatura española. 1. Spanish literature — History and criticism I. T.
PQ6032.D4913   860.9   LC 70-124524   ISBN 0814717756

Díez Echarri, Emiliano.   • **2.5086**
Historia de la literatura española e hispanoamericana [por] Emiliano Díez-Echarri y José María Roca Franquesa. Madrid, Aguilar, 1960. xxxiv, 1590 p. 25 cm. 1. Spanish literature — Hist. & crit. 2. Spanish American literature — Hist. & crit. I. Roca Franquesa, José María. joint author. II. T.
PQ 6032 D56   LC 0A 06-15505

Marín, Diego.   **2.5087**
✓ Breve historia de la literatura española. New York, Holt, Rinehart and Winston [1966] 394 p. 25 cm. 1. Spanish literature — History and criticism I. Río, Angel del, 1900-1962. joint author. II. T.
PQ6032.M3   LC 66-14651

Valbuena Prat, Angel, 1900-.   **2.5088**
✓ Historia de la literatura española / Angel Valbuena Prat. — 9a ed. ampliada y puesta al día / por Antonio Prieto. — Barcelona: G. Gili, 1981-1983. 6 v.; 20 cm. Vols. 5 and 6 edited by María del Pilar Palomo. Includes indexes. 1. Spanish literature — History and criticism I. Prieto, Antonio. II. Palomo, María del Pilar. III. T.
PQ6032.V3 1982   860/.9 19   LC 82-199254   ISBN 8425210712

Brenan, Gerald.   • **2.5089**
Literature of the Spanish people, from Roman times to the present day. 2d ed. Cambridge[Eng]: Cambridge U.P. 1953. xxii,495p. 1. Spanish literature — History and criticism I. T.
PQ6033.B7 1953   LC A54-10035

Mérimée, Ernest, 1846-1924.   **2.5090**
✓ A history of Spanish literature / by Ernest Mérimée; translated, revised and enlarged by S. Griswold Morley. — New York: Holt, c1930. xv, 635 p.: facsims., ports.; 22 cm. 1. Spanish literature — History and criticism I. T.
PQ6034.M42   LC 30-25447

Northup, George Tyler, 1874-.   **2.5091**
An introduction to Spanish literature. — 3d ed., rev. by Nicholson B. Adams. — [Chicago]: University of Chicago Press, [1960] 532 p.; 21 cm. 1. Spanish literature — History and criticism I. T.
PQ6037.N6 1960   860.9   LC 60-8127

Río, Angel del, 1900-1962.   • **2.5092**
✓ Historia de la literatura española. — Ed. rev. — New York: Holt, Rinehart and Winston, [1963, c1948] 2 v.: port.; 25 cm. 1. Spanish literature — History and criticism I. T.
PQ6037.R452   LC 63-18131

Alonso, Dámaso, 1898-.   **2.5093**
Del Siglo de Oro a este siglo de siglas; notas y artículos a través de 350 años de letras españolas. — 2. ed. — [Madrid] Editorial Gredos [c1968] 293 p. illus., facsims. 19 cm. — (Biblioteca románica hispánica. 7. Campo abierto)

Bibliography: p. [289]-290. 1. Spanish literature — Addresses, essays, lectures. I. T.
PQ6039.A43 1968   LC 65-79208

Salinas, Pedro, 1892-1951.   • **2.5094**
Ensayos de literatura hispánica: del 'Cantar del mío Cid' a García Lorca / Pedro Salinas; edición y prólogo de Juan Marichal. — Madrid: Aguilar, 1958. 404 p.; 21 cm. — (Ensayistas hispánicos) 1. Spanish literature — History and criticism I. Marichal, Juan. II. T.
PQ6039 S33   LC 59-852

Rudder, Robert S.   **2.5095**
✓ The literature of Spain in English translation: a bibliography / compiled and edited by Robert S. Rudder. — New York: Ungar, [1975] ix, 637 p.; 25 cm. Includes indexes. 1. Spanish literature — Translations into English — Bibliography. 2. English literature — Translations from Spanish — Bibliography. I. T.
Z2694.T7 R83 PQ6044   PQ6044 R84.   016.86/08   LC 75-761
    ISBN 0804432619

Fox-Lockert, Lucía, 1928-.   **2.5096**
Women novelists in Spain and Spanish America / Lucía Fox-Lockert. — Metuchen, N.J.: Scarecrow Press, 1979. viii, 347 p.; 23 cm. Includes index. 1. Spanish fiction — Women authors — History and criticism. 2. Spanish American fiction — Women authors — History and criticism. 3. Women in literature 4. Women and literature I. T.
PQ6055.F6   863/.03   LC 79-23727   ISBN 0810812703

PQ6057–6073 Special Periods

Alonso, Dámaso, 1898-.   • **2.5097**
De los siglos oscuros al de Oro; notas y artículos a través de 700 años de letras españolas. — 2. ed. — [Madrid] Editorial Gredos [1964] 293 p. 20 cm. — (Biblioteca románica hispánica. 7. Campo abierto) Bibliographical footnotes. 1. Spanish literature — Hist. & crit. I. T.
PQ6057.A4 1964   LC 66-48114

Barja, César.   • **2.5098**
Libros y autores clásicos. 4. ed. [New York] Las Américas Pub. Co., 1964. xii, 557 p. 18 cm. 1. Spanish literature — Early to 1500 — History and criticism. 2. Spanish literature — Classical period, 1500-1700 — History and criticism. I. T.
PQ6057.B3 1964   LC 64-55449

Castro, Américo, 1885-1972.   • **2.5099**
✓ Hacia Cervantes. 3. ed., considerablemente renovada. [Madrid] Taurus [1967] 499 p. 22 cm. (Persiles, 2) 1. Cervantes Saavedra, Miguel de, 1547-1616. 2. Spanish literature — History and criticism I. T.
PQ6057.C3 1967   860.9   LC 67-9331

Green, Otis Howard, 1898-.   **2.5100**
✓ Spain and the Western tradition; the Castilian mind in literature from El Cid to Calderón. Madison University of Wisconsin Press 1963-. v. 1. Spanish literature — Early to 1500 — History and criticism 2. Spanish literature — Classical period, 1500-1700 — History and criticism I. T.
PQ6057 G7   LC 63-13745

Deyermond, A. D.   • **2.5101**
✓ The middle ages, [by] A. D. Deyermond. — London: Benn; New York: Barnes & Noble, 1971. xix, 244 p.; 23 cm. — (A Literary history of Spain) 1. Spanish literature — To 1500 — History and criticism. I. T.
PQ6058.D4 1971   860.9/001   LC 70-871554   ISBN 0510322514

Green, Otis Howard, 1898-.   **2.5102**
✓ The literary mind of medieval & Renaissance Spain; essays, by Otis H. Green. Introd. by John E. Keller. — Lexington: University Press of Kentucky, 1970. xxvi, 252 p.; 24 cm. — (Studies in Romance languages, 1) 1. Spanish literature — To 1500 — Addresses, essays, lectures. 2. Spanish literature — Classical period, 1500-1700 — Addresses, essays, lectures. I. T.
PQ6059.G7   860.9   LC 74-111510   ISBN 0813112044

Jones, Royston Oscar, 1925-.   • **2.5103**
The golden age: prose and poetry: the sixteenth and seventeenth centuries, [by] R. O. Jones. — London: Benn; New York: Barnes & Noble, 1971. xvii, 233 p.;

23 cm. — (A literary history of Spain) 1. Spanish literature — Classical period, 1500-1700 — History and criticism. I. T.
PQ6064.J6 1971   860.9/003   LC 70-871546   ISBN 0389041912

Pfandl, Ludwig, 1881-.   • 2.5104
Historia de la literatura nacional española en la edad de oro; traducción del alemán por Jorge Rubió Balaguer. 2. ed. Barcelona, G. Gili, 1952. xv, 707, [2] p. illus., ports. 1. Spanish literature — History and criticism I. Rubió i Balaguer, Jordi, 1887-1982. tr. II. T.
PQ6064.P44x

Martinez Ruiz, Jos, 1873-1967.   • 2.5105
Al margen de los clásicos [por] Azorín [pseud.] Buenos Aires, Editorial Losada [1942] 166 p. 18 cm. (Biblioteca clásica y contemporanea.) 1. Spanish literature — Classical period, 1500-1700 2. Spanish literature — Addresses, essays, lectures. I. T.
PQ6065.M3 1942   LC 48-43207

Peers, E. Allison (Edgar Allison), 1891-1952.   2.5106
Spanish golden age poetry and drama. Edited by E. Allison Peers. New York, Phaeton Press, 1974. vii, 212 p. 22 cm. (Liverpool studies in Spanish literature, 2d ser.) (Studies in Hispanic literatures.) Reprint of the 1946 ed. published by Institute of Hispanic Studies, Liverpool, Eng. 1. Spanish poetry — Classical period, 1500-1700 — History and criticism — Addresses, essays, lectures. 2. Spanish drama — Classical period, 1500-1700 — History and criticism — Addresses, essays, lectures. I. T. II. Series. III. Series: Studies in Hispanic literatures.
PQ6065.P43 1974   860/.9/003   LC 74-5001   ISBN 0877530602

Vossler, Karl, 1872-1949.   • 2.5107
Introduccion a la literatura Española del siglo de oro, seis lecciones. Buenos Aires-México, Espasa-Calpe Argentina, S.A. [1945] 3 p. l., [9]-151 p. 18 cm. (Colección Austral. [511]) At head of title: Carlos Vossler. 'Versión del alemán, por Felipe González Vicén.' The tranlation is based on the author's elaborated translation, 'Einführung in die spanische dichtung des goldenen zeitalters,' of the original Spaish text published Madrid, 1934. cf. Prólogo. 'Primera edición: 28-IV-1945. Segunda edición: 12-XI-1945.' 1. Spanish literature — Classical period, 1500-1700 — History and criticism. I. González Vicen, Felipe. II. T.
PQ6065.V6x   861.309   LC a 47-3374

Shaw, Donald Leslie, 1930-.   2.5108
The nineteenth century [by] Donald L. Shaw. London, Benn; New York, Barnes & Noble, 1972. xxii, 200 p. 23 cm. (A literary history of Spain) 1. Spanish literature — 19th century — History and criticism. I. T.
PQ6070.S48 1972   860/.9/005   LC 72-186204   ISBN 0510322816
ISBN 0510322824

PQ6072–6073 20TH CENTURY

Barja, César.   • 2.5109
Libros y autores contemporáneos: Ganivet, Unamuno, Ortega y Gasset, Azorín, Baroja, Valle–Inclán, Antonio Machado, Pérez de Ayala. [Nueva ed.] New York, Las Américas Pub. Co., 1964. vii, 493 p. 19 cm. 'Concebidos estos capítulos, y originalmente escritos, como una continuación a los dos volumenes del autor, Libros y autores clásicos y Libros y autores modernos.'—Advertencia. Previous editions published under title: Literatura espanola: libros y autores contemporáneos. 1. Ganivet, Angel, 1865-1898. 2. Unamuno, Miguel de, 1864-1936. 3. Ortega y Gasset, José, 1883-1955. 4. Azorín, 1873-1967. 5. Baroja, Pío, 1872-1956. 6. Valle-Inclán, Ramón del, 1870-1936. 7. Machado, Antonio, 1875-1939. 8. Pérez de Ayala, Ramón, 1880-1962. I. T.
PQ6072.B33 1964   LC 64-55644

Brown, Gerald Griffiths.   • 2.5110
The twentieth century [by] G. G. Brown. — London: E. Benn; New York: Barnes & Noble, [1972] xv, 176 p.; 23 cm. — (A literary history of Spain) 1. Spanish literature — 20th century — History and criticism. I. T.
PQ6072.B75   860/.9/006   LC 72-188267   ISBN 038904623X

Salinas, Pedro, 1892-1951.   • 2.5111
Literatura española, siglo XX. 2. ed. aumentada. México, Antigua Librería Robredo, 1949. vii, 227 p. 19 cm. (Clásicos y modernos; creación y crítica literaria, 1) 'Una colección de artículos y ensayos escritos de 1932 a 1940.' 1. Spanish literature — 20th century — History and criticism. I. T. II. Series.
PQ6072.S3 1949   860.904   LC 49-52550

Schwartz, Kessel.   2.5112
Studies on twentieth–century Spanish and Spanish American literature / Kessel Schwartz. — Lanham, MD: University Press of America, c1983. x, 440 p.; 24 cm. 1. Spanish literature — 20th century — History and criticism — Addresses, essays, lectures. 2. Spanish American literature — 20th century — History and criticism — Addresses, essays, lectures. I. T.
PQ6072.S39 1983   860/.9/006 19   LC 83-5793   ISBN 0819131849

Bleiberg, Germán, 1915-.   • 2.5113
Spanish thought and letters in the twentieth century / Germán Bleiberg and E. Inman Fox, editors. — Nashville: Vanderbilt University Press, 1966. xvi, 610 p.: facsims.; 23 cm. English and Spanish. 1. Unamuno, Miguel de, 1864-1936. 2. Spanish literature — 20th century — Addresses, essays, lectures. I. Fox, E. Inman (Edward Inman), 1933- II. Unamuno, Miguel de, 1864-1936. III. Vanderbilt University. IV. American Council of Learned Societies. V. Hispanic Society of America. VI. T.
PQ6072.S67   860/.9006   LC 65-25181

Morris, C. B. (Cyril Brian)   2.5114
Surrealism and Spain, 1920–1936 [by] C. B. Morris. Cambridge [Eng.] Cambridge University Press, 1972. x, 291 p. illus. 23 cm. 1. Spanish literature — 20th century — History and criticism. 2. Surrealism I. T.
PQ6073.S9 M6   860/.9/1   LC 74-190414   ISBN 0521085292

PQ6076–6167 Special Forms

PQ6076–6098 POETRY

Alonso, Dámaso, 1898-.   • 2.5115
Ensayos sobre poesía española. — Madrid, Revista de Occidente [1944] 401 p.; 20 cm. I. T.
PQ6077.A4

Guillén, Jorge, 1893-.   • 2.5116
Language and poetry: some poets of Spain. — Cambridge: Harvard University Press, 1961. xi, 293 p. — (The Charles Eliot Norton lectures; 1957-1958.) 1. Spanish poetry — Addresses, essays, lectures. I. T.
PQ6077.G8   LC 60-15889

Trend, John Brande, 1887-.   2.5117
Lorca and the Spanish poetic tradition / by J. B. Trend. — Oxford: B. Blackwell, 1956. vii, 178 p.; 23 cm. 1. Spanish poetry — History and criticism — Addresses, essays, lectures. 2. Spanish American poetry — History and criticism — Addresses, essays, lectures. I. T.
PQ6077.T7   861/.009   LC 56-14705

Salinas, Pedro, 1892-1951.   • 2.5118
Reality and the poet in Spanish poetry, by Pedro Salinas. Baltimore, The Johns Hopkins press, 1940. ix, 165 p. 22 cm. 'The English text of these lectures is by Edith Fishtine Helman.' 1. Spanish poetry — History and criticism — Collected works. 2. Reality in literature — Collected works. I. Helman, Edith, tr. II. T.
PQ6078.S3   861.09   LC 40-6879

Alonso, Dámaso, 1898-.   • 2.5119
Poetas espanoles contemporánes. — Madrid: Gredos [1952] 446 p. ports.; 20 cm. — (Biblioteca románica hispánica. 2. Estudios y ensays; 6) 1. Bécquer, Gustavo Adolfo, 1836-1870. 2. Spanish poetry — 20th century — History and criticism. I. T.
PQ6085.A6 1952   LC A53-304

Cobb, Carl W.   2.5120
Contemporary Spanish poetry (1898–1963) / by Carl W. Cobb. — Boston: Twayne Publishers, c1976. 160 p.; 21 cm. (Twayne's world authors series; TWAS 373: Spain) Includes index. 1. Spanish poetry — 20th century — History and criticism. I. T.
PQ6085.C56   861/.6/209   LC 75-23016   ISBN 0805762027

Daydí-Tolson, Santiago.   2.5121
The post-civil war Spanish social poets / by Santiago Daydí–Tolson. — Boston: Twayne Publishers, c1983. 174 p.; 23 cm. — (Twayne's world authors series. TWAS 686) Includes index. 1. Spanish poetry — 20th century — History and criticism. 2. Literature and society — Spain. I. T. II. Series.
PQ6085.D37 1983   861/.64/09 19   LC 82-21178   ISBN 0805765336

Menéndez Pidal, Ramón, 1869-1968.   2.5122
[Épopée castillane à travers la littérature espagnole. Spanish] La epopeya castellana a través de la literatura española / Ramón Menéndez Pidal. — Madrid: Espasa-Calpe, [1974], c1945. 211 p.; 18 cm. — (Colección austral; no. 1561) Translation of L'épopée castillane a travers la littérature espagnole. 'Se compone de una serie de conferencias dadas, en francés, en la Universidad John's Hopkins de Baltimore, el año 1909.' 1. Epic poetry, Spanish — History and criticism. I. T.
PQ6088.M375 1974   861/.03   LC 76-475638   ISBN 8423915611

Foster, David William.　　　　　　　　　　　**2.5123**
The early Spanish ballad. New York, Twayne Publishers [c1971] 220 p. 21 cm. (Twayne's world authors series, TWAS 185. Spain) 1. Ballads, Spanish — History and criticism. 2. Spanish poetry — To 1500 — History and criticism. I. T.
PQ6090.F6　　　861/.04　　　*LC* 79-152012

Rennert, Hugo Albert, 1858-1927.　　　　　• **2.5124**
The Spanish pastoral romances. New York, Biblo and Tannen, 1968. 206 p. 21 cm. Reprint of the 1912 ed. 1. Pastoral poetry, Spanish — History and criticism. 2. Ballads, Spanish — History and criticism. I. T.
PQ6090.R3 1968　　　860.9/003　　　*LC* 67-29552

PQ6099–6129 Drama

Gerstinger, Heinz, 1919-.　　　　　　　　　**2.5125**
[Spanische Komödie. English] Lope de Vega and Spanish drama. Translated by Samuel R. Rosenbaum. New York, F. Ungar Pub. Co. [1974] vi, 170 p. illus. 21 cm. (World dramatists) Translation of Spanische Komödie. 1. Spanish drama — Classical period, 1500-1700 — History and criticism. I. T.
PQ6105.G413　　　862/.3/09　　　*LC* 72-90812　　　*ISBN* 0804422273

Leavitt, Sturgis Elleno, 1888-.　　　　　　　**2.5126**
Golden age drama in Spain: general consideration and unusual features, by Sturgis E. Leavitt. Chapel Hill, University of North Carolina Press [1972] 128 p. 24 cm. (University of North Carolina. Studies in the Romance languages and literatures, no. 121) 1. Spanish drama — Classical period, 1500-1700 — Addresses, essays, lectures. I. T.
PQ6105.L4　　　862/.3/09　　　*LC* 72-172082

Wilson, Edward Meryon, 1906-.　　　　　　• **2.5127**
The golden age: drama, 1492–1700, [by] Edward M. Wilson, Duncan Moir. — London: Benn, 1971. xviii, 171 p.; 23 cm. — (A Literary history of Spain) 1. Spanish drama — Classical period, 1500-1700 — History and criticism. I. Moir, Duncan W., joint author. II. T.
PQ6105.W48　　　862/.3/09　　　*LC* 73-888156　　　*ISBN* 0510322638

Wilson, Margaret, 1921 (Aug. 22)-.　　　　　**2.5128**
Spanish drama of the golden age. — [1st ed.]. — Oxford; New York: Pergamon Press, [1969] xi, 221 p.; 20 cm. — (The Commonwealth and international library. Pergamon Oxford Spanish division) 1. Spanish drama — Classical period, 1500-1700 — History and criticism. I. T.
PQ6105.W5 1969　　　862/.3/09　　　*LC* 74-78906　　　*ISBN* 0080139558

Ziomek, Henryk.　　　　　　　　　　　　　**2.5129**
A history of Spanish Golden Age drama / Henryk Ziomek. — Lexington, Ky.: University Press of Kentucky, c1984. x, 246 p.: ill.; 23 cm. (Studies in Romance languages (Lexington, Ky.) 29) Includes index. 1. Spanish drama — Classical period, 1500-1700 — History and criticism. I. T. II. Series.
PQ6105.Z56 1984　　　862/.3/09 19　　　*LC* 83-23309　　　*ISBN* 081311506X

Edwards, Gwynne.　　　　　　　　　　　　**2.5130**
Dramatists in perspective: Spanish theatre in the twentieth century / Gwynne Edwards. — New York: St. Martin's Press, 1985. 269 p.; 22 cm. Includes index. 1. Spanish drama — 20th century — History and criticism. I. T.
PQ6115.E35 1985　　　862/.6/09 19　　　*LC* 85-2216　　　*ISBN* 0312219504

Holt, Marion Peter.　　　　　　　　　　　**2.5131**
The contemporary Spanish theater (1949–1972) by Marion P. Holt. Boston, Twayne Publishers [1975] 189 p. 22 cm. (Twayne's world authors series, TWAS 336. Spain) 1. Spanish drama — 20th century — History and criticism. I. T.
PQ6115.H65　　　862/.6/409　　　*LC* 74-12472　　　*ISBN* 0805722432

Wardropper, Bruce Wear, 1919-.　　　　　• **2.5132**
Introducción al teatro religioso del Siglo de Oro; (la evolución del auto sacramental: 1500–1648) Madrid, Revista de Occidente [1953] 329 p. 1. Spanish drama — History and criticism 2. Mysteries and miracle-plays I. T.
PQ6121.R3W3　　　*LC* A54-2533

PQ6138–6147 Fiction

Alborg, Juan Luis.　　　　　　　　　　　**2.5133**
Hora actual de la novela española. — Madrid, Taurus [1958-1962] 2 v. ports. 22 cm. — (Colección Persiles, 6) 1. Spanish fiction — 20th cent. — Hist. & crit. 2. Novelists, Spanish I. T.
PQ6144.A7　　　*LC* 59-52573 rev

Eoff, Sherman Hinkle, 1900-.　　　　　　• **2.5134**
The modern Spanish novel; comparative essays examining the philosophical impact of science on fiction. — New York: New York University Press, 1961. 280 p.; 22 cm. 1. Spanish fiction — Addresses, essays, lectures. 2. Literature, Comparative — Addresses, essays, lectures. I. T.
PQ6144.E6　　　863.0903　　　*LC* 61-11261

Jones, Margaret E. W., 1938-.　　　　　　**2.5135**
The contemporary Spanish novel, 1939–1975 / by Margaret E.W. Jones. — Boston: Twayne Publishers, c1985. 159 p.; 22 cm. (Twayne's world authors series; TWAS 752. Spanish literature) Includes index. 1. Spanish fiction — 20th century — History and criticism. I. T.
PQ6144.J64 1985　　　863/.6/09 19　　　*LC* 84-13577　　　*ISBN* 0805766014

Landeira, Ricardo, 1944-.　　　　　　　　**2.5136**
The modern Spanish novel, 1898–1936 / by Ricardo Landeira. — Boston: Twayne Publishers, c1985. 163 p.; 23 cm. — (Twayne's world authors series; TWAS 764. Spanish literature) Includes index. 1. Spanish fiction — 20th century — History and criticism. I. T.
PQ6144.L36 1985　　　863/.62/09 19　　　*LC* 85-7678　　　*ISBN* 0805766030

Montesinos, José Fernández.　　　　　　• **2.5137**
Introducción a una historia de la novela en España en el siglo XIX: seguida de una bibliografía española de traducciones de novelas (1800–1850) / José F. Montesinos. — [Valencia]: Castalia, [1955] xvii, 345 p. — (Biblioteca de erudición y critica; 1) 1. Spanish fiction — 19th century — History and criticism. 2. Spanish fiction — 19th century — Translations from foreign literature — Bibliography. I. T.
PQ6144.M65　　　860/.9/005 19　　　*LC* 56-3334

García González de Nora, Eugenio, 1923-.　• **2.5138**
La novela española contemporánea [por] Eugenio G. de Nora. 2. ed. Madrid, Editorial Gredos [1958-62] 2 v. in 3. (Biblioteca románica hispánica. 2. Estudios y ensayos, 41) 1. Spanish fiction — 20th century — History and criticism. I. T.
PQ6144.N6　　　863.009 NOR　　　*LC* 59-4900

Schwartz, Ronald, 1937-.　　　　　　　　**2.5139**
Spain's new wave novelists, 1950–1974: studies in Spanish realism / by Ronald Schwartz. — Metuchen, N.J.: Scarecrow Press, 1976. x, 417 p.; 23 cm. Includes index. 1. Spanish fiction — 20th century — History and criticism. 2. Realism in literature I. T.
PQ6144.S38 1976　　　863/.03　　　*LC* 75-44366　　　*ISBN* 0810808544

Solé-Leris, Amadeu.　　　　　　　　　　**2.5140**
The Spanish pastoral novel / by Amadeu Solé–Leris. — Boston: Twayne Publishers, 1980. 171 p.; 21 cm. — (Twayne's world authors series; TWAS 575: Spain) Includes index. 1. Pastoral fiction, Spanish — History and criticism. 2. Spanish fiction — Classical period, 1500-1700 — History and criticism. I. T.
PQ6147.P3 S6　　　863/.03　　　*LC* 79-24897　　　*ISBN* 0805764178

Dunn, Peter N.　　　　　　　　　　　　**2.5141**
The Spanish picaresque novel / by Peter N. Dunn. — Boston: Twayne Publishers, 1979. 166 p.; 21 cm. — (Twayne's world authors series; TWAS 557: Spain) Includes index. 1. Spanish fiction — Classical period, 1500-1700 — History and criticism. 2. Picaresque literature — History and criticism. I. T.
PQ6147.P5 D8　　　863/.03　　　*LC* 79-1030　　　*ISBN* 0805763996

PQ6171–6269 Collections of Spanish Literature

Marín, Diego. comp.　　　　　　　　　　**2.5142**
Literatura española: selección / introducctiones y notas por Diego Marin; con la colaboración de Evelyn Rugg. — New York: Holt, Rinehart and Winston, [1968]. 2 v.; 26 cm. 1. Spanish literature (Selections: Extracts, etc.) I. Rugg, Evelyn. joint comp. II. T.
PQ6172.M35　　　*LC* 68-13505

Barnstone, Willis, 1927- comp.　　　　　　**2.5143**
Spanish poetry, from its beginnings through the nineteenth century; an anthology. Edited by Willis Barnstone. — New York: Oxford University Press, 1970. xxi, 526 p.; 25 cm. 1. Spanish poetry I. T.
PQ6176.B34　　　861/.008　　　*LC* 74-82982

Cohen, John Michael, 1903-, ed.　　　　　• **2.5144**
The Penguin book of Spanish verse. With plain prose translations of each poem. [Harmondsworth, Middx.] Penguin Books [1956] 441p. (The Penguin poets, D30) 1. Spanish poetry (Collections) 2. Spanish-American poetry(Collections) I. T.
PQ6176 C57

Peers, E. Allison (Edgar Allison), 1891-1952. ed.   • **2.5145**
A critical anthology of Spanish verse, compiled and edited by E. Allison Peers. New York, Greenwood Press, 1968. L, 741 p. 22 cm. Reprint of the 1949 ed. 1. Spanish poetry I. T.
PQ6176.P245 1968   861/.008   *LC* 69-10145

Rivers, Elias L. ed. and tr.   **2.5146**
Renaissance and baroque poetry of Spain, with English prose translations. Introduced and edited by Elias L. Rivers. — New York: Scribner, [1972? c1966] 351 p.; 21 cm. — (Lyceum editions) (Scribner library) Reprint, with a new pref., of the ed. published by Dell Pub. Co., New York, in the Spanish series of the Laurel language library. 1. Spanish poetry — Classical period, 1500-1700 2. Spanish poetry — Translations into English. 3. English literature — Translations from Spanish. I. T.
PQ6184.R5 1972   861/.3/08   *LC* 72-11297   *ISBN* 0684132869

Correa, Gustavo.   **2.5147**
Poesía española del siglo veinte: antología / estudio preliminar, selección y notas de Gustavo Correa. — New York: Appleton-Century-Crofts, 1972. xxii, 613 p. 1. Spanish poetry — 20th century I. T.
PQ6187 C65   PQ6187 C75.   861'.6'08   *LC* 70-188650   *ISBN* 0390211451

Alpern, Hymen, 1895-1967. comp.   **2.5148**
Diez comedias del Siglo de Oro; an annotated omnibus of ten complete plays by the most representative Spanish dramatists of the Golden Age, edited by José Martel and Hymen Alpern and revised by Leonard Mades. — 2d ed. — New York, Harper & Row [1968] xxix, 865 p. illus., ports. 22 cm. Compilers' names in reverse order in first edition. Includes bibliographies. 1. Spanish drama — Classical period, 1500-1700 2. Spanish drama (Comedy) I. Martel, José, 1883- joint comp. II. Mades, Leonard. ed. III. T.
PQ6217.A7 1968   862/.3/08   *LC* 68-10245

Resnick, Seymour. ed.   • **2.5149**
An anthology of Spanish literature in English translation. Edited by Seymour Resnick and Jeanne Pasmantier. — New York: F. Ungar Pub. Co., [1958] 2 v.; 23 cm. 1. Spanish literature — Translations into English. 2. English literature — Translations from Spanish. I. Pasmantier, Jeanne, joint ed. II. T.
PQ6267.E1 R4 1958a   860.82   *LC* 58-8467

Introduction to modern Spanish literature: an anthology of   **2.5150**
fiction, poetry, and essay / edited by Kessel Schwartz.
New York: Twayne Publishers, 1968. 336 p. 1. Spanish literature — 20th century 2. Spanish literature — Translations into English. 3. English literature — Translations from Spanish. I. Schwartz, Kessel.
PQ6267.E1 S3   860.8 19   *LC* 68-17229

Turnbull, Eleanor L. (Eleanor Laurelle) ed.   • **2.5151**
Ten centuries of Spanish poetry; an anthology in English verse with original texts, from the XIth century to the generation of 1898. Edited by Eleanor L. Turnbull. With introductions by Pedro Salinas. Baltimore, Johns Hopkins Press [1969, c1955] xv, 452 p. 21 cm. (Johns Hopkins paperback, JH-54) 1. Spanish poetry — Translations into English. 2. English poetry — Translations from Spanish. 3. Spanish poetry I. T.
PQ6267.E2 1969   861/.008   *LC* 72-5469

Roots and wings: poetry from Spain, 1900–1975: a bilingual   **2.5152**
anthology / Hardie St. Martin, editor.
1st ed. — New York: Harper & Row, c1976. xxiii, 528 p.; 25 cm. Includes indexes. 1. Spanish poetry — Translations into English. 2. English poetry — Translations from Spanish. 3. Spanish poetry — 20th century I. St. Martin, Hardie.
PQ6267.E2 1976   861/.6/408   *LC* 73-14293   *ISBN* 0060139765

Recent poetry of Spain: a bilingual anthology / translated and   **2.5153**
edited by Louis Hammer and Sara Schyfter.
1st ed. — Old Chatham, N.Y.: Sachem Press, c1983. xxii, 339 p.; 24 cm. English and Spanish. 1. Spanish poetry — 20th century — Translations into English. 2. English poetry — Translations from Spanish. 3. Spanish poetry — 20th century I. Hammer, Louis, 1931- II. Schyfter, Sara E.
PQ6267.E2 1983   861/.6/08 19   *LC* 83-11235   *ISBN* 093758407X

Turnbull, Eleanor L. (Eleanor Laurelle) ed. and tr.   • **2.5154**
Contemporary Spanish poetry; selections from ten poets, translated by Eleanor L. Turnbull. With Spanish originals and personal reminiscences of the poets by Pedro Salinas. — New York: Greenwood Press, [1968, c1945] xiii, 401 p.; 24 cm. Spanish and English. 1. Spanish poetry — 20th century 2. Spanish poetry — Translations into English. 3. English poetry — Translations from Spanish. I. T.
PQ6267.E3 T8 1968   861/.6/208   *LC* 69-14125

Bryant, Shasta M.   **2.5155**
The Spanish ballad in English, by Shasta M. Bryant. Lexington, University Press of Kentucky [c1973] 261 p. 24 cm. (Studies in Romance languages (Lexington, Ky.) 8) Includes ballad texts in Spanish with parallel English translation. 1. Ballads, Spanish — Spain — Texts. 2. Ballads, Spanish — Spain — History and criticism. I. T. II. Series.
PQ6267.E4 B23   861/.04   *LC* 72-81314   *ISBN* 081311280X

Cries from a wounded Madrid: poetry of the Spanish Civil War   **2.5156**
/ selected and translated by Carlos Bauer.
Bilingual ed. — Athens, Ohio: Ohio University, c1984. xv, 158 p.; 24 cm. Text in English and Spanish. 1. Spanish poetry — 20th century — Translations into English. 2. English poetry — Translations from Spanish. 3. Spanish poetry — 20th century 4. War poetry, Spanish 5. War poetry, Spanish — Translations into English. 6. War poetry, English — Translations from Spanish. 7. Spain — History — Civil War, 1936-1939 — Poetry I. Bauer, Carlos.
PQ6267.E5 W372 1984   861/.62/08 19

Corrigan, Robert Willoughby, 1927- comp.   **2.5157**
Masterpieces of the modern Spanish theatre. Edited by Robert W. Corrigan. — New York: Collier Books, [1967] 384 p.; 18 cm. — (Masterpieces of the modern theatre) 1. Spanish drama — 20th century — Translations into English. 2. English drama — Translations from Spanish. I. T.
PQ6267.E6 C65   862/.6/08   *LC* 66-24431

Holt, Marion Peter. comp.   **2.5158**
The modern Spanish stage: four plays. Edited by Marion Holt. [1st ed.] New York, Hill & Wang [1970] xxvi, 388 p. 19 cm. (A Mermaid dramabook) 1. Spanish drama — 20th century — Translations into English. 2. English drama — Translations from Spanish. I. T.
PQ6267.E6 H6   862/.6/208   *LC* 78-106966   *ISBN* 0809007460

Starkie, Walter, 1894- ed. and tr.   • **2.5159**
Eight Spanish plays of the golden age. Translated, edited, and with an introd., by Walter Starkie. New York, Modern Library [1964] xlviii, 328 p. 19 cm. (The Modern library of the world's best books, 345) 'The mystery play of Elche' (including music): p. [325]-328. 1. Spanish drama — Translations into English. 2. English drama — Translations from Spanish. 3. Spanish drama — Classical period, 1500-1700 I. T.
PQ6267.E6 S8   862.3082   *LC* 64-10292

PQ6271–6676 INDIVIDUAL AUTHORS AND WORKS

PQ6271–6498 To 1700

PQ6271–6279 A–C

Keller, John Esten.   **2.5160**
Alfonso X, el Sabio. New York, Twayne Publishers [1967] 198 p. 22 cm. (Twayne's world authors series, 12. Spain) 1. Alfonso X, King of Castile and Leon, 1221-1284. I. T.
PQ6273.A2 Z7   946/.02/0924   *LC* 66-29183

Darst, David H.   **2.5161**
Juan Boscán / by David H. Darst. — Boston: Twayne Publishers, c1978. 150 p.; 21 cm. (Twayne's world authors series; TWAS 475: Spain) Includes index. 1. Boscán, Juan, d. 1542 — Criticism and interpretation. I. T.
PQ6279.B6 D3   861/.3   *LC* 77-22158   *ISBN* 0805763163

PQ6280–6319 Calderón

Parker, Alexander Augustine.   **2.5162**
The allegorical drama of Calderón, an introduction to the Autos sacramentales, by Alexander A. Parker. — Oxford, Dolphin Book, 1968. 232 p.; 22 cm. 1. Calderón de la Barca, Pedro, 1600-1681. Autos sacramentales. I. T.
PQ6287.P3   862.35   862   *LC* 43-11230

Calderón de la Barca, Pedro, 1600-1681.   **2.5163**
Four plays, translated and with an introd. by Edwin Honig. With an appendix on Spanish golden age customs and drama by Norman Maccoll. — New York: Hill and Wang, [1961] 319 p.; 19 cm. — (A Mermaid dramabook, MD21) I. Honig, Edwin, tr. II. T.
PQ6292.A1 H6 1961   862.3   *LC* 61-14474

Calderón de la Barca, Pedro, 1600-1681.   **2.5164**
[Vida es sueño. English] Life is a dream; a play. Translated and with a foreword and introd. by Edwin Honig. [1st ed.] New York, Hill & Wang [1970] xxxv,

119 p. 21 cm. (A Mermaid dramabook) Translation of La vida es sueño. I. Honig, Edwin, tr. II. T.
PQ6292.V5 H6   862/.3   *LC* 74-116872   *ISBN* 0809065568

Hesse, Everett Wesley, 1908-.   • **2.5165**
Calderón de la Barca, by Everett W. Hesse. — New York: Twayne Publishers, [1967] 192 p.; 21 cm. — (Twayne's world authors series, 30. Spain) 1. Calderón de la Barca, Pedro, 1600-1681. I. T.
PQ6309.H4   862/.3   *LC* 67-25182

Edwards, Gwynne.   **2.5166**
The prison and the labyrinth: studies in Calderonian tragedy / Gwynne Edwards. — Cardiff: University of Wales Press, 1978. xl, 197 p.; 23 cm. Includes index. 1. Calderón de la Barca, Pedro, 1600-1681 — Tragedies. I. T.
PQ6312.E3   862/.3   *LC* 79-304637   *ISBN* 0708306888

Maraniss, James E., 1945-.   **2.5167**
On Calderón / James E. Maraniss. — Columbia: University of Missouri Press, 1978. 129 p.; 21 cm. Includes index. 1. Calderón de la Barca, Pedro, 1600-1681 — Criticism and interpretation. I. T.
PQ6312.M3   862/.3   *LC* 77-14034   *ISBN* 0826202373

PQ6321 Castro

Wilson, William Eade, 1900-.   • **2.5168**
Guillén de Castro, by William E. Wilson. New York, Twayne Publishers [1973] 166 p. 21 cm. (Twayne's world authors series, TWAS 253. Spain) 1. Castro, Guillén de, 1569-1631. I. T.
PQ6321.C7 Z9   862/.3   *LC* 72-2933

PQ6322–6361 Cervantes

Cervantes Saavedra, Miguel de, 1547-1616.   • **2.5169**
Don Quijote de la Mancha. Texto y notas de Martín de Riquer. New York, Las Américas Pub. Co., 1958. 1096 p. 19 cm. I. Riquer, Martín de, conde de Casa Dávalos, 1914- ed. II. T.
PQ6323.A1

El Saffar, Ruth S., 1941-.   **2.5170**
Novel to romance: a study of Cervantes's Novelas ejemplares [by] Ruth S. El Saffar. — Baltimore: Johns Hopkins University Press, [1974] xvi, 189 p.; 23 cm. 1. Cervantes Saavedra, Miguel de, 1547-1616. Novelas ejemplares. I. T.
PQ6324.Z5 E5   863/.3   *LC* 73-19332   *ISBN* 0801815452

Cervantes Saavedra, Miguel de, 1547-1616.   **2.5171**
The adventures of Don Quixote / by Miguel de Cervantes Saavedra; translated by J.M. Cohen. — Harmondsworth, England: Penguin Books, 1950. 940 p. — (Penguin classics) I. Cohen, J. M. (John Michael), 1903- II. T.
PQ6329 A2 1950   *ISBN* 0140440100

Cervantes Saavedra, Miguel de, 1547-1616.   **2.5172**
The ingenious gentleman Don Quixote de la Mancha; a new translation from the Spanish, with a critical text based upon the first editions of 1605 and 1615, and with variant readings, variorum notes, and an introduction by Samuel Putnam. New York, Modern Library [1964, c1949] xxx, 1043 p. I. Putnam, Samuel, 1892-1950. II. T. III. Title: Don Quixote de la Mancha.
PQ6329.A2 1964

Cervantes Saavedra, Miguel de, 1547-1616.   **2.5173**
[Don Quixote. English] Don Quixote: the Ormsby translation, revised, backgrounds and sources, criticism / Miguel de Cervantes; edited by Joseph R. Jones and Kenneth Douglas. — 1st ed. — New York: Norton, c1981. xiii, 1003 p.; 23 cm. — (A Norton critical edition) 1. Cervantes Saavedra, Miguel de, 1547-1616 Don Quixote — Addresses, essays, lectures. I. Ormsby, John, 1829-1895. II. Jones, Joseph Ramon, 1935- III. Douglas, Kenneth. IV. T.
PQ6329.A2 1981   863/.3   *LC* 79-20762   *ISBN* 0393045145

Cervantes Saavedra, Miguel de, 1547-1616.   • **2.5174**
Three exemplary novels / translated by Samuel Putnam. Illustrated by Luis Quintanilla. [1st ed.] New York: Viking Press, 1950. 232 p. illus. I. Putnam, Samuel, 1892-1950. II. T.
PQ6329.A6 P8   863.32   Fic   *LC* 50-10034

PQ6337–6361 Biography. Criticism

Byron, William.   **2.5175**
Cervantes, a biography / William Byron. — 1st ed. — Garden City, N.Y.: Doubleday, 1978. xiv, 583 p., [10] leaves of plates: ill.; 24 cm. Includes index. 1. Cervantes Saavedra, Miguel de, 1547-1616 — Biography. 2. Authors, Spanish — 17th century — Biography. I. T.
PQ6337.B9   863/.3 B   *LC* 74-33633   *ISBN* 0385002793

Durán, Manuel, 1925-.   **2.5176**
Cervantes. — New York: Twayne Publishers, [1974] 189 p.: port.; 21 cm. — (Twayne's world authors series, TWAS 329. Spain) 1. Cervantes Saavedra, Miguel de, 1547-1616. I. T.
PQ6337.D84   863/.3   *LC* 74-7006   *ISBN* 0805722068

Navarro y Ledesma, Francisco, 1869-1905.   **2.5177**
[Ingenioso hidalgo Miguel de Cervantes Saavedra. English] Cervantes, the man and the genius. Translated and rev. by Don and Gabriela Bliss. New York, Charterhouse [1973] xiv, 396 p. 24 cm. Translation of El ingenioso hidalgo Miguel de Cervantes Saavedra. 1. Cervantes Saavedra, Miguel de, 1547-1616. I. T.
PQ6337.N3 1973   863/.3   *LC* 72-84220

Predmore, Richard Lionel.   **2.5178**
Cervantes [by] Richard L. Predmore. — New York: Dodd, Mead, [1973] 224 p.: illus.; 27 cm. 1. Cervantes Saavedra, Miguel de, 1547-1616 — Biography. I. T.
PQ6337.P7   863/.3 B   *LC* 72-13587   *ISBN* 0396067972

Flores, Angel, 1900- ed.   **2.5179**
Cervantes across the centuries [essays] A quadricentennial volume edited by Angel Flores and M. J. Benardete. New York, Dryden Press, 1947 [i.e. 1948] vi, 371, [3] p. 25 cm. 'A selected bibliography': p. [373]-[374] 1. Cervantes Saavedra, Miguel de, 1547-1616 — Anniversaries, etc., 1947. I. Benardete, M. J. (Maír José), 1895- ed. II. T.
PQ6341.B47F6   863.32   *LC* 48-5819

Castro, Américo, 1885-1972.   • **2.5180**
El pensamiento de Cervantes, por Américo Castro. Madrid Impr. de la librería y casa editorial Hernando (s.a.) 1925. 406p. (Revista de filología española. Anejo 6) 1. Cervantes Saavedra, Miguel de, 1547-1616. I. T. II. Series.
PQ6351 C38

Madariaga, Salvador de, 1886-.   • **2.5181**
Don Quixote; an introductory essay in psychology, by Salvador de Madariaga. Oxford, At the Clarendon press, 1935. 159 p. 'This essay, written in Spanish and translated into English by the author and his wife, was first published in English in a limited edition by the Gregynog press, 1934.'—3d prelim. leaf. 1. Cervantes Saavedra, Miguel de, 1547-1616. Don Quixote I. Madariaga, Constance Helen Margaret Archibald de, tr. II. T.
PQ6352.M22x   *LC* a 35-1815

Unamuno, Miguel de, 1864-1936.   • **2.5182**
Vida de Don Quijote y Sancho según Miguel de Cervantes Saavedra; explicada y comentada por Miguel de Unamuno. 8. ed. Buenos Aires Espasa-Calpe Argentina [1938] 284p. (Colección Austral) 1. Cervantes Saavedra, Miguel de. Don Quixote I. T.
PQ6352 U5

Casalduero, Joaquín.   • **2.5183**
Sentido y forma del Quijote, 1605–1615. — [Madrid] Ediciones Insula, 1949. 392 p. 26 cm. 'Fe de erratas': leaf inserted. 1. Cervantes Saavedra, Miguel de. Don Quixote. I. T.
PQ6353.C33   863.32   *LC* 50-2684

PQ6366–6386 El Cid Campeador

El Cid Campeador.   **2.5184**
The poem of the Cid: a new critical edition of the Spanish text / with an introduction and notes by Ian Michael; together with a new prose translation by Rita Hamilton and Janet Perry. — Manchester: Manchester University Press; New York: Barnes & Noble, c1975. 242 p.: fold. map; 22 cm. — (Manchester medieval classics) Spanish and English on opposite pages. Includes bibliographical references. I. Michael, Ian. II. Hamilton, Rita. III. Perry, Janet. IV. T.
PQ6366.A1 1975   *LC* 75-17168   *ISBN* 0064947998

Cantar de mío Cid.   **2.5185**
Poema de mio Cid; edited with introduction and notes by Colin Smith. Oxford, Clarendon Press, 1972. xcviii, 184 p., leaf. facsim., map. 23 cm. Spanish text; introd. and notes in English. I. Smith, Colin, 1927- ed. II. Cid (Epic cycle) III. T.
PQ6366.A2 1972   *LC* 72-186260   *ISBN* 0198157088

El Cid Campeador.   **2.5186**
The poem of the Cid / translated by Lesley Byrd Simpson. — Berkeley: University of California Press, 1957. xvi, 139 p.: ill. I. Simpson, Lesley Byrd, 1891- II. T.
PQ6367.E3 S5   *LC* 57-10503   *ISBN* 0520011767

De Chasca, Edmund, 1903-.   **2.5187**
The poem of the Cid / by Edmund de Chasca. — Boston: Twayne Publishers, c1976. 189 p.; 21 cm. — (Twayne's world authors series; TWAS 378: Spain)

Includes index. 1. Cid, ca. 1043-1099 — Romances — History and criticism. 2. Cantar de mío Cid. I. T.
PQ6373.D4   861/.1   *LC* 75-30597   *ISBN* 0805761942

PQ6391–6424 G–Q

Garcilaso de la Vega, 1539-1616.   **2.5188**
Obras completas del Inca Garcilaso de la Vega / edición y estudio preliminanr del P. Carmelo Sáenz de Santa María. — Madrid; Ediciones Atlas, 1960. 4 v.; 26 cm. (Biblioteca de autores españoles desde la formación del lenguaje hasta nuestros días; t. 132-135) I. Sáenz de Santa María, Carmelo II. T.
PQ6391.A1 1960   *LC* 62-35806

Vega, Garcilaso de la, 1503-1536.   • **2.5189**
Obras completas / Garcilaso de la Vega; edición de Elias L. Rivers. — Edición de Elias L. Rivers. Columbus: Ohio State University Press, 1964. xxiv, 242 p.: facsims.; 24 cm. I. Rivers, Elias›L. II. T.
PQ6391.A1 1964   *LC* 65-6208

Gicovate, Bernard, 1922-.   **2.5190**
Garcilaso de la Vega / by Bernard Gicovate. — Boston: Twayne Publishers, [1975] 166 p.; 22 cm. — (Twayne's world authors series; TWAS 349: Spain) Includes index. 1. Vega, Garcilaso de la, 1503-1536. I. T.
PQ6392.G5   861.3   *LC* 74-28304   *ISBN* 0805723420

Góngora y Argote, Luis de, 1561-1627.   **2.5191**
[Soledades. English] The solitudes of Luis de Góngora. The Spanish text, with an English translation by Gilbert F. Cunningham. Pref. by A. A. Parker. Introd. by Elias L. Rivers. Baltimore, Johns Hopkins Press [1968] xxi, 146 p. 24 cm. I. Cunningham, Gilbert Farm, tr. II. T.
PQ6394.S6E5 1968   861/.3   *LC* 68-18492

Sturcken, H. Tracy.   **2.5192**
Don Juan Manuel, by H. Tracy Sturcken. — New York: Twayne Publishers, [1974] 162 p.; 21 cm. — (Twayne's world authors series, TWAS 303. Spain) 1. Juan Manuel, Infante of Castile, 1282-1347. I. T.
PQ6402.S8   863/.1   *LC* 73-15586   *ISBN* 0805725903

Lazarillo de Tormes. English.   **2.5193**
The life of Lazarillo of Tormes; his fortunes and misfortunes as told by himself. Translated and with an introd. by Robert S. Rudder. With a sequel by Juan de Luna. Translated by Robert S. Rudder with Carmen Criado de Rodríguez Puértolas. New York, Ungar [1973] xxi, 245 p. illus. 21 cm. 'The second part of the life of Lazarillo of Tormes' by Juan de Luna (p. [105]-245) I. Luna, Juan de, b. ca. 1585. La segunda parte de la vida de Lazarillo de Tormes. English. 1973. II. T. III. Title: Second part of the life of Lazarillo of Tormes.
PQ6408.E5 1973   863/.3   *LC* 70-125966   *ISBN* 0804427461 *ISBN* 0804467722

Fiore, Robert L.   **2.5194**
Lazarillo de Tormes / by Robert L. Fiore. — Boston: Twayne, c1984. 132 p.; 23 cm. — (Twayne's world authors series; TWAS 714. Spanish literature) Includes index. 1. Lazarillo de Tormes. I. T.
PQ6409.F56 1984   863/.3 19   *LC* 83-22633   *ISBN* 0805765611

León, Luis de, 1528?-1591.   **2.5195**
[Poems. English and Spanish. 1979] The unknown light: the poems of Fray Luis de León / introd. & translation. — Albany: State University of New York Press, c1979. 175 p.: port.; 24 cm. Poems in English and Spanish. I. Barnstone, Willis, 1927- II. T.
PQ6410.L3 A5 1979   861/.3   *LC* 79-15030   *ISBN* 0873953940

Bleznick, Donald William, 1924-.   **2.5196**
Quevedo, by Donald W. Bleznick. New York, Twayne [1972] 192 p. 21 cm. (Twayne's world authors series, TWAS 153: Spain) 1. Quevedo, Francisco de, 1580-1645 — Criticism and interpretation. I. T.
PQ6424.Z5 B5   868/.3/09   *LC* 71-120501

PQ6426–6428 Rojas

Rojas, Fernando de, d. 1541.   **2.5197**
La Celestina: tragicomedia de Calisto y Melibea / Fernando de Rojas. — Barcelona: Editorial Fama, 1955. 257 p.; 19 cm. I. T.
PQ6428.Cx

Dunn, Peter N.   **2.5198**
Fernando de Rojas / by Peter N. Dunn. — Boston: Twayne Publishers, c1975. 191 p.; 21 cm. (Twayne's world authors series; TWAS 368: Spain) Includes index. 1. Rojas, Fernando de, d. 1541. I. T.
PQ6428.D8   868/.2/09   *LC* 75-9838   *ISBN* 0805762183

Gilman, Stephen.   • **2.5199**
The art of La Celestina. Madison University of Wisconsin Press 1956. 261p. 1. Rojas, Fernando de, d. 1541. Celestina I. T.
PQ6428 G5

Gilman, Stephen.   **2.5200**
The Spain of Fernando de Rojas; the intellectual and social landscape of La Celestina. — [Princeton, N.J.]: Princeton University Press, [1972] xv, 559 p.; 25 cm. 1. Rojas, Fernando de, d. 1541. Celestina I. T.
PQ6428.G53   862/.2   *LC* 76-151530   *ISBN* 0691062021

PQ6429–6437 R–V

Ruiz, Juan, fl. 1343.   **2.5201**
Libro de buen amor. Edited, with an introd. and English paraphrase, by Raymond S. Willis. [Princeton, N.J.] Princeton University Press [1972] xcvi, 479 p. front. 23 cm. I. Willis, Raymond S. (Raymond Smith), 1906- ed. II. T.
PQ6430.A1 1972   861/.1   *LC* 79-134349   *ISBN* 069106086X

Lida de Malkiel, María Rosa.   **2.5202**
Two Spanish masterpieces: the Book of good love, and The Celestina. Urbana, University of Illinois Press, 1961. 106 p. 23 cm. 1. Ruiz, Juan, fl. 1343. 2. Rojas, Fernando de, d. 1541. Celestina I. T.
PQ6430.L5   *LC* 61-62764

Poesse, Walter.   • **2.5203**
Juan Ruiz de Alarcón. New York, Twayne [c1972.] 185 p. 21 cm. (Twayne's world authors series. Spain.) 1. Ruiz de Alarcón, Juan, 1580?-1639. I. T. II. Series.
PQ 6431 R8 Z7 P74 1972   *LC* 76-187625

Molina, Tirso de, 1571?-1648.   **2.5204**
El burlador de Sevilla y convidado de piedra; and La prudencia en la mujer / Tirso de Molina; introduction and notes by Raymond R. MacCurdy. — New York: Dell, c1965. 288 p.; 17 cm. — (Laurel language library; 8931. Spanish series) Texts in Spanish; introduction and notes in English. I. MacCurdy, Raymond R. II. Molina, Tirso de, 1571?-1648. Prudencia en la mujer. III. T. IV. Title: La prudencia en la mujer.
PQ6434.B8 1965   *LC* 65-1504

Wilson, Margaret, 1921 (Aug. 22)-.   **2.5205**
Tirso de Molina / by Margaret Wilson. — Boston: Twayne Publishers, c1977. 163 p.: ill.; 21 cm. (Twayne's world authors series; TWAS 445: Spain) Includes index. 1. Molina, Tirso de, 1571?-1648 — Criticism and interpretation. I. T.
PQ6436.W54   862/.3   *LC* 77-5947   *ISBN* 0805761817

Hatzfeld, Helmut Anthony, 1892-.   **2.5206**
Santa Teresa de Avila, by Helmut A. Hatzfeld. New York, Twayne Publishers [c1969] 200 p. 22 cm. (Twayne's world authors series, 79. Spain) 1. Teresa, of Avila, Saint, 1515-1582. I. T.
PQ6437.T3 Z7   868/.3/09   *LC* 68-57248

PQ6438–6492 Vega

Vega, Lope de, 1562-1635.   • **2.5207**
Fuente ovejuna / Lope de Vega; edición, estudio y notas por Tomás Garcia de la Santa. — 1. ed. — Zaragoza: Biblioteca Clásica Ebro, 1951. 108 p.: ill., facsim., port. — (Biblioteca Clásica Ebro. Clasicos españoles; 84) I. Garcia de la Santa, Tomás, ed. II. T.
PQ6439 F75 1951   *LC* 55-44592

Hayes, Francis C., 1904-.   • **2.5208**
Lope de Vega, by Francis C. Hayes. New York, Twayne Publishers [1967] 160 p. 21 cm. (Twayne's world authors series, 28. Spain) 1. Vega, Lope de, 1562-1635. I. T.
PQ6469.H3   826/.3   *LC* 67-19352

Rennert, Hugo Albert, 1858-1927.   **2.5209**
The life of Lope de Vega, 1562–1635. New York, B. Blom, 1968. xiii, 587 p. port. 20 cm. Reprint of the 1904 ed. 1. Vega, Lope de, 1562-1635. 2. Vega, Lope de, 1562-1635 — Bibliography. I. T.
PQ6469.R3 1968   862/.3   *LC* 67-13337

Larson, Donald R., 1935-.   **2.5210**
The honor plays of Lope de Vega / Donald R. Larson. — Cambridge: Harvard University Press, 1977. xi, 217 p.; 24 cm. 1. Vega, Lope de, 1562-1635 — Ethics. 2. Honor in literature I. T.
PQ6490.H7 L3   862/.3   *LC* 77-22950   *ISBN* 0674406281

PQ6495–6498 V–Z

Vicente, Gil, ca. 1470-ca. 1536.   **2.5211**
Farces and festival plays / Gil Vicente; edited by Thomas R. Hart. — Eugene: University of Oregon, 1972. 234 p. I. Hart, Thomas R. II. T.
PQ6496.V2 F3   PQ6496V2 F37 1972.

PQ6500–6576 Individual Authors, 1700–1868

PQ6501–6536 A–L

Alarcón, Pedro Antonio de, 1833-1891.   • **2.5212**
El sombrero de tres picos, y cuatro cuentos amatorios. Prólogo de Rafael Alberti, relación popular del corregidor y la molinera. Dibujos de Santiago Ontañón. Buenos Aires, Editorial Pleamar, 1944. 271 p. ill. 21 cm. (Colección El Ceibo y la encina) I. T.
PQ 6502 S69 1944   LC 61-56187

Alas, Leopoldo, 1852-1901.   **2.5213**
[Regenta. English] La regenta / Leopoldo Alas; translated with an introduction by John Rutherford. — Athens: University of Georgia Press, 1984. 734 p.; 24 cm. Translation of: La regenta. I. T.
PQ6503.A4 R313 1984   863/.5 19   LC 83-17886   ISBN 0820307009

Bécquer, Gustavo Adolfo, 1836-1870.   • **2.5214**
Obras completas. Con un prólogo, Semblanza de Bécquer, por Joaquín y Serafín Alvarez Quintero. Madrid Aguilar [1949] 1295 p. 14 cm. I. T.
PQ 6503 B3   LC 58-47060

Moore, John Aiken, 1920-.   **2.5215**
Ramón de la Cruz, by John A. Moore. New York, Twayne Publishers [1972] 181 p. 21 cm. (Twayne's world authors series, TWAS 179. Spain) 1. Cruz, Ramón de la, 1731-1794. I. T.
PQ6513.Z5 M6   862/.4   LC 70-153997

PQ6538–6576 M–Z

Cox, Ralph Merritt, 1939-.   **2.5216**
Juan Meléndez Valdés, by R. Merritt Cox. — New York: Twayne Publishers, [1974] 179 p.; 21 cm. — (Twayne's world authors series, TWAS 302. Spain) 1. Meléndez Valdés, Juan, 1754-1817. I. T.
PQ6538.M5 Z62   861/.4   LC 73-15583   ISBN 0805729186

Klibbe, Lawrence Hadfield, 1923-.   **2.5217**
José María de Pereda [by] Lawrence H. Klibbe. — New York: Twayne, [1975] 185 p.: port.; 21 cm. — (Twayne's world authors series, TWAS 354. Spain) 1. Pereda, José María de, 1833-1906. I. T.
PQ6554.P3 Z7   863/.5   LC 74-17390   ISBN 080572687X

Pérez Galdós, Benito, 1843-1920.   **2.5218**
Obras completas. Introd., biografia, bibliografia, notas y censo de personajes galdosianos por Federico Carlos Sainz de Robles. — [Madrid] Aguilar 1968-. v.: ill.; 18 cm. Contents.—t. 1-3. Episodios nacionales.—t. 4-5. Novelas.—t. 6. Novelas, teatro, miscelanea. I. Sáinz de Robles, Federico Carlos, 1898- II. T.
PQ6555.A1 1968   LC 77-234969

Pérez Galdós, Benito, 1843-1920.   **2.5219**
Doña Perfecta. Madrid, Liberia y Casa Editorial Hernando, S.A. 1965. 284 p.; 18 cm. (Novelas españolas contemporaneas.) I. T. II. Series.
PQ6555.D7x

Pérez Galdós, Benito, 1843-1920.   **2.5220**
Fortunata y Jacinta: dos historias de casadas / Benito Pérez Galdós; edición de Francisco Caudet. — Madrid: Catedra, 1983. 2 v.: ill. — (Letras hispánicas; 185-186) I. Caudet, Francisco, 1942- II. T.
PQ6555.F6   ISBN 8437604370

Pérez Galdós, Benito, 1843-1920.   **2.5221**
[Fortunata y Jacinta. English] Fortunata and Jacinta: two stories of married women / Benito Pérez Galdós; translated with an introduction by Agnes Moncy Gullón. — Athens: University of Georgia Press, c1986. xxiii, 818 p.; 25 cm. Translation of: Fortunata y Jacinta. I. T.
PQ6555.F7 E5 1986   863/.5 19   LC 84-28063   ISBN 0820307831

Pérez Galdós, Benito, 1843-1920.   **2.5222**
Miau / Benito Pérez Galdós. — 2a edición. — Buenos Aires: Espasa-Calpe, [1951] 269 p.; 18 cm. — (Colección Austral; 1024) I. T. II. Series.
PQ6555.M5 1951

Pérez Galdós, Benito, 1843-1920.   **2.5223**
Miau / edited by Edward R. Mulvihill and Roberto Sánches. — New York, Oxford University Press, 1970. xxiii, [2], 339 p. 21 cm. 1. Spanish language — Readers. I. Mulvihill, Edward R., ed. II. Sánchez, Roberto G., ed. III. T.
PQ6555.M5 1970   LC 72-82987

Casalduero, Joaquín.   • **2.5224**
Vida y obra de Galdós, 1843–1920. 2. ed., ampliada. Madrid, Editorial Gredos [1961] 278 p. 21 cm. (Biblioteca románica hispánica. Estudios y ensayos, 5) 1. Pérez Galdós, Benito, 1843-1920. I. T.
PQ6555.Z5Cx   LC 67-8917

Pattison, Walter Thomas, 1903-.   **2.5225**
Benito Pérez Galdós / by Walter T. Pattison. — Boston: Twayne Publishers, [1975] 181 p.: port.; 22 cm. (Twayne's world author's series; TWAS 341: Spain) Includes index. 1. Pérez Galdós, Benito, 1843-1920. I. T.
PQ6555.Z5 P28   863/.5   LC 74-20650   ISBN 0805726896

DeCoster, Cyrus Cole, 1914-.   **2.5226**
Juan Valera, by Cyrus DeCoster. New York, Twayne Publishers [1974] 186 p. port. 22 cm. (Twayne's world authors series, TWAS 316. Spain) 1. Valera, Juan, 1824-1905. I. T.
PQ6573.Z5 D4   868/.5/09   LC 74-3058   ISBN 0805729194

Zorilla, José, 1817-1893.   • **2.5227**
Don Juan Tenorio: drama religioso–fantastico en dos partes / by Don José Zorrilla . — Paris: Ediciones Magraner, 1947. xv, 244 p.: ill.; 23 cm. 1. Don Juan (Legendary character) — Drama. I. T.
PQ6575.D6   862/.5

PQ6600–6647 Individual Authors, 1868–1960

PQ6601–6603 A–B

Aleixandre, Vicente, 1898-.   **2.5228**
[Poems. English. 1979] A longing for the light: selected poems of Vicente Aleixandre / edited by Lewis Hyde. — 1st ed. — New York: Harper & Row, c1979. xviii, 281 p.; 24 cm. 1. Hyde, Lewis, 1945- II. T.
PQ6601.L26 A23 1979   861/.6/2   LC 78-2113   ISBN 0060100591

Aleixandre, Vicente, 1898-.   **2.5229**
Mis poemas mejores. [Madrid, Editorial Gredos, 1956] 206 p. (Biblioteca románica hispánica. 6. [serie]: Antología hispánica [6]) I. T. II. Series.
PQ6601.L26A6 1956

Alberti, Rafael, 1902-.   • **2.5230**
Selected poems. Edited and translated by Ben Belitt. Introd. by Luis Monguió. Berkeley, University of California Press, 1966. 219 p. illus. 21 cm. English and Spanish. I. Belitt, Ben, 1911- II. T.
PQ 6601 L43 A5 1966a   LC 65-25327

Donahue, Thomas John, 1943-.   **2.5231**
The theater of Fernando Arrabal: a garden of earthly delights / Thomas John Donahue. — New York: New York University Press, c1980. 153 p.; 24 cm. (The Gotham library of the New York University Press) Includes index. 1. Arrabal, Fernando — Criticism and interpretation. I. T.
PQ6601.R58 Z64   842/.9/14   LC 79-2598   ISBN 0814717713

Baroja, Pío, 1872-1956.   **2.5232**
El árbol de la ciencia: novela / Pio Baroja. New York: Las Américas Pub. Co., [1959] 397 p.; 18 cm. I. T.
PQ6603.A7 A9 1959

Patt, Beatrice P. (Shapiro) 1919-.   **2.5233**
Pío Baroja, by Beatrice P. Patt. New York, Twayne Publishers [1971] 208 p. 21 cm. (Twayne's world authors series, TWAS 146. Spain) 1. Baroja, Pío, 1872-1956. I. T.
PQ6603.A7 Z63   863/.62 19   LC 73-120479

Benavente, Jacinto, 1866-1954.   **2.5234**
Tres comedias: Sin querer, De pequeñas causas, Los intereses creados / por Jacinto Benavente; ed. by John Van Horne ... — Boston, New York [etc.] D. C. Heath & co. [c1918] 2 p.l., iii-xxxvi, 189 p. 17 cm. (Heath's modern language

series) 1. Contemporary Spanish tests. I. Van Horne, John, ed. II. T. III. Title: Sin querer. IV. Title: De pequeñas causas. V. Title: Los intereses creados.
PQ6603.E6 S5 1918   *LC* 18-19905

Peñuelas, Marcelino C., 1916-.   2.5235
Jacinto Benavente, by Marcelino C. Peñuelas. Translated by Kay Engler. New York, Twayne Publishers [c1968] 178 p. 22 cm. (Twayne's world authors series, 57. Spain) 1. Benavente, Jacinto, 1866-1954. I. T.
PQ6603.E6 Z78   862/.5   *LC* 68-9515

Blasco Ibáñez, Vicente, 1867-1928.   2.5236
La barraca / Vincente Blasco Ibáñez. — New York: Las Amércias Pub. Co., [1966?] 146 p.: port.; 18 cm. I. T.
PQ6603.L2 B15

Blasco Ibáñez, Vicente, 1867-1928.   2.5237
La barraca: novela / por Vicente Blasco Ibáñes; ed. with introduction, notes and vocabulary by Hayward Keniston. — New York: Holt, Rinehart and Winston, 1910. xiv, 325 p.: front. (port.); 18 cm. I. Keniston, Hayward, b. 1883. II. T.
PQ6603.L2 B2 1910   *LC* 10-15421

Blasco Ibáñez, Vicente, 1867-1928.   2.5238
The four horsemen of the Apocalypse: (Los cuatro jinetes del Apocalipsis) / from the Spanish of Vincente Blasco Ibáñez; authorized translation by Charlotte Brewster Jordan. — [New ed.] — New York: E. P. Dutton & company, [1941,c1918] 4 p., l., 3-489 p.; 20 cm. 1. World War, 1914-1918 — Fiction. I. Jordan, Charlotte Brewster, Mrs. II. T.
PZ3.B6125 Fo   PQ6603.L2 C813 1941.   *LC* 18-16490

Buero Vallejo, Antonio, 1916-.   • 2.5239
Historia de una escalera. — Barcelona: J. Janés, [1950] 156 p.; 17 cm. (Manantial que no cesa; 138) I. T.
PQ6603.U4 A19   *LC* 76-460646   *ISBN* 8423920038

Halsey, Martha T.   2.5240
Antonio Buero Vallejo, by Martha T. Halsey. — New York: Twayne, [1973] 178 p.; 22 cm. — (Twayne's world authors series, TWAS 260. Spain) 1. Buero Vallejo, Antonio, 1916- I. T.
PQ6603.U4 Z7   862/.6/4   *LC* 72-4656

PQ6605–6607 C–D

Cela, Camilo José, 1916-.   2.5241
La colmena / the complete novel edited with notes and vocabulary by José Ortega. — New York, Las Américas Pub. Co., 1966. 311 p. 22 cm. I. T.
PQ6605.E44 C6 1966   *LC* 66-31448

Cela, Camilo Jose.   2.5242
La familia de Pascual Duarte. — Lima, Peru: Ediciones Tawatinsuyu, 1960. 152 p.; 17 cm. (Festival de la literatura española contemporanea) I. T. II. Series.
PQ6605.E44.F3

Cela, Camilo José, 1916-.   • 2.5243
The family of Pascual Duarte. Translated and with an introd. by Anthony Kerrigan. [1st ed.] Boston, Little, Brown [1964] xx, 166 p. 20 cm. I. T.
PQ6605.E44F3x   *LC* 64-17474

McPheeters, D. W.   2.5244
Camilo José Cela, by D. W. McPheeters. — New York: Twayne Publishers, [1969] 178 p.; 22 cm. — (Twayne's world authors series, 67. Spain) 1. Cela, Camilo José, 1916- I. T.
PQ6605.E44 Z77   863/.6/4 B   *LC* 74-75876

Cernuda, Luis.   • 2.5245
The poetry of Luis Cernuda. Edited by Anthony Edkins & Derek Harris. — New York: New York University Press, 1971. xx, 171 p.; 24 cm. English and Spanish. I. T.
PQ6605.E7 A6 1971   861/.6/2   *LC* 74-173878   *ISBN* 0814721516

Jiménez Fajardo, Salvador.   2.5246
Luis Cernuda / by Salvador Jimenez–Fajardo. — Boston: Twayne Publishers, c1978. 174 p.: port.; 21 cm. — (Twayne's world authors series; TWAS 455: Spain) Includes index. 1. Cernuda, Luis — Criticism and interpretation. I. T.
PQ6605.E7 Z7   861/.6/2   *LC* 77-27247   *ISBN* 0805762922

Delibes, Miguel.   2.5247
El camino. New York, Holt [1960] 244 p. illus. 22 cm. I. T.
PQ6607.E45 C3 1960   *LC* 60-6136

PQ6613 Garcia Lorca

García Lorca, Federico, 1898-1936.   • 2.5248
Obras completas. Recopilación y notas de Arturo del Hoyo. Prólogo de Jorge Guillén; epílogo de Vicente Aleixandre. [8. ed. Madrid] Aguilar [1965] lxxix, 2018 p. ill., facsims., music, col. plates. 18 cm. I. T.
PQ6613.A763A1

García Lorca, Federico, 1898-1936.   • 2.5249
[Poems English and Spanish] Selected poems. Edited by Francisco García Lorca and Donald M. Allen. [Norfolk, Conn., New Directions, 1955] 180 p. 19 cm. (The New classics series) Spanish and English. I. T.
PQ6613.A763 A17 1955   861.6   *LC* 54-9872

García Lorca, Federico, 1898-1936.   • 2.5250
[Poems. English & Spanish. Selections] Lament for the death of a bullfighter and other poems: in the original Spanish / Federico García Lorca; with English translation by A.L. Lloyd. — New York: Oxford University Press, [1937] xv, 60 p.: port.; 26 cm. Lament for the death of a bullfighter was published in Spanish under title: Llanto por Ignacio Sánchez Mejías. 1. Sánchez Mejías, Ignacio, 1887-1934 — Poetry. I. Lloyd, A. L. (Albert Lancaster), 1908- II. T.
PQ6613.A763 A257 1937   861/.62 19   *LC* 81-466682

García Lorca, Federico, 1898-1936.   • 2.5251
[Plays. English] III tragedies: Blood wedding, Yerma, Bernarda Alba, in the authorized translations of Richard L. O'Connell and James Graham–Luján; with an introd. by the poet's brother, Francisco. [New York] New Directions [1947] 378 p. 21 cm. I. O'Connell, Richard L., tr. II. Graham Luján, James, joint tr. III. T.
PQ6613.A763 A27   862.6   *LC* 47-11626

García Lorca, Federico, 1898-1936.   • 2.5252
[Plays. English] Five plays; comedies and tragicomedies. Translated by James Graham–Lujan and Richard L. O'Connell. [Norfolk, Conn.] New Directions Book [c1963] vi, 246 p. music. 21 cm. Melodies used in the plays, with words: p. [237]-246. I. T.
PQ6613.A763 A275   862.62   *LC* 63-13642

García Lorca, Federico, 1898-1936.   2.5253
[Selections. English. 1980] Deep song and other prose / Federico García Lorca; edited and translated by Christopher Maurer. — New York: New Directions Pub. Corp., 1980. xiii, 143 p.; 21 cm. I. Maurer, Christopher. II. T.
PQ6613.A763 A258 1980   868/.6209   *LC* 80-394   *ISBN* 0811207641

García Lorca, Federico, 1898-1936.   • 2.5254
The gypsy ballads of Federico Garcia Lorca / tr. by Rolfe Humphries, with 3 historical ballads. — Bloomington: Indiana University Press, 1953. 64 p. — (Indiana University poetry series). I. T. II. Series.
PQ6613.A763P72   *LC* 53-9826   *ISBN* 025329902X

Cobb, Carl W.   2.5255
Lorca's Romancero gitano: a ballad translation and critical study / by Carl W. Cobb. — Jackson: University Press of Mississippi, c1983. xii, 116 p.; 27 cm. Includes index. 1. García Lorca, Federico, 1898-1936. Primer romancero gitano. I. García Lorca, Federico, 1898-1936. Primer romancero gitano. English. 1983. II. T.
PQ6613.A763 P7633 1983   861/.62 19   *LC* 82-17454   *ISBN* 0878051775

García Lorca, Federico, 1899-1936.   • 2.5256
Poet in New York / complete Spanish text, with a new translation by Ben Belitt. Introd. by Angel del Rio. New York, Grove Press [1957, c1955] 192 p. 21 cm. (Evergreen books, E-54) 1. Poetry of places — New York (N.Y.) 2. New York (N.Y.) — Description — Poetry. I. T.
PQ6613.A763Px   *LC* 57-5643

García Lorca, Federico, 1898-1936.   2.5257
[Correspondence. English. Selections] Selected letters / Federico García Lorca; edited and translated by David Gershator. — New York: New Directions Pub. Corp., 1983. xiv, 172 p., [6] p. of plates: ill., ports.; 21 cm. 1. García Lorca, Federico, 1898-1936. Correspondence 2. Authors, Spanish — 20th century — Correspondence. I. Gershator, David. II. T.
PQ6613.A763 Z48 1983   868/.6209 B 19   *LC* 83-4006   *ISBN* 0811208729

Durán, Manuel, 1925- ed.   • 2.5258
Lorca, a collection of critical essays. Englewood Cliffs, N.J., Prentice-Hall [1962] 181 p. 21 cm. (Twentieth century views, S-TC-14) (A Spectrum book) 1. García Lorca, Federico, 1898-1936 — Addresses, essays, lectures. I. T.
PQ6613.A763 Z626   868.62   *LC* 62-13724

Honig, Edwin.   2.5259
García Lorca. Norfolk, Conn., New directions books [1944] 3 p.l., v-xi, 232 p. front. (port.) 19 cm. 1. García Lorca, Federico, 1899-1936. I. T.
PQ6613.A763 Z73   *LC* 44-3382

PQ6613.I–U Gi–Gu

Gironella, José María.   • 2.5260
[Cipreses creen en Dios. English] The cypresses believe in God. Translated from
the Spanish by Harriet de Onís. [1st American ed.] New York, Knopf, 1955. 2 v.
(ix, 1010 p.) 22 cm. Sequel to One million dead. 1. Spain — History — Civil
War, 1936-1939 — Fiction. I. T.
PZ3.G4438 Cy   PQ6613.I88 C5x.   LC 54-7195

Gironella, José María, 1917-.   • 2.5261
One million dead. Translated from the Spanish by Joan MacLean. [1st ed.]
Garden City, N. Y., Doubleday, 1963. 684 p. 24 cm. Sequel to The cypresses
believe in God. 1. Spain — Hist. — Civil War, 1936-1939 — Fiction. I. T.
PQ6613.I88M5x   LC 63-18207

Goytisolo, Juan.   2.5262
Fiestas / Juan Goytisolo. — 2a edición. — Barcelona: Ediciones Destino, 1964.
235 p.: 18 cm. (Colección Destinolibro; 140) I. T.
PQ6613O79 F52 1964

Goytisolo, Juan.   2.5263
[Reivindicación del conde don Julian. English] Count Julian. Translated from
the Spanish by Helen R. Lane. New York, Viking Press [1974] 204 p. illus. 22
cm. Translation of Reivindicación del conde don Julian. I. T.
PZ4.G722 Co PQ6613.O79   863/.6/4   LC 73-3506   *ISBN*
0670244074

Goytisolo, Juan.   2.5264
Señas de indentidad. 3a ed. México: J. Mortiz, 1973. 422 p. 19 cm. (Novelistas
contemporáneos) I. T.
PQ 6613 O98 S4 1973

Guillén, Jorge, 1893-.   • 2.5265
Cántico, a selection [by] Jorge Guillén. Edited by Norman Thomas di
Giovanni. [1st ed.] Boston, Little, Brown [1965] 291 p. port. 23 cm. 'An
Atlantic Monthly press book.' Spanish and English. I. T.
PQ6613.U5C343   861.62   LC 64-10955

Guillén, Jorge, 1893-.   2.5266
Guillén on Guillén: the poetry and the poet / translated by Reginald Gibbons
(poetry), Anthony L. Geist (commentary). — Princeton, N.J.: Princeton
University Press, c1979. 220 p.; 23 cm. I. Gibbons, Reginald. II. Geist,
Anthony L., 1945- III. T.
PQ6613.U5 G78   861/.6/2   LC 78-70299   *ISBN* 0691063923

PQ6615–6631 H–Q

Nichols, Geraldine Cleary.   2.5267
Miguel Hernández / by Geraldine Cleary Nichols. — Boston: Twayne
Publishers, c1978. 201 p.: port.; 21 cm. — (Twayne's world authors series;
TWAS 464: Spain) Includes index. 1. Hernández, Miguel, 1910-1942. I. T.
PQ6615.E57 Z86   861/.6/2   LC 77-19102   *ISBN* 0805763015

Jiménez, Juan Ramón, 1881-1958.   • 2.5268
Platero y yo; elegía andaluza, 1907–1916. Con 50 ilus. de Rafael Alvarez
Ortega. Nota preliminar de Arturo del Hoyo. [9. ed. Madrid] Aguilar [1966]
349 p. illus. 21 cm. (Colección literaria: novelistas, dramaturgos, ensayistas,
poetas) I. T.
PQ6619.I4 P6 1966

Fogelquist, Donald F.   2.5269
Juan Ramón Jiménez / by Donald F. Fogelquist. Boston: Twayne Publishers,
c1976. 176 p.: port.; 22 cm. (Twayne's world authors series; TWAS 379: Spain)
Includes index. 1. Jiménez, Juan Ramón, 1881-1958. 2. Poets, Spanish — 20th
century — Biography. I. T.
PQ6619.I4 Z615   861/.6/2   LC 75-26547   *ISBN* 0805761802

Laforet, Carmen.   2.5270
Nada / Carmen Laforet. 18a. ed. Barcelona: Ediciones Destino, 1967, c1963.
295 p.; 19 cm. (Áncora y delfin 27) I. T.
PQ6621.A38.N3x 1967

Machado, Antonio, 1875-1939.   2.5271
Selected poems and prose / Antonio Machado; translated by Robert Bly, Will
Kirkland, Carmin Scholis and William Witherup: edited by Dennis Maloney.
Buffalo, NY: White Pine Press, 1983. — 66 p.; 21 cm. (White Pine journal; 26)
I. Maloney, Dennis. II. T. III. Series.
PQ 6623 A17 A6 E5 1983   *ISBN* 0934834342

Machado, Antonio, 1875-1939.   • 2.5272
Poesías completas. 9. ed. [Madrid] Espasa-Calpe [1962] 299 p. 18 cm.
(Colección austral, no. 149) LC 65-49673

Machado, Antonio, 1875-1939.   2.5273
[Poems English and Spanish] Eighty poems of Antonio Machado. The Spanish
text with translations by Willis Barnstone. Drawings by William Bailey with an
introd. by John dos Passos and a reminiscence by Juan Ramón Jiménez. New
York, Las Américas, 1959. 209 p. illus. 24 cm. (A Cypress book, C-2)
I. Barnstone, Willis, 1927- tr. II. T.
PQ6623.A3 A23   861.62   LC 58-11038

McVan, Alice Jane.   2.5274
Antonio Machado. With translations of selected poems. New York, Printed by
order of the Trustees, the Hispanic Society of America, 1959. 249 p. illus.
(Hispanic notes & monographs; essays, studies, and brief biographies) 'Selected
poems [in Spanish] with translations': p. [93]-231. 1. Machado, Antonio,
1875-1939. I. Machado, Antonio, 1875-1939. II. T.
PQ6623.A3 Z63   861.6   LC 59-4982

Glenn, Kathleen Mary.   2.5275
Azorín (José Martínez Ruiz) / by Kathleen M. Glenn. — Boston: Twayne
Publishers, 1981. 164 p.: port.; 21 cm. (Twayne's world authors series; TWAS
604: Spain) Includes index. 1. Azorín, 1873-1967 — Criticism and
interpretation. I. T.
PQ6623.A816 Z597   868/.62/09 19   LC 80-23267   *ISBN*
0805764461

Matute, Ana María, 1926-.   2.5276
Primera memoria. [4. ed.] Barcelona, Ediciones Destino [1966] 245 p., 19 cm.
(Her Los mercaderes, 1.) Ancora y delfin, 179. I. T.
PQ6623.A89.P7x

McKay, Douglas R.   2.5277
Miguel Mihura / by Douglas R. McKay. — Boston: Twayne Publishers, c1977.
154 p.: port.; 21 cm. — (Twayne's world authors series; TWAS 436: Spain)
Includes index. 1. Mihura, Miguel. 2. Authors, Spanish — 20th century —
Biography. I. T.
PQ6623.I35 Z77   868/.6/409   LC 76-54526   *ISBN* 0805761918

Zatlin-Boring, Phyllis.   2.5278
Elena Quiroga / by Phyllis Zatlin Boring. — Boston: Twayne Publishers,
c1977. 151 p.: port.; 21 cm. — (Twayne's world authors series; TWAS 459:
Spain) Includes index. 1. Quiroga, Elena — Criticism and interpretation. I. T.
PQ6631.U57 Z6   863/.6/4   LC 77-5953   *ISBN* 0805762965

PQ6633–6641 R–Z

Casona, Alejandro, 1903-1965.   • 2.5279
Obras completas. Prólogo de Federico Carlos Sainz de Robles. [9. ed., corr. y
ampliada. Madrid] Aguilar [1966] 2 v. illus., ports. 18 cm. (Biblioteca de
autores modernos) I. T.
PQ6633.O37 1966   LC 68-2074

Casona, Alejandro, 1903-1965.   • 2.5280
La dama del alba. La barca sin pescador. [Por] Alejandro Casona. Buenos
Aires, Editorial Losada [1964] 148 p. 18 cm. (Biblioteca contemporánea, 199)
I. T. II. Title: La barca sin pescador.
PQ6633.O37 D3 1964   LC 67-71722

Moon, Harold K., 1934-.   2.5281
Alejandro Casona / by Harold K. Moon. — Boston: Twayne Publishers, c1985.
157 p.: port.; 22 cm. (Twayne's world authors series; TWAS 748. Spanish
literature) Includes index. 1. Casona, Alejandro, 1903-1965 — Criticism and
interpretation. I. T.
PQ6633.O37 Z7 1985   862/.62 19   LC 84-15675   *ISBN*
0805765964

Anderson, Farris, 1938-.   2.5282
Alfonso Sastre. — New York: Twayne Publishers, [1971] 164 p.; 21 cm. —
(Twayne's world authors series, TWAS 155. Spain) 1. Sastre, Alfonso, 1926-
I. T.
PQ6635.A8 Z58   862/.6/4   LC 78-125251

Sender, Ramón José, 1901-.   2.5283
Requiem por un campesino español. Requiem for a Spanish peasant, novel.
Pref. by Maír José Benardete. English translation by Elinor Randall. — New
York, Las Americas Pub. Co. [1960] 123 p. 23 cm. — (A Cypress book) I. T.
II. Title: Requiem for a Spanish peasant.
PQ6635.E65R4 1960   863.62   LC 60-3604

King, Charles L.   2.5284
Ramón J. Sender, by Charles L. King. — New York: Twayne Publishers, [1974]
196 p.: port.; 22 cm. — (Twayne's world authors series, TWAS 307. Spain)
1. Sender, Ramón José, 1901- I. T.
PQ6635.E65 Z7   863/.6/2   LC 73-19612   *ISBN* 0805728155

Unamuno, Miguel de, 1864-1936.   **2.5285**
[Selections. Nozick.] Ficciones; four stories and a play. Translated by Anthony Kerrigan; with an introd. and notes by Martin Nozick. Princeton, N.J., Princeton University Press, c1976. xxix, 310 p. 21 cm. (Bollingen series. 85:7) (His Selected works, 7) 1. Unamuno, Miguel de, 1864-1936. 2. Unamuno, Miguel de, 1864-1936. I. T. II. Series.
PQ 6639 N17A6 E5 1976   *LC* 67-22341   *ISBN* 0691099308

Unamuno, Miguel de, 1864-1936.   **2.5286**
[Paz en la guerra. English] Peace in war: a novel / Miguel de Unamuno; translated by Allen Lacy and Martin Nozick with Anthony Kerrigan; annotated by Allen Lacy and Martin Nozick; with an introduction by Allen Lacy. — Princeton, N.J.: Princeton University Press, c1983. xl, 413 p.: 1 map; 21 cm. — (Bollingen series. 85:1) (Selected works of Miguel de Unamuno; v. 1) Translation of: Paz en la guerra. 1. Spain — History — Carlist War, 1873-1876 — Fiction. I. Lacy, Allen. II. Nozick, Martin, 1917- III. T. IV. Series.
PQ6639.N3 A25 vol. 1   863/.62 19   *LC* 82-61390   *ISBN* 069109926X

Unamuno, Miguel de, 1864-1936.   **2.5287**
[Selections. English. 1967] The private world: selections from the Diario íntimo and selected letters, 1890–1936 / Miguel de Unamuno; translated by Anthony Kerrigan, Allen Lacy, and Martin Nozick; annotated by Martin Nozick with Allen Lacy with an introduction by Allen Lacy. — Princeton, N.J.: Princeton University Press, c1984. xxxii, 358 p., [8] p. of plates: ill.; 21 cm. (Bollingen series. 85) (Selected works of Miguel de Unamuno; v. 2) 1. Unamuno, Miguel de, 1864-1936 — Diaries. 2. Unamuno, Miguel de, 1864-1936 — Religion. 3. Unamuno, Miguel de, 1864-1936 — Correspondence. 4. Authors, Spanish — 20th century — Biography. I. T. II. Series.
PQ6639.N3 A25 vol. 2   868/.6209 s 868/.6209 19   *LC* 83-43054
ISBN 0691099278

Unamuno, Miguel de, 1864-1936.   **2.5288**
Niebla. Englewood Cliffs, N.J., Prentice-Hall [1969, c1965] vii, 220 p. port. 23 cm. 1. Spanish language — Readers. I. Valdés, Mario J. ed. II. T.
PQ6639.N3 N5 1969   *LC* 69-17928

Unamuno, Miguel de, 1864-1936.   **2.5289**
Novela/Nivola / Miguel de Unamuno; translated, with an introduction, by Anthony Kerrigan, and with a foreword by Jean Casson, annotated by Martin Nozick and Anthony Kerrigan. — Princeton, N. J.: Princeton University Press, 1976. 517 p.; 24 cm. — (Bollingen series. 85:6) (Selected works of Miguel de Unamuno, v. 6) I. T. II. Series.
PQ6639.N3 N63 1976   863.6   *ISBN* 0691099294

Marías, Julián, 1914-.   **2.5290**
[Miguel de Unamuno. English] Miguel de Unamuno [by] Julián Marías. Translated by Frances M. López–Morillas. Cambridge, Mass., Harvard University Press, 1966. xii, 224 p. 22 cm. 1. Unamuno, Miguel de, 1864-1936. I. T.
PQ6639.N3 Z792   *LC* 66-18251

Valle-Inclán, Ramón del, 1870-1936.   **2.5291**
Luces de Bohemia = Bohemian lights: esperpento / Ramón del Valle–Inclán; translated by Anthony N. Zahareas and Gerald Gillespie; introd. and commentary by Anthony N. Zahareas. — Austin: University of Texas Press, c1976. xii, 266 p.; 21 cm. (Edinburgh bilingual library; 10) English and Spanish. I. T. II. Title: Bohemian lights. III. Series.
PQ6641.A47 L813 1976   862/.6/2   *LC* 75-36215   *ISBN* 0292746091

Valle-Inclán, Ramón del, 1870-1936.   **2.5292**
The pleasant memoirs of the Marquis de Bradomín; tr. from the Spanish by May Heywood Broun and Thomas Walsh. New York, Harcourt [1924] 316 p. (The European Library; ed. by J.E. Spingarn) I. Broun, May Heywood, tr. II. Walsh, Thomas. jt. tr. III. T.
PQ6641.A47M4x   *LC* 24-25745

Smith, Verity, 1939-.   **2.5293**
Ramón del Valle–Inclán. — New York: Twayne Publishers, [1973] 182 p.; 21 cm. — (Twayne's world authors series, TWAS 160. Spain) 1. Valle-Inclán, Ramón del, 1870-1936. I. T.
PQ6641.A47 Z84   868/.5/09   *LC* 73-120515

Zahareas, Anthony N.   **2.5294**
Ramón del Valle–Inclán; an appraisal of his life and works. [By] Anthony N. Zahareas, Rodolfo Cardona and Sumner Greenfield. New York Las Americas Publishing 1968. 856p. 1. Valle-Inclán, Ramón del, 1870-1936. I. Cardona, Rodolfo, 1924- II. Greenfield, Sumner. III. T.
PQ6641 A47 Z96

PQ6650–6676 Individual Authors, 1961–

Martín-Santos, Luis, 1924-1964.   **2.5295**
Tiempo de silencio / Luis Martín–Santos. — 9. ed. — Barcelona: Seix Barral, 1972. 240 p.; 20 cm. — (Biblioteca breve (Editorial Seix Barral); 209) I. T.
PQ6663.A7474 T52 1972   863.64   *ISBN* 843220109X

PQ7081–7082 History. Criticism

Anderson Imbert, Enrique, 1910-.   • **2.5296**
Historia de la literatura hispanoamericana / par Enrique Anderson Imbert. — Mexico: Fondo de cultura económica, [1954-61]. 2 v. — (Breviaros del Fondo de Cultura Económica; 89, 156) 1. Spanish American literature — History and criticism. I. T.
PQ7081.A5   LC 55-6941

Anderson-Imbert, Enrique.   **2.5297**
Spanish–American literature: a history / by Enrique Anderson–Imbert. — 2nd ed. (1969) / rev. and updated by Elaine Malley. — Detroit: Wayne State University Press, c1969. 2 v.; 21 cm. 'First edition (1963) translated from the Spanish by John V. Falconieri.' 1. Latin American literature — History and criticism. I. Malley, Elaine. II. T.
PQ7081.A56342   860.9   LC 70-75087   ISBN 0814313884

Fernández Moreno, César.   **2.5298**
[América Latina en su literature. English] Latin America in its literature / general editor, César Fernández Moreno, assistant editor, Julio Ortega; editor of the English edition, Iván A. Schulman; translated from the Spanish by Mary G. Berg. — New York: Holmes & Meier, 1980. 356 p.; 24 cm. — (Latin America in its culture; 1) Translation of América Latina en su literatura. Includes index. 1. Latin American literature — History and criticism. I. Ortega, Julio. II. Schulman, Iván A. III. T. IV. Series.
PQ7081.F3713 1980   860/.9   LC 79-26626   ISBN 0841905304

Foster, David William.   **2.5299**
Modern Latin American literature / compiled and edited by David William Foster, Virginia Ramos Foster. — New York: Ungar, 1975. 2 v.; 25 cm. (Library of literary criticism.) 1. Latin American literature — 20th century — Book reviews. I. Foster, Virginia Ramos. joint author. II. T. III. Series.
PQ7081.F63 1975   860/.9   LC 72-81713   ISBN 0804431396

Franco, Jean.   **2.5300**
Spanish American literature since Independence. — London, Ernest Benn Ltd; New York, Barnes and Noble, 1973. xiv, 306 p. 23 cm. — (A Literary history of Spain) 1. Spanish American literature — History and criticism. I. T.
PQ7081.F643 1973   860/.9   LC 73-157228   ISBN 0064922383

Gallagher, David Patrick.   **2.5301**
Modern Latin American literature [by] D. P. Gallagher. — London, Oxford University Press, 1973. 197 p. 21 cm. 1. Latin American literature — History and criticism. I. T.
PQ7081.G2 1973b   860/.9/98   LC 73-82887   ISBN 0198850719

Harss, Luis, 1936-.   **2.5302**
Into the mainstream, conversations with Latin–American writers [by] Luis Harss and Barbara Dohmann. — New York: Harper & Row, [1969, c1967] 385 p.; 21 cm. — (Harper colophon books; CN167) 1. Latin American fiction — Addresses, essays, lectures. I. Dohmann, Barbara, 1936- joint author. II. T.
PQ7081   PQ7081.H37.   863/.009   LC 79-8293

International Institute of Ibero-American Literature.   • **2.5303**
An outline history of Spanish American literature. 3d ed. Prepared under the auspices of the Instituto Internacional de Literatura Iberoamericana by a committee consisting of John E. Englekirk, chairman and editor [and others] New York, Appleton-Century-Crofts [1965] xiii, 252 p. maps (part fold. col.) 21 cm. 1. Latin American literature — Outlines, syllabi, etc. I. Englekirk, John Eugene, 1905- II. T.
PQ7081.I5 1965   LC 64-23888

Latin American literature in the 20th century: a guide.   **2.5304**
New York: Ungar, c1986. x, 278 p.; 21 cm. 'Based on the Encyclopedia of world literature in the 20th century, revised edition, Leonard S. Klein, general editor.' Includes index. 1. Latin American literature — 20th century — Bio-bibliography. 2. Latin American literature — 20th century — Dictionaries. I. Klein, Leonard S. II. Encyclopedia of world literature in the 20th century.
PQ7081.L36 1986   016.86/09/98 19   LC 85-24534   ISBN 0804463611

Leal, Luis, 1907-.   **2.5305**
Breve historia de la literatura hispanoamericana. New York, Knopf [1971.] 392 p. 24 cm. 1. Spanish American literature — History and criticism. I. T.
PQ 7081 L44 1971   LC 77-151900   ISBN 0394310152

McMurray, George R., 1925-.   **2.5306**
Spanish American writing since 1941: a critical survey / George R. McMurray. — New York: Ungar, 1987. xii, 340 p.; 22 cm. Includes index. 1. Spanish American literature — 20th century — History and criticism. I. T.
PQ7081.M373 1987   860/.9/98 19   LC 86-6908   ISBN 0804426236

Schwartz, Kessel.   • **2.5307**
A new history of Spanish American fiction. — Coral Gables, Fla.: University of Miami Press, [1972] 2 v.; 23 cm. 1. Spanish American fiction — History and criticism. I. T.
PQ7081.S34   863/.009   LC 71-161436   ISBN 087024227X

Guibert, Rita.   **2.5308**
Seven voices; seven Latin American writers talk to Rita Guibert. Translated from the Spanish by Frances Partridge. Introd. by Emir Rodríguez Monegal. — [1st ed.]. — New York: Knopf, 1973 [c1972] xvii, 436 p.: illus.; 22 cm. 1. Authors, Spanish American — Interviews. I. T.
PQ7081.3.G8 1972   860/.9/98   LC 72-2251   ISBN 0394468880

Dramatists in revolt: the new Latin American theater / edited by Leon F. Lyday & George W. Woodyard.   **2.5309**
Austin: University of Texas Press, c1976. xvi, 275 p.; 24 cm. — (The Texas pan-American series) Includes index. 1. Latin American drama — History and criticism — Addresses, essays, lectures. I. Lyday, Leon F., 1939- II. Woodyard, George William.
PQ7082.D7 D7 1976   862   LC 75-16078   ISBN 0292715102

Foster, David William.   **2.5310**
The 20th–century Spanish–American novel: a bibliographic guide / by David William Foster. — Metuchen, N.J.: Scarecrow Press, 1975. vii, 227 p.; 22 cm. Includes index. 1. Spanish American fiction — 20th century — History and criticism — Bibliography. I. T.
Z1609.F4 F68 PQ7082.N7   016.863   LC 75-25787   ISBN 0810808714

Alegría, Fernando, 1918-.   **2.5311**
Historia de la novela hispanoamericana. 4. ed. ampliada. México, Ediciones De Andrea, 1974. 319 p. 21 cm. (Historia literaria de Hispanoamérica; v. 1) First published under title Breve historia de la novela hispanoamericana. 1. Spanish American fiction — History and criticism. I. T. II. Series.
PQ7082.N7 A55 1974   LC 66-48116

Brotherston, Gordon.   **2.5312**
The emergence of the Latin American novel / Gordon Brotherston. — Cambridge; New York: Cambridge University Press, 1977. viii, 164 p. Includes index. 1. Spanish American fiction — 20th century — History and criticism. I. T.
PQ7082.N7 B66   PQ7082N7 B66.   863/.03   LC 76-40834   ISBN 0521214785

Brushwood, John Stubbs, 1920-.   **2.5313**
The Spanish American novel: a twentieth–century survey / John S. Brushwood. — Austin: University of Texas Press, [1975] xiv, 390 p.; 24 cm. (Texas Pan American series.) Includes index. 1. Spanish American fiction — 20th century — History and criticism. I. T. II. Series.
PQ7082.N7 B7   PQ7082N7 B7.   863   LC 74-32429   ISBN 0292775156

Contemporary Latin American fiction: Carpentier, Sabato, Onetti, Roa, Donoso, Fuentes, García Márquez: seven essays / edited by Salvador Bacarisse.   **2.5314**
Edinburgh: Scottish Academic Press, 1980. 109 p.; 24 cm. 1. Spanish American fiction — 20th century — History and criticism — Addresses, essays, lectures. I. Bacarisse, Salvador.
PQ7082.N7 C67   863 19   LC 80-500082   0707302553

Ortega, Julio.   **2.5315**
Poetics of change: the new Spanish–American narrative / Julio Ortega; translated from the Spanish by Galen D. Greaser in collaboration with the author. — 1st ed. — Austin: University of Texas Press, 1984. 192 p.; 24 cm. — (Texas Pan American series.) Includes index. 1. Spanish American fiction — 20th century — History and criticism — Addresses, essays, lectures. I. T. II. Series.
PQ7082.N7 O73 1984   863 19   LC 83-26110   ISBN 029276488X

Spell, Jefferson Rea, 1886-. 2.5316
Contemporary Spanish–American fiction. — New York: Biblo and Tannen, 1968 [c1944] ix, 323 p.; 24 cm. 1. Spanish American fiction — 20th century — History and criticism. I. T.
PQ7082.N7 S6 1968   863   LC 67-29553

Brotherston, Gordon. 2.5317
Latin American poetry: origins and presence / Gordon Brotherston. — Cambridge; New York: Cambridge University Press, 1975. 228 p.: map; 23 cm. Includes index. 1. Latin American poetry — History and criticism. I. T.
PQ7082.P7 B76   PQ7082P7 B76.   861   LC 75-2734   *ISBN* 0521207630

The Latin American short story: a critical history / Margaret 2.5318
Sayers Peden, editor.
Boston: Twayne Publishers, 1983. 160 p.; 23 cm. — (Twayne's critical history of the short story.) Includes index. 1. Short stories, Latin American — History and criticism. 2. Latin American fiction — 19th century — History and criticism. 3. Latin American fiction — 20th century — History and criticism. I. Peden, Margaret Sayers. II. Series.
PQ7082.S5 L35 1983   863/.01/098 19   LC 83-20   *ISBN* 0805793518

PQ7083–7087 COLLECTIONS

Anderson Imbert, Enrique, 1910-. • 2.5319
Literatura hispanoamericana: antologia e introduccion historica / por Enrique Anderson Imbert y Eugenio Florit. — New York: Holt, Rinehart and Winston 1960. 780 p. 1. Spanish-American literature (Selections, Extracts, etc.) I. Florit, Eugenio, 1903- II. T.
PQ7083.A65   LC 60-52107

International Institute of Ibero-American Literature. 2.5320
An anthology of Spanish American literature. Prepared by special committee [by] John E. Englekirk [and others] 2d ed. New York, Appleton-Century-Crofts [1968] xiv, 772 p. 26 cm. 'A companion volume to the third edition of the Outline history of Spanish American literature.' 1. Spanish American literature I. Englekirk, John Eugene, 1905- II. T.
PQ7083.I5 1968   860.8/098   LC 68-11957

Caillet Bois, Julio, comp. 2.5321
Antología de la poesía hispanoamericana. — Madrid, Aguilar, 1958. 1987 p. illus. 18 cm. 1. Spanish-American poetry (Collections) I. T.
PQ7084.C3

Anthology of contemporary Latin American literature, 2.5322
1960–1984 / edited by Barry J. Luby and Wayne H. Finke.
Rutherford [N.J.]: Fairleigh Dickinson University Press; London; Cranbury, NJ: Associated University Presses, c1986. 319 p.; 25 cm. Includes index. 1. Spanish American literature — 20th century — Translations into English. 2. English literature — Translations from Spanish. I. Luby, Barry J. II. Finke, Wayne.
PQ7087.E5 A56 1986   860/.9/98 19   LC 85-47789   *ISBN* 0838632556

The Borzoi anthology of Latin American literature / edited by 2.5323
Emir Rodríguez Monegal, with the assistance of Thomas
Colchie.
1st ed. — New York: Knopf, 1977. 2 v. (xv, 982 p.); 24 cm. 1. Latin American literature — Translations into English. 2. English literature — Translations from Spanish. 3. English literature — Translations from Portuguese. I. Rodríguez Monegal, Emir. II. Colchie, Thomas.
PQ7087.E5 B6   860/.8   LC 76-19126   *ISBN* 0394733010 pbk

Caracciolo Trejo, Enrique, comp. • 2.5324
The Penguin book of Latin American verse, edited by E. Caracciolo–Trejo; introduced by Henry Gifford; with plain prose translations [by Tom Raworth and others]. — Harmondsworth: Penguin, 1971. xlv, 425 p.; 19 cm. — (The Penguin poets) Spanish and Portugese texts, English translations, English introd. and notes. 1. Latin American poetry 2. Latin American poetry — Translations into English. 3. English prose literature — Translations from Spanish. 4. English prose literature — Translations from Portuguese. I. T.
PQ7087.E5 C28   861/.008   LC 72-176582   *ISBN* 014042136X

Oliver, William Irvin, 1926- comp. 2.5325
Voices of change in the Spanish American theater; an anthology. Edited and translated by William I. Oliver. — Austin: University of Texas Press, [1971] xviii, 294 p.; 24 cm. — (Texas pan-American series) 1. Spanish American drama — Translations into English. 2. English drama — Translations from Spanish. I. T.
PQ7087.E5 O4   862   LC 73-167285   *ISBN* 0292701233

PQ7100–8549 INDIVIDUAL COUNTRIES

PQ7100–7300 Mexico

Brushwood, John Stubbs, 1920-. 2.5326
Mexico in its novel; a nation's search for identity, by John S. Brushwood. — Austin: University of Texas Press, [1966] xii, 292 p.; 24 cm. — (The Texas Pan-American series) 1. Mexican fiction — History and criticism. I. T.
PQ7197.B69   863   LC 65-27534

Duncan, J. Ann. 2.5327
Voices, visions, and a new reality: Mexican fiction since 1970 / J. Ann Duncan. — Pittsburgh, Pa.: University of Pittsburgh Press, c1986. xi, 263 p.; 21 cm. — (Pitt Latin American series.) Includes index. 1. Mexican fiction — 20th century — History and criticism. I. T. II. Series.
PQ7203.D78 1986   863 19   LC 85-40853   *ISBN* 0822938154

Langford, Walter M. 2.5328
The Mexican novel comes of age [by] Walter M. Langford. — Notre Dame: University of Notre Dame Press, [c1971] x, 229 p.; 24 cm. 1. Mexican fiction — 20th century — History and criticism. I. T.
PQ7203.L3   863/.03   LC 77-160486   *ISBN* 0268004501

Sommers, Joseph, 1924-. 2.5329
After the storm; landmarks of the modern Mexican novel. — [1st ed. — Albuquerque]: University of New Mexico Press, [1968] xii, 208 p.; 22 cm. 1. Mexican fiction — 20th century — History and criticism. I. T.
PQ7203.S63   863   LC 68-23019

Read, John Lloyd, 1898-. 2.5330
The Mexican historical novel, 1826–1910. New York, Instituto de las Españas en los Estados Unidos, 1939. 3 p.l., ix-xiv, 337 p. 20 cm. 1. Mexican fiction — History and criticism. 2. Historical fiction I. Hispanic institute in the United States. II. T.
PQ7207.H5 R4 1939a   LC 40-3102

Rutherford, John David. 2.5331
Mexican society during the revolution: a literary approach, by John Rutherford. — Oxford: Clarendon P., 1972 (c1971). xii, 347 p.; 22 cm. Based on author's thesis, Oxford. 1. Historical fiction, Mexican 2. Literature and society — Mexico. 3. Mexico — History — 1910-1946 I. T.
PQ7207.H5 R8   863/.03   LC 72-175364   *ISBN* 0198271832

PQ7296–7298 Individual Authors, by Period

Juana Inés de la Cruz, Sister, 1651-1695. 2.5332
Obras completas. [1. ed.] Edición, prólogo y notas de Alfonso Méndez Plancarte. México, Fondo de Cultura Económica [1951-1957] 4 v. col. port., facsims. 22 cm. (Biblioteca americana. Serie de literatura colonial) Vol. 4, edición, introducción y notas de Alberto G. Salceda. I. T.
PQ7296.J6 1951   LC 52-68197

Azuela, Mariano, 1873-1952. • 2.5333
Los de abajo; novela de la Revolución mexicana. Edited with introd., notes and vocabulary by John E. Englekirk [and] Lawrence B. Kiddle. New York Crofts 1939. 181p. 1. Mexico — History — Revolution, 1910-1929 — Fiction 2. Spanish language — Chrestomathies and readers I. T.
PQ7297 A9 L6 1939

Azuela, Mariano, 1873-1952. 2.5334
The underdogs, a novel of the Mexican Revolution. Translated by E. Munguía, Jr. Illustrated by J. C. Orozco. With a foreword by Harriet de Onís. [New York] New American Library [1963, c1962] 151 p. illus. 18 cm. (A Signet classic, CP119) 1. Mexico — History — 1910-1946 — Fiction. I. T.
PQ7297.A9 L6 1963x   LC 63-2763

Robe, Stanley Linn, 1915-. 2.5335
Azuela and the Mexican underdogs / by Stanley L. Robe. — Berkeley: University of California Press, c1979. xiii, 233 p.: ill.; 27 cm. — (UCLA Latin American studies. v. 48) Includes the original Spanish text of Azuela's novel Los de abajo and its translation into English. 1. Azuela, Mariano, 1873-1952. Los de abajo. 2. Azuela, Mariano, 1873-1952 — Criticism, Textual.

3. Historical fiction, Mexican 4. Mexico — History — 1910-1946 5. Mexico — History — 1910-1946 — Fiction. I. Azuela, Mariano, 1873-1952. Los de abajo. English & Spanish. 1979. II. T. III. Series.
PQ7297.A9 L638   863   *LC* 76-20031   *ISBN* 0520032934

Leal, Luis, 1907-.   **2.5336**
Mariano Azuela. — New York: Twayne Publishers, [1971] 145 p.; 22 cm. — (Twayne's world authors series TWAS 119. Mexico) 1. Azuela, Mariano, 1873-1952. I. T.
PQ7297.A9 Z745   863   *LC* 72-120023

Carballido, Emilio.   **2.5337**
Teatro. [1. ed.] [México] Fondo de Cultura Económica [1960] 295p. (Letras mexicanas, 57) I. T.
PQ7297 C2482 T4

Castellanos, Rosario.   **2.5338**
Oficio de tinieblas. [1. ed. México, J. Mortiz, 1962] 368 p. 20 cm. I. T.
PQ7297.C2596 O3   *LC* 63-30898

Fuentes, Carlos.   **2.5339**
Cambio de piel. [1. ed. México] J. M[ortiz, 1967] 442 p. illus. 20 cm. (Novelistas contemporáneos) I. T.
PQ7297.F793 C28   *LC* 68-74156

Fuentes, Carlos.   • **2.5340**
La muerte de Artemio Cruz. — [1. ed.]. — México, Fondo de Cultura Económica [1962] 316 p. 17 cm. — (Colección popular, 34) I. T.
PQ7297.F793M8   *LC* 64-1174

Fuentes, Carlos.   **2.5341**
The death of Artemio Cruz / Carlos Fuentes; translated from the Spanish by Sam Hileman. — New York: Farrar, Straus, c1964. 306 p.; 21 cm. Translation of La muerte de Artemio Cruz. I. Hileman, Sam. II. Fuentes, Carlos. Muerte de Artemio Cruz. English. 1964. III. T.
PQ7297.F793 M83   *LC* 64-14685

Fuentes, Carlos.   • **2.5342**
La región más transparente. — [3. ed. México]. — México] Fondo de Cultura Económica [1960] 460 p. 18 cm. — (Letras mexicanas, 38) I. T.
PQ7297.F793R4   *LC* 58-38348

Fuentes, Carlos.   **2.5343**
Where the air is clear: a novel / by Carlos Fuentes; translated by Sam Hileman. — New York: Farrar, Straus and Giroux, c1960 (1984 printing). 376 p.; 20 cm. I. T.
PQ7297F793 R413 1960   *LC* 60-14898   *ISBN* 374509190

Fuentes, Carlos.   **2.5344**
Terra nostra / Carlos Fuentes. — 1. ed. — México: J. Mortiz, 1975. 783 p.: ill. (Novelistas contmporáneos) I. T.
PQ7297.F793 T4   PQ7297F793 T4 1975.

Fuentes, Carlos.   **2.5345**
[Terra nostra. English] Terra nostra / Carlos Fuentes; translated from the Spanish by Margaret Sayers Peden. — New York: Farrar, Straus, Giroux, 1976. 777 p.; 24 cm. I. T.
PZ4.F952 Te PQ7297.F793 T4x   863   *LC* 76-18238   *ISBN* 0374273278

Guzmán, Daniel de.   **2.5346**
Carlos Fuentes. — New York: Twayne Publishers, [1972] 171 p.; 21 cm. — (Twayne's world authors series, TWAS 151. Mexico) 1. Fuentes, Carlos. I. T.
PQ7297.F793 Z67   863   *LC* 73-120487

Paz, Octavio, 1914-.   **2.5347**
A draft of shadows, and other poems / Octavio Paz; edited and translated from the Spanish by Eliot Weinberger, with translations by Elizabeth Bishop and Mark Strand. — New York: New Directions, c1979. 186 p.; 21 cm. English and Spanish. 1. Weinberger, Eliot. I. T.
PQ7297.P285 A29   861   *LC* 79-15588   0811207382

Paz, Octavio, 1914-.   **2.5348**
Early poems, 1935–1955. Translated from the Spanish by Muriel Rukeyser and other poets, including Paul Blackburn [and others]. — Bloomington: Indiana University Press, [1974] 145 p.; 22 cm. — (UNESCO collection of representative works: Latin American series) English and Spanish. I. Rukeyser, Muriel, 1913- tr. II. T. III. Series.
PQ7297.P285 E2   861   *LC* 74-159081   *ISBN* 025331867X

Wilson, Jason, 1944-.   **2.5349**
Octavio Paz / by Jason Wilson. — Boston: Twayne Publishers, c1986. 165 p.: port.; 23 cm. — (Twayne's world authors series; TWAS 783. Latin American literature) Includes index. 1. Paz, Octavio, 1914- — Criticism and interpretation. I. T.
PQ7297.P285 Z97 1986   861 19   *LC* 86-9998   *ISBN* 0805766308

Rulfo, Juan.   **2.5350**
Obra completa: El llano en llamas, Pedro Páramo, otros textos / Juan Rulfo; prólogo y cronología, Jorge Ruffinelli; [diseño, Juan Fresán]. — [Caracas]: Biblioteca Ayacucho, [1977] xxxviii, 299 p.; 24 cm. — (Biblioteca Ayacucho; 13) I. Rulfo, Juan. El llano en llamas. 1977. II. Rulfo, Juan. Pedro Páramo. 1977. III. Ruffinelli, Jorge. IV. T.
PQ7297.R89 A6 1977   *LC* 79-128821

Rulfo, Juan.   **2.5351**
El llano en llamas. — [2. ed., corr. y aum.]. — México, Fondo de Cultura Económica [1970, c1953] 152 p. 17 cm. — (Colección popular, 1) I. T.
PQ7297.R89L6 1970   *LC* 55-1123

Rulfo, Juan.   **2.5352**
[Llano en llamas English] The burning plain, and other stories. Translated with an introd. by George D. Schade. Illustrated by Kermit Oliver. Austin, University of Texas Press [1967] xv, 175 p. illus. 22 cm. (Texas pan-American series) Translation of El llano en llamas. I. T.
PQ7297.R89 L6x   *LC* 67-25698

Rulfo, Juan.   **2.5353**
Pedro Páramo / por Juan Rulfo. — 7a ed. — México: Fondo de Cultura Económica, 1965, c1955. 152 p.; 18 cm. — (Letras mexicanas; 19) I. T.
PQ7297.R89 P4 1965

Rulfo, Juan.   **2.5354**
[Pedro Páramo. English] Pedro Páramo. Translated by Lysander Kemp. New York, Grove Press [1959] 123 p. 21 cm. I. T.
PQ7297.R89 P4x   863.64   *LC* 59-7435

Leal, Luis, 1907-.   **2.5355**
Juan Rulfo / by Luis Leal. — Boston: Twayne, c1983. 132 p.: port.; 23 cm. — (Twayne's world authors series. TWAS 692) Includes index. 1. Rulfo, Juan — Criticism and interpretation. I. T. II. Series.
PQ7297.R89 Z75 1983   863 19   *LC* 83-40   *ISBN* 0805765395

Usigli, Rodolfo.   **2.5356**
El gesticulador: pieza para demagogos en tres actos. / Edited by Rex Edward Ballinger. New York: Appleton-Century-Crofts, 1963. 178 p.: ill. 1. Spanish language — Chrestomathies and readers. I. Ballinger, Rex Edward. II. T.
PQ7297U85 G4 1963   *LC* 63-7433   *ISBN* 0390891657

Yáñez, Agustín, 1904-.   • **2.5357**
Al filo del agua; [novela] Prólogo de Antonio Castro Leal. 7. ed. México, Editorial Porrúa, 1967. xiii, 389 p. 19 cm. (Colección de escritores mexicanos, 72) I. T.
PQ7297.Y3 A67 1967   *LC* 67-8095

PQ7370–7390 Cuba

Cabrera Infante, G. (Guillermo), 1929-.   **2.5358**
Tres tristes tigres. Barcelona Editorial Seix Barral [1965] 451p. (Biblioteca breve) I. T.
PQ7389 C233 T7   *LC* 84-192708

Carpentier, Alejo, 1904-.   **2.5359**
El arpa y la sombra: novela / Alejo Carpentier. — México: Siglo Veintiuno Editores, 1983. 227 p.; 19 cm. — (Creación literaria.) 1. Carpentier, Alejo, 1904- I. T. II. Series.
PQ7389.C263 A88   863   *ISBN* 843230350X

Carpentier, Alejo, 1904-.   **2.5360**
Los pasos perdidos / Alejo Carpentier. — Madrid: Catedra, 1985. 332 p. — (Colección Letras Hispánicas) I. T.
PQ7389C263 P3 1985   *ISBN* 8437605024

Carpentier, Alejo, 1904-.   **2.5361**
The lost steps / by Alejo Carpentier; translated from the Spanish by Harriet de Onís. — 1st ed. — New York: Knopf, 1956. 278 p.; 22 cm. Translation of Los pasos perdidos. I. T.
PQ7389.C263 P313x   863.64   *LC* 56-8906

Carpentier, Alejo, 1904-.   **2.5362**
El reino de este mundo / Alejo Carpentier. — Mexico: ESIAPSA, 1949. 1 v. I. T.
PQ7389.C263 R4 1975   863

Shaw, Donald Leslie, 1930-.   **2.5363**
Alejo Carpentier / by Donald L. Shaw. — Boston: Twayne Publishers, c1985. 150 p.: port.; 23 cm. (Twayne's world authors series; TWAS 756. Latin

American literature) Includes index. 1. Carpentier, Alejo, 1904- — Criticism and interpretation. I. T.
PQ7389.C263 Z88 1985 863 19 *LC* 84-25297 *ISBN* 0805766065

Guillén, Nicolás, 1902-. 2.5364
Antología mayor / Nicolás Guillén. — 4a ed. — México: Editorial Diógenes, 1981. 291 p.; 18 cm. — (Escritores de lengua española) I. T.
PQ7389.G84 A6 1981 *ISBN* 9686021051

Lezama Lima, José. • 2.5365
Paradiso / José Lezama Lima. Ilus. de Rene Portocarrero. — 1. ed. — Mexico: Biblioteca Era, [1968]. 489 p.; 21 cm. 1. Spanish (Language of document). I. T.
PQ7389.L49 P3 1974

Martí, José, 1853-1895. 2.5366
José Martí, major poems: a bilingual edition / English translation by Elinor Randall; edited, with an introduction, by Philip S. Foner. — New York: Holmes & Meier Publishers, 1982. 173 p.; 23 cm. English and Spanish. I. Randall, Elinor. II. Foner, Philip Sheldon, 1910- III. T.
PQ7389.M2 A27 1982 861 19 *LC* 81-20016 *ISBN* 0841908346

Martí, José, 1853-1895. • 2.5367
Páginas escogidas: Selección, prólogo y notas de Fermin Estrella Gutiérrez. — Buenos Aires, Kapuelsz, [1954]. xii, 116 p.: port.; 15 cm. — (Biblioteca de grandes obras de la literatura universal; textos seleccionados y anotados para su usuo en las escuelas) I. T.
PQ7389.M2 A6 1954 *LC* 55-18865

PQ7471–7539 Central America

Asturias, Miguel Angel. • 2.5368
El señor presidente / Miguel Angel Asturias; translated from the Spanish by Frances Partridge. — [1st American ed.]. — New York; Atheneum, 1964 [c1963] 286 p. I. T.
PQ7499.A75 S4x *LC* 64-10908

Asturias, Miguel Angel, 1899-1974. 2.5369
El señor presidente / Miguel Angel Asturias. — 24. edición. — Buenos Aires: Losada, 1976,c1948. 298 p. — (Biblioteca clásica y contemporánea; 343) I. T.
PQ7499.A75 Sx

Callan, Richard J., 1932-. 2.5370
Miguel Angel Asturias, by Richard J. Callan. New York, Twayne Publishers [1970] 182 p. 21 cm. (Twayne's world author[s] series; TWAS 122. Guatemala) 1. Asturias, Miguel Angel. I. T.
PQ7499.A75 Z64 863 *LC* 70-99526

Cardenal, Ernesto. 2.5371
[Poems. Selections] Nueva antología poética / Ernesto Cardenal; [portada y viñetas de Anhelo Hernández]. — 2. ed. — México: Siglo Veintiuno Editores, 1979. 302 p.: ill.; 16 x 17 cm. — (La Creación literaria) I. T.
PQ7519.C34 N8 1979 861 *LC* 79-128114 *ISBN* 968230220X

Darío, Rubén, 1867-1916. 2.5372
Poesías completas. Edición, introducción y notas de Alfonso Méndez Plancarte. [9. ed.] Madrid Aguilar 1961. 1487p. I. Méndez Plancarte, Alfonso, 1909, ed. II. T.
PQ7519 D3 A17 1961

PQ7600–7799 Argentina

Foster, David William. 2.5373
Currents in the contemporary Argentine novel: Arlt, Mallea, Sabato, and Cortázar / David William Foster. — Columbia, Mo.: University of Missouri Press, 1978. xii, 155 p.; 24 cm. 1. Argentine fiction — 20th century — History and criticism. I. T.
PQ7703.F6 863/.03 *LC* 74-30083 *ISBN* 0826201768

Borges, Jorge Luis, 1900-. • 2.5374
[Collected works] Obras completas. [Buenos Aires] Emecé [1953-60] v. 1-3, 6, 9. I. T.
PQ7797.B635 1954 *LC* 55-20933

Borges, Jorge Luis, 1899-. 2.5375
[Selections. English. 1981] Borges, a reader: a selection from the writings of Jorge Luis Borges / edited by Emir Rodriguez Monegal and Alastair Reid. —

1st ed. — New York: Dutton, c1981. xi, 369 p.; 25 cm. I. Rodríguez Monegal, Emir. II. Reid, Alastair, 1926- III. T.
PQ7797.B635 A2 1981 868 19 *LC* 81-68076 *ISBN* 0525069984

Borges, Jorge Luis, 1899-. 2.5376
[Seis problemas para don Isidro Parodi. English] Six problems for Don Isidro Parodi / Jorge Luis Borges, Adolfo Bioy–Casares; translated by Norman Thomas di Giovanni. — 1st ed. — New York: Dutton, 1981. 160 p.; 25 cm. Translation of Seis problemas para don Isidro Parodi. I. Bioy Casares, Adolfo. joint author. II. T.
PQ7797.B635 S4413 1981 863 19 *LC* 80-20107 *ISBN* 0525204806

Barrenechea, Ana María. 2.5377
Borges, the labyrinth maker. Edited and translated by Robert Lima. — [New York] New York University Press, 1965. x, 175 p. 22 cm. Translation of La expresión de la irrealidad en la obra de Jorge Luis Borges. Bibliography: p. 155-166. 1. Borges, Jorge Luis, 1899- I. T.
PQ7797.B635Z633 868.62 *LC* 65-10764

Cortázar, Julio. 2.5378
[Todos los fuegos el fuego. English] All fires the fire, and other stories. Translated from the Spanish by Suzanne Jill Levine. [1st American ed.] New York, Pantheon Books [1973] 152 p. 22 cm. Translation of Todos los fuegos el fuego. I. T.
PZ3.C81929 Al3 PQ7797.C7145 863 *LC* 73-2937 *ISBN* 039446821X

Cortázar, Julio. 2.5379
[Queremos tanto a Glenda y otros relatos. English] We love Glenda so much and A change of light / Julio Cortázar; translated from the Spanish by Gregory Rabassa. — 1st Aventura ed. — New York: Vintage Books, 1984. 421 p.; 21 cm. (Aventura: the Vintage library of contemporary world literature) Translation of: Queremos tanto a Glenda y otros relatos. I. Cortázar, Julio. Change of light and other stories. 1984. II. T. III. Title: We love Glenda so much and other tales. IV. Title: Change of light.
PQ7797.C7145 A27 1984 863 19 *LC* 83-40387 *ISBN* 0394722973

Cortázar, Julio. 2.5380
[End of the game, and other stories] Blow–up, and other stories. Translated from the Spanish by Paul Blackburn. New York, Collier Books [1968, c1967] 248 p. 18 cm. First published in 1967 under title: End of the game, and other stories. I. T.
PZ3.C81929 Bl PQ7797.C7145 F5x 863 *LC* 68-7668

Cortázar, Julio. 2.5381
Los premios. Buenos Aires, Editorial Sudamericana [1960] 425 p. 19 cm. I. T.
PQ7797.C7145 P7 *LC* 61-37908

Cortázar, Julio. 2.5382
Queremos tanto a Glenda y otros relatos / Julio Cortázar. — Madrid: Ediciones Alfaguara, 1981, c1980. 166 p.; 20 cm. — (Literatura Alfaguara; 64) I. T.
PQ7797.C7145 Q4 1981 863 19 *LC* 81-160624 *ISBN* 842042126X

Cortázar, Julio. 2.5383
Rayuela. [5. ed.] Buenos Aires Editorial Sudamericana [1967] 635p. (Colección Novelistas latinoamericanos) I. T.
PQ7797 C7145 R3 1967

Cortázar, Julio. • 2.5384
[Rayuela. English] Hopscotch. Translated from the Spanish by Gregory Rabassa. New York, Pantheon Books [1966] 564 p. 22 cm. I. T.
PQ7797.C7145 R313x *LC* 66-10409

Cortázar, Julio. 2.5385
Relatos. [Buenos Aires] Editorial Sudamericana [1970] 647p. I. T.
PQ7797 C7145 R38

Garfield, Evelyn Picon. 2.5386
Julio Cortázar / Evelyn Picon Garfield. — New York: Ungar, [1975] xi, 164 p.; 21 cm. (Modern literature monographs) Includes index. 1. Cortázar, Julio — Criticism and interpretation. I. T.
PQ7797.C7145 Z684 863 *LC* 74-78440 *ISBN* 0804422249

Gálvez, Manuel, 1882-1962. 2.5387
Nacha Regules. 2. ed. Buenos Aires: Editorial Losada, 1960, c1950. 181 p. (Biblioteca contemporánea) I. T.
PQ7797.G25.N3

Lichtblau, Myron I., 1925-. 2.5388
Manuel Gálvez, by Myron I. Lichtblau. — New York: Twayne Publishers, [1972] 152 p.; 21 cm. — (Twayne's world authors series, TWAS 203. Argentina) 1. Gálvez, Manuel, 1882-1962. I. T.
PQ7797.G25 Z67 863 *LC* 71-169627

Güiraldes, Ricardo, 1886-1927.　　　　　　　　　　**2.5389**
Don Segundo Sombra. With an introd., notes, and glossary by P. R. Beardsell. — Oxford; New York: Pergamon Press, [1973] p. — (The Commonwealth and international library. Pergamon Oxford Latin-American series) Text in Spanish. 1. Sombra, Segundo, 1850 or 51-1936 — Fiction. 2. Spanish language — Readers. I. Beardsell, Peter R., 1940- ed. II. T.
PQ7797.G75 D6 1973　　468/.6/421　　*LC* 72-13207　　*ISBN* 0080170099

Güiraldes, Ricardo, 1886-1927.　　　　　　　　　　**2.5390**
Don Segundo Sombra; shadows on the pampas, by Ricardo Güiraldes. Translated from the Spanish by Harriet De Onis, with an introduction by Waldo Frank and decorations by Howard Willard. New York, Farrar & Rinehart [c1935] 270 p. illus. 20 cm. I. T.
PQ7797.G75 D613x　　868.6　　*LC* 35-27024

Hernández, José, 1834-1886.　　　　　　　　　　• **2.5391**
[Martín Fierro. English and Spanish] The gaucho Martín Fierro. Bilingual ed., English version by C. E. Ward. Annotated and rev. by Frank G. Carrino [and] Alberto J. Carlos. Coordinated, and with an introd., by Carlos Alberto Astiz. Illus. by Antonio Berni. [Albany] State University of New York Press [c1967] xvii, 507 p. 25 cm. Spanish and English. Added t.p. in Spanish. Prepared under the auspices of the Center for Inter-American Studies, State University of New York at Albany. I. Ward, Catherine Elena, 1935- tr. II. New York. State University, Albany. Center for Inter-American Studies. III. T.
PQ7797.H3 M3 1967　　*LC* 67-63759

Polt, John Herman Richard, 1929-.　　　　　　　　　**2.5392**
The writings of Eduardo Mallea. Berkeley, University of California Press, 1959. 132 p. 24 cm. 1. Mallea, Eduardo, 1903- I. T.
PQ7797.M22Z8x　　*LC* a 60-9001

Mallea, Eduardo, 1903-.　　　　　　　　　　　**2.5393**
Obras completas. Nota biobibliográfica y prólogo de Mariano Picón–Salas. — Buenos Aires, Emecé [1961-. v. port. Includes bibliographies. I. T.
PQ7797.M225 1961

Mallea, Eduardo, 1903-.　　　　　　　　　　　**2.5394**
Fiesta en noviembre, novela. Buenos Aires, Editorial Losada, s. a. [1942] 3 p.l., [9]-168 p. 18 cm. I. T.
PQ7797.M225 F5 1942　　*LC* 43-8219

Mallea, Eduardo, 1903-.　　　　　　　　　　　**2.5395**
Todo verdor perecerá / Eduardo Mallea. — Buenos Aires: Editorial Sudamericana, 1965. 209 p.; 18 cm. I. T.
PQ7797.M225 T6 1965　　863.6　　*LC* 67-42792

Lewald, H. Ernest (Herald Ernest)　　　　　　　　　**2.5396**
Eduardo Mallea / by H. Ernest Lewald. — Boston: Twayne Publishers, c1977. 118 p.: ill.; 21 cm. (Twayne's world authors series; TWAS 433: Argentina) Includes index. 1. Mallea, Eduardo, 1903- 2. Authors, Argentine — 20th century — Biography. I. T.
PQ7797.M225 Z73　　863 B　　*LC* 76-44804　　*ISBN* 0805762736

Sábato, Ernesto R.　　　　　　　　　　　　**2.5397**
Sobre héroes y tumbas / Ernesto Sabato. — 1. ed. definitiva en Biblioteca breve de la 18. ed. argentina corr. y rev. — Barcelona: Seix Barral, 1978. 558 p.; 20 cm. — (Biblioteca breve; 428: Novela) I. T.
PQ7797.S214 S6 1978　　863　　*LC* 78-370942　　*ISBN* 8432203327

Sábato, Ernesto R.　　　　　　　　　　　　**2.5398**
[Sobre héroes y tumbas. English] On heroes and tombs / Ernesto Sabáto [sic]; translated by Helen R. Lane. — Boston: Godine, 1981. 479 p.; 24 cm. Translation of: Sobre héroes y tumbas. I. T.
PQ7797.S214 S613 1981　　863 19　　*LC* 80-83957　　*ISBN* 0879233818

Sábato, Ernesto R., 1911-.　　　　　　　　　　　**2.5399**
El tunel / Ernesto Sabato. — 2ed. — Barcelona: Edhasa Sudamericana, 1977. 140 p. — (Pocket Edhasa; 10) I. T. II. Series.
PQ7797.S214 T8　　*ISBN* 8435001261

Puig, Manuel.　　　　　　　　　　　　　　**2.5400**
El beso de la mujer araña / Manuel Puig. — 1. ed. — Barcelona: Seix Barral, 1976. 287 p.; 20 cm. — (Nueva narrativa hispánica) I. T.
PQ7798.26U4B4　　PQ7798.26U4 B4.　　863　　*LC* 77-454355　　*ISBN* 8432213616

Puig, Manuel.　　　　　　　　　　　　　　**2.5401**
[Beso de la mujer araña. English] Kiss of the spider woman / by Manuel Puig; translated from the Spanish by Thomas Colchie. — 1st American ed. — New York: Knopf: distributed by Random House, 1979. 281 p.; 22 cm. Translation of El beso de la mujer araña. I. T.
PZ4.P9786 Ki 1979 PQ7798.26.U4B413x　　863　　*LC* 78-14307　　*ISBN* 039450366X

Puig, Manuel.　　　　　　　　　　　　　　**2.5402**
La traición de Rita Hayworth. [Buenos Aires] Editorial J. Alvarez [1968] 325p. (Colección Narradores argentinos) I. T.
PQ7798.26 U4 T7　　*LC* 68-132898

Puig, Manuel.　　　　　　　　　　　　　　**2.5403**
[Traición de Rita Hayworth. English] Betrayed by Rita Hayworth / by Manuel Puig; translated by Suzanne Jill Levine. — 1st Vintage Books ed. — New York: Random House, 1981. 222 p.; 19 cm. Translation of La traición de Rita Hayworth. Reprint of the ed. published by Dutton, New York. I. T.
PQ7798.26.U4 T713 1981　　863 19　　*LC* 80-6123　　*ISBN* 0394746597

PQ7900–8099 Chile

Barrios, Eduardo, 1884-1963.　　　　　　　　　　• **2.5404**
El hermano asno; unabridged text of the novel. Edited with introd., notes, historical and explanatory, and bibliography, by Carlos D. Hamilton and Alejandro Arratia. — New York, Las Americas Pub. Co., 1958. 143 p. 23 cm. I. T.
PQ8097.B36H4 1958　　*LC* 58-4680

Donoso, José, 1924-.　　　　　　　　　　　　**2.5405**
Coronación. [4. ed. Barcelona] Seix Barral [1972] 219 p., 2 l. 20 cm. I. T.
PQ8097.D617 C6 1972　　*LC* 74-314073

Donoso, José, 1924-.　　　　　　　　　　　　**2.5406**
El obsceno pájaro de la noche; [novela]. — [1. ed.]. — Barcelona, Seix Barral [1970] 543 p. 21 cm. — (Biblioteca breve) I. T.
PQ8097.D617O2　　*LC* 79-294342

McMurray, George R., 1925-.　　　　　　　　　　**2.5407**
José Donoso / by George R. McMurray. — Boston: Twayne Publishers, 1979. 178 p.; 21 cm. — (Twayne's world authors series; TWAS 517) Includes index. 1. Donoso, José, 1924- — Criticism and interpretation. I. T.
PQ8097.D617 Z77　　863　　*LC* 78-15574　　*ISBN* 0805763589

Mistral, Gabriela, 1889-1957.　　　　　　　　　　• **2.5408**
Selected poems of Gabriela Mistral. Translated and edited by Doris Dana. Woodcuts by Antonio Frasconi. — Baltimore: Published for the Library of Congress by the Johns Hopkins Press, [1971] xxix, 235 p.; 26 cm. — (Hispanic Foundation publications) Spanish and English. I. Dana, Doris, ed. II. T. III. Series.
PQ8097.G6 A6 1971　　861　　*LC* 77-137467　　*ISBN* 080181197X

Huidobro, Vicente, 1893-1948.　　　　　　　　　　**2.5409**
[Poems. English. Selections] The selected poetry of Vicente Huidobro / edited with an introduction by David M. Guss; translated by David M. Guss ... [et al.]. — New York: New Directions Pub. Corp., 1981. xxi, 234 p.: port.; 21 cm. Poetry in English translation, parallel Spanish and French texts. I. Guss, David M. II. T.
PQ8097.H8 A24 1981　　861 19　　*LC* 81-4305　　*ISBN* 0811208044

Neruda, Pablo, 1904-1973.　　　　　　　　　　　**2.5410**
[Poems. English and Spanish. 1972] Selected poems. Edited by Nathaniel Tarn. Translated by Anthony Kerrigan [and others. 1st American ed. New York] Delacorte Press [1972] 509 p. 24 cm. English and Spanish. I. Tarn, Nathaniel. ed. II. Kerrigan, Anthony. tr. III. T.
PQ8097.N4 A6 1972　　861　　*LC* 71-185016

Parra, Nicanor, 1914-.　　　　　　　　　　　　**2.5411**
Obra gruesa / Nicanor Parra. — 3. ed. — Santiago de Chile: Editorial Universitaria, 1973. 200 p.: facsims., port. — (Cormoran: Colección: Letras de América; 38) Poems. I. T.
PQ8097.P322 A6 1973

PQ8160–8180 Colombia

Isaacs, Jorge, 1837-1895.　　　　　　　　　　　• **2.5412**
María: novela presentación de Julio Caillet–Bois. — Buenos Aires: Editiorial Universitaria de Buenos Aires, [1963]. 272 p.; 18 cm. — (Serie del Nuevo Mundo; 2) I. T.
PQ8179.I8 M3 1963　　*LC* 64-41731

Rivera, José Eustasio, 1889-1928.　　　　　● 2.5413
La vorágine / José Eustasio Rivera; preliminar de Jordi Estrada. — Buenos Aires: Editorial Losada, 1976, c1942. 266 p.; 18 cm. (Biblioteca clásica y contemporánea; 94) I. T.
PQ8179.R54 V7 1975　　　LC 79-6414

Rivera, José Eustasio, 1889-1928.　　　　　2.5414
The vortex = La voragine / by José Eustasio Rivera; translated from the ninth Spanish edition by Earle K. James. — New York: Putnam, 1935. x, 320 p. Map on lining paper. Translation of La voragine. I. T.
PQ8179.R54 V7x

Silva, José Asunción, 1865-1896.　　　　　2.5415
[Poetry] Poesías completas, seguidas de prosas selectas; noticia biografica por Camilo de Brigard Silva; prólogo de Miguel de Unamuno. Madrid, Aguilar, 1952. 206 p. (Collección literaria novelistas, dramaturgos, ensayistas, poetas) I. Brigard Silva, Camilo de, ed. II. T.
PQ8179.S5 A17 1952

García Márquez, Gabriel, 1928-.　　　　　2.5416
[Short stories. English] Collected stories / Gabriel García Márquez. — 1st ed. — New York: Harper & Row, c1984. vi, 311 p.; 25 cm. Originally published separately in three volumes under the titles: Leaf storm, and other stories, c1972, No one writes to the Colonel, and other stories, c1968, Innocent Eréndira, and other stories, c1978. 1. García Márquez, Gabriel, 1928- — Translations, English. I. T.
PQ8180.17.A73 A27 1984　　　863 19　　　LC 84-47826　　　ISBN 0060153644

García Márquez, Gabriel, 1928-.　　　　　2.5417
Cien años de soledad. Buenos Aires, Editorial Sud-americana c1967. 351 p. 20 cm. (Coleccion Grandes novelas) I. T.
PQ8180.17.A73 C5　　　LC 67-100082

García Márquez, Gabriel, 1928-.　　　　　2.5418
[Cien años de soledad. English] One hundred years of solitude. Translated from the Spanish by Gregory Rabassa. [1st ed.] New York, Harper & Row [1970] 422 p. 22 cm. Translation of Cien años de soledad. I. T.
PZ4.G2164 On PQ8180.17.A73 C5x　　　863　　　LC 74-83632

Garcia Máiquez, Gabriel, 1928-.　　　　　2.5419
Crónica de una muerte anunciada / Gabriel Garcia Máiquez. — Barcelona: Bruguera, c1981. 192 p. (Narradores de hoy; 60) I. T.
PQ8180.17.A73 C68　　　ISBN 8402076939

García Márquez, Gabriel, 1928-.　　　　　2.5420
El otoño del patriarca / [por] Gabriel García Márquez. — Barcelona: Bruguera, 1981. 344 p.; 18 cm. — (CLUB Bruguera; 3) I. T. II. Series.
PQ8180.17.A73 O8 1980　　　863 19　　　ISBN 8402075444

García Márquez, Gabriel, 1928-.　　　　　2.5421
Todos los cuentos de Gabriel García Márquez (1947–1972). — 1. ed. — Esplugas de Llobregat: Plaza & Janés, 1975. 320 p.; 20 cm. (Novelistas del día) I. T.
PQ8180.17.A73 T6　　　LC 75-511402　　　ISBN 8401301599

PQ8200–8220 Ecuador

Icaza, Jorge, 1906-.　　　　　2.5422
Huasipungo; novela. 11. ed. Buenos Aires, Editorial Losada, 1977. 201 p. 18 cm. (Bibliotea clásica y contemporánea) I. T.
PQ 8219 I15 H8 1977

PQ8300–8499 Peru

Alegría, Ciro, 1909-1967.　　　　　● 2.5423
Novelas completas. Prólogo de Arturo del Hoyo. Con 10 ilus. — [3. ed. — Madrid] Aguilar [1968, c1967] 1018 p. illus., ports. 19 cm. — (Biblioteca de autores modernos) I. T. II. Series.
PQ8497.A56A6 1967　　　LC 65-7709

Alegría, Ciro, 1909-1967.　　　　　2.5424
Broad and alien is the world, by Ciro Alegría, translated from the Spanish by Harriet de Onís. New York, Toronto, Farrar & Rinehart [c1941] 434 p. 22 cm. Translation of El mundo es ancho y ajeno. I. De Onís, Harriet, 1899- tr. II. T.
PZ3.A3665Br PQ8497.A56M83 1941　　　863.6　　　LC 41-22353

Arguedas, José María.　　　　　2.5425
Los ríos profundos. Edited by William Rowe. — [1st English ed.]. — Oxford; New York: Pergamon Press, [1973] xxxv, 245 p. (Commonwealth and international library. Pergamon Oxford Latin-American series) Text in Spanish; introd. in English. I. Rowe, William, ed. II. T.
PQ8497.A65 R5 1973　　　PQ8497 A65 R5 1973.　　　863　　　LC 73-4524　　　ISBN 0080170153

Arguedas, José María.　　　　　2.5426
[Ríos profundos. English] Deep rivers / José María Arguedas; translated by Frances Horning Barraclough; introd. by John V. Murra; afterword by Mario Vargas Llosa. — Austin: University of Texas Press, c1978. xv, 248 p.; 24 cm. — (The Texas Pan American series) Translation of Los ríos profundos. I. T.
PZ4.A692 De PQ8497.A65 R5x　　　863　　　LC 77-26243　　　ISBN 0292715161

Vallejo, César, 1892-1938.　　　　　2.5427
[Poems] Poesía completa / César Vallejo. — Mexico: Premià Editora, S.A., 1978. 932 p.; 20 cm. (Biblioteca crítica) Includes index. I. T.
PQ8497.V35 A17 1978　　　861 19　　　LC 78-377010　　　ISBN 9684340060

Vargas Llosa, Mario, 1936-.　　　　　2.5428
La casa verde / Mario Vargas Llosa. — 14. ed. — Barcelona: Seix Barral, 1975. 430 p.; 20 cm. (Biblioteca Formentor) I. T.
PQ8498.32.A65C3x　　　ISBN 0843221872

Vargas Llosa, Mario, 1936-.　　　　　2.5429
The time of the hero. Translated by Lysander Kemp. New York, Grove Press [1966] 409 p. 22 cm. Translation of La ciudad y los perros. I. T.
PZ4.V297 Ti PQ8498.32.A65C513x　　　LC 65-14204

Vargas Llosa, Mario, 1936-.　　　　　2.5430
La ciudad y los perros. 7. ed. Barcelona: Editorial Seix Barral 1966. 343p. I. T.
PQ8498.32.A65 C5x

Vargas Llosa, Mario, 1936-.　　　　　2.5431
Conversación en la catedral. — [Barcelona]: Seix Barral, [1969] 2 v.; 21 cm. — (Nueva narrativa hispánica) I. T.
PQ8498.32.A65 C6　　　LC 75-259390

Vargas Llosa, Mario, 1936-.　　　　　2.5432
[Conversación en la catedral. English] Conversation in the cathedral. Translated from the Spanish by Gregory Rabassa. New York, Harper & Row [1975] 601 p. 22 cm. I. T.
PZ4.V297 Co PQ8498.32.A65C613x　　　863　　　LC 74-1892　　　ISBN 0060145021

Vargas Llosa, Mario, 1936-.　　　　　2.5433
La guerra del fin del mundo / Mario Vargas Llosa. — 1a ed. — Barcelona: Seix Barral, 1981. 531 p.: ill.; 23 cm. — (Biblioteca breve) 1. Brazil — History — Conselheiro Insurrection, 1897 — Fiction. I. T.
PQ8498.32.A65 G8 1981　　　863 19　　　LC 82-150225　　　ISBN 8432203963

Vargas Llosa, Mario, 1936-.　　　　　2.5434
[Guerra del fin del mundo. English] The war of the end of the world / Mario Vargas Llosa; translated by Helen R. Lane. — New York: Farrar Straus Giroux, c1984. 568 p.; 24 cm. Translation of: La guerra del fin del mundo. 1. Brazil — History — Conselheiro Insurrection, 1897 — Fiction. I. T.
PQ8498.32.A65 G813 1984　　　863 19　　　LC 84-10187　　　ISBN 0374286515

Vargas Llosa, Mario, 1936-.　　　　　2.5435
La tía Julia y el escribidor / Mario Vargas Llosa. — 1. ed. — Barcelona: Seix Barral, 1977. 447 p.; 20 cm. — (Biblioteca breve; 424: Novela) I. T.
PQ8498.32.A65 T5 1977　　　LC 77-574603　　　ISBN 8432203238

Vargas Llosa, Mario, 1936-.　　　　　2.5436
[Tía Julia y el escribidor. English] Aunt Julia and the scriptwriter / Mario Vargas Llosa; translated by Helen R. Lane. — New York: Farrar/Straus/Giroux, c1982. 374 p.; 24 cm. Translation of: La tía Julia y el escribidor. I. T.
PQ8498.32.A65 T513 1982　　　863 19　　　LC 82-5159　　　ISBN 0374106916

Gerdes, Dick.　　　　　2.5437
Mario Vargas Llosa / by Dick Gerdes. — Boston, Mass.: Twayne Publishers, c1985. 208 p.: port.; 23 cm. (Twayne's world authors series; TWAS 762. Latin American literature) Includes index. 1. Vargas Llosa, Mario, 1936- — Criticism and interpretation. I. T.
PQ8498.32.A65 Z668 1985　　　863 19　　　LC 85-5447　　　ISBN 080576612X

Mario Vargas Llosa: a collection of critical essays / edited by   **2.5438**
Charles Rossman and Alan Warren Friedman; [ill. by Barbara
Whitehead].
Austin: University of Texas Press, c1978. viii, 186 p.: ill.; 24 cm. 'Essays ...
previously published in Texas studies in literature and language, vol. 19, no. 4.'
1. Vargas Llosa, Mario, 1936- — Criticism and interpretation — Addresses,
essays, lectures. I. Rossman, Charles. II. Friedman, Alan Warren.
PQ8498.32.A65 Z715   863   *LC* 78-50821   *ISBN* 0292750390

PQ8510–8519 Uruguay

Onetti, Juan Carlos, 1909-.   **2.5439**
[Vida breve. English] A brief life / by Juan Carlos Onetti; translated from the
Spanish by Hortense Carpentier. — New York: Grossman Publishers, 1976.
viii, 292 p.; 22 cm. Translation of La vida breve. I. T.
PZ4.O557 Br PQ8519.O59   863   *LC* 75-28197   *ISBN* 0670190691

Onetti, Juan Carlos, 1909-.   **2.5440**
Obras completas / Juan Carlos Onetti; prólogo de Emir Rodríguez Monegal. —
2nd ed. — Madrid: Aguilar, 1979. 1431 p.: port. — (Biblioteca de autores
modernos) I. Rodríguez Monegal, Emir. II. T.
PQ8519.O59 1970   PQ8519 O57 1970.

Quiroga, Horacio, 1879-1937.   **2.5441**
Horacio Quiroga Sus mejores cuentos. Prólogo de Mario Rodríguez Fernández.
2nd ed. — Santiago de Chile Editorial Nascimento 1972. 150p. (Biblioteca
popular Nascimiento, 3) I. Rodríguez Fernández, Mario, 1933- II. T.
PQ8519 Q5 A6 1971   *LC* 74-217569

Quiroga, Horacio, 1878-1937.   **2.5442**
The decapitated chicken, and other stories / by Horacio Quiroga; selected &
translated by Margaret Sayers Peden; introd. by George D. Schade; ill. by Ed
Lindlof. — Austin: University of Texas Press, c1976. xviii, 195 p.: ill.; 21 cm. —
(The Texas Pan American series) I. T.
PZ3.Q5 De10 PQ8519.Q5 Ax   863   *LC* 75-40167   *ISBN*
0292775148

Rodó, José Enrique, 1872-1917.   **2.5443**
Ariel; edited with an introduction and notes by Gordon Brotherston. —
Cambridge, Cambridge U. P., 1967. vi, 106 p. 22 1/2 cm. In Spanish,
introduction in English. Bibliographical footnotes. 1. Social ethics
2. Democracy I. Brotherston, Gordon. ed. II. T.
PQ8519.R6A7 1967   868   *LC* 67-10988

Sánchez, Florencio, 1875-1910.   **2.5444**
La gringa and Barranca abajo. With notes and introd. by Giovanni Pontiero. —
Rutherford [N. J.] Fairleigh Dickinson University Press [1973, c1972] vi, 186 p.
22 cm. Spanish texts with introd. and notes in English. Bibliography: p. 50-52.
I. Sánchez, Florencio, 1875-1910. Barranca abajo. 1973. II. T. III. Title:
Barranca abajo.
PQ8519.S4G7 1973   862   *LC* 72-6355   *ISBN* 0828612644

PQ8530–8929 Venezuela

Gallegos, Rómulo, 1884-1969.   • **2.5445**
[Works. 1976] Obras completas / Rómulo Gallegos; prólogo de Jesús López
Pacheco. — 2a ed., 1a reimpresión. — Madrid: Aguilar, 1976. — 2 v.: ports.; 19
cm. — (Biblioteca de autores modernos) I. T. II. Series.
PQ8549.G24 1976   *ISBN* 8403049978

Shaw, Donald Leslie, 1930-.   **2.5446**
Gallegos: Donã Bárbara [by] D. L. Shaw. London, Grant and Cutler, 1972.
84 p. 21 cm. (Critical guides to Spanish texts, 4) 1. Gallegos, Rómulo,
1884-1969. Donã Bárbara. I. T.
PQ8549.G24 D6297   863   *LC* 73-158874   *ISBN* 0900411376

Gallegos, Rómulo, 1884-1969.   **2.5447**
Doña Barbara / by Rómula Gallegos; translated by Robert Malloy. — New
York: Peter Smith, 1948, c1931. vi, 440 p.; 20 cm. I. Malloy, Robert. II. T.
PQ8549.G24 D63 1948   *LC* 31-20843

Rizal, José, 1861-1896.   **2.5448**
[Noli me tangere. English] The lost Eden (Noli me tangere) A completely new
translation for the contemporary reader, by León Ma. Guerrero with his introd.
Foreword by James A. Michener. New York, Greenwood Press, 1968 [c1961]
xviii, 406 p. 22 cm. Sequel: The subversive. I. T.
PZ3.R5285 Lo4 PQ8897.R5   863   *LC* 68-9712

PQ9001–9999 Portuguese Literature

PQ9001–9187 History. Criticism. Collections

Bell, Aubrey F. G. (Aubrey Fitz Gerald), 1882-1950. • 2.5449
Portuguese literature, by Aubrey F. G. Bell. — Oxford: Clarendon Press, 1922. 375 p.; 23 cm. 1. Portuguese literature — History and criticism. I. T.
PQ9011.B4   869/.09   LC 22-12776

The Oxford book of Portuguese verse: XIIth century–XXth • 2.5450
century / chosen by Aubrey F. G. Bell; edited by B. Vidigal.
2. ed. — Oxford: Clarendon, 1952. 383 p. Poems in Portuguese text. 1. Portuguese poetry — Collections. I. Bell, Aubrey F. G. (Aubrey Fitz Gerald), 1882-1950.
PQ9150.O8 1952   869.1008   LC 53-12631

Contemporary Portuguese poetry: an anthology in English / 2.5451
selected by Helder Macedo and E. M. de Melo e Castro.
Manchester: Carcanet New Press, 1978. viii, 182 p.: ill.; 23 cm. 1. Portuguese poetry — 20th century — Translations into English. 2. English poetry — Translations from Portuguese. I. Macedo, Helder. II. Castro, Ernesto Manuel de Melo e.
PQ9163.E6 C66   869/.1/4208   LC 78-326236   ISBN 0856352446

PQ9191–9288 Individual Authors

Camões, Luís de, 1524?-1580. 2.5452
Os Lusiadas [by] Luis de Camões. Edited with an introduction and notes by Frank Pierce. Oxford [Eng.] Clarendon Press, 1973. xlv, 271 p. map. 23 cm. Introd. and notes in English. I. Pierce, Frank, 1915- ed. II. T.
PQ9198.A2 1973   869/.1/2   LC 73-175327   ISBN 0198157371

Camões, Luís de, 1524?-1580. • 2.5453
The Lusiads / Luis Vaz de Camoens; translated by William C. Atkinson. — Harmondsworth, Middlesex: Penguin, 1952. 248 p.: ill. — (The Penguin classics; L26) 'The present translation is believed to be the first ever made into English prose.' I. T.
PQ9199A2 A7 1952   LC 53-5415

Camões, Luís de, 1524?-1580. 2.5454
The Lusiads / Luis de Camões; in Sir Richard Fanshawe's translation; edited and with an introd. by Geoffrey Bullough. — London: Centaur Press, 1963. 352 p.: ports, facsims.; 26 cm. — (Centaur classics) 'Out of the Satyr of Petronius Arbiter' (Latin and English) p. [35]-53. With reproduction of t.p. of first English ed. dated 1655. 1. Portuguese poetry — Translations into English. 2. English poetry — Translations from Portuguese. I. T.
PQ9199.A2 F3 1963   869.12

Queirós, Eça de, 1845-1900. • 2.5455
The Maias / Eça de Queiroz; translated by Patricia McGowan Pinheiro and Ann Stevens. — New York: St. Martin's Press, 1965. 633 p.; 21 cm. I. T.
PQ9261.E3 M313   869/.3/3   LC 65-24582

Queirós, Eça de, 1845-1900. • 2.5456
Cousin Bazilio / translated by Roy Campbell. London, M. Reinhardt [1953] 295 p. I. Campbell, Roy, 1901-1957. tr. II. T.
PQ9261.E3 P6x

Coleman, Alexander. 2.5457
Eça de Queirós and European realism / Alexander Coleman. — New York: New York University Press, c1980. x, 330 p.; 24 cm. — (Gotham Library of the New York University Press) Includes index. 1. Queirós, Eça de, 1845-1900. 2. Novelists, Portuguese — 19th century — Biography. I. T.
PQ9261.E3 Z617   869/.3/3   LC 79-3011   ISBN 0814713785

Pessoa, Fernando, 1888-1935. 2.5458
[Selected works. English and Portugese] Selected poems by Fernando Pessoa, including poems by his heteronyms: Alberto Caeiro, Ricardo Reis [and] Alvaro de Campos, as well as some of his English sonnets and selections from his letters. Translated by Edwin Honig. With an introd. by Octavio Paz. Chicago, Swallow Press [1971] x, 170 p. port. 24 cm. I. T.
PQ9261.P417 A6 1971b   869/.1/41   LC 75-150758   ISBN 0804005206

Quental, Antero de, 1842-1891. • 2.5459
Sonnets and poems of Anthero de Quental. Translated by S. Griswold Morley. — Westport, Conn.: Greenwood Press, [1973] xxiv, 133 p.; 18 cm. I. Morley, Sylvanus Griswold, 1878- tr. II. T.
PQ9261.Q4 A26 1973   869/.1/3   LC 77-137073   ISBN 0837155363

Barreno, Maria Isabel, 1939-. 2.5460
[Novas cartas portuguesas. English] The three Marias: new Portuguese letters / Maria Isabel Barreno, Maria Teresa Horta, Maria Velho da Costa; translated from the Portuguese by Helen R. Lane. — 1st ed. — Garden City, N.Y.: Doubleday, 1975. 432 p.; 22 cm. Translation of Novas cartas portuguesas. I. Horta, Maria Teresa. II. Costa, Maria Velho da. III. T.
PQ9264.A74 N613   869/.08/09287   LC 74-2826   ISBN 0385018533

PQ9421–9999 Portuguese Literature Outside Portugal

PQ9500–9699 Brazil

Coutinho, Afrânio. • 2.5461
[Introdução à Literatura no Brasil. English] An introduction to literature in Brazil. Translated from the Portuguese by Gregory Rabassa. New York, Columbia University Press, 1969. xii, 326 p. 25 cm. Translation of Introdução à Literatura no Brasil. 1. Brazilian literature — History and criticism. 2. Literature — History and criticism I. T.
PQ9511.C6313   869/.09981   LC 69-15569

Putnam, Samuel, 1892-1950. • 2.5462
Marvelous journey; a survey of four centuries of Brazilian writing. — New York: Octagon Books, 1971 [c1948] xvi, 269, xii p.; 24 cm. 1. Brazilian literature — History and criticism. I. T.
PQ9511.P8 1971   869/.009   LC 73-159250   ISBN 0374967032

Sayers, Raymond S. • 2.5463
The Negro in Brazilian literature / Raymond S. Sayers. — New York: Hispanic Institute in the United States, 1956. 240 p.: illus., ports. 1. Negroes in literature 2. Brazilian literature — History and criticism I. T.
PQ9523.N4 S3   PQ9523N4 S3 1956.   869.09   LC 56-2175

Martins, Wilson. • 2.5464
[Modernismo. English] The modernist idea; a critical survey of Brazilian writing in the twentieth century. Translated by Jack E. Tomlins. New York, New York University Press, 1970 [c1971] xix, 345 p. 24 cm. Translation of O modernismo, 3d and updated ed., originally published as vol. 6 of A Literatura brasileira. 1. Brazilian literature — 20th century — History and criticism. 2. Modernism (Literature) — Brazil. I. T.
PQ9555.M313 1970   869   LC 79-124529   ISBN 0814702937

Nist, John A. • 2.5465
The modernist movement in Brazil; a literary study, by John Nist. Austin, University of Texas Press [1967] 223 p. 22 cm. (The Texas pan-American series) 1. Brazilian poetry — 20th century — History and criticism. 2. Modernism (Literature) — Brazil. I. T.
PQ9571.N5   869.1   LC 65-27537

Hulet, Claude L. (Claude Lyle), 1920- comp. 2.5466
Brazilian literature [edited by] Claude L. Hulet. Washington, Georgetown University Press [1974-. V. 24 cm. 'Prepared under the auspices of the Instituto Internacional de Literatura Iberoamericana.' Literary selections in Portuguese.

251

1. Brazilian literature 2. Brazilian literature — History and criticism. I. International Institute of Ibero-American Literature. II. T.
PQ9635.H8   869/.09   *LC* 74-16331   *ISBN* 0878400338

Bishop, Elizabeth, 1911-1979. comp.   2.5467
An anthology of twentieth–century Brazilian poetry. Edited, with introd., by Elizabeth Bishop and Emanuel Brasil. — [1st ed.]. — Middletown, Conn.: Wesleyan University Press, [1972] xxi, 181 p.; 24 cm. English and Portuguese. 'Sponsored by the Academy of American Poets.' 1. Brazilian poetry — 20th century 2. Brazilian poetry — 20th century — Translations into English. 3. English poetry — Translations from Portuguese. I. Brasil, Emanuel. joint comp. II. T.
PQ9658.B5   869/.1   *LC* 75-184359   *ISBN* 0819540447

PQ9697–9698 INDIVIDUAL AUTHORS

Amado, Jorge, 1912-.   • 2.5468
[Dona Flor e seus dois maridos. English] Dona Flor and her two husbands; a moral and amorous tale. Translated from the Portuguese by Harriet de Onís. [1st American ed.] New York, Knopf, 1969. 553 p. 23 cm. Translation of Dona Flor e seus dois maridos. I. T.
PZ3.A478 Do PQ9697.A647 D6x   869.3   *LC* 69-10710

Amado, Jorge, 1912-.   • 2.5469
[Terras do sem fim. English] The violent land. Translated from the Portuguese (Terras do sem fim) by Samuel Putnam. With a new foreword by the author. New York, Knopf, 1965. viii, 336 p. 22 cm. I. T.
PQ9697.A647 T4x   *LC* 65-15064

Lispector, Clarice.   2.5470
[Laços de família. English] Family ties. Translated with an introd. by Giovanni Pontiero. Austin, University of Texas Press [1972] 156 p. front. 22 cm. (Texas pan-American series) I. T.
PZ4.L769 Fam PQ9697.L585   869/.3   *LC* 72-412   *ISBN* 0292724047

Fitz, Earl E.   2.5471
Clarice Lispector / by Earl E. Fitz. — Boston: Twayne Publishers, c1985. 160 p.: port.; 23 cm. (Twayne's world authors series; TWAS 755. Latin American literature) Includes index. 1. Lispector, Clarice — Criticism and interpretation. I. T.
PQ9697.L585 Z66 1985   869.3 19   *LC* 84-25199   *ISBN* 0805766057

Machado de Assis, 1839-1908.   • 2.5472
[Selected works. English] The psychiatrist, and other stories. Translated by William L. Grossman & Helen Caldwell. Berkeley, University of California Press, 1963. 147 p. 22 cm. I. T.
PQ9697.M18 Ax 1963   *LC* 63-9407

Machado de Assis, 1839-1908.   2.5473
[Selected works. English. 1977] The Devil's Church and other stories / by Machado de Assis; translated by Jack Schmitt and Lorie Ishimatsu. — Austin: University of Texas Press, c1977. xiii, 152 p.: ill.; 24 cm. (The Texas Pan American series) I. T.
PZ3.M1817 De3 PQ9697.M18 Ax 1977   869/.3   *LC* 76-53828
ISBN 0292775350

Machado de Assis, 1839-1908.   • 2.5474
Dom Casmurro: a novel / by Machado de Assis; translated and by Helen Caldwell; with an introduction by Waldo Frank. — New York: Noonday Press, 1953. 283 p. I. T.
PZ3.M1817Do   PQ9697.M18 D63.   *LC* 53-9085

Machado de Assis, 1839-1908.   • 2.5475
[Mão e a luva. English] The hand & the glove. Translated by Albert I. Bagby, Jr. With a foreword by Helen Caldwell. [Lexington] University Press of Kentucky [1970] xxii, [1], 116 p. 23 cm. (Studies in Romance languages, 2) Translation of A mão e a luva. I. T.
PZ3.M1817 Han PQ9697.M18 M3x   869.3   *LC* 74-111502   *ISBN* 0813112117

Machado de Assis, 1839-1908.   • 2.5476
Epitaph of a small winner; translated from the Portuguese by William L. Grossman. Drawings by Shari Frisch. New York, Noonday Press, 1952. 223 p. illus. 21 cm. Translation of Memorias posthumas de Braz Cubas. I. T.
PQ9697.M18 M4x   869.3   *LC* 52-36198

Caldwell, Helen.   2.5477
Machado de Assis; the Brazilian master and his novels. Berkeley, University of California Press, 1970. 270 p. 23 cm. 1. Machado de Assis, 1839-1908. I. T.
PQ9697.M18 Z573   869.3   *LC* 76-89891   *ISBN* 0520016084

Ramos, Graciliano, 1892-1953.   • 2.5478
Anguish, by Graciliano Ramos; translated from the Portuguese by L.C. Kaplan. New York, Knopf, 1946. 259 p. 'Originally published in 1941 as Angustia.' I. T.
PQ9697.R254 A8x   869.34   *LC* 46-1914

PQ9900–9948 Africa

Hamilton, Russell G.   2.5479
Voices from an empire: a history of Afro–Portuguese literature / Russell G. Hamilton. — Minneapolis: University of Minnesota Press, c1975. x, 450 p.: map; 23 cm. (Minnesota monographs in the humanities; v. 8) Includes index. 1. African literature (Portuguese) I. T. II. Series.
PQ9900.H3   PQ9900 H3.   869/.09   *LC* 74-24416   *ISBN* 0816607451

PR English Literature

PR1–999 History. Criticism

Selected papers from the English Institute. 2.5480
no. 1- 1959- ; n. s. no. 1- 1977-. Baltimore, Johns Hopkins University Press. 21 cm. I. English Institute.
PR13.E51 n.s. *LC* sn 82-21865

Corbett, Edward P. J. comp. • 2.5481
Rhetorical analyses of literary works [edited by] Edward P. J. Corbett. — New York: Oxford University Press, 1969. xxviii, 272 p.; 23 cm. 1. English literature — History and criticism 2. American literature — History and criticism I. T.
PR14.C6 820.9 *LC* 68-56180

Browning, David Clayton, 1894- ed. 2.5482
Everyman's dictionary of literary biography. London, Dent; [1958] x, 752 p. 20 cm. 1. English literature — Bio-bibliography 2. American literature — Bio-bibliography. I. Cousin, John William, 1849-1910. A short biographical dictionary of English literature. II. T. III. Title: Dictionary of literary biography, English & American.
PR19.B7 *LC* a 58-2815

Browning, David Clayton, 1894-, ed. 2.5483
Everyman's dictionary of literary biography, English & American, compiled after John W. Cousin by D.C. Browning. London Dent [1958] 752p. (Everyman's reference library) 1. English literature — Bio-bibliography 2. American literature — Bio-bibliography I. Cousin, John William, 1849-1910. A short biographical dictionary of English literature II. T. III. Title: Dictionary of literary biography, English & American
PR19 B7

Dictionary of literary biography. 2.5484
Detroit: Gale Research Co., 1978-. v.: ill., ports.; 29 cm.
PR19.D5x

Drabble, Margaret, 1939-. • 2.5485
The Oxford companion to English literature. — 5th ed. / edited by Margaret Drabble. — Oxford; New York: Oxford University Press, 1985. xii, 1155 p.; 24 cm. Rev. ed. of: The Oxford companion to English literature / compiled and edited by Paul Harvey. 4th ed. 1969. 1. English literature — Dictionaries 2. English literature — Bio-bibliography 3. American literature — Dictionaries. 4. American literature — Bio-bibliography. I. Harvey, Paul, Sir, 1869-1948. Oxford companion to English literature. II. T.
PR19.D73 1985 820/.9 19 *LC* 84-27308 *ISBN* 0198661304

The New Century handbook of English literature, edited by • 2.5486
Clarence L. Barnhart with the assistance of William D. Halsey.
Rev. ed. — New York: Appleton-Century-Crofts, [1967] vii, 1167 p.; 25 cm. 1. English literature — Dictionaries I. Barnhart, Clarence Lewis, 1900- ed. II. Title: Century handbook of English literature.
PR19.N4 1967 820.3 *LC* 67-12396

Ruoff, James E. 2.5487
Crowell's handbook of Elizabethan & Stuart literature [by] James E. Ruoff. New York, Crowell [1975] ix, 468 p. 24 cm. 1. English literature — Early modern, 1500-1700 — Dictionaries. I. T. II. Title: Handbook of Elizabethan and Stuart literature.
PR19.R8 1975 820/.9/003 *LC* 73-22097 *ISBN* 0690226616

Spender, Stephen, 1909-. • 2.5488
The concise encyclopedia of English and American poets and poetry, edited by Stephen Spender and Donald Hall. New York, Hawthorn Books [1963] 415 p. illus. 26 cm. 1. English poetry — Dictionaries. 2. American poetry — Dictionaries. I. Hall, Donald, 1928- II. T. III. Title: Encyclopedia of English and American poets and poetry.
PR19.S6 821.003 *LC* 63-8015

Altick, Richard Daniel, 1915-. • 2.5489
The art of literary research. [1st ed.] New York, Norton [c1963] x, 276 p. 22 cm. The 3d vol. of the author's trilogy, the 1st of which is The scholar adventurers, the 2d of which is Selective bibliography for the study of English and American literature. 1. Literature — Research 2. English literature — Study and teaching 3. American literature — Study and teaching. I. T.
PR33.A4 807.2 *LC* 63-8025

Altick, Richard Daniel, 1915-. • 2.5490
The scholar adventurers. New York, Macmillan, c1950. viii, 338 p. 22 cm. 1. English literature — History and criticism 2. Literature — Research 3. Scholars I. T.
PR56.A7 820.72 *LC* 50-11053

PR57–79 Criticism

Erdman, David V. ed. • 2.5492
Evidence for authorship; essays on problems of attribution, with an annotated bibliography of selected readings, edited by David V. Erdman and Ephim G. Fogel. — Ithaca, N.Y.: Cornell University Press, [1966] xiv, 559 p.; 25 cm. Includes 8 papers presented at the English Institute, Columbia University, Sept., 1958. 1. English literature — Addresses, essays, lectures. 2. Authorship, Disputed — Addresses, essays, lectures. I. Fogel, Ephim Gregory, 1920- joint ed. II. English Institute. III. T.
PR61.E7 809 *LC* 65-24698

Gross, John J. 2.5493
The rise and fall of the man of letters: aspects of English literary life since 1800 [by] John Gross. — London: Weidenfeld & Nicolson, 1969. xiv, 322 p.: 32 plates, illus., facsim., ports.; 23 cm. 1. English literature — 19th century — History and criticism. 2. English literature — 20th century — History and criticism. 3. Criticism — Gt. Brit. — History. 4. Literature and society I. T.
PR63.G7 1969 820.9 *LC* 70-415648 *ISBN* 0297764942

Saintsbury, George, 1845-1933. • 2.5494
A history of English criticism; being the English chapters of A history of criticism and literary taste in Europe; rev., adapted, and supplemented, by George Saintsbury ... — Edinburgh and London, W. Blackwood and sons, 1911. xiii p., 1 l., 551 p. 21.5 cm. 'Bibliographical note': 1 leaf following p. xiii. 1. Criticism — Hist. 2. English literature — Hist. & crit. I. T.
PR63.S3 *LC* 12-16583

Thorpe, James Ernest, 1915-. • 2.5495
Principles of textual criticism, by James Thorpe. — San Marino, Calif.: Huntington Library, 1972. ix, 209 p.; 24 cm. 1. Criticism, Textual 2. English literature — Criticism, Textual 3. American literature — Criticism, Textual. I. T.
PR65.T5 801/.959 *LC* 72-179135

Brower, Reuben Arthur, 1908- ed. • 2.5496
In defense of reading; a reader's approach to literary criticism. Edited by Reuben A. Brower and Richard Poirier. — [1st ed.]. — New York, Dutton, 1962. 311 p. 22 cm. 1. English literature — Hist. & crit. 2. American literature — Hist. & crit. 3. Criticism I. Poirier, Richard. joint ed. II. T.
PR67.B7 801.9 *LC* 62-11512

Holmes, Charles S. ed. • 2.5497
The major critics; the development of English literary criticism, edited by Charles S. Holmes, Edwin Fussell [and] Ray Frazer. [1st ed.] New York, Knopf, 1957. 313 p. 20 cm. 1. English literature — History and criticism 2. Criticism — Great Britain. I. T.
PR67.H6 820.9 *LC* 57-5066

Jones, Edmund David, ed. • 2.5498
English critical essays (sixteenth, seventeenth, and eighteenth centuries) selected and ed. by Edmund D. Jones. — London; New York [etc.]: H. Milford, Oxford university press, [1922] viii, 460 p.; 16 cm. — (Half-title: The World's classics. CCXL) 1. Criticism — Great Britain. 2. Poetry 3. English poetry — History and criticism 4. English essays I. T.
PR67.J6 1922 *LC* 23-11958

English critical essays, twentieth century: first series / selected • 2.5499
with an introduction by Phyllis M. Jones.
London: Oxford University Press, 1933. [xv], 399 p.; 16 cm. — (World's classics. 405.) 1. English literature — History and criticism 2. Criticism 3. English essays I. Jones, Phyllis Maud. II. Series.
PR67.J65 320.4 *LC* 34-27029

Leavis, F. R. (Frank Raymond), 1895-. • 2.5500
Determination: critical essays / with an introduction by F.R. Leavis. — London: Chatto & Windus, 1934. 312 p.; 20 cm. Essays which originally

appeared in Scrutiny. 1. Criticism 2. English literature — History and criticism I. Scrutiny. II. T.
PR67.L4   *LC* 34-40330

2. Feminist literary criticism 3. English literature — History and criticism 4. Sex role in literature I. T.
PR77.R88 1984   801/.95/0941 19   *LC* 84-9592   *ISBN* 0521264545

PR69–78 By Period

English literary criticism: the Renaissance / O.B. Hardison, editor.   • **2.5501**
New York: Appleton-Century-Crofts, 1963. 337 p.; 21 cm. — (Goldentree books) 1. Criticism — Great Britain. 2. English literature — Early modern (to 1700) — Addresses, essays, lectures. I. Hardison, Osborne Bennett, 1928-. II. Series.
PR70.H3   *LC* 63-13837   *ISBN* 0390410500

Smith, G. Gregory (George Gregory), 1865-1932. ed.   • **2.5502**
Elizabethan critical essays;. — ed. with an introduction, by G. Gregory Smith ... — Oxford, Clarendon press, 1904. 2 v. 20.5 cm. 1. Poetry — Early works to 1800. 2. Criticism 3. English literature — Early modern (to 1700) — Hist. & crit. 4. English essays I. T.
PR70.S6   *LC* 04-17825

Critical essays of the seventeenth century / edited by Joel Spingarn.   • **2.5503**
Bloomington: Indiana University Press, 1957. 3 v. 1. English literature — Early modern (to 1700) — History and criticism. 2. Criticism — Great Britain. I. Spingarn, Joel Elias.
PR72.S65   *LC* 57-10727

Patey, Douglas Lane.   **2.5504**
Probability and literary form: philosophic theory and literary practice in the Augustan age / Douglas Lane Patey. — Cambridge [Cambridgeshire]; New York: Cambridge University Press, 1984. xiii, 380 p.; 22 cm. Includes index. 1. Criticism — Great Britain — History — 18th century. 2. English fiction — 18th century — History and criticism. 3. Literature — Philosophy 4. Probabilities I. T.
PR73.P38 1984   801/.95/0941 19   *LC* 83-7819   *ISBN* 0521254566

Elledge, Scott. ed.   • **2.5505**
Eighteenth–century critical essays. — Ithaca [N. Y.] Cornell University Press [1961] 2 v. (xxiii, 1225 p.) 25 cm. Bibliographical references included in 'Notes' (v. 1, p. [485]-570; v. 2, p. [1123]-1209) 1. Criticism — Gt. Brit. 2. English essays — 18th cent. 3. Literature — Addresses, essays, lectures. I. T.
PR74.E4   820.903   *LC* 61-7868

Hynes, Samuel Lynn. ed.   • **2.5506**
English literary criticism: restoration and 18th century. — New York, Appleton-Century-Crofts [1963] 322 p. 21 cm. — (Goldentree books) 1. Criticism — Gt. Brit. 2. English literature — Early modern (to 1700) — Addresses, essays, lectures. 3. English literature — 18th cent. — Addresses, essays, lectures. I. T.
PR74.H9   820.903   *LC* 63-13834

Orel, Harold, 1926-.   **2.5507**
Victorian literary critics: George Henry Lewes, Walter Bagehot, Richard Holt Hutton, Leslie Stephen, Andrew Lang, George Saintsbury, and Edmund Gosse / by Harold Orell. — New York: St. Martin's Press, 1984. ix, 243 p.: 8 ports.; 23 cm. Includes index. 1. Criticism — Great Britain — History — 19th century. 2. Critics — Great Britain — Biography. I. T.
PR75.O73 1984   801/.95/0941 19   *LC* 83-11093   *ISBN* 0312843046

Brack, M. comp.   • **2.5508**
Bibliography and textual criticism: English and American literature, 1700 to the present, edited by O. M. Brack, Jr. and Warner Barnes. With an introd. by O. M. Brack, Jr. — Chicago: University of Chicago Press, [c1969] x, 345 p.; 22 cm. — (Patterns of literary criticism) 1. Criticism, Textual — Addresses, essays, lectures. 2. English literature — Criticism, Textual 3. American literature — Criticism, Textual. I. Barnes, Milton. Warner, joint comp. II. T.
PR77.B7   820.9   *LC* 74-92463   *ISBN* 0226069842

National Council of Teachers of English. Committee on Literary Scholarship and the Teaching of English.   • **2.5509**
Contemporary literary scholarship: a critical review. Edited by Lewis Leary. — New York: Appleton-Century-Crofts, [1958] 474 p.; 22 cm. 1. English literature — History and criticism 2. American literature — History and criticism 3. Criticism — Great Britain — History. 4. Criticism — United States — History. I. Leary, Lewis Gaston, 1906- ed. II. T.
PR77.N3   820.4   *LC* 58-6939

Ruthven, K. K.   **2.5510**
Feminist literary studies: an introduction / K.K. Ruthven. — Cambridge [Cambridgeshire]; New York: Cambridge University Press, 1984. vii, 152 p.; 23 cm. Includes index. 1. Criticism — Great Britain — History — 20th century.

PR81–999 History of English Literature

Baugh, Albert Croll, 1891- ed.   • **2.5511**
A literary history of England; edited by Albert C. Baugh. — 2nd ed. — London: Routledge & K. Paul, 1967. xv, 1796, lxxx p.; 24 cm. 1. English literature — History and criticism I. T.
PR83.B3 1967b   820.9   *LC* 68-140788

The Cambridge history of English literature / edited by A.W. Ward ... and A.R. Waller.   • **2.5512**
Cambridge, [Eng]: The University Press, 1919-30. 15 v. Vols. 1-3, 5, reprints; v.4, 6-14, new impressions;v. 15, first edition. 1. English literature — History and criticism 2. English literature — Bibliography I. Ward, Adolphus William, Sir, 1837-1924. ed. II. Waller, Alfred Rayney, 1867-1922, jt. ed.
PR83.C22   *LC* 30-31831

Chambers, R. W. (Raymond Wilson), 1874-1942.   • **2.5513**
Man's unconquerable mind; studies of English writers, from Bede to A. E. Housman and W. P. Ker. — Philadelphia: A. Saifer, 1953. 414 p.: illus., facsims.; 24 cm. 1. English literature — Addresses, essays, lectures. I. T.
PR83.C37 1967   820.9   *LC* 54-712

Daiches, David, 1912-.   • **2.5514**
A critical history of English literature. — 2d ed. — New York: Ronald Press Co., [1970] 2 v. (1178 p.); 24 cm. 1. English literature — History and criticism I. T.
PR83.D29 1970   820.9   *LC* 70-112497

Eagleton, Terry, 1943-.   **2.5515**
Against the grain: essays 1975–1985 / Terry Eagleton. — London: Verso, 1986. 199 p. Includes index. 1. English literature — History and criticism I. T.
PR83.E2x   820.9 19   *ISBN* 0860911349

Renwick, W. L. (William Lindsay), 1889-.   **2.5518**
The beginnings of English literature to Skelton, 1509, by W. L. Renwick and Harold Orton. 3rd ed.; revised by Martyn F. Wakelin. London, Cresset, 1966. 493 p. 21 cm. (Introductions to English literature. v. 1) 1. English literature — Old English, ca. 450-1100 — History and criticism. 2. English literature — Old English, ca. 450-1100 — Bibliography. 3. English literature — Middle English, 1100-1500 — History and criticism. 4. English literature — Middle English, 1100-1500 — Bibliography. I. Orton, Harold, 1898-1975. joint author. II. T. III. Series.
PR83.I6 vol.1   820.9/001   *LC* 70-413797

Pinto, Vivian de Sola, 1895-.   **2.5519**
The English Renaissance 1510–1688, with a chapter on literature and music by Bruce Pattison. — 3rd ed. revised and reset. — London: Cresset P., 1966. 403 p.; 20 1/2 cm. — (Introductions to English literature. v. 2) 1. English literature — Early modern, 1500-1700 — History and criticism. 2. English literature — Early modern, 1500-1700 — Bibliography. I. T. II. Series.
PR83.I6 vol.2   820.9003   *LC* 67-70380

Dyson, H. V. D. (Henry Victor Dyson)   **2.5520**
Augustans and Romantics, 1689–1830 / by H.V.D. Dyson and John Butt; with chapters on art, economics and philosophy by Geoffrey Webb ... [et al.]. — London: Cresset Press, [1940] 317 p. — (Introductions to English literature, edited by Bonamy Dobrée;. 3) Includes index. 1. English literature — 18th century — History and criticism. 2. English literature — 19th century — History and criticism. 3. English literature — 18th century — Bibliography. 4. English literature — 19th century — Bibliography. I. Butt, John Everett, 1906-. II. Webb, Geoffrey. III. T.
PR83.I6 v.3   *LC* 41-7721

Batho, Edith Clara, 1895-.   **2.5521**
The Victorians and after, 1830–1914 / by Edith C. Batho and Bonamy Dobrée; with a chapter on the economic background by Guy Chapman. — 3rd ed., revised & reset. — London: Cresset, 1962. 360 p.; 21 cm. — (Introductions to English literature. v. 4) 1. English literature — 19th century — History and criticism. 2. English literature — 19th century — Bibliography. I. Dobrée, Bonamy, 1891- II. Chapman, Guy, 1887-. III. T. IV. Series.
PR83.I6 vol.4   *LC* 75-413777

Daiches, David, 1912-.   **2.5522**
The present age after 1920. — Rev. ed. — London: Cresset Press, 1962, c1958. x, 376 p. — (Introductions to English literature. 5) 1. English literature — 20th

century — History and criticism 2. English literature — 20th century Bibliography I. Muir, Edwin, 1887-1959. The present age from 1914 II. T. III. Title: The present age from 1914 IV. Series.
PR83.I6 vol.5

The New Pelican guide to English literature / edited by Boris 2.5523
Ford.
Rev. and expanded ed. — Harmondsworth, Middlesex, England; New York, N.Y.: Penguin Books, 1982-1983. 8 v.; 19 cm. Rev. ed. of: The Pelican guide to English literature. 3rd ed. [1973] 1. English literature — History and criticism. I. Ford, Boris.
PR83.N49 1982   820/.9 19   *LC* 82-231912   *ISBN* 0140222650

The Cambridge guide to English literature / [compiled by] 2.5524
Michael Stapleton.
Cambridge [Cambridgeshire]; New York: Cambridge University Press; Feltham, Middlesex: Newnes Books; Rushden, Northants: distributed for them by Hamlyn Pub. Group, 1983. xi, 992 p.: ill., ports.; 26 cm. 1. English literature — Dictionaries. 2. English literature — Bio-bibliography. 3. American literature — Dictionaries. 4. American literature — Bio-bibliography. 5. English literature — Commonwealth of Nations authors — Dictionaries. 6. English literature — Commonwealth of Nations authors — Bio-bibliography. I. Stapleton, Michael.
PR85.C28 1983   820/.9 B 19   *LC* 83-1967   *ISBN* 0521260221

A History of English literature. • 2.5525
New York: Oxford University Press, 1950. xiii, 697 p.: map (on lining papers); 24 cm. 1. English literature — History and criticism I. Anderson, George Kumler, 1901- Old and Middle English literature from the beginnings to 1485. II. Craig, Hardin, 1875-1968. Literature of the English Renaissance, 1485-1660. III. Bredvold, Louis Ignatius, 1888- Literature of the Restoration and the eighteenth century, 1660-1798. IV. Beach, Joseph Warren, 1880-1957. Literature of the nineteenth century and the early twentieth centuries, 1798 to the First World War. V. Craig, Hardin, 1875-1968. VI. Title: Old and Middle English literature from the beginnings to 1485. VII. Title: The literature of the English Renaissance, 1485-1660. VIII. Title: The literature of the Restoration and the eighteenth century, 1660-1798. IX. Title: The literature of the nineteenth and early twentieth centuries, 1798 to the First World War.
PR85.C68   *LC* 50-10467

Hazlitt, William, 1778-1830. • 2.5526
Hazlitt on English literature; an introduction to the appreciation of literature, by Jacob Zeitlin. — New York: AMS Press, [1970] lxxiii, 423 p.; 23 cm. Reprint of the 1913 ed. 1. English literature — History and criticism I. T.
PR85.H38 1970   820.9   *LC* 71-127904   *ISBN* 0404031935

Saintsbury, George, 1845-1933. • 2.5527
A short history of English literature / by George Saintsbury. — New York: Macmillan, 1937. xix, 818 p.; 19 cm. 'First edition 1898; reprinted, 1900 ... with corrections ... 1937.' 1. English literature — History and criticism I. T.
PR85.S2 1937

Sampson, George, 1873-1950. • 2.5528
The concise Cambridge history of English literature. — 3rd ed., revised throughout and with additional chapters on the literature of the United States of America and the mid twentieth-century literature of the English-speaking world by R. C. Churchill. — London: Cambridge U.P., 1970. xiii, 976 p.; 24 cm. Based on the Cambridge history of English literature. 1. English literature — History and criticism I. Churchill, Reginald Charles. II. The Cambridge history of English literature. III. T.
PR85.S34 1970   820.9   *LC* 69-16287   *ISBN* 0521073855

Jusserand, J. J. (Jean Jules), 1855-1932. • 2.5529
A literary history of the English people, from the origins to the end of the Middle Ages. — 3d ed. — New York: Gordian Press, 1969. 3 v.: illus.; 23 cm. Reprint of the 1926 ed. 1. English literature — History and criticism I. T.
PR93.J82 1969   820.9   *LC* 68-29336

Legouis, Émile Hyacinthe, 1861-1937. • 2.5530
A history of English literature: The Middle Ages and the Renascence (650–1660) by Émile Legouis, translated from the French by Helen Douglas Irvine; Modern times (1660–1950) by Louis Cazamian, translated from the French by W.D. MacInnes, and the author. Rev. ed. New York, Macmillan [1957] xxiii, 1427 p. 20 cm. 1. English literature — History and criticism I. Cazamian, Louis François, 1877-1965. II. T.
PR93.L43 1957

Taine, Hippolyte, 1828-1893. • 2.5531
[Histoire de la litterature anglaise. English] History of English literature [by] Hippolyte A. Taine. [Translated from the French by H. Van Laun] New York, F. Ungar Pub. Co. [1965] 4 v. 22 cm. 'Reprinted from the 1883 edition.' 1. English literature — History and criticism I. T.
PR93.T4 1965   820.9   *LC* 65-20501

PR99 COLLECTED ESSAYS OF INDIVIDUAL AUTHORS

PR99.A–L

Aiken, Conrad, 1889-1973. • 2.5532
A reviewer's ABC: collected criticism of Conrad Aiken from 1916 to the present / introduced by Rufus A. Blanshard. — [New York] Meridian Books [1958] 414 p. 22 cm. (Greenwich editions.) 'Checklist of Conrad Aiken's critical writings': p. [395]-408. 1. English literature — History and criticism — Addresses, essays, lectures 2. American literature — History and criticism — Addresses, essays, lectures. I. T. II. Series.
PR99.A46   820.9   *LC* 58-12328

Bagehot, Walter, 1826-1877. • 2.5533
Literary studies. — London, Dent; New York, Dutton [1911] 2 v. 18 cm. — (Everyman's library. Essays and belles lettres) Title within ornamental border. Introduction by George Sampson. Bibliography: v. 1, p. xviii. 1. English literature — Addresses, essays, lectures. I. T.
PR99.B15 1911   *LC* A 12-644

Cecil, David, Lord, 1902-. • 2.5534
The fine art of reading and other literary studies / Lord David Cecil. — Indianapolis: Bobbs-Merrill, c1957. 282 p.; 23 cm. 1. English literature — History and criticism — Addresses, essays, lectures. I. T.
PR99.C38   820.4   *LC* 57-9359

Bradley, A. C. (Andrew Cecil), 1851-1935. • 2.5535
A miscellany. Freeport, N.Y., Books for Libraries Press [1969] 267 p. 22 cm. (Essay index reprint series) Reprint of the 1929 ed. 1. English literature — Addresses, essays, lectures. I. T.
PR99.B66 1969   820.9   *LC* 72-76894   *ISBN* 0836900057

Greene, Graham, 1904-. • 2.5536
The lost childhood, and other essays. New York: Viking Press, 1952 [c1951] 191 p.; 22 cm. 1. English literature — History and criticism — Addresses, essays, lectures. I. T.
PR99.G6843 1952   820.4   *LC* 52-6427

Grierson, Herbert John Clifford, Sir, 1866-1960. • 2.5537
The Background of English literature, classical & romantic, and other collected essays & addresses / by Herbert Grierson. — [2nd ed.]. — New York: Barnes & Noble, 1960 [i.e. 1961]. ix, 290 p.; 21 cm. 1. English literature — History and criticism — Addresses, essays, lectures I. T.
PR99.G686 1961   *LC* 61-1003

Hazlitt, William, 1778-1830. • 2.5538
Lectures on the English comic writers, delivered at the Surry Institution. — New York: Russell & Russell, [1969] 343 p.; 21 cm. Reprint of the 1819 ed. 1. Hogarth, William, 1697-1764. 2. English wit and humor — History and criticism. 3. English literature — Early modern, 1500-1700 — History and criticism. 4. English literature — 18th century — History and criticism. I. T. II. Title: English comic writers.
PR99.H35 1969   820.9   *LC* 68-25078

Hunt, Leigh, 1784-1859. • 2.5539
Literary criticism. Edited by Lawrence Huston Houtchens and Carolyn Washburn Houtchens. With an essay in evaluation by Clarence DeWitt Thorpe. — New York, Columbia University Press, 1956. xiii, 732 p. ports. 24 cm. 1. English literature — History and criticism — Addresses, essays, lectures. I. Houtchens, Lawrence Huston, 1898-. II. T.
PR99.H838   820.4   *LC* 55-5598

Ker, W. P. (William Paton), 1855-1923. • 2.5540
On modern literature; lectures and addresses. Edited by Terence Spencer and James Sutherland. Oxford, Clarendon Press. — St. Clair Shores, Mich.: Scholarly Press, 1971. xviii, 281 p.; 22 cm. Reprint of the 1955 ed. 1. English literature — History and criticism — Addresses, essays, lectures. I. T.
PR99.K42 1971   820.9   *LC* 70-158500   *ISBN* 0403012996

Knights, L. C. (Lionel Charles), 1906-. 2.5541
Explorations 3 / L. C. Knights. — [Pittsburgh]: University of Pittsburgh Press, 1976. 196 p.; 23 cm. 1. English literature — History and criticism — Addresses, essays, lectures. I. T.
PR99.K57   820/.9   *LC* 75-29654   *ISBN* 0822911256

Lamb, Charles, 1775-1834. • 2.5542
[Selections] Lamb's criticism; a selection from the literary criticism of Charles Lamb. Edited with an introd. and short notes by E. M. W. Tillyard. Westport, Conn., Greenwood Press [1970] xvi, 114 p. 23 cm. Reprint of the 1923 ed. 1. English literature — History and criticism 2. Criticism I. T.
PR99.L27 1970   820/.9   *LC* 77-95108   *ISBN* 0837131219

Leavis, F. R. (Frank Raymond), 1895-.   • 2.5543
The common pursuit [by] F. R. Leavis. [New York] New York University Press, 1964 [c1952] 307 p. 23 cm. 1. English literature — History and criticism I. T.
PR99.L4 1952   820.9   LC 64-21836

Lewis, C. S. (Clive Staples), 1898-1963.   • 2.5544
Rehabilitations and other essays. Freeport, N.Y., Books for Libraries Press [1972] viii, 197 p. 23 cm. (Essay index reprint series) Reprint of the 1939 ed. 1. English literature — Addresses, essays, lectures. I. T.
PR99.L4 1972   820.9   LC 71-167377   ISBN 0836925599

PR99.M–Z

Murry, John Middleton, 1889-1957.   • 2.5545
Unprofessional essays. — London: Cape, [1956] 191 p. 1. English literature — History and criticism — Addresses, essays, lectures. 2. American literature — History and criticism — Addresses, essays, lectures. I. T.
PR99.M92   LC 56-3184

Nicolson, Marjorie Hope, 1894-.   • 2.5546
Science and imagination / by Marjorie Nicolson. — Ithaca, N. Y.: Great Seal Books [1956] ix, 238 p.; 19 cm. 1. Literature and science — Addresses, essays, lectures. 2. English literature — History and criticism — Addresses, essays, lectures. I. T.
PR99.N54   LC A 57-2874

Quiller-Couch, Arthur Thomas, Sir, 1863-1944.   • 2.5547
Cambridge lectures [by] Sir Arthur Quiller-Couch. — London, J. M. Dent & sons ltd.; New York, E. P. Dutton & co. inc. [1943] vii, 312 p.; 18 cm. (Half-title: Everyman's library, ed. by Ernest Rhys. Essays & belles-lettres. No. 974) 1. English literature — Addresses, essays, lectures. 2. Literature — Addresses, essays, lectures. I. T.
PR99.Q53   820.4   LC 43-51320

Quiller-Couch, Arthur Thomas, Sir, 1863-1944.   • 2.5548
Studies in literature, by Sir Arthur Quiller-Couch ... — New York, G. P. Putnam's sons, 1918. v, 324 p. 24 cm. 1. English literature — Hist. & crit. I. T.
PR99.Q6   LC 19-26163

Quiller-Couch, Arthur Thomas, Sir, 1863-1944.   • 2.5549
Studies in literature; second series. — Westport, Conn.: Greenwood Press, [1970] vii, 306 p.; 23 cm. Reprint of the 1922 ed. 1. English literature — History and criticism — Addresses, essays, lectures. I. T.
PR99.Q62 1970   821/.009   LC 76-100198   ISBN 0837139058

Quiller-Couch, Arthur Thomas, Sir, 1863-1944.   • 2.5550
Studies in literature, third series / by Sir Arthur Quiller-Couch ... — Cambridge [Eng.]: University Press, 1929. vi, 264 p.; 24 cm. 1. English liteature — History and criticism. I. T.
PR99.Q63   LC 30-4013

Sale, Roger.   2.5551
Modern heroism; essays on D. H. Lawrence, William Empson, & J. R. R. Tolkien. Berkeley, University of California Press, 1973. xi, 261 p. 23 cm. 1. Lawrence, D. H. (David Herbert), 1885-1930. 2. Empson, William, 1906- 3. Tolkien, J. R. R. (John Ronald Reuel), 1892-1973. I. T.
PR99.S25   823/.9/1209   LC 73-186106   ISBN 0520022084

Shaw, Bernard, 1856-1950.   2.5552
[Prose works. 1972] Bernard Shaw's nondramatic literary criticism. Edited by Stanley Weintraub. Lincoln, University of Nebraska Press [1972] xxvii, 246 p. 21 cm. (Regents critics series) 1. English literature — History and criticism — Addresses, essays, lectures. 2. Literature — Addresses, essays, lectures. I. Weintraub, Stanley, 1929- ed. II. T.
PR99.S52 1972   820/.9   LC 70-149739   ISBN 0803207956

Spitzer, Leo, 1887-1960.   • 2.5553
Essays on English and American literature. Edited by Anna Hatcher. Princeton, N.J., Princeton University Press, 1962. 290 p. 23 cm. 1. English literature — Addresses, essays, lectures. 2. American literature — Addresses, essays, lectures. I. T.
PR99.S6   821/.009 19   LC 63-7078

Stephen, Leslie, Sir, 1832-1904.   • 2.5554
Hours in a library. — New ed., with additions. New York, Putnam 1904. — Grosse Pointe, Mich.: Scholarly Press, 1968. 4 v.; 23 cm. 1. English literature — History and criticism I. T.
PR99.S7 1968   820.9   LC 76-2981

Tillotson, Geoffrey, 1905-1969.   • 2.5555
Essays in criticism and research. With a new pref. by the author. — [Hamden, Conn.]: Archon Books, 1967. xxxi, 214 p.; 22 cm. 1. English literature — History and criticism — Addresses, essays, lectures. I. T.
PR99.T54 1967   820.9   LC 67-11476

Tillyard, E. M. W. (Eustace Mandeville Wetenhall), 1889-1962.   • 2.5556
Essays, literary & educational. New York, Barnes & Noble [1962] 223 p. 23 cm. 1. English literature — History and criticism — Addresses, essays, lectures I. T.
PR99.T56   LC 62-52526

Tillyard, E. M. W. (Eustace Mandeville Wetenhall), 1889-1962.   • 2.5557
Some mythical elements in English literature. London, Chatto & Windus, 1961. St. Clair Shores, Mich., Scholarly Press, 1971. 142 p. 22 cm. (Clark lectures. 1959-60) 1. English literature — History and criticism — Addresses, essays, lectures. I. T. II. Series.
PR99.T57 1971   820.9   LC 78-158510   ISBN 040301302X

Williams, Raymond.   2.5558
Writing in society / Raymond Williams. — [S.l.]: NLB (dist. by Schocken), 1984. 268 p.; 21 cm. Includes index. 1. English literature — History and criticism — Addresses, essays, lectures. I. T.
PR99.W67   820/.9 19   LC 84-224995   ISBN 0860910725

PR103–119 BIOGRAPHY

Kunitz, Stanley, 1905- ed.   • 2.5559
British authors before 1800; a biographical dictionary, edited by Stanley J. Kunitz and Howard Haycraft. New York, Wilson, 1952. vi, 584 p. ports. 26 cm. (The Authors series) 1. Authors, English I. Haycraft, Howard, 1905- joint ed. II. T. III. Series.
PR105.K9   928.2   LC 52-6758

Stephen, Leslie, Sir, 1832-1904.   • 2.5560
Studies of a biographer. — Freeport, N.Y.: Books for Libraries Press, [1973-. p. — (Essay index reprint series) Reprint of the 1902 ed. 1. Authors, English — Biography 2. English literature — Addresses, essays, lectures. I. T.
PR105.S67 1973   820/.9   LC 72-10931   ISBN 0836972368

Eagle, Dorothy.   2.5561
The Oxford illustrated literary guide to Great Britain and Ireland / compiled and edited by Dorothy Eagle and Hilary Carnell. — 2nd ed. / rev. by Dorothy Eagle. — Oxford; New York: Oxford University Press, 1981. 312, [1] p., [47] p. of plates: ill., maps; 29 cm. Rev. ed. of: The Oxford literary guide to the British Isles. Includes index. 1. Literary landmarks — Great Britain. 2. Authors, English — Homes and haunts — Dictionaries. 3. British Isles — Description and travel — Guide-books. I. Carnell, Hilary. II. T.
PR109.E18 1981   914.1/048570248 19   LC 80-42051   ISBN 0198691254

Fisher, Lois H., 1936-.   2.5562
A literary gazetteer of England / by Lois H. Fisher. — New York: McGraw-Hill, c1980. x, 740 p.: ill.; 29 cm. Includes index. 1. Literary landmarks — England 2. England — Gazetteers. I. T.
PR109.F5   914.2/04/857 19   LC 79-22776   ISBN 0070210985

Gilbert, Sandra M.   2.5563
The madwoman in the attic: the woman writer and the nineteenth-century literary imagination / Sandra M. Gilbert and Susan Gubar. — New Haven: Yale University Press, 1979. xiv, 719 p.: ill.; 24 cm. 1. English literature — Women authors — History and criticism. 2. English literature — 19th century — History and criticism. 3. Women in literature 4. Women authors — Psychology. 5. English literature — Psychological aspects I. Gubar, Susan, 1944- joint author. II. T.
PR115.G5   820/.9/9287   LC 78-20792   ISBN 0300022867

Johnson, R. Brimley (Reginald Brimley), 1867-1932.   • 2.5564
The women novelists. Freeport, N.Y., Books for Libraries Press [1967] viii, 299 p. 22 cm. (Essay index reprint series) Reprint of the 1919 ed. 1. Women novelists — Great Britain. 2. English fiction — 18th century — History and criticism. 3. English fiction — 19th century — History and criticism. I. T.
PR115.J6 1967   823/.009   LC 67-23235

Showalter, Elaine.   2.5565
A literature of their own: British women novelists from Brontë to Lessing / Elaine Showalter. Princeton, N.J.: Princeton University Press, c1977. viii, 378 p.; 23 cm. Includes index. 1. English fiction — Women authors — History and criticism. 2. English fiction — 19th century — History and criticism. 3. English fiction — 20th century — History and criticism. 4. Women novelists, English — Biography. I. T.
PR115.S5   823/.03   LC 76-3018   ISBN 0691063184

Spacks, Patricia Ann Meyer.   2.5566
The female imagination / Patricia Meyer Spacks. — 1st ed. — New York: Knopf: distributed by Random House, 1975. 326, xii p.; 25 cm. Includes index. 1. Women and literature — Great Britain. 2. Women and literature — United States. I. T.
PR115.S6 1975   820/.9/9287   LC 74-21320   ISBN 039449184X

Stebbins, Lucy Poate, b. 1886. • 2.5567
A Victorian album; some lady novelists of the period. — New York: AMS Press, 1966 [c1946] x, 226 p.; 21 cm. 1. Women novelists — England. 2. English fiction — 19th century — History and criticism. I. T.
PR115.S8 1966   823/.03   *LC 76-182716*

Contemporary women novelists: a collection of critical essays / 2.5568
edited by Patricia Meyer Spacks.
Englewood Cliffs, N.J.: Prentice-Hall, c1977. viii, 183 p.; 21 cm. — (Twentieth century views) (A Spectrum book) 1. English fiction — Women authors — History and criticism — Addresses, essays, lectures. 2. American fiction — Women authors — History and criticism — Addresses, essays, lectures. 3. English fiction — 20th century — History and criticism — Addresses, essays, lectures. 4. American fiction — 20th century — History and criticism — Addresses, essays, lectures. 5. Women in literature — Addresses, essays, lectures. I. Spacks, Patricia Ann Meyer.
PR116.C6   823/.03   *LC 77-4503   ISBN 0131713302*

PR125–138 RELATIONS TO OTHER LITERATURES AND COUNTRIES

Tillyard, E. M. W. (Eustace Mandeville Wetenhall), 1889-1962. • 2.5569
The English epic and its background. — New York: Barnes & Noble, [1966, c1954] x, 548 p.; 21 cm. 1. Epic literature 2. English literature — History and criticism 3. Literature, Comparative I. T.
PR125.T5x   809/.13   *LC 67-2855*

Thomson, J. A. K. (James Alexander Kerr), 1879-1959. • 2.5570
The classical background of English literature. London, G. Allen & Unwin [1948] 272 p. 21 cm. 1. Classical literature — History and criticism. 2. Literature, Comparative — Classical and English. 3. Literature, Comparative — English and classical. 4. English literature — Classical influences I. T.
PR127.T5   820.9   *LC 48-3720*

Thomson, J. A. K. (James Alexander Kerr), 1879-1959. • 2.5571
Classical influences on English prose. — London, Allen & Unwin [1956] 306 p. 21 cm. 1. English prose literature — Hist. & crit. 2. Literature, Comparative — English and classical. 3. Literature, Comparative — Classical and English. I. T.
PR127.T55   820.9   *LC 56-3219*

Lee, Sidney, Sir, 1859-1926. • 2.5572
The French Renaissance in England; an account of the literary relations of England and France in the sixteenth century. — New York: Octagon Books, 1968. xxiv, 494 p.; 24 cm. Reprint of the 1910 ed. 1. Literature, Comparative — English and French. 2. Literature, Comparative — French and English. 3. Renaissance — England. I. T.
PR129.F8 L4 1968   820.9/002   *LC 68-23977*

Starkie, Enid. • 2.5573
From Gautier to Eliot; the influence of France on English literature, 1851–1939. Hutchinson of London. — St. Clair Shores, Mich.: Scholarly Press, 1971. 236 p.; 22 cm. Reprint of the 1960 ed. 1. Literature, Comparative — French and English. 2. Literature, Comparative — English and French. I. T.
PR129.F8 S8 1971   820.9/008   *LC 73-158509   ISBN 0403013038*

Spencer, T. J. B. (Terence John Bew), 1915-1978. • 2.5574
Fair Greece! Sad relic: literary philhellenism from Shakespeare to Byron / [by] Terence Spencer. London, Weidenfeld & Nicolson. — St. Clair Shores, Mich.: Scholarly Press, 1971. xi, 312 p.; ill.; 22 cm. Reprint of the 1954 ed. 1. English literature — History and criticism 2. Greece in literature. 3. Philhellenism — Great Britain. 4. Great Britain — Relations — Greece 5. Greece — Relations — Great Britain I. T.
PR129.G8 S6 1971   820.9/32   *LC 76-158507   ISBN 0403013070*

Praz, Mario, 1896-. • 2.5575
The flaming heart; essays on Crashaw, Machiavelli, and other studies in the relations between Italian and English literature from Chaucer to T. S. Eliot. — Gloucester, Mass., P. Smith, 1966 [c1958] 390 p. 21 cm. Bibliographical footnotes. 1. Literature, Comparative — English and Italian. 2. Literature, Comparative — Italian and English. I. T.
PR129.I8P7 1966   820.9   *LC 66-3061*

Sells, A. Lytton (Arthur Lytton), 1895-. • 2.5576
The Italian influence in English poetry, from Chaucer to Southwell, by A. Lytton Sells. Westport, Conn., Greenwood Press [1971] 346 p. illus. Reprint of the 1955 ed. 1. Literature, Comparative — English and Italian. 2. Literature, Comparative — Italian and English. 3. English poetry — History and criticism I. T.
PR129.I8 S44 1971   *LC 76-136893   ISBN 0837153360*

PR140–151 TREATMENT OF SPECIAL SUBJECTS

Fairchild, Hoxie Neale, 1894-. • 2.5577
The noble savage; a study in romantic naturalism. — New York, Russell & Russell, 1961 [c1955] 535 p. 22 cm. 1. Indians 2. Romanticism — England. 3. English literature — 18th cent. — Hist. & crit. 4. English literature — 19th cent. — Hist. & crit. I. T.
PR146.F3 1961   820.93   *LC 61-12130*

Gleckner, Robert F. ed. • 2.5578
Romanticism; points of view. Edited by Robert F. Gleckner [and] Gerald E. Enscoe. — 2d ed. — Englewood Cliffs, N.J., Prentice-Hall [1970] vi, 346 p. 22 cm. — (Prentice-Hall English literature series) 1. Romanticism — England — Addresses, essays, lectures. 2. Romanticism — Addresses, essays, lectures. I. Enscoe, Gerald E. joint ed. II. T.
PR146.G5 1970   820/.9/14   *LC 77-97922   ISBN 0137829795*

Quilligan, Maureen, 1944-. 2.5579
The language of allegory: defining the genre / Maureen Quilligan. — Ithaca: Cornell University Press, 1979. 305 p.; 22 cm. Includes index. 1. English literature — History and criticism 2. Allegory 3. American literature — History and criticism I. T.
PR149.A635 Q5   820/.9/15   *LC 78-74216   ISBN 0801411858*

Boyce, Benjamin, 1903-. • 2.5580
The Theophrastan character in England to 1642, with the assistance of notes by Chester Noyes Greenough. New York: Humanities Press [1967] ix, 324 p.; 22 cm. 1. Theophrastus. Characters 2. Characters and characteristics in literature 3. English literature — Early modern, 1500-1700 — History and criticism. I. Greenough, Chester Noyes, 1874-1938. II. T.
PR149.C37 B6x   *LC 67-18820*

Schofield, William Henry, 1870-1920. • 2.5581
Chivalry in English literature: Chaucer, Malory, Spenser, and Shakespeare. — New York: AMS Press, [1970] x, 294 p.; 23 cm. Reprint of the 1912 ed. 1. Chivalry in literature 2. English literature — Early modern, 1500-1700 — History and criticism. I. T.
PR149.C5 S4 1970   820.9/353   *LC 72-137289   ISBN 0404056210*

Drabble, Margaret, 1939-. 2.5582
A writer's Britain: landscape in literature / Margaret Drabble; photographed by Jorge Lewinski. — 1st American ed. — New York: Knopf, 1979. 281, [7] p.: ill. (some col.); 26 cm. Includes index. 1. English literature — History and criticism 2. Nature in literature 3. England in literature. 4. Literary landmarks — England I. Lewinski, Jorge. II. T.
PR149.L35 D7 1979   820/.9/36   *LC 79-2117   ISBN 039450819X*

Empson, William, 1906-. • 2.5583
[Some versions of pastoral] English pastoral poetry. Freeport, N.Y., Books for Libraries Press [1972] 298 p. 23 cm. (Essay index reprint series) Reprint of the 1938 ed. 1935 ed. has title: Some versions of pastoral. 1. Pastoral literature, English — History and criticism. I. T.
PR149.P3 E6 1972   821/.00914   *LC 74-177956   ISBN 0836925467*

Rosenberg, Edgar. • 2.5584
From Shylock to Svengali; Jewish stereotypes in English fiction. Stanford, Calif., Stanford University Press, 1960. 388 p. illus. 23 cm. 1. Jews in literature 2. English fiction — 19th century — History and criticism. I. T.
PR151.J5R6   823.093   *LC 60-8560*

The Authority of experience: essays in feminist criticism / 2.5585
edited by Arlyn Diamond and Lee R. Edwards.
Amherst: University of Massachusetts Press, 1977. xiv, 304 p.; 24 cm. 1. Women in literature — Addresses, essays, lectures. 2. English literature — History and criticism — Addresses, essays, lectures. 3. American literature — History and criticism — Addresses, essays, lectures. 4. Feminist literary criticism — Addresses, essays, lectures. I. Diamond, Arlyn, 1941- II. Edwards, Lee R. III. Title: Feminist criticism.
PR151.W6 A9   801/.95   *LC 76-8755   ISBN 0870232207*

What manner of woman: essays on English and American life 2.5586
and literature / edited by Marlene Springer.
New York: New York University Press, 1977. xx, 357 p.; 24 cm. — (The Gotham library) 1. English literature — History and criticism — Addresses, essays, lectures. 2. American literature — History and criticism — Addresses, essays, lectures. 3. Women in literature — Addresses, essays, lectures. I. Springer, Marlene.
PR151.W6 W5   820/.93/52   *LC 77-8331   ISBN 0814777775*

PR161–479 LITERARY HISTORY, BY PERIOD

Steadman, John M. 2.5587
Nature into myth: medieval and Renaissance moral symbols / by John M. Steadman. — 1st ed. — Pittsburgh: Duquesne University Press; Atlantic Highlands, N.J.: distributed by Humanities Press, c1979. xii, 308 p.: ill.; 24 cm. — (Duquesne studies. Language and literature series. v. 1) 1. English literature — History and criticism — Addresses, essays, lectures. 2. Symbolism in literature — Addresses, essays, lectures. I. T. II. Title: Medieval and Renaissance moral symbols. III. Series.
PR161.S8   821/.009/15   *LC* 77-25397   *ISBN* 0391007521

PR166–236 Anglo–Saxon (to 1066)

Anderson, George Kumler, 1901-. • 2.5588
The literature of the Anglo–Saxons / by George K. Anderson. — New York: Russell & Russell, 1962, c1949. ix, 431 p.: maps. 1. English literature — Old English, ca. 450-1100 — History and criticism. I. T.
PR173.A5 1962   *LC* 61-13776   *ISBN* 0846201097

Greenfield, Stanley B. • 2.5589
A critical history of Old English literature, by Stanley B. Greenfield. — [New York]: New York University Press, 1965. xi, 237 p.: illus., facsims., maps (on lining papers); 22 cm. 1. English literature — Old English, ca. 450-1100 — History and criticism. I. T.
PR173.G7   829.09   *LC* 65-19516

Old English literature in context: ten essays / edited by John 2.5590
D. Niles.
Cambridge [Eng.]: D. S. Brewer; Totowa, N.J.: Rowman & Littlefield, 1980. 184 p.: facsims.; 24 cm. 1. English literature — Old English, ca. 450-1100 — History and criticism — Addresses, essays, lectures. I. Niles, John D.
PR181.O4 1980   829/.09   *LC* 79-41515   085991061X

Sources and analogues of old English poetry II: the major 2.5591
Germanic and Celtic texts in translation / translated by Daniel
G. Calder ... [et al].
Cambridge [Cambridgeshire]: D.S. Brewer; Totowa, NJ: Barnes and Noble, 1983. xxiv, 222 p.: maps; 23 cm. Includes index. 1. English poetry — Old English, ca. 450-1100 — History and criticism — Sources. 2. Germanic literature — Translations into English. 3. Celtic literature — Translations into English. 4. English literature — Translations from other languages. 5. Literature, Comparative — Themes, motives I. Calder, Daniel Gillmore.
PR182.S66 1983   829/.1/09 19   *LC* 83-12288   *ISBN* 038920434X

Gardner, John, 1933-. 2.5592
The construction of Christian poetry in Old English / by John Gardner. — Carbondale: Southern Illinois University Press, [1975] xii, 147 p.; 24 cm. (Literary structures) 1. English poetry — Old English, ca. 450-1100 — History and criticism. 2. Christian poetry, English (Old) — History and criticism. I. T.
PR201.G37   829/.1   *LC* 74-28475   *ISBN* 0809307057

Pearsall, Derek Albert. 2.5593
Old English and Middle English poetry / Derek Pearsall. — London; Boston: Routledge & K. Paul, 1977. xiv, 352 p.; 24 cm. — (The Routledge history of English poetry; v. 1) 1. Anglo-Saxon poetry — History and criticism. 2. English poetry — Middle English, 1100-1500 — History and criticism. I. T. II. Series.
PR502.R58 vol. 1 PR201 P4x   PR255 P4.   821/.009 s 821/.1/09
LC 77-357401   *ISBN* 0710083963

Opland, Jeff, 1943-. 2.5594
Anglo–Saxon oral poetry: a study of the traditions / Jeff Opland. — New Haven: Yale University Press, 1980. xi, 289 p.; 25 cm. Includes indexes. 1. English poetry — Old English, ca. 450-1100 — History and criticism. 2. Folk poetry, English (Old) — History and criticism. 3. Oral tradition — England. I. T.
PR203.O6   829/.1   *LC* 79-24202   *ISBN* 0300024266

Wilson, James H. (James Harrison), 1920-. 2.5595
Christian theology and old English poetry / by James H. Wilson. — The Hague: Mouton, 1974. 196 p.; 22 cm. (Studies in English literature; v. 71) Includes index. 1. English poetry — Old English, ca. 450-1100 — History and criticism. 2. Christianity and literature I. T.
PR203.W5   829/.1   *LC* 74-78921

Cherniss, Michael D. 2.5596
Ingeld and Christ. Heroic concepts and values in Old English Christian poetry. [By] Michael D. Cherniss. — The Hague: Mouton, 1972 [1973]. 267 p.; 21 cm. — (Studies in English literature, v. 74) 1. English poetry — Old English, ca. 450-1100 — History and criticism. I. T.
PR205.C5 1973   829/.1   *LC* 72-88189

The Old English homily and its backgrounds / edited with an 2.5598
introd. by Paul E. Szarmach & Bernard F. Huppé.
Albany: State University of New York Press, 1978. vi, 267 p.; 22 cm. 1. English prose literature — Old English, ca. 450-1100 — History and criticism. 2. Sermons, English (Old) — History and criticism. 3. Preaching — England — History — Middle Ages, 600-1500. I. Szarmach, Paul E. II. Huppé, Bernard Felix, 1911-
PR226.O4   829   *LC* 77-21447   *ISBN* 0873953762

PR251–369 Medieval. Middle English (1066–1500)

Ackerman, Robert William, 1910-. • 2.5599
Backgrounds to medieval English literature [by] Robert W. Ackerman. New York, Random House [c1966] xviii, 171 p. 19 cm. (A Random House study in language and literature, SLL7) 1. English literature — Middle English, 1100-1500 — History and criticism. I. T.
PR255.A3   820.9/001   *LC* 66-26070

Bennett, H. S. (Henry Stanley), 1889-. • 2.5600
Chaucer and the fifteenth century. — Oxford: Clarendon Press, 1947. vi, 326 p.; 23 cm. — (Oxford history of English literature, v. 2, pt. 1) 1. Chaucer, Geoffrey, d. 1400. 2. English literature — Middle English, 1100-1500 — History and criticism. I. T. II. Series.
PR255.B43   821.17   *LC* 48-4950

Bennett, J. A. W. (Jack Arthur Walter) 2.5601
Middle English literature / J.A.W. Bennett; edited and completed by Douglas Gray. — Oxford: Clarendon Press; New York: Oxford University Press, 1986. xi, 496 p. — (The Oxford history of English literature) Includes index. 1. English literature — Middle English, 1100-1500 — History and criticism. I. Gray, Douglas. II. T. III. Series.
PR255.B45 1986   820/.9/001 19   *LC* 86-8741   *ISBN* 0198122144

Burrow, J. A. (John Anthony) 2.5602
Medieval writers and their work: Middle English literature and its background 1100–1500 / J.A. Burrow. — Oxford [Oxfordshire]; New York: Oxford University Press, 1982. 148 p.; 19 cm. — (OPUS) Includes index. 1. English literature — Middle English, 1100-1500 — History and criticism. I. T. II. Series.
PR255.B8 1982   820/.9/001 19   *LC* 81-16967   *ISBN* 0192191357

Everett, Dorothy, 1894-1953. • 2.5603
Essays on Middle English literature. Edited by Patricia Kean. — Oxford, Clarendon Press, 1955. xi, 179 p. 23 cm. 'Bibliography of writings by Dorothy Everett': p. [175]-176. 1. English literature — Middle English (1100-1500) — Addresses, essays, lectures. 2. Chaucer, Geoffrey — Criticism and interpretation. I. T.
PR255.E9   *LC* 55-14701

Kane, George. • 2.5604
Middle English literature; a critical study of the romances, the religious lyrics, Piers Plowman. London Methuen [1951] 252p. (Methuen's Old English library) 1. English literature — Middle English (1100-1500) — History and criticism I. T.
PR255 K3

Ker, W. P. (William Paton), 1855-1923. • 2.5605
[English literature; medieval] Medieval English literature [by] W. P. Kerr. [1st ed. reissued with bibliographical notes by Pamela Gradon.] London, New York, Oxford U.P., 1969. 143 p. 21 cm. (Oxford paperbacks university series, 43) First published in 1912 under title: English literature; medieval. 1. English literature — Old English, ca. 450-1100 — History and criticism. 2. English literature — Middle English, 1100-1500 — History and criticism. I. T.
PR255.K4 1969   820.9/001   *LC* 70-497374   *ISBN* 019888043X

Middle English prose: a critical guide to major authors and 2.5606
genres / edited by A.S.G. Edwards.
New Brunswick, N.J.: Rutgers University Press, c1984. xi, 452 p.; 24 cm. 1. English prose literature — Middle English, 1100-1500 — History and criticism. 2. English prose literature — Middle English, 1100-1500 — Bibliography. 3. English prose literature — Middle English, 1100-1500 — Manuscripts — Catalogs. 4. Manuscripts, English (Middle) — Catalogs. I. Edwards, A. S. G. (Anthony Stockwell Garfield), 1942-
PR255.M52 1984   828/.108/09 19   *LC* 83-2914   *ISBN* 0813510015

Wells, John Edwin, 1875-1943. • 2.5607
A manual of the writings in Middle English, 1050–1400 / by John Edwin Wells. — New Haven: Yale University Press; London: H. Milford, Oxford University Press, 1916. xv, 941 p. 'Published under the auspices of the Connecticut Academy of Arts and Sciences.' 1. English literature — Middle English, 1100-1500 — History and criticism. 2. English literature — Middle English,

1100-1500 — Bibliography. I. Connecticut Academy of Arts and Sciences. II. T.
PR255.W4   *LC* 16-12265

Fowler, David C., 1921-.   **2.5608**
The Bible in Middle English literature / by David C. Fowler. — Seattle: University of Washington Press, c1984. xiii, 326 p.: ill.; 24 cm. Includes index. 1. Bible — Influence — History. 2. English literature — Middle English, 1100-1500 — History and criticism. 3. Bible in literature 4. Christianity in literature I. T.
PR275.B5 F68 1984   820/.9/001 19   *LC* 84-7453   *ISBN* 0295954388

Coleman, Janet.   **2.5609**
Medieval readers and writers, 1350–1400 / Janet Coleman. — New York: Columbia University Press, 1981. 337 p.; 23 cm. 1. English literature — Middle English, 1100-1500 — History and criticism. 2. Didactic literature, English — History and criticism. 3. Middle classes — England — Books and reading. 4. England — Intellectual life — Medieval period, 1066-1485 5. Great Britain — History — 14th century I. T.
PR275.D53 C6 1981   820/.9/001 19   *LC* 81-10023   *ISBN* 0231053649

Benson, C. David.   **2.5610**
The history of Troy in Middle English literature: Guido delle Colonne's Historia Destructionis Troiae in medieval England / C. David Benson. — Woodbridge [Eng.]: D. S. Brewer; [Totawa, N.J.]: Rowman & Littlefield, 1980. 174 p.; 24 cm. 1. Colonne, Guido delle, 13th century. Historia trojana. 2. English literature — Middle English, 1100-1500 — History and criticism. 3. Troy — Legends — History and criticism. I. T.
PR275.T74 B46 1980   820/.9/358 19   *LC* 80-497628   *ISBN* 0859910598

Chambers, E. K. (Edmund Kerchever), 1866-1954.   • **2.5611**
English literature at the close of the middle ages / by E. K. Chambers. — With corrections. — Oxford, Eng.: Clarendon Press, [1947] 247 p.; 23 cm. — (The Oxford history of English literature; v. 2, pt. 2.) Includes index. 1. English literature — Middle English, 1100-1500 — History & criticism 2. English literature — Middle English, 1100-1500 — Bibliography. I. T. II. Series.
PR291.C5 1947   PR83.O9 v.2 pt.2.   820.902   *LC* 48-11011

Aers, David.   **2.5612**
Chaucer, Langland, and the creative imagination / David Aers. — London; Boston: Routledge & Kegan Paul, 1980. xii, 236 p.; 23 cm. 1. Chaucer, Geoffrey, d. 1400 — Criticism and interpretation. 2. Langland, William, 1330?-1400? Piers the Plowman 3. English poetry — Middle English, 1100-1500 — History and criticism. I. T.
PR311.A33   821/.1/09   *LC* 79-41239   *ISBN* 071000351X

Burrow, J. A. (John Anthony)   **2.5613**
Ricardian poetry: Chaucer, Gower, Langland, and the Gawain poet / J. A. Burrow. — New Haven: Yale University Press, 1971. x, 165 p., [1] leaf of plates: ill.; 23 cm. 1. English poetry — Middle English, 1100-1500 — History and criticism. 2. Great Britain — History — Richard II, 1377-1399 I. T.
PR311.B8 1971b   821/.1/09   *LC* 71-158136   *ISBN* 0300014929

Spearing, A. C.   **2.5614**
Criticism and medieval poetry [by] A. C. Spearing. — 2d ed. — New York: Barnes & Noble, [1972] vii, 198 p.; 21 cm. 1. English poetry — Middle English, 1100-1500 — History and criticism. I. T.
PR311.S68 1972   821/.1/0923   *LC* 72-169636   *ISBN* 0064964418

Speirs, John.   • **2.5615**
Medieval English poetry: the non–Chaucerian tradition. — London, Faber and Faber [1957] 406 p. 23 cm. 1. English poetry — Middle English (1100-1500) — Hist. & crit. I. T.
PR311.S7 1957   821.109   *LC* 57-59137

Muscatine, Charles.   **2.5616**
Poetry and crisis in the age of Chaucer. — Notre Dame, University of Notre Dame Press [1972] vii, 168 p. 22 cm. — (Ward-Phillips lectures in English language and literature. v. 4) 1. English poetry — Middle English (1100-1500) — Addresses, essays, lectures. I. T. II. Series.
PR313.M8   821/.1/09   *LC* 78-185409

Spearing, A. C.   **2.5617**
Medieval dream–poetry / A. C. Spearing. — Cambridge; New York: Syndics of the Cambridge University Press, 1976. vii, 236 p. Includes index. 1. English poetry — Middle English, 1100-1500 — History and criticism. 2. Dreams in literature I. T.
PR317.D7 S6   PR317D7 S6.   821/.1/09353   *LC* 75-46114
    ISBN 0521211948

Tuve, Rosemond, 1903-1964.   **2.5618**
Seasons and months; studies in a tradition of Middle English poetry. — [Cambridge, Eng.]: D. S. Brewer; [Totowa, N.J.]: Rowman and Littlefield,

[1975] 232 p.; 23 cm. Reprint of the 1933 ed. published by Librairie universitaire, Paris. Originally presented as the author's thesis, Bryn Mawr College, 1931. 1. English poetry — Middle English (1100-1500) — History and criticism. 2. Seasons in literature I. T.
PR317.S4 T8 1974   821/.009/33   *LC* 74-4052   *ISBN* 0874715407

Loomis, Laura Alandis (Hibbard) 1883-1960.   • **2.5619**
Mediaeval romance in England; a study of the sources and analogues of the non–cyclic metrical romances, by Laura A. Hibbard (Mrs. Laura Hibbard Loomis) New ed., with supplementary bibliographical index (1926-1959) [New York] B. Franklin [1969] viii, 350 p. 24 cm. (Burt Franklin research & source works series 17. Essays in literature & criticism, 36) Reprint of the 1960 ed. 1. Romances, English — History and criticism. I. T.
PR321.L6 1969   821/.1/09   *LC* 78-96857

Ramsey, Lee C., 1935-.   **2.5620**
Chivalric romances: popular literature in medieval England / Lee C. Ramsey. — Bloomington: Indiana University Press, c1983. 245 p.; 24 cm. 1. Romances, English — History and criticism. 2. English poetry — Middle English, 1100-1500 — History and criticism. 3. Chivalry in literature 4. Popular literature — England — History and criticism. I. T.
PR321.R35 1983   821/.1/09 19   *LC* 83-47659   *ISBN* 0253313600

Reiss, Edmund.   **2.5621**
The art of the Middle English lyric; essays in criticism. — Athens, University of Georgia Press [1972] xix, 173 p. 25 cm. 1. English poetry — Middle English (1100-1500) — Addresses, essays, lectures. I. T.
PR353.R4   821/.04   *LC* 74-169948   *ISBN* 0820302791

PR401 Modern (1500–

The Explicator.   **2.5622**
The Explicator cyclopedia / edited by Charles Child Walcutt and J. Edwin Whitesell. Chicago: Quadrangle Books, 1966-. 9 v. 1. English literature — Dictionaries. 2. American literature — History and criticism — Dictionaries. I. Walcutt, Charles Child, 1908- II. Whitesell, J. Edwin. III. T.
PR401.E9   PR401.E92.   *LC* 66-11875

Wellek, René, 1903-.   • **2.5623**
The rise of English literary history / by René Wellek. — Chapel Hill: The University of North Carolina Press, 1941. vii, 275 p.; 24 cm. Includes index. 1. English literature — Early modern, 1500-1700 — History and criticism. 2. English literature — 18th century — History and criticism. I. T.
PR401.W4   *LC* 41-10634

Berryman, John, 1914-1972.   **2.5624**
The freedom of the poet / John Berryman. — New York: Farrar, Straus & Giroux, c1976. x, 389 p.; 24 cm. 1. English literature — History and criticism — Addresses, essays, lectures. 2. American literature — History and criticism — Addresses, essays, lectures. I. T.
PR403.B4 1976   820/.9   *LC* 75-45162   *ISBN* 0374158487

McKillop, Alan Dugald, 1892-.   • **2.5625**
English literature from Dryden to Burns. — New York: Appleton-Century-Crofts, [1948] xii, 445 p.: illus., ports., maps (on lining-paper); 19 cm. — (Appleton-Century handbooks of literature) 1. English literature — Early modern, 1500-1700 — History and criticism. 2. English literature — 18th century — History and criticism. I. T. II. Series.
PR404.M3   820.9   *LC* 48-3527

Punter, David.   **2.5626**
The literature of terror: a history of Gothic fictions from 1765 to the present day / David Punter. — London; New York: Longmans, 1980. 449 p.; 23 cm. Includes index. 1. English literature — History and criticism 2. Gothic revival (Literature) 3. American literature — History and criticism I. T.
PR408.G68 P8 1980   823/.087209 19   *LC* 79-40934   *ISBN* 0582489210

Edel, Leon, 1907-.   **2.5627**
Stuff of sleep and dreams: experiments in literary psychology / Leon Edel. — 1st ed. — New York: Harper & Row, c1982. xi, 352 p.; 22 cm. 1. English literature — Psychological aspects 2. Authors, English — Psychology 3. American literature — History and criticism 4. Authors, American — Psychology. 5. Psychology and literature I. T.
PR408.P83 E3 1982   820/.9/353 19   *LC* 81-47787   *ISBN* 0060149299

Williams, Raymond.   **2.5628**
The country and the city. — New York: Oxford University Press, 1973. 335 p.; 23 cm. 1. English literature — History and criticism 2. City and town life in literature I. T.
PR409.C5 W5   820/.9/32   *LC* 72-98128   *ISBN* 0195197364

Hagstrum, Jean H. 2.5629
Sex and sensibility: ideal and erotic love from Milton to Mozart / Jean H. Hagstrum. — Chicago: University of Chicago Press, 1980. xiv, 350 p., [12] leaves of plates: ill.; 25 cm. 1. English literature — History and criticism 2. Love in literature 3. European literature — History and criticism. 4. Love in art 5. Arts I. T.
PR409.L67 H3   809/.933/54   LC 79-20657   ISBN 0226312895

PR411-429 16TH CENTURY. ELIZABETHAN ERA (1550-1640)

Lewis, C. S. (Clive Staples), 1898-1963. • 2.5630
English literature in the sixteenth century, excluding drama. — Oxford, Clarendon Press, 1954. vi, 696 p. 23 cm. — (The Clark lectures, Trinity College, Cambridge, 1944) The Oxford history of English literature, v. 3. Bibliography: p. [594]-685. 1. English literature — Early modern (to 1700) — Hist. & crit. I. T.
PR411.L4   820.903   LC 54-4883

Lyons, Bridget Gellert. 2.5631
Voices of melancholy; studies in literary treatments of melancholy in Renaissance England. — New York: Barnes & Noble, [1971] xvii, 189 p.: illus., facsim.; 23 cm. 1. English literature — Early modern, 1500-1700 — History and criticism. 2. Melancholy in literature I. T.
PR411.L9   820.9/353   LC 74-28481   ISBN 0389041688

Roston, Murray. 2.5632
Sixteenth-century English literature / Murray Roston. — 1st Amer. ed. — New York: Schocken Books, 1982. vi, 235 p., [12] p. of plates: ill.; 23 cm. — (History of literature series.) Includes index. 1. English literature — Early modern, 1500-1700 — History and criticism. I. T. II. Series.
PR411.R67 1982   820/.9/003 19   LC 82-5752   ISBN 0805238255

Campbell, Lily Bess, 1883-1967. • 2.5633
Divine poetry and drama in sixteenth-century England. — New York: Gordian Press, 1972. vii, 267 p.; 23 cm. Reprint of the 1959 ed. 1. English literature — Early modern, 1500 to 1700 — History and criticism. 2. Christian literature, English — History and criticism. I. T.
PR419.R4 C3 1972   820/.9/003   LC 79-148614   ISBN 0877521433

Craig, Hardin, 1875-1968. • 2.5634
The enchanted glass: the Elizabethan mind in literature. — Oxford: Blackwell, 1950. ix, 293 p.; 21 cm. Bibliography: p. 265-288. 1. English literature — Early modern (to 1700) — Hist. & crit. 2. Literature — Philosophy 3. Gt. Brit. — Intellectual life. 4. Renaissance — England. I. T. II. Title: The Elizabethan mind in literature.
PR421.C67 1950   820.903   LC 51-12021

Wilson, F. P. (Frank Percy), 1889-1963. • 2.5635
Elizabethan and Jacobean, by F. P. Wilson. Oxford, The Clarendon press, 1945. vi p., 1 l., 144 p. 20 cm. 'These lectures, the Alexander lectures in English, were delivered in University college, the University of Toronto, in November 1943.'—Pref. L.C. copy: First edition 1945. Reprinted 1946. 1. English literature — Early modern (to 1700) — History and criticism. I. T.
PR421.W5   820.903   LC a 46-3345

Wright, Louis B. (Louis Booker), 1899-. • 2.5636
Middle-class culture in Elizabethan England / by Louis B. Wright. — Ithaca, N.Y.: Published for the Folger Shakespeare Library by Cornell University Press, 1958. x, 733 p.; 24 cm. — (Folger Shakespeare Library publications) 1. English literature — Early modern, 1500-1700 — History and criticism. 2. Renaissance — England. 3. Middle classes — Great Britain. 4. England — Civilization — History. 5. Great Britain — Intellectual life I. T.
PR421.W95   PR421.W7 1958.

Bradbrook, M. C. (Muriel Clara), 1909-. 2.5637
The Artist and society in Shakespeare's England / M.C. Bradbrook. — Brighton, Sussex: Harvester Press; Totowa, N.J.: Barnes & Noble Books, c1982. x, 176 p.; 23 cm. — (The Collected papers of Muriel Bradbrook; v. 1) 1. Shakespeare, William, 1564-1616 — Criticism and interpretation — Addresses, essays, lectures. 2. English literature — Early modern, 1500-1700 — History and criticism — Addresses, essays, lectures. 3. Literature and society — Addresses, essays, lectures. I. T.
PR423.B7 1982   820/.9/003 19   LC 82-6645   ISBN 0389202940

Muir, Kenneth. • 2.5638
Introduction to Elizabethan literature. — New York: Random House, [1967] 207 p.; 19 cm. — (Studies in language and literature, SLL15) 1. English literature — Early modern, 1500-1700 — History and criticism. I. T. II. Title: Elizabethan literature.
PR424.M8   820.9/003   LC 67-20626

Anderson, Judith H. 2.5639
Biographical truth: the representation of historical persons in Tudor-Stuart writing / Judith H. Anderson. — New Haven: Yale University Press, c1984. ix,

243 p.; 25 cm. 1. English literature — Early modern, 1500-1700 — History and criticism. 2. Biography (as a literary form) I. T.
PR428.B55 A52 1984   820/.9/351 19   LC 83-14520   ISBN 0300030851

Tillyard, E. M. W. (Eustace Mandeville Wetenhall), 1889-1962. • 2.5640
The Elizabethan world picture, by E. M. W. Tillyard. New York, The Macmillan company, 1944. vii, [1], 108 p. 22 cm. 'First printing.' 1. English literature — Early modern (to 1700) — History and criticism. 2. Cosmology 3. Religious thought — 16th century 4. Philosophy — England — History. I. T.
PR428.P5 T5 1944   820.903   LC 44-2030

Matthiessen, F. O. (Francis Otto), 1902-1950. • 2.5641
Translation: an Elizabethan art. New York: Octagon Books, 1965. 232 p. 1. English literature — Translations from foreign literature — History & criticism. 2. English literature — Early modern (To 1700) — History & criticism. 3. Literature, Comparative 4. Translating and interpreting I. T.
PR428.T7 M3 1965   LC 65-16777

Woodbridge, Linda, 1945-. 2.5642
Women and the English Renaissance: literature and the nature of womankind, 1540 to 1620 / Linda Woodbridge. — Urbana: University of Illinois Press, c1984. 364 p.; 24 cm. Includes index. 1. English literature — Early modern, 1500-1700 — History and criticism. 2. Women in literature 3. Women — Great Britain — History — Renaissance, 1450-1600. I. T.
PR429.W64 W66 1984   820/.9/352042 19   LC 82-24792   ISBN 0252010272

PR431-439 17TH CENTURY

The Age of Milton: backgrounds to seventeenth-century 2.5643
literature / C. A. Patrides, Raymond B. Waddington, eds.
Manchester [Eng.]: Manchester University Press; Totowa, N.J.: Barnes and Noble, 1980. x, 438 p., [4] leaves of plates: ill.; 24 cm. 1. Milton, John, 1608-1674 — Contemporary England. 2. English literature — Early modern, 1500-1700 — History and criticism. 3. Great Britain — Intellectual life — 17th century I. Patrides, C. A. II. Waddington, Raymond B.
PR431.A37 1980   820/.9/003 19   LC 80-511211   ISBN 0389200514

Bush, Douglas, 1896-. • 2.5644
English literature in the earlier seventeenth century, 1600-1660. — 2d ed., rev. — Oxford: Clarendon Press, 1962. viii, 680 p.; 23 cm. — (Oxford history of English literature, 5) 1. English literature — Early modern (to 1700) — History and criticism. 2. English literature — Early modern (to 1700) — Bibliography. I. T. II. Series.
PR431.B8 1962   820.903   LC 62-51930

Grierson, Herbert John Clifford, Sir, 1866-1960. • 2.5645
Cross-currents in 17th century English literature: the world, the flesh, and the spirit, their actions and reactions. Gloucester, Mass., P. Smith, 1965 [c1958] 345 p. 21 cm. First published in 1929 under title: Cross currents in English literature of the XVIIth century. 1. English literature — Early modern, 1500-1700 — History and criticism. 2. Religion in literature 3. Great Britain — Intellectual life I. Grierson, Herbert John Clifford, Sir, 1866-1960. Cross currents in English literature of the XVIIth century. II. T. III. Title: Cross currents in English literature of the XVIIth century.
PR431.G7 1965   LC 66-401

King, Bruce Alvin. 2.5646
Seventeenth-century English literature / Bruce King. — 1st Amer. ed. — New York: Schocken Books, 1982. 295 p., [16] p. of plates: ill.; 23 cm. — (History of literature series.) Includes index. 1. English literature — Early modern, 1500-1700 — History and criticism. I. T. II. Series.
PR431.K48 1982   820/.9/004 19   LC 82-5750   ISBN 0805238263

Wedgwood, C. V. (Cicely Veronica), 1910-. • 2.5647
Seventeenth-century English literature, [by] C. V. Wedgwood. 2nd ed. London, New York, Oxford U.P., 1970. [7], 148 p. 21 cm. (Opus, 50) 1. English literature — Early modern, 1500-1700 — History and criticism. I. T.
PR431.W4 1970   820.9/004   LC 73-22016   ISBN 0198880502

Coleridge, Samuel Taylor, 1772-1834. • 2.5648
Coleridge on the seventeenth century. Edited by Roberta Florence Brinkley. Introd. by Louis I. Bredvold. — New York: Greenwood Press, 1968 [c1955] xxxviii, 704 p.; 24 cm. 1. English literature — Early modern, 1500-1700 — History and criticism. 2. Seventeenth century I. Brinkley, Roberta Florence. ed. II. T.
PR433.C6 1968   820.9/003   LC 69-10076

Knights, L. C. (Lionel Charles), 1906-. • 2.5649
Explorations; essays in criticism, mainly on the literature of the seventeenth century, by L. C. Knights. [New York] New York University Press, 1964 [c1955] 219 p. 21 cm. Bibliographical footnotes. 1. English literature — Early

modern (to 1700) — Addresses, essays, lectures. 2. English literature — Addresses, essays, lectures. I. T.
PR433.K5 1964   820.9   *LC* 64-22260

Jose, Nicholas, 1952-.   2.5650
Ideas of the Restoration in English literature, 1660–71 / Nicholas Jose. — Cambridge, Mass.: Harvard University Press, 1984. xvi, 205 p.; 23 cm. 1. English literature — Early modern, 1500-1700 — History and criticism. 2. Politics and literature — Great Britain. 3. Great Britain — History — Restoration, 1660-1688 I. T.
PR437.J67 1984   820/.9/004 19   *LC* 82-21292   *ISBN* 0674442768

Love, Harold, 1937-.   2.5651
Restoration literature; critical approaches; edited by Harold Love. — London: Methuen, [1972] xii, 322 p.; 22 cm. Distributed in the U.S.A. by Harper & Row Publishers Inc.; Barnes & Noble Import Division. 1. English literature — Early modern, 1500-1700 — Addresses, essays, lectures. I. T.
PR437.L65   820/.9/004   *LC* 72-93483   *ISBN* 0416662404

Sutherland, James Runcieman, 1900-.   • 2.5652
English literature of the late seventeenth century, by James Sutherland. — Oxford: Clarendon P., 1969. ix, 589 p.; 23 cm. — (The Oxford history of English literature, 6) 1. English literature — Early modern, 1500-1700 — History and criticism. 2. English literature — Early modern, 1500-1700 — Bibliography. I. T. II. Series.
PR437.S9 1969   820.9/004   *LC* 79-391852   *ISBN* 0198122101

Swedenberg, H. T. (Hugh Thomas), 1906-1978. comp.   • 2.5653
England in the Restoration and early eighteenth century; essays on culture and society. Edited by H. T. Swedenberg, Jr. Berkeley, University of California Press, 1972. xi, 231 p. illus. 25 cm. (Publications from the 17th and 18th Centuries Studies group, UCLA, 2) ([Publications from the Clark Library professorship, UCLA; 3]) 1. English literature — Early modern, 1500-1700 — Addresses, essays, lectures. 2. English literature — 18th century — Addresses, essays, lectures. 3. England — Intellectual life — Addresses, essays, lectures. I. T.
PR437.S94   820/.9/004   *LC* 72-149943   *ISBN* 0520019733

Trickett, Rachel, 1923-.   2.5654
The honest muse: a study in Augustan verse. — Oxford: Clarendon P., 1967. ix, 309 p.; 22 1/2 cm. 1. English poetry — Early modern, 1500-1700 — History and criticism. 2. English poetry — 18th century — History and criticism. I. T.
PR437.T7   *LC* 67-94468

Wilson, John Harold, 1900-.   • 2.5655
The court wits of the Restoration: an introduction. New York: Octagon Books, 1967 [c1948] vi, 264 p.: ports.; 21 cm. 1. English literature — Early modern (to 1700) — History& criticism. 2. English wit and humor — History & criticism. I. T.
PR437.W54 1967   *LC* 67-18791

PR441–449 18TH CENTURY

Beljame, Alexandre, 1843?-1906.   • 2.5656
[Public et les hommes de lettres en Angleterre. English] Men of letters and the English public in the eighteenth century, 1660–1744, Dryden, Addison, Pope / edited, with an introd. and notes by Bonamy Dobrée; translated by E. O. Lorimer. London, K. Paul, Trench, Trubner. St. Clair Shores, Mich., Scholarly Press, 1971. xxiv, 492 p. 22 cm. (International library of sociology and social reconstruction) Translation of Le public et les hommes de lettres en Angleterre au dix-huitième siècle, 1660-1744. 1. English literature — 18th century — History and criticism. 2. English literature — Social aspects 3. Great Britain — Civilization — 18th century I. T.
PR441.B37 1971   820.9/004   *LC* 71-159815   *ISBN* 0403013101

Butt, John Everett.   2.5657
The mid–eighteenth century / by John Butt; edited and completed by Geoffrey Carnall. — Oxford: Clarendon Press, 1979. vii, 671 p.; 23 cm. — (The Oxford history of English literature; v. 8) Spine title: English literature in the mid-eighteenth century. Includes index. 1. English literature — 18th century — History and criticism I. Carnall, Geoffrey. II. T. III. Title: English literature in the mid-eighteenth century. IV. Series.
PR441.B83   820/.9/006   *LC* 78-40253   *ISBN* 0198122128

The Eighteenth century / edited by Pat Rogers.   2.5658
New York: Holmes & Meier Publishers, 1978. xvi, 246 p., [8] leaves of plates: ill.; 22 cm. — (Context of English literature.) 1. English literature — 18th century — History and criticism. 2. Great Britain — Civilization — 18th century I. Rogers, Pat. II. Series.
PR441.E47 1978   820/.9   *LC* 78-15568   *ISBN* 0841904219

Novak, Maximillian E.   2.5659
Eighteenth–century English literature / Maximillian E. Novak. — 1st American ed. — New York: Schocken Books, 1984, c1983. ix, 227 p., [16] p. of

plates: ill.; 23 cm. — (History of literature series.) Includes index. 1. English literature — 18th century — History and criticism. I. T. II. Series.
PR441.N64 1984   820/.9/005 19   *LC* 83-16305   *ISBN* 0805238824

Addison and Steele, the critical heritage / edited by Edward A.   2.5660
Bloom and Lillian D. Bloom.
London; Boston: Routledge & K. Paul, 1980. xii, 480 p.; 23 cm. — (Critical heritage series) Includes index. 1. Addison, Joseph, 1672-1719 — Addresses, essays, lectures. 2. Steele, Richard, Sir, 1672-1729 — Addresses, essays, lectures. 3. English literature — 18th century — History and criticism — Addresses, essays, lectures. 4. Authors, English — 18th century — Biography — Addresses, essays, lectures. I. Bloom, Edward Alan, 1914- II. Bloom, Lillian D.
PR442.A3   824/.5/09 19   *LC* 80-40048   *ISBN* 0710003757

The Augustan milieu: essays presented to Louis A. Landa: 2.5661
edited by Henry Knight Miller, Eric Rothstein [and] G. S.
Rousseau.
Oxford, Clarendon P., 1970. viii, 359 p., plate. port. 23 cm. 1. English literature — 18th century — Addresses, essays, lectures. I. Landa, Louis A., 1901- II. Miller, Henry Knight, 1920- ed. III. Rothstein, Eric. ed. IV. Rousseau, G. S. (George Sebastian) ed.
PR442.A9   820.9/005   *LC* 70-20124   *ISBN* 0198116977

Augustan worlds / edited by J. C. Hilson, M. M. B. Jones and   2.5662
J. R. Watson.
[Leicester, Eng.]: Leicester University Press; [New York]: Harper and Row, 1978. 311 p.; 24 cm. Essays in honour of A. R. Humphreys. 'A.R. Humphreys: a check-list of his published work to 1976, compiled by J.C. Hilson': p. [299]-305. 1. Humphreys, A. R. (Arthur Raleigh), 1911- 2. English literature — 18th century — History and criticism — Addresses, essays, lectures. I. Hilson, J. C. II. Jones, M. Monica B. III. Watson, J. R. (John Richard), 1934- IV. Humphreys, A. R. (Arthur Raleigh), 1911-
PR442.A92 1978   820/.9/05   *LC* 78-313943   *ISBN* 071851159X

Champion, Larry S.   2.5663
Quick springs of sense; studies in the eighteenth century, edited by Larry S. Champion. — Athens: University of Georgia Press, [1974] viii, 254 p.; 25 cm. 1. English literature — 18th century — Addresses, essays, lectures. I. T.
PR442.C47   820/.9/005   *LC* 72-86783   *ISBN* 0820303135

Clifford, James Lowry, 1901-.   • 2.5664
Eighteenth–century English literature; modern essays in criticism. — New York: Oxford University Press, 1959. 351 p.; 21 cm. — (A Galaxy book, GB23) 1. English literature — 18th century — Addresses, essays, lectures. I. T.
PR442.C58   820.903   *LC* 59-5739

Clifford, James Lowry, 1901- ed.   • 2.5665
Pope and his contemporaries, essays presented to George Sherburn. Edited by James L. Clifford and Louis A. Landa. — Oxford, Clarendon Press, 1949. viii, 278 p. port. 23 cm. 'A list of the writings of George Sherburn': p. [260]-262. 1. Sherburn, George Wiley, 1884- 2. English literature — 18th cent. — Hist. & crit. I. Landa, Louis A., 1902- joint editor. II. T.
PR442.C6   820.4   *LC* 50-2790

David Nichol Smith Memorial Seminar. 4th, Canberra, 1976.   2.5666
Studies in the eighteenth century, IV: papers presented at the Fourth David Nichol Smith Memorial Seminar, Canberra, 1976 / edited by R. F. Brissenden and J. C. Eade. — Toronto: University of Toronto Press, 1979. x, 287 p., [4] leaves of plates: ill.; 23 cm. 1. English literature — 18th century 2. Civilization, Modern — 18th century — Congresses. I. Brissenden, R. F. II. Eade, J. C. (John Christopher) III. T.
PR442.D3   820/.9/005   *LC* 78-67481   *ISBN* 0708110665

David Nichol Smith Memorial Seminar. Canberra, 1966.   2.5667
Studies in the eighteenth century; papers presented at the David Nichol Smith Memorial Seminar, Canberra, 1966, edited by R. F. Brissenden. Canberra, Australian National University Press, 1968. xviii, 327 p. illus. 23 cm. Held at the Australian National University, 15-19 August 1966. 1. Smith, David Nichol, 1875-1962. 2. English literature — 18th century — Addresses, essays, lectures. I. Brissenden, R. F. ed. II. Australian National University. III. T.
PR442.D3 1966   820.9/005   *LC* 68-18428   *ISBN* 0708100694

David Nichol Smith Memorial Seminar. 2nd, Canberra, 1970.   2.5668
Studies in the eighteenth century; II. Papers presented at the second David Nichol Smith Memorial Seminar, Canberra, 1970. Edited by R. F. Brissenden. — Canberra: Australian National University Press, 1973. xiii, 419 p.: illus.; 23 cm. Held 23-29 August, 1970. Index. 1. English literature — 18th century — History and criticism — Congresses. 2. Eighteenth century — Congresses. I. Brissenden, R. F. II. T.
PR442.D3 1970   901.9/33   *LC* 73-177412   *ISBN* 0708100929

David Nichol Smith Memorial Seminar. 3d, Canberra, 1973.   2.5669
Studies in the eighteenth century, III: papers presented at the Third David Nichol Smith Memorial Seminar, Canberra, 1973 / edited by R. F. Brissenden and J. C. Eade. — Toronto; Buffalo: University of Toronto Press, 1976. xi,

262 p., [8] leaves of plates: ill.; 23 cm. English or French. Held 23-29 August, 1973. 1. English literature — 18th century — History and criticism — Addresses, essays, lectures. 2. Eighteenth century — Addresses, essays, lectures. I. Brissenden, R. F. II. Eade, J. C. (John Christopher) III. T.
PR442.D3 1973   809/.03/3   *LC* 76-364910   *ISBN* 0802022057

Ehrenpreis, Irvin, 1920-.   **2.5670**
Acts of implication: suggestion and covert meaning in the works of Dryden, Swift, Pope, and Austen / Irvin Ehrenpreis. — Berkeley: University of California Press, c1980. x, 158 p.; 23 cm. — (Beckman lectures. 1978) 1. English literature — 18th century — History and criticism — Addresses, essays, lectures. I. T. II. Series.
PR442.E38 1980   820/.9/006 19   *LC* 80-53161   *ISBN* 0520040473

Probability, time, and space in eighteenth–century literature /   **2.5671**
edited by Paula R. Backscheider.
New York: AMS Press, c1979. xv, 307 p.: ill.; 23 cm. Papers, most of them revised, of the 1973-76 sessions of a Modern Language Association group. 1. English literature — 18th century — History and criticism — Addresses, essays, lectures. 2. Philosophy, Modern — 18th century — Addresses, essays, lectures. 3. Literature and science — Addresses, essays, lectures. I. Backscheider, Paula. II. Modern Language Association of America.
PR442.P68   820/.9/005   *LC* 78-20850   *ISBN* 0404160468

A Provision of human nature: essays on Fielding and others in   **2.5672**
honor of Miriam Austin Locke / edited by Donald Kay.
University: University of Alabama Press, c1977. xi, 207 p.; port.; 25 cm. 1. Fielding, Henry, 1707-1754 — Addresses, essays, lectures. 2. Locke, Miriam Austin. 3. English literature — 18th century — History and criticism — Addresses, essays, lectures. I. Kay, Donald. II. Locke, Miriam Austin.
PR442.P7   823/.03   *LC* 76-40469   *ISBN* 0817374256

Tillotson, Geoffrey.   • **2.5673**
Augustan studies. — [London] University of London, Athlone Press, 1961. 266 p. 22 cm. 1. English literature — 18th cent. — Addresses, essays, lectures. I. T.
PR442.T47   820.903   *LC* 61-66195

The Age of Johnson; essays presented to Chauncey Brewster   **2.5674**
Tinker.
New Haven: Yale University Press, 1949. xi, 426 p. port. 24 cm. Editor: F. W. Hilles. 1. Johnson, Samuel, 1709-1784. 2. Tinker, Chauncey Brewster, 1876-1963. 3. English literature — 18th century — History and criticism. I. Hilles, Frederick Whiley, 1900- II. Tinker, Chauncey Brewster, 1876-1963.
PR442.T5   820.903   *LC* 49-8185 *

Reynolds, Joshua, Sir, 1723-1792.   • **2.5675**
Portraits; character sketches of Oliver Goldsmith, Samuel Johnson, and David Garrick, together with other manuscripts of Reynolds discovered among the Boswell papers and now first published. Prepared for the press with introductions and notes by Frederick W. Hilles. [1st ed.] New York, McGraw-Hill [1952] xvi, 197 p. illus. (on lining papers) ports., facsims. 25 cm. (The Yale editions of the private papers of James Boswell) 'References to sources': p. 185-190. 1. Johnson, Samuel, 1709-1784. 2. Goldsmith, Oliver, 1728-1774. 3. Gibbon, Edward, 1737-1794. 4. Garrick, David, 1717-1779. I. Hilles, Frederick Whiley, 1900- ed. II. T.
PR443.R4   *LC* 52-10851

Stephen, Leslie, Sir, 1832-1904.   • **2.5676**
English literature and society in the eighteenth century / by Leslie Stephen. — London: Duckworth, [1931]. vi, 224 p.; 18 cm. (Ford lectures. 1903) (The new readers library; 28.) 1. English literature — 18th century — History and criticism 2. England — Social life and customs I. T. II. Series.
PR443.S8   *LC* 33-37378

Battestin, Martin C.   **2.5677**
The providence of wit: aspects of form in Augustan literature and the arts / Martin C. Ballestin. — Oxford: Clarendon Press, 1974. x, 331, [6] leaves of plates: ill.; 23 cm. 1. English literature — 18th century — History and criticism. 2. Neoclassicism (Art) — Great Britain. 3. Aesthetics, British I. T.
PR445.B35   820/.9/004   *LC* 75-308945   *ISBN* 0198120524

Dobrée, Bonamy, 1891-.   • **2.5678**
English literature in the early eighteenth century, 1700–1740. — Oxford, Clarendon Press, 1959. xii, 701 p. 23 cm. — (The Oxford history of English literature, 7) Bibliography: p. [586]-696. 1. English literature — 18th cent. — Hist. & crit. I. T. II. Series.
PR445.D6   820.903   *LC* 60-95

Erskine-Hill, Howard.   **2.5679**
The Augustan idea in English literature / Howard Erskine–Hill. — London: E. Arnold, 1983. xvi, 379 p.; 25 cm. Includes index. 1. Augustus, Emperor of Rome, 63 B.C.-14 A.D. 2. English literature — 18th century — History and criticism. 3. Neoclassicism (Literature) I. T.
PR445.E7 1983   820/.9/351 19   *LC* 83-113105   *ISBN* 0713163739

Hagstrum, Jean H.   • **2.5680**
The sister arts; the tradition of literary pictorialism and English poetry from Dryden to Gray. — [Chicago] University of Chicago Press [1958] 336 p. illus. 25 cm. 1. English poetry — Early modern (to 1700) — Hist. & crit. 2. English poetry — 18th cent. — Hist. & crit. 3. Figures of speech 4. Art and literature 5. Painting — Hist. I. T.
PR445.H3   821.09   *LC* 58-11948

Weinbrot, Howard D.   **2.5681**
Augustan Caesar in 'Augustan' England: the decline of a classical norm / by Howard D. Weinbrot. — Princeton, N.J.: Princeton University Press, c1978. xi, 270 p.; 23 cm. 1. Augustus, Emperor of Rome, 63 B.C.-14 A.D. in fiction, drama, poetry, etc. 2. English literature — 18th century — History and criticism. 3. Classicism 4. Latin literature — History and criticism. I. T.
PR445.W4   820/.9/1   *LC* 77-72140   *ISBN* 0691063443

PR447 Romanticism

Bernbaum, Ernest, 1879-.   • **2.5682**
[Anthology of romanticism. v. 1] Guide through the romantic movement. 2d ed., rev. and enl. New York, Ronald Press [1949] xi, 351 p. 24 cm. First published in 1930 as v. 1 of the author's Anthology of romaticism. This ed. called 'a companion volume' to the 3d ed. of the Anthology. 1. English literature — 19th century — History and criticism. 2. English literature — 18th century — History and criticism. 3. Romanticism — England. I. T.
PR447.B55 1949   820.903   *LC* 49-8022

Elton, Oliver, 1861-1945.   • **2.5683**
A survey of English literature, 1780–1830, by Oliver Elton. 4th impression. London: E. Arnold & co., 1933. 2 v.; 23 cm. 1. English literature — 19th century — History and criticism. I. T.
PR447.E5   *LC* 33-21704

Frye, Northrop.   • **2.5684**
A study of English romanticism. — New York, Random House [1968] vi, 180 p. 19 cm. — (Studies in language and literature, SLL21) Rebound by Peter Smith. Includes bibliographical references. 1. English literature — 18th cent. — Hist. & crit. 2. English literature — 19th cent. — Hist. & crit. 3. Romanticism — England. I. T.
PR447.F7   820.9/1/4   *LC* 68-19748

Renwick, W. L. (William Lindsay), 1889-.   • **2.5685**
English literature, 1789–1815. — Oxford, Clarendon Press, 1963. 293 p. 23 cm. — (The Oxford history of English literature 9) Includes bibliography. 1. English literature — 18th cent. — Hist. & crit. 2. English literature — 19th cent. — Hist. & crit. I. T.
PR447.R4 1963   820.903   *LC* 63-3139

PR448 Special Topics, A–Z

Kenny, Virginia C.   **2.5686**
The country–house ethos in English literature, 1688–1750: themes of personal retreat and national expansion / Virginia C. Kenny. — Sussex: Harvester Press; New York: St. Martin's Press, 1984. xi, 236 p.; 22 cm. Includes index. 1. English literature — 18th century — History and criticism. 2. Country homes in literature. 3. Country life in literature 4. Upper classes in literature. 5. Imperialism in literature. 6. Solitude in literature 7. English literature — Early modern, 1500-1700 — History and criticism. 8. Literature and society — England. I. T.
PR448.C68 K4 1984   820/.9/005 19   *LC* 83-40586   *ISBN* 0312170343

Sitter, John E.   **2.5687**
Literary loneliness in mid–eighteenth–century England / John Sitter. — Ithaca, N.Y.: Cornell University Press, 1982. 230 p.; 23 cm. 1. English literature — 18th century — History and criticism. 2. Loneliness in literature 3. Social isolation in literature I. T.
PR448.L66 S5 1982   820/.9/353 19   *LC* 82-5105   *ISBN* 0801414997

Goldgar, Bertrand A., 1927-.   **2.5688**
Walpole and the wits: the relation of politics to literature, 1722–1742 / Bertrand A. Goldgar. Lincoln: University of Nebraska Press, c1976. 256 p.; 23 cm. 1. Walpole, Robert, Earl of Orford, 1676-1745. 2. English literature — 18th century — History and criticism. 3. Politics and literature 4. Politics in literature I. T.
PR448.P6 G6   820/.9/005   *LC* 76-6809   *ISBN* 0803208936

PR449 Treatment of Special Subjects, A–Z

Carnochan, W. B.   **2.5689**
Confinement and flight: an essay on English literature of the eighteenth century / W. B. Carnochan. — Berkeley: University of California Press, c1977. xi, 201 p.: ill.; 21 cm. Includes index. 1. English literature — 18th century —

History and criticism. 2. Flight in literature. 3. Imprisonment in literature.
I. T.
PR449.F47 C3   820/.9/005   LC 75-46034   ISBN 0520031881

Barrell, John.   **2.5690**
English literature in history, 1730–80: an equal, wide survey / John Barrell. —
New York: St. Martin's Press, 1983. 228 p.; 23 cm. 1. English literature — 18th
century — History and criticism. 2. History in literature 3. Great Britain —
History — 18th century I. T.
PR449.H56 B37 1983   820/.9/358 19   LC 83-16104   ISBN
0312254334

Byrd, Max.   **2.5691**
London transformed: images of the city in the eighteenth century / Max Byrd.
— New Haven: Yale University Press, 1978. x, 202 p.; 22 cm. 1. English
literature — 18th century — History and criticism. 2. London in literature.
I. T.
PR449.L65 B95   820/.9/32   LC 77-11875   ISBN 0300021666

Byrd, Max.   **2.5692**
Visits to Bedlam: madness and literature in the eighteenth century. — [1st ed.].
— Columbia: University of South Carolina Press, [1974] xvii, 200 p.: illus.; 22
cm. 1. English literature — 18th century — History and criticism. 2. Mental
illness in literature I. T.
PR449.M4 B9   820/.9/353   LC 73-19855   ISBN 0872493121

Rogers, Pat.   **2.5693**
Literature and popular culture in eighteenth century England / Pat Rogers. —
Sussex: Harvester Press; Totowa, N.J.: Barnes & Noble, 1985. xiv, 215 p.; 23
cm. 1. Pope, Alexander, 1688-1744 — Criticism and interpretation. 2. Defoe,
Daniel, 1661?-1731 — Criticism and interpretation. 3. English literature —
18th century — History and criticism. 4. Popular culture in literature.
5. Great Britain — Popular culture I. T.
PR449.P66 R64 1985   820/.9/005 19   LC 84-14645   ISBN
0710809816

Speck, W. A. (William Arthur), 1938-.   **2.5694**
Society and literature in England 1700–60 / W.A.Speck. — Atlantic Highlands,
New Jersey: Humanities Press, 1984 (c1983) 228 p.; 23 cm. 1. English
literature — 18th century 2. History in literature 3. Great Britain — History
— 18th century 4. Great Britain — Politics and government — 18th century
5. Great Britain — Social life and customs — 18th century I. T.
PR 449 .S63 S64   ISBN 0391029452

Nussbaum, Felicity.   **2.5695**
The brink of all we hate: English satires on women, 1660–1750 / Felicity A.
Nussbaum. — Lexington, KY: University Press of Kentucky, c1984. viii,
192 p.; 23 cm. 1. Women in literature 2. English literature — 18th century —
History and criticism. 3. English literature — Early modern, 1500-1700 —
History and criticism. 4. Satire, English — History and criticism. I. T.
II. Title: English satires on women, 1660-1750.
PR449.W65 N87 1984   827/.4/09352042 19   LC 83-10181   ISBN
0813114985

PR451–469 19TH CENTURY

Elton, Oliver, 1861-1945.   • **2.5696**
A survey of English literature, 1830–1880 / by Oliver Elton. — 3d impression.
— London: E. Arnold, 1932. 2 v.; 23 cm. Continuation of the author's Survey of
English literature, 1780-1830. 1. English literature — 19th century — History
and criticism. I. T.
PR451.E53 1932   LC 33-21705

Kunitz, Stanley, 1905- ed.   • **2.5697**
British authors of the nineteenth century, edited by Stanley J. Kunitz; associate
editor, Howard Haycraft. Complete in one volume with 1000 biographies and
350 portraits. New York, The H. W. Wilson company, 1936. 3 p.l., 677 p. illus.
(ports.) 26 cm. 1. Biography — Dictionaries. 2. Authors, English I. Haycraft,
Howard, 1905- joint ed. II. T.
PR451.K8 1936   928.2   LC 36-28581

Hough, Graham Goulden, 1908-.   • **2.5698**
Image and experience; studies in a literary revolution / by Graham Hough. —
Lincoln: University of Nebraska Press, 1964, c1960. ix, 228 p.; 21 cm. (A Bison
book) 1. English literature — 19th century — Addresses, essays, lectures.
2. English literature — 20th century — Addresses, essays, lectures. I. T.
PR453.H58 1964   LC 65-2758

Fairchild, Hoxie Neale, 1894-.   • **2.5699**
The romantic quest/ by Hoxie Neale Fairchild.— New York: Russell &
Russell; 1965 [1931] viii, 444 p.; 23 cm. 1. English literature — 18th century —
History and criticism 2. English literature — 19th century — History and
criticism 3. Romanticism — England I. T.
PR457 F3 1965   LC 65-18804

Jack, Ian Robert James.   • **2.5700**
English literature, 1815–1832. — Oxford, Clarendon Press, 1963. xii, 643 p. 22
cm. — (Oxford history of English literature, 10) Bibliography: p. [458]-631.
1. English literature — 19th cent. — Hist. & crit. I. T. II. Series.
PR457.J24   820.903   LC 63-25209

PR461–466 Victorian Era

Buckley, Jerome Hamilton.   • **2.5701**
The Victorian temper; a study in literary culture. — Cambridge, Mass.:
Harvard University Press, [1969, c1951] x, 282 p.: illus., ports.; 22 cm.
1. English literature — 19th century — History and criticism. I. T.
PR461.B75 1969   820.9/009/8   LC 74-89967   ISBN 0674936809

Chamberlin, J. Edward, 1943-.   **2.5702**
Ripe was the drowsy hour: the age of Oscar Wilde / J. E. Chamberlin. — New
York: Seabury Press, 1977. xiii, 222 p.; 22 cm. — (A Continuum book)
1. Wilde, Oscar, 1854-1900 — Biography. 2. English literature — 19th
century — History and criticism. 3. Arts, Victorian 4. Authors, English —
19th century — Biography. I. T.
PR461.C45   820/.9/008   LC 77-8072   ISBN 0816493081

Chesterton, G. K. (Gilbert Keith), 1874-1936.   • **2.5703**
The Victorian age in literature. — London, New York: Oxford University
Press, 1961. 159 p.; 17 cm. (Home university library of modern knowledge. 70)
1. English literature —- 19th century — History and criticism. I. T. II. Series.
PR461.C5

Dawson, Carl.   **2.5704**
Victorian noon: English literature in 1850 / Carl Dawson. — Baltimore: Johns
Hopkins University Press, c1979. xv, 268 p.: ill.; 24 cm. 1. English literature —
19th century — History and criticism. I. T.
PR461.D35   820/.9/008   LC 78-13939   ISBN 080182110X

Hicks, Granville, 1901-.   • **2.5705**
Figures of transition; a study of British literature at the end of the nineteenth
century. — Westport, Conn.: Greenwood Press, [1969, c1939] xv, 326 p.; 23
cm. 1. English literature — 19th century — History and criticism. I. T.
PR461.H5 1969   820.9/008   LC 70-90528   ISBN 0837127823

Jackson, Holbrook, 1874-1948.   • **2.5706**
The eighteen nineties: a review of art and ideas at the close of the nineteenth
century / by Holbrook Jackson. — New York: A.A. Knopf, c[1922]. 304 p.,
[24] leaves of plates: ill., port. 1. English literature — 19th century — History
and criticism 2. Art — Great Britain 3. Great Britain — Intellectual life I. T.
PR461.J22 1922   LC 22-25260

Parrott, Thomas Marc, 1866-1960.   • **2.5707**
A companion to Victorian literature / Thomas Marc Parrott and Robert
Bernard Martin. — New York: Scribner, 1955. 308 p.: ill.; 21 cm. 1. English
literature — 19th century — History and criticism. 2. Great Britain — History
— Victoria, 1837-1901 I. Martin, Robert Bernard, 1918-. II. T.
PR461.P3   LC 55-7295

Stewart, J. I. M. (John Innes Mackintosh), 1906-.   • **2.5708**
Eight modern writers, by J. I. M. Stewart. Oxford, Clarendon Press, 1963.
704 p. 23 cm. (The Oxford history of English literature, 12) 1. English
literature — 19th century — History and criticism. 2. English literature —
20th century. — History and criticism. I. T.
PR461.S8   820.904   LC 63-5783

Bibliographies of studies in Victorian literature for the ten years   • **2.5709**
1945–1954 / edited by Austin Wright; compiled by William
Frost ... [et al.].
Urbana: University of Illinois Press, 1956. 310 p.; 25 cm. 1. English literature
— 19th century — Bibliography. I. Wright, Austin. ed. II. Frost, William,
1917-
Z2013. B58   PR461.Z9 B49.   LC 56-5687

Buckler, William Earl, 1924-.   **2.5710**
The Victorian imagination: essays in aesthetic exploration / William E.
Buckler. — New York: New York University Press, c1980. x, 382 p.; 24 cm. —
(The Gotham library of the New York University Press) 1. Tennyson, Alfred
Tennyson, Baron, 1809-1892 — Criticism and interpretation — Addresses,
essays, lectures. 2. English literature — 19th century — History and criticism
— Addresses, essays, lectures. I. T.
PR463.B8   820/.9/008   LC 80-17571   ISBN 0814710328

Holloway, John.   • **2.5711**
The Victorian sage: studies in argument. Hamden, Conn.: Archon Books, 1962
[c1953] viii, 300 p.; 22 cm. 1. Caryle, Thomas, 1795-1881. 2. Disraeli,
Benjamin, Earl of Beaconsfield, 1804-1881. 3. Eliot, George, 1819-1880.
4. Arnold, Matthew, 1822-1888. 5. Hardy, Thomas, 1840-1928. 6. English
literature — 19th century — History and criticism. I. T.
PR463.H6 1962   LC 62-5610

Levine, Richard A. ed. 2.5712
Backgrounds to Victorian literature [by] Richard A. Levine. — San Francisco: Chandler Pub. Co, [1967] 338 p.; 21 cm. — (Chandler publications in backgrounds to literature) 1. English literature — 19th century — History and criticism. I. T.
PR463.L57 820.9/008 *LC* 67-12092

Tillotson, Geoffrey. • 2.5713
Criticism and the nineteenth century. Hamden, Conn.: Archon Books, 1967. xiii, 283 p.; 22 cm. 1. English literature — 19th century — History and criticism. 2. Criticism — Great Britain. I. T.
PR463.T5 1967 *LC* 67-17251

Wright, Austin. ed. • 2.5714
Victorian literature; modern essays in criticism. — New York: Oxford University Press, 1961. 377 p.; 21 cm. — (A Galaxy book, GB52) 1. English literature — 19th century — Addresses, essays, lectures. I. T.
PR463.W7 820.903 *LC* 61-5078

Welland, Dennis Sydney Reginald. • 2.5715
The Pre-Raphaelites in literature and art, by D. S. R. Welland. — Freeport, N.Y.: Books For Libraries Press, [1969] 215 [1] p.; 21 cm. — (Granger index reprint series) Reprint of the 1953 ed. 1. Preraphaelitism 2. English literature — 19th century I. T.
PR466.W43 1969 820.9/008 *LC* 72-76949 *ISBN* 0836960467

PR468–469 Special Topics. Treatment of Special Subjects

Henkle, Roger B. 2.5716
Comedy and culture: England 1820–1900 / Roger B. Henkle. — Princeton, N.J.: Princeton University Press, c1980. x, 373 p. 1. English literature — 19th century — History and criticism. 2. Comic, The 3. Middle classes — England. 4. Literature and society — England. I. T.
PR468.C65 H4 PR468C65 H4. 827/.8/09 *LC* 79-3214 *ISBN* 0691064288

Prickett, Stephen. 2.5717
Victorian fantasy / by Stephen Prickett. — Bloomington: Indiana University Press, c1979. xvi, 257 p., [12] leaves of plates: ill.; 22 cm. Includes index. 1. English literature — 19th century — History and criticism. 2. Fantastic literature, English — History and criticism. I. T.
PR468.F35 P7 820/.9/008 *LC* 78-21751 *ISBN* 0253174619

Vicinus, Martha. 2.5718
The industrial muse: a study of nineteenth century British working-class literature / Martha Vicinus. — New York: Barnes & Noble Books, 1974 i.e. [1975] x, 357 p., [8] leaves of plates: 32 ill.; 23 cm. Includes index. 1. English literature — 19th century — History and criticism. 2. Authors, Laboring class — Great Britain. 3. Labor and laboring classes — Great Britain I. T.
PR468.L3 V5 1975 820/.9/920623 *LC* 75-314327 *ISBN* 0064972100

Miles, Josephine, 1911-. • 2.5719
Pathetic fallacy in the nineteenth century: a study of a changing relation between object and emotion. New York: Octagon Books, 1965. ix, 122 p.; 24 cm. 1. Romanticism — England. 2. English literature — 19th century — History and criticism. 3. Nature in literature I. T.
PR468.N3 M5 1965 *LC* 65-16786

Reed, John Robert, 1938-. 2.5720
Victorian conventions / John R. Reed. — [Athens]: Ohio University Press, [1975] xiii, 561 p.: 24 cm. Includes index. 1. English literature — 19th century — History and criticism. 2. Great Britain — Social conditions — 19th century I. T.
PR468.S6 R4 820/.9/008 *LC* 73-92908 *ISBN* 0821401475

Bald, Marjory Amelia. • 2.5721
Women–writers of the nineteenth century. New York: Russell & Russell, 1963. 288 p.; 23 cm. 1. Women authors 2. English literature — 19th century — History and criticism I. T.
PR468.W6 B3 1963 *LC* 63-8356

Jackson, Holbrook, 1874-1948. • 2.5722
Dreamers of dreams; the rise and fall of 19th century idealism. London, Faber and Faber. — St. Clair Shores, Mich.: Scholarly Press, 1971. 283 p.; 22 cm. Reprint of the 1948 ed. 1. English literature — 19th century — History and criticism. 2. American literature — 19th century — History and criticism. 3. Idealism in literature I. T.
PR469.I3 J3 1971 820.9/13 *LC* 70-158496 *ISBN* 0403013143

Brandes, Georg Morris Cohen, 1842-1927. • 2.5723
Naturalism in nineteenth century English literature. — [New York]: Russell & Russell, 1957. vi, 366 p.; 22 cm. 1. English literature — 19th century — History and criticism. 2. Naturalism in literature I. T.
PR469.N3 B7 821.709 *LC* 57-8675

Brantlinger, Patrick, 1941-. 2.5724
The spirit of reform: British literature and politics, 1832–1867 / Patrick Brantlinger. Cambridge: Harvard University Press, 1977. ix, 293 p.: ill.; 24 cm. 1. English literature — 19th century — History and criticism. 2. Politics and literature I. T.
PR469.P6 B65 820/.9/008 *LC* 76-30537 *ISBN* 0674833155

Farrell, John Philip, 1939-. 2.5725
Revolution as tragedy: the dilemma of the moderate from Scott to Arnold / John P. Farrell. — Ithaca, N.Y.: Cornell University Press, 1980. 297 p.; 23 cm. 1. English literature — 19th century — History and criticism. 2. Authors, English — 19th century — Political and social views 3. Politics and literature 4. Literature and revolutions 5. Tragic, The I. T.
PR469.P6 F3 820/.9/007 *LC* 79-26000 *ISBN* 0801412781

Miller, J. Hillis (Joseph Hillis), 1928-. • 2.5726
The disappearance of God; five nineteenth–century writers. Cambridge, Mass., Belknap Press of Harvard University Press, 1963. ix, 367 p. 25 cm. 1. English literature — 19th century — History and criticism. 2. God in literature I. T.
PR469.R4 M5 820.93 *LC* 63-17206

Auerbach, Nina, 1943-. 2.5727
Woman and the demon: the life of a Victorian myth / Nina Auerbach. — Cambridge, Mass.: Harvard University Press, 1982. xi, 255 p.: ill.; 24 cm. 1. English literature — 19th century — History and criticism. 2. Women in literature 3. Feminism and literature 4. Women — England — History — 19th century. 5. Women in art 6. England — Popular culture. I. T.
PR469.W65 A93 1982 823/.8/09352042 19 *LC* 82-9298 *ISBN* 0674954068

Blake, Kathleen. 2.5728
Love and the woman question in Victorian literature: the art of self-postponement / Kathleen Blake. — Brighton, Sussex: Harvester Press; Totowa, N.J.: Barnes & Noble Books, 1983. xvii, 254 p.; 23 cm. Includes index. 1. English literature — 19th century — History and criticism. 2. Women in literature 3. Sex role in literature 4. Love in literature 5. Women artists in literature. 6. Feminism and literature I. T.
PR469.W65 B57 1983 820/.9/352042 19 *LC* 83-11918 *ISBN* 0389204250

Poovey, Mary. 2.5729
The proper lady and the woman writer: ideology as style in the works of Mary Wollstonecraft, Mary Shelley, and Jane Austen / Mary Poovey. — Chicago: University of Chicago Press, c1984. xxii, 287 p.; 24 cm. — (Women in culture and society). Includes index. 1. Wollstonecraft, Mary, 1759-1797 — Political and social views. 2. Shelley, Mary Wollstonecraft, 1797-1851 — Political and social views. 3. Austen, Jane, 1775-1817 — Political and social views. 4. Sex role in literature 5. Social ethics in literature. 6. English literature — 19th century — History and criticism. 7. English literature — Women authors — History and criticism. 8. Women in literature I. T. II. Series.
PR469.W65 P66 1984 823/.7/09352042 19 *LC* 83-3664 *ISBN* 0226675270

PR471–479 20TH CENTURY

Connolly, Cyril, 1903-1974. • 2.5730
Enemies of promise, and other essays; an autobiography of ideas. — 1st ed. Garden City, N.Y., Anchor Books, 1960. 421 p. 19 cm. (A Doubleday Anchor book, A194) 1. English literature — 20th century — History and criticism. I. T. II. Series.
PR471.C65 1960 *LC* 60-5920

Daiches, David, 1912-. • 2.5731
The present age in British literature / by David Daiches. — [1st American ed.] Bloomington: Indiana University Press, 1958. x, 376 p.; 22 cm. 1. English literature — 20th century — History and criticism. 2. English literature — 20th century — Bibliography. I. T.
PR471.D3 1969 820.90091 *LC* 58-6954

Fraser, G. S. (George Sutherland), 1915-. • 2.5732
The modern writer and his world; continuity and innovation in twentieth-century English literature [by] G. S. Fraser. New York, F. A. Praeger [1965, c1964] 426 p. 22 cm. Bibliography: p. 409-414. 1. English literature — 20th century — History and criticism. I. T.
PR471.F72 1965 820.904 *LC* 64-22924

Johnstone, John Keith, 1923-. • 2.5733
The Bloomsbury group: a study of E. M. Forster, Lytton Strachey, Virginia Woolf, and their circle / John Johnstone. — New York, Noonday Press, 1954.

383 p. 22 cm. 1. Forster, E. M. (Edward Morgan), 1879-1970. 2. Strachey, Lytton, 1880-1932. 3. Woolf, Virginia, 1882-1941. 4. English literature — 20th century — History and criticism. I. T.
PR471.J6 1954a   LC 54-11730

Swinnerton, Frank, 1884-.   • **2.5734**
The Georgian literary scene, 1910–1935: a panorama / by Frank Swinnerton; with nine illustrations from busts by Jo Davidson. — [6th ed.]. — New York: Farrar, Straus, [1950?] 415 p.: ports. Published also under title: The Georgian scene; a literary panorama. 1. English literature — 20th century — History and criticism. 2. Authors, English I. T. II. Title: The Georgian scene.
PR471.S8 1950   LC 51-969

Tindall, William York, 1903-.   • **2.5735**
Forces in modern British literature, 1885–1946. — Freeport, N.Y.: Books for Libraries Press, [1970, c1947] xiii, 385, xviii p.; 23 cm. — (Essay index reprint series) 1. English literature — 19th century — History and criticism. 2. English literature — 20th century — History and criticism. I. T.
PR471.T5 1970   820.9/00912   LC 79-117857   ISBN 0836917308

Blackmur, Richard P.   • **2.5736**
The expense of greatness, by R. P. Blackmur. New York: Arrow Editions, [c1940] 305 p.; 22 cm. 1. American literature — 20th century — History and criticism. 2. English literature — 20th century — History and criticism. I. T.
PR473.B56   820.4   LC 40-34148

Ford, Ford Madox, 1873-1939.   • **2.5737**
Portraits from life; memories and criticisms of Henry James, Joseph Conrad, Thomas Hardy, H.G. Wells, Stephen Crane, D.H. Lawrence, John Galsworthy, Ivan Turgenev, W.H. Hudson, Theodore Dreiser, Algernon Charles Swinburne. Boston, Houghton Mifflin, 1937. vi, 227 p. ports. 25 cm. London ed. (Allen & Unwin) has title: Mightier than the sword. 1. Authors, English 2. Authors, American 3. English literature — 19th century — History and criticism. 4. English literature — 20th century — History and criticism. I. T.
PR473.F64   820.4   LC 37-27254

Hoffman, Frederick John. ed.   • **2.5738**
Perspectives on modern literature. — Evanston, Ill., Row, Peterson [1962] 242 p. 21 cm. 1. Literature, Modern — 20th cent. — Hist. & crit. 2. English essays 3. American essays I. T.
PR473.H6   828.9109   LC 62-4217

Kermode, Frank, 1919-.   • **2.5739**
Puzzles and epiphanies; essays and reviews, 1958–1961, by Frank Kermode. With an introd. by William Phillips. New York, Chilmark Press [c1962] 234 p.; 23 cm. 1. English literature — 20th century — History and criticism — Addresses, essays, lectures. 2. Literature, Modern — 20th century — Addresses, essays, lectures. I. T.
PR473.K4   LC 62-15618

Temple, Ruth Zabriskie. comp.   • **2.5740**
Modern British literature, compiled and edited by Ruth Z. Temple [and] Martin Tucker. — New York: F. Ungar Pub. Co., [1966] 3 v.; 25 cm. — (Library of literary criticism.) 1. English literature — 20th century — History and criticism — Addresses, essays, lectures. I. Tucker, Martin. joint comp. II. T. III. Series.
PR473.T4   820/.9/0091   LC 65-16618   ISBN 0804432759

Fussell, Paul, 1924-.   **2.5741**
The Great War and modern memory / Paul Fussell. — New York: Oxford University Press, 1975. x, 363 p.: ill.; 24 cm. 1. English literature — 20th century — History and criticism. 2. World War, 1914-1918 — Literature and the war. 3. War and literature I. T.
PR478.E8 F8   820/.93   LC 75-7352   ISBN 0195019180

Hewison, Robert, 1943-.   **2.5742**
Under siege: literary life in London, 1939–1945 / Robert Hewison. — 1st American ed. — New York: Oxford University Press, 1977. x, 219 p., [8] leaves of plates: ill.; 23 cm. Includes index. 1. English literature — 20th century — History and criticism. 2. World War, 1939-1945 — Literature and the war 3. England — London. 4. London (England) — Intellectual life. I. T.
PR478.W67 H4 1977b   820/.9/00912   LC 77-79611   ISBN 0195199936

Hynes, Samuel Lynn.   **2.5743**
The Auden generation: literature and politics in England in the 1930's / Samuel Hynes. New York: Viking Press, 1977, c1976. 430 p.; 23 cm. 1. English literature — 20th century — History and criticism. 2. Politics and literature I. T.
PR479.P6 H9 1977   820/.9/12   LC 76-23104   ISBN 0670140449

PR500–976 LITERARY HISTORY, BY FORM

PR500–609 Poetry

Warton, Thomas, 1728-1790.   • **2.5744**
History of English poetry. — New York: Johnson Reprint Corp., 1968. 4 v. in 3.; 24 cm. — (Classics in art and literary criticism) A facsim. reproduction of the 1774-81 ed., with a new introd. by René Wellek and 'An index to The history of English poetry by Thomas Warton' ([96] p. at end of v. 4) previously published separately in 1806. 1. English poetry — History and criticism 2. Romances — History and criticism. 3. Learning and scholarship — England. I. T.
PR501.W3 1774a   821/.009   LC 68-15838

Barber, Charles Laurence.   **2.5745**
Poetry in English: an introduction / Charles Barber. — New York: St. Martin's Press, 1983. x, 220 p.; 23 cm. 1. English poetry — History and criticism 2. English poetry — Commonwealth of Nations authors — History and criticism. 3. American poetry — History and criticism. 4. Poetics I. T.
PR502.B27 1983   821/.009 19   LC 82-23099   ISBN 0312618883

Brooks, Cleanth, 1906-.   **2.5746**
The well wrought urn; studies in the structure of poetry. — New York: Harcourt, Brace, [1956? c1947] 300 p.; 19 cm. — (Harvest books, 11) 1. English poetry — Addresses, essays, lectures. 2. Poetry I. T.
PR502.B7x   821.04   LC 56-13729

Bush, Douglas, 1896-.   • **2.5747**
English poetry: the main currents from Chaucer to the present / Douglas Bush. — New York: Oxford University Press, 1952. 222 p.; 18 cm. 1. English poetry — History and criticism I. T.
PR502.B88   LC 52-13409

Davie, Donald.   • **2.5748**
Articulate energy; an inquiry into the syntax of English poetry. London, Routlege & Kegan Paul [1955]. — St. Clair Shores, Mich.: Scholarly Press, 1971. vii, 173 p.; 22 cm. 1. English poetry — History and criticism 2. English language — Syntax I. T.
PR502.D3 1971   821/.009   LC 77-158901   ISBN 040301316X

Dyson, A. E.   **2.5749**
Masterful images: English poetry from metaphysicals to romantics / A. E. Dyson and Julian Lovelock. New York: Barnes & Noble Books, 1976. 254 p.; 21 cm. Includes index. 1. English poetry — History and criticism I. Lovelock, Julian. joint author. II. T.
PR502.D9 1976b   821/.009   LC 76-366701   ISBN 0064918637

Graves, Robert, 1895-.   • **2.5750**
On English poetry: being an irregular approach to the psychology of this art, from evidence mainly subjective. — New York: Haskell House Publishers, 1972. 149 p.; 23 cm. Reprint of the 1922 ed. 1. English poetry — History and criticism I. T.
PR502.G7 1972   808.1   LC 78-185878   ISBN 0838313868

Grierson, Herbert John Clifford, Sir, 1866-1960.   • **2.5751**
A critical history of English poetry [by] Herbert J. C. Grierson and J. C. Smith. New York, Oxford university press, 1946. viii, 593 p. 22 cm. 'First American edition.' 1. English poetry — History and criticism I. T.
PR502.G76 1946   821.09   LC 46-11822

Hobsbaum, Philip.   **2.5752**
Tradition and experiment in English poetry / Philip Hobsbaum. — Totowa, N.J.: Rowman and Littlefield, 1979. xiii, 343 p.; 23 cm. Includes index. 1. English poetry — History and criticism I. T.
PR502.H55 1979   821/.009   LC 78-10954   ISBN 0847661288

Holloway, John, 1920-.   **2.5753**
The proud knowledge: poetry, insight and the self, 1620–1920 / John Holloway. — London; Boston: Routledge & Kegan Paul, 1977. 264 p.; 23 cm. Includes index. 1. English poetry — History and criticism I. T.
PR502.H58   821/.009   LC 77-372326   ISBN 0710085419

Knight, George Wilson, 1897-.   • **2.5754**
The burning oracle: studies in the poetry of action / by G. Wilson Knight. — London; New York [etc.]: Oxford University Press, 1939. vi p., 1 l., 292 p.; 22 cm. 1. English poetry — History and criticism 2. Poetry I. T.
PR502.K55   LC 40-4357

Miles, Josephine, 1911-.   **2.5755**
Poetry and change: Donne, Milton, Wordsworth, and the equilibrium of the present / Josephine Miles. — Berkeley: University of California Press, [1974]

243 p.; 22 cm. 1. English poetry — History and criticism 2. American poetry — History and criticism. I. T.
PR502.M49   821/.009   LC 73-84387   ISBN 0520025547

Pearsall, Derek Albert.   **2.5756**
Old English and Middle English poetry / Derek Pearsall. London; Boston: Routledge & K. Paul, 1977. xiv, 352 p.; 24 cm. (Routledge history of English poetry. v. 1) 1. English poetry — Old English, ca. 450-1100 — History and criticism. 2. English poetry — Middle English, 1100-1500 — History and criticism. I. T. II. Series.
PR502.R58 vol. 1 PR201   821/.009 s 821/.1/09   LC 77-357401
    ISBN 0710083963

Rothstein, Eric.   **2.5757**
Restoration and eighteenth–century poetry, 1660–1780 / Eric Rothstein. — Boston: Routledge & K. Paul, 1981. xiv, 242 p.; 24 cm. — (Routledge history of English poetry. v. 3) Includes index. 1. English poetry — Early modern, 1500-1700 — History and criticism. 2. English poetry — 18th century — History and criticism. I. T. II. Series.
PR502.R58 vol. 3 PR561   821/.009 s 821/.009 19   LC 80-41728
    ISBN 0710006608

Jackson, J. R. de J. (James Robert de Jager)   **2.5758**
Poetry of the Romantic period / J. R. de J. Jackson. — London; Boston: Routledge and Kegan Paul, 1980. xvi, 334 p.; 24 cm. — (The Routledge history of English poetry; v. 4) 1. English poetry — 18th century — History and criticism. 2. English poetry — 19th century — History and criticism. 3. Romanticism — Great Britain. I. T.
PR502.R58 vol. 4 PR571   821/.009 s 821/.7/09145 19   LC 79-40914
    ISBN 0710002890

Williams, Charles, 1886-1945.   • **2.5759**
The English poetic mind / by Charles Williams. — New York: Russell & Russell, 1963. 213 p; 23 cm. 1. Milton, John, 1608-1674 — Criticism and interpretation. 2. Wordsworth, William, 1770-1850. 3. Shakespeare, William, 1564-1616 — Criticism and interpretation 4. English poetry — History and criticism I. T.
PR502.W55 1963   821.09   LC 63-15188

PR503–504 Collected Essays

Blackmur, R. P. (Richard P.), 1904-1965.   • **2.5760**
Form and value in modern poetry. Garden City, N.Y., Doubleday. 1957 [c1952] 388 p. 18 cm. (Doubleday anchor books, A96) 1. English poetry — History and criticism 2. American poetry — History and criticism. I. T.
PR503.B55   821.09   LC 57-501

Eliot, T. S. (Thomas Stearns), 1888-1965.   • **2.5761**
The use of poetry and the use of criticism, studies in the relation of criticism to poetry in England. London, Faber and Faber [1970] 156 p. 20 cm. (Faber paper covered editions) 1. English poetry — History and criticism — Addresses, essays, lectures. 2. Criticism — Addresses, essays, lectures. I. T.
PR503.E45 1970   821/.009   LC 71-27234

Frye, Northrop.   • **2.5762**
Fables of identity; studies in poetic mythology. — New York: Harcourt, Brace & World, [1963] 264, [1] p.; 21 cm. 'H035.' 1. English poetry — Addresses, essays, lectures. 2. American poetry — Addresses, essays, lectures. 3. Criticism — Addresses, essays, lectures. I. T.
PR503.F7   821.09   LC 63-20974

Graves, Robert, 1895-.   • **2.5763**
The common asphodel; collected essays on poetry, 1922–1949. — New York: Haskell House, 1970. xi, 335 p.: illus.; 23 cm. Reprint of the 1949 ed. 1. English poetry — History and criticism 2. Poetry I. T.
PR503.G65 1970   809.1   LC 78-117590   ISBN 0838310230

Graves, Robert, 1895-.   • **2.5764**
The crowning privilege; collected essays on poetry. — Freeport, N.Y.: Books for Libraries Press, [1970, c1955] 311 p.; 23 cm. — (Essay index reprint series) 1. English poetry — History and criticism — Addresses, essays, lectures. I. T.
PR503.G66 1970   821/.009   LC 70-117797   ISBN 0836917510

Graves, Robert, 1895-.   • **2.5765**
Oxford addresses on poetry. — New York: Greenwood Press, 1968 [c1962] 141 p.; 22 cm. 1. English poetry — History and criticism — Addresses, essays, lectures. 2. Poetry — Addresses, essays, lectures. I. T.
PR503.G68 1968   809.1   LC 69-10102

Hazlitt, William, 1778-1830.   • **2.5766**
Lectures on the English poets, by William Hazlitt. Edited by his son. — New York: Russell & Russell, [1968] 407 p.; 19 cm. Reprint of the 3d ed., 1841. 1. English poetry — History and criticism I. Hazlitt, William, 1811-1893, ed. II. T.
PR503.H3 1968   821/.009   LC 68-25032

Leavis, F. R. (Frank Raymond), 1895-.   • **2.5767**
Revaluation: tradition and development in English poetry / F.R. Leavis. — London: Chatto and Windus, 1936. viii p., 1 l., 275, [1] p.; 22 cm. 1. English poetry — History and criticism I. T.
PR503.L4   LC 37-8370

Wasserman, Earl R. (Earl Reeves), 1913-.   • **2.5768**
The subtler language; critical readings of neoclassic and romantic poems / Earl R. Wasserman. — Baltimore: John Hopkins Press, [1959] 361 p.; 24 cm. 1. Shelley, Percy Bysshe, 1792-1822. 2. English poetry — History and criticism — Addresses,essays, lectures. I. T.
PR503.W35   821.0903   LC 59-10067

Bateson, Frederick Wilse, 1901-.   • **2.5769**
English poetry: a critical introduction / [by] Frederick Bateson. — [2d] ed. New York: Barnes & Noble [1966] x, 205 p. 23 cm. 1. English poetry — History and criticism I. T.
PR504.B36 1966a   LC 66-5718

De Sélincourt, Aubrey, 1894-1962.   • **2.5770**
Six great poets: Chaucer, Pope, Wordsworth, Shelley, Tennyson, the Brownings. — London: H. Hamilton, [1956] 247 p.: ports.; 19 cm. — (The 'Six great' series) 1. Chaucer, Geoffrey, d. 1400. 2. Pope, Alexander, 1688-1744. 3. Wordsworth, William, 1770-1850. 4. Shelley, Percy Bysshe, 1792-1822. 5. Tennyson, Alfred Tennyson, 1st Baron, 1809-1892. 6. Browning, Robert, 1812-1889. 7. Browning, Elizabeth Barrett, 1806-1861. 8. Poets, English I. T. II. Title: 6 great poets. III. Series.
PR504.D48   LC a 56-5237

PR505 Poets Laureate

Hopkins, Kenneth, 1914-.   • **2.5771**
The poets laureate. — Carbondale: Southern Illinois University Press, [1966] 295 p.; 21 cm. — (Arcturus books. AB30) 1. Poets laureate 2. English poetry I. T. II. Series.
PR505.H69 1966   821.09   LC 66-22824

PR507 Ballads

Booth, Mark W., 1943-.   **2.5772**
The experience of songs / Mark W. Booth. — New Haven: Yale University Press, c1981. ix, 226 p.: music; 22 cm. 1. Songs, English — History and criticism. I. T.
PR507.B63   821/.04/09 19   LC 81-972   ISBN 0300026226

Shepard, Leslie.   **2.5773**
The broadside ballad: a study in origins and meaning / by Leslie Shepard. — 1st American ed. — Hatboro, Pa.: Legacy Books, 1978. 205 p.: ill.; 25 cm. 'Grammophone records': p. [195]-202. Includes index. 1. Ballads, English — Great Britain — History and criticism. 2. Ballads, English — Great Britain — Texts. 3. Broadsides 4. Broadsides — Facsimiles. I. T.
PR507.S53 1978   821/.04   LC 78-50797   ISBN 0913714003. ISBN 0913714011 pbk

PR508 Special Topics, A–Z

Braden, Gordon, 1947-.   **2.5774**
The classics and English Renaissance poetry: three case studies / Gordon Braden. — New Haven: Yale University Press, 1978. xv, 303 p.; 24 cm. (Yale studies in English. 187) 'An earlier version of the whole book was submitted as a doctoral dissertation to the Yale Graduate School.' Includes indexes. 1. Golding, Arthur, 1536-1606 — Style. 2. Musaeus, Grammaticus. Hero and Leander 3. Herrick, Robert, 1591-1674 — Sources. 4. English poetry — Early modern, 1500-1700 — History and criticism. 5. Classical literature — History and criticism. I. T. II. Series.
PR508.C68 B7 1978   821/.3/09   LC 77-10888   ISBN 0300021542

Williams, Meg Harris, 1951-.   **2.5775**
Inspiration in Milton and Keats / Meg Harris Williams. — Totowa, N.J.: Barnes & Noble Books, c1982. xi, 212 p.; 22 cm. Includes index. 1. Milton, John, 1608-1674 — Criticism and interpretation. 2. Keats, John, 1795-1821 — Criticism and interpretation. 3. English poetry — History and criticism 4. Inspiration in literature. 5. Creation (Literary, artistic, etc.) I. T.
PR508.I48 W5 1982   821/.009/1 19   LC 81-12789   ISBN 038920109X

Partridge, A. C. (Astley Cooper)   • **2.5776**
The language of Renaissance poetry: Spenser, Shakespeare, Donne, Milton / [by] A. C. Partridge. — London: Deutsch 1971. 348 p.; 23 cm. — (Language library.) 1. English poetry — Early modern (to 1700) — History and criticism. 2. English language — Style I. T. II. Series.
PR508.L3 P3   821/.3/09   LC 72-177121   ISBN 0233962840

Bush, Douglas, 1896-.   ● **2.5777**
Mythology and the Renaissance tradition in English poetry. — New rev. ed. — New York: W. W. Norton, [1963] xiii, 372 p.; 22 cm. 1. English poetry — Early modern, 1500-1700 — History and criticism. 2. Mythology in literature 3. Literature, Comparative — Classical and English. 4. Literature, Comparative — English and classical. I. T.
PR508.M9 B8 1963   821.309   *LC* 63-15868

Bush, Douglas, 1896-.   ● **2.5778**
Mythology and the romantic tradition in English poetry. — Cambridge, Mass.: Harvard University Press, [1969] xxiv, 647 p.; 22 cm. First published in 1937. 'Reissued, with a new preface, 1969.' 1. English poetry — History and criticism 2. American poetry — History and criticism. 3. Mythology in literature 4. Romanticism — England. I. T.
PR508.M9 B85 1969   821   *LC* 72-85071   *ISBN* 0674598253

Nicolson, Marjorie Hope, 1894-.   ● **2.5779**
Mountain gloom and mountain glory: the development of the aesthetics of the infinite. — Ithaca, New York: Cornell University Press, [1959] xiii, 403 p. 20 cm. — 1. English poetry — History & criticism. 2. Mountains in literature 3. Infinite I. T.
PR508.N3 N5   809.93   *LC* 59-2804

Miller, J. Hillis (Joseph Hillis), 1928-.   **2.5780**
The linguistic moment: from Wordsworth to Stevens / by J. Hillis Miller. — Princeton, N.J.: Princeton University Press, c1985. xxi, 445 p.; 23 cm. 1. English poetry — History and criticism 2. Space and time in literature 3. Space and time in language 4. American poetry — 20th century — History and criticism. I. T.
PR508.S65 M5 1985   821/.009 19   *LC* 84-42894   *ISBN* 0691054428

PR509 Special Forms, A–Z

Sacks, Peter M.   **2.5781**
The English elegy: studies in the genre from Spenser to Yeats / Peter M. Sacks. — Baltimore: Johns Hopkins Press, c1985. xv, 375 p.; 24 cm. Includes index. 1. Elegiac poetry, English — History and criticism. I. T.
PR509.E4 S23 1985   821/.04/09 19   *LC* 84-23381   *ISBN* 0801832543

English Institute.   ● **2.5782**
Forms of lyric; selected papers from the English Institute. Edited with a foreword by Reuben A. Brower. — New York: Columbia University Press, 1970. x, 187 p.; 20 cm. Papers selected from two conferences of the English Institute, held in 1968 and 1969. 1. English poetry — History and criticism. — Addresses, essays, lectures. 2. American poetry — Addresses, essays, lectures. I. Brower, Reuben Arthur, 1908- ed. II. T.
PR509.L8 E5   821/.009/14   *LC* 78-121567   *ISBN* 023103413X

Langbaum, Robert Woodrow, 1924-.   ● **2.5783**
The poetry of experience: the dramatic monologue in modern literary tradition. — New York: Random House, 1957. 246 p.; 23 cm. 1. English poetry — History and criticism 2. Monologue I. T.
PR509.M6 L3   821.09   *LC* 56-8798

Shuster, George Nauman, 1894-.   ● **2.5784**
The English ode from Milton to Keats. New York: Columbia University Press, 1940. vi p., 2 l., [3]-314 p. 1 l.; 23 cm. (Columbia University studies in English and comparative literature, no. 150) 1. Odes 2. English poetry — History and criticism I. T. II. Series.
PR509 O3 S5

Greg, W. W. (Walter Wilson), 1875-1959.   ● **2.5785**
Pastoral poetry & pastoral drama; a literary inquiry, with special reference to the pre–Restoration stage in England. — New York, Russell & Russell, 1959. 464 p. 22 cm. 1. Pastoral poetry, English — Hist. & crit. 2. Pastoral poetry — Hist. & crit. 3. English poetry — Early modern (to 1700) — Hist. & crit. 4. English drama — Early modern and Elizabethan — Hist. & crit. I. T.
PR509.P3G7 1959   821.309   *LC* 59-14432

PR521–609 History of Poetry, by Period

PR521–539 16th Century. Elizabethan Era

Evans, Maurice.   **2.5786**
English poetry in the sixteenth century. — 2nd rev. ed. — New York: Norton, 1967. 184 p.; 22 cm. 1. English poetry — Early modern, 1500-1700 — History and criticism. I. T.
PR521.E9 1967   *LC* 67-81263

Wallerstein, Ruth Coons, 1893-.   ● **2.5787**
Studies in seventeenth–century poetic. — [Madison] University of Wisconsin Press, 1950. x, 421 p. illus. 24 cm. Bibliographical references included in 'Notes' (p. [371]-400) 1. Marvell, Andrew, 1621-1678. 2. English poetry — Early modern (to 1700) — Hist. & crit. 3. Elegiac poetry, English — Hist. & crit. I. T.
PR529.E4W3   821.409   *LC* 50-63463

Allen, Don Cameron, 1904-.   ● **2.5788**
Image and meaning: metaphoric traditions in Renaissance poetry. — New enl. ed. — Baltimore: Johns Hopkins Press, [1968] viii, 248 p.; 22 cm. 1. English poetry — Early modern, 1500-1700 — History and criticism. 2. Literature, Comparative 3. Metaphor I. T.
PR531.A4 1968   821/.009   *LC* 68-15444

Rivers, Isabel.   **2.5789**
Classical and Christian ideas in English Renaissance poetry: a students' guide / Isabel Rivers. — London; Boston: G. Allen & Unwin, 1979. 231 p.; 2 cm. Includes index. 1. English poetry — Early modern, 1500-1700 — Sources. 2. Classical literature — History and criticism. 3. Christianity and literature 4. Philosophy, Ancient 5. Bible in literature I. T.
PR532.R5   821/.3/093   *LC* 78-40853   *ISBN* 0048070025

Alpers, Paul J. comp.   ● **2.5790**
Elizabethan poetry; modern essays in criticism, edited by Paul J. Alpers. — New York, Oxford University Press, 1967. 524 p. illus. 21 cm. — (A Galaxy book, GB177) Includes bibliographical references. 1. Spenser, Edmund, 1552?-1599. Faerie queene 2. English poetry — Early modern (to 1700) — Addresses, essays, lectures. I. T.
PR533.A65   821/.3/09   *LC* 67-15124

Wasserman, Earl R. (Earl Reeves), 1913-.   ● **2.5791**
Elizabethan poetry in the eighteenth century. — Urbana: University of Illinois Press, 1947. 291 p.; 27 cm. — (Illinois studies in language and literature. v. 32, no. 2-3) 1. English poetry — Early modern, 1500-1700 — History and criticism. 2. Criticism — History. I. T. II. Series.
PR535.C7 W3   *LC* 47-11245

Freeman, Rosemary.   ● **2.5792**
English emblem books. — New York: Octagon Books, 1966. xiv, 256 p.: ill.; 24 cm. First published in 1948. 'Bibliography of English emblem books to 1700': p. 229-240. 1. Emblems 2. English poetry — Early modern (to 1700) — Hist. & crit. 3. Illustrated books 4. Emblems — Bibl. I. T.
PR535.E5F7 1966   821.00915   *LC* 66-18037

Tuve, Rosemond, 1903-1964.   ● **2.5793**
Elizabethan and metaphysical imagery; renaissance poetic and twentieth–century critics, by Rosemond Tuve. — Chicago, Ill.: The University of Chicago press, [1947] xiv, 442 p.; 24 cm. 1. English poetry — Early modern, 1500-1700 — History and criticism. 2. Figures of speech I. T.
PR535.F5 T8   821.309   *LC* 47-4244

Danby, John Francis.   ● **2.5794**
Poets on Fortune's Hill; studies in Sidney, Shakespeare, Beaumont & Fletcher, by John F. Danby. — Port Washington, N.Y.: Kennikat Press, [1966] 212 p.; 22 cm. First published in 1952. 1. Sidney, Philip, Sir, 1554-1586. 2. Shakespeare, William, 1564-1616. 3. Beaumont, Francis, 1584-1616. 4. Fletcher, John, 1579-1625. 5. English poetry — Early modern, 1500-1700 — History and criticism. I. T.
PR535.S6 D3 1966   821.309   *LC* 66-25905

Attridge, Derek.   **2.5795**
Well–weighed syllables: Elizabethan verse in classical metres / Derek Attridge. — London: Cambridge University Press, 1975 (c1974). viii, 258 p.; 23 cm. Includes index. 1. English poetry — Early modern, 1500-1700 — History and criticism. 2. English language — Early modern, 1500-1700 — Versification. 3. Latin poetry — History and criticism. I. T.
PR535.V4 A8   821/.3/09   *LC* 74-80362   *ISBN* 0521205301

Hulse, Clark, 1947-.   **2.5796**
Metamorphic verse: the Elizabethan minor epic / Clark Hulse. — Princeton, N.J.: Princeton University Press, c1981. xiv, 296 p.: ill.; 23 cm. 1. English poetry — Early modern, 1500-1700 — History and criticism. 2. Epic poetry, English — History and criticism. 3. Metamorphosis in literature I. T.
PR539.E64 H8   821/.03/09 19   *LC* 81-47135   *ISBN* 0691064830

Smith, A. J. (Albert James), 1924-.   **2.5797**
The metaphysics of love: studies in Renaissance love poetry from Dante to Milton / A.J. Smith. — Cambridge [Cambridgeshire]; New York: Cambridge University Press, 1985. ix, 349 p.; 23 cm. Includes index. 1. Love poetry, English — History and criticism. 2. English poetry — Early modern, 1500-1700 — History and criticism. 3. Love poetry, Italian — History and criticism. 4. English poetry — Italian influences I. T.
PR539.L7 S65 1985   809.1/9354 19   *LC* 84-14945   *ISBN* 0521259088

PR541–549 17th Century

Miner, Earl Roy.   2.5798
The restoration mode from Milton to Dryden, by Earl Miner. — Princeton, N.J.: Princeton University Press, 1974. xxiv, 587 p.; 22 cm. 'Limited paperback editions, LPE-19.' 1. English poetry — Early modern, 1500-1700 — History and criticism. I. T.
PR541.M5   821/.4/09   LC 73-14865   ISBN 0691100195

Williamson, George, 1898-1968.   2.5799
The Donne tradition: a study in English poetry from Donne to the death of Cowley / by George Williamson. — Cambridge: Harvard University Press, 1930. x, 264 p.; 21 cm. 1. Donne, John, 1572-1631. 2. English poetry — Early modern, 1500-1700 — History and criticism I. T.
PR541.W5   LC 30-12260

Leishman, J. B. (James Blair), 1902-1962.   2.5800
The metaphysical poets: Donne, Herbert, Vaughan, Traherne. — New York, Russell & Russell, 1963. 232 p. 23 cm. 1. Donne, John, 1573-1631. 2. Herbert, George, 1593-1633. 3. Vaughan, Henry, 1622-1695. 4. Traherne, Thomas, d. 1674. 5. English poetry — Early modern (to 1700) — Hist. & crit. I. T.
PR543.L4 1963   821.309   LC 63-9323

Martz, Louis Lohr.   2.5801
The wit of love: Donne, Carew, Crashaw, Marvell [by] Louis L. Martz. — Notre Dame [Ind.]: University of Notre Dame Press, [1969] 216 p.: illus. (part col.), ports.; 24 cm. — (University of Notre Dame. Ward-Phillips lectures in English language and literature, v. 3) 1. English poetry — Early modern, 1500-1700 — Addresses, essays, lectures. I. T.
PR544.M3   821/.4/09   LC 70-85345

Miles, Josephine, 1911-.   • 2.5802
The primary language of poetry in the 1640's. Berkeley: University of California Press, 1948. 160 p. 24 cm. (University of California publications in English, v. 19, no. 1) 1. English poetry — Early modern, 1500 to 1700 — History and criticism. 2. English language — Diction 3. Vocabulary I. T.
PR545.L3 M5   821/.4 9   LC 48-10316

Seelig, Sharon Cadman.   2.5803
The shadow of eternity: belief and structure in Herbert, Vaughan, and Traherne / Sharon Cadman Seelig. — Lexington, Ky.: University Press of Kentucky, 1981. 194 p.; 23 cm. 1. Herbert, George, 1593-1633 — Criticism and interpretation. 2. Vaughan, Henry, 1622-1695 — Criticism and interpretation. 3. Traherne, Thomas, d. 1674 — Criticism and interpretation. 4. English poetry — Early modern, 1500-1700 — History and criticism. I. T.
PR545.M4 S4 1981   821/.3/09 19   LC 80-51018   ISBN 0813114446

Nicolson, Marjorie Hope, 1894-.   • 2.5804
The breaking of the circle; studies in the effect of the 'new science' upon seventeenth-century poetry. — Rev. ed. — New York, Columbia University Press, 1960. 216 p. 21 cm. — 1. English poetry — Early modern, 1500-1700 — History and criticism. 2. Literature and science I. T.
PR545.S3 N5 1960   821.309   LC 60-12391

Martz, Louis Lohr.   • 2.5805
The poetry of meditation; a study in English religious literature of the seventeenth century. — [Rev. ed.]. — New Haven: Yale University Press [1962] xxv, 375 p. illus. 21 cm. — (Yale paperbound Y64) Includes bibliography. 1. English poetry — Early modern (to 1700) — Hist. & crit. 2. Religious poetry, English — Hist. & crit. I. T.
PR549.R4M32 1962b   821.309   LC 62-6601

White, Helen Constance, 1896-1967.   • 2.5806
The metaphysical poets: a study in religious experience / by Helen C. White. — New York: Macmillan, 1936. ix, 444 p.; 22 cm. 1. Donne, John, 1572-1631. 2. Herbert, George, 1593-1633. 3. Crashaw, Richard, 1613?-1649. 4. Vaughan, Henry, 1622-1695. 5. Traherne, Thomas, 1634?-1674. 6. English poetry — Early modern, 1500-1700 — History and criticism. 7. Religious poetry, English — History and criticism. 8. Religion in literature 9. Mysticism in literature I. T.
PR549.R4 W5   LC 36-35027

PR551–579 18th Century

Johnson, Samuel, 1709-1784.   • 2.5807
Lives of the English poets / by Samuel Johnson; edited by George Birkbeck Hill; with brief memoir of Birkbeck Hill by Harold Spencer Scott. — New York: Octagon Books, 1967. 3 v.; 24 cm. 1. Poets, English 2. English poetry — Early modern, 1500-1700 — History and criticism. 3. English poetry — 18th century — History and criticism. I. Hill, George Birkbeck Norman, 1835-1903. II. T.
PR553.J7 1967   821/.00922   LC 67-20301

Davie, Donald.   2.5808
Purity of diction in English verse. — New York: Schocken Books, [1967] viii, 217 p.; 21 cm. 1. English poetry — 18th century — History and criticism. 2. English poetry — 19th century — History and criticism. 3. English language — Diction I. T.
PR555.L3 D3 1967b   821/.009   LC 67-19424

Spacks, Patricia Ann Meyer.   • 2.5809
The insistence of horror; aspects of the supernatural in eighteenth-century poetry. — Cambridge, Harvard University Press, 1962. 244 p. 22 cm. 1. English poetry — 18th century — History and criticism.. 2. Supernatural in literature I. T.
PR555.S8 S65   809.93   LC 62-20252

Nicolson, Marjorie Hope, 1894-.   • 2.5810
Newton demands the muse: Newton's Opticks and the eighteenth century poets / by Marjorie Hope Nicolson. — Princeton: Princeton University Press, 1946. 178 p.; 21 cm. — (History of ideas series; 2) Includes index. 1. Newton, Isaac, Sir, 1642-1727. Opticks. 2. English poetry — 18th century — History and criticism. 3. Literature and science I. T. II. Series.
PR565.O6 N5 1946

Harvey, A. D. (Arnold D.)   2.5811
English poetry in a changing society, 1780–1825 / A.D. Harvey. — New York: St. Martin's Press, 1980. 195 p.; 22 cm. 1. English poetry — 18th century — History and criticism. 2. English poetry — 19th century — History and criticism. 3. Romanticism — Great Britain. 4. Literature and society — Great Britain. 5. Great Britain — History — 1789-1820 I. T.
PR575.H5 H3 1980   821/.7/09 19   LC 80-20221   ISBN 0312255020

Feingold, Richard.   2.5812
Nature and society: later eighteenth-century uses of the pastoral and georgic / Richard Feingold. — New Brunswick, N.J.: Rutgers University Press, c1978. ix, 209 p.; 24 cm. Based on the author's thesis, Columbia University. 1. Cowper, William, 1731-1800. The task. 2. Dyer, John, 1700?-1758. The fleece. 3. English poetry — 18th century — History and criticism. 4. Pastoral poetry, English — History and criticism. 5. Didactic poetry, English — History and criticism. 6. Great Britain — Economic conditions — 1760-1860 I. T.
PR579.P3 F4 1978   821/.6/09   LC 77-13418   ISBN 0813508479

PR581–599 19th Century

Foakes, R. A.   • 2.5813
The romantic assertion; a study in the language of nineteenth century poetry, by R. A. Foakes. — New York: Barnes & Noble, [1971] 186 p.; 23 cm. Reprint of the 1958 ed. 1. English poetry — 19th century — History and criticism. 2. Romanticism — England. 3. Figures of speech I. T.
PR585.L3 F6 1971   821/.7/09   LC 79-25014   ISBN 0389041475

Beach, Joseph Warren, 1880-1957.   • 2.5814
The concept of nature in nineteenth-century English poetry / by Joseph Warren Beach. — New York: Russell & Russell, 1966. 618 p. 23 cm. 1. Nature in literature 2. English poetry — 19th century — History and criticism. 3. American poetry — 19th century — History and criticism. I. T.
PR585.N3 B4 1966   LC 66-13163   ISBN 0846207168

Abrams, M. H. (Meyer Howard), 1912- ed.   • 2.5815
English romantic poets; modern essays in criticism. New York, Oxford University Press, 1960. 384 p. 21 cm. (A Galaxy book, GB35) 1. English poetry — 19th century — Addresses, essays, lectures. 2. Romanticism — England. I. T.
PR590.A2   821.709   LC 60-7058

Bostetter, Edward Everett, 1914-.   • 2.5816
The Romantic ventriloquists: Wordsworth, Coleridge, Keats, Shelley, Byron. — Seattle, University of Washington Press, 1963. xiii, 351 p. ports. 24 cm. Bibliography: p. 333-341. 1. English poetry — 19th cent. — Hist. & crit. 2. Romanticism — England. I. T.
PR590.B58   821.709   LC 63-10795

De Quincey, Thomas, 1785-1859.   • 2.5817
Reminiscences of the English Lake poets by Thomas De Quincey. London, J. M. Dent & sons, ltd.; New York, E. P. Dutton and co., inc., 1929. xi, 335 1 p. 18 cm. (Everyman's library. Biography, no. 163) 1. Lake poets I. T. II. Series.
PR590.D4 1907   LC 36-37028

The English romantic poets: a review of research and criticism /   2.5818
John Clubbe ... [et al.]; edited by Frank Jordan.
4th ed. — New York: Modern Language Association of America, 1985. xiii, 765 p.; 23 cm. (Reviews of research.) Includes index. 1. English poetry — 19th century — History and criticism. 2. Romanticism — England. 3. English

poetry — 19th century — History and criticism — Bibliography. I. Clubbe, John. II. Jordan, Frank, 1937- III. Series.
PR590.E5 1985   016.821/7/09 19   LC 85-7216   ISBN 087352263X

Hayden, John O. comp.   2.5819
Romantic bards and British reviewers; a selected edition of the contemporary reviews of the works of Wordsworth, Coleridge, Byron, Keats, and Shelley. Edited by John O. Hayden. — Lincoln: University of Nebraska Press, [1971] xix, 433 p.; 25 cm. 1. English poetry — 19th century — History and criticism. I. T.
PR590.H3 1971b   821/.7/09   LC 71-125670   ISBN 0803207735

Hough, Graham Goulden, 1908-.   • 2.5820
The romantic poets / Graham Hough. — 2d. ed. — London: Hutchinson University Library, 1957. 200 p.; 19 cm. (Hutchinson's university library: English literature) 1. English poetry — 19th century — History and criticism. 2. English poetry — 18th century — History and criticism. 3. Romanticism — England. I. T.
PR590.H57 1957   LC 60-27792

Kroeber, Karl, 1926-.   • 2.5821
Romantic narrative art. — Madison: University of Wisconsin Press, 1960. 225 p.; 25 cm. 1. English poetry — 19th century — History and criticism. 2. Romanticism — England. 3. Narrative poetry — History and criticism. I. T.
PR590.K7

Wain, John. ed.   • 2.5822
Contemporary reviews of romantic poetry. — Freeport, N.Y.: Books for Libraries Press, [1969] 240 p.; 23 cm. — (Essay index reprint series) Reprint of the 1953 ed. 1. English poetry — 19th century — History and criticism. 2. Romanticism — England. 3. Criticism — Gt. Brit. I. T.
PR590.W27 1969   821/.7/09   LC 75-76920   ISBN 0836900332

PR591–599 Victorian Era

Armstrong, Isobel. comp.   2.5823
Victorian scrutinies: reviews of poetry, 1830–1870. — London: Athlone Press, 1972. xi, 344 p.; 23 cm. 1. English poetry — 19th century — Addresses, essays, lectures. I. T.
PR593.A73   821/.8/09   LC 72-190491   ISBN 0485111314

Faverty, Frederic Everett, 1902- ed.   • 2.5824
The Victorian poets, a guide to research, edited by Frederic E. Faverty. 2d ed. Cambridge, Harvard University Press, 1968. 433 p. 25 cm. 1. English poetry — 19th century — History and criticism. I. T.
PR593.F3 1968   821/.8/09   LC 68-15636

Johnson, E. D. H. (Edward Dudley Hume)   • 2.5825
The alien vision of Victorian poetry: sources of the poetic imagination in Tennyson, Browning, and Arnold / Edward D. H. Johnson. — Hamden, Conn.: Archon, 1963, c1952. xvi, 224 p.; 22 cm. (Princeton University. Princeton studies in English; no. 34) 1. Tennyson, Alfred Tennyson, Baron, 1809-1892. 2. Browning, Robert, 1812-1889. 3. Arnold, Matthew, 1822-1888. I. T. II. Series.
PR593.J6 1963   LC 64-10457

The Victorian experience, the poets / edited by Richard A. Levine.   2.5826
Athens: Ohio University Press, c1982. x, 202 p.; 22 cm. 1. English poetry — 19th century — History and criticism — Addresses, essays, lectures. I. Levine, Richard A.
PR593.V48   821/.8/09 19   LC 81-4020   ISBN 0821404474

Stevenson, Lionel, 1902-1973.   2.5827
The Pre–Raphaelite poets. — Chapel Hill: University of North Carolina Press, [1972] 330 p.; 24 cm. 1. English poetry — 19th century — History and criticism. 2. Preraphaelitism I. T.
PR595.P7 S7   821/.8/09   LC 72-78151   ISBN 0807811963

Heath-Stubbs, John Francis Alexander, 1918-.   • 2.5828
The darkling plain: a study of the later fortunes of romanticism in English poetry from George Darley to W.B. Yeats. — London: Eyre & Spottiswoode, [1950] 221 p.; 23 cm. 1. English poetry — 19th century — History and criticism. 2. Romanticism — England. I. T.
PR595.R6 H4   LC 50-13507

PR601–611 20th Century

Deutsch, Babette, 1895-.   • 2.5829
Poetry in our time, a critical survey of poetry in the English–speaking world, 1900 to 1960. — 2d ed., rev. and enl. — Garden City, N.Y.: Doubleday, 1963. 457 p.; 18 cm. — (Anchor books) 1. English poetry — 20th century — History

and criticism. 2. American poetry — 20th century — History and criticism. I. T.
PR601.D43 1963   821.9109   LC 63-8763

Holbrook, David.   2.5830
Lost bearings in English poetry / David Holbrook. New York: Barnes & Noble, 1977. 255 p.; 23 cm. (Barnes & Noble critical studies) 'This volume incorporates the substance of the Sir D. Owen Evans memorial lectures delivered at the University College of Wales, Aberystwyth, during the session 1975-76.' Includes index. 1. English poetry — 20th century — History and criticism. 2. American poetry — 20th century — History and criticism. I. T.
PR601.H59 1977b   821/.9/09   LC 77-367321   ISBN 0064929345

Leavis, F. R. (Frank Raymond), 1895-.   • 2.5831
New bearings in English poetry: a study of the contemporary situation / F.R. Leavis. — Ann Arbor: University of Michigan Press, 1960. 238 p.; 21 cm. — (Ann Arbor paperbacks. AA-36) 1. English poetry — 20th century — History and criticism. I. Sward, Robert, 1933- II. T. III. Series.
PR601.L4 1960   LC 62-5386

Miller, J. Hillis (Joseph Hillis), 1928-.   • 2.5832
Poets of reality; six twentieth–century writers [by] J. Hillis Miller. Cambridge: Belknap Press of Harvard University Press, 1965. 369 p.; 25 cm. 1. English poetry — 20th century — History and criticism. 2. American poetry — 20th century — History and criticism. I. T.
PR601.M5   821.00912   LC 65-22055

Pinto, Vivian de Sola, 1895-.   2.5833
Crisis in English poetry, 1880–1940. — [S.l.]: Longmans, 1951. 228 p.; 20 cm. —(Hutchinson university library: English literature) 1. English poetry — 19th century — History and criticism. 2. English poetry — 20th century — History and criticism. I. T. II. Series.
PR601.P57   LC 52-357

Rosenthal, M. L. (Macha Louis), 1917-.   2.5834
The modern poetic sequence: the genius of modern poetry / M.L. Rosenthal and Sally M. Gall. — New York: Oxford University Press, 1983. xiv, 508 p.; 24 cm. Includes index. 1. English poetry — 20th century — History and criticism. 2. American poetry — History and criticism. I. Gall, Sally M. II. T.
PR601.R58 1983   821/.91/09 19   LC 82-14529   ISBN 0195031709

Contemporary poets / preface to the first edition, C. Day Lewis, preface to the third edition, Marjorie Perloff; editors, James Vinson and D.L. Kirkpatrick.   2.5835
4th ed. — New York: St. Martin's Press, 1985. xviii, 1071 p.; 26 cm. (Contemporary writers of the English language.) 1. English poetry — 20th century — Bio-bibliography. 2. American poetry — 20th century — Bio-bibliography. 3. English poetry — 20th century — History and criticism. 4. American poetry — 20th century — History and criticism. 5. Poets, English — 20th century — Biography — Dictionaries. 6. Poets, American — 20th century — Biography — Dictionaries. I. Vinson, James, 1933- II. Kirkpatrick, D. L. III. Series.
PR603.C6 1985   821/.91/09 B 19   LC 85-22249   ISBN 0312168373

Daiches, David, 1912-.   • 2.5836
Poetry and the modern world; a study of poetry in England between 1900 and 1939. — New York: Biblo and Tannen, 1969. x, 246 p.; 24 cm. Reprint of the 1940 ed. 1. English poetry — 20th century — History and criticism. I. T.
PR610.D25 1969   821/.912/09   LC 75-82812

Schmidt, Michael, 1947-.   2.5837
British poetry since 1960: a critical survey; edited by Michael Schmidt and Grevel Lindop. — [S.l.]: Dufour, 1972. [7], 289 p.; 24 cm. 1. English poetry — 20th century — History and criticism. I. Lindop, Grevel, 1948- joint author. II. T.
PR611.S3   821/.9/1409   LC 72-172222   ISBN 0902145738

PR621–739 Drama

Critical survey of drama: English language series / edited by Frank N. Magill.   2.5838
Englewood Cliffs, N.J.: Salem Press, c1985. 6 v. (xiv, 2575 p.); 24 cm. Includes index. 1. English drama — Bio-bibliography. 2. American drama — Bio-bibliography. 3. Dramatists, English — Biography — Dictionaries. 4. Dramatists, American — Biography — Dictionaries. 5. English drama — History and criticism — Collected works. 6. American drama — History and criticism — Collected works. 7. English drama — Commonwealth of Nations authors — History and criticism — Collected works. 8. Theater — Collected works. I. Magill, Frank Northen.
PR623.C75 1985   822/.009 19   LC 85-50962   ISBN 0893563757

Downer, Alan Seymour, 1912-.　　　　　● 2.5839
The British drama, a handbook and brief chronicle. — New York: Appleton-Century-Crofts, [1950] x, 397 p.: illus.; 22 cm. 1. English drama — History and criticism. I. T.
PR625.D55　　822.09　　*LC* 50-8678

Knight, George Wilson, 1897-.　　　　　● 2.5840
The Golden labyrinth: a study of British drama / by G. Wilson Knight. — New York: Norton, 1962. 402 p. 1. English drama — History and criticism. I. T.
PR625.K58　　*LC* 62-16987

Nicoll, Allardyce, 1894-.　　　　　● 2.5841
British drama / [by] Allardyce Nicoll. — 6th ed. revised and reset / revised by J. C. Trewin. — London: Harrap, 1978. viii, 311 p., [20] p. of plates: ill., facsim., ports.; 23 cm. Includes index. 1. English drama — History and criticism. 2. Theater — Great Britain — History. I. Trewin, J. C. (John Courtenay), 1908- II. T.
PR625.N5 1978　　822/.009　　*LC* 79-305452　　*ISBN* 0245532315

Nicoll, Allardyce, 1894-.　　　　　● 2.5842
A history of English drama, 1660–1900. — Cambridge [Eng.]: University Press, 1952-59. 6v.; 23 cm. 1. English drama — History & criticism. 2. Theater — Great Britain — History. I. T.
PR625.N52 1952　　822.09　　*LC* 52-14525

The Revels history of drama in English / general editors,　　2.5843
Clifford Leech & T. W. Craik.
London: Methuen; [New York]: distributed by Harper and Row Publishers, Barnes and Noble Import Division, 1976-1983. 8 v.: ill.; 24 cm. Includes index. 1. English drama — History and criticism. 2. American drama — History and criticism. 3. Theaters — Great Britain. 4. Theaters — United States I. Leech, Clifford. II. Craik, T. W. (Thomas Wallace) III. Barroll, J. Leeds (John Leeds), 1928- IV. Booth, Michael R.
PR625.R44　　822/.009　　*LC* 75-321430　　*ISBN* 0416130402

Salgādo, Gāmini, 1929-.　　　　　2.5844
English drama, a critical introduction / Gāmini Salgādo. — New York: St. Martin's Press, 1980. vi, 234 p.; 24 cm. Includes index. 1. English drama — History and criticism. I. T.
PR625.S2 1981　　822/.009 19　　*LC* 80-22444　　*ISBN* 0312254296

The English dramatic critics: an anthology, 1660–1932 /　　● 2.5845
assembled by James Agate.
New York: Hill and Wang, 1958. xii, 370 p. 'A drama book'. 1. English drama — History and criticism. 2. Theater — England. I. Agate, James, 1877-1947.
PR627.E484 1958　　*LC* 58-11370

Leech, Clifford.　　　　　● 2.5846
Shakespeare's tragedies, and other studies in seventeenth century drama. London Chatto and Windus 1950. 232p. 1. Tragedy 2. English drama — Early modern and Elizabethan — History and criticism 3. English drama — Restoration — History and criticism I. T.
PR633 L4 1950　　*LC* 50-11616

Clinton-Baddeley, V. C. (Victor Clinton), 1900-1970.　　2.5847
The burlesque tradition in the English theatre after 1660, by V. C. Clinton-Baddeley. London, Methuen, New York, Barnes & Noble Books [1973] xvi, 152 p. illus. 23 cm. Reprint of the 1952 ed. 1. English drama — History and criticism. 2. Burlesque (Literature) I. T.
PR635.B8 C5 1973　　822/.052　　*LC* 74-193369　　*ISBN* 0064712354

Singh, Sarup.　　　　　2.5848
Family relationships in Shakespeare and the Restoration comedy of manners / Sarup Singh. — Delhi: Oxford, 1983. x, 233 p.; 23 cm. Includes index. 1. Shakespeare, William, 1564-1616 — Knowledge — Manners and customs 2. English drama — History and criticism. 3. Family in literature 4. English drama (Comedy) — History and criticism. 5. English drama — Restoration, 1660-1700 — History and criticism. I. T.
PR635.F33 S56 1983　　822.3/3 19　　*LC* 83-904018　　*ISBN* 019561514X

Chambers, E. K. (Edmund Kerchever), 1866-1954.　　● 2.5849
The English folk–play / by E.K. Chambers. — Oxford, Eng.: Clarendon Press, 1933. vi, 248 p. 1. Mumming 2. Folk-drama, English I. T.
PR635.F6 C5　　*LC* 34-3298

PR641–739 BY PERIOD

PR641–644 Medieval

Craig, Hardin.　　　　　● 2.5850
English religious drama of the Middle Ages / by Hardin Craig. — Oxford: Clarendon Press, 1955. vi, 421 p.: ill.; 24 cm. Includes index. 1. Religious drama, English — History and criticism. 2. English drama — To 1500 —

History and criticism. 3. Mysteries and miracle-plays, English — History and criticism. I. T.
PR641.C7　　822.109　　*LC* 55-4054

Taylor, Jerome, 1918-.　　　　　2.5851
Medieval English drama; essays critical and contextual. Edited by Jerome Taylor and Alan H. Nelson. — Chicago: University of Chicago Press, [1972] vi, 351 p.: illus.; 24 cm. — (Patterns of literary criticism) 1. English drama — Medieval — History and criticism. I. Nelson, Alan H. II. T.
PR641.T3　　PR641 T3.　　822/.051　　*LC* 72-77479　　*ISBN* 0226791467

Wilson, F. P. (Frank Percy), 1889-1963.　　　　　● 2.5852
The English drama, 1485–1585, by F. P. Wilson; edited with a bibliography by G. K. Hunter. Oxford, Clarendon P., 1969. [7], 244 p. 23 cm. (The Oxford history of English literature, v. 4, pt. 1) 1. English drama — To 1500 — History and criticism. 2. English drama — Early modern and Elizabethan, 1500-1600 — History and criticism. I. Hunter, G. K. ed. II. T. III. Series.
PR641.W58 1969b　　822/.2/09　　*LC* 70-386045　　*ISBN* 0198122098

Kolve, V. A.　　　　　● 2.5853
The play called Corpus Christi / by V. A. Kolve. — Stanford, Calif.: Stanford University Press, 1966. viii, 337 p.; 24 cm. 1. Corpus Christi festival 2. Mysteries and miracle-plays, English — History & criticism. I. T.
PR643.C7 K6　　822/.1093　　*LC* 66-15301

Houle, Peter J.　　　　　2.5854
The English morality and related drama; a bibliographical survey [by] Peter J. Houle. — [Hamden, Conn.]: Archon Books, 1972. xviii, 195 p.; 22 cm. 1. Moralities, English — History and criticism. I. T.
PR643.M7 H6　　822/.051　　*LC* 70-38714　　*ISBN* 0208012648

Kelley, Michael R., 1940-.　　　　　2.5855
Flamboyant drama: a study of The castle of perseverance, Mankind, and Wisdom / by Michael R. Kelley; foreword by John Gardner. — Carbondale: Southern Illinois University Press, c1979. xiv, 162 p.: ill.; 22 cm. — (Literary structures.) Includes bibliographical references and index. 1. Moralities, English — History and criticism. 2. Castle of perseverance (Morality play) 3. Mankind (Morality play) 4. Wisdom (Morality play) I. T. II. Series.
PR643.M7 K4　　822/.2/09　　*LC* 78-31237　　*ISBN* 0809309157

Salter, Frederick Millet, 1895-1962.　　　　　● 2.5856
Mediaeval drama in Chester [by] F. M. Salter. — New York: Russell & Russell, [1968] ix, 138 p.; 23 cm. Reprint of the 1955 ed. 1. Chester plays. 2. English drama — To 1500 — History and criticism. I. T.
PR644.C4 S3 1968　　822/.05/1　　*LC* 68-25038

Travis, Peter W.　　　　　2.5857
Dramatic design in the Chester cycle / Peter W. Travis. — Chicago: University of Chicago Press, 1982. xv, 310 p.; 22 cm. Includes index. 1. Chester plays. 2. Mysteries and miracle-plays, English — History and criticism. 3. English drama — To 1500 — History and criticism. I. T.
PR644.C4 T7 1982　　822/.0516 19　　*LC* 81-13047　　*ISBN* 0226811646

Helterman, Jeffrey.　　　　　2.5858
Symbolic action in the plays of the Wakefield Master / Jeffrey Helterman. — Athens: University of Georgia Press, c1981. 202 p.; 22 cm. Includes index. 1. Towneley plays. 2. Mysteries and miracle-plays, English — History and criticism. 3. English drama — To 1500 — History and criticism. 4. Symbolism in literature I. T.
PR644.W3 H4　　822/.1 19　　*LC* 80-18273　　*ISBN* 0820305340

PR646–659 16th Century. Elizabethan Era

Bevington, David Martin.　　　　　● 2.5859
From Mankind to Marlowe: growth of structure in the popular drama of Tudor England. — Cambridge: Harvard University Press, 1962. 310 p.; 25 cm. 1. English drama — Early modern and Elizabethan, 1500-1600 — History and criticism. 2. Moralities, English — History and criticism. 3. Theater — Great Britain — History. I. T.
PR646.B4 1962　　822.209　　*LC* 62-9424

Boas, Frederick S. (Frederick Samuel), 1862-1957.　　● 2.5860
An introduction to Tudor drama / by Frederick S. Boas. — Oxford: Clarendon Press, 1933. vi, 176 p., [10] leaves of plates: ill.; 23 cm. 1. English drama — Early modern and Elizabethan, 1500-1600 — History and criticism. I. T.
PR646.B6　　822/.2/09　　*LC* 33-24344

Boas, Frederick S. (Frederick Samuel), 1862-1957.　　● 2.5861
University drama in the Tudor Age, by Frederick S. Boas. New York, B. Blom [1966] x, 414 p. facsims. 23 cm. 'First published 1914.' 1. English drama — Early modern and Elizabethan, 1500-1600 — History and criticism. I. T.
PR649.U6 B6 1966　　822/.3/09　　*LC* 65-20049

Boas, Frederick S. (Frederick Samuel), 1862-1957. • 2.5862
An introduction to Stuart drama / by Frederick S. Boas. — London; New York: Oxford University Press, c1946. viii, 443 p. 19 cm. 1. English drama — Early modern and Elizabethan, 1500-1600 — History and criticism. I. T.
PR651.B6   PR651.B63.   LC A 47-2869

Dessen, Alan C., 1935-. 2.5863
Elizabethan stage conventions and modern interpreters / Alan C. Dessen. — Cambridge [Cambridgeshire]; New York: Cambridge University Press, 1984. xi, 190 p.; 22 cm. Includes index. 1. Shakespeare, William, 1564-1616 — Dramatic production 2. English drama — Early modern and Elizabethan, 1500-1600 — History and criticism. 3. Theater — England — History — 16th century. 4. Stage directions I. T.
PR651.D45 1984   822/.3/09 19   LC 83-23970   ISBN 0521259126

Dessen, Alan C., 1935-. 2.5864
Elizabethan drama and the viewer's eye / Alan C. Dessen. — Chapel Hill: University of North Carolina Press, c1977. xi, 176 p. Includes index. 1. Shakespeare, William, 1564-1616 — Dramatic production 2. English drama — Early modern and Elizabethan, 1500-1600 — History and criticism. 3. Theater — England — History. I. T.
PR651.D4   PR651 D47.   822/.3/09   LC 76-26593   ISBN 0807812919

Doran, Madeleine, 1905-. • 2.5865
Endeavors of art: a study of form in Elizabethan drama. — Madison: University of Wisconsin Press, 1954. xv, 482 p.: illus.; 25 cm. 1. English drama — Early modern and Elizabethan, 1500-1600 — History and criticism. I. T.
PR651.D67   822.309   LC 53-13439

Ellis-Fermor, Una Mary, 1894-1958. • 2.5866
The Jacobean drama; an interpretation. — London, Methuen [1936] 336 p. 22 1/2 cm. 1. English drama — Early modern and Elizabethan — Hist. & crit. I. T.
PR651.E5 1965   822.309   LC 58-4145

Harrison, G. B. (George Bagshawe), 1894-. • 2.5867
Elizabethan plays and players / G. B. Harrison. — Ann Arbor: U. of Michigan P., 1956. 306 p.: fold. map; 21 cm. — (Ann Arbor books; 2.) 1. English drama — Early modern and Elizabethan — History and criticism. 2. Theater — London — History. I. T.
PR651.H37   LC A57-2358

Levin, Richard Louis, 1922-. 2.5868
New readings vs. old plays: recent trends in the reinterpretation of English Renaissance drama / Richard Levin. — Chicago: University of Chicago Press, 1979. xiv, 277 p.; 24 cm. Includes index. 1. Shakespeare, William, 1564-1616 — Criticism and interpretation — History — 20th century 2. English drama — Early modern and Elizabethan, 1500-1600 — History and criticism. 3. English drama — 17th century — History and criticism. 4. Criticism — History — 20th century. I. T.
PR651.L48   822/.3/09   LC 78-10695   ISBN 0226475204

Parrott, Thomas Marc, 1866-1960. • 2.5869
A short view of Elizabethan drama, together with some account of its principal playwrights and the conditions under which it was produced, by Thomas Marc Parrott and Robert Hamilton Ball. — New York: Scribner, [1958] 311 p.; 21 cm. 1. English drama — Early modern and Elizabethan, 1500-1600 — History and criticism. I. Ball, Robert Hamilton, 1902- joint author. II. T. III. Title: Elizabethan drama.
PR651.P3 1958   822.309   LC 58-4312

Schelling, Felix Emmanuel, 1858-1945. • 2.5870
Elizabethan drama, 1558–1642; a history of the drama in England from the accession of Queen Elizabeth to the closing of the theaters, to which is prefixed a résumé of the earlier drama from its beginnings. — New York: Russell & Russell, 1959 [c1935] 2 v.; 21 cm. 1. English drama — Early modern and Elizabethan, 1500-1600 — History and criticism. I. T.
PR651.S4 1959   822.309   LC 59-6230

Bradbrook, M. C. (Muriel Clara), 1909-. 2.5871
Aspects of dramatic form in the English and the Irish Renaissance / M.C. Bradbrook. — Brighton, Sussex: Harvester Press; Totowa, N.J.: Barnes & Noble Books, 1983. xvi, 186; 22 cm. — (The collected papers of Muriel Bradbrook; v. 3) 1. Shakespeare, William, 1564-1616 — Criticism and interpretation — Addresses, essays, lectures. 2. English drama — 17th century — History and criticism — Addresses, essays, lectures. 3. English drama — Early modern and Elizabethan, 1500-1600 — History and criticism — Addresses, essays, lectures. 4. English drama — Irish authors — History and criticism — Addresses, essays, lectures. I. T.
PR653.B67 1983   822/.3/09 19   LC 83-6014   ISBN 0710804067

Eliot, T. S. (Thomas Stearns), 1888-1965. • 2.5872
Essays on Elizabethan drama. — New York: Harcourt, Brace, [c1956] x, 178 p.; 19 cm. (Harvest book; 18.) 1. English drama — Early modern and Elizabethan,

1500-1600 — History and criticism — Addresses, essays, lectures. I. T. II. Title: Elizabethan drama.
PR653 E62   822.304   LC 56-14185

Kaufmann, Ralph James, 1924- ed. • 2.5873
Elizabethan drama; modern essays in criticism. — New York: Oxford University Press, 1961. 372 p.; 21 cm. — (A Galaxy book, GB63) 1. English drama — Early modern and Elizabethan, 1500-1600 — Addresses, essays, lectures. I. T.
PR653.K3   822.309   LC 61-13566

Maxwell, Baldwin, 1893-. • 2.5874
Studies in Beaumont, Fletcher, and Massinger / by Baldwin Maxwell. — New York: Octagon Books, 1966, c1939. vii, 238 p. 1. Beaumont, Francis, 1584-1616 — Criticism and interpretation. 2. Fletcher, John, 1579-1625 — Criticism and interpretation. 3. Massinger, Philip, 1583-1640 — Criticism and interpretation. I. T.
PR653.M35 1966   LC 66-18038

Simpson, Percy, 1865-1962. • 2.5875
Studies in Elizabethan drama. — Oxford, Clarendon Press, 1955. 265 p. 23 cm. 1. English drama — Early modern and Elizabethan — Hist. & crit. 2. Shakespeare, William — Criticism and interpretation. 3. Copyright — Unauthorized reprints — Great Britain. I. T. II. Title: Elizabethan drama.
PR654.S5   822.304   LC 55-2360

PR658 Special Topics, A–Z

Bradbrook, M. C. (Muriel Clara), 1909-. • 2.5876
The growth and structure of Elizabethan comedy. — London: Chatto & Windus, 1955. ix, 245 p. 1. English drama — Early modern and Elizabethan, 1500-1600 — History and criticism. 2. Comedy I. T.
PR651.B79   PR658.C6 B7.   LC a 55-10192

Ribner, Irving, 1921-. 2.5877
The English history play in the age of Shakespeare. — [Rev. ed.]. — New York: Barnes & Nobel, [1965] 356 p. 1. Historical drama, English — History and criticism. 2. English drama — Early modern and Elizabethan, 1500-1600 — History and criticism. 3. Historical drama, English — Bibliography. I. T.
PR658.H5 R5 1965   LC 65-29894

Cardozo, Jacob Lopes. 2.5878
The contemporary Jew in the Elizabethan drama. — New York: B. Franklin, [1968] xvi, 335, iv p.; 25 cm. — (Burt Franklin: research and source works series 175) (Essays in literature & criticism 5.) Reprint of the 1925 ed. 1. Jews in literature 2. English drama — Early modern and Elizabethan, 1500-1600 — History and criticism. I. T.
PR658.J4 C3 1968   822/.3/093   LC 68-4034

Stilling, Roger, 1938-. 2.5879
Love and death in Renaissance tragedy / Roger Stilling. — Baton Rouge: Louisiana State University Press, c1976. 303 p.; 24 cm. Includes index. 1. English drama — Early modern and Elizabethan, 1500-1600 — History and criticism. 2. English drama — 17th century — History and criticism. 3. Love in literature 4. Death in literature 5. English drama (Tragedy) — History and criticism. I. T.
PR658.L63 S8   822/.051   LC 74-27193   ISBN 0807101885

Nicoll, Allardyce, 1894-. • 2.5880
Stuart masques and the Renaissance stage. With 197 illus. — New York: B. Blom, [1963, c1938] 223 p.: illus., diagrs., plans.; 20 cm. 1. Jones, Inigo, 1573-1652. 2. Masques 3. Theaters — Stage-setting and scenery 4. Theater — England — History. I. T.
PR658.M3 N5 1963   792.02   LC 63-23186

Sutherland, Sarah P. 2.5881
Masques in Jacobean tragedy / Sarah P. Sutherland. — New York: AMS Press, c1983. xv, 148 p.; 23 cm. Includes index. 1. English drama — 17th century — History and criticism. 2. English drama (Tragedy) — History and criticism. 3. Masques I. T.
PR658.M3 S9 1983   822/.0512/09 19   LC 81-69122   ISBN 0404622798

Levin, Richard Louis, 1922-. • 2.5882
The multiple plot in English Renaissance drama [by] Richard Levin. Chicago, University of Chicago Press [1971] xiv, 277 p. 24 cm. 1. English drama — Early modern and Elizabethan, 1500-1600 — History and criticism. 2. Plots (Drama, novel, etc.) I. T.
PR658.P6 L4   822.3/09/24   LC 75-130306   ISBN 0226475263

Bowers, Fredson Thayer. • 2.5883
Elizabethan revenge tragedy, 1587–1642, by Fredson Thayer Bowers. — Princeton: Princeton university press, 1940. viii p., 2 l., [3]-288 p.; 33 cm. 1. English drama — Early modern and Elizabethan, 1500-1600 — History and

criticism. 2. Revenge in literature 3. Tragedy 4. English drama — 17th century — History and criticism. I. T.
PR658.T7 B6   822.309   LC 40-9732

Bradbrook, M. C. (Muriel Clara), 1909-.   • **2.5884**
Themes and conventions of Elizabethan tragedy, by M. C. Bradbrook ... Cambridge [Eng.] The University press, 1935. viii, 275, [1] p. 22.5 cm. 'Bibliographical note': p. [269] 1. English drama — Early modern and Elizabethan, 1500-1600 — History and criticism. 2. Theater — England — History and criticism. 3. Tragedy I. T.
PR658.T7B7   822.309   LC 35-9309

Kiefer, Frederick, 1945-.   **2.5885**
Fortune and Elizabethan tragedy / by Frederick Kiefer. — [San Marino, CA]: Huntington Library, 1983. xix, 354 p.: ill.; 24 cm. 1. English drama (Tragedy) — History and criticism. 2. English drama — Early modern and Elizabethan, 1500-1600 — History and criticism. 3. English drama — 17th century — History and criticism. 4. Fortune in literature. I. T.
PR658.T7 K5 1983   822/.0512/09 19   LC 82-15836   ISBN 0873281225

Ornstein, Robert.   • **2.5886**
The moral vision of Jacobean tragedy / Robert Ornstein. — Madison: University of Wisconsin Press, 1960. 299 p.; 25 cm. 1. English drama (Tragedy) — History and criticism. 2. English drama — Early modern and Elizabethan, 1500-1600 — History and criticism. I. T.
PR658.T7 O7   822.309   LC 60-9906

Ribner, Irving, 1921-.   • **2.5887**
Jacobean tragedy: the quest for moral order. New York: Barnes & Noble, 1962. 179 p.; 23 cm. 1. English drama — Early modern and Elizabethan, 1500-1600 — History and criticism. 2. English drama (Tragedy) — History and criticism. I. T.
PR658.T7 R5 1962a   LC 62-5963

Waith, Eugene M.   • **2.5888**
The Herculean hero in Marlowe, Chapman, Shakespeare and Dryden. — New York, Columbia University Press, 1962. 224 p. illus. 22 cm. 1. Marlowe, Christopher, 1564-1593. 2. Chapman, George, 1559?-1634. 3. Dryden, John, 1631-1700. 4. Shakespeare, William — Criticism and interpretation. 5. English drama (Tragedy) — Hist. & crit. 6. Heroes in literature 7. Hercules. I. T.
PR658.T7W3 1962a   809.93   LC 62-7592

PR671–698 17th Century

Harbage, Alfred, 1901-.   • **2.5889**
Cavalier drama: an historical and critical supplement to the study of the Elizabethan and Restoration stage / by Alfred Harbage. — New York: Russell & Russell, 1964. ix, 302 p. 1. English drama — Early modern and Elizabethan, 1500-1600 — History and criticism. 2. English drama — Restoration, 1660-1700 — History and criticism. I. T.
PR678.C3 H3 1964   LC 64-10388

Butler, Martin, Ph. D.   **2.5890**
Theatre and crisis, 1632–1642 / Martin Butler. -- Cambridge [Cambridgeshire]; New York: Cambridge University Press, 1984. xii, 340 p.: ill.; 23 cm. Revision of thesis (Ph. D.)—Cambridge University. Includes index. 1. English drama — 17th century — History and criticism. 2. Politics in literature 3. Theater — Great Britain — History — 17th century. 4. Theater — Political aspects 5. Great Britain — History — Charles I, 1625-1649 I. T.
PR678.P65 B8 1984   822/.4/09 19   LC 83-15250   ISBN 0521246326

Shepherd, Simon.   **2.5891**
Amazons and warrior women: varieties of feminism in seventeenth–century drama / Simon Shepherd. — New York: St. Martin's Press, 1981. 234 p.; 23 cm. Includes index. 1. English drama — 17th century — History and criticism. 2. Women in literature 3. Feminism in literature. I. T. II. Title: Warrior women.
PR678.W6 S5 1981   822/.4/09352042 19   LC 81-13579   ISBN 0312021550

Dobrée, Bonamy, 1891-.   • **2.5892**
Restoration comedy, 1660–1720 / by Bonamy Dobrée. — Oxford: Clarendon Press, 1924. 182 p. 1. English drama — Restoration, 1660-1700 — History and criticism. 2. English drama (Comedy) — History and criticism. I. T.
PR691.D6   LC 25-3113

Hume, Robert D.   **2.5893**
The development of English drama in the late seventeenth century / Robert D. Hume. Oxford [Eng.]: Clarendon Press, 1976. xv, 525 p.; 23 cm. 1. English drama — Restoration, 1660-1700 — History and criticism. I. T.
PR691.H8   822/.4/09   LC 76-365768   ISBN 019812063X

Krutch, Joseph Wood.   • **2.5894**
Comedy and conscience after the Restoration / Joseph Wood Krutch. — New York: Russell & Russell, 1967,c1949. 300p. "Originally published as a Columbia dissertation in 1924. Now being republished with two additions: an index, and the bibliography of relevant modern discussions prepared by G.S. Alleman." 1. Collier, Jeremy. 2. English drama (Comedy) — Restoration, 1660-1700 — History and criticism 3. Theater — Moral and religious aspects. I. T.
PR691.K7 1967   822.409   LC 67-15997

Lynch, Kathleen Martha.   **2.5895**
The social mode of restoration comedy. New York The Macmillan company 1926. 242p. (University of Michigan publications: Language and literature, v. 3) 1. English drama — Restoration — History and criticism 2. English drama (Comedy) — History and criticism I. T.
PR691 L84

Marshall, Geoffrey, 1938-.   **2.5896**
Restoration serious drama / by Geoffrey Marshall. — 1st ed. — Norman: University of Oklahoma Press, [1975] xx, 247 p.; 22 cm. 1. English drama — Restoration, 1660-1700 — History and criticism. I. T.
PR691.M37   822/.4/09   LC 74-15901   ISBN 080611259X

Milhous, Judith.   **2.5897**
Producible interpretation: eight English plays, 1675–1707 / Judith Milhous and Robert D. Hume. — Carbondale: Southern Illinois University Press, c1985. xv, 336 p.: ill.; 24 cm. 1. English drama — Restoration, 1660-1700 — History and criticism. 2. Theater — Production and direction I. Hume, Robert D. II. T.
PR691.M55 1985   822/.4/09 19   LC 84-5634

Palmer, John, 1885-1944.   **2.5898**
The comedy of manners. London G. Bell 1913. 308 p.: ill. 1. English drama — Restoration — History and criticism 2. English drama (Comedy) — History and criticism I. T.
PR691 P3

Powell, Jocelyn, 1938-.   **2.5899**
Restoration theatre production / Jocelyn Powell. — London; Boston: Routledge & Kegan Paul, 1984. xiv, 226 p., [24] p. of plates: ill.; 24 cm. (Theatre production studies.) Includes index. 1. English drama — Restoration, 1660-1700 — History and criticism. 2. Theater — Great Britain — History — 17th century. 3. Dramatists, English — Early modern, 1500-1700 I. T. II. Series.
PR691.P68 1984   792/.0942 19   LC 83-27250   ISBN 0710093217

Waith, Eugene M.   **2.5900**
Ideas of greatness; heroic drama in England [by] Eugene M. Waith. — New York: Barnes & Noble, [1971] xii, 292 p.: illus.; 23 cm. 1. English drama — Restoration — History and criticism. I. T.
PR691.W3 1971b   822/.0080353   LC 79-30481   ISBN 0389041815

Loftis, John Clyde, 1919- ed.   • **2.5901**
Restoration drama; modern essays in criticism, edited by John Loftis. — New York: Oxford University Press, 1966. xi, 371 p.; 21 cm. — (A Galaxy book, GB158) 1. English drama — Restoration, 1660-1700 — History and criticism. I. T.
PR693.L6   822.409   LC 66-10795

Miner, Earl Roy. ed.   • **2.5902**
Restoration dramatists; a collection of critical essays edited by Earl Miner. — Englewood Cliffs, N.J.: Prentice-Hall, [1966] 179 p.; 21 cm. — (Twentieth century views) (A Spectrum book.) 1. English drama — Restoration, 1660-1700 — History and criticism. I. T.
PR693.M5 1966   822.409   LC 66-28108

Restoration theatre.   **2.5903**
New York: St. Martin's Press, 1965. 240 p.: illus., port.; 23 cm. — (Stratford-upon-Avon studies. 6) 1. English drama — Restoration, 1660-1700 — Addresses, essays, lectures. I. Series.
PR693.R4   822.409   LC 64-8015

Loftis, John Clyde, 1919-.   **2.5904**
The Spanish plays of neoclassical England, by John Loftis. — New Haven: Yale University Press, 1973. xiii, 263 p.; 25 cm. 1. English drama — Restoration, 1660-1700 — History and criticism. 2. Literature, Comparative — Spanish and English. 3. Literature, Comparative — English and Spanish. I. T.
PR695.L6   822/.009   LC 73-77158   ISBN 0300013019

Staves, Susan, 1942-.   **2.5905**
Players' scepters: fictions of authority in the Restoration / Susan Staves. — Lincoln: University of Nebraska Press, c1979. xviii, 361 p.; 23 cm. 1. English drama — Restoration, 1660-1700 — History and criticism. 2. Authority in literature. 3. Great Britain — Intellectual life — 17th century I. T.
PR698.A98 S8   822/.4/09   LC 78-24346   ISBN 080324102X

Fujimura, Thomas Hikaru, 1919-. • 2.5906
The Restoration comedy of wit, by Thomas H. Fujimura. New York, Barnes & Noble [1968, c1952] viii, 232 p. 23 cm. 1. English drama (Comedy) — History and criticism. 2. English drama — Restoration, 1660-1700 — History and criticism. I. Fujimura, Thomas Hikaru, 1919- Comedy of wit, 1660-1710. II. T. III. Title: The Comedy of wit, 1660-1710.
PR698.C6 F8 1968   822.05/2   LC 68-23760

Harwood, John T. 2.5907
Critics, values, and Restoration comedy / by John T. Harwood. — Carbondale: Southern Illinois University Press, c1982. xvii, 177 p.: ill.; 22 cm. Includes index. 1. English drama — Restoration, 1660-1700 — History and criticism. 2. English drama (Comedy) — History and criticism. 3. Literature and morals 4. Criticism I. T.
PR698.C6 H3 1982   822/.0523 19   LC 81-18397   ISBN 080931049X

Smith, John Harrington. 2.5908
The gay couple in Restoration comedy. Cambridge Harvard University Press 1948. 252p. 1. English drama — Restoration — History and criticism I. T.
PR698 L6 S5

Dobrée, Bonamy, 1891-. • 2.5909
Restoration tragedy, 1660–1720, by Bonamy Dobrée. — Oxford, The Clarendon press, 1929. 189, [1] p. 20 cm. 1. English drama — Restoration — Hist. & crit. 2. English drama (Tragedy) — Hist. & crit. I. T.
PR698.T7D6   822.09   LC 30-14609

PR701–719 18th Century

Boas, Frederick S. (Frederick Samuel), 1862-1957. • 2.5910
An introduction to eighteenth–century drama, 1700–1780. — Oxford, Clarendon Press, 1953. x, 365 p. front. 19 cm. 1. English drama — 18th cent. — Hist. & crit. I. T.
PR703.B6   822.509   LC 53-8184

Bevis, Richard W. 2.5911
The laughing tradition: stage comedy in Garrick's day / Richard Bevis. — Athens: University of Georgia Press, c1980. x, 282 p.; 24 cm. Based on the author's thesis, University of California, Berkeley. 1. English drama — 18th century — History and criticism. 2. English drama (Comedy) — History and criticism. 3. Theater — England — History. I. T.
PR708.C6 B4 1980   822/.6/09   LC 79-48001   ISBN 0820305146

Hume, Robert D. 2.5912
The rakish stage: studies in English drama, 1660–1800 / Robert D. Hume. — Carbondale: Southern Illinois University Press, c1983. xvi, 382 p.; 24 cm. 1. English drama — 18th century — History and criticism — Addresses, essays, lectures. 2. English drama — Restoration, 1660-1700 — History and criticism — Addresses, essays, lectures. 3. English drama (Comedy) — History and criticism — Addresses, essays, lectures. I. T.
PR708.C6 H8 1983   822/.009 19   LC 82-16984   ISBN 0809311003

Bernbaum, Ernest, 1879-. • 2.5913
The drama of sensibility: a sketch of the history of English sentimental comedy and domestic tragedy, 1696–1780 / by Ernest Bernbaum. — Gloucester, Mass.: P. Smith, 19958. 288 p.; 21 cm. — (Harvard studies in English; v.3) 1. English drama — 18th century — History and criticism. 2. Sentimentalism in literature I. T. II. Series.
PR711.B45 1958   LC 63-6749

Bateson, Frederick Wilse, 1901-. • 2.5914
English comic drama, 1700–1750. — New York: Russell & Russell, 1963. 158 p.; 23 cm. 1. English drama — 18th century — History and criticism. 2. English drama (Comedy) — History and criticism. I. T.
PR714.C6 B3 1963   822.509   LC 63-8357

Loftis, John Clyde, 1919-. • 2.5915
The politics of drama in Augustan England. — Oxford, Clarendon Press, 1963. 173 p. 23 cm. Bibliographical footnotes. 1. English drama — Restoration — Hist. & crit. 2. English drama — 18th cent. — Hist. & crit. 3. Politics in literature I. T.
PR714.P6L6   822.509   LC 63-25966

Kern, Jean B. 2.5916
Dramatic satire in the age of Walpole, 1720–1750 / Jean B. Kern. — 1st ed. — Ames: Iowa State University Press, 1976. x, 189 p.; 22 cm. (A Replica edition) Includes index. 1. English drama — 18th century — History and criticism. 2. Satire, English — History and criticism. I. T.
PR714.S2 K4   822/.009   LC 75-32883   ISBN 0813804507

Loftis, John Clyde, 1919-. • 2.5917
Comedy and society from Congreve to Fielding. Stanford, Calif.: Stanford University Press, c1959. ix, 154 p.: map; 23 cm. (Stanford studies in language and literature; 19) 1. English drama — 18th century — History and criticism.

2. English drama (Comedy) — History and criticism. 3. Literature and society I. T. II. Series.
PR714.S6 L6   LC 59-10635

PR721–739 19th–20th Centuries

Nicoll, Allardyce, 1894-. • 2.5918
A history of late nineteenth century drama, 1850–1900 / by Allardyce Nicoll. — Cambridge: University Press, 1946. 2 v. (xii, 772 p.) 1. English drama — 19th century — History and criticism. 2. English drama — 19th century — Bibliography. 3. Theater — England — History. I. T.
PR721.N46   LC 47-5128

Booth, Michael R. 2.5919
English melodrama, by Michael R. Booth. — London: H. Jenkins, [1965] 223 p.: illus., facsims., plates.; 23 cm. 1. English drama — 19th century — History and criticism. 2. Melodrama I. T.
PR728.M4 B6   822.709   LC 66-5700

Taylor, John Russell. • 2.5920
The rise and fall of the well-made play. — [1st American ed.]. — New York: Hill and Wang, [1967] 175 p.; 23 cm. 1. English drama — 19th century — History and criticism. 2. English drama — 20th century — History and criticism. I. T.
PR731.T3 1967b   822/.8/09   LC 67-25684

Donoghue, Denis. • 2.5921
The third voice: modern British and American verse drama. — Princeton, N.J.: Princeton University Press, 1959. 286 p.; 23 cm. 1. Verse drama, English — History and criticism. 2. Verse drama, American — History and criticism. 3. English drama — 20th century — History and criticism. 4. American drama — 20th century — History and criticism. I. T.
PR736.D6   822.9109   LC 59-5595

Kerensky, Oleg, 1930-. 2.5922
The new British drama: fourteen playwrights since Osborne and Pinter / Oleg Kerensky. — New York: Taplinger Pub. Co., [1979] c1977. xx, 276 p.; 22 cm. Includes index. 1. English drama — 20th century — History and criticism. I. T.
PR736.K4 1979   822/.9/1409   LC 78-56986   ISBN 0800854993

Nightingale, Benedict, 1939-. 2.5923
A reader's guide to fifty modern British plays / by Benedict Nightingale. — London: Heinemann; Totowa, N.J.: Barnes & Noble, 1983 (c1982). 479 p.; 21 cm. — (Reader's guide series) Includes index. 1. English drama — 20th century — History and criticism. I. T.
PR736.N5 1982   822/.91/09 19   LC 82-11448   ISBN 0389202398

Taylor, John Russell. • 2.5924
[Anger, and after] The angry theatre; new British drama. Rev. and expanded ed. New York, Hill and Wang [1969] 391 p. illus., ports. 22 cm. First published in England under title: Anger, and after: a guide to the new British drama. 1. English drama — 20th century — History and criticism. 2. Theater — England. I. T.
PR736.T3 1969b   822/.9/1409   LC 78-88010   ISBN 0809026635

Taylor, John Russell. 2.5925
The second wave; British drama for the seventies. [1st American ed.] New York, Hill and Wang [1971] 236 p. 21 cm. 1. English drama — 20th century — History and criticism. 2. Theater — England. I. T.
PR736.T34 1971   822/.9/1409   LC 73-167983   ISBN 0809085186

Contemporary dramatists / with a preface by Ruby Cohn; editor, James Vinson; associate editor, D.L. Kirkpatrick. 2.5926
3rd ed. — New York: St. Martin's Press, 1982. xiv, 1104 p.; 24 cm. — (Contemporary writers of the English language.) Includes index. 1. English drama — 20th century — Bio-bibliography. 2. American drama — 20th century — Bio-bibliography. 3. English drama — 20th century — History and criticism — Addresses, essays, lectures. 4. American drama — 20th century — History and criticism — Addresses, essays, lectures. I. Vinson, James, 1933- II. Kirkpatrick, D. L. III. Series.
PR737.C57 1982   822/.914/09 19   LC 82-22994   ISBN 0312166648

Spanos, William V. 2.5927
The Christian tradition in modern British verse drama: the poetics of sacramental time [by] William V. Spanos. With a foreword by E. Martin Browne. — New Brunswick, N.J.: Rutgers University Press, [1967] xvi, 400 p.; 25 cm. 1. Verse drama, English — History and criticism 2. Religion in drama I. T.
PR739.R4 S6   822/.9/12093   LC 66-18882

Keyssar, Helene. 2.5928
Feminist theatre: an introduction to plays of contemporary British and American women / Helene Keyssar. — 1st Evergreen ed. — New York: Grove

Press, c1985. xvi, 223 p., [8] p. de planches: ill. — (Grove Press modern dramatists.) 1. English drama — Women authors — History and criticism. 2. American drama — 20th century — History and criticism. 3. American drama — Women authors — History and criticism. 4. Feminism in literature. 5. Feminist theater — United States. 6. Feminist theater — Great Britain. I. T. II. Series.
PR739.W62 K48   *LC* 85-70226   *ISBN* 0394620593

PR751–999 Prose

Gordon, Ian Alistair, 1908-.   **2.5929**
The movement of English prose / Ian A. Gordon; foreword by Randolph Quirk. — Bloomington: Indiana University Press, c1966. viii, 182 p. 1. English prose literature — History and criticism I. T.
PR751.G6 1967   *LC* 67-24520

Sutherland, James Runcieman, 1900-.   • **2.5930**
On English prose / by James Sutherland. — Toronto: University of Toronto Press, c1957. 123 p. (The Alexander lectures; 1956-57) 1. English prose literature — History and criticism. I. T.
PR753.S8   820.9   *LC* 58-251

Chambers, R. W. (Raymond Wilson), 1874-1942.   • **2.5931**
On the continuity of English prose from Alfred to More and his school / edited by E.V. Hitchcock and R.W. Chambers. — London: University Press for the Early English Text Society, 1932. xi, xlv-clxxiv p.; 22 cm. — 1. More, Thomas, Sir, Saint, 1478-1535. 2. English prose literature — History and criticism. I. Hitchcock, Elsie Vaughan. II. T.
PR767.C5   *LC* 33-1779

Krapp, George Philip, 1872-1934.   • **2.5932**
The rise of English literary prose / George Philip Krapp. — New York: F. Ungar, 1963. xiii, 551 p.; 22 cm. 1. English prose literature — Early modern, 1500-1700 — History and criticism. I. T.
PR767.K7 1963   828.209   *LC* 63-12909

Batten, Charles.   **2.5933**
Pleasurable instruction: form and convention in eighteenth-century travel literature / by Charles L. Batten, Jr. — Berkeley: University of California Press, c1978. xii, 170 p.: ill.; 24 cm. 1. English prose literature — 18th century — History and criticism. 2. Travel in literature 3. Voyages and travels — History. I. T.
PR769.B3   820/.9/005 19   *LC* 76-14316   *ISBN* 0520032608

Fish, Stanley Eugene. comp.   **2.5934**
Seventeenth-century prose; modern essays in criticism. Edited by Stanley E. Fish. — New York: Oxford University Press, 1971. xi, 572 p.; 21 cm. — (A Galaxy book, GB 348) 1. English prose literature — Early modern, 1500-1700 — Addresses, essays, lectures. I. T.
PR769.F5 1971   828/.3/0808   *LC* 75-141848   *ISBN* 0195013034

Williamson, George, 1898-1968.   • **2.5935**
The Senecan amble: a study in prose form from Bacon to Collier / George Williamson. — London: Faber and Faber, 1951. 377 p.; 23 cm. 1. English prose literature — Early modern, 1500-1700 — History and criticism. I. T.
PR769.W5 1951b   *LC* 53-1695

Cottom, Daniel.   **2.5936**
The civilized imagination: a study of Ann Radcliffe, Jane Austen, and Sir Walter Scott / Daniel Cottom. — Cambridge [Cambridgeshire]; New York: Cambridge University Press, 1985. ix, 229 p.; 22 cm. Includes index. 1. Radcliffe, Ann Ward, 1764-1823 — Aesthetics. 2. Austen, Jane, 1775-1817 — Aesthetics. 3. Scott, Walter, Sir, 1771-1832 — Aesthetics. 4. English fiction — 19th century — History and criticism. 5. Aesthetics in literature. 6. Social classes in literature 7. Literature and society — Great Britain. I. T.
PR778.A38 C68 1985   823/.7/09 19   *LC* 84-17002   *ISBN* 0521301726

Levine, George Lewis.   • **2.5937**
The art of Victorian prose, edited by George Levine & William Madden. — New York: Oxford University Press, 1968. xxi, 378 p.; 24 cm. 1. English prose literature — 19th century — Addresses, essays, lectures. I. Madden, William Anthony, 1923- joint author. II. T.
PR783.L4   828/.8/08   *LC* 68-15896

DeLaura, David J.   **2.5938**
Victorian prose; a guide to research. Edited by David J. DeLaura. — New York: Modern Language Association of America, 1973. xvi, 560 p.; 25 cm. 'Designed to join two ... earlier volumes: Victorian fiction: a guide to research (1964), edited by Lionel Stevenson, and The Victorian poets: a guide to research (2nd ed., 1968), edited by Frederic E. Faverty.' 1. English prose literature — 19th century — Bio-bibliography. I. T.
PR785.D4   820/.9/008   *LC* 73-80586   *ISBN* 0873522508

Approaches to Victorian autobiography / edited by George P. Landow.   **2.5939**
Athens, Ohio: Ohio University Press, 1979 (c1978). xlvi, 359 p.; 24 cm. 1. English prose literature — 19th century — History and criticism — Addresses, essays, lectures. 2. Autobiography — Addresses, essays, lectures. 3. Authors, English — 19th century — Biography — Addresses, essays, lectures. I. Landow, George P.
PR788.A95 A6   820/.9/08   *LC* 77-91505   *ISBN* 0821404008

PR820–888 PROSE FICTION. THE NOVEL

Allen, Walter Ernest, 1911-.   • **2.5940**
The English novel; a short critical history. — [1st American ed.]. — New York: Dutton, 1955 [c1954] 454 p.; 20 cm. 1. English fiction — History and criticism. I. T.
PR821.A4 1955   823.09   *LC* 55-8325

Baker, Ernest Albert, 1869-1941.   **2.5941**
The history of the English novel. repr. of 1924 ed. — New York Barnes & Noble [1950] 10 v. 1. English fiction — History and criticism I. T.
PR821 B3 1950

Bradbury, Malcolm, 1932-.   **2.5942**
Possibilities: essays on the state of the novel. — London; New York: Oxford University Press, 1973. xiii, 297 p.; 21 cm. 1. English fiction — History and criticism. I. T.
PR821.B7   823/.03   *LC* 73-168713   *ISBN* 0192121898

Day, Robert Adams.   **2.5943**
Told in letters: epistolary fiction before Richardson / Robert Adams Day. — Ann Arbor: University of Michigan Press, 1966. 281 p. Appendices (p. 237-270): A. A chronological list of English letter fiction, 1660-1740.—B. Notes on epistolary miscellanies.—C. A list of letter fiction in periodicals. 1. English fiction — Early modern, 1500-1700 — History and criticism. 2. English fiction — 18th century — History and criticism. I. T.
PR821.D3   823.009   *LC* 66-11077

Kettle, Arnold.   • **2.5944**
An introduction to the English novel. — London; New York: Hutchinson's University Library, [1951-53] 2 v.; 19 cm. — (Hutchinson's university library: English literature) 1. English fiction — History and criticism. I. T.
PR821.K4   820.09   *LC* 52-10810

Leavis, Q. D. (Queenie Dorothy)   • **2.5945**
Fiction and the reading public / Q.D. Leavis. — London: Chatto & Windus, 1932. xvi, 348 p.; 23 cm. 'Select bibliography': p. 336-343. 'The outline of popular fiction': p. 330-335. 1. English fiction — History and criticism 2. Books and reading I. T.
PR821 L4   *LC* 32-25568

Milligan, Ian.   **2.5946**
The novel in English: an introduction / Ian Milligan. — New York: St. Martin's Press, c1983. vi, 174 p.; 23 cm. Includes index. 1. English fiction — History and criticism. 2. American fiction — History and criticism. 3. Fiction — History and criticism I. T.
PR821.M54 1983   823/.009 19   *LC* 82-23100   *ISBN* 0312579675

Saintsbury, George, 1845-1933.   • **2.5947**
The English novel. London, J. M. Dent; New York, E. P. Dutton, 1913. St. Clair Shores, Mich., Scholarly Press, 1971. vii, 319 p. 22 cm. 1. English fiction — History and criticism. I. T.
PR821.S3 1971   823/.03   *LC* 78-145277   *ISBN* 0403011922

Stevenson, Lionel, 1902-1973.   • **2.5948**
The English novel, a panorama. — Boston, Houghton Mifflin [1960] 539 p. 23 cm. Includes bibliography. 1. English fiction — Hist. & crit. I. T.
PR821.S7   823.09   *LC* 60-16142

Van Ghent, Dorothy Bendon, 1907-.   • **2.5949**
The English novel, form and function. — New York: Rinehart, [1953] 276 p.; 24 cm. 1. English fiction — History and criticism. I. T.
PR821.V3   823.09   *LC* 53-9368

Scott, Walter, Sir, 1771-1832.   • **2.5950**
The lives of the novelists. London: Dent; New York: Dutton, [1910] xv, 408 p.; 18 cm. (Everyman's library, [v.331]) Introduction by George Saintsbury. 1. English fiction — History and criticism. 2. Novelists, English I. T.
PR823.S43 Lx   808.8

Twelve original essays on great English novels / edited by Charles Shapiro.   **2.5951**
Detroit: Wayne State University Press, 1960. 281 p.; 21 cm. 1. English fiction — History and criticism — Addresses, essays, lectures. I. Shapiro, Charles, 1926-. II. Title: 12 original essays on great English novels.
PR823.S5   820.9   823.09   *LC* 60-6374

Stevick, Philip.   • 2.5952
The chapter in fiction; theories of narrative division. [1st ed. Syracuse, N. Y.] Syracuse University Press [1970] 188 p. 22 cm. 1. English fiction — History and criticism 2. American fiction — History and criticism. I. T.
PR826.S73   823/.009   LC 75-125079   ISBN 815600704

Penzoldt, Peter.   2.5953
The supernatural in fiction. — [London]: P. Nevill, [1952] 271 p.; 23 cm. 1. Supernatural in literature 2. Short stories, English — History and criticism. 3. Short story I. T.
PR829.P4   LC 53-6698

PR830 Special Topics, A–Z

PR830.A–E

Buckley, Jerome Hamilton.   2.5954
Season of youth: the Bildungsroman from Dickens to Golding. Cambridge, Mass., Harvard University Press, 1974. x, 336 p. 22 cm. 1. English fiction — History and criticism. 2. Autobiographical fiction 3. Bildungsroman I. T.
PR830.A8 B8   823   LC 73-85887   ISBN 0674796403

Women writers and the city: essays in feminist literary criticism   2.5955
/ Susan Merrill Squier, editor.
Knoxville: University of Tennessee Press, c1984. 306 p.; 23 cm. Includes index. 1. English fiction — Women authors — History and criticism — Addresses, essays, lectures. 2. City and town life in literature — Addresses, essays, lectures. 3. American literature — Women authors — History and criticism — Addresses, essays, lectures. 4. French literature — Women authors — History and criticism — Addresses, essays, lectures. 5. Feminist literary criticism — Addresses, essays, lectures. I. Squier, Susan Merrill.
PR830.C53 W66 1984   809/.93321732 19   LC 83-17109   ISBN 0870494155

Butler, William Vivian, 1927-.   2.5956
The durable desperadoes; preface by Anthony Lejeune. — London: Macmillan, 1973. 288 p.; 21 cm. Includes index. 1. Detective and mystery stories, English — History and criticism. 2. English fiction — 20th century — History and criticism. 3. Outlaws in literature I. T.
PR830.D4 B86   823/.0872   LC 74-168988   ISBN 0333142179

Keating, H. R. F. (Henry Reymond Fitzwalter), 1926-.   2.5957
Murder must appetize / by H.R.F. Keating. — Rev. ed., 1st ed. in the U.S. — New York: Mysterious Press; London: Lemon Tree Press, 1981. 49, [18] p.; ill.; 22 cm. 1. Detective and mystery stories, English — History and criticism. I. T.
PR830.D4 K4 1981   823/.0872/09 19   LC 81-83116   ISBN 0892960523

Panek, LeRoy.   2.5958
Watteau's shepherds: the detective novel in Britain, 1914–1940 / LeRoy Panek. — Bowling Green, Ohio: Bowling Green University Popular Press, c1979. 232 p.: ill.; 24 cm. 1. Detective and mystery stories, English — History and criticism. I. T.
PR830.D4 P34   823/.0872   LC 79-83887   ISBN 0879721316

Routley, Erik.   2.5959
The puritan pleasures of the detective story: a personal monograph. — London: Gollancz, 1972. 253 p.; 22 cm. 1. Detective and mystery stories, English — History and criticism. 2. Detective and mystery stories, American — History and criticism. I. T.
PR830.D4 R6   823/.0872   LC 72-192225   ISBN 0575013842

Watson, Colin.   2.5960
Snobbery with violence: crime stories and their audience. — New York: St. Martin's Press, [1972, c1971] 256 p.: illus.; 23 cm. 1. Detective and mystery stories, English — History and criticism. I. T.
PR830.D4 W3 1972   823/.0872   LC 73-190584

Whodunit?: a guide to crime, suspense, and spy fiction / [edited   2.5961
by] H.R.F. Keating.
New York: Van Nostrand Reinhold Co., 1982. 320 p.: ill.; 24 cm. Includes index. 1. Detective and mystery stories, English — History and criticism. 2. Detective and mystery stories, American — History and criticism. 3. Crime and criminals in literature 4. Spy stories — History and criticism. 5. Fiction — Authorship I. Keating, H. R. F. (Henry Reymond Fitzwalter), 1926-
PR830.D4 W44 1982   823/.0872/09 19   LC 82-8616   ISBN 0442254385

Tillyard, E. M. W. (Eustace Mandeville Wetenhall), 1889-1962.   • 2.5962
The epic strain in the English novel. London, Chatto & Windus, 1958. 207 p. map. 23 cm. 1. Epic literature — History and criticism. 2. English fiction — History and criticism. I. T.
PR830.E6 T5 1958   LC A 58-5625

PR830.F–P

De Camp, L. Sprague (Lyon Sprague), 1907-.   2.5963
Literary swordsmen and sorcerers: the makers of heroic fantasy / L. Sprague de Camp. — Sauk City, Wis.: Arkham House, c1976. xxix, 313 p., [5] leaves of plates: ill.; 21 cm. 1. Fantastic fiction, English — History and criticism. 2. Fantastic fiction, American — History and criticism. I. T.
PR830.F3 D4   809/.933/7   LC 76-17991   ISBN 0870540769

Irwin, William Robert, 1915-.   2.5964
The game of the impossible: a rhetoric of fantasy / W. R. Irwin. Urbana: University of Illinois Press, c1976. xii, 215 p.; 24 cm. Includes index. 1. Fantastic fiction, English — History and criticism. 2. Fantastic fiction, American — History and criticism. I. T.
PR830.F3 I7   823/.8/0915   LC 76-13459   ISBN 0252005872

Little, T. E.   2.5965
The fantasts: studies in J.R.R. Tolkien, Lewis Carroll, Mervyn Peake, Nikolay Gogol, and Kenneth Grahame / by Edmund Little. — Amersham, England: Avebury, 1984. viii, 136 p.; 22 cm. 1. Fantastic fiction, English — History and criticism. 2. English fiction — 19th century — History and criticism. 3. English fiction — 20th century — History and criticism. I. T.
PR830.F3 L58 1984   823/.0876/09 19   LC 84-181608   ISBN 0861272129

Manlove, C. N. (Colin Nicholas), 1942-.   2.5966
The impulse of fantasy literature / C.N. Manlove. — Kent, Ohio: Kent State University Press, c1983. xiii, 174 p.; 22 cm. 1. Fantastic fiction, English — History and criticism. 2. Fantastic fiction, American — History and criticism. I. T.
PR830.F3 M28 1983   823/.0876/09 19   LC 82-15335   ISBN 0873382730

Manlove, C. N. (Colin Nicholas), 1942-.   2.5967
Modern fantasy: five studies / C. N. Manlove. — Cambridge; New York: Cambridge University Press, 1975. viii, 308 p.; 22 cm. 1. Fantastic fiction, English — History and criticism. 2. English fiction — 20th century — History and criticism. 3. English fiction — 19th century — History and criticism. I. T.
PR830.F3 M3   823/.0876   LC 74-31798   ISBN 0521207460

A Reference guide to modern fantasy for children / [editor] Pat   2.5968
Pflieger, Helen M. Hill, advisory editor.
Westport, Conn.: Greenwood Press, 1984. xvii, 690 p.; 25 cm. Includes index. 1. Fantastic fiction, English — Dictionaries. 2. Fantastic fiction, American — Dictionaries. 3. Children's stories, English — Dictionaries. 4. Children's stories, American — Dictionaries. I. Pflieger, Pat. II. Hill, Helen, 1915-
PR830.F3 R4 1984   823/.0876/09282 19   LC 83-10692   ISBN 0313228868

Tymn, Marshall B., 1937-.   2.5969
Fantasy literature: a core collection and reference guide / Marshall B. Tymn, Kenneth J. Zahorski, and Robert H. Boyer. — New York: R. R. Bowker Co., 1979. xiii, 273 p.; 24 cm. Includes index. 1. Fantastic fiction, English — History and criticism — Addresses, essays, lectures. 2. Fantastic fiction, American — History and criticism — Addresses, essays, lectures. 3. Fantastic fiction, English — Bibliography. 4. Fantastic fiction, American — Bibliography. I. Zahorski, Kenneth J., 1939- joint author. II. Boyer, Robert H., 1937- joint author. III. T.
PR830.F3 T9   016.823/0876   LC 79-1533   ISBN 0835211533

Brownstein, Rachel M.   2.5970
Becoming a heroine: reading about women in novels / Rachel M. Brownstein. — New York: Viking Press, 1982. xxviii, 332 p.; 24 cm. Includes index. 1. English fiction — History and criticism. 2. Heroines in literature 3. Women in literature 4. Women — Books and reading I. T.
PR830.H4 B76 1982   823/.009/352042 19   LC 81-24021   ISBN 0670154431

Cox, C. B.   • 2.5971
The free spirit, a study of liberal humanism in the novels of George Eliot, Henry James, E. M. Forster, Virginia Woolf [and] Angus Wilson. — London, New York, Oxford University Press, 1963. 195 p. 23 cm. Includes bibliography. 1. English fiction — 19th cent. — Hist. & crit. 2. English fiction — 20th cent. — Hist. & crit. 3. Humanism I. T.
PR830.H8C6   823.91209   LC 63-4598

Parry, Benita.   2.5972
Delusions and discoveries; studies on India in the British imagination, 1880-1930. — Berkeley: University of California Press, [1972] 368 p.; 23 cm. 1. English fiction — History and criticism. 2. British — India 3. India in literature. I. T.
PR830.I6 P3 1972b   823/.009/32   LC 70-186786   ISBN 0520022157

Cockshut, A. O. J.   2.5973
Man and woman: a study of love and the novel, 1740–1940 / A. O. J. Cockshut. — New York: Oxford University Press, 1978, c1977. 221 p.; 22 cm. 1. English fiction — History and criticism. 2. Love in literature I. T.
PR830.L69 C6 1978   823/.03   *LC* 77-18142   *ISBN* 0195200403

Alcorn, John, 1923-.   2.5974
The nature novel from Hardy to Lawrence / John Alcorn. New York: Columbia University Press, 1977. x, 139 p.; 23 cm. Includes index. 1. English fiction — History and criticism. 2. Nature in literature I. T.
PR830.N36 A4 1977   823/.03   *LC* 76-17552   *ISBN* 0231041225

Literature of the occult; a collection of critical essays / edited   2.5975
by Peter B. Messent.
Englewood Cliffs, N.J.: Prentice-Hall, c1981. xi, 188 p.; 21 cm. — (Twentieth century views) (A Spectrum book) 1. English fiction — History and criticism — Addresses, essays, lectures. 2. Occultism in literature — Addresses, essays, lectures. 3. Supernatural in literature — Addresses, essays, lectures. 4. American fiction — History and criticism — Addresses, essays, lectures. 5. Gothic revival (Literature) — Addresses, essays, lectures. 6. Ghost stories — History and criticism — Addresses, essays, lectures. I. Messent, Peter B.
PR830.O33 L57   823/.009/37 19   *LC* 80-26190   *ISBN* 0135377129

Wilding, Michael.   2.5976
Political fictions / Michael Wilding. — London; Boston: Routledge & Kegan Paul, 1980. ix, 266 p.; 22 cm. Includes index. 1. English fiction — History and criticism. 2. American fiction — History and criticism. 3. Politics and literature I. T.
PR830.P6 W5 1980   823/.8/09 19   *LC* 80-506746   *ISBN* 0710004575

PR830.S–T

Aldiss, Brian Wilson, 1925-.   2.5977
Trillion year spree: the history of science fiction / by Brian W. Aldiss; with David Wingrove. — 1st American ed. — New York: Atheneum, 1986. 511 p., [16] p. of plates: ill.; 25 cm. Reprint. Originally published: Billion year spree. London: Weidenfeld and Nicolson, 1973. Includes index. 1. Science fiction, English — History and criticism. 2. Science fiction, American — History and criticism. I. Wingrove, David. II. T.
PR830.S35 A38 1986   823/.0876/09 19   *LC* 86-47682   *ISBN* 0689118392

Amis, Kingsley.   2.5978
New maps of hell; a survey of science fiction. — [1st ed.]. — New York: Harcourt, Brace, [1960] 161 p.; 21 cm. 1. Science fiction, English — History and criticism. 2. Science fiction, American — History and criticism. 3. American fiction — History and criticism. I. T.
PR830.S35 A4   823.093   *LC* 60-5441

Parrinder, Patrick.   2.5979
Science fiction: its criticism and teaching / Patrick Parrinder. — London; New York: Methuen, 1980. xix, 166 p.; 21 cm. — (New accents) Includes index. 1. Science fiction, English — History and criticism. 2. Science fiction, American — History and criticism. 3. Science fiction — Study and teaching. I. T.
PR830.S35 P3 1980   823/.0876/09 19   *LC* 81-192471   *ISBN* 0416713904

Philmus, Robert M.   2.5980
Into the unknown; the evolution of science fiction from Francis Godwin to H. G. Wells [by] Robert M. Philmus. — Berkeley: University of California Press, 1970. ix, 174 p.; 24 cm. 1. Science fiction, English — History and criticism. I. T.
PR830.S35 P5   823/.0876   *LC* 70-84790   *ISBN* 0520013948

Scholes, Robert E.   2.5981
Structural fabulation: an essay on fiction of the future / Robert Scholes. — Notre Dame, Ind.: University of Notre Dame Press, [1975] xi, lll p.; 21 cm. (Ward-Phillips lectures in English language and literature. v. 7) Based on 4 lectures delivered at the University of Notre Dame in 1974, now extensively revised. Includes index. 1. Science fiction, English — History and criticism — Addresses, essays, lectures. 2. Science fiction, American — History and criticism — Addresses, essays, lectures. 3. English fiction — 20th century — History and criticism — Addresses, essays, lectures. 4. American fiction — 20th century — History and criticism — Addresses, essays, lectures. I. T. II. Series.
PR830.S35 S3   PR830S35 S3.   823/.0876   *LC* 74-30167   *ISBN* 0268005702

Street, Brian V.   2.5982
The savage in literature: representations of 'primitive' society in English fiction, 1858–1920 / Brian V. Street. — London; Boston: Routledge & K. Paul, 1975. xii, 207 p.; 23 cm. (International library of anthropology.) Includes index. 1. English fiction — 19th century — History and criticism. 2. English fiction

— 20th century — History and criticism. 3. Society, Primitive, in literature. I. T. II. Series.
PR830.S63 S7   823/.8/09352   *LC* 75-321131   *ISBN* 0710081103

Barclay, Glen St. John, 1930-.   2.5983
Anatomy of horror: the masters of occult fiction / Glen St. John Barclay. — New York: St. Martin's Press, 1979, c1978. 144 p.; 22 cm. Includes index. 1. Horror tales, English — History and criticism. 2. Horror tales, American — History and criticism. 3. Occultism in literature I. T.
PR830.T3 B37 1979   823/.0872   *LC* 78-70899   *ISBN* 0312034083

Summers, Montague, 1880-1948.   ● 2.5984
The Gothic quest: a history of the Gothic novel / by Montague Summers. — New York: Russell & Russell, 1964. 443 p.: ill., ports. 1. Lewis, M. G. (Matthew Gregory), 1775-1818. 2. English fiction — 18th century — History and criticism 3. Romanticism — England I. T.
PR830.T3 S9 1964   *LC* 64-8919

Wilt, Judith, 1941-.   2.5985
Ghosts of the gothic: Austen, Eliot, & Lawrence / Judith Wilt. — Princeton, N.J.: Princeton University Press, c1980. xii, 307 p., [2] leaves of plates: ill.; 23 cm. 1. Austen, Jane, 1775-1817 — Criticism and interpretation. 2. Eliot, George, 1819-1880 — Criticism and interpretation. 3. Lawrence, D. H. (David Herbert), 1885-1930 — Criticism and interpretation. 4. English fiction — History and criticism. 5. Gothic revival (Literature) — Great Britain. I. T.
PR830.T3 W5   823/.0872/09   *LC* 80-7559   *ISBN* 0691064393

PR830.W

Auerbach, Nina, 1943-.   2.5986
Communities of women: an idea in fiction / Nina Auerbach. — Cambridge, Mass.: Harvard University Press, 1978. 222 p.: ill.; 24 cm. 1. English fiction — History and criticism. 2. Women in literature 3. American fiction — 19th century — History and criticism. I. T.
PR830.W6 A9   823/.009/352   *LC* 77-21213   *ISBN* 0674151682

The Voyage in: fictions of female development / edited by   2.5987
Elizabeth Abel, Marianne Hirsch, and Elizabeth Langland.
Hanover, NH: Published for Dartmouth College by University Press of New England, 1983. vii, 366 p.; 22 cm. 'Fictions of female development cited in this volume': p. 357-359. 1. English fiction — Women authors — History and criticism — Addresses, essays, lectures. 2. Women in literature — Addresses, essays, lectures. 3. Sex role in literature — Addresses, essays, lectures. 4. Bildungsroman — Addresses, essays, lectures. 5. American fiction — Women authors — History and criticism — Addresses, essays, lectures. 6. Feminism and literature — Addresses, essays, lectures. I. Abel, Elizabeth. II. Hirsch, Marianne. III. Langland, Elizabeth.
PR830.W6 V69 1983   823/.009/9287 19   *LC* 82-40473   *ISBN* 0874512506

Newton, Judith Lowder.   2.5988
Women, power, and subversion: social strategies in British fiction, 1778–1860 / Judith Lowder Newton. — Athens: University of Georgia Press, c1981. xxi, 202 p.; 23 cm. Includes index. 1. English fiction — Women authors — History and criticism. 2. Women in literature 3. Power (Social sciences) in literature. 4. Feminism and literature 5. English fiction — 19th century — History and criticism. I. T.
PR830.W62 N4   823/.009/9287 19   *LC* 81-1068   *ISBN* 0820305642

Pratt, Annis.   2.5989
Archetypal patterns in women's fiction / Annis Pratt; with Barbara White, Andrea Loewenstein, Mary Wyer. — Bloomington: Indiana University Press, c1981. x, 211 p.; 25 cm. Includes index. 1. English fiction — Women authors — History and criticism. 2. American fiction — Women authors — History and criticism. 3. Myth in literature 4. Women and literature 5. Sex role in literature I. T.
PR830.W62 P7   823/.009/9287 19   *LC* 81-47167   *ISBN* 0253102529

Rigney, Barbara Hill, 1938-.   2.5990
Madness and sexual politics in the feminist novel: studies in Brontë, Woolf, Lessing, and Atwood / Barbara Hill Rigney. — Madison: University of Wisconsin Press, 1978. 148 p.; 23 cm. Includes index. 1. Atwood, Margaret Eleanor, 1939- — Criticism and interpretation. 2. English fiction — Women authors — History and criticism. 3. Mental illness in literature 4. Sex role in literature 5. Feminism and literature I. T.
PR830.W62 R5   823/.03   *LC* 78-53291   *ISBN* 0299077101

PR833 History of the Novel, by Period

Schlauch, Margaret, 1898-.   • **2.5991**
Antecedents of the English novel, 1400–1600: from Chaucer to Deloney.
Warszawa: PWN–Polish Scientific Publishers, 1963. viii, 264 p.; 22 cm.
1. English fiction — Early modern, 1500-1700 — History and criticism. I. T.
PR833.S3   LC 64-3786

Davis, Walter R.   **2.5992**
Idea and act in Elizabethan fiction, by Walter R. Davis. Princeton, N.J.:
Princeton University Press, 1969. viii, 301 p.; 23 cm. 1. English fiction — Early
modern, 1500-1700 — History and criticism. I. T.
PR836.D3   823/.3/09   LC 68-56307   ISBN 0691061629

Salzman, Paul.   **2.5993**
English prose fiction, 1558–1700: a critical history / Paul Salzman. — Oxford:
Clarendon Press; New York: Oxford University Press, 1985. xii, 391 p.; 23 cm.
Includes index. 1. English fiction — Early modern, 1500-1700 — History and
criticism. 2. Fiction — 15th and 16th centuries — History and criticism.
3. Fiction — 17th century — History and criticism. I. T.
PR836.S24 1985   823/.3/09 19   LC 84-12184   ISBN 0198128053

Kelly, Gary.   **2.5994**
The English Jacobin novel 1780–1805 / Gary Kelly. — Oxford [Eng.]; New
York: Clarendon Press, 1976. xi, 291 p.; 23 cm. Includes index. 1. Bage,
Robert, 1728-1801 — Criticism and interpretation. 2. Inchbald, Mrs.,
1753-1821 — Criticism and interpretation. 3. Holcroft, Thomas, 1745-1809 —
Criticism and interpretation. 4. Godwin, William, 1756-1836 — Criticism and
interpretation. 5. English fiction — 18th century — History and criticism.
I. T.
PR851.K4   823/.03   LC 77-352557   ISBN 0198120621

McKillop, Alan Dugald, 1892-.   • **2.5995**
The early masters of English fiction. — Lawrence: University of Kansas Press,
1956. 233 p.: illus., ports.; 24 cm. 1. English fiction — 18th century — History
and criticism. I. T.
PR851.M33   823.509   LC 55-11276

Richetti, John J.   **2.5996**
Popular fiction before Richardson: narrative patterns 1700–1739, by John J.
Richetti. — Oxford: Clarendon P., 1969. [9], 274 p.; 23 cm. 1. English fiction
— 18th century — History and criticism. I. T.
PR851.R5   823/.5/09   LC 71-422241   ISBN 0198116810

Rothstein, Eric.   **2.5997**
Systems of order and inquiry in later eighteenth–century fiction / Eric
Rothstein. — Berkeley: University of California Press, c1975. 274 p.; 23 cm.
1. English fiction — 18th century — History and criticism. I. T.
PR851.R6   823/.6/09   LC 74-16716   ISBN 0520028627

Tompkins, J. M. S. (Joyce Marjorie Sanxter), 1897-.   • **2.5998**
The popular novel in England, 1770–1800. Lincoln, University of Nebraska
Press, 1961. 388 p. 21 cm. (Bison book. BB121) 1. English fiction — 18th
century — History and criticism. I. T. II. Series.
PR851.T6 1961   823.609   LC 61-16192

Watt, Ian P.   • **2.5999**
The Rise of the novel: studies in Defoe, Richardson, and Fielding / by Ian Watt.
— Berkeley: University of California Press, c1957. 319 p.; 21 cm. 1. Defoe,
Daniel, 1661?-1731. 2. Richardson, Samuel, 1689-1761. 3. Fielding, Henry,
1707-1754. 4. English fiction — 18th century — History and criticism. I. T.
PR851.W3   LC 58-867   ISBN 0520013174

Williams, Ioan M. comp.   **2.6000**
Novel and romance, 1700–1800; a documentary record. Edited by Ioan
Williams. — New York: Barnes & Noble, [1970] xi, 484 p.; 23 cm. 1. English
fiction — 18th century — History and criticism. 2. Romances — History and
criticism. I. T.
PR852.W5   823/.6/09   LC 70-9802   ISBN 0389010634

Spector, Robert Donald. ed.   **2.6001**
Essays on the eighteenth–century novel. Bloomington, Indiana University Press
[1965] xii, 205 p. 20 cm. (A Midland book, MB-82) 1. English fiction — 18th
century — History and criticism. I. T.
PR853.S6   823.509   LC 65-11794

Howells, Coral Ann.   **2.6002**
Love, mystery, and misery: feeling in Gothic fiction / by Coral Ann Howells. —
London: University of London, The Athlone Press, 1978. 199 p.; 23 cm.
1. Gothic literature — England — History and criticism. 2. English fiction —
18th century — History and criticism. 3. English fiction — 19th century —
History and criticism. I. T.
PR 858 G6 H85 1978   ISBN 0485111810

Damrosch, Leopold.   **2.6003**
God's plot & man's stories: studies in the fictional imagination from Milton to
Fielding / Leopold Damrosch, Jr. — Chicago: University of Chicago Press,
1985. x, 343 p.: ill.; 24 cm. Includes index. 1. Milton, John, 1608-1674.
Paradise lost 2. English fiction — 18th century — History and criticism.
3. English fiction — Early modern, 1500-1700 — History and criticism.
4. Puritanism in literature. 5. Christianity in literature 6. Fiction — Stories,
plots, etc. I. T. II. Title: God's plot and man's stories.
PR858.P8 D3 1985   823/.4/09382 19   LC 84-8754   ISBN
0226135799

Foster, James Ralph, 1890-.   • **2.6004**
History of the pre-romantic novel in England / by James R. Foster. — New
York: Modern Language Association of America, 1949. xi, 294 p.: ill., ports.; 25
cm. (The Modern Language Association of America. Monograph series; 17)
1. English fiction — 18th century — History and criticism 2. French fiction —
History and criticism 3. Literature, Comparative — English and French
4. Literature, Comparative — French and English I. T. II. Series.
PR858R6 F6   LC 49-5698

Kiely, Robert.   **2.6005**
The romantic novel in England. — Cambridge: Harvard University Press, 1972.
vii, 275 p.; 24 cm. 1. English fiction — 18th century — History and criticism.
2. English fiction — 19th century — History and criticism. 3. Romanticism
I. T.
PR858.R73 K5   823/.085   LC 79-186677   ISBN 0674779355

PR861–868 19th Century

Brown, Julia Prewitt, 1948-.   **2.6006**
A reader's guide to the nineteenth century English novel / Julia Prewitt Brown.
— New York: Macmillan; London: Collier Macmillan, c1985. xx, 137 p., [1]
leaf of plates: ill.; 22 cm. Includes index. 1. English fiction — 19th century —
History and criticism. 2. Literature and society — Great Britain. 3. Great
Britain — Social conditions — 19th century I. T.
PR861.B76 1985   823/.7/09 19   LC 84-25001   ISBN 0025173707

Gindin, James Jack, 1926-.   **2.6007**
Harvest of a quiet eye: the novel of compassion [by] James Gindin. —
Bloomington: Indiana University Press, [1971] x, 370 p.; 25 cm. 1. English
fiction — 19th century — History and criticism. 2. English fiction — 20th
century — History and criticism. 3. American fiction — 19th century —
History and criticism. 4. American fiction — 20th century — History and
criticism. I. T.
PR861.G5   823/.03   LC 75-135006   ISBN 0253327059

Harris, Wendell V.   **2.6008**
British short fiction in the nineteenth century: a literary and bibliographic guide
/ by Wendell V. Harris. — Detroit: Wayne State University Press, 1979. 209 p.;
24 cm. Includes index. 1. Short stories, English — History and criticism.
2. English fiction — 19th century — History and criticism. 3. Short stories,
English — Bibliography. 4. English fiction — 19th century — Bibliography.
I. T.
PR861.H35   823/.01   LC 79-10810   ISBN 0814316360

Gill, Richard, 1922-.   **2.6009**
Happy rural seat; the English country house and the literary imagination. —
New Haven: Yale University Press, 1972. xix, 305 p.: illus.; 23 cm. 1. English
fiction — 19th century — History and criticism. 2. English fiction — 20th
century — History and criticism. 3. Architecture, Domestic, in literature I. T.
PR868.A7 G5 1972   823/.9/120932   LC 72-75192   ISBN
0300015240

Polhemus, Robert M.   **2.6010**
Comic faith: the great tradition from Austen to Joyce / Robert M. Polhemus.
— Chicago: University of Chicago Press, 1980. x, 398 p.; 24 cm. Includes index.
1. Joyce, James, 1882-1941 — Criticism and interpretation. 2. Comic, The
3. Religion in literature 4. English fiction — 19th century — History and
criticism. I. T.
PR868.C63 P6   823/.03   LC 79-24856   ISBN 0226673200

Irwin, Michael.   **2.6011**
Picturing: description and illusion in the nineteenth–century novel / Michael
Irwin. — London; Boston: Allen & Unwin, 1979. ix, 161 p.; 22 cm. 1. English
fiction — 19th century — History and criticism. 2. Description (Rhetoric)
I. T.
PR868.D39 I7   823/.03   LC 78-40883   ISBN 0048010219

Ousby, Ian, 1947-.   **2.6012**
Bloodhounds of heaven: the detective in English fiction from Godwin to Doyle
/ Ian Ousby. Cambridge, Mass.: Harvard University Press, 1976. x, 194 p.: ill.;
24 cm. 1. Detective and mystery stories, English — History and criticism.
2. English fiction — 19th century — History and criticism. 3. Detectives in
literature I. T.
PR868.D4 O9   823/.0872   LC 76-7069   ISBN 0674076575

Levine, George Lewis. 2.6013
The realistic imagination: English fiction from Frankenstein to Lady Chatterley / George Levine. — Chicago: University of Chicago Press, c1981. x, 357 p.; 24 cm. 1. English fiction — 19th century — History and criticism. 2. Realism in literature I. T.
PR868.R4 L48   823/.7/0912   *LC* 80-17444   *ISBN* 0226475506

PR871–878 Victorian Era

Cazamian, Louis François, 1877-1965. 2.6014
[Roman social en Angleterre, 1830-1850. English] The social novel in England, 1830–1850: Dickens, Disraeli, Mrs. Gaskell, Kingsley; translated, with a foreword, by Martin Fido. London, Boston, Routledge and Kegan Paul, 1973. xii, 369 p. 23 cm. Translation of Le roman social en Angleterre, 1830-1850. 1. English fiction — 19th century — History and criticism. 2. Literature and society — Great Britain. 3. Great Britain — Civilization — 19th century I. T.
PR871.C213 1973   823/.083   *LC* 72-95681   *ISBN* 0710072821

Halperin, John, 1941-. 2.6015
Egoism and self–discovery in the Victorian novel; studies in the ordeal of knowledge in the nineteenth century. Introd. by Walter Allen. New York, B. Franklin [1974] x, 293 p. ports. 23 cm. (Studies in literature and criticism, 1) 1. English fiction — 19th century — History and criticism. I. T.
PR871.H3 1974   823/.8/0935   *LC* 73-19510   *ISBN* 0833754858

Praz, Mario, 1896-. • 2.6016
[Crisi del'eroe nel romanzo vittoriano. English] The hero in eclipse in Victorian fiction; translated from the Italian by Angus Davidson. London, New York, Oxford U.P., 1969. [5], 478 p. 21 cm. (Oxford paperbacks, 175) Translation of La crisi del'eroe nel romanzo vittoriano.' 1. English fiction — 19th century — History and criticism. 2. Romanticism — England. 3. Middle classes in literature 4. Art and literature I. T.
PR871.P712 1969   823/.8/093   *LC* 79-495701   *ISBN* 019281060X

Stang, Richard, 1925-. • 2.6017
The theory of the novel in England, 1850–1870 / by Richard Stang. — New York: Columbia University Press, 1959. xii, 251 p.; 23 cm. Includes index. 1. English fiction — 19th century — History and criticism. 2. Fiction I. T. II. Title: The novel in England, 1850-1870.
PR871.S8 1959   *LC* 59-8115

Tillotson, Kathleen Mary. • 2.6018
Novels of the eighteen–forties. [With corrections. London] Oxford University Press [1961] 328 p. 20 cm. (Oxford paperbacks, no. 15) 1. English fiction — 19th century — History and criticism. I. T.
PR871.T5 1961   823.809   *LC* 61-3000

Victorian fiction: a second guide to research / edited by George 2.6019
H. Ford.
New York: Modern Language Association of America, 1978. xxv, 401 p.; 25 cm. Edition of 1964 edited by L. Stevenson. Includes index. 1. English fiction — 19th century — History and criticism. 2. English fiction — 19th century — Bibliography. I. Ford, George Harry, 1914- II. Stevenson, Lionel, 1902-1973. Victorian fiction.
PR871.V5 1978   823/.8/09 19   *LC* 77-83468   *ISBN* 0873522540

Williams, Raymond. 2.6020
The English novel from Dickens to Lawrence / Raymond Williams. — London: Hogarth Press, 1984, c1970. 196 p.; 20 cm. Reprint. Originally published: London: Chatto & Windus, 1970. Includes index. 1. English fiction — 19th century — History and criticism. 2. English fiction — 20th century — History and criticism. 3. England — Social life and customs — 19th century I. T.
PR871.W5x 1984   *LC* 86-672014   *ISBN* 070120558X

Cecil, David, Lord, 1902-. • 2.6021
Victorian novelists; essays in revaluation. With a new foreword by the author. — [Chicago] University of Chicago Press [1958] 311 p. 21 cm. First published in 1935 under title: Early Victorian novelists. 1. English fiction — 19th cent. — Hist. & crit. I. T.
PR873.C4 1958   823.809   *LC* 58-14686

Watt, Ian P. comp. 2.6022
The Victorian novel; modern essays in criticism, edited by Ian Watt. — London; New York: Oxford University Press, 1971. viii, 485 p.; 21 cm. — (A Galaxy book 351) 1. English fiction — 19th century — Addresses, essays, lectures. I. T.
PR873.W3 1971   823/.03   *LC* 77-135978   *ISBN* 0195013220

Reading the Victorian novel: detail into form / edited by Ian 2.6023
Gregor.
New York: Barnes & Noble Books, 1980. 314 p.; ill.; 23 cm. (Barnes & Noble critical studies) Imprint covered by label giving new place of publication: Totowa, N.J. 1. English fiction — 19th century — History and criticism —

Addresses, essays, lectures. 2. Fiction — Technique — Addresses, essays, lectures. 3. Reading — Addresses, essays, lectures. I. Gregor, Ian.
PR874.R4 1980   823/.8/09 19   *LC* 80-112099   *ISBN* 0064925420

Gilmour, Robin. 2.6024
The idea of the gentleman in the Victorian novel / Robin Gilmour. — London; Boston: Allen & Unwin, 1981. 190 p.; 23 cm. Includes index. 1. English fiction — 19th century — History and criticism. 2. Social ethics in literature. 3. Upper classes in literature. 4. Middle classes in literature 5. Men in literature 6. Great Britain — Gentry — History. I. T.
PR878.C64 G5   823/.8/0803520631 19   *LC* 81-10869   *ISBN* 0048000051

Cunningham, Valentine. 2.6025
Everywhere spoken against: dissent in the Victorian novel / Valentine Cunningham. Oxford: Clarendon Press, 1975. xii, 311 p.; 23 cm. Includes index. 1. English fiction — 19th century — History and criticism. 2. Dissenters in literature I. T.
PR878.D57 C8   823/.03   *LC* 76-365900   *ISBN* 0198120664

Beer, Gillian. 2.6026
Darwin's plots: evolutionary narrative in Darwin, George Eliot, and nineteenth–Century fiction / Gillian Beer. — London; Boston: Routledge & Kegan Paul, 1983. x, 303 p., [1] leaf of plates: ill.; 23 cm. Includes index. 1. Darwin, Charles, 1809-1882 — Influence. 2. Eliot, George, 1819-1880 — Criticism and interpretation. 3. Hardy, Thomas, 1840-1928 — Criticism and interpretation. 4. Evolution in literature. 5. English fiction — 19th century — History and criticism. 6. Literature and science I. T.
PR878.E95 B43 1983   823/.8/09357 19   *LC* 83-3103   *ISBN* 0710095058

Qualls, Barry V. 2.6027
The secular pilgrims of Victorian fiction: the novel as book of life / Barry V. Qualls. — Cambridge; New York: Cambridge University Press, 1982. xv, 217 p.: ill.; 22 cm. 1. English fiction — 19th century — History and criticism. 2. Pilgrims and pilgrimages in literature 3. Didactic fiction, English — History and criticism. I. T.
PR878.P53 Q3 1982   823/.8/0938 19   *LC* 82-1165   *ISBN* 0521244099

Sutherland, John, 1903-. 2.6028
Victorian novelists and publishers / J. A. Sutherland. — Chicago: University of Chicago Press, 1976. 251 p.; 23 cm. 1. English fiction — 19th century — History and criticism. 2. Publishers and publishing — Great Britain. 3. Authors and publishers — Great Britain. I. T.
PR878.P78 S9   823/.03   *LC* 76-8216   *ISBN* 0226780619

Wolff, Robert Lee. 2.6029
Gains and losses: novels of faith and doubt in Victorian England / by Robert Lee Wolff. — New York: Garland Pub., 1977. xiv, 537 p., [8] leaves of plates: ill.; 24 cm. Includes index. 1. English fiction — 19th century — History and criticism. 2. Religion in literature I. T.
PR878.R5 W6   823/.03   *LC* 75-641   *ISBN* 0824016173

Suvin, Darko, 1930-. 2.6030
Victorian science fiction in the UK: the discourses of knowledge and power / Darko Suvin. — Boston: G.K. Hall, 1983. xvii, 461 p.: ill.; 25 cm. (Reference publication in science fiction.) 1. English fiction — 19th century — History and criticism. 2. Science fiction, English — History and criticism. 3. English fiction — 19th century — Bio-bibliography. 4. Science fiction, English — Bio-bibliography. 5. Authors, English — 19th century — Biography. I. T. II. Series.
PR878.S35 S8 1983   823/.0876/09 19   *LC* 83-10768   *ISBN* 0816184356

Hughes, Winifred, 1948-. 2.6031
The maniac in the cellar: sensation novels of the 1860s / Winifred Hughes. — Princeton, N.J.: Princeton University Press, c1980. x, 211 p.; 23 cm. 1. English fiction — 19th century — History and criticism. 2. Sensationalism in literature 3. Popular literature — Great Britain — History and criticism. I. T.
PR878.S44 H8   823/.8/0916   *LC* 80-7530   *ISBN* 0691064415

Basch, Françoise. 2.6032
[Femmes victoriennes. English] Relative creatures: Victorian women in society and the novel / Françoise Basch; [translated by Anthony Rudolf]. — 1st Schocken ed. — New York: Schocken Books, 1974. xx, 360 p.: ill.; 21 cm. — (Studies in the life of women) Issued in French under title: Les femmes victoriennes. Includes index. 1. English fiction — 19th century — History and criticism. 2. Women in literature 3. Women — Great Britain — Social conditions. 4. Great Britain — Social conditions — 19th century I. T.
PR878.W6 B37 1974   823/.8/09352042 19   *LC* 74-8634   *ISBN* 0805204687

Cunningham, Gail. 2.6033
The new woman and the Victorian novel / Gail Cunningham. — New York: Barnes & Noble Books, 1978. 172 p.; 22 cm. Includes index. 1. English fiction

— 19th century — History and criticism. 2. Women in literature 3. Feminism in literature. I. T.
PR878.W6 C8 1978   823/.03   *LC* 78-6179   *ISBN* 0064913473

Foster, Shirley.   **2.6034**
Victorian women's fiction: marriage, freedom, and the individual / Shirley Foster. — Totowa, N.J.: Barnes & Noble Books, 1985. 240 p.; 23 cm. Includes index. 1. English fiction — 19th century — History and criticism. 2. Women in literature 3. English fiction — Women authors — History and criticism. 4. Women in literature 5. Marriage in literature I. T.
PR878.W6 F67 1985   823/.8/09352042 19   *LC* 84-24367   *ISBN* 0389205516

PR881–888 20th Century

Daiches, David, 1912-.   • **2.6035**
The novel and the modern world. — Rev. ed. — [Chicago]: University of Chicago Press, [1960] 220 p.: illus.; 23 cm. 1. English fiction — 20th century — History and criticism. I. T.
PR881.D3 1960   823.912   *LC* 60-11134

Frierson, William Coleman.   • **2.6036**
The English novel in transition, 1885–1940, by William C. Frierson. Norman, University of Oklahoma Press, 1942. xvi, 333, [1] p. 23 cm. 1. English fiction — 19th century — History and criticism. 2. English fiction — 20th century — History and criticism. I. T.
PR881.F8   823.809   *LC* 42-16403

Gindin, James Jack, 1926-.   • **2.6037**
Postwar British fiction: new accents and attitudes / by James Gindin. — Berkeley, University of California Press, 1962. x, 246 p. 24 cm. Notes on authors: p. [239]-246. 1. English fiction — 20th century — History and criticism. I. T.
PR881.G5   823.914   *LC* 62-17769

Hall, James, 1917-.   • **2.6038**
The tragic comedians: seven modern British novelists. — Bloomington: Indiana University Press, [1963] 174 p.; 22 cm. 1. English fiction — 20th century — History and criticism. I. T.
PR881.H3   823.9109   *LC* 63-9715

Karl, Frederick Robert, 1927-.   • **2.6039**
A reader's guide to the contemporary English novel [by] Frederick R. Karl. — Rev. ed. — [New York]: Farrar, Straus and Giroux, [1972] 375 p.; 21 cm. 1962 ed. published under title: The contemporary English novel. 1. English fiction — 20th century — History and criticism. I. T.
PR881.K25 1972   823/.03   *LC* 72-164536   *ISBN* 0374242011

Karl, Frederick Robert, 1927-.   • **2.6040**
A readers guide to great twentieth–century English novels [by] Frederick R. Karl & Marvin Magalaner. — New York: Noonday Press, [1959] 293 p.; 22 cm. 1. English fiction — 20th century — History and criticism. I. Magalaner, Marvin, 1920- joint author. II. T.
PR881.K3   823.9109   *LC* 59-15127

Mansfield, Katherine, 1888-1923.   • **2.6041**
Novels and novelists, by Katherine Mansfield, edited by J. Middleton Murry. New York, A.A. Knopf, 1930. 4 p. 1., 3-321 v p., 1 1 23 cm. A collection of book reviews, originally published in the Athenaeum from April 1919 to December 1929. of. Introductory note. 1. English fiction — 20th Century — History and criticism. 2. Books — Reviews I. Murry, John Middleton, 1889-1957. II. T.
PR881.M33   823.9104   *LC* 30-30203

Rabinovitz, Rubin.   **2.6042**
The reaction against experiment in the English novel, 1950–1960. — New York, Columbia University Press, 1967. ix, 243 p. 22 cm. Bibliography: p. [174]-221. 1. English fiction — 20th cent. — Hist. & crit. I. T.
PR881.R3   823/.91/09   *LC* 67-14064

Stevenson, Lionel, 1902-1973.   • **2.6043**
The history of the English novel: Volume XI: Yesterday and after. — New York: Barnes & Noble, [1967] 431 p.; 23 cm. Published as an additional volume in the 10 vol. series: History of the English novel, by Ernest A. Baker. 1. English fiction — 20th century — History and criticism. I. Baker, Ernest Albert, 1869-1941. The history of the English novel. II. T.
PR881.S7   823/.9/109   *LC* 67-25496

Contemporary novelists / editor, D.L. Kirkpatrick; consulting   **2.6044**
editor, James Vinson.
4th ed. — New York: St. Martin's Press, 1986. p. cm. (Contemporary writers of the English language.) On t.p. of earlier ed. (2nd, 1976) editors' names are in reverse order. 1. English fiction — 20th century — Bio-bibliography.

2. American literature — 20th century — Bio-bibliography. I. Kirkpatrick, D. L. II. Vinson, James, 1933- III. Series.
PR883.C64 1986   823/.914/09 19   *LC* 86-13904   *ISBN* 0312167318

Forms of modern British fiction / edited by Alan Warren   **2.6045**
Friedman.
Austin: University of Texas Press, [1975] viii, 247 p.: ill.; 21 cm. (Symposia in the arts and the humanities; no. 2) Papers presented at a symposium sponsored by the College of Humanities and the College of Fine Arts, the University of Texas at Austin. 1. English fiction — 20th century — History and criticism — Addresses, essays, lectures. I. Friedman, Alan Warren. II. University of Texas at Austin. College of Humanities. III. University of Texas at Austin. College of Fine Arts. IV. Series.
PR883.F6   823/.03   *LC* 75-16076   *ISBN* 0292724144

Lodge, David, 1935-.   **2.6046**
The novelist at the crossroads, and other essays on fiction and criticism. — Ithaca, N.Y.: Cornell University Press, [1971] xi, 297 p.; 23 cm. 1. English fiction — 20th century — History and criticism. 2. American fiction — 20th century — History and criticism. I. T.
PR883.L6   823/.03   *LC* 77-163130   *ISBN* 0801406749

Shapiro, Charles. ed.   **2.6047**
Contemporary British novelists. With a pref. by Harry T. Moore. — Carbondale: Southern Illinois University Press, [1965] xxi, 164 p.; 22 cm. — (Crosscurrents: modern critiques) 1. English fiction — 20th century — Addresses, essays, lectures. I. T.
PR883.S5   823.91409   *LC* 65-19772

Six contemporary British novelists / edited with an introd. by   **2.6048**
George Stade.
New York: Columbia University Press, 1976. x, 357 p.; 22 cm. 'First published as separate pamphlets for the series of Columbia essays on modern writers.' 1. English fiction — 20th century — History and criticism — Addresses, essays, lectures. I. Stade, George. II. Columbia essays on modern writers.
PR883.S53   823/.03   *LC* 76-3598   *ISBN* 0231040547

PR888 Special Topics, A–Z

Thompson, Raymond H. (Raymond Henry), 1941-.   **2.6049**
The return from Avalon: a study of the Arthurian legend in modern fiction / Raymond H. Thompson. — Westport, Conn.: Greenwood Press, 1985. 206 p.; 22 cm. (Contributions to the study of science fiction and fantasy. 0193-6875; no. 14) Includes index. 1. English fiction — 20th century — History and criticism. 2. Arthurian romances — History and criticism. 3. American fiction — 20th century — History and criticism. 4. Middle Ages in literature 5. Fantastic fiction — History and criticism. I. T. II. Series.
PR888.A76 T45 1985   823/.91/09351 19   *LC* 84-10853   *ISBN* 0313232911

Mahood, M. M. (Molly Maureen)   **2.6050**
The colonial encounter: a reading of six novels / M. M. Mahood. Totowa, N.J.: Rowman and Littlefield, 1977. 211 p.; 23 cm. Includes index. 1. English fiction — 20th century — History and criticism. 2. Colonies in literature I. T.
PR888.C6 M3   823/.9/1209   *LC* 76-151825   *ISBN* 0874719151

Twentieth–century crime and mystery writers / editor, John M.   • **2.6051**
Reilly.
2d. ed. — New York: St. Martin's Press, c1985. — xx, 1094 p.; 24 cm. — (Twentieth-century writers of the English language.) 1. Crime and criminals in literature 2. Authors — Biography I. Reilly, John M. II. Series.
PR888.D4 T8   823/.0872/09 19   *LC* 84-40813   *ISBN* 0312824181

Beja, Morris.   **2.6052**
Epiphany in the modern novel. — Seattle: University of Washington Press, [1971] 255 p.; 23 cm. 1. English fiction — 20th century — History and criticism. 2. American fiction — 20th century — History and criticism. 3. Epiphanies in literature I. T.
PR888.E64 B4 1971b   823/.03   *LC* 71-117725

Gray, Nigel.   **2.6053**
The silent majority; a study of the working class in post–war British fiction. — [London]: Vision, [1973] 227 p.; 23 cm. — (Vision critical studies) 1. English fiction — 20th century — History and criticism. 2. Labor and laboring classes in literature I. T.
PR888.L3 G7   823/.03   *LC* 74-159246   *ISBN* 0854780432

Stableford, Brian M.   **2.6054**
Scientific romance in Britain, 1890–1950 / Brian Stableford. — New York: St. Martin's Press, c1985. 372 p.; 23 cm. Includes index. 1. Science fiction, English — History and criticism. 2. English fiction — 20th century — History and criticism. 3. English fiction — 19th century — History and criticism. I. T.
PR888.S35 S73 1985   823/.0876/09 19   *LC* 85-14610   *ISBN* 0312703058

Panek, LeRoy. 2.6055
The special branch: the British spy novel, 1890–1980 / LeRoy L. Panek. — Bowling Green, Ohio: Bowling Green University Popular Press, c1981. 288 p.; 24 cm. 1. English fiction — 20th century — History and criticism. 2. Spy stories, English — History and criticism. I. T.
PR888.S65 P36   823/.0872/09 19   *LC* 81-80214   *ISBN* 0879721782

Morris, Robert K. 2.6056
Continuance and change; the contemporary British novel sequence [by] Robert K. Morris. With a pref. by Harry T. Moore. — Carbondale: Southern Illinois University Press, [1972] xx, 164 p.; 22 cm. — (Crosscurrents/modern critiques) 1. English fiction — 20th century — History and criticism. 2. Time in literature I. T.
PR888.T5 M6   823/.03   *LC* 74-175951   *ISBN* 0809305445

Gerber, Richard, 1924-. • 2.6057
Utopian fantasy: a study of English utopian fiction since the end of the nineteenth century / Richard Gerber. — London: Routledge and Paul, 1955. xii, 162 p.; 24 cm. "Annotated list of English utopian fantasies,1901-1951":p.143-157. 1. English fiction — 20th century — History and criticism. 2. Utopias — History and criticism. I. T.
PR888.U7 G4 1955   823.9109   *LC* 55-2866

Kaplan, Sydney Janet, 1939-. 2.6058
Feminine consciousness in the modern British novel / Sydney Janet Kaplan. — Urbana: University of Illinois Press, [1975] 182 p.; 24 cm. 1. English fiction — 20th century — History and criticism. 2. Women in literature 3. English fiction — Women authors — History and criticism. 4. Women's writings, English — History and criticism. I. T.
PR888.W6 K3   823/.03   *LC* 75-2179   *ISBN* 0252004639

Twentieth–century women novelists / edited by Thomas F. 2.6059
Staley.
Totowa, N.J.: Barnes & Noble Books, 1982. xvi, 224 p.; 23 cm. Includes index. 1. English fiction — Women authors — History and criticism. 2. English fiction — 20th century — History and criticism. I. Staley, Thomas F.
PR888.W62 T9 1982   823/.914/099287 19   *LC* 82-1740   *ISBN* 038920272X

PR901–978 Essays. Humor. Satire

Ketcham, Michael G. 2.6060
Transparent designs: reading, performance, and form in the Spectator papers / Michael G. Ketcham. — Athens: University of Georgia Press, c1985. 216 p.; 25 cm. Includes index. 1. Addison, Joseph, 1672-1719 — Criticism and interpretation. 2. Steele, Richard, Sir, 1672-1729 — Criticism and interpretation. 3. Spectator (London, 1711-14) 4. English essays — 18th century — History and criticism. 5. England — Social life and customs — 18th century I. T.
PR925.K38 1985   824/.5/09 19   *LC* 84-24046   *ISBN* 0820307718

Cazamian, Louis François, 1877-1965. • 2.6061
The development of English humor / by Louis Cazamian. — Durhan: Duke University Press, 1952. viii, 421 p. 24 cm. — (Duke University publications) 1. English wit and humor — History & criticism. 2. English literature — History & criticism. I. T.
PR931.C3 1952   827.09   *LC* 52-9795

Kantra, Robert A. 2.6062
All things vain: religious satirists and their art / Robert A. Kantra. — University Park: Pennsylvania State University Press, c1984. xviii, 231 p.: ill.; 24 cm. 1. Religious satire, English — History and criticism. 2. Religious satire — History and criticism. 3. Arts and religion I. T.
PR931.K3 1984   809.7/9382 19   *LC* 83-43029   *ISBN* 0271003588

Priestley, J. B. (John Boynton), 1894-. • 2.6063
The English comic characters. — London: Bodley Head, [1963] xiii, 242 p.; 19 cm. 1. Shakespeare, William, 1564-1616 — Characters 2. Dickens, Charles, 1812-1870 — Characters. 3. English wit and humor I. T.
PR931.P69 1963   *LC* 64-57214

Sutherland, James Runcieman, 1900-. • 2.6064
English satire. — Cambridge [Eng.] University Press, 1958. 173 p. 21 cm. — (The Clark lectures, 1956) 1. Satire, English — Hist. & crit. I. T.
PR931.S8   827.09   *LC* 58-1655

Sewell, Elizabeth, 1919-. • 2.6065
The field of nonsense. — London: Chatto and Windus, 1952. 198 p.; 21 cm. 1. English wit and humor — History and criticism. I. T.
PR932.S4   *LC* 53-1176

Kernan, Alvin B. 2.6066
The cankered muse: satire of the English Renaissance / Alvin Kernan. — New Haven: Yale University Press, 1959. x, 261 p. — (Yale studies in English. v. 142) Photocopy. 1. Satire, English — History and criticism. I. T. II. Series.
PR933.K4   *LC* 59-12815

Thackeray, William Makepeace, 1811-1863. • 2.6067
The English humourists; The four Georges, by W. M. Thackeray. — London, J. M. Dent & sons, ltd.; New York, E. P. Dutton & co. [1912] xviii, 423 p.; 17 cm. (Half-title: Everyman's library, ed. by Ernest Rhys. Essays and belles lettres. [no. 610]) Introduction signed: Walter Jerrold. Bibliography: p. xvii-xviii. 1. Humorists, English 2. English literature — 18th century — History and criticism. 3. Gt. Brit. — History — 1714-1837. 4. Gt. Brit. — Social life and customs. I. Jerrold, Walter, 1865-1929. ed. II. T. III. Title: The four Georges. AC1.E8 no. 610 1912   PR935.T5x.   827.509   *LC* A 13-916

Spufford, Margaret. 2.6068
Small books and pleasant histories: popular fiction and its readership in seventeenth century England / Margaret Spufford. — Athens, Ga.: University of Georgia Press, 1981. xxi, 275 p., [2] leaves of plates: ill.; 22 cm. 1. Chap-books, English — History and criticism. 2. English fiction — Early modern, 1500-1700 — History and criticism. 3. Books and reading — England — History. 4. Labor and laboring classes — England — Books and reading. 5. Book industries and trade — England — History. 6. Popular literature — England. I. T.
PR972.S65   398/.5/.0941 19   *LC* 81-11684   *ISBN* 0820305952

PR1100–1369 COLLECTIONS OF ENGLISH LITERATURE

Bernbaum, Ernest, 1879- ed. • 2.6069
Anthology of romanticism. — 3d ed., rev. and enl. — New York: Ronald Press Co., [1948] xxviii, 1238 p.; 24 cm. 1. English literature — 19th century 2. English literature — 18th century 3. Romanticism — England. I. T.
PR1105.B4 1948   820.82   *LC* 48-6845

The Oxford anthology of English literature / general editors, 2.6070
Frank Kermode and John Hollander.
Major authors ed. — New York: Oxford University Press, 1975. 2 v.: ill.; 22 cm. 1. English literature I. Kermode, Frank, 1919- II. Hollander, John.
PR1105.O9 1975   820/.8   *LC* 74-22882   *ISBN* 0195019008

Brooks, Cleanth, 1906- ed. 2.6071
Understanding poetry / Cleanth Brooks, Robert Penn Warren. — 4th ed. — New York: Holt, Rinehart and Winston, c1976. xxii, 602 p.; 24 cm. Includes index. 1. English poetry 2. American poetry I. Warren, Robert Penn, 1905- II. T.
PR1109.B676 1976   821/.008   *LC* 75-25539   *ISBN* 0030769809

The Norton anthology of English literature. The major authors 2.6072
/ M.H. Abrams, general editor.
5th ed. — New York: Norton, c1987. p. cm. A selection of writings of 34 authors from the 5th ed. of the 2-vol. Norton anthology of English literature, c1986. Includes index. 1. English literature I. Abrams, M. H. (Meyer Howard), 1912- II. Norton anthology of English literature.
PR1109.N64 1987   820/.8 19   *LC* 86-23646   *ISBN* 0393955621

First feminists: British women writers, 1578–1799 / edited and 2.6073
with an introduction by Moira Ferguson.
Bloomington: Indiana University Press; Old Westbury, N.Y.: Feminist Press, c1985. xiv, 461 p., 4 p. of plates: ports.; 24 cm. 1. Feminism — Literary collections. 2. Women — Literary collections 3. English literature — Women authors 4. English literature — Early modern, 1500-1700 5. English literature — 18th century I. Ferguson, Moira.
PR1111.F45 F57 1985   820/.8/09287 19   *LC* 84-42838   *ISBN* 0253322138

PR1119–1149 By Period

Cook, Albert S. (Albert Stanburrough), 1853-1927. • 2.6074
A literary Middle English reader; ed. by Albert Stanburrough Cook ... Boston, New York [etc.] Ginn and Company [c1915] xxviii, 554 p. 21 cm. Introduction: The literature. The language. Some useful books for the study of Middle English (p. xxvi-xxviii)—Romances.—Tales.—Chronicles.— Stories of travel.— Religious and didactic pieces.—Illustrations of life and manners.—

Translations.—Lyrics.— Plays. 1. English literature — Middle English, 1100-1500 2. English language — Middle English, 1100-1500 — Readers. I. T.
PR1120.C6   *LC* 15-20398

Gerould, Gordon Hall, 1877- ed.   ● **2.6075**
Old English and medieval literature. — New York: Greenwood Press, [1969, c1929] 351 p.; 23 cm. — (Nelson's English readings v. 1) 1. English literature — Middle English, 1100-1500 2. English literature — Old English, ca. 450-1100 I. T.
PR1120.G4 1969   820/.08   *LC* 78-95100   *ISBN* 0837127033

Haskell, Ann S. (Ann Sullivan) comp.   ● **2.6076**
A Middle English anthology / Edited by Ann S. Haskell. — [1st ed.] Garden City, N.Y.: Anchor Books, 1969. xii, 532 p.: ill.; 21 cm. 1. English literature — Middle English, 1100-1500 I. T.
PR1120.H36   820.8/001   *LC* 78-76988

Loomis, Roger Sherman, 1887-1966. ed.   ● **2.6077**
Medieval English verse and prose in modernized versions, by Roger Sherman Loomis and Rudolph Willard. — New York, Appleton-Century-Crofts [1948] xii, 557 p. 24 cm. 1. English literature — Middle English, 1100-1500 I. Willard, Rudolph, 1892- joint ed. II. T.
PR1120.L6   820.82   *LC* 48-7960

Matthews, William, 1905- ed.   ● **2.6078**
Later medieval English prose. — New York, Appleton-Century-Crofts [1963] 336 p. 21 cm. — (Goldentree books) Includes bibliography. 1. English literature — Middle English, 1100-1500 I. T.
PR1120.M28   828.1082   *LC* 63-9439

The Oxford book of late medieval verse and prose / edited by Douglas Gray; with a note on grammar and spelling in the fifteenth century by Norman Davis.   **2.6079**
Oxford: Clarendon Press, 1985. xxi, 586 p.; 23 cm. 1. English literature — Middle English, 1100-1500 I. Gray, Douglas.
PR1120.O93 1985   820/.8/002 19   *LC* 85-219422   *ISBN* 019812452X

Fourteenth century verse and prose.   ● **2.6080**
Oxford: Clarendon Press, [1928] xlvii, 292 p.: map. Editor: K. Sisam. Appendix: A Middle-English vocabulary, by J.R.R. Tolkien. 1. English literature — Middle English, 1100-1500 I. Sisam, Kenneth, 1887-. II. Title: 14th century verse and prose.
PR1120.S55   *LC* 33-21708

Harrison, G. B. (George Bagshawe), 1894- ed.   ● **2.6081**
England in Shakespeare's day / by George B. Harrison. — 2d ed. — Freeport, N.Y.: Books for Libraries Press, [1970] xiii, 239 p.; 22 cm. — (Library of English Renaissance literature) Reprint of the 1949 ed. 1. Shakespeare, William, 1564-1616 — Contemporary England 2. English literature — Early modern, 1500-1700 3. England — Social life and customs — 16th century — Literary collections. I. T.
PR1125.H3 1970   942.05/5   *LC* 76-119959   *ISBN* 0836954025

Hebel, John William, 1891-1934, ed.   ● **2.6082**
Tudor poetry and prose, selected from early editions and manuscripts and edited by J. William Hebel [and others]. — New York: Appleton-Century-Crofts, [1953] 1375 p.; 22 cm. '[Brings] together ... the material ... included in two books already published: (1) Hebel and Hudson's Poetry of the English Renaissance ... and (2) Hebel, Hudson, Johnson, and Green's Prose of the English Renaissance.' 1. English literature — Early modern, 1500-1700 I. T.
PR1125.H4   820.82   *LC* 53-10457

Lamson, Roy, 1908- ed.   **2.6083**
Renaissance England: poetry and prose from the Reformation to the Restoration / selected and edited by Roy Lamson and Hallett Smith. — New York: Norton, [1956] xx, 1128 p.: ill.; 24 cm. 'An expanded edition of the editors' ...The golden hind.' 1. English literature — Early modern, 1500-1700 I. Smith, Hallett Darius, 1907- joint ed. II. T.
PR1125.L3 1956a   820.82   *LC* 56-2208

Seventeenth–century prose and poetry / selected and edited by Alexander M. Witherspoon, Frank J. Warnke.   **2.6084**
2nd ed., enl. — New York: Harcourt Brace Jovanovich, c1982. xxvi, 1124 p.; 25 cm. Includes indexes. 1. English literature — Early modern, 1500-1700 I. Witherspoon, Alexander M. (Alexander Maclaren), 1894- II. Warnke, Frank J.
PR1127.S39 1982   820/.8/004 19   *LC* 82-83867   *ISBN* 0155802372

Seventeenth–century verse and prose [edited by] Helen C. White [and others].   ● **2.6085**
2d ed. — New York: Macmillan, [1971-. v.   ; 24 cm. 1951-52 ed. by H. C. White, R. C. Wallerstein, and R. Quintana is entered under White, Helen

Constance. 1. English literature — Early modern, 1500-1700 I. White, Helen Constance, 1896-1967, comp. Seventeenth-century verse and prose.
PR1127.S4   820.8/003   *LC* 70-115295

Witherspoon, Alexander M. (Alexander Maclaren), 1894- ed.   ● **2.6086**
Seventeenth–century prose and poetry, selected and edited by Alexander M. Witherspoon [and] Frank J. Warnke. — 2d ed. — New York, Harcourt, Brace & World [1963] xviii illus. 25 cm. First ed., 1929, edited by R. P. T. Coffin and A. M. Witherspoon, has title: A book of seventeenth-century prose. 1. English literature — Early modern (to 1700) I. Warnke, Frank J. joint ed. II. T.
PR1127.W55   820.82   *LC* 63-13251

Bredvold, Louis Ignatius, 1888- ed.   **2.6087**
Eighteenth century poetry & prose / edited by Louis I. Bredvold, Alan D. McKillop [and] Lois Whitney; prepared by John M. Bullitt. — 3d ed. — New York: Ronald Press Co., [1973] xxvii, 1493 p.; 25 cm. 1. English literature — 18th century I. McKillop, Alan Dugald, 1892- joint ed. II. Whitney, Lois, joint ed. III. Bullitt, John Marshall, 1921- ed. IV. T.
PR1134.B7 1973   820/.8   *LC* 72-96968

Pagliaro, Harold E. comp.   ● **2.6088**
Major English writers of the eighteenth century, edited by Harold E. Pagliaro. — New York: Free Press, [1969-. v.   ; 24 cm. 1. English literature — 18th century 2. English literature — 18th century — History and criticism — Bibliography. I. T.
PR1134.P3   820.8   *LC* 68-17520

Tillotson, Geoffrey, comp.   ● **2.6089**
Eighteenth–century English literature. Edited by Geoffrey Tillotson, Paul Fussell, Jr. [and] Marshall Waingrow. With the assistance of Brewster Rogerson. — New York: Harcourt, Brace & World, [1969] xxx, 1554 p.; 25 cm. 1. English literature — 18th century I. Fussell, Paul, 1924- joint comp. II. Waingrow, Marshall, joint comp. III. T.
PR1134.T5   820.8/005   *LC* 69-11483

Perkins, David, 1928- ed.   ● **2.6090**
English romantic writers. New York, Harcourt, Brace & World [1967] xxvi, 1265 p. facsims. 25 cm. 1. Romanticism — England. 2. English literature — 19th century I. T.
PR1139.P4   820.8   *LC* 67-10010

Harrison, Fraser. comp.   **2.6091**
The Yellow book: an illustrated quarterly: an anthology / edited by Fraser Harrison. — New York: St. Martin's Press, 1974. 308, 12 p.: ill.; 22 cm. 1. English literature — 19th century I. Yellow book. II. T.
PR1143.H3   820/.8/008   *LC* 74-80990

Heath, William Webster, 1929- comp.   **2.6092**
Major British poets of the romantic period. Edited by William Heath. — New York: Macmillan, [1973] xxiii, 1140 p.; 26 cm. 1. English poetry — 19th century I. T.
PR1143.H4   821/.7/08   *LC* 71-165242

PR1171–1369 By Form

PR1171–1225 POETRY

Everyman's book of English verse / edited by John Wain.   **2.6093**
London: J.M. Dent, 1981. 672 p.; 25 cm. 1. English poetry I. Wain, John.
PR1174.E9 1981   821/.008 19   *LC* 82-131481   *ISBN* 0460043692

Gardner, Helen Louise, Dame. comp.   **2.6094**
The new Oxford book of English verse, 1250–1950, chosen and edited by Helen Gardner. — New York: Oxford University Press, 1972. xii, 974 p.; 23 cm. — (The Oxford books of verse) 1. English poetry I. T.
PR1174.G3   821/.008   *LC* 72-93034   *ISBN* 0198121369

The Norton anthology of poetry / [edited by] Alexander W. Allison ... [et al.]; with an essay on ver[s]ification by Jon Stallworthy.   **2.6095**
3rd ed. — New York: Norton, c1983. liii, 1452 p.; 24 cm. Includes indexes. 1. English poetry 2. American poetry I. Allison, Alexander W. (Alexander Ward)
PR1174.N6 1983   821/.008 19   *LC* 83-13231   *ISBN* 0393952428

The Treasury of English poetry / edited and with an introduction by Mark Caldwell and Walter Kendrick.   2.6096
Garden City, N.Y.: Doubleday, c1984. xxxiv, 734 p.; 22 cm. Includes index. 1. English poetry I. Caldwell, Mark. II. Kendrick, Walter M.
PR1174.T73 1984   821/.008 19   *LC* 82-46028   *ISBN* 0385185332

Baylor, Robert. comp.   2.6097
Fine frenzy: enduring themes in poetry / Robert Baylor, Brenda Stokes. — 2d ed. — New York: McGraw-Hill, c1978. xxii, 393 p.; 21 cm. Includes index. 1. English poetry 2. American poetry I. Stokes, Brenda. II. T.
PR1175.B277 1978   821/.008   *LC* 77-5605   *ISBN* 0070041601

The Harper anthology of poetry / John Frederick Nims, [editor].   2.6098
New York: Harper & Row, c1981. xxxiv, 842 p.; 24 cm. 1. English poetry 2. American poetry I. Nims, John Frederick, 1913-
PR1175.H298 1981   821/.008 19   *LC* 80-27259   *ISBN* 0060448474

The New Oxford book of English light verse / chosen by Kingsley Amis.   2.6099
New York: Oxford University Press, 1978. xxxiv, 347 p.; 22 cm. 1. English poetry 2. Humorous poetry, English I. Amis, Kingsley.
PR1175.N37   821/.08   *LC* 77-25756   *ISBN* 0192118625

The Oxford book of English verse, 1250–1918, chosen and edited by Sir Arthur Quiller–Couch.   • 2.6100
New ed. — Oxford: The Clarendon press, 1939. xxviii, 1171, [1] p.; 20 cm. 'First published 1900; reprinted ... 1930; new edition 1939.' First edition has title: The Oxford book of English verse, 1250-1900. 1. English poetry I. Quiller-Couch, Arthur Thomas, Sir, 1863-1944. ed.
PR1175.O9 1939   821.0822   *LC* 40-27231

The Oxford book of light verse, chosen by W. H. Auden.   • 2.6101
Oxford, The Clarendon press, 1938. xxiv, 553, [1] p. 19 cm. 1. English poetry I. Auden, W. H. (Wystan Hugh), 1907-1973. ed.
PR1175.O93   821.0822   *LC* 38-29029

Palgrave, Francis Turner, 1824-1897. comp.   2.6102
The golden treasury of the best songs & lyrical poems in the English language / selected and arranged by Francis Turner Palgrave; with a 5th book selected by John Press. — 5th ed. London; New York: Oxford University Press, 1964. xxi, 615 p.; 23 cm. ([Oxford standard authors]) 'The Fifth book...contains works by poets who were alive in 1861, and by those born after that date.' 1. English poetry 2. Songs, English — Texts. I. Press, John. comp. II. T.
PR1175.P34 1964   821.008   *LC* 65-240

Untermeyer, Louis, 1885-1977. ed.   • 2.6103
A treasury of great poems, English and American, from the foundations of the English spirit to the outstanding poetry of our own time, with lives of the poets and historical settings selected and integrated by Louis Untermeyer. — Rev. and enl. — New York: Simon and Schuster, 1955. lviii, 1286 p.; 22 cm. 1. English poetry 2. American poetry I. T.
PR1175.U65 1955   821.082   *LC* 55-3994

Williams, Oscar, 1900-1964. ed.   • 2.6104
A little treasury of British poetry; the chief poets from 1500 to 1950. — New York: Scribner, 1951. 874 p.: illus.; 18 cm. — (The Little treasury series) 1. English poetry I. T.
PR1175.W564   821.082   *LC* 51-7409

Rowton, Frederic, 1818-1854.   2.6105
The female poets of Great Britain: chronologically arranged with copious selections and critical remarks / by Frederic Rowton; facsim. of the 1853 ed. with a critical introd. and bibliographical appendices by Marilyn L. Williamson. — Detroit: Wayne State University Press, 1981. lii, 565 p.; 24 cm. 1. English poetry — Women authors I. Williamson, Marilyn L., 1927- II. T.
PR1177.R7 1980   821/.008/09287 19   *LC* 80-22484   *ISBN* 0814316646

PR1181–1194 Poetry Collections: Special Forms. Special Subjects

Buchan, David, 1939- comp.   2.6106
A Scottish ballad book / edited by David Buchan. — London; Boston: Routledge & K. Paul, [1973] xi, 232 p.: music; 22 cm. (The Scottish series) 1. Ballads, English — Scotland — Texts. I. T.
PR1181.B88   821/.04   *LC* 73-82367   *ISBN* 0710075669

Child, Francis James, 1825-1896. ed.   • 2.6107
The English and Scottish popular ballads. New York: Cooper Square Publishers 1962-. v. in port.; 26 cm. ([The Cooper Square library of literary history and criticism]) 1. English ballads and songs 2. English ballads and songs — Bibliography 3. Scottish ballads and songs 4. Scottish ballads and songs — Bibliography I. T.
PR1181 C5

Friedman, Albert B. ed.   • 2.6108
The Viking book of folk ballads of the English–speaking world. — New York: Viking Press, 1956. xxxv, 473 p.; 22 cm. Includes unacc. melodies. 1. Ballads, English — Texts. 2. Ballads, English — History and criticism. 3. Ballads, English — Discography. I. T.
PR1181.F74   821.04   *LC* 56-7084

The Faber book of ballads / edited by Matthew Hodgart.   2.6109
London: Faber & Faber, 1965. 267 p. 1. Ballads, English — Texts. I. Hodgart, Matthew John Caldwell. II. Title: Book of ballads.
PR1181.H58   PN1376.H6.   *LC* 67-5157   *ISBN* 0571062369

Kinsley, James. comp.   • 2.6110
The Oxford book of ballads; newly selected and edited, by James Kinsley. [New ed.] Oxford, Clarendon P., 1969. xvi, 711 p. music. 19 cm. 'Replaces The Oxford book [of ballads] made by Sir Arthur Quiller-Couch in 1910.' 1. Ballads, English — England — Texts. 2. Ballads, English — Scotland — Texts. I. T.
PR1181.K55 1969   821/.04   *LC* 71-442618   *ISBN* 0198121334

Percy, Thomas, 1729-1811.   • 2.6111
Reliques of ancient English poetry: consisting of old heroic ballads, songs, and other pieces of our earlier poets, together with some few of later date / by Thomas Percy; edited with a general introduction, additional prefaces, notes, glossary, etc., by Henry B. Wheatley. — New York: Dover, 1966. 3 v.; 22 cm. Half-title: Percy's reliques. 1. Ballads, English — Texts. 2. English poetry — Middle English, 1100-1500 3. English poetry — Early modern, 1500-1700 4. English language — Early modern, 1500-1700. — Glossaries, vocabularies, etc. I. Wheatley, Henry Benjamin, 1838-1917. II. T. III. Title: Percy's reliques.
PR1181.P5 1966   *LC* 66-20326

Luria, Maxwell, 1932- comp.   2.6112
Middle English lyrics: authoritative texts, critical and historical backgrounds, perspectives on six poems / selected and edited by Maxwell S. Luria [and] Richard L. Hoffman. — [1st ed.]. — New York: Norton, [1974] xii, 360 p.; 22 cm. — (A Norton critical edition) 1. English poetry — Middle English, 1100-1500 2. English poetry — Middle English, 1100-1500 — History and criticism. 3. Lyric poetry I. Hoffman, Richard Lester. joint comp. II. T.
PR1187.L8   821/.04   *LC* 73-19768   *ISBN* 0393043797

Reeves, James. ed.   • 2.6113
The everlasting circle; English traditional verse. Edited with an introd. and notes from the manuscripts of S. Baring–Gould, H. E. D. Hammond, and George B. Gardiner. — London, Heinemann [1960] xv, 303 p. illus., ports., facsims. 23 cm. 1. English ballads and songs. I. T.
PR1187.R37 1960   821.04   *LC* 60-4337

Sharp, Cecil James, 1859-1924. comp.   • 2.6114
The idiom of the people: English traditional verse / edited with an introd. and notes from the MSS. of Cecil J. Sharp [by] James Reeves. — London: Heinemann [1958] 244 p.; 23 cm. 1. English ballads and songs. I. Reeves, James. ed. II. T.
PR1187.S26   821.04   *LC* 58-14883

Brown, Carleton Fairchild, 1869-1941, ed.   • 2.6115
Religious lyrics of the XVth century, edited by Carleton Brown. — Oxford, The Clarendon press, 1939. xxxi, [1], 394 p., 1 l. 19.5 cm. 1. English poetry — Middle English, 1100-1500 2. Religious poetry, English I. T.
PR1191.B75   821.20822   *LC* 40-3105

Gardner, Helen Louise, Dame. comp.   2.6116
A book of religious verse. Edited by Helen Gardner. — New York: Oxford University Press, 1972. 377 p.; 22 cm. 1. Religious poetry, English I. T.
PR1191.G33   821/.05   *LC* 72-171616   *ISBN* 019519666X

The Oxford book of English mystical verse / chosen by D.H.S. Nicholson and A.H.E. Lee.   • 2.6117
Oxford: Clarendon Press, [1917] xv, 644 p. 1. English poetry 2. Mysticism — Great Britain. 3. Mysticism in literature I. Nicholson, Daniel Howard. II. Lee, A.H.E.
PR1191.O8   821.008   *LC* 17-17649

Greene, Richard Leighton. ed.   2.6118
The early English carols / edited by Richard Leighton Greene. — 2d ed., rev. and enl. — Oxford: Clarendon Press, 1977. clxxii, 517 p., [1] leaf of plate; 25 cm. Includes index. 1. Carols, English — Texts. 2. English poetry — Middle English, 1100-1500 3. English poetry — Early modern, 1500-1700 I. T.
PR1195.C2 G7 1977   821/.04   *LC* 77-359272   *ISBN* 0198127154

Greene, Richard Leighton. ed.   **• 2.6119**
A selection of English carols. — Oxford, Clarendon Press, 1962. 279 p. illus. 19 cm. — (Clarendon medieval and Tudor series) 1. Carols, English 2. English poetry — Middle English, 1100-1500 I. T. II. Title: English carols.
PR1195.C2G73   821.0902   LC 62-4134

The New Oxford book of Christian verse / chosen and edited by   **2.6120**
Donald Davie.
Oxford; New York: Oxford University Press, 1981. xxix, 319 p.; 23 cm. 1. Christian poetry, English 2. Christian poetry, American I. Davie, Donald. PR1195.C48 N4   821/.008/0382 19   LC 80-49703   ISBN 0192134264

Poems on affairs of State; Augustan satirical verse, 1660–1714.   **• 2.6121**
Edited by George deF. Lord [and others]
New Haven, Yale University Press, 1963-75. 7 v. illus., ports., facsims. 24 cm. With reproduction of t.p. of 1st ed., London, 1689. 1. Political poetry, English 2. Verse satire, English 3. Great Britain — History — 1660-1714 — Poetry. I. Lord, George deForest, 1919- ed.
PR1195.H5 P62   821/.07   LC 63-7938   ISBN 0300017723

Anthology of Poems on affairs of state: Augustan satirical verse,   **2.6122**
1660–1714 / edited by George deF. Lord.
New Haven: Yale University Press, 1975. xxxii, 800 p., [15] leaves of plates: ill.; 24 cm. (A Yale paperbound) Includes indexes. 1. Political poetry, English 2. Verse satire, English 3. Great Britain — History — 1660-1714 — Poetry. I. Lord, George de Forest, 1919-
PR1195.H5 P623   821/.4/08031   LC 74-29735   ISBN 0300016204

Roberts, Michael, 1902-1948. comp.   **2.6123**
The Faber book of comic verse / edited by Michael Roberts. — New and revised ed. / with a supplement chosen by Janet Adam Smith. — London: Faber, 1974. 3-400 p.; 20 cm. Originally published in 1942. Includes index. 1. Humorous poetry, English I. Smith, Janet Adam. II. T.
PR1195.H8 R56 1974   821/.07   LC 75-300992   ISBN 0571048331

Fellowes, Edmund Horace, 1870-1951.   **• 2.6124**
English madrigal verse, 1588–1623 [by] E. H. Fellowes. 3rd ed. revised and enlarged by Frederick W. Sternfeld and David Greer. Oxford: Clarendon P., 1967 [i.e. 1968] xxx, 798 p.; 23 cm. 1. Madrigals 2. Songs, English — England — Texts. 3. Songs, English — Bibliography. I. Sternfeld, Frederick William, 1914- II. Greer, David Clive, 1937- III. T.
PR1195.M2 F4 1968   821/.3/08   LC 68-80676

The Oxford book of narrative verse / chosen and edited by Iona   **2.6125**
and Peter Opie.
Oxford [Oxfordshire]; New York: Oxford University Press, 1983. xiv, 407 p.; 23 cm. 1. Narrative poetry, English 2. Narrative poetry, American I. Opie, Iona Archibald. II. Opie, Peter.
PR1195.N2 O9 1983   821/.03/08 19   LC 82-22494   ISBN 0192141317

Kermode, Frank, 1919- ed.   **• 2.6126**
English pastoral poetry, from the beginnings to Marvell. Edited by Frank Kermode. New York, Norton [1972] 256 p. 20 cm. (The Norton library, N612) Original ed. issued in series: Life, literature, and thought library. 1. Pastoral poetry, English I. T.
PR1195.P3 K4 1972   821/.008/014   LC 72-7044   ISBN 0393006123

The Oxford book of satirical verse / chosen by Geoffrey   **2.6127**
Grigson.
Oxford; New York: Oxford University Press, 1980. xviii, 454 p.; 23 cm. 1. Verse satire, English 2. Verse satire, American I. Grigson, Geoffrey, 1905-
PR1195.S3 O9 1980   827/.009   LC 79-41738   ISBN 0192141104

Bender, Robert M.   **2.6128**
The Sonnet: a comprehensive anthology of British and American sonnets from the Renaissance to the present / edited with a critical introduction by Robert M. Bender and Charles L. Squier. — New York: Washington Square Press, 1965. 554 p.; 22 cm. 1. Sonnets, English 2. Sonnets, American I. Squier, Charles L. II. T.
PR1195.S5 B4   LC 65-22603

Lever, J. W. (Julius Walter) comp.   **2.6129**
Sonnets of the English Renaissance / selected and edited by J. W. Lever. — London: Athlone Press, 1974. [6], 186 p.; 21 cm. (Athlone Renaissance library) Distributed in the U.S. by Humanities Press, New York. 1. Sonnets, English 2. English poetry — Early modern, 1500-1700 I. T.
PR1195.S5 L4   821/.04   LC 75-305102   ISBN 048513604X

PR1203–1227 Poetry Collections: Special Periods

PR1203–1204 MEDIEVAL

Brown, Carleton Fairchild, 1869- ed.   **• 2.6130**
English lyrics of the XIIIth century, edited by Carleton Brown. — Oxford, The Clarendon press, 1932. xiii p., 1 l., 312 p. 19.5 cm. 1. English poetry — Middle English, 1100-1500 I. T.
PR1203.B68   821.10822   LC 33-5947

Brown, Carleton Fairchild, 1869-1941, ed.   **• 2.6131**
Religious lyrics of the XIVth century. — 2d ed., revised by G. V. Smithers. — Oxford, Clarendon Press [1952] xxii, 365 p. 19 cm. 'First edition 1924. Second edition reprinted ... from corrected sheets ... 1957.' 1. English poetry — Middle English, 1100-1500 2. Religious poetry, English I. T.
PR1203.B7 1957   821.2082   LC 52-4414

British Library. Manuscript. Cotton Nero A. x.   **2.6132**
The complete works of the Gawain–poet. In a modern English version with a critical introd. by John Gardner. Woodcuts by Fritz Kredel. Chicago, University of Chicago Press [1965] xii, 347 p. illus. 25 cm. I. Gardner, John, 1933- ed. II. Erkenwald, Saint. Legend. III. Pearl (Middle English poem) IV. Purity (Middle English poem) V. Patience (Middle English Poem) VI. Gawain and the Grene Knight. VII. T.
PR1203.C68   821/.1 19   LC 65-17291

Medieval English lyrics: a critical anthology / edited with an   **• 2.6133**
introd. and notes by R. T. Davies.
Evanston, Ill.: Northwestern University Press, 1964, c1963. 384 p.; 23 cm. 1. English poetry — Middle English, 1100-1500 I. Davies, Reginald Thorne.
PR1203.D28 1964   821.2   LC 64-10994   ISBN 0810100754

Gawain and the Grene Knight.   **2.6134**
Sir Gawain and the Green Knight, Pearl, and Sir Orfeo / translated by J. R. R. Tolkien. — 1st American ed. — Boston: Houghton Mifflin, 1975. 149 p.; 24 cm. 1. English poetry — Middle English, 1100-1500 — Modernized versions I. Tolkien, J. R. R. (John Ronald Reuel), 1892-1973. II. Pearl (Middle English poem). 1975. III. Sir Orfeo (Middle English poem). 1975. IV. T.
PR1203.G38 1975   821/.1/08   LC 75-20352   ISBN 0395219701

English verse between Chaucer and Surrey: being examples of   **• 2.6135**
conventional secular poetry, exclusive of romance, ballad, lyric,
and drama, in the period from Henry the Fourth to Henry the
Eighth / edited with introductions and notes.
New York: Octagon Books, 1965. xii, 591 p.; 26 cm. 1. English poetry — Middle English, 1100-1500 I. Hammond, Eleanor Prescott, 1866-1933.
PR1203.H3 1965   821.2008   LC 65-25568

The Harley lyrics, the Middle English lyrics of MS. Harley   **• 2.6136**
2253, edited by G. L. Brook.
[Manchester, Eng.] Manchester University Press, 1948. x, 125 p. facsim. 22 cm. — (Publications of the University of Manchester, no. 302. English series, no. 25.) The Ward Bequest. [Publications, v. 9] 'Select bibliography': p. 27-28. 1. English poetry — Middle English, 1100-1500 I. Brook, G. L. (George Leslie), 1910- ed. II. British Library. Manuscript. Harley 2253.
PR1203.H35   821.1082   LC 49-49683 *

British Library. Manuscript. Cotton Nero A. x.   **• 2.6137**
Pearl; [and], Cleanness; [and], Patience; [and], Sir Gawain and the Green Knight. — [New ed.] / edited with an introduction by A. C. Cawley and J. J. Anderson. — London: Dent; New York: Dutton, 1976. xxviii, 258 p.; 20 cm. — (Everyman's university library; no. 1346) Texts in Middle English; introd. and notes in Middle English. 'An Everyman paperback.' 1. English poetry — Middle English, 1100-1500 I. Cawley, A. C. (Arthur C.) II. Anderson, J. J. III. T.
PR1203.P39 1976   821/.1   LC 77-362970   ISBN 0460103466. ISBN 0460113461 pbk

Person, Henry Axel, 1903- ed.   **• 2.6138**
Cambridge Middle English lyrics, edited by Henry A. Person. — Rev. ed. — New York: Greenwood Press, [1969, c1962] viii, 92 p.; 23 cm. 1. English poetry — Middle English, 1100-1500 I. T.
PR1203.P47 1969   821/.1/08   LC 74-88919   ISBN 0837122422

Robbins, Rossell Hope, 1912- ed.   **• 2.6139**
Historical poems of the XIVth and XVth centuries. — New York, Columbia University Press, 1959. 440 p. 19 cm. 1. English poetry — Middle English, 1100-1500 2. Gt. Brit. — Hist. — Poetry. 3. Poetry of places — Gt. Brit. I. T.
PR1203.R58   821.1082   LC 59-6661

Robbins, Rossell Hope, 1912- ed. • 2.6140
Secular lyrics of the XIVth and XVth centuries. — 2d ed. — Oxford, Clarendon Press [1955] 331 p. 19 cm. 1. English poetry — Middle English, 1100-1500 I. T.
PR1203.R6 1955   821.1082   LC 56-13683

Sisam, Celia, comp. • 2.6141
The Oxford book of medieval English verse; chosen and edited by Celia and Kenneth Sisam. — Oxford: Clarendon P., 1970. xxiii, 617 p.; 20 cm. — ([The Oxford books of verse]) 1. English poetry — Middle English, 1100-1500 I. Sisam, Kenneth. joint comp. II. T.
PR1203.S55   821/.1/08   LC 73-536220   ISBN 0198121350

Stevick, Robert David, 1928-. • 2.6142
One hundred Middle English lyrics / edited with an introduction by Robert D. Stevick. — Indianapolis: Bobbs-Merrill Company, 1964. xxxiii, 188 p.; 21 cm. — (Library of literature) '7' 1. English poetry — Middle English, 1100-1500 I. T.
PR1203.S8   LC 62-20862

British Library. Manuscript. Cotton Nero A. x. 2.6143
The works of the Gawain–poet / [edited by] Charles Moorman. — Jackson: University Press of Mississippi, c1977. xii, 452 p.: ill.; 24 cm. 'Frequently cited sources': p. 63-65. 1. English poetry — Middle English, 1100-1500 I. Moorman, Charles. II. T.
PR1203.W67   821/.1   LC 76-40190   ISBN 0878050280

PR1205–1207 16TH CENTURY

Bender, Robert M., comp. 2.6144
Five courtier poets of the English Renaissance / edited by Robert M. Bender. — New York: Washington Square Press, 1967. xiv, 671 p.: ports.; 22 cm. 'The major works of Sir Thomas Wyatt; Henry Howard, Earl of Surrey; Sir Philip Sidney; Fulke Greville, Lord Brooke; Sir Walter Ralegh.' 1. English poetry — Early modern, 1500-1700 I. Wyatt, Thomas, Sir, 1503?-1542. II. Surrey, Henry Howard, Earl of, 1517?-1547. III. Sidney, Philip, Sir, 1554-1586. IV. Greville, Fulke, Baron Brooke, 1554-1628. V. Raleigh, Walter, Sir, 1552?-1618. VI. T.
PR1205.B4   821/.008   LC 67-26452

Bullett, Gerald William, 1893-1958. • 2.6145
Silver poets of the sixteenth century / edited with an introduction. — London: J.M. Dent, [1947] xix, 428 p. 18 cm. — (Everyman's library. Poetry, no. 985) Editor: G.W. Bullett. 1. English poetry — Early modern, 1500-1700 I. Davies, John, Sir, 1569-1626. II. Raleigh, Walter, Sir, 1552?-1618. III. Sidney, Philip, Sir, 1554-1586. IV. Surrey, Henry Howard, Earl of, 1517?-1547. V. Wyatt, Thomas, Sir, 1503?-1542. VI. T. VII. Series.
PR1205.B9   LC A 48-6358 *

Gardner, Helen Louise, Dame. comp. • 2.6146
The metaphysical poets / selected and edited by Helen Gardner. — 2nd ed. — London: Oxford U.P., 1967. xxxvi, 309 p.; 20 cm. 1. English poetry — Early modern, 1500-1700 I. T.
PR1205.G3 1967   821/.4/08   LC 67-102365

McClure, Norman Egbert, 1893-. • 2.6147
Sixteenth century English poetry. — New York: Harper, [1954] 623 p.; 25 cm. (Harper English literature series.) 1. English poetry — Early modern (to 1700). I. T.
PR1205.M35   821.08

The Oxford book of sixteenth century verse, chosen by E. K. • 2.6148
Chambers.
Oxford, The Clarendon press, 1932. xiii, 905, [1] p. 20 cm. 1. English poetry — Early modern, 1500-1700 I. Chambers, E. K. (Edmund Kerchever), 1866-1954. ed.
PR1205.O9   821.0822   LC 32-28157

Sylvester, Richard Standish. comp. 2.6149
The Anchor anthology of sixteenth–century verse. Edited with an introd. and notes by Richard S. Sylvester. — [1st ed.]. — Garden City, N.Y.: Anchor Press, 1974. xxxiv, 624 p.: facsim.; 21 cm. 1. English poetry — Early modern, 1500-1700 I. T.
PR1205.S78   821/.3/08   LC 73-8496   ISBN 0385002866

Tottel, Richard, d. 1594. • 2.6150
Tottel's miscellany (1557–1587) / Edited by Hyder Edward Rollins. — Rev. ed. — Cambridge: Harvard University Press, 1965. 2 v.: facsims.; 27 cm. I. Surrey, Henry Howard, Earl of, 1517?-1547. II. Wyatt, Thomas, Sir, 1503?-1542. III. Grimald, Nicholas, 1519-1562. IV. Rollins, Hyder Edward, 1889-1958. ed. V. T.
PR1205.T6 1965   821.2082   LC 64-22722

Ault, Norman, 1880-1950. • 2.6151
Elizabethan lyrics from the original texts. [3d ed.] New York, W. Sloane Associates [1949] xvii, 560 p. 22 cm. 1. English poetry — Early modern, 1500-1700 I. T.
PR1207.A8 1949   821.3082   LC 49-8434

Donno, Elizabeth Story, 1921-. • 2.6152
Elizabethan minor epics / edited with introd. by Elizabeth Story Donno. — New York: Columbia University Press, 1963. vii, 351 p. 1. Ovid, 43 B.C.-17 or 18 A.D — Influence. 2. English poetry — Early modern, 1500-1700 3. Love poetry I. T.
PR1207.D58 1963   LC 63-20343

England's Helicon, 1600, 1614 / edited by Hyder Edward • 2.6153
Rollins.
Cambridge, Mass.: Harvard University Press, 1935. 2 v.: ill. (coat of arms) facsims.; 25 cm. 1. English poetry — Early modern, 1500-1700 2. Pastoral poetry, English I. Rollins, Hyder Edward, 1889-1958.
PR1207.E3 1935   LC 35-3681

PR1209–1219 17TH–18TH CENTURIES

Ault, Norman, 1880-1950. ed. • 2.6154
Seventeenth century lyrics from the original texts. [2d ed.] New York, Sloane [1950] xv, 562 p. 22 cm. 'A short-title list of ... poetical collections mainly anonymous and of the XVIIth century': p. 519-527. 1. English poetry — Early modern (to 1700) I. T.
PR1209.A8 1950   821.3082   LC 50-7777

Cavalier poets: selected poems / edited with an introd. and notes 2.6155
by Thomas Clayton.
Oxford [Eng.]; New York: Oxford University Press, 1974. xxiii, 363 p.; 21 cm. Includes index. 1. English poetry — Early modern, 1500-1700 I. Clayton, Thomas, 1932-
PR1209.C27   821/.4/08   LC 77-30071   ISBN 0192541714

The English Spenserians: the poetry of Giles Fletcher, George 2.6155a
Wither, Michael Drayton, Phineas Fletcher, and Henry More / edited by William B. Hunter, Jr.
Salt Lake City: University of Utah Press, c1977. 453 p.: ill.; 27 cm. Includes index. 1. English poetry — Early modern, 1500-1700 I. Hunter, William Bridges, 1915-
PR1209.E5   821/.3/09   LC 75-30155   ISBN 0874801109

George Herbert and the seventeenth–century religious poets: 2.6156
authoritative texts criticism / selected and edited by Mario A. Di Cesare.
1st ed. — New York: Norton, c1978. xiv, 401 p.; 22 cm. — (A Norton critical edition) 1. English poetry — Early modern, 1500-1700 2. Christian poetry, English 3. English poetry — Early modern, 1500-1700 — History and criticism — Addresses, essays, lectures. 4. Religion in literature — Addresses, essays, lectures. I. Herbert, George, 1593-1633. II. Di Cesare, Mario A.
PR1209.G4 1978   821/.7/0931   LC 77-28074   ISBN 0393043983. ISBN 0393092542 pbk

Grierson, Herbert John Clifford, Sir, 1866-1960. • 2.6157
Metaphysical lyrics & poems of the seventeenth century: Donne to Butler / selected and ed., with an essay by Herbert J.C. Grierson. Oxford: The Clarendon press, 1921. lviii p., 1 l., 244 p. Oxford paperbacks, 102. 1. English poetry — Early modern (to 1700) I. T.
PR1209.G7   LC 22-2343

Howarth, Robert Guy, 1906-. • 2.6158
Minor poets of the seventeenth century. — London: Dent, [1959] xxviii, 386 p. — (Everyman's library. no. 873. Poetry and the drama.) Compiled by R.G. Howarth. 1. English poetry — Early modern, 1500-1700 I. T. II. Series.
PR1209.H6 1953   LC 64-9503

Martz, Louis Lohr. comp. 2.6159
The Anchor anthology of seventeenth–century verse / edited with an introd. and notes by Louis L. Martz. — [1st ed.]. — Garden City, N.Y.: Doubleday, 1969. 2 v.: ill.; 21 cm. — (The Anchor seventeenth-century series, ACO-13a-13b) Vol 1. is a rev. ed. of The meditative poem, by L. L. Martz, published in 1963. Vol. 2, edited with an introd. and notes, by R. S. Sylvester. 1. English poetry — Early modern, 1500-1700 I. Sylvester, Richard Standish. joint comp. II. T.
PR1209.M26 1969   821/.4/08   LC 68-29286

The Oxford book of seventeenth century verse, chosen by • 2.6160
H.J.C. Grierson and G. Bullough.
Oxford, Clarendon Press [1951] 974 p.; 20 cm. I. Grierson, Sir Herbert John Clifford, 1866-1960, ed. II. Bullough, Geoffrey, 1901-
PR1209.O8 1951

Parfitt, George A. E. comp.   2.6161
Silver poets of the seventeenth century, edited by G. A. E. Parfitt. — London: Dent; Totowa, N.J.: Rowman and Littlefield, [1975] xxi, 266 p.; 20 cm. 1. English poetry — Early modern, 1500-1700 I. T.
PR1209.P27   821/.008   *LC* 74-1167   *ISBN* 0874715172

Saintsbury, George, 1845-1933. ed.   • 2.6162
Minor poets of the Caroline period ... — ed. by George Saintsbury, M. A. — Oxford, At the Clarendon press, 1905-21. 3 v. front., plates. 23 cm. With reproductions of original title-pages. 1. English poetry — Early modern (to 1700) I. T. II. Title: Careline poets.
PR1209.S3   *LC* 05-33557

Pinto, Vivian de Sola, 1895-.   • 2.6163
Restoration carnival: five courtier poets: Rochester, Dorset, Sedley, Etherege & Sheffield. — London: Folio Society, 1954. 253 p.; 22 cm. Edited by Vivian de Sola Pinto. 1. English poetry — Early modern, 1500-1700 I. Pinto, Vivian de Sola, 1895- II. T.
PR1213.P5   *LC* 54-28381

The New Oxford book of eighteenth century verse / chosen and edited by Roger Lonsdale.   2.6164
Oxford; New York: Oxford University Press, 1984. xlii, 870 p.; 23 cm. Includes index. 1. English poetry — 18th century I. Lonsdale, Roger H.
PR1215.N48 1984   821/.5/08 19   *LC* 83-17477   *ISBN* 0192141228

The Oxford book of eighteenth century verse, chosen by David Nichol Smith.   • 2.6165
Oxford: The Clarendon press, 1926. xii, 727 p.; 20 cm. 1. English poetry — 18th century I. Smith, David Nichol, 1875-1962. ed.
PR1215.O85   *LC* 27-26382

Quintana, Ricardo. ed.   • 2.6166
English poetry of the mid and late eighteenth century: an historical anthology / edited by Ricardo Quintana & Alvin Whitley. — [1st ed.]. — New York: Knopf, 1963. ix, 368, v p.; 21 cm. — (The Borzoi series in eighteenth-century literature) 1. English poetry — 18th century I. Whitley, Alvin, joint ed. II. T.
PR1215.Q5   821.6082   *LC* 63-14613

Spacks, Patricia Ann Meyer. ed.   • 2.6167
Eighteenth–century poetry. Edited by Patricia Meyer Spacks. — Englewood Cliffs, N. J., Prentice-Hall [1964] lii, 451 p. 21 cm. — (Prentice-Hall English literature series) Includes bibliographies. 1. English poetry — 18th cent. I. T.
PR1215.S75   821.6082   *LC* 64-13245

Davie, Donald. ed.   • 2.6168
The late Augustans. London, New York, Heinemann [1963, c1958] xxxiii, 130 p. front. 19 cm. 1. English poetry — 18th century I. T.
PR1217.D3 1963   *LC* 66-83

PR1221–1223 19TH CENTURY

Buckley, Jerome Hamilton. comp.   • 2.6169
The Pre–Raphaelites. Edited with an introd. by Jerome H. Buckley. — New York: Modern Library, [1968] xxvii, 514 p.; illus.; 19 cm. — (Modern Library college editions) 1. English poetry — 19th century 2. English poetry — 19th century — History and criticism. I. T.
PR1221.B77   821/.8/08   *LC* 68-54722

Campbell, Oscar James, 1879-1970. ed.   • 2.6170
English poetry of the nineteenth century / by Oscar James Campbell and J. F. A. Pyre. — Westport, Conn.: Greenwood Press, [1971, c1929] xiv, 784 p.; 24 cm. 1. English poetry — 19th century I. Pyre, James Francis Augustin, 1871-1934. joint ed. II. T.
PR1221.C25 1971   821/.7/09   *LC* 75-154103   *ISBN* 083716074X

Campbell, Oscar James, 1879-1970. ed.   • 2.6171
Poetry and criticism of the romantic movement; editors: Oscar James Campbell ... J. F. A. Pyre ... [and] Bennett Weaver ... — New York: F. S. Crofts & co., 1932. xii, 849 p.; 24 cm. 1. English poetry — 19th century 2. English poetry — 19th century — History and criticism. 3. English literature — 19th century — History and criticism. 4. Criticism — History. 5. Romanticism — England. I. Pyre, James Francis Augustine, 1871-1934, joint ed. II. Weaver, Bennett, 1892- joint ed. III. T.
PR1221.C26   821.708   *LC* 32-14465

The Oxford book of nineteenth–century English verse, chosen by John Hayward.   • 2.6172
Oxford: Clarendon Press, 1964. xxxv, 969 p.; 20 cm. 1. English poetry — 19th century I. Hayward, John, 1905-1965. ed.
PR1221.O79   821.7082   *LC* 64-5255

The Oxford book of English verse of the Romantic period,   • 2.6173
1798–1837 / chosen by H. S. Milford.
Oxford: Clarendon Press, [1958]. viii, 887 p. 1. English poetry — 19th century I. Milford, Humphrey Sumner, Sir, 1877-1952. II. Title: Oxford book of regency verse. III. Title: Oxford book of romantic verse.
PR1221.O8 1935   *ISBN* 0198121237

Stephens, James, 1882-1950. ed.   • 2.6174
English romantic poets / edited by James Stephens, Edwin L. Beck [and] Royall H. Snow. — New York: American Book Co. [1952] 975 p.: ill.; 25 cm. 1. English poetry — 19th century I. T.
PR1221.S8 1952   *LC* 52-3737

Victorian poetry / edited by E. K. Brown and J. O. Bailey.   2.6175
2d ed. — New York: Ronald Press, 1962. xlv, 911 p. 1. English poetry — 19th century I. Bailey, James Osler. II. Brown, E. K. (Edward Killoran), 1905-1951. III. Bailey, James Osler, 1903- IV. Brown, E. K.
PR1223.B7 1962   821.8082   *LC* 62-13708

Davidson, Donald, 1893-1968. ed.   • 2.6176
British poetry of the eighteen–nineties. [1st ed.] Garden City, N.Y. Doubleday, Doran [1937] lxxii, 420 p.: front.; 25 cm. (The Doubleday-Doran series in literature) 1. English poetry — 19th century I. T.
PR1223 D3

Houghton, Walter Edwards, 1904- ed.   • 2.6177
Victorian poetry and poetics [by] Walter E. Houghton [and] G. Robert Stange. [Under the general editorship of Gordon N. Ray]. — 2d ed. — Boston: Houghton Mifflin, [1968] xxvi, 915 p.; 25 cm. 1. English poetry — 19th century 2. English poetry — History and criticism I. Stange, George Robert, 1919- joint ed. II. T.
PR1223.H6 1968   821/.8/08   *LC* 74-370

Martin, Robert Bernard.   2.6178
Victorian poetry; ten major poets: Tennyson, Browning, Arnold, Meredith, D. G. Rossetti, Christina Rossetti, Swinburne, Hardy, Hopkins, Housman. — New York: Random House, [1964] xxii, 845 p.; 22 cm. 1. English poetry — 19th century I. T.
PR1223.M36   821.8082   *LC* 64-14090

The Oxford book of Victorian verse, chosen by Arthur Quiller–Couch.   • 2.6179
Oxford: The Clarendon press, 1925. xv, 1023 p. 19 cm. First published 1912. 1. English poetry — 19th century I. Quiller-Couch, Arthur Thomas, Sir, 1863-1944. ed.
PR1223.O8   821.80822   *LC* 33-28868

Stephens, James, 1882-1950. ed.   • 2.6180
Victorian and later English poets, edited by James Stephens, Edwin L. Beck [and] Royall H. Snow. — New York: American Book Co., [1949] xiii, 1380 p.: facsims.; 25 cm. 1. English poetry — 19th century I. T.
PR1223.S74 1949   821.8082   *LC* 49-48232

Victorian poetry. [Edited and with a preface by Malcolm Bradbury and David Palmer.]   2.6181
[S.l.]: Crane, Russak; 1973. 304 p. illus. — (Stratford-upon-Avon studies. 15) Includes bibliographical references. 1. English poetry — 19th cent. — Collections. I. Bradbury, Malcolm, 1932- ed. II. Palmer, David, ed. III. Series.
PR1223.V5x   *LC* 72-87314

Woods, George Benjamin, 1878-1958, ed.   • 2.6182
Poetry of the Victorian period, selected and edited with critical and explanatory notes, brief biographies, and bibliographies [by] Jerome Hamilton Buckley [and] George Benjamin Woods. — 3d ed. — Chicago: Scott, Foresman, [1965] xvii, 1079 p.; 24 cm. First ed. by G. B. Woods; 2d ed. by G. B. Woods and J. H. Buckley. 1. English poetry — 19th century I. Buckley, Jerome Hamilton. joint author. II. T.
PR1223.W6 1965   821.8082   *LC* 65-11904

PR1224–1227 20TH CENTURY

Untermeyer, Louis, 1885-1977. ed.   • 2.6183
Modern British poetry. — New and enl. ed. — New York: Harcourt, Brace & World, [1962] 541 p.; 24 cm. 1. English poetry — 19th century 2. English poetry — 20th century I. T.
PR1224.U6 1962   821.082   *LC* 62-12184

The New poetry: an anthology / selected and introduced by A. Alvarez.   2.6184
Harmondsworth: Penguin, 1962. 188 p.; 18 cm. — (Penguin poets. D63) 1. English poetry — 20th century I. Alvarez, A. (Alfred), 1929- II. Series.
PR1225.A58 1962   *LC* 63-3573

Cecil, David, Lord, 1902- ed. • 2.6185
Modern verse in English, 1900–1950. Edited by David Cecil and Allen Tate, with critical introductions on British and American poetry, and biographical notes on the poets included. New York, Macmillan [1958] 689 p. 20 cm. 1. English poetry — 20th century 2. American poetry — 20th century I. Tate, Allen, 1899- joint ed. II. T.
PR1225.C4　　821.91082　　*LC* 58-13621

Conquest, Robert. • 2.6186
New lines: an anthology edited by Robert Conquest. — London: Macmillan, 1956-63. 2 v.; 22 cm. 1. English poetry — 20th century I. T.
PR1225.C59　　821.908　　*LC* 58-5987

Georgian poetry, 1920–1922. • 2.6187
London: The Poetry Bookshop, 1922. 207 p.; 20 cm. 'Prefatory note' signed: E.M. (i.e.E.H.) Marsh. 1. English poetry — 20th century I. Marsh, Edward Howard, Sir, 1872-1953.
PR1225.G4 1922　　*LC* 23-6782

Heath-Stubbs, John Francis Alexander, 1918- ed. 2.6188
The Faber book of twentieth–century verse / edited by John Heath–Stubbs & David Wright. — 3rd ed. — London: Faber, 1975. 3-347 p.; 20 cm. Includes index. 1. English poetry — 20th century I. Wright, David, 1920- joint ed. II. T.
PR1225.H4 1975　　821/.9/1208　　*LC* 76-352251　　*ISBN* 0571048846

Larkin, Philip. comp. 2.6189
The Oxford book of twentieth–century English verse; chosen by Philip Larkin. Oxford, Clarendon Press, 1973. l, 641 p. 23 cm. 1. English poetry — 20th century I. T.
PR1225.L3　　821/.9/108　　*LC* 73-159943　　*ISBN* 0198121377

The Oxford book of contemporary verse, 1945–1980 / chosen by 2.6190
D. J. Enright.
Oxford; New York: Oxford University Press, 1980. xxxii, 299 p.; 23 cm. Includes indexes. 1. English poetry — 20th century 2. American poetry — 20th century 3. English poetry — Commonwealth of Nations authors I. Enright, D. J. (Dennis Joseph), 1920-
PR1225.O89　　821/.008 19　　*LC* 80-506590　　*ISBN* 0192141082

The Oxford book of modern verse, 1892–1935, chosen by W. B. • 2.6191
Yeats.
New York: Oxford University Press, 1936. xiv, 450 p. 20 cm. 'First edition.' 1. English poetry — 20th cent. 2. English poetry — 19th cent. I. Yeats, W. B. (William Butler), 1865-1939. ed.
PR1225.O9 1936　　*LC* 36-28578

The Penguin book of contemporary British poetry / edited by 2.6192
Blake Morrison and Andrew Motion.
Harmondsworth: Penguin, 1982. 208 p.; 18 cm. 1. English poetry — 20th century I. Morrison, Blake, 1950- II. Motion, Andrew
PR1225　　PR1225 P35.　　821/.914/08 19　　*ISBN* 0140422838

The Faber book of modern verse / edited by Michael Roberts. 2.6193
4th ed. : rev. by Peter Porter. — London: Faber and Faber, 1982. 432 p.; 21 cm. — 1. English poetry — 20th century 2. American poetry — 20th century I. Porter, Peter. II. Roberts, Michael, 1902-1948.
PR1225 R58 1982.　　821/.9/108　　*ISBN* 0571180558

Williams, Oscar, 1900-1964. ed. 2.6194
A little treasury of modern poetry, English & American. — 3d ed. — New York: Scribner, [1970] liv, 937 p.: ports.; 19 cm. — (The Little treasury series) On cover: 3d College ed. 1. English poetry — 20th century 2. American poetry — 20th century I. T.
PR1225.W535 1970　　821/.008　　*LC* 75-91781

Some contemporary poets of Britain and Ireland: an anthology / 2.6195
edited by Michael Schmidt.
Manchester [Greater Manchester]: Carcanet Press, 1983. xv, 184 p.; 23 cm. Spine title: Some contemporary poets. 1. English poetry — 20th century 2. English poetry — Irish authors I. Schmidt, Michael, 1947- II. Title: Some contemporary poets.
PR1227.S647 1983　　821/.914/08 19　　*LC* 84-195688　　*ISBN* 0856354694

PR1240–1273 DRAMA

Jeffares, A. Norman (Alexander Norman), 1920- comp. 2.6196
Restoration comedy. Edited by A. Norman Jeffares. London, Folio Press: Totowa, N.J., Rowman and Littlefield, 1974. 4 v. illus. 26 cm. 1. English drama (Comedy) 2. English drama — Restoration, 1660-1700 I. T.
PR1248.J4　　822/.052　　*LC* 73-19769　　*ISBN* 0874714761

McMillin, Scott. comp. 2.6197
Restoration and eighteenth–century comedy. Authoritative texts of The country wife, The man of mode, The way of the world, The conscious lovers, The school for scandal; backgrounds, criticism. — [1st ed.]. — New York: Norton, [1973] x, 565 p.; 22 cm. — (A Norton critical edition) 1. English drama (Comedy) 2. English drama — Restoration, 1660-1700 3. English drama — 18th century I. T.
PR1248.M3　　822/.052　　*LC* 71-152309　　*ISBN* 0393043525

Richards, Stanley, 1918- comp. 2.6198
Best mystery and suspense plays of the modern theatre. Edited with an introductory note and prefaces to the plays, by Stanley Richards. — New York: Dodd, Mead, [1971] xi, 800 p.: illus.; 22 cm. 1. Detective and mystery plays, English 2. Detective and mystery plays, American I. T.
PR1259.D4 R5 1971　　822/.9/108　　*LC* 76-145393　　*ISBN* 0396063225

Richards, Stanley, 1918- comp. 2.6199
10 classic mystery and suspense plays of the modern theatre / edited with an introductory note and prefaces to the plays by Stanley Richards; illustrated with photos. from the original New York productions. — New York: Dodd, Mead [1973] xi, 887 p.: ill. 22 cm. 1. Detective and mystery plays, English 2. Detective and mystery plays, American I. T.
PR1259.D4 R55　　822/.9/1208　　*LC* 72-7755　　*ISBN* 0396067077

Best radio plays of ... 2.6200
1978-　　　. — London: Eyre Methuen, [c1979-. v.; 20-23 cm. Annual. 'The Giles Cooper award winners.' 1. Radio plays, English 2. English drama — 20th century
PR1259.R33 B46　　822/.02/08 19　　*LC* 85-641485

PR1260–1272 By Period

PR1260–1261 MEDIEVAL: MYSTERIES. MIRACLE PLAYS

Adams, Joseph Quincy, 1881-1946. ed. • 2.6201
Chief pre–Shakespearean dramas; a selection of plays illustrating the history of the English drama from its origin down to Shakespeare, by Joseph Quincy Adams. — Boston; New York [etc.]: Houghton Mifflin company, [c1924] vii, 712 p.: facsim.; 21 cm. 1. English drama — To 1500 2. Mysteries and miracle-plays, English 3. English drama — Early modern and Elizabethan, 1500-1600 I. T.
PR1260.A3　　*LC* 24-23608

Chester plays. 2.6202
The Chester mystery plays: seventeen pageant plays from the Chester craft cycle / adapted into modern English by Maurice Hussey. — 2nd ed. — London: Heinemann Educational, 1975. xxii, 170 p.; 19 cm. 1. Mysteries and miracle-plays, English I. Hussey, Maurice. II. T.
PR1260.C38 1975　　822/.1　　*LC* 79-304626　　*ISBN* 0435234153

English moral interludes / edited, with an introd., by Glynne 2.6203
Wickham.
London: Dent; Totowa, N.J.: Rowman and Littlefield, 1976. xvi, 213 p.; 20 cm. 1. Interludes, English. 2. Moralities, English I. Wickham, Glynne William Gladstone.
PR1260.E5 1976　　822/.051　　*LC* 75-25563　　*ISBN* 0874717663

English mystery plays: a selection / edited with an introd. and 2.6204
notes by Peter Happé.
Baltimore: Penguin Books, 1975. 713 p.; 18 cm. (The Penguin English library; EL93) 1. Mysteries and miracle-plays, English I. Happé, Peter.
PR1260.E53 1975b　　PR1260 E53 1975b.　　822/.051　　*LC* 76-361119　　*ISBN* 0140430938

Everyman, and medieval miracle plays, edited with an introd. by • 2.6205
A. C. Cawley.
London, Dent; New York, Dutton [1962] xxi, 266 p. 19 cm. (Everyman's library. 381) Apart from Everyman, this volume contains a completely new selection of Biblical pageants. 1. Mysteries and miracle-plays, English 2. English drama — To 1500 I. Cawley, A. C. (Arthur C.) ed. II. Series.
PR1260.E8x　　822.2　　*LC* 63-6778

Franklin, Alexander, ed. • 2.6206
Seven miracle plays. — [London, New York] Oxford University Press, 1963. 158 p. illus. 21 cm. Freely adapted versions. 1. Mysteries and miracle-plays, English 2. English drama — To 1500 I. T.
PR1260.F7　　822.1082　　*LC* 64-76

Pollard, Alfred W. (Alfred William), 1859-1944. ed. • 2.6207
English miracle plays, moralities and interludes: specimens of the pre-Elizabethan drama / edited, with an introduction, notes, and glossary, by

Alfred W. Pollard ... — 8th ed., rev. — Oxford: The Clarendon press, 1927. lxxi, 250 p.: front., ill., plates (1 double); 20 cm. 1. Mysteries and miracle-plays, English 2. Moralities, English 3. English drama — Medieval. I. T.
PR1260.P7 1927　　822.10822　　*LC* 40-20504

Thomas, R. George. ed.　　　　　　　　　　　**2.6208**
Ten miracle plays / [edited by] R. George Thomas. — Evanston, Ill.: Northwestern University Press, 1966. 166 p.; 21 cm. (York medieval texts) 1. Mysteries and miracle-plays, English 2. English drama — To 1500 I. Ludus Coventriae. II. T.
PR1260.T48　　822/.2/08　　*LC* 66-27881

Towneley plays.　　　　　　　　　　　　**• 2.6209**
Wakefield pageants in the Towneley cycle / edited by A.C. Cawley.— Manchester, Eng.: Manchester U.P., 1958. 187p.; 22 cm.— (Old and Middle English texts; 1.) 1. Mysteries and miracle-plays, English 2. English drama — Medieval. I. Cawley, A. C. (Arthur C.) ed. II. T.
PR1260 T58　　*LC* A60-3585　　*ISBN* 0719006066

Towneley plays.　　　　　　　　　　　　**• 2.6210**
The Wakefield mystery plays. Edited by Martial Rose. — [1st ed. in the U.S.A.]. — Garden City, N. Y., Doubleday, 1962 [c1961] 552 p. 22 cm. 1. Mysteries and miracle-plays, English 2. English drama — Medieval. I. Rose, Martial. ed. II. T.
PR1260.T6 1962　　822.1　　*LC* 62-11380

York plays.　　　　　　　　　　　　　　**2.6211**
The York cycle of mystery plays: a complete version / by J. S. Purvis. — London: S.P.C.K., 1957. 384 p. 1. Mysteries and miracle-plays, English 2. English drama — To 1500 I. Purvis, J. S. (John Stanley), 1890- II. T.
PR1260.Y6 1970　　PR1260 Y6 1957.　　*LC* 57-59008

Ludus Coventriae.　　　　　　　　　　　　**2.6212**
The Corpus Christi play of the English Middle Ages. An edition with introd. and notes by R. T. Davies. Totowa, N.J., Rowman and Littlefield [1972] 458 p. 23 cm. The text of the cycle of miracle plays commonly known as Ludus Coventriae (British Museum MSS Cottonian Vespasian D VIII), omitting a few episodes; includes also the texts of all extant versions of the play of Abraham and Isaac. 1. Mysteries and miracle-plays, English 2. English drama — To 1500 I. Davies, Reginald Thorne. ed. II. T.
PR1261.C6 1972　　822/.051　　*LC* 72-172754　　*ISBN* 087471124X

York plays.　　　　　　　　　　　　　　**2.6213**
The York plays / edited by Richard Beadle. — London: E. Arnold, 1982. 537 p.: ill.; 24 cm. — (York medieval texts. Second series.) 1. Mysteries and miracle-plays, English 2. English drama — To 1500 I. Beadle, Richard. II. T. III. Series.
PR1261.Y67 1982　　822/.0516/08 19　　*LC* 82-185833　　*ISBN* 0713163267

York plays. Selections.　　　　　　　　　　**2.6214**
York mystery plays: a selection in modern spelling / edited by Richard Beadle and Pamela M. King. — Oxford [Oxfordshire]: Clarendon Press; New York: Oxford University Press, 1984. xxxiii, 279 p.: map; 23 cm. 1. Mysteries and miracle-plays, English 2. English drama — To 1500 I. Beadle, Richard. II. King, Pamela M. III. T.
PR1261.Y67 1984　　822/.0516/08 19　　*LC* 84-3879　　*ISBN* 0198111894

PR1262–1266 16TH–17TH CENTURIES

Boas, Frederick S. (Frederick Samuel), 1862-1957. ed.　　　**• 2.6215**
Five pre–Shakespearean comedies, edited with an introd. by Frederick S. Boas. London, New York, Oxford University Press, 1970. xviii, 343 p. 20 cm. (Oxford paperbacks, 219) 1. English drama — Early modern and Elizabethan, 1500-1600 2. English drama (Comedy) I. T.
PR1262.B56 1970　　822/.2/08　　*LC* 73-485743　　*ISBN* 0192810855

Creeth, Edmund, ed.　　　　　　　　　　　**• 2.6216**
Tudor plays: an anthology of early English drama. — Garden City, N.Y.: Anchor Books, [1966]. xiv, 569 p.: ill.; 21 cm. (Anchor octavo AO-1) 1. English drama — Early modern and Elizabethan, 1500-1600 I. T.
PR1262.C68　　822.208　　*LC* 66-12240

Bald, R. C. (Robert Cecil), 1901-1965. ed.　　　　　　　**• 2.6217**
Six Elizabethan plays (1585–1635) Boston, Houghton Mifflin [1963] xvi, 469 p. 21 cm. 1. English drama — Early modern and Elizabethan, 1500-1600 2. English drama — 17th century I. T.
PR1263.B24　　822.3082　　*LC* 63-4440

Dodsley, Robert, 1703-1764. comp.　　　　　　　　　**• 2.6218**
A select collection of old English plays. — 4th ed., now first chronologically arr., rev., and enl., with the notes of all the commentators, and new notes, by W. Carew Hazlitt. — New York, B. Blom [1964] 15 v. in 7. 18 cm. Reprint of the 1874-76 ed. of a work first published in 1744. 'Glossarial index, by Richard

Morris': v. 15, p. [459]-509. Vol. 1 of Frost copy published: New York: Arno Press, 1979. 1. English drama (Collections) I. Hazlitt, William Carew, 1834-1913. ed. II. Morris, Richard, 1833-1894. III. T. IV. Title: Old English plays.
PR1263.D6x　　822.082　　*LC* 64-14702

Four Tudor comedies / edited with an introduction and notes by　　**2.6219**
William Tydeman.
Harmondsworth: Penguin, 1984. 440 p.; 20 cm. — (The Penguin English library) 1. English drama — Early modern and Elizabethan, 1500-1600 2. English drama (Comedy) I. Tydeman, William. II. Udall, Nicholas, 1505-1556. Ralph Roister Doister III. Stevenson, William, d. 1575. Gammer Gurton's nedle. IV. Lyly, John, 1554?-1606. Mother Bombie. V. Udall, Nicholas, 1505-1556. Jacke Jugeler. VI. Title: 4 tudor comedies. VII. Title: Roister Doister. VIII. Title: Gammer Gurton's nedle. IX. Title: Mother Bombie. X. Title: Jacke Jugeler.
PR1263.F66　　822/.052/08 19　　*ISBN* 0140432027

Harrier, Richard C., ed.　　　　　　　　　　　**• 2.6220**
The Anchor anthology of Jacobean drama / edited with an introd., notes, and variants by Richard C. Harrier. — [1st ed.]. — Garden City: N. Y., Anchor Books, 1963. 2 v.; 18 cm. — (The Anchor Seventeenth-Century Series) 1. English drama — Early modern and Elizabethan. I. T.
PR1263.H27 1963b　　822.3　　*LC* 63-8749 rev

Six Caroline plays/ ed. with an intro. by A.S. Knowland .　　**• 2.6221**
London: Oxford University Press, 1962. 553 p. — (World's classics.) 1. English drama — Early modern and Elizabethan, 1500-1600 I. Knowland, A. S. II. Title: 6 Caroline plays.
PR1263.K6　　82.08　　*LC* 62-4796

McIlwraith, A. K. (Archibald Kennedy) ed.　　　　　　**• 2.6222**
Five Stuart tragedies. — London, New York, Oxford University Press [1953] xxi, 497 p. 15 cm. — (World's classics, no. 526) 1. English drama — Early modern and Elizabethan, 1500-1600 I. T.
PR 1263 M16　　*LC* A 53-8184

McIlwraith, A. K. (Archibald Kennedy) comp.　　　　　**• 2.6223**
Five Elizabethan tragedies / edited with an introd. by A. K. McIlwraith. — London; New York: Oxford University Press, 1971. xx, 399 p.: ill.; 21 cm. (Oxford paperbacks, 266) Reprint of 1938 ed. 1. English drama — Early modern and Elizabethan, 1500-1600 I. T.
PR1263.M27 1971　　822.3/08　　*LC* 70-28236　　*ISBN* 0192811193

Nethercot, Arthur Hobart, 1895- comp.　　　　　　　**2.6224**
Elizabethan plays. Edited by Arthur H. Nethercot, Charles R. Baskervill [and] Virgil B. Heltzel. — [Rev. ed.] Rev. by Arthur H. Nethercot. — New York: Holt, Rinehart and Winston, [1971] xi, 845 p.; 25 cm. 'It was decided to publish this edition in two volumes, one to be entitled Elizabethan plays and the other Stuart plays.' 1934 ed., edited by C. R. Baskervill, V. B. Heltzel and A. H. Nethercot, published under title: Elizabethan and Stuart plays. 1. English drama — Early modern and Elizabethan, 1500-1600 I. Baskervill, Charles Read, 1872-1935. joint comp. II. Heltzel, Virgil Barney, 1896- joint comp. III. Baskervill, Charles Read, 1872-1935, ed. Elizabethan and Stuart plays. IV. T.
PR1263.N44 1971　　822/.3/08　　*LC* 79-161202　　*ISBN* 0030830303

Nethercot, Arthur Hobart, 1895- comp.　　　　　　　**2.6225**
Stuart plays. Edited by Arthur H. Nethercot, Charles R. Baskervill [and] Virgil B. Heltzel. [Rev. ed.] Rev. by Arthur H. Nethercot. New York, Holt, Rinehart and Winston [c1971] xi, 1038 p. 25 cm. 'It was decided to publish this edition in two volumes, one to be entitled Elizabethan plays and the other Stuart plays.' 1934 ed., edited by C. R. Baskervill, V. B. Heltzel, and A. H. Nethercot, published under title: Elizabethan and Stuart plays. 1. English drama — 17th century. I. Baskervill, Charles Read, 1872-1935, joint comp. II. Heltzel, Virgil B. (Virgil Barney), 1896- joint comp. III. Baskervill, Charles Read, 1872-1935, ed. Elizabethan and Stuart plays. IV. T.
PR1263.N46 1971　　822/.3/08　　*LC* 72-161203　　*ISBN* 003083029X

Elizabethan and Jacobean comedy: an anthology / edited by　　**• 2.6226**
Robert Ornstein and Hazelton Spencer.
Boston: Heath, c1964. xii, 315 p.: facsims.; 24 cm. 1. English drama (Comedy) 2. English drama — Early modern and Elizabethan, 1500-1600 I. Ornstein, Robert Evans. ed. II. Spencer, Hazelton, 1893-1944.
PR1263.O7　　PR1263 E563.　　822.3082　　*LC* 64-3948

Elizabethan and Jacobean tragedy: an anthology / edited by　　**• 2.6227**
Robert Ornstein and Hazelton Spencer.
Boston: Heath, 1964. xii, 308 p.: facsims.; 24 cm. 1. English drama — Early modern and Elizabethan, 1500-1600 2. English drama (Tragedy) I. Spencer, Hazelton, 1893-1944 II. Ornstein, Robert Evans.
PR1263.O72　　*LC* 64-3921

Nettleton, George Henry, 1874-1959. ed.　　　　　　　**2.6228**
British dramatists from Dryden to Sheridan, edited by George H. Nettleton and Arthur E. Case. Rev. by George Winchester Stone, Jr. — [2d ed.]. — Boston:

Houghton Mifflin, [1969] xvii, 958 p.; 25 cm. Libretto of the Beggar's opera by John Gay, with tunes for the airs and score of the overture by Pepusch: p. 531-565. Reprint of the 1939 ed. 1. English drama — Restoration, 1660-1700 2. English drama — 18th century I. Case, Arthur Ellicott, 1894-1946. joint ed. II. T.
PR1265.N4 1969   822/.008   LC 70-6981

Twelve famous plays of the restoration and eighteenth century; • 2.6229
introduction by Professor Cecil A. Moore.
New York: B. A. Cerf, D. S. Klopfer, The Modern library, [c1933] xxiii, 952 p.; 21 cm. — (The Modern library of the world's best books. [Modern library giants]) 'First Modern library edition, 1933.' 1. English drama — Restoration, 1660-1700 2. English drama — 18th century
PR1265.T8   822.0822   LC 33-10746

Lawrence, Robert Gilford, 1923- comp.   2.6230
Jacobean and Caroline comedies, edited with an introduction by Robert G. Lawrence. London, Dent, 1973. ii-xiv, 241 p. 20 cm. 1. English drama — 17th century 2. English drama (Comedy) I. Middleton, Thomas, d. 1627. A trick to catch the old one. 1973. II. Dekker, Thomas, ca. 1572-1632. The witch of Edmonton. 1973. III. Brome, Richard, d. 1652? A joviall crew. 1973. IV. T.
PR1265.5.L39   822/.3/08   LC 74-187828   ISBN 0460101463 ISBN 0460111469

Dobrée, Bonamy, 1891- ed.   • 2.6231
Five heroic plays. — London, Oxford University Press, 1960. xiii, 417 p. facsims. 16 cm. — (The World's classics, 576) 1. English drama — Restoration. I. T.
PR1266.D58   822.4   LC 61-282

Five restoration tragedies / edited with an introd. by Bonamy   • 2.6232
Dobrée.
London, Toronto: Oxford university press, c1928. xviii, 450 p. — (The World's classics; 313) 1. English drama — Restoration, 1660-1700 I. Dobrée, Bonamy, 1891-
PR1266.D6   PR1266.F55.   LC 29-13698

Harris, Brice, ed.   • 2.6233
Restoration plays. — New York: Modern Library, [1953] xx, 674 p.; 19 cm. — (The Modern library of the world's best books, 287) 1. English drama — Restoration, 1660-1700 I. T.
PR1266.H3   822.4082   LC 53-9766

PR1269–1272 18TH–20TH CENTURIES

Booth, Michael R. ed.   2.6234
Eighteenth century tragedy, edited with an introd. by Michael R. Booth. — London, New York, Oxford University Press, 1965. xiii, 394 p. 16 cm. — (The World's classics, 603) 1. English drama — 18th cent. 2. English drama (Tragedy) I. T.
PR1269.B6   822.082   LC 65-2301

Eighteenth–century plays / with an introd. by Ricardo   • 2.6235
Quintana.
New York: Modern Library, [1952] xxi, 484 p.; 19 cm. — (The Modern library of the world's best books [224]) 1. English drama — 18th century I. Quintana, Ricardo.
PR1269.E35   822.5   LC 52-5876

Plays by David Garrick and George Colman the elder / edited   2.6236
with an introduction and notes by E.R. Wood.
Cambridge; New York: Cambridge University Press, 1982. ix, 217 p.: ill.; 24 cm. — (British and American playwrights, 1750-1920.) 1. English drama — 18th century I. Garrick, David, 1717-1779. II. Colman, George, 1732-1794. III. Wood, E. R. (Edward Rudolf), 1907- IV. Series.
PR1269.P63 1982   822/.6 19   LC 81-17079   ISBN 0521235901

Taylor, William Duncan.   • 2.6237
Eighteenth century comedy; selected and introduced by W. D. Taylor. — [New ed.] Texts newly edited with annotation and an introduction to each play by Simon Trussler. — London; New York: Oxford U.P., 1969. xii, 370 p.: 5 facsims.; 21 cm. — (Oxford paperbacks, 181) 1. English drama (Comedy) 2. English drama — 18th century I. Trussler, Simon. II. T.
PR1269.T3 1969   822/.5/08   LC 70-455488   ISBN 0192810456

Six eighteenth–century plays / edited with an introduction by J. • 2.6238
H. Wilson.
Boston: Houghton-Mifflin, 1963. x, 374 p. (Riverside editions) 1. English drama — 18th century I. Wilson, John Harold, 1900- II. Title: 6 18th-century plays. III. Series.
PR1269.W5   822.6   LC 64-383

Booth, Michael R. comp.   • 2.6239
English plays of the nineteenth century; edited by Michael R. Booth. Oxford: Clarendon P., 1969-1976. 5 v.: plates, illus.; 23 cm. 1. English drama — 19th century I. T.
PR1271.B58   822/.009   LC 70-396661   ISBN 019811494X

Booth, Michael R. ed.   • 2.6240
Hiss the villain; six English and American melodramas. Edited, with an introd., by Michael Booth. — New York: B. Blom, [1964] 390 p.: illus., facsims.; 23 cm. 1. English drama — 19th century 2. American drama — 19th century. 3. Melodrama I. T.
PR1271.B6   822.8082   LC 65-16239

Kauvar, Gerald B. comp.   2.6241
Nineteenth–century English verse drama / With introductions and edited by Gerald B. Kauvar and Gerald C. Sorensen. — Rutherford [N.J.]: Fairleigh Dickinson University Press, [1973] 355 p.; 27 cm. 1. English drama — 19th century I. Sorensen. Gerald C., joint comp. II. T.
PR1271.K3   822/.7/09   LC 79-146163   ISBN 0838676316

Rowell, George. comp.   2.6242
Late Victorian plays, 1890–1914; edited with an introduction by George Rowell. 2nd ed. London, New York, University Press, 1972. xviii, 507 p. facsims. 21 cm. (Oxford paperbacks, 286) 1. English drama — 19th century 2. English drama — 20th century I. T.
PR1271.R66 1972   822/.9/1208   LC 73-150236   ISBN 0192811312

Rowell, George. ed.   • 2.6243
Nineteenth century plays. — London, New York, Oxford University Press [1953] xviii, 567 p. 16 cm. — (The World's classics, 533) 1. English drama — 19th cent. I. T.
PR1271.R68   822.7082   LC 53-13347

Salerno, Henry Frank, 1919- comp.   2.6244
English drama in transition, 1880–1920, edited by Henry F. Salerno. — New York: Pegasus, [1968] 544 p.; 20 cm. 'A Pegasus original.' 1. English drama — 19th century 2. English drama — 20th century I. T.
PR1271.S2   822/.008   LC 67-25504

Best plays of the seventies / edited with an introductory note   2.6245
and prefaces to the plays by Stanley Richards.
1st ed. — Garden City, N.Y.: Doubleday, 1980. 814 p.; 22 cm. 1. English drama — 20th century 2. American drama — 20th century. I. Richards, Stanley, 1918-
PR1272.B44   822/.914/08   LC 79-6634   ISBN 0385147392

Landmarks of modern British drama / with introductions by   2.6246
Roger Cornish and Violet Ketels.
London; New York: Methuen, c1985. p. cm. 1. English drama — 20th century I. Cornish, Roger, 1934- II. Ketels, Violet.
PR1272.L35 1985   822/.914/08 19   LC 85-18856   ISBN 0413590801

Popkin, Henry. ed.   2.6247
The new British drama / edited and with an introd. by Henry Popkin. — New York: Grove Press, 1964. 606 p.; 22 cm. 1. English drama — 20th century I. T.
PR1272 P67

PR1281–1309 PROSE: GENERAL

Shorter novels ...   • 2.6248
London & Toronto: J. M. Dent & sons, ltd.; New York: E. P. Dutton & co., [1929-30] 3 v.; 18 cm. — (Half-title: Everyman's library, ed. by Ernest Rhys. Fiction. [no. 824, 841, 856]) 1. English fiction — Collected works
PR1281.S5x   823.0822   LC 37-31196

Haight, Gordon Sherman. comp.   2.6249
The portable Victorian reader. Edited with an introd. by Gordon S. Haight. — New York: Viking Press, [1972] xivi, 658 p.; 19 cm. 1. English prose literature — 19th century 2. Great Britain — History — 19th century I. T. II. Title: Victorian reader.
PR1285.H27   828/.8/0808   LC 74-85862   ISBN 0670745987

The Oxford book of English prose / chosen & edited by Sir   • 2.6250
Arthur Quiller–Couch.
Oxford: Clarendon Press, 1925. — xx, 1092 p.; 20 cm. 1. English prose literature I. Quiller-Couch, Arthur Thomas, Sir, 1863-1944.
PR1285.O9   820.8   LC 26-26287

The Women's sharp revenge: five women's pamphlets from the   2.6251
Renaissance / edited by Simon Shepherd.
New York: St. Martin's Press, 1985. 208 p.; 22 cm. Includes indexes. 1. English prose literature — Women authors. 2. English prose literature — Early

modern, 1500-1700 3. Women — Literary collections 4. Feminism — Literary collections. 5. Women — Great Britain — History — Sources. 6. Pamphlets I. Shepherd, Simon.
PR1286.W6 W65 1985   828/.308/0809287 19   *LC* 85-2229   *ISBN* 0312887965

Ashley, Robert Paul, 1915- ed.   • **2.6252**
Elizabethan fiction, edited with an introd. and notes by Robert Ashley and Edwin M. Moseley. — New York: Rinehart, [1953] 443 p.; 19 cm. — (Rinehart editions, 64) 1. English fiction — Early modern, 1500-1700 I. Moseley, Edwin M., 1916- joint ed. II. T.
PR1293.A8x   *LC* 52-13061

Lawlis, Merritt E., 1918- comp.   • **2.6253**
Elizabethan prose fiction, edited by Merritt Lawlis. — New York, Odyssey Press [1967] xii, 649 p. 21 cm. Includes bibliographical references. 1. English fiction — Early modern (to 1700) I. T.
PR1293.L3   823/.3/08   *LC* 67-28286

Wilson, John Dover, 1881-1969. comp.   • **2.6254**
Life in Shakespeare's England: a book of Elizabethan prose. — New York: Barnes & Noble, [1969] xv, 291 p.: plates.; 23 cm. Reprint of the 1911 ed. 1. Shakespeare, William, 1564-1616 — Contemporary England 2. English prose literature — Early modern, 1500-1700 3. England — Social life and customs — 16th century I. T.
PR1293.W5 1969   942.05/5   *LC* 68-23765   *ISBN* 0389011681

English prose of the XVII century / selected and edited by   **2.6255**
Roberta Florence Brinkley.
[1st ed.] — New York: Norton, c1951. xii, 919 p.; 21 cm. 'Companion volume to English poetry of the seventeenth century.' 1. English prose literature — Early modern, 1500-1700 I. Brinkley, Roberta Florence.
PR 1295 B85 1951   PR1295.E5 1951.   *LC* 51-1284

Mish, Charles Carroll, 1913- comp.   **2.6256**
Restoration prose fiction, 1666–1700; an anthology of representative pieces, chosen and edited by Charles C. Mish. — Lincoln: University of Nebraska Press, [1970] xv, 289 p.: facsims.; 24 cm. 1. English fiction — Early modern, 1500-1700 I. T.
PR1295.M5   823/.4/08   *LC* 76-98095   *ISBN* 0803207131

Revolutionary prose of the English Civil War / edited by   **2.6257**
Howard Erskine–Hill and Graham Storey.
Cambridge; New York: Cambridge University Press, 1983. vii, 264 p.; 23 cm. — (Cambridge English prose texts.) 1. English prose literature — Early modern, 1500-1700 2. Revolutionary literature, English 3. Great Britain — History — Civil War, 1642-1649 — Pamphlets. I. Erskine-Hill, Howard. II. Storey, Graham, 1920- III. Series.
PR1295.R4 1983   828/.408/080358 19   *LC* 82-12904   *ISBN* 0521244048

Short fiction of the seventeenth century / selected and edited by   • **2.6258**
Charles C. Mish.
New York, W. W. Norton 1968, c1963. xvii, 458 p.: facsims. (The Norton Library seventeenth-century series; N437) 1. English fiction — Early modern, 1500-1700 I. Mish, Charles Carroll, 1913-
PR1295.S54   823.408

Eighteenth century prose / edited by Louis I. Bredvold, Robert   • **2.6259**
K. Root, George Sherburn.
New York: Ronald Press, 1932. xix, 942 p.; 22 cm. 1. English prose literature — 18th century I. Bredvold, Luis Ignatius, 1888- II. Root, Robert Kilburn, 1877-1950. III. Sherburn, George Wiley, 1884- IV. Title: 18th-century prose.
PR1297.E5 1932

McBurney, William Harlin.   • **2.6260**
Four before Richardson; selected English novels, 1720–1727. Lincoln, University of Nebraska Press [1963] xxxv, 373 p. 22 cm. 1. English fiction — 18th century I. T.
PR1297.M12   *LC* 63-9095

Pettit, Henry, 1906-.   • **2.6261**
A collection of English prose, 1660–1800. — New York: Harper, c1962. xi, 646 p.; 24 cm. 1. English prose literature — Early modern, 1500-1700 2. English prose literature — 18th century I. T.
PR1297 P4

Buckler, William Earl, 1924-.   • **2.6262**
Minor classics of nineteenth–century fiction, edited by William E. Buckler. Boston Houghton Mifflin [1967] (Riverside editions, b107-b108) 1. English fiction — 19th century I. T.
PR1301 B84

Woodring, Carl Ray, 1919-.   • **2.6263**
Prose of the romantic period / selected with an introduction and notes by Carl R. Woodring. — Boston: Houghton Mifflin, 1961. xxiv, 600 p.; 21 cm. — (Riverside editions; B57) 1. English prose literature — 19th century I. T.
PR1301.W6   *LC* 61-16304

Harold, Charles Frederick, ed. 1897-1948.   • **2.6264**
English prose of the Victorian era / chosen and edited by Charles Frederick Harold and William D. Templeman. — New York: Oxford U.P., 1938. lxxx, 1743 p.; 24 cm. 1. English prose literature — 19th century I. Templeman, William Darby, ed. II. T.
PR1304.H3   *LC* 38-37983

The Oxford book of short stories / chosen by V.S. Pritchett.   **2.6265**
New York: Oxford University Press, 1981. xiv, 547 p.; 23 cm. 1. Short stories, English 2. Short stories, American I. Pritchett, V. S. (Victor Sawdon), 1900-
PR1309.S5 O9 1981   823/.01/08 19   *LC* 81-156872   *ISBN* 0192141163

Sullivan, Nancy.   **2.6266**
The treasury of English short stories / selected and with an introduction by Nancy Sullivan. — Garden City, N.Y.: Doubleday, c1985. xxii, 672 p.; 22 cm. Includes indexes. 1. Short stories, English 2. Short stories, English — Commonwealth of Nations authors. I. T.
PR1309.S5 S84 1985   823/.01/08 19   *LC* 84-24647   *ISBN* 0385185383

PR1321–1329 ORATORY

McBath, James H. comp.   **2.6267**
British public addresses, 1828–1960. Edited by James H. McBath [and] Walter R. Fisher. Boston, Houghton Mifflin [1971] xii, 577 p. illus. 24 cm. 1. Speeches, addresses, etc., English 2. Great Britain — Politics and government — Addresses, essays, lectures. I. Fisher, Walter R. joint comp. II. T.
PR1322.M3   320.9 42/08   *LC* 72-141902   *ISBN* 0395048524

Strother, David Boyd, 1928- comp.   **2.6268**
Modern British eloquence, edited by David B. Strother. New York, Funk & Wagnalls [1969] xv, 492 p. ports. 24 cm. 1. Speeches, addresses, etc., English 2. Orators — Great Britain. 3. Great Britain — Politics and government — Addresses, essays, lectures. I. T.
PR1322.S7   942   *LC* 78-79249

PR1361–1369 ESSAYS

Miles, Josephine, 1911-.   • **2.6269**
Classic essays in English. 2d ed. Boston: Little, Brown, 1965. xxix, 434 p.; 21 cm. 1. English essays 2. American essays I. T.
PR1363.M53 1965   824.082   *LC* 65-16298

The Englishman: a political journal / by Richard Steele; edited   • **2.6270**
by Rae Blanchard.
Oxford: Clarendon Press, 1955. xxii, 497 p.: port., facsims.; 22 cm. Includes reproductions of original title pages. I. Steele, Richard, Sir, 1672-1729. ed. II. Blanchard, Rae, ed.
PR1365.E53   824.53   *LC* 55-2380

The Spectator.   • **2.6271**
Selections from the Spectator / with an introduction and noted by K. Deighton. — London: Macmillan; New York: St. Martin's Press, 1960. xix, 220 p.; 18 cm. (Macmillan's English classics.) All of the essays except one are by J. Addison. I. Deighton, K. II. Addison, Joseph, 1672-1719. III. T. IV. Series.
PR1365.S7 1960   *LC* 63-14488/CD

The Spectator. v. 1–5.   • **2.6272**
Oxford, Clarendon Press, 1965. 5 v. 23 cm. By Addison, Steele, and others. 'Edited, with an introduction and notes, by Donald F. Bond.' The original was issued in 635 numbers from Mar. 1, 1711 to Dec. 6, 1712 and June 18 to Dec. 20, 1714. Index in v. 5. I. Addison, Joseph, 1672-1719. II. Steele, Richard, Sir, 1672-1729. III. Bond, Donald Frederic, 1895- ed.
PR1365.S7 1965   824.5   *LC* 66-1187 rev

Bond, Richmond Pugh, 1899-.   • **2.6273**
The Tatler: the making of a literary journal [by] Richmond P. Bond. Cambridge, Mass.: Harvard University Press, 1971. 272 p. illus. 24 cm. 1. Tatler (London, England) I. T.
PR1365.T23 B6   824/.5/08   *LC* 77-154500   *ISBN* 0674868307

Steele, Richard, Sir, 1672-1729. • 2.6274
The Tatler / Edited by Lewis Gibbs [pseud.]. — London: Dent; New York:
Dutton, [1953] xiv, 304 p. 19 cm. The selections are chiefly Steele's
contributions to the Tatler. A few have been assigned, wholly or partly, to
Addison. Cf. p. 304. I. Addison, Joseph, 1672-1719. II. The Tatler. III. T.
PR1365.T2x   824.53   LC 53-9910

The Guardian / edited, with an introduction and notes by John   2.6275
Calhoun Stephens.
Lexington, Ky.: University Press of Kentucky, c1982. 825 p.; 25 cm. Originally
published in 175 daily no., London, Mar. 12-Oct. 1, 1713 by Steele, Addison,
and others. Basic copy-text for the 175 no. in this ed. is the set or original folio
half-sheets in the Lefferts Pope Collection in the Houghton Library, Harvard
University which have been compared and collated with original sheets
elsewhere. Includes bibliographical references and index. 1. English essays —
18th century I. Stephens, John Calhoun, 1916- II. Steele, Richard, Sir,
1672-1729. III. Addison, Joseph, 1672-1719.
PR1369.G8 1982   824/.5/08 19   LC 79-57559   ISBN 0813114225

Tatler (London, England)   2.6276
The Tatler / edited with an introduction and notes by Donald F. Bond. —
Oxford: Clarendon Press, 1985. 3 v. Includes index. 1. English essays — 18th
century I. Bond, Donald Frederic, 1898- II. T.
PR1369.T2 1985   824/.5/08 19   LC 84-9663   ISBN 0198124848

PR1490–1799 ANGLO–SAXON LITERATURE

PR1490–1508 Collections

The Anglo–Saxon poetic records, a collective editions. • 2.6277
[New York: Columbia University Press, 1931-53; v. 4, 1953] 6 v.: ill.; 23 cm.
Half title; each vol. has also special t.p. Vols. 1-2, 5, edited by G. P. Krapp; v. 3,
by G. P. Krapp and E. V. K. Dobbie; v. 4, 6, by E. V. K. Dobbie. 1. English
poetry — Old English, ca. 450-1100 I. Krapp, George Phillip, 1872-1934, ed.
II. Dobbie, Elliott Van Kirk, 1907- ed.
PR1502.A7   LC 62-55031

Bessinger, Jess B.   2.6278
A concordance to the Anglo–Saxon poetic records / edited by J. B. Bessinger,
Jr.; programmed by Philip H. Smith, Jr.; with an index of compounds compiled
by Michael W. Twomey. — Ithaca, N.Y.: Cornell University Press, 1978.
xxxvii, 1510 p.; 24 cm. — (Cornell concordances.) 1. English poetry — Old
English, ca. 450-1100 — Concordances. I. Smith, Philip H. II. T. III. Title:
The Anglo-Saxon poetic records. IV. Series.
PR1506.B47 1978   829/.1   LC 77-6186   ISBN 0801411467

The Anglo–Saxon world: an anthology / edited and translated   2.6279
by Kevin Crossley–Holland.
Oxford; New York: Oxford University Press, 1984. xii, 308 p.; 19 cm. — (The
World's classics) 1. English literature — Old English, ca. 450-1100 —
Translations into English. 2. English literature — Translations from Anglo-
Saxon. 3. Anglo-Saxons 4. Great Britain — History — Anglo Saxon period,
449-1066 I. Crossley-Holland, Kevin.
PR1508.A54 1984   829/.08 19   LC 83-17339   ISBN 0192816322

Cook, Albert S. (Albert Stanburrough), 1853-1927. ed. • 2.6280
Select translations from Old English poetry, edited with prefatory notes and
indexes by Albert S. Cook and Chauncey B. Tinker. Westport, Conn.,
Greenwood Press [1970] xi, 195 p. 23 cm. Reprint of the 1902 ed. 1. English
poetry — Old English, ca. 450-1100 — Translations into English. 2. English
poetry — Translations from Anglo-Saxon. I Tinker, Chauncey Brewster,
1876-1963. joint ed. II. T.
PR1508.C5 1970   829/.1   LC 73-89014   ISBN 0837130832

Cook, Albert S. (Albert Stanburrough), 1853-1927. • 2.6281
Select translations from Old English prose, ed. by Albert S. Cook ... and
Chauncey B. Tinker ... Boston, New York [etc.] Ginn & Company [c1908] vii,
296 p. 19 cm. Companion volume to the authors' 'Select translations from Old
English poetry.' 1. English literature — Old English, ca. 450-1100 —
Translations. I. Tinker, Chauncey Brewster, 1876-1963. II. T.
PR1508.C6   829.08   LC 08-3139

Kennedy, Charles William, 1882-1969, ed. and tr. • 2.6282
An anthology of Old English poetry, translated into alliterative verse by Charles
W. Kennedy. — New York: Oxford University Press, 1960. 174 p.; 21 cm.

1. English poetry — Old English, ca. 450-1100 — Translations into English.
2. English poetry — Translations from Anglo-Saxon. I. T.
PR1508.K36   829.1082   LC 59-11753

Poems of wisdom and learning in Old English / T. A. Shippey.   2.6283
Cambridge, Eng.: D. S. Brewer; Totowa, N.J.: Rowman and Littlefield, c1976.
152 p.; 23 cm. In English with text of poems in English and Old English on
facing pages. 1. English poetry — Old English, ca. 450-1100 — Translations
into English. 2. English poetry — Translations from Anglo-Saxon. 3. English
poetry — Old English, ca. 450-1100 4. Didactic poetry, English (Old)
I. Shippey, T. A.
PR1508.P6 1976   829/.1   LC 76-1824   ISBN 0874717892

Raffel, Burton. tr. • 2.6284
Poems from the Old English. Translated with an introd., by Burton Raffel.
Foreword by Robert P. Creed. — [2d ed.]. — Lincoln, University of Nebraska
Press [1964] xxii, 121 p. 22 cm. 1. English poetry — Old English, ca. 450-1100
— Translations into English. 2. English poetry — Translations from Anglo-
Saxon. I. T.
PR1508.R3 1964   829.1082   LC 64-3968

Swanton, Michael James. comp.   2.6285
Anglo–Saxon prose / edited and translated by Michael Swanton. — London:
Dent; Totowa, N.J.: Rowan and Littlefield, 1975. xxvi, 188 p.; 20 cm.
1. English prose literature — Old English, ca. 450-1100 — Translations into
English. 2. English prose literature — Translations from Anglo-Saxon. I. T.
PR1508.S9 1975b   829   LC 75-325253   ISBN 0460108093

PR1509–1799 Individual Authors and Works

PR1520–1538 Aelfric

Hurt, James, 1934-.   2.6286
Aelfric. — New York: Twayne Publishers, c1972. 152 p. — (Twayne's English
authors series) 1. Aelfric, Abbot of Enysham I. T.
PR1533 H8   LC 76-162871

PR1578 Beda Venerabilis

Hunter Blair, Peter, 1912-1982.   2.6287
The world of Bede. New York, St. Martin's Press, 1970. x, 340 p. 23 cm.
1. Bede, the Venerable, Saint, 673-735. 2. Great Britain — History — To 1066
I. T.
PR1578.H85   230/.924   LC 73-135524

PR1580–1588 Beowulf

Beowulf. • 2.6288
Beowulf and The fight at Finnsburg; edited, with introd., bibliography, notes,
glossary, and appendices, by Fr. Klaeber. — 3d ed., with 1st and 2d
supplements. — Boston, Heath [1950] clxxxvii, 471 p. illus. 21 cm. Includes
bibliographies. 1. Finnesburh. I. Klaeber, Friedrich, 1863- ed. II. T.
PR1580.K5 1950   829.3   LC 50-14865

Beowulf.   2.6289
Beowulf, with the Finnesburg fragment. Edited by C. L. Wrenn. Fully rev. by
W. F. Bolton. [3d ed. rev.] New York, St. Martin's Press, 1973. 301 p. 23 cm.
I. Wrenn, Charles Leslie, 1895- ed. II. Bolton, W. F. (Whitney French), 1930-
ed. III. Finnesburh. IV. T.
PR1580.W7 1973   829/.3   LC 72-86666

Beowulf. English & Anglo-Saxon.   2.6290
Beowulf: a dual–language edition / translated with an introd. and commentary
by Howell D. Chickering, Jr. — Garden City, N.Y.: Anchor Books, 1977. xiii,
390 p.; 21 cm. I. Chickering, Howell D. II. T.
PR1583.C48   829/.3   LC 72-21250   ISBN 0385062133

Beowulf. English.   2.6291
Beowulf: the Donaldson translation, backgrounds and sources, criticism /
edited by Joseph F. Tuso. — 1st ed. — New York: Norton, [1975] xvi, 205 p.:
ill.; 22 cm. — (A Norton critical edition) Includes index. 1. Beowulf —
Addresses, essays, lectures. 2. English poetry — Old English, ca. 450-1100 —
History and criticism — Addresses, essays, lectures. I. Donaldson, E. Talbot
(Ethelbert Talbot), 1910- II. Tuso, Joseph F. III. T.
PR1583.D6 1975   829/.3   LC 75-17991   ISBN 0393044130

Beowulf.   **2.6292**
Beowulf and its analogues; translated by G. N. Garmonsway and Jacqueline Simpson; including Archaeology and Beowulf, by Hilda Ellis Davidson. — London: Dent, 1968. xiii, 368 p.: 8 plates, illus., map, index.; 23 cm. I. Garmonsway, George Norman, tr. II. Simpson, Jacqueline. tr. III. Davidson, Hilda Roderick Ellis. Archaeology and Beowulf. IV. T.
PR1583.G28   829/.3   *LC* 77-383928   *ISBN* 0460038044

Beowulf. English.   **2.6293**
A readable Beowulf: the Old English epic newly translated / by Stanley B. Greenfield; with an introduction by Alain Renoir. — Carbondale [Ill.]: Southern Illinois University Press, c1982. x, 161 p.: ill.; 23 cm. I. Greenfield, Stanley B. II. Renoir, Alain. III. T.
PR1583.G73 1982   829/.3 19   *LC* 81-16933   *ISBN* 0809310597

Brodeur, Arthur Gilchrist, 1888-.   • **2.6294**
The art of Beowulf. — Berkeley: University of California Press, 1959. ix, 283 p.; 23 cm. 1. Beowulf. I. T.
PR1585.B68   829.3   *LC* 58-12828

Chambers, R. W. (Raymond Wilson), 1874-1942.   • **2.6295**
Beowulf; an introduction to the study of the poem with a discussion of the stories of Offa and Finn, by R. W. Chambers. With a supplement by C. L. Wrenn. — 3d ed. — Cambridge [Eng.]: University Press, 1959. xvii, 628 p.: geneal. tables.; 22 cm. 1. Offa, King of the Mercians, d. 796. 2. Beowulf. 3. Finnesburgh. 4. Offa saga. I. T.
PR1585.C5x   *LC* a 60-1942

Huppé, Bernard Felix, 1911-.   **2.6296**
The hero in the earthly city: a reading of Beowulf / by Bernard F. Huppé. — [Binghamton]: Medieval & Renaissance Texts & Studies, State University of New York at Binghamton, 1984. 201 p.; 25 cm. (Medieval & Renaissance texts & studies. v. 33) Includes a translation of Beowulf. 1. Augustine, Saint, Bishop of Hippo — Influence. 2. Beowulf. 3. Christianity in literature 4. Polarity in literature I. Beowulf. English. 1984. II. T. III. Series.
PR1585.H86 1984   829/.3 19   *LC* 84-674   *ISBN* 0866980679

Irving, Edward Burroughs, 1923-.   • **2.6297**
A reading of Beowulf [by] Edward B. Irving, Jr. New Haven: Yale University Press, 1968. ix, 256 p.; 21 cm. 1. Beowulf. I. T.
PR1585.I7   829/.3   *LC* 68-13911

Kiernan, Kevin S., 1945-.   **2.6298**
Beowulf and the Beowulf manuscript / Kevin S. Kiernan. — New Brunswick, N.J.: Rutgers University Press, c1981. xvi, 303 p., [1] leaf of plates: ill.; 24 cm. Includes index. 1. British Museum. Mss. (Cottonian Vitellius A. XV) 2. Beowulf. 3. Beowulf — Manuscripts 4. Nowell codex. 5. Manuscripts, Anglo-Saxon 6. Manuscript dating I. T.
PR1585.K5 1981   829/.3 19   *LC* 80-27635   *ISBN* 0813509254

Niles, John D.   **2.6299**
Beowulf: the poem and its tradition / John D. Niles. — Cambridge, Mass.: Harvard University Press, 1983. vi, 310 p.: ill.; 25 cm. 1. Beowulf. 2. Oral tradition I. T.
PR1585.N54 1983   829/.3 19   *LC* 83-4308   *ISBN* 0674067258

Ogilvy, J. D. A. (Jack David Angus), 1903-.   **2.6300**
Reading Beowulf: an introduction to the poem, its background, and its style / by J.D.A. Ogilvy and Donald C. Baker; drawings by Keith Baker. — 1st ed. — Norman: University of Oklahoma Press, c1983. xvii, 221 p.: ill.; 22 cm. Includes index. 1. Beowulf. I. Baker, Donald C. II. T.
PR1585.O37 1983   829/.3 19   *LC* 83-47835   *ISBN* 0806118482

Sisam, Kenneth.   • **2.6301**
The structure of Beowulf. — Oxford, Clarendon Press, 1965. 88 p. 19 cm. Bibliographical footnotes. 1. Beowulf. I. T.
PR1585.S5   *LC* 65-3079

Whitelock, Dorothy.   • **2.6302**
The audience of Beowulf. — Oxford: Clarendon Press, 1951. 111 p. 1. Beowulf. I. T.
PR1587.A8 W5   *LC* 51-6428

Robinson, Fred C.   **2.6303**
Beowulf and the appositive style / by Fred C. Robinson. — Knoxville: University of Tennessee Press, c1985. 106 p.; 23 cm. (Hodges lectures.) Includes index. 1. Beowulf. 2. English language — Old English, ca. 450-1100 — Apposition. 3. English language — Old English, ca. 450-1100 — Style. 4. Christianity in literature 5. Paganism in literature I. T. II. Series.
PR1588.R6 1985   829.3 19   *LC* 84-11889   *ISBN* 0870494449

PR1590–1799 Others, B–Z

Genesis (Anglo-Saxon poem)   **2.6304**
Genesis A: a new edition / [edited by] A. N. Doane. — Madison: University of Wisconsin Press, 1978. xiv, 416 p.; 24 cm. 1. Bible. O.T. Genesis — Poetry. I. Doane, Alger Nicolaus, 1938- II. T.
PR1611.A3 D6   829/.1   *LC* 77-77437   *ISBN* 0299074307

Cynewulf.   **2.6305**
The poems of Cynewulf / translated into English prose by Charles W. Kennedy; with an introduction, bibliography, and facsimile page of the Vercelli Ms. — New York: P. Smith, 1949. xii, 347 p.: facsim. I. Kennedy, Charles William, 1882- II. T.
PR1642.K4 1949   *LC* w 10-253

Calder, Daniel Gillmore.   **2.6306**
Cynewulf / by Daniel G. Calder. — Boston: Twayne Publishers, 1981. 189 p.: facsim.; 21 cm. — (Twayne's English author series; TEAS 327) Includes index. 1. Cynewulf — Criticism and interpretation. I. T. II. Series.
PR1664.C3   829/.4 19   *LC* 81-2343   *ISBN* 0805768149

Exeter book. English. Selections.   **2.6307**
A feast of creatures: Anglo–Saxon riddle–songs / translated with introduction, notes, and commentary by Craig Williamson. — Philadelphia: University of Pennsylvania Press, 1982. xii, 230 p.; 23 cm. Chiefly translations from: The Old English riddles of the Exeter book / edited by Craig Williamson. c1977. Includes indexes. 1. Riddles, English (Old) — Translations into English. 2. Songs, Anglo-Saxon — Texts. 3. English poetry — Old English, ca. 450-1100 — Translations into English. 4. English poetry — Translations from Anglo-Saxon. I. Williamson, Craig, 1943- II. T.
PR1762.W5 1982   829/.1 19   *LC* 82-4907   *ISBN* 0812278437

PR1804–6076 ENGLISH LITERATURE: INDIVIDUAL AUTHORS AND WORKS

PR1804–2165 Anglo–Norman Period. Early English

PR1806–1810 Ancren Riwle

Ancren riwle.   • **2.6308**
The Ancrene riwle (the Corpus ms.: Ancrene wisse) Translated into modern English by M. B. Salu. With an introd. by Gerard Sitwell and a Pref. by J. R. R. Tolkien. — London, Burns & Oates [1955] xxvii, 196 p. 21 cm. — (The Orchard books) Bibliographical footnotes. 1. Monasticism and religious orders for women 2. Monasticism and religious orders — Rules I. Salu, M. B., tr. II. T. III. Series.
PR1808.S3   271.9   *LC* 56-1929

Dobson, E. J. (Eric John)   **2.6309**
The origins of Ancrene wisse / by E. J. Dobson. — Oxford [Eng.]: Clarendon Press, 1976. 441 p.; 19 cm. 1. Ancren riwle. 2. Monastic and religious life of women — History — Middle Ages, 600-1500 4. Augustinians — England 5. Monasticism and religious orders for women — Rules I. T.
PR1810.D6   255/.901   *LC* 76-367043   *ISBN* 0198118643

PR1850–1954 Chaucer

Chaucer, Geoffrey, d. 1400.   • **2.6310**
Works. A facsimile of the William Morris Kelmscott Chaucer with the original 87 illus. by Edward Burne–Jones, together with an introd. by John T. Winterich and a glossary for the modern reader. Cleveland, World Pub. Co. [1958] xix p., facsim: 554 p. ill.; 34 cm. Original title page reads: The works of Geoffrey Chaucer, now newly imprinted. [Colophon: Here ends the Book of the works of Geoffrey Chaucer edited by F. S. Ellis; ornamented with pictures designed by Sir Edward Burne-Jones, and engraved on wood by W. H. Hooper. Printed by me William Morris at the Kelmscott Press, Upper Mall, Hammersmith, in the county of Middlesex. Finished on the 8th day of May, 1896] I. Burne-Jones, Edward Coley, Sir, 1833-1898. II. T.
PR1850 1896a   821.17   *LC* 58-4408

Chaucer, Geoffrey, d. 1400.   • **2.6311**
Major poetry. Albert C. Baugh, editor. — New York, Appleton-Century-Crofts [1963] 615 p. illus. 26 cm. Includes bibliography. I. Baugh, Albert Croll, 1891- ed. II. T.
PR1851.B3   821.1   LC 63-10513

Chaucer, Geoffrey, d. 1400.   **2.6312**
The Riverside Chaucer / general editor, Larry D. Benson. — 3rd ed. — Boston: Houghton Mifflin Co., 1987. xlvii, 1327 p.: port. 1. Chaucer, Geoffrey, d. 1400. I. Benson, Larry Dean, 1929- II. T.
PR1851.B4 1987   LC 86-81304   ISBN 0395290317

Chaucer, Geoffrey, d. 1400.   **2.6313**
A variorum edition of the works of Geoffrey Chaucer / Paul G. Ruggiers, general editor; Donald C. Baker, associate editor; Helen Storm Corsa ... [et al.] consultants. Norman: University of Oklahoma Press, 1979-. v.: facsims.; 30 cm. The Hengwrt manuscript serves as base text, with variants from other manuscripts. 1. Ruggiers, Paul G. 2. Baker, Donald C. I. Hengwrt manuscript. II. T.
PR1851.R98x 1979

Chaucer, Geoffrey, d. 1400.   • **2.6314**
Poetry; an anthology for the modern reader. Selected and edited by E. T. Donaldson. — New York, Ronald Press Co. [1958] 1001 p. 22 cm. I. Donaldson, E. T., comp. II. T.
PR1852.D6   821.17   LC 58-5855

Chaucer, Geoffrey, d. 1400.   • **2.6315**
[Works] 1938] The complete poetical works of Geoffrey Chaucer, now first put into modern English, by John S. P. Tatlock and Percy MacKaye. Illustrations by Warwick Goble. New York, The Macmillan company, 1938. xii p., 1 l., 607 p. col. plates. 26 cm. At head of title: The modern reader's Chaucer. 'Published September, 1912. Reprinted October, 1938.' Prose translation. I. Tatlock, John S. P. (John Strong Perry), 1876-1948. II. MacKaye, Percy, 1875-1956. III. Goble, Warwick. illus. IV. T.
PR1855.T3 1938   821.17   LC 41-3566

Chaucer, Geoffrey, d. 1400.   **2.6316**
The Canterbury tales / by Geoffrey Chaucer; edited from the Hengwrt manuscript by N.F. Blake. — London: Arnold, 1980. 707 p.; 24 cm. — (York medieval texts. Second series.) I. Blake, N. F. (Norman Francis) II. Hengwrt manuscript. III. T. IV. Series.
PR1866.B55 1980   821/.1 19   LC 81-127985   0713162176

Chaucer, Geoffrey, d. 1400.   **2.6317**
[Canterbury tales Selections] The Friar's, Summoner's, and Pardoner's tales from the Canterbury tales / Geoffrey Chaucer; edited by N. R. Havely. — New York: Holmes & Meier, 1976. vi, 165 p.; 22 cm. — (Medieval and Renaissance texts) I. Havely, N. R. II. T.
PR1867.H38 1976   821/.1   LC 75-19090   ISBN 0841902208. ISBN 0841902240 pbk

Chaucer, Geoffrey, d. 1400.   **2.6318**
[Canterbury tales. Prologue] The general prologue to the Canterbury tales and the Canon's yeoman's prologue and tale / Geoffrey Chaucer; edited by A. V. C. Schmidt. — New York: Holmes & Meier, 1976. vii, 175 p.; 22 cm. — (Medieval and Renaissance texts) I. Chaucer, Geoffrey, d. 1400. Canterbury tales. The canon yeoman's prologue and tale. 1975. II. Schmidt, A. V. C. III. T. IV. Series.
PR1868.P8 S3 1976   821/.1   LC 75-17975   ISBN 0841902194. ISBN 0841902232 pbk

Bowden, Muriel Amanda.   • **2.6319**
A commentary on the General prologue to the Canterbury tales. — 2d ed., with additional matter and new pref. — New York: Macmillan, [1967] xiii, 328 p.: facsim.; 22 cm. 1. Chaucer, Geoffrey, d. 1400. Canterbury tales. Prologue. I. T.
PR1868.P9 B6 1967   821/.1   LC 67-22153

Mann, Jill.   **2.6320**
Chaucer and medieval estates satire; the literature of social classes and the General Prologue to the Canterbury Tales. — Cambridge [Eng.]: University Press, 1973. xvii, 330 p.; 23 cm. Based on the author's thesis, Cambridge. 1. Chaucer, Geoffrey, d. 1400. Canterbury tales. Prologue 2. Social classes in literature 3. Literature, Medieval — History and criticism I. T.
PR1868.P9 M3   821/.1   LC 72-90490   ISBN 052120058X

Chaucer, Geoffrey, d. 1400.   **2.6321**
[Canterbury tales. The wife of Bath's tale] The wife of Bath's prologue and tale and the Clerk's prologue and tale from the Canterbury tales / Geoffrey Chaucer; edited by Gloria Cigman. — New York: Holmes & Meier, 1976, c1975. vi, 194 p.; 22 cm. — (Medieval and Renaissance texts) I. Chaucer, Geoffrey, d. 1400. Canterbury tales. The clerk's prologue and tale. 1976. II. Cigman, Gloria. III. T. IV. Series.
PR1868.W6 C5 1976   821/.1   LC 75-17976   ISBN 0841902259. ISBN 0841902267 pbk

Chaucer, Geoffrey, d. 1400.   • **2.6322**
[Canterbury tales Modern English. 1952.] The Canterbury tales / Geoffrey Chaucer; translated into modern English by Nevill Coghill. — Baltimore, Maryland: Penguin Books, 1952. 528 p.; 18 cm. — (Penguin classics) I. Coghill, Nevill, 1899- II. T.
PR1870.A1 C67 1952   821/.1   ISBN 0140440224 pbk

Cooper, Helen.   **2.6323**
The structure of the Canterbury tales / Helen Cooper. — Athens: University of Georgia Press, 1984, c1983. 256 p.; 25 cm. Includes index. 1. Chaucer, Geoffrey, d. 1400. Canterbury tales 2. Chaucer, Geoffrey, d. 1400 — Technique. I. T.
PR1874.C65 1984   821/.1 19   LC 83-13997   ISBN 0820306959

Howard, Donald Roy, 1927-.   **2.6324**
The idea of the Canterbury tales / Donald R. Howard. — Berkeley: University of California Press, c1976. xvi, 403 p.: ill.; 25 cm. 1. Chaucer, Geoffrey, d. 1400. Canterbury tales I. T.
PR1874.H65   PR1874 H65.   821/.1   LC 74-81433   ISBN 0520028163

Jones, Terry.   **2.6325**
Chaucer's knight: the portrait of a medieval mercenary / Terry Jones. — Baton Rouge: Louisiana State University Press, 1980. xi, 319 p.: ill. 1. Chaucer, Geoffrey, d. 1400. Canterbury tales. Knight's tale. I. T.
PR1874.J6   821   LC 79-67590   ISBN 0807106917

Owen, Charles Abraham, 1914- ed.   • **2.6326**
Discussions of the Canterbury tales. Edited with an introd. — Boston, Heath [1961] 110 p. 24 cm. — (Discussions of literature) 1. Chaucer, Geoffrey, d. 1400. Canterbury tales I. T.
PR1874.O9   821.1   LC 61-3444

Owen, Charles Abraham, 1914-.   **2.6327**
Pilgrimage and storytelling in the Canterbury tales: the dialectic of 'ernest' and 'game' / by Charles A. Owen, Jr. — 1st ed. — Norman: University of Oklahoma Press, c1977. ix, 253 p.: ill.; 23 cm. Includes index. 1. Chaucer, Geoffrey, d. 1400. Canterbury tales I. T.
PR1874.O93   821/.1   LC 76-53814

Pearsall, Derek Albert.   **2.6328**
The Canterbury tales / Derek Pearsall. — London; Boston: G. Allen & Unwin, 1985. xiv, 380 p.; 23 cm. — (Unwin critical library.) Includes index. 1. Chaucer, Geoffrey, d. 1400. Canterbury tales I. T. II. Series.
PR1874.P43 1985   821/.1 19   LC 85-6104   ISBN 0048000213

Ruggiers, Paul G.   • **2.6329**
The art of the Canterbury tales [by] Paul G. Ruggiers. — Madison: University of Wisconsin Press, 1965. xviii, 265 p.; 25 cm. 1. Chaucer, Geoffrey, d. 1400. The Canterbury tales. I. T.
PR1874.R8   821.1   LC 65-16365

Kolve, V. A.   **2.6330**
Chaucer and the imagery of narrative: the first five Canterbury tales / V.A. Kolve. — Stanford, Calif.: Stanford University Press, 1984. xiv, 551 p.: ill.; 26 cm. Includes index. 1. Chaucer, Geoffrey, d. 1400. Canterbury tales 2. Chaucer, Geoffrey, d. 1400 — Allegory and symbolism. 3. Narration (Rhetoric) 4. Art and literature 5. Art, Medieval — Themes, motives I. T.
PR1875.A44 K64 1984   821/.1 19   LC 80-50907   ISBN 0804711615

Bennett, J. A. W. (Jack Arthur Walter)   • **2.6331**
Chaucer's 'Book of fame': an exposition of 'The house of fame,' by J. A. W. Bennett. Oxford, Clarendon P., 1968. xiv, 191 p. plate, 1 illus. 23 cm. 1. Chaucer, Geoffrey, d. 1400. The hous of fame. I. T.
PR1878.B37   821/.1   LC 68-82962

Chaucer, Geoffrey.   • **2.6332**
Troilus and Criseyde / translated into modern English by Nevill Coghill. — Harmondsworth, Eng.: Penguin, 1971. xxvii, 332 p.; 19 cm. — (Penguin classics) I. Coghill, Nevill, 1899- II. Coghill, Nevill. III. T.
PR1895.C57   821/.1   LC 78-24282   ISBN 0940442391

Chaucer, Geoffrey, d. 1400.   **2.6333**
[Troilus and Criseyde] Chaucer's Troilus and Cressida: five books in present-day English / by James J. Donohue. — Dubuque, Iowa: Loras College Press, c1975. xviii, 201 p. I. Donohue, James John, 1906- II. T. III. Title: Troilus and Cressida.
PR1895.D6 1975   LC 75-29910

Chaucer, Geoffrey, d. 1400.   **2.6334**
Troilus and Criseyde and selected short poems / Geoffrey Chaucer; edited by Donald R. Howard and James Dean. — New York: New American Library, 1976. lvi, 327 p.: ill.; 18 cm. (The Signet classic poetry series) I. Howard, Donald Roy, 1927- II. Dean, James, 1943- III. T.
PR1895.H6   821/.1   LC 76-14707

Chaucer, Geoffrey, d. 1400.   • **2.6335**
The book of Troilus and Criseyde, by Geoffrey Chaucer, edited from all the known manuscripts by Robert Kilburn Root ... Princeton, Princeton university press, 1926. lxxxix, 1, 572, 1 p. 24 cm. I. Root, Robert Kilburn, 1877- ed. II. T. III. Title: Troilus and Criseyde.
PR1895.R6   LC 26-16058

Essays on Troilus and Criseyde / edited by Mary Salu.   **2.6336**
Cambridge [Cambridgeshire]: D.S. Brewer; Totowa, N.J.: Rowman & Littlefield, c1979. 143 p.; 24 cm. — (Chaucer studies. 3) 1. Chaucer, Geoffrey, d. 1400. Troilus and Criseyde 2. Troilus (Greek mythology) in literature. I. Salu, M. B. II. Series.
PR1896.E8   821/.1 19   LC 81-169026   ISBN 0847662365

Meech, Sanford Brown.   • **2.6337**
Design in Chaucer's Troilus [by] Sanford B. Meech. — New York: Greenwood Press, [1969, c1959] xii, 529 p.; 24 cm. 1. Chaucer, Geoffrey, d. 1400. Troilus and Criseyde 2. Boccaccio, Giovanni, 1313-1375. Filostrato. I. T.
PR1896.M4 1969   821/.1   LC 76-88981   ISBN 0837121183

PR1905–1921 Biography. Sources. Chronology

Chute, Marchette.   • **2.6338**
Geoffrey Chaucer of England / written and decorated by Marchette Chute. — New York: E. P. Dutton, 1946. 347 p., (map on lining papers); 22 cm. 1. Authors, English — Biography I. T.
PR1905.C45   821.17   LC 46-1426   ISBN 052511257X

Coghill, Nevill, 1899-.   • **2.6339**
The poet Chaucer. — 2nd ed. — London; New York [etc.]: Oxford U.P., 1967. xi, 145 p.; 21 cm. — (Oxford paperbacks, university series, opus 23) 1. Chaucer, Geoffrey, d. 1400 — Biography. I. T.
PR1905.C55 1967   821/.1   LC 68-97162

Crow, Martin Michael, 1901- ed.   **2.6340**
Chaucer life–records. — Oxford: Clarendon P., 1966. xxvi, 629 p.: tables; 25 cm. 1. Chaucer, Geoffrey, d. 1400. I. Olson, Clair Colby, 1901- joint ed. II. Manly, John Matthews, 1865-1940. III. T.
PR1905.C7   LC 66-71393

French, Robert Dudley, 1888-.   • **2.6341**
A Chaucer handbook / by Robert Dudley French. — 2d ed. — New York: F. S. Crofts & co., 1947. xi, 402 p.: front. (port.); 20 cm. 'First printing, August, 1927 ... Second edition, eighth printing. January 1947.' 1. Chaucer, Geoffrey, d. 1400. I. T.
PR1905.F7 1947   821.17   LC 47-849

Lowes, John Livingston, 1867-1945.   • **2.6342**
Geoffrey Chaucer, lectures delivered in 1932 on the William J. Cooper foundation in Swarthmore college, by John Livingston Lowes. Oxford: Clarendon P., 1944. 199 p.: ill. 1. Chaucer, Geoffrey, d. 1400. I. T.
PR1905.L6   821.17   LC 46-5100

Manly, John Matthews, 1865-1940.   • **2.6343**
Some new light on Chaucer. Lectures delivered at the Lowell Institute. New York P. Smith 1951. 305p. 1. Chaucer, Geoffrey, d. 1400. I. T.
PR1905 M3 1951

Tatlock, J. S. P.   • **2.6344**
The mind and art of Chaucer / by J. S. P. Tatlock. — New York: Gordian Press, 1966. ix, 114 p. I. T.
PR1905.T3   824.1   LC 66-19087

Brewer, Derek, 1923-.   • **2.6345**
Chaucer in his time. — London: Nelson, 1964, c1963. x, 243 p.: ill. 1. Chaucer, Geoffrey, d. 1400. 2. Great Britain — Social life and customs I. T.
PR1906.B7   LC 64-3055

Bryan, William Frank, 1879- ed.   • **2.6346**
Sources and analogues of Chaucer's Canterbury tales [by] Carleton Brown [and others] Edited by W. F. Bryan and Germaine Dempster. Humanities Press [1958] 765;. 'A collaborative undertaking by members of the Chaucer Group of the Modern Language Association of America.' Photo-offset from the 1941 ed. 1. Chaucer, Geoffrey, d. 1400 Canterbury tales — Sources. I. Dempster, Germaine (Collette) joint ed. II. Brown, Carleton Fairchild, 1869-1941. III. Modern Language Association of America. IV. T.
PR1912.A2 B7 1958   LC a 58-3943

Chaucer and the Italian trecento / edited by Piero Boitani.   **2.6347**
Cambridge [Cambridgeshire]; New York: Cambridge University Press, 1983. xii, 313 p., [1] leaf of plates: ill.; 24 cm. Includes index. 1. Chaucer, Geoffrey, d. 1400 — Sources. 2. Chaucer, Geoffrey, d. 1400 — Knowledge — Italy. 3. Italian literature — To 1400 — History and criticism. 4. Italy in literature. 5. Italy — Civilization — 1268-1559 I. Boitani, Piero.
PR1912.A3 C4 1983   821/.1 19   LC 82-17772   ISBN 0521239982

Chaucer: sources and backgrounds / edited by Robert P. Miller.   **2.6348**
New York: Oxford University Press, 1977. xv, 507 p.: ill.; 24 cm. 1. Chaucer, Geoffrey, d. 1400 — Sources. 2. Literature, Medieval I. Miller, Robert Parsons, 1923-
PR1912.A2 C48   PR1912A3 C48.   821/.1   LC 76-42673   ISBN 0195021665

Muscatine, Charles.   • **2.6349**
Chaucer and the French tradition; a study in style and meaning. — Berkeley, University of California Press, 1957. 282 p. 23 cm. 1. Chaucer, Geoffrey, d. 1400 — Sources. 2. Literature, Comparative — English and French. 3. Literature, Comparative — French and English. I. T.
PR1912.A3 M8   821.17   LC 57-5396

Severs, Jonathan Burke.   **2.6350**
The literary relationships of Chaucer's Clerkes tale, by J. Burke Severs. [Hamden, Conn.] Archon Books, 1972 [c1942] ix, 371 p. facsim. 23 cm. (Yale studies in English. v. 96) Includes the text of Petrarch's Historia Griseldis, with an anonymous French translation. 1. Chaucer, Geoffrey, d. 1400. Canterbury tales. Clerk's tale. 2. Chaucer, Geoffrey, d. 1400 — Sources. 3. Boccaccio, Giovanni, 1313-1375. Decamerone 4. Petrarca, Francesco, 1304-1374. Historia Griseldis. 5. Griselda (Legendary character) 6. Literature, Comparative — Themes, motives I. Petrarca, Francesco, 1304-1374. Historia Griseldis. French & Latin. 1972. II. T. III. Series.
PR1912.A3 S4 1972   821/.1   LC 74-179567   ISBN 0208011382

Shannon, Edgar Finley, 1874-1938.   • **2.6351**
Chaucer and the Roman poets. New York, Russell & Russell, 1964 [c1929] xxii, 401 p. 23 cm. (Harvard studies in comparative literature. 7) Bibliographical footnotes. 1. Chaucer, Geoffrey, d. 1400. 2. Ovid, 43 B.C.-17 or 18 A.D. 3. Literature, Comparative — Latin and English. 4. Literature, Comparative — English and Latin. I. T. II. Series.
PR1912.A3S5 1964   821.1   LC 64-10393

Boccaccio, Giovanni, 1313-1375.   **2.6352**
Chaucer's Boccaccio: sources of Troilus and the Knight's and Franklin's tales / edited and translated by N. R. Havely. — Woodbridge [Eng.]: D. S. Brewer; Totowa, N.J.: Rowman & Littlefield, c1980. 225 p.; 24 cm. — (Chaucer studies. 3 [i.e. 5]) Includes index. 1. Chaucer, Geoffrey, d. 1400 — Sources. 2. Troilus (Greek mythology) in literature. I. Havely, N. R. II. T. III. Series.
PR1912.B6 1980   821/.1   LC 79-41810

Tatlock, John S. P. (John Strong Perry), 1876-1948.   • **2.6353**
The development and chronology of Chaucer's works. — Gloucester, Mass., P. Smith, 1963. xiii, 233 p. 21 cm. Bibliographical footnotes. 1. Chaucer, Geoffrey — Chronology of works. I. T.
PR1921.T3 1963   821.1   LC 64-883

PR1924–1939 Criticism. Interpretation

Spurgeon, Caroline Frances Eleanor, 1869-1942. ed.   • **2.6354**
Five hundred years of Chaucer criticism and allusion, 1357–1900 ... with twenty–four collotype illustrations, introduction, notes, appendices and general index ... — New York, Russell & Russell, 1960. 3 v. plates, ports., facsims. 25 cm. 1. Chaucer, Geoffrey — Criticism and interpretation. I. T.
PR1924.A2 1960   821.1   LC 60-5339

Brewer, Derek, 1923-.   **2.6355**
Chaucer [by] D. S. Brewer. 3rd ed., extensively rev. and with additional material. London, Longmans [1973] 230 p. illus. 22 cm. 1. Chaucer, Geoffrey, d. 1400. I. T.
PR1924.B73 1973   821/.1 B   LC 73-179613   ISBN 0582485126

Brewer, Derek, 1923-.   **2.6356**
Tradition and innovation in Chaucer / Derek Brewer. — London: Macmillan, 1982. 181 p.; 23 cm. 1. Chaucer, Geoffrey, d. 1400 — Criticism and interpretation. I. T.
PR1924.B76   PR1924 B76.   ISBN 0333284275

Bronson, Bertrand Harris, 1902-.   • **2.6357**
In search of Chaucer. [Toronto] University Press [c1960] 117p. (The Alexander lectures, 1958-59) 1. Chaucer, Geoffrey, d. 1400. I. T.
PR1924 B8

Chaucer, the critical heritage / edited by Derek Brewer.   **2.6358**
London; Boston: Routledge & K. Paul, 1978. 2. v.; 23 cm. — (The Critical heritage series) 1. Chaucer, Geoffrey, d. 1400 — Criticism and interpretation — Addresses, essays, lectures. I. Brewer, Derek, 1923-
PR1924.C44   821/.1   LC 78-40016   ISBN 0710084978

David, Alfred, 1929-. **2.6359**
The strumpet muse: art and morals in Chaucer's poetry / Alfred David. — Bloomington: Indiana University Press, c1976. 280 p.: ill. 1. Chaucer, Geoffrey, d. 1400 — Criticism and interpretation. I. T.
PR1924.D3 1976   PR1924 D3 1976.   821/.1   LC 76-11939
ISBN 0253355176

Hussey, S. S., 1925-. **2.6360**
Chaucer: an introduction, [by] S. S. Hussey. London, Methuen, 1971. [9], 244 p. 22 cm. 1. Chaucer, Geoffrey, d. 1400 — Criticism and interpretation. I. T.
PR1924.H8   821/.1   LC 78-869391   ISBN 0416142206

Kane, George. **2.6361**
Chaucer / George Kane. — Oxford; New York: Oxford University Press, 1984. 122 p.; 22 cm. (Past masters.) Includes index. 1. Chaucer, Geoffrey, d. 1400 — Criticism and interpretation. I. T. II. Series.
PR1924.K33 1984   821/.1 19   LC 84-11230   ISBN 0192875965

Kean, P. M. (Patricia Margaret) **2.6362**
Chaucer and the making of English poetry. London Routledge and K. Paul 1972. 1. Chaucer, Geoffrey, d. 1400. I. T.
PR1924 K36

Kean, P. M. (Patricia Margaret) **2.6363**
Chaucer and the making of English poetry / [by] P. M. Kean. — London; Boston: Routledge and K. Paul, 1972. 2 v.: 3 ill. (1 col.); 24 cm. 1. Chaucer, Geoffrey, d. 1400. 2. Chaucer, Geoffrey, 1340?-1400. I. T.
PR1924.K36   821/.1   LC 72-193868

Kittredge, George Lyman, 1860-1941. **• 2.6364**
Chaucer and his poetry. — 55th anniversary ed., with an introd. by B. J. Whiting. — Cambridge: Harvard University Press, 1970 [c1915] xxxvi, 230 p.: ports.; 22 cm. 1. Chaucer, Geoffrey, d. 1400. I. T.
PR1924.K5 1970   821/.1   LC 78-135544   ISBN 0674112016

M. Madeleva (Mary Madeleva), Sister, 1887-1964. **• 2.6365**
A lost language, and other essays on Chaucer, by Sister M. Madeleva. New York, Russell & Russell [1967, c1951] 147 p. 20 cm. 1. Chaucer, Geoffrey, d. 1400. I. T.
PR1924.M23 1967   821/.1   LC 66-27123

Malone, Kemp, 1889-1971. **• 2.6366**
Chapters on Chaucer. — Baltimore, Johns Hopkins Press, 1951. ix, 240 p. 23 cm. 1. Chaucer, Geoffrey — Criticism and interpretation. I. T.
PR1924.M25   821.17   LC 51-2753

Patch, Howard Rollin, 1889-1963. **• 2.6367**
On rereading Chaucer, by Howard Rollin Patch. Cambridge, Mass., Harvard university press, 1939. xi p., 2 l., [3]-269 p. 22 cm. 1. Chaucer, Geoffrey, d. 1400 — Criticism and interpretation I. T.
PR1924.P3   821.17   LC 39-14338

Payne, Robert O. **• 2.6368**
The key of remembrance, a study of Chaucer's poetics. — New Haven, Published for the University of Cincinnati [by] Yale University Press, 1963. 246 p. 23 cm. Includes bibliography. 1. Chaucer, Geoffrey, d. 1400. I. T.
PR1924.P35   821.1   LC 63-7944

Root, Robert Kilburn, 1877-. **• 2.6369**
The poetry of Chaucer; a guide to its study and appreciation. Rev. ed. Boston Houghton Mifflin [1922] x, 306 p.; 20 cm. 1. Chaucer, Geoffrey, d. 1400 — Criticism and interpretation. I. T.
PR1924.R6 1922   LC 22-8997

Rowland, Beryl. **2.6370**
Companion to Chaucer studies / edited by Beryl Rowland. — Rev. ed. — New York: Oxford University Press, 1979. x, 516 p.; 21 cm. 1. Chaucer, Geoffrey, d. 1400 — Criticism and interpretation. 2. Chaucer, Geoffrey, d. 1400 — Criticism and interpretation — History. I. T.
PR1924.R68 1979   821/.1   LC 78-14542   ISBN 0195024893

Speirs, John. **• 2.6371**
Chaucer, the maker / by John Speirs. — [2d rev. ed.]. — London: Faber and Faber, 1960. 222 p. 1. Chaucer, Geoffrey, d. 1400. I. T.
PR1924.S57 1960   LC 61-1531

Winny, James. **2.6372**
Chaucer's dream-poems. — New York: Barnes & Noble, [1973] 158 p.; 23 cm. 1. Chaucer, Geoffrey, d. 1400 — Criticism and interpretation. I. T.
PR1924.W5   821/.1   LC 74-156818   ISBN 0064977692

Brewer, Derek, 1923-. **2.6373**
Chaucer, the poet as storyteller / Derek Brewer. — London: Macmillan, 1984. x, 150 p. 'This is a companion volume to Tradition and innovation in Chaucer....a Collection of essays...some not previously published.'—Pref.

1. Chaucer, Geoffrey, d. 1400 — Criticism and interpretation — Addresses, essays, lectures. I. T.
PR1925 B75 1984   ISBN 0333284283

Curry, Walter Clyde, 1887-. **• 2.6374**
Chaucer and the mediaeval sciences. Rev. and enl. [i.e. 2d] ed. New York, Barnes & Noble, 1960. 367 p. illus. 20 cm. 1. Chaucer, Geoffrey, d. 1400 — Knowledge — Science. 2. Chaucer, Geoffrey, d. 1400 — Knowledge — Astrology. I. T.
PR1933.S3 C8 1960   821.1   LC 60-9238

PR1940–1954 Language

Dempster, Germaine (Collette) **• 2.6375**
Dramatic irony in Chaucer. — New York, Humanities Press, 1959. 102 p. 24 cm. 1. Chaucer, Geoffrey — Style. 2. Chaucer, Geoffrey — Sources. 3. Irony in literature I. T.
PR1940.D4x   LC A 63-765

A Chaucer glossary / compiled by Norman Davis ... [et al.]. **2.6376**
Oxford: Clarendon Press; New York: Oxford University Press, 1979. xx, 185 p.; 23 cm. 1. Chaucer, Geoffrey, d. 1400 — Language — Glossaries, etc. 2. English language — Middle English, 1100-1500 — Glossaries, vocabularies, etc. I. Davis, Norman, 1913-
PR1941.C5   821/.1   LC 78-40245   ISBN 0198111681

Tatlock, John S. P. (John Strong Perry), 1876-1948. **• 2.6377**
A concordance to the complete works of Geoffrey Chaucer, and to the Romaunt of the Rose / by John S. P. Tatlock and Arthur G. Kennedy. — Gloucester, Mass.: Peter Smith, 1963. xiii, 1110 p. 1. Chaucer, Geoffrey — Concordances. 2. Roman de la Rose — Concordances. I. Kennedy, Arthur G., 1880-1954. II. T.
PR1941.T3 1963   821.1   LC 63-6086

Kökeritz, Helge, 1902-. **• 2.6378**
A guide to Chaucer's pronunciation. — Stockholm: Almquist & Wiksell; New Haven: Whitlock, [c1954] 32 p.; 21 cm. 1. Chaucer, Geoffrey, d. 1400. I. T.
PR1945.P7 K6   LC a 55-4786

Southworth, James Granville, 1896-. **• 2.6379**
The prosody of Chaucer and his followers: supplementary chapters to Verses of cadence. — Oxford: Blackwell, 1962. 96 p. 1. Chaucer, Geoffrey, d. 1400 — Versification. 2. English language — Middle English, 1100-1500 — Rhythm. I. T. II. Title: Verses of cadence.
PR1951.S6   LC 64-55110

Southworth, James Granville, 1896-. **• 2.6380**
Verses of cadence; an introduction to the prosody of Chaucer and his followers, by James G. Southworth. Oxford, B. Blackwell, 1954. — St. Clair Shores, Mich.: Scholarly Press, 1971. 94 p.; 22 cm. 1. Chaucer, Geoffrey, d. 1400 — Versification. 2. English language — Middle English, 1100-1500 — Rhythm. I. T.
PR1951.S6 1971   821/.1   LC 70-161954   ISBN 0403013321

PR1955–2008 C–L

Purity (Middle English poem) **2.6381**
Cleanness / edited by J. J. Anderson. — Manchester [Eng.]: Manchester University Press; New York: Barnes & Noble Books, c1977. ix, 177 p.: ill.; 22 cm. — (Old and Middle English texts) Middle English. Includes index. I. Anderson, J. J. II. T.
PR1964.A2 A5 1977   PR1964A2 A5 1977.   821/.1   LC 77-373063
ISBN 0064901785

Saint Erkenwald (Middle English poem) **2.6382**
St Erkenwald / edited by Ruth Morse. — Cambridge, Eng.: D. S. Brewer; Totowa, N.J.: Rowman and Littlefield, [1975] 111 p. 1. Erkenwald, Saint, Bp. of London, d. 693 — Legends. I. Morse, Ruth, ed. II. T.
PR1968.E4 1975   821/.1   LC 75-2128   ISBN 0874716861

Gower, John, 1325?-1408. **• 2.6383**
Selections from John Gower; with an introduction, notes, and glossary by J. A. W. Bennett. Oxford, Clarendon P., 1968. xxii, 189 p. plate. 19 cm. (Clarendon medieval and Tudor series) I. Bennett, J. A. W. (Jack Arthur Walter) ed. II. T.
PR1982.B4 1968   821/.1   LC 68-117337

Gower, John, 1325?-1408. **2.6384**
[Confessio amantis. Selections] Selected poetry / John Gower; edited by Carole Weinberg. — Manchester: Carcanet, 1983. 184 p.; 18 cm. — (Fyfield books.) Text in Middle English. Half title: John Gower's poetry. I. Weinberg, Carole. II. T. III. Title: John Gower's poetry. IV. Series.
PR1984.C62 1983   821/.1 19   LC 82-185805   ISBN 0856354155

Fisher, John H. • **2.6385**
John Gower, moral philosopher and friend of Chaucer / by John H. Fisher. — [New York]: New York University Press, 1964. ix, 378 p.: ill., coats of arms; 24 cm. 1. Gower, John, 1325?-1408. 2. Chaucer, Geoffrey, d. 1400. I. T. PR1986.F5 821.1 *LC* 64-21811

Henryson, Robert, 1430?-1506? **2.6386**
The poems of Robert Henryson / edited by Denton Fox. — Oxford: Clarendon Press; New York: Oxford University Press, 1981. cxxiii, 596 p.; 23 cm. — (Oxford English texts) I. Fox, Denton. II. T. PR1990.H4 A17 1981 821/.2 *LC* 79-40158 *ISBN* 0198127030

Gray, Douglas. **2.6387**
Robert Henryson / Douglas Gray. — Leiden: Brill, 1979. 283 p., 16 p. of photos: ill.; 21 cm. — (Medieval and Renaissance authors.) Includes index. 1. Henryson, Robert, 1430?-1506? — Criticism and interpretation. I. T. II. Series. PR1990.H4 Z66 821/.2 19 *LC* 80-487408 *ISBN* 9004059172

Stearns, Marshall Winslow. • **2.6388**
Robert Henryson. — New York: Columbia University Press, 1949. 155 p. 'A list of manuscript and printed editions of the Testament of Cresseid': p. [131]-133. 1. Henryson, Robert, 1430?-1506? I. T. PR1990.H4 Z8 *LC* 49-8094

Kempe, Margery, b. ca. 1373. **2.6389**
The book of Margery Kempe / translated by B.A. Windeatt. — Harmondsworth, Middlesex, England: Penguin; New York, N.Y., U.S.A.: Viking Penguin, 1985. 332 p.; 20 cm. (Penguin classics.) 1. Kempe, Margery, b. ca. 1373 — Biography. 2. Authors, English — Middle English, 1100-1500 — Biography. 3. Christian pilgrims and pilgrimages 4. Mysticism — England. I. T. II. Series. PR2007.K4 A3 1985 248.2/2/0924 B 19 *LC* 86-116367 *ISBN* 0140432515

PR2010-2024 Langland. Layamon

Langland, William, 1330?-1400? **2.6390**
[Piers the Plowman] Piers Plowman / by William Langland; an edition of the C-text by Derek Pearsall. — Berkeley: University of California Press, 1979, c1978. 416 p.; 24 cm. — (York medieval texts: 2d ser.) I. Pearsall, Derek Albert. II. T. PR2010.P4 1979 821/.1 *LC* 78-64463 *ISBN* 0520037936

Langland, William, 1330?-1400? **2.6391**
[Piers the Plowman] The vision of Piers Plowman / William Langland. — A critical edition of the B-text based on Trinity College Cambridge MS B.15.17, with selected variant readings, an introd., glosses, and a textual and literary commentary / by A. V. C. Schmidt. — London: J. M. Dent; New York: E. P. Dutton, 1978. xlvii, 364 p.; 20 cm. (Everyman's university library) Includes index. I. Schmidt, A. V. C. (Aubrey Vincent Carlyle) II. T. PR2010.S3 1978 821/.1 *LC* 79-307509 *ISBN* 046010571X

Langland, William, 1330?-1400? • **2.6392**
Visions from Piers Plowman, taken from the poem of William Langland and translated into modern English by Nevill Coghill. — New York: Oxford University Press, 1950. 143 p. plates. 22 cm. I. Coghill, Nevill, 1899- tr. II. T. PR2013.C6 1950 821.15 *LC* 50-9096

Langland, William, 1330?-1400? • **2.6393**
Piers the ploughman / William Langland; translated into modern English with an introduction by J.F. Goodridge. — Harmondsworth, [England]: Penguin Books, 1959. 365 p. — (The Penguin classics; L87.) 1. English poetry — Middle English, 1100-1500 I. Goodridge, Jonathan Francis, 1924- . II. T. PR2013.G6 821.1 *LC* 59-2627 *ISBN* 0140440879

Langland, William, 1330?-1400? **2.6394**
Piers Plowman: the three versions. General ed.: George Kane. [London] University of London, Athlone Press, 1960-75. v. 1-2.; 24 cm. SCAR lacks v. 2. Vol. 1: 'An edition in the form of Trinity College, Cambridge MS R.3.14 corrected from other manuscripts, with variant readings.' Vol. 2: 'An edition in the form of Trinity College Cambridge MS B.15.17, corrected and restored from the known evidence, with variant readings.' Bibliographical footnotes. I. Kane, George, ed. II. T. PR2013.K3x

Lansland, William, 1330?-1400? **2.6395**
Piers Plowman, the A version: Will's visions of Piers Plowman and Do-well: an edition in the form of Trinity College, Cambridge, Ms R. 3.14 / corrected from other manuscripts with variant readings by George Kane. — London: University of London, the Athlone Press, 1960. ix, 457 p.; 24 cm. — (Piers Plowman, the three versions / William Lansland; v. 1) I. Kane, George. II. T. III. Title: Will's visions of Piers Plowman and Do-well. PR2013.K3x vol. 1

Langland, William, 1330?-1400? **2.6396**
Piers Plowman / [by William Langland]; Will's visions of Piers Plowman, Do-well, Do-better and Do-best, [Vol.2]: The B version. An edition in the form of Trinity College Cambridge MS. B.15.17, corrected and restored from the known evidence, with variant readings / by George Kane and E. Talbot Donaldson. London: Athlone Press, 1975. ix, 681 p.; 24 cm. Middle English text, English introduction and notes. 1. English poetry I. Kane, George. II. Donaldson, E. Talbot (Ethelbert Talbot), 1910- III. T. PR2013.K3x vol. 2 821/.1 *ISBN* 0485135027

Bloomfield, Morton W. (Morton Wilfred), 1913-1987. • **2.6397**
Piers Plowman as a fourteenth-century apocalypse. — New Brunswick, N. J., Rutgers University Press [1961] 259 p. 22 cm. Includes bibliography. 1. Langland, William, 1330?-1400? Piers the Plowman I. T. PR2015.B5 821.1 *LC* 61-10254

Carruthers, Mary. **2.6398**
The search for St. Truth; a study of meaning in Piers Plowman. — Evanston [Ill.]: Northwestern University Press, 1973. x, 173 p.; 23 cm. 1. Langland, William, 1330?-1400? Piers the Plowman I. T. PR2015.C3 PR2015 C3. 821/.1 *LC* 73-80121 *ISBN* 0810104229

Donaldson, E. Talbot (Ethelbert Talbot) • **2.6399**
Piers plowman: the C-text and its poets / by E. Talbot Donaldson; with a new preface by the author. — Hamden, Conn.: Archon Books, 1966 c1949. xiv, 255 p. — (Yale studies in English. v.113) 1. Langland, William, 1330?-1400? Piers the Plowman I. T. II. Series. PR2015.D6 1966 821.1 *LC* 66-20230

Frank, Robert Worth, 1914-. • **2.6400**
Piers Plowman and the scheme of salvation; an interpretation of Dowel, Dobet, and Dobest, by Robert Worth Frank, Jr. — [Hamden, Conn.]: Archon Books, 1969 [c1957] xiv, 123 p.; 23 cm. — (Yale studies in English. v. 136) 1. Langland, William, 1330?-1400? Piers the Plowman I. T. II. Series. PR2015.F7 1969 821/.1 *LC* 69-15683 *ISBN* 0208007792

Kane, George. **2.6401**
Piers Plowman, the evidence for authorship. — [London]: University of London, Athlone Press, 1965. 72 p.: ill. Supplementary volume to the Athlone Press ed. of Piers Plowman. 1. Langland, William, 1330?-1400? Piers the Plowman I. T. PR2015.K3 1965 *LC* 65-4942

Kirk, Elizabeth D. **2.6402**
The dream thought of Piers Plowman, by Elizabeth D. Kirk. — New Haven, Yale University Press, 1972. x, 214 p. 21 cm. — (Yale studies in English. v. 178) 1. Langland, William, 1330?-1400? Piers the Plowman I. T. II. Series. PR2015.K5 821/.1 *LC* 72-75198 *ISBN* 0300015453

Lawlor, John. • **2.6403**
Piers Plowman; an essay in criticism. New York, Barnes & Noble [1962] 340 p. 22 cm. 1. Langland, William, 1330?-1400? Piers the Plowman I. T. PR2015.L3 1962 *LC* 62-52432

Salter, Elizabeth. • **2.6404**
Piers Plowman; an introduction. Cambridge, Harvard University Press, 1962. vii, 111 p. 23 cm. Bibliography: p. 109-110. 1. Langland, William, 1330?-1400? Piers the Plowman I. T. PR2015.S3 821.1 *LC* 62-4218

Fowler, David C., 1921-. • **2.6405**
Piers the Plowman: literary relations of the A and B texts. — Seattle, University of Washington Press, 1961. xiii, 260 p. 22 cm. — (University of Washington publications in language and literature, v. 16) Bibliographical references included in 'Notes' (p. 207-254) 1. Langland, William, 1330?-1400? Piers the Plowman I. T. PR2016.F6 821.1 *LC* 61-11575

Layamon, fl. 1200. **2.6406**
[Brut. Selections] Selections from Layamon's Brut / edited by G.L. Brook; with an introduction by C.S. Lewis. — Rev. ed. / revised by John Levitt. — [Exeter]: University of Exeter, 1983. xxii, 160 p.: facsim.; 18 cm. — (Exeter medieval English texts) Anglo-Saxon text, English introduction and notes. I. Brook, G. L. (George Leslie), 1910- II. Levitt, John. III. T. PR2024 B7 1983 821/.1 19 *ISBN* 0859891399

PR2040-2049 Malory

Malory, Thomas, Sir, 15th cent. • **2.6407**
Works [of] Malory; edited by Eugène Vinaver. — 2nd ed. reprinted, with corrections. — London: Oxford University Press, 1977, c1971. xv, 811 p.; 23 cm. — ([Oxford standard authors]) I. Vinaver, Eugène, 1899- ed. II. T. PR2041.V5 1971 PR2041 V5 1977. 823/.2 *LC* 72-591131 *ISBN* 0192541633

Malory, Thomas, Sir, 15th cent. • 2.6408
King Arthur and his knights: selections from the works of Sir Thomas Malory / edited with an introduction and notes by Eugène Vinaver. — Boston: Houghton Mifflin, 1956. xxi, 166 p.; 21 cm. — (Riverside editions; B8) 1. Arthurian romances I. Vinaver, Eugène, 1899- II. T. III. Series.
PR2042.V5 1968   823/.2   LC 56-14069

Benson, Larry Dean, 1929-. 2.6409
Malory's Morte d'Arthur / Larry D. Benson. — Cambridge: Harvard University Press, 1976. xi, 289 p.; 24 cm. Includes index. 1. Malory, Thomas, Sir, 15th cent. Morte d'Arthur I. T.
PR2045.B45   823/.2   LC 75-19233   ISBN 0674543939

Dillon, Bert. 2.6410
A Malory handbook / Bert Dillon. — Boston: G. K. Hall, c1978. xii, 196 p.; 24 cm. — (Reference publication in literature.) 1. Malory, Thomas, Sir, 15th cent. Le morte d'Arthur. 2. Malory, Thomas, Sir, 15th cent — Plots. 3. Arthurian romances — Stories, plots, etc. I. T. II. Series.
PR2045.D5   823/.2   LC 77-26240   ISBN 0816179646

Lumiansky, R. M. (Robert Mayer), 1913- ed. • 2.6411
Malory's originality; a critical study of Le morte Darthur. Edited by R. M. Lumiansky. — Baltimore, Johns Hopkins Press [1964] xii, 287 p. illus. 21 cm. Bibliographical footnotes. 1. Malory, Sir Thomas, 15th cent. Le morte d'Arthur. I. T.
PR2045.L8   823.2   LC 64-16311

Matthews, William, 1905-. 2.6412
The ill–framed knight: a skeptical inquiry into the identity of Sir Thomas Malory. Berkeley: University of California Press, 1966. 262p.,illus.,maps. 1. Malory, Thomas, Sir, 15th cent — Authorship. I. T.
PR2049 M3 1966   PR2045.M3.   823.2   LC 66-23179

PR2064–2125 Metrical Romances

Benson, Larry Dean, 1929- comp. 2.6413
King Arthur's death; the Middle English stanzaic Morte Arthur and alliterative Morte Arthure. Edited by Larry D. Benson. — Indianapolis: Bobbs-Merrill, [1974] xxxvi, 257 p.; 23 cm. — (The Library of literature, 29) 1. English poetry — Middle English, 1100-1500 2. Arthurian romances I. Le Morte Arthur. 1974. II. Morte Authure. 1974. III. T.
PR2064.B4   821/.1/08   LC 73-13545   ISBN 0672514532

Gawain and the Grene Knight. • 2.6414
Sir Gawain and the Green Knight; edited by J. R. R. Tolkien and E. V. Gordon. 2nd ed. revised by Norman Davis. Oxford, Clarendon P., 1967. xxviii, 232 p. front., plate (facsim.) 22 1/2 cm. Previous ed. 1925. 1. Gawain (Legendary character) — Romances. I. Tolkien, J. R. R. (John Ronald Reuel), 1892-1973. II. Gordon, E. V. (Eric Valentine), 1896-1938. III. Davis, Norman, 1913- IV. T.
PR2065.G3 1967b   821/.1   LC 68-78079

Barron, W. R. J. (William Raymond Johnston) 2.6415
Trawthe and treason: the sin of Gawain reconsidered: a thematic study of Sir Gawain and the Green Knight / W. R. J. Barron. — Manchester [Eng.]: Manchester University Press; Totowa, N.J.: distributed in the USA by Barnes and Noble Books, c1980. x, 150 p.; 23 cm. — (Publications of the Faculty of Arts of the University of Manchester; no. 25) 1. Gawain and the Grene Knight. 2. Gawain (Legendary character) — Romances — History and criticism. 3. Sin in literature I. T.
PR2065.G31 B37   821/.1 19   LC 80-513594   ISBN 0719012945

Borroff, Marie. • 2.6416
Sir Gawain and the Green Knight: a stylistic and metrical study. New York, Yale University Press, 1962. xii, 295 p. 24 cm. (Yale studies in English. v. 152) 1. Gawain and the Grene Knight. I. T. II. Series.
PR2065.G31 B6   821.1   LC 62-8235

Brewer, Elisabeth. comp. 2.6417
From Cuchulainn to Gawain; sources and analogues of Sir Gawain and the Green Knight, selected and translated by Elisabeth Brewer. — Totowa, N.J.: Rowman and Littlefield, 1974 (c1973). 101 p.; 21 cm. 1. Gawain and the Grene Knight — Sources. 2. Gawain (Legendary character) — Romances. I. T.
PR2065.G31 B7 1974   821/.1   LC 73-13641   ISBN 0874714435

Kittredge, George Lyman, 1860-1941. • 2.6418
A study of Gawain and the Green Knight. — Gloucester, Mass., P. Smith, 1960 [c1916] viii, 323 p. 21 cm. 'Bibliographical note': p. 290-306. 1. Gawain and the Grene Knight. I. T.
PR2065.G31K5 1960   821.1   LC 60-2793

Savage, Henry Lyttleton, 1892-. 2.6419
The Gawain–poet; studies in his personality and background. — Chapel Hill, University of North Carolina Press [1956] xviii, 236 p. 2 col. coats of arms. 22 cm. Bibliography: p. 219-228. 1. Gawain and the Grene Knight. I. T.
PR2065.G31S3   821.19   LC A 56-4712

Morte Arthure. 2.6420
The alliterative Morte Arthure: a critical edition / edited, with an introd., notes, and glossary, by Valerie Krishna; pref. by Rossell Hope Robbins. — New York: B. Franklin, c1976. xiv, 361 p., [8] leaves of plates: ill.; 24 cm. Includes index. 1. Arthurian romances I. Krishna, Valerie. II. T.
PR2065.M3 1976   PR2065 M3 1976.   821/.1   LC 76-28813   ISBN 089102039X

Morte Arthure. 2.6421
The alliterative Morte Arthure: a new verse translation / Valerie Krishna. — Washington, D.C.: University Press of America, c1983. xxx, 113 p.; 23 cm. 1. Arthurian romances I. Krishna, Valerie. II. T.
PR2065.M3 A34 1983   821/.1 19   LC 82-24838   ISBN 0819130354

Matthews, William, 1905-. • 2.6422
The tragedy of Arthur: a study of the alliterative 'Morte Arthure'. — Berkeley: University of California Press, 1960. 230 p.; 24 cm. 1. Morte Arthure. I. T.
PR2065.M3 M3 1960   LC 60-10359

The owl and the nightingale. • 2.6423
The owl and the nightingale, edited by Eric Gerald Stanley. — London, Nelson [1960] vi, 210 p. 19 cm. — (Nelson's medieval and Renaissance library) Imprint covered by label: New York, Barnes & Noble. Bibliography: p. 41-46. I. Stanley, Eric Gerald. ed. II. T.
PR2109.O7A15   821.1   LC 60-2619

Pearl (Middle English poem) 2.6424
Pearl: a new verse translation / by Marie Borroff. — 1st ed. — New York: W. W. Norton, c1977. xxi, 40 p. I. Borroff, Marie. II. T.
PR2111.A214 1977   PR2111 A214 1977.   821/.1   LC 76-43971   ISBN 0393044564

Pearl (Middle English poem) • 2.6425
Pearl / edited by E. V. Gordon. — Oxford: Clarendon Press, 1953. lx, 167 p.: front.; 19 cm. Final revision was made after the editor's death by his wife, Ida L. Gordon. Bibliography: p. [liii]—lvii. I. Gordon, E. V. (Eric Valentine), 1896-1938. ed. II. T.
PR2111.A243   821.1   LC 53-3076

Kean, P. M. (Patricia Margaret) 2.6426
The pearl; an interpretation [by] P. M. Kean. New York, Barnes & Noble [1967] x, 246 p. 23 cm. 1. Pearl (Middle English poem) I. T.
PR2111.K4 1967a   821.1   LC 67-5577

Rymes of Robyn Hood: an introduction to the English outlaw / 2.6427
[compiled by] R. B. Dobson and J. Taylor.
Pittsburgh: University of Pittsburgh Press, 1976. x, 330 p.: ill.; 24 cm. Includes index. 1. Robin Hood (Legendary character) — Legends. 2. English literature I. Dobson, R. B. (Richard Barrie) II. Taylor, John, 1925-
PR2125.D6 1976   820/.8/0351   LC 75-31564   ISBN 0822911264

PR2199–2405 English Renaissance (1500–1640) Prose. Poetry
(Drama: see: PR2411-3199)

PR2199 Anonymous Works

Mirrour for magistrates. • 2.6428
The mirror for magistrates, edited from original texts in the Huntington Library by Lily B. Campbell. New York, Barnes & Noble [1960] vii, 554 p. facsims. 25 cm. A collection of legends in verse originally published in 1559 as a continuation of Lydgate's 'Fall of princes,' by William Baldwin and others. Contains the text of the 1559 ed., with additions to the original, published in 1563, 1578, and 1587. With facsims. of original title pages. 1. Shakespeare, William, 1564-1616 — Sources 2. Great Britain — History — Poetry. I. Baldwin, William, ca. 1518-1563? II. Campbell, Lily Bess, 1883-1967. ed. III. T.
PR2199.M5 1960   821.3   LC 61-329

PR2200–2219 A–B

Ascham, Roger, 1515-1568.   • **2.6429**
English works: Toxophilus, Report of the affaires and state of Germany, The scholemaster / ed. by William Aldis Wright. — Cambridge: University press, 1904. xx, 304 p.; 20 cm. — (Half-title: Cambridge English classics) With reproductions of original title-pages of the Report of the affaires and state of Germany and The scholemaster. I. Wright, William Aldis, 1834-1914, ed. II. T.
PR2201.A2W7   LC 05-4512

Bacon, Francis, 1561-1626.   • **2.6430**
Essays by Francis Bacon, with an introduction by Geoffrey Grigson. London, Oxford university press [1940] xix, 269, [1] p. incl. facsim. 15 1/2 cm. (World's classics. 24) I. T. II. Series.
PR2206.A3 1940   824.3   LC 43-32694

Harris, Jesse W., 1900-.   • **2.6431**
John Bale: a study in the minor literature of the Reformation / by Jesse W. Harris. — Freeport, N.Y.: Books for Libraries Press [1970] 157 p.: facsim.; 24 cm. (Library of English Renaissance literature) Reprint of the 1940 ed. 'Facsimile of Bale's autobiography, 1536': p. 131-134. 1. Bale, John, 1495-1563 — Criticism and interpretation. I. T.
PR2209.B2 H28 1970   828/.2/09   LC 72-119958   ISBN 0836954017

Breton, Nicholas, 1545?-1626?   • **2.6432**
The works in verse and prose of Nicholas Breton. For the first time collected and edited: with memorial–introd., notes and illus., glossarial index, facsims. &c., by Alexander B. Grosart. — New York: AMS Press, 1966. 2 v.; 24 cm. — (Chertsey worthies' library.) Reprint of the 1879 ed. I. T. II. Series.
PR2214.B4 A14 1966   821/.3   LC 75-181917

Breton, Nicholas, 1545?-1626?   • **2.6433**
Poems / (Not hitherto reprinted) edited, with biography, canon, and notes, by Jean Robertson. Liverpool, University Press, 1952. — [Detroit, Mich.: Scholarly Press, 1971] clix, 229 p.: facsims., port.; 22 cm. — (Liverpool English texts & studies) I. T.
PR2214.B4 A17 1971   821/.3   LC 72-161960   ISBN 0403013356

Greville, Fulke, Baron Brooke, 1554-1628.   • **2.6434**
Poems and dramas of Fulke Greville first lord Brooke. Edited with introduction and notes by Geoffrey Bullough. — Edinburgh, Oliver and Boyd [1939] 2 v. front. (port.) facsims. 22 cm. I. Bullough, Geoffrey, 1901- ed. II. T.
PR2215.A1 1939   820.81   LC 40-3587

Rebholz, Ronald A.   • **2.6435**
The life of Fulke Greville: first Lord Brooke / [by] Ronald A. Rebholz. — Oxford: Clarendon Press, 1971. xxxv, 384 p., 2 plates (1 fold.): geneal. table, port.; 23 cm. 1. Greville, Fulke, Baron Brooke, 1554-1628. I. T.
PR2216.R38   821/.3 B   LC 78-874436   ISBN 0198120109

Waswo, Richard.   **2.6436**
The fatal mirror: themes and techniques in the poetry of Fulke Greville. — Charlottesville: University Press of Virginia [1972] ix, 181 p.; 25 cm. 1. Greville, Fulke, Baron Brooke, 1554-1628. I. T.
PR2216.W3   821/.3   LC 75-188603   ISBN 0813903920

PR2223–2224 Burton

Burton, Robert, 1577-1640.   • **2.6437**
The anatomy of melancholy. New York, Farrar & Rinehart incorporated [1929] xix, 1036 p.: ill.; 24 cm. — 1. Melancholy I. Smith, Paul Jordan, 1885- joint ed. II. Dell, Floyd, 1887-1969. ed. III. T.
PR2223.A1   LC 31-27057

Babb, Lawrence.   • **2.6438**
Sanity in bedlam: a study of Robert Burton's Anatomy of melancholy. — [East Lansing] Michigan State University Press, 1959. xi, 116 p. 24 cm. Bibliography: p. 111-113. 1. Burton, Robert, 1577-1640. 2. Burton, Robert, 1577-1640. The anatomy of melancholy. 3. Melancholy I. T.
PR2224.B3   828.3   LC 59-11689

Fox, Ruth A.   **2.6439**
The tangled chain: the structure of disorder in The anatomy of melancholy / Ruth A. Fox. — Berkeley: University of California Press, c1976. xiii, 282 p.; 22 cm. 1. Burton, Robert, 1577-1640. The anatomy of melancholy. I. T.
PR2224.F6   616.8/9   LC 75-17296   ISBN 0520030850

O'Connell, Michael, 1943-.   **2.6440**
Robert Burton / by Michael O'Connell. — Boston: Twayne Publishers, c1986. 130 p.; 23 cm. — (Twayne's English authors series. TEAS 426) Includes index. 1. Burton, Robert, 1577-1640 — Criticism and interpretation. I. T. II. Series.
PR2224.O36 1986   828/.309 19   LC 86-365   ISBN 0805769196

PR2228–2244 C–D

Campion, Thomas, 1567-1620.   **2.6441**
Campion's works / edited by Percival Vivian. — London: Routledge, [n.d.] 285 p. 1. Counterpoint. I. Vivian, Sylvanus Percival, Sir, 1880- II. T.
ML410.C3 V4 1966   PR2228.A1x 1966.   LC 67-110274/MN

Lowbury, Edward Joseph Lister.   • **2.6442**
Thomas Campion: poet, composer, physician / by Edward Lowbury, Timothy Salter, and Alison Young. — New York: Barnes & Noble [1970] viii, 195 p.: ill., facsims., music, 2 plates; 23 cm. 1. Campion, Thomas, 1567-1620. 2. Music and literature I. Salter, Timothy, 1942- joint author. II. Young, Alison, 1922- joint author. III. T.
PR2229.L6 1970b   784/.0924   LC 78-20216   ISBN 0389039993

Carew, Thomas, 1595?-1639?   • **2.6443**
The poems of Thomas Carew, with his masque Coelum Britannicum [sic] Edited with an introd. and notes by Rhodes Dunlap. — Oxford, Clarendon Press, 1949. lxxx, 297 p. ports., facsims. 23 cm. With facsimiles of original title pages. I. T.
PR2231.A27   821.49   LC 50-5566

Daniel, Samuel, 1562-1619.   • **2.6444**
Poems, and A defence of ryme. Edited by Arthur Colby Sprague. Cambridge Harvard University Press 1930. 215p. 1. Poetry — Early works to 1800 2. English language — Rime I. Sprague, Arthur Colby, 1895- ed. II. T. III. Title: A defence of ryme
PR2241 A17 1930

Davies, John, Sir, 1569-1626.   • **2.6445**
Orchestra; or, A poem of dancing. Edited with brief introd. and notes by E. M. W. Tillyard. London, Chatto & Windus, 1947. — St. Clair Shores, Mich.: Scholarly Press, 1971. 55 p.; 22 cm. — I. T.
PR2242.D2 A715 1971   821/.3   LC 70-161962   ISBN 040301333X

Sanderson, James L.   **2.6446**
Sir John Davies / by James L. Sanderson. — Boston: Twayne Publishers, [1975] 170 p.; 21 cm. (Twayne's English authors series; TEAS 175) Includes index. 1. Davies, John, Sir, 1569-1626. I. T.
PR2242.D2 S2   821/.3   LC 74-20817   ISBN 0805711411

Dekker, Thomas, ca. 1572-1632.   • **2.6447**
The gull's hornbook / edited by R. B. McKerrow. — New York: AMS Press [1971] viii, 107 p.; 24 cm. Reprint of the 1904 ed; original published in London, 1609. I. McKerrow, Ronald Brunlees, 1872-1940. ed. II. T.
PR2243.G8 1971   824/.3   LC 74-136374   ISBN 0404020690

Dekker, Thomas, ca. 1572-1632.   • **2.6448**
The plague pamphlets of Thomas Dekker. Edited by F. P. Wilson. Oxford, Clarendon Press, 1925. St. Clair Shores, Mich., Scholarly Press, 1971. xxxix, 268 p. facsims. 22 cm. 1. Plague — England — London. I. Wilson, F. P. (Frank Percy), 1889-1963. ed. II. T.
PR2243.P5 1971   828/.3/08   LC 73-161963   ISBN 0403013194

Deloney, Thomas, 1543?-1600.   **2.6449**
The works of Thomas Deloney, edited from the earliest extant editions & broadsides, with an introduction and notes, by Francis Oscar Mann. — Oxford, Clarendon Press, 1912. xliii, 600 p. 22.5 cm. With reproductions of original title-pages. I. Mann, Francis Oscar, ed. II. T.
PR2244.D2 1912   LC 12-12669

Deloney, Thomas, 1543?-1600.   • **2.6450**
Novels. Edited by Merritt E. Lawlis. — Bloomington, Indiana University Press, 1961. xxxii, 462 p. facsims. 24 cm. 'Editions ... used as copy texts: the Henry E. Huntington Library [copies of] ... Jack of Newbury and Thomas of Reading; the University of Sheffield Library [copy of] ... The gentle craft, part I; and the British Museum [copy of] ... The gentle craft, part II.' I. Lawlis, Merritt E., 1918- ed. II. T.
PZ3.D383No   PR2244.D2 Ax.   LC 59-10869

Lawlis, Merritt E., 1918-.   • **2.6451**
Apology for the middle class: the dramatic novels of Thomas Deloney. — Bloomington: Indiana University Press, 1960. 165 p.: ill.; 23 cm. — 1. Deloney, Thomas, 1543?-1600. I. T.
AS36.I385 no. 46   PR2244.D2 Z75.   LC 61-62779

PR2245–2248 Donne

Donne, John, 1572-1631.   • **2.6452**
The poems of John Donne / edited from the old editions and numerous manuscripts; with introd. and commentary, by Herbert J.C. Grierson. — Oxford: Clarendon Press, 1912. 2 v.: ill. With reproductions of original title-pages. I. Grierson, Herbert John Clifford, Sir, 1866-1960. II. T.
PR2245.A5 G6   LC 13-5442

Donne, John, 1572-1631.   2.6453
[Poems] The divine poems / John Donne; edited with introd. and commentary by Helen Gardner. — 2d ed. — Oxford [Eng.]; Clarendon Press; New York: Oxford University Press, 1978. xcviii, 158 p.; 23 cm. I. Gardner, Helen Louise, Dame. II. T.
PR2246.G26 1978   821/.3   LC 77-30283   ISBN 0198127456

Donne, John, 1572-1631.   • 2.6454
The elegies, and The songs and sonnets. Edited with introd. and commentary by Helen Gardner. — Oxford, Clarendon Press, 1965. xcix, 272 p. illus., ports. 23 cm. Includes unacc. melodies. I. Gardner, Helen Louise, ed. II. Donne, John, 1573-1631. Songs and sonnets. III. T.
PR2246.G27   821.3   LC 65-6720

Donne, John, 1573-1631.   • 2.6455
Poetry and prose: with Izaak Walton's Life, appreciations by Ben Jonson, Dryden, Coleridge / With an introduction and notes by H. W. Garrod. — Oxford: Clarendon, 1946. lviii,126 p.: ill. I. Walton, Izaak, 1593-1683. II. Garrod, Heathcote William, 1878-1960. III. T.
PR2246.G3   820.81   LC A47-722

Donne, John, 1572-1631.   2.6456
The epithalamions, anniversaries, and epicedes / John Donne; edited with introd. and commentary by W. Milgate. — Oxford [Eng.]: Clarendon Press, 1978. xlv, 237 p., [2] leaves of plates: ill.; 23 cm. I. Milgate, Wesley, 1916- II. T.
PR2246.M48   821/.3   LC 77-30423   ISBN 0198127294

Donne, John, 1573-1631.   2.6457
The satires, epigrams and verse letters / edited with introduction and commentary by W. Milgate. — Oxford: Clarendon P., 1967. lxxvii, 296 p.: 2 plates (ports.), tables, diagrs.; 22.5 cm. — ([Oxford English texts]) I. T.
PR2246.M5   821/.3   LC 67-111041

Donne, John, 1572-1631.   2.6458
Paradoxes and problems / John Donne; edited with introd. and commentary by Helen Peters. — Oxford: Clarendon Press; New York: Oxford University Press, 1980. c, 142 p., [1] leaf of plates: port.; 23 cm. — (Oxford English texts) 1. Paradoxes I. Peters, Helen. II. T.
PR2247.P3 1980   828/.3/08   LC 79-40844   ISBN 0198127537

PR2248 Biography. Criticism

Combs, Homer Carroll.   • 2.6459
A concordance to the English poems of John Donne / by Homer Carroll Combs and Zay Rusk Sullens. — New York: Haskell House, 1969. ix, 418 p.; 24 cm. Reprint of the 1940 ed. 1. Donne, John, 1572-1631 — Concordances. I. Sullens, Zay Rusk, joint author. II. T.
PR2248.A3 1969   821/.3   LC 74-92960   ISBN 0838309690

Bald, R. C. (Robert Cecil), 1901-1965.   2.6460
John Donne, a life [by] R. C. Bald. New York, Oxford University Press, 1970. x, [2], 627 p. illus., facsims., ports. 22 cm. 1. Donne, John, 1572-1631 — Biography. 2. Church of England — England — Clergy — Biography. 3. Poets, English — Early modern, 1500-1700 — Biography. I. T.
PR2248.B35 1970b   821/.3 B   LC 71-83007

Carey, John.   2.6461
John Donne, life, mind, and art / John Carey. — New York: Oxford University Press, 1981, c1980. 303 p.; 22 cm. Includes index. 1. Donne, John, 1572-1631. 2. Poets, English — Early modern, 1500-1700 — Biography. I. T.
PR2248.C34   821/.3 19   LC 81-125415   ISBN 0195202422

Fiore, Peter Amadeus, 1927-.   2.6462
Just so much honor: essays commemorating the four–hundredth anniversary of the birth of John Donne / edited by Peter Amadeus Fiore. — University Park: Pennsylvania State University Press, [1972] viii, 291 p.; 23 cm. 1. Donne, John, 1572-1631 — Addresses, essays, lectures. I. T.
PR2248.F5   821/.3   LC 79-157768   ISBN 0271005548

Gosse, Edmund, 1849-1928. ed.   2.6463
The life and letters of John Donne, dean of St. Paul's. New York, Dodd, Mead and company; London, W. Heinemann, 1899. 2 v. fronts., plates, ports., facsims. 23 cm. 1. Donne, John, 1572-1631. I. T.
PR2248.G6x   LC 02-2176

John Donne: the critical heritage / edited by A. J. Smith.   2.6464
London; Boston: Routledge & Paul, 1976 (c1975). xvii, 511 p.; 23 cm. (The Critical heritage series) Includes indexes. 1. Donne, John, 1572-1631 — Criticism and interpretation — History. 2. Donne, John, 1572-1631, in fiction, drama, poetry, etc. I. Smith, A. J. (Albert James), 1924-
PR2248.J63   821/.3   LC 76-351491   ISBN 0710082428

Leishman, J. B. (James Blair), 1902-1962.   • 2.6465
The Monarch of wit: an analytical and comparative study of the poetry of John Donne / by J.B.Leishman. — 7th ed. — London: Hutchinson, 1965. 287 p.: port; 24 cm. 1. Donne, John, 1573-1631 I. T.
PR2248.L44 1965   LC 67-882

Simpson, Evelyn Mary Spearing, 1885-1963.   • 2.6466
A study of the prose works of John Donne. — 2d ed. — Oxford: Clarendon Press, 1948. vii, 371 p.: facsim.; 24 cm. Appendices (p. [337]-360): A. List of manuscripts of Donne's prose works.—B. A chronological arrangements of Donne's sermons.—C. Prose works attributed to Donne. 1. Donne, John, 1573-1631. I. T.
PR2248.S5 1948   827.35   LC 49-3926 *

Stein, Arnold Sidney, 1915-.   • 2.6467
John Donne's lyrics: the eloquence of action. — Minneapolis: University of Minnesota Press, [1962] 244 p.; 23 cm. 1. Donne, John, 1572-1631. I. T.
PR2248.S7   821.3   LC 62-20644

Webber, Joan.   • 2.6468
Contrary music: the prose style of John Donne. — Madison, University of Wisconsin Press, 1963. 227 p.: ill.; 25 cm. Includes bibliography. 1. Donne, John, 1573-1631. I. T.
PR2248.W4   825.3   LC 63-8557

PR2250–2270 D–E

Douglas, Gawin, Bishop of Dunkeld, 1474?-1522.   2.6469
Selections from Gavin Douglas / with an introd., notes, and glossary by David F. C. Coldwell; appreciations by Thomas Warton [and others]. — Oxford: Clarendon Press, 1964. xxix, 161 p.: plate; 19 cm. — (Clarendon medieval and Tudor series) Includes extracts from the Aeneid of Virgil translated into Scottish verse by G. Douglas (p. 1-106) and extracts from The palice of honour, by G. Douglas (p. 107-115) I. Coldwell, David F. C. II. Virgil. Aeneis. Selections. English. III. T. IV. Title: The palice of honour. V. Title: The palace of honor. VI. Series.
PR2250.A5C6   873   LC 64-5751

Bawcutt, Priscilla J.   2.6470
Gavin Douglas: a critical study / Priscilla Bawcutt. — Edinburgh: University Press, c1976. xii, 245 p.; 22 cm. 1. Douglas, Gawin, 1474?-1522 — Criticism and interpretation. I. T.
PR2253.B38   821/.2   LC 77-352583   ISBN 0852242956

Drayton, Michael, 1563-1631.   • 2.6471
Works. [Corr. ed. of the Michael Drayton tercentenary edition.] Oxford: Published for the Shakespeare Head Press by Blackwell, 1961. 5 v.: ill., ports., fold. maps; 24 cm. I. Hebel, John William, 1891-1934, ed. II. T.
PR2255.A5 H4x   LC 63-6961

Elton, Oliver, 1861-1945.   • 2.6472
Michael Drayton, a critical study. — New York: Russell & Russell, 1966. xv, 216 p.: facsims., ports. 1. Drayton, Michael, 1563-1631 — Bibliography. 2. Drayton, Michael, 1563-1631. I. T.
PR2258.E6   LC 65-17891

Drummond, William, 1585-1649.   • 2.6473
[Poems. 1968] The poetical works of William Drummond of Hawthornden, with 'A Cypresse Grove.' Edited by L. E. Kastner. New York, Haskell House, 1968. 2 v. illus., facsims., ports. 24 cm. Reprint of the 1856 ed. I. Kastner, Leon Emile. ed. II. T.
PR2260.A5K3 1968   821/.3   LC 68-24906

Fogle, French Rowe.   • 2.6474
A critical study of William Drummond of Hawthornden. — New York: King's Crown Press, 1952. xvii, 236 p.; 21 cm. 1. Drummond, William, 1585-1649. I. T.
PR2263.F6   LC 52-7635

Dunbar, William, 1460?-1520?   2.6475
[Works. 1979] The poems of William Dunbar / edited by James Kinsley. — Oxford: Clarendon Press; New York: Oxford University Press, 1979. xvii, 508 p., [1] leaf of plates: port.; 23 cm. — (Oxford English texts) I. Kinsley, James. II. T.
PR2265.A5 K5 1979   821/.2   LC 78-40494   ISBN 0198118880

Baxter, John Walker.   • 2.6476
William Dunbar; a biographical study, by J. W. Baxter. Edinburgh, Oliver and Boyd. — St. Clair Shores, Mich.: Scholarly Press, 1971. viii, 254 p.; 22 cm. Reprint of the 1952 ed. 1. Dunbar, William, 1460?-1520? I. T.
PR2268.B3 1971b   821/.2   LC 78-161967   ISBN 0403013275

Scott, Tom, 1918-.   2.6477
Dunbar, a critical exposition of the poems. — Edinburgh: Oliver & Boyd, 1966. 389 p. 1. Dunbar, William, 1460?-1520? I. T.
PR2269.S3   LC 66-71430

PR2271–2298 F–L

Fletcher, Giles, 1588?-1623.   • 2.6478
Giles and Phineas Fletcher: poetical works / edited by Frederick S. Boas. — Grosse Pointe, Mich.: Scholarly Press, 1968. 2 v.: facsims.; 23 cm. (Cambridge English classics) Title on spine: Poetical works. I. Fletcher, Phineas, 1582-1650. II. Boas, Frederick S. (Frederick Samuel), 1862-1957. ed. III. T.
PR2271.A2 B6 1968   821/.3   LC 70-7883

Wooden, Warren W.   2.6479
John Foxe / by Warren W. Wooden. — Boston: Twayne Publishers, c1983. 144 p., [1] leaf of plates: port.; 21 cm. (Twayne's English authors series. TEAS 345) Includes index. 1. Foxe, John, 1516-1587 — Criticism and interpretation. I. T. II. Series.
PR2276.F7 Z93 1983   272/.6/0924 19   LC 82-15605   ISBN 0805768300

Gascoigne, George, 1542?-1577.   • 2.6480
The complete works / [edited by John W. Cunliffe. — Grosse Pointe, Mich.: Scholarly Press, 1969] 2 v.; 21 cm. — (Cambridge English classics) Reprint of the 1907-10 ed. Each volume has special t.p. I. Cunliffe, John William, 1865-1946. ed. II. T. III. Series.
PR2277.A25 1969   821/.3   LC 70-3982

Googe, Barnabe, 1540-1594.   • 2.6481
Selected poems / edited and with an introduction by Alan Stephens. — Denver: A. Swallow, [c1961] 61 p.; 23 cm. — (Books of the Renaissance; v. 7) I. T. II. Series.
PR2279.G4 A6 1961   LC 61-10506

Hall, Joseph, 1574-1656.   • 2.6482
The collected poems of Joseph Hall / edited by A. Davenport. Liverpool, University Press, 1949. — St. Clair Shores, Mich.: Scholarly Press, 1971. lxxxii, 309 p.; 22 cm. (Liverpool English texts & studies) I. Davenport, Arnold, 1910-1958, ed. II. T.
PR2283.H7 A17 1971   821/.3   LC 75-161969   ISBN 0403013402

Harington, John, Sir, 1560-1612.   • 2.6483
A new discourse of a stale subject, called The metamorphosis of Ajax. — A critical annotated ed. by Elizabeth Story Donno. — New York, Columbia University Press, 1962. xi, 278 p. illus., facsim., music. 23 cm. 'The copy-text used is that of the first edition, printed by Richard Field [in 1596] ... This has been collated with a microfilm copy of the MS used by the printer (BM Add. ms 46368) and with the second edition, also printed by Richard Field.'—p. 48. Bibliographical footnotes. 1. Outhouses I. Donno, Elizabeth Story, 1921- ed. II. T. III. Title: The metamorphosis of Ajax.
PR2284.N4 1962   827.3   LC 61-16779

Craig, D. H.   2.6484
Sir John Harington / by D.H. Craig. — Boston: Twayne, c1985. 168 p.: port.; 23 cm. (Twayne's English authors series. TEAS 386) Includes index. 1. Harington, John, Sir, 1560-1612. 2. Ariosto, Lodovico, 1474-1533. Orlando furioso. 3. Authors, English — Early modern, 1500-1700 — Biography. 4. Great Britain — Court and courtiers — Biography. I. T. II. Series.
PR2285.C7 1985   828/.309 19   LC 84-15807   ISBN 0805768726

Herbert of Cherbury, Edward Herbert, Baron, 1583-1648.   • 2.6485
The Poems, English & Latin, of Edward, Lord Herbert of Cherbury / edited by G.C. Moore Smith. — Oxford: Clarendon Press, 1923. xxxii, 169 p.: ill. With facsimile of the title page of the 1665 edition. I. Smith, G. C. Moore (George Charles Moore), 1858-1940. II. T.
PR2294.H2 1968   LC 37-21896   ISBN 0198118473

Lindsay, David, Sir, fl. 1490-1555.   • 2.6486
The works of Sir David Lindsay of the Mount, 1490–1555 / edited by Douglas Hamer. — Edinburgh; London: Printed for the Society by W. Blackwood & sons ltd., 1931-36. 4 v.: facsims.; 23 cm. (The Scottish text society. [Publications. 3d ser., 1-2,6,8]) 'The bibliographical notes prefixed to the poems are summarised from the editor's article, The bibliography of Sir David Lindsay (1490-1555), published in the Library (Transactions of the Bibliographical society), June 1929, vol. X., pp. 1-42, and from a full monograph and bibliography of Sir David Lindsay to be published by the London bibliographical society.'—Note, v. 1. 1. Lindsay, David, Sir, fl. 1490-1555 — Bibliography. I. Hamer, Douglas II. T.
PR2296.L6Ax   LC 31-15675

Lodge, Thomas, 1558?-1625.   • 2.6487
The complete works of Thomas Lodge, 1580–1623?. — New York, Russell & Russell, 1963. 4 v. facsims. 23 cm. 'Edition limited to 400 sets.' 'Bibliographical index': v. 1, p. 1-27. I. T.
PR2297.A1 1963   828.3   LC 63-15170

Paradise, Nathaniel Burton, 1895-1942.   • 2.6488
Thomas Lodge; the history of an Elizabethan. — [Hamden, Conn.]: Archon Books, 1970 [c1931] vii, 254 p.; 22 cm. 1. Lodge, Thomas, 1558?-1625. I. T.
PR2298.P3 1970   828/.3/09   LC 73-95028   ISBN 0208008381

Sisson, Charles Jasper, 1885-1966. ed.   • 2.6489
Thomas Lodge and other Elizabethans / edited by Charles J. Sisson. — New York: Octagon Books, 1966 [c1933] xii, 526 p.: ill., maps, geneal. tables; 24 cm. 1. Lodge, Thomas, 1558?-1625. 2. Barnes, Barnabe, 1569?-1609. 3. Bryskett, Lodowick, ca. 1545-ca. 1612. 4. Lyly, John, 1554?-1606. 5. Buck, George, Sir, d. 1623. I. Eccles, Mark. II. Jones, Deborah. III. T.
PR2298.S5 1966   820.9003   LC 66-18029

PR2300–2303 Lyly

Lyly, John, 1554?-1606.   • 2.6490
[Works. 1967] The complete works of John Lyly, now for the first time collected and edited from the earliest quartos, with life, bibliography, essays, notes, and index, by R. Warwick Bond. Oxford, Clarendon P., 1967. 3 v. fronts. 23 cm. 1. Lyly, John, 1554?-1606 — Bibliography. I. Bond, R. Warwick (Richard Warwick), 1857-1943. ed. II. T.
PR2300.A2 1967   828/.3/09   LC 67-91862

Winny, James.   • 2.6491
Descent of Euphues: three Elizabethan romance stories. — Cambridge: Cambridge University Press, 1957. 180 p. Edited by J. Winny. I. Lyly, John, 1554?-1606. Euphues. II. Greene, Robert, 1558?-1592. Pandosto III. Chettle, Henry, d. 1607? Piers Plainness. IV. T. V. Title: Euphues. VI. Title: Pandosto. VII. Title: Piers Plainness.
PR2302.E8 1957   PR1293.W52 1957.   823.3   LC 58-2619

Houppert, Joseph W.   2.6492
John Lyly / by Joseph W. Houppert. — Boston: Twayne Publishers, [1975] 169 p.; 22 cm. — (Twayne's English authors series; TEAS 177) Includes index. 1. Lyly, John, 1554?-1606 — Criticism and interpretation. I. T.
PR2303.H6   828/.3/09   LC 74-20932   ISBN 0805713492

Hunter, G. K.   • 2.6493
John Lyly: the humanist as coutier. Cambridge: Harvard University Press, 1962. ix, 376 p. 1. Lyly, John, 1554?-1606. I. T.
PR2303.H8 1962a   LC 62-51846

PR2315 Middleton
(see also: PR2710-2718)

Middleton, Thomas, d. 1627.   • 2.6494
The ghost of Lucrece / by Thomas Middleton; reproduced in facsimile from the unique copy in the Folger Shakespeare Library, with an introduction and an edited text by Joseph Quincy Adams. — New York; London: Scribner, 1937. xxxiii, [51], 43 p.: facsims.; 20 cm. — (Folger Shakespeare Library publications) I. Folger Shakespeare Library. II. T. III. Series.
PR2315.M5 G5 1937   PR2714.G5 1937.   LC 38-4985

PR2321–2322 More

More, Thomas, Sir, Saint, 1478-1535.   • 2.6495
[Works. 1963] The complete works of St. Thomas More. — New Haven: Yale University Press, 1963-. v.: ill., ports.; 25 cm. Half title: The Yale edition of the complete works of St. Thomas More / published by the St. Thomas More Project, Yale University, under the auspices of Gerald L. Carroll and Joseph B. Murray, trustees of the Michael P. Grace II, Trust. Text in English or Latin. I. T. II. Title: Complete works of Saint Thomas More. III. Title: Yale edition of the complete works of St. Thomas More.
PR2321.A1 1963   828/.209 19   LC 63-7949   ISBN 0300013027

Harpsfield, Nicholas, 1519-1575.   • 2.6496
The life and death of Sr Thomas Moore, knight, sometymes Lord high Chancellor of England / written in the tyme of Queen Marie by Nicholas Harpsfield; and now edited from eight manuscripts with collations, textual notes, etc., by Elsie Vaughan Hitchcock; with an introd. ... by R.W. Chambers. — London; Toronto: Published for the Early English Text Society by the Oxford University Press, 1932. ccxxxi, 400 p., [4] leaves of plates: ill., facsim., ports.; 23 cm. — (Original series - Early English Text Society; no. 186) Cover title: Harpsfield's life of More. 'Including the Rastell fragments ...' 1. More, Thomas, Sir, Saint, 1478-1535. 2. Harpsfield, Nicholas, 1519-1575. 3. English prose literature — History and criticism. I. Hitchcock, Elsie Vaughan.

II. Chambers, R. W. (Raymond Wilson), 1874-1942. III. T. IV. Title: Harpsfield's life of More.
PR1119.A2 no.186   PR2322.H3x.   *LC* 32-16959

PR2326 Nash
(see also: PR2721-2724)

Hibbard, G. R. (George Richard), 1915-.   • **2.6497**
Thomas Nashe; a critical introduction. Cambridge, Harvard University Press, 1962. 262 p. 23 cm. 1. Nash, Thomas, 1567-1601. I. T.
PR2326.N3 Z68   *LC* 62-2458

Nicholl, Charles.   **2.6498**
A cup of news: the life of Thomas Nashe / Charles Nicholl. — London; Boston: Routledge & Kegan Paul, 1984. ix, 342 p., [23] p. of plates: ill.; 25 cm. Includes index. 1. Nash, Thomas, 1567-1601 — Biography. 2. Authors, English — Early modern, 1500-1700 — Biography. 3. Pamphleteers — England — Biography. I. T.
PR2326.N3 Z78 1984   828/.309 B 19   *LC* 83-19048   *ISBN* 0710095171

PR2326–2338 N–S

Niccols, Richard, 1584-1616.   • **2.6499**
Sir Thomas Overbury's vision (1616): and other English sources of Nathaniel Hawthorne's 'The scarlet letter.' / facsimile reproductions, with an introd. by Alfred S. Reid. — Gainesville, Fla.: Scholars' Facsimiles & Reprints, 1957. xviii p.: facsims., 202 p.; 23 cm. Cover title: English sources of 'The scarlet letter.' 'Reproductions of these works are made from copies in ... the University of Florida Law Library, the University of Florida Library, Princeton University Library [and] Library of Congress.' 1. Overbury, Sir Thomas, 1581-1613. 2. Somerset, Frances Howard Carr, Countess of, 1593-1632. 3. Hawthorne, Nathaniel. The scarlet letter. I. T. II. Title: English sources of 'The scarlet letter.'
PR2326.N4 S5 1616   *LC* 57-6417

Overbury, Thomas, (Sir) 1581-1613.   **2.6500**
The Overburian characters, to which is added, A wife. Edited by W.J. Paylor. Oxford B. Blackwell 1936. 157p. (The Percy reprints, no. 13) 1. Characters and characteristics I. Paylor, Wilfrid, James, ed. II. T. III. Title: A wife
PR2326.O5 A16 1936

Raleigh, Walter, Sir, 1552?-1618.   • **2.6501**
The poems of Sir Walter Raleigh / edited with an introd. by Agnes M. C. Latham. — London: Routledge and Paul [1951] lxiii, 182 p.: ports.; 18 cm. I. T.
PR2334.A17 1951   *LC* 51-6586

Bradbrook, M. C. (Muriel Clara), 1909-.   • **2.6502**
The school of night; a study in the literary relationships of Sir Walter Raleigh, by M. C. Bradbrook. — New York, Russell & Russell, 1965. viii, 189 p. 23 cm. 'First published in 1936.' Bibliographical references included in 'Notes' (p. 179-186) 1. Raleigh, Walter, Sir, 1552?-1618. 2. English poetry — Early modern (to 1700) — Hist. & crit. I. T.
PR2335.B7 1965   821.309   *LC* 65-18791

Edwards, Philip.   • **2.6503**
Sir Walter Raleigh. — London, Longmans [1953] xii, 184 p. illus., port., facsim. 19 cm. — (Men and books) Bibliography: p. 177-179. 1. Raleigh, Walter, Sir, 1552?-1618. I. T. II. Series.
PR2335.E48   *LC* A 55-6956

Davis, Richard Beale.   • **2.6504**
George Sandys, poet–adventurer: a study in Anglo–American culture in the seventeenth century. — London: The Bodley Head; New York: Columbia University Press, 1955. 320 p.: ill., ports.; 23 cm. 1. Sandys, George, 1578-1644. I. T.
PR2338.D3 1955   *LC* 55-7835

PR2340–2343 Sidney

Sidney, Philip, Sir, 1554-1586.   • **2.6505**
The complete works / [edited by Albert Feuillerat]. — [Cambridge: University Press, 1912-1926] 4 v.: ill. — (Cambridge English classics) Each vol. has separate t.p. I. Feuillerat, Albert, 1874-1953. II. T. III. Series.
PR2340.A5 F4   *LC* 22-8855

Sidney, Philip, Sir, 1554-1586.   • **2.6506**
The poems of Sir Philip Sidney / edited by William A. Ringler, Jr. — Oxford: Clarendon Press, 1962. lxx, 578 p.: diagr., facsim., port. I. Ringler, William A., 1912- II. T.
PR2340.A5 R5   *LC* 62-52433   *ISBN* 0198118341

Sidney, Philip, Sir, 1554-1586.   **2.6507**
Miscellaneous prose of Sir Philip Sidney, edited by Katherine Duncan–Jones and Jan van Dorsten. — Oxford: Clarendon Press, 1973. x, 238 p.: front.; 23 cm. I. Duncan-Jones, Katherine. ed. II. Dorsten, J. A. van. ed. III. T.
PR2341.D78   821/.3   *LC* 74-162046   *ISBN* 0198118805

Sidney, Philip, Sir, 1554-1586.   **2.6508**
The Countess of Pembroke's Arcadia (the old Arcadia). Edited with introd. and commentary by Jean Robertson. — Oxford: Clarendon Press, 1973. lxxi, 514 p.: map.; 23 cm. I. Robertson, Jean, ed. II. T. III. Title: Arcadia.
PR2342.A5 1973   823/.3   *LC* 73-163390

Three studies in the Renaissance: Sidney, Jonson, Milton.   • **2.6509**
[Hamden, Conn.]: Archon Books, 1969 [c1958] vii, 283 p.: coat of arms.; 23 cm. — (Yale studies in English. v. 138) 1. Sidney, Philip, Sir, 1554-1586. Astrophel and Stella. 2. Jonson, Ben, 1573?-1637. 3. Milton, John, 1608-1674 — Criticism and interpretation. 4. Nature in literature I. Series.
PR2342.A8T5 1969   820.9/003   *LC* 69-15695   *ISBN* 0208007806

Buxton, John, 1912-.   • **2.6510**
Sir Philip Sidney and the English Renaissance. [2d ed.] London: Macmillan; New York: St. Martin's Press, [1964] t.p. 1965. xi, 283 p.: facsim., ports.; 23 cm. 1. Sidney, Philip, Sir, 1554-1586. 2. Renaissance — Great Britain. I. T.
PR2343.B87 1964   *LC* 64-14954

Kalstone, David.   **2.6511**
Sidney's poetry: contexts and interpretations. — Cambridge, Harvard University Press, 1965. viii, 195 p. 22 cm. Bibliographical references included in 'Noted' (p. 185-192) 1. Sidney, Philip, Sir, 1554-1586. I. T.
PR2343.K3   821.3   *LC* 65-13846

Montgomery, Robert Langford.   • **2.6512**
Symmetry and sense; the poetry of Sir Philip Sidney, by Robert L. Montgomery, Jr. — New York: Greenwood Press, [1969, c1961] vii, 134 p.; 24 cm. 1. Sidney, Philip, Sir, 1554-1586. I. T.
PR2343.M63 1969   821/.3   *LC* 75-88911   *ISBN* 0837121027

Myrick, Kenneth Orne, 1897-.   • **2.6513**
Sir Philip Sidney as a literary craftsman, by Kenneth Myrick. — [2d ed.]. — Lincoln, University of Nebraska Press [c1965] viii, 362 p. 21 cm. — (A Bison book, BB312) 'Bibliography of Sidney studies since 1935': p. 352-358. Bibliographical footnotes. 1. Sidney, Philip, Sir, 1554-1586. I. T.
PR2343.M9 1965   821.3   *LC* 66-2785

Nichols, J. G. (John Gordon), 1930-.   **2.6514**
The poetry of Sir Philip Sidney: an interpretation in the context of his life and times / J. G. Nichols. — New York: Barnes & Noble Books, 1974. x, 171 p., [1] leaf of plates: port.; 23 cm. (English texts and studies) Includes indexes. 1. Sidney, Philip, Sir, 1554-1586 — Criticism and interpretation. I. T.
PR2343.N5   821/.3   *LC* 74-6715   *ISBN* 0064951634

Rose, Mark.   • **2.6515**
Heroic love: studies in Sidney and Spenser. — Cambridge, Mass.: Harvard University Press, 1968. vii, 156 p.; 22 cm. 1. Sidney, Philip, Sir, 1554-1586. 2. Spenser, Edmund, 1552?-1599. 3. Love in literature I. T. II. Title: Studies in Sidney and Spenser.
PR2343.R6   821/.3/09   *LC* 68-29182

PR2345–2348 Skelton

Skelton, John, 1460?-1529.   **2.6516**
[Selections. 1983] John Skelton, the complete English poems / edited by John Scattergood. — New Haven: Yale University Press, 1983. 573 p.; 21 cm. (English poets.) I. Scattergood, V. J. II. T. III. Title: Complete English poems. IV. Series.
PR2346.S3 1983   821/.2 19   *LC* 82-16075   *ISBN* 0300029705

Edwards, H. L. R.   • **2.6517**
Skelton, the life and times of an early Tudor poet, by H. L. R. Edwards. — Freeport, N.Y.: Books for Libraries Press, [1971] 325 p.; 23 cm. — (Library of Old English and medieval literature) Reprint of the 1949 ed. 1. Skelton, John, 1460?-1529. I. T.
PR2348.E4 1971   821/.2 B   *LC* 77-148879   *ISBN* 0836956737

Fish, Stanley Eugene.   • **2.6518**
John Skelton's poetry / by Stanley Eugene Fish. — New Haven: Yale University Press, 1965. viii, 268 p.: ill. — (Yale studies in English. 157) 1. Skelton, John, 1460?-1529 — Criticism and interpretation. I. T. II. Series.
PR2348.F5   821/.2   *LC* 65-11177

Heiserman, Arthur Ray, 1929-.   • **2.6519**
Skelton and satire. — [Chicago]: University of Chicago Press [1961] 326 p.; 23 cm. Includes bibliography. 1. Skelton, John, 1460?-1529. 2. Satire, English — Hist. & crit. I. T.
PR2348.H4   827.2   *LC* 61-5606

PR2349 Southwell

Southwell, Robert, Saint, 1561?-1595.   2.6520
The poems of Robert Southwell, S.J.; edited by James H. McDonald and Nancy Pollard Brown. — Oxford: Clarendon P., 1967. cvi, 180 p.: front. (facsim.).; 22 1/2 cm. I. McDonald, James Harold, ed. II. Brown, Nancy Pollard, ed. III. T.
PR2349.S5 1967   LC 67-97908

Devlin, Christopher.   • 2.6521
The life of Robert Southwell, poet and martyr. — New York: Greenwood Press, [1969] x, 367 p.; 23 cm. 1. Southwell, Robert, 1561?-1595. I. T.
PR2349.S5 Z65   821/.3 B   LC 72-90498

PR2350–2368 Spenser

Spenser, Edmund, 1552?-1599.   • 2.6522
The works of Edmund Spenser. A variorum ed., edited by Edwin Greenlaw, Charles Grosvenor Osgood [and] Frederick Morgan Padelford. Baltimore, Johns Hopkins Press [1966, c1932-57] 11 v. illus., facsims., maps, plans, ports. 26 cm. Each vol. has also special t. p. With reproductions of original title pages. Vols. 5-11 have additional editor, Ray Heffner. Includes bibliographies. I. Greenlaw, Edwin Almiron, 1874-1931. ed. II. Osgood, Charles Grosvenor, 1871-1964. ed. III. Padelford, Frederick Morgan, 1875-1942. ed. IV. T.
PR2351.G65 1966   828/.3/09   LC 66-26133

Spenser, Edmund, 1552?-1599.   • 2.6523
The poetical works of Edmund Spenser / edited with critical notes by J. C. Smith and E. De Selincourt; with an introduction by E. De Selincourt, and a glossary. — London; New York [etc.]: H. Milfrod, Oxford University Press, 1924. lxvii, 736 p.: front. (port.) ill.; 20 cm. Includes the correspondence of Spenser and Harvey, printed from the original editions of 1580. I. Smith, J. C. (James Cruickshanks), 1867-1946. ed. II. De Selincourt, Ernest, 1870-1943. ed. III. T.
PR2351.S5   LC 46-44615

Spenser, Edmund, 1552?-1599.   • 2.6524
Spenser's minor poems / edited by Ernest De Sélincourt. — Oxford: Clarendon Press, 1910. xxxi, 528 p.: ill. — (The poetical works of Edmund Spenser: vol. 1) A companion volume to J.C. Smith's edition of The faerie queene. cf. Introduction. 'The aim of this volume is to present a trustworthy text ... based upon a collation of the editions published in the poet's lifetime with the folio of 1611.'—Introd. With reproductions of original title-pages. I. De Selincourt, Ernest, 1870-1943. II. T.
PR2352 D47 1910   LC 11-1754

Spenser, Edmund, 1552?-1599.   2.6525
The faerie queene / Edmund Spenser; edited by A. C. Hamilton. — 3d ed. — London; New York: Longman, 1977. xiii, 753 p.; 25 cm. — (Longman annotated English poets) I. Hamilton, A. C. (Albert Charles), 1921- II. T.
PR2358.A3 H27 1977   821/.3   LC 77-2738   ISBN 0582481066

Alpers, Paul J.   • 2.6526
The poetry of the Faerie queene, by Paul J. Alpers. [Princeton, N.J.] Princeton University Press, 1967. ix, 415 p. 1. Spenser, Edmund, 1552?-1599. Faerie queene I. T.
PR2358 A87   LC 67-14405

Brooks-Davies, Douglas.   2.6527
Spenser's Faerie queene: a critical commentary on books I and II / Douglas Brooks-Davies. — Manchester, Eng.: Manchester University Press; Totowa, N.J.: Rowman and Littlefield, 1978 (c1977). x, 198 p.: ill.; 20 cm. 1. Spenser, Edmund, 1552?-1599. The faerie queene. I. T.
PR2358.B75 1977   821/.3   LC 78-300630   ISBN 0874718295

Dunseath, T. K.   • 2.6528
Spenser's allegory of justice in book five of the Faerie queene, by T. K. Dunseath. — Princeton, N.J.: Princeton University Press, 1968. vii, 244 p.; 23 cm. 1. Spenser, Edmund, 1552?-1599. Faerie queene I. T.
PR2358.D8   821/.3   LC 68-10390

Freeman, Rosemary.   • 2.6529
The Faerie queene: a companion for readers. — Berkeley: University of California Press, 1970. 350 p.; 23 cm. 1. Spenser, Edmund, 1552?-1599. Faerie queene I. T.
PR2358.F7   821/.3   LC 70-116114   ISBN 0520017323

Giamatti, A. Bartlett.   2.6530
Play of double senses: Spenser's Faerie queene [by] A. Bartlett Giamatti. — Englewood Cliffs, N.J.: Prentice-Hall, [1975] xi, 140 p.; 21 cm. — (Landmarks in literature) 1. Spenser, Edmund, 1552?-1599. Faerie queene I. T.
PR2358.G5   821/.3   LC 74-18253   ISBN 0136833837

Hamilton, A. C.   • 2.6531
The structure of allegory in the Faerie queene. — Oxford, Clarendon Press, 1961. 227 p. 22 cm. A revision and expansion of the author's thesis, Cambridge University. Bibliographical footnotes. 1. Spenser, Edmund, 1552?-1599. Faerie queene 2. Allegory I. T.
PR2358.H28   821.3   LC 61-19484

Hankins, John Erskine, 1905-.   • 2.6532
Source and meaning in Spenser's allegory: a study of The faerie queene. — Oxford: Clarendon Press, 1971. viii, 337 p.; 23 cm. 1. Spenser, Edmund, 1552?-1599. Faerie queene — Sources. 2. Allegory I. T.
PR2358.H29   821/.3   LC 72-181312   ISBN 0198120133

Hough, Graham Goulden, 1908-.   • 2.6533
A preface to The faerie queene. — [1st American ed.]. — New York: Norton, [1963, c1962] 238 p.: ill.; 22 cm. 1. Spenser, Edmund, 1552?-1599. Faerie queene I. T.
PR2358.H6 1963   821.3   LC 63-9880

MacCaffrey, Isabel Gamble.   2.6534
Spenser's allegory: the anatomy of imagination / Isabel G. MacCaffrey. — Princeton, N.J.: Princeton University Press, c1976. xii, 445 p.; 23 cm. 1. Spenser, Edmund, 1552?-1599. Faerie queene 2. Spenser, Edmund, 1552?-1599 — Symbolism. 3. Allegory I. T.
PR2358.M3   821/.3   LC 75-30197   ISBN 0691063060

Parker, Pauline.   • 2.6535
The allegory of The Faerie Queene. — Oxford, Clarendon Press, 1960. 326 p. 23 cm. 1. Spenser, Edmund, 1552?-1599. Faerie queene I. T.
PR2358.P35   821.3   LC 60-2479

Rose, Mark.   2.6536
Spenser's art: a companion to book one of The faerie queene / Mark Rose. — Cambridge, Mass.: Harvard University Press, 1975. x, 159 p.; 22 cm. 1. Spenser, Edmund, 1552?-1599. Faerie queene I. T.
PR2358.R66   821/.3   LC 74-21229   ISBN 0674831934

Sale, Roger.   • 2.6537
Reading Spenser; an introduction to the Faerie queene. — New York: Random House, [1968] viii, 209 p.; 19 cm. — (Studies in language and literature, SLL20) 1. Spenser, Edmund, 1552?-1599. Faerie queene I. T.
PR2358.S2   821/.3   LC 68-13466

Warton, Thomas, 1728-1790.   • 2.6538
Observations on the Fairy queen of Spenser. — 2d ed., corr. and enl. — New York: Greenwood Press, [1968] 2 v.; 23 cm. Reprint of the 2d ed., 1762. 1. Spenser, Edmund, 1552?-1599. Faerie queene I. T.
PR2358.W3 1968   821/.3   LC 68-31011

Williams, Kathleen.   2.6539
Spenser's world of glass; a reading of the Faerie queene. — Berkeley, University of California Press, 1966. xx, 241 p. 23 cm. London ed. (Routledge & K. Paul) has title: Spenser's Faerie queene. Bibliographical footnotes. 1. Spenser, Edmund, 1552?-1599. Faerie queene I. T.
PR2358.W5 1966a   821.3   LC 66-19188

Cullen, Patrick, 1940-.   • 2.6540
Spenser, Marvell, and Renaissance pastoral. — Cambridge, Mass.: Harvard University Press, 1970. ix, 212 p.; 24 cm. 1. Spenser, Edmund, 1552?-1599. Shepheardes calender. 2. Marvell, Andrew, 1621-1678. 3. Pastoral poetry, English — History and criticism. I. T.
PR2359.C8   821/.00913   LC 76-123566   ISBN 0674831950

PR2362–2368 Biography. Criticism

Osgood, Charles Grosvenor, 1871-1964.   • 2.6541
A concordance to the poems of Edmund Spenser. — Gloucester, Mass.: P. Smith, 1963. xiii, 997 p.: port. 1. Spenser, Edmund, 1552?-1599 — Concordances. I. T.
PR2362.O7 1963   LC 63-6151

Bradner, Leicester, 1899-.   2.6542
Edmund Spenser and the Faerie Queene. — [Chicago]: Univ. of Chicago Press, [1948] xi, 189 p.; 20 cm. 1. Spenser, Edmund, 1552?-1599. I. T.
PR2363.B7   821.31   LC 48-6359 *

Jones, Harry Stuart Vedder, 1878-1942.   • 2.6543
A Spenser handbook / by H. S. V. Jones ... — New York: F. S. Crofts & co., 1930. viii p., 1 l., 419 p.: front. (port.); 20 cm. 1. Spenser, Edmund, 1552?-1599. I. T.
PR2363.J6   821.31   LC 31-3371 rev

Shire, Helena Mennie.   2.6544
A preface to Spenser / Helena Shire. — London; New York: Longman, 1979. xii, 196 p.: ill.; 22 cm. — (Preface books) Includes indexes. 1. Spenser,

Edmund, 1552?-1599. 2. Poets, English — Early modern, 1500-1700 — Biography. I. T.
PR2363.S5   821/.3 B   *LC* 76-23272   *ISBN* 0582315115

Nelson, William, 1908-.   ● **2.6545**
The poetry of Edmund Spenser: a study. — New York, Columbia University Press, 1963. 350 p. 23 cm. Includes bibliography. 1. Spenser, Edmund, 1552?-1599. I. T.
PR2364.N4   821.3   *LC* 63-9871

Ellrodt, Robert.   **2.6546**
Neoplatonism in the poetry of Spenser / Robert Ellrodt. — Folcroft, Pa.: Folcroft Library Editions, 1975. 246 p.; 26 cm. A revision of the author's thesis. Reprint of the 1960 ed. published by E. Droz, Geneva, which was issued as no. 35 of Travaux d'humanisme et Renaissance. Includes indexes. 1. Spenser, Edmund, 1552?-1599 — Criticism and interpretation. 2. Plato — Influence — Spenser. I. T.
PR2366.E4 1975   821/.3   *LC* 75-11942   *ISBN* 0841439915 lib. bdg

PR2369–2405 S–Z

Surrey, Henry Howard, Earl of, 1517?-1547.   ● **2.6547**
Poems. Appreciations by Thomas Warton [and others] With an introd., notes and glossary by Emrys Jones. — Oxford, Clarendon Press, 1964. xxxiv, 169 p. port. 19 cm. — (Clarendon medieval and Tudor series) Bibliographical references included in 'Biographical and textual notes' (p. xxvi-xxviii) and in 'Notes' (p. 103-160) I. Jones, Emrys Maldwyn, ed. II. T.
PR2370.A5J6   821.2   *LC* 64-6169

Wither, George, 1588-1667.   ● **2.6548**
The poetry of George Wither / edited by Frank Sidgwick. London, A. H. Bullen, 1902. — St. Clair Shores, Mich.: Scholarly Press, 1970. 2 v.: facsims., geneal. table.; 21 cm. I. Sidgwick, Frank. ed. II. T.
PR2390.A2 1970   821/.4   *LC* 71-107195   *ISBN* 0403002362

Wyatt, Thomas, Sir, 1503?-1542.   **2.6549**
[Complete poems] Sir Thomas Wyatt, The complete poems / edited by R. A. Rebholz. — New Haven: Yale University Press, 1981. 558 p; 20 cm. (The English poets; 5) Includes index. I. Rebholz, Ronald A. II. T.
PR2400.A5 R4 1981   821/.2 19   *LC* 80-53980   *ISBN* 0300026811

Hangen, Eva Catherine.   ● **2.6550**
A concordance to the complete poetical works of Sir Thomas Wyatt. Chicago, University of Chicago Press [c1941]. — New York: Johnson Reprint Corp., [1969] xviii, 527 p.; 20 cm. 1. Wyatt, Thomas, Sir, 1503?-1542 — Concordances. I. T.
PR2403.A3 H3 1969   821/.2   *LC* 72-6561

Thomson, Patricia.   ● **2.6551**
Sir Thomas Wyatt and his background / by Patricia Thomson. — Stanford, Calif.: Stanford University Press, 1965, c1964. xiv, 298 p. 1. Wyatt, Thomas, Sir, 1508?-1542. I. T.
PR2403.T4   *LC* 64-7650

Thomson, Patricia. comp.   **2.6552**
Wyatt, the critical heritage / edited by Patricia Thomson. — London; Boston: Routledge and K. Paul, 1974. ix, 186 p.; 23 cm. (The Critical heritage series) Includes index. 1. Wyatt, Thomas, Sir, 1503?-1542 — Criticism and interpretation — Addresses, essays, lectures. I. T.
PR2404.T5 1974   821/.2   *LC* 74-79362   *ISBN* 0710079079

PR2411–3199 English Renaissance (1500–1640) Drama

(Prose, Poetry: see: PR2199-2405)

PR2411 Anonymous Plays

Second maiden's tragedy.   **2.6553**
The second maiden's tragedy / edited by Anne Lancashire. — Manchester: Manchester University Press; Baltimore: Johns Hopkins University Press, 1978. xix, 317 p.; 21 cm. — (The Revels plays) Attributed to Thomas Middleton. Cf. introd. I. Lancashire, Anne Begor. II. Middleton, Thomas, d. 1627. III. T.
PR2411.S3 1978   PR2411 S3 1978.   822/.3   *LC* 77-4604   *ISBN* 0801820111

PR2420–2438 Beaumont. Fletcher

Beaumont, Francis, 1584-1616.   ● **2.6554**
The dramatic works in the Beaumont and Fletcher canon; general editor Fredson Bowers. Cambridge, Cambridge U.P., 1966-. v. table. 23 cm. I. Fletcher, John, 1579-1625. joint author. II. Bowers, Fredson Thayer. ed. III. T.
PR2420 1966   822.3 19   *LC* 66-74421

Beaumont, Francis, 1584-1616.   ● **2.6555**
A king and no king / Beaumont and Fletcher; edited by Robert K. Turner, Jr. — Lincoln: University of Nebraska Press, [1963] xxx, 154 p. 22 cm. — (Regents Renaissance drama series) I. Fletcher, John, 1579-1625. joint author. II. T.
PR2426.K5 1963   821.3   *LC* 63-14698

Beaumont, Francis, 1584-1616.   **2.6556**
Philaster [by] Beaumont and Fletcher. Edited by Dora Jean Ashe. — Lincoln: University of Nebraska Press, [1974] xxxii, 152 p.; 21 cm. — (Regents Renaissance drama series) I. Fletcher, John, 1579-1625. joint author. II. Ashe, Dora Jean. ed. III. T.
PR2429.A12   822/.3   *LC* 75-127980   *ISBN* 0803202911

Waith, Eugene M.   ● **2.6557**
The pattern of tragicomedy in Beaumont and Fletcher, by Eugene M. Waith. — [Hamden, Conn.]: Archon Books, 1969 [c1952] xiv, 212 p.; 23 cm. — (Yale studies in English. v. 120) 1. Beaumont, Francis, 1584-1616 — Criticism and interpretation. 2. Fletcher, John, 1579-1625 — Criticism and interpretation. I. T. II. Series.
PR2434.W285 1969   822/.3/09   *LC* 69-15694   *ISBN* 0208007776

Wallis, Lawrence Bergmann, 1897-.   ● **2.6558**
Fletcher, Beaumont & company; entertainers to the Jacobean gentry [by] Lawrence B. Wallis. — New York: Octagon Books, 1968 [c1947] xx, 315 p.; 24 cm. 1. Fletcher, John, 1579-1625. 2. Beaumont, Francis, 1584-1616. 3. English drama — Early modern and Elizabethan, 1500-1600 — History and criticism. I. T.
PR2434.W3 1968   822/.3/09   *LC* 68-22292

Wilson, John Harold, 1900-.   ● **2.6559**
The influence of Beaumont and Fletcher on Restoration drama. — New York: Haskell House, 1969. vii, 156 p.; 23 cm. Reprint of the 1928 ed. 1. Beaumont, Francis, 1584-1616. 2. Fletcher, John, 1579-1625. 3. English drama — Restoration — History and criticism. I. T.
PR2434.W5 1969   822/.3   *LC* 68-57458   *ISBN* 0838306454

PR2439.B5 Brome

Brome, Richard, d. 1652?   **2.6560**
[English Moor] The English Moore, or, The Mock–mariage / by Richard Brome; edited by Sara Jayne Steen. — Columbia: University of Missouri Press, 1983. x, 164 p.; 24 cm. Originally published as The English Moor. Includes index. I. Steen, Sara Jayne, 1949- II. T.
PR2439.B5 E5 1983   822/.4 19   *LC* 83-1095   *ISBN* 0826204031

PR2440–2458 Chapman

Chapman, George, 1559?-1634.   ● **2.6561**
The tragedies. Edited with introductions and notes by Thomas Marc Parrott. — New York, Russell & Russell, 1961. 2 v. (xiii, 730 p.) 22 cm. — (His Plays) Bibliographical references included in 'Notes' (p. [539]-730) I. Parrott, Thomas Marc, 1866-1960. ed. II. T.
PR2442.P33   822.3   *LC* 61-13786

Chapman, George, 1559?-1634.   ● **2.6562**
Poems / edited by Phyllis Brooks Bartlett. — New York: Russell & Russell, 1962, c1941. xii, 488 p.: port. I. Bartlett, Phyllis Brooks. II. T.
PR2450.P6 1962   *LC* 62-13830

Rees, Ennis.   ● **2.6563**
The tragedies of George Chapman: Renaissance ethics in action. Cambridge, Harvard University Press, 1954. 223 p. 22 cm. 1. Chapman, George, 1559?-1634. I. T.
PR2453.R4   *LC* 54-9333

PR2459–2499 C–D

Daniel, Samuel, 1562-1619.   ● **2.6564**
The tragedy of Philotas, by Samuel Daniel. Edited, with introd. and notes, by Laurence Michel. — [Hamden, Conn.]: Archon Books, 1970 [c1949] xi, 185 p.: facsim.; 24 cm. — (Yale studies in English. v. 110) 'In its original form ... submitted as [the editor's] ... dissertation ... at Fordham University.' Reprint of

the 1949 ed., with a new pref. by the editor. I. Michel. Laurence Anthony, ed. II. T. III. Series.
PR2464.P45 1970   822/.3   LC 72-120780   ISBN 020800923X

Rees, Joan. • **2.6565**
Samuel Daniel, a critical and biographical study. — [Liverpool]: Liverpool University Press, 1964. xiii, 183 p.: ill., facsim., ports. — (Liverpool English texts and studies) 1. Daniel, Samuel, 1562-1619. I. T. II. Series.
PR2466.R4   LC 66-33454

D'Avenant, William, Sir, 1606-1668. • **2.6566**
Dramatic works. With prefatory memoir and notes. — New York, Russell & Russell, 1964. 5 v. 23 cm. I. T.
PR2471.M3 1964   821.4   LC 64-23459

Harbage, Alfred, 1901-. • **2.6567**
Sir William Davenant, poet venturer, 1606–1668. — New York: Octagon Books, 1971 [c1935] 317 p.: port.; 24 cm. 1. D'Avenant, William, Sir, 1606-1668. I. T.
PR2476.H3 1971   821/.4 B   LC 75-120624   ISBN 0374936595

Dekker, Thomas, ca. 1572-1632. • **2.6568**
Dramatic works of Thomas Dekker. / Edited by Fredson Bowers. Cambridge, Eng.: University P., 1953-61. 4 v.: facsims. I. Bowers, Fredson Thayer. II. T.
PR2481.B6   822.3   LC 53-13115 rev.

Dekker, Thomas, ca. 1572-1632. • **2.6569**
The non–dramatic works of Thomas Dekker: For the first time collected and edited with memorial–introd. notes and illustrations, etc. / by Alexander B. Grosart. — New York: Russell & Russell, 1963. 5 v.: ill. — Limited ed. of 400 sets. I. Grosart, Alexander Balloch, 1827-1899. II. T.
PR2481 G76 1963   LC 63-15156

Dekker, Thomas, ca. 1572-1632. • **2.6570**
The shoemaker's holiday / Thomas Dekker; edited by J.B. Steane. — Cambridge: University Press, 1965. 140 p.: ill. I. Steane, J. B. II. T.
PR2490.A1 1965   822.3   LC 65-15305

Dekker, Thomas, ca. 1572-1632. **2.6571**
The shoemaker's holiday / Thomas Dekker; edited and with an introd. by Merritt Lawlis. — Woodbury, N.Y.: Barron's Educational Series, inc., c1979. xxvii, 82 p.; 20 cm. I. Lawlis, Merritt E., 1918- II. T.
PR2490.A1 1979b   822/.3   LC 78-14915   ISBN 0812003144

Price, George R. **2.6572**
Thomas Dekker, by George R. Price. New York, Twayne Publishers [1969] 189 p. 21 cm. (Twayne's English authors series, 71) 1. Dekker, Thomas, ca. 1572-1632. I. T.
PR2493.P7   822/.3   LC 68-17241

PR2500–2549 F–G

Leech, Clifford. • **2.6573**
The John Fletcher plays. — Cambridge, Harvard University Press, 1962. 179 p. 23 cm. 1. Fletcher, John, 1579-1625. I. T.
PR2514.L4   822.3   LC 62-144

Ford, John, 1586-ca. 1640. • **2.6574**
Five plays. Edited with an introd. and notes by Havelock Ellis. — New York: Hill and Wang, 1957. xvi, 427 p.; 19 cm. — (A Mermaid dramabook, MD4) I. Ellis, Havelock, 1859-1939. ed. II. T.
PR2522.E5 1957   822.38   LC 57-5839

Ford, John, 1586-ca. 1640. **2.6575**
'Tis pity she's a whore / John Ford; edited by Derek Roper. London: Methuen; [New York]: distributed by Harper & Row, 1975. lxxi, 146 p.: port.; 21 cm. (The Revels plays) I. Roper, Derek. II. T.
PR2524.T5 1975   822/.3   LC 76-365543   ISBN 0416670709

Anderson, Donald K., 1922-. **2.6576**
John Ford, by Donald K. Anderson, Jr. — New York: Twayne Publishers, [1972] 160 p.; 22 cm. — (Twayne's English authors series, TEAS 129) 1. Ford, John, 1586-ca. 1640. I. T.
PR2527.A5   822/.3   LC 74-180740

Leech, Clifford. • **2.6577**
John Ford and the drama of his time. — London, Chatto & Windus; [label: Fair Lawn, N. J., Essential Books] 1957. 144 p. 21 cm. 1. Ford, John, 1586-ca. 1640. I. T.
PR2527.L4   822.38   LC 57 1302

Oliver, H. J. (Harold James) • **2.6578**
The problem of John Ford. — [Carlton, Victoria] Melbourne University Press [1955] 146 p. 22 cm. 1. Ford, John, 1586-ca. 1640. I. T.
PR2527.O6   LC 56-309

Stavig, Mark. • **2.6579**
John Ford and the traditional moral order. — Madison: University of Wisconsin Press, 1968. xx, 225 p.; 23 cm. 1. Ford, John, 1586-ca. 1640. I. T.
PR2527.S7   828/.3/09   LC 68-14030

Farr, Dorothy Mary. **2.6580**
John Ford and the Caroline theatre / Dorothy M. Farr. — New York: Barnes & Noble Books, 1979. ix, 184 p.; 22 cm. Includes index. 1. Ford, John, 1586-ca. 1640 — Stage history. 2. Ford, John, 1586-ca. 1640 — Criticism and interpretation. 3. Theater — England — History. I. T.
PR2528.S75 F3 1979   822/.3   LC 78-12679   ISBN 0064920658

Prouty, Charles Tyler, 1909-. • **2.6581**
George Gascoigne, Elizabethan courtier, soldier, and poet / by C.T. Prouty. — New York: Benjamin Blom, 1966 [c1942] xii, 351 p. 1. Gascoigne, George, 1525?-1577. I. T.
PR2536.P7   LC 65-19620

Greene, Robert, 1558?-1592. • **2.6582**
The plays & poems of Robert Greene. Edited with introductions and notes, by J. Churton Collins. — Freeport, N.Y.: Books for Libraries Press, [1970] 2 v.: facsims.; 23 cm. — (Library of English Renaissance literature) Reprint of the 1905 ed. I. Collins, John Churton, 1848-1908. ed. II. T.
PR2541.C6 1970   823/.3/09   LC 79-119957   ISBN 0836954009

Jordan, John Clark, 1883-. **2.6583**
Robert Greene, by John Clark Jordan. New York, Columbia University Press, 1915. x p., 1 l., 231 p. 21 cm. (Columbia University studies in English and comparative literature) 1. Greene, Robert, 1558?-1592. I. T. II. Series.
PR2546.J6   LC 15-20972

PR2560–2578 J. Heywood. T. Heywood

Heywood, John, 1497?-1580? • **2.6584**
Works, and miscellaneous short poems / edited, with an introduction and notes, by Burton A. Milligan. — Urbana: University of Illinois Press, 1956. xi, 297 p.; 26 cm. — (Illinois studies in language and literature. v. 41) I. Milligan, Burton Alviere, 1903- II. T. III. Series.
PR2564.P7 1956   LC 56-5679

Heywood, Thomas, d. 1641. • **2.6585**
A woman killed with kindness. Edited by R. W. Van Fossen. — Cambridge, Harvard University Press [1961] lxxii, 122 p. facsim. 21 cm. — (The Revels plays) I. Van Fossen, R. W., ed. II. T.
PR2574.W8 1961   822.2   LC 61-65783

Baines, Barbara J. (Barbara Joan) **2.6586**
Thomas Heywood / by Barbara J. Baines. — Boston: Twayne, c1984. 178 p.: facsim.; 23 cm. (Twayne's English authors series. TEAS 388) Includes index. 1. Heywood, Thomas, d. 1641 — Criticism and interpretation. I. T. II. Series.
PR2577.B35 1984   822/.3 19   LC 84-10768   ISBN 0805768742

PR2600–2648 Jonson

Jonson, Ben, 1573?-1637. • **2.6587**
Ben Jonson / edited by C.H. Herford and Percy Simpson. Oxford: Clarendon P., 1925-52. 11v.illus. Vols. 6-11 edited by C.H. Herford, Percy and Evelyn Simpson. I. Herford, C.H. II. Simpson, Percy. III. Simpson, Evelyn. IV. T.
PR2601 H4   LC 25-21613

Jonson, Ben, 1573?-1637. **2.6588**
[Plays and masques] Ben Jonson's plays and masques: texts of the plays and masques, Jonson on his work, contemporary readers on Jonson, criticism / selected and edited by Robert M. Adams. — 1st ed. — New York: Norton, c1979. ix, 502 p.; 21 cm. — (A Norton critical edition) 1. Jonson, Ben, 1573?-1637 — Criticism and interpretation — Addresses, essays, lectures. I. Adams, Robert Martin, 1915- II. T.
PR2602.A3 1979   822/.3   LC 78-7325   ISBN 0393045064

Jonson, Ben, 1573?-1637. • **2.6589**
Bartholomew fair, edited by E. A. Horsman. London, Methuen [1968, c1960] xxxii, 176 p. 22 cm. (The Revels plays) I. Horsman, E. A. (Ernest Alan), 1918- ed. II. T.
PR2606.A16 1968   822/.3   LC 73-27631   ISBN 0416612806

Jonson, Ben, 1573?-1637. • **2.6590**
Every man in his humor, edited by Gabriele Bernhard Jackson. — New Haven: Yale University Press, 1969. ix, 250 p.; 22 cm. — (His The Yale Ben Jonson, 5) I. Jackson, Gabriele Bernhard, ed. II. T.
PR2613.A145   822/.3   LC 77-81419

Jonson, Ben, 1573?-1637. • 2.6591
Volpone. Edited by Alvin B. Kernan. — New Haven: Yale University Press, 1962. ix, 231 p.; 21 cm. — (The Yale Ben Jonson) I. T.
PR2622.A143   822.3   *LC* 61-14945

Jonson, Ben, 1573?-1637. 2.6592
The complete poems / Ben Jonson; edited by George Parfitt. — New Haven: Yale University Press, 1982. 634 p.; 21 cm. — (English poets.) Includes indexes. I. Parfitt, George A. E. II. T. III. Series.
PR2625.A2 1982   821/.3 19   *LC* 81-15948   *ISBN* 0300028253

Jonson, Ben, 1573?-1637. • 2.6593
Complete poetry. Edited with an introd., notes, and variants by William B. Hunter, Jr. [1st ed.] Garden City, N. Y., Anchor Books, 1963. xvi, 494 p. facsims. 20 cm. (The Anchor seventeenth-century series) Includes music. I. Hunter, William Bridges, 1915- ed. II. T. III. Series.
PR2625.A3H8   *LC* 63-8752

Jonson, Ben, 1573?-1637. • 2.6594
Timber; or, Discoveries [edited by] Ralph S. Walker. [Syracuse, N.Y.] Syracuse University Press, 1953. vi, 135 p. 23 cm. 1. Jonson, Ben, 1573?-1637. 2. Jonson, Ben, 1573?-1637. Conversations with William Drummond. I. Walker, Ralph Spence, 1904- II. T. III. Title: Discoveries.
PR2626.T5 1953   824.3   *LC* 53-13371

Chute, Marchette Gaylord, 1909-. • 2.6595
Ben Jonson of Westminster. — [1st ed.]. — New York: Dutton, 1953. 380 p.: illus.; 23 cm. I. Jonson, Ben, 1573?-1637. II. T.
PR2631.C53   928.2   *LC* 53-10335

Dutton, Richard, 1948-. 2.6596
Ben Jonson: to the first folio / Richard Dutton. — Cambridge [Cambridgeshire]; New York: Cambridge University Press, 1983. xi, 188 p.; 22 cm. — (British and Irish authors.) Includes index. 1. Jonson, Ben, 1573?-1637. 2. Authors, English — Early modern, 1500-1700 — Biography. I. T. II. Series.
PR2631.D8 1983   822/.3 19   *LC* 83-1819   *ISBN* 0521243130

Barton, Anne. 2.6597
Ben Jonson, dramatist / Anne Barton. — Cambridge; New York: Cambridge University Press, 1984. xiv, 370 p.; 24 cm. Includes index. 1. Jonson, Ben, 1573?-1637 — Criticism and interpretation. I. T.
PR2638.B28 1984   822/.3 19   *LC* 83-23196   *ISBN* 0521258839

Beaurline, Lester A. 2.6598
Jonson and Elizabethan comedy: essays in dramatic rhetoric / L. A. Beaurline. — San Marino, [Calif.]: Huntington Library, 1978. xi, 351 p.: ill.; 24 cm. 1. Jonson, Ben, 1573?-1637 — Criticism and interpretation. I. T.
PR2638.B4   PR2638 B4.   822/.3   *LC* 77-75148   *ISBN* 0873280717

Bryant, J. A. (Joseph Allen), 1919-. 2.6599
The compassionate satirist: Ben Jonson and his imperfect world [by] J. A. Bryant, Jr. Athens, University of Georgia Press [c1972] ix, 195 p. 24 cm. (South Atlantic Modern Language Association. Award study) 1. Jonson, Ben, 1573?-1637 — Criticism and interpretation. I. T.
PR2638.B7   822/.3   *LC* 73-81623   *ISBN* 082030316X

Dessen, Alan C., 1935-. • 2.6600
Jonson's moral comedy [by] Alan C. Dessen. — [Evanston, Ill.]: Northwestern University Press, 1971. ix, 256 p.; 22 cm. 1. Jonson, Ben, 1573?-1637 — Criticism and interpretation. I. T.
PR2638.D47   822/.3   *LC* 76-126900   *ISBN* 0810103184

Parfitt, George A. E. 2.6601
Ben Jonson, public poet and private man / George Parfitt. [New York]: Barnes & Noble Books, 1977, c1976. viii, 181 p.; 23 cm. Includes index. 1. Jonson, Ben, 1573?-1637 — Criticism and interpretation. I. T.
PR2638.P27 1977   822/.3   *LC* 76-40877   *ISBN* 0064953858

Partridge, Edward Bellamy, 1916-. • 2.6602
The broken compass; a study of the major comedies of Ben Jonson. — New York, Columbia University Press, 1958. 254 p. 23 cm. Issued in 1950 in microfilm form, as thesis, Columbia University, under title: The broken compass; a study of the imagery in Ben Jonson's comedies. Includes bibliography. 1. Jonson, Ben, 1573?-1637. 2. Figures of speech I. T.
PR2638.P3 1958   822.34   *LC* 58-59412

Summers, Claude J. 2.6603
Ben Jonson / by Claude J. Summers and Ted–Larry Pebworth. — Boston: Twayne Publishers, 1979. 233 p.: port.; 21 cm. — (Twayne's English authors series; TEAS 268) Includes index. 1. Jonson, Ben, 1573?-1637 — Criticism and interpretation. I. Pebworth, Ted-Larry. joint author. II. T.
PR2638.S69   822/.3   *LC* 79-12102   *ISBN* 0805767649

Trimpi, Wesley. • 2.6604
Ben Jonson's poems: a study of the plain style. — Stanford, Calif.: Stanford University Press, 1962. x, 292 p.; 24 cm. Includes indexes. 1. Jonson, Ben, 1573?-1637. I. T.
PR2638 T7   821.3   *LC* 62-9564

Barish, Jonas A. • 2.6605
Ben Jonson and the language of prose comedy / Jonas A. Barish. — Cambridge, Mass.: Harvard University Press, 1960. viii, 335 p.; 22 cm. 1. Jonson, Ben, 1573?-1637. 2. English drama (Comedy) — History and criticism. I. T.
PR2644.B3   *LC* 60-7987

PR2650–2658 Kyd. Lindsay

Kyd, Thomas, 1558-1594. • 2.6606
The works of Thomas Kyd. Ed. from the original texts, with introduction, notes, and facsimiles by Frederick S. Boas ... — Oxford, the Clarendon press, 1901. 2 p. l., [vii]-cxvi, 470 p., 1 l. 2 fold. facsim. (incl. front.) 23 cm. I. Boas, Frederick S. (Frederick Samuel), 1862-1957. ed. II. Ayrer, Jacob, d. 1605. III. Marlowe, Christopher, 1564-1593. IV. T.
PR2651.B6   *LC* 02-7537

Kyd, Thomas, 1598-1594. • 2.6607
The Spanish tragedy. Edited by Philip Edwards. Cambridge: Harvard University Press, 1959. ixx, 153 p.; 21 cm. (Revels plays.) Added t.p., facsim. of the 1615 ed. 'Abbreviations excluding texts': p. xiii-xv. 'Editions cited in the notes': p. lxix-lxx. I. Edwards, Philip. II. T. III. Series.
PR2654 S7 1959   *LC* 60-4133

Lindsay, David, Sir, fl. 1490-1555. 2.6608
[Satyre of the thrie estates] A satire of the three estates, by Sir David Lindsay: a play adapted by Matthew McDiarmid from the acting text made by Robert Kemp for Tyrone Guthrie's production at the Edinburgh Festival 1948 with music by Cedric Thorpe–Davie; introduction and notes by Matthew McDiarmid. [New ed.]. London, Heinemann, 1967. 171 p. 19 1/2 cm. Published in 1602 under title: Ane satyre of the thrie estaits. I. McDiarmid, Matthew P. II. Kemp, Robert, 1908- III. T.
PR2659.L5 A7 1967   822/.2   *LC* 67-88635

PR2660–2678 Marlowe

Marlowe, Christopher, 1564-1593. • 2.6609
The poems [of] Christopher Marlowe; edited by Millar MacLure. — London: Methuen, 1968. xliv, 271 p.: 3 facsims.; 21 cm. — (The Revels plays) The Revels edition of the works of Christopher Marlowe. I. MacLure, Millar, ed. II. T.
PR2662.M22   821/.3   *LC* 77-362432

Marlowe, Christopher, 1564-1593. • 2.6610
[Selected works. 1963] Complete plays. Edited, with an introd. and notes by Irving Ribner. New York, Odyssey Press [1963] xl, 432 p. facsims. 21 cm. I. Ribner, Irving. ed. II. T.
PR2662.R5 1963   822.3   *LC* 63-12619

Marlowe, Christopher, 1564-1593. • 2.6611
The tragical history of the life and death of Doctor Faustus / a conjectural reconstruction by W.W. Greg. Oxford: Clarendon Press, c1950. x, 66 p. I. T. II. Title: Doctor Faustus.
PR2664.A   *LC* 51-440

Marlowe, Christopher, 1564-1593. • 2.6612
Edward II: a play / edited by H. B. Charlton and R. D. Waller. New York: Gordian Press, 1966. ix, 226 p.; 23 cm. — (His Works and life; 6) 1. Edward II, King of England, 1284-1327 — Drama. I. Charlton, H. B. (Henry Buckley), 1890- ed. II. Waller, Ross Douglas. ed. III. T.
PR2665.A1 1966   *LC* 66-5191

Bakeless, John Edwin, 1894-. • 2.6613
The tragicall history of Christopher Marlowe, by John Bakeless. — Westport, Conn.: Greenwood Press, [1970, c1942] 2 v.: illus., facsims., map.; 23 cm. 1. Marlowe, Christopher, 1564-1593. I. T.
PR2673.B32 1970   822/.3 B   *LC* 70-106681   *ISBN* 0837133521

Boas, Frederick S. (Frederick Samuel), 1862-1957. • 2.6614
Christopher Marlowe, biographical and critical study / by Frederick S. Boas. — Oxford: Clarendon Press, 1940. x, 336 p.: ill., double map, facsims, (part double) 1. Marlowe, Christopher, 1564-1593. I. T.
PR2673.B58   *LC* 41-3078

Hotson, Leslie, 1897-. • 2.6615
The death of Christopher Marlowe, by J. Leslie Hotson. — New York: Russell & Russell, [1967] 76 p.: facsims., maps.; 22 cm. Reprint of the 1925 ed. 1. Marlowe, Christopher, 1564-1593. I. T.
PR2673.H6 1967   821/.3   *LC* 67-18292

Kocher, Paul Harold, 1907-.   • **2.6616**
Christopher Marlowe, a study of his thought, learning, and character. — New York: Russell & Russell, 1962 [c1946] 344 p.; 22 cm. 1. Marlowe, Christopher, 1564-1593. I. T.
PR2673.K6 1962   *LC* 61-13761

Levin, Harry, 1912-.   • **2.6617**
The overreacher, a study of Christopher Marlowe. — Cambridge: Harvard University Press, 1952. xii, 204 p.; 22 cm. 1. Marlowe, Christopher, 1564-1593. I. T.
PR2673.L4   822.32   *LC* 52-9392

Steane, J. B.   • **2.6618**
Marlowe: a critical study / by J.B. Steane. — Cambridge: University Press, 1964. viii, 381 p. 1. Marlowe, Christopher, 1564-1593 — Criticism and interpretation. I. T.
PR2673.S75   *LC* 64-2800

Wilson, F. P. (Frank Percy), 1889-1963.   • **2.6619**
Marlowe and the early Shakespeare. — Oxford: Clarendon Press, 1953. 144 p.; 20 cm. — (Clark lectures. 1951.) 1. Marlowe, Christopher, 1564-1593. 2. Shakespeare, William, 1564-1616 — Friends and associates I. T. II. Series.
PR2673.W5   *LC* 53-10120

Cole, Douglas.   • **2.6620**
Suffering and evil in the plays of Christopher Marlowe. — New York: Gordian Press, 1972 [c1962] x, 274 p.; 23 cm. 'Revision of a doctoral dissertation submitted to Princeton University in 1960.' 1. Marlowe, Christopher, 1564-1593. 2. Evil in literature I. T.
PR2674.C6 1972   822/.3   *LC* 70-148617   *ISBN* 0877521344

PR2690–2709 Marston. Massinger

Marston, John, 1575?-1634.   • **2.6621**
Poems / edited by Arnold Davenport. — Liverpool: Liverpool University Press, 1961. xv, 393 p.: facsims. — (Liverpool English texts and studies) Commentary: p.211-379. I. Davenport, Arnold. II. T. III. Series.
PR2691.D24   PR2691.D3.   *LC* 62-48971

Marston, John, 1575?-1634.   • **2.6622**
The plays of John Marston... edited from the earliest texts with introduction and notes by H. Harvey Wood. Edinburgh: Oliver and Boyd, 1934-1939. 3 v.: facsim.; 22 cm. — (The Blackfriars dramatists) I. Wood, Henry Harvey, 1903- II. T. III. Series.
PR2691.W6   822.39   *LC* 34-37467

Marston, John, 1575?-1634.   **2.6623**
Antonio's revenge / John Marston; edited by W. Reavley Gair. — Manchester [Eng.]: Manchester University Press; Baltimore: Johns Hopkins University Press, 1978. xv, 160 p.: ill.; 21 cm. — (The Revels plays) I. Gair, W. Reavley. II. T.
PR2694.A52 1978   PR2694 A52 1978.   822.3   *LC* 77-4605   *ISBN* 080182012X

Marston, John, 1575?-1634.   **2.6624**
The malcontent / John Marston; edited by George K. Hunter. — London: Methuen; [New York]: distributed by Harper & Row, 1975. lxxxiv, 171 p.: ill.; 21 cm. (Revels plays) I. Hunter, George Kirkpatrick. II. T. III. Series.
PR2694.M3 1975b   822/.3   *LC* 74-18548   *ISBN* 0416806902

Caputi, Anthony Francis, 1924-.   • **2.6625**
John Marston, satirist. — Ithaca, N. Y., Cornell University Press [1961] 289 p. 24 cm. Includes bibliography. 1. Marston, John, 1575?-1634. I. T.
PR2696.C3   827.3   *LC* 61-14952

Colley, John Scott.   **2.6626**
John Marston's theatrical drama / by John Scott Colley. — Salzburg: Inst. f. Engl. Sprache u. Literatur, Univ. Salzburg, 1974. ii, 202 p.; 21 cm. (Jacobean drama studies; 33) (Salzburg studies in English literature) Originally presented as the author's thesis, University of Chicago, 1969. 1. Marston, John, 1575?-1634 — Criticism and interpretation. I. T.
PR2697.C6 1974   822/.3   *LC* 74-192819

Finkelpearl, Philip J.   • **2.6627**
John Marston of the Middle Temple; an Elizabethan dramatist in his social setting [by] Philip J. Finkelpearl. Cambridge: Harvard University Press, 1969. xii, 275 p.; 25 cm. 1. Marston, John, 1575?-1634. 2. Middle Temple (London, England) 3. Inns of court I. T.
PR2697.F5   822/.3   *LC* 69-12722

Scott, Michael, 1949-.   **2.6628**
John Marston's plays: theme, structure and performance / Michael Scott. — New York: Barnes & Noble, 1978. 129 p.; 22 cm. 1. Marston, John, 1575?-1634 — Criticism and interpretation. I. T.
PR2697.S24 1978b   822/.3   *LC* 76-56045   *ISBN* 0064961281

Massinger, Philip, 1583-1640.   **2.6629**
[Selected works. 1976] The plays and poems of Philip Massinger / edited by Philip Edwards and Colin Gibson. — Oxford [Eng.]: Clarendon Press, 1976. 5 v.: ill.; 23 cm. I. Edwards, Philip. II. Gibson, Colin A. III. T.
PR2701.5.M3 1976   822/.3   *LC* 76-378032   *ISBN* 0198118945

Massinger, Philip, 1583-1640.   • **2.6630**
A new way to pay old debts: a comedy. Edited with an introd. and notes by M. St. Clare Byrne. — [London] University of London, Athlone Press [1956] 168 p. facsim. 19 cm. Imprint covered by label: New York, J. de Graff. I. T.
PR2704.N3 1956   822.37   *LC* 57-2419

Dunn, Thomas Alexander.   **2.6631**
Philip Massinger, the man and the playwright. — [London] Published on behalf of the University College of Ghana by T. Nelson [1957] 284 p. port., diagrs. 25 cm. Bibliography: p. 274-280. 1. Massinger, Philip, 1583-1640. I. T.
PR2706.D8   822.37   *LC* A 58-1100

PR2710–2718 Middleton
(see also: PR2315)

Middleton, Thomas, 1570?-1627.   • **2.6632**
The works of Thomas Middleton, ed. by A. H. Bullen. London, John C. Nimmo, 1885-86. 8 v. illus. (The English dramatists) I. T.
PR2711.B8   822.39

Middleton, Thomas, 17th cent.   **2.6633**
Thomas Middleton: three plays. Edited, with an introd., by Kenneth Muir. — London: Dent; Totowa, N.J.: Rowman & Littlefield, [1975] xix, 217 p. — (Everyman's university library) 1. English drama I. Middleton, Thomas. A chaste maid in Cheapside. 1975. II. Middleton, Thomas. Women beware women. 1975. III. Middleton, Thomas. The changeling. 1975. IV. T. V. Title: A Chaste maid in Cheapside. VI. Title: Women beware women. VII. Title: The Changeling.
PR2712.M8 1975   822/.3   *LC* 74-6889   *ISBN* 0460113682

Middleton, Thomas, d. 1627.   • **2.6634**
The changeling [by] Thomas Middleton & William Rowley. Edited by N.W. Bawcutt. Cambridge, Harvard University Press [1958] lxviii, 140 p. 21 cm. (The Revels plays) I. Rowley, William, 1585?-1642? joint author. II. T.
PR2714.C5 1958a   822.3   *LC* 60-94

Middleton, Thomas, d. 1627.   • **2.6635**
A game at chesse / edited by R.C. Bald. — Cambridge: University Press, 1929. 172 p.: ill., facsims., ports. I. Bald, R. C. (Robert Cecil), 1901-1965. II. T.
PR2714.G3 1929   *LC* 30-12424

Middleton, Thomas, d. 1627.   • **2.6636**
Hengist, king of Kent, or, The mayor of Queenborough / edited from the ms. in the Folger Shakespeare library, by R.C. Bald. — New York: For the trustees of Amherst college, Scribner, 1938. liv, 136 p.: facsims. — (Folger Shakespeare Library publications) I. Bald, R. C. (Robert Cecil), 1901-1965. II. T. III. Title: The mayor of Queenborough. IV. Series.
PR2714.H4 1938   *LC* 38-25309

Barker, Richard Hindry, 1902-.   • **2.6637**
Thomas Middleton. New York, Columbia University Press, 1958. viii, 216 p.; 23 cm. 1. Middleton, Thomas, d. 1627. I. T.
PR2716.B3   822.39   *LC* 58-11676

Rowe, George E., 1947-.   **2.6638**
Thomas Middleton & the new comedy tradition / George E. Rowe, Jr. — Lincoln: University of Nebraska Press, c1979. 239 p.; 23 cm. 1. Middleton, Thomas, d. 1627 — Criticism and interpretation. 2. Classical drama (Comedy) — History and criticism. I. T.
PR2717.R6   822/.3   *LC* 79-4289   *ISBN* 0803238533

Schoenbaum, S. (Samuel), 1927-.   • **2.6639**
Middleton's tragedies; a critical study. New York, Gordian Press, 1970 [c1955] ix, 275 p. 22 cm. 1. Middleton, Thomas, d. 1627 — Criticism and interpretation. I. T.
PR2717.S35 1970   822/.3   *LC* 71-128191   *ISBN* 0877521328

Heinemann, Margot.   **2.6640**
Puritanism and theatre: Thomas Middleton and opposition drama under the early Stuarts / Margot Heinemann. — Cambridge [Cambridgeshire]; New York: Cambridge University Press, 1980. ix, 300 p.; 23 cm. (Past and present publications) 1. Middleton, Thomas, d. 1627 — Criticism and interpretation. 2. Puritans — England. 3. English drama — 17th century — History and criticism. 4. Theater — England — History. 5. Great Britain — History — Early Stuarts, 1603-1649 I. T.
PR2718.P87 H44   822/.3   *LC* 79-14991   *ISBN* 0521226023

PR2721–2724 Nash
(see also: PR2336)

Nash, Thomas, 1567-1601. • **2.6641**
The works of Thomas Nashe / edited from the original texts by Ronald B. McKerrow; reprinted from the original edition with corrections and supplementary notes edited by F.P. Wilson. — Oxford: Blackwell, 1958. 5 v.: ill. I. McKerrow, Ronald Brunlees, 1872-1940. II. Wilson, F.P. III. T.
PR2721.M5x   828   LC 58-5628

Nash, Thomas, 1567-1601. • **2.6642**
Selected writings / edited by Stanley Wells. — Cambridge: Harvard University Press, 1965 [c1964] 374 p.: facsims. — (The Stratford-upon-Avon library) I. T. II. Series.
PR2722.W399   LC 65-3836

Nash, Thomas, 1567-1601. • **2.6643**
The unfortunate traveller; or, The life of Jack Wilton / newly edited, with an introd., by John Berryman; with six original ill. by Michael Ayrton. — New York: G.P.Putnam, 1960. 159 p.: ill.; 20 cm. (Capricorn books; 16) I. Nashe, Thomas. Life of Jack Wilton. II. T. III. Title: The life of Jack Wilton.
PR2724.U5 1960   PZ3.N1774Un2   LC 59-12690

PR2731–2737 Peele

Peele, George, 1556-1596. • **2.6644**
[Works. 1952] The life and works of George Peele. Charles Tyler Prouty, general editor. [New Haven, Yale University Press, 1952]-70. 3 v. illus. 24 cm. I. T.
PR2731.P76   LC 52-4943

Braunmuller, A. R., 1945-. **2.6645**
George Peele / by A.R. Braunmuller. — Boston: Twayne, c1983. 163 p.: facsim.; 23 cm. (Twayne's English authors series. TEAS 356) Includes index. 1. Peele, George, 1556-1596 — Criticism and interpretation. I. T. II. Series.
PR2737.B7 1983   822/.3 19   LC 83-199   ISBN 0805768424

PR2750–3120 Shakespeare

Shakespeare, William, 1564-1616. • **2.6646**
[Works. 1951.] The Arden edition of the works of William Shakespeare / [general editor, Una Ellis–Fermor]. — [1951 ed.]. — London: Methuen, 1951-. 39 v. Vols. revised frequently. I. Ellis-Fermor, Una Mary, 1894-1958. II. T. III. Title: The Arden Shakespeare. IV. Title: New Arden Shakespeare.
PR2753.C8 1951

Shakespeare, William, 1564-1616. • **2.6647**
[Works. 1871.] A new variorum edition of Shakespeare, edited by Horace Howard Furness ... Philadelphia, J.B. Lippincott & co., 1871-<c1980 >. v. < 1-29 >: ill.; 25 cm. Includes other editions of some volumes. Vols. 21-<29 > issued under the sponsorship of the Modern language association of America. Vols. 28-<29 > published by the Modern Language Association of America. I. Furness, Horace Howard, 1833-1912. II. Modern Language Association of America. III. T.
PR2753.F5   822.3/3 19   LC 04-13966

Shakespeare, William, 1564-1616. **2.6648**
[Works. 1984. Cambridge University Press] The new Cambridge Shakespeare. — Cambridge; New York: Cambridge University Press, 1984-. v. ; 24 cm. Each vol. has a special editor. General editor: Philip Brockbank. I. Brockbank, Philip. II. T.
PR2754.C3x

Shakespeare, William, 1564-1616. **2.6649**
[Works. 1974] The Riverside Shakespeare. Textual editor: G. Blakemore Evans. General introd.: Harry Levin. [Introductions and explanatory notes to the plays and poems by] Herschel Baker [and others] With an essay on stage history by Charles H. Shattuck. Boston, Houghton Mifflin, 1974. 2 v. (xvi, 1902 p.) illus. 27 cm. Issued in a case. I. Evans, G. Blakemore (Gwynne Blakemore), 1912- ed. II. T.
PR2754.E9 1974   822.3/3   LC 74-2007   ISBN 0395172268

Shakespeare, William, 1564-1616. **2.6650**
[Works. 1982] The Oxford Shakespeare. — Oxford: Clarendon Press; New York: Oxford University Press, 1982-. v.; 23 cm. Each volume has special editor. General editor: Stanley Wells. I. Wells, Stanley W. II. T.
PR2754.O9x

Shakespeare, William, 1564-1616. • **2.6651**
[Selections. 1979 English. 1953] Everyman's dictionary of Shakespeare quotations, compiled by D.C. Browning. London Dent [1953] 560p. (Everyman's reference library) 1. Shakespeare, William, 1564-1616 — Quotations I. Browning, David Clayton, 1894-, comp. II. T.
PR2768 B73

PR2800–2840 Individual Plays, A–Z

Saxo, Grammaticus, d. ca. 1204. **2.6652**
[Gesta Danorum. Liber 3, VI-4, II. English] Saxo Grammaticus and the life of Hamlet: a translation, history, and commentary / by William F. Hansen. — Lincoln: University of Nebraska Press, c1983. xiv, 202 p., [2] p. of plates: ill. Translation of: Gesta Danorum. Liber 3, VI-4, II. Includes index. 1. Shakespeare, William, 1564-1616. Hamlet — Sources 2. Hamlet — Legends. I. Hansen, William F., 1941- II. T.
PR2807.A77 E5 1983   PR2807A77 E5 1983.   948.9/01 19   LC 82-2671   ISBN 0803223188

Frye, Roland Mushat. **2.6653**
The Renaissance Hamlet: issues and responses in 1600 / Roland Mushat Frye. — Princeton, N.J.: Princeton University Press, c1984. xvi, 398 p.: ill.; 27 cm. Includes index. 1. Shakespeare, William, 1564-1616. Hamlet 2. Shakespeare, William, 1564-1616 — Contemporary England I. T.
PR2807.F79 1984   822.3/3 19   LC 83-42555   ISBN 0691065799

Jones, Ernest, 1879-1958. • **2.6654**
Hamlet and Œdipus. — Garden City, N.Y.: Doubleday, 1954 [c1949] 194 p.; 19 cm. — (Doubleday anchor books, A31) The revision of an essay published in 1910 in the American journal of psychology under the title: The Œdipus complex as an explanation of Hamlet's mystery. 1. Shakespeare, William, 1564-1616. Hamlet 2. Psychoanalysis in literature I. T.
PR2807.J63 1954   822.33   LC 54-3179

Knights, L. C. (Lionel Charles), 1906-. • **2.6655**
An approach to 'Hamlet.' — Stanford, Calif.: Stanford University Press, 1961, c1960. 90 p.; 23 cm. 1. Shakespeare, William, 1564-1616. Hamlet 2. Shakespeare, William, 1564-1616 — Criticism and interpretation I. T.
PR2807.K58   LC 61-6216

Levin, Harry, 1912-. • **2.6656**
The question of Hamlet. New York, Oxford University Press, 1959. 178 p. 21 cm. 1. Shakespeare, William, 1564-1616. Hamlet I. T.
PR2807.L39   822.33   LC 59-5784

Stoll, Elmer Edgar, 1874-1959. • **2.6657**
Hamlet; an historical and comparative study. New York, Gordian Press, 1968. 75 p. 24 cm. Reprint of the 1919 ed. 1. Shakespeare, William, 1564-1616. Hamlet I. T.
PR2807.S76 1968   822.3/3   LC 67-30880

Wilson, John Dover, 1881-1969. • **2.6658**
The manuscript of Shakespeare's Hamlet and the problems of its transmission: an essay in critical bibliography. — Cambridge, [Eng.]: University Press, 1963. 2 v. (xxx, 437 p.); 19 cm. First published 1934. Reprinted 1963. 1. Shakespeare, William, 1564-1616. Hamlet 2. Shakespeare, William, 1564-1616 — Bibliography. 3. Shakespeare, William — Criticism, Textual. I. T.
PR2807.W47 1963   PR2807.W5.   822.33   LC 64-101

Wilson, John Dover, 1881-1969. • **2.6659**
What happens in Hamlet. — Cambridge: University Press, 1959. 357 p.; 19 cm. 1. Shakespeare, William, 1564-1616. Hamlet I. T.
PR2807.W48   LC 59-65222

Ripley, John, 1936-. **2.6660**
Julius Caesar on stage in England and America, 1599–1973 / John Ripley. — Cambridge; New York: Cambridge University Press, 1980. xiii, 370 p.: ill.; 24 cm. Includes index. 1. Shakespeare, William, 1564-1616. Julius Caesar 2. Shakespeare, William, 1564-1616 — Stage history 3. Theater — England — History. 4. Theater — United States — History. I. T.
PR2808.R56   822.3/3   LC 79-10822   ISBN 052122781X

Schanzer, Ernest. • **2.6661**
The problem plays of Shakespeare; a study of Julius Caesar, Measure for measure, Antony and Cleopatra. — New York, Schocken Books [1963] 196 p. 23 cm. Includes bibliography. 1. Shakespeare, William, 1564-1616. Julius Caesar 2. Shakespeare, William, 1564-1616. Measure for measure. 3. Shakespeare, William, 1564-1616. Antony and Cleopatra I. T.
PR2808.S3   822.33   LC 63-9752

Colie, Rosalie Littell. **2.6662**
Some facets of King Lear; essays in prismatic criticism, edited by Rosalie L. Colie and F. T. Flahiff. — [Toronto; Buffalo]: University of Toronto Press, [1974] xi, 236 p.; 25 cm. 1. Shakespeare, William, 1564-1616. King Lear 2. Lear, King (Legendary character) — Legends — History and criticism — Addresses, essays, lectures. I. Flahiff, Frederick T., joint author. II. T.
PR2819.C6   822.3/3   LC 73-81755   ISBN 0802019986

Danby, John Francis. • **2.6663**
Shakespeare's doctrine of nature: a study of King Lear / by John F. Danby. London: Faber and Faber, 1949. 234p. 1. Shakespeare, William, 1564-1616. King Lear I. T.
PR2819.D33   822/.33   LC 49-6555   ISBN 0571045480

Heilman, Robert Bechtold, 1906-.   • **2.6664**
This great stage: image and structure in King Lear. — Baton Rouge, La.: Louisiana State University Press, 1948. xi, 339 p.; 22 cm. 1. Shakespeare, William, 1564-1616. King Lear I. T.
PR2819.H4   LC 48-8095

Rosenberg, Marvin.   **2.6665**
The masks of King Lear / by Marvin Rosenberg. — Berkeley: University of California Press, c1972. viii, 431 p.; 24 cm. 1. Shakespeare, William, 1564-1616. King Lear 2. Shakespeare, William, 1564-1616 — Stage history I. T.
PR2819.R65   822.3/3   LC 74-115492   ISBN 0520017188

Salgādo, Gāmini, 1929-.   • **2.6666**
King Lear / Gamini Salgado. — 2nd ed. — Atlantic Highlands, NJ: Humanities Press International, 1987, c1984. p. cm. — (Text and performance.) Includes index. 1. Shakespeare, William, 1564-1616. King Lear 2. Shakespeare, William, 1564-1616 — Stage history 3. Shakespeare, William, 1564-1616 — Film and video adaptations I. T. II. Series.
PR2819.S25 1987   822.3/3 19   LC 86-20902   ISBN 0391034936

Sharma, Ram Chandra, 1917-.   **2.6667**
An approach to King Lear / R. C. Sharma. — Delhi: Macmillan Co. of India, 1975. x, 295 p.; 22 cm. Includes index. 1. Shakespeare, William, 1564-1616. King Lear 2. Lear, King (Legendary character) — Legends — History and criticism. I. T.
PR2819.S47   822.3/3   LC 75-904387

Jorgensen, Paul A.   **2.6668**
Our naked frailties; sensational art and meaning in Macbeth [by] Paul A. Jorgensen. — Berkeley: University of California Press, 1971. viii, 234 p.; 24 cm. 1. Shakespeare, William, 1564-1616. Macbeth I. T.
PR2823.J6   822.3/3   LC 70-145788

Gless, Darryl J., 1945-.   **2.6669**
Measure for measure, the law, and the convent / Darryl J. Gless. — Princeton, N.J.: Princeton University Press, c1979. .xviii, 283 p.; 22 cm. Includes index. 1. Shakespeare, William, 1564-1616. Measure for measure. I. T.
PR2824.G5   822.3/3   LC 79-83990   ISBN 0691064032

Heilman, Robert Bechtold, 1906-.   • **2.6670**
Magic in the web: action and language in Othello / Robert B. Heilman. — Lexington: University of Kentucky Press, 1956. 298p. 1. Shakespeare, William, 1564-1616 Othello — Criticism and interpretation. I. T.
PR2829.H4   LC 56-6993

Rosenberg, Marvin.   • **2.6671**
The masks of Othello: the search for the identity of Othello, Iago, and Desdemona by three centuries of actors and critics. — Berkeley, University of California Press, 1961. ix, 313 p. illus. 24 cm. 1. Shakespeare, William, 1564-1616. Othello 2. Shakespeare, William, 1564-1616 — Stage history. I. T.
PR2829.R6 1961   822.33   LC 61-7521

PR2841–2849 Poems. Sonnets

Shakespeare, William, 1564-1616.   **2.6672**
[Sonnets] Shakespeare's Sonnets / edited with analytic commentary by Stephen Booth. — New Haven: Yale University Press, 1977. xix, 578 p.: ill.; 25 cm. 'The text of the 1609 quarto (Apsley imprint, the Huntington-Bridgewater copy) and an edited text printed in parallel': p. [1]-[133] Includes indexes. I. Booth, Stephen. II. T.
PR2848.A2 B6   821/.3   LC 76-56161   ISBN 0300019599

Shakespeare, William, 1564-1616.   • **2.6673**
The riddle of Shakespeare's sonnets: the text of the sonnets / with interpretive essays by Edward Hubler ... [et. al.]. — [1st ed.]. — New York: Basic Books, 1962. 346 p. 1. Shakespeare, William, 1564-1616. Sonnets I. Wilde, Oscar, 1854-1900. The portrait of Mr. W. H. II. Hubler, Edward. III. T.
PR2848.H78   LC 62-9372

Hubler, Edward.   • **2.6674**
The sense of Shakespeare's sonnets. — Princeton: Princeton University Press, 1952. 169 p.; 23 cm. — (Princeton studies in English, no. 33) 1. Shakespeare, William, 1564-1616. Sonnets I. T.
PR2848.H8   822.33   LC 52-5845

Knight, George Wilson, 1897-.   • **2.6675**
The mutual flame: on Shakespeare's Sonnets and The phoenix and the turtle. — London: Methuen, [1962] xi, 233 p. 1. Shakespeare, William, 1564-1616. Sonnets 2. Shakespeare, William, 1564-1616. Phoenix and the turtle I. T.
PR2848.K6   LC 62-51298

Leishman, J. B. (James Blair), 1902-1962.   • **2.6676**
Themes and variations in Shakespeare's sonnets. — London: Hutchinson, 1961. 254 p. 1. Shakespeare, William, 1564-1616. Sonnets I. T.
PR2848.L4   LC 61-65807

Muir, Kenneth.   **2.6677**
Shakespeare's sonnets / Kenneth Muir. — London; Boston: G. Allen & Unwin, 1979. 179 p.; 23 cm. (Unwin critical library.) Includes index. 1. Shakespeare, William, 1564-1616. Sonnets 2. Sonnets, English — History and criticism. I. T. II. Series.
PR2848.M8 1979   821/.3   LC 79-40008   ISBN 0048210420

Wilson, John Dover, 1881-1969.   • **2.6678**
An introduction to the sonnets of Shakespeare for the use of historians and others. — New York, Cambridge University Press, 1964 [c1963] 109 p. 20 cm. Cover title: Shakespeare's sonnets. Bibliographical footnotes. 1. Shakespeare, William, 1564-1616. Sonnets 2. Pembroke, William Herbert, 3d earl of, 1580-1630. I. T. II. Title: Shakespeare's sonnets.
PR2848.W5 1964   LC 64-25905

Arden of Feversham   **2.6679**
The tragedy of Master Arden of Faversham, edited by M. L. Wine. — London: Methuen [Distributed in the U.S.A. by Harper & Row Publishers, 1973] xcvi, 180 p.: illus.; 21 cm. — (The Revels plays) 1. Arden, Thomas, d. 1551 — Drama. I. Wine, Martin L., ed. II. T.
PR2854.A2 W5 1973   822/.3   LC 74-159342   ISBN 0416773109

PR2878–2880 Imitations. Paraphrases. Adaptations

Shakespeare, William, 1564-1616.   **2.6680**
The history of King Lear / [adapted from Shakespeare by] Nahum Tate; edited by James Black. — Lincoln: University of Nebraska Press, [1975] xxxvii, 111 p.; 21 cm. — (Regents Restoration drama series) 'A Bison book.' Text of the 1681 ed., printed for E. Flesher and sold by R. Bentley and M. Magnes, London, with textual variants from the 1689, 1699, 1702, and 1712 editions included. 1. Lear, King (Legendary character) — Drama. I. Tate, Nahum, 1652-1715. II. Black, James, 1932- ed. III. T.
PR2878.K4 T3 1975   822.3/3   LC 74-82562   ISBN 0803203829

PR2888–2890 Societies. Collections

Shakespeare survey.   • **2.6681**
1-. Cambridge [Eng.] New York, Cambridge University Press, 1948-. v. ill., facsims. 26 cm. Annual. 'An annual survey of Shakespearian study and production.' 1. Shakespeare, William, 1564-1616 — Criticism and interpretation 2. Shakespeare, William, 1564-1616 — Societies, periodicals, etc. 3. Shakespeare, William, 1564-1616 — Stage history I. Nicoll, Allardyce, 1894- ed.
PR2888.C3   822.33   LC 49-1639

Muir, Kenneth.   • **2.6682**
A new companion to Shakespeare studies, edited by Kenneth Muir and S. Schoenbaum. Cambridge [Eng.] University Press, 1971. v, 297 p. illus. 22 cm. 1. Shakespeare, William, 1564-1616 — Addresses, essays, lectures. I. Schoenbaum, S. (Samuel), 1927- joint author. II. T.
PR2890.M8   822.3/3   LC 78-118066   ISBN 0521079411

PR2892 Concordances. Dictionaries

Bartlett, John, 1820-1905.   • **2.6683**
A complete concordance or verbal index to words, phrases, and passages in the dramatic works of Shakespeare, with a supplementary concordance to the poems. London, Macmillan; New York, St Martin's Press [1966] 1910p. First ed. published in 1894 under title: A new and complete concordance or verbal index to words, phrases, and passages in the dramatic works of Shakespeare. 1. Shakespeare, William, 1564-1616 — Concordances I. T.
PR 2892.B34 1966   LC 67-2215

Campbell, Oscar James, 1879-1970. ed.   • **2.6684**
The reader's encyclopedia of Shakespeare, edited by Oscar James Campbell. Associate editor: Edward G. Quinn. — New York: Crowell, [1966] xv, 1014 p.: illus., facsims., geneal. tables, ports.; 26 cm. 1. Shakespeare, William, 1564-1616 — Dictionaries, indexes, etc. I. Quinn, Edward G., 1932- joint ed. II. T.
PR2892.C3   822.33   LC 66-11946

Onions, C. T. (Charles Talbut), 1873-1965.   **2.6685**
A Shakespeare glossary / C.T. Onions; enlarged and revised throughout by Robert D. Eagleson. — Oxford [Oxfordshire]: Clarendon Press, 1986. xvii, 326 p.; 21 cm. 1. Shakespeare, William, 1564-1616 — Language — Glossaries, etc. I. Eagleson, Robert D. II. T.
PR2892.O6 1986   822.3/3 19   LC 84-7912   ISBN 0198111991

Partridge, Eric, 1894-. • 2.6686
Shakespeare's bawdy: a literary & psychological essay and a comprehensive glossary. — [New popular ed., rev.] — New York: Dutton, [1955] ix, 226 p. 1. Shakespeare, William, 1564-1616 — Dictionaries, indexes, etc. 2. Vulgarity in literature 3. Sex in literature I. T.
PR2892.P27x   LC 55-12810

Spevack, Marvin.   2.6687
The Harvard concordance to Shakespeare. — Cambridge, Mass.: Belknap Press of Harvard University Press, 1973. ix, 1600 p.; 35 cm. 1. Shakespeare, William, 1564-1616 — Concordances 2. Shakespeare, William, 1564-1616 — Quotations I. T.
PR2892.S62   822.3/3/016   LC 73-76385   ISBN 0674374754

Stokes, Francis Griffin.   • 2.6688
A dictionary of the characters & proper names in the works of Shakespeare; with notes on the sources and dates of the plays and poems. — New York: Dover Publications, [1970] xv, 359 p.: geneal. tables.; 24 cm. Reprint of the 1924 ed. 1. Shakespeare, William, 1564-1616 — Dictionaries, indexes, etc. 2. Shakespeare, William, 1564-1616 — Characters 3. Names, Personal I. T.
PR2892.S67 1970   822.3/3   LC 77-116373   ISBN 0486222195

PR2893–2909 Biography

Chambers, E. K. (Edmund Kerchever), 1866-1954.   • 2.6689
Sources for a biography of Shakespeare. Oxford Clarendon Press 1946. 80p. 1. Shakespeare, William, 1564-1616 — Biography — Sources I. T.
PR2893 C5

Schoenbaum, S. (Samuel), 1927-.   2.6690
William Shakespeare: records and images / S. Schoenbaum. — New York: Oxford University Press, c1981. xviii, 276 p.: ill.; 36 cm. Includes index. 1. Shakespeare, William, 1564-1616 — Biography — Sources 2. Shakespeare, William, 1564-1616 — Biography 3. Dramatists, English — Early modern, 1500-1700 — Biography. I. T.
PR2893.S32 1981   822.3/3 19   LC 80-24538   ISBN 0195202341

Bentley, Gerald Eades, 1901-.   • 2.6691
Shakespeare; a biographical handbook. — New Haven, Yale University Press, 1961. 256 p. 21 cm. — (Yale Shakespeare supplements) Includes bibliography. 1. Shakespeare, William, 1564-1616 — Biography I. T.
PR2894.B4   928.2   LC 61-14997

Bradbrook, M. C. (Muriel Clara), 1909-.   2.6692
Shakespeare: the poet in his world / M. C. Bradbrook. — New York: Columbia University Press, 1978. ix, 272 p.; 22 cm. Includes index. 1. Shakespeare, William, 1564-1616. 2. Dramatists, English — Early modern, 1500-1700 — Biography. I. T.
PR2894.B69 1978   822.3/3   LC 78-7611   ISBN 0231046480

Chambers, E. K. (Edmund Kerchever), 1866-1954.   • 2.6693
William Shakespeare; a study of facts and problems, by E. K. Chambers ... — Oxford, The Clarendon press, 1930. 2 v. fronts., plates, ports., maps (part fold.) facsims. (part fold.) 22.5 cm. 1. Shakespeare, William, 1564-1616. 2. Shakespeare, William — Criticism and interpretation. 3. Shakespeare, William — Criticism, Textual. 4. Shakespeare, William — Stage history — To 1625. I. T.
PR2894.C44   822.33   LC 31-2409

White, Beatrice, 1902-.   • 2.6694
An index to 'The Elizabethan stage' and 'William Shakespeare' / by Sir Edmund Chambers. — New York: B. Blom, 1964. 161 p. I. Chambers, E. K. (Edmund Kerchever), 1866-1954. William Shakespeare: a study of facts and problems. II. Chambers, E. K. (Edmund Kerchever), 1866-1954. The Elizabethan stage. III. T.
PR2894.C442 1964   LC 64-14701

Chambers, Sir Edmund Kerchever, 1866-.   • 2.6695
A short life of Shakespeare: with the sources / abridged by Charles Williams from Sir Edmund Chambers's William Shakespeare: a study of facts and problems. — Oxford: Clarendon Press, 1933. 260 p.: ill. 1. Shakespeare, William, 1564-1616 — Biography 2. Shakespeare, William, 1564-1616 — Biography — Sources I. Williams, Charles, 1886-1945. II. T.
PR2894.C443   LC 33-13746

Granville-Barker, Harley, 1877-1946. ed.   • 2.6696
A companion to Shakespeare studies, edited by Harley Granville-Barker and G. B. Harrison. New York, The Macmillan company; Cambridge, Eng., The University press 1934. x p., 1 l., 408 p. illus. (incl. plans) facsims. 23 cm. 1. Shakespeare, William, 1564-1616. 2. Shakespeare, William, 1564-1616 — Criticism and interpretation I. Harrison, G. B. (George Bagshawe), 1894- joint ed. II. T.
PR2894.G7   822.33   LC 34-10408

Harrison, G. B. (George Bagshawe), 1894-.   • 2.6697
Introducing Shakespeare [by] G.B. Harrison. 3rd ed. Harmondsworth, Penguin, 1966. 232 p. front., illus. (incl. ports.) facsims., diagrs. 19 cm. 1. Shakespeare, William, 1564-1616. 2. Dramatists, English — Early modern, 1500-1700 — Biography. I. T.
PR2894.H353 1966   822.33   LC 66-78475

Schoenbaum, S. (Samuel), 1927-.   2.6698
William Shakespeare: a compact documentary life / S. Schoenbaum. — New York: Oxford University Press, 1977. xix, 376 p.: ill.; 22 cm. Abridged ed. of William Shakespeare, a documentary life. 1. Shakespeare, William, 1564-1616 — Biography 2. Dramatists, English — Early modern, 1500-1700 — Biography. I. T.
PR2894.S33 1977   822.3/3 B   LC 75-46358   ISBN 0195022114

Speaight, Robert, 1904-.   2.6699
Shakespeare, the man and his achievement / Robert Speaight. — New York: Stein and Day, 1977. 384 p., [8] leaves of plates: ill. Includes index. 1. Shakespeare, William, 1564-1616. I. T.
PR2894.S65   822.3/3   LC 76-12979   ISBN 0812820975

Brooke, Tucker, 1883-1946.   • 2.6700
Essays on Shakespeare and other Elizabethans. [Hamden, Conn.] Archon Books, 1969 [c1948] x, 220 p. 22 cm. 1. Shakespeare, William, 1564-1616 — Addresses, essays, lectures. 2. English literature — Early modern, 1500-1700 — History and criticism — Addresses, essays, lectures. I. T.
PR2899.B69 1969   822.3/3   LC 69-11554   ISBN 0208006133

Ellis-Fermor, Una Mary, 1894-1958.   • 2.6701
Shakespeare the dramatist. [Folcroft, Pa.] Folcroft Library Editions, 1973. 16 p. 34 cm. 'From the Proceedings of the British Academy. Volume XXXIV.' Reprint of the 1948 ed. published by G. Cumerlege, London, which was presented as the Annual Shakespeare lecture of the British Academy. 1. Shakespeare, William, 1564-1616 — Addresses, essays, lectures. 2. Drama — Addresses, essays, lectures. I. T.
PR2899.E5 1973   822.3/3   LC 73-2638   ISBN 0848419000

Sitwell, Edith, Dame, 1887-1964.   • 2.6702
A poet's notebook. — Westport, Conn.: Greenwood Press, [1972, c1950] xviii, 276 p.; 22 cm. Consists of portions of the author's A notebook on William Shakespeare and A poet's notebook. 1. Shakespeare, William, 1564-1616 — Criticism and interpretation 2. Poetry — History and criticism — Addresses, essays, lectures. 3. English poetry — History and criticism — Addresses, essays, lectures. I. T.
PR2899.S46 1972   822.3/3   LC 71-152605   ISBN 0837160405

Chute, Marchette Gaylord, 1909-.   • 2.6703
Shakespeare of London. — [1st ed.]. — New York: Dutton, 1949. xii, 397 p.: map (on lining-papers); 22 cm. 1. Shakespeare, William, 1564-1616. I. T.
PR2907.C5   928.2 822.33   LC 49-48602

Harrison, G. B. (George Bagshawe), 1894-.   • 2.6704
Shakespeare at work, 1592–1603. With a new pref. by the author. [Ann Arbor] University of Michigan Press [1958] 325 p. 21 cm. (Ann Arbor paperbacks, AA16) 1. Shakespeare, William, 1564-1616 — Criticism and interpretation 2. Shakespeare, William, 1564-1616 — Contemporary England 3. English drama — Early modern and Elizabethan, 1500-1600 — History and criticism. 4. Great Britain — History — Elizabeth I, 1558-1603. I. T.
PR2907.H3 1958   822.33   LC 58-895

PR2910–2920 The Age Of Shakespeare. Theaters

Rowse, A. L. (Alfred Leslie), 1903-.   2.6705
[Simon Forman] Sex and society in Shakespeare's age: Simon Forman the astrologer / A. L. Rowse. — New York: Scribner, 1976 (c1974). xiii, 315 p., [6] leaves of plates: ill.; 23 cm. First published in 1974 under title: Simon Forman. 1. Shakespeare, William, 1564-1616 — Contemporary England 2. Forman, Simon, 1552-1611. 3. Shakespeare, William, 1564-1616 — Contemporaries 4. England — Social life and customs — 16th century I. T.
PR2910.R76   309.1/42/055   LC 74-11678   ISBN 0684140519

Adams, John Cranford, 1903-.   • 2.6706
The Globe Playhouse: its design and equipment / by John Cranford Adams. — 2d ed. — New York: Barnes & Noble, 1961. x, 435 p.: ill. (some col.) 1. Globe Theatre (Southwark, London, England) I. T.
PR2920.A38 1961   LC 61-14744

Hodges, C. Walter (Cyril Walter), 1909-.   • 2.6707
The Globe restored: a study of the Elizabethan theater [by] C. Walter Hodges. [1st American ed.] New York, Coward-McCann [1968] xiv, 177 p. illus., 73 plates. 26 cm. 1. Shakespeare, William, 1564-1616 — Stage history 2. Globe Theatre (Southwark, London, England) I. T.
PR2920.H6 1968b   792/.09421/64   LC 68-19224

Hotson, Leslie, 1897-.   • **2.6708**
Shakespeare's wooden O. — New York: Macmillan, 1960, c1959. 335 p.: ill.; 22 cm. 1. Shakespeare, William, 1564-1616 — Stage history — To 1625 2. Globe Theatre (Southwark, London, England) 3. Theater — London — History. I. T.
PR2920.H65 1960   *LC* 60-10533

Orrell, John.   **2.6709**
The quest for Shakespeare's Globe / John Orrell. — Cambridge; New York: Cambridge University Press, 1983. xv, 187 p.: ill.; 26 cm. 1. Shakespeare, William, 1564-1616 — Stage history 2. Globe Theatre (Southwark, London, England) 3. Theaters — England — London — History — 17th century. 4. Theaters — England — London — Construction. I. T.
PR2920.O7 1983   792/.09421/64 19   *LC* 82-9445   *ISBN* 0521247519

PR2931–2933 Museums, Collections, etc

Schoenbaum, S. (Samuel), 1927-.   **2.6710**
Shakespeare, the Globe & the world / S. Schoenbaum. — New York: Oxford University Press, 1979. 208 p.: ill. (some col.); 31 cm. Prepared for a Folger Shakespeare Library exhibition held at various institutions Oct. 1979-Apr. 1981. Includes index. 1. Shakespeare, William, 1564-1616 — Exhibitions 2. Shakespeare, William, 1564-1616. 3. Folger Shakespeare Library. 4. Dramatists, English — Early modern, 1500-1700 — Biography. I. Folger Shakespeare Library. II. T.
PR2933.F64 S3   822.3/3   *LC* 79-3075   *ISBN* 0195026454

PR2937–2961 Authorship. Sources

Muir, Kenneth.   **2.6711**
The sources of Shakespeare's plays / by Kenneth Muir. — New Haven: Yale University Press, 1978, c1977. vi, 320 p.; 23 cm. 1. Shakespeare, William, 1564-1616 — Sources I. T.
PR2952.M84 1978   822.3/3   *LC* 77-10295   *ISBN* 0300022123

Bullough, Geoffrey, 1901- ed.   • **2.6712**
Narrative and dramatic sources of Shakespeare. — London: Routledge and Paul; New York: Columbia University Press, 1957-75. 8 v.; 23 cm. 1. Shakespeare, William, 1564-1616 — Sources I. T.
PR2952.5.B8   822.33   *LC* 57-9969   *ISBN* 0230088973

Thompson, Ann.   **2.6713**
Shakespeare's Chaucer: a study in literary origins / Ann Thompson. — New York: Barnes & Noble Books, 1978. x, 239 p.; 23 cm. (Liverpool English texts and studies) Includes index. 1. Shakespeare, William, 1564-1616 — Sources 2. Chaucer, Geoffrey, d. 1400 — Influence — Shakespeare. I. T. II. Series.
PR2955.C53 T5 1978   822.3/3   *LC* 78-106640   *ISBN* 0064968324

Holinshed, Raphael, d. 1580?   • **2.6714**
Holinshed's Chronicle as used in Shakespeare's plays / edited by Allardyce & Josephine Nicoll. — London: Dent; New York: Dutton, 1927. xiv, 233 p. — (Everyman's library; no. 800) Compiled by R. Holinshed. 1. Shakespeare, William, 1564-1616 — Sources I. Nicoll, Allardyce, 1894- II. Calina, Josephine. III. T.
PR2955.H7 E93   942   *LC* 27-283

Bentley, Gerald Eades, 1901-.   • **2.6715**
Shakespeare & Jonson: their reputations in the seventeenth century compared. — Chicago, University of Chicago press [1945] 2 v. — (Chicago. University. Committee on publications in the history of thought and culture. Publications) 1. Shakespeare, William, 1564-1616 — Allusions. 2. Jonson, Ben, 1573?-1637 — Allusions. I. T. II. Series.
PR2959.J6 B4   822.33

PR2965–2979 Criticism. Interpretation (General)
(Individual Plays: see: PR2800-2840)

Marder, Louis, 1915-.   • **2.6716**
His exits and his entrances: the story of Shakespeare's reputation / Louis Marder. — 1st. ed. — Philadelphia: Lippincott, c1963. 386 p. Limited edition. 1. Shakespeare, William, 1564-1616 — Appreciation I. T.
PR2965.M3   *LC* 63-11756

Johnson, Samuel, 1709-1784.   • **2.6717**
Johnson on Shakespeare; essays and notes selected and set forth with an introd. by Walter Raleigh. London H. Frowde 1908. 206p. 1. Shakespeare, William, 1564-1616 — Criticism and interpretation I. Raleigh, Walter Alexander, Sir, 1861-1922. ed. II. T.
PR2975 J62 1908

Stock, R. D. (Robert D.), 1941-.   **2.6718**
Samuel Johnson and neoclassical dramatic theory; the intellectual context of the Preface to Shakespeare, by R. D. Stock. Lincoln, University of Nebraska Press [1973] xxi, 226 p. 24 cm. 1. Johnson, Samuel, 1709-1784. Preface to Shakespeare. 2. Shakespeare, William, 1564-1616 — Criticism and interpretation — History — 18th century 3. English literature — 18th century — History and criticism. 4. Neoclassicism (Literature) I. T.
PR2975.J643 Z85   822.3/3   *LC* 72-77194   *ISBN* 0803208197

Barton, Anne.   • **2.6719**
Shakespeare and the idea of the play, [by] Anne Righter. New York, Barnes & Noble 1963, [c1962] 223 p. 23 cm. 1. Shakespeare, William, 1564-1616 — Criticism and interpretation 2. English drama — Early modern and Elizabethan, 1500-1600 — History and criticism. 3. Theater — England. I. T.
PR2976.B35   822.33   *LC* 63-2651

Berry, Ralph, 1931-.   **2.6720**
Shakespeare and the awareness of the audience / Ralph Berry. — New York: St. Martin's Press, 1985. xi, 157 p.; 23 cm. Includes index. 1. Shakespeare, William, 1564-1616 — Addresses, essays, lectures. 2. Shakespeare, William, 1564-1616 — Stage history — To 1625 — Addresses, essays, lectures. 3. Theater — Great Britain — History — Addresses, essays, lectures. 4. Theater audiences — England — London — Addresses, essays, lectures. 5. Masques — Addresses, essays, lectures. I. T.
PR2976.B423 1985   822.3/3 19   *LC* 84-9772   *ISBN* 0312714238

Bethell, Samuel Leslie.   • **2.6721**
Shakespeare and the popular dramatic tradition, by S. L. Bethell. Introd. by T. S. Eliot. — New York: Octagon Books, 1970 [c1944] xv, 209 p.: front.; 23 cm. — (Duke University publications) 1. Shakespeare, William, 1564-1616 — Criticism and interpretation I. T.
PR2976.B43 1970   822.3/3   *LC* 75-120230

Bradbrook, M. C. (Muriel Clara), 1909-.   **2.6722**
Muriel Bradbrook on Shakespeare / M.C. Bradbrook. — Totowa, N.J.: Barnes & Noble Books, 1984. viii, 166 p.; 22 cm. 1. Shakespeare, William, 1564-1616 — Criticism and interpretation — Addresses, essays, lectures. I. T.
PR2976.B568 1984   822/.3/3 19   *LC* 84-6273   *ISBN* 0389204870

Bradbrook, M. C. (Muriel Clara), 1909-.   • **2.6723**
Shakespeare and Elizabethan poetry; a study of his earlier work in relation to the poetry of the time. New York, Oxford University Press, 1952. viii, 279 p., illus., port. 20 cm. 1. Shakespeare, William — Criticism and interpretation 2. English poetry — Early modern, (to 1700) — History and criticism I. T.
PR2976.B59   822.33   *LC* 52-9906

Burckhardt, Sigurd, 1916-1966.   • **2.6724**
Shakespearean meanings / by Sigurd Burckhardt. — Princeton, N.J.: Princeton University Press, 1968. xi, 317 p.; 23 cm. 1. Shakespeare, William, 1564-1616 — Criticism and interpretation I. T.
PR2976.B77   822.3/3   *LC* 68-15765

Chambers, E. K. (Edmund Kerchever), 1866-1954.   • **2.6725**
Shakespeare: a survey. New York, Hill and Wang [1959?] 325 p. 19 cm. (A Dramabook, D14) 1. Shakespeare, William, 1564-1616 — Criticism and interpretation I. T.
PR2976.C35 1959   822.33   *LC* 58-11371

Coleridge, Samuel Taylor, 1772-1834.   • **2.6726**
Shakespearean criticism. Edited by Thomas Middleton Raysor. — [2d. ed.]. — London, Dent; New York, Dutton [1961-62, c1960] 2 v. 19 cm. — (Everyman's library, 162, 183. Essays) Includes bibliographical references. 1. Shakespeare, William — Criticism and interpretation. I. Raysor, Thomas Middleton, 1895- ed. II. T.
PR2976.C55x   822.33   *LC* A 62-5759

Colman, Ernest Adrian Mackenzie.   **2.6727**
The dramatic use of bawdy in Shakespeare [by] E. A. M. Colman. — [London]: Longman, [1974] xi, 230 p.; 23 cm. 1. Shakespeare, William, 1564-1616 — Criticism and interpretation 2. Vulgarity in literature 3. Sex in literature I. T.
PR2976.C57   822.3/3   *LC* 73-86132   *ISBN* 0582504562

Dean, Leonard Fellows, 1909- ed.   • **2.6728**
Shakespeare; modern essays in criticism, edited by Leonard F. Dean. Rev. ed. New York, Oxford University Press, 1967. x, 476 p. 21 cm. (A Galaxy book, GB46) 1. Shakespeare, William, 1564-1616 — Criticism and interpretation I. T.
PR2976.D4 1967   822.33   *LC* 67-10853

Lloyd Evans, Gareth.   **2.6729**
[Everyman's companion to Shakespeare] The Shakespeare companion / Gareth and Barbara Lloyd Evans. — New York: Scribner, c1978. xiv, 368 p., [12] leaves of plates: ill.; 24 cm. First published under title: Everyman's companion to Shakespeare. 1. Shakespeare, William, 1564-1616 — Criticism and

interpretation 2. Shakespeare, William, 1564-1616 — Handbooks, manuals, etc. I. Lloyd Evans, Barbara. joint author. II. T.
PR2976.E9 1978b   822.3/3   LC 78-54611   ISBN 0684158701

Fergusson, Francis.   2.6730
Trope and allegory: themes common to Dante and Shakespeare / Francis Fergusson. — Athens: University of Georgia Press, c1977. 164 p.; 23 cm. 1. Shakespeare, William, 1564-1616 — Criticism and interpretation 2. Dante Alighieri, 1265-1321 — Criticism and interpretation. I. T.
PR2976.F42   PR2976 F42.   809   LC 76-12684   ISBN 0820304107

Goddard, Harold Clarke, 1878-1950.   2.6731
The meaning of Shakespeare. [Chicago] University of Chicago Press [1951] xii, 690 p. 25 cm. 1. Shakespeare, William, 1564-1616 — Criticism and interpretation I. T.
PR2976.G57   822.33   LC 51-2298

Granville-Barker, Harley, 1877-1946.   2.6732
More prefaces to Shakespeare: A midsummer night's dream. A winter's tale. Twelfth night. Macbeth. 'From Henry V to Hamlet.' Edited by Edward M. Moore. Princeton, N.J., Princeton University Press [1974] 167 p. 23 cm. 1. Shakespeare, William, 1564-1616 — Criticism and interpretation 2. Prefaces I. T.
PR2976.G668 1974   822.3/3   LC 73-19312   ISBN 0691071667 ISBN 0691013136

Granville-Barker, Harley, 1877-1946.   • 2.6733
Prefaces to Shakespeare. — Princeton, Princeton University Press, 1946-47. 2 v. 22 cm. 1. Shakespeare, William — Criticism and interpretation. I. T.
PR2976.G673   822.33   LC A 47-347 *

Harbage, Alfred, 1901-.   • 2.6734
William Shakespeare, a reader's guide. — New York: Farrar, Straus, [1963] 498 p.; 22 cm. 1. Shakespeare, William, 1564-1616 — Criticism and interpretation I. T.
PR2976.H32   822.33   LC 63-9070

Hartwig, Joan.   2.6735
Shakespeare's tragicomic vision. — Baton Rouge, Louisiana State University Press [1972] 196 p. 22 cm. 1. Shakespeare, William, 1564-1616 — Criticism and interpretation I. T.
PR2976.H364   822.3/3   LC 79-181567   ISBN 0807100471

Modern Shakespearean criticism; essays on style, dramaturgy,   2.6736
and the major plays / edited by Alvin B. Kernan.
New York: Harcourt, Brace, Jovanovich, c1970. xi, 447 p.; 21 cm. 1. Shakespeare, William — Criticism and interpretation. I. Kernan, Alvin B.
PR2976.K47   822.3/3   LC 71-97863

Knight, George Wilson.   • 2.6737
The Shakespearian tempest: with a chart of Shakespeare's dramatic universe / by G. Wilson Knight. — 3d ed. — London: Methuen, 1953. xxiv, 332 p. 1. Shakespeare, William, 1564-1616 — Criticism and interpretation 2. Shakespeare, William, 1564-1616 — Knowledge — Music 3. Shakespeare, William, 1564-1616 — Knowledge — Natural history I. T.
PR2976.K5x   LC a 55-8672   ISBN 041654200X

Knight, George Wilson, 1897-.   • 2.6738
The crown of life; essays in interpretation of Shakespeare's final plays. London, Methuen [1961] 836 p. 23 cm. 1. Shakespeare, William — Criticism and interpretation. I. T.
PR2976.K618 1961   822.33   LC 62-53122

Knight, George Wilson, 1897-.   • 2.6739
Sovereign flower: on Shakespeare as the poet of royalism,together with related essays and indexes to earlier volumes. London: Methuen 1958 Reprinted 1966. 324 p. Reprinted with monor corrections and additions to Indexes A and C. 1. Shakespeare, William, 1564-1616 — Criticism and interpretation I. T.
PR2976.K619 1966   LC A59-1606

Knight, George Wilson, 1897-.   • 2.6740
The olive and the sword; a study of England's Shakespeare, by G. Wilson Knight... London, New York [etc.] Oxford university press, 1944. 4 p. leaves, 102 p., 1 leaf; 21 cm. 1. Shakespeare, William, 1564-1616 — Criticism and interpretation 2. Nationalism — Great Britain. I. T.
PR2976.K62   822.333   LC a 44-6033

Knights, L. C. (Lionel Charles), 1906-.   • 2.6741
Some Shakespearean themes / L.C. Knights. — Stanford: Stanford University Press, 1960. 183 p. — 1. Shakespeare, William, 1564-1616 — Criticism and interpretation I. T.
PR2976.K64   LC 60-15153

Leary, William Gordon.   2.6742
Shakespeare plain: the making and performing of Shakespeare's plays / William G. Leary. — New York: McGraw-Hill, c1977. xi, 298 p.; 21 cm. Includes index. 1. Shakespeare, William, 1564-1616 — Criticism and interpretation I. T.
PR2976.L38   822.3/3 19   LC 76-45776   ISBN 007036947X

Lloyd Evans, Gareth.   2.6743
The upstart crow: an introduction to Shakespeare's plays / Gareth Lloyd Evans; edited and revised by Barbara Lloyd Evans. — London: Dent, 1982. ix, 404 p.; 25 cm. Includes index. 1. Shakespeare, William, 1564-1616 — Criticism and interpretation I. Lloyd Evans, Barbara. II. T.
PR2976.L57 1982   822.3/3 19   LC 82-186072   ISBN 0460102567

Muir, Kenneth.   2.6744
The singularity of Shakespeare, and other essays / Kenneth Muir. — New York: Barnes & Noble Books, 1977. 235 p.; 22 cm. — (Liverpool English texts and studies) 1. Shakespeare, William, 1564-1616 — Criticism and interpretation — Addresses, essays, lectures. 2. Drama — History and criticism — Addresses, essays, lectures. I. T. II. Series.
PR2976.M754   822.3/3   LC 77-72251   ISBN 0064950182

Representing Shakespeare: new psychoanalytic essays / edited   2.6745
by Murray M. Schwartz and Coppélia Kahn.
Baltimore: Johns Hopkins University Press, c1980. xxi, 296 p.; 24 cm. Includes indexes. 1. Shakespeare, William, 1564-1616 — Criticism and interpretation — Addresses, essays, lectures. 2. Psychoanalysis and literature — Addresses, essays, lectures. I. Schwartz, Murray M. II. Kahn, Coppélia.
PR2976.R4   822.3/3   LC 79-3682   ISBN 0801823021

Ridler, Anne, 1912- ed.   • 2.6746
Shakespeare criticism, 1919–35, selected with an introduction by Anne Bradby. — London: Oxford University Press, 1936. xiv, 388 p.; 16 cm. (World's classics; 436) 1. Shakespeare, William — Criticism and interpretation. 2. Shakespeare, William — Appreciation. I. T.
PR2976.R48   822.33   LC 37-27117

Shakespeare criticism, 1935–60 / [edited by] Anne Ridler.   • 2.6747
London; New York: Oxford University Press, 1963. 401 p.; 16 cm. — (World's classics. 590.) 1. Shakespeare, William, 1564-1616 — Criticism and interpretation 2. Shakespeare, William, 1564-1616 — Appreciation I. Ridler, Anne, 1912- II. Series.
PR2976.S52 1963   PR2976.R482 1963.   822.33   LC 63-2557

Rossiter, Arthur Percival.   • 2.6748
Angel with horns, and other Shakespeare lectures. Edited by Graham Storey. — New York, Theatre Arts Books [1961] 316 p. 22 cm. 1. Shakespeare, William — Criticism and interpretation. I. T.
PR2976.R66   822.33   LC 61-19156

Shakespeare's craft: eight lectures / edited, with an introduction   2.6749
by Philip H. Highfill, Jr.
Carbondale: Published for the George Washington University by Southern Illinois University Press, c1982. viii, 177 p.; 23 cm. — (Tupper lectures on Shakespeare.) 1. Shakespeare, William, 1564-1616 — Criticism and interpretation — Addresses, essays, lectures. I. Highfill, Philip H. II. Series.
PR2976.S339   822.3/3 19   LC 81-9386   ISBN 0809310147

Shaw, Bernard, 1856-1950.   • 2.6750
[Prose works. 1971] Shaw on Shakespeare; an anthology of Bernard Shaw's writings on the plays and production of Shakespeare. Edited, and with an introd., by Edwin Wilson. Freeport, N.Y., Books for Libraries Press [1971, c1961] xxii, 284 p. 23 cm. (Essay index reprint series) 1. Shakespeare, William, 1564-1616 — Criticism and interpretation I. T.
PR2976.S35 1971   822.3/3   LC 77-134134   ISBN 0836921755

Tillyard, E. M. W. (Eustace Mandeville Wetenhall), 1889-1962.   • 2.6751
Shakespeare's last plays [by] E. M. W. Tillyard. New York, Barnes & Noble [1964] 85 p. 22 cm. A study of Cymbeline, The winter's tale, and The tempest. 1. Shakespeare, William, 1564-1616 — Criticism and interpretation I. T.
PR2976.T55 1964   822.33   LC 64-55773

Tillyard, E. M. W. (Eustace Mandeville Wetenhall), 1889-1962.   • 2.6752
Shakespeare's problem plays. London, Chatto & Windus, 1950. vi, 156 p. 22 cm. 1. Shakespeare, William — Criticism and interpretation. I. T.
PR2976.T57   LC 50-13421

Traversi, Derek Antona, 1912-.   • 2.6753
An approach to Shakespeare [by] D. A. Traversi. — 3d ed., rev. and expanded. — Garden City, N.Y.: Anchor Books, 1969. 2 v. (Doubleday Anchor book; A74a-A74b) 1. Shakespeare, William, 1564-1616 — Criticism and interpretation I. T.
PR2976.T75 1969   822.3/3   LC 68-17782

Van Doren, Mark, 1894-1972. • **2.6754**
Shakespeare. Garden City, N.Y., Doubleday, 1953 [c1939] 302 p. 18 cm. (Doubleday anchor books, A11) 1. Shakespeare, William, 1564-1616 — Criticism and interpretation I. T.
PR2976.V25 1953   822.33   *LC* 54-14938

Vickers, Brian. **2.6755**
Shakespeare; the critical heritage. — London; Boston: Routledge and K. Paul, 1974-1981. 6 v.; 23 cm. — (The Critical heritage series) 1. Shakespeare, William, 1564-1616 — Criticism and interpretation — Addresses, essays, lectures. 2. Shakespeare, William, 1564-1616 — Criticism and interpretation I. T.
PR2976.V5   822.3/3   *LC* 73-85430   *ISBN* 0710077165

Yates, Frances Amelia. **2.6756**
Shakespeare's last plays: a new approach / Frances A. Yates. — London: Routledge and Kegan Paul, 1975. xi, 140 p., 8 p. of plates: ill., ports.; 22 cm. This book contains four Lord Northcliffe lectures in Literature which were delivered in Jan. 1974, at University College, London. 1. Shakespeare, William, 1564-1616 — Criticism and interpretation — Addresses, essays, lectures. 2. Jonson, Ben, 1573?-1637. The alchemist. 3. Great Britain — History — James I, 1603-1625 I. T.
PR2976.Y3   PR2976 Y3.   822.3/3   *LC* 75-323687   *ISBN* 0710081006

Weimann, Robert. **2.6757**
Shakespeare and the popular tradition in the theater: studies in the social dimension of the dramatic form and function / by Robert Weimann; edited by Robert Schwartz. — Baltimore: Johns Hopkins University Press, c1978. xxii, 325 p. Revised English translation of Shakespeare und die Tradition des Volkstheaters. Includes index. 1. Shakespeare, William, 1564-1616 — Criticism and interpretation 2. Folk-drama, English — History and criticism. I. T.
PR2978.W413 1978   PR2978 W3713 1978.   822.3/3   *LC* 77-13673   *ISBN* 0801819857

PR2981 Comedies

Barber, C. L. (Cesar Lombardi) • **2.6758**
Shakespeare's festive comedy: a study of dramatic form and its relation to social custom / by C.L. Barber. — Princeton, N.J.: Princeton University Press, 1959. x, 265 p.; 25 cm. 1. Shakespeare, William, 1564-1616 — Comedies 2. English drama (Comedy) — History and criticism. 3. England — Social life and customs — 16th century I. T.
PR2981.B3   822.33   *LC* 59-5588

Charlton, H. B. (Henry Buckley), 1890-. • **2.6759**
Shakespearian comedy / by H. B. Charlton. — New York: Barnes & Noble, 1966. 303 p. 'Chapters 2 to 9 ... first published in numbers of the Bulletin of the John Rylands Library between July 1930 and October 1937.' 1. Shakespeare, William, 1564-1616 — Comedies 2. Shakespeare, William, 1564-1616 — Criticism and interpretation I. T.
PR2981.C5   *LC* 66-6944

Evans, Bertrand, 1912-. • **2.6760**
Shakespeare's comedies. — Oxford, Clarendon Press, 1960. xiii, 337 p. 22 cm. 1. Shakespeare, William — Comedies. 2. Shakespeare, William — Criticism and interpretation. I. T.
PR2981.E9   822.33   *LC* 60-50559

Frye, Northrop. **2.6761**
The myth of deliverance: reflections on Shakespeare's problem comedies / Northrop Frye. — Toronto; Buffalo: University of Toronto Press, c1983. viii, 90 p.; 22 cm. 'Based on the Tamblyn lectures, given at the University of Western Ontario on 25, 26, and 27 March 1981'—Pref. 1. Shakespeare, William, 1564-1616 — Comedies I. T. II. Title: Problem comedies.
PR2981.F68 1983   822.3/3 19   *LC* 83-181165   *ISBN* 0802065031

Muir, Kenneth. **2.6762**
Shakespeare's comic sequence / Kenneth Muir. — New York: Barnes & Noble Books, 1979. vii, 215 p.; 23 cm. 1. Shakespeare, William, 1564-1616 — Comedies I. T.
PR2981.M774   822.3/3   *LC* 79-52454   *ISBN* 0064950190

Pettet, E. C. • **2.6763**
Shakespeare and the romance tradition. With an introd. by H. S. Bennett. — [1st ed.]. — London, New York, Staples Press [1949] 208 p. 23 cm. Bibliography: p. 204. 1. Shakespeare, William — Comedies. 2. Shakespeare, William — Criticism and interpretation. 3. Romanticism — England I. T.
PR2981.P4   822.33   *LC* 50-58199

Traversi, Derek Antona, 1912-. • **2.6764**
Shakespeare: the last phase / Derek Antona Traversi. New York: Harcourt, [c1955]. 1 v. 1. Shakespeare, William, 1564-1616 — Criticism and interpretation I. T.
PR2981.T7x   822.33

Wilson, John Dover, 1881-1969. • **2.6765**
Shakespeare's happy comedies. — Evanston [Ill.]: Northwestern University Press, c1962. 224 p. 1. Shakespeare, William, 1564-1616 — Comedies 2. Shakespeare, William, 1564-1616 — Criticism and interpretation I. T.
PR2981.W5   *LC* 63-3499

PR2982 Histories

Berry, Edward I. **2.6766**
Patterns of decay: Shakespeare's early histories / Edward I. Berry. — Charlottesville: University Press of Virginia, 1975. x, 130 p.; 25 cm. 1. Shakespeare, William, 1564-1616 — Histories 2. Shakespeare, William, 1564-1616 — Criticism and interpretation I. T.
PR2982.B47   PR2982 B47.   822.3/3   *LC* 74-32400   *ISBN* 0813905958

Campbell, Lily Bess, 1883-1967. • **2.6767**
Shakespeare's 'Histories'; mirrors of Elizabethan policy, by Lily B. Campbell. San Marino, Calif., The Huntington Library, 1947. xi, 346 p. 2 facsim. (incl. front.) 24 cm. (Huntington Library publications.) 1. Shakespeare, William, 1564-1616 — Histories 2. Historiography I. T. II. Series.
PR2982.C3   822.33   *LC* 47-2108

Charney, Maurice. • **2.6768**
Shakespeare's Roman plays; the function of imagery in the drama. — Cambridge, Harvard University Press, 1961. 250 p. 22 cm. Bibliographical references included in 'Notes' (p. [219]-243) 1. Shakespeare, William — Histories. I. T.
PR2982.C45   822.33   *LC* 61-8838

Holderness, Graham. **2.6769**
Shakespeare's history / Graham Holderness. — Dublin: Gill and Macmillan; New York: St. Martin's Press, 1985. 243 p.; 23 cm. Includes index. 1. Shakespeare, William, 1564-1616 — Histories 2. Shakespeare, William, 1564-1616 — Stage history 3. Historical drama, English — History and criticism. 4. Great Britain — Historiography. I. T.
PR2982.H6 1985   822.3/3 19   *LC* 85-2413   *ISBN* 0312715811

MacCallum, Mungo William, Sir, 1854-1942. **2.6770**
Shakespeare's Roman plays and their background, by M. W. MacCallum. With a foreword by T. J. B. Spencer. — New York: Russell & Russell, 1967. xxiii, 666 p.; 23 cm. 1. Shakespeare, William, 1564-1616 — Tragedies 2. Shakespeare, William, 1564-1616 — Knowledge — Rome. 3. Shakespeare, William, 1564-1616 — Sources I. T.
PR2982.M2 1967   822.3/3   *LC* 64-13292

Prior, Moody Erasmus, 1901- . **2.6771**
The drama of power: studies in Shakespeare's history plays / Moody E. Prior. — Evanston, Ill.: Northwestern University Press, 1973. xvi, 410 p. I. T.
PR2982.P7   *LC* 73-76808   *ISBN* 0810104210 1312

Saccio, Peter. **2.6772**
Shakespeare's English kings: history, chronicle, and drama / Peter Saccio. — New York: Oxford University Press, 1977. viii, 268 p.: ill.; 22 cm. Includes index. 1. Shakespeare, William, 1564-1616 — Histories I. T.
PR2982.S2   PR2982 S2.   822.3/3   *LC* 76-42676   *ISBN* 019502155X

Tillyard, E. M. W. (Eustace Mandeville Wetenhall), 1889-1962. • **2.6773**
Shakespeare's history plays / by E.M.W.Tillyard. — New York: Barnes & Noble, 1964. viii, 336 p.; 22 cm. 1. Shakespeare, William, 1564-1616 — Histories I. T.
PR2982.T5 1964   *LC* 64-55772

Traversi, Derek Antona, 1912-. • **2.6774**
Shakespeare from Richard II to Henry V. / by Derek Traversi. — Stanford, Calif.: Stanford University Press, 1957. 198 p. 1. Shakespeare, William, 1564-1616 — Histories I. T.
PR2982.T7   822.333   *LC* 57-11673

Traversi, Derek Antona, 1912-. • **2.6775**
Shakespeare: the Roman plays. — Stanford: Stanford University Press, 1963. 288 p.; 23 cm. 1. Shakespeare, William, 1564-1616 — Histories I. T.
PR2982.T72   *LC* 63-15213

PR2983 Tragedies

Barroll, J. Leeds (John Leeds), 1928-. **2.6776**
Shakespearean tragedy: genre, tradition, and change in Antony and Cleopatra / J. Leeds Barroll. — Washington: Folger Books; London: Associated University Presses, c1984. 309 p.; 25 cm. Includes index. 1. Shakespeare, William, 1564-1616 — Tragedies 2. Shakespeare, William, 1564-1616. Antony and Cleopatra 3. Tragedy I. T.
PR2983.B29 1984   822.3/3 19   *LC* 82-49309   *ISBN* 0918016681

Bradley, A. C. (Andrew Cecil), 1851-1935.   2.6777
Shakespearean tragedy: Hamlet, Othello, King Lear, Macbeth; [lectures] New York, Meridian Books, 1955. 448 p. 18 cm. (Meridian books, M20) 1. Shakespeare, William, 1564-1616 — Tragedies I. T.
PR2983.B7 1955   822.33   LC 55-9704

Campbell, Lily Bess, 1883-1967.   • 2.6778
Shakespeare's tragic heroes, slaves of passion. With appendices on Bradley's interpretation of Shakespearean tragedy. — New York: Barnes & Noble, 1952. — xii, 296 p., [12] leaves of plates: ill.; 22 cm. 1. Shakespeare, William, 1564-1616 — Tragedies 2. Shakespeare, William, 1564-1616 — Philosophy 3. Tragedy 4. Ethics — History. 5. Emotions 6. English literature — Early modern (to 1700) — History and criticism. I. T.
PR2983.C3 1952   822.33   LC 52-13309

Champion, Larry S.   2.6779
Shakespeare's tragic perspective / Larry S. Champion. — Athens: University of Georgia Press, c1976. 279 p.; 24 cm. 1. Shakespeare, William, 1564-1616 — Tragedies 2. Shakespeare, William, 1564-1616 — Technique I. T.
PR2983.C33   PR2983 C4.   822.3/3   LC 74-75943   ISBN 0820303631

Charlton, H. B. (Henry Buckley), 1890-.   • 2.6780
Shakespearian tragedy. — Cambridge: University Press, 1952. 245 p. 1. Shakespeare, William, 1564-1616 — Criticism and interpretation 2. Shakespeare, William, 1564-1616 — Tragedies I. T.
PR2983.C5 1952

Farnham, Willard.   • 2.6781
Shakespeare's tragic frontier; the world of his final tragedies. — Berkeley, University of California Press, 1963. 289 p. 23 cm. Bibliographical references included in 'Notes' (p. [265]-280) 1. Shakespeare, William — Tragedies. I. T.
PR2983.F35 1963   822.33   LC 50-6566

Holloway, John, 1920-.   • 2.6782
The story of the night, studies in Shakespeare's major tragedies. Lincoln, University of Nebraska Press [1963, c1961] 187 p. 22 cm. 1. Shakespeare, William, 1564-1616 — Tragedies I. T.
PR2983.H6 1963   822.33   LC 63-8166

Honigmann, E. A. J.   2.6783
Shakespeare: seven tragedies: the dramatist's manipulation of response / E. A. J. Honigmann. New York: Barnes & Noble Books, 1976. viii, 215 p.; 23 cm. 1. Shakespeare, William, 1564-1616 — Tragedies 2. Shakespeare, William, 1564-1616 — Technique I. T.
PR2983.H63   822.3/3   LC 75-46319   ISBN 0064929655

Hunter, Robert Grams.   2.6784
Shakespeare and the mystery of God's judgments / Robert G. Hunter. — Athens: University of Georgia Press, c1976. 208 p.; 24 cm. 1. Shakespeare, William, 1564-1616 — Tragedies 2. Shakespeare, William, 1564-1616 — Religion 3. Christianity in literature I. T.
PR2983.H8   822.3/3   LC 75-11449   ISBN 0820303887

Knight, George Wilson, 1897-.   2.6785
The imperial theme: further interpretations of Shakespeare's tragedies, including the Roman plays / by G. Wilson Knight. — 3rd ed. reprinted with minor corrections and additional notes. — London: Methuen, 1968. xiii, 367 p.; 22 cm. 1. Shakespeare, William, 1564-1616 — Tragedies 2. Shakespeare, William, 1564-1616 — Criticism and interpretation I. T.
PR2983.K58 1968   ISBN 0416535801

Knight, George Wilson, 1897-.   2.6786
Shakespeare's dramatic challenge: on the rise of Shakespeare's tragic heroes / G. Wilson Knight. London: Croom Helm; New York: Barnes & Noble Books, c1977. 181 p.: port.; 23 cm. 1. Shakespeare, William, 1564-1616 — Tragedies 2. Shakespeare, William, 1564-1616 — Characters — Heroes 3. Shakespeare, William, 1564-1616 — Dramatic production I. T.
PR2983.K59 1977   822.3/3   LC 76-40875   ISBN 0064938239

Knight, George Wilson, 1897-.   • 2.6787
The wheel of fire; interpretations of Shakespearian tragedy, with three new essays, by G. Wilson Knight. — New York: Barnes and Noble, [1966] xx, 343 p.; 22 cm. 1. Shakespeare, William, 1564-1616 — Criticism and interpretation 2. Shakespeare, William, 1564-1616 — Tragedies I. T.
PR2983.K6 1966   822.33   LC 66-31509

Lawlor, John.   • 2.6788
The tragic sense in Shakespeare / by John Lawlor. — 1st American ed. — New York: Harcourt, Brace, 1960. 185 p. 1. Shakespeare, William, 1564-1616 — Tragedies 2. Tragic, The I. T.
PR2983.L3 1960   822.333   LC 60-10927

Long, Michael (Michael Dudley)   2.6789
The unnatural scene: a study in Shakespearean tragedy / Michael Long. — London: Methuen, 1976. viii, 266 p.; 21 cm. 1. Shakespeare, William, 1564-1616 — Tragedies I. T.
PR2983.L6   PR2983 L6.   822.3/3   LC 76-360072   ISBN 0416821308

Marsh, Derick R. C. (Derick Rupert Clement), 1928-.   2.6790
Passion lends them power: a study of Shakespeare's love tragedies / Derick R. C. Marsh. — Manchester [Eng.]: Manchester University Press; New York: Barnes & Noble, c1976. 239 p.; 23 cm. 1. Shakespeare, William, 1564-1616 — Tragedies 2. Love in literature I. T.
PR2983.M34   LC 76-375729   ISBN 0064945626

Rackin, Phyllis.   2.6791
Shakespeare's tragedies / Phyllis Rackin. — New York: Ungar, c1978. 184 p.: ill. — (World dramatists) Includes index. 1. Shakespeare, William, 1564-1616 — Tragedies I. T.
PR2983.R27   PR2983 R27.   822.3/3   LC 75-34216   ISBN 0804427062

Stirling, Brents, 1904-.   • 2.6792
Unity in Shakespearian tragedy; the interplay of theme and character. — New York, Gordian Press, 1966 [c1956] viii, 212 p. 23 cm. Bibliographical footnotes. 1. Shakespeare, William, 1564-1616 — Tragedies 2. Shakespeare, William, 1564-1616 — Criticism and interpretation I. T.
PR2983.S8 1966   822.33   LC 66-19086

PR2987 Study. Bibliography

Bergeron, David Moore.   2.6793
Shakespeare: a study and research guide / David M. Bergeron; M. Thomas Inge, general editor. — New York: St. Martin's Press, [1975] 145 p.; 21 cm. 1. Shakespeare, William, 1564-1616 — Bibliography 2. Shakespeare, William, 1564-1616 — Study and teaching I. T.
PR2987.B35x   822.3/3   LC 74-24940

Berman, Ronald.   • 2.6794
A reader's guide to Shakespeare's plays; a discursive bibliography / Ronald Berman. — Chicago: Scott, Foresman, [1965] 151 p.; 22 cm. 1. Shakespeare, William, 1564-1616 — Bibliography I. T.
PR2987.B4x   016.8223/3   LC 65-11910

Charney, Maurice.   2.6795
How to read Shakespeare. — [1st ed.]. — New York, McGraw-Hill [1971] x, 149 p. illus. 22 cm. 1. Shakespeare, William, 1564-1616 — Study and teaching I. T.
PR2987.C47   822.3/3   LC 78-169015   ISBN 007010655X

The Garland Shakespeare bibliographies.   2.6796
No. 1-   . — New York: Garland Pub., 1980-. v.; 23 cm.
PR2987. G3x   LC sn 84-10896

Quinn, Edward G., 1932-.   2.6797
The major Shakespearean tragedies; a critical bibliography [by] Edward Quinn, James Ruoff [and] Joseph Grennen. — New York: Free Press, [1973] viii, 293 p.; 24 cm. 1. Shakespeare, William, 1564-1616 — Criticism and interpretation — Bibliography. 2. Shakespeare, William, 1564-1616 — Bibliography I. Ruoff, James E. II. Grennen, Joseph E. III. T.
PR2987.Q5x Z8812.Q54   016.8223/3   LC 72-77284

Smith, Gordon Ross.   2.6798
A classified Shakespeare bibliography, 1936–1958. University Park, Pennyslvania State University Press, 1963. lviii, 784 p. 28 cm. 1. Shakespeare, William, 1564-1616 — Bibliography I. T.
PR2987.S6x   Z8811.S64   016.82233   LC 63-17265

Wells, Stanley W., 1930-.   2.6799
Shakespeare: select bibliographical guides; edited by Stanley Wells. — [London; New York]: Oxford University Press, 1973. 300 p.; 21 cm. 1. Shakespeare, William, 1564-1616 — Bibliography I. T.
PR2987.W4x   Z8811 W44.   016.8223/3   LC 74-159015   ISBN 0198710267

PR2989–2993 Characters

Garber, Marjorie B.   2.6800
Coming of age in Shakespeare / Marjorie Garber. — London; New York: Methuen, 1981. viii, 248 p.; 21 cm. 1. Shakespeare, William, 1564-1616 — Characters 2. Shakespeare, William, 1564-1616 — Knowledge — Psychology 3. Shakespeare, William, 1564-1616 — Knowledge — Manners and customs

4. Maturation (Psychology) in literature. 5. Rites and ceremonies in literature. 6. Life cycle, Human, in literature. I. T.
PR2989.G3   822.3/3 19   *LC* 80-41920   *ISBN* 0416303501

Hazlitt, William, 1778-1830.   ● **2.6801**
Characters of Shakespeare's plays. With an introd. by Sir Arthur Quiller–Couch. London Oxford University Press [1955] 276p. (The World's classics, no. 205) 1. Shakespeare, William, 1564-1616 — Characters I. Quiller-Couch, Arthur Thomas, Sir, 1863-1944. II. T.
PR2989 H3 1955

Kirschbaum, Leo, 1907-.   ● **2.6802**
Character and characterization in Shakespeare; [essays]. — Detroit, Wayne State University Press, 1962. 168 p. 21 cm. — (Wayne books, WB4) 1. Shakespeare, William — Characters. I. T.
PR2989.K5   *LC* 61-12265

Lewis, Wyndham, 1886-1957.   ● **2.6803**
The lion and the fox: the role of the hero in the plays of Shakespeare. New York: Barnes & Noble, 1966. 326 p. (University paperback; UP-68) 1. Shakespeare, William, 1564-1616 — Characters — Heroes 2. Shakespeare, William, 1564-1616 — Criticism and interpretation 3. Machiavelli, Niccolò, 1469-1527. 4. Heroes in literature I. T.
PR2989.L4   *LC* 66-7852

Palmer, John, 1885-1944.   **2.6804**
Political and comic characters of Shakespeare. London, Macmillan; New York, St Martin's Press, 1962. xii, 483 p. 23 cm. 1. Shakespeare, William, 1564-1616 — Characters I. T.
PR2989.P28 1962   822.33   *LC* 63-963

Schücking, Levin Ludwig, 1878-1964.   ● **2.6805**
Character problems in Shakespeare's plays: a guide to the better understanding of the dramatist. — London: Harrap, [1922] 269 p. 1. Shakespeare, William, 1564-1616 — Characters I. T.
PR2989.S3   *LC* 23-7709

Sewell, Arthur.   ● **2.6806**
Character and society in Shakespeare. Oxford: Clarendon Press, 1951. 149 p. 1. Shakespeare, William, 1564-1616 — Criticism and interpretation 2. Shakespeare, William, 1564-1616 — Characters 3. Shakespeare, William, 1564-1616 — Political and social views I. T.
PR2989.S45   *LC* 52-7043

Stoll, Elmer Edgar, 1874-1959.   ● **2.6807**
Shakespeare's young lovers; the Alexander lectures at the University of Toronto, 1935. — New York: AMS Press, 1966,c1937. 118 p.; 22 cm. Reprint of the 1937 ed. 1. Shakespeare, William, 1564-1616 — Characters — Women I. T.
PR2989.S7 1966   *LC* 75-182721

Dusinberre, Juliet.   **2.6808**
Shakespeare and the nature of women / Juliet Dusinberre. New York: Barnes & Noble Books, 1975. 329 p.; 23 cm. Includes index. 1. Shakespeare, William, 1564-1616 — Characters — Women 2. Shakespeare, William, 1564-1616 — Political and social views 3. Women in literature 4. Women — Great Britain — Social conditions. I. T.
PR2991.D8 1975b   822.3/3   *LC* 77-352949   *ISBN* 0064918424

The Woman's part: feminist criticism of Shakespeare / edited   **2.6809**
by Carolyn Ruth Swift Lenz, Gayle Greene, and Carol Thomas Neely.
Urbana: University of Illinois Press, c1980. x, 348 p.; 24 cm. Includes index. 1. Shakespeare, William, 1564-1616 — Characters — Women — Addresses, essays, lectures. 2. Women in literature — Addresses, essays, lectures. 3. Feminist literary criticism — Addresses, essays, lectures. I. Lenz, Carolyn Ruth Swift, 1928- II. Greene, Gayle, 1943- III. Neely, Carol Thomas, 1939- IV. Feminist criticism of Shakespeare.
PR2991.W6   822.3/3   *LC* 79-26896   *ISBN* 0252007514

Hotson, Leslie, 1897-.   ● **2.6810**
Shakespeare's motley. — New York: Haskell House, 1971. vii, 133 p.: illus.; 23 cm. Reprint of the 1952 ed. 1. Shakespeare, William, 1564-1616 — Characters — Fools 2. Armin, Robert, fl. 1610. 3. Motley I. T.
PR2992.F6 H6 1971   822.3/3   *LC* 75-117592   *ISBN* 0838310257

Brower, Reuben Arthur, 1908-.   **2.6811**
Hero & saint: Shakespeare and the Graeco–Roman heroic tradition, by Reuben A. Brower. — New York, Oxford University Press, 1971. xi, 424 p. 22 cm. 1. Shakespeare, William, 1564-1616 — Characters — Heroes 2. Shakespeare, William, 1564-1616 — Knowledge — Literature I. T.
PR2992.H4 B7   822.3/3   *LC* 72-176003   *ISBN* 0195015150

Spivack, Bernard.   ● **2.6812**
Shakespeare and the allegory of evil: the history of a metaphor in relation to his major villains. — New York, Columbia University Press, [c1958] ix, 508 p. 24 cm. Bibliographical references included in 'Notes' (p. [455]-481) 'Bibliography of morality plays': p. [483]-493. 1. Shakespeare, William — Characters — Villains. 2. Evil in literature 3. Moralities, English — Hist. & crit. 4. English dramas — Early modern and Elizabethan — Hist. & crit. I. T.
PR2992.V5S6   822.33   *LC* 57-12758

Wilson, John Dover, 1881-1969.   **2.6813**
The fortunes of Falstaff / by J. Dover Wilson. — Cambridge: University Press, 1943. viii, 143 p., [1] p.; 20 cm. — (George Rogers Clark lecture. 1943) 'Apart from the introduction and passages omitted here and there from later chapters ... the contents of this book weredelivered at Cambridge in May 1943 as five Clark lectures.' - Pref. 1. Shakespeare, William, 1564-1616 — Characters — Falstaff. I. T. II. Series.
PR2993.F2 W5 1943   *LC* 43-18292

PR2994–2997 Wit. Dramatic Art

Campbell, Oscar James, 1879-1970.   ● **2.6814**
Shakespeare's satire. — New York: Gordian Press, 1971 [c1943] xii, 227 p.; 23 cm. 1. Shakespeare, William, 1564-1616 — Humor, satire, etc. 2. Satire, English — History and criticism. I. T.
PR2994.C3 1971   822.3/3   *LC* 74-159036   *ISBN* 0877521506

Baker, George Pierce, 1866-1935.   ● **2.6815**
The development of Shakespeare as a dramatist. New York, AMS Press, 1965. x, 329 p. illus. 23 cm. First published in 1907. 1. Shakespeare, William, 1564-1616 — Technique 2. Shakespeare, William, 1564-1616 — Stage history — To 1625 I. T.
PR2995.B3 1965   822.33   *LC* 66-3647

Moulton, Richard Green, 1849-1924.   ● **2.6816**
Shakespeare as a dramatic artist; a popular illustration of the principles of scientific criticism, by Richard G. Moulton. With a new introd. by Eric Bentley. — New York: Dover Publications, [1966] xviii, 443 p.; 21 cm. 'Republication of the third revised and enlarged edition ... 1893.' 1. Shakespeare, William, 1564-1616 — Technique 2. Drama — Technique I. T.
PR2995.M7 1966   822.33   *LC* 66-14556

Quiller-Couch, Arthur Thomas, Sir, 1863-1944.   ● **2.6817**
Shakespeare's workmanship, by Sir Arthur Quiller–Couch. — New York, The Macmillan company; Cambridge, Eng., The University press, 1931. xiv, 309, [1] p. 18 cm. Printed in Great Britain. 'Papers ... first written as lectures and so spoken before an audience in the University of Cambridge.'—p. [vii] Published also under title: Notes on Shakespeare's workmanship, 1917. 1. Shakespeare, William — Technique. 2. Shakespeare, William — Criticism and interpretation. I. T.
PR2995.Q8 1931   822.33   *LC* 31-32231

Stoll, Elmer Edgar, 1874-1959.   ● **2.6818**
Art and artifice in Shakespeare: a study in dramatic contrast and illusion / by Elmer Edgar Stoll. — New York: Barnes & Noble, 1962. xiii, 178 p.; 22 cm. — (University paperbacks; UP-23) 1. Shakespeare, William, 1564-1616 — Technique 2. Shakespeare, William, 1564-1616 — Tragedies I. T.
PR2995.S7 1962   *LC* 62-12225

Mahood, M. M. (Molly Maureen)   ● **2.6819**
Shakespeare's wordplay [by] M. M. Mahood. London, Methuen, 1968. 192 p. 21 cm. (University paperbacks, UP242) 1. Shakespeare, William, 1564-1616 — Style 2. Play on words I. T.
PR2997.P8 M3 1968   822.3/3   *LC* 68-94266   *ISBN* 0416295606

Jones, Emrys, 1931-.   **2.6820**
Scenic form in Shakespeare. — Oxford, Clarendon Press, 1971. [9], 269 p. 23 cm. 1. Shakespeare, William, 1564-1616 — Dramatic production I. T.
PR2997.S3 J6   822.3/3   *LC* 71-887677   *ISBN* 0198120125

PR3000–3069 Treatment and Knowledge of Special Subjects

Whitaker, Virgil Keeble, 1908-.   ● **2.6821**
Shakespeare's use of learning; an inquiry into the growth of his mind & art. — San Marino, Calif., Huntington Library, 1953. ix, 366 p. 24 cm. — (Huntington Library publications) Bibliography: p. 347-360. 1. Shakespeare, William — Knowledge and learning. 2. Shakespeare, William — Sources. I. T.
PR3000.W5 1964   822.33   *LC* 53-9113

Curry, Walter Clyde, 1887-.   ● **2.6822**
Shakespeare's philosophical patterns. [2d ed.] Baton Rouge, Louisiana State University Press [1959] 261 p. 23 cm. Includes bibliography. 1. Shakespeare, William, 1564-1616 — Philosophy I. T.
PR3001.C8 1959   822.33   *LC* 59-14601

James, David Gwilym, 1905-1968. • **2.6823**
The dream of learning; an essay on the Advancement of learning, Hamlet, and King Lear. — Oxford, Clarendon Press, 1951. 126 p. 19 cm. 1. Bacon, Francis, viscount St. Albans. Advancement of learning. 2. Shakespeare, William, 1564-1616. Hamlet 3. Shakespeare, William, 1564-1616. King Lear I. T.
PR3001.J3   822.33   *LC* 52-7556

Harbage, Alfred, 1901-. • **2.6824**
As they liked it; an essay on Shakespeare and morality, by Alfred Harbage. — New York, The Macmillan company, 1947. xiii p., 1 l., 238 p. 21 cm. 'First printing.' Bibliographical references included in 'Notes' (p. [203]-222) 'List of works cited': p. 223-229. 1. Shakespeare, William — Religion and ethics. I. T.
PR3007.H3   822.33   *LC* 47-30198

Sisson, Charles Jasper, 1885-1966. • **2.6825**
Shakespeare's tragic justice. [Toronto] W.J. Gage [1961] 106p. 1. Shakespeare, William, 1564-1616 — Religion and ethics I. T.
PR3007 S5

Stauffer, Donald Alfred, 1902-1952. • **2.6826**
Shakespeare's world of images; the development of his moral ideas [by] Donald A. Stauffer. — [1st Midland book ed.]. — Bloomington, Indiana University Press [1966, c1949] 393 p. 20 cm. — (A Midland book, MB87) 1. Shakespeare, William, 1564-1616 — Religion and ethics. I. T.
PR3007.S8 1966   822.33   *LC* 66-12754

Root, Robert Kilburn, 1877-1950. • **2.6827**
Classical mythology in Shakespeare. — New York, Gordian Press, 1965. 134 p. 23 cm. — (Yale studies in English. v. 19) 1. Shakespeare, William, 1564-1616 — Knowledge — Folklore, mythology I. T. II. Series.
PR3009.R72   822.33   *LC* 65-24996

Frye, Roland Mushat. • **2.6828**
Shakespeare and Christian doctrine. Princeton, N.J., Princeton University Press, 1963. ix, 314 p. 23 cm. 1. Shakespeare, William, 1564-1616 — Religion 2. Christianity and literature I. T.
PR3011.F7   822.33   *LC* 63-9990

Kernan, Alvin B. **2.6829**
The playwright as magician: Shakespeare's image of the poet in the English public theater / Alvin B. Kernan. — New Haven: Yale University Press, 1979. vii, 164 p.; 22 cm. 1. Shakespeare, William, 1564-1616 — Knowledge — Performing arts 2. Theater — England — History. 3. Authors, English — Early modern, 1500-1700 I. T.
PR3034.K47   822.3/3   *LC* 79-10829   *ISBN* 0300023790

Thomson, J. A. K. (James Alexander Kerr), 1879-1959. • **2.6830**
Shakespeare and the classics.— New York: Barnes & Noble,; 1961. 254 p. 22 cm. 1. Shakespeare, William, 1564-1616 — Knowledge — Classical literature. 2. Literature, Comparative — English and classical. 3. Literature, Comparative — Classical and English. I. T.
PR 3037 T48   *LC* 52-2934

Speaight, Robert, 1904-. • **2.6831**
Nature in Shakespearian tragedy / by Robert Speaight. — London: Hollis & Carter, 1955. 179 p.; 22 cm. 1. Shakespeare, William, 1564-1616 — Knowledge — Natural history I. T.
PR3039.S63   *LC* 55-3369

Garber, Marjorie B. **2.6832**
Dream in Shakespeare; from metaphor to metamorphosis [by] Marjorie B. Garber. — New Haven: Yale University Press, 1974. x, 226 p.; 23 cm. 1. Shakespeare, William, 1564-1616 — Knowledge — Psychology I. T.
PR3069.D67 G3   PR3069 D67 G3.   822.3/3   *LC* 73-86895
ISBN 0300017065

Council, Norman. **2.6833**
When honour's at the stake; ideas of honour in Shakespeare's plays. New York, Barnes & Noble Books [1973] 165 p. 23 cm. 1. Shakespeare, William, 1564-1616 — Ethics I. T.
PR3069.H6 C6 1973b   822.3/3   *LC* 73-172834   *ISBN* 0064912922

Jorgensen, Paul A. • **2.6834**
Shakespeare's military world. — Berkeley, University of California, Press [1973] x, 345 p. 23 cm. — (California library reprint series) 1. Shakespeare, William, 1564-1616 — Knowledge — Military sciences 2. War and literature I. T.
PR3069.M5J6 1973   822.33   *LC* 56-9673   *ISBN* 0520250199

Sypher, Wylie. **2.6835**
The ethic of time: structures of experience in Shakespeare / Wylie Sypher. — New York: Seabury Press, c1976. xi, 216 p. — (A Continuum book) 1. Shakespeare, William, 1564-1616. 2. Time in literature I. T.
PR3069.T5 S9   PR3069T5 S9.   822.3/3   *LC* 76-13844   *ISBN* 0816492999

PR3070–3071 Textual Criticism

Bowers, Fredson Thayer. • **2.6836**
On editing Shakespeare [by] Fredson Bowers. — Charlottesville, University Press of Virginia [1966] ix, 210 p. 22 cm. 'On editing Shakespeare and the Elizabethan dramatists, comprising the first three articles of the present book, was published ... in 1955 by the University of Pennsylvania Library.' 1. Shakespeare, William, 1564-1616 — Criticism, Textual 2. English drama — Early modern and Elizabethan, 1500-1600 — History and criticism. 3. Editing I. T.
PR3071.B59   822.33   *LC* 66-26777

Greg, W. W. (Walter Wilson), 1875-1959. • **2.6837**
The editorial problem in Shakespeare: a survey of the foundation of the text. — 2nd ed. — Oxford: Clarendon Press, 1951. lv, 210 p.: ill. — (Clark lectures. 1939) 1. Shakespeare, William, 1564-1616 — Criticism, Textual I. T. II. Series.
PR3071.G7 1951   *LC* a 52-9294

Greg, W. W. (Walter Wilson), 1875-1959. • **2.6838**
Principles of emendation in Shakespeare. — St. Clair Shores, Mich.: Scholarly Press, 1972. 70 p.; 22 cm. Reprint of the 1928 ed., which was issued as the Annual Shakespeare lecture for 1928 of the British Academy. 1. Shakespeare, William, 1564-1616 — Criticism, Textual I. T.
PR3071.G75 1972   822.3/3   *LC* 73-131726   *ISBN* 0403006139

Hamilton, A. C. (Albert Charles), 1921-. **2.6839**
The early Shakespeare, by A. C. Hamilton. San Marino, Calif., Huntington Library, 1967. ix, 237 p. 24 cm. (Huntington Library publications.) 1. Shakespeare, William, 1564-1616 — Criticism and interpretation I. T. II. Series.
PR3071.H33   822.3/3   *LC* 67-12996

McKerrow, Ronald Brunlees, 1872-1940. • **2.6840**
The treatment of Shakespeare's text by his earlier editors, 1709–1768. — Freeport, N.Y.: Books for Libraries Press, [1970] 34 p.; 23 cm. — (British Academy. Annual Shakespeare lecture, 1933) (Library of Shakespearean biography and criticism, series 2, pt. C.) Reprint of the 1933 ed. 1. Shakespeare, William, 1564-1616 — Criticism, Textual — History. 2. Shakespeare, William, 1564-1616 — Editors I. T. II. Series.
PR3071.M25 1970   822.3/3   *LC* 79-109656

McKerrow, Ronald Brunlees, 1872-1940. • **2.6841**
Prolegomena for the Oxford Shakespeare; a study in editorial method. — Oxford: Clarendon Press, 1939. xiv, 110 p. With 2 specimen pages from the Oxford Shakespeare Richard III. 1. Shakespeare, William, 1564-1616 — Criticism, Textual I. T. II. Title: The Oxford Shakespeare.
PR3071.M26   *LC* 39-25837

PR3072–3088 Language. Style

Clemen, Wolfgang. • **2.6842**
The development of Shakespeare's imagery / with a preface by J. Dover Wilson. — Cambridge, Mass.: Harvard University Press, 1951. xii, 236 p. 1. Shakespeare, William, 1564-1616 — Style 2. Figures of speech I. T.
PR3072.C554   *LC* a 51-9877

Doran, Madeleine, 1905-. **2.6843**
Shakespeare's dramatic language: essays / by Madeleine Doran. — Madison: University of Wisconsin Press, 1976. x, 253 p.; 23 cm. 1. Shakespeare, William, 1564-1616 — Style I. T.
PR3072.D6   PR3072 D6.   822.3/3   *LC* 75-32072   *ISBN* 0299070107

Evans, B. Ifor (Benjamin Ifor), 1899-. • **2.6844**
The language of Shakespeare's plays. London, Methuen [1952] xiii, 190 p. 22 cm. 1. Shakespeare, William, 1564-1616 — Style I. T.
PR3072.E9   822.3/3   *LC* 52-2948

Miriam Joseph, Sister, 1898-. • **2.6845**
Rhetoric in Shakespeare's time; literary theory of Renaissance Europe. — New York: Harcourt, Brace & World, [1962] xii, 40, 286-421 p.; 21 cm. — (A Harbinger book; H012) 'Originally published ... as part of .... [the author's] Shakespeare's use of the arts of language.' 1. Shakespeare, William, 1564-1616 — Style 2. Rhetoric — 1500-1800 I. T.
PR3072.M48   808   *LC* 62-21466

Jorgensen, Paul Alfred, 1916-. • **2.6846**
Redeeming Shakespeare's words. Berkeley, University of California Press, 1962. x, 131 p. 23 cm. 1. Shakespeare, William, 1564-1616 — Language I. T.
PR3077.J6   822.33   *LC* 62-9940

Kökeritz, Helge, 1902-. • **2.6847**
Shakespeare's names: a pronouncing dictionary. — New Haven, Yale University Press, 1959. xvi, 100 p. 17 cm. — (Yale Shakespeare supplements)

1. Shakespeare, William — Language — Pronunciation. 2. Shakespeare, William — Dictionaries, indexes, etc. 3. Names — Pronunciation I. T.
PR3081.K57   822.33   *LC* A 59-6798

Kökeritz, Helge, 1902-.   • **2.6848**
Shakespeare's pronunciation. New Haven, Yale University Press, 1953. xv, 516 p. 25 cm. 1. Shakespeare, William, 1564-1616 — Language — Pronunciation 2. English language — Early modern, 1500-1700 — Pronunciation. I. T.
PR3081.K6   822.33   *LC* 52-12071

Spurgeon, Caroline Frances Eleanor, 1869-1942.   • **2.6849**
Shakespeare's imagery, and what it tells us, by Caroline F. E. Spurgeon ... with charts and illustrations ... Cambridge [Eng.] The University press, 1935. xv, [1], 408 p. front., pl., VII fold. diagr. 23 cm. 1. Shakespeare, William, 1564-1616 — Style 2. Figures of speech I. T.
PR3081.S64 1935   822.33   *LC* 35-24321

Halliday, F. E. (Frank Ernest), 1903-.   • **2.6850**
Poetry of Shakespeare's plays. New York: Barnes & Noble, 1964. 194 p. 1. Shakespeare, William, 1564-1616 — Versification 2. Shakespeare, William, 1564-1616 — Criticism and interpretation I. T.
PR3085 H3 1964   821.3   *LC* 64-22620

Crane, Milton, 1917-.   • **2.6851**
Shakespeare's prose / by Milton Crane. — Chicago, University of Chicago Press [1951] 219 p. 21 cm. Bibliography: p. 213-217. 1. Shakespeare, William, 1564-1616 — Prose 2. English drama — Early modern and Elizabethan, 1500-1600 I. T.
PR3087.C7 1963   822.33   *LC* 51-10894

PR3091–3112 Dramatic Representation of Shakespeare's Plays
(Music in Shakespeare: see: ML80.S5)

Brown, John Russell.   **2.6852**
Discovering Shakespeare: a new guide to the plays / John Russell Brown. — New York: Columbia University Press, 1981. viii, 168 p.; 23 cm. Includes index. 1. Shakespeare, William, 1564-1616 — Dramatic production 2. Shakespeare, William, 1564-1616 — Criticism and interpretation I. T.
PR3091.B68 1981   822.3/3 19   *LC* 81-10071   *ISBN* 0231053584

Eyewitnesses of Shakespeare: first hand accounts of performances, 1590–1890 / Gāmini Salgādo.   **2.6853**
New York: Barnes & Noble Books, 1975. 360 p.: ill.; 23 cm. 1. Shakespeare, William, 1564-1616 — Stage history I. Salgādo, Gāmini, 1929-
PR3091.E95   792/.09421   *LC* 74-28762   *ISBN* 0064960714

Harbage, Alfred, 1901-.   • **2.6854**
Shakespeare's audience, by Alfred Harbage. — New York: Columbia university press, 1941. ix, 201 p.; 23 cm. 1. Shakespeare, William, 1564-1616 — Stage history 2. Shakespeare, William, 1564-1616 — Appreciation I. T.
PR3091.H36   822.33   *LC* 41-26970

Harbage, Alfred, 1901-.   • **2.6855**
Theatre for Shakespeare. — [Toronto] University of Toronto Press [c1955] 118 p. 22 cm. — (The Alexander lectures, 1954-55) 1. Shakespeare, William — Stage history. I. T.
PR3091.H37   822.33   *LC* 56-1874

Knight, George Wilson, 1897-.   • **2.6856**
Principles of Shakespearian production with especial reference to the tragedies / by G. Wilson Knight. — London: Faber and Faber, [1936] 2 p. leaves, 7-246 p.; 23 cm. 1. Shakespeare, William, 1564-1616 — Stage history — 1800- I. T.
PR3091.K6 1936   *LC* 36-13059

Nagler, A. M. (Alois Maria), 1907-.   • **2.6857**
Shakespeare's stage. [Translated by Ralph Manheim] New Haven, Yale University Press, 1958. 117 p. illus. 18 cm. (Yale Shakespeare supplements) 1. Shakespeare, William, 1564-1616 — Stage history — To 1625 2. Theaters — England — London — History. 3. Theater — England — History. I. T.
PR3091.N313   792/.09421 19   *LC* 58-11256

Odell, George Clinton Densmore, 1866-1949.   • **2.6858**
Shakespeare: from Betterton to Irving. — New York, B. Blom [1963] 2 v. illus., ports., facsims. 24 cm. 1. Shakespeare, William — Stage history. 2. Theater — London — Hist. I. T.
PR3091.O4 1963   792.0942   *LC* 63-23277

Sprague, Arthur Colby, 1895-.   • **2.6859**
Shakespeare and the actors: the stage business in his plays, 1660–1905. — New York, Russell & Russell, 1963. 442 p. illus. 23 cm. Includes bibliography.

1. Shakespeare, William — Stage history. 2. Shakespeare, William — Dramaturgy. I. T.
PR3091.S65 1963   822.33   *LC* 63-11033

Trewin, J. C. (John Courtenay), 1908-.   **2.6860**
Going to Shakespeare / J. C. Trewin. — London; Boston: G. Allen & Unwin, 1978. 288 p.; 23 cm. Includes index. 1. Shakespeare, William, 1564-1616 — Dramatic production I. Shakespeare, William, 1564-1616. II. T.
PR3091.T72   822.3/3   *LC* 79-303273   *ISBN* 0047920106

Manvell, Roger, 1909-.   **2.6861**
Shakespeare and the film. — New York: Praeger, [1972] xvi, 172 p.: illus.; 25 cm. 1. Shakespeare, William, 1564-1616 — Film and video adaptations I. T.
PR3093.M3   822.3/3   *LC* 70-159966

Baldwin, Thomas Whitfield, 1890-.   • **2.6862**
The organization and personnel of the Shakespearean company. — New York, Russell & Russell, 1961 [c1954] xi, 463 p. tables. 25 cm. 1. Shakespeare, William — Theater — England — History. 3. Actors, English. I. T. II. Title: Shakespearean company.
PR3095.B3 1961   792.0942   *LC* 60-6036

Beckerman, Bernard.   • **2.6863**
Shakespeare at the Globe, 1599–1609. — New York: Macmillan, 1962. 254 p.; 22 cm. 1. Shakespeare, William, 1564-1616 — Stage history — To 1625 2. Shakespeare, William, 1564-1616 — Dramatic production 3. Southwark, Eng. Globe Theatre. I. T.
PR3095.B4   792.094216   *LC* 62-7159

Bradbrook, M. C. (Muriel Clara), 1909-.   • **2.6864**
Elizabethan stage conditions: a study of their place in the interpretation of Shakespeare's plays, by M. C. Bradbrook. London, Cambridge U.P., 1968. ix, 149 p. 19 cm. The Harness Prize essay, 1931. 1. Shakespeare, William, 1564-1616 — Stage history — To 1625 2. Shakespeare, William, 1564-1616 — Criticism and interpretation 3. Shakespeare, William, 1564-1616 — Technique I. University of Cambridge. Harness prize. II. T.
PR3095.B65 1968   792/.023   *LC* 68-30950   *ISBN* 0521095395

Thomson, Peter, 1938-.   **2.6865**
Shakespeare's theatre / Peter Thomson. — London; Boston: Routledge & Kegan Paul, 1983. xiii, 190 p., [8] p. of plates: ill.; 24 cm. (Theatre production studies.) Includes indexes. 1. Shakespeare, William, 1564-1616 — Stage history — To 1625 2. Lord Chamberlain's Servants (Theater company) 3. Globe Theatre (Southwark, London, England) 4. Theaters — England — London — History. I. T. II. Series.
PR3095.T48 1983   792/.09421/2 19   *LC* 82-25026   *ISBN* 0710094809

Hogan, Charles Beecher, 1906-.   • **2.6866**
Shakespeare in the theatre, 1701–1800. — Oxford: Clarendon Press, 1952-1957. 2 v. 1. Shakespeare, William, 1564-1616 — Stage history — 1625-1800 I. T.
PR3097.H6   *LC* 52-12229

Spencer, Hazelton, 1893-1944.   • **2.6867**
Shakespeare improved: the Restoration versions in quarto and on the stage / Hazelton Spencer. — New York: F. Ungar, 1963. xii, 406 p.: ill., facsim., ports. 1. Shakespeare, William, 1564-1616 — Adaptations 2. Shakespeare, William, 1564-1616 — Stage history — 1625-1800 3. Theater — London (England) — History. I. T.
PR3097.S7 1963   *LC* 63-21999

Hill, Errol.   **2.6868**
Shakespeare in sable: a history of black Shakespearean actors / Errol Hill; foreword by John Houseman. — Amherst: University of Massachusetts Press, 1984. xxviii, 216 p.: ill.; 24 cm. Includes index. 1. Shakespeare, William, 1564-1616 — Stage history — United States. 2. Afro-American actors — Biography. 3. Theater — United States — History. I. T. II. Title: Black Shakespearean actors.
PR3105.H54 1984   792.9/5 19   *LC* 83-18106   *ISBN* 0870234269

Shattuck, Charles Harlen, 1910-.   **2.6869**
Shakespeare on the American stage: from the Hallams to Edwin Booth / Charles H. Shattuck. — [Washington]: Folger Shakespeare Library, 1976. xiv, 170 p., [4] leaves of plates: ill. (some col.); 24 cm. 1. Shakespeare, William, 1564-1616 — Stage history — United States. 2. Actors — United States — Biography. 3. Theater — United States — History I. Folger Shakespeare Library. II. T.
PR3105.S5   792/.0973   *LC* 75-43999   *ISBN* 0813906512

Sprague, Arthur Colby, 1895-.   • **2.6870**
Shakespearian players and performances. With a new pref. to the Greenwood reprint by the author. — New York: Greenwood Press, [1969, c1953] 222 p.: illus.; 23 cm. 1. Shakespeare, William, 1564-1616 — Stage history 2. Shakespeare, William, 1564-1616 — Stage history — United States. 3. Actors — England. I. T.
PR3106.S6 1969   792/.028/0922   *LC* 69-14091

Trewin, J. C. (John Courtenay), 1908-.   ● **2.6871**
Shakespeare on the English stage, 1900–1964: a survey of productions illustrated from the Raymond Mander and Joe Mitchenson theatre collection / J.C. Trewin. — London: Barrie and Rockliff, 1964. xii, 328 p.: ill. Includes index. 1. Shakespeare, William, 1564-1616 — Stage history — 1800- I. T.
PR3106.T7   *LC* 64-54513

Grebanier, Bernard D. N., 1903-.   **2.6872**
Then came each actor: Shakespearean actors, great and otherwise, including players and princes, rogues, vagabonds and actors motley, from Will Kempe to Olivier and Gielgud and after / Bernard Grebanier. — New York: McKay, [1975] xii, 626 p., [16] leaves of plates: ill.; 24 cm. Includes index. 1. Shakespeare, William, 1564-1616 — Stage history 2. Actors — Biography I. T.
PR3112.G73   PR3112 G73.   791/.092/2   *LC* 74-82983   *ISBN* 0679505075

Shattuck, Charles Harlen, 1910-.   **2.6873**
The Hamlet of Edwin Booth [by] Charles H. Shattuck. — Urbana: University of Illinois Press, [1969] xxvii, 321 p.: illus., ports.; 24 cm. 1. Shakespeare, William, 1564-1616. Hamlet 2. Booth, Edwin, 1833-1893. I. T.
PR3112.S5   792/.028/0924   *LC* 71-76832   *ISBN* 0252000196

PR3135–3178 Shirley. Tourneur. Udall

Shirley, James, 1596-1666.   ● **2.6874**
Dramatic works and poems. Now first collected; with notes by William Gifford, and additional notes, and some account of Shirley and his writings, by Alexander Dyce. New York, Russell & Russell, 1966. 6 v. port.; 23 cm. 'Reproduced from the edition of 1833.' I. Giggord, William, 1756-1826, ed. II. Dyce, Alexander, 1798-1869. III. T.
PR3141.D8 1966

Lucow, Ben.   **2.6875**
James Shirley / by Ben Lucow. — Boston: Twayne Publishers, 1981. 176 p.; 21 cm. — (Twayne's English authors series; TEAS 321) Includes index. 1. Shirley, James, 1596-1666 — Criticism and interpretation. I. T.
PR3147.L8 1981   822/.4 19   *LC* 80-29503   *ISBN* 0805767169

Tourneur, Cyril, 1575?-1626.   ● **2.6876**
Works / edited by Allardyce Nicoll; with decorations by Frederick Carter. — New York: Russell & Russell, 1963. 344 p.: ill. I. Nicoll, Allardyce, 1894- II. T.
PR3170.A5 N5 1963   *LC* 63-15185

Udall, Nicholas, 1505-1556.   ● **2.6877**
The dramatic writings of Nicholas Udall, comprising Ralph Roister Doister: A note on Udall's lost plays: Note–book and word–list, ed. by John S. Farmer. London, Printed for subscribers, 1906. 160 p. (Early English dramatists) I. T.
PR3176.U3A14   822.22

PR3180–3188 Webster

Webster, John, 1580?-1625?   ● **2.6878**
Complete works. / Edited by F.L. Lucas. New York: Gordian P., 1966. 4v. (288, 372, 339, 274 p.) I. Lucas, F. L. (Frank Laurence), 1894-1967. ed. II. T.
PR3181.L8 1966   822.3   *LC* 66-20023

Webster, John, 1580?-1625?   ● **2.6879**
The Duchess of Malfi; edited by John Russell Brown. — London: Methuen, 1969. ix, 220 p.: facsim., music.; 21 cm. — (University paperback, UP263) (The Revels plays.) I. Brown, John Russell. ed. II. T.
PR3184.D8 1969   822/.3   *LC* 74-407606   *ISBN* 0416223603

Boklund, Gunnar.   ● **2.6880**
The Duchess of Malfi: sources, themes, characters. — Cambridge: Harvard University Press, 1962. viii, 189 p.; 22 cm. 1. Webster, John, 1580?-1625? Duchess of Malfi I. T.
PR3184.D83 B6

Webster, John, 1580?-1625?   ● **2.6881**
The white devil; edited by John Russell Brown. — London: Methuen, 1968. lxxiii, 203 p.; 21 cm. — (University paperback, UP 219) The Revels plays. I. Brown, John Russell. ed. II. T.
PR3184.W5 1968   822/.3   *LC* 73-407532   *ISBN* 0416698905

Berry, Ralph, 1931-.   ● **2.6882**
The art of John Webster. — Oxford: Clarendon Press, 1972. ix, 174 p.: illus.; 23 cm. 1. Webster, John, 1580?-1625? — Criticism and interpretation. I. T.
PR3187.B4   822/.3   *LC* 72-193341   *ISBN* 0198120230

Bogard, Travis.   ● **2.6883**
The tragic satire of John Webster. — New York, Russell & Russell, 1965 [c1955] xii, 158 p. 23 cm. Bibliographical references included in 'Notes' (p. 151-158) 1. Webster, John, 1580?-1625? I. T.
PR3187.B6 1965   822.3   *LC* 65-13952

Hunter, G. K. comp.   **2.6884**
John Webster: a critical anthology; edited by G. K. & S. K. Hunter. — Harmondsworth: Penguin, 1969. 328 p.; 19 cm. — (Penguin critical anthologies) 1. Webster, John, 1580?-1625? I. Hunter, S. K., joint comp. II. T.
PR3187.H8 1969b   822.3   *LC* 78-530038   *ISBN* 0140801359

Leech, Clifford.   ● **2.6885**
John Webster; a critical study. — New York: Haskell House, 1970. 122 p.; 23 cm. — (Hogarth lectures on literature, [16]) Reprint of the 1951 ed. 1. Webster, John, 1580?-1625? I. T.
PR3187.L4 1970   822/.3   *LC* 78-143481   *ISBN* 083830690X

PR3291–3784 17th–18th Centuries (1640–1770)

PR3291 Anonymous Works

The Adventures of Lindamira, a lady of quality / edited by Benjamin Boyce.   ● **2.6886**
Minneapolis: University of Minnesota Press, [1949] xvii, 167 p.; 23 cm. With facsimile of original t.p.: The adventures of Lindamira, a lady of quality. Written by her own hand, to her friend in the country. In IV. parts. Revised and corrected by Mr. Tho. Brown. London, Printed for R. Wellington, 1702. I. Boyce, Benjamin, 1903-. II. Brown, Thomas, 1663-1704. III. Title: Lindamira.
PR3291.A1 A36 1949   *LC* 49-8987

PR3300–3308 Addison

Addison, Joseph, 1672-1719.   ● **2.6887**
The Coverley papers from the Spectator / edited, with introd. and notes by O. M. Myers. — Corrected ed. Oxford: Clarendon Press, 1933. xx, 168 p. 19 cm. I. Myers, O. M., ed. II. Steele, Richard, Sir, 1672-1729. III. T.
PR3304.D4x

Addison, Joseph, 1672-1719.   ● **2.6888**
The letters of Joseph Addison / edited by Walter Graham. — Oxford: Clarendon Press, 1941. xxxvi, 527 p., [2] leaves of plates: ill. I. Graham, Walter James, 1885- II. T.
PR3306 A53

Smithers, Peter, Sir, 1913-.   ● **2.6889**
The life of Joseph Addison. — 2nd ed. — Oxford; London: Clarendon P., 1968. xvi, 499 p.: 5 plates, facsim., 4 ports.; 23 cm. 1. Addison, Joseph, 1672-1719 — Biography. I. T.
PR3306.S55 1968   824/.5 B   *LC* 68-105168   *ISBN* 0198116586

PR3310–3324 A–B

Akenside, Mark, 1721-1770.   ● **2.6890**
The poetical works of Mark Akenside. — London: W. Pickering, 1845. viii, 353 p.: port. — (Aldine edition of the British poets) 'Life of Akenside, by A. Dyce'. I. Dyce, Alexander, 1798-1869. II. T.
PR3310.A5 D8

Burney, Fanny, 1752-1840.   **2.6891**
Camilla; or, A picture of youth [by] Frances Burney; edited with an introduction by Edward A. Bloom and Lillian D. Bloom. London, New York, Oxford University Press, 1972. xxxiv, 956 p. 21 cm. (Oxford English novels) I. T.
PZ3.A665 Cam6 PR3316.A4 C3x   823/.6   *LC* 72-192391   *ISBN* 0192553275

Burney, Fanny, 1752-1840.   **2.6892**
Cecilia / by Fanny Burney; with a new introduction by Judith Simons. — London: Virago, 1986. [938] p.; 20 cm. (Virago modern classic) I. T.
PR3316.A4 C4x   823/.6 19   *ISBN* 0860687759

Burney, Fanny, 1752-1840.   **2.6893**
Evelina, or, The history of a young lady's entrance into the world [by] Frances Burney; edited and introduced by Edward A. Bloom. London, New York [etc.]

Oxford U.P., 1968. xliv, 436 p. 3 illus., facsim. 21 cm. (Oxford English novels) I. Bloom, Edward Alan, 1914- ed. II. T.
PZ3.A665 E23   PR3316.A4 E8x.   LC 68-73843

Burney, Fanny, 1752-1840.   **2.6894**
The journals and letters of Fanny Burney (Madame D'Arblay) / ed. by Joyce Hemlow and others. — Oxford, Clarendon Press, 1972- < 84 > . v. < 1-12 > illus., facsim., geneal. table, port. 23 cm. Vol. 2 edited by Joyce Hemlow and Althea Douglas. Vol. 12 edited by Joyce Hemlow, with Althea Douglas and Patricia Hawkins. 1. Burney, Fanny, 1752-1840. I. Hemlow, Joyce. II. Douglas, Althea. III. T.
PR3316.A4 Z552   823/.6 B   LC 72-189680   ISBN 0198114982

Gérin, Winifred.   • **2.6895**
The Young Fanny Burney.— London; New York: T. Nelson, 1961. 131p.: ill.; 23cm. 1. Burney, Fanny, 1752-1840. I. T.
PR3316.A4 Z643 1961   LC 61-19480

Hemlow, Joyce.   • **2.6896**
The history of Fanny Burney. — Oxford, Clarendon Press, 1958. 528 p. illus. 23 cm. 1. Burney, Fanny, 1752-1840. I. T.
PR3316.A4Z647   928.2   LC 58-963 rev

Kilpatrick, Sarah.   **2.6897**
Fanny Burney / Sarah Kilpatrick. — New York: Stein and Day, 1980. 232 p.: ill.; 25 cm. Includes index. 1. Burney, Fanny, 1752-1840 — Biography. 2. Novelists, English — 18th century — Biography. I. T.
PR3316.A4 Z664   823/.8 B 19   LC 80-5891   ISBN 0812827619

Steensma, Robert C., 1930-.   **2.6898**
Dr. John Arbuthnot / by Robert C. Steensma. — Boston: Twayne Publishers, 1979. 146 p.; 21 cm. — (Twayne's English authors series; TEAS 256) Includes index. 1. Arbuthnot, John, 1667-1735 — Criticism and interpretation. I. T.
PR3316.A5 Z87   828/.5/09   LC 78-24237   ISBN 0805767495

Behn, Aphra, 1640-1689.   • **2.6899**
The Works of Aphra Behn / edited by Montague Summers. — New York: Phaeton Press, 1967. 6 v.: port.; 22 cm. I. Summers, Montague, 1880-1948. II. T.
PR3317.A1 1967a   828/.4/09   LC 67-24964

Duffy, Maureen.   **2.6900**
The passionate shepherdess: Aphra Behn, 1640-89 / Maureen Duffy. — London: Cape, 1977. 324 p., [4] leaves of plates: ill.; 23 cm. Includes index. 1. Behn, Aphra, 1640-1689 — Biography. 2. Authors, English — Early modern, 1500-1700 — Biography. I. T.
PR3317.Z5 D8   822/.4 B   LC 78-301563   ISBN 0224013491

Goreau, Angeline.   **2.6901**
Reconstructing Aphra: a social biography of Aphra Behn / Angeline Goreau. — New York: Dial Press, c1980. x, 339 p., [8] leaves of plates: ill.; 24 cm. Includes index. 1. Behn, Aphra, 1640-1689 — Biography. 2. Authors, English — Early modern, 1500-1700 — Biography. I. T.
PR3317.Z5 G6   822/.4 B   LC 80-11495   ISBN 0803774788

PR3325 Boswell

Boswell, James, 1740-1795.   • **2.6902**
Boswell's column: being his seventy contributions to the London magazine under the pseudonym the Hypochondriack, from 1777 to 1783, here first printed in book form in England / introd. and notes by Margery Bailey. — 1st ed. — London: W. Kimber, 1951. xx, 359 p.: ill. I. Boswell, James, 1740-1795. Hypochondriack. II. T.
PR3325.A65 1951   LC 52-25238

Boswell, James, 1740-1795.   • **2.6903**
Letters of James Boswell / collected and edited by Chauncey Brewster Tinker. — Oxford: Clarendon Press, 1924. 2 v.: double facsim., port. 1. Boswell, James, 1740-1795 — Correspondence. I. Tinker, Chauncey Brewster, 1876-1963. II. T.
PR3325.A85 T5   LC 25-26165

Boswell, James, 1740-1795.   **2.6904**
The Yale edition of the private papers of James Boswell. — New York: McGraw-Hill, 1950-. v.; 25 cm. I. T.
PR3325.A88x

Brady, Frank.   **2.6905**
Boswell's political career. — New Haven, Yale University Press, 1965. xv, 200 p. 23 cm. — (Yale studies in English. v. 155) 'In its original form, this study was [the author's] ... Yale doctoral dissertation.' Bibliographical footnotes. 1. Boswell, James, 1740-1795. 2. Gt. Brit. — Pol. & govt. — 1760-1789. I. T. II. Series.
PR3325.B7   928.2   LC 65-11175

Brady, Frank.   **2.6906**
James Boswell, the later years, 1769-1795 / Frank Brady. — New York: McGraw-Hill, c1984. xvii, 609 p., [8] p. of plates: ill.; 25 cm. Includes index. 1. Boswell, James, 1740-1795 — Biography. 2. Johnson, Samuel, 1709-1784 — Biography. 3. Boswell, James, 1740-1795. Life of Samuel Johnson 4. Authors, Scottish — 18th century — Biography. 5. Authors, English — 18th century — Biography. I. T.
PR3325.B72 1984   828/.609 B 19   LC 83-9400   ISBN 0070505586

Dowling, William C.   **2.6907**
The Boswellian hero / by William C. Dowling. — Athens: University of Georgia Press, c1979. xvi, 202 p.; 24 cm. Includes index. 1. Boswell, James, 1740-1795 — Criticism and interpretation. 2. Johnson, Samuel, 1709-1784. in fiction, drama, poetry, etc. 3. Heroes in literature 4. Biography (as a literary form) I. T.
PR3325.D6 1979   828/.6/09   LC 78-5885   ISBN 0820304611

Pottle, Frederick Albert, 1897-.   • **2.6908**
James Boswell; the earlier years, 1740-1769 [by] Frederick A. Pottle. — [1st ed.]. — New York, McGraw-Hill [1966] xix, 606 p. illus., ports. 24 cm. Bibliographical references included in 'Notes' (p. 443-568). 1. Boswell, James, 1740-1795. I. T.
PR3325.P62   828.608 (B)   LC 65-27779

PR3326 Brome. Brooke

Brome, Alexander, 1620-1666.   **2.6909**
Poems / Roman R. Dubinski, editor. — Toronto; Buffalo: University of Toronto Press, c1982. 2 v.: ill.; 25 cm. Includes index. I. Dubinski, Roman R. (Roman Rudolph), 1936- II. T.
PR3326.B36 A17 1982   821/.4 19   LC 83-107902   ISBN 0802055354

Brooke, Henry, 1703?-1783.   **2.6910**
The fool of quality, by Henry Brooke; with a biographical preface by Charles Kingsley, and a new life of the author by E. A. Baker. London, Routledge, New York, Dutton [1906] lix, 427 p. port., fold. geneal. tab. 21 cm. (Library of early novelists, v. 7) 1. Brooke, Henry, 1703?-1783. 2. Brooks family 3. Brooke, Henry, 1703?-1783 — Bibliography. I. Baker, Ernest Albert, 1869-1941. II. Kingsley, Charles, 1819-1875. III. T.
PZ1.L6143 vol. 7   PR3326.B4 F6x 1906.   LC a 10-1072

PR3327 Browne

Browne, Thomas, Sir, 1605-1682.   • **2.6911**
Works / edited by Geoffrey Keynes. New ed. Chicago: University of Chicago Press, 1964. 4 v. I. Keynes, Geoffrey Langdon, 1887-. II. T.
PR3327.A143   LC 61-14539

Browne, Thomas, Sir, 1605-1682.   • **2.6912**
Religio medici, and other works / edited by L.C. Martin. — Oxford: Clarendon P., 1964. xxvii, 383 p.: ill., facsims., group port.; 23 cm. 1. Religion 2. Christian life 3. Christian ethics I. Martin, Leonard Cyril, 1886-. II. T.
PR3327.A15   828.3   LC 64-6939

Browne, Thomas, Sir, 1605-1682.   **2.6913**
[Pseudodoxia epidemica] Sir Thomas Browne's Pseudodoxia epidemica / edited by Robin Robbins. — Oxford: Clarendon Press; New York: Oxford University Press, 1981. 2 v. (lxi, 1198 p., [7] p. of plates): ill.; 23 cm. — (Oxford English texts) 1. Natural history — Pre-Linnean works 2. Errors, Popular 3. Superstition 4. Learning and scholarship I. Robbins, Robin Hugh A. II. T.
PR3327.A27   001.9/6 19   LC 80-41787   ISBN 0198127065

Bennett, Joan Frankau.   • **2.6914**
Sir Thomas Browne, a man of achievement in literature. — Cambridge [Eng.] University Press, 1962. 254 p. 23 cm. Includes bibliography. 1. Browne, Thomas, Sir, 1605-1682. I. T.
PR3327.B4   828.3   LC 62-52250

PR3329-3332 Bunyan

Bunyan, John, 1628-1688.   • **2.6915**
Grace abounding to the chief of sinners; &, The life & death of Mr. Badman / by John Bunyan. — London; Toronto: Dent; New York: Dutton, [1911?] xv, 304 p. 17 1/2 cm. — (Everyman's library Theology & philosophy; [no. 815]) 'Introduction by G. B. Harrison.' 1. Bunyan, John, 1628-1688. I. Bunyan, John, 1628-1688. Relation of the imprisonment of Mr. John Bunyan. II. Bunyan, John, 1628-1688. Continuation of Mr. Bunyan's life. III. Bunyan, John, 1628-1688. Life and death of Mr. Badman. IV. Harrison, G. B. (George Bagshawe), 1894- V. T. VI. Title: The life and death of Mr. Badman. VII. Title: A relation of the imprisonment of Mr. John Bunyan. VIII. Title: A continuation of Mr. Bunyan's life. IX. Series.
AC1.E8 no. 815   PR3329.G1 1911.   928.2   LC 37-5632

Bunyan, John, 1628-1688.   • **2.6916**
Grace abounding to the chief of sinners, and, The pilgrim's progress from this world to that which is to come, edited with an introduction by Roger Sharrock. — London; New York [etc.]: Oxford U.P., 1966. xi, 412 p. front (port.) 3 facsims. 22.5 cm. — (Oxford standard authors) I. T.
PR3329.G1 1966   LC 66-72516

Bunyan, John, 1628-1688.   **2.6917**
The holy war: made by Shaddai upon Diabolus for the regaining of the metropolis of the world; or, The losing and taking again of the town of Mansoul / edited by Roger Sharrock and James F. Forrest. — Oxford: Clarendon Press; New York: Oxford University Press, 1980. xlviii, 288 p., [1] leaf of plates: facsim. — (Oxford English texts) Includes index. I. Sharrock, Roger. II. Forrest, James F. III. T. IV. Title: The losing and taking again of the town of Mansoul.
PR3329.H1 1980   823/.4   LC 79-40264   ISBN 0198118872

Bunyan, John, 1628-1688.   • **2.6918**
The pilgrim's progress from this world to that which is to come. Edited by James Blanton Wharey. — 2d ed., rev. by Roger Sharrock. — Oxford, Clarendon Press, 1960. cxviii, 365 p. illus., port., facsims. 23 cm. 1. Bunyan, John. The pilgrim's progress — Bibl. I. Wharey, James Blanton, 1872-1946. ed. II. T.
PR3330.A2W5 1960   823.4   LC 60-1990

The Pilgrim's progress: critical and historical views / edited by   **2.6919**
Vincent Newey.
Totowa, N.J.: Barnes & Noble Books, 1980. xiii, 302 p.; 23 cm. 1. Bunyan, John, 1628-1688 The Pilgrim's progress — Addresses, essays, lectures. I. Newey, Vincent.
PR3330.A9 P5 1980   828/.407 19   LC 80-140328   ISBN 0389200166

Sharrock, Roger.   • **2.6920**
John Bunyan. — [New ed.; with revised bibliography]. — London; Melbourne [etc.]: Macmillan; New York: St. Martin's P., 1968. 163 p.; 21 cm. 1. Bunyan, John, 1628-1688. I. T.
PR3331.S47 1968   823/.4 B   LC 68-22423

Tindall, William York, 1903-.   • **2.6921**
John Bunyan, mechanick preacher. — New York, Russell & Russell, 1964 [c1934] xii, 309 p. 23 cm. — (Columbia University studies in English and comparative literature) Issued also as thesis, Columbia University. Bibliography: p. [291]-295. 1. Bunyan, John, 1628-1688. I. T. II. Series.
PR3331.T5 1964   828.4   LC 64-23462

Winslow, Ola Elizabeth.   **2.6922**
John Bunyan. — New York: Macmillan, 1961. 242 p.: illus.; 22 cm. 1. Bunyan, John, 1628-1688. I. T.
PR3331.W62   928.2   LC 61-6890

PR3338 Butler

Butler, Samuel, 1612-1680.   • **2.6923**
Satires and miscellaneous poetry and prose / edited by René Lamar. — Cambridge: University Press, 1928. xxi, 503 p. — (Cambridge English classics) I. Lamar, René, 1889-. II. T. III. Series.
PR3338.A15   LC 28-18057

Butler, Samuel, 1612-1680.   **2.6924**
Characters, edited with an introd. and notes by Charles W. Daves. — Cleveland: Press of Case Western Reserve University, 1970. xiii, 330 p.; 24 cm. I. Daves, Charles W. ed. II. T.
PR3338.A64 1970   828/.4/08   LC 73-84487

Butler, Samuel, 1612-1680.   • **2.6925**
Hudibras; edited with an introduction and commentary by John Wilders. — Oxford: Clarendon P., 1967. lxi, 463 p.: front., plate (port.); 23 cm. — (Oxford English texts) I. Wilders, John. ed. II. T.
PR3338.A7 1967   821/.4   LC 67-110276

Butler, Samuel, 1612-1680.   **2.6926**
Prose observations / Samuel Butler; edited with an introd. and commentary by Hugh De Quehen. — Oxford: Clarendon Press; New York: Oxford University Press, 1979. lx, 429 p.: ill.; 23 cm. — (Oxford English texts) 1. Commonplacebooks I. Quehen, Hugh de. II. T.
PR3338.A76 1979   823/.4   LC 77-30357   ISBN 0198127286

Wasserman, George Russell, 1927-.   **2.6927**
Samuel 'Hudibras' Butler / by George R. Wasserman. — Boston: Twayne Publishers, c1976. 146 p.; 21 cm. — (Twayne's English authors series; TEAS 193) Includes index. 1. Butler, Samuel, 1612-1680 — Criticism and interpretation. I. T.
PR3338.W3   821/.4   LC 76-24859   ISBN 0805766677

PR3339–3359 C

Carey, Henry, 1687?-1743.   • **2.6928**
The poems of Henry Carey / edited with an introduction and notes by Frederick T. Wood. — London: Scholartis Press, [1930] 261 p.; 23 cm. I. Wood, Frederick Thomas, 1905-.
PR3339.C23 A17 1930   LC 30-25470

Cary, Patrick, fl. 1651.   **2.6929**
The poems of Patrick Cary / edited by Veronica Delany with biographical and critical introduction. — Oxford [Eng.]: Clarendon Press, 1978. xcvi, 128 p.: ill.; 23 cm. I. Delany, Veronica. II. T.
PR3339.C43 1978   821/.4   LC 77-30206   ISBN 0198125666

Centlivre, Susanna, 1667?-1723.   **2.6930**
The plays of Susanna Centlivre / edited with an introduction by Richard C. Frushell. — New York: Garland Pub., 1982. 3 v.; 23 cm. — (Eighteenth-century English drama.) Reprint of works originally published 1700-1723. I. Frushell, Richard C. II. T. III. Series.
PR3339.C6 A116 1982   822/.5 19   LC 78-66629   ISBN 082403581X

Centlivre, Susanna, 1667?-1723.   **2.6931**
A bold stroke for a wife. Edited by Thalia Stathas. — Lincoln: University of Nebraska Press, [1968] xxvi, 112 p.; 21 cm. — (Regents renaissance drama series BB267) 'A Bison book.' I. Stathas, Thalia, ed. II. T.
PR3339.C6 A65 1968   822/.5   LC 67-12640

Lock, F. P.   **2.6932**
Susanna Centlivre / by F. P. Lock. — Boston: Twayne Publishers, 1979. 155 p.: port.; 21 cm. — (Twayne's English authors series; TEAS 254) Includes index. 1. Centlivre, Susanna, 1667?-1723 — Criticism and interpretation. I. T.
PR3339.C6 L6 1979   822/.5 19   LC 78-24405   ISBN 0805767444

Chatterton, Thomas, 1752-1770.   • **2.6933**
The complete works of Thomas Chatterton: a bicentenary edition; edited by Donald S. Taylor in association with Benjamin B. Hoover. — Oxford: Clarendon Press, 1971. 2 v. (xlv, 1265, vii p. 27 plates (1 fold.)): illus., facsims., maps.; 23 cm. I. Taylor, Donald S., ed. II. Hoover, Benjamin Beard, 1921- ed. III. T.
PR3340.A2 1971   821/.6   LC 72-584147   ISBN 0198118481

Churchill, Charles, 1731-1764.   • **2.6934**
Poetical works. Edited with an introd. and notes by Douglas Grant. — Oxford, Clarendon Press, 1956. xxii, 587 p. facsims. 23 cm. Includes bibliographical references. 'Each poem is prefixed by a type-facsimile of the title-page to the edition chosen.' I. T.
PR3346.C8 1956   827.61   LC 57-553

Smith, Raymond J.   **2.6935**
Charles Churchill / by Raymond J. Smith. Boston: Twayne Publishers, c1977. 156 p.: port.; 21 cm. (Twayne's English authors series; TEAS 197) Includes index. 1. Churchill, Charles, 1731-1764 — Criticism and interpretation. I. T.
PR3346.C8 S55   821/.6   LC 76-42988   ISBN 0805766693

Cibber, Colley, 1671-1757.   **2.6936**
Colley Cibber, three sentimental comedies: Love's last shift: or, The fool in fashion. The careless husband. The lady's last stake; or, The wife's resentment. Edited, with an introd. and notes, by Maureen Sullivan. — New Haven: Yale University Press, 1973. li, 352 p.: illus.; 24 cm. — (Yale studies in English. 184) I. T. II. Series.
PR3347.A6 1973   822/.5   LC 73-77168   ISBN 0300015321

Barker, Richard Hindry, 1902-.   **2.6937**
Mr. Cibber of Drury Lane, by Richard Hindry Barker. New York, Columbia university press, 1939. 5 p. l., [3]-278 p. 24 cm. (Columbia university studies in English and comparative literature. no. 143) Issued also as thesis (PH.D.) Columbia university. 1. Cibber, Colley, 1671-1757. I. T.
PR3347.B3 1939a   LC 40-4155

Cleland, John, 1709-1789.   **2.6938**
John Cleland's Memoirs of a woman of pleasure, with an introduction for modern readers by Peter Quennell. —. — 1st paparback ed. [New York] Putnam, 1963. xxviii, 228 p.; 18 cm. Cover title: Fanny Hill. First published 1749 under title: Memoires of a woman of pleasure. I. T. II. Title: Fanny Hill III. Title: Memoirs of a woman of pleasure
PR3348.C65 M4x 1963b   LC 63-9656

Collins, William, 1721-1759.   **2.6939**
The works of William Collins / edited by Richard Wendorf and Charles Ryskamp. — Oxford: Clarendon Press; New York: Oxford University Press, 1979. xxxvii, 234 p., [2] leaves of plates: ill.; 23 cm. — (Oxford English texts) I. Wendorf, Richard. II. Ryskamp, Charles. III. T.
PR3350.A2 1979   821/.5   LC 78-40758   ISBN 0198127499

Wendorf, Richard. 2.6940
William Collins and eighteenth–century English poetry / Richard Wendorf. — Minneapolis: University of Minnesota Press, c1981. xiii, 227 p.: ill.; 24 cm. 1. Collins, William, 1721-1759 — Criticism and interpretation. I. T.
PR3354.W46　　823/.8 19　　*LC* 81-14674　　*ISBN* 0816610584

Collop, John, fl. 1640-1660. ● 2.6941
Poems / edited by Conrad Hilberry. — Madison, Univ. of Wisconsin Press, 1962. xii, 227 p. I. Hilberry, Conrad. II. T.
PR3356.C5 H5　　*LC* 61-5905

Page, Eugene Richard, 1903-. ● 2.6942
George Colman, the elder; essayist, dramatist, and theatrical manager, 1732–1794. New York Columbia University Press 1935. 334p. (Columbia university studies in English and comparative literature, no. 120) 1. Colman, George, 1732-1794. 2. Theater — London I. T. II. Series.
PR3358 Z5 P3

PR3360–3368 Congreve

Congreve, William, 1670-1729. 2.6943
The works of Congreve: Comedies: Incognita: Poems; edited by F.W. Bateson. London, P. Davies [1930] xxviii, 507 p. 19 cm. I. Bateson, Frederick Wilse, 1901- II. T.
PR3361.B3x

Congreve, William, 1670-1729. ● 2.6944
The complete plays of William Congreve. Edited by Herbert Davis. Chicago, University of Chicago Press [1967] vii, 501 p. 25 cm. (Curtain playwrights) Includes bibliographical references. I. Davis, Herbert John, 1893-1967. ed. II. T.
PR3362.D3 1967　　*LC* 66-20598

Congreve, William, 1670-1729. ● 2.6945
Comedies,. — by William Congreve; ed., with introduction and notes, by Bonamy Dobrée. — London, New York [etc.] H. Milford, Oxford university press [1925] xxviii p., 1 l., 441, [1] p. 15.5 cm. — (Half-title: The World's classics, 276) I. Dobrée, Bonamy, 1891- ed. II. T.
PR3362.D6　　*LC* 26-13750

Congreve, William, 1670-1729. ● 2.6946
The mourning bride, poems, & miscellanies, edited, with introd. by Bonamy Dobrée. London Oxford University Press [1928] 540p. (The World's classics, 277) I. Dobrée, Bonamy, 1891- ed. II. T.
PR3364 M68 1928

Taylor, Daniel Crane, 1897-. 2.6947
William Congreve, by D. Crane Taylor. London, Milford, 1931. 252 p. front. (port.) 23 cm. 1. Congreve, William, 1670-1729. I. T.
PR3366.T3x

Love, Harold, 1937-. 2.6948
Congreve / Harold Love. — Totowa, N.J.: Rowman and Littlefield, 1975, c1974. 131 p.; 23 cm. (Plays & playwrights series) Includes index. 1. Congreve, William, 1670-1729 — Criticism and interpretation. I. T.
PR3367.L6 1975　　822/.4　　*LC* 74-23234　　*ISBN* 0874716233

Williams, Aubrey L. 2.6949
An approach to Congreve / Aubrey L. Williams. — New Haven: Yale University Press, 1979. xiii, 234 p.; 22 cm. 1. Congreve, William, 1670-1729 — Religion. I. T.
PR3368.R4 W5　　822/.4　　*LC* 78-10381　　*ISBN* 0300023049

Avery, Emmett Langdon, 1903-. ● 2.6950
Congreve's plays on the eighteenth–century stage. — New York, Modern Language Association of America, 1951. viii, 226 p. 25 cm. — (Modern Language Association of America. Monograph series, 18) Bibliographical footnotes. 1. Congreve, William, 1670-1729. 2. Theater — London — Hist. I. T. II. Series.
PR3368.S8A8　　822.46　　*LC* 51-9620

PR3369–3373 Corbet. Cotton. Cowley

Corbet, Richard, Bp. of Norwich, 1582-1635. ● 2.6951
Poems. Edited by J. A. W. Bennett and H. R. Trevor–Roper. — Oxford, Clarendon Press, 1955. lxv, [1], 177 p. port. 23 cm. 'Previous editions of Corbett's poems': p. xli—li. 'The manuscripts': p. lvii—lxv. 'Other references and abbreviations': p. [lxvi] I. T.
PR3369.C2 1955　　821.39　　*LC* 55-14700

Cotton, Charles, 1630-1687. ● 2.6952
Poems. Edited, with an introd. by John Buxton. Cambridge, Harvard University Press [1958] xliv, 286 p. port. 17 cm. (The Muses' library) I. Buxton, John. ed. II. T.
PR3369.C3 A1x

Cowley, Abraham, 1618-1667. ● 2.6953
Poetry & prose, with Thomas Sprat's life, and observations by Dryden, Addison, Johnson and others. With an introd. and notes by L. C. Martin. — Oxford, Clarendon Press, 1949. xlvii, 128 p. port. 19 cm. Bibliography: p. [xiv] I. Sprat, Thomas, 1635-1713. II. T.
PR3371.M3　　*LC* A 50-5306

Cowley, Abraham, 1618-1667. ● 2.6954
Essays, plays and sundry verses / text edited by A.R. Waller. — Cambridge: University Press, 1906. 499 p. — (Cambridge English classics) 'A supplement of notes, biographical, bibliographical and critical ... will be published ... at no very distant date.' - Pref. I. Waller, Alfred Rayney, 1867-1922. II. T. III. Series.
PR3371.W3　　*LC* 07-23868

Cowley, Abraham, 1618-1667. 2.6955
The civil war. Edited by Allan Pritchard. — [Toronto; Buffalo]: University of Toronto Press, [1973] x, 196 p.; 25 cm. — (University of Toronto. Dept. of English. Studies and texts, 20) 1. Great Britain — History — Civil War, 1642-1649 — Poetry. I. Pritchard, Allan, ed. II. T.
PR3372.C5 1973　　821/.4　　*LC* 75-185731　　*ISBN* 0802052630

Nethercot, Arthur Hobart, 1895-. ● 2.6956
Abraham Cowley: the muse's Hannibal / by Arthur H. Nethercot. — New York: Russell & Russell, [1967] vii, 367 p.: illus., ports.; 22 cm. 'First published in 1931, reissued, 1967, with additional notes.' 1. Cowley, Abraham, 1618-1667.
PR3373.N4 1967　　821/.4　　*LC* 66-24739

PR3380–3384 Cowper

Cowper, William, 1731-1800. 2.6957
The poems of William Cowper / edited by John D. Baird and Charles Ryskamp. — Oxford: Clarendon Press; New York: Oxford University Press, 1980-. v.; 23 cm. — (Oxford English texts) I. Baird, John D. II. Ryskamp, Charles. III. T.
PR3380.A2 1980　　821/.6　　*LC* 78-40749　　*ISBN* 0198118759

Cowper, William, 1731-1800. ● 2.6958
The poetical works of William Cowper, edited by H.S. Milford. 4th ed. London,: Oxford university press, 1934. xxx, 684 p. : ill.; 19 cm. 'List of chief editions consulted:' xx-xxiii. I. Milford, Humphrey Sumner, Sir, 1877-1952. II. T.
PR3380.A5 M5　　*LC* 36-8492

Cowper, William, 1731-1800. 2.6959
Selected poems and letters, chosen and edited by A. Norman Jeffares. [London] Oxford University Press 1963. 222p. (New Oxford English series) I. T.
PR3381 J4

Cowper, William, 1731-1800. 2.6960
The letters and prose writings of William Cowper / edited by James King and Charles Ryskamp. — Oxford: Clarendon Press; New York: Oxford University Press, 1979-1986. 5 v.: port.; 23 cm. 1. Cowper, William, 1731-1800 — Correspondence. 2. Poets, English — 18th century — Correspondence. I. King, James. II. Ryskamp, Charles. III. T.
PR3383.A3 K5 1979　　821/.6 B　　*LC* 78-40495　　*ISBN* 0198118635

Nicholson, Norman, 1914-. 2.6961
William Cowper. — London: J. Lehmann, 1951. 167 p.: port. 1. Cowper, William, 1731-1800. I. T.
PR3383.N5 1951　　*LC* 51-6592

Ryskamp, Charles. ● 2.6962
William Cowper of the Inner Temple, Esq.; a study of his life and works to the year 1768. — Cambridge [Eng.] University Press, 1959. xvii, 274 p. illus. 24 cm. Includes bibliography. 1. Cowper, William, 1731-1800. I. T.
PR3383.R9　　830.81　　*LC* 59-16274

Newey, Vincent. 2.6963
Cowper's poetry: a critical study and reassessment / by Vincent Newey. — Totowa, NJ: Barnes & Noble, 1982. xx, 358 p.; 23 cm. — (Liverpool English texts and studies; 20) 1. Cowper, William, 1731-1800 — Criticism and interpretation. I. T.
PR3384.N4 1982　　821/.6 19　　*LC* 82-6843　　*ISBN* 0389200794

PR3386 Crashaw. Crown

Crashaw, Richard, 1613?-1649.   **2.6964**
The complete poetry of Richard Crashaw. Edited, with an introd. and notes, by George Walton Williams. — [1st ed.]. — Garden City, N.Y.: Anchor Books, 1970. xxvi, 707 p.: illus.; 21 cm. — (The Anchor seventeenth-century series, ACO-12) English, Latin, Italian, and Greek. I. Williams, George Walton, 1922- ed. II. T.
PR3386.A185   821/.4   *LC* 68-14177

Bertonasco, Marc F., 1934-.   **2.6965**
Crashaw and the Baroque, by Marc F. Bertonasco. — University: University of Alabama Press, [1971] vii, 158 p.; 21 cm. 1. Crashaw, Richard, 1613?-1649. 2. Emblems I. T.
PR3386.B4   821/.4   *LC* 70-148692   *ISBN* 081737308X

Parrish, Paul A., 1944-.   **2.6966**
Richard Crashaw / by Paul A. Parrish. — Boston: Twayne Publishers, 1980. 189 p.: ill.; 21 cm. — (Twayne's English authors series; TEAS 299) Includes index. 1. Crashaw, Richard, 1613?-1649 — Criticism and interpretation. I. T.
PR3386.P3 1980   821/.4   *LC* 80-14468   *ISBN* 0805767916

Crown, Mr. (John), 1640?-1712.   **2.6967**
City politiques. Edited by John Harold Wilson. Lincoln, University of Nebraska [1967] xix, 159 p. 21 cm. (Regents restoration drama series) I. Wilson, John Harold, 1900- ed. II. T.
PR3388.C2 C5 1967   *LC* 67-12641

PR3401–3408 Defoe

Defoe, Daniel, 1661?-1731.   **2.6968**
The versatile Defoe: an anthology of uncollected writings / by Daniel Defoe; edited and introduced by Laura Ann Curtis. — Totowa, N.J.: Rowman and Littlefield, 1979. ix, 469 p.: ill.; 24 cm. I. Curtis, Laura Ann. II. T.
PR3401.C8 1979b   828/.408   *LC* 79-114904   *ISBN* 0847661490

Defoe, Daniel, 1661?-1731.   • **2.6969**
[Selections. 1927] The Shakespeare Head edition of the novels and selected writings of Daniel Defoe. [Oxford, Basil Blackwell, publishers to the Shakespeare head press of Stratford-upon-Avon, 1927-28] 14 v.; 20 cm. Half-title; each volume has also special t.-p. Maps on lining papers, v.11, 13. I. T.
PR3401.S5x   *LC* a 40-2511

Defoe, Daniel, 1661?-1731.   • **2.6970**
[Robinson Crusoe] The life and strange surprizing adventures of Robinson Crusoe of York, mariner: who lived eight and twenty years all alone in an un-inhabited island on the coast of America, near the mouth of the great river of Oroonoque, having been cast on shore by shipwreck wherein all the men perished but himself [i.e. Daniel Defoe]; edited with an introduction by J. Donald Crowley. London, New York, Oxford University Press, 1972. xxx, 316 p., [2] leaves. map. 21 cm. (Oxford English novels) I. Crowley, J. Donald (Joseph Donald) ed. II. T.
PZ3.D362 R220 PR3403.A1x   823/.5   *LC* 72-172417   *ISBN* 0192553593

Defoe, Daniel, 1661?-1731.   **2.6971**
The history and remarkable life of the truly honourable Col. Jacque, commonly call'd Col. Jack ... Edited with an introd. by Samuel Holt Monk. — London; New York: Oxford University Press, 1965. xxx, 317 p.; 21 cm. — (Oxford English novels.) Title on cover: Colonel Jack. I. Monk, Samuel Holt. II. T. III. Title: Colonel Jack. IV. Series.
PZ3.D362 Hi5   PR3404.C5 1965.   *LC* 65-29730

Defoe, Daniel, 1661?-1731.   **2.6972**
Memoirs of a cavalier or a military journal of the wars in Germany, and the wars in England; from the year 1632, to the year 1648. Written threescore years ago by an English gentleman... / Daniel Defoe; edited with an introduction by James T. Boulton. — London: Oxford University Press, 1972. xxii, 318 p. — (Oxford English novels) 1. Thirty Years' War, 1618-1648 — Fiction. 2. Great Britain — History — Civil War, 1642-1649 — Fiction. I. Boulton, James T. II. T. III. Series.
PR3404.M4 B6   *ISBN* 0192553631

Defoe, Daniel, 1661?-1731.   **2.6973**
Moll Flanders / Daniel Defoe; edited with an introd. and notes by James Sutherland. Boston: Houghton Mifflin, 1959. xxi, 297 p. (Riverside editions; B31.) I. T.
PR3404 M6 1959   PR3404 M6 1959.   *LC* 59-16265

Defoe, Daniel, 1661?-1731.   **2.6974**
Roxana, the fortunate mistress, or, A history of the life and vast variety of fortunes of Mademoiselle de Beleau, afterwards called the Countess de Wintselshcim in Germany, being the person he Lady Roxana in the time of Charles II / edited, with an introduction by Jane Jack. — London, New York,

Oxford University Press, 1964. xviii, 333 p. 21 cm. — (Oxford English novels.) I. Jack, Jane. II. T. III. Title: The fortunate mistress. IV. Series.
PZ3.D362Rk12   PR3404.R6 1964.   *LC* 64-56215

Defoe, Daniel, 1661?-1731.   • **2.6975**
[Correspondence] Letters. Edited by George Harris Healey. Oxford, Clarendon Press, 1955. xxi, 506 p. port. 23 cm. I. Healey, George Harris, ed. II. T.
PR3406.A53   *LC* a 55-2092

Moore, John Robert, 1890-.   **2.6976**
Daniel Defoe, citizen of the modern world / by John Robert Moore. — Chicago; London: University of Chicago Press, 1958. xv, 409 p., [4] leaves of plates: ill., maps, port.; 25 cm. 1. Defoe, Daniel, 1661?-1731. 2. Novelists, English — 18th century — Biography I. T.
PR3406.M58   *LC* 58-11950   *ISBN* 0226535770

Starr, George A.   • **2.6977**
Defoe & spiritual autobiography, by G. A. Starr. — Princeton, N. J., Princeton University Press, 1965. xiii, 203 p. 21 cm. Bibliographical footnotes. 1. Defoe, Daniel, 1661?-1731. I. T.
PR3406.S72   823.5   *LC* 66-10273

Richetti, John J.   **2.6978**
Defoe's narratives; situations and structures / John J. Richetti. — Oxford [Eng.]: Clarendon Press, 1975. viii, 244 p.; 23 cm. Includes index. 1. Defoe, Daniel, 1661?-1731 — Criticism and interpretation. I. T.
PR3407.R5   823/.5   *LC* 76-356072   *ISBN* 0198120672

Shinagel, Michael.   • **2.6979**
Daniel Defoe and middle–class gentility. — Cambridge, Mass.: Harvard University Press, 1968. xi, 279 p.; 24 cm. 1. Defoe, Daniel, 1661?-1731. I. T.
PR3407.S5   823/.5   *LC* 68-14273

Sutherland, James Runcieman, 1900-.   • **2.6980**
Daniel Defoe; a critical study [by] James Sutherland. — Cambridge, Mass.: Harvard University Press, 1971. vii, 259 p.; 22 cm. 1. Defoe, Daniel, 1661?-1731. I. T.
PR3407.S8   823/.5   *LC* 70-159532   *ISBN* 0674190807

Novak, Maximillian E.   • **2.6981**
Economics and the fiction of Daniel DeFoe. — Berkeley, University of California Press, 1962. 185 p. 24 cm. — (University of California publications. English studies, 24) Includes bibliography. 1. Defoe, Daniel, 1661?-1731 — Political and social views. 2. Economics in literature I. T.
PR3408.E35N6   823.5   *LC* 62-63115

Alkon, Paul K. (Paul Kent)   **2.6982**
Defoe and fictional time / Paul K. Alkon. — Athens: University of Georgia Press, c1979. 276 p.; 23 cm. 1. Defoe, Daniel, 1661?-1731 — Criticism and interpretation. 2. Time in literature I. T.
PR3408.T54 A5   823/.5   *LC* 78-6021   *ISBN* 0820305481

PR3409 Denham. Diaper

Denham, John, Sir, 1615-1669.   • **2.6983**
The poetical works. Edited with notes and introd. by Theodore Howard Banks. — 2d ed. — [Hamden, Conn.]: Archon Books, 1969. xviii, 362 p.: geneal. table.; 23 cm. Critical ed. based on the author's Poems and translations, 1688. I. Banks, Theodore Howard, 1895- ed. II. T.
PR3409.D2 1969   821/.4   *LC* 69-11555   *ISBN* 0208001557

Diaper, William, d. 1717.   • **2.6984**
Complete works / edited with an introduction by Dorothy Broughton. — London: Routledge and Paul, [1952] lxxvii, 363 p.: facsims.; 18 cm. — (The Muses' library) Erratum slip inserted. I. Broughton, Dorothy. II. T. III. Series.
PR3409.D47 1952   *LC* 52-956

PR3410–3428 Dryden

Dryden, John, 1631-1700.   • **2.6985**
The works of John Dryden / [General editors:Edward Niles Hooker,H.T.Swedenberg,Jr.] Berkeley: University of California Press, 1956-. v.: ill., facsims.; 25 cm. I. Hooker, Edward Niles. II. Swedenberg,H.T. III. T.
PR3410 F56   821.48   *LC* 55-7149   *ISBN* 0520021207

Dryden, John, 1631-1700.   • **2.6986**
The prologues and epilogues of John Dryden: a critical edition by William Bradford Gardner. — New York: Published for the University of Texas by Columbia University Press, 1951. xx, 361 p.: ill.; 24 cm. I. Gardner, William Bradford. II. T.
PR3412.G3   *LC* 51-9220

Dryden, John, 1631-1700. • 2.6987
Poetry, prose and plays; selected by Douglas Grant. Cambridge Harvard University Press 1952. 896p. (The Reynard library) I. Grant, Douglas, 1921-, comp. II. T.
PR3412 G7 1952

Dryden, John, 1631-1700. • 2.6988
Poems. Edited by James Kinsley. — Oxford, Clarendon Press, 1958. 4 v. (xxi, 2104 p.) port. 23 cm. Bibliography: v. 1, p. [xix]-xxi. I. T.
PR3412.K5   821.48   LC 58-3883

Dryden, John, 1631-1700. • 2.6989
[Selections] Selected poetry and prose of John Dryden. Edited, with an introd. and notes, by Earl Miner. [New York, Random House, 1969] xxxix, 554 p. 19 cm. (Modern library college editions) I. Miner, Earl Roy. ed. II. T.
PR3412.M47   821/.4   LC 69-17414

Dryden, John, 1631-1700. 2.6990
Marriage à la mode / John Dryden; edited by Mark S. Auburn. — Lincoln: University of Nebraska Press, c1981. xxxi, 144 p.; 22 cm. — (Regents restoration drama series.) I. Auburn, Mark S. II. T. III. Series.
PR3415.M3 1981   822/.4 19   LC 80-51043   ISBN 0803203861

Schilling, Bernard Nicholas. • 2.6991
Dryden and the conservative myth, a reading of Absalom and Achitophel. — New Haven, Yale University Press, 1961. viii, 329 p. facsim. 23 cm. Includes the text of Absalom and Achitophel, reprinted from George Noyes' The poetical works of John Dryden, with a facsimile reproduction of the t. p. of the 2d ed., augm. and rev., published in London in 1681. 'Bibliographical notes': p. [307]-318. I. Dryden, John, 1631-1700. Absalom and Achitophel II. T.
PR3416.A23S3   821.4   LC 61-14437

Dryden, John, 1631-1700. • 2.6992
Of dramatic poesy, and other critical essays. Edited with an introd. by George Watson. — London, J. M. Dent; New York, Dutton [1962] 2 v. 19 cm. — (Everyman's library, 568-569: Essays & belles lettres) Includes bibliography. 1. Literature — Addresses, essays, lectures. I. T.
PR3417.A1 1962   824.4   LC 62-5615

PR3422–3428 Biography. Criticism

Montgomery, Guy, comp. • 2.6993
Concordance to the poetical works of John Dryden, edited by Guy Montgomery. Assisted by Mary Jackman and Helen S. Agoa. Pref. by Josephine Miles. — New York: Russell & Russell, [1967, c1957] 722 p.; 29 cm. 'Based on the Cambridge edition of the Poetical works of John Dryden, edited by George Rapall Noyes ... revised and enlarged in 1950.' 1. Dryden, John, 1631-1700 — Concordances. I. T.
PR3422.M6 1967   821/.4   LC 66-27126

Dryden, John, 1631-1700. • 2.6994
The letters of John Dryden: with letters addressed to him / collected and edited by Charles E. Ward. — [Durham, N.C.]: Duke University Press, 1942. xvii, 196 p., [1] leaf of plates: port.; 22 cm. I. Ward, Charles Eugene, 1902- II. T.
PR3423 A4 1942

Bredvold, Louis Ignatius, 1888-. • 2.6995
The intellectual milieu of John Dryden; studies in some aspects of seventeenth-century thought. Ann Arbor: University of Michigan Press, 1956. 185 p. , 21 cm. (Ann Arbor books; AA3) 1. Dryden, John, 1631-1700. 2. Philosophy — History — England. 3. Religious thought — 17th century 4. Seventeenth century I. T.
PR3423.B7   LC 58-6356

Osborn, James Marshall. • 2.6996
John Dryden: some biographical facts and problems, by James M. Osborn. — Rev. ed. — Gainesville, University of Florida Press, 1965. xvi, 316 p. facsims., ports. 24 cm. Bibliographical footnotes. 1. Dryden, John, 1631-1700. 2. Dryden, John, 1631-1700 — Bibl. I. T.
PR3423.O7 1965   828.409   LC 65-29104

Scott, Walter, Sir, 1771-1832. • 2.6997
The life of John Dryden. Edited with an introd. by Bernard Kreissman. — Lincoln, University of Nebraska Press [1963] xix, 471 p. 21 cm. 1. Dryden, John, 1631-1700. I. Kreissman, Bernard. II. T.
PR3423.S34 1963   821.4   LC 63-8121

Smith, David Nichol, 1875-1962. • 2.6998
John Dryden. — [Hamden, Conn.]: Archon Books, 1966. 92 p. — (The Clark lectures on English literature; 1948-9) 1. Dryden, John, 1631-1700. I. T.
PR3423.S6 1966   LC 66-20232

Ward, Charles Eugene. • 2.6999
The life of John Dryden. — Chapel Hill, University of North Carolina Press [1961] 380 p. illus. 24 cm. 1. Dryden, John, 1631-1700. I. T.
PR3423.W3   928.2   LC 61-18582

Wykes, David. 2.7000
A preface to Dryden / David Wykes. London; New York: Longman, 1977. xix, 236 p.: ill.; 22 cm. (Preface books) Includes index. 1. Dryden, John, 1631-1700. I. T.
PR3423.W9   821/.4 B   LC 76-12598   ISBN 0582351014

Miner, Earl Roy. • 2.7001
Dryden's poetry, by Earl Miner. — Bloomington: Indiana University Press, 1967. xx, 354 p.: illus., port.; 25 cm. 1. Dryden, John, 1631-1700 — Criticism and interpretation. I. T.
PR3424.M53   821/.4   LC 67-10108

Miner, Earl Roy. 2.7002
John Dryden, edited by Earl Miner. — [Athens]: Ohio University Press, 1972. xxvi, 363 p.: illus.; 23 cm. — (Writers and their background) 1. Dryden, John, 1631-1700 — Criticism and interpretation. I. T.
PR3424.M54 1972b   821/.4   LC 72-95818   ISBN 082140119X

Ramsey, Paul, 1924-. • 2.7003
The art of John Dryden. Lexington, University of Kentucky Press, 1969. 213 p. 21 cm. (South Atlantic Modern Language Association. Award study) 1. Dryden, John, 1631-1700 — Criticism and interpretation. I. T.
PR3424.R3   821/.4   LC 70-80088   ISBN 0813111846

Van Doren, Mark, 1894-1972. • 2.7004
John Dryden, a study of his poetry / Mark Van Doren. — Bloomington: Indiana University Press, 1960, c1946. 298 p. — (Midland books; MB-22) First published in 1920 under title: The poetry of John Dryden. 1. Dryden, John, 1631-1700. I. T.
PR3424.V2 1960   LC 62-5532

Hughes, Derek, 1944-. 2.7005
Dryden's heroic plays / Derek Hughes. — Lincoln: University of Nebraska Press, c1981. xi, 195 p.; 23 cm. 1. Dryden, John, 1631-1700 — Criticism and interpretation. 2. Heroes in literature I. T.
PR3427.H4 H8 1981   821/.4 19   LC 80-19109   ISBN 0803223145

McFadden, George, 1916-. 2.7006
Dryden, the public writer, 1660-1685 / George McFadden. — Princeton, N.J.: Princeton University Press, c1978. xi, 305 p.; 23 cm. Includes index. 1. Dryden, John, 1631-1700 — Political and social views. 2. Dryden, John, 1631-1700 — Friends and associates. 3. Authors, English — Early modern, 1500-1700 — Biography. I. T.
PR3427.P6 M3   821/.4   LC 77-85551   ISBN 0691063508

Zwicker, Steven N. 2.7007
Dryden's political poetry; the typology of king and nation [by] Steven N. Zwicker. — Providence: Brown University Press, [1972] xiii, 154 p.; 25 cm. 1. Dryden, John, 1631-1700. 2. Politics in literature 3. Bible in literature I. T.
PR3427.P6 Z9   821/.4   LC 70-188832   ISBN 0870571346

PR3429–3443 D'Urfey. Etheredge. Farquhar

D'Urfey, Thomas, 1653-1723. 2.7008
[Madam Fickle] Two comedies / by Thomas D'Urfey; edited, with introductions and notes, by Jack A. Vaughn. — Rutherford: Fairleigh Dickinson University Press, c1976. 301 p.: port.; 22 cm. I. Vaughn, Jack A., 1935- II. D'Urfey, Thomas, 1653-1723. A fond husband. 1975. III. T.
PR3431.D3 M27 1976   822/.4   LC 73-21191   ISBN 0838614787

Etherege, George, Sir, 1635?-1691. 2.7009
[Plays (Cordner)] The plays of Sir George Etherege / edited by Michael Cordner. — Cambridge [Cambridgeshire]; New York: Cambridge University Press, 1982. xix, 341 p.; 22 cm. — (Plays by Renaissance and Restoration dramatists.) I. Cordner, Michael. II. T. III. Series.
PR3432.A133 1982   822/.4 19   LC 82-1180   ISBN 0521246547

Etherege, George, Sir, 1635?-1691. • 2.7010
Poems. Edited by James Thorpe. — Princeton, N. J., Princeton University Press, 1963. xiv, 149 p. 24 cm. Bibliographical references included in 'Notes' (p. 67-145) I. Thorpe, James Ernest, 1915- ed. II. T.
PR3432.A69 1963   821.4   LC 63-9987

Etherege, George, Sir, 1635?-1691. 2.7011
Letters of Sir George Etherege. Edited by Frederick Bracher. — Berkeley: University of California Press, [1973, c1974] xxv, 324 p.; 24 cm. 1. Etherege, George, Sir, 1635?-1691 — Correspondence. I. T.
PR3432.A83 1974   822/.4 B   LC 70-187870   ISBN 0520022181

Holland, Norman Norwood, 1927-.   • 2.7012
The first modern comedies; the significance of Etherege, Wycherley, and
Congreve. — Cambridge, Mass., Harvard University Press, 1959. 274 p. 25 cm.
1. Etherege, George, Sir, 1635?-1691. 2. Wycherley, William, 1640-1716.
3. Congreve, William, 1670-1729. I. T.
PR3432.H6   822.409   LC 59-7654

Underwood, Dale.   • 2.7013
Etherege and the seventeenth–century comedy of manners. — [Hamden,
Conn.]: Archon Books, 1969 [c1957] ix, 165 p.; 23 cm. — (Yale studies in
English. v. 135) Condensed version of the author's thesis, Yale. 1. Etherege,
George, Sir, 1635?-1691. 2. English drama — Restoration, 1660-1700 —
History and criticism. I. T. II. Series.
PR3432.U5 1969   822/.4   LC 69-15693   ISBN 0208007644

Farquhar, George, 1677?-1707.   2.7014
[Works. 1986] The works of George Farquhar / edited by Shirley Strum Kenny.
— Oxford [Oxfordshire]: Clarendon Press; New York: Oxford University
Press, 1986. 2 v.: ill., 2 ports.; 22 cm. Includes indexes. I. Kenny, Shirley
Strum. II. T.
PR3435.A5 K44 1986   822/.4 19   LC 85-25942   ISBN
0198118589

Farquhar, George, 1677?-1707.   2.7015
The beaux' stratagem / George Farquhar; edited by Charles N. Fifer. —
Lincoln: University of Nebraska Press, c1977. xxxvi, 145 p.; 21 cm. — (Regents
restoration drama series) I. Fifer, Charles N., 1922- II. T.
PR3437.B4 1977   822/.4   LC 77-89834   ISBN 0803253842

Farquhar, George.   2.7016
The recruiting officer / George Farquhar; edited by Michael Shugrue. —
Lincoln, Nebraska: University of Nebraska Press, 1965. xxi, 137 p.; 22 cm. —
(Regents Restoration drama series) 'A Bison book.' I. Shugrue, Michael
Francis. II. T.
PR3437.R4 1965   822.4   LC 65-15341

Rothstein, Eric.   • 2.7017
George Farquhar. — New York: Twayne Publishers, [1967] 206 p.; 21 cm. —
(Twayne's English authors series, 58) 1. Farquhar, George, 1677?-1707. I. T.
PR3438.R6   822/.4   LC 67-19355

PR3450–3458 Fielding

Fielding, Henry, 1707-1754.   2.7018
The Wesleyan edition of the works of Henry Fielding. — Middletown, Conn.:
Wesleyan University Press, 1972-. v.; 25 cm. I. T.
PR3450.F72x

Fielding, Henry, 1707-1754.   • 2.7019
The Covent–Garden journal / by Sir Alexander Drawcansir, knt. censor of
Great Britain (Henry Fielding); edited by Gerard Edward Jensen. — New
Haven: Yale University Press, 1915. 2 v.: ill., ports. I. Jensen, Gerard Edward,
1884- II. T.
PR3454.C5 1915a

Fielding, Henry, 1707-1754.   2.7020
The history of the adventures of Joseph Andrews, and of his friend Mr.
Abraham Adams; and, An apology for the life of Mrs. Shamela Andrews [by]
Henry Fielding edited with an introduction by Douglas Brooks. — London;
New York: Oxford U.P., 1970. xxviii, 394 p.; 21 cm. — (Oxford English
novels.) An apology for the life of Mrs. Shamela Andrews is a parody of Samuel
Richardson's 'Pamela.' 1. Richardson, Samuel, 1689-1761. Pamela I. Brooks,
Douglas. II. Fielding, Henry, 1707-1754. Apology for the life of Mrs. Shamela
Andrews. III. T. IV. Title: An apology for the life of Mrs. Shamela Andrews.
V. Series.
PZ3.F46 Ad40 PR3454.H5x   823/.5   LC 78-548668   ISBN
0192553232

Fielding, Henry, 1707-1754.   • 2.7021
The life of Jonathan Wild. London: H. Milford, Oxford University Press, [1932]
289 p. (World's classics. 382.) 1. Wild, Jonathan, 1682?-1725 — Fiction. I. T.
II. Title: Jonathan Wild. III. Series.
PR3454.J58 1932   823.5   LC 32-26088

Fielding, Henry, 1707-1754.   • 2.7022
The tragedy of tragedies, or, The life and death of Tom Thumb the Great: with
the annotations of H. Scriblerus Secundus / edited by James T. Hillhouse. — St.
Clair Shores, Mich.: Scholarly Press, 1970. viii, 223 p.: illus.; 22 cm.
I. Hillhouse, James Theodore, 1890-1956. II. Fielding, Henry, 1707-1754.
Tom Thumb III. T. IV. Title: Tom Thumb. V. Title: The life and death of
Tom Thumb the Great.
PR3454.T6 1970c   822/.5   LC 71-131704   ISBN 0403005914

Fielding, Henry, 1707-1754.   2.7023
[History of Tom Jones] Tom Jones: an authoritative text, contemporary
reactions, criticism, edited by Sheridan Baker. [1st ed.] New York, Norton
[1973] viii, 934 p. 23 cm. (A Norton critical edition) I. Baker, Sheridan
Warren, 1918- comp. II. T.
PZ3.F46 To3 PR3454.T6x   823/.5   LC 72-7320   ISBN
0393043592 ISBN 0303093938

Cross, Wilbur Lucius, 1862-1948.   2.7024
The history of Henry Fielding / by Wilbur L. Cross. — New Haven: Yale
University Press; London: Oxford University Press, 1918. 3 v.: ill., ports.,
facsims., music ; 23 cm. Includes index. 'Published on the foundation
established in memory of William McKean Brown.' 1. Fielding, Henry,
1707-1754 — Criticism and interpretation. I. T.
PR3456.C8   LC 18-20882

Hunter, J. Paul, 1934-.   2.7025
Occasional form: Henry Fielding and the chains of circumstance / J. Paul
Hunter. — Baltimore: Johns Hopkins University Press, 1976 (c1975). xiv,
263 p.; 24 cm. 1. Fielding, Henry, 1707-1754 — Criticism and interpretation.
I. T.
PR3457.H8   823/.5   LC 75-11337   ISBN 0801816726

Miller, Henry Knight, 1920-.   • 2.7026
Essays on Fielding's Miscellanies: a commentary on volume one. — Princeton,
N. J., Princeton University Press, 1961. xv, 474 p. 23 cm. Bibliographical
footnotes. 1. Fielding, Henry, 1707-1754. I. T.
PR3457.M5   828.5   LC 61-7410

Rawson, Claude Julien.   2.7027
Henry Fielding and the Augustan ideal under stress: 'Nature's dance of death'
and other studies, [by] C. J. Rawson. — London; Boston: Routledge and Kegan
Paul, 1972. xiii, 266 p.; 23 cm. 1. Fielding, Henry, 1707-1754. 2. English
literature — 18th century — History and criticism. I. T.
PR3457.R3   823/.5   LC 73-153055   ISBN 0710074549

Cleary, Thomas R. (Thomas Raymond), 1940-.   2.7028
Henry Fielding: political writer / Thomas R. Cleary. — Waterloo, Ont.: Wilfrid
Laurier University Press; Gerrards Cross: Colin Smythe, c1984. xviii, 347 p.; 23
cm. I. T.
PR3458.P6 C6x   823/.5 19   ISBN 0889201315

McCrea, Brian.   2.7029
Henry Fielding and the politics of mid–eighteenth–century England / Brian
McCrea. — Athens: University of Georgia Press, c1981. xiii, 257 p.; 22 cm.
(South Atlantic Modern Language Association award study) Includes index.
1. Fielding, Henry, 1707-1754 — Political and social views. 2. Politics and
literature — Great Britain. 3. Politics in literature 4. Authors, English — 18th
century — Biography. 5. Great Britain — Politics and government —
1727-1760 I. T.
PR3458.P6 M3 1981   823/.5   LC 80-14711   ISBN 0820305316

Fielding, Sarah, 1710-1768.   2.7030
The adventures of David Simple: containing an account of his travels through
the Cities of London and Westminster in the search of a real friend; edited with
an introduction by Malcolm Kelsall. London, New York [etc.] Oxford U.P.,
1969. xxviii, 436 p. illus. 21 cm. (Oxford English novels) I. Kelsall, M. M.
(Malcolm Miles), 1938- II. T.
PZ3.F4604 Ad7 PR3459.F3   823/.5   LC 78-385732   ISBN
0192553208

PR3465–3476 Garrick. Gay. Gibbon

Garrick, David, 1717-1779.   2.7031
[Plays] The plays of David Garrick: a complete collection of the social satires,
French adaptations, pantomimes, Christmas and musical plays, preludes,
interludes, and burlesques, to which are added the alterations and adaptations
of the plays of Shakespeare and other dramatists from the sixteenth to the
eighteenth centuries / edited with commentary and notes by Harry William
Pedicord and Fredrick Louis Bergmann. — Carbondale: Southern Illinois
University Press, c1980-c1982. 7 v.: facsims., ports.; 25 cm. I. Pedicord, Harry
William. II. Bergmann, Fredrick Louis, 1916- III. T.
PR3465.A5 P4 1980   822/.6 19   LC 79-28443   ISBN 0809308622

Dircks, Phyllis T.   2.7032
David Garrick / by Phyllis T. Dircks. — Boston: Twayne, c1985. 152 p.; ill.; 23
cm. (Twayne's English authors series. TEAS 403) Includes index. 1. Garrick,
David, 1717-1779 — Criticism and interpretation. I. T. II. Series.
PR3469.D56 1985   822/.6 19   LC 84-15818   ISBN 0805768939

Gay, John, 1685-1732.   2.7033
Poetry and prose of John Gay / edited by Vinton A. Dearing with the assistance
of Charles E. Beckwith. — Oxford: Clarendon Press, 1974 [i.e. 1975] 2 v.; 23
cm. Includes index. I. Dearing, Vinton A. (Vinton Adams), 1920- II. T.
PR3473.A1 1975   821/.5   LC 75-310986   ISBN 019811897X

Gay, John, 1685-1732. • 2.7034
The poetical works of John Gay, including Polly, The beggar's opera, and selections from the other dramatic work. Edited by G. C. Faber. — New York: Russell & Russell, [1969] xlvii, 700 p.: port.; 22 cm. Reprint of the 1926 ed. I. Faber, Geoffrey Cust, Sir, 1889-1961, ed. II. T.
PR3473.A3 1969   828/.5/09   LC 68-15124

Gay, John, 1685-1732. 2.7035
[Selections. 1983] John Gay, dramatic works / edited by John Fuller. — Oxford: Clarendon Press; New York: Oxford University Press, 1983. 2 v.; 23 cm. I. Fuller, John. II. T.
PR3473.A4 1983   822/.5 19   LC 81-18973   ISBN 0198127014

Armens, Sven M. • 2.7036
John Gay, social critic. New York: Octagon Books, 1966, [c1954] 262 p. Based on thesis, Harvard University. 1. Gay, John, 1685-1732. I. T.
PR3474.A7 1966   828.5   LC 66-18053

Gay, John, 1685-1732. • 2.7037
The letters of John Gay / edited by C. F. Burgess. — Oxford: Clarendon Press, 1966. xxviii, 142 p.: port. I. Burgess, C. F. (Chester Francis) II. T.
PR3474.B8   826.5   LC 66-68249

Spacks, Patricia Ann Meyer. • 2.7038
John Gay, by Patricia Meyer Spacks. — New York: Twayne Publishers, [1965] 176 p.; 21 cm. — (Twayne's English authors series, 22) 1. Gay, John, 1685-1732. I. T.
PR3474.S67   828.509   LC 65-18223

Gibbon, Edward, 1737-1794. 2.7039
The English essays of Edward Gibbon, edited by Patricia B. Craddock. — Oxford: Clarendon Press, 1973 (c1972). xix, 650 p.; 23 cm. I. T.
PR3476.A16   824/.6   LC 73-158897   ISBN 0198124961

Gibbon, Edward, 1737-1794. • 2.7040
Autobiography; as originally edited by Lord Sheffield. With an introd. by J.B. Bury. London: Oxford University Press, [1959] 339p. (The World's classics, 139) I. Sheffield, John Holroyd, Earl of, 1735-1821. II. T.
PR3476 A82

PR3480–3498 Goldsmith

Goldsmith, Oliver, 1728-1774. • 2.7041
Collected works; edited by Arthur Friedman. — Oxford, Clarendon P., 1966. 5 v. front. (port.) tables. 23 cm. I. Friedman, Arthur, 1906- ed. II. T.
PR3481.F7   828.609   LC 66-70092

Goldsmith, Oliver, 1728-1774. • 2.7042
The complete poetical works of Oliver Goldsmith, ed. with introduction and notes by Austin Dobson. London, H. Frowde 1911. xxxvi, 278 p. ill., ports. 19 cm. At head of title: Oxford edition. Spine title: The poetical works of Goldsmith. I. Dobson, Austin, 1840-1921. II. T. III. Title: Poetical works of Goldsmith
PR 3482 D65 1911

Goldsmith, Oliver, 1728-1774. • 2.7043
Selected works / chosen by Richard Garnett. — London: R. Hart-Davis, 1950. 847 p.; 21 cm. — (The Reynard library) I. T. II. Series.
PR3482.G3   LC 51-10564

Goldsmith, Oliver, 1728-1774. • 2.7044
Essays on Goldsmith by Scott, Macaulay, and Thackeray, and selections from his writings; with an introduction by G. E. Hadow ... and notes by C. B. Wheeler, M. A. — Oxford, The Clarendon press; London, New York [etc.] H. Milford, 1918. 212 p. 19.5 cm. 'Selections': p. [62]-168. I. Hadow, Grace Eleanor, 1875- ed. II. Wheeler, Charles Bickersteth, 1862- III. Scott, Walter, Sir, 1771-1832. IV. Macaulay, Thomas Babington Macaulay, 1st baron, 1800-1859. V. Thackeray, William Makepeace, 1811-1863. VI. T.
PR3482.H25   LC 19-17833

Goldsmith, Oliver, 1728-1774. • 2.7045
The vicar of Wakefield, and other writings. Edited, with an introd. and notes by Frederick W. Hilles. — New York: Modern Library, [1955] xxv, 580 p.; 19 cm. — (The Modern library of the world's best books [291]) I. Hilles, Frederick Whiley, 1900- ed. II. T.
PR3482.H5   823.64   LC 55-6394

Goldsmith, Oliver, 1728-1774. • 2.7046
New essays. Now first collected and edited with an introd. and notes by Ronald S. Crane. — New York: Greenwood Press, [1968, c1927] xli, 147 p.; 23 cm. 'Eighteen essays ... appeared originally, between January, 1760 and June, 1762, as anonymous contributions to the British magazine, the Royal magazine, the Public ledger, the Lady's magazine, and Lloyd's evening post ... here for the first time ascribed to Oliver Goldsmith.' I. Crane, Ronald Salmon, 1886- ed. II. T.
PR3487.E9 1968   824/.6   LC 68-57605

Goldsmith, Oliver, 1728-1774. • 2.7047
She stoops to conquer / edited with introduction and notes by G. A. F. M. Chatwin. — Oxford: Clarendon Press, 1912. 100 p. I. Chatwin, G. A. F. M., ed. II. T.
PR3488.A1x   822.6   LC 13-840

Paden, William Doremus, 1903- ed. • 2.7048
A concordance to the poems of Oliver Goldsmith, compiled and edited by William Doremus Paden and Clyde Kenneth Hyder. — Gloucester, Mass.: P. Smith, 1966 [c1940] xii, 180 p.; 29 cm. 'Based exclusively upon The poetical works of Oliver Goldsmith, edited by Austin Dobson ... 1906.' 1. Goldsmith, Oliver, 1728-1774 — Concordances. I. Hyder, Clyde Kenneth, 1902- joint ed. II. T.
PR3492.P3 1966   821.6   LC 66-9077

Goldsmith, Oliver, 1728-1774. • 2.7049
The collected letters of Oliver Goldsmith, edited by Katharine C. Balderston. Cambridge [Eng.] University Press, 1928. 189 p. 1. Goldsmith, Oliver, 1728-1774. I. Balderston, Katharine Canby, 1895- II. T.
PR3493.A3 1928   828.6

Wardle, Ralph Martin, 1909-. • 2.7050
Oliver Goldsmith, by Ralph M. Wardle. — [Unaltered and unabridged ed. — Hamden, Conn.]: Archon Books, 1969 [c1957] 330 p.: illus., ports.; 23 cm. 1. Goldsmith, Oliver, 1728-1774. I. T.
PR3493.W3 1969   828/.6/09 B   LC 69-13631   ISBN 0208007555

The art of Oliver Goldsmith / edited by Andrew Swarbrick. 2.7051
London: Vision; Totowa, NJ: Barnes & Noble, 1984. 200 p.; 23 cm. — (Critical studies series.) 1. Goldsmith, Oliver, 1728-1774 — Criticism and interpretation — Addresses, essays, lectures. I. Swarbrick, Andrew. II. Series.
PR3494.A77 1984   828/.609 19   LC 84-374   ISBN 0389204625

PR3499–3505 Graves. Gray. Green

Graves, Richard, 1715-1804. 2.7052
The spiritual Quixote, or The summer's ramble of Mr. Geoffrey Wildgoose: a comic romance; edited with an introduction by Clarence Tracy. — London; New York [etc.]: Oxford U.P., 1967. xxvii, 504 p.: front., illus.; 21 cm. — (Oxford English novels) I. Tracy, Clarence Rupert. ed. II. T. III. Title: The summer's ramble of Mr. Geoffrey Wildgoose.
PR3499.G7x   PZ3.G7873 Sp5   LC 67-93705

Gray, Thomas, 1716-1771. • 2.7053
The complete poems of Thomas Gray; English, Latin and Greek; edited by H. W. Starr and J. R. Hendrickson. — Oxford: Clarendon P., 1966. xv, 284 p.: front. (port.); 23 cm. 1. Gray, Thomas, 1716-1771. I. Starr, Herbert Willmarth, 1916- ed. II. Hendrickson, John Raymond, ed. III. T.
PR3500.A2 1966   821.6   LC 66-72617

Gray, Thomas, 1716-1771. • 2.7054
Gray: poetry & prose / with essays by Johnson, Goldsmith and others; with an introduction and notes by J. Crofts. — Oxford: Clarendon Press, 1926. xii, 176 p.: port. I. Johnson, Samuel, 1709-1784. II. Goldsmith, Oliver, 1728-1774. III. Crofts, J. IV. T.
PR3501.C7   LC 27-24021

Gray, Thomas, 1716-1771. • 2.7055
Correspondence of Thomas Gray, edited by Paget Toynbee and Leonard Whibley. With corrections and additions by H. W. Starr. — Oxford: Clarendon Press, [1971] 3 v.: illus., fold. maps.; 23 cm. Reprint of 1935 ed. 1. Gray, Thomas, 1716-1771. I. Toynbee, Paget Jackson, 1855-1932. ed. II. Whibley, Leonard, 1862 or 3-1941, ed. III. Starr, Herbert Willmarth, 1916- ed. IV. T.
PR3503.A3 1971   821/.6   LC 78-24999

Ketton-Cremer, Robert Wyndham, 1906-. • 2.7056
Thomas Gray: a biography. Cambridge, Eng.: University Press, 1955. 309 p.: ill.; 23 cm. 1. Gray, Thomas, 1716-1771 — Biography. I. T.
PR3503.K4 1955   LC 55-14583

Cook, Albert S. (Albert Stanburrough), 1853-1927. • 2.7057
A concordance to the English poems of Thomas Gray. Gloucester, Mass., P. Smith, 1967 [c1908] x, 160 p. 21 cm. 1. Gray, Thomas, 1716-1771 — Concordances. I. T.
PR3504.C6 1967   821/.6   LC 67-8967

Green, Matthew, 1696-1737. • 2.7058
The spleen / by Matthew Green; edited with introduction, notes, and appendices by W.H. Williams. — London: Methuen, 1936. xxiv, 88 p. I. Winchilsea, Anne Kingsmill Finch, Countess of, 1661-1720. II. Williams, William Henry. III. T.
PR3505.G27 S7 1936   LC 36-32963

PR3505–3508 Habington. Herbert

Habington, William, 1605-1654. • **2.7059**
The poems of William Habington / edited with introduction and commentary by Kenneth Allott. — London: University Press of Liverpool, 1948. lxviii, 208 p.: facsims.; 22 cm. (Liverpool English texts & studies) I. Allott, Kenneth, 1920-. II. T. III. Series.
PR3505.H3 1948   LC 68-1232

Herbert, George, 1593-1633. • **2.7060**
The poems of George Herbert; with an introd. by Arthur Waugh. — London New York: Oxford University Press, 1934. xxvii, 277 p.: port. — (The World's classics; 109) I. T.
PR3507.A25

Herbert, George, 1593-1633. • **2.7061**
The works of George Herbert, edited with a commentary by F. E. Hutchinson. Oxford, The Clarendon press, 1941. lxxvii, 619, [1] p. front., facsims. 23 cm. 'The main object of this edition is to establish the text of The temple by providing a more complete and more accurate collection of the evidence than has been hitherto available.'—Pref. I. Hutchinson, Francis Ernest, 1871-1947. ed. II. T.
PR3507.A33 1941   820.81 821.38   LC 41-18566

Fish, Stanley Eugene. **2.7062**
The living temple: George Herbert and catechizing / Stanley Fish. — Berkeley: University of California Press, c1978. ix, 201 p.: ill.; 21 cm. Includes index. 1. Herbert, George, 1593-1633. The temple. 2. Herbert, George, 1593-1633 — Criticism and interpretation. 3. Catechetics in literature. I. T.
PR3507.T43 F57   821/.3   LC 73-90664   ISBN 0520026578

Bloch, Chana, 1940-. **2.7063**
Spelling the word: George Herbert and the Bible / Chana Bloch. — Berkeley: University of California Press, c1985. xiv, 324 p.; 22 cm. 1. Herbert, George, 1593-1633 — Criticism and interpretation. 2. Bible in literature 3. Christian poetry, English — History and criticism. I. T.
PR3508.B5 1985   821/.3 19   LC 84-123   ISBN 0520051211

Charles, Amy Marie. **2.7064**
A life of George Herbert / Amy M. Charles. — Ithaca, N.Y.: Cornell University Press, 1977. 242 p.: ill.; 23 cm. 1. Herbert, George, 1593-1633 — Biography. 2. Poets, English — Early modern, 1500-1700 — Biography. I. T.
PR3508.C48   821/.3 B   LC 77-3116   ISBN 0801410142

George Herbert, the critical heritage / edited by C.A. Patrides. **2.7065**
London; Boston: Routledge & Kegan Paul, 1983. xix, 390 p.: music; 23 cm. — (Critical heritage series.) 'Seventeenth-century musical settings of lyrics by Herbert'—P. 357-373. 1. Herbert, George, 1593-1633 — Criticism and interpretation — Addresses, essays, lectures. I. Patrides, C. A. II. Series.
PR3508.G48 1983   821/.3 19   LC 82-22959   ISBN 0710092407

Mann, Cameron, bp., 1851-1932, comp. • **2.7066**
A concordance to the English poems of George Herbert. Boston, Houghton Mifflin, 1927. — St. Clair Shores, Mich.: Scholarly Press, 1972. xii, 277 p.; 21 cm. 1. Herbert, George, 1593-1633 — Concordances. I. T.
PR3508.M3 1972   821/.3   LC 70-145161   ISBN 0403010896

Stein, Arnold Sidney, 1915-. • **2.7067**
George Herbert's lyrics [by] Arnold Stein. — Baltimore: Johns Hopkins Press, [1968] xliv, 221 p.; 24 cm. 1. Herbert, George, 1593-1633. I. T.
PR3508.S7   821/.3   LC 68-12898

Strier, Richard. **2.7068**
Love known: theology and experience in George Herbert's poetry / Richard Strier. — Chicago: University of Chicago Press, 1983. xxi, 277 p.; 24 cm. Includes indexes. 1. Herbert, George, 1593-1633 — Criticism and interpretation. 2. Christian poetry, English — History and criticism. 3. Theology, Protestant, in literature. 4. Justification — History of doctrines 5. Protestantism and literature I. T.
PR3508.S75 1983   821/.3 19   LC 83-6798   ISBN 0226777162

Summers, Joseph H. (Joseph Holmes), 1920-. • **2.7069**
George Herbert, his religion and art. Cambridge, Harvard University Press 1954. 246p. I. Herbert, George, 1593-1633. II. T.
PR3508.S8x   LC a 54-3214

PR3510–3517 Herrick. Holcroft. Hurd

Herrick, Robert, 1591-1674. • **2.7070**
Poetical works, edited by L. C. Martin. — Oxford, Clarendon Press, 1956. xi, 631 p. port. 23 cm. I. T.
PR3510.A5M3   821.43   LC 56-2924

Herrick, Robert, 1591-1674. • **2.7071**
The complete poetry of Robert Herrick. Edited with an introd., notes and a new foreword by J. Max Patrick. — New York: Norton, [1968] xvi, 579 p.: illus.; 20 cm. — (The Norton library seventeenth-century series, N435) I. Patrick, John Max, 1911- ed. II. T.
PR3510.A5 P3 1968   821/.4   LC 68-2296

Herrick, Robert, 1591-1674. • **2.7072**
Poems from Hesperides and Noble numbers. Selected and introduced by John Hayward. Baltimore: Penguin Books, [1962,c1961] 220 p.; 19 cm. (The Penguin poets, D58.) I. Hayward, John, 1905-1965. ed. II. T.
PR3511.H3 1962   LC 62-2288

MacLeod, Malcolm, 1901-. • **2.7073**
A concordance to the poems of Robert Herrick / compiled and edited by Malcolm MacLeod. — New York: Oxford University Press, 1936. xviii, 299 p.; 26 cm. 1. Herrick, Robert, 1591-1674 — Concordances. I. T.
PR3513.A3 M2   LC 36-24656

Scott, George Walton. **2.7074**
Robert Herrick, 1591–1674. — New York: St. Martin's Press, [1974] 200 p.: illus.; 23 cm. 1. Herrick, Robert, 1591-1674. I. T.
PR3513.S3 1974   821/.4 B   LC 73-94380

Robert Herrick Memorial Conference, University of Michigan, Dearborn, 1974. **2.7075**
'Trust to good verses': Herrick tercentenary essays / Roger B. Rollin, J. Max Patrick, editors. — Pittsburgh: University of Pittsburgh Press, c1978. vi, 291 p.; 21 cm. Includes index. 1. Herrick, Robert, 1591-1674 — Congresses. I. Rollin, Roger B. II. Patrick, John Max, 1911- III. T.
PR3514.A24 1974   821/.4   LC 77-74547   ISBN 0822933535

Holcroft, Thomas, 1745-1809. **2.7076**
Anna St Ives; edited with an introduction by Peter Faulkner. — London; New York: Oxford U.P., 1970. xx, 495 p.; 21 cm. — (Oxford English novels) I. T.
PR3515.H2 A8 1970   823/.6   LC 71-496041   ISBN 0192553399

Hurd, Richard, Bp. of Worcester, 1720-1808. • **2.7077**
Hurd's Letters on chivalry and romance, with the third Elizabethan dialogue; edited with introd. by Edith J. Morley. London: H. Frowde; 1911. 176 p.; 18 cm. 1. Dialogue 2. Chivalry 3. Romanticism I. Morley, Edith Julia, 1875-, ed. II. T.
PR3517 H78 A16 1911

PR3521–3538 Johnson

Johnson, Samuel, 1709-1784. • **2.7078**
[Works] The Yale edition of the works of Samuel Johnson. [New Haven, Yale University Press, 1958-. v.: facsims.; 23 cm. Editors vary. Vol. 15 has bibliographical references and index. I. T.
PR3521.Y3   824.63   LC 57-11918

Johnson, Samuel, 1709-1784. **2.7079**
Samuel Johnson / edited by Donald Greene. — Oxford [Oxfordshire]; New York: Oxford University Press, 1984. xxxii, 840 p.; 23 cm. — (Oxford authors.) Includes index. I. Greene, Donald Johnson. II. T. III. Series.
PR3522.G73 1984   828/.609 19   LC 83-17280   ISBN 019254179X

Johnson, Samuel, 1709-1784. • **2.7080**
The poems of Samuel Johnson, edited by David Nichol Smith and Edward L. McAdam. — Oxford, The Clarendon press, 1941. xxvi, 420 p. 23 cm. With reproductions of original title-pages. I. Smith, David Nichol, 1875-1962. ed. II. McAdam, Edward Lippincott, jr., joint ed. III. T.
PR3522.S6   821.69   LC A 42-1656

Johnson, Samuel, 1709-1784. • **2.7081**
[Rasselas] The history of Rasselas, Prince of Abissinia; edited with an introduction by Geoffrey Tillotson and Brian Jenkins. London, New York, Oxford University Press, 1971. xxx, 145 p. 21 cm. (Oxford English novels) I. Tillotson, Geoffrey, ed. II. Jenkins, Brian, ed. III. T.
PZ3.J637 R60 PR3529.A1x   823/.6   LC 76-562416   ISBN 0192553429

PR3532–3538 Biography. Criticism

Johnson, Samuel, 1709-1784. • **2.7082**
The letters of Samuel Johnson, with Mrs. Thrale's genuine letters to him. Collected & edited by R. W. Chapman. — Oxford, Clarendon Press, 1952. 3 v. facsims. 23 cm. I. Piozzi, Hester Lynch, 1741-1821. II. T.
PR3533.A2 1952   928.2   LC 53-6169

Bate, Walter Jackson, 1918-.   • 2.7083
The achievement of Samuel Johnson. — New York: Oxford University Press, 1955. xi, 248 p.: port.; 21 cm. 1. Johnson, Samuel, 1709-1784 — Criticism and interpretation. I. T.
PR3533.B33   928.2   LC 55-9707

Bate, Walter Jackson, 1918-.   2.7084
Samuel Johnson / W. Jackson Bate. — 1st ed. — New York: Harcourt Brace Jovanovich, c1977. xxii, 646 p., [9] leaves of plates: ill.; 25 cm. Includes index. 1. Johnson, Samuel, 1709-1784. 2. Authors, English — 18th century — Biography. I. T.
PR3533.B334   828/.6/09 B   LC 77-73044   ISBN 0151792607

Boswell, James, 1740-1795.   • 2.7085
Life of Johnson, together with Journal of a tour to the Hebrides and Johnson's Diary of a journey into North Wales / Edited by George Birkbeck Hill. — Rev. and enl. ed. by L. F. Powell. — Oxford: Clarendon Press, 1934-64. 6 v. illus., facsims., fold. map, ports. 23 cm. Vols. 5-6, with revisions by L. F. Powell, first published in 1950; republished in 1964 as 2d ed., with further revisions. Errata slips inserted. 1. Johnson, Samuel, 1709-1784. 2. Hebrides — Descr. & trav. I. Boswell, James, 1740-1795. Journal of a tour to the Hebrides. II. Johnson, Samuel, 1709-1784. Diary of a journey into North Wales. III. Hill, George Birkbeck Norman, 1835-1903. ed. IV. Powell, Lawrence Fitzroy, 1881- ed. V. T.
PR3533.B6 1934   LC 34-32393 rev

Boswell, James, 1740-1795.   • 2.7086
[Life of Samuel Johnson] Life of Johnson; edited by R. W. Chapman; a new edition corrected by J. D. Fleeman. New ed. London, New York, Oxford U.P., 1970. xxiv, 1492 p. 21 cm. (Oxford paperbacks, 204) 1. Johnson, Samuel, 1709-1784 — Biography. I. Chapman, R. W. (Robert William), 1881-1960. ed. II. T.
PR3533.B6 1970   828/.6/09 B   LC 78-515717

Clifford, James Lowry, 1901-.   • 2.7087
Young Sam Johnson. New York: McGraw-Hill [1955] 377 p.: ill.; 21 cm. 1. Johnson, Samuel, 1709-1784. I. T.
PR3533.C6   928.2   LC 54-12672

Shaw, William, 1749-1831.   2.7088
Memoirs of the life and writings of the late Dr. Samuel Johnson [by] William Shaw. Anecdotes of the late Samuel Johnson, LL.D., during the last twenty years of his life [by] Hesther Lynch Piozzi. Edited with an introd. by Arthur Sherbo. London, New York, Oxford University Press, 1974. xxii, 201 p. illus. 25 cm. (Oxford English memoirs and travels) Half title: Memoirs and anecdotes of Dr. Johnson. On spine: Memoirs of Dr. Johnson. 1. Johnson, Samuel, 1709-1784. I. Piozzi, Hester Lynch, 1741-1821. Anecdotes of the late Samuel Johnson. 1974. II. T. III. Title: Anecdotes of the late Samuel Johnson. IV. Title: Memoirs and anecdotes of Dr. Johnson. V. Title: Memoirs of Dr. Johnson. VI. Series.
PR3533.S5 1974   828/.6/09 B   LC 74-177118   ISBN 0192554166

Wain, John.   2.7089
Samuel Johnson / John Wain. — London: Macmillan, c1974. 388 p., [8] leaves of plates: ill.; 24 cm. 1. Johnson, Samuel, 1709-1784. I. T.
PR3533.W33 1974   828/.6/09 B   LC 75-305050   ISBN 0333132009

Hardy, J. P. (John P.), 1933-.   2.7090
Samuel Johnson: a critical study / J. P. Hardy. — London; Boston: Routledge & Kegan Paul, 1979. 228 p.; 23 cm. 1. Johnson, Samuel, 1709-1784 — Criticism and interpretation. I. T.
PR3534.H3   828/.609   LC 79-40038   ISBN 0710002912

Sherbo, Arthur, 1918-.   • 2.7091
Samuel Johnson, editor of Shakespeare / with an essay on The Adventurer. — Urbana: University of Illinois Press, 1956. xi, 181 p.: ill.; 26 cm. — (Illinois studies in language and literature. v. 42) 1. Shakespeare, William, 1564-1616 — Criticism and interpretation 2. Johnson, Samuel, 1709-1784. 3. The Adventurer. I. T. II. Series.
PR3534.S4   LC 56-5689

Folkenflik, Robert, 1939-.   2.7092
Samuel Johnson, biographer / Robert Folkenflik. — Ithaca: Cornell University Press, 1978. 237 p.; 23 cm. Includes index. 1. Johnson, Samuel, 1709-1784 — Criticism and interpretation. 2. Biography (as a literary form) I. T.
PR3537.B54 F64   828/.6/09   LC 78-58050   ISBN 0801409683

PR3539-3545 K–M

King, Henry, 1592-1669.   • 2.7093
Poems / edited by Margaret Crum. — Oxford: Clarendon Press, 1965. xiii, 264 p.; 23 cm. I. Crum, Margaret. II. T.
PR3539.K65 A6 1965   LC 66-4956

Lee, Nathaniel, 1653?-1692.   • 2.7094
Works. Edited with introd. and notes by Thomas B. Stroup and Arthur L. Cooke. — New Brunswick, N. J., Scarecrow Press, 1954-55 [i. e. 1954] 2 v. facsims. 23 cm. Bibliographical references included in 'Notes.' I. T.
PR3540.A1 1954   822.49   LC 54-14766 rev

Lennox, Charlotte, ca. 1729-1804.   2.7095
The female Quixote, or, The adventures of Arabella; edited with an introduction by Margaret Dalziel; Chronology and appendix by Duncan Isles. London, New York, Oxford U.P., 1970. xxiii, 2-427 p. illus. 21 cm. (Oxford English novels) I. T. II. Title: The adventures of Arabella.
PZ3.L548 Fe8 PR3541.L27F4x   823/.6   LC 73-526120   ISBN 0192553305

Lillo, George, 1693-1739.   2.7096
The plays of George Lillo / [edited with an introd. by Trudy Drucker]. — New York: Garland Pub., 1979. v.; 19 cm. — (Eighteenth-century English drama. 27) Reprint of the 1775 ed. published by T. Davies, London, under title: The works of George Lillo, with some accounts of his life. I. Drucker, Trudy. II. T. III. Series.
PR3541.L5 1979   822/.5   LC 78-66658

Lovelace, Richard, 1618-1658.   2.7097
The poems of Richard Lovelace; edited by C. H. Wilkinson. — Oxford, The Clarendon press, [1953] lxxxvii, 367 p. Pages also numbered lxxx, 367. 'Reprinted lithographically from corrected sheets of the first edition (1930)' I. Wilkinson, Cyril Hackett, 1888-1960. ed. II. T.
PR3542.L2   LC 26-14708

Hartmann, Cyril Hughes, 1896-.   2.7098
The Cavalier spirit and its influence on the life and work of Richard Lovelace (1618–1658) / by Cyril Hughes Hartmann. — London: G. Routledge; New York; E.P Dutton, 1925. xv, 158 p., [7] leaves of plates: ill.; 23 cm. 1. Lovelace, Richard, 1618-1658 — Biography. 2. Poets, English — Early modern, 1500-1700 — Biography. 3. Great Britain — History — Charles I, 1625-1649 I. T.
PR3542.L2 H3   821/.4 B   LC 25-22026

Mackenzie, Henry, 1745-1831.   2.7099
The man of feeling / Henry MacKenzie; edited with an introduction by Brian Vickers. — Oxford; New York: Oxford University Press, 1987. xxx, 137 p.; 19 cm. (World's classics.) I. Vickers, Brian. II. T. III. Series.
PR3543.M2 M3 1987   823/.6 19   LC 86-32428   ISBN 0192817760

Macpherson, James, 1736-1796.   • 2.7100
The poems of Ossian; translated by James Macpherson, to which are prefixed a preliminary discourse and dissertation on the era and poems of Ossian. Boston, Phillips, Sampson, 1851. St. Clair Shores, Mich., Scholarly Press, 1970. 492 p. illus. 21 cm. 'A critical dissertation on the poems of Ossian ... by Hugh Blair': p. 88-188. 1. Ossian, 3rd cent. — Poetry. I. Blair, Hugh, 1718-1800. II. T.
PR3544.A1 1970   821/.6 19   LC 76-107180   ISBN 040300036X

Saunders, Thomas Bailey, 1860-1928.   • 2.7101
The life and letters of James Macpherson; containing a particular account of his famous quarrel with Dr. Johnson, and a sketch of the origin and influence of the Ossianic poems, by Bailey Saunders. — New York: Greenwood Press, [1969] xi, 327 p.: port.; 23 cm. Reprint of the 1894 ed. 1. Macpherson, James, 1736-1796. I. T.
PR3544.S2 1969   821/.6   LC 69-14071   ISBN 0837123909

Cook, Richard I.   2.7102
Bernard Mandeville [by] Richard I. Cook. New York, Twayne Publishers [1974] 174 p. facsim. 22 cm. (Twayne's English authors series, TEAS 170) 1. Mandeville, Bernard, 1670-1733 — Criticism and interpretation. I. T.
PR3545.M6 Z6   192   LC 73-21513   ISBN 0805713719

PR3546 Marvell

Marvell, Andrew, 1621-1678.   2.7103
The poems and letters of Andrew Marvell; edited by H. M. Margoliouth. — 3d ed. rev. by Pierre Legouis with the collaboration of E. E. Duncan-Jones. — Oxford: Clarendon Press, 1971. 2 v.: illus., 2 facsims., 2 ports.; 23 cm. Previous ed. 1952. I. Margoliouth, Herschel Maurice, 1887- ed. II. T.
PR3546.A1 1971   821/.4   LC 72-183209   ISBN 0198118538

Marvell, Andrew, 1621-1678.   2.7104
[Complete poems] The complete English poems. Edited by Elizabeth Story Donno. [New York] St. Martin's Press [1974, c1972] 314 p. 21 cm. Published in 1972 under title: The complete poems. I. Donno, Elizabeth Story, 1921- ed. II. T.
PR3546.A1 1974   821/.4   LC 73-86828

Bradbrook, Muriel Clara. • 2.7105
Andrew Marvell, by M.C. Bradbrook and M.G. Lloyd Thomas. Cambridge, Eng.: Cambridge University Press, 1940. 161p. illus. 1. Marvell, Andrew, 1621-1678. I. Lloyd Thomas, Mary Gwyneth. II. T.
PR3546.B7   LC 41-10835

Hunt, John Dixon. 2.7106
Andrew Marvell: his life and writings / John Dixon Hunt. — Ithaca, N.Y.: Cornell University Press, 1978. 206 p.: ill.; 25 cm. 1. Marvell, Andrew, 1621-1678. 2. Poets, English — Early modern, 1500-1700 — Biography. I. T.
PR3546.H8 1978   821/.4   LC 78-57689   ISBN 0801412021

Legouis, Pierre, 1891-. 2.7107
[André Marvell. English] Andrew Marvell: poet, puritan, patriot. 2nd ed. Oxford, Clarendon P., 1968. iii-xv, 262 p. 23 cm. Abridged version of a French book published in 1928 under title: André Marvell, poète, puritain, patriote, 1621-1678. 1. Marvell, Andrew, 1621-1678. I. T.
PR3546.L423 1968   821/.4 B   LC 70-374771   ISBN 0198710143

Patterson, Annabel M. 2.7108
Marvell and the civic crown / Annabel M. Patterson. — Princeton, N.J.: Princeton University Press, c1978. x, 264 p.: ill.; 23 cm. 1. Marvell, Andrew, 1621-1678 — Criticism and interpretation. I. T.
PR3546.P3   824/.4   LC 77-85555   ISBN 0691063567

Wallace, John M. (John Malcolm), 1928-. • 2.7109
Destiny his choice: the loyalism of Andrew Marvell, by John M. Wallace. — London: Cambridge U.P., 1968. x, 266 p.; 23 cm. 1. Marvell, Andrew, 1621-1678. I. T.
PR3546.W3   821/.4   LC 68-10334   ISBN 0521067251

PR3550–3598 Milton

Milton, John, 1608-1674. • 2.7110
The works of John Milton. — New York: Columbia University Press, 1931-1938. 18 v. in 21: ports., facsims.; 24 cm. 'Of the Columbia University edition of The works of John Milton there have been printed for sale two thousand copies on rag paper and one hundred and fifty numbered copies on handmade paper.' This copy not numbered. 'Frank Allen Patterson, general editor.' Vols. 1-3 in two parts each; vols. 4-18 one part each. I. Patterson, Frank Allen, 1878-1944. II. T.
PR3550.F31   LC 31-10596

Milton, John, 1608-1674. 2.7111
Complete poetical works. Edited by Douglas Bush. — [Cambridge edition]. — Boston, Houghton Mifflin [1965] xxxiii, 570 p. facsims., ports. 25 cm. The translations of the Latin, Greek, and Italian poems are by the editor. I. Bush, Douglas, 1896- ed. II. T.
PR3551.B87   821.4   LC 65-2686

Milton, John, 1608-1674. 2.7112
[Poems] The poems of John Milton, edited by John Carey and Alastair Fowler. [London] Longman [New York] Norton [1972, c1968] xxii, 1181 p. illus. 21 cm. (Annotated English poets) I. Carey, John. ed. II. Fowler, Alastair. ed. III. T.
PR3551.C3 1972   821/.4   LC 75-178128   ISBN 0393043606

Milton, John. • 2.7113
Poems. / Edited by Helen Darbishire. — [London]: Oxford University Press, 1961. x, 679 p.: facsims; 19 cm. English or Latin. Includes reproductions of original title pages. 1. English poetry 2. English poetry — Early modern (to 1700) I. Darbishire, Helen. II. T.
PR3551.D3 1961   821.4   LC 61-66591

Milton, John. • 2.7114
The complete English poetry of John Milton: excluding his translations of Psalms 80–88 / arranged in chronological order with an introduction, notes, variants, and literal translations of the foreign language poems by John T. Shawcross. — 1st ed. — Garden City, N.Y.: Anchor Books, 1963. xv, 574 p.; 19 cm. — (The Anchor seventeenth-century series) Includes index. I. Shawcross, John Thomas. II. T.
PR3551.S4   821.4   LC 63-7688

Milton, John, 1608-1674. • 2.7115
Poetical works / edited by Helen Darbishire; with translations of the Italian, Latin and Greek poems from the Columbia University edition. — London: Oxford University Press [1958] xii, 628 p. facsims. 23 cm. — (Oxford Standard Authors)
PR3552.D3 1958   821.47   LC 58-2543

Milton, John, 1608-1674. • 2.7116
[Works] Complete poems and major prose. Edited by Merritt Y. Hughes. Notes and introductions by the editor. [1st ed.] New York, Odyssey Press [1957] xix, 1059 p. illus., maps, facsims. 24 cm. I. Hughes, Merritt Yerkes, 1893- ed. II. T.
PR3552.H74   821.47   LC 57-4209

Fletcher, Angus John Stewart, 1930-. 2.7117
The transcendental masque; an essay on Milton's Comus, by Angus Fletcher. — Ithaca [N.Y.]: Cornell University Press, [1972, c1971] xiv, 261 p.: col. illus.; 22 cm. 'Blake's illustrations for Comus in eight scenes' [18] p., inserted between p. 256-257. 1. Milton, John, 1608-1674. Comus 2. Masques I. Blake, William, 1757-1827. II. T.
PR3557.F5 1972   822/.4   LC 78-148019   ISBN 080140620X

PR3560–3565 Paradise Lost. Paradise Regained

Milton, John, 1608-1674. • 2.7118
Paradise lost: a poem in twelve books / John Milton; edited by Merritt Y. Hughes. — New ed. — [New York]: Odyssey Press, c1962. lx, 324 p.: ill.; 21 cm. I. Hughes, Merritt Yerkes, 1893- II. T.
PR3560 1962   821.4   LC 62-11937   ISBN 067263080X

Milton, John, 1608-1674. 2.7119
Paradise lost: an authoritative text, backgrounds and sources, criticism / John Milton; edited by Scott Elledge. — 1st ed. — New York: Norton, [1975] xxix, 546 p.; 22 cm. (A Norton critical edition) I. Elledge, Scott. II. T.
PR3560 1975   821/.4   LC 75-12732   ISBN 0393044068

Behrendt, Stephen C., 1947-. 2.7120
The moment of explosion: Blake and the illustration of Milton / Stephen C. Behrendt. — Lincoln: University of Nebraska Press, c1983. x, 211 p., [27] p. of plates: ill. (some col.); 29 cm. Includes index. 1. Milton, John, 1608-1674. Paradise lost 2. Milton, John, 1608-1674 Paradise lost — Illustrations. 3. Blake, William, 1757-1827. I. T.
PR3562.B38 1983   821/.4 19   LC 82-13561   ISBN 0803211694

Crosman, Robert, 1940-. 2.7121
Reading Paradise lost / Robert Crosman. — Bloomington: Indiana University Press, c1980. xi, 262 p.; 24 cm. 1. Milton, John, 1608-1674. Paradise lost I. T.
PR3562.C68   821/.4   LC 79-3035   ISBN 0253151562

Crump, Galbraith M. (Galbraith Miller), 1929-. 2.7122
The mystical design of Paradise lost. Lewisburg [Pa.] Bucknell University Press [1975] 194 p. 21 cm. 1. Milton, John, 1608-1674. Paradise lost I. T.
PR3562.C7   821/.4   LC 74-202   ISBN 0838715192

Danielson, Dennis Richard, 1949-. 2.7123
Milton's good God: a study in literary theodicy / Dennis Richard Danielson. — Cambridge [Cambridgeshire]; New York: Cambridge University Press, 1982. xi, 292 p.: ill.; 23 cm. Based upon the author's thesis (doctoral) Includes index. 1. Milton, John, 1608-1674. Paradise lost 2. Milton, John, 1608-1674 — Religion. 3. God in literature 4. Good and evil in literature. I. T.
PR3562.D28 1982   821/.4 19   LC 81-15535   ISBN 0521237440

Davies, Stevie. 2.7124
Images of kingship in Paradise lost: Milton's politics and Christian liberty / Stevie Davies. — Columbia: University of Missouri Press, 1983. 248 p.; 22 cm. Includes index. 1. Milton, John, 1608-1674. Paradise lost 2. Milton, John, 1608-1674 — Symbolism. 3. Milton, John, 1608-1674 — Political and social views. 4. Kings and rulers in literature I. T.
PR3562.D36 1983   821/.4 19   LC 82-17485   ISBN 0826203922

Demaray, John G. 2.7125
Milton's theatrical epic: the invention and design of Paradise lost / John G. Demaray. — Cambridge: Harvard University Press, 1980. xviii, 161 p., [4] leaves of plates: ill.; 24 cm. 1. Milton, John, 1608-1674. Paradise lost 2. Theater — History — 16th century 3. Theater — History — 17th century. I. T.
PR3562.D44   821/.4   LC 79-23139   ISBN 0674576152

Ferry, Anne. • 2.7126
Milton's epic voice; the narrator in Paradise lost. — Cambridge, Harvard University Press, 1963. xv, 187 p. 22 cm. Bibliographical references included in 'Notes' (p. [183]-187) 1. Milton, John, 1608-1674. Paradise lost. I. T.
PR3562.F4   821.4   LC 63-11419

Fiore, Peter Amadeus, 1927-. 2.7127
Milton and Augustine: patterns of Augustinian thought in Paradise lost / Peter A. Fiore. — University Park: Pennsylvania State University, c1981. 118 p.; 23 cm. Includes index. 1. Milton, John, 1608-1674. Paradise lost 2. Augustine, Saint, Bishop of Hippo — Theology. 3. Milton, John, 1608-1674 — Religion and ethics. 4. Fall of man in literature I. T.
PR3562.F47   821/.4   LC 80-17854   ISBN 0271002697

Fish, Stanley Eugene. 2.7128
Surprised by sin: the reader in 'Paradise lost.'. — Toronto, Macmillan; London, St.Martin's Press, 1967. xi, 344 p. 22.5 cm. 1. Milton, John, 1608-1674. Paradise lost I. T.
PR3562.F5 1967   821/.4   LC 67-14191

Hamlet, Desmond M.　　　　　　　　**2.7129**
One greater man: justice and damnation in Paradise lost / Desmond M. Hamlet. — Lewisburg, [Pa.]: Bucknell University Press, c1976. 224 p.; 22 cm. Based on the author's thesis, University of Illinois at Urbana-Champaign, 1973. Includes index. 1. Milton, John, 1608-1674. Paradise lost 2. Milton, John, 1608-1674 — Knowledge — Religion. 3. Justice in literature I. T.
PR3562.H32　　821/.4　　LC 74-27670　　ISBN 0838716741

Hunter, G. K.　　　　　　　　**2.7130**
Paradise lost / G.K. Hunter. — London; Boston: Allen and Unwin, 1980. 213 p.; 23 cm. — (Unwin critical library.) Includes index. 1. Milton, John, 1608-1674. Paradise lost I. T. II. Series.
PR3562.H85　　821/.4 19　　LC 79-41772　　ISBN 0048000043

Lewis, C. S. (Clive Staples), 1898-1963.　　　● **2.7131**
A preface to Paradise lost, being the Ballard Matthews Lectures delivered at University College, North Wales, 1941. Rev. and enl. / by C.S. Lewis. — London: Oxford University Press, 1942. vii, 139 p. — (Wales, North. University College of North Wales, Bangor. Ballard Matthews Lectures) 1. Milton, John, 1608-1674. Paradise lost 2. Epic poetry — Histoy and criticism. I. T.
PR3562.L4　　LC 43-1806

Lieb, Michael, 1940-.　　　　　　　　**2.7132**
Poetics of the holy: a reading of Paradise lost / by Michael Lieb. — Chapel Hill: University of North Carolina Press, c1981. xxi, 442 p.: ill.; 24 cm. Includes index. 1. Milton, John, 1608-1674. Paradise lost 2. Religion and poetry I. T.
PR3562.L52　　821/.4 19　　LC 80-29159　　ISBN 0807814792

MacCaffrey, Isabel Gamble.　　　　　　**2.7133**
Paradise lost as 'myth.'. — Cambridge, Harvard University Press, 1959. 229 p. 22 cm. Includes bibliography. 1. Milton, John, 1608-1674. Paradise lost I. T.
PR3562.M18　　821.4　　LC 59-9282

McColley, Diane Kelsey, 1934-.　　　　　**2.7134**
Milton's Eve / Diane Kelsey McColley. — Urbana: University of Illinois Press, c1983. viii, 232 p., [8] p. of plates: ill.; 24 cm. 1. Milton, John, 1608-1674. Paradise lost 2. Milton, John, 1608-1674 — Characters — Eve. 3. Eve (Biblical figure) in fiction, drama, poetry, etc. 4. Women in literature 5. Fall of man in literature I. T.
PR3562.M34 1983　　821/.4 19　　LC 83-1313　　ISBN 0252009800

Revard, Stella Purce.　　　　　　　　**2.7135**
The war in heaven: Paradise lost and the tradition of Satan's rebellion / Stella Purce Revard. — Ithaca, N. Y.: Cornell University Press, 1980. 315 p.; 23 cm. Includes index. 1. Milton, John, 1608-1674. Paradise lost 2. Devil in literature 3. War in literature I. T.
PR3562.R4　　821/.4　　LC 79-23297　　ISBN 0801411386

Ricks, Christopher B.　　　　　　　　● **2.7136**
Milton's grand style. — Oxford, Clarendon Press, 1963. 154 p. 23 cm. Bibliographical footnotes. 1. Milton, John. Paradise lost. I. T.
PR3562.R54　　821.4　　LC 63-6009

Roston, Murray.　　　　　　　　**2.7137**
Milton and the baroque / Murray Roston. — Pittsburgh: University of Pittsburgh Press, 1980. ix, 192 p., [6] leaves of plates: ill.; 23 cm. 1. Milton, John, 1608-1674. Paradise lost 2. Milton, John, 1608-1674 — Style. 3. Baroque literature — History and criticism. 4. Art, Baroque I. T.
PR3562.R6 1980　　821/.4　　LC 79-21611　　ISBN 0822911388

Shawcross, John T.　　　　　　　　**2.7138**
With mortal voice: the creation of Paradise lost / John T. Shawcross. — Lexington, Ky.: University Press of Kentucky, c1982. x, 198 p.; 23 cm. 1. Milton, John, 1608-1674. Paradise lost I. T.
PR3562.S48 1982　　821/.4 19　　LC 80-51944　　ISBN 0813114500

Stein, Arnold Sidney, 1915-.　　　　　● **2.7139**
Answerable style: essays on Paradise lost. — Minneapolis: University of Minnesota Press, [1953] 166 p.; 23 cm. 1. Milton, John, 1608-1674. Paradise lost I. T.
PR3562.S7　　821.47　　LC 53-5944

Summers, Joseph H. (Joseph Holmes), 1920-.　　● **2.7140**
The muse's method: an introduction to Paradise Lost / Joseph H. Summers. — London: Chatto & Windus, c1962. — x, 227 p. Includes index. 1. Milton, John, 1608-1674. Paradise lost I. T.
PR3562 S8　　821.4　　LC 62-5100

Webber, Joan.　　　　　　　　**2.7141**
Milton and his epic tradition / by Joan Malory Webber. — Seattle: University of Washington Press, c1979. xiv, 244 p.; 21 cm. 1. Milton, John, 1608-1674. Paradise lost 2. Milton, John, 1608-1674. Paradise regained 3. Epic poetry — History and criticism. I. T.
PR3562.W34　　821/.4　　LC 78-4368　　ISBN 0295956186

PR3566–3570 Other Works

Milton, John, 1608-1674.　　　　　　● **2.7142**
Samson Agonistes / Milton; edited by F. T. Prince. — London: Oxford University Press, 1957. 144 p.; 23 cm. 1. Samson (Biblical judge) — Poetry. I. T.
PR3566 1957　　LC 57-3821

Radzinowicz, Mary Ann.　　　　　　**2.7143**
Toward Samson Agonistes: the growth of Milton's mind / Mary Ann Radzinowicz. — Princeton, N.J.: Princeton University Press, c1978. xxiii, 436 p.: ill.; 25 cm. Includes index. 1. Milton, John, 1608-1674. Samson Agonistes 2. Milton, John, 1608-1674 — Criticism and interpretation. I. T.
PR3566.R3　　821/.4　　LC 77-85559　　ISBN 0691063575

Milton, John, 1608-1674.　　　　　　● **2.7144**
Prose selections, ed. by Merritt Y. Hughes. — [1st ed.]. — New York: Odyssey Press [1947] cxci, 454 p. facsim. 19 cm. — (Odyssey series in literature) Bibliography: p. cxxv—cxlvii. I. Hughes, Merritt Yerkes, 1893- ed. II. T.
PR3569.H8　　828.4　　LC 47-30552 *

Milton, John, 1608-1674.　　　　　　**2.7145**
[Prose works. Selections] Selected prose / John Milton; edited by C.A. Patrides. — New and rev. ed. — Columbia: University of Missouri Press, 1985. 462, [1] p.; 19 cm. I. Patrides, C. A. II. T.
PR3569.P34 1985　　824/.4 19　　LC 85-1027　　ISBN 0826204848

Milton, John, 1608-1674.　　　　　　**2.7146**
Complete prose works / [Don M. Wolfe, general editor] New Haven: Yale University Press, 1953-1982. 8 v. in 10: facsims. I. Wolfe, Don Marion, 1902- II. T.
PR3569.W6　　828.4　　LC 52-5371 rev

PR3579–3586 Biography. Criticism (General)

A Milton encyclopedia / edited by William B. Hunter, Jr.,　　**2.7147**
general editor, John T. Shawcross and John M. Steadman, co-editors, Purvis E. Boyette and Leonard Nathanson, associate editors.
Lewisburg: Bucknell University Press, c1978-c1983. 9 v.; 26 cm. 1. Milton, John, 1608-1674 — Dictionaries, indexes, etc. I. Hunter, William Bridges, 1915-
PR3580.M5　　821/.4　　LC 75-21896　　ISBN 0838718345

French, Joseph Milton, 1895- ed.　　　● **2.7148**
The life records of John Milton. Edited by J. Milton French. New York: Gordian Press, 1966 [c1949-58] 5 v.: ports.; 24 cm. — (Rutgers studies in English, no. 7) 1. Milton, John, 1608-1674. I. T.
PR3581.F72　　828.403　　LC 66-20024

Hanford, James Holly, 1882-.　　　　● **2.7149**
John Milton, Englishman / James Holly Hanford. — New York: Crown Publishers, [1949] xi, 272 p.: illus., ports.; 24 cm. 1. Milton, John, 1608-1674. I. T.
PR3581.H25　　PR3581.H25 1949a.　　928.2　　LC 49-11254

Lieb, Michael, 1940-.　　　　　　　**2.7150**
Achievements of the left hand: essays on the prose of John Milton. Edited by Michael Lieb and John T. Shawcross. — Amherst: University of Massachusetts Press, [1974] viii, 396 p.; 25 cm. 1. Milton, John, 1608-1674. 2. Milton, John, 1608-1674 — Prose. I. Shawcross, John T. joint author. II. T.
PR3581.L47　　824/.4　　LC 73-79506　　ISBN 0870231251

Parker, William Riley, 1906-1968.　　　● **2.7151**
Milton: a biography. — Oxford: Clarendon P., 1968. 2 v. (xxi, 1489 p.): plates, facsim., 3 ports. (1 col.).; 23 cm. 1. Milton, John, 1608-1674 — Biography. I. T.
PR3581.P27　　821/.4 B　　LC 68-141367

Thorpe, James Ernest, 1915-.　　　　**2.7152**
John Milton: the inner life / by James Thorpe. — San Marino, CA: Huntington Library, 1983. x, 191 p.: port.; 24 cm. 1. Milton, John, 1608-1674. 2. Poets, English — Early modern, 1500-1700 — Biography. I. T.
PR3581.T49 1983　　821/.4 19　　LC 83-12602　　ISBN 0873280792

Wolfe, Don Marion, 1902-.　　　　　**2.7153**
Milton and his England, by Don M. Wolfe. — Princeton, N.J.: Princeton University Press, 1971. 1 v. (unpaged): illus.; 29 cm. 1. Milton, John, 1608-1674. 2. Milton, John, 1608-1674 — Contemporary England. 3. Great Britain — History — Stuarts, 1603 1714 I. T.
PR3581.W6　　821/.4 B　　LC 76-146646　　ISBN 0691062005

Parker, William Riley, 1906-1968.　　　● **2.7154**
Milton's contemporary reputation; an essay, together with A tentative list of printed allusions to Milton, 1641–1674, and facsimile reproductions of five

contemporary pamphlets written in answer to Milton. — New York: Haskell House Publishers, 1971. ix, 299 p.; 22 cm. Reprint of the 1940 ed. 1. Milton, John, 1608-1674 — Contemporaries. 2. Milton, John, 1608-1674 — Allusions. I. T.
PR3583.P3 1971   821/.4   LC 70-122996   *ISBN* 0838311296

PR3588 Criticism. Interpretation

Hanford, James Holly, 1882-.   • **2.7155**
A Milton handbook [by] James Holly Hanford & James G. Taaffe. — 5th ed. — New York: Appleton-Century-Crofts, [1970] xii, 374 p.: illus., facsims., ports.; 22 cm. 1. Milton, John, 1608-1674. I. Taaffe, James G. joint author. II. T.
PR3588.H2 1970   821/.4   LC 77-98702   *ISBN* 0390408700

Havens, Raymond Dexter, 1880-1954.   • **2.7156**
The influence of Milton on English poetry. — New York: Russell & Russell, 1961 [c1922] xii, 722 p.; 24 cm. 1. Milton, John, 1608-1674 — Influence. 2. English poetry — History and criticism I. T.
PR3588.H3 1961   821.4   LC 61-5717

Martz, Louis Lohr.   **2.7157**
Poet of exile: a study of Milton's poetry / by Louis L. Martz. — New Haven, Conn.: Yale University Press, 1980. x, 356 p.: ill.; 24 cm. 1. Milton, John, 1608-1674 — Criticism and interpretation — Addresses, essays, lectures. I. T.
PR3588.M376   821/.4   LC 79-64079   *ISBN* 0300023936

Miller, David M.   **2.7158**
John Milton: poetry / by David M. Miller. — Boston: Twayne, 1978. 199 p.: port.; 21 cm. — (Twayne's English authors series; TEAS 242) Includes index. 1. Milton, John, 1608-1674 — Criticism and interpretation. I. T.
PR3588.M47   821/.4   LC 78-18800   *ISBN* 080576724X

Tuve, Rosemond, 1903-1964.   • **2.7159**
Images & themes in five poems by Milton / Rosemond Tuve. — Cambridge, [Mass.]: Harvard University Press, 1957. 161 p. 1. Milton, John, 1608-1674 — Criticism and interpretation. 2. Figures of speech I. T.
PR3588.T8   LC 57-7619

Woodhouse, A. S. P. (Arthur Sutherland Pigott), 1895-1964.   **2.7160**
The heavenly muse; a preface to Milton. Edited by Hugh MacCallum. — [Toronto; Buffalo]: University of Toronto Press, [1972] xii, 373 p.: port.; 25 cm. — (University of Toronto. Dept. of English. Studies and texts, no. 21) 1. Milton, John, 1608-1674 — Criticism and interpretation. I. MacCallum, Hugh Reid, ed. II. T.
PR3588.W59   821/.4   LC 79-185724   *ISBN* 0802052479

PR3592 Treatment of Special Subjects

Frye, Roland Mushat.   **2.7161**
Milton's imagery and the visual arts: iconographic tradition in the epic poems / Roland Mushat Frye. — Princeton, N.J.: Princeton University Press, c1978. 260 p: plates., ill. Includes index. 1. Milton, John, 1608-1674 — Knowledge — Art. 2. Milton, John, 1608-1674. Paradise lost 3. Milton, John, 1608-1674. Paradise regained 4. Christian art and symbolism 5. Arts, Renaissance I. T.
PR3592.A66 F78   821/.4   LC 77-24541   *ISBN* 0691063494

Hill, Christopher, 1912-.   **2.7162**
Milton and the English Revolution / by Christopher Hill. — New York: Viking Press, 1978, c1977. xviii, 541 p.; 25 cm. Includes index. 1. Milton, John, 1608-1674 — Political and social views. 2. Milton, John, 1608-1674 — Religion. 3. Great Britain — History — Puritan Revolution, 1642-1660 I. T.
PR3592.P64 H5 1978   821/.4   LC 77-21548   *ISBN* 0670476129

Milner, Andrew.   **2.7163**
John Milton and the English Revolution: a study in the sociology of literature / Andrew Milner. — Totowa, N.J.: Barnes & Noble Books, 1981. vii, 248 p.; 23 cm. Includes index. 1. Milton, John, 1608-1674 — Political and social views. 2. Literature and society 3. Great Britain — Politics and government — 1642-1660 I. T.
PR3592.P64 M5 1981   821/.4 19   LC 81-124809   *ISBN* 0389201235

Stavely, Keith W.   **2.7164**
The politics of Milton's prose style / Keith W. Stavely. — New Haven: Yale University Press, 1975. ix, 136 p.; 23 cm. (Yale studies in English. 185) Includes index. 1. Milton, John, 1608-1674 — Political and social views. 2. Milton, John, 1608-1674 — Style. 3. Milton, John, 1608-1674 — Prose. I. T. II. Series.
PR3592.P64 S8   821/.4   LC 74-20086   *ISBN* 0300018045

Barker, Arthur Edward, 1911-.   • **2.7165**
Milton and the Puritan dilemma, 1641–1660 / by Arthur Barker. — Toronto: University of Toronto Press, 1942. xxiv, 440 p. — (University of Toronto. Department of English studies and texts; no. 1) 1. Milton, John, 1608-1674 —
Political and social views. 2. Milton, John, 1608-1674 — Religion and ethics. 3. Great Britain — History — Puritan Revolution, 1642-1660 I. T. II. Series.
PR3592.P7 B3   LC 43-2578   *ISBN* 0802050255

Christopher, Georgia B., 1932-.   **2.7166**
Milton and the science of the saints / Georgia B. Christopher. — Princeton, N.J.: Princeton University Press, c1982. xii, 264 p.; 22 cm. 1. Milton, John, 1608-1674 — Religion. 2. Reformation in literature 3. Theology, Puritan, in literature. 4. Calvinism in literature. I. T.
PR3592.R4 C56 1982   821/.4 19   LC 81-47911   *ISBN* 069106508X

Empson, William, 1906-.   • **2.7167**
Milton's God. — [Norfolk, Conn.] New Directions [1962] 280 p. 23 cm. 1. Milton, John — Religion and ethics. 2. God — History of doctrines I. T.
PR3592.R4E55 1962   821.4   LC 61-13123

PR3593 Textual Criticism

A Variorum commentary on the poems of John Milton. [Merritt   • **2.7168**
Y. Hughes, general editor].
New York: Columbia University Press, 1970-. v.   ; 23 cm. 1. Milton, John, 1608-1674 — Criticism, Textual. I. Hughes, Merritt Yerkes, 1893- ed. II. Bush, Douglas, 1896-
PR3593.V3   821/.4   LC 70-129962   *ISBN* 0231088795

PR3594–3598 Language. Style

Fletcher, Harris Francis, 1892-.   • **2.7169**
The use of the Bible in Milton's prose, with an index of the Biblical quotations and citations arranged in the chronological order of the prose works; another index of all quotations and citations in the order of the books of the Bible; and an index of the quotations and citations in the De doctrina. — New York: Haskell House, 1970. 176 p.; 23 cm. Reprint of the 1929 ed. 1. Milton, John, 1608-1674 — Prose. 2. Milton, John, 1608-1674. De doctrina christiana. 3. Bible in literature I. T.
PR3594.F5 1970   828/.4/08   LC 75-95425   *ISBN* 0838309747

Ingram, William.   • **2.7170**
A concordance to Milton's English poetry; edited by William Ingram and Kathleen Swaim. — Oxford: Clarendon Press, 1972. xvii, 683 p.; 26 cm. 1. Milton, John, 1608-1674 — Concordances. I. Milton, John, 1608-1674. II. Swaim, Kathleen M. joint author. III. T.
PR3595.I55   821/.4   LC 72-186436   *ISBN* 019811138X

Bridges, Robert Seymour, 1844-1930.   • **2.7171**
Milton's prosody. With a chapter on accentual verse & notes. Rev. final ed. Oxford [University Press] 1921. 119p. 1. Milton, John, 1608-1674 — versification I. T.
PR3597 B7 1921

PR3600–3618 M–P

Montagu, Mary Wortley, Lady, 1689-1762.   **2.7172**
Essays and poems and simplicity, a comedy / Lady Mary Wortley Montagu; edited by Robert Halsband and Isobel Grundy. — Oxford [Eng.]: Clarendon, 1977. viii, 412 p., [4] leaves of plates: ill.; 23 cm. I. Halsband, Robert, 1914- II. Grundy, Isobel. III. T.
PR3604.A6 1977   821/.5   LC 77-361583   *ISBN* 0198124449

O'Keeffe, John, 1747-1833.   **2.7173**
Wild oats: or, The strolling gentlemen: a comedy in five acts / by John O'Keeffe; the text as prepared and directed by Clifford Williams for the Royal Shakespeare Company; with an introduction and editorial material by the director. — London: Heinemann Educational, 1977. xvi, 88 p.; 19 cm. — (The Hereford plays) I. Williams, Clifford John. II. Royal Shakespeare Company. III. T.
PR3605.O3 A77 1977   822/.6   LC 77-368276   *ISBN* 0435237225

Oldham, John.   • **2.7174**
Poems / With an introd. by Bonamy Dobrée. — [Carbondale]: Southern Illinois University Press, [c1960] 266 p. (Centaur classics) I. T.
PR3605.O4 1960   LC 60-9250

Zigerell, James.   **2.7175**
John Oldham / by James Zigerell. — Boston: Twayne Publishers, c1983. 145 p.: port.; 23 cm. — (Twayne's English authors series. TEAS 372) Includes index. 1. Oldham, John, 1653-1683 — Criticism and interpretation. I. T. II. Series.
PR3605.O4 Z98 1983   821/.4 19   LC 83-10722   *ISBN* 0805768580

Otway, Thomas, 1652-1685.   • **2.7176**
The works of Thomas Otway; plays, poems, and love letters / edited by J.C. Ghosh. — Oxford: Clarendon Press, 1932. 2 v.: facsims. Xerox copy (Ann

Arbor, Mich., University microfilms, 1967) 'With the exception of ... the Prologue to Constantine the Great ... the first edition of every work has been used as the basis of the present text' - v. 1, p. 89. I. Ghosh, Jyotish Chandra. II. T.
PR3610.A5 G5

Otway, Thomas, 1652-1685.   2.7177
The orphan / Thomas Otway; edited by Aline Mackenzie Taylor. — Lincoln: University of Nebraska Press, c1976. xxx, 118 p.; 22 cm. (Regents restoration drama series) Based on 'The history of Brandon, part I of the English adventures, written presumably by Roger Boyle, Earl of Orrery, and published in May 1676.' I. Taylor, Aline Mackenzie. II. Orrery, Roger Boyle, Earl of, 1621-1679. III. T.
PR3612.O7 1976   822/.4   *LC* 75-13067   *ISBN* 0803203837

Ham, Roswell Gray, 1891-.   • 2.7178
Otway and Lee; biography from a baroque age. — New York: Greenwood Press, [1969, c1931] xiv, 250 p.: illus., ports.; 24 cm. 1. Otway, Thomas, 1652-1685. 2. Lee, Nathaniel, 1653?-1692. 3. English drama — Restoration, 1660-1700 — History and criticism. I. T.
PR3613.H3 1969   822/.4/09   *LC* 69-13923

Paltock, Robert, 1697-1767.   2.7179
The life and adventures of Peter Wilkins. Edited with an introd. by Christopher Bentley. — London; New York: Oxford University Press, 1973. xviii, [6], 388 p.: illus.; 21 cm. — (Oxford English novels) Reprint of the 1751 ed. published by J. Robinson and R. Dodsley, London. I. T. II. Title: Peter Wilkins.
PZ3.P188 L30 PR3615.P5   823/.6   *LC* 74-163872   *ISBN* 0192553291

PR3618.P2 Pepys
(see also: DA447.P4)

Ollard, Richard Lawrence.   2.7180
Pepys: a biography, by Richard Ollard. — New York: Holt, Rinehart and Winston, 1975. 368 p.: illus.; 24 cm. 1. Pepys, Samuel, 1633-1703 — Biography. I. T.
PR3618.P2 O5 1975   914.2/03/660924 B   *LC* 74-5541   *ISBN* 0030131464

Percy, Thomas, 1729-1811.   • 2.7181
The Percy letters / David Nichol Smith & Cleanth Brooks, general editors ... [Baton Rouge]: Louisiana State University Press, 1944-. v.; 24 cm. 1. Percy, Thomas, 1729-1811 — Correspondence. I. Brooks, Cleanth, 1906- II. Smith, David Nichol, 1875-1962. III. T.
PR3618.P5 A84   826.6   *LC* 44-9765

Philips, Ambrose, 1674-1749.   • 2.7182
The poems of Ambrose Philips. Edited by M. G. Segar. — New York: Russell & Russell, [1969] lvi, 192, [4] p.: facsims., geneal. table; 21 cm. Reprint of the 1937 ed. I. Segar, Mary Gertrude, ed. II. T.
PR3619.P2 A17 1969   821/.5   *LC* 71-80955

Piozzi, Hester Lynch, 1741-1821.   • 2.7183
Thraliana: the diary of Mrs. Hester Lynch Thrale (later Mrs. Piozzi) 1776–1809 / edited by Katharine C. Balderston; Published in co-operation with the Huntington Library. — 2nd ed. — Oxford: Clarendon Press, 1951. 2 v. (xxxii, 1191 p.) 1. Piozzi, Hester Lynch, 1741-1821 — Biography. 2. Johnson, Samuel, 1709-1784. I. T.
PR3619.P5 A16   *LC* a 52-4370

Piozzi, Hester Lynch, 1741-1821.   2.7184
The Thrales of Streatham Park / [edited by] Mary Hyde. — Cambridge: Harvard University Press, c1977. xvii, 373 p.: ill.; 25 cm. Annotated journal of Hester Thrale. 1. Piozzi, Hester Lynch, 1741-1821 — Biography. 2. Thrall family. 3. Salusbury family. 4. England — Social life and customs — 18th century I. Hyde, Mary Morley Crapo. II. T.
PR3619.P5 A827 1977   828/.6/09 B   *LC* 77-24922   *ISBN* 0674887468

Clifford, James Lowry, 1901-.   • 2.7185
Hester Lynch Piozzi (Mrs. Thrale) / by James L. Clifford. — 2nd ed. — Oxford: Clarendon Press, 1952. 493 p.: ill.; 23 cm. Without thesis note. 1. Piozzi, Hester Lynch, 1741-1821. I. T.
PR3619.P5 C5 1952   *LC* 53-3106

PR3620–3638 Pope

Pope, Alexander, 1688-1744.   2.7186
The Twickenham edition of the poems of Alexander Pope. General editor: John Butt. London: Methuen; New Haven: Yale University Press, [1961-69] 10 v. in 11. illus. General editor of v. 7-10: Maynard Mack. Editors of individual volumes vary. I. Homer. Odyssey. English II. Butt, John Everett. III. Mack, Maynard, 1909- IV. Homer. Iliad. English V. T.
PR3621.B82

Pope, Alexander, 1688-1744.   • 2.7187
Poems: a one-volume edition of the Twickenham text with selected annotations / edited by John Butt. — New Haven: Yale University Press, c1963. 850 p. I. Butt, John Everett. ed. II. T.
PR3621.B83   *LC* 63-25056

Pope, Alexander, 1688-1744.   2.7188
Literary criticism of Alexander Pope. Edited by Bertrand A. Goldgar. — Lincoln, University of Nebraska Press [1965] xxxv, 181 p. 21 cm. — (Regents critics series) Bibliography: p. xxxv. Bibliographical footnotes. 1. Literature — History and criticism I. Goldgar, Bertrand A., 1927- ed. II. T.
PR3621.G6   809.1   *LC* 64-17231

Pope, Alexander, 1688-1744.   2.7189
The last and greatest art: some unpublished poetical manuscripts of Alexander Pope / transcribed and edited by Maynard Mack. — Newark: University of Delaware Press, c1984. 454 p.: facsims.; 32 cm. 1. Pope, Alexander, 1688-1744 — Manuscripts — Facsimiles. I. Mack, Maynard, 1909- II. T.
PR3622.M3 1984   821/.5 19   *LC* 82-4772   *ISBN* 0874131839

Williams, Aubrey L.   • 2.7190
Pope's Dunciad; a study of its meaning, by Aubrey L. Williams. — [Hamden, Conn.]: Archon Books, 1968. ix, 162 p.: map.; 21 cm. 1. Pope, Alexander, 1688-1744. Dunciad. I. T.
PR3625.W5 1968   821/.5   *LC* 68-11258

Pope, Alexander, 1688-1744.   • 2.7191
Memoirs of the extraordinary life, works, and discoveries of Martinus Scriblerus / Written in collaboration by the members of the Scriblerus Club – John Arbuthnot, Alexander Pope ... [et al.]; Edited by Charles Kerby–Miller. — New Haven: Published for Wellesley college by Yale Univ. Press, 1950. ix, 408 p. 'Published in Dublin [in 1741] as a separate ... volume by George Faulkner, and in the following two years ... issued by Pope ... as part of an octavo edition of his works. In all these editions the work was identified as by Pope and Dr. Arbuthnot.' - p. 65. 'The 1723 Memoirs': p. [374]-385. I. Arbuthnot, John, 1667-1735. II. Kerby-Miller, Charles ed. III. Scriblerus Club, London. IV. T.
PR3630.M4 1950   *LC* 50-7238

Pope, Alexander, 1688-1744.   • 2.7192
Epistle to Bathurst; a critical reading, with an edition of the manuscripts, by Earl R. Wasserman. — Baltimore, Johns Hopkins Press [1960] 145 p. facsims. 29 cm. Includes a complete photographic reproduction of the 3 Huntington Library manuscripts, with each page of photos. accompanied by a facing transcription, and a reproduction of the 1st ed., 1732, with title: Of the use of riches, an epistle to the Right Honorable Allen Lord Bathurst. Includes bibliographies. I. Wasserman, Earl R. (Earl Reeves), 1913- ed. II. Henry E. Huntington Library and Art Gallery. III. T.
PR3630.O45 1960   827.5   *LC* 60-12741

Halsband, Robert, 1914-.   2.7193
The rape of the lock and its illustrations, 1714–1896 / Robert Halsband. — Oxford: Clarendon Press; New York: Oxford University Press, 1980. xvi, 160 p., [5] leaves of plates: ill. (some col.); 25 cm. Includes index. 1. Pope, Alexander, 1688-1744 The rape of the lock — Illustrations. I. T.
PR3631.5.H34   821/.5   *LC* 79-40481   *ISBN* 0198120982

PR3632–3638 Biography. Criticism

Bedford, Emmett G.   2.7194
A concordance to the poems of Alexander Pope, compiled by Emmett G. Bedford and Robert J. Dilligan. Detroit, Gale Research Co. [1974] 2 v. port. 29 cm. Based on the Twickenham ed. of the Poems of Alexander Pope. 1. Pope, Alexander, 1688-1744 — Concordances. I. Dilligan, Robert J. joint author. II. Pope, Alexander, 1688-1744. Poems III. T.
PR3632.B4   821/.5   *LC* 74-852   *ISBN* 0810310082

Pope, Alexander, 1688-1744.   • 2.7195
Correspondence. Edited by George Sherburn. Oxford, Clarendon Press, 1956. 5v. illus., ports., facsim. I. T.
PR3633.A4   *LC* 57-528

Ault, Norman, 1880-1950.   • 2.7196
New light on Pope, with some additions to his poetry hitherto unknown. — [Hamden, Conn.]: Archon Books, 1967. viii, 379 p.: port.; 22 cm. 'First published in 1949.' 1. Pope, Alexander, 1688-1744. I. T.
PR3633.A7 1967   821.5   *LC* 67-11471

Gordon, I. R. F.   **2.7197**
A preface to Pope / I. R. F. Gordon. — London; New York: Longman, 1976. xiii, 195 p.: ill.; 22 cm. (Preface books) Includes indexes. 1. Pope, Alexander, 1688-1744. I. T.
PR3633.G6   821/.5   *LC* 75-25572   *ISBN* 0582315050

Mack, Maynard, 1909-.   **2.7198**
Alexander Pope: a life / Maynard Mack. — 1st ed. — New Haven: Yale University Press in association with W.W. Norton, New York, 1985. xii, 975 p.: ill., ports.; 24 cm. Includes index. 1. Pope, Alexander, 1688-1744 — Biography. 2. Poets, English — 18th century — Biography. I. T.
PR3633.M27 1985   821/.5 B 19   *LC* 85-2941   *ISBN* 0300033915

Mack, Maynard, 1909-.   **2.7199**
The garden and the city; retirement and politics in the later poetry of Pope, 1731–1743. — [Toronto]: University of Toronto Press, [1969] xviii, 341 p.: illus., ports.; 26 cm. 1. Pope, Alexander, 1688-1744. 2. Pope, Alexander, 1688-1744 — Homes and haunts — Twickenham. I. T.
PR3633.M33   821/.5   *LC* 69-18883   *ISBN* 0802052096

Sherburn, George Wiley, 1884-.   • **2.7200**
The early career of Alexander Pope, by George Sherburn. — Oxford: Clarendon P., 1968. vi, 326 p.: illus.; 23 cm. 'First published 1934.' 1. Pope, Alexander, 1688-1744. I. T.
PR3633.S45 1968   821/.5 B   *LC* 76-401360   *ISBN* 0198116756

Brower, Reuben Arthur, 1908-.   • **2.7201**
Alexander Pope: the poetry of allusion, by Reuben A. Brower. — London; New York, [etc.]: Oxford U.P., 1968. xiii, 368 p.; 21 cm. — (Oxford paperbacks, no. 149) 1. Pope, Alexander, 1688-1744 — Criticism and interpretation. I. T.
PR3634.B7 1968   821/.5   *LC* 73-413763   *ISBN* 0198811497

Jackson, Wallace, 1930-.   **2.7202**
Vision and re–vision in Alexander Pope / Wallace Jackson. — Detroit: Wayne State University Press, 1983. 204 p.; 24 cm. 1. Pope, Alexander, 1688-1744 — Criticism and interpretation. I. T.
PR3634.J3 1983   821/.5 19   *LC* 82-20179   *ISBN* 0814317294

Morris, David B.   **2.7203**
Alexander Pope, the genius of sense / David B. Morris. — Cambridge, Mass.: Harvard University Press, 1984. xii, 370 p., [1] p. of plates: ill.; 25 cm. 1. Pope, Alexander, 1688-1744 — Criticism and interpretation. I. T.
PR3634.M67 1984   821/.5 19   *LC* 83-18577   *ISBN* 0674015223

Tillotson, Geoffrey, 1905-1969.   • **2.7204**
On the poetry of Pope / by Geoffrey Tillotson. — 2nd ed. — Oxford: Clarendon Press, 1950. 179 p.; 20 cm. 1. Pope, Alexander, 1688-1744. I. T.
PR3634.T5 1950   821.53   *LC* 51-6506   *ISBN* 0198115806

Brownell, Morris R.   **2.7205**
Alexander Pope & the arts of Georgian England / Morris R. Brownell. — Oxford [Eng.]: Clarendon Press, 1978. xxvi, 401 p., [24] leaves of plates: ill.; 26 cm. 1. Pope, Alexander, 1688-1744 — Aesthetics. 2. Pope, Alexander, 1688-1744 — Homes and haunts — Twickenham. 3. Art, English — History. 4. Landscape architecture — England — History. I. T.
PR3637.A35 B7   821/.5   *LC* 77-23988   *ISBN* 0198173385

PR3639–3658 Prior. Quarles. Ramsay. Reeve

Prior, Matthew, 1664-1721.   • **2.7206**
The literary works of Matthew Prior. Edited by H. Bunker Wright and Monroe K. Spears. — Oxford, Clarendon Press, 1959. 2 v. (liii, 1094 p.) port., facsim. 23 cm. Includes bibliographical references. I. Wright, Harold Bunker, 1907- ed. II. Spears, Monroe Kirklyndorf. ed. III. T.
PR3640.A2 1959   821.5   *LC* 59-1258

Eves, Charles Kenneth, 1888-.   • **2.7207**
Matthew Prior, poet and diplomatist. — New York: Octagon Books, 1973 [c1939] 436 p.: ports.; 24 cm. Originally presented as the author's thesis, Columbia. Original ed. issued as no. 144 of Columbia University studies in English and comparative literature. 1. Prior, Matthew, 1664-1721. I. T.
PR3643.E9 1973   821/.5 B   *LC* 73-1151   *ISBN* 0374926468

Quarles, Francis, 1592-1644.   • **2.7208**
The complete works in prose and verse, of Francis Quarles; now for the first time collected and edited: with memorial–introduction, notes and illustrations, portrait, emblems, facsimiles &c., by the Rev. Alexander B. Grosart ... — [Edinburgh], Printed for private circulation [by T. and A. Constable], 1880. 3 v. front. (port.) plates, facsims. 26 cm. — (Chertsey worthies' library) I. Grosart, Alexander Balloch, 1827-1899. ed. II. T.
PR3650.A5G7   *LC* 03-30557

Ramsay, Allan, 1685-1758.   **2.7209**
The works of Allan Ramsay. — Edinburgh: Printed for the Scottish Text Society by W. Blackwood, 1951-1974. 6 v.; 23 cm. — (Scottish Text Society.

Publications; 3d ser., 19-20, 29, 4th ser., 6-8) Volumes 1-2 edited by B. Martin; vols. 3-6 edited by A.M. Kinghorn and A. Law. I. Martin, Burns, 1895-. II. Kinghorn, Alexander Manson. III. Law, Alexander. IV. T.
PR3657.A1 1951

Martin, Burns.   **2.7210**
Allan Ramsay, a study of his life and works. — Westport, Conn.: Greenwood Press, [1973] vi, 203 p.: front.; 19 cm. Reprint of the 1931 ed. 1. Ramsay, Allan, 1685-1758. I. T.
PR3657.M3 1973   821/.5   *LC* 72-605   *ISBN* 0837158303

Reeve, Clara, 1729-1807.   **2.7211**
The old English baron: a Gothic story / Clara Reeve; edited with an introduction by James Trainer. — London; Toronto: Oxford University Press, 1967. xviii, 153 p.: ill., facsims., port.; 21 cm. — (Oxford English novels.) I. Trainer, James II. T. III. Series.
PZ 3.R257. O 15   PR3658.R5 O4 1967.   *LC* 67-109149

PR3660–3667 Richardson

Richardson, Samuel, 1689-1761.   • **2.7212**
The novels of Samuel Richardson. Complete and unabridged. [New York, AMS Press, 1970] 19 v. illus., ports., facsims. 23 cm. Reprint of the 1902 ed. 'With a life of the author, and introductions by William Lyon Phelps. I. Phelps, William Lyon, 1865-1943. II. T.
PR3661.P5 1970   823/.6   *LC* 75-114357   *ISBN* 0404053106

Richardson, Samuel, 1689-1761.   **2.7213**
Selected letters of Samuel Richardson / edited, with an introduction by John Carroll. — Oxford: Clarendon Press, [1965] t.p. 1964. 350 p.: port.; 23 cm. 1. Richardson, Samuel, 1689-1761 — Correspondence. I. Carroll, John J. II. T.
PR3664.C3   826.6   *LC* 65-1191

Richardson, Samuel, 1689-1761.   **2.7214**
Clarissa, or, The history of a young lady / Samuel Richardson; edited with an introd. and notes by Angus Ross. — Harmondsworth, Eng.: Viking, 1985. 1533 p.: music. I. Ross, Angus. II. T. III. Title: The history of a young lady
PR3664 C43 1985   *LC* 85-51071   *ISBN* 0670808296

Castle, Terry.   **2.7215**
Clarissa's ciphers: meaning & disruption in Richardson's 'Clarissa' / Terry Castle. — Ithaca, N.Y.: Cornell University Press, 1982. 201 p.; 23 cm. Includes index. 1. Richardson, Samuel, 1689-1761. Clarissa 2. Women in literature 3. Reader-response criticism I. T.
PR3664.C43 C37 1982   823/.6 19   *LC* 82-2460   *ISBN* 0801414954

Eagleton, Terry, 1943-.   **2.7216**
The rape of Clarissa: writing, sexuality, and class struggle in Samuel Richardson / Terry Eagleton. — Minneapolis: University of Minnesota Press, c1982. ix, 109 p.; 23 cm. 1. Richardson, Samuel, 1689-1761. Clarissa 2. Richardson, Samuel, 1689-1761 — Political and social views. I. T.
PR3664.C43 E2 1982   823/.6 19   *LC* 82-243008   *ISBN* 0816612048

Goldberg, Rita, 1949-.   **2.7217**
Sex and Enlightenment: women in Richardson and Diderot / Rita Goldberg. — Cambridge [Cambridgeshire]; New York: Cambridge University Press, 1984. xi, 239 p.; 23 cm. Includes index. 1. Richardson, Samuel, 1689-1761. Clarissa 2. Richardson, Samuel, 1689-1761 — Characters — Women. 3. Diderot, Denis, 1713-1784. Religieuse. 4. Diderot, Denis, 1713-1784 — Characters — Women. 5. Women in literature 6. Sex in literature 7. Enlightenment I. T.
PR3664.C43 G58 1984   823/.6 19   *LC* 83-23210   *ISBN* 0521260698

Warner, William Beatty.   **2.7218**
Reading Clarissa: the struggles of interpretation / William Beatty Warner. — New Haven: Yale University Press, 1979. xiii, 274 p.; 24 cm. 1. Richardson, Samuel, 1689-1761. Clarissa 2. Richardson, Samuel, 1689-1761 — Criticism and interpretation — History. I. T.
PR3664.C43 W3   823/.5   *LC* 79-1475   *ISBN* 0300023219

Richardson, Samuel, 1689-1761.   **2.7219**
Pamela, or, Virtue rewarded / Samuel Richardson; edited by Peter Sabor, with an introduction by Margaret A. Doody. — Harmondsworth: Penguin Books, 1980. 537 p. — (Penguin English library) I. T.
PR3664 P35 1980   *ISBN* 0140431403

Kreissman, Bernard.   • **2.7220**
Pamela–Shamela: a study of the criticisms, burlesques, parodies, and adaptations of Richardson's Pamela. — [Lincoln]: University of Nebraska Press, 1960. 98 p.; 23 cm. 1. Richardson, Samuel, 1689-1761. Pamela I. T.
PR3664.P4 K7 1960   *LC* 60-36321

Richardson, Samuel, 1689-1761.   2.7221
The history of Sir Charles Grandison; edited with an introduction by Joselyn Harris. — London; New York: Oxford University Press, 1972. 3 v. (xliii, 482 p.; [5], 681 p.; [5], 485 p.); 21 cm. — (Oxford English novels) I. T. II. Title: Sir Charles Grandison.
PZ3.R396 Hi3 PR3664.S5x   823/.6   LC 73-152832   ISBN 0192553585

Eaves, T. C. Duncan (Thomas Cary Duncan), 1918-.   • 2.7222
Samuel Richardson: a biography, by T. C. Duncan Eaves and Ben D. Kimpel. Oxford, Clarendon Press, 1971. xvii, 728 p., 12 plates. facsims., ports. 24 cm. 1. Richardson, Samuel, 1689-1761. I. Kimpel, Ben D., joint author. II. T.
PR3666.E2   823/.6 B   LC 78-27067   ISBN 0198124317

Doody, Margaret Anne.   2.7223
A natural passion: a study of the novels of Samuel Richardson / by Margaret Anne Doody. — [S.l.]: Oxford, 1975 (c1974) viii, 410 p., [3] leaves of plates: ill.; 23 cm. Includes indexes. 1. Richardson, Samuel, 1689-1761 — Criticism and interpretation. I. T.
PR3667.D57   823/.6   LC 75-307628   ISBN 019812029X

Kinkead-Weekes, Mark.   2.7224
Samuel Richardson; dramatic novelist. — Ithaca, N.Y.: Cornell University Press, [1973] ix, 506 p.; 22 cm. 1. Richardson, Samuel, 1689-1761 — Criticism and interpretation. I. T.
PR3667.K5   823/.6   LC 72-13385   ISBN 080140777X

McKillop, Alan Dugald, 1892-.   2.7225
Samuel Richardson, printer and novelist, by Alan Dugald McKillop. Chapel Hill, The University of North Carolina Press, 1936. xi, 357 p. 24 cm. 1. Richardson, Samuel, 1689-1761. I. T.
PR3667.M25   LC 36-32602

PR3668–3678 R–S

Rochester, John Wilmot, Earl of, 1647-1680.   • 2.7226
Poems / edited with an introd. and notes by Vivian de Sola Pinto. — [2d ed.]. — Cambridge: Harvard University Press, 1964, c1953. lxix, 247 p.; 17 cm. — (Muses' library) I. Pinto, Vivian de Sola, 1895- II. T.
PR3669.R2 1964   LC 64-2324

Rochester, John Wilmot, Earl of, 1647-1680.   • 2.7227
[Poems] The complete poems of John Wilmot, earl of Rochester. Edited by David M. Vieth. New Haven, Yale University Press, 1968. lxix, 256 p. 24 cm. I. Vieth, David M. ed. II. T.
PR3669.R2 1968   821/.4   LC 68-27768

Rochester, John Wilmot, Earl of, 1647-1680.   2.7228
The letters of John Wilmot, Earl of Rochester / edited and annotated with an introd. by Jeremy Treglown. — Chicago: University of Chicago Press; Oxford: Basil Blackwell, 1980. xii, 275 p., [4] leaves of plates: ill.; 24 cm. 1. Rochester, John Wilmot, Earl of, 1647-1680 — Correspondence. 2. Poets, English — Early modern, 1500-1700 — Correspondence. I. Treglown, Jeremy. II. T.
PR3669.R2 A83 1980   821/.4 19   LC 80-20592   ISBN 0226811816

Farley-Hills, David.   2.7229
Rochester's poetry / David Farley–Hills. — Totowa, N.J.: Rowman and Littlefield, 1978. viii, 230 p.; 23 cm. 1. Rochester, John Wilmot, Earl of, 1647-1680 — Criticism and interpretation. I. T.
PR3669.R2 F34 1978   821/.4   LC 79-100289   ISBN 0847660788

Griffin, Dustin H.   2.7230
Satires against man; the poems of Rochester [by] Dustin H. Griffin. Berkeley, University of California Press [c1973] xiii, 317 p. 21 cm. 1. Rochester, John Wilmot, Earl of, 1647-1680 — Criticism and interpretation. I. T.
PR3669.R2 G7   821/.4   LC 72-95304   ISBN 0520023943

Pinto, Vivian de Sola, 1895-.   • 2.7231
Enthusiast in wit; a portrait of John Wilmot, earl of Rochester 1647–1680. Lincoln, University of Nebraska Press, 1962. xxii, 246 p. illus. 23 cm. An extensive revision, rewriting, and supplementation of the original text published in 1935 under title: Rochester: portrait of a Restoration poet. 1. Rochester, John Wilmot, 2d earl, 1647-1680. I. T.
PR3669.R2 P5 1962   LC 62-8539 REV

Spirit of wit: reconsiderations of Rochester / edited by Jeremy Treglown.   2.7232
Hamden, Conn.: Archon Books, 1982. viii, 199 p.; 23 cm. 1. Rochester, John Wilmot, Earl of, 1647-1680 — Criticism and interpretation — Addresses, essays, lectures. I. Treglown, Jeremy.
PR3669.R2 S65 1982   821/.4 19   LC 82-13751   ISBN 0208020128

Rowe, Nicholas, 1674-1718.   2.7233
Three plays: Tamerlane, The fair penitent, Jane Shore / by Nicholas Rowe; edited by J. R. Sutherland, with introduction, bibliography, and notes. —

London: Scholartis Press, 1929. 352 p.: facsims. I. Sutherland, James Runcieman, 1900- II. T. III. Title: Tamerlane. IV. Title: The fair penitent. V. Title: Jane Shore.
PR3671.R5 A765   PR3671.R5 A765.   LC 29-20329

Rowe, Nicholas, 1674-1718.   2.7234
[Jane Shore] The tragedy of Jane Shore. Edited by Harry William Pedicord. Lincoln, University of Nebraska Press [1974] xxvii, 97 p. 21 cm. (Regents Restoration drama series) 1. Shore, Jane, d. 1527? — Drama. I. Pedicord, Harry William. ed. II. T.
PR3671.R5 A68 1974   822/.5   LC 73-85439   ISBN 0803203810

Jenkins, Annibel.   2.7235
Nicholas Rowe / by Annibel Jenkins. Boston: Twayne Publishers, c1977. 167 p.: port.; 21 cm. (Twayne's English authors series; TEAS 200) Includes index. 1. Rowe, Nicholas, 1674-1718 — Criticism and interpretation. I. T.
PR3671.R5 J4   822/.5   LC 76-53826   ISBN 0805766634

Rymer, Thomas, 1641-1713.   • 2.7236
The critical works of Thomas Rymer. Edited with an introd. and notes by Curt A. Zimansky. — Westport, Conn.: Greenwood Press, [1971, c1956] li, 299 p.; 23 cm. 1. Drama — History and criticism 2. Literature — History and criticism I. Zimansky, Curt Arno, ed. II. T.
PR3671.R7 1971   822/.051   LC 70-156207   ISBN 0837161576

Savage, Richard, d. 1743.   • 2.7237
Poetical works. Edited with notes and commentaries by Clarence Tracy. — Cambridge [Eng.] University Press, 1962. 276 p. 23 cm. I. Tracy, Clarence Rupert. ed. II. T.
PR3671.S2A17 1962   821.5   LC 62-52507

Sedley, Charles, Sir, 1639?-1701.   • 2.7238
The poetical and dramatic works of Sir Charles Sedley. Collected and edited from the old editions. With a pref. on the text, explanatory and textual notes, an appendix containing works of doubtful authenticity, and a bibliography, by V. de Sola Pinto. — New York: AMS Press, [1969] 2 v.: illus., facsims., ports.; 23 cm. Reprint of the 1928 ed. I. Pinto, Vivian de Sola, 1895- ed. II. T.
PR3671.S4 1969   828/.4/09   LC 70-85905

Shadwell, Thomas, 1642?-1692.   2.7239
The virtuoso. Edited by Marjorie Hope Nicolson and David Stuart Rodes. — Lincoln, University of Nebraska Press [1966] xxvi, 153 p. 22 cm. — (Regents Restoration drama series) I. Nicolson, Marjorie Hope, 1894- ed. II. Rodes, David Stuart. ed. III. T.
PR3671.S8A79 1966   822.4   LC 65-19466

Shenstone, William, 1714-1763.   • 2.7240
The poetical works. With life, critical dissertation, and explanatory notes, by George Gilfillan. — New York: Greenwood Press, 1968. xxviii, 284 p.; 23 cm. Reprint of the 1854 ed. I. Gilfillan, George, 1813-1878. II. T.
PR3677.A1 1968   821/.5   LC 68-54436

Shenstone, William, 1714-1763.   • 2.7241
The letters of William Shenstone, arranged and edited with introduction, notes and index by Marjorie Williams. — Oxford, B. Blackwell, 1939. xxvii, [1], 700 p. front. (port.) pl., fold. facsim. 22.5 cm. I. Williams, Marjorie. ed. II. T.
PR3677.A83 1939a   928.2   LC 39-30578

Humphreys, A. R. (Arthur Raleigh), 1911-.   • 2.7242
William Shenstone; an eighteenth–century portrait, by A. R. Humphreys. — Cambridge, The University press, 1937. 135 p. 1. Shenstone, William, 1714-1763. I. T.
PR3677.H8   928.2   LC 38-6938

PR3679–3684 Sheridan

Sheridan, Frances Chamberlaine, 1724-1766.   2.7243
[Plays] The plays of Frances Sheridan / edited by Robert Hogan and Jerry C. Beasley. — Newark: University of Delaware Press; London; Cranbury, NJ: Associated University Presses, c1984. 209 p.: ill.; 24 cm. I. Hogan, Robert Goode, 1930- II. Beasley, Jerry C. III. T.
PR3679.S5 A19 1984   822/.6 19   LC 82-49304   ISBN 0874132436

Sheridan, Richard Brinsley, 1751-1816.   • 2.7244
The plays of Richard Brinsley Sheridan. — London: J. M. Dent & Co.; New York: E. P. Dutton & Co., 1931. viii, 411 p. — (Everyman's library, ed. by Ernest Rhys. Poetry and the drama, [no. 95].) I. T. II. Series.
PR 3680.A5 M6   LC 36-37097

Sheridan, Richard Brinsley, 1751-1816.   2.7245
[Works. 1973] The dramatic works of Richard Brinsley Sheridan; edited by Cecil Price. Oxford, Clarendon Press, 1973. 2 v. illus., facsims., port. 23 cm. (Oxford English texts) Includes index. I. Price, Cecil John Layton. ed. II. T.
PR3680.A5 P7   822/.6   LC 73-176171   ISBN 0198118562

Sheridan, Richard Brinsley, 1751-1816. • 2.7246
Plays & poems. Edited with introductions, appendices and bibliographies by R. Crompton Rhodes. — New York, Russell & Russell, 1962. 3 v. illus., port. 23 cm. Includes bibliographies. 1. Sheridan, Richard Brinsley, 1751-1816 — Bibl. I. Rhodes, R. Crompton (Raymond Crompton) ed. II. T.
PR3680.A5R4 1962   828.6   *LC* 62-13850

Sheridan, Richard Brinsley, 1751-1816. • 2.7247
The Letters of Richard Brinsley Sheridan / edited by Cecil Price. — Oxford: Clarendon Press, 1966. 3 v.: front. (port.); 23 cm. I. Price, Cecil John Layton. II. T.
PR3683.A4 1966   *LC* 66-73161

Darlington, William Aubrey, 1890-. • 2.7248
Sheridan, by W. A. Darlington. [Reprinted with additions to bibliography. London] Published for the British Council and the National Book League by Longmans, Green [1966] 31 p. port. 22 cm. (Bibliographical series of supplements to British book news on writers and their work, no. 18) 1. Sheridan, Richard Brinsley, 1751-1816. I. T. II. Series.
PR3683.D3 1966   822/.6   *LC* 76-507230

Sheridan, Betsy, 1758-1837. • 2.7249
Betsy Sheridan's journal; letters from Sheridan's sister, 1784–1786, and 1788–1790. Edited by William LeFanu. — New Brunswick, N. J., Rutgers University Press [1960] 223 p. illus. 23 cm. 1. Sheridan, Richard Brinsley, 1751-1816. I. Le Fanu, W. R. (William Richard), 1904- ed. II. T.
PR3683.L4 1960a   920.7   *LC* 60-51999

Moore, Thomas, 1779-1852. • 2.7250
Memoirs of the life of the Rt. Hon. Richard Brinsley Sheridan. New York, Greenwood Press [1968] 2 v. port. 23 cm. Reprint of the 1858 ed. On spine: Life of Sheridan. 1. Sheridan, Richard Brinsley, 1751-1816. I. T. II. Title: Life of Sheridan.
PR3683.M6 1968   822/.6 B   *LC* 69-14001

Rhodes, R. Crompton (Raymond Crompton) • 2.7251
Harlequin Sheridan, the man and the legends: with a bibliography and appendices / by R. Crompton Rhodes. — Oxford: Blackwell, 1933. xvii, 305 p.: ill. 1. Sheridan, Richard Brinsley, 1751-1816 — Biography. I. T.
PR3683.R5   *LC* 33-25226

Auburn, Mark S. 2.7252
Sheridan's comedies, their contexts and achievements / Mark S. Auburn. — Lincoln: University of Nebraska Press, c1977. ix, 221 p.; 23 cm. 1. Sheridan, Richard Brinsley, 1751-1816 — Criticism and interpretation. I. T.
PR3684.A9   822/.6   *LC* 77-7205   *ISBN* 0803209142

Loftis, John Clyde, 1919-. 2.7253
Sheridan and the drama of Georgian England / John Loftis. — Cambridge, Mass.: Harvard University Press, c1977. xi, 174 p.; 23 cm. Includes index. 1. Sheridan, Richard Brinsley, 1751-1816 — Criticism and interpretation. I. T.
PR3684.L6   822/.6   *LC* 76-27161   *ISBN* 0674806323

PR3687–3688 Smart. Smith

Smart, Christopher, 1722-1771. 2.7254
The poetical works of Christopher Smart / edited with an introd. by Karina Williamson. — Oxford: Clarendon Press; New York: Oxford University Press, 1980-1983. 2 v.: port.; 23 cm. Includes indexes. I. Williamson, Karina. II. T.
PR3687.S7 A6 1980   821/.6   *LC* 79-41319   *ISBN* 0198118694

Sherbo, Arthur, 1918-. • 2.7255
Christopher Smart, scholar of the university. — [East Lansing]: Michigan State University Press, 1967. 303 p.: port.; 24 cm. 'Books in use at Cambridge about the year 1730, for arithmetic, algebra, geometry, physics, mechanics, and hydrostatics.': p. 273-277. 1. Smart, Christopher, 1722-1771. I. T.
PR3687.S7 Z8   821/.6 B   *LC* 67-12575

Smith, Charlotte (Turner) Mrs. 1749-1806. 2.7256
Emmeline: the orphan of the castle [by] Charlotte Smith; edited with an introduction by Anne Henry Ehrenpreis. — London; New York: Oxford University Press, 1971. xxvii, 531 p.: illus.; 21 cm. — (Oxford English novels) I. T.
PZ3.S6445 Em7 PR3688.S4   823/.6   *LC* 77-591127   *ISBN* 0192553224

Smith, Charlotte Turner, 1749-1806. 2.7257
The old manor house [by] Charlotte Smith; edited with an introduction by Anne Henry Ehrenpreis. — London: Oxford U.P., 1969. xxx, 544 p.: 1 illus., port.; 21 cm. — (Oxford English novels) I. Ehrenpreis, Anne Henry, ed. II. T.
PZ3.S6445 Ol5 PR3688.S4   823/.6   *LC* 79-378200   *ISBN* 0192553178

PR3690–3699 Smollett. Southerne

Smollett, Tobias George. 2.7258
The works of Tobias Smollett / [O. M. Brack, Jr., editor]. — Newark: University of Delaware Press; London: Associated University Presses, c1980-. 6 v.: ill. Includes index. I. Brack, M. II. T.
PR3691.A1x   823/.6

Smollett, Tobias George, 1721-1771. 2.7259
The adventures of Roderick Random / Tobias Smollett; edited with an introd. by Paul–Gabriel Boucé. — Oxford; New York: Oxford University Press, 1979. xlviii, 481 p.; 21 cm. — (Oxford English novels) I. Boucé, Paul-Gabriel. II. T.
PZ3.S6665 Acf 1979 PR3694.A4x   823/.6   *LC* 78-41108   *ISBN* 0192553704

Smollett, Tobias George, 1721-1771. 2.7260
[Adventures of Sir Launcelot Greaves] The life and adventures of Sir Launcelot Greaves; edited with an introd. by David Evans. London, New York, Oxford University Press, 1973. xxvii, 234 p. illus. 21 cm. (Oxford English novels) First published in book-form in 1762 under title: The Adventures of Sir Launcelot Greaves. I. T.
PZ3.S6665 Li PR3694.A5x   823/.6   *LC* 74-162185   *ISBN* 019255364X

Smollett, Tobias George, 1721-1771. 2.7261
The expedition of Humphrey Clinker / edited with an introduction by Lewis M. Knapp. — London; New York: Oxford University Press, 1966. xxii, 375 p.: front. (map); 21 cm. — (Oxford English novels.) I. Knapp, Lewis Mansfield, 1894-. II. T. III. Title: Humphrey Clinker. IV. Series.
PZ3.S6665 H34 PR3694.E9x   823/.6   *LC* 66-66694   *ISBN* 0192811320

Smollett, Tobias George, 1721-1771. 2.7262
The Adventures of Peregrine Pickle: in which are included Memoirs of a lady of quality / by Tobias Smollett; edited with an introduction by James L. Clifford. — London: Oxford University Press, 1964. xxxiv, 805 p.; 21 cm. (Oxford English novels.) I. Clifford, James Lowry, 1901- II. T. III. Title: Peregrine Pickle. IV. Series.
PR3694.P4 1964   *LC* 64-56171

Smollett, Tobias George, 1721-1771. 2.7263
The letters of Tobias Smollett; edited by Lewis M. Knapp. — Oxford: Clarendon P., 1970. xxiv, 161 p., 3 plates.: ports.; 23 cm. 1. Smollett, Tobias George, 1721-1771 — Correspondence. I. Knapp, Lewis Mansfield, 1894-. II. T.
PR3696.A45 1970   823.6   *LC* 71-19277   *ISBN* 0198124171

Boucé, Paul-Gabriel. 2.7264
[Romans de Smollett. English] The novels of Tobias Smollett / Paul–Gabriel Boucé; translated by Antonia White in collaboration with the author. — London; New York: Longman, 1976. ix, 405 p.; 24 cm. Translation of Les romans de Smollett, which was originally presented as the author's thesis, Sorbonne, 1971. Includes index. 1. Smollett, Tobias George, 1721-1771. I. T.
PR3696.B613   823/.6   *LC* 75-31687   *ISBN* 0582500230

Jones, Claude Edward, 1907-. • 2.7265
Smollett studies / by Claude E. Jones. New York: Phaeton Press, 1970. xi, 31-133 p. 23 cm. (University of California publications in English, v. 9, no. 2) Reprint of the 1942 ed. 1. Smollett, Tobias George, 1721-1771 — Knowledge — Military sciences. 2. Smollett, Tobias George, 1721-1771 — Knowledge — Literature. 3. Great Britain. Royal Navy — History. 4. Critical review; or, Annals of literature. I. T.
PR3696.J6 1970   823/.6   *LC* 70-128188   *ISBN* 0877530483

Martz, Louis Lohr. • 2.7266
The later career of Tobias Smollett / by Louis Martz. — New Haven: Yale University Press; London: H. Milford, Oxford University Press, 1942. ix, 213 p.; 24 cm. (Yale studies in English. v. 97) 1. Smollett, Tobias George, 1721-1771. I. T. II. Series.
PR3696 M35

Tobias Smollett; bicentennial essays presented to Lewis M. 2.7267
Knapp. Edited by G. S. Rousseau and P.–G. Boucé.
New York, Oxford University Press, 1971. 260 p. illus. 24 cm. 1. Smollett, Tobias George, 1721-1771. I. Knapp, Lewis M. (Lewis Mansfield) II. Rousseau, G. S. (George Sebastian) ed. III. Boucé, Paul-Gabriel. ed.
PR3697.T6   823/.6   *LC* 70-146954   *ISBN* 0195013700

Southerne, Thomas, 1660-1746. 2.7268
Oroonoko / Thomas Southerne; edited by Maximillian E. Novak and David Stuart Rodes. Lincoln: University of Nebraska Press, c1976. xlii, 143 p.; 21 cm. (Regents restoration drama series) Present text based on 1st ed. printed for H. Playford, B. Tooke, and S. Buckley, London, in Dec. 1695, with 1696 t.p. date. 1. Slavery — Surinam — Drama. I. Novak, Maximillian E. II. Rodes, David Stuart. III. T.
PR3699.S3 O6 1976   822/.5   *LC* 75-38054   *ISBN* 0803203853

PR3700–3708 Steele

Steele, Richard, Sir, 1672-1729.   • 2.7269
The plays of Richard Steele; edited by Shirley Strum Kenny. — Oxford: Clarendon Press, 1971. xv, 443 p., plate, port.; 23 cm. I. Kenny, Shirley Strum. ed. II. T.
PR3701.K4   822/.5   LC 79-27567   ISBN 0198124147

Steele, Richard, Sir, 1672-1729.   • 2.7270
Occasional verse. Edited by Rae Blanchard. — Oxford, Clarendon Press, 1952. xxiv, 137 p. facsims. 23 cm. I. Blanchard, Rae. II. T.
PR3702.B54   821.59   LC 52-11844

Steele, Richard, Sir, 1672-1729.   • 2.7271
Richard Steele's periodical journalism, 1714–16. Edited by Rae Blanchard. — Oxford, Clarendon Press, 1959. xxviii, 346 p. facsims. 23 cm. I. Blanchard, Rae. II. Steele, Richard, Sir, 1672-1729. Lover. III. Steele, Richard, Sir, 1672-1729. Reader. IV. Steele, Richard, Sir, 1672-1729. Town-talk in a letter to a lady in the country. V. Steele, Richard, Sir, 1672-1729. Chit-chat in a letter to a lady in the country. VI. T. VII. Title: The lover. VIII. Title: The reader. IX. Title: Town-talk in a letter to a lady in the country. X. Title: Chit-chat in a letter to a lady in the country.
PR3702.B545   824.5   LC 59-3638

Steele, Richard, Sir, 1672-1729.   • 2.7272
Tracts and pamphlets. Edited with notes and commentary by Rae Blanchard. — New York: Octagon Books, 1967. xvii, 663 p.: illus., facsims., map.; 24 cm. Reprint of the 1944 ed. I. Blanchard, Rae, ed. II. T.
PR3702.B55 1967   828/.5/08   LC 67-18751

Steele, Richard, Sir, 1672-1729.   • 2.7273
The correspondence of Richard Steele / edited by Rae Blanchard. — London: Oxford University Press, 1941. xxviii, 562 p.: front., pl., ports., fold. facsim.; 23 cm. 1. Steele, Richard, Sir, 1672-1729 — Correspondence. I. Blanchard, Rae. II. T.
PR3706.A2 1941   LC a 42-3852

Aitken, George Atherton, 1860-1917.   2.7274
The life of Richard Steele. by George A. Aitken ... Boston: Houghton Mifflin, 1889. 2 v. fronts., ports., facsims., geneal. tables (1 fold.) 24 cm. Appendices (v.2. p. [347]-428): I. The Steeles of Cheshire, and others.—II. Fords of St. Michael's parish, Barbadoes.—III. Performances of Steele's plays.—IV. Music for Steele's songs.—V. Bibliography. 1. Steele, Richard, Sir, 1672-1729. I. T.
PR3706.A7 1889

PR3710–3716 Sterne

Sterne, Laurence, 1713-1768.   2.7275
[Works. 1978] The Florida edition of the works of Laurence Sterne / edited by Melvyn New and Joan New. — [Gainesville]: University Presses of Florida, 1978-. v.; 24 cm. 'A University of Florida book.' I. New, Melvyn. II. New, Joan. III. T.
PR3710.F78   823/.6   LC 77-20621   ISBN 0813005809

Sterne, Laurence, 1713-1768.   • 2.7276
[Selections. 1968] A sentimental journey through France and Italy, by Mr. Yorick; to which are added The Journal to Eliza and A political romance; edited with introductions by Ian Jack. London; New York [etc.]: Oxford U.P., 1968. xxvi, 241 p.; 21 cm. (Oxford English novels) 1. France — Social life and customs I. Jack, Ian Robert James. ed. II. T. III. Title: The journal to Eliza. IV. Title: A political romance.
PR3714.S4 1968   823/.6   LC 70-353180

Sterne, Laurence, 1713-1768.   • 2.7277
The life and opinions of Tristram Shandy, gentleman / Laurence Sterne; edited by James Aiken Work. — New York: Odyssey Press, 1940. lxxv, 647 p.: ill.; 19 cm. — Includes facsimiles of title-pages of the first and second editions. I. Work, James Aiken. II. T. III. Title: Tristram Shandy.
PZ3.S839 T30   PR3714.T7 1940.   LC 40-34600   ISBN 0672631288

Laurence Sterne: riddles and mysteries / edited by Valerie Grosvenor Myer.   2.7278
Totowa, N.J.: Barnes & Noble Books, 1984. 184 p.; 22 cm. — (Critical studies series) Includes index. 1. Sterne, Laurence, 1713-1768 Life and opinions of Tristram Shandy, gentleman — Addresses, essays, lectures. I. Myer, Valerie Grosvenor.
PR3714.T73 L38 1984   823/.6 19   LC 84-2845   ISBN 0389204730

Swearingen, James E., 1939-.   2.7279
Reflexivity in Tristram Shandy: an essay in phenomenological criticism / James E. Swearingen. — New Haven: Yale University Press, 1977. xiii, 271 p.; 22 cm. Includes index. 1. Sterne, Laurence, 1713-1768. The life and opinions of Tristram Shandy, gentleman. I. T. II. Title: Phenomenological criticism.
PR3714.T73 S9   823/.6   LC 77-5515   ISBN 0300021232

Sterne, Laurence, 1713-1768.   • 2.7280
Letters of Laurence Sterne; edited by Lewis Perry Curtis ... — Oxford: The Clarendon press, 1935. xxxiv, 495, [1] p. illus., plates, ports., fold. map, fold. plan, facsim. 23 cm. Includes Sterne's 'Memoirs of the life and family of the late Rev. Mr. Laurence Sterne' and letters relating to Sterne and his family. I. Curtis, Lewis Perry, 1900- ed. II. T.
PR3716.A35   928.2   LC 35-6762

Cash, Arthur H. (Arthur Hill), 1922-.   2.7281
Laurence Sterne, the early & middle years / [by] Arthur H. Cash. — London: Methuen, 1975. xxvii, 333 p., leaf of plate, [12] p. of plates: ill., geneal. table, ports. (1 col.); 25 cm. Ill. on lining papers. Distributed in the USA by Harper & Row, Barnes & Noble Import Division, N.Y. 1. Sterne, Laurence, 1713-1768 — Biography. I. T.
PR3716.C29 1975   823/.6 B   LC 75-328064   ISBN 041682210X

Cash, Arthur H. (Arthur Hill), 1922-.   2.7282
Sterne's comedy of moral sentiments; the ethical dimension of the journey. Foreword by Herbert Read. — Pittsburgh, Duquesne University Press [1966] 152 p. 26 cm. — (Duquesne studies. Philological series, 6) A Modern Humanities Research Association monograph. 1. Sterne, Laurence, 1713-1768. I. T. II. Series.
PR3716.C3   823.6   LC 65-13007

Cross, Wilbur Lucius, 1862-1948.   2.7283
The life and times of Laurence Sterne, by Wilbur L. Cross ... — 3rd ed. / with alterations and additions. — New Haven: Yale University Press; London: H. Milton, Oxford University Press, 1929. xxvi, 670 p.: ill., facsims., ports.; 24 cm. 1. Sterne, Laurence, 1713-1768 — Biography. I. Yale University. William McKean Brown Memorial Publication Fund. II. T.
PR3716.C7 1929   LC 29-30567

Howes, Alan B.   • 2.7284
Yorick and the critics; Sterne's reputation in England, 1760–1868, by Alan B. Howes. — [Hamden, Conn.]: Archon Books, 1971 [c1958] x, 186 p.; 23 cm. — (Yale studies in English. v. 139) Originally presented as the author's thesis, Yale University. 1. Sterne, Laurence, 1713-1768. I. T. II. Series.
PR3716.H6 1971   823/.6   LC 75-163005   ISBN 0208011293

Sterne, the critical heritage / edited by Alan B. Howes.   2.7285
London; Boston: Routledge and K. Paul, 1974. xxiv, 488 p.; 23 cm. (The Critical heritage series) Includes indexes. 1. Sterne, Laurence, 1713-1768 — Criticism and interpretation. I. Howes, Alan B.
PR3716.S84   823/.6   LC 73-89196   ISBN 0710077882

PR3718 Suckling

Suckling, John, Sir, 1609-1642.   2.7286
[Works. 1971] The works of Sir John Suckling. Oxford, Clarendon Press, 1971. 2 v. plates, illus., facsims., ports. 23 cm. (Oxford English texts) I. Clayton, Thomas, 1932- ed. II. Beaurline, Lester A. ed. III. T.
PR3718.A1 1971   821/.4   LC 76-30160   ISBN 0198118503

Suckling, John, Sir, 1609-1642.   • 2.7287
Sir John Suckling's poems and letters from manuscript, by Herbert Berry. — London, Ont.: Humanities Departments of the University of Western Ontario, 1960. 124 p.: map, facsims.; 23 cm. (University of Western Ontario studies in the humanities, no. 1) I. Berry, Herbert. II. T.
PR3718.A6 1960   LC 61-65583

Squier, Charles L.   2.7288
Sir John Suckling / by Charles L. Squier. — Boston: Twayne, 1978. 171 p.: port.; 21 cm. — (Twayne's English authors series; TEAS 218) Includes index. 1. Suckling, John, Sir, 1609-1642 — Criticism and interpretation. I. T.
PR3718.Z5 S6   821/.4   LC 78-6429   ISBN 0805767215

PR3720–3728 Swift

Swift, Jonathan, 1667-1745.   • 2.7289
The prose works of Jonathan Swift / edited by Herbert Davis. — Oxford: Printed at the Shakespeare Head Press and pub. for the Press by Blackwell, 1939-1968. 14 v.: ports., facsims.; 21 cm. Vol. 8 edited by Herbert Davis and Irvin Ehrenpreis; v.14, Index, compiled by Willim J. Kunz, Steven Hollander and Susan Staves. I. Davis, Herbert John, 1893-1967. II. Ehrenpreis, Irvin, 1920- III. Kunz, William J. IV. Hollander, Steven. V. Staves, Susan. VI. T.
PR3721.D3   LC 39-5505   ISBN 063100310X

Swift, Jonathan, 1667-1745.   2.7290
[Poems] Jonathan Swift, the complete poems / edited by Pat Rogers. — New Haven: Yale University Press, 1983. 956 p.; 21 cm. — (The English poets; 14) Includes indexes. I. Rogers, Pat. II. T.
PR3721.R63 1983   821/.5 19   LC 82-13547   ISBN 0300029667

Swift, Jonathan, 1667-1745. • 2.7291
Poems. Edited by Harold Williams. — 2d ed. — Oxford, Clarendon Press, 1958. 3 v. (lxii, 1242 p.) facsims. 23 cm. 'Bibliographical summary': p. xlviii-lxii. I. Williams, Harold Herbert, Sir, 1880-1964. ed. II. T.
PR3721.W5 1958   827.52   *LC* 58-4369

Swift, Jonathan, 1667-1745. 2.7292
[Gulliver's travels] The annotated Gulliver's travels: Gulliver's travels / by Jonathan Swift; edited with a biographical introd. and notes by Isaac Asimov. — New York: C. N. Potter: distributed by Crown Publishers, c1980. xxi, 298 p.: ill.; 29 cm. Includes index. I. Asimov, Isaac, 1920- II. T. III. Title: Gulliver's travels.
PR3724.G7 1980b   823/.5   *LC* 80-15032   *ISBN* 0517539497

Case, Arthur Ellicott, 1894-1946. • 2.7293
Four essays on Gulliver's travels / by Arthur E. Case. — Princeton: Princeton University Press, 1945. 5 p. leaves, 133 p.: fold. map.; 22 cm. 1. Swift, Jonathan, 1667-1745 Gulliver's travels — Addresses, essays, lectures. I. T. II. Title: 4 essays on Gulliver's travels.
PR3724.G8 C3   *LC* a 46-568

Swift, Jonathan, 1667-1745. • 2.7294
A tale of a tub, to which is added The battle of the books, and the Mechanical operation of the spirit. Together with The history of Martin, Wotton's Observations upon the Tale of a tub, Curll's Complete key, etc. The whole edited with an introd. and notes historical and explanatory, by A. C. Guthkelch and D. Nichol Smith. — 2d ed. — Oxford: Clarendon Press, 1958. lxxvii, 374 p.: illus., facsims.; 23 cm. I. Guthkelch, Adolph Charles Louis, d. 1916, ed. II. Smith, David Nichol, 1875-1962. ed. III. T.
PR3724.T3 1958   827.52   *LC* 58-1241

Harth, Phillip, 1926-. • 2.7295
Swift and Anglican rationalism: the religious background of A tale of a tub / Phillip Harth. — Chicago: University of Chicago Press, 1961. 171 p. 1. Swift, Jonathan, 1667-1745. A tale of a tub 2. Church of England — Doctrinal and controversial works 3. Rationalism I. T.
PR3724.T33 H3   *LC* 61-15934

Paulson, Ronald. • 2.7296
Theme and structure in Swift's Tale of a tub. — [Hamden, Conn.]: Archon Books, 1972 [c1960] x, 259 p.; 22 cm. Original ed. issued as v. 143 of Yale studies in English. Based on the author's thesis, Yale. 1. Swift, Jonathan, 1667-1745. A tale of a tub. I. T.
PR3724.T33 P3 1972   823/.5   *LC* 72-6570   *ISBN* 0208011331

PR3726–3728 Biography. Criticism

Swift, Jonathan, 1667-1745. • 2.7297
The correspondence of Jonathan Swift / edited by Harold Williams. — Oxford, Clarendon Press, 1963-1965. 5 v.: facsims., ports. 1. Swift, Jonathan, 1667-1745 — Correspondence. I. Williams, Harold Herbert, Sir, 1880-1964. II. T.
PR3726.A5 1963   PR3726.A4 1963.   *LC* 64-580 rev

Swift, Jonathan, 1667-1745. • 2.7298
Journal to Stella / edited by Harold Williams. — Oxford: Clarendon Press, 1948. 2 v. (lxii, 801 p.): facsim., ports. 1. Johnson, Esther, 1681-1728. I. Williams, Harold Herbert, Sir, 1880-1964. II. T.
PR3726.A65 1948   *LC* a 49-2389

Ehrenpreis, Irvin, 1920-. • 2.7299
The personality of Jonathan Swift. — New York: Barnes & Noble, [1969] 179 p.; 23 cm. Reprint of the 1958 ed. 1. Swift, Jonathan, 1667-1745. I. T.
PR3726.E35 1969   827/.5   *LC* 74-9613   *ISBN* 0389010731

Ehrenpreis, Irvin, 1920-. • 2.7300
Swift: the man, his works, and the age. Cambridge: Harvard University Press, 1962-. v.; 23 cm. 1. Swift, Jonathan, 1667-1745. I. T.
PR3726.E37   828.5   *LC* 62-51793   *ISBN* 0674858352

Landa, Louis A., 1901-. • 2.7301
Swift and the Church of Ireland. — Oxford: Clarendon Press, 1954. xvi, 206 p.; 23 cm. 1. Swift, Jonathan, 1667-1745 — Religion and ethics. 2. Church of Ireland — History. I. T.
PR3726.L3   828/.509 19   *LC* a 55-4540

Murry, John Middleton, 1889-1957. • 2.7302
Jonathan Swift, a critical biography. — New York: Noonday Press, 1955. 508 p.: illus.; 22 cm. 1. Swift, Jonathan, 1667-1745 — Biography. I. T.
PR3726.M8 1955   928.2   *LC* 55-12009

Quintana, Ricardo. • 2.7303
The mind and art of Jonathan Swift. London: Oxford University Press, 1953. xvi, 400 p., 22 cm. 1. Swift, Jonathan, 1667-1745. I. T.
PR3726.Q8   *LC* 54-489

The Character of Swift's satire: a revised Focus / edited by 2.7304
Claude Rawson.
Newark: University of Delaware Press; London: Associated University Presses, c1983. 343 p.; 24 cm. Includes essays reprinted with revisions from: Swift / edited by C.J. Rawson. London: Sphere, 1971. (Focus) Includes index. 1. Swift, Jonathan, 1667-1745 — Criticism and interpretation — Addresses, essays, lectures. I. Rawson, Claude Julien.
PR3727.C47 1983   828/.509 19   *LC* 81-72062   *ISBN* 0874132096

Davis, Herbert John, 1893-1967. • 2.7305
Jonathan Swift, essays on his satire and other studies / Herbert John Davis. — New York: Oxford U.P., 1964. vi, 292 p.; 21 cm. (Galaxy book. GB 106) 1. Swift, Jonathan, 1667-1745. I. T. II. Series.
PR3727.D29 1964   *LC* 64-10062

Davis, Herbert John, 1893-1967. • 2.7306
The satire of Jonathan Swift / by Herbert Davis. New York: Macmillan, 1947. 109 p. (Smith College lectures; 1946) 'Three lectures delivered at Smith College in May, 1946.' 1. Swift, Jonathan, 1667-1745 — Criticism and interpretation — Addresses, essays, lectures. I. T. II. Series.
PR3727.D3   827.5   *LC* 47-2180

Ferguson, Oliver Watkins, 1924-. • 2.7307
Jonathan Swift and Ireland. — Urbana: University of Illinois Press, 1962. viii, 217 p.; 24 cm. 1. Swift, Jonathan, 1667-1745. 2. Ireland — Politics and government — 18th century I. T.
PR3727.F4   *LC* 62-8610

Barnett, Louise K. 2.7308
Swift's poetic worlds / Louise K. Barnett. — Newark: University of Delaware Press, 1982. 225 p.; 22 cm. Includes index. 1. Swift, Jonathan, 1667-1745 — Poetic works. I. T.
PR3728.P58 B35   821/.5 19   *LC* 80-54538   *ISBN* 0874131871

Downie, J. A. (James Alan), 1951-. 2.7309
Jonathan Swift, political writer / J.A. Downie. — London; Boston: Routledge & K. Paul, 1984. xv, 391 p.; 23 cm. Includes index. 1. Swift, Jonathan, 1667-1745 — Political and social views. 2. Swift, Jonathan, 1667-1745. 3. Authors, Irish — 18th century — Biography. 4. Ireland — Politics and government — 18th century I. T.
PR3728.P6 D6 1984   828/.509 B 19   *LC* 83-19194   *ISBN* 0710096453

Lock, F. P. 2.7310
Swift's tory politics / F.P. Lock. — 1st American ed. — Newark: University of Delaware Press, 1984, (c1983). viii, 189 p.; 23 cm. 1. Swift, Jonathan, 1667-1745 — Political and social views. 2. Great Britain — Politics and government — 18th century I. T.
PR3728.P6 L62   828/.509 19   *LC* 83-8155   *ISBN* 0874132525

Fabricant, Carole. 2.7311
Swift's landscape / Carole Fabricant. — Baltimore: Johns Hopkins University Press, 1983 (c1982). xi, 307 p.: ill.; 24 cm. 1. Swift, Jonathan, 1667-1745 — Settings. 2. Swift, Jonathan, 1667-1745 — Knowledge — Ireland. 3. Ireland in literature. 4. Authors, Irish — 18th century — Biography. I. T.
PR3728.S46 F3   828/.509 19   *LC* 82-165   *ISBN* 0801827213

PR3729–3744 T–V

Taylor, Jeremy, Bp. of Down and Connor, 1613-1667. • 2.7312
The Golden grove: selected passages from the sermons and writings of Jeremy Taylor / edited by Logan Pearsall Smith; with a bibliography of the works of Jeremy Taylor by Robert Gathorne–Hardy. — Oxford, The Clarendon press, 1930. lxiii, 330 p., 1 l. incl. front. port. 20 cm. 1. Taylor, Jeremy, Bp. of Down and Connor, 1613-1667 — Bibliography. I. Smith, Logan Pearsall, 1865-1946. II. Gathorne-Hardy, Robert, 1902- III. T.
PR3729.T13 A6 1930   208.1   *LC* 31-3379

Temple, William, Sir, 1628-1699. • 2.7313
Five miscellaneous essays. Edited, with an introd., by Samuel Holt Monk. — Ann Arbor, University of Michigan Press [1963] xlii, 203 p. 24 cm. I. Monk, Samuel Holt. II. T. III. Title: 5 miscellaneous essays.
PR3729.T2 F5 1963   824.4   *LC* 63-9897

Thomson, James, 1700-1748. • 2.7314
The complete poetical works of James Thomson / edited, with notes, by J. Logie Robertson, M. A. London; New York: Oxford university press, 1908. xxiii, 516 p. 19 cm. (Oxford standard authors) I. Robertson, J. Logie (James Logie), 1846-1922. ed. II. T. III. Series.
PR3730.A2 1908   *LC* 10-427

Thomson, James, 1700-1748. 2.7315
Liberty; The castle of indolence, and other poems / James Thomson; edited with introduction and commentary by James Sambrook. — Oxford: Clarendon, 1986. ix, 452 p.; 22 cm. (Oxford English texts.) A companion to Sambrook's

edition of Thomson's The Seasons, 1981. Includes indexes. I. Sambrook, James. II. Thomson, James, 1700-1748. Castle of indolence. III. T. IV. Series.
PR3732.L5 1986   *ISBN* 0198127596

Thomson, James, 1700-1748.   2.7316
The seasons / James Thomson; edited with introd. and commentary by James Sambrook. — Oxford: Clarendon Press; New York: Oxford University Press, 1981. xcv, 405 p., [3] leaves of plates: ill.; 23 cm. 1. Seasons — Poetry. I. Sambrook, James. II. T.
PR3732.S4 1981   821/.5   *LC* 79-41094   *ISBN* 0198127138

McKillop, Alan Dugald, 1892-.   • 2.7317
The background of Thomson's Seasons. — Hamden, Conn., Archon Books, 1961 [c1942] vi, 191 p. 23 cm. Includes bibliographical references. 1. Thomson, James, 1700-1748. The seasons. I. T.
PR3732.S5M3 1961   821.5   *LC* 61-4999

Thomson, James, 1700-1748.   • 2.7318
Letters and documents. Edited by Alan Dugald McKillop. Lawrence, University of Kansas Press, 1958. xi, 225 p. ports., facsim. 24 cm. 1. Thomson, James, 1700-1748. I. T.
PR3733.A45 1958   *LC* 57-11249

Campbell, Hilbert H.   2.7319
James Thomson / by Hilbert H. Campbell. — Boston: G. K. Hall, 1979. 175 p.: port.; 21 cm. — (Twayne's English authors series; TEAS 269) Includes index. 1. Thomson, James, 1700-1748. 2. Poets, Scottish — 18th century — Biography. I. T.
PR3733.C3   821/.5   *LC* 79-2508   *ISBN* 0805767150

Traherne, Thomas, d. 1674.   • 2.7320
The poetical works of Thomas Traherne, faithfully reprinted from the author's original manuscript, together with Poems of felicity, reprinted from the Burney manuscript, and poems from various sources / Edited with pref. and notes by Gladys I. Wade. New York: Cooper Square Publishers, 1965. 305 p.: facsim.; 23cm. Reprint of the 1932 ed. I. Wade, Gladys Irene, 1895-   ed. II. Traherne, Philip, d.1723. III. T.
PR3736.T7 1965   *LC* 65-24605

Day, Malcolm M.   2.7321
Thomas Traherne / by Malcolm M. Day. — Boston: Twayne, c1982. 176 p.; 21 cm. — (Twayne's English authors series. TEAS 342) Includes index. 1. Traherne, Thomas, d. 1674 — Criticism and interpretation. I. T. II. Series.
PR3736.T7 Z64 1982   821/.4 19   *LC* 81-6728   *ISBN* 0805767428

Vanbrugh, John, Sir, 1664-1726.   • 2.7322
The complete works of Sir John Vanbrugh the plays edited by Bonamy Dobrée; the letters edited by Geoffrey Webb... Bloomsbury [London] The Nonesuch press, 1927-28. 4 v. illus. Text of the plays is that of the first edition, collated with one or more subsequent editions, while the letters have been taken from the originals as far as possible. With views and plans of Blenheim and other buildings designed by Vanbrugh. 1. England — Historic houses, etc. I. Dobrée, Bonamy, 1891- II. Webb, Geoffrey Fairbank, 1898- III. T.
PR3737.A1 1927   822.47   *LC* 28-18054

Vanbrugh, John, Sir, 1664-1726.   2.7323
The provoked husband [by] Sir John Vanbrugh and Colley Cibber. Edited by Peter Dixon. — Lincoln: University of Nebraska Press, [1973] xxvii, 176 p.; 22 cm. — (Regents Restoration drama series) I. Cibber, Colley, 1671-1757. joint author. II. T.
PR3737.P69 1973   822/.4   *LC* 79-128911   *ISBN* 0803203780

Vanbrugh, John, Sir, 1664-1726.   2.7324
The relapse. Edited by Curt A. Zimansky. — Lincoln: University of Nebraska Press, [1970] xxiii, 159 p.; 21 cm. — (Regents Restoration drama series) 'A Bison book.' I. Zimansky, Curt Arno, ed. II. T.
PR3737.R4 1970   822/.4   *LC* 70-107279   *ISBN* 0803253753

Vaughan, Henry, 1622-1695.   • 2.7325
Works / edited by L. C. Martin. 2d. ed. Oxford: Clarendon Press, 1957. xxviii, 771 p. : facsims. 23 cm. I. Martin, Leonard Cyril, 1886- II. T.
PR 3740 A2 1957   821/.49   *LC* 58-1198

Calhoun, Thomas O.   2.7326
Henry Vaughan, the achievement of Silex scintillans / Thomas O. Calhoun. — Newark [Del.]: University of Delaware Press, c1981. 265 p.; 24 cm. Includes index. 1. Vaughan, Henry, 1622-1695. Silex scintillans. I. T.
PR3742.S43 C3   821/.4   *LC* 79-51851   *ISBN* 0874131650

Hutchinson, Francis Ernest, 1871-1947.   • 2.7327
Henry Vaughan, a life and interpretation. — Oxford, Clarendon Press, 1947. viii p., [2] l., 260 p. plates, map. 23 cm. 'Works of Henry Vaughan': 2d leaf. 1. Vaughan, Henry, 1622-1695. I. T.
PR3743.H8   928.2   *LC* 47-5970 *

Blunden, Edmund, 1896-1974.   • 2.7328
On the poems of Henry Vaughan; characteristics and intimations. With his principal Latin poems carefully translated into English verse, by Edmund Blunden. New York, Russell & Russell [1969] 64 p. facsim. 20 cm. 'First published in 1927.' 1. Vaughan, Henry, 1622-1695. I. T.
PR3744.B6 1969   821/.4   *LC* 72-83854

PR3750–3784 W–Z

Waller, Edmund, 1606-1687.   • 2.7329
Poems, 1645, together with poems from Bodleian MS Don d 55. — Menston: Scolar Press, 1971. [248] p.; 23 cm. Facsim. of Poems originally published, London, Printed by T. W. for Humphrey Mosley, 1645. Wing W 512. I. T.
PR3750.A1 1645ab   821/.4   *LC* 72-185143   *ISBN* 0854175431

Gilbert, Jack Glenn.   2.7330
Edmund Waller / by Jack G. Gilbert. — Boston: Twayne Publishers, 1979. 161 p.: port.; 21 cm. — (Twayne's English author series; TEAS 266) Includes index. 1. Waller, Edmund, 1606-1687. 2. Poets, English — Early modern, 1500-1700 — Biography. I. T.
PR3753.G5   821/.4 B   *LC* 78-31322   *ISBN* 0805767630

Walpole, Horace, 1717-1797.   2.7331
The castle of Otranto: a Gothic story / edited with an introd. by W.S. Lewis. — London; New York: Oxford University Press, 1964. xviii, 110 p.: ill., facsim. — (Oxford English novels) I. Lewis, Wilmarth Sheldon, 1895- II. T.
PR3757.W2 C3 1964   *LC* 64-56281

Walpole, Horace, 1717-1797.   2.7332
[Miscellany] Horace Walpole's Miscellany, 1786–1795 / edited, introduced and annotated by Lars E. Troide. — New Haven: Yale University Press, 1978. xli, 174 p.: ill.; 22 cm. (Yale studies in English. 188) Originally presented as the editor's thesis, Yale. Includes index. I. Troide, Lars E., 1942- II. T. III. Series.
PR3757.W2 M5 1978   828/.6/09   *LC* 77-14117   *ISBN* 0300021054

Cooper, John Rex, 1912-.   • 2.7333
The art of The compleat angler [by] John R. Cooper. — Durham, N. C.: Duke University Press, 1968. vii, 200 p.; 23 cm. Bibliography: p. 186-196. 1. Walton, Izaak, 1593-1683. The compleat angler. I. T.
PR3757.W6C633   799.1/2   *LC* 67-29870

Ryley, Robert M.   2.7334
William Warburton / by Robert M. Ryley. — Boston: Twayne Publishers, c1984. 136 p.; 23 cm. — (Twayne's English authors series. TEAS 361) Includes index. 1. Warburton, William, Bp. of Gloucester, 1698-1779 — Criticism and interpretation. I. T. II. Series.
PR3757.W7 R94 1984   230/.3/0924 19   *LC* 83-22686   *ISBN* 0805768475

Vance, John A., 1947-.   2.7335
Joseph and Thomas Warton / by John A. Vance. — Boston: Twayne, c1983. 152 p.: ports.; 23 cm. — (Twayne's English authors series. TEAS 380) Includes index. 1. Warton, Joseph, 1722-1800 — Criticism and interpretation. 2. Warton, Thomas, 1728-1790 — Criticism and interpretation. 3. English poetry — 18th century — History and criticism. 4. Criticism — England — History — 18th century. I. T. II. Series.
PR3759.W2 Z93 1983   821/.6/09 19   *LC* 83-6659   *ISBN* 0805768661

Wesley, Charles, 1707-1788.   • 2.7336
Representative verse of Charles Wesley / selected and edited with an introduction by Frank Baker. — London: Epworth Press, 1962. lxi, 413 p., [4] leaves of plates: facsims., port. I. Baker, Frank, 1910- II. T.
PR3763W4 A6 1962

Winchilsea, Anne Kingsmill Finch, Countess of, 1661-1720.   2.7337
Selected poems of Anne Finch, Countess of Winchilsea / edited by Katharine M. Rogers. — New York: Ungar, c1979. xxiv, 167 p.; 21 cm. Includes index. I. Rogers, Katharine M. II. T.
PR3765.W57 A17 1979   821/.5 19   *LC* 78-20953   *ISBN* 0804427410

Wycherley, William, 1640-1716.   2.7338
The plays of William Wycherley / edited by Arthur Friedman. — Oxford [Eng.]: Clarendon Press; New York: Oxford University Press, 1979. xix, 543 p.; 23 cm. — (Oxford English texts) I. Friedman, Arthur, 1906- II. T.
PR3771.F7 1979   822/.4   *LC* 77-30450   *ISBN* 0198118619

Wycherley, William, 1640-1716.   2.7339
The country wife / William Wycherley; edited by David Cook and John Swannell. — London: Methuen; [New York]: distributed by Harper & Row, Barnes & Noble Import Division, 1975. lxxviii, 175 p., [3] leaves of plates: ill.; 21 cm. (The Revels plays) I. T.
PR3774.C6 1975   822/.4   *LC* 75-326743   *ISBN* 0416814301

McCarthy, B. Eugene, 1934-. 2.7340
William Wycherley: a biography / B. Eugene McCarthy. — Athens: Ohio University Press, c1979. xii, 255 p.: port.; 24 cm. 1. Wycherley, William, 1640-1716. 2. Dramatists, English — Early modern, 1500-1700 — Biography. I. T.
PR3776.M3 1979 822/.4 B *LC* 79-9210 *ISBN* 0821404105

Zimbardo, Rose A. • 2.7341
Wycherley's drama: a link in the development of English satire / by Rose A. Zimbardo. — New Haven: Yale University Press, 1965. viii, 174 p. — (Yale studies in English. 156) 1. Wycherley, William, 1640-1716. I. T. II. Series.
PR3776.Z5 *LC* 65-11191

Chadwick, William Rowley. 2.7342
The four plays of William Wycherley: a study in the development of a dramatist / by W. R. Chadwick. — The Hague: Mouton, 1975. 208 p., [1] leaf of plates: ill.; 22 cm. (Studies in English literature; v. 83) 1. Wycherley, William, 1640-1716 — Criticism and interpretation. I. T.
PR3777.C5 822/.4 *LC* 75-322399 *ISBN* 9027930813

Rogers, Katharine M. 2.7343
William Wycherley, by Katharine M. Rogers. — New York: Twayne, [1972] 174 p.; 21 cm. — (Twayne's English authors series, TEAS 127) 1. Wycherley, William, 1640-1716. I. T.
PR3777.R6 822/.4 *LC* 76-161823

Young, Edward, 1683-1765. • 2.7344
The poetical works of Edward Young. — Westport, Conn.: Greenwood Press, [1970] 2 v.; 23 cm. — (The Aldine edition of the British poets) Reprint of the 1844 ed. 'Life of Young, by the Rev. J. Mitford': v. 1, p. [ix]-lvii. I. Mitford, John, 1781-1859. II. T. III. Series.
PR3780.A2 1970 821/.5 *LC* 73-98882 *ISBN* 0837129214

PR3991–5999 19th Century (1770/1800–1891/1900)

Ainsworth, William Harrison, 1805-1882. • 2.7345
Rookwood, by William Harrison Ainsworth. London & Toronto, J.M. Dent & sons, ltd. New York, E.P. Dutton & co. [1931] xvi, 394 pages 18 cm. (Everyman's library, ed. by Ernest Rhys. [no. 870].) Title with ornamental border. Introuction by Frank Swinnerton. 1. Turpin, Richard, 1706-1739. I. T.
PR4002.R6x *LC* 32-158

PR4020–4024 Arnold

Arnold, Matthew, 1822-1888. • 2.7346
Poems. Edited by Kenneth Allott. — New York: Barnes & Noble [1965] xxiv, 624 p. facsim., port. 23 cm. — (Longmans annotated English poets) I. Allott, Kenneth. ed. II. T.
PR4020.A5A4 1965 821.8 *LC* 65-4583

Arnold, Matthew, 1822-1888. • 2.7347
[Selections] The portable Matthew Arnold; edited and with an introd. by Lionel Trilling. New York, Viking Press, 1949. viii, 659 p. 17 cm. (The Viking portable library, 45) I. Trilling, Lionel, 1905-1975. ed. II. T.
PR4020.A5 T7 824.85 *LC* 49-9982

Arnold, Matthew, 1822-1888. • 2.7348
Poetry and criticism of Matthew Arnold / edited with an introd. and notes by A. Dwight Culler. — Boston: Houghton Mifflin, 1961. 528 p.; 21 cm. — (Riverside editions, B55.) 1. English poetry — 19th century — Individual authors. I. Culler, A. Dwight. II. T.
PR4021 C8 828.8 *LC* 61-19991

Arnold, Matthew, 1822-1888. • 2.7349
Essays, letters, and reviews. Collected and edited by Fraser Neiman. — Cambridge: Harvard University Press, 1960. xv, 398 p.: ill.; 25 cm. I. Neiman, Fraser. II. T.
PR4021.N4 824.8 *LC* 60-7998

Arnold, Matthew, 1822-1888. • 2.7350
[Selected works. English] Complete prose works. [Edited by R. H. Super. Ann Arbor, University of Michigan Press, 1960-1977. 11 v.; 22 cm. I. Super, R. H. (Robert Henry), 1914- ed. II. T.
PR4021.S8 824.8 *LC* 60-5018

Arnold, Matthew, 1822-1888. • 2.7351
Poetical works, edited by C. B. Tinker and H. F. Lowry. — London; New York: Oxford University Press, 1950. xxxii, 509 p.; 19 cm. — I. T.
PR4021.T5 821.89 *LC* 50-4748

Parrish, Stephen Maxfield. • 2.7352
A concordance to the poems of Matthew Arnold / edited by Stephen Maxfield Parrish. — Ithaca, N.Y.: Cornell University Press, 1959. xxi, 965 p.; 25 cm. — (Cornell concordances.) 1. Arnold, Matthew, 1822-1888 — Concordances. I. T. II. Series.
PR4023.A3 P3 *LC* 59-4899

Arnold, Matthew, 1822-1888. 2.7353
Letters, 1848–1888. Collected and arranged by George W. E. Russell. New York, Macmillan, 1895. — Grosse Pointe, Mich.: Scholarly Press, 1968. 2 v.; 19 cm. 1. Arnold, Matthew, 1822-1888 — Correspondence. I. Russell, George William Erskine, 1853-1919. ed. II. T.
PR4023.A43 1968 826/.8 *LC* 78-2979

Honan, Park. 2.7354
Matthew Arnold, a life / Park Honan. — New York: McGraw-Hill, c1981. xii, 496 p., [8] leaves of plates; 24 cm. 1. Arnold, Matthew, 1822-1888. 2. Poets, English — 19th century — Biography. 3. Critics — England — Biography. I. T.
PR4023.H6 821/.8 B 19 *LC* 80-26131 *ISBN* 0070296979

Trilling, Lionel, 1905-1975. • 2.7355
Matthew Arnold. [2d ed.] New York, Columbia Univ. Press, 1949. 465 p. port. 23 cm. Includes bibliographies. 1. Arnold, Matthew, 1822-1888. I. T.
PR4023.T7 1949 928.2 *LC* 49-8833 *

ApRoberts, Ruth. 2.7356
Arnold and God / Ruth apRoberts. — Berkeley: University of California Press, 1984. xi, 299 p.; 24 cm. 1. Arnold, Matthew, 1822-1888 — Religion. 2. Bible — Criticism, interpretation, etc. 3. God in literature 4. Religion in literature I. T.
PR4024.A54 821/.8 19 *LC* 82-10847 *ISBN* 0520047478

Culler, A. Dwight (Arthur Dwight), 1917-. • 2.7357
Imaginative reason; the poetry of Matthew Arnold [by] A. Dwight Culler. New Haven, Yale University Press, 1966. 303 p. port. 23 cm. 1. Arnold, Matthew, 1822-1888 — Criticism and interpretation. I. T.
PR4024.C8 821.8 *LC* 66-12493

Dawson, Carl. comp. 2.7358
Matthew Arnold, the poetry: the critical heritage, edited by Carl Dawson. — London; Boston: Routledge and Kegan Paul, 1973. xiv, 466 p.; 23 cm. — (The Critical heritage series) 1. Arnold, Matthew, 1822-1888 — Criticism and interpretation. I. T.
PR4024.D28 1973 821/.8 *LC* 73-81596 *ISBN* 0710075650

Faverty, Frederic Everett, 1902-. • 2.7359
Matthew Arnold, the ethnologist, by Frederic E. Faverty. New York, AMS Press [1968] vii, 241 p. 22 cm. (Humanities series no. 27) Reprint of the 1951 ed. 1. Arnold, Matthew, 1822-1888. I. T.
PR4024.F38 1968 828/.8/09 *LC* 68-54264

Johnson, Wendell Stacy, 1927-. • 2.7360
The voices of Matthew Arnold; an essay in criticism. — New Haven, Published for Smith College by the Yale University Press, 1961. 146 p. 21 cm. 1. Arnold, Matthew, 1822-1888. I. T.
PR4024.J6 821.8 *LC* 61-6316

Matthew Arnold, prose writings: the critical heritage / edited by Carl Dawson and John Pfordresher. 2.7361
London; Boston: Routledge & K. Paul, 1979. xv, 458 p.; 23 cm. — (Critical heritage series) Includes index. 1. Arnold, Matthew, 1822-1888 — Prose works — Addresses, essays, lectures. I. Dawson, Carl. II. Pfordresher, John.
PR4024.M38 821/.8 *LC* 79-40780 *ISBN* 0710002440

Raleigh, John Henry, 1920-. • 2.7362
Matthew Arnold and American culture. — Berkeley, University of California Press, 1957. x, 301 p. 24 cm. University of California publications, English studies, 17. Bibliographical references included in 'Notes' (p. 269-293) 1. Arnold, Matthew, 1822-1888. 2. Criticism — U.S. — Hist. 3. Literature, Comparative — English and American. 4. Literature, Comparative — American and English. I. T.
PR4024.R3 824.85 *LC* A 57-9870

Tinker, Chauncey Brewster, 1876-1963. • 2.7363
The poetry of Matthew Arnold; a commentary, by C. B. Tinker and H. F. Lowry. — New York: Russell & Russell, [1970] xv, 404 p.; map; 20 cm. Reprint of the 1940 ed. 'The scholar-gipsy country, by Sir Francis Wylie': p. 351-373. 1. Arnold, Matthew, 1822-1888 — Criticism and interpretation. I. Lowry,

Howard Foster, 1901-1967. joint author. II. Wylie, Francis James, Sir, 1865-1952. III. T.
PR4024.T5 1970   821/.8   *LC* 75-81480

PR4030–4038 Austen

Austen, Jane, 1775-1817.   • 2.7364
Novels. The text based on collation of the early editions, by R. W. Chapman. With notes, indexes, and illus. from contemporary sources. — 3d ed. — London, New York, Oxford University Press [1952]-54 [v. , 1953] 6 v. illus. 20 cm. Vol. 6, without ed. statement has title: Works. I. T.
PZ3.A93A24   PR4031.C3x.   *LC* 54-12216

Bradbrook, Frank W.   • 2.7365
Jane Austen: Emma. — Great Neck, N.Y.: Barron's Educational series, 1961. 64 p.; 19 cm. (Studies in English literature, 3) 1. Austen, Jane, 1775-1817. Emma. I. T. II. Series.
PR4034.B6 B7   *LC* 62-19946

Austen, Jane, 1775-1817.   • 2.7366
Volume the second / by Jane Austen; edited by B.C. Southam. — Oxford: Clarendon Press, 1963. xii, 236 p.: ill., facsim., ports.; 19 cm. I. Southam, Brian Charles. II. Austen, Jane, 1775-1817. Love & Freindship. III. Austen, Jane, 1775-1817. Love & friendship. IV. T.
PR4034.L6 1963   *LC* 64-1075

Austen, Jane, 1775-1817.   • 2.7367
Pride and prejudice; text, backgrounds, criticism / Bradford A. Booth compiler. New York: Harcourt, Brace and World, 1963. vii, 228 p.; 24 cm. (Harbrace sourcebooks.) I. Booth, Bradford Allen, comp. II. T.
PR4034.P7 1963   *LC* 63-14766

Austen, Jane, 1775-1817.   • 2.7368
Jane Austen's letters to her sister Cassandra and others / collected and edited by R.W.Chapman. 2d ed. London: Oxford University Press, 1952. xlv, 519, [163] p.: ill., maps. 1. Austen, Cassandra, 1773-1845 — Correspondence. 2. Austen, Jane, 1775-1817 — Correspondence. 3. Austen family. I. T.
PR4036.A55 1952   928.2   *LC* 53-1415

Austen-Leigh, James Edward, 1798-1874.   • 2.7369
Memoir of Jane Austen, by her nephew James Edward Austen–Leigh, with introduction, notes, & index by R. W. Chapman. — Oxford, The Clarendon press, 1926. xvi, 235 p.: ill., port.; 19 cm. 1. Austen, Jane, 1775-1817. I. Chapman, R. W. (Robert William), 1881-1960. II. T.
PR4036.A8 1926   *LC* 27-20619

Austen-Leigh, William.   • 2.7370
Jane Austen, her life and letters: a family record / by William Austen–Leigh and Richard Arthur Austen–Leigh. — 2nd ed. — New York: Russell & Russell, 1965. –. xv, 437 p.: genealogical table, port.; 22 cm. — 1. Austen, Jane, 1775-1817. I. Austen-Leigh, Richard Arthur, 1872-1961. II. T.
PR4036.A86 1965   *LC* 65-13949

Bush, Douglas, 1896-.   2.7371
Jane Austen. New York, Macmillan Pub. Co. [1975] xv, 205 p. 21 cm. (Masters of world literature series, 14) 1. Austen, Jane, 1775-1817. I. T.
PR4036.B8   823/.7 B   *LC* 73-18765   *ISBN* 0025196006 *ISBN* 0020492502

Chapman, R. W. (Robert William), 1881-1960.   • 2.7372
Jane Austen; facts and problems. Oxford, Clarendon Press [1949] viii, 224 p. illus. 20 cm. (The Clark lectures, Trinity College, Cambridge University, 1948) 1. Austen, Jane, 1775-1817. I. T. II. Series.
PR4036.C5   *LC* 49-9230

Halperin, John, 1941-.   2.7373
The life of Jane Austen / John Halperin. — Baltimore, Md.: Johns Hopkins University Press, 1984. xiii, 399 p., [8] p. of plates: ill.; 23 cm. Includes index. 1. Austen, Jane, 1775-1817 — Biography. 2. Novelists, English — 19th century — Biography. I. T.
PR4036.H24 1984b   823/.7 B 19   *LC* 84-9741   *ISBN* 0801823358

Jenkins, Elizabeth, 1907-.   • 2.7374
Jane Austen / by Elizabeth Jenkins. New York: Farrar, Straus and Cudahy [1959, c1949] 410 p. port. 22 cm. Includes index. 1. Austen, Jane, 1775-1817. I. T.
PR4036.J4 1959   928.2   *LC* 49-48867 *

Lascelles, Mary.   • 2.7375
Jane Austen and her art / by Mary Lascelles. — Oxford: Clarendon Press, 1939. vii, 225 p.; 23 cm. Includes index. 1. Austen, Jane, 1775-1817. I. T.
PR4036.L35   *LC* 39-31338

Pinion, F. B.   2.7376
A Jane Austen companion: a critical survey and reference book, [by] F. B. Pinion. — London: Macmillan; New York: St. Martin's Press, 1973. xiii, 342, [19] p.: illus., geneal. tables, maps, ports.; 23 cm. 1. Austen, Jane, 1775-1817. I. T.
PR4036.P53   823/.7   *LC* 72-88426   *ISBN* 0333124898

Babb, Howard S.   • 2.7377
Jane Austen's novels; the fabric of dialogue, by Howard S. Babb. — [Hamden, Conn.]: Archon Books, 1967. x, 244 p.; 23 cm. First published in 1962. 1. Austen, Jane, 1775-1817 — Criticism and interpretation. I. T. II. Title: The fabric of dialogue.
PR4037.B3 1967   823/.7   *LC* 67-28550

Brown, Lloyd Wellesley, 1938-.   2.7378
Bits of ivory; narrative techniques in Jane Austen's fiction [by] Lloyd W. Brown. — Baton Rouge, Louisiana State University Press [1973] 239 p. 23 cm. 1. Austen, Jane, 1775-1817. I. T.
PR4037.B74   823/.7   *LC* 72-89112   *ISBN* 0807102245

Hardy, Barbara Nathan.   2.7379
A reading of Jane Austen / Barbara Hardy. — New York: New York University Press, 1979. 192 p.; 22 cm. — (The Gotham library) 1. Austen, Jane, 1775-1817 — Criticism and interpretation. I. T.
PR4037.H3 1979   823/.7   *LC* 75-39852   *ISBN* 0814733972

Liddell, Robert, 1908-.   • 2.7380
The novels of Jane Austen / Robert Liddell. — London: Longmans, 1963. xiii, 174 p.; 23 cm. Includes index. 1. Austen, Jane, 1775-1817. I. T.
PR4037.L5   *LC* 64-1786

Litz, A. Walton.   • 2.7381
Jane Austen, a study of her artistic development [by] A. Walton Litz. — New York: Oxford University Press, 1965. x, 198 p.; 21 cm. 1. Austen, Jane, 1775-1817 — Criticism and interpretation. I. T.
PR4037.L57   823.7   *LC* 65-12466

Mudrick, Marvin.   • 2.7382
Jane Austen; irony as defense and discovery. — Princeton, Princeton University Press, 1952. viii, 267 p. 23 cm. Bibliographical footnotes. 1. Austen, Jane, 1775-1817. I. T.
PR4037.M8   823.74   *LC* 52-5823

Southam, B. C.   • 2.7383
Jane Austen: the critical heritage; edited by B. C. Southam. — London: Routledge & K. Paul; New York: Barnes & Noble, 1968. x, 276 p.; 22 cm. — (Critical heritage series) 1. Austen, Jane, 1775-1817. I. T.
PR4037.S59 1968   823/.7   *LC* 68-77814   *ISBN* 071002942X

Watt, Ian P. ed.   • 2.7384
Jane Austen, a collection of critical essays. Englewood Cliffs, N.J., Prentice-Hall [1963] 184 p. 21 cm. (A Spectrum book: Twentieth century views, S-TC-26) 1. Austen, Jane, 1775-1817 — Criticism and interpretation. I. T.
PR4037.W35   823.7   *LC* 63-9516

Weldon, Fay.   2.7385
Letters to Alice on first reading Jane Austen / Fay Weldon. — New York: Taplinger Pub. Co., 1985, c1984. 127 p.; 24 cm. 1. Austen, Jane, 1775-1817 — Criticism and interpretation. 2. Fiction 3. Books and reading I. T.
PR4037.W45 1985   823/.7 19   *LC* 84-24077   *ISBN* 0800847431

Wright, Andrew H.   • 2.7386
Jane Austen's novels: a study in structure [by] Andrew H. Wright. — [2nd ed.]. — Harmondsworth: Penguin, 1972. 206 p.; 20 cm. — (Pelican books) 1. Austen, Jane, 1775-1817. I. T.
PR4037.W7 1972   823/.7   *LC* 73-155270   *ISBN* 0140214836

Smith, LeRoy W.   2.7387
Jane Austen and the drama of woman / LeRoy W. Smith. — New York: St. Martin's Press, 1983. ix, 206 p.; 23 cm. Includes index. 1. Austen, Jane, 1775-1817 — Criticism and interpretation. 2. Austen, Jane, 1775-1817 — Characters — Women. 3. Women in literature 4. Sex role in literature 5. Social problems in literature I. T.
PR4038.W6 S6 1983   823/.7 19   *LC* 82-10680   *ISBN* 0312439911

PR4049–4135 B

Barrie, James Matthew, bart., Sir.   2.7388
Plays in one volume: edited by A. E. Wilson. — Rev. ed. London: Hodder and Stoughton, 1942. 1272 p. I. Wilson, Albert Edward, ed. II. T.
PR4070.F42   *LC* 43-5728

Barrie, J. M. (James Matthew), 1860-1937.   **2.7389**
The works of J. M. Barrie. Peter Pan ed. New York: AMS Press, 1975. 18 v.: ill.;
19 cm. Reprint of the 1929-41 ed. published by Scribner, New York. I. T.
PR4070.F75   828/.9/1209   *LC* 79-146660   *ISBN* 0404087809

Barrie, J. M. (James Matthew), 1860-1937.   • **2.7390**
Letters / edited by Viola Meynell. — New York: C. Scribner's Sons, 1947. vii,
311 p.: port.; 21 cm. 1. Barrie, J. M. (James Matthew), 1860-1937 —
Correspondence. I. Meynell, Viola, 1886-1956. II. T.
PR4076.A4 1947   *LC* 47-30928

Green, Roger Lancelyn.   • **2.7391**
J. M. Barrie. [1st American ed.] New York, H. Z. Walck [1961, c1960] 64 p.:
ill.; 19 cm. 1. Barrie, J. M. (James Matthew), 1860-1937. I. T.
PR4076.G7 1961   *LC* 61-8577

Wright, Allen.   **2.7392**
J. M. Barrie: glamour of twilight / [by] Allen Wright. — Edinburgh: Ramsay
Head Press, 1976. 96 p.; 19 cm. — (New assessments) 1. Barrie, J. M. (James
Matthew), 1860-1937. 2. Authors, Scottish — 20th century — Biography.
I. T.
PR4076.W73   828/.9/1209 B   *LC* 77-363590   *ISBN* 0902859374

Disraeli, Benjamin, Earl of Beaconsfield, 1804-1881.   • **2.7393**
Coningsby; or, The new generation. With an introd. by Malcolm Elwin.
London, Heron Books [1968] xv, 503 p. illus., port. 21 cm. (The Literary
heritage collection) I. T. II. Title: New generation.
PZ3.B356 C29 PR4084.Cx   823/.8   *LC* 76-504630

Disraeli, Benjamin, Earl of Beaconsfield, 1804-1881.   **2.7394**
Lothair / Benjamin Disraeli; edited with an introd. by Vernon Bogdanor. —
London; New York: Oxford University Press, 1975. xxv, 387 p.; 21 cm. —
(Oxford English novels) I. T.
PZ3.B356 Lo20 PR4084.Lx   823/.8   *LC* 75-329012   *ISBN*
0192553569

Disraeli, Benjamin, Earl of Beaconsfield, 1804-1881.   • **2.7395**
Sybil: or, The two nations / by Benjamin Disraeli. — London; New York:
Oxford university press, 1925. xiii, 431 p.; 15 cm — . (The World's classics; 291)
Introduction signed: Walter Sichel. I. Sichel, Walter Sydney, 1855-1933. II. T.
PR4084.S9   *LC* 27-26169   *ISBN* 0192502913

Braun, Thom.   **2.7396**
Disraeli the novelist / Thom Braun. — London; Boston: Allen & Unwin, 1981.
vii, 149 p.; 23 cm. 1. Disraeli, Benjamin, Earl of Beaconsfield, 1804-1881 —
Criticism and interpretation. I. T.
PR4087.B7   823/.8 19   *LC* 81-190227   *ISBN* 0048090174

Beckford, William, 1760-1844.   **2.7397**
[Vathek. English] Vathek; edited with an introduction by Roger Lonsdale.
London, Oxford U.P., 1970. xliii, 187 p. 1 illus. 21 cm. (Oxford English novels)
Translated from the French. I. Lonsdale, Roger H. ed. II. T.
PR4091.V313x 1970   843/.5 19   *LC* 76-487817   *ISBN* 0192553372

Gemmett, Robert J.   **2.7398**
William Beckford / by Robert J. Gemmett. Boston: Twayne Publishers, c1977.
189 p.: port.; 21 cm. (Twayne's English authors series; TEAS 204) Includes
index. 1. Beckford, William, 1760-1844 — Criticism and interpretation. I. T.
PR4092.G4   828/.6/09   *LC* 76-43256   *ISBN* 080576674X

Beddoes, Thomas Lovell, 1803-1849.   • **2.7399**
The works of Thomas Lovell Beddoes / edited with an introd. by H. W.
Donner. — London: Oxford University Press, 1935. lxiv, 834 p., [13] leaves of
plates: ill.; 23 cm. I. Donner, Henry Wolfgang. II. T.
PR4097.A27 1935   821/.7

Besant, Walter, Sir, 1836-1901.   • **2.7400**
Autobiography of Sir Walter Besant. With a prefatory note by S. Squire
Sprigge. New York, Dodd, Mead, 1902. — St. Clair Shores, Mich.: Scholarly
Press, 1971. xxvii, 294 p.: port.; 22 cm. — 1. Besant, Walter, Sir, 1836-1901.
PR4106.A6 1971   823/.8 B   *LC* 76-144877   *ISBN* 0103008646

Blackmore, R. D. (Richard Doddridge), 1825-1900.   • **2.7401**
Lorna Doone: a romance of Exmoor; illustrated by John Austen. New York:
Heritage Press [1943] xv, 549 p.: ill.; 24 cm. 1. Monmouth's Rebellion, 1685 —
Fiction. I. T.
PR4132.L67 B5   *LC* 30-29832

Sutton, Max Keith.   **2.7402**
R. D. Blackmore / by Max Keith Sutton; [front. photo. by Frederick Jenkins].
— Boston: Twayne Publishers, 1979. 156 p.: port.; 21 cm. — (Twayne's English
authors series; TEAS 265) Includes index. 1. Blackmore, R. D. (Richard
Doddridge), 1825-1900 — Criticism and interpretation. I. T.
PR4134.S9   823/.8   *LC* 78-31885   *ISBN* 0805767568

PR4140–4148 Blake

Blake, William, 1757-1827.   **2.7403**
[Works. Bentley] William Blake's writings / edited by G.E. Bentley Jr.. —
Oxford: Clarendon Press, 1978. 2 v.: ill., facsims., maps, ports.; 22 cm.
I. Bentley, G. E. (Gerald Eades), 1930- II. T.
PR 4141 B47 1978   *ISBN* 0198118856

Blake, William, 1757-1827.   **2.7404**
[Works. 1982] The complete poetry and prose of William Blake / edited by
David V. Erdman; commentary by Harold Bloom. — Newly rev. ed., 1st Calif.
ed. — Berkeley: University of California Press, 1982. xxvi, 990 p.: ill.; 25 cm.
First published in 1965 under title: Poetry and prose of William Blake. Includes
index of titles and first lines. I. Erdman, David V. II. Bloom, Harold. III. T.
PR4141.E7 1982b   821/.7 19   *LC* 81-40323   *ISBN* 0520044738

Blake, William, 1757-1827.   **2.7405**
[Selected works. 1979] Blake's poetry and designs: authoritative texts,
illuminations in color and monochrome, related prose, criticism / selected and
edited by Mary Lynn Johnson, John E. Grant. — 1st ed. — New York: Norton,
c1979. xlviii, 618 p.: ill.; 22 cm. — (A Norton critical edition) Includes indexes.
I. Johnson, Mary Lynn, 1937- II. Grant, John Ernest. III. T.
PR4141.5.J64 1979   821/.7   *LC* 78-20958   *ISBN* 0393044874

Blake, William, 1757-1827.   **2.7406**
[Selected works. 1977] The complete poems [of] William Blake / edited by
Alicia Ostriker. — Harmondsworth; New York [etc.]: Penguin, 1977. 1071 p.;
19 cm. — (Penguin English poets) Includes indexes. I. Ostriker, Alicia. II. T.
PR4141.5.O8   821/.7   *LC* 78-306649   *ISBN* 0140422153

Blake, William, 1757-1827.   **2.7407**
The notebook of William Blake; a photographic and typographic facsimile,
edited by David V. Erdman, with the assistance of Donald K. Moore. —
Oxford: Clarendon Press, 1973. xiii, 105 p.: illus., 240 p. of plates.; 28 cm.
1. Blake, William, 1757-1827 — Manuscripts — Facsimiles. I. Erdman, David
V. II. Moore, Donald K. III. T.
PR4142.A5 1973   821/.7   *LC* 74-162276   *ISBN* 0198124600

Doskow, Minna.   **2.7408**
William Blake's Jerusalem: structure and meaning in poetry and picture /
Minna Doskow. — Rutherford: Fairleigh Dickinson University Press; London:
Associated University Presses, c1982. 283 p.: 100 facsims.; 25 cm. Includes
indexes. 1. Blake, William, 1757-1827. Jerusalem. I. T.
PR4144.J43 D67 1982   821/.7 19   *LC* 81-65463   *ISBN*
0838630901

Wicksteed, Joseph Hartley, 1870-.   • **2.7409**
Blake's Innocence and Experience; a study of the songs and manuscripts
'shewing the two contrary states of the human soul,' by Joseph H. Wicksteed.
London, J. M. Dent; New York, E. P. Dutton, 1928. St. Clair Shores, Mich.,
Scholarly Press, 1972. p. Includes facsimile texts of Blake's Songs of innocence
and of his Songs of experience, 3 pages from the MS 'An island in the moon,'
and 17 pages from his sketch book known as the Rossetti MS. 1. Blake,
William, 1757-1827. Songs of innocence. 2. Blake, William, 1757-1827. Songs
of experience. I. T.
PR4144.S63 W5 1972   821/.7   *LC* 70-145370   *ISBN* 0403012759

PR4146–4148 Biography. Criticism

Blake, William, 1757-1827.   • **2.7410**
The letters of William Blake; edited by Geoffrey Keynes. 2nd ed., revised and
amplified. London, Hart-Davis, 1968. 224 p. 13 plates, illus., facsims., ports. 23
cm. 1. Blake, William, 1757-1827 — Correspondence. 2. Poets, English —
19th century — Correspondence. 3. Artists — England — Correspondence.
I. Keynes, Geoffrey, Sir, 1887- ed.
PR4146.A5 1968   826/.7   *LC* 79-374000   *ISBN* 0246636564

Bronowski, Jacob, 1908-1974.   • **2.7411**
William Blake, 1757–1827; a man without a mask, by J. Bronowski. — New
York: Haskell House Publishers, 1967. 153 p.: port.; 24 cm. Half title: A man
without a mask. 1. Blake, William, 1757-1827. I. Title: A man without a mask.
PR4146.B67 1967   828/.7/09   *LC* 67-30809

Damon, S. Foster (Samuel Foster), 1893-1971.   • **2.7412**
William Blake, his philosophy and symbols. — New York: P. Smith, 1947. xiv,
487 p.: front.; 26 cm. 1. Blake, William, 1757-1827. I. T.
PR4146.D3

Frye, Northrop. ed.   • **2.7413**
Blake; a collection of critical essays. — Englewood Cliffs, N.J.: Prentice-Hall,
[1966] 183 p.; 21 cm. — (A Spectrum book: Twentieth century views) 1. Blake,
William, 1757-1827.
PR4146.F7   828.709   *LC* 66-16346

Margoliouth, Herschel Maurice, 1887-.   • **2.7414**
William Blake [by] H. M. Margoliouth. — [Hamden, Conn.]: Archon Books, 1967. 184 p.: illus.; 17 cm. Reprint of the 1961 ed. 1. Blake, William, 1757-1827.
PR4146.M3 1967   821/.7   *LC* 67-26654

Nurmi, Martin K.   **2.7415**
William Blake / by Martin K. Nurmi. U.S. ed. — [Kent, Ohio]: Kent State University Press, 1976. 175 p., [2] leaves of plates: ill.; 22 cm. Includes index. 1. Blake, William, 1757-1827. I. T.
PR4146.N8 1976   821/.7   *LC* 76-25476   *ISBN* 0873381912

Raine, Kathleen, 1908-.   • **2.7416**
William Blake [by] Kathleen Raine. New York, Praeger [1971, c1970] 216 p. illus. (part col.), ports. 22 cm. (Praeger world of art series) 1. Blake, William, 1757-1827 — Criticism and interpretation.
PR4146.R32 1971 · 769/.924   *LC* 70-121081

Schorer, Mark, 1908-.   • **2.7417**
William Blake, the politics of vision / Mark Schorer. — New York, H. Holt and company [1946] xvi, 524 p.: ill.; 22 cm. 'First printing' 1. Blake, William, 1757-1827. I. T.
PR4146.S4   821.69   *LC* 46-6649

Symons, Arthur, 1865-1945.   • **2.7418**
William Blake. — New York: Cooper Square Publishers, 1970. [14], 433 p.; 23 cm. Reprint of the 1907 ed. 1. Blake, William, 1757-1827.
PR4146.S8 1970   760/.0924   *LC* 79-115694   *ISBN* 0815403259

William Blake: the critical heritage / edited by G. E. Bentley, Jr.   **2.7419**
London; Boston: Routledge & K. Paul, 1975. xix, 294 p., [8] leaves of plates: ill.; 23 cm. (The Critical heritage series) Includes index. 1. Blake, William, 1757-1827. I. Bentley, G. E. (Gerald Eades), 1930-
PR4146.W47   760/.092/4   *LC* 75-331134   *ISBN* 0710082347

Wilson, Mona, 1872-.   • **2.7420**
The life of William Blake. — 3rd ed.; edited by Geoffrey Keynes. — London; New York: Oxford University Press, 1971. xiv, 415 p., plate; 1 illus., facsim., port.; 21 cm. 1. Blake, William, 1757-1827 — Biography. I. T.
PR4146.W5 1971   700/.924 B   *LC* 78-853448   *ISBN* 0192117076

Wright, Thomas, 1859-1936.   **2.7421**
The life of William Blake. — Chicheley [Eng.]: P. P. B. Minet [distributed by A. Schram, New York], 1972. 2 v. in 1.: illus.; 25 cm. Reprint of the 1929 ed. published by T. Wright, Olney, Eng. 1. Blake, William, 1757-1827 — Biography. I. T.
PR4146.W7 1972   760/.092/4 B   *LC* 74-180550   *ISBN* 0856090212

Adams, Hazard, 1926-.   • **2.7422**
William Blake; a reading of the shorter poems. — Seattle: University of Washington Press, [1963] xiv, 337 p.: illus., diagrs.; 27 cm. 1. Blake, William, 1757-1827 — Criticism and interpretation.
PR4147.A63   821.7   *LC* 63-16384

Beer, John B.   • **2.7423**
Blake's visionary universe [by] John Beer. — [Manchester]: Manchester University Press; New York: Barnes & Noble, [c1969] xiv, 394 p.: illus.; 22 cm. 1. Blake, William, 1757-1827 — Criticism and interpretation. I. T.
PR4147.B4   760/.0924   *LC* 72-455136   *ISBN* 0389010936

Bloom, Harold.   • **2.7424**
Blake's apocalypse; a study in poetic argument. — Ithaca, N.Y.: Cornell University Press, [1970, c1963] 454 p.; 22 cm. 1. Blake, William, 1757-1827 — Criticism and interpretation. I. T.
PR4147.B5 1970   821/.7   *LC* 70-11249   *ISBN* 0801405688

Erdman, David V.   • **2.7425**
Blake, prophet against empire; a poet's interpretation of the history of his own times, by David V. Erdman. — [2d] rev. ed. — Princeton, N.J.: Princeton University Press, 1969. xxii, 546 p.: illus., map.; 23 cm. 1. Blake, William, 1757-1827 — Political and social views. 2. Eighteenth century I. T.
PR4147.E7 1969   760/.092/4   *LC* 69-18055   *ISBN* 069106010X

Frye, Northrop.   • **2.7426**
Fearful symmetry; a study of William Blake. — [Princeton, N.J.]: Princeton University Press, [1969] 462 p.: illus.; 22 cm. — (Princeton paperbacks) 1. Blake, William, 1757-1827 — Criticism and interpretation. I. T.
PR4147.F7 1969   821.7   *LC* 74-5945   *ISBN* 0691012911

Gardner, Stanley.   • **2.7427**
Infinity on the anvil: a critical study of Blake's poetry. — Oxford: Blackwell, 1954. 160 p.: ill. 1. Blake, William, 1757-1827. I. T.
PR4147.G35   *LC* 54-44573

Gleckner, Robert Francis, 1925-.   • **2.7428**
The piper & the bard; a study of William Blake. — Detroit, Wayne State University Press, c1959. xii, 322 p. 24 cm. 1. Blake, William, 1757-1827. I. T.
PR4147.G55   821.7   *LC* 59-9651

Interpreting Blake: essays / selected and edited by Michael Phillips.   **2.7429**
Cambridge [Eng.]; New York: Cambridge University Press, 1978. ix, 269 p.: ill.; 26 cm. Except for two essays, revised papers previously presented at a May 1974 symposium on William Blake, held at the Institute for Advanced Studies in the Humanities of the University of Edinburgh. 1. Blake, William, 1757-1827 — Criticism and Interpretation — Addresses, essays, lectures. I. Phillips, Michael Curtis. II. University of Edinburgh. Institute for Advanced Studies in the Humanities.
PR4147.I5   821/.7   *LC* 78-8322   *ISBN* 0521221765

Murry, John Middleton, 1889-1957.   • **2.7430**
William Blake. — New York: Haskell House Publishers, 1971. 380 p.; 23 cm. Reprint of the 1933 ed. 1. Blake, William, 1757-1827 — Criticism and interpretation.
PR4147.M8 1971   760/.0924   *LC* 71-173845   *ISBN* 0838313442

Pinto, Vivian de Sola, 1895- ed.   • **2.7431**
The divine vision; studies in the poetry and art of William Blake, born November 28th, 1757, by Kathleen Raine [and others] and with an introductory poem by Walter de la Mare. Collected and edited for the William Blake Bicentenary Committee. — London, V. Gollancz, 1957. 216 p. illus. 22 cm. 1. Blake, William, 1757-1827. I. Raine, Kathleen J. II. William Blake Bicentenary Committee. III. T.
PR4147.P5   821.79   *LC* 58-14610

Rudd, Margaret, 1925-.   • **2.7432**
Organiz'd innocence: the story of Blake's prophetic books. London: Routledge & Paul, 1956. 266 p.: ill.; 22 cm. 1. Blake, William, 1757-1827. I. T.
PR4147.R83   *LC* 56-14627

William Blake and the moderns / Robert J. Bertholf and Annette S. Levitt, editors.   **2.7433**
Albany: State University of New York Press, c1982. xv, 294 p.; 24 cm. 1. Blake, William, 1757-1827 — Influence — Addresses, essays, lectures. 2. Literature, Modern — 20th century — History and criticism — Addresses, essays, lectures. 3. Philosophy, Modern — 20th century — Addresses, essays, lectures. I. Bertholf, Robert J. II. Levitt, Annette S., 1938-
PR4148.I52 W5 1982   821/.7 19   *LC* 82-656   *ISBN* 087395615X

Fairchild, B. H.   **2.7434**
Such holy song: music as idea, form, and image in the poetry of William Blake / by B.H. Fairchild. — Kent, Ohio: Kent State University Press, c1980. 114 p.; 24 cm. Includes index. 1. Blake, William, 1757-1827 — Criticism and interpretation. 2. Blake, William, 1757-1827 — Knowledge — Music. 3. Music in literature. I. T.
PR4148.M74 F3 1980   821/.7   *LC* 79-92809   *ISBN* 0873382382

White, Helen Constance, 1896-1967.   • **2.7435**
The Mysticism of William Blake / by Helen C. White. — New York: Russell & Russell, 1964, c1927. 276 p.; 22 cm. — (University of Wisconsin studies in language and literature; no. 23) 1. Blake, William, 1757-1827. 2. Mysticism I. T.
PR4148.M8 W5 1964   *LC* 64-10715

Beer, John B.   • **2.7436**
Blake's humanism [by] John Beer. — Manchester: Manchester U.P.; New York: Barnes & Noble, 1968. xiii, 269 p.: 23 plates, illus., facsims., port.; 23 cm. 1. Blake, William, 1757-1827 — Political and social views. I. T.
PR4148.P6 B4   821/.7   *LC* 68-92577   *ISBN* 0719003008

PR4150-4161 Borrow. Boucicault

Collie, Michael.   **2.7437**
George Borrow, eccentric / Michael Collie. — Cambridge [Cambridgeshire]; New York: Cambridge University Press, 1982. ix, 275 p., [1] leaf of plates: port.; 24 cm. 1. Borrow, George Henry, 1803-1881. 2. Authors, English — 19th century — Biography. 3. Eccentrics and eccentricities — England — Biography. I. T.
PR4156.C6 1982   828/.809 B 19   *LC* 82-4397   *ISBN* 0521246156

Boucicault, Dion, 1820-1890.   **2.7438**
[Selections. 1984] Plays / by Dion Boucicault; edited with an introduction and notes by Peter Thomson. — Cambridge [Cambridgeshire]; New York: Cambridge University Press, 1984. xi, 238 p.: ill.; 24 cm. (British and American playwrights, 1750-1920.) I. Thomson, Peter, 1938- II. T. III. Series.
PR4161.B2 A6 1984   822/.8 19   *LC* 83-20897   *ISBN* 0521239974

PR4162–4174 The Brontës

Brontë, Anne, 1820-1849. • **2.7439**
The complete poems of Anne Brontë / edited by Clement Shorter; now for the
first time collected; with a bibliographical introduction by C.W. Hatfield. —
New York: Doran [1924] xxiii, 153 p.; 22 cm. I. Shorter, Clement King,
1857-1926. II. Hatfield, Charles William. III. T.
PR4162.A2 S5   *LC* 21-7215

Brontë, Anne, 1820-1849. • **2.7440**
Agnes Grey. — London: Oxford University Press, [1959] viii, 208 p.; 16 cm. —
(The World's classics; 141) I. T.
PR4162.A5

Brontë, Anne, 1820-1849. • **2.7441**
The tenant of Wildfell Hall / Anne Brontë. — London: Zodiac Press, 1954.
409 p.; 22 cm. I. T.
PR4162.T4   *ISBN* 0701112387

Gérin, Winifred. • **2.7442**
Anne Brontë / Winifred Gerin. — London; New York: Nelson, 1959. xv,
368 p.: ill.; 23 cm. 1. Brontë, Anne, 1820-1849. I. T.
PR4163.G4   928.2   *LC* 59-4263

Harrison, Ada M. • **2.7443**
Anne Brontë, her life and work [by] Ada Harrison and Derek Stanford. —
[Unaltered and unabridged ed. — Hamden, Conn.]: Archon Books, 1970
[c1959] 252 p.: port.; 23 cm. 1. Brontë, Anne, 1820-1849. I. Stanford, Derek.
PR4163.H3 1970   823.8 B   *LC* 73-121756   *ISBN* 0208009876

The Clarendon edition of the novels of the Brontës. **2.7444**
Oxford: Clarendon Press; New York: Oxford University Press, 1969-. v.; 22 cm.
I. Brontë, Charlotte, 1816-1855. II. Brontë, Emily, 1818-1848. III. Brontë,
Anne, 1820-1849.
PR4165.A1x

Brontë, Charlotte, 1816-1855. **2.7445**
[Poems. Selections] The poems of Charlotte Brontë: a new text and commentary
/ edited by Victor A. Neufeldt. — New York: Garland Pub., 1985. xlvii, 497 p.;
23 cm. (Garland English texts. no. 9) Includes index. I. Neufeldt, Victor A.
II. T. III. Series.
PR4166.N48 1985   821/.8 19   *LC* 84-48884   *ISBN* 0824087429

Brontë, Charlotte, 1816-1855. • **2.7446**
The professor; Tales from Angria; Emma: a fragment Together with a selection
of poems by Charlotte, Emily and Anne Brontë. Ed., with an introd. and
biography by Phyllis Bentley. — [London]: Collins, [1954]. 480 p.: ill.; 19 cm.
— (Collins classics; 436) I. T. II. Title: Tales from Angria. III. Title: Emma.
PR4166.P7x

Brontë, Charlotte, 1816-1855. **2.7447**
[Poems. Selections] The poems of Charlotte Brontë / edited by Tom Winnifrith.
— Oxford; New York, N.Y.: Published for the Shakespeare Head Press by B.
Blackwell, 1984. xxxiv, 429 p.; 24 cm. 'A new annotated and enlarged edition of
the Shakespeare Head Brontë.' Includes index. I. Winnifrith, Tom.
II. Shakespeare Head Brontë. III. T.
PR4166.W5 1984   821/.8 19   *LC* 84-8859   *ISBN* 0631125639

Spark, Muriel. ed. • **2.7448**
The letters of the Brontës; a selection. [1st American ed.] Norman, University
of Oklahoma Press [1954] 208 p. 21 cm. London ed. (Nevill) has title: The
Brontë letters. 1. Brontë family I. T.
PR4168.A4 S6 1954a   928.2   *LC* 54-10062

Allott, Miriam Farris. comp. **2.7449**
The Brontës, the critical heritage / edited by Miriam Allott. — London;
Boston: Routledge and Kegan Paul, 1974. xx, 475 p.; 23 cm. — (The Critical
heritage series) Includes index. 1. Brontë, Charlotte, 1816-1855. 2. Brontë,
Emily, 1818-1848. 3. Brontë, Anne, 1820-1849. I. T.
PR4168.A7 1974   823/.8/09 B   *LC* 73-85426   *ISBN* 0710077017

Gaskell, Elizabeth Cleghorn, 1810-1865. • **2.7450**
The life of Charlotte Brontë / by Elizabeth C. Gaskell; with an introd. by
Clement Shorter. — London: Oxford University Press, 1919. xxii, 476 p.: ill.; 16
cm. (The world's classics) Printing date varies. 1. Brontë, Charlotte,
1816-1855. 2. Authors, English — 19th century — Biography I. T.
PR4168.G3 1919   823.8   *ISBN* 019250214x

Gérin, Winifred. • **2.7451**
Charlotte Brontë: the evolution of genius. — Oxford: Clarendon P., 1967. xvi,
617 p.: front., 10 plates (incl. ports.); 22 1/2 cm. 1. Brontë, Charlotte,
1816-1855. I. T.
PR4168.G4   823/.8 B   *LC* 67-92825

Lloyd Evans, Barbara. **2.7452**
The Scribner companion to the Brontës / Barbara and Gareth Lloyd Evans. —
U.S. ed. — New York: C. Scribner's Sons, 1982. xviii, 400 p., [16] p. of plates:
ill.; 25 cm. 'Published in Great Britain by J.M. Dent & Sons Ltd. as Everyman's
companion to the Brontës'—T.p. verso. 1. Brontë family 2. Brontë, Charlotte,
1816-1855. 3. Brontë, Emily, 1818-1848. 4. Brontë, Anne, 1820-1849.
5. Novelists, English — 19th century — Biography. 6. English fiction — 19th
century — History and criticism. I. Lloyd Evans, Gareth. II. T.
PR4168.L56 1982b   823/.8/09 19   *LC* 82-50257   *ISBN*
0684176629

Peters, Margot. **2.7453**
Unquiet soul: a biography of Charlotte Brontë / Margot Peters. — 1st ed. —
Garden City, N.Y.: Doubleday, 1975. xv, 460 p.: ill.; 24 cm. Includes index.
1. Brontë, Charlotte, 1816-1855 — Biography. I. T.
PR4168.P38   PR4168 P38.   823/.8   *LC* 74-9461   *ISBN*
0385066228

Ratchford, Fannie Elizabeth, 1888-. • **2.7454**
The Brontës' web of childhood / by Fannie Elizabeth Ratchford. — New York:
Russell & Russell, 1964. xviii, 293 p., [9] l. of plates: ill., facsims., map, ports.
1. Brontë family I. T.
PR4168.R3 1964   *LC* 64-18601   *ISBN* 0846204878

Knies, Earl A. • **2.7455**
The art of Charlotte Brontë, by Earl A. Knies. — Athens: Ohio University
Press, 1969. x, 234 p.; 22 cm. 1. Brontë, Charlotte, 1816-1855. I. T.
PR4169.K6   823/.8   *LC* 69-15917   *ISBN* 0821400522

Linder, Cynthia A., 1923-. **2.7456**
Romantic imagery in the novels of Charlotte Brontë / Cynthia A. Linder. —
New York: Barnes & Noble Books, 1978. 138 p.; 22 cm. Includes index.
1. Brontë, Charlotte, 1816-1855 — Style. 2. Figures of speech 3. Romanticism
— England. I. T.
PR4169.L5 1978b   823/.8   *LC* 78-2903   *ISBN* 0064942805

Brontë, Emily, 1818-1848. • **2.7457**
The complete poems of Emily Jane Brontë, edited from the manuscripts by C.
W. Hatfield. New York, Columbia university press, 1941. xxi p., 2 l., [3]-262 p.
front., facsims. 24 cm. 'Facsimile manuscripts': p. [20]-21. 'Sources from which
the text of the poems has been derived': p. [24]-26. I. Hatfield, Charles William,
ed.
PR4172.A1 1941   821.89   *LC* 41-21750

Brontë, Emily, 1818-1848. • **2.7458**
Gondal's queen; a novel in verse. Arranged, with an introd. and notes by Fannie
E. Ratchford. Austin, University of Texas Press, 1955. 207 p.: facsims., port.;
24 cm. I. T.
PR4172.G6 1955   821.89   *LC* 54-10044

Brontë, Emily, 1818-1848. • **2.7459**
Wuthering Heights, revised; an authoritative text, with essays in criticism.
Edited by William M. Sale, Jr. New York, Norton [1972] ix, 382 p. 22 cm. (A
Norton critical edition) I. Sale, William Merritt, 1899- ed. II. T.
PZ3.B7902 W73 PR4172 Wx   823/.8   *LC* 76-38631   *ISBN*
0393094006 *ISBN* 0393042308

Gérin, Winifred. **2.7460**
Emily Brontë: a biography. Oxford, Clarendon Press, 1971. xviii, 290 p., 10
plates. illus., facsims., ports. 23 cm. 1. Brontë, Emily, 1818-1848 — Biography.
I. T.
PR4173.G4   823/.8 B   *LC* 79-881328   *ISBN* 0198120184

Gérin, Winifred. • **2.7461**
Branwell Brontë. — London ; New York: T. Nelson, [1961] xi, 338 p.: ill.,
maps, ports., facsims.; 23 cm. 1. Brontë, Patrick Branwell, 1817-1848. I. T.
PR4174.B2 G4   *LC* 61-65127

PR4174 Brown

Brown, George Douglas, 1869-1902. **2.7462**
The house with the green shutters / [by] George Douglas; edited by John T.
Low. — Edinburgh: Holmes McDougall, 1975. v. (The First novel library, 11)
I. T.
PZ3.B8156 H15   PR4174.B6 Hx.   *LC* 68-85813   *ISBN*
0901824720

PR4180–4198 Elizabeth Barrett Browning

Browning, Elizabeth Barrett, 1806-1861. • **2.7463**
[Works. 1973] The complete works of Elizabeth Barrett Browning, edited with
introductions and notes by Charlotte Porter and Helen A. Clarke. New York,

Crowell, 1900. [New York, AMS Press, 1973] 6 v. illus. 19 cm. I. Porter, Charlotte Endymion, 1859-1942. ed. II. Clarke, Helen Archibald, d. 1926. ed.
PR4180.F73   821/.8   *LC* 74-148759   *ISBN* 0404088406

Browning, Elizabeth Barrett, 1806-1861.   **2.7464**
[Poems. 1978] Aurora Leigh, and other poems / [by] Elizabeth Barrett Browning. — [1st ed. reprinted]; introduced by Cora Kaplan. — London: The Women's Press, 1979, c1977. 416 p.; 21 cm. Reprint of the 1856 ed. I. Kaplan, Cora. II. T.
PR4185.A1 1978   821/.8   *LC* 79-304439   *ISBN* 0704328208

Browning, Elizabeth Barrett, 1806-1861.   **2.7465**
A variorum edition of Elizabeth Barrett Browning's Sonnets from the Portuguese / by Miroslava Wein Dow. — Troy, N.Y.: Whitston Pub. Co., 1980. xxx, 173 p.; 24 cm. 'Originally a doctoral dissertation,' University of Maryland. '500 casebound copies.' Includes index. 1. Sonnets, English I. Dow, Miroslava Wein. II. T.
PR4189.A1 1980b   821/.8 19   *LC* 80-125695   *ISBN* 0878751793

Browning, Elizabeth Barrett, 1806-1861.   • **2.7466**
Diary by E. B. B.; the unpublished diary of Elizabeth Barrett Barrett, 1831–1832. Edited with an introd. and notes by Philip Kelley and Ronald Hudson. Including psychoanalytical observations by Robert Coles. — Athens: Ohio University Press, 1969. xlvii, 358 p.: illus., facsims., maps (1 fold.), port.; 26 cm. 1. Browning, Elizabeth Barrett, 1806-1861. I. Kelley, Philip. ed. II. Hudson, Ronald. ed. III. T.
PR4193.A2   821.8 B   *LC* 68-18390

Browning, Elizabeth Barrett, 1806-1861.   • **2.7467**
Twenty–two unpublished letters of Elizabeth Barrett Browning and Robert Browning: addressed to Henrietta and Arabella Moulton–Barrett. New York, The United feature syndicate, 1935. 89, [1] p., illus. '1188 copies printed by hand..at Crosby Gaige's Watch Hill press, Peekskill, New York.' 1. Barrett, Arabella, d. 1868. 2. Browning, Robert, 1812-1889. Correspondence 3. Browning, Elizabeth Barrett, 1806-1861 — Correspondence. 4. Cook, Henrietta Barrett, d. 1860. I. Browning, Robert, 1812-1889. II. T. III. Title: 22 unpublished letters of Elizabeth Barrett Browning and Robert Browning.
PR4193.A353   821.82   *LC* 36-5644

Browning, Elizabeth Barrett, 1806-1861.   **2.7468**
[Correspondence. 1972] Invisible friends; the correspondence of Elizabeth Barrett Barrett and Benjamin Robert Haydon, 1842–1845. Edited by Willard Bissell Pope. Cambridge, Harvard University Press, 1972. xviii, 200 p. illus. 24 cm. 1. Browning, Elizabeth Barrett, 1806-1861. I. Haydon, Benjamin Robert, 1786-1846. II. Pope, Willard Bissell. ed. III. T.
PR4193.A36 1972   821/.8 B   *LC* 72-80659   *ISBN* 0674465865

Browning, Elizabeth Barrett, 1806-1861.   • **2.7469**
Elizabeth Barrett to Miss Mitford; the unpublished letters of Elizabeth Barrett Barrett to Mary Russell Mitford. Edited and introduced by Betty Miller. — [1st ed.]. — London, J. Murray, 1954. xviii, 284 p. illus., ports. 23 cm. 'The manuscripts of this correspondence are in the ... library of Wellesley College, Massachusetts.' 1. Browning, Elizabeth Barrett, 1806-1861 — Correspondence. 2. Mitford, Mary Russell, 1787-1855 — Correspondence. I. Mitford, Mary Russell, 1787-1855. II. Miller, Betty Bergson Spiro, 1910-. III. T.
PR4193.A374 1954   928.2   *LC* 54-3636

PR4200–4248 Robert Browning

Browning, Robert, 1812-1889.   • **2.7470**
Works / with introductions by F.G. Kenyon. — [Centenary ed.]. — New York: Barnes & Noble, [1966] 10 v.: ports; 22 cm. I. Kenyon, Frederic G. (Frederic George), Sir, 1863-1952. II. T.
PR4200.F66   *LC* 66-28309

Browning, Robert, 1812-1889.   **2.7471**
[Poems] The complete works of Robert Browning, with variant readings & annotations. Editorial board: Roma A. King, Jr. [and others] Athens, Ohio University Press, 1969-<1985 >. v. <1, 3-5, 7 > port. 25 cm. Vol. 7: general editor, Jack W. Herring. I. King, Roma A. (Roma Alvah), 1914- ed. II. Herring, Jack W., 1925- III. T.
PR4201.K5 1969   821/.8   *LC* 68-18389   *ISBN* 0821402307

Browning, Robert, 1812-1889.   **2.7472**
[Poems. Selections] The poetry of Robert Browning. Edited, with an introd. and notes, by Jacob Korg. Indianapolis, Bobbs-Merrill Co. [1971] xlii, 588 p. illus., maps, port. 21 cm. (The Library of literature 25) I. T.
PR4202.K6 1971   821/.8   *LC* 77-122683

Browning, Robert, 1812-1889.   **2.7473**
[Poems. Selections] Robert Browning's poetry: authoritative texts, criticism / selected and edited by James F. Loucks. — 1st ed. — New York: Norton, c1979. xvi, 604 p.; 22 cm. (A Norton critical edition) Includes index.

1. Browning, Robert, 1812-1889 — Criticism and interpretation — Addresses, essays, lectures. I. Loucks, James F. II. T.
PR4202.L59 1979   821/.8   *LC* 79-10295   *ISBN* 0393044750

Browning, Robert, 1812-1889.   **2.7474**
[Poems] The poetical works of Robert Browning / edited by Ian Jack and Margaret Smith. — Oxford [Oxfordshire]: Clarendon Press; New York: Oxford University Press, 1983-<1984 >. v. <1-2 >; 23 cm. I. Jack, Ian Robert James. II. Smith, Margaret, 1931- III. T.
PR4203.J3 1983   821/.8 19   *LC* 82-12603   *ISBN* 0198118937

Buckler, William Earl, 1924-.   **2.7475**
Poetry and truth in Robert Browning's The ring and the book / William E. Buckler. — New York: New York University Press, 1985. x, 293 p.; 24 cm. (The Gotham library of the New York University Press) 1. Browning, Robert, 1812-1889. Ring and the book 2. Franceschini, Guido, conte, 1657-1698. in fiction, drama, poetry, etc. 3. Franceschini, Pompilia, 1680-1698. in fiction, drama, poetry, etc. 4. Italy in literature. I. T.
PR4219.B8 1985   821/.8 19   *LC* 84-22808   *ISBN* 0814710727

The Old yellow book, source of Browning's The ring and the   • **2.7476**
book. A new translation with explanatory notes and critical chapters upon the poem and its source, by John Marshall Gest.
New York, Haskell House, 1970. xv, 699 p. 23 cm. 'The Old yellow book is a collection of pamphlets relating to the trial of Guido Franceschini.' Reprint of the 1925 ed. 1. Browning, Robert, 1812-1889. The ring and the book. 2. Franceschini, Pompilia, 1680-1698. 3. Cenci, Beatrice, 1577-1599. 4. Law — Italy I. Gest, John Marshall, 1859-1934. ed. II. Franceschini, Guido, conte, 1657-1698. defendant.
PR4219.O6x.   340/.0945   *LC* 78-92953   *ISBN* 0838310583

Berdoe, Edward, 1836-1916.   • **2.7477**
The Browning cyclopaedia; a guide to the study of the works of Robert Browning. With copious explanatory notes and references on all difficult passages. [2d ed.] London Allen & Unwin [1931] xviii, 577 p.; 20 cm. 1. Browning, Robert, 1812-1889 — Dictionaries, indexes, etc. I. T.
PR4230 B4

Browning, Robert, 1812-1889.   • **2.7478**
New letters; edited with introd. and notes, by William Clyde De Vane and Kenneth Leslie Knickerbocker. New Haven, Yale University Press, 1950. vi, 413 p.; 25 cm. 1. Browning, Robert, 1812-1889. Correspondence I. De Vane, William Clyde, 1898-1965. II. Knickerbocker, Kenneth Leslie, 1905-. III. T.
PR4231.A3 1950   821.8   *LC* 50-10538

Browning, Robert, 1812-1889.   • **2.7479**
Dearest Isa; Robert Browning's letters to Isabella Blagden. Edited and with an introd. by Edward C. McAleer. — Westport, Conn.: Greenwood Press, [1970, c1951] xxxiii, 402 p.: illus., ports., maps.; 23 cm. 1. Browning, Robert, 1812-1889. Correspondence 2. Blagden, Isa Jane, 1816-1873. I. Blagden, Isa Jane, 1816-1873. II. McAleer, Edward C. ed. III. T.
PR4231.A33 1970   821/.8   *LC* 76-100218   *ISBN* 0837130360

Browning, Robert, 1812-1889.   **2.7480**
[Correspondence] The Brownings' correspondence / edited by Philip Kelley & Ronald Hudson. — Winfield, KS: Wedgestone Press, c1984-<c1985 >. v. <1-3 >: ill. (some col.); 24 cm. Correspondence written by and to Robert and Elizabeth Barrett Browning. 1. Browning, Robert, 1812-1889. Correspondence 2. Browning, Elizabeth Barrett, 1806-1861 — Correspondence. 3. Poets, English — 19th century — Correspondence. I. Browning, Elizabeth Barrett, 1806-1861. II. Kelley, Philip. III. Hudson, Ronald. IV. T.
PR4231.A4 1984   821/.8 B 19   *LC* 84-5287   *ISBN* 091145909X

Chesterton, G. K. (Gilbert Keith), 1874-1936.   • **2.7481**
Robert Browning / by G.K. Chesterton. — London: Macmillan, 1951. 207 p.; 18 cm. — (Macmillan's pocket library) 1. Browning, Robert, 1812-1889. I. T.
PR4231 C4   *LC* 52-33885

De Vane, William Clyde, 1898-.   • **2.7482**
A Browning handbook. — 2d ed. — New York, Appleton-Century-Crofts [c1955] 594 p. illus. 22 cm. Includes bibliography. 1. Browning, Robert, 1812-1889. I. T.
PR4231.D45 1955   821.83   *LC* 54-9558

Griffin, W. Hall.   • **2.7483**
The life of Robert Browning: with notices of his writings, his family & his friends / ompleted and edited by Harry Christopher Minchin. Hamden, Conn.: Archon Books, 1966. x 344 p.: port.; 22 cm. 1. Browning, Robert, 1812-1889. I. Minchin, Harry Christopher, 1861-1941. II. T.
PR4231.G7 1966   *LC* 66-15388

Irvine, William, 1906-1964.   **2.7484**
The book, the ring, & the poet; a biography of Robert Browning [by] William Irvine & Park Honan. — New York: McGraw-Hill, [1974] xi, 607 p.: illus.; 24

cm. 1. Browning, Robert, 1812-1889 — Biography. I. Honan, Park. joint author. II. T.
PR4231.I7   821/.8 B   *LC* 72-12604   *ISBN* 0070320454

Litzinger, Boyd.   • **2.7485**
The Browning critics [by] Boyd Litzinger and K. L. Knickerbocker. — [Lexington]: University of Kentucky Press, [1965] xxii, 426 p.; 23 cm. 1. Browning, Robert, 1812-1889. I. Knickerbocker, K. L. (Kenneth Leslie) joint author. II. T.
PR4231.L57   821.8   *LC* 65-27008

Litzinger, Boyd. comp.   **2.7486**
Browning: the critical heritage. Edited by Boyd Litzinger and Donald Smalley. — New York: Barnes & Noble, [1970] xviii, 550 p.; 23 cm. — (The Critical heritage series) 1. Browning, Robert, 1812-1889. I. Smalley, Donald Arthur, 1907- joint comp. II. T.
PR4231.L58 1970   821/.8   *LC* 79-12803   *ISBN* 0389010243

Miller, Betty Bergson Spiro, 1910-.   • **2.7487**
Robert Browning, a portrait. [1st ed.]. — London: Murray, 1952. xv, 302 p.: ill., ports.; 22 cm. 1. Browning, Robert, 1812-1889. 2. Browning, Elizabeth Barrett, 1806-1861. I. T.
PR4231.M5 1952   928.2 B   *LC* 53-228

Gridley, Roy E.   **2.7488**
Browning, by Roy E. Gridley. — London; Boston: Routledge and Kegan Paul, 1972. viii, 192 p.; 22 cm. — (Routledge author guides) 1. Browning, Robert, 1812-1889. I. T.
PR4238.G67   821/.8   *LC* 73-154087   *ISBN* 0710073682

Honan, Park.   • **2.7489**
Browning's characters; a study in poetic technique. — [Hamden, Conn.]: Archon Books, 1969 [c1961] xiv, 327 p.; 23 cm. 1. Browning, Robert, 1812-1889. 2. Monologue I. T.
PR4238.H6 1969   821/.8   *LC* 69-19215   *ISBN* 0208007938

Jack, Ian Robert James.   **2.7490**
Browning's major poetry, by Ian Jack. — Oxford: Clarendon Press, 1973. xiv, 308 p.; 23 cm. 1. Browning, Robert, 1812-1889 — Criticism and interpretation. I. T.
PR4238.J3   821/.8   *LC* 74-155507   *ISBN* 0198120486

Raymond, William Ober, 1880-.   • **2.7491**
The infinite moment, and other essays in Robert Browning, by William O. Raymond. — 2d [enl.] ed. — [Toronto] University of Toronto Press [1965] vi, 264 p. 24 cm. Bibliographical references included in 'Notes' (p. [247]-260) 1. Browning, Robert, 1812-1889. I. T.
PR4238.R35 1965   821.8   *LC* 65-1834

Ryals, Clyde de L., 1928-.   **2.7492**
Becoming Browning: the poems and plays of Robert Browning, 1833–1846 / Clyde de L. Ryals. — Columbus: Ohio State University Press, c1983. x, 292 p.: ill.; 23 cm. Includes index. 1. Browning, Robert, 1812-1889 — Criticism and interpretation. I. T.
PR4238.R86 1983   821/.8 19   *LC* 83-4140   *ISBN* 0814203523

Ryals, Clyde de L., 1928-.   **2.7493**
Browning's later poetry, 1871–1889 / Clyde de L. Ryals. — Ithaca, N.Y.: Cornell University Press, 1975. 262 p.; 23 cm. Includes index. 1. Browning, Robert, 1812-1889 — Criticism and interpretation. I. T.
PR4238.R87   821/.8   *LC* 75-16927   *ISBN* 0801409640

Tucker, Herbert F.   **2.7494**
Browning's beginnings: the art of disclosure / Herbert F. Tucker, Jr. — Minneapolis, Minn.: University of Minnesota Press, c1980. x, 257 p.; 24 cm. Includes index. 1. Browning, Robert, 1812-1889 — Criticism and interpretation. I. T.
PR4238.T8   821/.8   *LC* 80-17727   *ISBN* 0816609462

Broughton, Leslie Nathan, 1877-1952.   • **2.7495**
A concordance to the poems of Robert Browning, by Leslie N. Broughton and Benjamin F. Stelter. — New York: Haskell House Publishers, 1970. 4 v.; 29 cm. 'First published 1924-25.' 1. Browning, Robert, 1812-1889 — Concordances. I. Stelter, Benjamin Franklin. joint author. II. T.
PR4245.B7 1970   821/.8   *LC* 77-92950   *ISBN* 0838311016

Hatcher, Harlan Henthorne, 1898-.   • **2.7496**
The versification of Robert Browning. — Folcroft, Pa.: Folcroft Press, [1969, c1928] ix, 195 p.; 22 cm. Original ed. issued as no. 5 of Ohio State University Contributions in languages and literatures. 1. Browning, Robert, 1812-1889 — Versification. I. T.
PR4247.H3 1969   821/.8   *LC* 72-194441

PR4300–4348 Burns

Burns, Robert, 1759-1796.   **2.7497**
[Poems (Kinsley)] The poems and songs of Robert Burns / edited by James Kinsley. — Oxford: Clarendon P., 1968. 3 v.: 3 plates, music, 3 ports.; 23 cm. ([Oxford English texts]) I. Kinsley, James. ed. II. T.
PR4300 1968.O9   821/.6   *LC* 68-108513   *ISBN* 0198118430

Burns, Robert, 1759-1796.   **2.7498**
Poems. Selected and edited by Laurence Brander. London, Oxford Univ. Press [1957] 333 p. 16 cm. (The World's classics, 515) I. Brander, Laurence, 1903- ed. II. T.
PR4302.B7x

Burns, Robert, 1759-1796.   **2.7499**
Selected poetry and prose / edited with an introd., glossary, and notes by Robert D. Thornton. — Boston: Houghton Mifflin [1966] xxvi, 307 p.; 21 cm. (Riverside editions, B100) Includes unacc. melodies. I. Thornton, Robert D. (Robert Donald), 1917- ed. II. T.
PR4302.T48   828.609   *LC* 66-31295

Lindsay, Maurice, 1918-.   **2.7500**
The Burns encyclopedia / [by] Maurice Lindsay. — 3rd ed. — New York: St Martin's Press; London: Hale, 1980. [11], 426 p., 16 p. of plates: ill., facsim., ports.; 24 cm. I. T.
PR4330.L5 1980   821/.6   *LC* 79-2534   *ISBN* 0709183232 *ISBN* 0312108664

Ross, John Dawson, 1853-1939.   • **2.7501**
A Burns handbook.. — Stirling, [Scot.]: E. Mackay, [1931] 378 p.: map.; 18 cm. 1. Burns, Robert, 1759-1796 — Dictionaries, indexes, etc. I. T.
PR4330.R57   821/.6

Burns, Robert, 1759-1796.   **2.7502**
[Correspondence] The letters of Robert Burns / J. De Lancey Ferguson. — 2nd ed. / edited by G. Ross Roy. — Oxford [Oxfordshire]: Clarendon Press, 1985. 2 v.: ill.; 23 cm. Includes indexes. 1. Burns, Robert, 1759-1796. Correspondence 2. Poets, Scottish — 18th century — Correspondence. I. Ferguson, J. De Lancey (John De Lancey), 1888- II. Roy, G. Ross (George Ross), 1924- III. T.
PR4331.A4 1985   821/.6 B 19   *LC* 83-26741   *ISBN* 0198124783

Daiches, David, 1912-.   • **2.7503**
Robert Burns. — [Rev. ed.]. — New York: Macmillan, [1967, c1966] 334 p.; 23 cm. 1. Burns, Robert, 1759-1796. I. T.
PR4331.D25 1967   821.6   *LC* 66-26244

Ferguson, J. De Lancey (John De Lancey), 1888-.   **2.7504**
Pride and passion, Robert Burns, 1759–1796 / by DeLancey Ferguson. — 1st ed. — New York: Oxford University Press, 1939. xix, 321 p. 1. Burns, Robert, 1759-1796 — Biography. 2. Authors, Scottish — Biography. I. T.
PR4331.F4   *LC* 39-8763

Hecht, Hans, 1876-.   **2.7505**
[Robert Burns. English] Robert Burns: the man and his work: translated [from the German] by Jane Lymburn; foreword by Sir Patrick J. Dollan. Bath, Cedric Chivers Ltd, 1971. xix, 301 p. 22 cm. (Portway reprints) Appendix: 'A memoir of the life of the late Robert Burns, by R. Heron ... Edinburgh, T. Brown, 1797:' p. 257-282. 1. Burns, Robert, 1759-1796. I. Heron, Robert, 1764-1807. Memoir of the life of the late Robert Burns. 1971. II. T.
PR4331.H313   821/.6   *LC* 72-172094   *ISBN* 085594028X

Lockhart, J. G. (John Gibson), 1794-1854.   • **2.7506**
Life of Robert Burns / by J.G. Lockhart. — London; Toronto: J.M. Dent; New York: E.P. Dutton, [1933] xv, 322 p.; 18 cm. — (Everyman's library. Biography; [no. 156]) Contains also Select letters and journals of Burns and his Border tour and Highland tour. 1. Burns, Robert, 1759-1796 — Biography. I. Burns, Robert, 1759-1796. II. T. III. Series.
PR4331.L6

Snyder, Franklyn Bliss, 1884-1958.   • **2.7507**
The life of Robert Burns. — [Hamden, Conn.]: Archon Books, 1968 [c1932] xiii, 524 p.: facsims., maps, port.; 24 cm. 1. Burns, Robert, 1759-1796 — Biography. I. T.
PR4331.S6 1968   821/.6 B   *LC* 68-16336

Crawford, Thomas.   **2.7508**
Burns; a study of the poems and songs. Stanford, Calif., Stanford University Press, 1960. 400 p. 23 cm. 1. Burns, Robert, 1759-1796. I. T.
PR4338.C77 1960a   *LC* 60-15880

Low, Donald A.   **2.7509**
Robert Burns: the critical heritage / edited by Donald A. Low. — London; Boston: Routledge & K. Paul, [1974] xvi, 447 p.; 23 cm. (The Critical heritage series) 1. Burns, Robert, 1759-1796 — Criticism and interpretation. I. T.
PR4338.L6   821/.6   *LC* 73-91033   *ISBN* 0710077971

Reid, J. B. • 2.7510
A complete word and phrase concordance to the poems and songs of Robert Burns, incorporating a glossary of Scotch words, with notes, index, and appendix of readings. Compiled and edited by J. B. Reid. — New York: B. Franklin, [1968] 568 p.; 26 cm. — (Burt Franklin bibliography & reference series 252) Title on spine: Concordance to poems and songs of Robert Burns. Reprint of the 1889 ed. 1. Burns, Robert, 1759-1796 — Concordances. I. T. II. Title: Concordance to poems and songs of Robert Burns.
PR4345.R4 1968 821/.6 *LC* 68-58477

PR4349.B7 Butler

Butler, Samuel, 1835-1902. • 2.7511
[Works. 1968] The Shrewsbury edition of the works of Samuel Butler. Edited by Henry Festing Jones and A. T. Bartholomew. [1st AMS ed. New York, AMS Press, 1968] 20 v. illus. 24 cm. On spine: The works of Samuel Butler. Half title. Reprint of the 1923-26 ed. I. Jones, Henry Festing, 1851-1928. ed. II. Bartholomew, Augustus Theodore, 1882-1933, ed. III. T.
PR4349.B7 1968 828/.8/09 *LC* 77-181920

Butler, Samuel, 1835-1902. 2.7512
Erewhon; Erewhon revisited / Samuel Butler; introduction by Desmond MacCarthy. — London: Dent, 1932. xv, 389 p.: music; 19 cm. — (Everyman's library. Fiction; no.881.) 1. Utopias I. Butler, Samuel, 1835-1902. Erewhon revisited. II. T. III. Title: Erewhon revisited. IV. Series.
PR4349.B7 E7 1932b *LC* 37-31201

Butler, Samuel, 1835-1902. • 2.7513
Notebooks; selections / edited by Geoffrey Keynes and Brian Hill. London, Cape. 1951. 327 p.; 21 cm. I. Keynes, Geoffrey, ed. II. Hill, Brian. ed. III. T.
PR4349.B7 N6 1951 828.8 *LC* 51-7518

Butler, Samuel, 1835-1902. • 2.7514
Further extracts from the note-books of Samuel Butler / chosen and edited by A.T. Bartholomew. — London: Cape, [1934] 414 p.: ill; 20 cm. 1. Butler, Samuel, 1835-1902. I. Bartholomew, Augustus Theodore, 1882-1933. II. T.
PR4349.B7 N7 *LC* 34-16411

Butler, Samuel, 1835-1902. 2.7515
The way of all flesh / Samuel Butler. — New York: Garland Pub., 1975. v, 423 p.; 19 cm. (Victorian fiction: Novels of faith and doubt) Reprint of the 1903 ed. published by G. Richards, London. I. T. II. Series.
PZ3.B9779 W58 PR4349.B7Wx 823/.8 *LC* 75-1540 *ISBN* 0824016114

Butler, Samuel, 1835-1902. • 2.7516
The family letters of Samuel Butler, 1841–1886. Selected, edited, and introduced by Arnold Silver. Stanford, Calif., Stanford University Press, 1962. 295 p. illus. 23 cm. I. T.
PR4349.B7 Z537 928.2 *LC* 62-9882

Furbank, Philip Nicholas. • 2.7517
Samuel Butler, 1835–1902, by P. N. Furbank. — [2d ed. — Hamden, Conn.]: Archon Books, 1971. 124 p.; 21 cm. 1. Butler, Samuel, 1835-1902. I. T.
PR4349.B7 Z726 1971 828/.8/09 *LC* 76-131373

PR4350–4398 Byron

Byron, George Gordon Noël Byron, 6th baron, 1788-1824. • 2.7518
[Works. English. 1966] Poetical works. London Oxford University Press [1966] ix, 923 p.; 19 cm. (Oxford standard authors) I. T.
PR4350 F52 1966

Byron, George Gordon Byron, Baron, 1788-1824. 2.7519
The complete poetical works / Lord Byron; edited by Jerome J. McGann. — Oxford: Clarendon Press; New York: Oxford University Press, 1980- < 1986 >. v. < 1-4 >; 22 cm. (Oxford English texts) I. McGann, Jerome J. II. T.
PR4351.M27 821/.7 19 *LC* 81-105172 *ISBN* 0198118902

Ridenour, George M. • 2.7520
The style of Don Juan, by George M. Ridenour. [Hamden, Conn.] Archon Books, 1969 [c1960] xiv, 168 p. 22 cm. (Yale studies in English. v. 144) 1. Byron, George Gordon Byron, Baron, 1788-1824. Don Juan. I. T. II. Series.
PR4359.R5 1969 821/.7 *LC* 69-15690 *ISBN* 0208007814

Byron, George Gordon Byron, Baron, 1788-1824. 2.7521
[Letters and journals] Byron's letters and journals: the complete and unexpurgated text of all the letters available in manuscript and the full printed version of all others / edited by Leslie A. Marchand. — Cambridge, Mass.: Belknap Press of Harvard University Press, 1973- < 1981 >. v. < 1-11 >: ports.; 23 cm. 1. Byron, George Gordon Byron, Baron, 1788-1824 — Correspondence. 2. Byron, George Gordon Byron, Baron, 1788-1824 —

Diaries. 3. Poets, English — 19th century — Biography. I. Marchand, Leslie Alexis, 1900- II. T.
PR4381.A3 M35 1973 821/.7 19 *LC* 73-81853 *ISBN* 0674089405

Byron, George Gordon Byron, Baron, 1788-1824. • 2.7522
Byron, a self-portrait; letters and diaries, 1798 to 1824, with hitherto unpublished letters. Edited by Peter Quennell. New York, Scribner [1950] 2 v. (xv, 803 p.) fronts. 22 cm. Errata slip inserted in v. 2. I. Quennell, Peter, 1905- II. T.
PR4381.A3 Q4 928.2 *LC* 50-6875

Byron, George Gordon Byron, Baron, 1788-1824. 2.7523
Lord Byron: selected letters and journals / edited by Leslie A. Marchand. — Cambridge, Mass.: Belknap Press of Harvard University Press, 1982. 400 p.: port.; 25 cm. Includes index. 1. Byron, George Gordon Byron, Baron, 1788-1824 — Correspondence. 2. Byron, George Gordon Byron, Baron, 1788-1824 — Diaries. 3. Poets, English — 19th century — Biography. I. Marchand, Leslie Alexis, 1900- II. T.
PR4381.A385 1982 821/.7 B 19 *LC* 82-9720 *ISBN* 067453915X

Knight, George Wilson, 1897-. • 2.7524
Lord Byron; Christian virtues, by G. Wilson Knight. New York: Barnes & Noble, 1967. xiii,304 p.; 23 cm. 1. Byron, George Gordon Byron, Baron, 1788-1824 — Religion and ethics. I. T.
PR4381.K55 1967 *LC* 67-760

Longford, Elizabeth Harman Pakenham, Countess of, 1906-. 2.7525
The life of Byron / by Elizabeth Longford. — 1st ed. — Boston: Little, Brown, c1976. xii, 237 p.; 21 cm. — (The Library of world biography) Includes index. 1. Byron, George Gordon Byron, Baron, 1788-1824 — Biography. I. T.
PR4381.L6 821/.7 B *LC* 76-22714 *ISBN* 0316531928

Marchand, Leslie Alexis, 1900-. • 2.7526
Byron; a biography. [1st ed.] New York, Knopf, 1957. 3 v. illus., ports., fold. map. 24 cm. Issued in a case. 1. Byron, George Gordon Byron, Baron, 1788-1824 — Biography. I. T.
PR4381.M33 928.2 *LC* 57-7547

Marchand, Leslie Alexis, 1900-. • 2.7527
Byron's poetry; a critical introduction [by] Leslie A. Marchand. Boston, Houghton Mifflin [1965] vii, 261 p. 21 cm. (Riverside studies in literature, L5) 1. Byron, George Gordon Byron, Baron, 1788-1824. I. T.
PR4381.M332 821.7 *LC* 65-6991

Maurois, André, 1885-1967. • 2.7528
Byron / by André Maurois; [translated from the French by Hamish Miles]. — New York: F. Ungar Publishing Company,, 1964, c1930. xv, 596 p., plates, ill., facsims., ports.; 24 cm. Translation of Don Juan; ou, La vie de Byron. Includes index. 1. Byron, George Gordon Noël Byron, 6th Baron, 1788-1824 — Biography. I. T.
PR4381.M35 1964

Moore, Doris Langley-Levy, 1903-. • 2.7529
The late Lord Byron; posthumous dramas. [1st ed.] Philadelphia, Lippincott [1961] viii, 542 p. plates, ports. 24 cm. 1. Byron, George Gordon Byron, Baron, 1788-1824. I. T.
PR4381.M67 1961a 928.2 *LC* 61-8670

Origo, Iris, 1902-. • 2.7530
The last attachment; the story of Byron and Teresa Guiccioli as told in their unpublished letters and other family papers [by] Iris Origo. New York, Scribner [1972] 533 p. 23 cm. Originally published in 1949. 1. Byron, George Gordon Byron, Baron, 1788-1824 — Relations with women. 2. Guiccioli, Teresa Gamba, Contessa, afterwards Boissy, 1800?-1873. 3. Byron, George Gordon Byron, Baron, 1788-1824 — Correspondence. I. Byron, George Gordon Byron, Baron, 1788-1824. II. Guiccioli, Teresa (Gamba) contessa, afterwards Boissy, 1800?-1873. III. T.
PR4381.O7 1972 821/.7 B *LC* 72-179132 *ISBN* 0684126753

Chapman, John Stewart. 2.7531
Byron and the Honourable Augusta Leigh / John S. Chapman. — New Haven: Yale University Press, 1975. xxiv, 282 p., [2] leaves of plates: ports.; 22 cm. Includes index. 1. Byron, George Gordon Byron, Baron, 1788-1824 — Relations with women. 2. Leigh, Augusta, 1784-1851. 3. England — Social life and customs I. T.
PR4382.C45 821/.7 *LC* 74-29714 *ISBN* 0300018762

Elwin, Malcolm, 1902-. • 2.7532
Lord Byron's wife. [1st American ed.] New York, Harcourt, Brace & World [1963, c1962] 556 p. illus. 25 cm. 1. Byron, Anne Isabella Milbanke Byron, Baroness, 1792-1860. 2. Byron, George Gordon Byron, Baron, 1788-1824. I. T.
PR4382.E4 1963 *LC* 63-8083

Moore, Doris Langley-Levy, 1903-.   **2.7533**
Ada, Countess of Lovelace: Byron's legitimate daughter / Doris Langley Moore. — 1st u.s. ed. — New York: Harper & Row, c1977. 397 p., [6] leaves of plates: ill., ports.; 24 cm. I. Lovelace, Ada King, Countess of Lovelace, 1815-1852. 2. Byron, George Gordon Byron, Baron, 1788-1824 — Biography — Descendants. I. T.
PR4382.M66   821.7   *LC* 72-26246   *ISBN* 0060130121

His very self and voice; collected conversations of Lord Byron.   • **2.7534**
Edited with an introd. and notes by Ernest J. Lovell, Jr.
New York, Macmillan, 1954. xlvi, 676 p. 25 cm. 1. Byron, George Gordon Byron, Baron, 1788-1824 — Biography. 2. Byron, George Gordon Byron, Baron, 1788-1824 — Friends and associates. 3. Poets, English — 19th century — Biography. I. Byron, George Gordon Byron, Baron, 1788-1824. II. Lovell, Ernest James, 1918- ed.
PR4383.H57 1954   821/.7 B 19   *LC* 54-13156

Marshall, William Harvey, 1925-.   • **2.7535**
The structure of Byron's major poems / by William H. Marshall. — Philadelphia: University of Pennsylvania Press, 1962. 191 p.; 21 cm. Includes index. 1. Byron, George Gordon Noël Byron, 6th Baron, 1788-1824. I. T.
PR4388.M3 1974   PR4388.M3.   821.7   *LC* 62-17305   *ISBN* 0812210786 Pbk

Martin, Philip W.   **2.7536**
Byron, a poet before his public / Philip W. Martin. — Cambridge [Cambridgeshire]; New York: Cambridge University Press, 1982. x, 253 p.: ill.; 23 cm. Revision of thesis (doctoral)—University of Exeter. Includes index. 1. Byron, George Gordon Byron, Baron, 1788-1824 — Criticism and interpretation. 2. Authors and readers I. T.
PR4388.M35 1982   821/.7 19   *LC* 81-21598   *ISBN* 0521241863

Rutherford, Andrew. comp.   **2.7537**
Byron: the critical heritage. New York, Barnes & Noble [1970] xvii, 513 p. 23 cm. (The Critical heritage series) 1. Byron, George Gordon Byron, Baron, 1788-1824 — Criticism and interpretation. I. T.
PR4388.R83 1970   821/.7   *LC* 72-12804   *ISBN* 0389016950

Thorslev, Peter Larsen.   • **2.7538**
The Byronic hero: types and prototypes / Peter Larsen Thorslev. — Minneapolis: U. of Minnesota P., 1962. 228 p.; 23 cm. 1. Byron, George Gordon Noël Byron, 6th Baron, 1788-1824. 2. Heroes in literature 3. Romanticism I. T.
PR4389.T45 1962   821.7   *LC* 62-16632

Vassallo, Peter.   **2.7539**
Byron, the Italian literary influence / Peter Vassallo. — New York: St. Martin's Press, 1984. x, 192 p.; 23 cm. Includes index. 1. Byron, George Gordon Byron, Baron, 1788-1824 — Knowledge — Italy. 2. Byron, George Gordon Byron, Baron, 1788-1824 — Knowledge — Literature. 3. Byron, George Gordon Byron, Baron, 1788-1824 — Books and reading. 4. Italian literature — History and criticism 5. Italy in literature. 6. English poetry — Italian influences I. T.
PR4392.I82 V37 1984   821/.7 19   *LC* 82-23174   *ISBN* 0312111258

PR4416–4438 Carleton. Carlyle

Carleton, William, 1794-1869.   **2.7540**
Traits and stories of the Irish peasantry / William Carleton. — New York: Garland Pub., 1979. 2 v. (xii, 275, 304 p., [4] leaves of plates): ill.; 19 cm. — (Ireland, from the Act of Union, 1800, to the death of Parnell, 1891. 34) Reprint of the 1830 ed. published by W. Curry, Jr., Dublin. I. T. II. Series.
PR4416.T7 1979b   823/.7   *LC* 79-9573   *ISBN* 082403483X

Wolff, Robert Lee.   **2.7541**
William Carleton, Irish peasant novelist: a preface to his fiction / Robert Lee Wolff. — New York: Garland Pub., 1980. 156 p.; 23 cm. 1. Carleton, William, 1794-1869 — Criticism and interpretation. I. T.
PR4417.W6   823/.7   *LC* 79-4399   *ISBN* 0824035275

Carlyle, Jane Welsh, 1801-1866.   **2.7542**
I too am here: selections from the letters of Jane Welsh Carlyle / with an introd. and notes by Alan and Mary McQueen Simpson. — Cambridge; New York: Cambridge University Press, 1977. xvii, 306 p., [4] leaves of plates: ill.; 24 cm. Includes index. 1. Carlyle, Jane Welsh, 1801-1866 — Correspondence. I. T.
PR4419.C5 A83 1977   824/.8 B   *LC* 76-11093   *ISBN* 0521213045

Hanson, Lawrence.   • **2.7543**
Necessary evil: the life of Jane Welsh Carlyle / by Lawrence and Elisabeth Hanson. — New York: Macmillan, 1952. 618 p.: ports.; 22 cm. 1. Carlyle, Thomas, 1795-1881. 2. Carlyle, Jane Welsh, 1801-1866. I. Hanson, Elizabeth M. II. T.
PR4419.C5 H3 1952a   *LC* 52-10222

Carlyle, Thomas, 1795-1881.   • **2.7544**
[Works 1896] The works of Thomas Carlyle / with introduction by H.D. Traill. — Centenary ed. — New York: C. Scribner's Sons, 1898-1901. 30 v.: ill., ports., maps (some folded); 21 cm. I. Traill, H. D. (Henry Duff), 1842-1900. II. T.
PR 4420 E96   *LC* 01-9337

Carlyle, Thomas, 1795-1881.   • **2.7545**
A Carlyle reader; selections from the writings of Thomas Carlyle. Edited by G. B. Tennyson. New York, Modern Library [1969] xlvi, 497 p. 19 cm. (Modern Library college editions, T102) On spine: Thomas Carlyle: Selections from his writings. I. Tennyson, G. B. ed. II. T.
PR4422.T4   824/.8 19   *LC* 68-54721

Carlyle, Thomas, 1795-1881.   • **2.7546**
On heroes, hero-worship and the heroic in history / by Thomas Carlyle. — London: Oxford University Press, [1928] 245 p.; 16 cm. — (The world's classics; 62.) 1. Heroes I. T.
PR4426.A1

Carlyle, Thomas, 1795-1881.   • **2.7547**
Sartor resartus; the life and opinions of Herr Teufelsdröckh. Edited by Charles Frederick Harrold. [1st ed.] Garden City, N.Y. Doubleday, Doran [1937] lxxvi, 352 p.: port.; 19 cm. (Doubleday-Doran series in literature) I. Harrold, Charles Frederick, 1897-, ed. II. T.
PR4429 A1 1937

Tennyson, G. B.   • **2.7548**
Sartor called resartus: the genesis, structure, and style of Thomas Carlyle's first major work / by G. B. Tennyson. — Princeton, N. J.: Princeton University Press, 1965. viii, 354 p.; 21 cm. Includes index. 1. Carlyle, Thomas, 1795-1881. Sartor resartus. I. T.
PR4429.T4   824.8   *LC* 65-17162

Carlyle, Thomas, 1795-1881.   • **2.7549**
[Correspondence] The collected letters of Thomas and Jane Welsh Carlyle. general editor: Charles Richard Sanders. Duke-Edinburgh ed. Durham, N.C., Duke University Press, 1970-< 1985 > . v. < 1-12 > illus., fold. map, ports. 24 cm. 1. Carlyle, Thomas, 1795-1881. Correspondence. 2. Carlyle, Jane Welsh, 1801-1866 — Correspondence. I. Sanders, Charles Richard, 1904- II. Carlyle, Jane Welsh, 1801-1866. Correspondence. 1970. III. T.
PR4433.A4 1970   824/.8 B   *LC* 71-101132   *ISBN* 0822302403

Froude, James Anthony, 1818-1894.   • **2.7550**
Thomas Carlyle; a history of the first forty years of his life, 1795–1835. New York, Scribner, 1882;. — St. Clair Shores, Mich.: Scholarly Press, 1970. 2 v.; 22 cm. 1. Carlyle, Thomas, 1795-1881 — Biography. I. T.
PR4433.F73 1970   824/.8 B   *LC* 79-121334   *ISBN* 0403002109

Froude, James Anthony, 1818-1894.   • **2.7551**
Thomas Carlyle; a history of his life in London, 1834–1881. — New ed. London, Longmans, Green, 1897. — St. Clair Shores, Mich.: Scholarly Press, [1970?] 2 v.: port.; 22 cm. 1. Carlyle, Thomas, 1795-1881 — Biography — London life. I. T.
PR4433.F74 1970   824/.8 B   *LC* 72-108483   *ISBN* 0403001919

Froude, James Anthony, 1818-1894.   **2.7552**
[Thomas Carlyle] Froude's Life of Carlyle / abridged and edited by John Clubbe. — Columbus: Ohio State University Press, c1979. xxvi, 725 p.: ill.; 24 cm. Abridgement of the author's Thomas Carlyle, a history of the first forty years of his life, 1795-1835 and Thomas Carlyle, a history of his life in London, 1834-1881. 1. Carlyle, Thomas, 1795-1881 — Biography. 2. Authors, Scottish — 19th century — Biography. I. Clubbe, John. II. T. III. Title: Life of Carlyle.
PR4433.F742 1979   824/.8 B   *LC* 78-19158   *ISBN* 0814202748

Kaplan, Fred, 1937-.   **2.7553**
Thomas Carlyle: a biography / Fred Kaplan. — Ithaca, N.Y.: Cornell University Press, 1983. 614 p.: ill.; 25 cm. 1. Carlyle, Thomas, 1795-1881 — Biography. 2. Authors, Scottish — 19th century — Biography. I. T.
PR4433.K3 1983   824/.8 19   *LC* 83-5364   *ISBN* 080141508X

Neff, Emery Edward, 1892-.   **2.7554**
Carlyle. — New York: Norton, [1932] 282 p.: port. 1. Carlyle, Thomas, 1795-1881. I. T.
PR4433.N4   *LC* 32-5610

Carlyle past and present: a collection of new essays / edited by   **2.7555**
K. J. Fielding and Rodger L. Tarr.
New York: Barnes & Noble, 1976. 279 p.; 23 cm. (Barnes & Noble critical studies) 1. Carlyle, Thomas, 1795-1881 — Addresses, essays, lectures. I. Fielding, K. J. II. Tarr, Rodger L.
PR4434.C3 1976b   824/.8   *LC* 75-35036   *ISBN* 006492078X

Harrold, Charles Frederick, 1897-1948.   • **2.7556**
Carlyle and German thought: 1819–1834. Hamden: Archon Books, 1963 [c1934] xii, 340 p.; 23 cm. 1. Carlyle, Thomas, 1795-1881. 2. Literature,

Comparative — English and German 3. Literature, Comparative — German and English I. T.
PR4434.H3 1963   *LC* 63-19635

LaValley, Albert J.   • 2.7557
Carlyle and the idea of the modern; studies in Carlyle's prophetic literature and its relation to Blake, Nietzsche, Marx, and others, by Albert J. LaValley. — New Haven: Yale University Press, 1968. x, 351 p.; 22 cm. 1. Carlyle, Thomas, 1795-1881. I. T.
PR4434.L3   828/.8/08   *LC* 68-13916

Seigel, J. P. (Jules Paul) comp.   2.7558
Thomas Carlyle: the critical heritage. New York, Barnes & Noble [1971] xv, 526 p. 23 cm. (The Critical heritage series) 1. Carlyle, Thomas, 1795-1881. I. T.
PR4434.S45 1971b   824/.8   *LC* 72-178789   *ISBN* 0389042072

Calder, Grace J.   • 2.7559
The writing of Past and present: a study of Carlyle's manuscripts. New Haven Yale Univ. Press 1949. viii, 216 p.: facsims.; 25 cm. — (Yale studies in English. v. 112) 1. Carlyle, Thomas, 1795-1881. Past and present 2. Carlyle, Thomas, 1795-1881 — Style. I. T. II. Series.
PR4435.C35 PR13 Y3 vol.112   *LC* 49-9274

PR4453.C4 Chesterton

Chesterton, G. K. (Gilbert Keith), 1874-1936.   2.7560
[Works. 1986] The collected works of G.K. Chesterton. — San Francisco: Ignatius Press, c1986-<c1987 >. v. <1-2, 4, 27-28 >; 21 cm. I. T.
PR4453.C4 1986   828/.91209 19   *LC* 85-81511   *ISBN* 0898700779

Chesterton, G. K. (Gilbert Keith), 1874-1936.   2.7561
The Father Brown omnibus. — New & rev. ed. — New York: Dodd, Mead, [c1951] xii, 993 p. Includes an introduction about the origin of Father Brown by R.T. Bond. I. Chesterton, G. K. (Gilbert Keith), 1874-1936. Father Brown stories. II. Chesterton, G. K. (Gilbert Keith), 1874-1936. Secret of Father Brown. III. Chesterton, G. K. (Gilbert Keith), 1874-1936. Incredulity of Father Brown. IV. Chesterton, G. K. (Gilbert Keith), 1874-1936. Wisdom of Father Brown. V. Chesterton, G. K. (Gilbert Keith), 1874-1936. Innocence of Father Brown. VI. T. VII. Title: The Father Brown stories. VIII. Title: The secret of Father Brown. IX. Title: The incredulity of Father Brown. X. Title: The wisdom of Father Brown. XI. Title: The innocence of Father Brown.
PR4453.C4 F3 1951   *LC* 51-11019

Chesterton, G. K. (Gilbert Keith), 1874-1936.   2.7562
The Napoleon of Notting Hill / G. K. Chesterton; introd. by Andrew M. Greeley. — New York: Paulist Press, [1978] xvii, 197 p.: ill.; 21 cm. I. T.
PZ3.C4265 Nap 1978 PR4453.C4 N3x   823/.9/12   *LC* 77-99307
ISBN 0809120968

Chesterton, G. K. (Gilbert Keith), 1874-1936.   • 2.7563
The autobiography of G. K. Chesterton. New York: Sheed & Ward, 1936 [i.e. 1939] vii, 360 p. front., plates, ports. 22 cm. 'Seventh printing, April, 1939.' I. T.
PR4453.C4Z5 1939   324.91   *LC* 36-30892

Belloc, Hilaire, 1870-1953.   • 2.7564
On the place of Gilbert Chesterton in English letters. — London: Sheed & Ward, 1940. 84 [4] p.; 19 cm. 1. Chesterton, G. K. (Gilbert Keith), 1874-1936. I. T.
PR4453.C4 Z53   *LC* a 41-613

Dale, Alzina Stone, 1931-.   2.7565
The outline of sanity: a biography of G.K. Chesterton / by Alzina Stone Dale. — Grand Rapids, Mich.: Eerdmans, c1982. xvi, 354 p., [12] p. of plates: ill.; 24 cm. Includes index. 1. Chesterton, G. K. (Gilbert Keith), 1874-1936. 2. Authors, English — 20th century — Biography. I. T.
PR4453.C4 Z588 1982   828/.91209 B 19   *LC* 82-11452   *ISBN* 0802835503

Ward, Maisie, 1889-.   • 2.7566
Gilbert Keith Chesterton / by Maisie Ward. — London: Sheed & Ward, 1944. viii, 574 p.: ill.; 23 cm. 1. Chesterton, G. K. (Gilbert Keith), 1874-1936. I. T.
PR4453.C4 Z84 1944   *LC* 44-7853

Wills, Garry, 1934-.   • 2.7567
Chesterton, man and mask. — New York, Sheed & Ward [1961] 243 p. 22 cm. 1. Chesterton, G. K. (Gilbert Keith), 1874-1936. I. T.
PR4453.C4 Z88   928.2   *LC* 61-7283

PR4453.C6–4459 Clare. Clarke. Clough

Clare, John, 1793-1864.   • 2.7568
The prose of John Clare. Edited by J. W. and Anne Tibble. — New York: Barnes & Noble, [1970] xii, 302 p.: illus., map.; 23 cm. Reprint of the 1951 ed. I. T.
PR4453.C6 A16 1970   828/.8/08   *LC* 73-9846   *ISBN* 0389010227

Clare, John, 1793-1864.   2.7569
[Selections. 1984] John Clare / edited by Eric Robinson and David Powell. — Oxford [Oxfordshire]; New York: Oxford University Press, 1984. xxix, 530 p.; 23 cm. (Oxford authors.) Includes index. I. Robinson, Eric, 1924- II. Powell, David, 1925- III. T. IV. Series.
PR4453.C6 A6 1984   821/.7 19   *LC* 83-13382   *ISBN* 0192541919

Clare, John, 1793-1864.   • 2.7570
[Letters] The letters of John Clare. Edited by J. W. and Anne Tibble. New York, Barnes & Noble [1970] 379 p. col. port. 23 cm. Reprint of the 1951 ed. I. T.
PR4453.C6 Z52 1970   821/.7 B 19   *LC* 79-9747   *ISBN* 0389010219

Howard, William James.   2.7571
John Clare / by William Howard. — Boston: Twayne Publishers, 1981. 205 p.: port.; 21 cm. — (Twayne's English authors series; TEAS 312) Includes index. 1. Clare, John, 1793-1864 — Criticism and interpretation. I. T.
PR4453.C6 Z73   821/.3 19   *LC* 80-19278   *ISBN* 0805767347

Storey, Edward.   2.7572
A right to song: the life of John Clare / Edward Storey; photographs by John Baguley. — London: Methuen, 1982. 330 p., [9] p. of plates: ill.; 24 cm. Includes index. 1. Clare, John, 1793-1864. 2. Poets, English — 19th century — Biography. I. T.
PR4453.C6 Z89 1982   821/.7 19   *LC* 82-176526   *ISBN* 0413399400

Storey, Mark. comp.   2.7573
Clare; the critical heritage. — London; Boston: Routledge & K. Paul, [1973] xvii, 453 p.; 22 cm. — (The Critical heritage series) 1. Clare, John, 1793-1864. I. T.
PR4453.C6 Z9   821/.7   *LC* 72-96509   *ISBN* 0710073895

Storey, Mark.   2.7574
The poetry of John Clare: a critical introduction / Mark Storey. — New York: St Martin's Press, 1974. xii, 228 p.; 23 cm. Includes index. 1. Clare, John, 1793-1864. I. T.
PR4453.C6 Z92 1974   821/.7   *LC* 74-75012

Altick, Richard Daniel, 1915-.   • 2.7575
The Cowden Clarkes / by Richard D. Altick. — London: Oxford University Press, 1948. xiii, 268 p.: ports.; 22 cm. 1. Clarke, Mary Cowden, 1809-1898. 2. Clarke, Charles Cowden, 1787-1877. I. T.
PR4453.C69 Z6   *LC* 49-7626

Clarke, Mary Cowden, 1809-1898.   • 2.7576
My long life; an autobiographic sketch. New York, Dodd, Mead, 1896. — Grosse Pointe Mich.: Scholarly Press, 1968. 276 p.: ports.; 20 cm. — 1. Clarke, Mary Cowden, 1809-1898. I. T.
PR4453.C8 A82 1968   822.3/3   *LC* 76-3946

Clough, Arthur Hugh, 1819-1861.   2.7577
[Poems] The poems of Arthur Hugh Clough. — 2d ed. / edited by F. L. Mulhauser; translations edited by Jane Turner. — Oxford: Clarendon Press, 1974. xxix, 822 p.; 23 cm. I. Mulhauser, Frederick, ed. II. T.
PR4456.M8 1974   821/.8   *LC* 74-190044   *ISBN* 0198118988

Clough, Arthur Hugh, 1819-1861.   • 2.7578
Selected prose works / edited by Buckner B. Trawick. — University: University of Alabama Press, [1964] 351 p.; 21 cm. I. Trawick, Buckner B. II. T.
PR4456.T7-   *LC* 64-8048

Clough, Arthur Hugh, 1819-1861.   • 2.7579
Correspondence. Edited by Frederick L. Mulhauser. — Oxford, Clarendon Press, 1957. 2 v. (xxiii, 655 p.) 23 cm. 1. Clough, Arthur Hugh, 1819-1861 — Correspondence. 2. Authors — Correspondence, reminiscences, etc. I. T.
PR4458.A4 1957   928.2   *LC* 57-59593

Chorley, Katharine Campbell Hopkinson Chorley, Baroness, 1897-.   • 2.7580
Arthur Hugh Clough, the uncommitted mind; a study of his life and poetry. — Oxford: Clarendon Press, 1962. 372 p.: ill.; 23 cm. 1. Clough, Arthur Hugh, 1819-1861 — Biography. I. T.
PR4458.C5   *LC* 62-1613

Greenberger, Evelyn Barish.   2.7581
Arthur Hugh Clough; the growth of a poet's mind. — Cambridge, Mass.: Harvard University Press, 1970. ix, 270 p.; 24 cm. 1. Clough, Arthur Hugh, 1819-1861. I. T.
PR4458.G7   821/.8   *LC* 78-116735   *ISBN* 0674048490

Harris, Wendell V.   2.7582
Arthur Hugh Clough, by Wendell V. Harris. — New York: Twayne Publishers, [1970] 175 p.; 22 cm. — (Twayne's English authors series, 97) 1. Clough, Arthur Hugh, 1819-1861. I. T.
PR4458.H3   821/.8   *LC* 76-99530

Timko, Michael, 1925-.   2.7583
Innocent Victorian; the satiric poetry of Arthur Hugh Clough. — [Athens] Ohio University Press [1966] xvi, 198 p. port. 22 cm. Bibliography: p. [177]-192. 1. Clough, Arthur Hugh, 1819-1861. I. T.
PR4458.T5   821.8   *LC* 66-11301

Houghton, Walter Edwards, 1904-.   • 2.7584
The poetry of Clough: an essay in revaluation / by Walter E. Houghton. New Haven: Yale University Press, 1963. 236 p.; 25 cm. 1. Clough, Arthur Hugh, 1819-1861. I. T.
PR4459.H6   *LC* 63-7936

Thorpe, Michael. comp.   2.7585
Clough: the critical heritage. — New York: Barnes & Noble, [1972] xvii, 411 p.; 23 cm. — (The Critical heritage series) 1. Clough, Arthur Hugh, 1819-1861. I. T.
PR4459.T5 1972b   821/.8   *LC* 72-187962   *ISBN* 038904508X

PR4470–4488 Samuel Taylor Coleridge

Coleridge, Samuel Taylor, 1772-1834.   2.7586
[Works. 1969] The collected works of Samuel Taylor Coleridge. [London] Routledge and K. Paul; [Princeton] Princeton University Press [c1969- <c1984 >. <v. 1-4, 6-7, 10, 12, pt. 1-2, 13; in 14 > ill. 23 cm. (Bollingen series. 75) I. T. II. Series.
PR4470.F69   821/.7   *LC* 68-10201

Coleridge, Samuel Taylor, 1772-1834.   • 2.7587
The poems of Samuel Taylor Coleridge: including poems and versions of poems herein published for the first time / edited, with textual and bibliographical notes, by Ernest Hartley Coleridge. — London: H. Milford, Oxford University Press, 1935. xxiii, 614 p., [1] leaf of plates: port.; 19 cm. Includes index. I. Coleridge, Ernest Hartley, 1846-1920. II. T.
PR4471.C59

Coleridge, Samuel Taylor, 1772-1834.   • 2.7588
Inquiring spirit; a new presentation of Coleridge from his published and unpublished prose writings, edited by Kathleen Colburn. — New York, Pantheon Books [1951] 454 p. 23 cm. Bibliography: p. 413. 1. Coleridge, Samuel Taylor, 1772-1834. I. T.
PR4472.C6 1951a   828.7   *LC* 51-7691

Coleridge, Samuel Taylor, 1772-1834.   2.7589
Imagination in Coleridge / edited by John Spencer Hill. — Totowa, N.J.: Rowman and Littlefield, 1978. xvii, 232 p.; 23 cm. Includes index. 1. Imagination — Collected works. I. Hill, John Spencer, 1943- II. T.
PR4472.H5 1978   821/.7   *LC* 77-16310   *ISBN* 0847660265

Nethercot, Arthur Hobart, 1895-.   • 2.7590
The road to Tryermaine: a study of the history, background, and purposes of Coleridge's 'Christabel.' — New York: Russell & Russell, 1962 [c1939] 230 p.; 23 cm. 1. Coleridge, Samuel Taylor, 1772-1834. Christabel. I. T.
PR4480.C52 N4 1962   *LC* 62-10693

Schneider, Elisabeth Wintersteen, 1897-.   • 2.7591
Coleridge, opium, and Kubla Khan, by Elisabeth Schneider. — New York, Octagon Books, 1966 [c1953] xi, 377 p. 24 cm. Bibliographical references included in 'Notes' (p. 307-363) 1. Coleridge, Samuel Taylor, 1772-1834. 2. Opium — Physiological effect. I. T.
PR4480.K83S4 1966   821.7   *LC* 66-17512

PR4482–4488 Biography. Criticism

Logan, Eugenia.   • 2.7592
A concordance to the poetry of Samuel Taylor Coleridge / edited by Sister Eugenia Logan. — Saint-Mary-of-the-Woods, Ind., 1940. xvi, 901 p.; 27 cm. 'Limited edition of 525 copies.' Privately printed. 1. Coleridge, Samuel Taylor, 1772-1834 — Concordances. I. T.
PR4482.L6   *LC* 40-5258

Coleridge, Samuel Taylor, 1772-1834.   2.7593
Notebooks / edited by Kathleen Coburn. — [Complete ed.]. — Princeton: Princeton University Press, [1957-. v. in ; ill.; 24 cm. — (Bollingen series. 50.) 1. Coleridge, Samuel Taylor, 1772-1834. I. Coburn, Kathleen, 1905- II. T. III. Series.
PR4483.A25

Coleridge, Samuel Taylor, 1772-1834.   2.7594
Collected letters, edited by Earl Leslie Griggs. — Oxford, Clarendon Press, 1956-1971. 6 v. ports. 23 cm. Includes bibliographical references. I. T.
PR4483.A428   928.2   *LC* 56-2923

Bate, Walter Jackson, 1918-.   • 2.7595
Coleridge. — New York: Macmillan, [1968] xii, 244 p.; 22 cm. — (Masters of world literature series) 1. Coleridge, Samuel Taylor, 1772-1834. I. T.
PR4483.B3   821/.7   *LC* 68-12395

Beer, John Bernard.   • 2.7596
Coleridge, the visionary / by J.B. Beer. — London: Chatto & Windus, 1959. 366 p.; 23 cm. Includes index. 1. Coleridge, Samuel Taylor, 1772-1834. I. T.
PR4483.B37   *LC* 59-4562

Doughty, Oswald.   2.7597
Perturbed spirit: the life and personality of Samuel Taylor Coleridge / Oswald Doughty. — Rutherford [N.J.]: Fairleigh Dickinson University Press; East Brunswick, N.J.: Associated University Presses, c1981. 565 p.; 24 cm. Includes index. 1. Coleridge, Samuel Taylor, 1772-1834 — Biography. 2. Poets, English — 19th century — Biography. 3. Critics — England — Biography. I. T.
PR4483.D6 1981   821/.7 19   *LC* 78-66792   *ISBN* 0838623530

Barfield, Owen, 1898-.   2.7598
What Coleridge thought. — [1st ed.]. — Middletown, Conn.: Wesleyan University Press, [1971] xii, 285 p.; 24 cm. 1. Coleridge, Samuel Taylor, 1772-1834. I. T.
PR4484.B3   821/.7   *LC* 73-153100   *ISBN* 0819540404

Fogle, Richard Harter, 1911-.   • 2.7599
The idea of Coleridge's criticism. Berkeley, University of California Press, 1962. xiv, 185 p. 22 cm. (Perspectives in criticism, 9) 1. Coleridge, Samuel Taylor, 1772-1834. I. T. II. Series.
PR4484.F6   *LC* 62-10824

Fruman, Norman.   • 2.7600
Coleridge, the damaged archangel. — New York: G. Braziller, [1971] xxiii, 607 p.; 24 cm. 1. Coleridge, Samuel Taylor, 1772-1834. I. T.
PR4484.F7   821/.7 B   *LC* 71-148734   *ISBN* 0807606073

Lowes, John Livingston.   • 2.7601
The road to Xanadu: a study in the ways of the imagination / John Livingston Lowes. — Rev. ed. — Boston: Houghton Mifflin, [1964], c1927. xvi, 614 p.: ill.; 21 cm. — (Sentry edition; SE 41) 1. Coleridge, Samuel Taylor, 1772-1834. The rime of the ancient mariner. 2. Coleridge, Samuel Taylor, 1772-1834. Kubla Khan 3. Coleridge, Samuel Taylor, 1772-1834. 4. Imagination I. T.
PR4484.L6 1964   821.7   *LC* 64-6070

Mileur, Jean-Pierre.   2.7602
Vision and revision: Coleridge's art of immanence / Jean–Pierre Mileur. — Berkeley: University of California Press, c1982. xi, 184 p.; 23 cm. 1. Coleridge, Samuel Taylor, 1772-1834 — Criticism and interpretation. I. T.
PR4484.M5 1982   821/.7 19   *LC* 81-2487   *ISBN* 0520044479

Reading Coleridge: approaches and applications / edited by Walter B. Crawford.   2.7603
Ithaca: Cornell University Press, 1979. 288 p.: port.; 23 cm. 1. Coleridge, Samuel Taylor, 1772-1834 — Criticism and interpretation — Addresses, essays, lectures. 2. Griggs, Earl Leslie, 1899- I. Crawford, Walter Byron.
PR4484.R4   821/.7   *LC* 79-7616   *ISBN* 0801412196

PR4489.C2 Sara Coleridge

Coleridge, Sara Coleridge, 1802-1852.   2.7604
Phantasmion: Prince of Palmland. — [s.l.]: S. Colman, 1839. 2 v. I. T.
PR4489.C2 P5

PR4490–4514 Collins. Crabbe

Collins, Wilkie, 1824-1889.   • 2.7605
Armadale. New York, P. F. Collier. — St. Clair Shores, Mich.: Scholarly Press, 1972. 2 v.: illus.; 21 cm. — (The works of Wilkie Collins, v. 8-9) I. T.
PZ3.C697 Ar10 PR4494.A7x   823/.8   *LC* 70-107168   *ISBN* 0403004330

Collins, Wilkie, 1824-1889. • 2.7606
The moonstone / by Wilkie Collins; with an introduction by T. S. Eliot. —
[London]: Oxford University Press: H. Milford, [1928] xx, 552 p.; 16 cm. —
(The World's classics, CCXVI.) I. T.
PR4494.Mx

Collins, Wilkie, 1824-1889. • 2.7607
No name. — New York: Stein and Day, [1967] 593 p.; 23 cm. — (The Doughty
library no. 2) I. T.
PZ3.C697 No20 PR4494.N6x. LC 66-24803

Collins, Wilkie, 1824-1889. • 2.7608
Poor Miss Finch; a novel. New York, Harper. — St. Clair Shores, Mich.:
Scholarly Press, 1971. 454 p.: illus.; 22 cm. Reprint of the 1873 ed. I. T.
PZ3.C697 Po13 PR4494.P6x 823/.8 LC 77-131672 ISBN
0403005590

Collins, Wilkie, 1824-1889. • 2.7609
The woman in white, by Wilkie Collins. London, Dent; New York, Dutton
[1932] xii, 569 p.; 18 cm. — (Everyman's library. Fiction [no. 464]) I. T.
PR4494.W6x

Davis, Nuel Pharr, 1915-. • 2.7610
The life of Wilkie Collins / introduction by Gordon N. Ray. — Urbana:
University of Illinois Press, 1956. 360 p.: ill.; 24 cm. 1. Collins, Wilkie,
1824-1889 — Biography. I. T.
PR4496.D3 LC 56-8418

Marshall, William Harvey. 2.7611
Wilkie Collins, by William H. Marshall. — New York: Twayne Publishers,
[1970] 159 p.; 21 cm. — (Twayne's English authors series, 94) 1. Collins,
Wilkie, 1824-1889. I. T.
PR4496.M3 823/.8 LC 70-79393

Robinson, Kenneth, 1911-. • 2.7612
Wilkie Collins, a biography. — London: Bodley Head, [1951] 348 p.: ill., ports.;
22 cm. 1. Collins, Wilkie, 1824-1889 — Biography. I. T.
PR4496.R6 LC 52-1002

Page, Norman. comp. 2.7613
Wilkie Collins: the critical heritage / edited by Norman Page. — London;
Boston: Routledge & Kegan Paul, 1974. xvi, 288 p.; 23 cm. (The Critical
heritage series) Includes index. 1. Collins, Wilkie, 1824-1889 — Criticism and
interpretation. I. T.
PR4497.P3 823/.8 LC 73-92987 ISBN 0710078439

Crabbe, George, 1754-1832. • 2.7614
The poetical works of George Crabbe, edited by A. J. Carlyle and R. M. Carlyle.
London, Oxford University Press, 1914. — St. Clair Shores, Mich.: Scholarly
Press, 1972. p. — I. T.
PR4510.A5 C3 1972 821/.7 LC 33-27214 ISBN 0403009081

Crabbe, George, 1754-1832. • 2.7615
Poems / edited by Adolphus William Ward. — Cambridge: University Press,
1905-1907. 3 v.; 20 cm. — (Cambridge English classics) I. Ward, Adolphus
William, Sir, 1837-1924. II. Bartholomew, Augustus Theodore, 1882-1933.
III. T. IV. Series.
PR4510.A5 W3 LC 07-23869

Crabbe, George, 1785-1857. • 2.7616
The life of George Crabbe / by his son with an introduction by Edmund
Blunden. — London: Cresset Press, 1947. xxx, 286 p.; 20 cm. — (The Cresset
library) 1. Crabbe, George, 1754-1832 — Biography. 2. Poets, English — 18th
century — Biography. 3. Poets, English — 19th century — Biography. I. T.
PR4513.C7 1947 928.2 LC 48-22870

Haddakin, Lilian. • 2.7617
The poetry of Crabbe. — London, Chatto & Windus, 1955. 175 p. 21 cm.
1. Crabbe, George, 1754-1832. I. T.
PR4513.H3 821.79 LC 55-3811

Bareham, Tony. 2.7618
George Crabbe / Terence Bareham. — New York: Barnes & Noble Books,
1977. 245 p.; 23 cm. — (Barnes & Noble critical studies) Includes index.
1. Crabbe, George, 1754-1832 — Criticism and interpretation. I. T.
PR4514.B35 821/.7 LC 77-154876 ISBN 0064903052

Pollard, Arthur. comp. 2.7619
Crabbe: the critical heritage. London, Boston, Routledge and K. Paul, 1972.
xiii, 495 p. 23 cm. (The Critical heritage series) 1. Crabbe, George, 1754-1832
— Criticism and interpretation — Addresses, essays, lectures. I. T.
PR4514.P6 1972 821/.7 LC 72-95294 ISBN 0710072589

PR4525–4538 Davidson. De Quincey

Davidson, John, 1857-1909. 2.7620
The poems of John Davidson / edited by Andrew Turnbull. — Edinburgh:
Scottish Academic Press, [1973]. 2 v. (xxxiv, 551 p.); 23 cm. — (Association for
Scottish Literary Studies. [Publications] no. 2-3) I. T.
PR4525.D5 A17 1973b 821/.8 LC 74-170500 ISBN 0701119888

Townsend, James Benjamin, 1918-. • 2.7621
John Davidson, poet of Armageddon. — New Haven: Yale University Press,
1961. 555 p.: ill.; 23 cm. — (Yale studies in English. v. 148) 1. Davidson, John,
1857-1909. I. T. II. Series.
PR4525.D5 Z83 LC 61-10188

DeQuincey, Thomas, 1785-1859. 2.7622
The collected writings / edited by David Masson. — London A. & C. Black
1896-97. 14 v. I. Masson, David, 1822-1907. II. T.
PR4530 E96 LC a 12-431

Lindop, Grevel, 1948-. 2.7623
The opium-eater, a life of Thomas De Quincey / Grevel Lindop. — New York:
Taplinger Pub. Co., 1982 (c1981). xiv, 433 p.; 24 cm. Includes index. 1. De
Quincey, Thomas, 1785-1859 — Biography. 2. Authors, English — 19th
century — Biography. 3. Opium habit — England. I. T.
PR4536.L5 828/.809 B 19 LC 81-5662 ISBN 0800858417

PR4550–4598 Dickens

Dickens, Charles, 1812-1870. 2.7624
The Clarendon Dickens; ed. by Kathleen Tillotson [and] John Butt. Oxford,
Clarendon Press, 1966-. v. illus., map. 23 cm. Half-title: The Clarendon
Dickens. I. Tillotson, Kathleen Mary. ed. II. T.
PR4550.Fx

Dickens, Charles, 1812-1870. 2.7625
The New Oxford illustrated Dickens. [London, New York, Oxford University
Press, 1951-59] 21 v. illus. 19 cm. All the plates in this issue have been remade
from the original drawings by 'Phiz (Hablot K. Browne) and others, which
appeared in the first edition.—cf. book jackets. Half title: each volume has
special t.p. I. T.
PR4550.Fx

Dickens, Charles, 1812-1870. 2.7626
The public readings / Charles Dickens; edited by Philip Collins. — Oxford
[Eng.]: Clarendon Press, 1975. lxix, 486 p., [3] leaves of plates: ill.; 23 cm.
I. Collins, Philip Arthur William. II. T.
PR4553.C6 1975 823/.8 LC 76-354076 ISBN 0198125011

Dickens, Charles, 1812-1870. 2.7627
Dickens on America & the Americans / edited by Michael Slater. — Austin:
University of Texas Press, c1978. 245 p.: ill.; 26 cm. 1. Dickens, Charles,
1812-1870 — Quotations. 2. United States — Collected works. I. Slater,
Michael. II. T.
PR4553.S58 1978 823/.8 LC 78-9313 ISBN 029271517X

Dickens, Charles, 1812-1870. 2.7628
Bleak house: an authoritative and annotated text, illustrations, a note on the
text, genesis and composition, backgrounds, criticism / Charles Dickens; edited
by George Ford, Sylvère Monod. — 1st ed. — New York: Norton, c1977. xx,
986 p., [2] leaves of plates: ill.; 22 cm. — (A Norton critical edition) I. Ford,
George Harry, 1914- II. Monod, Sylvère, 1921- III. T.
PZ3.D55 Bl73 PR4556.F5 823/.8 LC 77-7783 ISBN 0393043746

Newsom, Robert, 1944-. 2.7629
Dickens on the romantic side of familiar things: Bleak house and the novel
tradition / by Robert Newsom. — New York: Columbia University Press,
1977. xiv, 173 p.; 22 cm. Includes index. 1. Dickens, Charles, 1812-1870. Bleak
house. I. T.
PR4556.N45 823/.8 LC 77-23476 ISBN 0231042442

Collins, Philip Arthur William. 2.7630
Charles Dickens, David Copperfield / by Philip Collins. — London: Edward
Arnold, 1977. 64 p.; 20 cm. — (Studies in English literature; no. 67) Includes
index. 1. Dickens, Charles, 1812-1870. David Copperfield. I. T.
PR4558.C64 823/.8 LC 77-370347 ISBN 0713159359

Dickens, Charles, 1812-1870. 2.7631
The annotated Christmas carol: a Christmas carol / by Charles Dickens;
illustrated by John Leech; with an introd., notes, and bibliography by Michael
Patrick Hearn. — 1st ed. — New York: C.N. Potter: distributed by Crown
Publishers, c1976. 182 p.: ill.; 29 cm. Includes index. I. Hearn, Michael
Patrick. II. T. III. Title: Christmas carol.
PZ3.D55 An5 PR4572.G85 823/.8 LC 76-21345 ISBN
0517527413

Dickens, Charles, 1812-1870.   2.7632
Charles Dickens' book of memoranda: a photographic and typographic
facsimile of the notebook begun in January 1855 / transcribed and annotated by
Fred Kaplan from the original manuscript in the Berg Collection of English and
American literature. — 1st ed. — [New York]: New York Public Library,
Astor, Lenox and Tilden Foundations: Distributed by Readex Books, 1982. x,
107 p.: facsims.; 24 cm. — (Harcourt Brace Jovanovich Fund publication. no.
2) 1. Dickens, Charles, 1812-1870 — Manuscripts — Facsimiles. I. Kaplan,
Fred, 1937- II. T. III. Series.
PR4572.M37 1981   828/.803 B 19   LC 81-18872   *ISBN*
0871042797

Dickens, Charles, 1812-1870.   • 2.7633
Speeches. Edited by K. J. Fielding. Oxford: Clarendon Press, 1960. xxiv, 456 p.;
22 cm. I. T.
PR4572.S6 1960   LC 60-1170

PR4579–4598 Biography. Criticism

Philip, Alexander John, 1879-.   • 2.7634
A Dickens dictionary, by Alex. J. Philip. 2d ed. rev. and greatly enl. by Alex. J.
Philip and W. Laurence Gadd. New York, B. Franklin [1970] xxii, 375 p. illus.,
port. 24 cm. (Essays in literature and criticism, 48) (Burt Franklin bibliography
& reference series, 313.) Reprint of the 1928 ed. 'Index to originals': p. 325-370.
1. Dickens, Charles, 1812-1870 — Dictionaries, indexes, etc. I. Gadd, William
Laurence, 1862- joint author. II. T.
PR4580.P5 1970   823/.8   LC 73-114560

Dickens, Charles, 1812-1870.   • 2.7635
The letters of Charles Dickens / edited by Madeline House & Graham Storey;
associate editors: W. J. Carlton ... [et al.]. — Pilgrim ed. — Oxford: Clarendon
Press, 1965-. v.: facsims., ports.; 24 cm. Editors vary. 1. Dickens, Charles,
1812-1870. Correspondence 2. Dickens, Charles, 1812-1870. 3. Authors,
English — 19th century — Correspondence I. House, Madeline. II. Storey,
Graham. III. T.
PR4581.A3 H6   LC 65-2115   *ISBN* 0198124740

Fielding, Kenneth Joshua.   • 2.7636
Charles Dickens, a critical introduction. — 2nd ed. enl. — [London]:
Longmans, [1965] 269 p.; 19 cm. 1. Dickens, Charles, 1812-1870. I. T.
PR4581.F46 1965   LC 65-4924

Forster, John, 1812-1876.   • 2.7637
The life of Charles Dickens, by John Forster ... — London, J. M. Dent & sons,
ltd.; New York, E. P. Dutton & co. [1927] 2 v. illus. (incl. facsims.) 18 cm. —
(Half-title: Everyman's library, ed. by Ernest Rhys. Biography. [no. 781-782])
First issue of this edition, 1927. Introduction by G. K. Chesterton.
'Bibliography of John Forster': v. 1, p. xiii-xiv. 'Biographies of Dickens by other
authors': v. 1, p. xiv. 1. Dickens, Charles, 1812-1870. I. T.
AC1.E8 no. 781-782   PR4581.F7x.   928.2   LC A 27-281

Johnson, Edgar.   • 2.7638
Charles Dickens, his tragedy and triumph. — Boston: Little, Brown, 1965,
c1952. 2 v.: ill., facsim., geneal. tables, ports.; 22 cm. 1. Dickens, Charles,
1812-1870. I. T.
PR4581.J6 1965   LC 65-328

Kaplan, Fred, 1937-.   2.7639
Dickens and mesmerism: the hidden springs of fiction / Fred Kaplan. —
Princeton, N.J.: Princeton University Press, [1975] xiv, 249 p., 4 leaves of
plates: ill.; 23 cm. 1. Dickens, Charles, 1812-1870. 2. Mesmerism — England.
I. T.
PR4581.K27   823/.8   LC 75-2994

Maurois, André, 1885-1967.   • 2.7640
[Essai sur Dickens. English] Dickens. [Translated from the French by Hamish
Miles] New York, Ungar Pub. Co. [1967] 183 p. 20 cm. First published in 1934.
Translation of Un essai sur Dickens. 1. Dickens, Charles, 1812-1870. I. Miles,
Hamish, 1894-1937, tr. II. T.
PR4581.M46 1967   823.8   LC 66-26514

Priestley, J. B. (John Boynton), 1894-.   • 2.7641
Charles Dickens, a pictorial biography. New York, Viking Press [1962, c1961]
144 p. illus., ports., facsims. 24 cm. (A Studio book) 1. Dickens, Charles,
1812-1870. I. T.
PR4581.P67 1962   928.2   LC 61-15437

Smith, Grahame.   2.7642
Dickens, money, and society. — Berkeley, Calif.: University of California Press,
1968. 226 p.; 23 cm. 1. Dickens, Charles, 1812-1870. I. T.
PR4581.S62   823/.8   LC 68-19192

Nisbet, Ada.   • 2.7643
Dickens & Ellen Ternan; with a foreword by Edmund Wilson. — Berkeley:
University of California Press, 1952. xvi, 89 p.; 21 cm. 1. Dickens, Charles,
1812-1870. 2. Ternan, Ellen Lawless, 1839-1914. I. T.
PR4582.N5   928.2   LC 52-14405

Slater, Michael.   2.7644
Dickens and women / Michael Slater. — Stanford, Calif.: Stanford University
Press, 1983. xii, 465 p., [8] p. of plates: ill.; 25 cm. Includes indexes. 1. Dickens,
Charles, 1812-1870 — Relations with women. 2. Dickens, Charles, 1812-1870
— Characters — Women. 3. Dickens, Charles, 1812-1870. 4. Women —
England — Biography. 5. Women in literature I. T.
PR4582.S4 1983   823/.8 19   LC 82-62351   *ISBN* 0804711801

House, Humphrey, 1908-1955.   • 2.7645
The Dickens world / by Humphrey House. — 2d ed. — London: Oxford
University Press, 1960. 231 p.; 20 cm. — (Oxford paperbacks; 9) 1. Dickens,
Charles, 1812-1870 — Criticism and interpretation. I. T.
PR4583.H65 1960   823.8   LC 60-51570   *ISBN* 0192810022 Pbk

Patten, Robert L.   2.7646
Charles Dickens and his publishers / by Robert L. Patten. — Oxford [Eng.]:
Clarendon Press; New York: Oxford University Press, 1978. xiv, 502 p., [4]
leaves of plates: ill.; 22 cm. Includes index. 1. Dickens, Charles, 1812-1870 —
Friends and associates. 2. Authors and publishers 3. Serial publication of
books 4. Novelists, English — 19th century — Biography. I. T.
PR4583.P29 1978   823/.8 B   LC 77-30164   *ISBN* 0198120761

Steig, Michael, 1936-.   2.7647
Dickens and Phiz / by Michael Steig. — Bloomington: Indiana University
Press, c1978. x, 340 p.: ill.; 24 cm. 1. Dickens, Charles, 1812-1870 — Friends
and associates. 2. Dickens, Charles, 1812-1870 — Illustrations. 3. Browne,
Hablot Knight, 1815-1882. I. T.
PR4583.S8   823/.8   LC 77-23645   *ISBN* 0253317053

Schwarzbach, F. S., 1949-.   2.7648
Dickens and the city / F.S. Schwarzbach. — London: Athlone Press; [Atlantic
Highlands, N.J.]: distributed by Humanities Press, 1979. xii, 258 p., [4] leaves of
plates: ill.; 23 cm. Includes index. 1. Dickens, Charles, 1812-1870 — Homes
and haunts — England — London. 2. London in literature. 3. Cities and towns
in literature 4. Novelists, English — 19th century — Biography. I. T.
PR4584.S3   823/.8 B   LC 79-306781   *ISBN* 0485111748

Butt, John Everett, 1906-.   • 2.7649
Dickens at work / John Butt and Kathleen Tillotson. — London: Methuen,
[1957] 238 p.: facsims.; 22 cm. 1. Dickens, Charles, 1812-1870. I. Tillotson,
Kathleen Mary. II. T.
PR4588.B8   LC 57-4323

Charles Dickens, new perspectives / edited by Wendell Stacy   2.7650
Johnson.
Englewood Cliffs, N.J.: Prentice-Hall, c1982. viii, 194 p.; 21 cm. — (Twentieth
century views.) 'A Spectrum book.' Includes index. 1. Dickens, Charles,
1812-1870 — Criticism and interpretation — Addresses, essays, lectures.
I. Johnson, Wendell Stacy, 1927- II. Series.
PR4588.C36 1982   823/.8 19   LC 82-440   *ISBN* 0131281577

Chesterton, G. K. (Gilbert Keith), 1874-1936.   • 2.7651
Charles Dickens. Introd. by Steven Marcus. Schocken Books [c1965] xviii,
302 p.; 21 cm. (Schocken paperbacks, SB91) I. Dickens, Charles, 1812-1870.
II. T.
PR4588.C5 1965   LC 65-14824

Cockshut, A. O. J.   • 2.7652
The imagination of Charles Dickens / A. O. J. Cockshut. — [New York]: New
York University Press, 1962, c1961. 192 p.; 22 cm. 1. Dickens, Charles,
1812-1870. I. T.
PR4588.C63 1962   828.8   LC 62-51655

DeVries, Duane.   2.7653
Dickens's apprentice years: the making of a novelist / Duane DeVries.
Hassocks, Eng.: Harvester Press; New York: Barnes & Noble Books, 1976.
195 p.; 24 cm. Includes index. 1. Dickens, Charles, 1812-1870 — Technique.
I. T.
PR4588.D4 1976   823/.8   LC 76-372615   *ISBN* 0064916723

Ford, George Harry, 1914-.   • 2.7654
Dickens and his readers; aspects of novel–criticism since 1836. [Princeton, N.J.]
Published for the University of Cincinnati by Princeton University Press, 1955.
318 p.: ill; 23 cm. 1. Dickens, Charles, 1812-1870. 2. English fiction — History
and criticism 3. Criticism — Great Britain. I. T.
PR4588.F6   PR4588.F6.   823.8   LC 55-6692

Ford, George Harry, 1914- ed.   • 2.7655
The Dickens critics, edited by George H. Ford and Lauriat Lane, Jr. —
Westport, Conn.: Greenwood Press, [1972, c1961] x, 417 p.; 22 cm. 1. Dickens,

Charles, 1812-1870 — Criticism and interpretation. I. Lane, Lauriat, joint ed. II. T.
PR4588.F63 1972　　823/.8　　*LC* 72-152596　　*ISBN* 0837160294

Garis, Robert.　　● **2.7656**
The Dickens theatre, a reassessment of the novels / by Robert Garis. — Oxford: Clarendon Press, 1965. 259 p.; 23 cm. 1. Dickens, Charles, 1812-1870. I. T.
PR4588.G28　　*LC* 65-4243

Gissing, George, 1857-1903.　　● **2.7657**
Charles Dickens; a critical study. New York, Dodd, Mead, 1904. St. Clair Shores, Mich., Scholarly Press, 1972 [c1898] 293 p. 22 cm. 1. Dickens, Charles, 1812-1870 — Criticism and interpretation. I. T.
PR4588.G5 1972　　823/.8　　*LC* 75-145043　　*ISBN* 0403009898

Gross, John J.　　● **2.7658**
Dickens and the twentieth century / edited by John Gross and Gabriel Pearson. — Toronto: University of Toronto Press, [c1962] xxiv, 244 p.; 23 cm. 1. Dickens, Charles, 1812-1870. I. Pearson, Gabriel II. T.
PR4588.G7 1962a　　*LC* 63-6397

Hardy, Barbara Nathan.　　● **2.7659**
The moral art of Dickens; essays, by Barbara Hardy. — New York: Oxford University Press, 1970. xiii, 155 p.; 21 cm. 1. Dickens, Charles, 1812-1870. I. T.
PR4588.H3 1970b　　823/.8　　*LC* 76-19901

Kincaid, James R. (James Russell)　　**2.7660**
Dickens and the rhetoric of laughter [by] James R. Kincaid. Oxford, Clarendon Press, 1971. ix, 264 p. 23 cm. 1. Dickens, Charles, 1812-1870 — Criticism and interpretation. 2. Laughter I. T.
PR4588.K5　　823/.8　　*LC* 72-179306　　*ISBN* 0198120168

Leavis, F. R. (Frank Raymond), 1895-.　　● **2.7661**
Dickens, the novelist, by F. R. Leavis and Q. D. Leavis. [1st American ed.] New York, Pantheon Books [1971, c1970] xviii, 371 p. 23 cm. 1. Dickens, Charles, 1812-1870. I. Leavis, Q. D. (Queenie Dorothy) joint author. II. T.
PR4588.L36 1971　　823/.8　　*LC* 77-135367　　*ISBN* 0394468600

Miller, J. Hillis (Joseph Hillis), 1928-.　　● **2.7662**
Charles Dickens: the world of his novels. Cambridge, Harvard University Press, 1958. 346 p. 22 cm. 1. Dickens, Charles, 1812-1870. I. T.
PR4588.M5　　823.83　　*LC* 58-10402

Page, Norman.　　**2.7663**
A Dickens companion / Norman Page. — 1st American ed. — New York: Schocken Books, 1984. xv, 369 p., [12] p. of plates: ill.; 23 cm. Includes indexes. 1. Dickens, Charles, 1812-1870 — Handbooks, manuals, etc. I. T.
PR4588.P33 1984　　823/.8 19　　*LC* 83-16306　　*ISBN* 0805238832

Thomas, Deborah A., 1943-.　　**2.7664**
Dickens and the short story / Deborah A. Thomas. — Philadelphia: University of Pennsylvania Press, 1982. xii, 196 p.; 24 cm. Includes index. 1. Dickens, Charles, 1812-1870 — Criticism and interpretation. 2. Dickens, Charles, 1812-1870 — Technique. 3. Short story I. T.
PR4591.T5 1982　　823/.8 19　　*LC* 81-43523　　*ISBN* 0812278283

PR4592 Special Topics, A–Z

Moss, Sidney Phil, 1917-.　　**2.7665**
Charles Dickens' quarrel with America / Sidney P. Moss. — Troy, N.Y.: Whittson Pub. Co., 1984. 356 p.: ill.; 24 cm. 1. Dickens, Charles, 1812-1870 — Knowledge — United States. 2. Dickens, Charles, 1812-1870 — Journeys — United States. 3. Dickens, Charles, 1812-1870 — Appreciation — United States. 4. Copyright — United States — History — 19th century. 5. United States in literature. 6. Novelists, English — 19th century — Biography. 7. Books and reading — United States — History — 19th century. I. T.
PR4592.A54 M67 1984　　823/.8 19　　*LC* 82-50401　　*ISBN* 0878752552

Welsh, Alexander.　　**2.7666**
The city of Dickens. Oxford, Clarendon Press, 1971. xi, 233 p., 12 plates; illus., facsims. 23 cm. 1. Dickens, Charles, 1812-1870 — Criticism and interpretation. 2. Cities and towns in literature 3. Christian ethics in literature. 4. Good and evil in literature. 5. Home in literature I. T.
PR4592.C56 W45 1971　　823/.8　　*LC* 73-851703　　*ISBN* 0198120087

Collins, Philip Arthur William.　　● **2.7667**
Dickens and crime. — London: Macmillan; New York: St. Martin's Press, 1962. 371 p.; 23 cm. — (Cambridge studies in criminology. v. 17) 1. Dickens, Charles, 1812-1870. 2. Crime and criminals in literature I. T. II. Series.
PR4592.C7 C6 1962　　*LC* 62-52224

Collins, Philip Arthur William.　　● **2.7668**
Dickens and education. London: Macmillan; New York: St. Martin's Press, 1963. ix, 258 p.; 23 cm. 1. Dickens, Charles, 1812-1870. 2. Education — Philosophy I. T.
PR4592.E4 C62　　*LC* 63-23870

Stone, Harry, 1926-.　　**2.7669**
Dickens and the invisible world: fairy tales, fantasy, and novel–making / Harry Stone. — Bloomington: Indiana University Press, c1979. xi, 370 p.; 24 cm. Includes index. 1. Dickens, Charles, 1812-1870 — Criticism and interpretation. 2. Fairy tales — History and criticism. 3. Fantasy in literature 4. Children's literature — History and criticism. I. T.
PR4592.F35 S7　　823/.8　　*LC* 78-20281　　*ISBN* 0253183669

Adrian, Arthur A., 1906-.　　**2.7670**
Dickens and the parent–child relationship / Arthur A. Adrian. — Athens, Ohio: Ohio University Press, c1984. xii, 169 p.; 24 cm. Includes index. 1. Dickens, Charles, 1812-1870 — Political and social views. 2. Parent and child in literature. 3. Parents in literature. 4. Children in literature 5. Child abuse in literature. 6. Family in literature I. T.
PR4592.P34 A37 1984　　823/.8 19　　*LC* 83-19505　　*ISBN* 082140735X

Pope, Norris, 1945-.　　**2.7671**
Dickens and charity / Norris Pope. — New York: Columbia University Press, 1978. xi, 303 p., [8] leaves of plates: ill.; 23 cm. 1. Dickens, Charles, 1812-1870 — Religion. 2. Dickens, Charles, 1812-1870 — Political and social views. 3. Evangelicalism — England. 4. Great Britain — Social conditions — 19th century I. T.
PR4592.R4 P65 1978　　823/.8　　*LC* 78-3867　　*ISBN* 023104478X

Stewart, Garrett.　　**2.7672**
Dickens and the trials of imagination / Garrett Stewart. — Cambridge: Harvard University Press, 1974. xxiii, 260 p.; 25 cm. 1. Dickens, Charles, 1812-1870 — Style. I. T.
PR4594.S8　　823/.8　　*LC* 74-77086　　*ISBN* 0674204409

PR4611–4612 Dodgson (Lewis Carroll)

Carroll, Lewis, 1832-1898.　　**2.7673**
[Selections. 1982] The complete illustrated works of Lewis Carroll / edited by Edward Guiliano; illustrated by John Tenniel ... [et al.]. — New York: Avenel Books: Distributed by Crown Publishers, 1982. xxii, 868 p.: ill.; 24 cm. I. Guiliano, Edward. II. Tenniel, John, Sir, 1820-1914. III. T.
PR4611.A4 1982　　828/.809 19　　*LC* 82-13878　　*ISBN* 051738566X

Phillips, Robert S. comp.　　**2.7674**
Aspects of Alice; Lewis Carroll's dreamchild as seen through the critics' looking-glasses, 1865–1971. Edited by Robert Phillips. Illus. by Sir John Tenniel and Lewis Carroll. New York, Vanguard Press [1971] xxvii, 450 p. illus. 25 cm. 1. Carroll, Lewis, 1832-1898. Alice's adventures in Wonderland. 2. Carroll, Lewis, 1832-1898. Through the looking-glass I. T.
PR4611.A73P5　　823/.8　　*LC* 70-178822　　*ISBN* 0814907008

Carroll, Lewis, 1832-1898.　　● **2.7675**
[Alice's adventures in Wonderland.] The annotated Alice: Alice's adventures in Wonderland & Through the looking glass, by Lewis Carroll [pseud.] Illustrated by John Tenniel. With an introd. and notes by Martin Gardner. [1st ed.] New York, C. N. Potter [1960] 351 p. illus. 28 cm. I. Gardner, Martin, 1914- ed. II. T. III. Title: Alice's adventures in Wonderland. IV. Title: Through the looking glass.
PR4611.Ax　　*LC* 60-7341

Carroll, Lewis, 1832-1898.　　**2.7676**
Alice's adventures in Wonderland; and, Through the looking–glass and what Alice found there [by] Lewis Carroll; with illustrations by John Tenniel; edited with an introduction by Roger Lancelyn Green. London, New York, Oxford University Press, 1971. xxxiii, 277 p. illus. 21 cm. (Oxford English novels) I. Green, Roger Lancelyn. ed. II. T. III. Title: Through the looking-glass.
PR4611.Ax　　823/.8　　*LC* 70-881320　　*ISBN* 0192553410

Carroll, Lewis, 1832-1898.　　● **2.7677**
The annotated Snark: the full text of Lewis Carroll's great nonsense epic, The hunting of the snark, and the original illustrations by Henry Holiday. With an introd. and notes by Martin Gardner. — New York: Simon and Schuster, 1962. –. 111 p.: ill.; 26 cm. — I. Gardner, Martin, 1914- II. T. III. Title: The hunting of the snark.
PR4611.H8 1962　　821.8　　*LC* 61-16553

Hudson, Derek.　　**2.7678**
Lewis Carroll: an illustrated biography / by Derek Hudson. — 1st American ed. — New York: C. N. Potter: distributed by Crown Publishers, 1977. 272 p.: ill.; 27 cm. Includes index. 1. Carroll, Lewis, 1832-1898 — Biography. 2. Authors, English — 19th century — Biography. I. T.
PR4612.H8 1977　　828/.8/09 B　　*LC* 77-1482　　*ISBN* 0517530783

PR4613–4638 Dowson. Doyle. Du Maurier

Dowson, Ernest Christopher, 1867-1900. 2.7679
[Poetical works of Ernest Christopher Dowson] The poetry of Ernest Dowson. Edited, with an introd., by Desmond Flower. [1st American ed.] Rutherford [N.J.] Fairleigh Dickinson University Press 1967. 295 p. 22 cm. First published in England in 1934 under title: The poetical works of Ernest Christopher Dowson. I. Flower, Desmond, 1907- ed. II. T.
PR4613.D5 A17 1967 821/.8 LC 75-88560 ISBN 0838675514

Doyle, Arthur Conan, Sir, 1859-1930. 2.7680
The annotated Sherlock Holmes; the four novels and the fifty–six short stories complete. Edited, with an introd., notes, and bibliography by William S. Baring–Gould. Illustrated ... by Charles Doyle [and others. 1st ed.] New York, C. N. Potter; Distributed by Crown Publishers [1967] 2 v. ill., coat of arms, facsims., maps, ports. 29 cm. 1. Holmes, Sherlock (Fictitious character) — Fiction. 2. Detective and mystery stories, English I. Baring-Gould, William Stuart, 1913- ed. II. T.
PR4620.A5 B3 1967 823/.8 19 LC 67-22406

Doyle, Arthur Conan, Sir, 1859-1930. • 2.7681
The complete Sherlock Holmes; with a pref. by Christopher Morley. New York, Doubleday, [195-?]. 2 v. (xvii, 1323 p.); 22 cm. I. T.
PR4621.C6x Fic LC 53-1290

Doyle, Arthur Conan, Sir, 1859-1930. 2.7682
The complete Professor Challenger stories / Arthur Conan Doyle. London: J. Murray, 1976. vi, 577 p.; 19 cm. First published in 1952. I. T.
PZ3.D772 Cnp10 PR4622 Cx 823/.9/12 LC 77-351884 ISBN 0719503604

Hardwick, Michael, 1924-. • 2.7683
The Sherlock Holmes companion / Michael and Mollie Hardwick; ill. by Sidney Paget. — Garden City, N.Y.: Doubleday, [1963, c1962] ix, 232 p.: ill.; 21 cm. 1. Doyle, Arthur Conan, Sir, 1859-1930 — Dictionaries, indexes, etc. I. Hardwick, Mollie. joint author II. T.
PR4623.A3H3 823.8 LC 62-52932

Du Maurier, George, 1834-1896. • 2.7684
Trilby [by] George Du Maurier. — London, J. M. Dent & sons, ltd.; New York, E. P. Dutton & co., inc. [1931] xii, 362 p.: ill.; 18 cm. (Half-title: Everyman's library, ed. by Ernest Rhys. Fiction. [no. 863]) Bibliography: p. viii. I. T.
AC1.E8 no. 863 PR4634.T7x. LC 37-5591

PR4640–4648 Edgeworth

Edgeworth, Maria, 1767-1849. • 2.7685
Tales and novels. — New York: Harper, 1835-1836. 20 v. in 10.: ill.; 20 cm. Added t.-p. engr.: Novels and tales. New York, Harper, 1832-34. At head of title: Harper's stereotype ed. I. T. II. Title: Harper's stereotype ed.
PR4640.E32a

Edgeworth, Maria, 1767-1849. • 2.7686
Castle Rackrent / edited with an introduction by George Watson. — London: Oxford University Press, 1964. xxxv, 130 p.; 21 cm. — (Oxford English novels.) I. Watson, George, 1927- II. T. III. Series.
PR4644.C3 1964 LC 64-56170

Butler, Marilyn. 2.7687
Maria Edgeworth: a literary biography. — Oxford: Clarendon Press, 1972. x, 531, [7] p.: illus., facsim., ports.; 23 cm. 1. Edgeworth, Maria, 1767-1849. I. T.
PR4646.B85 823/.7 LC 72-190759

Newby, P. H. (Percy Howard), 1918-. • 2.7688
Maria Edgeworth, by P.H. Newby. Denver, A. Swallow [1950] 98 p. 19 cm. (The English novelists. Denver) 1. Edgeworth, Maria, 1767-1849. I. T.
PR4646.N4 823/.7 LC 50-8858 ISBN 0841423644

Harden, O. Elizabeth McWhorter (Oleta Elizabeth McWhorter), 1935-. 2.7689
Maria Edgeworth / by Elizabeth Harden. — Boston: Twayne Publishers, c1984. 149 p.; 23 cm. (Twayne's English authors series. TEAS 375) Includes index. 1. Edgeworth, Maria, 1767-1849 — Criticism and interpretation. I. T. II. Series.
PR4647.H26 1984 823/.7 19 LC 84-8571 ISBN 0805768793

PR4650–4698 Eliot

Eliot, George, 1819-1880. • 2.7690
[Works. 1970] The writings of George Eliot. New York, AMS Press [1970] 25 v. illus., facsims., ports. 23 cm. Reprint of the 1907-08 ed. I. T.
PR4650.F70 823/.8 LC 74-114748 ISBN 0404022804

Eliot, George, 1819-1880. 2.7691
A writer's notebook, 1854–1879, and uncollected writings / George Eliot; edited by Joseph Wiesenfarth. — Charlottesville: Published for the Bibliographical Society of the University of Virginia by the University Press of Virginia, 1981. xli, 301 p., [8] leaves of plates: ill.; 29 cm. I. Wiesenfarth, Joseph. II. T.
PR4653.W53 1981 823/.8 19 LC 80-23271 ISBN 0813908876

Eliot, George, 1819-1880. • 2.7692
Essays. Edited by Thomas Pinney. — New York, Columbia University Press [1963] xii, 476 p. 23 cm. Includes a list of the author's essays, reviews, and attributions. 1. Literature — Addresses, essays, lectures. I. Pinney, Thomas. ed. II. T.
PR4659.E7 1963a 828.8 LC 63-20344

Eliot, George, 1819-1880. • 2.7693
Middlemarch: an authoritative text, backgrounds, reviews and criticism / George Eliot; edited by Bert G. Hornback. — 1st ed. — New York: Norton, c1977. xiv, 770 p.; 22 cm. — (A Norton critical edition) I. Hornback, Bert G., 1935- II. T.
PZ3.E43 Mi30 PR4662.A1 823/.8 LC 76-22805 ISBN 0393044300. ISBN 0393092100 pbk

Beaty, Jerome, 1924-. • 2.7694
Middlemarch from notebook to novel; a study of George Eliot's creative method. — Urbana, University of Illinois Press, 1960. ix, 134 p. facsims. 26 cm. — (Illinois studies in language and literature. v. 47) 1. Eliot, George, 1819-1880. Middlemarch. I. T. II. Series.
PR4662.B4 823.8 LC 59-10550

Hardy, Barbara Nathan. • 2.7695
Middlemarch: critical approaches to the novel [by] Mark Schorer [and others], edited by Barbara Hardy. — London, Athlone P., 1967. [7], 192 p. 22 1/2 cm. Bibliography included in 'Notes' (p. 184-190) 1. Eliot, George, 1819-1880. Middlemarch. I. Schorer, Mark, 1908- II. T.
PR4662.H3 1967b 823/.8 LC 67-112527

McSweeney, Kerry, 1941-. 2.7696
Middlemarch / Kerry McSweeney. — London; Boston: G. Allen & Unwin, 1984. 167 p.; 22 cm. — (Unwin critical library.) Includes index. 1. Eliot, George, 1819-1880. Middlemarch. I. T. II. Series.
PR4662.M39 1984 823/.8 19 LC 84-2982 ISBN 0048000310

Mintz, Alan L. 2.7697
George Eliot & the novel of vocation / Alan Mintz. — Cambridge, Mass.: Harvard University Press, 1978. xi, 193 p.; 24 cm. 1. Eliot, George, 1819-1880. Middlemarch. 2. Vocation in literature. I. T.
PR4662.M5 823/.8 LC 77-15510 ISBN 0674348737

PR4679–4698 Biography. Criticism

Eliot, George, 1819-1880. 2.7698
[Letters] The George Eliot letters, edited by Gordon S. Haight. New Haven, Yale University Press, 1954-78. 9 v. 25 cm. 1. Eliot, George, 1819-1880 — Correspondence. 2. Novelists, English — 19th century — Correspondence. I. Haight, Gordon Sherman. ed. II. T.
PR4681.A4 1954 823/.8 B LC 52-12063

Eliot, George, 1819-1880. 2.7699
[Correspondence. Selections] Selections from George Eliot's letters / edited by Gordon S. Haight. — New Haven [Conn.]: Yale University Press, c1985. x, 567 p.: port; 25 cm. This is a condensation of The George Eliot letters originally published in nine volume, 1954-78. Includes index. 1. Eliot, George, 1819-1880 — Correspondence. 2. Novelists, English — 19th century — Correspondence. I. Haight, Gordon Sherman. II. T.
PR4681.A4 1985 823/.8 19 LC 84-13222 ISBN 0300033265

Bennett, Joan (Frankau). • 2.7700
George Eliot, her mind and her art. — Cambridge [Eng.] University Press, 1948. xv, 202 p. 21 cm. 'List of the books referred to in the text': p. 197-198. 1. Eliot, George, 1819-1880. I. T.
PR4681.B4 823.88 LC 49-1008 *

George Eliot, a centenary tribute / edited by Gordon S. Haight and Rosemary T. VanArsdel. 2.7701
Totowa, N.J.: Barnes & Noble, 1982. x, 174 p.; 22 cm. Selected papers from the George Eliot Centennial Conference, held at the University of Puget Sound, Apr. 10-12, 1980. 1. Eliot, George, 1819-1880 — Criticism and interpretation — Congresses. I. Haight, Gordon Sherman. II. VanArsdel, Rosemary T. III. George Eliot Centennial Conference (1980: University of Puget Sound)
PR4681.G46 1982 823/.8 19 LC 81-19088 ISBN 0389202525

Haight, Gordon Sherman.   • 2.7702
George Eliot; a biography [by] Gordon S. Haight. New York, Oxford University Press [1968] xvi, 616 p. ports. 22 cm. 1. Eliot, George, 1819-1880 — Biography. I. T.
PR4681.H27   823/.8 B   *LC* 68-9440

Knoepflmacher, U. C.   • 2.7703
George Eliot's early novels; the limits of realism [by] U. C. Knoepflmacher. Berkeley, University of California Press, 1968. xi, 269 p. 23 cm. 1. Eliot, George, 1819-1880. I. T.
PR4681.K6   823/.8   *LC* 68-23005

Laski, Marghanita, 1915-.   2.7704
George Eliot and her world. New Jersey: Transatlantic Arts, 1973. 119 p. illus., facsims., geneal. table, maps, ports. 24 cm. 1. Eliot, George, 1819-1880 — Biography. I. T.
PR4681.L3   823/.8 B   *ISBN* 0500130434

Haight, Gordon Sherman.   • 2.7705
George Eliot & John Chapman, with Chapman's Diaries, by Gordon S. Haight. 2d ed. [Hamden, Conn.] Archon Books, 1969. xi, 285 p. port. 23 cm. 1. Eliot, George, 1819-1880. 2. Chapman, John, 1822-1894. I. Chapman, John, 1822-1894. II. T.
PR4683.H3 1969   823/.8   *LC* 69-10924   *ISBN* 020800503X

Carroll, David. comp.   2.7706
George Eliot: the critical heritage. London, Routledge & K. Paul, 1971. xv, 511 p. 23 cm. (The Critical heritage series) 1. Eliot, George, 1819-1880 — Addresses, essays, lectures. I. T.
PR4688.C3 1971   823/.8   *LC* 77-574450   *ISBN* 0710069367

Hardy, Barbara Nathan.   • 2.7707
The novels of George Eliot; a study in form. [London] University of London, Athlone Press; [label: Fair Lawn, N.J., Essential Books] 1959. 242 p. 23 cm. 1. Eliot, George, 1819-1880. I. T.
PR4688.H27   823.8   *LC* 59-2660

Harvey, W. J. (William John), 1925-1967.   • 2.7708
The art of George Eliot. — New York, Oxford University Press, 1962 [c1961] 254 p. 23 cm. 1. Eliot, George, pseud., i. e. Marian Evans, afterwards Cross, 1819-1880. I. T.
PR4688.H28   823.8   *LC* 62-16015

Roberts, Neil.   2.7709
George Eliot: her beliefs and her art / Neil Roberts. — [Pittsburgh]: University of Pittsburgh Press, 1975. 240 p.; 23 cm. Includes index. 1. Eliot, George, 1819-1880 — Criticism and interpretation. I. T.
PR4688.R6 1975   823/.8   *LC* 75-956   *ISBN* 0822911213

Thale, Jerome.   • 2.7710
The novels of George Eliot. New York, Columbia University Press, 1959. 175 p. 22 cm. 1. Eliot, George, 1819-1880. I. T.
PR4688.T5   823.8   *LC* 59-8377

Doyle, Mary Ellen, 1932-.   2.7711
The sympathetic response: George Eliot's fictional rhetoric / Mary Ellen Doyle. — Rutherford: Fairleigh Dickinson University Press; London: Associated University Presses, c1981. 183 p.; 22 cm. Includes index. 1. Eliot, George, 1819-1880 — Technique. I. T.
PR4691.D6   823/.8 19   *LC* 80-65908   *ISBN* 0838630650

Witemeyer, Hugh.   2.7712
George Eliot and the visual arts / Hugh Witemeyer. — New Haven: Yale University Press, 1979. xiii, 238 p., [17] leaves of plates: ill.; 22 cm. 1. Eliot, George, 1819-1880 — Knowledge — Art. 2. Art in literature I. T.
PR4692.A66 W5   823/.8   *LC* 78-15580   *ISBN* 0300022816

Graver, Suzanne.   2.7713
George Eliot and community: a study in social theory and fictional form / Suzanne Graver. — Berkeley: University of California Press, c1984. xi, 340 p.; 24 cm. Includes index. 1. Eliot, George, 1819-1880 — Political and social views. 2. Eliot, George, 1819-1880 — Criticism and interpretation. 3. Social values in literature. 4. Community in literature. 5. Social history — 19th century I. T.
PR4692.S58 G7 1984   823/.8 19   *LC* 82-13548   *ISBN* 0520048024

Mudge, Isadore Gilbert, 1875-1957.   • 2.7714
A George Eliot dictionary; the characters and scenes of the novels, stories, and poems alphabetically arranged, by Isadore G. Mudge and M. E. Sears. — New York: Haskell House Publishers, 1972. xlvii, 260 p.; 23 cm. 1. Eliot, George, 1819-1880 — Dictionaries, indexes, etc. I. Sears, Minnie Earl, 1873-1933. joint author. II. T.
PR4695.M8 1972   823/.8   *LC* 72-762   *ISBN* 0838313507

PR4699–4708 Ferguson. Galt

Brown, Malcolm Johnston, 1910-.   2.7715
Sir Samuel Ferguson [by] Malcolm Brown. — Lewisburg [Pa.]: Bucknell University Press, [c1973] 101 p.; 21 cm. — (The Irish writers series) 1. Ferguson, Samuel, Sir, 1810-1886. I. T.
PR4699.F2 Z57   821/.8   *LC* 72-3599   *ISBN* 0838710832

Galt, John, 1779-1839.   2.7716
The last of the lairds: or, The life and opinions of Malachi Mailings Esq., of Auldbiggings / [by] John Galt; edited from the original manuscript by Ian A. Gordon. Edinburgh: Scottish Academic Press; London: Distributed by Chatto and Windus, 1976. xx, 170 p.; 23 cm. I. T. II. Title: The life and opinions of Malachi Mailings Esq., of Auldbiggings.
PZ3.G14 Las14 PR4708.G2   823/.7   *LC* 77-352255   *ISBN* 0701121750

Galt, John, 1779-1839.   • 2.7717
Annals of the parish, or, The chronicle of Dalmailing during the ministry of the Rev. Micah Balwhidder, written by himself / John Galt; edited with an introd. by James Kinsley. — London; New York: Oxford University Press, 1967. xxvi, 242 p.; 21 cm. — (Oxford English novels.) I. Kinsley, James. II. T. III. Title: The chronicle of Dalmailing. IV. Series.
PR4708.G2 A8 1967   *LC* 67-107172

Scott, P. H. (Paul Henderson), 1920-.   2.7718
John Galt / P.H. Scott. — Edinburgh: Scottish Academic Press, 1985. 130 p.; 18 cm. (Scottish writers; 5) 1. Galt, John, 1779-1839 — Criticism and interpretation. 2. Scotland in literature. I. T.
PR4708.G2 Z87 1985   823/.7 19   *LC* 85-167934   *ISBN* 0707303648

PR4710–4714 Gaskell. Gilbert

Gaskell, Elizabeth Cleghorn, 1810-1865.   2.7719
The novels and tales of Mrs. Gaskell / edited by Clement Shorter. — Oxford: Oxford University Press, 1906-1919. 11 v. I. Shorter, Clement K. II. T.
PR4710.AA2S5x

Gaskell, Elizabeth Cleghorn, 1810-1865.   • 2.7720
Cranford; The cage at Cranford; The moorland cottage. — London: Oxford Univ. Press, 1934. 411 p.; 16 cm. — (The world's classics; 110.) Three stories in one volume. I. T.
PR4710.C7x

Gaskell, Elizabeth Cleghorn, 1810-1865.   2.7721
Mary Barton: a tale of Manchester life, by Elizabeth Gaskell; edited with an introduction by Stephen Gill. Harmondsworth, Penguin, 1970. [1], 487 p. ports. 19 cm. (Penguin English library) I. T.
PZ3.G212 M48 PR4710.M3x   823/.8   *LC* 76-18825   *ISBN* 0140430539

Gaskell, Elizabeth Cleghorn, 1810-1865.   2.7722
North and South; edited by Dorothy Collin, with an introduction by Martin Dodsworth. Harmondsworth, Penguin, 1970. [1], 540 p. port. 19 cm. (Penguin English library) I. T.
PZ3.G212 N10 PR4710.N6x   823/.8   *LC* 74-19240   *ISBN* 0140430555

Gaskell, Elizabeth Cleghorn, 1810-1865.   • 2.7723
Wives and daughters [by] Elizabeth Gaskell; edited by Frank Glover Smith, with an introduction by Laurence Lerner. Harmondsworth, Penguin, 1969. [1], 713 p. facsim., port. 18 cm. (The Penguin English library) I. T.
PZ3.G212 W45 PR4710.W5x   823/.8   *LC* 75-468638   *ISBN* 0140430466

Chapple, J. A. V. (John Alfred Victor), 1928-.   2.7724
Elizabeth Gaskell: a portrait in letters / J.A.V. Chapple assisted by John Geoffrey Sharps. — Manchester: Manchester University Press, c1980. xviii, 172 p., [8] p. of plates: ill., facsims., ports.; 24 cm. 1. Novelists, English — 19th century — Correspondence. I. Sharps, John Geoffrey. II. Gaskell, Elizabeth Cleghorn, 1810-1865. III. T.
PR4711.A3   823/.8 18   823/.8 19   *ISBN* 0719007992

Gérin, Winifred.   2.7725
Elizabeth Gaskell: a biography / Winifred Gérin. — Oxford: Clarendon Press, 1976. xiv, 318 p., [9] leaves of plates: ill.; 22 cm. Includes index. 1. Gaskell, Elizabeth Cleghorn, 1810-1865 — Biography. 2. Novelists, English — 19th century — Biography. I. T.
PR4711.G4   823/.8 B   *LC* 76-375703   *ISBN* 0198120702

Lansbury, Coral.   2.7726
Elizabeth Gaskell / by Coral Lansbury. — Boston: Twayne Publishers, c1984. 130 p.: port.; 23 cm. — (Twayne's English authors series. TEAS 371) Includes

index. 1. Gaskell, Elizabeth Cleghorn, 1810-1865 — Criticism and interpretation. I. T. II. Series.
PR4711.L29 1984   823/.8 19   *LC* 84-3780   *ISBN* 0805768572

Gilbert, W. S. (William Schwenck), 1836-1911.   2.7727
[Selections. 1982] Plays by W.S. Gilbert: The palace of truth, Sweethearts, Princess Toto, Engaged, Rosencrantz and Guildenstern / edited with an introduction and notes by George Rowell. — Cambridge; New York: Cambridge University Press, 1982. ix, 189 p.: ill., ports.; 24 cm. — (British and American playwrights, 1750-1920.) I. Rowell, George. II. T. III. Series.
PR4713.A4 1982   822/.8 19   *LC* 81-12248   *ISBN* 0521235898

Gilbert, W. S. (William Schwenck), 1836-1911.   • 2.7728
The Bab ballads. Edited by James Ellis. Cambridge, Mass., Belknap Press of Harvard University Press, 1970. ix, 366 p. 360 illus. 25 cm. I. T.
PR4713.B3 1970   821/.8   *LC* 77-102668   *ISBN* 0674058003

Pearson, Hesketh, 1887-1964.   • 2.7729
Gilbert, his life and strife. — New York: Harper, [1957] 276 p.: ill.; 22 cm. 1. Gilbert, W. S. (William Schwenck), 1836-1911 — Biography. I. T.
PR4714.P4   *LC* 58-67

PR4716–4717 Gissing

Gissing, George, 1857-1903.   2.7730
Born in exile / George Gissing; edited and with an introd. and notes by Pierre Coustillas. — Hassocks [Eng.]: Harvester Press, 1978. xxi, 521 p.; 20 cm. I. Coustillas, Pierre. II. T.
PZ3.G45 Bo 1978 PR4716.B6x   823/.8   *LC* 79-313660   *ISBN* 0855278722

Gissing, George, 1857-1903.   2.7731
Demos; a story of English socialism. Edited with an introd. by Pierre Coustillas. [Brighton, Eng.] Harvester Press, 1972. xxvii, 477, xxix-xliv p. 19 cm. (Society & the Victorians, no. 10) First published in 1886; reprint of the 1897 ed. I. T. II. Series.
PZ3.G45 D7 PR4716.D4x   823/.8   *LC* 70-183643   *ISBN* 0901759201 *ISBN* 0901759333

Gissing, George, 1857-1903.   2.7732
The emancipated / George Gissing; edited and with a new introd. by Pierre Coustillas. — 1st ed. reprinted. — Hassocks [Eng.]: Harvester Press, 1977. xix, 469 p.; 19 cm. — (Society and the Victorians; 32) Reprint of the 1890 ed. published by R. Bentley, London. I. Coustillas, Pierre. II. T. III. Series.
PZ3.G45 Em 1977 PR4716.E6x   823/.8   *LC* 78-311704   *ISBN* 0855277394

Gissing, George, 1857-1903.   2.7733
In the year of jubilee / George Gissing; with a new introd. by Gillian Tindall; and textual notes by P. F. Kropholler. — Hassocks, Eng.: Harvester Press, 1976. xx, 457 p.; 20 cm. — (Society and the Victorians; no. 27) Reprint of the 1895 ed. published by Lawrence & Bullen, London. Includes original t.p. I. T. II. Series.
PZ3.G45 In10 PR4716.I6x   823/.8   *LC* 77-354710   *ISBN* 0855270640

Gissing, George, 1857-1903.   2.7734
New Grub Street / George Gissing. — 1st Modern Library ed. — New York: Modern Library, 1985. 425 p.; 21 cm. Reprint. Originally published: New York: Houghton Mifflin, 1962. I. T.
PR4716.N48 1985   823/.8 19   *LC* 84-25542   *ISBN* 039460525X

Gissing, George, 1857-1903.   2.7735
The nether world: a novel / [by] George Gissing. — [New ed. reprinted] edited with an introduction by John Goode. Brighton: Harvester Press, 1974. xviii, iii-viii, 392 p.; 20 cm. (Society and the Victorians, no. 20) Reprint of the 1890 ed. published by Smith, Elder, & Co., London. I. T. II. Series.
PZ3.G45 N7 PR4716.N4x   823/.8   *LC* 74-168620   *ISBN* 0901759104 *ISBN* 0901759740

Gissing, George, 1857-1903.   2.7736
The odd women / George Gissing; introduction by Margaret Walters. — London: Virago, 1980. 336 p.; 20 cm. (Virago modern classics) I. T.
PR4716.O3x 1980   *LC* 85-673379   *ISBN* 0860681408

Gissing, George, 1857-1903.   2.7737
The private papers of Henry Ryecroft / George Gissing; introduction by John Stewart Collis; with bibliographical notes by Pierre Coustillas. — Brighton, Sussex, England: Harvester Press, 1982. xxxi, xiv, 298, 6 p.; 19 cm. Reprint. Originally published: Westminister [London, England]: A. Constable, 1903. With new introd. and bibliographical notes. I. T.
PR4716.P7 1982   823/.8 19   *LC* 83-195367   *ISBN* 0710803966

Gissing, George, 1857-1903.   2.7738
The unclassed / George Gissing; edited with an introd. by Jacob Korg. — Rev. ed. — Hassocks, Eng.: Harvester Press, 1976. xxiii, viii, 322 p.; 19 cm. — (Society and the Victorians; no. 26) Reprint of the 1895 ed. published by Lawrence and Bullen, London. I. T. II. Series.
PZ3.G45 Un10 PR4716.U6x   823/.8   *LC* 77-362950   *ISBN* 0855270543

Gissing, George, 1857-1903.   2.7739
The whirlpool / George Gissing; edited and with a new introd. and notes by Patrick Parrinder. — Hassocks [Eng.]: Harvester Press, c1977. xxii, 467 p.; 19 cm. Reprint of the 1897 ed. published by Lawrence and Bullen, London. I. Parrinder, Patrick. II. T.
PZ3.G45 Wh 1977 PR4716.W5x   823/.8   *LC* 77-80329   *ISBN* 0855277890

Gissing, George, 1857-1903.   2.7740
Workers in the dawn / George Gissing; edited with an introduction by Pierre Coustillas. — Brighton, Sussex: Harvester Press, 1985. cii, 436 p.; 20 cm. I. Coustillas, Pierre. II. T.
PR4716.W67 1985   823/.8   *ISBN* 0710805284

Gissing, George, 1857-1903.   • 2.7741
Letters of George Gissing to members of his family. Collected and arr. by Algernon and Ellen Gissing. With a pref. by his son. New York, Haskell House, 1970. vii, 414 p. facsim., port. 23 cm. I. Gissing, Algernon, 1860-1937, ed. II. Gissing, Ellen, 1867- ed. III. T.
PR4717.A3 1970   823/.8 B   *LC* 77-130257   *ISBN* 083831158X

Gissing, George, 1857-1903.   • 2.7742
Letters of George Gissing to Eduard Bertiz, 1887–1903. Edited by Arthur C.Young. New Brunswick,N.J.: Rutgers U.P. 1961. 337 p.; 22 cm. 1. Bertz, Eduard, 1853-1931. I. Young, Arthur C. ed. II. T.
PR4717.A33   928.2   *LC* 60-14209

Collie, Michael.   2.7743
George Gissing: a biography / Michael Collie. — Folkestone, Eng.: Dawson; Hamden, Conn.: Archon Books, 1977. 189 p.; 23 cm. Includes index. 1. Gissing, George, 1857-1903. 2. Novelists, English — 19th century — Biography. I. T.
PR4717.C58   823/.8 B   *LC* 78-309185   *ISBN* 071290770X

Coustillas, Pierre. comp.   2.7744
Gissing, the critical heritage; edited by Pierre Coustillas and Colin Partridge. London, Boston, Routledge and Kegan Paul, 1972. xvii, 563 p. 23 cm. (The Critical heritage series) 1. Gissing, George, 1857-1903. I. Partridge, C. J. joint comp. II. T.
PR4717.C645   823/.8   *LC* 72-81444   *ISBN* 0710073674

Goode, John Allen.   2.7745
George Gissing, ideology and fiction / John Goode. — New York: Barnes & Noble, 1979, c1978. 205 p.; 22 cm. — (Barnes & Noble critical studies) 1. Gissing, George, 1857-1903 — Criticism and interpretation. I. T.
PR4717.G66 1979   823/.8   *LC* 79-107803   *ISBN* 0064924882

Korg, Jacob, 1922-.   • 2.7746
George Gissing, a critical biography. — Seattle: University of Washington Press, 1963. 311 p.: ill.; 24 cm. 1. Gissing, George, 1857-1903 — Biography. I. T.
PR4717.K6   *LC* 63-9938

PR4720–4727 Godwin. Gosse. Grahame

Godwin, William, 1756-1836.   2.7747
[Things as they are] Caleb Williams / edited with an introduction by David McCracken. — London; New York: Oxford U.P., 1970. xxxi, 351 p. facsim. 21 cm. (Oxford English novels) First ed., London, 1794 has title: Things as they are; or, The adventures of Caleb Williams. I. McCracken, David. ed. II. T.
PZ3.G548 Cal 20 PR4722.T4x   823/.6   *LC* 76-478320   *ISBN* 0192553313

Gosse, Edmund, 1849-1928.   • 2.7748
Father and son: a study of two temperaments; with introduction and notes by Cecil Ballantine. London, Heinemann Educational, 1970. xxix, 224 p. 19 cm. 1. Gosse, Edmund, 1849-1928 — Biography — Youth. 2. Gosse, Philip Henry, 1810-1888. I. Ballantine, Cecil. II. T.
PR4725.G7 Z52 1970   828/.809 B   *LC* 72-495631   *ISBN* 0435133500

Thwaite, Ann.   2.7749
Edmund Gosse: a literary landscape, 1849–1928 / Ann Thwaite. — Chicago: University of Chicago Press, 1984. vii, 567 p., [32] p. of plates: ill.; 25 cm.

Includes index. 1. Gosse, Edmund, 1849-1928 — Biography. 2. Authors, English — 19th century — Biography. I. T.
PR4725.G7 Z84 1984   828/.809 19   *LC* 83-18076   *ISBN* 0226801365

Grahame, Kenneth, 1859-1932.   • 2.7750
The wind in the willows / by Kenneth Grahame; illustrations by Arthur Rackham; introduction by A.A. Milne. — New York: Heritage Press [1959, c1940] xiv, 190 p. [12] leaves of plates: ill. (some col.); 25 cm. — (The Heritage illustrated bookshelf) I. Rackham, Arthur, 1867-1939. II. T. III. Series.
PR4726.W5x   823

Green, Peter, 1924-.   • 2.7751
Kenneth Grahame, a biography. [1st ed.] Cleveland, World Pub. Co. [1959] xvi, 400 p. illus. 23 cm. 1. Grahame, Kenneth, 1859-1932. I. T.
PR4727.G7   928.2   *LC* 59-7751

PR4728.G5 Gregory

Gregory, Lady, 1852-1932.   • 2.7752
Selected plays / Lady Gregory; chosen and introduced by Elizabeth Coxhead; foreword by Sean O'Casey. — [1st American ed.] New York: Hill and Wang [1963] 269 p.; 23 cm. I. Coxhead, Elizabeth, 1909- II. T.
PR4728.G5A6 1963   822   *LC* 63-11055

Gregory, Lady, 1852-1932.   • 2.7753
Irish folk–history plays. New York, Putnam, 1912. St. Clair Shores, Mich., Scholarly Press, 1971. 2 v. 22 cm. I. T.
PR4728.G5 I7 1971   822/.9/12   *LC* 70-145063   *ISBN* 0403010063

Gregory, Lady, 1852-1932.   • 2.7754
Lady Gregory's Journals, 1916–1930 / edited by Lennox Robinson. — [London]: Putnam, 1946. 343 p.; 22 cm. I. Robinson, Lennox, 1886-1958. II. T.
PR4728 G5Z53 1946

Gregory, Lady, 1852-1932.   2.7755
Seventy years: being the autobiography of Lady Gregory / edited and with a foreword by Colin Smythe. — 1st American ed. — New York: Macmillan, 1976, c1974. xiv, 583 p., [8] leaves of plates: ill.; 22 cm. Includes index. 1. Gregory, Lady, 1852-1932 — Biography. I. T.
PR4728.G5 Z534 1976   822/.9/12 B   *LC* 75-23329   *ISBN* 0025455508

Coxhead, Elizabeth, 1909-.   • 2.7756
Lady Gregory, a literary portrait. [1st ed.] New York, Harcourt, Brace & World [1961] 241 p. illus. 23 cm. 1. Gregory, Lady, 1852-1932. I. T.
PR4728.G5Z55 1961a   *LC* 61-13965

Kohfeldt, Mary Lou.   2.7757
Lady Gregory: the woman behind the Irish renaissance / Mary Lou Kohfeldt. — 1st ed. — New York: Atheneum, 1985. xiii, 366 p., [8] p. of plates: ill., ports.; 24 cm. Includes index. 1. Gregory, Lady, 1852-1932 — Biography. 2. Authors, Irish — 20th century — Biography. I. T.
PR4728.G5 Z625 1985   822/.914 B 19   *LC* 84-45044   *ISBN* 0689114869

PR4731–4735 Haggard. Hallam

Haggard, H. Rider (Henry Rider), Sir, 1856-1925.   2.7758
Three adventure novels of H. Rider Haggard. — New York: Dover Publications, 1951. 636 p. I. T.
PR4731.A1 1951   *LC* 60-20211   *ISBN* 0486206432

Hallam, Arthur Henry, 1811-1833.   2.7759
The letters of Arthur Henry Hallam / edited by Jack Kolb. — Columbus: Ohio State University Press, c1981. xix, 841 p.: facsim.; 24 cm. Includes index. 1. Hallam, Arthur Henry, 1811-1833 — Correspondence. 2. Tennyson family 3. Authors, English — 19th century — Correspondence. I. Kolb, Jack, 1946- II. T.
PR4735.H4 Z53 1981   824/.7 B   *LC* 79-13490   *ISBN* 0814203000

PR4739–4758 Hardy

Gittings, Robert.   2.7760
The second Mrs. Hardy / by Robert Gittings and Jo Manton. — London: Heinemann; Seattle: University of Washington Press, 1979. x, 150 p.: ill.; 24 cm. 1. Hardy, Florence Emily, 1881-1937 — Biography. 2. Hardy, Thomas, 1840-1928 — Biography — Marriage. 3. Authors, English — 20th century — Biography. 4. Wives — England — Biography. I. Manton, Jo, 1919- joint author. II. T.
PR4739.H774 Z67   823/.8 B   *LC* 79-63567   *ISBN* 0435183664

Hardy, Thomas, 1840-1928.   2.7761
The New Wessex edition. — London: Macmillan; New York: St. Martin's Press, 1977-. v.; 22 cm. I. T.
PR4740.F77

Hardy, Thomas, 1840-1928.   2.7762
The complete poetical works of Thomas Hardy, volume 1: Wessex poems, Poems of the past and the present, Time's laughingstocks / edited by Samuel Hynes. — Oxford [Oxfordshire]: Clarendon Press; New York: Oxford University Press, 1982. 403 p.; 23 cm. I. Hynes, Samuel Lynn. II. T. III. Title: Wessex poems. IV. Title: Poems of the past and the present. V. Title: Time's laughingstocks.
PR4741.H9 1982   821/.8 19   *LC* 81-22456   *ISBN* 0198127081

Hardy, Thomas, 1840-1928.   2.7763
Jude the obscure: an authoritative text, backgrounds and sources, criticism / Thomas Hardy; edited by Norman Page. — 1st ed. — New York: Norton, c1978. xii, 468 p.: map; 22 cm. — (A Norton critical edition) 1. Hardy, Thomas, 1840-1928. Jude the obscure. I. T.
PZ3.H222 Ju 1978 PR4746.J8x   823/.8   *LC* 77-14056   *ISBN* 0393044734

Paterson, John, 1887-.   • 2.7764
The making of The return of the native. — Berkeley: University of California Press, 1960. 168 p.: ill.; 24 cm. (California. University. Publications. English studies; 19) 1. Hardy, Thomas, 1840-1928. Return of the native. I. T. II. Series.
PR4747.P3   *LC* 60-64161

Hardy, Thomas, 1840-1928.   • 2.7765
The dynasts; an epic–drama of the war with Napoleon. With an introd. by John Wain. — London, Macmillan; New York, St. Martin's Press, 1965. xxxvii, 525 p. 18 cm. — (Papermac, P120) 1. Napoleon I, Emperor of the French, 1769-1821 — Drama I. T.
PR4750.D7 1965   822.8   *LC* 66-677

Hardy, Thomas, 1840-1928.   2.7766
The mayor of Casterbridge: an authoritative text, backgrounds criticism / Thomas Hardy; edited by James K. Robinson. — 1st ed. — New York: Norton, c1977. viii, 436 p.: ill.; 22 cm. — (A Norton critical edition) I. Robinson, James K. II. T.
PZ3.H222 M47 PR4750.M3x   823/.8   *LC* 76-57983   *ISBN* 0393044599

Jackson, Arlene M., 1938-.   2.7767
Illustration and the novels of Thomas Hardy / Arlene M. Jackson. — Totowa, N.J.: Rowman and Littlefield, c1981. xiii, 151 p., [32] leaves of plates: ill.; 24 cm. Includes index. 1. Hardy, Thomas, 1840-1928 — Illustrations. 2. Hardy, Thomas, 1840-1928 — Technique. 3. Hardy, Thomas, 1840-1928 — Knowledge — Art. 4. Art and literature 5. Serialized fiction — England — Illustrations. I. T.
PR4751.5.J3   823/.8   *LC* 80-10548   *ISBN* 0847662756

PR4752–4758 Biography. Criticism

Saxelby, F. Outwin.   • 2.7768
A Thomas Hardy dictionary: the characters and scenes of the novels and poems alphabetically arranged and described / by F. Outwin Saxelby. — London: Routledge; New York: Dutton, 1911. lxxviii, 238 p.: maps; 23 cm. 1. Hardy, Thomas, 1840-1928 — Dictionaries, indexes, etc. I. T.
PR4752.A27   *LC* 12-516

Pinion, F. B.   • 2.7769
A Hardy companion: a guide to the works of Thomas Hardy and their background [by] F. B. Pinion. — London; Melbourne [etc.]: Macmillan; New York: St. Martin's P., 1968. xviii, 555 p.: 32 plates, illus., facsims., maps.; 22 cm. Map on lining papers. 1. Hardy, Thomas, 1840-1928 — Dictionaries, indexes, etc. I. T.
PR4752.P5   828/.8/09   *LC* 68-19810

Hardy, Thomas, 1840-1928.   2.7770
The life and work of Thomas Hardy / by Thomas Hardy; edited by Michael Millgate. — Athens: University of Georgia Press, 1985. xxxvii, 604 p., [16] p. of plates: ill.; 23 cm. 'An edition on new principles of the materials previously drawn upon for The early life of Thomas Hardy, 1840-1891, and The later years of Thomas Hardy, 1892-1928, published over the name of Florence Emily Hardy.' Includes index. 1. Hardy, Thomas, 1840-1928. 2. Authors, English — 19th century — Biography. I. Millgate, Michael. II. Hardy, Florence Emily, 1881-1937. Early life of Thomas Hardy, 1840-1891. III. Hardy, Florence Emily, 1881-1937. Later years of Thomas Hardy, 1892-1928 IV. T.
PR4753.A28 1985   823/.8 B 19   *LC* 84-16185

Hardy, Thomas, 1840-1928.   • 2.7771
Notebooks and some letters from Julia Augusta Martin / Thomas Hardy; edited with notes by Evelyn Hardy. — New York: St. Martin's Press [c1955]

135 p.: ill., port.; 21 cm. 1. Martin, Julia Augusta, 1810-1893. 2. Hardy, Thomas, 1840-1928. I. Martin, Julia Augusta, 1810-1893. II. Hardy, Evelyn, 1902- III. T.
PR4753.A3 1955   *LC* 55-12774

Hardy, Thomas, 1840-1928.   2.7772
The collected letters of Thomas Hardy, Vol.1: 1840–1892 / edited by Richard Little Purdy and Michael Millgate. — Oxford: Clarendon Press, 1978. xxii, 293 p., plate: facsim.; 24 cm. 1. Novelists, English — 19th century — Correspondence. I. Purdy, Richard Little. II. Millgate, Michael. III. T.
PR4753.A42 1978   823/.8   *LC* 77-30355   *ISBN* 0198124708

Hardy, Thomas, 1840-1928.   • 2.7773
'Dearest Emmie,' Thomas Hardy's letters to his first wife. Edited by Carl J. Weber. — London, Macmillan; New York, St Martin's Press, 1963. xvi, 111 p. port. 23 cm. I. Hardy, Emma Lavinia Gifford, 1840-1912. II. T.
PR4753.A425 1963   928.2   *LC* 63-14999

Bailey, James Osler, 1903-.   • 2.7774
The poetry of Thomas Hardy: a handbook and commentary, by J. O. Bailey. — Chapel Hill: University of North Carolina Press, [1970] xxviii, 712 p.; 24 cm. 1. Hardy, Thomas, 1840-1928 — Handbooks, manuals, etc. I. T.
PR4753.B27   821/.8   *LC* 77-97015   *ISBN* 0807811351

Gittings, Robert.   2.7775
Thomas Hardy's later years / by Robert Gittings. — 1st American ed. — Boston: Little, Brown, c1978. xv, 244 p., [8] leaves of plates: ill.; 24 cm. 'An Atlantic Monthly Press book.' Includes index. 1. Hardy, Thomas, 1840-1928 — Biography. 2. Authors, English — 20th century — Biography. I. T.
PR4753.G49 1978   823/.8 B   *LC* 77-19236   *ISBN* 0316314544

Gittings, Robert.   2.7776
Young Thomas Hardy / by Robert Gittings. — 1st American ed. — Boston: Little, Brown, 1975. xi, 259 p., [8] leaves of plates: ill.; 24 cm. Sequel: The older Hardy. 'An Atlantic Monthly Press book.' Includes index. 1. Hardy, Thomas, 1840-1928 — Biography — Youth. 2. Authors, English — 19th century — Biography — Youth. I. T.
PR4753.G5 1975   823/.8 B   *LC* 75-5555   *ISBN* 0316314536

Hardy, Evelyn, 1902-.   • 2.7777
Thomas Hardy; a critical biography. — New York: Russell & Russell, [1970] 342 p.: illus., port.; 23 cm. Reprint of the 1954 ed. 1. Hardy, Thomas, 1840-1928. I. T.
PR4753.H28 1970   823/.8   *LC* 75-83860

Hardy, Florence Emily, 1881-1937.   • 2.7778
The life of Thomas Hardy, 1840–1928. Compiled largely from contemporary notes, letters, diaries, and biographical memoranda, as well as from oral information in conversations extending over many years. New York, St. Martin's Press, 1962. 470 p. illus. 23 cm. 'Brings together ... The early life of Thomas Hardy, 1840-1891, and The later years of Thomas Hardy, 1892-1928.' 1. Hardy, Thomas, 1840-1928. I. T.
PR4753.H35 1962   928.2   *LC* 62-4705

Millgate, Michael.   2.7779
Thomas Hardy, a biography / Michael Millgate. — 1st American ed. — New York: Random House, c1982. xvi, 637 p., [32] p. of plates: ill., ports.; 25 cm. 1. Hardy, Thomas, 1840-1928 — Biography. 2. Authors, English — 19th century — Biography. I. T.
PR4753.M54 1982   823/.8 19   *LC* 81-15873   *ISBN* 0394488024

Weber, Carl Jefferson, 1894-1966.   • 2.7780
Hardy of Wessex, his life and literary career, by Carl J. Weber. — [Rev. ed.]. — New York: Columbia University Press, [1965] x, 324 p.: port.; 23 cm. 1. Hardy, Thomas, 1840-1928. I. T.
PR4753.W27 1965   823.8 B   *LC* 65-20474

Webster, Harvey Curtis, 1906-.   • 2.7781
On a darkling plain; the art & thought of Thomas Hardy. — [Hamden, Conn.] Archon Books [1964, c1947] 239 p. 19 cm. Bibliographical references included in 'Notes' (p. 217-233) 1. Hardy, Thomas, 1840-1928. I. T.
PR4753.W35 1964   828.8   *LC* 64-24718

Abercrombie, Lascelles, 1881-1938.   • 2.7782
Thomas Hardy, a critical study. — New York: Russell & Russell, 1964. 224 p.: port.; 23 cm. 1. Hardy, Thomas, 1840-1928. I. T.
PR4754.A2 1964   828.8   *LC* 64-8920

Beach, Joseph Warren, 1880-1957.   • 2.7783
The technique of Thomas Hardy. — New York: Russell & Russell, 1962 [c1949] 255 p.; 22 cm. 1. Hardy, Thomas, 1840-1928. I. T.
PR4754.B4 1962   823.8   *LC* 61-14870

Blunden, Edmund, 1896-1974.   • 2.7784
Thomas Hardy. — London: Macmillan, 1951. 286 p.; 18 cm. — (Macmillan's pocket library) 1. Hardy, Thomas, 1840-1928. I. T. II. Series.
PR4754.B57 1951

Cecil, David, Lord, 1902-.   • 2.7785
Hardy, the novelist; an essay in criticism. Mamaroneck, N.Y., P. P. Appel, 1972 [c1946] 235 p. 23 cm. Original ed. issued in series: The Clark lectures at Trinity College, Cambridge, 1942. 1. Hardy, Thomas, 1840-1928. I. T.
PR4754.C3 1972   823/.8   *LC* 76-162488   *ISBN* 0911858105

Chase, Mary Ellen, 1887-1973.   • 2.7786
Thomas Hardy from serial to novel / by Mary Ellen Chase. — New York: Russell & Russell, 1964, c1927. 210 p.; 23 cm. 1. Hardy, Thomas, 1840-1928 — Criticism and interpretation. I. T.
PR4754.C36 1964   823.8   *LC* 64-18595   *ISBN* 0846204827

Grundy, Joan.   2.7787
Hardy and the sister arts / Joan Grundy. — New York: Barnes & Noble, 1979. xii, 204 p.; 22 cm. 1. Hardy, Thomas, 1840-1928 — Criticism and interpretation. 2. Arts in literature I. T.
PR4754.G75 1979   823/.8   *LC* 78-20834   *ISBN* 0064925765

Guérard, Albert J. (Albert Joseph), 1914- ed.   • 2.7788
Hardy; a collection of critical essays. Englewood Cliffs, N.J., Prentice-Hall [1963] 180 p. 21 cm. (Twentieth century views, S-TC-25) (A Spectrum book) 1. Hardy, Thomas, 1840-1928. I. T.
PR4754.G78   823.8   *LC* 63-9520

Guérard, Albert J. (Albert Joseph), 1914-.   • 2.7789
Thomas Hardy / Albert J. Guérard. — [New York: New Directions, 1964] xi, 207 p.; 21 cm. — (New Directions paperbook. 185) 1. Hardy, Thomas, 1840-1928. I. T. II. Series.
PR4754.G8 1964   *LC* 64-23651

Hynes, Samuel Lynn.   • 2.7790
The pattern of Hardy's poetry. — Chapel Hill: University of North Carolina Press, 1961 [c1956] 193 p.; 23 cm. 1. Hardy, Thomas, 1840-1928. I. T.
PR4754.H9   *LC* 61-3336

Johnson, Lionel Pigot, 1867-1902.   • 2.7791
The art of Thomas Hardy / by Lionel Johnson: to which is added a chapter on the poetry by J.E. Barton and a bibliography by John Lane; together with a new portrait by Vernon Hill and the etched portrait by William Sprang. — New York: Russell & Russell, 1965. xiii, 367 p.: ports.; 23 cm. 'William Barnes, a biographical note, by Thomas Hardy': p. 359-367. 1. Hardy, Thomas, 1840-1928. 2. Hardy, Thomas, 1840-1928 — Bibliography. 3. Barnes, William, 1801-1886. I. Hardy, Thomas, 1840-1928. William Barnes. II. T. III. Title: William Barnes.
PR4754.J6 1965   *LC* 65-18811

Kramer, Dale, 1936-.   2.7792
Thomas Hardy: the forms of tragedy. — Detroit: Wayne State University Press, 1975. 190 p.; 24 cm. 1. Hardy, Thomas, 1840-1928 — Criticism and interpretation. 2. Tragedy I. T.
PR4754.K7   823/.8   *LC* 74-17084   *ISBN* 0814315305

Marsden, Kenneth.   2.7793
The poems of Thomas Hardy, a critical introduction. — New York: Oxford University Press, 1969. ix, 247 p.; 21 cm. 1. Hardy, Thomas, 1840-1928. I. T.
PR4754.M3   821/.8   *LC* 72-6352

Miller, J. Hillis (Joseph Hillis), 1928-.   • 2.7794
Thomas Hardy, distance and desire [by] J. Hillis Miller. Cambridge, Mass., Belknap Press of Harvard University Press, 1970. xvi, 282 p. 22 cm. 1. Hardy, Thomas, 1840-1928. I. T.
PR4754.M5   823/.8   *LC* 75-102670   *ISBN* 0674885058

Millgate, Michael.   2.7795
Thomas Hardy: his career as a novelist. — [1st American ed.]. — New York: Random House, [1971] 428 p.; 22 cm. 1. Hardy, Thomas, 1840-1928. I. T.
PR4754.M54 1971b   823/.8   *LC* 79-117656   *ISBN* 0394461215

Page, Norman.   2.7796
Thomas Hardy / by Norman Page. — London; Boston: Routledge & Kegan Paul, 1977. xiii, 195 p.; 23 cm. 1. Hardy, Thomas, 1840-1928 — Criticism and interpretation. I. T.
PR4754.P3   823/.8   *LC* 77-369063   *ISBN* 0710086148

Pinion, F. B.   2.7797
A commentary on the poems of Thomas Hardy / F. B. Pinion. New York: Barnes & Noble Books, 1977, c1976. xviii, 293 p., [4] leaves of plates: ill.; 23 cm. 1. Hardy, Thomas, 1840-1928 — Criticism and interpretation. I. T.
PR4754.P5 1977   821/.8   *LC* 76-15684   *ISBN* 0064955729

Pinion, F. B. 2.7798
Thomas Hardy, art and thought / F. B. Pinion. Totowa, N.J.: Rowman and Littlefield, 1977. 214 p.; 23 cm. 1. Hardy, Thomas, 1840-1928 — Criticism and interpretation — Addresses, essays, lectures. 2. Hardy, Thomas, 1840-1928 — Books and reading — Addresses, essays, lectures. I. T.
PR4754.P56   823/.8   *LC* 77-151788   *ISBN* 0874719755

Thomas Hardy, the writer and his background / edited by 2.7799
Norman Page.
New York: St. Martin's Press, 1980. 275 p.; 23 cm. Includes index. 1. Hardy, Thomas, 1840-1928 — Criticism and interpretation — Addresses, essays, lectures. I. Page, Norman.
PR4754.T4 1980   823/.8   *LC* 80-5188   *ISBN* 0312801327

Kay-Robinson, Denys. 2.7800
The landscape of Thomas Hardy / Denys Kay-Robinson; with photographs by Simon McBride. — Salem, NH: Salem House, c1984. 240 p.: ill. (some col.); 26 cm. Includes indexes. 1. Hardy, Thomas, 1840-1928 — Settings. 2. Landscape in literature. 3. Literary landmarks — England 4. England in literature. 5. England — Description and travel I. McBride, Simon. II. T. III. Title: Thomas Hardy.
PR4757.S46 K3 1984b   823/.8 19   *ISBN* 0906671728

Springer, Marlene. 2.7801
Hardy's use of allusion / Marlene Springer. — Lawrence, Kan.: University Press of Kansas, 1983. ix, 207 p.; 23 cm. Includes index. 1. Hardy, Thomas, 1840-1928 — Style. 2. Hardy, Thomas, 1840-1928 — Characters. I. T.
PR4757.S8 S67 1983   823/.8 19   *LC* 82-21977   *ISBN* 0700602313

Elliott, Ralph Warren Victor. 2.7802
Thomas Hardy's English / Ralph W.V. Elliott. — Oxford, England: B. Blackwell in association with André Deutsch, 1984. 387 p.; 23 cm. — (Language library.) Includes indexes. 1. Hardy, Thomas, 1840-1928 — Language. 2. Hardy, Thomas, 1840-1928 — Style. I. T. II. Series.
PR4758.E4 1984   823/.8 19   *LC* 84-133469   *ISBN* 0631136592

PR4759–4773 Harris. Hazlitt

Harris, Frank, 1855-1931. • 2.7803
My life and loves / by Frank Harris; edited, and with an introd. by John. F. Gallagher. — New York: Grove Press, [1963] 5 v. in 1 (xviii, 983 p.): port.; 24 cm. 1. Harris, Frank, 1855-1931 — Biography. I. Gallagher, John F. II. T.
PR4759.H37 Z5 1963   *LC* 63-16996

Hazlitt, William, 1778-1830. • 2.7804
The complete works of William Hazlitt, edited by P. P. Howe after the edition of A. R. Waller and Arnold Glover ... Centenary ed. — London; Toronto: J.M. Dent, [1930-1934] 21 v. front. (v. 1, col.; v. 21, fold.; incl. ports., facsim.) 23 cm. 'Limited to one thousand sets for sale in England and the United States of America.' The general index and index of quotations were compiled by James Thornton. I. Howe, P. P. (Percival Presland), 1886-1944. II. Waller, Alfred Rayney, 1867-1922. III. Glover, Arnold, 1865-1905. IV. Thornton, James. V. T.
PR4770.A2 1930   824.76   *LC* 31-3084

Hazlitt, William, 1778-1830. • 2.7805
Hazlitt on theatre / edited by William Archer and Robert Lowe; introduction by William Archer. — New York: Hill and Wang, 1957? xxxviii, 211 p. — (A dramabook: D7) 1. Hazlitt, William, 1778-1830. I. Archer, William, 1856-1924. II. Lowe, Robert William, 1853-1902. III. T.
PR4771.A8 1957

Hazlitt, William, 1778-1830. • 2.7806
Selected writings. Edited with an introd. by Ronald Blythe. — Baltimore, Md.: Penguin Books, [1970] 509 p.: port.; 19 cm. — (The Penguin English library) I. T.
PR4771.B6   824/.7   *LC* 71-15783   *ISBN* 0140430504

Hazlitt, William, 1778-1830. • 2.7807
Table talk, or, Original essays / by William Hazlitt. — London: Dent; New York: Dutton, [1980] ix, 337 p.; 18 cm. — (Everyman's library.) Includes index I. T. II. Title: Original essays. III. Series.
PR4772.T3 1908   *LC* a 10-2166

Baker, Herschel Clay, 1914-. • 2.7808
William Hazlitt / Herschel Baker. — Cambridge, Mass.: Belknap Press of Harvard University Press, 1962. xiv, 530 p.: plates (incl. ports.) facsims.; 26 cm. 1. Hazlitt, William, 1778-1830. I. T.
PR4773.B3   828.7   *LC* 62-13260

Kinnaird, John, 1924-. 2.7809
William Hazlitt, critic of power / John Kinnaird. — New York: Columbia University Press, 1978. xv, 429 p.: ill.; 24 cm. 1. Hazlitt, William, 1778-1830.

2. Hazlitt, William, 1778-1830 — Knowledge — Literature. 3. Criticism — England — History. 4. Authors, English — 19th century — Biography. I. T.
PR4773.K5   824/.7   *LC* 78-14523   *ISBN* 0231046006

Park, Roy. 2.7810
Hazlitt and the spirit of the age: abstraction and critical theory / [by] Roy Park. — [S.l.]: Oxford University Press, 1971. x, 259 p.; 23 cm. 1. Hazlitt, William, 1778-1830. I. T.
PR4773.P3   801   *LC* 73-875630   *ISBN* 0198120141

Wardle, Ralph Martin, 1909-. 2.7811
Hazlitt / by Ralph M. Wardle. — Lincoln: University of Nebraska Press, [1971] xiii, 530 p.: ill., ports. 1. Hazlitt, William, 1778-1830. I. T.
PR4773.W3   *LC* 75-130870   *ISBN* 0803207905

PR4779–4799 Henley. Hogg. Hood

Henley, William Ernest, 1849-1903. 2.7812
[Works. 1970] The works of W. E. Henley. [New York, AMS Press, 1970] 7 v. port. 19 cm. Half title; each vol. has also special t.p. On spine: The works of Henley. Reprint of the 1908 ed. I. Stevenson, Robert Louis, 1850-1894. joint author. II. T.
PR4783.A1 1970   828/.8/09   *LC* 78-132384   *ISBN* 0404032907

Buckley, Jerome Hamilton. • 2.7813
William Ernest Henley; a study in the 'counter-decadence' of the 'nineties. — New York: Octagon Books, 1971 [c1945] xi, 234 p.: illus., ports.; 23 cm. 1. Henley, William Ernest, 1849-1903. I. T.
PR4784.B8 1971   828/.8/09 B   *LC* 74-120238

Hogg, James, 1770-1835. 2.7814
Selected poems [of] James Hogg; edited by Douglas S. Mack. — Oxford: Clarendon Press, 1970. xxix, 183 p., plate.: port.; 23 cm. I. Mack, Douglas S. ed. II. T.
PR4791.A4 1970   821/.7   *LC* 76-563133   *ISBN* 0198124279

Hogg, James, 1770-1835. • 2.7815
The private memoirs and confessions of a justified sinner: written by himself, with a detail of curious traditionary facts and other evidence by the editor / edited with an introduction by John Carey. — London; New York [etc.]: Oxford U.P., 1969. xxxiii, 262 p.: facsim.; 21 cm. — (Oxford English novels) I. Carey, John. ed. II. T.
PR4791.P7 1969   823.7   *LC* 74-382669   *ISBN* 0192553194

Gifford, Douglas. 2.7816
James Hogg / [by] Douglas Gifford. Edinburgh: The Ramsay Head Press, 1976. 240 p.; 19 cm. (New assessments) 1. Hogg, James, 1770-1835 — Criticism and interpretation. I. T.
PR4792.G5   821/.7   *LC* 77-354723   *ISBN* 0902859358

Simpson, Louis Aston Marantz, 1923-. • 2.7817
James Hogg; a critical study. New York, St. Martin's Press [1962] vi, 222 p. 23 cm. 1. Hogg, James, 1770-1835. I. T.
PR4792.S48 1962   *LC* 61-11537

Hood, Thomas, 1799-1845. • 2.7818
The Complete poetical works of Thomas Hood / edited, with notes, by Walter Jerrold. — [Oxford ed.] London, New York [etc.]: H. Frowde, 1911. xv, 773 p.: front (port.); 19 cm. I. Jerrold, Walter, 1865-1929. II. T.
PR4795.A2   821/.7

Hood, Thomas, 1799-1845. • 2.7819
Letters of Thomas Hood, from the Dilke papers in the British Museum. Edited with an introd. and notes by Leslie A. Marchand. — New York: Octagon Books, 1972 [c1945] viii, 104 p.; 23 cm. Letters written to Mr. and Mrs. Dilke. Original ed. issued as v. 4 of Rutgers University studies in English. 1. Hood, Thomas, 1799-1845. I. Dilke, Charles Wentworth, 1789-1864. II. Dilke, Maria Dover (Walker) d. 1850. III. T.
PR4798.A44 1972   821/.7 B   *LC* 75-159193   *ISBN* 0374939365

Brander, Laurence, 1903-. • 2.7820
Thomas Hood / by Laurence Brander. London: Published for the British Council and the National Book League by Longmans, Green, 1963. 47 p.: port.; 22 cm. (Writers and their work. no. 159) 1. Hood, Thomas, 1799-1845. I. T. II. Series.
PR4798.B7   PR105.B5 no.159.   *LC* 64-2695

Jerrold, Walter, 1865-1929. • 2.7821
Thomas Hood: his life and times. — New York: Greenwood Press, [1969] ix, 420 p.: illus., ports.; 23 cm. Reprint of the 1907 ed. 1. Hood, Thomas, 1799-1845. I. T.
PR4798.J5 1969   821/.7   *LC* 69-13953   *ISBN* 0837110432

Jeffrey, Lloyd N.   2.7822
Thomas Hood, by Lloyd N. Jeffrey. — New York: Twayne Publishers, [1972] 176 p.; 21 cm. — (Twayne's English authors series, TEAS 137) 1. Hood, Thomas, 1799-1845. I. T.
PR4799.J4   821/.7   LC 72-185453

PR4803.H44 Hopkins

Hopkins, Gerard Manley, 1844-1889.   • 2.7823
Journals and papers / edited by Humphry House; completed by Graham Storey. — London; New York: Oxford University Press, 1959. xxxii, 579 p.: illus.,ports.,maps,facsims.,music; 23 cm.. "This volume and The sermons and devotional writings edited by Christopher Devlin together constitute the second edition,revised and enlarged,of [the author's] Note-books and papers edited by Humphry House,1937." 1. Hopkins, Gerard Manley, 1844-1889. I. T.
PR4803.H44 A12 1959   828.8   LC 59-830

Hopkins, Gerard Manley, 1844-1889.   • 2.7824
Sermons and devotional writings. Edited by Christopher Devlin. — London, New York, Oxford University Press, 1959. xiv, 369 p.: ill.; 23 cm. 'This volume and 'The journals and papers of Gerard Manley Hopkins,' edited by Humphry House and completed by Graham Storey, together constitute the second edition, revised and enlarged, of 'The note-books and papers of Gerard Manley Hopkins,' edited by Humphry House, 1937.' 1. Sermons, English 2. Devotional literature I. Devlin, Christopher. II. T.
PR4803.H44 A16 1959   828.8   LC 59-1014

Hopkins, Gerard Manley, 1844-1889.   • 2.7825
The poems of Gerard Manley Hopkins. 4th ed. based on the 1st ed. of 1918 and enlarged to incorporate all known poems and fragments; edited with additional notes, a foreword on the revised text, and a new biographical and critical introduction by W. H. Gardner and N. H. MacKenzie. London, New York [etc.] Oxford U.P., 1967. lxvi, 362 p. 22 cm. I. Gardner, W. H. (William Henry), 1902- II. MacKenzie, N. H., ed. III. T.
PR4803.H44 A17 1967   LC 67-26002

Hopkins, Gerard Manley, 1844-1889.   • 2.7826
A Hopkins reader, selected and with an introd. by John Pick. New York, Oxford University Press, 1953. 317 p. illus. 23 cm. I. Pick, John, 1911- ed. II. T.
PR4803.H44 A6 1953   820.81   LC 53-6436

Hopkins, Gerard Manley, 1844-1889.   • 2.7827
The letters of Gerald Manley Hopkins to Robert Bridges / edited with notes & an introduction by Claude Colleer Abbott. — London: Oxford University Press, [1955] xlvii, 324 p.: ill.; 23 cm. 'The correspondence of Gerard Manley Hopkins and Richard Watson Dixon is referred to throughout as volume II. The appendixes, and also the index to both volumes ... will be found there.' 1. Hopkins, Gerard Manley, 1844-1889 — Correspondence. 2. Bridges, Robert Seymour, 1844-1930 — Correspondence. I. Bridges, Robert Seymour, 1844-1930. II. Abbott, Claude Colleer, 1889-. III. T.
PR4803.H44 Z55 1955   LC 55-14502

Hopkins, Gerard Manley, 1844-1889.   • 2.7828
Further letters of Gerard Manley Hopkins, including his correspondence with Coventry Patmore / edited with notes and an introduction by Claude Colleer Abbott. — 2d ed., rev. and enl. London, New York: Oxford University Press, 1956. xliii, 465 p.: ill.; 23 cm. 1. Hopkins, Gerard Manley, 1844-1889 — Correspondence. 2. Patmore, Coventry Kersey Dighton, 1823-1896 — Correspondence. I. Patmore, Coventry Kersey Dighton, 1823-1896. II. Abbott, Claude Colleer, 1889-. III. T.
PR4803.H44 Z56 1956   LC 57-206

Hartman, Geoffrey H.   • 2.7829
Hopkins; a collection of critical essays, edited by Geoffrey H. Hartman. — Englewood Cliffs, N.J.: Prentice-Hall, [1966] viii, 182 p.; 21 cm. — (Twentieth century views) (A Spectrum book.) 1. Hopkins, Gerard Manley, 1844-1889. I. T.
PR4803.H44 Z647   821.8   LC 66-16341

Heuser, Alan.   • 2.7830
The shaping vision of Gerard Manley Hopkins. — [Hamden, Conn.]: Archon Books, 1968. viii, 128 p.; 22 cm. Reprint of the 1958 ed. 1. Hopkins, Gerard Manley, 1844-1889. I. T.
PR4803.H44 Z648 1968   821/.8   LC 68-15346

Holloway, Marcella Marie, Sister, 1913-.   • 2.7831
The prosodic theory of Gerard Manley Hopkins. — Washington: Catholic University of America Press, [c1947] 121 p.; 23 cm. 1. Hopkins, Gerard Manley, 1844-1889. 2. Versification I. T.
PR4803.H44 Z649   LC a 48-7100

Immortal diamond; studies in Gerard Manley Hopkins. Edited   • 2.7832
by Norman Weyand with the assistance of Raymond V. Schoder. Introd. by John Pick.
New York: Octagon Books, 1969 [c1949] xxvi, 451 p.: port.; 23 cm. 'Anniversary tribute to commemorate the one hundredth anniversary of the poet's birth on July 28, 1944.' 1. Hopkins, Gerard Manley, 1844-1889. I. Weyand, Norman T., ed.
PR4803.H44 Z65 1969   821/.8   LC 76-86289

Gardner, W. H.   • 2.7833
Gerard Manley Hopkins (1844–1889); a study of poetic idiosyncrasy in relation to poetic tradition. With a foreword by Gerard Hopkins. London, Oxford University Press [1958] 2 v. ill. 23 cm. 1. Hopkins, Gerard Manley, 1844-1889. I. T.
PR 4803 H44 Z7 G2 1958   LC 58-3066   ISBN 192121138

MacKenzie, Norman H.   2.7834
A reader's guide to Gerard Manley Hopkins / Norman H. MacKenzie. — Ithaca, N.Y.: Cornell University Press, 1981. 256 p.; 21 cm. Includes indexes. 1. Hopkins, Gerard Manley, 1844-1889 — Criticism and interpretation. I. T.
PR4803.H44 Z716   821/.8 19   LC 80-69275   ISBN 0801413494

Pick, John.   • 2.7835
Gerard Manley Hopkins, priest and poet / John Pick. — 2d ed. — London: Oxford University Press, 1966. xii, 169 p.: front. plate (port.); 20 cm. — (Oxford paperbacks) 1. Hopkins, Gerard Manley, 1844-1889. I. T.
PR4803.H44 Z77 1966   821.8   LC 66-73650

Gerard Manley Hopkins, by the Kenyon critics.   • 2.7836
Norfolk, Conn., New Directions Books [c1945] 144 p. port.; 19 cm. (Makers of modern literature)
PR4803.H44 Zx

PR4809–4828 Housman. Hughes. Hunt. Jones

Housman, A. E. (Alfred Edward), 1859-1936.   2.7837
Complete poems; centennial ed., with an introd. by Basil Davenport and a history of the text by Tom Burns Haber. [1st ed.] New York, Holt, 1959. 268 p.: ill.; 22 cm. Holograph annotations by Robert Sward. I. Sward, Robert, 1933- II. T.
PR4809.H15 A17 1959   821.912   LC 59-8788

Housman, A. E. (Alfred Edward), 1859-1936.   2.7838
The classical papers of A. E. Housman. Collected and edited by J. Diggle & F. R. D. Goodyear. [London] Cambridge University Press, 1972-. v. port. 24 cm. I. Diggle, James, ed. II. Goodyear, Francis Richard David. ed. III. T.
PR4809.H15 A6 1972   880   LC 74-158552   ISBN 0521082439

Page, Norman.   2.7839
A.E. Housman, a critical biography / Norman Page. — 1st American ed. — New York: Schocken Books, 1983. xi, 236 p., [8] p. of plates: ill., ports.; 23 cm. 1. Housman, A. E. (Alfred Edward), 1859-1936. 2. Poets, English — 19th century — Biography. 3. Classicists — England — Biography. I. T.
PR4809.H15 P33 1983   821/.912 B 19   LC 83-4510   ISBN 0805238727

Hughes, Thomas, 1822-1896.   • 2.7840
Tom Brown at Oxford / Thomas Hughes. — London, New York: T. Nelson, [n.d.] 574 p.; 17 cm. (The Nelson classics.) Sequel to School days at Rugby (Tom Brown's schooldays). I. T.
PR4809.H8 T64

Hughes, Thomas, 1822-1896.   • 2.7841
Tom Brown's schooldays; illustrated with 19 line drawings and 8 colour-plates by S. Van Abbé. London, Dent; New York, Dutton [1951] 340 p. illus. 21 cm. (Children's illustrated classics.) 1. Schools — Fiction. I. Van Abbé, S. (Salomon), 1883- illus. II. T. III. Series.
PR4809.H8 Tx   [Fic]   LC 52-8383

Hunt, Leigh, 1784-1859.   • 2.7842
The Poetical works of Leigh Hunt / edited by H. S. Milford. — London: Oxford University Press, 1923. lvi, 776 p.: port.; 21 cm. I. Milford, Humphrey Sumner, Sir, 1877-1952. II. T.
PR4810.A2 1923   LC 23-8592

Hunt, Leigh, 1784-1859.   • 2.7843
Essays (selected) / by Leigh Hunt. — London: J.M. Dent; New York: E.P. Dutton, 1929. xiv, 360 p.; 18 cm. — (Everyman's library. Essays and belles lettres; no.829) I. T.
PR4812.E6 1929   824.7   LC 30-61

Hunt, Leigh, 1784-1859.   • **2.7844**
The autobiography of Leigh Hunt / edited and with an introd. and notes by J.E. Morpurgo. — London: Cresset Press, 1949. xxviii, 512 p.; 21 cm. — (The Cresset library) 1. Hunt, Leigh, 1784-1859 — Biography. I. T. II. Series.
PR4813.A4 1949   LC 49-4667

Blainey, Ann, 1935-.   **2.7845**
Immortal boy: a portrait of Leigh Hunt / Ann Blainey. — New York: St. Martin's Press, c1985. 210 p., [8] p. of plates: ill.; 23 cm. Includes index. 1. Hunt, Leigh, 1784-1859 — Biography. 2. Authors, English — 19th century — Biography. I. T.
PR4813.B55 1985   828/.709 B 19   LC 84-27582   ISBN 0312409451

Blunden, Edmund, 1896-1974.   • **2.7846**
Leigh Hunt and his circle. — New York: Harper, 1930. xiii, 402 p.: front., plates, ports.; 23 cm. 1. Hunt, Leigh, 1784-1859 — Biography. I. Blunden, Edmund, 1896-1974. Leigh Hunt, a biography. II. T. III. Title: Leigh Hunt, a biography.
PR4813.B6   LC 30-30013

Jones, Henry Arthur, 1851-1929.   **2.7847**
[Plays. Selections] Plays / by Henry Arthur Jones; edited with an introduction and notes by Russell Jackson. — Cambridge [Cambridgeshire]; New York: Cambridge University Press, 1982. x, 228 p.: ill.; 24 cm. — (British and American playwrights, 1750-1920.) I. Jackson, Russell, 1949- II. T. III. Series.
PR4827.A4 1982   822/.912 19   LC 81-18047   ISBN 0521233690

PR4830–4838 Keats

Keats, John, 1795-1821.   • **2.7848**
Poems / edited with an introduction [by] E. de Selincourt. — London: Methuen, [1961] lxvii, 639 p.: port.; 23 cm. I. De Selincourt, Ernest, 1870-1943. II. T.
PR4830.F26   LC 64-9163

Keats, John, 1795-1821.   • **2.7849**
Poetical works / edited by H.W.Garrod. — London: Oxford University Press, [1956] xxviii, 477 p.; 19 cm. — (Oxford editions of standard authors) I. Garrod,Heathcote William. II. T.
PR4830.F56   LC 56-59184   ISBN 0192541323

Keats, John, 1795-1821.   **2.7850**
[Poems] The poems of John Keats / edited by Jack Stillinger. — Cambridge, Mass.: Belknap Press of Harvard University Press, 1978. xv, 769 p.; 24 cm. Includes index. I. Stillinger, Jack. II. T.
PR4831.S75 1978   821/.7   LC 78-4490   ISBN 0674677307

Keats, John, 1795-1821.   • **2.7851**
Selected poems and letters / chosen and edited by Roger Sharrock. — [London]: Oxford University Press, 1964. iv, 220 p.; 19 cm. — (New Oxford English series) 1. Keats, John, 1795-1821. I. Sharrock, Roger. II. T. III. Series.
PR4832.S5   LC 65-6291

PR4836–4838 Biography. Criticism

Baldwin, Dane Lewis.   • **2.7852**
A concordance to the poems of John Keats / compiled and edited by Dane Lewis Baldwin .. [et al.]. — Gloucester, Mass.: P. Smith, 1963. xxi, 437 p.: port.; 28 cm. 1. Keats, John, 1795-1821 — Concordances. I. T.
PR4836.A3 1963   LC 63-6084

Keats, John, 1795-1821.   • **2.7853**
The letters of John Keats, 1814–1821. Edited by Hyder Edward Rollins. — Cambridge, Harvard University Press, 1958. 2 v. illus., ports., maps (on lining papers) facsims. 24 cm. Includes bibliographical references. I. Rollins, Hyder Edward, 1889-1958. ed. II. T.
PR4836.A5776   928.2   LC 58-5597

Keats, John, 1795-1821.   • **2.7854**
The life and letters of John Keats / by Lord Houghton. — London: Oxford University Press, 1951. 282 p.; 16 cm. (World's classics) I. Houghton, Richard Monckton Milnes, 1st baron, 1809-1885. II. T.
PR4836.A62 1951   821.7   928.2 B

Bate, Walter Jackson, 1918-.   • **2.7855**
John Keats. — Cambridge: Belknap Press of Harvard University Press, 1963. xvii, 732 p.: illus., ports., map (on lining papers) facsims.; 24 cm. 1. Keats, John, 1795-1821. I. T.
PR4836.B3   821.7   LC 63-17194

Bush, Douglas, 1896-.   • **2.7856**
John Keats, his life and writings. — New York: Macmillan, [1966] 224 p.; 21 cm. — (Masters of world literature series) 1. Keats, John, 1795-1821. I. T.
PR4836.B79   821.7 B   LC 66-11583

Gittings, Robert.   • **2.7857**
The mask of Keats: a study of problems / by Robert Gittings. — Cambridge: Harvard University Press, 1956. x, 177 p., [4] leaves of plates: ill.; 22 cm. 1. Keats, John, 1795-1821. 2. Authors, English — 19th century — Biography. I. T.
PR4836.G52   LC 57-643

Hilton, Timothy, 1941-.   **2.7858**
Keats and his world. — New York: Viking Press, [1971] 144 p.: illus., facsims., ports.; 24 cm. — (A Studio book) 1. Keats, John, 1795-1821. I. T.
PR4836.H58 1971   821/.7 B   LC 78-146972   ISBN 0670411965

Rollins, Hyder Edward, 1889-1958. ed.   • **2.7859**
The Keats circle; letters and papers, and more letters and poems of the Keats circle. — 2d ed. — Cambridge, Harvard University Press, 1965. 2 v. illus., facsims., ports. 24 cm. Selected principally from the Keats Collection in the Houghton Library of Harvard University. 1. Keats, John, 1795-1821 — Friends and associates. I. Houghton Library. II. T.
PR4836.R54 1965   821.7 (B)   LC 65-13632 rev

Ward, Aileen.   • **2.7860**
John Keats; the making of a poet. — New York: Viking Press, [1963] 450 p.: illus.; 24 cm. 1. Keats, John, 1795-1821. I. T.
PR4836.W3   928.2   LC 63-15218

Ford, George Harry, 1914-.   • **2.7861**
Keats and the Victorians; a study of his influence and rise to fame, 1821–1895. — Hamden [Conn.] Archon Books, 1962 [c1944] xii, 197 p. illus. 23 cm. — (Yale studies in English. v. 101) 'In its original form, this study ... was presented to the Graduate School of Yale University ... for the degree of doctor of philosophy [1942]' Bibliography: p. [182]-191. 1. Keats, John, 1795-1821. I. T. II. Series.
PR4837.F6x

Garrod, Heathcote William, 1878-1960.   • **2.7862**
Keats / by H.W. Garrod ... — 2nd ed. — Oxford: Clarendon Press, [1939] 155 p.; 20 cm. 1. Keats, John, 1795-1821. I. T.
PR4837.G3 1939   LC 40-31155

Little, Judy, 1941-.   **2.7863**
Keats as a narrative poet: a test of invention / Judy Little. — Lincoln: University of Nebraska Press, [1975] viii, 167 p.; 22 cm. Includes index. 1. Keats, John, 1795-1821 — Criticism and interpretation. I. T.
PR4837.L56   821/.7   LC 74-81365   ISBN 0803208464

Matthews, G. M., comp.   • **2.7864**
Keats: the critical heritage, edited by G.M. Matthews. New York, Barnes & Noble, 1971. xiii, 430 p. 23 cm. (Critical heritage series.) 1. Keats, John, 1795-1821. I. T. II. Series.
PR4837.M27   ISBN 0389044407

Murry, John Middleton, 1889-1957.   • **2.7865**
[Studies in Keats] Keats. [4th ed., rev. and enl. New York] Minerva Press [1968, c1955] 322 p. 21 cm. First ed. Published in 1930 under title: Studies in Keats. 1. Keats, John, 1795-1821. I. T.
PR4837.M8 1968   821/.7   LC 72-5635

Pettet, Ernest Charles.   • **2.7866**
On the poetry of Keats . — Cambridge: University Press, 1957. viii, 395 p.; 22 cm. 1. Keats, John, 1795-1821. I. T.
PR4837.P4   LC a 57-6328

Sperry, Stuart M.   **2.7867**
Keats the poet [by] Stuart M. Sperry. — [Princeton, N.J.]: Princeton University Press, [1973] xi, 350 p.: illus.; 23 cm. 1. Keats, John, 1795-1821. I. T.
PR4837.S57   821/.7   LC 72-6516   ISBN 069106220X

Vendler, Helen Hennessy.   **2.7868**
The odes of John Keats / Helen Vendler. — Cambridge, Mass.: Belknap Press of Harvard University Press, 1983. viii, 330 p.: ill.; 24 cm. 1. Keats, John, 1795-1821 — Criticism and interpretation. I. T.
PR4837.V43 1983   821/.7 19   LC 83-158   ISBN 0674630750

Wasserman, Earl R. (Earl Reeves), 1913-.   • **2.7869**
The finer tone: Keats' major poems. Baltimore, Johns Hopkins Press, 1953. 228 p. 23 cm. 1. Keats, John, 1795-1821 — Criticism and interpretation. I. Keats, John, 1795-1821. II. T.
PR4837.W3   821.78   LC 53-6494

Van Ghent, Dorothy Bendon, 1907-.   **2.7870**
Keats, the myth of the hero / by Dorothy Van Ghent; revised and edited by Jeffrey Cane Robinson. — Princeton, N.J.: Princeton University Press, c1983. vii, 277 p.; 23 cm. 1. Keats, John, 1795-1821 — Criticism and interpretation. 2. Keats, John, 1795-1821 — Knowledge — Folklore, mythology. 3. Heroes in literature 4. Myth in literature I. Robinson, Jeffrey Cane, 1943- II. T.
PR4838.H4 V36 1983   821/.7 19   *LC* 82-61391   *ISBN* 0691065691

Gradman, Barry, 1944-.   **2.7871**
Metamorphosis in Keats / Barry Gradman. — New York: New York University Press, c1980. xx, 140 p.; 24 cm. — (Gotham library of the New York University Press) Includes index. 1. Keats, John, 1795-1821 — Criticism and interpretation. 2. Metamorphosis in literature I. T.
PR4838.M47 G7   821/.7 19   *LC* 79-3756   *ISBN* 0814729770

Sharp, Ronald A.   **2.7872**
Keats, skepticism, and the religion of beauty / Ronald A. Sharp. — Athens: University of Georgia Press, c1979. x, 198 p.; 23 cm. Includes index. 1. Keats, John, 1795-1821 — Religion. 2. Keats, John, 1795-1821 — Aesthetics. I. T.
PR4838.R4 S5   821/.7   *LC* 78-21463   *ISBN* 0820304700

Bate, Walter Jackson, 1918-.   • **2.7873**
The Stylistic development of Keats / by Walter Jackson Bate. — New York: Humanities Press, 1958. x, 214 p.; 22 cm. 1. Keats, John, 1795-1821. I. T.
PR4838.S8 B3 1958   *LC* 60-4775

PR4839–4845 Keble. Kingsley

Keble, John, 1792-1866.   • **2.7874**
The Christian year / by John Keble. — London: Dent; New York: Dutton, [n.d.] xxx, 254 p.; 17 cm. — (Everyman's library. Theology & philosophy) 1. Church year — Poetry. I. T.
PR4839.K15 C4   821/.7

Kingsley, Charles, 1819-1875.   • **2.7875**
Alton Locke, tailor and poet; an autobiography. New York, Harper, 1858. — St. Clair Shores, Mich.: Scholarly Press, 1972. 371 p.; 21 cm. — I. T.
PZ3.K614 Al6 PR4842.A5x   823/.8   *LC* 78-145120   *ISBN* 040301056X

Kingsley, Charles, 1819-1875.   • **2.7876**
Hereward the Wake [by] Charles Kingsley. London, Dent; New York, Dutton [1935] xvi, 424 p. 18 cm. (Everyman's library. Fiction. [no. 296]) First published in this edition, 1908; reprinted ... 1935. Bibliography: p. xi. 1. Great Britain — History — To 1066 — Fiction. I. T.
PR4842.H4x   *LC* 36-37147

Kinglsey, Charles, 1819-1875.   • **2.7877**
The poems of Charles Kingsley. — London & Toronto, J. M. Dent & sons, ltd.: New York, E. P. Dutton & co. [1927] xvi, 236 p., 1 l: 18 cm. — (Everyman's library, ed. by Ernest Rhys. Poetry and drama [no. 793]) 'First issue in this edition, 1927.' Introduction by Ernest Rhys. Bibliography: p. [xiii]-xiv. I. T. II. Series.
PR4842.P5x   821.89   *LC* A 27-284

Kingsley, Charles.   • **2.7878**
Westward ho!: or the voyages and adventures of Sir Amyas Leigh / Charles Kingsley. London & Toronto: Dent; New York: Dutton [1934] 633 p.;16 cm. — (Everyman's library. Fiction. [no. 20]) I. T.
PR4842.W4x

Kingsley, Charles, 1819-1875.   • **2.7879**
American notes: letters from a lecture tour, 1874 / edited by Robert Bernard Martin. — Princeton, N.J.: Princeton University Library, 1958. 62 p.: ill., ports., facsims.; 24 cm. — (Friends of the Princeton Library. Occasional publications) 1. Canada — Description and travel — 1867-1950 2. United States — Description and travel — 1865-1909. I. T. II. Series.
PR4843.A5 1958   *LC* 58-10725

Martin, Robert Bernard.   • **2.7880**
The dust of combat: a life of Charles Kingsley. — 1st American ed. — New York: Norton, 1960. 308 p.: ill; 23 cm. 1. Kingsley, Charles, 1819-1875. I. T.
PR4843.M3 1960   *LC* 60-2623

Pope-Hennessy, Una Birch, Dame, 1876-1949.   • **2.7881**
Canon Charles Kingsley: a biography / by Una Pope–Hennessy. — London; Chatto & Windus, 1948. 294 p., leaves of plates: ports.;22 cm. 1. Kingsley, Charles, 1819-1875 — Biography. I. T.
PR4843.P6   *LC* 49-3111

Kingsley, Henry, 1830-1876.   • **2.7882**
Austin Elliot. — Uniform ed. — New York: Scribner, 1895. 331 p.; 18 cm. — (His Novels; v. 1) I. T.
PR4845.K5 A8   *LC* 32-11740

Kingsley, Henry, 1830-1876.   • **2.7883**
The recollections of Geoffry Hamlyn. London & Toronto: J .M. Dent & Sons; New York: E. P. Dutton [1924] xii, 475 p.; 18 cm. — (Everyman's library, [v.416]) List of his novels and other stories, p. vii. I. T.
PR 4845 K5 R3 1909   808.8

Kingsley, Henry, 1830-1876.   • **2.7884**
Ravenshoe. Edited with an introd. by William H. Scheuerle. — Lincoln: University of Nebraska Press, [1967] xl, 453 p.; 21 cm. — (A Bison book, BB365) I. Scheuerle, William H., ed. II. T.
PZ3.K615 R5   PR4845.K5 R3x.   *LC* 67-12117

Scheuerle, William H.   **2.7885**
The neglected brother; a study of Henry Kingsley [by] William H. Scheuerle. — Tallahassee: Florida State University Press, 1971. ix, 185 p.; 24 cm. 1. Kingsley, Henry, 1830-1876. I. T.
PR4845.K5 Z83   823/.8 B   *LC* 77-149955

PR4850–4858 Kipling

Kipling, Rudyard, 1865-1936.   • **2.7886**
[Works] The collected works of Rudyard Kipling. [1st AMS ed.] New York, AMS Press [1970] 28 v. illus., facsims., maps, port. 23 cm. Half-title: The Burwash edition of the complete works in prose and verse of Rudyard Kipling. I. T.
PR4850.F70   828/.8/09   *LC* 75-120920   *ISBN* 0404037402

Kipling, Rudyard, 1865-1936.   • **2.7887**
Rudyard Kipling's verse. — Definitive ed. — New York, Doubleday, Doran and co., inc., 1940. xv, [1], 852 p. front. (port.) 24 cm. 'First edition.' I. T.
PR4851 1940a   821.89   *LC* 40-29931

Kipling, Rudyard, 1865-1936.   • **2.7888**
A choice of Kipling's verse, made by T.S. Eliot, with an essay on Rudyard Kipling. London Faber and Faber [1941] 306 p.; 21 cm. First published 1912. I. Eliot, T. S. (Thomas Stearns), 1888-1965. II. T.
PR4851 1941

Kipling, Rudyard, 1865-1936.   • **2.7889**
[Selected works. 1956] Kipling, a selection of his stories and poems, by John Beecroft. Illustrated by Richard M. Powers. Garden City, N.Y., Doubleday [1956] 2 v. illus. 22 cm. I. T.
PR4852.B4   823.89   *LC* 56-6647

Kipling, Rudyard, 1865-1936.   • **2.7890**
[Selected works. 1961] The best short stories of Rudyard Kipling. Edited by Randall Jarrell. [1st ed.] Garden City, N.Y., Hanover House [1961] 693 p. 22 cm. I. T.
PZ3.K629 Bh   PR4852.J3x.   *LC* 61-14717

Young, William Arthur, 1867-1955.   • **2.7891**
A dictionary of the characters and scenes in the stories and poems of Rudyard Kipling 1886–1911. New York, B. Franklin [1969] xxx, 231 p. 24 cm. (Essays in literature & criticism, 38) (Burt Franklin bibliography & reference series, 291) Reprint of the 1911 ed. Revised ed. published in 1967 under title: A Kipling dictionary. 1. Kipling, Rudyard, 1865-1936 — Dictionaries, indexes, etc. 2. Kipling, Rudyard, 1865-1936 — Bibliography. I. T.
PR4856.A28 1969   828/.8/09   *LC* 73-104696

Carrington, Charles Edmund, 1897-.   • **2.7892**
Rudyard Kipling, his life and work / Charles Edmund Carrington. — London: Macmillan, 1955. xxii, 549 p.: ill.; 23 cm. 1. Kipling, Rudyard, 1865-1936 — Biography. I. T.
PR4856.C353   928.2   *LC* 55-12629

Gilbert, Elliot L. ed.   • **2.7893**
Kipling and the critics / edited and with an introduction by Elliot L Gilbert. New York: New York University Press, 1965. xxii, 183 p.; 22 cm. 1. Kipling, Rudyard, 1865-1936. I. T.
PR4856.G5   828.8   *LC* 65-13208

Gross, John J. comp.   **2.7894**
The age of Kipling. Edited by John Gross. — New York: Simon and Schuster, [1972] xii, 178 p.: illus.; 26 cm. London ed. (Weidenfeld & Nicolson) published under title: Rudyard Kipling: the man, his work and his world. 1. Kipling, Rudyard, 1865-1936. I. T.
PR4856.G7 1972b   828/.8/09 B   *LC* 72-83900   *ISBN* 0671214055

Tompkins, J. M. S. (Joyce Marjorie Sanxter), 1897-.   • **2.7895**
The art of Rudyard Kipling [by] J. M. S. Tompkins. [2d ed.] Lincoln, University of Nebraska Press [1965] xiv, 277 p. 21 cm. (A Bison Book, BB332) 'List of tales and poems': p. 260-269. 1. Kipling, Rudyard, 1865-1936. I. T.
PR4856.T6 1965   828.809   *LC* 65-26135

Wilson, Angus. 2.7896
The strange ride of Rudyard Kipling: his life and works / Angus Wilson. — New York: Viking Press, 1978, c1977. xviii, 370 p., [28] leaves of plates: ill.; 25 cm. 1. Kipling, Rudyard, 1865-1936. 2. Authors, English — 19th century — Biography. I. T.
PR4856.W54 1978　　828/.8/09 B　　LC 77-21543　　ISBN 0670677019

Dobrée, Bonamy, 1891-. • 2.7897
Rudyard Kipling: realist and fabulist. — London; New York [etc.]: Oxford U.P., 1967. x, 244 p.: front. (port.).; 22 1/2 cm. 1. Kipling, Rudyard, 1865-1936 — Criticism and interpretation. I. T.
PR4857.D6 1967　　LC 67-87161

Rutherford, Andrew. ed. • 2.7898
Kipling's mind and art, selected critical essays. — Stanford, Calif.: Stanford University Press, 1964. x, 278 p.; 22 cm. 1. Kipling, Rudyard, 1865-1936 — Criticism and interpretation. I. T.
PR4857.R8　　823.8　　LC 64-15164

PR4860–4864 Lamb

Lamb, Charles, 1775-1834. • 2.7899
The works of Charles and Mary Lamb. Edited by E. V. Lucas. London, Methuen, 1903. St. Clair Shores, Mich., Scholarly Press, 1971. 7 v. illus., facsims., maps, ports. 22 cm. I. Lamb, Mary, 1764-1847. II. Lucas, E. V. (Edward Verrall), 1868-1938. ed. III. T.
PR4860.A2 1971b　　824/.7/08　　LC 70-115252　　ISBN 0403003660

Lamb, Charles, 1775-1834. 2.7900
Lamb as critic / edited by Roy Park. — Lincoln: University of Nebraska Press, ç1980. xi, 367 p.; 23 cm. — (The Routledge critics series) I. Park, Roy. II. T.
PR4860.A3 1980　　809　　LC 78-73572　　ISBN 0803287003

Lamb, Charles, 1775-1834. • 2.7901
The portable Charles Lamb / edited, and with an introd., by John Mason Brown. New York: Viking Press, 1949. x, 594 p.; 17 cm. — (Viking portable library. 43) 1. Lamb, Charles, 1775-1834. I. Brown, John Mason, 1900-1969. II. T. III. Series.
PR4860.A4 B7　　828.7　　LC 49-8063 *　　ISBN 067001043X

Lamb, Charles, 1775-1834. 2.7902
[Correspondence. 1968. The letters of Charles Lamb] The letters of Charles Lamb: to which are added those of his sister, Mary Lamb / Edited by E. V. Lucas. — [1st AMS ed. London] J. M. Dent. New York: AMS Press [1968] 3 v.: ill.; 24 cm. Reprint of the 1935 London) ed. 1. Lamb, Charles, 1775-1834 — Correspondence. 2. Lamb, Mary Ann, 1764-1847. 3. Lamb, Charles, 1775-1834. I. Lamb, Mary, 1764-1847. II. Lucas, E. V. (Edward Verrall), 1868-1938. ed. III. T.
PR4863.A33 1968　　824/.7 B　　LC 68-59268

Barnett, George Leonard. 2.7903
Charles Lamb / by George L. Barnett. Boston: Twayne Publishers, c1976. 272 p.: port.; 21 cm. (Twayne's English authors series; TEAS 195) Includes index. 1. Lamb, Charles, 1775-1834. 2. Authors, English — 19th century — Biography. I. T.
PR4863.B327　　824/.7 B　　LC 76-47526　　ISBN 0805766685

Barnett, George Leonard. • 2.7904
Charles Lamb: the evolution of Elia. Bloomington, Ind., Indiana University Press, c1964. xi, 286 p.: facsims.; 23 cm. (Indiana University humanities series no. 53) 1. Lamb, Charles, 1775-1834 — Criticism and interpretation. I. T.
PR4863.B33　　LC 64-63001

Blunden, Edmund, 1896-1974. • 2.7905
Charles Lamb and his contemporaries, by Edmund Blunden. — [Hamden, Conn.] Archon Books, 1967. ix, 215 p. 19 cm. — (The Clark lectures, Trinity College, Cambridge, 1932) First published 1933. 1. Lamb, Charles, 1775-1834 — Friends and associates. I. T.
PR4863.B6 1967　　824/.7　　LC 67-19516

Courtney, Winifred F., 1918-. 2.7906
Young Charles Lamb, 1775–1802 / Winifred F. Courtney. — New York: New York University Press, 1982. xviii, 411 p., [9] p. of plates: ill.; 23 cm. — (The Gotham library of the New York University Press) Includes index. 1. Lamb, Charles, 1775-1834 — Biography — Youth. 2. Authors, English — 19th century — Biography. I. T.
PR4863.C6 1982　　824/.7 B 19　　LC 81-14021　　ISBN 0814713823

Lucas, E. V. (Edward Verrall), 1868-1938. • 2.7907
The life of Charles Lamb. [5th ed., rev.] London Methuen [1921] 2 v.: ports.; 18 cm. 1. Lamb, Charles, 1775-1834. I. T.
PR4863 L8 1921

McKenna, Wayne. 2.7908
Charles Lamb and the theatre / Wayne McKenna. — New York: Barnes & Noble Books, 1978. 134 p.; 23 cm. 1. Lamb, Charles, 1775-1834 — Knowledge — Performing arts. 2. Lamb, Charles, 1775-1834 — Dramatic works. 3. Dramatic criticism — England — History — 19th century. 4. Theater — England — History — 19th century. I. T.
PR4864.M3　　822/.009　　LC 77-82139　　ISBN 0064947076

PR4870–4948 L

Landor, Walter Savage, 1775-1864. 2.7909
Poetry & prose: with Swinburne's poem and essays by Ernest De Selincourt, Walter Raleigh & Oliver Elton / Landor; with an introd. and notes by E. K. Chambers. — New York: AMS Press, [1948] xxxvi, 185 p.; 18 cm. Reprint of the 1946 ed. published at the Clarendon Press, Oxford, Eng. I. Chambers, E. K. (Edmund Kerchever), 1866-1954. II. T.
PR4871.C47 1948　　828/.7/09　　LC 76-29435　　ISBN 0404153143

Lear, Edward, 1812-1888. • 2.7910
The Complete nonsense of Edward Lear / edited and introduced by Holbrook Jackson. — New York: Dover Publications, 1951. 288 p.: ill.; 21 cm. I. Jackson, Holbrook. II. T.
PR4879.L2 N5 1951 PZ8.3.L43　　LC 51-14566　　ISBN 0486201678

Le Fanu, Joseph Sheridan, 1814-1873. 2.7911
Best ghost stories of J.S. Le Fanu / edited and with an introduction by E.F. Bleiler. — Dover ed. — New York: Dover, 1964. xi, 467 p.: ill. I. Bleiler, Everett Franklin, 1920- II. T.
PR4879.L7 A15 1964　　LC 64-13463　　ISBN 0486204154

Lewis, M. G. (Matthew Gregory), 1775-1818. 2.7912
The monk, a romance [by] Matthew Lewis; edited with an introd. by Howard Anderson. London, Oxford University Press, 1973. xxx, 455 p. 21 cm. (Oxford English novels) I. Anderson, Howard Peter, ed. II. T.
PZ3.L588 M19 PR4887.M7　　823/.7　　LC 73-179618　　ISBN 0192553623

Peck, Louis Francis, 1904-. • 2.7913
A life of Matthew G. Lewis. — Cambridge: Harvard University Press, 1961. ix, 331 p.: facsims., ports.; 25 cm. 1. Lewis, M. G. (Matthew Gregory), 1775-1818 — Biography. I. T.
PR4888.P4　　LC 61-11027

Lytton, Edward George Earl Lytton Bulwer-Lytton: 1st baron, 1803-1873. • 2.7914
The last days of Pompeii / Introduction By Charles Dwoskin.— New York: Fine Editions Press, [c1956] 359 p; 21 cm. I. T.
PR4912.A1x　　LC 57-951

Lytton, Edward Bulwer Lytton, Baron, 1803-1873. • 2.7915
Rienzi, the last of the Roman tribunes. Philadelphia, Lippincott, 1885. St. Clair Shores, Mich., Scholarly Press, 1971. xx, 366 p. front. 22 cm. At head of title: The Lord Lytton edition. 1. Rienzo, Cola di, d. 1354 — Fiction. I. T.
PZ3.L998 R25 PR4919.A1x　　823/.8　　LC 70-145150　　ISBN 0403010799

Lytton, Edward Bulwer Lytton, Baron, 1803-1873. 2.7916
A strange story / by Lord Lytton. — 2nd Ed. London: Low, 1862. 407 p.: port.; 16 cm. I. T.
PR 4920 A1

Lytton, Edward Bulwer Lytton, Baron, 1803-1873. • 2.7917
Bulwer and Macready: a chronicle of the early Victorian theatre. — Urbana: University of Illinois Press, 1958. 278 p.: ill; 27 cm. Correspondence of Bulwer, Macready, and Forster, augmented by diary notes and other memorabilia. 1. Theater — London — History. I. Macready, William Charles,1793-1873. II. Forster, John, 1812-1876. III. Shattuck, Charles Harlen, 1910- IV. T.
PR4931.A3　　792.0942　　LC 57-6957

PR4963–4979 Macaulay. Macdonald. Mallock. Marryat

Macaulay, Thomas Babington Macaulay, Baron, 1800-1859. 2.7918
[Works. 1897] The works of Lord Macaulay, complete. Edited by his sister Lady Trevelyan. London, Longmans, Green, 1897. 8 v. port. 23 cm. I. Trevelyan, Hannah More (Macaulay) Lady, 1810-1873, ed. II. T.
PR4963.A1 1897　　901.9　　LC 78-15522

Macaulay, Thomas Babington Macaulay, Baron, 1800-1859. • 2.7919
Prose and poetry; selected by G.M. Young. London R. Hart-Davis 1952. 864 p.; 21 cm. — (The Reynard library) I. Young, G. M. (George Malcolm), 1882-1959. II. T.
PR4963 A1 1952

Macaulay, Thomas Babington Macaulay, 1st baron, 1800-1859. • 2.7920
Miscellaneous essays and The lays of ancient Rome. London: Dent; New York:
Dutton [1932] xvi, 528 p.; 18 cm. (Everyman's library) I. T. II. Title: The lays
of ancient Rome
PR4963 A16

Macaulay, Thomas Babington Macaulay, 1st baron, 1800-1859. • 2.7921
Critical & historical essays. [Newly arr. by A.J. Grieve] London & Toronto:
Dent; New York: Dutton [1930-31] 2 v.; 18 cm. — (Everyman's library. Essays
and belles lettres [225-226]) 1. Great Britain — History — Addresses, essays,
lectures 2. English literature — History and criticism I. Grieve, Alexander
James, 1874-, ed. II. T.
PR4963 A16 1930

Macdonald, George, 1824-1905. • 2.7922
George Macdonald, an anthology / by C.S. Lewis. — London: G. Bles:
Centenary Press, 1946. 128 p. I. T.
PR4966.L4 LC a 46-4930

Macdonald, George, 1824-1905. • 2.7923
Visionary novels: Lilith, Phantastes / edited by Anne Fremantle, with an
introduction by W.H. Auden. — New York: Noonday Press, [1954] 434 p.; 22
cm. I. Fremantle, Anne. II. T. III. Title: Lilith. IV. Title: Phantastes.
PZ3.M144 Vj PR4967.V5. LC 54-11729

Mallock, William Hurrell, 1849-1923. • 2.7924
The new Republic, or, Culture, faith, and philosophy in an English country
house / edited with notes and an introduction by J. Max Patrick. — Gainesville:
University of Florida Press, 1950. xxxvi, 237 p.; 23 cm. I. Patrick, John Max,
1911-. II. T. III. Title: Culture, faith, and philosophy in an English country
house.
PR4972.M5 N4 PZ3.M296Ner10. LC 50-9045

Marryat, Frederick, 1792-1848. • 2.7925
Masterman Ready / Captain Marryat. — London: Dent; New York: Dutton,
1930. xii, 340 p.; 18 cm. — (Everyman's library. no. 160) I. T. II. Series.
PZ3.M349 M20 PR4977.M3x 823/.7 LC 79-553283 ISBN
0460001604

Marryat, Frederick, 1928-1848. • 2.7926
Mr. Midshipman Easy / Captain Marryat. — London: Dent; New York:
Dutton, 1907. viii, 406 p.; 18 cm. — (Eveyman's Library; 82) I. T.
PR4977.M5x ISBN 0460000829

Marryat, Frederick, 1792-1848. • 2.7927
A diary in America: with remarks on its institutions / edited, with notes and an
introduction by Sydney Jackman. — [1st Borzoi ed.]. — New York: Knopf,
1962. xxvi, 487, ix p.: port; 22 cm. 1. United States — Description and travel —
1783-1848 2. United States–Social life and customs. I. Jackman, S. W. (Sydney
Wayne), 1925- II. T.
PR4978.A4 1962 LC 61-18120

PR4984–4989 Martineau. Maturin. Braddon. Mayhew

Martineau, Harriet, 1802-1876. 2.7928
Harriet Martineau's autobiography / with memorials by Maria Weston
Chapman. — Brookfield, Ut.: Gregg International, 1877. 3 v.: ill., facsims.,
ports. 1. Martineau, Harriet, 1802-1876. I. Chapman, Maria Weston,
1806-1885. II. T.
PR4984.M5 Z462 1877b

Pichanick, Valerie Kossew, 1936-. 2.7929
Harriet Martineau, the woman and her work, 1802–76 / Valerie Kossew
Pichanick. — Ann Arbor: University of Michigan Press, c1980. 301 p.: port.; 24
cm. — (Women and culture series.) Includes index. 1. Martineau, Harriet,
1802-1876. 2. Authors, English — 19th century — Biography. I. T. II. Series.
PR4984.M5 Z78 1980 823/.8 B LC 80-15322 0472100024

Thomas, Gillian. 2.7930
Harriet Martineau / by Gillian Thomas. — Boston: Twayne, c1985. 144 p.:
port.; 23 cm. (Twayne's English authors series. TEAS 404) Includes index.
1. Martineau, Harriet, 1802-1876 — Criticism and interpretation. I. T.
II. Series.
PR4984.M5 Z85 1985 823/.8 19 LC 84-12911 ISBN 0805768947

Webb, R. K. (Robert Kiefer), 1922-. • 2.7931
Harriet Martineau; a radical Victorian. — New York, Columbia University
Press, 1960. xiii, 385 p. illus., ports., facsims. 23 cm. Bibliography: p. 368-377.
1. Martineau, Harriet, 1802-1876. I. T.
PR4984.M5Z93 1960a 928.2 LC 59-11698

Maturin, Charles Robert, 1780-1824. • 2.7932
Melmoth the Wanderer: a tale; edited with an introduction by Douglas Grant.
— London; New York [etc.]: Oxford U.P., 1968. xx, 560 p.; 21 cm. — (Oxford
English novels) I. T.
PZ3.M4375 Me8 PR4987.M7 823/.7 LC 70-362058 ISBN
0192553186

Wolff, Robert Lee. 2.7933
Sensational Victorian: the life and fiction of Mary Elizabeth Braddon / Robert
Lee Wolff. — New York: Garland Pub., 1979. xiv, 529 p., [32] leaves of plates:
ill.; 24 cm. 1. Braddon, M. E. (Mary Elizabeth), 1837-1915. 2. Novelists,
English — 19th century — Biography. I. T.
PR4989.B727 Z9x 823/.8 LC 76-52717 ISBN 0824016181

Braddon, M. E. (Mary Elizabeth), 1837-1915. 2.7934
Lady Audley's secret / Mary Elizabeth Braddon; edited with an introduction
by David Skilton. — Oxford [Oxfordshire]; New York: Oxford University
Press, 1986. xxxiv, 455 p. — (The World's classics) I. Skilton, David. II. T.
PR4989.M4 L2 1986 823/.8 19 LC 86-12486 ISBN
0192817418(pbk.)

Humpherys, Anne. 2.7935
Henry Mayhew / by Anne Humpherys. — Boston: Twayne Publishers, c1984.
191 p.: port.; 23 cm. — (Twayne's English authors series. TEAS 396) Includes
index. 1. Mayhew, Henry, 1812-1887. 2. Authors, English — 19th century —
Biography. 3. Sociologists — England — Biography. 4. Labor and laboring
classes — England — London — History. 5. London (England) — Poor —
History. I. T. II. Series.
PR4989.M48 Z687 1984 808/.0092/4 B 19 LC 83-22729 ISBN
0805768823

PR5000–5018 Meredith

Meredith, George, 1828-1909. • 2.7936
The works of George Meredith. — Memorial ed. ... — [New York: C. Scribner's
sons, 1909-1912] 29 v.: ill., facsims. (some fold.) ports.; 22 cm. Half-title.
1. Meredith, George, 1828-1909. I. T.
PR5000.F09 LC 10-36017

Meredith, George, 1828-1909. 2.7937
The egoist: an annotated text, backgrounds criticism / George Meredith; edited
by Robert M. Adams. — 1st ed. — New York: Norton, c1979. ix, 561 p.; 21 cm.
— (A Norton critical edition) 1. Meredith, George, 1828-1909. The egoist.
I. Adams, Robert Martin, 1915- II. T.
PZ3.M54 Eg 1979 PR5006.E5x 823/.8 LC 77-25313 ISBN
0393044319

Meredith, George, 1828-1909. • 2.7938
Selected poems / edited with an introduction by Graham Hough. — London:
Oxford University Press, 1962. 95 p.; 20 cm. I. Hough, Graham Goulden,
1908- II. T.
PR5007.A1 1962 LC 62-4132

Meredith, George, 1828-1909. 2.7939
[Poems. 1978] The poems of George Meredith / edited by Phyllis B. Bartlett. —
New Haven: Yale University Press, 1978. 2 v. (xlix, 1253 p.).: ill.; 25 cm.
Includes indexes. I. Bartlett, Phyllis Brooks. II. T.
PR5007.A1 1978 821/.8 LC 73-77142 ISBN 0300012837

Meredith, George, 1828-1909. • 2.7940
The letters of George Meredith; edited by C. L. Cline. — Oxford [Eng.]:
Clarendon Press, 1970. 3 v. (xlii, 1786 p.); 23 cm. I. Cline, Clarence Lee. ed.
II. T.
PR5013.A43 1970 823/.8 B LC 79-499447 ISBN 0198114737

Lindsay, Jack, 1900-. • 2.7941
George Meredith, his life and work. — London: Bodley Head, [1956] 420 p.:
ports.; 23 cm. 1. Meredith, George, 1828-1909 — Biography. I. T.
PR5013.L5 LC 56-3861

Priestley, J. B. (John Boynton), 1894-. • 2.7942
George Meredith, by J. B. Priestley. New York, Macmillan, 1926. St. Clair
Shores, Mich., Scholarly Press, 1970. vi, 204 p. 21 cm. (English men of letters)
1. Meredith, George, 1828-1909. I. T.
PR5013.P7 1970 823/.8 LC 70-131807 ISBN 0403006945

Sassoon, Siegfried, 1886-1967. • 2.7943
Meredith. Port Washington, N.Y., Kennikat Press [1969, c1948] 269 p. port. 22
cm. 1. Meredith, George, 1828-1909. I. T.
PR5013.S3 1969 823/.8 B LC 68-26214

Stevenson, Lionel, 1902-1973. • 2.7944
The ordeal of George Meredith; a biography. — New York: Russell & Russell,
[1967, c1953] viii, 368 p.: port.; 24 cm. 1. Meredith, George, 1829-1909. I. T.
PR5013.S7 1967 823/.8 B LC 66-27156

Beer, Gillian. • 2.7945
Meredith: a change of masks: a study of the novels. — London: Athlone P., 1970. x, 214 p.; 23 cm. Distributed in the U.S.A. by Oxford University Press, New York. 1. Meredith, George, 1828-1909 — Criticism and interpretation. I. T.
PR5014.B4 1970   823/.8   *LC* 70-546357   *ISBN* 0485111225

Fletcher, Ian. • 2.7946
Meredith now: some critical essays; edited by Ian Fletcher. — London: Routledge and K. Paul, 1971. xiv, 317 p.; 23 cm. 1. Meredith, George, 1828-1909 — Criticism and interpretation — Addresses, essays, lectures. I. T.
PR5014.F5   823/.8   *LC* 72-178535   *ISBN* 0710070616

Pritchett, V. S. (Victor Sawdon), 1900-. • 2.7947
George Meredith [by] V. S. Pritchett. [1st American ed.] New York, Random House [1970, c1969] 123 p. 22 cm. (The Clark lectures for 1969) 1. Meredith, George, 1828-1909 — Criticism and interpretation. I. T.
PR5014.P7 1970   823/.8   *LC* 77-119899

Williams. Ioan M., comp. 2.7948
Meredith, the critical heritage. Edited by Ioan Williams. — New York: Barnes & Noble, [1971] xiii, 535 p.; 23 cm. — (The Critical heritage series) 1. Meredith, George, 1828-1909 — Criticism and interpretation — Addresses, essays, lectures. I. T.
PR5014.W5 1971   823/.8   *LC* 73-27406   *ISBN* 0389041068

Wilt, Judith, 1941-. 2.7949
The readable people of George Meredith / by Judith Wilt. — Princeton, N.J.: Princeton University Press, [1975] 253 p.; 23 cm. 1. Meredith, George, 1828-1909 — Criticism and interpretation. I. T.
PR5014.W55   823/.8   *LC* 74-25610   *ISBN* 0691062757

Wright, Walter Francis, 1912-. • 2.7950
Art and substance in George Meredith: a study in narrative. — [Lincoln]: University of Nebraska Press, 1953. 211 p.; 23 cm. 1. Meredith, George, 1828-1909. I. T.
PR5014.W7   *LC* 53-7702

Beach, Joseph Warren, 1880-1957. • 2.7951
The comic spirit in George Meredith: an interpretation. — New York: Russell & Russell, 1963 [c1911] 230 p.; 23 cm. 1. Meredith, George, 1828-1909. I. T.
PR5017.H8 B4 1963   *LC* 62-16694

PR5021–5043 Meynell. Moore

Meynell, Alice Christiana Thompson, 1847-1922. • 2.7952
Prose and poetry. Centenary volume edited by F. P. [and others] With a biographical & critical introd. by V. Sackville–West. — Freeport, N.Y.: Books for Libraries Press, [1970] 394 p.: ports.; 23 cm. — (Essay index reprint series) Reprint of the 1947 ed. I. T.
PR5021.M3 A723 1970   824/.8   *LC* 76-117824   *ISBN* 0836919831

Meynell, Viola, 1886-1956. • 2.7953
Alice Meynell; a memoir. New York, Scribner, 1929. — St. Clair Shores, Mich.: Scholarly Press, 1971. 354 p.: illus., ports.; 22 cm. 1. Meynell, Alice Christiana Thompson, 1847-1922. I. T.
PR5021.M3 M4 1971   821/.8 B   *LC* 79-145182   *ISBN* 0403008042

Moore, George, 1852-1933. 2.7954
The bending of the bough; a play in five acts. — Chicago: De Paul University, 1969. 87 p.; 22 cm. — (Irish drama series, v. 3) I. T. II. Series.
PR5042.B4 1969   822   *LC* 75-9273

Moore, George, 1852-1933. 2.7955
Confessions of a young man. Edited by Susan Dick. — Montreal: McGill-Queen's University Press, 1972. viii, 266 p.; 23 cm. I. Dick, Susan. ed. II. T.
PZ3.M783 Co6 PR5042.C6x   828/.8/03   *LC* 70-183725   *ISBN* 0773500979

Moore, George, 1852-1933. • 2.7956
Esther Waters, an English story, by George Moore. New York, Liveright, inc. [c1932] 442 p.; 23 cm. ([The black and gold library]) Illustrated lining-papers. I. T.
PR5042.E8   *LC* 32-17147

Moore, George, 1852-1933. 2.7957
Hail and farewell: ave, salve, vale / George Moore. — 1st annotated ed. / edited by Richard Cave. — Toronto: Macmillan of Canada, 1976. 774 p., [8] leaves of plates: ill.; 24 cm. Includes index. I. T.
PR5042.H3 1976   823/.8   *LC* 77-361833   *ISBN* 0770514677

Moore, George, 1852-1933. • 2.7958
Letters to Lady Cunard, 1895–1933 / edited with an introduction and notes by Rupert Hart–Davis. — London: R. Hart-Davis, 1957. 208 p.: facsims., ports.;

23 cm. 1. Moore, George, 1852-1933 — Correspondence. 2. Cunard, Maud Alice Burke, Lady, 1872-1948. I. Hart-Davis, Rupert, 1907- II. T.
PR5043.A47   *LC* a 58-1420

Dunleavy, Janet Egleson. 2.7959
George Moore: the artist's vision, the storyteller's art. — Lewisburg: Bucknell University Press, [1973] 156 p.; 22 cm. 1. Moore, George, 1852-1933. I. T.
PR5043.D8   823/.8   *LC* 75-125793   *ISBN* 0838777570

PR5070–5088 Morris

Morris, William, 1834-1896. • 2.7960
Collected works. With introductions by his daughter, May Morris. Russell & Russell, 1966. 24 v.: ill., facsims. maps, ports.; 25 cm. Reprint of the 1910-15 ed. I. Morris, May, 1862 — ed.
PR5071.S6 1966   *LC* 66-15432

Morris, William, 1834-1896. • 2.7961
Selected writings and designs. Edited with an introd. by Asa Briggs. With a suppl. by Graeme Shankland on William Morris, designer. — Baltimore, Penguin Books [1963, c1962] 308 p. illus. 18 cm. — (Pelican books. A521) I. T. II. Series.
PR5072.B7   821.8   *LC* 63-516

Morris, William, 1834-1896. • 2.7962
Stories in prose, stories in verse, shorter poems, lectures and essays / edited by G.D.H. Cole. — Centenary ed. — Bloomsbury [London]: Nonesuch Press; New York: Random House, 1934. xxiv, 671 p.: ill. Illustrated lining-papers. I. Cole, G. D. H. (George Douglas Howard), 1889-1959. II. Nonesuch Press. III. T.
PR5072.C6 1934   *LC* 34-20557

Morris, William, 1834-1896. 2.7963
Three works: A dream of John Ball; The pilgrims of hope; News from nowhere. With an introd. by A. L. Morton. — London, Lawrence and Wishart, 1973. 401 p. 19 cm. I. T.
PR5072.M6   828/.8/09   *LC* 68-3268

Morris, William, 1834-1896. 2.7964
The well at the world's end. — London: Longmans, Green, 1896. 2 v. I. T.
PR5079.W4 1896   *LC* 04-16567

Morris, William, 1834-1896. 2.7965
On art and socialism; essays and lectures, selected with an introd. by Holbrook Jackson. [London]: J. Lehmann, 1947. 335p. (The Chiltern library) 1. Socialism and art I. Jackson, Holbrook, 1874-1948. ed. II. T. III. Series.
PR5080 O55 1947

Morris, William, 1834-1896. • 2.7966
The letters of William Morris to his family and friends / edited with introduction and notes by Philip Henderson. — London; New York: Longmans, Green, [1950] lxvii, 406 p.: ill., ports.; 23 cm. 1. Morris, William, 1834-1896. Correspondence I. Henderson, Philip, 1906- II. T.
PR5083.A4 1950   *LC* 50-11163

Morris, William, 1834-1896. 2.7967
[Correspondence] The collected letters of William Morris / edited by Norman Kelvin. — Princeton, N.J.: Princeton University Press, c1984. 626 p.: ill. 1. Morris, William, 1834-1896. Correspondence 2. Authors, English — 19th century — Correspondence. 3. Artists — England — Correspondence. 4. Socialists — England — Correspondence. I. Kelvin, Norman. II. T.
PR5083.A4 1984   821/.8 B 19   *LC* 82-47604   *ISBN* 0691065012

Faulkner, Peter. 2.7968
Against the age: an introduction to William Morris / Peter Faulkner. — London; Boston: Allen & Unwin, 1980. xi, 193 p., [8] p. of plates: ill.; 23 cm. Includes index. 1. Morris, William, 1834-1896. 2. Authors, English — 19th century — Biography. 3. Artists — England — Biography. 4. Socialists — England — Biography. I. T.
PR5083.F29   821/.8 B 19   *LC* 80-40460   *ISBN* 0048090123

Faulkner, Peter. • 2.7969
William Morris and W.B. Yeats. — Dublin: Dolmen Press; [distributed outside Ireland by the Oxford University Press], 1962. 30 p.; 21 cm. Limited ed. of 1050 copies. 1. Yeats, W. B. (William Butler), 1865-1939. 2. Morris, William, 1834-1896. I. Dolmen Press, Dublin. II. T.
PR5083.F3   *LC* 63-2833

Mackail, J. W. (John William), 1859-1945. • 2.7970
The life of William Morris. New York, Haskell House, 1970. 2 v. illus., port. 23 cm. Reprint of the 1899 ed. 1. Morris, William, 1834-1896. I. T.
PR5083.M25 1970   709.24 B   *LC* 79-118180   *ISBN* 0838310702

Thompson, E. P. (Edward Palmer), 1924-. 2.7971
William Morris: romantic to revolutionary / E. P. Thompson. — New edition. New York: Pantheon Books, 1961. x, 829 p.; 25 cm. 1. Morris, William, 1834-1896. 2. Authors, English — 19th century — Biography. 3. Socialism — Great Britain I. T.
PR5083.T6 821/.8 B *LC* 76-62712 *ISBN* 0394411366

Faulkner, Peter. comp. 2.7972
William Morris: the critical heritage; edited by Peter Faulkner. — London; Boston: Routledge and Kegan Paul, 1973. xiii, 465 p.; 23 cm. — (The Critical heritage series) 1. Morris, William, 1834-1896. I. T.
PR5084.F3 1973 828/.8/09 *LC* 72-93518 *ISBN* 0710075200

Silver, Carole G. 2.7973
The romance of William Morris / by Carole Silver. — Athens, Ohio: Ohio University Press, c1982. xviii, 233 p.: ill.; 23 cm. Includes index. 1. Morris, William, 1834-1896 — Criticism and interpretation. 2. Romances, English — History and criticism. I. T.
PR5084.S5 1982 821/.8 19 *LC* 82-2278 *ISBN* 0821406515

PR5105–5115 Newman. Oliphant. O'Shaugnessy

Newman, John Henry, 1801-1890. • 2.7974
Prose and poetry, selected by Geoffrey Tillotson. Cambridge: Harvard University Press, 1957. 842 p.; 21 cm. (The Reynard library) I. Tillotson, Geoffrey, ed. II. T.
PR5106 T5

Oliphant, Mrs. (Margaret), 1828-1897. • 2.7975
A beleaguered city; being a narrative of certain recent events in the city of Semur, in the Department of the Haute Bourgogne, a story of the seen and the unseen, by Mrs. Oliphant. Westport, Conn., Greenwood Press [1970] viii, 267 p. 23 cm. I. T.
PZ3.O48 Be8 PR5113.B4x 823/.8 *LC* 79-98862 *ISBN* 0837131375

Oliphant, Mrs. (Margaret), 1828-1897. 2.7976
Miss Marjoribanks / with an introduction by Q. D. Leavis. — London: Chatto & Windus (Zodiac P.), 1969. vi, 499 p.; 22 cm. (Her Chronicles of Carlingford) I. T.
PZ3.O48 Mip4 PR5113.M5x 823/.9/12 *LC* 70-487530 *ISBN* 0701115033

Oliphant, Mrs. (Margaret), 1828-1897. 2.7977
Autobiography and letters of Mrs. Margaret Oliphant, edited by Mrs. Harry Coghill, with an introduction by Q. D. Leavis. [Leicester] Leicester University Press [distributed in North America by Humanities Press, New York, 1974] 464 p. illus. 23 cm. (The Victorian library) Reprint of the 1899 ed. published by William Blackwood and Sons, Edinburgh. 1. Oliphant, Mrs. (Margaret), 1828-1897 — Biography. 2. Oliphant, Mrs. (Margaret), 1828-1897 — Correspondence. 3. Oliphant, Mrs. (Margaret), 1828-1897 — Bibliography. I. Coghill, Annie Louisa Walker, d. 1907, ed. II. T.
PR5114.A3 1974 823/.8 B *LC* 74-183200 *ISBN* 0718550196

O'Shaughnessy, Arthur William Edgar, 1844-1881. • 2.7978
Poems of Arthur O'Shaughnessy; selected and edited by William Alexander Percy. New Haven, Yale University Press, 1923. vi, 104 p. 24 cm. 'Published on the Kingsley Trust Association publication fund.' I. Percy, William Alexander, 1885-1942. ed. II. Kingsley Trust Association. III. T.
PR5115.O4 A6 1923 *LC* 23-7743

PR5130–5138 Pater

Pater, Walter, 1839-1894. • 2.7979
Selected works / edited by Richard Aldington with an introduction. — London: W. Heinemann [1948] 557 p.; 23 cm. I. Aldington, Richard, 1892-1962. II. T.
PR5132.A4 *LC* 48-28141

Pater, Walter, 1839-1894. • 2.7980
Marius the Epicurean; his sensations and ideas. Edited and with an introd. by Harold Bloom. New York, New American Library [1970] 286, [1] p. 18 cm. (A Signet classic, CY476) I. T.
PZ3.P272 M12 PR5134.M3x 823/.8 *LC* 72-97499

Pater, Walter, 1839-1894. • 2.7981
Letters of Walter Pater; edited by Lawrence Evans. Oxford, Clarendon P., 1970. iii-xlvii, 182 p. 9 plates. facsims., port. 23 cm. 1. Pater, Walter, 1839-1894. I. Evans, Lawrence, 1935- ed. II. T.
PR5136.A43 1970 824/.8 *LC* 73-504920 *ISBN* 0198124066

Benson, Arthur Christopher, 1862-1925. • 2.7982
Walter Pater / by A.C. Benson. — Detroit: Gale Research, 1968. vii, 226 p.; 23 cm. — (The Gale library of lives and letters: British writers series) 1. Pater, Walter, 1839-1894. 2. Authors, English — 19th century — Biography. I. T.
PR5136.B4 1968 *LC* 67-23876

Cecil, David, Lord, 1902-. • 2.7983
Walter Pater, the scholar–artist. — Cambridge: University Press, 1955. 29 p.; 19 cm. — (Rede lecture. 1955) 1. Pater, Walter, 1839-1894. I. T. II. Series.
PR5136.C43 *LC* 56-4331

Levey, Michael. 2.7984
The case of Walter Pater / Michael Levey. — [London]: Thames and Hudson, c1978. 232 p., [4] leaves of plates: ill.; 25 cm. Includes index. 1. Pater, Walter, 1839-1894 — Biography. 2. Authors, English — 19th century — Biography. I. T.
PR5136.L4 824/.8 B *LC* 78-322216 *ISBN* 0500011931

Walter Pater, the critical heritage / edited by R. M. Seiler. 2.7985
London; Boston: Routledge & Kegan Paul, 1980. xvi, 449 p.; 23 cm. (The critical heritage series) Includes index. 1. Pater, Walter, 1839-1894 — Criticism and interpretation — Addresses, essays, lectures. I. Seiler, R. M. (Robert Morris)
PR5137.W34 824/.8 B *LC* 79-42837 *ISBN* 0710003803

PR5140–5144 Patmore

Patmore, Coventry Kersey Dighton, 1823-1896. • 2.7986
The poems of Coventry Patmore / edited, with an introduction, by Frederick Page. — London: Oxford University Press, 1949. xxvii, 506 p.: port.; 19 cm. Includes index. I. Page, Frederick, 1879- II. T.
PR5140.A2 1949 *LC* 49-11371

Oliver, Edward James, 1911-. • 2.7987
Coventry Patmore. New York, Sheed & Ward, 1956. 211 p.; 21 cm. 1. Patmore, Coventry Kersey Dighton, 1823-1896. I. T.
PR5143.O4 821.89 *LC* 56-6824

Patmore, Derek, 1908-. • 2.7988
Portrait of my family, 1783–1896. [1st ed.] New York: Harper; 1935. x p., 2 l., 270 p., 1 l. front., pl., ports. 23 cm. 1. Patmore, Coventry Kersey Dighton, 1823-1896. 2. Patmore family. I. T.
PR5143.P35 *LC* 35-22363

Patmore, Derek, 1908-. • 2.7989
The life and times of Coventry Patmore. — London, Constable [1949] xii, 249 p. illus., ports. 22 cm. 1. Patmore, Coventry Kersey Dighton, 1823-1896 — Biography. I. Patmore, Derek, 1908- Portrait of my family. II. T. III. Title: Portrait of my family.
PR5143.P35 1949 928.2 *LC* 49-6556 *

Gosse, Edmund, 1849-1928. • 2.7990
Coventry Patmore. New York, Greenwood Press [1969] viii, 213 p. illus. 23 cm. (Literary lives) Reprint of the 1905 ed. 1. Patmore, Coventry Kersey Dighton, 1823-1896. I. T. II. Series.
PR5144.G6 1969 821/.8 B *LC* 69-13915 *ISBN* 0837119804

Reid, John Cowie, 1916-. • 2.7991
The mind and art of Coventry Patmore. — London: Routledge & K. Paul, [1957] 358 p.: ill.; 23 cm. 1. Patmore, Coventry Kersey Dighton, 1823-1896. I. T.
PR5144.R4 *LC* 57-2660

PR5160–5204 Peacock. Pinero. Radcliffe

Peacock, Thomas Love, 1785-1866. 2.7992
The works of Thomas Love Peacock. — New York: AMS Press, 1967. 10 v.: fronts.; 23 cm. Half-title: The Halliford edition ... edited by H. F. B. Brett-Smith & C. E. Jones. Reprint of 1924-34 ed. I. Brett-Smith, Herbert Francis Brett, ed. II. Jones, Clifford Ernest, ed. III. T.
PR5160.A2 1967 823/.7 *LC* 71-181967

Butler, Marilyn. 2.7993
Peacock displayed: a satirist in his context / Marilyn Butler. — London; Boston: Routledge & K. Paul, 1979. ix, 361 p.; 22 cm. Includes index. 1. Peacock, Thomas Love, 1785-1866 — Criticism and interpretation. I. T.
PR5164.B8 823/.7 *LC* 79-40541 *ISBN* 0710002939

Pinero, Arthur Wing, Sir, 1855-1934. • 2.7994
The social plays of Arthur Wing Pinero. Edited with a general introd. and critical pref. to each play, by Clayton Hamilton. — [Authorized library ed.]. — New York: AMS Press, 1967 [c1917-22] 4 v.: ports.; 23 cm. I. T.
PR5180.A2 1967 822/.8 *LC* 79-181969

Pinero, Arthur Wing, Sir, 1855-1934.   **2.7995**
[Selections. 1985] Three plays / Arthur Wing Pinero; with introductions by Stephen Wyatt. — London; New York: Methuen, c1985. xx, 245 p.; 18 cm. (Master playwrights.) I. T. II. Series.
PR5181 1985   822/.8 19   LC 85-151501   ISBN 0413572900

Lazenby, Walter.   **2.7996**
Arthur Wing Pinero. New York, Twayne Publishers [1972] 173 p. 21 cm. (Twayne's English authors series, TEAS 150) 1. Pinero, Arthur Wing, Sir, 1855-1934. I. T.
PR5184.L3   822/.8   LC 72-937

Radcliffe, Ann Ward, 1764-1823.   • **2.7997**
The mysteries of Udolpho, a romance: interspersed with some pieces of poetry / edited, with an introduction, by Bonamy Dobrée. — London: Oxford University Press, 1966. xxii, 672 p.; 21 cm. — (Oxford English novels.) Includes reproduction of original title page, 1794. I. Dobrée, Bonamy, 1891- II. T. III. Series.
PR5202.M8 1966   LC 66-2628

Grant, Aline.   • **2.7998**
Ann Radcliffe, a biography. — Denver: A. Swallow, [1951] 153 p.; 23 cm. 1. Radcliffe, Ann Ward, 1764-1823 — Biography. I. T.
PR5203.G7   LC 51-14495

PR5210–5235 R

Reade, Charles, 1814-1884.   **2.7999**
The works of Charles Reade. — New York: AMS Press, [1970-. v.   : illus., ports.; 23 cm. 'Library edition.' Comprised of reprints, originally published separately, 1895- I. T.
PR5210 1970   823/.8   LC 73-118070   ISBN 0404052606

Burns, Wayne, 1918-.   **2.8000**
Charles Reade; a study in Victorian authorship. — New York: Bookman Associates, [1961] 360 p.: illus.; 23 cm. 1. Reade, Charles, 1814-1884. I. T.
PR5216.B8   823.8   LC 61-7182

Reynolds, George W. M. (George William MacArthur), 1814-1879.   **2.8001**
Wagner, the wehr–wolf / by G. W. M. Reynolds; edited by E. F. Bleiler; with 24 ill. by Henry Anelay. — New York: Dover Publications, 1972. xviii, 160 p.: ill.; 28 cm. I. Bleiler, Everett Franklin, 1920- II. T.
PZ3.R3356 Wag10 PR5221.R35   823/.8   LC 74-78971   ISBN 0486220052

Gérin, Winifred.   **2.8002**
Anne Thackeray Ritchie: a biography / Winifred Gérin. — Oxford; New York: Oxford University Press, 1981. xiv, 310 p., [16] p. of plates: ill., ports.; 22 cm. Includes index. 1. Ritchie, Anne Thackeray, 1837-1919 — Biography. 2. Thackeray, William Makepeace, 1811-1863 — Biography. 3. Novelists, English — 19th century — Biography. I. T.
PR5227.R7 G47 1981   823/.8 19   LC 80-49704   ISBN 0198126646

Roberts, Charles George Douglas, Sir, 1860-1943.   **2.8003**
Selected poetry and critical prose. Edited with an intro. and notes by W. J. Keith. — [Toronto; Buffalo]: University of Toronto Press, [1974] xxxix, 326 p.; 23 cm. — (Literature of Canada: poetry and prose in reprint) I. T.
PR5231.A6 1974   811/.5/2   LC 73-91558   ISBN 0802020763

Robertson, T. W. (Thomas William), 1829-1871.   **2.8004**
Six plays / T.W. Robertson; with an introduction by Michael R. Booth. — [S.l.]: Humanities, 1981, c1980. 138 p.: ill. I. T.
PR5232.R5 A6 1981   822/.8 19   ISBN 0906399165

Rogers, Samuel, 1763-1855.   • **2.8005**
Recollections of the table–talk of Samuel Rogers / first collected by Alexander Dyce. edited.with an introd., by Morchard Bishop. — London: Richards Press, 1952. 248 p.: ill.; 21 cm. 1. Rogers, Samuel, 1763-1855. I. Dyce, Alexander, 1798-1869. II. T.
PR5235.A4 1856b   LC 53-2229

PR5236–5248 The Rossettis

Troxell, Janet Camp.   • **2.8006**
Three Rossettis: unpublished letters to and from Dante Gabriel, Christina, William / collected and edited by Janet C. Troxell. — Cambridge: Harvard University Press, 1937. 216 p.: ill.; 26 cm. 1. Rossetti family I. Troxell, Janet Camp. II. Rossetti, William Michael, 1829-1919. III. Rossetti, Christina Georgina, 1830-1894. IV. Rossetti, Dante Gabriel, 1828-1882. V. T. VI. Title: 3 Rossettis.
PR5236.R9 A4   LC 38-1069

Rossetti, Christina Georgina, 1830-1894.   **2.8007**
The complete poems of Christina Rossetti / edited, with textual notes and introductions, by R. W. Crump. — A variorum ed. — Baton Rouge: Louisiana State University Press, c1979. 2 v.: port.; 24 cm. I. Crump, R. W. (Rebecca W.), 1944- II. T.
PR5237.A1 1979   821/.8   LC 78-5571   ISBN 0807103586

Rossetti, Christina Georgina, 1830-1894.   • **2.8008**
The poetical works of Christina Georgina Rossetti / with memoir and notes &c by William Michael Rossetti. — New York: Macmillan, 1906. lxxiii, 507 p.: front.; 20 cm. I. Rossetti, William Michael, 1829-1919. II. T.
PR5237.A47   821/.8   LC 77-3038   ISBN 0841472041 lib. bdg

Rossetti, Christina Georgina, 1830-1894.   • **2.8009**
The family letters of Christina Georgina Rossetti; with some supplementary letters and appendices. Edited by William Michael Rossetti. — New York: Haskell House, 1968. xxii, 242 p.: illus.; 24 cm. 'Haskell House catalogue item #237.' Reprint of the 1908 ed. 1. Rossetti, Christina Georgina, 1830-1894. I. Rossetti, William Michael, 1829-1919. ed. II. T.
PR5238.A3 1968   826.8   LC 68-24915

Battiscombe, Georgina.   **2.8010**
Christina Rossetti, a divided life / Georgina Battiscombe. — London: Constable, 1981. 233 p. [12] p. of plates: ill.; 24 cm. 'An owl book.' Includes index. 1. Rossetti, Christina Georgina, 1830-1894 — Biography. 2. Poets, English — 19th century — Biography. I. T.
PR5238.B32 1981   821/.8 B 19   LC 81-47451

Bellas, Ralph A.   **2.8011**
Christina Rossetti / by Ralph A. Bellas. Boston: Twayne Publishers, c1977. 139 p.; 21 cm. (Twayne's English authors series; TEAS 201) Includes index. 1. Rossetti, Christina Georgina, 1830-1894. I. T.
PR5238.B44 1977   821/.8 B   LC 76-29711   ISBN 0805766715

Charles, Edna Kotin, 1921-.   **2.8012**
Christina Rossetti, critical perspectives, 1862–1982 / Edna Kotin Charles. — Selinsgrove [Pa.]: Susquehanna University Press; London: Associated University Presses, c1985. 187 p.: ill.; 24 cm. Includes index. 1. Rossetti, Christina Georgina, 1830-1894 — Criticism and interpretation — History. I. T.
PR5238.C48 1985   821/.8 19   LC 84-40392   ISBN 0941664066

Rossetti, Dante Gabriel, 1828-1882.   • **2.8013**
The collected works of Dante Gabriel Rossetti / edited with preface and notes by William M. Rossetti. — London: Ellis and Elvey, 1890. 2 v.; 20 cm. I. Rossetti, William Michael, 1829-1919. II. T.
PR5240.E90   821/.8   LC 03-15539

Rossetti, Dante Gabriel, 1828-1882.   • **2.8014**
Poems & translations, 1850–1870, together with the prose story 'Hand and soul,' by Dante Gabriel Rossetti. — London; New York [etc.]; Milford: Oxford university press, [1914] xvii, [2], 492 p.; 16 cm. — (The World's classics. 185) '... The present volume in the 'World's classics' was first published in 1914.'—p. [iv] 1. Italian poetry — Translations into English. 2. English poetry — Translations from Italian. I. T. II. Title: Hand and soul.
PR5240.F14   LC 24-28796

Rossetti, Dante Gabriel, 1828-1882.   • **2.8015**
Poems, ballads and sonnets; selections from the posthumous poems and from his translations; Hand and soul, edited by Paull Franklin Baum. — [1st ed.] Garden City, N.Y.: Doubleday, Doran [1937] lxii, 399 p.; 19 cm. — (The Doubleday-Doran series in literature.) I. Baum, Paull F. (Paull Franklin), 1886- II. T.
PR5241.B3   LC 37-27270

Rossetti, Dante Gabriel, 1828-1882.   **2.8016**
Poems / Dante Gabriel Rossetti; edited with an introduction and notes by Oswald Doughty. — London: J. M. Dent, 1957. 328 p.; 20 cm. I. T.
PR5241.D6   LC 57-59297

Rossetti, Dante Gabriel, 1828-1882.   • **2.8017**
Letters. Edited by Oswald Doughty and John Robert Wahl. — Oxford, Clarendon Press, 1965-. v. illus. 23 cm. Includes bibliographical references. I. Doughty, Oswald. ed. II. Wahl, John Robert, ed. III. T.
PR5246.A4   826.8   LC 66-1718

Dobbs, Brian.   **2.8018**
Dante Gabriel Rossetti. an alien Victorian / [by] Brian and Judy Dobbs. — London: Macdonald and Jane's, 1977. ix, 257 p., [16] p. of plates: ill., ports.; 24 cm. 1. Rossetti, Dante Gabriel, 1828-1882 — Biography. 2. Poets, English — 19th century — Biography. 3. Painters — Great Britain — Biography. I. Dobbs, Judy. joint author. II. T.
PR5246.D57   759.2 B   LC 78-311073   ISBN 0345040324

Doughty, Oswald. • **2.8019**
A Victorian romantic: Dante Gabriel Rossetti. — 2nd ed. — London: Oxford University Press, 1960. 712 p.: ill.; 22 cm. 1. Rossetti, Dante Gabriel, 1828-1882. I. T.
PR5246.D6 1960   LC 60-51824

Howard, Ronnalie Roper. **2.8020**
The dark glass; vision and technique in the poetry of Dante Gabriel Rossetti. — [Athens]: Ohio University Press, [1972] xiii, 218 p.; 22 cm. 1. Rossetti, Dante Gabriel, 1828-1882 — Criticism and interpretation. I. T.
PR5247.H6   821/.8   LC 70-158176

Rossetti, William Michael, 1829-1919. **2.8021**
The diary of W. M. Rossetti 1870–1873 / edited with an introd. and notes by Odette Bornand. — Oxford [Eng.]: Clarendon Press, 1977. xxiii, 302 p., [1] leaf of plates: port.; 22 cm. 1. Rossetti, William Michael, 1829-1919 2. Rossetti Family. 3. Critics — England — Biography. 4. Art critics — England — Biography. 5. Poets, English — 19th century — Biography. I. Bornand, Odette. II. T.
PR5249.R2 A799 1977   700/.92/4 B   LC 78-312738   ISBN 0198124589

Rossetti, William Michael, 1829-1919. **2.8022**
Some reminiscences. — London: Brown Langham, 1906. 2 v. (578 p.): ill., facsim., ports. 1. Rossetti, William Michael, 1829-1919 — Biography. I. T.
PR5249.R2 A8   LC 06-45370

PR5250–5268 Ruskin

Ruskin, John, 1819-1900. • **2.8023**
The works of John Ruskin / edited by E.T. Cook and Alexander Wedderburn. — Library ed. — London: Allen; New York: Longman's Green, 1903-1912. 39 v.: ill. (some col., some fold.), facsims., plans, ports.; 26 cm. Half title: The complete works of John Ruskin. 'Two thousand and sixty-two copies of this edition—of which two thousand are for sale in England and America—have been printed at the Ballantyne press, Edinburgh, and the type has been distributed.' I. Cook, Edward Tyas, Sir, 1857-1919. II. Wedderburn, Alexander Dundas Oligvy, 1854-. III. T. IV. Title: The complete works of John Ruskin.
PR5250.F03   LC 05-37354

Ruskin, John, 1819-1900. **2.8024**
The literary criticism of John Ruskin / selected, edited, and with an introduction by Harold Bloom. — Garden City, N.Y.: Anchor Books, 1965. xxvii, 398 p. 1. Literature — History and criticism 2. English literature — History and criticism 3. Aesthetics I. Bloom, Harold. II. T.
PR5252.B6   LC 65-20057

Ruskin, John, 1819-1900. • **2.8025**
Ruskin today. Chosen and annotated by Kenneth Clark. [1st ed.] New York, Holt, Rinehart and Winston [1965, c1964] xxi, 362 p. plates. 23 cm. I. Clark, Kenneth, 1903- ed. II. T.
PR5252.C48   828.8   LC 64-21912

Ruskin, John, 1819-1900. • **2.8026**
The genius of John Ruskin: selections from his writings / edited with an introd. by John D. Rosenberg. New York: G. Braziller, [1963] 560 p.; 22 cm. I. Rosenberg, John D. II. T.
PR5252.R64   828.8   LC 63-17875

Ruskin, John, 1819-1900. **2.8027**
The Brantwood diary of John Ruskin, together with selected related letters and sketches of persons mentioned. Edited and annotated by Helen Gill Viljoen. — New Haven: Yale University Press, 1971. xv, 632 p.: illus.; 25 cm. — 1. Ruskin, John, 1819-1900. I. T.
PR5263.A13 1971   828/.8/09 B   LC 72-99844   ISBN 0300012276

Ruskin, John, 1819-1900. • **2.8028**
The diaries of John Ruskin / selected and edited by Joan Evans and John Howard Whitehouse. — Oxford: Clarendon Press, 1956-59. 3 v. (xii, 1210 p.): ill., ports.,; 25 cm. 1. Ruskin, John, 1819-1900 — Diaries. I. Evans, Joan, 1893- II. Whitehouse, John Howard, 1873- III. T.
PR5263.A15   PR5263.A32.   LC 56-14657 rev

Ruskin, John, 1819-1900. • **2.8029**
Praeterita: outlines of scenes and thoughts perhaps worthy of memory in my past life / John Ruskin; with an introduction by Kenneth Clark. — London: R. Hart-Davis, 1949. xxii, 592 p.; 21 cm. 1. Ruskin, John, 1819-1900. I. T.
PR5263.A2 1949   LC 50-11443

Ruskin, John, 1819-1900. • **2.8030**
The gulf of years: letters from John Ruskin to Kathleen Olander / commentary by Kathleen Prynne; edited and with a preface by Rayner Unwin. — London:

Allen & Unwin, [1953] 95, [1] p.: ill., ports.; 21 cm. 1. Prynne, Kathleen Olander. 2. Ruskin, John, 1819-1900 — Correspondence. I. T.
PR5263.A327   LC 53-12000

Ruskin, John, 1819-1900. **2.8031**
Ruskin's letters from Venice, 1851–1852. By John Lewis Bradley. New Haven, Yale University Press, 1955. xx, 330 p.: ill.; 24 cm. — (Yale studies in English. v. 129) The editor's thesis-Yale University. Without thesis statement. 'Daily letters from Ruskin to his father.' 1. Ruskin, John James. 2. Ruskin, John, 1819-1900 — Correspondence. I. Bradley, John Lewis. II. T. III. Title: Letters from Venice, 1851-1852. IV. Series.
PR5263.A37   824.86   LC 55-9436

Abse, Joan, 1926-. **2.8032**
John Ruskin, the passionate moralist / Joan Abse. — 1st American ed. — New York: Knopf: Distributed by Random House, 1981, c1980. 363 p., 8 p. of plates; 25 cm. Includes index. 1. Ruskin, John, 1819-1900 — Biography. 2. Authors, English — 19th century — Biography. I. T.
PR5263.A54 1981   828/.809 B 19   LC 81-47483   ISBN 039451596X

Bradley, John Lewis. **2.8033**
An introduction to Ruskin [by] John L. Bradley. — Boston: Houghton Mifflin, [1971] xvi, 137 p.; 21 cm. — (Riverside studies in literature) 1. Ruskin, John, 1819-1900. I. T.
PR5263.B66   828/.8/09   LC 76-23385   ISBN 0395042267

Evans, Joan, 1893-. • **2.8034**
John Ruskin. — New York: Haskell House Publishers, 1970. 447 p.: illus., ports.; 23 cm. 1. Ruskin, John, 1819-1900. I. T.
PR5263.E9 1970   828/.8/09 B   LC 70-117998   ISBN 0838310532

Leon, Derrick, 1908-1944. **2.8035**
Ruskin, the great Victorian / Derrick Leon. — London: Routledge and Paul, 1949. xx, 595 p., [11] leaves of plates: ports; 23 cm. 1. Ruskin, John, 1819-1900. I. T.
PR5263.L4   928.2   LC 49-48959   ISBN 0710065213

Lutyens, Mary, 1908- ed. **2.8036**
Millais and the Ruskins. — New York: Vanguard Press, [c1967] xiii, 296 p.: illus., ports.; 24 cm. Consists largely of letters written by John Ruskin, Euphemia Millais, and John Millais. I. Ruskin, John, 1819-1900. II. Millais, Euphemia Chalmers Gray, Lady, 1828-1897. III. Millais, John Everett, Sir, 1829-1896. IV. T.
PR5263.L8 1967   828/.8/09   LC 68-8086

Quennell, Peter, 1905-. • **2.8037**
John Ruskin, the portrait of a prophet. New York, Viking Press, 1949. xiv, 289 p. illus., ports. 22 cm. 'Selected bibliography': p. xiii-xiv. 1. Ruskin, John, 1819-1900. I. T.
PR5263.Q4   928.2   LC 49-11240

Rosenberg, John D. • **2.8038**
The darkening glass; a portrait of Ruskin's genius. New York, Columbia University Press, 1961. 274 p. illus. 24 cm. Includes bibliography. 1. Ruskin, John, 1819-1900. I. T.
PR5263.R6   828.8   LC 61-16678

Kirchhoff, Frederick, 1942-. **2.8039**
John Ruskin / by Frederick Kirchhoff. — Boston: Twayne Publishers, c1984. 161 p.; 23 cm. — (Twayne's English authors series. TEAS 369) Includes index. 1. Ruskin, John, 1819-1900 — Criticism and interpretation. I. T. II. Series.
PR5264.K57 1984   828/.809 19   LC 83-22698   ISBN 0805768556

Landow, George P. **2.8040**
The aesthetic and critical theories of John Ruskin, by George P. Landow. — Princeton, N.J.: Princeton University Press, 1971. xii, 468 p.: illus.; 23 cm. 1. Ruskin, John, 1819-1900 — Aesthetics. I. T.
PR5264.L3   828/.8/08   LC 76-120757   ISBN 069106198X

PR5300–5348 Scott

Scott, Walter, Sir, 1771-1832. **2.8041**
The Waverley novels. Dryburgh ed. [London, Edinburgh, A. and C. Black; etc., etc., 1892-94] 25 v. fronts., plates, facsims. (part fold.) plan. 22 cm. Half-title. I. T.
PR5300.E92   LC 04-15333

Scott, Walter, Sir, 1771-1832. **2.8042**
Poetical works / selected and edited, with introd. and notes by Andrew Lang. — Dryburgh ed. London, Edinburgh: A. and C. Black, 1895. 2 v.; 22 cm. I. Lang, Andrew, 1844-1912. II. T.
PR5305.E95x

Scott, Walter, Sir, 1771-1832.   **2.8043**
[Selections. 1972] Selected poems; edited by Thomas Crawford. Oxford, Clarendon Press, 1972. xxviii, 302 p. 2 maps. 21 cm. (Oxford paperback English texts) I. Crawford, Thomas. ed. II. T.
PR5305.F72   821/.7   *LC* 72-192883   *ISBN* 0198710593

Scott, Walter, Sir, 1771-1832.   **2.8044**
Waverley: or, 'Tis sixty years since / Walter Scott; edited by Claire Lamont. — Oxford: Clarendon Press; New York: Oxford University Press, c1981. xlii, 470 p.; 23 cm. 1. Jacobite Rebellion, 1745-1746 — Fiction. I. Lamont, Claire. II. T. III. Title: 'Tis sixty years since.
PR5322.W4 1981   823/.7   *LC* 79-41313   *ISBN* 0198126433

Husband, Margaret Fair Anderson.   • **2.8045**
A dictionary of the characters in the Waverley novels of Sir Walter Scott. — New York: Humanities Press, 1962. xvi, 287 p.; 24 cm. 1. Scott, Walter, Sir, 1771-1832 — Dictionaries, indexes, etc. 2. Scott, Walter, Sir, 1771-1832. Waverley novels. I. T. II. Title: Characters in the Waverley novels.
PR5331.H8   *LC* 62-6138

Buchan, John, 1875-1940.   • **2.8046**
Sir Walter Scott. — New York: Coward-McCann, [c1932] 384 p.: front. (port.); 25 cm. 1. Scott, Walter, Sir, 1771-1832. I. T.
PR5332.B83   *LC* 32-22094

Grierson, Herbert John Clifford, Sir, 1866-1960.   • **2.8047**
Sir Walter Scott, bart. New York, Haskell House, 1969. xii, 320 p. port. 23 cm. Reprint of the 1938 ed. I. Scott, Walter, Sir, 1771-1832. II. T.
PR5332.G73 1969   828/.7/09 B   *LC* 72-95427   *ISBN* 0838309771

Johnson, Edgar.   • **2.8048**
Sir Walter Scott; the great unknown. [New York] Macmillan [1970] 2 v. (xxvi, 1397 p.)) illus., plan, ports. 24 cm. 1. Scott, Walter, Sir, 1771-1832. I. T.
PR5332.J6   828/.7/09   *LC* 75-84431

Pearson, Hesketh, 1887-1964.   • **2.8049**
Sir Walter Scott, his life and personality. New York, Harper [1954] 295 p. illus. 22 cm. London ed. (Methuen) has title: Walter Scott, his life and personality. 1. Scott, Walter, Sir, 1771-1832. I. T.
PR5332.P4 1954a   928.2   *LC* 54-8982

Pope-Hennessy, Una Birch, Dame, 1876-1949.   • **2.8050**
Sir Walter Scott / by Una Pope-Hennessy. — Denver: A. Swallow [1949] 101 [2] p.; 19 cm. (The English novelists) 1. Scott, Walter, Sir, 1771-1832. I. T.
PR5332.P62   *LC* 49-50397

Wilson, A. N., 1950-.   **2.8051**
The Laird of Abbotsford: a view of Sir Walter Scott / A. N. Wilson. — Oxford; New York: Oxford University Press, 1980. xvi, 197 p.; 23 cm. Includes index. 1. Scott, Walter, Sir, 1771-1832. 2. Novelists, Scottish — 19th century — Biography. I. T.
PR5332.W5 1980   823/.7 B   *LC* 79-41270   *ISBN* 0192117564

Scott, Walter, Sir, 1771-1832.   **2.8052**
The journal of Sir Walter Scott / Edited by W. E. K. Anderson. — Oxford: Clarendon Press, 1972. xlvi, 812 p.: ill.; 24 cm. 1. Scott, Walter, Sir, 1771-1832. I. Anderson, W. E. K., ed. II. T.
PR5334.A2 1972   828/.7/03 B   *LC* 72-188235   *ISBN* 0198124384

Scott, Walter, Sir, 1771-1832.   • **2.8053**
The letters of Sir Walter Scott. Edited by H. J. C. Grierson. Assisted by Davidson Cook, W. M. Parker and others. London, Constable, 1932–37. [New York, AMS Press, 1971] 12 v. 23 cm. 'Centenary edition.' 1. Scott, Walter, Sir, 1771-1832 — Correspondence. 2. Scott, Walter, Sir, 1771-1832. I. Grierson, Herbert John Clifford, Sir, 1866-1960. ed. II. Cook, Davidson, 1874-1941, ed. III. Parker, William Mathie, 1891- ed. IV. T.
PR5334.A6 1971   828/.7/09   *LC* 72-144431   *ISBN* 0404056504

Corson, James Clarkson.   **2.8054**
Notes and index to Sir Herbert Grierson's edition of the letters of Sir Walter Scott / by James C. Corson. — Oxford [Eng.]; New York: Clarendon Press, 1979. xv, 699 p.; 23 cm. 1. Scott, Walter, Sir, 1771-1832 — Correspondence. 2. Novelists, Scottish — 19th century — Biography. I. Scott, Walter, Sir, 1771-1832. Letters of Sir Walter Scott. II. Grierson, Herbert John Clifford, Sir, 1866-1960. III. T.
PR5334.A63 C6   828/.7/09   *LC* 77-30289   *ISBN* 0198127189

Cockshut, A. O. J.   • **2.8055**
The achievement of Walter Scott [by] A. O. J. Cockshut. [1st U.S. ed. New York] New York University Press, 1969. 216 p. 22 cm. 1. Scott, Walter, Sir, 1771-1832 — Criticism and interpretation. I. T.
PR5341.C58 1969b   823/.7   *LC* 70-84604

Crawford, Thomas.   **2.8056**
Scott / Thomas Crawford. — Edinburgh: Scottish Academic Press, 1983 (c1982). viii, 132 p.; 19 cm. — (Scottish writers.) 1. Scott, Walter, Sir, 1771-1832 — Criticism and interpretation. I. T. II. Series.
PR5341.C66 1982   828/.709 19   *LC* 82-227945   *ISBN* 0707303052

Davie, Donald.   • **2.8057**
The heyday of Sir Walter Scott. New York: Barnes & Noble [1961] 168 p.; 22 cm. 1. Scott, Walter, Sir, 1771-1832. I. T.
PR5341.D3   *LC* 61-3076

Hayden, John O. comp.   **2.8058**
Scott: the critical heritage, edited by John O. Hayden. New York, Barnes & Noble [1970] xiv, 554 p. 24 cm. (The Critical heritage series) 1. Scott, Walter, Sir, 1771-1832 — Criticism and interpretation. I. T.
PR5341.H35 1970b   823/.7   *LC* 73-21709   *ISBN* 0389013315

Hillhouse, James Theodore, 1890-1956.   • **2.8059**
The Waverley novels and their critics, by James T. Hillhouse. New York, Octagon Books, 1968 [c1964] xi, 357 p. 24 cm. 1. Scott, Walter, Sir, 1771-1832 — Waverley novels. I. T.
PR5341.H5 1968   823/.7   *LC* 68-22297

Millgate, Jane.   **2.8060**
Walter Scott: the making of the novelist / Jane Millgate. — Toronto: University of Toronto Press, 1984. xii, 223 p.; 24 cm. 1. Scott, Walter, Sir, 1771-1832 — Criticism and interpretation. I. T.
PR5341.M54   823/.7 19   *ISBN* 0802025277

Wilt, Judith, 1941-.   **2.8061**
Secret leaves: the novels of Walter Scott / Judith Wilt. — Chicago: University of Chicago Press, 1985. vii, 231 p.; 23 cm. (A Chicago original paperback) Includes index. 1. Scott, Walter, Sir, 1771-1832 — Criticism and interpretation. I. T.
PR5341.W55 1985   823/.7 19   *LC* 85-8615   *ISBN* 0226901610

Welsh, Alexander.   • **2.8062**
The hero of the Waverley novels. — New Haven: Yale University Press, 1963. xiv, 273 p.; 23 cm. — (Yale studies in English. v. 154) 1. Scott, Walter, Sir, 1771-1832 — Characters. 2. Scott, Walter, Sir, 1771-1832. Waverly novels. 3. Heroes in literature I. T. II. Series.
PR5342.A2 W4   *LC* 63-7954

PR5360–5368 Shaw

Shaw, Bernard, 1856-1950.   • **2.8063**
The collected works of Bernard Shaw. — Ayot St. Lawrence ed. New York: W.H. Wise, 1930-. v.: front., port.; 24 cm. Each volume has special title page. Limited to 1790 sets. I. T.
PR5360.F30   *LC* 30-29359

Shaw, Bernard, 1856-1950.   • **2.8064**
[Plays. 1962] Complete plays, with prefaces. New York, Dodd, Mead, 1962. 6 v. ports. 22 cm. I. T.
PR5360.F62   822.912   *LC* 62-13608

Shaw, Bernard, 1856-1950.   • **2.8065**
Selected non-dramatic writings. Edited by Dan H. Laurence. Boston, Houghton Mifflin [1965] xiv, 455 p. 21 cm. (Riverside editions, B71) I. Laurence, Dan H. ed. II. T.
PR5361.L3   828.91208   *LC* 65-4708

Shaw, Bernard, 1856-1950.   • **2.8066**
Selected prose / selected by Diarmuid Russell. — New York: Dodd, Mead, c1952. 1004 p.; 22 cm. I. T.
PR5361.R8   *LC* 52-11523

Shaw, Bernard, 1856-1950.   **2.8067**
The complete prefaces of Bernard Shaw. London, Paul Hamlyn [1965] vii, 948 p. 25 cm. I. T.
PR5364.P7x   *LC* 66-83980

PR5366–5368 Biography. Criticism

Broad, Lewis, 1900-.   • **2.8068**
Dictionary to the plays and novels of Bernard Shaw, with bibliography of his works and of the literature concerning him, with a record of the principal Shavian play productions, by C. Lewis Broad and Violet M. Broad. St. Clair Shores, Mich., Scholarly Press, 1972. xi, 230 p. port. 22 cm. Reprint of the 1929 ed. 1. Shaw, Bernard, 1856-1950 — Dictionaries, indexes, etc. 2. Shaw, Bernard, 1856-1950 — Bibliography. I. Broad, Violet M. joint author. II. T.
PR5366.A23 1972   822/.9/12   *LC* 76-131645   *ISBN* 0403005329

Shaw, Bernard, 1856-1950. • 2.8069
Collected letters. Edited by Dan H. Laurence. New York, Dodd, Mead [1965-.
v. illus. facsim. ports 25 cm. I. Laurence, Dan H. ed. II. T.
PR5366.A4 1965 826.912 LC 65-22550

Shaw, Bernard, 1856-1950. • 2.8070
[Correspondence. Selections. English. 1952] Bernard Shaw and Mrs. Patrick
Campbell: their correspondence / edited by Alan Dent. — 1st American ed. —
New York: A.A. Knopf, 1952. xvii, 385, xiii p.; 22 cm. 1. Shaw, Bernard,
1856-1950 — Correspondence 2. Campbell, Patrick, Mrs., 1865-1940.
I. Campbell, Patrick, Mrs., 1865-1940. II. Dent, Alan. III. T.
PR5366.A42 1952 LC 52-6411

Shaw, Bernard, 1856-1950. • 2.8071
Letters to Granville Barker / edited by C. B. Purdom with commentary and
notes. — New York: Theatre Arts Books, [c1957] viii, 206 p.: ill.; 22 cm.
1. Shaw, Bernard, 1856-1950 — Correspondence. 2. Granville-Barker,
Harley, 1877-1946 — Correspondence. I. Purdom, C.B. II. Granville-Barker,
Harley, 1877-1946. III. T.
PR5366.A463 LC 56-9608

Shaw, Bernard, 1856-1950. • 2.8072
[Essays. 1969] Shaw; an autobiography, selected from his writings by Stanley
Weintraub. New York, Weybright and Talley [1969-70] 2 v. illus., ports. 25 cm.
1. Shaw, Bernard, 1856-1950. I. Weintraub, Stanley, 1929- comp. II. T.
PR5366.A5 1969 822/.9/12 B LC 74-84621

Brown, Ivor John Carnegie, 1891-. • 2.8073
Shaw in his time / Ivor Brown. — [London]: Nelson, [1965] 212 p.: ill., ports.;
23 cm. 1. Shaw, Bernard, 1856-1950. I. T.
PR5366.B7 LC 66-31903

Chappelow, Allan, ed. 2.8074
Shaw the villager and human being, a biographical symposium, assembled and
narrated by Allan Chappelow. Foreword by Sybil Thorndike. New York,
Macmillan, 1962 [c1961] xxvi, 354 p. illus., ports., facsims. 24 cm. 1. Shaw,
Bernard, 1856-1950. I. T.
PR5366.C5 1962 928.2 LC 62-51710

Ervine, St. John G. (St. John Greer), b. 1883. • 2.8075
Bernard Shaw, his life, work, and friends. — New York: Morrow, 1956. 628 p.:
ill.; 25 cm. 1. Shaw, Bernard, 1856-1950. I. T.
PR5366.E7 1956a LC 56-9717

Kaufmann, Ralph James, 1924- ed. • 2.8076
G. B. Shaw; a collection of critical essays, edited by R. J. Kaufmann.
Englewood Cliffs, N.J., Prentice Hall [1965] 182 p. 21 cm. (Twentieth century
views) 'A Spectrum book.' 1. Shaw, Bernard, 1856-1950. I. T.
PR5366.K28 822.912 LC 65-23295

Ohmann, Richard Malin. • 2.8077
Shaw: the style and the man / by Richard M. Ohmann. — 1st ed. Middletown,
Conn.: Wesleyan University Press, 1962. 200 p.: ill.; 22 cm. 1. Shaw, Bernard,
1856-1950 — Biography. 2. Authors, English — Biography I. T.
PR5366.O45 828.912 LC 62-18343

Pearson, Hesketh, 1887-1964. • 2.8078
George Bernard Shaw: his life and personality. — New York, Atheneum, 1963.
480 p. 19 cm. — (Atheneum paperbacks, 36) First published in London in 1942
under title: Bernard Shaw: his life and personality. 1. Shaw, Bernard,
1856-1950. I. T.
PR5366.P4 1963 928.2 LC 63-4164

Peters, Margot. 2.8079
Bernard Shaw and the actresses / Margot Peters. — 1st ed. — Garden City,
N.Y.: Doubleday, 1980. xiv, 461 p., [12] leaves of plates: ill.; 25 cm. Includes
index. 1. Shaw, Bernard, 1856-1950 — Relations with women. 2. Dramatists,
English — 19th century — Biography. 3. Actresses — Great Britain —
Biography. I. T.
PR5366.P45 1980 822/.912 B LC 79-7205 ISBN 0385120516

Bentley, Eric, 1916-. • 2.8080
Bernard Shaw [by] Eric Bentley. 2nd ed. London, Methuen, 1967. xviii, 204 p.
21 1/2 cm. 1. Shaw, Bernard, 1856-1950 — Criticism and interpretation. I. T.
PR5367.B4 1967 822/.9/12 LC 67-100979

Berst, Charles A. 2.8081
Bernard Shaw and the art of drama [by] Charles A. Berst. — Urbana:
University of Illinois Press, [1973] xx, 343 p.; 24 cm. 1. Shaw, Bernard,
1856-1950 — Criticism and interpretation. I. T.
PR5367.B44 822/.9/12 LC 72-93625 ISBN 025200258X

Chesterton, G. K. (Gilbert Keith), 1874-1936. • 2.8082
George Bernard Shaw. [New ed., with additional chapter] London, Bodley
Head [1948] 295 p.; 18 cm. Sullivan 15, note. 1. Shaw, Bernard, 1856-1950.
I. T.
PR5367.C5 1948

Gibbs, A. M. (Anthony Matthews), 1933-. 2.8083
The art and mind of Shaw: essays in criticism / A.M. Gibbs. — New York: St.
Martin's Press, 1983. ix, 224 p.; 23 cm. 1. Shaw, Bernard, 1856-1950 —
Criticism and interpretation. I. T.
PR5367.G48 1983 822/.912 19 LC 82-19158 ISBN 0312049927

MacCarthy, Desmond, 1878-1952. • 2.8084
Shaw's plays in review. — New York: Thames and Hudson, [c1951] 217 p.; 22
cm. 1. Shaw, Bernard, 1856-1950. I. T.
PR5367.M3 LC 52-596

Meisel, Martin. • 2.8085
Shaw and the nineteenth-century theater. Princeton, N.J., Princeton University
Press, 1963. 477 p. illus. 23 cm. 1. Shaw, Bernard, 1856-1950 — Criticism and
interpretation. 2. English drama — 19th century — History and criticism.
I. T.
PR5367.M38 822.912 LC 63-7074

Purdom, C. B. (Charles Benjamin), 1883-. • 2.8086
A guide to the plays of Bernard Shaw / by C.B. Purdom. — New York:
Crowell, 1963. 344 p.; 21 cm. 1. Shaw, Bernard, 1856-1950. I. T.
PR5367.P8 1963a LC 63-18410

Valency, Maurice Jacques, 1903-. 2.8087
The cart and the trumpet; the plays of George Bernard Shaw [by] Maurice
Valency. New York, Oxford University Press, 1973. ix, 467 p. 24 cm. 1. Shaw,
Bernard, 1856-1950 — Criticism and interpretation. 2. English drama — 19th
century — History and criticism. I. T.
PR5367.V3 822/.9/12 LC 72-92301 ISBN 019501636X

Chappelow, Allan. 2.8088
Shaw—'the Chucker-Out'; a biographical exposition and critique, and a
companion to and commentary on 'Shaw the villager'. Foreword by Vera
Brittain. New York, AMS Press, 1971. xx, 558 p. illus. 24 cm. 1. Shaw,
Bernard, 1856-1950 — Political and social views. I. T.
PR5368.P6 C47 1971 822/.912 B 19 LC 74-152559 ISBN
0404083595

Hummert, Paul A., 1918-. 2.8089
Bernard Shaw's Marxian romance [by] Paul A. Hummert. Lincoln, University
of Nebraska Press [c1973] xiv, 227 p. 24 cm. 1. Shaw, Bernard, 1856-1950 —
Political and social views. 2. Marx, Karl, 1818-1883. I. T.
PR5368.P6 H93 822/.9/12 LC 75-144815 ISBN 0803207743

Mander, Raymond, comp. 2.8090
Theatrical companion to Shaw; a pictorial record of the first performances of
the plays of George Bernard Shaw, by Raymond Mander & Joe Mitchenson.
London Rockliff [1955] 343p. 1. Shaw, Bernard, 1856-1950 — Stage history
I. Mitchenson, Joe. jt. comp. II. T.
PR5368 S75 M3 1955

PR5397–5398 Mary Wollstonecraft Shelley

Shelley, Mary Wollstonecraft, 1797-1851. • 2.8091
[Frankenstein] Frankenstein; or The modern Prometheus [by] Mary W.
Shelley. [1831 ed.]; edited with an introduction by M. K. Joseph. London, New
York, Oxford U.P., 1969. xxv, 241 p. 1 illus. 21 cm. (Oxford English novels)
I. Joseph, M. K. ed. II. T.
PR5397.F7 1969 823/.7 LC 71-432987 ISBN 0192553259

The Endurance of Frankenstein: essays on Mary Shelley's novel 2.8092
/ edited by George Levine and U. C. Knoepflmacher.
Berkeley: University of California Press, c1979. xx, 341 p.: ill.; 24 cm. Includes
index. 1. Shelley, Mary Wollstonecraft, 1797-1851 Frankenstein — Addresses,
essays, lectures. I. Levine, George Lewis. II. Knoepflmacher, U. C.
PR5397.F73 E5 823/.7 LC 77-20325 ISBN 0520036123

Shelley, Mary Wollstonecraft, 1797-1851. • 2.8093
Mary Shelley's journal, ed. by Frederick L. Jones. [1st ed.] Norman, Univ. of
Oklahoma Press, 1947. xxi, 247 p.; 24 cm. 'The text ... is taken from the Modern
Language Association rotograph of Dowden's copy of Shelley and Mary.'-p.xii.
1. Shelley, Percy Bysshe, 1792-1822. I. Jones, Frederick Lafayette, 1901-
II. T.
PR5398.A28 1947 823.79 LC 47-31418

Shelley, Mary Wollstonecraft, 1797-1851.   • 2.8094
The letters of Mary W. Shelley, collected and edited by Frederick L. Jones.
Norman, University of Oklahoma press, 1944. 2 v.: ill.; 24 cm. 'First edition.'
I. Jones, Frederick Lafayette, 1901- II. T.
PR5398.A42   823.79   LC 44-9875

Neumann, Bonnie Rayford.   2.8095
The lonely muse: a critical biography of Mary Wollstonecraft Shelley / by
Bonnie Rayford Neumann. — Salzburg, Austria: Institut für Anglistik und
Amerikanistik, Universität Salzburg, 1979. 283 p.; 21 cm. (Romantic
reassessment; 85) (Salzburg studies in English literature) 1. Shelley, Mary
Wollstonecraft, 1797-1851. 2. Authors, English — 19th century — Biography.
I. T.
PR5398.N4   823/.7 B   LC 80-482016

PR5400–5448 Percy Bysshe Shelley

Shelley, Percy Bysshe, 1792-1822.   2.8096
The complete poetical works of Percy Bysshe Shelley; edited by Neville Rogers.
— Oxford: Clarendon Press, 1972-. v. : facsim.; 23 cm. I. Rogers, Neville. ed.
II. T.
PR5402 1972   821/.7   LC 73-150180   ISBN 0198118546

Shelley, Percy Bysshe, 1792-1822.   2.8097
[Selections. 1977] Shelley's Poetry and prose: authoritative texts, criticism /
selected and edited by Donald H. Reiman and Sharon B. Powers. — 1st ed. —
New York: Norton, c1977. xix, 700 p.; 22 cm. (A Norton critical edition)
Includes index. I. Reiman, Donald H. II. Powers, Sharon B. III. T.
PR5403.R4   821/.7   LC 76-26929   ISBN 039304436X. ISBN
0393091643 pbk

PR5429–5448 Biography. Criticism

Shelley, Percy Bysshe, 1792-1822.   • 2.8098
Letters / Edited by Frederick L. Jones. Oxford, Clarendon P. 1964. 2 v.; 23 cm.
I. Jones, Frederick Lafayette, 1901-. II. T.
PR5431.A3 1964   928.2   LC 64-1836

Blunden, Edmund, 1896-1974.   • 2.8099
Shelley, a life story, by Edmund Blunden ... — New York, The Viking press,
1947. xii, 388 p. 22 cm. First published in London in 1946. Bibliographical
references in 'Appendix: Some Shelleyana' (p. 371-379) 1. Shelley, Percy
Bysshe, 1792-1822. I. T.
PR5431.B5 1947   928.2   LC 47-30070

Cameron, Kenneth Neill.   2.8100
Shelley: the golden years. — Cambridge: Harvard University Press, 1974. x,
669 p.; 26 cm. Continuation of the author's The young Shelley. 1. Shelley,
Percy Bysshe, 1792-1822. I. T.
PR5431.C29   821/.7 B   LC 73-80566   ISBN 0674031601

Hodgart, Patricia.   2.8101
A preface to Shelley / Patricia Hodgart. — London; New York: Longman,
1985. xii, 204 p.: ill.; 22 cm. (Preface books) Includes indexes. 1. Shelley, Percy
Bysshe, 1792-1822. 2. Poets, English — 19th century — Biography. I. T.
PR5431.H58 1985   821/.7 B 92 19   LC 84-7190   ISBN
058235370X

Hogg, Thomas Jefferson, 1792-1862.   • 2.8102
The life of Percy Bysshe Shelley. With an introd. by Edward Dowden. London,
G. Routledge; New York, E. P. Dutton, 1906. — St. Clair Shores, Mich.:
Scholarly Press, 1970. xx, 585 p.; 21 cm. First published in 1858. 1. Shelley,
Percy Bysshe, 1792-1822 — Biography. I. T.
PR5431.H6 1970   821/.7 B   LC 76-145089   ISBN 0403007542

Maurois, André, 1885-1967.   • 2.8103
[Ariel; ou, la vie de Shelley. English] Ariel; the life of Shelley. [Translated by
Ella D'Arcy] New York, F. Ungar Pub. Co. [c1952] 335 p. 22 cm. 1. Shelley,
Percy Bysshe, 1792-1822. I. T.
PR5431.M32 1952   928.2   LC 57-12326

White, Newman Ivey, 1892-1948.   • 2.8104
Shelley. — New York: Octagon Books, 1972 [c1940] 2 v.: illus.; 24 cm.
1. Shelley, Percy Bysshe, 1792-1822. I. T.
PR5431.W5 1972   821/.7 B   LC 72-7385   ISBN 0374984263

White, Newman Ivey, 1892-1948.   • 2.8105
Portrait of Shelley / by Newman Ivey White. — [1st ed.] New York: Knopf,
1945. 482, xxiii p., [1] leaf of plates: col. port.; 22 cm. Typography and binding
design by W.A. Dwiggins. Includes index. 1. Shelley, Percy Bysshe, 1792-1822.
I. T.
PR5431.W52   LC 45-2732

Cameron, Kenneth Neill.   • 2.8106
The young Shelley; genesis of a radical. — New York: Octagon Books, 1973
[c1950] xii, 437 p.; 23 cm. Continued by the author's Shelley: the golden years.
Reprint of the ed. published by Macmillan, New York. 1. Shelley, Percy
Bysshe, 1792-1822 — Political and social views. I. T.
PR5432.C3 1973   821/.7 B   LC 73-8660   ISBN 0374912556

Baker, Carlos, 1909-1987.   • 2.8107
Shelley's major poetry: the fabric of a vision. — New York, Russell & Russell,
1961 [c1948] 307 p. 25 cm. Includes bibliography. 1. Shelley, Percy Bysshe,
1792-1822. I. T.
PR5438.B26 1961   821.7   LC 61-12127

Bloom, Harold.   • 2.8108
Shelley's mythmaking. — New Haven: Yale University Press, 1959. 279 p.; 24
cm. — (Yale studies in English. v. 141) This study, in its initial form, was
presented to Yale University as a doctoral dissertation. 1. Shelley, Percy
Bysshe, 1792-1822. I. T. II. Series.
PR5438.B55   821.7   LC 59-6793

Curran, Stuart.   2.8109
Shelley's annus mirabilis: the maturing of an epic vision / by Stuart Curran. —
San Marino, Calif.: Huntington Library, 1975. xxii, 255 p.: ill.; 24 cm.
1. Shelley, Percy Bysshe, 1792-1822 — Criticism and interpretation. I. T.
PR5438.C8   821/.7   LC 75-318514   ISBN 0873280644

King-Hele, Desmond, 1927-.   2.8110
Shelley: his thought and work. — 2d ed. — Teaneck [N.J.]: Fairleigh Dickinson
University Press, [1971] vii, 394 p.: maps.; 23 cm. 1. Shelley, Percy Bysshe,
1792-1822 — Criticism and interpretation. I. T.
PR5438.K5 1971   821/.7   LC 73-163306   ISBN 0838610226

Wasserman, Earl R. (Earl Reeves), 1913-.   2.8111
Shelley: a critical reading [by] Earl R. Wasserman. Baltimore, Johns Hopkins
Press [1971] xiii, 507 p. 25 cm. 1. Shelley, Percy Bysshe, 1792-1822 —
Criticism and interpretation. I. T.
PR5438.W3   821/.7   LC 70-138036   ISBN 0801812127

Webb, Timothy.   2.8112
The violet in the crucible: Shelley and translation / Timothy Webb. Oxford:
Clarendon Press, 1976. xii, 364 p.; 23 cm. Includes index. 1. Shelley, Percy
Bysshe, 1792-1822 — Knowledge — Literature. 2. European literature —
Translations into English — History and criticism. 3. English literature —
Translations from foreign languages — History and criticism I. T. II. Title:
Shelley and translation.
PR5442.L5 W4   821/.7   LC 77-362953   ISBN 0198120591

Keach, William, 1942-.   2.8113
Shelley's style / William Keach. — New York: Methuen, 1985. xvii, 269 p.: 1
facsim.; 25 cm. Includes indexes. 1. Shelley, Percy Bysshe, 1792-1822 — Style.
I. T.
PR5444.K4 1984   821/.7 19   LC 84-1151   ISBN 041630320X

PR5473.S6 Stephen

Stephen, Leslie, Sir, 1832-1904.   2.8114
Some early impressions / Leslie Stephen. — New York: B. Franklin, [1968]
192 p.; 23 cm. — (Burt Franklin research & source work series; no. 172)
1. Authors, English — Correspondence, reminiscences, etc. I. T. II. Series.
PR5473.S6 A67   LC 68-4623

Stephen, Leslie, Sir, 1832-1904.   2.8115
[Mausoleum book] Sir Leslie Stephen's Mausoleum book / with an introd. by
Alan Bell. — Oxford [Eng.]: Clarendon Press, 1977. xxxiii, 118 p., [4] leaves of
plates: ports.; 23 cm. Includes index. 1. Stephen, Leslie, Sir, 1832-1904 —
Biography — Marriage. 2. Authors, English — 19th century — Biography.
I. T. II. Title: Mausoleum book.
PR5473.S6 A815 1977   828/.8/09 B   LC 77-10887   ISBN
0198120842

Annan, Noel Gilroy Annan, Baron, 1916-.   2.8116
Leslie Stephen: the Godless Victorian / Noel Annan. — 1st American ed. —
New York: Random House, c1984. xv, 432 p., [8] p. of plates: ill.; 24 cm.
Includes index. 1. Stephen, Leslie, Sir, 1832-1904 — Biography. 2. Authors,
English — 19th century — Biography. 3. Atheists — Great Britain —
Biography. I. T.
PR5473.S6 A88 1984   828/.809 B 19   LC 84-42512   ISBN
0394530616

PR5480–5498 Stevenson

Stevenson, Robert Louis, 1850-1894. • **2.8117**
The works of Robert Louis Stevenson. — New York: C. Scribner, 1921-23. 26 v.: front. (port.), facsim. Each volume has also special title page. I. T.
PR5480.F21 *LC* 21-21632

Stevenson, Robert Louis, 1850-1894. • **2.8118**
Novels and stories: selected with an introd. by V.S. Pritchett. London, Pilot Press, 1945 [i.e. 1946] 615 p. 23 cm. (Pilot omnibus 2) I. Pritchett, V. S. (Victor Sawdon), 1900- comp. II. T.
PZ3.S848 No PR5481.Px. *LC* 48-4119

The Definitive Dr. Jekyll and Mr. Hyde companion / edited by **2.8119**
Harry M. Geduld.
New York: Garland, 1983. xi, 219 p.: ill.; 27 cm. 1. Stevenson, Robert Louis, 1850-1894 Strange case of Dr. Jekyll and Mr. Hyde — Addresses, essays, lectures. 2. Stevenson, Robert Louis, 1850-1894 — Adaptations — Addresses, essays, lectures. 3. Split self in literature — Addresses, essays, lectures. 4. Horror in mass media — Addresses, essays, lectures. I. Geduld, Harry M.
PR5485.D4 1983 823/.8 19 *LC* 82-48271 *ISBN* 0824094697

Stevenson, Robert Louis, 1850-1894. • **2.8120**
Collected poems. Edited, with an introd. and notes, by Janet Adam Smith. — 2d ed. — New York: Viking Press, [1971] 572 p.: illus.; 21 cm. — I. T.
PR5489.A2 1971 821/.8 *LC* 79-144343 *ISBN* 0670229091

Stevenson, Robert Louis, 1850-1894. • **2.8121**
RLS: Stevenson's letters to Charles Baxter / edited by De Lancey Ferguson and Marshall Waingrow. — New Haven: Yale University Press, 1956. xxvi, 385 p.: ill., port., facsims. I. Baxter, Charles, 1848-1919 II. Ferguson, J. De Lancey (John De Lancey), 1888- III. Waingrow, Marshall IV. T.
PR5493 A3 1956 PR5493 A3 1956. 928.2 *LC* 56-7119

Stevenson, Robert Louis, 1850-1894. • **2.8122**
[Correspondence] The letters of Robert Louis Stevenson / edited by Sidney Colvin. — A new ed. rearranged in four volumes with 150 new letters. New York: Greenwood Press [1969] 4 v.; 23 cm. At head of title: Biographical edition. Reprint of the 1911 ed. 1. Stevenson, Robert Louis, 1850-1894. I. Colvin, Sidney, Sir, 1845-1927. ed. II. T.
PR5493.A3 1969b 828/.8/09 B *LC* 69-14101 *ISBN* 0837114403

Daiches, David, 1912-. **2.8123**
Robert Louis Stevenson and his world. — New Jersey: Transatlantic Arts, 1974, c1973. 128 p.: illus.; 24 cm. 1. Stevenson, Robert Louis, 1850-1894 — Biography. I. T.
PR5493.D22 828/.8/09 B *ISBN* 0500130450

Eigner, Edwin M. **2.8124**
Robert Louis Stevenson and romantic tradition / by Edwin M. Eigner. — Princeton, N.J.: Princeton University Press, 1966. xii, 258 p.; 23 cm. 1. Stevenson, Robert Louis, 1850-1894 — Biography. I. T.
PR5493.E35 823.8 *LC* 66-11969

Furnas, J. C. (Joseph Chamberlain), 1905-. **2.8125**
Voyage to windward; the life of Robert Louis Stevenson. — New York, Sloane [1951] x, 566 p. illus., ports. 22 cm. Bibliography: p. 473-492. 1. Stevenson, Robert Louis, 1850-1894. I. T.
PR5493.F8 928.2 *LC* 51-12678

Pope-Hennessy, James. **2.8126**
Robert Louis Stevenson / James Pope Hennessy. — New York: Simon and Schuster, [1975] c1974. 320 p., [8] leaves of plates: ill.; 22 cm. Includes index. 1. Stevenson, Robert Louis, 1850-1894 — Biography. I. T.
PR5493.P6 1975 828/.8/09 *LC* 74-23350 *ISBN* 0671219731 lib. bdg

Swearingen, Roger G., 1944-. **2.8127**
The prose writings of Robert Louis Stevenson: a guide / by Roger G. Swearingen. — Hamden, Conn.: Archon Books, 1980. xxiii, 217 p.; 24 cm. Includes index. 1. Stevenson, Robert Louis, 1850-1894 — Chronology. 2. Stevenson, Robert Louis, 1850-1894 — Bibliography. I. Stevenson, Robert Louis, 1850-1894. II. T.
PR5493.S9 1980 828/.8/09 *LC* 79-26612 *ISBN* 0208018263

Daiches, David, 1912-. • **2.8128**
Robert Louis Stevenson. Norfolk, Conn., New Directions Books [c1947] x, 196 p.: port.; 19 cm. — (The Makers of modern literature.) 1. Stevenson, Robert Louis, 1850-1894. I. T.
PR5496.D3 *LC* 47-11770

Robert Louis Stevenson, the critical heritage / edited by Paul **2.8129**
Maixner.
London; Boston: Routledge & Kegan Paul, 1981. xxiii, 532 p.; 23 cm. — (Critical heritage series.) Includes indexes. 1. Stevenson, Robert Louis, 1850-1894 — Criticism and interpretation. I. Maixner, Paul. II. Series.
PR5496.R6 828/.809 19 *LC* 80-42296 *ISBN* 0710005059

PR5499 Surtees

Surtees, Robert Smith, 1805-1864. • **2.8130**
Jorrocks' jaunts and jollities; with an introduction by Alex Hamilton. — London: Cassell, 1968. xvii, 231 p.; 18 cm. — (The first novel library, 16) I. T.
PZ3.S9627 Jo6 PR5499.S4 823/.8 *LC* 73-407776 *ISBN* 0304930741

Surtees, Robert Smith, 1805-1864. **2.8131**
Handley Cross: or, Mr. Jorrocks's hunt / by the author of 'Mr. Sponge's sporting tour,' 'Ask mamma,' 'Plain or ringlets?' etc., etc.; with ill. by John Leech. — New York: AMS Press, 1979. p. cm. Reprint of the 1930 ed. published by Viking Press, New York. I. Leech, John, 1817-1864. II. Mr. Sponge's sporting tour, Author of. III. T. IV. Title: Mr. Jorrocks's hunt.
PZ3.S9627 Han 1979 PR5499.S4 Hx 823/.8 *LC* 75-41268 *ISBN* 0404146147

Surtees, Robert Smith, 1805-1864. **2.8132**
Mr. Facey Romford's hounds / R.S. Surtees; with an introduction by Jeremy Lewis. — Oxford; New York: Oxford University Press, 1984. xxiii 438 p.; 19 cm. (The World's classics) (Oxford paperbacks) I. T. II. Title: Mister Facey Romford's hounds.
PR5499.S4 M48 1984 823/.8 19 *LC* 83-23737 *ISBN* 0192816578

Surtees, Robert Smith, 1805-1864. **2.8133**
Mr. Sponge's sporting tour / R.S. Surtees; with an introduction by Joyce Cary; and the original illustrations by John Leech. — Oxford [Oxfordshire]; New York: Oxford University Press, 1982. xxv, 500 p.: ill.; 19 cm. — (The World's classics) Originally published: London: Oxford University Press, 1958. I. T.
PR5499.S4 M5 1982 823/.8 19 *LC* 81-18737 *ISBN* 0192815210

PR5500–5518 Swinburne

Swinburne, Algernon Charles, 1837-1909. **2.8134**
New writings by Swinburne: a medley of poems, critical essays, hoaxes & burlesques / edited by Cecil Y. Lang. — [Syracuse] Syracuse University Press, 1964. xv, 253 p. 24 cm. I. Lang, Cecil Y. ed. II. T.
PR5502.L3 *LC* 64-8669

Swinburne, Algernon Charles, 1837-1909. **2.8135**
The poems of Algernon Charles Swinburne. London, Chatto & Windus, 1904–05. — [New York: AMS Press, 1972] 6 v.; 19 cm. I. T.
PR5505 1972 821/.8 *LC* 77-148312 *ISBN* 0404089305

Swinburne, Algernon Charles, 1837-1909. **2.8136**
[Love's cross-currents] The novels of A. C. Swinburne / with an introd. by Edmund Wilson. — Westport, Conn.: Greenwood Press, 1978, c1962. 377 p.; 23 cm. Reprint of the ed. published by Farrar, Straus and Cudahy, New York. I. Swinburne, Algernon Charles, 1837-1909. Lesbia Brandon. 1978. II. T.
PZ3.S977 No 1978 PR5510.A1x 823/.8 *LC* 77-20107 *ISBN* 0313200106

Swinburne, Algernon Charles, 1837-1909. • **2.8137**
Letters / edited by Cecil Y. Lang. — New Haven: Yale University Press, 1959-1962. 6 v.: facsims., port.; 25 cm. — (The Yale edition of the Swinburne letters) 1. Swinburne, Algernon Charles, 1837-1909 — Correpondence. 2. Swinburne, Algernon Charles, 1837-1909. I. Lang, Cecil Y. II. T. III. Series.
PR5513.A32 *LC* 59-12698

Henderson, Philip, 1906-. **2.8138**
Swinburne; portrait of a poet. — [1st American ed.]. — New York: Macmillan, [1974] xiii, 305 p.: illus.; 24 cm. 1. Swinburne, Algernon Charles, 1837-1909 — Biography. I. T.
PR5513.H38 821/.8 *LC* 74-478 *ISBN* 0025509608

Connolly, Thomas Edmund, 1918-. • **2.8139**
Swinburne's theory of poetry / Thomas E. Connolly. — [Albany]: State University of New York, 1964. 144 p. 22 cm. 1. Swinburne, Algernon Charles, 1837-1909. I. T.
PR5514.C6 801.9 *LC* 64-17576

McGann, Jerome J. **2.8140**
Swinburne; an experiment in criticism [by] Jerome J. McGann. — Chicago: University of Chicago Press, [1972] xi, 321 p.; 24 cm. 1. Swinburne, Algernon Charles, 1837-1909 — Criticism and interpretation. I. T.
PR5514.M27 821/.8 *LC* 72-77598 *ISBN* 0226558460

Riede, David G.   **2.8141**
Swinburne: a study of romantic mythmaking / David G. Riede. — Charlottesville: University Press of Virginia, 1978. x, 227 p.; 24 cm. 1. Swinburne, Algernon Charles, 1837-1909 — Criticism and interpretation. 2. Myth in literature I. T.
PR5517.M82 R5   821/.8   *LC* 78-4940   *ISBN* 0813907454

PR5520–5534 Symonds. Synge

Symonds, John Addington, 1840-1893.   **2.8142**
The memoirs of John Addington Symonds / edited and introduced by Phyllis Grosskurth. — New York: Random House, c1984. 318 p., [12] p. of plates: ill., ports.; 25 cm. Includes index. 1. Symonds, John Addington, 1840-1893 — Biography. 2. Authors, English — 19th century — Biography. 3. Gay men — England — Biography. I. Grosskurth, Phyllis. II. T.
PR5523.A425 1984   828/.809 B 19   *LC* 84-42676   *ISBN* 0394540859

Grosskurth, Phyllis.   **2.8143**
The woeful Victorian; a biography of John Addington Symonds. — [1st ed.]. — New York, Holt, Rinehart and Winston [1965, c1964] x, 370 p. illus., ports. 22 cm. First published in 1964 under title: John Addington Symonds. Bibliographical references included in 'Notes' (p. 329-355) Bibliography: p. 357-361. 1. Symonds, John Addington, 1840-1893. I. T.
PR5523.G7 1965   928.2   *LC* 65-14446

Synge, J. M. (John Millington), 1871-1909.   • **2.8144**
The complete works of John M. Synge. New York, Random House [c1935] 5 p. l., 7-625 p. 20 cm. I. T.
PR5530.A2 1935   820.81 822.91   *LC* 35-27153

Synge, J. M. (John Millington), 1871-1909.   • **2.8145**
The plays and poems of J. M. Synge / Edited with an introd. and notes by T. R. Henn. — London: Methuen, [1963] xi, 363 p.; 21 cm. I. Henn, T. R. II. T.
PR5530.A2 1963   828.912   *LC* 65-1566   *ISBN* 041626500X

Synge, J. M. (John Millington), 1871-1909.   • **2.8146**
Collected works / [general editor: Robin Skelton]. — London: Oxford University Press, 1962-68. 4 v.: port., facsims; 22 cm. I. Skelton, Robin, 1925-. II. T.
PR5530.A5 S5   *LC* 63-804

Synge, J. M. (John Millington), 1871-1909.   **2.8147**
[Correspondence] The collected letters of John Millington Synge: vol. 1: 1871–1907 / edited by Ann Saddlemyer. — Oxford [Oxfordshire]: Clarendon Press; New York: Oxford University Press, 1983. 385 p. 1. Dramatists, Irish — 20th century — Correspondence. I. Saddlemyer, Ann. II. T.
PR5533.A44 1983   822/.912 B 19   *LC* 82-14535   *ISBN* 0198126786

Greene, David Herbert, 1913-.   • **2.8148**
J. M. Synge, 1871–1909, by David H. Greene and Edward M. Stephens. New York, Macmillan, 1959. 321 p.: ill.; 22 cm. 1. Synge, J. M. (John Millington), 1871-1909. I. Stephens, Edward M., d. 1955. II. T.
PR5533.G7   822.91   *LC* 59-7443

Skelton, Robin.   • **2.8149**
J. M. Synge and his world. New York, Viking Press [1971] 144 p. illus., facsims., map, ports. 24 cm. (A Studio book) 1. Synge, J. M. (John Millington), 1871-1909. I. T.
PR5533.S5   822/.9/12 B   *LC* 75-142147   *ISBN* 0670407291

Thornton, Weldon.   **2.8150**
J. M. Synge and the Western mind / Weldon Thornton. — New York: Harper & Row, 1979. 169 p.; 23 cm. (Irish literary studies. 4) Includes index. 1. Synge, J. M. (John Millington), 1871-1909. 2. Authors, Irish — 19th century — Biography. I. T. II. Series.
PR5533.T55 1979   822/.9/12   *LC* 78-13301   *ISBN* 0064968790

Grene, Nicholas.   **2.8151**
Synge: a critical study of the plays / Nicholas Grene. — Totowa, N.J.: Rowman and Littlefield, 1976 (c1975). 202 p.; 22 cm. Includes index. 1. Synge, J. M. (John Millington), 1871-1909 — Criticism and interpretation. I. T.
PR5534.G7   822/.9/2   *LC* 75-29091   *ISBN* 0874717752

Price, Alan Frederick.   **2.8152**
Synge and Anglo–Irish drama [by] Alan Price. New York, Russell & Russell [1972, c1961] xi, 236 p. 23 cm. 1. Synge, J. M. (John Millington), 1871-1909. 2. English drama — Irish authors — History and criticism. I. T.
PR5534.P7 1972   822/.9/12   *LC* 70-173554

PR5550–5598 Tennyson

Tennyson, Alfred Tennyson, Baron, 1809-1892.   **2.8153**
[Works. 1987] The poems of Tennyson / edited by Christopher Ricks. — 2nd ed. — Berkeley: University of California Press, 1987. 3 v.; 23 cm. Includes indexes. I. Ricks, Christopher B. II. T.
PR5550 1987   821/.8 19   *LC* 86-30726   *ISBN* 0520060121

Tennyson, Alfred Tennyson, Baron, 1809-1892.   • **2.8154**
Poetical works, including the plays / Alfred Tennyson. — London: Oxford University Press, 1953. xvi, 867 p.; 19 cm. I. T.
PR5550.F53   821.8   *LC* 54-8589

Tennyson, Alfred Tennyson, Baron, 1809-1892.   • **2.8155**
[Works. 1970] The works of Tennyson. [Annotated by Alfred Lord Tennyson. Edited by Hallam, Lord Tennyson. Westport, Conn., Greenwood Press, 1970] 9 v. illus., facsims., ports. 17 cm. Cover title. 'The Eversley edition.' Reprint of the 1907-08 ed. I. Tennyson, Hallam Tennyson, Baron, 1852-1928. ed. II. T.
PR5550.F70b   821/.8   *LC* 73-118673   *ISBN* 0837145708

Tennyson, Alfred Tennyson, 1st Baron, 1809-1892.   • **2.8156**
Poems / selected with an introduction and notes by Jerome Hamilton Buckley. — Boston: Houghton Mifflin, [c1958] 542 p. — (Riverside editions; B26) I. Buckley, Jerome Hamilton, 1917-. II. T. III. Series.
PR5551 1958   *LC* 58-14851

Buckler, William Earl, 1924-.   **2.8157**
Man and his myths: Tennyson's Idylls of the king in critical context / William E. Buckler. — New York: New York University Press, 1984. xiii, 360 p.; 24 cm. — (Gotham library of the New York University Press) Includes index. 1. Tennyson, Alfred Tennyson, Baron, 1809-1892. Idylls of the king. 2. Arthurian romances — History and criticism. 3. Myth in literature I. T.
PR5560.B8 1984   821/.8 19   *LC* 84-8430   *ISBN* 081471059X

Jump, John Davies, 1913- comp.   • **2.8158**
Tennyson: the critical heritage; edited by John D. Jump. — London, Routledge & K. Paul; New York, Barnes & Noble, 1967. x, 464 p. 23 cm. — (The Critical heritage series) I. T.
PR5560.J8   821/.8   *LC* 67-110235

Staines, David, 1946-.   **2.8159**
Tennyson's Camelot: The idylls of the King and its medieval sources / David Staines. — Ontario: Wilfrid Laurier University Press; Gerrards Cross: Distributed by Smythe, c1982. xviii, 218 p.; 24 cm. I. T.
PR5560.S7x   821/.8 19   *ISBN* 0889201153

Tennyson, Alfred Tennyson, Baron, 1809-1892.   **2.8160**
In memoriam; an authoritative text, backgrounds and sources, criticism. Selected and edited by Robert H. Ross. — [1st ed.]. — New York: Norton, [1973] x, 261 p.; 22 cm. — (A Norton critical edition) 1. Ross, Robert H. ed. II. T.
PR5562.A1 1973   821/.8   *LC* 72-13041   *ISBN* 0393043657

Tennyson, Alfred Tennyson, Baron, 1809-1892.   **2.8161**
In Memoriam / Tennyson; edited by Susan Shatto and Marion Shaw. — Oxford: Clarendon Press; New York: Oxford University Press, 1982. xvi, 397 p., [4] p. of plates: ill.; 22 cm. I. Shatto, Susan. II. Shaw, Marion. III. T.
PR5562.A1 1982   821/.8 19   *LC* 82-188984   *ISBN* 0198127472

Bradley, A. C. (Andrew Cecil), 1851-1935.   • **2.8162**
A commentary on Tennyson's In memoriam. — 3d ed., rev. — Hamden, Conn., Archon Books, 1966. xviii, 251 p. 19 cm. Reprint of work published in 1910. 1. Tennyson, Alfred Tennyson, Baron, 1809-1892. In memoriam. I. T.
PR5562.B7 1966   821.8   *LC* 66-12319

Rader, Ralph Wilson, 1930-.   • **2.8163**
Tennyson's Maud: the biographical genesis. — Berkeley, University of California Press, 1963. x, 155 p. 22 cm. — (Perspectives in criticism; 15) 1. Tennyson, Alfred Tennyson, 1st Baron, 1809-1892. Maud. I. T. II. Series.
PR5567.R3   821.8   *LC* 63-20984

Killham, John.   • **2.8164**
Tennyson and The princess: reflections of an age. — [London]: University of London, Athlone Press, 1958. 299 p.; 23 cm. 1. Tennyson, Alfred Tennyson, 1st Baron, 1809-1892. Princess. 2. Women — Great Britain I. T.
PR5571.K5   *LC* 59-730

PR5579–5598 Biography. Criticism

Baker, Arthur Ernest, 1876-.   • **2.8165**
A Tennyson dictionary; the characters and place–names contained in the poetical and dramatic works of the poet, alphabetically arranged and described with synopses of the poems and plays. — London: Routledge; New York:

Dutton [1916] vii, 296 p.; 23 cm. 1. Tennyson, Alfred Tennyson, baron, 1809-1892 — Dictionaries, indexes, etc. I. T.
PR5580.B4   821/.8   *LC* 16-17515

Tennyson, Emily Sellwood Tennyson, Baroness, 1813-1896.   **2.8166**
The letters of Emily Lady Tennyson. Edited with an introd. by James O. Hoge. — University Park: Pennsylvania State University Press, [1974] 404 p.: illus.; 24 cm. 1. Tennyson, Alfred Tennyson, Baron, 1809-1892. 2. Tennyson, Emily Sellwood Tennyson, Baroness, 1813-1896. I. T.
PR5581.A3 1974   821/.8 B   *LC* 73-12629   *ISBN* 0271011238

Tennyson, Alfred Tennyson, Baron, 1809-1892.   **2.8167**
The letters of Alfred Lord Tennyson / edited by Cecil Y. Lang and Edgar F. Shannon, Jr. — Cambridge, Mass.: Harvard University Press, 1981-. v.; 24 cm. 1. Tennyson, Alfred Tennyson, Baron, 1809-1892. Correspondence 2. Poets, English — 19th century — Correspondence. I. Lang, Cecil Y. II. Shannon, Edgar Finley, 1918- III. T.
PR5581.A4 1981b   821/.8 B 19   *LC* 80-25764   *ISBN* 0674525833

Benson, Arthur Christopher, 1862-1925.   • **2.8168**
Alfred Tennyson. — New York: Greenwood Press, [1969] x, 243 p.: illus.; ports.; 23 cm. Reprint of the 1907 ed. 1. Tennyson, Alfred Tennyson, Baron, 1809-1892. I. T.
PR5581.B45 1969   821/.8   *LC* 69-13820   *ISBN* 0837110718

Buckley, Jerome Hamilton.   • **2.8169**
Tennyson; the growth of a poet. — Cambridge: Harvard University Press, 1960. 298 p.; 22 cm. 1. Tennyson, Alfred Tennyson, Baron, 1809-1892. I. T.
PR5581.B8   821.8   *LC* 60-13298

Martin, Robert Bernard.   **2.8170**
Tennyson, the unquiet heart / Robert Bernard Martin. — Oxford: Clarendon Press; New York: Oxford University Press, 1980. xii, 643 p., [11] leaves of plates: ill.; 25 cm. Includes index. 1. Tennyson, Alfred Tennyson, Baron, 1809-1892 — Biography. 2. Poets, English — 19th century — Biography. I. T.
PR5581.M3 1980   821/.8 B   *LC* 79-41802   *ISBN* 0198120729

Pinion, F. B.   **2.8171**
A Tennyson companion: life and works / F.B. Pinion. — New York: St. Martin's Press, 1984. ix, 267 p., 16 p. of plates: ill.; 23 cm. Includes index. 1. Tennyson, Alfred Tennyson, Baron, 1809-1892. 2. Poets, English — 19th century — Biography. I. T.
PR5581.P5 1984   821/.8 B 19   *LC* 84-4786   *ISBN* 0312791070

Ricks, Christopher B.   • **2.8172**
Tennyson [by] Christopher Ricks. — New York: Macmillan, [1972] xii, 349 p.; 23 cm. — (Masters of world literature series) 1. Tennyson, Alfred Tennyson, Baron, 1809-1892. I. T.
PR5581.R54   821/.8   *LC* 76-165569

Tennyson, Charles, Sir, 1879-.   • **2.8173**
Alfred Tennyson, by his grandson, Charles Tennyson. — [Hamden, Conn.]: Archon Books, 1968 [i.e. 1969, c1949] xv, 580 p.: illus., ports.; 23 cm. 1. Tennyson, Alfred Tennyson, Baron, 1809-1892. I. T.
PR5581.T38 1969   821.8 B   *LC* 74-2856

Tennyson, Emily Sellwood Tennyson, Baroness, 1813-1896.   **2.8174**
Lady Tennyson's journal / edited with an introd. by James O. Hoge. — Charlottesville: University Press of Virginia, 1981. 401 p., [1] leaf of plates: ill.; 24 cm. 1. Tennyson, Alfred Tennyson, Baron, 1809-1892 — Biography. 2. Tennyson, Emily Sellwood Tennyson, Baroness, 1813-1896. 3. Tennyson family 4. Poets, English — 19th century — Biography. 5. Wives — Great Britain — Biography. I. Hoge, James O. II. T.
PR5581.T39 1981   821/.8 B 19   *LC* 80-21387   *ISBN* 0813908760

Tennyson, Hallam Tennyson, Baron, 1852-1928.   • **2.8175**
Alfred Lord Tennyson; a memoir, by his son. — New York: Greenwood Press, [1969, c1897] 2 v.: illus., geneal. table., ports.; 23 cm. 1. Tennyson, Alfred Tennyson, Baron, 1809-1892. I. T.
PR5581.T4 1969   821/.8 B   *LC* 69-14111

Culler, A. Dwight (Arthur Dwight), 1917-.   **2.8176**
The poetry of Tennyson / A. Dwight Culler. — New Haven: Yale University Press, 1977. x, 276 p.; 24 cm. 1. Tennyson, Alfred Tennyson, Baron, 1809-1892 — Criticism and interpretation. I. T.
PR5588.C8   821/.8   *LC* 76-48899   *ISBN* 0300020848

Killham, John, comp.   • **2.8177**
Critical essays on the poetry of Tennyson, edited by John Killham. — London: Routledge & K. Paul, 1967. viii, 263 p.; 21 1/2 cm. — (Routledge paperback, 69) 1. Tennyson, Alfred Tennyson, baron, 1809-1892 — Criticism and interpretation. I. T.
PR5588.K5 1967   821/.8   *LC* 67-86619

Marshall, George O.   • **2.8178**
A Tennyson handbook. — New York: Twayne Publishers, [c1963] 291 p.; 22 cm. 1. Tennyson, Alfred Tennyson, Baron, 1809-1892. I. T.
PR5588.M3   821.8   *LC* 63-17403

Palmer, D. J. (David John), 1935-.   **2.8179**
Tennyson / Edited by D. J. Palmer. — [Athens]: Ohio University Press, 1973. xvi, 279 p.: illus.; 23 cm. — (Writers and their background) Includes index. 1. Tennyson, Alfred Tennyson, Baron, 1809-1892. I. T.
PR5588.P3   821/.8   *LC* 72-95819   *ISBN* 0821401165

Shannon, Edgar Finley, 1918-.   • **2.8180**
Tennyson and the reviewers; a study of his literary reputation and of the influence of the critics upon his poetry, 1827–1851. — [Hamden, Conn.] Archon Books, 1967 [c1952] ix, 232 p. 22 cm. 1. Tennyson, Alfred Tennyson, Baron, 1809-1892 — Appreciation. 2. Criticism — Great Britain. I. T.
PR5588.S48 1967   821/.8   *LC* 67-14498

Tennyson, Charles, Sir, 1879-.   • **2.8181**
Six Tennyson essays. — London: Cassell, [1954] 197 p.; 22 cm. 1. Tennyson, Alfred Tennyson, 1st Baron, 1809-1892 — Addresses, essays, lectures. I. T. II. Title: 6 Tennyson essays.
PR5588.T4 1954   *LC* 54-2048

Turner, Paul, 1917-.   **2.8182**
Tennyson / by Paul Turner. London; Boston: Routledge and Kegan Paul, 1976. xiv, 198 p.; 23 cm. (Routledge author guides) Includes index. 1. Tennyson, Alfred Tennyson, Baron, 1809-1892. I. T.
PR5588.T8   821/.8   *LC* 76-380784   *ISBN* 0710083718

PR5600–5648 Thackeray

Thackeray, William Makepeace, 1811-1863.   **2.8183**
The Works of William Makepeace Thackeray. — Centenary biographical edition. — London: Smith, Elder, 1910-1911. 26 v. I. T.
PR5600 1910

Thackeray, William Makepeace, 1811-1863.   **2.8184**
The book of snobs / William Makepeace Thackeray; edited by John Sutherland. — New York: St. Martin's Press, 1978. 22, 237 p.: ill.; 22 cm. 1. Snobs and snobbishness I. Sutherland, John, 1903- II. T.
PR5610.A1 1978   828/.8/07   *LC* 78-54067   *ISBN* 0312090110

Mudge, Isadore Gilbert, 1875-1957.   • **2.8185**
A Thackeray dictionary; the characters and scenes of the novels and short stories alphabetically arranged, by Isadore Gilbert Mudge and M. Earl Sears. New York, Humanities Press, 1962. xlv, 304 p. geneal. tables. 24 cm. Bibliography: p. xli—xlii. 1. Thackeray, William Makepeace, 1811-1863 — Dictionaries, indexes, etc. I. Sears, Minnie Earl, 1873-1933. joint author. II. T.
PR5630.M7 1962   823.8   *LC* 62-6137

Thackeray, William Makepeace, 1811-1863.   • **2.8186**
The letters and private papers of William Makepeace Thackeray; collected and edited by Gordon N. Ray ... — Cambridge, Mass., Harvard University Press, 1945-46. 4 v. fronts., illus., plates, ports., maps, facsims., geneal. tables. 24 cm. Part of the illustrative matter is folded. Bibliographical foot-notes. I. Ray, Gordon Norton, 1915- ed. II. T.
PR5631.A3R3   928.2   *LC* A 45-5303 rev

Ray, Gordon Norton, 1915-.   • **2.8187**
The buried life; a study of the relation between Thackeray's fiction and his personal history, by Gordon N. Ray. Cambridge, Harvard University Press, 1952. vi, 148 p. fold. geneal. table, port. 22 cm. 1. Thackeray, William Makepeace, 1811-1863. I. T.
PR5631.R3   928.2   *LC* 52-11301

Ray, Gordon Norton, 1915-.   • **2.8188**
Thackeray [by] Gordon N. Ray. — New York: Octagon Books, 1972 [c1958] 2 v.: illus.; 23 cm. 1. Thackeray, William Makepeace, 1811-1863. I. T.
PR5631.R33 1972   823/.8   *LC* 72-8078   *ISBN* 0374967229

Stevenson, Lionel, 1902-1973.   • **2.8189**
The showman of Vanity Fair; the life of William Makepeace Thackeray. New York, C. Scribner's sons, 1947. 405 p.: ill.; 24 cm. 1. Thackeray, William Makepeace, 1811-1863 — Biography. I. T.
PR5631.S73   823.823   *LC* 47-30056

Trollope, Anthony, 1815-1882.   • **2.8190**
Thackeray. — New York: AMS Press, [1968] vi, 210 p.; 22 cm. — (English men of letters) Reprint of the 1887 ed. 1. Thackeray, William Makepeace, 1811-1863. I. T.
PR5631.T7 1968   823/.8   *LC* 68-58404

✓**Welsh, Alexander. comp.**   • **2.8191**
Thackeray; a collection of critical essays. — Englewood Cliffs, N.J.: Prentice-Hall, [1968] v, 184 p.; 21 cm. — (Twentieth century views) (A Spectrum book.) 1. Thackeray, William Makepeace, 1811-1863. I. T.
PR5631.W4   823/.8   *LC* 68-14482

Colby, Robert Alan, 1920-.   **2.8192**
Thackeray's canvass of humanity: an author and his public / Robert A. Colby. — Columbus: Ohio State University Press, 1979. xiv, 485 p.: ill.; 24 cm. 1. Thackeray, William Makepeace, 1811-1863 — Criticism and interpretation. I. T.
PR5638.C6   823/.8   *LC* 78-27465   *ISBN* 0814202829

Ferris, Ina.   **2.8193**
William Makepeace Thackeray / by Ina Ferris. — Boston: Twayne Publishers, c1983. 148 p.: ill.; port.; 23 cm. — (Twayne's English authors series. TEAS 365) Includes index. 1. Thackeray, William Makepeace, 1811-1863 — Criticism and interpretation. I. T. II. Series.
PR5638.F47 1983   823/.8 19   *LC* 83-184   *ISBN* 0805768513

Rawlins, Jack P.   **2.8194**
✓Thackeray's novels: a fiction that is true / Jack P. Rawlins. — Berkeley: University of California Press, c1974. xi, 244 p.; 21 cm. Includes index. 1. Thackeray, William Makepeace, 1811-1863 — Criticism and interpretation. I. T.
PR5638.R3   823/.8   *LC* 73-84393   *ISBN* 0520025628

✓**Tillotson, Geoffrey, 1905-1969.**   • **2.8195**
Thackeray, the novelist / by Geoffrey Tillotson. — London: Cambridge University Press, 1954. 311 p.: ill.; 21 cm. 1. Thackeray, William Makepeace, 1811-1863. I. T.
PR5638.T5   *LC* 54-13290

✓**Tillotson, Geoffrey.**   • **2.8196**
Thackeray: the critical heritage; edited by Geoffrey Tillotson and Donald Hawes. — London: Routledge & K. Paul; New York: Barnes & Noble, 1968. xv, 392 p.; 22 cm. — (The Critical heritage series) 1. Thackeray, William Makepeace, 1811-1863. I. Hawes, Donald. joint author. II. T.
PR5648.T5   823/.8   *LC* 68-79649   *ISBN* 0710029438

PR5650–5671 Thomson. Trelawny

Thomson, James, 1834-1882.   • **2.8197**
Poems and some letters / edited, with a biographical and critical introd. and textual notes, by Anne Ridler. — Carbondale: Southern Illinois University Press, 1963. xlv, 278 p.: port., facsim.; 23 cm. (Centaur classics) Bibliography: p. 258. I. Ridler, Anne, 1912- ed. II. T.
PR5655.A2 1963   821.8   *LC* 62-14999

Walker, Imogene B., 1906-.   • **2.8198**
✓James Thomson (B.V.), a critical study [by] Imogene B. Walker. — Westport, Conn.: Greenwood Press, [1970, c1950] ix, 212 p.; 23 cm. 1. Thomson, James, 1834-1882. I. T.
PR5658.W3 1970   821/.8   *LC* 70-108847   *ISBN* 0837137381

Trelawny, Edward John, 1792-1881.   **2.8199**
Adventures of a younger son / Edward John Trelawny; edited with an introd. by William St. Clair. — London; New York: Oxford University Press, 1974. xxiv, 477 p.: map; 21 cm. (Oxford English novels) Originally published in 3 vols. in 1831. I. T.
PZ3.T719 Ad72 PR5671.T5   823/.7   *LC* 74-189509   *ISBN* 0192553615

PR5680–5688 Trollope

Trollope, Anthony, 1815-1882.   **2.8200**
[Short stories] The complete short stories / Anthony Trollope; edited, with introduction, by Betty Jane Breyer. — Fort Worth, Tex.: Texas Christian University Press, c1979-c1983. 5 v.; 24 cm. I. Breyer, Betty Jane. II. T.
PR5682.B73   823/.8 19   *LC* 79-15519   *ISBN* 091264656X

Trollope, Anthony, 1815-1882.   • **2.8201**
The American senator, by Anthony Trollope ... — London, H. Milford, Oxford university press [1931] vii, 557, [1] p. 16 cm. — (Half-title: The World's classics. 391) I. T.
PZ3.T75Am7   PR5684.A6x   *LC* 31-28507

Trollope, Anthony, 1815-1882.   • **2.8202**
Ayala's angel. — London, Oxford University Press, H. Milford [1935] vii, 631 p. 16 cm. — (The world's classics, 342) I. T.
PR5684.A9   *LC* A 36-719

Trollope, Anthony, 1815-1882.   • **2.8203**
Barchester Towers. — London, New York [etc.]: H. Milford [1925] vii, 506 p.; 16 cm. — (World's classics, 343.) I. T. II. Series.
PR5684.B3 1925

Trollope, Anthony, 1815-1882.   • **2.8204**
The Belton estate, by Anthony Trollope. — London, New York [etc.] H. Milford, Oxford university press [1923] vi, 432 p. 15.5 cm. — (Half-title: The World's classics, CCLI) I. T.
PZ3.T75Be   PR5684.B4x.   *LC* A 25-288

Trollope, Anthony, 1815-1882.   • **2.8205**
Can you forgive her? — London: Oxford University Press, H. Milford [1938] 2 v.; 16 cm. (The World's classics; 468) I. T.
PZ3T75C15   PR5684.C3x.   *LC* 39-2769

Trollope, Anthony, 1815-1882.   • **2.8206**
The Claverings, by Anthony Trollope. — London, New York [etc.]: H. Milford [1924] xvi, 514 p. 16 cm. — (The world's classics, 252) I. T.
PZ3.T75Cl5 PR5684.C57   *LC* 25-2849

Trollope, Anthony, 1815-1882.   • **2.8207**
The Duke's children / by Anthony Trollope. — London: Oxford University Press, H. Milford [1938] 2 v.; 17 cm. (The world's classics; 462-463.) 'In the World's classics ... first published in 1938. I. T.
PZ3.T75Du50   PR5684.D9x.   *LC* 38-27978

Trollope, Anthony, 1815-1882.   • **2.8208**
Doctor Thorne, by Anthony Trollope. — London, New York [etc.]: H. Milford, Oxford University Press [1931] vii, 569 p. 19 cm.   (Half-title: The world's classics. 298) I. T.
PZ3.T75D 38   PR5684.Dx.   *LC* 33-36727

Trollope, Anthony, 1815-1882.   • **2.8209**
Dr. Wortle's school, by Anthony Trollope ... — London: Oxford University Press, H. Milford [1928] vi, 273, [1] p. 16 cm. — (Half-title: The World's classics. CCCXVII) First published in 1881. I. T.
PZ3.T75Do 9   PR5684.Dx.   *LC* 29-15487

Trollope, Anthony, 1815-1882.   **2.8210**
The Eustace diamonds / Anthony Trollope; edited with an introduction by W.J. McCormack; with illustrations by Blair Hughes–Stanton. — Oxford [Oxfordshire]; New York: Oxford University Press, 1983. xliv, 361, 414 p.: ill.; 19 cm. — (The Centenary edition of Anthony Trollope's Palliser novels) (The World's classics) (Oxford paperbacks) I. McCormack, W. J. II. T.
PR5684.E7 1983   823/.8 19   *LC* 82-14348   *ISBN* 0192815881

Trollope, Anthony, 1815-1882.   **2.8211**
Framley Parsonage / Anthony Trollope; edited with an introduction and notes by David Skilton and Peter Miles. — Harmondsworth, Middlesex, England; New York, N.Y., U.S.A.: Penguin Books, 1984. 573 p.; 19 cm. (Penguin English library) I. Skilton, David. II. Miles, Peter. III. T.
PR5684.F7 1984   823/.8 19   *LC* 85-111471   *ISBN* 0140432132

Trollope, Anthony, 1815-1882.   **2.8212**
Kept in the dark / by Anthony Trollope. New York: Dover Publications, 1978. 92 p.; 24 cm. 'Unabridged republication of the work as it originally appeared in eight installments in Good words, published by Isbister and Company, Limited, London, 1882.' I. T.
PZ3.T75 Ke 1978 PR5684   PR5684.K47 1978.   823/.8   *LC* 77-20469   *ISBN* 0486236099

Trollope, Anthony, 1815-1882.   • **2.8213**
The last chronicle of Barset, by Anthony Trollope ... — London: H. Milford, Oxford University Press [1932] 2 v.; 16 cm. (The World's classics, 398, 399.) I. T.
PZ3.T75Las45   PR5684.Lx.   *LC* 32-26674

Trollope, Anthony, 1815-1882.   **2.8214**
Marion Fay: a novel / by Anthony Trollope; with illustrations by William Small; R.H. Super, editor. — Ann Arbor: University of Michigan Press, c1982. xxxvi, 451 p.: ill.; 24 cm. Originally published: London: Chapman & Hall, 1882. I. Super, R. H. (Robert Henry), 1914- II. T.
PR5684.M37 1982   823/.8 19   *LC* 82-7036   *ISBN* 0472100238

Trollope, Anthony, 1815-1882.   **2.8215**
✓The New Zealander, edited with an introduction by N. John Hall. — Oxford: Clarendon Press, 1972. xlv, 226 p.: ill.; 23 cm. 1. Great Britain — Politics and government — 1837-1901 2. England — Civilization — 19th century I. Hall, N. John. II. T.
DA560.T76 1972   PR5684.N48.   914.2/03/81   *LC* 72-188453   *ISBN* 0198124422

Trollope, Anthony, 1815-1882.   • **2.8216**
Nina Balatka. Linda Tressel. London, Oxford Univ. Press [1946] 383 p.; 16 cm. (The World's classics, 505) I. T. II. Title: Linda Tressel.
PR5684.Nx   823.8   LC 48-94

Trollope, Anthony, 1815-1882.   • **2.8217**
Orley farm. — London: Oxford University Press, H. Milford [1935] 2 v.; 16 cm. (Half-title: The world's classics. 423) I. T.
PZ3.T75Or20   PR5684.Ox.   LC 35-27163

Trollope, Anthony, 1815-1882.   • **2.8218**
Phineas Finn, the Irish member. — London: Oxford University Press, H. Milford [1937] 2 v.; 16 cm. — (The world's classics, 447-448.) I. T.
PZ3.T75P45 PR5684.P5   LC 37-28541

Trollope, Anthony, 1815-1882.   • **2.8219**
Phineas redux. — London: Oxford University Press, H. Milford [1937] p. — 2 v.; 15 1/2 cm. — (The World's classics, 450, 451.) I. T.
PR5684.P53x

Trollope, Anthony, 1815-1882.   • **2.8220**
The Prime Minister. — London: Oxford University Press, H. Milford [1938] 2 v.; 16 cm. — (The World's classics, 454-455.) 'The third of the 'Political' novels'.' I. T. II. Series.
PR5684.P7 1938   LC 38-27560

Trollope, Anthony, 1815-1882.   • **2.8221**
Rachel Ray. London, New York [etc]: H. Milford [1924] vi, 403 p.; 15 1/2 cm. (The World's classics, 279) I. T.
PR5684 R3 1924

Trollope, Anthony, 1815-1882.   • **2.8222**
Ralph the heir. — London: Oxford University Press, H. Milford [1939] 2 v.; 16 cm. — (World's classics. 475-476.) I. T. II. Series.
PR5684.R35 1939

Trollope, Anthony, 1815-1882.   • **2.8223**
The small house at Allington. — London: H. Milford, Oxford University Press [1939] 2 v.; 16 cm. (The world's classics, 472-473.) I. T.
PZ3.T75Sm45   PR5684.S55x.   LC 39-27704

Trollope, Anthony, 1815-1882.   • **2.8224**
The three clerks. With an introd. by W. Teignmouth Shore. London: H. Milford, Oxford University Press [1929] xvi, 567 p.; 16 cm. — (The World's classics, 140) I. Shore, W. Teignmouth (William Teignmouth), 1865-1932. ed. II. T.
PR5684 T4

Trollope, Anthony, 1815-1882.   • **2.8225**
The vicar of Bullhampton / by Anthony Trollope. — London, New York [etc.]: H. Milford [1924] xi, 527 p.; 16 cm. (The World's classics; 272) I. T.
PZ3.T75 Vi 7   PR5684.V5x.   823

Trollope, Anthony, 1815-1882.   • **2.8226**
The warden. With an introd. by Ronald Knox. Illus. by Edward Ardizzone. London, Oxford University Press, 1952. 290 p.: ill.; 21 cm. — (The Oxford Trollope. Crown ed.) I. T.
PR5684.W25x   823.8   LC 52-14819

Trollope, Anthony, 1815-1882.   • **2.8227**
The way we live now. — London: Oxford University Press, H. Milford [1941] 2 v.; 16 cm. — (World's classics. 484-485.) I. T. II. Series.
PR5684.W35 1941

PR5686–5688 Biography. Criticism

Gerould, Winifred Gregory, 1885-.   • **2.8228**
A guide to Trollope, by Winifred Gregory Gerould and James Thayer Gerould. Drawings by Florence W. Ewing. — Westport, Conn.: Greenwood Press, [1970, c1948] xxv, 256 p.: maps, plans.; 23 cm. 1. Trollope, Anthony, 1815-1882 — Dictionaries, indexes, etc. I. Gerould, James Thayer, 1872- joint author. II. T.
PR5686.A24 1970   823/.8   LC 70-100227   ISBN 0837130344

Trollope, Anthony, 1815-1882.   **2.8229**
[Correspondence] The letters of Anthony Trollope / edited by N. John Hall with the assistance of Nina Burgis. — Stanford, Calif.: Stanford University Press, 1983. 2 v. (xxxvii, 1082 p.); 24 cm. 1. Trollope, Anthony, 1815-1882. Correspondence 2. Novelists, English — 19th century — Correspondence. I. Hall, N. John. II. Burgis, Nina. III. T.
PR5686.A4 1983   823/.8 B 19   LC 79-64213   ISBN 0804710767

Trollope, Anthony, 1815-1882.   • **2.8230**
An autobiography / by Anthony Trollope; with an introd. by Michael Sadleir. — London, New York [etc.]: H. Milford, Oxford University Press [1923] xxiv, 335 p.; 15 cm. — (The world's classics; 239) Preface signed: Henry M. Trollope.

1. Trollope, Anthony, 1815-1882. I. Trollope, Henry Meripale, 1846- II. Sadleir, Michael, 1888-1957. III. T.
PR5686.A5 1923   PR5686.A31 1923.   LC 23-18080

Booth, Bradford Allen, 1909-.   • **2.8231**
Anthony Trollope; aspects of his life and art. Bloomington, Indiana University Press [c1958] xi, 258 p.; 24 cm. 1. Trollope, Anthony, 1815-1882. I. T.
PR5686.B6   LC 58-6953

Cockshut, A. O. J.   • **2.8232**
Anthony Trollope; a critical study, by A. O. J. Cockshut. — [1st U.S. ed. — New York]: New York University Press, 1968 [c1955] 256 p.: port.; 22 cm. 1. Trollope, Anthony, 1815-1882. I. T.
PR5686.C6 1968   823/.8   LC 68-18402

Pope-Hennessy, James.   • **2.8233**
Anthony Trollope. — [1st American ed.]. — Boston: Little, Brown, [c1971] 400 p.: illus.; 24 cm. 1. Trollope, Anthony, 1815-1882. I. T.
PR5686.P63 1971b   823/.8 B   LC 74-183856

Sadleir, Michael, 1888-1957.   • **2.8234**
Trollope, a commentary. With portrait, four facsimiles and charts. — New York, Farrar, Straus and company, 1947. 435 p. front. (port.) illus. 22 cm. 'Revised American edition, 1947.' 'Anthony's mother': p. 37-[116] 'Bibliography of Frances Trollope': p. 403-405. 'Bibliography of Anthony Trollope': p. 414-416. 1. Trollope, Anthony, 1815-1882. 2. Trollope, Frances Milton, 1780-1863. I. T.
PR5686.S3 1947   928.2   LC 47-1170

Snow, C. P. (Charles Percy), 1905-.   **2.8235**
Trollope, his life and art / C. P. Snow. — New York: Scribner, c1975. 191 p., [12] leaves of plates: ill. (some col.); 26 cm. 1. Trollope, Anthony, 1815-1882. I. T.
PR5686.S5   823/.8   LC 75-4088   ISBN 0684144018

Stebbins, Lucy Poate, b. 1886.   • **2.8236**
The Trollopes; the chronicle of a writing family, by Lucy Poate Stebbins and Richard Poate Stebbins. — New York: AMS Press, 1966 [c1945] 394 p.: ports.; 23 cm. 1. Trollope, Anthony, 1815-1882. 2. Trollope family. I. Stebbins, Richard Poate, 1913- joint author. II. T.
PR5686.S8 1966   823/.8 B   LC 71-182720

Walpole, Hugh, Sir, 1884-1941.   • **2.8237**
Anthony Trollope. — Freeport, N.Y.: Books for Libraries Press, [1971] vii, 205 p.; 23 cm. Reprint of the 1928 ed. 1. Trollope, Anthony, 1815-1882. I. T.
PR5686.W3 1971   823/.8   LC 75-161000   ISBN 0836958683

ApRoberts, Ruth.   **2.8238**
The moral Trollope. — [Athens]: Ohio University Press, 1971. 203 p.; 23 cm. 1. Trollope, Anthony, 1815-1882. I. T.
PR5687.A6   823/.8   LC 75-141383   ISBN 0821400894

Edwards, Peter David.   **2.8239**
Anthony Trollope, his art and scope / P. D. Edwards. — New York: St. Martin's Press, [1978,c1977] x, 234 p.; 22 cm. 1. Trollope, Anthony, 1815-1882 — Criticism and interpretation. I. T.
PR5687.E3   823/.8   LC 77-27915   ISBN 031204271X

Pollard, Arthur.   **2.8240**
Anthony Trollope / by Arthur Pollard. — London; Boston: Routledge & Kegan Paul, 1978. xi, 208 p.; 23 cm. Includes index. 1. Trollope, Anthony, 1815-1882 — Criticism and interpretation. I. T.
PR5687.P57   823/.8   LC 77-30497   ISBN 0710088116

Smalley, Donald Arthur, 1907- comp.   • **2.8241**
Trollope: the critical heritage, edited by Donald Smalley. — London: Routledge & K. Paul; New York: Barnes & Noble, 1969. xviii, 572 p.; 23 cm. — (The Critical heritage series) 1. Trollope, Anthony, 1815-1882. I. T.
PR5687.S6 1969   823/.8   LC 79-391304   ISBN 0710061536

Trollope, Frances (Milton), 1780-1863.   **2.8242**
The widow Barnaby. / By Frances Trollope. — New York: AMS Press, 1839. 3 v. I. T.
PR5699.T3 W5   LC 79-8208

Heineman, Helen, 1936-.   **2.8243**
Frances Trollope / by Helen Heineman. — Boston: Twayne, c1984. 163 p.; 22 cm. (Twayne's English authors series. TEAS 370) Includes index. 1. Trollope, Frances Milton, 1780-1863 — Criticism and interpretation. I. T. II. Series.
PR5699.T3 Z714 1984   823/.7 19   LC 84-3771   ISBN 0805768564

PR5710–5718 Ward

Ward, Humphry, Mrs., 1851-1920.   • **2.8244**
Robert Elsmere / by Mrs. Humphry Ward; edited with an introd. by Clyde de L. Ryals. — Lincoln: University of Nebraska Press, [1967] xli, 636 p.; 21 cm. — (Bison book.) I. Ryals, Clyde de L., 1928- II. T. III. Series.
PR5714.R6   *LC* 67-12116

Peterson, William S.   **2.8245**
Victorian heretic: Mrs Humphry Ward's Robert Elsmere / by William S. Peterson. — [Leicester]: Leicester University Press, 1976. xi, 259 p.: port.; 23 cm. Includes index. 1. Ward, Humphry, Mrs., 1851-1920. Robert Elsmere. I. T.
PR5714.R63 P4   823/.8   *LC* 77-350068   *ISBN* 0718511476

Smith, Esther Marian Greenwell.   **2.8246**
Mrs. Humphry Ward / by Esther Marian Greenwell Smith. — Boston: Twayne Publishers, 1980. 163 p.; 21 cm. (Twayne's English authors series; TEAS no. 288) Includes index. 1. Ward, Humphry, Mrs., 1851-1920 — Criticism and interpretation. I. T.
PR5717.S6   823/.8   *LC* 79-24476   *ISBN* 0805767665

PR5770–5778 Wells

Wells, H. G. (Herbert George), 1866-1946.   **2.8247**
Seven science fiction novels. New York, Dover Publications, 1950 [c1934] 1015 p. 21 cm. Published in 1934 under title: Seven famous novels. I. T.
PR5770.F50   *LC* 51-2132

Wells, H. G. (Herbert George), 1866-1946.   **2.8248**
The complete short stories of H. G. Wells. — 22nd. impression. London: E. Benn; New York: St. Martin's Press, [1974] vi, 9-1038 p.; 20 cm. Originally published under title: The short stories. I. T.
PZ3.W465 Cm6 PR5772.A1x   823/.9/12   Fic   *LC* 79-145813
    ISBN 0510403018

Wells, H. G. (Herbert George), 1866-1946.   **2.8249**
Kipps / H.G. Wells; introduced by Benny Green. — Oxford; New York: Oxford University Press, 1984. 330 p.; 20 cm. (Twentieth-century classics.) I. T. II. Series.
PR5774.K65 1984   823/.912 19   *LC* 84-9711   *ISBN* 019281477X

Wells, H. G. (Herbert George), 1866-1946.   **2.8250**
Mr. Britling sees it through / by H. G. Wells ... with frontispiece. — New York: Macmillan Co., 1916. 4 p. l., 3-443 p.: ill.; 20 cm. 1. World War, 1914-1918 — Fiction. I. T.
PR5774.M5 1916   *LC* 16-18291

Wells, H.G. (Herbert George, 1886-1946.   **2.8251**
The sea lady. — New York: D. Appleton, 1902. vii, 300 p., [7] leaves of plates: ill. I. T.
PR5774.S39 1902

Wells, H. G. (Herbert George), 1866-1946.   **2.8251a**
Tono–Bungay / H. G. Wells; with notes by Bernard Bergonzi. — Lincoln: University of Nebraska Press, 1978, c1909. 317 p.: ill.; 21 cm. 'A Bison book.' Reprint of the 1966 ed. published by Houghton Mifflin, Boston, which was issued as B101 of Riverside editions. I. T.
PZ3.W465 To 1978 PR5774.Tx   823/.9/12   *LC* 77-28027   *ISBN* 0803247028. *ISBN* 0803297017

Wells, H. G. (Herbert George), 1866-1946.   **2.8252**
Experiment in autobiography: discoveries and conclusions of a very ordinary man (since 1866) by H.G. Wells; with drawings by the author. — Boston: Little, Brown, [1984?], c1934. x, 718 p.: ill., port.; 24 cm. 1. Wells, H. G. (Herbert George), 1866-1946. 2. Authors, English — 20th century — Biography. I. T.
PR5776.A34 1984   823/.912 B 19   *LC* 84-81815   *ISBN* 0316930318

Bergonzi, Bernard.   • **2.8253**
The early H. G. Wells: a study of the scientific romances. — Toronto: University of Toronto Press, 1961. 226 p. illus. 21 cm. Includes bibliography. 1. Wells, H. G. (Herbert George), 1866-1946. I. T.
PR5776.B42   823.912   *LC* 62-52983

The H. G. Wells scrapbook: articles, essays, letters, anecdotes, illustrations, photographs and memorabilia about the prophetic genius of the twentieth century / edited by Peter Haining , foreword by Jack Williamson.   **2.8254**
London: C. N. Potter, c1978. 144 p.: ill., maps, ports., facsim.; 30 cm. 1. Wells, Herbert George, 1866-1946. 2. Authors, English — 20th century — Biography I. Haining, Peter.
PR5776.H15 1978   *LC* 78-73102   *ISBN* 051753722

MacKenzie, Norman Ian.   **2.8255**
H. G. Wells; a biography, by Norman and Jeanne MacKenzie. New York, Simon and Schuster [1973] xvi, 487 p. illus. 25 cm. 1. Wells, H. G. (Herbert George), 1866-1946 — Biography. I. MacKenzie, Jeanne. joint author. II. T.
PR5776.M3 1973b   823/.9/12 B   *LC* 73-1184   *ISBN* 0671215205

West, Anthony, 1914-.   **2.8256**
H.G. Wells: aspects of a life / Anthony West. — New York: Random House, c1984. 405 p., [40 p. of plates]: ill. Includes index. 1. Wells, H. G. (Herbert George), 1866-1946 — Biography 2. Novelists, English — 20th century — Biography I. T.
PR5776.W46 1984   823/.912 19   *LC* 83-3074   *ISBN* 0394531965

Hillegas, Mark Robert, 1926-.   **2.8257**
The future as nightmare; H. G. Wells and the anti–utopians [by] Mark R. Hillegas. New York, Oxford University Press, 1967. xi, 200 p. 22 cm. 1. Wells, H. G. (Herbert George), 1866-1946 — Criticism and interpretation. 2. Science fiction — History and criticism 3. Dystopias in literature. 4. Future in literature I. T.
PR5777.H5   823/.9/12   *LC* 67-28128

McConnell, Frank D., 1942-.   **2.8258**
The science fiction of H. G. Wells / Frank McConnell. — New York: Oxford University Press, 1981. ix, 235 p.: ill.; 20 cm. (Science-fiction writers.) Includes index. 1. Wells, H. G. (Herbert George), 1866-1946 — Criticism and interpretation. 2. Science fiction, English — History and criticism. I. T. II. Series.
PR5777.M3 1981   823/.912 19   *LC* 80-19675   *ISBN* 0195028112

Parrinder, Patrick. comp.   **2.8259**
H. G. Wells: the critical heritage; edited by Patrick Parrinder. London; Boston, Routledge and Kegan Paul, 1972. xv, 351 p. 23 cm. (The Critical heritage series) 1. Wells, H. G. (Herbert George), 1866-1946 — Criticism and interpretation. I. T.
PR5777.P37 1972   823/.9/12   *LC* 72-83659   *ISBN* 0710073879

Kemp, Peter.   **2.8260**
H.G. Wells and the culminating ape / Peter Kemp. — New York: St. Martin's Press, 1982. 225 p.; 23 cm. Includes index. 1. Wells, H. G. (Herbert George), 1866-1946 — Knowledge — Biology. 2. Biology in literature. I. T.
PR5778.B55 K4 1982   823/.912 19   *LC* 81-13598   *ISBN* 0312355920

Reed, John Robert, 1938-.   **2.8261**
The natural history of H.G. Wells / by John R. Reed. — Athens: Ohio University Press, c1982. x, 294 p.; 24 cm. 1. Wells, H. G. (Herbert George), 1866-1946 — Philosophy. 2. Wells, H. G. (Herbert George), 1866-1946 — Criticism and interpretation. 3. Philosophy in literature I. T.
PR5778.P5 R4 1982   823/.912 19   *LC* 81-11261   *ISBN* 0821406280

PR5795.W7 White (Mark Rutherford)

White, William Hale, 1831-1913.   • **2.8262**
The autobiography of Mark Rutherford, dissenting minister / edited by his friend Reuben Shapcott; with a memorial introduction by H.W. Massingham. — London: Oxford University Press, 1936. xxxvi, 166 p.: port.; 19 cm. I. T.
PR5795.W7 A9 1936   *LC* 37-3826

White, William Hale, 1831-1913.   **2.8263**
Catharine Furze; Clara Hopgood / William Hale White. — New York: Garland Pub., 1976. 189, 298 p.; 19 cm. (Victorian fiction: Novels of faith and doubt) Reprint of two of the author's works originally published by T. F. Unwin, London, in 1893 and 1896, respectively. I. White, William Hale, 1831-1913. Clara Hopgood. 1976. II. T. III. Title: Catherine Furze. IV. Series.
PZ3.W5862 Catl5 PR5795.W7C3x   823/.8   *LC* 75-1516   *ISBN* 0824015894

White, William Hale, 1831-1913.   **2.8264**
The revolution in Tanner's Lane; Miriam's schooling / William Hale White. — New York: Garland Pub., 1975. viii, 388, 194 p.; 19 cm. — (Victorian fiction: Novels of faith and doubt; no. 64) Reprint of 2 works, the 1st published in 1887 by Trübner, London; the 2d published in 1890 by K. Paul, Trench, Trübner, London. I. White, William Hale, 1831-1913. Miriam's schooling. 1975. II. T. III. Title: Revolution in Tanner's Lane. IV. Series.
PZ3.W5862 Re16 PR5795.W7P4x   823/.8   *LC* 75-1515   *ISBN* 0824015886

Stock, Irvin, 1920-.   • **2.8265**
William Hale White (Mark Rutherford); a critical study. Foreword by Lionel Trilling. — Freeport, N.Y.: Books for Libraries Press, [1970] xii, 268 p.; 23 cm. Reprint of the 1956 ed. 1. White, William Hale, 1831-1913. I. T.
PR5795.W7 Z78 1970   823/.8 B   *LC* 72-126260   *ISBN* 0836954874

PR5810–5828 Wilde

Wilde, Oscar, 1854-1900. • **2.8266**
Complete works of Oscar Wilde / with an introduction by Vyvyan Holland. — New ed. — London: Collins, 1966. 1216 p.; 22 cm. I. Holland, Vyvyan Beresford, 1886-1967. II. T.
PR5810.F66 1966   ISBN 0004105419

Wilde, Oscar, 1854-1900. • **2.8267**
The first collected edition of the works of Oscar Wilde, 1908–1922. Edited by Robert Ross. — New York: Barnes & Noble, [1969] 15 v.; 22 cm. Reprint of the 1908 ed. in 14 v. with For the love of the king (originally published in 1922) as an additional volume. I. Ross, Robert Baldwin, 1869-1918. ed. II. T.
PR5810.F69   LC 76-9852   ISBN 0389011517

Wilde, Oscar, 1854-1900. • **2.8268**
[Selections. 1946] The portable Oscar Wilde, selected and edited by Richard Aldington. New York, The Viking press, 1946. viii, 690 p. illus. (facsims.) 17 cm. (The Viking portable library) I. Aldington, Richard, 1892-1962. ed. II. T.
PR5811.A4   820.81   LC 46-3202

Wilde, Oscar, 1854-1900. • **2.8269**
De profundis, being the first complete and accurate version of 'Epistola: in carcere et vinculis,' the last prose work in English of Oscar Wilde. — New York: Philosophical Library, [1960] 127 p.; 19 cm. — I. T.
PR5818.D4x   828/.8/03   LC 77-502

Wilde, Oscar, 1854-1900. **2.8270**
The picture of Dorian Gray, edited with an introd. by Isobel Murray. — London; New York: Oxford University Press, 1974. xxxiv, 249 p.; 21 cm. — (Oxford English novels) I. T.
PZ3.W645 P36 PR5819.P5x   823/.8   LC 74-180250   ISBN 0192553682

Wilde, Oscar, 1854-1900. • **2.8271**
[Salomé. English] Salome; a tragedy in one act. Translated from the French of Oscar Wilde by Lord Alfred Douglas. Pictured by Aubrey Beardsley. New York, Dover Publications [1967] xviii, 66 p. 20 illus. 28 cm. 'An unabridged republication of the first edition of the work originally published in 1894 ... with ... additions.' I. Beardsley, Aubrey, 1872-1898. illus. II. T.
PR5820.S2 1967   822/.8   LC 67-24337

PR5822–5828 Biography. Criticism

Wilde, Oscar, 1854-1900. • **2.8272**
Letters. Edited by Rupert Hart–Davis. [1st American ed.] New York, Harcourt, Brace, & World [1962] xxv, 958 p. illus., ports., facsims. 24 cm. I. Hart-Davis, Rupert II. T.
PR5823.A27 1962   928.2   LC 60-10942

Bentley, Joyce. **2.8273**
The importance of being Constance / Joyce Bentley. — 1st American ed. — New York: Beaufort Books, c1983. 160 p., [8] p. of plates: ill.; 22 cm. Includes index. 1. Wilde, Constance, 1858-1898. 2. Wilde, Oscar, 1854-1900 — Biography — Marriage. 3. Wives — England — Biography. 4. Authors, Irish — 19th century — Biography. I. T.
PR5823.B43 1983b   828/.809 B 19   LC 84-11102   ISBN 082530248X

Douglas, Alfred Bruce, Lord, 1870-1945. • **2.8274**
Oscar Wilde, a summing up. — London: Duckworth, [1940] 143 p.; 22 cm. 1. Wilde, Oscar, 1854-1900. 2. Douglas, Alfred Bruce, Lord, 1870-1945. I. T.
PR5823.D58   LC 40-31761

Fido, Martin. **2.8275**
Oscar Wilde. — New York: Viking Press, [1973] 144 p.: illus.; 31 cm. — (A Studio book) 1. Wilde, Oscar, 1854-1900 — Biography. 2. Great Britain — Intellectual life — 19th century I. T.
PR5823.F47   828/.8/09 B   LC 73-993   ISBN 0670529079

Gide, André, 1869-1951. • **2.8276**
Oscar Wilde: in memorium (reminiscences) De profundis / translated from the French by Bernard Frechtman. — New York: Philosophical Library, 1949. xii, 50 p.; 23 cm. 1. Wilde, Oscar, 1854-1900. I. T.
PR5823.G514   LC 49-8466

Harris, Frank, 1855-1931. • **2.8277**
Oscar Wilde, including My memories of Oscar Wilde, by George Bernard Shaw. And an introductory note by Lyle Blair. [East Lansing] Michigan State University Press, 1959. ix, 358 p. 24 cm. 1. Wilde, Oscar, 1854-1900. I. Shaw, Bernard, 1856-1950. II. T.
PR5823.H3 1959   928.2   LC 59-6709

Holland, Vyvyan Beresford, 1886-1967. • **2.8278**
Oscar Wilde, a pictorial biography. New York, Viking Press [1960] 144 p. illus. 24 cm. (A Studio book) 1. Wilde, Oscar, 1854-1900. I. T.
PR5823.H58   LC 61-2371

Holland, Vyvyan Beresford, 1886-1967. • **2.8279**
Son of Oscar Wilde. 1st American ed. New York, Dutton, 1954. 237 p. illus. 21 cm. 1. Wilde, Oscar, 1854-1900. I. T.
PR5823.H6 1954   928.2   LC 54-10920

Hyde, H. Montgomery (Harford Montgomery), 1907-. **2.8280**
Oscar Wilde: a biography / by H. Montgomery Hyde. — New York: Farrar, Straus, and Giroux, 1975. xii, 410 p., [12] leaves of plates: ill.; 24 cm. Includes index. 1. Wilde, Oscar, 1854-1900 — Biography. 2. Authors, Irish — 19th century — Biography. I. T.
PR5823.H88   828/.8/09 B   LC 75-22439   ISBN 0374227470

Hyde, H. Montgomery (Harford Montgomery), 1907-. • **2.8281**
Oscar Wilde: the aftermath / by H. Montgomery Hyde. — New York: Farrar, Straus c1963. xxi, 221 p. facsim. 22 cm. Bibliographical footnotes. 1. Wilde, Oscar, 1854-1900. I. T.
PR5823.H9 1963a   928.2   LC 63-20020

Oscar Wilde: interviews and recollections / edited by E. H. Mikhail. **2.8282**
New York: Barnes & Noble, 1979. 2 v. (xxiv, 502 p.); 22 cm. Includes index. 1. Wilde, Oscar, 1854-1900 — Interviews. 2. Wilde, Oscar, 1854-1900 — Anecdotes. 3. Authors, Irish — 19th century — Biography — Addresses, essays, lectures. I. Mikhail, E. H.
PR5823.O66 1979b   828/.8/09 B   LC 77-16829   ISBN 0064948153

Pearson, Hesketh, 1887-1964. • **2.8283**
Oscar Wilde, his life and wit / by Hesketh Pearson ... — 1st ed. — New York: Harper, [1946] 345 p.: front., pl., ports.; 22 cm. Includes index. 1. Wilde, Oscar, 1854-1900 — Biography. I. Pearson, Hesketh, 1887-1964. Life of Oscar Wilde. II. T. III. Title: The life of Oscar Wilde.
PR5823.P4   928.2   LC 46-5458

Ellmann, Richard, 1918- comp. • **2.8284**
Oscar Wilde; a collection of critical essays. — Englewood Cliffs, N.J.: Prentice-Hall, [1969] viii, 180 p.; 21 cm. — (A Spectrum book, S-TC-87: Twentieth century views) 1. Wilde, Oscar, 1854-1900 — Criticism and interpretation. I. T.
PR5824.E4   828/.8/09   LC 70-79445   ISBN 0139594787

Miller, Robert Keith, 1949-. **2.8285**
Oscar Wilde / Robert Keith Miller. — New York: Ungar, c1982. xii, 167 p.; 21 cm. — (Modern literature series.) Includes index. 1. Wilde, Oscar, 1854-1900 — Criticism and interpretation. I. T. II. Series.
PR5824.M5 1982   828/.809 B 19   LC 81-70734   ISBN 0804426295

Nassaar, Christopher S. **2.8286**
Into the demon universe; a literary exploration of Oscar Wilde [by] Christopher S. Nassaar. — New Haven: Yale University Press, 1974. xiii, 191 p.: front.; 23 cm. Based on the author's thesis, University of Wisconsin. 1. Wilde, Oscar, 1854-1900 — Criticism and interpretation. I. T.
PR5824.N27 1974   828/.8/09   LC 73-86910   ISBN 0300016840

San Juan, E. (Epifanio), 1938-. • **2.8287**
The art of Oscar Wilde. Princeton, N.J., Princeton University Press, 1967. ix, 238 p. 22 cm. 1. Wilde, Oscar, 1854-1900 — Criticism and interpretation. I. T.
PR5824.S3   828/.8/09   LC 66-21840

Shewan, Rodney. **2.8288**
Oscar Wilde: art and egotism / Rodney Shewan. Barnes & Noble Books, c1977. xix, 239 p., [4] leaves of plates: ill. Includes index. 1. Wilde, Oscar, 1854-1900 — Criticism and interpretation. I. T.
PR5824.S5   LC 77-536   ISBN 0064962385

Bird, Alan. **2.8289**
The plays of Oscar Wilde / Alan Bird. — New York: Barnes & Noble Books, 1977. 220 p.; 23 cm. — (Barnes & Noble critical studies) Includes index. 1. Wilde, Oscar, 1854-1900 — Dramatic works. I. T.
PR5827.D7 B5 1977b   822/.8   LC 78-100316   ISBN 0064904156

Cohen, Philip K., 1943-. **2.8290**
The moral vision of Oscar Wilde / Philip K. Cohen. — Rutherford: Fairleigh Dickinson University Press, c1978. 287 p.: ill.; 22 cm. Includes index. 1. Wilde, Oscar, 1854-1900 — Ethics. I. T.
PR5827.R4 C6   828/.8/09   LC 76-50283   ISBN 0838620523

PR5841–5842 Wollstonecraft. Wood

Wollstonecraft, Mary, 1759-1797.   **2.8291**
A Wollstonecraft anthology / edited, with an introd., by Janet M. Todd. —
Bloomington: Indiana University Press, c1977. x, 269 p.: ill.; 24 cm. I. Todd,
Janet M., 1942- II. T.
PR5841.W8 A6 1977   828/.6/09   LC 77-72192   ISBN 0253366054

Ferguson, Moira.   **2.8292**
Mary Wollstonecraft / by Moira Ferguson and Janet Todd. — Boston: Twayne
Publishers, c1984. 158 p., [1] leaf of plates: ill.; 23 cm. — (Twayne's English
authors series. TEAS 381) Includes index. 1. Wollstonecraft, Mary, 1759-1797
— Criticism and interpretation. I. Todd, Janet M., 1942- II. T. III. Series.
PR5841.W8 Z67 1984   828/.609 19   LC 83-18342   ISBN
080576867X

Tomalin, Claire.   **2.8293**
The life and death of Mary Wollstonecraft. — 1st American ed. — New York:
Harcourt Brace Jovanovich, [1975] c 1974. 316 p.: illus.; 22 cm.
1. Wollstonecraft, Mary, 1759-1797 — Biography. I. T.
PR5841.W8 Z84 1975   301.41/2/0924 B   LC 74-14816   ISBN
0151515395

Wood, Henry, Mrs., 1814-1887.   **2.8294**
East Lynne / by Mrs. Henry Wood; with an introduction by Sally Mitchell. —
New Brunswick, N.J.: Rutgers University Press, c1984. xviii, [1], 525 p.; 21 cm.
I. T.
PR5842.W8 E3 1984   823/.8 19   LC 83-23041   ISBN 0813510414

PR5849 Dorothy Wordsworth

Wordsworth, Dorothy, 1771-1855.   • **2.8295**
The poetry of Dorothy Wordsworth, edited from the Journals, by Hyman
Eigerman. — Westport, Conn.: Greenwood Press, [1970, c1940] [117] p.; 23
cm. I. Eigerman, Hyman, ed. II. T.
PR5849.A6 1970   821/.7   LC 78-100193   ISBN 0837134366

Wordsworth, Dorothy, 1771-1855.   • **2.8296**
Journals of Dorothy Wordsworth / edited by E. De Selincourt. London:
Macmillan & co., ltd., c1941. 2 v.; 22 cm. Maps on lining-papers.
1. Wordsworth, William, 1770-1850. 2. Wordsworth, Dorothy, 1771-1855.
I. De Selincourt, Ernest, 1870-1943. II. T.
PR5849.A8 1941   LC 42-3963

Gittings, Robert.   **2.8297**
Dorothy Wordsworth / Robert Gittings and Jo Manton. — Oxford
[Oxfordshire]: Clarendon Press, 1985. viii, 318 p., [12] p. of plates: ill.; 23 cm.
Includes index. 1. Wordsworth, Dorothy, 1771-1855. 2. Wordsworth family.
3. Authors, English — 19th century — Biography. 4. Lake District (Eng.) —
Biography. I. Manton, Jo, 1919- II. T.
PR5849.G5 1985   821/.7 B 19   LC 85-174718   ISBN 0198185197

PR5850–5898 William Wordsworth

Wordsworth, William, 1770-1850.   • **2.8298**
The poetical works of William Wordsworth. Edited from the manuscripts with
textual and critical notes by E.de Selincourt. Oxford, Clarendon [1940-. v.; 23
cm. Vol.4 ed. by E. de Selincourt and Helen Darbishire. I. De Selincourt,
Ernest, 1870-1943. ed. II. Darbishire, Helen, 1881-1961. joint ed. III. T.
PR5850.F40

Wordsworth, William, 1770-1850.   **2.8299**
The Cornell Wordsworth / General editor, Stephen Parrish; associate editor,
Mark L. Reed. — Ithaca, N.Y.: Cornell University Press, 1975-. v.; 24 cm.
I. Parrish, Stephen. II. Reed, Mark L. III. T.
PR5850.F75x

Wordsworth, William, 1770-1850.   **2.8300**
The prose works of William Wordsworth. Edited by W. J. B. Owen and Jane
Worthington Smyser. — Oxford: Clarendon Press, 1974. 3 v.; 23 cm. I. Owen,
W. J. B. (Warwick Jack Burgoyne) ed. II. Smyser, Jane Worthington, ed.
III. T.
PR5851.O9 1974   828/.7/08   LC 74-166513   ISBN 0198124368

Wordsworth, William, 1770-1850.   • **2.8301**
Literary criticism, edited by Paul M. Zall. — Lincoln: University of Nebraska
Press, [1966] xvii, 212 p.; 21 cm. — (Regents critics series) 1. Wordsworth,
William, 1770-1850 — Correspondence. 2. Authors, English —
Correspondence. 3. Literature — Philosophy I. Zall, Paul M. ed. II. T.
PR5851.Z3   809.1   LC 66-10447

Wordsworth, William, 1770-1850.   **2.8302**
The pedlar: Tintern Abbey: The two–part prelude / William Wordsworth;
edited with a critical introduction and notes by Jonathan Wordsworth. —
Cambridge [Cambridgeshire]: Cambridge University Press, c1985. 76 p. cm.
I. Wordsworth, Jonathan. II. T. III. Title: Tintern Abbey IV. Title: Two-
part prelude
PR5852.W67 1985   821/.7 19   LC 84-12126   ISBN 0521265266

Wordsworth, William, 1770-1850.   **2.8303**
The ruined cottage; The brothers; Michael / William Wordsworth; edited with
a critical introduction and notes by Jonathan Wordsworth. — Cambridge
[Cambridgeshire]; New York: Cambridge University Press, c1985. 82 p.
I. Wordsworth, Jonathan. II. T. III. Title: The brothers. IV. Title: Michael.
PR5852.W68 1985   821/.7 19   LC 84-12126   ISBN 0521265266

Wordsworth, William, 1770-1850.   **2.8304**
[Selections. 1984] William Wordsworth / edited by Stephen Gill. — Oxford
[Oxfordshire]; New York: Oxford University Press, 1984. xxxii, 752 p.; 23 cm.
— (Oxford authors.) Includes index. I. Gill, Stephen Charles. II. T.
III. Series.
PR5853.G54 1984   821/.7 19   LC 83-17278   ISBN 0192541757

Holt, Ted, 1943-.   **2.8305**
A commentary on Wordsworth's Prelude, books I–V / Ted Holt John Gilroy.
— London; Boston: Routledge & Kegan Paul, 1983. xi, 124 p.; 22 cm.
1. Wordsworth, William, 1770-1850. The prelude. I. Gilroy, John, 1946-
II. T.
PR5864.H64 1983   821/.7 19   LC 83-10897   ISBN 0710095694

McConnell, Frank D., 1942-.   **2.8306**
The confessional imagination: a reading of Wordsworth's Prelude [by] Frank
D. McConnell. — Baltimore: Johns Hopkins University Press, [1974] ix, 211 p.;
23 cm. 1. Wordsworth, William, 1770-1850. The prelude. 2. Confession in
literature I. T.
PR5864.M25   821/.7   LC 73-19333   ISBN 0801815746

Wordsworth, William, 1770-1850.   • **2.8307**
The Ecclesiastical sonnets. — A critical ed. / by Abbie Findlay Potts. — New
York: Yale University Press, 1922. x, 316 p.: ill.; 23 cm. — (Cornell studies in
English.) I. Potts, Abbie Findlay, 1884-1964. II. T. III. Series.
PR13.C6 v.7   PR5866.P6.   LC 23-5009

Wordsworth, William, 1770-1850.   • **2.8308**
Lyrical ballads / [by] Wordsworth and Coleridge; the text of the 1798 ed. with
the additional 1800 poems and the prefaces; edited with introd., notes and
appendices by R. L. Brett and A. R. Jones. — New York: Barnes & Noble,
[1963] L, 339 p.; 21 cm. — I. Coleridge, Samuel Taylor, 1772-1834. II. Brett,
R. L. III. T.
PR5869.L9 1963   821/.7   LC 63-24405

Jacobus, Mary.   **2.8309**
Tradition and experiment in Wordsworth's lyrical ballads (1798) / Mary
Jacobus. — Oxford: Clarendon Press, 1976. x, 301 p.; 23 cm. Includes index.
1. Wordsworth, William, 1770-1850. Lyrical ballads. 2. Wordsworth,
William, 1770-1850 — Criticism and interpretation. I. T.
PR5869.L93 J3   821/.7   LC 76-357140   ISBN 0198120699

Jordan, John Emory, 1919-.   **2.8310**
Why the Lyrical ballads?: The background, writing, and character of
Wordsworth's 1798 Lyrical ballads / by John E. Jordan. Berkeley: University of
California Press, c1976. xii, 212 p.; 23 cm. Includes index. 1. Wordsworth,
William, 1770-1850. Lyrical ballads. I. T.
PR5869.L93 J65   821/.7   LC 75-27926   ISBN 0520031245

PR5879–5898 Biography. Criticism

Davies, Hunter, 1936-.   **2.8311**
William Wordsworth: a biography / Hunter Davies. — 1st American ed. —
New York: Atheneum, 1980. xiii, 367 p., [8] leaves of plates: ill.; 25 cm.
Includes index. 1. Wordsworth, William, 1770-1850 — Biography. 2. Poets,
English — 19th century — Biography. I. T.
PR5881.D34 1980b   821/.7 19   LC 80-66004   ISBN 0689110871

Harper, George McLean, 1863-1947.   • **2.8312**
William Wordsworth, his life, works, and influence. — New York, Russell &
Russell, 1960. 2 v. illus. 25 cm. 1. Wordsworth, William, 1770-1850. I. T.
PR5881.H3 1960   928.2   LC 60-11020

Havens, Raymond Dexter, 1880-1954.   • **2.8313**
The mind of a poet: a study of Wordsworth's thought with particular reference
to The prelude / by Raymond Dexter Havens. — Baltimore: Johns Hopkins
Press, 1941. xviii, 670 p., [1] leaf of plates: fold. maps; 24 cm. —
1. Wordsworth, William, 1770-1850. 2. Wordsworth, William, 1770-1850.
Prelude I. T.
PR5881.H35   821/.7   LC 42-1043

Moorman, Mary Trevelyan, 1905-.   • 2.8314
William Wordsworth, a biography / by Mary Moorman. — Oxford: Clarendon Press, 1957-65. 2 v.: ill.; 23 cm. 1. Wordsworth, William, 1770-1850 — Biography. I. T.
PR5881.M6   *LC* 57-2574rev

Purkis, John Arthur, 1933-.   2.8315
A preface to Wordsworth. — New York: Scribner, [1972, c1970] 208 p.: illus.; 23 cm. — (Preface books) 1. Wordsworth, William, 1770-1850. I. T.
PR5881.P8 1972   821/.7   *LC* 79-38526   *ISBN* 0684128497

Legouis, Émile Hyacinthe, 1861-1937.   • 2.8316
The early life of William Wordsworth, 1770–1798; a study of 'The prelude' by Émile Legouis ... tr. by J. W. Matthews with a prefatory note by Leslie Stephen. London and Toronto, J. M. Dent & co., ltd.; New York, E. P. Dutton & Co., inc. [1932] xvi, 481, [1] p. front. (port.) 23 cm. 'First published in this edition, 1897; reprinted, with additional appendix, 1921, 1932.' 1. Wordsworth, William, 1770-1850. I. Matthews, J. W. II. T.
PR5882.L5   928.2   *LC* 37-3806

Margoliouth, Herschel Maurice, 1887-.   • 2.8317
Wordsworth and Coleridge, 1795–1834 [by] H. M. Margoliouth. [Hamden, Conn.] Archon Books, 1966. vii, 206 p.; 17 cm. First published in 1953. 1. Wordsworth, William, 1770-1850. 2. Coleridge, Samuel Taylor, 1772-1834. I. T.
PR5883.M3 1966   *LC* 66-20231

Abrams, M. H. (Meyer Howard), 1912- comp.   2.8318
Wordsworth: a collection of critical essays. Edited by M. H. Abrams. Englewood Cliffs, N.J., Prentice-Hall [1972] x, 214 p. 21 cm. (Twentieth century views) (A Spectrum book) 1. Wordsworth, William, 1770-1850 — Criticism and interpretation — Addresses, essays, lectures. I. T.
PR5888.A27   821/.7   *LC* 72-4888   *ISBN* 0139650797 *ISBN* 013965061X

Hartman, Geoffrey H.   • 2.8319
Wordsworth's poetry, 1787–1814, by Geoffrey H. Hartman. — New Haven: Yale University Press, 1964. xii, 418 p.; 24 cm. 1. Wordsworth, William, 1770-1850 — Criticism and interpretation. I. T.
PR5888.H37   821.7   *LC* 64-20920

Jones, John, 1924-.   • 2.8320
The egotistical sublime: a history of Wordsworth's imagination. — London: Chatto & Windus, 1954. ix, 212 p.; 21 cm. 1. Wordsworth, William, 1770-1850. I. T.
PR5888.J6   *LC* 65-41603   *ISBN* 0701108614

Logan, James Venable, 1901-.   • 2.8321
Wordsworthian criticism, a guide and bibliography. — Columbus, Ohio State University Press, 1961. xiv, 304 p. 24 cm. 1. Wordsworth, William, 1770-1850. 2. Wordsworth, William, 1770-1850 — Bibl. 3. Criticism — Hist. I. T.
PR5888.L6 1961   821.7   *LC* 61-3121

Sheats, Paul D.   2.8322
The making of Wordsworth's poetry, 1785–1798 [by] Paul D. Sheats. — Cambridge, Mass.: Harvard University Press, 1973. xvii, 301 p.; 22 cm. 1. Wordsworth, William, 1770-1850. I. T.
PR5888.S47   821/.7   *LC* 72-90645   *ISBN* 0674543750

Beer, John B.   2.8323
Wordsworth and the human heart / John Beer. — New York: Columbia University Press, 1978. xx, 277 p.; 22 cm. 1. Wordsworth, William, 1770-1850 — Criticism and interpretation. 2. Emotions in literature I. T.
PR5892.E5 B43   821/.7   *LC* 78-17567   *ISBN* 0231046464

Grob, Alan.   2.8324
The philosophic mind: a study of Wordsworth's poetry and thought, 1797–1805. — Columbus: Ohio State University Press, [1973] xii, 279 p.; 21 cm. 1. Wordsworth, William, 1770-1850 — Philosophy. I. T.
PR5892.P5 G7 1973   821/.7   *LC* 72-13783   *ISBN* 0814201784

Perkins, David.   • 2.8325
The quest for permanence: the symbolism of Wordsworth, Shelley and Keats / David Perkins. — Cambridge, Mass.: Harvard University Press, 1959. viii, 305 p.; 22 cm. 1. Wordsworth, William, 1770-1850. 2. Shelley, Percy Bysshe, 1792-1822. 3. Keats, John, 1795-1821. 4. Symbolism in literature I. T.
PR5892.P5 P4   *LC* 59-11515

Brantley, Richard E.   2.8326
Wordsworth's 'natural Methodism' / Richard E. Brantley. — New Haven: Yale University Press, 1975. xvi, 205 p.; 23 cm. 1. Wordsworth, William, 1770-1850 — Religion. 2. Evangelicalism in literature. I. T.
PR5892.R4 B7   821/.7   *LC* 74-20078   *ISBN* 0300018347

Baker, Jeffrey, 1925-.   2.8327
Time and mind in Wordsworth's poetry / Jeffrey Baker. — Detroit: Wayne State University Press, 1980. 212 p.; 24 cm. Includes index. 1. Wordsworth, William, 1770-1850 — Criticism and interpretation. 2. Time in literature I. T.
PR5892.T5 B3 1980   821/.7   *LC* 80-11947   *ISBN* 0814316557

Ward, John Powell, 1937-.   2.8328
Wordsworth's language of men / J.P. Ward. — Brighton, Sussex: Harvester Press; Totowa, N.J.: Barnes & Noble, 1984. xii, 235 p.; 22 cm. Includes index. 1. Wordsworth, William, 1770-1850 — Language. 2. Wordsworth, William, 1770-1850 — Style. 3. Languages — Philosophy 4. Poetry I. T.
PR5894.W37 1984   821/.7 19   *LC* 84-11076   *ISBN* 0389205001

PR5900–5908 Yeats

Yeats, W. B. (William Butler), 1865-1939.   • 2.8329
The variorum edition of the poems of W. B. Yeats. Edited by Peter Allt and Russell K. Alspach. New York, Macmillan, 1957. xxxv, 884 p. 25 cm. I. T.
PR5900.A3 1957   821.91   *LC* 57-5974

Yeats, W. B. (William Butler), 1865-1939.   2.8330
The poems / W.B. Yeats. — New ed. / edited by Richard J. Finneran. — New York: Macmillan, c1983. xxv, 747 p.; 22 cm. I. Finneran, Richard J. II. T.
PR5900.A3 1983   821/.8 19   *LC* 83-17567   *ISBN* 0026329409

Yeats, W. B. (William Butler), 1865-1939.   • 2.8331
Collected plays. New ed., with 5 additional plays. New York, Macmillan, 1953 [c1952] 446 p. port. 22 cm. I. T.
PR5900.A4 1953   822.91   *LC* 53-10132

Yeats, W. B. (William Butler), 1865-1939.   • 2.8332
The variorum edition of the plays of W. B. Yeats. Edited by Russell K. Alspach assisted by Catharine C. Alspach. New York, Macmillan, 1966. xxv, 1336 p. 25 cm. I. T.
PR5900.A4 1966   822.912   *LC* 64-8597

Yeats, W. B. (William Butler), 1865-1939.   2.8333
Essays and introductions. New York, Macmillan, 1961. xi, 530 p. ports. 24 cm. Settings of 6 poems by Florence Farr: p. 23-27. 1. Literature — Addresses, essays, lectures. I. T.
PR5900.A5 1961   824.912   *LC* 61-8106

Yeats, W. B. (William Butler), 1865-1939.   2.8334
Uncollected prose / by W. B. Yeats; collected and edited by John P. Frayne and C. Johnson. — New York: Columbia University Press, 1970-1976. 2 v.: ill., ports.; 24 cm. Errata note for v.1 included in v.2 on p. [516]. I. Frayne, John P., ed.
PR5900.A5 1970   828   *LC* 74-101295   *ISBN* 0231028458

Yeats, W. B. (William Butler), 1865-1939.   • 2.8335
Mythologies. New York, Macmillan, 1959. 368 p.: ill.; 25 cm. I. T.
PR5902.M27   828.912   *LC* 59-12014

Yeats, W. B. (William Butler), 1865-1939.   • 2.8336
Explorations. Selected by Mrs. W. B. Yeats. — New York, Macmillan [c1962] viii, 452 p. port. 25 cm. I. T.
PR5902.Y4   828.912   *LC* 63-9338

Vendler, Helen Hennessy.   2.8337
Yeats's Vision and the later plays. — Cambridge, Harvard University Press, 1963. 286 p. 22 cm. Includes bibliography. 1. Yeats, W. B. (William Butler), 1865-1939. A vision. 2. Yeats, W. B. (William Butler), 1865-1939. 3. Symbolism in literature I. T.
PR5904.V53V4   822.912   *LC* 63-9565

Yeats, W. B. (William Butler), 1865-1939.   • 2.8338
A vision. A reissue with the author's final revisions. — New York, Macmillan, 1956 [c1938] 305 p. illus., port., diagrs. 21 cm. 1. Mysticism 2. Astrology I. T.
PR5904.V5x   828.91   *LC* 56-2713

PR5906–5908 Biography. Criticism

Yeats, W. B. (William Butler), 1865-1939.   2.8339
[Autobiography] Memoirs. Transcribed and edited by Denis Donoghue. [1st American ed.] New York, Macmillan [1973, c1972] 318 p. 22 cm. Consists of the 1st draft of the Autobiography written in 1915 and 1916, and the Journal written from 1908-1930. 1. Yeats, W. B. (William Butler), 1865-1939. I. Yeats, W. B. (William Butler), 1865-1939. Journal. 1973. II. T.
PR5906.A552 1973   821/.8 B   *LC* 72-11279

Yeats, W. B. (William Butler), 1865-1939.   • 2.8340
Autobiography: consisting of Reveries over childhood and youth. The trembling of the veil, and Dramatis personae. New York, Macmillan 1953 [c1944] 344 p. illus. 22 cm. 1. Yeats, W. B. (William Butler), 1865-1939. I. T.

II. Title: Reveries over childhood and youth. III. Title: The trembling of the veil. IV. Title: Dramatis personae.
PR5906.A5x   928.2   *LC* 53-12858

Yeats, W. B. (William Butler), 1865-1939.   ● **2.8341**
Letters / edited by Allan Wade. — New York: Macmillan, 1955 [c1954] 938 p.: ill.; 24 cm. 1. Yeats, W. B. (William Butler), 1865-1939 — Correspondence. I. Wade, Allan, 1881-1955. II. T.
PR5906.A63 1955   *LC* 55-732

Ellmann, Richard, 1918-.   ● **2.8342**
The identity of Yeats / by Richard Ellmann. — 2d ed. — New York: Oxford University Press, 1964. xxiv, 342 p.: ill.; 21 cm. — (Galaxy book.) 1. Yeats, W. B. (William Butler), 1865-1939. I. T. II. Series.
PR5906.E39 1964   *LC* 64-7098

Ellmann, Richard, 1918-.   ● **2.8343**
Yeats, the man and the masks. — London: Macmillan, 1949. ix, 336 p.: port.; 23 cm. 1. Yeats, W. B. (William Butler), 1865-1939. I. T.
PR5906.E4 1949   *LC* 50-22656

Jeffares, A. Norman (Alexander Norman), 1920-.   ● **2.8344**
W. B. Yeats, man and poet, by A. Norman Jeffares. New York, Barnes & Noble [1966] ix, 365 p. illus., ports. 23 cm. 1. Yeats, W. B. (William Butler), 1865-1939. I. T.
PR5906.J42 1966   821   *LC* 66-31815

Malins, Edward Greenway.   **2.8345**
A preface to Yeats / Edward Malins. — New York: Scribner, 1975 (c1974). xii, 212 p.: ill.; 23 cm. (Preface books) 1. Yeats, W. B. (William Butler), 1865-1939. I. T.
PR5906.M296   821/.8   *LC* 74-11930   *ISBN* 0684140764

Archibald, Douglas N.   **2.8346**
Yeats / Douglas Archibald. — 1st ed. — Syracuse: Syracuse University Press, 1983. xiv, 280 p.; 24 cm. (Irish studies) Includes index. 1. Yeats, W. B. (William Butler), 1865-1939 — Criticism and interpretation. I. T.
PR5907.A72 1983   821/.8 19   *LC* 82-19638   *ISBN* 0815622635

Bloom, Harold.   **2.8347**
Yeats / Harold Bloom. — London; New York: Oxford University Press, 1972. xii, 500 p.: port.; 21 cm. 'A Galaxy book' 1. Yeats, W. B. (William Butler), 1865-1939. I. T.
PR5907.B55 1972   821/.8   *LC* 70-100365   *ISBN* 0195016033

Eddins, Dwight, 1939-.   **2.8348**
Yeats: the nineteenth century matrix. University, University of Alabama Press [1971] x, 173 p. 22 cm. 1. Yeats, W. B. (William Butler), 1865-1939. I. T.
PR5907.E3   821/.8   *LC* 73-148693   *ISBN* 0817373098

Hall, James, 1917-.   ● **2.8349**
The permanence of Yeats; selected criticism edited by James Hall and Martin Steinmann. New York, Macmillan, 1950. vi, 414 p. 22 cm. 1. Yeats, W. B. (William Butler), 1865-1939. I. Steinmann, Martin, 1915- II. T.
PR5907.H3   821.91   *LC* 50-5401

Harper, George Mills.   **2.8350**
The mingling of heaven and earth: Yeats's theory of theatre / George Mills Harper. — Dublin: Dolmen Press; Atlantic Highlands, N.J.: distributed by Humanities Press, 1975. 48 p.: ill.; 25 cm. (New Yeats papers. 10) 'This paper is a development of a lecture delivered to the Yeats International Summer School at Sligo on 26 August 1965.' 1. Yeats, W. B. (William Butler), 1865-1939 — Criticism and interpretation — Addresses, essays, lectures. 2. Theater — Ireland. I. T. II. Series.
PR5907.H32   821/.8   *LC* 76-356054   *ISBN* 085105269X

Jeffares, A. Norman (Alexander Norman), 1920-.   **2.8351**
A new commentary on the poems of W.B. Yeats / A. Norman Jeffares. — Stanford, Calif.: Stanford University Press, 1984. xxxv, 543 p., [3] p. of plates: ill.; 24 cm. Includes indexes. Rev. ed. of: A commentary on the collected poems of W.B. Yeats. 1968. 1. Yeats, W. B. (William Butler), 1865-1939 — Criticism and interpretation. I. Yeats, W. B. (William Butler), 1865-1939. II. Jeffares, A. Norman (Alexander Norman), 1920- A commentary on the collected poems of W.B. Yeats. III. T.
PR5907.J39 1984   821/.8 19   *LC* 83-40105   *ISBN* 0804712212

Koch, Vivienne.   ● **2.8352**
W. B. Yeats, the tragic phase; a study of the last poems. [Hamden, Conn.] Archon Books, 1969. 151 p. 22 cm. Reprint of the 1951 ed. 1. Yeats, W. B. (William Butler), 1865-1939. I. T.
PR5907.K6 1969   821   *LC* 69-19228   *ISBN* 0208008055

MacNeice, Louis, 1907-1963.   ● **2.8353**
The poetry of W. B. Yeats. London, New York [etc.] Oxford university press, 1941. xi, 242 p. 22 cm. 1. Yeats, W. B. (William Butler), 1865-1939 — Criticism and interpretation. I. T.
PR5907.M25 1941   821.91   *LC* 41-5731

Parrish, Stephen Maxfield.   ● **2.8354**
A concordance to the poems of W. B. Yeats. Programmed by James Allan Painter. Ithaca, N. Y., Cornell University Press [1963] xxxvii, 967 p. 24 cm. (Cornell concordances.) 1. Yeats, W. B. (William Butler), 1865-1939 — Concordances. I. Painter, James Allan. II. T. III. Series.
PR5907.P35   821.912   *LC* 63-11493

Stallworthy, Jon.   ● **2.8355**
Between the lines: Yeat's poetry in the making / Jon Stallworthy. — Oxford: Clarendon Press, 1963. x, 261 p.: ill.; 23 cm. 1. Yeats, W. B. (William Butler), 1865-1939. I. T.
PR5907.S75   *LC* 63-5092

Sultan, Stanley.   **2.8356**
Yeats at his last / Stanley Sultan. — Dublin: Dolmen Press; Atlantic Highlands, N.J.: distributed by Humanities Press, 1975. 48 p.: 1 ill. facsim.; 25 cm. (New Yeats papers. 11) 1. Yeats, W. B. (William Butler), 1865-1939 — Criticism and interpretation. I. T. II. Series.
PR5907.S87   821/.8   *LC* 76-355047   *ISBN* 0851052711

Unterecker, John Eugene, 1922-.   ● **2.8357**
A reader's guide to William Butler Yeats [by] John Unterecker. New York, Octagon Books, 1971 [c1959] 310 p. 22 cm. 1. Yeats, W. B. (William Butler), 1865-1939. Collected poems. I. T.
PR5907.U5 1971   821/.8   *LC* 72-154661   *ISBN* 0374980489

Unterecker, John Eugene, 1922- ed.   ● **2.8358**
Yeats: a collection of critical essays. Englewood Cliffs, N.J., Prentice-Hall [1963] 180 p. 21 cm. (Twentieth century views) (A Spectrum book, S-TC-23.) 1. Yeats, W. B. (William Butler), 1865-1939. I. T.
PR5907.U53   821.912   *LC* 62-19408

Ure, Peter.   **2.8359**
Yeats and Anglo–Irish literature: critical essays / Peter Ure; edited by C. J. Rawson; with a memoir by Frank Kermode. — [New York]: Barnes & Noble, 1974. xvi, 292 p.; 23 cm. (English texts and studies) 1. Yeats, W. B. (William Butler), 1865-1939 — Criticism and interpretation — Addresses, essays, lectures. 2. English literature — 20th century — History and criticism — Addresses, essays, lectures. I. T.
PR5907.U69   821/.8   *LC* 74-194800   *ISBN* 0064971120

Ure, Peter, 1919-.   ● **2.8360**
Yeats, the playwright: a commentary on character and design in the major plays. — London: Routledge & K. Paul, [1963] vii, 182 p.; 23 cm. 1. Yeats, W. B. (William Butler), 1865-1939. I. T.
PR5907.U72   *LC* 63-23802

Ure, Peter.   ● **2.8361**
Towards a mythology; studies in the poetry of W.B. Yeats. [Liverpool] Univ. Press of Liverpool, 1946. 123 p.; 23 cm. 1. Yeats, W. B. (William Butler), 1865-1939. 2. Mythology in literature I. T.
PR5907.U9   *LC* a 47-3892

W. B. Yeats: the critical heritage / edited by A. Norman Jeffares.   **2.8362**
London; Boston: Routledge and Kegan Paul, 1977. xvi, 483 p.; 23 cm. (The Critical heritage series) Includes index. 1. Yeats, W. B. (William Butler), 1865-1939 — Criticism and interpretation — Addresses, essays, lectures. I. Jeffares, A. Norman (Alexander Norman), 1920-
PR5907.W2   821/.8   *LC* 77-30043   *ISBN* 0710084803

Jeffares, A. Norman (Alexander Norman), 1920-.   **2.8363**
A commentary on the collected plays of W. B. Yeats / A. Norman Jeffares and A. S. Knowland. — Stanford, Calif.: Stanford University Press, 1975. xxi, 310 p.: ill.; 21 cm. Includes index. 1. Yeats, W. B. (William Butler), 1865-1939 — Dramatic works. I. Knowland, A. S. joint author. II. T.
PR5908.D7 J4   822/.8   *LC* 74-82993   *ISBN* 0804708754

Taylor, Richard, 1935-.   **2.8364**
A reader's guide to the plays of W.B. Yeats / Richard Taylor. — New York: St. Martin's Press, 1984. ix, 197 p.: ill.; 23 cm. Includes index. 1. Yeats, W. B. (William Butler), 1865-1939 — Dramatic works. I. T. II. Title: Plays of W.B. Yeats.
PR5908.D7 T38 1984   822/.8 19   *LC* 81-21295   *ISBN* 0312664567

Olney, James.   **2.8365**
The rhizome and the flower: the perennial philosophy, Yeats and Jung / James Olney. — Berkeley: University of California Press, c1980. xv, 379 p.; 23 cm. 1. Yeats, W. B. (William Butler), 1865-1939 — Philosophy. 2. Jung, C. G.

(Carl Gustav), 1875-1961. 3. Plato — Influence. 4. Philosophy, Modern — 20th century I. T.
PR5908.P5 O45   801/.92   *LC* 78-62834   *ISBN* 0520037480

O'Driscoll, Robert. 2.8366
Symbolism and some implications of the symbolic approach: W. B. Yeats during the eighteen–nineties / Robert O'Driscoll. — Dublin: Dolmen Press; New York: distributed in the U.S.A. and in Canada by Humanities Press, 1975. 84 p.: 1 ill.; 25 cm. (New Yeats papers. 9) 1. Yeats, W. B. (William Butler), 1865-1939 — Symbolism. 2. Symbolism in literature I. T. II. Series.
PR5908.S95 O3   821/.8   *LC* 76-355055   *ISBN* 0851052703

PR5910–5914 Yonge

Yonge, Charlotte Mary, 1823-1901. 2.8367
Heartsease, or, The brother's wife. — New York: AMS Press, 1979. v. I. T. II. Title: The brother's wife.
PR5912.H4 1855

Yonge, Charlotte Mary, 1823-1901. 2.8368
The heir of Redclyffe / illustrated by Kate Greenaway. — London: Macmillan, 1882. 463 p.: ill. I. T.
PR5912.H45

PR5921–5922 Zangwill

Zangwill, Israel, 1864-1926. 2.8369
[Works] The works of Israel Zangwill. [New York, AMS Press, 1969] 14 v. illus., port. 23 cm. 'Edition de luxe.' Reprint of the 1925 ed. I. T.
PR5922.A2 1969   823/.8   *LC* 73-99252

PR6000–6049 20th Century (1900–1960)

PR6001 A–As

Abse, Dannie. 2.8370
Collected poems, 1948–1976 / Dannie Abse. — [Pittsburgh, Pa.]: University of Pittsburgh Press, 1977. ix, 204 p.; 21 cm. — (Pitt poetry series; 126) 'An International Poetry Forum selection'. I. T.
PR6001.B7 A17 1977   821/.9/14   *LC* 76-21049   *ISBN* 0822933332

The Poetry of Dannie Abse: critical essays and reminiscences / 2.8371
edited with an introduction by Joseph Cohen.
London: Robson Books, 1984 (c1983). 187 p.; 23 cm. 1. Abse, Dannie — Criticism and interpretation — Addresses, essays, lectures. I. Cohen, Joseph, 1926-
PR6001.B7 Z83   821/.914 19   *LC* 83-200531   *ISBN* 0860512436

✓ **Richard Aldington, an intimate portrait, edited by Alister** 2.8372
Kershaw and Frédéric–Jacques Temple.
Carbondale, Southern Illinois University Press [1965] xxi, 186 p. ports. 21 cm. 1. Aldington, Richard, 1892-1962. I. Temple, Frédéric Jacques. II. Kershaw, Alister.
PR6001.L4A65   828.91209   *LC* 65-16539

Aldington, Richard, 1892-1962. • 2.8373
The complete poems of Richard Aldington. — London: A. Wingate, 1948. 365 p.; 22 cm. I. T.
PR6001.L4 A7 1948   *LC* 49-6437

Aldington, Richard, 1892-1962. 2.8374
The Colonel's daughter / Richard Aldington; new introduction by Anthony Burgess. — London: Hogarth, 1986. [384] p.; 20 cm. I. T.
PR6001.L4 C6x   823/.912 19   *ISBN* 0701206012

Aldington, Richard, 1892-1962. 2.8375
Death of a hero / Richard Aldington; new introduction by Christopher Ridgway. — London: Hogarth Press, 1984. 375 p.; 20 cm. 1. World War, 1914-1918 — Fiction. I. T.
PR6001.L4 D4 1984   823/.912 19   *LC* 84-249509   *ISBN* 0701206047

Gates, Norman T. 2.8376
The poetry of Richard Aldington: a critical evaluation and an anthology of uncollected poems [by] Norman T. Gates. — University Park: Pennsylvania

State University Press, [1975] xiv, 362 p.; 24 cm. 'A Rider College publication.' 1. Aldington, Richard, 1892-1962. I. Aldington, Richard, 1892-1962. II. T.
PR6001.L4 Z6   821/.9/12   *LC* 73-6877   *ISBN* 027101119X

Smith, Richard Eugene. 2.8377
Richard Aldington / by Richard Eugene Smith. — Boston: Twayne Publishers, c1977. 204 p.: port.; 21 cm. — (Twayne's English authors series; TEAS 222) Includes index. 1. Aldington, Richard, 1892-1962 — Criticism and interpretation. I. T.
PR6001.L4 Z79   821/.9/12   *LC* 77-24042   *ISBN* 080576691X

Allingham, Margery, 1904-1966. • 2.8378
The tiger in the smoke, a novel. [1st ed.] Garden City, N.Y., Doubleday, 1952. 254 p. 22 cm. I. T.
PZ3.A4372Ti2 PR6001.L678T5   *LC* 52-10048

Ambler, Eric, 1909-. 2.8379
A coffin for Dimitrios / Eric Ambler; with introduction by Elleston Trevor; annotated bibliography by James Sandoe; illustrations by Karl Nicholason. — San Diego, Ca.: University of California; Del Mar, Ca.: Publisher's inc., c1977. xii, 289 p.: ill., ports. — (The mystery library; 6) Includes appendices. Published in England under the title of The mask of Dimitrios. I. T.
PR6001.M47 C6

Ambler, Eric, 1909-. • 2.8380
Epitaph for a spy / with a footnote by the author. New York: Knopf, 1952. 259 p.; 20 cm. 'First Borzoi edition.' I. T.
PZ3.A48E6 1952p3 PR6001.M48Ex   *LC* 51-13217

Ambler, Eric, 1909-. • 2.8381
Intrigue: the great spy novels of Eric Ambler / by Eric Ambler. — New York: A. A. Knopf, 1943. [1146] p.; 20 cm. I. T. II. Title: Journey into fear. III. Title: A coffin for Dimitrios. IV. Title: Cause for alarm. V. Title: Background to danger.
PR6001.M481x   *LC* 43-2963

Amis, Kingsley. 2.8382
Collected poems, 1944–1979 / Kingsley Amis. — New York: Viking Press, 1980. 154 p.; 21 cm. — I. T.
PR6001.M6 A17 1980   821/.9/14   *LC* 79-23238   *ISBN* 0670229105

✓ **Amis, Kingsley.** • 2.8383
Lucky Jim, a novel. — [1st ed.]. — Garden City, N.Y.: Doubleday, 1954 [c1953] 256 p.; 22 cm. — I. T.
PZ4.A517 Lu   PR6001.M6 Lx.   *LC* 54-5356

Amis, Kingsley. • 2.8384
That uncertain feeling. — [1st American ed.]. — New York: Harcourt, Brace [1956, c1955] 247 p. 22 cm. I. T.
PR6001.M6T48 1956   PZ4.A517Th2.   *LC* 56-5331

Gardner, Philip. 2.8385
Kingsley Amis / by Philip Gardner. — Boston: Twayne Publishers, 1981. 174 p.; 21 cm. — (Twayne's English authors series; TEAS 319) Includes index. 1. Amis, Kingsley — Criticism and interpretation. I. T.
PR6001.M6 Z67   828/.91409 19   *LC* 80-22104   *ISBN* 0805768092

Arden, John. 2.8386
Serjeant Musgrave's dance: an unhistorical parable. — New York: Grove Press, [1962, c1960] 104 p.: ill.; 21 cm. (Evergreen original, E-312) I. T.
PR6001.R44 S4 1962   822.914   *LC* 62-9780

Arlen, Michael, 1895-1956. 2.8387
The green hat / by Michael Arlen. — New York: G.H. Doran Co., [c1924] 350 p.; 20 cm. I. T.
PR6001.R7 G7x   *LC* 24-22007

Keyishian, Harry. 2.8388
Michael Arlen / by Harry Keyishian. — Boston: Twayne Publishers, [1975] 150 p.: port.; 22 cm. (Twayne's English authors series; TEAS 174) Includes index. 1. Arlen, Michael, 1895-1956. I. T.
PR6001.R7 Z68   823/.9/12   *LC* 74-20819   *ISBN* 0805710116

Ashford, Daisy. • 2.8389
The young visiters: or, Mr. Salteena's plan / by Daisy Ashford; illustrated by William Pene Du Bois. — Garden City, N.Y.: Doubleday, 1951. 92 p.: ill.; 20 cm. I. T.
PZ3.A8245 Y2   PR6001.S44 Yx.

PR6001 Auden

Auden, W. H. (Wystan Hugh), 1907-1973.   **2.8390**
Collected poems / W. H. Auden; edited by Edward Mendelson. — 1st trade ed.
— New York: Random House, c1976. 696 p. I. Mendelson, Edward. II. T.
PR6001.U4 A17 1976   821/.9/12   *LC* 75-36263   *ISBN*
0394408950

Auden, W. H. (Wystan Hugh), 1907-1973.   **2.8391**
The English Auden: poems, essays, and dramatic writings, 1927–1939 / by W.
H. Auden; edited by Edward Mendelson. — 1st ed. — New York: Random
House, 1978 (c1977). xxiii, 469 p.; 25 cm. Includes index. I. Mendelson,
Edward. II. T.
PR6001.U4 A6   821/.912 19   *LC* 77-5968   *ISBN* 0394420497

Auden, W. H. (Wystan Hugh), 1907-1973.   • **2.8392**
The ascent of F6: a tragedy in two acts / by W.H. Auden and Christopher
Isherwood. — London: Faber & Faber, [1936] 123 p.; 23 cm. I. Isherwood,
Christopher, 1904- II. T. III. Title: A tragedy in two acts.
PR6001.U4 A8 1936   *LC* 46-39392

Auden, W. H. (Wystan Hugh), 1907-1973.   • **2.8393**
The dog beneath the skin, or, Where is Francis? A play in three acts / by W.H.
Auden and Christopher Isherwood. — London: Faber and Faber, [1935] 180 p.;
23 cm. I. Isherwood, Christopher, 1904- II. T. III. Title: Where is Francis?
PR6001.U4 D6 1935   *LC* 35-13653

Auden, W. H. (Wystan Hugh), 1907-1973.   • **2.8394**
The double man / W.H. Auden. — New York: Random House, c1941. 189 p.;
23 cm. Prose and poetry. I. T.
PR6001.U4 D65 1941   *LC* 41-6863

Auden, W. H. (Wystan Hugh), 1907-1973.   • **2.8395**
The dyer's hand, and other essays. New York, Random House [1962] 527 p. 22
cm. I. T.
PR6001.U4 D9   828.912   *LC* 62-16290

Auden, W. H. (Wystan Hugh), 1907-1973.   • **2.8396**
For the time being / by W.H. Auden. — New York: Random [1944] 132 p.; 21
cm. Contains two poems: The sea and mirror, a commentary on Shakespeare's
The tempest, and For the time being, a Christmas oratorio. 1. Shakespeare,
William, 1564-1616. Tempest I. Auden, W. H. (Wystan Hugh), 1907-1973. Sea
and the mirror. II. T. III. Title: The sea and the mirror.
PR6001.U4 F6   *LC* 45-4866

Auden, W. H. (Wystan Hugh), 1907-1973.   • **2.8397**
Letters from Iceland, by W. H. Auden, and Louis MacNeice. New York,
Random House [1969] 253 p. illus., map. 22 cm. 1. Iceland — Description and
travel — 1945- I. MacNeice, Louis, 1907-1963. joint author. II. T.
PR6001.U4 L4 1969   914.91/2/044   *LC* 70-3939

Auden, W. H. (Wystan Hugh), 1907-1973.   • **2.8398**
On the frontier: a melodrama in three acts / by W.H. Auden and Christopher
Isherwood. — 1st ed. — New York: Random House, c1938. 120 p.; 24 cm.
I. Isherwood, Christopher, 1904- II. T.
PR6001.U4 O5 1938a   *LC* 39-7727

Auden, W. H. (Wystan Hugh), 1907-1973.   • **2.8399**
The orators; an English study [by] W. H. Auden. [1st American ed.] New York,
Random House [1967, c1966] viii, 85 p. illus. 22 cm. I. T.
PR6001.U4 O7 1967   828/.9/1209   *LC* 67-22628

Biography. Criticism

Beach, Joseph Warren, 1880-1957.   • **2.8400**
The making of the Auden canon. New York, Russell & Russell [1971, c1957]
viii, 315 p. 23 cm. 'Facts in regard to W. H. Auden's procedure in making up
the texts of the Collected poetry, Random House, 1945, and the Collected
shorter poems, Faber and Faber, 1950.' 1. Auden, W. H. (Wystan Hugh),
1907-1973. I. T.
PR6001.U4 Z58 1971   821/.9/12   *LC* 74-139901

Callan, Edward, 1917-.   **2.8401**
Auden, a carnival of intellect / Edward Callan. — New York: Oxford
University Press, 1983. xii, 299 p.; 22 cm. 1. Auden, W. H. (Wystan Hugh),
1907-1973. 2. Poets, English — 20th century — Biography. I. T.
PR6001.U4 Z633 1983   821/.912 19   *LC* 82-2167   *ISBN*
0195031687

Carpenter, Humphrey.   **2.8402**
W.H. Auden, a biography / by Humphrey Carpenter. — 1st American ed. —
Boston: Houghton Mifflin Co., 1981. xvi, 495 p., [24] p. of plates: ill.; 24 cm.

Includes indexes. 1. Auden, W. H. (Wystan Hugh), 1907-1973 — Biography.
2. Poets, English — 20th century — Biography. I. T.
PR6001.U4 Z636 1981   821/.912 B 19   *LC* 81-6756   *ISBN*
0395308534

Duchêne, François.   **2.8403**
The case of the helmeted airman; a study of W. H. Auden's poetry. Totowa,
N.J., Rowman and Littlefield [1972] 228 p. 23 cm. 1. Auden, W. H. (Wystan
Hugh), 1907-1973. I. T.
PR6001.U4 Z66   821/.9/12   *LC* 72-196005   *ISBN* 0874711142

Fuller, John.   • **2.8404**
A reader's guide to W. H. Auden. [1st U.S. ed.] New York, Farrar, Straus &
Giroux [1970] 288 p. 21 cm. ([The Reader's guide series]) 1. Auden, W. H.
(Wystan Hugh), 1907-1973. 2. Auden, W. H. (Wystan Hugh), 1907-1973 —
Bibliography. I. T.
PR6001.U4 Z69 1970   821/.9/12   *LC* 75-105621

Greenberg, Herbert J.   • **2.8405**
Quest for the necessary; W. H. Auden and the dilemma of divided
consciousness. Cambridge, Mass.: Harvard University Press, 1968. viii, 209 p.
22 cm. 1. Auden, W. H. (Wystan Hugh), 1907-1973. I. T.
PR6001.U4 Z7   821/.9/12   *LC* 68-54019

Hoggart, Richard, 1918-.   • **2.8406**
Auden, an introductory essay / by Richard Hoggart. — London: Chatto &
Windus, 1951. 256 p.: port.; 22 cm. Includes index. 1. Auden, W. H. (Wystan
Hugh), 1907-1973. I. T.
PR6001.U4 Z74 1951   *LC* 51-6435

Johnson, Richard, 1937-.   **2.8407**
Man's place; an essay on Auden. Ithaca [N.Y.] Cornell University Press [1973]
xvi, 251 p. 22 cm. 1. Auden, W. H. (Wystan Hugh), 1907-1973. I. T.
PR6001.U4 Z754   821/.9/12   *LC* 72-12406   *ISBN* 0801407648

Mendelson, Edward.   • **2.8408**
Early Auden / Edward Mendelson. — New York: Viking Press, 1981. xxiii,
407 p.; 24 cm. 1. Auden, W. H. (Wystan Hugh), 1907-1973 — Criticism and
interpretation. I. T.
PR6001.U4 Z758 1981   821/.912 19   *LC* 80-54084   *ISBN*
0670287121

Spears, Monroe Kirklyndorf.   • **2.8409**
The poetry of W. H. Auden; the disenchanted island. New York: Oxford
University Press, 1963. x, 394 p.; 21 cm. 1. Auden, W. H. (Wystan Hugh),
1907-1973. I. T.
PR6001.U4 Z83   821.912   *LC* 63-17739

Spears, Monroe Kirklyndorf. ed.   • **2.8410**
Auden; a collection of critical essays. Edited by Monroe K. Spears. Englewood
Cliffs, N.J., Prentice-Hall [1964] 184 p. 22 cm. (Twentieth century views) (A
Spectrum book.) 1. Auden, W. H. (Wystan Hugh), 1907-1973. I. T.
PR6001.U4 Z84   821.912   *LC* 64-19682

PR6003 B–Ba

Bagnold, Enid.   • **2.8411**
The chalk garden / by Enid Bagnold. — New York: Random House, c1956.
165 p., [2] leaves of plates: ill.; 21 cm. — (A Random House play) I. T.
PR6003.A35 C5   *LC* 55-12484

Bailey, Henry Christopher, 1878-1961.   **2.8412**
Mr. Fortune objects / by H.C. Bailey. — Garden City, N.Y.: Doubleday, 1935.
1 v. Short stories. I. T.
PR6003. A4x

Barker, George, 1913-.   • **2.8413**
Collected poems, 1930–1955. New York: Criterion Books [1958,c1957] 245 p.;
21 cm. I. T.
PR6003.A68 A17 1958   *LC* 58-10616

Fielding, Gabriel, 1916-.   • **2.8414**
The birthday king: a romance / by Gabriel Fielding [pseud.]. — New York:
Morrow, 1963 [c1962] 383 p.: 21 cm. — First published by Hutchinson,
London in 1962. 1. World War, 1939-1945 — Fiction I. T.
PZ4.B2635 Bi2   PR6003.A74 B5x.   *LC* 63-7877

Borrello, Alfred.   **2.8415**
Gabriel Fielding. New York, Twayne Publishers [1974] 165 p. port. 22 cm.
(Twayne's English authors series, TEAS 162) 1. Fielding, Gabriel, 1916- I. T.
PR6003.A74 Z6   823/.9/14   *LC* 73-16101   *ISBN* 0805711945

PR6003 Beckett
(see also PQ2603)

Beckett, Samuel, 1906-.   **2.8416**
[Poems. Selections] Collected poems, 1930–1978 / Samuel Beckett. — London: J. Calder, 1984. ix, 179 p.; 21 cm. In English, French, or French and English (some of the poems in the last category being works of French poets with English versions by Beckett). Updated version of: Collected poems in English and French. 1977. 1. French poetry — Translations into English. 2. English poetry — Translations from French. I. T.
PR6003.E282 A17 1984   841/.914 19   *LC* 84-116487   *ISBN* 0714540528

Beckett, Samuel, 1906-.   • **2.8417**
A Samuel Beckett reader; edited by John Calder. — London: New English Library, 1967. 192 p.; 18 cm. — (NEL Signet modern classics) I. T.
PR6003.E282 A6 1967b   828   *LC* 68-72947

Beckett, Samuel, 1906-.   **2.8418**
[Plays. Selections] Collected shorter plays / Samuel Beckett. — 1st hardcover ed. — New York: Grove Press, 1984. 316 p.: ill.; 22 cm. 1. Beckett, Samuel, 1906- — Translations, English. I. T.
PR6003.E282 A6 1984   822/.912 19   *LC* 83-49371   *ISBN* 0394538501

Beckett, Samuel, 1906-.   • **2.8419**
All that fall. — New York: Grove Press, [1957] 59 p.; 22 cm. A play. I. T.
PR6003.E282 A79 1957   822.91   *LC* 57-11485

Beckett, Samuel, 1906-.   • **2.8420**
Happy days; a play in two acts. — New York: Grove Press, [1961] 64 p.; 21 cm. — (Evergreen original, E-318) I. T.
PR6003.E282 H3   822   *LC* 61-16911

Beckett, Samuel, 1906-.   **2.8421**
I can't go on, I'll go on: a selection from Samuel Beckett's work / Samuel Beckett; edited and introduced by Richard W. Seaver. New York: Grove Press; distributed by Random House, 1976. xlviii, 621 p.; 22 cm. I. T.
PR6003.E282 I2 1976   848/.9/1409   *LC* 75-43432   *ISBN* 0394406699

Beckett, Samuel, 1906-.   • **2.8422**
Krapp's last tape, and other dramatic pieces. — New York: Grove Press, [1960] 141 p.; 21 cm. — (Evergreen original E-226) I. T.
PR6003.E282 K7   822   *LC* 60-8388

Beckett, Samuel, 1906-.   **2.8423**
More pricks than kicks. New York, Grove Press [1970] 191 p. 21 cm. (His Collected works) First published: London: Chatto and Windus, 1934. I. T.
PR6003.E282 M6 1970   823/.9/12   *LC* 72-119923

Beckett, Samuel, 1906-.   • **2.8424**
Murphy. — New York: Grove Press, [1957] 282 p.; 22 cm. A novel. I. T.
PZ3.B38868 Mu   PR6003.E282 M8x.   *LC* 57-6939

Beckett, Samuel, 1906-.   • **2.8425**
Watt. — [1st American ed.]. — New York: Grove Press, [1959] 254 p.; 21 cm. A novel. I. T.
PZ3.B38868 Wat2   PR6003.E282 W3x.   *LC* 58-9097

Bair, Deirdre.   **2.8426**
Samuel Beckett: a biography / Deirdre Bair. — 1st ed. — New York: Harcourt Brace Jovanovich, c1978. xiv, 736 p., [12] leaves of plates: ill.; 24 cm. 1. Beckett, Samuel, 1906- — Biography. 2. Authors, Irish — 20th century — Biography. I. T.
PR6003.E282 Z564 1978   848/.9/1409 B   *LC* 77-92527   *ISBN* 0151792569

Coe, Richard N.   • **2.8427**
Samuel Beckett / [by] Richard N. Coe. — New York, Grove Press [1964] 118 p. 18 cm. (Evergreen pilot books; EP29.) 1. Beckett, Samuel, 1906- I. T.
PR6003.E282 Z6 1964   *LC* 64-18116

Esslin, Martin. ed.   • **2.8428**
Samuel Beckett: a collection of critical essays. — Englewood Cliffs, N.J.: Prentice-Hall, [1965] viii, 182 p.; 21 cm. — (A Spectrum book: Twentieth century views) 1. Beckett, Samuel, 1906- — Criticism and interpretation. I. T.
PR6003.E282 Z64   828.91409   *LC* 65-23302

Fletcher, John, 1937-.   • **2.8429**
The novels of Samuel Beckett. New York, Barnes & Noble [1964] 256 p. 23 cm. 1. Beckett, Samuel, 1906- I. T.
PR6003.E282 Z66 1964   *LC* 64-7219

Kenner, Hugh.   • **2.8430**
Samuel Beckett, a critical study. — New ed., with a supplementary chapter. — Berkeley: University of California Press, 1968. 226 p.: port.; 21 cm. 1. Beckett, Samuel, 1906- — Criticism and interpretation. I. T.
PR6003.E282 Z76 1968   828/.9/1209   *LC* 68-4862

Mercier, Vivian, 1919-.   **2.8431**
Beckett/Beckett / Vivian Mercier. — New York: Oxford University Press, 1977. xv, 254 p.; 22 cm. 1. Beckett, Samuel, 1906- — Criticism and interpretation. I. T.
PR6003.E282 Z7813   848/.9/1409   *LC* 76-42658   *ISBN* 019502186X

Rabinovitz, Rubin.   **2.8432**
The development of Samuel Beckett's fiction / Rubin Rabinovitz. — Urbana: University of Illinois Press, c1984. x, 231 p.; 24 cm. 1. Beckett, Samuel, 1906- — Fictional works. I. T.
PR6003.E282 Z7887 1984   823/.912 19   *LC* 83-4850   *ISBN* 0252010957

Samuel Beckett now; critical approaches to his novels, poetry,   • **2.8433**
and plays. Edited with an introd. by Melvin J. Friedman.
[Chicago] University of Chicago Press [1970] xii, 275 p. 23 cm. With the exception of three essays, an earlier form of this book appeared in French as Configuration critique de Samuel Beckett. 1. Beckett, Samuel, 1906- I. Friedman, Melvin J. ed.
PR6003.E282 Z82   848/.9/1409   *LC* 77-99052   *ISBN* 0226263460

Samuel Beckett, the critical heritage / edited by Lawrence   **2.8434**
Graver and Raymond Federman.
London; Boston: Routledge & Kegan Paul, 1979. xx, 372 p.; 23 cm. — (The Critical heritage series) Includes index. 1. Beckett, Samuel, 1906- — Criticism and interpretation. I. Graver, Lawrence, 1931- II. Federman, Raymond.
PR6003.E282 Z822   828/.9/1209   *LC* 78-40719   *ISBN* 0710089481

PR6003 Beerbohm

Beerbohm, Max, Sir, 1872-1956.   • **2.8435**
The incomparable Max: a collection of writings of Sir Max Beerbohm. — New York: Dodd, Mead [1962] 395 p.; 22 cm. I. T.
PR6003.E4 A6 1962   *LC* 62-20642

Beerbohm, Max, Sir, 1872-1956.   • **2.8436**
And even now / by Max Beerbohm. — New York: E.P. Dutton, 1950. ix, 320 p.; 20 cm. I. T.
PR6003.E4 A8 1950

Beerbohm, Max, Sir, 1872-1956.   • **2.8437**
Yet again. — London: W. Heinemann, [1951] 334 p. I. T.
PR6003.E4 Y4 1951   *LC* a 63-5048

Beerbohm, Max, Sir, 1872-1956.   • **2.8438**
Zuleika Dobson, by Max Beerbohm; introduction by Francis Hackett. — New York: The Modern library [1926] xi, 358 p.; 17 cm. (Half-title: The modern library of the world's best books) I. T.
PZ3.B3958Z25   PR6003.E4 Z1x.   *LC* 36-29319

Behrman, S. N. (Samuel Nathaniel), 1893-1973.   • **2.8439**
Portrait of Max; an intimate memoir of Sir Max Beerbohm. New York, Random House [1960] 317 p. illus., port. 24 cm. 'Originated in the New Yorker as a series of articles.' 1. Beerbohm, Max, Sir, 1872-1956. I. T.
PR6003.E4 Z56   928.2   *LC* 60-5529

Felstiner, John.   **2.8440**
The lies of art; Max Beerbohm's parody and caricature. — [1st ed.]. — New York: Knopf, 1972. xx, 283, xi p.: illus.; 22 cm. 1. Beerbohm, Max, Sir, 1872-1956. I. T.
PR6003.E4 Z66   828/.9/1209   *LC* 76-171162   *ISBN* 0394472276

Riewald, Jacobus Gerhardus. comp.   **2.8441**
The surprise of excellence: modern essays on Max Beerbohm. Edited, with an introd., by J. G. Riewald. — [Hamden, Conn.]: Archon Books, 1974. xiii, 265 p.: port.; 23 cm. 1. Beerbohm, Max, Sir, 1872-1956 — Criticism and interpretation. I. T.
PR6003.E4 Z782   824/.9/12   *LC* 74-5181   *ISBN* 0208014438

PR6003 Be

Behan, Brendan.   • **2.8442**
The quare fellow, and The hostage; two plays. — New York: Grove Press, [1964] 182 p.; 18 cm. — (An Evergreen black cat book, BC-79) I. Behan, Brendan. The hostage. II. T. III. Title: The hostage.
PR6003.E417 Q3 1964   822   *LC* 65-3106

Behan, Brendan.   • 2.8443
Borstal boy. — [1st American ed.]. — New York: Knopf, 1959. 372 p.; 22 cm.
Autobiographical. 1. Behan, Brendan. I. T.
PR6003.E417 Z52   365.94264   *LC* 59-6223

Bell, Clive, 1881-1964.   • 2.8444
Old friends: personal recollections. [1st American ed.] New York: Harcourt,
Brace [1957, c1956] 199 p.: ill.; 22 cm. I. T.
PR6003.E425 O4 1957   828.91   *LC* 57-13597

Belloc, Hilaire, 1870-1953.   • 2.8445
Selected essays / with an introduction by J.B. Morton. — London: Methuen,
[1948] xv, 303 p.; 19 cm. I. T.
PR6003.E45 A16 1948   *LC* a 52-5387

Belloc, Hilaire, 1870-1953.   • 2.8446
Stories, essays, and poems [by] Hilaire Belloc. — London, J. M. Dent & sons
ltd. 1941. xiv, 454 p.; 18 cm. — (Half-title: Everyman's library, ed. by Ernest
Rhys. Essays & belles-lettres. [No. 948]) 'This collection first published in 1938.
Last reprinted 1941.' Bibliography: p. xi. I. T. II. Series.
PR6003.E45A6 1941   820.81   *LC* 42-25411

Belloc, Hilaire, 1870-1953.   • 2.8447
Hilaire Belloc, an anthology of his prose and verse, selected by W. N.
Roughead. London, R. Hart-Davis, 1951. 283 p.: music, ports.; 23 cm.
I. Roughead, William Nicol. II. T.
PR6003.E45 A6 1951   820.81   *LC* 51-6715

Markel, Michael H.   2.8448
Hilaire Belloc / by Michael H. Markel. — Boston: Twayne Publishers, c1982.
175 p., [1] p. of plates: port.; 21 cm. — (Twayne's English authors series. TEAS
347) Includes index. 1. Belloc, Hilaire, 1870-1953 — Criticism and
interpretation. I. T. II. Series.
PR6003.E45 Z77 1982   828/.91209 19   *LC* 82-8518   *ISBN*
0805768335

Morton, John Bingham, 1893-.   • 2.8449
Hilaire Belloc: a memoir / by J.B. Morton. — New York: Sheed & Ward,
c1955. 185 p. 1. Belloc, Hilaire, 1870-1953. I. T.
PR6003E45 Z8 1955a   PR6003E45 Z8.   928.2   *LC* 55-10499

Speaight, Robert, 1904-.   • 2.8450
The life of Hilaire Belloc. — Freeport, N.Y.: Books for Libraries Press, [1970,
c1957] xv, 552 p.: illus., ports.; 23 cm. — (Biography index reprint series)
1. Belloc, Hilaire, 1870-1953 — Biography. I. T.
PR6003.E45 Z85 1970   828/.9/1209   *LC* 78-136655   *ISBN*
0836980506

Wilson, A. N., 1950-.   2.8451
Hilaire Belloc / A.N. Wilson. — 1st American ed. — New York: Atheneum,
1984. x, 398 p., [16] p. of plates: ill.; 25 cm. 1. Belloc, Hilaire, 1870-1953 —
Biography. 2. Authors, English — 20th century — Biography. I. T.
PR6003.E45 Z893 1984   828/.91209 B 19   *LC* 83-45504   *ISBN*
0689114400

PR6003 Bennett

Bennett, Arnold, 1867-1931.   • 2.8452
Anna of the Five Towns / Arnold Bennett. — London: Methuen, 1961. 254 p.
I. T.
PZ3.B438 An15 PR6003.E6 A6x   823/.9/12   *LC* 74-5320   *ISBN*
051819082X

Bennett, Arnold, 1867-1931.   • 2.8453
The Clayhanger family: I. Clayhanger. II. Hilda Lessways. III. These Twain.
By Arnold Bennett. — London: Methuen & Co. [1925] ix, 1302 p.; 20 cm. I. T.
II. Title: Clayhanger. III. Title: These Twain. IV. Title: Hilda Lessways.
PR6003.E6C55

Bennett, Arnold, 1867-1931.   • 2.8454
A man from the north. New York: Doran, 1911. 264 p. I. T.
PR6003.E6Mx PZ3B438Ma   *LC* 11-26258

Bennett, Arnold, 1867-1931.   • 2.8455
The old wives' tale / by Arnold Bennett; with an introduction by J. B. Priestley.
— New York: Harper, c1950. xxii, 612 p.; 21 cm. — (Harper's modern classics)
I. T.
PR6003.E6 O4 1950   *LC* 50-6257

Bennett, Arnold, 1867-1931.   • 2.8456
Riceyman Steps. — 11th ed., 2nd impression. — London: Cassell, 1968. 304 p.;
19 cm. — I. T.
PZ3.B438 Ri5 PR6003.E6R5x   *LC* 75-358278   *ISBN* 0304931527

Bennett, Arnold, 1867-1931.   • 2.8457
The journals; selected and edited by Frank Swinnerton. Harmondsworth:
Penguin, 1971. 599 p.; 18 cm. (Penguin modern classics) The Journals
originally published London, Cassell, 1930-1933. 'Now published with the
addition of Journal volume 6, newly discovered, covering the period 21
September 1906-18 July 1907, and Florentine journal, covering the period 1
April 1910 - 25 May 1910.' 1. Bennett, Arnold, 1867-1931. I. Swinnerton,
Frank, 1884- II. T.
PR6003.E6 Z45 1971   828/.9/1203 B   *LC* 70-874485   *ISBN*
0140032843

Drabble, Margaret, 1939-.   2.8458
Arnold Bennett: a biography / by Margaret Drabble. — 1st American ed. —
New York: Knopf, 1974. xiv, 396 p., [12] leaves of plates: ill.; 25 cm.
1. Bennett, Arnold, 1867-1931 — Biography. I. T.
PR6003.E6 Z715 1974b   823/.9/12 B   *LC* 73-20773   *ISBN*
039448794X

Lucas, John, 1937-.   2.8459
Arnold Bennett: a study of his fiction / by John Lucas. — London: Methuen;
[New York]: distributed by Harper & Row Publishers, 1975 (c1974). 235 p.; 22
cm. Includes index. 1. Bennett, Arnold, 1867-1931 — Criticism and
interpretation. I. T.
PR6003.E6 Z778   823/.9/12   *LC* 75-307589   *ISBN* 0416757707

PR6003 Be–Bo

Bentley, E. C. (Edmund Clerihew), 1875-1956.   2.8460
Trent's last case / E. C. Bentley; with introd. and annotations by Aaron Marc
Stein; bibliography by Charles Shibuk; ill. by Darrel Millsap. — San Diego:
University Extension, University of California, San Diego, c1977. xxv, 269 p.:
ill.; 21 cm. — (The Mystery library; 5) I. T. II. Series.
PZ3.B4443 Tr 1977 PR6003.E7247   823/.9/12   *LC* 76-50690
ISBN 0891630309

Bentley, E. C. (Edmund Clerihew), 1875-1956.   • 2.8461
Trent's case book [comprising] Trent's last case, Trent's own case: with H.
Warner [and] Trent intervenes / [by] E. C. Bentley; with an introd. by Ben Ray
Redman. — New York, Knopf, 1953. 187 p. 249, 188 p. 22 cm. I. T.
PZ3.B4443 To   PR6003.E7247 T7x.   *LC* 52-12213

Betjeman, John, Sir, 1906-.   2.8462
Collected poems. Compiled by the Earl of Birkenhead. Introd. by Philip Larkin.
— Enl. ed. — Boston: Houghton Mifflin, 1971. xli, 366 p.; 19 cm. — I. T.
PR6003.E77 A6 1971   821/.9/12   *LC* 77-162003   *ISBN*
039512705X

Betjeman, John, Sir, 1906-.   • 2.8463
A ring of bells: poems / introduced and selected by Irene Slade; illustrated by
Edward Ardizzone. — [1st American ed.] Boston: Houghton Mifflin, 1963
[c1962]. 129 p.: ill.; 23 cm. I. T.
PR6003.E77 R5   *LC* 63-10654

Betjeman, John, Sir, 1906-.   • 2.8464
Summoned by bells. Boston: Houghton Mifflin [c1960] 97 p.; 22 cm.
Autobiography in verse. I. T.
PR6003.E77 Z52   *LC* 60-14977

Blackwood, Algernon, 1869-1951.   2.8465
Best ghost stories of Algernon Blackwood. Selected with an introd. by E. F.
Bleiler. — New York: Dover Publications, [c1973] xviii, 366 p.: port.; 22 cm.
1. Ghost stories, English I. T.
PZ3.B5683 Be PR6003.L3   823/.9/12   *LC* 73-75877   *ISBN*
0486229777

Bolt, Robert.   • 2.8466
A man for all seasons; a play in two acts. — New York: Random House, [1962]
163 p.: illus.; 22 cm. 1. More, Thomas, Sir, Saint, 1478-1535 — Drama. I. T.
PR6003.O474 M3 1962   822.914   *LC* 62-13648

Bolt, Robert.   2.8467
The tiger and the horse; a play in three acts. London, Heinemann [1963] xxii,
97 p. (The Hereford Plays series) I. T.
PR6003.O474 Tx

PR6003 Bowen

Bowen, Elizabeth, 1899-1973.   2.8468
The collected stories of Elizabeth Bowen / with an introd. by Angus Wilson. —
1st American ed. — New York: Knopf, 1981. 784 p.: ill.; 22 cm. I. T.
PR6003.O6757 A15 1981   823/.912 19   *LC* 80-8729   *ISBN*
0394516664

Bowen, Elizabeth, 1899-1973.   • **2.8469**
Collected impressions. — New York, Knopf, 1950. ix, 269 p.; 23 cm.
1. Literature — History and criticism I. T.
PR6003.O6757 A16 1950   824.91   LC 50-4637

Bowen, Elizabeth, 1899-1973.   • **2.8470**
The death of the heart [by] Elizabeth Bowen. New York, A. A. Knopf, 1939.
418 p.; 21 cm. 'First American edition.' . I. T.
PZ3.B6738De2 PR6003.O6757D4   LC 38-29084

Bowen, Elizabeth, 1899-1973.   • **2.8471**
Eva Trout; or, Changing scenes. [1st ed.] New York, Knopf, 1968. 302 p. 22 cm.
I. T.
PR6003.O6757.E9 1968   823/.9/12   LC 68-12685

Bowen, Elizabeth, 1899-1973.   **2.8472**
The heat of the day. [1st ed.] New York, A. A. Knopf, 1949 [c1948] 372 p. 20
cm. I. T.
PR6003.O6757 H4 1949   LC 49-420

Bowen, Elizabeth, 1899-1973.   • **2.8473**
The house in Paris, by Elizabeth Bowen. New York, A. A. Knopf, 1936. 268 p.;
20 cm. 'First American edition.' I. T.
PR6003.O6757 H6 1936   LC 36-4991

Bowen, Elizabeth, 1899-1973.   • **2.8474**
The hotel. Westport, Conn., Greenwood Press [1972, c1928] 294 p. 22 cm. I. T.
PR6003.O6757 H6 1972   823/.912 19   LC 73-141416   ISBN
0837146852

Bowen, Elizabeth, 1899-1973.   • **2.8475**
The last September / Elizabeth Bowen. — New York: Knopf, 1952. 303 p.; 20
cm. I. T.
PZ3.B6738 La PR6003.O6757 L38   823/.9/12

Bowen, Elizabeth, 1899-1973.   • **2.8476**
The little girls. — [1st ed.]. — New York, A. Knopf, 1964 [1963] 306 p.; 22 cm.
I. T.
PR6003.O6757 L5   LC 63-20834

Bowen, Elizabeth, 1899-1973.   • **2.8477**
A time in Rome. — [1st ed.]. — New York: Knopf, 1960 [c1959] 241 p.; 21 cm.
1. Rome (Italy) — Description. I. T.
PR6003.O6757 T5   LC 60-5185

Bowen, Elizabeth, 1899-1973.   • **2.8478**
To the north / Elizabeth Bowen. 1st American ed. New York, N.Y.: Knopf,
1933. 306 p.; 21 cm. I. T.
PR6003.O6757 Tx   LC 33-3924

Bowen, Elizabeth, 1899-1973.   • **2.8479**
A world of love / Elizabeth Bowen. — 1st ed. — New York: Knopf, 1955,
c1954. 244 p.; 22 cm. I. T.
PZ3.B6738Wo   PR6003.O6757 Wx.   LC 55-5209

Bowen, Elizabeth, 1899-1973.   • **2.8480**
Seven winters. Dublin, Cuala Press, 1942. [Shannon, Irish University Press,
1971] 57 p. 22 cm. I. T.
PR6003.O6757 Z52 1971   823/.9/12 B   LC 70-25218   ISBN
0716513978

Blodgett, Harriet.   **2.8481**
Patterns of reality: Elizabeth Bowen's novels / by Harriet Blodgett. — The
Hague: Mouton, 1975. 213 p.; 24 cm. (De proprietatibus litterarum: Series
practica; 84) Includes index. 1. Bowen, Elizabeth, 1899-1973 — Criticism and
interpretation. I. T. II. Series.
PR6003.O6757 Z58   823/.9/12   LC 76-353796   ISBN 9027933111

Heath, William Webster, 1929-.   • **2.8482**
Elizabeth Bowen, an introduction to her novels. — Madison, University of
Wisconsin Press, 1961. 180 p.; 25 cm. 1. Bowen, Elizabeth, 1899-1973. I. T.
PR6003.O6757 Z67   823.91   LC 61-10688

Kenney, Edwin J.   **2.8483**
Elizabeth Bowen [by] Edwin J. Kenney, Jr. — Lewisburg [Pa.]: Bucknell
University Press, 1975. 107 p.; 21 cm. — (The Irish writers series) 1. Bowen,
Elizabeth, 1899-1973. I. T.
PR6003.O6757 Z675   823/.9/12   LC 74-168810   ISBN
0838779395

Lee, Hermione.   **2.8484**
Elizabeth Bowen, an estimation / by Hermione Lee. — London: Vision Press;
Totowa, N.J.: Barnes & Noble, 1981. 255 p.; 23 cm. — (Critical studies series.)

Includes index. 1. Bowen, Elizabeth, 1899-1973 — Criticism and
interpretation. I. T. II. Series.
PR6003.O6757 Z677 1981   823/.912 19   LC 81-188192   ISBN
0389202045

PR6003 Br–By

Brooke, Rupert, 1887-1915.   • **2.8485**
The poetical works of Rupert Brooke; edited by Geoffrey Keynes. 2nd ed.
London, Faber and Faber Ltd., 1970. 216 p., 2 plates. 2 ports. 21 cm.
I. Keynes, Geoffrey, Sir, 1887- ed. II. T.
PR6003.R4 1970   821/.9/12   LC 70-597949   ISBN 0571047084

Brooke, Rupert, 1887-1915.   • **2.8486**
The letters of Rupert Brooke. Chosen and edited by Geoffrey Keynes. [1st
American ed.] New York, Harcourt, Brace & World [1968] xv, 709 p. ports. 25
cm. 1. Brooke, Rupert, 1887-1915 — Correspondence. I. Keynes, Geoffrey,
Sir, 1887- ed. II. T.
PR6003.R4 Z515 1968b   826/.9/12   LC 68-24401

Hassall, Christopher, 1912-1963.   • **2.8487**
Rupert Brooke; a biography. [1st American ed.] New York: Harcourt, Brace &
World [1964] 556 p.: ill., ports.; 25 cm. 1. Brooke, Rupert, 1887-1915. I. T.
PR6003.R4 Z67 1964   LC 63-8099

Buchan, John, 1875-1940.   • **2.8488**
The four adventures of Richard Hannay / recounted by John Buchan. —
London: Hodder and Stoughton, [1933] x, 1204 p.; 20 cm. I. Buchan, John,
1875-1940. Thirty-nine steps. II. Buchan, John, 1875-1940. Greenmantle.
III. Buchan, John, 1875-1940. Mr. Standfast. IV. Buchan, John, 1875-1940.
Three hostages. V. T. VI. Title: The three hostages. VII. Title: Greenmantle.
VIII. Title: Mr. Standfast. IX. Title: The thirty-nine steps. X. Title: The 3
hostages. XI. Title: The 39 steps. XII. Title: The 4 adventures of Richard
Hannay.
PR6003.U13 F6 1933   LC 33-9290

Buchan, John, 1875-1940.   **2.8489**
The thirty-nine steps / John Buchan; with introduction by Michael F. Gilbert;
bibliography by Janet Adam Smith; illustrations by Karl Nicholason. — San
Diego: University Extension University of California, 1978. xiv, 207 p.: ill.,
ports. — (The Mystery library; 8) 1. Detective and mystery stories I. T.
II. Title: 39 steps. III. Series.
PR6003.U13 T48 1978   LC 78-57084   ISBN 0891630457

Bunting, Basil.   **2.8490**
Collected poems / Basil Bunting. — New ed. — Oxford [Eng.]; New York:
Oxford University Press, 1978. 152 p.; 25 cm. I. T.
PR6003.U36 1978   821/.9/14   LC 77-30657   ISBN 0192118781

PR6005 C–Ca

Calder-Marshall, Arthur.   **2.8491**
The scarlet boy. — New York: Harper, [c1961] 1 v. I. T.
PR6005.A3 S25   Fic   LC 62-7899

Carroll, Paul Vincent, 1900-1968.   • **2.8492**
Irish stories and plays. — New York: Devin-Adair, 1958. 278 p.; 21 cm. I. T.
PR6005.A74 I7   823.914   LC 58-9753

PR6005 Cary

Cary, Joyce, 1888-1957.   • **2.8493**
The African witch. New York: Harper [1962, c1936] 313 p.; 22 cm. I. T.
PR6005.A77 A4x   LC 62-9919

Cary, Joyce, 1888-1957.   • **2.8494**
Aissa saved. [1st American ed.] New York: Harper & Row, [1962?]. 219 p.; 22
cm. I. T.
PR6005.A77 A5x   LC 62-20121

Cary, Joyce, 1888-1957.   • **2.8495**
An American visitor. New York: Harper [1961] 247 p.; 22 cm. I. T.
PR6005.A77 A6x   LC 61-10241

Cary, Joyce, 1888-1957.   • **2.8496**
The captive and the free: a novel / Introd. by David Cecil; editor's note by
Winifred Davin. — [1st ed.] New York: Harper [1959] 369 p.; 22 cm. I. T.
PZ3.C25884Cap PR6005.A77C3   823.91   LC 58-8885

Cary, Joyce, 1888-1957.   • **2.8497**
Castle Corner / by Joyce Cary. — 1st U.S. ed. — New York: Harper & Row,
1963. 424 p.; 22 cm. I. T.
PR6005.A77 C37x   LC 63-20302

Cary, Joyce, 1888-1957. • **2.8498**
Charley is my darling / by Joyce Cary. — New York: Harper, [1960] 342 p.; 22 cm. I. T.
PZ3.C25884 Ch2 PR6005.A77 C5x. *LC* 59-13306

Cary, Joyce, 1888-1957. • **2.8499**
Except the Lord, a novel. [1st ed.] New York: Harper [1953] 276 p.; 22 cm. The 2d vol. of the author's trilogy, the 1st of which is Prisoner of grace and the 3d, Not honour more. I. T.
PZ3.C25884 Ex PR6005.A77 Ex. 823/.912 19 *LC* 53-7728

Cary, Joyce, 1888-1957. • **2.8500**
A fearful joy: a novel / Joyce Cary. — [1st ed.] New York: Harper, [c1949] 343 p.; 22 cm. I. T.
PR6005.A77 F4x *LC* 50-14742

Cary, Joyce, 1888-1957. • **2.8501**
First trilogy: Herself surprised. To be a pilgrim. The horse's mouth. — [1st ed.]. — New York: Harper, [1958] 275, 343, 289 p.; 22 cm. I. T. II. Title: Herself surprised. III. Title: To be a pilgrim. IV. Title: The horse's mouth.
PZ3.C25884 Fi PR6005.A77 F5x. *LC* 57-8201

Cary, Joyce, 1888-1957. • **2.8502**
A house of children. [With a prefatory essay by the author] London, M. Joseph [1951] 239 p. (Carfax edition) I. T.
PR6005.A77 H6x 823.91 *ISBN* 0718101839

Cary, Joyce, 1888-1957. • **2.8503**
Mister Johnson: a novel. — [1st ed.]. — New York: Harper, [1951?] 261 p.; 22 cm. I. T.
PR6005.A77 M5x *LC* 51-12810

Cary, Joyce, 1888-1957. • **2.8504**
Not honour more, a novel. [1st ed.] New York, Harper [1955] 309 p. 22 cm. I. T.
PZ3.C25884No PR6005.A77N6 *LC* 55-6570

Cary, Joyce, 1888-1957. • **2.8505**
Prisoner of grace. — New York: Harper & Brothers, c1952. 301 p.; 21 cm. I. T.
PZ3.C25884 Pr 1978 PR6005.A77 P7x 823/.9/12 *LC* 52-7281
ISBN

Adams, Hazard, 1926-. **2.8506**
Joyce Cary's trilogies: pursuit of the particular real / Hazard Adams. — Tallahassee: University Presses of Florida, c1983. xvi, 280 p.; 24 cm. 'A Florida State University book.' Includes index. 1. Cary, Joyce, 1888-1957 — Criticism and interpretation. I. T.
PR6005.A77 Z58 1983 823/.912 19 *LC* 83-3461 *ISBN* 0813007593

Bloom, Robert, 1930-. **2.8507**
The indeterminate world: a study of the novels of Joyce Cary. Philadelphia, University of Pennsylvania Press [1963, c1962] 212 p. 22 cm. 1. Cary, Joyce, 1888-1957. I. T.
PR6005.A77 Z63 *LC* 62-10745

Echeruo, Michael J. C. **2.8508**
Joyce Cary and the dimensions of order / Michael J. C. Echeruo. — New York: Barnes & Noble, 1979. x, 175 p.; 23 cm. Includes index. 1. Cary, Joyce, 1888-1957 — Philosophy. I. T.
PR6005.A77 Z647 1979 823/.9/12 *LC* 78-9857 *ISBN* 0064918750

Fisher, Barbara. **2.8509**
Joyce Cary: the writer and his theme / Barbara Fisher. — Atlantic Highlands, N.J.: Humanities Press, 1980. xiii, 414 p. 1. Cary, Joyce, 1888-1957 — Criticism and interpretation. I. T.
PR6005.A77 Z74 *ISBN* 0391017632

Mahood, M. M. (Molly Maureen) **2.8510**
Joyce Cary's Africa / M. M. Mahood. — London: Methuen, 1964. viii, 206 p.: ill., facsims, maps (on lining papers); 21 cm. 1. Cary, Joyce, 1888-1957. 2. Nigeria in literature I. T.
PR6005.A77 Z77 823.912 *LC* 64-56031

Wolkenfeld, Jack. **2.8511**
Joyce Cary: the developing style. — New York: New York University Press, 1968. xiii, 200 p.; 22 cm. 1. Cary, Joyce, 1888-1957. I. T.
PR6005.A77 Z79 823/.9/12 *LC* 68-16830

Wright, Andrew H. • **2.8512**
Joyce Cary: a preface to his novels [by] Andrew Wright. — Westport, Conn.: Greenwood Press, [1972] 186 p.; 22 cm. Reprint of the 1958 ed. 1. Cary, Joyce, 1888-1957. I. T.
PR6005.A77 Z8 1972 823/.9/12 *LC* 72-138602 *ISBN* 0837158044

PR6005 Ch–Co

Childers, Erskine, 1870-1922. **2.8513**
The riddle of the sands: a record of secret service / by Erskine Childers; with a new introd. by Norman Donaldson. — New York: Dover Publications, 1976. 284 p.: maps; 22 cm. Reprint of the 1903 ed. published by Smith, Elder, London. I. T.
PZ3.C4376 Ri14 PR6005.H52 R5x 823/.9/12 *LC* 75-36077
ISBN 0486232808

Christie, Agatha, 1890-1976. • **2.8514**
The murder of Roger Ackroyd / by Agatha Christie. — New York: Dodd, Mead, 1926. vii, 306 p.; 20 cm. 1. Detective and mystery stories I. T.
PR6005.H66 M85x

Christie, Agatha, 1890-1976. **2.8515**
The murder at the vicarage: a detective story / by Agatha Christie. — New York: Dodd, Mead, 1930. 319 p. I. T.
PR6005.H66 M8x Fic *LC* 30-29830

Christie, Agatha, 1890-1976. • **2.8516**
The nursery rhyme murders; including: A pocket full of rye, Hickory dickory death. The crooked house, by Agatha Christie. New York, Dodd, Mead [1970] 505 p. 22 cm. I. T. II. Title: A pocket full of rye. III. Title: Hickory dickory death. IV. Title: The crooked house.
PZ3.C4637 Nu 1970 PR6005.H66N8x 823/.9/12 *LC* 72-117622

Christie, Agatha, 1890-1976. • **2.8517**
The mysterious Mr. Quin. By Agatha Christie. New York, Dodd, Mead, 1930. 290 p. 20 cm. I. T.
PR 6005 H89 M995 1930 *LC* 30-11715

Clarke, Arthur Charles, 1917-. • **2.8518**
Childhood's end. New York, Harcourt, Brace & World [1963, c1953] 216 p. 21 cm. I. T.
PZ3.L36C49 1963 PR6005.L36 C5x. *LC* 63-2407

Clarke, Arthur Charles, 1917-. **2.8519**
2001; a space odyssey, by Arthur C. Clarke. [New York] New American Library [c1968] 221 p. 22 cm. 'Based on a screenplay by Stanley Kubrick and Arthur C. Clarke.' Sequel: 2010, odyssey 2. I. T.
PZ3.C551205 Tw3 PR6005.L36 823/.9/14 *LC* 68-29754

Clarke, Austin, 1896-1974. **2.8520**
Collected poems / Austin Clarke; edited by Liam Miller. — 1st collected ed. — Dublin: Dolman Press; London; New York: distributed outside Ireland by Oxford University Press, 1974. xvi, 568 p.; 22 cm. Includes indexes. I. T.
PR6005.L37 A17 1974 821/.9/12 *LC* 75-314851 *ISBN* 0192118455

Clarke, Austin, 1896-1974. • **2.8521**
Collected plays. — [Dublin]: Dolmen Press: [distributed outside Ireland by the Oxford University Press, 1963] 402 p. 21 cm. I. Dolmen Press, Dublin. II. T.
PR6005.L37 A19 1963 822.912 *LC* 63-25006

Tapping, G. Craig. **2.8522**
Austin Clarke: a study of his writings / G. Craig Tapping. — Totowa, N.J.: Barnes & Noble, 1981. 362 p. 1. Clarke, Austin, 1896-1974 — Criticism and interpretation I. T.
PR6005L37 Z87 1981

Colum, Padraic, 1881-1972. • **2.8523**
Three plays / by Padraic Colum. — Dublin: A. Figgis, 1963. 188 p.; 16 cm. — (An Chomhairle ealaíon series of Irish authors; no. 3) I. T. II. Title: The land. III. Title: The fiddler's home. IV. Title: Thomas Muskerry. V. Series.
PR6005.O38 822/.9/12 *LC* 64-7320

Colum, Padraic, 1881-1972. • **2.8524**
Collected poems of Padraic Colum. New York: Devin-Adair, 1953. vi, 214 p.; 22 cm. I. T.
PR6005.O38 A17 1953 821.91 *LC* 53-13044

Colum, Padraic, 1881-1972. **2.8525**
[Short stories. Selections] Selected short stories of Padraic Colum / edited by Sanford Sternlicht. — Syracuse, N.Y.: Syracuse University Press, 1985. xxvi, 130 p.: 1 port.; 21 cm. (Irish studies) I. Sternlicht, Sanford V. II. T.
PR6005.O38 A6 1985 823/.912 19 *LC* 84-20522 *ISBN* 0815623275

Comfort, Alex, 1920-. • **2.8526**
Darwin and the naked lady: discursive essays on biology and art. — New York: G. Braziller, 1962 [c1961] xi, 174 p.: ill.; 22 cm. I. T.
PR6005.O388 D3 1962 *LC* 62-8015

PR6005 Compton–Burnett

Compton-Burnett, I. (Ivy), 1884-1969.   • **2.8527**
Darkness and day. — [1st American ed.] New York: Knopf, 1951. 298 p.; 22 cm. I. T.
PR6005.O3895 Dx   Fic

Compton-Burnett, I. (Ivy), 1884-1969.   • **2.8528**
A family and a fortune, and More women than men; two novels by I. Compton-Burnett. New York, Simon And Schuster, 1965. 523 p. 21 cm. (An Essandess paperback) I. Compton-Burnett, I. (Ivy), 1884-1969. More women than men. II. T. III. Title: More women than men.
PZ3.C7375Fam 2 PR6005.O3895F3   LC 65-10942

Compton-Burnett, I. (Ivy), 1892-1969.   • **2.8529**
Bullivant and the Lambs / Ivy Compton–Burnett. — New York: Knopf, 1948. 299 p. London ed. has title: Manservant and maidservant. I. T. II. Title: Manservant and maidservant.
PR6005.O3895Mx   823.91

Compton-Burnett, I. (Ivy), 1884-1969.   • **2.8530**
Pastors and masters, by I. Compton–Burnett. London, Gollancz, 1967. 126 p. 19 1/2 cm. ([Her Reissue of works by I. Compton-Burnett, 8]) I. T.
PZ3.C7375 Pas7 PR6005.O3895P3x   823/.9/12   *LC* 77-374352

Compton-Burnett, I. (Ivy), 1884-1969.   • **2.8531**
Two worlds and their ways, by I. Compton–Burnett. London, Gollancz, 1969. 285 p. 20 cm. ([Her reissue of works by I. Compton-Burnett, 10]) I. T.
PZ3.C7375 Tw6 PR6005.O3895T9x   823/.9/12   *LC* 73-408339
     ISBN 0575002808

Baldanza, Frank.   **2.8532**
Ivy Compton–Burnett. New York, Twayne Publishers [1964] 142 p. 21 cm. (Twayne's English authors series, 11) 1. Compton-Burnett, I. (Ivy), 1884-1969. I. T.
PR6005.O3895 Z585 1964   823.912   *LC* 64-8325

Burkhart, Charles, comp.   **2.8533**
The art of I. Compton–Burnett: a collection of critical essays; edited by Charles Burkhart. London, Gollancz, 1972. 207 p. 23 cm. 1. Compton-Burnett, I. (Ivy), 1884-1969. I. T.
PR6005.O3895 Z59   823/.9/12   *LC* 73-330768   *ISBN* 0575014024

Johnson, Pamela Hansford, 1912-.   • **2.8534**
I. Compton-Burnett / by Pamela Hansford Johnson. — London Published for the British Council and the National Book League by Longmans, Green [1951] 44 p.: port.; 22 cm. (Writers and their work. no. 20) 1. Compton-Burnett, I. (Ivy), 1884-1969 — Criticism and interpretation. I. T. II. Series.
PR6005.O3895 Z68   823.912   *LC* 53-6487

Nevius, Blake.   **2.8535**
Ivy Compton–Burnett. New York, Columbia University Press, 1970. 48 p. 21 cm. (Columbia essays on modern writers, 47) 1. Compton-Burnett, I. (Ivy), 1884-1969. I. T. II. Series.
PR6005.O3895 Z8   823/.9/12   *LC* 74-110600   *ISBN* 0231029888

Spurling, Hilary.   **2.8536**
[Ivy when young] Ivy, the life of I. Compton–Burnett / Hilary Spurling. — 1st American ed. — New York: Knopf, 1984. xv, 621 p., [20] p. of plates: ill.; 24 cm. First published in Great Britain as two works with titles: Ivy when young and Secrets of a woman's heart. Includes index. 1. Compton-Burnett, I. (Ivy), 1884-1969 — Biography. 2. Novelists, English — 20th century — Biography. I. Spurling, Hilary. Secrets of a woman's heart. 1984. II. T.
PR6005.O3895 Z93 1984   823/.912 B 19   *LC* 83-49028   *ISBN* 039447029X

PR6005 Con

Connolly, Cyril, 1903-1974.   • **2.8537**
The condemned playground: essays: 1927–1944. — New York: Macmillan Co., 1946. xiii, 287 p.: ill., port.; 21 cm. 1. English literature — History and criticism — Addresses, essays, lectures 2. Books — Reviews I. T.
PR6005.O393 C6   *LC* 46-5046

Connolly, Cyril, 1903-1974.   • **2.8538**
The rock pool. — New York: Atheneum, 1968. xii, 178 p.; 21 cm. — I. T.
PZ3.C76274 Ro4   PR6005.O393 Rx.   *LC* 68-55799

Connolly, Cyril, 1903-1974.   • **2.8539**
The unquiet grave: word cycle / by Palinurus; revised edition with an introduction by Cyril Connolly. — 1st Persea ed. — London: Hamish Hamilton, 1951. xvi, 142 p.: ill.; 20 cm. Includes index. I. T.
PR6005.O393 U5 1981   828/.912/08 19   *LC* 81-82929   *ISBN* 0241023424

Connor, Tony.   • **2.8540**
With love somehow, poems. — London, New York, Oxford University Press, 1962. 64 p.; 22 cm. I. T.
PR6005.O3935 W5   821.914   *LC* 63-107

PR6005 Conrad

Conrad, Joseph, 1857-1924.   • **2.8541**
The Works of Joseph Conrad. — New collected edition. — London: Dent, 1923-1938. 22 v.: ill., facsim., ports.; 22 cm. Each volume has also special t.-p. I. Ford, Ford Madox, 1873-1939. II. T.
PR6005.O4 1923

Conrad, Joseph, 1857-1924.   • **2.8542**
The portable Conrad. Edited, and with an introd. and notes, by Morton Dauwen Zabel. — Rev. [ed.] by Frederick R. Karl. — New York: Viking Press, [1969] vi, 762 p.; 19 cm. — (Viking portable library, P33) I. Zabel, Morton Dauwen, 1901-1964. ed. II. Karl, Frederick Robert, 1927- ed. III. T.
PZ3.C764 Ps5 PR6005.O4A6 1969   823/.9/12   *LC* 78-4800   *ISBN* 0670010332

Conrad, Joseph, 1857-1924.   **2.8543**
[Selected works. 1978] Congo diary and other uncollected pieces / by Joseph Conrad; edited and with comments by Zdzislaw Najder. — 1st ed. — Garden City, N.Y.: Doubleday, 1978. viii, 158 p.; 22 cm. I. Najder, Zdzisław. II. T.
PR6005.O4 A6 1978   823/.9/12 B   *LC* 72-89333   *ISBN* 038500771X

Conrad, Joseph, 1857-1924.   **2.8544**
The nigger of the 'Narcissus': an authoritative text, backgrounds and sources, reviews and criticism / Joseph Conrad; edited by Robert Kimbrough. — 1st ed. — New York: Norton, c1979. xi, 370 p.; 21 cm. — (Norton critical editions) 1. Conrad, Joseph, 1857-1924. The nigger of the Narcissus. I. Kimbrough, Robert. II. T.
PR6005.O4 N5638 1979   823/.9/12   *LC* 78-15249   *ISBN* 039304517X

Conrad, Joseph, 1857-1924.   • **2.8545**
Conrad's prefaces to his works; with an introductory essay by Edward Garnett, and a biographical note on his father by David Garnett. — Freeport, N.Y.: Books for Libraries Press, [1971] viii, 218 p.; 23 cm. Reprint of the 1937 ed. I. Garnett, Edward, 1868-1937. II. T.
PR6005.O4 P7 1971   823/.9/12   *LC* 72-160963   *ISBN* 0836958314

Conrad, Joseph, 1857-1924.   • **2.8546**
Romance / Joseph Conrad and F.M. Hueffer. — Garden City, N.Y.: Doubleday, 1950 [c1903] 541 p.; 21 cm. I. Ford, Ford Madox, 1873-1939. II. T.
PR6005.O4 R6 1903   *LC* 50-14824

Biography. Criticism

Conrad, Joseph, 1857-1924.   **2.8547**
[Correspondence] The collected letters of Joseph Conrad / edited by Frederick R. Karl and Laurence Davies. — Cambridge ed. — Cambridge [Cambridgeshire]; New York: Cambridge University Press, 1983. v. < 1 > : ill.; 23 cm. English and French. 1. Conrad, Joseph, 1857-1924. Correspondence 2. Novelists, English — 20th century — Biography. I. Karl, Frederick Robert, 1927- II. Davies, Laurence, 1943- III. T.
PR6005.O4 Z48 1983   823/.912 19   *LC* 82-14643   *ISBN* 0521242169

International Conference on Conrad, Canterbury, Eng., 1974.   **2.8548**
Joseph Conrad: a commemoration: papers from the 1974 International Conference on Conrad / edited by Norman Sherry. New York: Barnes & Noble Books, 1977 (c1976). xvi, 224 p.; 23 cm. 1. Conrad, Joseph, 1857-1924 — Congresses. I. Sherry, Norman. II. T.
PR6005.O4 Z489 1974   823/.9/12   *LC* 76-24069   *ISBN* 0064962334

Conrad, Joseph, 1857-1924.   • **2.8549**
Letters from Joseph Conrad, 1895–1924; edited with introduction and notes by Edward Garnett. — Indianapolis: The Bobbs-Merrill company, 1928. 312 p.: port. (incl. front.) facsims.; 22 cm. Includes index. 1. Conrad, Joseph, 1857-1924. Correspondence I. Garnett, Edward, 1868-1937. II. T.
PR6005.O4 Z53   *LC* 28-8754

Conrad's Polish background: letters to and from Polish friends / translated by Halina Carroll.   **2.8550**
London: Oxford University Press, 1964. 313 p.: geneal. tables. 1. Conrad, Joseph, 1857-1924. Correspondence I. Najder, Zdzisław. II. Conrad, Joseph, 1857-1924. III. Bobrowski, Tadeusz, 1829-1894.
PR6005.O4 Z532   *LC* 64-4657

Conrad, Joseph, 1857-1924.   • 2.8551
Letters to William Blackwood and David S. Meldrum / Joseph Conrad; edited by William Blackburn. — Durham, N.C.: Duke University Press, 1958. 209 p.: ill.; 23 cm. 1. Conrad, Joseph, 1857-1924 — Correspondence. 2. Blackwood, William, 1836-1912 — Correspondence. 3. Meldrum, David Storrar, 1865- — Correspondence. 4. Authors, English — 19th century — Correspondence 5. Authors, English — 20th century — Correspondence. I. Blackwood, William, 1836-1912. II. T.
PR6005.O4 Z5335   928.2   LC 58-12588

Conrad, Joseph, 1857-1924.   2.8552
Joseph Conrad's letters to R. B. Cunninghame Graham; edited by C. T. Watts. London, Cambridge U.P., 1969. xiii, 222 p. plate, illus., port. 22 cm. Based on editor's thesis, Cambridge. I. Cunninghame Graham, R. B. (Robert Bontine), 1852-1936. II. Watts, Cedric Thomas. ed. III. T.
PR6005.O4 Z535   823/.9/12   LC 69-16288   ISBN 0521072131

Conrad, Joseph, 1857-1924.   • 2.8553
Letters of Joseph Conrad to Marguerite Poradowska, 1890–1920 / translated from the French and edited, with an introduction, notes, and appendices, by John A. Gee and Paul J. Sturm. — New Haven: Yale University Press, 1940. xxiv, 147 p.: geneal. tab. front., ports., facsims.; 19 cm. Contains an annotated English translation of letters now in the Rare Book Room of Yale University Library, and, in an appendix, the original text of five of the letters. Published on the Louis Stern Memorial Fund. 1. Conrad, Joseph, 1857-1924. Correspondence 2. Poradowska, Marguerite Gachet. I. Gee, John Archer. II. Sturm, Paul Jones. III. T.
PR6005.O4 Z538   LC 41-475

Conrad, Joseph, 1857-1924.   • 2.8554
Joseph Conrad, life and letters / by G. Jean–Aubry. — Garden City, N.Y.: Doubleday, Page, 1927. 2 v.: ill., facsims., ports.; 25 cm. Editor: G. Jean-Aubry. 1. Conrad, Joseph, 1857-1924 — Biography. 2. Authors, English — 20th century — Biography. 3. Authors, English — 20th century — Correspondence. I. Jean-Aubry, G. (Georges), 1882-1950. II. T.
PR6005.O4 Z54   LC 27-20475

Baines, Jocelyn, 1924-.   • 2.8555
Joseph Conrad, a critical biography. London: Weidenfeld and Nicolson [1960] 507 p.: ill., facsim., ports.; 25 cm. 1. Conrad, Joseph, 1857-1924. I. T.
PR6005 O4 Z554   LC 65-8309

Bradbrook, M. C. (Muriel Clara), 1909-.   • 2.8556
Joseph Conrad: Józef Teodor Konrad Nałęcz Korzeniowski, Poland's English genius, by M. C. Bradbrook. — New York: Russell & Russell, 1965. 79 p.; 23 cm. 'First published in 1941.' Bibliography: p. [78]-79. 1. Conrad, Joseph, 1857-1924. I. T.
PR6005.O4Z565 1965   823.912   LC 65-18792

Conrad, Jessie George, d. 1936.   • 2.8557
Joseph Conrad and his circle, by Jessie Conrad; with 31 illustrations. New York: E. P. Dutton, [c1935] 283 p. front., plates, ports. 25 cm. Includes index. 1. Conrad, Joseph, 1857-1924. I. T.
PR6005.O4 Z578 1935a   LC 35-16452

Conrad, Jessie (George).   • 2.8558
Joseph Conrad as I knew him, by Jessie Conrad. — Freeport, N.Y.: Books for Libraries Press, [1970, c1925] xxi, 162 p.; 23 cm. 1. Conrad, Joseph, 1857-1924 — Biography. I. T.
PR6005.O4 Z58 1970   823/.9/12   LC 76-128877   ISBN 0836954971

Conrad under familial eyes: texts / selected and edited by   2.8559
Zdzisław Najder; translated by Halina Carroll–Najder.
Cambridge [Cambridgeshire]; New York: Cambridge University Press, 1984 (c1983). xxi, 282 p.; 22 cm. Translated from the Polish. 1. Conrad, Joseph, 1857-1924 — Biography — Sources. 2. Novelists, English — 20th century — Biography — Sources. I. Najder, Zdzisław, 1930- II. Carroll-Najder, Halina. PR6005.O4 Z5811813   823/.912 19   LC 83-5187   ISBN 052125082X

Cox, Clyde H. C. B.   2.8560
Joseph Conrad, the modern imagination / C. B. Cox. — London: J. M. Dent; Totowa, N.J.: Rowman & Littlefield, 1974. vii, 191 p.; 22 cm. Includes index. 1. Conrad, Joseph, 1857-1924 — Criticism and interpretation. I. T.
PR6005.O4 Z585 1974   823/.9/12   LC 74-186948   ISBN 0460105744

Daleski, H. M. (Hillel Matthew), 1926-.   2.8561
Joseph Conrad, the way of dispossession / by H. M. Daleski. — New York: Holmes & Meier, 1976. 234 p.; 23 cm. 1. Conrad, Joseph, 1857-1924 — Criticism and interpretation. I. T.
PR6005.O4 Z653   823/.9/12   LC 76-12992   ISBN 0841902100

Fleishman, Avrom.   2.8562
Conrad's politics; community and anarchy in the fiction of Joseph Conrad. — Baltimore: Johns Hopkins Press, [1967] xiii, 267 p.: ports.; 24 cm. 1. Conrad, Joseph, 1857-1924 — Political and social views. I. T.
PR6005.O4 Z68   823/.9/12   LC 67-19479

Fogel, Aaron, 1947-.   2.8563
Coercion to speak: Conrad's poetics of dialogue / Aaron Fogel. — Cambridge, Mass.: Harvard University Press, 1985. 284 p.; 25 cm. Includes index. 1. Conrad, Joseph, 1857-1924 — Technique. 2. Dialogue 3. Speech in literature.
PR6005.O4 Z69 1985   823/.912 19   LC 85-775   ISBN 067413639X

Ford, Ford Madox, 1873-1939.   • 2.8564
Joseph Conrad: a personal remembrance, by Ford Madox Ford (Ford Madox Hueffer) New York: Octagon Books, 1965 [c1924] vii, 276 p.: port.; 21 cm. 1. Conrad, Joseph, 1857-1924. I. T.
PR6005.O4 Z72   928.2   LC 65-16772

Geddes, Gary.   2.8565
Conrad's later novels / Gary Geddes. — Montreal: McGill-Queen's University Press, c1980. x, 223 p.; 23 cm. Includes index. 1. Conrad, Joseph, 1857-1924 — Criticism and interpretation. I. T.
PR6005.O4 Z7253   823/.912 19   LC 80-499300   ISBN 0773503579

Guérard, Albert J. (Albert Joseph), 1914-.   • 2.8566
Conrad the novelist. Cambridge: Harvard University Press, 1958. xiv, 322 p. 22 cm. 1. Conrad, Joseph, 1857-1924. I. T.
PR6005.O4 Z737   823.91   LC 58-8995

Hay, Eloise Knapp.   2.8567
The political novels of Joseph Conrad, a critical study. — Chicago: University of Chicago Press, [1963] 350 p.: illus.; 24 cm. 1. Conrad, Joseph, 1857-1924 — Criticism and interpretation. 2. Conrad, Joseph, 1857-1924 — Political and social views. 3. Politics in literature I. T.
PR6005.O4 Z743   823.912   LC 63-13066

Karl, Frederick Robert, 1927-.   2.8568
Joseph Conrad: the three lives / a biography by Frederick R. Karl. — 1st ed. — New York: Farrar, Straus, and Giroux, 1979. xvi, 1008 p., [32] leaves of plates: ill.; 24 cm. Includes index. 1. Conrad, Joseph, 1857-1924 — Biography. 2. Novelists, English — 20th century — Biography. I. T.
PR6005.O4 Z759   823/.9/12 B   LC 78-13515   ISBN 0374180148

Karl, Frederick Robert, 1927-.   • 2.8569
A reader's guide to Joseph Conrad, by Frederick R. Karl. — Rev. ed. — New York: Farrar, Straus and Giroux, [1969] 310 p.; 22 cm. — ([The Reader's guide series]) 1. Conrad, Joseph, 1857-1924. I. T.
PR6005.O4 Z76 1969   823/.9/12   LC 72-87218

Morf, Gustav.   2.8570
The Polish shades and ghosts of Joseph Conrad / by Gustav Morf. — New York: Astra Books; Boston: distributed by Twayne Publishers, 1977 (c1976). 334 p.: ill.; 23 cm. Includes index. 1. Conrad, Joseph, 1857-1924 — Homes and haunts — Poland. 2. Conrad, Joseph, 1857-1924 — Political and social views. 3. Novelists, English — 20th century — Biography. I. T.
PR6005.O4 Z7815   823/.9/12 B   LC 75-18281   ISBN 0913994200

Moser, Thomas Colborn, 1923-.   • 2.8571
Joseph Conrad: achievement and decline / by Thomas Moser. — Hamden, Conn.: Archon Books, 1966, c1957. viii, 227 p.; 22 cm. 1. Conrad, Joseph, 1857-1924. I. T.
PR6005.O4 Z784 1966   LC 66-12321

Najder, Zdzisław.   2.8572
[Życie Conrada-Korzeniowskiego. English] Joseph Conrad, a chronicle / by Zdzisław Najder. — New Brunswick, N.J.: Rutgers University Press, c1983. xxi, 647 p., [32] p. of plates: ill.; 26 cm. Translation of: Życie Conrada-Korzeniowskiego. Includes indexes. 1. Conrad, Joseph, 1857-1924. 2. Conrad, Joseph, 1857-1924 — Knowledge — Poland. 3. Authors, English — 20th century — Biography. 4. Poland in literature. I. T.
PR6005.O4 Z7844313 1983   823/.912 19   LC 82-10193   ISBN 0813509440

Sherry, Norman.   2.8573
Conrad's Eastern world. — London: Cambridge U.P., 1966. xii, 340 p.: 16 plates (incl. ports., facsims.) 3 maps, table.; 23 cm. Facsims. on endpapers. 1. Conrad, Joseph, 1857-1924. I. T.
PR6005.O4 Z793   823.912   LC 66-11282

Sherry, Norman. 2.8574
Conrad's Western world. — Cambridge [Eng.]: University Press, 1971. xiv, 455 p.: illus., facsim., maps, plan, ports.; 22 cm. 1. Conrad, Joseph, 1857-1924. I. T.
PR6005.O4 Z793 1971   823/.9/12   LC 70-130910   ISBN 0521079721

Stewart, J. I. M. (John Innes Mackintosh), 1906-. 2.8575
Joseph Conrad, by J. I. M. Stewart. London: Longman's, Green, and Co. Ltd., 1968. 272 p. port. 21 cm. 1. Conrad, Joseph, 1857-1924. I. T.
PR6005.O4 Z82   823/.9/12 B   LC 68-15412

Tennant, Roger. 2.8576
Joseph Conrad / Roger Tennant. — 1st ed. — New York: Atheneum, 1981. x, 276 p., [8] p. of plates: ill.; 25 cm. Includes index. 1. Conrad, Joseph, 1857-1924 — Biography. 2. Novelists, English — 20th century — Biography. I. T.
PR6005.O4 Z882 1981   823/.912 B 19   LC 80-69393   ISBN 0689111525

Thorburn, David. 2.8577
Conrad's romanticism. — New Haven: Yale University Press, 1974. xvi, 201 p.; 22 cm. 1. Conrad, Joseph, 1857-1924. I. T.
PR6005.O4 Z883   823/.9/12   LC 73-86919   ISBN 0300016905

Watt, Ian P. 2.8578
Conrad in the nineteenth century / Ian Watt. — Berkeley: University of California Press, 1980 (c1979). xvii, 375 p.; 25 cm. 1. Conrad, Joseph, 1857-1924 — Criticism and interpretation. I. T.
PR6005.O4 Z923   823/.912   LC 78-54804   ISBN 0520036832

Yelton, Donald Charles. 2.8579
Mimesis and metaphor. An inquiry into the genesis and scope of Conrad's symbolic imagery. By Donald C. Yelton. The Hague; Paris: Mouton, 1973. 336 p. 21 cm. (Studies in English literature, v. 39) Revision of author's thesis, Symbol and Metaphor in Conrad's Fiction, Columbia University, 1962. 1. Conrad, Joseph, 1857-1924. I. T.
PR6005.O4 Z95   LC 67-27213

PR6005 Cor–Cz

Cornford, Frances Darwin, 1886-1960. • 2.8580
Collected poems. London: Cresset Press, 1954. 116 p.; 22 cm. I. T.
PR6005.O67 A6 1954   LC 55-15407

Coward, Noel, 1899-1973. • 2.8581
Collected short stories. — London: Heinemann, 1962. 507 p.; 21 cm. I. T.
PR6005.O85Ax   LC 63-27271

Coward, Noel, 1899-1973. • 2.8582
Play parade. — London: Heinemann, 1961-. v.; 21 cm. At head of title: The Collected works of Noël Coward 1. English drama — 20th century — Collected works. I. Title: Pacific 1860. III. Title: 'Peace in our time.' IV. Title: Relative values. V. Title: Quadrille. VI. Title: Blithe spirit. VII. Title: The collected works of Noël Coward
PR6005.O85 Px   822.912

Coward, Noel Pierce, 1899-. • 2.8583
Tonight at 8:30; plays by Noel Coward. — Garden City, N.Y., Doubleday, Doran and company, inc., 1936. vii p., 3 l., 5-283 p. 21 cm. 'First edition.' I. T.
PR6005.O85T6 1936a   822.91   LC 36-28576

Coward, Noel, 1899-1973. • 2.8584
Present indicative / Noel Coward. — London; Toronto: W. Heinemann, 1937. 431 p., [15] leaves of plates: ill., ports. Autobiography. 1. Coward, Noel, 1899-1973 — Biography. I. T.
PR6005.085 Z5 1937   928/.2   LC 37-4195

Coward, Noel, 1899-1973. • 2.8585
Future indefinite / Noël Coward. — London; Toronto: Heineman, 1954. 336 p., [19] leaves of plates: ill.; 23 cm. Autobiographical. 1. Coward, Noël Pierce, 1899-1973 — Biography. 2. Authors, English — 20th century — Biography. I. T.
PR6005.O85 Z52 1954   928.2   LC 54-2161

Berkeley, Anthony. 2.8586
Before the fact: a murder story for ladies / by Francis Iles. — London: Gollancz, c1932. 352 p.; 20 cm. I. T.
PR6005.O9B4x   ISBN 0575024607

Creasey, John. 2.8587
Gideon's day. [1st ed.] New York: Harper [1955] 216 p. 22 cm. I. T.
PR6005.R517 G5x   LC 55-8046

Crichton Smith, Iain. 2.8588
Selected poems, 1955–1980 / Iain Crichton Smith; selected by Robin Fulton. — Loanhead, Midlothian: Macdonald Publishers, 1981. xiii, 233 p.; 23 cm. I. Fulton, Robin II. T.
PR6005.R58 A6 1981   ISBN 0904265552

Crofts, Freeman Wills, 1879-1957. 2.8589
The cask / by Freeman Wills Crofts. — London: Collins, 1920. 1 v. I. T.
PZ3.C8747 Ca15 PR6005.R675   823/.9/12

Cronin, A. J. (Archibald Joseph), 1896-1981. • 2.8590
The citadel, by A. J. Cronin. — Boston, Little, Brown, 1937. 401 p. 20 cm. I. T.
PR6005.R68 Cx   PZ3.C8772Cl2   LC 37-27496

PR6007 D–Du

Davie, Donald. 2.8591
Collected poems, 1950–1970. — New York: Oxford University Press, 1972. xiii, 316 p.; 23 cm. — I. T.
PR6007.A667 A17 1972b   821/.9/14   LC 72-82671   ISBN 0195197127

Davie, Donald. 2.8592
[Poems. Selections] Collected poems, 1970–1983 / Donald Davie. — Manchester: Carcanet New Press; Notre Dame, Ind.: University of Notre Dame Press, 1983. 172 p.; 22 cm. I. T.
PR6007.A667 A6 1983   821/.914 19   LC 83-235811   ISBN 0268007454

Davie, Donald. 2.8593
In the stopping train & other poems / [by] Donald Davie. — Manchester: Carcanet New Press, 1978 (c1977). 55 p.; 23 cm. — I. T.
PR6007.A667 I5   821/.9/14   LC 78-302977   ISBN 0856352242

Day Lewis, C. (Cecil), 1904-1972. • 2.8594
Collected poems. — [London]: Cape, 1954. 370 p. 23 cm. I. T.
PR6007.A95A17 1954   821.91   LC 55-1888

Blake, Nicholas. 2.8595
The beast must die/ Nicholas Blake. — New York: Harper & Row, c1938. 1. Mystery and detective stories. I. T.
PR6007.A95 B38   LC 38-18282

De la Mare, Walter, 1873-1956. • 2.8596
The complete poems of Walter de la Mare. [1st American ed.] New York, Knopf, 1970 [c1969] xv, 948 p. ports. 24 cm. I. T.
PR6007.E3 A17 1970   821/.9/12   LC 79-97061

De la Mare, Walter, 1873-1956. • 2.8597
Memoirs of a midget, by Walter de la Mare, with a foreword by Carl Van Doren. [New York] The Press of the Readers Club [c1941] ix, 379 p.; 22 cm. I. T.
PZ3.D3702Me11 PR6007.E3M4   LC 42-2416

Forster, E. M. (Edward Morgan), 1879-1970. • 2.8598
Goldsworthy Lowes Dickinson / by E. M. Forster. — London: E. Arnold, 1934. x, 277 p.: front., pl., ports., facsims.; 23 cm. 1. Dickinson, Goldsworthy Lowes, 1862-1932. 2. Authors, English — 20th century — Biography. I. Balfour, Ronald Edmond. II. T.
PR6007.I35 Z7 1934   PR6011.O58 G6 1934.   LC 34-17231

Donleavy, J. P. (James Patrick), 1926-. 2.8599
The ginger man. Complete and unexpurgated ed. New York, Delacorte Press, 1965. 347 p. 22 cm. (Seymour Lawrence books) I. T.
PR6007.O6 G5x   LC 65-26495

Douglas, Alfred Bruce, Lord, 1870-1945. • 2.8600
The autobiography of Lord Alfred Douglas. — Freeport, N.Y.: Books for Libraries Press, [1970] xiv, 340 p.: port.; 23 cm. Reprint of the 'new edition,' first published 1931. I. T.
PR6007.O86 Z5 1970   821/.9/12 B   LC 76-124232   ISBN 0836954211

Douglas, Keith Castellain, 1920-1944. 2.8601
Complete poems [of] Keith Douglas / edited by Desmond Graham. — Oxford [Eng.]; New York: Oxford University Press, 1978 (c1977). xiii, 145 p. I. Graham, Desmond, 1940- II. T.
PR6007.O872 A17   PR6007O872 A17 1978.   821/.9/12   LC 77-30095   ISBN 0192118765

Graham, Desmond, 1940-. 2.8602
Keith Douglas, 1920–1944; a biography. — London; New York: Oxford University Press, 1974. xii, 295 p.: illus.; 24 cm. 1. Douglas, Keith Castellain, 1920-1944 — Biography. 2. Poets, English — 20th century — Biography. I. T.
PR6007.O872 Z67   821/.9/12   LC 74-174164   ISBN 0192117165

DuMaurier, Daphne, Dame, 1907-.   • **2.8603**
Three romantic novels of Cornwall: Rebecca, Frenchman's Creek, and Jamaica Inn. 1st ed. — Garden City, N.Y.: Doubleday, 1961. 704 p.; 22 cm. I. T. II. Title: Rebecca. III. Title: Frenchman's creek. IV. Title: Jamaica Inn. PR6007.U47x   *LC* 61-3701

Dunsany, Edward John Moreton Drax Plunkett, 18th Baron,   **2.8604**
1878-1957.
The king of Elfland's daughter. With a front. in photogravure by S.H. Sime. London, G.P. Putnam's Sons [1924] [14], 301 p. facsim., plate. 'First printed May 1924.' I. T.
PR6007.U6   *LC* 24-24254

PR6007 Durrell

Durrell, Lawrence.   **2.8605**
Collected poems, 1931–1974 / Lawrence Durrell; edited by James A. Brigham. — New York: Viking Press, 1980. 350 p.; 23 cm. I. Brigham, James A. II. T.
PR6007.U76 A17 1980   821/.912   *LC* 80-5041   *ISBN* 0670227927

Durrell, Lawrence.   • **2.8606**
The Alexandria quartet: Justine, Balthazar, Mountolive, Clea. New York: Dutton [1962] 884 p.; 23 cm. I. T. II. Title: Justine. III. Title: Balthazar. IV. Title: Mountolive. V. Title: Clea.
PR6007.U76 A7   *LC* 62-53350   *ISBN* 0571086098

Friedman, Alan Warren.   **2.8607**
Lawrence Durrell, and the Alexandria quartet; art for love's sake. [1st ed.] Norman, University of Oklahoma Press, 1970] xxv, 221 p. 22 cm. 1. Durrell, Lawrence. Alexandria quartet 2. Durrell, Lawrence. I. T.
PR6007.U76 A734   828/.9/1209   *LC* 69-16728   *ISBN* 0806108711

Durrell, Lawrence, 1912-.   • **2.8608**
The black book / Lawrence Durrell. — [1st American ed.] New York: Dutton, 1960. 250 p.; 21 cm. I. T.
PZ3.D9377 B12   PR6007.U76 B6 1960.

Durrell, Lawrence.   • **2.8609**
The dark labyrinth / by Lawrence Durrell. — New York: Dutton, 1962. 266 p. I. T.
PR6007.U76 D37 1962   *LC* 62-7808

Durrell, Lawrence, 1912-.   **2.8610**
Vega and other poems / Lawrence Durrell. — Woodstock, N.Y.: Overlook Press, 1974 (c1973). 3-54 p.; 23 cm. — I. T.
PR6007.U76 V4   821/.9/12   *LC* 73-75122   *ISBN* 0879510099

Durrell, Lawrence.   • **2.8611**
Lawrence Durrell [and] Henry Miller: a private correspondence / Edited by George Wickes. — [1st ed.]. — New York: Dutton, 1963. 400 p.: illus.; 22 cm. I. Miller, Henry, 1891- II. T.
PR6007.U76 Z53   928.2   *LC* 62-14726

The world of Lawrence Durrell / edited by Harry T. Moore.   • **2.8612**
Carbondale: Southern Illinois University Press, 1962. xix, 239 p. — (Crosscurrents: modern critiques) I. Moore, Harry T.
PR6007.U76 Z75   823.914   *LC* 62-7230

PR6009 E

Eddison, Eric Rucker, 1882-1945.   **2.8613**
The Worm Ouroboros: a romance / by E. R. Eddison; illustrated by Keith Henderson; with an introd. by Orville Prescott. — New York: Dutton, 1952. 445 p.: ill. I. T.
PR6009.D3 W6 1967   823.912

Kavan, Anna, 1904-1968.   **2.8614**
Eagles' nest: a novel / Anna Kavan. — London: P. Owen, 1957. 179 p.; 20 cm. I. T.
PR6009.D45E2x   *LC* 57-37941   *ISBN* 0720628350

Kavan, Anna, 1904-1968.   **2.8615**
Asylum piece and other stories / by Anna Kavan [i.e. H. W. Edmonds]. — New York, N.Y.: M. Kesend Pub., [1980] c1972. x, 206 p.; 22 cm. Originally published by P. Owen, London. 1. Mental illness — Fiction. I. T.
PZ3.E241 As 1980 PR6009.D63A8x   823/.912   *LC* 79-28536

Kavan, Anna, 1904-1968.   **2.8616**
Ice [by] Anna Kavan. Introd. by Brian W. Aldiss. [1st ed. in the U.S.A.] Garden City, N.Y., Doubleday, 1970. xiii, 176 p. 22 cm. (Doubleday science fiction) I. T.
PZ3.E241 Ic4 PR6009.D63I3x   823/.9/12   *LC* 70-126384

Kavan, Anna, 1904-1968.   **2.8617**
Julia and the bazooka, and other stories / by Anna Kavan [i.e. H. W. Edmonds]; edited by Rhys Davies, with an introd. by Rhys Davies. — 1st American ed. — New York: Knopf: distributed by Random House, 1975, c1970. xii, 155 p.; 22 cm. I. T.
PZ3.E241 Ju5 PR6009.D63J8x   823/.9/12   *LC* 74-21336   *ISBN* 0394494458

Kavan, Anna, 1904-1968.   **2.8618**
Who are you!: a novel / Anna Kavan [i.e. H. W. Edmonds]. — London: Owen, 1975. 3-117 p.; 19 cm. I. T.
PZ3.E241 Wh3 PR6009.D63W5x   823/.9/12   *LC* 75-326422   *ISBN* 0720602335

Kavan, Anna, 1904-1968.   **2.8619**
Sleep has his house / by Anna Kavan [i.e. H. W. Edmonds]. — New York: M. Kesend Pub. Co., [1980] c1948. 182 p.; 21 cm. 1. Kavan, Anna, 1904-1968 — Biography. 2. Novelists, American — 20th century — Biography. I. T.
PR6009.D63 Z52 1980   823/.912 B   *LC* 79-26730   *ISBN* 0935576002

Ellis, Havelock, 1859-1939.   • **2.8620**
Selected essays / Havelock Ellis. — London: Dent, [1936] xi, 340 p.; 18 cm. (Everyman's library. Philosophy & theology; no. 930) Introduction by J.S. Collis. I. T. II. Series.
PR6009.L8 A6 1936   *LC* 37-142

Ellis, Havelock, 1859-1939.   • **2.8621**
The dance of life, by Havelock Ellis ... Boston: Houghton Mifflin, 1923. xiv, 377 p.; 23 cm. I. T.
PR6009.L8D3 1923a   *LC* 23-9889

Ellis, Havelock, 1859-1939.   • **2.8622**
My life: autobiography of Havelock Ellis. — Boston: Houghton Mifflin, 1939. xii, 647 p.: front., pl., ports.; 22 cm. 1. Ellis, Havelock, 1859-1939 — Biography. I. T.
PR6009.L8 Z5 1939   928.2   *LC* 39-27979

Collis, John Stewart, 1900-.   • **2.8623**
Havelock Ellis: artist of life; a study of his life and work / by John Collis. — New York: W. Sloane Associates, 1959. 223 p. 22 cm. 'First published in Great Britain under the title An artist of life.' 1. Ellis, Havelock, 1859-1939. I. T.
PR6009.L8 Z63 1959   *LC* 59-7409

Empson, William, 1906-.   **2.8624**
Collected poems / William Empson. — London: Hogarth, 1984. 119 p. I. T.
PR6009.M7 Ax   821/.912 19   *ISBN* 0701205555

PR6011 F–Fl

Firbank, Ronald, 1886-1926.   • **2.8625**
The complete Ronald Firbank / with a preface by Anthony Powell. — London: G. Duckworth, [1961] 766 p. port. 20 cm. I. T.
PR6011.I7 1961   823.912   *LC* 61-16205

Firbank, Ronald, 1886-1926.   • **2.8626**
The new rythum, and other pieces. — [Norfolk, Conn.]: New Directions [1963, c1962] 134 p.: ill.; 23 cm. I. T.
PZ3.F514Ne2   PR6011.I7 N4x.   *LC* 63-8814

Flecker, James Elroy, 1884-1915.   • **2.8627**
The collected poems of James Elroy Flecker / edited with an introduction by Sir John Squire. [3rd ed. rev.]. — London: Secker and Warburg, [1946] xxx, 162 p.; 22 cm. I. Squire, John Collings, Sir, 1884-1958. II. T.
PR6011.L4 A17 1946

PR6011 Ford

Ford, Ford Madox, 1873-1939.   • **2.8628**
Collected poems / by Ford Madox Ford; with an introduction by William Rose Benét. — [1st ed.] New York: Oxford University Press, 1936. xvi, 348 p.; 23 cm. I. T.
PR6011.O53 A17 1936   *LC* 36-23887

Ford, Ford Madox, 1873-1939.   **2.8629**
The Bodley Head Ford Madox Ford / [edited and introduced by Graham Greene]. — London: Bodley Head, [1962-. v.; 20 cm. I. Greene, Graham, 1904-II. T.
PR6011.O53 A6 1962

Ford, Ford Madox, 1873-1939.   • **2.8630**
The fifth queen / Ford Madox Ford. — New York: Vanguard Press, [1963] 592 p.; 23 cm. 1. Catharine Howard, Consort of Henry VIII, d. 1542 — Fiction. I. Ford, Ford Madox, 1873-1939. Privy seal. II. Ford, Ford Madox,

1873-1939. Fifth queen crowned. III. T. IV. Title: Privy seal. V. Title: The fifth queen crowned. VI. Title: The 5th queen. VII. Title: The 5th queen crowned.
PZ3.F7518 Fg   PR6011.O53 F542.   823   LC 63-13786   ISBN 0814900992

Ford, Ford Madox, 1873-1939.   • 2.8631
The good soldier, a tale of passion. With an interpretation by Mark Schorer. New York: Vintage Books, 1957 [c1951] xxii, 256 p.; 19 cm. (A Vintage book) First Vintage Book printing, 1957? I. T.
PZ3.F7518Go PR6011.O53G6 1957   823/.9/12   LC 57-1046

Ford, Ford Madox, 1873-1939.   • 2.8632
Parade's end. With an introd. by Robie Macauley. [1st Borzoi ed.] New York: Knopf, 1950. xxii, 836 p.; 22 cm. I. T. II. Title: Some do not. III. Title: No more parades. IV. Title: A man could stand up. V. Title: The last post.
PR6011.O53 P3 1950   LC 50-9209

Ford, Ford Madox, 1873-1939.   • 2.8633
Memories and impressions; a study in atmospheres, by Ford Madox Hueffer. New York, Harper, 1911. St. Clair Shores, Mich., Scholarly Press, 1971. xviii, 335 p. ports. 22 cm. 1. Ford, Ford Madox, 1873-1939 — Contemporary England. 2. Ford, Ford Madox, 1873-1939 — Biography — Youth. 3. Preraphaelites — England. 4. Authors, English — 20th century — Biography. 5. England — Civilization — 19th century 6. England — Civilization — 20th century I. T.
PR6011.O53 Z466 1971   828/.9/1203   LC 75-145019   ISBN 0403009669

Cassell, Richard A., 1921-.   • 2.8634
Ford Madox Ford, a study of his novels. Baltimore: Johns Hopkins Press, [1962, c1961] 307 p.; 23 cm. 1. Ford, Ford Madox, 1873-1939. I. T.
PR6011.O53 Z58 1962a   823.912   LC 61-17069

Green, Robert, 1940-.   2.8635
Ford Madox Ford: prose and politics / Robert Green. — Cambridge [Eng.]; New York: Cambridge University Press, 1981. xv, 218 p.; 23 cm. Includes index. 1. Ford, Ford Madox, 1873-1939 — Criticism and interpretation. 2. Ford, Ford Madox, 1873-1939 — Political and social views. I. T.
PR6011.O53 Z64 1981   823/.912 19   LC 80-41566   ISBN 052123610X

MacShane, Frank. comp.   • 2.8636
Ford Madox Ford: the critical heritage. — London; Boston: Routledge and K. Paul, 1972. xiii, 271 p.; 23 cm. — (The Critical heritage series) 1. Ford, Ford Madox, 1873-1939. I. T.
PR6011.O53 Z74   823/.912 19   LC 72-188232   ISBN 071006957X

Mizener, Arthur.   • 2.8637
The saddest story; a biography of Ford Madox Ford. — New York: World Pub. Co., [1971] xxiii, 616 p.: illus., facsims., ports.; 24 cm. 1. Ford, Ford Madox, 1873-1939. I. T.
PR6011.O53 Z78   823/.912 B 19   LC 73-124285

Moser, Thomas C.   2.8638
The life in the fiction of Ford Madox Ford / Thomas C. Moser. — Princeton, N.J.: Princeton University Press, 1981 (c1980). 349 p. Includes index. 1. Ford, Ford Madox, 1873-1939 — Criticism and interpretation. 2. Autobiographical fiction I. T.
PR6011.O53 Z795   823/.912   LC 80-7548   ISBN 0691064458

Stang, Sondra J.   2.8639
Ford Madox Ford / Sondra J. Stang. — New York: Ungar, c1977. xiii, 157 p.; 21 cm. — (Modern literature monographs) Includes index. 1. Ford, Ford Madox, 1873-1939 — Criticism and interpretation. I. T.
PR6011.O53 Z9   828/.9/1209   LC 77-41   ISBN 0804428328

PR6011 Forester

Forester, C. S. (Cecil Scott), 1899-1966.   • 2.8640
The African queen, by C. S. Forester; with a new foreword by the author. New York, The Modern library [1940] 5 p. l., 3-307, [1] p. 19 cm. (The Modern library of the world's best books) 'First Modern library edition, 1940.' I. T.
PZ3.F75956 Af3   PR6011.O56 Ax.   LC 40-27677

PR6011 Forster

Forster, E. M. (Edward Morgan), 1879-1970.   2.8641
[Works. 1972] The Abinger edition of E. M. Forster, edited by Oliver Stallybrass. [London, Edward Arnold, 1972-<1978 >. v. <3a, 4a, 6, 6a, 8, 11-12 > 23 cm. I. Stallybrass, Oliver. ed. II. T.
PR6011.O58 1972   823/.9/12   LC 73-331075   ISBN 0713156511

Forster, E. M. (Edward Morgan), 1879-1970.   • 2.8642
The collected tales of E.M. Forster. — New York: A.A. Knopf, 1947. ix, 308 p.; 20 cm. Previously published in 2 v. under titles: The celestial omnibus and The eternal moment. I. T. II. Title: Story of a panic. III. Title: Other side of the Hedge. IV. Title: Celestial omnibus. V. Title: Other kingdom. VI. Title: Curate's friend. VII. Title: Road from Colonus. VIII. Title: Machine stops. IX. Title: Point of it. X. Title: Mr. Andrews. XI. Title: Co-ordination. XII. Title: Story of the siren. XIII. Title: Eternal moment.
PR6011.O58 A15 1947a   LC 47-4482

Forster, E. M. (Edward Morgan), 1879-1970.   • 2.8643
Albergo Empedocle, and other writings. Edited with an introd. and notes by George H. Thomson. New York, Liveright [1971] xii, 273 p. 22 cm. I. Thomson, George H., 1924- ed. II. T.
PR6011.O58 A6 1971   823/.9/12   LC 79-162435   ISBN 0871405407

Forster, E. M. (Edward Morgan), 1879-1970.   • 2.8644
Abinger harvest. New York: Harcourt, Brace, [1947] x, 363 p.; 21 cm. 'Articles, essays, reviews [and] poems.' I. T.
PR6011.O58.A63 1964   LC 47-31225

Forster, E. M. (Edward Morgan), 1879-1970.   2.8645
Howards End. New York: Knopf, 1921. 393 p. 19 cm. I. T.
PR6011.O58 H6   LC 21-17626

Widdowson, Peter.   2.8646
E. M. Forster's Howards End: fiction as history / Peter Widdowson. — London: Chatto & Windus for Sussex University Press, 1977. 124 p.; 20 cm. — (Text and context) 1. Forster, E. M. (Edward Morgan), 1879-1970. Howards End. 2. Forster, E. M. (Edward Morgan), 1879-1970 — Political and social views. I. T.
PR6011.O58 H6384   823/.9/12   LC 77-364055   ISBN 0856210676

Forster, E. M. (Edward Morgan), 1879-1970.   2.8647
The life to come, and other short stories. New York, W. W. Norton [1973, c1972] xxi, 240 p. 22 cm. I. T.
PZ3.F7735 Li4 PR6011.O58L5x   823/.9/12   LC 72-13127   ISBN 0393083810

Forster, E. M. (Edward Morgan), 1879-1970.   • 2.8648
The longest journey, by E. M. Forster. New York, A. A. Knopf, 1922. 327 p. 20 cm. I. T.
PZ3.F7735 Lo4   PR6011.O58 L6x.   LC 22-13322

Forster, E. M. (Edward Morgan), 1879-1970.   • 2.8649
Maurice; a novel. New York, Norton [1971] 256 p. 22 cm. I. T.
PR6011.O58 M3   PZ3.F7735 Mau   823/.9/12   LC 76-170181   ISBN 0393086577

Forster, E. M. (Edward Morgan), 1879-1970.   • 2.8650
A passage to India, by E. M. Forster. New York, Harcourt, Brace and company [c1924] 322 p.; 20 cm. I. T.
PZ3.F7735 Pa2   PR6011.O58 P3x.   LC 24-19334

Forster, E. M. (Edward Morgan), 1879-1970.   • 2.8651
Pharos and Pharillon / E.M. Forster. — New York: Knopf, 1961 [i.e. 1962, c1923] 97 p.; 21 cm. I. T.
PR6011.O58 P5 1962   LC 62-1459/L

Forster, E. M. (Edward Morgan), 1879-1970.   • 2.8652
A room with a view / E. M. Foster. — New York: Knopf, c1923. 318 p.; 20 cm. I. T.
PR6011.O58 Rx   LC 23-904

Forster, E. M. (Edward Morgan), 1879-1970.   • 2.8653
Two cheers for democracy. — [1st American edition] New York: Harcourt, Brace & World, c1951. xvi, 363 p.; 21 cm. — (Harvest book.) Essays, articles, broadcasts, etc. 1. Democracy I. T. II. Title: 2 cheers for democracy. III. Series.
PR6011.O58 T8 1951a   LC 51-13652

Forster, E. M. (Edward Morgan), 1879-1970.   • 2.8654
Where angels fear to tread, by E. M. Forster. New York: Knopf, 1920. 283 p.; 19 cm. I. T.
PZ3.F7735 W4   PR6011.O58 Wx.   LC 20-3575

Biography. Criticism

Forster, E. M. (Edward Morgan), 1879-1970.   2.8655
[Correspondence. Selections] Selected letters of E.M. Forster / edited by Mary Lago and P.N. Furbank. — Cambridge, Mass.: Belknap Press of Harvard University Press, 1983. 344 p.: ill. Includes indexes. 1. Forster, E. M. (Edward

Morgan), 1879-1970 — Correspondence. 2. Novelists, English — 20th century — Correspondence. I. Lago, Mary. II. Furbank, Philip Nicholas. III. T.
PR6011.O58 Z48 1983   823/.912 B 19   *LC* 83-4376   *ISBN* 0674798252

Bradbury, Malcolm, 1932- ed.   • 2.8656
Forster; a collection of critical essays. Englewood Cliffs, N.J., Prentice-Hall [1966] 180 p. 22 cm. (A Spectrum book: Twentieth century views series, S-TC-59) 1. Forster, E. M. (Edward Morgan), 1879-1970. I. T.
PR6011.O58 Z64 1966   823.912   *LC* 66-16350

Colmer, John.   2.8657
E. M. Forster: the personal voice / John Colmer. — London; Boston: Routledge & K. Paul, 1975. xii, 243 p.; 22 cm. Includes index. 1. Forster, E. M. (Edward Morgan), 1879-1970. I. T.
PR6011.O58 Z647   823/.9/12 B   *LC* 75-328968   *ISBN* 0710082096

Crews, Frederick C.   • 2.8658
E. M. Forster: the perils of humanism. Princeton, N.J., Princeton University Press, 1962. 187 p. 23 cm. Based on thesis, Princeton University. 1. Forster, E. M. (Edward Morgan), 1879-1970. I. T.
PR6011.O58 Z65 1962   823.912   *LC* 62-7036

Das, G. K.   2.8659
E. M. Forster's India / G. K. Das; foreword by John Beer. — Totowa, N.J.: Rowman and Littlefield, 1978 (c1977). xix, 170 p.; 23 cm. Based on the author's thesis, Cambridge. Includes index. 1. Forster, E. M. (Edward Morgan), 1879-1970 — Knowledge — India. I. T.
PR6011.O58 Z652   823/.9/12   *LC* 77-2901   *ISBN* 0874719771

E. M. Forster, a human exploration: centenary essays / edited   2.8660
by G. K. Das and John Beer.
New York: New York University Press, 1979. xvii, 314 p.: ill.; 22 cm. — (The Gotham Library of the New York University Press) 1. Forster, E. M. (Edward Morgan), 1879-1970 — Criticism and interpretation — Addresses, essays, lectures. I. Das, G. K. II. Beer, John B.
PR6011.O58 Z653 1979b   823/.912   *LC* 79-84339   *ISBN* 0814717683

E.M. Forster, centenary revaluations / edited by Judith Scherer   2.8661
Herz and Robert K. Martin.
Toronto; Buffalo: University of Toronto Press, 1982. xiii, 337 p.; 22 cm. 1. Forster, E. M. (Edward Morgan), 1879-1970 — Criticism and interpretation — Congresses. I. Forster, E. M. (Edward Morgan), 1879-1970. II. Herz, Judith Scherer. III. Martin, Robert K., 1941-
PR6011.O58 Z6535 1982   823/.912 19   *LC* 82-152647   *ISBN* 0802024548

Gardner, Philip. comp.   2.8662
E. M. Forster, the critical heritage; edited by Philip Gardner. London, Boston, Routledge and Kegan Paul, 1973. 498 p. 23 cm. (The Critical heritage series) Includes index. 1. Forster, E. M. (Edward Morgan), 1879-1970 — Criticism and interpretation. I. T.
PR6011.O58 Z657   823/.9/12   *LC* 73-77562   *ISBN* 071007641X

Gillie, Christopher.   2.8663
A preface to Forster / Christopher Gillie. — Harlow, Essex; New York: Longman, 1983. xii, 196 p.: ill.; 22 cm. — (Preface books) Includes index. 1. Forster, E. M. (Edward Morgan), 1879-1970 — Criticism and interpretation. I. T.
PR6011.O58 Z666 1983   823/.912 19   *LC* 81-12366   *ISBN* 0582353157

McDowell, Frederick P. W.   2.8664
E.M. Forster / by Frederick P.W. McDowell. — Rev. ed. — Boston: Twayne Publishers, c1982. 174 p.: port.; 21 cm. — (Twayne's English authors series. TEAS 89) Includes index. 1. Forster, E. M. (Edward Morgan), 1879-1970 — Criticism and interpretation. I. T. II. Series.
PR6011.O58 Z822 1982   823/.912 19   *LC* 81-6735   *ISBN* 0805768173

Martin, Richard, M.A.   2.8665
The love that failed; ideal and reality in the writings of E.M. Forster. The Hague, Mouton, 1974. 231 p. 22 cm. (Studies in English literature, v. 84) 1. Forster, E. M. (Edward Morgan), 1879-1970 — Criticism and interpretation. I. T.
PR6011.O58 Z8225   823/.9/12   *LC* 73-79280

Stone, Wilfred Healey, 1917-.   • 2.8666
The cave and the mountain; a study of E.M. Forster [by] Wilfred Stone. Stanford, Calif., Stanford University Press, 1966. viii, 436 p. illus., ports. 24 cm. 1. Forster, E. M. (Edward Morgan), 1879-1970. I. T.
PR6011.O58 Z845   823.912   *LC* 65-21493

Summers, Claude J.   2.8667
E.M. Forster / Claude J. Summers. — New York: Ungar, c1983. x, 406 p.; 21 cm. — (Literature and life series.) Includes index. 1. Forster, E. M. (Edward Morgan), 1879-1970 — Criticism and interpretation. I. T. II. Series.
PR6011.O58 Z8464 1983   823/.912 19   *LC* 82-40624   *ISBN* 0804428492

Trilling, Lionel, 1905-1975.   • 2.8668
E. M. Forster. [2d rev. ed. New York, New Directions Pub. Corp., 1965, c1964] 194 p. 18 cm. 1. Forster, Edward Morgan, 1897- I. T.
PR6011.O58 Z85 1965   *LC* 64-23845

Wilde, Alan.   • 2.8669
Art and order: a study of E. M. Forster. — [New York]: New York University Press, 1964. ix, 179 p.; 22 cm. 1. Forster, E. M. (Edward Morgan), 1879-1970. I. T.
PR6011.O58 Z93   823.912   *LC* 64-12911

PR6011 Fr–Fz

Freeman, R. Austin (Richard Austin), 1862-1943.   2.8670
The Dr. Thorndyke omnibus / 38 of his criminal investigations as set down by R. Austin Freeman. — New York: Dodd, Mead, 1932. 5 v. in 1. I. T.
PR6011.R43 D6   *LC* 32-3421

Fry, Christopher.   2.8671
[Plays. Selections] Selected plays / Christopher Fry. — Oxford [Oxfordshire]; New York: Oxford University Press, 1985. 365 p.; 20 cm. (Oxford paperbacks) I. T.
PR6011.R9 A6 1985   822/.914 19   *LC* 84-25407   *ISBN* 0192818732

Fry, Christopher.   • 2.8672
The dark is light enough: a winter comedy / Christopher Fry. — London; Toronto: Oxford University Press, 1954. 103 p.; 20 cm. 'Melodies arranged and composed by Leslie Bridgewater': p.103. I. T.
PR6011.R9 D3   *LC* 54-10014

Fry, Christopher.   • 2.8673
Thor, with angels: a play / Christopher Fry. — London; Toronto: Oxford University Press, 1949. 54 p.; 19 cm. I. T.
PR6011.R9 T5 1949   *LC* 49-9706

Fry, Christopher, 1907-.   • 2.8674
Venus observed: a play / Christopher Fry. — London; New York: Oxford University Press, 1950 [c1949] vii, 99 p.; 20 cm. In verse. I. T.
PR6011.R9 V4   *LC* 50-21670

Stanford, Derek.   • 2.8675
Christopher Fry: an appreciation / by Derek Stanford. — London: P. Nevill, c1951. 222 p., [5] leaves of plates: ports.; 22 cm. 1. Fry, Christopher, 1907- I. T.
PR6011.R9 Z8 1951   *LC* 51-6420

Fuller, Roy Broadbent, 1912-.   • 2.8676
Collected poems, 1936–1961. — Philadelphia: Dufour Editions, 1962. 248 p.; 23 cm. I. T.
PR6011.U55A17 1962   821.912   *LC* 62-51612

PR6013 G–Gi

Galsworthy, John, 1867-1933.   • 2.8677
End of the chapter. New York, Scribner [1970?] 836 p. 22 cm. (His The Forsyte chronicles, v. 7-9) I. T.
PR6013.A5 E6 1970   823/.912 19   *LC* 72-112973

Galsworthy, John, 1867-1933.   • 2.8678
The Forsyte saga, by John Galsworthy. — New York: C. Scribner's sons, 1922. xvi, 870 p.: fold. geneal. tab.; 20 cm. Combines into one novel of the Forsyte family of three generations, three of Mr. Galsworthy's novels—'The man of property,' 'In chancery' and 'To let'—and two stories—'The Indian summer of a Forsyte' and 'Awakening.' I. T.
PZ3.G139 Fo   PR6013.A5 Fx.   *LC* 22-6520

Galsworthy, John, 1867-1933.   • 2.8679
A modern comedy, by John Galsworthy. — New York: C. Scribner's sons, 1929. xvii, 798 p.; 20 cm. I. T.
PZ3.G139 Md   PR6013.A5 Mx.   *LC* 29-26919

Galsworthy, John, 1867-1933.   • 2.8680
On Forsyte 'change, by John Galsworthy. — New York: C. Scribner's sons, 1930. 6 p.l., 3-285 p.; 20 cm. Nineteen stories relating to the great family of Forsyte. I. T.
PZ3.G139 On   PR6013.A5 Ox.   823.91   *LC* 30-27763

Galsworthy, John, 1867-1933. • 2.8681
Representative plays / by John Galsworthy; with an introduction by George P. Baker. — New York; Chicago: C. Scribner's Sons, 1924. xxi, 469 p.; 20 cm. I. T.
PR6013.A5 R4 1924   LC 24-24259

Dupré, Catherine. 2.8682
John Galsworthy: a biography / Catherine Dupré. 1st American ed. — New York: Coward, McCann & Geoghegan, 1976. 315 p., [4] leaves of plates: ill.; 24 cm. Includes index. 1. Galsworthy, John, 1867-1933 — Biography. 2. Authors, English — 20th century — Biography. I. T.
PR6013.A5 Z5655 1976   823/.9/12 B   LC 76-13473   ISBN 0698107152

Fréchet, Alec. 2.8683
[John Galsworthy. English] John Galsworthy: a reassessment / Alec Fréchet; translated from the French by Denis Mahaffey. — Totowa, N.J.: Barnes & Noble Books, 1982. x, 229 p.; 23 cm. Includes index. 1. Galsworthy, John, 1867-1933. 2. Novelists, English — 20th century — Biography. I. T.
PR6013.A5 Z56613 1982   823/.912 19   LC 81-22900   ISBN 0389202770

Garnett, David, 1892-. • 2.8684
Lady into fox, and A man in the zoo, / illustrated with wood engravings by R.A. Garnett. — London: Chatto & Windus, 1929. 189 p.: ill. (The Phoenix library. [no. 7]) I. T.
PR6013.A66 L3

Gibbons, Stella, 1902-. • 2.8685
Cold Comfort Farm. Illustrated by Charles Saxon. New York, Dial Press, 1964. ix, 254 p.: ill.; 21 cm. I. T.
PZ3.G3527 Co20   PR6013.I24 Cx.   LC 64-11905

Gilbert, Michael Francis. 2.8686
Game without rules / Michael Francis Gilbert. — New York: Harper & Row, 1967. 243 p. I. T.
PR6013.I3335 G3x   LC 67-13703

PR6013 Go

Godden, Rumer, 1907-. • 2.8687
Black narcissus / Rumer Godden. — [1st Modern Library ed.] New York: Modern Library [1947] 294 p.; 19 cm. I. T.
PR6013.O2 Bx   ISBN 0432060014

Godden, Rumer, 1907-. 2.8688
The greengage summer, a novel. New York Viking Press 1958. 218p. I. T.
PR6013 O2 G7

Godden, Rumer, 1907-. 2.8689
In this house of Brede. — New York: Viking Press, [1969] 376 p.; 23 cm. — I. T.
PZ3.G5422 In PR6013.O2I6x   823/.9/12   LC 78-83231

Gogarty, Oliver St. John, 1878-1957. • 2.8690
Collected poems. — [New York]: Devin-Adair Co., [1954] xxvii, 212 p.: port.; 22 cm. I. T.
PR6013.O28 A17 1954   LC 54-9300

Gogarty, Oliver St. John, 1878-1957. • 2.8691
As I was going down Sackville Street, by Oliver St. J. Gogarty ... New York, Reynal & Hitchcock [1937] x, 342 p. front., illus., ports. 25 cm. At head of title: A phantasy in fact. 1. Gogarty, Oliver St. John, 1878-1957. I. T.
PR6013.O28 A8 1937   LC 37-4752

O'Connor, Ulick. • 2.8692
The times I've seen: Oliver St. John Gogarty, a biography. — New York: I. Obolensky, [1963] 365 p.: ports.; 24 cm. 1. Gogarty, Oliver St. John, 1878-1957 — Biography. I. T.
PR6013.O28 Z8   LC 63-12375

PR6013 Golding

Golding, William, 1911-. • 2.8693
The brass butterfly, a play in three acts. — London, Faber and Faber [1958] 80 p. 21 cm. Based on the author's Envoy extraordinary. I. T.
PR6013.O35B7   822.91   LC 58-42465

Golding, William, 1911-. 2.8694
Close quarters / William Golding. — New York: Farrar, Straus & Giroux, c1987. 281 p.; 21 cm. I. T.
PR6013.O35 C5 1987   823/.914 19   LC 87-5351   ISBN 0374125104

Golding, William, 1911-. 2.8695
Darkness visible / William Golding. — 1st American ed. — New York: Farrar Straus Giroux, 1979. 265 p.; 21 cm. I. T.
PZ4.G63 Dar 1979 PR6013.O35D3x   823/.9/14   LC 79-19206   ISBN 0374135029

Golding, William, 1911-. • 2.8696
Free fall. [1st American ed.] New York: Harcourt, Brace [1960, c1959] 253 p. 21 cm. I. T.
PZ4.G63 Fr2   PR6013.O35 Fx.   LC 60-5431

Golding, William, 1911-. • 2.8697
The hot gates, and other occasional pieces / by William Golding. — 1st American ed. — New York: Harcourt, Brace & World, [1966, c1965] 175 p.: 21 cm. I. T.
PR6013.O35.H6 1966   824/.914   LC 66-12363

Golding, William, 1911-. • 2.8698
The inheritors. [1st American ed.] New York, Harcourt, Brace & World [1962, c1955] 233 p. 21 cm. I. T.
PZ4.G63 In5   PR6013.O35 Ix.   LC 62-16724

Golding, William, 1911-. • 2.8699
Lord of the flies / William Golding; introduced by E. M. Forster. — New York: Coward-McCann, 1962. 243 p.: ill.; 23 cm. I. T.
PR6013.O35 Lx   LC 62-51372   ISBN 0698102193

Golding, William, 1911-. 2.8700
A moving target / William Golding. — 1st American ed. — New York: Farrar, Straus, Giroux, 1982. ix, 202 p.; 22 cm. I. T.
PR6013.O35 M6 1982   824/.914 19   LC 82-5026   ISBN 0374215731

Golding, William, 1911-. 2.8701
The paper men / William Golding. — 1st Harvest/HBJ ed. — San Diego: Harcourt Brace Jovanovich, 1985. 191 p.; 21 cm. 'A Harvest/HBJ book.' I. T.
PR6013.O35 P3 1985   823/.914 19   LC 84-1636   ISBN 0156708000

Golding, William, 1911-. • 2.8702
The pyramid [by] William Golding. [1st American ed.] New York, Harcourt, Brace & World [1967] 183 p. 21 cm. I. T.
PZ4.G63 Py2   PR6013.O35 Px.   LC 67-19198

Golding, William, 1911-. 2.8703
Rites of passages / William Golding. — New York: Farrar, Straus, Giroux, 1980. 278 p.; 21 cm. I. T.
PR6013.O35 R5 1980   823/.914   LC 80-16809   ISBN 0374250863

Golding, William, 1911-. 2.8704
The scorpion god; three short novels [by] William Golding. [1st American ed.] New York, Harcourt Brace Jovanovich [1972, c1971] 178 p. 21 cm. I. Golding, William, 1911- Clonk clonk. 1972. II. Golding, William, 1911- Envoy extraordinary. 1972. III. T.
PZ4.G63 Sc3 PR6013.O35S2x   823/.9/14   LC 70-174508   ISBN 0151364109

Golding, William, 1911-. • 2.8705
Sometime, never: three tales of imagination / by William Golding, John Wyndham, Mervyn Peake. — London: Eyre & Spottiswoode, 1956. 224 p.; 19 cm. I. Golding, William, 1911- Envoy extraordinary. II. Wyndham, John, 1903-1969. Consider her ways. III. Peake, Mervyn Laurence, 1911-1968. Boy in darkness. IV. T. V. Title: Envoy extraordinary. VI. Title: Consider her ways. VII. Title: Boy in darkness.
PR6013.O35S6x   LC 57-18342

Golding, William, 1911-. • 2.8706
The spire. [1st American ed.] New York, Harcourt, Brace & World [1964] 215 p. 21 cm. I. T.
PZ4.G63 Sp   PR6013.O35 S6x.   LC 63-15314

Golding, William, 1911-. • 2.8707
The two deaths of Christopher Martin. [1st American ed.] New York, Harcourt, Brace [1957, c1956] 208 p. 21 cm. I. T.
PZ4.G63 Tw   PR6013.O35 Tx.   LC 57-10059

Biography. Criticism

Babb, Howard S. • 2.8708
The novels of William Golding [by] Howard S. Babb. [Columbus] Ohio State University Press [1970] 210 p. 21 cm. 1. Golding, William, 1911- I. T.
PR6013.O35 Z58   823/.9/14   LC 74-83143   ISBN 0814200001

Biles, Jack I., 1920-.   **2.8709**
Talk: conversations with William Golding [by] Jack I. Biles. Foreword by William Golding. [1st ed.] New York, Harcourt Brace Jovanovich [1970] xii, 112 p. 21 cm. 1. Golding, William, 1911- 2. Interviews I. Golding, William, 1911- II. T.
PR6013.O35 Z595   823/.9/14   LC 73-117570   ISBN 0151879869

Crompton, Don.   **2.8710**
A view from the spire: William Golding's later novels / Don Crompton; edited and completed by Julia Briggs. — Oxford, OX, UK; New York, NY, USA: B. Blackwell, 1985. vi, 199 p.; 23 cm. Includes index. 1. Golding, William, 1911- — Criticism and interpretation. I. Briggs, Julia. II. T.
PR6013.O35 Z597 1985   823/.914 19   LC 84-16742   ISBN 0631138269

Dick, Bernard F.   **2.8711**
William Golding, by Bernard F. Dick. New York, Twayne Publishers [1967] 119 p. 21 cm. (Twayne's English authors series, 57) 1. Golding, William, 1911- I. T.
PR6013.O35 Z6   821/.9/14   LC 67-19351

Kinkead-Weekes, Mark.   • **2.8712**
William Golding: a critical study, by Mark Kinkead–Weekes and Ian Gregor. London, Faber, 1967. 3-257 p. 22 cm. 1. Golding, William, 1911- — Criticism and interpretation. I. Gregor, Ian. joint author. II. T.
PR6013.O35 Z7   823/.9/14   LC 67-83103

Oldsey, Bernard Stanley, 1923-.   **2.8713**
The art of William Golding [by] Bernard S. Oldsey & Stanley Weintraub. [1st ed.] New York, Harcourt, Brace & World [1965] 178 p. 21 cm. 1. Golding, William, 1911- I. Weintraub, Stanley, 1929- joint author. II. T.
PR6013.O35 Z8   828.914   LC 65-23971

Tiger, Virginia.   **2.8714**
William Golding: the dark fields of discovery / by Virginia Tiger. — London: Calder & Boyars, 1975. 244 p.; 22 cm. Includes index. 1. Golding, William, 1911- — Criticism and interpretation. I. T.
PR6013.O35 Z92   823/.9/14   LC 75-306940   ISBN 0714510122

Cunninghame Graham, R. B. (Robert Bontine), 1852-1936.   **2.8715**
The Scottish sketches of R.B. Cunninghame Graham / selected and edited with introduction, notes, glossary and bibliography by John Walker. — Edinburgh: Scottish Academic Press, c1982. xii, 204 p.; 24 cm. 1. Scotland — Literary collections. 2. Scotland — Addresses, essays, lectures. I. Walker, John, 1933- II. T.
PR6013.R19 S36 1982   823/.912 19   LC 82-218324   ISBN 0707302889

Watts, Cedric Thomas.   **2.8716**
Cunninghame Graham: a critical biography / by Cedric Watts and Laurence Davies. — Cambridge [Eng.]; New York: Cambridge University Press, 1979. xiii, 333 p.: ill.; 23 cm. Includes index. 1. Cunninghame Graham, R. B. (Robert Bontine), 1852-1936. 2. Authors, Scottish — 20th century — Biography. 3. Politicians — Scotland — Biography. I. Davies, Laurence, 1943- joint author. II. T.
PR6013.R19 Z88   828/.8/09   LC 78-18107   ISBN 0521224675

PR6013 Graves

Graves, Robert, 1895-.   • **2.8717**
More poems, 1961. London, Cassell [1961] 45 p. 23 cm. 'Supplement to Collected poems, 1959.' I. T.
PR6013.R35 A17 1961   821.912   LC 61-4311

Graves, Robert, 1895-.   • **2.8718**
Collected poems, 1966 / Robert Graves. — Garden City, N.Y.: Anchor Books [1966] xxi, 447 p.; 18 cm. (Anchor books; A517) I. T. II. Title: Collected poems, nineteen sixty-six. III. Series.
PR6013.R35A17 1966   821.912   LC 66-21011

Graves, Robert, 1895-.   **2.8719**
New collected poems / Robert Graves; introduction by James McKinley. — 1st ed. in the U.S.A. — Garden City, N.Y.: Doubleday, 1977. xxxi, 442 p., [8] leaves of plates: ill.; 22 cm. Includes indexes. I. T.
PR6013.R35 A17 1977   821/.9/12   LC 76-14051   ISBN 0385115075

Graves, Robert, 1895-.   • **2.8720**
Claudius, the god and his wife Messalina. New York, H. Smith and R. Haas, 1935. 583 p. illus. (map) fold. geneal. tables. 22 cm. At head of title: By Robert Graves. 1. Claudius, Emperor of Rome, 10 B.C.-54 A.D — Fiction. 2. Messalina, Valeria, d. 48 — Fiction. I. T.
PZ3.G7876 Cl2   PR6013.R35 C5x.   LC 35-27093

Graves, Robert, 1895-.   • **2.8721**
Count Belisarius / by Robert Graves. — [1st ed.] London: Cassell, [1938] ix, 526 p.: front., maps.; 20 cm. 1. Belisarius, 505 (ca.)-565 — Fiction. I. T.
PR6013.R35 C67   LC 38-36266

Graves, Robert, 1895-.   • **2.8722**
Hercules, my shipmate: a novel / by Robert Graves. — New York: Creative Age Press, inc. [1945] x, 464 p.: front. (map) geneal. tab.; 21 cm. 1. Argonauts — Fiction. I. T.
PZ3.G7876 He   PR6013.R35 Hx.   LC 45-8179

Graves, Robert, 1895-.   • **2.8723**
I, Claudius; from the autobiography of Tiberius Claudius, born B.C. 10, murdered and deified A.D. 54, by Robert Graves. — New York: The Modern library, [1937] x, 427 p.; 17 cm. — (The Modern library of the world's best books) 1. Claudius, Emperor of Rome, 10 B.C.-54 A.D — Fiction. I. T.
PZ3.G7876 I12   PR6013.R35 Ix.   LC 37-27271

Graves, Robert, 1895-.   • **2.8724**
Occupation: writer / by Robert Graves. — New York: Creative Age Press, 1950. ix, 320 p.; 22 cm. 'A collection of [the author's]... short stories, plays, and miscellaneous essays.' I. T.
PR6013.R35 O2   828   LC 50-5991

Graves, Robert, 1895-.   • **2.8725**
Wife to Mr. Milton; the story of Marie Powell, by Robert Graves. [1st American ed.]. — New York, Creative Age Press [c1944] viii, 380 p.; 21 cm. Written in the form of an autobiography. 1. Milton, Mary Powell, d. 1652 — Fiction I. Graves, Robert, 1895- Story of Marie Powell. II. T. III. Title: The story of Marie Powell.
PZ3.G7876   PR6013.R35 Wx.   LC 44-47871

Graves, Robert, 1895-.   • **2.8726**
Good–bye to all that. New ed., rev., with a prologue and an epilogue. Garden City, N.Y., Doubleday, 1957. 347 p. 18 cm. (Doubleday anchor books, A123) Autobiography. 1. World War, 1914-1918 — Personal narratives, English. I. T.
PR6013.R35 Z5 1957   940.48142   LC 57-12294

Day, Douglas.   • **2.8727**
Swifter than reason; the poetry and criticism of Robert Graves. — [Chapel Hill, University of North Carolina Press, 1963] xxi, 228 p. 23 cm. Bibliography: p. [218]-223. 1. Graves, Robert, 1895- I. T.
PR6013.R35Z67   821.912   LC 63-22117

Kirkham, Michael.   • **2.8728**
The poetry of Robert Graves. — New York: Oxford University Press, 1969. viii, 284 p.; 23 cm. 1. Graves, Robert, 1895- I. T.
PR6013.R35 Z73   821/.9/12   LC 70-3328

Seymour-Smith, Martin.   **2.8729**
Robert Graves, his life and work / Martin Seymour–Smith. — 1st American ed. — New York: Holt, Rinehart and Winston, 1983, c1982. xvi, 609 p., [2] leaves of plates: ill.; 24 cm. 1. Graves, Robert, 1895- 2. Authors, English — 20th century — Biography. I. T.
PR6013.R35 Z783 1983   828/.91209 B 19   LC 82-48031   ISBN 0030221714

PR6013 Green

Green, Henry, 1905-1974.   • **2.8730**
Back: a novel / by Henry Green. — London: Hogarth Press, 1946. 208 p.; 21 cm. I. T.
PR6013.R416 B2   ISBN 0701200758

Green, Henry, 1905-1974.   • **2.8731**
Blindness, by Henry Green. New York, E. P. Dutton & company [c1926] vii, 286 p. 20 cm. I. T.
PR6013.R416 B57   PZ3.G8235 Bl   LC 26-18388

Green, Henry, 1905-1974.   • **2.8732**
Caught; a novel. New York, A. M. Kelley, 1970. 196 p. 21 cm. (Viking reprint editions) I. T.
PZ3.G8235 Cau5 PR6013.R416C3x   823/.9/12   LC 70-83158

Green, Henry, 1905-1974.   • **2.8733**
Concluding; a novel. New York, A. M. Kelley, 1970 [c1948] 254 p. 22 cm. (Viking reprint editions) I. T.
PZ3.G8235 Co10 PR6013.R416C6x   823/.9/12   LC 73-122055

Bassoff, Bruce, 1941-.   **2.8734**
Toward loving: the poetics of the novel and the practice of Henry Green / by Bruce Bassoff. — 1st ed. — Columbia: University of South Carolina Press,

1975. x, 179 p.; 23 cm. Includes index. 1. Green, Henry, 1905-1974 — Criticism and interpretation. I. T.
PR6013.R416 Z58   823/.9/12   *LC* 75-22071   *ISBN* 0872493245

Odom, Keith C.   **2.8735**
Henry Green / by Keith C. Odom. — Boston: Twayne, c1978. 155 p.: port.; 21 cm. — (Twayne's English authors series; TEAS 235) Includes index. 1. Green, Henry, 1905-1974 — Criticism and interpretation. I. Green, Henry, 1905-1974. II. T.
PR6013.R416 Z78   823/.9/12   *LC* 77-18068   *ISBN* 0805767061

Weatherhead, Andrew Kingsley, 1923-.   **2.8736**
A reading of Henry Green / by A. Kingsley Weatherhead. — Seattle: University of Washington Press, 1961. x, 170 p.; 23 cm. 1. Green, Henry, 1905-1974 — Criticism and interpretation. I. T.
PR6013.R416 Z93   *LC* 61-8767

PR6013 Greene

Greene, Graham, 1904-.   • **2.8737**
Loser takes all. — Harmondsworth: Penguin, 1971. 124 p.; 19 cm. First published in 1955. I. T.
PZ3.G8319 Lo5 PR6013.R44   823/.9/12   *LC* 72-184803   *ISBN* 0140032770

Greene, Graham, 1904-.   • **2.8738**
Collected essays. — New York: Viking Press, [1969] 463 p.; 21 cm. — I. T.
PR6013.R44 A16 1969b   824/.9/12   *LC* 79-75644

Greene, Graham, 1904-.   **2.8739**
The collected plays of Graham Greene. — Harmondsworth: Penguin, 1985. 414 p.; 20 cm. I. T.
PR6013.R44 Ax   822/.912 19   *ISBN* 0140074791

Greene, Graham, 1904-.   **2.8740**
Collected stories, including May we borrow your husband? A sense of reality, Twenty-one stories. — New York: Viking Press, 1973. xii, 561 p.; 21 cm. — I. T.
PZ3.G8319 Ck3 PR6013.R44Ax   823/.9/12   *LC* 73-2334   *ISBN* 0670229113

Greene, Graham, 1904-.   • **2.8741**
Brighton rock; an entertainment. New York, The Viking press [c1938] 358 p.; 21 cm. 'Published in June 1938.' I. T.
PR6013.R44 B7x   *LC* 38-15724

Greene, Graham, 1904-.   • **2.8742**
A burnt-out case. — New York: Viking Press, 1961. 248 p.; 21 cm. — I. T.
PZ3.G8319 Bu   PR6013.R44 B8x.   *LC* 61-6090

Greene, Graham, 1904-.   • **2.8743**
The confidential agent, an entertainment [by] Graham Greene. New York, The Viking Press, 1939. 302 p.; 20 cm. I. T.
PR6013.R44 C65x   *LC* 39-23873

Greene, Graham, 1904-.   • **2.8744**
The comedians. — New York: Viking Press, [1966] 309 p.; 22 cm. — I. T.
PZ3.G8319 Cm   PR6013.R44 C6x.   *LC* 66-12636

Greene, Graham, 1904-.   **2.8745**
Doctor Fischer of Geneva: or, The bomb party / Graham Greene. — New York: Simon and Schuster, c1980. 156 p.; 22 cm. — I. T.
PZ3.G8319 Do 1980 PR6013.R44D6x   823/.912 19   *LC* 80-10314   *ISBN* 0671254677

Greene, Graham, 1904-.   • **2.8746**
The end of the affair. New York: Viking Press, 1951. 240 p.; 22 cm. I. T.
PZ3.G8319 El2   PR6013.R44 E35x.   *LC* 51-13559

Greene, Graham, 1904-.   • **2.8747**
England made me: a novel / by Graham Greene. — London; Toronto: W. Heinemann [1935] 314 p.; 19 cm. I. T.
PR6013.R44E5   *LC* 35-15473

Greene, Graham, 1904-.   • **2.8748**
The heart of the matter. — [1st ed.]. — New York: Viking Press, 1948. 306 p.; 22 cm. — I. T.
PZ3.G8319 He2   PR6013.R44 H4x.   *LC* 48-7530

Greene, Graham, 1904-.   **2.8749**
The honorary consul. — New York: Simon and Schuster, [1973] 315 p.; 25 cm. — I. T.
PZ3.G8319 Hو PR6013.R44H6x   823/.9/12   *LC* 73-5254   *ISBN* 0671215698

Greene, Graham, 1904-.   **2.8750**
The human factor / Graham Greene. — 1st U.S. ed. — New York: Simon and Schuster, c1978. 347 p.; 25 cm. — I. T.
PZ3.G8319 Hu 1978 PR6013.R44H8x   823/.9/12   *LC* 77-17169   *ISBN* 0671240854

Green, Graham, 1904-.   • **2.8751**
It's a battlefield. New York, Viking Press [1962] 214 p. 21 cm. I. T.
PZ3.G8319 It12   PR6013.R44 Ix.   *LC* 62-19606

Greene, Graham, 1904-.   • **2.8752**
The man within / by Graham Greene. — London: W. Heinemann, 1929. 354 p.; 20 cm. I. T.
PZ3.G8319Man   PR6013.R44 M3x.

Greene, Graham, 1904-.   • **2.8753**
The ministry of fear, an entertainment by Graham Greene. New York, The Viking press, 1943. 4 p. l., 3-239 p. 21 cm. I. T.
PR6013.R44 M5   *LC* 43-8250

Greene, Graham, 1904-.   **2.8754**
Our man in Havana / Graham Greene. — New York: Viking, 1958. 245 p.: ill.; 20 cm. — I. T.
PR6013.R44 O9   823/.912 19   *LC* 82-144130

Greene, Graham, 1904-.   **2.8755**
The portable Graham Greene. Edited by Philip Stratford. — New York: Viking Press, [1973] xxiii, 610 p.; 19 cm. — (Viking portable library) I. T.
PR6013.R44 P57   828/.9/1209   *LC* 72-78990   *ISBN* 0670565660

Greene, Graham, 1904-.   • **2.8756**
The power and the glory. — New York: The Viking press, 1946. 301 p.; 21 cm. 'First published in March 1940 under the title: The labyrinthine ways. Reissued in January 1946 under its original English title: The power and the glory.' I. T.
PZ3.G8319 Po2   PR6013.R44 Px.   *LC* 46-1198

Greene, Graham, 1904-.   • **2.8757**
The quiet American. — New York: Viking Press, 1956 [c1955] 249 p.; 21 cm. — I. T.
PZ3.G8319 Qui2   PR6013.R44 Qx.   *LC* 56-6281

Greene, Graham, 1904-.   **2.8758**
The shipwrecked / Graham Greene. New York: Viking Press, 1982. 1 v. I. T. II. Title: England made me
PR6013.R44 S5x   *ISBN* 0670640387

Greene, Graham, 1904-.   • **2.8759**
Stamboul train / by Graham Greene. — London, W. Heinemann, ltd. [1932] 6 p.l., 3-307 p. 19 cm. I. T.
PZ3.G8319 St   PR6013.R44 Sx.   *LC* 33-2642

Greene, Graham, 1904-.   **2.8760**
The tenth man / Graham Greene. — New York: Simon and Schuster, 1985. 157 p.; 25 cm. 1. World War, 1939-1945 — Fiction. I. T.
PR6013.R44 T4 1985   823/.912 19   *LC* 84-29830   *ISBN* 067150794X

Greene, Graham, 1904-.   **2.8761**
This gun for hire / Graham Greene. — New York: Viking, 1952. 227 p.; 20 cm. I. T.
PR6013.R44 T44   *ISBN* 0670701726

Greene, Graham, 1904-.   **2.8762**
The third man; Loser takes all / Graham Greene. — [Uniform ed.]. — New York: Viking Press, 1983. 209 p. I. Greene, Graham, 1904- Loser takes all. II. T. III. Title: Loser takes all.
PR6013.R44 T5   823/.912 19   *ISBN* 0670700843

Greene, Graham, 1904-.   • **2.8763**
Triple pursuit; a Graham Greene omnibus. — New York: Viking Press, [1971, c1958] 435 p.; 22 cm. I. T.
PZ3.G8319 Tt PR6013.R44T75x   823/.9/12   *LC* 70-146055   *ISBN* 0670731269

Greene, Graham, 1904-.   • **2.8764**
Travels with my aunt; a novel. — New York: Viking Press, [1969] 244 p.; 23 cm. — I. T.
PZ3.G8319 Tr3 PR6013.R44T7x   823/.9/12   *LC* 72-94848   *ISBN* 0670725242

Biography. Criticism

Greene, Graham, 1904-.   **2.8765**
[Autre et son double. English] The other man: conversations with Graham Greene / by Marie-Françoise Allain; translated from the French by Guido

Waldman. — New York: Simon and Schuster, c1983. 176 p.; 23 cm. Translation of: L'Autre et son double. 1. Greene, Graham, 1904- Interviews. 2. Authors, English — 20th century — Interviews. I. Allain, Marie-Françoise. II. T.
PR6013.R44 Z4613 1983   823/.912 B 19   *LC* 82-19652   *ISBN* 067144767X

Greene, Graham, 1904-.   • 2.8766
In search of a character: two African journals / by Graham Greene. — New York: Viking Press, [1962, c1961]. 93 p.; 24 cm. 1. Africa, West — Description and travel I. T.
PR6013.R44 Z5   916.6/03   *LC* 61-17938

Greene, Graham, 1904-.   • 2.8767
A sort of life. New York, Simon and Schuster [1971] 220 p. 22 cm. Continued by: Ways of escape. I. T.
PR6013.R44 Z52   828/.9/1209 B   *LC* 77-156146   *ISBN* 0671210106

Greene, Graham, 1904-.   2.8768
Ways of escape and A fuller life / Graham Greene. — New York: Simon and Schuster, c1980. 320 p.; 23 cm. Continues: A sort of life. 1. Greene, Graham, 1904- — Biography. 2. Authors, English — 20th century — Biography. I. T.
PR6013.R44 Z54 1980   828/.91209 B 19   *LC* 80-20336   *ISBN* 0671412191

Allott, Kenneth.   • 2.8769
The art of Graham Greene, by Kenneth Allott and Miriam Farris. New York: Russell & Russell [1963] 253 p.: ill.; 23 cm. 1. Greene, Graham, 1904- I. Allott, Miriam Farris. joint author. II. T.
PR6013.R44 Z6 1963   *LC* 63-15146

Atkins, John Alfred, 1916-.   • 2.8770
Graham Greene, by John Atkins. — New revised ed. — London: Calder & Boyars, 1966. xiv, 9-257 p.; 21 cm. 1. Greene, Graham, 1904- I. T.
PR6013.R44 Z63 1966   823.912   *LC* 66-78769

De Vitis, A. A.   2.8771
Graham Greene / by A.A. DeVitis. — Rev. ed. — Boston: Twayne Publishers, c1986. 218 p.: port.; 23 cm. (Twayne's English authors series. TEAS 3) Includes index. 1. Greene, Graham, 1904- — Criticism and interpretation. I. T. II. Series.
PR6013.R44 Z632 1986   823/.912 19   *LC* 85-17612   *ISBN* 0805769110

Evans, Robert Owen, 1919- ed.   • 2.8772
Graham Greene; some critical considerations [by] Harvey Curtis Webster [and others. — Lexington] University of Kentucky Press [c1963] xviii, 286 p. 23 cm. Bibliography: p. [245]-276. 1. Greene, Graham, 1904- I. Webster, Harvey Curtis, 1906- II. T.
PR6013.R44Z633   *LC* 63-22005

Gaston, Georg, 1938-.   2.8773
The pursuit of salvation: a critical guide to the novels of Graham Greene / Georg M.A. Gaston. — Troy, N.Y.: Whitston Pub. Co., 1984. vi, 164 p.; 24 cm. Includes index. 1. Greene, Graham, 1904- — Criticism and interpretation. 2. Salvation in literature I. T.
PR6013.R44 Z6334 1984   823/.912 19   *LC* 84-50635   *ISBN* 0878752897

Hynes, Samuel Lynn. comp.   2.8774
Graham Greene: a collection of critical essays. Edited by Samuel Hynes. — Englewood Cliffs, N.J.: Prentice-Hall, [1973] vi, 183 p.; 21 cm. — (Twentieth century views) (A Spectrum book) 1. Greene, Graham, 1904- — Criticism and interpretation. I. T.
PR6013.R44 Z6335   828/.9/1209   *LC* 72-8640   *ISBN* 0133622517

Kelly, Richard Michael, 1937-.   2.8775
Graham Greene / Richard Kelly. — New York: F. Ungar, 1985 (c1984). 195 p.; 21 cm. Includes index. 1. Greene, Graham, 1904- — Criticism and interpretation. I. T.
PR6013.R44 Z6345   823/.912 19   *LC* 84-8595   *ISBN* 0804424640

Kohn, Lynette.   2.8776
Graham Greene, the major novels. — Stanford, Calif., 1961. 54 p. — (Stanford honors essay in humanities. no. 4) 1. Greene, Graham, 1904- I. T. II. Series.
PR6013.R44 Z635   *LC* 61-15644

Kunkel, Francis Leo, 1921-.   2.8777
The labyrinthine ways of Graham Greene, by Francis L. Kunkel. — Rev. expanded ed. — Mamaroneck, N.Y.: P. P. Appel, 1973 [c1959] x, 212 p.; 23 cm. Issued in microfilm form as the author's thesis, Columbia, 1959, under title: A critical study of Graham Greene. 1. Greene, Graham, 1904- I. T.
PR6013.R44 Z64 1973   828/.9/1209   *LC* 73-75125   *ISBN* 0911858253

Lodge, David, 1935-.   • 2.8778
Graham Greene. — New York: Columbia University Press, 1966. 48 p.; 21 cm. — (Columbia essays on modern writers, no. 17) 1. Greene, Graham, 1904- I. T. II. Series.
PR6013.R44 Z645   823.912   *LC* 66-19553

Rai, Gangeshwar.   2.8779
Graham Greene: an existential approach / Gangeshwar Rai. — Atlantic Highlands, N.J.: Humanities Press, c1983. viii, 162 p.; 22 cm. Includes index. 1. Greene, Graham, 1904- — Criticism and interpretation. I. T.
PR6013.R44 Z85   823.912   *ISBN* 0391028359

PR6013 Grieve (MacDiarmid)

MacDiarmid, Hugh, 1892-.   2.8780
[Poems 1978] Complete poems, 1920–1976 / Hugh MacDiarmid [i.e. C. M. Grieve]; edited by Michael Grieve and W. R. Aitken. — London: Martin Brian & O'Keeffe, 1978. 2 v. (xxii, 1485 p.); 23 cm. Includes indexes. I. Grieve, Michael. II. Aitken, William Russell. III. T.
PR6013.R735 A17 1978   821/.9/12   *LC* 79-319786   *ISBN* 0856164402

MacDiarmid, Hugh, 1892-.   2.8781
The Hugh MacDiarmid anthology: poems in Scots and English / edited by Michael Grieve and Alexander Scott. — London; Boston: Routledge and K. Paul, 1972. xxiii, 295 p.; 23 cm. — (The Scottish series) I. Grieve, Michael, 1920-. II. Scott, Alexander. III. T. IV. Series.
PR6013.R735 A6 1972   821/.9/12   *LC* 72-83662   *ISBN* 0710074328

MacDiarmid, Hugh, 1892-.   2.8782
A drunk man looks at the thistle, by Hugh MacDiarmid. Edited by John C. Weston. — [Amherst]: University of Massachusetts Press, 1971. xiv, 122 p.; 23 cm. — I. Weston, John Charles. II. T.
PR6013.R735 D7 1971   821/.9/12   *LC* 70-103473   *ISBN* 087023059X

MacDiarmid, Hugh, 1892-.   2.8783
[Correspondence. Selections] The letters of Hugh MacDiarmid / edited with an introduction by Alan Bold. — Athens: University of Georgia Press, 1984. xxxv, 910 p., [16] p. of plates: ports.; 24 cm. Includes index. Errata slip inserted. 1. MacDiarmid, Hugh, 1892- — Correspondence. 2. Poets, Scottish — 20th century — Correspondence. I. Bold, Alan Norman, 1943- II. T.
PR6013.R735 Z48 1984   821/.912 B 19   *LC* 84-8723   *ISBN* 0820307351

MacDiarmid, Hugh, 1892-.   2.8784
Lucky poet: a self-study in literature and political ideas: being the autobiography of Hugh MacDiarmid (Christopher Murray Grieve). — Berkeley, University of California Press, 1972. xxiv, 436 p., leaf. port. 23 cm. Reprint of the 1943 ed. 1. MacDiarmid, Hugh, 1892- I. T.
PR6013.R735 Z5 1972b   821/.9/12   *LC* 73-152431   *ISBN* 0224007157

The age of MacDiarmid: essays on Hugh MacDiarmid and his influence on contemporary Scotland / edited by P.H. Scott & A.C. Davis.   2.8785
[S.l.]: Barnes & Noble Books, 1980. 268 p.; 23 cm. 1. MacDiarmid, Hugh, 1892- — Criticism and interpretation — Addresses, essays, lectures. 2. Scotland — Civilization — 20th century — Addresses, essays, lectures. I. MacDiarmid, Hugh, 1892- II. Scott, P.H. III. Davis, A. C., fl. 1980-
PR6013.R735 Z564 1980   821/.912 19   *LC* 80-146761   *ISBN* 0906391121

Bold, Alan Norman, 1943-.   2.8786
MacDiarmid: the terrible crystal / Alan Bold. — London; Boston: Routledge & K. Paul, 1983. xx, 252 p.; 23 cm. Includes indexes. 1. MacDiarmid, Hugh, 1892- — Criticism and interpretation. I. T.
PR6013.R735 Z585 1983   821/.912 19   *LC* 83-3075   *ISBN* 0710094930

Buthlay, Kenneth.   2.8787
Hugh MacDiarmid / Kenneth Buthlay. — Edinburgh: Scottish Academic Press, 1982, c1981. 143 p.; 19 cm. — (Scottish writers. 2) 1. MacDiarmid, Hugh, 1892- — Criticism and interpretation. I. T. II. Series.
PR6013.R735 Z59 1982   821/.912 19   *LC* 83-101629   *ISBN* 0707303079

Glen, Duncan, 1933- comp.   2.8788
Hugh MacDiarmid; a critical survey. New York, Barnes & Noble [1972] ix, 241 p. 23 cm. 1. MacDiarmid, Hugh, 1892- — Criticism and interpretation — Addresses, essays, lectures. I. T.
PR6013.R735 Z67   821/.9/12   *LC* 73-161069   *ISBN* 0064924327

Gish, Nancy K., 1942-. 2.8789
Hugh MacDiarmid, the man and his work / Nancy K. Gish. — [S.l.]: Salem House (dist. by Merrimack Publishers' Circle), 1984. vii, 235 p., [1] p. of plates: ill.; 23 cm. Includes index. 1. MacDiarmid, Hugh, 1892- 2. Poets, Scottish — 20th century — Biography. I. T.
PR6013.R735 Z734 1984   821/.912 19   *LC* 85-116199   *ISBN* 0333294734

PR6013 Grigson. Gunn

Grigson, Geoffrey, 1905-. • 2.8790
Collected poems, 1924–1962. — London: Phoenix House, [1963] 268 p.; 21 cm. I. T.
PR6013.R744 A17 1963   *LC* 64-6734

Gunn, Neil Miller. 2.8791
Highland river / Neil M. Gunn. — London: Hutchinson Library Services, 1974. 256 p. I. T.
PR6013.U64 H57   *ISBN* 0091198801

Neil M. Gunn; the man and the writer. Edited by Alexander Scott & Douglas Gifford. 2.8792
New York, Barnes & Noble, 1973. 400 p. illus. 23 cm. 1. Gunn, Neil Miller, 1891-1973. I. Gunn, Neil Miller, 1891-1973. II. Scott, Alexander, 1920- ed. III. Gifford, Douglas.
PR6013.U64 Z7 1973   *ISBN* 0064961354

Gunn, Thom. 2.8793
Selected poems, 1950–1975 / Thom Gunn. — New York: Farrar, Straus, Giroux, c1979. ix, 131 p.; 22 cm. I. T.
PR6013.U65 A6 1979   821/.9/14   *LC* 79-9158   *ISBN* 0374258651

Gunn, Thom. • 2.8794
Fighting terms. — Rev. — New York: Hawk's Well Press, 1958. 46 p.; 18 cm. Poems. I. T.
PR6013.U65 F5 1962   *LC* 59-20699

Gunn, Thom. 2.8795
Moly, and My sad captains. — New York: Farrar, Straus and Giroux, [1973] 91 p.; 21 cm. Poems. I. Gunn, Thom. My sad captains. 1973. II. T. III. Title: My sad captains.
PR6013.U65 M6 1973   821/.9/14   *LC* 72-96312

Gunn, Thom. • 2.8796
The sense of movement: [poems. — Chicago]: University of Chicago Press [1959, c1957] 62 p.; 23 cm. I. T.
PR6013.U65 S4 1957   *LC* 59-8734   *ISBN* 0571055435

PR6015 H–Ho

Hartley, L. P. (Leslie Poles), 1895-1972. • 2.8797
Eustace and Hilda: a trilogy. London: Putnam; New York: British Book Centre, 1958. 736 p.; 20 cm. I. T. II. Title: The shrimp and the anemone. III. Title: Hilda's letter. IV. Title: The sixth heaven.
PZ3.H2537 Eu   PR6015.A6723 Ex.   *LC* 59-3545

Jones, Edward Trostle. 2.8798
L. P. Hartley / by Edward T. Jones. — Boston: Twayne Publishers, c1978. 221 p.: port.; 21 cm. — (Twayne's English authors series; TEAS 232) Includes index. 1. Hartley, L. P. (Leslie Poles), 1895-1972 — Criticism and interpretation. I. T.
PR6015.A6723 Z72 1978   823/.9/12   *LC* 78-4564   *ISBN* 0805767037

Mulkeen, Anne, 1927-. 2.8799
Wild thyme, winter lightning; the symbolic novels of L. P. Hartley. — Detroit: Wayne State University Press, 1974. xiv, 193 p.: port.; 23 cm. 1. Hartley, L. P. (Leslie Poles), 1895-1972. I. T.
PR6015.A6723 Z78   823/.9/12   *LC* 73-18047   *ISBN* 0814314945

Hill, Geoffrey. 2.8800
Somewhere is such a kingdom: poems 1952–1971 / Geoffrey Hill; with an introd. by Harold Bloom. — 1st American ed. — Boston: Houghton Mifflin, 1975. xxv, 130 p.; 21 cm. I. T.
PR6015.I4735 S6 1975   821/.9/14   *LC* 75-11949   *ISBN* 0395207134

Hilton, James, 1900-1954. • 2.8801
Good–bye, Mr. Chips, by James Hilton. — Boston: Little, Brown, 1934. 125 p.; 20 cm. I. T.
PZ3.H5677Go3   PR6015.I53 G6x.   *LC* 34-27174

Hilton, James, 1900-1954. • 2.8802
Lost horizon / by James Hilton. — Author's ed. New York, W. Morrow & company, 1936. ix, 277 p. col. front., col. plates. 21 cm. I. T.
PZ3.H5677 Lo18   PR6015.I53 L6x.   *LC* 36-23004

Hilton, James, 1900-1954. • 2.8803
Random harvest. [1st ed.] Boston, Little, Brown and company, 1941. 4 p.l., 3-326, [1] p. 21 cm. ('An Atlantic monthly press book.') I. T.
PZ3.H5677 Ran   PR6015.I53 R3x.   *LC* 41-51508

Hodgson, William Hope, 1875-1918. 2.8804
Carnacki: the ghost-finder / William Hope Hodgson. — Sauk City, Wis.: Mycroft and Moran, 1947. 241 p. I. T.
PR6015.O253 C3   PZ3.H6685 Cd.   *LC* 48-5230

Hodgson, William Hope, 1875-1918. 2.8805
The night land: a love tale / by William Hope Hodgson. — Westport, Conn.: Hyperion Press, 1976, c1912. 583 p.; 22 cm. — (Classics of science fiction) Reprint, with new introd., of the ed. published by E. Nash, London. I. T.
PZ3.H6685 Ni8 PR6015.O253N5x   823/.9/12   *LC* 75-28858   *ISBN* 0883553724

Hope, Alec Derwent, 1907-. • 2.8806
Poems / by A.D. Hope. — New York: Viking Press, 1961 [i.e.1962, c1960] 120 p.; 23 cm. I. T.
PR6015.O597 P6 1962   *LC* 62-4418

Hornung, E. W. (Ernest William), 1866-1921. 2.8807
Raffles, the amateur cracksman / by Ernest William Hornung; illustrated by F. C. Yohn. — Lincoln: University of Nebraska Press, c1976. xvii, 244 p., [2] leaves of plates: ill.; 21 cm. 'A Bison book.' Reprint, with new introd., of the 1899 ed. published by Scribner, New York. 1. Raffles (Fictitious character) — Fiction. I. T.
PZ3.H786 Raf12 PR6015.O687R3x   823/.8   *LC* 75-38587   *ISBN* 0803208693. *ISBN* 0803258364 pbk

PR6015 Hudson. Hughes

Hudson, W. H. (William Henry), 1841-1922. • 2.8808
Green mansions: a romance of the tropical forest / by W. H. Hudson; introd. by John Galsworthy. — New York, The Modern Library [1920] xi, 289 p.; 17 cm. (The Modern library of the world's best books) I. T.
PR6015.U23 Gx

Hudson, W. H. (William Henry), 1841-1922. • 2.8809
The purple land: being the narrative of one Richard Lamb's adventures in the Banda Oriental in South America as told by himself / by W. H. Hudson. — London & Toronto: Dent; New York: Dutton, 1922. vii, 366 p.: front. (port.); 23 cm. (The collected works of W.H. Hudson.) 1. Uruguay — Description and travel I. T.
PR6015.U23 P8   *LC* 27-6056

Hughes, Richard Arthur Warren, 1900-1976. • 2.8810
A high wind in Jamaica / Richard Hughes. London: Chatto and Windus, c1929. 283 p.; 20 cm. I. T.
PR6015.U35 Hx   *LC* 30-26402

Thomas, Peter, 1939-. 2.8811
Richard Hughes [by] Peter Thomas. — [Cardiff]: University of Wales Press [for] the Welsh Arts Council, 1973. [3], 104 p., leaf, port.; 25 cm. — (Writers of Wales) Limited ed. of 1000 numbered copies; no. 22. 1. Hughes, Richard Arthur Warren, 1900- — Criticism and interpretation. I. Welsh Arts Council. II. T.
PR6015.U35 Z9   823/.9/12   *LC* 74-163123   *ISBN* 0708304648

PR6015 Huxley

Huxley, Aldous, 1894-1963. • 2.8812
Collected short stories. New York, Harper [c1957] 397 p. 22 cm. I. T.
PR6015.U9 A15 1957   *LC* 57-11799

Huxley, Aldous, 1894-1963. • 2.8813
Collected essays. New York, Harper [1959] 399 p. 22 cm. I. T.
PR6015.U9 A16 1959   824.912   *LC* 59-10583

Huxley, Aldous, 1894-1963. • 2.8814
The collected poetry of Aldous Huxley. Edited by Donald Watt. With an introd. by Richard Church. [1st U.S. ed.] New York, Harper & Row [1971] 168 p. 22 cm. (A Cass Canfield book) I. T.
PR6015.U9 A17 1971b   821/.9/12   *LC* 77-138736   *ISBN* 0060120517

Huxley, Aldous, 1894-1963.   • **2.8815**
After many a summer dies the swan, by Aldous Huxley. New York, Harper & Row [1965, c1939] 246 p. 19 cm. (A Harper perennial classic) I. T.
PR6015.U9 A4x   823/.9/12   *LC* 65-9705

Huxley, Aldous, 1894-1963.   • **2.8816**
Antic hay and The Gioconda smile / by Aldous Huxley; with an introd. by Charles J. Rolo. — New York: Harper [1957] xvii, 280 p.; 21 cm. I. T. II. Title: The Gioconda smile.
PR6015.U9 A6x   *LC* 56-12646

Huxley, Aldous, 1894-1963.   • **2.8817**
Brave new world: a novel. — New York: Modern Library [1956, c1946] 310 p.; 19 cm. (The Modern library of the world's best books; 48.) I. T.
PR6015.U9 B65   *LC* 56-8833

Firchow, Peter Edgerly, 1937-.   **2.8818**
The end of Utopia: a study of Aldous Huxley's Brave new world / Peter Edgerly Firchow. — Lewisburg [Pa.]: Bucknell University Press; London: Associated University Presses, c1984. 154 p.; 25 cm. Includes index. 1. Huxley, Aldous, 1894-1963. Brave new world. 2. Huxley, Aldous, 1894-1963 — Political and social views. 3. Utopias in literature 4. Dystopias in literature. 5. Forecasting in literature. I. Huxley, Aldous, 1894-1963. Brave new world. II. T.
PR6015.U9 B674 1984   823/.912 19   *LC* 82-74490   *ISBN* 0838750583

Huxley, Aldous, 1894-1963.   • **2.8819**
Crome yellow, by Aldous Huxley. New York: George H. Doran company [c1922] 307 p. 20 cm. I. T.
PZ3.H981 Cr   PR6015.U9 Cx.   *LC* 22-6512

Huxley, Aldous, 1894-1963.   • **2.8820**
Eyeless in Gaza, by Aldous Huxley. New York: Harper, 1936. 3 p. l., 473, [1] p. 22 cm. 'First edition.' I. T.
PZ3.H981Ey2 PR6015.U9E9 1936   *LC* 36-14923

Huxley, Aldous, 1894-1963.   • **2.8821**
Point counter point, by Aldous Huxley ... New York, The Modern library [1930] 3 p. l., 514 p. 17 cm. (Half-title: The Modern library of the world's best books) I. T.
PZ3.H981Po5 PR6015.U9P6   823.91   *LC* 31-26121

Huxley, Aldous, 1894-1963.   • **2.8822**
Time must have a stop, by Aldous Huxley ... New York: Harper, 1944. 3 p. l., 311 p., 1 l. 22 cm. 'First edition.' I. T.
PZ3.H981Ti PR6015.U9T47   *LC* 44-7463

Huxley, Aldous, 1894-1963.   • **2.8823**
Letters of Aldous Huxley. Edited by Grover Smith. [1st U.S. ed.] New York, Harper & Row [1970, c1969] 992 p. port. 25 cm. I. Smith, Grover Cleveland, 1923- ed. II. T.
PR6015.U9 Z53 1970   823/.9/12   *LC* 69-15263

Aldous Huxley, the critical heritage / edited by Donald Watt.   **2.8824**
London; Boston: Routledge & K. Paul, 1975. xxiv, 493 p.; 23 cm. — (The Critical heritage series) 1. Huxley, Aldous, 1894-1963 — Criticism and interpretation. I. Watt, Donald, 1938-
PR6015.U9 Z555   823/.9/12   *LC* 75-317517   *ISBN* 0710081146

Atkins, John Alfred, 1916-.   • **2.8825**
Aldous Huxley; a literary study, by John Atkins. New and rev. ed. New York, Orion Press [1968, c1967] xxxvii, 218 p. 21 cm. 1. Huxley, Aldous, 1894-1963 — Criticism and interpretation. I. T.
PR6015.U9 Z56 1968   823/.9/14   *LC* 68-18181

Bowering, Peter.   • **2.8826**
Aldous Huxley: a study of the major novels. New York, Oxford University Press, 1969 [c1968] 242 p. 22 cm. Originated in author's thesis, University of London. 1. Huxley, Aldous, 1894-1963 — Criticism and interpretation. I. T.
PR6015.U9 Z565 1969   823/.9/12   *LC* 74-1169

Firchow, Peter Edgerly, 1937-.   **2.8827**
Aldous Huxley, satirist and novelist. Minneapolis, University of Minnesota Press [1972] viii, 203 p. 23 cm. (Minnesota monographs in the humanities, v. 6) 1. Huxley, Aldous, 1894-1963. I. T. II. Series.
PR6015.U9 Z63 1972   823/.9/12   *LC* 74-187165   *ISBN* 0816606358

Kuehn, Robert E., 1932- comp.   **2.8828**
Aldous Huxley: a collection of critical essays. Edited by Robert E. Kuehn. Englewood Cliffs, N.J., Prentice-Hall [1974] iv, 188 p. 21 cm. (A Spectrum book, S-TC-118) (Twentieth century views) 1. Huxley, Aldous, 1894-1963 — Criticism and interpretation. I. T.
PR6015.U9 Z745   823/.9/12   *LC* 74-11444   *ISBN* 0134486149 *ISBN* 0134485068

May, Keith M.   **2.8829**
Aldous Huxley. New York: Barnes & Noble, 1973 (c1972). 251 p. (Novelists and their world) 1. Huxley, Aldous, 1894-1963. I. T. II. Series.
PR6015.U9 Z758   *ISBN* 006494669X

Meckier, Jerome.   • **2.8830**
Aldous Huxley; satire and structure. New York, Barnes & Noble [1969] 223 p. 23 cm. 1. Huxley, Aldous, 1894-1963. 2. Lawrence, D. H. (David Herbert), 1885-1930. I. T.
PR6015.U9 Z76 1969b   823/.9/12   *LC* 79-8451   *ISBN* 0389010316

Woodcock, George, 1912-.   **2.8831**
Dawn and the darkest hour; a study of Aldous Huxley. New York, Viking Press [1972] 299 p. 22 cm. 1. Huxley, Aldous, 1894-1963 — Criticism and interpretation. I. T.
PR6015.U9 Z96   823/.9/12   *LC* 72-183511   *ISBN* 0670258598

PR6017 Isherwood

Isherwood, Christopher, 1904-.   • **2.8832**
All the conspirators: a novel / by Christopher Isherwood. — [New York] New Directions [1958] 255 p.; 20 cm. I. T.
PZ3.I814 Al   PR6017.S5 Ax.   *LC* 58-12798

Isherwood, Christopher, 1904-.   • **2.8833**
The Berlin stories: The last of Mr. Norris [and] Goodbye to Berlin. With a new pref. by the author. — [New York]: J. Laughlin, [1954] 207 p.; 21 cm. — (A New Directions book) I. T. II. Title: The last of Mr. Norris. III. Title: Goodbye to Berlin.
PZ3.I814 Be3   PR6017.S5 Bx.   *LC* 55-2508

Isherwood, Christopher.   **2.8834**
Exhumations: stories, articles, verses / Christopher Isherwood. — New York: Simon and Schuster, 1966. 254 p. I. T.
PR6017.S5E9 1966a   828.91209   *LC* 66-17601

Isherwood, Christopher, 1904-.   • **2.8835**
Lions and shadows; an education in the twenties. Norfolk, Conn., New Directions [c1947] 312 p.: port.; 22 cm. I. T.
PR6017.S5 L5 1947   *LC* 47-11810

Isherwood, Christopher, 1904-.   **2.8836**
A meeting by the river. New York, Simon and Schuster [1967] 191 p. 21 cm. I. T.
PR6017.S5 M38   *LC* 67-13030

Isherwood, Christopher, 1904-.   • **2.8837**
The memorial; portrait of a family. — Westport, Conn.: Greenwood Press, [1970, c1946] 294 p.; 23 cm. — I. T.
PZ3.I814 Me7   PR6017.S5 M4x.   823/.9/12   *LC* 72-106718 *ISBN* 0837135443

Isherwood, Christopher, 1904-.   • **2.8838**
Prater Violet: a novel / Christopher Isherwood. — [1st ed.] New York: Random House, 1945. 127 p.; 20 cm. I. T.
PZ3.I814 Pr PR6017.S5P7x   823/.9/12   *LC* 45-9732

Isherwood, Christopher, 1904-.   • **2.8839**
Sally Bowles. — London: Published by L. and Virginia Woolf at the Hogarth Press, 1937. 150 p.; 17 cm. I. T.
PR6017.S5 S2 1937   *LC* 38-20990

Isherwood, Christopher, 1904-.   **2.8840**
Christopher and his kind, 1929–1939 / Christopher Isherwood. 1st ed. — New York: Farrar, Straus Giroux, 1976. 339 p.; 22 cm. 1. Isherwood, Christopher, 1904- — Biography. 2. Authors, English — 20th century — Biography. I. T.
PR6017.S5 Z498   823/.9/12 B   *LC* 76-42228

Summers, Claude J.   **2.8841**
Christopher Isherwood / Claude J. Summers. — New York: Ungar, c1980. x, 182 p.; 21 cm. — (Modern literature monographs) Includes index. 1. Isherwood, Christopher, 1904- — Criticism and interpretation. I. T.
PR6017.S5 Z85   823/.912 19   *LC* 80-5335   *ISBN* 0804428468

Wilde, Alan.   **2.8842**
Christopher Isherwood. — New York: Twayne Publishers, [1971] 171 p.; 22 cm. — (Twayne's United States authors series, 173) 1. Isherwood, Christopher, 1904- I. T.
PR6017.S5 Z9   823/.9/12   *LC* 75-120013

PR6019 J–Jo

James, M. R. (Montague Rhodes), 1862-1936. • **2.8843**
The collected ghost stories of M.R. James. — London: E. Arnold, 1947. xii, 647 p.; 18 cm. 1. Ghost stories I. T.
PR6019.A565x

Jameson, Storm, 1891-. **2.8844**
Journey from the north; autobiography of Storm Jameson. [1st U.S. ed.] New York, Harper & Row [c1970] 792 p. illus., ports. 22 cm. (A Cass Canfield book) I. T.
PR6019.A67 Z52 1970   823/.9/12 B   LC 78-138739

Johnson, E. Pauline, 1861-1913. **2.8845**
Flint and feather: collected verse / by E. Pauline Johnson (Tekahionwake); with introduction by Theodore Watts–Dunton; illustrated by J.R. Seavey. — Rev. and enl. ed. — Toronto: Musson Book Co., 1913. xxx, 165 p. [8] leaves of plates: ill., port.; 23 cm. 'Biographical sketch': p. xxiii-xxx. 1. Johnson, E. Pauline, 1861-1913. I. Watts-Dunton, Theodore, 1832-1914. II. T. III. T.
PR6019.O391x

Johnson, Pamela Hansford, 1912-. **2.8846**
Cork Street, next to the hatter's: a novel in bad taste. — New York: Scribner's, 1965. 247 p. I. T.
PR6019.O3938 C68

Johnson, Pamela Hansford, 1912-. **2.8847**
Night and silence, who is here?: an American comedy / Pamela Hansford Johnson. — New York: Scribner, 1963. 246p. I. T.
PR6019.O3938Nx   LC 63-14895

Johnson, Pamela Hansford, 1912-. • **2.8848**
The unspeakable Skipton. [1st American ed.] New York, Harcourt, Brace [1959] 249 p. 21 cm. I. T.
PR6019.O3938 U5   LC 59-6420

Johnston, Denis, 1901-. **2.8849**
[Plays] The dramatic works of Denis Johnston. — Atlantic Highlands, N.J.: Humanities Press, 1979-. 2 v.: ill.; 23 cm. I. T.
PR6019.O397 A19 1979   822/.9/12   LC 79-11257   ISBN 0391010034

Ferrar, Harold. **2.8850**
Denis Johnston's Irish theatre / by Harold Ferrar. — Dublin: Dolmen Press; [London]: Distributed by Oxford University Press, 1975 (c1973). 144 p.; 22 cm. (Irish theatre series; 5) Distributed in the U.S. by Humanities Press, New York. 1. Johnston, Denis, 1901- — Criticism and interpretation. I. T.
PR6019.O397 Z65   822/.9/12   LC 76-353145   ISBN 0851052088

Jones, David Michael, 1895-1974. • **2.8851**
Epoch and artist: selected writings / by David Jones; edited by Harman Grisewood. London: Faber and Faber, [1959] 320 p.; 20 cm. 1. Literature — Addresses, essays, lectures. 2. Art — Addresses, essays, lectures. I. Grisewood, Harman, 1906- II. T.
PR6019.O53 A6   941   LC 60-1029

Jones, David Michael, 1895-1974. • **2.8852**
The anathemata; fragments of an attempted writing. New York, Chilmark Press [1963?] 243 p.: ill.; 23 cm. Published also by Faber. I. T.
PR6019.O53 A8 1963   LC 63-3658

Corcoran, Neil. **2.8853**
The song of deeds: a study of The anathemata of David Jones / Neil Corcoran. — Cardiff: University of Wales Press, 1983. xi, 120 p.; 22 cm. Includes index. 1. Jones, David Michael, 1895-1974. Anathemata. I. T.
PR6019.O53 A832   821/.912 19   LC 82-152684   ISBN 0708308066

Hague, René. **2.8854**
A commentary on The anathemata of David Jones / by René Hague. — Toronto: University of Toronto Press, 1978 (c1977). xii, 264 p., [1] leaf of plates: facsim., port.; 23 cm. 1. Jones, David Michael, 1895-1974. The anathemata. I. T.
PR6019.O53 A834   ISBN 0802022979

Summerfield, Henry. **2.8855**
An introductory guide to The anathemata and The sleeping lord sequence of David Jones / by Henry Summerfield. — Victoria, B.C.: Sono Nis Press, 1979. 192 p.: ill.; 23 cm. 1. Jones, David Michael, 1895-1974. The anathemata. 2. Jones, David Michael, 1895-1974. The sleeping lord. I. T.
PR6019.O53 A838   821/.9/12   LC 79-320257   ISBN 0919462685

Jones, David Michael, 1895-1974. • **2.8856**
In parenthesis; seinnyessit e gledyf ym penn mameu. — New York: Chilmark Press [1962, c1961] 224 p. illus. 23 cm. 1. World War, 1914-1918 I. T.
PR6019.O53I6 1962   828.912   LC 61-17876

Jones, David Michael, 1895-1974. **2.8857**
The sleeping lord, and other fragments / by David Jones. — New York: Chilmark Press: distributed by Random House, c1974. 111p. I. T.
PR6019.O53 S5   821/.9/12   LC 73-91950   ISBN 394463087

Jones, David Michael, 1895-1974. **2.8858**
Dai Greatcoat: a self-portrait of David Jones in his letters / edited by René Hague. — London; Boston: Faber and Faber, 1980. 273 p., [4] leaves of plates; 23 cm. Includes index. 1. Jones, David Michael, 1895-1974 — Correspondence. 2. Authors, English — 20th century — Correspondence. 3. Artists — England — Correspondence. I. Hague, René. II. T.
PR6019.O53 Z48 1980   821/.912 19   LC 80-670267   ISBN 0571115403

Hague, René. **2.8859**
David Jones / [by] René Hague. — [Cardiff]: University of Wales Press [for] the Welsh Arts Council, 1975. [3], 92 p., plate: port.; 25 cm. (Writers of Wales) 1. Jones, David Michael, 1895-1974. I. Welsh Arts Council. II. T.
PR6019.O53 Z67   821/.9/12   LC 76-353392   ISBN 0708306039

Rees, Samuel, 1936-. **2.8860**
David Jones / by Samuel Rees. — Boston: Twayne, 1978. 154 p.: port.; 21 cm. — (Twayne's English authors series; TEAS 246) Includes index. 1. Jones, David Michael, 1895-1974 — Criticism and interpretation. I. T.
PR6019.O53 Z86 1978   821/.9/12   LC 78-9768   ISBN 0805767266

Jones, Gwyn, 1907-. **2.8861**
Selected short stories. — London; New York: Oxford University Press, 1974. xi, 173 p.; 20 cm. — (Oxford paperbacks 323) I. T.
PZ3.J7166 Se PR6019.O593   823/.9/12   LC 74-175073   ISBN 0192811622

PR6019 Joyce

Joyce, James, 1882-1941. • **2.8862**
Collected poems / James Joyce. — New York: Viking Press, 1957. — 63 p.; 22 cm. I. T.
PR6019.O9 A17

Joyce, James, 1882-1941. • **2.8863**
Introducing James Joyce: a selection of Joyce's prose / by T.S. Eliot; with an introductory note. — London: Faber, 1952. 146 p.; 19 cm. I. Eliot, T. S. (Thomas Stearns), 1888-1965. II. T.
PR6019.09 A6   LC 43-1388

Joyce, James, 1882-1941. • **2.8864**
The portable James Joyce, with an introduction & notes by Harry Levin. — New York: The Viking Press, 1947. vi, 760 p.; 17 cm. — (The Viking portable library) 1. Levin, Harry, 1912- ed. I. T.
PR6019.O9 A6 1947   823.91   LC 47-1424

Joyce, James, 1882-1941. • **2.8865**
Critical writings. Edited by Ellsworth Mason and Richard Ellmann. — New York: Viking Press, 1959. 288 p.; 22 cm. 1. Literature — Addresses, essays, lectures. I. T.
PR6019.O9 A6 1959   824.912   LC 59-6868

Joyce, James, 1882-1941. • **2.8866**
Chamber music; edited with an introd. and notes by William York Tindall. New York, Columbia University Press, c1954. 236 p.; 21 cm. — (Columbia bicentennial editions and studies) Poems. I. Tindall, William York, 1903- II. T.
PR6019.O9 C5 1954   LC 54-5333

Joyce, James, 1882-1941. • **2.8867**
Dubliners: the corrected text / with an explanatory note by Robert Scholes and fifteen drawings by Robin Jacques. — London: Cape, [1967] 261 p.: ill.; 21 cm. I. T.
PR6019.O9 D8 1967   LC 67-104013

Joyce, James, 1882-1941. • **2.8868**
Exiles: a play in three acts / James Joyce; including hitherto unpublished notes by the author, discovered after his death, and an introd. by Padraic Colum. — [1st ed.] — New York: Viking Press, 1951. 127 p.; 20 cm. — I. T.
PR6019.O9 E9 1951   822.912   LC 52-212

Atherton, James Stephen. **2.8869**
The books at the wake: a study of literary allusions in James Joyce's Finnegans wake / by James S. Atherton. — Expanded and corrected ed. — Mamaroneck,

N. Y.: P. P. Appel, 1974, c1959. 314 p. — 1. Joyce, James, 1882-1941 Finnegans wake — Sources. 2. Joyce, James, 1882-1941 — Allusions. I. T.
PR6019.O9 F55 1974

Campbell, Joseph, 1904-. • 2.8870
A skeleton key to Finnegans wake, by Joseph Campbell & Henry Morton Robinson. 1st ed. — New York, Harcourt, Brace and company [1944] xiii, 365 p.; 21 cm. 1. Joyce, James, 1882-1941. Finnegan's wake I. Robinson, Henry Morton, 1898-1961. II. T.
PR6019.O9 F57   823.91   LC 44-6502

Glasheen, Adaline. 2.8871
Third census of Finnegans wake: an index of the characters and their roles / by Adaline Glasheen. Rev. and expanded from the second census. — Berkeley: University of California Press, c1977. lxxi, 314 p.; 24 cm. Published in 1963 under title: A second census of Finnegans wake. 1. Joyce, James, 1882-1941. Finnegans wake. I. T.
PR6019.O9 F59 1977   823/.9/12   LC 75-3770   ISBN 0520029801

Hart, Clive. • 2.8872
A concordance to Finnegan's wake / Clive Hart. — Minneapolis: University of Minnesota Press, 1963. 516 p.; 29 cm. 1. Joyce, James, 1882-1941 Finnegans wake — Concordances. I. T.
PR6019.O9 F592   LC 63-8226

McHugh, Roland. 2.8873
Annotations to Finnegans wake / Roland McHugh. — Baltimore: Johns Hopkins University Press, c1980. xii, 628 p.; 26 cm. 1. Joyce, James, 1882-1941. Finnegans wake. I. T.
PR6019.O9 F59357   823/.9/12   LC 79-18419   ISBN 0801822599

McHugh, Roland. 2.8874
The sigla of Finnegans wake / Roland McHugh. Austin: University of Texas Press, c1977 (c1976). vi, 150 p.: ill.; 23 cm. Includes index. 1. Joyce, James, 1882-1941. Finnegans wake. I. T.
PR6019.O9 F5936   823/.9/12 B   LC 76-13577   ISBN 0292775288

Joyce, James, 1882-1941. 2.8875
A shorter Finnegans wake. Edited by Anthony Burgess. New York, Viking Press [1967, c1966] xxviii, 256 p. 22 cm. I. Burgess, Anthony, 1917- II. T. III. Title: Finnegans wake.
PR6019.O9F59x   LC 67-11267

Joyce, James, 1882-1941. • 2.8876
Finnegans wake. — New York: Viking Press, [1957, c1939] 643 p.; 25 cm. — I. T.
PZ3.J853 Fi6   PR6019.O9 Fx.   LC 59-354

Joyce, James, 1882-1941. • 2.8877
A portrait of the artist as a young man / by James Joyce. — New York: The Viking Press & B. W. Huebsch, 1925. 299 p.; 19 cm. — I. T.
PR6019.O9 P63   LC 28-10873

Joyce, James, 1882-1941. 2.8878
[Portrait of the artist as a young man] Stephen hero; edited from the MS. in the Harvard College Library by Theodore Spencer. A new ed., incorporating the additional MS. pages in the Yale University Library and the Cornell University Library, edited by John J. Slocum and Herbert Cahoon. [Norfolk, Conn., New Directions, 1963] 253 p. group port., facsims. 21 cm. ([A New Directions paperbook, 133]) 'The surviving pages of the early draft of A portrait of the artist as a young man.' I. T.
PR6019.O9 P63 1963   823.912   LC 63-14454

Connolly, Thomas Edmund, 1918- ed. • 2.8879
Joyce's Portrait, criticisms & critiques. — New York, Appleton-Century-Crofts [1962] 335 p. 21 cm. — (Goldentree books) 1. Joyce, James, 1882-1941. A portrait of the artist as a young man. I. T.
PR6019.O9P644   823.912   LC 62-14861

Ulysses

Joyce, James, 1882-1941. 2.8880
Ulysses: the corrected text / prepared by Hans Walter Gabler with Wolfhard Steppe and Claus Melchior. — New York: Random House, 1986. xiii, 649 p.; 24 cm. I. Gabler, Hans Walter, 1938- II. Steppe, Wolfhard. III. Melchior, Claus. IV. T.
PR6019.O9 U4 1986   823/.912 19   LC 85-28279   ISBN 039455373X

Joyce, James, 1882-1941. • 2.8881
Ulysses / by James Joyce; with a foreword by Morris L. Ernst and the decision of the United States District Court rendered by Judge John M. Woolsey. — New York: Modern Library, 1942. xvii, 767 p.: ill., (music); 21 cm. I. Ernst, Morris L. II. Woolsey, John M. III. T.
PR6019.O9 U41x   LC 44-679

Thornton, Weldon. 2.8882
Allusions in Ulysses; an annotated list. — Chapel Hill: University of North Carolina Press, [1968] viii, 554 p.; 24 cm. 1. Joyce, James, 1882-1941 Ulysses — Concordances. I. T.
PR6019.O9 U49 1968   823/.9/12   LC 68-14359

Hanley, Miles Lawrence, comp. • 2.8883
Word index to James Joyce's Ulysses, by Miles L. Hanley, assisted by Martin Joos and others. Madison, University of Wisconsin Press, 1951. xxiii, 392 p. 28 cm. 1. Joyce, James, 1882-1941. Ulysses. I. T.
PR6019.O9 U4x

Adams, Robert Martin, 1915-. • 2.8884
Surface and symbol: the consistency of James Joyce's Ulysses / Robert Martin Adams. — New York: Oxford University Press, 1962. xix, 290 p.; 21 cm. Includes index. 1. Joyce, James, 1882-1941. Ulysses. I. T.
PR6019.O9 U515 1962   LC 62-16573

Budgen, Frank Spencer Curtis, 1882-. • 2.8885
James Joyce and the making of Ulysses. With a portrait of James Joyce and four drawings to Ulysses by the author. — Bloomington, Indiana University Press [1960] 339 p. illus. 21 cm. 1. Joyce, James, 1882-1941. Ulysses. I. T.
PR6019.O9U63 1960a   823.912   LC 61-3004

Delaney, Frank, 1942-. • 2.8886
James Joyce's Odyssey: a guide to the Dublin of Ulysses / Frank Delaney; photographed by Jorge Lewinski. — 1st American ed. — New York: Holt, Rinehart and Winston, 1982, c1981. 192 p.: ill., maps; 24 cm. Maps on lining papers. Includes index. 1. Joyce, James, 1882-1941. Ulysses. 2. Joyce, James, 1882-1941 — Homes and haunts — Ireland — Dublin (Dublin) 3. Dublin (Dublin) in literature. 4. Authors, Irish — 20th century — Biography. 5. Literary landmarks — Ireland — Dublin (Dublin) 6. Dublin (Dublin) — Description — Guide-books. I. Lewinski, Jorge. II. T.
PR6019.O9 U638 1982   823/.912 19   LC 81-83276   ISBN 0030604575

Ellmann, Richard, 1918-. • 2.8887
Ulysses on the Liffey. — New York: Oxford University Press, 1972. xvii, 208 p.: illus.; 22 cm. 1. Joyce, James, 1882-1941. Ulysses. I. T.
PR6019.O9 U64 1972b   823/.9/12   LC 79-190477   ISBN 0195196651

Gifford, Don. 2.8888
Notes for Joyce; an annotation of James Joyce's Ulysses [by] Don Gifford, with Robert J. Seidman. [1st ed.] New York, Dutton, 1974. xiv, 554 p. illus. 25 cm. Running title: Notes on Ulysses. 1. Joyce, James, 1882-1941. Ulysses. 2. Joyce, James, 1882-1941 — Handbooks, manuals, etc. I. Joyce, James, 1882-1941. Ulysses. II. T.
PR6019.O9 U647   823/.9/12   LC 74-157897   ISBN 0525473149

Gilbert, Stuart. • 2.8889
James Joyce's Ulysses: a study / by Stuart Gilbert. — 2d ed., rev. — New York: Knopf, 1952. 407 p.; 22 cm. 1. Joyce, James, 1882-1941. Ulysses. I. T.
PR6019.O9 U65 1952   823.912   LC 51-11996

Groden, Michael. 2.8890
Ulysses in progress / Michael Groden. — Princeton, N.J.: Princeton University Press, c1977. xiv, 235 p.; 23 cm. Includes index. 1. Joyce, James, 1882-1941. Ulysses. 2. Joyce, James, 1882-1941 — Technique. I. T.
PR6019.O9 U6533   823/.9/12   LC 77-1217   ISBN 0691063389

Hart, Clive. 2.8891
James Joyce's Ulysses; critical essays, edited by Clive Hart and David Hayman. — Berkeley: University of California Press, [1974] xiv, 433 p.; 24 cm. 1. Joyce, James. Ulysses. I. Hayman, David. joint author. II. T.
PR6019.O9 U6542   823/.9/12   LC 73-76108   ISBN 0520024443

Kain, Richard Morgan, 1908-. • 2.8892
Fabulous voyager: James Joyce's Ulysses / by Richard M. Kain. — Chicago: University of Chicago Press, 1947. xii, 299 p. [1] feuillet de planches; 22 cm. 1. Joyce, James, 1882-1941. Ulysses. I. T.
PR6019.O9 U67   823.91   LC 47-2073

Kenner, Hugh. 2.8893
Joyce's voices / Hugh Kenner. — Berkeley: University of California Press, c1978. xiii, 120 p.: ill.; 21 cm. — (A Quantum book) Most of the book is derived from the author's four T. S. Eliot memorial lectures entitled Objectivity and after, and delivered in May 1975 at the University of Kent at Canterbury. Includes index. 1. Joyce, James, 1882-1941. Ulysses. I. T.
PR6019.O9 U672   823/.9/12   LC 76-3887   ISBN 0520032063

Kenner, Hugh. 2.8894
Ulysses / Hugh Kenner. — London; Boston: G. Allen & Unwin, 1980. 182 p.; 23 cm. — (Unwin critical library.) Includes index. 1. Joyce, James, 1882-1941. Ulysses. I. T. II. Series.
PR6019.O9 U6723   823/.912 19   LC 79-41773   ISBN 0048000035

Lawrence, Karen, 1949-.   **2.8895**
The odyssey of style in Ulysses / Karen Lawrence. — Princeton, N.J.: Princeton University Press, c1981. xi, 229 p.; 23 cm. Includes index. 1. Joyce, James, 1882-1941. Ulysses. I. T.
PR6019.O9 U6743 1981   823/.912 19   *LC* 81-47142   *ISBN* 0691064873

Litz, A. Walton.   **• 2.8896**
The art of James Joyce: method and design in Ulysses and Finnegans wake. — London, New York, Oxford University Press, 1961. 152 p. illus. 23 cm. Includes bibliography. 1. Joyce, James, 1882-1941. Ulysses. 2. Joyce, James, 1882-1941. Finnegans wake. I. T.
PR6019.O9U675 1961   823.912   *LC* 61-2855

Steppe, Wolfhard.   **2.8897**
A handlist to James Joyce's Ulysses: a complete alphabetical index to the critical reading text / prepared by Wolfhard Steppe, with Hans Walter Gabler. — New York: Garland Pub., 1985. x, 300 p.; 29 cm. (Garland reference library of the humanities; vol. 582) 1. Joyce, James, 1882-1941 Ulysses — Indexes. I. Gabler, Hans Walter, 1938- II. Joyce, James, 1882-1941. Ulysses. III. T.
PR6019.O9 U725 1985   823/.912 19   *LC* 84-48862   *ISBN* 0824087534

Sultan, Stanley.   **2.8898**
The argument of Ulysses. — [Columbus] Ohio State University Press [1965, c1964] 485 p. 24 cm. Includes bibliographical references. 1. Joyce, James, 1882-1941. Ulysses. I. T.
PR6019.O9U73   823.912   *LC* 64-22634

Ulysses: fifty years. Edited and with an introd. by Thomas F.   **2.8899**
Staley.
Bloomington, Indiana University Press [1974] ix, 190 p. illus. 22 cm. 'The essays in this volume were first presented at a colloquium in the Graduate Institute of Modern Letters at the University of Tulsa in July of 1972.' 1. Joyce, James, 1882-1941. Ulysses. I. Staley, Thomas F. ed. II. University of Tulsa. Graduate Institute of Modern Letters.
PR6019.O9 U75   823/.9/12   *LC* 73-16538   *ISBN* 0253361605

Biography. Criticism

Joyce, James, 1882-1941.   **• 2.8900**
Letters; edited by Stuart Gilbert. New York, Viking Press, 1957-[66] 3 v. facsims., ports. 25 cm. Vols. 2-3 edited by Richard Ellmann. 'A chronology of the life of James Joyce, by Richard Ellmann': v. 1, p. 43-50. 1. Joyce, James, 1882-1941 — Correspondence. I. Gilbert, Stuart. ed. II. Ellmann, Richard, 1918- ed. III. T.
PR6019.O9 Z52   928.2   *LC* 57-5129

Joyce, James, 1882-1941.   **2.8901**
Selected letters of James Joyce / edited by Richard Ellmann. New York: Viking Press, 1975. xxix, 440 p.; 24 cm. 1. Joyce, James, 1882-1941 — Correspondence. 2. Novelists, Irish — Correspondence. I. T.
PR6019.O9 Z52 1975   823/.9/12 B   *LC* 71-83240   *ISBN* 0670631906

Adams, Robert Martin, 1915-.   **2.8902**
After Joyce: studies in fiction after Ulysses / Robert Martin Adams. New York: Oxford University Press, 1977. xiii, 201 p.; 22 cm. 1. Joyce, James, 1882-1941 — Influence. 2. Fiction — 20th century — History and criticism I. T.
PR6019.O9 Z5228   809.3   *LC* 76-51707   *ISBN* 0195021681

Benstock, Shari, 1944-.   **2.8903**
Who's he when he's at home: a James Joyce directory / Shari Benstock and Bernard Benstock. — Urbana: University of Illinois Press, c1980. 234 p.; 24 cm. 1. Joyce, James, 1882-1941 — Characters 2. Joyce, James, 1882-1941 — Dictionaries, indexes, etc. I. Benstock, Bernard. joint author. II. T.
PR6019.O9 Z5259   823/.9/12 19   *LC* 79-17947   *ISBN* 0252007565

Colum, Mary (Maguire)   **• 2.8904**
Our friend James Joyce / by Mary and Padraic Colum. — 1st ed. — Garden City, N. Y.: Doubleday, 1958. 239 p.; 22 cm. 1. Joyce, James, 1882-1941. 2. Authors, Irish — Biography. I. Colum, Padraic, 1881- II. T.
PR6019.O9Z527   928.2   *LC* 58-8086

A Companion to Joyce studies / edited by Zack Bowen and   **2.8905**
James F. Carens.
Westport, Conn.: Greenwood Press, 1984. xiv, 818 p.; 25 cm. 1. Joyce, James, 1882-1941 — Criticism and interpretation. I. Bowen, Zack R. II. Carens, James F. (James Francis), 1927-
PR6019.O9 Z52717 1984   823/.912 19   *LC* 83-1479   *ISBN* 0313228329

Ellmann, Richard, 1918-.   **2.8906**
James Joyce / Richard Ellmann. — New and rev. ed. — New York: Oxford University Press, 1982. xviii, 887 p., 54 leaves of plates: ill.; 24 cm. 1. Joyce, James, 1882-1941. 2. Authors, Irish — 20th century — Biography. I. T.
PR6019.O9 Z5332 1982   823/.912 B 19   *LC* 81-22455   *ISBN* 0195031032

Gifford, Don.   **2.8907**
Joyce annotated: notes for Dubliners and A portrait of the artist as a young man / Don Gifford. — 2d ed., rev. and enl. — Berkeley: University of California Press, c1982. ix, 308 p.: maps; 24 cm. 'Maps were drawn by Peggy Diggs.' Edition for 1967 published under title: Notes for Joyce: Dubliners and A portrait of the artist as a young man. Includes index. 1. Joyce, James, 1882-1941 — Handbooks, manuals, etc. 2. Joyce, James, 1882-1941. Dubliners. 3. Joyce, James, 1882-1941. Portrait of the artist as a young man I. Joyce, James, 1882-1941. Dubliners. II. Joyce, James, 1882-1941. Portrait of the artist as a young man III. T.
PR6019.O9 Z5335 1982   823/.912 19   *LC* 80-29448   *ISBN* 0520041895

Gorman, Herbert Sherman, 1893-1954.   **• 2.8908**
James Joyce: a definitive biography / by Herbert Gorman. — London: J. Lane, 1941. 354 p.: ill. 1. Joyce, James, 1882-1941. I. T.
PR6019.O9 Z548   *LC* 41-12166

Joyce, James, 1882-1941.   **• 2.8909**
Dublin diary / edited by George Harris Healey. Ithaca, N.Y.: Cornell University Press, 1962. 119 p.; 23 cm. I. T.
PR6019.O9 Z648   *LC* 62-51465

Joyce, Stanislaus.   **• 2.8910**
My brother's keeper: James Joyce's early years / by Stanislaus Joyce; edited with an introd. and notes by Richard Ellmann, pref. by T. S. Eliot. 1st ed. — New York: Viking Press, 1958. 266 p.: ill.; 22 cm. 1. Joyce, James, 1882-1941. I. Ellmann, Richard, 1918- II. T.
PR6019.O9 Z649   928.2   *LC* 58-5403

Kenner, Hugh.   **• 2.8911**
Dublin's Joyce. — Bloomington: Indiana University Press, 1956. xi, 372 p.: port.; 23 cm. 1. Joyce, James, 1882-1941. I. T.
PR6019.O9 Z67   823.91   *LC* 56-5486

Levin, Harry, 1912-.   **• 2.8912**
James Joyce, a critical introduction. — Rev. and augm. ed. — [Norfolk, Conn.: New Directions, 1960] 256 p.; 18 cm. — (A New Directions paperbook, no. 87) 1. Joyce, James, 1882-1941 — Criticism and interpretation. I. T.
PR6019.O9 Z7 1960   823.912   *LC* 60-9222

A James Joyce miscellany / edited for the James Joyce   **2.8913**
Society, 1947–1957.
[New York: James Joyce Society, [1957] 77 p.: ports. Editor: M. Magalaner. 1. Joyce, James, 1882-1941. I. Magalaner, Marvin, 1920-. II. James Joyce Society.
PR6019.O9 Z7191

Magalaner, Marvin, 1920- ed.   **• 2.8914**
A James Joyce miscellany. Second series. — Carbondale, Southern Illinois University Press, 1959. xvi, 232 p. ports., facsims. 23 cm. 'Prepared under the sponsorship of the James Joyce Society in New York.' Includes bibliographical references. 1. Joyce, James, 1882-1941. I. James Joyce Society. II. T.
PR6019.O9Z7192   823.912   *LC* 59-6903

Magalaner, Marvin, 1920- ed.   **2.8915**
A James Joyce miscellany. Third series. — Carbondale, Southern Illinois University Press [1962] 293 p. illus. 23 cm. 1. Joyce, James, 1882-1941. I. T.
PR6019.O9Z7193   823.912   *LC* 62-15002

Magalaner, Marvin, 1920-.   **• 2.8916**
Joyce, the man, the work, the reputation [by] Marvin Magalaner and Richard M. Kain. New York, New York University Press, 1956. xi, 377 p. port. 24 cm. 1. Joyce, James, 1882-1941 — Criticism and interpretation — Addresses, essays, lectures. I. Kain, Richard Morgan, 1908- joint author. II. T.
PR6019.O9 Z72   823.91   *LC* 56-6292

Manley, Seon. comp.   **• 2.8917**
James Joyce: two decades of criticism by Eugene Jolas [and others] Edited, with a new introd., by Seon Givens. — New York: Vanguard Press, [1963] xxxviii, 486 p.: illus., port.; 24 cm. 1. Joyce, James, 1882-1941 — Criticism and interpretation. I. Jolas, Eugène, 1894-1952. II. T.
PR6019.O9 Z726 1963   823.912   *LC* 63-21852

Portraits of the artist in exile: recollections of James Joyce by   **2.8918**
Europeans / edited by Willard Potts.
Seattle: University of Washington Press, 1979 (c1978). xvi, 304 p.: ill.; 25 cm. Translated from various languages. 1. Joyce, James, 1882-1941 — Biography

— Addresses, essays, lectures. 2. Authors, Irish — 20th century — Biography — Addresses, essays, lectures. I. Potts, Willard, 1929-
PR6019.O9 Z7823   823/.9/12   LC 78-4367   ISBN 0295956143

Staley, Thomas F. ed. • 2.8919
James Joyce today: essays on the major works, commemorating the twenty-fifth anniversary of his death. Edited with a pref. by Thomas F. Staley. Bloomington, Indiana University Press, 1966. viii, 183 p. 22 cm. 1. Joyce, James, 1882-1941 — Criticism and interpretation. I. T.
PR6019.O9 Z812   828   LC 66-22447

Tindall, William York, 1903-. • 2.8920
James Joyce, his way of interpreting the modern world. — New York: Scribner, 1950. ix, 134 p.; 21 cm. 1. Joyce, James, 1882-1941. I. T.
PR6019.O9Z83   820.81   LC 50-5299

Tindall, William York, 1903-. • 2.8921
The Joyce country. New York, Schocken Books [1972] 182 p. (chiefly illus.) 16 cm. 1. Joyce, James, 1882-1941 — Homes and haunts. 2. Literary landmarks — Dublin. 3. Dublin (Dublin) — Description — Views. I. T.
PR6019.O9 Z832 1972   823/.9/12   LC 72-83501   ISBN 0805203478

Tindall, William York, 1903-. • 2.8922
A reader's guide to James Joyce. — New York: Octagon Books, 1971 [c1959] 304 p.; 22 cm. 1. Joyce, James, 1888-1941. I. T.
PR6019.O9 Z833 1971   823/.9/12   LC 78-168558   ISBN 0374979472

Work in progress: Joyce centenary essays / edited by Richard 2.8923
F. Peterson, Alan M. Cohn, and Edmund L. Epstein.
Carbondale: Southern Illinois University Press, c1983. vi, 153 p.; 22 cm. 1. Joyce, James, 1882-1941 — Criticism and interpretation — Addresses, essays, lectures. I. Joyce, James, 1882-1941. II. Peterson, Richard F. III. Cohn, Alan M., 1926- IV. Epstein, Edmund L.
PR6019.O9 Z957 1983   823/.912 19   LC 82-16943   ISBN 0809310945

PR6021 K

Kavanagh, Patrick, 1904-1967. • 2.8924
The green fool. New York, Harper, 1939. 350 p.; 22 cm. Published also by M. Joseph. I. T.
PR6021.A74 G7 1939

Kavanagh, Patrick, 1905-1967. • 2.8925
A soul for sale: poems. — London: Macmillan, 1947. v, 54 p.; 22 cm. I. T.
PR6021.A74 S65 1947

Kavanagh, Patrick, 1904-1967. • 2.8926
Tarry Flynn, a novel. New York, Devin-Adair Co., 1949. 256 p. 22 cm. I. T.
PR6021.A74 T3x   LC 49-11429

Nemo, John. 2.8927
Patrick Kavanagh / by John Nemo. — Boston: Twayne Publishers, 1979. 166 p.: port.; 21 cm. — (Twayne's English authors series; TEAS 267) Includes index. 1. Kavanagh, Patrick, 1904-1967 — Criticism and interpretation. I. T.
PR6021.A74 Z79   821/.9/12   LC 79-11031   ISBN 0805767703

Keane, Molly, 1904-. 2.8928
Good behaviour / Molly Keane. — 1st American ed. — New York: Knopf: distributed by Random House, 1981. 245 p.; 22 cm. I. T.
PR6021.E33 G6 1981   823/.912 19   LC 80-8792   ISBN 0394518187

Keane, Molly, 1904-. 2.8929
Time after time / Molly Keane. — 1st American ed. — New York: Knopf, 1984, c1983. 249 p.; 22 cm. I. T.
PR6021.E33 T5 1984   823/.914 19   LC 83-47966   ISBN 0394532805

Kiely, Benedict. 2.8930
Nothing happens in Carmincross / by Benedict Kiely. — 1st ed. — Boston: D.R. Godine, c1985. 279 p.; 22 cm. I. T.
PR6021.I24 N6 1985   823/.914 19   LC 85-70139   ISBN 0879235853

Kiely, Benedict. 2.8931
The state of Ireland: a novella & seventeen stories / by Benedict Kiely; with an introd. by Thomas Flanagan. — Boston: D.R. Godine, 1980. 389 p.: ill.; 22 cm. 1. Ireland — Fiction. I. T.
PR6021.I24 S8 1980   823/.914   LC 79-92210   ISBN 0879233206

Kinsella, Thomas, 1928-. • 2.8932
Downstream: [poems] — Dublin: Dolmen Press, 1962. 63 p.; 22 cm. — (Poetry Book Society choice.) I. T. II. Series.
PR6021.I35 D6   LC 66-81

Kinsella, Thomas. 2.8933
Notes from the land of the dead, and other poems. — [1st ed.]. — New York: Knopf; [distributed by Random House], 1973. viii, 89 p.; 24 cm. — I. T.
PR6021.I35 N66 1973   821/.9/14   LC 73-7275   ISBN 0394487826

Kinsella, Thomas. 2.8934
Peppercanister poems, 1972–1978 / Thomas Kinsella. — Winston-Salem, N.C.: Wake Forest University Press, 1979. 159 p.: ill.; 23 cm. — I. T.
PR6021.I35 P4 1979   821/.914 19   LC 79-63669   ISBN 0916390098

Kinsella, Thomas. • 2.8935
Poems & translations / Thomas Kinsella. — 1st ed. — New York: Atheneum, 1961. 89 p.; 22 cm. I. T.
PR6021.I35 P6   LC 61-9256

Harmon, Maurice. 2.8936
The poetry of Thomas Kinsella: 'with darkness for a nest' / Maurice Harmon. Atlantic Highlands, N.J.: Humanities Press, 1975. 126 p.; 22 cm. Includes index. 1. Kinsella, Thomas — Criticism and interpretation. I. T.
PR6021.I35 Z7 1975   821/.9/14   LC 75-9875   ISBN 0391003860

Kirkup, James, 1918-. • 2.8937
The prodigal son: poems, 1956–1959. — London: Oxford University Press, 1959. 105 p.; 22 cm. I. T.
PR6021.I64 P7   LC 60-132

Kirkup, James, 1918-. • 2.8938
Refusal to conform: last and first poems. — London: Oxford University Press, 1963. xi, 121 p.; 22 cm. I. T.
PR6021.I64 R4   LC 64-3702

Koestler, Arthur, 1905-. • 2.8939
Darkness at noon / by Arthur Koestler; translated by Daphne Hardy. — New York: Modern Library, 1946. 267 p.; 19 cm. I. T.
PZ3.K8194 Da8 PR6021.O4D3x   823/.9/12

PR6023 Larkin. Lavin

Larkin, Philip. • 2.8940
A girl in winter, a novel. New York, St Martin's Press [1963, c1957] 248 p. 19 cm. I. T.
PZ4.L328 Gi2   PR6023.A66 Gx.   LC 62-17790

Larkin, Philip. 2.8941
High windows. — New York: Farrar, Straus and Giroux, [1974] 42 p.; 21 cm. — I. T.
PR6023.A66 H5 1974   821/.9/14   LC 74-9800   ISBN 0374170002

Larkin, Philip. 2.8942
Jill: a novel / by Philip Larkin. — Woodstock, N.Y.: Overlook Press; 1976, c1946. 247 p. I. T.
PR6023.A66 J54 1976   823/.9/14   LC 75-27292   ISBN 0879510382

Larkin, Philip. • 2.8943
The less deceived; poems. [4th ed. Hessle, East Yorkshire] Marvell Press [1958] 45 p. 23 cm. I. T.
PR6023.A66 L4 1958   LC 58-14856

Larkin, Philip. 2.8944
Required writing: miscellaneous pieces, 1955–1982 / Philip Larkin. — New York: Farrar Straus Giroux, [1984], c1983. 328 p.; 22 cm. I. T.
PR6023.A66 R4 1984   824/.914 19   LC 84-4099   ISBN 0374249482

Motion, Andrew, 1952-. 2.8945
Philip Larkin / Andrew Motion. — London; New York: Methuen, 1982. 92 p.; 20 cm. — (Contemporary writers.) 1. Larkin, Philip — Criticism and interpretation. I. T. II. Series.
PR6023.A66 Z77 1982   821/.914 19   LC 82-7988   ISBN 0416322700

Petch, Simon. 2.8946
The art of Philip Larkin / Simon Petch. — [Sydney]: Sydney University Press; Beaverton, OR, U.S.A.: International Scholarly Book Services, 1981. xiii, 108 p.; 23 cm. (Sydney studies in literature.) 1. Larkin, Philip — Criticism and interpretation. I. T. II. Series.
PR6023.A66 Z814x 1981   LC 81-670204   ISBN 0424000903

Lavin, Mary, 1912-. 2.8947
The house in Clewe Street / by Mary Lavin; new introduction Augustine Martin. — London: Virago, 1987. [476] p.; 20 cm. (Virago modern classics) Originally published: London: Joseph, 1945. I. T.
PR6023.A914 *LC* gb87-16149 *ISBN* 086068718X

Lavin, Mary, 1912-. 2.8948
Mary O'Grady / Mary Lavin; with a new afterword by Augustine Martin. — New York, N.Y., U.S.A.: Penguin Books—Virago Press, 1986, c1950. 391 p.; 20 cm. — (Virago modern classics) I. T.
PR6023.A914 M37 1986 823/.912 19 *LC* 86-210513 *ISBN* 0140161333

Bowen, Zack R. 2.8949
Mary Lavin / Zack Bowen. — Lewisburg [Pa.]: Bucknell University Press, [1975] 77 p.; 21 cm. (The Irish writers series) 1. Lavin, Mary, 1912- I. T.
PR6023.A914 Z68 1975 823/.9/12 *LC* 73-126002 *ISBN* 0838777627

Kelly, A. A. (Angeline A.) 2.8950
Mary Lavin, quiet rebel: a study of her short stories / A. A. Kelly. — New York: Barnes & Noble Books, c1980. 200 p.: port.; 21 cm. 1. Lavin, Mary, 1912- — Criticism and interpretation. I. T.
PR6023.A914 Z75 1980 823/.912 19 *LC* 79-55699 *ISBN* 0064936171

Peterson, Richard F. 2.8951
Mary Lavin / by Richard F. Peterson. — Boston: Twayne Publishers, c1978. 171 p.: port.; 21 cm. — (Twayne's English authors series; TEAS 239) Includes index. 1. Lavin, Mary, 1912- — Criticism and interpretation. I. T.
PR6023.A914 Z83 823/.9/12 *LC* 78-329 *ISBN* 080576707X

PR6023 Lawrence

Lawrence, D. H. (David Herbert), 1885-1930. • 2.8952
Phoenix; the posthumous papers of D. H. Lawrence. Edited and with an introd. by Edward D. McDonald. New York, Viking Press [1972, c1936] xxvii, 852 p. 20 cm. (A Viking compass book, C359) I. T.
PR6023.A93 A116 1972 828/.9/1208 *LC* 72-169016 *ISBN* 0670552119 *ISBN* 067000359X

Lawrence, D. H. (David Herbert), 1885-1930. • 2.8953
Short novels. — London: Heinemann, 1956. 2 v.; 19 cm. (The Phoenix edition of D. H. Lawrence) I. T.
PR6023.A93 A15 1956 *LC* 57-1407

Lawrence, D. H. (David Herbert), 1885-1930. • 2.8954
The tales of D. H. Lawrence. London, W. Heinemann. St. Clair Shores, Mich., Scholarly Press, 1971. 2 v. (1138 p.) 21 cm. 'This volume contains the whole of Lawrence's shorter fiction from The Prussian officer, published in 1914, to The man who died, posthumously published in 1931.' I. T.
PZ3.L4345 Tal5 PR6023.A93A15 1971 823/.9/12 *LC* 73-145135 *ISBN* 0403010683

Lawrence, D. H. (David Herbert), 1885-1930. • 2.8955
Selected literary criticism, edited by Anthony Beal. New York, Viking Press, 1956 [c1955] 435 p. 22 cm. 1. Literature — Addresses, essays, lectures. 2. Books — Reviews I. T.
PR6023.A93 A16 1956 824.91 *LC* 56-11064

Lawrence, D. H. (David Herbert), 1885-1930. • 2.8956
Complete poems / collected and edited with an introd. and notes by Vivian de Sola Pinto and Warren Roberts. — New York: Viking Press, 1964. 2 v. (1072 p.): facsim., port.; 22 cm. Includes indexes. I. Pinto, Vivian de Sola, 1895- II. Roberts, Warren, 1916- III. T.
PR6023.A93 A17 821/.9/12 *LC* 64-11226 *ISBN* 014042220X

Lawrence, D. H. (David Herbert), 1885-1930. • 2.8957
Selected poems / with an introduction by Kenneth Rexroth. — [New York: New Directions, 1948, c1947] viii, 148 p., 19 cm. — (The New classics series) I. Rexroth, Kenneth, 1905- II. T. III. Series.
PR6023.A93 A17 1948 821.91

Lawrence, D.H. (David Herbert) 2.8958
The Cambridge edition of the letters and works of D.H. Lawrence. — Cambridge [Cambridgeshire]; New York: Cambridge University Press, 198-. v.; 23 cm. I. T.
PR6023.A93A1x

Lawrence, D. H. (David Herbert), 1885-1930. • 2.8959
Stories, essays, and poems / [by] D. H. Lawrence. — London: Dent [1939] xiii, 412 p. 18 cm. (Everyman's library. Essays & belles-lettres; [No. 958]) I. Hawkins, Desmond, 1908- ed. II. T.
PR6023.A93 A6 1939 *LC* 42-25412

Lawrence, D. H. (David Herbert), 1885-1930. • 2.8960
The portable D. H. Lawrence, edited, and with an introduction, by Diana Trilling. New York, The Viking press, 1947. vii, 692 p. 17 cm. (The Viking portable library) I. Trilling, Diana. ed. II. T.
PR6023.A93 A6 1947 820.81 *LC* 47-30029

Lawrence, D. H. (David Herbert), 1885-1930. • 2.8961
The later D.H. Lawrence. [The best novels, stories, essays, 1925–1930; selected, with introductions, by William York Tindall. 1st collected ed.] New York, Knopf, 1952. xx, 449 p.; 22 cm. I. Tindall, William York, 1903- II. T.
PR6023.A93 A6 1952 828 *LC* 51-11982

Lawrence, D. H. (David Herbert), 1885-1930. • 2.8962
Aaron's rod. — The Phoenix edition of D. H. Lawrence. London: Heinemann [1954] 290 p.; 19 cm. I. T.
PR6023.A93 A65 *LC* 57-2836

Lawrence, D. H. (David Herbert), 1885-1930. • 2.8963
The boy in the bush [by] D. H. Lawrence and M. L. Skinner. Pref. by Harry T. Moore. New York, Viking Press [1972, c1924] xxviii, 370 p. 20 cm. (A Viking compass book, C331) I. Skinner, M. L. (Mary Louisa), 1876-1955. joint author. II. T.
PZ3.L4345 Bo3 PR6023.A93B6x 823/.9/12 *LC* 72-197184 *ISBN* 067000331X

Lawrence, D. H. (David Herbert), 1885-1930. • 2.8964
Kangaroo. — London: M. Secker, [1923] v, 402 p.; 20 cm. I. T.
PR6023.A93 K3 1923

Lawrence, D. H. (David Herbert), 1885-1930. • 2.8965
The first Lady Chatterley / by D.H. Lawrence. — New York: Dial Press, 1944. xvii, 320 p.; 21 cm. I. T.
PZ3.L4345 Fi PR6023.A93 L2 1944. PR6023A93 L2 1944. *LC* 44-3755

Lawrence, D. H. (David Herbert), 1885-1930. • 2.8966
Lady Chatterley's lover. With an introd. by Mark Schorer. [3d manuscript version] New York: Grove Press [1959] 368 p.; 21 cm. I. T.
PR6023.A93 L2 1959 823.912 *LC* 59-1656

Lawrence, D. H. (David Herbert), 1885-1930. 2.8967
[Lady Chatterley's lover] John Thomas and Lady Jane. New York, Viking Press [1972] ix, 372 p. 22 cm. 'The second version of Lady Chatterley's lover.' I. T.
PZ3.L4345 Jo PR6023.A93L2 1972 823/.9/12 *LC* 70-185281 *ISBN* 0670408123

Penguin (Firm) defendant. • 2.8968
The trial of Lady Chatterley: Regina v. Penguin Books Limited / the transcript of the trial edited by C.H. Rolph; with ill. by Paul Hogarth and a selection of cartoons. — Harmondsworth, Penguin, 1961. 249 p.: ill., ports.; 18 cm. — (Penguin special. S192) "Lady Chatterley's lover [was] ... the first novel to be prosecuted under the new Obscene publications act ... This account of the historic trial [Oct. 20-Nov. 2, 1960] ... is taken from the official Old Bailey transcript.'—p. [4] of cover. 1. Lawrence, D. H. (David Herbert), 1885-1930. Lady Chatterley's lover. 2. Trials (Obscenity) — Great Britain. 3. Prohibited books I. Hewitt, Cecil Rolph. II. Hogarth, Paul, 1917- III. Great Britain. Central Criminal Court. IV. T. V. Series.
PR6023.A93 L36 823.912 *LC* 61-2694

Lawrence, D. H. (David Herbert), 1885-1930. • 2.8969
The Plumed Serpent, Quetzalcoatl. Introd. by William York Tindall. — New York: Knopf, 1951. xvi, 445 p.; 22 cm. I. T.
PZ3.L4345Pl2 PR6023.A93 P5x. *LC* 51-3154

Lawrence, D. H. (David Herbert), 1885-1930. • 2.8970
The rainbow, by D.H. Lawrence. — New York: Modern Library, [1927]. 467 p.; 18 cm. I. T.
PZ3.L4345R8 PR6023.A93 R1x. *LC* 27-26627

Balbert, Peter, 1942-. 2.8971
D. H. Lawrence and the psychology of rhythm: the meaning of form in The rainbow / by Peter Balbert. — The Hague: Mouton, 1974. 130 p.; 22 cm. (Studies in English literature; v. 99) Includes index. fl24.00 1. Lawrence, D. H. (David Herbert), 1885-1930. The rainbow. 2. Lawrence, D. H. (David Herbert), 1885-1930 — Style. I. T.
PR6023.A93 R332 *LC* 74-84240

Barrett, Gerald R. comp. 2.8972
From fiction to film: D. H. Lawrence's 'The rocking–horse winner.' [Compiled by] Gerald R. Barrett [and] Thomas L. Erskine. Encino, Calif., Dickenson Pub. Co. [1974] vii, 238 p. illus. 22 cm. (The Dickenson literature and film series) Includes the text of Lawrence's short story, the final shooting script of the film, and critical essays. 1. Lawrence, D. H. (David Herbert), 1885-1930. The rocking-horse winner. 2. The Rocking-horse winner. [Motion picture] I. Erskine, Thomas L. joint comp. II. Lawrence, D. H. (David Herbert),

1885-1930. The rocking-horse winner. 1974. III. The Rocking-horse winner. [Motion picture] IV. T.
PR6023.A93 R633   823/.9/12   *LC* 73-92475   *ISBN* 0822101305

Lawrence, D. H. (David Herbert), 1885-1930.   ● **2.8973**
Sex literature and censorship; essays, edited by Harry T. Moore. New York, Twayne Publishers [1953] 122 p. 23 cm. 1. Sex 2. Sex in literature I. T.
PR6023.A93S4   824.91   *LC* 53-13129

Lawrence, D. H. (David Herbert), 1885-1930.   **2.8974**
Sons and lovers: a facsimile of the manuscript / D. H. Lawrence; edited, and with an introd., by Mark Schorer. — Berkeley: University of California Press, 1978 (c1977). 624 p.: chiefly facsims.; 37 cm. 1. Lawrence, D. H. (David Herbert), 1885-1930 — Manuscripts — Facsimiles. I. T.
PR6023.A93 S6   823/.9/12   *LC* 75-46037   *ISBN* 0520031903

Lawrence, D. H. (David Herbert), 1885-1930.   ● **2.8975**
Sons and lovers. With an introd. by Alfred Kazin. New York: Modern Library [c1962] 420 p. 19 cm. (The Modern library of the world's best books, 333) I. T.
PZ3.L4345 So29   PR6023.A93 Sx.   *LC* 63-1407

Lawrence, D. H. (David Herbert), 1885-1930.   ● **2.8976**
The virgin and the gipsy, by D. H. Lawrence. — New York, A. A. Knopf, 1930. 175 p.; 20 cm. 'This work lacks the author's final revision, and has been printed from the manuscript exactly as it stands.' I. T.
PR6023.A93V5   PZ3.L4345Vi.   *LC* 30-30568

Lawrence, D. H. (David Herbert), 1885-1930.   ● **2.8977**
Women in love, by D. H. Lawrence; with a foreword by the author. New York, The Modern library [1937] 548 p.; 18 cm. (The Modern library of the world's best books) 'First Modern library edition.' I. T.
PZ3.L4345 Wo17   PR6023.A93 Wx.   *LC* 37-27406

Biography. Criticism

Lawrence, D. H. (David Herbert), 1885-1930.   ● **2.8978**
The collected letters of D. H. Lawrence / edited with an introd. by Harry T. Moore. — New York: Viking Press, 1962. 2 v. (lvi, 1307 p.); 22 cm. Includes indexes. 1. Lawrence, D. H. (David Herbert), 1885-1930. Correspondence. 2. Novelists, English — 20th century — Biography. I. T.
PR6023.A93 Z5315   823/.9/12   *LC* 62-9685

Lawrence, D. H. (David Herbert), 1885-1930.   **2.8979**
Letters to Thomas and Adele Seltzer / D. H. Lawrence; edited by Gerald M. Lacy. — Santa Barbara, CA: Black Sparrow Press, 1976. xiv, 284 p.: ill.; 24 cm. 1. Lawrence, D. H. (David Herbert), 1885-1930. Correspondence. 2. Seltzer, Thomas. 3. Seltzer, Adele Szold, 1876- 4. Authors, English — 20th century — Correspondence. I. Seltzer, Thomas. II. Seltzer, Adele Szold, 1876- III. Lacy, Gerald M. IV. T.
PR6023.A93 Z5354 1976   823/.9/12 B   *LC* 76-10782   *ISBN* 087685224X

Ben-Ephraim, Gavriel, 1946-.   **2.8980**
The Moon's dominion: narrative dichotomy and female dominance in Lawrence's earlier novels / Gavriel Ben-Ephraim. — Rutherford [N.J.]: Fairleigh Dickinson University Press; London: Associated University Presses, c1981. 255 p.; 22 cm. Originally presented as the author's thesis, Hebrew University. Includes index. 1. Lawrence, D. H. (David Herbert), 1885-1930 — Criticism and interpretation. 2. Lawrence, D. H. (David Herbert), 1885-1930 — Characters — Women. 3. Sex role in literature I. T.
PR6023.A93 Z5668 1981   823/.912   *LC* 78-75172   *ISBN* 0838622666

Bynner, Witter, 1881-1968.   ● **2.8981**
Journey with genius; recollections and reflections concerning the D. H. Lawrences. — New York, J. Day Co. [1951] xv, 361 p. illus., ports. 22 cm. 1. Lawrence, D. H. (David Herbert), 1885-1930. 2. Lawrence, Frieda von Richthofen, 1879-1956. I. T.
PR6023.A93Z58   928.2   *LC* 51-11710

Carswell, Catherine MacFarlane, 1879-1946.   ● **2.8982**
The savage pilgrimage; a narrative of D. H. Lawrence. St. Clair Shores, Mich., Scholarly Press, 1972. xii, 307 p. 22 cm. Reprint of the 1951 ed. 1. Lawrence, D. H. (David Herbert), 1885-1930. I. T.
PR6023.A93 Z6 1972   823/.9/12 B   *LC* 75-144937   *ISBN* 0403008999

Delavenay, Emile.   **2.8983**
[D. H. Lawrence, l'homme et la genèse de son œuvre, les années de formation, 1885-1919. English] D. H. Lawrence, the man and his work; the formative years: 1885–1919. Translated from the French by Katharine M. Delavenay. Carbondale, Southern Illinois University Press [1972] xvi, 592 p. illus. 25 cm. Translation of D. H. Lawrence, l'homme et la genèse de son œuvre, les années

de formation, 1885-1919. 1. Lawrence, D. H. (David Herbert), 1885-1930. I. T.
PR6023.A93 Z623613   823/.9/12 B   *LC* 70-190586   *ISBN* 0809306034

Draper, Ronald P., 1928- comp.   **2.8984**
D. H. Lawrence: the critical heritage. Edited by R. P. Draper. New York, Barnes & Noble [1970] 377 p. 23 cm. (The Critical heritage series) 1. Lawrence, D. H. (David Herbert), 1885-1930. I. T.
PR6023.A93 Z6245 1970b   823/.9/12   *LC* 77-15554   *ISBN* 038901088X

Hough, Graham Goulden, 1908-.   ● **2.8985**
The dark sun: a study of D. H. Lawrence. — New York: Macmillan, 1957 [c1956] 265 p. 22 cm. 1. Lawrence, D. H. (David Herbert), 1885-1930. I. T.
PR6023.A93 Z6318 1957   *LC* 57-7262

Leavis, F. R. (Frank Raymond), 1895-.   ● **2.8986**
D. H. Lawrence, by F. R. Leavis. New York, Haskell House Publishers, 1972. 33 p. 23 cm. Reprint of the 1930 ed. 1. Lawrence, D. H. (David Herbert), 1885-1930 — Criticism and interpretation. I. T.
PR6023.A93 Z65 1972   823/.9/12   *LC* 72-3172   *ISBN* 0838315410

Meyers, Jeffrey.   **2.8987**
D.H. Lawrence and the experience of Italy / Jeffrey Meyers. — Philadelphia: University of Pennsylvania Press, 1982. xv, 189 p.: ill., maps, ports.; 24 cm. 1. Lawrence, D. H. (David Herbert), 1885-1930 — Knowledge — Italy. 2. Authors, English — 20th century — Biography. 3. Italy in literature. I. T.
PR6023.A93 Z679 1982   823/.912 B 19   *LC* 82-60261   *ISBN* 0812278615

Miller, Henry, 1891-.   **2.8988**
The world of Lawrence: a passionate appreciation / Henry Miller; edited with an introd. and notes by Evelyn J. Hinz and John J. Teunissen. — Santa Barbara, Calif.: Capra Press, 1980. 272 p.: ill.; 24 cm. 1. Lawrence, D. H. (David Herbert), 1885-1930 — Criticism and interpretation. I. T.
PR6023.A93 Z6814   823/.912   *LC* 79-27735   *ISBN* 0884961478

Moore, Harry Thornton. ed.   ● **2.8989**
A D. H. Lawrence miscellany. — Carbondale, Southern Illinois University Press, 1959. xxvi, 395 p. illus., group port., facsims. (incl. music) 23 cm. Bibliographical footnotes. 1. Lawrence, D. H. (David Herbert), 1885-1930. I. T.
PR6023.A93Z683   828.912   *LC* 59-11268

Moore, Harry Thornton.   ● **2.8990**
D. H. Lawrence, his life and works. [Rev. ed.] New York, Twayne Publishers [1964] 330 p. illus., ports., map (on lining papers) 22 cm. 1. Lawrence, D. H. (David Herbert), 1885-1930. I. T.
PR6023.A93 Z687 1964   *LC* 63-18498

Moynahan, Julian, 1925-.   **2.8991**
The deed of life; the novels and tales of D. H. Lawrence. Princeton, N.J., Princeton University Press, 1963. 229 p. 23 cm. 1. Lawrence, D. H. (David Herbert), 1885-1930. I. T.
PR6023.A93 Z689 1963   823.912   *LC* 63-9986

Nehls, Edward, ed.   ● **2.8992**
D. H. Lawrence: a composite biography, gathered, arranged, and edited by Edward Nehls. — Madison, University of Wisconsin Press, 1957-59. 3 v. illus., ports. 24 cm. Bibliography: v. 1, p. 535-540. 'Notes and sources': v. 1, p. 541-600. 1. Lawrence, D. H. (David Herbert), 1885-1930. I. T.
PR6023.A93Z73   928.2   *LC* 57-9817

Murry, John Middleton, 1889-1957.   ● **2.8993**
D. H. Lawrence: son of woman / by J. Middleton Murry. — London: Cape [1954] 397 p.; 21 cm. 1. Lawrence, D. H. (David Herbert), 1885-1930. I. T. II. Title: Son of woman.
PR6023.A93 Z787S

Sagar, Keith M.   **2.8994**
D. H. Lawrence, a calendar of his works / Keith Sagar; with a checklist of the manuscripts of D. H. Lawrence by Lindeth Vasey. — Austin: University of Texas Press, c1979. ix, 294 p.; 22 cm. Includes indexes. 1. Lawrence, D. H. (David Herbert), 1885-1930 — Chronology. 2. Lawrence, D. H. (David Herbert), 1885-1930 — Manuscripts. 3. Authors, English — 20th century — Biography. I. T.
PR6023.A93 Z862 1979b   823/.912   *LC* 78-65562   *ISBN* 0292715196

Sanders, Scott R. (Scott Russell), 1945-.   **2.8995**
D. H. Lawrence: the world of the five major novels. New York, Viking Press [1974] 224 p. 22 cm. 1. Lawrence, D. H. (David Herbert), 1885-1930 — Criticism and interpretation. I. T.
PR6023.A93 Z865 1974   823/.9/12   *LC* 73-3500   *ISBN* 0670271314

Spender, Stephen, 1909- comp. 2.8996
D. H. Lawrence: novelist, poet, prophet. [1st U.S. ed.] New York, Harper & Row [1973] 250 p. illus. 26 cm. 1. Lawrence, D. H. (David Herbert), 1885-1930. I. T.
PR6023.A93 Z9175 1973b   823/.9/12 B   *LC* 73-2000   *ISBN* 0060139560

Spilka, Mark. ed. • 2.8997
D. H. Lawrence: a collection of critical essays. Englewood Cliffs, N.J., Prentice-Hall [1963] 182 p. 21 cm. (A Spectrum book. Twentieth century views, S-TC-24) 1. Lawrence, D. H. (David Herbert), 1885-1930 — Criticism and interpretation. I. T.
PR6023.A93 Z918   828.912   *LC* 63-9517

Spilka, Mark. • 2.8998
The love ethic of D. H. Lawrence. Bloomington, Indiana University Press, 1955. 244 p. 21 cm. 1. Lawrence, D. H. (David Herbert), 1885-1930. I. T.
PR6023.A93 Z92   823.91   *LC* 55-8447

Tindall, William York, 1903-. • 2.8999
D. H. Lawrence & Susan his cow [by] William York Tindall ... — New York, Columbia University Press, 1939. xiv, 231 p.; 23 cm. 'An effort to account for Lawrence historically, to place him in the intellectual, social, and literary movements of his time, to show how his response to his personal problems took its character from what was going on around him.'—Pref. Bibliography: p. [213]-219. 1. Lawrence, D. H. (David Herbert), 1885-1930. I. T.
PR6023.A93 Z93   928.2   *LC* 39-30216

Vivas, Eliseo. • 2.9000
D. H. Lawrence; the failure and the triumph of art. — Evanston, Northwestern University Press [1960] xvii, 302 p. 22 cm. Bibliographical references included in 'Notes' (p. 293-300) 1. Lawrence, D. H. (David Herbert), 1885-1930. I. T.
PR6023.A93Z94   823.912   *LC* 60-10049

Lawrence, Frieda von Richthofen, 1879-1956. • 2.9001
'Not I, but the wind ...' New York, Viking Press, 1934. St. Clair Shores, Mich., Scholarly Press, 1972. xi, 297 p. illus. 22 cm. The author's memoirs together with letters and some material written by her husband, D. H. Lawrence. I. Lawrence, D. H. (David Herbert), 1885-1930. II. T.
PR6023.A934 Z5 1972   823/.9/12 B   *LC* 77-145136   *ISBN* 040300764X

Lawrence, Frieda von Richthofen, 1879-1956. • 2.9002
Frieda Lawrence; the memoirs and correspondence. Edited by E. W. Tedlock, Jr. — [1st American ed.]. — New York, Knopf, 1964. xix, 481 p. ports. 22 cm. 1. Lawrence, D. H. (David Herbert), 1885-1930. I. T.
PR6023.A934Z52 1964   828.912   *LC* 64-12307

O'Donnell, Thomas J., 1938-. 2.9003
The confessions of T. E. Lawrence: the romantic hero's presentation of self / by Thomas J. O'Donnell. — Athens: Ohio University Press, c1979. x, 196 p.: port.; 24 cm. Includes index. 1. Lawrence, T. E. (Thomas Edward), 1888-1935 — Criticism and interpretation. 2. Confession in literature I. T.
PR6023.A937 Z83   828/.9/1209   *LC* 77-92257   *ISBN* 0821403702

PR6023 Lehmann

Lehmann, John, 1907-. 2.9004
Thrown to the Woolfs / John Lehmann. — 1st American ed. — New York: Holt, Rinehart, and Winston, 1979, c1978. xx, 164 p., [4] leaves of plates: ill.; 22 cm. Includes index. 1. Lehmann, John, 1907- — Biography. 2. Woolf, Leonard, 1880-1969 — Friends and associates. 3. Woolf, Virginia, 1882-1941 — Friends and associates. 4. Hogarth Press. 5. Authors, English — 20th century — Biography. I. T.
PR6023.E4 Z519 1979   821/.9/12 B   *LC* 79-1925   *ISBN* 0030521912

Lehmann, Rosamond, 1901-. • 2.9005
The ballad and the source. New York, Reynal and Hitchcock [1945] 250 p. 20 cm. I. T.
PZ3.L5282 Bal   PR6023.E42 Bx.   *LC* 46-4661

Lehmann, Rosamond, 1901-. • 2.9006
Dusty answer, by Rosamond Lehmann. New York, Reynal & Hitchcock [1947] 375 p. 20 cm. I. T.
PR6023.E42 Dx

Lehmann, Rosamond, 1901-. • 2.9007
Invitation to the waltz. New York: Reynal & Hitchcock, [1947,c1932] 189 p.; 20 cm. — I. T.
PR6023 E42 I5

LeStourgeon, Diana E. 2.9008
Rosamond Lehmann, by Diana E. LeStourgeon. New York, Twayne Publishers [1965] 157 p. 21 cm. (Twayne's English authors series, 16) 1. Lehmann, Rosamond, 1901- I. T.
PR6023.E42 Z75   823.912   *LC* 64-8331

PR6023 Lessing

Lessing, Doris May, 1919-. • 2.9009
African stories, by Doris Lessing. — New York: Simon and Schuster, [1965] 636 p.; 22 cm. — I. T.
PZ3.L56684 Af2   PR6023.E833 Ax.   *LC* 65-23003

Lessing, Doris May, 1919-. 2.9010
Stories / Doris Lessing. — 1st ed. — New York: Knopf: distributed by Random House, 1978. 625 p.; 22 cm. — I. T.
PZ3.L56684 St 1978 PR6023.E833Ax   823/.9/14   *LC* 77-20797   *ISBN* 0394500091

Lessing, Doris May, 1919-. 2.9011
Briefing for a descent into Hell [by] Doris Lessing. — [1st ed.]. — New York: Knopf, 1971. 308 p.; 22 cm. — I. T.
PR6023.E833 B7   PZ3.L56684 Br3   823/.9/14   *LC* 71-136325   *ISBN* 0394421981

Lessing, Doris May, 1919-. • 2.9012
Children of violence / Doris Lessing. — New York: Simon and Schuster, 1964-. v.; 23 cm. I. T. II. Title: A ripple from the storm. III. Title: Landlocked.
PR6023.E833 C5x   *LC* 64-22409

Lessing, Doris May, 1919-. 2.9013
Documents relating to the sentimental agents in the Volyen Empire / Doris Lessing. — 1st ed. — New York: Knopf: Distributed by Random House, 1983. 178 p.; 25 cm. — (Canopus in Argos—archives) I. T.
PR6023.E833 D59 1983   823/.914 19   *LC* 82-25172   *ISBN* 0394529685

Lessing, Doris May, 1919-. 2.9014
The diary of Jane Somers / Jane Somers. — 1st American ed. — New York: Knopf, 1983. 253 p.; 22 cm. I. T.
PR6023.E833 D5x   823/.914 19   *LC* 82-48739   *ISBN* 0394529707

Lessing, Doris May, 1919-. 2.9015
The good terrorist / Doris Lessing. — 1st American ed. — New York: Knopf: Distributed by Random House, 1985. 375 p.; 22 cm. I. T.
PR6023.E833 G66 1985   823/.914 19   *LC* 85-40214   *ISBN* 0394543394

Lessing, Doris May, 1919-. • 2.9016
The golden notebook. — New York: Simon and Schuster, 1962. 567 p.; 25 cm. — I. T.
PZ3.L56684 Go   PR6023.E833 G6x.   *LC* 62-12412

Lessing, Doris May, 1919-. • 2.9017
The grass is singing / Doris Lessing. — London: M. Joseph, 1950. 256 p.; 19 cm. I. T.
PR6023.E833 G7   *LC* 50-25216

Lessing, Doris May. • 2.9018
The habit of loving / Doris Lessing. — New York: Crowell, c1957. 311 p.; 22 cm. I. T.
PR6023.E833 H3x   *LC* 58-9187   *ISBN* 0690005016

Lessing, Doris May, 1919-. • 2.9019
A man and two women: stories / by Doris Lessing. — New York: Simon and Schuster, 1963. 316 p.; 22 cm. I. T.
PR6023.E833 M3 1963   *LC* 63-19277

Lessing, Doris May, 1919-. 2.9020
The making of the representative for Planet 8 / Doris Lessing. — 1st ed. — New York: Knopf: distributed by Random House, 1982. 144 p.; 25 cm. — (Canopus in Argos—archives) I. T.
PR6023.E833 M34 1982   823/.914 19   *LC* 80-29073   *ISBN* 039451906X

Lessing, Doris May, 1919-. 2.9021
The marriages between zones three, four, and five (as narrated by the chroniclers of zone three) / Doris Lessing. — 1st ed. — New York: Knopf: distributed by Random House, 1980. 244 p.; 25 cm. — (Canopus in Argos—archives) I. T.
PZ3.L56684 Map 1980 PR6023.E833M37x   823/.9/14   *LC* 79-16515   *ISBN* 0394509145

Lessing, Doris May, 1919-. 2.9022
The memoirs of a survivor / Doris Lessing. — 1st American ed. — New York: Knopf: distributed by Random House, 1975, c1974. 213 p.; 22 cm. I. T.
PZ3.L56684 Me3 PR6023.E833M4x 823/.9/14 *LC* 74-21294 *ISBN* 0394496337

Lessing, Doris May, 1919-. 2.9023
The Sirian experiments: the report by Ambien II, of the five / Doris Lessing. — 1st ed. — New York: Knopf: distributed by Random House, 1981. viii, 288 p.; 25 cm. — (Canopus in Argos—archives) I. T.
PR6023.E833 S57 1981 823/.914 *LC* 79-27710 *ISBN* 0394512316

Lessing, Doris May, 1919-. 2.9024
Shikasta: re, colonised planet 5: personal, psychological, historical documents relating to visit by Johor (George Sherban) emissary (grade 9) 87th of the period of the last days / Doris Lessing. — 1st American ed. — New York: Knopf: distributed by Random House, 1979. x, 364 p.; 25 cm. — (Canopus in Argos—archives) I. T.
PZ3.L56684 Sh 1979 PR6023.E833S5x 823/.9/14 *LC* 79-11295 *ISBN* 0394507320

Lessing, Doris May, 1919-. 2.9025
The summer before the dark [by] Doris Lessing. — [1st. American ed.]. — New York: Knopf; [distributed by Random House], 1973. 273 p.; 22 cm. — I. T.
PR6023.E833 S8 PZ3.L56684 Su3 823/.9/14 *LC* 72-11044 *ISBN* 0394484282

Lessing, Doris May, 1919-. • 2.9026
In pursuit of the English. New York, Simon and Schuster, 1961 [c1960] 239 p. 23 cm. Autobiographical. 1. London (England) — Social life and customs I. T.
PR6023.E833 Z5 *LC* 61-7007

Lessing, Doris May, 1919-. 2.9027
A small personal voice [by] Doris Lessing. Essays, reviews, interviews, edited and introduced by Paul Schlueter. — [1st ed.]. — New York: Knopf; [distributed by Random House], 1974. x, 171 p.; 22 cm. 1. Lessing, Doris May, 1919- I. T.
PR6023.E833 Z52 1974 823/.9/14 *LC* 74-7724 *ISBN* 039449329X

Brewster, Dorothy, 1883-. 2.9028
Doris Lessing. — New York: Twayne Publishers, [1965] 173 p.; 21 cm. — (Twayne's English authors series, 21) 1. Lessing, Doris May, 1919- I. T.
PR6023.E833 Z58 823.914 *LC* 65-18222

Draine, Betsy, 1945-. 2.9029
Substance under pressure: artistic coherence and evolving form in the novels of Doris Lessing / Betsy Draine. — Madison, Wis.: University of Wisconsin Press, 1983. xv, 224 p.; 24 cm. Includes index. 1. Lessing, Doris May, 1919- — Criticism and interpretation. I. T.
PR6023.E833 Z63 1983 823/.914 19 *LC* 82-70556 *ISBN* 0299092305

Knapp, Mona. 2.9030
Doris Lessing / Mona Knapp. — New York: Frederick Ungar Pub. Co., 1985 (c1984). xviii, 210 p.; 21 cm. (Literature and life series.) Includes index. 1. Lessing, Doris May, 1919- — Criticism and interpretation. I. T. II. Series.
PR6023.E833 Z735 823/.914 19 *LC* 84-131 *ISBN* 0804424918

Notebooks, memoirs, archives: reading and rereading Doris Lessing / edited by Jenny Taylor. 2.9031
Boston: Routledge & Kegan Paul, 1982. xi, 251 p.; 22 cm. Includes index. 1. Lessing, Doris May, 1919- — Criticism and interpretation — Addresses, essays, lectures. I. Taylor, Jenny, 1949-
PR6023.E833 Z78 1982 823/.914 19 *LC* 82-5476 *ISBN* 0710090331

Rubenstein, Roberta, 1944-. 2.9032
The novelistic vision of Doris Lessing: breaking the forms of consciousness / Roberta Rubenstein. — Urbana: University of Illinois Press, c1979. 271 p.; 24 cm. Includes index. 1. Lessing, Doris May, 1919- — Criticism and interpretation. 2. Psychology in literature I. T.
PR6023.E833 Z87 823/.9/14 *LC* 78-25916 *ISBN* 0252007069

Sage, Lorna. 2.9033
Doris Lessing / Lorna Sage. — London; New York: Methuen, 1983. 91 p.; 20 cm. — (Contemporary writers.) 1. Lessing, Doris May, 1919- — Criticism and interpretation. I. T. II. Series.
PR6023.E833 Z878 1983 823/.914 19 *LC* 82-20846 *ISBN* 0416317308

Schlueter, Paul, 1933-. 2.9034
The novels of Doris Lessing. With a pref. by Harry T. Moore. — Carbondale: Southern Illinois University Press, [1973] x, 144 p.; 22 cm. — (Crosscurrents/ Modern critiques) On spine: Doris Lessing. 1. Lessing, Doris May, 1919- I. T.
PR6023.E833 Z88 823/.9/14 *LC* 72-10281 *ISBN* 0809306123

Singleton, Mary Ann. 2.9035
The city and the veld: the fiction of Doris Lessing / Mary Ann Singleton. — Lewisburg [Pa.]: Bucknell University Press, c1977. 243 p. Includes index. 1. Lessing, Doris May, 1919- — Criticism and interpretation. I. T.
PR6023.E833 Z89 823/.9/14 *LC* 75-5145 *ISBN* 0838716520

PR6023 Leverson. Lewis

Leverson, Ada, 1865-1936. • 2.9036
The little Ottleys: Love's shadow; Tenterhooks; Love at second sight / with a foreword by Colin MacInnes. — New York: Norton [1962] 543 p.; 23 cm. I. Leverson, Ada, 1865-1936. Love's shadow. II. Leverson, Ada, 1865-1936. Tenterhooks. III. Leverson, Ada, 1865-1936. Love at second sight. IV. T. V. Title: Love's shadow. VI. Title: Tenterhooks. VII. Title: Love at second sight.
PR6023.E87 A6 1962 *LC* 62-52081

Lewis, C. S. (Clive Staples), 1898-1963. • 2.9037
The literary impact of the Authorised version / by C.S. Lewis. — London: University of London, 1950. 26 p.; 22 cm. — (Ethel M. Wood lecture; 1950) 1. Bible as literature 2. Versions. I. T. II. Series.
PR6023.E926 L5 1950 *LC* a 51-7248

Lewis, C. S. (Clive Staples), 1898-1963. 2.9038
On stories, and other essays on literature / C.S. Lewis; edited by Walter Hooper. — 1st ed. — New York: Harcourt Brace Jovanovich, c1982. xxi, 153 p.; 21 cm. I. Hooper, Walter. II. T.
PR6023.E926 O5 1982 809 19 *LC* 81-48014 *ISBN* 015169964X

Lewis, C. S. (Clive Staples), 1898-1963. • 2.9039
Out of the silent planet / C. S. Lewis. — London: Lane [1943] 263 p.; 19 cm. The 1st vol. of the author's trilogy, the 2d of which is Perelandra, the 3d, That hideous strength. I. T.
PR6023.E926 O6

Lewis, C. S. (Clive Staples), 1898-1963. 2.9040
Perelandra: a novel. — New York: Macmillan, [1968, c1944] 238 p. 'A sequel to Out of the silent planet.'- Pref. I. T.
PR6023.E926 P4 1968

Lewis, C. S. (Clive Staples), 1898-1963. • 2.9041
That hideous strength; a modern fairy–tale for grownups. New York, Macmillan [1968, c1946] 382 p. 22 cm. The third of a trilogy, the title of the first being Out of the silent planet and that of the second Perelandra. I. T.
PZ3.L58534 Th4 PR6023.E926T4x 823/.9/12 *LC* 68-7663

Lewis, C. S. (Clive Staples), 1898-1963. • 2.9042
Till we have faces; a myth retold. [1st American ed.] New York, Harcourt, Brace [1957, c1956] 313 p. illus. 22 cm. 1. Psyche (Greek deity) — Fiction. 2. Cupid (Roman deity) — Fiction. I. T.
PZ3.L58534 Ti2 PR6023.E926 T5x. *LC* 56-11300

Lewis, Wyndham, 1884-1957. • 2.9043
Tarr. — [Rev. ed.]. — London: Chatto and Windus, [1935] 4 p. l., 326 p., 1 l.; 17 1/2 cm. — (The Phoenix library) I. T. II. Series.
PR6023.E97 T3

Lewis, Wyndham, 1882-1957. • 2.9044
Letters. Edited by W. K. Rose. Norfolk, Conn., New Directions [1964, c1963] xxvii, 580 p. illus. (part col.) ports., facsims. 21 cm. I. Rose, William K., ed. II. T.
PR6023.E97 Z54 1964 826.912 *LC* 61-10121

Jameson, Fredric. 2.9045
Fables of aggression: Wyndham Lewis, the modernist as fascist / Fredric Jameson. — Berkeley: University of California Press, c1979. 190 p.; 23 cm. Errata slip inserted. 1. Lewis, Wyndham, 1882-1957 — Criticism and interpretation. I. T.
PR6023.E97 Z68 828/.9/1209 *LC* 78-64462 *ISBN* 0520037928

Kenner, Hugh. • 2.9046
Wyndham Lewis. — Norfolk, Conn., New Directions Books [1954] 169 p. illus. 19 cm. — (The Makers of modern literature) 1. Lewis, Wyndham, 1886-1957. I. T.
PR6023.E97Z7 928.2 *LC* 54-9869

Materer, Timothy, 1940-. 2.9047
Wyndham Lewis, the novelist / Timothy Materer. — Detroit: Wayne State University Press, 1976. 189 p.: port.; 24 cm. Includes index. 1. Lewis, Wyndham, 1882-1957. I. T.
PR6023.E97 Z74   823/.9/12   *LC* 75-29310   *ISBN* 0814315445

Meyers, Jeffrey. 2.9048
The enemy: a biography of Wyndham Lewis / Jeffrey Meyers. — London: Routledge & Kegan Paul, c1980. xiii, 391 p.; 24 cm. Includes index. 1. Lewis, Wyndham, 1882-1957 — Biography. 2. Authors, English — 20th century — Biography. 3. Artists — England — Biography. I. T.
PR6023.E97 Z75   828/.91209 19   *LC* 81-169344   *ISBN* 0710005148

PR6023 Li–Lo

Lindsay, Maurice, 1918-. 2.9049
Collected poems / by Maurice Lindsay. — Edinburgh: P. Harris Pub., 1979. 128 p.; 23 cm. I. T.
PR6023.I58114 Ax

Lindsay, David, 1876-1945. 2.9050
A voyage to Arcturus / David Lindsay; with a new introd. by Van A. Mensing. — Boston: Gregg Press, 1977. xvii, 303 p.; 21 cm. — (The Gregg Press science fiction series) Reprint of the 1920 ed. published by Methuen, London. I. T.
PZ3.L6495 Vo10 PR6023.I58115V6x   823/.9/12   *LC* 77-8471   *ISBN* 0839823754

Linklater, Eric, 1899-1974. 2.9051
White–maa's saga. — London: J. Cape, [1929] 283 p. I. T.
PR6023.I582 W4

Llewellyn, Richard. • 2.9052
How green was my valley. — New York: The Macmillan company, 1940. 4 p., l., 495 p.; 22 cm. 'First printing.' The 1st vol. of a trilogy. The 2d is Up, into the singing mountain; the 3d, Down where the moon is small. I. T.
PZ3.L7714 Ho9   PR6023.L47 H6x.   *LC* 40-27043

Lowndes, Marie Adelaide Belloc, 1868-1947. 2.9053
The lodger, by Mrs. Belloc Lowndes. — New York: Scribner, 1913. 1 v. I. T.
PZ3.L954 Lo15 PR6023.O95L6   823/.9/12

PR6023 Lowry

Lowry, Malcolm, 1909-1957. • 2.9054
Selected poems of Malcolm Lowry / edited by Earle Birney; with the assistance of Margerie Lowry. — San Francisco: City Lights Books, 1962. 79 p.: ill.; 16 cm. — (Pocket poets series. no. 17) I. Birney, Earle, 1904- II. T. III. Series.
PR6023.O96 A6 1962   PS8523.O9 A6 1962.   *LC* 62-51260

Lowry, Malcolm, 1909-1957. • 2.9055
Dark as the grave wherein my friend is laid. Edited by Douglas Day & Margerie Lowry. — [New York]: New American Library, [1968] xxiii, 255 p.; 22 cm. I. Day, Douglas. ed. II. Lowry, Margerie Bonner. ed. III. T.
PZ3.L9563 Dar   PR6023.O96 Dx.   *LC* 68-26029

Lowry, Malcolm, 1909-1957. • 2.9056
Hear us O Lord from heaven thy dwelling place: short stories / Malcolm Lowry. — 1st ed. — Philadelphia: Lippincott, 1961. 283 p.; 21 cm. I. T.
PZ3.L9563He   PR6023.O96 Hx.   *LC* 61-8688

Lowry, Malcolm, 1909-1957. • 2.9057
Ultramarine: a novel / by Malcolm Lowry. — 1st American ed. — Philadelphia: Lippincott, c1962. 203 p. I. T.
PR6023.O96 U458 1962   *LC* 62-15207

Lowry, Malcolm, 1909-1957. • 2.9058
Under the volcano / Malcolm Lowry. — New York: Reynal & Hitchcock, c1947. 375 p.; 21 cm. I. T.
PZ3.L9563 Un   PS8523.O9 U5 1947.   PR6023.O96 Ux.   *LC* 47-1776

Binns, Ronald, 1948-. 2.9059
Malcolm Lowry / Ronald Binns. — London; New York: Methuen, 1984. 96 p.; 20 cm. (Contemporary writers.) 1. Lowry, Malcolm, 1909-1957 — Criticism and interpretation. I. T. II. Series.
PR6023.O96 Z568 1984   813/.54 19   *LC* 84-1080   *ISBN* 0416377505

Bradbrook, M. C. (Muriel Clara), 1909-. 2.9060
Malcolm Lowry: his art & early life; a study in transformation [by] M. C. Bradbrook. [London] Cambridge University Press [1974] xiii, 170 p. maps 21 cm. 1. Lowry, Malcolm, 1909-1957. I. T.
PR6023.O96 Z57   813/.5/4   *LC* 74-76945   *ISBN* 0521204739

Costa, Richard Hauer. • 2.9061
Malcolm Lowry. — New York: Twayne Publishers, [1972] 208 p.; 21 cm. — (Twayne's world authors series, TWAS 217. Canada) 1. Lowry, Malcolm, 1909-1957. I. T.
PR6023.O96 Z59   813/.5/4   *LC* 75-185451

Day, Douglas. 2.9062
Malcolm Lowry; a biography. — New York: Oxford University Press, 1973. xiii, 483 p.: illus.; 24 cm. 1. Lowry, Malcolm, 1909-1957. I. T.
PR6023.O96 Z598   813/.5/4 B   *LC* 73-82665   *ISBN* 0195017110

Grace, Sherrill, 1944-. 2.9063
The voyage that never ends: Malcolm Lowry's fiction / Sherrill E. Grace. — Vancouver: University of British Columbia Press, c1982. xvi, 152 p.; 24 cm. Includes index. 1. Lowry, Malcolm, 1909-1957 — Criticism and interpretation. I. T.
PR6023.O96 Z65 1982   813/.54 19   *LC* 83-135782   *ISBN* 0774801549

Woodcock, George, 1912- comp. • 2.9064
Malcolm Lowry: the man and his work. — Vancouver: University of British Columbia Press, [1971] ix, 174 p.; 25 cm. — (Canadian literature series, 3) 1. Lowry, Malcolm, 1909-1957. I. T.
PR6023.O96 Z88   813/.5/4   *LC* 79-857301   *ISBN* 0774800062

PR6023 Lu

Lustgarten, Edgar, 1907-1978. 2.9065
One more unfortunate. — New York: Scribner, 1947. 202 p. I. T.
PR6023.U73 O5   *LC* 47-11093

PR6025 Mac–Mack

Macaulay, Rose, Dame. • 2.9066
The towers of Trebizond. London, Collins, 1956. 287 p. 21 cm. I. T.
PR6025.A16 Tx   PZ3.M1215 Tr5   *LC* 56-44142

Macaulay, Rose, Dame. 2.9067
The world my wilderness / Rose Macaulay; with a new introduction by Penelope Fitzgerald. — London: Virago, 1983. xiv, 253 p.; 20 cm. — (Virago modern classics) I. T.
PR6025.A16 W6 1983   823/.912 19   *LC* 83-113126   *ISBN* 0860683400

MacCaig, Norman, 1910-. 2.9068
[Poems] Collected poems / Norman MacCaig. — London: Chatto & Windus: Hogarth Press, 1985. xii, 390 p.; 24 cm. Includes index. I. T.
PR6025.A1628 A17 1985   821/.912 19   *LC* 85-239500   *ISBN* 0701139536

MacCarthy, Desmond, 1878-1952. • 2.9069
Memories. Forewords by Raymond Mortimer & Cyril Connolly. New York, Oxford University Press, 1953. 223 p. 22 cm. I. T.
PR6025.A164Z52 1953a   824.91   *LC* 53-11095

Macdonell, Archibald Gordon, 1895-1941. • 2.9070
England, their England. — London: Macmillan; New York: St. Martin's Press, 1957. 249 p.; 18 cm. — (St. Martin's library) I. T. II. Series.
PR6025.A222 E5

Machen, Arthur, 1863-1947. 2.9071
The great god Pan, and, The inmost light. Freeport, N.Y.: Books for Libraries Press, 1970. 177 p. I. T. II. Title: The inmost light
PR6025 A245 G68

Mackenzie, Compton, Sir, 1883-1972. 2.9072
Sinister street / by Compton Mackenzie. — London, M. Secker, 1913-14. 2 v. 20 cm. I. T.
PR6025.A2526 S5   PZ3.M1974 Si   *LC* 13-20828

Young, Kenneth, 1916-. 2.9073
Compton Mackenzie. London, Longmans, Green, 1968. 32 p. front. (port.) 23 cm. (Bibliographical series of supplements to British book news on writers and their work, no. 202) 1. Mackenzie, Compton, Sir, 1883-1972. I. British Council. II. National Book League. III. T. IV. Series.
PR6025.A2526 Z9   828/.9/1209   *LC* 68-105258

PR6025 MacNeice

MacNeice, Louis, 1907-1963. • 2.9074
Collected poems. Edited by E. R. Dodds. — New York: Oxford University Press, 1967. 575 p.; 22 cm. — I. T.
PR6025.A316 A17 1967   821.912   *LC* 67-793

MacNeice, Louis, 1907-1963.   ● **2.9075**
Christopher Columbus, a radio play. — [1st ed.] [London]: Faber & Faber, [1944] 92 p.; 23 cm. 'Introduction: Some comments on radio drama': p. 7-19. 1. Colombo, Christoforo — Drama. 2. Radio plays — Technique I. T.
PR6025.A316 C5 1944   *LC* 44-4602

MacNeice, Louis, 1907-1963.   ● **2.9076**
The dark tower, and other radio scripts / by Louis MacNeice. — London: Faber and Faber, 1947. 202 p.; 23 cm. Cover title: The dark tower, and other broadcast plays. I. T.
PR6025.A316 D3   *LC* 47-29050

McKinnon, William T.   ● **2.9077**
Apollo's blended dream: a study of the poetry of Louis MacNeice [by] William T. McKinnon. — London; New York: Oxford University Press, 1971. xiv, 241 p., plate:; port.; 23 cm. 1. MacNeice, Louis, 1907-1963. I. T.
PR6025.A316 Z8   821/.9/12   *LC* 70-859466   *ISBN* 0192112996

Press, John.   ● **2.9078**
Louis MacNeice. — [London] Published for the British Council and the National Book League by Longmans, Green [1965] 47 p. port. 22 cm. — (Bibliographical series of supplements to British book news on writers and their work, 187) Bibliography: p. 45-47. 1. MacNeice, Louis, 1907-1963. I. T.
PR6025.A316Z9   828.91209   *LC* 66-8144

PR6025 Mansfield

Mansfield, Katherine, 1888-1923.   ● **2.9079**
Journal / edited by J. Middleton Murry. — Definitive ed. — London: Constable, 1954. 336 p.: port. I. T.
PR6025.A57 Z4 1954   *LC* 55-1185

Mansfield, Katherine, 1888-1923.   **2.9080**
The collected letters of Katherine Mansfield / edited by Vincent O'Sullivan and Margaret Scott. — Oxford [Oxfordshire]: Clarendon Press, 1984. xxx, 376 p.: facsim.; 25 cm. 1. Mansfield, Katherine, 1888-1923. Correspondence 2. Authors, New Zealand — 20th century — Correspondence. I. O'Sullivan, Vincent James. II. Scott, Margaret, 1928- III. T.
PR9639.3.M258 Z48 1984   PR6025.A57 Z48.   823/.912 B 19   *LC* 83-12189   *ISBN* 0198126131

Mansfield, Katherine, 1888-1923.   ● **2.9081**
The letters of Katherine Mansfield / edited by J. Middleton Murry. — New York: Knopf, 1929. 2 v.; 23 cm. 1. Mansfield, Katherine, 1888-1923. Correspondence I. Murry, John Middleton, 1889-1957. II. T.
PR6025.A57 Z5 1929   *LC* 29-5743

Mansfield, Katherine, 1888-1923.   ● **2.9082**
Katherine Mansfield's letters to John Middleton Murry, 1913–1922 / edited by John Middleton Murry. — 1st American ed. — New York: Knopf, 1951. 701 p.: ports.; 22 cm. 1. Mansfield, Katherine, 1888-1923. Correspondence 2. Murry, John Middleton, 1889-1957 — Correspondence. 3. Authors, New Zealand — 20th century — Correspondence. I. Murry, John Middleton, 1889-1957. II. T. III. Title: Letters to John Middleton Murry, 1913-1922.
PR6025.A57 Z556 1951   *LC* 51-12071

Alpers, Antony, 1919-.   ● **2.9083**
Katherine Mansfield: a biography / Antony Alpers. — 1st American ed. — New York: Knopf, 1953. xvi, 376 p.: ill., ports.; 22 cm. 1. Mansfield, Katherine, 1888-1923. 2. Authors, New Zealand — 20th century — Biography. I. T.
PR6025.A57 Z557   *LC* 52-12181

Alpers, Antony, 1919-.   **2.9084**
The life of Katherine Mansfield / Antony Alpers. — New York: Viking Press, 1980. xxvi, 466 p., [8] leaves of plates: ill., ports. Includes index. 1. Mansfield, Katherine, 1888-1923 — Biography. 2. Authors, New Zealand — 20th century — Biography. I. T.
PR9639.3.M258 Z58   PR6025A57 Z559.   823/.9/12   *LC* 79-12088   *ISBN* 0670428051

Mansfield, Katherine, 1888-1923.   **2.9085**
[Short stories] Collected stories of Katherine Mansfield. — [London]: Constable, 1945. 793 p.; 19 cm. I. T.
PR6025.A57x   823/.912 19   *LC* 82-192030

Hanson, Clare.   **2.9086**
Katherine Mansfield / Clare Hanson and Andrew Gurr. — New York, NY: St. Martin's Press, 1981. 146 p.; 20 cm. Includes index. 1. Mansfield, Katherine, 1888-1923 — Criticism and interpretation. I. Gurr, Andrew. joint author. II. T.
PR6025.A57 Z6x   823/.912 19   *LC* 80-24334   *ISBN* 0312450931

Magalaner, Marvin, 1920-.   **2.9087**
The fiction of Katherine Mansfield. With a pref. by Harry T. Moore. — Carbondale: Southern Illinois University Press, [1971] viii, 148 p.; 22 cm. — (Crosscurrents: modern critiques) 1. Mansfield, Katherine, 1888-1923. I. T.
PR6025.A57 Z79   823   *LC* 74-132489   *ISBN* 0809304783

PR6025 Mar–Mas

Marsh, Ngaio, 1899-.   **2.9088**
Died in the wool. [Boston]: Little, Brown, 1945. 270p. I. T.
PR6025 A6387 D5

Martyn, Edward.   **2.9089**
Maeve: a psychological drama in two acts [and] the last feast of the Fianna, a dramatic legend / by Edward Martyn and Alice Milligan. — Chicago: DePaul University Press, 1967. (Irish Drama Series; v. 2.) I. Milligan, Alice. II. T. III. Title: The last feast of the Fianna. IV. Series.
PR6025.A74 M3x

Masefield, John, 1878-1967.   ● **2.9090**
Poems. [Complete ed., with recent poems.] New York, Macmillan, 1953. 685 p. I. T.
PR6025.A77 1953   821.91   *LC* 53-4222 rev.

Masefield, John, 1878-1967.   **2.9091**
[Letters from the front, 1915-1917] John Masefield's Letters from the front, 1915–1917 / edited by Peter Vansittart. — New York: F. Watts, c1984. 307 p.: ill.; 24 cm. Includes index. 1. Masefield, John, 1878-1967 — Correspondence. 2. Masefield, Constance, d. 1960. 3. Authors, English — 20th century — Correspondence. 4. World War, 1914-1918 — Personal narratives, English. 5. World War, 1914-1918 — Campaigns — France 6. World War, 1914-1918 — Medical care — France. 7. World War, 1914-1918 — War work — Red Cross. I. Vansittart, Peter. II. T. III. Title: Letters from the front, 1915-1917.
PR6025.A77 Z487   828/.91209 B 19   *LC* 84-51644   *ISBN* 0531097765

Mason, A. E. W. (Alfred Edward Woodley), 1865-1948.   **2.9092**
The house of the arrow. — New York: Doran, 1924. 1 v. I. T.
PR6025.A79 H68 1924

PR6025 Maugham

Maugham, W. Somerset (William Somerset), 1874-1965.   ● **2.9093**
Collected plays. London, Heinemann, [1952] 3 v. 21 cm. I. T.
PR6025.A86 A19 1952   *LC* 54-4008

Maugham, W. Somerset (William Somerset), 1874-1965.   ● **2.9094**
The Maugham reader. With an introd. by Glenway Wescott. — [1st ed.]. — Garden City, N. Y., Doubleday, 1950. xxvi, 1217 p. 22 cm. I. T.
PR6025.A86A6 1950   823.91   *LC* 50-9916

Maugham, W. Somerset (William Somerset), 1874-1965.   ● **2.9095**
[Selected works. 1952] Complete short stories. Garden City, N.Y., Doubleday, 1952. 2 v. 22 cm. Vol. 1 first published in 1934: Vol. 2 issued separately in 1952. I. T. II. Title: East and West. III. Title: World over.
PR6025.A86 A6 1952   PZ3.M442 Cm   *LC* 52-11626

Maugham, W. Somerset (William Somerset), 1874-1965.   ● **2.9096**
Ashenden: or, The British agent / W. Somerset Maugham. — 1st ed. — London: Heinemann, 1928. 304 p. I. T. II. Title: The British agent.
PR6025A86 A82   *LC* 46-32271   *ISBN* 0434456055

Maugham, W. Somerset (William Somerset), 1874-1965.   ● **2.9097**
Cakes and ale / W. S. Maugham. — New York: Modern lib. 1950. 272p. (Modern library of the world's best books 270) I. T.
PR6025.A86 C3 1950   *LC* 50-6793

Maugham, W. Somerset (William Somerset), 1874-1965.   ● **2.9098**
Liza of Lambeth. London, Heinemann [1956] 171 p. (The Collected edition of his works, 1) I. T.
PR6025.A86 L5x   823.91

Maugham, W. Somerset (William Somerset), 1874-1965.   ● **2.9099**
The moon and sixpence / by W. Somerset Maugham. — New York: Modern library, [1935] 341 p.; 18 cm. — (The Modern library of the world's best books) I. T.
PR6025.A86 M66 1935   *LC* 36-18159

Maugham, W. Somerset (William Somerset), 1874-1965.   ● **2.9100**
Of human bondage, by W. Somerset Maugham ... New York, The Modern library [1930] 766 p. 17 cm. (Half-title: The modern library of the world's best books) I. T.
PR6025.A86O4 1930   823.01   *LC* 31-26122

Maugham, W. Somerset (William Somerset), 1874-1965. • **2.9101**
The painted veil. — New York: Doran, [1925] 289 p. I. T.
PR6025.A86 P3   *LC* 25-7084

Maugham, W. Somerset (William Somerset), 1874-1965. • **2.9102**
The razor's edge, a novel. Garden City, New York, Doubleday, Doran & co., inc., 1944. 4 p.l., 343 p. 22 cm. I. T.
PR6025.A86 R3 1944   *LC* 44-6503

Maugham, W. Somerset (William Somerset), 1874-1965. • **2.9103**
The travel books. — London: Heinemann, [1955] xv, 148, 170, 146 p. I. Maugham, W. Somerset (William Somerset), 1874-1965. On a Chinese screen. II. Maugham, W. Somerset (William Somerset), 1874-1965. Gentleman in the parlour. III. Maugham, W. Somerset (William Somerset), 1874-1965. Don Fernando. IV. T. V. Title: On a Chinese screen. VI. Title: The gentleman in the parlour. VII. Title: Don Fernando.
PR6025.A86 T63   *LC* 56-1946

Maugham, W. Somerset (William Somerset), 1874-1965. • **2.9104**
A writer's notebook. Westport, Conn., Greenwood Press [1970, c1949] xvi, 367 p. port. 23 cm. I. T.
PR6025.A86 W7 1970   828/.9/1208   *LC* 73-110048   *ISBN* 0837144337

Burt, Forrest D. **2.9105**
W. Somerset Maugham / by Forrest D. Burt. — Boston: Twayne, c1985. 157 p.: port.; 23 cm. (Twayne's English authors series. TEAS 399) Includes index. 1. Maugham, W. Somerset (William Somerset), 1874-1965 — Criticism and interpretation. I. T. II. Series.
PR6025.A86 Z5585 1985   823/.912 19   *LC* 84-25288   *ISBN* 0805768858

Calder, Robert Lorin. **2.9106**
W. Somerset Maugham and the quest for freedom / Robert Lorin Calder. — Garden City, N.Y.: Doubleday, 1973. -. xii, 324 p.; 22 cm. — 1. Maugham, W. Somerset (William Somerset), 1874-1965. I. T.
PR6025.A86 Z559 1973   823/.9/12   *ISBN* 0385046987

Cordell, Richard Albert. • **2.9107**
Somerset Maugham, a writer for all seasons; a biographical and critical study, by Richard A. Cordell. [2d ed.] Bloomington, Indiana University Press [1969] 308 p. illus., ports. 22 cm. 1. Maugham, W. Somerset (William Somerset), 1874-1965. I. T.
PR6025.A86 Z56 1969   823/.9/12 B   *LC* 78-3602

The Maugham enigma; an anthology. • **2.9108**
New York, Citadel Press [1954] 217 p. ill. Compiled by K.W. Jonas. 1. Maugham, W. Somerset (William Somerset), 1874-1965. I. Jonas, Klaus Werner.
PR6025.A86 Z63   823.91   *LC* 53-13462

Jonas, Klaus W. ed. • **2.9109**
The world of Somerset Maugham; an anthology, edited by Klaus W. Jonas. Westport, Conn., Greenwood Press [1972, c1959] 200 p. ports. 22 cm. 1. Maugham, W. Somerset (William Somerset), 1874-1965 — Addresses, essays, lectures. I. T.
PR6025.A86 Z64 1972   823/.9/12   *LC* 73-156196   *ISBN* 0837161479

PR6025 Mi

Milne, A. A. (Alan Alexander), 1882-1956. • **2.9110**
Toad of Toad Hall; a play from Kenneth Grahame's book. New York, Scribner [1965? c1929] xi, 175 p. 21 cm. I. Grahame, Kenneth, 1859-1932. Wind in the willows II. T.
PR6025.I65 T65 1965   822   *LC* 65-2685

Milne, A. A. (Alan Alexander), 1882-1956. • **2.9111**
The World of Pooh; the complete Winnie-the-Pooh and The house at Pooh Corner. With decorations and new illus. in full color by E.H. Shepard. [New York]: Dutton, [1957] 314 p.: ill. I. Shepard, Ernest H. (Ernest Howard), 1879-1976. II. Milne, A. A. (Alan Alexander), 1882-1956. Winnie-the-Pooh. III. Milne, A. A. (Alan Alexander), 1882-1956. House at Pooh Corner. IV. T. V. Title: Winnie the Pooh. VI. Title: The house at Pooh Corner.
PR6025.I65 W6 1957a   PZ7.M552 Wo   *LC* 57-8986   *ISBN* 0525433201

Crews, Frederick C. • **2.9112**
The Pooh perplex, a freshman casebook. [1st ed.] New York, Dutton, 1963. x, 150 p. illus. 21 cm. 1. Milne, A. A. (Alan Alexander), 1882-1956. Winnie-the-Pooh. 2. Criticism — Anecdotes, facetiae, satire, etc. I. T.
PR6025.I65 W65   823.912   *LC* 63-15770

Milne, A. A. (Alan Alexander), 1882-1956. • **2.9113**
The world of Christopher Robin; the complete When we were very young and Now we are six. With decorations and new illus. in full color by E. H. Shepard. [New York] Dutton [1958] 234 p. illus. 24 cm. Verses for children. I. T. II. Title: When we were very young. III. Title: Now we are six.
PR6025.I65 W6x   PZ8.3.M6354 Wo   *LC* 58-9571

Milne, A. A. (Alan Alexander), 1882-1956. • **2.9114**
Autobiography, by A. A. Milne ... — New York, E. P. Dutton & co., inc. [c1939] 315 p. front. (port.) 23 cm. 'Published serially in the Atlantic monthly under the title 'What luck.' 'First edition.' I. T.
PR6025.I65Z5 1939   928.2   *LC* 39-27813

Mitchell, James Leslie, 1901-1935. **2.9115**
A Scots quair: a trilogy of novels / Lewis Grassic Gibbon [i.e. J. L. Mitchell]; with a foreword by Ivor Brown. — New York: Schocken Books, 1977, c1946. 496 p.; 24 cm. Reprint of the 1950 ed. published by Hutchinson, London. I. T.
PZ3.M6932 Sc8 PR6025.I833S2x   823/.9/12   *LC* 77-4988   *ISBN* 0805236619

Mitford, Nancy, 1904-1973. • **2.9116**
The blessing. — New York, Random House [1951] 305 p. 21 cm. I. T.
PZ3.M6972Bl2   PR6025.I88 Bx.   *LC* 51-13267

Mitford, Nancy, 1904-1973. • **2.9117**
Don't tell Alfred. [1st ed.] New York, Harper [1961, c1960] 247 p. 22 cm. I. T.
PZ3.M6972 Do2   PR6025.I88 Dx.   *LC* 61-6462

Mitford, Nancy, 1904-1973. • **2.9118**
Love in a cold climate, a novel. New York, Random House [1949] 304 p. 21 cm. I. T.
PR6025.I88 Lx   PZ3.M6972 Lo   *LC* 49-9848

Mitford, Nancy, 1904-1973. • **2.9119**
The pursuit of love: a novel / Nancy Mitford. — Garden City, N.Y.: Sun Dial Press, [1947,c1945]. 247 p.; 21 cm. I. T.
PR6025I88 P9 1947   823/.9/1   *ISBN* 0850467454

Mitford, Nancy, 1904-1973. **2.9120**
A talent to annoy: essays, articles and reviews, 1929–1968 / by Nancy Mitford; edited by Charlotte Mosley. — London: Hamilton, 1986. xi, 217 p.; 23 cm. I. Mosley, Charlotte. II. T.
PR6025.I88 Tx   828/.91208 19   *ISBN* 0241119162

Mittelhölzer, Edgar, 1909-. **2.9121**
A morning at the office, a novel. London Hogarth Press 1950. 246p. I. T.
PR6025.I89 M6

Mittelhölzer, Edgar. **2.9122**
Shadows move among them / Edgar Mittelhölzer. — Philadelphia: Lippincott, [c1951]. 334 p. I. T.
PR6025I89 S5   *LC* 51-8454

PR6025 Mo–Mz

Montgomery, Bruce, 1921-1978. **2.9123**
The case of the gilded fly / by Edmund Crispin [i.e. R. B. Montgomery]. — London: Gollancz, [1944]. 223 p. I. T.
PZ3.M7681 Cas 1979 PR6025.O46 C3x

Moore, T. Sturge (Thomas Sturge), 1870-1944. • **2.9124**
The poems of T. Sturge Moore. — Collected ed. — London: Macmillan, 1931-1932. 2 v.: port.; 22 cm. I. T.
PR6025.O58 A17 1931   821/.9/12   *LC* 32-17899

Moraes, Dom F., 1938-. • **2.9125**
Poems. — London: Eyre & Spottiswoode, [1960] 48 p. I. T.
PR6025.O62 A17   *LC* a 61-2329

Muir, Edwin, 1887-1959. • **2.9126**
Collected poems. — [2d ed.]. — New York: Oxford University Press, 1965. 310 p.: port.; 21 cm. — I. T.
PR6025.U6 A17 1965   821.912   *LC* 65-6179

Muir, Edwin, 1887-1959. • **2.9127**
An autobiography / Edwin Muir. — London: Hogarth Press, 1954. 287 p.: ill., map., ports.; 23 cm. Includes index. 1. Muir, Edwin, 1887-1959 — Biography. I. Hogarth Press. II. T.
PR6025.U6 Z46 1954   *LC* 54-41959

Butter, Peter H. • **2.9128**
Edwin Muir / P.H. Butter. — New York: Grove Press, 1962. 120 p. (Evergreen pilot books; EP17) 1. Muir, Edwin, 1887-1959. I. T.
PR6025.U6 Z58 1962   *LC* 61-12359

Knight, Roger.   2.9129
Edwin Muir: an introduction to his work / Roger Knight. — London; New
York: Longman, 1980. 210 p.; 22 cm. — (A Longman paperback) Includes
index. 1. Muir, Edwin, 1887-1959 — Criticism and interpretation. I. T.
PR6025.U6 Z72   828/.91209   LC 79-42832   ISBN 0582489016

Phillips, Michael Joseph.   2.9130
Edwin Muir: a master of modern poetry / Michael J. Phillips. — Indianapolis:
Hackett Pub. Co., 1979 (c1978). 161 p.; 24 cm. 1. Muir, Edwin, 1887-1959 —
Criticism and interpretation. I. T.
PR6025.U6 Z8   821/.9/12   LC 78-67103   ISBN 0915144549

Wiseman, Christopher.   2.9131
Beyond the labyrinth: a study of Edwin Muir's poetry / Christopher Wiseman.
— Victoria, B.C.: Sono Nis Press, 1978. 252 p.; 24 cm. Includes index. 1. Muir,
Edwin, 1887-1959 — Criticism and interpretation. I. T.
PR6025.U6 Z97   821/.9/12   LC 79-305016   ISBN 0919462669

Saki, 1870-1916.   2.9132
The complete works of Saki / H. H. Munro; with an introd. by Noël Coward. —
1st ed. — Garden City, N.Y.: Doubleday, 1976. xiv, 944 p.; 24 cm. I. T.
PR6025.U675 1976   828/.9/1209   LC 74-33655   ISBN 0385053738

Saki, 1870-1916.   • 2.9133
The short stories of Sake (H.H. Munro) / complete with an introduction by
Christopher Morley. — New York: Viking Press, 1930. xiii, 718 p.: ill. I. T.
PR6025.U675 A15 1958

Langguth, A. J., 1933-.   2.9134
Saki, a life of Hector Hugh Munro: with six short stories never before collected
/ A.J. Langguth. — New York: Simon and Schuster, c1981. 366 p., [8] p. of
plates: ill.; 22 cm. Includes index. 1. Saki, 1870-1916. 2. Authors, English —
20th century — Biography. I. Saki, 1870-1916. II. T.
PR6025.U675 Z76   823/.912 B 19   LC 81-5607   ISBN 0671247158

Murphy, Richard, 1927-.   • 2.9135
Sailing to an island; [poems] New York, Chilmark Press; [distributed by
Random House, 1963] 63 p. 23 cm. I. T.
PR6025.U6973 S3   LC 63-12779

Murry, John Middleton, 1889-1957.   • 2.9136
The autobiography of John Middleton Murry: between two worlds. — New
York: J. Messner, c1936. 500 p., [4] p. of plates: ports. 1. Murry, John
Middleton, 1889-1957. I. T. II. Title: Between two worlds.
PR6025.U8 Z52 1935

Lea, Frank Alfred, 1915-.   • 2.9137
The life of John Middleton Murry. New York: Oxford University Press, 1960.
378 p.: ill.; 28 cm. 1. Murry, John Middleton, 1889-1957. 2. Mansfield,
Katherine, 1888-1923. I. T.
PR6025.U8 Z75

PR6027 N

Newby, P. H. (Percy Howard), 1918-.   2.9138
Kith / P. H. Newby. — 1st American ed. — Boston: Little, Brown, c1977.
143 p.; 22 cm. I. T.
PZ3.N4294 Ki3 PR6027.E855 K5x   823/.9/14   LC 77-5204   ISBN
0316604208

Newby, P. H. (Percy Howard), 1918-.   • 2.9139
A lot to ask [by] P. H. Newby. London, Faber, 1973. 3-247 p. 21 cm. I. T.
PR6027.E855 L6   823/.9/14   LC 73-163500   ISBN 057110293X

Bufkin, E. C.   2.9140
P. H. Newby / by E. C. Bufkin. — Boston: Twayne Publishers, [1975] 144 p.:
port.; 22 cm. (Twayne's English authors series; TEAS 176) Includes index.
1. Newby, P. H. (Percy Howard), 1918- — Criticism and interpretation. I. T.
PR6027.E855 Z6   823/.9/14   LC 74-22324   ISBN 0805714146

Lees-Milne, James.   2.9141
Harold Nicolson: a biography, 1930–1968. v. 2 / by James Lees-Milne. —
Hamden, Conn.: Archon Books, 1984. 403 p.: ill. Includes indexes.
1. Nicolson, Harold George, Sir, 1886-1968 — Biography. 2. Authors, English
— 20th century — Biography. 3. Diplomats — Great Britain — Biography.
I. T.
PR6027.I4 Z77 1982   828/.91209 B 19   LC 82-135213   ISBN
0208020764

Noyes, Alfred, 1880-1958.   • 2.9142
Collected poems in one volume. — London: Murray, [1950]. 415 p. —
1. English poetry I. T.
PR6027.O8 1966   821.912   821   LC 66-16190

PR6029 O'B–O'C

O'Brien, Kate, 1897-1974.   2.9143
Without my cloak / by Kate O'Brien; with a new introduction by Desmond
Hogan. — London: Virago, 1986. [490] p.; 20 cm. (Virago modern classics)
I. T.
PR6029.B65 W5x   823/.912 19   ISBN 0860687600

O'Casey, Sean, 1884-1964.   • 2.9144
Collected plays. — London, Macmillan, 1949-52. [v.2, 1952] 4 v. 21 cm.
Includes songs with music. I. T.
PR6029.C33A19 1949   822.91   LC 50-617 rev

O'Casey, Sean, 1880-1964.   • 2.9145
Selected plays of Sean O'Casey / selected and with a foreword by the author;
introd. by John Gassner. — New York: G.Braziller, 1954. xxix, 799 p. I. T.
PR6029C33A19 1954   822.91   LC 54-14533

O'Casey, Sean, 1880-1964.   • 2.9146
The Sean O'Casey reader: plays, autobiographies, opinions. Edited with an
introd. by Brooks Atkinson. — New York: St. Martin's Press, 1968. xxiv,
1008 p.; 25 cm. 'Plays: Juno and the paycock, The plough and the stars, The
silver tassie, Within the gates, Purple dust, Red roses for me, Cock-a-doodle
dandy, Bedtime story, The drums of Father Ned': p. 1-529. I. T.
PR6029.C33 A6 1968   828   LC 68-29125

O'Casey, Sean, 1880-1964.   • 2.9147
Behind the green curtains; Figuro in the night; The moon shines on Kylenamoe.
New York, St. Martin's Press [1961] 157 p. illus. 22 cm. I. T. II. Title: Figuro
in the night. III. Title: The moon shines on Kylenamoe.
PR6029.C33 B4   LC 61-13378

O'Casey, Sean, 1880-1964.   • 2.9148
The Bishop's bonfire; a sad play within the tune of a polka. New York:
Macmillan, 1955. 124 p.: ill.; 21 cm. I. T.
PR6029.C33 B5 1955a   822.91   LC 55-3558

O'Casey, Sean, 1880-1964.   • 2.9149
The drums of Father Ned; [play] New York, St. Martin's Press [1960] 109 p.
illus. 22 cm. I. T.
PR6029.C33D7   822.912   LC 60-8769

O'Casey, Sean, 1880-1964.   • 2.9150
Feathers from the Green Crow, Sean O'Casey, 1905–1925. Edited by Robert
Hogan. Columbia, University of Missouri Press [1962] 342 p. illus. 23 cm. I. T.
PR6029.C33F4   822.912   LC 62-9508

O'Casey, Sean, 1880-1964.   • 2.9151
Under a colored cap: articles merry and mournful with comments and a song.
New York, St. Martin's Press, 1963. 276 p. 21 cm. Autobiographical. I. T.
PR6029.C33Z585 1963   828.912   LC 63-11345

Benstock, Bernard.   2.9152
Paycocks and others: Sean O'Casey's world / Bernard Benstock. — Dublin:
Gill and Macmillan; New York: Barnes & Noble, 1976. x, 318 p.; 23 cm.
Includes index. 1. O'Casey, Sean, 1880-1964 — Characters. 2. O'Casey, Sean,
1880-1964 — Criticism and interpretation. I. T.
PR6029.C33 Z5888   822/.9/12   LC 75-36767   ISBN 006490363X

Fallon, Gabriel.   • 2.9153
Sean O'Casey, the man I knew. — [1st American ed.]. — Boston: Little, Brown,
[1965] 213 p.: illus., ports.; 22 cm. 1. O'Casey, Sean, 1880-1964. I. T.
PR6029.C33 Z63 1965   822.912   LC 65-21349

Krause, David, 1917-.   2.9154
Sean O'Casey and his world / David Krause. New York: Scribner, [1976].
128 p.: ill.; 24 cm. Includes index. 1. O'Casey, Sean, 1880-1964 — Biography.
2. Dramatists, Irish — 20th century — Biography. I. T.
PR6029.C33 Z678 1976b   822/.9/12 B   LC 76-7182   ISBN
0684147270

O'Riordan, John.   2.9155
A guide to O'Casey's plays: from the plough to the stars / John O'Riordan. —
New York: St. Martin's Press, 1985 (c1984). xi, 419 p.; 22 cm. Includes index.
1. O'Casey, Sean, 1880-1964 — Criticism and interpretation. I. T.
PR6029.C33 Z783   822/.912 19   LC 83-40587   ISBN 0312353006

O'Connor, Frank, 1903-1966.   2.9156
Collected stories / Frank O'Connor; introduction by Richard Ellmann. — 1st
ed. — New York: Knopf, 1981. xiii, 701 p.; 25 cm. I. T.
PR6029.D58 A15 1981   823/.912 19   LC 81-1253   ISBN
0394516028

O'Connor, Frank, 1903-1966. • 2.9157
An only child [by] Frank O'Connor [pseud. 1st ed.] New York, Knopf, 1961. 275 p. illus. 22 cm. Autobiography. 1. O'Connor, Frank, 1903-1966. I. T.
PR6029.D58 Z52   928.2   *LC* 60-15873

O'Connor, Frank, 1903-1966. • 2.9158
My father's son [by] Frank O'Connor. [1st American ed.] New York, Knopf, 1969 [c1968] 235 p. ports. 22 cm. 1. O'Connor, Frank, 1903-1966 — Biography. 2. O'Connor, Frank, 1903-1966. 3. Authors, Irish — 20th century — Biography. I. T.
PR6029.D58 Z523 1969   821 B   *LC* 70-79323

Tomory, William M. 2.9159
Frank O'Connor / by William M. Tomory. — Boston: Twayne Publishers, 1980. 198 p.: port.; 21 cm. (Twayne's English author series; TEAS 297) Includes index. 1. O'Connor, Frank, 1903-1966 — Criticism and interpretation. I. T.
PR6029.D58 Z89   823/.912   *LC* 80-10308   *ISBN* 0805767894

PR6029 O'F–Or

O'Faoláin, Seán, 1900-. • 2.9160
Finest stories. [1st ed.] Boston, Little, Brown [1957] 385 p. 22 cm. I. T.
PZ3.O32 Fi   PR6029.F3 F5x.   *LC* 57-5828

O'Faoláin, Seán, 1900-. 2.9161
Foreign affairs, and other stories / Sean O'Faolain. — 1st ed. — Boston: Little, Brown, 1976. 226 p.; 21 cm. 'An Atlantic Monthly Press book.' Five stories appeared in Playboy, one in Winter's tales (London), and one in the Atlantic monthly. I. T.
PZ3.O32 Fo3 PR6029.F3 F6x   823/.9/12   *LC* 75-25713   *ISBN* 0316632937

O'Faoláin, Seán, 1900-. • 2.9162
A nest of simple folk / Seán O'Faoláin. — New York: Viking Press, 1934. 398 p.: geneal. table; 22 cm. I. T.
PZ3.O32 Ne2   PR6029.F3 N4.   *LC* 33-27269

O'Faoláin, Seán, 1900-. • 2.9163
The talking trees, and other stories. — [1st ed.]. — Boston: Little, Brown, [1970] 279 p.; 22 cm. 'An Atlantic Monthly Press book.' I. T.
PR6029.F3 T3   PZ3.O32 Tal   823   *LC* 74-121428

O'Faoláin, Seán, 1900-. • 2.9164
Vive moi! / by Sean O'Faolain. — 1st ed. — Boston: Litle, Brown, 1964. 374 p.: port.; 22 cm. — (Atlantic Monthly Press book.) 1. O'Faoláin, Seán, 1900- — Biography. 2. Authors, English — 20th Century — Biography. I. T. II. Series.
PR6029.F3 Z5   *LC* 64-18784

O'Faoláin, Seán, 1900-. • 2.9165
I remember! I remember! Stories. [1st ed.] Boston: Little, Brown, [1962, c1961] 240 p. 21 cm. I. T.
PZ3.O32I2 PR6029.F3512   *LC* 61-66313

O'Flaherty, Liam, 1896-. • 2.9166
Stories / Liam O'Flaherty; introduced by Vivan Mercier. — New York: Devin-Adair, 1956. 419 p.; 22 cm. I. T.
PR6029.F5 S7

Kelly, A. A. (Angeline A.) 2.9167
Liam O'Flaherty the storyteller / A. A. Kelly. — New York: Barnes & Noble Books, 1977 (c1976). xiii, 154 p.; 23 cm. Includes index. 1. O'Flaherty, Liam, 1896- — Criticism and interpretation. I. T.
PR6029.F5 Z73   823/.9/12   *LC* 75-43225   *ISBN* 0064936163

Zneimer, John. 2.9168
The literary vision of Liam O'Flaherty. [1st ed. Syracuse, N.Y.] Syracuse University Press [1970] xiii, 207 p. 24 cm. 1. O'Flaherty, Liam, 1896- I. T.
PR6029.F5 Z9   823/.9/12   *LC* 74-130981   *ISBN* 0815600739

O'Brien, Flann, 1911-1966. • 2.9169
At Swim–Two–Birds, by Flann O'Brien. New York, Walker [1966] 315 p. 22 cm. 1. O'Brien, Flann, 1911-1966. I. T.
PZ3.O589 At7   PR6029.N56 Ax.   *LC* 66-17221

O'Brien, Flann, 1911-1966. 2.9170
[Béal boċt. English] The poor mouth: a bad story about the hard life / by Flann O'Brien [i.e. B. O'Nolan]; translated by Patrick C. Power; illustrated by Ralph Steadman. — New York: Viking Press, 1974, c1973. 128 p.: ill.; 25 cm. 'A Richard Seaver book.' Translation of An béal boċt. I. T.
PR6029.N56B4x   891.6/2/34   *LC* 74-4797   *ISBN* 0670564419

O'Brien, Flann, 1911-1966. 2.9171
A Flann O'Brien reader / edited and with an introd. by Stephen Jones. — New York: Viking Press, 1978. xxix, 447 p.; 24 cm. 'A Richard Seaver book.' I. T.
PR6029.N56 F55 1978   828/.9/1209   *LC* 76-46968   *ISBN* 0670317403

Orczy, Emmuska Orczy, Baroness, 1865-1947. 2.9172
The old man in the corner: twelve mysteries / The Baroness Orczy; with an introd. by E. F. Bleiler. — New York: Dover Publications, 1980. ix, 162 p.; 22 cm. A collection of stories originally published in Royal magazine, 1901-1905. 1. Detective and mystery stories I. T.
PZ3.O65 Ok 1980 PR6029.R25 O6x   823/.912 19   *LC* 79-55295   *ISBN* 0486239721

PR6029 Orwell

Orwell, George, 1903-1950. • 2.9173
The collected essays, journalism, and letters of George Orwell. Edited by Sonia Orwell and Ian Angus. — [1st ed.]. — New York: Harcourt, Brace & World, [1968] 4 v.: facsims., ports.; 23 cm. I. T.
PR6029.R8 A6 1968   *LC* 68-12591

Orwell, George, 1903-1950. 2.9174
[Selections. 1985] Orwell, the lost writings / George Orwell; edited with an introduction by W.J. West. — New York: Arbor House, [1985] 304 p.; 24 cm. I. West, W. J. (William J.) II. T.
PR6029.R8 A6 1985   828/.91209 19   *LC* 85-9194   *ISBN* 0877957452

Orwell, George, 1903-1950. 2.9175
Orwell, the war commentaries / edited with an introduction by W.J. West. — New York: Pantheon Books, [1986] c1985. 253 p.: maps; 24 cm. 1. World War, 1939-1945 I. West, W. J. (William J.) II. T. III. Title: War commentaries.
PR6029.R8 A6 1986   940.53 19   *LC* 86-5057   *ISBN* 0394557018

Orwell, George, 1903-1950. • 2.9176
Animal farm; illustrated by Joy Batchelor and John Halas. New York, Harcourt, Brace [1954] 155 p. illus. 21 cm. I. T.
PR6029.R8A63 1954   *LC* 54-11330

Orwell, George, 1903-1950. • 2.9177
Burmese days; a novel. [New ed.] New York, Harcourt, Brace [1950, c1934] 287 p. 21 cm. I. T.
PZ3.O793Bu5 PR6029.R8B8 1950   *LC* 50-3534

Orwell, George, 1903-1950. • 2.9178
A clergyman's daughter / George Orwell. — New York: Harcourt, Brace, [1960] 320 p.; 21 cm. I. T.
PZ3.O793 Cl4   PR6029.R8 C4 1960.   *LC* 60-10943

Orwell, George, 1903-1950. • 2.9179
Coming up for air / George Orwell. — New York: Harcourt, Brace, Jovanovich, 1950. 278 p. A Harvest/HBJ book I. T.
PR6029.R8 C6 1950   *LC* 50-5002   *ISBN* 0156196255

Orwell, George, 1903-1950. • 2.9180
Down and out in Paris and London. — New York: Harper, 1933. 292 p.: ill. Illustrated lining-papers in color. 'First edition.' 1. Paris (France) — Social conditions. 2. Paris (France) — Poor. 3. London (England) — Social conditions. 4. London (England) — Poor. I. T.
PR6029.R8 D6 1933   *LC* 33-17928

Orwell, George, 1903-1950. • 2.9181
Keep the aspidistra flying / George Orwell. — New York: Harcourt, Brace, Jovanovich, [1956] 248 p.; 21 cm. — (A Harvest/HBJ book.) I. T.
PZ3.O793 Ke3   PR6029.R8 K44.   *ISBN* 0156468999

Orwell, George, 1903-1950. • 2.9182
The lion and the unicorn: socialism and the English genius. — London: Secker & Warburg, 1941. 126 p.; 19 cm. (Searchlight books; no. 1) 1. Socialism — Great Britain 2. Great Britain — Civilization 3. Great Britain — Social conditions I. T. II. Series.
PR6029.R8 L5 1941   *LC* a 41-3680

Hynes, Samuel Lynn. comp. 2.9183
Twentieth century interpretations of 1984; a collection of critical essays. Edited by Samuel Hynes. Englewood Cliffs, N.J., Prentice-Hall [1971] vi, 117 p. 21 cm. (Twentieth century interpretations) (A Spectrum book) 1. Orwell, George, 1903-1950. Nineteen eighty-four I. T.
PR6029.R8 N5346 1971   823/.9/12   *LC* 78-160533   *ISBN* 0136226051 *ISBN* 0136225977

On Nineteen eighty–four / edited by Peter Stansky.   **2.9184**
New York: W.H. Freeman, c1983. xi, 226 p.: ill.; 24 cm. 1. Orwell, George, 1903-1950 Nineteen eighty-four — Addresses, essays, lectures. I. Stansky, Peter. II. Title: On 1984.
PR6029.R8 N644 1983   823/.912 19   *LC* 83-20502   *ISBN* 0716716127

Orwell, George, 1903-1950.   **2.9185**
Nineteen eighty–four / George Orwell; with a critical introduction and annotations by Bernard Crick. — Oxford: Clarendon Press; New York: Oxford University Press, [1984] xi, 460 p.; 23 cm. Includes indexes. 1. Orwell, George, 1903-1950. Nineteen eighty-four I. Crick, Bernard R. II. T. III. Title: 1984.
PR6029.R8 N647 1984   823/.912 19   *LC* 83-17337   *ISBN* 0198185219

Steinhoff, William R.   **2.9186**
George Orwell and the origins of 1984 / William Steinhoff. — Ann Arbor: University of Michigan Press, [1975] 288 p.; 24 cm. Includes index. 1. Orwell, George, 1903-1950. Nineteen eighty-four I. T.
PR6029.R8 N67   823/.9/12   *LC* 74-78989   *ISBN* 0472874004

Orwell, George, 1903-1950.   • **2.9187**
The Orwell reader; fiction, essays, and reportage. With an introd. by Richard H. Rovere. — [1st ed.]. — New York: Harcourt, Brace, [1956] 456 p.; 22 cm. — I. T.
PR6029.R8 O7   828.91   *LC* 56-9137

Biography. Criticism

Brander, Laurence, 1903-.   • **2.9188**
George Orwell / L. Brander. — London: Longmans, Green, 1954. 212 p.: port. 1. Orwell, George, 1903-1950. I. T.
PR6029.R8 Z57   *LC* A55-2892

Alldritt, Keith.   • **2.9189**
The making of George Orwell; an essay in literary history. — New York: St. Martin's Press, [1969]. 181 p.; 23 cm. 1. Orwell, George, 1903-1950. I. T.
PR6029.R8 Z57 1969b   828/.9/1209   *LC* 69-17404

Bolton, W. F. (Whitney French), 1930-.   **2.9190**
The language of 1984: Orwell's English and ours / W.F. Bolton. — Knoxville: University of Tennessee Press, [1984] 252 p.; 23 cm. Includes indexes. 1. Orwell, George, 1903-1950 — Language. 2. English language — 20th century I. T.
PR6029.R8 Z588 1984   823/.912 19   *LC* 83-21671   *ISBN* 0870494120

Calder, Jenni.   **2.9191**
Chronicles of conscience; a study of George Orwell and Arthur Koestler. — [Pittsburgh]: University of Pittsburgh Press, [1968] 303 p.; 20 cm. — (Critical essays in modern literature) (Pitt paperback, 49.) 1. Orwell, George, 1903-1950. 2. Koestler, Arthur, 1905- I. T.
PR6029.R8 Z6 1968b   823/.9/1209   *LC* 69-12146

Crick, Bernard R.   **2.9192**
George Orwell, a life / Bernard Crick. — 1st American ed. — Boston: Little, Brown, 1981 (c1980). xxx, 473 p., [16] p. of plates: ill.; 24 cm. 'An Atlantic Monthly Press book.' 1. Orwell, George, 1903-1950 — Biography. 2. Authors, English — 20th century — Biography. I. T.
PR6029.R8 Z627   828/.91209 B 19   *LC* 80-85096   *ISBN* 0316161128

George Orwell: the critical heritage / edited by Jeffrey Meyers.   **2.9193**
London; Boston: Routledge & K. Paul, 1975. xiv, 392 p.; 23 cm. (The Critical heritage series) Includes index. 1. Orwell, George, 1903-1950 — Criticism and interpretation — Addresses, essays, lectures. I. Meyers, Jeffrey.
PR6029.R8 Z64   828/.9/1209   *LC* 75-332644   *ISBN* 071008255X

Hammond, J. R. (John R.), 1933-.   **2.9194**
A George Orwell companion: a guide to the novels, documentaries, and essays / J.R. Hammond. — New York: St. Martin's Press, 1982. xii, 278 p., [4] leaves of plates: ill.; 23 cm. Includes index. 1. Orwell, George, 1903-1950 — Criticism and interpretation. I. T.
PR6029.R8 Z663 1982   828/.91209 19   *LC* 82-875   *ISBN* 0312324529

Atkins, John Alfred, 1916-.   • **2.9195**
George Orwell; a literary study, by John Atkins. London, J. Calder [1954] 348 p. 22 cm. 1. Orwell, George, 1903-1950. I. T.
PR6029.R8 Z67 1954   820.81   *LC* a 55-3453

Hollis, Christopher, 1902-1977.   • **2.9196**
A study of George Orwell: the man and his works. — London: Hollis and Carter, [1956] 212 p.; 23 cm. 1. Orwell, George, 1903-1950. I. T.
PR6029.R8 Z68 1956a   *LC* 57-3398

Lief, Ruth Ann.   **2.9197**
Homage to Oceania; the prophetic vision of George Orwell. — [Columbus]: Ohio State University Press, [1969] viii, 162 p.; 25 cm. 1. Orwell, George, 1903-1950. I. T.
PR6029.R8 Z73   823/.9/12   *LC* 68-28811

Remembering Orwell / conceived and compiled by Stephen   **2.9198**
Wadhams; introduction by George Woodcock.
Markham, Ont.: Penguin Canada, 1984. xix, 227 p. Based on interviews recorded for the CBC radio program 'George Orwell: a radio biography', broadcast Jan. 1984. Includes index. 1. Orwell, George, 1903-1950. 2. Authors, English — 20th century — Biography. I. Wadhams, Stephen.
PR6029.R8 Z749   828/.91209 19   *ISBN* 0140074589

Sandison, Alan.   **2.9199**
George Orwell: after 1984 / Alan Sandison. — 2nd ed. — Houndmills, Basingstoke, Hampshire: Macmillan; Dover, N.H.: Longwood Academic, 1986. 232 p.; 23 cm. — (Macmillan studies in twentieth-century literature.) Rev. ed. of: The last man in Europe. 1974. Includes index. 1. Orwell, George, 1903-1950 — Criticism and interpretation. I. Sandison, Alan. Last man in Europe. II. T. III. Series.
PR6029.R8 Z78 1986   828/.91209 19   *LC* 85-19893   *ISBN* 0333386256

Smyer, Richard I., 1935-.   **2.9200**
Primal dream and primal crime: Orwell's development as a psychological novelist / Richard I. Smyer. — Columbia: University of Missouri Press, 1979. viii, 187 p.; 24 cm. Includes index. 1. Orwell, George, 1903-1950 — Criticism and interpretation. I. T.
PR6029.R8 Z789   823/.9/12   *LC* 79-4840   *ISBN* 0826202829

Stansky, Peter.   **2.9201**
Orwell, the transformation / Peter Stansky and William Abrahams. — 1st American ed. — New York: Knopf, 1980, c1979. 302 p., [2] leaves of plates: ill.; 22 cm. The second half of Orwell's biography, begun with The unknown Orwell. 1. Orwell, George, 1903-1950. 2. Authors, English — 20th century — Biography. I. Abrahams, William Miller, 1919- joint author. II. T.
PR6029.R8 Z7898 1980   828/.9/1209 B   *LC* 79-3490   *ISBN* 0394473949

Stansky, Peter.   **2.9202**
The unknown Orwell [by] Peter Stansky and William Abrahams. — [1st ed.]. — New York: Knopf, 1972. xx, 316, xiii p.: illus.; 22 cm. 1. Orwell, George, 1903-1950. I. Abrahams, William Miller, 1919- joint author. II. T.
PR6029.R8 Z79   828/.9/1209 B   *LC* 72-2245   *ISBN* 0394473930

Williams, Raymond. comp.   **2.9203**
George Orwell; a collection of critical essays. — Englewood Cliffs, N.J.: Prentice-Hall, [1974] viii, 182 p.; 21 cm. — (A Spectrum book. Twentieth century views) 1. Orwell, George, 1903-1950 — Criticism and interpretation. I. T.
PR6029.R8 Z865   828/.9/1209   *LC* 74-11153   *ISBN* 0136477194

Woodcock, George, 1912-.   • **2.9204**
The crystal spirit; a study of George Orwell. — [1st ed.]. — Boston: Little, Brown, [1966] vii, 366 p.; 22 cm. 1. Orwell, George, 1903-1950. I. T.
PR6029.R8 Z9   828.91208   *LC* 66-20803

The World of George Orwell / Edited by Miriam Gross.   **2.9205**
New York: Simon and Schuster, [1972, c1971] 182 p.: ill.; 26 cm. 1. Orwell, George, 1903-1950. 2. Authors, English — 20th century — Biography. I. Gross, Miriam, ed.
PR6029.R8 Z92 1972   828/.91209 B   *LC* 73-164705   *ISBN* 0671211242

Zwerdling, Alex.   **2.9206**
Orwell and the Left / Alex Zwerdling. — New Haven: Yale University Press, 1974. xii, 215 p.; 22 cm. 1. Orwell, George, 1903-1950 — Political and social views. I. T.
PR6029.R8 Z97   828/.9/1209   *LC* 74-75951   *ISBN* 0300016867

PR6029 Osborne

Osborne, John, 1929-.   • **2.9207**
The entertainer: a play / John Osborne. — New York: Criterion Books, 1958. 89 p. I. T.
PR6029.S39.E6 1958a   822.91   *LC* 58-6810

Osborne, John, 1929-.   • **2.9208**
Epitaph for George Dillon: a play in three acts / by John Osborne and Anthony Creighton. New York: Criterion Books [1958]. 94 p. I. Creighton, Anthony. II. T.
PR6029.S39 E64   822   *LC* 58-13808

Osborne, John, 1929-.   • **2.9209**
Inadmissible evidence; a play. — New York: Grove Press, [1965] 115 p.: illus.;
21 cm. — I. T.
PR6029.S39 I5 1965   822.914   LC 65-27394

Osborne, John, 1929-.   • **2.9210**
Look back in anger, a play in three acts. — New York: Criterion Books, [1957]
96 p.; 21 cm. — I. T.
PR6029.S39 L6 1957a   822.91   LC 57-9161

Osborne, John, 1929-.   • **2.9211**
Luther, a play. — [1st American ed.]. — New York: Criterion Books, [1962,
c1961] 102 p.; 21 cm. 1. Luther, Martin — Drama.
PR6029.S39 L8 1962   822.914   LC 62-8939

Osborne, John, 1929-.   • **2.9212**
Plays for England: The blood of the Bambergs [and] Under plain cover. The
world of Paul Slickey. New York, Grove Press [1966] 217 p. 18 cm. I. T.
II. Title: The blood of the Bambergs. III. Title: Under plain cover. IV. Title:
The world of Paul Slickey.
PR6029.S39 P5 1966   LC 66-14105

Osborne, John, 1929-.   • **2.9213**
A subject of scandal and concern, a play for television. — London, Faber and
Faber [1961] 47 p. 20 cm. I. T.
PR6029.S39 S8   LC A 62-336

Osborne, John, 1929-.   • **2.9214**
West of Suez. A patriot for me. Time present. The hotel in Amsterdam. Four
plays by John Osborne. — New York: Dodd, Mead, [1973] 311 p.; 22 cm. —
I. T.
PR6029.S39 W4 1973   822/.9/14   LC 72-3920   ISBN 0396066593

Trussler, Simon.   • **2.9215**
The plays of John Osborne: an assessment. — London, Gollancz, 1969. 252 p.
21 cm. 1. Osborne, John, 1929- I. T.
PR6029.S39 Z9   822/.9/14   LC 73-409379   ISBN 575002670 42/-

PR6029 Owen

Owen, Wilfred.   **2.9216**
The complete poems and fragments / Wilfred Owen; edited by Jon Stallworthy.
— 1st American ed. — New York: W.W. Norton, 1984. 2 v. (xxvi, 560 p.)
I. Stallworthy, Jon. II. T.
PR6029.W4 Ax   821/.912 19   ISBN 039301830X

Owen, Wilfred, 1893-1918.   • **2.9217**
Collected letters / edited by Harold Owen and John Bell. — London: Oxford
University Press, 1967. — 629 p.: ill., facsims., geneal. table.; 26 cm. 1. Owen,
Wilfred, 1893-1918. I. Owen, William Harold, 1897- II. Bell, John. III. T.
PR6029.W4 Z48 1967   LC 67-114870

Owen, William Harold, 1897-.   • **2.9218**
Journey from obscurity: Wilfred Owen, 1893–1918: memoirs of the Owen
family. — London, New York, Oxford University Press, 1963-1965. 3 v.: ill.; 23
cm. 1. Owen, Wilfred, 1893-1918. 2. Owen family I. T.
PR6029.W4 Z8   928.2   LC 63-5999

Welland, Dennis Sydney Reginald.   • **2.9219**
Wilfred Owen; a critical study. London, Chatto & Windus, 1960. 158 p. 21 cm.
1. Owen, Wilfred, 1893-1918. I. T.
PR 6029 W46Z7 W44 1960   LC 61-1940

PR6031 P–Pl

Peake, Mervyn Laurence, 1911-1968.   **2.9220**
The Gormenghast trilogy [by] Mervyn Peake. — [Rev. ed.]. — New York:
Weybright and Talley, [1967] 3 v.: illus.; 24 cm. I. T. II. Title: Titus Groan.
III. Title: Gormenghast. IV. Title: Titus alone.
PR6031.E183 G6x   LC 67-26053

Pearse, Padraic, 1879-1916.   **2.9221**
Collected works of Pádraic H. Pearse: plays, stories, poems. — 1st AMS ed. —
New York: AMS Press, 1978. xix, 340, viii p.: port.; 19 cm. Reprint of the 1917
ed. published by Phoenix Pub. Co., Dublin. I. T.
PR6031.E2 1978   828/.9/1209   LC 75-28838   ISBN 0404138276

Porter, Raymond J.   **2.9222**
P. H. Pearse, by Raymond J. Porter. — New York: Twayne, [1973] 168 p.; 22
cm. — (Twayne's English authors series, TEAS 154) 1. Pearse, Padraic,
1879-1916 — Criticism and interpretation. I. T.
PR6031.E2 Z83   828/.9/1209   LC 72-13377

Plomer, William, 1903-1973.   • **2.9223**
Collected poems / William Plomer. — London: J. Cape, 1960. 225 p. I. T.
PR6031.L7 A6 1960   LC 60-4557

Plomer, William, 1903-1973.   **2.9224**
The autobiography of William Plomer / with a postscript by Simon Nowell–
Smith. — New York: Taplinger Pub. Co., 1976, c1975. 455 p., [6] leaves of
plates: ill.; 23 cm. 1. Plomer, William, 1903-1973 — Biography. I. T.
PR6031.L7 Z524 1976   828 B 19   LC 75-10548   ISBN 0800805437

PR6031 Powell

Powell, Anthony, 1905-.   • **2.9225**
A dance to the music of time: A question of upbringing. A buyer's market. The
acceptance world. Boston, Little, Brown [1962] 229, 274, 214 p. 21 cm. I. T.
II. Title: A question of upbringing. III. Title: A buyer's market. IV. Title: The
acceptance world.
PZ3.P867Dan PR6031.O74D3   LC 62-8063

Powell, Anthony, 1905-.   • **2.9226**
A dance to the music of time: second movement / by Anthony Powell. —
Boston: Little, Brown, 1964. 239, 229, 254 p. — (The Music of time) I. Powell,
Anthony, 1905- At Lady Molly's. II. Powell, Anthony, 1905- Casanova's
Chinese restaurant. III. Powell, Anthony, 1905- The kindly ones. IV. T.
V. Series.
PR6031.O74 D3 1962   LC 64-11443   ISBN 0316715360

Powell, Anthony, 1905-.   **2.9227**
A dance to the music of time: third movement. — Boston: Little, Brown, [1971]
242, 227, 243 p.; 21 cm. — (His The music of time) 1. World War, 1939-1945
— Fiction. I. T.
PR6031.O74 D33   823/.9/12   LC 70-161417

Powell, Anthony, 1905-.   **2.9228**
A dance to the music of time: fourth movement / by Anthony Powell. — 1st ed.
— Boston: Little, Brown, [1976] 240, 280, 272 p.; 21 cm. I. T.
PZ3.P867 Daq3 PR6031.O74 D4x   823/.9/12   LC 75-34418
     ISBN 0316715484

Powell, Anthony, 1905-.   **2.9229**
The strangers all are gone. — New York: Holt, 1983. 208 p., [16] p. of plates:
ill.; 24 cm. — (To keep the ball rolling: the memoirs of Anthony Powell; v. 4)
Includes index. 1. Powell, Anthony, 1905- — Biography. 2. Novelists, English
— 20th century — Biography. I. T.
PR6031.O74 Z476 1983   823/.912 B 19   LC 82-23363

Powell, Anthony, 1905-.   **2.9230**
Faces in my time. — New York: Holt, Rinehart and Winston, 1981, c1980. viii,
230 p., [8] leaves of plates: ill.; 24 cm. — (His The memoirs of Anthony Powell;
v. 3) Includes index. 1. Powell, Anthony, 1905- — Biography. 2. Novelists,
English — 20th century — Biography. I. T.
PR6031.O74 Z514 1981   823/.912 B   LC 80-14843   ISBN
0030210011

Powell, Anthony, 1905-.   **2.9231**
Infants of the spring. — New York: Holt, Rinehart and Winston, 1977, c1976.
214 p. [8] p.: ill.; 24 cm. — (His The memoirs of Anthony Powell; [1]) Includes
index. 1. Powell, Anthony, 1905- — Biography. 2. Novelists, English — 20th
century — Biography. I. T. II. Title: Memoirs of Anthony Powell.
PR6031.O74 Z516 1977   823/.912 B 19   LC 77-71357   ISBN
0030209919

Powell, Anthony, 1905-.   **2.9232**
Messengers of day. — New York: Holt, Rinehart, and Winston, 1978. 209 p.,
[8] leaves of plates: ill.; 24 cm. (His The memoirs of Anthony Powell; v. 2)
Includes index. 1. Powell, Anthony, 1905- — Biography — London life.
2. Novelists, English — 20th century — Biography. 3. London (England) —
Intellectual life I. T. II. Title: Memoirs of Anthony Powell.
PR6031.O74 Z52 1978   823/.9/12 B   LC 78-4703   ISBN
003020996X

Russell, John David.   **2.9233**
Anthony Powell, a quintet, sextet, and war [by] John Russell. — Bloomington:
Indiana University Press, [1970] xi, 238 p.; 22 cm. 1. Powell, Anthony, 1905-
I. T.
PR6031.O74 Z9   823/.9/12   LC 71-126217   ISBN 0253104106

Morris, Robert K.   **2.9234**
The novels of Anthony Powell / [by] Robert K. Morris. — [Pittsburgh]:
University of Pittsburgh Press, [1968]. xi, 252 p.; 20 cm. — (Critical essays in
modern literature.) (Pitt paperbacks; 32) 1. Powell, Anthony, 1905- I. T.
II. Series. III. Series: Pitt paperbacks; 32
PR6031.O86 Z74   823.912   LC 68-12728

PR6031 Powys

Powys, John Cowper, 1872-1963. • 2.9235
A Glastonbury romance. London: Macdonald, 1955. 1120 p. , 21 cm. I. T.
PZ3.P8758 G12   PR6031.O867 Gx.   *LC* 56-1864

Powys, John Cowper, 1872-1963. • 2.9236
Wolf Solent; a novel. New York, Simon and Schuster, 1929. — St. Clair Shores, Mich.: Scholarly Press, 1971. 2 v. (966 p.); 22 cm. — I. T.
PZ3.P8758 Wol15 PR6031.O867 W6x   823/.9/12   *LC* 75-145244
ISBN 0403011590

Powys, John Cowper, 1872-1963. • 2.9237
Autobiography. [New York] New Directions, 1960. 652 p. illus. 23 cm. I. T.
PR6031.O867 Z5 1960   *LC* 60-9295

Brebner, John Alexander. 2.9238
The demon within; a study of John Cowper Powys's novels [by] John A. Brebner. — New York: Barnes & Noble, 1974 [c1973] xi, 248 p.; 23 cm. 1. Powys, John Cowper, 1872-1963 — Criticism and interpretation. I. T.
PR6031.O867 Z58 1973b   823/.9/12   *LC* 74-160964   *ISBN* 006490654X

Cavaliero, Glen, 1927-. 2.9239
John Cowper Powys: novelist. — Oxford: Clarendon Press, 1973. ix, 195 p.; 22 cm. 1. Powys, John Cowper, 1872-1963 — Criticism and interpretation. I. T.
PR6031.O867 Z63   823/.9/12   *LC* 74-156784   *ISBN* 0198120494

Hopkins, Kenneth. 2.9240
The Powys brothers; a biographical appreciation. — Rutherford, N.J.: Fairleigh Dickinson University Press, [1967] x, 275 p.: illus., ports.; 24 cm. 1. Powys, John Cowper, 1872-1963. 2. Powys, Llewelyn, 1884-1939. 3. Powys, Theodore Francis, 1875-1953. I. T.
PR6031.O876 Z73 1967b   820.9/0091/2   *LC* 68-10855

PR6031 Pr

Press, John. • 2.9241
Uncertainties and other poems. London, Oxford University Press, 1956. 103 p. English poetry. I. T.
PR6031.R4 U5   821

Priestley, J. B. (John Boynton), 1894-. • 2.9242
Plays. — London: Heinemann, [1948-1950] 3 v. I. T.
PR6031.R6 A19   *LC* a 51-8183

Priestley, J. B. (John Boynton), 1894-. • 2.9243
Angel pavement, by J. B. Priestley. Boston, Little, Brown [1967, c1930] xii, 608 p. 21 cm. 'An Atlantic Monthly Press book.' I. T.
PR6031.R6 Ax   PZ3.P934 An15   *LC* 67-11214

Priestley, J. B. (John Boynton), 1894-. • 2.9244
Delight, by J. B. Priestley. Freeport, N.Y., Books for Libraries Press [1971, c1949] xvi, 170 p. 23 cm. (Essay index reprint series) I. T.
PR6031.R6 D38 1971   824/.9/12   *LC* 70-117828   *ISBN* 0836920155

Priestley, J. B. (John Boynton), 1894-. • 2.9245
Festival. [1st American ed.] New York, Harper [1951] 607 p. This story is published in England under the title of Festival at Farbridge. I. T.
PR6031.R6 Fx   *LC* 51-2104

Priestley, J. B. (John Boynton), 1894-. • 2.9246
The good companions, by J. B. Priestley. New York, Harper & Brothers, 1929. 640 p. 22 cm. I. T.
PR6031.R6 G6   *LC* 30-38

Priestley, J. B. (John Boynton), 1894-. • 2.9247
The image men [by] J. B. Priestley. [1st American ed.] Boston, Little, Brown [1969] xi, 492 p. 25 cm. 'An Atlantic Monthly Press book.' I. T.
PZ3.P934 Im3 PR6031.R6   823/.9/12   *LC* 69-15075

Priestley, J. B. (John Boynton), 1894-. • 2.9248
Midnight on the desert, being an excursion into autobiography during a winter in America, 1935-36. New York, Harper, 1937. 310 p. 1. West (U.S.) — Description and travel I. T.
PR6031.R6 M5 1937a   928.2   *LC* 37-4255

Priestley, J. B. (John Boynton), 1894-. • 2.9249
Rain upon Godshill: a further chapter of autobiography / by J. B. Priestley. London: Heinemann, [1939] 330 p.; 22 cm. 1. Priestley, J. B. (John Boynton), 1894- I. T.
PR6031.R6 R3 1939   *LC* 39-30218

Priestley, J. B. (John Boynton), 1894-. • 2.9250
Margin released; a writer's reminiscences and reflections. [1st ed.] New York, Harper & Row [c1962] 236 p. illus. 22 cm. 1. Authors — Correspondence, reminiscences, etc. I. T.
PR6031.R6 Z52   828.912   *LC* 62-20114

Atkins, John Alfred, 1916-. 2.9251
J. B. Priestley: the last of the sages / by John Atkins. — London: J. Calder; New York: Riverrun Press, 1981. ix, 309 p.: ports.; 23 cm. Includes index. 1. Priestley, J. B. (John Boynton), 1894- — Biography. 2. Authors, English — 20th century — Biography. I. T.
PR6031.R6 Z557   828/.91209 B   *LC* 79-41354   *ISBN* 0714538043

Hughes, David, 1930-. • 2.9252
J. B. Priestley, an informal study of his work. Freeport, N.Y., Books for Libraries Press [1970, c1958] 226 p. port. 23 cm. 1. Priestley, J. B. (John Boynton), 1894- I. T.
PR6031.R6 Z57 1970   813/.5/2   *LC* 73-128879   *ISBN* 0836954998

Pritchett, V. S. (Victor Sawdon), 1900-. 2.9253
A man of letters: selected essays / V.S. Pritchett. — 1st American ed. — New York: Random House, c1985. xii, 305 p. 1. Books — Reviews 2. Literature, Modern — Book reviews. I. T.
PR6031.R7 A6 1985b   809/.03 19   *LC* 85-25757   *ISBN* 0394549821

Pritchett, V. S. (Victor Sawdon), 1900-. • 2.9254
A cab at the door; a memoir, by V. S. Pritchett. New York, Random House [1968] 244 p. 22 cm. I. T.
PR6031.R7 Z5 1968b   828/.9/1203   *LC* 68-14504

Pritchett, V. S. (Victor Sawdon), 1900-. 2.9255
Midnight oil. — New York: Random House, c1972. 271 p. (HIS autobiography, v.2) 1. Pritchett, V. S. (Victor Sawdon), 1900- I. T.
PR6031.R7 Z52x   *LC* 76-37074   *ISBN* 0394474759

PR6033 Q

Quennell, Peter, 1905-. • 2.9256
The sign of the fish. New York, Viking Press [1960] 255 p. illus. 22 cm. 1. Authors — Correspondence, reminiscences, etc. 2. Literature — Addresses, essays, lectures. I. T.
PR6033.U4 S5   *LC* 60-6786

PR6035 R–Re

Raine, Kathleen, 1908-. • 2.9257
Collected poems. — London, H. Hamilton [1956] xv, 175 p. 21 cm. I. T.
PR6035.A37 A6 1956   821.91   *LC* 56-4285

Rattigan, Terence, 1911-. • 2.9258
The collected plays of Terence Rattigan. — London: H. Hamilton, [1953-1964] 3 v. I. T.
PR6035.A75 1953   *ISBN* 0241899966

Read, Herbert Edward, Sir, 1893-1968. • 2.9259
Collected poems, by Herbert Read. 1st American ed. New York: Horizon Press, 1966. 286 p.; 21 cm. I. T.
PR6035.E24 A17 1966   *LC* 66-16298

Read, Herbert Edward, Sir, 1893-1968. • 2.9260
The green child / Herbert Read; with an introd. by Kenneth Rexroth. — New York: New Directions, [1948] 193 p.; 21 cm. — (A New Directions book) I. T.
PR6035.E24 G7 1948   *LC* 48-9595

Redgrove, Peter. 2.9261
Sons of my skin: Redgrove's selected poems, 1954–1974 / chosen and introduced by Marie Peel. — London; Boston: Routledge & Paul, 1975. 200 p.; 23 cm. Includes index. I. T.
PR6035.E267 A17 1975   821/.9/14   *LC* 75-324416   *ISBN* 0710080735

Reeves, James. 2.9262
[Poems. Selections] Collected poems, 1929–1959 / James Reeves. — London: Heinemann, 1960. 191 p., [1] leaf of plates: port.; 22 cm. Includes indexes. I. T.
PR6035.E38 A6 1960   821/.912 19   *LC* 82-182277

Reid, Alastair, 1926-. • 2.9263
Passwords: places, poems, preoccupations. — [1st ed.]. — Boston: Little, Brown, [1963] 238 p.; 22 cm. I. T.
PR6035.E4 P3   *LC* 63-13981

Renault, Mary.   2.9264
The mask of Apollo. [1st American ed.] New York, Pantheon Books [1966]
371 p. 22 cm. 1. Greece — History — To 146 B.C. — Fiction. I. T.
PZ3.R2913 Mas2   PR6035.E53.M3.   *LC* 66-24894

Renault, Mary.   2.9265
Fire from heaven. New York, Pantheon Books [1969] 375 p. map (on lining
papers) 22 cm. 1. Alexander, the Great, 356-323 B.C — Fiction. 2. Philip II,
King of Macedonia, 382-336 B.C — Fiction. I. T.
PZ3.R2913 Fi PR6035.E55   823/.9/12   *LC* 72-98035

Renault, Mary.   • 2.9266
The bull from the sea. [New York] Pantheon Books [1962] 343 p. 22 cm.
1. Theseus (Greek mythology) — Fiction. I. T.
PZ3.R2913 Bu   PR6035.E55 Bx.   *LC* 62-8924

Renault, Mary.   • 2.9267
The last of the wine. — [New York]: Pantheon, [1956] 389 p.: illus.; 22 cm.
1. Greece — History — Fiction. I. T.
PZ3.R2913 Las2   PR6035.E55 Lx.   *LC* 56-10409

Renault, Mary.   2.9268
The Persian boy. [1st ed.] New York, Pantheon Books [1972] 419 p. maps. 22
cm. 1. Alexander, the Great, 356-323 B.C — Fiction. I. T.
PZ3.R2913 Pe PR6035.E55 P4x   823/.9/12   *LC* 72-3407   *ISBN*
0394481917

Dick, Bernard F.   2.9269
The Hellenism of Mary Renault [by] Bernard F. Dick. With a pref. by Harry T.
Moore. — Carbondale: Southern Illinois University Press, [1972] xix, 135 p.; 22
cm. — (Crosscurrents/modern critiques) 1. Renault, Mary. I. T.
PR6035.E55 Z63   823/.9/12   *LC* 71-188696   *ISBN* 0809305763

Wolfe, Peter, 1933-.   2.9270
Mary Renault. — New York: Twayne Publishers, [c1969] 198 p.; 21 cm. —
(Twayne's English authors series, 98) 1. Renault, Mary, pseud. — Criticism
and interpretation. I. T.
PR6035.E55 Z95   823/.9/12 B   *LC* 70-98029

PR6035 Rh–Rz

Rhys, Jean.   2.9271
[Novels. 1985] Jean Rhys, the complete novels. — New York: Norton, 1985. p.
cm. I. T.
PR6035.H96 A15 1985   823/.912 19   *LC* 85-4996

Rhys, Jean.   • 2.9272
After leaving Mr. Mackenzie. — New York: Harper & Row, [1972, c1931]
191 p.; 22 cm. — I. T.
PZ3.R3494 Af8 PR6035.H96 A4x   823/.9/12   *LC* 79-160658
    ISBN 0060135344

Rhys, Jean.   2.9273
Jean Rhys: the collected short stories / introduction by Diana Athill. — New
York, London: Norton, 1987. 403 p.; 21 cm. — I. T.
PR6035.H96 Ax   *ISBN* 0393023753

Rhys, Jean.   • 2.9274
Good morning, midnight. [1st U.S. ed.] New York, Harper & Row [1970?]
189 p. 22 cm. I. T.
PR6035.H96G6 1970   823/.9/12   *LC* 78-96002

Rhys, Jean.   • 2.9275
Voyage in the dark / Jean Rhys. — London: Constable, [1934] 218 p.; 19 cm.
I. T.
PR6035.H96 V6 1934   823/.912 19   *LC* 35-945

Rhys, Jean.   • 2.9276
Wide Sargasso Sea. Introd. by Francis Wyndham. New York, Norton [1967,
c1966] 189 p. 22 cm. I. T.
PR6035.H96 Wx   PZ7.R3478Wi   *LC* 67-15822

Rhys, Jean.   2.9277
[Correspondence] The letters of Jean Rhys / selected and edited by Francis
Wyndham and Diana Melly. — 1st American ed. — New York, NY: Viking,
1984. 315 p.; 24 cm. 'Elisabeth Sifton books.' Includes indexes. 1. Rhys, Jean.
Correspondence 2. Novelists, English — 20th century — Correspondence.
I. Wyndham, Francis. II. Melly, Diana. III. T.
PR6035.H96 Z48 1984   823/.912 B 19   *LC* 83-40244   *ISBN*
0670427268

Angier, Carole, 1943-.   2.9278
Jean Rhys / Carole Angier. — New York, N.Y., U.S.A.: Viking, 1985. 125,
[1] p., [8] p. of plates: ill.; 23 cm. (Lives of modern women.) 1. Rhys, Jean.

2. Novelists, English — 20th century — Biography. 3. Women in literature
I. T. II. Series.
PR6035.H96 Z62 1985   823/.912 B 19   *LC* 85-51189   *ISBN*
0670806269

James, Louis.   2.9279
Jean Rhys / [by] Louis James. — London: Longman, 1978. [6], 74 p.; 21 cm. —
(Critical studies of Caribbean writers) 1. Rhys, Jean — Criticism and
interpretation. I. T. II. Series.
PR6035.H96 Z73   823/.9/12   *LC* 79-310602   *ISBN* 0582785057

Nebeker, Helen.   2.9280
Jean Rhys, woman in passage: a critical study of the novels of Jean Rhys /
Helen Nebeker. — 1st ed. — Montréal; St. Albans, Vt.: Eden Press Women's
Publications, c1981. xi, 223 p.: port.; 21 cm. Includes index. 1. Rhys, Jean —
Criticism and interpretation. I. T.
PR6035.H96 Z8 1981   823/.912 19   *LC* 81-165107   *ISBN*
0920792049

Staley, Thomas F.   2.9281
Jean Rhys, a critical study / Thomas F. Staley. — Austin: University of Texas
Press, 1980 (c1979). xiii, 140 p.; 23 cm. Includes index. 1. Rhys, Jean —
Criticism and interpretation. I. T.
PR6035.H96 Z87   823/.912   *LC* 79-88248   *ISBN* 029274014X

Richards, I. A. (Ivor Armstrong), 1893-.   2.9282
New & selected poems / [by] I. A. Richards. — Manchester: Carcanet New
Press, 1978. 124 p.; 20 cm. Stamped on t.p.: Distributed in the U.S. by Dufour
Editions, Inc. I. T.
PR6035.I337 N4   821/.9/12   *LC* 78-317055   *ISBN* 0856352411

Richardson, Dorothy Miller, 1873-1957.   • 2.9283
Pilgrimage [by] Dorothy M. Richardson. With an introd. by Walter Allen. —
New York: Knopf, 1967. 4 v.; 21 cm. I. T.
PR6035.I34 Px   PZ3.R3937 Pi5   *LC* 66-22423

Fromm, Gloria G., 1931-.   2.9284
Dorothy Richardson: a biography / Gloria G. Fromm. — Urbana: University
of Illinois Press, c1977. xix, 451 p.: ill.; 24 cm. Includes index. 1. Richardson,
Dorothy Miller, 1873-1957. 2. Novelists, English — 20th century —
Biography. I. T.
PR6035.I34 Z68   823/.9/12 B   *LC* 77-8455   *ISBN* 0252006313

Hanscombe, Gillian E.   2.9285
The art of life: Dorothy Richardson and the development of feminist
consciousness / Gillian E. Hanscombe. — Athens, Ohio: Ohio University
Press, 1983, c1982. 200 p.; 23 cm. 1. Richardson, Dorothy Miller, 1873-1957.
Pilgrimage. 2. Richardson, Dorothy Miller, 1873-1957 — Political and social
views. 3. Feminism and literature I. T.
PR6035.I34 Z72 1983   823/.912 19   *LC* 82-22589   *ISBN*
0821407392

Staley, Thomas F.   2.9286
Dorothy Richardson / by Thomas F. Staley. — Boston: Twayne Publishers,
c1976. 145 p.; 21 cm. (Twayne's English authors series; TEAS 187) Includes
index. 1. Richardson, Dorothy Miller, 1873-1957 — Criticism and
interpretation. I. T.
PR6035.I34 Z93   823/.9/12   *LC* 76-8009   *ISBN* 0805766626

Ridler, Anne, 1912-.   • 2.9287
Selected poems. New York, Macmillan, 1961. 96 p. 22 cm. I. T.
PR6035.I54 A17 1961   *LC* 61-11095

Rosenberg, Isaac, 1890-1918.   2.9288
The collected works of Isaac Rosenberg: poetry, prose, letters, paintings, and
drawings / with a foreword by Siegfried Sassoon; edited with an introd. and
notes by Ian Parsons. — New York: Oxford University Press, 1979. xxxii,
320 p., [16] leaves of plates: ill.; 25 cm. Includes indexes. I. Parsons, I. M. (Ian
Macnaghten) II. T.
PR6035.O67 1979b   821/.9/12   *LC* 78-78341

Russell, George William, 1867-1935.   • 2.9289
Collected poems / by A.E. — London: Macmillan, 1913. xv, 275 p.; 20 cm.
Title page has embossed seal: 'Presentation copy.' I. T.
PR6035.U7 A17 1913   *LC* a 14-2514

Russell, George William, 1867-1935.   2.9290
Deirdre, a legend in three acts. Introd. by Herbert V. Fackler. — Chicago: De
Paul University, 1970. 34 p.; 22 cm. — (Irish drama series, v. 4) I. Fackler,
Herbert V. II. T.
PR6035.U7 D4 1970   822   *LC* 72-18457

Russell, George William, 1867-1935.   • 2.9291
Vale and other poems / by A.E. — London: Macmillan, 1931. viii, 56 p.; 20 cm.
I. T.
PR6035.U7 V3 1931   *LC* 31-6127

Russell, George William, 1867-1935.   2.9292
Letters from AE. / selected and edited by Alan Denson; with a foreword by Monk Gibbon. — London; New York: Abelard-Schuman, [1962, c1961]. 288 p.: ill.; 23 cm. Includes index. 1. Russell, George William, 1867-1935 — Correspondence. I. Denson, Alan. II. T.
PR6035.U7 Z54   928.2   *LC* 60-13700

Summerfield, Henry.   2.9293
That myriad–minded man; a biography of George William Russell 'A. E.,' 1867-1935. Totowa, N.J.: Rowman and Littlefield, 1976 (c1975) xiii, 354 p.: illus.; 23 cm. 1. Russell, George William, 1867-1935 — Biography. I. T.
PR6035.U7 Z83   828/.8/09 B   *LC* 74-2161   *ISBN* 0874715369

PR6037 S–Sa

Sackville-West, V. (Victoria), 1892-1962.   2.9294
All passion spent / by V. Sackville–West. — [1st ed.]. — Garden City, N.Y.: Doubleday, Doran, 1931. 294 p.; 22 cm. I. T.
PR6037.A35 Ax   *LC* 31-28061

Sackville-West, V. (Victoria), 1892-1962.   2.9295
The Edwardians. Garden City, N.Y. Doubleday, Doran & company, inc., 1930. 5 p. l., 314 p. 21 cm. I. T.
PR6037.A35 Ex   *LC* 30-26888

Sackville-West, V. (Victoria), 1892-1962.   2.9296
[Correspondence. Selections] The letters of Vita Sackville–West to Virginia Woolf / edited by Louise DeSalvo and Mitchell A. Leaska; with an introduction by Mitchell A. Leaska. — 1st ed. — New York: Morrow, c1985. 448 p.: ill.; 25 cm. Includes index. 1. Sackville-West, V. (Victoria), 1892-1962 — Correspondence. 2. Woolf, Virginia, 1882-1941. Correspondence 3. Authors, English — 20th century — Correspondence. I. Woolf, Virginia, 1882-1941. II. DeSalvo, Louise A., 1942- III. Leaska, Mitchell Alexander. IV. T.
PR6037.A35 Z497 1985   823/.912 B 19   *LC* 84-60758   *ISBN* 0688039634

Glendinning, Victoria.   2.9297
Vita: the life of V. Sackville–West / Victoria Glendinning. — 1st American ed. — New York: Knopf, 1983. xviii, 436 p., [32] p. of plates: ill.; 25 cm. 1. Sackville-West, V. (Victoria), 1892-1962 — Biography. 2. Authors, English — 20th century — Biography. I. T.
PR6037.A35 Z68 1983   823/.912 B 19   *LC* 83-47961   *ISBN* 0394520238

Nicolson, Nigel.   2.9298
Portrait of a marriage. [1st ed.] New York, Atheneum, 1973. xi, 249 p. illus. 25 cm. 1. Sackville-West, V. (Victoria), 1892-1962 — Biography. 2. Sackville-West, V. (Victoria), 1892-1962 — Relations with women — Violet Keppel Trefusis. 3. Trefusis, Violet Keppel, 1886-1968 — Biography. 4. Nicolson, Harold George, Sir, 1886-1968 — Biography. 5. Authors, English — 20th century — Biography. I. T.
PR6037.A35 Z8   821/.9/12 B   *LC* 73-80754   *ISBN* 0689105746

Stevens, Michael.   2.9299
V. Sackville–West: a critical biography. New York, Scribners [1974] xvi, 192 p. illus. 24 cm. Originally presented as the author's thesis, Uppsala. 1. Sackville-West, V. (Victoria), 1892-1962. I. T.
PR6037.A35 Z87 1974   821/.9/12 B   *LC* 73-19357   *ISBN* 0684136775

Watson, Sara Ruth.   2.9300
V. Sackville–West. New York, Twayne Publishers [1972] 164 p. 21 cm. (Twayne's English authors series. TEAS 134) 1. Sackville-West, V. (Victoria), 1892-1962. I. T.
PR6037.A35 Z96   823/.9/12   *LC* 77-169631

Sansom, William, 1912-.   • 2.9301
The stories of William Sansom. With an introd. by Elizabeth Bowen. — Freeport, N.Y.: Books for Libraries Press, [1971, c1963] 421 p.; 23 cm. — (Short story index reprint series) I. T.
PZ3.S2278 St5 PR6037.A75 Ax   823/.9/14   *LC* 77-144171   *ISBN* 0836937864

Chalpin, Lila K.   2.9302
William Sansom / by Lila Chalpin. — Boston: Twayne Publishers, 1980. 155 p.: port.; 21 cm. (Twayne's English authors series; TEAS 287) Includes index. 1. Sansom, William, 1912- — Criticism and interpretation. I. T.
PR6037.A75 Z6   823/.9/14   *LC* 79-21075   *ISBN* 0805767819

Sayers, Dorothy L. (Dorothy Leigh), 1893-1957.   • 2.9303
Lord Peter; a collection of all the Lord Peter Wimsey stories. Compiled and with an introd. by James Sandoe. Coda by Carolyn Heilbrun. Codetta by E. C.

Bentley. [1st ed.] New York, Harper & Row [1971, c1972] xii, 464 p. 23 cm. I. T.
PZ3.S2738 Lm3 PR6037.A95 Ax   823/.9/12   *LC* 68-28234   *ISBN* 0060137878

Sayers, Dorothy L. (Dorothy Leigh), 1893-1957.   • 2.9304
Busman's honeymoon; a love story with detective interruptions. New York, Harper [1960, c1937] 381 p. 20 cm. I. T.
PZ3.S2738 Bu7   PR6037.A95 Bx.   *LC* 60-9116

Sayers, Dorothy L. (Dorothy Leigh), 1893-1957.   • 2.9305
Gaudy night / by Dorothy L. Sayers. — New York: Harper & Row, [1960], 1936. 469 p.; 20 cm. I. T.
PZ3.S2738 Gau8   PR6037.A95 Gx.   823.912   *LC* 60-9117

Sayers, Dorothy L. (Dorothy Leigh), 1893-1957.   • 2.9306
The nine tailors; changes rung on an old theme in two short touches and two full peals, by Dorothy L. Sayers. — New York: Harcourt, Brace, [c1934] vii, 331 p.: front., illus. (map, plan); 20 cm. — I. T.
PR6037.A95 Nx   PZ3.S2738 Ni3   *LC* 34-6048

Sayers, Dorothy L. (Dorothy Leigh), 1893-1957.   • 2.9307
Strong poison. New York, Harper [1958] 252 p. 20 cm. I. T.
PR6037.A95 Sx   PZ3.S2738 St8   *LC* 58-8893

As her whimsey took her: critical essays on the work of   2.9308
Dorothy L. Sayers / edited by Margaret P. Hannay.
Kent, Ohio: Kent State University Press, c1979. xvi, 301 p.; 24 cm. 'Dorothy L. Sayer's manuscripts and letters in public collections in the United States [by] Joe R. Christopher ... [et al.]': p. 215-278. Includes index. 1. Sayers, Dorothy L. (Dorothy Leigh), 1893-1957 — Criticism and interpretation — Addresses, essays, lectures. I. Hannay, Margaret P., 1944-
PR6037.A95 Z6   823/.9/12   *LC* 79-10933   *ISBN* 0873382277

Brabazon, James.   2.9309
Dorothy L. Sayers: a biography / by James Brabazon; with a preface by Anthony Fleming; foreword by P.D. James. — New York: Scribner, c1981. xviii, 308 p., [8] p. of plates: ill., ports.; 24 cm. Includes index. 1. Sayers, Dorothy L. (Dorothy Leigh), 1893-1957 — Biography. 2. Authors, English — 20th century — Biography. I. T.
PR6037.A95 Z62   823/.914 B 19   *LC* 81-4831   *ISBN* 0684168642

Durkin, Mary Brian.   2.9310
Dorothy L. Sayers / by Mary Brian Durkin. — Boston: Twayne, c1980. 204 p.: port.; 21 cm. — (Twayne's English authors series. TEAS 281) Includes index. 1. Sayers, Dorothy L. (Dorothy Leigh), 1893-1957 — Criticism and interpretation. I. T. II. Series.
PR6037.A95 Z65   823/.9/12   *LC* 79-21271   *ISBN* 0805767789

Hone, Ralph E.   2.9311
Dorothy L. Sayers: a literary biography / by Ralph E. Hone. — Kent, Ohio: Kent State University Press, c1979. xvii, 217 p., [4] leaves of plates: ill.; 24 cm. 1. Sayers, Dorothy L. (Dorothy Leigh), 1893-1957. 2. Authors, English — 20th century — Biography. I. T.
PR6037.A95 Z73   823/.9/12 B   *LC* 79-9783   *ISBN* 0873382285

PR6037 Sc–Si

Shaffer, Peter, 1926-.   2.9312
[Plays] The collected plays of Peter Shaffer. — 1st ed. — New York: Harmony Books, c1982. xviii, 558 p.; 24 cm. I. T.
PR6037.H23 A6 1982   822/.914 19   *LC* 82-11793   *ISBN* 0517546809

Silkin, Jon.   • 2.9313
The re–ordering of the stones. — [London]: Chatto and Windus, 1961. 56 p. — (Phoenix living poets.) I. T. II. Series.
PR6037.I49 R4   *LC* 62-4541

Silkin, Jon.   2.9314
The little time–keeper: poems / by Jon Silkin. — 1st American ed. — New York: Norton, 1977, c1976. 75 p.; 22 cm. — I. T.
PR6037.I5 L5 1977   821/.9/14   *LC* 77-21668   *ISBN* 0393044866

Silkin, Jon.   2.9315
The principle of water. — Chealde: Carcanet Press, 1974. 96 p.; 23 cm. Poems. I. T.
PR6037.I5 P7   821/.9/14   *LC* 74-180734   *ISBN* 0856351016

Sillitoe, Alan.   2.9316
Down from the hill / Alan Sillitoe. — London: Granada, 1984. 218 p. I. T.
PR6037.I55 D6x   823/.914 19   *ISBN* 0246125179

Sillitoe, Alan. • 2.9317
The loneliness of the long–distance runner. [1st American ed.] New York, Knopf, 1960 [c1959] 176 p. 21 cm. I. T.
PZ4.S5723Lo2 PR6037.I55L59 1960 *LC* 60-8227

Sillitoe, Alan. • 2.9318
Saturday night and Sunday morning. — [1st American ed.]. — New York: Knopf, 1959 [c1958] 239 p.; 22 cm. — I. T.
PR6037.I55 S3 1959 *LC* 59-9260

Sillitoe, Alan. 2.9319
The second chance, and other stories / Alan Sillitoe. — New York: Simon and Schuster, c1981. 219 p.; 23 cm. I. T.
PR6037.I55 S4 1981 823/.914 19 *LC* 80-27643 *ISBN* 067142761X

Simpson, N. F. (Norman Frederick), 1919-. 2.9320
One way pendulum; a farce in a new dimension. New York, Grove Press, [1961, c1960] 93 p. illus. 21 cm. (Evergreen original E-325) I. T.
PR6037.I712 O5 *LC* 61-11778

Simpson, N. F. (Norman Frederick), 1919-. 2.9321
A resounding tinkle: a comedy, by N. F. Simpson. — London: Faber, 1968. 3-74 p.; 19 cm. — (Faber paper covered editions) I. T.
PR6037.I712 R4 1968 822/.9/14 *LC* 76-398279

Sinclair, May. • 2.9322
Mary Olivier: a life. — Westport, Conn.: Greenwood Press, [1972, c1919] 380 p.; 22 cm. — I. T.
PZ3.S6155 Mar7 PR6037.I73 M3x 823/.9/12 *LC* 74-169850 *ISBN* 0837162440

Boll, Theophilus Ernest Martin, 1902-. 2.9323
Miss May Sinclair: novelist; a biographical and critical introduction, by Theophilus E. M. Boll. — Rutherford [N.J.]: Fairleigh Dickinson University Press, [1973] 332 p.: illus.; 25 cm. 1. Sinclair, May. I. T.
PR6037.I73 Z58 1973 823/.9/12 B *LC* 72-414 *ISBN* 0838611567

Zegger, Hrisey D. 2.9324
May Sinclair / by Hrisey Dimitrakis Zegger. — Boston: Twayne Publishers, c1976. 176 p.: port; 21 cm. — (Twayne's English authors series. TEAS 192) Includes index. 1. Sinclair, May — Criticism and interpretation. I. T. II. Series.
PR6037.I73 Z9 823/.9/12 *LC* 76-18853 *ISBN* 0805766669

Sisson, C. H. (Charles Hubert), 1914-. 2.9325
Collected poems, 1943–1983 / C.H. Sisson. — Manchester [Greater Manchester]: Carcanet Press, 1984. 383 p.; 23 cm. Includes index. I. T.
PR6037.I78 A17 1984 821/.914 19 *LC* 84-116491 *ISBN* 0856354988

PR6037 The Sitwells

Sitwell, Edith, Dame, 1887-1964. • 2.9326
Collected poems. — New York: Vanguard Press, [1954] L, 442 p.; 25 cm. — I. T.
PR6037.I8 A17 1954 821.91 *LC* 54-11518

Brophy, James D. 2.9327
Edith Sitwell: the symbolist order [by] James D. Brophy. With a pref. by Harry T. Moore. — Carbondale: Southern Illinois University Press, [1968] xvii, 170 p.; 22 cm. — (Crosscurrents: modern critiques) 1. Sitwell, Edith, Dame, 1887-1964. I. T.
PR6037.I8 Z57 821/.9/12 *LC* 68-10118

Glendinning, Victoria. 2.9328
Edith Sitwell, a unicorn among lions / Victoria Glendinning. — 1st ed. — New York: Knopf, 1981. xiv, 393, [20] p. of plates: ill.; 25 cm. Includes index. 1. Sitwell, Edith, Dame, 1887-1964 — Biography. 2. Poets, English — 20th century — Biography. I. T.
PR6037.I8 Z59 1981 821/.912 19 *LC* 80-2721 *ISBN* 0394504399

Sitwell, Osbert, 1892-1969. • 2.9329
Collected stories / Osbert Sitwell. — [1st ed.]. — London: G. Duckworth, 1953. xviii, 540 p.; 23 cm. I. T.
PR6037.I83 A15 1953 PZ3 S625 Co *LC* 53-30248

Sitwell, Osbert, 1892-1969. 2.9330
The collected satires and poems of Osbert Sitwell. New York: AMS Press, 1976. xii, 292 p.; 18 cm. Reprint of the 1931 ed. published by Duckworth, London. Includes indexes. I. T.
PR6037.I83 A17 1976 821/.9/12 *LC* 75-41252 *ISBN* 0404146023

Sitwell, Osbert, 1892-1969. • 2.9331
Selected poems, old and new. — London: Duckworth, [1943] 163 p. I. T.
PR6037.I83 A6 1943 *LC* a 44-562

Sitwell, Osbert, 1892-1969. 2.9332
Left hand, right hand! An autobiography by Osbert Sitwell. London, Macmillan, 1957. xv, 304 p. 18 cm. (St. Martin's library) 1. Sitwell family. I. T.
PR6037.I83 Z512x

Sitwell, Osbert, Sir, bart, 1892-1969. • 2.9333
The scarlet tree / Sir Osbert Sitwell. — Boston: Little, Brown, 1946. x, 381 p.; 23 cm. (An Atlantic monthly press book) 1. Sitwell, Osbert, 1892-1969 — Biography. 2. Sitwell family. I. Sitwell, Osbert, Sir, bart., 1892-1969. Left hand, right hand! II. T. III. Series.
PR6037.I83 Z513 *LC* 46-4925

Sitwell, Osbert, 1892-1969. • 2.9334
Great morning!. — Westport, Conn.: Greenwood Press, [1972, c1947] xv, 360 p.; 22 cm. A continuation of the autobiographies, Left hand, right hand! and The scarlet tree. 1. Sitwell, Osbert, 1892-1969. I. T.
PR6037.I83 Z514 1972 828/.9/1209 B *LC* 79-156212 *ISBN* 0837161622

Sitwell, Osbert, 1892-1969. • 2.9335
Laughter in the next room. — Westport, Conn.: Greenwood Press, [1972, c1948] 400 p.; 23 cm. A continuation of the autobiographies, Left hand, right hand! The scarlet tree, and Great morning! 1. Sitwell, Osbert, 1892-1969. I. T.
PR6037.I83 Z515 1972 828/.9/1209 B *LC* 79-152607 *ISBN* 0837160421

Sitwell, Osbert, 1892-1969. • 2.9336
Tales my father taught me; an evocation of extravagant episodes. [1st ed.] Boston, Little, Brown [1962] 206 p. illus. 22 cm. 1. Sitwell, George Reresby, Sir, bart., 1800-1943. I. T.
PR6037.I83 Z518 928.2 *LC* 62-9554

Wykes-Joyce, Max. • 2.9337
The triad of genius. — London: P. Owen, [1953-. v.: ill., ports. 1. Sitwell, Edith, Dame, 1887-1964. I. T.
PR6037.I83 Z9 *LC* 54-8670

Sitwell, Sacheverell, 1897-. • 2.9338
Collected poems. With a long introductory essay by Edith Sitwell. [London] Duckworth 1936. 593 p. 1. Sitwell, Edith, Dame, 1887-1964. I. T.
PR6037.I85 A17 1936

Sitwell, Sacheverell, Sir, bart., 1897-. • 2.9339
Selected Poems / by Sacheverell Sitwell; with a preface by Osbert Sitwell. — London: Duckworth, 1948. 192 p.; 19 cm. I. T.
PR6037.I85 A6 1948 *LC* 49-3306

Sitwell, Sacheverell, Sir, bart., 1897-. • 2.9340
Selected works. London, R. Hale [1955] 300 p.: ill.; 22 cm. I. T.
PR6037.I85 A6 1955 828.91 *LC* 56-1223

PR6037 Sk–So

Skelton, Robin. • 2.9341
The dark window; poems. — London, Oxford University Press, 1962. 96 p. 23 cm. I. T.
PR6037.K38D3 1962 821.914 *LC* 62-4561

Bramah, Ernest. 2.9342
Max Carrados / by Ernest Bramah. — London: Methuen, 1914. 1 v. I. T.
PR6037.M425

Bramah, Ernest, pseud. 2.9343
The wallet of Kai Lung / Ernest Bramah [i.e. E.B. Smith]. — Boston: L.C. Page, 1900. 4 p. l., 337 p.; 20 cm. First American edition; composed of the English sheets with a title page printed for the American edition. I. T.
PR6037.M425 W 823/.9/1 FS

Smith, Stevie, 1902-1971. 2.9344
The collected poems of Stevie Smith [i.e. F. M. Smith]. — New York: Oxford University Press, 1976. 591 p.: ill.; 23 cm. Includes indexes. I. T.
PR6037.M43 A17 1976 821/.9/12 *LC* 75-4322 *ISBN* 0195198166

Smith, Sydney Goodsir, 1915-1975. 2.9345
Collected poems, 1941–1975 / Sydney Goodsir Smith; with an introd. by Hugh McDiarmid. London: J. Calder, 1976 (c1975). xvi, 269 p.: port.; 23 cm. (The Scottish library.) Text in Scots dialect. 'Books by Sydney Goodsir Smith': p. xiii-xiv. I. T.
PR6037.M58 A17 1975 *LC* 76-358513 *ISBN* 0714511066

Snow, C. P. (Charles Percy), 1905-.   **2.9346**
Strangers and brothers [by] C. P. Snow. [Omnibus ed.] New York, Scribner [1972] 3 v. 24 cm. Sequence of 11 novels originally issued separately, 1940-70. I. T.
PZ3.S6737 St6 PR6037.N58 S8x   823/.9/12   LC 74-37229   ISBN 0684128624

Karl, Frederick Robert, 1927-.   **2.9347**
C.P. Snow, the politics of conscience / with a preface by Harry T. Moore. — Carbondale: Southern Illinois U.P., 1963. 162 p.; 22 cm. — (Crosscurrents. Modern critiques) 1. Snow, Charles Percy, Sir, 1905- I. T. II. Title: Politics of conscience. III. Series.
PR6037N58 Z7   823.912   LC 63-8905

Shusterman, David.   **2.9348**
C. P. Snow / by David Shusterman. — Boston: Twayne Publishers, [1975] 161 p.: port.; 22 cm. (Twayne's English authors series; TEAS 179) Includes index. 1. Snow, C. P. (Charles Percy), 1905- I. T.
PR6037.N58 Z87   823/.9/12   LC 74-23949   ISBN 080571510X

Somerville, E. Œ. (Edith Œnone), 1858-1949.   **2.9349**
The Irish R. M. complete; all the stories in one volume. By E. Œ. Somerville and Martin Ross [pseud.] London, Faber and Faber, 1956. 437 p. Collected edition first published 1928 under title The Irish R. M. and his experiences. The stories are reprinted from the authors' Some experiences of an Irish R. M., Further experiences of an Irish R. M., and In Mr. Knox's country. I. Martin, Violet Florence, 1865-1915, joint author. II. T.
PR6037.O6 I7x PZ3.S6962 Ix

Somerville, Edith Anna OEnone, 1861-1949.   • **2.9350**
The real Charlotte / by E.OE. Somerville & Martin Ross. — London: Longmans, Green, 1911. 384 p. I. Martin, Violet Florence, 1865-1915. II. T.
PR6037.O6 R43 1911

Collis, Maurice, 1889-.   **2.9351**
Somerville and Ross: a biography. London, Faber, 1968. 3-286 p. 19 plates, illus., ports. 23 cm. 1. Somerville, E. Œ. (Edith Œnone), 1858-1949. 2. Ross, Martin, 1862-1915. I. T.
PR6037.O6 Z59   823 B   LC 68-118569   ISBN 0571084303

Robinson, Hilary.   **2.9352**
Somerville & Ross: a critical appreciation / Hilary Robinson. — New York: St. Martin's Press, 1980. 217 p.; 23 cm. 1. Somerville, E. Œ. (Edith Œnone), 1858-1949 — Criticism and interpretation. 2. Ross, Martin, 1862-1915 — Criticism and interpretation. I. T.
PR6037.O6 Z79 1980   823/.8/09   LC 80-44   ISBN 0312744269

Cummins, Geraldine Dorothy, 1890-.   **2.9353**
Dr. E. Œ. Somerville, a biography. Being the first biography of the leading member of the famous literary partnership of E. Œ. Somerville and Martin Ross, with a new bibliography of first editions compiled by Robert Vaughan and a pref. by Lennox Robinson. London, Dakers [1952] 271 p. illus. 22 cm. 1. Somerville, Edith Œnone, 1861-1949 — Biography. I. T.
PR6037.O6 Z7x   LC 52-68252

PR6037 Sp

Spark, Muriel.   • **2.9354**
Voices at play / by Muriel Spark. — Philadelphia: Lippincott, 1962. 247 p. Short stories and radio plays. I. T.
PR6037.P29 A6 1962   LC 62-9244

Spark, Muriel.   **2.9355**
The Abbess of Crewe. — New York: Viking Press, [1974] 116 p.; 22 cm. — I. T.
PZ4.S735 Ab3 PR6037.P29 Ax   823/.9/14   LC 74-16161   ISBN 0670100293

Spark, Muriel.   • **2.9356**
The bachelors / by Muriel Spark. — Philadelphia: Lippincott, 1961, c1960. 219 p. I. T.
PR6037.P29 B2x   PZ4.S735Bac 2   LC 61-6333

Spark, Muriel.   • **2.9357**
Doctors of philosophy: a play. New York: Knopf, 1966. v, 110 p.; 23 cm. I. T.
PR6037 P29 D6   LC 66-490

Spark, Muriel.   **2.9358**
The driver's seat. [1st American ed.] New York, Knopf, 1970. 117 p. 22 cm. 'This novel first appeared in the New Yorker.' I. T.
PR6037.P29D7 1970   823/.9/14   LC 79-111242

Spark, Muriel, 1918-.   • **2.9359**
The girls of slender means. — [1st ed.]. — New York, Knopf, 1963. 176 p. I. T.
PR6037.P29 G5 1963   LC 63-14614

Spark, Muriel.   • **2.9360**
A Muriel Spark trio: The comforters, The ballad of Peckham Rye, Memento mori. — Philadelphia: Lippincott, 1962. 608 p.; 21 cm. I. T. II. Title: The comforters. III. Title: The ballad of Peckham Rye. IV. Title: Memento mori.
PR6037.P29 M8x   LC 62-14653

Spark, Muriel.   • **2.9361**
The prime of Miss Jean Brodie / by Muriel Spark. — Philadelphia: Lippincott, 1962, [c1961]. 187 p.; 21 cm. A novel. I. T.
PR6037.P29 P7x   LC 62-7182

Spark, Muriel.   • **2.9362**
The public image. — [1st American ed.]. — New York: Knopf, 1968. 144 p.; 22 cm. Originally serialized in Cosmopolitan magazine. I. T.
PR6037.P29 P8x   PZ4.S735 Pu3   LC 68-23954

Spark, Muriel, 1918-.   • **2.9363**
Robinson: a novel / by Muriel Spark. — Philadelphia: Lippincott, [1963, c1958] 185 p. illus. 20 cm. I. T.
PR6037.P29 R6 1963   LC 63-22881

Spark, Muriel.   **2.9364**
[Short stories] The stories of Muriel Spark / Muriel Spark. — 1st ed. — New York: Dutton, c1985. 314 p.; 25 cm. I. T.
PR6037.P29 S8 1985   823/.914 19   LC 85-10355   ISBN 0525243305

Muriel Spark: an odd capacity for vision / edited by Alan Bold.   **2.9365**
London: Vision; Totowa, N.J.: Barnes & Noble, 1984. 208 p.; 22 cm. (Critical studies series.) 1. Spark, Muriel — Criticism and interpretation — Addresses, essays, lectures. I. Bold, Alan Norman, 1943- II. Series.
PR6037.P29 Z82 1984   823/.914 19   LC 84-2830   ISBN 038920482X

Stanford, Derek.   • **2.9366**
Muriel Spark, a biographical and critical study. With a bibliography by Bernard Stone. — Fontwell, Centaur Press, 1963. 184 p. port. 22 cm. Bibliography: p. 167-184. 1. Spark, Muriel. I. T.
PR6037.P29Z9   LC 64-39181

Whittaker, Ruth.   **2.9367**
The faith and fiction of Muriel Spark / Ruth Whittaker. — New York: St. Martin's Press, 1982. 168 p.; 23 cm. Includes index. 1. Spark, Muriel — Criticism and interpretation. I. T.
PR6037.P29 Z97 1982   823/.914 19   LC 81-21296   ISBN 0312279639

Spencer, Bernard, 1909-.   • **2.9368**
Aegean Islands, and other poems. [London]: Editions Poetry London, [1946] 47 p.; 23 cm. I. T.
PR6037.P42 A7   LC 47-24234

Spender, Stephen, 1909-.   **2.9369**
[Poems] Collected poems, 1928–1985 / Stephen Spender. — 1st ed. — New York: Random House, c1986. 204 p.; 22 cm. Updated ed. of: Collected poems, 1928-1953. 1955. Includes index. I. Spender, Stephen, 1909- Poems II. T.
PR6037.P47 A17 1985   821/.912 19   LC 85-2323   ISBN 0394546016

Spender, Stephen, 1909-.   • **2.9370**
Engaged in writing; and, The fool and the princess. New York: Farrar, Straus and Cudahy, 1958. 239 p. I. Spender, Stephen, 1909- Fool and the princess. II. T. III. Title: The fool and the princess.
PR6037.P47 E5   LC 58-10544

Spender, Stephen, 1909-.   **2.9371**
The thirties and after: poetry, politics, people 1933–1970 / Stephen Spender. — 1st ed. — New York: Random House, c1978. xiv, 236 p.; 24 cm. — I. T.
PR6037.P47 T5   824/.9/12   LC 77-90247   ISBN 039450173X

Spender, Stephen, 1909-.   • **2.9372**
World within world: the autobiography of Stephen Spender. — London: Hamish Hamilton, 1951. ix, 349 p., [1] leaf of plate: port.; 22 cm. 'Book Society choice.' Includes index. 1. Spender, Stephen, 1909- — Biography. I. T.
PR6037.P47 Z55   LC 51-6587

Sprigg, C. St. John (Christopher St. John), 1907-1937.   • **2.9373**
Poems / Christopher Caudwell. — London: John Lane, [1939] 96 p. I. T.
PR6037.P65 P6   LC 40-13375

PR6037 Sq–Sz

Squire, John Collings, Sir, 1884-1958. • **2.9374**
Collected poems / by J.C. Squire; with a preface by John Betjeman. — London: Macmillan, 1959. 241 p.: ill.; 23 cm. Includes index. I. Betjeman, John, 1906-. II. T.
PR6037.Q5 A6 1959   *LC* 60-363

Howarth, Patrick. • **2.9375**
Squire, 'most generous of men'. London, Hutchinson [1963] 307 p.: port.; 22 cm. 1. Squire, John Collings, Sir, 1884-1958. I. T.
PR6037.Q5 Z6   828.912   *LC* 64-41737

Stallworthy, Jon. **2.9376**
The apple barrel: selected poems, 1955–63. — London; New York: Oxford University Press, 1974. [8], 64 p.; 22 cm. — I. T.
PR6037.T1615 A6 1974   821/.9/14   *LC* 74-177277   *ISBN* 0192118374

Stallworthy, Jon. **2.9377**
Hand in hand. — New York: Oxford University Press, 1974. 48 p.; 22 cm. Poems. I. T.
PR6037.T1615 H3 1974b   821/.9/14   *LC* 73-93710   *ISBN* 019519778X

Stallworthy, Jon. • **2.9378**
Out of bounds. — London: Oxford University Press, 1963. 61 p. I. T.
PR6037.T1615 O8   *LC* 63-25553

Stapledon, Olaf, 1886-1950. **2.9379**
Last and first men, & Star maker; two science–fiction novels. New York, Dover Publications [1968] 438 p. illus. 22 cm. Each work previously published separately in 1931 and 1937 respectively. I. T. II. Title: Star maker.
PR6037.T18 L3x   PZ3.S7944 Las5   *LC* 68-19448

Stapledon, Olaf, 1886-1950. **2.9380**
To the end of time / Olaf Stapledon; [selection and introd. by Basil Davenport]; with a new introd. by Curtis C. Smith. — Boston: Gregg Press, 1975. xi, xiv, 775 p.; 21 cm. (The Gregg Press science fiction series) Reprint of the 1953 ed. published by Funk & Wagnalls, New York. 1. Science fiction, English I. Davenport, Basil, 1905-1966. II. T.
PZ3.S7944 To4 PR6037.T18 T6x   823/.9/12   *LC* 75-5744   *ISBN* 0839823126

Stephens, James, 1882-1950. • **2.9381**
Collected poems. New, rev. and enl. ed. New York, Macmillan [c1954] 363 p.; 22 cm. I. T.
PR6037.T4 A17 1954a   *LC* 54-12526

Stephens, James, 1882-1950. • **2.9382**
The crock of gold by James Stephens, with twelve illustrations in colour and decorative headings and tailpieces by Thomas Mackenzie. New York: Macmillan, 1926. 227 p.: ill.; 21 cm. I. Mackenzie, Thomas. illus. II. T.
PZ3.S8337Cr13 PR6037.T4C7 1956   *LC* 27-26089

Stephens, James, 1882-1950. **2.9383**
Deirdre, by James Stephens. — New York: The Macmillan company, 1923. 3 p. l., 286 p.; 20 cm. 1. Deirdre — Fiction. I. Longes mac nUsnig. II. T.
PZ3.S8337 D   PR6037.T4 Dx.   *LC* 23-12751

Stephens, James, 1882-1950. • **2.9384**
A James Stephens reader. Selected and with an introd. by Lloyd Frankenberg. Pref. by Padraic Colum. New York, Macmillan, 1962. 467 p. 22 cm. I. T.
PR6037.T4 J3   828.912   *LC* 62-8597

Pyle, Hilary. **2.9385**
James Stephens, his work and an account of his life. — New York: Barnes & Noble, [1965] xi, 196 p.: ill., ports. 1. Stephens, James, 1882-1950. I. T.
PR6037.T4 Z83 1965a   828.912   *LC* 65-67233

Innes, Michael, 1906-. **2.9386**
Lament for a maker [by] Michael Innes. New York: Dodd, 1938. 278 p. 21 cm. I. T.
PZ3.S85166 Lam9 PR6037.T466 L3 1938   823/.9/12   *LC* 38-20118

Stoker, Bram, 1847-1912. **2.9387**
[Dracula] The annotated Dracula: [annotated ed. of] Dracula / by Bram Stoker; introd., notes, and bibliography by Leonard Wolf; art by Sätty. — 1st ed. — New York: C. N. Potter: distributed by Crown Publishers, [1975] xviii, 362 p.: ill.; 29 cm. Includes index. 1. Stoker, Bram, 1847-1912. Dracula. 2. Dracula, Count (Fictitious character) I. Wolf, Leonard. ed. II. T.
PZ3.S8743 An4 PR6037.T617 D7x   823/.8   *LC* 75-4544   *ISBN* 0517520176

Strachey, Lytton, 1880-1932. **2.9388**
The shorter Strachey / selected and introduced by Michael Holroyd and Paul Levy. — Oxford; New York: Oxford University Press, 1980. xii, 274 p.; 20 cm. Includes index. I. Holroyd, Michael. II. Levy, Paul, 1941- III. T.
PR6037.T73 A6 1980   828/.9/1209   *LC* 79-40997   *ISBN* 0192122118

Strachey, Lytton, 1880-1932. **2.9389**
The really interesting question, and other papers. Edited and with an introd. and commentaries by Paul Levy. [1st American ed.] New York, Coward, McCann & Geoghegan [1973, c1972] xiv, 176 p. 23 cm. I. T.
PR6037.T73 R4 1973   824/.9/12   *LC* 72-87481   *ISBN* 0698105079

Holroyd, Michael. • **2.9390**
Lytton Strachey; a critical biography. [1st ed.] New York, Holt, Rinehart and Winston [1968, c1967] 2 v. illus. (part col.), ports. 25 cm. 1. Strachey, Lytton, 1880-1932. I. T.
PR6037.T73 Z69 1968   828/.9/1209 B   *LC* 68-10061

Swinnerton, Frank, 1884-. • **2.9391**
Figures in the foreground; literary reminiscences, 1917–1940 [by] Frank Swinnerton. Freeport, N.Y., Books for Libraries Press [1970, c1963] 272 p. 23 cm. (Essay index reprint series) Sequel to Background with chorus. 1. Swinnerton, Frank, 1884- 2. Authors — Correspondence, reminiscences, etc. 3. English literature — 20th century — History and criticism. I. T.
PR6037.W85 Z54 1970   820.9/009/12   *LC* 73-117850   *ISBN* 0836917243

Symons, Julian, 1912-. • **2.9392**
The plain man / Julian Symons. — New York: Harper and Row, 1962. 181 p. I. T.
PR6037.Y5 P5x   *LC* 62-17130

Symons, Julian. **2.9393**
The progress of a crime. — New York: Harper, c1960. 211p. I. T.
PR6037.Y5 P7x   *LC* 60-10452

PR6039 T–Ta

Taylor, Elizabeth, 1912-1975. • **2.9394**
The blush, and other stories. New York, Viking Press [1959] 217 p. 21 cm. I. T.
PR6039.A928 B5x   *LC* 59-6737

Taylor, Elizabeth, 1912-1975. • **2.9395**
A dedicated man, and other stories. — New York: Viking Press, [1965] 223 p. I. T.
PR6039.A928 D35x   *LC* 65-21151

Taylor, Elizabeth, 1912-1975. **2.9396**
[Short stories. Selections] The devastating boys and other stories. New York, Viking Press [1972] 179 p. 21 cm. I. Taylor, Elizabeth, 1912-1975. Devastating boys and other stories. II. T.
PR6039.A928 D4   823/.9/14   *LC* 79-181977   *ISBN* 0670270679

Taylor, Elizabeth, 1912-1975. **2.9397**
A game of hide and seek / by Elizabeth Taylor; with a new introduction by Elizabeth Jane Howard. — London [England]: Virago, 1986. xi, 259 p.; 20 cm. — (Virago modern classic.) I. T. II. Series.
PR6039.A928 G3x   823/.914 19   *ISBN* 086068556X

Taylor, Elizabeth, 1912-1975. **2.9398**
Mrs. Palfrey at the Claremont. — New York: Viking Press, [1971] 178 p.; 21 cm. — I. T.
PR6039.A928 Mx   823/.9/14   *LC* 70-150119   *ISBN* 0670494976

PR6039 Thomas

Thomas, Caitlin. • **2.9399**
Not quite posthumous letter to my daughter. [1st American ed.] Boston, Little, Brown [1963] 174 p. 22 cm. I. T.
PR6039.H5 N6 1963a   *LC* 63-8964

Thomas, Dylan, 1914-1953. **2.9400**
[Short stories] The collected stories / Dylan Thomas. — New York: New Directions, 1984. xv, 362 p.; 24 cm. I. T.
PR6039.H52 A15 1984   823/.912 19   *LC* 84-6822   *ISBN* 0811209180

Thomas, Dylan, 1914-1953. **2.9401**
The poems of Dylan Thomas. Edited with an introd. and notes by Daniel Jones. — [New York: New Directions Pub. Corp., 1971] xix, 291 p.; 23 cm. — (A New directions book) I. Jones, Daniel. ed. II. T.
PR6039.H52 A17 1971   821/.9/12   *LC* 79-145935

Thomas, Dylan, 1914-1953.   • 2.9402
Selected writings / introduction by John L. Sweeney. — [New York]: New
Directions, [c1946] xxiii, 184 p.: port. I. T.
PR6039.H52 A6 1946   *LC* 47-1886

Thomas, Dylan, 1914-1953.   • 2.9403
Quite early one morning. — [New York]: New Directions, [c1954] viii, 240 p.;
21 cm. — I. T.
PR6039.H52 A6 1954   828.91   *LC* 54-12907

Thomas, Dylan, 1914-1953.   • 2.9404
Adventures in the skin trade, and other stories. — [Norfolk] Conn.: New
Directions, [1955] 275 p.; 21 cm. — I. T.
PZ4.T455 Ad   *LC* 55-7367

Thomas, Dylan, 1914-1953.   • 2.9405
The beach of Falesá / by Dylan Thomas; based on a story by Robert Louis
Stevenson. — New York: Stein and Day, c1963. 126 p.; 22 cm. I. Stevenson,
Robert Louis, 1850-1894. The beach of Falesá. II. T.
PR6039.H52 B4 1963   *LC* 63-20057

Thomas, Dylan, 1914-1953.   • 2.9406
A child's Christmas in Wales. Illustrated by Fritz Eichenberg. [New York, New
Directions Pub. Corp., 1969, c1954] 31 p. illus. 21 x 28 cm. (A New Directions
book) I. Eichenberg, Fritz, 1901- illus. II. T.
PR6039.H52 C48 1969   821/.9/12   *LC* 77-88732

Thomas, Dylan, 1914-1953.   • 2.9407
Deaths and entrances: poems / by Dylan Thomas. — London: J.M. Dent, 1946.
66 p.; 15 cm. I. T.
PR6039.H52 D4   *LC* 46-4321

Thomas, Dylan, 1914-1953.   • 2.9408
The doctor and the devils. From the story by Donald Taylor. (Norfolk,Conn.)
New Directions [1953] 138 p. 20 cm. 'Dramatic story, written in the form of a
film scenario.' I. Taylor, Donald Fraser. II. T.
PR6039.H52 Dx   *LC* 53-12848

Thomas, Dylan, 1914-1953.   • 2.9409
In country sleep, and other poems. — [New York: J. Laughlin, 1952.] 34 p.
illus. 23 cm. (New Directions books) I. T. II. Series.
PR6039.H52 I6x   *LC* 52-7569

Thomas, Dylan, 1914-1953.   • 2.9410
A prospect of the sea, and other stories and prose writings. Edited by Daniel
Jones. — London: Dent, [1955] vii, 136 p.: group port.; 19 cm. — I. T.
PR6039.H52 P76 1955   823/.912 19   *LC* a 56-1095

Thomas, Dylan, 1914-1953.   • 2.9411
Under milk wood, a play for voices. — [New York]: New Directions, [1954] xiv,
107 p.: illus.; 21 cm. 'The first half of this play was published in an earlier form
as Llareggub in Botteghe oscure, IX.' 'Music for the songs': p. 100-107. I. T.
PR6039.H52 U6   822.91   *LC* 54-9641

Thomas, Dylan, 1914-1953.   2.9412
[Correspondence] The collected letters / Dylan Thomas; edited by Paul Ferris.
— New York: Macmillan, c1985. xxiii, 982 p.: ill.; 24 cm. 1. Thomas, Dylan,
1914-1953. Correspondence 2. Poets, Welsh — 20th century —
Correspondence. I. Ferris, Paul, 1929- II. T.
PR6039.H52 Z48 1985   821/.912 B 19   *LC* 85-23684   *ISBN*
0026176300

Thomas, Dylan, 1914-1953.   • 2.9413
Portrait of the artist as a young dog, by Dylan Thomas. — Norfolk, Conn.: New
directions, [c1940] 186 p., 1 l.; 23 cm. Autobiography. I. T.
PR6039.H52 Z5 1940   928.2   *LC* 40-34154

Ackerman, John.   • 2.9414
Dylan Thomas, his life and work. — London, New York, Oxford University
Press, 1964. 201 p. facsims., port. 23 cm. Bibliography: p. [191]-194.
1. Thomas, Dylan, 1914-1953. I. T.
PR6039.H52Z55   828.912   *LC* 65-435

Brinnin, John Malcolm, 1916- ed.   • 2.9415
A casebook on Dylan Thomas. — New York: Crowell, [1960] xiii, 322 p.; 22
cm. 1. Thomas, Dylan, 1914-1953. I. T.
PR6039.H52 Z59   821.912   *LC* 60-9937

Brinnin, John Malcolm, 1916-.   • 2.9416
Dylan Thomas in America, an intimate journal. With photos. — [1st ed.]. —
Boston, Little, Brown [1955] 303 p. illus. 21 cm. — (An Atlantic Monthly Press
book) 1. Thomas, Dylan, 1914-1953. I. T.
PR6039.H52Z6   928.2   *LC* 55-10768

Ferris, Paul, 1929-.   2.9417
Dylan Thomas / by Paul Ferris. — New York: Dial Press, c1977. 399 p., [8]
leaves of plates: ill.; 24 cm. Includes index. 1. Thomas, Dylan, 1914-1953 —
Biography. 2. Authors, Welsh — 20th century — Biography. I. T.
PR6039.H52 Z637   821/.9/12 B   *LC* 76-54936   *ISBN* 0803719477

FitzGibbon, Constantine, 1919-.   • 2.9418
The life of Dylan Thomas. — [1st American ed.]. — Boston: Little, Brown,
[1965] xi, 370 p.: facsims., ports.; 25 cm. 'An Atlantic monthly press book.'
1. Thomas, Dylan, 1914-1953 — Biography. I. T.
PR6039.H52 Z643 1965   821.912 B   *LC* 65-20748

Holbrook, David.   • 2.9419
Llareggub revisited; Dylan Thomas and the state of modern poetry. —
[London] Bowes and Bowes, 1962. 255 p. illus. 23 cm. 1. Thomas, Dylan,
1914-1953. 2. English poetry — Hist. & crit. I. T.
PR6039.H52Z68   821.912   *LC* 62-52982

Moynihan, William T.   • 2.9420
The craft and art of Dylan Thomas [by] William T. Moynihan. — Ithaca, N. Y.,
Cornell University Press [1966] xvi, 304 p. 23 cm. Bibliographical footnotes.
1. Thomas, Dylan, 1914-1953. I. T.
PR6039.H52Z78   821.912   *LC* 65-28600

Olson, Elder, 1909-.   • 2.9421
The poetry of Dylan Thomas. — [Chicago]: University of Chicago, [1954] vii,
163 p. 1. Thomas, Dylan, 1914-1953. I. T.
PR6039.H52 Z79 1954   *LC* 54-9580

Tindall, William York, 1903-.   • 2.9422
A reader's guide to Dylan Thomas. — New York: Farrar, Straus and Cudahy,
[1962] 305 p.; 22 cm. 1. Thomas, Dylan, 1914-1953. I. T.
PR6039.H52 Z865   821.912   *LC* 62-11525

Thomas, Edward, 1878-1917.   2.9423
The collected poems of Edward Thomas / edited and introduced by R. George
Thomas. — Oxford: Clarendon Press; New York: Oxford University Press,
1978. xxxii, 486 p.; 22 cm. Includes index. I. Thomas, R. George. II. T.
PR6039.H55 A17 1978   821/.912 19   *LC* 78-40077   *ISBN*
0198125674

Thomas, Edward, 1878-1917.   2.9424
A language not to be betrayed: selected prose of Edward Thomas / selected and
with introduction by Edna Longley. — 1st American ed. — New York: Persea
Books, c1981. xxii, 290 p.; 23 cm. Includes index. I. Longley, Edna. II. T.
PR6039.H55 A6 1981   828/.91208 19   *LC* 81-80915   *ISBN*
0892550562

Coombes, H.   2.9425
Edward Thomas; a critical study [by] H. Coombes. — New York: Barnes &
Noble Books, 1973. 256 p.: front.; 21 cm. 1. Thomas, Edward, 1878-1917 —
Criticism and interpretation. I. T.
PR6039.H55 Z66 1973   821/.9/12   *LC* 73-163364   *ISBN*
0064912728

Moore, John, 1907-1967.   • 2.9426
The life and letters of Edward Thomas. — London: Heinemann, [1939] xvii,
343 p. 1. Thomas, Edward, 1878-1917. I. T.
PR6039.H55 Z76   *LC* 40-11179

Thomas, R. S. (Ronald Stuart), 1913-.   2.9427
[Prose. Works. Selections] Selected prose / R.S. Thomas; edited by Sandra
Anstey; with an introduction by Ned Thomas. — Bridgend, Mid Glamorgan:
Poetry Wales Press, 1984 (c1983). 187 p.: ill., 1 port.; 23 cm. 1. Poetry —
Addresses, essays, lectures. 2. Wales — Addresses, essays, lectures. I. Anstey,
Sandra. II. T.
PR6039.H618 A6   828/.91408 19   *LC* 83-243686   *ISBN*
0907476279

Thomas, R. S. (Ronald Stuart), 1913-.   2.9428
Selected poems, 1946–1968 [by] R. S. Thomas. New York, St. Martin's [1974,
c1973] 134 p. 23 cm. I. T.
PR6039.H618 A6 1973   821/.9/14   *LC* 73-87573

PR6039–6043 Th–Tr

Thwaite, Anthony.   • 2.9429
The owl in the tree, poems. — London; New York: Oxford University Press,
1963. 59 p.; 23 cm. I. T.
PR6039.H97 O9 1963   *LC* 63-5897

Thwaite, Anthony.   2.9430
The stones of emptiness; poems 1963–66. — London, New York, Oxford University Press, 1967. ix, 58 p.; 22 1/2 cm. I. T.
PR6070.H9S7   PR6039.H97 S7 1967.   821.914   *LC* 67-90988
ISBN

Tolkien, J. R. R. (John Ronald Reuel), 1892-1973.   2.9431
The hobbit; or, There and back again, by J. R. R. Tolkien. Illus. by the author. Boston, Houghton Mifflin, 1938. 310 p. col. front., illus., plates (part col.) 21 cm. Illustrated lining-papers. I. T.
PR6039.O32 H6x   PZ8.T52 Ho2   *LC* 38-5859

Tolkien, J. R. R. (John Ronald Reuel), 1892-1973.   • 2.9432
The lord of the rings, by J. R. R. Tolkien. — 2d ed. — Boston: Houghton Mifflin, 1967 [c1966-. 3v.: fold. col. map.; 23 cm. Each vol. has also special t.p. I. T. II. Title: The fellowship of the ring. III. Title: The two towers. IV. Title: The return of the king.
PR6039.O32 Lx   PZ3.T576 Lo5   Fic   *LC* 67-12274

Tolkien, J. R. R. (John Ronald Reuel), 1892-1973.   2.9433
The Silmarillion / J. R. R. Tolkien; edited by Christopher Tolkien. — 1st American ed. — Boston: Houghton Mifflin, 1977. 365 p.: map (1 fold.); 24 cm. Includes index. I. T.
PZ3.T576 Si3 PR6039.O32   823/.9/12   *LC* 77-8025   *ISBN* 0395257301

Foster, Robert, 1949-.   2.9434
The complete guide to Middle–earth: from The hobbit to The Silmarillion / Robert Foster. — Rev. & enl. ed. — New York: Ballantine Books, 1978. xvi, 575 p.; 22 cm. 'A Del Rey book.' Published in 1971 under title: A guide to Middle-earth. 1. Tolkien, J. R. R. (John Ronald Reuel), 1892-1973 — Dictionaries, indexes, etc. I. T.
PR6039.O32 Z49 1978   823/.9/12   *LC* 77-26825   *ISBN* 0345275209

Rogers, Deborah Webster.   2.9435
J.R.R. Tolkien / by Deborah Webster Rogers and Ivor A. Rogers. — Boston: Twayne Publishers, 1980. 164 p.: port.; 21 cm. (Twayne's English authors series; TEAS 304) Includes index. 1. Tolkien, J. R. R. (John Ronald Reuel), 1892-1973 — Criticism and interpretation. I. Rogers, Ivor A. joint author. II. T.
PR6039.O32 Z816   828/.91209   *LC* 80-11518   *ISBN* 0805767967

Tomlinson, Charles, 1927-.   2.9436
[Poems. Selections] Selected poems, 1951–1974 / Charles Tomlinson. — Oxford; New York: Oxford University Press, 1978. xiii, 149 p.; 23 cm. I. T.
PR6039.O349 A17 1978   821/.9/14   *LC* 77-30466   *ISBN* 019211882X

Tomlinson, Charles, 1927-.   • 2.9437
A peopled landscape; poems. — London, New York, Oxford University Press, 1963. 51 p. 23 cm. I. T.
PR6039.O349P4   821.914   *LC* 63-4900

Tomlinson, Charles, 1927-.   • 2.9438
Seeing is believing: poems. — New York: McDowell, Obolensky, [c1958] viii, 59 p.; 22 cm. I. T.
PR6039.O349 S4   *LC* 58-8704

Tomlinson, H. M. (Henry Major), 1873-1958.   • 2.9439
The day before; a romantic chronicle. New York G.P. Putnam [c1939] 297p. I. T.
PR6039 O35 D3

Toynbee, Philip.   • 2.9440
Prothalamium, a cycle of the Holy Graal; a novel. — Westport, Conn.: Greenwood Press, [1970, c1947] 127 p.; 23 cm. London ed. (Horizon) has title: Tea with Mrs. Goodman. I. T.
PZ3.T6693 Pr5 PR6039.O8 P7x   823/.9/14   *LC* 75-110839   *ISBN* 0837124743

Treece, Henry, 1911-1966.   • 2.9441
Collected poems by Henry Treece. 'First American edition.' New York, A.A. Knopf, 1946. xi, 155 p.: port.; 22 cm. I. T.
PR6039.R38 A17 1946   821.91   *LC* 46-4926

Treece, Henry, 1911-1966.   • 2.9442
The dark island. — New York: Random House, 1952. 314 p. I. T.
PR6039.R38 Dx

Treece, Henry, 1911-1966.   2.9443
The green man; a novel. New York, Putnam [1966] 255 p. 22 cm. Based on a text by Saxo Grammaticus entitled Amleth's revenge, a portion of the Gesta Danorum. I. Saxo, Grammaticus, d. ca. 1204. Gesta Danorum II. T.
PR6039.R38 G8x   *LC* 66-15592

Tressell, Robert, 1870-1911.   • 2.9444
The ragged trousered philanthropists / by Robert Tressell [pseud.] — New York: Monthly Review Press, [1962] 633 p.: ill. I. T.
PR6039.R4x   *LC* 62-11421

Trevor, Elleston.   2.9445
The Quiller memorandum. — New York: Simon & Schuster, 1965. 224 p. I. T. II. Title: The Berlin memorandum
PR6039.R518 Q5   *LC* 65-12589

PR6043 V

Van Druten, John, 1901-1957.   • 2.9446
I am a camera, a play in three acts. Adapted from the Berlin stories of Christopher Isherwood. New York, Random House [1952] 182 p. illus. 21 cm. I. T.
PR6043.A4I13   822.91   *LC* 52-5920

Vickers, Roy.   2.9447
The Department of Dead Ends: 14 detective stories / by Roy Vickers; selected and introduced by E. F. Bleiler. — New York: Dover Publications, c1978. viii, 277 p.; 21 cm. A selection of stories originally published 1935-1958. 1. Detective and mystery stories, English I. Bleiler, Everett Franklin, 1920- II. T.
PZ3.V6643 Df PR6043.I183 D4x   823/.9/14   *LC* 78-52587

PR6045 W–Wal

Wain, John.   • 2.9448
Contenders; a novel. New York: St.Martin's P., 1958. 278p. I. T.
PR6045.A249 C6   *LC* 58-8593

Wain, John, 1925-.   • 2.9449
Hurry on down / John Wain. — London: Secker & Warburg, 1978, c1953. 240 p.; 23 cm. I. T.
PR6045.A249 H9 1978   *LC* 53-39049   *ISBN* 0436560607

Wain, John, 1925-.   • 2.9450
Living in the present, a novel. London, Secker & Warburg, 1955. 248 p.; 21 cm. I. T.
PR6045.A249 L5   823.914   *LC* 55-44865

Wain, John.   • 2.9451
Nuncle, and other stories. London: Macmillan; New York: St. Martin's Press, 1960. 245 p. 20 cm. I. T.
PR6045.A249 Nx

Wain, John.   • 2.9452
Strike the father dead: a novel / by John Wain. — New York: St. Martin's Press, 1962. 328 p. I. T.
PR6045.A249 S7

Wain, John, 1925-.   • 2.9453
A travelling woman: a novel. — New York: St. Martin's Press [1959] 207 p. I. T.
PR6045.A249 T7   *LC* 59-10162

Wain, John.   • 2.9454
Weep before God; poems. New York, St. Martin's Press [1961] 45 p. 22 cm. I. T.
PR6045.A249 W4   *LC* 61-19764

Wain, John.   • 2.9455
A winter in the hills. — New York: Viking Press, [1970] 383 p.; 23 cm. — I. T.
PZ4.W14 Wi3 PR6045.A249 W5x   823/.9/14   *LC* 70-119783
    ISBN 0670774510

Wain, John, 1925-.   • 2.9456
A word carved on a sill. — London: Routledge & K. Paul, [1956] 54 p. Poems. I. T.
PR6045.A249 W6   *LC* 56-36059

Wain, John.   • 2.9457
Sprightly running: part of an autobiography / by John Wain. — London: Macmillan; New York: St. Martin's Press, 1962. ix, 264 p.; 22 cm. 1. Wain, John. I. T.
PR6045.A249 Z53 1963a

Salwak, Dale.   2.9458
John Wain / by Dale Salwak. — Boston: Twayne Publishers, 1981. 155 p.: port.; 21 cm. — (Twayne's English authors series; TEAS, 316) Includes index. 1. Wain, John — Criticism and interpretation. I. T.
PR6045.A249 Z87   828/.914/09 19   *LC* 80-22135   *ISBN* 0805768068

Wallace, Edgar, 1875-1932.   **2.9459**
The murder book of J.G. Reeder / by Edgar Wallace. — New York: Dover,
1982. 109 p.; 22 cm. Reprint. Originally published: Garden City, N.Y.:
Published for the Crime Club by Doubleday, Doran, 1929. I. T.
PR6045.A327 M8 1982   823/.912 19   *LC* 82-9486   *ISBN*
0486243745

Walpole, Hugh, Sir, 1884-1941.   **• 2.9460**
The cathedral; a novel, by Hugh Walpole ... New York, George H. Doran
company [c1922] x p., 1 l., 13-459 p. 20 cm. I. T.
PZ3.W1655Cat PR6045.A34C29   *LC* 22-26984

Walpole, Hugh, Sir, 1884-1941.   **• 2.9461**
Fortitude, by Hugh Walpole; introduction by Hugh Walpole ... New York, The
Modern library [1930] 3 p. l., v-x p., 2 l., 11-484 p. 17 cm. (Half-title: The
modern library of the world's best books) I. T.
PZ3.W1655Fo5 PR6045.A34F59 1930   *LC* 31-26123

Hart-Davis, Rupert.   **• 2.9462**
Hugh Walpole, a biography. — London, Macmillan, 1952. xiv, 503 p. illus.,
ports., map, geneal. table. 23 cm. 'List of books by Hugh Walpole': p. 481-483.
Bibliography: p. 484. 1. Walpole, Hugh, Sir, 1884-1941. I. T.
PR6045.A34Z58   928.2   *LC* 52-2174

Rohmer, Sax, 1883-1959.   **2.9463**
The mystery of Dr. Fu Manchu / Sax Rohmer; introduced by D.J. Enright. —
London: Dent, 1985 (c1913). xv, 237 p.; 20 cm. (Classic thrillers) First
published in 1913. I. T.
PR6045.A37 M9x   823/.912 19   *ISBN* 0460022903

PR6045 War–Wat

Warner, Rex, 1905-.   **• 2.9464**
Imperial Caesar. [1st ed.]. — Boston, Little, Brown [1960] 343 p.: ill.; 22 cm.
1. Caesar, Julius — Fiction. I. T.
PR6045.A78 I5   823.91   *LC* 60-6532

Warner, Rex, 1905-.   **• 2.9465**
Poems and contradictions / Rex Warner. — [London]: John Lane, [1945] 55 p.;
23 cm. I. T.
PR6045.A78 P65 1945   *LC* 45-10590

Warner, Rex, 1905-.   **• 2.9466**
The professor. — London: Boriswood, 1938. — 294 p.; 20 cm. — I. T.
PR6045.A78 Px

Warner, Rex, 1905-.   **• 2.9467**
The wild goose chase: a novel. — London: Boriswood, [1937] 442 p.; 23 cm.
First ed. of author's first novel. I. T.
PR6045.A78 W54 1937

Warner, Rex, 1905-.   **• 2.9468**
The young Caesar. Boston, Little, Brown [1958] 353 p. 21 cm. 1. Caesar, Julius
— Fiction. I. T.
PZ3.W2466Yo PR6045.A78Y6   *LC* 58-6031

Warner, Sylvia Townsend, 1893-.   **2.9469**
Kingdoms of Elfin / Sylvia Townsend Warner. New York: Viking Press, 1977.
221 p.: map (on lining papers); 22 cm. 1. Fairies — Fiction. I. T.
PZ3.W2473 Ki3 PR6045.A812 K5x   823/.9/12   *LC* 76-41753
     ISBN 067041350X

Warner, Sylvia Townsend, 1893-.   **• 2.9470**
Mr. Fortune's maggot. New York Viking Press 1927. 241p. I. T.
PR6045 A812 M5 1927

Warner, Sylvia Townsend, 1893-.   **• 2.9471**
A spirit rises; stories. New York, Viking, 1962. 210 p. I. T.
PR6045.A812 S7x   *LC* 62-11675

Warner, Sylvia Townsend, 1893-.   **• 2.9472**
Winter in the air and other stories / by Sylvia Townsend Warner. — London:
Chatto & Windus, 1955. 249 p. I. T.
PR6045.A812 Wx

Watkins, Vernon Phillips, 1906-1967.   **• 2.9473**
Selected poems. — [Norfolk, Conn.]: New Directions, [1948] 92 p. I. T.
PR6045.A825 A6 1948   *LC* 48-7510

Watkins, Vernon Phillips, 1906-1967.   **• 2.9474**
Affinities: poems. — 1st U.S. ed. — [Norfolk, Conn.: New Directions, 1963,
c1962] 99 p. I. T.
PR6045.A825 A73 1963   *LC* 63-10008

Watkins, Vernon Phillips, 1906-1967.   **• 2.9475**
Ballad of the Mari Lwyd, and other poems / by Vernon Watkins. — [2d ed.]
London: Faber and Faber, [1947] 90 p.; 23 cm. I. T.
PR6045.A825 B3 1947   *LC* 48-24881

Watkins, Vernon Phillips, 1906-1967.   **2.9476**
I that was born in Wales: a new selection from the poems of Vernon Watkins /
chosen and introduced by Gwen Watkins and Ruth Pryor. Cardiff: University
of Wales Press, 1976. 73 p.; 23 cm. Poems. I. Watkins, Gwen. II. Pryor, Ruth.
III. T.
PR6045.A825 I2 1976   821/.9/12   *LC* 76-376727   *ISBN*
0708306152

Watkins, Vernon Phillips, 1906-1967.   **2.9477**
Unity of the stream: selected poems / Vernon Watkins. — Redding Ridge, CT:
Black Swan Books, [1983], c1978. 123 p.; 22 cm. — (Literary series.) I. T.
II. Series.
PR6045.A825 U55 1983   821/.912 19   *LC* 83-7652   *ISBN*
0933806051

Polk, Dora.   **2.9478**
Vernon Watkins and the spring of vision / Dora Polk. — Swansea: Christopher
Davies, 1978 (c1977). 161 p.; 22 cm. 1. Watkins, Vernon Phillips, 1906-1967 —
Criticism and interpretation. I. T.
PR6045.A825 Z8   821/.9/12   *LC* 78-320241   *ISBN* 0715403494

PR6045 Waugh

Waugh, Alec, 1898-.   **• 2.9479**
My place in the bazaar. New York, Farrar, Straus [1961] 233 p. 21 cm. I. T.
PR6045.A95 Mx   PZ3.W355 My   *LC* 61-10440

Waugh, Alec.   **• 2.9480**
The early years of Alec Waugh. — New York: Farrar, Straus, 1963, c1962. xii,
312 p.: port. 1. Waugh, Alec, 1898- — Biography. 2. Authors, English — 20th
century — Biography. I. T.
PR6045.A95Z52   928.2   *LC* 63-6040

Waugh, Evelyn, 1903-1966.   **• 2.9481**
The world of Evelyn Waugh. Selected and edited by Charles J. Rolo. [1st ed.]
Boston, Little, Brown [1958] 411 p. 22 cm. 1. Waugh, Evelyn, 1903-1966.
I. Rolo, Charles James, 1916- II. T.
PR6045.A97 A6   *LC* 58-7852

Waugh, Evelyn, 1903-1966.   **2.9482**
The essays, articles, and reviews of Evelyn Waugh / edited by Donat Gallagher.
— 1st American ed. — Boston: Little, Brown, c1984, c1983. xxv, 662 p.; 24 cm.
Includes index. I. Gallagher, Donat. II. T.
PR6045.A97 A6 1983   828/.91208 19   *LC* 83-82436   *ISBN*
0316926434

Waugh, Evelyn, 1903-1966.   **• 2.9483**
Basil Seal rides again, or, The rake's regress / frontispiece by Kathleen Hale. —
Boston: Little, Brown, [1963] 49 p.: col. ill.; 26 cm. Limited to 1,000 signed and
numbered copies. I. T. II. Title: The rake's regress.
PR6045.A97 B3 1963   *LC* 63-17422

Waugh, Evelyn, 1903-1966.   **• 2.9484**
Brideshead revisited: the sacred and profane memories of Captain Charles
Ryder: a novel. — London: Chapman & Hall, 1960. 381 p. I. T.
PR6045.A97 B7x   *LC* 61-2044

Waugh, Evelyn, 1903-1966.   **• 2.9485**
Black mischief. Boston, Little, Brown, 1946 [c1932] 312 p. map. 20 cm. I. T.
PR6045.A97 Bx   *LC* a 48-7366

Waugh, Evelyn.   **• 2.9486**
Decline and fall. London, Chapman & Hall ltd., 1928. xii, 288 p. incl. front.,
plates. 19 cm. I. T.
PR6045.A97 Dx   PZ3.W256 De   *LC* 28-28961

Waugh, Evelyn, 1903-1966.   **• 2.9487**
A handful of dust. [New York] New Directions [1945] 308 p. 18 cm. (New
classics series) I. T.
PZ3.W356Han PR6045.A97H3 1945   *LC* A 48-6348 *

Waugh, Evelyn, 1903-1966.   **• 2.9488**
Helena, a novel. [1st ed.] Boston, Little, Brown, 1950. xiii, 247 p. 20 cm.
1. Helena, Saint, ca. 255-ca. 330 — Fiction. I. T.
PR6045.A97 H4x   PZ3.W356 He   *LC* 50-10054

Waugh, Evelyn, 1903-1966.   **• 2.9489**
Love among the ruins: a romance of the near future. — London: Chapman &
Hall, 1953. 51 p.: ill. I. T.
PR6045.A97 L6x   *LC* 53-2951

Waugh, Evelyn, 1903-1966. • 2.9490
The loved ones, an Anglo–American tragedy. — [1st ed.]. — Boston: Little,
Brown, 1948. 164 p.; 20 cm. — I. T.
PR6045.A97 Lx   PZ3.W356 Lo   *LC* 48-7279

Waugh, Evelyn, 1903-1966. • 2.9491
Ordeal of Gilbert Pinfold: a conversation piece / by Evelyn Waugh. — Boston:
Little,Brown 1957. 232 p. I. T.
PR6045.A97 O7 1957   *LC* 57-9369

Waugh, Evelyn, 1903-1966. • 2.9492
Put out more flags. Boston: Little, Brown and Co., 1942. 286 p. I. T.
PR6045.A97 P8   *LC* 42-11453

Waugh, Evelyn, 1903-1966. • 2.9493
Scott–King's modern Europe. — [1st American ed.]. — Boston: Little, Brown,
1949. 89 p.: ill. I. T. II. Title: A sojourn in Neutralia.
PR6045.A97 S36 1949   *LC* 49-419

Waugh, Evelyn, 1903-1966. • 2.9494
Sword of honour: a final version of the novels Men at arms (1952) Officers and
gentlemen (1955) and End of the battle (1962). — Boston: Little, Brown, [1966,
c1961] 796 p. 1. World War, 1939-1945 — Fiction. I. Waugh, Evelyn,
1903-1966. Men at arms. II. Waugh, Evelyn, 1903-1966. Officers and
gentleman. III. Waugh, Evelyn, 1903-1966. The end of the battle. IV. T.
V. Title: Men at arms. VI. Title: Officers and gentlemen. VII. Title: End of the
battle.
PR6045.A97 S95 1961   *LC* 66-25514

Waugh, Evelyn, 1903-1966. • 2.9495
Scoop, a novel about journalists. London, Chapman & Hall [1938] 308 p. I. T.
PR6045.A97 Sx   823.91   *LC* 38-15720

Waugh, Evelyn, 1903-1966. • 2.9496
Tactical exercise. — Freeport, N.Y.: Books For Libraries Press, [1971, c1954]
289 p.; 21 cm. — (Short story index reprint series) I. T.
PZ3.W356 Tac5 PR6045.A97 T3x   823/.9/12   *LC* 78-167471
ISBN 0836939972

Waugh, Evelyn, 1903-1966. • 2.9497
Vile bodies / Evelyn Waugh. — Boston: Little, Brown, 1946. x, 321 p.; 20 cm.
I. T.
PZ3.W356 Vi PR6045.A97 V5x

Biography. Criticism

Waugh, Evelyn, 1903-1966. 2.9498
When the going was good / by Evelyn Waugh. — Boston: Little, Brown, 1984,
c1962. 297 p.; 22 cm. Condensation of the author's four books written between
1929 and 1935: Labels, Remote people, Ninety-two days, and Waugh in
Abyssinia. 1. Waugh, Evelyn, 1903-1966 — Journeys. 2. Authors, English —
20th century — Biography. 3. Africa — Description and travel 4. South
America — Description and travel 5. Middle East — Description and travel.
I. T.
PR6045.A97 Z477 1984   910.4/1 19   *LC* 84-80133   *ISBN*
0316926469

Waugh, Evelyn, 1903-1966. 2.9499
The diaries of Evelyn Waugh / edited by Michael Davie. — Boston: Little,
Brown, [1977] 818 p. cm. Includes index. 1. Waugh, Evelyn, 1903-1966 —
Diaries. 2. Novelists, English — 20th century — Biography. I. Davie,
Michael. II. T.
PR6045.A97 Z498 1977   823/.9/12 B   *LC* 77-16214   *ISBN*
0316174505

Waugh, Evelyn, 1903-1966. • 2.9500
A Little learning; an autobiography: the early years / by Evelyn Waugh. — 1st
American ed. — Boston: Little, Brown, c1964. 234 p., [6] leave of plates: ill.,
ports., geneaological table. I. T.
PR6045.A97 Z5   PR6045A97 Z5 1964.   928.2   *LC* 64-23290

Waugh, Evelyn, 1903-1966. 2.9501
The letters of Evelyn Waugh / edited by Mark Amory. — New Haven: Ticknor
& Fields, 1980. xx, 664 p.; 24 cm. Includes index. 1. Waugh, Evelyn,
1903-1966. Correspondence 2. Authors, English — 20th century —
Correspondence. I. Amory, Mark, 1941- II. T.
PR6045.A97 Z53 1980   823/.912 B   *LC* 80-17818   *ISBN*
0899190219

Carens, James F. (James Francis), 1927-. • 2.9502
The satiric art of Evelyn Waugh, by James F. Carens. Seattle, University of
Washington Press, 1966. xvi, 195 p. 22 cm. 1. Waugh, Evelyn, 1903-1966. I. T.
PR6045.A97 Z62   823.912   *LC* 66-13540

Davis, Robert Murray. 2.9503
Evelyn Waugh, writer / Robert Murray Davis. — 1st ed. — Norman, Okla.:
Pilgrim Books, c1981. xv, 342 p.; 24 cm. 1. Waugh, Evelyn, 1903-1966 —
Criticism and interpretation. I. T.
PR6045.A97 Z64 1981   823/.912 19   *LC* 81-1098   *ISBN*
0937664006

Evelyn Waugh, the critical heritage / edited by Martin 2.9504
Stannard.
London; Boston: Routledge & Kegan Paul, 1984. xxii, 537 p.; 22 cm. (Critical
heritage series.) Includes index. 1. Waugh, Evelyn, 1903-1966 — Criticism and
interpretation — Addresses, essays, lectures. I. Stannard, Martin, 1947-
II. Series.
PR6045.A97 Z683 1984   823/.912 19   *LC* 83-21172   *ISBN*
0710095481

Heath, Jeffrey M. 2.9505
The picturesque prison: Evelyn Waugh and his writing / Jeffrey Heath. —
Kingston [Ont.]: McGill-Queen's University Press, c1982. xviii, 334 p.: port.;
24 cm. 1. Waugh, Evelyn, 1903-1966 — Criticism and interpretation. I. T.
PR6045.A97 Z69 1982   823/.912 19   *LC* 82-211598   *ISBN*
0773503773

Pryce-Jones, David, 1936-. 2.9506
Evelyn Waugh and his world. Edited by David Pryce–Jones. — [1st American
ed.]. — Boston: Little, Brown, [1973] viii, 248 p.: illus.; 26 cm. 1. Waugh,
Evelyn, 1903-1966. 2. Authors, English — 20th century — Biography. I. T.
PR6045.A97 Z76 1973   823/.912 B   *LC* 73-5746

Stopp, Frederick J. • 2.9507
Evelyn Waugh; portrait of an artist. Boston, Little, Brown [c1958] 254p. illus.
Bibliography: p.238-240. 1. Waugh, Evelyn, 1903-1966. I. T.
PR6045.A97 Z8 1958a   *LC* 59-5157

Sykes, Christopher, 1907-. 2.9508
Evelyn Waugh: a biography / Christopher Sykes. — 1st American ed. —
Boston: Little, Brown, [1975] xii, 462 p., [6] leaves of plates: ill.; 24 cm.
1. Waugh, Evelyn, 1903-1966 — Biography. I. T.
PR6045.A97 Z83 1975   823/.9/12 B   *LC* 75-25721   *ISBN*
0316826006

PR6045 We–Wi

Webb, Mary Gladys (Meredith) 1883-1927. • 2.9509
Precious bane, by Mary Webb; with an introduction by Stanley Baldwin. New
York, The Modern library [1938] xvi, 356 p. 19 cm. (The Modern library of the
world's best books) 'First published, 1926 ... first Modern library edition, 1938.'
I. T.
PR6045.E2 Px   *LC* 38-27818

West, Rebecca, Dame, 1892-. 2.9510
Rebecca West, a celebration / selected from her writings by her publishers with
her help; critical introd. by Samuel Hynes. — New York: Viking Press, 1977.
xix, 780 p.; 25 cm. Includes index. I. T.
PR6045.E8 A6 1977   828/.9/1209   *LC* 76-21281   *ISBN*
0670590614

West, Rebecca. • 2.9511
The birds fall down. New York, Viking Press, 1966. 435 p. 22 cm. I. T.
PR6045.E8 B5x   *LC* 67-10214

West, Rebecca, Dame, 1892-. 2.9512
The return of the soldier / by Rebecca West; new introduction by Victoria
Glendinning. — Rev. ed. — London: Virago, 1980. 187 p.; 20 cm. (Virago
modern classics) I. T.
PR6045.E8 R4x 1980   *LC* 84-673740   *ISBN* 0860681440

West, Rebecca, Dame, 1892-. 2.9513
This real night / Rebecca West. — 1st American ed. — New York, N.Y.,
U.S.A.: Viking, 1985, c1984. 265 p.; 23 cm. I. T.
PR6045.E8 T5 1985   823/.912 19   *LC* 84-40467   *ISBN*
0670804320

Deakin, Motley F. 2.9514
Rebecca West / by Motley F. Deakin. — Boston: Twayne Publishers, 1980.
183 p.: port.; 21 cm. (Twayne's English authors series; TEAS 296) Includes
index. 1. West, Rebecca, Dame, 1892- — Criticism and interpretation. I. T.
PR6045.E8 Z63   828/.91209   *LC* 79-27601   *ISBN* 0805767886

Orel, Harold, 1926-. 2.9515
The literary achievement of Rebecca West / Harold Orel. — New York: St.
Martin's Press, 1986. xii, 235 p.; 23 cm. Includes index. 1. West, Rebecca,
Dame, 1892- — Criticism and interpretation. I. T.
PR6045.E8 Z83 1986   828/.91209 19   *LC* 85-12510   *ISBN*
0312487444

Weldon, Fay.   2.9516
Rebecca West / Fay Weldon. — New York, U.S.A.: Viking, 1985. 107 p., [4] p. of plates: ill.; 23 cm. (Lives of modern women.) 1. West, Rebecca, Dame, 1892- — Biography. 2. Authors, English — 20th century — Biography. I. T. II. Series.
PR6045.E8 Z88 1985   828/.91209 B 19   *LC* 85-51188   *ISBN* 0670806277

White, Antonia, 1899-.   2.9517
As once in May: the early autobiography of Antonia White and other writings / edited by Susan Chitty. — London: Virago, 1983. 340 p.: ill.; 23 cm. 1. White, Antonia, 1899- — Biography. 2. Authors, English — 20th century — Biography. I. Chitty, Susan, Lady. II. T.
PR6045.H15634 A6 1983   823/.912 19   *LC* 83-197218   *ISBN* 0860683524

White, Antonia, 1899-.   2.9518
Beyond the glass / Antonia White. — London: Eyre & Spottiswoode, 1954. 285 p.; 20 cm. I. T.
PR6045.H15634 B49 1981   823/.912 19   *LC* 80-39826   *ISBN* 0803706707

White, T. H. (Terence Hanbury), 1906-1964.   • 2.9519
The once and future king. — New York: Putnam, c1958. 677 p.; 22 cm. 1. Arthurian romances I. T. II. Title: The sword in the stone. III. Title: The queen of air and darkness. IV. Title: The ill-made knight. V. Title: The candle in the wind.
PR6045.H2 O5 1958   813   *LC* 58-10760   *ISBN* 0399105972

Whiting, John Robert, 1917-1963.   • 2.9520
The devils: a play / based on a book [The devils of Loudun] by Aldous Huxley. — New York: Hill and Wang, [1962, c1961] 128 p. — (A Spotlight dramabook; SD5) 1. Grandier, Urbain, 1590-1634 — Drama. I. T. II. Series.
PR6045.H35 D4   *LC* 62-15211

PR6045 Williams

Williams, Charles, 1886-1945.   • 2.9521
The image of the city, and other essays / selected by Anne Ridler, with a critical introduction. — London; New York: Oxford University Press, 1958. lxxii, 199 p. ill. 23 cm. 1. Williams, Charles, 1886-1945. 2. English literature — History and criticism — Addresses, essays, lectures. 3. Religion — Addresses, essays, lectures. I. Ridler, Anne, 1912- II. T.
PR6045.I45 A16 1958   *LC* 58-4749

Williams, Charles, 1886-1945.   • 2.9522
Selected writings / Charles Williams; chosen by Anne Ridler. — London: Oxford University Press, 1961. viii, 244 p.; 20 cm. — (Oxford paperbacks. no. 21) I. Ridler, Anne, 1912- II. T. III. Series.
PR6045.I5 A6   *LC* 61-3078

Williams, Charles, 1886-1945.   • 2.9523
All Hallow's eve. — London: Faber & Faber, [1945] 240 p. I. T.
PR6045.I5 A64 1945

Williams, Charles, 1886-1945.   2.9524
The Arthurian poems of Charles Williams. — Woodbridge: Boydell & Brewer, 1982. — 61 p.; 18 cm. I. Williams, Charles, 1886-1945. Region of the summer stars. II. Williams, Charles, 1886-1945. Taliessin through Logres. III. T.
PR6045.I5 A8 1982   821/.9/12 18   821/.912 19   *ISBN* 085991089X

Williams, Charles, 1886-1945.   • 2.9525
Descent into hell. New York, Pellegrini & Cudahy [1949] 248 p. 21 cm. I. T.
PR6045.I5 Dx   PZ3.W67144 De   *LC* 49-7643

Williams, Charles, 1886-1945.   • 2.9526
The greater trumps. New York, Pellegrinin & Cudahy [1950] x, 268 p. 21 cm. I. T.
PR6045.I5 Gx   PZ3.W67144 Gr 3   *LC* 50-6710

Williams, Charles, 1886-1945.   • 2.9527
Many dimensions. — New York: Pellegrini & Cudahy, [1949] 308 p.; 21 cm. — I. T.
PR6045.I5 M3x   PZ3.W67144 Man4   *LC* 49-10010

Williams, Charles, 1886-1945.   • 2.9528
The place of the lion. — New York, Pellegrini & Cudahy [1951] 236 p. 21 cm. I. T.
PR6045.I5 Px   PZ3.W67144Pl3   *LC* 51-9847

Williams, Charles, 1886-1945.   • 2.9529
War in heaven. — New York: Pellegrini & Cudahy, 1949. 290 p.; 21 cm. I. T.
PR6045.I5 W3 1949   *LC* 49-10011

Cavaliero, Glen, 1927-.   2.9530
Charles Williams, poet of theology / Glen Cavaliero. — Grand Rapids, Mich.: Eerdmans, 1983. x, 199 p.; 22 cm. Includes index. 1. Williams, Charles, 1886-1945 — Criticism and interpretation. 2. Theology in literature. 3. Christianity in literature I. T.
PR6045.I5 Z6 1983   828/.91209 19   *LC* 82-11420   *ISBN* 0802835791

Howard, Thomas.   2.9531
The novels of Charles Williams / Thomas Howard. — New York: Oxford University Press, 1983. xii, 220 p.; 22 cm. 1. Williams, Charles, 1886-1945 — Criticism and interpretation. I. T.
PR6045.I5 Z77 1983   828/.91209 19   *LC* 82-18902   *ISBN* 0195032470

Moorman, Charles.   • 2.9532
Arthurian triptych; mythic materials in Charles Williams, C. S. Lewis, and T. S. Eliot. — Berkeley, University of California Press, 1960. ix, 163 p. 23 cm. — (Perspectives in criticism, 5) Bibliographical references included in 'Notes' (p. 157-163) 1. Williams, Charles, 1886-1945. 2. Lewis, C. S. (Clive Staples), 1898-1963. 3. Eliot, Thomas Sterns, 1888-1965. 4. Arthur, King. 5. Mythology in literature I. T. II. Series.
PR6045.I5Z85   820.993   *LC* 59-14476

Williams, Emlyn.   • 2.9533
The collected plays. — New York: Random house, 1961. 1 v. 1. English drama I. T.
PR6045.I52 1961   822   822.912

PR6045 Wil–Win

Wilson, Angus.   • 2.9534
Anglo–Saxon attitudes: a novel. New York: Viking Press, 1956. 410 p. I. T.
PR6045.I577 A5   *LC* 56-9740

Wilson, Angus.   • 2.9535
A bit of the map, and other stories. New York, Viking Press, 1957. 193 p. 21 cm. I. T.
PR6045.I577 B5x   PZ3.W68895 Bi   *LC* 57-12615

Wilson, Angus.   • 2.9536
Hemlock and after. — London, Secker & Warburg [1952] 246 p. 19 cm. I. T.
PZ3.W68895He 25   PR6045.I577 Hx.   *LC* 52-41131

Wilson, Angus.   • 2.9537
The middle age of Mrs. Eliot, a novel. New York, Viking Press [1959, c1958] 439 p. 21 cm. I. T.
PZ3.W68895Mi2 PR6045.I577M5 1959   *LC* 59-6869

Wilson, Angus.   • 2.9538
The mulberry bush, a play in three acts. — London, Secker & Warburg, 1956. 112 p. 19 cm. I. T.
PR6045.I577M8 1956   822.91   *LC* 56-27536

Wilson, Angus.   • 2.9539
No laughing matter. New York, Viking Press [1967] 496 p. 23 cm. I. T.
PZ3.W68895No PR6045.I577N6   *LC* 67-26185

Wilson, Angus.   • 2.9540
The old men at the zoo. — New York, Viking, 1961. 352 p. 21 cm. I. T.
PZ3.W68895Ol PR6045.I577O43   *LC* 61-13729

Wilson, Angus, 1913-.   • 2.9541
Such darling dodos, and other stories. — New York: Morrow, 1951. 187 p. I. T.
PR6045.I577 S8   *LC* 51-319

Wilson, Angus.   • 2.9542
The wild garden = or, Speaking of writing. — Berkeley: University of California Press, 1963. 149 p. 1. Fiction — Addresses, essays, lectures I. T. II. Title: Speaking of writing
PR6045.I577W5 1963   823.914   *LC* 63-22841

Wilson, Angus, 1913-.   • 2.9543
The Wrong set and other stories / by Angus Wilson. — New York: William Morrow and Company, 1950, c1949. 239 p. I. T.
PR6045.I577 W7   *LC* 50-6169

Critical essays on Angus Wilson / [compiled by] Jay L. Halio.   2.9544
Boston, Mass.: G.K. Hall, c1985. viii, 236 p.; 25 cm. (Critical essays on modern British literature.) Includes index. 1. Wilson, Angus — Criticism and interpretation — Addresses, essays, lectures. I. Halio, Jay L. II. Series.
PR6045.I577 Z6 1985   823/.914 19   *LC* 84-15841   *ISBN* 081618691X

Faulkner, Peter.   **2.9545**
Angus Wilson, mimic and moralist / Peter Faulkner. — New York: Viking Press, c1980. xii, 225, [1] p.; 22 cm. 1. Wilson, Angus — Criticism and interpretation. I. T.
PR6045.I577 Z66   823/.914   LC 80-15035   ISBN 0670126926

Gardner, Averil.   **2.9546**
Angus Wilson / by Averil Gardner. — Boston: Twayne Publishers, c1985. 140 p.: port.; 23 cm. (Twayne's English authors series. TEAS 401) Includes index. 1. Wilson, Angus — Criticism and interpretation. I. T. II. Series.
PR6045.I577 Z67 1985   823/.914 19   LC 84-23986   ISBN 0805768912

Wilson, Ethel, 1890-.   • **2.9547**
Love and salt water. London: Macmillan; New York: St. Martin's Press, 1957. ix, 202 p. , 21 cm. I. T.
PR6045.I593 Lx   PZ3.W6922 L6   LC 59-1064

Winter, Ella, 1898-.   • **2.9548**
And not to yield, an autobiography. [1st ed.] New York, Harcourt, Brace & World [1963] xii, 308 p. illus., ports. 22 cm. I. T.
PR6045.I726 Z5   LC 63-15320

PR6045 Wo

Wodehouse, P. G. (Pelham Grenville), 1881-1975.   • **2.9549**
The most of P. G. Wodehouse. — New York: Simon and Schuster, 1960. 666 p.; 22 cm. — I. T.
PZ3.W817 Mnr   PR6045.O53 A6 1960.   LC 60-12584

Wodehouse, P. G. (Pelham Grenville), 1881-1975.   • **2.9550**
The code of the Woosters. New York, Simon and Schuster [1969, c1938] 222 p. 21 cm. (A P. G. Wodehouse classic) I. T.
PZ3.W817 Clo7 PR6045.O53 C6x   823/.9/12   LC 76-4718   ISBN 067120307X

Wodehouse, P. G. (Pelham Grenville), 1881-1975.   • **2.9551**
Heavy weather / by P.G. Wodehouse. — Boston: Little,Brown, 1933. 314 p.; 20 cm. I. T.
PR6045.O53 H4 1933

Wodehouse, P. G. (Pelham Grenville), 1881-1975.   • **2.9552**
The ice in the bedroom / P. G. Wodehouse. New York: Simon and Schuster, 1961. 246 p.; 21 cm. 'First printing.' I. T.
PR6045.O53 Ix

Wodehouse, P. G. (Pelham Grenville), 1881-1975.   • **2.9553**
Jeeves / by P.G. Wodehouse. — New York: Doran [c1923] 288 p.; 20 cm. I. T.
PR6045.O53 J4 1923.   LC 23-13575

Wodehouse, Pelham Grenville, Sir, 1881-.   • **2.9554**
Leave it to Psmith / by P.G. Wodehouse. — New York: H. Doran, c1924. 347 p. I. T.
PR6045.O53 L4 1924   LC 24-8571

Wodehouse, P. G. (Pelham Grenville), 1881-1975.   • **2.9555**
Money in the bank. Garden City, N. Y., Doubleday, Doran, 1942. 300 p. 20 cm. 'First edition.' I. T.
PR6045.O53 Mx   PZ3.W817 Mo   LC 42-36025

Wodehouse, P. G. (Pelham Grenville), 1881-1975.   • **2.9556**
Summer lightning. — London: H. Jenkins, [1935?] 318 p. I. T.
PR6045.O53 S79 1935   LC 35-28594

Wodehouse, P. G. (Pelham Grenville), 1881-1975.   • **2.9557**
Summer moonshine / P. G. Wodehouse. — New York: Doubleday, Doran, 1938. 322 p.; 20 cm. I. T.
PZ3.W817 Sum6 PR6045.O53 S8x   823/.9/12   LC 39-25330

Wodehouse, P. G. (Pelham Grenville), 1881-1975.   • **2.9558**
Uncle Fred in the springtime. New York, Simon and Schuster [1969, c1939] 220 p. 22 cm. (A P. G. Wodehouse classic) I. T.
PZ3.W817 Um6 PR6045.O53 U6x   823/.9/12   LC 72-4717   ISBN 0671203096

Connolly, Joseph.   **2.9559**
P.G. Wodehouse: an illustrated biography: with complete bibliography and collector's guide / Joseph Connolly. — London: Orbis Pub., 1979. 160 p.: ill.; 26 cm. Includes index. 1. Wodehouse, P. G. (Pelham Grenville), 1881-1975 — Biography. 2. Authors, English — 20th century — Biography. I. T.
PR6045.O53 Z6   823/.912 B   LC 80-451543   ISBN 0856132357

Sharma, Maha Nand.   **2.9560**
Wodehouse: the fictionist / Maha Nand Sharma. — Atlantic Highlands, N.J.: Humanities Press, 1982. ix, 224 p.; 23 cm. Original imprint covered by label:

Meerut: Meenakshī Prakashan. 1. Wodehouse, P. G. (Pelham Grenville), 1881-1975 — Criticism and interpretation I. T.
PR6045.O53 Z935

Wodehouse, P. G. (Pelham Grenville), 1881-1975.   • **2.9561**
Selected stories. Introd. by John W. Aldridge. — [New York] Modern Library [1958] 382 p. 19 cm. — (Modern library of the world's best books. [126]) I. T. II. Series.
PR6045.O53x   PZ3.W817Se   LC 58-11472

PR6045 Woolf

Woolf, Leonard, 1880-1969.   • **2.9562**
The village in the jungle [by] Leonard Woolf. London Hogarth Press 1961. 307p. I. T.
PR6045 O68 V5 1961

Woolf, Leonard, 1880-1969.   • **2.9563**
Sowing, an autobiography of the years 1880 to 1904. [1st American ed.] New York, Harcourt, Brace [1960] 224 p. illus. 22 cm. 1. Woolf, Leonard, 1880-1969. 2. Authors, English — Biography I. T.
PR6045.O68 Z5   928.2   LC 60-12726

Woolf, Leonard, 1880-1969.   • **2.9564**
Growing; an autobiography of the years 1904–1911. [1st American ed.] New York, Harcourt, Brace & World [1962,c1961] 256 p. illus. 22 cm. 1. Woolf, Leonard, 1880-1969. 2. Sri Lanka — Description and travel. I. T.
PR6045.O68 Z51x   915.489   LC 61-15815

Woolf, Leonard, 1880-1969.   • **2.9565**
Beginning again; an autobiography of the years 1911 to 1918 [by] Leonard Woolf. — 1st American ed. . — New York: Harcourt, Brace & World, 1964. 263 p.: illus., ports.; 22 cm. Continuation of Growing; an autobiography of the years, 1904-1911. 1. Woolf, Leonard, 1880-1969 — Biography. I. Sward, Robert, 1933- II. T.
JA94.W6 A26 1964   PR6045.O68 Z52x.   928.2   LC 64-11545

Woolf, Leonard, 1880-1969.   • **2.9566**
Downhill all the way: an autobiography of the years 1919–1939 [by] Leonard Woolf. [1st American ed.] New York, Harcourt, Brace & World [1967] 259 p. illus., ports. 21 cm. Continuation of Beginning again; an autobiography of the years 1911-1918. Continued by The journey not the arrival matters: an autobiography of the years 1939-1969. I. T.
PR6045.O68 Z53x   655.5/92/0924   LC 67-20326

Woolf, Leonard, 1880-1969.   • **2.9567**
The journey, not the arrival matters; an autobiography of the years, 1939–1969 [by] Leonard Woolf. [1st American ed.] New York, Harcourt, Brace & World [1970, c1969] 217 p. illus., ports. 21 cm. 1. Woolf, Leonard, 1880-1969. I. T.
PR6045.O68 Z54x JA94.W6 A29 1970   655.5/92/0924

Woolf, Virginia, 1882-1941.   **2.9568**
[Short stories] The complete shorter fiction of Virginia Woolf / edited by Susan Dick. — 1st American ed. — San Diego: Harcourt Brace Jovanovich, c1985. 313 p.; 22 cm. I. Dick, Susan. II. T.
PR6045.O72 A15 1985   823/.912 19   LC 85-17719   ISBN 0151189838

Woolf, Virginia, 1882-1941.   • **2.9569**
Collected essays. [1st American ed.] New York, Harcourt, Brace & World [1967, c1966] 4 v. 21 cm. I. T.
PR6045.O72 A16 1967   824/.9/12   LC 67-20327

Woolf, Virginia, 1882-1941.   • **2.9570**
Between the acts. — New York: Harcourt,Brace & World, [c1941] 219 p. I. Woolf, Leonard, 1880-1969. II. T.
PR6045.O72 B4 1941   PR6045.O72 B42 1941.   LC 41-51933   ISBN 0151119392

Woolf, Virginia Stephen, 1882-1941.   • **2.9571**
Flush, a biography / by Virginia Woolf. — 1st ed. — New York: Harcourt, Brace, c1933. 185 p.: ill., ports. 1. Browning, Elizabeth Barrett, 1806-1861 — Fiction. 2. Dogs — Biography 3. Flush (Dog) I. T.
PR4194.W66   PR6045.O72 F55 1933.   LC 33-27336

Woolf, Virginia, 1882-1941.   • **2.9572**
A haunted house, and other short stories / by Virginia Woolf. — 1st American ed. — New York, Harcourt, Brace and company [1944] vii, 148 p. 21 cm. I. Woolf, Leonard, 1880-1969. II. T.
PZ3.W884Hau2 PR6045.O72H3 1944   LC 44-40070

Woolf, Virginia, 1882-1941.   • **2.9573**
Jacob's room. London Published by L. & V. Woolf at the Hogarth Press 1922. 290p. I. T.
PR6045 O72 J3 1922

Woolf, Virginia, 1882-1941.   • **2.9574**
Mrs. Dalloway / by Virginia Woolf. — New York: Harcourt, Brace, Jovanovich, [1964], c1953. 296 p.; 19 cm. — (A Harvest book; HB81) I. T.
PR6045.O72 M5 1964   813   *ISBN* 0156628635 pbk

Woolf, Virginia, 1882-1941.   • **2.9575**
Night and day. London, Duckworth [1919] [4], 538 p. First edition. I. T.
PR6045.O72 Nx

Woolf, Virginia, 1882-1941.   • **2.9576**
Orlando; a biography. Ninth impression. London Hogarth Press 1960. 299p. I. T.
PR6045 O72 O7 1960

Woolf, Virginia, 1882-1941.   • **2.9577**
Three guineas / Virginia Woolf. — London: Hogarth Press; Toronto: Clarke, Irwin, 1938. 329 p.: ill., ports.; 21 cm. In response to three requests for donations (to a peace society; to a woman's college rebuilding fund; to a society for obtaining employment for professional women) the author proposes that 'the daughters of educated men' unite in opposition to man-made war. 1. War 2. Peace I. Hogarth Press. II. T. III. Title: 3 guineas.
PR6045.O72 T5x   *LC* 38-21271

Woolf, Virginia, 1882-1941.   • **2.9578**
To the lighthouse. — New York: Harcourt, Brace, [c1927] 310 p. I. T.
PR6045.O72 T6 1927a   *LC* 27-10646

Woolf, Virginia, 1882-1941.   • **2.9579**
The voyage out / by Virginia Woolf. — New York: Harcourt, Brace & Co., [1920] 375 p.; 20 cm. I. T.
PR6045.O72 V68   823/.912 19

Woolf, Virginia, 1882-1941.   • **2.9580**
The waves. — [1st ed.]. — New York: Harcourt, Brace, [c1931] 297 p. I. T.
PR6045.O72 W4 1931   *LC* 31-30698

Woolf, Virginia, 1882-1941.   • **2.9581**
The years [by] Virginia Woolf. London: Hogarth Press, [1937] 469 p.; 19 cm. I. T.
PZ3.W884Ye PR6045.O72Y4   *LC* 37-3929

Biography. Criticism

Woolf, Virginia, 1882-1941.   **2.9582**
The diary of Virginia Woolf / edited by Anne Olivier Bell; introd. by Quentin Bell. — 1st American ed. — New York: Harcourt Brace Jovanovich, 1977-c1984. 5 v.; 25 cm. Includes indexes. 1. Woolf, Virginia, 1882-1941 — Diaries. 2. Authors, English — 20th century — Biography. I. T.
PR6045.O72 Z494 1977   828/.91203 B 19   *LC* 77-73111   *ISBN* 0151255970

Woolf, Virginia, 1882-1941.   **2.9583**
Moments of being: unpublished autobiographical writings / Virginia Woolf; edited and with an introd. and notes by Jeanne Schulkind. — 1st American ed. — New York: Harcourt Brace Jovanovich, 1977 (c1976). 207 p.; 22 cm. 1. Woolf, Virginia, 1882-1941 — Biography. 2. Authors, English — 20th century — Biography. I. T.
PR6045.O72 Z496   823/.9/12 B   *LC* 76-27410   *ISBN* 0151620342

Woolf, Virginia, 1882-1941.   • **2.9584**
A writer's diary: being extracts from the diary of Virginia Woolf / edited by Leonard Woolf. — [1st American ed.]. — New York: Harcourt, Brace, c1954. x, 356 p.; 22 cm. 1. Woolf, Virginia, 1882-1941. I. Woolf, Leonard, 1880-1969. II. T.
PR6045.O72 Z5 1954   *LC* 54-5257

Bennett, Joan Frankau, 1896-.   • **2.9585**
Virginia Woolf, her art as a novelist / by Joan Bennett ... — Cambridge [Eng.]: University Press, 1945. viii, 131, [1] p.; 19 cm. 1. Woolf, Virginia, 1882-1941. I. T.
PR6045.O72 Z52 1945   *LC* a 45-2941

Woolf, Virginia, 1882-1941.   **2.9586**
[Correspondence] The letters of Virginia Woolf / editor, Nigel Nicolson, assistant editor, Joanne Trautmann. — 1st American ed. — New York: Harcourt Brace Jovanovich, 1975-c1980. 6 v.: ports.; 24 cm. 1. Woolf, Virginia, 1882-1941. Correspondence 2. Authors, English — 20th century — Correspondence. I. Nicolson, Nigel. II. Trautmann, Joanne. III. T.
PR6045.O72 Z525 1975   823/.9/12 B   *LC* 75-25538   *ISBN* 0151509247

Woolf, Virginia, 1882-1941.   • **2.9587**
Letters: Virginia Woolf & Lytton Strachey. Edited by Leonard Woolf & James Strachey. [1st American ed.] New York, Harcourt, Brace [c1956] vii, 166 p. 21 cm. I. Strachey, Lytton, 1880-1932. II. T.
PR6045.O72 Z53 1956a   928.2   *LC* 56-11962

Apter, T. E.   **2.9588**
Virginia Woolf, a study of her novels / T. E. Apter. — New York: New York University Press, 1979. viii, 167 p.; 23 cm. (Gotham library of the New York University Press) Includes index. 1. Woolf, Virginia, 1882-1941 — Criticism and interpretation. I. T.
PR6045.O72 Z539 1979   823/.9/12   *LC* 78-78175

Bazin, Nancy Topping, 1934-.   **2.9589**
Virginia Woolf and the androgynous vision. New Brunswick, N.J., Rutgers University Press [1973] xii, 251 p. illus. 22 cm. 1. Woolf, Virginia, 1882-1941 — Criticism and interpretation. I. T.
PR6045.O72 Z543   823/.9/12   *LC* 72-4198   *ISBN* 0813507359

Bell, Quentin.   **2.9590**
Virginia Woolf; a biography. [1st American ed.] New York, Harcourt Brace Jovanovich [1972] xv, 216, 314 p. illus. 23 cm. 1. Woolf, Virginia, 1882-1941 — Biography. I. T.
PR6045.O72 Z545 1972   823/.9/12 B   *LC* 72-79926   *ISBN* 0151937656

Blackstone, Bernard, 1911-.   • **2.9591**
Virginia Woolf; a commentary. New York, Harcourt, Brace, 1949. 255 p. 1. Woolf, Virginia, 1882-1941. I. T.
PR6045.O72 Z56   *LC* 49-9253

Brewster, Dorothy, 1883-.   • **2.9592**
Virginia Woolf. [New York] New York University Press, 1962. 184 p. 22 cm. 1. Woolf, Virginia, 1882-1941. I. T.
PR6045.O72 Z562   823.912   *LC* 62-19050

Brewster, Dorothy, 1883-.   • **2.9593**
Virginia Woolf's London. [New York] New York University Press, 1960. 120 p. 21 cm. 1. Woolf, Virginia, 1882-1941. 2. London (England) — Description. I. T.
PR6045.O72Z563 1960   823.912   *LC* 60-5178

Daiches, David, 1912-.   • **2.9594**
Virginia Woolf. [Rev. ed. New York, New Directions, 1963] 169 p. 19 cm. (A New Directions paperbook, 96) 1. Woolf, Virginia, 1882-1941. 2. Novelists, English — 20th century — Biography. I. T.
PR6045.O72 Z58 1963   828.912   *LC* 62-16926

Fleishman, Avrom.   **2.9595**
Virginia Woolf: a critical reading / Avrom Fleishman. — Baltimore: Johns Hopkins University Press, [1975] xiii, 232 p.; 23 cm. 1. Woolf, Virginia, 1882-1941 — Criticism and interpretation. I. T.
PR6045.O72 Z63 1975   823/.9/12   *LC* 74-24375   *ISBN* 0801816165

Gordon, Lyndall.   **2.9596**
Virginia Woolf, a writer's life / Lyndall Gordon. — New York: Norton, 1985 (c1984). 341 p., [8] p. of plates: ill.; 22 cm. Includes index. 1. Woolf, Virginia, 1882-1941 — Biography. 2. Novelists, English — 20th century — Biography. I. T. II. Title: Writer's life.
PR6045.O72 Z653   823/.912 B 19   *LC* 84-25424   *ISBN* 0393018911

Guiguet, Jean.   **2.9597**
[Virginia Woolf et son oeuvre. English] Virginia Woolf and her works / by Jean Guiguet; translated by Jean Stewart. — New York: Harcourt Brace Jovanovich, 1976. 487 p.; 21 cm. (A Harvest book; HB 342) Includes index. 1. Woolf, Virginia, 1882-1941. I. T.
PR6045.O72 Z673 1976   823/.9/12 B   *LC* 76-14812   *ISBN* 0156936305 pbk

Kelley, Alice van Buren.   **2.9598**
The novels of Virginia Woolf: fact and vision / Alice van Buren Kelley. — Chicago: University of Chicago Press, 1973. vii, 279 p.; 23 cm. Includes index. 1. Woolf, Virginia, 1882-1941 — Criticism and interpretation. I. T.
PR6045.O72 Z75   823/.9/12   *LC* 73-77134   *ISBN* 0226429857

Leaska, Mitchell Alexander.   **2.9599**
The novels of Virginia Woolf: from beginning to end / by Mitchell A. Leaska. — 1st ed. — New York: John Jay Press, c1977. xiii, 264 p.; 24 cm. Includes index. 1. Woolf, Virginia, 1882-1941 — Criticism and interpretation. I. T.
PR6045.O72 Z773   823/.9/12   *LC* 77-5012   *ISBN* 0894440055

Love, Jean O., 1920-.   **2.9600**
Virginia Woolf: sources of madness and art / Jean O. Love. — Berkeley: University of California Press, 1978 (c1977) 379 p. Includes index. 1. Woolf,

Virginia, 1882-1941 — Biography. 2. Authors, English — 20th century —
Biography. I. T.
PR6045.O72 Z812   823/.9/12 B   *LC* 76-48004   *ISBN* 0520033582

Love, Jean O., 1920-.   **2.9601**
Worlds in consciousness; mythopoetic thought in the novels of Virginia Woolf,
by Jean O. Love. Berkeley, University of California Press, 1970. xvi, 268 p. 23
cm. 1. Woolf, Virginia, 1882-1941. I. T.
PR6045.O72 Z813   823/.9/12   *LC* 72-93185   *ISBN* 0520016068

Moore, Madeline.   **2.9602**
The short season between two silences: the mystical and the political in the
novels of Virginia Woolf / Madeline Moore. — Boston: G. Allen & Unwin,
1984. xiv, 189 p., [5] of plates: ill.; 23 cm. Includes index. 1. Woolf, Virginia,
1882-1941 — Criticism and interpretation. 2. Mysticism in literature
3. Politics in literature I. T.
PR6045.O72 Z822 1984   823/.912 19   *LC* 83-73007   *ISBN*
0048000221

Naremore, James.   **2.9603**
The world without a self; Virginia Woolf and the novel. New Haven, Yale
University Press, 1973. 259 p. 22 cm. 1. Woolf, Virginia, 1882-1941 — Style.
I. T.
PR6045.O72 Z826   823/.9/12   *LC* 72-91315   *ISBN* 0300015941

Rose, Phyllis, 1942-.   **2.9604**
Woman of letters: a life of Virginia Woolf / Phyllis Rose. — New York: Oxford
University Press, 1978. xxii, 298 p.: ill.; 22 cm. 1. Woolf, Virginia, 1882-1941.
2. Authors, English — 20th century — Biography. I. T.
PR6045.O72 Z867   823/.9/12   *LC* 77-16489   *ISBN* 0195023706

Silver, Brenda R., 1942-.   **2.9605**
Virginia Woolf's reading notebooks / Brenda R. Silver. — Princeton, N.J.:
Princeton University Press, c1983. xv, 384 p.; 24 cm. 1. Woolf, Virginia,
1882-1941 — Books and reading. 2. Woolf, Virginia, 1882-1941 —
Manuscripts — Facsimiles. I. Woolf, Virginia, 1882-1941. II. T.
PR6045.O72 Z8764 1983   828/.91203 B 19   *LC* 81-47156   *ISBN*
0691061793

Sprague, Claire. comp.   **2.9606**
Virginia Woolf; a collection of critical essays. Englewood Cliffs, N.J., Prentice-
Hall [1971] iv, 185 p. 21 cm. (A Spectrum book: Twentieth century views)
1. Woolf, Virginia, 1882-1941. I. T.
PR6045.O72 Z878   823/.9/12   *LC* 73-133057   *ISBN* 0139628371

Squier, Susan Merrill.   **2.9607**
Virginia Woolf and London: the sexual politics of the city / Susan M. Squier. —
Chapel Hill: University of North Carolina Press, c1985. xii, 220 p.: ill.; 24 cm.
Includes index. 1. Woolf, Virginia, 1882-1941 — Homes and haunts —
England — London. 2. Woolf, Virginia, 1882-1941 — Knowledge — England.
3. London (England) in literature. 4. Cities and towns in literature
5. Novelists, English — 20th century — Biography. 6. London (England) —
Biography. I. T.
PR6045.O72 Z8785 1985   823/.912 19   *LC* 84-17376   *ISBN*
080781637X

Virginia Woolf: a feminist slant / edited by Jane Marcus.   **2.9608**
Lincoln: University of Nebraska Press, 1984 (c1983). xv, 281 p.; 23 cm.
1. Woolf, Virginia, 1882-1941 — Criticism and interpretation — Addresses,
essays, lectures. 2. Feminist literary criticism — Addresses, essays, lectures.
I. Marcus, Jane.
PR6045.O72 Z892   823/.912 19   *LC* 82-24787   *ISBN* 0803230818

Virginia Woolf, new critical essays / edited by Patricia   **2.9609**
Clements and Isobel Grundy.
Totowa, N.J.: Barnes & Noble Books, 1983. 224 p.; 23 cm. — (Critical studies
series.) 1. Woolf, Virginia, 1882-1941 — Criticism and interpretation —
Addresses, essays, lectures. I. Clements, Patricia. II. Grundy, Isobel.
III. Series.
PR6045.O72 Z8938 1983   823/.912 19   *LC* 83-6374   *ISBN*
0389203750

PR6047 Young

Young, E. H. (Emily Hilda), 1880-1949.   • **2.9610**
Miss Mole / E.H. Young. — New York: Harcourt, Brace [c1930] 293 p.; 20 cm.
I. T.
PR6047.O465 M5 1930   823/.912 19   *LC* 30-30566

PR6051–6076 20th Century (1961–)

PR6051 A

Adams, Richard, 1920-.   **2.9611**
Watership Down [by] Richard Adams. New York, Macmillan [1974, c1972] ix,
429 p. maps. 24 cm. I. T.
PR6051.D345 W3x   [Fic]   *LC* 73-6044   *ISBN* 0027000303

Aldiss, Brian Wilson, 1925-.   **2.9612**
Barefoot in the head; a European fantasia [by] Brian W. Aldiss. — [1st ed. in the
U.S.A.]. — Garden City, N.Y.: Doubleday, 1970 [c1969] 281 p.; 22 cm. — I. T.
PZ4.A363 Bar3 PR6051.L3 B3x   823/.9/14   *LC* 74-97644

Aldiss, Brian Wilson, 1925-.   **2.9613**
The Malacia tapestry / Brian W. Aldiss. New York: Harper & Row,
1977,c1976. 313 p.: ill.; 21 cm. I. T.
PZ4.A363 Mal PR6051.L3 M3x   823/.9/14   *LC* 76-50166   *ISBN*
0060100532

Ayckbourn, Alan, 1939-.   **2.9614**
The Norman conquests: a trilogy of plays / Alan Ayckbourn. — 1st black cat
ed. — New York: Grove Press: distributed by Random House, 1979, c1975.
226 p.; 19 cm. (A Black cat book) Reprint of the ed. published by Chatto and
Windus, London. I. T.
PR6051.Y35 N6 1979   822/.9/14   *LC* 78-73051   *ISBN*
0394170822

PR6052 B–Bo

Bainbridge, Beryl, 1933-.   **2.9615**
The bottle factory outing / Beryl Bainbridge. — New York: G. Braziller, 1975,
c1974. 219 p.; 22 cm. I. T.
PZ4.B162 Bo4 PR6052.A3195 B6x   823/.9/14   *LC* 74-25294
ISBN 0807607819

Bainbridge, Beryl, 1933-.   **2.9616**
A quiet life: a novel / by Beryl Bainbridge. New York: G. Braziller, 1977,
c1976. 210 p.; 22 cm. I. T.
PZ4.B162 Qi3 PR6052.A3195 Q8x   823/.9/14   *LC* 76-55837
ISBN 0807608467

Ballard, J. G., 1930-.   **2.9617**
[Atrocity exhibition] Love and napalm: export U.S.A. [by] J. G. Ballard. Pref.
by William S. Burroughs. [1st American ed.] New York, Grove Press [1972,
c1969] 156 p. 21 cm. First published in 1970 under title: The atrocity exhibition.
I. T.
PZ4.B1893 Lo3 PR6052.A46 A8x   823/.9/14   *LC* 72-81790   *ISBN*
0394482778

Ballard, J. G., 1930-.   **2.9618**
Vermilion sands [by] J. G. Ballard. London, Cape, 1973. 208 p. 21 cm. I. T.
PZ4.B1893 Ve PR6052.A46 V4x   823/.9/14   *LC* 74-154893   *ISBN*
0224008943

Barnes, Peter, 1931-.   **2.9619**
Collected plays / Peter Barnes. — London: Heinemann, c1981. ix, 468 p.; 22
cm. I. T.
PR6052.A668 A6 1981   822/.914 19   *LC* 81-160715   *ISBN*
0435182811

Bennett, Alan, 1934-.   • **2.9620**
Beyond the fringe / by Alan Bennett [and others]. — New York: Random
House, 1963. viii, 88 p.: ill., group port.; 22 cm. I. T.
PR6052.E5 B4   *LC* 63-16854

Bond, Edward.   **2.9621**
Plays / Edward Bond. — London: Methuen, 1977. 312 p.; 18 cm. — (Master
playwrights.) I. T. II. Series.
PR6052.O5 A19 1977   822/.9/14   *LC* 77-378582   *ISBN*
041345410X

Bond, Edward.   **2.9622**
[Bingo] Bingo & The sea: two plays / by Edward Bond. — New York: Hill and
Wang, [1975] xviii, 124 p.; 21 cm. — (A Mermaid dramabook) 1. Shakespeare,

William, 1564-1616, in fiction, drama, poetry, etc. I. Bond, Edward. The Sea. 1975. II. T.
PR6052.O5 A6 1975   822/.9/14   *LC* 75-15990   *ISBN* 0809030306. *ISBN* 0809012332 pbk

Bond, Edward.   **2.9623**
Lear. — [1st American ed.]. — New York: Hill and Wang, [1972] xiv, 88 p.; 21 cm. — (A Dramabook) 1. Lear, King — Drama. I. T.
PR6052.O5 L4 1972   822/.9/14   *LC* 72-81289   *ISBN* 0809064898

Hay, Malcolm.   **2.9624**
Bond, a study of his plays / by Malcolm Hay and Philip Roberts. — London: Eyre Methuen, 1981 (c1980). 319 p., [8] leaves of plates: ill.; 20 cm. — (Methuen's modern theatre profiles) Includes index. 1. Bond, Edward — Criticism and interpretation. I. Roberts, Philip, 1942- joint author. II. T. III. Series.
PR6052.O5 Z677 1980   822/.914 19   *LC* 80-146896   *ISBN* 0413382907

PR6052 Br

Bradbury, Malcolm, 1932-.   **2.9625**
Eating people is wrong: a comedy / by Malcolm Bradbury. — 1st American ed. New York: Knopf, 1960,c1949. 275 p.; 21 cm. — I. T.
PR6052.R246 E2x   823   *LC* 59-15589

Bradbury, Malcolm, 1932-.   **2.9626**
The history man: a novel / by Malcolm Bradbury. — 1st American ed. — Boston: Houghton Mifflin, 1976, c1975. 230 p.; 22 cm. I. T.
PZ4.B7977 Hi3 PR6052.R246 H5x   823/.9/14   *LC* 75-33236
    ISBN 0395240859

Bradbury, Malcolm, 1932-.   **2.9627**
Rates of exchange / Malcolm Bradbury. — 1st American ed. — New York: Knopf: Distributed by Random House, 1983. 309 p.; 22 cm. I. T.
PR6052.R246 R3 1983   823/.914 19   *LC* 83-47787   *ISBN* 0394532686

Bradbury, Malcolm, 1932-.   **2.9628**
Stepping westward; a novel. [1st American ed.] Boston Houghton Mifflin 1966. 390p. I. T.
PR6052.R246 S7x   *LC* 66-11228

Braine, John.   • **2.9629**
Room at the top, a novel. Boston, Houghton Mifflin, 1957. 301 p. 21 cm. I. T.
PZ4.B814Ro2 PR6052.R265R6 1957   *LC* 57-11710

Brookner, Anita.   **2.9630**
The debut / Anita Brookner. — New York: Linden Press, 1981. 192 p.; 22 cm. British ed. has title: A start in life. I. T.
PR6052.R5875 D4 1981   823/.914 19   *LC* 80-39772   *ISBN* 0671426265

Brookner, Anita.   **2.9631**
Family and friends / Anita Brookner. — New York: Pantheon Books, 1985. p. cm. I. T.
PR6052.R5875 F3 1985   823/.914 19   *LC* 85-6373   *ISBN* 0394546164

Brookner, Anita.   **2.9632**
Hotel du Lac / Anita Brookner. — 1st American ed. — New York: Pantheon Books, c1984. 184 p.; 22 cm. I. T.
PR6052.R5875 H6 1984   823/.914 19   *LC* 84-20641   *ISBN* 0394542150

Brookner, Anita.   **2.9633**
Look at me / Anita Brookner. — 1st American ed. — New York: Pantheon Books, c1983. 192 p.; 22 cm. I. T.
PR6052.R5875 L6 1983   823/.914 19   *LC* 82-18968   *ISBN* 0394529448

Brookner, Anita.   **2.9634**
Providence / Anita Brookner. — 1st American ed. — New York: Pantheon Books, [1984], c1982. 183 p.; 22 cm. Reprint. Originally published: London: J. Cape, 1982. I. T.
PR6052.R5875 P7 1984   823/.914 19   *LC* 83-19449   *ISBN* 0394529456

Brunner, John, 1934-.   **2.9635**
Stand on Zanzibar. — [1st ed.]. — Garden City, N.Y.: Doubleday, 1968. xvii, 505 p.; 24 cm. — (Doubleday science fiction) Sequel: The sheep look up. I. T.
PR6052.R8 S8x   *LC* 68-22631

Brunner, John, 1934-.   **2.9636**
The traveler in black / John Brunner. — New York: Ace Books, 1977, (c1971) 181 p.; 21 cm. (Methuen paperback) I. T.
PR6052.R8 T7x   823/.9/1

Brutus, Dennis, 1924-.   **2.9637**
Stubborn hope: new poems, and selections from China poems and Strains / Dennis Brutus. — Washington: Three Continents Press, c1978. 98 p., [1] leaf of plates: port.; 23 cm. — I. T.
PR6052.R84 S84   821   *LC* 77-90993   *ISBN* 0914478257

PR6052 Bu

Burgess, Anthony, 1917-.   • **2.9638**
Nothing like the sun, a story of Shakespeare's love–life [by] Anthony Burgess. — New York: W. W. Norton, [1964] 234 p.; 22 cm. 1. Shakespeare, William, 1564-1616, in fiction, drama, poetry, etc. I. T.
PZ4.B953 No 1964 PR6052.U638   823/.914 19   *LC* 64-20416

Burgess, Anthony, 1917-.   **2.9639**
A clockwork orange [by] Anthony Burgess. — [1st American ed.]. — New York: W. W. Norton, [1963, c1962] 184 p.; 22 cm. — I. T.
PZ4.B953 Cl 1963 PR6052.U638 C5x   *LC* 63-7983

Burgess, Anthony, 1917-.   • **2.9640**
Cyrano de Bergerac, by Edmond Rostand. Translated and adapted for the modern stage by Anthony Burgess. — [1st ed.]. — New York: Knopf, 1971. xiv, 174 p.; 22 cm. I. Rostand, Edmond, 1868-1918. Cyrano de Bergerac. II. T.
PR6052.U638 C9 1971   822/.9/14   *LC* 76-161405   *ISBN* 039447239X

Burgess, Anthony, 1917-.   **2.9641**
Earthly powers / Anthony Burgess. — New York, N.Y.: Simon and Schuster, c1980. 607 p.; 24 cm. — I. T.
PR6052.U638 E2 1980   823/.914 19   *LC* 80-20978   *ISBN* 0671414909

Burgess, Anthony, 1917-.   **2.9642**
The end of the world news: an entertainment / Anthony Burgess. — New York: McGraw-Hill, c1983. x, 388 p.; 24 cm. 1. Freud, Sigmund, 1856-1939 — Fiction. 2. Trotsky, Leon, 1879-1940 — Fiction. I. T.
PR6052.U638 E5 1983   823/.914 19   *LC* 82-17159   *ISBN* 0070089655

Burgess, Anthony, 1917-.   **2.9643**
Enderby's dark lady, or, No end to Enderby / by Anthony Burgess. — New York: McGraw-Hill, c1984. 160 p.; 23 cm. I. T. II. Title: Enderby's dark lady. III. Title: No end to Enderby.
PR6052.U638 E56 1984   823/.914 19   *LC* 84-762   *ISBN* 0070089698

Burgess, Anthony, 1917-.   **2.9644**
Enderby, by Anthony Burgess. — New York: W. W. Norton, [1968] 412 p.; 22 cm. — I. T.
PZ4.B953 En 1968 PR6052.U638 E5x   *LC* 68-13483

Burgess, Anthony, 1917-.   **2.9645**
Honey for the bears [by] Anthony Burgess. — [1st American ed.]. — New York: W. W. Norton, [1964, c1963] 255 p.; 22 cm. — I. T.
PZ4.B953 Ho 1964 PR6052.U638 H6x   *LC* 64-10565

Burgess, Anthony, 1917-.   • **2.9646**
The wanting seed [by] Anthony Burgess. — [1st American ed.]. — New York: W. W. Norton, [1963, c1962] 285 p.; 22 cm. — I. T.
PZ4.B953 Wan 1963 PR6052.U638 W3x   *LC* 63-15877

Burgess, Anthony, 1917-.   **2.9647**
Little Wilson and big God / Anthony Burgess. — 1st American ed. — New York: Weidenfeld & Nicolson, c1986. ix, 460 p.; 24 cm. 1. Burgess, Anthony, 1917- — Biography. 2. Authors, English — 20th century — Biography. I. T.
PR6052.U638 Z464 1986   823/.914 19   *LC* 86-26721   *ISBN* 1555841007

Aggeler, Geoffrey, 1939-.   **2.9648**
Anthony Burgess: the artist as novelist / Geoffrey Aggeler. — University: University of Alabama Press, c1979. 245 p.: music; 25 cm. 1. Burgess, Anthony, 1917- — Criticism and interpretation. I. T.
PR6052.U638 Z53   823/.9/14   *LC* 78-12200   *ISBN* 0817371060

De Vitis, A. A.   **2.9649**
Anthony Burgess, by A. A. DeVitis. — New York: Twayne Publishers, [1972] 179 p.; 21 cm. — (Twayne's English authors series, TEAS 132) 1. Burgess, Anthony, 1917- — Criticism and interpretation. I. T.
PR6052.U638 Z6   823/.9/14   *LC* 72-161806

PR6053 C

Cadet, J. M., 1935-. 2.9650
The Ramakien: the Thai epic [by] J. M. Cadet. Illustrated with the bas–reliefs of Wat Phra Jetubon, Bangkok. — [1st ed.]. — Tokyo; Palo Alto, Calif.: Kodansha International, [1971] 256 p.: illus.; 30 cm. A retelling of the Thai version of Vālmīkī's Rāmāyana. I. Vālmīki. Rāmāyana. English II. Rāmmakīan. English. III. T.
PZ4.C1274 Ram PR6053.A335 PL4202.R3x 294.5/922 *LC* 70-128685 *ISBN* 0870111345

Carter, Angela, 1940-. 2.9651
[Infernal desire machines of Doctor Hoffman] The war of dreams. [1st American ed.] New York, Harcourt Brace Jovanovich [1974, c1972] 285 p. 21 cm. First published in 1972 under title: The infernal desire machines of Doctor Hoffman. I. T.
PZ4.C3232 War3 PR6053.A73 823/.9/14 *LC* 74-1157 *ISBN* 0151443750

Carter, Angela, 1940-. 2.9652
The bloody chamber / Angela Carter. — 1st U.S. ed. — New York: Harper & Row, c1979. 164 p.; 22 cm. I. T.
PR6053.A73 B5 1979 823/.9/14 *LC* 79-2645 *ISBN* 0060107081

Carter, Angela, 1940-. 2.9653
Nights at the circus / Angela Carter. — 1st American ed. — New York, N.Y.: Viking, 1985, c1984. 294 p.; 22 cm. I. T.
PR6053.A73 N5 1985 823/.914 19 *LC* 84-40459 *ISBN* 0670803758

Churchill, Caryl. 2.9654
Plays / Caryl Churchill. — London; New York: Methuen, 1985-. v. < 1 >; 18 cm. (A Methuen paperback) I. T.
PR6053.H786 A19 1985 822/.914 19 *LC* 85-186277 *ISBN* 0413566706

Colegate, Isabel. 2.9655
The shooting party / Isabel Colegate. — New York: Viking Press, 1981, c1980. 195 p.; 22 cm. — I. T.
PR6053.O414 S5 1981 823/.914 19 *LC* 80-54194 *ISBN* 0670640646

PR6054 D

Deane, Seamus, 1940-. 2.9656
Rumours / [by] Seamus Deane. — Dublin: Dolmen Press, 1978 (c1977). 54, [1] p.; 22 cm. Poems. Distributed in the U.S. by Humanities Press Inc., Atlantic Highlands, N.J. I. T.
PR6054.E22 R8 821/.9/14 *LC* 78-301258 *ISBN* 0851053203

Drabble, Margaret, 1939-. • 2.9657
The Garrick year. New York: Morrow, 1965, c1964. 221 p. I. T.
PR6054.R25 Gx *LC* 65-14949

Drabble, Margaret, 1939-. 2.9658
The ice age / Margaret Drabble. — 1st American ed. — New York: Knopf, 1977. 295 p.; 22 cm. — I. T.
PZ4.D756 Ic3 PR6054.R25 I3x 823/.9/14 *LC* 77-3319 *ISBN* 0394417909

Drabble, Margaret, 1939-. • 2.9659
Jerusalem the golden. — New York: Morrow, 1967. 240 p.; 22 cm. — I. T.
PR6054.R25 Jx PZ4.D756 Je2 *LC* 67-20186

Drabble, Margaret, 1939-. 2.9660
The middle ground / Margaret Drabble. — 1st American ed. — New York: Knopf, 1980. 277 p.; 22 cm. — I. T.
PR6054.R25 M5 1980 823/.914 *LC* 80-7630 *ISBN* 0394512243

Drabble, Margaret, 1939-. • 2.9661
The millstone; a novel. New York, Morrow, 1966 [c1965] 192 p. 21 cm. I. T.
PR6054.R25 Mx PZ4.D756 Mi2 *LC* 66-16401

Drabble, Margaret, 1939-. 2.9662
The needle's eye, a novel. — [1st American ed.]. — New York: Knopf, 1972. 368 p.; 22 cm. — I. T.
PZ4.D756 Ne3 PR6054.R25 N4x 823/.9/14 *LC* 79-178957 *ISBN* 0394479661

Drabble, Margaret, 1939-. 2.9663
The realms of gold / Margaret Drabble. — 1st American ed. — New York: Knopf, 1975. 354 p.; 22 cm. I. T.
PZ4.D756 Re3 PR6054.R25 R4x 823/.9/14 *LC* 75-8229 *ISBN* 0394498771

Drabble, Margaret, 1939-. • 2.9664
A summer bird–cage / Margaret Drabble. — New York: Morrow, 1964 [c1962] 224 p.; 21 cm. I. T.
PR6054.R25 S9 1964 823/.914 19 *LC* 64-16446

Drabble, Margaret, 1939-. • 2.9665
The waterfall. — [1st American ed.]. — New York: Knopf, 1969. 290 p.; 22 cm. — I. T.
PZ4.D756 Wat3 PR6054.R25 W3x 823/.9/14 *LC* 72-79321 5.95

Creighton, Joanne V., 1942-. 2.9666
Margaret Drabble / Joanne V. Creighton. — London; New York: Methuen, 1985. 127 p.; 20 cm. (Contemporary writers.) 1. Drabble, Margaret, 1939- — Criticism and interpretation. I. T. II. Series.
PR6054.R25 Z63 1985 823/.914 19 *LC* 85-2928 *ISBN* 0416383904

Critical essays on Margaret Drabble / [edited by] Ellen Cronan Rose. 2.9667
Boston, Mass.: G.K. Hall, c1985. vii, 205 p.; 24 cm. (Critical essays on modern British literature.) Includes index. 1. Drabble, Margaret, 1939- — Criticism and interpretation — Addresses, essays, lectures. I. Rose, Ellen Cronan, 1938- II. Series.
PR6054.R25 Z64 1985 823/.914 19 *LC* 84-19812 *ISBN* 0816187525

Margaret Drabble—golden realms / edited by Dorey Schmidt; associate editor, Jan Seale. 2.9668
Edinburg, Tex.: Pan American University, School of Humanities, c1982. 195 p.; 23 cm. — (Living author series. no. 4) 1. Drabble, Margaret, 1939- — Criticism and interpretation — Addresses, essays, lectures. I. Schmidt, Dorey. II. Seale, Jan. III. Series.
PR6054.R25 Z75x 1982 *LC* 84-673178 *ISBN* 0938738038

Moran, Mary Hurley, 1947-. 2.9669
Margaret Drabble, existing within structures / Mary Hurley Moran. — Carbondale: Southern Illinois University Press, c1983. ix, 133 p.; 22 cm. — (Crosscurrents/modern critiques. New series.) 'Selected bibliography of Drabble's works': p. 126-127. 1. Drabble, Margaret, 1939- — Criticism and interpretation. I. T. II. Series.
PR6054.R25 Z76 1983 823/.914 19 *LC* 83-332 *ISBN* 0809310805

Myer, Valerie Grosvenor. 2.9670
Margaret Drabble: puritanism and permissiveness / Valerie Grosvenor Myer. 1st U.S. ed. New York: Barnes & Noble, 1974. 200 p. (Barnes & Noble critical studies) Includes index. 1. Drabble, Margaret, 1939-. I. T.
PR6054.R25Z78 1974 *ISBN* 0064950549

Rose, Ellen Cronan, 1938-. 2.9671
The novels of Margaret Drabble: equivocal figures / Ellen Cronan Rose. — Totowa, N.J.: Barnes & Noble, 1980. xi, 141 p.: 1 ill.; 23 cm. Includes index. 1. Drabble, Margaret, 1939- — Criticism and interpretation. I. T.
PR6054.R25 Z87 1980 823/.914 19 *LC* 81-100527 *ISBN* 0389200069

Dunn, Douglas. 2.9672
Elegies / Douglas Dunn. — London; Boston: Faber and Faber, 1985. 64 p.; 21 cm. 'Poetry Book Society choice'—Jkt. 1. Elegiac poetry, English I. T.
PR6054.U54 E4 1985 821/.914 19 *LC* 84-25880 *ISBN* 0571135706

PR6055 E

Ewart, Gavin. 2.9673
The collected Ewart, 1933–1980: poems / by Gavin Ewart. — London: Hutchinson, 1980. 412 p.; 22 cm. Includes index. I. T.
PR6055.W3 A6 1980 821/.914 19 *LC* 80-500954 *ISBN* 0091410002

PR6056 F

Fenton, Edward. 2.9674
Scorched earth / Edward Fenton. — London: Sinclair Browne, 1984. I. T.
PR6056.E4 823/.914 19 *ISBN* 0863000444

Figes, Eva. 2.9675
Nelly's version / Eva Figes. — London: Secker & Warburg, 1977. 218 p.; 23 c.. — I. T.
PZ4.F4695 Ne PR6056.I46 823/.9/14 *LC* 77-374132 *ISBN* 0436156016

Figes, Eva.   **2.9676**
Waking / Eva Figes. — 1st American ed. — New York: Pantheon, c1981. 88 p.; 20 cm. I. T.
PR6056.I46 W3 1981   823/.914 19   *LC* 81-14078   *ISBN* 0394722272

Fitzgerald, Penelope.   **2.9677**
The bookshop / Penelope Fitzgerald. — London: Duckworth, 1978. 118 p.; 23 cm. — I. T.
PZ4.F555 Bo PR6056.I86   823/.9/14   *LC* 78-325826   *ISBN* 0715613200

Fitzgerald, Penelope.   **2.9678**
Offshore / Penelope Fitzgerald. — London: Collins, 1979. 141 p.; 22 cm. — I. T.
PZ4.F555 Of PR6056.I86   *LC* 79-321649   *ISBN* 0002216140

Fitzgerald, Penelope.   **2.9679**
At Freddie's / Penelope Fitzgerald. — Boston: D.R. Godine, 1985, c1982. 213 p.; 20 cm. I. T.
PR6056.I86 A92 1985   823/.914 19   *LC* 82-3143   *ISBN* 0879234393

Fleming, Ian, 1908-1964.   **2.9680**
Casino Royale. London: J. Cape [1953] 218 p. 20 cm. I. T.
PZ4.F598 Cas   PR6056.L4 C3.   *LC* 53-31362

Forster, Margaret.   **2.9681**
Georgy girl: a novel / by Margaret Forster. — London: Secker & Warburg, 1965. 217 p. I. T.
PR6056.O695 G4x   Fic   *LC* 65-1981   *ISBN* 043616101X

Fowles, John, 1926-.   • **2.9682**
The collector. — [1st American ed.]. — Boston: Little, Brown, [1963] 305 p.; 21 cm. — I. T.
PR6056.O85 Cx   PZ4.F788 Co2   *LC* 63-13451

Fowles, John, 1926-.   **2.9683**
Daniel Martin / John Fowles. — Boston: Little, Brown, c1977. 629 p.; 24 cm. A novel. I. T.
PZ4.F788 Dan3 PR6056.O85 D3x   823/.9/14   *LC* 77-23343   *ISBN* 0316289590

Fowles, John, 1926-.   **2.9684**
The ebony tower. — [1st ed.]. — Boston: Little, Brown, [1974] 312 p.; 25 cm. I. T.
PZ4.F788 Eb3 PR6056.O85 E2x   823/.9/14   *LC* 74-10952   *ISBN* 0316290939

Fowles, John, 1926-.   **2.9685**
The French lieutenant's woman / John Fowles; illustrated by Elaine Raphael and Don Bolognese. — Limited ed. — Franklin Center, Pa.: Franklin Library, 1979. 489 p.: col. ill.; 24 cm. 'Privately printed.' Accompanied by 'Notes from the editors' (22 p.) I. Raphael, Elaine. II. Bolognese, Don. III. T.
PR6056.O85 F7 1979   823/.914   *LC* 80-459698

Fowles, John, 1926-.   **2.9686**
A maggot / by John Fowles. — Boston: Little, Brown, c1985. 455 p.; 25 cm. I. T.
PR6056.O85 M28 1985   823/.914 19   *LC* 85-15937   *ISBN* 0316289949

Fowles, John, 1926-.   **2.9687**
The magus: a revised version / John Fowles; with a foreword by the author. — 1st American ed. — Boston: Little, Brown, 1978, c1977. 656 p.; 25 cm. — I. T.
PZ4.F788 Mag 1978 PR6056.O85 M32x   823/.9/14   *LC* 77-17343   *ISBN* 0316290920

Fowles, John, 1926-.   **2.9688**
Mantissa / John Fowles. — 1st ed. — Boston: Little, Brown, c1982. 195 p.; 24 cm. I. T.
PR6056.O85 M35 1982   823/.914 19   *LC* 82-7234   *ISBN* 0316289809

Fowles, John, 1926-.   **2.9689**
Poems. — [New York]: Ecco Press, [1973] xi, 116 p.; 22 cm. — I. T.
PR6056.O85 P6 1973   821/.9/14   *LC* 72-96853   *ISBN* 0912946024

Fowles, John, 1926-.   **2.9690**
The tree / John Fowles. — New York: Ecco Press, 1983, c1979. 91 p.; 21 cm. Reproduction of the 1979 ed. by Little, Brown and Co., Boston; without the photos, and pref. by Frank Horvat. 1. Fowles, John, 1926- — Knowledge — Natural history. 2. Trees 3. Trees in literature I. T.
PR6056.O85 Z474 1983   823/.914 19   *LC* 83-11555   *ISBN* 0880010401

Huffaker, Robert, 1936-.   **2.9691**
John Fowles / by Robert Huffaker. — Boston: Twayne Publishers, 1980. 166 p.: port.; 21 cm. — (Twayne's English authors series; TEAS 292) Includes index. 1. Fowles, John, 1926- — Criticism and interpretation. I. T.
PR6056.O85 Z69 1980   823/.914   *LC* 79-27531   *ISBN* 0805767851

Loveday, Simon, 1949-.   **2.9692**
The romances of John Fowles / Simon Loveday. — New York: St. Martin's Press, 1985. xiii, 174 p.: ill.; 23 cm. Includes index. 1. Fowles, John, 1926- Criticism and interpretation. I. T.
PR6056.O85 Z74 1985   823/.914 19   *LC* 84-13396   *ISBN* 0312691076

Olshen, Barry N.   **2.9693**
John Fowles / Barry N. Olshen. — New York: F. Ungar, 1979 (c1978). xii, 140 p.; 21 cm. — (Modern literature monographs) Includes index. 1. Fowles, John, 1926- — Criticism and interpretation. I. T.
PR6056.O85 Z79   823/.9/14   *LC* 78-3149   *ISBN* 0804426551

Palmer, William J.   **2.9694**
The fiction of John Fowles: tradition, art, and the loneliness of selfhood / William J. Palmer. — Columbia: University of Missouri Press, [1974] 113 p.; 21 cm. (A Literary frontiers edition) 1. Fowles, John, 1926- — Criticism and interpretation. I. T.
PR6056.O85 Z82   823/.9/14   *LC* 74-80389   *ISBN* 0826201660

Wolfe, Peter, 1933-.   **2.9695**
John Fowles, magus and moralist / Peter Wolfe. — Lewisburg: Bucknell University Press, [1976] 178 p. cm. Includes index. 1. Fowles, John, 1926- — Criticism and interpretation. I. T.
PR6056.O85 Z9 1976   823/.9/14   *LC* 75-5149   *ISBN* 0838717004

Francis, Dick.   **2.9696**
Dead cert / by Dick Francis. — New York: Holt, Rinehart and Winston, 1962. 220 p. I. T.
PR6056.R27 D4x   *LC* 62-17561

Friel, Brian.   **2.9697**
Philadelphia, here I come! / Brian Friel. — London: Faber and Faber, 1965. 110 p. I. T.
PR6056.R5 P5   822.91   *LC* 66-35156

PR6057 G

Garioch, Robert.   **2.9698**
[Poems. English & Lowlands Scots] Complete poetical works / Robert Garioch; edited by Robin Fulton. — Edinburgh: Macdonald Publishers, 1983. xxxii, 326 p.: ill.; 23 cm. I. Fulton, Robin II. T.
PR6057.A638 A17 1983   821/.914 19   *LC* 83-220217   *ISBN* 0904265935

George, Peter, 1924-1966.   **2.9699**
Dr. Strangelove: or, How I learned to stop worrying and love the bomb; a novel by Peter George, based on the screenplay by Stanley Kubrick, Peter George and Terry Southern. New York Bantam Books 1964. 145p. I. Kubrick, Stanley. Dr. Strangelove II. T. III. Title: How I learned to stop worrying and love the bomb
PR6057 E76 D6

Gray, Simon, 1936-.   **2.9700**
Butley [by] Simon Gray. New York, Viking Press [1972, c1971] 78 p. 20 cm. (A Viking compass book, C372) A play. 'A Richard Seaver book.' I. T.
PR6057.R33 B8 1972   822/.9/14   *LC* 72-80998   *ISBN* 0670197653 *ISBN* 0670003727

Griffiths, Trevor.   **2.9701**
Comedians / by Trevor Griffiths. — New York: Grove Press, 1976. 69 p.; 21 cm. Play. I. T.
PR6057.R52 C6 1976   822/.9/14   *LC* 76-16727   *ISBN* 0802140092

PR6058 H

Heaney, Seamus.   **2.9702**
Poems, 1965–1975 / Seamus Heaney. — New York: Farrar, Straus, and Giroux, c1980. ix, 228 p.; 22 cm. I. T.
PR6058.E2 A17 1980   821/.914 19   *LC* 80-68753   *ISBN* 0374234965

Heaney, Seamus.   **2.9703**
Field work: [poems] / Seamus Heaney. — New York: Farrar, Straus, Giroux, 1979 (c1976). 65 p.; 22 cm. — I. T.
PR6058.E2 F5 1979   821/.9/14   *LC* 79-20556   *ISBN* 0374154821

Heaney, Seamus. 2.9704
Sweeney astray: a version from the Irish / by Seamus Heaney. — New York: Farrar, Straus, Giroux, 1983. 85 p.; 24 cm. 'This version of Buile Suibhne is based on J.G. O'Keeffe's bilingual edition, which was published by the Irish Texts Society in 1913'—Introd. 1. Suibhne Geilt — Poetry. 2. Magh Rath, Battle of, 637 — Poetry. I. Buile Suibhne Geilt. II. T.
PR6058.E2 S9   821/.914 19   LC 84-1512   ISBN 0374272212

Buttel, Robert. 2.9705
Seamus Heaney / Robert Buttel. — Lewisburg [Pa.]: Bucknell University Press, [1975] 88 p.; 21 cm. (The Irish writers series) 1. Heaney, Seamus. I. T.
PR6058.E2 Z57   821/.9/14   LC 74-3616   ISBN 0838715672

Hill, Susan, 1942-. 2.9706
A bit of singing and dancing. — London: Hamilton, 1973. vii, 196 p.; 21 cm. I. T.
PZ4.H6488 Bj PR6058.I45   823/.9/14   LC 73-169613   ISBN 0241023114

Hill, Susan, 1942-. 2.9707
I'm the king of the castle. — New York: Viking Press, [1970] 252 p.; 21 cm. — I. T.
PZ4.H6488 Im PR6058.I45   823/.9/14   LC 75-119771   ISBN 0670390704

Holdstock, Robert. 2.9708
Mythago wood / by Robert Holdstock. — New York: Arbor House, c1984. 252 p.; 22 cm. I. T.
PR6058.O442 M9 1984   823/.914 19   LC 85-7429   ISBN 0877957614

Hughes, Richard Arthur Warren, 1900-1976. 2.9709
The fox in the attic. — [1st ed.]. — New York: Harper, [1962, c1961] 352 p.; 22 cm. 'The first of a group of novels, The human predicament, which is conceived as a long historical novel of ... [our] own times culminating in the Second World War.' I. T.
PR6058.U35 F6x   LC 61-12232

Hughes, Richard Arthur Warren, 1900-1976. 2.9709a
The wooden shepherdess [by] Richard Hughes. — [1st U.S. ed.]. — New York: Harper & Row, [1973] ix, 389 p.; 21 cm. — (His The human predicament, 2) I. T.
PR6058.U375W6x   823/.9/12   LC 76-181656   ISBN 0060119861

Hughes, Ted, 1930-. 2.9710
New selected poems / Ted Hughes. — 1st ed. — New York: Harper & Row, c1982. xii, 242 p.; 24 cm. Includes index. I. T.
PR6058.U37 A6 1982   821/.914 19   LC 80-8207   ISBN 0060909250

Hughes, Ted, 1930-. 2.9711
Cave birds: an alchemical cave drama / poems by Ted Hughes; and drawings by Leonard Baskin. — New York: Viking Press, 1979. 60 p.: ill.; 23 x 29 cm. I. Baskin, Leonard, 1922- II. T.
PR6058.U37 C3   821/.914 19   LC 78-6662   ISBN 0670209279

Hughes, Ted, 1930-. • 2.9712
Crow: from the life and songs of the crow. — [1st U.S. ed]. — New York: Harper & Row, [1971] viii, 84 p.; 22 cm. 1. Crows — Poetry. I. T.
PR6058.U37 C67 1971   821/.9/14   LC 70-125352   ISBN 0060119896

Hughes, Ted, 1930-. • 2.9713
The earth–owl and other moon–people / by Ted Hughes; illustrated by R. A. Brandt. — London, Faber and Faber [1963] 46 p. illus. 22 cm. Poems. I. T.
PR6058.U37 E2x   LC 64-4066

Hughes, Ted, 1930-. 2.9714
Gaudete: [poems] / by Ted Hughes. — 1st U.S. ed. — New York: Harper & Row, c1977. 200 p.; 24 c.. — I. T.
PR6058.U37 G3 1977   821/.9/14   LC 77-3753   ISBN 006012007X

Hughes, Ted, 1930-. • 2.9715
The hawk in the rain / Ted Hughes. — [1st ed.]. — New York: Harper, 1957. 52 p.; 20 cm. Poems. I. T.
PR6058.U37 H3x   LC 57-11106

Hughes, Ted, 1930-. • 2.9716
Lupercal. New York: Harper, [1960] 63 p. 23 cm. Poems. I. T.
PR6058.U37 L8x   821.914   LC 60-10407

Hughes, Ted, 1930-. 2.9717
Season songs. Pictures by Leonard Baskin. — [1st ed.]. — New York: Viking Press, 1975. 77 p.: illus.; 29 cm. 1. Seasons — Juvenile poetry. I. Baskin, Leonard, 1922- II. T.
PR6058.U37 S37 1975   821/.9/14   LC 74-18280   ISBN 0670627259

The Achievement of Ted Hughes / edited by Keith Sagar. 2.9719
Athens: University of Georgia Press, 1983. vi, 377 p.; 25 cm. 1. Hughes, Ted, 1930- — Criticism and interpretation — Addresses, essays, lectures. I. Sagar, Keith M.
PR6058.U37 Z52 1983   821/.914 19   LC 82-13522   ISBN 0820306509

Sagar, Keith M. 2.9720
The art of Ted Hughes / Keith Sagar. — Cambridge [Eng.]; New York: Cambridge University Press, 1975. 213 p., [1] leaf of plates: 1 ill.; 23 cm. Includes indexes. 1. Hughes, Ted, 1930- — Criticism and interpretation. I. T.
PR6058.U37 Z87   821/.9/14   LC 74-31787   ISBN 0521207142

PR6060–6061 J–K

James, P. D. 2.9721
The black tower / by P. D. James. — New York: Scribner, c1975. 271 p.; 21 cm. I. T.
PZ4.J2847 Bl3 PR6060.A467   823/.9/14   LC 75-15120   ISBN 0684142635

James, P. D. 2.9722
Shroud for a nightingale, by P. D. James. — New York: Scribner, [1971] 296 p.; 21 cm. — I. T.
PZ4.J2847 Sh PR6060.A467   823/.9/14   LC 70-143933   ISBN 068412372X

James, P. D. 2.9723
An unsuitable job for a woman [by] P. D. James. — New York: Scribner, [1973, c1972] 216 p.; 21 cm. — I. T.
PZ4.J2847 Up3 PR6060.A467   823/.9/14   LC 72-11140   ISBN 068413280X

James, P. D. 2.9724
A taste for death / P.D. James. — 1st American ed. — New York: Knopf, 1986. 459 p.; 25 cm. I. T.
PR6060.A467 T3 1986   823/.914 19   LC 86-45273   ISBN 039455583X

Jenkins, Robin, 1912-. 2.9725
Fergus Lamont / Robin Jenkins. — Edinburgh: Canongate, 1979. 293 p.; 23 cm. — A novel. I. T.
PZ4.J52 Fe 1979 PR6060.E5194   PR6019.E46 F47.   823/.9/14   ISBN 0903937549

Jhabvala, Ruth Prawer, 1927-. 2.9726
An experience of India [by] R. Prawer Jhabvala. — New York: Norton, [1972] 220 p.; 22 cm. — I. T.
PZ4.J6 Ex3 PR6060.H3 E9x   823   LC 70-163372   ISBN 0393086593

Jhabvala, Ruth Prawer, 1927-. 2.9727
Heat and dust / Ruth Prawer Jhabvala. — 1st U.S. ed. — New York: Harper & Row, 1976, c1975. 181 p.; 21 cm. I. T.
PZ4.J6 He3 PR6060.H3 H4x   823   LC 72-25088   ISBN 0060121971

Jhabvala, Ruth Prawer, 1927-. 2.9728
How I became a holy mother, and other stories / Ruth Prawer Jhabvala. 1st U.S. ed. — New York: Harper & Row, c1976. 218 p.; 21 cm. I. T.
PR6060.H3 H6x   823   LC 76-9206   ISBN 006012198X

Shahane, Vasant Anant, 1923-. 2.9729
Ruth Prawer Jhabvala / Vasant A. Shahane. — New Delhi: Arnold-Heinemann Publishers (India), 1976. 198 p.; 19 cm. — (Indian writers series; v. 11) Includes index. 1. Jhabvala, Ruth Prawer, 1927- — Criticism and interpretation. I. T.
PR9499.3.J5 Z88   PR6060H3 Z88.   823   LC 76-901173
Rs20.00

Johnston, Jennifer, 1930-. 2.9730
The captains and the kings. — London: Hamilton, 1972. 142 p.; 21 cm. — I. T.
PZ4.J7225 Cap PR6060.O394   823/.9/14   LC 72-192895   ISBN 0241021146

Johnston, Jennifer, 1930-. 2.9731
The gates. — London: Hamilton, 1973. 171 p.; 21 cm. — I. T.
PZ4.J7225 Gat PR6060.O394 823/.9/14 LC 73-330783 ISBN
0241022851

Johnston, Jennifer, 1930-. 2.9732
How many miles to Babylon? A novel. — [1st ed. in the U.S.]. — Garden City,
N.Y.: Doubleday, 1974. 156 p.; 22 cm. — I. T.
PZ4.J7225 Ho3 PR6060.O394 823/.9/14 LC 74-1502 ISBN
0385056907

Johnston, Jennifer, 1930-. 2.9733
The old jest / Jennifer Johnston. — 1st ed. in the U.S.A. — Garden City, N.Y.:
Doubleday, 1980, c1979. 203 p.; 22 cm. — I. T.
PZ4.J7225 Ol 1980 PR6060.O394 823/.9/14 LC 79-7518 ISBN
038515447X

Johnston, Jennifer, 1930-. 2.9734
Shadows on our skin / Jennifer Johnston. — 1st ed. in the United States of
America. — Garden City, N.Y.: Doubleday, 1978, c1977. 198 p.; 22 cm. —
I. T.
PZ4.J7225 Sh 1978 PR6060.O394 823/.9/14 LC 77-72415 ISBN
0385131259

Johnston, Jennifer, 1930-. 2.9735
The Christmas tree / Jennifer Johnston. — 1st U.S. ed. — New York: W.
Morrow, 1982, c1981. 167 p.; 22 cm. — I. T.
PR6060.O394 C5 1982 823/.914 19 LC 81-18972 ISBN
0688011330

Casey, Daniel J., 1937-. 2.9736
Benedict Kiely [by] Daniel J. Casey. — Lewisburg: Bucknell University Press,
1975 (c1974). 107 p.; 22 cm. — (The Irish writers series) 1. Kiely, Benedict.
I. T.
PR6061.I329 Z58 828/.9/1409 LC 74-168802 ISBN 0838779360

PR6062 L

Le Carré, John, 1931-. 2.9737
The spy who came in from the cold. [1st American ed.] New York: Coward-
McCann [1964] 256 p. 22 cm. A novel. I. T.
PZ4.L4526 Sp3 PR6062.E33 823/.9/14 Fic LC 64-10430

Lee, Tanith. 2.9738
Death's master / by Tanith Lee. — New York: DAW Books, c1979. 348 p.; 18
cm. 1. Science fiction 2. Fantasy I. T.
PR6062.E4163 D4x ISBN 0879774419

Lee, Tanith. 2.9739
Night's master / Tanith Lee; illustrated by George Barr. — New York: Daw
Books, 1978. 188 p.; 18 cm. I. T.
PR6062.E4163 N5x 813.54 ISBN 0879974141

PR6063 M–Mo

MacBeth, George. 2.9740
Collected poems, 1958–1970. — [1st American ed.]. — New York: Atheneum,
1972 [c1971] 254 p.; 23 cm. — I. T.
PR6063.A13 A6 1972 821/.9/14 LC 78-183613

McShane, Mark. 2.9741
Seance / Mark McShane. — New York: Doubleday, 1962. 189 p. I. T.
PR6063.A278 S4x LC 62-11750

Manning, Olivia. 2.9742
The Balkan trilogy / Olivia Manning. — Middlesex, England; New York, N.Y.:
Penguin Books, 1981 (1982 printing) 924 p.; 20 cm. 1. World War, 1939-1945
— Fiction. I. Manning, Olivia. Great fortune. 1981. II. Manning, Olivia.
Spoilt city. 1981. III. Manning, Olivia. Friends and heroes. 1981. IV. T.
PR6063.A384 B27 1982 823/.914 19 LC 82-167331 ISBN
0140059369

Manning, Olivia. 2.9743
The Levant trilogy / Olivia Manning. — Harmondsworth, England: Penguin
Books, 1982. 3 v. in 1 I. T. II. Title: The danger tree. III. Title: The battle lost
and won. IV. Title: The sum of things.
PR6063.A384 L4x ISBN 0140059628

Moorcock, Michael, 1939-. 2.9744
Gloriana: or, The unfulfill'd queen: being a romance / by Michael Moorcock. —
New York: Avon Books, 1979, c1978. — 311 p.: ill.; 21 cm. I. T. II. Title: The
unfulfill'd queen.
PZ4.M8185 Gl 1978 PR6063.O59 823/.9/14 LC 78-71781 ISBN
0380429861

Moorcock, Michael, 1939-. 2.9745
Byzantium endures: a novel / by Michael Moorcock. — 1st American ed. —
New York: Random House, c1981. 373 p.: ill.; 25 cm. I. T.
PR6063.O59 B9 1981 823/.914 19 LC 81-40210 ISBN
0394519728

Mortimer, Penelope, 1918-. 2.9746
The handyman / Penelope Mortimer. — 1st U.S. ed. — New York, NY: St.
Martin's Press, [1985] c1983. 198 p.; 22 cm. 'A Joan Kahn book.' I. T.
PR6063.O815 H3 1985 823/.914 19 LC 85-11792 ISBN
0312358636

Mortimer, Penelope, 1918-. 2.9747
The pumpkin eater. New York, McGraw-Hill [1963, c1962] 222 p. 21 cm. I. T.
PR6063.O815P8x LC 62-22084

PR6063 Mu

Murdoch, Iris. 2.9748
An accidental man. — New York: Viking Press, [1971] 442 p.; 22 cm. — I. T.
PZ4.M974 Ac PR6063.U7 A3x 823/.9/14 LC 79-171893 ISBN
0670102083

Murdoch, Iris. • 2.9749
The bell, a novel. New York, Viking Press, 1958. 342 p. 21 cm. I. T.
PZ4.M974Be PR6063.U7B4 LC 58-12380

Murdoch, Iris. 2.9750
The black prince. — New York: Viking Press, [1973] xviii, 366 p.; 22 cm. —
I. T.
PZ4.M974 Bl3 PR6063.U7 B5x 823/.9/14 LC 72-91828 ISBN
0670172863

Murdoch, Iris. 2.9751
Bruno's dream. — New York: Viking Press, [1969] 311 p.; 22 cm. — I. T.
PZ4.M974 Br PR6063.U7 B7x 823/.9/14 LC 69-11725 ISBN
0670192686

Murdoch, Iris. • 2.9752
A fairly honourable defeat. — New York: Viking Press, [1970] 436 p.; 23 cm. —
I. T.
PZ4.M974 Fai 1970 PR6063.U7 F3x 823/.914 LC 75-89509
ISBN 0670305332

Murdoch, Iris. • 2.9753
The flight from the enchanter. — London, Chatto & Windus, 1956. 316 p. 21
cm. I. T.
PZ4.M974Fl2 PR6063.U7 F5x. LC 56-32361

Murdoch, Iris. 2.9754
The good apprentice / Iris Murdoch. — 1st American ed. — New York, N.Y.:
Viking, 1986, c1985. 522 p.; 24 cm. I. T.
PR6063.U7 G6 1986 823/.914 19 LC 85-40635 ISBN
0670809403

Murdoch, Iris. 2.9755
Henry and Cato / Iris Murdoch. New York: Viking Press, 1977, c1976. 375 p.;
22 cm. I. T.
PZ4.M974 He3 PR6063.U7 H4x 823/.9/14 LC 76-27653 ISBN
0670366978

Murdoch, Iris, 1919-. 2.9756
The Italian girl: a novel. — New York: Viking Press, [1964] 213 p. I. T.
PR6063.U7 I8x LC 64-18481

Murdoch, Iris, 1919-. • 2.9757
The nice and the good / by Iris Murdoch. — London: Chatto & Windus, 1968.
350 p.; 21 cm. I. T.
PZ4.M974 Ni3 PR6063.U7 N5x. LC 68-75865 ISBN
0701112611

Murdoch, Iris. 2.9758
Nuns and soldiers / Iris Murdoch. — New York: Viking Press, c1980. 505 p.;
24 cm. I. T.
PR6063.U7 N8 823/.914 LC 80-16935 ISBN 0670518263

Murdoch, Iris. 2.9759
The philosopher's pupil / Iris Murdoch. — New York: Viking Press, 1983.
576 p.; 23 cm. I. T.
PR6063.U7 P44 1983 823/.914 19 LC 82-45901 ISBN
0670551864

Murdoch, Iris, 1919-.   **2.9760**
The red and the green / Iris Murdoch. — New York: Viking Press, [1965]
311 p. I. T.
PR6063.U7 R4x

Murdoch, Iris.   **2.9761**
The sacred and profane love machine. — New York: Viking Press, [1974]
374 p.; 22 cm. — I. T.
PZ4.M974 Sac3 PR6063.U7 S3x   823/.9/14   LC 73-22649   ISBN
0670614335

Murdoch, Iris.   • **2.9762**
The sandcastle, a novel. New York, Viking Press, 1957. 342 p. 21 cm. I. T.
PR6063.U7 S3x   PZ4.M974 San   LC 57-7554

Murdoch, Iris.   **2.9763**
The sea, the sea / Iris Murdoch. — New York: Viking Press, 1978. 502 p.; 23
cm. — I. T.
PZ4.M974 Sd PR6063.U7 S4x   823/.9/14   LC 78-13516   ISBN
0670626511

Murdoch, Iris.   • **2.9764**
A severed head, a novel. New York, Viking Press, 1961. 248 p. 21 cm. I. T.
PR6063.U7 S42x   PZ4.M974 Se   LC 61-7278

Murdoch, Iris.   **2.9765**
The three arrows and The servants and the snow: plays / by Iris Murdoch. —
New York: Viking Press, 1974. 221 p.; 21 cm. I. Murdoch, Iris. The servants
and the snow. 1974. II. T.
PR6063.U7 T5 1974   822/.9/14   LC 73-8328   ISBN 0670706388

Murdoch, Iris, 1919-.   **2.9766**
The time of the angels. New York: Viking Press [1966] 245 p. 22 cm. I. T.
PZ4.M974Ti PR6063.U7T55x   LC 66-24208

Murdoch, Iris.   • **2.9767**
Under the net: a novel / by Iris Murdoch. — New York: Viking Press, 1954.
279 p. I. T.
PR6063.U7 U4x   LC 54-7053

Murdoch, Iris.   • **2.9768**
An unofficial rose, a novel. New York, Viking Press [1962] 344 p. 21 cm. I. T.
PZ4.M974Uq PR6063.U7U56   LC 62-11669

Murdoch, Iris, 1919-.   • **2.9769**
The unicorn: a novel / Iris Murdoch. — New York: Viking Press, 1963. 311 p.
I. T.
PZ4.M974 Up   PR6063.U7 U5x.   LC 63-11857

Murdoch, Iris.   **2.9770**
A word child. — New York: Viking Press, [1975] 390 p.; 22 cm. — I. T.
PZ4.M974 Wo3 PR6063.U7 W6x   823/.9/14   LC 75-1418   ISBN
067078236X

Baldanza, Frank.   **2.9771**
Iris Murdoch. New York, Twayne Publishers [1974] 187 p. port. 21 cm.
(Twayne's English authors series, TEAS 169) 1. Murdoch, Iris. I. T.
PR6063.U7 Z58   823/.9/14   LC 73-22302   ISBN 0805714103

Byatt, A. S. (Antonia Susan), 1936-.   **2.9772**
Degrees of freedom. [New York] Barnes & Noble [1965] 224 p. 23 cm.
1. Murdoch, Iris. I. T.
PR6063.U7 Z6 1965   LC 65-6364

Dipple, Elizabeth.   **2.9773**
Iris Murdoch, work for the spirit / Elizabeth Dipple. — Chicago: University of
Chicago Press, 1982. xi, 356 p.; 24 cm. Includes indexes. 1. Murdoch, Iris —
Criticism and interpretation. 2. Murdoch, Iris — Religion. I. T.
PR6063.U7 Z64   823/.914 19   LC 81-52553   ISBN 0226153630

Gerstenberger, Donna Lorine.   **2.9774**
Iris Murdoch / Donna Gerstenberger. — Lewisburg [Pa.]: Bucknell University
Press, [1974] c1975. 85 p.; 21 cm. — (The Irish writers series) 1. Murdoch, Iris
— Criticism and interpretation. I. T.
PR6063.U7 Z66 1975   823/.9/14   LC 72-126290   ISBN
0838777740

Hague, Angela.   **2.9775**
Iris Murdoch's comic vision / Angela Hague. — Selinsgrove [Pa.]:
Susquehanna University Press, c1984. 164 p.; 22 cm. Includes index.
1. Murdoch, Iris — Criticism and interpretation. 2. Comic, The, in literature.
I. T.
PR6063.U7 Z67 1984   823/.914 19   LC 82-42638   ISBN
0941664007

Todd, Richard.   **2.9776**
Iris Murdoch / Richard Todd. — London; New York: Methuen, 1985 (c1984).
112 p.; 20 cm. (Contemporary writers.) 1. Murdoch, Iris — Criticism and
interpretation. I. T. II. Series.
PR6063.U7 Z924   823/.914 19   LC 84-1155   ISBN 0416354203

Wolfe, Peter, 1933-.   **2.9777**
The disciplined heart: Iris Murdoch and her novels. — Columbia: University of
Missouri Press, [1966] x, 220 p.; 25 cm. 1. Murdoch, Iris — Criticism and
interpretation. I. T.
PR6063.U7 Z95   823.914   LC 66-21761

Murphy, Richard, 1927-.   **2.9778**
The price of stone & earlier poems / Richard Murphy. — Winston-Salem, N.C.:
Wake Forest University Press, c1985. xii, 190 p.; 24 cm. I. T. II. Title: Price of
stone and earlier poems.
PR6063.U735.P72 1985   LC 85-51492   ISBN 0916390241

Richard Murphy: poet of two traditions: interdisciplinary studies   **2.9779**
/ edited by Maurice Harmon.
Dublin: Wolfhound Press, 1978. 128 p.: ill.; 24 cm. 1. Murphy, Richard, 1927-
— Criticism and interpretation — Addresses, essays, lectures. I. Murphy,
Richard, 1927- II. Harmon, Maurice.
PR6063.U735 Z88   821/.9/14   LC 78-319567   ISBN 0905473175

PR6064–6065 N–O

Nichols, Peter, 1927-.   **2.9780**
Plays, one / Peter Nichols. — London: Methuen, 1987. xv, 376 p.; 18 cm. —
(Methuen world dramatists) (A Methuen paperback) I. T.
PR6064.I2 A19 1987   822/.914   LC gb86-23273   ISBN
0413423301

Nichols, Peter, 1927-.   **2.9781**
[Day in the death of Joe Egg] Joe Egg; [play] New York, Grove Press [c1967]
87 p. 20 cm. (An Evergreen original, E462) First published in 1967 under title:
A day in the death of Joe Egg. I. T.
PR6064.I2 D3 1967b   822/.9/14   LC 68-21264

Nichols, Peter, 1927-.   **2.9782**
Passion play / Peter Nichols. — London: Eyre Methuen, 1981. 106 p.; 20 cm.
I. T.
PR6064.I2 P37   822/.914 19   LC 81-127672   ISBN 0413479102

Nichols, Peter, 1927-.   **2.9783**
A piece of my mind / Peter Nichols. — London: Methuen, 1987. [vi, 80] p.; 19
cm. (A Methuen modern play) I. T.
PR6064.I2   822/.914 19   ISBN 0413173607

O'Brien, Edna.   **2.9784**
The country girls. [1st ed.] New York, Knopf, 1960. 242 p. 21 cm. (Borzoi
books) I. T.
PR6065.B7 C8x 1960   LC 60-7490

O'Brien, Edna.   **2.9785**
Girls in their married bliss. — New York: Simon & Schuster, c1968, [1964]
191 p.; 21 cm. I. T.
PR6065.B7.G4x   LC 65-10455

O'Brien, Edna.   **2.9786**
The lonely girl. New York, Random House [1962] 244 p. 21 cm. I. T.
PR6065.B7 L6x   PZ4.O129 Lo   LC 62-8438

Eckley, Grace.   **2.9787**
Edna O'Brien. — Lewisburg [Pa.]: Bucknell University Press, [1974] 88 p.; 20
cm. — (The Irish writers series) 1. O'Brien, Edna. I. T.
PR6065.B7 Z65   823/.9/14   LC 79-168806   ISBN 0838778380

O'Faolain, Julia.   **2.9788**
Women in the wall / Julia O'Faolain. — New York: Viking Press, [1975] 326 p.:
ill.; 22 cm. 1. Radegonde, Saint, d. 587 — Fiction. 2. France — History — To
987 — Fiction. I. T.
PZ4.O312 Wo3 PR6065.F3 W6x   823/.9/14   LC 75-1355   ISBN
0670778532

Orton, Joe.   **2.9789**
The complete plays / Joe Orton; introduced by John Lahr. New York: Grove
Press: distributed by Random House, 1977. 448 p.; 19 cm. (A Black cat book)
I. T.
PR6065.R7 A19 1977   822/.9/14   LC 76-54475   ISBN
0802140416

Lahr, John, 1941-.   **2.9790**
Prick up your ears: the biography of Joe Orton / John Lahr. — 1st ed. — New
York: Knopf: distributed by Random House, 1978. xiii, 302 p., [8] leaves of

plates: ill.; 25 cm. 1. Orton, Joe. 2. Dramatists, English — 20th century —
Biography. I. T.
PR6065.R7 Z77   822/.9/14 B   *LC* 78-7130   *ISBN* 0394501535

PR6066–6068 P–R

Pinter, Harold, 1930-.   **2.9791**
[Works. 1977] Complete works: with an introduction 'Writing for the theatre' /
Harold Pinter. — 1st Black cat ed. — New York: Grove Press: distributed by
Random House, 1977-<1981> c1976-<c1981>. v. <1-4>; 19 cm. Vol. 3
lacks ed. statement. I. T.
PR6066.I53 1977   812/.5/4   *LC* 77-2449   *ISBN* 0802140882

Esslin, Martin.   **2.9792**
Pinter: a study of his plays / by Martin Esslin. Expanded ed. — New York:
Norton, 1976. 273 p., [4] leaves of plates: ill.; 19 cm. (The Norton library; N819)
First ed. published in 1970 under title: The peopled wound. Includes index.
1. Pinter, Harold, 1930- — Criticism and interpretation. I. T.
PR6066.I53 Z643 1976   822/.9/14   *LC* 76-17904   *ISBN*
0393008193

Ganz, Arthur F., 1928- comp.   **2.9793**
Pinter, a collection of critical essays, edited by Arthur Ganz. — Englewood
Cliffs, N.J.: Prentice-Hall, [1972] vi, 184 p.; 21 cm. — (A Spectrum book:
Twentieth century views, S-TC-103) 1. Pinter, Harold, 1930- — Criticism and
interpretation — Addresses, essays, lectures. I. T.
PR6066.I53 Z647   822/.9/14   *LC* 72-8031   *ISBN* 0136763871

Hinchliffe, Arnold P., 1930-.   **2.9794**
Harold Pinter / by Arnold P. Hinchliffe. — Rev. ed. — Boston: Twayne
Publishers, 1981. 177 p.: port.; 21 cm. — (Twayne's English authors series;
TEAS 51) Includes index. 1. Pinter, Harold, 1930- — Criticism and
interpretation. I. T.
PR6066.I53 Z675 1981   822/.914 19   *LC* 80-24903   *ISBN*
0805767843

Hollis, James R., 1930-.   • **2.9795**
Harold Pinter; the poetics of silence [by] James R. Hollis. Pref. by Harry T.
Moore. — Carbondale, Southern Illinois University Press [1970] xii, 143 p. 22
cm. — (Crosscurrents/modern critiques) 1. Pinter, Harold, 1930- I. T.
PR6066.I53 Z678   822/.9/14   *LC* 77-86186   *ISBN* 809304503 4.95

Pomerance, Bernard.   **2.9796**
The elephant man: a play / by Bernard Pomerance. — 1st ed. — New York:
Grove Press: distributed by Random House, 1979. vi, 71 p.; 21 cm. 1. Merrick,
Joseph Carey, 1862 or 3-1890 — Drama. I. T.
PR6066.O48 E4 1979   822/.9/14   *LC* 79-7792

Porter, Peter.   **2.9797**
Preaching to the converted. — London: Oxford University Press, 1973 (c1977)
[9], 61 p.; 22 cm. Poems. I. T.
PR6066.O73 P7   821/.9/14   *LC* 72-172564   *ISBN* 0192118218

Postgate, Raymond William, 1896-1971.   **2.9798**
Verdict of twelve [by] Raymond Postgate. — Garden City, N.Y.: Doubleday,
1940. 1 v. I. T.
PZ3.P8483 Ve18   PR6066.O74 V47.

Pym, Barbara.   **2.9799**
Excellent women / Barbara Pym. — London: J. Cape, 1952. 256 p.; 21 cm.
I. T.
PR6066.Y58 E9x   *ISBN* 0224015532

Pym, Barbara.   **2.9800**
A glass of blessings / Barbara Pym. — London: J. Cape, 1958. 255 p.; 20 cm. —
I. T.
PR6066.Y58 G5 1958   823/.914 19   *LC* 81-185756

Pym, Barbara.   **2.9801**
Less than angels / Barbara Pym. — London: J. Cape, 1955. 256 p.; 21 cm.
1. Anthropologists — Fiction 2. Love stories I. T.
PR6066.Y58.L6x   823   *ISBN* 0224016504

Pym, Barbara.   **2.9802**
Quartet in autumn / Barbara Pym. — London: Macmillan, 1977. 218 p.; 21 cm.
— I. T.
PZ4.P9965 Qar PR6066.Y58 Q3x   823/.9/14   *LC* 77-379168
    ISBN 0333227786

Raine, Craig.   **2.9803**
A Martian sends a postcard home / Craig Raine. — Oxford; New York: Oxford
University Press, 1979. v, 46 p.; 22 cm. I. T.
PR6068.A313 M3   821/.9/14   *LC* 79-41074   *ISBN* 019211896X

Raine, Craig.   **2.9804**
The onion, memory / Craig Raine. — Oxford; New York: Oxford University
Press, 1978. vi, 84 p.; 22 cm. Poems. I. T.
PR6068.A313 O5   821/.9/14   *LC* 77-30527   *ISBN* 0192118773

Rendell, Ruth, 1930-.   **2.9805**
A demon in my view / Ruth Rendell. 1st ed. in the U.S.A. — Garden City,
N.Y.: Doubleday, 1977, c1976. 182 p.; 22 cm. I. T.
PZ4.R4132 De3 PR6068.E63   823/.9/14   *LC* 76-9486   *ISBN*
0385121105

Roberts, Keith, 1935-.   **2.9806**
The chalk giants / [by] Keith Roberts. — London: Hutchinson, 1974. 271 p.; 23
cm. I. T.
PZ4.R6447 Ch PR6068.O15   823/.9/14   *LC* 75-325249   *ISBN*
0091178800

PR6069 S

Scott, Paul, 1920-.   **2.9807**
The Raj quartet / by Paul Scott. New York: Morrow, 1976. 1922 p. in various
pagings; 25 cm. 1. India — History — 20th century — Fiction. I. T.
PZ4.S428 Raj3 PR6069.C596   823/.9/14   *LC* 76-13249   *ISBN*
0688030653

Tedesco, Janis, 1950-.   **2.9808**
Introduction to the Raj quartet / Janis Tedesco, Janet Popham. — Lanham,
MD: University Press of America, c1985. xxiv, 271 p.; 23 cm. 1. Scott, Paul,
1920- Raj quartet. 2. India in literature. I. Popham, Janet, 1948- II. T.
III. Title: Raj quartet.
PR6069.C596 R3437 1985   823/.914 19   *LC* 85-623   *ISBN*
081914570X

Swinden, Patrick.   **2.9809**
Paul Scott, images of India / Patrick Swinden. — New York: St. Martin's Press,
1980. xii, 123 p.; 23 cm. Includes index. 1. Scott, Paul, 1920- — Criticism and
interpretation. 2. India in literature. I. T.
PR6069.C596 Z86 1980   823/.914   *LC* 79-28281   *ISBN*
031259822X

Scott, Paul, 1920-.   • **2.9810**
The love pavilion. New York, Morrow, 1960. 313 p. 21 cm. 'Published in Great
Britain under the title The Chinese love pavilion.' I. T.
PR6069.C6x   *LC* 60-11706

Shaw, Bob.   **2.9811**
Other days, other eyes. London: Gollancz, 1972. 160 p.; 21 cm. — I. T.
PZ4.S53356 Ot PR6069.H364   823/.9/14   *LC* 73-162306   *ISBN*
0575014857

Sheed, Wilfrid.   • **2.9812**
The morning after; selected essays and reviews. With a foreword by John
Leonard. — [1st ed.]. — New York: Farrar, Straus & Giroux, [1971] xx, 303 p.;
23 cm. — I. T.
PR6069.H396 M6   PS3537.H56 M6.   824/.9/14   *LC* 76-161369
    ISBN 0374213054

Stoppard, Tom.   **2.9813**
On the razzle / Tom Stoppard; adapted from Einen Jux will er sich machen by
Johann Nestroy. — London; Boston: Faber and Faber, 1981. 79 p.; 20 cm. —
(Faber paperbacks) I. Nestroy, Johann, 1801-1862. Jux will er sich machen.
II. T.
PR6069.T6 O5 1981   822/.914 19   *LC* 82-140750   *ISBN*
0571118356

Stoppard, Tom.   **2.9814**
The real Inspector Hound. — New York: Grove Press, [1969, c1968] 58 p.; 21
cm. — (Evergreen original E-489) A play. I. T.
PR6069.T6 R4 1969   822/.9/14   *LC* 68-57490

Stoppard, Tom.   **2.9815**
The real thing / Tom Stoppard. — Reprinted with revisions. — London;
Boston: Faber and Faber, 1983. 84 p.; 21 cm. Originally published in 1982. I. T.
PR6069.T6 R43 1983   822/.914 19   *LC* 84-210058   *ISBN*
0571132006

Stoppard, Tom.   **2.9816**
Rosencrantz & Guildenstern are dead. New York, Grove Press [1967] 126 p. 21
cm. (An Evergreen book, E455) I. T.
PR6069.T6 R6 1967b   822/.9/14   *LC* 67-30108

Stoppard, Tom.   **2.9817**
Travesties: [a play] / by Tom Stoppard. — New York: Grove Press: distributed
by Random House, 1975. 99 p.; 21 cm. (An Evergreen book; E-661) 1. Carr,

Henry Wilfred, 1894-1962 — Drama. 2. Joyce, James, 1882-1941. in fiction, drama, poetry, etc. 3. Lenin, Vladimir Il'ich, 1870-1924 — Drama. I. T.
PR6069.T6 T7 1975b   822/.9/14   *LC* 75-13552   *ISBN* 039417884X

Bigsby, C. W. E.   **2.9818**
Tom Stoppard / by C. W. E. Bigsby; edited by Ian Scott–Kilvert. Harlow [Eng.]: Published for the British Council by Longman Group, 1976. 32 p.: port.; 22 cm. (Writers and their work. 250) 'Tom Stoppard, a select bibliography': p. 30-32. 1. Stoppard, Tom — Criticism and interpretation. I. T. II. Series.
PR6069.T6 Z58   822/.9/14 B   *LC* 76-378638   *ISBN* 0582012627

Londré, Felicia Hardison, 1941-.   **2.9819**
Tom Stoppard / Felicia Hardison Londré. — New York: F. Ungar Pub. Co., c1981. xii, 180 p.; 21 cm. — (Modern literature series) Includes index. 1. Stoppard, Tom — Criticism and interpretation. I. T.
PR6069.T6 Z75   822/.914 19   *LC* 80-53698   *ISBN* 0804425388

Storey, David, 1933-.   • **2.9820**
This sporting life. — London: Longmans, 1960. 256 p.; 19 cm. (The heritage of literature series, section B, no. 98) I. Halson, Geoffrey. II. T. III. Series.
PZ4.S8815 Th5 PR6069.T65   823/.9/12   *LC* 60-26348

Storey, David, 1933-.   **2.9821**
[Plays. Selections] Early days; Sisters; and Life class / David Storey. — Harmondsworth, Middlesex, England; New York, N.Y.: Penguin, 1980. 236 p.; 20 cm. — (Penguin plays) I. T.
PR6069.T65 A6 1980   822/.914 19   *LC* 81-141016   *ISBN* 0140481656

Storey, David, 1933-.   **2.9822**
[Plays. Selections] Home; The changing room; and Mother's day / David Storey. — Harmondsworth, Middlesex, England; New York, N.Y., U.S.A.: Penguin Books, 1984. 268 p.; 20 cm. (Penguin plays) I. T. II. Title: Home. III. Title: Changing room. IV. Title: Mother's day.
PR6069.T65 A6 1984   822/.914 19   *LC* 84-252311   *ISBN* 0140481451

Storey, David, 1933-.   **2.9823**
In celebration; The contractor; The restoration of Arnold Middleton; The farm / David Storey. — Harmondsworth: Penguin, 1982. 223 p.; 18 cm. — (Penguin plays) I. Storey, David, 1933- The contractor. II. Storey, David, 1933- The restoration of Arnold Middleton. III. Storey, David, 1933- The farm. IV. T.
PR6069.T65 I5 1982   822/.9/14   *LC* 73-164041   *ISBN* 0140481664

Storey, David, 1933-.   **2.9824**
A prodigal child / David Storey. — New York: E.P. Dutton, c1982. 319 p.; 22 cm. I. T.
PR6069.T653 P7 1982b   823/.914 19   *LC* 82-73605   *ISBN* 0525241604

PR6070–6073 T–W

Thomas, D. M.   **2.9825**
The flute–player: a novel / by D. M. Thomas. — 1st American ed. — New York: Dutton, 1979. 192 p.; 22 cm. 'A Henry Robbins book.' I. T.
PZ4.T4544 Fl 1979 PR6070.H58   823/.9/14   *LC* 79-2582   *ISBN* 0525107274

Tracy, Honor, 1915-.   • **2.9826**
The first day of Friday; a novel. New York, Random House [1963] 246 p. 22 cm. I. T.
PZ4.T762 Fi2   PR6070.R25 Fx.   *LC* 63-11622

Tracy, Honor, 1915-.   • **2.9827**
The straight and narrow path: a novel / by Honor Tracy. — London: Methuen, [1956] 228 p.; 19 cm. I. T.
PZ4.T762St   PR6039.R32 S8 1956.   PR6070.R25 Sx.   *LC* 56-33344

Wesker, Arnold, 1932-.   **2.9828**
The plays of Arnold Wesker. — 1st ed. — New York: Harper & Row, c1976-1977. 2 v. I. T.
PR6073.E75 A19 1976   *LC* 75-25104   *ISBN* 0060145676

Wilson, Colin, 1931-.   • **2.9829**
Adrift in Soho. — Boston: Houghton Mifflin, 1961. 229 p.; 21 cm. I. T.
PR6073.I44 A3x   *LC* 61-15179

Tredell, Nicolas.   **2.9830**
The novels of Colin Wilson / by Nicolas Tredell. — London: Vision; Totowa, NJ: Barnes & Noble Books, 1982. 157 p.; 23 cm. — (Critical studies series.)

Includes index. 1. Wilson, Colin, 1931- — Criticism and interpretation. I. T. II. Series.
PR6073.I44 Z87 1982   823/.914 19   *LC* 82-13913   *ISBN* 0854780351

Weigel, John A.   **2.9831**
Colin Wilson / John A. Weigel. — Boston: Twayne Publishers, [1975] 157 p.: port.; 22 cm. (Twayne's English authors series; TEAS 181) Includes index. 1. Wilson, Colin, 1931- — Criticism and interpretation. I. T.
PR6073.I44 Z9   828/.9/1409   *LC* 74-28137   *ISBN* 0805715754

PR8300 REGIONAL LITERATURES IN ENGLISH. ANGLO–IRISH LITERATURE

PR8500–8697 Scotland

(Literary History and Collections. For individual authors see main PR period lists.)

Royle, Trevor.   **2.9832**
Companion to Scottish literature / Trevor Royle. — Detroit, Mich.: Gale Research Co., c1983. xi, 322 p.; 24 cm. British ed. published under title: The Macmillan companion to Scottish literature. London: Macmillan Reference Books, 1983. Includes index. 1. Scottish literature — Dictionaries. 2. English literature — Scottish authors — Dictionaries. 3. Scottish literature — Bio-bibliography. 4. English literature — Scottish authors — Bio-bibliography. 5. Authors, Scottish — Biography — Dictionaries. 6. Scotland in literature — Dictionaries. I. T.
PR8506.R69 1983   820/.9/9411 19   *LC* 83-5493   *ISBN* 0810305194

Craig, David, 1932-.   • **2.9833**
Scottish literature and the Scottish people, 1680–1830. — London, Chatto & Windus, 1961. 339 p. 23 cm. 'Work on this subject was originally done for a thesis accepted for the Cambridge Ph. D.' 1. Scottish literature — Hist. & crit. 2. Scotland — Civilization I. T.
PR8511.C7   820.9   *LC* 62-6437

MacDiarmid, Hugh, 1892-.   **2.9834**
Contemporary Scottish studies: 1st series / by Christopher Grieve. — London: Parsons, 1926. 343 p.; 23 cm. 1. Scottish literature — Biobibliography. 2. Scottish literature — History and criticism. 3. English literature — Scottish authors I. T.
PR8511.G7x

Lindsay, Maurice, 1918-.   **2.9835**
History of Scottish literature / Maurice Lindsay. — London: Hale, 1977. 496 p.; 25 cm. Includes index. 1. Scottish literature — History and criticism. I. T.
PR8511.L5   820/.9   *LC* 77-360000   *ISBN* 0709156421

Wittig, Kurt, 1914-.   • **2.9836**
The Scottish tradition in literature. — Edinburgh: Oliver and Boyd, 1958. 352 p.; 23 cm. 1. Scottish literature — History and criticism. I. T.
PR8511.W5   *LC* 58-3514

Jack, Ronald D. S.   **2.9837**
The Italian influence on Scottish literature / [by] R. D. S. Jack. — Edinburgh: Edinburgh University Press, 1972. vii, 256 p.; 23 cm. 1. Scottish literature — History and criticism. 2. Literature, Comparative — Scottish and Italian. 3. Literature, Comparative — Italian and Scottish. I. T.
PR8519.J3   820/.9   *LC* 74-182903   *ISBN* 085224214X

Scottish poetry: a critical survey.   **2.9838**
London: Cassell, [1955] ix, 329 p.; 23 cm. 1. Scottish poetry — History and criticism. 2. English peotry — Scottish authors — History and criticism. I. Kinsley, James.
PR8561.K5   *LC* 56-2090

Buchan, David, 1939-.   **2.9839**
The ballad and the folk [by] David Buchan. London, Boston, Routledge and K. Paul, 1972. xii, 326 p., leaf. illus., map. 23 cm. 1. Ballads, English — Scotland — History and criticism. 2. Scotland — Civilization I. T.
PR8580.B8   398/.042/09411   *LC* 72-169448   *ISBN* 0710073224

Hart, Francis Russell.   2.9840
The Scottish novel: from Smollett to Spark / Francis Russell Hart. — Cambridge, Mass.: Harvard University Press, 1978. xii, 442 p.; 24 cm. 1. Scottish fiction — History and criticism. 2. English fiction — Scottish authors — History and criticism. I. T.
PR8597.H37   823/.03   LC 77-20680   ISBN 0674795849

Murray, Isobel.   2.9841
Ten modern Scottish novels / Isobel Murray and Bob Tait. — Aberdeen: Aberdeen University Press: Atlantic Highlands, N.J.: Distributed in the U.S.A. by Humanities Press, 1984. vii, 243 p.; 22 cm. Distributor from label on t.p. 1. Scottish fiction — 20th century — History and criticism. 2. English fiction — Scottish authors — History and criticism. 3. Scotland in literature. I. Tait, Bob. II. T.
PR8603.M87 1984c   823/.912/09 19   LC 86-109163   ISBN 0080284949

MacQueen, John. ed.   • 2.9842
The Oxford book of Scottish verse; chosen by John MacQueen and Tom Scott. Oxford, Clarendon P., 1966. xxix, 633 p. 19 1/2 cm. 1. Scottish poetry I. Scott, Tom, 1918- joint ed. II. T.
PR8650.M3   LC 66-68550

Eyre-Todd, George, 1862-1937. ed.   • 2.9843
Early Scottish poetry: Thomas the Rhymer, John Barbour, Androw of Wyntoun, Henry the minstrel. Edited by George Eyre–Todd. Westport, Conn., Greenwood Press [1971] 220 p. 23 cm. Reprint of the 1891 ed. 1. Scottish poetry — To 1700 2. English poetry — Middle English, 1100-1500 3. English poetry — Scottish authors I. Thomas, the Rhymer, 1220?-1297? II. Barbour, John, d. 1395. III. Andrew, of Wyntoun, 1350?-1420? IV. Henry, the Minstrel, fl. 1470-1492. V. T.
PR8655.E87 1971   821/.1/08   LC 77-98753   ISBN 0837130948

Bruce, George, 1909- comp.   • 2.9844
The Scottish literary revival: an anthology of twentieth–century poetry. — London: Collier-Macmillan; New York: Macmillan, 1968. xi, 130 p.: index.; 23 cm. 1. Scottish poetry — 20th century I. T.
PR8658.B7 1968   821/.008   LC 67-17497

King, Charles, 1919- comp.   2.9845
Twelve modern Scottish poets. London: University of London Press, 1971. 205 p.; 22 cm. 1. Scottish poetry — 20th century 2. Scottish poetry — 20th century — Bio-bibliography. I. T.
PR8658.K5   821/.9/1208   LC 72-169391   ISBN 0340147741

MacCaig, Norman, 1910-.   2.9846
Contemporary Scottish verse, 1959–1969 / edited by Norman MacCaig & Alexander Scott. — London: Calder & Boyars, 1970. 271 p.; 21 cm. — (The Scottish library) Includes poetry in Gaelic. 1. Scottish poetry — 20th century 2. English poetry — Scottish authors I. Scott, Alexander, 1920- joint author. II. T.
PR8658.M28   821/.9/1408   LC 70-510243   ISBN 0714501786

Twelve more modern Scottish poets / edited by Charles King   2.9847
and Iain Crichton–Smith.
London: Hodder and Stoughton, 1986. 176 p.: ill., ports.; 22 cm. Includes poems in Gaelic with English translation. 1. English poetry — Scottish authors 2. Scottish poetry — 20th century I. King, Charles, 1919- II. Crichton Smith, Iain. III. Title: 12 more modern Scottish poets.
PR8658.T94   821/.914/0809411 19   ISBN 0340403632

Modern Scottish short stories / edited by Fred Urquhart and   2.9848
Giles Gordon.
London: H. Hamilton, 1978. 212 p.; 23 cm. 1. Short stories, Scottish. 2. Short stories, English — Scottish authors 3. English fiction — 20th century I. Urquhart, Fred, 1912- II. Gordon, Giles, 1940-
PR8675.M6x   823/.01   LC 79-304737   ISBN 0241100585

Reid, James Macarthur, 1901-1970.   • 2.9849
Scottish short stories / selected with an introd. by J.M. Reid. — London; Toronto: Oxford University Press, c1963. xiii, 328 p. — 'The World's classics;595' 1. Short stories, Scottish. 2. English fiction — Scottish authors I. T.
PR8676.R4x   PZ1.R27 Sc   LC 63-25061   ISBN 0192505955

PR8700–8897 Ireland

(Literary History and Collections. For individual authors see main PR period lists.)

Dictionary of Irish literature / Robert Hogan, editor–in–chief;   2.9850
Zack Bowen, William J. Feeney, James Kilroy, advisory editors;
Mary Rose Callaghan, Richard Burnham, associate editors.
Westport, Conn.: Greenwood Press, 1979. xviii, 815 p.; 25 cm. Includes index. 1. English literature — Irish authors — Dictionaries. 2. English literature — Irish authors — Bio-Bibliography. 3. Authors, Irish — Biography. I. Hogan, Robert Goode, 1930-
PR8706.D5 1979   820/.9/9415 B   LC 78-20021   ISBN 0313207186

Jeffares, A. Norman (Alexander Norman), 1920-.   2.9851
Anglo–Irish literature / A. Norman Jeffares. — 1st American ed. — New York: Schocken Books, 1983 (c1982). vi, 349 p.; 23 cm. — (History of literature series.) Includes index. 1. English literature — Irish authors — History and criticism. 2. Ireland in literature. I. T. II. Series.
PR8711.J4   820/.9/9415 19   LC 82-5753   ISBN 080523828X

McHugh, Roger Joseph.   2.9852
Short history of Anglo–Irish literature from its origins to the present day / Roger McHugh and Maurice Harmon. — Totowa, N.J.: Barnes & Noble Books, 1982. 377 p.: ill.; 23 cm. Includes index. 1. English literature — Irish authors — History and criticism. 2. Ireland in literature. I. Harmon, Maurice. II. T.
PR8711.M35 1982   820/.9/9415 19   LC 82-8765   ISBN 0389203165

Anglo–Irish literature: a review of research / edited by Richard   2.9853
J. Finneran.
New York: Modern Language Association of America, 1976. xv, 596 p.; 24 cm. Includes index. 1. English literature — Irish authors — History and criticism. 2. English literature — Irish authors — Bibliography. I. Finneran, Richard J.
PR8712.A5   820/.9/9415 19   LC 74-31959   ISBN 0873522524

Recent research on Anglo–Irish writers / edited by Richard J.   2.9854
Finneran.
New York: Modern Language Association of America, 1983. xvi, 361 p.; 24 cm. Supplement to: Anglo-Irish literature. Includes index. 1. English literature — Irish authors — History and criticism. 2. English literature — Irish authors — Bibliography. I. Finneran, Richard J. II. Title: Anglo-Irish literature.
PR8712.R4 1983   820/.9/9415 19   LC 82-12575   ISBN 0873522591

Fallis, Richard.   2.9855
The Irish renaissance / Richard Fallis. — 1st ed. — Syracuse, N.Y.: Syracuse University Press, 1977. xvi, 319 p.; 23 cm. Includes index. 1. English literature — Irish authors — History and criticism. I. T.
PR8750.F34   820/.9   LC 77-24576   ISBN 0815621868

Kenner, Hugh.   2.9856
A colder eye: the modern Irish writers / Hugh Kenner. — 1st ed. — New York, N.Y.: Knopf, 1983. xiv, 301 p.; 25 cm. 1. English literature — Irish authors — History and criticism. 2. Ireland in literature. 3. English literature — 20th century — History and criticism. 4. English literature — 19th century — History and criticism. 5. Ireland — Intellectual life. I. T.
PR8750.K46 1983   820/.9/9415 19   LC 82-48723   ISBN 0394422252

Ussher, Arland.   2.9857
Three great Irishmen: Shaw, Yeats, Joyce; with portraits by Augustus John. — New York: Devin-Adair, 1953 (c1952) 160 p.: ill. 1. Shaw, Bernard, 1856-1950. 2. Yeats, W. B. (William Butler), 1865-1939. 3. Joyce, James, 1882-1941. I. T.
PR8750 U7 1953   LC 53-10682

Costello, Peter.   2.9858
The heart grown brutal: the Irish Revolution in literature from Parnell to the death of Yeats, 1891–1939. — Dublin: Gill & Macmillan; Totowa, N.J.: Rowman & Littlefield, 1978 (c1977). xiii, 330 p., [4] leaves of plates. ill.; 23 cm. Includes index. 1. English literature — Irish authors — History and criticism. 2. English literature — 20th century — History and criticism. 3. Authors, Irish — 20th century — Political and social views. 4. Literature and revolutions. 5. Ireland — History — 20th century I. T.
PR8753.C67   820/.99415   LC 78-312181   ISBN 0847660079

Contemporary Irish writing / edited by James D. Brophy, Raymond J. Porter. 2.9859
[New Rochelle, N.Y.]: Iona College Press; Boston, Mass.: Twayne Publishers, c1983. 174 p.; 23 cm. — (Library of Irish studies. 2) Sequel to: Modern Irish literature. 1. English literature — Irish authors — History and criticism — Addresses, essays, lectures. 2. English literature — 20th century — History and criticism — Addresses, essays, lectures. 3. Ireland in literature — Addresses, essays, lectures. I. Brophy, James D. II. Porter, Raymond J. III. Series.
PR8754.C66 1983   820/.9/89162 19   *LC* 83-113   *ISBN* 0805790160

Hogan, Robert Goode, 1930-. 2.9860
The modern Irish drama: a documentary history / by Robert Hogan and James Kilroy. — Dublin: Dolmen Press; Atlantic Highlands, N.J.: Humanities Press, 1975-. v.   ; 23 cm. — (The Irish theatre series; 6-) 1. English drama — Irish authors — History and criticism. I. Kilroy, James. joint author. II. T.
PR8789.H62   792/.09415   *LC* 76-20588   *ISBN* 0391006096

Maxwell, D. E. S. (Desmond Ernest Stewart), 1925-. 2.9861
A critical history of modern Irish drama, 1891–1980 / D.E.S. Maxwell. — Cambridge [Cambridgeshire]; New York: Cambridge University Press, 1985 (c1984). xvii, 250 p.: ill.; 24 cm. Spine title: Modern Irish drama, 1891-1980. Includes index. 1. English drama — Irish authors — History and criticism. 2. English drama — 20th century — History and criticism. 3. Ireland in literature. I. T. II. Title: Modern Irish drama, 1891-1980.
PR8789.M39   822/.91/099415 19   *LC* 84-5801   *ISBN* 0521225329

Glassie, Henry H. 2.9862
All silver and no brass: an Irish Christmas mumming / Henry Glassie; illustrated by the author. — Bloomington: Indiana University Press, c1975. xx, 192 p., [4] leaves of plates: ill.; 25 cm. Includes index. 1. Folk drama, Irish — History and criticism. 2. Mumming plays I. T.
PR8793.F6 G6   398.2/36   *LC* 75-9132   *ISBN* 0253304709

The Irish short story: a critical history / James F. Kilroy, editor. 2.9863
Boston, Mass.: Twayne Publishers, 1984. xiii, 251 p.; 23 cm. — (Twayne's critical history of the short story.) Includes index. 1. Short stories, English — Irish authors — History and criticism. 2. Ireland in literature. I. Kilroy, James. II. Series.
PR8804.I74 1984   823/.01/099415 19   *LC* 84-670   *ISBN* 0805793542

Averill, Deborah M. 2.9864
The Irish short story from George Moore to Frank O'Connor / Deborah M. Averill. — Washington, D.C.: University Press of America, c1982. x, 328 p.; 23 cm. Includes index. 1. Short stories, English — Irish authors — History and criticism. I. T.
PR8807.S5 A9 1982   823/.01/099417 19   *LC* 81-40188   *ISBN* 0819121339

Montague, John. comp. 2.9865
[Faber book of Irish verse] The book of Irish verse: an anthology of Irish poetry from the sixteenth century to the present / edited by John Montague. — 1st American ed. — New York: Macmillan, 1977, c1974. 400 p.; 22 cm. Edition of 1974 published under title: The Faber book of Irish verse. Includes indexes. 1. Irish poetry I. T.
PR8851.M6   821/.008   *LC* 75-30593

The Penguin book of Irish verse / introduced and edited by Brendan Kennelly. 2.9866
2nd ed. — Harmondsworth, Middlesex; New York: Penguin Books, 1981. 470 p.; 19 cm. 1. English poetry — Irish authors 2. English poetry — Translations from Irish. 3. Irish poetry — Translations into English. 4. Ireland — Poetry. I. Kennelly, Brendan.
PR8851.P4 1981   821/.008 19   *LC* 82-139765   *ISBN* 0140421211

Contemporary Irish poetry: an anthology / edited with introd. and notes by Anthony Bradley. 2.9867
Berkeley: University of California Press, 1980 (c1979). xvii, 430 p.: ports.; 24 cm. Includes indexes. 1. English poetry — Irish authors 2. English poetry — 20th century I. Bradley, Anthony, 1942-
PR8858.C65   821/.9/1208   *LC* 76-50244   *ISBN* 0520033892

Simmons, James, 1933- comp. 2.9868
Ten Irish poets: an anthology of poems by George Buchanan ... [et al.] / edited by James Simmons. — 1st ed. — Cheadle Hulme, [Eng.]: Carcanet Press, 1974. 92 p.; 22 cm. 1. English poetry — Irish authors 2. English poetry — 20th century I. T.
PR8858.S54   821/.9/108   *LC* 74-194718   *ISBN* 0856350818

Modern Irish short stories / edited by Ben Forkner; pref. by Anthony Burgess. 2.9869
New York: Viking Press, 1980. 557 p.; 21 cm. 1. Short stories, English — Irish authors. I. Forkner, Ben.
PR8875.M6 1980b   823/.01/08   *LC* 80-16071   *ISBN* 0670483249

Mercier, Vivian, 1919- ed. 2.9870
Great Irish short stories. [New York, Dell, 1964] 384 p. 18 cm. (Laurel edition) (Laurel great short stories) 1. Short stories, Irish I. T.
PR 8876 M57 1964   *LC* 64-4630

Dublin / compiled by Benedict Kiely. 2.9871
Oxford [Oxfordshire]; New York: Oxford University Press, 1983. vi, 112 p.: ill.; 21 cm. — (Small Oxford books) Includes index. 1. English literature — Irish authors 2. Literary landmarks — Ireland — Dublin (Dublin) 3. Dublin (Dublin) — Literary collections. I. Kiely, Benedict.
PR8892.D8 D8 1983   820/.8/0941835 19   *LC* 82-12545   *ISBN* 0192141244

PR8900–8997 Wales

(Literary History and Collections. For individual authors see main PR period lists. See also PB.)

Anglo–Welsh poetry, 1480–1980 / edited and introduced by Raymond Garlick & Roland Mathias. 2.9872
Bridgend, Mid Glamorgan: Poetry Wales Press; Chester Springs, PA: dist. by Dufour Editions, Inc., 1985. 377 p.; 22 cm. Includes indexes. Distributor from label of t.p. 1. English poetry — Welsh authors 2. Wales — Poetry. I. Garlick, Raymond. II. Mathias, Roland.
PR8964.A5 1985   PR8956.A64 1985.   821/.008/09429 19

The Penguin book of Welsh short stories / edited by Alun Richards. 2.9873
Harmondsworth, Eng.; Baltimore: Penguin, 1976. 358 p.; 18 cm. 1. Short stories, English — Welsh authors. 2. Short stories, Welsh — Translations into English. 3. Short stories, English — Translations from Welsh. I. Richards, Alun.
PZ1.P375 PR8980.P4x   PR1307.P36.   823/.01   *LC* 76-372041   *ISBN* 0140040617 pbk

PR9080–9899 ENGLISH LITERATURE OUTSIDE EUROPE
(Except United States: see PS)

Awakened conscience: studies in Commonwealth literature / edited by C. D. Narasimhaiah. 2.9874
Atlantic Highlands, N.J.: Humanities Press, 1978. xxxi, 450 p.; 25 cm. First published 1978, by Sterling, New Delhi. 1. English literature — Commonwealth of Nations authors — History and criticism — Congresses. 2. English literature — 20th century — History and criticism — Congresses. I. Narasimhaiah, C. D.
PR9080.A9   820/.9   *ISBN* 0391009206

King, Bruce Alvin. 2.9875
Literatures of the world in English, edited by Bruce King. — London; Boston: Routledge and Kegan Paul, 1974. xi, 225 p.; 23 cm. 1. English literature — Commonwealth of Nations authors — History and criticism. I. T.
PR9080.K5   820/.9   *LC* 73-89197   *ISBN* 0710077874

King, Bruce Alvin. 2.9876
The new English literatures: cultural nationalism in a changing world / Bruce King. — New York: St. Martin's Press, 1980. xi, 248 p.; 20 cm. 1. English literature — Commonwealth of Nations authors — History and criticism. 2. English literature — 20th century — History and criticism. 3. Nationalism and literature 4. Civilization, Modern — 20th century — English influences I. T.
PR9080.K53 1980   820/.9   *LC* 80-36847   *ISBN* 0312566557

Modern Commonwealth literature / compiled and edited by   2.9877
John H. Ferres, Martin Tucker.
New York: Ungar, c1977. xxiv, 561 p.; 24 cm. — (Library of literary criticism.)
1. English literature — Commonwealth of Nations authors — History and criticism. I. Ferres, John H. II. Tucker, Martin. III. Series.
PR9080.M6   820/.9   *LC* 75-35425   *ISBN* 0804430802

PR9180–9199.3 Canada

(For French Canadian literature see
PQ3900-3919)

PR9180–9191 LITERARY HISTORY AND CRITICISM

Canadian writers and their works: fiction series, volume 1 /   2.9878
edited by Robert Lecker, Jack David, Ellen Quigley.
Downsview, Ont.: ECW Press, 1983. 256 p. Includes index. 1. Brooke, Frances, 1724?-1789. 2. Moodie, Susanna, 1803-1852. 3. Richardson, John, 1796-1852. 4. Traill, Catharine Parr, 1802-1899. 5. Leprohon, Mrs., 1829-1879. 6. De Mille, James, 1837-1880. 7. Machar, Agnes Maule, 1837-1927. 8. Canadian fiction — History and criticism. 9. Authors, Canadian — Biography. I. Lecker, Robert, 1951- II. David, Jack, 1946- III. Quigley, Ellen, 1955-
PR9180.C36 1983   C813/.009 19   *ISBN* 0920802451

The Oxford companion to Canadian literature / general editor,   2.9879
William Toye.
Toronto; New York: Oxford University Press, 1983. xviii, 843 p.; 24 cm.
1. Canadian literature — Dictionaries. 2. Canadian literature — Bio-bibliography. 3. Authors, Canadian — Biography. I. Toye, William.
PR9180.2.O94 1983   809/.8971 19   *LC* 84-145212   *ISBN* 0195402839

Story, Norah.   • 2.9880
The Oxford companion to Canadian history and literature. — Toronto; New York [etc.]: Oxford University Press, 1967. xi, 935 p.; 24 cm. 1. Canadian literature — Dictionaries. 2. Canadian literature — Bio-bibliography. I. T.
PR9180.2.S7x   810/.3   *LC* 67-31959

Atwood, Margaret Eleanor, 1939-.   2.9881
Survival: a thematic guide to Canadian literature [by] Margaret Atwood. — Toronto: Anansi, 1972. 287 p.; 21 cm. 1. Canadian literature — History and criticism. I. T.
PR9184.3.A8   810/.9/971   *LC* 72-91501   *ISBN* 0887847137

Klinck, Carl Frederick, 1908- ed.   2.9882
Literary history of Canada: Canadian literature in English / general editor, Carl F. Klinck; editors, Alfred G. Bailey ... [et al.]. — 2d ed. — Toronto; Buffalo: University of Toronto Press, 1976. 3 v.; 24 cm. 1. Canadian literature — History and criticism. I. T.
PR9184.3.K5 1976   810/.9/005   *LC* 76-12353   *ISBN* 0802022111

Mandel, Eli, 1922- comp.   2.9883
Contexts of Canadian criticism. Edited and with an introd. by Eli Mandel. Chicago, University of Chicago Press [1971] vii, 304 p. 22 cm. (Patterns of literary criticism, 9) 1. Canadian literature — History and criticism. 2. Criticism — Canada. 3. Canada — History — Addresses, essays, lectures. I. T.
PR9184.3.M3x   801/.95/0971   *LC* 78-143280   *ISBN* 0226502988
ISBN 0226502996

Stouck, David, 1940-.   2.9884
Major Canadian authors: a critical introduction / David Stouck. — Lincoln: University of Nebraska Press, c1984. xii, 308 p.: ports.; 23 cm. Includes index. 1. Canadian literature — History and criticism — Addresses, essays, lectures. I. T.
PR9184.3.S84 1984   810/.9/971 19   *LC* 83-10216   *ISBN* 0803241194

Waterston, Elizabeth, 1922-.   2.9885
Survey; a short history of Canadian literature, by Elizabeth Waterston. Toronto, Methuen [1973] 215 p. illus. 18 cm. (Methuen Canadian literature series) 1. Canadian literature — History and criticism. I. T.
PR9184.3.W3   810/.9/971   *LC* 72-97553   *ISBN* 0458909505 *ISBN* 0458909300

The Search for English–Canadian literature: an anthology of   2.9886
critical articles from the nineteenth and early twentieth centuries / edited and introduced by Carl Ballstadt.
Toronto; Buffalo: University of Toronto Press, [1975] l, 214 p.; 23 cm. (Literature of Canada; 16) 1. Canadian literature — History and criticism — Addresses, essays, lectures. I. Ballstadt, Carl, 1931-
PR9184.6.S4   810/.9/971   *LC* 75-15779   *ISBN* 0802021778

Crossing frontiers: papers in Canadian Western literature /   2.9887
edited by Dick Harrison.
Edmonton: University of Alberta Press, 1979. 174 p.; 23 cm. Papers given at a conference held in Banff, Alta., April 1978, sponsored by the Dept. of English, Univ. of Alta. and the Dept. of History, Idaho State Univ. at Pocatello. 1. Canadian literature — History and criticism — Congresses. 2. West (U.S.) in literature — Congresses. 3. American literature — West (U.S.) — History and criticism — Congresses. I. Harrison, Dick, 1937- II. University of Alberta. Dept. of English. III. Idaho State University. Dept. of History.
PR9185.5.W45 C7   810/.9/3278   *LC* 80-451207   *ISBN* 0888640587

Who's who in Canadian literature 1983–1984 / [editors], Gordon   2.9888
Ripley, Anne V. Mercer.
Toronto: Reference Press, 1983. xix, 425 p. Includes indexes. 1. Authors, Canadian — 20th century — Biography. 2. Canadian literature — 20th century — Bio-bibliography. I. Ripley, Gordon, 1946- II. Mercer, Anne V., 1953-
PR9186.2.W5x   C810/.9/005 19   *ISBN* 0919981003

Woodcock, George, 1912-.   2.9889
The world of Canadian writing: critiques & recollections / George Woodcock. — Vancouver, B.C.: Douglas & McIntyre; Seattle: University of Washington Press, 1980. xi, 306 p.; 22 cm. Includes index. 1. Canadian literature — 20th century — History and criticism. I. T.
PR9189.6.W6 1980   810/.9/0054   *LC* 80-15497   *ISBN* 0295957212

Marshall, Tom, 1938-.   2.9890
Harsh and lovely land: the major Canadian poets and the making of a Canadian tradition / Tom Marshall. — Vancouver: University of British Columbia Press, c1979. xiv, 184 p.; 24 cm. 1. Canadian poetry — History and criticism. I. T.
PR9190.25.M37   811/.009   *LC* 79-318888   *ISBN* 0774801077

Woodcock, George, 1912- comp.   2.9891
Colony and confederation: early Canadian poets and their background / edited by George Woodcock; with an introd. by Roy Daniells. — Vancouver, [B.C.]: University of British Columbia Press, [1974] vii, 218 p.; 25 cm. (Canadian literature series; 6) 1. Canadian poetry — History and criticism — Addresses, essays, lectures. I. T.
PR9190.25.W6   811/.4/09   *LC* 75-322823   *ISBN* 0774800313

Woodcock, George, 1912- comp.   2.9892
Poets and critics: essays from Canadian literature, 1966–1974 / edited by George Woodcock. — Toronto: Oxford University Press, 1974. x, 246 p.; 21 cm. 1. Canadian poetry — 20th century — History and criticism — Addresses, essays, lectures. I. Canadian literature. II. T.
PR9190.5.W66   811/.5/409   *LC* 74-196959   *ISBN* 0195402243

New, William H. comp.   2.9893
Dramatists in Canada; selected essays, edited by William H. New. — Vancouver: University of British Columbia Press, [1972] vii, 204 p.; 25 cm. — (Canadian literature series, 4) Most of the essays were originally published in Canadian literature. 1. Canadian drama — 20th century — Addresses, essays, lectures. 2. French-Canadian drama — 20th century — Addresses, essays, lectures. I. Canadian literature. II. T.
PR9191.5.N4   809.2   *LC* 72-93104   *ISBN* 077480016X

PR9194–9197 COLLECTIONS

Dewart, Edward Hartley, 1828-1903, ed.   2.9894
Selections from Canadian poets. Introd. by Douglas Lochhead. — [Toronto and Buffalo]: University of Toronto Press, [1973] xix, 304 p.; 22 cm. — (Literature of Canada; poetry and prose in reprint) Reprint of the 1864 edition printed by J. Lovell, Montreal. 1. Canadian poetry I. T.
PR9194.D4 1973   811/.008   *LC* 72-91691   *ISBN* 0802019528

Richler, Mordecai, 1931- comp.   • 2.9895
Canadian writing today. — Harmondsworth: Penguin, 1970. 331 p.; 20 cm. — (Writing today) Includes translations from French. 1. Canadian literature — 20th century. 2. French-Canadian literature — Translations into English. 3. Canadian literature — Translations from French. I. T.
PR9194.9.R5x   808.8/9971   *LC* 75-566309   *ISBN* 0140030379

The New Oxford book of Canadian verse in English / chosen **2.9896**
and with an introduction by Margaret Atwood.
Toronto; New York: Oxford University Press, 1982. xl, 477 p.; 23 cm. Includes index. 1. Canadian poetry I. Atwood, Margaret Eleanor, 1939-
PR9195.25.N48 1982   811/.008/0971 19   LC 83-208695   ISBN 0195403967

The Oxford book of Canadian verse, in English and French. **2.9897**
Chosen and with an introd. by A. J. M. Smith.
Toronto, New York, Oxford University Press, 1960. 445 p. 19 cm. 1. Canadian poetry 2. French-Canadian poetry I. Smith, A. J. M. (Arthur James Marshall), 1902- ed.
PR9195.25.O9x   LC 60-50007

Smith, A. J. M. (Arthur James Marshall), 1902- comp.   • **2.9898**
Modern Canadian verse in English and French [compiled by] A. J. M. Smith.
Toronto, Oxford University Press, 1967. xxvi, 426 p. 19 cm. 1. Canadian poetry I. T.
PR9195.25 S65x   808.81   LC 68-31903

Smith, A. J. M. (Arthur James Marshall), 1902- ed.   • **2.9899**
The book of Canadian poetry: a critical and historical anthology. — 3d ed., rev. and enl. — Toronto: W. J. Gage [c1957] xxv, 532 p.; 24 cm. Bibliography: p. 505-521. 1. Canadian poetry (Collections) I. T.
PR9195.25.S6x   811.082   LC 59-20696

15 Canadian poets plus 5 / edited by Gary Geddes and Phyllis **2.9900**
Bruce.
Toronto: Oxford University Press, 1978. xviii, 420 p.: ports.; 21 cm. Enl. ed. of: 15 Canadian poets. Includes index. 1. Canadian poetry — 20th century I. Geddes, Gary. II. Bruce, Phyllis. III. Title: Fifteen Canadian poets plus five.
PR9195.7.A14x 1978   LC 83-672073   ISBN 0195402898

Canadian short stories, third series / selected by Robert **2.9901**
Weaver.
Toronto; New York: Oxford University Press, 1978. xi, 362 p.: ill.; 18 cm. 1. Short stories, Canadian 2. Canadian fiction — 20th century I. Weaver, Robert, 1921-
PZ1.C1586 PR9197.3.C3 1978   813/.01   LC 79-313105   ISBN 019540291X

Canadian short fiction anthology / selected and edited by Cathy **2.9902**
Ford; foreword by Audrey Thomas.
Vancouver: Intermedia Press, 1976. 230 p.; 22 cm. 1. Short stories, Canadian 2. Canadian fiction — 20th century I. Ford, Cathy.
PZ1.C1584 PR9197.3.C3x   813/.01   LC 78-320801   ISBN 0889560404

Weaver, Robert, 1921-.   • **2.9903**
Canadian short stories / selected and with an introd. by Robert Weaver. — London: Oxford University Press, c1960. xiii, 420 p.; 16 cm. (The World's classics; 573) 1. Short stories, Canadian I. T.
PR9197.3.W4x   LC 84-246932

PR9199.2–9199.3 INDIVIDUAL AUTHORS, A-Z

PR9199.2 19th Century

Howe, Joseph, 1804-1873.   **2.9904**
Poems and essays. Introd. by M. G. Parks. — [Toronto; Buffalo]: University of Toronto Press, [1973] xxxvi, 341 p.; 23 cm. — (Literature of Canada; poetry and prose in reprint) I. T.
PR9199.2.H6 A6 1973   811/.4   LC 73-78943   ISBN 0802020828

McLachlan, Alexander, 1820-1896.   **2.9905**
The poetical works of Alexander McLachlan / introd. by E. Margaret Fulton. — Toronto; Buffalo: University of Toronto Press, c1974. xxiii, 448 p.; 22 cm. — (Literature of Canada; Poetry and prose in reprint; 13) 'Originally published in 1900 by William Briggs, Toronto.' Includes index. I. T.
PR9199.2.M33 1974   811/.3   LC 73-82589   ISBN 0802021271

PR9199.3 20th Century

PR9199.3 A–C

Atwood, Margaret Eleanor, 1939-.   **2.9906**
The handmaid's tale / Margaret Atwood. — Boston: Houghton Mifflin, 1986. 311 p.; 24 cm. I. T.
PR9199.3.A8 H3 1986   813/.54 19   LC 85-21944   ISBN 0395404258

Atwood, Margaret Eleanor, 1939-.   **2.9907**
Lady oracle / Margaret Atwood. — New York: Simon and Schuster, c1976. p. cm. I. T.
PZ4.A889 Lad3 PR9199.3.A8L3x   813/.5/4   LC 76-15612   ISBN 0671223399

Atwood, Margaret Eleanor, 1939-.   **2.9908**
Life before man / Margaret Atwood. — New York: Simon & Schuster, c1979. 317 p.; 24 cm. — I. T.
PZ4.A889 Li 1979 PR9199.3.A8L5x   813/.5/4   LC 79-20281   ISBN 0671251155

Atwood, Margaret Eleanor, 1939-.   **2.9909**
Surfacing [by] Margaret Atwood. — New York: Simon and Schuster, [1973, c1972] 224 p.; 21 cm. — I. T.
PR9199.3.A8 S8x   813/.5/4   LC 72-86983   ISBN 0671214500

Atwood, Margaret Eleanor, 1939-.   **2.9910**
You are happy: [poems] / Margaret Atwood. — 1st U.S. ed. — New York: Harper & Row, c1974. 96 p.; 22 cm. I. T.
PR9199.3.A8 Y6 1974   811/.5/4   LC 74-1787   ISBN 0060101644

The Art of Margaret Atwood: essays in criticism / edited by **2.9911**
Arnold E. Davidson & Cathy N. Davidson.
Toronto: Anansi, c1981. 304 p.; 23 cm. 1. Atwood, Margaret Eleanor, 1939- Criticism and interpretation — Addresses, essays, lectures. I. Davidson, Arnold E., 1936- II. Davidson, Cathy N., 1949-
PR9199.3.A8 Z54   813/.54 19   LC 81-191842   ISBN 0887840809

Rosenberg, Jerome H.   **2.9912**
Margaret Atwood / Jerome H. Rosenberg. — Boston: Twayne Publishers, c1984. 184 p., [1] leaf of plates: port.; 23 cm. — (Twayne's world authors series; TWAS 740. Canadian literature) Includes index. 1. Atwood, Margaret Eleanor, 1939- — Criticism and interpretation. I. T.
PR9199.3.A8 Z85 1984   818/.5409 19   LC 84-4672   ISBN 0805765867

Birney, Earle, 1904-.   **2.9913**
Spreading time: remarks on Canadian writing and writers / Earle Birney. — Montreal: Véhicule Press, 1980-. v.; 22 cm. 1. Birney, Earle, 1904- 2. Canadian literature — 20th century — History and criticism. I. T.
PR9199.3.B44   C810/.9   ISBN 0919890253

Aichinger, Peter, 1933-.   **2.9914**
Earle Birney / by Peter Aichinger. — Boston: Twayne Publishers, 1979. 180 p.: port; 21 cm. — (Twayne's world authors series; TWAS 538: Canada) Includes index. 1. Birney, Earle, 1904- — Criticism and interpretation. I. T.
PR9199.3.B44 Z553   818/.5/209   LC 79-10808   ISBN 0805763805

Davey, Frank, 1940-.   **2.9915**
Earle Birney [by] Frank Davey. [Toronto] Copp Clark Pub. Co. [c1971] vii, 128 p. 18 cm. (Studies in Canadian literature, 11) 1. Birney, Earle, 1904- I. T.
PR9199.3.B44Z7x   818/.5/209 B   LC 72-192973

Callaghan, Morley, 1903-.   • **2.9916**
The loved and the lost: a novel / Morley Callaghan. — Toronto: Macmillan of Canada, 1951. 234 p. I. T.
PR9199.3.C27 L6x   LC 51-9921

Callaghan, Morley, 1903-.   • **2.9917**
The many colored coat / Morley Callaghan. — New York, Coward-McCann, 1960. 318 p.; 22 cm. I. T.
PR9199.3.C27 M3x   819.32   LC 60-11285/L

Callaghan, Morley, 1903-.   • **2.9918**
That summer in Paris; memories of tangled friendships with Hemingway, Fitzgerald, and some others. New York, Coward-McCann, 1963. 255 p. illus. 22 cm. 1. Callaghan, Morley, 1903- — Friends and associates. 2. Hemingway, Ernest, 1899-1961 — Friends and associates. 3. Fitzgerald, F. Scott (Francis Scott), 1896-1940 — Friends and associates. 4. Novelists, Canadian — 20th century — Biography. 5. Novelists, American — 20th century — Biography. I. T.
PR9199.3.C27 Z52   818.52   LC 63-7319

Conron, Brandon.   • **2.9919**
Morley Callaghan. — New York: Twayne Publishers, [1966] 188 p.; 21 cm. — (Twayne's world authors series, 1. Canada) 1. Callaghan, Morley, 1903- I. T.
PR9199.3.C27 Z6x   813.52   *LC* 66-16118

Scobie, Stephen.   **2.9920**
Leonard Cohen / Stephen Scobie. — Vancouver: Douglas & McIntyre, c1978. xii, 192 p.; 22 cm. — (Studies in Canadian literature; 12) 1. Cohen, Leonard, 1934- — Criticism and interpretation. I. T.
PR9199.3.C57 Z88   811/.5/4   *LC* 79-317983   *ISBN* 0888941943

PR9199.3 D–G

Dabydeen, Cyril, 1945-.   **2.9921**
Still close to the island / Cyril Dabydeen. — 1st ed. — Ottawa, Ont.: Commoner's Publishing, 1980. 111 p. I. T.
PR9199.3.D2x   819.32   *ISBN* 0889700362

Davies, Robertson, 1913-.   **2.9922**
Fifth business; a novel by Robertson Davies. Toronto, Macmillan of Canada [1970] 314 p. 22 cm. The first of three linked novels, the others being The manticore (1972) and World of wonders (c1975). I. T.
PR9199.3.D3 F5x   PZ4.D258 Fi PR6007.A814   813/.5/4   *LC* 77-567099

Davies, Robertson, 1913-.   • **2.9923**
Leaven of malice / Robertson Davies. — New York: Scribner, 1955, c1954. 312 p.; 21 cm. I. T.
PR9199.3.D3 L4x   *LC* 55-8566

Davies, Robertson, 1913-.   **2.9924**
The manticore [by] Robertson Davies. New York, Viking Press [1972] 310 p. 22 cm. The second of three linked novels, the first being Fifth business (1970), and the third being World of wonders (c1975). I. T.
PR9199.3.D3M3x   813/.5/4   *LC* 72-81120   *ISBN* 0670453137

Davies, Robertson, 1913-.   • **2.9925**
A mixture of frailties. New York, Scribner [1958] 379 p. 22 cm. I. T.
PR9199.3.D3M5x   *LC* 58-10526

Davies, Robertson, 1913-.   **2.9926**
One half of Robertson Davies. — New York: Viking Press, 1978, c1977. 286 p.; 22 cm. I. T.
PR9199.3.D3 O5 1978b   814/.5/4   *LC* 78-2395   *ISBN* 0670526088

Davies, Robertson, 1913-.   **2.9927**
World of wonders / Robertson Davies. — New York: Viking Press, 1976, c1975. 358 p.; 22 cm. The last of three linked novels, the first being Fifth business (1970) and the second being The manticore (1972). I. T.
PZ4.D258 Wo3 PR9199.3.D3W6x   813/.5/4   *LC* 75-38778   *ISBN* 0670788120

Stone-Blackburn, Susan, 1941-.   **2.9928**
Robertson Davies, playwright: a search for the self on the Canadian stage / Susan Stone–Blackburn. — Vancouver: University of British Columbia Press, 1985. 249 p.; 24 cm. 1. Davies, Robertson, 1913- — Dramatic works. I. T.
PR9199.3.D3 Z8 1985   812/.54 19   *LC* 85-157720   *ISBN* 0774802111

Studies in Robertson Davies' Deptford trilogy / edited by   **2.9929**
Robert G. Lawrence and Samuel L. Macey; with an introductory essay by Robertson Davies.
Victoria, B.C.: English Literary Studies, University of Victoria, 1980. 123 p.; 23 cm. — (ELS monograph series. no. 20) 1. Davies, Robertson, 1913- — Criticism and interpretation — Addresses, essays, lectures. I. Lawrence, Robert Gilford, 1923- II. Macey, Samuel L. III. Davies, Robertson, 1913- IV. Series.
PR9199.3.D3 Z83   813/.54 19   *LC* 81-109003   *ISBN* 0920604382

De La Roche, Mazo, 1885-1961.   • **2.9930**
Jalna / by Mazo De La Roche. — Boston: Little, Brown, 1928. 347 p.;20 cm. I. T.
PR9199.3.D42J3x   *LC* 27-20930

De La Roche, Mazo, 1885-1961.   • **2.9931**
Whiteoaks of Jalna. — Whiteoak ed. — Boston: Little, Brown, [1957] 423 p.: geneal. table; 20 cm. I. T.
PR9199.3.D42W5x

Hambleton, Ronald, 1917-.   • **2.9932**
Mazo De La Roche of Jalna. — [1st ed.]. — New York: Hawthorn Books, [1966] 239 p.: illus., map, ports.; 24 cm. 1. De La Roche, Mazo, 1885-1961. I. T.
PR9199.3.D42Zx   813.52 B   *LC* 66-22660

Gustafson, Ralph, 1909-.   **2.9933**
At the ocean's verge: selected poems / Ralph Gustafson. — 1st ed. — Redding Ridge, CT: Black Swan Books, c1984. xiv, 155 p.; 23 cm. (Literary series.) Includes index. I. T. II. Series.
PR9199.3.G8 A6 1984   811/.52 19   *LC* 84-6290   *ISBN* 0933806167

PR9199.3 H–L

Klein, A. M. (Abraham Moses), 1909-1972.   **2.9934**
Short stories / A.M. Klein; edited by M.W. Steinberg. — Toronto: University of Toronto Press, c1983. xxv, 338 p.: port.; 25 cm. — (Collected works of A.M. Klein; v. 2) I. Steinberg, M. W. (Moses Wolfe), 1918-. II. T.
PR9199.3.K48Ax   C813/.52 19   *ISBN* 0802055982

Kroetsch, Robert, 1927-.   **2.9935**
[Poems] Field notes: 1–8 a continuing poem: the collected poetry of Robert Kroetsch. — New York: Beaufort Books, 1981. 144 p.; 23 cm. — (Spectrum poetry series.) I. T. II. Series.
PR9199.3.K7 A17 1981   811/.54 19   *LC* 81-2635   *ISBN* 0825300746

Lampman, Archibald, 1861-1899.   **2.9936**
The poems of Archibald Lampman (including At the Long Sault). Introd. by Margaret Coulby Whitridge. [Toronto] University of Toronto Press [1974] xxxviii, xxv, 473, 45 p. 23 cm. (Literature of Canada: poetry and prose in Reprint, 12) Reprint of The poems of Archibald Lampman (Morang, 1900), and At the Long Sault and other new poems (Ryerson, 1943). I. Lampman, Archibald, 1861-1899. At the Long Sault. 1974. II. T. III. Title: At the Long Sault.
PR9199.3.L29 A6 1974   811/.4 19   *LC* 73-92517   *ISBN* 0802020747 *ISBN* 0802062040

Laurence, Margaret.   • **2.9937**
A bird in the house; stories. — [1st American ed.]. — New York: Knopf, 1970. 207 p.; 22 cm. I. T.
PZ4.L377 Bi3 PR9199.3.L33B5x   813/.5/4   *LC* 70-98659

Laurence, Margaret.   **2.9938**
The diviners. — [1st ed.]. — New York: Knopf; [distributed by Random House], 1974. 382 p.: music.; 25 cm. — I. T.
PR9199.3.L33 D5x   813/.5/4   *LC* 73-20740   *ISBN* 0394491564

Laurence, Margaret.   • **2.9939**
The fire–dwellers. — [1st American ed.]. — New York: Knopf, 1969. 308 p.; 22 cm. — I. T.
PR9199.3.L33 F5x   813/.5/4   *LC* 69-14736

Laurence, Margaret.   • **2.9940**
A jest of God / Margaret Laurence. — [1st American ed.]. — New York: Knopf, 1966. –. 240 p.; 22 cm. — I. T.
PR9199.3.L33 J4x   *LC* 66-14920

Morley, Patricia A.   **2.9941**
Margaret Laurence / by Patricia Morley. — Boston: Twayne Publishers, 171 p.: port.; 21 cm. — (Twayne's world authors series; TWAS 591: Canada) Includes index. 1. Laurence, Margaret — Criticism and interpretation. I. T.
PR9199.3.L33 Z79 1981   813/.54 19   *LC* 80-27501   *ISBN* 080576433X

Thomas, Clara.   **2.9942**
The Manawaka world of Margaret Laurence / Clara Thomas. — Toronto: McClelland and Stewart, [1975] 212 p.: ill.; 22 cm. 1. Laurence, Margaret. I. T.
PR9199.3.L33 Z9   813/.5/4   *LC* 76-351741   *ISBN* 0771084609

Layton, Irving, 1912-.   • **2.9943**
The collected poems of Irving Layton. — Toronto: McClelland and Stewart, [1971] 589 p.; 24 cm. Errata sheet inserted. I. T.
PR9199.3.L35 Ax   811/.5/4   *LC* 72-183480   *ISBN* 0771048378

Layton, Irving, 1912-.   **2.9944**
Taking sides: the collected social and political writings / Irving Layton; edited and introduced by Howard Aster. — Oakville, Ont.: Mosaic Press/Valley Editions, c1977. 222 p.; 24 cm. I. Aster, Howard. II. T.
PR9199.3.L35 T3   818/.5/407   *ISBN* 088962058X

Irving Layton, the poet and his critics / edited and with an   **2.9945**
introd. by Seymour Mayne.
Toronto; New York: McGraw-Hill Ryerson, c1978. viii, 291 p.; 23 cm. — (Critical views on Canadian writers) 1. Layton, Irving, 1912- — Criticism and interpretation — Addresses, essays, lectures. I. Mayne, Seymour, 1944-
PR9199.3.L35 Z7   811/.5/4   *LC* 78-324623   *ISBN* 0070827117

Leacock, Stephen, 1869-1944.　　　　　　　　　2.9946
The Bodley Head Leacock / edited and introduced by J.B. Priestley. — London: Bodley Head, [c1957] 464 p. I. Priestley, J. B. (John Boynton), 1894- II. T.
PR9199.3.L367Ax

Leacock, Stephen, 1869-1944.　　　　　　　　• 2.9947
Nonsense novels. — New York: Dover Publications, [1971] 102 p.; 21 cm. 'An unabridged and unaltered republication of the work originally published by the John Lane Company in 1912.' I. T.
PR9199.3.L367 N6x　　　818/.5/207　　LC 78-166423　　ISBN 0486227596

PR9199.3 M–P

Moore, Brian, 1921-.　　　　　　　　　　　• 2.9948
The luck of Ginger Coffey, a novel. — [1st ed.]. — Boston: Little, Brown, [1960] 243 p.; 21 cm. — I. T.
PZ4.M819 Lu PR9199.3.M6L8x　　813/.5/4　　LC 60-6533

Moore, Brian, 1921-.　　　　　　　　　　　• 2.9949
The emperor of ice–cream, a novel. — [New York: Viking Press, [1965] 250 p.; 21 cm. — I. T.
PZ4.M819 Em PR9199.3.M617　　813/.5/4　　LC 65-20780

Moore, Brian, 1921-.　　　　　　　　　　　2.9950
The lonely passion of Judith Hearne. — [1st American ed.]. — Boston: Little, Brown, [1956, c1955] 228 p.; 20 cm. First published in London in 1955 under title: Judith Hearne. I. T.
PZ4.M819 Lo 1956 PR9199.3.M617 L57x　　813/.5/4 19　　LC 56-7053

Dahlie, Hallvard.　　　　　　　　　　　　2.9951
Brian Moore / by Hallvard Dahlie. — Boston: Twayne Publishers, c1981. 168 p.: port.; 22 cm. — (Twayne's world authors series; TWAS 632: Canada) Includes index. 1. Moore, Brian, 1921- — Criticism and interpretation. I. T.
PR9199.3.M617 Z63 1981　　813/.54 19　　LC 80-27502　　ISBN 0805764755

Munro, Alice.　　　　　　　　　　　　　2.9952
[Who do you think you are?] The beggar maid: stories of Flo and Rose / by Alice Munro. — 1st American ed. — New York: Knopf: distributed by Random House, 1979, c1978. 210 p.; 22 cm. First published in 1978 under title: Who do you think you are? I. T.
PZ4.M969 Be 1979 PR9199.3.M8 Bx　　813/.5/4　　LC 79-63809
　　ISBN 0394506820

Munro, Alice.　　　　　　　　　　　　　2.9953
The moons of Jupiter: stories / by Alice Munro. — 1st ed. — New York: Knopf: Distributed by Random House, 1983, c1982. 233 p.; 22 cm. I. T.
PR9199.3.M8 M66 1983　　813/.54 19　　LC 82-48734　　ISBN 0394529529

Munro, Alice.　　　　　　　　　　　　　2.9954
Something I've been meaning to tell you...; thirteen stories. — Toronto; New York: McGraw-Hill Ryerson, [1974] 246 p.; 23 cm. — I. T.
PZ4.M969 So PR9199.3.M8 Sx　　813/.5/4　　LC 74-187　　ISBN 0070777608

Probable fictions: Alice Munro's narrative acts / edited by　　2.9955
Louis K. MacKendrick.
Downsview, Ont.: ECW Press, c1983. 193 p.; 22 cm. 1. Munro, Alice — Criticism and interpretation — Addresses, essays, lectures. 2. Narration (Rhetoric) — Addresses, essays, lectures. I. MacKendrick, Louis King, 1941- PR9199.3.M8 Z83 1983　　813/.54 19　　LC 84-132359　　ISBN 0920802729

Ondaatje, Michael, 1943-.　　　　　　　　　2.9956
Coming through slaughter / Michael Ondaatje. — New York: Norton, c1976. 156 p.: ill.; 22 cm. 1. Bolden, Buddy, 1877-1931 — Fiction. I. T.
PZ4.O5398 Co3 PR9199.3.O5C6x　　813/.5/4　　LC 77-23225　　ISBN 0393087654

Ondaatje, Michael, 1943-.　　　　　　　　　2.9957
There's a trick with a knife I'm learning to do: poems, 1963–1978 / Michael Ondaatje. — 1st ed. — New York: Norton, c1979. xi, 107 p.; 22 cm. — I. T.
PR9199.3.O5 T5 1979　　811/.5/4　　LC 78-25709　　ISBN 0393011917

Patterson, Nancy-Lou.　　　　　　　　　　2.9958
Apple staff and silver crown: a fairy tale / Nancy-Lou Patterson. — Erin, Ont.: Porcupine's Quill; Scarborough, Ont.: Distributed in Canada and the U.S. by Firefly Books, c1985. 223 p.: ill.; 23 cm. I. T.
PR9199.3.P3x　　[Fic] 19　　LC 85-240064　　ISBN 088984075X

Pratt, E. J. (Edwin John), 1882-1964.　　　　　• 2.9959
The collected poems of E.J. Pratt / edited with an introduction by Northrop Frye. — 2d ed. — Toronto: Macmillan Co. of Canada, 1958. xxviii, 395 p.: ill.; 24 cm. Includes indexes. 1. Canadian poetry I. Frye, Northrop. II. T.
PR9199.3.P7 Ax　　811.52　　LC 59-30932

Djwa, Sandra, 1939-.　　　　　　　　　　2.9960
E.J. Pratt: the evolutionary vision / Sandra Djwa. — Vancouver: Copp Clark Pub.; Montreal: McGill-Queen's University Press, c1974.. viii, 160 p.; 18 cm. — (Studies in Canadian literature.) I. T. II. Series.
PR9199.3.P7Z6　　C811/.5/2　　LC 73-92935　　ISBN 0773030115 pa

Pitt, David G. (David George), 1921-.　　　　　2.9961
E.J. Pratt, the truant years, 1882–1927 / David G. Pitt. — Toronto; Buffalo: University of Toronto Press, c1984. xix, 414 p., [14] p. of plates: ill.; 24 cm. Includes index. 1. Pratt, E. J. (Edwin John), 1883-1964 — Biography. 2. Poets, Canadian — 20th century — Biography. I. T.
PR9199.3.P7 Z835 1984　　811/.52 B 19　　LC 85-114711　　ISBN 0802056601

PR9199.3 R–Z

Richler, Mordecai, 1931-.　　　　　　　　　• 2.9962
The apprenticeship of Duddy Kravitz: a novel / by Mordecai Richler. — 1st ed. — Boston: Little, Brown, [1959]. 377 p.; 22 cm. I. T.
PR9199.3.R5Ax　　LC 59-11885L

Richler, Mordecai, 1931-.　　　　　　　　　• 2.9963
Cocksure; a novel. — Toronto; Montreal: McClelland and Stewart, [c1968] 250 p.; 21 cm. — I. T.
PR9199.3.R5 C6x　　813/.5/4　　LC 71-367215

Richler, Mordecai, 1931-.　　　　　　　　　• 2.9964
St. Urbain's horseman; a novel. — [1st ed.]. — New York: Knopf, 1971. 467 p.; 22 cm. — I. T.
PR9199.3.R5 S2x　　813/.5/4　　LC 76-136329　　ISBN 0394444736

Richler, Mordecai, 1931-.　　　　　　　　　2.9965
Home sweet home: my Canadian album / Mordecai Richler. — 1st ed. — New York: Knopf: Distributed by Random House, 1984. 291 p.; 22 cm. 1. Richler, Mordecai, 1931- — Biography. 2. Novelists, Canadian — 20th century — Biography. 3. Canada — Civilization — 1945-. I. T.
PR9199.3.R5 Z468 1984　　813/.54 B 19　　LC 83-49026　　ISBN 0394537564

Richler, Mordecai, 1931-.　　　　　　　　　2.9966
The street / Mordecai Richler. — Washington: The New Republic Book Co., 1975, c1969. 128 p.; 22 cm. 1. Richler, Mordecai, 1931- — Biography — Youth. 2. Jews — Québec (Province) — Montréal 3. Novelists, Canadian — 20th century — Biography. I. T.
PR9199.3.R5 Z52 1975　　813/.5/4 B　　LC 75-15771　　ISBN 0915220040

Davidson, Arnold E., 1936-.　　　　　　　　2.9967
Mordecai Richler / Arnold E. Davidson. — New York: F. Ungar Pub. Co., c1983. v, 203 p.; 21 cm. — (Literature and life series.) Includes index. 1. Richler, Mordecai, 1931- — Criticism and interpretation. I. T. II. Series.
PR9199.3.R5 Z63 1983　　813/.54 19　　LC 82-40282　　ISBN 0804421404

Ramraj, Victor J.　　　　　　　　　　　　2.9968
Mordecai Richler / by Victor J. Ramraj. — Boston: Twayne Publishers, c1983. 154 p.: port.; 23 cm. — (Twayne's world authors series. TWAS 707) Includes index. 1. Richler, Mordecai, 1931- — Criticism and interpretation. I. T. II. Series.
PR9199.3.R5 Z84 1983　　813/.54 19　　LC 83-10668　　ISBN 0805765549

Ross, Sinclair, 1908-.　　　　　　　　　　• 2.9969
As for me and my house: a novel / by Sinclair Ross. — New York: Reynal and Hitchcock, c1941. 3 prelim. leaves, 296 p.; 20.6 x 13.7 cm. I. T.
PZ3.R7336 A5　　PR9199.3.R6A8x.　　LC 41-3337

Ross, Sinclair.　　　　　　　　　　　　　• 2.9970
The lamp at noon and other stories. Introd.: Margaret Laurence. — [Toronto]: McClelland and Stewart, [c1968] 134 p.; 19 cm. — (New Canadian library, no. 62) I. T.
PZ3.R7366 Lam3 PR9199.3.R6L3x　　813/.5/2　　LC 70-397414

Waddington, Miriam.　　　　　　　　　　2.9971
The price of gold / Miriam Waddington. Toronto: Oxford University Press, 1976. 112 p.; 22 cm. Poems. I. T.
PR9199.3.W3 P7　　811/.5/4　　LC 76-377898　　ISBN 0195402650

Wayman, Tom, 1945-.   **2.9972**
Introducing Tom Wayman: selected poems, 1973–80. — Princeton, N.J.: Ontario Review Press; New York, N.Y.: distributed by Persea Books, c1980. 134 p.; 23 cm. (Ontario Review Press poetry series) I. T.
PR9199.3.W39 A17 1980   811/.54 19   *LC* 80-20260   *ISBN* 0865380031

Wevill, David, 1935-.   **2.9973**
Firebreak; poems. London, Macmillan; New York, St. Martin's Press, 1971. ix, 68 p. 21 cm. I. T.
PR9199.3.W4257 F5 1971   811/.5/4   *LC* 76-160136   *ISBN* 0333123565 *ISBN* 0333123573

PR9210–9218 West Indies, General

Critics on Caribbean literature: readings in literary criticism /   **2.9974**
edited by Edward Baugh.
New York: St. Martin's Press, 1978. 164 p.; 23 cm. 1. West Indian literature (English) — History and criticism — Addresses, essays, lectures. I. Baugh, Edward.
PR9210.C7   810/.9   *LC* 76-21943   *ISBN* 0312176058

James, Louis.   **2.9975**
The islands in between: essays on West Indian literature; edited, with an introduction, by Louis James. London, Ibadan [etc.] Oxford U.P., 1968. [8], 166 p. 4 plates, 8 ports. 19 cm. (Three crown books) 1. West Indian literature (English) — History and criticism. I. T.
PR9210.J3x   820   *LC* 68-94794

West Indian literature / edited by Bruce King.   **2.9976**
Hamden, Conn.: Archon Books, 1979. 247 p.; 20 cm. 1. Caribbean literature (English) — History and criticism — Addresses, essays, lectures. I. King, Bruce Alvin.
PR9210.W4 1979b   810/.9/9729 19   *LC* 79-1255   *ISBN* 020801814X

Brown, Lloyd Wellesley, 1938-.   **2.9977**
West Indian poetry / by Lloyd W. Brown. — Boston: Twayne Publishers, c1977. 192 p. — (Twayne's world authors series; TWAS 422: West Indies) Includes index. 1. West Indian poetry (English) — History and criticism. I. T.
PR9212.B7   PR9212 B7.   811/.009   *LC* 77-21613   *ISBN* 0805762620

Gilkes, Michael.   **2.9978**
The West Indian novel / Michael Gilkes. — Boston: Twayne, c1981. 168 p.; 21 cm. — (Twayne's world authors series; TWAS 592. West Indies) Includes index. 1. West Indian fiction (English) — History and criticism. I. T.
PR9214.G5   823/.009/9729 19   *LC* 81-973   *ISBN* 0805764348

Ramchand, Kenneth.   **2.9979**
The West Indian novel and its background / by Kenneth Ramchand. — 2nd ed. — London: Heinemann, 1983. xii, 310 p.; 22 cm. (Studies in Caribbean literature.) Revision of thesis (Ph. D.)—University of Edinburgh. 1. West Indian fiction (English) — 20th century — History and criticism. 2. Literature and society — West Indies. I. T. II. Series.
PR9214.R36 1983   813/.009/9729 19   *LC* 83-196677   *ISBN* 0435986651

Caribbean narrative: an anthology of West Indian writing /   **2.9980**
edited and introduced by O. R. Dathorne.
London: Heinemann, 1966. 247 p. 1. Caribbean fiction I. Dathorne, O. R., 1934-
PR9215.C3x   823.00809   *LC* 66-73862   *ISBN* 0435982214

Dathorne, O. R., 1934-.   **2.9981**
Caribbean verse: an anthology; edited and introduced by O. R. Dathorne. — London: Heinemann, 1967. xi, 131 p.; 18 1/2 cm. 1. Caribbean poetry I. T.
PR9216.D3x   *LC* 67-92134

Figueroa, John J. comp.   **2.9982**
Caribbean voices. — Combined ed. Selected by John Figueroa. — Washington: R. B. Luce Co., [1973, c1971] 2 v. in 1.; 22 cm. Poems. 1. West Indian poetry (English) 2. English poetry — 20th century I. T.
PR9216.F5 1973   821/.008   *LC* 73-76298

Salkey, Andrew. comp.   **2.9983**
[Breaklight: an anthology of Caribbean poetry] Breaklight: the poetry of the Caribbean. Edited and with an introd. by Andrew Salkey. Garden City, N.Y., Doubleday, 1972 [c1971] xix, 265 p. 22 cm. First published in London under title: Breaklight: an anthology of Caribbean poetry. 1. West Indian poetry (English) 2. English poetry — 20th century I. T.
PR9216.S3 1972   811   *LC* 79-178835

Salkey, Andrew. ed.   **2.9984**
West Indian stories. — London: Faber, 1960. 3-224 p.; 19 cm. — 1. Short stories, West Indian (English) I. T.
PZ1.S1494 We   PR9217.5/.S3.   823/.008   *LC* 65-1560

PR9230–9230.9 Barbados

Brathwaite, Edward.   **2.9985**
The arrivants; a new world trilogy. London, New York, Oxford University Press, 1973. 275 p. 21 cm. (Oxford paperbacks, 318) Poems. I. T.
PR9230.9.B68 A6 1973   811   *LC* 73-181354   *ISBN* 0192811541

Brathwaite, Edward.   **2.9986**
Mother poem / Edward Kamau Brathwaite. — Oxford; New York: Oxford University Press, 1977. 122 p.; 22 cm. 1. Barbados — Poetry. I. T.
PR9230.9.B68 M6   811   *LC* 77-30091   *ISBN* 0192118595

Brathwaite, Edward.   **2.9987**
Other exiles / Edward Brathwaite. — London; New York: Oxford University Press, 1975. 52 p.; 21 cm. Poems. I. T.
PR9230.9.B68 O8x   811   *LC* 76-353799   *ISBN* 0192118552

Brathwaite, Edward.   **2.9988**
Rights of passage. — London; New York [etc.]: Oxford U.P., 1967. [8], 86 p.; 22 1/2 cm. — I. T.
PR9230.9.B68 R5x   811   *LC* 67-75397

Lamming, George, 1927-.   ● **2.9989**
The emigrants. — New York McGraw-Hill [1955, c1954] 282p. I. T.
PR9230.9.L3 E6x

Lamming, George, 1927-.   ● **2.9990**
In the castle of my skin / with an introduction by Richard Wright; end papers and port. of the author by Denis Williams. — New York: McGraw-Hill, [1953] 313 p. . ill. , 22 cm. I. T.
PR9230.9.L3 I6x   *LC* 53-9014

Lamming, George, 1927-.   ● **2.9991**
Water with berries. — New York: Holt, Rinehart and Winston, [1972, c1971] 248 p.; 22 cm. — I. T.
PR9230.9.L3 W3x   823/.9/14   *LC* 72-78097   *ISBN* 0030014069

Paquet, Sandra Pouchet.   **2.9992**
The novels of George Lamming / Sandra Pouchet Paquet. — London: Heinemann, 1982. 130 p.; 22 cm. — (Studies in Caribbean literature.) Includes index. 1. Lamming, George, 1927- — Criticism and interpretation. I. T. II. Series.
PR9230.9.L3 Zx   823/.914 19   *LC* 82-176490   *ISBN* 0435918311

PR9265–9265.9 Jamaica

Jamaica woman: an anthology of poems / edited by Pamela   **2.9993**
Mordecai and Mervyn Morris.
Kingston, Jamaica: Heinemann Educational Books (Caribbean), 1980. xii, 110 p.; 18 cm. Includes index. 1. Jamaican poetry — Women authors. I. Mordecai, Pamela. II. Morris, Mervyn.
PR9265.6.J3   811 19   *LC* 81-213053

Hearne, John, 1925-.   **2.9994**
[The faces of love. English] The eye of the storm. [1st American ed.] Boston: Little, Brown [1958, c1957] 328 p.; 22 cm. I. T.
PR9265.9.H4Fx   *LC* 58-7858

Hearne, John, 1925-.   **2.9995**
Land of the living / John Hearne. — New York: Harper, 1962. 280 p. I. T.
PR9265.9.H4 L3x   *LC* 62-15725

Mais, Roger.   **2.9996**
The three novels of Roger Mais. With an introduction by the Hon. Norman W. Manley. London J. Cape [1966] [various pagings] I. T. II. Title: The hills were joyful together III. Title: Brother man IV. Title: Black lightning
PR9265.9.M3 Ax

PR9272.9 Individual Authors, A–Z

A–N

Anthony, Michael, 1932-. 2.9997
Cricket in the road. — [London]: A. Deutsch, [1973] 143 p.; 20 cm. — I. T.
PZ4.A629 Cr PR9272.9.A5 813 *LC* 73-176257 *ISBN* 0233964363

Anthony, Michael, 1932-. 2.9998
The year in San Fernando. Introd. by Paul Edwards & Kenneth Ramchand. — [London]: Heinemann in association with Andre Deutsch, [1970] xxii, 184 p.; 19 cm. — (Caribbean writers series. 1) Label mounted on t.p.: Humanities Press, New York. I. T. II. Series.
PR9272.9.A5 Y4x 813 *LC* 74-17262 *ISBN* 0435980319

Hodge, Merle, 1944-. 2.9999
Crick crack, monkey / Merle Hodge; introduction by Roy Narinesingh. — London: Heinemann, 1981. xiv, 112 p.; 19 cm. — (Caribbean writers series. 24) I. T. II. Series.
PR9272.9.H6 C7 1981 823 19 *LC* 81-143132 *ISBN* 0435984012

Lovelace, Earl, 1935-. 2.10000
The dragon can't dance / Earl Lovelace. — London: A. Deutsch, c1979. 240 p. I. T.
PR9272.9.L6 D7x *ISBN* 0233970681

Lovelace, Earl, 1935-. 2.10001
The schoolmaster. London Collins 1968. 224p. I. T.
PR9272.9.L6 S3x

Lovelace, Earl, 1935-. 2.10002
The wine of astonishment / Earl Lovelace. — London: Deutsch, 1982. 146 p.; 23 cm. I. T.
PR9272.9.L6 W5 1982 813 19 *LC* 82-145284 *ISBN* 0233972188

Naipaul, Shiva, 1945-. 2.10003
The chip-chip gatherers. — [1st American ed.]. — New York: Knopf; [distributed by Random House], 1973. 319 p.; 22 cm. — I. T.
PR9272.9.N3 C5x 823 *LC* 72-11045 *ISBN* 0394483456

Naipaul, Shiva, 1945-. 2.10004
Fireflies. — [1st American ed.]. — New York: Knopf, 1971 [c1970] 436 p.; 22 cm. — I. T.
PR9272.9.N3 F5x 813 *LC* 79-136327 *ISBN* 039442493X

Naipaul, Shiva, 1945-. 2.10005
Love and death in a hot country / Shiva Naipaul. — New York: Viking Press, 1984, c1983. 185 p.; 22 cm. I. T.
PR9272.9.N3 L6 1984 813 19 *LC* 83-40245 *ISBN* 0670442119

Naipaul, V. S. (Vidiadhar Surajprasad), 1932-. 2.10006
Three novels / V.S. Naipaul. — 1st ed. — New York: Knopf, 1982. 502 p.; 25 cm. I. T.
PR9272.9.N32 A6 1982 823/.914 19 *LC* 82-47819 *ISBN* 0394528476

Naipaul, V. S. (Vidiadhar Surajprasad), 1932-. 2.10007
A bend in the river / V. S. Naipaul. — 1st ed. — New York: Knopf; distributed by Random House, 1979. 278 p.; 22 cm. I. T.
PZ4.N155 Be 1979 PR9272.9.N32 B4x 823/.9/14 *LC* 78-21591 *ISBN* 0394505735

Naipaul, V. S. (Vidiadhar Surajprasad), 1932-. 2.10008
Guerrillas / V. S. Naipaul. — 1st American ed. — New York: Knopf, 1975. 248 p.; 23 cm. I. T.
PZ4.N155 Gu3 PR9272.9.N32 G8x 823 *LC* 75-8236 *ISBN* 0394498984

Naipaul, V. S. (Vidiadhar Surajprasad), 1932-. • 2.10009
A house for Mr. Biswas. New York, McGraw-Hill [c1961] 531 p. 21 cm. I. T.
PR9272.9.N32 H6x *LC* 62-10904

Naipaul, V. S. (Vidiadhar Surajprasad), 1932-. 2.10010
In a free state [by] V. S. Naipaul. [1st American ed.] New York, Knopf, 1971. 256 p. 22 cm. I. T.
PR9272.9.N32 I6x 823 *LC* 79-154916 *ISBN* 0394471857

Naipaul, V. S. (Vidiadhar Surajprasad), 1932-. 2.10011
The mimic men [by] V. S. Naipaul. [1st American ed.] New York, Macmillan [1967] 300 p. 21 cm. I. T.
PR9272.9.N32 M4x *LC* 67-22616

Naipaul, Vidiadhar Surajprasad, 1932-. • 2.10012
Mr. Stone and the knights companion / V. S. Naipaul. — London: Andre Deutsch, 1963. 159 p. I. T.
PR9272.9.N32 M5x *LC* 63-6280

Walsh, William, 1916-. 2.10013
V. S. Naipaul. New York, Barnes & Noble Books [1973] 94 p. 20 cm. (Modern writers) 1. Naipaul, V. S. (Vidiadhar Surajprasad), 1932- I. T.
PR9272.9.N32 Z95 1973b 823 B *LC* 73-175222 *ISBN* 0064974057

White, Landeg. 2.10014
V. S. Naipaul: a critical introduction / Landeg White. — New York: Barnes & Noble Books, 1975. 217 p.; 23 cm. 1. Naipaul, V. S. (Vidiadhar Surajprasad), 1932- — Criticism and interpretation. I. T.
PR9272.9.N32 Z97 1975b 823 *LC* 75-321026 *ISBN* 0064976173

Theroux, Paul. 2.10015
V. S. Naipaul, an introduction to his work. New York, Africana Pub. Corp. [1972] 144 p. 23 cm. 1. Naipaul, V. S. (Vidiadhar Surajprasad), 1932- I. T.
PR9272.9.N32 Z9x 823 *LC* 72-88268 *ISBN* 0841901309

S–Z

Selvon, Samuel. 2.10016
A brighter sun, a novel. London A. Wingate [1952] 236p. I. T.
PR9272.9S4 B7

Selvon, Samuel, 1924-. 2.10017
The lonely Londoners / by Samuel Selvon. — New York: St. Martin's Press, c1956. 171 p. I. T.
PR9272.9.S4 L6 1956 *LC* 57-10886

Selvon, Samuel. 2.10018
Turn again Tiger / Samuel Selvon. — New York: St. Martin's Press, 1959. 246 p. I. T.
PR9272.9.S4 T8x *LC* 59-8089

Walcott, Derek. 2.10019
[Poems. Selections] Collected poems, 1948–1984 / Derek Walcott. — 1st ed. — New York: Farrar, Straus & Giroux, 1986. 515 p.; 23 cm. I. T.
PR9272.9.W3 A17 1986 811 19 *LC* 85-20688 *ISBN* 0374126267

Walcott, Derek. 2.10020
Another life. — New York: Farrar, Straus and Giroux, [1973] 151 p.; 23 cm. Verse. I. T.
PR9272.9.W3A1x 811 *LC* 70-183233 *ISBN* 0374105243

Walcott, Derek. 2.10021
Dream on Monkey Mountain, and other plays. — New York: Farrar, Straus and Giroux, [1970] 326 p.; 22 cm. — I. T.
PR9272.9.W3 D7x 812 *LC* 74-122827 *ISBN* 0374143684

Walcott, Derek. 2.10022
[Joker of Seville] The joker of Seville & O Babylon!: Two plays / Derek Walcott. — New York: Farrar, Straus and Giroux, c1978. 275 p.; 21 cm. '[The joker of Seville] based on Tirso de Molina's El burlador de Sevilla.' I. Walcott, Derek. O Babylon! 1978. II. Molina, Tirso de, 1571?-1648. El burlador de Sevilla. III. T.
PR9272.9.W3 J6 1978 812 *LC* 78-1363 *ISBN* 0374179980

Walcott, Derek. 2.10023
[Remembrance] Remembrance & Pantomime: two plays / Derek Walcott. — New York: Farrar, Straus, and Giroux, c1980. 169 p.; 22 cm. I. Walcott, Derek. Pantomime. 1980. II. T.
PR9272.9.W3 R4 1980 812 *LC* 79-29680 *ISBN* 0374249121

Walcott, Derek. 2.10024
Sea grapes / Derek Walcott. New York: Farrar, Straus and Giroux, c1976. viii, 83 p.; 22 cm. I. T.
PR9272.9.W3 S4 1976 811 *LC* 76-13850 *ISBN* 0374255245

Walcott, Derek. 2.10025
The star–apple kingdom / Derek Walcott. — New York: Farrar, Straus, and Giroux, c1979. 57 p.; 22 cm. — I. T.
PR9272.9.W3 S7 1979 813 *LC* 78-11323 *ISBN* 0374269742

PR9289 Honduras

Edgell, Zee. 2.10026
Beka Lamb / Zee Edgell. — London: Heinemann, 1982. 171 p.; 19 cm. — (Caribbean writers series. 26) I. T. II. Series.
PR9289.9.E33 B4 1982 813 19 *LC* 82-182704 *ISBN* 0435984004

PR9320–9320.9 Guyana

Harris, Wilson.   **2.10027**
Ascent to Omai. — London: Faber, 1970. 3-128 p.; 21 cm. — I. T.
PR9320.9.H3 A8x   813   *LC* 77-487418   *ISBN* 0571090591

Harris, Wilson.   **2.10028**
Da Silva da Silva's cultivated wilderness: and, Genesis of the clowns / by
Wilson Harris. — London: Faber, 1977. 148 p.: ill.; 21 cm. I. Harris, Wilson.
Genesis of the clowns. 1977. II. T.
PZ4.H318 Da PR9320.9.H3 D3x   813   *LC* 77-367264   *ISBN*
0571108199

Harris, Wilson.   **2.10029**
Explorations: a selection of talks and articles, 1966–1981 / Wilson Harris;
edited with an introduction by Hena Maes–Jelinek. — Mundelstrup, Denmark:
Dangaroo Press, 1981. 145 p.: ill.; 24 cm. I. T.
PR9320.9.H3 E95   *ISBN* 8788213005

Harris, Wilson.   **2.10030**
Palace of the peacock / Wiilson Harris. — London: Faber and Faber, [1960].
152 p. I. T.
PR9320.9.H3 P3x   *LC* 61-24895   *ISBN* 0571089305

Harris, Wilson.   **2.10031**
The secret ladder / Wilson Harris. — London: Faber and Faber, 1963. 127 p.
I. T.
PR9320.9.H3 S4   *LC* 64-30798

Harris, Wilson.   **2.10032**
The tree of the sun / by Wilson Harris. — London: Faber and Faber, 1978.
94 p.; 21 cm. — I. T.
PZ4.H318 Tr PR9320.9.H3 T7x   813   *LC* 78-314415   *ISBN*
0571111815

Maes-Jelinek, Hena.   **2.10033**
Wilson Harris / by Hena Maes–Jelinek. — Boston: Twayne Publishers, c1982.
191 p.: port.; 21 cm. — (Twayne's world authors series. TWAS 663) Includes
index. 1. Harris, Wilson — Criticism and interpretation. I. T. II. Series.
PR9320.9.H3 Z77 1982   813 19   *LC* 82-12082   *ISBN* 0805765069

PR9340–9348 Africa, General

(see also: PL8000-8844)

Brown, Lloyd Wellesley, 1938-.   **2.10034**
Women writers in Black Africa / Lloyd W. Brown. — Westport, Conn.:
Greenwood Press, 1981. 204 p.; 22 cm. — (Contributions in women's studies.
no. 21 0147-104X) Includes index. 1. African literature (English) — Women
authors — History and criticism. I. T. II. Series.
PR9340.B7   820 19   *LC* 80-1710   *ISBN* 0313225400

Ngũgĩ wa Thiong'o, 1938-.   **2.10035**
Homecoming: essays on African and Caribbean literature, culture and politics /
Ngugi Wa Thiong' O (James Ngugi). — New York: L. Hill, 1973, c1972. xix,
155 p.; 21 cm. 1. African literature (English) — Addresses, essays, lectures.
2. English literature — West Indian authors — Addresses, essays, lectures.
3. Africa — Civilization — Addresses, essays, lectures. 4. Kenya — Politics
and government — Addresses, essays, lectures. 5. West Indies — Civilization
I. T.
PR9340.N4 1973   *LC* 72-96592   *ISBN* 0882080350

Roscoe, Adrian A.   **2.10036**
Uhuru's fire: African literature east to south / Adrian Roscoe. — Cambridge
[Eng.]; New York: Cambridge University Press, 1977. 281 p.; 24 cm. 1. African
literature (English) — History and criticism. I. T.
PR9340.R6   820/.9   *LC* 76-3038   *ISBN* 0521212952

Achebe, Chinua.   **2.10037**
Morning yet on creation day: essays / Chinua Achebe. — 1st ed. in the U.S.A.
— Garden City, N.Y.: Anchor Press, 1975. xiii, 175 p.; 22 cm. 1. African
literature (English) — History and criticism — Addresses, essays, lectures.
2. African literature — History and criticism — Addresses, essays, lectures.
I. T.
PR9340.5.A3 1975   PR9340.5 A3 1975.   820/.9/96   *LC* 74-33603
   ISBN 0385017030

The Writing of East and Central Africa / edited by G.D.   **2.10038**
Killam.
London; Exeter, N.H., USA: Heinemann, 1984. x, 274 p.; 22 cm. (Studies in
African literature.) 1. African literature (English) — Africa, Eastern —

History and criticism. 2. African literature (English) — Africa, Central —
History and criticism. 3. Africa, Eastern, in literature. 4. Africa, Central, in
literature. I. Killam, G. D. II. Series.
PR9340.5.W75 1984   820/.9/96 19   *LC* 84-187181   *ISBN*
0435916718

Goodwin, K. L.   **2.10039**
Understanding African poetry: a study of ten poets / K.L. Goodwin. —
London; Exeter, N.H., USA: Heinemann, 1982. xix, 204 p.; 23 cm. 1. African
poetry (English) — History and criticism. I. T.
PR9342.G66 1982   821 19   *LC* 84-146951   *ISBN* 0435913255

Etherton, Michael.   **2.10040**
The development of African drama / Michael Etherton. — New York:
Africana Pub. Co., 1982. 368 p.: ill.; 22 cm. Includes index. 1. African drama
(English) — History and criticism. 2. Theater — Africa — History. I. T.
PR9343.E86 1982   822/.009/96 19   *LC* 82-8870   *ISBN*
0841908125

South African writing today; edited by Nadine Gordimer and   **2.10041**
Lionel Abrahams.
Harmondsworth, Penguin, 1967. 264 p. 20 cm. 1. South African literature
(English) I. Abrahams, Lionel. II. Gordimer, Nadine, 1923-
PR9347.5.G6S6   PZ1.G6527So.   *LC* 67-108261

Nichols, Lee.   **2.10042**
African writers at the microphone / Lee Nichols. — 1st ed. — Washington,
D.C.: Three Continents Press, 1984. 281 p.: ill., ports. 'An original by three
Continents'. 1. Authors, African — 20th century — Interviews 2. African
literature (English) — History and criticism I. T.
PR9348 N44 1984   *LC* 83-50539   *ISBN* 0894101641

Pieterse, Cosmo, 1930- comp.   **2.10043**
African writers talking; a collection of radio interviews. Edited by Cosmo
Pieterse & Dennis Duerden. — New York: Africana Pub. Corp., [1972] ix,
195 p.: ports.; 23 cm. 1. English literature — African authors — Interviews.
I. Duerden, Dennis. joint comp. II. T.
PR9348.P5x   820/.9 B   *LC* 72-75255   *ISBN* 084190118X

PR9350–9369.3 Union of South Africa

Palmer, Eustace.   • **2.10044**
An introduction to the African novel; a critical study of twelve books by Chinua
Achebe, James Ngugi, Camara Laye, Elechi Amadi, Ayi Kwei Armah, Mongo
Beti, and Gabriel Okara. — New York: Africana Pub. Corp., [1972] xv, 176 p.;
23 cm. — (Studies in African literature.) 1. Camara, Laye. 2. English fiction —
African authors — History and criticism. 3. English fiction — 20th century —
History and criticism. I. T. II. Series.
PR9352.2.P3x   809.3/3   *LC* 76-183208   *ISBN* 0841901120

Gray, Stephen, 1941-.   **2.10045**
Southern African literature: an introduction / Stephen Gray. — New York:
Barnes & Noble, 1979. 209 p., [4] leaves of plates: ill.; 23 cm. 1. South African
literature (English) — History and criticism. 2. South African literature —
History and criticism. 3. Africa, Southern, in literature. I. T.
PR9354.3.G7   820/.9   *LC* 79-53358   *ISBN* 0064925307

Cook, David, 1929- comp.   **2.10046**
Poems from East Africa, edited by David Cook & David Rubadiri. — London,
Heinemann Educational, 1971. xvi, 206 p. 19 cm. (African writers series, 96)
(An HEB paperback) 1. East African poetry (English) I. Rubadiri, David,
joint comp. II. T.
PR9355.25.C6x   821   *LC* 72-176796   *ISBN* 043590096X

Litto, Fredric M., 1939- comp.   • **2.10047**
Plays from black Africa. Edited and with an introd. by Frederic M. Litto. [1st
ed.] New York, Hill and Wang [1968] xvii, 316 p. 19 cm. (A Mermaid
dramabook, MD42) 1. African drama (English) I. T.
PR9356.3.L5x   822   *LC* 68-30770

Alvarez-Péreyre, Jacques.   **2.10048**
[Guetteurs de l'aube. English] The poetry of commitment in South Africa /
Jacques Alvarez–Pereyre; translated from the French by Clive Wake. —
London; Portsmouth, N.H., USA: Heinemann, 1984. viii, 278 p.; 22 cm.
(Studies in African literature.) Translation of Guetteurs de l'aube. Includes
index. 1. Protest poetry, South African (English) — History and criticism.
2. South African poetry (English) — 20th century — History and criticism.
3. South Africanpoetry (English) — Black authors — History and criticism.
4. Race relations in literature. 5. Social problems in literature 6. Politics in
literature I. T. II. Series.
PR9360.9.P76 A4813 1984   821 19   *LC* 84-218616   *ISBN*
0435910566

A Book of South African verse / selected, and introduced by Guy Butler.   2.10049
Cape Town: Oxford University Press, [1959] xli, 228 p.; 19 cm. Includes five poems by John Peter. Includes index. 1. South African poetry (English) I. Butler, Guy, 1918- II. Peter, John Desmond, 1921-.
PR9365.25.B6x   821.91082   *LC* 59-3258

Cope, Jack, 1913-.   2.10050
The Penguin book of South African verse; compiled and introduced by Jack Cope and Uys Krige. — Harmondsworth: Penguin, 1968. 331 p.; 18 cm. — (The Penguin poets) 1. South African poetry (English) I. Krige, Uys, 1910- joint author. II. T.
PR9365.25.C6x   821/.008   *LC* 76-405528

Macnab, Roy Martin, 1923- ed.   2.10051
Poets in South Africa; an anthology edited by Roy Macnab. — [2nd imp.]. — Cape Town: Maskew Miller, [1968] [xiv], 111 p.; 22 cm. 1. South African poetry (English) I. T.
PR9365.25.M2x   821/.008   *LC* 70-405627

Royston, Robert. comp.   2.10052
Black poets in South Africa / edited by Robert Royston. — London: Heinemann Educational, 1973. 3-96 p.; 19 cm. (African writers series; 164) First published in 1973 under title: To whom it may concern. 1. South African poetry (English) — Black authors I. T.
PR9365.35.N4 R6 1974   821

Hooper, Alfred Gifford, comp.   2.10053
Short stories from Southern Africa, selected by A. G. Hooper. — [5th imp.]. — Cape Town; New York: Oxford University Press, [1970] xi, 148 p.; 22 cm. 1. Short stories, South African I. T.
PR9367.32.H6x   823/.01   *LC* 72-184073

South African stories / edited by David Wright.   2.10054
London: Faber, 1960. 234 p. 1. Short stories, South African I. Wright, David, 1920-
PR9367.32.S6x   *LC* 60-4810

PR9369.2–9369.3 INDIVIDUAL AUTHORS, A–Z

PR9369.2 To 1900

Schreiner, Olive, 1855-1920.   2.10055
The story of an African farm / by Olive Schreiner. — Chicago: Cassandra Editions, 1977. 304 p., [1] leaf of plates: ill.; 15 cm. Reprint of the 1924 ed. published by Collins, London. I. T.
PZ3.S378 St 1977 PR9369.2.S37   823   *LC* 77-21221   *ISBN* 091586424X

First, Ruth.   2.10056
Olive Schreiner / Ruth First and Ann Scott. — New York: Schocken Books, 1980. 383 p., [4] leaves of plates: ill.; 24 cm. Includes index. 1. Schreiner, Olive, 1855-1920 — Biography. 2. Authors, South African — 19th century — Biography. 3. Feminists — Biography. I. Scott, Ann, 1950- joint author. II. T.
PR9369.2.S37 Z64 1980   823 B   *LC* 80-13190

PR9369.3 20th Century

A–F

Abrahams, Peter, 1919-.   • 2.10057
Tell freedom; memories of Africa. — [1st American ed.]. — New York: Knopf, 1954. 370 p.; 22 cm. — I. T.
PR9369.3.A2 T4x   928.2   *LC* 54-5266

Abrahams, Peter, 1919-.   • 2.10058
A wreath for Udomo / by Peter Abrahams. — New York: Knopf, 1956. 356 p.; 22 cm. I. T.
PR9369.3.A2 W7   *LC* 56-5768

Campbell, Roy, 1901-1957.   • 2.10059
Collected poems. — Chicago: H. Regnery Co., 19. v.; 22 cm. Publisher varies: v. 2, The Bodley Head, London. Vol. 3: Translations; with a foreword by Edith Sitwell. I. Sitwell, Dame Edith, 1887-1964. II. T.
PR9369.3.C35 Ax   *LC* 57-59279

Campbell, Roy, 1901-1957.   • 2.10060
Light on a dark horse: an autobiography, 1901-1935; with line illustrations by the author. — London: Hollis & Carter, 1969. viii, 348 p.: illus.; 23 cm. — I. T.
PR9369.3.C35 Z52x   821 B   *LC* 77-433503   *ISBN* 037001314X

Campbell, Roy, 1901-1957.   • 2.10061
Broken record: reminiscences. — London: Boriswood, 1934. 208 p.; 20 cm. 1. Campbell, Roy, 1901-1957 — Biography. I. T.
PR9369.3.C35 Z5x   *LC* 35-3571

Povey, John.   2.10062
Roy Campbell / by John Povey. — Boston: Twayne Publishers, c1977. 233 p.: port.; 21 cm. — (Twayne's world authors series. TWAS 439: South Africa) Includes index. 1. Campbell, Roy, 1901-1957 — Criticism and interpretation. I. T. II. Series.
PR9369.3.C35 Z85   821   *LC* 77-1358   *ISBN* 0805762779

Cope, Jack.   2.10063
The fair house / Jack Cope. — London: MacGibbon & Kee, 1955. 1 v. I. T.
PR9369.3.C6 F3x   *LC* 55-32125

Fugard, Athol.   2.10064
Boesman and Lena and other plays / Athol Fugard. — Oxford; New York: Oxford University Press, 1978. xxv, 299 p.; 20 cm. — (Oxford paperbacks) I. T.
PR9369.3.F8 A19 1978   822   *LC* 77-30721   *ISBN* 0192812424

Fugard, Athol.   • 2.10065
The blood knot: a play in seven scenes / by Athol Fugard. — New York: Odyssey Press, 1964. 131 p.; 20 cm. I. T.
PR9369.3.F8 B5x   *LC* 64-25778

Fugard, Athol.   2.10066
A lesson from Aloes: a play / by Athol Fugard. — 1st ed. — New York: Random House, c1981. xv, 79 p.; 22 cm. — I. T.
PR9369.3.F8 L4 1981   822 19   *LC* 80-6040   *ISBN* 0394518985

Fugard, Athol.   2.10067
'Master Harold'— and the boys / Athol Fugard. — 1st ed. — New York: A.A. Knopf: Distributed by Random House, 1982. 60 p.; 22 cm. I. T.
PR9369.3.F8 M3 1982   822 19   *LC* 82-48027   *ISBN* 0394528743

Fugard, Athol.   2.10068
Sizwe Bansi is dead and The island / by Athol Fugard, John Kani, and Winston Ntshona. — New York: Viking Press, 1976. 79 p., [5] leaves of plates: ill.; 22 cm. Plays. I. Kani, John, joint author. II. Ntshona, Winston, joint author. III. Fugard, Athol. The island. 1976. IV. T.
PR9369.3.F8 S5 1976   822   *LC* 75-45066   *ISBN* 0670647845

Fugard, Athol.   2.10069
Statements: [three plays] / devised by Athol Fugard, John Kani, and Winston Ntshona. — London: Oxford University Press, 1974. 109 p.; 20 cm. (Oxford paperbacks; 345) I. Kani, John. II. Ntshona, Winston. III. T.
PR9369.3.F8 S8   822   *LC* 75-301105   *ISBN* 0192113852

G–H

Gordimer, Nadine.   2.10070
The conservationist. — New York: Viking Press, [1975, c1974] 252 p.; 22 cm. — I. T.
PR9369.3.G6 C6x   823   *LC* 74-7768   *ISBN* 067023883X

Gordimer, Nadine.   • 2.10071
Friday's footprint: and other stories / by Nadine Gordimer. — New York: Viking Press, 1960. 244 p.; 21 cm. I. T.
PR9369.3.G6 F7 1960   *LC* 60-5857

Gordimer, Nadine.   2.10072
July's people / Nadine Gordimer. — New York: Viking Press, 1981. 160 p.; 22 cm. — I. T.
PR9369.3.G6 J8 1981   823 19   *LC* 80-24877   *ISBN* 0670410489

Gordimer, Nadine.   • 2.10073
Livingstone's companions; stories. — New York: Viking Press, [1971] 248 p.; 23 cm. I. T.
PR9369.3.G6 L5x   PR6057.O63 L5x.   823   *LC* 78-158415   *ISBN* 0670435708

Gordimer, Nadine.   • 2.10074
The lying days, a novel. New York, Simon and Schuster, 1953. 340 p. 22 cm. I. T.
PR9369.3.G6 L9x   *LC* 53-10813

Gordimer, Nadine, 1923-.   • 2.10075
Occasion for loving: a novel / Nadine Gordimer. — New York: Viking Press, 1963. 308 p.; 22 cm. I. T.
PR9369.3.G6 O3 1963   *LC* 63-8852

Gordimer, Nadine.   • 2.10076
The soft voice of the serpent, and other stories. New York, Simon and Schuster,
1952. 244 p. 22 cm. I. T.
PR9369.3.G6 S57x   *LC* 52-9515

Gordimer, Nadine.   2.10077
A soldier's embrace: stories / by Nadine Gordimer. — New York: Viking Press,
1980. 144 p.; 23 cm. — I. T.
PR9369.3.G6 S6 1980   823   *LC* 79-56266   *ISBN* 0670656380

Gordimer, Nadine.   • 2.10078
A world of strangers. New York, Simon and Schuster, 1958. 312 p. 22 cm. I. T.
PR9369.3.G6 W6x   *LC* 58-9049

Haugh, Robert F.   2.10079
Nadine Gordimer, by Robert F. Haugh. — New York: Twayne Publishers,
[1974] 174 p.: port.; 22 cm. — (Twayne's world authors series, TWAS 315.
South Africa) 1. Gordimer, Nadine. I. T.
PR9369.3.G6 Z5x   823   *LC* 74-1350   *ISBN* 0805723870

Head, Bessie, 1937-.   2.10080
A question of power; a novel. — [1st American ed.]. — New York: Pantheon
Books, [c1973] 206 p.; 22 cm. — I. T.
PZ4.H4323 Qe3 PR9369.3.H4 Q8x   823

Head, Bessie, 1937-.   2.10081
When rain clouds gather; a novel. — New York: Simon and Schuster, [1969,
c1968] 188 p.; 22 cm. — I. T.
PR9369.3.H4 W5x   823   *LC* 69-12089

J–Z

Jacobson, Dan.   2.10082
Evidence of love / Dan Jacobson. — Boston: Little, Brown, c1960. 242 p. I. T.
PR9369.3.J3 E8x   [Fic]   *LC* 60-5873

Jacobson, Dan.   2.10083
The Zulu and the zeide: short stories / by Dan Jacobson. — 1st ed. — Boston,
Little, Brown c1959. 247 p. 21 cm. (An Atlantic Monthly Press book.) I. T.
PZ4.J175Zu PR6060.A3Z4   PR9369.3.J3Z81x.   *LC* 59-7336

Roberts, Sheila, 1942-.   2.10084
Dan Jacobson / by Sheila Roberts; Bernth Lindfors, editor. — Boston: Twayne
Publishers, c1984. 144 p.: port.; 23 cm. — (Twayne's world authors series.
TWAS 720) Includes index. 1. Jacobson, Dan — Criticism and interpretation.
I. Lindfors, Bernth. II. T. III. Series.
PR9369.3.J3 Z86 1984   823/.912 19   *LC* 83-12910   *ISBN*
0805765670

Jordan, A. C.   2.10085
Tales from southern Africa. Translated and retold by A. C. Jordan. Foreword
by Z. Pallo Jordan. Introd. and commentaries by Harold Scheub. Illus. by Feni
Dumile. — Berkeley: University of California Press, 1973. xxiii, 277 p.: illus.; 23
cm. — (Perspectives on Southern Africa. 4) I. T. II. Series.
PZ4.J817 Tal3 PR9369.J6   PR9369.3J62 T35.   823   *LC* 76-145787
ISBN 0520019113

Abrahams, Cecil Anthony.   2.10086
Alex La Guma / by Cecil A. Abrahams. — Boston: Twayne, c1985. 159 p.;
port.; 23 cm. (Twayne's world authors series; TWAS 743. African literature)
Includes index. 1. La Guma, Alex — Criticism and interpretation. I. T.
PR9369.3.L3 Z58 1985   823 19   *LC* 84-15653   *ISBN* 0805765891

Paton, Alan.   • 2.10087
Cry, the beloved country. With an introd. by Lewis Gannett. New York:
Scribner, [1960, c1950] 283 p.; 21 cm. (Modern standard authors.) I. T.
II. Series.
PR9639.3.P37 C7x

Paton, Alan.   2.10088
Knocking on the door: shorter writings / Alan Paton; selected and edited by
Colin Gardner. — New York: Scribner, c1975. viii, 296 p.; 24 cm. I. Gardner,
Colin Oxenham. II. T.
PR9369.3.P37 K6 1975b   823   *LC* 75-39502   *ISBN* 0684144298

Paton, Alan.   • 2.10089
Too late the phalarope. New York, Scribner, 1953. 276 p. 21 cm. I. T.
PR9369.3.P37Tx   *LC* 53-11549

Callan, Edward, 1917-.   2.10090
Alan Paton / by Edward Callan. — Rev. ed. — Boston: Twayne Publishers,
c1982. 143 p.: port.; 21 cm. — (Twayne's world authors series. TWAS 40)
Includes index. 1. Paton, Alan — Criticism and interpretation. I. T. II. Series.
PR9369.3.P37 Z6 1982   823 19   *LC* 82-11970   *ISBN* 0805765123

Smith, Pauline.   2.10091
The beadle. London: Cape, 1926. 288p. I. T.
PR9369.3.S656 B4x   *LC* 27-2151

Smith, Pauline.   2.10092
The Little Karoo. With an introd. by Arnold Bennett and a pref. by William
Plomer. — London, Cape [1925] 188p. I. T.
PR9369.3.S656 L5x   823.912

Haresnape, Geoffrey, 1939-.   2.10093
Pauline Smith. — New York: Twayne Publishers, [c1969] 198 p.; 21 cm. —
(Twayne's world authors series, 80. South Africa) 1. Smith, Pauline. I. T.
PR9369.3.S656 Zx   823 B   *LC* 67-19346

Themba, Can, 1924-1968.   2.10094
The will to die; selected by Donald Stuart and Roy Holland. — London,
Heinemann, 1972. xi, 115 p. 19 cm. — (African writers series, 104) Imprint
covered by label: Distributed in the U.S.A. by Humanities Press, New York.
I. T.
PR9369.3.T55 W5x   828   *LC* 72-187987   *ISBN* 0435901044

PR9379 Ghana

Fraser, Robert, 1947-.   2.10095
The novels of Ayi Kwei Armah: a study in polemical fiction / [by] Robert
Fraser. — London: Heinemann, 1980. xiii, 113 p.; 22 cm. — (Studies in African
literature.) Includes index. 1. Armah, Ayi Kwei, 1939- — Criticism and
interpretation. I. T. II. Series.
PR9379.9.A7 Z65   823   *LC* 80-470459   *ISBN* 0435913018

PR9381–9381.9 Kenya

Angira, Jared.   2.10096
Silent voices; poems. London, Heinemann [1972] vi, 88 p. 19 cm. (African
writers series, 111) I. T.
PR9381.9.A5 S5x   821   *LC* 73-151269   *ISBN* 0435901117

Cook, David, 1929-.   2.10097
Ngugi wa Thiong'o, an exploration of his writings / David Cook, Michael
Okenimkpe. — London: Heinemann, 1983. 250 p.; 22 cm. — (Studies in
African literature.) 1. Ngũgĩ wa Thiong'o, 1938- — Criticism and
interpretation. I. Okenimkpe, Michael. II. T. III. Series.
PR9381.9.N45 Z562 1983   823 19   *LC* 83-212850   *ISBN*
0435911740

Critical perspectives on Ngugi wa Thiong'o / edited by G.D.   2.10098
Killam.
1st ed. — Washington: Three Continents Press, c1984. 321 p.: ill., map; 23 cm.
(Critical perspectives. 13) 1. Ngũgĩ wa Thiong'o, 1938- — Criticism and
interpretation. I. Killam, G. D. II. Series.
PR9381.9.N45 Z57 1984   823 19   *LC* 81-51673   *ISBN* 0894100653

PR9387–9387.9 Nigeria

Introduction to Nigerian literature / Edited by Bruce King.   2.10099
[New York]: Africana Pub. Corp., [1972, c1971] 216 p.; 23 cm. 1. Nigerian
literature (English) — History and criticism — Addresses, essays, lectures.
2. Nigerian literature — History and criticism — Addresses, essays, lectures.
I. King, Bruce Alvin. ed.
PR9387.I7x   *LC* 73-180669   *ISBN* 0841901112

Obiechina, Emmanuel N., 1933-.   2.10100
An African popular literature: a study of Onitsha market pamphlets [by]
Emmanuel Obiechina. Cambridge [Eng.] University Press, 1973. x, 246 p.
facsims. 22 cm. Includes three pamphlets in facsimile: Our modern ladies
character towards boys, by Highbred Maxwell; Elizabeth, my lover, by Okenwa
Olisah; and What women are thinking about men, by J. O. Nnadozie.
1. Nigerian literature (English) — Nigeria — Onitsha — History and criticism.
2. Popular literature — Nigeria — Onitsha — History and criticism. 3. Social
problems in literature 4. Nigerian literature (English) — Nigeria — Onitsha.
5. Popular literature — Nigeria — Onitsha. 6. Chap-books, Nigerian I. T.
PR9387.85.O5 O3   820/.8   *LC* 72-83668   *ISBN* 0521200156 *ISBN*
0521097444

PR9387.9 INDIVIDUAL AUTHORS, A–Z

A–M

Achebe, Chinua.   2.10101
Arrow of God / Chinua Achebe. — 2d ed. — London: Heinemann, 1974. 230 p. — (African writers series; 16) On cover: Revised edition. I. T.
PR9387.9.A25 A7 1974

Achebe, Chinua.   2.10102
Christmas in Biafra, and other poems. — Garden City, N.Y.: Anchor Books, 1973. 92 p.; 21 cm. — I. T.
PR6051.C5 C5 1973b   PR9387.9.A3 C45.   821   LC 73-157441
   ISBN 0385008406

Achebe, Chinua.   2.10103
Girls at war, and other stories / by Chinua Achebe. — Garden City, N.Y.: Doubleday, 1973. –. x, 129 p.; 22 cm. — I. T.
PR9387.9.A3 G5x   823   LC 72-85361   ISBN 038500852X

Achebe, Chinua.   • 2.10104
A man of the people: a novel / Chinua Achebe. — New York: J. Day, 1966. 166 p. I. T.
PR9387.9.A3 M3x   PR6021.C5 M3x.   LC 66-22929

Achebe, Chinua.   • 2.10105
No longer at ease. New York, I. Obolensky [1961, c1960] 170 p. 21 cm. I. T.
PR9387.9.A3 N6x   PR6051.C5N6x.   LC 61-7356

Achebe, Chinua.   • 2.10106
Things fall apart. — New York: McDowell, Obolensky, [1959] 215 p.; 22 cm. — I. T.
PR9387.9.A3 T5x   PR6051.C5 T5x.   813.5   LC 59-7114

Critical perspectives on Chinua Achebe / edited by C. L. Innes   2.10107
& Bernth Lindfors.
1st ed. — Washington: Three Continents Press, c1978. 315 p., [1] leaf of plates: ill.; 24 cm. — (Critical perspectives; 4) Includes index. 1. Achebe, Chinua — Criticism and interpretation — Addresses, essays, lectures. I. Innes, Catherine Lynette. II. Lindfors, Bernth.
PR9387.9.A3 Z63   823   LC 77-9163   ISBN 0914478451

Clark, J. P., 1935-.   • 2.10108
Three plays: Song of a goat, The masquerade, The raft [by] J. P. Clark. — London, Oxford University Press, 1964. 134 p. 19 cm. — (A Three crowns book) I. T. II. Title: Song of a goat. III. Title: The masquerade. IV. Title: The raft.
PR9387.9.C55 T5x   822.914   LC 66-4358

Emecheta, Buchi.   2.10109
The slave girl / Buchi Emecheta. — New York: G. Braziller, [1977]. 179 p. I. T.
PZ4.E525 Sl3 PR9387.9.E387   823   LC 77-77559   ISBN 0807608726

Ekwensi, Cyprian.   2.10110
People of the city. — [Rev. ed.]. — London: Heinemann Educational Books, 1963. 156 p.: ill.; 19 cm. — (African writers series; 5) I. T.
PR9387.9.E5 P4x   LC 56-4629

N–Z

Soyinka, Wole.   2.10111
Collected plays. — London; New York: Oxford University Press, 1973-. v. ; 20 cm. — (A Galaxy book; 392) I. T.
PR9387.9.S6 1973   822   LC 74-156793   ISBN 0192811363

Soyinka, Wole.   • 2.10112
Idanre & other poems. — [1st American ed.]. — New York: Hill and Wang, [1968, c1967] 88 p.; 21 cm. — I. T.
PR9387.9.S6 I3x   821   LC 68-30761

Soyinka, Wole.   2.10113
The interpreters / Wole Soyinka. — New York: Africana Pub., 1972. 253 p.; 21 cm. I. T.
PR9387.9S6 I5 1972   LC 72-76610   ISBN 084190121X

Soyinka, Wole.   2.10114
Aké: the years of childhood / Wole Soyinka. — New York: Random House, [1982] 230 p. 1. Nigeria — Social life and customs. I. T.
PR9387.9.S6 Z462 1982   822 B 19   LC 82-40148   ISBN 0394528077

Jones, Eldred D.   2.10115
The writing of Wole Soyinka / Eldred Durosimi Jones. — Rev. ed. — London; Exeter, N.H., USA: Heinemann, 1983, c1973. xvi, 222 p.; 22 cm. (Studies in African literature.) Includes index. 1. Soyinka, Wole — Criticism and interpretation. I. T. II. Series.
PR9387.9.S6 Z7 1983   822 19   LC 84-230969   ISBN 0435916459

Moore, Gerald, 1924-.   2.10116
Wole Soyinka. — New York: Africana Pub. Corp., [1971] xii, 114 p.: ill.; 19 cm. — (Modern African writers) 1. Soyinka, Wole. I. T. II. Series.
PR9387.9.S6 Z77x   828   LC 74-176321   ISBN 0841900957

Tutuola, Amos.   • 2.10117
The palm–wine drinkard and his dead palm–wine tapster in the Dead's Town. — Westport, Conn.: Greenwood Press, [1970, c1953] 130 p.; 23 cm. — I. T.
PR9387.9.T8 P3x   823   LC 78-104255   ISBN 0837140447

Tutuola, Amos.   2.10118
The witch–herbalist of the remote town / Amos Tutuola. — London; Boston: Faber and Faber, 1981. 205 p.; 21 cm. I. T.
PR9387.9.T8 W5 1981   823 19   LC 82-670146   ISBN 0571117031

Critical perspectives on Amos Tutuola / edited by Bernth   2.10119
Lindfors.
1st ed. — Washington: Three Continents Press, c1975. xiv, 318 p.; 24 cm. (Critical perspectives) 1. Tutuola, Amos — Criticism and interpretation — Addresses, essays, lectures. I. Lindfors, Bernth.
PR9387.9.T8 Z6   823   LC 75-13706   ISBN 0914478052

PR9410–9418 Asia, General

Ahmed-ud-Din, Feroz.   2.10120
This handful of dust / Feroz Ahmed–ud–Din; foreword by A. G. Stock. — Calcutta: Writers Workshop; [Thompson], Conn.: agents in U.S., Inter Culture Associates, c1974. 31 p.; 22 cm. ('A Writers Workshop redbird book.') I. T.
PR9420.9.A4 T5   PR9420.9A4 T5.   821   LC 75-903788

Srinivasa Iyengar, K. R.   • 2.10121
Indian writing in English / K. R. Srinivasa Iyengar. — Bombay: Asia Pub. House, 1962. xi, 440 p. 1. Indic literature (English) — History and criticism I. T.
PR9480.3.S7x   LC 62-3123

PR9490–9499 India

Lal, P. comp.   2.10122
Modern Indian poetry in English: the Writers Workshop selection; an anthology & a credo. Edited by P. Lal. — Calcutta: Writers Workshop, 1973. 733 p.: ill. 'Writers Workshop redbird book.' 1. Indic poetry (English) 2. English poetry — 20th century I. T.
PR9495.25.L3x   ISBN 0882532721

Ten twentieth–century Indian poets / chosen and edited by R.   2.10123
Parthasarathy.
Delhi; New York: Oxford University Press, 1976. xiv, 114 p.; 22 cm. — (New poetry in India) (Three crowns books) Includes indexes. 1. Indic poetry (English) — 20th century. I. Parthasarathy, R II. Series.
PR9495.7.T4   PR9495.7 T4.   821/.008   LC 77-375533   ISBN 0195606655

Anand, Mulk Raj, 1905-.   • 2.10124
Coolie. — New revised ed.; with an introduction by Saros Cowasjee. — London: Bedley Head, 1972. 320 p.; 21 cm. — I. T.
PZ3.A535 Co7 PR9499.3.A5 C6x   823   LC 72-192575   ISBN 0370014103

Anand, Mulk Raj, 1905-.   • 2.10125
Private life of an Indian prince; with an introduction by Saros Cowasjee. — Revised ed. — London: Bodley Head, 1970. 365 p.; 21 cm. — I. T.
PZ3.A535 Pr3 PR9499.3.A5 P7x   823   LC 71-488837   ISBN 0370014073

Taylor, Kamala (Purnaiya), 1924-.   • 2.10126
Nectar in a sieve, a novel by Kamala Markandaya. [1st American ed.] New York, J. Day Co. [1955, c1954] 248 p. 21 cm. I. T.
PR9499.3.M367N4x   PR6063.A642 N4x.   LC 55-5937

Markandaya, Kamala, 1924-.   **2.10127**
Two virgins; a novel. — New York: John Day Co., [1973] 250 p.; 22 cm. — I. T.
PR9499.3.M367 T8x   823/.9/14   *LC* 73-4293   *ISBN* 0381982440

Nahal, Chaman Lal, 1927-.   **2.10128**
Azadi / Chaman Nahal. — 1st American ed. — Boston: Houghton Mifflin, 1975. 371 p.: map (on lining papers); 22 cm. 1. India — History — 1947- — Fiction. I. T.
PZ4.N149 Az3 PR9499.3.N25   823   *LC* 75-4580   *ISBN* 0395194016

Nandy, Pritish.   **2.10129**
Riding the midnight river: selected poems of Pritish Nandy. — New Delhi: Arnold Heinemann, 1975. 144 p. I. T.
PR9499.3.N28 R5   PR9499.3N26 R5.

Raja Rao.   • **2.10130**
Kanthapura / by Raja Rao. — New York: New Directions, 1963. viii, 244 p.; 21 cm. I. T.
PR9499.3.R3 K3x   PR6035.A4 K3x.   *LC* 63-18637

Raja Rao.   • **2.10131**
The serpent and the rope. [1st American ed. New York] Pantheon Books [1963, c1960] 407 p. 22 cm. I. T.
PR9499.3.R3 S4 1963   *LC* 62-14261 rev

Rama Rau, Santha, 1923-.   • **2.10132**
Remember the house. — [1st ed.]. — New York: Harper, [1956] 241 p.; 22 cm. — I. T.
PR9499.3.R33x   PR6035.A425.   *LC* 55-10715

Rushdie, Salman.   **2.10133**
Midnight's children: a novel / by Salman Rushdie. — 1st American ed. — New York: Knopf, 1981, c1980. 446 p.; 25 cm. — I. T.
PR9499.3.R8 M5 1981   823 19   *LC* 80-2712   *ISBN* 039451470X

PR9550 Philippines

Essays on the Philippine novel in English / edited by Joseph A. Galdon.   **2.10134**
[S.l.]: Cellar, 1980. vii, 168 p. 1. Philippine fiction — History and criticism. I. Galdon, Joseph A.
PR9550.5 E88

Philippine short stories, 1925–1940 / selected and edited with a critical introduction by Leopoldo Y. Yabes.   **2.10135**
Quezon City: University of the Philippines Press, 1975. xlv, 545 p.; 24 cm. 1. Short stories, Philippine (English) I. Yabes, Leopoldo Y.
PR9550.8.S5 P5   823/.01   *LC* 77-370520

Philippine short stories, 1941–1955 / selected and edited with a critical introduction by Leopoldo Y. Yabes.   **2.10136**
Quezon City, Philippines: University of the Philippines Press, 1981. 2 v. (xxxiii, 1383 p.): ill.; 23 cm. 1. Short stories, Philippine (English) I. Yabes, Leopoldo Y.
PR9550.8.S5 P52 1981   823 19   *LC* 82-163561   *ISBN* 0824807677

PR9570 Singapore

The Poetry of Singapore / editors, Edwin Thumboo ... [et al.].   • **2.10137**
Singapore: Published under the sponsorship of the ASEAN Committee on Culture and Information, c1985. 560 p.: maps; 24 cm. — (Anthology of ASEAN literatures. v. 1) Text in English, Chinese, Malay or Tamil; some with translations. Spine title: ASEAN literatures. Maps on lining papers. 1. Singapore poetry (English) 2. Singapore poetry (English) — Translations from other languages 3. Chinese poetry — Singapore 4. Malay poetry — Singapore 5. Tamil poetry — Singapore I. Thumboo, Edwin, 1933- II. Title: ASEAN literatures. III. Series.
PR9570.S52 P63   *ISBN* 997188089X

PR9600–9619.3 Australia

The Oxford history of Australian literature / edited by Leonie Kramer; with contributions by Adrian Mitchell ... [et al.].   **2.10138**
Melbourne; New York: Oxford University Press, 1981. vi, 509 p.; 22 cm. Includes index. 1. Australian literature — History and criticism. I. Kramer,

Leonie Judith Gibson. II. Mitchell, Adrian Christopher William. III. Title: History of Australian literature.
PR9604.3.O9 1981   820/.9/994 19   *LC* 81-162174   *ISBN* 0195505905

Moore, T. Inglis (Tom Inglis), 1901-1978.   **2.10139**
Social patterns in Australian literature [by] T. Inglis Moore. Berkeley, University of California Press, 1971. viii, 350 p. 25 cm. 1. Australian literature — History and criticism. 2. Literature and society — Australia. I. T.
PR9605.2.M6x   820/.9   *LC* 71-133027   *ISBN* 0520018281

Studies in the recent Australian novel / edited by K. G. Hamilton.   **2.10140**
St. Lucia, Q.: University of Queensland Press, c1978. ix, 257 p.; 22 cm. 'From the Australian Studies Centre, University of Queensland.' 1. Australian fiction — 20th century — History and criticism — Addresses, essays, lectures. I. Hamilton, K. G. (Kenneth Gordon), 1921-
PR9609.6.S74   823/.03   *LC* 79-307752   *ISBN* 0702212474

A Map of Australian verse / [by] James McAuley.   **2.10141**
Melbourne; New York: Oxford University Press, 1975. x, 342 p.; 23 cm. 1. Australian poetry — 20th century — History and criticism. I. McAuley, James Phillip, 1917-
PR9610.5.M3   821   *LC* 76-358517   *ISBN* 0195504720

Argyle, Barry.   **2.10142**
An introduction to the Australian novel, 1830–1930. — Oxford: Clarendon Press, 1972. [9], 265 p.; 23 cm. 1. Australian fiction — History and criticism. I. T.
PR9612.2.A7x   823/.03   *LC* 72-196854   *ISBN* 0198120095

Jones, Joseph Jay, 1908-.   **2.10143**
Australian fiction / by Joseph and Johanna Jones. — Boston: Twayne Publishers, c1983. 177 p.; 23 cm. (Twayne's world authors series. TWAS 735) Includes index. 1. Australian fiction — History and criticism. I. Jones, Johanna. II. T. III. Series.
PR9612.2.J66 1983   823/.009/994 19   *LC* 83-12691   *ISBN* 0805764720

Who is she? / edited by Shirley Walker.   **2.10144**
New York: St. Martin's Press, 1983. xi, 219 p.; 22 cm. 1. Australian fiction — History and criticism — Addresses, essays, lectures. 2. Women in literature — Addresses, essays, lectures. 3. Women — Australia — Addresses, essays, lectures. I. Walker, Shirley, 1927-
PR9612.6.W6 W48 1983b   823/.009/352042 19   *LC* 83-47740   *ISBN* 0312870159

The Oxford anthology of Australian literature / edited by Leonie Kramer and Adrian Mitchell.   **2.10145**
Melbourne; New York: Oxford University Press, 1985. xi, 589 p.: ill.; 23 cm. Includes index. 1. Australian literature I. Kramer, Leonie Judith Gibson. II. Mitchell, Adrian Christopher William.
PR9614.4.O85 1985   820/.8/0994 19   *LC* 85-228185   *ISBN* 0195544773

Classic Australian short stories / selected and introduced by Judah Waten and Stephen Murray–Smith.   **2.10146**
North Pomfret, Vt.: David & Charles, 1975, c1974. x, 352 p.; 22 cm. 1. Short stories, Australian I. Waten, Judah L. II. Murray-Smith, Stephen.
PZ1.C564 PR9617.3.Cx   823/.01   *LC* 75-307748   *ISBN* 0858850370

PR9619.2–9619.3 Individual Authors, A–Z

PR9619.2 To 1900

Andrews, B. G.   **2.10147**
Price Warung (William Astley) / by Barry Andrews. Boston: Twayne Publishers, c1976. 197 p.: port.; 21 cm. (Twayne's world authors series; TWAS 383: Australia) Includes index. 1. Warung, Price, 1855-1911. 2. Novelists, Australian — 19th century — Biography. I. T.
PR9619.2.A76 Z57   823   *LC* 75-29305   *ISBN* 0805762256

Furphy, Joseph, 1843-1912.   • **2.10148**
Such is life, being certain extracts from the diary of Tom Collins. — [Sydney]: Angus and Robertson, [1962] vii, 371 p.; 21 cm. — (Sirius books) I. T.
PR9619.2.F82 S8x   *LC* 68-52335

Furphy, Joseph, 1843-1912.   **2.10149**
Joseph Furphy / edited with an introduction by John Barnes. — St. Lucia [Brisbane]; New York: University of Queensland Press, c1981. xxv, 439 p.: 1 map; 19 cm. — (Portable Australian authors.) I. Barnes, John, 1931- II. T. III. Series.
PR9619.2.F87 A6 1981   823 19   *LC* 81-4819   *ISBN* 0702216127

Lawson, Henry, 1867-1922. • 2.10150
Poetical works of Henry Lawson; with preface and introduction by David McKee Wright. — Sydney: Angus & Robertson, 1925. 3 v.; 19 cm. Includes index. I. T.
PR9619.2.L3 A6   821 19   *LC* 80-490839   *ISBN* 0207122172

Lawson, Henry, 1867-1922. • 2.10151
Henry Lawson's best stories, chosen by Cecil Mann. [Sydney] Angus and Robertson [1966] viii, 273 p. 23 cm. I. Mann, Cecil, ed. II. T.
PR9619.2.L3 Ax   *LC* 66-28938

Roderick, Colin Arthur. • 2.10152
Henry Lawson, poet and short story writer. — [Sydney]: Angus and Robertson, [1966] 70 p.: ill., port. 1. Lawson, Henry, 1867-1922. I. T.
PR9619.2.L3 Zx   *LC* 66-66959

PR9619.3 20th Century

A-P

Astley, Thea, 1925-. 2.10153
An item from the late news / Thea Astley. — Ringwood, Vic.; Harmondsworth: Penguin, 1984, c1982. 200 p.; 19 cm. I. T.
PR9619.3.A75 I8 1984   823 19   *ISBN* 0140069488

Brennan, Christopher John, 1870-1932. 2.10154
[Selections. 1984] Christopher Brennan / edited with an introduction and notes by Terry Sturm. — St. Lucia, Queensland, Australia: University of Queensland Press; Lawrence, Mass.: Distributed in the USA and Canada by Technical Impex Corp., c1984. xxxii, 477 p.; 20 cm. (Portable Australian authors.) I. Sturm, Terry. II. T. III. Series.
PR9619.3.B68 A6 1984   821 19   *LC* 84-3696   *ISBN* 0702217352

Day, A. Grove (Arthur Grove), 1904-. 2.10155
Eleanor Dark / by A. Grove Day. — Boston: Twayne Publishers, c1976. 168 p.: port.; 21 cm. — (Twayne's world authors series; TWAS 382: Australia) Includes index. 1. Dark, Eleanor, 1901- Criticism and interpretation. I. T.
PR9619.3.D38 E5   823   *LC* 75-23369   *ISBN* 0805762248

Day, A. Grove (Arthur Grove), 1904-. 2.10156
Robert D. FitzGerald, by A. Grove Day. New York, Twayne [1974] 192 p. 22 cm. (Twayne's world authors series. TWAS 286. Australia) 1. FitzGerald, Robert David, 1902- I. T.
PR9619.3.F48 Z63   821   *LC* 73-15877   *ISBN* 0805723110

Hetherington, John Aikman, 1907-. • 2.10157
Norman Lindsay. — [2nd ed.]. — Melbourne: Lansdowne Press, [1961] 48 p.: port. — (Australian writers and their work.) 1. Lindsay, Norman, 1879-1969. I. T. II. Series.
PR9619.3.L5 Zx

Malouf, David, 1934-. 2.10158
Harland's half acre / David Malouf. — 1st American ed. — New York: Knopf, 1984. 230 p.; 22 cm. I. T.
PR9619.3.M265 H3 1984   821 19   *LC* 84-47680   *ISBN* 0394539192

Manning, Frederic. 2.10159
The middle parts of fortune: Somme & Ancre, 1916 / Frederic Manning. — New York: St. Martin's Press, 1978. 246 p.; 23 cm. 1. World War, 1914-1918 — Fiction. 2. Somme, Battle of the, 1916 — Fiction. I. T.
PZ3.M3206 Mi 1977 PR9619.3.M267   823/.9/12   *LC* 77-72368   *ISBN* 0312531850

Smith, Vivian Brian. 2.10160
Vance and Nettie Palmer, by Vivian Smith. — New York: Twayne Publishers, [1975] 154 p.: port.; 22 cm. — (Twayne's world authors series, TWAS 332. Australia) 1. Palmer, Vance, 1885-1959. 2. Palmer, Nettie, 1885-1964. I. T.
PR9619.3.P27 Z8   828   *LC* 74-9791   *ISBN* 0805726675

Porter, Hal. 2.10161
Hal Porter / selected and edited with an introd. and bibliography by Mary Lord. — St. Lucia, Australia: University of Queensland Press, 1980. xxxi, 408 p.; 20 cm. — (Portable Australian authors.) I. Lord, Mary. II. T. III. Series.
PR9619.3.P56 A6 1980   823 19   *LC* 80-509181   *ISBN* 0702214655

Porter, Hal. • 2.10162
The watcher on the cast–iron balcony: an Australian autobiography / Hal Porter. — London: Faber and Faber, 1963. 255 p. I. T.
PR9619.3.P63 W3 1963   *LC* 64-57899

R-U

Slessor, Kenneth, 1901-1971. • 2.10163
Poems. / Kenneth Slessor. — Sydney: Angus and Robertson, 1962. ix, 116 p. — (Sirius books) I. T.
PR9619.3.S534 P6   *LC* 64-56033

Stead, Christina, 1902-. 2.10164
A Christina Stead reader / selected by Jean B. Read. — 1st ed. — New York: Random House, c1978. viii, 369 p.; 24 cm. I. Read, Jean B. II. T.
PZ3.S7986 Ch 1978 PR9619.3.S75   823   *LC* 78-57134   *ISBN* 0394500954

Stead, Christina, 1902-. • 2.10165
House of all nations. New York: Holt, Rinehart and Winston, [1972, c1938] viii, 787 p.; 22 cm. — I. T.
PZ3.S7986 Ho5 PR9619.3.S75   823   *LC* 72-80210   *ISBN* 003001946X

Stead, Christina, 1902-. 2.10166
The little hotel: a novel / Christina Stead. New York: Holt, Rinehart and Winston, 1975, c1973. 191 p.; 22 cm. I. T.
PZ3.S7986 Lg4 PR9619.3.S75   823   *LC* 74-6943   *ISBN* 0030132266

Stead, Christina, 1902-. 2.10167
Miss Herbert (the suburban wife) / Christina Stead. — 1st ed. — New York: Random House, c1976. 308 p.; 22 cm. I. T.
PZ3.S7986 Mi PR9619.3.S75   823   *LC* 75-40561   *ISBN* 039440517X

Stead, Christina, 1902-. • 2.10168
Dark places of the heart / Christina Stead. — 1st ed. — New York: Holt, Rinehart and Winston, 1966. 352 p. British ed. has title: Cotter's England. I. T. II. Title: Cotter's England.
PR9619.3.S75 D3   *LC* 66-21616

Stead, Christina, 1902-. • 2.10169
A little tea, a little chat. New York, Harcourt, Brace [1948] 394 p. 21 cm. I. T.
PR9619.3.S75 L5x   *LC* 48-8364

Stead, Christina, 1902-. • 2.10170
The man who loved children / Christina Stead; introd. by Randall Jarrell. — New York: Holt, Rinehart and Winston, 1965. xii, 527 p. I. T.
PR9619.3.S75 M3x   *LC* 65-10128

Stead, Christina, 1902-. 2.10171
Ocean of story: the uncollected stories of Christina Stead / Christina Stead; edited with an afterword by R.G. Geering. — Ringwood, Vic., Australia; New York, N.Y., U.S.A.: Viking, 1985. 552 p.; 23 cm. Spine title: Christina Stead: ocean of story. I. Geering, R. G. II. T. III. Title: Christina Stead, ocean of story.
PR9619.3.S75 O25 1985   823 19   *LC* 86-159098   *ISBN* 0670809969

Stead, Christina, 1902-. • 2.10172
The puzzleheaded girl: four novellas / Christina Stead. — 1st ed. — New York: Holt, Rinehart and Winston, 1967. 255 p.; 22 cm. I. Stead, Christina, 1902- Dianas. II. Stead, Christina, 1902- Rightangled creek. III. Stead, Christina, 1902- Girl from the beach. IV. T. V. Title: The Dianas. VI. Title: The rightangled creek. VII. Title: Girl from the beach.
PR9619.3.S75 P8   *LC* 67-17992

Stead, Christina, 1902-. • 2.10173
The Salzburg tales / by Christina Stead. — New York: D. Appleton-Century, 1934. vi, 415 p. I. T.
PR9619.3.S75 S3   *LC* 34-20399

Geering, R. G. 2.10174
Christina Stead, by R. G. Geering. New York, Twayne Publishers [c1969] 181 p. 22 cm. (Twayne's world authors series, 95. Australia) 1. Stead, Christina, 1902- I. T.
PR9619.3.S75 Z6x   *LC* 68-17240

Lidoff, Joan. 2.10175
Christina Stead / Joan Lidoff. — New York: F. Ungar Pub. Co., c1982. ix, 255 p.; 21 cm. — (Literature and life series.) Includes index. 1. Stead, Christina, 1902- — Criticism and interpretation. I. T. II. Series.
PR9619.3.S75 Z7 1982   823 19   *LC* 82-40283   *ISBN* 0804425205

Semmler, Clement. 2.10176
Douglas Stewart. — New York: Twayne Publishers, [1975, c1974] 170 p.: port.; 22 cm. — (Twayne's world authors series, TWAS 327. Australia) 1. Stewart, Douglas Alexander, 1913- — Criticism and interpretation. I. T.
PR9619.3.S8 Z88 1975   821   *LC* 74-7389   *ISBN* 0805728635

Upfield, Arthur William, 1888-1964.   2.10177
Death of a lake / Arthur Upfield. — New York: Doubleday, 1954. 249 p. I. T.
PR9619.3.U6 D42   Fic

W–Z

White, Patrick, 1912-.   • 2.10178
The aunt's story / Patrick White. — New York: Viking Press, 1948. 281 p.; 21 cm. I. T.
PR9619.3.W5 A8x   LC 48-5103   ISBN 0670141682

White, Patrick, 1912-.   2.10179
The cockatoos; stories. — New York: Viking Press, [1975, c1974] 307 p.; 21 cm. I. T.
PZ3.W58469 Co3 PR9619.3.W5C6x   823   LC 74-3792   ISBN 0670226483

White, Patrick, 1912-.   2.10180
The eye of the storm. — New York: Viking Press, [1974, c1973] 608 p.; 23 cm. — I. T.
PZ3.W58469 Ey3 PR9619.3.W5E9x   823   LC 73-3501   ISBN 0670303747

White, Patrick, 1912-.   2.10181
Fringe of leaves. New York: Viking Press, [1977] c1976. 405 p. I. T.
PR9619.3W5 F7 1977   823   LC 76-18961   ISBN 0670330736

White, Patrick, 1912-.   • 2.10182
The living and the dead / Patrick White. — New York: Viking Press, 1941. 383 p.; 23 cm. I. T.
PZ3.W58469 Li 1979 PR9619.3.W5L5x   823   LC 41-1591

White, Patrick, 1912-.   • 2.10183
Riders in the chariot / Patrick White. — New York, Viking Press, 1961. 532 p. 22 cm. I. T.
PZ3.W58469 Ri PR9619.3.W5R5x   823

White, Patrick, 1912-.   • 2.10184
The tree of man / Patrick White. — New York: Viking Press, 1955. 499 p.; 22 cm. I. T.
PR9619.3.W5 T7

White, Patrick.   2.10185
The Twyborn affair / Patrick White. — New York: Viking Press, 1980, c1979. 432 p.; 24 cm. I. T.
PZ3.W58469 Tw 1980 PR9619.3.W5T8x   823   LC 79-26242   ISBN 0670737895

White, Patrick, 1912-.   • 2.10186
Voss, a novel. — New York, Viking Press, 1957. 442 p. 21 cm. I. T.
PR9619.3.W5 V6x   LC 57-9493

Beatson, Peter.   2.10187
The eye in the mandala: Patrick White: a vision of man and God / Peter Beatson. New York: Barnes & Noble Books, 1976. xii, 172 p.; 23 cm. 1. White, Patrick, 1912- — Criticism and interpretation. I. T.
PR9619.3.W5 Z57   823   LC 76-13072   ISBN 0064903311

Kiernan, Brian.   2.10188
Patrick White / Brian Kiernan. — New York: St. Martin's Press, 1980. 147 p.; 20 cm. Includes index. 1. White, Patrick, 1912- — Criticism and interpretation. I. T.
PR9619.3.W5 Z75 1980   823   LC 80-5098   ISBN 0312598076

McCulloch, A. M. (Ann M.), 1949-.   2.10189
A tragic vision: the novels of Patrick White / A.M. McCulloch. — St. Lucia, [Qld.]; New York: University of Queensland Press, c1983. 206 p.; 22 cm. — (University of Queensland Press scholars' library.) Includes index. 1. White, Patrick, 1912- — Criticism and interpretation. I. T. II. Series.
PR9619.3.W5 Z77 1983   823 19   LC 82-19986   ISBN 0702217727

Walsh, William, 1916-.   2.10190
Patrick White's fiction / William Walsh. — Totowa, N.J.: Rowman and Littlefield, 1977. 136 p.; 22 cm. Includes index. 1. White, Patrick, 1912- — Criticism and interpretation. I. T.
PR9619.3.W5 Z94 1977   823   LC 78-304002   ISBN 0847660117

Weigel, John A.   2.10191
Patrick White / by John A. Weigel. — Boston: Twayne Publishers, c1983. 142 p.: port.; 23 cm. — (Twayne's world authors series. Australian literature. TWAS 711.) Includes index. 1. White, Patrick, 1912- — Criticism and interpretation. I. T. II. Series.
PR9619.3.W5 Z944 1983   823 19   LC 83-12599   ISBN 0805765581

Wolfe, Peter, 1933-.   2.10192
Laden choirs: the fiction of Patrick White / Peter Wolfe. — Lexington, Ky.: University Press of Kentucky, c1983. 248 p.; 24 cm. 1. White, Patrick, 1912- — Criticism and interpretation. I. T.
PR9619.3.W5 Z95 1983   823 19   LC 83-6831   ISBN 0813115019

Wright, Judith.   2.10193
Collected poems, 1942–1970. — [Sydney]: Angus and Robertson, [1971] xvi, 302 p.; 23 cm. — I. T.
PR9619.3.W7 Ax   821   LC 76-857930   ISBN 0207121664

PR9620–9639.3 New Zealand

McCormick, E. H. (Eric Hall), 1906-.   2.10194
New Zealand literature, a survey. London Oxford University Press 1959. 173p. 1. New Zealand literature — History and criticism I. T.
PR9624.3.M2x

Reid, John Cowie.   2.10195
Creative writing in New Zealand, a brief critical history. Auckland Printed for the Author by Whitcombe and Tombs 1946. 93p. 1. New Zealand literature — History and criticism I. T.
PR9624.3.R4x

Curnow, Wystan, 1939- comp.   2.10196
Essays on New Zealand literature. — [Auckland, N.Z.]: Heinemann Educational Books, [1973] viii, 192 p.; 23 cm. 1. New Zealand literature — Addresses, essays, lectures. I. T.
PR9624.6.C8   820   LC 74-179530   ISBN 0435181955

McNaughton, Howard Douglas.   2.10197
New Zealand drama / by Howard McNaughton. — Boston: Twayne Publishers, 1981. 168 p.; 21 cm. — (Twayne's world authors series; TWAS 626: New Zealand) Includes index. 1. New Zealand drama — History and criticism. I. T.
PR9631.2.M27   822/.009/9931 19   LC 80-27870   ISBN 0805764682

Jones, Joseph Jay, 1908-.   2.10198
New Zealand fiction / by Joseph and Johanna Jones. — Boston: Twayne, c1983. 114 p.; 23 cm. — (Twayne's world authors series. TWAS 643) Includes index. 1. New Zealand fiction — History and criticism. I. Jones, Johanna. II. T. III. Series.
PR9632.2.J6 1983   823/.009/9931 19   LC 83-12662   ISBN 0805763686

New Zealand short stories / selected with an introd. by D. M. Davin.   2.10199
London: Oxford University Press, 1953. ix, 426 p.; 15 cm. — (World's classics. 534) 1. Short stories, New Zealand I. Davin, Dan, 1913- II. Series.
PR9632.2.N49   LC a 54-474

The Oxford book of New Zealand writing since 1945 / chosen by MacDonald P. Jackson and Vincent O'Sullivan.   2.10200
Auckland, New Zealand; New York: Oxford University Press, 1983. xxxvi, 679 p.; 24 cm. Includes index. 1. New Zealand literature — 20th century I. Jackson, MacDonald P. (MacDonald Pairman) II. O'Sullivan, Vincent. III. Title: New Zealand writing since 1945.
PR9634.9.O93 1983   820 19   LC 83-204994   ISBN 0195580974

Stevens, Joan.   2.10201
The New Zealand novel, 1860–1965 / by Joan Stevens. — 2nd ed. rev. to 1965. — Wellington: A.H. & A.W. Reed, 1966. 159 p.; 22 cm. Includes index. 1. New Zealand fiction — History and criticism. I. T.
PR9635.S7 1966   823.9

The Penguin book of New Zealand verse / selected with an introd. and notes by Allen Curnow.   2.10202
Harmondsworth: Penguin Books, 1960. 339 p. — (Penguin poets. D45) Includes index. 1. New Zealand poetry — Collections. I. Curnow, Allen, 1911- II. Series.
PR9635.25.P4x   LC 61-66264

The Oxford book of contemporary New Zealand poetry / chosen by Fleur Adcock.   2.10203
Auckland: Oxford University Press, 1983. xiv, 146 p.; 21 cm. Spine title: Contemporary New Zealand poetry. Includes index. 1. New Zealand poetry — 20th century I. Adcock, Fleur. II. Title: Contemporary New Zealand poetry.
PR9635.7.O9 1982   821 19   LC 83-159347   ISBN 0195580923

New Zealand love poems / chosen by James Bertram.   2.10204
Dunedin: J. McIndoe, 1977. 72 p.; 23 cm. Includes indexes. 1. Love poetry, New Zealand. I. Bertram, James M.
PR9635.82.N4   821/.008   LC 78-317409   ISBN 0908565313

Some other country: New Zealand's best short stories / chosen **2.10205**
by Marion McLeod and Bill Manhire.
Wellington; Boston: Unwin Paperbacks with the Port Nicholson Press, 1984.
246 p.; 21 cm. 1. Short stories, New Zealand. 2. New Zealand fiction — 20th
century. I. McLeod, Marion. II. Manhire, Bill, 1946-
PR9636.S66 1984   823/.01/08 19   *LC* 85-159263   *ISBN*
086861484X

PR9639.3 INDIVIDUAL AUTHORS, A–Z

A–L

Ashton-Warner, Sylvia. **2.10206**
Incense to idols / Sylvia Ashton–Warner. — New York: Simon and Schuster,
1960. 312 p. I. T.
PR9639.3.A8 I6x   PR6051.S55 I6x.   *LC* 60-10988   *ISBN*

Ashton-Warner, Sylvia. **2.10207**
Myself / Sylvia Ashton–Warner. — New York: Simon & Schuster, 1967.
239 p.: ill. 1. Ashton-Warner, Sylvia. 2. Teachers — Biography. I. T.
PR9639.3.A8 M9x   828.914

Ashton-Warner, Sylvia. **2.10208**
Spinster, a novel. — New York: Simon and Schuster, 1959 [c1958] 242 p.; 22
cm. — I. T.
PR9639.3.A8 S6x   PR6051.S55 S6x.   *LC* 59-5492

Baxter, James K. **2.10209**
Collected poems / James K. Baxter; edited by J.E. Weir. — Wellington; New
York: Oxford University Press in association with Price Milburn, c1979. xxvii,
656 p.; 24 cm. Includes index. I. Weir, J. E. (John Edward), 1935- II. T.
PR9639.3.B3 A127   821 19   *LC* 81-156943   *ISBN* 0195580370

Baxter, James K. **2.10210**
[Plays] Collected plays / James K. Baxter; edited by Howard McNaughton. —
Auckland; New York: Oxford University Press, 1982. xvi, 336 p.; 25 cm.
I. McNaughton, Howard Douglas. II. T.
PR9639.3.B3 A19 1982   822 19   *LC* 83-165413   *ISBN* 0195580931

Baxter, James K. **2.10211**
The labyrinth: some uncollected poems 1944–72 / by James K. Baxter. —
Wellington; New York: Oxford University Press, [1974] 75 p.; 23 cm. I. T.
PR9639.3.B3 L3   821   *LC* 75-303172

Doyle, Charles, 1928-. **2.10212**
James K. Baxter / by Charles Doyle. — Boston: Twayne Publishers, c1976.
189 p.: port.; 21 cm. — (Twayne's world authors series; TWAS 384: New
Zealand) Includes index. 1. Baxter, James K — Criticism and interpretation.
I. T.
PR9639.3.B3 Z63   821   *LC* 75-33781   *ISBN* 0805762272

Brasch, Charles. **2.10213**
[Poems] Collected poems / Charles Brasch; edited by Alan Roddick. —
Auckland; New York: Oxford University Press, 1984. xiv, 256 p.; 24 cm.
Includes index. I. Roddick, Alan. II. T. III. Title: Charles Brasch.
PR9639.3.B67 A17 1984   821 19   *LC* 84-199930   *ISBN*
0195581059

Finlayson, Roderick. **2.10214**
D'Arcy Cresswell. — New York: Twayne Publishers, [1972] 132 p.; 21 cm. —
(Twayne's world authors series, TWAS 205. New Zealand literature)
1. Cresswell, Walter D'Arcy, 1896-1960. I. T.
PR9639.3.C65Zx   821   *LC* 74-169625

Cross, Ian, 1925-. **2.10215**
The God boy: a novel / Ian Cross. — New York: Harcourt Brace, 1957. 180 p.;
21 cm. I. T.
PR9639.3.C68 G64 1957   823   *LC* 57-10063

Cross, Ian, 1925-. **2.10216**
After Anzac Day. London, A. Deutsch, 1961. 235 p. 19 cm. I. T.
PR9639.3.C69 A7x   *LC* 61-59746

Frame, Janet. **2.10217**
Faces in the water / Janet Frame. — Paperback reprint ed. — New York: G.
Braziller, 1982. 254 p.; 21 cm. I. T.
PR9639.3.F7 F3 1982   823   *LC* 79-25441   *ISBN* 0807609579

Frame, Janet. **2.10218**
Intensive care; a novel. — New York: G. Braziller, [1970] 342 p.; 22 cm. —
I. T.
PR9639.3.F7 I6x   823   *LC* 78-110305   *ISBN* 0807605557

Frame, Janet. **2.10219**
Owls do cry: a novel / by Janet Frame. — Paperback reprint ed. — New York:
G. Braziller, 1982. 210 p.; 21 cm. I. T.
PR9639.3.F7 O94 1982   823   *LC* 79-28167   *ISBN* 0807609560

Frame, Janet. **2.10220**
The pocket mirror; poems. — New York: G. Braziller, [1967] 121 p.; 22 cm. —
I. T.
PR9639.3.F7 P6 1967b   811/.5/4 19   *LC* 67-18210

Frame, Janet. **2.10221**
Scented gardens for the blind: a novel / Janet Frame. — New York: G.
Braziller, c1964. 252 p.; 21 cm. I. T.
PR9639.3.F7 S3x   *LC* 64-10786

Frame, Janet. **2.10222**
An angel at my table: an autobiography / Janet Frame. — New York: G.
Braziller, c1984. 195 p.; 24 cm. 'Volume two.' Continues: To the is-land.
Continued by: Envoy from mirror city. 1. Frame, Janet — Biography.
2. Authors, New Zealand — 20th century — Biography. I. T.
PR9639.3.F7 Z463 1984   823 19   *LC* 85-158468   *ISBN*
0807610429

Frame, Janet. **2.10223**
The envoy from mirror city: an autobiography / Janet Frame. — New York: G.
Braziller, 1985. 176 p.; 24 cm. Continues: An angel at my table. 'Volume three.'
1. Frame, Janet — Biography. 2. Authors, New Zealand — 20th century —
Biography. I. T.
PR9639.3.F7 Z464 1985   823 B 19   *LC* 85-7834   *ISBN*
0807611247

Frame, Janet. **2.10224**
To the is–land: an autobiography / by Janet Frame. — New York: G. Braziller,
c1982. 253 p.; 22 cm. Continued by: Angel at my table. 1. Frame, Janet —
Biography. 2. Authors, New Zealand — 20th century — Biography. I. T.
PR9639.3.F7 Z477 1982   823 B 19   *LC* 82-1350   *ISBN*
0807610429

Evans, Patrick David, 1944-. **2.10225**
Janet Frame / by Patrick Evans. — Boston: Twayne, c1977. 228 p.: port.; 21
cm. — (Twayne's world authors series; TWAS 415: New Zealand) Includes
index. 1. Frame, Janet — Criticism and interpretation. I. T.
PR9639.3.F7 Z645   823   *LC* 77-4752   *ISBN* 080576254X

Hulme, Keri. **2.10226**
The bone people: a novel / by Keri Hulme. — U.S. ed. — Baton Rouge:
Louisiana State University Press, 1985, c1983. 450 p.; 24 cm. 1. Maoris —
Fiction. I. T.
PR9639.3.H75 B6 1985   823 19   *LC* 85-12937   *ISBN* 0807112844

Ihimaera, Witi Tame, 1944-. **2.10227**
Tangi [by] Witi Ihimaera. — [London]: Heinemann, [1973] 207 p.; 22 cm. —
I. T.
PZ4.I24 Tan3 PR9639.3.I5   823   *LC* 74-173974

M–Z

Turner, Dorothea, 1910-. **2.10228**
Jane Mander. — New York: Twayne Publishers, [1972] 164 p.; 21 cm. —
(Twayne's world authors series, TWAS 178. New Zealand) 1. Mander, Jane.
I. T.
PR9639.3.M25x   823   *LC* 76-120493

Satchell, William. **2.10229**
[Thomas de Quincey, his life and work] The greenstone door / [by] William
Satchell. — Auckland: Golden Press in association with Whitcombe & Tombs,
1973. viii, 400 p.; 22 cm. — (New Zealand classics) First published in 1914.
1. New Zealand — History — 1843-1870 — Fiction. I. T.
PZ3.S2535 Gr6 PR9639.3.S34   823   *LC* 75-300186   *ISBN*
0855582852

Wilson, Phillip John. **2.10230**
William Satchell, by Phillip Wilson. — New York: Twayne Publishers, [1968]
168 p.; 22 cm. — (Twayne's world authors series, TWAS 35. New Zealand)
1961 ed published under title: The Maorilander. 1. Satchell, William. I. T.
PR9639.3.S34 Zx   813   *LC* 67-25198

Shadbolt, Maurice. **2.10231**
Strangers and journeys. — New York: St. Martin's Press, [c1972] 636 p.; 22 cm.
— I. T.
PZ4.S5235 St3 PR9639.3.S5   823   *LC* 72-94597

PS American Literature

PS1–478 HISTORY. CRITICISM

American literary scholarship. • 2.10232
Durham, N.C.: Duke University Press. v.; 22 cm. Annual. Began in 1963. Description based on: 1980.
PS3.A47   810 11   *LC* sn 85-9247

Hart, James David, 1911-. 2.10233
The Oxford companion to American literature / James D. Hart. — 5th ed. — New York: Oxford University Press, 1983. 896 p.; 25 cm. 'Chronological index': p. 861-896. 1. American literature — Dictionaries. 2. American literature — Bio-bibliography. I. T.
PS21.H3 1983   810/.9 19   *LC* 81-22469   *ISBN* 0195030745

Kunitz, Stanley, 1905- ed. • 2.10234
American authors, 1600–1900: a biographical dictionary of American literature / edited by Stanley J. Kunitz and Howard Haycraft. — New York: The H. W. Wilson company, 1938. vi, 846 p.: ill. (ports.); 26 cm. Complete in one volume with 1300 biographies and 400 portraits. 1. Authors, American 2. United States — Biography — Dictionaries. I. Haycraft, Howard, 1905- joint ed. II. T.
PS21.K8   928.1   *LC* 38-27938

Kazin, Alfred, 1915-. • 2.10235
Starting out in the thirties. — [1st ed.]. — Boston: Little, Brown, [1965] 166 p.; 22 cm. 'An Atlantic Monthly Press book.' 1. Kazin, Alfred, 1915- 2. Critics — United States — Biography. I. T.
PS29.K38 A38 1965   809 B   *LC* 65-20740

Jones, Howard Mumford, 1892-. • 2.10236
The theory of American literature / Howard Mumford Jones; reissued, with a new concluding chapter and revised bibliography. — Ithaca, N.Y.: Cornell University Press, 1966. xi, 225 p. — (Cornell paperbacks; CP-24) 1. American literature — History and criticism 2. Literature — History and criticism — Theory, etc. I. T.
PS31.J6 1966

PS55–79 Criticism

Wilson, Edmund, 1895-1972. ed. • 2.10237
The shock of recognition; the development of literature in the United States recorded by the men who made it. — [2d ed.]. — New York: Farrar, Straus and Cudahy, [1955] 1290 p.: illus.; 20 cm. 1. American literature — History and criticism 2. American literature I. T.
PS55.W5 1955   810.82   *LC* 55-12140

Miller, Perry, 1905-1963. • 2.10238
The raven and the whale; the war of words and wits in the era of Poe and Melville. — [1st ed.]. — New York: Harcourt, Brace, [1956] viii, 370 p.: ports. (on lining papers); 25 cm. 1. Poe, Edgar Allan, 1809-1849. 2. Melville, Herman, 1819-1891. 3. Criticism — United States — History. 4. American literature — 19th century — History and criticism. I. T.
PS74.M5   810.903   *LC* 56-6659

Borklund, Elmer. 2.10239
Contemporary literary critics / Elmer Borklund. — 2nd ed. — Detroit, Mich.: Gale Research Co., 1982. 600 p.; 24 cm. 1. Criticism — United States. 2. Criticism — United States — Bio-bibliography. 3. Criticism — Great Britain. 4. Criticism — Great Britain — Bio-bibliography. 5. Critics — United States — Biography. 6. Critics — Great Britain — Biography. I. T.
PS78.B56 1982   801/.95/0922 B 19   *LC* 82-245089   *ISBN* 0810304430

Criticism in America: its function and status / essays by Irving • 2.10240
Babbitt ... [et al.].
New York: Harcourt, Brace and Co., 1924. 330 p. 1. Criticism — United States — Addresses, essays, lectures. I. Babbitt, Irving, 1865-1933.
PN99.U5 C7   PS78.C7.   *LC* 24-3993

Foerster, Norman, 1887-. • 2.10241
Towards standards; a study of the present critical movement in American letters, by Norman Foerster... New York, Farrar & Rinehart incorporated [1930] xiv, 224 p. 20 cm. 1. Criticism 2. Humanism 3. American literature — 20th century — History and criticism I. T.
PS78.F6   *LC* 30-29023

Fraiberg, Louis, 1913-. • 2.10242
Psychoanalysis & American literary criticism. Detroit: Wayne State University Press, 1960. 263 p.; 24 cm. 1. Psychoanalysis in literature 2. Psychoanalysis 3. American literature — 20th century — History and criticism. 4. Criticism — United States. I. T. II. Title: American literary criticism.
PS78.F7   *LC* 59-11980

Lewis, R. W. B. (Richard Warrington Baldwin). 2.10243
Trials of the word: essays in American literature and the humanistic tradition / R.W.B. Lewis. — New Haven: Yale University Press, 1965. x, 239 p. 1. American literature — History and criticism — Addresses, essays, lectures. I. T.
PS78.L47   810.9   *LC* 65-22331

PS85–478 History of American Literature

Aaron, Daniel, 1912-. 2.10244
The unwritten war; American writers and the Civil War. — [1st ed.]. — New York: Knopf; distributed by Random House], 1973. xix, 385, xiv p.; 25 cm. — (Impact of the Civil War.) 1. American literature — History and criticism 2. United States — History — Civil War, 1861-1865 — Literature and the war I. T. II. Series.
PS88.A18   810/.9/3   *LC* 73-5982   *ISBN* 0394465830

Bode, Carl, 1911- ed. • 2.10245
The young rebel in American literature. New York: Praeger [1960, c1959] 170 p.; 21 cm. 1. American literature — Addresses, essays, lectures. I. T.
PS88.B64   *LC* 60-12700

Canby, Henry Seidel, 1878-1961. • 2.10246
Classic Americans; a study of eminent American writers from Irving to Whitman, with an introductory survey of the colonial background of our national literature. — New York: Russell & Russell, 1959 [c1958] 371 p.; 22 cm. 1. American literature — 19th century — History and criticism. 2. American literature — Colonial period, ca. 1600-1775 — History and criticism. I. T.
PS88.C35 1959   928.1   *LC* 59-7257

Cargill, Oscar, 1898-. • 2.10247
Intellectual America; ideas on the march. — New York: Cooper Square Publishers, 1968 [c1941] xxi, 777 p.; 24 cm. 1. American literature — History and criticism 2. American literature — 20th century — History and criticism. 3. U.S. — Intellectual life. I. T.
PS88.C37 1968   810.9   *LC* 68-29659

Foerster, Norman, 1887- ed. • 2.10248
The reinterpretation of American literature: some contributions toward the understanding of its historical development / edited for the American Literature Group of the Modern Language Association. — New York: Russell & Russell, 1959. 213 p.; 20 cm. 1. American literature — Hist. & crit. I. Modern Language Association of America. American Literature Group. II. T.
PS88.F6 1959   810.9   *LC* 59-6876

Horton, Rod William, 1910-. • 2.10249
Backgrounds of American literary thought / Rod W. Horton and Herbert W. Edwards. — New York: Appleton-Century-Crofts, 1952. 425 p. — (Appleton-Century handbooks of literature) 1. American literature — History and criticism 2. United States — Civilization 3. United States — Intellectual life I. T.
PS88.H6   *LC* 52-12730

Kolodny, Annette, 1941-. 2.10250
The lay of the land: metaphor as experience and history in American life and letters / by Annette Kolodny. — Chapel Hill: University of North Carolina

Press, [1975] xiii, 185 p.; 24 cm. Includes index. 1. American literature —
History and criticism 2. Nature in literature 3. United States — History —
Philosophy I. T.
PS88.K65   810/.9/36   *LC* 74-23950   *ISBN* 0807812412

Krieger, Murray, 1923-.   • 2.10251
The classic vision: the retreat from extremity in modern literature. —
Baltimore: Johns Hopkins Press, [1971] xiv, 376 p.; 24 cm. 1. American
literature — History and criticism 2. English literature — History and
criticism I. T.
PS88.K7   820.9   *LC* 77-167984   *ISBN* 0801813123

Literary history of the United States. Editors: Robert E. Spiller   2.10252
[and others].
4th ed., rev. — New York: Macmillan, [1974] 2 v.; 24 cm. 1. American
literature — History and criticism 2. American literature — Bibliography
I. Spiller, Robert Ernest, 1896- ed.
PS88.L522 1974   810/.9   *LC* 73-14014   *ISBN* 0026131609

Parrington, Vernon Louis, 1871-1929.   • 2.10253
Main currents in American thought; an interpretation of American literature
from the beginnings to 1920, by Vernon Louis Parrington ... — [New York,
Harcourt, Brace and company, 1927-30] 3 v. 23 cm. Each volume has special t.-
p. Bibliography at end of each volume. 1. American literature 2. United States
— Civilization 3. Philosophy, American 4. United States — Religion
5. United States — Pol. & govt. I. T.
PS88.P3   *LC* 27-8440

Perry, Bliss, 1860-1954.   • 2.10254
The American spirit in literature; a chronicle of great interpreters, by Bliss
Perry. — New Haven, Yale university press; [etc., etc.] 1920. ix, 281 p. col.
front. 18 cm. — (The chronicles of America series, Allen Johnson, editor ... v.
34) 'Graduates' edition.' 'Bibliographical note': p. 269-272. 1. American
literature — History and criticism I. T.
E173.C56 vol. 34   PS88.P4x.   *LC* 22-12156

Poirier, Richard.   • 2.10255
A world elsewhere: the place of style in American literature. — New York:
Oxford University Press, 1966. xi, 257 p.; 21 cm. 1. American literature —
History and criticism I. T.
PS88.P6   810.9   *LC* 66-24438

Quinn, Arthur Hobson, 1875-1960. ed.   • 2.10256
The literature of the American people, an historical and critical survey. — New
York, Appleton-Century-Crofts [1951] xix, 1172 p. 25 cm. Bibliography: p.
[985]-1107. 1. American literature — Hist. & crit. I. T.
PS88.Q5   810.9   *LC* 51-10789

Spiller, Robert Ernest, 1896-.   • 2.10257
The cycle of American literature; an essay in historical criticism, by Robert E.
Spiller. — New York: Free Press, [1967, c1955] xii, 243 p.; 21 cm. — (A Free
Press paperback) 1. American literature — History and criticism I. T.
PS88.S6 1967   810.9   *LC* 68-7396

Tanner, Tony.   2.10258
The reign of wonder, naivety and reality in American literature. — Cambridge
[Eng.]: University Press, 1965. viii, 388 p.; 23 cm. 1. American literature —
History and criticism I. T.
PS88.T25   810.9   *LC* 65-15304

Wasserstrom, William.   2.10259
The ironies of progress: Henry Adams and the American dream / William
Wasserstrom. — Carbondale: Southern Illinois University Press, c1984. xiii,
269 p.; 24 cm. Includes index. 1. Adams, Henry, 1838-1918 — Criticism and
interpretation. 2. American literature — History and criticism 3. United
States — Civilization I. T.
PS88.W3 1984   818/.409 19   *LC* 83-16990   *ISBN* 0809311550

Wendell, Barrett, 1855-1921.   • 2.10260
A literary history of America. — New York: Greenwood Press, [1968, c1900]
574 p.; 24 cm. 1. American literature — History and criticism I. T.
PS88.W4 1968c   810.9   *LC* 69-14144

Cunliffe, Marcus.   2.10261
The literature of the United States / Marcus Cunliffe. — 4th ed. — New York,
N.Y., U.S.A.: Penguin Books, 1986. 512 p.; 20 cm. — (Pelican books) Includes
index. 1. American literature — History and criticism I. T.
PS92.C8 1986   810/.9 19   *LC* 86-175396   *ISBN* 0140225145

Reconstructing American literary history / edited by Sacvan   2.10262
Bercovitch.
Cambridge, Mass.: Harvard University Press, 1986. xii, 351 p.; 22 cm. (Harvard
English studies. 13) 1. American literature — History and criticism —
Addresses, essays, lectures. I. Bercovitch, Sacvan. II. Series.
PS92.R4 1986   810/.9 19   *LC* 85-21972   *ISBN* 0674750853

PS121-152 COLLECTED ESSAYS.
COLLECTIVE BIOGRAPHY

Blackmur, R. P. (Richard P.), 1904-1965.   2.10263
The lion and the honeycomb: essays in solicitude and critique. — [1st ed.]. —
New York: Harcourt, Brace [1955] 309 p.; 22 cm. 1. American literature —
Addresses, essays, lectures. 2. Criticism — Addresses, essays, lectures. I. T.
PS121.B59   814.5   *LC* 55-5638

Brooks, Van Wyck, 1886-1963.   • 2.10264
America's coming-of-age. — [Rev. ed.]. — Garden City, N.Y.: Doubleday,
1958. xii, 183 p. (Doubleday anchor books; A-129) 1. National characteristics,
American 2. American literature — History and criticism 3. United States —
Intellectual life I. Brooks, Van Wyck, 1886-1963. Three essays on America.
II. T. III. Title: Three essays on America. IV. Title: 3 essays on America.
E169.1.B7985 1975   PS121.B74 1958.   973   *LC* 58-33

Browne, Ray Broadus. ed.   2.10265
Critical approaches to American literature. Edited by Ray B. Browne & Martin
Light. — New York: Crowell, [1965] 2 v.; 22 cm. 1. American literature —
History and criticism I. Light, Martin. joint ed. II. T.
PS121.B77   810.9   *LC* 65-22675

James, Henry, 1843-1916.   • 2.10266
The American essays / Henry James; edited with an introd. by Leon Edel. —
1st ed. — New York: Vintage Books, 1956. xx, 288, viii p. — (Vintage books,
K-40) Includes index. 1. American literature — Addresses, essays, lectures
I. Edel, Leon, 1907- II. T.
PS121 J3   PS121 J3.   814.4   *LC* 56-58002

Jones, Howard Mumford, 1892-.   • 2.10267
Ideas in America, by Howard Mumford Jones ... Cambridge, Mass., Harvard
university press, 1944. xi p., 1 l., 304 p. 20 cm. Bibliographical references
included in 'Notes' (p. 237-304) 1. American literature — History and
criticism 2. American literature — 20th century — History and criticism.
3. United States — Intellectual life I. T.
PS121.J6   810.9   *LC* A 44-1981

Lawrence, D. H. (David Herbert), 1885-1930.   • 2.10268
The symbolic meaning: the uncollected versions of Studies in classic American
literature / edited by Armin Arnold; with a pref. by Harry T. Moore. —
[Fontwell, Arundel, Eng.]: Centaur Press [1962] xi, 264 p.; 23 cm.
Bibliographical footnotes. 1. American literature — Hist. & crit. I. Arnold,
Armin. ed. II. T.
PS121.L3 1962   810.9   *LC* 63-776

Lawrence, D. H. (David Herbert), 1885-1930.   • 2.10269
Studies in classic American literature. New York, Viking Press [1964, c1961]
viii, 177 p. 22 cm. 1. American literature — History and criticism I. T.
PS121.L3 1964a   810.9   *LC* 64-4884

Matthiessen, F. O. (Francis Otto), 1902-1950.   • 2.10270
The responsibilities of the critic: essays and reviews / selected by John Rackliffe.
— New York: Oxford University Press, 1952. xvi, 282 p.; 22 cm. 1. Criticism
2. American literature — Hist. & crit. I. T.
PS121.M3   810.4   *LC* 52-12569

New dimensions in popular culture. Edited by Russel B. Nye.   2.10271
Bowling Green, Ohio: Bowling Green University Popular Press, [1972] iii,
246 p.; 23 cm. Essays from an English graduate seminar in literature and
popular culture, given at Michigan State University. 1. American literature —
History and criticism — Addresses, essays, lectures. 2. United States —
Popular culture I. Nye, Russel Blaine, 1913- ed.
PS121.N4   *LC* 72-88412   *ISBN* 0879720468

Spiller, Robert Ernest, 1896-.   2.10272
Late harvest: essays and addresses in American literature and culture / Robert
E. Spiller. — Westport, Conn.: Greenwood Press, 1981. xi, 280 p.; 22 cm. —
(Contributions in American studies; no. 49 0084-9227) Includes index.
1. American literature — History and criticism — Addresses, essays, lectures.
2. United States — Study and teaching — Addresses, essays, lectures. I. T.
PS121.S55   810/.9   *LC* 80-543   *ISBN* 0313220239

Warren, Robert Penn, 1905-.   • 2.10273
Selected essays. — New York: Random House, [1958] 305 p.; 20 cm.
1. American literature — Addresses, essays, lectures. I. T.
PS121.W3   810.4   *LC* 58-7674

Whicher, George Frisbie, 1889-1954.   • 2.10274
Poetry and civilization; essays. Collected and edited by Harriet Fox Whicher.
— New York: Russell & Russell, [1968, c1955] xvii, 142 p.: port.; 23 cm.
1. American literature — Addresses, essays, lectures. 2. Education —
Addresses, essays, lectures. I. T.
PS121.W47 1968   810.9   *LC* 68-10955

Winters, Yvor, 1900-1968.　　　　　　　　　　● 2.10275
In defense of reason. Primitivism and decadence: a study of American
experimental poetry. Maule's curse: seven studies in the history of American
obscurantism. The anatomy of nonsense. The significance of The bridge by Hart
Crane, or What are we to think of Professor X? By Yvor Winters. — New York:
The Swallow press & W. Morrow and company, 1947. viii, 611 p.; 22 cm.
1. Criticism 2. American literature — History and criticism I. T. II. Title:
Primitivism and decadence. III. Title: Maule's curse. IV. Title: The anatomy
of nonsense.
PS121.W53　　　801　　　LC 47-2236

Bewley, Marius.　　　　　　　　　　　　　　　● 2.10276
The complex fate: Hawthorne, Henry James, and some other American writers
/ with an introd. and two interpolations by F. R. Leavis. — New York: Gordian
Press, 1967 [c1952] xvi, 247 p.; 21 cm. 1. American poetry — 20th century —
History and criticism. I. T.
PS124.B45 1967　　　810.9　　　LC 67-28474

Vision and refuge: essays on the literature of the Great Plains /　　2.10277
edited by Virginia Faulkner with Frederick C. Luebke.
Lincoln: Published by the University of Nebraska Press for the Center for Great
Plains Studies, University of Nebraska—Lincoln, c1982. xiv, 146 p.; 23 cm.
1. American fiction — History and criticism — Addresses, essays, lectures.
2. Great Plains in literature — Addresses, essays, lectures. I. Faulkner,
Virginia, 1913- II. Luebke, Frederick C., 1927- III. University of Nebraska—
Lincoln. Center for Great Plains Studies.
PS124.V5　　　810/.9/978 19　　　LC 81-10418　　　ISBN 0803219601

American writers: a collection of literary biographies / Leonard　　2.10278
Unger, editor in chief.
New York: Scribner, 1974. 4 v.; 29 cm. The 4-vol. main set consists of 97 of the
pamphlets originally published as the University of Minnesota pamphlets on
American writers; some have been rev. and updated. The supplements cover
writers not included in the original series. 1. American literature — History
and criticism 2. American literature — Bio-bibliography. 3. Authors,
American — Biography. I. Unger, Leonard. ed. II. University of Minnesota.
Pamphlets on American writers.
PS129.A55　　　810/.9 B　　　LC 73-1759　　　ISBN 0684136627

First person singular: writers on their craft / compiled by Joyce　　2.10279
Carol Oates.
Princeton, N.J.: Ontario Review Press; New York, NY: Distributed by Persea
Books, c1983. viii, 280 p.; 24 cm. 1. Authors, American — 20th century —
Interviews. 2. Authorship — Addresses, essays, lectures. I. Oates, Joyce
Carol, 1938-
PS129.F5 1983　　　810/.9/0054 19　　　LC 83-21927　　　ISBN 0865380376

LeClair, Tom, 1944-.　　　　　　　　　　　　　2.10280
Anything can happen: interviews with contemporary American novelists /
conducted and edited by Tom LeClair and Larry McCaffery. — Urbana:
University of Illinois Press, c1983. 305 p.: ill.; 24 cm. Includes index.
1. Novelists, American — 20th century — Interviews. I. McCaffery, Larry,
1946- II. T.
PS129.L36 1983　　　813/.54/09 19　　　LC 82-2867　　　ISBN 0252009703

Parry, Albert, 1901-.　　　　　　　　　　　　● 2.10281
Garrets and pretenders; a history of Bohemianism in America. — Rev. ed., with
a new chapter, 'Enter Beatniks,' by Harry T. Moore. — New York: Dover
Publications, [c1960] 422 p.: illus.; 22 cm. 1. Bohemianism — United States.
2. Authors, American I. T.
PS138.P3 1960　　　917.3　　　LC 61-549

Ehrlich, Eugene H.　　　　　　　　　　　　　2.10282
The Oxford illustrated literary guide to the United States / Eugene Ehrlich and
Gorton Carruth. — New York: Oxford University Press, 1982. xiv, 464 p.: ill.;
29 cm. 'A Hudson Group book.' Includes indexes. 1. Literary landmarks —
United States. 2. Authors, American — Homes and haunts. 3. United States
— Description and travel — 1981- — Guide-books. I. Carruth, Gorton. II. T.
PS141.E74 1982　　　917.3/04 19　　　LC 82-8034　　　ISBN 0195031865

PS147-152 Women Authors

American women writers: a critical reference guide from　　2.10283
colonial times to the present / edited by Lina Mainiero.
New York: Ungar, c1979-c1982. 4 v.; 24 cm. 1. American literature — Women
authors — History and criticism. 2. Women authors, American — Biography.
3. American literature — Women authors — Bibliography. I. Mainiero, Lina.
PS147.A4　　　810/.9/9287 19　　　LC 78-20945　　　ISBN 0804431515

Ostriker, Alicia.　　　　　　　　　　　　　　2.10284
Stealing the language: the emergence of women's poetry in America / Alicia
Suskin Ostriker. — Boston, Mass.: Beacon Press, c1986. 1 v. Includes index.
1. American poetry — Women authors — History and criticism. 2. American
poetry — 20th century — History and criticism. 3. Women in literature

4. Women and literature — United States. 5. Feminism and literature —
United States. 6. Women — United States — Language. I. T.
PS147.O8 1986　　　811/.009/9287 19　　　LC 85-47949　　　ISBN
0807063029

Walker, Cheryl, 1947-.　　　　　　　　　　　2.10285
The nightingale's burden: women poets and American culture before 1900 /
Cheryl Walker. — 1st Midland book ed. — Bloomington: Indiana University
Press, c1982. xvi, 189 p.: ports.; 24 cm. Includes index. 1. American poetry —
Women authors — History and criticism. 2. American poetry — 19th century
— History and criticism. 3. Women in literature 4. Feminism and literature
I. T.
PS147.W27 1982　　　811/.009/9287 19　　　LC 81-48514　　　ISBN
0253340659

Watts, Emily Stipes.　　　　　　　　　　　　2.10286
The poetry of American women from 1632 to 1945 / by Emily Stipes Watts.
Austin: University of Texas Press, c1977. xvi, 218 p.; 24 cm. (The Dan
Danciger publication series) Includes index. 1. American poetry — Women
authors — History and criticism. 2. Women poets, American — Biography.
I. T.
PS147.W3　　　811/.009/352　　　LC 76-43282　　　ISBN 0292764359

Baym, Nina.　　　　　　　　　　　　　　　2.10287
Woman's fiction: a guide to novels by and about women in America, 1820–1870
/ Nina Baym. — Ithaca, N.Y.: Cornell University Press, 1978. 320 p.; 23 cm.
Includes index. 1. American fiction — Women authors — History and
criticism. 2. American fiction — 19th century — History and criticism.
3. Women in literature I. T.
PS149.B38　　　813/.03　　　LC 77-90897　　　ISBN 0801411289

Papashvily, Helen Waite.　　　　　　　　　　● 2.10288
All the happy endings: a study of the domestic novel in America, the women
who wrote it, the women who read it, in the nineteenth century. — Port
Washington, N.Y.: Kennikat Press [1972, c1956] xvii, 231 p.; 22 cm. (Essay and
general literature index reprint series) 1. American fiction — 19th century —
History and criticism. 2. Women authors, American I. T.
PS149.P3 1972　　　813/.03　　　LC 76-153255　　　ISBN 0804614970

Coming to light: American women poets in the twentieth century　　2.10289
/ edited by Diane Wood Middlebrook and Marilyn Yalom.
Ann Arbor: University of Michigan Press, c1985. viii, 270 p.; 23 cm. (Women
and culture series.) 'Prepared under the auspices of the Center for Research on
Women, Stanford University.' 1. American poetry — Women authors —
History and criticism — Addresses, essays, lectures. 2. American poetry —
20th century — History and criticism — Addresses, essays, lectures. 3. Women
in literature — Addresses, essays, lectures. I. Middlebrook, Diane Wood.
II. Yalom, Marilyn. III. Stanford University. Center for Research on Women.
IV. Series.
PS151.C65 1985　　　811/.5/099287 19　　　LC 85-1145　　　ISBN
047208061X

Juhasz, Suzanne, 1942-.　　　　　　　　　　2.10290
Naked and fiery forms: modern American poetry by women: a new tradition /
Suzanne Juhasz. New York: Octagon Books, 1976. x, 212 p.; 21 cm.
1. American poetry — Women authors — History and criticism. 2. American
poetry — 20th century — History and criticism. 3. Women poets, American —
20th century — Biography. I. T.
PS151.J8 1976　　　811/.5/09　　　LC 76-16672　　　ISBN 0374944504

Douglas, Ann, 1942-.　　　　　　　　　　　　2.10291
The feminization of American culture / Ann Douglas. 1st ed. — New York:
Knopf, 1977. x, 403 p.; 25 cm. 1. American literature — 19th century —
History and criticism. 2. Women — United States 3. Clergy — United States.
4. American literature — Women authors — History and criticism. 5. United
States — Civilization — 19th century I. T.
PS152.D6 1977　　　810/.9　　　LC 76-47923　　　ISBN 0394405323

Feminist criticism and social change: sex, class and race in　　2.10292
literature and culture / edited by Judith Newton and Deborah
Rosenfelt.
New York: Methuen, c1985. xxxix, 291 p. 1. American literature — History
and criticism 2. Feminist literary criticism 3. Marxist criticism 4. English
literature — History and criticism 5. Social history in literature. 6. Sex role in
literature 7. Social classes in literature 8. Race relations in literature.
I. Newton, Judith Lowder. II. Rosenfelt, Deborah Silverton.
PS152.F46 1985　　　810/.9 19　　　LC 85-15209　　　ISBN 0416387004

PS153 Other Special Groups of Authors, A–Z

PS153 A–M

Kim, Elaine H.   **2.10293**
Asian American literature, an introduction to the writings and their social context / Elaine H. Kim. — Philadelphia: Temple University Press, 1982. xix, 363 p.; 24 cm. Includes index. 1. American literature — Asian-American authors — History and criticism. 2. Asian Americans in literature. I. T.
PS153.A84 K55 1982   810/.9/895 19   LC 82-5987   ISBN 0877222606

Brinkmeyer, Robert H.   **2.10294**
Three Catholic writers of the modern South / by Robert H. Brinkmeyer, Jr. — Jackson: University Press of Mississippi, c1985. xvi, 190 p.; 23 cm. Includes index. 1. Tate, Allen, 1899- — Criticism and interpretation. 2. Gordon, Caroline, 1895- — Criticism and interpretation. 3. Percy, Walker, 1916- — Criticism and interpretation. 4. American literature — Catholic authors — History and criticism. 5. American literature — Southern States — History and criticism. 6. American literature — 20th century — History and criticism. 7. Theology, Catholic, in literature. 8. Southern States in literature. I. T.
PS153.C3 B75 1985   810/.9/382 19   LC 84-19641   ISBN 0878052461

Larson, Charles R.   **2.10295**
American Indian fiction / Charles R. Larson. — 1st ed. — Albuquerque: University of New Mexico Press, c1978. vii, 208 p.; 24 cm. Includes index. 1. American fiction — Indian authors — History and criticism. 2. American fiction — 20th century — History and criticism. 3. Indians in literature I. T.
PS153.I52 L3   813/.009   LC 78-55698   ISBN 082630477X

Lincoln, Kenneth.   **2.10296**
Native American renaissance / Kenneth Lincoln. — Berkeley: University of California Press, 1983. x, 313 p. Includes index. 1. American literature — Indian authors — History and criticism. 2. American literature — 20th century — History and criticism. 3. Indians in literature I. T.
PS153.I52 L6 1983   PS153I52 L6 1983.   810/.9/897 19   LC 82-17450   ISBN 0520048571

Recovering the word: essays on native American literature /   **2.10297**
edited by Arnold Krupat and Brain Swann.
Berkeley: University of California Press, c1987. p. cm. Includes index. 1. American literature — Indian authors — History and criticism. 2. Indian literature — History and criticism. 3. Oral tradition — United States. 4. Indians in literature I. Krupat, Arnold. II. Swann, Brian.
PS153.I52 R43 1987   897 19   LC 86-19150   ISBN 0520059646

Studies in American Indian literature: critical essays and course   **2.10298**
designs / edited by Paula Gunn Allen.
New York, N.Y.: Modern Language Association of America, c1983. xiv, 384 p.; 24 cm. Includes index. 1. American literature — Indian authors — Study and teaching. 2. American literature — Indian authors — History and criticism. 3. Indian literature — Study and teaching. 4. Indian literature — History and criticism. 5. Indians in literature I. Allen, Paula Gunn.
PS153.I52 S8 1983   PS153I52 S8 1983.   810/.9/897 19   LC 82-12516   ISBN 0873523547

Guttmann, Allen.   **• 2.10299**
The Jewish writer in America; assimilation and the crisis of identity. — New York: Oxford University Press, 1971. x, 256 p.; 22 cm. 1. American literature — Jewish authors — History and criticism. 2. Jews in literature I. T.
PS153.J4 G8   810.9/8/924   LC 74-161887   ISBN 0195014472

Malin, Irving. comp.   **2.10300**
Contemporary American–Jewish literature; critical essays. — Bloomington: Indiana University Press, [1973] viii, 302 p.; 22 cm. 1. American literature — Jewish authors — History and criticism. 2. American literature — 20th century — History and criticism. I. T.
PS153.J4 M3 1973   810/.9/005   LC 72-75393   ISBN 0253314208

Chicano literature: a reference guide / edited by Julio A.   **2.10301**
Martínez and Francisco A. Lomelí.
Westport, Conn.: Greenwood Press, 1985. xiv, 492 p.; 24 cm. Includes index. 1. American literature — Mexican American authors — Dictionaries. 2. American literature — Mexican American authors — History and criticism. 3. American literature — Mexican American authors — Bio-bibliography. 4. Mexican Americans in literature — Dictionaries. I. Martínez, Julio A. II. Lomelí, Francisco A.
PS153.M4 C46 1985   810/.9/86872073 19   LC 83-22583   ISBN 0313236917

Modern Chicano writers: a collection of critical essays / edited   **2.10302**
by Joseph Sommers and Tomás Ybarra–Frausto.
Englewood Cliffs, N.J.: Prentice-Hall, c1979. xii, 190 p.; 21 cm. (Twentieth-century views) (A Spectrum book) 1. American literature — Mexican American authors — History and criticism — Addresses, essays, lectures. 2. American literature — 20th century — History and criticism — Addresses, essays, lectures. 3. Mexican American literature (Spanish) — History and criticism — Addresses, essays, lectures. I. Sommers, Joseph, 1924- II. Ybarra-Frausto, Tomás, 1938-
PS153.M4 M6   810/.9/0052   LC 78-25605   ISBN 0135897211

Sánchez, Marta Ester.   **2.10303**
Contemporary Chicana poetry: a critical approach to an emerging literature / Marta Ester Sánchez. — Berkeley: University of California Press, c1985. xi, 377 p.; 24 cm. Includes index. 1. American poetry — Mexican American authors — History and criticism. 2. American poetry — Women authors — History and criticism. 3. American poetry — 20th century — History and criticism. 4. Mexican American women in literature. I. T.
PS153.M4 S26 1985   811/.54/0986872073 19   LC 84-8816   ISBN 0520052625

Three American literatures: essays in Chicano, Native American,   **2.10304**
and Asian–American literature for teachers of American
literature / edited by Houston A. Baker, Jr.; with an
introduction by Walter J. Ong.
New York: Modern Language Association of America, 1982. 265 p.; 21 cm. 1. American literature — Minority authors — History and criticism — Addresses, essays, lectures. 2. American literature — Mexican American authors — History and criticism — Addresses, essays, lectures. 3. American literature — Indian authors — History and criticism — Addresses, essays, lectures. 4. American literature — Asian-American authors — History and criticism — Addresses, essays, lectures. 5. Minorities in literature — Addresses, essays, lectures. 6. United States — Literatures — History and criticism — Addresses, essays, lectures. I. Baker, Houston A.
PS153.M56 T5 1982   810/.9/920693 19   LC 82-6342   ISBN 0873523520

PS153.N5 AFRO–AMERICAN AUTHORS

Afro–American literature: the reconstruction of instruction /   **2.10305**
edited by Dexter Fisher and Robert B. Stepto for the
Commission on the Literatures and Languages of America.
New York: Modern Language Association of America, 1979, c1978. viii, 256 p.; 21 cm. Based on a two-week seminar held at Yale University in June 1977. 1. American literature — Afro-American authors — History and criticism — Congresses. 2. American literature — Afro-American authors — Study and teaching (Higher) — Congresses. 3. Afro-Americans — Study and teaching (Higher) — Congresses. I. Fisher, Dexter. II. Stepto, Robert B. III. Modern Language Association of America. Commission on the Literatures and Languages of America.
PS153.N5 A35 1979   PS153N5 A35 1979.   810/.9/896073   LC 78-62061   ISBN 0873523512

The Afro–American novel since 1960 / edited by Peter Bruck,   **2.10306**
Wolfgang Karrer.
Amsterdam: Grüner, 1982. vii, 327 p.; 23 cm. 'Checklist of Afro-American novels, 1945-1980': p. 307-325. 1. American fiction — Afro-American authors — History and criticism — Addresses, essays, lectures. 2. American fiction — 20th century — History and criticism — Addresses, essays, lectures. 3. Afro-Americans in literature — Addresses, essays, lectures. I. Bruck, Peter. II. Karrer, Wolfgang, 1941-
PS153.N5 A37 1982   PS153N5 A37 1982.   813/.54/09896073 19   LC 82-203278   ISBN 9060322193

Baker, Houston A.   **2.10307**
Blues, ideology, and Afro–American literature: a vernacular theory / Houston A. Baker, Jr. — Chicago: University of Chicago Press, 1985 (c1984). xi, 227 p.: ill. 1. American literature — Afro-American authors — History and criticism. 2. Blues (Music) — United States — History and criticism. I. T.
PS153.N5 B23 1984   810/.9/896073 19   LC 84-2655   ISBN 0226035360

Baker, Houston A.   **2.10308**
The journey back: issues in Black literature and criticism / Houston A. Baker, Jr. — Chicago: University of Chicago Press, c1980. xvii, 198 p. 1. American literature — Afro-American authors — History and criticism. I. T.
PS153.N5 B24   PS153N5 B24.   810/.9/896073   LC 79-20861   ISBN 0226035344

Baker, Houston A.   **2.10309**
Singers of daybreak: studies in Black American literature / [by] Houston A. Baker, Jr. — Washington: Howard University Press, 1974. xi, 109 p.; 24 cm. 1. American literature — Negro authors — Addresses, essays, lectures. I. T.
PS153.N5 B27   PS153N5 B27.   810/.9/896073   LC 74-11006   ISBN 0882580175

Bigsby, C. W. E. comp.   • **2.10310**
The Black American writer / edited by C. W. E. Bigsby. — Deland, Fla.: Everett/Edwards, [c1969] 2 v.; 25 cm. — 1. American literature — Negro authors — Addresses, essays, lectures. I. T.
PS153.N5 B5   *LC* 79-89569

Black literature and literary theory / edited by Henry Louis   **2.10311**
Gates, Jr.; [contributors, Sunday O. Anozie ... et al.].
New York: Methuen, 1984. 328 p.: ill.; 23 cm. Includes bibliographies and index. 1. American fiction — Afro-American authors — History and criticism — Addresses, essays, lectures. 2. African fiction (English) — Black authors — History and criticism — Addresses, essays, lectures. 3. Caribbean fiction (English) — Black authors — History and criticism — Addresses, essays, lectures. 4. Literature — History and criticism — Theory, etc. — Addresses, essays, lectures. 5. Criticism — Addresses, essays, lectures. I. Gates, Henry Louis. II. Anozie, Sunday Ogbonna.
PS153.N5 B555 1984   813/.009/896073 19   *LC* 84-6636   *ISBN* 0416372406

Black women writers (1950–1980): a critical evaluation / edited   **2.10312**
by Mari Evans.
1st ed. — Garden City, N.Y.: Anchor Press/Doubleday, 1984, c1983. xxviii, 543 p.; 22 cm. 1. American literature — Afro-American authors — History and criticism. 2. American literature — Women authors — History and criticism. 3. American literature — 20th century — History and criticism. I. Evans, Mari, 1923-
PS153.N5 B558 1984   810/.9/9287 19   *LC* 81-43914   *ISBN* 0385171242

Black women writers at work / edited by Claudia Tate.   **2.10313**
New York: Continuum, 1983. xxvi, 213 p. 1. Afro-American authors — Interviews. 2. Women authors, American — Interviews. 3. Authors, American — 20th century — Interviews. 4. American literature — Afro-American authors — History and criticism. 5. American literature — Women authors — History and criticism. 6. American literature — 20th century — History and criticism. 7. Authorship I. Tate, Claudia. ed.
PS153.N5 B56 1983   PS153N5 B56 1983.   810/.9/9287 19   *LC* 82-23546   *ISBN* 0826402321

Bone, Robert A.   • **2.10314**
The Negro novel in America / [by] Robert Bone. — [Rev. ed.] — New Haven: Yale University Press, [1965] x, 289 p.; 21 cm. 1. American literature — Negro authors — History and criticism. 2. American fiction — History and criticism. I. T.
PS153.N5 B6 1965   *LC* 65-9819

Bontemps, Arna Wendell, 1902-1973.   • **2.10315**
The Harlem renaissance remembered: essays / edited, with a memoir, by Arna Bontemps. — New York: Dodd, Mead [1972] viii, 310 p.: ports.; 22 cm. 1. American literature — Afro-American authors — Addresses, essays, lectures. 2. American literature — 20th century — History and criticism — Addresses, essays, lectures. 3. Harlem Renaissance I. T.
PS153.N5 B63   810/.9896073 19   *LC* 72-723   *ISBN* 0396065171

Brown, Sterling Allen, 1901-.   **2.10316**
Negro poetry and drama: and The Negro in American fiction / [by] Sterling Brown; with a new pref. by Robert Bone. — New York: Atheneum, 1969 [c1937] 142, 209 p.; 21 cm. (Studies in American Negro life. Atheneum, NL 12) 1. American literature — Afro-American authors — History and criticism. 2. Afro-Americans in literature I. Brown, Sterling Allen, 1901- The Negro in American fiction. 1969. II. T.
PS153.N5 B68 1969   810.9   *LC* 69-15521

Christian, Barbara, 1943-.   **2.10317**
Black feminist criticism: perspectives on Black women writers / Barbara Christian. — New York: Pergamon Press, c1985. xv, 261 p.; 24 cm. (Athene series.) 1. American literature — Afro-American authors — History and criticism — Addresses, essays, lectures. 2. American literature — 20th century — History and criticism — Addresses, essays, lectures. 3. Afro-American women — Addresses, essays, lectures. 4. Feminism and literature — Addresses, essays, lectures. I. T. II. Series.
PS153.N5 C47 1985   810/.9/9287 19   *LC* 84-22805   *ISBN* 0080319564

Conjuring: black women, fiction, and literary tradition / edited   **2.10318**
by Marjorie Pryse and Hortense J. Spillers.
Bloomington: Indiana University Press, c1985. 266 p.: ill.; 24 cm. (Everywoman.) (Midland book) 1. American literature — Afro-American authors — History and criticism — Addresses, essays, lectures. 2. American literature — Women authors — History and criticism — Addresses, essays, lectures. 3. Afro-American women in literature — Addresses, essays, lectures. 4. Women in literature — Addresses, essays, lectures. I. Pryse, Marjorie, 1948- II. Spillers, Hortense J. III. Series.
PS153.N5 C63 1985   810/.9/896 19   *LC* 84-43171   *ISBN* 0253314070

Davis, Arthur Paul, 1904-.   **2.10319**
From the dark tower: Afro-American writers, 1900 to 1960 / by Arthur P. Davis. — Washington: Howard University Press, 1974. xiv, 306 p.: ports.; 25 cm. 1. American literature — Afro-American authors — History and criticism. 2. American literature — 20th century — History and criticism. I. T.
PS153.N5 D33   810/.9/896073   *LC* 73-88969   *ISBN* 0882580043

Ellison, Ralph.   **2.10320**
Shadow and act. — New York: Random House, [1964] xxii, 317 p.; 22 cm. 1. Afro-American authors I. T.
PS153.N5 E4 1964   809.8   *LC* 64-18928

Hill, Herbert, 1924- ed.   • **2.10321**
Anger, and beyond: the Negro writer in the United States. — [1st ed.] — New York: Harper & Row, [1966] xxii, 227 p.; 22 cm. 1. Negro authors. 2. American literature — Negro authors. I. T.
PS153.N5 H5   *LC* 65-14654

Jackson, Blyden.   **2.10322**
The waiting years: essays on American Negro literature / Blyden Jackson. — Baton Rouge: Louisiana State University Press, [1976] 216 p. 1. American literature — Negro authors — History and criticism — Addresses, essays, lectures. I. T.
PS153.N5 J34   PS153N5 J34.   810/.9/896073   *LC* 74-82001   *ISBN* 0807101737

Johnson, Abby Arthur.   **2.10323**
Propaganda and aesthetics: the literary politics of Afro-American magazines in the twentieth century / Abby Arthur Johnson and Ronald Maberry Johnson. — Amherst: University of Massachusetts Press, 1979. 248 p. Includes index. 1. American literature — Afro-American authors — Periodicals — History. 2. Afro-American periodicals — History. 3. American literature — 20th century — History and criticism. 4. Afro-Americans — Race identity 5. Little magazines — United States. I. Johnson, Ronald Maberry. joint author. II. T.
PS153.N5 J6   PS153N5 J6.   810/.8/0052   *LC* 78-19692   *ISBN* 087023269X

Kent, George E.   **2.10324**
Blackness and the adventure of Western culture / by George E. Kent. — [1st ed.] Chicago: Third World Press [c1972] 210 p.; 23 cm. 1. American literature — Afro-American authors — History and criticism — Addresses, essays, lectures. 2. American literature — 20th century — History and criticism — Addresses, essays, lectures. 3. Afro-Americans in literature I. T.
PS153.N5 K4   810/.9/896073   *LC* 76-171225

Loggins, Vernon, 1893-.   • **2.10325**
The Negro author, his development in America to 1900. — Port Washington, N.Y.,: Kennikat Press, [1964,c1959] ix, 480 p.; 22 cm. — (Columbia University studies in English and comparative literature) 1. American literature — Negro authors — History and criticism. 2. Negro authors. 3. American literature — Negro authors — Bibliography. I. T. II. Series.
PS153.N5 L65 1964   *LC* 64-15540

Margolies, Edward.   • **2.10326**
Native sons: a critical study of twentieth-century Negro American authors. — [1st ed.] — Philadelphia: Lippincott, [1968] 210 p.; 24 cm. 1. American literature — Negro authors — History and criticism. 2. American literature — 20th century — History and criticism. I. T.
PS153.N5 M26   *LC* 68-24135

O'Brien, John.   **2.10327**
Interviews with Black writers. — New York: Liveright, [1973] xiii, 274 p.: ports.; 22 cm. 1. American literature — Afro-American authors — Interviews. I. T.
PS153.N5 O2   810/.9/896073   *LC* 72-97488   *ISBN* 087140561X

Ostendorf, Berndt.   **2.10328**
Black literature in white America / Berndt Ostendorf. — Totowa, N.J.: Barnes & Noble Books, 1982. ix, 171 p. 1. American literature — Afro-American authors — History and criticism. 2. Afro-Americans — Race identity I. T.
PS153.N5 O8   810/.9/896073 19   *LC* 81-19089   *ISBN* 0389202576

Redding, J. Saunders (Jay Saunders), 1906-.   **2.10329**
To make a poet black [by] J. Saunders Redding. Chapel Hill, University of North Carolina Press, 1939. x, 142 p. 22 cm. 1. American poetry — Afro-American authors — History and criticism. 2. American literature — Afro-American authors — History and criticism. I. T.
PS153.N5 R4   *LC* 39-27275

Sherman, Joan R.   **2.10330**
Invisible poets: Afro-Americans of the nineteenth century / [by] Joan R. Sherman. — Urbana: University of Illinois Press, [1974] xxxii, 270 p.: ill.; 24 cm. 1. American poetry — Afro-American authors — History and criticism. 2. American poetry — 19th century — History and criticism. I. T.
PS153.N5 S48   811/.009   *LC* 73-81569   *ISBN* 025200325X

Turner, Darwin T., 1931-. **2.10331**
In a minor chord: three Afro–American writers and their search for identity / [by] Darwin T. Turner; with a pref. by Harry T. Moore. — Carbondale: Southern Illinois University Press, [1971] xxii, 153 p.; 22 cm. — (Crosscurrents/modern critiques) 1. Toomer, Jean, 1894-1967. 2. Cullen, Countee, 1903-1946. 3. Hurston, Zora Neale. I. T.
PS153.N5 T8   810.9/005/2   LC 72-132491   *ISBN* 0809304813

Wagner, Jean, 1919-. **2.10332**
[Poètes Nègres des États-Unis. English] Black poets of the United States: from Paul Laurence Dunbar to Langston Hughes / translated by Kenneth Douglas. — Urbana: University of Illinois Press [1973] xxiii, 561 p.; 23 cm. (An Illini book) Translation of Les poètes Nègres des États-Unis. Originally presented as the author's thesis, Sorbonne, 1963. 1. American literature — Afro-American authors — History and criticism. 2. Afro-Americans in literature I. T.
PS153.N5 W313   811/.009   LC 72-75141   *ISBN* 025200292X
ISBN 0252003411

Williams, Sherley Anne, 1944-. • **2.10333**
Give birth to brightness: a thematic study in neo–Black literature. — New York: Dial Press, 1972. 252 p.; 21 cm. 1. American literature — Negro authors — History and criticism. I. T.
PS153.N5 W54   LC 74-37446

Young, James O. **2.10334**
Black writers of the thirties / [by] James O. Young. — Baton Rouge: Louisiana State University Press, 1974 (c1973) xiii, 257 p.; 24 cm. 'The original draft was prepared as a doctoral dissertation in history at the University of Southern California.' 1. American literature — Afro-American authors — History and criticism. 2. American literature — 20th century — History and criticism. 3. Afro-Americans — Intellectual life. 4. Afro-Americans in literature I. T.
PS153.N5 Y6 1973   810/.9/896073   LC 72-96402   *ISBN* 0807100609

PS153 P–Z

Franklin, H. Bruce (Howard Bruce), 1934-. **2.10335**
The victim as criminal and artist: literature from American prison / by H. Bruce Franklin. — New York: Oxford University Press, 1978. xxii, 337 p. Includes index. 1. American literature — History and criticism 2. Prisoners' writings, American — History and criticism. 3. American literature — Afro-American authors — History and criticism. 4. Prisons in literature 5. Slavery in the United States in literature. I. T.
PS153.P74 F7   PS153P74 F7.   820/.9   LC 76-57284   *ISBN* 0195022440

PS157–159 Relations to Other Literatures and Countries

The American writer and the European tradition / [edited by] • **2.10336**
Margaret Denny and William H. Gilman.
Minneapolis: published for the University of Rochester by the University of Minnesota Press, [1950] xi, 192 p.; 23 cm. 1. American literature — History and criticism — Addresses, essays, lectures. I. Gilman, William Henry, 1911- II. Denny, Margaret.
PS157.D4   810.9   LC 50-13091

Yu, Beongcheon. **2.10337**
The great circle: American writers and the Orient / Beongcheon Yu. — Detroit: Wayne State University Press, 1984 (c1983). 266 p.; 24 cm. 1. American literature — Oriental influences. 2. American literature — History and criticism 3. Civilization, Oriental, in literature. 4. Exoticism in literature I. T.
PS157.Y8 1983   810/.9/325 19   LC 83-14811   *ISBN* 0814317375

Gohdes, Clarence Louis Frank, 1901-. • **2.10338**
American literature in nineteenth century England. — Carbondale: Southern Illinois University Press, [1963?, c1944] 191 p.; 21 cm. 1. American literature — 19th century — History and criticism. 2. Literature, Comparative — American and English. 3. Literature, Comparative — English and American. I. T.
PS159.G8 G6 1963   PS159.G8 G6 1944.   810.903   LC 63-9473

Brown, Deming, 1919-. • **2.10339**
Soviet attitudes toward American writing. — Princeton, N. J.: Princeton University Press, 1962. 338 p.; 23 cm. Includes bibliography. 1. American literature — 20th cent. — Hist. & crit. 2. Criticism — Russia. 3. Russia — Relations (general) with the U.S. 4. U.S. — Relations (general) with Russia. I. T.
PS159.R8B7   810.904   LC 62-11954

Williams, Stanley Thomas, 1888-1956. • **2.10340**
The Spanish background of American literature. [Hamden, Conn.] Archon Books, 1968 [c1955] 2 v. illus., facsims., map, ports. 24 cm. 1. American literature — History and criticism 2. United States — Relations — Spain 3. Spain — Relations — United States 4. United States — Relations — Latin America 5. Latin America — Relations — United States I. T.
PS159.S7 W5 1968   810.9   LC 68-16337

PS163–173 Treatment of Special Subjects

Foerster, Norman, 1887-. • **2.10341**
Nature in American literature: studies in the modern view of nature. — New York: Russell & Russell, [1958] 324 p.; 20 cm. 1. Nature in literature 2. American literature — 19th century — History and criticism. I. T.
PS163.F6 1958   810.903   LC 58-12864

Hintz, Howard William, 1903-. • **2.10342**
The Quaker influence in American literature, by Howard W. Hintz. Westport, Conn., Greenwood Press [1970, c1940] 96 p. 23 cm. 1. Society of Friends. 2. American literature — History and criticism I. T.
PS166.H5 1970   810.9/92/286   LC 74-104238   *ISBN* 0837139457

Puritan influences in American literature / edited by Emory **2.10343**
Elliott.
Urbana: University of Illinois Press, c1979. xx, 212 p.: map; 24 cm. — (Illinois studies in language and literature. 65) 1. American literature — History and criticism — Addresses, essays, lectures. 2. Puritans — United States — Addresses, essays, lectures. 3. National characteristics, American, in literature — Addresses, essays, lectures. I. Elliott, Emory, 1942- II. Series.
PS166.P8   810/.9/3   LC 79-12270   *ISBN* 0252007336

The American autobiography: a collection of critical essays / **2.10344**
edited by Albert E. Stone.
Englewood Cliffs, N.J.: Prentice-Hall, c1981. viii, 184 p.; 21 cm. (Twentieth century views.) 'A Spectrum book.' Includes index. 1. American literature — History and criticism — Addresses, essays, lectures. 2. Autobiography — Addresses, essays, lectures. I. Stone, Albert E. II. Series.
PS169.A95 A5   810/.9/351 19   LC 81-10530   *ISBN* 0130246387

Tichi, Cecelia, 1942-. **2.10345**
New world, new earth: environmental reform in American literature from the Puritans through Whitman / Cecelia Tichi. — New Haven: Yale University Press, 1979. xii, 290 p.; 24 cm. 1. American literature — History and criticism 2. Ecology in literature. 3. Nature in literature I. T. II. Title: Environmental reform in American literature from the Puritans through Whitman.
PS169.E25 T5   810/.9/36   LC 78-15809   *ISBN* 0300022875

Boynton, Percy Holmes, 1875-1946. • **2.10346**
The rediscovery of the frontier. — New York: Greenwood Press, [1968, c1931] ix, 184 p.; 22 cm. 1. American literature — History and criticism 2. American fiction — History and criticism. 3. Frontier and pioneer life — U.S. I. T.
PS169.F7 B6 1968   813/.0093   LC 69-13836

Hazard, Lucy Lockwood, 1890-. • **2.10347**
The frontier in American literature. — New York: F. Ungar Pub. Co., [1961] 308 p.; 21 cm. — (American classics) 1. American literature — History and criticism 2. Frontier and pioneer life — United States. I. T.
PS169.F7 H3 1961   810   LC 60-13981

Gross, Theodore L. • **2.10348**
The heroic ideal in American literature [by] Theodore L. Gross. — New York: Free Press, [1971] xvi, 304 p.; 22 cm. 1. American literature — History and criticism 2. Heroes in literature I. T.
PS169.H4 G7   810.9/352   LC 72-142366

Nigro, August J., 1934-. **2.10349**
The diagonal line: separation and reparation in American literature / August J. Nigro. — Selinsgrove [Pa.]: Susquehanna University Press, c1984. 190 p.; 24 cm. Includes index. 1. American literature — History and criticism 2. Separation in literature 3. Reparation in literature. 4. Myth in literature 5. Fall of man in literature I. T.
PS169.S43 N53 1984   810/.9/3 19   LC 83-50945   *ISBN* 0941664023

Lynen, John F. • **2.10350**
The design of the present; essays on time and form in American literature [by] John F. Lynen. — New Haven: Yale University Press, 1969. ix, 456 p.; 25 cm. 1. American literature — History and criticism 2. Time in literature I. T.
PS169.T5 L9   810.9   LC 69-15451

Stout, Janis P.   **2.10351**
The journey narrative in American literature: patterns and departures / Janis P. Stout. — Westport, Conn.: Greenwood Press, 1983. xiii, 272 p.; 22 cm. Includes index. 1. American literature — History and criticism 2. Travel in literature 3. Narration (Rhetoric) 4. Escape in literature 5. Quests in literature I. T.
PS169.T74 S7 1983   810/.9/355 19   *LC* 82-24256   *ISBN* 0313232350

Fussell, Edwin S.   **2.10352**
Frontier: American literature and the American West, by Edwin Fussell. Princeton, N.J., Princeton University Press, 1965. xv, 450 p. 25 cm. 1. West (U.S.) in literature. 2. American literature — 19th century — History and criticism. I. T.
PS169.W4 F8   810.93   *LC* 64-12181

The Westering experience in American literature: Bicentennial   **2.10353**
essays / edited by Merrill Lewis and L. L. Lee.
Bellingham: Bureau for Faculty Research, Western Washington University, c1977. vi, 224 p.: ill.; 23 cm. 1. American literature — History and criticism — Addresses, essays, lectures. 2. West (U.S.) in literature — Addresses, essays, lectures. I. Lewis, Merrill. II. Lee, L. L. (Lawrence L.)
PS169.W4 W4   810/.9/32   *LC* 77-80814   *ISBN* 0930216016

Watts, Emily Stipes.   **2.10354**
The businessman in American literature / Emily Stipes Watts. — Athens, Ga.: University of Georgia Press, c1982. x, 183 p.; 23 cm. Includes index. 1. American literature — History and criticism 2. Businessmen in literature 3. Capitalism in literature. I. T.
PS173.B87 W3 1982   810/.9/352338 19   *LC* 81-21977   *ISBN* 0820306169

Harap, Louis.   **2.10355**
The image of the Jew in American literature: from early Republic to mass immigration / Louis Harap. — 1st ed. — Philadelphia: Jewish Publication Society of America, c1974. xiii, 586 p.; 24 cm. 1. Jews in literature 2. American literature — Jewish authors — History and criticism. I. T.
PS173.J4 H3   810/.9/8924   *LC* 74-12887   *ISBN* 0827600542

Liptzin, Solomon, 1901-.   • **2.10356**
The Jew in American literature / by Sol Liptzin. — New York: Bloch, c1966. 251 p.; 23 cm. 1. American literature — History and criticism 2. Jews in literature I. T.
PS173.J4 L5   810.93   *LC* 66-21078

Tatum, Charles M.   **2.10357**
Chicano literature / by Charles M. Tatum. — Boston: Twayne Publishers, c1982. 214 p.; 21 cm. — (Twayne's United States authors series. 433) Includes index. 1. American literature — Mexican American authors — History and criticism. 2. Mexican American literature (Spanish) — History and criticism. I. T. II. Series.
PS173.M39 T36 1982   810/.9/86872073 19   *LC* 82-1059   *ISBN* 0805773738

Davis, Charles T. (Charles Twitchell), 1918-1981.   **2.10358**
Black is the color of the cosmos: essays on Afro–American literature and culture, 1942–1981 / Charles T. Davis; edited by Henry Louis Gates, Jr.; foreword by A. Bartlett Giamatti. — New York: Garland Pub., 1982. xxxv, 376 p., [6] leaves of plates: ports.; 23 cm. — (Critical studies on Black life and culture. v. 1) Includes index. 1. American literature — Afro-American authors — History and criticism. 2. American literature — 20th century — History and criticism. 3. Afro-Americans in literature — History and criticism. I. Gates, Henry Louis. II. T. III. Series.
PS173.N4 D38 1982   PS173N4 D38 1982.   810/.9/896073 19   *LC* 80-9042   *ISBN* 0824093151

Gross, Seymour Lee.   • **2.10359**
Images of the Negro in American literature / edited by Seymour L. Gross and John Edward Hardy. — Chicago: University of Chicago Press, [1966] x, 321 p.; 21 cm. — (Patterns of literary criticism) 1. American literature — History and criticism 2. Negroes in literature. I. Hardy, John Edward. joint ed. II. T.
PS173.N4 G7   *LC* 66-23689

Klotman, Phyllis Rauch.   **2.10360**
Another man gone: the Black runner in contemporary Afro–American literature / Phyllis R. Klotman. — Port Washington, N.Y.: Kennikat Press, 1977.. 160 p. (Kennikat Press national university publications: Literary criticism series) Includes index. 1. American literature — Afro-American authors — History and criticism. 2. Afro-Americans in literature 3. American literature — History and criticism I. T.
PS173.N4 K55   PS173N4 K55 1977.   810/.9/896073   *LC* 76-18826   *ISBN* 0804691495

Yellin, Jean Fagan.   • **2.10361**
The intricate knot: Black figures in American literature, 1776–1863. — New York: New York University Press, 1972. ix, 260 p.; 24 cm. 1. Afro-Americans in literature 2. American literature — Revolutionary period, 1775-1783 —

History and criticism. 3. American literature — 19th century — History and criticism. I. T.
PS173.N4 Y4   813/.009/352   *LC* 72-76556   *ISBN* 0814796508 *ISBN* 0814796516

McIlwaine, Shields, 1902-.   • **2.10362**
The southern poor–white from Lubberland to Tobacco road. — New York: Cooper Square Publishers, 1970 [c1967] xxv, 274 p.: illus.; 23 cm. 1. Americans in literature 2. Southern States — Social conditions I. T.
PS173.P7 M3 1970   810.9/352   *LC* 75-132690   *ISBN* 0815403534

Jessup, Josephine Lurie.   • **2.10363**
The faith of our feminists: a study in the novels of Edith Wharton, Ellen Glasgow, Willa Cather. — New York: R. R. Smith, 1950. 128 p.; 22 cm. 1. Wharton, Edith Newbold Jones, 1862-1937. 2. Glasgow, Ellen Anderson Gholson, 1874-1945 3. Cather, Willa, 1873-1947. 4. American fiction — 20th century — History and criticism 5. Women in literature I. T.
PS173 W6 J4   *LC* 50-6823

PS185–228 LITERARY HISTORY, BY PERIOD

PS185–195 17th–18th Centuries

American writers before 1800: a biographical and critical   **2.10364**
dictionary / edited by James A. Levernier and Douglas R. Wilmes.
Westport, Conn.: Greenwood Press, 1983. 3 v.; 25 cm. 1. American literature — Colonial period, ca. 1600-1775 — History and criticism. 2. American literature — Revolutionary period, 1775-1783 — History and criticism. 3. American literature — 1783-1850 — History and criticism. 4. American literature — Colonial period, ca. 1600-1775 — Bio-bibliography. 5. Authors, American — 18th century — Biography. 6. Authors, American — To 1700 — Biography. I. Levernier, James. II. Wilmes, Douglas R.
PS185.A4 1983   810/.9/001 19   *LC* 82-933   *ISBN* 0313222290

Tyler, Moses Coit, 1835-1900.   • **2.10365**
A history of American literature, 1607–1765. — Ithaca: Cornell University Press, 1949. xxxiii, 551 p.: facsim.; 24 cm. 1. American literature — Colonial period, ca. 1600-1775 — History and criticism. I. T.
PS185.T8 1949   810.9   *LC* 49-11766

Tyler, Moses Coit, 1835-1900.   • **2.10366**
The literary history of the American Revolution, 1763–1783. — New York: F. Ungar Pub. Co., [1957] 2 v.; 25 cm. — (American classics) 1. American literature — Revolutionary period, 1775-1783 — History and criticism. I. T.
PS185.T8x   810.9   *LC* 57-6634

American literature, 1764–1789: the Revolutionary years /   **2.10367**
Everett Emerson, editor.
Madison: University of Wisconsin Press, 1977. xvi, 301 p.; 24 cm. 1. American literature — Revolutionary period, 1775-1783 — History and criticism. I. Emerson, Everett H., 1925-
PS193.A4   810/.9/001   *LC* 75-32073   *ISBN* 0299072703

Elliott, Emory, 1942-.   **2.10368**
Revolutionary writers: literature and authority in the New republic, 1725–1810 / Emory Elliott. — New York: Oxford University Press, 1982. x, 324 p.; 22 cm. Includes index. 1. American literature — Colonial period, ca. 1600-1775 — History and criticism. 2. American literature — Revolutionary period, 1775-1783 — History and criticism. 3. American literature — 1783-1850 — History and criticism. 4. Authority in literature. 5. Literature and society — United States. 6. United States — Intellectual life — 18th century I. T.
PS193.E4 1982   810/.9/001 19   *LC* 81-4016   *ISBN* 0195029992

Howard, Leon, 1903-.   • **2.10369**
The Connecticut wits. — Chicago: University of Chicago Press, [1943] xiii, 453 p. 1. Barlow, Joel, 1754-1812. 2. Dwight, Timothy, 1752-1817. 3. Humphreys, David, 1752-1818. 4. Trumbull, John, 1750-1831. I. T.
PS193.H6   *LC* 43-808

Murdock, Kenneth Ballard, 1895-1975.   **2.10370**
Literature & theology in colonial New England. Cambridge, Mass.: Harvard University Press, [1949] xi, 235 p. 21 cm. 'The substance of this book was presented in a course of lectures given for the Lowell Institute in King's Chapel, Boston, in March and April, 1944, as one of the institute's annual series on 'Current topics in theology." 1. American literature — Colonial period, ca. 1600-1775 — History and criticism — Addresses, essays, lectures. 2. American literature — New England — History and criticism — Addresses, essays, lectures. 3. Religion and literature I. T.
PS195.R4 M8   810.903   *LC* 49-10048 *

PS201–214 19th Century

Anderson, Quentin, 1912-. • 2.10371
The imperial self: an essay in American literary and cultural history. — [1st ed.]. — New York: Knopf, 1971. xiii, 274, vii p.; 22 cm. 1. American literature — 19th century — History and criticism. I. T.
PS201.A5 820.9/003 LC 75-136318 ISBN 0394414586

Brooks, Van Wyck, 1886-1963. • 2.10372
The times of Melville and Whitman. — New York: Dutton, 1953. viii, 499 p.; 19 cm. (Everyman's library, 648A. Essays and belles-lettres) 1. American literature — 19th century — History and criticism 2. United States — Civilization I. T.
PS201.B72 810.903 LC 53-6065

Eight American authors; a review of research and criticism, • 2.10373
edited by James Woodress. Essays by Jay B. Hubbell [and others]
Rev. ed. New York, Norton [c1971] xix, 392 p. 24 cm. 'Sponsored by the American Literature Section of the Modern Language Association.' Previous ed. edited by F. Stovall. 1. American literature — 19th century — History and criticism. I. Woodress, James Leslie. ed. II. Hubbell, Jay B. (Jay Broadus), 1885-1979. III. Stovall, Floyd, 1896- ed. Eight American authors.
PS201.E4 1971 810/.9/003 LC 73-160485

Lewis, R. W. B. (Richard Warrington Baldwin). • 2.10374
The American Adam; innocence, tragedy, and tradition in the nineteenth century. — [Chicago]: University of Chicago Press, [1955] ix, 204 p.; 24 cm. Issued also in microfilm form as thesis, University of Chicago. 1. American literature — 19th century — History & criticism. 2. United States — Intellectual life — 1783-1865 3. United States — Intellectual life — 1865-1918 I. T.
PS201.L4 810.902 LC 55-5133

Matthiessen, F. O. (Francis Otto), 1902-1950. • 2.10375
American renaissance: art and expression in the age of Emerson and Whitman / [by] F. O. Matthiessen. — London; New York [etc.]: Oxford University Press [c1941] xxiv p., 2 l., 3-678 p.: front., plates, ports.; 25 cm. 1. American literature — 19th century — History and criticism. I. T.
PS201.M3 810.903 LC 41-9633

Rees, Robert A. • 2.10376
Fifteen American authors before 1900; bibliographic essays on research and criticism, edited by Robert A. Rees and Earl N. Harbert. — Madison: University of Wisconsin Press, [1971] xvii, 442 p.; 25 cm. 1. American literature — 19th century — History and criticism. I. Harbert, Earl N., 1934- joint author. II. T.
PS201.R38 016.8109 LC 77-157395 ISBN 0299059103

Stovall, Floyd, 1896- ed. • 2.10377
Eight American authors, a review of research and criticism, by Jay B. Hubbell [and others] New York, Modern Language Association of America, 1956. 418 p. 21 cm. (Revolving fund series, no. 19) 1. American literature — 19th century — History and criticism. I. Hubbell, Jay B. (Jay Broadus), 1885-1979. II. T.
PS201.S8 810.903 LC a 57-3059

Ziff, Larzer, 1927-. 2.10378
Literary democracy: the declaration of cultural independence in America / Larzer Ziff. — New York: Viking Press, 1981. xxv, 333 p.; 24 cm. 1. American literature — 19th century — History and criticism. 2. Literature and society — United States. 3. United States — Civilization — 1783-1865 I. T.
PS201.Z5 1981 810/.9/003 19 LC 80-54085 ISBN 0670430269

Cowley, Malcolm, 1898-. • 2.10379
A many-windowed house: collected essays on American writers and American writing / edited, with an introd. by Henry Dan Piper. — Carbondale: Southern Illinois University Press, [1970] xviii, 261 p.; 23 cm. 1. American literature — 19th century — History and criticism. 2. American literature — 20th century — History and criticism. I. Piper, Henry Dan. ed. II. T.
PS203.C64 810.9 LC 74-112384 ISBN 0809304449

Brooks, Van Wyck, 1886-1963. • 2.10380
The world of Washington Irving. New York, Dutton, 1950. 514 p. 19 cm. (Everyman's library, 642A. Essays and belles-lettres) 1. American literature — Early 19th cent. — History and criticism. I. T.
PS208.B7 1950 AC1.E8 no. 642A 810.903 LC 50-58259

Wilson, Edmund, 1895-1972. • 2.10381
Patriotic gore; studies in the literature of the American Civil War. — New York: Oxford University Press, 1962. 816 p.; 20 cm. 1. American literature — 19th century — History and criticism. 2. United States — History — Civil War, 1861-1865 — Literature and the war I. T.
PS211.W5 810.9 LC 62-9834

Berthoff, Warner. 2.10382
The ferment of realism: American literature, 1884-1919 / Warner Berthoff. — Cambridge; New York: Cambridge University Press, 1981. xix, 330 p.; 22 cm. Originally published: New York: Free Press, 1965. Includes indexes. 1. American literature — 19th century — History and criticism. 2. American literature — 20th century — History and criticism. 3. Realism in literature I. T.
PS214.B4 1981 810/.9/12 19 LC 80-42335 ISBN 0521240921

Brooks, Van Wyck, 1886-1963. • 2.10383
The confident years: 1885-1915. New York: Dutton, 1955. viii, 620 p.; 19 cm. (His Makers and finders: a history of the writer in America, 1800-1915 [5]) Everyman's library, 650A. Essays and belles-lettres. 1. American literature — 19th century — History and criticism 2. American literature — 20th century — History and criticism. I. T.
PS214.B7 1955 810.903 LC 54-8848

Hicks, Granville, 1901-. • 2.10384
The great tradition: an interpretation of American literature since the civil war / by Granville Hicks. — Rev. ed. New York: The Macmillan company, 1935. xv p., 1 l., 341 p.; 23 cm. 1. American literature — 19th century — History and criticism. 2. American literature — 20th century — History and criticism. I. T.
PS214.H5 1935 810.9 LC 36-27042

Martin, Jay. • 2.10385
Harvests of change: American literature, 1865-1914. — Englewood Cliffs, N. J., Prentice-Hall [1967] 382 p. 24 cm. Bibliographical footnotes. 1. American literature — 19th cent. — Hist. & crit. 2. American literature — 20th cent. — Hist. & crit. I. T.
PS214.M35 810.9/004 LC 67-14850

Pizer, Donald. • 2.10386
Realism and naturalism in nineteenth-century American literature / with a pref. by Harry T. Moore. — Carbondale: Southern Illinois University Press [1966] xv, 176 p.; 22 cm. (Crosscurrents: modern critiques) 1. American fiction — 19th century — History and criticism — Addresses, essays, lecture. 2. Realism in literature — Addresses, essays, lectures. 3. Naturalism in literature — Addresses, essays, lectures. I. T.
PS214.P5 810.912 LC 66-10058

Ziff, Larzer, 1927-. • 2.10387
The American 1890s; life and times of a lost generation [by] Larzer Ziff. — New York, Viking Press [1966] viii, 376 p. 22 cm. Bibliographical references included in 'Notes' (p. [351]-365) 1. American literature — 19th cent. — Hist. & crit. I. T.
PS214.Z5 810.9004 LC 66-15885

Kaplan, Harold, 1916-. 2.10388
Democratic humanism and American literature. — Chicago: University of Chicago Press, [1972] xix, 298 p.; 24 cm. 1. American literature — 19th century — History and criticism. 2. Humanism in literature I. T.
PS217.H8 K3 810/.9/38 LC 71-184508 ISBN 0226424227

Ferguson, Robert A., 1942-. 2.10389
Law and letters in American culture / Robert A. Ferguson. — Cambridge, Mass.: Harvard University Press, 1984. viii, 417 p.: ill.; 24 cm. Includes index. 1. American literature — 1783-1850 — History and criticism. 2. Law and literature — United States. 3. Law in literature 4. Lawyers as authors 5. American literature — Revolutionary period, 1775-1783 — History and criticism. 6. United States — Intellectual life — 1783-1865 I. T.
PS217.L37 F47 1984 810/.9/92344 19 LC 84-8940 ISBN 0674514653

Richardson, Robert D., 1934-. 2.10390
Myth and literature in the American renaissance / Robert D. Richardson, Jr. — Bloomington: Indiana University Press, c1978. viii, 309 p.; 22 cm. Includes index. 1. American literature — 19th century — History and criticism. 2. Myth in literature I. T.
PS217.M93 R5 810/.9/37 19 LC 77-22638 ISBN 0253339650

McWilliams, John P. 2.10391
Hawthorne, Melville, and the American character: a looking-glass business / John P. McWilliams, Jr. — Cambridge [Cambridgeshire]; New York: Cambridge University Press, 1984. xi, 261 p.; 24 cm. — (Cambridge studies in American literature and culture.) 1. Hawthorne, Nathaniel, 1804-1864 — Knowledge — History. 2. Melville, Herman, 1819-1891 — Knowledge — History. 3. United States in literature. 4. American literature — 19th century — History and criticism. 5. National characteristics, American, in literature. I. T. II. Series.
PS217.N38 M38 1984 813/.3/09 19 LC 83-15235 ISBN 0521259002

Ideology and classic American literature / [edited by] Sacvan 2.10392
Bercovitch and Myra Jehlen.
Cambridge [Cambridgeshire]; New York: Cambridge University Press, 1986.
xii, 451 p.: ill.; 24 cm. — (Cambridge studies in American literature and
culture.) Includes index. 1. American literature — 19th century — History and
criticism. 2. Politics in literature I. Bercovitch, Sacvan. II. Jehlen, Myra.
III. Series.
PS217.P64 I36 1986   810/.9/358 19   *LC* 85-21247   *ISBN*
0521252210

Gilmore, Michael T. 2.10393
American romanticism and the marketplace / Michael T. Gilmore. — Chicago:
University of Chicago Press, c1985. ix, 177 p.; 23 cm. Includes index.
1. American literature — 1783-1850 — History and criticism. 2. American
literature — 19th century — History and criticism. 3. Romanticism — United
States. 4. Authors and readers — United States. 5. Authors, American — 19th
century — Biography. I. T.
PS217.R6 G54 1985   810/.9/003 19   *LC* 84-23936   *ISBN*
0226293955

Rosenthal, Bernard, 1934-. 2.10394
City of nature: journeys to nature in the age of American romanticism /
Bernard Rosenthal. — Newark: University of Delaware Press, c1980. 273 p.,
[1] leaf of plates: ill.; 22 cm. Includes index. 1. American literature — 19th
century — History and criticism. 2. Romanticism — United States. 3. Nature
in literature I. T.
PS217.R6 R64   810/.9/14   *LC* 78-68879   *ISBN* 0874131472

Buell, Lawrence. 2.10395
Literary transcendentalism; style and vision in the American Renaissance. —
Ithaca: Cornell University Press, [1973] viii, 336 p.; 22 cm. 1. American
literature — 19th century — History and criticism. 2. Transcendentalism
(New England) I. T.
PS217.T7 B8   810/.9/38   *LC* 73-8409   *ISBN* 0801407877

Critical essays on American transcendentalism / [compiled by] 2.10396
Philip F. Gura and Joel Myerson.
Boston, Mass.: G.K. Hall, c1982. li, 638 p.; 25 cm. — (Critical essays on
American literature.) 1. American literature — History and criticism —
Addresses, essays, lectures. 2. Transcendentalism in literature — Addresses,
essays, lectures. I. Gura, Philip F., 1950- II. Myerson, Joel. III. Series.
PS217.T7 C7 1982   810/.9/13 19   *LC* 81-7269   *ISBN* 0816184666

PS221–228 20th Century

Aldridge, John W. • 2.10397
In search of heresy: American literature in an age of conformity / by John W.
Aldridge. — New York: McGraw-Hill, c1956. ix, 208 p.; 21 cm. 1. American
literature — 20th century — History and criticism. 2. Criticism — United
States. 3. Conformity I. T.
PS221.A64 1974   813/.03   *LC* 56-8166   *ISBN* 083717452X

Brooks, Van Wyck, 1886-1963. • 2.10398
Three essays on America. New York Dutton 1934. 216p. 1. American
literature — History and criticism 2. United States — Intellectual life
3. National characteristics, American I. T.
PS221 B77   *LC* 34-14327

Cooperman, Stanley. • 2.10399
World War I and the American novel. Baltimore, Johns Hopkins Press [1967]
xii, 273 p. 24 cm. 1. World War, 1914-1918 — Literature and the war.
2. American literature — 20th century — History and criticism. I. T.
PS221.C63   810.9/005   *LC* 66-28506

Cowley, Malcolm, 1898- ed. • 2.10400
After the genteel tradition: American writers, 1910–1930 / with a pref. by
Harry T. Moore. — Carbondale: Southern Illinois University Press, [1964] x,
210 p.; 22 cm. — (Crosscurrents; modern critiques) 1. American literature —
20th century — History and criticism. I. T.
PS221.C645 1964   801.904   *LC* 64-11608

Cowley, Malcolm, 1898-. 2.10401
And I worked at the writer's trade: chapters of literary history, 1918–1978 /
Malcolm Cowley. — New York: Viking Press, c1978. xi, 276 p.; 23 cm.
Includes index. 1. American literature — 20th century — History and criticism
— Addresses, essays, lectures. 2. Authors, American — 20th century —
Biography — Addresses, essays, lectures. I. T.
PS221.C646   810/.9/005   *LC* 77-28713   *ISBN* 0670122912

Cowley, Malcolm, 1898-. • 2.10402
Exile's return; a literary odyssey of the 1920s. — [New ed.]. — New York:
Viking Press, 1951. vi, 322 p.; 22 cm. 1. Cowley, Malcolm, 1898- — Biography

— Youth. 2. Authors, American — 20th century — Biography. 3. American
literature — 20th century — History and criticism. I. T.
PS221.C65 1951   810.904   *LC* 51-4022

Critics of culture: literature and society in the early twentieth 2.10403
century / edited by Alan Trachtenberg.
New York: Wiley, c1976. vi, 287 p.; 22 cm. (Wiley sourcebooks in American
social thought) 1. American literature — 20th century — History and criticism
— Addresses, essays, lectures. 2. United States — Intellectual life
I. Trachtenberg, Alan. II. Series.
PS221.C7   810/.9/005   *LC* 75-31838   *ISBN* 0471881465

Curley, Dorothy Nyren. comp. • 2.10404
Modern American literature / Compiled and edited by Dorothy Nyren Curley,
Maurice Kramer [and] Elaine Fialka Kramer. — 4th enl. ed. — New York: F.
Ungar Pub. Co., 1969. 3 v.; 25 cm. — (A Library of literary criticism) Vol. 4:
Supplement to the fourth edition. 1. American literature — 20th century —
History and criticism. 2. Criticism — United States. I. Kramer, Maurice, joint
comp. II. Kramer, Elaine Fialka, joint comp. III. T.
PS221.C8 1969   810.9/005   *LC* 76-76599   *ISBN* 0804430462

De Voto, Bernard Augustine, 1897-1955. • 2.10405
The literary fallacy. — Port Washington, N.Y.: Kennikat Press, [1969, c1944]
175 p.: port.; 21 cm. — (The Patten lectures, 1944) (Essay and general literature
index reprint series.) 1. American literature — 20th century — History and
criticism. I. T. II. Series.
PS221.D4 1969   810.9/005   *LC* 69-16484   *ISBN* 080460519X

Sixteen modern American authors: a survey of research and 2.10406
criticism / edited by Jackson R. Bryer.
[Rev. ed.]. — Durham, N.C.: Duke University Press, 1974. xx, 673 p.; 25 cm.
First ed. published in 1969 under title: Fifteen modern American authors.
1. American literature — 20th century — History and criticism. I. Bryer,
Jackson R. ed.
PS221.F45 1974   810/.9/0052   *LC* 72-97454   *ISBN* 0822302977

French, Warren G., 1922- comp. 2.10407
The fifties: fiction, poetry, drama. Edited by Warren French. — Deland, Fla.:
Everett/Edwards, [c1970] xii, 316 p.; 25 cm. 1. American literature — 20th
century — History and criticism. I. T.
PS221.F66   810.9/005/4   *LC* 73-125030

French, Warren G., 1922-. 2.10408
The Forties: fiction, poetry, drama. Edited by Warren French. — Deland, Fla.:
Everett/Edwards, [1969] ix, 330 p.; 25 cm. 1. American literature — 20th
century — History and criticism. I. T.
PS221.F67   810/.9005   *LC* 69-10440

French, Warren G., 1922-. 2.10409
The thirties: fiction, poetry, drama / edited by Warren French. — 2d ed., rev. —
Deland, Fla.: Everett/Edwards, c1976. ix, 259 p.; 24 cm. Includes index.
1. American literature — 20th century — History and criticism — Addresses,
essays, lectures. I. T.
PS221.F68 1976   810/.9/0052   *LC* 75-45270   *ISBN* 0912112085

French, Warren G., 1922-. 2.10410
The twenties: fiction, poetry, drama / edited by Warren French. — 1st. ed. —
Deland, Fla.: Everett/Edwards, [1975] xvii, 532 p.; 24 cm. Includes index.
1. American literature — 20th century — History and criticism — Addresses,
essays, lectures. I. T.
PS221.F69   810/.9/0052   *LC* 74-24534   *ISBN* 0912112050

Frohock, W. M. (Wilbur Merrill), 1908-. • 2.10411
Strangers to this ground; cultural diversity in contemporary American writing.
— Dallas, Southern Methodist University Press [1961] x, 180 p. 23 cm.
1. American literature — 20th cent. — Hist. & crit. 2. Individuality
3. National characteristics, American I. T.
PS221.F7   810.904   *LC* 61-17183

Harvard guide to contemporary American writing / Daniel 2.10412
Hoffman, editor; with essays by Leo Braudy ... [et al.].
Cambridge, Mass.: Belknap Press of Harvard University Press, 1979. 618 p.; 24
cm. Includes index. 1. American literature — 20th century — History and
criticism — Addresses, essays, lectures. I. Hoffman, Daniel, 1923- II. Braudy,
Leo.
PS221.H357   810/.9/0054   *LC* 79-10930   *ISBN* 0674375351

Hassan, Ihab Habib, 1925-. 2.10413
Contemporary American literature, 1945–1972: an introduction / [by] Ihab
Hassan. — New York: Ungar, [1973] xi, 194 p.; 22 cm. 1. American literature
— 20th century — History and criticism. I. T.
PS221.H36   810/.9/0054   *LC* 72-81701   *ISBN* 0804431213

Hoffman, Frederick John. 2.10414
The twenties; American writing in the postwar decade. New, rev. ed. New
York, Collier Books [1962] 516 p. 18 cm. (Collier books, BS106) 1. American

literature — 20th century — History and criticism. 2. United States — History — 1919-1933 I. T.
PS221.H58 1962   810.904   *LC* 62-17574

Josephson, Matthew, 1899-1978.   • **2.10415**
Life among the surrealists: a memoir. — [1st ed.] New York: Holt, Rinehart and Winston, [1962] 403 p.: ill.; 22 cm. Includes bibliography. 1. Authors, American 2. Americans — France — Paris 3. Broom. 4. Paris (France) — Intellectual life. I. T.
PS221.J65   818.52   *LC* 62-7704 rev

Kenner, Hugh.   **2.10416**
A homemade world: the American modernist writers / by Hugh Kenner. — New York: Morrow, 1975. xviii, 221, ix p.; 21 cm. 1. American literature — 20th century — History and criticism. I. T.
PS221.K4 1975   810/.9/005   *LC* 75-10969   *ISBN* 0688079628 pbk

Kostelanetz, Richard.   **2.10417**
The end of intelligent writing: literary politics in America / Richard Kostelanetz. — New York: Sheed and Ward, [1974] xviii, 480 p.; 24 cm. Includes index. 1. American literature — 20th century — History and criticism. 2. Publishers and publishing — United States. 3. Authors and publishers — United States. I. T.
PS221.K64   810/.9/0054   *LC* 73-9098   *ISBN* 0836205545

Kramer, Dale.   • **2.10418**
Chicago renaissance; the literary life in the Midwest, 1900–1930. — [1st ed.]. — New York: Appleton-Century, [1966] x, 369 p.; 25 cm. 1. American literature — Chicago. 2. American literature — 20th century — History and criticism. 3. Bohemianism — Chicago. I. T.
PS221.K67   810.9005   *LC* 66-22240

Madden, David, 1933-.   **2.10419**
American dreams, American nightmares, edited by David Madden. With a pref. by Harry T. Moore. — Carbondale: Southern Illinois University Press, [1970] xlii, 229 p.; 22 cm. — (Crosscurrents: modern critiques) 1. American literature — 20th century — Addresses, essays, lectures. 2. U.S. — Civilization — Addresses, essays, lectures. I. T.
PS221.M25   810.9/3   *LC* 70-93885   *ISBN* 0809304465

Millett, Fred Benjamin, 1890-.   • **2.10420**
Contemporary American authors; a critical survey and 219 bio–bibliographies [by] Fred B. Millett. New York: Harcourt, Brace and Co., 1940. xiii, 716 p.; 22 cm. Based on Contemporary American literature, bibliographies and study outlines, by J. M. Manly and Edith Rickert; 1st ed., 1922, 2d ed., 1929. cf. Foreword. 1. American literature — 20th century — Bio-bibliography 2. American literature — 20th century — History and criticism. I. Manly, John Matthews, 1865-1940. Contemporary American literature. II. Rickert, Edith, 1871-1938. Contemporary American literature. III. T.
PS 221 M65   *LC* 40-27229

Poirier, Richard.   • **2.10421**
The performing self: compositions and decompositions in the languages of contemporary life. — New York: Oxford University Press, 1971. xv, 203 p.; 22 cm. 1. American literature — 20th century — Addresses, essays, lectures. 2. English literature — 20th century — Addresses, essays, lectures. I. T.
PS221.P64   820.9/009/1   *LC* 76-140914   *ISBN* 0195013889

Spiller, Robert Ernest, 1896- ed.   • **2.10422**
A time of harvest, American literature, 1910–1960. — New York: Hill and Wang, [1962] 173 p.; 21 cm. (American century series, AC50) 1. American literature — 20th century — Addresses, essays, lectures. I. T.
PS221.S66   810.904   *LC* 62-9492

Thorp, Willard, 1899-.   • **2.10423**
American writing in the twentieth century. — Cambridge: Harvard University Press, 1960. 353 p.; 22 cm. — (The Library of Congress series in American civilization) 1. American literature — 20th century — History & criticism. I. T.
PS221.T48   810.904   *LC* 59-14739

Times (London, England) Literary supplement.   • **2.10424**
American writing today: its independence and vigor, edited by Allan Angoff. — [New York] New York University Press, 1957. 433 p. 22 cm. 'Appeared originally in the Times (London) Literary supplement [Sept. 17, 1954]' 1. American literature — 20th cent. — Hist. & crit. I. Angoff, Allan. ed. II. T.
PS221.T5 1957   810.904   *LC* 56-10779

Wilson, Edmund, 1895-1972.   • **2.10425**
Classics and commercials: a literary chronicle of the forties. New York, Farrar, Straus [1950] x, 534 p. 20 cm. 'A selection of ... literary articles written during the nineteen forties.' 1. American literature — 20th century — Addresses, essays, lectures. 2. Literature, Modern — Addresses, essays, lectures. I. T.
PS221.W55   804   *LC* 50-10620

Wilson, Edmund, 1895-1972.   • **2.10426**
The shores of light: a literary chronicle of the twenties and thirties. — New York: Farrar, Straus and Young, [1952] 814 p.; 20 cm. 1. American literature — 20th century — Addresses, essays, lectures. 2. Literature, Modern — Addresses, essays, lectures. I. T.
PS221.W56   804   *LC* 52-13935

Kiernan, Robert F.   **2.10427**
American writing since 1945: a critical survey / Robert F. Kiernan. — New York: F. Ungar, c1983. x, 178 p.; 22 cm. Includes index. 1. American literature — 20th century — History and criticism. I. T.
PS225.K48 1983   810/.9/0054 19   *LC* 83-828   *ISBN* 0804424586

Prescott, Peter S.   **2.10428**
Never in doubt: critical essays on American books, 1972–1985 / Peter S. Prescott. — New York: Arbor House, c1986. x, 302 p.; 24 cm. 1. American literature — 20th century — History and criticism — Addresses, essays, lectures. I. T.
PS225.P74 1986   810/.9/0054 19   *LC* 85-28773   *ISBN* 0877958033

PS228 SPECIAL TOPICS, A–Z

Higgs, Robert J., 1932-.   **2.10429**
Laurel & thorn: the athlete in American literature / Robert J. Higgs. — Lexington, Ky.: University Press of Kentucky, c1981. 196 p.; 23 cm. Based on the author's thesis (doctoral—University of Tennessee) 1. American literature — 20th century — History and criticism. 2. Athletes in literature 3. Sports stories — History and criticism. I. T. II. Title: Laurel and thorn.
PS228.A83 H5   810/.9/355 19   *LC* 80-51014   *ISBN* 0813114128

Tytell, John.   **2.10430**
Naked angels: the lives & literature of the Beat generation / by John Tytell. — New York: McGraw-Hill, c1976. 273 p., [4] leaves of plates: ill.; 21 cm. Includes index. 1. Burroughs, William S., 1914- 2. Ginsberg, Allen, 1926- 3. Kerouac, Jack, 1922-1969. 4. Bohemianism — United States. I. T.
PS228.B6 T9   813/.5/409   *LC* 75-22206   *ISBN* 0070657238. *ISBN* 0070657246 pbk

Aaron, Daniel, 1912-.   • **2.10431**
Writers on the left, episodes in American literary communism. [1st ed.] New York, Harcourt, Brace & World [1961] xvi, 460 p. 22 cm. (Communism in American life) 1. American literature — 20th century — History and criticism. 2. Communism and literature 3. Authors, American — 20th century — Political and social views. I. T. II. Series.
PS228.C6 A2   810.904   *LC* 61-13349

Thomas, F. Richard.   **2.10432**
Literary admirers of Alfred Stieglitz / F. Richard Thomas. — Carbondale: Southern Illinois University Press, c1983. xiv, 102 p., 16 p. of plates: ill.; 24 cm. Includes index. 1. Stieglitz, Alfred, 1864-1946—Influence. 2. Stein, Gertrude, 1874-1946 — Criticism and interpretation. 3. Williams, William Carlos, 1883-1963 — Criticism and interpretation. 4. Crane, Hart, 1899-1932 — Criticism and interpretation. 5. Anderson, Sherwood, 1876-1941 — Criticism and interpretation. 6. American literature — 20th century — History and criticism. 7. Photography in literature. 8. Literature and photography I. T.
PS228.P48 T5 1983   810/.9/0052 19   *LC* 82-10543   *ISBN* 080931097X

Beidler, Philip D.   **2.10433**
American literature and the experience of Vietnam / Philip D. Beidler. — Athens, Ga.: University of Georgia Press, c1982. xiv, 220 p.; 22 cm. 1. American literature — 20th century — History and criticism. 2. Vietnamese Conflict, 1961-1975 — Literature and the war. I. T.
PS228.V5 B4 1982   810/.9/358 19   *LC* 81-19845   *ISBN* 0820306126

Walsh, Jeffrey.   **2.10434**
American war literature, 1914 to Vietnam / Jeffrey Walsh. — New York: St. Martin's Press, 1982. xii, 218 p.; 23 cm. 1. American literature — 20th century — History and criticism. 2. War in literature 3. World War, 1914-1918 — Literature and the war. 4. World War, 1939-1945 — Literature and the war 5. Vietnamese Conflict, 1961-1975 — Literature and the war. I. T.
PS228.W37 W3 1982   810/.9/3   *LC* 79-22409   *ISBN* 0312031289

DuPlessis, Rachel Blau.   **2.10435**
Writing beyond the ending: narrative strategies of twentieth–century women writers / by Rachel Blau DuPlessis. — Bloomington: Indiana University Press, c1985. xvi, 253 p.; 25 cm. (Everywoman: studies in history, literature, and culture) Includes index. 1. American literature — Women authors — History and criticism. 2. Women in literature 3. American literature — 20th century — History and criticism. 4. English literature — Women authors — History and criticism. 5. English fiction — 20th century — History and criticism. 6. Narration (Rhetoric) 7. Feminism and literature I. T.
PS228.W65 D86 1985   810/.9/9287 19   *LC* 83-49512   *ISBN* 0253367050

PS241–286 LITERARY HISTORY: SPECIAL REGIONS

PS243 New England

Brooks, Van Wyck, 1886-1963.   • **2.10436**
The flowering of New England. — New York: Dutton, 1952. viii, 563 p.; 19 cm. — (Everyman's library 654A. Essays and belleslettres) Sequel: New England: Indian summer, 1865-1915. 1. American literature — New England. 2. American literature — 19th century — History and criticism. 3. New England — Civilization. I. T.
AC1.E8 no. 645A   PS243.B7 1952.   810.903   *LC* 52-5308

Brooks, Van Wyck, 1886-1963.   • **2.10437**
New England: Indian summer. — New York: Dutton, 1950. 569 p.; 19 cm. — (Everyman's library, 641A. Essays and belleslettres) Sequel to The flowering of New England. Sequel: The world of Washington Irving. 1. American literature — New England — History and criticism. 2. American literature — 19th century — History and criticism. 3. American literature — 20th century — History and criticism. 4. New England — Civilization. I. T.
AC1.E8 no. 641A   PS243.B72 1950.   810.903   *LC* 50-7352

Buell, Lawrence.   **2.10438**
New England literary culture from revolution through renaissance / Lawrence Buell. — Cambridge [Cambridgeshire]; New York, NY, USA: Cambridge University Press, 1986. xii, 513 p.; 24 cm. (Cambridge studies in American literature and culture.) Includes index. 1. American literature — New England — History and criticism. 2. New England in literature. 3. Puritans — New England. 4. New England — Civilization. I. T. II. Series.
PS243.B84 1986   810/.9/974 19   *LC* 85-14893   *ISBN* 0521302064

Lowance, Mason I., 1938-.   **2.10439**
The language of Canaan: metaphor and symbol in New England from the Puritans to the trancendentalists / Mason I. Lowance, Jr. — Cambridge, Mass.: Harvard University Press, 1980. x, 335 p.; 24 cm. 1. Bible — Language, style 2. American literature — New England — History. 3. Puritans — New England. 4. Transcendentalism (New England) 5. Christian art and symbolism I. T.
PS243.L6   810/.9/15   *LC* 79-21179   *ISBN* 0674509498

Simpson, Lewis P.   **2.10440**
The man of letters in New England and the South: essays on the history of the literary vocation in America / [by] Lewis P. Simpson. — Baton Rouge: Louisiana State University Press, [1973] xii, 255 p.; 23 cm. 1. American literature — New England — Addresses, essays, lectures. 2. American literature — Southern States — Addresses, essays, lectures. I. T.
PS243.S48   810/.9/974   *LC* 72-94151   *ISBN* 0807102164

Westbrook, Perry D.   **2.10441**
Acres of flint: Sarah Orne Jewett and her contemporaries / by Perry D. Westbrook. — Rev. ed. — Metuchen, N.J.: Scarecrow Press, 1981. xi, 184 p., [4] leaves of plates: ill.; 22 cm. Includes index. 1. Jewett, Sarah Orne, 1849-1909 — Criticism and interpretation. 2. American literature — New England — History and criticism. 3. American literature — 19th century — History and criticism. 4. American literature — Women authors — History and criticism. 5. New England in literature. I. T.
PS243.W4 1981   810/.9/974 19   *LC* 80-20501   *ISBN* 0810813572

Westbrook, Perry D.   **2.10442**
The New England town in fact and fiction / Perry D. Westbrook. — Rutherford [N.J.]: Fairleigh Dickinson University Press; London: Associated University Presses, c1982. 286 p.; 24 cm. Includes index. 1. American literature — New England — History and criticism. 2. Cities and towns in literature 3. New England in literature. 4. City and town life — New England — History. 5. New England — Historiography. I. T.
PS243.W43 1982   810/.9/3274 19   *LC* 80-67077   *ISBN* 0838630111

PS261–267 The South

Bradbury, John M.   • **2.10443**
The Fugitives: a critical account / by John M. Bradbury. — Chapel Hill: University of North Carolina Press, 1958. xiv, 300 p. 1. The Fugitives. 2. American literature — Southern States — History. I. T.
PS261.B62   *LC* 58-14633

Bradbury, John M.   • **2.10444**
Renaissance in the South; a critical history of the literature, 1920-1960. — Chapel Hill: University of North Carolina Press, [1963] 222 p.; 24 cm. 1. American literature — Southern States — History and criticism. I. T.
PS261.B624   810.975   *LC* 63-21072

Cook, Sylvia Jenkins, 1943-.   **2.10445**
From Tobacco Road to Route 66: the southern poor white in fiction / Sylvia Jenkins Cook. — Chapel Hill: University of North Carolina Press, c1976. xiv, 208 p.; 23 cm. Includes index. 1. American fiction — Southern States — History and criticism. 2. American fiction — 20th century — History and criticism. 3. Poor in literature. I. T.
PS261.C57   813/.03   *LC* 75-35822   *ISBN* 0807812641

Cowan, Louise, 1916-.   • **2.10446**
The Fugitive group: a literary history. — Baton Rouge: Louisiana State University Press [1959] xxiii, 277 p. illus., ports. 24 cm. 1. Fugitives (Group) 2. The Fugitive. 3. American literature — Southern States — History and criticism. I. T.
PS261.C6   810.975   *LC* 59-14394

Gray, Richard J.   **2.10447**
The literature of memory: modern writers of the American South / by Richard Gray. — Baltimore: Johns Hopkins University Press, c1977. xi, 377 p.; 24 cm. Includes index. 1. American literature — Southern States — History and criticism. 2. American literature — 20th century — History and criticism. I. T.
PS261.G68   810/.9/0052   *LC* 76-18941   *ISBN* 0801818036

**The History of Southern literature / general editor, Louis D.   2.10448
Rubin, Jr.; senior editors, Blyden Jackson ... [et al.]; associate editor, Mary Ann Wimsatt.**
Baton Rouge: Louisiana State University Press, c1985. xiv, 626 p.; 24 cm. Includes index. 1. American literature — Southern States — History and criticism. 2. Southern States in literature. I. Rubin, Louis Decimus, 1923-
PS261.H53 1985   810/.9/975/ 19   *LC* 85-10183   *ISBN* 0807112518

Hobson, Fred C., 1943-.   **2.10449**
Tell about the South: the southern rage to explain / Fred Hobson. — Baton Rouge: Louisiana State University Press, c1983. xii, 391 p.; 24 cm. — (Southern literary studies.) 'Winner of the Jules F. Landry award for 1983'—P. [ii] Includes index. 1. American literature — Southern States — History and criticism. 2. Southern States in literature. 3. Confession in literature I. T. II. Series.
PS261.H54 1983   810/.9/975 19   *LC* 83-5477   *ISBN* 0807111120

Holman, C. Hugh (Clarence Hugh), 1914-.   **2.10450**
The immoderate past: the southern writer and history / by C. Hugh Holman. — Athens: University of Georgia Press, c1977. ix, 118 p.; 23 cm. — (The Lamar lectures at Wesleyan College; 1976) Includes index. 1. American fiction — Southern States — History and criticism — Addresses, essays, lectures. 2. History in literature — Addresses, essays, lectures. I. T.
PS261.H64   813/.03   *LC* 76-58439   *ISBN* 0820304190

Holman, C. Hugh (Clarence Hugh), 1914-.   **2.10451**
The roots of Southern writing; essays on the literature of the American South [by] C. Hugh Holman. Athens, University of Georgia Press [1972] xiii, 236 p. 25 cm. 1. American literature — Southern States — Addresses, essays, lectures. I. T.
PS261.H65   810/.9   *LC* 74-184774   *ISBN* 0820302902

Hubbell, Jay B. (Jay Broadus), 1885-1979.   • **2.10452**
The South in American literature, 1607-1900. — [Durham, N. C.] Duke University Press, 1954. xix, 987 p. 25 cm. Bibliography: p. [883]-974. 1. American literature — Southern States — Hist. & crit. I. T.
PS261.H78   810.9   *LC* 54-9434

King, Richard H.   **2.10453**
A Southern Renaissance: the cultural awakening of the American South, 1930-1955 / Richard H. King. — New York: Oxford University Press, 1980. xi, 350 p.; 22 cm. 1. American literature — Southern States — History and criticism. 2. American literature — 20th century — History and criticism. 3. Southern States — Civilization 4. Southern States — Intellectual life — 1865- I. T.
PS261.K45   810/.9/975   *LC* 79-9470   *ISBN* 0195026640

MacKethan, Lucinda Hardwick.   **2.10454**
The dream of Arcady: place and time in Southern literature / Lucinda Hardwick MacKethan. — Baton Rouge: Louisiana State University Press, c1980. 229 p.; 23 cm. Includes index. 1. American literature — Southern States — History and criticism. 2. Pastoral literature, American — Southern States — History and criticism. 3. Southern states in literature. I. T.
PS261.M25   810/.9/32   *LC* 79-16543   *ISBN* 0807105996

Ridgely, Joseph Vincent.   **2.10455**
Nineteenth-century Southern literature / J. V. Ridgely. — Lexington, Ky.: University Press of Kentucky, c1980. x, 128 p.; 23 cm. (New perspectives on the South.) Includes index. 1. American literature — Southern States — History and criticism. 2. American literature — 19th century — History and criticism. 3. Southern States in literature. I. T. II. Series.
PS261.R44   810/.9/975   *LC* 79-4011   *ISBN* 0813103010

Rubin, Louis Decimus, 1923-. 2.10456
A gallery of Southerners / Louis D. Rubin, Jr. — Baton Rouge: Louisiana State University Press, c1982. xxi, 233 p.; 24 cm. 1. American literature — Southern States — History and criticism — Addresses, essays, lectures. 2. American literature — 20th century — History and criticism — Addresses, essays, lectures. I. T.
PS261.R64 1982   810/.9/975 19   LC 82-64   ISBN 0807109975

Rubin, Louis Decimus, 1923-. • 2.10457
South: modern Southern literature in its cultural setting, edited by Louis D. Rubin, Jr. and Robert D. Jacobs. [1st ed.] Garden City, N.Y., Doubleday [1961] 440 p. 19 cm. (Dolphin books, C316) 1. American literature — Southern States — Addresses, essays, lectures. I. Jacobs, Robert D., 1918- II. T.
PS261.R65   810.904   LC 61-15071

Rubin, Louis Decimus, 1923- ed. • 2.10458
Southern renascence: the literature of the modern South, edited by Louis D. Rubin, Jr. and Robert D. Jacobs. — Baltimore: Johns Hopkins Press, 1953. xii, 450 p.; 24 cm. 1. American literature — Southern States — History and criticism. I. Jacobs, Robert D., 1918- joint ed. II. T.
PS261.R67   810.9   LC 53-11174

Skaggs, Merrill Maguire. 2.10459
The folk of Southern fiction / by Merrill Skaggs. — Athens: University of Georgia Press, 1973 (c1972) xiii, 280 p.; 25 cm. 1. American fiction — Southern States — History and criticism. 2. Local color in literature 3. American fiction — 19th century — History and criticism. 4. American fiction — 20th century — History and criticism. I. T.
PS261.S48   813/.009/32   LC 76-190050   ISBN 0820302945

Southern literary study: problems and possibilities / edited by 2.10460
Louis D. Rubin, Jr. and C. Hugh Holman.
Chapel Hill: University of North Carolina Press, [1975] xiii, 235 p.; 20 cm. Proceedings of a conference sponsored by the English Department of the University of North Carolina, held Nov. 30-Dec. 2, 1972, at Chapel Hill. 1. American literature — Southern states — History and criticism — Congresses. I. Rubin, Louis Decimus, 1923- II. Holman, C. Hugh (Clarence Hugh), 1914- III. North Carolina. University. Dept. of English.
PS261.S528   810/.9/975   LC 75-11553   ISBN 0807812528

Southern writers: a biographical dictionary / edited by Robert 2.10461
Bain, Joseph M. Flora, and Louis D. Rubin, Jr.
Baton Rouge: Louisiana State University Press, c1979, 1980 printing. xxvii, 515 p.; 24 cm. — (Southern literary studies.) 1. American literature — Southern States — Bio-bibliography. 2. Authors, American — Southern States — Biography. I. Bain, Robert. II. Flora, Joseph M. III. Rubin, Louis Decimus, 1923- IV. Series.
PS261.S59   810/.9/975 B   LC 78-25899   ISBN 0807103543

Sullivan, Walter, 1924-. 2.10462
Death by melancholy; essays on modern Southern fiction. — Baton Rouge: Louisiana State University Press, [1972] xi, 133 p.; 23 cm. — (Southern literary studies.) 1. American fiction — Southern States — Addresses, essays, lectures. 2. American fiction — 20th century — Addresses, essays, lectures. I. T. II. Series.
PS261.S9   813/.009   LC 72-79339   ISBN 0807102369

Sullivan, Walter, 1924-. 2.10463
A requiem for the renascence: the state of fiction in the modern south / Walter Sullivan. — Athens: University of Georgia Press, c1976. xxiv, 81 p.; 23 cm. (Mercer University Lamar memorial lectures; no. 18) 1. American fiction — Southern States — History and criticism — Addresses, essays, lectures. 2. American fiction — 20th century — History and criticism — Addresses, essays, lectures. I. T.
PS261.S93   813/.009   LC 75-21176   ISBN 0820303909

Women writers of the contemporary South / edited by Peggy 2.10464
Whitman Prenshaw.
Jackson: University Press of Mississippi, c1984. xii, 323 p.: ports.; 24 cm. — (Southern quarterly series.) Includes index. 1. American fiction — Southern States — History and criticism — Addresses, essays, lectures. 2. American fiction — Women authors — History and criticism — Addresses, essays, lectures. 3. American fiction — 20th century — History and criticism — Addresses, essays, lectures. 4. Southern States in literature — Addresses, essays, lectures. I. Prenshaw, Peggy Whitman. II. Series.
PS261.W65 1984   813/.54/093287 19   LC 84-5165   ISBN 0878052224

Stewart, John Lincoln, 1917-. 2.10465
The burden of time: the fugitives and agrarians; the Nashville groups of the 1920's and 1930's, and the writing of John Crowe Ransom, Allen Tate, and Robert Penn Warren, by John L. Stewart. — Princeton, N. J., Princeton University Press, 1965. xi, 551 p. 25 cm. 1. Ransom, John Crowe, 1888-1974.

2. Tate, Allen, 1899- 3. Warren, Robert Penn, 1905- 4. American literature — Tennessee — Nashville — History and criticism. I. T.
PS266.N3 S7   810.904   LC 65-12994

Davis, Richard Beale. 2.10466
Literature and society in early Virginia, 1608-1840. — Baton Rouge: Louisiana State University Press, [1973] xxiv, 332 p.; 23 cm. — (Southern literary studies.) 1. American literature — Virginia — Addresses, essays, lectures. 2. Virginia — Intellectual life. I. T. II. Series.
PS266.V5 D3   810/.997/55   LC 72-89896   ISBN 0807102156

Watson, Ritchie Devon. 2.10467
The cavalier in Virginia fiction / Ritchie Devon Watson, Jr. — Baton Rouge: Louisiana State University Press, c1985. xii, 298 p.: ill.; 24 cm. (Southern literary studies.) Includes index. 1. American fiction — Virginia — History and criticism. 2. Virginia in literature. 3. Aristocracy in literature 4. Men in literature 5. Social ethics in literature. 6. Historical fiction, American — Virginia. 7. Plantation life in literature. I. T. II. Series.
PS266.V5 W3 1985   813/.009/3520621 19   LC 84-21306   ISBN 0807112127

PS271-286 The West. Midwest

Haslam, Gerald W. comp. 2.10468
Western writing / Gerald W. Haslam, editor. — 1st. ed. — Albuquerque: University of New Mexico Press, [1974] 156 p.; 24 cm. 1. American literature — West (U.S.) — History and criticism — Addresses, essays, lectures. 2. West (U.S.) in literature. I. T.
PS271.H3   813/.5/40932   LC 74-83389   ISBN 0826303536

Fairbanks, Carol, 1935-. 2.10469
Prairie women: images in American and Canadian fiction / Carol Fairbanks. — New Haven: Yale University Press, c1986. xi, 300 p.: ill.; 25 cm. Includes index. 1. American fiction — Middle West — History and criticism. 2. Canadian fiction — Prairie Provinces — History and criticism. 3. Rural women in literature. 4. Women pioneers in literature. 5. Women in literature 6. Prairies in literature. 7. Frontier and pioneer life in literature. 8. American fiction — Women authors — History and criticism. 9. Canadian fiction — Women authors — History and criticism. 10. Feminism and literature I. T.
PS273.F34 1986   813/.009/352042 19   LC 85-22616   ISBN 0300033745

Rusk, Ralph Leslie, 1888-. • 2.10470
The literature of the middle western frontier. — New York: F. Ungar Pub. Co., [1962, label c1953] 2 v.; 22 cm. — (American classics) 1. American literature — Middle West — History and criticism. 2. American literature — Middle West — Bibliography. I. T.
PS273.R8 1962   810.977   LC 61-13639

Major, Mabel, 1894-. • 2.10471
Southwest heritage: a literary history with bibliography / Mabel Major, Rebecca W. Smith and T.M. Pearce. — [Rev. ed.]. — Albuquerque: Universtiy of New Mexico Press, 1948. 199 p. 1. American literature — Southwest, New — History and criticism. 2. American literature — Southwest, New — Bibliography. 3. Southwest, New — Bibliography. I. Smith, Rebecca Washington, 1894- II. Pearce, T. M. (Thomas Matthews), 1902- III. T.
PS277.M3 1948   LC 39-27090

Duffey, Bernard I., 1917-. • 2.10472
The Chicago renaissance in American letters: a critical history. — [East Lansing]: Michigan State College Press, 1954. 285 p.; 22 cm. 1. American literature — Illinois — Chicago — History and criticism. I. T.
PS285.C47 D8   LC 54-11828

Smith, Carl S. 2.10473
Chicago and the American literary imagination, 1880-1920 / Carl S. Smith. — Chicago: University of Chicago Press, 1984. xiv, 232 p.: ill.; 23 cm. Includes index. 1. American literature — Illinois — Chicago — History and criticism. 2. Chicago (Illinois) in literature. 3. American literature — 19th century — History and criticism. 4. American literature — 20th century — History and criticism. 5. City and town life in literature I. T.
PS285.C47 S6 1984   810/.9/3277311 19   LC 83-9311   ISBN 0226763714

PS301-478 LITERARY HISTORY, BY FORM

PS301-326 Poetry

Gelpi, Albert. 2.10474
The tenth muse: the psyche of the American poet / Albert Gelpi. — Cambridge: Harvard University Press, 1975. xx, 327 p.; 24 cm. 1. American poetry — History and criticism. 2. United States — Intellectual life I. T.
PS303.G4   811/.009   LC 74-25038   *ISBN* 0674874412

Pearce, Roy Harvey. • 2.10475
The continuity of American poetry. — Princeton, N.J.: Princeton University Press, 1961. xv, 442 p.; 25 cm. 1. American poetry — History and criticism. I. T.
PS303.P4   811.09   LC 61-7424

Waggoner, Hyatt Howe. 2.10476
American poets, from the Puritans to the present / Hyatt H. Waggoner. — Rev. ed. — Baton Rouge: Louisiana State University Press, 1984. xxiv, 735 p.; 22 cm. Includes index. 1. American poetry — History and criticism. I. T.
PS303.W3 1984   811/.009 19   LC 83-19624   *ISBN* 0807111465

Martin, Wendy. 2.10477
An American triptych: Anne Bradstreet, Emily Dickinson, Adrienne Rich / by Wendy Martin. — Chapel Hill: University of North Carolina Press, c1984. x, 272 p.; 24 cm. Includes bibliographical references and index. 1. Bradstreet, Anne, 1612?-1672 — Criticism and interpretation. 2. Dickinson, Emily, 1830-1886 — Criticism and interpretation. 3. Rich, Adrienne Cecile — Criticism and interpretation. 4. American poetry — Women authors — History and criticism. 5. Feminism in literature. 6. Theology in literature. 7. Puritans in literature. I. T.
PS310.F45 M3 1984   811/.009/9287 19   LC 83-6864   *ISBN* 080781573X

Martin, Robert K., 1941-. 2.10478
The homosexual tradition in American poetry / by Robert K. Martin. — Austin: University of Texas Press, c1979. xx, 259 p.; 24 cm. Includes index. 1. American poetry — History and criticism. 2. Homosexuality in literature 3. Gays' writings, American — History and criticism. I. T.
PS310.H66 M3   811/.009/352   LC 79-16769   *ISBN* 0292730098

Coffman, Stanley K. • 2.10479
Imagism; a chapter for the history of modern poetry, by Stanley K. Coffman, Jr. — New York: Octagon Books, 1972 [c1951] xi, 235 p.; 22 cm. Reprint of the 1st ed. 1. Imagist poetry — History and criticism. 2. American poetry — 20th century — History and criticism. 3. English poetry — 20th century — History and criticism. I. T.
PS310.I5 C6 1972   821/.9/1209   LC 72-4262   *ISBN* 0374917930

Modern Black poets: a collection of critical essays / edited by 2.10480
Donald B. Gibson.
Englewood Cliffs, N.J.: Prentice-Hall, [1973] viii, 181 p.; 22 cm. — (Twentieth century views.) (Spectrum book.) 1. American poetry — Negro authors — History and criticism 2. American poetry — 20th century — History and criticism 3. American poetry — Afro-American authors — History and criticism — Addresses, essays, lectures. 4. American poetry — 20th century — History and criticism — Addresses, essays, lectures. I. Gibson, Donald B. II. Series. III. Series: Spectrum book.
PS310 N4 G5   PS310.N4 G5.   811/.5/09   LC 72-12811   *ISBN* 013588392X

Wald, Alan M., 1946-. 2.10481
The revolutionary imagination: the poetry and politics of John Wheelwright and Sherry Mangan / Alan M. Wald. — Chapel Hill: University of North Carolina Press, c1983. xix, 288 p.: ill.; 23 cm. 1. Wheelwright, John, 1897-1940. 2. Mangan, Sherry, 1904- 3. Revolutionary poetry, American — History and criticism. 4. Radicalism in literature. 5. Socialism in literature 6. American poetry — 20th century — History and criticism. 7. Politics and literature — United States. 8. Poets, American — 20th century — Political activity. I. T.
PS310.P6 W34 1983   811/.5/09358 19   LC 82-8498   *ISBN* 0807815357

Beach, Joseph Warren, 1880-1957. • 2.10482
Obsessive images: symbolism in poetry of the 1930's and 1940's / J.W. Beach; edited by William Van O'Connor. — Minneapolis: University of Minnesota Press, 1960. 396 p.; 23 cm. 1. American poetry — 20th century — History and criticism. 2. Symbolism in literature 3. Figures of speech I. O'Connor, William Van, 1915-1966. II. T.
PS310.S9 B4   LC 60-15381

Waggoner, Hyatt Howe. 2.10483
American visionary poetry / Hyatt H. Waggoner. — Baton Rouge: Louisiana State University Press, c1982. xii, 226 p.; 23 cm. Includes index. 1. American poetry — History and criticism. 2. Vision in literature. 3. Visual perception in literature. I. T.
PS310.V57 W33 1982   811/.009/1 19   LC 82-8987   *ISBN* 0807110515

Shakespeare's sisters: feminist essays on women poets / edited, 2.10484
with an introd. by Sandra M. Gilbert and Susan Gubar.
Bloomington: Indiana University Press, c1979. xxvi, 337 p.; 25 cm. 1. American poetry — Women authors — History and criticism — Addresses, essays, lectures. 2. English poetry — Women authors — History and criticism — Addresses, essays, lectures. 3. Feminist literary criticism — Addresses, essays, lectures. I. Gilbert, Sandra M. II. Gubar, Susan, 1944-
PS310.W64 S5   821/.009   LC 78-9510   *ISBN* 0253112583

Daly, Robert. 2.10485
God's altar: the world and the flesh in Puritan poetry / Robert Daly. — Berkeley: University of California Press, c1978. ix, 253 p.; 23 cm. 1. American poetry — Colonial period, ca. 1600-1775 — History and criticism. 2. Puritans — New England. 3. Christian poetry, American — History and criticism. 4. American poetry — Puritan authors — History and criticism. I. T.
PS312.D3   811/.1/09   LC 77-76182   *ISBN* 0520034805

Donoghue, Denis. • 2.10486
Connoisseurs of chaos; ideas of order in modern American poetry. — New York: Macmillan, [1965] 254 p.; 22 cm. 'Given [in briefer form] as the George Elliston Lectures at the University of Cincinnati in January, 1965.' 1. American poetry — 19th century — History and criticism. 2. American poetry — 20th century — History and criticism. I. T.
PS316.D65   811.009   LC 65-17830

PS323-326 20TH CENTURY

Berke, Roberta Elzey. 2.10487
Bounds out of bounds: a compass for recent American and British poetry / Roberta Berke. — New York: Oxford University Press, 1981. vii, 203 p.; 22 cm. 1. American poetry — 20th century — History and criticism. 2. English poetry — 20th century — History and criticism. I. T.
PS323.5.B4   821/.91/09 19   LC 80-20886   *ISBN* 0195028724

Borroff, Marie. 2.10488
Language and the poet: verbal artistry in Frost, Stevens, and Moore / Marie Borroff. — Chicago: University of Chicago Press, 1979. ix, 198 p.; 24 cm. Includes indexes. 1. Frost, Robert, 1874-1963 — Style. 2. Stevens, Wallace, 1879-1955 — Style. 3. Moore, Marianne, 1887-1972 — Style. 4. American poetry — 20th century — History and criticism. 5. English language — Style I. T.
PS323.5.B64   811/.5/409   LC 78-14567   *ISBN* 0226066517

Breslin, James E. B., 1935-. 2.10489
From modern to contemporary: American poetry, 1945-1965 / James E.B. Breslin. — Chicago: University of Chicago Press, 1984. xvi, 272 p.; 24 cm. 1. American poetry — 20th century — History and criticism. I. T.
PS323.5.B7 1984   811/.54/09 19   LC 83-17869   *ISBN* 0226074080

Contemporary poetry in America: essays and interviews / edited 2.10490
by Robert Boyers.
New York: Schocken Books, 1975, c1974. viii, 370 p.: ports.; 22 cm. 1. American poetry — 20th century — History and criticism — Addresses, essays, lectures. 2. Authors, American — 20th century — Interviews. I. Boyers, Robert.
PS323.5.C6   PS323.5 C6 1975.   811/.5/409   LC 74-22501

Forrest-Thomson, Veronica. 2.10491
Poetic artifice: a theory of twentieth-century poetry / Veronica Forrest-Thomson. — New York: St. Martin's Press, 1979 (c1978). xiv, 168 p.; 23 cm. 1. American poetry — 20th century — History and criticism. 2. English poetry — 20th century — History and criticism. 3. Poetics I. T.
PS323.5.F6   821/.9/109   LC 78-15847   *ISBN* 0312617984

Howard, Richard, 1929-. 2.10492
Alone with America: essays on the art of poetry in the United States since 1950. — Enl. ed. — New York: Atheneum, 1980. xiii, 687 p.; 24 cm. 1. American poetry — 20th century — History and criticism. I. T.
PS323.5.H6 1980   811/.54/09 19   LC 79-64718   *ISBN* 0689110006

Miller, James Edwin, 1920-. 2.10493
The American quest for a supreme fiction. Whitman's legacy in the personal epic / James E. Miller, Jr. — Chicago: University of Chicago Press, 1979. xvi, 360 p.; 24 cm. 1. Whitman, Walt, 1819-1892 — Influence. 2. American poetry — 20th century — History and criticism. 3. Epic poetry, American — History and criticism. I. T.
PS323.5.M45   811/.03 19   LC 78-15176   *ISBN* 0226526119

Modern American poetry / edited by R.W. (Herbie) Butterfield. 2.10494
London: Vision; Totowa, NJ: Barnes & Noble, 1984. 239 p.; 22 cm. — (Critical studies series.) 1. American poetry — 20th century — History and criticism. I. Butterfield, R. W. II. Series.
PS323.5.M53 1984   811/.5/09 19   LC 83-27507   *ISBN* 0389204609

Molesworth, Charles, 1941-. 2.10495
The fierce embrace: a study of contemporary American poetry / Charles Molesworth. — Columbia: University of Missouri Press, 1979. x, 214 p.; 23 cm. Includes index. 1. American poetry — 20th century — History and criticism. I. T.
PS323.5.M55   811/.5/409   *LC* 79-1561   *ISBN* 0826202780

Pritchard, William H. 2.10496
Lives of the modern poets / William H. Pritchard. — New York: Oxford University Press, 1980. xii, 316 p.; 22 cm. Includes index. 1. American poetry — 20th century — History and criticism — Addresses, essays, lectures. 2. English poetry — 19th century — History and criticism — Addresses, essays, lectures. I. T.
PS323.5.P7   821/.9/12   *LC* 79-17615   *ISBN* 019502690X

Rexroth, Kenneth, 1905-. 2.10497
American poetry in the twentieth century. — New York: Herder and Herder, [1971] 180 p.; 21 cm. 1. American poetry — 20th century — History and criticism. I. T.
PS323.5.R4   811/.5/09   *LC* 76-150308

Spears, Monroe Kirklyndorf. • 2.10498
Dionysus and the city; modernism in twentieth-century poetry [by] Monroe K. Spears. — New York: Oxford University Press, 1970. ix, 278 p.; 22 cm. 1. American poetry — 20th century — History and criticism. 2. English poetry — 20th century — History and criticism. 3. Modernism (Literature) I. T.
PS323.5.S65   821/.9/09   *LC* 79-83017

Diggory, Terence, 1951-. 2.10499
Yeats & American poetry: the tradition of the self / Terence Diggory. — Princeton, N.J.: Princeton University Press, c1983. xix, 262 p.; 22 cm. 1. Yeats, W. B. (William Butler), 1865-1939 — Influence. 2. American poetry — 20th century — History and criticism. 3. Self in literature. I. T. II. Title: Yeats and American poetry.
PS324.D53 1983   811/.52/09 19   *LC* 82-15070   *ISBN* 0691065586

Lowell, Amy, 1874-1925. • 2.10500
Poetry and poets; essays. — New York: Biblo and Tannen, 1971 [c1930] vi, 232 p.; 21 cm. 1. American poetry — 20th century — Addresses, essays, lectures. 2. English poetry — 20th century — History and criticism — Addresses, essays, lectures. 3. Poetry — History and criticism I. T.
PS324.L75 1971   821/.009   *LC* 77-162298   *ISBN* 0819602744

Mills, Ralph J. • 2.10501
Contemporary American poetry / by Ralph J. Mills, Jr. — New York: Random House, 1965. vi, 262 p. — (Random House studies in language and literature; SLL2) 1. American poetry — 20th century — History and criticism. I. T.
PS324.M5   *LC* 65-17446

Nemerov, Howard. ed. 2.10502
Poets on poetry. — New York: Basic Books, [1966] xii, 250 p.; 22 cm. 'Originated in the Voice of America 'Forum' series.'—Dust jacket. 1. American poetry — 20th century — History and criticism. I. T.
PS324.N4   811.509   *LC* 65-27338

O'Connor, William Van, 1915-1966. • 2.10503
Sense and sensibility in modern poetry. — New York: Gordian Press, 1973 [c1948] xii, 278 p.; 23 cm. Reprint of the ed. published by University of Chicago Press. Originally presented as the author's thesis, Columbia University. 1. American poetry — 20th century — History and criticism. 2. English poetry — 20th century — History and criticism. I. T.
PS324.O3 1973   821/.9/1209   *LC* 71-180986   *ISBN* 0877521573

Schwartz, Sanford, 1948-. 2.10504
The matrix of modernism: Pound, Eliot, and early twentieth-century thought / Sanford Schwartz. — Princeton, N.J.: Princeton University Press, c1985. x, 235 p.; 23 cm. Includes index. 1. Pound, Ezra, 1885-1972 — Criticism and interpretation. 2. Eliot, T. S. (Thomas Stearns), 1888-1965 — Criticism and interpretation. 3. American poetry — 20th century — History and criticism. 4. Modernism (Literature) 5. English poetry — 20th century — History and criticism. 6. Philosophy, Modern — 20th century 7. Philosophy in literature I. T.
PS324.S38 1985   811/.52/091 19   *LC* 85-42702   *ISBN* 0691066515

Tate, Allen, 1899-. 2.10505
The poetry reviews of Allen Tate, 1924–1944 / edited, with an introduction, by Ashley Brown and Frances Neel Cheney. — Baton Rouge: Louisiana State University Press, c1983. xii, 214 p.; 24 cm. — (Southern literary studies.)

Includes index. 1. American poetry — 20th century — Book reviews. 2. English poetry — 20th century — Book reviews. I. Brown, Ashley, 1923- II. Cheney, Frances Neel, 1906- III. T. IV. Series.
PS324.T25 1983   811/.52/09 19   *LC* 82-12687   *ISBN* 0807110574

Altieri, Charles, 1942-. 2.10506
Enlarging the temple: new directions in American poetry during the 1960's / Charles Altieri. — Lewisburg [Pa.]: Bucknell University Press, c1979. 258 p.; 24 cm. Includes index. 1. American poetry — 20th century — History and criticism. 2. Poetics I. T.
PS325.A37   811/.5/209   *LC* 77-89773   *ISBN* 0838721273

Altieri, Charles, 1942-. 2.10507
Self and sensibility in contemporary American poetry / Charles Altieri. — Cambridge [Cambridgeshire]; New York: Cambridge University Press, 1984. viii, 237 p.; 24 cm. — (Cambridge studies in American literature and culture.) Includes index. 1. Creeley, Robert, 1926- — Criticism and interpretation. 2. Ashbery, John — Criticism and interpretation. 3. Rich, Adrienne Cecile — Criticism and interpretation. 4. Self in literature. 5. American poetry — 20th century — History and criticism. I. T. II. Series.
PS325.A38 1984   811/.54/09353 19   *LC* 83-7855   *ISBN* 0521253969

Jackson, Richard, 1946-. 2.10508
Acts of mind: conversations with contemporary poets / by Richard Jackson. — University: University of Alabama Press, c1983. x, 222 p.; 25 cm. Includes index. 1. Poets, American — 20th century — Interviews. 2. American poetry — 20th century — History and criticism — Addresses, essays, lectures. 3. Poetics — Addresses, essays, lectures. I. T.
PS325.J3 1983   811/.54/09 19   *LC* 82-4767   *ISBN* 0817301224

Kalstone, David. 2.10509
Five temperaments: Elizabeth Bishop, Robert Lowell, James Merrill, Adrienne Rich, John Ashbery / David Kalstone. — New York: Oxford University Press, 1977. 212 p.; 22 cm. 1. American poetry — 20th century — History and criticism. 2. Autobiography in literature. I. T.
PS325.K35   811/.5/209   *LC* 76-42655   *ISBN* 0195022602

Lieberman, Laurence. 2.10510
Unassigned frequencies: American poetry in review, 1964–77 / Laurence Lieberman. — Urbana: University of Illinois Press, 1979, c1977. xi, 296 p.; 24 cm. 1. American poetry — 20th century — Addresses, essays, lectures. 2. American poetry — 20th century — Book reviews. I. T.
PS325.L5   811/.5/409   *ISBN* 0252004779

Rosenthal, M. L. (Macha Louis), 1917-. • 2.10511
The new poets: American and British poetry since World War II / M. L. Rosenthal. — New York: Oxford University Press, 1967. xi, 350 p. 1. American poetry — 20th century — History and criticism. 2. English poetry — 20th century — History and criticism. I. T.
PS326.R6   821/.9/1409   *LC* 67-15134

PS330–351 Drama

Meserve, Walter J. 2.10512
An emerging entertainment: the drama of the American people to 1828 / Walter J. Meserve. — Bloomington: Indiana University Press, c1977. x, 342 p. Includes indexes. 1. American drama — History and criticism. I. T.
PS332.M39   PS332 M39.   812/.009   *LC* 77-74444   *ISBN* 0253370078

Quinn, Arthur Hobson, 1875-1960. 2.10513
A history of the American drama, from the beginning to the civil war, by Arthur Hobson Quinn ... — 2d ed. — New York: F. S. Crofts & co., 1943. xvi p., 1 l., 530 p.; 22 cm. 'First printing, November, 1923.' 'A list of American plays': p. [423]-497. 1. American drama — History and criticism. I. T.
PS332.Q5 1943   812.09   *LC* 43-11974

Quinn, Arthur Hobson, 1875-1960. • 2.10514
A history of the American drama from the Civil war to the present day, by Arthur Hobson Quinn ... — New York: F. S. Crofts & co., 1936. xxv, 296, 432 p.: ill. The text of the two volume edition of 1927, with an added chapter (The new decade, 1927-1936) The bibliography and play list have been completely revised and reset. cf. Foreword to the revised edition. 1. American drama — History and criticism. 2. American drama — Bibliography. I. T.
PS332.Q55 1936   812.09   *LC* 36-27316

Mitchell, Loften. 2.10515
Black drama: the story of the American Negro in the theatre. — [1st ed.]. — New York: Hawthorn Books, [1967] 248 p.: ill., ports.; 24 cm. 1. Negroes in literature. 2. Theater — United States 3. Negroes — Moral and social conditions I. T.
PS338.N4 M5   PS338N4 M5.   792/.0973   *LC* 66-22313

Goldstein, Malcolm.   **2.10516**
The political stage: American drama and theater of the great depression. — New York: Oxford University Press, 1974. x, 482 p.: illus.; 24 cm. 1. American drama — 20th century — History and criticism. 2. Political plays, American — History and criticism. 3. Theater — United States I. T.
PS338.P6 G6   812/.5/2093   LC 73-87609

Brown, Janet, 1952-.   **2.10517**
Feminist drama: definition & critical analysis / Janet Brown. — Metuchen, N.J.: Scarecrow Press, 1979. v, 161 p.; 23 cm. Includes index. 1. American drama — 20th century — History and criticism. 2. Feminism in literature. 3. American drama — Women authors — History and criticism. 4. Feminist theater — United States. I. T.
PS338.W6 B7   812/.5/4093   LC 79-22382   ISBN 0810812673

Abramson, Doris E.   • **2.10518**
Negro playwrights in the American theatre, 1925–1959 [by] Doris E. Abramson. New York, Columbia University Press, 1969. xii, 335 p. 23 cm. 1. American drama — Afro-American authors — History and criticism. 2. American drama — 20th century — History and criticism. 3. Theater — United States I. T.
PS351.A2   812/.5/09   LC 69-19457

Auerbach, Doris.   **2.10519**
Sam Shepard, Arthur Kopit, and the Off Broadway theater / by Doris Auerbach. — Boston: Twayne Publishers, c1982. 145 p.; 21 cm. — (Twayne's United States authors series. TUSAS 432) Includes index. 1. Shepard, Sam, 1943- — Criticism and interpretation. 2. Kopit, Arthur L — Criticism and interpretation. 3. American drama — 20th century — History and criticism. 4. Off-Broadway theater I. T. II. Series.
PS351.A9 1982   812/.54/09 19   LC 82-11975   ISBN 0805773711

Bigsby, C. W. E.   **2.10520**
A critical introduction to twentieth–century American drama / C.W.E. Bigsby. — Cambridge [Cambridgeshire]; New York: Cambridge University Press, 1982-1985. 3 v.: ill.; 24 cm. 1. American drama — 20th century — History and criticism. 2. Theater — United States — History — 20th century. I. T.
PS351.B483 1982   812/.52/09 19   LC 81-18000   ISBN 0521242274

Dickinson, Thomas Herbert, 1877-.   • **2.10521**
Playwrights of the new American theater, by Thomas H. Dickinson. — St. Clair Shores, Mich.: Scholarly Press, 1972. vi, 331 p.; 22 cm. Reprint of the 1925 ed. 1. American drama — 20th century — History and criticism. I. T.
PS351.D5 1972   812/.5/209   LC 77-144975   ISBN 040300943X

Downer, Alan Seymour, 1912-.   • **2.10522**
Fifty years of American drama, 1900–1950. — Chicago: Regnery, 1951. 158 p.; 22 cm. — (Twentieth-century literature in America) 1. American drama — 20th century — History and criticism. I. T.
PS351.D6   812.509   LC 51-13185

Gagey, Edmond McAdoo, 1901-.   • **2.10523**
Revolution in American drama [by] Edmond M. Gagey. — Freeport, N.Y.: Books for Libraries Press, [1971, c1947] viii, 315 p.; 23 cm. — (Essay index reprint series) 1. American drama — 20th century — History and criticism. 2. Theater — U.S. — History. I. T.
PS351.G3 1971   812/.5/09   LC 75-167343   ISBN 0836924983

Krutch, Joseph Wood, 1893-1970.   • **2.10524**
The American drama since 1918; an informal history. — [Rev. ed.]. — New York: G. Braziller, 1957. 344 p.; 21 cm. 1. American drama — 20th century — History and criticism. I. T.
PS351.K7 1957   812.509   LC 57-1458

Weales, Gerald Clifford, 1925-.   • **2.10525**
American drama since World War II. — [1st ed.]. — New York: Harcourt, Brace & World, [1962] 246 p.; 21 cm. 1. American drama — 20th century — History and criticism. I. T.
PS351.W4   812.5409   LC 62-14467

Weales, Gerald Clifford, 1925-.   • **2.10526**
The jumping–off place; American drama in the 1960's [by] Gerald Weales. — [New York]: Macmillan, [1969] xii, 306 p.; 22 cm. 1. American drama — 20th century — History and criticism. I. T.
PS351.W43 1969   812/.5/409   LC 69-10544

PS362–379 Prose

Bercovitch, Sacvan.   **2.10527**
The American jeremiad / Sacvan Bercovitch. — Madison: University of Wisconsin Press, 1978. xvi, 239 p.; 23 cm. 1. American prose literature — History and criticism. 2. Preaching — United States — History. 3. Oratory —

United States — History. 4. Puritans — New England. 5. Christianity and politics — History. 6. United States — Civilization I. T.
PS362.B43   810/.9/38   LC 78-53283   ISBN 0299073505

Brownell, William Crary, 1851-1928.   • **2.10528**
American prose masters: Cooper, Hawthorne, Emerson, Poe, Lowell, Henry James. Edited by Howard Mumford Jones. — Cambridge: Belknap Press of Harvard University Press, 1963. xx, 295 p.; 22 cm. — (The John Harvard library) 1. American prose literature — 19th century — History and criticism. I. T.
PS362.B7 1963   818.309   LC 63-11415

Minter, David L.   **2.10529**
The interpreted design as a structural principle in American prose [by] David L. Minter. — New Haven: Yale University Press, 1969. x, 246 p.; 23 cm. — (Yale publications in American studies, 15) 1. American prose literature — History and criticism. I. T. II. Series.
PS362.M5   810.9   LC 69-15453

Foster, Frances Smith.   **2.10530**
Witnessing slavery: the development of ante–bellum slave narratives / Frances Smith Foster. — Westport, Conn.: Greenwood Press, c1979. xi, 182 p. — (Contributions in Afro-American and African studies. no. 46 0069-9624) Includes index. 1. American prose literature — Afro-American authors — History and criticism. 2. Slavery and slaves in literature 3. Slaves — United States — Biography. 4. Autobiography I. T. II. Series.
PS366.A35 F6   PS366A35 F6.   813/.009/352   LC 78-22137   ISBN 0313208212

Stepto, Robert B.   **2.10531**
From behind the veil: a study of Afro–American narrative / Robert B. Stepto. — Urbana: University of Illinois Press, c1979. xv, 203 p. Includes index. 1. American prose literature — Afro-American authors — History and criticism. 2. Narration (Rhetoric) 3. Autobiography 4. Afro-Americans in literature I. T.
PS366.A35 S7   PS366A35 S7.   813/.009/352   LC 79-11283   ISBN 0252007522

Lindberg, Gary H., 1941-.   **2.10532**
The confidence man in American literature / Gary Lindberg. — New York: Oxford University Press, 1982. x, 319 p.; 24 cm. 1. American prose literature — History and criticism. 2. Swindlers and swindling in literature 3. Swindlers and swindling — United States. 4. United States — Civilization I. T.
PS366.S95 L5   810/.9/355 19   LC 80-29233   ISBN 0195029399

PS371–379 Prose Fiction. The Novel

Åhnebrink, Lars.   • **2.10533**
The beginnings of naturalism in American fiction: a study of the works of Hamlin Garland, Stephen Crane, and Frank Norris; with special reference to some European influences, 1891–1903. — New York: Russell & Russell, 1961. xi, 505 p.; 22 cm. — (Essays and studies on American language and literature, 9) 1. Garland, Hamlin, 1860-1940. 2. Crane, Stephen, 1871-1900. 3. Norris, Frank, 1870-1902. 4. American fiction — History and criticism. I. T.
PS371.A2 1961   813.409   LC 61-13093

Bewley, Marius.   • **2.10534**
The eccentric design; form in the classic American novel. — New York: Columbia University Press, 1959. 327 p.; 23 cm. 1. American fiction — History and criticism. I. T.
PS371.B4   LC 59-13769

Bridgman, Richard.   • **2.10535**
The colloquial style in America. — New York: Oxford University Press, 1966. 254 p.; 22 cm. 1. American fiction — History and criticism. I. T.
PS371.B7 1966   818.0809   LC 66-14473

Chase, Richard Volney, 1914-1962.   • **2.10536**
The American novel and its tradition. — [1st ed.]. — Garden City, N.Y.: Doubleday, 1957. 266 p.; 18 cm. — (Doubleday anchor books, A116) A Doubleday anchor original. 1. American fiction — History and criticism. I. T.
PS371.C5   813.09   LC 57-11412

Cowie, Alexander, 1896-.   • **2.10537**
The rise of the American novel. — New York, American Book Co. [1948] xii, 877 p. 23 cm. — (American literature series) Bibliography: p. 861-862. 1. American fiction — Hist. & crit. I. T.
PS371.C73 1951   813.09   LC 51-2714

Maxwell, D. E. S. (Desmond Ernest Stewart), 1925-.   • **2.10538**
American fiction; the intellectual background. — New York, Columbia University Press, 1963. 306 p. 22 cm. 1. American fiction — Hist. & crit. I. T.
PS371.M3 1963   813.09   LC 63-14926

Stegner, Wallace Earle, 1909- ed. 2.10539
The American novel: from James Fenimore Cooper to William Faulkner. Edited by Wallace Stegner. New York, Basic Books [1965] xiii, 236 p. 22 cm. '[Essays originally] designed ... for oral presentation over the Voice of America.'
1. American fiction — History and criticism. I. T.
PS371.S73 813.03 *LC* 65-14125

Tuttleton, James W. 2.10540
The novel of manners in America, by James W. Tuttleton. — Chapel Hill: University of North Carolina Press, [1972] xiv, 304 p.; 24 cm. 1. American fiction — History and criticism. I. T.
PS371.T9 813/.03 *LC* 70-174787 *ISBN* 0807811882

Wagenknecht, Edward, 1900-. • 2.10541
Cavalcade of the American novel: from the birth of the Nation to the middle of the twentieth century. — New York: Holt, [1952] 575 p.: ill.; 22 cm. 1. American fiction — History and criticism. I. T.
PS371.W3 813.09 *LC* 52-7022

Young, Philip, 1918-. • 2.10542
Three bags full; essays in American fiction. — [1st ed.]. — New York: Harcourt Brace Jovanovich, [1972] xvi, 231 p.; 21 cm. 1. American fiction — Addresses, essays, lectures. I. T.
PS372.Y6 813/.009 *LC* 73-174517 *ISBN* 0151901740

PS374 Fiction: Special Topics, A–Z

PS374 A–L

Umphlett, Wiley Lee, 1931-. 2.10543
The sporting myth and the American experience; studies in contemporary fiction. — Lewisburg [Pa.]: Bucknell University Press, [1974, c1975] 205 p.; 22 cm. 1. American fiction — 20th century — History and criticism. 2. Athletes in literature I. T.
PS374.A85 U5 813/.083 *LC* 73-8306 *ISBN* 0838713637

Dunlap, George Arthur, 1893-. • 2.10544
The city in the American novel, 1789–1900: a study of American novels portraying contemporary conditions in New York, Philadelphia, and Boston / George Arthur Dunlap. — New York: Russell & Russell, 1965. 187 p.; 22 cm. 1. American fiction — History and criticism. 2. Cities and towns in literature 3. Social problems in literature I. T.
PS374.C5 D8 1965 813.093 *LC* 65-17889

Geherin, David, 1943-. 2.10545
The American private eye: the image in fiction / David Geherin. — New York: F. Ungar Pub. Co., c1985. xi, 228 p.; 22 cm. Includes index. 1. Detective and mystery stories, American — History and criticism. 2. Detectives in literature 3. American fiction — 20th century — History and criticism. I. T.
PS374.D4 G39 1985 813/.0872/09 19 *LC* 84-15251 *ISBN* 0804422435

Kramer, John E., 1935-. 2.10546
College mystery novels: an annotated bibliography, including a guide to professional series–character sleuths / John E. Kramer, Jr., John E. Kramer, III. — New York: Garland Pub., 1983. xvii, 356 p.; 22 cm. — (Garland reference library of the humanities. v. 360) Includes indexes. 1. Detective and mystery stories, American — Bibliography. 2. Detective and mystery stories, English — Bibliography. 3. College stories, American — Bibliography. 4. College stories, English — Bibliography. 5. College teachers in literature — Bibliography. 6. Education, Higher, in literature — Bibliography. 7. Bibliography — Books issued in series. I. Kramer, John E. II. T. III. Series.
Z1231.F4 K73 1983 PS374.D4 K73 016.813/0872 19 *LC* 82-48291 *ISBN* 0824092376

Nevins, Francis M. comp. 2.10547
The mystery writer's art / Francis M. Nevins, Jr., editor. — Bowling Green, Ohio: Bowling Green University Popular Press, [c1970]. xii, 338 p.; 24 cm. 1. Detective and mystery stories, American — Addresses, essays, lectures. 2. Detective and mystery stories, English — Addresses, essays, lectures. I. T.
PS374.D4 N4 823/.0872 823.08 *LC* 77-147820

Pronzini, Bill. 2.10548
Gun in cheek / by Bill Pronzini. — New York: Coward, McCann & Geoghegan, c1982. Includes index. 1. Detective and mystery stories, American — History and criticism. 2. Detective and mystery stories, English — History and criticism. 3. Crime and criminals in literature I. T.
PS374.D4 P7 1982 813/.0872/09 19 *LC* 82-5172 *ISBN* 069811180X

May, John R. 2.10549
Toward a new earth; apocalypse in the American novel [by] John R. May. — Notre Dame: University of Notre Dame Press, [1972] ix, 254 p.; 22 cm. 1. American fiction — History and criticism. 2. Eschatology in literature I. T.
PS374.E83 M3 813/.009/35 *LC* 72-3510

Attebery, Brian, 1951-. 2.10550
The fantasy tradition in American literature: from Irving to Le Guin / Brian Attebery. — Bloomington: Indiana University Press, c1980. viii, 212 p.; 25 cm. 1. Fantastic fiction, American — History and criticism. I. T.
PS374.F27 A86 813/.0876/09 19 *LC* 80-7670 *ISBN* 0253356652

Meyer, Roy Willard, 1925-. • 2.10551
The middle western farm novel in the twentieth century, by Roy W. Meyer. — Lincoln, University of Nebraska Press [1965] vii, 265 p. 24 cm. Based on thesis, State University of Iowa. 'An annotated bibliography of middle western farm fiction, 1891-1962': p. 200-242. Bibliography: p. 243-252. 1. American fiction — Middle West — Hist. & crit. 2. American fiction — 20th cent. — Hist. & crit. 3. Farm life in literature I. T.
PS374.F3M4 1965 813.5093 *LC* 64-17221

Rosinsky, Natalie M. (Natalie Myra) 2.10552
Feminist futures—contemporary women's speculative fiction / by Natalie M. Rosinsky. — Ann Arbor, Mich.: UMI Research Press, c1984. 146 p.; 24 cm. — (Studies in speculative fiction. no. 1) Revision of thesis—University of Wisconsin, Madison, 1982. Includes index. 1. American fiction — 20th century — History and criticism. 2. Future in literature 3. Feminism in literature. 4. American fiction — Women authors — History and criticism. 5. Science fiction, American — Women authors — History and criticism. 6. Utopias in literature 7. Sex role in literature I. T. II. Series.
PS374.F86 R6 1984 813/.0876/099287 19 *LC* 84-2762 *ISBN* 0835715787

Henderson, Harry B. 2.10553
Versions of the past: the historical imagination in American fiction / Harry B. Henderson III. — New York: Oxford University Press, 1974. xx, 344 p.; 22 cm. 1. American fiction — History and criticism. 2. Historical fiction, American I. T.
PS374.H5 H46 813/.081 *LC* 74-79624

Leisy, Ernest Erwin, 1887-. • 2.10554
The American historical novel. — [1st ed.]. — Norman: University of Oklahoma Press, c1950. x, 280 p.; 22 cm. 1. American fiction — History and criticism. 2. Historical fiction 3. United States — History — Fiction — Bibliography. 4. United States — History — Fiction I. T.
PS374.H5 L4 813.09 *LC* 50-5331 *ISBN* 0806102012

Austen, Roger. 2.10555
Playing the game: the homosexual novel in America / by Roger Austen. — Indianapolis: Bobbs-Merrill, c1977. xv, 240 p.; 24 cm. Includes index. 1. American fiction — 20th century — History and criticism. 2. Homosexuality in literature 3. Gays' writings, American — History and criticism. I. T.
PS374.H63 A9 813/.5/09352 *LC* 76-46228 *ISBN* 067252287X

Girgus, Sam B., 1941-. 2.10556
The new covenant: Jewish writers and the American idea / Sam B. Girgus. — Chapel Hill: University of North Carolina Press, c1984. xi, 220 p.; 22 cm. Includes index. 1. American fiction — Jewish authors — History and criticism. 2. American fiction — 20th century — History and criticism. 3. Jews in literature 4. Jews — United States — Intellectual life. 5. United States — Civilization — Jewish influences I. T.
PS374.J48 G57 1984 813/.5/098924 19 *LC* 83-12458 *ISBN* 0807815772

Fiedler, Leslie A. • 2.10557
Love and death in the American novel [by] Leslie A. Fiedler. — Rev. ed. — New York: Stein and Day, 1966. 512 p.; 22 cm. 1. American fiction — History and criticism. 2. National characteristics, American 3. Love in literature I. T.
PS374.L6 F5 1966 813.03 *LC* 66-14948

PS374 N–R

Pizer, Donald. 2.10558
Twentieth–century American literary naturalism: an interpretation / by Donald Pizer. — Carbondale: Southern Illinois University Press, c1982. xiii, 171 p.; 22 cm. — (Crosscurrents/modern critiques. New series.) Includes index. 1. American fiction — 20th century — History and criticism. 2. Naturalism in literature I. T. II. Series.
PS374.N29 P5 813/.5/0912 19 *LC* 81-5606 *ISBN* 0809310279

Christian, Barbara. 2.10559
Black women novelists: the development of a tradition, 1892–1976 / Barbara Christian. — Westport, Conn.: Greenwood Press, c1980. xiv, 275 p. — (Contributions in Afro-American and African studies 0069-9624; no. 52)

Includes index. 1. American fiction — Afro-American authors — History and criticism. 2. American fiction — Women authors — History and criticism. 3. American fiction — 20th century — History and criticism. 4. Afro-American women in literature. I. T. II. Series.
PS374.N4 C5   PS374N4 C5.   813/.09/9287   *LC* 79-8953   *ISBN* 031320750X

Rosenblatt, Roger.   **2.10560**
Black fiction / Roger Rosenblatt. — Cambridge, Mass.: Harvard University Press, 1974. 211 p.; 24 cm. Includes index. 1. American fiction — Afro-American authors — History and criticism. I. T.
PS374.N4 R6   813/.009   *LC* 74-81387   *ISBN* 0674076206

Singh, Amritjit.   **2.10561**
The novels of the Harlem renaissance: twelve black writers, 1923–1933 / Amritjit Singh. — University Park: Pennsylvania State University Press, 1976. 175 p. Includes index. 1. American fiction — Afro-American authors — History and criticism. 2. American fiction — 20th century — History and criticism. 3. Afro-Americans in literature I. T.
PS374.N4 S5   PS374N4 S5.   813/.03   *LC* 75-27170   *ISBN* 0271012080

Tischler, Nancy Marie Patterson.   ● **2.10562**
Black masks: negro characters in modern Southern fiction / [by] Nancy M. Tischler. — University Park: Pennsylvania State University Press, [1969] 223 p.; 23 cm. 1. Negroes in literature. 2. American fiction — Southern States — History and criticism. 3. American fiction — 20th century — History and criticism. I. T.
PS374.N4 T5   *LC* 68-8187

Zavarzadeh, Mas'ud, 1938-.   **2.10563**
The mythopoeic reality: the postwar American nonfiction novel / Mas'ud Zavarzadeh. Urbana: University of Illinois Press, 1977 (c1976). ix, 262 p.; 24 cm. Includes index. 1. Nonfiction novel 2. American fiction — 20th century — History and criticism. I. T.
PS374.N6 Z3   818/.5/407   *LC* 76-49509   *ISBN* 0252005236

Blotner, Joseph Leo, 1923-.   ● **2.10564**
The modern American political novel, 1900–1960, by Joseph Blotner. — Austin: University of Texas Press, [1966] x, 424 p.; 24 cm. 1. American fiction — 20th century — History and criticism. 2. Political fiction, American — History and criticism. 3. Politics in literature I. T.
PS374.P6 B55   813.5093   *LC* 65-27533

Rosenberg, Betty.   **2.10565**
Genreflecting: a guide to reading interests in genre fiction / Betty Rosenberg. — 2nd ed. — Littleton, Colo.: Libraries Unlimited, 1986. xxviii, 298 p.; 25 cm. Includes indexes. 1. American fiction — Stories, plots, etc. 2. English fiction — Stories, plots, etc. 3. Popular literature — United States. 4. Reading interests 5. Fiction — Bibliography. 6. Fiction — Handbooks, manuals, etc. I. T.
PS374.P63 R67 1986   016.813/009 19   *LC* 86-21489   *ISBN* 087287530X

American realism: new essays / edited by Eric J. Sundquist.   **2.10566**
Baltimore: Johns Hopkins University Press, c1982. ix, 298 p.; 24 cm. 1. American fiction — History and criticism — Addresses, essays, lectures. 2. Realism in literature — Addresses, essays, lectures. I. Sundquist, Eric J.
PS374.R37 A47 1982   813/.009/12 19   *LC* 82-3010   *ISBN* 0801827965

Cady, Edwin Harrison.   ● **2.10567**
The light of common day; realism in American fiction [by] Edwin H. Cady. — Bloomington: Indiana University Press, [1971] 224 p.; 22 cm. 1. Realism in literature 2. American fiction — 19th century — Addresses, essays, lectures. I. T.
PS374.R37 C3   813/.00912   *LC* 70-159725   *ISBN* 0253334306

Habegger, Alfred.   **2.10568**
Gender, fantasy, and realism in American literature / Alfred Habegger. — New York: Columbia University Press, 1982. xiii, 378 p.; 24 cm. 1. Howells, William Dean, 1837-1920 — Criticism and interpretation. 2. James, Henry, 1843-1916 — Criticism and interpretation. 3. Sex role in literature 4. Fantasy in literature 5. American fiction — 19th century — History and criticism. 6. Realism in literature 7. Women and literature — United States. I. T.
PS374.R37 H3 1982   813/.4/0912 19   *LC* 82-1239   *ISBN* 0231053967

Kort, Wesley A.   **2.10569**
Shriven selves: religious problems in recent American fiction / [by] Wesley A. Kort. — Philadelphia: Fortress Press, [1972] x, 149 p.; 21 cm. 1. American fiction — 20th century — History and criticism. 2. Religion in literature I. T.
PS374.R47 K6   813/.03   *LC* 78-171499   *ISBN* 0800604083

Reynolds, David S., 1949-.   **2.10570**
Faith in fiction: the emergence of religious literature in America / David S. Reynolds. — Cambridge, Mass.: Harvard University Press, 1981. 269 p.; 24 cm. Includes index. 1. American fiction — 19th century — History and criticism. 2. Religion in literature I. T.
PS374.R47 R49   813/.009/382 19   *LC* 80-20885   *ISBN* 0674291727

PS374 S–T

Clareson, Thomas D.   **2.10571**
Some kind of paradise: the emergence of American science fiction / Thomas D. Clareson. — Westport, Conn.: Greenwood Press, 1985. xiv, 248 p.; 24 cm. (Contributions to the study of science fiction and fantasy. 0193-6875; no. 16) Includes index. 1. Science fiction, American — History and criticism. 2. American fiction — 20th century — History and criticism. I. T. II. Series.
PS374.S35 C56 1985   813/.0876 19   *LC* 84-29060   *ISBN* 0313231672

Ketterer, David.   **2.10572**
New worlds for old: the apocalyptic imagination, science fiction, and American literature. — Bloomington: Indiana University Press, [1974] xii, 347 p.; 22 cm. 1. Science fiction, American — History and criticism. I. T.
PS374.S35 K4   813/.0876   *LC* 73-16717   *ISBN* 0253340527

Science fiction writers: critical studies of the major authors   **2.10573**
from the early nineteenth century to the present day / E.F. Bleiler, editor.
New York: Scribner, c1982. xv, 623 p.; 29 cm. 1. Science fiction, American — History and criticism. 2. Science fiction, English — History and criticism. 3. Science fiction, American — Bio-bibliography. 4. Science fiction, English — Bio-bibliography. I. Bleiler, Everett Franklin, 1920-
PS374.S35 S36 1982   823/.0876/09 19   *LC* 81-51032   *ISBN* 0684167409

Wolfe, Gary K., 1946-.   **2.10574**
The known and the unknown: the iconography of science fiction / Gary K. Wolfe. — Kent, Ohio: Kent State University Press, c1979. xvii, 250 p.; 24 cm. 1. Science fiction, American — History and criticism. 2. Science fiction, English — History and criticism. I. T.
PS374.S35 W6   823/.0876   *LC* 79-88606   *ISBN* 0873382315

The American short story, 1900–1945: a critical history / Philip   **2.10575**
Stevick, editor.
Boston, Mass.: Twayne Publishers, 1984. xi, 209 p.; 23 cm. — (Twayne's critical history of the short story.) 1. Short stories, American — History and criticism. 2. American fiction — 20th century — History and criticism. I. Stevick, Philip. II. Series.
PS374.S5 A366 1984   813/.01/09 19   *LC* 84-641   *ISBN* 0805793534

The American short story, 1945–1980: a critical history /   **2.10576**
Gordon Weaver, editor.
Boston: Twayne, 1983. 150 p.; 23 cm. — (Twayne's critical history of the short story.) Includes index. 1. Short stories, American — History and criticism. 2. American fiction — 20th century — History and criticism. I. Weaver, Gordon. II. Series.
PS374.S5 A37 1983   813/.01/09 19   *LC* 82-23423   *ISBN* 080579350X

Bone, Robert A.   **2.10577**
Down home: a history of Afro–American short fiction from its beginnings to the end of the Harlem Renaissance / by Robert Bone. — New York: Putnam, [1975] xxii, 328 p.; 22 cm. (New perspectives on Black America) Includes index. 1. Short stories, American — History and criticism. 2. American fiction — Negro authors — History and criticism. 3. Pastoral fiction, American — History and criticism. 4. Southern States in literature. I. T. II. Series.
PS374.S5 B6   PS374S5 B6.   813/.01   *LC* 75-19111   *ISBN* 0399116028

Gerlach, John C.   **2.10578**
Toward the end: closure and structure in the American short story / John Gerlach. — University, Ala.: University of Alabama Press, c1985. ix, 193 p.; 22 cm. Includes index. 1. Short stories, American — History and criticism. 2. Fiction — Technique 3. Plots (Drama, novel, etc.) I. T.
PS374.S5 G37 1985   813/.01/09 19   *LC* 84-2509   *ISBN* 0817302344

Pattee, Fred Lewis, 1863-1950.   ● **2.10579**
The development of the American short story: an historical survey / by Fred Lewis Pattee. — New York: Harper, 1923. v, 388 p.; 21 cm. 1. Short story I. T.
PS374.S5 P3   813.01   *LC* 23-4306

Peden, William Harwood, 1913-. • **2.10580**
The American short story; front line in the national defense of literature, by William Peden. — Boston: Houghton Mifflin, 1964. viii, 213 p.; 22 cm. 1. Short stories, American — History and criticism. 2. American fiction — 20th century — History and criticism. I. T.
PS374.S5 P4 813.509 LC 64-17360

West, Ray Benedict, 1908-. • **2.10581**
The short story in America. — Chicago: Gateway Editions; distributed by H. Regnery Co., 1956, c1952. 128 p. — (A Gateway edition; 6037) 1. Short stories, American — History and criticism. I. T.
PS374.S5 W4 LC 56-14026

Kaul, A. N. • **2.10582**
The American vision; actual and ideal society in nineteenth–century fiction. — New Haven: Yale University Press, 1963. xi, 340 p.; 23 cm. — (Yale publications in American studies, 7) 1. American fiction — 19th century — History and criticism. 2. Social problems in literature I. T. II. Series.
PS374.S7 K3 1963 813.309 LC 63-9309

Taylor, Walter Fuller, 1900-. • **2.10583**
The economic novel in America. — New York: Octagon Books, 1964 [c1942] xi, 378 p.; 24 cm. 1. American fiction — 19th century — History and criticism. 2. Social problems in literature 3. United States — Social conditions I. T.
PS374.S7 T35 1964 813.4093 LC 64-24845

Tompkins, Jane P. **2.10584**
Sensational designs: the cultural work of American fiction, 1790–1860 / Jane Tompkins. — New York: Oxford University Press, 1985. xix, 236 p.; 22 cm. Includes index. 1. American fiction — 19th century — History and criticism. 2. American fiction — 18th century — History and criticism. 3. Social problems in literature 4. Literature and society — United States. I. T.
PS374.S7 T66 1985 813/.2/09355 19 LC 85-4925 ISBN 0195035658

Berman, Neil David, 1947-. **2.10585**
Playful fictions and fictional players: game, sport, and survival in contemporary American fiction / Neil David Berman. — Port Washington, N.Y.: Kennikat Press, 1981. 112 p.; 23 cm. — (Literary criticism series) (National university publications) Includes index. 1. American fiction — 20th century — History and criticism. 2. Sports in literature 3. Play in literature I. T.
PS374.S76 B4 813/.54/09355 19 LC 80-20230 ISBN 0804692653

Messenger, Christian K., 1943-. **2.10586**
Sport and the spirit of play in American fiction: Hawthorne to Faulkner / Christian K. Messenger. — New York: Columbia University Press, 1981. xv, 369 p.; 24 cm. 1. American fiction — History and criticism. 2. Sports in literature 3. Athletes in literature 4. Play in literature 5. Sports stories — History and criticism. I. T.
PS374.S76 M4 813/.009/355 19 LC 81-4843 ISBN 0231051689

The Haunted dusk: American supernatural fiction, 1820–1920 / **2.10587**
edited by Howard Kerr, John W. Crowley, and Charles L. Crow.
Athens, Ga.: University of Georgia Press, c1983. vi, 236 p.: ill.; 24 cm. 1. American fiction — History and criticism — Addresses, essays, lectures. 2. Supernatural in literature — Addresses, essays, lectures. 3. Occultism in literature — Addresses, essays, lectures. 4. Ghost stories, American — History and criticism — Addresses, essays, lectures. I. Kerr, Howard. II. Crowley, John William, 1945- III. Crow, Charles L.
PS374.S83 H3 1983 813/.0872/09 19 LC 82-7011 ISBN 0820306304

Lenz, William E. **2.10588**
Fast talk & flush times: the confidence man as a literary convention / William E. Lenz. — Columbia: University of Missouri Press, 1985. 237 p.; 23 cm. Includes index. 1. American fiction — 19th century — History and criticism. 2. Trickster in literature 3. Deception in literature 4. Swindlers and swindling in literature I. T. II. Title: Fast talk and flush times.
PS374.T7 L46 1985 813/.3/09355 19 LC 84-2200 ISBN 0826204503

Wadlington, Warwick, 1938-. **2.10589**
The confidence game in American literature / Warwick Wadlington. — Princeton, N.J.: Princeton University Press, [1975] xii, 331 p.; 23 cm. Includes index. 1. American fiction — History and criticism. 2. Trickster in literature 3. Deception in literature I. T.
PS374.T7 W3 813/.009 LC 75-3480 ISBN 0691062943

PS374 U–Z

Lyons, John Ormsby, 1927-. • **2.10590**
The college novel in America / with a pref. by Harry T. Moore. — Carbondale: Southern Illinois University Press [1962] 208 p.; 22 cm. (Crosscurrents:

Modern critiques) 1. Universities and colleges in literature 2. American fiction — History and criticism. I. T. II. Series.
PS374.U52 L9 813.09 LC 62-17619

Women and utopia: critical interpretations / edited by Marleen **2.10591**
Barr, Nicholas D. Smith.
Lanham, Md.: University Press of America, c1983. 171 p.; 23 cm. 1. Lessing, Doris May, 1919- — Criticism and interpretation — Addresses, essays, lectures. 2. Utopias in literature — Addresses, essays, lectures. 3. American fiction — Women authors — History and criticism — Addresses, essays, lectures. 4. Women in literature — Addresses, essays, lectures. 5. Sex role in literature — Addresses, essays, lectures. 6. Feminism and literature — Addresses, essays, lectures. 7. American fiction — History and criticism — Addresses, essays, lectures. I. Barr, Marleen S. II. Smith, Nicholas D.
PS374.U8 W65 1983 813/.009/372 19 LC 83-16920 ISBN 0819135585

Critical essays on the western American novel / William T. **2.10592**
Pilkington.
Boston, Mass.: G.K. Hall, c1980. xviii, 275 p.; 24 cm. (Critical essays on American literature.) 1. Western stories — History and criticism — Addresses, essays, lectures. 2. American fiction — West (U.S.) — History and criticism — Addresses, essays, lectures. I. Pilkington, William T. II. Series.
PS374.W4 C7 1980 813/.0874/09 LC 80-18223 ISBN 0816183511

Fiedler, Leslie A. • **2.10593**
The return of the vanishing American, by Leslie A. Fiedler. New York, Stein and Day [1968] 192 p. 22 cm. 1. American fiction — History and criticism. 2. West (U.S.) in literature. I. T.
PS374.W4 F5 813/.0093 LC 68-15433

Folsom, James K. • **2.10594**
The American western novel, by James K. Folsom. — New Haven, College & University Press [1966] 224 p. 21 cm. Bibliography: p. 213-220. 1. American fiction — Hist. & crit. 2. The West in literature. I. T.
PS374.W4F6 813.0874 LC 66-14825

American novelists revisited: essays in feminist criticism / **2.10595**
edited by Fritz Fleischmann.
Boston, Mass.: G.K. Hall, c1982. 415 p.; 24 cm. (Publication in women's studies.) 1. American fiction — History and criticism — Addresses, essays, lectures. 2. Women in literature — Addresses, essays, lectures. 3. Feminist literary criticism — Addresses, essays, lectures. 4. Feminism in literature — Addresses, essays, lectures. I. Fleischmann, Fritz, 1950- II. Series.
PS374.W6 A45 1982 813/.009 19 LC 82-6097 ISBN 0816190445

Fetterley, Judith, 1938-. **2.10596**
The resisting reader: a feminist approach to American fiction / Judith Fetterley. — Bloomington: Indiana University Press, c1978. xxvi, 198 p.; 21 cm. 1. American fiction — History and criticism. 2. Women in literature 3. Feminist literary criticism I. T.
PS374.W6 F4 813/.009/352042 LC 78-3242 ISBN 0253310784

Fryer, Judith, 1939-. **2.10597**
The faces of Eve: women in the nineteenth century American novel / Judith Fryer. — New York: Oxford University Press, 1976. x, 294 p., [3] leaves of plates: ill.; 22 cm. Includes index. 1. American fiction — 19th century — History and criticism. 2. Women in literature I. T.
PS374.W6 F7 813/.009/352 LC 75-32345 ISBN 0195020251

Huf, Linda. **2.10598**
A portrait of the artist as a young woman: the writer as heroine in American literature / Linda Huf. — New York: F. Ungar Pub. Co., c1983. 196 p.: ports.; 22 cm. Includes index. 1. American fiction — Women authors — History and criticism. 2. Women artists in literature. 3. Women authors in literature. I. T.
PS374.W6 H78 1983 813/.009/9287 19 LC 82-40263 ISBN 0804424063

Jones, Anne Goodwyn. **2.10599**
Tomorrow is another day: the woman writer in the South, 1859–1936 / Anne Goodwyn Jones. — Baton Rouge: Louisiana State University Press, c1981. xvii, 413 p.: ill.; 24 cm. Includes index. 1. American fiction — Women authors — History and criticism. 2. American fiction — Southern States — History and criticism. 3. Women in literature 4. Southern States in literature. 5. Women authors, American — Southern States. I. T.
PS374.W6 J6 813/.4/099287 19 LC 80-29123 ISBN 080710776X

Stewart, Grace. **2.10600**
A new mythos: the novel of the artist as heroine, 1877–1977 / Grace Stewart. — St. Alban's, Vt.: Eden Press, c1979. 200 p.; 22 cm. — (Monographs in women's studies.) 1. American fiction — Women authors — History and criticism. 2. Women artists in literature. 3. English fiction — Women authors — History and criticism. I. T. II. Series.
PS374.W6 S76 813/.03 LC 78-74840 ISBN 0888310307

Westling, Louise Hutchings. • **2.10601**
Sacred groves and ravaged gardens: the fiction of Eudora Welty, Carson McCullers, and Flannery O'Connor / Louise Westling. — Athens: University of Georgia Press, c1985. xi, 217 p.: ill.; 24 cm. Includes index. 1. Welty, Eudora, 1909- — Criticism and interpretation. 2. McCullers, Carson, 1917-1967 — Criticism and interpretation. 3. O'Connor, Flannery — Criticism and interpretation. 4. American fiction — 20th century — History and criticism. 5. Women in literature 6. American fiction — Women authors — History and criticism. 7. American fiction — Southern States — History and criticism. 8. Southern States in literature. 9. Landscape in literature. I. T.
PS374.W6 W4 1985   813/.5/099287 19   *LC* 84-16434   *ISBN* 0820307467

Witham, W. Tasker. • **2.10602**
The adolescent in the American novel, 1920–1960. — New York: Ungar, [1964] vi, 345 p.; 24 cm. 1. Youth in literature 2. American fiction — 20th century — History and criticism. I. T.
PS374.Y6 W5   813.5093   *LC* 63-8849

PS375–379 History of Fiction, by Period

Petter, Henri. • **2.10603**
The early American novel / by Henri Petter. — [Columbus]: Ohio State University Press, [1971] xiii, 500 p.; 25 cm. 1. American fiction — 18th century — History and criticism. I. T.
PS375.P4   813/.03   *LC* 73-114737   *ISBN* 0814201458

Spiller, Robert, 1896-. • **2.10604**
The American literary revolution, 1783–1837, edited with a pref. and explanatory notes by Robert E. Spiller. — Garden City, N.Y.: Anchor Books, 1967. x, 500 p.; 18 cm. — (Documents in American civilization series) 1. American prose literature — Revolutionary period. I. T. II. Series.
PS375.S65   810.9/002/08   *LC* 67-12851

Bell, Michael Davitt. **2.10605**
The development of American romance: the sacrifice of relation / Michael Davitt Bell. — Chicago: University of Chicago Press, 1981 (c1980). xiv, 291 p.; 24 cm. Includes index. 1. American fiction — 19th century — History and criticism. 2. Romanticism — United States. I. T.
PS377.B4   813/.2/09   *LC* 80-12241   *ISBN* 0226042111

Brown, Herbert Ross, 1902-. • **2.10606**
The sentimental novel in America, 1789–1860. — Freeport, N.Y.: Books for Libraries Press, [1970] ix, 407 p.; 23 cm. — (Essay index reprint series) 'First published in 1940.' 1. American fiction — 19th century — History and criticism. 2. Sentimentalism in literature 3. National characteristics, American I. T.
PS377.B7 1970   813/.03   *LC* 75-107685   *ISBN* 0836914902

Fisher, Philip, 1941-. **2.10607**
Hard facts: setting and form in the American novel / Philip Fisher. — New York: Oxford University Press, 1985. vii, 191 p.; 22 cm. 1. American fiction — 19th century — History and criticism. 2. Popular literature — United States — History and criticism. 3. Setting (Literature) 4. Historical fiction, American 5. Sentimentalism in literature 6. Slavery and slaves in literature 7. Naturalism in literature 8. Cities and towns in literature I. T.
PS377.F55 1985   813/.009 19   *LC* 84-18999   *ISBN* 0195035283

Hoffman, Daniel, 1923-. **2.10608**
Form and fable in American fiction. New York, Norton [1973, c1961] xvi, 368 p. 20 cm. (The Norton library, N673) 1. American fiction — 19th century — History and criticism. 2. Literature and folklore — United States. 3. Folklore in literature — United States. I. T.
PS377.H6 1973   813/.3/09   *LC* 72-12502   *ISBN* 0393006735

Pizer, Donald. **2.10609**
Realism and naturalism in nineteenth–century American literature / Donald Pizer. — Rev. ed. — Carbondale: Southern Illinois University Press, c1984. xiv, 227 p.; 23 cm. — (Crosscurrents/modern critiques/new series) Includes index. 1. American fiction — 19th century — History and criticism — Addresses, essays, lectures. 2. Realism in literature — Addresses, essays, lectures. 3. Naturalism in literature — Addresses, essays, lectures. I. T.
PS377.P5 1984   810/.9/12 19   *LC* 83-20406   *ISBN* 0809311259

Smith, Henry Nash. **2.10610**
Democracy and the novel: popular resistance to classic American writers / Henry Nash Smith. — New York: Oxford University Press, 1978. viii, 204 p.; 22 cm. 1. American fiction — 19th century — History and criticism. 2. Literature and society 3. United States — Popular culture I. T.
PS377.S55   813/.03   *LC* 78-1290   *ISBN* 0195023978

PS379 20th Century

PS379 A–J

Aldridge, John W. • **2.10611**
After the lost generation; a critical study of the writers of two wars. — New York, Noonday Press [1958] 263 p. 21 cm. 1. American fiction — 20th cent. — Hist. & crit. I. T.
PS379.A5 1958   813.509   *LC* 58-4468

Avery, Evelyn Gross, 1940-. **2.10612**
Rebels and victims: the fiction of Richard Wright and Bernard Malamud / Evelyn Gross Avery. — Port Washington, N.Y.: Kennikat Press, 1979. x, 116 p.; 23 cm. (Literary criticism series) (National university publications) Includes index. 1. Wright, Richard, 1908-1960 — Criticism and interpretation. 2. Malamud, Bernard — Criticism and interpretation. 3. American fiction — 20th century — History and criticism. 4. Afro-Americans in literature 5. Jews in literature 6. Victims in literature I. T.
PS379.A9   813/.5/09 19   *LC* 79-4362   *ISBN* 0804692343

Beach, Joseph Warren, 1880-1957. • **2.10613**
American fiction, 1920–1940: John Dos Passos, Ernest Hemingway, William Faulkner, Thomas Wolfe, Erskine Caldwell, James T. Farrell, John P. Marquand [and] John Steinbeck. New York, Russell & Russell, 1960 [c1941] 371 p. 22 cm. 1. American fiction — 20th century — History and criticism. 2. Novelists, American — 20th century. I. T.
PS379.B38 1960   813.5209   *LC* 60-8197

Bradbury, Malcolm, 1932-. **2.10614**
The modern American novel / Malcolm Bradbury. — Oxford [Oxfordshire]; New York: Oxford University Press, 1983. viii, 209 p.; 22 cm. — (OPUS) Includes index. 1. American fiction — 20th century — History and criticism. I. T. II. Series.
PS379.B67 1983   813/.5/09 19   *LC* 82-12567   *ISBN* 0192125915

Cowley, Malcolm, 1898-. **2.10615**
A second flowering; works and days of the lost generation. — New York: Viking Press, [1973] x, 276 p.: illus.; 22 cm. 1. Authors, American — 20th century. 2. American literature — 20th century — Addresses, essays, lectures. I. T.
PS379.C7   813/.5/209   *LC* 72-78992   *ISBN* 0670628263

Eisinger, Chester E. • **2.10616**
Fiction of the forties. — Chicago: University of Chicago Press, [1963] 392 p.; 23 cm. 1. American fiction — 20th century — History and criticism. I. T.
PS379.E4   813.509   *LC* 63-20904

Frohock, W. M. (Wilbur Merrill), 1908-. • **2.10617**
The novel of violence in America. — [2d ed., rev. and enl.]. — Dallas: Southern Methodist University Press, [1958, c1957] 238 p.; 24 cm. First ed. published in 1950 under title: The novel of violence in America, 1920-1950. 1. American fiction — 20th century — History and criticism. I. T.
PS379.F7 1958   813.509   *LC* 57-14767

Galloway, David D. **2.10618**
The absurd hero in American fiction: Updike, Styron, Bellow, Salinger / by David Galloway. — 2nd rev. ed. — Austin: University of Texas Press, c1981. xv, 265 p.; 24 cm. Includes index. 1. American fiction — 20th century — History and criticism. 2. Heroes in literature 3. Absurd (Philosophy) in literature I. T.
PS379.G24 1981   813/.54/09352 19   *LC* 80-54119   *ISBN* 0292703562

Geismar, Maxwell David, 1909-. • **2.10619**
American moderns, from rebellion to conformity. — New York: Hill and Wang, [1958] 265 p.; 21 cm. 'A collection of articles and reviews written in the nineteen-forties and fifties.' 1. American fiction — 20th century — History and criticism. I. T.
PS379.G35   813.509   *LC* 58-8403

Geismar, Maxwell David, 1909-. • **2.10620**
The last of the provincials; the American novel, 1915–1925: H. L. Mencken, Sinclair Lewis, Willa Cather, Sherwood Anderson, F. Scott Fitzgerald. [2d ed.] Boston, Houghton Mifflin [c1949] xi, 404 p. 22 cm. Bibliography: p. [379]-[389] 1. American fiction — 20th century — History and criticism. I. T.
PS379.G36 1949   813.509   *LC* 50-5185

Geismar, Maxwell David, 1909-. • **2.10621**
Rebels and ancestors: the American novel, 1890–1915: Frank Norris, Stephen Crane, Jack London, Ellen Glasgow [and] Theodore Dreiser. — Boston: Houghton Mifflin, 1953. xii, 435 p.; 22 cm. — (His The novel in America) 1. American fiction — 20th century — History & criticism. 2. American fiction — 19th century — History & criticism. I. T.
PS379.G38   813.409   *LC* 53-5730

Geismar, Maxwell David, 1909-. • 2.10622
Writers in crisis; the American novel, 1925–1940: Ring Lardner, Ernest Hemingway, John Dos Passos, William Faulkner, Thomas Wolfe, John Steinbeck. — New York: Hill and Wang [1961] 308 p.; 21 cm. (American century series, AC38) 1. American fiction — 20th century — History and criticism. I. T.
PS379.G4 1961   *LC* 61-9966

Harper, Howard M. • 2.10623
Desperate faith; a study of Bellow, Salinger, Mailer, Baldwin, and Updike [by] Howard M. Harper, Jr. Chapel Hill, University of North Carolina Press [1967] 200 p. 1. American fiction — 20th century — History & criticism I. T.
PS379 H27   *LC* 67-17034

Harris, Charles B. • 2.10624
Contemporary American novelists of the absurd, by Charles B. Harris. — New Haven, Conn.: College & University Press, [c1971] 159 p.; 21 cm. 1. American fiction — 20th century — History and criticism. I. T.
PS379.H28   813/.03   *LC* 70-147308

Hassan, Ihab Habib, 1925-. • 2.10625
Radical innocence, studies in the contemporary American novel. — Princeton, N.J.: Princeton University Press, 1961. 362 p.; 23 cm. 1. American fiction — 20th century — History and criticism. I. T.
PS379.H32   813.509   *LC* 61-7416

Hatcher, Harlan Henthorne, 1898-. • 2.10626
Creating the modern American novel / by Harlan Hatcher. — New York: Russell & Russell, 1965, [c1962] x, 307 p.; 23 cm. 1. American fiction — 20th cent. — History and criticism. 2. Novelists, American I. T.
PS379.H34 1962   813/.509   *LC* 65-17899

Hicks, Granville, 1901-. • 2.10627
The Living novel: a symposium / edited by Granville Hicks. — New York: Macmillan, 1957. xii, 230 p.; 22 cm. 1. American fiction — History and criticism — Addresses, essays, lectures. I. Hicks, Granville. II. T.
PS379.H5   813.504   *LC* 57-12221

Hoffman, Frederick John. • 2.10628
The modern novel in America, 1900–1950. — Chicago: Regnery, 1951. viii, 216 p.; 22 cm. — (Twentieth-century literature in America) 1. American fiction — 20th century — History and criticism. I. T.
PS379.H6   813.509   *LC* 51-13723

PS379 K–Z

Karl, Frederick Robert, 1927-. 2.10629
American fictions, 1940–1980: a comprehensive history and critical evaluation / Frederick R. Karl. — 1st ed. — New York: Harper & Row, c1983. xiv, 637 p.; 25 cm. 1. American fiction — 20th century — History and criticism. I. T.
PS379.K24 1983   813/.54/09 19   *LC* 81-47659   *ISBN* 0060149396

Kazin, Alfred, 1915-. 2.10630
Bright book of life: American novelists and storytellers from Hemingway to Mailer. — [1st ed.]. — Boston: Little, Brown, [1973] 334 p.; 22 cm. 'An Atlantic Monthly Press book.' 1. American fiction — 20th century — History and criticism. I. T.
PS379.K25 1973   813/.5/209   *LC* 72-13748   *ISBN* 0316484180

Kazin, Alfred, 1915-. • 2.10631
On native grounds, an interpretation of modern American prose literature. — [Abridged, with a new postscript]. — Garden City, N.Y.: Doubleday, 1956. 425 p.; 18 cm. — (Doubleday anchor books, A69) 1. American prose literature — 20th century — History and criticism. I. T.
PS379.K3 1956   810.9   *LC* 56-5972

Kennard, Jean E., 1936-. 2.10632
Number and nightmare, forms of fantasy in contemporary fiction / Jean E. Kennard. — Hamden, Conn.: Archon Books, 1975. 244 p.; 22 cm. Includes index. 1. American fiction — 20th century — History and criticism. 2. English fiction — 20th century — History and criticism. 3. Existentialism in literature I. T.
PS379.K4   823/.9/1409   *LC* 74-28448   *ISBN* 0208014861

Klein, Marcus. • 2.10633
After alienation; American novels in mid–century. — Freeport, N.Y.: Books for Libraries Press, [1970, c1964] 307 p.; 23 cm. — (Essay index reprint series) 1. American fiction — 20th century — History and criticism. I. T.
PS379.K5 1970   813/.5/09   *LC* 70-128267   *ISBN* 0836919696

Klinkowitz, Jerome. 2.10634
Literary disruptions: the making of a post–contemporary American fiction / Jerome Klinkowitz. — Urbana: University of Illinois Press, [1975] x, 241 p.; 24 cm. 1. American fiction — 20th century — History and criticism. I. T.
PS379.K55   813/.5/409   *LC* 75-4806   *ISBN* 0252005147

Klinkowitz, Jerome. 2.10635
The self–apparent word: fiction as language/language as fiction / Jerome Klinkowitz. — Carbondale: Southern Illinois University Press, c1984. x, 153 p.; 23 cm. 1. American fiction — 20th century — History and criticism. I. T.
PS379.K553 1984   813/.54/09 19   *LC* 83-20071   *ISBN* 080931164X

Madden, David, 1933-. 2.10636
Tough guy writers of the thirties, edited by David Madden. With a pref. by Harry T. Moore. Carbondale, Southern Illinois University Press [1968] xxxix, 247 p. 22 cm. (Crosscurrents: modern critiques) 1. American fiction — 20th century — History and criticism — Addresses, essays, lectures. 2. Violence in literature — Addresses, essays, lectures. 3. Detective and mystery stories, American — History and criticism — Addresses, essays, lectures. I. T.
PS379.M26   813/.5/209   *LC* 68-10115

Malin, Irving. • 2.10637
New American Gothic. With a pref. by Harry T. Moore. — Carbondale: Southern Illinois University Press, [1962] 175 p.; 22 cm. — (Crosscurrents, modern critiques) 1. American fiction — 20th century — History and criticism. I. T.
PS379.M28   813.5409   *LC* 62-15005

Millgate, Michael. • 2.10638
American social fiction, James to Cozzens. — New York: Barnes & Noble, [1964] x, 217 p.; 23 cm. 1. American fiction — 20th century — History and criticism. 2. American fiction — 19th century — History and criticism. 3. Social problems in literature I. T.
PS379.M48   813.093   *LC* 64-5659

Newman, Charles Hamilton, 1938-. 2.10639
The post–modern aura: the act of fiction in an age of inflation / by Charles Newman; with a preface by Gerald Graff. — Evanston: Northwestern University Press, 1985. iii, 203 p. 1. American fiction — 20th century — History and criticism 2. American literature — 20th century — History and criticism I. T. II. Title: The act of fiction in an age of inflation
PS379 N48 1985   *LC* 84-61438   *ISBN* 081010668X

Olderman, Raymond M. • 2.10640
Beyond the waste land: a study of the American novel in the nineteen–sixties / by Raymond M. Olderman. — New Haven: Yale University Press, 1972. xi, 258 p.; 22 cm. 1. American fiction — 20th century — History and criticism. I. T.
PS379.O5   813/.03   *LC* 73-182210   *ISBN* 0300015437

Pearce, Richard, 1932-. 2.10641
The novel in motion: an approach to modern fiction / Richard Pearce. — Columbus: Ohio State University Press, c1983. xiv, 155 p.; 24 cm. 1. American fiction — 20th century — History and criticism. 2. English fiction — 20th century — History and criticism. I. T.
PS379.P36 1983   813/.5/09 19   *LC* 82-24565   *ISBN* 0814203450

Rideout, Walter Bates. • 2.10642
The radical novel in the United States, 1900–1954: some interrelations of literature and society. — Cambridge: Harvard University Press, 1956. 339 p.; 24 cm. 'The first version ... was written as a doctoral dissertation [Harvard University, under title: The proletarian novel in the United States]' 1. American fiction — 20th century — History and criticism. 2. Social problems in literature 3. Politics in literature 4. United States — Civilization — 20th century I. T.
PS379.R5   813.509   *LC* 56-10162

Searles, George J. (George John), 1944-. 2.10643
The fiction of Philip Roth and John Updike / George J. Searles. — Carbondale [Ill.]: Southern Illinois University Press, c1985. ix, 197 p.; 23 cm. — (Crosscurrents/modern critiques/new series) Includes index. 1. Roth, Philip — Criticism and interpretation. 2. Updike, John — Criticism and interpretation. 3. American fiction — 20th century — History and criticism. I. T.
PS379.S398 1985   813/.54/09 19   *LC* 84-1269   *ISBN* 0809311755

Tanner, Tony. • 2.10644
City of words: American fiction, 1950–1970. — [1st U.S. ed.]. — New York: Harper & Row, [1971] 463 p.; 22 cm. 1. American fiction — 20th century — History and criticism. I. T.
PS379.T3   813/.03   *LC* 70-156554   *ISBN* 0060142170

Von Hallberg, Robert, 1946-. 2.10645
American poetry and culture, 1945–1980 / Robert von Hallberg. — Cambridge, Mass.: Harvard University Press, 1985. 276 p.; 24 cm. Includes index. 1. Creeley, Robert, 1926- — Criticism and interpretation. 2. Merrill, James Ingram — Criticism and interpretation. 3. Lowell, Robert, 1917-1977 — Criticism and interpretation. 4. Dorn, Edward — Criticism and interpretation. 5. American poetry — 20th century — History and criticism. 6. Literature and society — United States. I. T.
PS379.V58 1985   811/.54/09 19   *LC* 84-22387   *ISBN* 0674030117

Walcutt, Charles Child, 1908-. • 2.10646
American literary naturalism, a divided stream. — Minneapolis: University of
Minnesota Press, [c1956] 332 p.; 23 cm. 1. American fiction — 20th century —
History and criticism. 2. Naturalism in literature I. T.
PS379.W28   813.509   LC 56-12465

Weinberg, Helen. • 2.10647
The new novel in America; the Kafkan mode in contemporary fiction. —
Ithaca, N.Y.: Cornell University Press, [1970] xvii, 248 p.; 22 cm. 1. Kafka,
Franz, 1883-1924. 2. American fiction — 20th century — History and
criticism. 3. Heroes in literature I. T.
PS379.W39   813/.5/409   LC 70-87011   ISBN 0801405378

Wright, Austin McGiffert, 1922-. • 2.10648
The American short story in the twenties. — [Chicago]: University of Chicago
Press, [1961] 425 p.; 25 cm. Includes bibliography. 1. Short stories, American
— Hist. & crit. 2. American fiction — 20th cent. — Hist. & crit. I. T.
PS379.W7   813.5209   LC 61-14535 rev

PS400–438 Oratory. Wit. Humor

Speech Association of America. • 2.10649
History and criticism of American public address / William Norwood
Brigance, editor. — New York: Russell & Russell, 1960- [c1943-. v.
; 24 cm.
Vol. 3: Marie Kathryn Hochmuth, editor; W. Norwood Brigance, Donald
Bryant, associates. 1. Speeches, addresses, etc., American — History and
criticism. I. Brigance, William Norwood, 1896-1960, ed. II. T. III. Title:
American public address.
PS400.S662   815.09   LC 60-8199

Blair, Walter, 1900-. 2.10650
America's humor: from Poor Richard to Doonesbury / Walter Blair, Hamlin
Hill. — New York: Oxford University Press, 1978. xvi, 559 p.; ill.; 24 cm.
Includes index. 1. American wit and humor — History and criticism. I. Hill,
Hamlin Lewis, 1931- joint author. II. T.
PS430.B495   817/.009   LC 77-23829   ISBN 0195023269

Blair, Walter, 1900-. • 2.10651
Horse sense in American humor, from Benjamin Franklin to Ogden Nash. —
New York: Russell & Russell, [1962, c1942] 341 p.: illus.; 21 cm. 1. American
wit and humor — History and criticism. I. T.
PS430.B5 1962   817.09   LC 62-10227

Critical essays on American humor / [edited by] William 2.10652
Bedford Clark, W. Craig Turner.
Boston, Mass.: G.K. Hall, c1984. viii, 232 p.; 25 cm. (Critical essays on
American literature.) 1. American wit and humor — History and criticism —
Addresses, essays, lectures. I. Clark, William Bedford. II. Turner, W. Craig.
III. Series.
PS430.C7 1984   817/.009 19   LC 84-4489   ISBN 0816186847

DeMuth, James, 1943-. 2.10653
Small town Chicago: the comic perspective of Finley Peter Dunne, George Ade,
Ring Lardner / James DeMuth. — Port Washington, N.Y.: Kennikat Press,
1980. 122 p.; 22 cm. (Interdisciplinary urban series) (National university
publications) 1. Dunne, Finley Peter, 1867-1936 — Humor, satire, etc. 2. Ade,
George, 1866-1944 — Humor, satire, etc. 3. Lardner, Ring, 1885-1933 —
Humor, satire, etc. 4. American wit and humor — History and criticism.
5. Chicago in literature. 6. City and town life in literature 7. American
newspapers — Illinois — Chicago — History. I. T.
PS430.D44   817/.5/20932   LC 79-19853   ISBN 0804692521

Hauck, Richard Boyd, 1936-. • 2.10654
A cheerful nihilism; confidence and 'the absurd' in American humorous fiction.
— Bloomington: Indiana University Press, [1971] xiv, 269 p.; 25 cm.
1. American fiction — History and criticism. 2. American wit and humor —
History and criticism. I. T.
PS430.H27   813/.00917   LC 79-135007   ISBN 0253313457

Rourke, Constance, 1885-1941. 2.10655
American humor: a study of the national character / Constance Rourke;
introduction and bibliographical essay by W.T. Lhamon, Jr. — Tallahassee:
University Presses of Florida: Florida State University Press, 1986. p. cm.
Reprint. Originally published: New York: Harcourt, Brace, c1931. Includes
index. 1. American wit and humor — History and criticism. 2. National
characteristics, American 3. American literature — History and criticism
I. Lhamon, W. T. II. T.
PS430.R6 1986   817/.009 19   LC 85-26428   ISBN 0813008379

Rubin, Louis Decimus, 1923-. 2.10656
The comic imagination in American literature. Edited by Louis D. Rubin, Jr.
New Brunswick, N.J., Rutgers University Press [1973] xii, 430 p. 23 cm. Based

on a series of lectures prepared for the Voice of America. 1. American wit and
humor — History and criticism. I. Voice of America (Organization). II. T.
PS430.R8   810/.9/17   LC 73-7921   ISBN 0813507588

Comic relief: humor in contemporary American literature / 2.10657
edited by Sarah Blacher Cohen.
Urbana: University of Illinois Press, c1978. 339 p.; 24 cm. 1. American
literature — 20th century — History and criticism — Addresses, essays,
lectures. 2. American wit and humor — History and criticism — Addresses,
essays, lectures. I. Cohen, Sarah Blacher.
PS438.C6 1978   817/.5/409   LC 78-16510   ISBN 0252005767

Yates, Norris Wilson. 2.10658
The American humorist: conscience of the twentieth century. — Ames: Iowa
State University Press, [1964] 410 p.: ill.; 22 cm. 1. American wit and humor —
History and criticism. 2. Humorists, American 3. American literature — 20th
century — History and criticism. I. T. II. Title: Conscience of the twentieth
century.
PS438.Y3   817.509   LC 63-22161

PS451–478 Folk Literature
(see also: GR110-113)

Hoffman, Daniel Gerard, 1923-. • 2.10659
Paul Bunyan, last of the frontier demigods. — Philadelphia: University of
Pennsylvania Press for Temple University Publications, 1952. xiv, 213 p. 24 cm.
1. Bunyan, Paul (Legendary character) I. T.
PS461.B8 H6   398.22   LC 52-12005

The critics & the ballad: readings / selected and edited by • 2.10660
MacEdward Leach and Tristram P. Coffin.
Carbondale: Southern Illinois University Press, 1961. xii, 284 p.: music; 20 cm.
— 1. Ballads, English — History and criticism. 2. Ballads — History and
criticism. 3. Ballads, American — History and criticism. 4. Ballads, Scottish
— History and criticism. I. Leach, MacEdward, 1896-1967. II. Coffin,
Tristram Potter, 1922-
PS476.L4   PR976.C75.   784.4/942   LC 61-7439

Jackson, Bruce. comp. 2.10661
Get your ass in the water and swim like me: narrative poetry from Black oral
tradition / [compiled by] Bruce Jackson. — Cambridge, Mass.: Harvard
University Press, 1974. xvi, 244 p.; 24 cm. & phonodisc (2 s.: 6 in.; 33 1/3 rpm.
microgroove) in pocket. Includes indexes. 1. Folk poetry, American 2. Toasts
(Afro-American folk poetry) 3. Narrative poetry, American 4. American
poetry — Afro-American authors 5. Afro-Americans — Poetry. I. T.
PS477.5.T6 J3   811/.008   LC 74-81626   ISBN 0674354206

PS501–690 Collections of American Literature

The Pushcart prize. 2.10662
1st- ed.; 1976/77-. [Yonkers, N.Y.] Pushcart Press. v. 25 cm. Annual. 'Best of
the small presses.' 1. American literature — 20th century — Collected works.
2. Little presses — United States — Collected works. I. Henderson, Bill, 1941-
PS501.P87   810/.8 19   LC 76-58675

Brooks, Cleanth, 1906- comp. 2.10663
American literature; the makers and the making [compiled by] Cleanth Brooks,
R. W. B. Lewis [and] Robert Penn Warren. New York, St. Martin's Press
[c1973] 2 v. 25 cm. 1. American literature 2. American literature — History
and criticism I. Lewis, R. W. B. (Richard Warrington Baldwin). joint comp.
II. Warren, Robert Penn, 1905- joint comp. III. T.
PS504.B7   810/.9   LC 72-95981

Anthology of American literature / general editor, George 2.10664
McMichael; advisory editors, Frederick Crews ... [et al.].
3rd ed. — New York: Macmillan; London: Collier Macmillan, <c1985 >. v.
<2 >; 24 cm. Includes index. 1. American literature I. McMichael, George
L., 1927- II. Crews, Frederick C.
PS507.A68 1985   810/.8 19   LC 84-874   ISBN 0023793201

Bradley, Sculley, 1897- comp. 2.10665
The American tradition in literature, edited by Sculley Bradley, Richmond
Croom Beatty [and] E. Hudson Long. 3d ed. New York, Norton [1967] 2 v. 22
cm. 1. American literature I. Beatty, Richmond Croom, 1905- joint comp.
II. Long, E. Hudson (Eugene Hudson), 1908- III. T.
PS507.B74 1967   810.8   LC 67-11076

Cady, Edwin Harrison. ed.   • **2.10666**
Literature of the early Republic. — 2d ed. Edited with an introd. and notes by Edwin H. Cady. — New York: Holt, Rinehart and Winston, [1969] xiv, 686 p.; 21 cm. — (Rinehart editions, 44) 1. American literature — Revolutionary period, 1775-1783 2. American literature — Early 19th century. I. T.
PS507.C2 1969   810.8/002   LC 69-19909   ISBN 0030803357

Harper's magazine.   • **2.10667**
Gentlemen, scholars, and scoundrels: a treasury of the best of Harper's magazine from 1850 to the present / edited by Horace Knowles. — New York: Harper [1959] 696 p.; 24 cm. 1. American literature I. Knowles, Horace. ed. II. T.
PS507.H23   810.82   LC 58-8831

Library of America.   **2.10668**
New York: Literary Classics of the United States; New York: distributed by Viking Press, 1982-. v.; 21 cm. 1. American literature (Collections)
PS507.L5x

The Norton anthology of American literature / [compiled by]   **2.10669**
Ronald Gottesman ... [et al.].
Shorter ed., 2nd ed. — New York: Norton, c1986. p. cm. 1. American literature I. Gottesman, Ronald.
PS507.N65 1986   810/.8 19   LC 85-25861   ISBN 0393953890

Tidwell, James Nathan. ed.   • **2.10670**
A treasury of American folk humor; a rare confection of laughter, tall tales, jests, and other gems of merriment of the American people, edited with an introd. — New York: Crown Publishers, [1956] 620 p.; 22 cm. 1. American literature 2. American wit and humor I. T.
PS507.T55   817.082   LC 56-11371

PS508 Special Classes of Authors, A–Z

Wand, David Hsin-Fu.   **2.10671**
Asian–American heritage: an anthology of prose and poetry / edited by David Hsin–Fu Wand. — New York: Washington Square Press, 1974. xii, 308 p.: ill.; 18 cm. 1. American literature — Asian-American authors 2. American literature — 20th century 3. Asians in the United States. I. T.
PS508.A8 A85   810.8089   ISBN 0671487566

Koch, Kenneth, 1925-.   **2.10672**
Rose, where did you get that red? Teaching great poetry to children. — [1st ed.]. — New York: Random House, [1973] xvi, 360 p.: facsims.; 22 cm. 1. Children's writings, American 2. Poetry — Study and teaching I. T.
PS508.C5 K58   811/.5/408   LC 72-11415   ISBN 0394483200

Koch, Kenneth, 1925-.   **2.10673**
Wishes, lies and dreams; teaching children to write poetry, by Kenneth Koch and the students of P.S. 61 in New York City. — New York: Chelsea House Publishers, [1970] 309 p.: illus., facsims.; 22 cm. 1. Children's writings, American 2. Poetry — Study and teaching I. New York (City). Public School 61. II. T.
PS508.C5 K6   811/.5/408   LC 74-111920

Hispanics in the United States: an anthology of creative   **2.10674**
literature / edited by Francisco Jiménez and Gary D. Keller.
Ypsilanti, Mich.: Bilingual Review/Press, 1980-82. 2 v. (The bilingual review = La revista bilingüe; v. 8, no. 2-3 (Nov-Dec 1981) English and Spanish. 1. American literature — Hispanic American authors 2. Hispanic Americans — Literary collections. 3. American literature — 20th century I. Jiménez, Francisco, 1943- II. Keller, Gary D.
PS508.H57 H57 1982   810/.8/086873 19   LC 80-66273   ISBN 0916950298

Earth power coming: short fiction in native American literature **2.10675**
/ edited by Simon J. Ortiz.
Tsaile, Ariz.: Navajo Community College Press, c1983. ix, 289 p.; 23 cm. 1. Short stories, American — Indian authors. 2. Indians of North America — Fiction I. Ortiz, Simon J., 1941-
PS508.I5 E23 1983   813/.01/08897 19   LC 83-60959   ISBN 0912586508

Haslam, Gerald W.   **2.10676**
Forgotten pages of American literature [by] Gerald W. Haslam. — Boston: Houghton Mifflin, [1970] xiii, 398 p.; 22 cm. 1. American literature — Indian authors 2. American literature — Asian authors. 3. American literature —

Latin American authors 4. American literature — Afro-American authors I. T.
PS508.I5 H3   810.8/09174   LC 70-15946

The Remembered earth: an anthology of contemporary Native   **2.10677**
American literature / edited by Geary Hobson.
Albuquerque, N.M.: Red Earth Press, c1979. xi, 427 p.: ill.; 24 cm. 1. American literature — Indian authors 2. American literature — 20th century 3. Indians of North America — Literary collections. I. Hobson, Geary.
PS508.I5 R4   810/.8/0897   LC 79-110061   ISBN 0918434033

Velie, Alan R., 1937-.   **2.10678**
Four American Indian literary masters: N. Scott Momaday, James Welch, Leslie Marmon Silko, and Gerald Vizenor / by Alan R. Velie. — 1st ed. — Norman: University of Oklahoma Press, c1982. xi, 164 p.; 22 cm. Includes index. 1. American literature — Indian authors — History and criticism. I. T.
PS508.I5 V4 1982   810/.9/897 19   LC 81-43642   ISBN 0806116498

Gross, Theodore L. comp.   **2.10679**
The literature of American Jews / edited by Theodore L. Gross. — New York: Free Press, [1973] xvii, 510 p.: ill.; 24 cm. 1. American literature — Jewish authors 2. Jews in literature I. T.
PS508.J4 G7   810/.8/08924   LC 72-93311   ISBN 0029131901

Malin, Irving. ed.   **2.10680**
Breakthrough: a treasury of contemporary American–Jewish literature / edited by Irving Malin and Irwin Stark. — [1st ed.]. — New York: McGraw-Hill, [1964] viii, 376 p.; 22 cm. 1. American literature — Jewish authors I. Stark, Irwin, 1912- joint ed. II. T.
PS508.J4 M3   810.82   LC 63-13261

Chicano voices / [edited by] Carlota Cárdenas de Dwyer; Tino **2.10681**
Villanueva, editorial adviser.
Boston: Houghton Mifflin, c1975. xi, 189 p.: ill.; 21 cm. — (Multi-ethnic literature) Includes index. 1. American literature — Mexican American authors I. Dwyer, Carlota Cárdenas de.
PS508.M4 C55   810/.8/0868   LC 75-13954   ISBN 0395205794

Harth, Dorothy E., comp.   **2.10682**
Voices of Aztlan: Chicano literature of today / edited by Dorothy E. Harth and Lewis M. Baldwin. — New York: New American Library [1974] 246 p.; 18 cm. (A Mentor book, 451 MJ1296) 1. American literature — Mexican American authors 2. American literature — 20th century I. Baldwin, Lewis M., joint comp. II. T.
PS508.M4 H3   810/.8/086872   LC 73-93824

Ludwig, Ed, 1920- comp.   **2.10683**
The Chicanos: Mexican American voices. Edited by Ed Ludwig and James Santibañez. — Baltimore: Penguin Books, [1971] ix, 286 p.; 19 cm. 1. American literature — Mexican American authors 2. American literature — 20th century I. Santibañez, James, 1931- joint comp. II. T.
PS508.M4 L8   810.8/005/4   LC 74-29454   ISBN 0140213562

Ortego y Gasca, Philip D. comp.   **2.10684**
We are Chicanos: an anthology of Mexican–American literature. Edited by Philip D. Ortego. New York, Washington Square Press [1973] xxi, 330 p. illus. 18 cm. 1. American literature — Mexican American authors 2. American literature — 20th century I. T.
PS508.M4 O7   810/.8/086872   LC 73-168248   ISBN 0671481304

Afro–American writing: an anthology of prose and poetry /   **2.10685**
edited by Richard A. Long and Eugenia W. Collier.
2nd and enl. ed. — University Park: Pennsylvania State University Press, c1985. xlv, 736 p.; 24 cm. Includes index. 1. American literature — Afro-American authors 2. American literature — 20th century I. Long, Richard A., 1927- II. Collier, Eugenia W.
PS508.N3 A37 1985   810/.8/0896073 19   LC 83-43224   ISBN 027100374X

Baker, Houston A. comp.   **2.10686**
Black literature in America [by] Houston A. Baker, Jr. — New York: McGraw-Hill, [1971] xvi, 443 p.; 23 cm. 1. American literature — Afro-American authors I. T.
PS508.N3 B27   810.9/8/96073   LC 72-143442   ISBN 007003365X

Baraka, Imamu Amiri, 1934- comp.   • **2.10687**
Black fire; an anthology of Afro–American writing, edited by LeRoi Jones and Larry Neal. New York, Morrow, 1968. xviii, 670 p. illus. 22 cm. 1. American literature — Afro-American authors 2. American literature — 20th century I. Neal, Larry, 1937- joint comp. II. T.
PS508.N3 B33   810.8/005/4   LC 68-23914

Brawley, Benjamin Griffith, 1882-1939. ed.   • 2.10688
Early Negro American writers; selections with biographical and critical
introductions. — New York: Dover Publications, [1970] ix, 305 p.; 22 cm.
Reprint of the 1935 ed. 1. American literature — Afro-American authors I. T.
PS508.N3 B7 1970   810.8/08/96073   LC 78-127946   ISBN
0486226239

Brown, Sterling Allen, 1901- ed.   2.10689
The Negro caravan, edited by Sterling A. Brown, Arthur P. Davis, and Ulysses
Lee. — New York: Arno Press, 1969 [c1941] xviii, 1082 p.; 24 cm. —
(American Negro, his history and literature.) (Afro-American culture series.)
1. American literature — Afro-American authors I. Davis, Arthur Paul,
1904- joint ed. II. Lee, Ulysses Grant, joint ed. III. T. IV. Series. V. Series:
Afro-American culture series.
PS508.N3 B75 1969   810.9/9174/96   LC 69-18584

Chant of saints: a gathering of Afro–American literature, art,   2.10690
and scholarship / edited by Michael S. Harper and Robert B.
Stepto.
Urbana: University of Illinois Press, c1979. xviii, 486 p., [4] leaves of plates: ill.
(some col.); 23 cm. 1. American literature — Afro-American authors
2. American literature — Afro-American authors — History and criticism —
Addresses, essays, lectures. 3. Afro-American arts I. Harper, Michael S.,
1938- II. Stepto, Robert B.
PS508.N3 C49   810/.8/0896073   LC 79-117219   ISBN 0252007123

Chapman, Abraham. comp.   • 2.10691
Black voices; an anthology of Afro–American literature. Edited, with an introd.
and biographical notes, by Abraham Chapman. — New York: St. Martin's
Press, [1970, c1968] 718 p.; 21 cm. 1. American literature — Afro-American
authors I. T.
PS508.N3 C5 1970   810.8/09174/96   LC 74-10383

Chapman, Abraham. comp.   2.10692
New Black voices; an anthology of contemporary Afro–American literature.
Edited, with an introd. and biographical notes, by Abraham Chapman. New
York, New American Library [1972] 606 p. 18 cm. (A Mentor book, MW1116)
1. American literature — Afro-American authors 2. American literature —
20th century I. T.
PS508.N3 C53   810/.8/0054   LC 74-181598

Confirmation, an anthology of African American women /   2.10693
[compiled by] Amiri Baraka (LeRoi Jones) & Amina Baraka.
1st Quill ed. — New York: Quill, 1983. 418 p.; 24 cm. 1. American literature —
Afro-American authors 2. American literature — Women authors
3. American literature — 20th century 4. Afro-American women — Literary
collections. I. Baraka, Imamu Amiri, 1934- II. Baraka, Amina. III. Title:
Confirmation, an anthology of African American women.
PS508.N3 C66 1983b   810/.8/09287 19   LC 82-21425   ISBN
0688015824

Davis, Arthur Paul, 1904- comp.   2.10694
Cavalcade; Negro American writing from 1760 to the present. Edited by Arthur
P. Davis [and] Saunders Redding. — Boston: Houghton Mifflin, [1971] xviii,
905 p.: illus.; 24 cm. 1. American literature — Negro authors. 2. American
literature — Negro authors — History and criticism. I. Redding, J. Saunders
(Jay Saunders), 1906- joint comp. II. T.
PS508.N3 D27   PS508N3 D27.   810.8/08/96   LC 70-20257
     ISBN 039504345X

Davis, Arthur Paul, 1904- comp.   2.10695
The new Negro renaissance: an anthology / edited by Arthur P. Davis and
Michael W. Peplow. — New York: Holt, Rinehart and Winston, c1975. xxxi,
538 p.; 21 cm. — (Rinehart editions; 153) 1. American literature — Afro-
American authors 2. American literature — 20th century 3. Afro-American
authors — Biography. I. Peplow, Michael W. joint comp. II. T.
PS508.N3 D28   810/.8/0896073   LC 75-2238   ISBN 0030140668

Davis, Charles T. (Charles Twitchwell), 1918-1981, comp.   2.10696
On being black; writings by Afro–Americans from Frederick Douglass to the
present. Edited by Charles T. Davis and Daniel Walden. Greenwich, Conn.,
Fawcett Publications [1970] 383 p. 18 cm. (A Fawcett premier book M473)
1. American literature — Afro-American authors I. Walden, Daniel, 1922-
joint comp. II. T.
PS508.N3 D3   810.8/0917496   LC 71-117295

Emanuel, James A. comp.   2.10697
Dark symphony: Negro literature in America / edited by James A. Emanuel
and Theodore L. Gross. — New York: Free Press, [1968] xviii, 604 p.; 21 cm.
1. American literature — Negro authors. I. Gross, Theodore L. joint comp.
II. T.
PS508.N3 E4   810.8/09   LC 68-54984

Hill, Herbert, 1924- ed.   • 2.10698
Soon, one morning: new writing by American Negroes, 1940–1962 / selected
and edited, with an introd. and biographical notes, by Herbert Hill. — [1st ed.]

New York: Knopf, 1963. 617 p.; 22 cm. 1. American literature — Afro-
American authors I. T.
PS508.N3 H5   810.89   LC 62-15567

Porter, Dorothy Burnett, 1905- comp.   2.10699
Early Negro writing, 1760–1837. Selected and introduced by Dorothy Porter.
— Boston: Beacon Press, [1971] xiii, 658 p.: port.; 21 cm. 1. American
literature — Afro-American authors I. T.
PS508.N3 P6   810.8/08/96073   LC 71-101325   ISBN 0807054526

Levine, Stephen, 1937-.   2.10700
Death Row: an affirmation of life. Compiled & edited by Stephen Levine with
the assistance of Dovie C. Mathis and the inspiration of Jack Rainsberger. San
Francisco, Glide Publications [1972] xxv, 241 p. illus. 23 cm. 1. Prisoners'
writings, American 2. American literature — 20th century I. Mathis, Dovie
C., joint comp. II. T.
PS508.P7 L4   810/.8/0054   LC 72-176239   ISBN 0912078127

The Norton anthology of literature by women: the tradition in   2.10701
English / [compiled by] Sandra M. Gilbert, Susan Gubar.
1st ed. — New York: Norton, c1985. xxxiv, 2457 p.; 22 cm. Includes index.
1. American literature — Women authors 2. English literature — Women
authors I. Gilbert, Sandra M. II. Gubar, Susan, 1944-
PS508.W7 N67 1985   820/.8/09287 19   LC 84-27276   ISBN
0393019403

This bridge called my back: writings by radical women of color   2.10702
/ editors, Cherríe Moraga, Gloria Anzaldúa; foreword, Toni
Cade Bambara.
2d ed. — New York: Kitchen Table, Women of Color Press, [1983, c1981] xxvi,
261 p.: ill.; 22 cm. Originally published: Watertown, Mass.: Persephone Press,
1981. 1. Feminism — Literary collections. 2. American literature — Women
authors 3. American literature — Minority authors 4. American literature —
20th century I. Moraga, Cherríe. II. Anzaldúa, Gloria.
PS509.F44 T5 1983   810/.8/09287 19   ISBN 091317503X

The Ethnic image in modern American literature, 1900–1950 /   2.10703
edited by Philip Butcher.
Washington, D.C.: Howard University Press, 1984. 2 v.; 24 cm. Includes index.
1. American literature — 20th century 2. Minorities — United States —
Literary collections. 3. American literature — Minority authors 4. United
States — Ethnic relations — Literary collections. I. Butcher, Philip, 1918-
PS509.M5 E86 1984   810/.9/3520693 19   LC 83-8440   ISBN
0882581104

Voices from the Harlem renaissance / edited by Nathan Irvin   2.10704
Huggins.
New York: Oxford University Press, 1976. 438 p.: ill.; 23 cm. 1. Afro-
Americans — Literary collections. 2. American literature — Afro-American
authors 3. Afro-American arts — New York (City) 4. American literature —
20th century 5. The arts, Modern — 20th century — New York (N.Y.)
6. Harlem Renaissance 7. Harlem (New York, N.Y.). I. Huggins, Nathan
Irvin, 1927-
PS509.N4 V6   810/.8/89607307471   LC 75-16912   ISBN
0195019555

Vietnam literature anthology, a balanced perspective: three   2.10705
views of Vietnam, and a chapter from a forthcoming novel / by
Jack Strahan, Peter Hollenbeck, and R.L. Barth; edited by J.
Topham.
College ed. — New York: American Poetry and Literature Press, 1984. x, 83 p.;
22 cm. Includes indexes. 1. Vietnamese Conflict, 1961-1975 — Literary
collections. 2. American literature — 20th century I. Strahan, Jack, 1951-
II. Hollenbeck, Peter. III. Barth, R. L. (Robert L.). IV. Topham, J.
PS509.V53 1984 PL4378.V53x   810/.8/0358 19   LC 84-11029
     ISBN 093348674X

PS530–536.2 By Period

Laughter in the wilderness: early American humor to 1783 /   2.10706
edited, with an introd., by W. Howland Kenney.
[Kent, Ohio]: Kent State University Press, c1976. ix, 236 p.; 24 cm.
1. American literature — Colonial period, ca. 1600-1775 2. American wit and
humor I. Kenney, William Howland.
PS530.L35   817/.1/08   LC 75-44710   ISBN 0873381858

Miller, Perry, 1905-1963. ed.   • 2.10707
The American Puritans, their prose and poetry. [1st ed.] Garden City, N.Y.,
Doubleday, 1956. 346 p. illus. 18 cm. (Doubleday anchor books, A80)

1. Puritans — United States. 2. American literature — Colonial period, ca. 1600-1775 3. American literature — Puritan authors. I. T.
PS530.M48   810.82   LC 56-7536

Miller, Perry, 1905-1963. ed.   • 2.10708
The Puritans / [by] Perry Miller and Thomas H. Johnson; bibliographies rev. for the Torchbook ed. by George McCandlish. — Rev. ed. New York: Harper & Row [1963] 2 v.: ill.; 21 cm. (Harper torchbooks. The Academy library) 1. Puritans — United States — Literary collections. 2. American literature — Colonial period, ca. 1600-1775 3. American literature — Puritan authors. I. Johnson, Thomas Herbert. joint ed. II. T.
PS531.M5 1963   810.82   LC 63-1710

Untermeyer, Louis, 1885-1977.   2.10709
50 modern American & British poets, 1920–1970 / Edited, with a biographical and critical commentary, by Louis Untermeyer. — New York: McKay, [1973] xxv, 358 p.; 22 cm. 1. American poetry — 20th century 2. English poetry — 20th century 3. American poetry — 20th century — History and criticism. 4. English poetry — 20th century — History and criticism. I. T.
PS535.5.U5   821/.9/1208   LC 72-89118

Waldman, Anne, 1945- comp.   2.10710
Another World; a second anthology of works from the St. Mark's poetry project. Indianapolis, Bobbs-Merrill [1971] xix, 387 p. illus. 22 cm. 'Works from issues 12-23 of The World.' 1. American literature — 20th century I. World (New York, 1966-) II. T.
PS535.5.W3   810.8/005/4   LC 75-142494

The American mercury reader: a selection of distinguished   2.10711
articles, stories, and poems published in the American mercury
during the past twenty years / edited by Lawrence E. Spivak
and Charles Angoff.
1st AMS ed. — New York: AMS Press, 1979. 378 p.: ill.; 23 cm. Reprint of the 1944 ed. published by Blakiston, Philadelphia. 1. American literature — 20th century I. Spivak, Lawrence Edmund, 1900- II. Angoff, Charles, 1902- III. American mercury.
PS536.A56 1979   810/.8/0054   LC 75-41009   ISBN 0404147658

American harvest: twenty years of creative writing in the United   • 2.10712
States / edited by Allen Tate and John Peale Bishop.
New York: L.B. Fischer, 1942. 544 p. 1. American literature — 20th century I. Tate, Allen, 1899- II. Bishop, John Peale, 1892-1944.
PS536 A64 1942   LC 42-23613

Filler, Louis, 1912- ed.   • 2.10713
The anxious years: America in the nineteen thirties; a collection of contemporary writings. New York, Putnam [1963] 375 p. 23 cm. 1. American literature — 20th century 2. Social problems — Literary collections. I. T.
PS536.F5   810.82   LC 62-18266

The Little review anthology. Edited by Margaret Anderson.   • 2.10714
New York: Hermitage House, 1953. 383 p. 1. American literature — 20th century 2. Literature — History and criticism I. Anderson, Margaret C. II. The Little review.
PS536.L57   810.8/0054

New directions in prose and poetry (Norfolk, Conn.: 1936)   2.10715
New directions in prose and poetry. — [No. 1]-. Norfolk, CT.: New Directions, 1936-1941. v.: ill.; 24 cm. Annual. 1. American literature — 20th century — Periodicals. 2. Literature, Modern — 20th century — Periodicals. 3. American literature — 20th century 4. Literature, Modern — 20th century I. Laughlin, James, 1914- II. T.
PS536.N37   810/.8/005/2 19   LC 37-1751

Salzman, Jack. comp.   • 2.10716
The survival years; a collection of American writings of the 1940's. — New York: Pegasus, [1969] 352 p.; 21 cm. 1. American literature — 20th century I. T.
PS536.S12   810.8/0052   LC 73-77129

Jones, LeRoi, ed.   • 2.10717
The moderns: an anthology of new writing in America / edited with an introd. by LeRoi Jones. — New York: Corinth Books, 1963. xvi, 351 p.; 22 cm. 1. American literature — 20th century I. T.
PS536.2.B29 1963   813.54082   LC 63-11408

PS538–572 By Region

The Literary humor of the urban Northeast, 1830–1890 / edited,   2.10718
with an introduction, by David E.E. Sloane.
Baton Rouge: Louisiana State University Press, c1983. xii, 319 p.: ill.; 24 cm. 1. American literature — Northeastern States. 2. American wit and humor — Northeastern States. 3. American literature — 19th century 4. City and town life — Literary collections. 5. City and town life — Anecdotes, facetiae, satire, etc. 6. Northeastern States — Literary collections. I. Sloane, David E. E., 1943-
PS538.L57 1983   817/.3/080974 19   LC 82-12688   ISBN 0807110558

Brooks, Van Wyck, 1886-1963.   • 2.10719
A New England reader. [1st ed.] New York, Atheneum, 1962. 427 p. 25 cm. 1. American literature — New England. I. T.
PS541.B7   810.82   LC 62-17283

Miller, Perry, 1905-1963. ed.   • 2.10720
The American transcendentalists, their prose and poetry. Garden City, N.Y., Doubleday, 1957. 388 p. 19 cm. 1. American literature — New England. 2. American literature — 19th century 3. Transcendentalism (New England) I. T.
PS541.M5   810.82   LC 57-11433

Untermeyer, Louis, 1885-1977. ed.   • 2.10721
An anthology of the New England poets from colonial times to the present day / ed., with biographical and critical commentaries, by Louis Untermeyer. — [New York]: Random House, [1948] xx, 636 p.; 22 cm. 1. American poetry — New England. I. T.
PS541.U5   811.082   LC 48-7220

The literary South / [compiled by] Louis D. Rubin, Jr.   2.10722
New York: Wiley, c1979. xvi, 735 p.; 24 cm. Includes index. 1. American literature — Southern States. 2. Southern States — Literary collections. I. Rubin, Louis Decimus, 1923-
PS551.L55   810/.8/0975   LC 78-24221   ISBN 0471046590

Randolph, Vance, 1892-.   • 2.10723
We always lie to strangers: tall tales from the Ozarks / by Vance Randolph; illustrated by Glenn Rounds. — New York: Columbia University Press, 1951. viii, 309 p.: ill.; 23 cm. 1. American wit and humor 2. Folklore — Arkansas. I. T.
PS558.A8 R3   LC 51-10537

Taylor, J. Golden. comp.   • 2.10724
The literature of the American West / edited by J. Golden Taylor. — Boston: Houghton Mifflin [1971] ix, 592 p.; 24 cm. 1. American literature — West (U.S.) I. T.
PS561.T38   810.8/032   LC 71-132448   ISBN 0395054583

Flanagan, John Theodore, 1906- ed.   2.10725
America is West, an anthology of middlewestern life and literature. Edited by John T. Flanagan. — Westport, Conn.: Greenwood Press, [1970, c1945] vii, 677 p.: illus.; 23 cm. 1. American literature 2. Middle West I. T.
PS563.F5 1970   810.8/032   LC 71-106687   ISBN 0837133580

Cohen, Hennig. ed.   2.10726
Humor of the old Southwest / edited with an introd. by Hennig Cohen and William B. Dillingham. — 2d ed. — Athens: University of Georgia Press, [1975] c1964. xxviii, 427 p.; 22 cm. 1. American literature — Southwest, Old. 2. American wit and humor — Southwest, Old. I. Dillingham, William B. II. T.
PS566.C6 1975   817/.3/08   LC 74-13512   ISBN 0820303585

Meine, Franklin Julius, 1896-1968. ed.   2.10727
Tall tales of the Southwest: an anthology of southern and southwestern humor, 1830–1860 / edited by Franklin J. Meine. — St. Clair Shores, Mich.: Scholarly Press, 1977, c1930. xxxii, 456 p.; 22 cm. Reprint of the ed. published by Knopf, New York, in series: Americana deserta. 1. American literature — Southwest, Old. 2. Tall tales — Southwest, Old. 3. American wit and humor — Southwest, Old. 4. American literature — 19th century I. T.
PS566.M4 1977   817/.5/208   LC 76-51493   ISBN 0403072131

Southwest: a contemporary anthology / Karl and Jane Kopp,   2.10728
general editors; Bart Lanier Stafford III, fiction editor.
Albuquerque, N.M.: Red Earth Press, c1977. xii, 418 p.: ill.; 24 cm. 1. American literature — Southwestern States. 2. American literature — 20th century 3. Southwestern States — Literary collections. I. Kopp, Karl, 1934- II. Kopp, Jane.
PS566.S59   810/.8/0978   LC 77-80002   ISBN 0918434017

PS580–688 By Form

PS580–619 POETRY

Allen, Gay Wilson, 1903- ed.   **2.10729**
American poetry / [edited by] Gay Wilson Allen, Walter B. Rideout [and] James K. Robinson. — New York: Harper & Row [1965] xxxiv, 1274 p.; 21 cm. Bibliographical references included in 'Notes' (p. [1071]-1243) Bibliography: p. [1245]-1246. 1. American poetry (Collections) I. Rideout, Walter Bates, joint ed. II. Robinson, James K. joint ed. III. T.
PS583.A5   811.008   LC 65-19490

The Oxford book of American verse; chosen and with an introd. • **2.10730**
by F. O. Matthiessen.
New York, Oxford University Press, 1950. lvi, 1132 p. 19 cm. 1. American poetry I. Matthiessen, F. O. (Francis Otto), 1902-1950. comp.
PS583.O82   811.082   LC 50-9826

New American poets of the 80's / edited by Jack Myers &   **2.10731**
Roger Weingarten.
1st ed. — Green Harbor, MA: Wampeter Press, 1984. xv, 435 p. Contributor notes: p. 411-424. 1. American poetry — 20th century I. Myers, Jack. II. Weingarten, Roger.
PS584 N38 1984   ISBN 0931694353

The New Oxford book of American verse / chosen and edited   **2.10732**
by Richard Ellmann.
New York: Oxford University Press, 1976. liv, 1076 p.; 23 cm. Includes index. 1. American poetry I. Ellmann, Richard, 1918-
PS584.N4   811/.008   LC 75-46354

Treasury of American poetry / selected and with an introd. by   **2.10733**
Nancy Sullivan.
Garden City, N.Y.: Doubleday, [1978] p. cm. 1. American poetry I. Sullivan, Nancy.
PS584.T7   811/.008   LC 77-92232   ISBN 038512032X

Ciardi, John, 1916-.   **2.10734**
How does a poem mean? / John Ciardi, Miller Williams. — 2d. ed. — Boston: Houghton, Mifflin, [1975] xxiii, 408 p.; 24 cm. Includes indexes. 1. American poetry 2. English poetry 3. Poetics I. Williams, Miller. joint author. II. T.
PS586.C53 1975   821/.008   LC 74-11592   ISBN 0395204402

The Oxford book of American light verse / chosen and edited   **2.10735**
by William Harmon.
New York: Oxford University Press, 1979. l, 540 p.; 23 cm. Includes index. 1. American poetry 2. Humorous poetry, American I. Harmon, William, 1938-
PS586.O95   811/.07   LC 78-12356   ISBN 0195025091

Van Doren, Mark, 1894-1972.   • **2.10736**
American poets, 1630–1930, edited by Mark Van Doren. Boston, Little, Brown, 1932. 698 p. 1. American poetry I. T.
PS586 V3   811.008   LC 32-27285

Williams, Oscar, 1900-1964.   **2.10737**
The mentor book of major American poets: from Edward Taylor and Walt Whitman to Hart Crane and W.H. Auden / Edited by Oscar Williams and Edwin Honig, with an introd. and notes on the poets. — [New York] New American Library [1962]. — 535p.; 18 cm. 1. American poetry — Collected works. I. T.
PS586.W52   LC 62-14316

The Oxford book of children's verse in America / edited by   **2.10738**
Donald Hall.
New York: Oxford University Press, 1985. xxxviii, 319 p.; 23 cm. Companion volume to: The Oxford book of children's verse. Includes indexes. 1. Children's poetry, American I. Hall, Donald, 1928-
PS586.3.O94 1985   811/.008/09282 19   LC 84-20755   ISBN 0195035399

The Random House book of poetry for children / selected and   **2.10739**
introduced by Jack Prelutsky; illustrated by Arnold Lobel.
New York: Random House, c1983. 248 p.: ill. (some col.); 28 cm. 'Opening poems for each section especially written for this anthology by Jack Prelutsky. Includes indexes. 1. Children's poetry, American 2. Children's poetry, English

I. Prelutsky, Jack. II. Lobel, Arnold. ill. III. Title: Book of poetry for children.
PS586.3.R36 1983   811/.008/09282 19   LC 83-2990   ISBN 0394850106

Howe, Florence. comp.   **2.10740**
No more masks! An anthology of poems by women. Edited by Florence Howe & Ellen Bass. Introd by Florence Howe. — Garden City, N.Y.: Doubleday, 1973. xxix, 396 p.; 21 cm. 1. Women's writings, American. 2. American poetry — 20th century I. Bass, Ellen. joint comp. II. T.
PS589.H6   811/.008/0352   LC 72-89675   ISBN 038502553X

PS591–595 Special Poets, Forms, Subjects

Day, A. Grove.   **2.10741**
The sky clears; poetry of the American Indians. New York: Macmillan, 1951. xv, 204 p. 22 cm. 1. Indians of North America — Poetry I. T.
PS 591 I55 D27 1964   LC 51-347

New and old voices of Wah'kon–tah / edited by Robert K.   **2.10742**
Dodge and Joseph B. McCullough; with a foreword by Vine
Deloria, Jr.
New York: International Publishers, c1985. xv, 139 p.; 22 cm. 1. American poetry — Indian authors 2. American poetry — 20th century 3. Indians of North America — Poetry I. Dodge, Robert K. II. McCullough, Joseph B.
PS591.I55 N4 1985   811/.54/080897 19   LC 85-14445   ISBN 0717806308

Niatum, Duane, 1938- comp.   **2.10743**
Carriers of the dream wheel: contemporary native American poetry / edited by Duane Niatum. — 1st ed. — New York: Harper & Row, [1975] xx, 300 p., [8] leaves of plates: ill.; 21 cm. 1. American poetry — Indian authors 2. American poetry — 20th century I. T.
PS591.I55 N5 1975   811/.5/408   LC 74-5986   ISBN 0064511510

Songs from this Earth on turtle's back: contemporary American   **2.10744**
Indian poetry / edited by Joseph Bruchac.
1st ed. — Greenfield Center, N.Y.: Greenfield Review Press, c1983. xvi, 294 p.: ill.; 23 cm. 1. American poetry — Indian authors 2. American poetry — 20th century 3. Indians of North America — Poetry I. Bruchac, Joseph, 1942-
PS591.I55 S66 1983   811/.54/080897 19   LC 82-82420   ISBN 0912678585

Fiesta in Aztlan: anthology of Chicano poetry / Toni   **2.10745**
Empringham, editor.
Santa Barbara: Capra Press, 1981. 128 p.; 23 cm. 1. American poetry — Mexican American authors 2. American poetry — Pacific States. 3. American poetry — 20th century I. Empringham, Toni.
PS591.M49 C5   811/.5/080868073 19   LC 80-25891   ISBN 0884961648

The Next world: poems / by 32 Third World Americans; edited   **2.10746**
by Joseph Bruchac.
Trumansburg, N.Y.: Crossing Press, c1978. 238 p.: ports.; 21 cm. — (The Crossing Press series of contemporary anthologies) 1. American poetry — Minority authors 2. American poetry — 20th century I. Bruchac, Joseph, 1942-
PS591.M54 N44   811/.5/408   LC 78-1923   ISBN 0895940086

Adoff, Arnold. comp.   **2.10747**
The poetry of Black America: anthology of the 20th century / introd. by Gwendolyn Brooks. — [1st ed.]. — New York: Harper & Row, [1973] xxxi, 552 p.; 24 cm. 1. American poetry — Afro-American authors I. T.
PS591.N4 A32   811/.5/408   LC 72-76518   ISBN 0060200898

Stetson, Erlene, 1949-.   **2.10748**
Black sister: poetry by black American women, 1746–1980 / edited with an introduction by Erlene Stetson. — Bloomington: Indiana University Press, c1981. xxiv, 312 p.; 25 cm. 1. American poetry — Afro-American authors 2. American poetry — Women authors I. T.
PS591.N4 B525   811/.008/09287 19   LC 80-8847   ISBN 0253305128

Bontemps, Arna Wendell, 1902-1973. ed.   **2.10749**
American Negro poetry. Edited and with an introd. by Arna Bontemps. Rev. ed. New York, Hill and Wang [1974] xx, 231 p. 21 cm. (American century series) 1. American poetry — Afro-American authors 2. American poetry — 20th century I. T.
PS591.N4 B58 1974   811/.5/08   LC 72-95044   ISBN 0809025213
ISBN 080900108X

Brooks, Gwendolyn, 1917- comp. • 2.10750
A broadside treasury. [1st ed.]. — Detroit, Mich.: Broadside Press, [1971]
188 p.; 22 cm. Poems. 1. American poetry — Afro-American authors
2. American poetry — 20th century I. T.
PS591.N4 B66   811/.5/408   LC 70-142061   ISBN 0910296510

Cullen, Countee, 1903-1946. ed. 2.10751
Caroling dusk; an anthology of verse by negro poets, edited by Countee Cullen;
decorations by Aaron Douglas. — New York; London: Harper & brothers,
1927. xxii p., 1 l., 237, [1] p.; 22 cm. 'The biographical notices carried with these
poems have been written by the poets themselves save in three cases.'—
Foreword. 1. American poetry — Afro-American authors I. T.
PS591.N4 C8   LC 27-23175

Hayden, Robert Earl. comp. 2.10752
Kaleidoscope; poems by American Negro poets, edited and with an introd. by
Robert Hayden. — [1st ed.]. — New York, Harcourt, Brace & World [1967]
xxiv, 231 p. ports. (on lining papers) 20 cm. — (Curriculum-related books)
1. American poetry — Negro authors. I. T.
PS591.N4 H3   811/.5/208   LC 67-18543

Henderson, Stephen Evangelist, 1925- comp. 2.10753
Understanding the new Black poetry; Black speech and Black music as poetic
references, by Stephen Henderson. New York: Morrow, 1973. xxii, 394 p.; 21
cm. 'An Institute of the Black World book.' 1. American poetry — Afro-
American authors I. T.
PS591.N4 H37   811/.008   LC 79-170234   ISBN 0688001394

Johnson, James Weldon, 1871-1938. ed. • 2.10754
The book of American Negro poetry, chosen and edited, with an essay on the
Negro's creative genius, by James Weldon Johnson. New York, Harcourt,
Brace and company [c1931] vii, 300 p. illus. (music) 20 cm. 'Revised edition.'
1. American poetry — Afro-American authors I. T.
PS591.N4 J6 1931   811.08   LC 31-26811

Rottmann, Larry, 1942- comp. 2.10755
Winning hearts and minds; war poems by Vietnam veterans. Edited by Larry
Rottmann, Jan Barry [and] Basil T. Paquet. — Brooklyn, N.Y.: 1st Casuality
Press, [1972] viii, 116 p.: illus.; 21 cm. 1. Veterans' writings, American
2. American poetry — 20th century I. Barry, Jan, 1943- joint comp.
II. Paquet, Basil T., 1944- joint comp. III. T.
PS591.V4 R6   811/.5/408   LC 72-185861

Emrich, Duncan, 1908- comp. 2.10756
American folk poetry: an anthology. — [1st ed.] Boston: Little, Brown [1974]
xxxi, 831 p.: ill.; 24 cm. 1. Folk poetry, American 2. Folk-songs, English —
United States — Texts. I. T.
PS593.L8 E5   811/.04   LC 74-3499   ISBN 0316237221

Text—sound texts / edited by Richard Kostelanetz. 2.10757
1st Morrow Quill paperback ed. — New York: Morrow, 1980. 441 p.: ill.; 23
cm. 1. Sound poetry 2. American poetry — 20th century 3. Canadian poetry
— 20th century 4. Performance art I. Kostelanetz, Richard.
PS593.S67 T4 1980   811/.54/08 19   LC 79-93246   ISBN
0688086160

Lomax, John Avery, 1867-1948. comp. 2.10758
Cowboy songs and other frontier ballads. Rev. and enl. Collected by John A.
Lomax and Alan Lomax. New York: The Macmillan company, 1938. xxxviii,
431 p. incl. facsims.; 24 cm. Some of the ballads with music (unaccompanied
melodies) Music edited by Edward N. Waters. 1. Folk-songs, English — West
(U.S.) — Texts. 2. Cowboys — Poetry. 3. Ballads, English — West (U.S.) —
Texts. I. Lomax, Alan, 1915- joint comp. II. Waters, Edward N. (Edward
Neighbor), 1906- III. T.
PS595.C6 L6 1938   784.4/978 19   LC 38-27656

The Gift outright: America to her poets / edited by Helen 2.10759
Plotz.
New York: Greenwillow Books, c1977. xv, 204 p.; 24 cm. Indexes.
1. American poetry 2. United States — Poetry. I. Plotz, Helen.
PS595.U5 G5   811/.008   LC 77-8555   ISBN 0688801099

PS601–615 Special Periods

Meserole, Harrison T. comp. 2.10760
Seventeenth–century American poetry / edited with an introd., notes, and
comments by Harrison T. Meserole. — [New York]: New York University
Press, 1968. xxxvi, 541 p.; 24 cm. — (The Stuart editions) 1. American poetry
— Colonial period, ca. 1600-1775 I. T.
PS601.M4 1968b   811/.1/08   LC 68-29435

Silverman, Kenneth. comp. 2.10761
Colonial American poetry, edited with introductions. — New York: Hafner
Pub. Co., 1968. xv, 449 p.; 24 cm. 1. American poetry — Colonial period, ca.
1600-1775 I. T.
PS601.S5   811/.1/08   LC 68-18556

Early American poetry: Selections from Bradstreet, Taylor, 2.10762
Dwight, Freneau, and Bryant / [edited by] Jane Donahue
Eberwein.
Madison: University of Wisconsin Press, 1978. xiii, 383 p.; 23 cm. 1. American
poetry — 1783-1850 2. American poetry — Colonial period, ca. 1600-1775
I. Eberwein, Jane Donahue, 1943-
PS609.E2 1978   811/.1/08   LC 77-91051   ISBN 0299074404

Untermeyer, Louis, 1885-1977. ed. • 2.10763
Modern American poetry. — New and enl. ed. — New York: Harcourt, Brace
& World, [1962] 701 p.; 24 cm. 1. American poetry — 19th century
2. American poetry — 20th century I. T.
PS611.U6 1962   811.082   LC 62-12183

Carruth, Hayden, 1921- comp. 2.10764
The voice that is great within us: American poetry of the twentieth century. —
Toronto; New York: Bantam Books, [1970] xlv, 722 p.; 18 cm. — (A Bantam
classic) 1. American poetry — 20th century I. T.
PS613.C3   811/.5/08   LC 77-22250

Contemporary American poetry / edited by A. Poulin, Jr. 2.10765
4th ed. — Boston: Houghton Mifflin Co., c1985. xxix, 727 p.: ill.; 24 cm.
1. American poetry 2. American poetry — 20th century —
History and criticism. I. Poulin, A.
PS613.C66 1985   811/.5408 19   LC 84-81715   ISBN 0395358051

Ellmann, Richard, 1918- comp. 2.10766
The Norton anthology of modern poetry, edited by Richard Ellmann and
Robert O'Clair. — [1st ed.]. — New York: Norton, [1973] xlvi, 1456 p.; 24 cm.
1. American poetry — 20th century 2. English poetry — 20th century
3. American poetry — 19th century 4. English poetry — 19th century
I. O'Clair, Robert, joint comp. II. T.
PS613.E4 1973   821/.008   LC 73-6587   ISBN 0393093573

Fifty years of American poetry: anniversary volume for the 2.10767
Academy of American Poets / introduction by Robert Penn
Warren; wood engravings by Barry Moser.
New York: H.N. Abrams, 1984. 260 p.: ill.; 27 cm. Includes index. 1. American
poetry — 20th century I. Warren, Robert Penn, 1905- II. Academy of
American Poets. III. Title: 50 years of American poetry.
PS613.F5 1984   811/.5/08 19   LC 84-11024   ISBN 0810909340

Hall, Donald, 1928- ed. • 2.10768
Contemporary American poetry. Selected and introduced by Donald Hall. —
2d ed., rev. and expanded. — [Harmondsworth, Eng.; Baltimore]: Penguin
Books, [1972, c1971] 280 p.; 18 cm. — (Penguin poets) 1. American poetry —
20th century I. T.
PS613.H3 1971   811/.5/408   LC 72-181803   ISBN 0140420673

The Longman anthology of contemporary American poetry, 2.10769
1950–1980 / [edited by] Stuart Friebert, David Young.
New York: Longman, c1983. xxx, 592 p.: ports.; 23 cm. 1. American poetry —
20th century I. Friebert, Stuart, 1931- II. Young, David, 1930-
PS613.L6 1983   811/.54/08 19   LC 81-15630   ISBN 0582282632

The Poetry anthology, 1912–1977: sixty–five years of America's 2.10770
most distinguished verse magazine / edited by Daryl Hine &
Joseph Parisi.
Boston: Houghton Mifflin, 1978. xlvii, 555 p.; 21 cm. — (Sentry edition; 86)
Includes index. 1. American poetry — 20th century I. Hine, Daryl. II. Parisi,
Joseph, 1944- III. Poetry (Chicago)
PS613.P64   811/.5/208   LC 78-8042   ISBN 0395265487

Auden, W. H. (Wystan Hugh), 1907-1973. • 2.10771
The Faber book of modern American verse / edited by W.H. Auden. —
London: Faber and Faber, [1956] 336 p.; 21 cm. 1. American poetry — 20th
century I. T.
PS614.A815   LC 56-59056

Ciardi, John, 1916- ed. • 2.10772
Mid–century American poets. — New York: Twayne, [1950] xxx, 300 p.; 22
cm. — ([The Twayne library of modern poetry, 7]) 1. American poetry — 20th
century I. T.
PS614.C515   811.5082   LC 50-6746

The Generation of 2000: contemporary American poets / edited   2.10773
by William Heyen.
Princeton, N.J.: Ontario Review Press; New York, N.Y.: Distributed by Persea Books, c1984. xxii, 364 p.: ports.; 23 cm. (Ontario Review Press poetry series.) 1. American poetry — 20th century I. Heyen, William, 1940- II. Series.
PS615.G38 1984   811/.5/08 19   *LC* 84-14745   *ISBN* 0865380422

The Harvard book of contemporary American poetry / edited   2.10774
by Helen Vendler.
Cambridge, Mass.: Belknap Press of Harvard University Press, 1985. 440 p.; 24 cm. Includes indexes. 1. American poetry — 20th century I. Vendler, Helen Hennessy. II. Title: Contemporary American poetry.
PS615.H37 1985   811/.5/08 19   *LC* 85-5473   *ISBN* 0674373405

Monaco, Richard.   2.10775
New American poetry / photography by Philip Friedman. — New York: McGraw-Hill, [1973] xiii, 208 p.: ill.; 23 cm. 1. American poetry — 20th century I. T.
PS615.M55   811/.5/408   *LC* 72-6571   *ISBN* 0070426783

The New naked poetry: recent American poetry in open forms /   2.10776
edited by Stephen Berg and Robert Mezey.
Indianapolis: Bobbs-Merrill, 1976. xxvii, 478 p.: ports.; 23 cm. Includes index. 1. American poetry — 20th century I. Berg, Stephen. II. Mezey, Robert.
PS615.M58   811/.5/408   *LC* 75-12999   *ISBN* 0672613549

The Morrow anthology of younger American poets / edited by   2.10777
Dave Smith & David Bottoms.
New York: William Morrow & Co., 1985. 784 p.: ports.; 24 cm. 1. American poetry — 20th century I. Smith, Dave, 1942- II. Bottoms, David. III. Title: Anthology of younger American poets.
PS615.M64 1985b   811/.54/08 19   *LC* 84-20537

The Postmoderns: the new American poetry revised / edited and   2.10778
with a new preface by Donald Allen & George F. Butterick.
1st Evergreen ed. — New York: Grove Press, 1982. 436 p.; 21 cm. 1. American poetry — 20th century 2. American poetry — 20th century — Bio-bibliography. I. Allen, Donald Merriam. II. Butterick, George F.
PS615.P67 1982   811/.54/08 19   *LC* 79-52054   *ISBN* 0394174585

PS623–635 DRAMA

Halline, Allan Gates, ed.   2.10779
American plays; selected and edited, with critical introductions and bibliographies, by Allan Gates Halline... New York, Cincinnati [etc.] American book company [c1935] vii, 787 p. 24 cm. (American literature series) 1. American drama I. T.
PS623.H3   812.0822   *LC* 35-5220

Moody, Richard, 1911- ed.   • 2.10780
Dramas from the American theatre, 1762–1909. — Cleveland: World Pub. Co., [1966] xiii 873 p.: illus., facsims.; 26 cm. — (New World literature series, v. 1) 1. American drama 2. Theater — United States I. T.
PS623.M66   812.008   *LC* 66-13958

Moses, Montrose Jonas, 1878-1934. ed.   • 2.10781
Representative plays by American dramatists, edited with an introd. to each play, by Montrose J. Moses. New York E.P. Dutton [1918-[25] 3 v.: ports., facsim.; 25 cm. 1. American drama (Collections) I. T.
PS623 M67   *LC* 11-8005466

Gassner, John, 1903-1967. comp.   2.10782
Best plays of the early American theatre; from the beginning to 1916. Edited, with introductions, by John Gassner in association with Mollie Gassner. — New York: Crown Publishers, [1967] xlviii, 716 p.: front.; 25 cm. 1. American drama I. Gassner, Mollie, joint comp. II. T.
PS625.G3   812/.008   *LC* 67-6995

The Longman anthology of American drama / edited by Lee A.   2.10783
Jacobus.
New York: Longman, c1982. ix, 690 p.; 26 cm. — (Longman English and humanities series.) 1. American drama I. Jacobus, Lee A. II. Series.
PS625.L66 1982   822/.008 19   *LC* 80-21895   *ISBN* 058228242X

Contemporary Chicano theatre / Roberto J. Garza, editor.   2.10784
Notre Dame: University of Notre Dame Press, c1976. viii, 248 p.; 24 cm. 1. American drama — Mexican American authors 2. American drama — 20th century. I. Garza, Roberto J., 1934-
PS628.M4 C6   812/.5/408   *LC* 75-19876   *ISBN* 0268007098

Hatch, James Vernon, 1928- comp.   2.10785
Black theater, U.S.A.; forty-five plays by Black Americans, 1847-1974. James V. Hatch, editor. Ted Shine, consultant. — New York: Free Press, [1974] x,

886 p.; 27 cm. 1. American drama — Afro-American authors I. Shine, Ted. II. T.
PS628.N4 H3   812/.008/0352   *LC* 75-169234   *ISBN* 0029141605

King, Woodie. comp.   2.10786
Black drama anthology. Edited by Woodie King and Ron Milner. — New York: Columbia University Press, 1972. 671 p.; 21 cm. 1. American drama — Afro-American authors 2. American drama — 20th century. I. Milner, Ron, joint comp. II. T.
PS628.N4 K5   812/.5/4080352   *LC* 77-181833   *ISBN* 0231036442

Oliver, Clinton F., comp.   2.10787
Contemporary Black drama: from 'A raisin in the sun' to 'No place to be somebody.' / selected and edited with introductions by Clinton F. Oliver; Stephanie Sills, co–editor. — New York: Scribner, [1971] xii, 451 p.; 24 cm. 1. American drama — Afro-American authors 2. American drama — 20th century. I. Sills, Stephanie, ed. II. T.
PS628.N4 O4   812/.5/408   *LC* 77-132574   *ISBN* 0684414325

Patterson, Lindsay. comp.   2.10788
Black theater; a 20th century collection of the work of its best playwrights. Compiled with an introd. by Lindsay Patterson. — New York: Dodd, Mead, [1971] ix, 493 p.; 24 cm. 1. American drama — Negro authors. 2. American drama — 20th century. I. T.
PS628.N4 P3   PS628N4 P3.   812/.5/08   *LC* 75-135538   *ISBN* 0396062547

A Century of plays by American women / edited with an introd.   2.10789
by Rachel France.
1st ed. — New York: Richards Rosen Press, 1979. 223 p.: ill.; 29 cm. 1. American drama — Women authors 2. American drama — 20th century. 3. One-act plays, American I. France, Rachel, 1936-
PS628.W6 C4   812/.041   *LC* 78-12347   *ISBN* 0823904725

The New women's theatre: ten plays by contemporary American   2.10790
women / edited and with an introd., by Honor Moore.
1st ed. — New York: Vintage Books, 1977. xxxvii, 537 p.; 21 cm. 1. American drama — Women authors 2. American drama — 20th century. I. Moore, Honor, 1945-
PS628.W6 N4   812/.5/408   *LC* 76-58261   *ISBN* 039472206X

Plays by American women, 1900–1930 / edited and with an   2.10791
introduction by Judith E. Barlow.
New York, N.Y.: Applause Theatre Book Publishers, 1985. xxxiii, 261 p.; 22 cm. Rev. ed. of: Plays by American women. c1981. 1. American drama — Women authors 2. American drama — 20th century. I. Barlow, Judith E. II. Plays by American women.
PS628.W6 P59 1985   812/.52/0809287 19   *LC* 84-24606   *ISBN* 0879102268

Ballet, Arthur H., comp.   2.10792
Playwrights for tomorrow: a collection of plays / edited, with an introd. by Arthur H. Ballet. — Minneapolis: University of Minnesota Press, [1966-. v.   ; 23 cm. A project of the Office for Advanced Drama Research of the University of Minnesota. 1. American drama — 20th century. I. Minnesota. University. Office for Advanced Drama Research. II. T.
PS634.B32   812/.5/408   *LC* 66-19124   *ISBN* 0816605807

Best American plays.   • 2.10793
[1st]-   ser.; 1939-. New York, Crown Publishers. v. 1. American drama — 20th century. I. Title: Twenty best plays of the modern American theatre. II. Title: Best plays of the modern American theatre.
PS634.B4   *LC* 57-12830

Cerf, Bennett, 1898-1971. comp.   2.10794
Plays of our time, edited by Bennett Cerf. New York, Random House [1967] 782 p. 25 cm. 1. American drama — 20th century. I. T.
PS634.C4169   812/.5/208   *LC* 67-22665

Cerf, Bennett, 1898-1971. ed.   • 2.10795
Six American plays for today / selected and with biographical notes by Bennett Cerf. — New York: Modern Library [1961] 599 p.; 19 cm. (The Modern library of the world's best books [38]) 1. American drama — 20th century. I. T.
PS634.C418   812.5082   *LC* 61-11189

Cerf, Bennett, 1898-1971.   • 2.10796
24 favorite one-act plays / edited by Bennett Cerf and Van H. Cartmell. — 1st ed. — Garden City, N.Y.: Doubleday, 1958. 455 p.; 22 cm. 1. American drama — 20th century. 2. English drama — 20th century I. Cartmell, Van Henry, 1896- II. T.
PS634.C43   *LC* 58-13274

Couch, William, comp.   • 2.10797
New Black playwrights: an anthology / edited and with an introd. by William Couch, Jr. — Baton Rouge: Louisiana State University Press, [1968] xxiii,

258 p.; 24 cm. 1. American drama — Negro authors. 2. American drama — 20th century. I. T.
PS634.C684   *LC* 68-31137

Gaver, Jack. ed.   • **2.10798**
Critics's choice: New York Drama Critics' Circle prize plays, 1935–55. — Freeport, N.Y.: Books for Libraries Press, [1971, c1955] 661 p.; 27 cm. — (Play anthology reprint series) 1. American drama — 20th century. I. New York Drama Critics' Circle. II. T.
PS634.G35 1971   812/.5/08   *LC* 70-173622   *ISBN* 0836982215

The Most popular plays of the American theatre: ten of   **2.10799**
Broadway's longest–running plays / edited with an introd. and notes by Stanley Richards.
New York: Stein and Day, 1979. 703 p., [7] leaves of plates: ill.; 25 cm. 1. American drama — 20th century. I. Richards, Stanley, 1918-
PS634.M66   812/.5/08   *LC* 79-65112   *ISBN* 0812826825

New American plays / edited and with an introd. by Robert W.   **2.10800**
Corrigan.
[1st ed.]. — New York: Hill and Wang, [1965-. v.   ; 19-21 cm. — (A Mermaid dramabook; MD 34, 41) Vol. 2 edited and with an introd. by William M. Hoffman. 1. American drama — 20th century. I. Corrigan, Robert Willoughby, 1927- II. Hoffman, William M., 1939-
PS634.N36   812.54082   *LC* 65-14530   *ISBN* 0809007452

New plays USA.   **2.10801**
1-   . — [New York, N.Y.]: Theatre Communications Group/TCG, c1982-. v.; 24 cm. Annual. I. Theatre Communications Group.
PS634.N413   812/.008 19   *LC* 83-645685

The Obie winners: the best of Off–Broadway / edited and with   **2.10802**
an introd. by Ross Wetzsteon.
Garden City, N.Y.: Doubleday, c1980. xii, 803 p., [4] leaves of plates: ill.; 22 cm. 1. American drama — 20th century. 2. Off-Broadway theater 3. Drama — 20th century I. Wetzsteon, Ross.
PS634.O2   812/.5408   *LC* 79-6096   *ISBN* 038517005X

Orzel, Nick, ed.   • **2.10803**
Eight plays from Off–Off Broadway, edited by Nick Orzel and Michael Smith. With an introd. by Michael Smith. — Indianapolis: Bobbs-Merrill, [1966] 281 p.: illus.; 20 cm. I. Smith, Michael Townsend, 1938- joint ed. II. T.
PS634.O7   812/.5/408   *LC* 66-27887

Richards, Stanley, 1918- comp.   • **2.10804**
Best plays of the sixties. Edited with an introductory note and prefaces to the plays [by] Stanley Richards. — [1st ed.]. — Garden City, N.Y.: Doubleday, 1970. xiii, 1036 p.: ports.; 22 cm. 1. American drama — 20th century. 2. English drama — 20th century I. T.
PS634.R5   822/.9/1408   *LC* 73-97684

Six modern American plays; introd. by Allan G. Halline.   • **2.10805**
New York: Modern Library, [1951] 419 p.; 19 cm. — (The Modern library of the world's best books, 276) 1. American drama — 20th century. I. Halline, Allan Gates.
PS634.S57   812.5082   *LC* 51-8900

Smith, Michael Townsend, 1938- comp.   • **2.10806**
More plays from Off–Off Broadway / edited by Michael Smith. — Indianapolis: Bobbs-Merrill Co., [1972] xii, 409 p.: ports.; 22 cm. 1. American drama — 20th century. I. T.
PS634.S593   812/.5/408   *LC* 77-142473

Word plays: an anthology of new American drama.   **2.10807**
[1]-   . — New York: Performing Arts Journal Publications, c1980-. v.; 23 cm. (PAJ playscripts.) 1. American drama — 20th century — Collected works. I. Series.
PS634.W658   812 11   *LC* sc 84-7858

PS642–659 PROSE

Blackmur, R. P. (Richard P.), 1904-1965. ed.   • **2.10808**
American short novels. New York, Crowell [1960] 398 p. 24 cm. (American literary forms) 1. American fiction I. T. II. Series.
PS643.B5x   *LC* 60-6314

Best American short stories and the Yearbook of the American   • **2.10809**
short story.
Boston: Houghton Mifflin, [1916-] v. Editor: 1915-1941   E.J. O'Brien. Imprint varies. Editor: 1941-   Martha Foley. 1. Short stories, American 2. Short stories — Bibliography. I. O'Brien, Edward Joseph Harrington,

1890-1941. II. Foley, Martha. III. Title: Yearbook of the American short story.
PS645.B45   PZ1.B4.   *LC* 16-11387

Warren, Robert Penn, 1905-.   • **2.10810**
A Southern harvest: short stories by southern writers / edited by Robert Penn Warren. — Boston: Houghton, Mifflin, c1937. xv, 359 p.; 24 cm. Biographical notes. 1. Short stories, American 2. American literature — Southern States. I. T.
PZ1.W28 So7 PS551   PS645.W37.   813/.01   *LC* 37-35187

PS647 Special Groups of Authors, A–Z

Rosen, Kenneth, comp.   **2.10811**
The man to send rain clouds; contemporary stories by American Indians. Edited and with an introd. by Kenneth Rosen. Illus. by R. C. Gorman & Aaron Yava. — New York: Viking Press, [1974] xiv, 178 p.: illus.; 21 cm. 'A Richard Seaver book.' 1. American fiction — Indian authors 2. American fiction — 20th century I. T.
PS647.I5 R6x   813/.01   *LC* 73-6086   *ISBN* 0670453315

Cuentos Chicanos: a short story anthology / edited by Rudolfo   **2.10812**
A. Anaya and Antonio Márquez.
Rev. ed. — Albuquerque: Published for New America by the University of New Mexico Press, c1984. viii, 186 p.; 24 cm. English and Spanish. 1. Short stories, American — Mexican American authors 2. American fiction — 20th century I. Anaya, Rudolfo A. II. Márquez, Antonio, 1940-
PS647.M49 C8 1984   813/.01/0886872073 19   *LC* 84-13066   *ISBN* 082630771X

Clarke, John Henrik, 1915- ed.   **2.10813**
American Negro short stories. [1st ed.] New York, Hill and Wang [1966] xix, 355 p. 21 cm. 1. Short stories, American 2. American literature — Afro-American authors I. T.
PS647.N35C5x   *LC* 66-23863

Hughes, Langston, 1902-1967. ed.   **2.10814**
The best short stories by Negro writers; an anthology from 1899 to the present. — [1st ed.]. — Boston: Little, Brown, [1967] xvii, 508 p.; 22 cm. 1. Short stories, American I. T.
PS647.N35H8x   *LC* 67-11221

King, Woodie. comp.   • **2.10815**
Black short story anthology. New York: Columbia University Press, 1972. 381 p.; 21 cm. 1. Short stories, American 2. American fiction — Afro-American authors I. T.
PZ1.K582 Bl PS647.N35K5x   813/.01   *LC* 72-6773   *ISBN* 0231037112

Stadler, Quandra Prettyman, comp.   **2.10816**
Out of our lives: a selection of contemporary Black fiction. — Washington: Howard University Press, 1975. xvi, 298 p.; 22 cm. 1. American fiction — Afro-American authors I. T.
PS647.N35 S8x   813/.01   *LC* 74-7092   *ISBN* 0882580272

Turner, Darwin T., 1931- comp.   • **2.10817**
Black American literature: fiction / edited by Darwin T. Turner. — Columbus, Ohio: C. E. Merrill Pub. Co., [1969] ix, 142 p.; 23 cm. — (Charles E. Merrill program in American literature. Charles E. Merrill literary texts) 1. American essays — Negro authors 2. American fiction — Afro-American authors 3. Short stories, American I. T. II. Title: Black American literature essays
PS683 N4 T8   PZ1.T865 Bl PS647.N35T8x.   813/.5/08   *LC* 79-82446   *ISBN* 067509500X

Classic American women writers: Sarah Orne Jewett, Kate   **2.10818**
Chopin, Edith Wharton, Willa Cather / edited with an introd., chronologies and bibliographies Cynthia Griffin Wolff.
1st ed. — New York: Harper & Row, c1980. vi, 406 p.; 18 cm. — (Perennial library; P 502) 1. Short stories, American — Women authors I. Wolff, Cynthia Griffin.
PS647.W6 C58   813/.01   *LC* 79-2743   *ISBN* 0060805021

Companions of our youth: stories by women for young people's   **2.10819**
magazines, 1865–1900 / edited by Jane Benardete and Phyllis Moe.
New York: F. Ungar Pub. Co., c1980. viii, 216 p.: ill.; 24 cm. 1. Children's stories, American I. Benardete, Jane. II. Moe, Phyllis.
PS647.W6C6x   *LC* 80-14573   *ISBN* 0804420432

Hidden hands: an anthology of American women writers,   **2.10820**
1790–1870 / edited by Lucy M. Freibert and Barbara A. White.
New Brunswick, N.J.: Rutgers University Press, c1985. xv, 409 p.: ports.; 24 cm. (Douglass series on women's lives and the meaning of gender.) Includes

index. 1. American fiction — Women authors 2. American fiction — 19th century I. Freibert, Lucy M., 1922- II. White, Barbara Anne. III. Series.
PS647.W6 H5 1985   810/.8/09287 19   *LC* 84-22884   *ISBN* 0813510880

Provisions: a reader from 19th–century American women / 2.10821
edited with an introduction and critical commentary by Judith Fetterley.
Bloomington: Indiana University Press, c1985. viii, 467 p.; 25 cm. (Everywoman.) 1. American prose literature — Women authors 2. American prose literature — 19th century. 3. Women — United States — Literary collections. I. Fetterley, Judith, 1938- II. Series.
PS647.W6 P7 1985   818/.308/0809287 19   *LC* 84-42840   *ISBN* 0253170400

PS648 Special Forms, Topics, A–Z

Adolescence in literature / Thomas West Gregory, [editor]. 2.10822
New York: Longman, c1978. xix, 411 p.; 23 cm. (English and humanities series) 1. Adolescence — Fiction. 2. Short stories, American I. Gregory, Thomas West. II. Series.
PZ1.A2294 PS648.A34   813/.01   *LC* 77-17719   *ISBN* 0582280451

Great detectives: a century of the best mysteries from England 2.10823
and America / edited by David Willis McCullough.
1st ed. — New York: Pantheon Books, c1984. xv, 728 p.; 24 cm. 1. Detective and mystery stories, American 2. Detective and mystery stories, English I. McCullough, David W.
PS648.D4 G68 1984   813/.0872/08 19   *LC* 84-42707   *ISBN* 0394540654

Shaw, Joseph Thompson, 1874-. 2.10824
The hard–boiled omnibus; early stories from Black mask, edited, and with an introduction, by Joseph T. Shaw. New York, Simon and Schuster [1946] 468 p. 21 cm. 1. Detective and mystery stories, American I. Black mask. II. T.
PS 648 D4 H25 1946   *LC* 46-8293

Southwest, towards the twenty–first century: tales of terror, 2.10825
mystery, and mercy / [editing, Karl and Jane Kopp].
1st ed. — Corrales, N.M.: Red Earth Press, c1981. 232 p.; 21 cm. 1. American fiction — Southwest, New. 2. American fiction — 20th century 3. Detective and mystery stories, American I. Kopp, Karl, 1934- II. Kopp, Jane.
PS648.D4 S59 1981   813/.0872/08979 19   *LC* 82-118927   009183405X

Don't bet on the prince: contemporary feminist fairy tales in 2.10826
North America and England / [edited by] Jack Zipes.
New York: Methuen, 1986. xiv, 270 p.: ill.; 23 cm. 1. Feminism — Fiction. 2. Women — Fiction. 3. Short stories, American 4. Short stories, English 5. Fairy tales 6. Fairy tales — History and criticism. 7. Feminist literary criticism 8. Women in literature I. Zipes, Jack David.
PS648.F4 D66 1986   813/.01/08352042 19   *LC* 85-29794   *ISBN* 0416013716

The Handicapped in literature: a psychosocial perspective / 2.10827
edited by Eli M. Bower.
Denver: Love Pub. Co., c1980. xi, 407 p.; 23 cm. 1. Handicapped — Literary collections. 2. American prose literature — 20th century. 3. English prose literature — 20th century I. Bower, Eli Michael.
PS648.H23 H36   813/.54/0803520816 19   *LC* 79-57278   *ISBN* 0891080988

Asimov, Isaac, 1920- comp. 2.10828
Before the Golden Age; a science fiction anthology of the 1930s. [1st ed.] Garden City, N.Y., Doubleday, 1974. xix, 986 p. 25 cm. (Doubleday science fiction) 1. Science fiction, American I. T.
PZ1.A815 Be PS648.S3A7x   813/.0876   *LC* 73-10965   *ISBN* 0385024193

Conklin, Groff, 1904-1968. ed. 2.10829
The golden age of science fiction / edited with an introd. by Groff Conklin; pref. by John W. Campbell, Jr. — Bonanza 1980 ed. — New York: Bonanza Books, [1980] c1963. xxx, 785 p.; 24 cm. Reprint of the ed. published by Bonanza, New York, under title: The best of science fiction. 1. Science fiction, American 2. Science fiction, English I. T.
PS648.S3 C6 1980   813/.0876/08 19   *LC* 80-27208   *ISBN* 0517334860

Ellison, Harlan. 2.10830
Dangerous visions; 33 original stories. Illus. by Leo and Diane Dillon. — [1st ed.]. — Garden City, N.Y.: Doubleday, 1967. xxix, 520 p.: illus.; 25 cm. — (Doubleday science fiction) Sequel: Again, dangerous visions. 1. Science fiction I. T.
PS648.S3 E4x   *LC* 67-19078

Machines that think: the best science fiction stories about robots 2.10831
and computers / edited by Isaac Asimov, Patricia S. Warrick, Martin H. Greenberg.
1st ed. — New York: Holt, Rinehart, and Winston, 1984, c1983. 627 p.; 24 cm. 1. Science fiction, American 2. Androids — Fiction. 3. Computers — Fiction. I. Asimov, Isaac, 1920- II. Warrick, Patricia S. III. Greenberg, Martin Harry.
PS648.S3 M27 1984   813/.0876/08356 19   *LC* 83-245   *ISBN* 0030614988

Mohs, Mayo. comp. 2.10832
Other worlds, other gods; adventures in religious science fiction. — [1st ed.]. — Garden City, N.Y.: Doubleday, 1971. 264 p.; 22 cm. 1. Science fiction, American I. T.
PZ1.M743 Ot PS648.S3M6x   813/.0876   *LC* 76-144282

Superfiction: or, The American story transformed: an anthology 2.10833
/ edited by Joe David Bellamy.
New York: Random House, 1975. 293 p.: ill.; 19 cm. — (Vintage Book) 1. Short stories, American I. Bellamy, Joe David. II. Title: The American story transformed.
PS648.S5 Bx   813/.01   *LC* 75-13368   *ISBN* 0394715233

Foley, Martha. comp. 2.10834
200 years of great American short stories / edited by Martha Foley. — Boston: Houghton Mifflin, 1975. xii, 968 p.; 24 cm. 1. Short stories, American I. T.
PZ1.F688 Tw PS648.S5 Fx   813/.01   *LC* 75-1107   *ISBN* 039520447X

The Graywolf annual. 2.10835
[1]-   . — Port Townsend, Wash.: Graywolf Press, 1985-. v.; 22 cm. (Graywolf short fiction series.) Annual. Published: St. Paul, Minn., c1986- 1. Short stories, American — Periodicals 2. American fiction — 20th century — Periodicals. 3. Short stories — Periodicals. I. Series.
PS648.S5 G7   813/.01/08 19   *LC* 86-658048

The Treasury of American short stories / selected and with an 2.10836
introduction by Nancy Sullivan.
1st ed. — Garden City, N.Y.: Doubleday, c1981. xvii, 748 p.; 22 cm. Includes indexes. 1. Short stories, American I. Sullivan, Nancy.
PS648.S5 T7   813/.01/08 19   *LC* 80-2438   *ISBN* 0385171390

Freimarck, Vincent, comp. 2.10837
Race and the American romantics / edited by Vincent Freimarck & Bernard Rosenthal. — New York: Schocken Books, 1972 (c1971) xi, 328 p.; 22 cm. — (Sourcebooks in Negro history) 1. American prose literature — 19th century. 2. Slavery in the United States. I. Rosenthal, Bernard, 1934- joint comp. II. T. III. Series.
PS648.S55 F7   818/.3/0808   *LC* 73-163330   *ISBN* 0805234179

The Arbor House treasury of great Western stories / edited by 2.10838
Bill Pronzini and Martin Greenberg; [introduction by John Jakes].
New York: Arbor House, c1982. 455 p.; 24 cm. 'Priam books'—Cover. 1. American fiction — 20th century 2. Western stories I. Pronzini, Bill. II. Greenberg, Martin Harry.
PS648.W4 A7 1982   813/.0874/08 19   *LC* 82-72052   *ISBN* 0877954100

PS651–659 By Period

American Colonial prose: John Smith to Thomas Jefferson / 2.10839
edited by Mary Ann Radzinowicz.
Cambridge [Cambridgeshire]; New York: Cambridge University Press, 1984. ix, 285 p.; 23 cm. — (Cambridge English prose texts.) 1. American prose literature — Colonial period, ca. 1600-1775 I. Radzinowicz, Mary Ann. II. Series.
PS651.A5 1984   818/.108 19   *LC* 83-20873   *ISBN* 0521244269

Dorson, Richard Mercer, 1916- ed. • 2.10840
America begins; early American writing. Edited, with an introd., by Richard M. Dorson. — Freeport, N.Y.: Books for Libraries Press, [1972, c1950] x, 438 p.: illus.; 22 cm. — (Essay index reprint series) 1. American prose literature — Colonial period, ca. 1600-1775 I. T.
PS651.D6 1972   081   *LC* 72-5802   *ISBN* 0836929861

The Mirth of a nation: America's great dialect humor / edited 2.10841
by Walter Blair and Raven I. McDavid, Jr.
Minneapolis, MN: University of Minnesota Press, [1983] p. cm. Includes index. 1. American fiction — 19th century 2. American wit and humor I. Blair, Walter, 1900- II. McDavid, Raven Ioor.
PS653.M5   813/.3/09 19   *LC* 81-16403   *ISBN* 0816610223

Pizer, Donald. comp. • 2.10842
American thought and writing: the 1890's. — Boston: Houghton Mifflin, [1972] xiii, 561 p.; 21 cm. — (Riverside editions, A125) 1. American prose literature — 19th century. I. T.
PS658.P5   810/.8/004   *LC* 76-177497   *ISBN* 0395134935

Burnett, Whit, 1899- comp. 2.10843
Black hands on a white face; a time–piece of experiences in a Black and white America. An anthology. — New York: Dodd, Mead, [c1971] xiv, 392 p.; 22 cm. 1. American prose literature — 20th century. 2. Race relations in literature. I. T.
PS659.B8   818/.08   *LC* 73-160860   *ISBN* 0396063748

Elkin, Stanley, 1930- comp. 2.10844
Stories from the sixties / edited with a pref. by Stanley Elkin. — [1st ed.]. — Garden City, N.Y.: Doubleday, 1971. 400 p.; 22 cm. 1. Short stories, American 2. American fiction — 20th century I. T.
PS659.E5x   813/.01   *LC* 71-144262

55 short stories from the New Yorker. • 2.10845
New York: Simon and Schuster, 1949. viii, 480 p.; 24 cm. 1. Short stories, American I. The New Yorker (New York, 1925-)
PS659.N4 F5x   *LC* 49-11777

Short stories from the New Yorker. • 2.10846
New York: Simon and Schuster, 1940. 3 p., l., ix-xii, 438 p.; 24 cm. 'The sixty-eight stories in this collection were chosen from those appearing in 'The New Yorker' during its first fifteen and a half years of publication—February, 1925, to September, 1940.' 1. Short stories, American 2. American literature — 20th century I. The New Yorker (1925-)
PS659.N4 S5x   *LC* 40-27816

Stories from the New Yorker, 1950–1960. • 2.10847
New York: Simon and Schuster, 1960. 780 p.; 24 cm. 1. Short stories, American I. The New Yorker (New York, 1925-)
PS659.N4 S8x   *LC* 60-12590

The Ploughshares reader: new fiction for the eighties / edited 2.10848
and with an introduction by DeWitt Henry.
Wainscott, New York: Pushcart Press, 1985. 514 p. 1. Short stories, American — 20th century. I. Henry, DeWitt. II. Ploughshares
PS659 P65 1985   *LC* 84-62095   *ISBN* 0916366308

Prize stories. • 2.10849
1947-. Garden City, N. Y., Doubleday. v. 22 cm. Annual. The O. Henry awards. None published 1952-53. 1. Short stories, American — Collected works.
PS659.P7x   813/.01/08 19   *LC* 21-9372

Salzman, Jack. comp. • 2.10850
Years of protest; a collection of American writings of the 1930's, edited by Jack Salzman. Barry Wallenstein, assistant editor. — New York, Pegasus [1967] 448 p. illus., facsims. 21 cm. Bibliography: p. 447-448. 1. American fiction — 20th cent. I. Wallenstein, Barry. joint comp. II. T.
PS659.S3x   *LC* 67-13489

Statements 2: new fiction / edited by Jonathan Baumbach and 2.10851
Peter Spielberg; with an introd. by Robert Coover.
1st ed. — New York: Fiction Collective: distributed by G. Braziller, c1977. 217 p.; 23 cm. 1. American fiction — 20th century I. Baumbach, Jonathan. II. Spielberg, Peter.
PS659.S8 1977x   813/.01   *LC* 76-56053   *ISBN* 0914590367

Statements: new fiction from the Fiction Collective / [assembled 2.10852
by Jonathan Baumbach].
New York: G. Braziller, [1975] 208 p.; 23 cm. (A Venture book) 1. American fiction — 20th century I. Baumbach, Jonathan. II. Fiction Collective (U.S.)
PS659.S8x   813/.01   *LC* 74-25083   *ISBN* 0807607770

PS660–688 ORATORY. ESSAYS

Baird, Albert Craig, 1883- ed. • 2.10853
American public addresses, 1740–1952. New York: McGraw-Hill, 1956. 301 p.; 24 cm. (McGraw-Hill series in speech) 1. Speeches, addresses, etc., American 2. United States — Politics and government — Addresses, essays, lectures. I. T.
PS662.B27   815.082   *LC* 55-11553

Hurd, Charles, 1903-1968, ed. • 2.10854
A treasury of great American speeches. Rev. and edited by Andrew Bauer. New and rev. ed. New York, Hawthorn Books [1970] 411 p. 24 cm. 1. Speeches,

addresses, etc., American 2. United States — History — Addresses, essays, lectures. I. T.
PS662.H8 1970   815/.01   *LC* 77-107901

Potter, David, 1915- comp. 2.10855
The colonial idiom. Edited by David Potter and Gordon L. Thomas. Carbondale, Southern Illinois University Press [1970] xiii, 639 p. 24 cm. (Landmarks in rhetoric and public address.) 1. Speeches, addresses, etc., American 2. United States — History — Colonial period, ca. 1600-1775 — Addresses, essays, lectures. I. Thomas, Gordon L., 1914- joint comp. II. T. III. Series.
PS662.P6   815/.1/08   *LC* 71-83669   *ISBN* 0809304317

Wrage, Ernest J., ed. • 2.10856
American forum: speeches on historic issues, 1788–1900, edited by Ernest J. Wrage [and] Barnet Baskerville. New York, Harper [1960] 377 p. 25 cm. 1. Speeches, addresses, etc., American 2. United States — Civilization — Addresses, essays, lectures. I. Baskerville, Barnet. joint ed. II. T.
PS662.W7   815.082   *LC* 60-7019

O'Neill, Daniel J., comp. 2.10857
Speeches by Black Americans, edited and compiled by Daniel J. O'Neill. Encino, Calif., Dickenson Pub. Co. [1971] xii, 274 p. illus., ports. 23 cm. 1. Speeches, addresses, etc., American — Afro-American authors. 2. Afro-American orators 3. Afro-Americans — Civil rights — Addresses, essays, lectures. I. T.
PS663.N4 O5   815/.008   *LC* 76-152850

American rhetoric from Roosevelt to Reagan: a collection of 2.10858
speeches and critical essays / [edited by] Halford Ross Ryan.
Prospect Heights, Ill.: Waveland Press, c1983. xv, 309 p.; 23 cm. 1. Speeches, addresses, etc., American 2. Political oratory — United States — Addresses, essays, lectures. I. Ryan, Halford Ross.
PS668.A43 1983   815/.01/08358 19   *LC* 83-151860   *ISBN* 0881330159

Representative American speeches. 2.10859
1937/38-. New York, H. W. Wilson Co. v. 21 cm. (Reference shelf.) Annual. 1. Speeches, addresses, etc., American 2. Speeches, addresses, etc. I. Baird, Albert Craig, 1883- ed. II. Thonssen, Lester, 1904- ed. III. Braden, Waldo Warder, 1911- ed. IV. Peterson, Owen, 1924- ed. V. Series.
PS668.B3   815.5082   *LC* 38-27962

Miller, Perry, 1905-1963. ed. • 2.10860
American thought: Civil War to World War I. — New York: Rinehart, [1954] 345 p.; 19 cm. — (Rinehart editions, 70) 1. American essays 2. United States — Civilization — Addresses, essays, lectures. I. T.
PS682.M5   814.4082   *LC* 54-7243

The Penguin book of contemporary American essays / Maureen 2.10861
Howard, editor.
New York, N.Y., U.S.A.: Viking, 1984. xxix, 283 p.; 24 cm. 1. American essays — 20th century. I. Howard, Maureen, 1930- II. Title: Contemporary American essays.
PS688.P44 1984   814/.54/08 19   *LC* 84-40265   *ISBN* 0670239836

PS700–3576 INDIVIDUAL AUTHORS

PS700–893 Colonial Period (17th–18th Centuries)

PS708–739 Brackenridge. Bradstreet. St John de Crèvecoeur

Brackenridge, H. H. (Hugh Henry), 1748-1816. • 2.10862
A Hugh Henry Brackenridge reader, 1770–1815. Edited, with an introd., by Daniel Marder. [Pittsburgh] University of Pittsburgh Press [1970] x, 407 p. 24 cm. I. Marder, Daniel. ed. II. T.   *LC* 69-12332   *ISBN* 0822931842
PS708.B5 A6 1970   818/.2/09

Brackenridge, H. H. (Hugh Henry), 1748-1816. 2.10863
Modern chivalry: containing the adventures of Captain John Farrago and Teague O'Regan, his servant / edited for the modern reader by Lewis Leary. — New Haven: College & University Press, 1965. 335 p.; 21 cm. — (Masterworks

of literature series.) 'Reproduced here are the first four volumes ... those of 1792, 1793, and 1797.' I. Leary, Lewis Gaston, 1906- II. T. III. Series.
PS708.B5 M6 1965   *LC* 65-28257

Bradstreet, Anne, 1612?-1672.   • **2.10864**
The works of Anne Bradstreet / edited by Jeannine Hensley; foreword by Adrienne Rich. — Cambridge, Mass.: Belknap Press of Harvard University Press, 1967. xxxvii, 320 p.: facsim.; 22 cm. — (John Harvard library.) Bibliographical footnotes. I. Hensley, Jeannine, ed. II. T. III. Series.
PS711.A1 1967   811/.1   *LC* 67-17312

Bradstreet, Anne, 1612?-1672.   **2.10865**
The complete works of Anne Bradstreet / edited by Joseph R. McElrath, Jr. and Allan P. Robb. — Boston: Twayne Publishers, 1981. xlii, 536 p.; 25 cm. I. McElrath, Joseph R. II. Robb, Allan P. III. T.
PS711.A1 1981   811/.1   *LC* 79-27242   *ISBN* 0805785337

Critical essays on Anne Bradstreet / [edited by] Pattie Cowell   **2.10866**
and Ann Stanford.
Boston, Mass.: G.K. Hall, c1983. xxv, 286 p.: ill.; 24 cm. — (Critical essays on American literature.) 1. Bradstreet, Anne, 1612?-1672 — Criticism and interpretation — Addresses, essays, lectures. I. Cowell, Pattie. II. Stanford, Ann. III. Series.
PS712.C7 1983   811/.1 19   *LC* 82-21339   *ISBN* 081618643X

Stanford, Ann.   **2.10867**
Anne Bradstreet, the worldly Puritan: an introduction to her poetry / by Ann Stanford. — New York: B. Franklin, 1974. xiv, 170 p.: ill.; 23 cm. Includes index. 1. Bradstreet, Anne, 1612?-1672. I. T.
PS712.S8   811/.1   *LC* 74-22319   *ISBN* 0891020306

Philbrick, Thomas.   **2.10868**
St. John de Crèvecoeur. New York: Twayne Publishers [1970] 178 p.; 21 cm. (Twayne's United States authors series, 154) 1. St. John de Crèvecoeur, J. Hector, 1735-1813. I. T.
PS737.C5 Z85   818/.2/09   *LC* 73-99532

PS745–752 Franklin
(see also: E302.F82; E302.6.F7-.F8)

Granger, Bruce Ingham, 1920-.   • **2.10869**
Benjamin Franklin, an American man of letters. Ithaca, N.Y., Cornell University Press 1964. ix, 264 p. 23 cm. 1. Franklin, Benjamin, 1706-1790. I. T.
PS751.G7   818.1   *LC* 64-23360

The Oldest revolutionary: essays on Benjamin Franklin / edited   **2.10870**
by J. A. Leo Lemay.
[Philadelphia]: University of Pennsylvania Press, 1976. x, 165 p.; 24 cm. 1. Franklin, Benjamin, 1706-1790 — Addresses, essays, lectures. I. Lemay, J. A. Leo (Joseph A. Leo), 1935-
PS752.O4   973.3/092/4   *LC* 75-41618   *ISBN* 0812277074

PS755–759 Freneau

Adkins, Nelson Frederick, 1897-.   • **2.10871**
Philip Freneau and the cosmic enigma; the religious and philosophical speculations of an American poet, by Nelson F. Adkins. — New York: Russell & Russell, [1971, c1949] 84 p.; 23 cm. 1. Freneau, Philip Morin, 1752-1832. I. T.
PS758.A6 1971   811/.2   *LC* 75-139892

Axelrad, Jacob.   • **2.10872**
Philip Freneau, champion of democracy. — Austin: University of Texas Press, [1967] xii, 480 p.; 24 cm. 1. Freneau, Philip Morin, 1752-1832 — Political and social views. I. T.
PS758.A9   811/.2 B   *LC* 66-15699

Bowden, Mary Weatherspoon.   **2.10873**
Philip Freneau / by Mary Weatherspoon Bowden. — Boston: Twayne Publishers, c1976. 194 p.; 21 cm. (Twayne's United States authors series; TUSAS 260) Includes index. 1. Freneau, Philip Morin, 1752-1832. I. T.
PS758.B6   811/.2 B   *LC* 75-30651   *ISBN* 0805771611

PS805–855 Mather. Taylor. Tompson.
Trumbull. Tyler

Levy, Babette May, 1907-.   **2.10874**
Cotton Mather / by Babette M. Levy. — Boston: Twayne Publishers, 1979. 188 p.: port.; 21 cm. — (Twayne's United States authors series; TUSAS 328)

Includes index. 1. Mather, Cotton, 1663-1728 — Criticism and interpretation. I. T.
PS805.Z5 L4   973.2/092/4 B   *LC* 78-23445   *ISBN* 0805772618

Taylor, Edward, 1642-1729.   **2.10875**
Poems; edited by Donald E. Stanford. With a foreword by Louis L. Martz. — New Haven: Yale University Press, 1960. lxii, 543 p.: facsim.; 23 cm. I. Stanford, Donald E., 1913- ed. II. T.
PS850.T2 A6 1960   811.1   *LC* 60-6432

Keller, Karl, 1933-.   **2.10876**
The example of Edward Taylor / by Karl Keller. — Amherst: University of Massachusetts Press, 1975. 319 p., [4] leaves of plates: ill.; 24 cm. 1. Taylor, Edward, 1642-1729. I. T.
PS850.T2 Z74   811/.1 B   *LC* 74-21240   *ISBN* 087023174X

Tompson, Benjamin, 1642-1714.   **2.10877**
Benjamin Tompson, colonial bard: a critical edition / Peter White. — University Park: Pennsylvania State University Press, 1981 (c1980). xi, 218 p.; 24 cm. Includes index. I. White, Peter, 1947- II. T.
PS850.T45 A6   811/.1   *LC* 79-21367   *ISBN* 0271002506

Trumbull, John, 1750-1831.   **2.10878**
Satiric poems: The progress of dulness and M'Fingal; edited with a preface and notes by Edwin T. Bowden. — Austin: University of Texas Press, [1962] 229 p.: ill.; 23 cm. 'The text here is ... an accurate reproduction of the first complete edition of each poem.' I. Bowden, Edwin T. II. T. III. Title: M'Fingal. IV. Title: The progress of dulness.
PS852.P7 1962   *LC* 61-15829

Gimmestad, Victor E.   **2.10879**
John Trumbull, by Victor E. Gimmestad. New York, Twayne Publishers [1974] 183 p. 21 cm. (Twayne's United States authors series, TUSAS 240) 1. Trumbull, John, 1750-1831. I. T.
PS853.G5   811/.2   *LC* 73-17016   *ISBN* 0805707468

Tyler, Royall, 1757-1826.   • **2.10880**
The contrast; a comedy in five acts. With a history of George Washington's copy by James Benjamin Wilbur. — New York: AMS Press, [1970] xxxviii, 120 p.: illus.; 23 cm. Reprint of the 1920 ed. I. Wilbur, James Benjamin, 1856-1929, ed. II. T.
PS855.T7 C6 1970   812/.2   *LC* 74-130232   *ISBN* 0404065635

Carson, Ada Lou.   **2.10881**
Royall Tyler / by Ada Lou Carson and Herbert L. Carson. — Boston: Twayne Publishers, 1979. 172 p.: port; 21 cm. — (Twayne's United States authors series; TUSAS 344) Includes index. 1. Tyler, Royall, 1757-1826 — Criticism and interpretation. I. Carson, Herbert L. joint author. II. T.
PS855.T7 Z6   818/.2/09   *LC* 79-4621   *ISBN* 0805772812

PS858–866 Ward. Wheatley

Ward, Nathaniel, 1578-1652.   • **2.10882**
The simple cobler of Aggawam in America / edited by P. M. Zall. — Lincoln: University of Nebraska Press [1969] xviii, 81 p.: map (on lining papers); 22 cm. 1. Freedom of religion — Great Britain. 2. Great Britain — Church history — 17th century 3. Great Britain — Politics and government — 1642-1649 I. Zall, Paul M. ed. II. T.
PS858.W2 S5 1969   274.2   *LC* 69-19107

Wheatley, Phillis.   • **2.10883**
Poems / edited with an introd., by Julian D. Mason, Jr. — Chapel Hill: University of North Carolina Press, 1966. viii, 113 p.: ill.; 23 cm. I. Mason, Julian Dewey, 1931- ed. II. T.
PS866.W5 1966   *LC* 66-15510

Critical essays on Phillis Wheatley / [edited by] William H.   **2.10884**
Robinson.
Boston, Mass.: G.K. Hall, c1982. xii, 236 p.; 25 cm. — (Critical essays on American literature.) 1. Wheatley, Phillis, 1753-1784 — Criticism and interpretation — Addresses, essays, lectures. I. Robinson, William Henry, 1922- II. Series.
PS866.W5 Z583 1982   811/.1 19   *LC* 81-23757   *ISBN* 0816183368

Robinson, William Henry, 1922-.   **2.10885**
Phillis Wheatley and her writings / William H. Robinson. — New York: Garland, 1984. xiii, 464 p.: ill.; 23 cm. — (Critical studies on Black life and culture. v. 12) Includes a reprinting of Phillis Wheatley's Poems on various subjects, religious and moral. Includes index. 1. Wheatley, Phillis, 1753-1784. 2. Poets, American — 18th century — Biography. I. Wheatley, Phillis, 1753-1784. Poems on various subjects religious and moral. 1983. II. T. III. Series.
PS866.W5 Z688 1984   811/.1 B 19   *LC* 82-21027   *ISBN* 0824093461

Robinson, William Henry, 1922-.   **2.10886**
Phillis Wheatley in the Black American beginnings / by William H. Robinson.
— 1st ed. — Detroit: Broadside Press, [1975] 95 p.; 22 cm. (Broadside critics series; no. 5) 1. Wheatley, Phillis, 1753-1784. I. T. II. Series.
PS866.W5 Z69   811/.1   LC 75-312984   ISBN 0910296189. ISBN 0910296278 pbk

---

PS991–3390 19th Century

PS1004 Henry Adams

(see also: E175.5)

Adams, Henry, 1838-1918.   • **2.10887**
A Henry Adams reader, edited and with an introd. by Elizabeth Stevenson. — [1st ed.]. — Garden City, N. Y., Doubleday, 1958. 392 p. 22 cm. (Doubleday anchor books) I. T.
AC8.A22   PS1004.A4 A6 1958.   081   LC 58-5929

Adams, Henry, 1838-1918.   • **2.10888**
Democracy: an American novel. — New York: Farrar, [1952?] 246 p.; 22 cm. I. T.
PZ3.A2137D12 PS1004.A4D4 1952   LC 52-3211

Adams, Henry, 1838-1918.   • **2.10889**
Esther, a novel, by Henry Adams (Francis Snow Compton) with an introduction by Robert E. Spiller ... New York, Scholars' facsimiles & reprints, 1938. xxv, 302 p. 18 cm. (Scholars' facsimiles & reprints) Facsimile of the original (1884) edition. I. Spiller, Robert Ernest, 1896- II. T.
PS1004.A4 E8 1884a   LC 38-18393

**Critical essays on Henry Adams / [collected by] Earl N.   2.10890
Harbert.**
Boston, Mass.: G.K. Hall, c1981. 262 p.; 25 cm. — (Critical essays on American literature.) 1. Adams, Henry, 1838-1918 — Criticism and interpretation — Addresses, essays, lectures. I. Harbert, Earl N., 1934- II. Series.
PS1004.A4 Z63 1981   818/.409 19   LC 81-2699   ISBN 0816182809

PS1006 Ade

Ade, George, 1866-1944.   • **2.10891**
The America of George Ade, 1866–1944: fables, short stories, essays / edited with an introd. by Jean Shepherd. — New York: Putnam, [c1961] 284 p.: ill.; 22 cm. I. T.
PS1006.A6 A6 1961   LC 61-2525

Ade, George, 1866-1944.   • **2.10892**
Artie; and, Pink Marsh: two novels / drawings by John T. McCutcheon; introduction by James T. Farrell. — Chicago: University of Chicago Press, [1963] xi, 224 p.: ill.; 22 cm. — (Chicago in fiction) I. Ade, George, 1866-1944. Pink Marsh. II. T. III. Title: Pink Marsh. IV. Series.
PZ3.A228 As   PS1006.A6 A85.   LC 63-22584

Ade, George, 1866-1944.   • **2.10893**
Chicago stories / illustrated by John T. McCutcheon and others; selected and edited, with an introduction by Franklin J. Meine. — Chicago: H. Regnery Co., 1963. xxx, 278 p.: ill.; 27 cm. 1. Chicago — Social life and customs. I. McCutcheon, John Tinney, 1870-1949. II. Ade, George, 1866-1944. Stories of the streets and of the town. III. T. IV. Title: Stories of the streets and of the town.
PS1006.A6 S7 1963   LC 63-21830

Coyle, Lee.   • **2.10894**
George Ade. New York, Twayne Publishers [1964] 159 p. 21 cm. (Twayne's United States authors series, 63) 1. Ade, George, 1866-1944. I. T.
PS1006.A6 Z6   817.4   LC 64-20713

Kelly, Fred C. (Fred Charters), 1882-1959.   • **2.10895**
George Ade, warmhearted satirist / by Fred C. Kelly. — 1st ed. — Indianapolis; New York: The Bobbs-Merrill, [1947] 282 p.: ill., facsims., ports.; 22 cm. 1. Ade, George, 1866-1944 — Biography. 2. Authors, American — 19th century — Biography. I. T.
PS1006.A6 Z7   LC 47-30196

PS1010–1038 The Alcotts. Allen

Bedell, Madelon.   **2.10896**
The Alcotts: biography of a family Madelon Bedell. — 1st ed. — New York: C. N. Potter: distributed by Crown Publishers, c1980. xv, 400 p., [16] p. of plates: ill., facsims., ports. 1. Alcott family. I. T.
PS1013.B4   PS1013 B4.   141/.3/0922 B   LC 79-26741   ISBN 0517540312

Alcott, Louisa May, 1832-1888.   **2.10897**
Behind a mask: the unknown thrillers of Louisa May Alcott / edited and with an introd. by Madeleine Stern. — New York: Morrow, 1975. xxxiii, 277 p., [2] leaves of plates: ill.; 24 cm. Contains an introd. by M. B. Stern and four stories by L. M. Alcott: Behind a mask; or, A woman's power, The abbot's ghost; or, Maurice Treherne's temptation, Pauline's passion and punishment, and The mysterious key and what it opened. The first two of these were published under the pseud. of A. M. Barnard. I. Stern, Madeleine B., 1912- II. T.
PZ3.A355 Be PS1017   PS1017 B4 1975.   813/.4   LC 74-31046   ISBN 0688003389

Alcott, Louisa May, 1832-1888.   **2.10898**
Jo's boys. London, Dent; New York, Dutton [c1960] 325 p. (The children's illustrated classics) I. T.
PS1017.Jx   LC 60-16166

Alcott, Louisa May, 1832-1888.   **2.10899**
Little women / Louisa M. Alcott; introduction by Madelon Bedell. — 1st ed. — New York: Modern Library, c1983. lv, 603 p.; 19 cm. (Modern Library college editions) I. Bedell, Madelon. II. T.
PS1017.L5 1983   813/.4 19   LC 83-810   ISBN 0394331877

Alcott, Louisa May, 1832-1888.   **2.10900**
Little men / by Louisa M. Alcott; illustrated by Harry Toothill. London: J.M. Dent, 1957. xi, 335 p.: ill.; 23 cm. (Children's illustrated classics) I. T.
PS1017.Lx

Alcott, Louisa May, 1832-1888.   **2.10901**
Work: a story of experience / Louisa May Alcott; introd. by Sarah Elbert. — New York: Schocken Books, 1977. xliv, 443 p.: ill.; 21 cm. — (Studies in the life of women) Originally published in 1892; with new introd. I. T.
PZ3.A355 Wo4 PS1017.W6x   813/.4   LC 76-48849   ISBN 0805205632

**Critical essays on Louisa May Alcott / [edited by] Madeleine   2.10902
B. Stern.**
Boston, Mass.: G.K. Hall, c1984. x, 295 p.; 25 cm. (Critical essays on American literature.) 1. Alcott, Louisa May, 1832-1888 — Criticism and interpretation — Addresses, essays, lectures. I. Stern, Madeleine B., 1912- II. Series.
PS1018.C7 1984   813/.4 19   LC 84-4499   ISBN 0816186863

Saxton, Martha.   **2.10903**
Louisa May: a modern biography of Louisa May Alcott / Martha Saxton. — Boston: Houghton Mifflin, 1977. 428 p.: ill. Includes index. 1. Alcott, Louisa May, 1832-1888 — Biography. 2. Novelists, American — 19th century — Biography. I. T.
PS1018.S2   PS1018 S2.   813/.4 B   LC 77-23750   ISBN 0395257204

Stern, Madeleine B., 1912-.   • **2.10904**
Louisa May Alcott. — [1st ed.]. — Norman: University of Oklahoma Press, 1950. 424 p.: ill., ports.; 21 cm. 1. Alcott, Louisa May, 1832-1888. I. T.
PS1018.S75   928.1   LC 50-6953

Allen, James Lane, 1849-1925.   • **2.10905**
A Kentucky cardinal & Aftermath / by James Lane Allen; edited for school use by Jane C. Tunnell. — New York: Macmillan, 1924. xiii, 268 p.: plates; 20 cm. I. Tunnell, Jane C., ed. II. T. III. Title: Aftermath.
PS1034.Kx PZ3.A427K 14   LC 24-30860

Knight, Grant Cochran, 1893-1956.   • **2.10906**
James Lane Allen and the genteel tradition, by Grant C. Knight. Chapel Hill, The University of North Carolina Press, 1935. xiii, 313 p. front. (port.) 23 cm. 1. Allen, James Lane, 1849-1925. I. T.
PS1036.K6   928.1   LC 35-9575

PS1086–1181 Bellamy. Bierce. Brown. Bryant

Bellamy, Edward, 1850-1898.   **2.10907**
Looking backward, 2000–1887 / by Edward Bellamy; edited with an introduction by Cecelia Tichi. — Harmondsworth, Middlesex, England; New York, N.Y.: Penguin Books, 1982. 234 p.: port.; 19 cm. — (Penguin American library) I. Tichi, Cecelia, 1942- II. T. III. Series.
PS1086.L6 1982   813/.4 19   LC 82-14986   ISBN 0140390189

Bowman, Sylvia E.   2.10908
Edward Bellamy / by Sylvia E. Bowman. — Boston: Twayne Publishers, c1986. 157 p.: port.; 23 cm. — (Twayne's United States authors series. TUSAS 500) Includes index. 1. Bellamy, Edward, 1850-1898 — Criticism and interpretation. I. T. II. Series.
PS1087.B58 1986   813/.4 19   *LC* 86-242   *ISBN* 0805774602

Bierce, Ambrose, 1842-1914?   • 2.10909
[Selected works. 1946] The collected writings of Ambrose Bierce, with an introduction by Clifton Fadiman. New York, The Citadel press [1946] 2 p., l., vii-xix, 810 p. 22 cm. I. Fadiman, Clifton, 1904- II. T.
PS1097.A1 1946   818.4   *LC* 47-30068

Bierce, Ambrose, 1842-1914?   • 2.10910
The devil's dictionary / Ambrose Bierce. — New York: Dover Publications, 1958. 145 p. I. T.
PS1097 D4 1958a   PS1097 D4 1958.   817.4   *LC* A62-8606

Grenander, M. E. (Mary Elizabeth), 1918-.   2.10911
Ambrose Bierce, by M. E. Grenander. New York, Twayne Publishers [1971] 193 p. 22 cm. (Twayne's United States authors series. TUSAS 180) 1. Bierce, Ambrose, 1842-1914? I. T.
PS1097.Z5 G75   813/.4   *LC* 78-120519

Brown, Charles Brockden, 1771-1810.   2.10912
[Novels] The novels and related works of Charles Brockden Brown / [Sydney J. Krause, general editor, Alexander Cowie, contributing editor, S.W. Reid, textual editor]. — Bicentennial ed. — [Kent, Ohio]: Kent State University Press, c1977-<c1984 >. v. <1-4 >: ill.; 25 cm. I. T.
PZ3.B814 Nr5 PS1130.B7x   813/.2 19   *LC* 74-79474   *ISBN* 0873381602

Axelrod, Alan, 1952-.   2.10913
Charles Brockden Brown, an American tale / by Alan Axelrod. — 1st ed. — Austin: University of Texas Press, 1983. xx, 203 p.; 24 cm. 'Primarily a study of four novels by Charles Brockden Brown ... Wieland, Ormond, Arthur Mervyn, and Edgar Huntly'—Pref. 1. Brown, Charles Brockden, 1771-1810 — Criticism and interpretation. I. T.
PS1137.A9 1983   813/.2 19   *LC* 82-13405   *ISBN* 0292710763

Critical essays on Charles Brockden Brown / [edited by]   2.10914
Bernard Rosenthal.
Boston, Mass.: G.K. Hall, c1981. vii, 246 p.; 25 cm. — (Critical essays on American literature.) 1. Brown, Charles Brockden, 1771-1810 — Criticism and interpretation — Addresses, essays, lectures. I. Rosenthal, Bernard, 1934- II. Series.
PS1137.C7   813/.2 19   *LC* 80-27488   *ISBN* 0816182558

Bryant, William Cullen, 1794-1878.   2.10915
The poetical works of William Cullen Bryant / with chronologies of Bryant's life and poems and a bibliography of his writings by Henry C. Sturges; and a memoir of his life by Richard Henry Stoddard. — Roslyn edition. — New York: AMS Press, 1969. cxxx, 418 p.: ill., port.; 22 cm. — I. Sturges, Henry Cady, 1846- II. Stoddard, Richard Henry, 1825-1903. III. T.
PS1150.F03   *LC* 79-85192   *ISBN* 0404011438

Bryant, William Cullen, 1794-1878.   2.10916
The letters of William Cullen Bryant / edited by William Cullen Bryant, II, and Thomas G. Voss. — 1st ed. — New York: Fordham University Press, 1975-<1984 >. v. <1-4 >: ill.; 24 cm. Includes indexes. 1. Bryant, William Cullen, 1794-1878 — Correspondence. I. Bryant, William Cullen, 1908- II. Voss, Thomas G. III. T.
PS1181.A4 1975   811/.3 B   *LC* 74-27169   *ISBN* 0823209911

Brown, Charles Henry, 1910-.   • 2.10917
William Cullen Bryant / [by] Charles H. Brown. — New York: Scribner, [1971] 576 p.: ill.; 25 cm. 1. Bryant, William Cullen, 1794-1878. I. T.
PS1181.B74   811/.3 B   *LC* 79-143949   *ISBN* 0684123703

PS1240–1294 Cable. Chambers. Chesnutt. Chopin

Cable, George Washington, 1844-1925.   • 2.10918
The Grandissimes; a story of Creole life. New York, Sagamore Press, 1957. 339 p. 21 cm. 1. Southern States — Social life and customs — 1775-1865 I. T.
PZ3.C11 Gr15   PS1244.G6x.   *LC* 57-12445

Cable, George Washington, 1844-1925.   • 2.10919
Old Creole days. With an introd. and notes by Arlin Turner. — New York: Garrett Press, 1970. xxx, 229 p.: port.; 19 cm. — (The works of George W. Cable) Reprint of the 1879 ed. I. T.
PS1244.O6x   813/.4   *LC* 73-96486   *ISBN* 0512000654

Bikle, Lucy Leffingwell (Cable)   • 2.10920
George W. Cable; his life and letters. — New York, Russell & Russell [1967] xvi, 306 p. illus., facsims., ports. 22 cm. Reprint of the 1928 ed. 1. Cable, George Washington, 1844-1925. I. T.
PS1246.B5 1967   818/.4/08   *LC* 66-27039

Critical essays on George W. Cable / [edited by] Arlin Turner.   2.10921
Boston: Hall, c1980. xxviii, 251 p.; 25 cm. — (Critical essays on American literature.) 1. Cable, George Washington, 1844-1925 — Criticism and interpretation — Addresses, essays, lectures. I. Turner, Arlin. II. Series.
PS1246.C7   813/.4   *LC* 79-17229   *ISBN* 0816182566

Rubin, Louis Decimus, 1923-.   • 2.10922
George W. Cable: the life and times of a Southern heretic [by] Louis D. Rubin, Jr. — New York: Pegasus, [1969] viii, 304 p.: port.; 21 cm. — (Pegasus American authors) 1. Cable, George Washington, 1844-1925. I. T.
PS1246.R8   813/.4 B   *LC* 76-77135

Turner, Arlin, 1909-.   • 2.10923
George W. Cable, a biography. — Durham, N.C.: Duke University Press, 1956. 391 p.: ill.; 24 cm. 1. Cable, George Washington, 1844-1925. I. T.
PS1246.T8   *LC* 56-9165

Chambers, Robert W. (Robert William), 1865-1933.   2.10924
The king in yellow, and other horror stories. Selected with an introd. by E. F. Bleiler. New York, Dover Publications [1970] xiii, 287 p. 22 cm. 1. Horror tales I. T.
PZ3.C355 Ki13 PS1284.K5x   813/.5/2   *LC* 70-98301   *ISBN* 0486225003

Chesnutt, Charles Waddell, 1858-1932.   2.10925
The short fiction of Charles W. Chesnutt / edited and with introd. by Sylvia Lyons Render. — Washington: Howard University Press, 1974. 422 p. I. Render, Sylvia Lyons. II. T.
PZ3.C4253 Sh PS1292.C6 Ax   813/.4   *LC* 73-88973   *ISBN* 0882580124

Chesnutt, Charles Waddell, 1858-1932.   • 2.10926
The conjure woman. New introd. by Robert M. Farnsworth. — [1st ed.]. — Ann Arbor: University of Michigan Press, [1969] xix, 229 p.; 21 cm. — (Ann Arbor paperbacks) 'Originally published in 1899.' I. T.
PZ3.C4253 Co6 PS1292.C6 C6x   813/.4   *LC* 70-8946

Andrews, William L., 1946-.   2.10927
The literary career of Charles W. Chesnutt / William L. Andrews. — Baton Rouge: Louisiana State University Press, c1980. xiii, 292 p.: port. — (Southern literary studies.) Includes index. 1. Chesnutt, Charles Waddell, 1858-1932 — Criticism and interpretation. I. T. II. Series.
PS1292.C6 Z53   PS1292C6 Z53.   813/.4   *LC* 79-25875   *ISBN* 0807106739

Heermance, J. Noel.   2.10928
Charles W. Chesnutt; America's first great Black novelist, by J. Noel Heermance. — [Hamden, Conn.]: Archon Books, 1974. xiii, 258 p.; 22 cm. 1. Chesnutt, Charles Waddell, 1858-1932. I. T.
PS1292.C6 Z7   813/.4 B   *LC* 73-14595   *ISBN* 0208013806

Keller, Frances Richardson, 1917-.   2.10929
An American crusade: the life of Charles Waddell Chesnutt / Frances Richardson Keller. — Provo, Utah: Brigham Young University Press, c1978. xvi, 304 p.: ill.; 24 cm. Includes index. 1. Chesnutt, Charles Waddell, 1858-1932 — Biography. 2. Novelists, American — 19th century — Biography. I. T.
PS1292.C6 Z75   813/.4 B   *LC* 77-14608   *ISBN* 0842508376

Render, Sylvia Lyons.   2.10930
Charles W. Chesnutt / by Sylvia Lyons Render. — Boston: Twayne Publishers, 1981 (c1980). 186 p.: port.; 22 cm. — (Twayne's United States authors series; TUSAS 373) Includes index. 1. Chesnutt, Charles Waddell, 1858-1932 — Criticism and interpretation. I. T.
PS1292.C6 Z85   813/.4 19   *LC* 80-24234   *ISBN* 0805772723

Chopin, Kate, 1851-1904.   2.10931
The awakening / Kate Chopin; an authoritative text, contexts, criticism, edited by Margaret Culley. — 1st ed. — New York: Norton, c1976. viii, 229 p.; 22 cm. (A Norton critical edition) I. Culley, Margaret. II. T.
PZ3.C456 Aw20 PS1294.C63   813/.4   *LC* 76-55321   *ISBN* 0393044343. *ISBN* 0393091724 pbk

Chopin, Kate, 1851-1904.   2.10932
[Works] The complete works of Kate Chopin. Edited and with an introd. by Per Seyersted. Foreword by Edmund Wilson. Baton Rouge, Louisiana State University Press [1970, c1969] 2 v. (1032 p.) port. 24 cm. (Southern literary studies.) I. Seyersted, Per, 1921- ed. II. T. III. Series.
PS1294.C63 1970   813/.4   *LC* 73-80043   *ISBN* 0807108499

Seyersted, Per, 1921-. • 2.10933
Kate Chopin. A critical biography. Oslo, Universitetsforlaget; Baton Rouge, Louisiana State University Press 1969. 246 p. 2 plates. 23 cm. (Publications of the American Institute, University of Oslo) 1. Chopin, Kate, 1851-1904. 2. Authors, American — 19th century — Biography. I. T.
PS1294.C63 S4   813/.4 B   LC 77-88740   ISBN 0807109150

Skaggs, Peggy. 2.10934
Kate Chopin / by Peggy Skaggs. — Boston: Twayne Publishers, c1985. 130 p.: port.; 23 cm. — (Twayne's United States authors series. TUSAS 485) Includes index. 1. Chopin, Kate, 1851-1904 — Criticism and interpretation. I. T. II. Series.
PS1294.C63 S55 1985   813/.4 19   LC 84-27977   ISBN 0805774394

PS1300–1348 Clemens (Mark Twain)

Twain, Mark, 1835-1910. 2.10935
The Mark Twain papers. Editorial board: Walter Blair, Donald Coney [and] Henry Nash Smith. Associate editor: Frederick Anderson. [Berkeley, University of California Press, 1967-. v. ports. 24 cm. I. T.
PS1300.F67x

Twain, Mark, 1835-1910. 2.10936
The works of Mark Twain. — Berkeley: Published for the Iowa Center for Textual Studies by the University of California Press, 1972-. v.: ill.; 24 cm. I. Iowa Center for Textual Studies. II. T.
PS1300.F72   818/.4/09   LC 72-190706   ISBN 0520020189

Twain, Mark, 1835-1910. 2.10937
Mark Twain's Notebooks & journals / Mark Twain [i.e. S. L. Clemens]; edited by Frederick Anderson, Michael B. Frank, and Kenneth M. Sanderson. — Berkeley: University of California Press, 1976 (c1975). 2 v. I. Anderson, Frederick, 1926- II. T.
PS1302.A48 1975   818/.4/09   LC 72-87199   ISBN 0520025423

Twain, Mark, 1835-1910. • 2.10938
The portable Mark Twain, edited by Bernard De Voto. New York, The Viking press, 1946. vii, 786 p. 17 cm. (The Viking portable library) I. De Voto, Bernard Augustine, 1897-1955. ed. II. T.
PS1302.D4   817.44   LC 46-6686

Twain, Mark, 1835-1910. • 2.10939
Mark Twain of the Enterprise: newspaper articles & other documents, 1862–1864 / edited by Henry Nash Smith with the assistance of Frederick Anderson. — Berkeley: University of California Press, 1957. 240 p.: ill., ports., facsims.; 25 cm. I. Smith, Henry Nash, 1906-. II. Anderson, Frederick, 1926- III. Territorial enterprise and Virginia City news. IV. T.
PS1302.S5   LC 57-6543

Twain, Mark, 1835-1910. 2.10940
The Devil's race–track: Mark Twain's great dark writings: the best from Which was the Dream? and Fables of man / edited by John S. Tuckey. — Berkeley: University of California Press, c1980. xx, 385 p.: facsims.: 24 cm. I. Tuckey, John Sutton, 1921- II. T.
PS1302.T8 1980   818/.409 19   LC 78-62865   ISBN 0520037804

Twain, Mark, 1835-1910. 2.10941
[Adventures of Huckleberry Finn.] The annotated Huckleberry Finn: Adventures of Huckleberry Finn / by Mark Twain (Samuel L. Clemens); with an introduction, notes, and bibliography by Michael Patrick Hearn. — New York: C.N. Potter; distributed by Crown Publishers, c1981. 378 p.: ill.; 29 cm. Includes index. I. Hearn, Michael Patrick. II. T.
PS1305.A2 H4 1981   813/.4 19   LC 81-5904   ISBN 0517530317

Twain, Mark, 1835-1910. 2.10942
Adventures of Huckleberry Finn: an authoritative text, backgrounds and sources, criticism / Samuel Langhorne Clemens; edited by Sculley Bradley, Richmond Croom Beatty, E. Hudson Long [and] Thomas Cooley. 2d ed. — New York: Norton, c1977. xi, 452 p. (A Norton critical edition) I. Bradley, Sculley, 1897-II. Beatty, Richmond Croom, 1905-1961. III. Long, E. Hudson (Eugene Hudson), 1908- IV. Cooley, Thomas, 1942- V. T.
PZ3.C59 A86 PS1305.A2 7x   813/.4   LC 76-30648   ISBN 0393044548

Blair, Walter, 1900-. 2.10943
Mark Twain & Huck Finn. Berkeley, University of California Press [1973, c1960] xvi, 436 p. illus. 24 cm. (Library reprint series) 1. Twain, Mark, 1835-1910. The adventures of Huckleberry Finn. 2. Twain, Mark, 1835-1910. I. T.
PS1305.B5 1973   813/.4   LC 73-87552   ISBN 0520025210

Egan, Michael. 2.10944
Mark Twain's Huckleberry Finn: race, class and society / [by] Michael Egan. — London: Chatto and Windus for Sussex University Press, 1977. 135 p.; 20 cm. — (Text and context) 1. Twain, Mark, 1835-1910. The adventures of Huckleberry Finn. 2. Twain, Mark, 1835-1910 — Political and social views. I. T.
PS1305.E35   813/.4   LC 77-361174   ISBN 0856210609. ISBN 0856210617 pbk

Norton, Charles A. 2.10945
Writing Tom Sawyer: the adventures of a classic / by Charles A. Norton. — Jefferson, N.C.: McFarland, 1983. viii, 160 p.: ill.; 24 cm. Includes index. 1. Twain, Mark, 1835-1910. Adventures of Tom Sawyer. I. T.
PS1306.N67 1983   813/.4 19   LC 82-17164   ISBN 0899500676

Twain, Mark, 1835-1910. 2.10946
[Pudd'nhead Wilson] Pudd'nhead Wilson and Those extraordinary twins: authoritative texts, textual introduction and tables of variants criticism / Samuel Langhorne Clemens; edited by Sidney E. Berger. — 1st ed. — New York: Norton, c1980. xii, 384 p.; 22 cm. — (A Norton critical edition) 1. Twain, Mark, 1835-1910. Pudd'nhead Wilson. 2. Twain, Mark, 1835-1910. Those extraordinary twins. I. Twain, Mark, 1835-1910. Those extraordinary twins. 1980. II. Berger, Sidney E. III. T.
PS1317.B4 1980   813/.4   LC 79-23679   ISBN 0393013375

PS1329–1348 Biography. Criticism

Twain, Mark, 1835-1910. • 2.10947
[Autobiography] The autobiography of Mark Twain [pseud.] including chapters now published for the first time, as arr. and edited, with an introd. and notes, by Charles Neider. New York, Harper [1959] 388 p. illus. 25 cm. I. T.
PS1331.A2 1959   928.1   LC 59-6005

Twain, Mark, 1835-1910. • 2.10948
Mark Twain's letters: arranged with comment / by Albert Bidelow Paine ... New York; London: Harper & brothers, [c1917] 2 v. (855 p.): ill., ports., facsims; 21 cm. I. Paine, Albert Bigelow, 1861-1937. II. T.
PS1331.A3 1917   928.1   LC 17-30756

Twain, Mark, 1835-1910. • 2.10949
Mark Twain–Howells letters: the correspondence of Samuel L. Clemens and William D. Howells, 1872–1910 / edited by Henry Nash Smith and William M. Gibson with the assistance of Frederick Anderson. — Cambridge: Belknap Press of Harvard University Press, 1960. 2 v. (xxv, 948 p.): ill., ports., facsims., geneal. tables; 25 cm. Bibliographical references included in 'Note on editorial practice' (v. 1, p. xxi—xxv) 'Calendar of letters': v. 2, p. 883-903. 'Index of works by Samuel L. Clemens and William D. Howells': v. 2, p. 943-948. I. Howells, William Dean, 1837-1920. II. Smith, Henry Nash. ed. III. Gibson, William Merriam, 1912- ed. IV. T.
PS1331.A3H6   928.1   LC 60-5397

Brooks, Van Wyck, 1886-1963. • 2.10950
The ordeal of Mark Twain / by Van Wyck Brooks. — New and rev. ed. — New York: Dutton, 1933. 325 p. 1. Twain, Mark, 1835-1910. 2. Authors, American — 19th century — Biography. I. T.
PS1331.B7 1933   818/.4/03   LC 33-3197

Brooks, Van Wyck, 1886-1963. 2.10951
The ordeal of Mark Twain / Van Wyck Brooks; introd. by Malcolm Cowley. — New York: Meridian Books, 1955,[c1948]. 256 p. (Meridian books,; M14) 1. Twain, Mark, 1835-1910. I. T.
PS1331.B7x 1955   [B]   LC 55-9699

Budd, Louis J. 2.10952
Our Mark Twain: the making of his public personality / Louis J. Budd. — Philadelphia: University of Pennsylvania Press, 1983. xv, 266 p.: ill.; 24 cm. 1. Twain, Mark, 1835-1910 — Biography. 2. Authors, American — 19th century — Biography. 3. Humorists, American — Biography. I. T.
PS1331.B9 1983   818/.409 B 19   LC 82-23758   ISBN 081227881X

Cox, James Melville, 1925-. • 2.10953
Mark Twain: the fate of humor [by] James M. Cox. Princeton, N.J., Princeton University Press, 1966. viii, 321 p. 23 cm. 1. Twain, Mark, 1835-1910. I. T.
PS1331.C6   817.4   LC 66-11966

Critical essays on Mark Twain, 1910–1980 / [edited by] Louis J. Budd. 2.10954
Boston, Mass.: G.K. Hall, c1983. viii, 241 p.; 24 cm. — (Critical essays on American literature.) 1. Twain, Mark, 1835-1910 — Addresses, essays, lectures. 2. Authors, American — 19th century — Biography — Addresses, essays, lectures. I. Budd, Louis J. II. Series.
PS1331.C76 1983   818/.409 19   LC 83-4400   ISBN 0816186529

De Voto, Bernard Augustine, 1897-1955. • 2.10955
Mark Twain's America. Illustrated by M. J. Gallagher. Cambridge, Houghton Mifflin Co., 1951 [c1932] xvi, 351 p. illus. 22 cm. Bibliography: p. [323]-339. 1. Twain, Mark, 1835-1910. I. T.
PS1331.D4 1951   817.44   LC 51-6160

Emerson, Everett H., 1925-. 2.10956
The authentic Mark Twain: a literary biography of Samuel L. Clemens / Everett Emerson. — Philadelphia: University of Pennsylvania Press, 1984. xiii, 330 p., [12] p. of plates: ill., ports. Includes indexes. 1. Twain, Mark, 1835-1910. 2. Authors, American — 19th century — Biography. I. T.
PS1331.E47 1983   818/.409 B 19   *LC* 83-10626   *ISBN* 0812278976

Howells, William Dean, 1837-1920. • 2.10957
My Mark Twain: reminiscences and criticisms. Edited and with an introd. by Marilyn Austin Baldwin. — Baton Rouge, Louisiana State University Press [1967] xviii, 189 p. group port. 23 cm. Bibliographical references included in 'Notes' (p. 165-184) 1. Twain, Mark, 1835-1910. I. Baldwin, Marilyn Austin, ed. II. T.
PS1331.H6 1967   817/.4   *LC* 67-21374

Kaplan, Justin. 2.10958
Mark Twain and his world / Justin Kaplan. — New York: Simon and Schuster, [1974] 224 p., [16] leaves of plates: ill.; 26 cm. 1. Twain, Mark, 1835-1910. 2. United States — Civilization — 19th century I. T.
PS1331.K325 1974   PS1331 K325 1974.   818/.4/09   *LC* 72-87659
ISBN 0671214624

Kaplan, Justin. • 2.10959
Mr. Clemens and Mark Twain, a biography. New York, Simon and Schuster [1966] 424 p. illus., ports. 24 cm. 1. Twain, Mark, 1835-1910. I. T.
PS1331.K33   817.4 B   *LC* 66-17603

Paine, Albert Bigelow, 1861-1937. • 2.10960
Mark Twain: a biography: the personal and literary life of Samuel Langhorne Clemens / by Albert Paine; with letters, comments and incidental writings hitherto unpublished; also new episodes, anecdotes, etc. — Centenary ed. New York and London: Harper & brothers [1935] 4 v. in 2.: ill., plates, facsims.; 21 cm. 1. Twain, Mark, 1835-1910. I. T.
PS1331.P3 1935   *LC* 35-27375

Smith, Henry Nash. ed. • 2.10961
Mark Twain; a collection of critical essays. Englewood Cliffs, N.J., Prentice-Hall [1963] 179 p. 22 cm. (Twentieth century views) (A Spectrum book.) 'S-TC-30.' 1. Twain, Mark, 1835-1910. I. T.
PS1331.S548 1963   818.4   *LC* 63-11599

Smith, Henry Nash. • 2.10962
Mark Twain: the development of a writer. Cambridge: Belknap Press of Harvard University Press, 1962. ix, 212 p.; 25 cm. 1. Twain, Mark, 1835-1910. I. T.
PS1331.S55 1962   818.4   *LC* 62-19224

Wagenknecht, Edward, 1900-. • 2.10963
Mark Twain; the man and his work, with a commentary on Mark Twain criticism and scholarship since 1960 [by] Edward Wagenknecht. 3d ed. Norman, University of Oklahoma Press [1967] xiii, 302 p. port. 1. Twain, Mark, 1835-1910. I. T.
PS1331 W34 1967   *LC* 67-15630

Hill, Hamlin Lewis, 1931-. 2.10964
Mark Twain. God's fool, by Hamlin Hill. [1st ed.] New York, Harper & Row [1973] xxviii, 308 p. illus. 25 cm. 1. Twain, Mark, 1835-1910. I. T.
PS1332.H5   818/.4/09 B   *LC* 72-9754   *ISBN* 0060118938

Macnaughton, William R., 1939-. 2.10965
Mark Twain's last years as a writer / William R. Macnaughton. — Columbia: University of Missouri Press, 1979. x, 254 p.; 23 cm. Includes index. 1. Twain, Mark, 1835-1910. 2. Twain, Mark, 1835-1910 — Biography — Last years and death. 3. Authors, American — 19th century — Biography. I. T.
PS1332.M34   818/.4/09 B   *LC* 78-19846   *ISBN* 0826202640

De Voto, Bernard Augustine, 1897-1955. • 2.10966
Mark Twain at work / by Bernard De Voto. — Cambridge, Mass.: Harvard university press, 1942. ix, 144 p.: port., 2 facsim.; 25 cm. 'Boy's manuscript' is a sketch by Mark Twain from which his Tom Sawyer was subsequently developed. Lib. copy: photographic reprint. 1. Twain, Mark, 1835-1910. I. T.
PS1336.D4   *LC* a 42-3264

Anderson, Frederick, 1926- comp. • 2.10967
Mark Twain: the critical heritage. Edited by Frederick Anderson with the assistance of Kenneth M. Sanderson. New York, Barnes & Noble [1971] xvi, 347 p. 23 cm. (The Critical heritage series) 1. Twain, Mark, 1835-1910. I. T.
PS1338.A5 1971b   818/.4/09   *LC* 72-177519   *ISBN* 0389042137

Gibson, William Merriam, 1912-. 2.10968
The art of Mark Twain / William M. Gibson. — New York: Oxford University Press, 1976. xiv, 230 p.; 22 cm. 1. Twain, Mark, 1835-1910 — Criticism and interpretation. I. T.
PS1338.G5   818/.4/09   *LC* 75-25455   *ISBN* 0195019938

The Mythologizing of Mark Twain / edited by Sara deSaussure 2.10969
Davis and Philip D. Beidler; [contributions by John C. Gerber ... et al.].
University: University of Alabama Press, c1984. xix, 186 p.: ill.; 24 cm. Essays presented at the Eighth Alabama Symposium on English and American Literature, Oct. 15-17, 1981, University of Alabama. Includes index. 1. Twain, Mark, 1835-1910 — Criticism and interpretation — Congresses. I. Davis, Sara deSaussure, 1943- II. Beidler, Philip D. III. Gerber, John C. IV. Alabama Symposium on English and American Literature. (8th: 1981: University of Alabama)
PS1338.M9 1984   818/.409 19   *LC* 83-9166   *ISBN* 0817302018

Sloane, David E. E., 1943-. 2.10970
Mark Twain as a literary comedian / David E. E. Sloane. — Baton Rouge: Louisiana State University Press, c1979. 221 p.; 24 cm. — (Southern literary studies.) Includes index. 1. Twain, Mark, 1835-1910 — Criticism and interpretation. 2. Comic, The 3. American wit and humor — History and criticism. I. T. II. Series.
PS1338.S55   818/.4/09   *LC* 78-11125   *ISBN* 0807104604

Pettit, Arthur G. 2.10971
Mark Twain & the South / Arthur G. Pettit. — Lexington: University Press of Kentucky, [1974] ix, 223 p.; 24 cm. 1. Twain, Mark, 1835-1910 — Political and social views. 2. Southern States in literature. 3. Race relations in literature. I. T.
PS1342.P64 P47   818/.4/09 B   *LC* 73-86405   *ISBN* 0813113105

PS1400–1448 Cooper

Cooper, James Fenimore, 1789-1851. 2.10972
The writings of James Fenimore Cooper / James Franklin Beard, editor-in-chief; James P. Elliot, textual editor. — Albany: State University of New York Press, 1980-. v.: ill.; 24 cm. Half title. Each volume has special t.p. Includes indexes. I. Beard, James Franklin, 1919- II. T.
PS1400.F8x

Cooper, James Fenimore, 1789-1851. • 2.10973
Letters and journals / Edited by James Franklin Beard. — Cambridge: Belknap Press of Harvard University Press, 1960-68. 6 v.: ill., ports., facsims.; 25 cm. I. T.
PS1431.A3 1960   818/.2/08   *LC* 60-5388

Dekker, George. comp. 2.10974
Fenimore Cooper—the critical heritage, edited by George Dekker and John P. McWilliams. — London; Boston: Routledge and Kegan Paul, 1973. xi, 306 p.; 23 cm. — (Critical heritage series) Includes index. 1. Cooper, James Fenimore, 1789-1851 — Criticism and interpretation. I. McWilliams, John P. joint comp. II. T.
PS1438.D38   813/.2   *LC* 73-77039   *ISBN* 0710076355

James Fenimore Cooper, a collection of critical essays / edited 2.10975
by Wayne Fields.
Englewood Cliffs, N.J.: Prentice-Hall, c1979. viii, 197 p.; 21 cm. — (Twentieth century views) (A Spectrum book) 1. Cooper, James Fenimore, 1789-1851 — Criticism and interpretation — Addresses, essays, lectures. I. Fields, Wayne.
PS1438.J3 1979   813/.2   *LC* 79-12869   *ISBN* 0135099439

Peck, H. Daniel. 2.10976
A world by itself: the pastoral moment in Cooper's fiction / H. Daniel Peck. New Haven: Yale University Press, 1977. xiv, 213 p.; 22 cm. Includes index. 1. Cooper, James Fenimore, 1789-1851 — Criticism and interpretation. I. T.
PS1438.P4   813/.2   *LC* 76-25868   *ISBN* 0300020279

Ringe, Donald A. • 2.10977
James Fenimore Cooper. — New York: Twayne Publishers, [1962] 175 p.; 21 cm. — (Twayne's United States authors series, 11) 1. Cooper, James Fenimore, 1789-1851. I. T.
PS1438.R5   813.2   *LC* 61-18068

PS1449 Crane

Crane, Stephen, 1871-1900. 2.10978
The red badge of courage: an authoritative text, backgrounds and sources, criticism / Stephen Crane; edited by Sculley Bradley, Richmond Croom Beatty, E. Hudson Long. — 2d ed. / rev. by Donald Pizer. — New York: Norton, c1976. viii, 364 p.; 21 cm. (A Norton critical edition) 1. United States — History — Civil War, 1861-1865 — Fiction. I. Bradley, Sculley, 1897- II. Beatty, Richmond Croom, 1905-1961. III. Long, E. Hudson (Eugene Hudson), 1908- IV. Pizer, Donald. V. T.
PZ3.C852 Re 1976 PS1449.C85   813/.4   *LC* 76-18237   *ISBN* 0393044351. *ISBN* 0393091821

Crane, Stephen, 1871-1900.   **2.10979**
[Works. 1969] The University of Virginia edition of the works of Stephen Crane. [Charlottesville, University Press of Virginia, 1969-1975. 10 v.: fronts.; 25 cm. Half title; each vol. has also special t.p. Title on spine: The works of Stephen Crane. I. University of Virginia. II. T.
PS1449.C85 1969   813/.4   *LC* 68-8536   *ISBN* 0813902584

Crane, Stephen, 1871-1900.   • **2.10980**
[Selections. 1969] The portable Stephen Crane. Edited, with an introd. and notes, by Joseph Katz. New York, Viking Press [1969] xxvi, 550 p. 18 cm. (Viking portable library, P68) I. Katz, Joseph. ed. II. T.
PS1449.C85 A6 1969   813.4   *LC* 69-18738   *ISBN* 0670010685

Crane, Stephen, 1871-1900.   **2.10981**
Maggie, a girl of the streets: (a story of New York) / Stephen Crane; an authoritative text, backgrounds and sources, the author and the novel, reviews and criticism, edited by Thomas A. Gullason. — 1st ed. — New York: Norton, c1979. xiii, 258 p.: maps; 22 cm. — (A Norton critical edition) I. Gullason, Thomas A. II. T.
PZ3.C852 Maf 1979 PS1449.C85   813/.4   *LC* 78-24596   *ISBN* 0393012220

Bassan, Maurice, comp.   • **2.10982**
Stephen Crane; a collection of critical essays. — Englewood Cliffs, N.J.: Prentice-Hall, [1967] 184 p.; 21 cm. — (A Spectrum book: Twentieth century views, S-TC-66) 1. Crane, Stephen, 1871-1900 — Criticism and interpretation. I. T.
PS1449.C85 Z548   818/.4/09   *LC* 67-14842

Berryman, John, 1914-1972.   • **2.10983**
Stephen Crane. [New York] Sloane [1950] xv, 347 p. port. 22 cm. (The American men of letters series) 1. Crane, Stephen, 1871-1900. I. T.
PS1449.C85 Z56   928.1   *LC* 50-10964

Cady, Edwin Harrison.   **2.10984**
Stephen Crane / by Edwin H. Cady. — Rev. ed. — Boston: Twayne Publishers, 1980. 175 p.: port.; 21 cm. — (Twayne's United States authors series; TUSAS 23) Includes index. 1. Crane, Stephen, 1871-1900 — Criticism and interpretation. I. T.
PS1449.C85 Z575 1980   813/.4   *LC* 79-26608   *ISBN* 0805772995

Hoffman, Daniel, 1923-.   • **2.10985**
The poetry of Stephen Crane. — New York: Columbia University Press, 1957 [c1956] xiii, 304 p.; 21 cm. 1. Crane, Stephen, 1871-1900 — Criticism and interpretation. I. T.
PS1449.C85 Z65   811.49   *LC* 57-11017

Nagel, James.   **2.10986**
Stephen Crane and literary impressionism / James Nagel. — University Park: Pennsylvania State University Press, c1980. x, 190 p.; 24 cm. 1. Crane, Stephen, 1871-1900 — Criticism and interpretation. 2. Impressionism I. T.
PS1449.C85 Z75   813/.4   *LC* 80-16051

Solomon, Eric.   **2.10987**
Stephen Crane, from parody to realism. — Cambridge: Harvard University Press, 1966. 301 p.; 22 cm. 1. Crane, Stephen, 1871-1900. I. T.
PS1449.C85 Z848   813.4   *LC* 66-21347

Stallman, R. W. (Robert Wooster), 1911-.   **2.10988**
Stephen Crane; a biography, by R. W. Stallman. New York, G. Braziller [1968] xvi, 664 p. illus., facsims., ports. 24 cm. 1. Crane, Stephen, 1871-1900. I. T.
PS1449.C85 Z9   813/.8   *LC* 68-16110

PS1485-1533 Curtis. Daly. Davis. DeForest. Deland

Curtis, George William, 1824-1892.   • **2.10989**
From the easy chair. — New York: Greenwood Press, [1969, c1891-94] 3 v.: ports.; 18 cm. — I. T.
PS1485.A1 1969   814.3   *LC* 69-13870

Daly, Augustin, 1838-1899.   **2.10990**
[Plays. Selections] Plays / by Augustin Daly; edited with an introduction and notes by Don B. Wilmeth and Rosemary Cullen. — Cambridge [Cambridgeshire]; New York: Cambridge University Press, 1984. xi, 208 p.: ill.; 24 cm. — (British and American playwrights, 1750-1920.) I. Wilmeth, Don B. II. Cullen, Rosemary. III. T. IV. Series.
PS1499.D85 A6 1984   812/.4 19   *LC* 83-18929   *ISBN* 0521240905

Davis, Rebecca Harding, 1831-1910.   **2.10991**
Life in the iron mills, and other stories / by Rebecca Harding Davis; edited and with a biographical interpretation by Tillie Olsen. — Rev. and expanded ed. —

Old Westbury, N.Y.: Feminist Press, 1985. 242 p.; 18 cm. I. Olsen, Tillie. II. T.
PS1517.L5 1985   813/.4 19   *LC* 84-25908   *ISBN* 0935312390

De Forest, John William, 1826-1906.   • **2.10992**
Miss Ravenel's conversion from secession to loyalty / edited with an introd. by Gordon S. Haight. — New York: Rinehart, 1955. 485 p.; 19 cm. (Rinehart editions; 74.) 1. United States — History — Civil War, 1861-1865 — Fiction. I. T.
PZ3.D363 Mi2 PS1525.D5   813/.3   *LC* 55-8419

Deland, Margaret Wade Campbell, 1857-1945.   • **2.10993**
Dr. Lavendar's people / Illustrated by Lucius Hitchcock. New York, Harper, 1903. — St. Clair Shores, Mich.: Scholarly Press, 1970. vii, 369 p.: ill.; 21 cm. I. T.
PZ3.D371 D8 PS1532 Dx   813/.4   *LC* 77-129345   *ISBN* 0403004780

PS1541 Dickinson

Dickinson, Emily, 1830-1886.   • **2.10994**
The poems of Emily Dickinson: including variant readings critically compared with all known manuscripts / edited by Thomas H. Johnson. — Cambridge: Belknap Press of Harvard University Press, 1955. — 3v. (lxviii, 1266 p.): facsims.; 24 cm. Includes indexes. I. Johnson, Thomas H. II. T.
PS1541.A1 1955   811.49   *LC* 54-8631   *ISBN* 0674676009

Dickinson, Emily, 1830-1886.   **2.10995**
The letters of Emily Dickinson / edited by Thomas H. Johnson; associate editor, Theodora Ward. — Cambridge, Mass.: Belknap Press of Harvard University Press, 1958. 3 v. (xxvii, 999 p.): ill., ports., facsims. 1. Dickinson, Emily, 1830-1886 — Correspondence. I. Johnson, Thomas Herbert. II. Ward, Theodora Van Wagenen, 1890- III. T.
PS1541.Z5 A3   928.1   *LC* 58-5594   *ISBN* 0674526252

Anderson, Charles Roberts, 1902-.   **2.10996**
Emily Dickinson's poetry: stairway of surprise / by Charles R. Anderson. — Westport, Conn.: Greenwood, 1982, c1960. xviii, 334 p.; 23 cm. Reprint. Originally published: London: Heineman, 1963, c1960. 1. Dickinson, Emily, 1830-1886 — Criticism and interpretation. I. Dickinson, Emily, 1830-1886. II. T.
PS1541.Z5 A63 1982   811/.4 19   *LC* 82-15844   *ISBN* 0313237336

Diehl, Joanne Feit, 1947-.   **2.10997**
Dickinson and the Romantic imagination / Joanne Feit Diehl. — Princeton, N.J.: Princeton University Press, c1981. ix, 205 p.; 23 cm. Includes index. 1. Dickinson, Emily, 1830-1886 — Criticism and interpretation. 2. Romanticism 3. Influence (Literary, artistic, etc.) 4. Feminism and literature I. T.
PS1541.Z5 D5   811/.4 19   *LC* 81-47121   *ISBN* 0691064784

Eberwein, Jane Donahue, 1943-.   **2.10998**
Dickinson, strategies of limitation / Jane Donahue Eberwein. — Amherst: University of Massachusetts Press, 1985. 308 p.: ill.; 24 cm. Includes indexes. 1. Dickinson, Emily, 1830-1886 — Criticism and interpretation. 2. Dickinson, Emily, 1830-1886 — Technique. I. T.
PS1541.Z5 E34 1985   811/.4 19   *LC* 84-16335   *ISBN* 0870234730

Feminist critics read Emily Dickinson / edited with an   **2.10999**
introduction by Suzanne Juhasz.
Bloomington: Indiana University Press, c1983. vii, 184 p.; 24 cm. Includes index. 1. Dickinson, Emily, 1830-1886 — Criticism and interpretation — Addresses, essays, lectures. 2. Feminist literary criticism — Addresses, essays, lectures. I. Juhasz, Suzanne, 1942-
PS1541.Z5 F36 1983   811/.4 19   *LC* 82-48265   *ISBN* 0253321700

Ferlazzo, Paul J.   **2.11000**
Emily Dickinson / by Paul J. Ferlazzo. — Boston: Twayne, c1976. 168 p.: port.; 21 cm. — (Twayne's United States authors series; TUSAS 280) Includes index. 1. Dickinson, Emily, 1830-1886. 2. Poets, American — 19th century — Biography. I. T.
PS1541.Z5 F4   811/.4 B   *LC* 76-48304   *ISBN* 0805771808

Gelpi, Albert.   **2.11001**
Emily Dickinson: the mind of the poet / Albert J. Gelpi. — Cambridge: Harvard University Press, 1965. xiii, 201 p.; 22 cm. — 1. Dickinson, Emily, 1830-1886. I. T.
PS1541.Z5 G4   *LC* 65-13844

Johnson, Thomas Herbert.   **2.11002**
Emily Dickinson: an interpretive biography. — New York: Atheneum, 1967, c1955. 276 p.: illus.; 24 cm. 1. Dickinson, Emily, 1830-1886 — Biography. I. T.
PS1541.Z5 J6   811.49   *LC* 55-9439   *ISBN* 0689701136 pa

Juhasz, Suzanne, 1942-. 2.11003
The undiscovered continent: Emily Dickinson and the space of the mind / Suzanne Juhasz. — Bloomington: Indiana University Press, c1983. ix, 189 p.; 25 cm. 1. Dickinson, Emily, 1830-1886 — Criticism and interpretation. 2. Imagination 3. Solitude 4. Feminism and literature I. T.
PS1541.Z5 J8 1983   811/.4 19   *LC* 82-49014   *ISBN* 0253361648

Lindberg-Seyersted, Brita. 2.11004
The voice of the poet; aspects of style in the poetry of Emily Dickinson. — Cambridge: Harvard University Press, 1968. 290 p.; 24 cm. 1. Dickinson, Emily, 1830-1886. I. T.
PS1541.Z5 L5 1968b   811/.4   *LC* 68-31985

McNeil, Helen, 1942-. 2.11005
Emily Dickinson / Helen McNeil. — 1st American ed. — New York: Pantheon Books, c1986. xvi, 208 p.; 21 cm. — (Virago Pantheon pioneers.) Includes index. 1. Dickinson, Emily, 1830-1886 — Biography. 2. Poets, American — 19th century — Biography. I. T. II. Series.
PS1541.Z5 M25 1986   811/.4 B 19   *LC* 86-42618   *ISBN* 0394747666

Porter, David T. 2.11006
Dickinson, the modern idiom / David Porter. — Cambridge, Mass.: Harvard University Press, 1981. ix, 316 p.; 24 cm. 1. Dickinson, Emily, 1830-1886 — Criticism and interpretation. I. T.
PS1541.Z5 P626   811/.4 19   *LC* 80-24322   *ISBN* 0674204441

Sewall, Richard Benson. ed. • 2.11007
Emily Dickinson, a collection of critical essays. Englewood Cliffs, N.J., Prentice-Hall [1963] 183 p. 22 cm. (A Spectrum book: Twentieth century views, S-TC-28) 1. Dickinson, Emily, 1830-1886. I. T.
PS1541.Z5 S4   811.4   *LC* 63-9307

Sewall, Richard Benson. 2.11008
The life of Emily Dickinson, by Richard B. Sewall. — New York: Farrar, Straus and Giroux, [1974] 2 v. (xxvii, 821 p.): illus.; 24 cm. 1. Dickinson, Emily, 1830-1886 — Biography. I. T.
PS1541.Z5 S42   811/.4 B   *LC* 74-8764   *ISBN* 0374186960

St. Armand, Barton Levi. 2.11009
Emily Dickinson and her culture: the soul's society / Barton Levi St. Armand. — Cambridge [Cambridgeshire]; New York: Cambridge University Press, c1984. xii, 368 p.: ill.; 24 cm. (Cambridge studies in American literature and culture.) 1. Dickinson, Emily, 1830-1886 — Criticism and interpretation. I. T. II. Series.
PS1541.Z5 S7 1984   811/.4 19   *LC* 84-3188   *ISBN* 0521262674

Whicher, George Frisbie, 1889-1954. 2.11010
This was a poet; a critical biography of Emily Dickinson. New York, Scribner's, 1938. xiii, 337 p. illus., 2 port. (incl. front.) facsims. 24 cm. 1. Dickinson, Emily, 1830-1886. I. T.
PS1541.Z5 W5   928.1   *LC* 38-28929

PS1545–1583 Dunbar. Eggleston

Dunbar, Paul Laurence, 1872-1906. • 2.11011
The complete poems of Paul Laurence Dunbar / with the introduction to 'Lyrics of lowly life.' by W. D. Howells. — New York: Dodd, Mead and Company, 1913. xxxii, 289 p.: ill; 21 cm. I. T.
PS1556.A1 1913   *LC* 13-25781

Dunbar, Paul Laurence, 1872-1906. • 2.11012
The best stories of Paul Laurence Dunbar / selected and edited with an introduction by Benjamin Brawley. — New York: Dodd, Mead, 1938. xvii, 258 p.: ill; 21 cm. I. Brawley, Benjamin Griffith, 1882-1939. ed. II. T.
PS1556.Ax   *LC* 38-5603

Brawley, Benjamin Griffith, 1982-1939. • 2.11013
Paul Laurence Dunbar: poet of his people. — Port Washington, N.Y.: Kennikat Press, [1967,c1936] xi, 159 p.: ill; 21 cm. 'Appendix. The praise of Dunbar': p. 127-140. 1. Dunbar, Paul Laurence, 1872-1906. I. T.
PS1557.B7 1967   *LC* 67-27578

Revell, Peter. 2.11014
Paul Laurence Dunbar / by Peter Revell. — Boston: Twayne Publishers, 1979. 197 p.: port.; 21 cm. — (Twayne's United States authors series; TUSAS 298) Includes index. 1. Dunbar, Paul Laurence, 1872-1906 — Criticism and interpretation. I. T.
PS1557.R4   811/.4   *LC* 78-31608   *ISBN* 0805772138

Eggleston, Edward, 1837-1902. • 2.11015
The circuit rider: a tale of the heroic age / edited for the modern reader by William Randel. — New Haven: College & University Press, [c1966] 251 p.: ill.;

21 cm. — (Masterworks of literature series) I. Randel, William Peirce, 1909- II. T. III. Series.
PZ3.E29 C12   PS1582.C5 1966.   *LC* 66-24153

Eggleston, Edward, 1837-1902. 2.11016
The Hoosier school-master: a novel / by Edward Eggleston; introduction by B. Edward McClellan; illustrated by Frank Beard. — 1st Midland book ed. — Bloomington: Indiana University Press, 1984. 226 p.: ill.; 22 cm. — (Library of Indiana classics.) Reprinted from the original 1871 edition and includes the original Frank Beard illustrations'—Introd. I. McClellan, B. Edward (Bernard Edward), 1939-. II. T. III. Series.
PS1582.H62 1984   813/.4 19   *LC* 83-49054   *ISBN* 0253328500

PS1600–1648 Emerson

Emerson, Ralph Waldo, 1803-1882. • 2.11017
[Works. 1971] The collected works of Ralph Waldo Emerson / introductions and notes by Robert E. Spiller; text established by Alfred R. Ferguson. — Cambridge, Mass.: Belknap Press, 1971-. v.: ill.; 24 cm. Vol. 2-: Introduction and notes by Joseph Slater; text established by Alfred R. Ferguson and Jean Ferguson Carr. I. Spiller, Robert Ernest, 1896-. II. Ferguson, Alfred Riggs. III. Slater, Joseph, 1916- IV. Carr, Jean Ferguson. V. T.
PS1600.F71   814/.3 19   *LC* 70-158429   *ISBN* 0674139704

Emerson, Ralph Waldo, 1803-1882. 2.11018
Selected prose and poetry. Edited with an introd. by Reginald L. Cook. — 2d ed. — New York: Holt, Rinehart and Winston, [1969] xxii, 568 p.; 21 cm. — (Rinehart editions) I. Cook, Reginald Lansing, 1903- ed. II. T.
PS1602.C6 1969   814/.3   *LC* 69-14253   *ISBN* 0030771404

Sealts, Merton M. comp. 2.11019
Emerson's Nature: origin, growth, meaning / edited by Merton M. Sealts, Jr. and Alfred R. Ferguson. — 2d ed., enl. — Carbondale: Southern Illinois University Press, 1979. xi, 225 p.; 24 cm. 1. Emerson, Ralph Waldo, 1803-1882. Nature. 2. Nature in literature — Addresses, essays, lectures. I. Ferguson, Alfred Riggs. joint comp. II. Emerson, Ralph Waldo, 1803-1882. Nature. 1979. III. T.
PS1613.S4 1979   191   *LC* 78-13945   *ISBN* 0809308916

Emerson, Ralph Waldo, 1803-1882. • 2.11020
The letters of Ralph Waldo Emerson ... edited by Ralph L. Rusk ... — New York, Columbia university press, 1939. 6 v. fronts. (facsims.) 24.5 cm. I. Rusk, Ralph Leslie, 1888- ed. II. T.
PS1631.A3 1939   928.1   *LC* 39-12289

Emerson, Ralph Waldo, 1803-1882. • 2.11021
Journals and miscellaneous notebooks / edited by William H. Gilman [and others] — Cambridge: Belknap Press of Harvard University Press, 1960-. v.: ill., facsims.; 25 cm. Vols. 8, 11-12 accompanied by separate 'Emendations and departures from the manuscript,' by the editors. I. Gilman, William Henry, 1911-1976, ed. II. T.
PS1631.A3 1960   928.1   *LC* 60-11554   *ISBN* 0674484703

Emerson, Ralph Waldo, 1803-1882. 2.11022
[Journals and miscellaneous notebooks. Selections] Emerson in his journals / selected and edited by Joel Porte. — Cambridge, Mass.: Belknap Press of Harvard University Press, 1982. xvii, 588 p.: ports., facsims.; 25 cm. Selected from the Journals and miscellaneous notebooks. Includes index. 1. Emerson, Ralph Waldo, 1803-1882 — Diaries. 2. Authors, American — 19th century — Biography. I. Porte, Joel. II. T.
PS1631.A33 1982   814/.3 19   *LC* 81-20255   *ISBN* 0674248619

Emerson, Ralph Waldo, 1803-1882. 2.11023
The correspondence of Emerson and Carlyle / edited by Joseph Slater. — New York: Columbia University Press, 1964. viii, 622 p.; 25 cm. 1. Carlyle, Thomas, 1795-1881. Correspondence 2. Emerson, Ralph Waldo, 1803-1882 — Correspondence. 3. Emerson, Ralph Waldo, 1803-1882. I. Slater, Joseph Locke. II. Carlyle, Thomas, 1795-1881. III. T.
PS1631.A35 C3   *LC* 63-17539

Allen, Gay Wilson, 1903-. 2.11024
Waldo Emerson: a biography / by Gay Wilson Allen. — New York: Viking Press, 1981. xxiv, 751 p., [16] p. of plates: ill.; 24 cm. 1. Emerson, Ralph Waldo, 1803-1882. 2. Authors, American — 19th century — Biography. 3. Transcendentalists (New England) — Biography. I. T.
PS1631.A7   814/.3 B 19   *LC* 81-65275   *ISBN* 0670748668

Konvitz, Milton Ridvas, 1908- ed. 2.11025
Emerson: a collection of critical essays. Edited by Milton R. Konvitz and Stephen E. Whicher. Englewood Cliffs, N.J., Prentice-Hall [1962] 184 p. 21 cm. (Twentieth century views) (A Spectrum book, S-TC-12) 1. Emerson, Ralph Waldo, 1803-1882 — Criticism and interpretation. I. Whicher, Stephen E., joint ed. II. T.
PS1631.K6   818.3   *LC* 62-14850

Porte, Joel. 2.11026
Representative man: Ralph Waldo Emerson in his time / Joel Porte. — New York: Oxford University Press, 1979. xxvi, 361 p.: port.; 22 cm. 1. Emerson, Ralph Waldo, 1803-1882. 2. Authors, American — 19th century — Biography. I. T.
PS1631.P65　　814/.3 B　　*LC* 78-5818　　*ISBN* 0195024362

Whicher, Stephen E. 2.11027
Freedom and fate: an inner life of Ralph Waldo Emerson. — Philadelphia: University of Pennsylvania Press, 1953. 203 p.; 23 cm. 1. Emerson, Ralph Waldo, 1803-1882. I. T.
PS1631.W5　　*LC* 53-9552

Critical essays on Ralph Waldo Emerson / [collected by] Robert 2.11028
E. Burkholder and Joel Myerson.
Boston, Mass.: G.K. Hall, c1983. ix, 530 p.; 24 cm. — (Critical essays on American literature.) 1. Emerson, Ralph Waldo, 1803-1882 — Criticism and interpretation — Addresses, essays, lectures. I. Burkholder, Robert E. II. Myerson, Joel. III. Series.
PS1638.C74 1983　　814/.3 19　　*LC* 82-15831　　*ISBN* 0816183058

Paul, Sherman, 1920-. • 2.11029
Emerson's angle of vision; man and nature in American experience. Cambridge: Harvard University Press, 1952. viii, 268 p.: ill.; 22 cm. 1. Emerson, Ralph Waldo, 1803-1882. I. T.
PS1638.P3　　814.36　　*LC* 52-5039

Waggoner, Hyatt Howe. 2.11030
Emerson as poet [by] Hyatt H. Waggoner. — [Princeton]: Princeton University Press, 1975 (c1974) xiii, 211 p.; 23 cm. 1. Emerson, Ralph Waldo, 1803-1882 — Criticism and interpretation. I. T.
PS1638.W3　　811/.3　　*LC* 74-2983　　*ISBN* 0691062692

Yannella, Donald. 2.11031
Ralph Waldo Emerson / by Donald Yannella. — Boston: Twayne Publishers, c1982. 147 p., [1] leaf of plates: port.; 21 cm. — (Twayne's United States authors series. TUSAS 414) Includes index. 1. Emerson, Ralph Waldo, 1803-1882 — Criticism and interpretation. I. T. II. Series.
PS1638.Y36 1982　　814/.3 19　　*LC* 81-20321　　*ISBN* 0805773444

Bishop, Jonathan. 2.11032
Emerson on the soul. Cambridge, Mass.: Harvard University Press, 1964. 248 p.; 24 cm. 1. Emerson, Ralph Waldo, 1803-1882. 2. Soul I. T.
PS1642.R4 B5　　818/.3　　*LC* 64-25052

PS1705-1768 Frederic. Freeman. Garland. Gilman. Guiney

Frederic, Harold, 1856-1898. • 2.11033
The damnation of Theron Ware / Edited by Everett Carter. — Cambridge: Belknap Press of Harvard University Press, 1960. xxiv, 355 p.; 22 cm. — (The John Harvard library) I. T.
PZ3.F873D11　　PS1707.D3x.　　*LC* 60-11553

Freeman, Mary Eleanor Wilkins, 1852-1930. 2.11034
[Short stories. Selections] Selected stories of Mary E. Wilkins Freeman / edited with an introduction by Marjorie Pryse. — New York: W.W. Norton, c1983. xix, 344 p.: port.; 21 cm. I. Pryse, Marjorie, 1948- II. T.
PS1711.P7 1983　　813/.4 19　　*LC* 82-21179　　*ISBN* 0393017265

Garland, Hamlin, 1860-1940. • 2.11035
Main-travelled roads / with a new pref. by B.R. McElderry, Jr., and the 1893 introd. by William Dean Howells. — New York: Harper, [1956] 247 p.; 21 cm. (Harper's modern classics.) Short stories. I. T. II. Series.
PZ3.G18 M20 PS1732.M3　　813/.4　　*LC* 56-6980

Garland, Hamlin, 1860-1940. 2.11036
Rose of Dutcher's Coolly. Introduced and edited by Donald Pizer. — Lincoln: University of Nebraska Press, [1969] xxxiii, 404 p.; 21 cm. 'A Bison book.' Reprint of the 1895 ed. I. T.
PS1732.R6x　　PZ3.G18 R6 PS1733　　813/.5/2　　*LC* 79-82509

Garland, Hamlin, 1860-1940. • 2.11037
Companions on the trail: a literary chronicle / by Hamlin Garland; decorations by Constance Garland. — New York: Macmillan, 1931. 539 p.: port.; 23 cm. 1. Authors, American — 19th century — Correspondence, reminiscences, etc. I. T.
PS1733.A39 1931　　813/.5/2 B　　*LC* 31-25190

Garland, Hamlin, 1860-1940. • 2.11038
A daughter of the middle border. — New York: Sagamore, 1957. 337 p.: ports.; 22 cm. — (American century series; S-11) A continuation of the author's autobiography, A son of the middle border. 1. Garland, Hamlin, 1860-1940. I. T.
PS1733.A42 1957　　813/.5/2 B　　*LC* 57-9763

Garland, Hamlin, 1860-1940. • 2.11039
A son of the middle border / by Hamlin Garland. New York: Macmillan, 1956 [c1923] 466 p.; 20 cm. 1. Garland, Hamlin, 1860-1940. 2. Frontier and pioneer life — Northwestern States. I. McComb, Ernest Hacket Kemper 1873- ed. II. T.
PS1733.A4x

McCullough, Joseph B. 2.11040
Hamlin Garland / by Joseph B. McCullough. — Boston: Twayne Publishers, c1978. 143 p.: ill.; 21 cm. — (Twayne's United States authors series: TUSAS 299) Includes index. 1. Garland, Hamlin, 1860-1940 — Criticism and interpretation. I. T.
PS1733.M27　　813/.5/2 B　　*LC* 77-15002　　*ISBN* 0805772030

Gilman, Charlotte Perkins, 1860-1935. 2.11041
The Charlotte Perkins Gilman reader: The yellow wallpaper, and other fiction / edited and introduced by Ann J. Lane. — 1st ed. — New York: Pantheon Books, 1980. xlii, 208 p.; 22 cm. I. Lane, Ann J., 1931- II. T. III. Title: Yellow wallpaper, and other fiction.
PS1744.G57 A15 1980　　813/.4　　*LC* 80-7711　　*ISBN* 0394510852

Gilman, Charlotte Perkins, 1860-1935. • 2.11042
The living of Charlotte Perkins Gilman: an autobiography. — New York: Arno Press, 1972 [c1935] xxxviii, 341 p.: ports.; 23 cm. (American women: images and realities) 1. Gilman, Charlotte Perkins, 1860-1935. I. T. II. Series.
PS1744.G57 Z5 1972　　309.1/2/4 B　　*LC* 72-2604　　*ISBN* 0405044593

Scharnhorst, Gary. 2.11043
Charlotte Perkins Gilman / by Gary Scharnhorst. — Boston: Twayne Publishers, c1985. 143 p.: port.; 23 cm. (Twayne's United States authors series. TUSAS 482) Includes index. 1. Gilman, Charlotte Perkins, 1860-1935 — Criticism and interpretation. I. T. II. Series.
PS1744.G57 Z85 1985　　828/.409 19　　*LC* 84-19208　　*ISBN* 0805774351

Guiney, Louise Imogen, 1861-1920. • 2.11044
Happy ending; the collected lyrics of Louise Imogen Guiney. — New ed., with newly collected poems. — Boston: Houghton Mifflin Co., 1927. xiv, 194 p. I. T.
PS1767.H3 1970　　*LC* 27-21050

PS1770-1838 G.W. Harris. J.C. Harris. Harte

Harris, George Washington, 1814-1869. 2.11045
High times and hard times; sketches and tales. Edited, with introductory essays, by M. Thomas Inge. Drawings by Mary Alice Bahler. — [Nashville]: Vanderbilt University Press, 1967. x, 348 p.: illus.; 25 cm. I. Inge, M. Thomas. ed. II. T.
PS1799.H87 A6 1967　　813/.3　　*LC* 67-21655

Rickels, Milton. • 2.11046
George Washington Harris. — New York: Twayne Publishers, [1966, c1965] 159 p.; 21 cm. — (Twayne's United States authors series, TUSAS 91) 1. Harris, George Washington, 1814-1869. I. T.
PS1799.H87 Z85 1966　　817.3　　*LC* 65-24244

Harris, Joel Chandler, 1848-1908. • 2.11047
The complete tales of Uncle Remus / compiled by Richard Chase; with illus. by Arthur Burdette Frost [and others] — Boston: Houghton Mifflin, 1955. xxxii, 875 p.: ill.; 22 cm. I. T.
PZ7.H242 Co　　PS1801.Cx.　　*LC* 54-12233　　*ISBN* 0395067995

Harris, Joel Chandler, 1848-1908. • 2.11048
The favorite Uncle Remus / by Joel Chandler Harris; illustrated by A. B. Frost; selected, arranged, & edited by George Van Santvoord and Archibald C. Coolidge. — [Boston]: Houghton Mifflin, c1948. 308 p.: ill. I. Frost, A. B. (Arthur Burdett), 1851-1928. II. Van Santvoord, George, 1891- III. Coolidge, Archibald Cary, 1866-1928. IV. T.
PZ7.H24 Fa　　PS1808x.　　813　　*LC* 48-1944　　*ISBN* 0395068002

Bickley, R. Bruce, 1942-. 2.11049
Joel Chandler Harris / by R. Bruce Bickley, Jr. — Boston: Twayne Publishers, c1978. 174 p.: port.; 21 cm. (Twayne's United States authors series; TUSAS 308) Includes index. 1. Harris, Joel Chandler, 1848-1908. 2. Authors, American — 19th century — Biography. 3. Remus, Uncle (Fictitious character) 4. Folklore in literature 5. Afro-Americans in literature I. T.
PS1813.B53 1978　　818/.4/09　　*LC* 77-25919　　*ISBN* 0805772154

Cousins, Paul M. • 2.11050
Joel Chandler Harris; a biography, by Paul M. Cousins. — Baton Rouge: Louisiana State University Press, [1968] xiv, 237 p.: illus., ports.; 24 cm. —

(Southern literary studies.) 1. Harris, Joel Chandler, 1848-1908. I. T. II. Series.
PS1813.C6   817/.4 B   *LC* 68-13452

Harris, Julia Florida (Collier) 1875-.   • 2.11051
The life and letters of Joel Chandler Harris, by Julia Collier Harris. Boston, Houghton Mifflin, 1918. — [New York: AMS Press, 1973] ix, 620 p.: illus.; 23 cm. 1. Harris, Joel Chandler, 1848-1908. I. T.
PS1813.H3 1973   818/.4/09 B   *LC* 72-168247   *ISBN* 0404000592

**Critical essays on Joel Chandler Harris / [compiled by] R.   2.11052
Bruce Bickley, Jr.**
Boston, Mass.: G.K. Hall, c1981. xxiv, 240 p.; 24 cm. — (Critical essays on American literature.) Errata slip inserted. 1. Harris, Joel Chandler, 1848-1908 — Criticism and interpretation. I. Bickley, R. Bruce, 1942- II. Series.
PS1814.C7   818/.409 19   *LC* 81-6816   *ISBN* 0816183813

Brookes, Stella Brewer, 1903-.   • 2.11053
Joel Chandler Harris, folklorist. Athens: University of Georgia Press, 1950. xv, 182 p.; 23 cm. 1. Harris, Joel Chandler, 1848-1908 — Biography. 2. Folk-lore, Afro-American. 3. Authors, American — 19th century — Biography. I. T.
PS1817.F6 B7   813.49   *LC* 50-12631

Harte, Bret, 1836-1902.   2.11054
The best of Bret Harte, selected by Wilhelmina Harper and Aimée M. Peters; illus. by Paul Brown. Boston, Houghton Mifflin Co., 1947. xiii, 434 p. illus. 22 cm. I. Harper, Wilhelmina. comp. II. T.
PS1829.B43   *LC* 47-11050

Stewart, George Rippey, 1895-.   2.11055
Bret Harte, argonaut and exile: being an account of the life of the celebrated American humorist ... compiled from new and original sources / by George R. Stewart, Jr. — Port Washington, N.Y.: Kennikat Press, [1964?] xi, 384 p.: ill. facsims., ports.; 24 cm. Includes index. 1. Harte, Bret, 1836-1902. I. T.
PS1833.S7   *LC* 64-24470

PS1850–1898 Hawthorne

Hawthorne, Nathaniel, 1804-1864.   • 2.11056
The centenary edition of the works of Nathaniel Hawthorne / [editors]: William Charvat, and others. — Columbus: Ohio State University Press, 1963-c1962-. v.: ill.; 25 cm. 1. Charvat, William, 1905-1966. ed. I. Ohio State Center for Textual Studies. II. T.
PS1850.F63   *LC* 63-750

Hawthorne, Nathaniel, 1804-1864.   2.11057
[Selected works. 1977] The portable Hawthorne. — Rev. and expanded ed. / edited by Malcolm Cowley. — New York: Penguin Books, 1977, c1969. vi, 698 p.; 18 cm. I. Cowley, Malcolm, 1898- II. T.
PS1852.C6 1977   813/.3   *LC* 77-21031   *ISBN* 0140150382

Hawthorne, Nathaniel, 1804-1864.   2.11058
The Blithedale romance: an authoritative text, backgrounds and sources, criticism / Nathaniel Hawthorne; edited by Seymour Gross and Rosalie Murphy. — 1st ed. — New York: Norton, c1978. x, 418 p.; 21 cm. — (A Norton critical edition) 1. Hawthorne, Nathaniel, 1804-1864. The Blithedale romance. I. Gross, Seymour Lee, 1926- II. Murphy, Rosalie. III. T.
PZ3.H318 Bl 1978 PS1855.A1x   813/.3   *LC* 77-24887   *ISBN* 0393044491

Hawthorne, Nathaniel, 1804-1864.   2.11059
The house of the seven gables / edited by Seymour L. Gross. — New York: Norton, [1967] x, 484 p. — (Norton critical editions) An authoritative text, backgrounds and sources, essays in criticism. I. Gross, Seymour Lee, 1926- II. T.
PS1861.A3 G7   PZ3.H318 Ho82.   PS1861.A1 1967.   *LC* 67-11080

Hawthorne, Nathaniel.   2.11060
The scarlet letter: an authoritative text, backgrounds and sources, criticism / Nathaniel Hawthorne; edited by Sculley Bradley ... [et al.]. — 2nd ed. — New York: Norton, c1978. x, 439 p.; 22 cm. — (A Norton critical edition) 1. Hawthorne, Nathaniel. Scarlet letter. I. Bradley, Sculley, 1897- II. T.
PZ3.H318 Sc 1978 PS1868.A1x   813/.3   *LC* 77-24583   *ISBN* 0393044955

Gerber, John C. comp.   2.11061
Twentieth century interpretations of The scarlet letter; a collection of critical essays, edited by John C. Gerber. — Englewood Cliffs, N.J.: Prentice-Hall, [1968] viii, 120 p.; 21 cm. — (Twentieth century interpretations) (A Spectrum book, S-820.) 1. Hawthorne, Nathaniel, 1804-1864. The scarlet letter. I. T. II. Title: The scarlet letter.
PS1868.G38   813/.4   *LC* 68-23438

Crews, Frederick C.   • 2.11062
The sins of the fathers: Hawthorne's psychological themes [by] Frederick C. Crews. — New York: Oxford University Press, 1966. viii, 279 p.; 23 cm. 1. Hawthorne, Nathaniel, 1804-1864. I. T.
PS1881.C7 1966   813.3   *LC* 66-16011

Kaul, A. N. ed.   • 2.11063
Hawthorne; a collection of critical essays, edited by A. N. Kaul. — Englewood Cliffs, N.J.: Prentice-Hall, [1966] 182 p.; 21 cm. — (A Spectrum book) (Twentieth century views.) 1. Hawthorne, Nathaniel, 1804-1864. I. T.
PS1881.K3 1966   813.3   *LC* 66-14704

Stewart, Randall, 1896-1964.   • 2.11064
Nathaniel Hawthorne, a biography. — [Hamden, Conn.]: Archon Books, 1970, [c1948] 279 p.; 22 cm. 1. Hawthorne, Nathaniel, 1804-1864 — Biography. I. T.
PS1881.S67 1970   813/.3 B   *LC* 74-114425   *ISBN* 0208008292

Turner, Arlin.   2.11065
Nathaniel Hawthorne, a biography / Arlin Turner. — New York: Oxford University Press, 1980. xii, 457 p.: ill.; 24 cm. 1. Hawthorne, Nathaniel, 1804-1864 — Biography. 2. Novelists, American — 19th century — Biography. I. T.
PS1881.T79   813/.3 B   *LC* 78-21988   *ISBN* 0195025474

Bell, Michael Davitt.   2.11066
Hawthorne and the historical romance of New England. — Princeton, N.J.: Princeton University Press, 1971. xii, 253 p.; 23 cm. 1. Hawthorne, Nathaniel, 1804-1864. 2. Historical fiction, American 3. New England in literature. I. T.
PS1888.B4   813/.3   *LC* 72-148169   *ISBN* 069106136X

Brodhead, Richard H., 1947-.   2.11067
Hawthorne, Melville, and the novel / Richard H. Brodhead. — Chicago: University of Chicago Press, 1976. x, 216 p.; 23 cm. 1. Hawthorne, Nathaniel, 1804-1864 — Criticism and interpretation. 2. Melville, Herman, 1819-1891 — Criticism and interpretation. 3. Fiction — 19th century — History and criticism. I. T.
PS1888.B7 1976   813/.3/09   *LC* 75-5071   *ISBN* 0226075222

Crowley, J. Donald (Joseph Donald) comp.   2.11068
Hawthorne: the critical heritage; edited by J. Donald Crowley. — London: Routledge & K. Paul, [1970] xvi, 532 p.; 23 cm. — (The Critical heritage series) 1. Hawthorne, Nathaniel, 1804-1864 — Criticism and interpretation — Addresses, essays, lectures. I. T.
PS1888.C7   813/.3   *LC* 77-552816   *ISBN* 0710068867

Doubleday, Neal Frank.   2.11069
Hawthorne's early tales; a critical study. — Durham, N.C.: Duke University Press, 1972. ix, 262 p.; 25 cm. 1. Hawthorne, Nathaniel, 1804-1864. I. T.
PS1888.D6   813/.3   *LC* 76-185462   *ISBN* 0822302675

Fogle, Richard Harter.   • 2.11070
Hawthorne's fiction: the light & the dark. — [Rev. ed.]. — Norman: University of Oklahoma Press, [1964] xiii, 240 p.; 21 cm. 1. Hawthorne, Nathaniel, 1804-1864. I. T.
PS1888.F6 1964   813.3   *LC* 64-23334

Martin, Terence.   2.11071
Nathaniel Hawthorne / by Terence Martin. — Rev. ed. — Boston: Twayne Publishers, c1983. 221 p.; 22 cm. — (Twayne's United States authors series. TUSAS 75) Includes index. 1. Hawthorne, Nathaniel, 1804-1864 — Criticism and interpretation. I. T. II. Series.
PS1888.M34 1983   813/.3 19   *LC* 82-23419   *ISBN* 0805773843

Waggoner, Hyatt Howe.   • 2.11072
Hawthorne: a critical study. — Rev ed. — Cambridge, Mass.: Belknap Press of Harvard University Press, 1963. 278 p.; 22 cm. 1. Hawthorne, Nathaniel, 1804-1864. I. T.
PS1888.W3 1963   813.3   *LC* 63-17215

Stoehr, Taylor, 1931-.   2.11073
Hawthorne's mad scientists: pseudoscience and social science in nineteenth-century life and letters / by Taylor Stoehr. — Hamden, Conn.: Archon Books, 1978. 313 p.; 23 cm. 1. Hawthorne, Nathaniel, 1804-1864 — Characters — Scientists. 2. Scientists in literature. 3. Quacks and quackery in literature. 4. Social reformers in literature. 5. United States — Civilization — 1783-1865 I. T.
PS1889.S7   813/.3   *LC* 78-50   *ISBN* 0208017100

Colacurcio, Michael J.   2.11074
The province of piety: moral history in Hawthorne's early tales / Michael J. Colacurcio. — Cambridge, Mass.: Harvard University Press, 1984. viii, 669 p.; 24 cm. Includes index. 1. Hawthorne, Nathaniel, 1804-1864 — Knowledge — History. 2. Hawthorne, Nathaniel, 1804-1864 — Ethics. 3. Historical fiction, American 4. Ethics in literature. I. T.
PS1892.H5 C6 1984   813/.3 19   *LC* 83-26586   *ISBN* 0674719573

PS1905–2014 Hayne. Hearn. Holmes. Howe

Hayne, Paul Hamilton, 1830-1886.　　　　　　　　　**2.11075**
A man of letters in the nineteenth–century South: selected letters of Paul Hamilton Hayne / edited by Rayburn S. Moore. — Baton Rouge: Louisiana State University Press, c1982. xviii, 345 p.; 24 cm. — (Southern literary studies.) Includes index. 1. Hayne, Paul Hamilton, 1830-1886 — Correspondence. 2. Poets, American — 19th century — Correspondence. I. Moore, Rayburn S., 1920- II. T. III. Series.
PS1908.A44 1982　　811/.3 B 19　　LC 82-271　　　*ISBN* 0807110256

Hearn, Lafcadio, 1850-1904.　　　　　　　　　• **2.11076**
Selected writings / edited by Henry Goodman; with an introd. by Malcolm Cowley. — New York: Citadel Press, [1949] viii, 566 p.; 22 cm. Bibliography: p. 564-566. I. Goodman, Henry, 1893- ed. II. T.
PS1916.G6　　　813.49　　*LC* 49-11635 *

Hearn, Lafcadio, 1850-1904.　　　　　　　　　• **2.11077**
Glimpses of unfamiliar Japan. — Boston: Houghton Mifflin Co., [c1894] 2 v. (x, 699 p.) 1. Japan — Description and travel I. T.
PS1917.G57 1894　　*LC* 04-16699

Stevenson, Elizabeth, 1919-.　　　　　　　　　**2.11078**
Lafcadio Hearn. New York, Macmillan, 1961. 362 p. illus. 24 cm. 'First printing.' 1. Hearn, Lafcadio, 1850-1904. I. T.
PS1918.S75　　*LC* 61-10337

Holmes, Oliver Wendell, 1809-1894.　　　　　　**2.11079**
The works of Oliver Wendell Holmes. Standard library ed. [St. Clair Shores, Mich., Scholarly Press, 1972, c1892] 13 v. illus. 22 cm. Half title. Each v. has special t. p. I. T.
PS1950.F72　　818/.3/09　　*LC* 73-108494　　*ISBN* 0403004721

Holmes, Oliver Wendell, 1809-1894.　　　　　　• **2.11080**
Representative selections, with introduction, bibliography, and notes. New York, Cincinnati [etc.] American book company [c1939] cxxix, 472 p. front. (port.) 19 cm. I. Hayakawa, S. I. (Samuel Ichiyé), 1906- ed. II. Jones, Howard Mumford, 1892- joint ed. III. T.
PS1953.H4　　*LC* 39-21102

Small, Miriam Rossiter.　　　　　　　　　• **2.11081**
Oliver Wendell Holmes. New York: Twayne Publishers [1963, c1962] 176 p.; 21 cm. (Twayne's United States authors series, 29) 1. Holmes, Oliver Wendell, 1809-1894. I. T.
PS1981.S5 1963　　　818.3　　*LC* 62-19473

Howe, Julia Ward, 1819-1910.　　　　　　　　**2.11082**
Reminiscences, 1819–1899, by Julia Ward Howe ... Boston; New York: Houghton, Mifflin, 1899. 465 p.: ill., facsim., ports.; 21 cm. 1. Howe, Julia Ward, 1819-1910 — Biography. I. T.
PS2018.A4　　*LC* 00-54

Clifford, Deborah Pickman.　　　　　　　　　**2.11083**
Mine eyes have seen the glory: a biography of Julia Ward Howe / by Deborah Pickman Clifford. — 1st ed. — Boston: Little, Brown, c1979. 313 p., [4] leaves of plates: ill.; 24 cm. 'An Atlantic Monthly Press book.' Includes index. 1. Howe, Julia Ward, 1819-1910 — Biography. 2. Authors, American — 19th century — Biography. I. T.
PS2018.C55　　818/.4/09 B　　*LC* 78-10379　　*ISBN* 0316147478

PS2020–2038 Howells

Howells, William Dean, 1837-1920.　　　　　　**2.11084**
[Selected works. 1968] A selected edition of W. D. Howells. Bloomington: Indiana University Press, 1968-. v.: facsims., ports.; 25 cm. Vols. 4, 9, 19, 24, 28, and [31] published by Twayne Publishers, Boston. They lack a general t.p.; instead, special t.p. versos state: This volume of Selected letters is also published as volume ... of A selected edition of W.D. Howells. Vol. 31 is incorrectly numbered 28. I. T.
PS2020.F68　　*LC* 68-3215

Howells, William Dean, 1837-1920.　　　　　　**2.11085**
Selected writings of William Dean Howells / edited, with an introduction, by Henry Steele Commager. — New York: Random House, 1950. xvii, 946 p.: port. 1. Twain, Mark, 1835-1910. I. Commager, Henry Steele, 1902- II. T.
PS2022.C6 1950　　*LC* 50-9450

Howells, William Dean, 1837-1920.　　　　　　**2.11086**
Editor's study / by William Dean Howells; edited, with an introd. by James W. Simpson. — Troy, N.Y.: Whitston Pub. Co., 1983. xlvii, 417 p. I. Simpson, James W. II. T.
PS2028 E34 1983　　*LC* 81-50049　　*ISBN* 0878752137

Howells, William Dean, 1837-1920.　　　　　　**2.11087**
W. D. Howells as critic / edited by Edwin H. Cady. — London; Boston: Routledge & Kegan Paul, 1973. xvi, 493 p.; 23 cm. — (The Routledge critics series) Includes index. 1. Literature, Modern — History and criticism — Addresses, essays, lectures. I. Cady, Edwin Harrison. II. T.
PS2028.W14 1973　　809　　*LC* 73-83119　　*ISBN* 0710076762

Howells, William Dean, 1837-1920.　　　　　　• **2.11088**
Life in letters of William Dean Howells. Edited by Mildred Howells. — New York: Russell & Russell, [1968, c1928] 2 v.: illus., ports.; 25 cm. I. Howells, Mildred, 1872- ed. II. T.
PS2033.A67 1968　　816/.4　　*LC* 68-10928

Brooks, Van Wyck, 1886-1963.　　　　　　　　• **2.11089**
Howells, his life and world. [1st ed.]. — New York, Dutton, 1959. 296 p.: ill.; 22 cm. 1. Howells, William Dean, 1837-1920. I. T.
PS2033.B7　　813.4　　*LC* 59-10782

Carter, Everett.　　　　　　　　　　　　　　• **2.11090**
Howells and the age of realism. — Hamden, Conn., Archon Books, 1966 [c1954] 307 p. 22 cm. Bibliographical references included in 'Notes' (p. 277-298) 1. Howells, William Dean, 1837-1920. 2. Realism in literature I. T.
PS2033.C3 1966　　818.409　　*LC* 66-15384

Lynn, Kenneth Schuyler.　　　　　　　　　　**2.11091**
William Dean Howells; an American life [by] Kenneth S. Lynn. — [1st ed.]. — New York: Harcourt Brace Jovanovich, [1971] 372 p.: illus., ports.; 26 cm. 1. Howells, William Dean, 1837-1920. I. T.
PS2033.L9　　818/.4/09 B　　*LC* 71-142091　　*ISBN* 0151421773

Critical essays on W.D. Howells, 1866–1920 / [compiled by]　　**2.11092**
Edwin H. Cady & Norma W. Cady.
Boston, Mass.: G.K. Hall, c1983. xxxii, 267 p.; 24 cm. — (Critical essays on American literature.) 1. Howells, William Dean, 1837-1920 — Criticism and interpretation — Addresses, essays, lectures. I. Cady, Edwin Harrison. II. Cady, Norma W. III. Series.
PS2034.C7 1983　　818/.409 19　　*LC* 83-6089　　*ISBN* 0816186510

Eble, Kenneth Eugene.　　　　　　　　　　　**2.11093**
William Dean Howells / by Kenneth E. Eble. — 2nd ed. — Boston: Twayne Publishers, c1982. 225 p.; 22 cm. — (Twayne's United States authors series. TUSAS 16) Includes index. 1. Howells, William Dean, 1837-1920 — Criticism and interpretation. I. T. II. Series.
PS2034.E24 1982　　818/.409 19　　*LC* 82-11876　　*ISBN* 080577372X

PS2050–2098 Irving

Irving, Washington, 1783-1859.　　　　　　　　**2.11094**
The complete works of Washington Irving / edited by Henry A. Pochman. — Madison: University of Wisconsin Press, 1969-. v. I. Pochman, Henry A. II. T.
PS2050.Fx

A Century of commentary on the works of Washington Irving,　　**2.11095**
1860–1974 / edited by Andrew B. Myers.
Tarrytown, N.Y.: Sleepy Hollow Restorations, c1976. xxxviii, 504 p.: ill.; 22 cm. Includes index. 1. Irving, Washington, 1783-1859 — Addresses, essays, lectures. 2. Authors, American — 19th century — Biography — Addresses, essays, lectures. I. Myers, Andrew B.
PS2081.C4　　818/.2/09 B　　*LC* 74-7843　　*ISBN* 091288228X

Hedges, William L.　　　　　　　　　　　　• **2.11096**
Washington Irving: an American study, 1802–1832. Baltimore: Johns Hopkins Press, 1965. xiv, 274 p.; 24 cm. (The Goucher College Series) 1. Irving, Washington, 1783-1859 — Criticism and interpretation. I. T.
PS2081.H35　　818.2　　*LC* 65-11663

Williams, Stanley Thomas, 1888-1956.　　　　　• **2.11097**
The life of Washington Irving. — New York: Octagon Books, 1971 [c1935] 2 v.: illus.; 24 cm. 1. Irving, Washington, 1783-1859. I. T.
PS2081.W45 1971　　818/.2/09 B　　*LC* 73-154672　　*ISBN* 0374986304

Bowden, Mary Weathersmoon.　　　　　　　　**2.11098**
Washington Irving / by Mary Weathersmoon Bowden. — Boston: Twayne Publishers, 1981. 201 p.: port.; 21 cm. — (Twayne's United States authors series; TUSAS 379) Includes index. 1. Irving, Washington, 1783-1859 — Criticism and interpretation. I. T.
PS2088.B66　　818/.209 19　　*LC* 80-21364　　*ISBN* 0805773142

Roth, Martin, 1934-.　　　　　　　　　　　　**2.11099**
Comedy and America: the lost world of Washington Irving / Martin Roth. — Port Washington, N.Y.: Kennikat Press, 1976. xiv, 205 p.; 22 cm. (Literary criticism series) (National university publications) 1. Irving, Washington, 1783-1859 — Criticism and interpretation. 2. Irving, Washington, 1783-1859.

A history of New York. 3. Comedy — History and criticism. 4. New York (State) — History — Colonial period, ca. 1600-1775 I. T.
PS2088.R6   818/.2/09   *LC* 76-6870   *ISBN* 0804691320

PS2110–2128 James

James, Henry, 1843-1916.   **2.11100**
[Selections. 1907] The novels and tales of Henry James. New York ed. ... New York: A.M. Kelley, 1971. 26 v. fronts. (v. 1: port.) 22 cm. Half-title; each volume has special t.-p. Vol. 1-24 have critical prefaces by the author; v. 25-26, left unfinished at the author's death, are edited by Percy Lubbock. Reprint of 1907-1917 ed. published by Scribner. I. Lubbock, Percy, 1879- II. T.
PS2110.F07   813/.4 19

Jámes, Henry, 1843-1916.   • **2.11101**
The complete plays of Henry James / ed. by Leon Edel. — [1st ed.]. — Philadelphia: J. B. Lippincott Co., [1949] 846 p.: ill., ports.; 25 cm. I. Edel, Leon Joseph, 1907- ed. II. T.
PS2111.E4   812.4   *LC* 49-10769 *

James, Henry, 1843-1916.   **2.11102**
The art of the novel: critical prefaces / by Henry James; with a foreword by R.W.B. Lewis and an introduction by R.P. Blackmur. — 50th anniversary ed., Northeastern University Press ed. — Boston: Northeastern University Press, 1984. xlvii, 352 p.; 21 cm. Reprint. Originally published: New York: Scribner, 1934. Includes index. 1. James, Henry, 1843-1916 — Technique — Addresses, essays, lectures. 2. Fiction — Technique — Addresses, essays, lectures. I. T.
PS2112 1984   813/.4 19   *LC* 84-5619   *ISBN* 093035060X

James, Henry, 1843-1916.   • **2.11103**
[Short stories] The complete tales of Henry James / edited, with an introd., by Leon Edel. — Philadelphia: Lippincott [1962-65, c1964] 12 v.; 21cm. I. Edel, Leon, 1907- ed. II. T.
PS2112.E3 1962   813/.4 19   *LC* 62-11335

James, Henry, 1843-1916.   **2.11104**
The portable Henry James / edited, and with an introd., by Morton Dauwen Zabel. — Rev. in 1968 / by Lyall H. P. Powers. — New York: Penguin Books, [1977] c1968. viii, 696 p.; 18 cm. — (The Viking Portable library) I. Zabel, Morton Dauwen, 1901-1964. II. T.
PS2112.Z3 1977   813/.4   *LC* 77-2390   *ISBN* 0140150552

James, Henry, 1843-1916.   **2.11105**
The ambassadors: an authoritative text, the author on the novel, criticism. Edited by S. P. Rosenbaum. — [1st ed.]. — New York: W. W. Norton, [1963, c1964] viii, 486 p.; 21 cm. — (Norton critical editions) 'N309.' I. Rosenbaum, S. P. (Stanford Patrick), 1929- II. T.
PZ3.J234 Amb17   PS2116.A46 1964.   *LC* 63-8035   *ISBN* 0393096130

Stone, Albert E. comp.   **2.11106**
Twentieth century interpretations of The ambassadors; a collection of critical essays, edited by Albert E. Stone, Jr. — Englewood Cliffs, N.J.: Prentice-Hall, [1969] iv, 121 p.; 21 cm. — (Twentieth century interpretations) (A Spectrum book.) 1. James, Henry, 1843-1916. The ambassadors. I. T.
PS2116.A53 S8   813/.4   *LC* 69-15349   *ISBN* 0130239372

James, Henry, 1843-1916.   **2.11107**
The American: an authoritative text, backgrounds and sources, criticism / Henry James; edited by James W. Tuttleton. — 1st ed. — New York: Norton, c1978. x, 496 p.; 22 cm. — (A Norton critical edition) 1. James, Henry, 1843-1916. The American. I. Tuttleton, James W. II. T.
PZ3.J234 Ame 1978   PS2116.Ax   813/.4   *LC* 77-27622   *ISBN* 0393044769. *ISBN* 0393090914 pbk

Buitenhuis, Peter. comp.   **2.11108**
Twentieth century interpretations of The portrait of a lady; a collection of critical essays, edited by Peter Buitenhuis. — Englewood Cliffs, N.J.: Prentice-Hall, [1968] vi, 122 p.; 21 cm. — (Twentieth century interpretations) (A Spectrum book.) 1. James, Henry, 1843-1916. The portrait of a lady. I. T.
PS2116.P63 B8   813/.4   *LC* 68-23697

James, Henry, 1843-1916.   **2.11109**
The portrait of a lady: an authoritative text, Henry James and the novel, reviews and criticism. Edited by Robert D. Bamberg. — [1st ed.]. — New York: Norton, [1975] ix, 755 p.; 22 cm. — (A Norton critical edition) 1. James, Henry, 1843-1916. The portrait of a lady. I. Bamberg, Robert D., ed. II. T.
PZ3.J234 Po50   PS2116.P62x   813/.4   *LC* 74-19457   *ISBN* 0393043851

James, Henry, 1843-1916.   **2.11110**
The turn of the screw. An authoritative text, backgrounds and sources, essays in criticism. Edited by Robert Kimbrough. — [1st ed.]. — New York: W. W.

Norton, [1966] x, 276 p.; 20 cm. — (A Norton critical edition) I. Kimbrough, Robert. ed. II. T.
PS2116.T8 1966   813.4   *LC* 66-11786

James, Henry, 1843-1916.   **2.11111**
The wings of the dove / Henry James; edited by J. Donald Crowley and Richard A. Hocks. — 1st ed. — New York: W. W. Norton, c1978. viii, 583 p.; 22 cm. (A Norton critical edition) 1. James, Henry, 1843-1916. Wings of the dove. I. Crowley, J. Donald (Joseph Donald) II. Hocks, Richard A., 1936- III. T.
PZ3.J234 Wi 1978   PS2116.W5   813/.4   *LC* 77-19062   *ISBN* 0393044785. *ISBN* 0393090884 pbk

James, Henry, 1843-1916.   • **2.11112**
Literary reviews and essays, on American, English, and French literature / edited by Albert Mordell. — New York: Twayne Publishers, [c1957] 409 p.; 24 cm. Includes bibliographical references. 1. French literature — 19th century — Addresses, essays, lectures. 2. American literature — 19th century — Addresses, essays, lectures. 3. English literature — 19th century — Addresses, essays, lectures. 4. Books — Reviews I. T.
PS2120.L5 1957   814.4   *LC* 58-249

James, Henry, 1843-1916.   • **2.11113**
Henry James, autobiography / edited with an introduction by Frederick W. Dupee. — New York: Criterion Books, 1956. xiv, 622 p.: ill., ports.; 24 cm. Includes index. 1. James, Henry, 1843-1916 — Biography. I. Dupee, F. W. (Frederick Wilcox), 1904- II. James, Henry, 1843-1916. Small boy and others. III. James, Henry, 1843-1916. Notes of a son and brother. IV. James, Henry, 1843-1916. Middle years. V. T. VI. Title: A small boy and others. VII. Title: Notes of a son and brother. VIII. Title: The middle years.
PS2123.A3 1956   *LC* 56-6211

James, Henry, 1843-1916.   **2.11114**
The complete notebooks of Henry James / edited with introductions and notes by Leon Edel and Lyall H. Powers. — New York: Oxford University Press, 1987. xxix, 633 p., [8] p. of plates: ill.; 24 cm. Includes index. 1. James, Henry, 1843-1916 — Notebooks, sketchbooks, etc. 2. James, Henry, 1843-1916 — Diaries. 3. Novelists, American — 19th century — Diaries. I. Edel, Leon, 1907- II. Powers, Lyall Harris, 1924- III. T.
PS2123.A3 1987   818/.403 19   *LC* 86-21680   *ISBN* 0195037820

James, Henry, 1843-1916.   **2.11115**
Letters / Henry James; edited by Leon Edel. — Cambridge, Mass.: Belknap Press of Harvard University Press, 1974-1984. 4 v.: ill.; 22 cm. 1. James, Henry, 1843-1916 — Correspondence. I. Edel, Leon, 1907- II. T.
PS2123.A42 1974   813/.4 B   *LC* 74-77181   *ISBN* 0674387805

Dupee, F. W. (Frederick Wilcox), 1904-.   • **2.11116**
Henry James. — [New York]: Sloane, 1951. xiii, 301 p.: port.; 22 cm. — (American men of letters series.) 1. James, Henry, 1843-1916. I. T. II. Series.
PS2123.D8   *LC* 51-2012

Edel, Leon, 1907-.   • **2.11117**
Henry James. — [1st ed.]. — Philadelphia: Lippincott, c1953-1972. 5 v.: illus.; 22 cm. 1. James, Henry, 1843-1916. I. T.
PS2123.E385 1953   813.4   *LC* 53-5421

Pirie, Gordon.   **2.11118**
Henry James / Gordon Pirie. — London: Evans Bros., 1974. 152 p.: ill., facsim., port.; 20 cm. (Literature in perspective) Includes indexes. 1. James, Henry, 1843-1916. I. T.
PS2123.P5   813/.4   *LC* 75-322529   *ISBN* 0237350262

Blackmur, R. P. (Richard P.), 1904-1965.   **2.11119**
Studies in Henry James / R.P. Blackmur; edited with an introduction by Veronica A. Makowsky. — New York: New Directions, c1983. 250 p.; 21 cm. Includes index. 1. James, Henry, 1843-1916 — Criticism and interpretation — Addresses, essays, lectures. I. T.
PS2124.B54 1983   813/.4 19   *LC* 82-18911   *ISBN* 081120863X

Edel, Leon, 1907- ed.   **2.11120**
Henry James; a collection of critical essays. — Englewood Cliffs, N.J.: Prentice-Hall, [c1963] vi, 185 p.; 21 cm. — (A Spectrum book: Twentieth century views) 'S-TC-34.' 1. James, Henry, 1843-1916 — Criticism and interpretation. I. T.
PS2124.E38   813.4   *LC* 63-20365

Gard, Roger, comp.   • **2.11121**
Henry James: the critical heritage. — London: Routledge & K. Paul; New York: Barnes & Noble, 1968. xxi, 566 p.; 23 cm. — (The Critical heritage series) 1. James, Henry, 1843-1916 — Criticism and interpretation. I. T.
PS2124.G35 1968   813/.4   *LC* 68-121918   *ISBN* 0710060688

Krook, Dorothea.   **2.11122**
The ordeal of consciousness in Henry James. — Cambridge [Eng.] University Press, 1962. xiii, 422 p. 23 cm. Bibliographical footnotes. 1. James, Henry, 1843-1916. I. T.
PS2124.K7   818.4   *LC* 62-5617

Long, Robert Emmet.   **2.11123**
Henry James, the early novels / by Robert Emmet Long. — Boston: Twayne Publishers, c1983. 195 p., [1] leaf of plates: port.; 21 cm. — (Twayne's United States authors series. TUSAS 440) Includes index. 1. James, Henry, 1843-1916 — Criticism and interpretation. I. T. II. Series.
PS2124.L62 1983   813/.4 19   LC 82-18721   ISBN 0805773797

Matthiessen, F. O. (Francis Otto), 1902-1950.   • **2.11124**
Henry James, the major phase / by F.O. Matthiessen. — London: Oxford University Press, 1944. xvi, 190 p.: port. 1. James, Henry, 1843-1916. I. T.
PS2124.M3   LC 44-47752

Poirier, Richard.   • **2.11125**
The comic sense of Henry James, a study of the early novels. New York: Oxford University Press, 1960. 260 p. 23 cm. 1. James, Henry, 1843-1916. I. T.
PS2124.P6 1960   813.4   LC 60-3811

Samuels, Charles Thomas, 1936-1974.   **2.11126**
The ambiguity of Henry James / by Charles Samuels. — Urbana: University of Illinois Press, [1971] x, 235 p.; 24 cm. 1. James, Henry, 1843-1916 — Criticism and interpretation. I. T.
PS2124.S2   813/.4   LC 70-140035   ISBN 0252001737

Sears, Sallie.   **2.11127**
The negative imagination; form and perspective in the novels of Henry James. — Ithaca, N.Y.: Cornell University Press, [1968] xiii, 231 p.; 22 cm. 1. James, Henry, 1843-1916 — Criticism and interpretation. I. T.
PS2124.S4   813/.4   LC 68-9754

Tompkins, Jane P. comp.   **2.11128**
Twentieth century interpretations of The turn of the screw, and other tales; a collection of critical essays. Edited by Jane P. Tompkins. — Englewood Cliffs, N.J.: Prentice-Hall, [1970] v, 115 p.; 21 cm. — (Twentieth century interpretations) (A Spectrum book.) 1. James, Henry, 1843-1916 — Criticism and interpretation. I. T.
PS2124.T6   813/.4   LC 73-126815   ISBN 0139330445

Veeder, William R.   **2.11129**
Henry James: the lessons of the master: popular fiction and personal style in the nineteenth century / William Veeder. — Chicago: University of Chicago Press, 1975. xiii, 287 p., [4] leaves of plates: ill.; 24 cm. 1. James, Henry, 1843-1916 — Criticism and interpretation. I. T.
PS2124.V43   813/.4   LC 75-8957   ISBN 0226852237

Ward, J. A. (Joseph Anthony), 1931-.   **2.11130**
The search for form; studies in the structure of James's fiction, by J. A. Ward. Chapel Hill, University of North Carolina Press [1967] xiv, 228 p. 23 cm. 1. James, Henry, 1843-1916. I. T.
PS2124.W3   813/.4   LC 67-23497

Sharp, Corona.   **2.11131**
The confidante in Henry James: evolution and moral value of a fictive character. Notre Dame, Ind.: University of Notre Dame Press, 1963. xxx, 305 p.; 22 cm. 1. James, Henry, 1843-1916. 2. Confidant in literature I. T.
PS2127.C6 S5   813.4   LC 63-19326

Sicker, Philip.   **2.11132**
Love and the quest for identity in the fiction of Henry James / Philip Sicker. — Princeton, N.J.: Princeton University Press, c1980. xv, 196 p.; 23 cm. Includes index. 1. James, Henry, 1843-1916 — Criticism and interpretation. 2. Love in literature 3. Identity (Psychology) in literature. I. T.
PS2127.L65 S5   813/.4   LC 79-17311   ISBN 0691064172

PS2130–2133 Jewett

Jewett, Sarah Orne, 1849-1909.   • **2.11133**
Stories and tales / by Sarah Orne Jewett. — Boston: Houghton Mifflin, [1910] 7 v.: ill.; 17 cm. I. T.
PS2130.A6 1910   LC A11-1493

Cary, Richard, 1909-.   **2.11134**
Sarah Orne Jewett. New York: Twayne Publishers [1962] 175 p.; 21 cm. (Twayne's United States authors series, 19) 1. Jewett, Sarah Orne, 1849-1909. I. T.
PS2133.C3   813.4   LC 62-13673

Matthiessen, F. O. (Francis Otto), 1902-1950.   • **2.11135**
Sarah Orne Jewett. — Boston: Houghton Mifflin, 1929. 159 p.: ill., ports., facsims. 1. Jewett, Sarah Orne, 1849-1909. I. T.
PS2133.M3   LC 29-9532

PS2160–2248 Kennedy. King. Lanier

Kennedy, John Pendleton, 1795-1870.   • **2.11136**
Horse-shoe Robinson, by John Pendleton Kennedy; edited, with introduction, chronology, and bibliography, by Ernest E. Leisy ... New York; Cincinnati [etc.]: American Book Company [c1937] xxxii, 550 p.: front. (port.) pl., map, facsims.; 21 cm. (Half-title: American fiction series; general editor, H. H. Clark) 'Selected bibliography': p. xxix-xxxii. 1. United States — History — Revolution — Fiction. I. Leisy, Ernest Erwin, 1887- ed. II. T.
PS2162.H6 1937   LC 37-4088

Kennedy, John Pendleton, 1795-1870.   **2.11137**
Swallow barn, or, A sojourn in the Old Dominion / John Pendleton Kennedy; with an introduction by Lucinda H. MacKethan. — Baton Rouge: Louisiana State University Press, c1986. xxxix, 506 p.: ill.; 22 cm. — (Library of Southern civilization.) I. MacKethan, Lucinda Hardwick. II. T. III. Title: Swallow barn. IV. Title: Sojourn in the Old Dominion. V. Series.
PS2162.S93 1986   813/.3 19   LC 85-23215   ISBN 0807113220

King, Grace Elizabeth, 1852-1932.   **2.11138**
Grace King of New Orleans; a selection of her writings. Edited with introd. and notes by Robert Bush. — Baton Rouge: Louisiana State University Press, [1973] xiv, 404, [1] p.; 24 cm. — (Southern literary studies.) I. T. II. Series.
PS2176.G7 1973   813/.4   LC 72-96399   ISBN 0807100552

Bush, Robert, 1917-.   **2.11139**
Grace King: a southern destiny / Robert Bush. — Baton Rouge: Louisiana State University Press, c1983. xv, 317 p.: ill., ports.; 24 cm. — (Southern literary studies.) 1. King, Grace Elizabeth, 1852-1932. 2. Authors, American — 19th century — Biography. 3. New Orleans (La.) in literature. I. T. II. Series.
PS2178.B87 1983   813/.4 B 19   LC 83-9849   ISBN 0807111112

Lanier, Sidney, 1842-1881.   **2.11140**
The centennial edition of the works of Sidney Lanier. [Baltimore, The Johns Hopkins press, 1945] 10 v.: ill. (incl. music), facsims. (incl. music), ports.; 24 cm. Half-title. Each volume has special t.-p. Frontispiece of v. 10 accompanied by guard sheet with descriptive letterpress. 'General editor: Charles R. Anderson.' 1. Lanier, Sidney, 1842-1881 — Bibliography. 2. Lanier, Sidney, 1842-1881 — Correspondence. I. Anderson, Charles Roberts, 1902- II. Baum, Paull F. (Paull Franklin), 1886- III. Malone, Kemp, 1889-1971. IV. Gohdes, Clarence Louis Frank, 1901- V. Greever, Garland, 1883- VI. Graham, Philip, 1898- VII. Starke, Aubrey Harrison. VIII. Thies, Frieda Charlotte, 1880- IX. T.
PS2200.F45   PS2200.F45.   810.81   LC a 46-2793

Lanier, Sidney, 1842-1881.   **2.11141**
Sidney Lanier: poems and letters. With an introd. and notes by Charles R. Anderson. — Baltimore: Johns Hopkins Press, [1969] ix, 227 p.; 21 cm. — (Johns Hopkins paperback, JH-59) Selections drawn from the text and notes of the Centennial edition of the works of Sidney Lanier, 1945. I. Anderson, Charles Roberts, 1902- ed. II. T.
PS2202.A5   811/.4   LC 76-83323   ISBN 0801810841

Mims, Edwin, 1872-1959.   • **2.11142**
Sidney Lanier. Port Washington, N.Y., Kennikat Press [1968, c1905] vii, 386 p. 19 cm. 1. Lanier, Sidney, 1842-1881. I. T.
PS2213.M5 1968   811/.4 B   LC 68-16281

Starke, Aubrey Harrison.   • **2.11143**
Sidney Lanier: a biographical and critical study. — New York: Russell & Russell, 1964 [c1933] xvi, 525 p.: ill., ports., facsims., music. 22 cm. Bibliography: p. [455]-473. Bibliographical references included in 'Notes' (p. [475]-508) 1. Lanier, Sidney, 1842-1881. I. T.
PS2213.S7 1964   811.4   LC 64-10713

PS2250–2348 Longfellow. Lowell

Longfellow, Henry Wadsworth, 1807-1882.   • **2.11144**
The poems of Longfellow: including Evangeline, The song of Hiawatha, The courtship of Miles Standish, Tales of a wayside inn. — New York: B.A. Cerf, D.S. Klopfer, [1932] xi, 678 p.; 17 cm. (The Modern library of the world's best books) 'First Modern library edition, 1932.' I. T.
PS2250.F32   811.34   LC 32-26750

Arvin, Newton, 1900-1963.   **2.11145**
Longfellow: his life and work. — [1st ed.]. — Boston: Little, Brown, [1963] 338 p.: illus.; 22 cm. 1. Longfellow, Henry Wadsworth, 1807-1882. 2. Poets, American — 19th century — Biography. I. T.
PS2281.A6   811.4   LC 63-8312

Lowell, James Russell, 1819-1891.   • **2.11146**
James Russell Lowell: representative selections / with introduction, bibliography, and notes, by Harry Hayden Clark and Norman Foerster. — New

York; Cincinnati [etc.]: American Book Company [1947] clxvi, 498 p.: front. (port.); 19 cm. 1. Clark, Harry Hayden, 1901-1971. ed. I. T.
PS2302.C5   *LC 47-671*

Duberman, Martin B.   **2.11147**
James Russell Lowell [by] Martin Duberman. — Boston: Houghton Mifflin, 1966. xxii, 516 p.: illus., facsims., ports.; 22 cm. 1. Lowell, James Russell, 1819-1891. I. T.
PS2331.D8   811.3 B   *LC 66-19835*

PS2380–2388 Melville

Melville, Herman, 1819-1891.   • **2.11148**
[Works. 1968] The writings / [Editors: Harrison Hayford, Hershel Parker, G. Thomas Tanselle] The Northwestern-Newberry ed. [Evanston, Ill.: Northwestern University Press, 1968-. v.; 25 cm. Edition originated under the auspices of the Center for Editions of American Authors (Modern Language Association of America) I. Hayford, Harrison. II. Parker, Hershel. III. Tanselle, G. Thomas (George Thomas), 1934- IV. T.
PS2380.F68   818/.3/09   *LC 68-2173*

Melville, Herman, 1819-1891.   **2.11149**
Selected writings of Herman Melville: complete short stories, Typee [and] Billy Budd, foretopman. — New York: Modern Library, [1952] 903 p.; 21 cm. — (The Modern library of the world's best books) I. T.
PS2382.M6   813.36   *LC 51-14537*

Melville, Herman, 1819-1891.   • **2.11150**
Billy Budd, sailor (an inside narrative) Reading text and genetic text, edited from the manuscript with introd. and notes by Harrison Hayford and Merton M. Sealts, Jr. — [Chicago]: University of Chicago Press, [1962] ix, 431 p.: facsims., tables.; 24 cm. I. Hayford, Harrison. II. Sealts, Merton M. III. T.
PZ3.M498 Bl   PS2384.B7 H39 1962.   *LC 62-17135*

Vincent, Howard Paton, 1904- comp.   **2.11151**
Twentieth century interpretations of Billy Budd; a collection of critical essays, edited by Howard P. Vincent. — Englewood Cliffs, N.J.: Prentice-Hall, [1971] vi, 112 p.; 21 cm. — (Twentieth century interpretations) (A Spectrum book) 1. Melville, Herman, 1819-1891. Billy Budd. I. T. II. Title: Billy Budd.
PS2384.B7 V5   813/.3   *LC 76-133055*   *ISBN* 0130847151

Melville, Herman, 1819-1891.   • **2.11152**
Clarel: a poem and pilgrimage in the Holy Land / by Herman Melville; edited by Walter E. Bezanson. — New York: Hendricks House, 1960. cxvii, 652 p.: maps. 1. Poetry of places — Palestine. 2. Palestine — Description and travel — Poetry. I. T.
PS2384.C5 1960   *LC 61-569*

Kenny, Vincent S.   **2.11153**
Herman Melville's Clarel; a spiritual autobiography, [by] Vincent Kenny. — [Hamden, Conn.]: Archon Books, 1973. xvi, 272 p.; 22 cm. 1. Melville, Herman, 1819-1891. Clarel. I. T.
PS2384.C53 K4 1973   811/.3   *LC 73-3074*   *ISBN* 0208012265

Melville, Herman, 1819-1891.   **2.11154**
The confidence–man: his masquerade; an authoritative text, backgrounds and sources, reviews, criticism [and] an annotated bibliography. Edited by Hershel Parker. — New York: Norton, [1971] xvii, 376 p.; 21 cm. — (A Norton critical edition) 'Slightly corrected reprinting of the first American edition,' published in 1857. I. T.
PZ3.M498 Cp4 PS2384.Cx   813/.3   *LC 71-141591*   *ISBN* 0393043452

Melville, Herman, 1819-1891.   • **2.11155**
Moby–Dick: An authoritative text / reviews and letters by Melville; analogues and sources; criticism; edited by Harrison Hayford [and] Hershel Parker; pictorial materials prepared by John B. Putnam. — [1st ed.]. — New York: W. W. Norton, [1967] xviii, 728 p.: ill., maps; 20 cm. — (Norton critical edition.) I. Hayford, Harrison. II. Parker, Hershel. III. T. IV. Series.
PZ3.M498 Mo76   PS2384.M62 1967.   *LC 66-11309*

Approaches to teaching Melville's Moby Dick / edited by   **2.11156**
Martin Bickman.
New York: Modern Language Association of America, 1985. x, 157 p.; 23 cm. (Approaches to teaching masterpieces of world literature. 8) Includes index. 1. Melville, Herman, 1819-1891 Moby Dick — Addresses, essays, lectures. 2. Melville, Herman, 1819-1891 — Study and teaching — Addresses, essays, lectures. I. Bickman, Martin, 1945- II. Series.
PS2384.M62 A66 1985   813/.3 19   *LC 85-4892*   *ISBN* 087352490X

Herbert, T. Walter (Thomas Walter), 1938-.   **2.11157**
Moby–Dick and Calvinism: a world dismantled / T. Walter Herbert, Jr. — New Brunswick, N.J.: Rutgers University Press, c1977. xii, 186 p.; 23 cm.

1. Melville, Herman, 1819-1891. Moby Dick. 2. Melville, Herman, 1819-1891 — Religion. 3. Calvinism in literature. I. T.
PS2384.M62 H37   813/.3   *LC 76-56252*   *ISBN* 0813508290

Twentieth century interpretations of Moby–Dick: a collection of   **2.11158**
critical essays / edited by Michael T. Gilmore.
Englewood Cliffs, N.J.: Prentice-Hall, c1977. iv, 123 p.; 21 cm. (A Spectrum book) 1. Melville, Herman, 1819-1891. Moby-Dick. I. Gilmore, Michael T.
PS2384.M62 T9   813/.3   *LC 76-44426*   *ISBN* 0135860571

Melville, Herman, 1819-1891.   **2.11159**
The letters of Herman Melville / edited by Merrell R. Davis and William H. Gilman. — New Haven: Yale University Press, 1960. xxxi, 398 p.: ill., facsims.; 25 cm. 1. Melville, Herman, 1819-1891 — Correspondence. I. Davis, Merrell Rees, 1912- II. Gilman, William Henry, 1911-1976. III. T.
PS2386.A57   *LC 60-7822*

Berthoff, Warner.   • **2.11160**
The example of Melville. — Princeton, N.J.: Princeton University Press, 1962. 218 p.; 23 cm. 1. Melville, Herman, 1819-1891. I. T.
PS2386.B4   813.3   *LC 63-7065*

Hillway, Tyrus.   **2.11161**
Herman Melville / by Tyrus Hillway. — Rev. ed. — Boston: Twayne Publishers, 1979. 177 p.: port.; 21 cm. — (Twayne's United States authors series; TUSAS 37) Includes index. 1. Melville, Herman, 1819-1891. 2. Authors, American — 19th century — Biography. I. T.
PS2386.H5 1979   813/.3 B   *LC 78-11937*   *ISBN* 0805772561

Howard, Leon.   • **2.11162**
Herman Melville: a biography. — Berkeley: University of California Press, 1951. xi, 354 p.: ill. 1. Melville, Herman, 1819-1891. I. T.
PS2386 H6   *LC 51-62667*

Miller, Edwin Haviland.   **2.11163**
Melville / Edwin Haviland Miller. — New York: G. Braziller, c1975. 382 p., [4] leaves of plates: ill.; 25 cm. (A Venture book) Includes index. 1. Melville, Herman, 1819-1891 — Biography. I. T.
PS2386.M49   813/.3 B   *LC 75-7958*   *ISBN* 0807607878

Mumford, Lewis, 1895-.   **2.11164**
Herman Melville: a study of his life and vision / Lewis Mumford. — Rev. ed. — New York: Harcourt, Brace & World, 1962. xvi, 256 p.; 22 cm. 1. Melville, Herman, 1819-1891. I. T.
PS2386.M8 1962   928.1   *LC 62-21847*

Bowen, Merlin, 1910-.   **2.11165**
The long encounter; self and experience in the writings of Herman Melville. [Chicago] University of Chicago Press [1960] 282 p. 23 cm. 1. Melville, Herman, 1819-1891 — Criticism and interpretation. 2. Self I. Bowen, Merlin, 1910- Self and experience in the writings of Herman Melville. II. T. III. Title: Self and experience in the writings of Herman Melville.
PS2387.B6 1960   813.3   *LC 60-7232*

Branch, Watson Gailey, comp.   **2.11166**
Melville, the critical heritage / edited by Watson G. Branch. — London; Boston: Routledge & K. Paul, 1974. xix, 444 p.; 23 cm. (The Critical heritage series) Includes index. 1. Melville, Herman, 1819-1891 — Criticism and interpretation. I. T.
PS2387.B66 1974   813/.3   *LC 73-86570*   *ISBN* 0710077742

Chase, Richard Volney, 1914-1962. ed.   • **2.11167**
Melville: a collection of critical essays. — Englewood Cliffs, N.J.: Prentice-Hall, [1962] 168 p.; 21 cm. — (Twentieth century views) (A Spectrum book, S-TC-13.) 1. Melville, Herman, 1819-1891 — Criticism and interpretation. I. T.
PS2387.C45   818.3   *LC 62-14917*

Dillingham, William B.   **2.11168**
An artist in the rigging: the early work of Herman Melville [by] William B. Dillingham. — Athens: University of Georgia Press, [1972] xi, 157 p.; 23 cm. 1. Melville, Herman, 1819-1891. I. T.
PS2387.D5   813/.3   *LC 79-156038*   *ISBN* 0820302767

Dillingham, William B.   **2.11169**
Melville's later novels / William B. Dillingham. — Athens, Ga.: University of Georgia Press, c1986. xii, 430 p.; 23 cm. 1. Melville, Herman, 1819-1891 — Criticism and interpretation. I. T.
PS2387.D525 1986   813/.3 19   *LC 85-1192*   *ISBN* 0820307998

Dillingham, William B.   **2.11170**
Melville's short fiction, 1853–1856 / William B. Dillingham. — Athens: University of Georgia Press, c1977. 390 p.; 23 cm. Includes index. 1. Melville, Herman, 1819-1891 — Criticism and interpretation. I. T.
PS2387.D53   813/.3   *LC 76-28922*   *ISBN* 0820304115

New perspectives on Melville / edited by Faith Pullin.   **2.11171**
Kent, Ohio: Kent State University Press, 1979 (c1978). xii, 314 p.; 20 cm.
1. Melville, Herman, 1819-1891 — Criticism and interpretation — Addresses, essays, lectures. I. Pullin, Faith.
PS2387.N48   813/.3   LC 78-16505   ISBN 0873382269

Rosenberry, Edward H.   **2.11172**
Melville / by Edward H. Rosenberry. — London; Boston: Routledge & K. Paul, 1979. xii, 170 p., [2] leaves of plates: ill.; 23 cm. Includes index.
1. Melville, Herman, 1819-1891 — Criticism and interpretation. I. T.
PS2387.R636   813/.3   LC 78-40838   ISBN 0710089899

Shurr, William.   **2.11173**
The mystery of iniquity; Melville as poet, 1857–1891 [by] William H. Shurr. [Lexington, Ky.] University Press of Kentucky [c1972] 283 p. 25 cm. (South Atlantic Modern Language Association. Award study) 1. Melville, Herman, 1819-1891. I. T.
PS2387.S5   811/.3   LC 70-190535   ISBN 0813112761

PS2410–2458 Mitchell. Moody. More. Murfree (Charles Egbert Craddock)

Mitchell, S. Weir (Silas Weir), 1829-1914.   • **2.11174**
Hugh Wynne, free Quaker; sometime brevet lieutenant–colonel on the staff of His Excellency General Washington, by S. Weir Mitchell. New York, Century Co., 1898 [c1896] Grosse Pointe, Mich., Scholarly Press, 1968. 2 v. ports. 19 cm. 1. United States — History — Revolution, 1775-1783 — Fiction I. T.
PZ3.M695 Hu20 PS2414.H8x   813/.4   LC 75-3261

Moody, William Vaughn, 1869-1910.   • **2.11175**
The poems and plays of William Vaughn Moody. With an introd. by John M. Manly. — New York: AMS Press, [1969] 2 v.: port.; 23 cm. Reprint of the 1912 ed. I. T.
PS2425.A2 1969   818/.5/209   LC 70-80719

Brown, Maurice F., 1928-.   **2.11176**
Estranging dawn: the life and works of William Vaughn Moody, by Maurice F. Brown. — Carbondale: Southern Illinois University Press, [1973] xiii, 321 p.: ill.; 25 cm. 1. Moody, William Vaughn, 1869-1910. I. T.
PS2428.B7   818/.5/209 B   LC 73-252   ISBN 0809306182

Halpern, Martin.   • **2.11177**
William Vaughn Moody. New York: Twayne Publishers [1964] 208 p.; 21 cm. (Twayne's United States authors series, 64) 1. Moody, William Vaughn, 1869-1910. I. T.
PS2428.H3   811.52   LC 64-20714

More, Paul Elmer, 1864-1937.   **2.11178**
The essential Paul Elmer More; a selection of his writings. Edited with an introd. and notes by Byron C. Lambert. Foreword by Russell Kirk. — New Rochelle, N.Y.: Arlington House, [1972] 353 p.; 24 cm. I. Lambert, Byron Cecil, 1923- ed. II. T.
PS2431.A6 1972   818/.5/209   LC 79-189372   ISBN 0870001620

Dakin, Arthur Hazard, 1905-.   **2.11179**
Paul Elmer More. — Princeton, N.J.: Princeton University Press, 1960. 416 p.: ill. 1. More, Paul Elmer, 1864-1937. I. T.
PS2432.D8   818.509   LC 59-11076

Duggan, Francis X.   • **2.11180**
Paul Elmer More, by Francis X. Duggan. — New York: Twayne Publishers, [1967, c1966] 174 p.; 21 cm. — (Twayne's United States authors series, 106) 1. More, Paul Elmer, 1864-1937. I. T.
PS2432.D8   818.509   LC 66-24144

Murfree, Mary Noailles, 1850-1922.   • **2.11181**
In the Tennessee mountains / by Charles Egbert Craddock (Mary Ann Murfree). — Ridgewood, N.J.: Gregg Press, [1968] 322 p. — (Americans in fiction; [v. 46]) Short stories. I. T. II. Series.
PZ3.M943 It6   PS2454.I6x.   813/.4   LC 68-20019

Murfree, Mary Noailles, 1850-1922.   • **2.11182**
The prophet of the Great Smoky Mountains, by Charles Egbert Craddock. — New York: AMS Press, [1970] 308 p.; 23 cm. Reprint of the 1885 ed. I. T.
PZ3.M943 Pr10 PS2454.P7x   813/.4   LC 76-110350

Parks, Edd Winfield, 1906-1968.   • **2.11183**
Charles Egbert Craddock (Mary Noailles Murfree). — Port Washington, N.Y.: Kennikat Press, [1972, c1941] x, 258 p.: facsim., ports.; 21 cm. 1. Murfree, Mary Noailles, 1850-1922. I. T.
PS2456.P3 1972   813/.4 B   LC 75-159098   ISBN 0804616418

PS2470–2473 Norris. Norton

Norris, Frank, 1870-1902.   **2.11184**
Complete works of Frank Norris. — Port Washington, NY: Kennikat Press, 1967, c1928. 10 v.: ill., ports. Each vol. has special t.p. only, general title from jacket. Reprint. Originally published: Garden City N.Y.:Doubleday, Doran, 1928. I. T.
PS2470.A2 1928

Critical essays on Frank Norris / [compiled by] Don Graham.   **2.11185**
Boston, Mass.: G.K. Hall, c1980. li, 231 p.; 24 cm. — (Critical essays on American literature.) 1. Norris, Frank, 1870-1902 — Criticism and interpretation — Addresses, essays, lectures. I. Graham, Don, 1940- II. Series.
PS2473.C7   813/.4 19   LC 80-21426   ISBN 0816183074

French, Warren G., 1922-.   **2.11186**
Frank Norris. New York, Twayne Publishers [1962] 160 p. 21 cm. (Twayne's United States authors series, 25) 1. Norris, Frank, 1870-1902. I. T.
PS2473.F7   813.4   LC 62-16820

Pizer, Donald.   **2.11187**
The novels of Frank Norris. Bloomington, Indiana University Press 1966. xiii, 209 p. 22 cm. 1. Norris, Frank, 1870-1902. I. T.
PS2473.P5   813.4   LC 66-12734

Vanderbilt, Kermit.   **2.11188**
Charles Eliot Norton, apostle of culture in a democracy. — Cambridge, Mass.: Belknap Press, 1959. xiii, 286 p.: ill., facsim., ports.; 22 cm. 1. Norton, Charles Eliot, 1827-1908. I. T. II. Title: Apostle of culture in a democracy.
PS2478.V3   818/.4/09 s 813/.4   LC 59-10321

PS2500–2533 Fuller (Ossoli). Page. Payne

Fuller, Margaret, 1810-1850.   **2.11189**
Margaret Fuller, American romantic; a selection from her writings and correspondence. Edited by Perry Miller. Gloucester, Mass., Peter Smith, 1969 [c1963] xxxi, 319 p. 21 cm. I. Miller, Perry, 1905-1963. ed. II. T.
PS2502.M5 1969   818/.3/09   LC 74-8135

Fuller, Margaret, 1810-1850.   **2.11190**
The letters of Margaret Fuller / edited by Robert N. Hudspeth. — Ithaca, N.Y.: Cornell University Press, 1983. 2 v.: ill.; 25 cm. 1. Fuller, Margaret, 1810-1850 — Correspondence. 2. Authors, American — 19th century — Correspondence. I. Hudspeth, Robert N. II. T.
PS2506.A4 1983   818/.309 B 19   LC 82-22098   ISBN 0801413869

Wade, Mason, 1913-.   • **2.11191**
Margaret Fuller: whetstone of genius / by Margaret Fuller. — Clifton [N.J.]: A. M. Kelley, 1973 [c1940] xvi, 304 p.: ill.; 23 cm. (Viking reprint editions) 1. Fuller, Margaret, 1810-1850. I. T.
PS2506.W3 1973   818/.3/09 B   LC 72-122077   ISBN 0678031789

Critical essays on Margaret Fuller / [compiled by] Joel Myerson.   **2.11192**
Boston: G. K. Hall, c1980. xvi, 289 p.; 25 cm. (Critical essays on American literature.) 1. Fuller, Margaret, 1810-1850 — Criticism and interpretation — Addresses, essays, lectures. I. Myerson, Joel. II. Series.
PS2507.C7   818/.3/09   LC 79-17244

Page, Thomas Nelson, 1853-1922.   • **2.11193**
In ole Virginia: or, Marse Chan and other stories / with an introd. by Kimball King. — Chapel Hill: University of North Carolina Press, [1969] xxxvi, 230 p.; 21 cm. — (Southern literary classics series) (Chapel Hill books, chb-40.) Reprint of the 1887 ed. I. T.
PZ3.P145 In13 PS2514.I6x   813/.4   LC 71-77316

Gross, Theodore L.   • **2.11194**
Thomas Nelson Page, by Theodore L. Gross. — New York: Twayne Publishers, [1967] 175 p. 21 cm. — (Twayne's United States authors series; TUSAS 111) 1. Page, Thomas Nelson, 1853-1922. 2. Authors, American — 19th century — Biography. I. T.
PS2517.G7a   813.4   LC 67-13176

Overmyer, Grace.   • **2.11195**
America's first Hamlet / by Grace Overmyer. — Washington Square, [N.Y.]: New York University Press, 1957. 439 p. [1] p. of plates: port.; 23 cm. 1. Payne, John Howard, 1791-1852. I. T.
PS2533.O84 [1957]   812/.3   LC 56-12391

PS2600–2648 Poe

Poe, Edgar Allan, 1809-1849.   **2.11196**
Collected works of Edgar Allan Poe / edited by Thomas Ollive Mabbott; with the assistance of Eleanor D. Kewer and Maureen C. Mabbott. — Cambridge,

Mass.: Belknap Press of Harvard University Press, 1978. 2 v.: facsims., ports.; 24 cm. Includes bibliography. I. Mabbott, Thomas Ollive, 1898-1968. II. T.
PS2600 F69   *ISBN* 0674139364

Poe, Edgar Allan, 1809-1849.   2.11197
Collected writings of Edgar Allan Poe. — New York: Gordian Press, 1981-. v.; 24 cm. Vol. 1 has imprint: Boston, Twayne Publishers, 1981. I. T.
PS2600.F81

Woodson, Thomas. comp.   2.11198
Twentieth century interpretations of The fall of the house of Usher; a collection of critical essays. — Englewood Cliffs, N.J.: Prentice-Hall, [1969] iii, 122 p.; 22 cm. — (Twentieth century interpretations) (A Spectrum book.) 1. Poe, Edgar Allan, 1809-1849. The fall of the house of Usher. I. T. II. Title: The fall of the house of Usher.
PS2614.W6   813/.3   *LC* 69-15343   *ISBN* 0133017214

Poe, Edgar Allan, 1809-1849.   2.11199
[Essays. Selections.] Selections from the critical writings of Edgar Allan Poe / edited, with an introd. and notes, by F.C. Prescott; new pref. by J. Lesley Dameron; new introd. by Eric W. Carlson. — New York: Gordian Press, 1981. li, 348 p.; 23 cm. 'Second edition.' Reprint of the 1909 ed. published by Holt, New York, in series: English-readings. 1. Poe, Edgar Allan, 1809-1849 — Aesthetics — Addresses, essays, lectures. 2. American literature — 19th century — History and criticism — Addresses, essays, lectures. I. Prescott, Frederick Clarke, 1871-1957. II. T.
PS2619.A1 1981   818/.309 19   *LC* 80-24488   *ISBN* 0877521824

Poe, Edgar Allan, 1809-1849.   • 2.11200
Letters. Edited by John Ward Ostrom. With new foreword and supplementary chapter. — New York: Gordian Press, 1966 [c1948] 2 v. (xxviii, 730 p.): illus., ports.; 24 cm. 1. Poe, Edgar Allan, 1809-1849 — Correspondence. I. Ostrom, John Ward, 1903- ed. II. T.
PS2631.A33 1966   816.3   *LC* 66-20025

Baudelaire, Charles, 1821-1867.   2.11201
Baudelaire on Poe; critical papers, translated and edited by Lois and Francis E. Hyslop. State College, Pa.: Bald Eagle Press, 1952. 175 p.; 24 cm. 1. Poe, Edgar Allan, 1809-1849. I. T.
PS2631.B3   *LC* 51-14209

Bittner, William Robert.   2.11202
Poe, a biography. — [1st ed.] Boston, Little, Brown [1962] 306 p. illus. 22 cm. 1. Poe, Edgar Allan, 1809-1849 — Biography. I. T.
PS2631.B55   928.1   *LC* 62-16955

Quinn, Arthur Hobson, 1875-1960.   • 2.11203
Edgar Allan Poe, a critical biography. — New York: Cooper Square, 1969 [c1941] xvi, 804 p.; illus., facsims., ports.; 24 cm. 1. Poe, Edgar Allan, 1809-1849. I. T.
PS2631.Q5 1969   818/.3/09 B   *LC* 76-97465   *ISBN* 0815403135

Regan, Robert, ed.   2.11204
Poe; a collection of critical essays. — Englewood Cliffs, N.J.: Prentice-Hall, [1967] 183 p.; 21 cm. — (A Spectrum book: Twentieth century views) 1. Poe, Edgar Allan, 1809-1849. I. T.
PS2631.R38   818/.3/09   *LC* 67-14087

Buranelli, Vincent.   2.11205
Edgar Allan Poe / by Vincent Buranelli. — 2d ed. — Boston: Twayne, c1977. 166 p.: port.; 21 cm. — (Twayne's United States author series; TUSAS 4) Includes index. 1. Poe, Edgar Allan, 1809-1849 — Criticism and interpretation. I. T.
PS2638.B87 1977   818/.3/09   *LC* 77-7265   *ISBN* 0805771891

Davidson, Edward Hutchins.   • 2.11206
Poe: a critical study. — Cambridge: Belknap Press of Harvard University Press, 1957. x, 296 p.; 22 cm. 1. Poe, Edgar Allan, 1809-1849. I. T.
PS2638.D3   811.32   *LC* 57-12965

Edgar Allan Poe: the critical heritage / edited by I.M. Walker.   2.11207
London; New York: Routledge & K. Paul, 1986. xvii, 419 p.; 23 cm. — (Critical heritage series.) 1. Poe, Edgar Allan, 1809-1849 — Criticism and interpretation — Addresses, essays, lectures. I. Walker, I. M. (Ian Malcolm) II. Series.
PS2638.E35 1986   818/.309 19   *LC* 85-14531   *ISBN* 0710098553

Hoffman, Daniel, 1923-.   2.11208
Poe Poe Poe Poe Poe Poe Poe. [1st ed.] Garden City, N.Y., Doubleday, 1972. xvi, 339 p. 22 cm. 1. Poe, Edgar Allan, 1809-1849 — Criticism and interpretation. I. T.
PS2638.H57   818/.3/09   *LC* 72-171397

Howarth, William L., 1940- comp.   2.11209
Twentieth century interpretations of Poe's tales; a collection of critical essays. Edited by William L. Howarth. — Englewood Cliffs, N.J.: Prentice-Hall, [1971] x, 116 p.; 21 cm. — (Twentieth century interpretations) (A Spectrum book.)

1. Poe, Edgar Allan, 1809-1849 — Criticism and interpretation. I. T. II. Title: Poe's tales.
PS2638.H6   813/.3   *LC* 69-15337   *ISBN* 0136846548

Krutch, Joseph Wood, 1893-1970.   2.11210
Edgar Allan Poe, a study in genius. — New York: Russell & Russell, 1965 [c1926] x, 244 p.: illus., facsims., ports.; 22 cm. 1. Poe, Edgar Allan, 1809-1849. I. T.
PS2638.K7 1965   928.1   *LC* 65-13945

PS2649 Porter (O. Henry). Posey

Henry, O., 1862-1910.   • 2.11211
The complete works of O. Henry [i.e. W.S. Porter] / foreword by Harry Hansen. — Garden City, N.Y.: Doubleday, 1953. 2 v. (xiii, 1692 p.); 22 cm. — I. T.
PS2649.P5 1953   817.5   *LC* 53-6098

Current-García, Eugene.   2.11212
O. Henry (William Sydney Porter) New Haven, Conn.: College & University Press, [c1965] 192 p. 21 cm. (Twayne's United States authors series, 77) 1. Henry, O., 1862-1910. I. T.
PS2649.P5 Z64   817.52   *LC* 65-12997

Posey, Alexander Lawrence, 1873-1908.   2.11213
Poems of Alexander Lawrence Posey, Creek Indian bard. Originally collected and arranged by Mrs. Minnie H. Posey. Memoir by William Elsey Connely. Rev. by Okmulgee Cultural Foundation [and the] Five Civilized Tribes Heritage Foundation. Illus. by Joan Hill. — [1st rev. ed. — Muskogee, Okla.: Printed by Hoffman Printing Co., 1969] 213 p.: illus., port.; 22 cm. Issued in a case. 1. Posey, Minnie (Harris) ed. II. Connelley, William Elsey, 1855-1930. III. Okmulgee Cultural Foundation. IV. Five Civilized Tribes Heritage Foundation. V. T.
PS2649.P55 1969   811/.4   *LC* 75-259784

PS2656–2736 Prescott. Ridge. Robins. Rowson

Prescott, William Hickling, 1796-1859.   • 2.11214
William Hickling Prescott: representative selections / With introduction, bibliography, and notes by William Charvat and Michael Kraus. — New York: American Book Co., [1943] cxiii, 466 p.: ill., port. — (American writers series) I. Charvat, William, 1905-1966. II. Kraus, Michael, 1901- III. T. IV. Series.
PS2656.A4C46   *LC* 43-1590

Darnell, Donald G.   2.11215
William Hickling Prescott / Donald G. Darnell. — Boston: Twayne Publishers, [1975] 140 p.: port.; 22 cm. (Twayne's United States authors series; TUSAS 251) Includes index. 1. Prescott, William Hickling, 1796-1859. I. T.
PS2657.D3   907/.2/024   *LC* 74-26789   *ISBN* 0805705988

Ridge, John Rollin, 1827-1867.   2.11216
Poems. — San Francisco: H. Payot, 1868. 137 p.: ill.; 19 cm. I. T.
PS2699.R7x

Robins, Elizabeth, 1862-1952.   2.11217
The convert / Elizabeth Robins; introduced by Jane Marcus. — London: Women's Press; Old Westbury, N.Y.: Feminist Press, 1980. xvi, 304 p.; 20 cm. I. T.
PS2719.R4 C6 1980   *ISBN* 0912670835

Rowson, Mrs., 1762-1824.   2.11218
Charlotte Temple / Susanna Haswell Rowson; edited with an introduction by Cathy N. Davidson. — New York: Oxford University Press, 1986. xxxx, 120 p.: facsims.; 21 cm. — (Oxford paperbacks) 'First American edition, under the title: Charlotte, a tale of truth, 1794'–Verso t.p. I. Davidson, Cathy N., 1949- II. T.
PS2736.R3 C5 1986   813/.2 19   *LC* 86-18012   *ISBN* 0195042387

PS2770–2934 Santayana. Simms. Stoddard

Santayana, George, 1863-1952.   • 2.11219
The last Puritan: a memoir in the form of a novel / by George Santayana. — New York: C. Scribner's sons [1936] 4 p.: l., 3-602 p.; 21 cm. (Scribner library, SL23) I. T.
PZ3.S2284Las2 PS2772.L3 1936   *LC* 36-27119

Simms, William Gilmore, 1806-1870.   2.11220
[Works. 1969] The writings of William Gilmore Simms. Centennial edition. [1st ed.] Columbia, University of South Carolina Press [1969-. v. facsim. 24 cm. Vols. :Introductions and explanatory notes and texts established by J. C. Guilds. Vol. : Introd. and explanatory notes by S. E. Meats. Text established by K. Butterworth. I. T.
PS2840.A1 1969   813/.3   *LC* 68-9190   *ISBN* 0872491404

Simms, William Gilmore, 1806-1870. 2.11221
Woodcraft, or, Hawks about the dovecote; a story of the South at the close of the Revolution / ed. for the modern reader by Charles S. Watson. — [S.l.]: New College & University Press, 1984, c1983. 537 p. — (The masterworks of literature series) 1. South Carolina — History — Revolution, 1775-1783 — Fiction. I. Simms, William Gilmore, 1806-1870. Sword and the distaff. II. T. III. Title: Hawks about the dovecote. IV. Title: The sword and the distaff
PZ3.S592 Wo10   PS2848.W6x.   LC 80-68192   ISBN 0808404237

Simms, William Gilmore, 1806-1870. • 2.11222
The Yemassee; a romance of Carolina. Edited for the modern reader by Joseph V. Ridgely. — New York: Twayne Publishers, [1964] 415 p.; 22 cm. — (Twayne's United States classics series) 1. Indians of North America — Fiction 2. South Carolina — History — Colonial period, ca. 1600-1775 — Fiction. I. Ridgely, Joseph Vincent. II. T. III. Series.
PZ3.S592 Y42   PS2848.Y5 1964.   LC 62-10274

Simms, William Gilmore, 1806-1870. • 2.11223
Views and reviews in American literature, history and fiction: first series. Cambridge, Belknap Press of Harvard University Press, 1962. xliii, 292 p. 22 cm. 1. American literature — History and criticism I. T.
PS2850.V52   LC 62-17226

Simms, William Gilmore, 1806-1870. • 2.11224
[Correspondence] Letters of William Gilmore Simms / collected and edited by Mary C. Simms Oliphant, Alfred Taylor Odell, T.C. Duncan Eaves; introduction by Donald Davidson; biographical sketch by Alexander S. Salley. — Columbia: University of South Carolina Press, 1952-56. 5 v.: ill., maps, ports.; 24 cm. 1. Simms, William Gilmore, 1806-1870. Correspondence 2. Authors, American — 19th century — Correspondence. I. Oliphant, Mary C. Simms (Mary Chevillette Simms), 1891- II. Odell, Alfred Taylor. III. Eaves, T. C. Duncan (Thomas Cary Duncan), 1918- IV. T.
PS2853.A4 1952   818/.309 B 19   LC 52-2352   ISBN 0872494136

Ridgely, Joseph Vincent. • 2.11225
William Gilmore Simms. New York, Twayne Publishers [c1962] 144 p. 22 cm. (Twayne's United States authors series, 28) 1. Simms, William Gilmore, 1806-1870. I. T.
PS2853.R5   813.3   LC 62-16823

Wakelyn, Jon L. 2.11226
The politics of a literary man: William Gilmore Simms [by] Jon L. Wakelyn. Westport, Conn., Greenwood Press [1973] xiv, 306 p. port. 22 cm. (Contributions in American studies, no. 5) 1. Simms, William Gilmore, 1806-1870 — Political and social views. 2. Southern States — History — 1775-1865 I. T.
PS2853.W33   818/.3/09   LC 72-845   ISBN 0837164141

Stoddard, Elizabeth, 1823-1902. 2.11227
The Morgesons and other writings, published and unpublished / by Elizabeth Stoddard; edited, with a critical introduction, by Lawrence Buell and Sandra A. Zagarell. — Philadelphia: University of Pennsylvania Press, 1984. xxxiv, 362 p.: ill.; 24 cm. I. Buell, Lawrence. II. Zagarell, Sandra A. III. T.
PS2934.S3 A6 1984   813/.4 19   LC 83-23439   ISBN 0812279247

PS2950–2958 Stowe

Stowe, Harriet Beecher, 1811-1896. • 2.11228
Dred; tale of the great Dismal Swamp. Boston, Phillips, Sampson, 1856. Grosse Pointe, Mich., Scholarly Press, 1968. 2 v. 20 cm. I. T.
PZ3.S89 D7 PS2954.D7x   813/.3   LC 70-5460

Stowe, Harriet Beecher, 1811-1896. • 2.11229
Oldtown folks. Edited by Henry F. May. Cambridge, Belknap Press of Harvard University Press, 1966. viii, 614 p. 25 cm. (John Harvard library.) 'The text followed is that of the first edition, published in 1869.' I. May, Henry Farnham, 1915- ed. II. T. III. Series.
PZ3.S89 O9   PS2954.Ox.   LC 66-18257

Gossett, Thomas F., 1916-. 2.11230
Uncle Tom's cabin and American culture / Thomas F. Gossett. — Dallas, Tex.: Southern Methodist University Press, 1985. xi, 484 p., [16] p. of plates: ill., ports.; 24 cm. Includes index. 1. Stowe, Harriet Beecher, 1811-1896. Uncle Tom's cabin. 2. Slavery and slaves in literature 3. Afro-Americans in literature 4. Race relations in literature. I. T.
PS2954.U6 G67 1985   813/.3 19   LC 83-17245   ISBN 0870741896

Stowe, Harriet Beecher, 1811-1896. • 2.11231
Uncle Tom's cabin / introduced by Howard Mumford Jones. — Columbus, Ohio: C. E. Merrill Pub. Co. [1969] xviii, x, 322 p.: ill.; 23 cm. (Charles E. Merrill program in American literature) (Charles E. Merrill standard editions.) 1. Slavery in the United States — Fiction. I. T.
PZ3.S89 Un96 PS2954.U6x   813/.3   LC 74-92333   ISBN 0675094143

Adams, John R., 1900-. • 2.11232
Harriet Beecher Stowe. New York, Twayne Publishers [c1963] 172 p. 21 cm. (Twayne's United States authors series, 42) 1. Stowe, Harriet Beecher, 1811-1896. I. T.
PS2956.A6   813.3   LC 63-17370

Wilson, Robert Forrest, 1883-1942. • 2.11233
Crusader in crinoline; the life of Harriet Beecher Stowe. Westport, Conn., Greenwood Press [1972, c1941] 706 p. illus. 23 cm. 1. Stowe, Harriet Beecher, 1811-1896. I. T.
PS2956.W5 1972   818/.3/09 B   LC 70-159717   ISBN 0837161916

Critical essays on Harriet Beecher Stowe / [edited by] Elizabeth Ammons. 2.11234
Boston: G. K. Hall, c1980. xviii, 307 p.; 25 cm. (Critical essays on American literature.) Includes index. 1. Stowe, Harriet Beecher, 1811-1896 — Criticism and interpretation — Addresses, essays, lectures. I. Ammons, Elizabeth. II. Series.
PS2957.C68   813/.3 19   LC 79-17596   ISBN 0816182604

Crozier, Alice C. • 2.11235
The novels of Harriet Beecher Stowe [by] Alice C. Crozier. New York, Oxford University Press, 1969. x, 235 p. 22 cm. 1. Stowe, Harriet Beecher, 1811-1896. I. T.
PS2957.C7   813/.3   LC 73-83010

PS2970–3014 Tarkington. Thayer

Tarkington, Booth, 1869-1946. • 2.11236
Alice Adams. New York: Grosset & Dunlap [1961, c1921] 434 p.; 20 cm. I. T.
PS2972.Ax   LC cd 62-177

Tarkington, Booth, 1869-1946. • 2.11237
The gentleman from Indiana. New York, Doubleday & McClure, 1899. — St. Clair Shores, Mich.: Scholarly Press, 1970. viii, 384 p.; 21 cm. — I. T.
PZ3.T175 Gen25 PS2972.G4x   813/.5/2   LC 75-129453   ISBN 0403004837

Tarkington, Booth, 1869-1946. • 2.11238
Growth, by Booth Tarkington. Garden City, N.Y., Doubleday, Page, 1927. 887 p. 20 cm. I. T. II. Title: The magnificent Ambersons. III. Title: The turmoil. IV. Title: National avenue.
PS2972.Gx   PZ3.T175 Gr   LC 27-27696

Tarkington, Booth, 1869-1946. • 2.11239
The magnificent Ambersons. New York, Sagamore Press, 1957. 248 p. 21 cm. (American century series, S-2) I. T.
PZ3.T175Ma8 PS2972.M25 1957   LC 57-9754

Tarkington, Booth, 1869-1946. • 2.11240
Penrod: his complete story; Penrod, Penrod and Sam, Penrod Jashber. / Illustrated by Gordon Grant. — Garden City, N. Y.: Doubleday, 1937. xii, 590 p.: illus.; 22 cm. I. T. II. Title: Penrod and Sam. III. Title: Penrod Jashber.
PS2972.Px

Tarkington, Booth, 1869-1946. • 2.11241
Seventeen: a tale of youth and summer time and the Baxter family especially William / by Booth Tarkington; illustrated by Edwin Tunis. — New York: Harper, 1932. x, 288 p., [14] leaves of plates: ill. I. T.
PZ3 T175 Se   PS2972.Sx.

Fennimore, Keith J. 2.11242
Booth Tarkington, by Keith J. Fennimore. New York, Twayne Publishers [1974] 167 p. 21 cm. (Twayne's United States authors series, TUSAS 238) 1. Tarkington, Booth, 1869-1946. I. T.
PS2973.F4   813/.5/2   LC 73-16403   ISBN 0805707158

Woodress, James Leslie. 2.11243
Booth Tarkington: gentleman from Indiana. — [1st ed.]. — Philadelphia: Lippincott, [1955]. 350 p.: ill.; 22 cm. 1. Tarkington, Booth, 1869-1946. I. T.
PS2973.W6   LC 55-6307

Murdock, Eugene Converse. 2.11244
Mighty Casey, all-American / Eugene C. Murdock. — Westport, Conn.: Greenwood, c1984. xii, 164 p., [7] p. of plates: ill.; 24 cm. (Contributions to the study of popular culture. 0198-9871; no. 7) 1. Thayer, Ernest Lawrence, 1863-1940. 2. Casey at the bat 2. Thayer, Ernest Lawrence, 1863-1940 — Parodies, travesties, etc. 3. Baseball in literature. 4. Baseball — Poetry. 5. American poetry I. T. II. Series.
PS3014.T3 C336 1984   811/.52 19   LC 83-16338   ISBN 0313240752

PS3040-3058 Thoreau

Thoreau, Henry David, 1817-1862.   • 2.11245
Walden, and Civil disobedience: authoritative texts, background, reviews, and essays in criticism / edited by Owen Thomas. — [1st ed.]. — New York: W. W. Norton, [1966] vi, 424 p.; 21 cm. — (A Norton critical edition) 1. Government, Resistance to I. Thoreau, Henry David, 1817-1862. Civil disobedience. 1966. II. Thomas, Owen Paul. ed. III. T. IV. Title: Civil disobedience.
PS3048.A1 1966   818.308   LC 66-11310

Thoreau, Henry David, 1817-1862.   2.11246
The writings of Henry D. Thoreau / editor-in-chief, Walter Harding. — Princeton, N.J.: Princeton University Press, 1971-. v. : ill.; 21 cm. I. Harding, Walter Roy, 1917- II. T.
PS3048.A1 1971   818/.3/03   LC 72-120764   ISBN 0691061947

Ruland, Richard, 1932- comp.   2.11247
Twentieth century interpretations of Walden; a collection of critical essays, edited by Richard Ruland. Englewood Cliffs, N.J., Prentice-Hall [1968] viii, 119 p. 21 cm. (Twentieth century interpretations) (A Spectrum book.) 1. Thoreau, Henry David, 1817-1862. Walden I. T.
PS3048.R8   818/.3/08   LC 68-14480

Cameron, Sharon.   2.11248
Writing nature: Henry Thoreau's Journal / Sharon Cameron. — New York: Oxford University Press, 1985. x, 173 p.; 22 cm. Includes index. 1. Thoreau, Henry David, 1817-1862. Journal 2. Thoreau, Henry David, 1817-1862. Walden 3. Nature in literature I. T.
PS3053.C296 1985   818/.303 B 19   LC 85-13598   ISBN 0195035704

Harding, Walter Roy, 1917-.   2.11249
The days of Henry Thoreau: a biography / Walter Harding. — Princeton, N.J.: Princeton University Press, 1982. xx, 498 p., [8] p. of plates: ill.; 23 cm. Originally published: New York: Dover Publications, 1982. 1. Thoreau, Henry David, 1817-1862 — Biography. 2. Authors, American — 19th century — Biography. I. T.
PS3053.H3 1982b   818/.309 B 19   LC 82-230890   ISBN 0691065551

Harding, Walter Roy, 1917-.   2.11250
The new Thoreau handbook / Walter Harding, Michael Meyer. — New York: New York University Press, c1980. xvii, 238 p.; 24 cm. (The Gotham library of the New York University Press) An earlier version published under title: A Thoreau handbook. Includes index. 1. Thoreau, Henry David, 1817-1862. 2. Thoreau, Henry David, 1817-1862 — Bibliography. 3. Authors, American — 19th century — Biography. I. Meyer, Michael, 1945- joint author. II. T.
PS3053.H32 1980   818/.3/09   LC 79-53078   ISBN 0814734014

Krutch, Joseph Wood, 1893-1970.   • 2.11251
Henry David Thoreau. [New York]: W. Sloane Associates [1948] xiii, 298 p.: port; 22 cm. (The American men of letters series) 1. Thoreau, Henry David, 1817-1862. I. T.
PS3053.K7   928.1   LC 48-8483 *

Lebeaux, Richard, 1946-.   2.11252
Thoreau's seasons / Richard Lebeaux. — Amherst: University of Massachusetts Press, 1984. xviii, 410 p.; 25 cm. — ([New England writers]) Series statement from jacket. Includes index. 1. Thoreau, Henry David, 1817-1862 — Biography — Psychology. 2. Seasons in literature 3. Authors, American — 19th century — Biography. I. T.
PS3053.L35 1984   818/.309 B 19   LC 83-17982   ISBN 0870234013

Lebeaux, Richard, 1946-.   2.11253
Young man Thoreau / Richard Lebeaux. — Amherst: University of Massachusetts Press, 1977. 262 p.; 24 cm. Includes index. 1. Thoreau, Henry David, 1817-1862 — Biography — Psychology. 2. Authors, American — 19th century — Biography. I. T.
PS3053.L37   818/.3/09 B   LC 76-44851   ISBN 0870232312

Paul, Sherman. ed.   • 2.11254
Thoreau: a collection of critical essays. — Englewood Cliffs, N.J.: Prentice-Hall, [1962] 188 p.; 20 cm. — (Twentieth century views) (A Spectrum book, S-TC-10.) 1. Thoreau, Henry David, 1817-1862. I. T.
PS3053.P33   818.3   LC 62-13605

Bridgman, Richard.   2.11255
Dark Thoreau / Richard Bridgman. — Lincoln: University of Nebraska Press, c1982. xvi, 306 p.: port.; 23 cm. 1. Thoreau, Henry David, 1817-1862 — Criticism and interpretation. I. T.
PS3054.B7 1982   818/.309 19   LC 81-4788   ISBN 0803211678

Garber, Frederick.   2.11256
Thoreau's redemptive imagination / Frederick Garber. — New York: New York University Press, 1977. x, 229 p.; 24 cm. — (The Gotham library of the

New York University Press) 1. Thoreau, Henry David, 1817-1862 — Criticism and interpretation. I. T.
PS3054.G3   818/.3/09   LC 77-73031   ISBN 0814729657

Schneider, Richard J.   2.11257
Henry David Thoreau / by Richard J. Schneider. — Boston: Twayne Publishers, c1987. 179 p.: ill.; 23 cm. — (Twayne's United States authors series. TUSAS 497) Includes index. 1. Thoreau, Henry David, 1817-1862 — Criticism and interpretation. I. T. II. Series.
PS3054.S36 1987   818/.309 19   LC 86-31826   ISBN 0805774955

PS3070-3109 Timrod. Tuckerman

Timrod, Henry, 1828-1867.   • 2.11258
Collected poems / edited by Edd Winfield Parks and Aileen Wells Parks. — A variorum ed. Athens: University of Georgia Press [1965] x, 206 p.; 23 cm. I. Parks, Edd Winfield, 1906-1968. ed. II. Parks, Aileen Wells. ed. III. T.
PS3070 A2 1965   LC 65-25289

Timrod, Henry, 1828-1867.   • 2.11259
The essays of Henry Timrod / edited with an introduction by Edd Winfield Parks. — Athens: University of Georgia Press, 1942. 184 p. 1. Poetics I. Parks, Edd Winfield, 1906-1968. II. T.
PS3071.P3   LC 42-18682

Parks, Edd Winfield, 1906-1968.   • 2.11260
Henry Timrod. New York, Twayne Publishers [1964] 158 p. 21 cm. (Twayne's United States authors series, 53) 1. Timrod, Henry, 1828-1867. I. T.
PS3073.P3   811.3   LC 63-20607

Tuckerman, Frederick Goddard, 1821-1873.   • 2.11261
Complete poems / edited, with an introd. by N. Scott Momaday; with a critical foreword by Yvor Winters. — New York: Oxford University Press, 1965. xxviii, 217 p.; 23 cm. I. Momaday, Natachee Scott. II. T.
PS3104.T5 1965   811/.3   LC 65-12467

PS3125-3159 Very. Wallace. Westcott

Very, Jones, 1813-1880.   • 2.11262
Selected poems / edited with an introd. by Nathan Lyons. — New Brunswick, N. J.: Rutgers University Press [1966] ix, 143 p.: ports.; 22 cm. 'Selected bibliography': p. 135-138. I. Lyons, Nathan. ed. II. T.
PS3126.L9   811.3   LC 66-18878

Wallace, Lew, 1827-1905.   • 2.11263
Ben-Hur, a tale of the Christ / by Lew Wallace. — New York: Harper, [1959] 624 p.; 21 cm. 1. Jesus Christ — Fiction I. T.
PZ3.W154B59   PS3134.B45 1959.   813.4   LC 59-15325

Westcott, Edward Noyes, 1847-1898.   • 2.11264
David Harum; a story of American life / illustrated by B West Clinedinst. — New York, Dover Publications [1960] xiv, 258 p. illus. 21 cm. I. T.
PZ3.W522 D15 PS3159.W12 D38 1960   LC 60-50769

PS3200-3248 Whitman

Whitman, Walt, 1819-1892.   • 2.11265
Complete poetry and selected prose. Edited with an introd. and glossary by James E. Miller, Jr. — Boston: Houghton Mifflin, [1959] 516 p.; 21 cm. — (Riverside editions, A34) I. T.
PS3200.F59   811.3   LC 59-2805

Whitman, Walt, 1819-1892.   2.11266
Collected writings. General editors: Gay Wilson Allen and E. Sculley Bradley. Advisory Editorial Board: Roger Asselineau [and others. New York, New York University Press, 1961-. v. ports., facsims. 27 cm. I. T.
PS3200.F61   928.1   LC 60-15980

Whitman, Walt, 1819-1892.   2.11267
Leaves of grass: authoritative texts, prefaces, Whitman on his art, criticism. Edited by Sculley Bradley [and] Harold W. Blodgett. New York, Norton [1973] lx, 1008 p. ports., facsims. 22 cm. (A Norton Critical edition) I. Bradley, Sculley, 1897- ed. II. Blodgett, Harold William, 1900- ed. III. T.
PS3201 1973   811/.3   LC 72-5156   ISBN 0393043541 ISBN 0393093883

Whitman, Walt, 1819-1892.   • 2.11268
Whitman's manuscripts: Leaves of grass (1860): a parallel text / edited with notes and introduction by Fredson Bowers. — Chicago: University of Chicago Press, 1955. lxxiv, 264 p.: facsims., port.; 25 cm. Most of the mss. transcribed are from the library of Clifton Waller Barrett, presented by him to the

University of Virginia Library. 1. Whitman, Walt, 1819-1892 — Manuscripts. 2. Whitman, Walt, 1819-1892. I. Bowers, Fredson Thayer, 1905- II. T.
PS3201.A1 1955　　*LC* 55-7313

Whitman, Walt, 1819-1892.　　　　　　　　　　2.11269
Walt Whitman of the New York Aurora; editor at twenty–two. A collection of recently discovered writings, edited by Joseph Jay Rubin [and] Charles H. Brown. — Westport, Conn.: Greenwood Press, [1972, c1950] viii, 147 p.; 22 cm. I. New York Aurora. II. T.
PS3203.R8 1972　　818/.3/07　　*LC* 72-5277　　*ISBN* 0837157242

Whitman, Walt, 1819-1892.　　　　　　　　　　2.11270
Specimen days. — Boston: D. R. Godine, 1971. xxiv, 197 p.: ill., ports.; 31 cm. — I. T.
PS3220.A1 1971　　811/.3 B　　*LC* 76-104907

Whitman, Walt, 1819-1892.　　　　　　　　　　2.11271
Walt Whitman's Camden conversations / selected and arranged with an introd. by Walter Teller. — New Brunswick, N.J.: Rutgers University Press, [1973] xii, 215 p.: ill.; 21 cm. Selections from With Walt Whitman in Camden, by H. Traubel. I. Teller, Walter Magnes, 1910- ed. II. Traubel, Horace, 1858-1919. With Walt Whitman in Camden. 1973. III. T.
PS3222.W3 1973　　811/.3　　*LC* 73-8509　　*ISBN* 0813507677

Allen, Gay Wilson, 1903-.　　　　　　　　　• 2.11272
The solitary singer: a critical biography of Walt Whitman / by Gay Wilson Allen. — New York: Macmillan, 1955. xii, 616 p.: ill., maps, ports.; 23 cm. Includes index. 1. Whitman, Walt, 1819-1892 — Biography. 2. Poets, American — 19th century — Biography. I. T.
PS3231.A69　　811/.3　　*LC* 55-114

Allen, Gay Wilson, 1903-.　　　　　　　　　　2.11273
The new Walt Whitman handbook / Gay Wilson Allen. — New York: New York University Press, 1975. xxi, 423 p.: ill.; 24 cm. Edition for 1946 published under title: Walt Whitman handbook. Includes index. 1. Whitman, Walt, 1819-1892. I. T.
PS3231.A7 1975　　811/.3　　*LC* 74-21595　　*ISBN* 0814705561

Asselineau, Roger.　　　　　　　　　　　　• 2.11274
The evolution of Walt Whitman / by Roger Asselineau; [translated by Richard P. Adams and the author]. — Cambridge: Belknap Press of Harvard University Press, 1960-62. 2 v. 22 cm. 1. Whitman, Walt, 1819-1892. I. T.
PS3231.A833　　811.3　　*LC* 60-13297

Chase, Richard Volney, 1914-1962.　　　　　• 2.11275
Walt Whitman reconsidered. — New York: William Sloane Associates, [1955] 191 p. 1. Whitman, Walt, 1819-1892. I. T.
PS3231.C47　　811.38　　*LC* 55-6326

Kaplan, Justin.　　　　　　　　　　　　　2.11276
Walt Whitman, a life / Justin Kaplan. — New York: Simon and Schuster, c1980. 432 p., [16] leaves of plates: ill.; 24 cm. 1. Whitman, Walt, 1819-1892. 2. Poets, American — 19th century — Biography. I. T.
PS3231.K3　　811/.3 B　　*LC* 80-16538　　*ISBN* 0671225421

Zweig, Paul.　　　　　　　　　　　　　　2.11277
Walt Whitman: the making of the poet / Paul Zweig. — New York: Basic Books, c1984. xi, 372 p.: port.; 25 cm. 1. Whitman, Walt, 1819-1892. 2. Poets, American — 19th century — Biography. I. T.
PS3231.Z87 1984　　811/.3 B 19　　*LC* 83-45258　　*ISBN* 0465090591

Hindus, Milton. comp.　　　　　　　　　　2.11278
Walt Whitman, the critical heritage. — London: Routledge and K. Paul, [1971] xi, 292 p.; 23 cm. — (The Critical heritage series) 1. Whitman, Walt, 1819-1892. I. T.
PS3238.H5　　811/.3　　*LC* 75-30929　　*ISBN* 071007087X

Miller, Edwin Haviland. comp.　　　　　　• 2.11279
A century of Whitman criticism. — Bloomington: Indiana University Press, [1969] xliii, 368 p.: port.; 22 cm. 1. Whitman, Walt, 1819-1892. I. T.
PS3238.M44 1969　　811/.3　　*LC* 78-85094　　*ISBN* 0253111153

Pearce, Roy Harvey. ed.　　　　　　　　　2.11280
Whitman, a collection of critical essays. — Englewood Cliffs, N.J.: Prentice-Hall, [1962] 183 p.; 21 cm. — (Twentieth century views) (A Spectrum book, S-TC-5.) 1. Whitman, Walt, 1819-1892. I. T.
PS3238.P4　　811.3　　*LC* 62-9310

Walt Whitman—the measure of his song / edited by Jim　　2.11281
Perlman, Ed Folsom, & Dan Campion; introduction by Ed Folsom.
Minneapolis: Holy Cow! Press, 1981. liii, 394 p.: ports.; 23 cm. 1. Whitman, Walt, 1819-1892 — Addresses, essays, lectures. 2. Whitman, Walt, 1819-1892. in fiction, drama, poetry, etc. I. Perlman, Jim, 1951- II. Folsom, Ed, 1947- III. Campion, Dan, 1949-
PS3238.W37　　811/.3 19　　*LC* 80-85268　　*ISBN* 0930100093

Hollis, C. Carroll (Charles Carroll), 1911-.　　　2.11282
Language and style in Leaves of grass / C. Carroll Hollis. — Baton Rouge: Louisiana State University Press, c1983. xiii, 277 p.; 24 cm. Includes index. 1. Whitman, Walt, 1819-1892. Leaves of grass. 2. Whitman, Walt, 1819-1892 — Style. I. T.
PS3244.H6 1983　　811/.3 19　　*LC* 82-20881　　*ISBN* 0807110965

PS3250–3298 Whittier

Whittier, John Greenleaf, 1807-1892.　　　　　2.11283
[Poems. 1975] The poetical works of Whittier: Cambridge edition / with a new introd. by Hyatt H. Waggoner. — Boston: Houghton Mifflin, 1975. xxxii, 538 p.: port.; 25 cm. Text of the Cambridge ed. of 1894, which was edited by H. E. Scudder, and published under title: The complete poetical works of John Greenleaf Whittier. Includes indexes. I. T.
PS3250.F75　　811/.3　　*LC* 75-25974　　*ISBN* 0395215994

Whittier, John Greenleaf, 1807-1892.　　　　　2.11284
[Poems. 1971] John Greenleaf Whittier's poetry; an appraisal and a selection, by Robert Penn Warren. Minneapolis, University of Minnesota Press [1971] 208 p. 23 cm. I. Warren, Robert Penn, 1905- II. T.
PS3253.W3　　811/.3　　*LC* 79-152299　　*ISBN* 0816606048

Whittier, John Greenleaf, 1807-1892.　　　　　2.11285
The letters of John Greenleaf Whittier / edited by John B. Pickard. — Cambridge, Mass.: Belknap Press of Harvard University Press, 1975. 3 v.: ill.; 25 cm. 1. Whittier, John Greenleaf, 1807-1892 — Correspondence. I. T.
PS3281.A3 1975　　811/.3 B　　*LC* 73-88055　　*ISBN* 0674528301

Critical essays on John Greenleaf Whittier / [compiled by]　2.11286
Jayne K. Kribbs.
Boston, Mass.: G. K. Hall, c1980. xl, 228 p.; 25 cm. — (Critical essays on American literature.) 1. Whittier, John Greenleaf, 1807-1892 — Criticism and interpretation — Addresses, essays, lectures. I. Kribbs, Jayne K. II. Series.
PS3288.C7 1980　　811/.3　　*LC* 80-14207　　*ISBN* 0816183082

PS3334–3346 Wilson. Wister

Wilson, Harriet E., 1808-ca. 1870.　　　　　　2.11287
Our Nig, or, Sketches from the life of a free Black, in a two–story white house, north, showing that slavery's shadows fall even there / by 'Our Nig'. — 2nd ed. — New York: Random House, c1983. 173 p. Reprint. Originally published: Boston: G.C. Rand & Avery, 1859. With a new introd. I. T.
PS3334.W39 O9 1983　　813/.3 19　　*LC* 82-42908　　*ISBN* 0394532104

Wister, Owen, 1860-1938.　　　　　　　　　2.11288
The Virginian: a horseman of the plains / by Owen Wister; with illustrations by Charles M. Russell and drawings from western scenes by Frederic Remington. — New York: Macmillan, c1929. 434 p., [10] leaves of plates: ill. 1. Western stories. 2. Wyoming — Social life and customs — Fiction. I. T.
PS3345.V5x

Cobbs, John L.　　　　　　　　　　　　　2.11289
Owen Wister / by John L. Cobbs. — Boston: Twayne Publishers, c1984. 140 p.: port.; 23 cm. — (Twayne's United States authors series. TUSAS 475) Includes index. 1. Wister, Owen, 1860-1938 — Criticism and interpretation. I. T. II. Series.
PS3346.C6 1984　　813/.52 19　　*LC* 84-4688　　*ISBN* 0805774165

Payne, Darwin.　　　　　　　　　　　　　2.11290
Owen Wister, chronicler of the West, gentleman of the East / by Darwin Payne. — Dallas, Tex.: Southern Methodist University Press, 1985. xiv, 377 p., [20] p. of plates: ill., ports.; 24 cm. Includes index. 1. Wister, Owen, 1860-1938. 2. Authors, American — 19th century — Biography. 3. Western stories — History and criticism. I. T.
PS3346.P39 1985　　813/.52 B 19　　*LC* 85-1989　　*ISBN* 0870742051

PS3500–3549 20th Century (1900–1950)

PS3501 Adams. Agee

Adams, Léonie, 1899-.　　　　　　　　　　• 2.11291
Poems, a selection. — New York: Funk & Wagnalls, 1954. 128 p. I. T.
PS3501.D285 A6 1954　　*LC* 54-6356

Agee, James, 1909-1955.   • **2.11292**
The collected poems of James Agee. Edited and with an introd. by Robert Fitzgerald. — Boston: Houghton Mifflin, 1968. xii, 179 p.; 23 cm. — I. T.
PS3501.G35 A17 1968   811/.5/2   LC 68-30683

Agee, James, 1909-1955.   **2.11293**
[Prose works. Selections] James Agee, selected journalism / edited, with an introduction, by Paul Ashdown. — Knoxville: University of Tennessee Press, c1985. xliv, 183 p.: ill.; 23 cm. I. Ashdown, Paul, 1944- II. T.
PS3501.G35 A6 1985   814/.52 19   LC 85-710   ISBN 087049466X

Agee, James, 1909-1955.   • **2.11294**
A death in the family. — New York: Grosset & Dunlap, [1967, c1957] 339 p.; 22 cm. — I. T.
PZ4   PS3501.G35Dx.   LC 67-6299

Agee, James, 1909-1955.   • **2.11295**
Permit me voyage; with a foreword by Archibald MacLeish. New Haven, Yale University Press, 1934. 59 p. 22 cm. (The Yale series of younger poets, 33) I. T.
PS3501.G35 P4x   LC 34-38156

Agee, James.   • **2.11296**
Letters of James Agee to Father Flye / James Agee. — New York: Braziller, 1962. 235 p.: ill. 1. Agee, James, 1909-1955. 2. Authors, American — Correspondence. I. Flye, James Harold. II. T.
PS3501.G35Z54 1962   816.52

Bergreen, Laurence.   **2.11297**
James Agee: a life / Laurence Bergreen. — 1st ed. — New York: Dutton, c1984. xii, 467 p., [16] p. of plates: port.; 24 cm. Includes index. 1. Agee, James, 1909-1955 — Biography. 2. Authors, American — 20th century — Biography. I. T.
PS3501.G35 Z59 1984   818/.5209 B 19   LC 83-25496   ISBN 0525242538

Kramer, Victor A.   **2.11298**
James Agee / by Victor A. Kramer. — Boston: Twayne Publishers, [1975] 182 p.: port.; 22 cm. (Twayne's United States authors series; TUSAS 252) Includes index. 1. Agee, James, 1909-1955 — Criticism and interpretation. I. T.
PS3501.G35 Z74   818/.5/209   LC 74-23882   ISBN 0805700064

PS3501 Aiken. Algren

Aiken, Conrad, 1889-1973.   • **2.11299**
Collected short stories. Pref. by Mark Schorer. — [1st ed.]. — Cleveland: World Pub. Co., [1960] xiv, 566 p.; 22 cm. — I. T.
PZ3.A2912 Ck   PS3501.I5 A15 1960.   LC 60-10537

Aiken, Conrad, 1889-1973.   • **2.11300**
The collected novels of Conrad Aiken / introduction by R.P. Blackmur. — 1st ed. — New York: Holt, Rinehart and Winston, 1964. 575 p.; 24 cm. I. Aiken, Conrad, 1889-1973. Blue voyage. II. Aiken, Conrad, 1889-1973. Great circle. III. Aiken, Conrad, 1889-1973. King Coffin. IV. Aiken, Conrad, 1889-1973. Heart for the gods of Mexico. V. Aiken, Conrad, 1889-1973. Conversation. VI. T. VII. Title: Blue voyage. VIII. Title: Great circle. IX. Title: King Coffin. X. Title: A heart for the gods of Mexico. XI. Title: Conversation.
PZ3.A2912Cf   PS3501.I5 A15 1964.   LC 63-20431

Aiken, Conrad, 1889-1973.   • **2.11301**
Collected poems [by] Conrad Aiken. 2d ed. New York, Oxford University Press, 1970. xiv, 1049 p. port. 22 cm. I. T.
PS3501.I5 A17 1970   811/.5/2   LC 79-120179

Aiken, Conrad, 1889-1973.   **2.11302**
Selected letters of Conrad Aiken / edited by Joseph Killorin. — New Haven: Yale University Press, 1978. xxv, 350 p., [10] leaves of plates: ill.; 24 cm. 1. Aiken, Conrad, 1889-1973 — Correspondence. 2. Authors, American — 20th century — Correspondence. I. Killorin, Joseph, 1926- II. T.
PS3501.I5 Z48 1978   818/.52/09 B   LC 77-20620   ISBN 0300021801

Hoffman, Frederick John.   • **2.11303**
Conrad Aiken. New York: Twayne Publishers [1962] 172 p.; 22 cm. (Twayne's United States authors series, 17) 1. Aiken, Conrad, 1889-1973. I. T.
PS3501.I5 Z68   818.52   LC 62-13671

Lorenz, Clarissa M.   **2.11304**
Lorelei Two: my life with Conrad Aiken / Clarissa M. Lorenz. — Athens: University of Georgia Press, c1983. 231 p., [8] p. of plates: ill.; 25 cm. Includes index. 1. Aiken, Conrad, 1889-1973 — Biography — Marriage. 2. Lorenz, Clarissa M. 3. Authors, American — 20th century — Biography. 4. Wives — United States — Biography. 5. Wives — England — Biography. I. T.
PS3501.I5 Z74 1983   818/.5209 19   LC 82-17347   ISBN 0820306614

Martin, Jay.   • **2.11305**
Conrad Aiken, a life of his art. Princeton, N.J., Princeton University Press, 1962. 280 p. 23 cm. 1. Aiken, Conrad, 1889-1973. I. T.
PS3501.I5 Z75   811.52   LC 62-11958

Algren, Nelson, 1909-.   • **2.11306**
The neon wilderness. — Garden City, N.Y.: Doubleday, 1947. 286 p. Short stories. I. T.
PS3501.L43 N4   LC 47-772

Algren, Nelson, 1909-.   • **2.11307**
The man with the golden arm: a novel. — [1st ed.]. — Garden City, N.Y.: Doubleday, 1949. 343 p.; 22 cm. — I. T.
PZ3.A396 Man   PS3501.L4625 Mx.   LC 49-10533

Algren, Nelson, 1909-.   • **2.11308**
A walk on the wild side. — New York: Farrar, Straus, and Cudahy, 1956. 346 p. I. T.
PS3501.L4625 W3 1956   LC 56-8623

Cox, Martha Heasley.   **2.11309**
Nelson Algren, by Martha Heasley Cox and Wayne Chatterton. — Boston: Twayne Publishers, [1975] 163 p.: port.; 21 cm. — (Twayne's United States authors series, TUSAS 249) 1. Algren, Nelson, 1909- — Criticism and interpretation. I. Chatterton, Wayne. joint author. II. T.
PS3501.L4625 Z66   813/.5/2   LC 74-19223   ISBN 0805700145

PS3501 Am–An

Ammons, A. R., 1926-.   • **2.11310**
Collected poems, 1951–1971. — [1st ed.]. — New York: Norton, [1972] xvii, 396 p.; 21 cm. — I. T.
PS3501.M6 A17 1972   811/.5/4   LC 72-5811   ISBN 0393042413

Anderson, Maxwell, 1888-1959.   • **2.11311**
Eleven verse plays [by] Maxwell Anderson, 1929–1939. — [New York]: Harcourt, Brace and company, [1940] [1321] p.: illus.; 21 cm. Each play has separate paging. I. T.
PS3501.N256 1940   812.5   LC 40-27679

Anderson, Maxwell, 1888-1959.   **2.11312**
Both your houses: a play in three acts / Maxwell Anderson. — New York: S. French, 1933. 180 p.; 20 cm. I. T.
PS3501.N256 B6 1933   LC 33-10095

Anderson, Maxwell, 1888-1959.   • **2.11313**
Three American plays, by Maxwell Anderson and Laurence Stallings. New York, Harcourt, c1926. 263 p. 23 cm. I. Stallings, Laurence, 1894-1968. II. Anderson, Maxwell, 1888-1959. What price glory. III. Anderson, Maxwell, 1888-1959. What price glory. IV. Anderson, Maxwell, 1888-1959. Buccaneer. V. T. VI. Title: What price glory. VII. Title: First flight. VIII. Title: The buccaneer. IX. Title: 3 American plays. X. Title: 1st flight.
PS3501.N256 T5 1926   LC 26-17652

Anderson, Maxwell, 1888-1959.   **2.11314**
Dramatist in America: letters of Maxwell Anderson, 1912–1958 / edited by Laurence G. Avery. — Chapel Hill: University of North Carolina Press, c1977. lxxxiii, 366 p.; 24 cm. Includes index. 1. Anderson, Maxwell, 1888-1959 — Correspondence. 2. Dramatists, American — 20th century — Correspondence. I. Avery, Laurence G. II. T.
PS3501.N256 Z53 1977   812/.5/2 B   LC 77-4491   ISBN 0807813095

Bailey, Mabel Driscoll, 1904-.   • **2.11315**
Maxwell Anderson, the playwright as prophet. — London: Abelard-Schuman, [1957] 200 p. 1. Anderson, Maxwell, 1888-1959. I. T.
PS3501.N256 Z57   LC 57-6380

Adler, Thomas P.   **2.11316**
Robert Anderson / by Thomas P. Adler. — Boston: Twayne Publishers, c1978. 184 p.: port.; 21 cm. — (Twayne's United States authors series; 300) Includes index. 1. Anderson, Robert Woodruff, 1917- — Criticism and interpretation. I. T.
PS3501.N34 Z56   812/.5/4   LC 77-15103   ISBN 0805772049

PS3501 Sherwood Anderson

Anderson, Sherwood, 1876-1941.   **2.11317**
Marching men; a critical text. Edited with an introd. by Ray Lewis White. — Cleveland: Press of Case Western Reserve University, 1972. xxvii, 290 p.; 24 cm. — (His The major fiction of Sherwood Anderson) Includes selected essays, 1902-1914, and The rabbit-pen. I. White, Ray Lewis. ed. II. T.
PZ3.A55 Mar6 PS3501.N4   813/.5/2   LC 73-149169   ISBN 0829502165

Anderson, Sherwood, 1876-1941. • 2.11318
Death in the woods, and other stories. — New York: Liveright, [c1933] 298 p.
I. T.
PS3501.N4 D4 LC 33-23673

Anderson, Sherwood, 1876-1941. • 2.11319
Dark laughter. With an introd. by Howard Mumford Jones. — New York:
Liveright Pub. Corp., [1960] 319 p.; 22 cm. — I. T.
PZ3.A55 Da 12 PS3501.N4 Dx. LC 60-53556

Anderson, Sherwood, 1876-1941. • 2.11320
Poor white: a novel / with an introd. by Walter B. Rideout. — New York:
Viking Press, 1966. xx, 363 p.; 20 cm. (Compass books) I. Rideout, Walter
Bates. II. T.
PZ3.A55 Po8 PS3501.N4 P6 1966. LC 66-1691

Anderson, Sherwood, 1876-1941. • 2.11321
The triumph of the egg: a book of impressions from American life in tales and
poems / by Sherwood Anderson; in clay by Tennessee Mitchell; photographs by
Eugene Hutchinson. — New York: B.W. Huebsch, 1921. xi, 269 p.: ill. I. T.
PS3501.N4 T7 LC 21-21097

Anderson, Sherwood, 1876-1941. • 2.11322
Windy McPherson's son / Sherwood Anderson; introd. by Wright Morris. —
Chicago: University of Chicago Press, 1965. xix, 330 p. — (Chicago in fiction)
I. T. II. Series.
PZ3.A55 W6 PS3501.N4 W48 1965. LC 65-17280

Anderson, Sherwood, 1876-1941. • 2.11323
Winesburg, Ohio. Introd. by Malcolm Cowley. [New ed.] New York, Viking
press, 1960. 247 p. 21 cm. I. T.
PS3501.N4 W5 1960 LC 60-10867

Anderson, Sherwood, 1876-1941. • 2.11324
A story teller's story. Pref. by Walter B. Rideout. New York, Viking Press
[1969] 442 p. 20 cm. (A Viking compass book) Reprint of the 1924 ed. with new
pref. Autobiographical. 1. Anderson, Sherwood, 1876-1941 — Biography.
2. Authors, American — 20th century — Biography. I. T.
PS3501.N4 Z5 1969 811/.5/2 LC 74-10403

Anderson, Sherwood, 1876-1941. • 2.11325
Tar: a Midwest childhood; a critical text. Edited with an introd. by Ray Lewis
White. Cleveland, Press of Case Western Reserve University, 1969. xx, 257 p.
24 cm. (His the major fiction of Sherwood Anderson) Autobiographical.
1. Anderson, Sherwood, 1876-1941 — Biography. 2. Anderson, Sherwood,
1876-1941. 3. Authors, American — 20th century — Biography. I. White,
Ray Lewis. ed. II. T.
PS3501.N4 Z52 1969 813/.5/2 LC 69-17680 ISBN 0829501592

Anderson, Sherwood, 1876-1941. • 2.11326
[Memoirs] Sherwood Anderson's memoirs: a critical edition / newly edited
from the original manuscripts by Ray Lewis White. — Chapel Hill: University
of North Carolina Press [1969] xxxix, 579 p.: port.; 27 cm. 1. Anderson,
Sherwood, 1876-1941. I. White, Ray Lewis. ed. II. T.
PS3501.N4 Z524 1969 811/.5/2 B LC 73-80019

Anderson, Sherwood, 1876-1941. • 2.11327
Letters of Sherwood Anderson / Selected and edited by Howard Mumford
Jones in association with Walter B. Rideout. — 'First ed.' Boston, Mass.: Little,
Brown, c1953. xxii 467 p.: ill., ports. Includes index. 1. Anderson, Sherwood,
1876-1941. I. Jones, Howard Mumford, 1892- II. Rideout, Walter Bates,
1917- III. T.
PS3501.N4 Z54 LC 52-12649

Anderson, David D. • 2.11328
Sherwood Anderson; an introduction and interpretation [by] David D.
Anderson. — New York: Holt, Rinehart and Winston, [1967] x, 182 p.: ports.;
21 cm. — (American authors and critics series) 1. Anderson, Sherwood,
1876-1941. I. T.
PS3501.N4 Z548 818/.5/208 LC 67-11297

Howe, Irving. • 2.11329
Sherwood Anderson. — Stanford, Calif.: Stanford University Press, [1966,
c1951] xv, 271 p.; 23 cm. 1. Anderson, Sherwood, 1876-1941. I. T.
PS3501.N4 Z65 1966 818.5209 LC 66-26240

White, Ray Lewis. ed. • 2.11330
The achievement of Sherwood Anderson: essays in criticism. — Chapel Hill:
University of North Carolina Press, [1966] 270 p.; 24 cm. 1. Anderson,
Sherwood, 1876-1941. I. T.
PS3501.N4 Z95 818.5209 LC 66-25354

PS3501 An–Az

Everson, William, 1912-. • 2.11331
The hazards of holiness: poems, 1957–1960 / by Brother Antoninus.
— Garden City, N. Y.: Doubleday, 1962. 94 p. I. T.
PS3501.N77 H3 LC 62-15940

Everson, William, 1912-. • 2.11332
The residual years: poems 1934–1948: the pre–Catholic poetry of Brother
Antoninus / William Everson [i.e. Brother Antoninus]; with an introduction by
Kenneth Rexroth. — [New York: New Directions, 1968] xvii, 238 p.; 21 cm. —
(New Directions book.) I. Rexroth, Kenneth, 1905- II. Antoninus, Brother.
Crooked lines of God. III. T. IV. Series.
PS3501.N77 R4 811/.5/2 LC 68-25545

Arnow, Harriette Louisa (Simpson) • 2.11333
The dollmaker. New York: Macmillan, 1954. 549 p. I. T.
PZ3.A7654 Do PS3501.R64Dx. LC 54-9223

Ashbery, John. • 2.11334
The double dream of spring. — [1st ed.]. — New York: Dutton, 1970. 95 p.; 21
cm. Poems. I. T.
PS3501.S475 D6 811/.5/4 LC 77-87191

Ashbery, John. 2.11335
Self–portrait in a convex mirror: poems / by John Ashbery. — New York:
Viking Press, 1975. 83 p.; 22 cm. I. T.
PS3501.S475 S4 811/.5/4 LC 75-1095 ISBN 067063283X

Ashbery, John. 2.11336
Shadow train: poems / John Ashbery. — New York: Viking Press, 1981. 50 p.;
21 cm. — I. T.
PS3501.S475 S5 1981b 811/.54 19 LC 80-27030 ISBN
0670637866

Ashbery, John. • 2.11337
The tennis court oath: a book of poems / by John Ashbery. — Middletown,
Conn.: Wesleyan University Press, c1962. 94 p. I. T.
PS3501.S475 T4 LC 62-10569 ISBN 0819520136

Beyond amazement: new essays on John Ashbery / edited by 2.11338
David Lehman.
Ithaca, N.Y.: Cornell University Press, 1980. 294 p.; 22 cm. Includes indexes.
1. Ashbery, John — Criticism and interpretation — Addresses, essays,
lectures. I. Lehman, David, 1948-
PS3501.S475 Z59 811/.54 LC 79-6850 ISBN 0801412358

Shapiro, David, 1947-. 2.11339
John Ashbery, an introduction to the poetry / David Shapiro. — New York:
Columbia University Press, 1979. xx, 190 p.: ill.; 21 cm. — (Columbia
introductions to twentieth-century American poetry.) Includes index.
1. Ashbery, John — Criticism and interpretation. I. T. II. Series.
PS3501.S475 Z85 811/.5/4 LC 79-4420 ISBN 0231040903

Auchincloss, Louis. • 2.11340
I come as a thief. — Boston: Houghton Mifflin, 1972. 231 p.; 23 cm. I. T.
PZ3.A898 Iac PS3501.U25I2 813/.5/4 LC 77-190053 ISBN
0395139392

Auchincloss, Louis. • 2.11341
Portrait in brownstone. Boston, Houghton Mifflin [1962] 371 p. 22 cm. I. T.
PZ3.A898Po PS3501.U25P6 LC 62-8116

Auchincloss, Louis. • 2.11342
The rector of Justin. — Boston: Houghton Mifflin, 1964. 341 p.; 23 cm. — I. T.
PZ3.A898 Re PS3501.U25 Rx. LC 64-14523

PS3503 B–Be

Babbitt, Irving, 1865-1933. • 2.11343
Spanish character and other essays: with a bibliography of his publications and
an index to his collected works / edited by Frederick Manchester [et al.]. —
Boston: Houghton Mifflin, 1940. 360 p. I. Manchester, Frederick Alexander,
1882- II. T.
PS3503.A125 S7 LC 40-32716

Baker, Dorothy Dodds, 1907-. • 2.11344
Young man with a horn. — Boston: Houghton, Mifflin, c1938. 243 p.; 21 cm.
I. T.
PS3503.A54156 Y6 LC 38-13334

Barnes, Djuna. • 2.11345
Selected works: Spillway; The antiphon; Nightwood. — New York, Farrar, Straus and Cudahy [1962] 366 p. 22 cm. I. T. II. Title: Spillway. III. Title: The antiphon. IV. Title: Nightwood,
PS3503.A614A6 1962   818.52   *LC* 62-7185

Barry, Philip, 1896-. • 2.11346
The Philadelphia story: a comedy in three acts / by Philip Barry. — New York: Coward-McCann, inc. [c1939] 5 p. l., 3-206 p.; 21 cm. I. T.
PS3503.A648 P5 1939   812.5   *LC* 40-11146

Behrman, S. N. (Samuel Nathaniel), 1893-1973. • 2.11347
4 plays: The second man, Biography, Rain from heaven, End of summer / by S.N. Behrman. — New York: Random House, [1955, c1952] 370 p.; 20 cm. I. T. II. Title: The second man. III. Title: Biography. IV. Title: Rain from heaven. V. Title: End of summer.
PS3503.E37 F6   812.5   *LC* 55-8150

PS3503 Bellow

Bellow, Saul. • 2.11348
The adventures of Augie March: a novel. — New York: Viking Press, 1953. 536 p.; 23 cm. I. T.
PS3503.E4488 A66 1953   813/.52 19   *LC* 53-7953

Bellow, Saul. • 2.11349
Dangling man. New York, The Vanguard press [1944] 191 p. 21 cm. I. T.
PS3503.E4488 D3 1944   813/.52 19   *LC* 44-3681

Bellow, Saul. • 2.11350
Herzog. New York, Viking Press [1964] 341 p. 22 cm. I. T.
PS3503.E4488 H45 1964   813/.52 19   *LC* 64-19794

Bellow, Saul. • 2.11351
Henderson, the rain king; a novel. — New York: Viking Press, 1959. 341 p.; 23 cm. — I. T.
PS3503.E4488 H4x   *LC* 59-5649

Bellow, Saul. 2.11352
Him with his foot in his mouth and other stories / Saul Bellow. — 1st ed. — New York: Harper & Row, c1984. 294 p. I. Bellow, Saul. What kind of a day did you have? II. Bellow, Saul. Zetland: by a character witness III. Bellow, Saul. Silver dish IV. T.
PS3503.E4488 H56T 1984   813/.52 19   *LC* 84-48322   *ISBN* 006015179X

Bellow, Saul. 2.11353
Humboldt's gift / Saul Bellow. — New York: Viking Press, 1975. 487 p.; 24 cm. I. T.
PS3503.E4488 H8x   813/.5/2   *LC* 75-12595   *ISBN* 0670386553

Bellow, Saul. • 2.11354
Mr. Sammler's planet. — New York: Viking Press, [1970] 313 p.; 22 cm. 'Originally appeared in Atlantic monthly in a different form.' I. T.
PZ3.B41937 Mi   PS3503.E4488 M4.   813/.5/2   *LC* 74-87248   *ISBN* 0670333190

Bellow, Saul. • 2.11355
Mosby's memoirs and other stories. — New York: Viking Press, [1968] 184 p.; 23 cm. I. T.
PS3503.E4488 M6   *LC* 68-31395   *ISBN* 0670489654

Bellow, Saul. • 2.11356
Seize the day, with three short stories and a one–act play. — New York: Viking Press, 1956. 211 p.; 22 cm. — I. T.
PS3503.E4488 S4   813.5   *LC* 56-10686

Bellow, Saul. • 2.11357
The victim. New York: Vanguard Press [1947] [5] l., 3-294 p.; 22 cm. I. T.
PS3503.E4488 V5 1947   813/.52 19   *LC* 47-12088

Bradbury, Malcolm, 1932-. 2.11358
Saul Bellow / Malcolm Bradbury. — London: Methuen, 1982. 110 p. — (Contemporary writers.) 1. Bellow, Saul — Criticism and interpretation I. T. II. Series.
PS3503E4488 Z58   *LC* 81-22500   *ISBN* 0416316506

Cohen, Sarah Blacher. 2.11359
Saul Bellow's enigmatic laughter. — Urbana: University of Illinois Press, [1974] 242 p.; 24 cm. 1. Bellow, Saul — Style. 2. Comic, The I. T.
PS3503.E4488 Z614   813/.5/2   *LC* 73-5408   *ISBN* 0252004019

Dutton, Robert R. • 2.11360
Saul Bellow, by Robert R. Dutton. — New York: Twayne Publishers, [1971] 177 p.; 22 cm. — (Twayne's United States authors series, TUSAS 181) 1. Bellow, Saul. I. T.
PS3503.E4488 Z66   813/.5/2   *LC* 74-120518

Fuchs, Daniel, 1934-. 2.11361
Saul Bellow, vision and revision / Daniel Fuchs. — Durham, N.C.: Duke University Press, 1984. 345 p.; 25 cm. 1. Bellow, Saul — Criticism and interpretation. 2. Bellow, Saul — Technique. I. T.
PS3503.E4488 Z665 1984   813/.52 19   *LC* 83-9061   *ISBN* 0822305038

Opdahl, Keith Michael. • 2.11362
The novels of Saul Bellow: an introduction. — University Park: Pennsylvania State University Press, [1967] 200 p.; 23 cm. Bibliography: p. [181]-193. 1. Bellow, Saul. I. T.
PS3503.E4488Z8   813/.5/2   *LC* 67-16197

Porter, M. Gilbert. 2.11363
Whence the power?: The artistry and humanity of Saul Bellow / M. Gilbert Porter. — Columbia: University of Missouri Press, 1974. ix, 209 p.; 23 cm. 1. Bellow, Saul — Criticism and interpretation. I. T.
PS3503.E4488 Z82   813/.5/2   *LC* 74-79165   *ISBN* 0826201652

PS3503 Be

Bemelmans, Ludwig, 1898-1962. • 2.11364
The world of Bemelmans: an omnibus / by Ludwig Bemelmans. — New York: Viking Press, 1955. 503 p.: ill. I. T.
PS3503E475 A6 1955   PS3503E475 A6 1955.   810.81   *LC* 55-10472

Benchley, Robert, 1889-1945. • 2.11365
The Benchley roundup / a selection by Nathaniel Benchley of his favorites; drawings by Gluyas Williams. — [1st ed.] New York: Harper [1954] 333 p.: ill.; 22 cm. 1. Benchley, Nathaniel, 1915- comp. I. T.
PS3503.E49 B46   817.5   *LC* 54-8937

Benchley, Nathaniel, 1915-. • 2.11366
Robert Benchley: a biography / by Nathaniel Benchley; foreword by Robert E. Sherwood. — New York; Toronto: McGraw-Hill, c1955. xvii, 258 p., [8] p. of plates: ports. 1. Benchley, Robert, 1889-1945. 2. Authors, American — Biography. I. T.
PS3503.E49 Z6   *LC* 55-10402

Benét, Stephen Vincent, 1898-1943. • 2.11367
Ballads and poems, 1915–1930 / Stephen Vincent Benét. — 1st ed. — Garden City, N.Y.: Doubleday, Doran, 1931. xii, 229 p.; 21 cm. 'This book is, in the main, a selection from three earlier books of verse, all now out of print.' I. T.
PS3503.E5325 A6

Benét, Stephen Vincent, 1898-1943. • 2.11368
Selected works of Stephen Vincent Benét. — New York: Farrar & Rinehart, inc., 1942. 2 v.; 22 cm. I. T.
PS3503.E5325 A6 1942   810.81   *LC* 42-15523

Benét, Stephen Vincent, 1898-1943. • 2.11369
The devil and Daniel Webster / illustrated by Harold Denison. — New York; Toronto: Farrar & Rinehart, [1937] 4 p. l., 13-16 p.: ill.; 21 cm. 1. Webster, Daniel, 1782-1852 — Fiction. I. Denison, Harold, 1887- illus. II. T.
PS3503.E5325 D4 1937a   813.5   *LC* 38-5407

Benét, Stephen Vincent, 1898-1943. • 2.11370
John Brown's body / Stephen Vincent Benét; with illustrations by Fritz Kredel and Warren Chappell. — New York: Rinehart, 1954. xvi, 368 p.: col. ill.; 25 cm. I. T.
PS3503.E5325J6   *LC* 54-9619

Benét, Stephen Vincent, 1898-1943. • 2.11371
Selected letters / edited by Charles A. Fenton. — New Haven: Yale University Press, 1960. 436 p.: ill.; 21 cm. 1. Benét, Stephen Vincent, 1898-1943 — Correspondence. I. Fenton, Charles A. II. T.
PS3503.E5325 Z54   *LC* 60-11231

Fenton, Charles A. • 2.11372
Stephen Vincent Benét: the life and times of an American man of letters, 1898–1943. — New Haven: Yale University Press, 1958. xv, 436 p.: ill., ports.; 21 cm. 1. Benét, Stephen Vincent, 1898-1943 — Biography. I. T.
PS3503.E5325 Z62   *LC* 58-11252

Stroud, Parry Edmund, 1917-.   • **2.11373**
Stephen Vincent Benét / by Parry Stroud. — New York: Twayne Publishers, [1963, c1962] 173 p.; 21 cm. (Twayne's United States authors series, 27) 1. Benét, Stephen Vincent, 1898-1943. I. T.
PS3503.E5325 Z77 1963   818.52   *LC* 62-16822

Benét, William Rose, 1886-1950.   • **2.11374**
Golden fleece: a collection of poems and ballads old and new / [by] William Rose Benét. — New York: Dodd, Mead & company, [c1935] xi p., 1 l., 224 p.; 22 cm. I. T.
PS3503.E533 G6 1935   *LC* 35-2997

Benét, William Rose, 1886-1950.   • **2.11375**
The dust which is God, a novel in verse. New York, A.A. Knopf, 1945. 559 p. 22 cm. I. T.
PS 3503 E584 D97 1945   *LC* 45-4100

Berryman, John, 1914-1972.   • **2.11376**
Berryman's sonnets. — New York: Farrar, Straus and Giroux, [1967] ix, 115 p.; 21 cm. — I. T.
PS3503.E744 B4   811/.5/4   *LC* 67-15007

Berryman, John, 1914-1972.   **2.11377**
The dream songs. — New York: Farrar, Straus and Giroux, [1969] xx, 427 p.; 22 cm. Previously published separately under titles: 77 dream songs (1964) and His toy, his dream, his rest (1968) I. T.
PS3503.E744 D7 1969   811/.5/4   *LC* 74-93811

Berryman, John, 1914-1972.   **2.11378**
Henry's fate & other poems, 1967–1972 / John Berryman. New York: Farrar, Straus and Giroux, 1977. xviii, 93 p.; 23 cm. I. T.
PS3503.E744 H4 1977   811/.5/4   *LC* 76-52950   *ISBN* 0374169500

Berryman, John, 1914-1972.   • **2.11379**
Homage to Mistress Bradstreet; [poem] With pictures by Ben Shahn. — New York: Farrar, Straus & Cudahy, [1956] 57 p.: ill.; 25 cm. 1. Bradstreet, Anne, 1612?-1672 — in fiction, drama, poetry, etc. I. Shahn, Ben, 1898-1969. II. T.
PS3503.E744 H6   811.5   *LC* 56-6168

Berryman, John, 1914-1972.   • **2.11380**
Short poems. — New York: Farrar, Straus & Giroux, [1967] 120 p.; 22 cm. — I. T.
PS3503.E744 S5   811/.5/4   *LC* 67-28940

Haffenden, John.   **2.11381**
John Berryman, a critical commentary / John Haffenden. — New York: New York University Press, c1980. vii, 216 p.; 23 cm. — (The Gotham library of the New York University Press) Includes index. 1. Berryman, John, 1914-1972 — Criticism and interpretation. I. T.
PS3503.E744 Z58   811/.54 19   *LC* 79-3893   *ISBN* 0814734049

Haffenden, John.   **2.11382**
The life of John Berryman / John Haffenden. — Boston: Routledge & K. Paul, 1982. xiii, 451 p.; 24 cm. Includes index. 1. Berryman, John, 1914-1972. 2. Poets, American — 20th century — Biography. I. T.
PS3503.E744 Z59 1982   811/.54 B 19   *LC* 81-23501   *ISBN* 0710092164

PS3503 Bi

Biggers, Earl Derr, 1884-1933.   **2.11383**
The house without a key. Indianapolis: Bobbs-Merrill [c1925] 316 p. I. T.
PS3503I54 H6   813.5

Bishop, Elizabeth, 1911-1979.   **2.11384**
[Poems] The complete poems, 1927–1979 / Elizabeth Bishop. — New York: Farrar Straus Giroux, c1983. 287 p.; 25 cm. Includes indexes. I. T.
PS3503.I785 1983   811/.54 19   *LC* 82-21119   *ISBN* 0374127476

Bishop, Elizabeth, 1911-1979.   **2.11385**
[Prose works] The collected prose / Elizabeth Bishop; edited, with an introduction, by Robert Giroux. — New York: Farrar, Straus, Giroux, c1984. xxii, 278 p.; 25 cm. I. Giroux, Robert. II. T.
PS3503.I785 A15 1984   818/.5408 19   *LC* 83-16418   *ISBN* 0374126283

Elizabeth Bishop and her art / edited by Lloyd Schwartz and   **2.11386**
Sybil P. Estess; foreword by Harold Bloom.
Ann Arbor: University of Michigan Press, c1983. xix, 341 p., [1] leaf of plates: ill.; 21 cm. — (Under discussion.) 1. Bishop, Elizabeth, 1911-1979. 2. Poets, American — 20th century — Biography — Addresses, essays, lectures. I. Schwartz, Lloyd, 1941- II. Estess, Sybil P., 1942- III. Series.
PS3503.I785 Z65 1983   811/.54 19   *LC* 82-20235   *ISBN* 047206343X

Stevenson, Anne, 1933 Jan. 3.   • **2.11387**
Elizabeth Bishop. New York, Twayne Publishers [1966] 143 p. 21 cm. (Twayne's United States authors series, 105) 1. Bishop, Elizabeth, 1911-1979. I. T.
PS3503.I785 Z87   811.54   *LC* 66-17066

Bishop, John Peale, 1892-1944.   • **2.11388**
The collected essays of John Peale Bishop / ed. with an introd. by Edmund Wilson. — New York: Scribner, 1948. xviii, 508 p.: port. I. Wilson, Edmund, 1895-1972. II. T.
PS3503.I79 A17 1948   *LC* 48-8528

Bishop, John Peale, 1892-1944.   • **2.11389**
The collected poems of John Peale Bishop / edited with a pref. and a personal memoir by Allen Tate. — New York: Scribner, 1948. xxiii, 277 p.: port. I. Tate, Allen, 1899- ed. II. T.
PS3503.I79 A17 1948   *LC* 48-4117

White, Robert Lee, 1928-.   • **2.11390**
John Peale Bishop / by Robert L. White. — New York: Twayne Publishers, [1966] 176 p.; 21 cm. — (Twayne's United States authors series, 99) 1. Bishop, John Peale, 1892-1944. I. T.
PS3503.I79 Z9   818.5209   *LC* 66-12050

PS3503 Bl–Bo

Blish, James.   **2.11391**
Black Easter; The day after judgment / James Blish; with an new introd. by David G. Hartwell. — Boston: Gregg Press, 1980. x, 165, 166 p.; 21 cm. — (The Gregg Press science fiction series) Reprint of the 1968 and 1971 editions published by Doubleday, Garden City, N.Y. respectively. 1. Science fiction, American I. T.
PS3503.L64 B59 1980   813/.54   *LC* 80-17971   *ISBN* 0839826443

Blish, James.   **2.11392**
A case of conscience / James Blish. — New York: Ballantine Books, c1958. 188 p.; 18 cm. — 'A Del Roy Book'. I. T.
PZ3.B61987 Cas3 PS3503.L64   PS3503.L64 C3.   813/.5/4   *LC* 58-8569   *ISBN* 0345280237 pbk

Bogan, Louise, 1897-1970.   • **2.11393**
Collected poems, 1923–1953. — New York, Noonday Press [1954] 126 p. 22 cm. I. T.
PS3503.O195A17 1954   811.5   *LC* 54-9946

Bontemps, Arna Wendell, 1902-1973.   **2.11394**
Black thunder, by Arna Bontemps. With an introd. for this ed. by the author. — Boston: Beacon Press, [1968] xv, 9-224 p.; 21 cm. — (Beacon paperback no. 305.) I. T.
PS3503.O474 B5 1968   *LC* 68-31383

Bontemps, Arna Wendell, 1902-1973.   **2.11395**
Arna Bontemps–Langston Hughes letters, 1925–1967 / selected and edited by Charles H. Nichols. — New York: Dodd, Mead, c1980. 529 p.: ill.; 25 cm. 1. Bontemps, Arna Wendell, 1902-1973 — Correspondence. 2. Hughes, Langston, 1902-1967 — Correspondence. 3. Afro-American authors — Correspondence 4. Authors, American — 20th century — Correspondence. I. Hughes, Langston, 1902-1967. joint author. II. Nichols, Charles Harold. III. T.
PS3503.O474 Z486 1980   816/.5/208   *LC* 79-17341   *ISBN* 0396076874

Booth, Philip F.   **2.11396**
Available light / Philip Booth. — New York: Viking Press, 1976. ix, 83 p.; 23 cm. Poems. I. T.
PS3503.O532 A95   811/.5/4   *LC* 75-38875   *ISBN* 0670143103

Bourjaily, Vance Nye.   • **2.11397**
Confessions of a spent youth: a novel / by Vance Bourjaily. — New York: Dial Press, 1960. 434 p.; 21 cm. I. T.
PS3503.O77 C6   *LC* 60-14690

Bourne, Randolph Silliman, 1886-1918.   • **2.11398**
History of a literary radical and other essays / edited with an introd. by Van Wyck Brooks. — New York: Biblo and Tannen, 1969 [c1920] xxxv, 343 p.; 23 cm. I. Brooks, Van Wyck, 1886-1963. ed. II. T.
PS3503.O8 H5 1969   814/.5/2   *LC* 69-17713

Clayton, Bruce.   **2.11399**
Forgotten prophet: the life of Randolph Bourne / Bruce Clayton. — Baton Rouge: Louisiana State University Press, c1984. x, 275 p.: port.; 23 cm. 1. Bourne, Randolph Silliman, 1886-1918 — Biography. 2. Authors, American — 20th century — Biography. I. T.
PS3503.O8 Z6 1984   818/.5209 B 19   *LC* 84-5748   *ISBN* 0807111694

Bowen, Catherine Drinker.   • 2.11400
Adventures of a biographer / by Catherine Drinker Bowen. — Boston: Little, Brown, 1959. xi, 235 p. 1. Bowen, Catherine Drinker — Biography. 2. Biography (as a literary form) 3. Biographers — Biography. I. T.
PS3503O814Z52   920.002   LC 59-11888

Bowles, Jane Auer, 1917-1973.   • 2.11401
Collected works / with an introd. by Truman Capote.— 1st American print. — New York: Farrar, Straus & Giroux, 1966. ix, 431 p.; 21 cm. I. 2 serious ladies. II. Bowles, Jane Auer, 1917-1973. Two serious ladies. III. Bowles, Jane Auer, 1917-1973. In the summer house. IV. Bowles, Jane Auer, 1917-1973. Plain pleasures. V. T. VI. Title: Two serious ladies. VII. Title: In the summer house. VIII. Title: Plain pleasures.
PZ3.B6816Co   PS3503.O837 1966.   LC 66-22592

Boyle, Kay, 1902-.   • 2.11402
Collected poems. [1st ed.] New York, Knopf, 1962. 105 p., 22 cm. I. T.
PS3503.O9357 A17   LC 62-14759

Boyle, Kay, 1902-.   2.11403
Fifty stories / Kay Boyle. — Garden City, N.Y.: Doubleday, 1980. 648 p. — I. T.
PZ3.B69796 Fh PS3503.O9357   PS3503O9357 F54.   813/.52 19
    LC 78-22151   ISBN 0385149964

Boyle, Kay, 1902-.   • 2.11404
Generation without farewell / Kay Boyle. — 1st ed. — New York: Knopf, 1960, c1959. 300 p.; 21 cm. I. T.
PZ3.B69796Gc   PS3503.O9357 G46.   LC 59-11822

Boyle, Kay, 1902-.   • 2.11405
Plagued by the nightingale / Kay Boyle; preface by Harry T. Moore; a note on the text by Matthew J. Bruccoli. — Carbondale: Southern Illinois University Press, c1966. x, 203 p.; 22 cm. — (Crosscurrents: modern fiction) I. T. II. Series.
PS 3503 O9357 P6 1966   LC 65-19774

Boyle, Kay, 1902-.   2.11406
The underground woman. — [1st ed.]. — Garden City, N.Y.: Doubleday, 1975. 264 p.; 22 cm. — I. T.
PZ3.B69796 Un   PS3503O9357 U5.   813/.5/2   LC 72-186008
    ISBN 0385070470

PS3503 Br

Bradbury, Ray, 1920-.   2.11407
The stories of Ray Bradbury / with an introd. by the author. — 1st ed. — New York: Knopf: distributed by Random House, 1980. xx, 884 p. — (A Borzoi book) I. T.
PZ3.B72453 St 1980 PS3503.R167 A6 1980   813/.54   LC 80-7655
    ISBN 0394513355

Bradbury, Ray, 1920-.   • 2.11408
Dandelion wine, a novel / Ray Bradbury. — New York: Bantam, 1957. 184 p. I. T.
PZ3.B72453 Dan   PS3503.R167 D3.   LC 57-7824

Bradbury, Ray, 1920-.   2.11409
Fahrenheit 451; illustrated by Joe Mugnaini. — New York: Ballantine Books, [1953] 199 p.: illus.; 21 cm. Short stories. I. T.
PS3503.R167 F3 1953x   LC 53-11280

Bradbury, Ray, 1920-.   2.11410
Something wicked this way comes, a novel. New York, Simon and Schuster, 1962. 317 p. 22 cm. I. T.
PS 3503 R167 S69 1962   LC 62-9604

Braithwaite, William Stanley, 1878-1962.   2.11411
The William Stanley Braithwaite reader / edited by Philip Butcher. — Ann Arbor: University of Michigan Press [1972] xiii, 322 p.: port.; 24 cm. I. T.
PS3503.R246 W5 1972   818/.5/209   LC 72-84343   ISBN 0472081942

Brautigan, Richard.   2.11412
The abortion: an historical romance 1966. — New York: Simon and Schuster, [1971] 226 p.; 21 cm. — I. T.
PZ4.B826 Ab PS3503.R2736 A3x   813/.5/4   LC 78-150949   ISBN 0671208721

Brautigan, Richard.   2.11413
Trout fishing in America, The pill versus the Springhill mine disaster, and In watermelon sugar. — New York: Delacorte Press, [1969] 112, 108, 138 p.: illus.; 22 cm. 'A Seymour Lawrence book.' I. T. II. Title: The pill versus the Springhill mine disaster. III. Title: In watermelon sugar.
PS3503.R2736 A6 1969   813/.5/4   LC 77-90905

Brautigan, Richard.   2.11414
Loading mercury with a pitchfork: [poems] / Richard Brautigan. — New York: Simon and Schuster, c1976. 127 p.; 21 cm. I. T.
PS3503.R2736 L6   811/.5/4   LC 76-2001   ISBN 0671222635

Foster, Edward Halsey.   2.11415
Richard Brautigan / by Edward Halsey Foster. — Boston: Twayne Publishers, c1983. 142 p.: port.; 21 cm. — (Twayne's United States authors series. TUSAS 439) Includes index. 1. Brautigan, Richard — Criticism and interpretation. I. T. II. Series.
PS3503.R2736 Z66 1983   813/.54 19   LC 82-15682   ISBN 0805773789

Bromfield, Louis, 1896-1956.   • 2.11416
A Bromfield galaxy: The green bay tree; Early autumn; A good woman / by Louis Bromfield. — New York: Harper, c1957. 639 p.; 22 cm. I. T. II. Title: The green bay tree. III. Title: Early autumn. IV. Title: A good woman.
PS3503.R66 B7 1957   LC 57-7802

Bromfield, Louis, 1896-1956.   2.11417
The farm. New York: Harper, 1933. 346 p. I. T.
PS3503.R66 F3   LC 33-21276

Brooks, Gwendolyn, 1917-.   2.11418
Selected poems. — [1st ed.]. — New York: Harper & Row, [1963] x, 127 p.; 22 cm. — I. T.
PS3503.R7244 A6 1963   811.54   LC 63-16503

Brooks, Gwendolyn, 1917-.   • 2.11419
The world of Gwendolyn Brooks. — [1st ed.]. — New York: Harper & Row, [1971] xiii, 426 p.; 22 cm. I. T.
PS3503.R7244 A6 1971   811/.5/4   LC 74-160646   ISBN 0060105380

Brooks, Gwendolyn, 1917-.   2.11420
Annie Allen. — Westport, Conn.: Greenwood Press, [1971, c1949] x, 60 p.: port.; 23 cm. Poems. I. T.
PS3503.R7244 A7 1971   811/.5/4   LC 78-138207   ISBN 0837155614

Brooks, Gwendolyn, 1917-.   • 2.11421
Report from part one / prefaces by Don L. Lee and George Kent. — [1st ed.] Detroit: Broadside Press, [c1972] 215 p.: ill.; 23 cm. Autobiographical. I. Brooks, Gwendolyn, 1917- II. T.
PS3503.R7244 Z524   LC 72-77308

Brooks, Van Wyck, 1886-1963.   • 2.11422
From a writer's notebook. — 1st ed. — New York: Dutton, 1958. 182 p. I. T.
PS3503.R7297 F7 1958   818   LC 58-5066

O'Connor, Richard, 1915-1975.   2.11423
Heywood Broun: a biography / by Richard O'Connor. — New York: Putnam, [1975] 249 p., [4] leaves of plates: ill.; 22 cm. Includes index. 1. Broun, Heywood, 1888-1939 — Biography. I. T.
PS3503.R76 Z74   070/.92/4 B   LC 74-30572   ISBN 039911503X

Brown, Fredric, 1906-1972.   2.11424
The deep end. New York: Dutton, 1952. 220 p. (Guilt edged mystery) I. T.
PS3503.R8135 D4 1983   813.54   LC 52-12155

Brown, Harry, 1917-1986.   • 2.11425
A walk in the sun / by Harry Brown. — New York: A. A. Knopf, 1944. 3 p.: 3-187 p.; 19 cm. I. T.
PZ3.B81589Wal PS3503.R81565W3   LC 44-5274

Brown, Sterling Allen, 1901-.   2.11426
The collected poems of Sterling A. Brown / selected by Michael S. Harper. — New York: Harper and Row, 1980. xii, 257 p. — (National poetry series.) I. Harper, Michael S. II. T. III. Series.
PS3503R833 A17 1980   LC 79-5221   ISBN 0060105178

PS3503 Bu–Bz

Buck, Pearl S. (Pearl Sydenstricker), 1892-1973.   • 2.11427
Dragon seed, by Pearl S. Buck. Garden City, N.Y.: The Sun Dial Press, [1943] 3 p. l., 3-378 p. 22 cm. 1. China — History — 1937-1945 — Fiction. I. T.
PZ3.B8555 Dr   PS3503.U198 Dx.

Buck, Pearl S. (Pearl Sydenstricker), 1892-1973.   • 2.11428
The good earth, by Pearl S. Buck; with a foreword by the author. New York, The Modern library [1944] 313 p., 19 cm. (The modern library of the world's best books) I. T.
PS3503.U198 G6x   LC 34-27027

Buck, Pearl S. (Pearl Sydenstricker), 1892-1973. • **2.11429**
A house divided / by Pearl S. Buck. — New York: Reynal & Hitchcock, [c1935] 353 p.; 22 cm. 'A John Day book.' I. T.
PS3503.U198 H6   LC 35-1591

Buck, Pearl S. (Pearl Sydenstricker), 1892-1973. • **2.11430**
Letter from Peking, a novel. — New York: J. Day Co., [1957] 252 p.; 21 cm. — I. T.
PZ3.B8555 Le   PS3503.U198 L4.   LC 57-9389

Buck, Pearl S. (Pearl Sydenstricker), 1892-1973. • **2.11431**
Sons. New York, The John Day company [1932] 4 p. l., 3-467, [1] p. 22 cm. I. T.
PZ3.B8555So25 PS3503.U198S6   LC 32-27061

Buck, Pearl S. (Pearl Sydenstricker), 1892-1973. • **2.11432**
My several worlds: a personal record. — New York: Day, [1954] 407 p.; 22 cm. I. T.
PS3503.U198 Z5   928.1   LC 54-10460

Doyle, Paul A. • **2.11433**
Pearl S. Buck / by Paul A. Doyle. — New York: Twayne Publishers, [1965] 175 p.; 21 cm. (Twayne's United States authors series, 85) 1. Buck, Pearl S. (Pearl Sydenstricker), 1892-1973 — Criticism and interpretation. I. T.
PS3503.U198 Z64   813.52   LC 65-18904

Burdick, Eugene, 1918-. • **2.11434**
Fail-safe, by Eugene Burdick & Harvey Wheeler. — New York: McGraw-Hill, [1962] 286 p.; 22 cm. I. Wheeler, Harvey, 1918- II. T.
PZ4.B94 Fai   PS3503.U52 F3.   LC 62-19642

Burgess, Gelett, 1866-1951. • **2.11435**
The purple cow and other nonsense: being a collection of the humorous masterpieces of Gelett Burgess ... adorned with less than a million heart-rending illustrations / by the author. — New York: Dover, 1961. 113 p.: ill.; 21 cm. 1. Nonsense-verses 2. Wit and humor I. T. II. Title: The Burgess nonsense book
PS3503.U6 P8   LC 61-19211   ISBN 0486207722 175

Burke, Kenneth, 1897-. • **2.11436**
The complete white oxen; collected short fiction. Berkeley, University of California Press, 1968. xvii, 310 p. I. T. II. Title: The white oxen.
PS3503.U6134 W5x   LC 68-17692

Rueckert, William H. (William Howe), 1926- comp. • **2.11437**
Critical responses to Kenneth Burke, 1924–1966 / William H. Rueckert, editor. — Minneapolis: University of Minnesota Press, [1969] x, 523 p.: port.; 25 cm. On spine: Kenneth Burke. 1. Burke, Kenneth, 1897- I. T.
PS3503.U6134 Z84   818/.5/209   LC 71-75973

Burroughs, Edgar Rice, 1875-1950. **2.11438**
A princess of Mars / by Edgar Rice Burroughs; illustrated by Frank E. Schoonover. — Chicago: A.C. McClurg; 1917. xii, 326 p.: ill.; 19 cm. I. T.
PS3503.U687 P7 1917

Bynner, Witter, 1881-1968. **2.11439**
Prose pieces / edited, and with an introd. by James Kraft. — New York: Farrar, Straus, Giroux, c1979. xxiii, 407 p.: port.; 22 cm. — (The Works of Witter Bynner) I. Kraft, James. II. T.
PS3503.Y45 A16 1979   814/.5/2   LC 78-11441   ISBN 0374238332

Bynner, Witter, 1881-1968. **2.11440**
Selected poems / Witter Bynner; edited and with a critical introd. by Richard Wilbur; biographical introd. by James Kraft. — New York: Farrar, Straus, Giroux, c1978. cxxviii, 254 p.: port.; 22 cm. — (The Works of Witter Bynner) I. Wilbur, Richard, 1921- II. T.
PS3503.Y45 A17 1978   811/.5/2   LC 77-21365   ISBN 0374258635

Bynner, Witter, 1881-1968. **2.11441**
Light verse and satires / Witter Bynner; edited, and with an introd., by William Jay Smith. — New York: Farrar, Straus, Giroux, c1978. lviii, 301 p.: ill; 22 cm. — (The works of Witter Bynner) I. T.
PS3503.Y45 L48 1978   811/.5/2   LC 77-11158   ISBN 0374187401

PS3505 Cabell

Cabell, James Branch, 1879-1958. • **2.11442**
Beyond life: dizain des démiurges / with a new introd. and bibliography by William Leigh Godshalk. — New York: Johnson Reprint Corp., 1970. xxxvi, 270 p.; 19 cm. — (Series in American studies) Reprint of the 1927 ed. I. T. II. Series.
PS3505.A153 B4 1970   818/.5/208   LC 70-107855

Cabell, James Branch, 1879-1958. • **2.11443**
The cream of the jest; a comedy of evasions, by James Branch Cabell. New York, R. M. McBride, 1917. xv, 280 p. incl. front. 20 cm. I. T.
PS3505.A153 C7 1917   LC 17-24970

Cabell, James Branch, 1879-1958. • **2.11444**
Figures of earth: a comedy of appearances. — New York: R.M. McBride, 1927. 293 p. — (His Works; 2) Storisende edition. Limited edition. Copy no. 446. I. T.
PS3505.A153 F5 1969

Cabell, James Branch, 1879-1958. • **2.11445**
Jurgen; a comedy of justice, by James Branch Cabell ... New York, R. M. McBride & co., [c1919] 368 p. 20 cm. I. T.
PZ3.O107Ju PS3505.A153J8   LC 19-14946

Cabell, James Branch, 1879-1958. • **2.11446**
The rivet in Grandfather's neck: a comedy of limitations. — New York: R.M. McBride, 1929. xxvi, 319 p.; 24 cm. — (Works of James Branch Cabell; 14) Storisende edition, XIV. 'Of this...volume fifteen hundred and ninety copies have been printed...This copy is number 1589.' I. T.
PS3505.A153 R5 1929

Cabell, James Branch, 1879-1958. **2.11447**
The letters of James Branch Cabell. Edited by Edward Wagenknecht. [1st ed.] Norman, University of Oklahoma Press [1975] xvii, 277 p. illus. 24 cm. 1. Cabell, James Branch, 1879-1958 — Correspondence. 2. Authors, American — Correspondence. I. T.
PS3505.A153 Z53 1975   813/.5/2 B   LC 74-5963   ISBN 0806111204

Davis, Joe Lee. • **2.11448**
James Branch Cabell. New York, Twayne Publishers [1962] 174 p. 21 cm. (Twayne's United States authors series, 21) 1. Cabell, James Branch, 1879-1958. I. T.
PS3505.A153 Z62   818.52   LC 62-16816

Tarrant, Desmond. • **2.11449**
James Branch Cabell, the dream and the reality. [1st ed.] Norman, University of Oklahoma Press [1967] xii, 292 p. 1. Cabell, James Branch, 1879-1958. 2. Mythology in literature I. T.
PS3505A153 Z73   LC 67-15595

PS3505 Ca

Cain, James M. (James Mallahan), 1892-1977. • **2.11450**
The postman always rings twice. — New York: A.A. Knopf, 1934. 4 p. l., 3-187, [1] p.; 19 1/2 cm. — First edition. Three novels in one. I. T.
PS3505.A3113 P6 1934   LC 34-2906

Caldwell, Erskine, 1903-. **2.11451**
Annette. — New York: New American Library, [1973] 170 p.; 22 cm. — I. T.
PS3505.A322 A84   PZ3.C12734 An   813/.5/2   LC 73-80322

Caldwell, Erskine, 1903-. • **2.11452**
Complete stories. [1st ed.] New York: Duell, Sloan and Pearce [1953] 664 p. 22 cm. I. T.
PZ3.C12734 Cn   PS3505.A322Ax.   LC 53-10243

Caldwell, Erskine, 1903-. • **2.11453**
God's little acre / by Erskine Caldwell; with a new introd. by the author. — 'First Modern library edition'. New York: Modern Library, c1933. ix, 303 [7] p.; 17 cm. I. T.
PZ3.C12734 Go   PS3505.A322 G6 1937.   LC 34-10388

Caldwell, Erskine, 1903-. • **2.11454**
Journeyman. — [1st rev. ed.]. — New York: Viking Press, 1938. 234 p. I. T.
PS3505.A322 J6 1938   LC 38-5280

Caldwell, Erskine, 1903-. • **2.11455**
Tragic ground / by Erskine Caldwell. — New York: Duell, Sloan and Pearce, 1944. 237 p. I. T.
PZ3.C12734 Tq   PS3505.A322 T66.   LC 45-1137

Caldwell, Erskine, 1903-. • **2.11456**
Trouble in July. New York: Duell, Sloan & Pearce, [c1940] 4 p.: l., 3-241 p.; 21 cm. 'First edition.' I. T.
PZ3.C12734Tr PS3505.A322T7   LC 40-27204

Caldwell, Erskine, 1903-. • **2.11457**
Tobacco road / by Erskine Caldwell. — New York: Modern Library [1947] 241 p. 19 cm. — (The Modern library of the world's best books) I. T.
PS3505.A322Tx   LC A 48-9238 *

Critical essays on Erskine Caldwell / [edited by] Scott **2.11458**
MacDonald.
Boston, Mass.: G-K. Hall, c1981. xxxvii, 400 p.; 25 cm. — (Critical essays on American literature.) 1. Caldwell, Erskine, 1903- — Criticism and interpretation — Collected works. I. MacDonald, Scott, 1942- II. Series.
PS3505.A322 Z54   813/.52 19   *LC* 80-28914   *ISBN* 081618299X

Devlin, James E., 1938-. **2.11459**
Erskine Caldwell / by James E. Devlin. — Boston: Twayne, c1984. 165 p.: port.; 23 cm. (Twayne's United States authors series. TUSAS 469) Includes index. 1. Caldwell, Erskine, 1903- — Criticism and interpretation. I. T. II. Series.
PS3505.A322 Z56 1984   813/.52 19   *LC* 83-26538   *ISBN* 0805774106

March, William, 1893-1954. • **2.11460**
A William March omnibus. With an introd. by Alistair Cooke. New York, Rinehart [c1956] 397 p. 22 cm. I. T.
PZ3.C1553Wi PS3505.A53157A6 1956   *LC* 56-5630

March, William, 1893-1954. • **2.11461**
Company K / by William March (pseud.). — New York: Sagamore Press; New York: Hill & Wang, 1957. 183 p. — (American century series; S-9.) 1. European War, 1914-1918 — Fiction I. T.
PS3505.A53157 C6 1957   *LC* 57-9761

Simmonds, Roy S. **2.11462**
The two worlds of William March / Roy S. Simmonds. — [University, Ala.]: University of Alabama Press, c1984. xviii, 367 p.: port.; 25 cm. Includes index. 1. March, William, 1893-1954. 2. Novelists, American — 20th century — Biography. I. T.
PS3505.A53157 Z85 1984   813/.52 B 19   *LC* 83-1100   *ISBN* 0817301674

PS3505 Capote

Capote, Truman, 1924-. • **2.11463**
Breakfast at Tiffany's: a short novel and three stories. — New York: Random House, [1958] 179 p.; 21 cm. — I. T.
PZ3.C1724 Br   PS3505.A59 B7 1958.   *LC* 58-10956

Capote, Truman, 1924-. • **2.11464**
The grass harp /by Truman Capote. — New York: Random House, 1951. 181 p.; 21 cm. I. T.
PS3505.A59 G7   *LC* 51-13101

Capote, Truman, 1924-. **2.11465**
Music for chameleons: new writing / by Truman Capote. — 1st ed. — New York: Random House, c1980. xix, 262 p.; 22 cm. I. T.
PS3505.A59 M8   813/.54   *LC* 79-5532   *ISBN* 0394508262

Capote, Truman, 1924-. • **2.11466**
Other voices, other rooms. — New York: Random House, [1948] 231 p.; 22 cm. — I. T.
PS3505.A59 O7 1948   PZ3.C1724 Ot   *LC* 48-5135

Capote, Truman, 1924-. • **2.11467**
A tree of night, and other stories. New York, Random House [1949] 209 p. 21 cm. 1. Short stories I. T.
PZ3.C1724 Tr   PS3505.A59Tx.   *LC* 49-7722

Nance, William L. • **2.11468**
The worlds of Truman Capote [by] William L. Nance. — New York: Stein and Day, [1970] 256 p.; 22 cm. 1. Capote, Truman, 1924- I. T.
PS3505.A59 Z7 1970   813/.5/4 B   *LC* 78-110940   *ISBN* 0812813022

Reed, Terry, 1937-. **2.11469**
Truman Capote / by Kenneth T. Reed. — Boston: Twayne Publishers, 1981. 145 p.: port.; 21 cm. (Twayne's United States authors series; TUSAS 388) Includes index. 1. Capote, Truman, 1924- — Criticism and interpretation. I. T.
PS3505.A59 Z84   813/.54 19   *LC* 80-26056   *ISBN* 0805773215

PS3505 Carr

Carr, John Dickson, 1906-1977. **2.11470**
The crooked hinge / John Dickson Carr; introd., with notes, and checklist by Robert E. Briney; ill. by Dick Conner. [San Diego]: University Extension, University of California, San Diego, [1976] c1938. xv, 283 p.: ill.; 21 cm. (The Mystery library; 2) I. T. II. Series.
PZ3.C2317 Cr8 PS3505.A763 C7x   813/.5/2   *LC* 76-56880   *ISBN* 0891630260

PS3505 Cather

Cather, Willa, 1873-1947. • **2.11471**
Collected short fiction, 1892–1912 / edited by Virginia Faulkner; introd. by Mildred R. Bennett. — [Rev. ed.] Lincoln: University of Nebraska Press [1970] xli, 600 p.; 25 cm. I. T.
PZ3.C2858 Co5 PS3505.A87 Ax   813/.5/2   *LC* 73-126046   *ISBN* 0803207700

Cather, Willa, 1873-1947. • **2.11472**
The novels and stories of Willa Cather ... Library ed. [Boston, Houghton Mifflin company, 1937-41] 13 v. 9 front. (v. 6, 8-11: facsims.) illus., port. 22 cm. Half-title; each volume has special t.-p. I. T.
PS3505.A87 Ax   *LC* a 43-1040

Cather, Willa, 1873-1947. **2.11473**
The troll garden / Willa Cather. — A definitive ed. / edited by James Woodress; with introduction, notes, textual commentary, emendations, and table of revisions. — Lincoln: Published by the University of Nebraska Press for the Center for Great Plains Studies, University of Nebraska—Lincoln, c1983. xxx, 176 p.; 23 cm. I. Woodress, James Leslie. II. University of Nebraska—Lincoln. Center for Great Plains Studies. III. T.
PS3505.A87 T7 1983   813/.52 19   *LC* 82-20138   *ISBN* 0803214170

Bloom, Edward Alan, 1914-. • **2.11474**
Willa Cather's gift of sympathy / [by] Edward A. Bloom and Lillian D. Bloom; with a pref. by Harry T. Moore. — Carbondale: Southern Illinois University Press, [1962] 260 p.; 22 cm. (Crosscurrents: modern critiques) 1. Cather, Willa, 1873-1947. I. Bloom, Lillian D. joint author. II. T.
PS3505.A87 Z583   813.52   *LC* 62-7231

Brown, E. K. (Edward Killoran), 1905-1951. • **2.11475**
Willa Cather, a critical biography [by] E. K. Brown; completed by Leon Edel. — [1st ed.]. — New York, Knopf, 1953. xxiv, 351 p. port. 22 cm. 1. Cather, Willa, 1873-1947. I. T.
PS3505.A87 Z584   928.1   *LC* 52-12204

Critical essays on Willa Cather / [compiled by] John J. **2.11476**
Murphy.
Boston, Mass.: G.K. Hall, c1984. viii, 310 p.; 25 cm. — (Critical essays on American literature.) 1. Cather, Willa, 1873-1947 — Criticism and interpretation — Collected works. I. Murphy, John J. (John Joseph), 1933- II. Series.
PS3505.A87 Z593 1984   813/.52 19   *LC* 83-12612   *ISBN* 0816186766

Randall, John Herman, 1923-. • **2.11477**
The landscape and the looking glass: Willa Cather's search for value / by John H. Randall III. — Boston: Houghton Mifflin, 1960. xv, 425 p.: ill.; 22 cm. 1. Cather, Willa, 1873-1947. I. T.
PS3505.A87 Z78 1973   813/.5/2   *LC* 60-6225

Sergeant, Elizabeth Shepley, 1881-. • **2.11478**
Willa Cather, a memoir. [n.p.] University of Nebraska Press [1963] 303 p. illus. 21 cm. (A Bison book) 1. Cather, Willa, 1873-1947. I. T.
PS3505.A87 Z83 1963   928.1   *LC* 63-3155

PS3505 Ch

Chandler, Raymond, 1888-1959. • **2.11479**
The Raymond Chandler omnibus: four famous classics / foreword by Lawrence Clark Powell. — 1st collected ed. — New York: Knopf: distributed by Random House, 1964. viii, 625 p. — I. T.
PS3505.H3224 Ax

Durham, Philip, 1912-. • **2.11480**
Down these mean streets a man must go; Raymond Chandler's knight. [Chapel Hill, University of North Carolina Press, 1963] viii, 173 p.; 22 cm. 1. Chandler, Raymond, 1888-1959. I. T.
PS3505.H3224 Z64   818.52   *LC* 63-21075

MacShane, Frank. **2.11481**
The life of Raymond Chandler / Frank MacShane. — 1st ed. — New York: E. P. Dutton, c1976. xii, 306 p., [8] leaves of plates: ill.; 25 cm. 1. Chandler, Raymond, 1888-1959 — Biography. 2. Authors, American — 20th century — Biography. I. T.
PS3505.H3224 Z7   813/.5/2 B   *LC* 75-38791   *ISBN* 0525145524

Chase, Mary Ellen, 1887-1973. • **2.11482**
The edge of darkness. [1st ed.] New York: Norton, 1957. 235 p.; 22 cm. I. T.
PS3505H48 E3 1957   *LC* 57-10637

Chase, Mary Ellen, 1887-1973.   **2.11483**
Mary Peters, by Mary Ellen Chase. New York, The Macmillan company, 1934.
377 p.; 20 cm. I. T.
PZ3.C3901 Mar PS3505.H48M3   *LC* 34-27262

Chase, Mary Ellen, 1887-1973.   • **2.11484**
Silas Crockett / by Mary Ellen Chase. — New York: The Macmillan company,
1935. x, 404 p.: ill.; 21 cm. I. T.
PZ3.C3901 Si   PS3505.H48 S5.   *LC* 35-25387

Chase, Mary Ellen, 1887-1973.   • **2.11485**
Windswept, by Mary Ellen Chase. — New York: Macmillan, 1944 [c1941]
440 p.: ill.; 22 cm. I. T.
PZ3.C3901 Wi   PS3505.H48 W54.   *LC* 41-21397

Westbrook, Perry D.   • **2.11486**
Mary Ellen Chase / by Perry D. Westbrook. — New York: Twayne Publishers,
[1965] 176 p.; 21 cm. (Twayne's United States authors series, 86) 1. Chase,
Mary Ellen, 1887-1973. I. T.
PS3505.H48 Z96   818.52   *LC* 65-18905

Chayefsky, Paddy, 1923-.   **2.11487**
Altered states: a novel / by Paddy Chayevsky. — 1st ed. — New York: Harper &
Row, c1978. 184 p.; 22 cm. — I. T.
PZ4.C5136 Al 1978 PS3505.H632   813/.5/4   *LC* 77-11542   *ISBN*
0060107278

Chayefsky, Paddy, 1923-.   • **2.11488**
The tenth man, a new play. — New York: Random House, [1960] 154 p.: illus.;
22 cm. — I. T.
PS3505.H632 T4   812.54   *LC* 60-8375

Clum, John M.   **2.11489**
Paddy Chayefsky / by John M. Clum. Boston: Twayne Publishers, c1976.
149 p.: port.; 21 cm. (Twayne's United States authors series; TUSAS 272)
1. Chayefsky, Paddy, 1923- I. T.
PS3505.H632 Z56   812/.5/4   *LC* 76-7363   *ISBN* 0805771727

Cheever, John.   **2.11490**
The stories of John Cheever. — 1st ed. — New York: Knopf, 1978. viii, 693 p.;
25 cm. Short stories, published 1946-75. I. T.
PZ3.C3983 St PS3505.H6428 Ax   813/.5/2   *LC* 78-160   *ISBN*
0395500873

Cheever, John.   • **2.11491**
Bullet Park: a novel. — [1st ed.]. — New York: Knopf, 1969. 245 p.; 22 cm. —
I. T.
PS3505.H6428 B8   813/.5/2   *LC* 69-14730

Cheever, John.   **2.11492**
Falconer / John Cheever. — 1st ed. — New York: Knopf, 1977. 211 p.; 22 cm.
— I. T.
PZ3.C3983 Fal3 PS3505.H6428F3   813/.5/2   *LC* 76-19382   *ISBN*
0394483472

Cheever, John, 1912-.   • **2.11493**
The Wapshot chronicle. — [1st ed.]. — New York: Harper, [1957] 307 p.; 22
cm. — I. T.
PS3505.H6428 W3x   *LC* 56-11100

Cheever, John, 1912-.   • **2.11494**
The Wapshot scandal. — New York: Harper & Row, [c1964] 309 p.; 22 cm. —
I. T.
PS3505.H6428 W4x   *LC* 63-20301

Cheever, John.   • **2.11495**
The world of apples. — [1st ed.]. — New York: Knopf, 1973. 174 p.; 22 cm. —
I. T.
PZ3.C3983 Wo PS3505.H6428 W6x   813/.5/2   *LC* 72-11018
     ISBN 0394483464

Cheever, Susan.   **2.11496**
Home before dark / Susan Cheever. — Boston: Houghton Mifflin, 1984. x,
243 p., [16] p. of plates: ill.; 22 cm. 1. Cheever, John — Biography.
2. Novelists, American — 20th century — Biography. I. T.
PS3505.H6428 Z59 1984   813/.52 B 19   *LC* 84-9057   *ISBN*
0395352975

Hunt, George W., 1937-.   **2.11497**
John Cheever, the hobgoblin company of love / George W. Hunt. — Grand
Rapids: Eerdmans, c1983. xxi, 326 p.; 24 cm. 1. Cheever, John — Criticism
and interpretation. I. T.
PS3505.H6428 Z69 1983   813/.52 19   *LC* 83-1560   *ISBN*
0802835767

PS3505 Ci–Cl

Ciardi, John, 1916-.   **2.11498**
[Poems. Selections] Selected poems / John Ciardi. — Fayetteville: University of
Arkansas Press, c1984. xi, 222 p.; 24 cm. I. T.
PS3505.I27 A6 1984   811/.52 19   *LC* 83-24254   *ISBN* 0938626299

Ciardi, John, 1916-.   • **2.11499**
As if: poems new and selected. — New Brunswick, N.J.: Rutgers University
Press, 1955. 143 p.; 22 cm. — I. T.
PS3505.I27 A75   811.5   *LC* 55-9956

Ciardi, John, 1916-.   • **2.11500**
In the stoneworks: poems. New Brunswick, N.J.: Rutgers University Press,
c1961. 83 p. Poems. I. T.
PS3505.I27 I5   *LC* 61-10256

Ciardi, John, 1916-.   **2.11501**
The little that is all. — New Brunswick, N.J.: Rutgers University Press, [1974]
x, 86 p.; 22 cm. Poems. I. T.
PS3505.I27 L47   811/.5/2   *LC* 74-6238   *ISBN* 0813507766

Ciardi, John, 1916-.   • **2.11502**
39 poems. — New Brunswick, N.J.: Rutgers University Press, 1959. 86 p.; 22
cm. — I. T.
PS3505.I27 T5   811.52   *LC* 59-15628

Clark, Walter Van Tilburg, 1909-1971.   • **2.11503**
The city of trembling leaves / [by] Walter Van Tilburg Clark. — [1st ed.] New
York: Random House, [c1945] 690 p.; 20 cm. I. T.
PS3505.L376 C5   813.5   *LC* 45-35081

Clark, Walter Van Tilburg, 1909-1971.   • **2.11504**
The Ox–Bow incident. — New York: Random House, [1957] 309 p.; 19 cm. —
(Modern library paperbacks, P31) I. T.
PZ3.C5483 Ox4   PS3505.L376 Ox.   *LC* 57-11399

Clark, Walter Van Tilburg, 1909-1971.   • **2.11505**
The track of the cat: a novel. — New York: Random House, [1949] 404 p.; 22
cm. I. T.
PS3505.L376 T73   *LC* 49-9031

Clark, Walter Van Tilburg, 1909-1971.   • **2.11506**
The watchful gods, and other stories. New York, Random House [1950] 306 p.
21 cm. I. T.
PS3505.L376 W3   813.5   *LC* 50-9687

PS3505 Co

Coffin, Robert Peter Tristram, 1892-1955.   • **2.11507**
Collected poems. New and enl. ed. New York, Macmillan, 1948. xxxiii, 446 p.
port. 22 cm. I. T.
PS3505.O234 A17 1948   *LC* 48-2263

Colum, Mary (Maguire)   **2.11508**
Life and the dream [by] Mary Colum. — [Rev. ed. with additional material. —
Chester Springs, Pa.]: Dufour Editions, [1966] 378 p.: port.; 26 cm.
Autobiographical. I. T.
PS3505.O3765 Z5 1966a   818/.5/203   *LC* 66-15455

Connelly, Marc, 1890-.   • **2.11509**
The green pastures: a fable, suggested by Roark Bradford's southern sketches,
'Ol' man Adam an' his chillun' / by Marc Connelly. — New York: Farrar &
Rinehart, [1930] xvi, 173 p.; 20 cm. In dramatic form, with cast of characters as
presented at the Mansfield theatre, New York, 1930. Attempts 'to present
certain aspects of a living religion in the terms of its believers ... thousands of
negroes in the deep South.'—p. xv. 1. Afro-Americans — Religion 2. Afro-
American folk-lore I. T.
PS3505.O4814 G7 1930   *LC* 30-19513

Cowley, Malcolm, 1898-.   • **2.11510**
Blue Juniata; collected poems. — New York: Viking Press, [1968] x, 149 p.; 22
cm. — I. T.
PS3505.O956 B6 1968   811/.5/2   *LC* 68-28027

Cowley, Malcolm, 1898-.   **2.11511**
The dream of the golden mountains: remembering the 1930s / by Malcolm
Cowley. — New York: Viking Press, 1980 [c1979] xii, 328 p., [4] leaves of
plates: ill.; 22 cm. Includes index. 1. Cowley, Malcolm, 1898- — Biography.
2. Communism and literature 3. Authors, American — 20th century —
Biography. 4. United States — Civilization — 1918-1945 I. T.
PS3505.O956 Z464 1980   811/.52 B 19   *LC* 79-18485   *ISBN*
0670284742

Cozzens, James Gould, 1903-.   • 2.11512
Ask me tomorrow: or, The pleasant comedy of young fortunatus. — New York: Harcourt, Brace & World, [c1968] 342 p.; 22 cm. I. T. II. Title: The pleasant comedy of young fortunatus.
PZ3.C83983 As5 PS3505.O99 A8x   813/.5/2   LC 70-1358

Cozzens, James Gould, 1903-.   • 2.11513
By love possessed. — [1st ed.]. — New York: Harcourt, Brace, [1957] 570 p.; 22 cm. — I. T.
PZ3.C83983 By   PS3505.O99 B8.   LC 57-10062

Cozzens, James Gould, 1903-.   • 2.11514
Castaway. — New York: Harcourt, Brace & World, 1967 (c1962). 115 p.; 21 cm. I. T.
PS3505.O99 C3   LC 67-19207

Cozzens, James Gould, 1903-.   • 2.11515
Guard of honor. — [1st ed.]. — New York: Harcourt, Brace, [1948] 631 p.; 21 cm. 1. World War, 1939-1945 — Fiction. I. T.
PZ3.C83983 Gu   PS3505.O99 G7.   LC 48-8544

Cozzens, James Gould, 1903-.   • 2.11516
The just and the unjust. — 1st ed. — New York: Harcourt, Brace and company, [1942] 3-434 p.; 21 cm. I. T.
PZ3.C83983 Ju   PS3505.O99 J8.   LC 42-17992

Cozzens, James Gould, 1903-.   • 2.11517
The last Adam. [1st ed.] New York: Harcourt, Brace, [1956? c1933] 314 p.; 19 cm. (Harvest books, 12.) I. T.
PS3505.O99 L3   LC 33-1357

Cozzens, James Gould, 1903-.   • 2.11518
Men and brethren. — New York: Harcourt Brace Jovanovich, [1970, c1936] 185 p.; 21 cm. — I. T.
PZ3.C83983 Me6 PS3505.O99 M4x   813/.5/2   LC 70-16039
ISBN 0151591369

Cozzens, James Gould, 1903-.   • 2.11519
Morning, noon, and night. — [1st ed.]. — New York: Harcourt, Brace & World, [1968] 408 p.; 21 cm. — I. T.
PS3505.O99 M66   LC 68-20064

Cozzens, James Gould.   • 2.11520
The son of perdition / by James Gould Cozzens. — New York: William Morrow & Co., 1929. 304 p.; 20 cm. I. T.
PS3505.O99 Sx

Cozzens, James Gould, 1903-.   • 2.11521
S. S. San Pedro. — New York: Harcourt, Brace & World, [1967, c1931] 85 p.; 20 cm. — I. T.
PZ3.C83983 S2   PS3505.O99 Sx.   LC 67-19206

Bruccoli, Matthew Joseph, 1931-.   2.11522
James Gould Cozzens: a life apart / Matthew J. Bruccoli. — 1st ed. — San Diego: Harcourt Brace Jovanovich, c1983. xxiii, 343 p.: ill.; 24 cm. 1. Cozzens, James Gould, 1903- — Biography. 2. Novelists, American — 20th century — Biography. I. T.
PS3505.O99 Z59 1983   813/.52 19   LC 82-23312   ISBN 0151460485

PS3505 Cr

Crane, Hart, 1899-1932.   • 2.11523
The complete poems and selected letters and prose of Hart Crane; edited with an introduction and notes by Brom Weber. — 1st ed. reprinted lithographically. — London: Oxford U.P., 1968. xvii, 302 p.: ports.; 23 cm. I. Weber, Brom, 1917- II. T.
PS3505.R272 1968   818/.5/209   LC 77-376085   ISBN 0192125443

Hanley, Alfred, 1942-.   2.11524
Hart Crane's holy vision, White buildings / by Alfred Hanley. — 1st ed. — Pittsburgh, Pa.: Duquesne University Press, c1981. 194 p.; 22 cm. 1. Crane, Hart, 1899-1932. White buildings. 2. Crane, Hart, 1899-1932 — Religion. I. T.
PS3505.R272 W534   811/.52 19   LC 81-12656   ISBN 0820701513

Crane, Hart, 1899-1932.   2.11525
Letters of Hart Crane and his family. Edited by Thomas S. W. Lewis. — New York: Columbia University Press, 1974. xxiv, 675 p.; 23 cm. 1. Crane, Hart, 1899-1932 — Biography. 2. Crane family I. T.
PS3505.R272 Z54 1974   811/.5/2 B   LC 73-21675   ISBN 0231037406

Butterfield, R. W.   • 2.11526
The broken arc: a study of Hart Crane [by] R. W. Butterfield. — Edinburgh: Oliver & Boyd, 1969. xii, 276 p.; 23 cm. — (Biography and criticism, 13) 1. Crane, Hart, 1899-1932. I. T.
PS3505.R272 Z6   811/.5/2   LC 70-438054

Hart Crane: a collection of critical essays / edited by Alan   2.11527
Trachtenberg.
Englewood Cliffs, NJ: Prentice-Hall, c1982. iv, 224 p.; 21 cm. — (A Spectrum book) 1. Crane, Hart, 1899-1932 — Criticism and interpretation — Addresses, essays, lectures. I. Trachtenberg, Alan.
PS3505.R272 Z673   811/.52 19   LC 80-25616   ISBN 0133839354

Leibowitz, Herbert A.   • 2.11528
Hart Crane; an introduction to the poetry [by] Herbert A. Leibowitz. — New York: Columbia University Press, 1968. 308 p.; 20 cm. 1. Crane, Hart, 1899-1932. I. T.
PS3505.R272 Z73   LC 68-13559

Lewis, R. W. B. (Richard Warrington Baldwin).   • 2.11529
The poetry of Hart Crane; a critical study [by] R. W. B. Lewis. — Princeton, Princeton University Press, 1967. 426 p. 25 cm. Bibliographical footnotes. 1. Crane, Hart, 1899-1932. I. T.
PS3505.R272Z74   811/.5/2   LC 67-14411

Paul, Sherman.   2.11530
Hart's Bridge. — Urbana: University of Illinois Press, [1972] viii, 315 p.; 24 cm. 1. Crane, Hart, 1899-1932. I. T.
PS3505.R272 Z76   811/.5/2   LC 76-188133   ISBN 0252002571

Unterecker, John Eugene, 1922-.   • 2.11531
Voyager; a life of Hart Crane, by John Unterecker. — New York: Farrar, Straus and Giroux, [1969] xii, 787 p.: illus.; 25 cm. 1. Crane, Hart, 1899-1932 — Biography. I. T.
PS3505.R272 Z797   811/.5/2 B   LC 69-11575

Dickie, Margaret, 1935-.   2.11532
Hart Crane: the patterns of his poetry [by] M. D. Uroff. — Urbana: University of Illinois Press, [1974] 236 p.; 24 cm. 1. Crane, Hart, 1899-1932 — Criticism and interpretation. I. T.
PS3505.R272 Z798   PS3505 R272 Z798.   811/.5/2   LC 74-8906
ISBN 0252003934

Creeley, Robert, 1926-.   2.11533
[Poems. Selections] The collected poems of Robert Creeley, 1945-1975. — Berkeley: University of California Press, 1983 (c1982). x, 671 p.; 22 cm. Includes index. I. T.
PS3505.R43 A17 1982   811/.54 19   LC 81-19668   ISBN 0520042433

Creeley, Robert, 1922-.   • 2.11534
The gold diggers, and other stories. New York, Scribner [1965] 158 p. 21 cm. I. T.
PZ4.C9134Go PS3505.R43G6   LC 65-23982

PS3505 Cu–Cz

Cullen, Countee, 1903-1946.   • 2.11535
On these I stand: an anthology of the best poems of Countee Cullen / selected by himself and including six new poems never before published. — New York; London: Harper & brothers, [1947] x, 197, [1] p.; 21 cm. 'First edition.' I. T.
PS3505.U334 1968   PS3505.U287 A6 1947.   811.5   LC 47-30109

Cullen, Countee, 1903-1946.   2.11536
Color. — New York: Arno Press, 1969 [c1925] xvii, 108 p.; 21 cm. — (The American Negro, his history and literature) (Afro-American culture series.) Poems. I. T. II. Series. III. Series: Afro-American culture series.
PS3505.U287 C6 1969   811/.5/2   LC 70-101515

Cummings, E. E. (Edward Estlin), 1894-1962.   • 2.11537
E. E. Cummings: a miscellany revised / edited with an introd. and notes, by George J. Firmage; foreword by the author. — [1st ed.] New York: October House [1965] viii, 335 p.: ill., port.; 23 cm. A republication of E. E. Cummings: a miscellany, with additional material.
PS3505.U334 A16 1965   818.52   LC 64-13163

Cummings, E. E. (Edward Estlin), 1894-1962.   • 2.11538
Complete poems, 1913-1962. [1st American ed.] New York, Harcourt, Brace, Jovanovich [1972] xxvi, 866 p. 24 cm. I. T.
PS3505.U334 A17 1972   811/.5/2   LC 72-78457   ISBN 0151210608

Cummings, E. E. (Edward Estlin), 1894-1962. • 2.11539
Eimi. 4th ed. New York: Grove Press, [1958, c1933] xix, 432 p.; 21cm. Author's diary,May 10-June 14,1931,recorded during his trip to Russia and Turkey. I. T.
PS3505.U334 E5 1958a   817.5   LC 58-11213

Cummings, E. E. (Edward Estlin), 1894-1962. • 2.11540
i: six nonlectures / E.E. Cummings. — [1st ed.]. — Cambridge: Harvard University Press, c1953. 118 p.; 24 cm. (Charles Eliot Norton lectures. 1952-1953.) I. T. II. Series.
PS3505.U334 Z5   818.5   LC 53-10472   ISBN 0674440102

Cummings, E. E. (Edward Estlin), 1894-1962. • 2.11541
Selected letters of E. E. Cummings / edited by F. W. Dupee and George Stade. — [1st ed.] New York: Harcourt, Brace & World, [1969] xxiv, 296 p.: ill., ports.; 24 cm. I. Dupee, F. W. (Frederick Wilcox), 1904- ed. II. Stade, George. ed. III. T.
PS3505.U334 Z53   811/.5/2   LC 69-12032

Friedman, Norman. comp. • 2.11542
E. E. Cummings: a collection of critical essays. Englewood Cliffs, N.J., Prentice-Hall [1972] vi, 185 p. 21 cm. (A Spectrum book: Twentieth century views) 1. Cummings, E. E. (Edward Estlin), 1894-1962. I. T.
PS3505.U334 Z64   811/.5/2   LC 74-163857   ISBN 0131955527
ISBN 0131955454

Friedman, Norman. • 2.11543
E. E. Cummings, the art of his poetry. Baltimore, Johns Hopkins Press [1960] 195 p. facsim. 22 cm. 1. Cummings, E. E. (Edward Estlin), 1894-1962. I. T.
PS3505.U334 Z65   811.52   LC 60-9771

Norman, Charles, 1904-. • 2.11544
The magic-maker, E. E. Cummings. New York: Macmillan, 1958. 400 p.: ill.; 22 cm. 1. Cummings, E. E. (Edward Estlin), 1894-1962. I. T.
PS3505.U334 Z8   928.1   LC 58-12439

Wegner, Robert E. • 2.11545
The poetry and prose of E. E. Cummings [by] Robert E. Wegner. [1st ed.] New York, Harcourt, Brace & World [1965] ix, 177 p. 21 cm. 1. Cummings, E. E. (Edward Estlin), 1894-1962. I. T.
PS3505.U334 Z95   811.52   LC 64-11544

Cunningham, J. V. (James Vincent), 1911-. 2.11546
The collected essays of J. V. Cunningham. 1st ed. — Chicago: Swallow Press, 1977. xi, 463 p.; 24 cm. 1. English literature — History and criticism — Addresses, essays, lectures. 2. American poetry — History and criticism — Addresses, essays, lectures. I. T.
PS3505.U435 A16 1976   814/.5/4   LC 75-21800   ISBN 0804006709

PS3507 Da

Dahlberg, Edward, 1900-1977. • 2.11547
Bottom dogs / with an introduction by D.H. Lawrence. — New York: Simon and Schuster, 1930. xvii, 269 p. I. T.
PZ3.D1374 Bo   PS3507.A33 B6.   813/.5/2   LC 30-6431

Dahlberg, Edward, 1900-1977. • 2.11548
Can these bones live / with 42 drawings by James Kearns and a pref. by Herbert Read. — Rev. ed. New York: New Directions, 1960. 177 p.: ill.; 23 cm. I. Dahlberg, Edward, 1900-1977. Do these bones live. II. Kearns, James. III. Read, Herbert Edward, Sir, 1893-1968. IV. T. V. Title: Do these bones live.
PS3507.A33 D6 1960   LC 60-9220

Dahlberg, Edward, 1900-1977. • 2.11549
From Flushing to Calvary / by Edward Dahlberg. — New York: Harcourt, Brace, [c1932] 293 p.; 21 cm. I. T.
PS3507.A33 Fx   LC 32-28968

Dahlberg, Edward, 1900-1977. • 2.11550
Those who perish / Edward Dahlberg. — New York: John Day Company, c1934. 242 p.; 20 cm. I. T.
PZ3.D1374 Th   PS3507.A33 T46.   LC 34-28620

Dahlberg, Edward, 1900-1977. • 2.11551
Because I was flesh: the autobiography of Edward Dahlberg. — [New York]: New Directions, c1963. 234 p.; 21 cm. 1. Dahlberg, Edward, 1900-1977 — Biography. I. T.
PS3507.A33 Z5   LC 64-10079

Moramarco, Fred S., 1938-. • 2.11552
Edward Dahlberg, by Fred Moramarco. — New York: Twayne Publishers, [1972] 171 p.; 21 cm. — (Twayne's United States authors series, 206) 1. Dahlberg, Edward, 1900-1977. I. T.
PS3507.A33 Z7   818/.5/209   LC 75-187606

Davidson, Donald, 1893-1968. • 2.11553
Poems, 1922–1961. Minneapolis: University of Minnesota, [1966] 183 p.; 23 cm. I. T.
B945.Q54 D38 1969   PS3507.A666 A6 1966.   LC 66-13261

Young, Thomas Daniel, 1919-. • 2.11554
Donald Davidson, by Thomas Daniel Young and M. Thomas Inge. New York, Twayne Publishers [c1971] 173 p. 21 cm. (Twayne's United States authors series, TUSAS 190) 1. Davidson, Donald, 1893-1968. I. Inge, M. Thomas. joint author. II. T.
PS3507.A666 Z89   818/.5/209   LC 72-125815

Day, Clarence, 1874-1935. • 2.11555
The best of Clarence Day: including God and my father, Life with mother, Life with father, This simian world, and selections from Thoughts without words. — [1st ed.]. — New York: A. A. Knopf, 1948. x, 451 p.: ill.; 22 cm. — I. T.
PS3507.A858 B4   818.5   LC 48-6580

PS3507 De–Di

De La Torre, Lillian, 1902-. 2.11556
Dr. Sam: Johnson, detector; being a light–hearted collection of recently reveal'd episodes in the career of the great lexicographer narrated as from the pen of James Boswell ... By Lillian De La Torre. — New York: A. A. Knopf, 1946. xi, 257, [1] p.: col. ill.; 19 cm. — (Borzoi book.) 1. Johnson, Samuel, 1709-1784. in fiction, drama, poetry, etc. I. T. II. Series.
PZ3.D37615 Do   PS3507.E45 D63.   LC 46-6547

Derleth, August William, 1909-1971. • 2.11557
Wind over Wisconsin. New York: Grosset & Dunlap, [c1938] 391 p.; 21 cm. I. T.
PS3507.E69 Wx   813.5

Deutsch, Babette, 1895-. • 2.11558
The collected poems. — [1st ed.]. — Garden City, N.Y.: Doubleday, 1969. xxii, 230 p.; 22 cm. — I. T.
PS3507.E84 A17 1969   811/.5/2   LC 68-22508

De Voto, Bernard Augustine, 1897-1955. • 2.11559
The easy chair. — Boston: Houghton Mifflin, [c1955] xi, 356 p.; 21 cm. 1. United States. I. T.
PS3507.E867 E2   LC 55-9969

Stegner, Wallace Earle, 1909-. 2.11560
The uneasy chair: a biography of Bernard DeVoto / [by] Wallace Stegner. — [1st ed.]. — Garden City, N.Y.: Doubleday, 1974. xi, 464 p.: ill.; 24 cm. 1. De Voto, Bernard Augustine, 1897-1955 — Biography. I. T.
PS3507.E867 Z9   818/.5/209 B   LC 73-81985   ISBN 0385078846

De Vries, Peter. • 2.11561
The blood of the lamb: a novel. — Boston: Little, Brown, [1961] 246 p. I. T.
PS3507.E8673 B56   LC 62-8060

De Vries, Peter. • 2.11562
The Mackerel plaza / by Peter De Vries. — Boston; Toronto: Little, Brown, 1958. 260 p. I. T.
PZ3.D4998Mac   PS3507.E8673 M34.   LC 58-6032

De Vries, Peter. • 2.11563
The tents of wickedness. Boston, Little, Brown, 1959. 276 p. I. T.
PS3507.E8673 T4   LC 59-11106

De Vries, Peter. • 2.11564
The tunnel of love / Peter De Vries. — Boston: Little Brown, 1954. 246 p. I. T.
PS3507.E8673 T85   LC 54-6879

De Vries, Peter. • 2.11565
Without a stitch in time: a selection of the best humorous short pieces. — [1st ed.]. — Boston: Little, Brown, [1972] viii, 328 p.; 21 cm. Short stories. I. T.
PZ3.D4998 Wi   PS3507.E8673 Wx.   813/.5/2   LC 72-5163
ISBN 0316181862

Di Donato, Pietro, 1911-. • 2.11566
Christ in concrete: a novel / by Pietro di Donato. — Indianapolis: Bobbs-Merrill, [1939]. 311 p.; 22 cm. I. T.
PS3507.I37 C57 1939   LC 39-10762   ISBN 067252161X

PS3507 Do

Doolittle, Hilda, 1866-1961. • 2.11567
Selected poems / H.D. [i.e. H. Doolittle]. — New York: Grove Press, 1957.
128 p.; 22 cm. I. T.
PS3507.O726 A6 1957   811.52   *LC* 57-8646 rev.

H. D. (Hilda Doolittle), 1886-1961. 2.11568
[Poems. Selections] Collected poems, 1912–1944 / H.D.; edited by Louis L.
Martz. — New York: New Directions, 1983. xxxvi, 629 p.; 24 cm. I. Martz,
Louis Lohr. II. T.
PS3507.O726 A6 1983   811/.52 19   *LC* 83-6380   *ISBN*
0811208761

H. D. (Hilda Doolittle), 1886-1961. • 2.11569
Bid me to live: a madrigal / by H.D. New York: Grove Press [1960] 184 p.; 21
cm. I. T.
PS3507.O726 B5   813.5   *LC* 60-6345

H. D. (Hilda Doolittle), 1886-1961. 2.11570
The gift / H.D. — New York: New Directions, c1982. xv, 142 p.: ports.; 21 cm.
I. T.
PS3507.O726 G5 1982   813/.52 19   *LC* 82-8207   *ISBN*
0811208532

H. D. (Hilda Doolittle), 1886-1961. • 2.11571
Helen in Egypt / by H. D.; introd. by Horace Gregory. — New York: Grove
Press, c1961. xi, 315 p. Poem. 1. Helen of Troy — Poetry. I. T.
PS3507.O726 H37   811   *LC* 61-12764

H. D. (Hilda Doolittle), 1886-1961. • 2.11572
Hermetic definition / by H.D.; [foreword by Norman Holmes Pearson]. —
[New York: New Directions Pub. Corp., 1972] [v], 117 p.; 21 cm. — (New
Directions book.) Poems. I. T. II. Series.
PS3507.O726 H44 1972   811/.5/2

H. D. (Hilda Doolittle), 1886-1961. 2.11573
Trilogy: The walls do not fall, Tribute to the angels, The flowering of the rod /
by H. D. — [New York: New Directions, 1973] xii, 172 p.; 21 cm. (A New
Directions book) I. T.
PS3507.O726 T74 1973   811/.5/2   *LC* 73-78848   *ISBN*
0811204901

Quinn, Vincent Gerard, 1926-. • 2.11574
Hilda Doolittle (H. D.) by Vincent Quinn. New York, Twayne Publishers
[1968, c1967] 160 p. 21 cm. (Twayne's United States authors series, 126) 1. H.
D. (Hilda Doolittle), 1886-1961. I. T.
PS3507.O726 Z84   818/.5/209   *LC* 67-28856

Dorn, Edward. 2.11575
Selected poems / Edward Dorn; pref. by Robert Creeley; edited by Donald
Allen. — Bolinas, Calif.: Grey Fox Press, c1978. viii, 92 p.; 22 cm. Includes
index. I. Allen, Donald Merriam, 1912- II. T.
PS3507.O73277 A17 1978   811/.5/4   *LC* 78-2925   *ISBN*
0912516321

Dorn, Edward. 2.11576
Slinger / by Edward Dorn. — 1st ed. — Berkeley, Calif.: Wingbow Press:
distributed by Bookpeople, 1975. [206] p.; 23 cm. Title on spine: Gunslinger. A
poem consisting of 5 pts.: Book 1-4, and Cycle; all were previously published
except Book 4; Book 1-3 were originally published under title: Gunslinger 1-3.
I. T. II. Title: Gunslinger.
PS3507.O73277 S5   811/.5/4   *LC* 75-3658   *ISBN* 0914728067

Dos Passos, John, 1896-1970. 2.11577
Century's ebb: the thirteenth chronicle / by John Dos Passos. — Boston:
Gambit, 1975. xiii, 474 p.; 22 cm. I. T.
PZ3.D74 Ce3 PS3507.O743 C4x   813/.5/2   *LC* 75-920   *ISBN*
0876450893

Dos Passos, John, 1896-1970. • 2.11578
Chosen country. Boston: Houghton Mifflin. 1951. 485 p. I. T.
PS3507.O743 C5   *LC* 51-7856

Dos Passos, John, 1896-1970. • 2.11579
District of Columbia. — Boston: Houghton Mifflin, 1952. xii, 342, 248, 446 p.
I. Dos Passos, John, 1896-1970. Adventures of a young man. II. Dos Passos,
John, 1896-1970. Number one. III. Dos Passos, John, 1896-1970. Grand
design. IV. T. V. Title: Adventures of a young man. VI. Title: Number one.
VII. Title: The grand design.
PS3507.O743 D5 1952   *LC* 52-7617

Dos Passos, John, 1896-1970. • 2.11580
First encounter. — New York: Philosophical Library, [1945] 160 p.
1. European War, 1914-1918 — Fiction. I. T. II. Title: 1st encounter.
PS3507.O743 F5 1945   *LC* a 45-5412

Dos Passos, John, 1896-1970. • 2.11581
The great days. — New York: Sagamore Press, [1958] 312 p.; 22 cm. I. T.
PS3507.O743 G7 1958   PZ3.D74 Gt.   *LC* 58-6966

Dos Passos, John, 1896-1970. • 2.11582
Manhattan transfer. Boston: Houghton Mifflin [1963? c1953] 404 p.; 20 cm.
(Sentry edition) I. T.
PS3507.O743M3 1963   *LC* 64-9120

Dos Passos, John, 1896-1970. • 2.11583
Midcentury. Boston, Houghton Mifflin, 1961. 496 p. 23 cm. I. T.
PZ3.D74Mi PS3507.O743M5   *LC* 61-5359

Dos Passos, John, 1896-1970. • 2.11584
Most likely to succeed. Boston: Houghton Mifflin, 1966 [c1954] 310 p.; 22 cm.
I. T.
PS3507.O743 M6 1966   *LC* 66-17513

Dos Passos, John, 1896-1970. • 2.11585
Three soldiers / introduction by John Dos Passos. — [New York]: Modern
Library, [c1932] 471 p. — (Modern library of the world's best books.) 1. World
War, 1914-1918 — Fiction. I. T. II. Title: 3 soldiers. III. Series.
PS3507.O743 T48 1932   *LC* 32-33154

Dos Passos, John, 1896-1970. • 2.11586
U. S. A. I. The 42nd parallel. II. Nineteen nineteen. III. The big money. By
John Dos Passos. New York, The Modern library [1939] [1473] p. 21 cm.
Various pagings. 'First Modern library giant edition. I. T. II. Title: 42nd
parallel. III. Title: Nineteen nineteen. IV. Title: Big money.
PS3507.O743Ux   *LC* 39-21677

Becker, George Joseph. 2.11587
John Dos Passos / George J. Becker. — New York: F. Ungar Pub. Co., [1974]
ix, 133 p.; 21 cm. (Modern literature monographs) Includes index. 1. Dos
Passos, John, 1896-1970. I. T.
PS3507.O743 Z5456   813/.5/2   *LC* 74-78437   *ISBN* 0804420345

Hook, Andrew. comp. 2.11588
Dos Passos: a collection of critical essays. — Englewood Cliffs, N.J.: Prentice-
Hall, [1974] vi, 186 p.; 21 cm. — (Twentieth century views) (A Spectrum book)
1. Dos Passos, John, 1896-1970 — Criticism and interpretation. I. T.
PS3507.O743 Z58   813/.5/2   *LC* 73-21561   *ISBN* 0132188678

Wrenn, John H. • 2.11589
John Dos Passos. — New York: Twayne Publishers, [1962, c1961] 208 p.; 21
cm. — (Twayne's United States authors series, 9) 1. Dos Passos, John,
1896-1970. I. T.
PS3507.O743 Z93 1962   813.52   *LC* 61-15669

PS3507 Dreiser

Dreiser, Theodore, 1871-1945. • 2.11590
Best short stories. With an introd. by James T. Farrell. — Cleveland: World
Pub. Co., [c1956] 349 p.; 21 cm. — I. T.
PS3507.R55 A15 1956   PZ3.D814 Be3   *LC* 56-5948

Dreiser, Theodore, 1871-1945. • 2.11591
An American tragedy / illustrated by Grant Reynard; introd. by H. L.
Mencken. — New York: World Pub. Co., [1971, c1948] 874 p.: ill.; 21 cm. I. T.
PZ3.D814 Am 35 PS3507.R55 A6x   813/.5/2   *LC* 75-31583

Dreiser, Theodore, 1871-1945. • 2.11592
The bulwark: a novel / Theodore Dreiser. — [1st ed.]. — Garden City, New
York: Doubleday & company inc., 1946. viii, 337 p. I. T.
PZ3.D814 Bu   PS3507.R55 B8 1946.   *LC* 46-25076

Dreiser, Theodore, 1871-1945. • 2.11593
The financier. Cleveland, World Pub. Co., 1946. 503 p. 21 cm. I. T.
PS3507.R55F5 1946   *LC* A 48-7665

Dreiser, Theodore, 1871-1945. • 2.11594
The 'genius' / Theodore Dreiser. — New York: Boni and Liveright, [1925]
736 p. — I. T.
PS3507.R55 Gx PZ3.D814 Ge8   *LC* 26-22295

Dreiser, Theodore, 1871-1945. • 2.11595
Jennie Gerhardt. Cleveland, World Pub. Co. [1946, c1926] 430 p. 21 cm. I. T.
PZ3.D814 J25   PS3507.R55 Jx.   *LC* 51-31791

Dreiser, Theodore, 1871-1945. • 2.11596
Sister Carrie: an authoritative text, backgrounds, and sources criticism / edited by Donald Pizer. — [1st ed.]. — New York: Norton, [1970] x, 591 p.; 22 cm. — (A Norton critical edition) I. T.
PZ3.D814 S41 PS3507.R55 S5x   813/.5/2   LC 73-116120   ISBN 0393043258

Dreiser, Theodore, 1871-1945. • 2.11597
The stoic. Cleveland: World Pub. Co., [1952, c1947] 310 p.; 21 cm. The 3d vol. of the author's trilogy, the 1st of which is The financier, and the 2d, The Titan. I. T.
PS3507.R55 S86   LC 52-9798

Dreiser, Theodore, 1871-1945. • 2.11598
The Titan. — Cleveland: World Pub. Co. 1946, c1925. 551 p.; 21 cm. The 2d vol. of the author's trilogy, the 1st of which is The financier and 3d, The stoic. I. T.
PZ3.D814 Ti20   PS3507.R55 T5 1946.   LC 49-54858

Critical essays on Theodore Dreiser / [compiled by] Donald Pizer. 2.11599
Boston, Mass.: G.K. Hall, c1981. xiii, 343 p.; 25 cm. — (Critical essays on American literature.) 1. Dreiser, Theodore, 1871-1945 — Criticism and interpretation — Collected works. I. Pizer, Donald. II. Series.
PS3507.R55 Z576   813/.52 19   LC 80-29495   ISBN 0816182574

Elias, Robert Henry, 1914-. • 2.11600
Theodore Dreiser, apostle of nature / [by] Robert H. Elias. — Emended ed. with a survey of research and criticism. — Ithaca: Cornell University Press, [1970] x, 435 p.: port.; 22 cm. 1. Dreiser, Theodore, 1871-1945. I. T.
PS3507.R55 Z63 1970   813/.5/2   LC 70-129563   ISBN 080140603X

Kazin, Alfred, 1915- ed. • 2.11601
The stature of Theodore Dreiser; a critical survey of the man and his work. Edited by Alfred Kazin and Charles Shapiro; with an introd. by Alfred Kazin. — Bloomington: Indiana University Press, [1955] 303 p.; 24 cm. 1. Dreiser, Theodore, 1871-1945. I. Shapiro, Charles. joint ed. II. T.
PS3507.R55 Z64   813.5   LC 55-8446

Lehan, Richard Daniel, 1930-. • 2.11602
Theodore Dreiser: his world and his novels [by] Richard Lehan. — Carbondale: Southern Illinois University Press, [1969] xiv, 280 p.: illus., ports.; 24 cm. 1. Dreiser, Theodore, 1871-1945. I. T.
PS3507.R55 Z66   813/.5/2   LC 69-19748   ISBN 0809303825

Matthiessen, F. O. (Francis Otto), 1902-1950. • 2.11603
Theodore Dreiser. [New York]: Sloane, [1951] 267 p.: port.; 22 cm. (American men of letters series.) 1. Dreiser, Theodore, 1871-1945. I. T. II. Series.
PS3507.R55 Z7   928.1   LC 51-1734

Moers, Ellen, 1928-. • 2.11604
Two Dreisers. New York, Viking Press [1969] xvii, 404 p. 22 cm. 1. Dreiser, Theodore, 1871-1945. I. T.
PS3507.R55 Z74   813/.5/2 B   LC 69-15660

Salzman, Jack. comp. 2.11605
Theodore Dreiser: the critical reception. Edited with an introd. by Jack Salzman. — [1st ed.]. — New York: D. Lewis, 1972. xxxvii, 741 p.; 25 cm. — (The American critical tradition) 1. Dreiser, Theodore, 1871-1945 — Criticism and interpretation — Addresses, essays, lectures. I. T.
PS3507.R55 Z816   813/.5/2   LC 73-78882

Swanberg, W. A., 1907-. • 2.11606
Dreiser / by W. A. Swanberg. — New York: Scribner, [1965] xvii, 614 p.: ill., ports.; 25 cm. 1. Dreiser, Theodore, 1871-1945. I. T.
PS3507.R55 Z84   928.1   LC 65-13661

Warren, Robert Penn, 1905-. 2.11607
Homage to Theodore Dreiser, August 27, 1871–December 28, 1945, on the centennial of his birth. — [1st ed.]. — New York: Random House, [1971] 173 p.: port.; 22 cm. 1. Dreiser, Theodore, 1871-1945. I. T.
PS3507.R55 Z86   813/.5/2   LC 73-156965   ISBN 0394410270

PS3507 Dr–Dz

Drury, Allen, 1918-. • 2.11608
Advise and consent / drawings by Arthur Shilstone. — [1st ed.]. — Garden City, N.Y.: Doubleday, 1959. 616 p.: ill.; 25 cm. I. T.
PZ4.D794 Ad   PS3507.R925 A3 1959.   LC 59-9137

Rampersad, Arnold. 2.11609
The art and imagination of W. E. B. Du Bois / Arnold Rampersad. — Cambridge, Mass.: Harvard University Press, 1976. viii, 325 p.; 24 cm. 1. Du Bois, W. E. B. (William Edward Burghardt), 1868-1963. 2. Authors, American — 20th century — Biography. I. T.
PS3507.U147 Z85   301.24/2/0924 B   LC 76-10295

Dunbar-Nelson, Alice Moore, 1875-1935. 2.11610
Give us each day: the diary of Alice Dunbar–Nelson / edited with a critical introduction and notes by Gloria T. Hull. — 1st ed. — New York: W.W. Norton, c1984. 480 p.; 22 cm. Includes index. 1. Dunbar-Nelson, Alice Moore, 1875-1935 — Diaries. 2. Authors, American — 20th century — Biography. I. Hull, Gloria T. II. T.
PS3507.U6228 Z465 1984   818/.5203 B 19   LC 84-6055   ISBN 0393018938

Duncan, Robert Edward, 1919-. • 2.11611
Selected poems. San Francisco, City Lights Books, 1959. 79 p. (Pocket poets series. no. 10) I. T. II. Series.
PS3507.U629 A6 1959   811.54   LC 59-9263

Duncan, Robert Edward, 1919-. 2.11612
Caesar's gate: poems / Robert Duncan; with paste–ups by Jess. — [Berkeley, Calif.]: Sand Dollar, 1972. xlix, 73 p.: ill.; 23 cm. I. Jess, 1923- II. T.
PS3507.U629 C3   811/.5/4   LC 77-368620

Duncan, Robert Edward, 1919-. 2.11613
The opening of the field, by Robert Duncan. — Rev. ed. — New York: New Directions Pub. Corp., 1973. 96 p.; 21 cm. — (New Directions paperbook NDP 356) (A New Directions book) Poems. I. T.
PS3507.U629 O6 1973   811/.5/4   LC 72-93976   ISBN 0811204804

Duncan, Robert Edward. 2.11614
Roots and branches; poems / by Robert Duncan. — New York: Scribner, 1964. xi, 176 p.; 20 cm. — (Scribner first editions.) I. T.
PS3507.U629 R6   811.54   LC 64-24233

Duncan, Robert Edward, 1919-. 2.11615
The years as catches: first poems, 1939–1946 / by Robert Duncan. — Berkeley: Oyez, 1966. xi, 93, [6] p.: port.; 23 cm. I. T.
PS3507.U629 Y4   811/.5/4   LC 67-3614

Dunne, Finley Peter, 1867-1936. • 2.11616
Mr. Dooley remembers: the informal memoirs of Finley Peter Dunne / edited with an introd. and commentary by Philip Dunne. — [1st ed.]. — Boston: Little, Brown, [1963] viii, 307 p.: illus., ports. 'An Atlantic Monthly Press book.' I. T.
PS3507.U6755 Z5 1963   PS3507 U6755 Z5 1963.   817.52   LC 63-18509

Eckley, Grace. 2.11617
Finley Peter Dunne / by Grace Eckley. — Boston: Twayne, 1981. 173 p.: port.; 22 cm. — (Twayne's United States authors series; TUSAS 402) Includes index. 1. Dunne, Finley Peter, 1867-1936 — Criticism and interpretation. I. T.
PS3507.U6755 Z57   818/.5207 19   LC 80-20446   ISBN 0805772952

Fanning, Charles. 2.11618
Finley Peter Dunne & Mr. Dooley: the Chicago years / Charles Fanning. — Lexington: University Press of Kentucky, c1978. x, 286 p., [4] leaves of plates: ill., maps (on lining papers); 24 cm. Includes excerpts from articles by Dunne which appeared in Chicago newspapers. 1. Dunne, Finley Peter, 1867-1936 — Criticism and interpretation. I. Dunne, Finley Peter, 1867-1936. II. T.
PS3507.U6755 Z63   818/.5/207   LC 77-75483   ISBN 0813113652

Schaaf, Barbara C. 2.11619
Mr. Dooley's Chicago / by Barbara C. Schaaf. 1st ed. — Garden City, N.Y.: Anchor Press, 1977. 399 p., [8] leaves of plates: ill.; 22 cm. Includes index. 1. Dunne, Finley Peter, 1867-1936 — Criticism and interpretation. 2. Chicago in literature. 3. Chicago — Anecdotes, facetiae, satire, etc. I. T.
PS3507.U6755 Z88   818/.5/207   LC 76-23793   ISBN 0385020236

PS3509 E–El

Eastlake, William. • 2.11620
Castle keep. — New York, Simon and Schuster, 1965. 382 p. 21 cm. I. T.
PS3509.A85 C3   LC 65-11975

Eberhart, Richard, 1904-. • 2.11621
Collected verse plays. Chapel Hill: University of North Carolina Press, [c1962] 167 p.; 23 cm. I. T.
PS3509.B456 A19 1962   LC 62-16088

Eberhart, Richard, 1904-. 2.11622
Collected poems, 1930–1976: including 43 new poems / Richard Eberhart. — New York: Oxford University Press, 1976. xvi, 364 p.; 21 cm. I. T.
PS3509.B456 A6 1976   811/.5/2   LC 76-7288   ISBN 0195198492

Roache, Joel, 1941-. • **2.11623**
Richard Eberhart; the progress of an American poet. — New York: Oxford University Press, 1971. xxix, 299 p.: illus., ports.; 22 cm. 1. Eberhart, Richard, 1904- I. T.
PS3509.B456 Z85   811/.5/2 B   *LC* 75-83016

Edmonds, Walter Dumaux, 1903-. • **2.11624**
Drums along the Mohawk, by Walter D. Edmonds. Boston, Little, Brown, and company, 1936. xiii, 592 p. 22 cm. Maps on lining-papers. 1. Mohawk River Valley (N.Y.) — History — Revolution, 1775-1783 — Fiction. I. T.
PZ3.E242 Dr   PS3509.D564 Dx.   *LC* 36-16924

Edmonds, Walter Dumaux, 1903-. • **2.11625**
Rome haul / by Walter D. Edmonds; with an introduction by the author. — New York: The Modern Library, [1938] 347 p. (The Modern library of the world's best books) 'First Modern library edition.' Dramatized under the title of 'The farmer takes a wife.' I. T.
PS3509.D564 Rx PZ3.E242 Ro 6   *LC* 38-4884

PS3509 Eliot

Eliot, T. S. (Thomas Stearns), 1888-1965. • **2.11626**
Collected poems, 1909-1962. [1st American ed.] New York, Harcourt, Brace & World [1963] 221 p. 25 cm. I. T.
PS3509.L43 A17 1963   821.912   *LC* 63-21424

Eliot, T. S. (Thomas Stearns), 1888-1965. • **2.11627**
The complete plays. [1st American ed. New York] Harcourt, Brace & World [1969? c1967] 355 p. 22 cm. I. T.
PS3509.L43 A19 1969   822/.9/12   *LC* 71-3603

Eliot, T. S. (Thomas Stearns), 1888-1965. • **2.11628**
Old Possum's book of practical cats / T.S. Eliot. — 1st American ed. — [New York]: Harcourt, Brace, [c1939] 46 p.: ill.; 23 cm. I. T.
PS3509.L43 O55   *LC* 39-33125

Eliot, T. S. (Thomas Stearns), 1888-1965. • **2.11629**
To criticize the critic, and other writings. New York, Farrar, Straus & Giroux [1965] 188 p. 24 cm. 1. Literature — History and criticism I. T.
PS3509.L43 T6   809   *LC* 65-25139

Bantock, G. H. (Geoffrey Herman), 1914-. • **2.11630**
T. S. Eliot & education / [by] G. H. Bantock. — New York: Random House, [1969] 117 p.; 19 cm. (Studies in the Western educational tradition, SED 18) 1. Eliot, T. S. (Thomas Stearns), 1888-1965 — Knowledge — Education. 2. Eliot, T. S. (Thomas Stearns), 1888-1965 — Political and social views. I. T.
PS3509.L43 Z63   821/.9/12   *LC* 70-81346

Bodelson, Carl Adolf Gottlieb, 1894-. • **2.11631**
T.S. Eliot's Four quartets: a commentary. — [Copenhagen]: Copenhagen University Publications Fund, 1958. 128 p. 1. Eliot, T. S. (Thomas Stearns), 1888-1965. Four quartets. I. T.
PS3509.L43 Z65x   *LC* 60-45717

Frye, Northrop. • **2.11632**
T.S. Eliot. — 1st Evergreen ed. — New York: Grove Press, c1963. 106 p. — (Evergreen Pilot books; EP26) 1. Eliot, T. S. (Thomas Stearns), 1888-1965. I. T.
PS3509.L43 Z674 1963   *LC* 63-9402

Gardner, Helen Louise, Dame. • **2.11633**
The art of T.S. Eliot / Helen Gardner. New York: Dutton, 1950. 185 p.; 23cm. 1. Eliot, T. S. (Thomas Stearns), 1888-1965. I. T.
PS3509.L43 Z675 1950   *LC* 50-9034

Gray, Piers. **2.11634**
T.S. Eliot's intellectual and poetic development, 1909-1922 / Piers Gray. — Brighton, Sussex: Harvester Press; Atlantic Highlands, N.J.: Humanities Press, 1982. xii, 273 p.; ill.; 22 cm. Includes index. 1. Eliot, T. S. (Thomas Stearns), 1888-1965 — Criticism and interpretation. I. T.
PS3509.L43 Z6798 1982   821/.912 19   *LC* 81-208217   *ISBN* 0391025066

Jones, Genesius. • **2.11635**
Approach to the purpose; a study of the poetry of T. S. Eliot. New York, Barnes & Noble [1965, c1964] 351 p. 23 cm. 'List of works consulted': p. 342-346. 1. Eliot, T. S. (Thomas Stearns), 1888-1965. I. T.
PS3509.L43Z686 1965   812.912   *LC* 65-3788

Kenner, Hugh. ed. • **2.11636**
T. S. Eliot; a collection of critical essays. Englewood Cliffs, N.J., Prentice-Hall [1962] 210 p. 21 cm. (A Spectrum book: Twentieth century views, S-TC-2) 1. Eliot, T. S. (Thomas Stearns), 1888-1965 — Addresses, essays, lectures. I. T.
PS3509.L43 Z6913   811.52   *LC* 62-9290

Kirk, Russell. • **2.11637**
Eliot and his age: T. S. Eliot's moral imagination in the twentieth century. — [1st ed.] New York: Random House, [c1971] xii, 462 p.; 25 cm. 1. Eliot, T. S. (Thomas Stearns), 1888-1965 — Criticism and interpretation. I. T.
PS3509.L43 Z6914   821/.9/12   *LC* 76-159354   *ISBN* 0394472365

Kojecký, Roger. • **2.11638**
T. S. Eliot's social criticism. [1st American ed.] New York, Farrar, Straus and Giroux [1972, c1971] 255 p. 23 cm. 1. Eliot, T. S. (Thomas Stearns), 1888-1965. I. T.
PS3509.L43 Z69153 1972   828/.9/1208   *LC* 72-181289   *ISBN* 0374272433

Matthiessen, F. O. (Francis Otto), 1902-1950. • **2.11639**
The achievement of T. S. Eliot; an essay on the nature of poetry. With a chapter on Eliot's later work by C. L. Barber. 3d ed. New York, Oxford University Press, 1958. 248 p. 22 cm. 1. Eliot, T. S. (Thomas Stearns), 1888-1965. 2. Poetry I. T.
PS3509.L43 Z74 1958   811.5   *LC* 58-12348

Smith, Grover Cleveland, 1923-. • **2.11640**
T. S. Eliot's poetry and plays: a study in sources and meaning. — [Chicago]: University of Chicago Press, [1956] xii, 338 p.; 25 cm. 1. Eliot, T. S. (Thomas Stearns), 1888-1965 — Criticism and interpretation.
PS3509.L43 Z868   811.5   *LC* 56-11001

Southam, B. C. • **2.11641**
A student's guide to the Selected poems of T. S. Eliot, [by] B. C. Southam. London, Faber and Faber [1968] 136 p. 19 cm. 1. Eliot, T. S. (Thomas Stearns), 1888-1965. Poems. Selections I. T.
PS3509.L43 Z869   821/.9/12   *LC* 77-369843   *ISBN* 0571083781

T.S. Eliot, the critical heritage / edited by Michael Grant. **2.11642**
London; Boston: Routledge & Kegan Paul, 1982. 2 v. (xx, 769 p.) — (The Critical heritage series) Includes index. 1. Eliot, T. S. (Thomas Stearns), 1888-1965 — Criticism and interpretation — Addresses, essays, lectures. I. Grant, Michael, 1940-
PS3509L43 Z8732 1982   PS3509L43 Z8732 1982.   821/.912 19   *LC* 82-3842   *ISBN* 0710092245

Tate, Allen, 1899- ed. • **2.11643**
T. S. Eliot: the man and his work; a critical evaluation by twenty–six distinguished writers. New York, Delacorte Press [1966] vi, 400 p. ports. 21 cm. 'A Seymour Lawrence book.' 1. Eliot, T. S. (Thomas Stearns), 1888-1965. I. T.
PS3509.L43 Z874   828.91209   *LC* 66-20994

Unger, Leonard. **2.11644**
Eliot's compound ghost: influence and confluence / Leonard Unger. — University Park, Pa.: Pennsylvania State University Press, c1981. 131 p.; 24 cm. 1. Eliot, T. S. (Thomas Stearns), 1888-1965 — Knowledge — Literature. 2. Eliot, T. S. (Thomas Stearns), 1888-1965 — Sources. I. T.
PS3509.L43 Z8819   821/.912 19   *LC* 81-47173   *ISBN* 0271002921

Williamson, George, 1898-1968. • **2.11645**
A reader's guide to T. S. Eliot; a poem–by–poem analysis. New York, Farrar, Straus & Giroux [1965, c1953] 248 p. 22 cm. 1. Eliot, T. S. (Thomas Stearns), 1888-1965. I. T.
PS3509.L43 Z898 1965   821.912   *LC* 66-13470

PS3509 En–Ez

Engle, Paul, 1908-. • **2.11646**
American song, a book of poems, by Paul Engle. [1st ed.] Garden City, N.Y., Doubleday, Doran & Company, inc., 1934. xvi, 102 p. 20 cm. I. T.
PS3509.N44 A7 1934   811.5   *LC* 34-27209

PS3511 Farrell. Fast

Farrell, James T. (James Thomas), 1904-1979. **2.11647**
The death of Nora Ryan / James T. Farrell. — 1st ed. — Garden City, N.Y.: Doubleday, 1978. 402 p.; 22 cm. I. T.
PZ3.F2465 De PS3511.A738 D4x   813/.5/2   *LC* 77-83935   *ISBN* 0385134509

Farrell, James T. (James Thomas), 1904-1979. • **2.11648**
Father and son / James T. Farrell. — New York: The Vanguard Press, [c1940] 616 p.; 21 cm. I. T.
PZ3.F2465Fat PS3511.A738F37 1940   *LC* 40-32291

Farrell, James T. (James Thomas), 1904-1979. **2.11649**
Face of time. New York: Vanguard, 1953. 1 v. I. T.
PS3511.A738 F3x   *LC* 53-1085

Farrell, James T. (James Thomas), 1904-1979. • 2.11650
My days of anger / by James T. Farrell. — New York: The Vanguard Press,
[1943] 5 p. l., 3-403 p.; 22 cm. I. T.
PZ3.F2465 My   PS3511.A738 Mx.   *LC* 43-16086

Farrell, James T. (James Thomas), 1904-1979. • 2.11651
No star is lost / James T. Farrell. — New York, Vanguard Press [c1938] 637 p.;
21 cm. I. T.
PS3511.A738 N6   813.5   *LC* 38-17566

Farrell, James T. (James Thomas), 1904-1979. 2.11652
Olive and Mary Anne / James T. Farrell; [ill. by Joseph Graham]. — New
York: Stonehill Pub. Co., c1977. 212 p.: ill.; 22 cm. I. T.
PZ3.F2465 Ol PS3511.A738 O5x   813/.52   *LC* 77-81172   *ISBN*
0883730715

Farrell, James T. (James Thomas), 1904-1979. • 2.11653
Studs Lonigan; a trilogy containing Young Lonigan, The young manhood of
Studs Lonigan, Judgment day. With a new introduction by the author. New
York, The Modern library [1938] [1113] p. 21 cm. (The Modern library of the
world's best books) At head of title: James T. Farrell. Various pagings. 'First
Modern library giant edition.' I. T. II. Title: Young Lonigan. III. Title: The
young manhood of Studs Lonigan. IV. Title: Judgment day.
PS3511.A738Sx   *LC* 38-31286

Farrell, James T. (James Thomas), 1904-1979. • 2.11654
A world I never made, by James T. Farrell. [1st ed.] New York, Vanguard Press
[1936] 508 p.; 21 cm. I. T.
PS3511.A738 W6 1936   813.5   *LC* 36-24944

Farrell, James T. (James Thomas), 1904-1979. • 2.11655
An omnibus of short stories. — New York: Vanguard press, 1956. 313 p.; 23
cm. I. T.
PS3511.A77 O5   *LC* 56-12033

Fast, Howard, 1914-. • 2.11656
The Howard Fast reader: a collection of stories and novels. — New York:
Crown Publishers, [1960] 628 p. I. T.
PS3511.A784 A15 1960   *LC* 60-8629

PS3511 Faulkner

Faulkner, William, 1897-1962. • 2.11657
Collected stories. — New York: Random House, [1950] 900 p.; 22 cm. — I. T.
PZ3.F272 Co   PS3511.A86 A16 1950.   *LC* 50-9187

Faulkner, William, 1897-1962. • 2.11658
Essays, speeches & public letters. Edited by James B. Meriwether. — New
York: Random House, [1966, c1965] xv, 233 p.; 21 cm. I. Meriwether, James
B. ed. II. T.
PS3511.A86 A6 1966   818.5208   *LC* 64-20036

Faulkner, William, 1897-1962. • 2.11659
Absalom, Absalom! Introd. by Harvey Breit. — New York: Modern Library,
[1951] xii, 378 p.: map; 19 cm. — (Modern library of the world's best books.
271) I. T. II. Series.
PZ3.F272 Ab4   PS3511.A86 A63 1951.   *LC* 51-10393

William Faulkner's As I lay dying: a critical casebook / [edited 2.11660
by] Dianne L. Cox.
New York: Garland Pub., 1985. xxix, 216 p.; 24 cm. (Garland Faulkner
casebooks; vol. 3) 1. Faulkner, William, 1897-1962 As I lay dying —
Addresses, essays, lectures. I. Cox, Dianne L.
PS3511.A86 A869 1985   813/.52 19   *LC* 84-13793   *ISBN*
0824092287

Faulkner, William, 1897-1962. • 2.11661
Bear, man, & God: seven approaches to William Faulkner's The bear / edited
by Francis Lee Utley, Lynn Z. Bloom [and] Arthur F. Kinney. — New York:
Random House, [1964] xii, 429 p.: geneal. tables.; 22 cm. Includes complete text
of The bear, Delta autumn, and selections from other works by W. Faulkner.
'William Faulkner's canon: p. [428]-429. 1. Faulkner, William, 1897-1962.
Bear I. Faulkner, William, 1897-1962. Bear II. Bloom, Lynn Z., 1934-
III. Kinney, Arthur F., 1933- IV. Utley, Francis Lee, 1907- V. T. VI. Title:
The bear.
PS3511.A86 B439 1964   813.52   *LC* 63-8263

Faulkner, William, 1897-1962. • 2.11662
A fable. [New York] Random House [1954] 437 p. 22 cm. 1. World War,
1914-1918 — Fiction. I. T.
PS3511.A86 F3   PZ3.F272 Fab   *LC* 54-6651

Faulkner, William, 1897-1962. • 2.11663
Go down, Moses. — New York: Modern Library, [1955] 389 p.; 19 cm. — (The
Modern library of the world's best books [175]) I. T.
PZ3.F272 Go3   PS3511.A86Gx.   *LC* 55-6391

Faulkner, William, 1897-1962. • 2.11664
The hamlet / William Faulkner. — New York: Random House, [1956, c1940]
373 p. — (Modern library paperbacks; P18) The 1st vol. of the author's trilogy,
Snopes, the 2d of which is The town; the 3d, The mansion. I. T.
PS3511.A86Hx PZ3

Faulkner, William, 1897-1962. • 2.11665
Intruder in the dust. — New York: Random House, [1948] 247 p.; 21 cm. —
I. T.
PZ3.F272 In   PS3511.A86 Ix.   *LC* 48-8519

Faulkner, William, 1897-1962. • 2.11666
Knight's gambit. — New York: Random House, c1949. 246 p.; 21 cm. Short
stories. I. T.
PZ3.F272 Kn   PS3511.A86 K6.   *LC* 49-11472

Faulkner, William, 1897-1962. 2.11667
Light in August. — New York: Random House, [1967, c1959] 480 p.; 21 cm. —
I. T.
PZ3.F272 Li14   PS3511.A86Lx.   *LC* 67-12716

Faulkner, William, 1897-1962. 2.11668
Mayday / by William Faulkner; with introd. by Carvel Collins. — [Notre
Dame, Ind.]: University of Notre Dame Press, 1980 (c1976). 87 p. Cover title.
1. Faulkner, William, 1897-1962 — Manuscripts — Facsimiles. I. T.
PS3511.A86 M36   813/.5/2   *LC* 77-376384

Faulkner, William, 1897-1962. • 2.11669
The mansion. — New York: Random House, [1959] 436 p.; 21 cm. The 3d vol.
of the author's trilogy, Snopes, the 1st of which is The hamlet, and the 2d, The
town. I. T.
PS3511.A86 M3x   *LC* 59-10811

Faulkner, William, 1897-1962. • 2.11670
Mosquitoes: a novel / by William Faulkner. — New York: Liveright, c1927.
349 p. I. T.
PS3511.A86 M6 1927   *LC* 27-10732   *ISBN* 0871409364

Faulkner, William, 1897-1962. • 2.11671
Pylon. New York, Random House [1965, c1935] 315 p. 21 cm. I. T.
PZ3.F272 Py6   PS3511.A86Px.   *LC* 65-8629

Faulkner, William, 1897-1962. • 2.11672
The reivers, a reminiscence. — New York: Random House, [1962] 305 p.; 21
cm. — I. T.
PS3511.A86 R38   PZ3.F272 Re   *LC* 62-10335

Faulkner, William, 1897-1962. • 2.11673
Requiem for a nun. — New York: Random House, [1951] 286 p.; 21 cm. —
I. T.
PS3511.A86 R4 1951   813.5   *LC* 51-12731

Faulkner, William, 1897-1962. • 2.11674
Sartoris [by] William Faulkner. — New York: Harcourt, Brace and company,
[c1929] 380 p.; 20 cm. — I. T.
PZ3.F272 Sar   PS3511.A86 S32.   *LC* 29-3496

Faulkner, William, 1897-1962. • 2.11675
Sanctuary. New York: Random House [1962, c1958] 309 p. 21 cm. I. T.
PS3511.A86 S4 1962   *LC* 62-15256

Twentieth century interpretations of Sanctuary: a collection of 2.11676
critical essays / edited by J. Douglas Canfield.
Englewood Cliffs, N.J.: Prentice-Hall, c1982. 145 p.; 21 cm. — (Twentieth
century interpretations.) 'A Spectrum book.' 1. Faulkner, William, 1897-1962
Sanctuary — Addresses, essays, lectures. I. Canfield, J. Douglas (John
Douglas), 1941- II. Series.
PS3511.A86 S438 1982   813/.52 19   *LC* 82-7573   *ISBN*
0137912285

Faulkner, William, 1897-1962. • 2.11677
Soldiers' pay. — New York: Liveright, [1970, c1954] 319 p.; 21 cm. — I. T.
PZ3.F272 So9 PS3511.A86 S5x   813/.5/2   *LC* 79-114374   2.47

Faulkner, William, 1897-1962. • 2.11678
The sound and the fury; &, As I lay dying / by William Faulkner; with a new
appendix and a foreword by the author. — New York: The Modern library,
[1946] 532 p.; 20 cm. — (Modern library of the world's best books. [187]) 'First
Modern library edition, 1946.' I. Faulkner, William, 1897-1962. As I lay dying.
II. T. III. Title: As I lay dying. IV. Series.
PZ3.F272 Sou6   PS3511.A86 S6.   *LC* 47-1273

Bleikasten, André.   2.11679
The most splendid failure: Faulkner's The sound and the fury / André Bleikasten. — Bloomington: Indiana University Press, c1976. xi, 275 p.; 22 cm. Includes index. 1. Faulkner, William, 1897-1962. The sound and the fury. I. T.
PS3511.A86 S78 1976   813/.5/2   LC 75-22638   ISBN 0253338778

Faulkner, William, 1897-1962.   • 2.11680
The town. — New York: Random House, [1957] 371 p.; 21 cm. I. Faulkner, William, 1897-1962. Snopes. II. Faulkner, William, 1897-1962. Hamlet. III. T.
PS3511.A86 T6   PZ3.F272 To   LC 57-6656

Faulkner, William, 1897-1962.   • 2.11681
The unvanquished; drawings by Edward Shenton. New York, Random House, 1938. 5 p. l., 3-293 p. illus. 21 cm. Seven short stories forming a continuous novel. 1. United States — History — Civil war — Fiction. I. T.
PS3511.A86 U5   LC 38-27161

Faulkner, William, 1897-1962.   2.11682
Vision in spring / William Faulkner; with an introduction by Judith L. Sensibar. — 1st ed. — Austin: University of Texas Press, 1984. 88, xlvi p.: ill.; 26 cm. I. T.
PS3511.A86 V57 1984   811/.52 19   LC 83-21888   ISBN 029278712X

Faulkner, William, 1897-1962.   • 2.11683
The wild palms, by William Faulkner. New York, Random House [c1939] 339 p.; 21 cm. I. T.
PZ3.F272W PS3511.A86W5   LC 39-1750

Biography. Criticism

Adams, Richard Perrill, 1917-.   • 2.11684
Faulkner: myth and motion [by] Richard P. Adams. — Princeton, N.J.: Princeton University Press, 1968. xiv, 260 p.; 23 cm. 1. Faulkner, William, 1897-1962. I. T.
PS3511.A86 Z556   813/.5/2   LC 68-29382

Blotner, Joseph Leo, 1923-.   2.11685
Faulkner: a biography / Joseph Blotner. — One vol. ed., 1st ed., [rev., updated, condensed]. — New York: Random House, c1984. xix, 778 p., [40] p. of plates: ill., facsims, ports. Includes index. 1. Faulkner, William, 1897-1962 — Biography. 2. Novelists, American — 20th century — Biography. I. T.
PS3511.A86 Z63 1984   813/.52 B 19   LC 83-17663   ISBN 0394504135

Brooks, Cleanth, 1906-.   • 2.11686
William Faulkner; the Yoknapatawpha country. New Haven, Yale University Press, 1963. xiv, 499 p. map, geneal. tables. 24 cm. 1. Faulkner, William, 1897-1962. 2. Yoknapatawpha County (Imaginary place) I. T. II. Title: The Yoknapatawpha country.
PS3511.A86 Z64   813.52   LC 63-17023

Brooks, Cleanth, 1906-.   2.11687
William Faulkner: toward Yoknapatawpha and beyond / Cleanth Brooks. — New Haven: Yale University Press, 1978. xviii, 445 p.; 24 cm. 1. Faulkner, William, 1897-1962 — Criticism and interpretation. I. T.
PS3511.A86 Z642   813/.5/2   LC 77-10898   ISBN 0300022042

Broughton, Panthea Reid.   2.11688
William Faulkner: the abstract and the actual / Panthea Reid Broughton. — Baton Rouge: Louisiana State University Press, [1974] xviii, 222 p.; 23 cm. 1. Faulkner, William, 1897-1962 — Criticism and interpretation. I. T.
PS3511.A86 Z644   813/.5/2   LC 74-77324   ISBN 0807100838

Cowley, Malcolm, 1898-.   • 2.11689
The Faulkner–Cowley file; letters and memories, 1944–1962. — New York: Viking Press, [1966] 184 p.; 22 cm. 1. Faulkner, William, 1897-1962. I. Faulkner, William, 1897-1962. II. T.
PS3511.A86 Z77   818.5203   LC 66-15884

Critical essays on William Faulkner: the Compson family /   2.11690
[edited by] Arthur F. Kinney.
Boston, Mass.: G.K. Hall, c1982. xi, 433 p.: ill.; 25 cm. — (Critical essays on American literature.) 1. Faulkner, William, 1897-1962. Sound and the fury I. Kinney, Arthur F., 1933- II. Series.
PS3511.A86 Z777 1982   813/.52 19   LC 82-3111   ISBN 081618464X

Cullen, John B.   2.11691
Old times in the Faulkner country / by John B. Cullen; in collaboration with Floyd C. Watkins. — Baton Rouge: Louisiana State University Press, 1975,

c1961. xvi, 132 p.; 23 cm. Reprint of the ed. published by the University of North Carolina Press, Chapel Hill. 1. Faulkner, William, 1897-1962. I. T.
PS3511.A86 Z78 1975   813/.5/2   LC 75-309704   ISBN 0807100994

Davis, Thadious M., 1944-.   2.11692
Faulkner's 'Negro': art and the southern context / Thadious M. Davis. — Baton Rouge: Louisiana State University Press, c1983. xii, 266 p.; 24 cm. — (Southern literary studies.) Includes index. 1. Faulkner, William, 1897-1962 — Criticism and interpretation. 2. Faulkner, William, 1897-1962 — Characters 3. Afro-Americans in literature 4. Race relations in literature. 5. Southern States in literature. I. T. II. Series.
PS3511.A86 Z7817 1983   813/.52 19   LC 82-7327   ISBN 0807110477

Hoffman, Frederick John.   • 2.11693
William Faulkner. — New York: Twayne Publishers, [1961] 134 p.; 21 cm. — (Twayne's United States authors series, 1) 1. Faulkner, William, 1897-1962. I. T.
PS3511.A86 Z79   813.52   LC 61-9856

Howe, Irving.   • 2.11694
William Faulkner: critical study. — 2d ed., rev. and expanded. — New York: Vintage Books [1962] 299 p. 19 cm. 1. Faulkner, William, 1897-1962. I. T.
PS3511.A86Z84 1962   813.52   LC 62-2290

Kerr, Elizabeth Margaret, 1905-.   2.11695
William Faulkner's Yoknapatawpha: 'a kind of keystone in the universe' / Elizabeth M. Kerr. — New York: Fordham University Press, 1983. 438 p.; 24 cm. 1. Faulkner, William, 1897-1962 — Symbolism. 2. Faulkner, William, 1897-1962 — Religion. 3. Symbolism in literature 4. Myth in literature 5. Man (Christian theology) in literature. 6. Humanism in literature 7. Yoknapatawpha County (Imaginary place) I. T.
PS3511.A86 Z8598 1983   813/.52 19   LC 82-83490   ISBN 0823211002

Levins, Lynn Gartrell.   2.11696
Faulkner's heroic design: the Yoknapatawpha novels / Lynn Gartrell Levins. — Athens: University of Georgia Press, c1976. x, 202 p.; 23 cm. 1. Faulkner, William, 1897-1962 — Criticism and interpretation. 2. Yoknapatawpha County (Imaginary place) I. T.
PS3511.A86 Z877   813/.5/2   LC 74-18585   ISBN 0820303747

Minter, David L.   2.11697
William Faulkner, his life and work / David Minter. — Baltimore, MD: Johns Hopkins University Press, c1980. xvi, 325 p.; 24 cm. 1. Faulkner, William, 1897-1962. 2. Novelists, American — 20th century — Biography. I. T.
PS3511.A86 Z913   813/.52 B   LC 80-13089   ISBN 0801823471

Peters, Erskine.   2.11698
William Faulkner, the Yoknapatawpha world and black being / by Erskine Peters. — Darby, Pa.: Norwood Editions, 1983. xvi, 265 p.; 24 cm. Includes index. 1. Faulkner, William, 1897-1962 — Criticism and interpretation. 2. Faulkner, William, 1897-1962 — Characters — Afro-Americans. 3. Race relations in literature. 4. Afro-Americans in literature 5. Yoknapatawpha County (Imaginary place) I. T. II. Title: Yoknapatawpha world and black being.
PS3511.A86 Z94615 1983   813/.52 19   LC 82-24657   ISBN 0848256751

Reed, Joseph W., 1932-.   2.11699
Faulkner's narrative, by Joseph W. Reed, Jr. — New Haven: Yale University Press, 1973. x, 303 p.; 25 cm. 1. Faulkner, William, 1897-1962. I. T.
PS3511.A86 Z947   813/.5/2   LC 72-91304   ISBN 0300015909

Rollyson, Carl E. (Carl Edmund)   2.11700
Uses of the past in the novels of William Faulkner / by Carl E. Rollyson, Jr. — Ann Arbor, Mich.: UMI Research Press, c1984. 224 p.; 24 cm. — (Studies in modern literature. no. 37) Revision of thesis–University of Toronto, 1975. Includes index. 1. Faulkner, William, 1897-1962 — Knowledge — History. 2. History in literature 3. Time in literature 4. Memory in literature 5. Historical fiction, American I. T. II. Series.
PS3511.A86 Z962 1984   813/.52 19   LC 84-2745   ISBN 083571554X

Sensibar, Judith L. (Judith Levin), 1941-.   2.11701
The origins of Faulkner's art / by Judith L. Sensibar. — Austin: University of Texas Press, c1984. xxi, 290 p.: ill.; 24 cm. Includes index. 1. Faulkner, William, 1897-1962 — Criticism and interpretation. 2. Faulkner, William, 1897-1962 — Poetic works. I. T.
PS3511.A86 Z9665 1984   813/.52 19   LC 83-23382   ISBN 0292790201

Taylor, Walter, 1927-. 2.11702
Faulkner's search for a South / Walter Taylor. — Urbana: University of Illinois Press, c1983. x, 242 p.; 24 cm. Includes index. 1. Faulkner, William, 1897-1962 — Criticism and interpretation. 2. Southern States in literature. I. T.
PS3511.A86 Z975 1983   813/.52 19   *LC* 81-16127   *ISBN* 0252009436

Thompson, Lawrance Roger, 1906-1973. • 2.11703
William Faulkner: an introduction and interpretation / [by] Lawrance Thompson. — New York: Barnes & Noble, [1963]. 184 p.: ill.; 22 cm. — (American authors and critics series no. 10) 1. Faulkner, William, 1897-1962. I. T. II. Series.
PS3511.A86 Z977 1967   *LC* 63-15356

Vickery, Olga W. • 2.11704
The novels of William Faulkner; a critical interpretation, by Olga W. Vickery. — [Rev. ed. — Baton Rouge]: Louisiana State University Press, [1964] ix, 318 p.; 23 cm. 1. Faulkner, William, 1897-1962. I. T.
PS3511.A86 Z98 1964   813.52   *LC* 64-23150

Volpe, Edmond Loris. • 2.11705
A reader's guide to William Faulkner, by Edmond L. Volpe. — New York: Farrar, Straus, [1964] x, 427 p.: illus., geneal. table.; 21 cm. 1. Faulkner, William, 1897-1962. I. T.
PS3511.A86 Z983   813.52   *LC* 64-17120

Warren, Robert Penn, 1905- ed. • 2.11706
Faulkner; a collection of critical essays, edited by Robert Penn Warren. — Englewood Cliffs, N.J.: Prentice-Hall, [1966] 311 p.; 21 cm. — (A Spectrum book: Twentieth century views.) 1. Faulkner, William, 1897-1962. I. T.
PS3511.A86 Z9853   813.52   *LC* 66-28113

Bassett, John Earl, 1942-. 2.11707
William Faulkner: the critical heritage / edited by John Bassett. — London; Boston: Routledge and K. Paul, 1975. xvi, 422 p.; 23 cm. (The Critical heritage series) Includes index. 1. Faulkner, William, 1897-1962 — Criticism and interpretation. I. T.
PS3511.A86 Z985616   813/.5/2   *LC* 75-318841   *ISBN* 0710081243

PS3511 Fa–Fi

Fauset, Jessie Redmon. 2.11708
There is confusion. — New York: Boni and Liveright, 1924. 297 p.; 23 cm. — I. T.
PZ3.F276 Th5 PS3511.A864 T5x   813/.5/2   *LC* 73-18575   *ISBN* 0404113869

Fearing, Kenneth, 1902-1961. • 2.11709
Collected poems of Kenneth Fearing. — 1st ed. — New York: Random House, [c1940] 149 p. I. T.
PS3511.E115 A17 1940   *LC* 40-33832

Fearing, Kenneth, 1902-1961. • 2.11710
New and selected poems. — Bloomington: Indiana University Press, [1956] 143 p.; 24 cm. — (Indiana University poetry series) I. T. II. Series.
PS3511.E115A6 1956   811.5   *LC* 56-12003

Fearing, Kenneth, 1902-1961. 2.11711
The big clock. — [1st ed.]. — New York: Harcourt, Brace, [1946] 175 p. I. T.
PS3511.E115 B54   *LC* 46-6954

Ferber, Edna, 1887-1968. • 2.11712
Cimarron [by] Edna Ferber. Garden City, N. Y., Doubleday, Doran and company, inc. [1930] 388 p. 22 cm. I. T.
PZ3.F380Ci PS3511.E46C5   *LC* 30-8609

Ferber, Edna, 1887-1968. • 2.11713
Show boat [by] Edna Ferber. — Garden City, N.Y.: Doubleday, Page & co., c1926. 3 p. l., 398 p.; 20 cm. Title on two leaves. I. T.
PZ3.F380Sh2 PS3511.E46S5 1926   *LC* 26-16053

Ferber, Edna, 1887-1968. • 2.11714
So–Big, by Edna Ferber. Garden City, N.Y., Doubleday, Page & company, 1924. 3 p. l., 360 p. 20 cm. I. T.
PZ3.F380So PS3511.E46S6   *LC* 24-26188

Ferlinghetti, Lawrence. • 2.11715
A Coney Island of the mind, poems. — [New York]: New Directions, [1958] 93 p.; 21 cm. — (New Directions paperback no. 74) I. T.
PS3511.E557 C6   811.5   *LC* 58-7150

Ferlinghetti, Lawrence, 1919-. • 2.11716
Her. — New York: New Directions, [c1960] 156 p. — (New Directions paperbook. 88) 'Semi-autobiographical'. Cover drawing by author. I. T. II. Series.
PS3511.E557 H4 1960

Ferlinghetti, Lawrence. • 2.11717
Unfair arguments with existence: seven plays for a new theatre. — [New York: New Directions Books, 1963] ix, 118 p.; 21 cm. — (A New Directions paperbook) 'ND 143.' I. T.
PS3511.E557 U5 1963   812.54   *LC* 63-21384

Field, Rachel, 1894-1942. 2.11718
All this, and heaven too / by Rachel Field. — New York: Macmillan, 1940. 596 p.; 22 cm. 'Motion picture edition, illustrated with stills from Warner bros. pictures, inc., production ... published June 1940.' I. T.
PS3511.I25 A4   [Fic]   *ISBN* 0025376802

Finney, Charles G. (Charles Grandison), 1905-. 2.11719
The circus of Dr. Lao. by Charles G. Finney, with drawings by Boris Artzybasheff. New York, The Viking press, 1935. 154 p. plates. 24 cm. Illustrated lining-papers. I. Artzybasheff, Boris, 1899- illus. II. T.
PS3511.I64C5 1935   818.5   *LC* 35-10889

PS3511 Fitzgerald

Fitzgerald, F. Scott (Francis Scott), 1896-1940. • 2.11720
The Bodley Head Scott Fitzgerald / with an introd. by J. B. Priestley. — London: Bodley Head, [1958-63] 6 v.; 20 cm. I. T.
PS3511.I9 A6 1960   *LC* 61-188

Fitzgerald, F. Scott (Francis Scott), 1896-1940. • 2.11721
The crack–up: with other uncollected pieces, note–books and unpublished letters, together with letters to Fitzgerald from Gertrude Stein, Edith Wharton, T.S. Eliot, Thomas Wolfe, and John Dos Passos, and essays and poems by Paul Rosenfeld...[et al.] / edited by Edmund Wilson. — [New York: J. Laughlin, 1956,c1945] 347 p.; 19 cm. — (New Directions paperbook. no. 54) I. Wilson, Edmund, 1895-1972. II. T. III. Series.
PS3511.I9 C7 1956   PS3511.I9 C7 1945.   *LC* 56-13361   *ISBN* 0811200515

Critical essays on F. Scott Fitzgerald's The great Gatsby / 2.11722
[edited by] Scott Donaldson.
Boston, Mass.: G.K. Hall, c1984. viii, 277 p.; 25 cm. — (Critical essays on American literature) 1. Fitzgerald, F. Scott (Francis Scott), 1896-1940 Great Gatsby — Addresses, essays, lectures. I. Donaldson, Scott. II. Series.
PS3511.I9 G832 1984   813/.52 19   *LC* 83-18646   *ISBN* 0816186790

Fitzgerald, F. Scott (Francis Scott), 1896-1940. 2.11723
The vegetable: or, From President to postman / by F. Scott Fitzgerald. — A new ed., with unpublished scenes and corrections and an introd. / by Charles Scribner III. — New York: Scribner, [1976] c1923. 202 p. in various pagings; 21 cm. I. T.
PS3511.I9 V4 1976   812/.5/2   *LC* 76-2633   *ISBN* 0684146223

Fitzgerald, F. Scott (Francis Scott), 1896-1940. • 2.11724
The letters of F. Scott Fitzgerald / edited by Andrew Turnbull. — New York: Scribner, 1963. xviii, 615 p.: ports.; 24 cm. I. Turnbull, Andrew. II. T.
PS3511.I9Z54   928.1   *LC* 63-16755

Fitzgerald, F. Scott (Francis Scott), 1896-1940. • 2.11725
Scott Fitzgerald: letters to his daughter / edited by Andrew Turnbull; with an introd. by Frances Fitzgerald Lanahan. — New York: Scribner, [1965] xvii, 172 p.; 21 cm. I. Turnbull, Andrew, 1921- ed. II. Smith, Scottie Fitzgerald. III. T. IV. Title: Letters to his daughter.
PS3511.I9 Z55   816.52   *LC* 65-23983

Bruccoli, Matthew Joseph, 1931- comp. • 2.11726
F. Scott Fitzgerald in his own time: a miscellany. Edited by Matthew J. Bruccoli [and] Jackson R. Bryer. [1st ed. Kent, Ohio] Kent State University Press [1971] xxii, 481 p. facsims. 24 cm. 1. Fitzgerald, F. Scott (Francis Scott), 1896-1940. I. Bryer, Jackson R. joint comp. II. T.
PS3511.I9 Z559   813/.5/2   *LC* 76-126919   *ISBN* 0873381084

Donaldson, Scott. 2.11727
Fool for love: F. Scott Fitzgerald / by Scott Donaldson. — 1st ed. — New York: Congdon & Weed: Distributed by St. Martin's Press, c1983. xi, 262 p.: ports.; 24 cm. 1. Fitzgerald, F. Scott (Francis Scott), 1896-1940 — Biography. 2. Novelists, American — 20th century — Biography. I. T.
PS3511.I9 Z59 1983   813/.52 B 19   *LC* 83-7439   *ISBN* 0865530858

Eble, Kenneth Eugene. 2.11728
F. Scott Fitzgerald / by Kenneth Eble. — Rev. ed. — Boston: Twayne
Publishers, c1977. 187 p.: port.; 21 cm. — (Twayne's United States authors
series; TUSAS 36) Includes index. 1. Fitzgerald, F. Scott (Francis Scott),
1896-1940. 2. Authors, American — 20th century — Biography. I. T.
PS3511.I9 Z6 1977   813/.5/2 B   *LC* 77-429   *ISBN* 0805771832

Graham, Sheilah. 2.11729
The real F. Scott Fitzgerald thirty–five years later / by Sheilah Graham. —
New York: Grosset & Dunlap, c1976. 287 p.: ill.; 22 cm. 'Appendix' (p.
236-281) consists of Act I, scenes 1 and 2 of Dame Rumor (an unpublished play
by S. Graham and F. S. Fitzgerald) and of a facsim. of the manuscript of Not in
the script (a short story by S. Graham) Includes index. 1. Fitzgerald, F. Scott
(Francis Scott), 1896-1940 — Relations with women — Sheilah Graham.
2. Graham, Sheilah. I. T.
PS3511.I9 Z642   813/.5/2 B   *LC* 74-18880   *ISBN* 0448118750

Hindus, Milton. • 2.11730
F. Scott Fitzgerald: an introduction and interpretation. — New York: Holt,
Rinehart and Winston [1968] xi, 129 p.: port.; 21 cm. (American authors and
critics series) 1. Fitzgerald, F. Scott (Francis Scott), 1896-1940. I. T.
II. Series.
PS3511.I9 Z66   813/.5/2   *LC* 68-13614

Kazin, Alfred, 1915- ed. • 2.11731
F. Scott Fitzgerald: the man and his work. [1st ed.] Cleveland, World Pub. Co.
[1951] 219 p. 22 cm. 1. Fitzgerald, F. Scott (Francis Scott), 1896-1940. I. T.
PS3511.I9 Z67   928.1   *LC* 51-10640

Lehan, Richard Daniel, 1930-. • 2.11732
F. Scott Fitzgerald and the craft of fiction / [by] Richard D. Lehan; with a pref.
by Harry T. Moore. — Carbondale: Southern Illinois University Press, [1966]
xv, 206 p.; 22 cm. (Crosscurrents: modern critiques) 1. Fitzgerald, F. Scott
(Francis Scott), 1896-1940. I. T.
PS3511.I9 Z68   813.52   *LC* 66-15059

Mellow, James R. 2.11733
Invented lives: F. Scott and Zelda Fitzgerald / James R. Mellow. — Boston:
Houghton Mifflin, 1984. xxi, 569 p., [16] p. of plates: ill.; 24 cm. Includes index.
1. Fitzgerald, F. Scott (Francis Scott), 1896-1940 — Biography. 2. Fitzgerald,
Zelda, 1900-1948 — Biography. 3. Authors, American — 20th century —
Biography. I. T.
PS3511.I9 Z686 1984   813/.52 B 19   *LC* 84-9002   *ISBN*
0395344123

Miller, James Edwin, 1920-. • 2.11734
F. Scott Fitzgerald, his art and his technique, by James E. Miller, Jr. [New
York] New York University Press, 1964. xiv, 173 p. 22 cm. 1. Fitzgerald, F.
Scott (Francis Scott), 1896-1940 — Criticism and interpretation. I. T.
PS3511.I9 Z688   813.52   *LC* 64-16900

Mizener, Arthur ed. • 2.11735
F. Scott Fitzgerald, a collection of critical essays. Englewood Cliffs, N.J.,
Prentice-Hall [1963] 174 p. 21 cm. (A Spectrum book: Twentieth century views,
S-TC-27) 'S-TC-27.' 1. Fitzgerald, F. Scott (Francis Scott), 1896-1940 —
Criticism and interpretation. I. T.
PS3511.I9 Z698   813.52   *LC* 63-9306

Mizener, Arthur. 2.11736
The far side of paradise: a biography of F. Scott Fitzgerald / by Arthur
Mizener; illustrated. — 2nd ed. — Boston: Houghton Mifflin, 1965. xxviii,
416 p., [4] leaves of plates: port. — (Sentry edition; 46) 1. Fitzgerald, F. Scott
(Francis Scott), 1896-1940 — Biography. 2. Authors, American — 20th
century — Biography. I. T.
PS3511I9Z7   813.52   *LC* 65-19307   *ISBN* 0395083958 PB

Piper, Henry Dan. • 2.11737
F. Scott Fitzgerald: a critical portrait. — [1st ed.] New York: Holt, Rinehart
and Winston, [1965] xi, 334 p.; 24 cm. 1. Fitzgerald, F. Scott (Francis Scott),
1896-1940. I. T.
PS3511.I9 Z82   813.52   *LC* 65-14435

The Short stories of F. Scott Fitzgerald: new approaches in 2.11738
criticism / edited by Jackson R. Bryer.
Madison, Wis.: University of Wisconsin Press, 1982. xx, 390 p.; 23 cm.
1. Fitzgerald, F. Scott (Francis Scott), 1896-1940 — Criticism and
interpretation — Addresses, essays, lectures. I. Bryer, Jackson R.
PS3511.I9 Z853 1982   813/.52 19   *LC* 81-69815   *ISBN*
0299090809

Stern, Milton R. • 2.11739
The golden moment: the novels of F. Scott Fitzgerald [by] Milton R. Stern.
Urbana, University of Illinois Press [1970] xiii, 462 p. 24 cm. 1. Fitzgerald, F.
Scott (Francis Scott), 1896-1940 — Criticism and interpretation. I. T.
PS3511.I9 Z87   813/.5/2   *LC* 70-110422   *ISBN* 0252001079

Turnbull, Andrew, 1921-. • 2.11740
Scott Fitzgerald. New York: Scribner, [1962] 364 p.: ill.; 24 cm. 1. Fitzgerald,
F. Scott (Francis Scott), 1896-1940. I. T.
PS3511.I9 Z88   928.1   *LC* 62-9315

Milford, Nancy. • 2.11741
Zelda; a biography. New York, Harper & Row [1970] xiv, 424 p. illus.; ports. 25
cm. 1. Fitzgerald, Zelda, 1900-1948 — Biography. 2. Authors, American —
20th century — Biography. I. T.
PS3511.I9234 Z8 1970   813/.5/2 B   *LC* 66-20742

PS3511 Fl–Fo

Fletcher, John Gould, 1886-1950. • 2.11742
Selected poems / by John Gould Fletcher. — New York, Toronto: Farrar &
Rinehart, [c1938] xii, 237 p.; 22 cm. I. T.
PS3511.L457 A6 1938   *LC* 38-14768

Foote, Shelby. • 2.11743
Shiloh, a novel. — New York: Dial Press, [c1952] 226 p. 1. Shiloh, Battle of,
1862 — Fiction. I. T.
PS3511.O348 S45   *LC* 52-5614

White, Helen, 1914-. 2.11744
Shelby Foote / by Helen White and Redding S. Sugg, Jr. — Boston: Twayne
Publishers, c1982. 150 p.: port.; 21 cm. — (Twayne's United States authors
series. TUSAS 431) Includes index. 1. Foote, Shelby — Criticism and
interpretation. I. Sugg, Redding S. II. T. III. Series.
PS3511.O348 Z94   813/.54 19   *LC* 82-3071   *ISBN* 0805773665

Forbes, Esther. • 2.11745
O genteel lady! Boston and New York, Houghton Mifflin company, 1926. 4 p.l.,
296, [1] p. 20 cm. I. T.
PS3511.O35Ox   *LC* 26-9023

Forbes, Esther, 1894-. • 2.11746
A mirror for witches in which is reflected the life, machinations, and death of
famous Doll Bilby: who, with a more than feminine perversity, preferred a
demon to a mortal lover: here is also told how and why a righteous and most
awful judgment befell her, destroying both corporeal body and immortal soul /
with woodcuts by Robert Gibbings. — Boston: Houghton Mifflin, [c1928]
213 p.: front., ill., plates.; 24 cm. 1. Witchcraft — Massachusetts — Salem.
I. T.
PS3511.O585 M57 1928   *LC* 28-12074

PS3511 Frost

Frost, Robert, 1874-1963. 2.11747
Complete poems of Robert Frost, 1949. — New York: H. Holt, [1949] xxi,
642 p.: port.; 25 cm. 'Limited to five hundred copies ... signed by the author ... '
I. T.
PS3511.R94 1949   811.5   *LC* 49-9497

Frost, Robert, 1874-1963. • 2.11748
The poetry of Robert Frost. Edited by Edward Connery Lathem. [1st ed.] New
York, Holt, Rinehart and Winston [1969] xx, 607 p., port. 22 cm. I. Lathem,
Edward Connery. ed. II. T.
PS3511.R94 1969   811/.5/2   *LC* 68-24759   *ISBN* 0030725356

Frost, Robert, 1874-1963. • 2.11749
Selected prose. Edited by Hyde Cox and Edward Connery Lathem. — [1st ed.].
— New York: Holt, Rinehart and Winston, [1966] 119 p.; 22 cm. I. Cox, Hyde.
ed. II. Lathem, Edward Connery. ed. III. T.
PS3511.R94 A16 1966   811.52   *LC* 66-10268

Frost, Robert, 1874-1963. • 2.11750
Selected letters. Edited by Lawrance Thompson. — [1st ed.]. — New York:
Holt, Rinehart and Winston, [1964] lxiv, 645 p.: facsims.; 25 cm. I. Thompson,
Lawrance Roger, 1906-1973. ed. II. T.
PS3511.R94 Z52 1964   928.1   *LC* 64-10767

Frost, Robert, 1874-1963. • 2.11751
Family letters of Robert and Elinor Frost. Edited by Arnold Grade. Foreword
by Lesley Frost. — [1st ed.]. — Albany: State University of New York Press,
1972. xxi, 293 p.: illus.; 25 cm. I. Frost, Elinor, 1873-1938. II. Grade, Arnold
E., ed. III. T.
PS3511.R94 Z52 1972   811/.5/2 B   *LC* 71-152518   *ISBN*
0873950879

Brower, Reuben Arthur, 1908-. • 2.11752
The poetry of Robert Frost; constellations of intention. — New York: Oxford
University Press, 1963. 246 p.; 21 cm. 1. Frost, Robert, 1874-1963 — Criticism
and interpretation. I. T.
PS3511.R94 Z556   811.52   *LC* 63-8466

Cook, Reginald Lansing, 1903-. • **2.11753**
The dimensions of Robert Frost / [by] Reginald L. Cook. — New York; Toronto: Rinehart, [1959, c1958] xii, 241 p.; 23 cm. 1. Frost, Robert, 1874-1963. I. T.
PS3511.R94 Z585 1968   811.5   *LC* 58-9351

Cox, James Melville, 1925- ed. • **2.11754**
Robert Frost; a collection of critical essays. Englewood Cliffs, N.J., Prentice-Hall [1962] 205 p. 21 cm. (A Spectrum book: Twentieth century views, S-TC-3) 1. Frost, Robert, 1874-1963 — Criticism and interpretation. I. T.
PS3511.R94 Z588   811.52   *LC* 62-9283

Cox, Sidney, 1889-1952. • **2.11755**
A swinger of birches: a portrait of Robert Frost / with an introd. by Robert Frost. — New York: New York University Press, 1957. 177 p.; 21 cm. 1. Frost, Robert, 1874-1963. I. T.
PS3511.R94 Z59   928.1   *LC* 57-6372

Poirier, Richard. **2.11756**
Robert Frost: the work of knowing / Richard Poirier. — New York: Oxford University Press, 1977. xvii, 322 p.; 22 cm. 1. Frost, Robert, 1874-1963 — Criticism and interpretation. I. T.
PS3511.R94 Z87   811/.5/2   *LC* 76-57259   *ISBN* 0195022165

Pritchard, William H. **2.11757**
Frost: a literary life reconsidered / William H. Pritchard. — New York: Oxford University Press, 1984. xix, 286 p.: ports.; 22 cm. Includes index. 1. Frost, Robert, 1874-1963. 2. Poets, American — 20th century — Biography. I. T.
PS3511.R94 Z89 1984   811/.52 B 19   *LC* 84-11239   *ISBN* 0195034627

Sergeant, Elizabeth Shepley, 1881-1965. • **2.11758**
Robert Frost; the trial by existence. — [1st ed.]. — New York: Holt, Rinehart and Winston, [1960] xxvii, 451 p.: illus., ports.; 22 cm. Prose and poems. 1. Frost, Robert, 1874-1963. I. T.
PS3511.R94 Z92   811.52   *LC* 60-8792

Squires, Radcliffe, 1917-. • **2.11759**
The major themes of Robert Frost. — Ann Arbor: University of Michigan Press, [1963] 119 p.; 23 cm. 1. Frost, Robert, 1874-1963 — Criticism and interpretation. I. T.
PS3511.R94 Z925   811.52   *LC* 63-9902

Thompson, Lawrance Roger, 1906-1973. • **2.11760**
Fire and ice; the art and thought of Robert Frost. — New York: Russell & Russell, 1961 [c1942] 241 p.; 22 cm. 1. Frost, Robert, 1874-1963 — Criticism and interpretation. I. T.
PS3511.R94 Z93 1961   811.52   *LC* 61-15326

Thompson, Lawrance Roger, 1906-1973. • **2.11761**
Robert Frost, by Lawrance Thompson. — [1st ed.]. — New York: Holt, Rinehart and Winston, [1966-76] 3 v.: illus., ports.; 24 cm. 1. Frost, Robert, 1874-1963. I. T.
PS3511.R94 Z953   811.52 B   *LC* 66-20523

Thompson, Lawrance Roger, 1906-1973. **2.11762**
Robert Frost, a biography / by Lawrance Thompson and R.H. Winnick. — 1st ed. — New York: Holt, Rinehart and Winston, 1982, c1981. xiii, 543 p., [8] leaves of plates: ill.; 24 cm. 'The authorized life of the poet condensed into a single volume edited by Edward Connery Lathem.' Includes index. 1. Frost, Robert, 1874-1963 — Biography. 2. Poets, American — 20th century — Biography. I. Winnick, R. H. joint author. II. Lathem, Edward Connery. III. T.
PS3511.R94 Z954 1982   811/.52 B 19   *LC* 80-28337

PS3511 Fu–Fz

Futrelle, Jacques, 1875-1912. **2.11763**
The thinking machine; being a true and complete statement of several intricate mysteries which came under the observation of Professor Augustus S.F.X. Van Duesen, PH.D., LL. D., F.R.S., M.D., etc. By Jacques Futrelle. Illus. by the Kinneys. New York, Dodds, Mead, 1907. 342 p. illus. I. T.
PS3511.U98 T5x   813.52

PS3513 G–Gi

Gale, Zona, 1874-1938. • **2.11764**
Birth / by Zona Gale. — New York: The Macmillan company, 1918. 402 p.; 20 cm. I. T.
PS3513.A34 Bx PZ3.G1319 B   *LC* 18-20940

Gale, Zona, 1874-1938. • **2.11765**
Miss Lulu Bett / edited by Lella B. Kelsey. — New York: Appleton-Century, [1928] xii, 278 p.: port. — (Appleton modern literature series) I. Kelsey, Lella B. II. T. III. Series.
PS3513.A34 M5 1928   *LC* 28-5567

Gardner, Erle Stanley, 1889-1970. **2.11766**
The case of the sulky girl. New York: W. Morrow and company, 1933. 4 p bl., 303 p. 20 cm. I. T.
PZ3.G1714 Cap   PS3513.A6322.   *LC* 33-23930

Garrigue, Jean, 1912-1972. • **2.11767**
The monument rose: poems. — New York: Noonday Press, 1953. 58 p.; 25 cm. I. T.
PS3513.A7217 M6   811.5   *LC* 53-10701

Gibson, William. **2.11768**
Neuromancer / William Gibson. — New York: [Berkley Publishing Group], c1984. x, 271 p.; 18 cm. 'Ace science fiction books.' I. T.
PS3513.I2824   823/.914 19   *ISBN* 0441569579

Gill, Brendan, 1914-. **2.11769**
Here at the New Yorker / Brendan Gill. — 1st ed. — New York: Random House, [1975] 406 p.: ill.; 25 cm. Autobiographical. Includes index. 1. Gill, Brendan, 1914- — Biography. 2. New Yorker (New York, 1925-) I. T.
PS3513.I468 Z52   818/.5/209 B   *LC* 74-23927   *ISBN* 0394489896

Ginsberg, Allen, 1926-. • **2.11770**
[Poems] Collected poems, 1947–1980 / Allen Ginsberg. — 1st ed. — New York: Harper & Row, c1984. xxi, 837 p.: ill.; 24 cm. Includes indexes. I. T.
PS3513.I74 A17 1984   811/.54 19   *LC* 84-47573   *ISBN* 0060153415

Merrill, Thomas F. • **2.11771**
Allen Ginsberg / by Thomas F. Merrill. — New York: Twayne Publishers, [c1969] 183 p.; 21 cm. — (Twayne's United States author series, 161) 1. Ginsberg, Allen, 1926- I. T.
PS3513.I74 Z8   811/.5/4   *LC* 74-99535

PS3513 Glasgow

Glasgow, Ellen Anderson Gholson, 1874-1945. • **2.11772**
Works. Virginia ed. New York: C. Scribner's sons, 1938. 12 v.: ill. 25 cm. I. T. II. Title: Barren ground. III. Title: The miller of Old Church. IV. Title: Vein of iron. V. Title: The sheltered life. VI. Title: The romantic comedians. VII. Title: They stooped to folly. VIII. Title: The battle ground. IX. Title: The deliverance. X. Title: Virginia. XI. Title: The voice of the people. XII. Title: Romance of a plain man. XIII. Title: Life and Gabriella.
PS3513.L34 1938   *LC* 38-24704

Glasgow, Ellen Anderson Gholson, 1874-1945. • **2.11773**
Collected stories. Edited by Richard K. Meeker. — [Baton Rouge]: Louisiana State University Press, [1963] 254 p.; 24 cm. I. Meeker, Richard Kilburn, 1925-. II. T.
PZ3.G464 Co   PS3513.L34 A16.   *LC* 63-13240

Glasgow, Ellen Anderson Gholson, 1874-1945. • **2.11774**
A certain measure; an interpretation of prose fiction, by Ellen Glasgow. — New York, Harcourt, Brace and company [1943] 272 p. 1. Glasgow, Ellen Anderson Gholson, 1874-1945. 2. Fiction — Technique I. T.
PS3513.L34 C4   813.59   *LC* 43-15827

Glasgow, Ellen Anderson Gholson, 1874-1945. • **2.11775**
The freeman, and other poems / by Ellen Glasgow. — New York: Doubleday, Page, 1902. 56 p.; 22 cm. I. T.
PS3573L34 F7 1902   PS3513.L34 F7 1902.

Glasgow, Ellen Anderson Gholson, 1873-1945. • **2.11776**
In this our life / by Ellen Glasgow. New York: Harcourt, Brace and Company [c1941] 5 p., 3-467 p. 21 cm. 'First edition.' I. T.
PS3513.L34 I5   PZ3.G464 In   *LC* 41-51629

Glasgow, Ellen Anderson Gholson, 1873-1945. • **2.11777**
The woman within / Ellen Glasgow. — New York: Harcourt, Brace, 1954. xii, 307 p.: ill., facsim., ports. I. T.
PS3513.L34 Z5   928.1   *LC* 54-11329

Ellen Glasgow: centennial essays / edited by M. Thomas Inge. **2.11778**
Charlottesville: University Press of Virginia, 1976. 232 p., [1] leaf of plates: port.; 25 cm. Nine essays, 6 of which were read at the centennial symposium held at Mary Baldwin College on Oct. 19, 1973 and at the Richmond Public Library on Oct. 20, 1973. Includes index. 1. Glasgow, Ellen Anderson Gholson, 1873-1945 — Addresses, essays, lectures. I. Inge, M. Thomas. II. Mary Baldwin College, Staunton, Va.
PS3513.L34 Z653   813/.5/2   *LC* 75-15976   *ISBN* 0813906202

McDowell, Frederick Peter Woll, 1915-.　• 2.11779
Ellen Glasgow and the ironic art of fiction / by Frederick P.W. McDowell. — Madison: University of Wisconsin Press, 1960. xi, 292 p.; 25 cm. Includes index. 1. Glasgow, Ellen Anderson Gholson, 1873-1945. 2. Irony in literature I. T.
PS3513.L34 Z68　　813　　LC 60-9551

Raper, Julius Rowan, 1938-.　2.11780
Without shelter; the early career of Ellen Glasgow [by] J. R. Raper. Baton Rouge, Louisiana State University Press [1971] xii, 273 p. 24 cm. (Southern literary studies.) 1. Glasgow, Ellen Anderson Gholson, 1873-1945. 2. Novelists, American — 20th century — Biography. I. T. II. Series.
PS3513.L34 Z75　　813/.5/2 B　　LC 74-142337　　ISBN 0807109045

Rouse, Blair.　• 2.11781
Ellen Glasgow. New York, Twayne Publishers [c1962] 160 p. 21 cm. (Twayne's United States authors series, 26) 1. Glasgow, Ellen Anderson Gholson, 1873-1945. I. T.
PS3513.L34 Z79　　813.52　　LC 62-16821

Santas, Joan Foster.　• 2.11782
Ellen Glasgow's American dream. — Charlottesville: University Press of Virgia [1965] 248 p.; 25 cm. 1. Glasgow, Ellen Anderson Gholson, 1874-1945. I. T.
PS3513.L34 Z85　　813.52　　LC 65-23998

Thiébaux, Marcelle.　2.11783
Ellen Glasgow / Marcelle Thiebaux. — New York: F. Ungar Pub. Co., c1982. xiii, 222 p.; 21 cm. — (Modern literature series.) Includes index. 1. Glasgow, Ellen Anderson Gholson, 1873-1945 — Criticism and interpretation. I. T. II. Series.
PS3513.L34 Z9 1982　　813/.52 19　　LC 81-70128　　ISBN 0804428727

PS3513 Gl–Go

Glaspell, Susan, 1882-1948.　2.11784
Alison's house: a play in three acts. — New York: French, 1930. 155 p. I. T.
PS3513.L35 A7　　LC 31-226

Waterman, Arthur E., 1926-.　• 2.11785
Susan Glaspell, By Arthur E. Waterman. — New York: Twayne Publishers, [1966] 144 p.; 21 cm. — (Twayne's United States authors series, 101) 1. Glaspell, Susan, 1882-1948. I. T.
PS3513.L35 Z93　　818.5209　　LC 66-17062

Gordon, Caroline, 1895-.　2.11786
The collected stories of Caroline Gordon / with an introd. by Robert Penn Warren. — New York: Farrar, Straus, Giroux, c1981. xiii, 352 p.; 24 cm. I. T.
PS3513.O5765 A6 1981　　813/.52 19　　LC 80-28675　　ISBN 0374126305

Gordon, Caroline, 1895-.　• 2.11787
The garden of Adonis / by Caroline Gordon. — New York: C. Scribner's Sons, 1937. 299 p.; 22 cm. I. T.
PZ3.G6525 Gar　　PS3513.O5765 G3.　　LC 37-33903

Gordon, Caroline, 1895-.　• 2.11788
Green centuries / by Caroline Gordon. — New York: Scribner, 1941. 469 p.; 22 cm. — I. T.
PZ3.G6525 Gr5 PS3513.O5765 G7x　　813/.5/2　　LC 41-22068

Gordon, Caroline, 1895-.　• 2.11789
Penhally. — New York: Scribner, [1931] 282 p.; 22 cm. — I. T.
PZ3.G6525 Pe5 PS3513.O5765 P4x　　813/.5/2

Gordon, Caroline, 1895-.　• 2.11790
The strange children. — New York: Cooper Square Publishers, 1971 [c1951] 303 p.; 22 cm. — I. T.
PZ3.G6525 St5 PS3513.O5765 S8x　　813/.5/2　　LC 71-164525
ISBN 0815403941

Gordon, Caroline, 1895-.　• 2.11791
The women on the porch. — New York: Cooper Square Publishers, 1971 [c1944] 316 p.; 22 cm. — I. T.
PZ3.G6525 Wo5 PS3513.O5765 W6x　　813/.5/2　　LC 78-164524
ISBN 0815403933

Gordon, Caroline, 1895-.　2.11792
The Southern mandarins: letters of Caroline Gordon to Sally Wood, 1924-1937 / edited by Sally Wood; foreword by Andrew Lytle. — Baton Rouge: Louisiana State University Press, c1984. xx, 218 p.; 24 cm. — (Southern literary studies.) 1. Gordon, Caroline, 1895- — Correspondence. 2. Wood, Sally — Correspondence. 3. Tate, Allen, 1899- — Biography — Marriage. 4. Authors,

American — 20th century — Correspondence. I. Wood, Sally. II. T. III. Series.
PS3513.O5765 Z497 1984　　813/.52 B 19　　LC 83-16229　　ISBN 0807111376

Fraistat, Rose Ann C., 1952-.　2.11793
Caroline Gordon as novelist and woman of letters / Rose Ann C. Fraistat. — Baton Rouge: Louisiana State University Press, c1984. xi, 181 p.; 22 cm. — (Southern literary studies.) Includes index. 1. Gordon, Caroline, 1895- 2. Novelists, American — 20th century — Biography. I. T. II. Series.
PS3513.O5765 Z63 1984　　813/.52 19　　LC 83-19963　　ISBN 0807111511

Goyen, William.　• 2.11794
The house of breath. New York, Random House [1950] 181 p. 21 cm. I. T.
PZ3.G7484 Ho　　PS3513.O97 H6x.　　LC 50-9448

Phillips, Robert S.　2.11795
William Goyen / by Robert Phillips. — Boston: Twayne Publishers, 1979. 157 p.: port.; 21 cm. — (Twayne's United States authors series; TUSAS 329) Includes index. 1. Goyen, William — Criticism and interpretation. I. T.
PS3513.O97 Z8　　813/.5/4　　LC 78-27472　　ISBN 0805772693

PS3513 Gr–Gz

Green, Paul, 1894-1981.　• 2.11796
The field god, and In Abraham's bosom / by Paul Green. — New York: R. M. McBride & company, 1927. 317 p.; 20 cm. I. T.
PS3513.R452 F5 1927　　LC 27-8921

Green, Paul, 1894-1981.　• 2.11797
The lost colony: a symphonic drama of American history. — Roanoke Island ed. Chapel Hill: University of North Carolina Press, 1954. 70 p.: ill.; 23 cm. 1. Raleigh's Roanoke colonies, 1584-1590 — Drama. 2. Roanoke Island (N.C.) — History — Drama. I. T.
PS3513.R452 L7 1954　　812.5　　LC 54-3678

Green, Paul, 1894-1981.　• 2.11798
This body the earth. — New York: Harper, 1935. 422 p. I. T.
PS3513.R452 T45　　LC 35-19876

Gregory, Horace, 1898-.　• 2.11799
Collected poems. — [1st ed.] New York, Holt, Rinehart and Winston, [1964] 226 p.; 22 cm. I. T.
PS3513.R558 A6 1964　　LC 64-14359

Grey, Zane, 1872-1939.　• 2.11800
Riders of the purple sage: a novel / by Zane Grey; illustrated by Douglas Duer. — New York: Grosset & Dunlap, [1920] 3 p. l., 334, [1] p.: front., plates.; 19 cm. I. T.
PS3513.R6545 Rx　　LC 21-13692

Gruber, Frank, 1904-1969.　• 2.11801
Zane Grey; a biography. — New York: World Pub. Co., [1970] xi, 284 p.: illus., ports.; 22 cm. 1. Grey, Zane, 1872-1939. I. T.
PS3513.R6545 Z65 1970　　813/.5/2 B　　LC 75-75879

Guthrie, A. B. (Alfred Bertram), 1901-.　• 2.11802
The big sky / [by] A. B. Guthrie, Jr. — [rev. ed.] Boston: Houghton Mifflin [196-? c1947] 349 p.: ill.; 21 cm. I. T.
PZ3　　PS3513.U855 Bx.　　LC 64-57397

Guthrie, A. B. (Alfred Bertram), 1901-.　• 2.11803
The way west. New York, W. Sloane Associates [1949] 340 p. maps. 22 cm. I. T.
PS3513.U855 W3 1949　　LC 49-11198

Ford, Thomas W.　• 2.11804
A. B. Guthrie, Jr. / by Thomas W. Ford. — Austin, Tex.: Steck-Vaughn Co., [1968] ii, 44 p.; 21 cm. (Southwest writers series. no. 15) 1. Guthrie, A. B. (Alfred Bertram), 1901- — Criticism and interpretation. I. T. II. Series.
PS3513.U855 Z65　　813/.5/2　　LC 68-22976

Guthrie, Ramon, 1896-.　2.11805
Maximum security ward and other poems / Ramon Guthrie; edited, with an introduction by Sally M. Gall. — New York: Persea Books, c1984. xxi, 213 p.; 23 cm. (Persea lamplighter titles.) I. Gall, Sally M. II. T. III. Series.
PS3513.U875 A6 1984　　811/.52 19　　LC 83-22067　　ISBN 0892550791

Gall, Sally M.　2.11806
Ramon Guthrie's Maximum security ward: an American classic / Sally M. Gall. — Columbia: University of Missouri Press, 1984. 91 p.; 21 cm. —

(Literary frontiers edition.) 1. Guthrie, Ramon, 1896- Maximum security ward. I. T. II. Series.
PS3513.U875 M334 1984   811/.52 19   *LC* 83-16836   *ISBN* 0826204309

PS3515 H–He

Hall, Donald, 1928-.   • **2.11807**
Exiles and marriages / by Donald Hall. — New York: Viking Press, 1955. x, 118 p.; 22 cm. Poems. 1. Poetry I. T.
PS3515.A3152 E9   *LC* 56-5073

Hall, Donald, 1928-.   **2.11808**
The weather for poetry: essays, reviews, and notes on poetry, 1977–81 / Donald Hall. — Ann Arbor: University of Michigan Press, c1982. xvi, 335 p.; 21 cm. — (Poets on poetry.) 1. Poetry — Addresses, essays, lectures. 2. American poetry — 20th century — History and criticism — Addresses, essays, lectures. 3. English poetry — 20th century — History and criticism — Addresses, essays, lectures. I. T. II. Series.
PS3515.A3152 W4 1982   811/.009 19   *LC* 82-8544   *ISBN* 0472063405

Hammett, Dashiell, 1894-1961.   **2.11809**
The big knockover: selected stories and short novels / Dashiell Hammett; edited and with an introd. by Lillian Hellman. — New York: Random House, 1966. xxi, 355 p.; 22 cm. I. T.
PS3515.A4347 Ax

Hammett, Dashiell, 1894-1961.   • **2.11810**
Novels. — New York: Knopf, 1965. 726 p.; 22 cm. 1. Detective and mystery stories, American I. T.
PZ3.H1884 No   PS3515.A4347 Ax.   *LC* 65-20520

Hammett, Dashiell, 1894-1961.   **2.11811**
The Continental Op. Selected and with an introd. by Steven Marcus. — [1st ed.]. — New York: Random House, [1974] xxix, 287 p.; 22 cm. 1. Detective and mystery stories, American I. T.
PZ3.H1884 Cq6 PS3515.A4347 C6x   813/.5/2   *LC* 74-9050   *ISBN* 0394487044

Gregory, Sinda, 1947-.   **2.11812**
Private investigations: the novels of Dashiell Hammett / Sinda Gregory. — Carbondale: Southern Illinois University Press, c1985. xiv, 205 p.; 23 cm. Includes index. 1. Hammett, Dashiell, 1894-1961 — Criticism and interpretation. 2. Detective and mystery stories, American — History and criticism. I. T.
PS3515.A4347 Z68 1985   813/.52 19   *LC* 84-1389   *ISBN* 0809311658

Hansberry, Lorraine, 1930-1965.   • **2.11813**
A raisin in the sun: a drama in three acts. — New York: Random House, [1959] 142 p.: ill; 21 cm. — (A Random House play) I. T.
PS3515.A515 R3   *LC* 59-10834

Hansberry, Lorraine, 1930-1965.   **2.11814**
The sign in Sidney Brustein's window: a drama in three acts. — New York: Random House, [1965] lxi, 143 p.: ports.; 22 cm. I. T.
PS3515.A515 S5 1965   812.54   *LC* 65-18311

Hardwick, Elizabeth.   **2.11815**
Bartleby in Manhattan: and other essays / Elizabeth Hardwick. — New York: Random House, 1985. x, 292 p.; 22 cm. I. T.
PS3515.A5672 B3 1983   814/.52 19   *LC* 82-42796   *ISBN* 0394528808

Hardwick, Elizabeth.   **2.11816**
The ghostly lover / Elizabeth Hardwick. — New York: Ecco Press, 1982, c1945. 278 p.; 22 cm. Originally published: New York: Harcourt, Brace, 1945. I. T.
PS3515.A5672 G47 1982   813/.52 19   *LC* 81-9679   *ISBN* 0912946954

Hawkes, John, 1925-.   • **2.11817**
The cannibal. [New York, New Directions, 1949] xiv, 223 p.; 17 cm. (The Direction series; 13) I. T. II. Series.
AP2.D583 no. 13   PS3515.A92 C3.   813.5   *LC* 49-48130 rev*

Hawkes, John, 1925-.   • **2.11818**
Second skin / John Hawkes. — [New York]: New Directions, [1964] 210 p.; 21 cm. I. T. II. Title: 2nd skin.
PS3515.A92 S43   *LC* 64-10674   *ISBN*

Hayden, Robert Earl.   **2.11819**
Angle of ascent: new and selected poems / by Robert Hayden. — 1st ed. — New York: Liveright, [1975] 131 p.; 21 cm. I. T.
PS3515.A9363 A6 1975   811/.5/2   *LC* 75-20493   *ISBN* 0871406136

Hayden, Robert Earl.   **2.11820**
[Prose works. Selections] Collected prose / Robert Hayden; foreword by William Meredith; edited by Frederick Glaysher. — Ann Arbor: University of Michigan Press, 1984. xii, 203 p.; 21 cm. (Poets on poetry.) 1. Poetry — Addresses, essays, lectures. I. Glaysher, Frederick, 1954- II. T. III. Series.
PS3515.A9363 A6 1984   818/.5208 19   *LC* 84-3602   *ISBN* 0472063510

Fetrow, Fred M.   **2.11821**
Robert Hayden / by Fred M. Fetrow. — Boston: Twayne Publishers, c1984. 159 p.: port.; 23 cm. — (Twayne's United States authors series. TUSAS 471) Includes index. 1. Hayden, Robert Earl — Criticism and interpretation. I. T. II. Series.
PS3515.A9363 Z66 1984   811/.52 19   *LC* 83-26581   *ISBN* 0805774122

Hecht, Ben, 1893-1964.   • **2.11822**
A treasury of Ben Hecht: collected stories and other writings. — New York: Crown Publishers, [c1959] xii, 397 p. I. T.
PS3515.E18 A6 1959   *LC* 59-9170

Hecht, Ben, 1893-1964.   • **2.11823**
Erik Dorn, a novel. Introd. by Nelson Algren. Chicago, University of Chicago Press [1963] xix, 409 p. — (Chicago in fiction) I. T. II. Series.
PS3515.E18 E7 1963   813.5   *LC* 63-22588

Hecht, Ben, 1893-1964.   • **2.11824**
Gargoyles. — New York: Boni and Liveright, [1922] 346 p. I. T.
PS3515.E18 G3   *LC* 22-18299

Hecht, Ben, 1893-1964.   • **2.11825**
A child of the century / Ben Hecht. — New York: Simon and Schuster, 1954. 654 p.: ill. — Autobiography. I. T.
PS3515.E18.Z5   *LC* 53-9699

Heggen, Thomas, 1919-1949.   • **2.11826**
Mister Roberts, by Thomas Heggen, illustrated by Samuel Hanks Bryant. — Boston: Houghton Mifflin Company, 1946. xvii, 221 p.: illus.; 21 cm. — I. T.
PZ3.H3614 Mi   PS3515.E263 Mx.   *LC* 46-25229

Heinlein, Robert A. (Robert Anson), 1907-.   **2.11827**
Glory road: a novel. New York: Putnam, 1963. 288 p.; 22 cm. I. T.
PS3515.E288 G5   *LC* 63-16185

Heinlein, Robert A. (Robert Anson), 1907-.   • **2.11828**
Stranger in a strange land. New York, Putnam [1961] 408 p. 22 cm. I. T.
PZ3.H364 St   PS3515.E288 Sx.   *LC* 61-11702

Heinlein, Robert A. (Robert Anson), 1907-.   **2.11829**
The past through tomorrow: 'future history stories' / Robert A. Heinlein. — New York: Putnam, 1967. 337 p.; 22 cm. — (His Future history series) I. T.
PS3515.E33 P38   *LC* 67-15112/AC/r852   *ISBN* 0399106200

Hellman, Lillian, 1906-.   • **2.11830**
The collected plays. [1st ed.] Boston, Little, Brown [1972] 815 p. 25 cm. I. T.
PS3515.E343 A6 1972   812/.52 19   *LC* 79-175482

Hellman, Lillian, 1906-.   **2.11831**
Pentimento. — [1st ed.]. — Boston: Little, Brown, [1973] 297 p.; 25 cm. 1. Hellman, Lillian, 1906- 2. Dramatists, American — 20th century — Biography. I. T.
PS3515.E343 Z498   812/.52 B 19   *LC* 73-7747   *ISBN* 0316355208

Hellman, Lillian, 1905-.   **2.11832**
Scoundrel time / Lillian Hellman. — 1st ed. — Boston: Little, Brown, c1976. 155 p., 6 leaves of plates: ill. 1. Hellman, Lillian, 1905- — Biography. I. T.
PS3515.E343 Z499   PS3515E343 Z499.   812/.5/2 B   *LC* 76-220   *ISBN* 0316355151

Hellman, Lillian, 1906-.   • **2.11833**
An unfinished woman; a memoir. — [1st ed.]. — Boston: Little, Brown, [1969] 280 p.: ports.; 25 cm. Autobiographical. I. T.
PS3515.E343 Z5   812/.52 B 19   *LC* 76-75019

Wright, William, 1930-.   **2.11834**
Lillian Hellman: the image, the woman / by William Wright. — New York: Simon and Schuster, c1986. 507 p., [16] p. of plates; 25 cm. Includes index.

1. Hellman, Lillian, 1906- — Biography. 2. Dramatists, American — 20th century — Biography. I. T.
PS3515.E343 Z96 1986   812/.52 B 19   *LC* 86-17794   *ISBN* 0671526871

PS3515 Hemingway

Hemingway, Ernest, 1899-1961.   • **2.11835**
The fifth column, and four stories of the Spanish Civil War. — New York: Scribner, [1969] 151 p.; 22 cm. 1. Spain — History — Civil War, 1936-1939 — Drama 2. Spain — History — Civil War, 1936-1939 — Fiction. I. T.
PS3515.E37 A15 1969   813/.5/2   *LC* 69-17057

Hemingway, Ernest, 1899-1961.   **2.11836**
Three stories & ten poems / Ernest Hemingway. — [Bloomfield Hills, Mich.: Bruccoli Clark Books, 1977] 58 p.; 18 cm. I. T.
PS3515.E37 A15 1977

Hemingway, Ernest, 1899-1961.   **2.11837**
By–line: Ernest Hemingway; selected articles and dispatches of four decades / edited by William White. — New York: Scribner, 1967. xiv, 489 p. 1. Hemingway, Ernest, 1899-1961. I. White, William, 1910- I. T.
PS3515.E37 A16 1967   818   *LC* 67-15483   *ISBN* 0684717956 pbk

Hemingway, Ernest, 1899-1961.   **2.11838**
Dateline, Toronto: the complete Toronto star dispatches, 1920–1924 / Ernest Hemingway; edited by William White. — New York: Scribner's, c1985. xxxi, 478 p.; 24 cm. I. White, William, 1910- II. Toronto daily star. III. Toronto star weekly. IV. T.
PS3515.E37 A6 1985   814/.54 19   *LC* 85-14439   *ISBN* 0684185156

Hemingway, Ernest, 1899-1961.   • **2.11839**
Across the river and into the trees. — New York: Scribner, 1950. 308 p.; 22 cm. — I. T.
PZ3.H3736 Ac   PS3515.E37 A7.   *LC* 50-9370

Hemingway, Ernest, 1899-1961.   • **2.11840**
Short stories. — New York: Scribner, [1956] viii, 499 p.; 22 cm. This collection originally published in 1938, with the play 'The fifth column' in the same vol. I. T.
PS3515.E37 Ax   *LC* a 57-5738

Hemingway, Ernest, 1899-1961.   • **2.11841**
A farewell to arms / by Ernest Hemingway . — New York, Scribner, 1953, c1929. 342 p. 22 cm. I. T.
PS3515.E37F3x   *LC* 53-7687 rev

Hemingway, Ernest, 1899-1961.   • **2.11842**
For whom the bell tolls. New York: Scribner, 1940. 471 p.; 22 cm. 1. Spain — History — Civil War, 1936-1939 — Fiction. I. T.
PS3515.E37 F6x   *LC* 40-27732

Hemingway, Ernest, 1899-1961.   **2.11843**
The garden of Eden / Ernest Hemingway. — New York: C. Scribner's, 1986. 247 p.; 22 cm. I. T.
PS3515.E37 G37 1986   813/.52 19   *LC* 86-3701   *ISBN* 0684186934

Hemingway, Ernest, 1899-1961.   **2.11844**
In our time / by Ernest Hemingway. — [Bloomfield Hills, Mich.: Bruccoli Clark Books], c1977. 30 p.: port.; 27 cm. Facsim. of the 1924 ed.; original imprint reads: Paris: Printed at the Three Mountains Press and for sale at Shakespeare & Company ...; London: William Jackson. I. T.
PZ3.H3736 Il 1924a PS3515.E37 I53   813/.5/2   *LC* 78-113212

Hemingway, Ernest, 1899-1961.   • **2.11845**
Islands in the stream. — New York: Scribner, [1970] 466 p.: map (on lining papers); 24 cm. — I. T.
PZ3.H3736 Is PS3515.E37 I8x   813/.5/2   *LC* 71-123834   10.00

Hemingway, Ernest, 1899-1961.   • **2.11846**
The Nick Adams stories / pref. by Philip Young. — New York: Scribner, [1972] 268 p.; 24 cm. Eight of these stories never before published. I. T.
PS3515.E37 N5   PZ3.H3736 Ni   813/.5/2   *LC* 77-159759   *ISBN* 0684124858

Hemingway, Ernest, 1899-1961.   • **2.11847**
The old man and the sea. — New York: Scribner, 1952. 140 p.; 22 cm. — I. T.
PZ3.H3736 Ol   PS3515.E37 O4.   *LC* 52-11935

Hemingway, Ernest, 1899-1961.   • **2.11848**
The sun also rises. — New York: Scribner, 1956 [c1954] 247 p.; 22 cm. — I. T.
PZ3.H3736 Su12   PS3515.E37 Sx.   *LC* 57-4130

Hemingway, Ernest, 1899-1961.   • **2.11849**
To have and have not. — New York: Scribner, 1937. 262 p.; 21 cm. — I. T.
PS3515.E37 T6 1937   PZ3.H3736 Tn   *LC* 37-23935

Biography. Criticism

Hemingway, Ernest, 1899-1961.   **2.11850**
The dangerous summer / Ernest Hemingway; introduction by James A. Michener. — New York: Scribner, c1985. ix, 228 p., [16] p. of plates: ill., map; 24 cm. Includes index. 1. Hemingway, Ernest, 1899-1961 — Journeys — Spain. 2. Ordóñez Araujo, Antonio, 1932- 3. Dominguín, Luis Miguel, 1926- 4. Bullfights — Spain. 5. Bullfighters — Spain — Biography. 6. Authors, American — 20th century — Biography. 7. Spain — Description and travel — 1951-1980 I. T.
PS3515.E37 Z464 1985   818/.5203 B 19   *LC* 84-27578   *ISBN* 0684183552

Hemingway, Ernest, 1899-1961.   • **2.11851**
A moveable feast. New York: Scribner, [1964] 211 p.: ports.; 22 cm. 1. Authors — Correspondence, reminiscences, etc. 2. Paris (France) — Social life and customs — 20th century I. T.
PS3515.E37 Z475 1964   818/.5203 19   *LC* 64-15441

Hemingway, Ernest, 1899-1961.   **2.11852**
[Correspondence. Selections] Ernest Hemingway, selected letters, 1917–1961 / edited by Carlos Baker. — New York: Scribner, 1981. xxvii, 948 p.; 24 cm. 1. Hemingway, Ernest, 1899-1961. Correspondence. Selections 2. Novelists, American — 20th century — Correspondence. I. Baker, Carlos, 1909-1987. II. T.
PS3515.E37 Z53 1981   813/.52 19   *LC* 80-39773   *ISBN* 0684167654

Baker, Carlos, 1909-1987.   • **2.11853**
Ernest Hemingway; a life story, by Carlos Baker. — New York: Scribner, [1969] xvi, 697 p.: illus., ports.; 23 cm. 1. Hemingway, Ernest, 1899-1961 — Biography. I. T.
PS3515.E37 Z575 1969   813/.5/2 B   *LC* 68-57079

Baker, Carlos, 1909-1987. ed.   • **2.11854**
Hemingway and his critics: an international anthology / edited, with an introd. and a checklist of Hemingway criticism. — New York: Hill and Wang, [1961] 298 p.; 21 cm. (American century series, AC36) 1. Hemingway, Ernest, 1899-1961. I. T.
PS3515.E37 Z577   813.52   *LC* 61-7565

Baker, Carlos, 1909-1987.   • **2.11855**
Hemingway, the writer as artist. — [4th ed.]. — Princeton, N.J.: Princeton University Press, [1972] xx, 438 p.; 23 cm. 'A working check-list of Hemingway's prose, poetry, and journalism, with notes': p. [409]-426. 1. Hemingway, Ernest, 1899-1961. I. T.
PS3515.E37 Z58 1972   813/.5/2   *LC* 70-170253   *ISBN* 0691062315

Baker, Sheridan Warner, 1918-.   • **2.11856**
Ernest Hemingway: an introduction and interpretation / [by] Sheridan Baker. — New York: Holt, Rinehart and Winston, [1967] ix, 150 p.: ports.; 21 cm. — (American authors and critics series) 1. Hemingway, Ernest, 1899-1961. I. T. II. Series.
PS3515.E37 Z582   813/.5/2   *LC* 67-11298

Buckley, Peter.   **2.11857**
Ernest / by Peter Buckley. — New York: Dial Press, c1978. 256 p.: ill. 1. Hemingway, Ernest, 1899-1961 — Biography. 2. Novelists, American — 20th century — Biography. I. T.
PS3515.E37 Z58414   813/.5/2   *LC* 78-17729   *ISBN* 080372392X

Donaldson, Scott.   **2.11858**
By force of will: the life and art of Ernest Hemingway / Scott Donaldson. — New York: Viking Press, c1977. xiv, 367 p.; 24 cm. 1. Hemingway, Ernest, 1899-1961. 2. Novelists, American — 20th century — Biography. I. T.
PS3515.E37 Z5857   813/.5/2 B   *LC* 76-18306   *ISBN* 0670198242

Hemingway, Gregory H., 1931-.   **2.11859**
Papa: a personal memoir / Gregory H. Hemingway; with a preface by Norman Mailer. — Boston: Houghton Mifflin, 1976. xv, 119 p., [4] leaves of plates: ill.; 22 cm. 1. Hemingway, Ernest, 1899-1961 — Biography. I. T.
PS3515.E37 Z617   813/.5/2 B   *LC* 76-6933   *ISBN* 0395243483

Hemingway, Mary Welsh, 1908-.   **2.11860**
How it was / Mary Welsh Hemingway. 1st ed. — New York: Knopf: distributed by Random House, 1976. vi, 537, xi p., [12] leaves of plates: ill.; 25 cm. Autobiographical. Includes index. 1. Hemingway, Ernest, 1899-1961 — Biography — Marriage. 2. Hemingway, Mary Welsh, 1908- I. T.
PS3515.E37 Z6175   813/.5/2   *LC* 76-13672   *ISBN* 0394401093

Hemingway, the critical heritage / edited by Jeffrey Meyers. **2.11861**
London; Boston: Routledge & Kegan Paul, 1982. xvi, 611 p.; 23 cm. — (Critical heritage series.) Includes index. 1. Hemingway, Ernest, 1899-1961 — Criticism and interpretation — Addresses, essays, lectures. I. Meyers, Jeffrey. II. Series.
PS3515.E37 Z6196 1982   813/.52 19   *LC* 81-20998   *ISBN* 0710009291

Laurence, Frank M. **2.11862**
Hemingway and the movies / Frank M. Laurence. — Jackson: University Press of Mississippi, c1981. xix, 329 p.: ill.; 24 cm. Originally presented as the author's thesis, University of Pennsylvania. 1. Hemingway, Ernest, 1899-1961 — Film adaptations. 2. Film adaptations I. T.
PS3515.E37 Z689 1981   813/.52   *LC* 79-56697   *ISBN* 0878051155

Meyers, Jeffrey. **2.11863**
Hemingway, a biography / Jeffrey Meyers. — 1st ed. — New York: Harper & Row, c1985. xv, 644 p., [16] p. of plates: ill.; 24 cm. Includes index. 1. Hemingway, Ernest, 1899-1961 — Biography. 2. Novelists, American — 20th century — Biography. I. T.
PS3515.E37 Z7418 1985   813/.52 B 19   *LC* 84-48611   *ISBN* 0060154373

The short stories of Ernest Hemingway: critical essays / edited, **2.11864**
with an overview and checklist, by Jackson J. Benson.
Durham, N.C.: Duke University Press, 1975. xv, 375 p.; 25 cm. 1. Hemingway, Ernest, 1899-1961 — Criticism and interpretation — Addresses, essays, lectures. 2. Hemingway, Ernest, 1899-1961 — Bibliography. I. Benson, Jackson J.
PS3515.E37 Z8274   813/.5/2   *LC* 74-75815   *ISBN* 0822303205

Waldhorn, Arthur, 1918-. • **2.11865**
A reader's guide to Ernest Hemingway. — New York: Farrar, Straus and Giroux, [1972] xiv, 284 p.; 21 cm. 1. Hemingway, Ernest, 1899-1961. I. T.
PS3515.E37 Z92   813/.5/2   *LC* 75-179795   *ISBN* 0374242992

Weeks, Robert Percy, 1915- ed. • **2.11866**
Hemingway: a collection of critical essays. Englewood Cliffs, N.J., Prentice-Hall [1962] 180 p. 21 cm. (Twentieth century views. A Spectrum book, S-TC-8) 1. Hemingway, Ernest, 1899-1961 — Criticism and interpretation. I. T.
PS3515.E37 Z94   813.52   *LC* 62-13652

PS3515 He–Ho

Herbst, Josephine, 1897-1969. **2.11867**
Rope of gold: a novel of the thirties / Josephine Herbst; with an introduction by Alice Kessler–Harris and Paul Lauter and an afterword by Elinor Langer. — 1st Feminist Press ed. — Old Westbury, N.Y.: Feminist Press, 1984. xvi, 449 p.; 21 cm. (Novels of the thirties series.) Reprint. Originally published: New York: Harcourt, Brace, c1939. I. T. II. Series.
PS3515.E596 R6 1984   813/.52 19   *LC* 84-18793   *ISBN* 0935312331

Hersey, John, 1914-. **2.11868**
A bell for Adano [by] John Hersey. New York, A. A. Knopf, 1944. vii, 269, [1] p. 21 cm. 'First edition.' 1. World War, 1939-1945 — Fiction. I. T.
PS3515.E7715 B5 1944   *LC* 44-164

Hersey, John, 1914-. • **2.11869**
The wall. [1st ed.] New York: Knopf, 1950. 632 p.; 22 cm. I. T.
PS3515.E7715 W3   PZ3.H4385 Wal   *LC* 50-5697

Heyward, Du Bose, 1885-1940. • **2.11870**
Mamba's daughters / by Du Bose Heyward. — Garden City, N.Y.: Doubleday, Doran & company, 1929. 311 p.; 20 cm. I. T.
PS3515.E98 M3   *LC* 29-3497

Heyward, Du Bose, 1885-1940. • **2.11871**
Porgy / Du Bose Heyward. — Garden City, N.Y.: Doubleday, 1953. 158 p. I. T.
PZ3.H1586 Po   PS3515.E98Px.   813.5   *LC* 53-9814

Hillyer, Robert, 1895-1961. • **2.11872**
Collected poems. New York: Knopf, 1961. 235 p. I. T.
PS3515.I69 A17   *LC* 61-8531

Himes, Chester B., 1909-. **2.11873**
If he hollers let him go / Chester B. Himes. — Garden City, N. Y.: Doubleday, 1946 [c1945] 249 p.; 20 cm. I. T.
PS 3515.I713 I23 1945   *LC* 45-10120

Himes, Chester B., 1909-. **2.11874**
The third generation. [1st ed.] Cleveland, World Pub. Co. [1954] 350 p. 21 cm. I. T.
PZ3.H57 Th   PS3515.I713 T4x.   *LC* 52-13247

Hobson, Laura Keane Zametkin, 1900-. • **2.11875**
Gentleman's agreement: a novel / by Laura Z. Hobson. — New York: Simon & Schuster, 1947. 275 p.; 21 cm. I. T.
PS3515.O1515 G4   *LC* 47-30138

Hollander, John. • **2.11876**
A crackling of thorns / foreword by W.H. Auden. — New Haven: Yale University Press, 1958. 71 p. — (Yale series of younger poets. v. 54) I. T. II. Series.
PS3515.O3485 C7   *LC* 58-6538

Hollander, John. • **2.11877**
The night mirror: poems / by John Hollander. — [1st ed.]. — New York: Atheneum, 1971. 81 p.; 23 cm. — I. T.
PS3515.O3485 N5   811/.5/4   *LC* 72-162968

Hollander, John. **2.11878**
Reflections on espionage: the question of Cupcake / by John Hollander. — 1st ed. — New York: Atheneum, 1976. 76 p.; 24 cm. I. T.
PS3515.O3485 R4 1976   811/.5/4   *LC* 75-33826   *ISBN* 0689107048

Hollander, John. **2.11879**
Spectral emanations: new and selected poems / by John Hollander. — 1st ed. — New York: Atheneum, 1978. xi, 238 p.; 23 cm. — I. T.
PS3515.O3485 S6   811/.5/4   *LC* 77-20645   *ISBN* 0689108885

Irish, William, 1903-1968. **2.11880**
Phantom lady / by William Irish. — Philadelphia: Lippincott, [c1942] 291 p. — (A Story press book) I. T.
PS3515.O6455 P43   PS3545O777 P43.   *LC* 42-21645

Horgan, Paul, 1903-. • **2.11881**
A distant trumpet. — New York: Farrar, Straus and Cudahy, [1960] 629 p.; 22 cm. — I. T.
PS3515.O6583Dx   *LC* 60-7628

Horgan, Paul, 1903-. • **2.11882**
Everything to live for. — New York: Farrar, Straus and Giroux, [1968] 215 p.; 22 cm. — I. T.
PS3515.O6583 E8x   *LC* 68-23740

Horgan, Paul, 1903-. • **2.11883**
Mountain standard time: Main line west, Far from Cibola [and] The common heart / introd. by D. W. Brogan. — New York: Farrar, Straus and Cudahy, [1962] 595 p.; 22 cm. I. T. II. Title: Main line west. III. Title: Far from Cibola. IV. Title: The common heart.
PS3515.O6583 M68   813.5   *LC* 62-13072

Hough, Emerson, 1857-1923. • **2.11884**
The covered wagon / by Emerson Hough; illustrated with scenes from the photoplay, a Paramount picture. New York: Grosset & Dunlap, [1923]. 378 p.: plates; 20 cm. Plates opposite t.-p., pp. 36, 188, 300. I. T.
PS3515.O7593 Cx   *LC* 24-24985

Howard, Robert Ervin, 1906-1936. **2.11885**
Conan the conqueror [by] Robert E. Howard. New York, Gnome Press, c1950. 255 p. (His The Hyperborean Age) I. T.
PS3515.O842 C6x   813.52

PS3515 Hughes

Hughes, Langston, 1902-1967. • **2.11886**
Five plays / edited with an introd. by Webster Smalley. — Bloomington: Indiana University Press, [1963] 258 p.; 21 cm. I. T.
PS3515U274A19 1963   *LC* 63-7169

Hughes, Langston, 1902-1967. • **2.11887**
The Langston Hughes reader. — New York: G. Braziller, 1958. 501 p.; 22 cm. I. T.
PS3515.U274 A6 1958   *LC* 58-7871

Hughes, Langston, 1902-1967. • **2.11888**
Selected poems. Drawings by E. McKnight Kauffer. — [1st ed.]. — New York: Knopf, 1959. 297 p.: illus.; 25 cm. — I. T.
PS3515.U274 A6 1959   811.52   *LC* 58-10967

Hughes, Langston, 1902-1967. **2.11889**
Langston Hughes in the Hispanic world and Haiti / edited by Edward J. Mullen. — Hamden, Conn.: Archon Books, 1977. 193 p.; 23 cm. 'Langston Hughes's works translated into Spanish': p. 47-65. Includes index. 1. Hughes, Langston, 1902-1967 — Criticism and interpretation — Addresses, essays,

lectures. 2. Civilization, Hispanic — Literary collections. I. Mullen, Edward J., 1942- II. T.
PS3515.U274 A6 1977   818/.5/209   *LC* 77-3388   *ISBN* 0208016341

Hughes, Langston, 1902-1967.   • 2.11890
Ask your mama: 12 moods for jazz. — [1st ed.] — New York: Knopf, 1961. 92 p.; 19 x 23 cm. 'Poem.' I. T.
PS3515.U274 A8   *LC* 61-15039

Hughes, Langston, 1902-1967.   2.11891
Fine clothes to the Jew. — New York: Knopf, 1927. 89 p.; 20 cm. Poems. I. T.
PS3515.U274 F5 1927   *LC* 27-2880

Hughes, Langston, 1902-1967.   2.11892
Good morning, revolution: uncollected social protest writings / edited and with an introd. by Faith Berry; foreword by Saunders Redding. — [1st ed.]. — New York: L. Hill, [1973] xiv, 145 p.; 22 cm. I. T.
PS3515.U274 G6 1973   818/.5/209   *LC* 73-81747   *ISBN* 0882080237

Hughes, Langston, 1902-1967.   • 2.11893
Laughing to keep from crying. — New York: Holt, [1952] 206 p.; 21 cm. Short stories. I. T.
PS3515.U274 Lx   *LC* 52-7952

Hughes, Langston, 1902-1967.   2.11894
Not without laughter / by Langston Hughes. — New York; London: A. A. Knopf, 1930. viii, 324 p., 1 l.; 20 cm. — I. T.
PS3515.U274 N6   PZ3.H87313 No   *LC* 30-19627

Hughes, Langston, 1902-1967.   • 2.11895
Simple speaks his mind. — [New York]: Simon and Schuster, [1950] 231 p.; 20 cm. I. T.
PS3515.U274 S53   *LC* 50-7299

Hughes, Langston, 1902-1967.   • 2.11896
Simple's Uncle Sam. — New York: Hill and Wang, [1965] x, 180 p.; 21 cm. I. T.
PS3515.U274 S6   *LC* 65-24717

Hughes, Langston, 1902-1967.   2.11897
The ways of white folks [by] Langston Hughes. — New York: A. A. Knopf, 1934. 7 p. 1., 3-248 p., 1 l.; 20 cm. Short stories. 'First edition.' I. T.
PS3515.U274 W3   PZ3.H87313 Way   *LC* 34-27175

Hughes, Langston, 1902-1967.   • 2.11898
The weary blues / by Langston Hughes; with an introduction by Carl Van Vechten. — New York: A. A. Knopf, 1926. 109 p.; 20 cm. — Poems. I. T.
PS3515.U274 W4 1926   *LC* 26-4730

Biography. Criticism

Hughes, Langston, 1902-1967.   • 2.11899
The big sea, an autobiography. — New York: Hill and Wang, [1963, c1940] 335 p.; 21 cm. — (American century series) 'AC65.' 1. Hughes, Langston, 1902-1967. I. T.
PS3515.U274 Z5 1963   928.1   *LC* 63-18485

Hughes, Langston, 1902-1967.   • 2.11900
I wonder as I wander: an autobiographical journey. — New York: Rinehart, [1956] 405 p.; 24 cm. I. T.
PS3515.U274 Z58   *LC* 56-7254

Barksdale, Richard.   2.11901
Langston Hughes / Richard K. Barksdale. — Chicago: American Library Association, 1977. xii, 155 p.; 25 cm. — (The Poet and his critics) Includes index. 1. Hughes, Langston, 1902-1967 — Poetic works. 2. Hughes, Langston, 1902-1967 — Criticism and interpretation — History. I. T.
PS3515.U274 Z615   811/.5/2   *LC* 77-8599   *ISBN* 0838902375

Berry, Faith.   2.11902
Langston Hughes, before and beyond Harlem / Faith Berry. — Westport, Conn.: L. Hill, c1983. xiv, 376 p.; 24 cm. 1. Hughes, Langston, 1902-1967. 2. Poets, American — 20th century — Biography. I. T.
PS3515.U274 Z617 1983   818/.5209 B 19   *LC* 82-24971   *ISBN* 088208156X

Emanuel, James A.   • 2.11903
Langston Hughes / by James A. Emanuel. — New York: Twayne Publishers, [1967] 192 p.; 21 cm. — (Twayne's United States authors series, TUSAS 123) 1. Hughes, Langston, 1902-1967. I. T.
PS3515.U274 Z64   *LC* 67-24764

PS3515 Hu

Hugo, Richard F.   2.11904
Making certain it goes on: the collected poems of Richard Hugo. — 1st ed. — New York: Norton, c1984. xxi, 456 p.; 22 cm. Includes index. I. T.
PS3515.U3 A17 1984   811/.54 19   *LC* 83-8016   *ISBN* 0393017842

Hugo, Richard F.   2.11905
31 letters and 13 dreams: poems / by Richard Hugo. — 1st ed. — New York: Norton, c1977. 71 p.; 22 cm. — I. T.
PS3515.U3 T5   811/.5/4   *LC* 77-22156   *ISBN* 0393044815

Humphries, Rolfe, 1894-1969.   • 2.11906
Collected poems. — Bloomington: Indiana University Press, 1965. xv, 261 p. (Indiana University. Poetry series; no. 28) I. T. II. Series.
PS3515.U4835 A6 1965   811.52   *LC* 65-19700

McBain, Ed.   2.11907
87th precinct / by Ed McBain; introd. by Anthony Boucher. — New York: Simon and Schuster, 1959. 1 v. I. T.
PS3515.U582 Ex

Hurston, Zora Neale.   2.11908
I love myself when I am laughing ... and then again when I am looking mean and impressive: a Zora Neale Hurston reader / edited by Alice Walker; introd. by Mary Helen Washington. — Old Westbury, N.Y.: The Feminist Press, c1979. 313 p.: ports.; 23 cm. 1. Hurston, Zora Neale. in fiction, drama, poetry, etc. I. Walker, Alice, 1944- II. T.
PS3515.U789 A6 1979   813/.5/2   *LC* 79-17582   *ISBN* 0912670568

Hurston, Zora Neale.   2.11909
Spunk: the selected stories of Zora Neale Hurston. — Berkeley: Turtle Island Foundation, 1985. 106 p. I. T.
PS3515.U789 S6x   *ISBN* 0913666793

Hurston, Zora Neale.   2.11910
Their eyes were watching God; a novel. — New York: Negro Universities Press, [1969, c1937] 286 p.; 23 cm. — I. T.
PZ3.H9457 Th4 PS3515.U789 T5x   813/.5/2   *LC* 70-88437   *ISBN* 0837118859

Hurston, Zora Neale.   2.11911
Dust tracks on a road: an autobiography / with an introd. by Larry Neal. — Philadelphia: Lippincott, 1971 [c1942] xxv, 286 p.; 21 cm. — I. T.
PS3515.U789 Z5 1971   813/.5/2 B   *LC* 73-166497

Hemenway, Robert E., 1941-.   2.11912
Zora Neale Hurston: a literary biography / Robert E. Hemenway; with a foreword by Alice Walker. — Urbana: University of Illinois Press, c1977. xxvi, 371 p., [5] leaves of plates: ill.; 24 cm. Includes index. 1. Hurston, Zora Neale. 2. Novelists, American — 20th century — Biography. I. T.
PS3515.U789 Z7   813/.5/2 B   *LC* 77-9605   *ISBN* 0252006526

Howard, Lillie P.   2.11913
Zora Neale Hurston / by Lillie P. Howard. — Boston: Twayne Publishers, c1980. 192 p.: port.; 22 cm. — (Twayne's United States authors series; TUSAS 381) Includes index. 1. Hurston, Zora Neale — Criticism and interpretation. I. T.
PS3515.U789 Z73   813/.52 19   *LC* 80-24907   *ISBN* 0805772960

PS3517 I

Ignatow, David, 1914-.   • 2.11914
Poems, 1934–1969. — [1st ed.]. — Middletown, Conn.: Wesleyan University Press, [1970] xvii, 262 p.; 24 cm. — I. T.
PS3517.G53 A6 1970   811/.5/4   *LC* 79-105500   *ISBN* 0819540145

Inge, William.   • 2.11915
Summer brave, and eleven short plays. New York: Random House, [1962] 299 p.; 20 cm. 'The rewritten and final version of the romantic comedy Picnic.' I. T.
PS3517.N265 P5 1962   812.54   *LC* 62-12730

Inge, William.   2.11916
Splendor in the grass: a screenplay / by William Inge. — New York: Bantam Books, 1961. 121 p. — (A Bantam book; J2204) I. T.
PS3517N265 S6   PS3517N265 S6.   *LC* 61-65785

PS3519 J–Je

Jackson, Laura (Riding), 1901-.   • 2.11917
Collected poems. New York Random House [1938] 477p. I. T.
PS3519.A363 A17 1938

Jackson, Laura (Riding), 1901-.   2.11918
[Poems Selections] Selected poems: in five sets [by] Laura Riding. [1st American ed.] New York, Norton [1973, c1970] 94 p. 21 cm. I. T.
PS3519.A363 A17 1973   811/.5/2   LC 74-156823   ISBN 0393043789 ISBN 0393007014

Jackson, Shirley, 1919-1965.   • 2.11919
Hangsaman / Shirley Jackson. — [New York]: Farrar, Straus and Young, 1951. 280 p. I. T.
PS3519.A392 H34   LC 51-10525

Jackson, Shirley, 1919-1965.   • 2.11920
The haunting of Hill House. — New York: Viking Press, 1959. 246 p.; 21 cm. — I. T.
PZ3.J14763 Hau   PS3519.A392 Hx.   LC 59-13414

Jackson, Shirley, 1920-   • 2.11921
The lottery: or, The adventures of James Harris. — New York: Farrar, Straus, 1949. 306 p.; 21 cm. Short stories. I. T.
PZ3.J14763Lo PS3519.A392L67   LC 49-8263

Jackson, Shirley, 1919-1965.   • 2.11922
We have always lived in the castle. — New York: Viking Press, [1962] 214 p.; 21 cm. A novel. I. T.
PS3519.A392Wx   LC 62-17935

Jarrell, Randall, 1914-1965.   • 2.11923
The third book of criticism. — New York: Farrar, Straus & Giroux, [1969] viii, 333 p.; 21 cm. 1. Literature, Modern — Addresses, essays, lectures. I. T.
PS3519.A86 A16 1969   809   LC 79-87217

Jarrell, Randall, 1914-1965.   • 2.11924
The complete poems. — New York: Farrar, Strauss & Giroux, [1969] xvi, 507 p.; 25 cm. — I. T.
PS3519.A86 A17 1969   811/.5/2   LC 68-29469

Jarrell, Randall, 1914-1965.   2.11925
Kipling, Auden & Co.: essays and reviews, 1935–1964 / Randall Jarrell. — 1st ed. — New York: Farrar, Straus and Giroux, 1980. xii, 381 p.; 24 cm. Includes index. I. T.
PS3519.A86 K5 1980   811/.52 19   LC 80-80161   ISBN 0374181535

Jarrell, Randall, 1914-1965.   • 2.11926
Pictures from an institution, a comedy. — [1st ed.]. — New York: Knopf, 1954. 277 p.; 22 cm. A novel. I. T.
PZ4.J37 Pi   PS3519.A86 P5.   LC 54-5973

Jarrell, Randall, 1914-1965.   • 2.11927
A sad heart at the supermarket; essays & fables. — [1st ed.]. — New York: Atheneum, 1962. 211 p.; 21 cm. — I. T.
PS3519.A86 S3   814.52   LC 62-11681

Critical essays on Randall Jarrell / [edited by] Suzanne Ferguson.   2.11928
Boston, Mass.: G.K. Hall, c1983. ix, 327 p.; 25 cm. — (Critical essays on American literature.) 1. Jarrell, Randall, 1914-1965 — Criticism and interpretation — Addresses, essays, lectures. I. Ferguson, Suzanne, 1939- II. Series.
PS3519.A86 Z62 1983   811/.52 19   LC 82-12100   ISBN 0816184860

Jeffers, Robinson, 1887-1962.   • 2.11929
The selected poetry of Robinson Jeffers. — New York: Random House, [c1938] xviii, 622 p.; port.; 24 cm. 'First edition.' I. T.
PS3519.E27 A6 1938   811.5   LC 38-28958

Jeffers, Robinson, 1887-1962.   • 2.11930
The selected letters of Robinson Jeffers, 1897–1962 / edited by Ann N. Ridgeway; foreword by Mark Van Doren; photos. by Leigh Wiener. — Baltimore: Johns Hopkins Press, [1968] xx, 407 p.; ill., facsims., geneal. table, ports.; 24 cm. I. Ridgeway, Ann N., ed. II. T.
PS3519.E27 Z53   816/.5/2   LC 67-29318

Carpenter, Frederic Ives, 1903-.   • 2.11931
Robinson Jeffers. New York, Twayne Publishers [1962] 159 p. 21 cm. (Twayne's United States authors series, 22) 1. Jeffers, Robinson, 1887-1962. I. T.
PS3519.E27 Z575   818.52   LC 62-16817

Monjian, Mercedes Cunningham.   • 2.11932
Robinson Jeffers, a study in inhumanism. — [Pittsburgh]: University of Pittsburgh Press, [1958] 103 p.; 19 cm. — (Critical essays in English and American literature; no. 3) 1. Jeffers, Robinson, 1887-1962. I. T. II. Series.
PS3519.E27 Z66   LC 58-11145

Powell, Lawrence Clark, 1906-.   • 2.11933
Robinson Jeffers: the man & his work. A foreword by Robinson Jeffers. Decorations by Rockwell Kent. Los Angeles, Primavera Press. — New York: Haskell House, 1970. xviii, 215 p.: illus., ports.; 24 cm. Reprint of the 1934 ed. 1. Jeffers, Robinson, 1887-1962. I. T.
PS3519.E27 Z7 1970   811/.5/2   LC 68-54176   ISBN 0838306756

Squires, James Radcliffe, 1917-.   • 2.11934
The loyalties of Robinson Jeffers. Ann Arbor: University of Michigan Press, 1956. 202 p.; 22 cm. 1. Jeffers, Robinson, 1887-1962. I. T.
PS3519.E27 Z78   LC 56-11031

PS3519 Jo–Jz

Johnson, James Weldon, 1871-1938.   2.11935
Saint Peter relates an incident. New York, The Viking press, 1935. ix p., 1 l., 13-105 p. 24 cm. I. T.
PS3519.O2625 A6 1935   LC 35-22368

Johnson, James Weldon, 1871-1938.   • 2.11936
The autobiography of an ex–coloured man / [by] James Weldon Johnson with an introduction by Carl Van Vechten. — New York & London: A. A. Knopf, 1927. xii, 211 p.; 21 cm. — (Blue jade library) 1. Mulattoes 2. Negroes. I. T.
PS3519.O2625 Ax   LC 27-18249

Johnson, James Weldon, 1871-1938.   • 2.11937
God's trombones: seven negro sermons in verse / by James Weldon Johnson; drawings by Aaron Douglas; lettering by C. B. Falls. — New York: Viking, 1927. 56 p.: ill.; 23 cm. I. T. II. Title: Negro sermons in verse.
PS3519.O2625 G6 1927   LC 27-12269

Levy, Eugene D.   2.11938
James Weldon Johnson, Black leader, Black voice [by] Eugene Levy. — Chicago: University of Chicago Press, [1973] xiii, 380 p.: port.; 23 cm. — (Negro American biographies and autobiographies) 1. Johnson, James Weldon, 1871-1938 — Biography. I. T. II. Series.
PS3519.O2625 Z7   818/.5/209 B   LC 72-95134   ISBN 0226476030

Justice, Donald Rodney, 1925-.   2.11939
Selected poems / Donald Justice. — 1st ed. — New York: Atheneum, 1979. ix, 137 p.; 25 cm. — I. T.
PS3519.U825 A17 1979   811/.54   LC 79-52416   ISBN 0689110162

Justice, Donald Rodney, 1925-.   • 2.11940
Night light: [poems] / by Donald Justice. — [1st ed.] Middletown, Conn.: Wesleyan University Press, [1967] 77 p.; 21 cm. (Wesleyan poetry program.) I. T. II. Series.
PS3519.U825 N5   LC 67-15229

PS3521 K–Ke

Kanin, Garson, 1912-.   • 2.11941
Born yesterday: a comedy / by Garson Kanin. — New York: The Viking press, 1946. 141 p.: ill.; 20 cm. I. T.
PS3521.A45 B6 1946   812.52   LC 47-289

Kantor, MacKinlay, 1904-.   • 2.11942
Andersonville / MacKinlay Kantor. — Cleveland: World, 1955. 767 p.: ill.; 24 cm. 1. Andersonville (Ga.) Military Prison. — Fiction 2. United States — Civil War, 1861-1865 — Fiction. I. T.
PZ3.K142 An   PS3521.A47 A5.   LC 55-8257

Kantor, MacKinlay, 1904-.   2.11943
Long remember / by MacKinlay Kantor; decorations by Will Crawford. — New York: Coward-McCann, [c1934] 411 p.: ill., map. 1. Gettysburg, Battle of, 1863 — Fiction. I. T.
PS3521.A47 L6   LC 34-27082

Kaufman, George S. (George Simon), 1889-1961.   • 2.11944
Six plays by Kaufman and Hart / with an introduction by Brooks Atkinson. — New York: The Modern library [c1942] xxxii, 586 p.; 19 cm. — (Half-title: The Modern library of the world's best books) I. Hart, Moss, 1904-1961. joint author. II. T.
PS3521.A727S5 1942a   812.5   LC 44-8784

Kazin, Alfred, 1915-.   • 2.11945
Contemporaries. [Essays. 1st ed.] Boston, Little, Brown [1962] 513 p. 22 cm. Rev. ed. published as: Contemporaries, from the 19th century to the present. New and rev. ed. c1982. 1. Literature, Modern — Addresses, essays, lectures. I. T.
PS3521.A995 C6   809.03   LC 62-10528

Kees, Weldon, 1914-1955?   **2.11946**
The collected poems of Weldon Kees / edited by Donald Justice. — Rev. ed. —
Lincoln: University of Nebraska Press, [1975] xvii, 180 p.; 21 cm. 'A Bison
book.' I. T.
PS3521.E285 A6 1975   811/.5/2   *LC* 75-3567   *ISBN* 0803208642

Kees, Weldon, 1914-1955?   **2.11947**
The ceremony & other stories / Weldon Kees; edited & with an introduction by
Dana Gioia. — Port Townsend, Wash.: Graywolf Press, 1984. xvii, 147 p.; 22
cm. — (Graywolf short fiction series.) I. Gioia, Dana. II. T. III. Title: The
ceremony and other stories. IV. Series.
PS3521.E285 C4 1984   813/.52 19   *LC* 83-83186   *ISBN*
0915308452

Ross, William T.   **2.11948**
Weldon Kees / by William T. Ross. — Boston: Twayne Publishers, c1985.
149 p.: ill.; 23 cm. (Twayne's United States authors series. TUSAS 484)
Includes index. 1. Kees, Weldon, 1914-1955? — Criticism and interpretation.
I. T. II. Series.
PS3521.E285 Z87 1985   811/.52 19   *LC* 84-15734   *ISBN*
0805774378

Kelley, Edith Summers.   **2.11949**
Weeds / with an introd. by Matthew J. Bruccoli. — Carbondale: Southern
Illinois University Press, [1972, c1923] xiii, 335 p.; 22 cm. — (Crosscurrents/
Modern fiction) I. T.
PZ3.K2868 We6 PS3521.E4117   813/.5/2   *LC* 72-75333   *ISBN*
0809305879

Kerouac, Jack, 1922-1969.   • **2.11950**
The Dharma bums / by Jack Kerouac. — New York: Viking Press, 1958.
244 p.; 21cm. I. T.
PS3521.E735 D5   *LC* 58-11734

Kerouac, Jack, 1922-1969.   • **2.11951**
Doctor Sax; Faust part three. New York Grove Press [c1959] 245p. (Evergreen
original, E-160) I. T.
PS3521 E735 D6   *LC* 59-9806

Kerouac, Jack, 1922-1969.   **2.11952**
Heaven & other poems / Jack Kerouac. — Bolinas, Calif.: Grey Fox Press;
Berkeley, Calif.: distributed by Bookpeople, c1977. vii, 59 p.: ill.; 21 cm. I. T.
PS3521.E735 H4 1977   811/.5/4   *LC* 77-6233   *ISBN* 0912516305

Kerouac, Jack, 1922-1969.   • **2.11953**
On the road / by Jack Kerouac. — [Viking compass ed.] New York: Viking
Press, c1957. 310 p.; 22 cm. — 1. American fiction I. T.
PZ3.K4596 On   PS3521.E735 O5 1957.   *LC* 57-9425   *ISBN*
0670000477

Kerouac, Jack, 1922-1969.   • **2.11954**
The subterraneans. — New York: Grove Press, [c1958] 111 p. — (Evergreen
original; E-99) I. T. II. Series.
PS3521.E735 S8 1958   *LC* 58-6703

Kerouac, Jack.   **2.11955**
Visions of Cody [by] Jack Kerouac. Introd. by Allen Ginsberg. New York,
McGraw Hill [1972] xii, 398 p. illus. 24 cm. I. T.
PS3521.E735V5 1972   813/.5/4   *LC* 72-3847   *ISBN* 0070342016

Charters, Ann.   **2.11956**
Kerouac; a biography. [San Francisco, Straight Arrow Books, 1973] 419 p.
illus. 24 cm. 1. Kerouac, Jack, 1922-1969 — Biography. I. T.
PS3521.E735 Z6   813/.5/4 B   *LC* 72-95055   *ISBN* 0879320559

Clark, Tom, 1941-.   **2.11957**
Jack Kerouac / by Tom Clark. — 1st ed. — San Diego: Harcourt Brace
Jovanovich, c1984. xviii, 254 p.: ill.; 24 cm. — (HBJ album biographies.)
Includes index. 1. Kerouac, Jack, 1922-1969 — Biography. 2. Authors,
American — 20th century — Biography. 3. Bohemianism — United States —
Biography. I. T. II. Series.
PS3521.E735 Z62 1984   813/.54 B 19   *LC* 83-22628   *ISBN*
0156456621

Gifford, Barry, 1946-.   **2.11958**
Jack's book: an oral biography of Jack Kerouac / by Barry Gifford & Lawrence
Lee. — New York: St. Martin's Press, c1978. 339 p.: ill.; 24 cm. Includes index.
1. Kerouac, Jack, 1922-1969 — Biography. 2. Authors, American — 20th
century — Biography. 3. Bohemianism — United States. I. Lee, Lawrence,
1941- II. T.
PS3521.E735 Z635   813/.5/4 B   *LC* 77-15824   *ISBN* 0312439423

Hipkiss, Robert A., 1935-.   **2.11959**
Jack Kerouac, prophet of the new romanticism: a critical study of the published
works of Kerouac and a comparison of them to those of J. D. Salinger, James
Purdy, John Knowles, and Ken Kesey / Robert A Hipkiss. — Lawrence:

University Press of Kansas, c1976. ix, 150 p.; 23 cm. 1. Kerouac, Jack,
1922-1969. I. T.
PS3521.E735 Z67   813/.5/4 B   *LC* 76-14817   *ISBN* 0700601511

McNally, Dennis.   **2.11960**
Desolate angel: Jack Kerouac, the Beat generation, and America / Dennis
McNally. — 1st ed. — New York: Random House, c1979. xi, 400 p., [8] leaves
of plates: ill.; 24 cm. Includes index. 1. Kerouac, Jack, 1922-1969 —
Biography. 2. Authors, American — 20th century — Biography.
3. Bohemianism — United States. I. T.
PS3521.E735 Z775   813/.5/4 B   *LC* 78-23786   0394300113

Kesselring, Joseph.   • **2.11961**
Arsenic and old lace: a comedy / by Joseph Kesselring. — New York: Random
House, [c1941] 187 p.; 21 cm. 'First printing.' I. T.
PS3521.E775 A8 1941   812.5   *LC* 41-51666

PS3521 Ki–Kz

Kinnell, Galway, 1927-.   **2.11962**
[Poems. Selections] Selected poems / Galway Kinnell. — Boston: Houghton
Mifflin, 1982. 160 p.; 22 cm. — I. T.
PS3521.I582 A6 1982   811/.54 19   *LC* 81-20254   *ISBN*
0395320453

Kinnell, Galway, 1927-.   **2.11963**
The avenue bearing the initial of Christ into the New World: poems 1946–1964.
— Boston: Houghton Mifflin, 1974. ix, 177 p.; 21 cm. — I. T.
PS3521.I582 A95   811/.5/4   *LC* 74-1109   *ISBN* 0395186285

Kinnell, Galway, 1927-.   • **2.11964**
What a kingdom it was. Boston, Houghton Mifflin, 1960. 83 p. 22 cm. Poems.
I. T.
PS3521.I582 W5   *LC* 59-8860

Knowles, John, 1926-.   • **2.11965**
A separate peace; a novel. — New York: Macmillan, 1960 [c1959] 186 p.; 21
cm. — I. T.
PZ4.K745 Se2   PS3521.N6 S46.   *LC* 60-5312

Koch, Kenneth, 1925-.   • **2.11966**
Ko, or, A season on earth. — New York: Grove Press, [1960, c1959] 115 p. —
(Evergreen original; E-194) A narrative poem. I. T. II. Title: A season on
earth. III. Series.
PS3521.O27 K6

Kreymborg, Alfred, 1883-1966.   • **2.11967**
Troubadour: an autobiography / Alfred Kreymborg. — New York: Boni and
Liveright, 1925. 415 p. 1. Kreymborg, Alfred, 1883-1966. 2. Authors,
American — 20th century — Biography. I. T.
PS3521.R55 Z5 1925   812.52   *LC* 25-8503

Kumin, Maxine, 1925-.   **2.11968**
The designated heir [by] Maxine Kumin. New York, Viking Press [1974] 174 p.
22 cm. I. T.
PZ4.K9647 De PS3521.U638   813/.5/4   *LC* 73-18915   *ISBN*
0670268968

Kumin, Maxine, 1925-.   **2.11969**
House, bridge, fountain, gate / Maxine Kumin. — New York: Viking Press,
1975. 98 p.; 21 cm. (A Viking compass book; C592) Poems. I. T.
PS3521.U638 H6   811/.5/4   *LC* 75-1353   *ISBN* 0670379964.
ISBN 0670005924 pbk

Kumin, Maxine, 1925-.   **2.11970**
The retrieval system: poems / by Maxine Kumin. — New York: Viking, 1978.
viii, 69 p.; 21 cm. Poems. I. T.
PS3521.U638 R4 1978   811/.5/4   *LC* 77-28201   *ISBN* 0670595764

Kumin, Maxine, 1925-.   **2.11971**
Up country; poems of New England, new and selected, by Maxine Kumin.
Drawings by Barbara Swan. [1st ed.] New York, Harper & Row [1972] 83 p.
illus. 22 cm. I. T.
PS3521.U638 U6   811/.5/4   *LC* 72-79680   *ISBN* 0060124733

Kunitz, Stanley, 1905-.   **2.11972**
The poems of Stanley Kunitz, 1928–1978. — 1st ed. — Boston: Little, Brown,
c1979. xvii, 249 p.; 22 cm. 'An Atlantic Monthly Press book.' Includes index.
I. T.
PS3521.U7 P6   811/.5/2   *LC* 79-463   *ISBN* 0316507113

Kuttner, Henry.   **2.11973**
Mutant, by Lewis Padgett [pseud.] 1st ed. New York Gnome Press [1953]
210 p. 21 cm. I. T.
PS3521.U87 M8x   *LC* 53-12601

Vance, Jack, 1916-.   **2.11974**
The dying earth / Jack Vance. — New York: Pocket Books, 1982,c1950. 156 p.; 18 cm. 'A kangaroo book' I. T.
PS 3521 U93 D99   *ISBN* 0671831526

PS3523 L–Le

La Farge, Oliver, 1901-1963.   • **2.11975**
All the young men: stories / by Oliver La Farge. — Boston: Houghton Mifflin, 1935. 272 p.; 21 cm. 1. Navajo Indians — Fiction. I. T.
PS3523.A2263 A61   *LC* 35-13561

La Farge, Oliver, 1901-1963.   • **2.11976**
Laughing Boy, by Oliver La Farge. [Boston] Houghton Mifflin [1929] xii, 302 p. 21 cm. 1. Navajo Indians — Fiction. I. T.
PZ3.L129Lau PS3523.A2663L3   *LC* 29-23247   *ISBN* 0395078741

Lardner, John, 1912-1960.   • **2.11977**
The world of John Lardner / edited by Roger Kahn; with a pref. by Walt Kelly. — New York: Simon and Schuster, 1961. 224 p.; 22 cm. I. Kahn, Roger. II. T.
PS3523.A677 A6   817.12   *LC* 61-12847

Lardner, Ring, 1885-1933.   • **2.11978**
How to write short stories (with samples) New York, Scribner, 1924. St. Clair Shores, Mich., Scholarly Press, 1971. x, 359 p. 22 cm. I. T.
PZ3.L323 Ho6 PS3523.A7   813/.5/2   *LC* 75-145130   *ISBN* 0403010632

Lardner, Ring, 1885-1933.   • **2.11979**
The portable Ring Lardner / edited and with an introduction by Gilbert Seldes. — New York: Viking Press, 1946. vii, 756 p. — (Viking portable library.) I. Seldes, Gilbert Vivian, 1893- II. T. III. Series.
PS3523.A7 A6 1946   818.52

Lardner, Ring, 1885-1933.   • **2.11980**
The best short stories of Ring Lardner. — New York: Scribner, [1957] 346 p.; 22 cm. — I. T.
PZ3.L323 Be   PS3523.A7 A6 1957.   *LC* 57-13394

Lardner, Ring, 1885-1933.   • **2.11981**
The love nest, and other stories / by Ring W. Lardner; with an introduction by Sarah E. Spooldripper. — New York: C. Scribner's sons, 1926. xvi p., 2 l., 3-232 p. 19 1/2 cm. I. T.
PS3523.A7 L6   *LC* 26-9020 Rev

Lardner, Ring, 1885-1933.   **2.11982**
Some champions: sketches & fiction / by Ring Lardner; edited by Matthew J. Bruccoli & Richard Layman; with a foreword by Ring Lardner, Jr. — New York: Scribner, c1976. xv, 205 p.; 24 cm. Previously uncollected sketches and stories. 1. Lardner, Ring, 1885-1933 — Biography — Journalistic career — Addresses, essays, lectures. I. T.
PS3523.A7 Z518 1976   818/.5/209 B   *LC* 75-38544   *ISBN* 0684145820

Lardner, Ring, 1885-1933.   **2.11983**
Letters from Ring / edited by Clifford M. Caruthers. — Flint, Mich.: Walden Press, c1979. vi, 305 p., [5] leaves of plates: ill.; 23 cm. Includes index. 1. Lardner, Ring, 1885-1933 — Correspondence. 2. Authors, American — 20th century — Correspondence. I. Caruthers, Clifford M., 1935- II. T.
PS3523.A7 Z53 1979   818/.5209   *LC* 80-105353   *ISBN* 0911938087

Evans, Elizabeth, 1935-.   **2.11984**
Ring Lardner / Elizabeth Evans. — New York: F. Ungar, c1979. x, 150 p.; 21 cm. (Modern literature monographs) Includes index. 1. Lardner, Ring, 1885-1933 — Criticism and interpretation. I. T.
PS3523.A7 Z655   818/.5/209 B   *LC* 79-4829   *ISBN* 0804421854

Geismar, Maxwell David, 1909-.   • **2.11985**
Ring Lardner and the portrait of folly, by Maxwell Geismar. New York, Crowell [1972] 166 p. 21 cm. (Twentieth-century American writers) 1. Lardner, Ring, 1885-1933. I. T.
PS3523.A7 Z68   818/.5/209   *LC* 77-175105   *ISBN* 0690702345

Patrick, Walton R.   • **2.11986**
Ring Lardner. New York: Twayne Publishers [1963] 175 p.; 22 cm. (Twayne's United States authors series, 32) 1. Lardner, Ring, 1885-1933. I. T.
PS3523.A7 Z82   817.52   *LC* 62-19476

Yardley, Jonathan.   **2.11987**
Ring: a biography of Ring Lardner / by Jonathan Yardley. — 1st ed. — New York: Random House, c1977. 415 p., [8] leaves of plates: ill.; 25 cm. Includes index. 1. Lardner, Ring, 1885-1933 — Biography. 2. Authors, American — 20th century — Biography. I. T.
PS3523.A7 Z9   818/.5/209   *LC* 77-1661   *ISBN* 0394498119

Larsen, Nella.   **2.11988**
Passing. — New York: Collier Books, [1971] 189 p.; 18 cm. — (African/American library) Originally published in 1929. I. T. II. Series.
PZ3.L33 Pas10 PS3523.A7225   813/.5/2   *LC* 74-146616

Larsen, Nella.   **2.11989**
Quicksand. — New York: Negro Universities Press, [1969] 301 p.; 18 cm. — I. T.
PZ3.L33 Qu5 PS3523.A7225   813/.5/2   *LC* 74-75553

Lavin, Mary, 1912-.   **2.11990**
Collected stories. With an introd. by V. S. Pritchett. — Boston: Houghton Mifflin, 1971. xiii, 425 p.; 22 cm. — I. T.
PZ3.L393 Co PS3523.A914 A6 1971   823/.9/12   *LC* 73-132790   *ISBN* 0395120993

Lea, Tom, 1907-.   • **2.11992**
The brave bulls: a novel / by Tom Lea. — [1st ed.] Boston: Little, Brown [1949] xvii, 270 p.: ill.; 20 cm. I. T.
PZ3.L4645Br PS3523.E1142B7   PS3523.E32 B7.   *LC* 49-7577 *

Lea, Tom, 1907-.   • **2.11993**
The wonderful country: a novel / with drawings by the author. — [1st ed.]. — Boston: Little, Brown, [1952] 387 p.: ill.; 21 cm. — I. T.
PZ3.L4645 Wo   PS3523.E32 W65 1952.   *LC* 52-9093

Lederer, William Julius, 1912-.   **2.11994**
The ugly American / [by] William J. Lederer and Eugene Burdick. — [1st ed.]. — New York: Norton, [1958] 285 p.; 22 cm. I. Burdick, Eugene, 1918-. II. T.
PZ4.L468 Ug   PS3523.E35 U5.   *LC* 58-7388

Lee, Harper, 1926-.   • **2.11995**
To kill a mockingbird. — [1st ed.]. — Philadelphia: Lippincott, [1960] 296 p.; 21 cm. — A novel. I. T.
PZ4.L4778 To   PS3523.E4 T6.   *LC* 60-7847

Leiber, Fritz, 1910-.   **2.11996**
Our lady of darkness / by Fritz Leiber. New York: Berkley Pub. Corp.: distributed by Putnam, c1977. 185 p.; 22 cm. I. T.
PZ3.L5293 Ou PS3523.E4583   813/.5/4   *LC* 76-20735   *ISBN* 0399118721

Leiber, Fritz, 1910-.   **2.11997**
The green millennium / [by] Fritz Leiber. — London: Abelard Press; 1953. 192 p. — I. T.
PS3523.E4583 G7   823/.9/1

Levin, Meyer, 1905-.   **2.11998**
The settlers: a novel. — New York: Simon and Schuster, [1972] 832 p.; 23 cm. — I. T.
PZ3.L578 Se   PS3523.E7994 S4.   813/.5/2   *LC* 74-179591   *ISBN* 0671211544

Levin, Meyer, 1905-.   **2.11999**
Compulsion. — New York: Simon and Schuster, 1956. 495 p.; 22 cm. 1. Leopold, Nathan Freudenthal, 1904 or 5- — Fiction. 2. Loeb, Richard A., 1905 or 6-1936 — Fiction. I. T.
PZ3.L578 Co   PS3523.E8 C6.   *LC* 56-9911

PS3523 Lewis

Lewis, Sinclair, 1885-1951.   • **2.12000**
Ann Vickers / by Sinclair Lewis. — New York: Doubleday, 1933. 562 p.; 21 cm. I. T.
PS3523.E94 A68 1933

Lewis, Sinclair, 1885-1951.   • **2.12001**
Arrowsmith / Edited by Barbara Grace Spayd. Text ed. New York Chicago: Harcourt, Brace and company, [c1945] xxv, 486 p.; 19 cm. 'Library aids for research studies': p. 465-466. 'Foreign editions of Sinclair Lewis's novels': p. 484-486. 1. Spayd, Barbara Grace, ed. I. T.
PZ3.L5884 Ar15   PS3523.E94 Ax.   *LC* 45-5016

Lewis, Sinclair, 1885-1951.   • **2.12002**
Babbitt / by Sinclair Lewis. — New York: Harcourt, Brace & World, c1922. 401 p.; 21 cm. I. T.
PS3523.E94 B3 1922   *LC* 22-14419

Lewis, Sinclair, 1885-1951.   • **2.12003**
Cass Timberlane, a novel of husbands and wives. — [1st Modern library ed.]. — New York: [Random House, 1957, c1945] 390 p.; 19 cm. — (The Modern library of the world's best books [221]) I. T.
PZ3.L5884 Cas3   PS3523.E94 Cx.   *LC* 57-11171

Lewis, Sinclair, 1885-1951.   • **2.12004**
Dodsworth: a novel / with a foreword by Clifton Fadiman. — [1st Modern Library ed.] New York: Modern Library, [1947] vii, 377 p.; 19 cm. (The modern library of the world's best books]) I. T.
PZ3.L5884Do6 PS3523.E94D6 1947   *LC* 48-84

Lewis, Sinclair, 1885-1951.   • **2.12005**
Elmer Gantry, by Sinclair Lewis. — New York: Harcourt, Brace and company, [c1927] 4 p. l., 432 p.; 20 cm. — I. T.
PZ3.L5884 El   PS3523.E94 E4 1976.   *LC* 27-4761

Lewis, Sinclair, 1885-1951.   • **2.12006**
Free air / by Sinclair Lewis. — New York: Harcourt, Brace & Howe, 1919. 370 p.; 22 cm. — I. T.
PZ3.L5884 Fr5 PS3523.E94 F7x   813/.5/2

Lewis, Sinclair.   • **2.12007**
It can't happen here: a novel / by Sinclair Lewis. — 1st. ed. — Garden City, N.Y.: Doubleday, Doran, 1935. 458 p. I. T.
PS3523.E94Ix   *LC* 35-19689

Lewis, Sinclair, 1885-1951.   • **2.12008**
The man from Main Street: a Sinclair Lewis reader: selected essays and other writings, 1904–1950 / edited by Harry E. Maule and Melville H. Cane; assisted by Philip Allan Friedman. — New York: Random House, [c1953] xvi, 371 p.: port. 22 cm. I. T.
PS3523.E94 M3   814.5   *LC* 52-5158

Lewis, Sinclair, 1885-1951.   • **2.12009**
Main Street. — New York: Harcourt, Brace, c1920. 451 p.; 21 cm. — (Harbrace modern classics) I. T.
PZ3.L5884 Mai2   PS3523.E94 M3 1920.   *LC* 57-52248

Lewis, Sinclair, 1885-1951.   • **2.12010**
Work of art / Sinclair Lewis. — Garden City, N.Y.: Doubleday, Doran, c1934. 452 p. l. T.
PS3523.E94 W6 1934   *LC* 33-27268

Lewis, Sinclair, 1885-1951.   • **2.12011**
From Main Street to Stockholm: letters of Sinclair Lewis, 1919–1930 / edited and with an introduction by Harrison Smith. — 1st ed. — New York: Harcourt, Brace, 1952. xii, 307 p.: port.; 23 cm. I. Smith, Harrison, 1888- II. T.
PS3523.E94 Z48   *LC* 52-6449

Dooley, D. J. (David Joseph), 1921-.   • **2.12012**
The art of Sinclair Lewis, by D. J. Dooley. Lincoln, University of Nebraska Press [1967] xvi, 286 p. 22 cm. 1. Lewis, Sinclair, 1885-1951. I. T.
PS3523.E94 Z566   813/.5/2   *LC* 65-17173

Schorer, Mark, 1908- ed.   • **2.12013**
Sinclair Lewis: a collection of critical essays. — Englewood Cliffs, N.J.: Prentice-Hall, [1962] 174 p.; 21 cm. — (Twentieth century views) (A Spectrum book, S-TC-6.) 1. Lewis, Sinclair, 1885-1951. I. T.
PS3523.E94 Z77   813.52   *LC* 62-9311

Schorer, Mark, 1908-.   • **2.12014**
Sinclair Lewis: an American life. — [1st ed.]. — New York: McGraw-Hill, [1961] 867 p.: ill.; 25 cm. 1. Lewis, Sinclair, 1885-1951. I. T.
PS3523.E94 Z78   928.1   *LC* 61-12961

PS3523 Li

Lindsay, Vachel, 1879-1931.   **2.12015**
The poetry of Vachel Lindsay: complete & with Lindsay's drawings / newly edited by Dennis Camp. — 1st ed. — Peoria, Ill.: Spoon River Poetry Press, 1984-c1985. 2 v. (xxii, 817 p.): ill. (some col.); 24 cm. I. Camp, Dennis. II. T.
PS3523.I58 A17 1984   811/.52 19   *LC* 84-197091   *ISBN* 0933180454

Masters, Edgar Lee, 1868-1950.   • **2.12016**
Vachel Lindsay; a poet in America. New York, Biblo and Tannen, 1969 [c1935] ix, 392 p. illus., ports. 24 cm. 1. Lindsay, Vachel, 1879-1931. I. T.
PS3523.I58 Z73 1969   811/.5/2 B   *LC* 68-56452

Ruggles, Eleanor, 1916-.   • **2.12016a**
The west-going heart: a life of Vachel Lindsay / Eleanor Ruggles. — 1st ed.— New York: Norton, 1959. 448 p., [8] p. of plates: ill., ports; 22 cm. 1. Lindsay, Vachel, 1879-1931. I. T.
PS3523.I58 Z76   928.1   *LC* 59-11337

Linebarger, Paul Myron Anthony, 1913-1966.   **2.12017**
The best of Cordwainer Smith [i.e. P. M. A. Linebarger] / edited, with introd. and notes, by J. J. Pierce. — Garden City, N.Y.: Nelson Doubleday, [1975] 342 p.; 22 cm. 1. Science fiction, American I. T.
PZ3.L654038 Be4 PS3523.I629   813/.5/4   *LC* 75-19108   *ISBN* 0345245814

Smith, Cordwainer, 1913-1966.   **2.12018**
Norstrilia / Cordwainer Smith. New York: Ballantine Books, 1975. 277 p. 'A Del Ray Book'. I. T.
PS3523.I629 N67 1975   813   *ISBN* 0345323009

PS3523 London

London, Jack, 1876-1916.   • **2.12019**
The Bodley Head Jack London / Edited and introduced by Arthur Calder-Marshall. — London: Bodley Head, [1963-. v.: map.; 20 cm. I. Calder-Marshall, Arthur, 1908- II. T.
PZ3.L846Bo   PS3523.O46 1963.   *LC* 66-3327 rev

London, Jack, 1876-1916.   • **2.12020**
Best short stories of Jack London. — Garden City, N.Y.: The Sun dial press, [1945] 4 p., l., 311 p.; 21 cm. — I. T.
PS3523.O46A6 1945x   *LC* 45-3930

London, Jack, 1876-1916.   **2.12021**
[Selections. 1979] No mentor but myself: a collection of articles, essays, reviews, and letters on writing and writers / Jack London; edited by Dale L. Walker; foreword by Howard Lachtman. — Port Washington, N.Y.: Kennikat Press, 1979. xv, 197 p.; 23 cm. — (Literary criticism series) (Kennikat Press national university publications) I. Walker, Dale L. II. T.
PS3523.O46 A6 1979   818/.5/209   *LC* 78-21238   *ISBN* 0804692270

London, Jack, 1876-1916.   **2.12022**
[Short stories. Selections] Curious fragments: Jack London's tales of fantasy fiction / edited by Dale L. Walker; pref. by Philip José Farmer. — Port Washington, N.Y.: Kennikat Press, 1975. x, 223 p.; 23 cm. — (National university publications) 1. Fantastic fiction, American I. Walker, Dale L. II. T.
PZ3.L846 Cu3 PS3523.O46 Ax   813/.5/2   *LC* 75-29450   *ISBN* 0804691142

London, Jack, 1876-1916.   **2.12023**
The call of the wild: a casebook with text, background sources, reviews, critical essays, and bibliography / by Jack London; compiled with an introd. by Earl J. Wilcox. — Chicago: Nelson-Hall, c1980. 254 p.; 23 cm. Includes index. 1. London, Jack, 1876-1916. The call of the wild. I. Wilcox, Earl J., 1933- II. T.
PS3523.O46 C3 1980   813/.5/2   *LC* 79-21647   *ISBN* 0882293818

London, Jack, 1876-1916.   • **2.12024**
The iron heel / introd. by Max Lerner. — New York: Sagamore Press, 1957. 303 p.; 21 cm. — (American century series, S-23) I. T.
PZ3.L846 Ir17   PS3523.O46 I7.   *LC* 57-12443

London, Jack, 1876-1916.   • **2.12025**
Martin Eden / by Jack London. — New York: Macmillan, 1957, c1936. 381 p.; 20 cm. I. T.
PS3523.O46 M3   *LC* 57-734

London, Jack, 1876-1916.   • **2.12026**
The sea-wolf. New York: Macmillan, 1958. 366 p.; 21 cm. I. T.
PZ3.L846 Se20   PS3523.O46 Sx.   *LC* 59-1892

London, Jack, 1876-1916.   • **2.12027**
Tales of adventure. Edited by Irving Shepard. — [1st ed.]. — Garden City, N.Y.: Hanover House, [1956] 531 p.; illus.; 25 cm. — I. T.
PS3523.O46 T28   813.5   *LC* 56-5714

London, Jack, 1876-1916.   • **2.12028**
White Fang / by Jack London. — New York: Macmillan, 1914. vii, 327 p.: col. front., col. plates; 20 cm. I. T.
PZ3.L846Whi 80   PS3523.O46 W48 1914.   *LC* 06-35449

London, Jack, 1876-1916.   • **2.12029**
Letters from Jack London: containing an unpublished correspondence between London and Sinclair Lewis / edited by King Hendricks and Irving Shepard. New York: Odyssey Press, [1965] 502 p.: ill., facsim., ports. 1. London, Jack, 1876-1916 — Correspondence. 2. Lewis, Sinclair, 1885-1951 — Correspondence. I. Lewis, Sinclair, 1885-1951. II. Hendricks, King, 1900-. III. Shepard, Irving. IV. T.
PS3523.O46 Z53   *LC* 65-22039

Calder-Marshall, Arthur, 1908-. • **2.12030**
Lone wolf: the story of Jack London / illustrated by Biro. — [1st ed.] — New York: Duell, Sloan and Pearce, [1961] 167 p.: ill. 1. London, Jack, 1876-1916. I. T.
BX5199.N76C3   PS3523.O46 Z62.   922.342   *LC* 62-15477

Foner, Philip Sheldon, 1910-. • **2.12031**
Jack London, American rebel. [Rev. ed.] New York: Citadel Press, [1964] iv, 155 p.; 21 cm. 1. London, Jack, 1876-1916. I. T.
PS3523.O46 Z624 1964   *LC* 64-2837

Franchere, Ruth. • **2.12032**
Jack London: the pursuit of a dream / Ruth Franchere. — New York: Crowell, 1962. 264 p. 1. London, Jack, 1876-1916. 2. Authors, American — Biography. I. T.
PS3523.O46Z625   813.5

Kingman, Russ. **2.12033**
A pictorial life of Jack London / by Russ Kingman; foreword by Irving Stone. — New York: Crown Publishers, c1979. 288 p.: ill.; 29 cm. Includes index. 1. London, Jack, 1876-1916 — Pictorial works. 2. Authors, American — 20th century — Biography. I. T.
PS3523.O46 Z665 1979   818/.5/209 B   *LC* 79-17998   *ISBN* 0517531631

O'Connor, Richard, 1915-1975. • **2.12034**
Jack London, a biography. — [1st ed.]. — Boston: Little, Brown, [1964] x, 430 p.: ports.; 22 cm. 1. London, Jack, 1876-1916. I. T.
PS3523.O46 Z84   928.1   *LC* 64-21486

Sinclair, Andrew. **2.12035**
Jack: a biography of Jack London / Andrew Sinclair. — 1st ed. — New York: Harper & Row, c1977. xv, 297 p.: ill.; 25 cm. Includes index. 1. London, Jack, 1876-1916 — Biography. 2. Novelists, American — 20th century — Biography. I. T.
PS3523.O46 Z876   818/.5/209 B   *LC* 76-57899   *ISBN* 0060138998

PS3523 Lo

Loos, Anita, 1894-1981. • **2.12036**
Gentlemen prefer blondes; the illuminating diary of a professional lady / by Anita Loos; intimately illustrated by Ralph Barton. — New York: Liveright, 1973, c1963. xvi, 11-217 p.: ill. I. T.
PS3523.O557 G4 1973   *LC* 63-9284

Lovecraft, Howard Phillips. **2.12037**
The case of Charles Dexter Ward / H. P. Lovecraft. — New York: Ballantine Books, 1971 (c1943). 127 p.; 18 cm. I. T.
PS3523.O833 C3x   *ISBN* 0345251180 pa

Lowell, Amy, 1874-1925. • **2.12038**
Complete poetical works. With an introd. by Louis Untermeyer. — Boston: Houghton Mifflin, 1955. xxix, 607 p.; 22 cm. — I. T.
PS3523.O88 1955   811.5   *LC* 55-6949

Damon, S. Foster (Samuel Foster), 1893-1971. • **2.12039**
Amy Lowell: a chronicle with extracts from her correspondence / by S. Foster Damon. — Hamden, Conn.: Archon Books, 1966. xxi, 773 p.: ill., facsims., ports: 23 cm. 'A chronological arrangement of the first printing of poems and prose by Amy Lowell': p. [729]-742. 1. Lowell, Amy, 1874-1925. I. T.
PS3523.O88Z64 1966   *LC* 66-15386

Gregory, Horace, 1898-. • **2.12040**
Amy Lowell: portrait of the poet in her time. — Freeport, N.Y.: Books for Libraries Press, [1969, c1958] ix, 213 p.: ill., ports.; 23 cm. — (Select bibliographies reprint series) 1. Lowell, Amy, 1874-1925. 2. Poets, American I. T.
PS3523.O88 Z67 1969   811/.5/2 B   *LC* 69-16855

PS3523 Robert Lowell

Lowell, Robert, 1917-1977. **2.12041**
Selected poems / Robert Lowell. — [Rev. ed.] New York: Farrar Straus and Giroux, [1977] xvi, 255 p.: port.; 24 cm. Includes indexes. I. T.
PS3523.O89 A17 1977   811/.5/2   *LC* 76-2000   *ISBN* 0374258694

Lowell, Robert, 1917-1977. **2.12042**
Notebook. — [3d ed. rev. and expanded]. — New York: Farrar, Straus and Giroux, [1970] 265 p.: front.; 22 cm. Poems. First-2d ed. published in 1969 under title: Notebook 1967-68. I. T.
PS3523.O89 A6 1970   811/.5/2   *LC* 71-122829   *ISBN* 0374223254

Lowell, Robert, 1917-1977. **2.12043**
Day by day / Robert Lowell. New York: Farrar, Straus and Giroux, c1977. 137 p.; 22 cm. Poems. I. T.
PS3523.O89 D39 1977   811/.5/2   *LC* 77-6799   *ISBN* 0374135258

Lowell, Robert, 1917-1977. **2.12044**
The dolphin. — New York: Farrar, Straus and Giroux, [1973] 78 p.; 23 cm. Poems. I. T.
PS3523.O89 D6 1973   811/.5/2   *LC* 72-96315   *ISBN* 0374141401

Lowell, Robert, 1917-1977. **2.12045**
For Lizzie and Harriet. — New York: Farrar, Straus and Giroux, [1973] 48 p.; 23 cm. Poems. I. T.
PS3523.O89 F56 1973   811/.5/2   *LC* 72-96316   *ISBN* 0374157294

Lowell, Robert, 1917-1977. • **2.12046**
For the Union dead. — New York: Farrar, Straus & Giroux, [1964] xii, 72 p.; 22 cm. Poems. I. T.
PS3523.O89 F6   811.52   *LC* 64-21495

Lowell, Robert, 1917-1977. **2.12047**
History. — New York: Farrar, Straus and Giroux, [1973] 207 p.; 22 cm. Poems. I. T.
PS3523.O89 H5 1973   811/.5/2   *LC* 72-96314   *ISBN* 0374170444

Lowell, Robert, 1917-1977. • **2.12048**
The Old Glory. — Rev. ed. — New York: Farrar, Straus & Giroux, [1968] 223 p.; 22 cm. Theater trilogy based on stories by Hawthorne and a novella by Melville. I. Hawthorne, Nathaniel, 1804-1864. II. Melville, Herman, 1819-1891. Benito Cereno. 1968. III. T.
PS3523.O89 O4 1968   812/.5/2   *LC* 68-54690

Axelrod, Steven Gould, 1944-. **2.12049**
Robert Lowell: life and art / Steven Gould Axelrod. — Princeton, N.J.: Princeton University Press, c1978. xiii, 286 p., [4] leaves of plates: ill.; 23 cm. 1. Lowell, Robert, 1917-1977. 2. Poets, American — 20th century — Biography. I. T.
PS3523.O89 Z56   811/.5/2   *LC* 78-51155   *ISBN* 069106363X

Staples, Hugh B. • **2.12050**
Robert Lowell: the first twenty years. — New York: Farrar, Straus and Cudahy, [1962] 120 p.; 23 cm. 1. Lowell, Robert, 1917-1977. I. T.
PS3523.O89 Z56   811/.5/2   *LC* 62-8843

Hamilton, Ian, 1938-. **2.12051**
Robert Lowell: a biography / Ian Hamilton. — 1st ed. — New York: Random House, c1982. xii, 527 p., [16] p. of plates: ill.; 24 cm. Includes index. 1. Lowell, Robert, 1917-1977. 2. Poets, American — 20th century — Biography. I. T.
PS3523.O89 Z68 1982   811/.52 B 19   *LC* 82-40121   *ISBN* 039450965X

Mazzaro, Jerome. • **2.12052**
The poetic themes of Robert Lowell. — Ann Arbor: University of Michigan Press, [1965] viii, 145 p.; 23 cm. 1. Lowell, Robert, 1917-1977. I. T.
PS3523.O89 Z77   811.52   *LC* 65-20349

Parkinson, Thomas Francis, 1920- comp. • **2.12053**
Robert Lowell: a collection of critical essays. — Englewood Cliffs, N.J.: Prentice-Hall, [1968] xii, 176 p.; 20 cm. (Twentieth century views. S-TC-79) (A Spectrum book.) 1. Lowell, Robert, 1917-1977. I. T. II. Series. III. Series: A Spectrum book.
PS3523.O89 Z8   811/.5/2   *LC* 68-7920

Perloff, Marjorie. **2.12054**
The poetic art of Robert Lowell [by] Marjorie G. Perloff. — Ithaca: Cornell University Press, [1973] xiii, 209 p.; 22 cm. 1. Lowell, Robert, 1917-1977. I. T.
PS3523.O89 Z82   811/.5/2   *LC* 72-12412   *ISBN* 0801407710

Procopiow, Norma. **2.12055**
Robert Lowell, the poet and his critics / Norma Procopiow. — Chicago: American Library Association, 1984. xv, 335 p.; 24 cm. — (Poet and his critics.) 1. Lowell, Robert, 1917-1977 — Criticism and interpretation. I. T. II. Series.
PS3523.O89 Z835 1984   811/.52 19   *LC* 84-467   *ISBN* 0838904114

PS3523 Lu–Lz

Lumpkin, Grace. **2.12056**
The wedding / by Grace Lumpkin; with an afterword by Lillian Barnard Gilkes and a postscript by Grace Lumpkin [and textual note by Matthew J. Bruccoli]. — Carbondale: Southern Illinois University Press, [1976] c1939. 322 p.; 20 cm.

(Lost American fiction) Reprint of the ed. published by L. Furman, New York.
I. T.
PZ3.L9712 We5 PS3523.U54   813/.5/2   *LC* 75-28481   *ISBN*
0809307677

Lytle, Andrew Nelson, 1902-.   • **2.12057**
The velvet horn / by Andrew Lytle. — New York: McDowell, Obolensky,
[c1957] 373 p. I. T.
PS3523.Y85 V45   *LC* 57-10518

Lytle, Andrew Nelson, 1902-.   • **2.12058**
At the Moon's inn / by Andrew Lytle. — [1st ed.] — Indianapolis: Bobbs-
Merrill, [c1941] 400 p.; 23 cm. Map on lining-papers. I. T.
PS3523.Y88Ax PZ3.L9977At

Lytle, Andrew Nelson, 1902-.   • **2.12059**
The long night / by Andrew Lytle. — [1st ed.] Indianapolis: Bobbs-Merrill,
1936. 331 p.; 21 cm. I. T.
PZ3.L9977 Lo   PS3523.Y88Lx.   *LC* 36-27451

PS3525 M–McC

McAlmon, Robert, 1895-1956.   • **2.12060**
Being geniuses together: an autobiography. — London: Secker & Warburg,
[1938] 373 p.; 23 cm. I. T.
PS3525.A1143 Z5 1938   818.5   *LC* 39-12296

McCarthy, Mary, 1912-.   • **2.12061**
The writing on the wall: and other literary essays / [by] Mary McCarthy. —
New York: Harcourt, Brace & World [1970] 213 p.; 21 cm. I. T.
PS3525.A1435 A16 1970   809   *LC* 70-100498

McCarthy, Mary, 1912-.   • **2.12062**
Cast a cold eye. New York: Harcourt, Brace and World, 1950. 212 p.: 21 cm.
Short stories. I. T.
PS3525.A1435 C3x 1950   813.5   *LC* 50-9761

McCarthy, Mary, 1912-.   • **2.12063**
A charmed life. — [1st ed.]. — New York: Harcourt,Brace, 1955. 313 p.: 21cm.
I. T.
PS3525.A1435 C5x   *LC* 55-10153

McCarthy, Mary, 1912-.   • **2.12064**
The company she keeps. [New York] Simon and Schuster, 1942. 304 p. 21 cm.
I. T.
PZ3.M1272 Co   PS3525.A1435 C6x.

McCarthy, Mary, 1912-.   • **2.12065**
Memories of a Catholic girlhood. [1st ed.] New York, Harcourt, Brace [1957]
245 p. illus. 21 cm. I. T.
PS3525.A1435Z55   818.5   *LC* 57-8842

McCarthy, Mary, 1912-.   • **2.12066**
The groves of academe / Mary McCarthy. — New York: Harcourt, Brace,
1952. 302 p.; 21 cm. I. T.
PS3525.A176 G73x   *LC* 52-7255

McCarthy, Mary, 1912-.   • **2.12067**
The group. — [1st ed.]. — New York: Harcourt, Brace & World, [1963] 378 p.;
23 cm. A novel. I. T.
PZ3.M1272 Gs   PS3525.A176 G7x.   *LC* 63-15316

McCarthy, Mary, 1912-.   • **2.12068**
The oasis. — New York: Random House [1949] 181 p.; 21 cm. I. McCarthy,
Mary, 1912- Source of embarrassment. II. T. III. Title: A source of
embarrassment.
PS3525.A176 O2x   PZ3.M1272Oas.   *LC* 49-10152 rev*

McCoy, Horace, 1897-1955.   • **2.12069**
They shoot horses, don't they? / by Horace McCoy. — New York: Simon and
Schuster, 1935. 186 p.; 21 cm. I. T.
PS3525.A1769 T45   PS3525A168 T45.   *LC* 35-10855

PS3525 McCullers

McCullers, Carson, 1917-1967.   • **2.12070**
The ballad of the sad café; the novels and stories of Carson McCullers. —
Boston: Houghton Mifflin, 1951. 791 p.; 21 cm. I. T.
PZ3.M13884 Bal   PS3525.A1772 B3.   *LC* 51 10969

McCullers, Carson, 1917-1967.   • **2.12071**
Clock without hands. — Boston: Houghton Mifflin, 1961. 241 p.; 22 cm. — A
novel. I. T.
PZ3.M13884 Cl   PS3525.A1772 C55.   *LC* 61-10351

McCullers, Carson, 1917-1967.   • **2.12072**
The heart is a lonely hunter / by Carson McCullers. Boston: Houghton Mifflin
company, 1940. 3 p., l., [3]-356 p. 21 cm. I. T.
PS3525.A1772 H4 1940   *LC* 40-10298

McCullers, Carson, 1917-1967.   • **2.12073**
The member of the wedding, a play. [New York, 1951] 118 p. front. 21 cm. 'A
New Directions book.' Based on the author's novel of the same title. I. T.
PS3525.A1772 M5 1951   812.5   *LC* 51-10532

McCullers, Carson, 1917-1967.   **2.12074**
The mortgaged heart. Edited by Margarita G. Smith. Boston: Houghton
Mifflin, 1971. xix, 292 p.; 22 cm. 'The previously uncollected writings of Carson
McCullers.'—dust jacket. I. T.
PS3525.A1772 M6 1971   813/.5/2   *LC* 70-120829   *ISBN*
0395109531

McCullers, Carson, 1917-1967.   • **2.12075**
Reflections in a golden eye / introduction by Tennessee Williams. — [New
York: New Directions, 1950, c1941] 182 p. — (The New classics series) I. T.
II. Series.
PS3525.A1772 R4   *LC* 50-6225

McCullers, Carson, 1917-1967.   • **2.12076**
The square root of wonderful: a play / by Carson McCullers. — Boston:
Houghton Mifflin, 1958. 159 p.; 19 cm. I. T.
PS3525.A1772 S63 1958   *LC* 58-6501

Carr, Virginia Spencer.   **2.12077**
The lonely hunter: a biography of Carson McCullers / by Virginia Spencer
Carr. — 1st ed. — Garden City, N.Y.: Doubleday, 1975. xix, 600 p., [24] leaves
of plates: ill.; 24 cm. Includes index. 1. McCullers, Carson, 1917-1967 —
Biography. I. T.
PS3525.A1772 Z58   813/.5/2 B   *LC* 74-9478   *ISBN* 0385040288

McDowell, Margaret B.   **2.12078**
Carson McCullers / by Margaret B. McDowell. — Boston: Twayne Publishers,
1980. 158 p.: port.; 22 cm. (Twayne's United States authors series; TUSAS 354)
Includes index. 1. McCullers, Carson, 1917-1967 — Criticism and
interpretation. I. T.
PS3525.A1772 Z76   813/.5/2   *LC* 79-13361

PS3525 McG–McK

McGinley, Phyllis, 1905-.   • **2.12079**
Times three: selected verse from three decades, with seventy new poems /
foreword by W.H. Auden. — New York: Viking Press, 1960. xvi, 304 p. I. T.
PS3525.A23293.T5 1960   811.52   *LC* 60-11911

Wagner, Linda Welshimer.   • **2.12080**
Phyllis McGinley. — New York: Twayne Publishers, [1971] 128 p.; 21 cm. —
(Twayne's United States authors series, 170) 1. McGinley, Phyllis, 1905- I. T.
PS3525.A23293 Z9   811/.5/2   *LC* 74-120010

McKay, Claude, 1890-1948.   **2.12081**
The passion of Claude McKay: selected poetry and prose, 1912–1948 / edited
with an introd. and notes by Wayne F. Cooper. — New York: Schocken Books,
[1973] vii, 363 p.: ill.; 22 cm. — (Sourcebooks in Negro history) I. T. II. Series.
PS3525.A24785 A6 1973   818/.5/209   *LC* 72-95662   *ISBN*
0805234985

McKay, Claude, 1890-1948.   **2.12082**
Banana Bottom. — Chatham, N.J.: Chatham Bookseller, [1970, c1933] 317 p.;
22 cm. — I. T.
PZ3.M1926 Bam7 PS3525.A24785 B33x   813/.5/2   *LC* 78-129549

McKay, Claude, 1890-1948.   **2.12083**
Banjo: a story without a plot. — New York: Harper, 1929. 326 p. I. T.
PS3525.A24785 B35   *LC* 29-10435

McKay, Claude, 1890-1948.   **2.12084**
Home to Harlem, by Claude McKay. — New York: Harper, 1928. 340 p.; 20
cm. I. T.
PZ3.M1926Ho PS3525.A24785H6   *LC* 28-6523

McKay, Claude, 1890-1948.   **2.12085**
A long way from home. Introd. by St. Clair Drake. — New York: Harcourt,
Brace & World, [1970] xxi, 354 p.; 21 cm. — (A Harvest book, HB 172) An
autobiography. 1. McKay, Claude, 1890-1948. I. T.
PS3525.A24785 Z5 1970   818/.5/209 B   *LC* 76-11560

McKenney, Ruth, 1911-.   • **2.12086**
My sister Eileen / Ruth McKenney. — New York: Harcourt, Brace & Co.,
1938. xiii, 226 p.; 29 cm. — I. T.
PS3525.A25x   *LC* 38-17844

PS3525 MacLeish

MacLeish, Archibald, 1892-. • 2.12087
A time to speak: the selected prose of Archibald MacLeish. — Boston: Houghton Mifflin, 1941. 209 p.; 22 cm. I. T.
PS3525.A27 A16 1941 *LC* 41-51701

MacLeish, Archibald, 1892-. 2.12088
[Poems] Collected poems, 1917–1982 / Archibald MacLeish; with a prefatory note to the newly collected poems by Richard B. McAdoo. — Boston: Houghton Mifflin, 1985. 524 p.; 22 cm. I. T.
PS3525.A27 A17 1985 811/.52 19 *LC* 85-14392 *ISBN* 0395394171

MacLeish, Archibald, 1892-. • 2.12089
A continuing journey. — Boston: Houghton Mifflin, 1968 [c1967] x, 374 p.; 22 cm. Essays. I. T.
PS3525.A27 C69 814/.5/2 *LC* 67-26606

MacLeish, Archibald, 1892-. • 2.12090
'J.B.', a play in verse. — Boston: Houghton Mifflin, [1958] 153 p. I. T.
PS3525.A27 J2 *LC* 58-1148

MacLeish, Archibald, 1892-. 2.12091
Scratch. Suggested by Stephen Vincent Benét's short story 'The devil and Daniel Webster.'. — Boston: Houghton Mifflin, 1971. ix, 116 p.; 22 cm. A play. 1. Webster, Daniel, 1782-1852 — Drama. I. T.
PS3525.A27 S3 812/.5/2 *LC* 73-145912 *ISBN* 0395123461

McNickle, D'Arcy, 1904-1977. 2.12092
The surrounded / D'Arcy McNickle; introd. by Lawrence W. Towner. — Albuquerque: University of New Mexico Press, [1978] c1936. xiii, 297 p.; 20 cm. — (A Zia book) Reprint of the ed. published by Dodd, Mead, New York. 1. Salish Indians — Fiction. I. T.
PZ3.M2353 Su 1978 PS3525.A2844 813/.5/2 *LC* 77-91886 *ISBN* 0826304699

PS3525 Mailer

Mailer, Norman, 1923-. • 2.12093
An American dream. — New York: Dial Press, 1965. 270 p.; 22 cm. — I. T.
PZ3.M2815 Am PS3525.A4152A6x. *LC* 64-20280

Mailer, Norman. 2.12094
The armies of the night: history as a novel, the novel as history. — [New York]: New American Library, [1968] 288 p.; 22 cm. 1. Vietnamese Conflict, 1961-1975 — Public opinion. I. T.
PS3525.A4152 A8 818/.5/403 *LC* 68-23406

Mailer, Norman, 1923-. • 2.12095
Barbary shore. New York, Rinehart [1951] 312 p. 22 cm. I. T.
PS3525.A4152 B3x *LC* 51-10764

Mailer, Norman, 1923-. • 2.12096
The deer park. New York: Putnam, [1955] 375 p.; 22 cm. I. T.
PS3525.A4152 D4 PZ3.M2815 De. *LC* 55-10093

Mailer, Norman. 2.12097
The executioner's song / Norman Mailer. — 1st ed. — Boston: Little, Brown, c1979. 1056 p.; 24 cm. 1. Gilmore, Gary — Fiction. I. T.
PZ3.M2815 Ex PS3525.A4152E8x 813/.5/2 *LC* 79-17193 *ISBN* 0316544175

Mailer, Norman. 2.12098
Existential errands. — [1st ed.]. — Boston: Little, Brown, [1972] xv, 365 p.; 21 cm. I. T.
PS3525.A4152 E9 813/.5/4 *LC* 76-175476

Mailer, Norman. • 2.12099
The naked and the dead. New York, Rinehart [1948] 721 p. map. 22 cm. 1. World War, 1939-1945 — Fiction. I. T.
PS3525.A4152 N34 1948 *LC* 48-6633

Mailer, Norman. 2.12100
Pieces and pontifications / Norman Mailer. — 1st ed. — Boston: Little, Brown, c1982. x, 208, xiii, 192 p.; 24 cm. 1. Mailer, Norman — Interviews. 2. Authors, American — 20th century — Interviews. I. T.
PS3525.A4152 P5 1982 813/.54 19 *LC* 82-214 *ISBN* 0316544183

Mailer, Norman. • 2.12101
Why are we in Vietnam?: a novel. — New York: Putnam, [1967] 208 p.; 22 cm. I. T.
PS3525.A4152W49 *LC* 67-23133

Mailer, Norman. • 2.12102
Advertisements for myself. New York, Putnam [1959] 532 p. 22 cm. A collection of the author's short stories, articles, and essays, connected by an autobiographical narrative. I. T.
PS3525.A4152Z52 928.1 *LC* 59-11020

Adams, Laura. 2.12103
Existential battles: the growth of Norman Mailer / Laura Adams. — Athens: Ohio University Press, c1976. vii, 192 p.; 22 cm. Includes index. 1. Mailer, Norman — Criticism and interpretation. I. T.
PS3525.A4152 Z56 813.5/4 *LC* 74-27710 *ISBN* 0821401823

Braudy, Leo. comp. 2.12104
Norman Mailer, a collection of critical essays, edited by Leo Braudy. Englewood Cliffs, N.J., Prentice-Hall [1972] v, 185 p. 21 cm. (Twentieth century views) (A Spectrum book, S-TC-101) 1. Mailer, Norman. I. T.
PS3525.A4152 Z6 813/.5/4 *LC* 72-2673 *ISBN* 0135455332 *ISBN* 0135455413

Mailer, his life and times / [edited] by Peter Manso. 2.12105
New York: Simon and Schuster, c1985. 718 p.: ill.; 24 cm. Includes index. 1. Mailer, Norman. 2. Authors, American — 20th century — Biography. I. Manso, Peter.
PS3525.A4152 Z76 1985 813/.52 19 *LC* 84-27569 *ISBN* 0671442643

Poirier, Richard. • 2.12106
Norman Mailer. — New York: Viking Press, [1972] xiv, 176 p.; 20 cm. — (Modern masters) 1. Mailer, Norman, 1923- I. T. II. Series.
PS3525.A4152 Z84 813/.5/4 *LC* 75-185983 *ISBN* 0670515035

PS3525 Marquand

Marquand, John P. (John Phillips), 1893-1960. • 2.12107
H. M. Pulham, esquire, by John P. Marquand. Boston, Little, Brown and company, 1941. 431 p. 21 cm. 'First edition, after the printing of 950 copies for presentation. Published February, 1941.' 'A serial version of this story appeared in McCall's under the title of Gone tomorrow.' I. T.
PS3525.A6695H2 1941 *LC* 41-51574

Marquand, John Phillips. • 2.12108
Late George Apley: a novel in the form of a memoir. New York: Modern Library, 1940. 354 p. (Modern library of the world's best books.) I. T. II. Series.
PS3525A6695 L35 1940 *LC* 40-27102

Marquand, John P. (John Phillips), 1893-1960. • 2.12109
Sincerely, Willis Wayde. [1st ed.] Boston: Little, Brown, [c1955] 511 p.; 21 cm. I. T.
PZ3.M34466 Si PS3525.A6695 Sx. *LC* 55-5534

Marquand, John P. (John Phillips), 1893-1960. • 2.12110
So little time and Point of no return: two complete novels. — Boston: Little, Brown [1961?] 792 p.; 22 cm. I. Marquand, John P. (John Phillips), 1893-1960. Point of no return. II. T. III. Title: Point of no return.
PZ3.M34466 So4 PS3525.A6695 Sx. *LC* 61-14546

Marquand, John P. (John Phillips), 1893-1960. • 2.12111
Wickford Point. Boston, Little, Brown [c1939] 458 p. I. T.
PS3525.A6695 W5 813.5 *LC* 39-27145

Bell, Millicent. 2.12112
Marquand: an American life / Millicent Bell. — 1st ed. — Boston: Little, Brown, c1979. xv, 537 p., [8] leaves of plates: ill.; 24 cm. 'An Atlantic Monthly Press book.' 1. Marquand, John P. (John Phillips), 1893-1960 — Biography. 2. Authors, American — 20th century — Biography. I. T.
PS3525.A6695 Z57 818/.5/209 B *LC* 79-12818 *ISBN* 0316088285

Birmingham, Stephen. • 2.12113
The late John Marquand; a biography. [1st ed.] Philadelphia, Lippincott [1972] xiii, 322 p. illus. 25 cm. 1. Marquand, John P. (John Phillips), 1893-1960. I. T.
PS3525.A6695 Z59 818/.5/209 B *LC* 76-39182 *ISBN* 0397008864

Gross, John J., 1912-. • 2.12114
John P. Marquand. New York, Twayne Publishers [1963] 191 p. 22 cm. (Twayne's United States authors series, 33) 1. Marquand, John P. (John Phillips), 1893-1960. I. T.
PS3525.A6695 Z68 813.52 *LC* 62-19477

PS3525 Ma–Me

Marquis, Don, 1878-1937.   • **2.12115**
The lives and times of Archy and Mehitabel / with pictures by George Herriman and an introd. by E. B. White. — Garden City, N.Y.: Doubleday, [1950] xxiv, 19-477 p.: ill.; 20 cm. In prose and verse. I. T. II. Title: Archy and Mehitabel. III. Title: Archy's Life of Mehitabel. IV. Title: Archy does his part.
PS3525.A67 L5 1950   817.5   *LC* 50-5335

Anthony, Edward, 1895-.   • **2.12116**
O rare Don Marquis: a biography / by Edward Anthony. — 1st ed. — Garden City, N.Y.: Doubleday, 1962. 670 p.: ill., ports.; 22 cm. 1. Marquis, Don, 1878-1937 — Biography. I. T.
PS3525.A67 Z57   *LC* 62-7596

Marquis, Don, 1878-1937.   • **2.12117**
The best of Don Marquis / with an introduction by Christopher Morley; and with illustrations by George Herriman. — 1st ed. Garden City; New York: Doubleday & company, inc., 1946. xxx, 670 p.: ill.; 20 cm. I. T.
PS 3525 A78 A6 1946   *LC* 46-8219

Masters, Edgar Lee, 1868-1950.   • **2.12118**
Spoon River anthology / Woodcuts by John Ross and Clare Romano Ross. New York: Macmillan [1963, c1944] xiv, 297 p. illus. 25 cm. I. T.
PS3525.A83 S5 1963   811.52   *LC* 63-9624

Masters, Edgar Lee, 1868-1950.   • **2.12119**
Across Spoon River; an autobiography. New York: Octagon Books, 1969 [c1936] 426 p.: ill., ports.; 24 cm. I. T.
PS3525.A83 Z5 1969   811/.5/2 B   *LC* 70-96162

Mathews, John Joseph, 1895-.   **2.12120**
Sundown / John Joseph Mathews; with a new introd. by Priscilla Oaks. — Boston: Gregg Press, 1979, c1934. xi, 312 p.; 23 cm. — (The Gregg Press western fiction series) Reprint of the ed. published by Longmans, Green, London, New York. 1. Osage Indians — Fiction. I. T.
PZ3.M4247 Su 1979 PS3525.A8477   813/.5/2   *LC* 79-9365   *ISBN* 0839825889

Maxwell, William, 1908-.   • **2.12121**
The folded leaf, by William Maxwell. New York and London, Harper & brothers, 1945. 5 p. l., 3-310 p., 1 l. 21 cm. 'Eighth edition.' I. T.
PZ3.M4518Fo2 PS3525.A9464F6 1945   *LC* 45-3288

Maxwell, William.   • **2.12122**
They came like swallows / William Maxwell. — New York: Harper & Brothers, c1937. 267 p.; 23 cm. I. T.
PS3525.A9464T5x

PS3525 Mencken

Mencken, H. L. (Henry Louis), 1880-1956.   • **2.12123**
Letters / selected and annotated by Guy J. Forgue; with a personal note by Hamilton Owens. — [1st ed.]. — New York: Knopf, 1961. xxxviii, 506, xxii p.: port.; 25 cm. 1. Mencken, H. L. (Henry Louis), 1880-1956. I. T.
PS3525.E43 A16 1961   *LC* 61-12312

Mencken, H. L. (Henry Louis), 1880-1956.   • **2.12124**
H. L. Mencken's Smart set criticism / selected and edited by William H. Nolte. — Ithaca, N.Y.: Cornell University Press, [1968] xxxvii, 349 p.: port.; 24 cm. I. Nolte, William Henry, 1928- ed. II. T. III. Title: Smart set criticism.
PS3525.E43 A6 1968   818/.5/209   *LC* 68-16387

Mencken, H. L. (Henry Louis), 1880-1956.   • **2.12125**
The American scene, a reader. Selected and edited, and with an introd. and commentary by Huntington Cairns. [1st ed.] New York, Knopf, 1965. xxvii, 542 p. 25 cm. I. Cairns, Huntington, 1904- ed. II. T.
PS3525.E43 A75 1965   818.52   *LC* 65-11127

Mencken, H. L. (Henry Louis), 1880-1956.   • **2.12126**
The bathtub hoax and other blasts and bravos: from the Chicago Tribune / by H.L. Mencken; edited with an introd. and notes, by Robert McHugh. — 1st ed. — New York: Knopf, 1958. xvi, 286 p. 1. United States — Civilization — Addresses, essays, lectures I. Chicago Tribune, The II. T.
PS3525.E43B3   *LC* 58-12629

Mencken, H. L. (Henry Louis), 1880-1956.   • **2.12127**
Prejudices / a selection made by James T. Farrell and with an introduction by him. — New York: Vintage Books, 1958. 258 p.; 19 cm. — (Vintage book; 58) I. T.
PS3525.E43 P9 1958   *LC* 58-797

Mencken, H. L. (Henry Louis), 1880-1956.   • **2.12128**
Happy days, 1880–1892 / [by] H.L. Mencken. — New York: A.A. Knopf, 1940. –. xi, 313 p., 1 l. front. (port.); 23 cm. — Reminiscences. - I. T.
PS3525.E43Z52 1940b   928.1   *LC* 40-27046

Mencken, H. L. (Henry Louis), 1880-1956.   • **2.12129**
Newspaper days, 1899–1906. New York, A. A. Knopf, 1941. xi p., 3 l., 3-313 p., 1 l. front. (port.) 23 cm. I. T.
PS3525.E43 Z53   *LC* 41-16367

Mencken, H. L. (Henry Louis), 1880-1956.   **2.12130**
The new Mencken letters / edited by Carl Bode. — New York: Dial Press, 1977. 635 p.; 24 cm. Includes index. 1. Mencken, H. L. (Henry Louis), 1880-1956 — Correspondence. 2. Authors, American — 20th century — Correspondence. I. Bode, Carl, 1911- II. T.
PS3525.E43 Z53 1977   818/.5/209 B   *LC* 76-44850   *ISBN* 0803713797

Mencken, H. L. (Henry Louis), 1880-1956.   • **2.12131**
Heathen days, 1890–1936 / H. L. Mencken. — New York: A. A. Knopf, 1943. x, 299 p.: port. Reminiscences. I. T.
PS3525.E43 Z533   *LC* 43-249

Angoff, Charles, 1902-.   • **2.12132**
H.L. Mencken, a portrait from memory. — New York: T. Yoseloff, [1956] 240 p.; 22 cm. I. T.
PS3525.E43 Z539   *LC* 56-9094

Bode, Carl, 1911-.   • **2.12133**
Mencken. Carbondale: Southern Illinois University Press, [1969] ix, 452 p.: ill., ports.; 25 cm. 1. Mencken, H. L. (Henry Louis), 1880-1956 — Biography. 2. Authors, American — 20th century — Biography. I. T.
PS3525.E43 Z5398   818/.5/209 B   *LC* 69-16116   *ISBN* 0809303760

Goldberg, Isaac, 1887-1938.   • **2.12134**
The man Mencken: a biographical and critical survey. — New York: Simon and Schuster, 1925. xiv, 338 p.: ill; facsims., ports. 1. Mencken, H. L. (Henry Louis), 1880-1956. I. T.
PS3525.E43 Z57   *LC* 25-23719

Manchester, William Raymond, 1922-.   • **2.12135**
Disturber of the peace: the life of H.L. Mencken / with an introduction by Gerald W. Johnson. — New York: Harper, [1951] xiv, 336 p.: ports. 1. Mencken, H. L. (Henry Louis), 1880-1956 — Biography. I. Manchester, William Raymond, 1922- Sage of Baltimore. II. T. III. Title: The sage of Baltimore.
PS3525.E43 Z67 1951   *LC* 51-9028

Nolte, William Henry, 1928-.   • **2.12136**
H.L. Mencken, literary critic / by William H. Nolte. — Middletown, Conn.: Wesleyan University Press, c1966. xiii, 282 p.; 23 cm. 1. Mencken, H. L. (Henry Louis), 1880-1956. I. T.
PS3525.E43 Z73   *LC* 66-18117

PS3525 Me

Meredith, William, 1919-.   • **2.12137**
The open sea, and other poems. — New York: Knopf, 1958 [c1957] vii, 60 p.; 22 cm. I. T.
PS3525.E588 O6   *LC* 58-5824

Merrill, James Ingram.   • **2.12138**
Selected poems. [London]: Chatto and Windus, 1961. 63 p.; 23 cm. (The Phoenix living poets) I. T.
PS3525 E6645 A17 1961   *LC* 62-695

Merrill, James Ingram.   • **2.12139**
Braving the elements; poems, by James Merrill. — [1st ed.]. — New York: Atheneum, 1972. 73 p.; 23 cm. — I. T.
PS3525.E6645 B7   811/.5/4   *LC* 72-78488

Merrill, James Ingram.   **2.12140**
Divine comedies: poems / by James Merrill. — 1st ed. — New York: Atheneum, 1976. 136 p.; 24 cm. The book of Ephraim is pt. 1 of the author's trilogy; the other two pts. are Mirabell, books of number and Scripts for the pageant. I. T.
PS3525.E6645 D5 1976   811/.5/4   *LC* 75-33404   *ISBN* 068910703X

Merrill, James Ingram.   • **2.12141**
The (Diblos) notebook / [by] James Merrill. — [1st ed.] New York: Atheneum, 1965. 147 p.; 21 cm. I. T.
PZ4.M567 No   PS3525.E6645 Dx.   *LC* 65-12401

Merrill, James Ingram.   **2.12142**
Mirabell, books of number / James Merrill. — 1st ed. — New York: Atheneum, 1978. 182 p.; 24 cm. Pt. 2 of the author's trilogy; the other two pts. are The book of Ephraim, included in Divine comedies, and Scripts for the pageant. I. T.
PS3525.E6645 M5 1978   811/.5/4   *LC* 78-4350   *ISBN* 0689109016

Merrill, James Ingram.   • **2.12143**
Nights and days; poems, by James Merrill. — [1st ed.]. — New York, Atheneum, 1966. 56 p. 21 cm. I. T.
PS3525.E6645 N5 1966   811.54   *LC* 66-11395

Merrill, James Ingram.   **2.12144**
Scripts for the pageant / James Merrill. — 1st ed. — New York: Atheneum, 1980. 235 p.; 24 cm. Pt. 3 of the author's trilogy; the other two pts. are The book of Ephraim, included in Divine comedies, and Mirabell, books of number. I. T.
PS3525.E6645 S3 1980   811/.54   *LC* 79-55588   *ISBN* 0689110537

Merritt, Abraham, 1882-1943.   **2.12145**
The ship of Ishtar / by A. Merritt; illustrated by Virgil Finlay. — New York: Putnam, 1926. 1 v. I. T.
PS3525.E676 S5x

Merton, Thomas, 1915-1968.   • **2.12146**
A Thomas Merton reader / edited by Thomas P. McDonnell. — [1st ed.]. — New York: Harcourt, Brace & World, [1962] 553; 22 cm. 1. Monastic and religious life I. McDonnell, Thomas P. II. T.
PS3525.E7174 A6 1962   *LC* 62-16737

Merwin, W. S. (William Stanley), 1927-.   **2.12147**
The compass flower: poems / by W. S. Merwin. — 1st ed. — New York: Atheneum, 1977. 94 p.; 23 cm. I. T.
PS3525.E719 C6x   811/.5/4   *LC* 76-27345   *ISBN* 0689107684

Merwin, W. S. (William Stanley), 1927-.   • **2.12148**
The dancing bears / by W.S. Merwin. — New Haven: Yale University Press, 1954. 88 p.; 19 cm. Poems. I. T.
PS3525.E719 D3 1970

Merwin, W. S. (William Stanley), 1927-.   • **2.12149**
The drunk in the furnace / by W.S. Merwin. — New York: Macmillan, 1960. viii, 54 p.; 21 cm. — (The Macmillan poets; 35) Poems. I. T.
PS3525.E719 D7 1960   *LC* 60-14768

Merwin, W. S. (William Stanley), 1927-.   • **2.12150**
Green with beasts. — New York: Knopf, 1956. 85 p. Poems. I. T.
PS3525.E719 G7   *LC* 56-14287

PS3525 Mi

Michener, James A. (James Albert), 1907-.   • **2.12151**
Selected writings / with a special foreword by the author. — New York: Modern Library, [1957] 425 p.; 19 cm. (The Modern library of the world's best books, 296) I. T.
PS3525.I19 A6   813.5   *LC* 57-6493

Michener, James A. (James Albert), 1907-.   • **2.12152**
The bridges at Toko–ri. [New York] Random House [1953] 146 p. 24 cm. 1. Korean War, 1950-1953 — Fiction. I. T.
PS3525.I19Bx   *LC* 52-7129

Michener, James A. (James Albert), 1907-.   • **2.12153**
The fires of spring / [by] James A. Michener. — New York: Random House, [1949] 495 p.; 22 cm. I. T.
PZ3.M583 Fi   PS3525.I19 Fx.   *LC* 49-7426

Michener, James A. (James Albert), 1907-.   • **2.12154**
Hawaii. New York, Random House [1959] 937 p. 23 cm. A novel. 1. Hawaii — History — Fiction. I. T.
PS3525.I19Hx   *LC* 59-10815

Michener, James A. (James Albert), 1907-.   • **2.12155**
Tales of the south Pacific / by James A. Michener. — New York: The Macmillan company, 1947. v p., 1 l., 326 p.; 22 cm. 'First printing.' 1. World War, 1939-1945 — Fiction. I. T.
PS3525.I19 T3 1947   *LC* 47-30127

Becker, George Joseph.   **2.12156**
James A. Michener / George J. Becker. — New York: F. Ungar Pub. Co., c1983. ix, 199 p.; 21 cm. — (Literature and life series.) Includes index. 1. Michener, James A. (James Albert), 1907- — Criticism and interpretation. I. T. II. Series.
PS3525.I19 Z56 1983   813/.54 19   *LC* 82-40279   *ISBN* 0804420440

Miles, Josephine, 1911-.   **2.12157**
[Poems. Selections] Collected poems, 1930–83 / Josephine Miles. — Urbana: University of Illinois Press, c1983. xvi, 260 p.; 24 cm. Includes index. I. T.
PS3525.I4835 A6 1983   811/.52 19   *LC* 82-11014   *ISBN* 0252010175

Macdonald, Ross, 1915-.   **2.12158**
The Galton case / Ross Macdonald. — New York: Knopf, 1959. 242 p.; 20 cm. I. T.
PS3525.I486 G3 1959   813/.52 19

Speir, Jerry, 1946-.   **2.12159**
Ross Macdonald / by Jerry Speir. — New York: F. Ungar Pub. Co., c1978. ix, 182 p.; 22 cm. — (Recognitions) Includes index. 1. Macdonald, Ross, 1915- — Criticism and interpretation. 2. Detective and mystery stories, American — History and criticism. I. T.
PS3525.I486 Z87   813/.5/2   *LC* 78-4297   *ISBN* 0804428247

Millay, Edna St. Vincent, 1892-1950.   • **2.12160**
Collected poems. Edited by Norma Millay. — New York: Harper, [1956] 738 p.; 22 cm. — I. T.
PS3525.I495 A17 1956   811.5   *LC* 56-8756

Millay, Edna St. Vincent, 1892-1950.   • **2.12161**
Letters / edited by Allan Ross Macdougall. — New York: Harper, 1952. xii, 384 p.: facsims., port.; 22 cm. 1. Millay, Edna St. Vincent, 1892-1950 — Correspondence. I. Macdougall, Allan Ross, 1893- II. T.
PS3525.I495 Z53 1952   811/.5/2 B   *LC* 52-7291

Brittin, Norman A.   • **2.12162**
Edna St. Vincent Millay, by Norman A. Brittin. — New York: Twayne Publishers, [1967] 192 p.; 21 cm. — (Twayne's United States authors series, TUSAS 116) 1. Millay, Edna St. Vincent, 1892-1950. I. T.
PS3525.I495 Z62   818/.5/209   *LC* 67-13181

Gould, Jean, 1909-.   • **2.12163**
The poet and her book: a biography of Edna St. Vincent Millay. — New York: Dodd, Mead, [1969] xii, 308 p.: ill., ports.; 24 cm. 1. Millay, Edna St. Vincent, 1892-1950. I. T.
PS3525.I495 Z64   811/.5/2 B   *LC* 69-17603

Gurko, Miriam.   • **2.12164**
Restless spirit; the life of Edna St. Vincent Millay. — New York: Crowell, [1962] 271 p.; 21 cm. 1. Millay, Edna St. Vincent, 1892-1950. I. T.
PS3525.I495 Z67   928.1   *LC* 62-16544

Sheean, Vincent, 1899-.   • **2.12165**
The indigo bunting: a memoir of Edna St. Vincent Millay. — New York: Harper, [1951] 131 p.: ill. 1. Millay, Edna St. Vincent, 1892-1950 — Biography. I. T.
PS3525.I495 Z8   *LC* 51-13495

PS3525 Arthur Miller

Miller, Arthur, 1915-.   • **2.12166**
Collected plays. With an introd. — New York: Viking Press, 1957. 439 p.; 22 cm. 1. American drama I. T.
PS3525.I5156 A19 1957   812.5   *LC* 57-8405

Miller, Arthur, 1915-.   • **2.12167**
After the fall: a play. — New York: Viking Press, [1964] 129 p.; 22 cm. — I. T.
PS3525.I5156 A66   812.52   *LC* 63-19605

Ferres, John H. comp.   **2.12168**
Twentieth century interpretations of The crucible: a collection of critical essays / edited by John H. Ferres. — Englewood Cliffs, N.J.: Prentice-Hall [1972] vi, 122 p.; 21 cm. (Twentieth century interpretations) (A Spectrum book, S-884) 1. Miller, Arthur, 1915- The Crucible — Addresses, essays, lectures. 2. Witchcraft in literature — Addresses, essays, lectures. 3. Salem (Mass.) — History — Colonial period, ca. 1600-1775 — Addresses, essays, lectures. I. T.
PS3525.I5156 C734   812/.5/2   *LC* 72-4734   *ISBN* 0131948601 *ISBN* 0131948520

Miller, Arthur, 1915-.   **2.12169**
Salesman in Beijing / Arthur Miller; photographs by Inge Morath. — New York: Viking Press, 1984. xii, 254 p.: ill.; 22 cm. 1. Miller, Arthur, 1915- Death of a salesman. 2. Miller, Arthur, 1915- — Stage history — China — Peking. 3. Miller, Arthur, 1915- — Diaries. 4. Pei-ching jen min i shu chü yüan. 5. Theater — China — Peking. 6. Dramatists, American — 20th century — Biography. 7. Theatrical producers and directors — United States — Biography. 8. China — Social life and customs — 1976- I. Miller, Arthur, 1915- Death of a salesman. II. T.
PS3525.I5156 D4356 1984   812/.52 19   *LC* 83-47999   *ISBN* 067061601X

Twentieth century interpretations of Death of a salesman: a   2.12170
collection of critical essays / edited by Helene Wickham Koon.
Englewood Cliffs, N.J.: Prentice-Hall, c1983. 115 p.; 21 cm. 'A Spectrum book.'
1. Miller, Arthur, 1915- Death of a salesman — Addresses, essays, lectures.
I. Koon, Helene, 1925-
PS3525.I5156 D4377 1983   812/.52 19   *LC* 82-18518   *ISBN*
0131981358

Miller, Arthur, 1915-.   • 2.12171
Focus. New York, Reynal & Hitchcock [1945] 3 p. l., 217 p. 20 cm. I. T.
PZ3.M61224Fo PS3525.I5156F6   *LC* 45-9586

Miller, Arthur, 1915-.   • 2.12172
I don't need you any more: stories / by Arthur Miller. — New York: Viking
Press [1967] xiii, 240 p.; 22 cm. I. T.
PS3525.I5156 I17 1967   813/.52 19   *LC* 67-11269

Miller, Arthur, 1915-.   • 2.12173
Incident at Vichy; a play. New York, Viking Press [1965] 70 p. 22 cm. 1. World
War, 1939-1945 — Drama. I. T.
PS3525.I5156 I5   812.52   *LC* 65-12025

Miller, Arthur, 1915-.   • 2.12174
The misfits. New York, Viking Press [1961] 132 p. 24 cm. Written as a guide to
the director and the artists in the making of the 1961 motion picture. 'A story
conceived as a film'—Author's note. Based on the short story published in
Esquire in 1957. Cf. Arthur Miller / R. Hayman. 1972. P. 84. I. Misfits
(Motion picture) II. T.
PS3525.I5156 M5 1961   813/.52 19   *LC* 61-6089

Miller, Arthur, 1915-.   2.12175
The theater essays of Arthur Miller / edited and with an introd. by Robert A.
Martin; foreword by Arthur Miller. — New York: Viking Press, 1978. xliv,
401 p.; 22 cm. Includes index. 1. Drama — Addresses, essays, lectures.
I. Martin, Robert A. II. T.
PS3525.I5156 T5   809/.2   *LC* 77-20281   *ISBN* 0670698016

Corrigan, Robert Willoughby, 1927- comp.   • 2.12176
Arthur Miller: a collection of critical essays / edited by Robert W. Corrigan. —
Englewood Cliffs, N.J.: Prentice-Hall, [1969] vii, 176 p.; 22 cm. — (Twentieth
century views) (A Spectrum book.) 1. Miller, Arthur, 1915- I. T.
PS3525.I5156 Z6   812/.5/2   *LC* 69-15344

Evans, Richard Isadore, 1922-.   2.12177
Psychology and Arthur Miller [by] Richard I. Evans. — [1st ed.]. — New York:
Dutton, 1969. xvii, 136 p.; 21 cm. — (His Dialogues with notable contributors
to personality theory, v. 5) 1. Miller, Arthur, 1915- 2. Psychoanalysis.
I. Miller, Arthur, 1915- II. T.
PS3525.I5156 Z63 1969   812/.5/2   *LC* 69-13344

Hayman, Ronald, 1932-.   • 2.12178
Arthur Miller. — New York: Ungar, [1972] vii, 141 p.: ill.; 21 cm. — (World
dramatists) 1. Miller, Arthur, 1915- I. T.
PS3525.I5156 Z69 1972   812/.5/2   *LC* 75-153122   *ISBN*
0804423741

Huftel, Sheila.   • 2.12179
Arthur Miller: the burning glass. — [1st ed.]. — New York: Citadel Press,
[1965] 256 p.: illus., ports.; 22 cm. 1. Miller, Arthur, 1915- I. T.
PS3525.I5156 Z7   812.52   *LC* 65-15492

Moss, Leonard, 1931-.   • 2.12180
Arthur Miller. — New York: Twayne Publishers, [1967] 160 p.; 21 cm. —
(Twayne's United States authors series, TUSAS 115) 1. Miller, Arthur, 1915-
I. T.
PS3525.I5156 Z77   812/.5/2   *LC* 67-13180

PS3525 Henry Miller

Miller, Henry, 1891-.   • 2.12181
The widsom of the heart. — Norfolk, Conn.: New Directions Books, [c1941]
256 p. Short stories and essays. I. T.
PS3525.I545 W5 1941

Mailer, Norman.   2.12182
Genius and lust: a journey through the major writings of Henry Miller / by
Norman Mailer. — New York: Grove Press, 1976. xi, 576 p.; 24 cm. Includes
excerpts from Miller's writings. 1. Miller, Henry. I. Miller, Henry. II. T.
PS3525.I545Z7x   *ISBN* 0802101275

Miller, Henry, 1891-.   • 2.12183
The Henry Miller reader. Edited by Lawrence Durrell. — Freeport, N.Y.:
Books for Libraries Press, [1972, c1959] xvi, 397 p.; 23 cm. — (Essay index
reprint series) I. T.
PS3525.I5454 A6 1972   818/.5/209   *LC* 73-38712   *ISBN*
0836926641

Miller, Henry, 1891-.   • 2.12184
The cosmological eye. — Norfolk, Conn.: New [Directions, c1939] 363 p.: ill.
Short stories, sketches, essays, and an autobiographical note. I. T.
PS3525.I5454 C6   *LC* 40-8233

Miller, Henry, 1891-.   • 2.12185
Tropic of Cancer. — New York: Grove Press, [1961] 318 p.; 22 cm. — I. T.
PS3525.I5454 T7 1961   818.52   *LC* 61-15597

Miller, Henry, 1891-.   • 2.12186
Tropic of Capricorn. — New York: Grove Press, [1962, c1961] 348 p.; 22 cm.
— I. T.
PS3525.I5454 T8 1962   *LC* 62-6073

Miller, Henry, 1891-.   • 2.12187
The books in my life. — [New York: New Directions Pub. Corp, 1969-. v.   :
illus.; 21 cm. — (A New Directions book) I. T.
PS3525.I5454 Z52 1969   809   *LC* 71-88728

Miller, Henry, 1891-.   2.12188
My life and times. — [Chicago]: Playboy Press, [1972] 204 p.: illus.; 32 cm. —
(Gemini-Smith book.) I. T. II. Series.
PS3525.I5454 Z524   818/.5/209 B   *LC* 79-151843

Miller, Henry, 1891-.   • 2.12189
The rosy crucifixion. — New York: Grove Press, [c1965] 3 v. Autobiography.
I. Miller, Henry, 1891- Sexus. II. Miller, Henry, 1891- Plexus. III. Miller,
Henry, 1891- Nexus. IV. T. V. Title: Sexus. VI. Title: Plexus. VII. Title:
Nexus.
PS3525.I5454 Z558 1965   *LC* 65-23919

Baxter, Annette Kar.   • 2.12190
Henry Miller, expatriate. Pittsburgh: University of Pittsburgh Press, [c1961].
201 p. (Critical essays in English and American litterature, 5) 1. Miller, Henry,
1891- I. T. II. Series.
PS3525.I5454 Z65   *LC* 61-9393

Gordon, William A.   • 2.12191
The mind and art of Henry Miller [by] William A. Gordon. — [Baton Rouge]:
Louisiana State University Press, [1967] xxxii, 232 p.; 23 cm. 1. Miller, Henry,
1891- I. T.
PS3525.I5454 Z68   813/.5/2   *LC* 67-12215

Martin, Jay.   2.12192
Always merry and bright: the life of Henry Miller: an unauthorized biography /
Jay Martin. — Santa Barbara, Calif.: Capra Press, 1978. xi, 560 p.: ill.; 24 cm.
1. Miller, Henry, 1891- — Biography. 2. Authors, American — 20th century
— Biography. I. T.
PS3525.I5454 Z716   813/.52 B 19   *LC* 78-6912   *ISBN*
088496082X

Mitchell, Edward B., comp.   2.12193
Henry Miller; three decades of criticism. Edited and with an introd. by Edward
Mitchell. — New York: New York University Press, 1971. xviii, 216 p.; 24 cm.
1. Miller, Henry, 1891- 2. Miller, Henry, 1891- — Bibliography. I. T.
PS3525.I5454 Z72   813/.52 19   *LC* 78-181513   *ISBN* 0814753566

Wickes, George, ed.   • 2.12194
Henry Miller and the critics / with a pref. by Harry T. Moore. — Carbondale:
Southern Illinois University Press / [1963] xviii, 194 p.; 22 cm. (Crosscurrents:
modern critiques) 'Major books by Henry Miller': p. [193]-194. 1. Miller,
Henry, 1891- I. T.
PS3525.I5454Z9   818.52   *LC* 63-14289

PS3525 Mi–Mo

Miller, Walter M., 1923-.   2.12195
A canticle for Leibowitz; a novel. [1st ed.] Philadelphia, Lippincott, 1960
[c1959] 320 p. 21 cm. I. T.
PS3525.I577C3   *LC* 60-5735

Mitchell, Margaret, 1900-1949.   • 2.12196
Gone with the wind. — New York: Macmillan, 1936. 1037 p.; 22 cm. 1. United
States — History — Civil War, 1861-1865 — Fiction. I. T.
PS3525.I972 G6 1936   PZ3.M69484 Go   *LC* 36-27334

Recasting: 'Gone with the wind' in American culture / edited by   **2.12197**
Darden Asbury Pyron.
Miami: University Presses of Florida, c1983. x, 232 p.; 23 cm. 'A Florida International University book.' Includes index. 1. Mitchell, Margaret, 1900-1949 Gone with the wind — Addresses, essays, lectures. 2. Gone with the wind (Motion picture) 3. Southern States in literature — Addresses, essays, lectures. I. Pyron, Darden Asbury.
PS3525.I972 G687 1983   813/.52 19   *LC* 82-20310   *ISBN* 081300747X

Mitchell, Margaret, 1900-1949.   **2.12198**
[Gone with the wind letters, 1936-1949] Margaret Mitchell's Gone with the wind letters, 1936–1949 / edited by Richard Harwell. — New York: Macmillan, c1976. xxxvi, 441 p., [16] leaves of plates: ill.; 24 cm. Includes index. 1. Mitchell, Margaret, 1900-1949 — Correspondence. I. Harwell, Richard Barksdale. II. T. III. Title: Gone with the wind letters, 1936-1949.
PS3525.I972 Z53 1976   813/.5/2 B   *LC* 76-13190   *ISBN* 0025486500

PS3525 Marianne Moore

Moore, Marianne, 1887-1972.   • **2.12199**
The complete poems of Marianne Moore. New York: Macmillan [1967] xiv, 305 p.; 24 cm. I. T.
PS3525.O5616 A17 1967   811/.5/2   *LC* 67-26082

Moore, Marianne, 1887-1972.   • **2.12200**
A Marianne Moore reader. — New York: Viking Press, 1961. xviii, 301 p.; 20 cm. — (A Viking Compass book; C181) Includes index. I. T. II. Series.
PS3525.O5616 M3 1965   818

Engel, Bernard F.   • **2.12201**
Marianne Moore / by Bernard F. Engel. — New York: Twayne Publishers, [1964] 176 p.; 21 cm. (Twayne's United States authors series, 54) 1. Moore, Marianne, 1887-1972. I. T.
PS3525.O5616 Z65   811.52   *LC* 63-20613

Hall, Donald, 1928-.   • **2.12202**
Marianne Moore; the cage and the animal. New York: Pegasus [1970] x, 199 p.: port.; 21 cm. (Pegasus American authors) 1. Moore, Marianne, 1887-1972. I. T.
PS3525.O5616 Z68   811/.5/2   *LC* 71-114171

Nitchie, George Wilson, 1921-.   • **2.12203**
Marianne Moore; an introduction to the poetry [by] George W. Nitchie. New York, Columbia University Press, 1969. viii, 205 p. 20 cm. 1. Moore, Marianne, 1887-1972. I. T.
PS3525.O5616 Z7   811/.5/2   *LC* 79-96998   *ISBN* 023103119X

Tomlinson, Charles, 1927- comp.   • **2.12204**
Marianne Moore; a collection of critical essays. Englewood Cliffs, N.J., Prentice-Hall [1970, c1969] vi, 185 p. 22 cm. (A Spectrum book) 1. Moore, Marianne, 1887-1972. I. T.
PS3525.O5616 Z86   811/.5/2   *LC* 69-17374   *ISBN* 0135560438

PS3525 Mo–Mz

Morley, Christopher, 1890-1957.   • **2.12205**
The haunted bookshop / illustrated by Douglas Gorsline. — Philadelphia: Lippincott [1955] 253 p.: ill.; 22 cm. I. T.
PS3525.O71 Hx   *LC* 55-7993

Morley, Christopher, 1890-1957.   **2.12206**
Kitty Foyle. Philadelphia, New York [etc.] J.B. Lippincott Company [c1939] 339, [1] p. 21 cm. 'First edition.' At head of title: Christopher Morley. I. T.
PS3525.O71 K5   *LC* 39-27954

Morley, Christopher, 1890-1957.   • **2.12207**
Parnassus on wheels; illustrated by Douglas Gorsline. Philadelphia, Lippincott [1955] 160 p. illus. 22 cm. I. T.
PS3525.O71Px   *LC* 55-7994

Morley, Christopher, 1890-1957.   • **2.12208**
Thunder on the left by Christopher Morley. — Garden City, N.Y.: Doubleday, Page, 1936. 273 p.; 20 cm. I. T.
PZ3.M8265Th   PS3525.O71 T47.   *LC* 25-27460

Oakley, Helen McKelvey.   **2.12209**
Three hours for lunch: the life and times of Christopher Morley: a biography / by Helen McK. Oakley. — 1st ed. — New York: Watermill Publishers, c1976. xv, 382 p.: ill.; 23 cm. 1. Morley, Christopher, 1890-1957 — Biography. 2. Authors, American — 20th century — Biography. I. T.
PS3525.O71 Z8 1976   818/.5209 B 19   *LC* 75-39492   0883700058

Morris, Wright, 1910-.   **2.12210**
Ceremony in Lone Tree. — [1st ed.]. — New York: Atheneum, 1960. 304 p. I. T.
PZ3.M8346Ce   PS3525.O7475C4x.   *LC* 60-7775

Morris, Wright, 1910-.   • **2.12211**
The field of vision. — New York: Harcourt, Brace, [c1956] 251 p. A novel. I. T.
PS3525.O7475 F5x   *LC* 56-8525

Morris, Wright, 1910-.   **2.12212**
Here is Einbaum. — Los Angeles: Black Sparrow Press, 1973. 81 p.; 23 cm. I. T.
PZ3.M8346 He PS3525.O7475 H4x   813/.5/2   *LC* 73-11149   *ISBN* 0876851642

Morris, Wright, 1910-.   • **2.12213**
The huge season: a novel / by Wright Morris. — New York: Viking Press, c1954. 306 p. I. T.
PS3525.O7475 H8x   [Fic]   *LC* 54-10858

Morris, Wright, 1910-.   **2.12214**
A life. — [1st ed.]. — New York: Harper & Row, [1973] 152 p.; 22 cm. — I. T.
PS3525.O7475L5x   813/.5/2   *LC* 73-4155   *ISBN* 0060130792

Morris, Wright, 1910-.   • **2.12215**
Love among the cannibals. — [1st ed.]. — New York: Harcourt, Brace, [1957] 253 p. I. T.
PS3525.O7475 L6x   *LC* 57-10060

Morris, Wright, 1910-.   • **2.12216**
My uncle Dudley. — New York: Harcourt, Brace, [1942] 210 p.; 21 cm. — I. T.
PZ3.M8346 My5 PS3525.O7475 M9x   813/.5/2   *LC* 71-110050   *ISBN* 0837144353

Morris, Wright, 1910-.   **2.12217**
Real losses, imaginary gains / Wright Morris. 1st ed. — New York: Harper & Row, c1976. 186 p.; 24 cm. I. T.
PZ3.M8346 Re PS3525.O7475 R4x   813/.5/2   *LC* 75-33473   *ISBN* 0060130989

Morris, Wright, 1910-.   • **2.12218**
The world in the attic. New York: C. Scribner's Sons, 1949. 189 p.; 21 cm. I. T.
PS3525.O7475 W6x   *LC* 49-5058 *

Crump, Gail Bruce, 1942-.   **2.12219**
The novels of Wright Morris: a critical interpretation / by G. B. Crump. — Lincoln: University of Nebraska Press, c1978. 258 p.; 23 cm. Includes index. 1. Morris, Wright, 1910- — Criticism and interpretation. I. T.
PS3525.O7475 Z63   813/.5/2   *LC* 77-15796   *ISBN* 0803209622

Madden, David, 1933-.   • **2.12220**
Wright Morris. New York: Twayne Publishers [1965, c1964] 191 p.; 21 cm. (Twayne's United States authors series, 71) 1. Morris, Wright, 1910- I. T.
PS3525.O7475 Z7   813.52   *LC* 64-20721

Morrison, Theodore, 1901-.   • **2.12221**
The stones of the house. New York: Viking Press, 1953. 375 p.; 22 cm. I. T.
PS 3525 O75 S89 1953   *LC* 53-5319

Morrison, Theodore, 1901-.   • **2.12222**
The dream of Alcestis / Illustrated by Marvin Bileck. New York: Viking Press, 1950. 119 p.: ill.; 22 cm. In verse. I. T.
PS3525.O759 D7   811.52   *LC* 50-10245

Mourning Dove, 1888-1936.   **2.12223**
Cogewea, the half blood: a depiction of the great Montana cattle range / by Hum–ishu–ma, 'Mourning Dove,' given through Sho–pow–tan; with notes and biographical sketch by Lucullus Virgil McWhorter. — Lincoln: University of Nebraska Press, c1981. xxix, 302 p.: port.; 21 cm. Reprint of the 1927 ed. published by Four Seas Co., Boston. 1. Okinagan Indians — Fiction. I. Sho-pow-tan. II. McWhorter, Lucullus Virgil, 1860-1944. III. T.
PS3525.O872 C6 1981   813/.52 19   *LC* 80-29687   *ISBN* 0803230699

PS3527 Nabokov
(see also PG3476.N3)

Nabokov, Vladimir Vladimirovich, 1899-1977.   **2.12224**
Ada: or, Ardor, a family chronicle / Vladimir Nabokov. — New York: McGraw-Hill, c1969. 626 p.; 22 cm. I. T. II. Title: Ardor, a family chronicle.
PZ3.N121 Ad4 PS3527.A15 A652x   813/.5/4   *LC* 77-350160

Boyd, Brian. 2.12225
Nabokov's Ada: the place of consciousness / Brian Boyd. — Ann Arbor: Ardis, c1985. xi, 245 p.; 24 cm. 1. Nabokov, Vladimir Vladimirovich, 1899-1977. Ada. I. T.
PS3527.A15 A6533 1985   813/.54 19   *LC* 84-28357   *ISBN* 0882339060

Nabokov, Vladimir Vladimirovich, 1899-1977. • 2.12226
Lolita. — New York: Putnam, [1958, c1955] 319 p.; 23 cm. I. T.
PZ3.N121 Lo2   PS3527.A15 Lx.   *LC* 58-10755

Nabokov, Vladimir Vladimirovich, 1899-1977. • 2.12227
Nabokov's dozen: a collection of thirteen stories. — [1st ed.]. — Garden City, N.Y.: Doubleday, 1958. 214 p. I. T.
PS3527.A15 N2x   *LC* 58-10032

Nabokov, Vladimir Vladimirovich, 1899-1977. • 2.12228
Pale fire: a novel. — New York: Putnam, [1962] 315 p.; 22 cm. I. T.
PS3527.A15 P3x   *LC* 62-7351

Nabokov, Vladimir Vladimirovich, 1899-1977. • 2.12229
Pnin. — [1st ed.]. — Garden City, N.Y.: Doubleday, 1957. 191 p.; 22 cm. A novel. I. T.
PS3527.A15 P6x   *LC* 57-6299

Nabokov, Vladimir Vladimirovich, 1899-1977. • 2.12230
The real life of Sebastian Knight / Vladimir Nabokov. — Norfolk, Conn.: New Directions, c1959. 205 p.; 22 cm.. I. T.
PG3476.N3 R4   PS3527.A15 R4x.   *LC* 59-9489

Nabokov, Vladimir Vladimirovich, 1899-1977. 2.12231
Strong opinions [by] Vladimir Nabokov. — New York: McGraw-Hill, [1973] xiii, 335 p.; 22 cm. I. T.
PS3527.A15 S7   809   *LC* 73-6604   *ISBN* 0070457379

Fowler, Douglas. 2.12232
Reading Nabokov / Douglas Fowler. — Ithaca, N.Y.: Cornell University Press, 1974. 224 p.; 21 cm. Includes index. 1. Nabokov, Vladimir Vladimirovich, 1899-1977 — Criticism and interpretation. I. T.
PS3527.A15 Z7   813/.5/4   *LC* 73-20798   *ISBN* 0801408288

Nabokov, Vladimir Vladimirovich, 1899-1977. • 2.12233
Speak, memory; an autobiography revisited, by Vladimir Nabokov. — [Rev. ed.]. — New York: Putnam, 1966. 316 p.: ill., col. map (on lining papers), ports. 1. Nabokov, Vladimir Vladimirovich, 1899-1977 — Biography. I. Nabokov, Vladimir Vladimirovich, 1899-1977. Conclusive evidence. II. T. III. Title: Conclusive evidence.
PS3527.A15 Z5x   891.7/8/4203 B   *LC* 66-23330   *ISBN* 0398502203

PS3527 Na–Ne

Nash, Ogden, 1902-1971. 2.12234
I wouldn't have missed it: selected poems of Ogden Nash / selected by Linell Smith and Isabel Eberstadt; introd. by Archibald MacLeish. — 1st ed. — Boston: Little, Brown, [1975] xxiii, 407 p.: ill.; 24 cm. I. T.
PS3527.A637 A6 1975   811/.5/2   *LC* 75-14008   *ISBN* 0316598305

Nash, Ogden, 1902-1971. 2.12235
The old dog barks backwards. Illustrated by Robert Binks. — [1st ed.]. — Boston: Little, Brown, [1972] 129 p.: illus.; 20 cm. Poems. I. T.
PS3527.A637 O4 1972   811/.5/2   *LC* 76-186967   *ISBN* 0316598046

Nathan, George Jean, 1882-1958. • 2.12236
The world of George Jean Nathan / selected and edited, with an introd., by Charles Angoff. — [1st ed.]. — New York: Knopf, 1952. xxviii, 489 p.; 22 cm. I. Angoff, Charles, 1902- II. T.
PS3527.A72 A6 1952   810.81   *LC* 51-11986

Nathan, Robert, 1894-. • 2.12237
The adventures of Tapiola. — New York: Knopf, 1950. 121, 137 p.: ill. I. Nathan, Robert, 1894- Journey of Tapiola. II. Nathan, Robert, 1894- Tapiola's brave regiment. III. T. IV. Title: Journey of Tapiola. V. Title: Tapiola's brave regiment.
PS3527.A74 A7   *LC* a 52-7597

Nathan, Robert, 1894-. • 2.12238
The enchanted voyage. — 1st ed. — New York: Knopf, 1936. 187 p. I. T.
PS3527.A74 E5 1936   *LC* 36-18874

Nathan, Robert, 1894-. • 2.12239
One more spring / Robert Nathan. — 1st ed. — New York: Knopf, 1933. 212 p. I. T. II. Title: 1 more spring.
PS3527.A74 O5 1933   *LC* 33-3086

Nathan, Robert, 1894-. • 2.12240
Portrait of Jennie, by Robert Nathan. — New York: A. A. Knopf, 1940. 4 p., l., 3-212 p., 1 l.; 21 cm. 'First edition.' I. T.
PZ3.N195 Po   PS3527.A74 Px.   *LC* 40-27011

Nathan, Robert, 1894-. • 2.12241
Winter in April. — [1st ed.]. — New York: Knopf, 1938. 4, 228 p.; 21 cm. I. T.
PS3527.A74 W4 1938   Fic   *LC* 38-27028

Neihardt, John Gneisenau, 1881-1973. • 2.12242
Collected poems of John G. Neihardt. — New York: Macmillan, 1926. 2 v.: port.; 25 cm. 'Of this edition of collected poems five hundred copies have been printed, each signed by the author.' I. T.
PS3527.E35 1926   811/.5/2   *ISBN* 031321025X

Nemerov, Howard. 2.12243
The collected poems of Howard Nemerov. — Chicago: University of Chicago Press, 1977. xviii, 516 p.; 24 cm. Includes index. I. T.
PS3527.E5 A17 1977   811/.5/4   *LC* 77-544   *ISBN* 0226572587

Nemerov, Howard, 1920-. • 2.12244
A commodity of dreams & other stories / by Howard Nemerov. — New York: Simon and Schuster, 1959. 245 p. I. T.
PZ3.N343 Co   PS3527.E5 C6 1959.   *LC* 59-6015

Nemerov, Howard, 1920-. • 2.12245
The homecoming game: a novel / by Howard Nemerov. — New York: Simon and Schuster, 1957. 246 p. I. T.
PS3527.E5 H6   *LC* 57-5679

Nemerov, Howard. • 2.12246
Stories, fables & other diversions / by Howard Nemerov. — Boston: Godine, 1971. 121 p.; 25 cm. I. T. II. Title: Stories, fables, and other diversions.
PS3527.E5 S8   813/.54 19   *LC* 75-143388

PS3527 Ni–No

Nims, John Frederick, 1913-. • 2.12247
Knowledge of the evening: poems,1950–1960. — New Brunswick: Rutgers University Press, 1960. 96p. I. T.
PS3527.I863 K6   811.54   *LC* 60-11524

Nin, Anaïs, 1903-1977. 2.12248
Anaïs Nin reader. Edited by Philip K. Jason. Introd. by Anna Balakian. — [1st ed.]. — Chicago: Swallow Press, [1973] 316 p.; 23 cm. — I. T.
PS3527.I865 A6 1973   813/.5/2   *LC* 72-91913   *ISBN* 0804005958

Nin, Anaïs, 1903-1977. 2.12249
A woman speaks: the lectures, seminars, and interviews of Anaïs Nin / edited with an introd. by Evelyn J. Hinz. 1st ed. — Chicago: Swallow Press, 1976 (c1975). xviii, 270 p.; 22 cm. Includes index. I. Hinz, Evelyn J. II. T.
PS3527.I865 A6 1975   818/.5/209   *LC* 75-15111   *ISBN* 0804006938

Nin, Anaïs, 1903-1977. • 2.12250
Cities of the interior / Anaïs Nin; line engravings by Ian Hugo. — Denver: A. Swallow, [1959-. ca. 950 p.: ill.; 23 cm. I. T.
PS3527.I865 C5   *LC* 61-65506

Nin, Anaïs, 1903-1977. • 2.12251
House of incest. / Photomontages by Val Telberg. — Denver: A. Swallow, [1961,c1958] 72 p.: ill. (A Swallow paperbook) I. T.
PS3527.I865 H6   *LC* 61-65487

Nin, Anaïs, 1903-1977. • 2.12252
Under a glass bell: and other stories. — New York: Dutton, 1948. 221 p. I. T.
PZ3.N617 Up7 PS3527.I865 U6x   813/.5/2   *LC* 48-605

Nin, Anaïs, 1903-1977. • 2.12253
Winter of artifice: three novelettes / with engravings by Ian Hugo. — Denver: A. Swallow, [1961] 175 p.: ill. I. T.
PS3527.I865 W5   *LC* 61-17530

Nin, Anaïs, 1903-1977. 2.12254
The diary of Anaïs Nin. Edited, and with an introd., by Gunther Stuhlmann. [1st ed.]. — New York: Swallow Press, [1966-80] 7 v.: illus.; 22 cm. Vol. 3 has imprint: New York, Harcourt, Brace & World; v. 4-7: New York, Harcourt, Brace, Jovanovich. 1. Nin, Anaïs, 1903-1977 — Diaries. 2. Authors, American — 20th century — Biography. I. Stuhlmann, Gunther. II. T.
PS3527.I865 Z5   818/.5203 B 19   *LC* 66-12917   *ISBN* 0151255938

Evans, Oliver Wendell, 1915-. • 2.12255
Anaïs Nin, [by] Oliver Evans. With a pref. by Harry T. Moore. Carbondale, Southern Illinois University Press [1968] xvii, 221 p. 22 cm. (Crosscurrents: modern critiques) 1. Nin, Anaïs, 1903-1977. I. T.
PS3527.I865 Z6　　813/.5/2　　LC 67-11703

Nordhoff, Charles, 1887-1947. • 2.12256
Mutiny on the Bounty, by Charles Nordhoff and James Norman Hall. Boston, Little, Brown, and company, 1932. xii, 396 p. 21 cm. 1. Bligh, William, 1754-1817 — Fiction. 2. Bounty (Ship) I. Hall, James Norman, 1887-1951. joint author. II. T.
PS3527.O437M8x　　LC 32-25596

PS3529 O–Oh

Odets, Clifford, 1906-1963. • 2.12257
The big knife / by Clifford Odets. — New York: Random House, c1949. 147 p.; 21 cm. I. T.
PS3529.D46 B5 1949b　　812

Odets, Clifford, 1906-1963. • 2.12258
The country girl: a play in three acts / by Clifford Odets. — New York: Viking Press, 1951. 124 p.; 21 cm. I. T.
PS3529.D46 C6　　PS3529D46 C6.　　LC 51-1860

Odets, Clifford, 1906-1963. • 2.12259
Six plays of Clifford Odets, with a preface by the author. — New York: The Modern library, [1939] x, 433 p.; 19 cm. — (The Modern library of the world's best books) 'First Modern library edition 1939.' I. T.
PS3529.D46 S5 1939　　812.5　　LC 39-27816

Cantor, Harold, 1926-. 2.12260
Clifford Odets, playwright–poet / by Harold Cantor. — Metuchen, N.J.: Scarecrow Press, 1978. viii, 235 p.; 22 cm. Includes index. 1. Odets, Clifford, 1906-1963 — Criticism and interpretation. I. T.
PS3529.D46 Z6　　812/.5/4　　LC 77-27284　　ISBN 0810811073

Murray, Edward. • 2.12261
Clifford Odets: the thirties and after. — New York: F. Ungar Pub. Co., [1968] ix, 229 p.; 21 cm. 1. Odets, Clifford, 1906-1963. I. T.
PS3529.D46 Z77　　812/.5/4　　LC 68-9397

Shuman, R. Baird (Robert Baird), 1929-. • 2.12262
Clifford Odets. New York, Twayne Publishers [c1962] 160 p. 22 cm. (Twayne's United States authors series, 30) 1. Odets, Clifford, 1906-1963. I. T.
PS3529.D46 Z87　　818.54　　LC 62-19474

O'Hara, Frank. • 2.12263
The collected poems of Frank O'Hara. Edited by Donald Allen. With an introd. by John Ashbery. — [1st ed.]. — New York: Knopf, 1971. xxix, 586 p.: port.; 26 cm. I. Allen, Donald Merriam, 1912- ed. II. T.
PS3529.H28 1971　　811/.5/4　　LC 70-111237　　ISBN 0394439015

O'Hara, Frank. 2.12264
Poems retrieved / Frank O'Hara; edited by Donald Allen. Bolinas, Calif.: Grey Fox Press; Berkeley, Calif.: distributed by Book People, c1977. xvi, 242 p.; 23 cm. Includes index. I. T.
PS3529.H28 P6　　811/.5/4　　LC 77-554　　ISBN 0912516186

Perloff, Marjorie. 2.12265
Frank O'Hara: poet among painters / Marjorie Perloff. — New York: G. Braziller, c1977. 234 p.: [4] leaves of plates: ill.; 22 cm. Includes indexes. 1. O'Hara, Frank — Criticism and interpretation. 2. O'Hara, Frank — Knowledge — Art. I. T.
PS3529.H28 Z8　　811/.5/4　　LC 76-16636　　ISBN 0807608351

O'Hara, John, 1905-1970. • 2.12266
Appointment in Samarra; with a new foreword by the author. — New York: Modern Library, [1953] 301 p.; 19 cm. — (The Modern library of the world's best books, 42) I. T.
PZ3.O3677 Ap5　　PS3529.H29 Ax.　　LC 53-5341

O'Hara, John, 1905-1970. • 2.12267
Butterfield 8: a novel. — New York: Harcourt, Brace, [c1935] 310 p. I. T.
PS3529.H29 B8　　LC 35-19688

O'Hara, John, 1905-1970. 2.12268
The Ewings. — [1st ed.]. — New York: Random House, [1972] 310 p.; 22 cm. I. T.
PS3529.H29 E8　　PZ3.O3677 Ew　　813/.5/2　　LC 78-31494
ISBN 039447404X

O'Hara, John, 1905-1970. • 2.12269
From the terrace, a novel. — New York: Random House, [1958] 897 p.; 23 cm. — I. T.
PS3529.H29Fx　　LC 58-12336

O'Hara, John, 1905-1970. 2.12270
Good Samaritan, and other stories. — [1st ed.]. — New York: Random House, [1974] ix, 296 p.; 22 cm. I. T.
PS3529.H29Gx　　813/.5/2　　LC 74-1483　　ISBN 0394490703

O'Hara, John, 1905-1970. • 2.12271
Ourselves to know, a novel. — New York: Random House, [1960] 408 p.; 22 cm. — I. T.
PZ3.O3677 Ou　　PS3529.H29 Ox.　　LC 60-5528

O'Hara, John, 1905-1970. • 2.12272
Pal Joey. [1st ed.] New York, Duell, Sloan and Pearce [c1940] 195 p. 21 cm. I. T.
PS3529.H29 P3 1940　　LC 40-33705

O'Hara, John, 1905-1970. • 2.12273
A rage to live. — New York: Random House, [c1949] 590 p. I. T.
PS3529.H29 R3　　LC 49-10363

O'Hara, John, 1905-1970. • 2.12274
Ten North Frederick. — New York: Random House, [1955] 408 p.; 22 cm. — I. T.
PZ3.O3677 Te　　PS3529.H29 Tx.　　LC 55-8167

O'Hara, John, 1905-1970. 2.12275
Selected letters of John O'Hara / edited by Matthew J. Bruccoli. — 1st ed. — New York: Random House, c1978. xxi, 538 p.; 25 cm. Includes index. 1. O'Hara, John, 1905-1970 — Correspondence. 2. Novelists, American — 20th century — Correspondence. I. Bruccoli, Matthew Joseph, 1931- II. T.
PS3529.H29 Z48 1978　　813/.5/2 B　　LC 77-90249　　ISBN 0394421337

Bruccoli, Matthew Joseph, 1931-. 2.12276
The O'Hara concern: a biography of John O'Hara / by Matthew J. Bruccoli. — 1st ed. — New York: Random House, 1975. xxix, 417 p.: ill., maps (on lining papers); 25 cm. Includes index. 1. O'Hara, John, 1905-1970. I. T.
PS3529.H29 Z59　　813/.5/2 B　　LC 75-9736　　ISBN 0394484460

O'Hara, John, 1905-1970. • 2.12277
Selected short stories. With an introd. by Lionel Trilling. [1st Modern library ed.] New York, Modern Library [1956] 303 p. 19 cm. (The Modern library of the world's best books, 211]) I. T.
PZ3.O3677 Se　　PS3529.H29x.　　LC 56-8834

PS3529 Ol

Olson, Charles, 1910-1970. • 2.12278
Archaeologist of morning. — New York: Grossman Publishers, 1973. [245] p.; 23 cm. Poems. I. T.
PS3529.L655 A17 1973　　811/.5/4　　LC 73-160764　　ISBN 0670130354

Olson, Charles, 1910-1970. • 2.12279
Selected writings of Charles Olson / edited, with an introd. by Robert Creeley. — New York: New Directions, 1967, c1966. 280 p. — (A New Directions paper book) I. T.
PS3529.L655 A6 1967　　LC 66-27613

Olson, Charles, 1910-1970. • 2.12280
The distances: poems. — New York: Grove Press, [1960] 96 p. — (Evergreen original; E-274) I. T. II. Series.
PS3529.L655 D5　　LC 60-12563

Olson, Charles, 1910-1970. 2.12281
The Maximus poems / Charles Olson; edited by George F. Butterick. — Berkeley: University of California Press, c1983. 652 p.: ill.; 29 cm. Includes index. I. Butterick, George F. II. T.
PS3529.L655 M3 1983　　811/.54 19　　LC 79-65759　　ISBN 0520040155

Olson, Elder, 1909-. • 2.12282
Collected poems. — Chicago: University of Chicago Press, [1963] xiii, 194 p.; 21 cm. I. T.
PS3529.L66 A17 1963　　LC 63-22589

PS3529 O'Neill

O'Neill, Eugene, 1888-1953. • **2.12283**
Plays ... — New York, Random House [c1955] 3 v. 21 cm. I. T.
PS3529.N5A6 1955   812.5   *LC* A 41-2908

O'Neill, Eugene, 1888-1953. • **2.12284**
Ten 'lost' plays. With a foreword by Bennett Cerf. New York, Random House
[1964] 303 p. 21 cm. I. T.
PS3529.N5 A6 1964   812.52   *LC* 64-17937

O'Neill, Eugene, 1888-1953. **2.12285**
'Children of the sea,' and three other unpublished plays. Edited by Jennifer
McCabe Atkinson. Foreword by Frank Durham. Washington, NCR Microcard
Editions [1972] xviii, 214 p. 24 cm. 'A Bruccoli Clark book.' I. T.
PS3529.N5 A6 1972   812/.5/2   *LC* 77-183148   *ISBN* 0910972141
ISBN 091097215X

O'Neill, Eugene, 1888-1953. • **2.12286**
Long day's journey into night. [1st ed.] New Haven, Yale University Press,
1956 [c1955] 176 p. 25 cm. A play. I. T.
PS3529.N5 L6   812.5   *LC* 56-5944

O'Neill, Eugene, 1888-1953. • **2.12287**
A moon for the misbegotten, a play in four acts. [1st ed.] New York, Random
House [1952] 177 p. 21 cm. I. T.
PS3529.N5 M68 1952   812.5   *LC* 52-6668

O'Neill, Eugene, 1888-1953. • **2.12288**
More stately mansions / by Eugene O'Neill; shortened from the author's partly
rev. script by Karl Ragner Gierow and edited by Donald Gallup. — New
Haven: Yale University Press, 1964. 194 p.: ill.; 25 cm. I. T.
PS3529.N5 M73 1964   *LC* 64-12655

Biography. Criticism

Bogard, Travis. • **2.12289**
Contour in time; the plays of Eugene O'Neill. New York, Oxford University
Press, 1972. xx, 491 p. illus. 24 cm. 1. O'Neill, Eugene, 1888-1953. I. T.
PS3529.N5 Z568   812/.5/2 B   *LC* 74-186499   *ISBN* 0195015738

Cargill, Oscar, 1898- ed. • **2.12290**
O'Neill and his plays, four decades of criticism, edited by Oscar Cargill, N.
Bryllion Fagin [and] William J. Fisher. [New York] New York University
Press, 1961. xi, 528 p. 25 cm. 1. O'Neill, Eugene, 1888-1953 — Criticism and
interpretation. I. T.
PS3529.N5 Z576   812.52   *LC* 61-17631

Critical essays on Eugene O'Neill / [compiled by] James J. **2.12291**
Martine.
Boston, Mass.: G.K. Hall, c1984. vii, 214 p.; 25 cm. (Critical essays on
American literature.) Includes index. 1. O'Neill, Eugene, 1888-1953 —
Criticism and interpretation — Addresses, essays, lectures. I. Martine, James
J. II. Series.
PS3529.N5 Z62727 1984   812/.52 19   *LC* 83-26540   *ISBN*
0816186839

Engel, Edwin A, 1907-. • **2.12292**
The Haunted heroes of Eugene O'Neill. — Cambridge, Harvard University
Press, 1953. 310 p. 1. O'Neill, Eugene, 1888-1953. I. T.
PS3529N5Z63   812.59   *LC* 53-5068

Falk, Doris V. • **2.12293**
Eugene O'Neill and the tragic tension; an interpretive study of the plays. New
Brunswick, N.J., Rutgers University Press, 1958. 211 p. 22 cm. 1. O'Neill,
Eugene, 1888-1953 — Criticism and interpretation. I. T.
PS3529.N5 Z64   812.5   *LC* 58-10830

Gassner, John, 1903-1967. ed. • **2.12294**
O'Neill, a collection of critical essays. Englewood Cliffs, N.J., Prentice-Hall
[1964] viii, 180 p. 21 cm. (Twentieth century views, S-TC-39) (A Spectrum
book). 1. O'Neill, Eugene, 1888-1953 — Criticism and interpretation. I. T.
PS3529.N5 Z648   812.52   *LC* 64-19679

Gelb, Arthur, 1924-. **2.12295**
O'Neill / [by] Arthur & Barbara Gelb. Rev. ed. — New York: Harper & Row
[1974] xx, 990 p.: ill.; 24 cm. 1. O'Neill, Eugene, 1888-1953. I. Gelb, Barbara.
joint author. II. T.
PS3529.N5 Z653 1974   812/.5/2 B   *LC* 73-6760   *ISBN*
0060114878

Raleigh, John Henry, 1920-. • **2.12296**
The plays of Eugene O'Neill. With a pref. by Harry T. Moore. Carbondale,
Southern Illinois University Press [1965] xvi, 304 p. 22 cm. (Crosscurrents:
modern critiques) 1. O'Neill, Eugene, 1888-1953. I. T.
PS3529.N5 Z79   812.52   *LC* 65-12387

Sheaffer, Louis. **2.12297**
O'Neill: son and artist. [1st ed.] Boston, Little, Brown [1973] xviii, 750 p. illus.
25 cm. 1. O'Neill, Eugene, 1888-1953. I. T.
PS3529.N5 Z797   812/.5/2   *LC* 73-8610   *ISBN* 0316783366

Sheaffer, Louis. • **2.12298**
O'Neill, son and playwright. — [1st. ed.]. — Boston: Little, Brown, [1968] xx,
543 p.: illus., facsim., ports.; 24 cm. 1. O'Neill, Eugene, 1888-1953. I. T.
PS3529.N5 Z798   812/.5/2 B   *LC* 68-17278

PS3529 Op–Oz

Oppen, George. **2.12299**
The collected poems of George Oppen. — New York: New Directions Pub.
Corp., 1975. 263 p.; 21 cm. (A New Directions book) Includes index. I. T.
PS3529.P54 1975   811/.5/2   *LC* 75-6965   *ISBN* 0811205835

Oskison, John Milton, 1874-. **2.12300**
Black Jack Davey. — New York: D. Appleton, 1926. 311 p.; 20 cm. I. T.
PS3529.S7x   *LC* 26-15737

PS3531 P–Po

Parker, Dorothy, 1893-1967. • **2.12301**
The collected poetry of Dorothy Parker. New York: The Modern Library,
[1944] xii, 210 p.; 19 cm. (The Modern library of the world's best books) I. T.
PS3531.A5855 A17 1944   811.5   *LC* 45-35009

Parker, Dorothy, 1893-1967. • **2.12302**
Dorothy Parker, with an introduction by W. Somerset Maugham. New York,
The Viking press, 1944. 3 p. l., 9-544 p. 18 cm. (The Viking portable library)
Published in 1973 under title: The portable Dorothy Parker. A collection of
poems and stories. I. T.
PS3531.A5855 A6 1944   818.5   *LC* 44-4169

Parker, Dorothy, 1893-1967. **2.12303**
The portable Dorothy Parker. Rev. and enl. ed. With a new introd. by Brendan
Gill. New York, Viking Press [1973] xxvii, 610 p. 19 cm. (The Viking portable
library) Published in 1944 under title: ... Dorothy Parker. I. T.
PS3531.A5855 A6 1973   818/.5/209   *LC* 74-180479   *ISBN*
0670540161 *ISBN* 067001074X

Patchen, Kenneth, 1911-1972. • **2.12304**
The collected poems of Kenneth Patchen. — [1st ed. — New York: New
Directions Pub. Corp., 1968] 504 p.; 21 cm. — (A New Directions book) I. T.
PS3531.A764 A6 1968   811./5/4   *LC* 67-23487

Patchen, Kenneth, 1911-1972. • **2.12305**
The Journal of Albion Moonlight / Kenneth Patchen. — New York: New
Directions, 1961, c1941. 313 p.; 21 cm. (A New Directions paperback; 99) I. T.
PS3531.A764 J6 1961   818.54   *LC* 61-19730

Patchen, Kenneth, 1911-1972. • **2.12306**
The memoirs of a shy pornographer: an amusement. — [New York: J.
Laughlin, c1945] 242 p. — (New Directions book.) I. T. II. Series.
PS3531.A764 M45   *LC* 45-8438

Patchen, Kenneth, 1911-1972. • **2.12307**
Sleepers awake. — [New York: Padell Book Co., 1946] 389 p.: ill. I. T.
PS3531.A764 S5   *LC* 46-21856

Pennell, Joseph Stanley, 1908-1963. **2.12308**
The history of Rome Hanks and kindred matters. — Sag Harbor, N.Y.: Second
Chance Press, 1982. 363 p.; 23 cm. Reprint. Originally published: New York:
Scribner, 1944. 1. United States — History — Civil War, 1861-1865 — Fiction.
I. T.
PS3531.E4259 H5 1982   813/.52 19   *LC* 81-85726   *ISBN*
0933256329

Perelman, S. J. (Sidney Joseph), 1904-. • **2.12309**
Perelman's home companion: a collector's item (the collector being S.J.
Perelman) of 36 otherwise unavailable pieces by himself. — New York: Simon
and Schuster, 1955. 239 p. I. T.
PS3531.E6544 P4   *LC* 55-10046

Peterkin, Julia Mood, 1880-1961.   • **2.12310**
Collected short stories of Julia Peterkin. Selected and edited and with an introd.
by Frank Durham. — [1st ed.]. — Columbia: University of South Carolina
Press, [1970] xii, 384 p.; 23 cm. I. T.
PZ3.P436 Co PS3531.E77   813/.5/2   LC 70-120576   ISBN
0872491846

Peterkin, Julia Mood, 1880-1961.   • **2.12311**
Scarlet sister Mary, by Julia Peterkin ... Indianapolis, The Bobbs-Merrill
Company [c1928] 4 p. L., 11-345 p. 20 cm. I. T.
PZ3.P436 Sc   PS3531 E77Sx.   LC 28-24477

Peterkin, Julia Mood, 1880-1961.   • **2.12312**
Black April: a novel / by Julia Peterkin. — Indianapolis: Bobbs-Merril, [c1927]
315 p. 20 cm. I. T.
PS 3531 E82 B62 1927   LC 27-5080

Petry, Ann Lane, 1911-.   **2.12313**
The street / Ann Petry. — Boston: Beacon Press, 1985, c1974. 435 p.; 21 cm.
Reprint. Originally published: Boston: Houghton Mifflin, 1946. I. T.
PS3531.E933 S75 1985   813/.54 19   LC 85-47522   ISBN
0807063576

Phillips, David Graham, 1867-1911.   • **2.12314**
The second generation. New York: D. Appleton, [1927] 334 p.; 20cm.
(Appleton dollar library) I. T.
PS3531 H5 S4 1927

Phillips, David Graham, 1867-1911.   • **2.12315**
Susan Lenox, her fall and rise. New York [etc.] D. Appleton 1917. 2 v. illus.
I. T.
PZ3.P543Su   PS3531.H5 S9 1917.   LC 17-6327

Porter, Katherine Anne, 1890-1980.   • **2.12316**
Collected stories. [1st American ed.] New York: Harcourt, Brace & World
[1965] viii, 495 p. 22 cm. I. T.
PS3531.O752 A6 1965   PZ3.P8315 Co   LC 65-14706

Porter, Katherine Anne, 1890-1980.   **2.12317**
Ship of fools. — Boston: Little, Brown, [1962] 497 p. I. T.
PS3531.O752 S5   LC 62-9557

Givner, Joan, 1936-.   **2.12318**
Katherine Anne Porter: a life / Joan Givner. — New York: Simon and
Schuster, c1982. 572 p., [8] leaves of plates: ill., ports.; 24 cm. 1. Porter,
Katherine Anne, 1890-1980 — Biography. 2. Authors, American — 20th
century — Biography. I. T.
PS3531.O752 Z64 1982   813/.52 19   LC 82-10626   ISBN
0671432079

Katherine Anne Porter: a collection of critical essays / edited   **2.12319**
by Robert Penn Warren.
Englewood Cliffs, N.J.: Prentice-Hall, c1979. xii, 195 p.; 21 cm. (Twentieth
century views) (A Spectrum book) 1. Porter, Katherine Anne, 1890-1980 —
Criticism and interpretation — Addresses, essays, lectures. I. Warren, Robert
Penn, 1905-
PS3531.O752 Z715   813/.5/2   LC 78-21453   ISBN 0135146798

Lopez, Enrique Hank.   **2.12320**
Conversations with Katherine Anne Porter, refugee from Indian Creek / by
Enrique Hank Lopez. — 1st ed. — Boston: Little, Brown, c1981. xix, 326 p.:
ill.; 24 cm. 1. Porter, Katherine Anne, 1890-1980 — Biography. 2. Authors,
American — 20th century — Biography. I. Porter, Katherine Anne,
1890-1980. II. T.
PS3531.O752 Z76 1981   813/.52 19   LC 80-28331   ISBN
0316531995

Unrue, Darlene Harbour.   **2.12321**
Truth and vision in Katherine Anne Porter's fiction / Darlene Harbour Unrue.
— Athens: University of Georgia Press, c1985. xiv, 267 p.; 24 cm. Includes
index. 1. Porter, Katherine Anne, 1890-1980 — Criticism and interpretation.
I. T.
PS3531.O752 Z83 1985   813/.52 19   LC 84-23925   ISBN
0820307688

Post, Melville Davisson, 1871-1930.   **2.12322**
The complete Uncle Abner / Melville Davisson Post; with introd. and
annotated bibliography by Allen J. Hubin; ill. by Darrel Millsap. — San Diego:
University Extension, University of California, c1977. xvi, 423 p.: ill.; 21 cm. —
(The Mystery library; 4) 1. Detective and mystery stories, American I. T.
II. Series.
PZ3.P844 Cm 1977 PS3531.O76427   813/.5/2   LC 76-50688
ISBN 0891630287

PS3531 Pound

Pound, Ezra, 1885-1972.   **2.12323**
Collected early poems of Ezra Pound / edited by Michael John King; with an
introd. by Louis L. Martz. — New York: New Directions Pub. Corp., 1976.
xxii, 330 p.: ill.; 24 cm. (A New Directions book) Includes indexes. I. T.
PS3531.O82 A17 1976   811/.5/2   LC 76-7086   ISBN 0811206084

Pound, Ezra, 1885-1972.   • **2.12324**
Selected poems. — [New York: New Directions, 1949] viii, 184 p.; 19 cm. (The
New classics series) I. T. II. Series.
PS3531.O82 A6 1949   LC 49-11526

Pound, Ezra, 1885-1972.   **2.12325**
Selected prose, 1909–1965. Edited, with an introd. by William Cookson. [New
York, New Directions Pub. Corp., 1973] 475 p. 22 cm. I. T.
PS3531.O82 A6 1973b   814/.5/2   LC 72-93978   ISBN 0811204650

Pound, Ezra, 1885-1972.   **2.12326**
[Cantos. Canto 1-117,120] The cantos of Ezra Pound. [New York, New
Directions Pub. Corp., 1972] 803 p. port. 22 cm. (A New Directions book) I. T.
PS3531.O82 C24 1972   811/.5/2   LC 73-160490   ISBN
0811203506

Dekker, George.   • **2.12327**
The cantos of Ezra Pound; a critical study. New York, Barnes & Noble [1963]
xvi, 207 p. 23 cm. First published in 1963 under title: Sailing after knowledge.
Bibliographical footnotes. 1. Pound, Ezra, 1885-1972. Cantos I. T.
PS3531.O82C284 1963   811.52   LC 63-23827

Furia, Philip, 1943-.   **2.12328**
Pound's Cantos declassified / Philip Furia. — University Park: Pennsylvania
State University Press, c1984. x, 153 p.; 24 cm. Includes index. 1. Pound, Ezra,
1885-1972. Cantos I. T.
PS3531.O82 C2853 1984   811/.52 19   LC 83-43227   ISBN
0271003731

Terrell, Carroll Franklin.   **2.12329**
A companion to the Cantos of Ezra Pound / by Carroll F. Terrell. — Orono:
National Poetry Foundation, University of Maine at Orono; Berkeley:
University of California Press, c1980-c1984. 2 v. (xv, 791 p.); 27 cm. 1. Pound,
Ezra, 1885-1972. Cantos I. Pound, Ezra, 1885-1972. Cantos II. T.
PS3531.O82 C289   811/.52 19   LC 78-54802   ISBN 0520036875

Woodward, Anthony.   **2.12330**
Ezra Pound and The Pisan cantos / by Anthony Woodward. — London;
Boston: Routledge & Kegan Paul, 1980. xi, 128 p.; 23 cm. Includes index.
1. Pound, Ezra, 1885-1972. The cantos. I. T.
PS3531.O82 C2897 1980   811/.52   LC 79-41446   ISBN
0710003722

Watts, Harold Holliday, 1906-.   • **2.12331**
Ezra Pound and The cantos. — Chicago: H. Regnery Co., 1952. 132 p.
1. Pound, Ezra, 1885-1972. Cantos I. T.
PS3531.O82 C29 1952a   LC 53-1720

Flory, Wendy Stallard.   **2.12332**
Ezra Pound and The cantos: a record of struggle / Wendy Stallard Flory. —
New Haven: Yale University Press, 1980. xv, 321 p.: ill.; 24 cm. 1. Pound,
Ezra, 1885-1972. Cantos I. T.
PS3531.O82 C2935   811/.5/2   LC 79-23904   ISBN 0300023928

Kearns, George.   **2.12333**
Guide to Ezra Pound's Selected cantos / George Kearns. — New Brunswick,
N.J.: Rutgers University Press, c1980. x, 306 p.; 21 cm. Includes index.
1. Pound, Ezra, 1885-1972. Cantos I. Pound, Ezra, 1885-1972. Cantos.
Selections. II. T.
PS3531.O82 C294   811/.52   LC 80-10306   ISBN 081350886X

Biography. Criticism

Surette, Leon.   **2.12334**
A light from Eleusis: a study of Ezra Pound's Cantos / Leon Surette. — Oxford:
Clarendon Press; New York: Oxford University Press, 1979. xiv, 306 p.; 23 cm.
1. Pound, Ezra, 1885-1972. The cantos. I. T.
PS3531.O82 C297   811/.5/2   LC 79-311244   ISBN 0198120893

Pound, Ezra, 1885-1972.   **2.12335**
Ezra Pound and Dorothy Shakespear, their letters, 1909–1914 / edited by
Omar Pound and A. Walton Litz. — New York: New Directions, 1984. xv,
399 p.; 24 cm. Includes index. 1. Pound, Ezra, 1885-1972. Correspondence
2. Pound, Dorothy. 3. Poets, American — 20th century — Correspondence.
I. Pound, Dorothy. II. Pound, Omar S. III. Litz, A. Walton. IV. T.
PS3531.O82 Z4895 1984   811/.52 19   LC 84-11545   ISBN
0811209008

Pound, Ezra, 1885-1972. • 2.12336
Letters, 1907–1941 / edited by D.D. Paige. — New York: Harcourt, Brace, [1950] xxv, 358 p. 1. Pound, Ezra, 1885-1972 — Correspondence. I. T.
PS3531.O82 Z53   LC 50-10346

Alexander, Michael J. 2.12337
The poetic achievement of Ezra Pound / Michael Alexander. — Berkeley: University of California Press, c1979. 247 p.; 23 cm. Includes index. 1. Pound, Ezra, 1885-1972 — Criticism and interpretation. I. T.
PS3531.O82 Z539   811/.5/2   LC 78-59449   ISBN 0520037391

Brooker, Peter. 2.12338
A student's guide to the Selected poems of Ezra Pound / Peter Brooker. — London; Boston: Faber & Faber, 1979. 367 p.: map; 20 cm. 1. Pound, Ezra, 1885-1972. Poems. Selections 2. Pound, Ezra, 1885-1972 — Handbooks, manuals, etc. I. Pound, Ezra, 1885-1972. Poems. Selections II. T.
PS3531.O82 Z5513   811/.5/2   LC 79-670305   ISBN 0571110118

Davie, Donald. • 2.12339
Ezra Pound: poet as sculptor. New York, Oxford University Press, 1964. viii, 261 p. port. 21 cm. 1. Pound, Ezra, 1885-1972. I. T.
PS3531.O82 Z58   811.52   LC 64-24860

Davie, Donald. 2.12340
[Pound] Ezra Pound / Donald Davie; edited by Frank Kermode. — New York: Viking Press, 1976, c1975. x, 134 p.; 22 cm. (Modern masters) British ed. published in 1975 under title: Pound. Includes index. 1. Pound, Ezra, 1885-1972 — Criticism and interpretation. I. T.
PS3531.O82 Z582 1976   811/.5/2   LC 76-112   ISBN 0670303925

H. D. (Hilda Doolittle), 1886-1961. 2.12341
End to torment: a memoir of Ezra Pound / by H. D.; edited by Norman Holmes Pearson and Michael King; with the poems from 'Hilda's book' by Ezra Pound. — New York: New Directions Pub. Corp., 1979. xii, 84 p.: ill.; 21 cm. 1. Pound, Ezra, 1885-1972 — Biography. 2. H. D. (Hilda Doolittle), 1886-1961. 3. Poets, American — 20th century — Biography. I. Pound, Ezra, 1885-1972. II. Pearson, Norman Holmes, 1909-1975. III. King, Michael John. IV. T.
PS3531.O82 Z595 1979   811/.5/2 B   LC 78-27149   ISBN 0811207196

Froula, Christine, 1950-. 2.12342
A guide to Ezra Pound's selected poems / Christine Froula. — New York: New Directions, 1983. xiv, 258 p.; 21 cm. Includes index. 1. Pound, Ezra, 1885-1972 — Criticism and interpretation. I. T.
PS3531.O82 Z632 1983   811/.52 19   LC 82-18776   ISBN 0811208567

Heymann, C. David (Clemens David), 1945-. 2.12343
Ezra Pound, the last rower: a political profile / by C. David Heymann. — New York: Viking Press, 1976. xii, 372 p.: ill.; 24 cm. 'A Richard Seaver book.' 1. Pound, Ezra, 1885-1972 — Biography. 2. Pound, Ezra, 1885-1972 — Political and social views. I. T.
PS3531.O82 Z645   811/.5/2 B   LC 74-4803   ISBN 0670303917

Homberger, Eric. comp. • 2.12344
Ezra Pound: the critical heritage. — London; Boston: Routledge and Kegan Paul, 1972. xix, 500 p.; 23 cm. (The Critical heritage series) 1. Pound, Ezra, 1885-1972. I. T.
PS3531.O82 Z647   811/.5/2   LC 72-90114   ISBN 0710072600

Kenner, Hugh, 1923-. • 2.12345
The poetry of Ezra Pound. — Norfolk, Conn.: New Directions, [1951] 342 p. 1. Pound, Ezra, 1885-1972. I. T.
PS3531.O82 Z7   LC 51-12356

Kenner, Hugh. • 2.12346
The Pound era. Berkeley, University of California Press, 1971. xiv, 606 p. illus. 24 cm. 1. Pound, Ezra, 1885-1972. 2. Twentieth century I. T.
PS3531.O82 Z712   811/.5/2   LC 72-138349   ISBN 0520018605

Levy, Alan. 2.12347
Ezra Pound, the voice of silence / by Alan Levy. — Sag Harbor, N.Y.: Permanent Press, c1983. ix, 149 p.: ports.; 22 cm. Includes index. 1. Pound, Ezra, 1885-1972. 2. Pound, Ezra, 1885-1972 — Bibliography. 3. Poets, American — 20th century — Biography. I. T.
PS3531.O82 Z738 1983   811/.52 19   LC 82-83126   ISBN 093296625X

Norman, Charles, 1904-. • 2.12348
Ezra Pound. Rev. ed. New York, Funk & Wagnalls [1969] xvi, 493 p. illus., ports. 22 cm. 1. Pound, Ezra, 1885-1972. I. T.
PS3531.O82 Z773 1969   811/.5/2 B   LC 69-18876

Quinn, Mary Bernetta. 2.12349
Ezra Pound: an introduction to the poetry. — New York: Columbia University Press, 1973 (c1972). xiv, 191 p.; 20 cm. (Columbia introductions to twentieth-century American poetry.) 1. Pound, Ezra, 1885-1972. I. T. II. Series.
PS3531.O82 Z788   811/.5/2   LC 72-6830   ISBN 023103282X

Simpson, Louis Aston Marantz, 1923-. 2.12350
Three on the tower: the lives and works of Ezra Pound, T. S. Eliot, and William Carlos Williams / by Louis Simpson. — New York: Morrow, 1975. ix, 373 p.; 24 cm. Includes index. 1. Pound, Ezra, 1885-1972. 2. Eliot, T. S. (Thomas Stearns), 1888-1965. 3. Williams, William Carlos, 1883-1963. I. T.
PS3531.O82 Z836   811/.5/209   LC 74-26952   ISBN 0688028993

Stock, Noel. 2.12351
The life of Ezra Pound. [1st American ed.] New York, Pantheon Books [1970] xvii, 472 p. illus., facsims., ports. 25 cm. 1. Pound, Ezra, 1885-1972. I. T.
PS3531.O82 Z839   811/.5/2 B   LC 73-110127

Stock, Noel. ed. • 2.12352
Ezra Pound perspectives; essays in honor of his eightieth birthday. Edited with an introd. by Noel Stock. Chicago: H. Regnery Co., 1965. xiii, 219 p.: ill., facsims., ports.; 25 cm. 1. Pound, Ezra, 1885-1972. I. T.
PS3531.O82 Z842   811/.52   LC 65-26903

Sutton, Walter. ed. • 2.12353
Ezra Pound, a collection of critical essays. Englewood Cliffs, N.J., Prentice-Hall [1963] 184 p. 21 cm. (A Spectrum book: Twentieth century views, STC-29) 1. Pound, Ezra, 1885-1972. I. T.
PS3531.O82 Z85   811.52   LC 63-10448

PS3531 Po–Pr

Pratt, Fletcher, 1897-1956. 2.12354
The well of the unicorn / George U. Fletcher [i.e. F. Pratt]. — New York: Garland Pub., 1975, c1948. xii, 338 p.: ill.; 18 cm. (The Garland Library of science fiction) Reprint of the ed. published by W. Sloane Associates, New York. I. T. II. Series.
PZ3.P88896 We5 PS3531.R23   813/.5/2   LC 75-405   ISBN 0824014103

Prokosch, Frederic, 1908-. • 2.12355
The Asiatics; a novel. With an introd. by Carl Van Doren. — Westport, Conn.: Greenwood Press, [1972, c1935] vii, 371 p.: map; 22 cm. — I. T.
PZ3.P9424 As8 PS3531.R78   813/.5/2   LC 70-138620   ISBN 0837157323

Purdy, James. • 2.12356
Cabot Wright begins. — New York: Farrar, Straus & Giroux, [1964] 228 p. I. T.
PS3531.U426 C3x   LC 62-8754

Purdy, James. • 2.12357
Children is all. — [New York, New Directions, 1962] 183 p. 22 cm. I. T.
PS3531.U426C5   818.54   LC 62-16923

Purdy, James. • 2.12358
Color of darkness: eleven stories and a novella. — [New York: New Directions, [1957] 175 p. I. Purdy, James Malcolm. 63, dream palace. II. T. III. Title: Sixty-three, dream palace. IV. Title: 63, dream palace.
PS3531.U426 C6x   LC 57-12947

Purdy, James. • 2.12359
Eustace Chisholm and the works. New York, Farrar, Straus & Giroux [1967] 241 p. I. T.
PS3531.U426 E8x   LC 67-15008

Purdy, James. • 2.12360
The nephew. — New York: Farrar, Straus & Cudahy, [1960] 210 p. I. T.
PS3531.U426 N4x   LC 60-15672

Adams, Stephen D. 2.12361
James Purdy / Stephen D. Adams. — New York: Barnes & Noble Books, 1977 (c1976). 166 p.; 23. — (Barnes & Noble critical studies) 1. Purdy, James — Criticism and interpretation. I. T.
PS3531.U426 Z57   813/.5/4   LC 76-40878   ISBN 0064900142

Chupack, Henry. 2.12362
James Purdy / by Henry Chupack. — Boston: Twayne Publishers, [1975] 144 p.: port.; 22 cm. (Twayne's United States authors series; TUSAS 248) Includes index. 1. Purdy, James — Criticism and interpretation. I. T.
PS3531.U426 Z67   813/.5/4   LC 74-22438   ISBN 0805706011

PS3533 Q

Queen, Ellery.   **2.12363**
Calamity town: a novel. Boston: Little, Brown, 1942. 4 p. l., [3]-318 p. 21 cm.
I. T.
PZ3.Q295 Cal   PS3533.U4 C3.   *LC* 42-9585

Queen, Ellery.   **2.12364**
The glass village: a novel / by Ellery Queen. — Boston: Little, Brown, c1954.
217 p.: ill. (on lining papers) I. T.
PS3533.U4 G6 1976   PS3533U4 G6 1954.

Quinn, Seabury.   **2.12365**
The Devil's Bride / by Seabury Quinn. — New York: Popular Library, 1976.
254 p.: ill.; 18 cm. I. T.
PS3533.U69 D4x   *ISBN* 044500424X

PS3535 R–Re

Rand, Ayn, 1905-.   • **2.12366**
Atlas shrugged. — New York: Random House, [c1957] 1168 p. I. T.
PS3535.A547 A8   *LC* 57-10033

Rand, Ayn.   • **2.12367**
The fountainhead / by Ayn Rand. — New York: Indianapolis: Bobbs, [1943]
760 p. I. T.
PZ3.R152 Fo   PS3535.A547 F6 1943.   *LC* 43-7230

Ransom, John Crowe, 1888-1974.   • **2.12368**
[Poems. Selections] Selected poems. 3d ed., rev. and enl. New York: Knopf,
1969. viii, 159 p.; 24 cm. I. T.
PS3535.A635 A6 1969   811/.5/2   *LC* 69-14732

Ransom, John Crowe, 1888-1974.   **2.12369**
[Correspondence. Selections] Selected letters of John Crowe Ransom / edited,
with an introduction, by Thomas Daniel Young and George Core. — Baton
Rouge: Louisiana State University Press, c1985. 430 p.; 24 cm. (Southern
literary studies.) Includes index. 1. Ransom, John Crowe, 1888-1974 —
Correspondence. 2. Poets, American — 20th century — Correspondence.
3. Critics — United States — Correspondence. 4. Editors — United States —
Correspondence. I. Young, Thomas Daniel, 1919- II. Core, George. III. T.
IV. Series.
PS3535.A635 Z48 1985   811/.52 B 19   *LC* 84-10006   *ISBN*
0807111686

Buffington, Robert.   • **2.12370**
The equilibrist; a study of John Crowe Ransom's poems, 1916–1963. —
Nashville: Vanderbilt University Press, 1967. ix, 160 p.; 24 cm. 1. Ransom,
John Crowe, 1888-1974. I. T.
PS3535.A635 Z59   811/.5/2   *LC* 67-27550

Knight, Karl F.   • **2.12371**
The poetry of John Crowe Ransom: a study of diction, metaphor, and symbol /
by Karl F. Knight. — The Hague: Mouton, 1964. 133 p. — (Studies in
American literature; 2) 1. Ransom, John Crowe, 1888-1974. I. T.
PS3535.A635 Z7   *LC* 66-31535

Williams, Miller.   **2.12372**
The poetry of John Crowe Ransom. — New Brunswick, N.J.: Rutgers
University Press, [1972] 125 p.: port.; 22 cm. 1. Ransom, John Crowe,
1888-1974. I. T.
PS3535.A635 Z9   811/.5/2   *LC* 78-184566   *ISBN* 081350712X

Young, Thomas Daniel, 1919-.   **2.12373**
Gentleman in a dustcoat: a biography of John Crowe Ransom / Thomas Daniel
Young. Baton Rouge: Louisiana State University Press, c1976. xx, 528 p., [5]
leaves of plates: ill.; 23 cm. (Southern literary studies.) 1. Ransom, John Crowe,
1888-1974 — Biography. 2. Authors, American — 20th century — Biography.
I. T. II. Series.
PS3535.A635 Z9185   811/.5/2 B   *LC* 75-27667   *ISBN* 0807101907

Young, Thomas Daniel, 1919-.   • **2.12374**
John Crowe Ransom: critical essays and a bibliography. — Baton Rouge:
Louisiana State University Press, 1968. xii, 290 p. — (Southern literary
studies.) 1. Ransom, John Crowe, 1888-1974. 2. Ransom, John Crowe,
1888-1974 — Bibliography. I. T. II. Series.
PS3535.A635 Z93   *LC* 68-15428

Rawlings, Marjorie Kinnan, 1896-1953.   • **2.12375**
The yearling / decorations by Edward Shenton. — New York: Scribner, 1938.
428 p.: ill. I. T.
PS3535.A845 Y4   *LC* 38-27280

Rexroth, Kenneth, 1905-.   • **2.12376**
The collected shorter poems. — [New York]: New Directions, [1967, c1966]
348 p.; 21 cm. — I. T.
PS3535.E923 A17 1967   811/.5/2   *LC* 66-17818

Rexroth, Kenneth, 1905-.   • **2.12377**
The collected longer poems. — [New York]: New Directions, [1968] 307 p.; 21
cm. — I. T.
PS3535.E923 A17 1968   811/.5/2   *LC* 68-25549

Rexroth, Kenneth, 1905-.   • **2.12378**
Beyond the mountains: [plays]. — [New York: New Directions, 1951] 190 p. —
(Direction; 20) I. Rexroth, Kenneth, 1905- Phaedra. II. Rexroth, Kenneth,
1905- Iphigenia. III. Rexroth, Kenneth, 1905- Hermios. IV. Rexroth,
Kenneth, 1905- Berenike. V. T. VI. Title: Phaedra. VII. Title: Iphigenia.
VIII. Title: Hermios. IX. Title: Berenike. X. Series.
PS3535.E923 B45 1951   *LC* 51-9631

Rexroth, Kenneth, 1905-.   • **2.12379**
Bird in the bush: obvious essays. — [New York]: New Directions, [c1959] x,
246 p. I. T.
PS3535.E923 B5   *LC* 58-13437

Rexroth, Kenneth, 1905-.   • **2.12380**
An autobiographical novel. — Garden City, N.Y.: Doubleday, 1966. xi, 367 p.
I. T.
PS3535.E923 Z5

PS3535 Ri

Rice, Elmer L., 1892-1967.   • **2.12381**
Seven plays. — New York: Viking Press, 1950. 524 p. I. T.
PS3535.I224 S45 1950   *LC* 50-10796

Rice, Elmer L., 1892-1967.   • **2.12382**
Minority report: an autobiography / by Elmer Rice. — New York: Simon and
Schuster, 1963. 474 p. 1. Rice, Elmer L., 1892-1967 — Biography. 2. Theater
— United States I. T.
PS3535.I224 Z5   *LC* 63-15364

Rich, Adrienne Cecile.   **2.12383**
Poems: selected and new, 1950–1974 / Adrienne Rich. — New York: Norton,
[1975] xvi, 256 p.; 21 cm. — I. T.
PS3535.I233 A17 1975   811/.5/4   *LC* 74-10781   *ISBN* 0393043924

Rich, Adrienne Cecile.   **2.12384**
Adrienne Rich's poetry: texts of the poems: the poet on her work: reviews and
criticism / selected and edited by Barbara Charlesworth Gelpi, Albert Gelpi. —
1st ed. — New York: Norton, [1975] xiii, 215 p.; 22 cm. (A Norton critical
edition) Includes index. 1. Rich, Adrienne Cecile — Criticism and
interpretation — Addresses, essays, lectures. I. Gelpi, Barbara Charlesworth.
II. Gelpi, Albert. III. T.
PS3535.I233 A6 1975   811/.5/4   *LC* 75-315494   *ISBN*
0393043991. *ISBN* 0393092410 pbk

Rich, Adrienne Cecile.   **2.12385**
The dream of a common language: poems, 1974–1977 / Adrienne Rich. — 1st
ed. — New York: Norton, c1978. 77 p.; 22 cm. 'Twenty-one love poems': p.
25-36. 1. Women — Poetry. I. Rich, Adrienne Cecile. Twenty-one love poems.
1978. II. T.
PS3535.I233 D7 1978   811/.5/4   *LC* 77-28156   *ISBN* 0393045021

Rich, Adrienne Cecile.   **2.12386**
On lies, secrets, and silence: selected prose, 1966–1978 / Adrienne Rich. — 1st
ed. — New York: Norton, c1979. 310 p.; 22 cm. I. T.
PS3535.I233 O6 1979   814/.5/4   *LC* 78-26432   *ISBN* 0393012336

Rich, Adrienne Cecile.   • **2.12387**
The will to change; poems 1968–1970 [by] Adrienne Rich. — [1st ed.]. — New
York: Norton, [1971] 67 p.; 22 cm. — I. T.
PS3535.I233 W5   811/.5/4   *LC* 78-146842   *ISBN* 0393043460

Richter, Conrad, 1890-1968.   • **2.12388**
The aristocrat. — [1st ed.]. — New York: Knopf, 1968. 180 p.; 22 cm. — I. T.
PZ3.R417 Ar   PS3535.I429 A7x.   *LC* 68-23945

Richter, Conrad, 1890-1968.   • **2.12389**
The awakening land: I. The trees; II. The fields; III. The town. New York,
Knopf, [c1966] ix, 630 p. 22 cm. I. T. II. Title: The trees. III. Title: The fields.
IV. Title: The town.
PS3535.I429 A9x   *LC* 66-21362

Richter, Conrad, 1890-1968.   ● **2.12390**
The light in the forest. — [1st ed.]. — New York: Knopf, 1953. 179 p.; 20 cm. — I. T.
PS3535.I429L5x   LC 52-12207

Richter, Conrad, 1890-1968.   ● **2.12391**
The sea of grass, by Conrad Richter. — New York: A. A. Knopf, 1937. 4 p. l., 3-149, [2]; 20 cm. 'First edition.' I. T.
PS3535.I429S4x   LC 37-27107

Richter, Conrad, 1890-1968.   ● **2.12392**
A simple honorable man. — New York: Knopf, 1962. 309 p. I. T.
PS3535.I429 S5   LC 62-11047

Richter, Conrad, 1890-1968.   ● **2.12393**
The waters of Kronos. — New York: Knopf, 1960. 175 p. I. T.
PS3535.I429 W3   LC 60-7297

Edwards, Clifford D.   ● **2.12394**
Conrad Richter's Ohio trilogy. Its ideas, themes, and relationship to literary tradition. By Clifford D. Edwards. — The Hague: Mouton, 1970. 210 p.; 22 cm. — (Studies in American literature, v. 18) 1. Richter, Conrad, 1890-1968. I. T.
PS3535.I429 Z65   813/.5/2   LC 79-85902

Gaston, Edwin W.   ● **2.12395**
Conrad Richter, by Edwin W. Gaston, Jr. New York, Twayne Publishers [1965] 176 p. 22 cm. (Twayne's United States authors series, 81) 1. Richter, Conrad, 1890-1968. I. T.
PS3535.I429 Z68   813.52   LC 65-13001

PS3535 Ro

Roberts, Elizabeth Madox, 1881-1941.   ● **2.12396**
The great meadow, by Elizabeth Madox Roberts. — New York: The Viking press, 1930. 4 p.l., 3-338 p.; 20 cm. Maps on lining-papers. I. T.
PZ3.R54145 Gr PS3535.O172   LC 30-7676

Roberts, Elizabeth Madox, 1881-1941.   ● **2.12397**
The time of man, a novel, by Elizabeth Madox Roberts. — New York: The Viking press, 1926. 4 p.l., 382 p.; 19 cm. — I. T.
PZ3.R54145 Ti PS3535.O172   LC 26-15401

Roberts, Elizabeth Madox, 1886-.   ● **2.12398**
The haunted mirror: stories / by Elizabeth Madox Roberts. — New York: Viking Press [c1932] 288 p.; 20 cm. I. T.
PS3535 O172 H3   LC 32-32267

Roberts, Elizabeth Madox, 1886-1941.   ● **2.12399**
Not by strange gods: stories. — New York: Viking Press, 1941. 244 p. I. T.
PS3535.O172 N6   LC 41-5114

McDowell, Frederick P. W.   ● **2.12400**
Elizabeth Madox Roberts. New York: Twayne Publishers [1963] 176 p. 22 cm. (Twayne's United States authors series, 38) 1. Roberts, Elizabeth Madox, 1886-1941. I. T.
PS3535.O172 Z7   813.52   LC 63-10955

Roberts, Kenneth Lewis, 1885-1957.   **2.12401**
Northwest passage / Kenneth Roberts. — Special 1st ed. — Garden City, N.Y.: Doubleday, Doran, 1937 (Garden City, N.Y.: Country Life Press) 734p.: maps (on lining papers) 'Book I of this novel appeared serially under the title of Rogers' rangers.' 1. Stephens, Samuel, fl. 1759. 2. Rogers, Robert, 1731-1795 — Fiction. 3. Rogers' rangers — Fiction. I. T.
PS3535.O176 N6 1937   813.5   LC 37-27401

Robinson, Edwin Arlington, 1869-1935.   ● **2.12402**
Selected letters of Edwin Arlington Robinson. [Introd. by Ridgely Torrence.] New York, Macmillan, 1940. x, 191 p.: port.; 22 cm. 1. Robinson, Edwin Arlington, 1869-1935 — Correspondence. I. Torrence, Ridgely, 1875-1950. II. T.
PS 3535 O18 Z5 1940   LC 40-27180

Robinson, Edwin Arlington, 1869-1935.   ● **2.12403**
Collected poems by Edwin Arlington Robinson. — New York: The Macmillan company, 1937. xii, 1498 p.: front. (port.); 21 cm. 'Complete edition with additional poems. Published April, 1937.' I. T.
PS3535.O25 A17 1937   811.5   LC 37-27280

Anderson, Wallace Ludwig, 1917-.   ● **2.12404**
Edwin Arlington Robinson; a critical introduction [by] Wallace L. Anderson. — Boston: Houghton Mifflin, [1967] xvi, 175 p.; 21 cm. — (Riverside studies in literature) 1. Robinson, Edwin Arlington, 1869-1935 — Criticism and interpretation. I. T.
PS3535.O25 Z553   811/.5/2   LC 67-5760

Coxe, Louis Osborne, 1918-.   ● **2.12405**
Edwin Arlington Robinson; the life of poetry [by] Louis Coxe. — New York: Pegasus, [1969] 188 p.: port.; 22 cm. 1. Robinson, Edwin Arlington, 1869-1935 — Criticism and interpretation. I. T.
PS3535.O25 Z64   811/.52 B   LC 69-15698

Fussell, Edwin S.   ● **2.12406**
Edwin Arlington Robinson; the literary background of a traditional poet, by Edwin S. Fussell. — New York: Russell & Russell, [1970, c1954] x, 211 p.; 23 cm. 1. Robinson, Edwin Arlington, 1869-1935. I. T.
PS3535.O25 Z66 1970   811/.5/2   LC 74-102493

Neff, Emery Edward, 1892-.   ● **2.12407**
Edwin Arlington Robinson / Emery Neff. — New York: William Sloane Associates, 1948. xviii, 286 p.: port.; 22 cm. — (American men of letters series.) Includes index. 1. Robinson, Edwin Arlington, 1869-1935. I. T. II. Series.
PS3535.O25 Z74   LC 48-8640

Smith, Chard Powers, 1894-.   ● **2.12408**
Where the light falls; a portrait of Edwin Arlington Robinson. — New York: Macmillan, [1965] xx, 420 p.: illus., ports.; 22 cm. 1. Robinson, Edwin Arlington, 1869-1935. I. T.
PS3535.O25 Z85   928.1   LC 65-11479

Winters, Yvor, 1900-1968.   ● **2.12409**
Edwin Arlington Robinson. — [Rev. ed.]. — [New York]: New Directions Pub. Corp., [1971, c1946] 180 p.: port.; 22 cm. — (A New Directions book) 1. Robinson, Edwin Arlington, 1869-1935. I. T. II. Series.
PS3535.O25 Z94 1971   811/.5/2   LC 71-159744

Roethke, Theodore, 1908-1963.   ● **2.12410**
Collected poems. — [1st ed.]. — Garden City, N.Y.: Doubleday, 1966. xi, 274 p.; 21 cm. — I. T.
PS3535.O39 1966   811.54   LC 65-23784

Roethke, Theodore, 1908-1963.   ● **2.12411**
Selected letters. Edited with an introd. by Ralph J. Mills, Jr. — Seattle: University of Washington Press, [1968] xxii, 273 p.: ports.; 24 cm. I. Mills, Ralph J. ed. II. T.
PS3535.O39 Z54   816/.5/4   LC 68-11045

Malkoff, Karl.   ● **2.12412**
Theodore Roethke: an introduction to the poetry. — New York: Columbia University Press, 1966. viii, 245 p.; 20 cm. 1. Roethke, Theodore, 1908-1963 — Criticism and interpretation. I. T.
PS3535.O39 Z67   811.54   LC 66-23967

Seager, Allan, 1906-1968.   ● **2.12413**
The glass house; the life of Theodore Roethke. — [1st ed.]. — New York: McGraw-Hill, [1968] 301 p.; 23 cm. 1. Roethke, Theodore, 1908-1963. I. T.
PS3535.O39 Z83   811/.5/4 B   LC 68-15741

Stein, Arnold Sidney, 1915- ed.   ● **2.12414**
Theodore Roethke: essays on the poetry / edited by Arnold Stein. — Seattle: University of Washington press [1965] xx, 199 p.: port.; 22 cm. 1. Roethke, Theodore, 1908-1963. I. T.
PS3535.O39 Z87   LC 65-23914

Rosenberg, Harold.   **2.12415**
The tradition of the new / Harold Rosenberg. — New York: Horizon Press, 1959. 285 p.; 22 cm. I. T.
PS3535.O698 T69 1965   814/.5/2   LC 59-9254

Rosten, Leo Calvin, 1908-.   ● **2.12416**
The education of H*y*m*a*n K*a*p*l*a*n, by Leonard Q. Ross [pseud.]. — New York: Harcourt, Brace and company, [1938] 7 p.l., 3-176 p.; 21 cm. 'Tenth printing, January, 1938.' I. T.
PZ3.R7386 Ed10   PS3535.O7577 Ex.   LC 38-6588

Roth, Henry.   ● **2.12417**
Call it sleep, a novel. With a history by Harold U. Ribalow. A critical introd. by Maxwell Geismar; and a personal appreciation by Meyer Levin. — Paterson, N.J.: Pageant Books, 1960 [c1934] 599 p.; 22 cm. — I. T.
PZ3.R74274 Cal5   PS3535.O785 Cx.   LC 60-13694

PS3535 Ru

Rukeyser, Muriel, 1913-.   **2.12418**
The collected poems / Muriel Rukeyser. — New York: McGraw-Hill, c1978. xx, 588 p.; 24 cm. Includes index. I. T.
PS3535.U4 A17 1978   811/.5/2   LC 78-7633   ISBN 0070542708

Kertesz, Louise, 1939-.   **2.12419**
The poetic vision of Muriel Rukeyser / Louise Kertesz; foreword by Kenneth Rexroth. — Baton Rouge: Louisiana State University Press, c1980. xviii,

412 p., [5] leaves of plates: ill.; 24 cm. Includes index. 1. Rukeyser, Muriel, 1913- — Criticism and interpretation. I. T.
PS3535.U4 Z74   811/.5/2   *LC* 79-1131   *ISBN* 080710552X

Runyon, Damon, 1880-1946.   • **2.12420**
A treasury of Damon Runyon / selected, with an introd. by Clark Kinnaird. — New York: Modern Library, [1958] 428 p.; 19 cm. — (The Modern library of the world's best books [58]) I. T.
PS3535.U52 A6 1958   817.5   *LC* 58-6363

Runyon, Damon, 1880-1946.   • **2.12421**
Guys and dolls / by Damon Runyon. — Philadelphia: Lippincott, [1950?] 505 p.; 21 cm. Three volumes in one: Guys and dolls, Money from home, Blue plate special. I. T. II. Title: Money from home. III. Title: Blue plate special.
PS3535.U52 Gx   *LC* 50-9056

Hoyt, Edwin Palmer.   • **2.12422**
A gentleman of Broadway / Edwin P. Hoyt. — 1st ed. — Boston: Little, Brown, c1964. 369 p., [8] p. of plates: ports. 'Runyon checklist': p. [335]-340. 1. Runyon, Damon, 1880-1946. I. T.
PS3535.U52 Z65   *LC* 64-21492

PS3537 Salinger

Salinger, J. D. (Jerome David), 1919-.   • **2.12423**
The catcher in the rye / by J.D. Salinger. — New York: Modern Library, c1951. 277 p. 19 cm. I. T.
PZ4.S165 Cat3   PS3537.A426 Cx.   *LC* 58-11471

Salinger, Jerome David, 1919-.   • **2.12424**
Franny and Zooey. — Boston: Little, Brown, [1961] 201 p. I. T.
PS3537.A426 F7x   *LC* 61-14542

Salinger, Jerome David, 1919-.   • **2.12425**
Nine stories. — [1st ed.]. — New York: Modern Library, [1959] 302 p.; 19 cm. — (Modern library of the world's best books. [301]) I. T. II. Series.
PS3537.A426 N5x   *LC* 59-10908

Salinger, J. D. (Jerome David), 1919-.   • **2.12426**
Raise high the roof beam, carpenters; and, Seymour, an introduction. — Boston: Little, Brown, [1963] 248 p. I. Salinger, Jerome David, 1919- Seymour, an introduction. II. T. III. Title: Seymour, an introduction.
PS3537.A426 R3x   *LC* 63-8969

French, Warren G., 1922-.   • **2.12427**
J. D. Salinger. New York, Twayne Publishers [1963] 191 p. 22 cm. (Twayne's United States authors series, 40) 1. Salinger, J. D. (Jerome David), 1919- I. T.
PS3537.A426 Z6   813.54   *LC* 63-10957

Gwynn, Frederick Landis, 1916-.   • **2.12428**
The fiction of J. D. Salinger / [by] Frederick L. Gwynn and Joseph L. Blotner. — [Pittsburgh]: University of Pittsburgh Press, [1958] 59 p.; 19 cm. (Critical essays in English and American literature, 4) 1. Salinger, J. D. (Jerome David), 1919- I. Blotner, Joseph Leo, 1923- joint author. II. T.
PS3537.A426 Z64   813.54   *LC* 58-14389

Lundquist, James.   2.12429
J. D. Salinger / James Lundquist. — New York: F. Ungar Pub. Co., c1979. ix, 194 p.; 20 cm. (Modern literature monographs) Includes index. 1. Salinger, J. D. (Jerome David), 1919- — Criticism and interpretation. I. T.
PS3537.A426 Z73   813/.5/4   *LC* 78-4301   *ISBN* 0804425604

PS3537 Sandburg

Sandburg, Carl, 1878-1967.   • **2.12430**
The complete poems of Carl Sandburg. — Rev. and expanded ed. — New York: Harcourt Brace Jovanovich, [1970] xxxi, 797 p.; 24 cm. — I. T.
PS3537.A618 1970   811/.5/2   *LC* 76-78865   *ISBN* 0151207739

Sandburg, Carl, 1878-1967.   • **2.12431**
Remembrance rock. — New York: Harcourt, Brace, [1948] 1067 p. I. T.
PS3537.A618 R4   *LC* 48-28125

Sandburg, Carl, 1878-1967.   • **2.12432**
The letters of Carl Sandburg. Edited by Herbert Mitgang. — [1st ed.]. — New York: Harcourt, Brace & World, [1968] xiv, 577 p.; 24 cm. I. Mitgang, Herbert. ed. II. T.
PS3537.A618 Z53   *LC* 68-12588

Crowder, Richard.   • **2.12433**
Carl Sandburg. New York: Twayne Publishers [1964] 176 p. 21 cm. (Twayne's United States authors series, 47) 1. Sandburg, Carl, 1878-1967. I. T.
PS3537.A618 Z555   928.1   *LC* 63-20606

Detzer, Karl William, 1891-.   • **2.12434**
Carl Sandburg; a study in personality and background, by Karl Detzer, with four photographs by Edward Steichen. New York, Harcourt, Brace and Company c1941. 210 p. ill., ports. 22 cm. 'First edition.' 1. Sandburg, Carl, 1878-1967. I. Steichen, Edward, 1879-1973. ill. II. T.
PS3537.A618 Z56   928.1   *LC* 41-15748

Van Doren, Mark, 1894-1972.   2.12435
Carl Sandburg. With a bibliography of Sandburg materials in the collections of the Library of Congress. Washington, Published for the Library of Congress by the Gertrude Clarke Whittall Poetry and Literature Fund; [for sale by the Supt. of Docs., U.S. Govt. Print. Off.] 1969. vi, 83 p. 24 cm. Lecture delivered Jan. 8, 1968, under the auspices of the Gertrude Clarke Whittall Poetry and Literature Fund. 1. Sandburg, Carl, 1878-1967. 2. Sandburg, Carl, 1878-1967 — Bibliography. I. Library of Congress. Reference Dept. II. Gertrude Clarke Whittall Poetry and Literature Fund. III. T.
PS3537.A618 Z878   811/.5/2   *LC* 71-600851

PS3537 Sa–Sc

Saroyan, William, 1908-.   2.12436
Best stories. — London: Faber and Faber, [1942] 318 p. I. T.
PS3537.A826 A16 1942   *LC* 43-4861

Saroyan, William, 1908-.   • **2.12437**
[Selected works. 1958] The William Saroyan reader. Introd. by William Saroyan. [1st ed.] New York, G. Braziller, 1958. 498 p. 22 cm. I. T.
PS3537.A826 A6 1958   818.5   *LC* 58-10541

Saroyan, William, 1908-.   • **2.12438**
The daring young man on the flying trapeze and other stories / by William Saroyan. — New York: Random House, 1934. 270 p.; 24 cm. I. T.
PS3537.A826 D3   *LC* 34-34422

Saroyan, William, 1908-.   • **2.12439**
The human comedy / illustrated by Don Freeman. — New York: Harcourt, Brace [1944] 299p. I. T.
PS3537 A826 H8

Saroyan, William, 1908-.   • **2.12440**
Three plays: My heart's in the Highlands, The time of your life, Love's old sweet song. New York, Harcourt, Brace and company [c1940] 4 p. l., 121, 200, 146 p. 22 cm. 'First edition.' I. T. II. Title: My heart's in the Highlands. III. Title: The time of your life. IV. Title: Love's old sweet song.
PS3537.A826 T47 1940   *LC* 40-30799

Sarton, May, 1912-.   2.12441
Collected poems (1930–1973). — [1st ed.]. — New York: Norton, [1974] 416 p.; 21 cm. — I. T.
PS3537.A832 A17 1974   811/.5/2   *LC* 74-1259   *ISBN* 039304386X

Sarton, May, 1912-.   • **2.12442**
The birth of a grandfather. New York, Rinehart [1957] 277 p. I. T.
PS3537.A832 B5   813.5   *LC* 57-9630

Sarton, May, 1912-.   • **2.12443**
Faithful are the wounds. — New York: Norton, [1972, c1955] 281 p.; 21 cm. — I. T.
PZ3.S249 Fai5 PS3537.A832F3x   813/.5/2   *LC* 72-1812   *ISBN* 0393084396

Sarton, May, 1912-.   • **2.12444**
A shower of summer days. — New York: Norton, [1970, c1952] 244 p.; 21 cm. — I. T.
PZ3.S249 Shc4 PS3537.A832S51x   813/.5/2   *LC* 72-11247   *ISBN* 0393085996

Sarton, May, 1912-.   • **2.12445**
The small room: a novel / May Sarton. — New York: Norton, 1961. 249 p. I. T.
PS3537.A832 S53   *LC* 61-11347

Sarton, May, 1912-.   • **2.12446**
I knew a phoenix; sketches for an autobiography. New York, W. W. Norton [1969, c1959] 222 p. illus. 22 cm. 1. Sarton, May, 1912- — Biography. 2. Authors, American — 20th century — Biography. I. T.
PS3537.A832 Z52 1969   818/.5/203   *LC* 74-957

Scarborough, Dorothy, 1878-1935.   2.12447
The wind / by Dorothy Scarborough; foreword by Sylvia Ann Grider. — Austin: University of Texas Press, [1979] xvii, 337 p.; 21 cm. (Barker Texas

History Center series; 4) Reprint of the 1925 ed. published by Harper, New York; with new foreword. I. T.
PZ3.S284 Wi 1979 PS3537.C16   *LC* 78-24225   *ISBN*
0292790120

Schulberg, Budd Wilson, 1914-.   • **2.12448**
The disenchanted. — New York: Random House, [1950] 388 p. A novel. I. T.
PS3537.C7114 D5   *LC* 50-10247

Schulberg, Budd.   • **2.12449**
What makes Sammy run? With a new introd. by the author. — New York: Modern Library, [1952] 303 p.; 19 cm. — (The Modern library of the world's best books) I. T.
PS3537.C7114Wx   *LC* 52-5877

Peplow, Michael W.   **2.12450**
George S. Schuyler / by Michael W. Peplow. — Boston: Twayne Publishers, 1981 (c1980). 144 p.: port.; 21 cm. — (Twayne's United States authors series; TUSAS 349) Includes index. 1. Schuyler, George Samuel, 1895- — Criticism and interpretation. I. T.
PS3537.C76 Z83   813/.5/2   *LC* 79-21363   *ISBN* 0805772898

Schwartz, Delmore, 1913-1966.   • **2.12451**
Successful love, and other stories. — New York: Corinth Books, 1961. 242 p. I. T.
PS3537.C79 S79   *LC* 61-14981

Schwartz, Delmore, 1913-1966.   • **2.12452**
Summer knowledge; new and selected poems, 1938–1958. — [1st ed.]. — Garden City, N.Y.: Doubleday, 1959. 240 p.; 22 cm. — I. T.
PS3537.C79 S8   811.52   *LC* 59-10689

Schwartz, Delmore, 1913-1966.   • **2.12453**
The world is a wedding. — [Norfolk, Conn.]: New Directions, [1948] 196 p. Short stories. I. T.
PS3537.C79 W6   *LC* 48-7957

Atlas, James.   **2.12454**
Delmore Schwartz: the life of an American poet / by James Atlas. — New York: Farrar, Straus and Giroux, c1977. xiii, 417 p., [8] leaves of plates: ill.; 24 cm. 1. Schwartz, Delmore, 1913-1966. 2. Poets, American — 20th century — Biography. I. T.
PS3537.C79 Z56   811/.5/2 B   *LC* 77-23852   *ISBN* 0374137617

McDougall, Richard.   **2.12455**
Delmore Schwartz. New York, Twayne Publishers [1974] 156 p. port. 22 cm. (Twayne's United States authors series, TUSAS 243) 1. Schwartz, Delmore, 1913-1966. I. T.
PS3537.C79 Z77   818/.5/209   *LC* 73-17285   *ISBN* 0805706577

Scott, Winfield Townley, 1910-1968.   • **2.12456**
New and selected poems. Selected and edited by George P. Elliott. — [1st ed.]. — Garden City, N.Y.: Doubleday, 1967. xiii, 154 p.; 22 cm. — I. T.
PS3537.C943 A6 1967   811/.5/2   *LC* 67-19106

PS3537 Se–Sh

Sexton, Anne.   **2.12457**
The complete poems / Anne Sexton; with a foreword by Maxine Kumin. — Boston: Houghton Mifflin, 1981. xxxiv, 622 p.; 22 cm. Includes index. I. T.
PS3537.E915 A17 1981   811/.54 19   *LC* 81-2482   *ISBN* 0395294754

Sexton, Anne.   **2.12458**
Words for Dr. Y.: uncollected poems with three stories / Anne Sexton; edited by Linda Gray Sexton. — Boston: Houghton Mifflin, 1978. vii, 101 p.; 22 cm. I. Sexton, Linda Gray, 1953- II. T.
PS3537.E915 W6   811/.5/4   *LC* 78-7543   *ISBN* 0395270812

Sexton, Anne.   **2.12459**
Anne Sexton: a self-portrait in letters / edited by Linda Gray Sexton and Lois Ames. — Boston: Houghton Mifflin, 1977. xiv, 433 p., [12] leaves of plates: ill.; 25 cm. Includes index. 1. Sexton, Anne — Correspondence. 2. Poets, American — 20th century — Correspondence. I. Sexton, Linda Gray, 1953- II. Ames, Lois. III. T.
PS3537.E915 Z53 1977   816/.5/4   *LC* 77-21355   *ISBN* 0395257271

Anne Sexton: the artist and her critics / edited by J. D. **2.12460**
McClatchy.
Bloomington: Indiana University Press, c1978. xv, 297 p.; 22 cm. 1. Sexton, Anne — Criticism and interpretation — Addresses, essays, lectures. I. McClatchy, J. D., 1945-
PS3537.E915 Z57   811/.5/4   *LC* 77-23646   *ISBN* 0253307481

Shapiro, Karl Jay, 1913-.   **2.12461**
Collected poems 1940–1978 / Karl Shapiro. — 1st ed. — New York: Random House, c1978. x, 341 p.; 25 cm. Includes indexes. I. T.
PS3537.H27 A17 1978   811/.5/2   *LC* 77-90251   *ISBN* 039442543X

Shapiro, Karl Jay, 1913-.   • **2.12462**
Essay on rime. — New York: Reynal & Hitchcock, [1945] 72 p. 1. Poetics 2. English poetry — History and criticism — Addresses, essays, lectures. 3. American poetry — History and criticism — Addresses, essays, lectures. I. T.
PS3537.H27 E8   *LC* 45-9654

Sherwood, Robert E. (Robert Emmet), 1896-1955.   • **2.12463**
Abe Lincoln in Illinois: a play in twelve scenes / with a foreword by Carl Sandburg. — New York: Scribner, [1939] xii, 250 p. 1. Lincoln, Abraham, 1809-1865 — Drama I. T.
PS3537.H825 A63   *LC* 39-27098

Sherwood, Robert E. (Robert Emmet), 1896-1955.   • **2.12464**
Idiot's delight, by Robert Emmet Sherwood. New York, C. Scribner's sons; London, C. Scribner's sons, ltd., 1936. viii p., 2 l., 3-190 p. 20 cm. A play. I. T.
PS3537.H825I4 1936   812.5   *LC* 36-8866

Sherwood, Robert E. (Robert Emmet), 1896-1955.   • **2.12465**
The petrified forest. — New York: Scribner, 1936. 176 p. I. T.
PS3537.H825 P4   *LC* 36-33958

Sherwood, Robert E. (Robert Emmet), 1896-1955.   • **2.12466**
There shall be no night. — New York: Scribner, 1940. xxx, 178 p. I. T.
PS3537.H825 T45   *LC* 40-27741

Brown, John Mason, 1900-1969.   • **2.12467**
The worlds of Robert E. Sherwood; mirror to his times, 1896–1939. [1st ed.] New York, Harper & Row [1965] xviii, 409 p. illus., ports. 22 cm. 1. Sherwood, Robert E. (Robert Emmett), 1896-1955 — Biography. 2. Dramatists, American — 20th century — Biography. I. T.
PS3537.H825 Z63   812.52   *LC* 65-20424

Shirer, William L. (William Lawrence), 1904-.   **2.12468**
20th century journey: a memoir of a life and the times / by William L. Shirer. — New York: Simon and Schuster, c1976- <c1984 >. v. <1-2 >: ill.; 24 cm. Vol. 2 has imprint: Boston: Little, Brown. 1. Shirer, William L. (William Lawrence), 1904- — Biography. 2. Novelists, American — 20th century — Biography. 3. Journalists — United States — Biography. I. T.
PS3537.H913 Z52   070/.92/4 B   *ISBN* 0671221957

Shulman, Max.   • **2.12469**
Barefoot boy with cheek / by Max Shulman; pictures by Will Crawford. Garden City, N. Y.: Doubleday, Doran and company, inc., 1943. 6 p. l., 207 p. incl. front., illus. 21 cm. 'First edition.' I. T.
PZ3.S56264 Bar   PS3537.H9919 Bx.   *LC* 43-6576

PS3537 Si

Simak, Clifford D., 1904-.   **2.12470**
City / by Clifford D. Simak. — New York: Gnome Press; 1952. 267 p. I. T.
PS3537I54   PS3537I54 C5 1960.   813'.5'4   *LC* 52-10460/L

Simon, Neil.   **2.12471**
The comedy of Neil Simon / with an introd. by Neil Simon. — New York: Random House, c1971. 657 p.: port.; 25 cm. Vol. 1 of The collected plays of Neil Simon. I. T.
PS3537.I663 A6 1971   PS3537.I663 A6 1971.   812/.5/4   *LC* 70-159374   *ISBN* 0394473647

Simon, Neil.   **2.12472**
The collected plays of Neil Simon, volume II / with an introd. by Neil Simon. — 1st ed. — New York: Random House, c1979. 737 p.; 25 cm. 'A companion The comedy of Neil Simon.' I. T.
PS3537.I663 A6 1979   PS3537.I663 A6 1979.   812/.5/4   *LC* 79-5081   *ISBN* 0394507703

Simpson, Louis Aston Marantz, 1923-.   • **2.12473**
Adventures of the letter I [by] Louis Simpson. — [1st ed.]. — New York: Harper & Row, [c1971] viii, 69 p.; 21 cm. Poems. I. T.
PS3537.I75 A66 1971b   811/.5/4   *LC* 74-138762   *ISBN* 006013884X

Simpson, Louis Aston Marantz, 1923-.   **2.12474**
At the end of the open road: poems. — [1st ed.]. — Middletown, Conn.: Wesleyan University Press, [1963] 70 p.; 21 cm. — (Wesleyan poetry program.) I. T. II. Series.
PS3537.I75 A9   *LC* 63-17792

Simpson, Louis Aston Marantz, 1923-. • 2.12475
North of Jamaica [by] Louis Simpson. — [1st U.S. ed.]. — New York: Harper & Row, [1972] 285 p.; 22 cm. 1. Simpson, Louis Aston Marantz, 1923- I. T.
PS3537.I75 Z5 1972b 811/.5/4 B *LC* 72-181647 *ISBN* 0060138874

Moran, Ronald. • 2.12476
Louis Simpson. — New York: Twayne Publishers, [1972] 187 p.; 22 cm. — (Twayne's United States authors series, TUSAS 210) 1. Simpson, Louis Aston Marantz, 1923- I. T.
PS3537.I75 Z8 811/.5/4 *LC* 74-185266

Sinclair, Upton, 1878-1968. • 2.12477
Boston; a novel. New York, Albert & Charles Boni, 1928. St. Clair Shores, Mich., Scholarly Press, 1970. 2 v. (755 p.) 22 cm. 1. Sacco-Vanzetti case — Fiction. I. T.
PZ3.S616 Bo8 PS3537.I85 813/.5/2 *LC* 78-115273 *ISBN* 0403002958

Sinclair, Upton, 1878-1968. 2.12478
Dragon's teeth / [by] Upton Sinclair. New York: The Viking Press, 1942. viii, 631 p.; 22 cm. 1. Germany — History — 1933-1945 — Fiction. I. T.
PZ3.S616 Dr 1977 PS3537.I85 813/.5/2 *LC* 42-106

Sinclair, Upton, 1878-1968. • 2.12479
The jungle. With the author's 1946 introd. Cambridge, Mass., R. Bentley, 1971 [c1946] viii, 342 p. 22 cm. I. T.
PZ3.S616 Ju29 PS3537.I85 J8x 813/.5/2 *LC* 79-151835 *ISBN* 0837604001

Sinclair, Upton, 1878-1968. • 2.12480
American outpost; a book of reminiscences. Port Washington, N.Y., Kennikat Press [1969, c1932] 380 p. port. 21 cm. I. T.
PS3537.I85 Z5 1969 813/.5/2 *LC* 76-93072 *ISBN* 0804606854

Sinclair, Upton, 1878-1968. • 2.12481
Autobiography. [1st ed.] New York, Harcourt, Brace & World [1962] 342 p. illus. 22 cm. I. T.
PS3537.I85 Z517 928.1 *LC* 62-19592

Sinclair, Upton, 1878-1968. • 2.12482
My lifetime in letters / Upton Sinclair. — Columbia: University of Missouri Press, 1960. xxi, 412 p., [1] l. of plates; port. 1. Authors — Correspondence I. T.
PS3537.I85 Z54 PS3537.I85 Z48 1960. *LC* 59-14141

Dell, Floyd. 2.12483
Upton Sinclair: a study in social protest. — N.Y., G.H. Doran [1927] 194 p.: front. (port.) (The Murray Hill biographies) 1. Sinclair, Upton, 1878-1968. I. T.
PS3537.I85 Z6 1927 813

Harris, Leon A. 2.12484
Upton Sinclair, American rebel / by Leon Harris. — New York: Crowell, [1975] x, 435 p., [11] leaves of plates: ill.; 24 cm. Includes index. 1. Sinclair, Upton, 1878-1968 — Biography. 2. Novelists, American — 20th century — Biography. I. T.
PS3537.I85 Z64 813/.5/2 B *LC* 74-23582 *ISBN* 0690006713

PS3537 Sk–St

Skinner, B. F. (Burrhus Frederic), 1904-. • 2.12485
Walden Two. New York, Macmillan Co., 1948. 266 p. 22 cm. I. T.
PZ3.S62825 Wal PS3537.K527 813/.5/4 *LC* 48-2440

Skinner, Cornelia Otis, 1901-. • 2.12486
Our hearts were young and gay, by Cornelia Otis Skinner and Emily Kimbrough; drawings by Alajálov. — New York: Dodd, Mead & company, 1942. 4 p., l., 247 p.: illus.; 21 cm. I. Kimbrough, Emily, 1899- joint author. II. Alajalov, Constantin, 1900- illus. III. T.
PS3537.K533 O8 817.5 *LC* 42-36388

Smith, Betty, 1904-. • 2.12487
A tree grows in Brooklyn: a novel / by Betty Smith; with drawings by Richard Bergere. — New York: Harper & Row, c1947, c1943. vii, 420 p.: ill.; 22 cm. I. T.
PZ3.S64335 Tr2 PS3537.M2895 T7 1947. *LC* 47-11189

Smith, Clark Ashton. 2.12488
Zothique / by Ashton Smith; ed. by Lin Carter. — New York: Ballantine, 1970. 1 v. I. T.
PS3537.M335 Z6x

Smith, Lillian Eugenia, 1897-1966. • 2.12489
Strange fruit: a novel. — New York: Reynal & Hitchcock, [1944] 314 p. I. T.
PS3537.M653 S8 *LC* 44-4605

Smith, Lillian Eugenia, 1897-1966. 2.12490
The winner names the age: a collection of writings / by Lillian Smith; edited by Michelle Cliff; pref. by Paula Snelling. — 1st ed. — New York: Norton, c1978. 218 p.; 22 cm. 1. Cliff, Michelle. II. T.
PS3537.M653 W5 1978 814/.5/2 *LC* 78-7222 *ISBN* 039308826X

Smith, Thorne, 1893-. 2.12491
Topper: an improbable adventure, by Thorne Smith. New York, R. M. McBride & company, 1926. 5 p. l., 292 p. 20 cm. I. T.
PS3537.M835bT6x *LC* 26-5828//r

Snodgrass, W. D. (William De Witt), 1926-. • 2.12492
Heart's needle / W.D. Snodgrass. [1st ed.] New York: Knopf 1959. 62 p.; 22 cm. Poems. I. T.
PS3537.N32 H4 811.54 *LC* 59-5430 *ISBN* 0394403606

Spencer, Elizabeth. • 2.12493
Fire in the morning. — New York: McGraw-Hill, [1968, c1948] 275 p.; 20 cm. — I. T.
PZ3.S74614 Fi5 PS3537.P4454Fx. *LC* 68-20057

Spencer, Elizabeth. • 2.12494
The voice at the back door. — New York: McGraw-Hill, [1956] 334 p.; 21 cm. — I. T.
PZ3.S74614 Vo PS3537.P4454Vx. *LC* 56-11727

Spencer, Elizabeth. • 2.12495
The light in the piazza. — [1st ed.] New York: McGraw-Hill, [1960] 110 p.; 21 cm. I. T.
PS3537.P48 L54 *LC* 60-15005

Spillane, Mickey, 1918-. 2.12496
I, the jury, by Mickey Spillane. [1st ed.] New York, E. P. Dutton, 1947. 218 p. 21 cm. I. T.
PS3537.P653 Ix *LC* 47-5468

Stafford, Jean, 1915-. • 2.12497
The collected stories of Jean Stafford. — New York: Farrar, Straus, and Giroux, [1969] 463 p.; 22 cm. — I. T.
PS3537.T135 Ax 813/.5/4 *LC* 68-29471

Stafford, Jean, 1915-. • 2.12498
Boston adventure / by Jean Stafford. — New York: Harcourt, Brace and World, [1944] 496 p. I. T.
PS3537.T135 B6x *LC* 44-40176

Stafford, Jean, 1915-. • 2.12499
The Catherine wheel: a novel / by Jean Stafford. — New York: Harcourt, Brace, c1952. 281 p. I. T.
PS3537.T135 C3 *LC* 52-6161

Stafford, Jean, 1915-. • 2.12500
The mountain lion. — New York: Harcourt, Brace, 1947. 231 p.; 21 cm. I. T.
PS3537.T135 M6x *LC* 47-1963

Stafford, William, 1914-. 2.12501
Smoke's way: poems from limited editions, 1968–1981 / William Stafford. — Port Townsend, Wash.: Graywolf Press, c1983. 112 p.; 21 cm. I. T.
PS3537.T143 S58 1983 811/.54 19 *LC* 83-80525 *ISBN* 0915308401

Stafford, William, 1914-. 2.12502
Stories that could be true: new and collected poems / by William Stafford. — 1st ed. — New York: Harper & Row, c1977. xvii, 267 p.; 25 cm. Includes indexes. I. T.
PS3537.T143 S7 811/.5/4 *LC* 77-3775 *ISBN* 0060139889

Stegner, Wallace Earle, 1909-. • 2.12503
All the little live things [by] Wallace Stegner. — New York: Viking Press, [1967] 345 p.; 22 cm. — I. T.
PS3537.T316Ax *LC* 67-13499

Stegner, Wallace Earle, 1909-. • 2.12504
The big rock candy mountain. — New York: Duell, Sloan and Pearce, [1943] 515 p. I. T.
PS3537.T316 B5 *LC* 43-51281

Stegner, Wallace Earle, 1909-.   • 2.12505
The city of the living, and other stories. — Boston: Houghton, Mifflin, 1956. 206 p. I. T.
PS3537.T316 C48   LC 56-12088

Stegner, Wallace Earle, 1909-.   • 2.12506
The women on the wall. Boston, Houghton Mifflin [1950] vi, 277 p. 22 cm. I. T.
PS3537.T316Wx   LC 49-50344

PS3537 Stein

Stein, Gertrude, 1874-1946.   • 2.12507
Selected writings of Gertrude Stein / edited, with an introduction and notes, by Carl Van Vechten. — New York: Random House, [1946] xv, 622 p.: port. I. Van Vechten, Carl, 1880-1964. II. T.
PS3537.T323 A6 1946   LC 46-11965

Stein, Gertrude, 1874-1946.   • 2.12508
Selected operas and plays of Gertrude Stein. Edited and with an introd. by John Malcolm Brinnin. — [Pittsburgh]: University of Pittsburgh Press, [1970] xvii, 325 p.; 22 cm. I. T.
PS3537.T323 A6 1970   812/.5/2   LC 70-101196   ISBN 0822931958

Stein, Gertrude, 1874-1946.   • 2.12509
A primer for the gradual understanding of Gertrude Stein. Edited by Robert Bartlett Haas. — Los Angeles: Black Sparrow Press, 1971. 158 p.; 24 cm. 1. Stein, Gertrude, 1874-1946. I. Haas, Robert Bartlett. ed. II. T.
PS3537.T323 A6 1971   818/.5/209   LC 75-32292   ISBN 0876851367

Stein, Gertrude, 1874-1946.   2.12510
The Yale Gertrude Stein: selections / with an introd. by Richard Kostelanetz. — New Haven: Yale University Press, c1980. xxxi, 464 p. Selected from the Yale edition of the unpublished writings of Gertrude Stein. I. Kostelanetz, Richard. II. T.
PS3537.T323 A6 1980   818/.5209   LC 80-5398   ISBN 0300025742

Stein, Gertrude, 1874-1946.   • 2.12511
Ida: a novel / Gertrude Stein. — 1st ed. — New York: Random House, c1941. 154 p.; 24 cm. I. T.
PS3537.T323 I4 1941   LC 41-4374

Stein, Gertrude, 1874-1946.   • 2.12512
Lucy Church, amiably. — Paris: Imprimerie 'Union', 1930. 240 p.; 19 cm. At head of title: A novel of romantic beauty and nature, and which looks like an engraving. I. T.
PS3537.T323 L86 1930   LC 34-38297

Stein, Gertrude, 1874-1946.   • 2.12513
The making of Americans: being a history of a family's progress / written by Gertrude Stein, 1906–1908. — [Paris: Contact editions, 1925] 925 p.; 25 cm. I. T.
PS3537.T323 M3 1925   LC 44-10190

Stein, Gertrude, 1874-1946.   • 2.12514
Tender buttons: objects, food, rooms. New York: Claire Marie, 1914. 78, [1] p.; 18 1/2 cm. At head of title: Gertrude Stein. Printed wrappers. cf. Sawyer,pg. 37. Publisher's advertisement: 1 p. (at end) I. T.
PS3537.T323 T4 1914   LC 14-12312

Stein, Gertrude, 1874-1946.   • 2.12515
Three lives. Norfolk, Conn., New directions [1941] 1 p.l., v-xi p., 3 l., 11-279 p. 19 cm. I. T.
PZ3.S8194 T15   PS3537.T323 Tx.   LC 44-39873

Stein, Gertrude, 1874-1946.   • 2.12516
The autobiography of Alice B. Toklas. — 1st ed. New York: Harcourt, Brace and company [c1933] vii, 310 p.: front., plates, ports., facsim.; 23 cm. The life of Gertrude Stein written by herself as though it were the autobiography of her secretary, Alice B. Toklas. 'First edition' 1. Toklas, Alice B. 2. Paris (France) — Intellectual life I. T.
PS3537.T323 Z5   LC 33-22918

Bridgman, Richard.   • 2.12517
Gertrude Stein in pieces. — New York: Oxford University Press, 1970 [i.e. 1971] xvi, 411 p.; 24 cm. 1. Stein, Gertrude, 1874-1946. I. T.
PS3537.T323 Z56 1971   818/.5/209   LC 71-123609

Brinnin, John Malcolm, 1916-.   • 2.12518
The third rose: Gertrude Stein and her world. — [1st ed.] — Boston: Little, Brown, [1959] 427 p.: ill.; 22 cm. 1. Stein, Gertrude, 1874-1946. I. T.
PS3537.T323 Z57   LC 59-13732

Sprigge, Elizabeth, 1900-.   • 2.12519
Gertrude Stein, her life and work. — London: H. Hamilton, [1957] 277 p.: ill. 1. Stein, Gertrude, 1874-1946. I. T.
PS3537.T323 Z825   LC 57-1002

Sutherland, Donald, 1915-.   • 2.12520
Gertrude Stein, a biography of her work. New Haven Yale University Press 1951. 218 p.; 21 cm. 1. Stein, Gertrude, 1874-1946. I. T.
PS3537 T323 Z83   LC 51-12323

Toklas, Alice B.   2.12521
Staying on alone; letters of Alice B. Toklas. Edited by Edward Burns. With an introd. by Gilbert A. Harrison. New York, Liveright [1973] xxii, 426 p. illus. 24 cm. 1. Stein, Gertrude, 1874-1946. 2. Toklas, Alice B. 3. Authors, American — 20th century — Biography. I. T.
PS3537.T323 Z84   818/.5/209 B   LC 72-82424   ISBN 0871405695

Toklas, Alice B..   • 2.12522
What is remembered. — [1st ed.]. — New York: Holt, Rinehart and Winston [1963] 186 p.: ill.; 22 cm. 1. Stein, Gertrude, 1874-1946. 2. Paris — Intellectual life. I. T.
PS3537.T323Z85   928.1   LC 63-7274

Stein, Leo, 1872-1947.   • 2.12523
Journey into the self: being the letters, papers & journals of Leo Stein / edited by Edmund Fuller; introduction by Van Wyck Brooks. — New York: Crown Publishers, [1950] xiv, 331 p.: ill.; 24 cm. I. Fuller, Edmund, 1914- II. T.
PS3537.T3232 Z52   LC 50-8701

PS3537 Steinbeck

Steinbeck, John, 1902-1968.   • 2.12524
[Selections. 1946] The portable Steinbeck, selected by Pascal Covici. Enl. ed. With an introduction by Lewis Gannett. New York, The Viking press, 1946. xxx, 609 p. 17 cm. (The Viking portable library) 'Revised edition issued in January 1946.' First edition, 1943, published under title: Steinbeck. I. Covici, Pascal, 1885-1964, comp. II. T.
PS3537.T3234A6 1946x   LC 46-25068

Steinbeck, John, 1902-1968.   • 2.12525
Short novels: Tortilla Flat, The red pony, Of mice and men, The moon is down, Cannery Row, The pearl. With an introd. by Joseph Henry Jackson. — New York: Viking Press, 1953. xiii, 407 p.; 22 cm. — I. T.
PZ3.S8195 Sh   PS3537.T3234 A6 1953.   LC 53-9196

Steinbeck, John, 1902-1968.   • 2.12526
East of Eden. [Autographed 1st ed.] New York, Viking Press, 1952. 602 p. 24 cm. I. T.
PS3537.T3234 E3 1952   813.5   LC 52-4118

Steinbeck, John, 1902-1968.   • 2.12527
The grapes of wrath [by] John Steinbeck. — New York: The Viking press, [c1939] 4 p. l., 3-619 p.; 21 cm. Songs with music on lining-papers. 'First published in April 1939.' I. T.
PS3537.T3234 G8 1939   LC 39-27282

Steinbeck, John, 1902-1968.   • 2.12528
In dubious battle/ by John Steinbeck. — New York: Modern Library, [c1936]. — 343 p.; 19cm. — (Modern library of the world's best books.) I. T. II. Series.
PS3537.T3234 I5   LC 39-27817

Steinbeck, John, 1902-1968.   • 2.12529
The long valley. — New York: The Viking press, 1938. 303 p.; 21 cm. Short stories. 'Second printing September 1938.' I. T.
PZ3.S8195 Lo2   PS3537.T3234 L6 1938.   LC 38-27754

Steinbeck, John, 1902-1968.   2.12530
The Pastures of heaven. — New York: Brewer, Warren & Putnam, 1932. 294 p. I. T.
PS3537.T3234 P3 1932   LC 32-30511

Steinbeck, John, 1902-1968.   • 2.12531
The short reign of Pippin IV; a fabrication. New York, Viking Press, 1957. 188 p. illus. 21 cm. I. T.
PS3537.T3234S5x   LC 57-7555

Steinbeck, John, 1902-1968.   • 2.12532
Sweet Thursday. — New York: Viking Press, 1954. x, 273 p.; 22 cm. — I. T.
PS3537.T3234S8x   LC 54-7983

Steinbeck, John, 1902-1968.   • 2.12533
To a God unknown. The Pearl. Original illus. by David W. Whitfield. — [London]: Distributed by Heron Books, [1971] 308 p.: illus.; 21 cm. I. Steinbeck, John, 1902-1968. The Pearl. 1971. II. III. Title: The Pearl.
PZ3.S8195 To5 PS3537.T3234 T6x   813/.5/2   LC 72-27943

Steinbeck, John, 1902-1968. • 2.12534
The wayward bus [by] John Steinbeck. — New York: The Viking Press, 1947.
5 p., l., 3-312 p.; 21 cm. — I. T.
PS3537.T3234W3x   813.5   *LC* 47-30085

Steinbeck, John, 1902-1968. • 2.12535
The winter of our discontent. — [1st ed.]. — New York: Viking Press, 1961.
311 p.; 22 cm. '500 copies.' I. T.
PS3537.T3234 W5   PZ3.S8195 Wi   *LC* 61-6793

French, Warren G., 1922-. • 2.12536
John Steinbeck. — New York: Twayne Publishers, [1961] 190 p.; 21 cm. —
(Twayne's United States authors series, 2) 1. Steinbeck, John, 1902-1968 —
Criticism and interpretation. I. T.
PS3537.T3234 Z65   813.52   *LC* 61-9853

Levant, Howard. 2.12537
The novels of John Steinbeck: a critical study / Howard Levant; with an introd.
by Warren French. — Columbia: University of Missouri Press, 1974. xxii,
304 p.; 23 cm. 'Selected works by John Steinbeck': p. [303]-304. 1. Steinbeck,
John, 1902-1968 — Criticism and interpretation. I. T.
PS3537.T3234 Z717   813/.5/2   *LC* 74-76251   *ISBN* 0826201644

Lisca, Peter. • 2.12538
The wide world of John Steinbeck. — New Brunswick, N.J.: Rutgers University
Press, 1958. 326 p.; 22 cm. 1. Steinbeck, John, 1902-1968. I. T.
PS3537.T3234 Z72   813.5   *LC* 57-10965

Moore, Harry Thornton. • 2.12539
The novels of John Steinbeck; a first critical study. — 2d ed., with a
contemporary epilogue. — Port Washington, N.Y.: Kennikat Press, [1968]
106 p.: map.; 21 cm. 1. Steinbeck, John, 1902-1968 — Criticism and
interpretation. I. T.
PS3537.T3234 Z75 1968   813/.5/2   *LC* 67-27627

PS3537 Sterling

Sterling, George, 1869-1926. • 2.12540
Selected poems. New York, Holt, 1923. — St. Clair Shores, Mich.: Scholarly
Press, 1970. 232 p.; 21 cm. — I. T.
PS3537.T42 A6 1970   811/.5/2   *LC* 74-131840   *ISBN* 0403007275

PS3537 Stevens

Stevens, Wallace, 1879-1955. • 2.12541
Collected poems. — [1st collected ed.]. — New York: Knopf, 1954. xv, 534,
v p.: port.; 25 cm. — I. T.
PS3537.T4753 1954   811.5   *LC* 54-11750

Stevens, Wallace, 1879-1955. • 2.12542
Opus posthumous / by Wallace Stevens; edited, with an introd. by Samuel
French Morse. — New York: Knopf, c1957. xxxvii, 300 p. Poems, plays, prose.
I. T.
PS3537.T4753 A6 1957   *LC* 57-7548

Stevens, Wallace, 1879-1955. • 2.12543
Letters. Selected and edited by Holly Stevens. [1st ed.] New York, A. A. Knopf,
1966. xxxviii, 890, xxxix p. illus., facsims., ports. 25 cm. 1. Stevens, Wallace,
1879-1955 — Correspondence. 2. Poets, American — 20th century —
Correspondence. I. Stevens, Holly. ed. II. T.
PS3537.T4753 Z53   811/.52 B 19   *LC* 66-19401

Baird, James. • 2.12544
The dome and the rock; structure in the poetry of Wallace Stevens. —
Baltimore: Johns Hopkins Press, [1968] xxxi, 334 p.; 24 cm. 1. Stevens,
Wallace, 1879-1955 — Criticism and interpretation. I. T.
PS3537.T4753 Z59   811/.5/2   *LC* 68-19701

Borroff, Marie. ed. • 2.12545
Wallace Stevens; a collection of critical essays. Englewood Cliffs, N.J., Prentice-
Hall [1963] 181 p. 21 cm. (A Spectrum book: Twentieth century views, S-
TC-33) 1. Stevens, Wallace, 1879-1955 — Criticism and interpretation. I. T.
PS3537.T4753 Z6   811.52   *LC* 63-19419

Burney, William A. • 2.12546
Wallace Stevens. New York, Twayne Publishers [1968] 190 p. 21 cm.
(Twayne's United States authors series, 127) 1. Stevens, Wallace, 1879-1955.
I. T.
PS3537.T4753 Z6216   811/.5/2   *LC* 67-28857

Kermode, Frank, 1919-. • 2.12547
Wallace Stevens. — New York: Grove Press, 1961, c1960. 134 p. — (Evergreen
pilot books; EP4) 1. Stevens, Wallace, 1879-1955. I. T.
PS3537.T4753 Z67 1961   *LC* 61-6598

Morse, Samuel French, 1916-. • 2.12548
Wallace Stevens: poetry as life. — New York: Pegasus, [1970] 232 p.; 22 cm. —
(Pegasus American authors) 1. Stevens, Wallace, 1879-1955. I. T.
PS3537.T4753 Z68   811/.5/2 B   *LC* 78-114170

Pack, Robert, 1929-. • 2.12549
Wallace Stevens; an approach to his poetry and thought. — New York:
Gordian Press, 1968. xvi, 203 p.; 23 cm. Reprint of the 1958 ed. 1. Stevens,
Wallace, 1879-1955 — Criticism and interpretation. I. T.
PS3537.T4753 Z73 1968   811/.5/2   *LC* 68-24044

Pearce, Roy Harvey. • 2.12550
The act of the mind: essays on the poetry of Wallace Stevens / edited by Roy
Harvey Pearce and J. Hills Miller. — Baltimore: Johns Hopkins Press, [1965]
xi, 287 p. Errata slip inserted. 1. Stevens, Wallace, 1879-1955. I. Miller, J.
Hillis (Joseph Hillis), 1928- II. T.
PS3537.T4753 Z75   *LC* 65-11666

Riddel, Joseph N. • 2.12551
The clairvoyant eye: the poetry and poetics of Wallace Stevens / Joseph N.
Riddel. — Baton Rouge: Louisiana State University Press, 1965. 308 p. 'Index
to Stevens titles': p. 299-303. 1. Stevens, Wallace, 1879-1955. I. T.
PS3537.T4753 Z775   *LC* 65-24679

Vendler, Helen Hennessy. • 2.12552
On extended wings: Wallace Stevens' longer poems. — Cambridge, Mass.:
Harvard University Press, 1969. x, 334 p.; 22 cm. 1. Stevens, Wallace,
1879-1955. I. T.
PS3537.T4753 Z8   811/.5/2   *LC* 70-82299   *ISBN* 0674634357

Wells, Henry Willis, 1895-. • 2.12553
Introduction to Wallace Stevens / Henry W. Wells. — Bloomington: Indiana
University Press, 1964, c1963. 218 p. 1. Stevens, Wallace, 1879-1955. I. T.
PS3537.T4753 Z93   *LC* 64-10833

PS3537 St–Sz

Stewart, George Rippey, 1895-. • 2.12554
Storm: a novel / by George R. Stewart; with a new introd. by the author. — New
York: Modern Library, c1947. ix, 349 p. — (Modern library of the world's best
books. 254.) 1st Modern Library ed. I. T. II. Series.
PS3537.T49 S98   *LC* 48-243

Stickney, Trumbull, 1874-1904. • 2.12555
The poems of Trumbull Stickney. Edited and with an introd., by Amberys R.
Whittle. Foreword by Edmund Wilson. — [1st ed.]. — New York: Farrar,
Straus and Giroux, [1972] xlix, 316 p.: port.; 22 cm. 'The text is based primarily
upon The poems of Trumbull Stickney (Boston, 1905).' I. Whittle, Amberys
R., ed. II. T.
PS3537.T525 1972b   811/.4   *LC* 78-139342   *ISBN* 0374235376

Stone, Irving, 1903-. 2.12556
The origin: a biographical novel of Charles Darwin / by Irving Stone; edited by
Jean Stone. — 1st ed. — New York: Doubleday, 1980. 743 p.: maps; 24 cm.
1. Darwin, Charles, 1809-1882 — Fiction. I. Stone, Jean. II. T.
PS3537.T669 O74   813/.52   *LC* 79-6655   *ISBN* 0385120648

Stout, Rex, 1886-1975. 2.12557
And be a villain / by Rex Stout. — New York: Viking Press, 1948. 216 p. 'A
Nero Wolfe novel.' I. T.
PS3537.T733 A5   *LC* 48-8378

Stribling, T. S. (Thomas Sigismund), 1881-1965. 2.12558
Clues of the Caribbees: being certain criminal investigations of Henry Poggioli,
Ph.D. / T. S. Stribling. — New York: Dover Publications, 1977, c1929. 314 p.:
ill.; 22 cm. 1. Detective and mystery stories, American I. T.
PZ3.S9166 Cl 1977 PS3537.T836   813/.5/2   *LC* 76-56999   *ISBN*
048623486X

Stuart, Jesse, 1907-. • 2.12559
Man with a bull–tongue plow / [by] Jesse Stuart. New York: E. P. Dutton &
co., inc. [1934] 6 p. l., 3-361 p. 22 cm. Title on two leaves. Sonnets. I. T.
PS3537.T92516 M3 1934   811.5   *LC* 34-34715

Stuart, Jesse, 1907-. • 2.12560
Taps for Private Tussie [by] Jesse Stuart, illustrated by Thomas Benton. New
York, Books, inc., distributed by E. P. Dutton & company, inc. [1943] 303 p.
incl. col. front., col. plates. 22 cm. I. Benton, Thomas Hart, 1889-1975. illus.
II. T.
PZ3.S9306Tap2 PS3537.T92516T3 1943   *LC* 43-17838

LeMaster, J. R., 1934-. 2.12561
Jesse Stuart, Kentucky's chronicler–poet / J. R. LeMaster. — [Memphis, Tenn.]: Memphis State University Press, c1980. xii, 218 p.; 24 cm. Includes index. 1. Stuart, Jesse, 1907- — Criticism and interpretation. I. T.
PS3537.T92516 Z76   811/.52   *LC* 79-28224   *ISBN* 0878700498

Suckow, Ruth, 1892-1960. 2.12562
Children and older people. — New York: Knopf, 1931. 277 p. I. T.
PS3537.U34 C5x   *LC* 31-21755

Suckow, Ruth, 1892-1960. • 2.12563
Country people / Ruth Suckow. — New York: A.A. Knopf, 1924. 213 p.; 20 cm. I. T.
PS3537.U35 C6   PS3537.U34 Cx.   *LC* 24-12281

Suckow, Ruth, 1892-1960. 2.12564
Iowa interiors / Ruth Suckow; with a new introduction by Elizabeth Hardwick. — New York: Arno Press, 1977 [c1926] 283 p.; 21 cm. — (Rediscovered fiction by American women) Reprint of the ed. published by Knopf, New York. I. T. II. Series.
PZ3.S942 Io12 PS3537.U34   813/.5/2   *LC* 76-51679   *ISBN* 0405100574

Hamblen, Abigail Ann. 2.12565
Ruth Suckow / by Abigail Ann Hamblen. — Boise: Boise State University, c1978. 48 p.; 21 cm. — (Boise State University Western writers series; no. 34) 1. Suckow, Ruth, 1892-1960 — Criticism and interpretation. 2. Middle West in literature. I. T.
PS3537.U34 Z68   813/.5/2   *LC* 78-52563   *ISBN* 0884300587

Omrčanin, Margaret Stewart. 2.12566
Ruth Suckow: a critical study of her fiction. — Philadelphia: Dorrance, [1972] 218 p.; 22 cm. 1. Suckow, Ruth, 1892-1960. I. T.
PS3537.U34 Z86   813/.5/2   *LC* 70-184135   *ISBN* 080591658X

Swann, Thomas Burnett. 2.12567
Wolfwinter / by Thomas Swann. — New York: Ballantine, 1972. 205 p.; 18 cm. I. T.
PS3537.W3713 W6x

Swenson, May. • 2.12568
To mix with time, new and selected poems. — New York, Scribner [1963] 183 p. 21 cm. I. T.
PS3537.W4786A6 1963   811.54   *LC* 63-10635

Swenson, May. 2.12569
New & selected things taking place: poems / by May Swenson. — 1st ed. — Boston: Little, Brown, c1978. ix, 301 p.; 23 cm. 'An Atlantic Monthly Press book.' Includes index. I. T.
PS3537.W4786 N4   811/.5/4   *LC* 78-16671   *ISBN* 0316825204

PS3539 T–Th

Tomkins, Mary E. 2.12570
Ida M. Tarbell, by Mary E. Tomkins. New York, Twayne Publishers [1974] 182 p. port. 22 cm. (Twayne's United States authors series, TUSAS 247) 1. Tarbell, Ida M. (Ida Minerva), 1857-1944. I. T.
PS3539.A58 Z9   070.9/24   *LC* 73-22293   *ISBN* 080570714X

Tate, Allen, 1899-. 2.12571
Collected poems, 1919–1976 / Allen Tate. — New York: Farrar Straus Giroux, c1977. x, 217 p.; 24 cm. I. T.
PS3539.A74 A17 1977   811/.5/2   *LC* 77-11132   *ISBN* 0374125392

Tate, Allen, 1899-. 2.12572
The fathers, and other fiction / Allen Tate; introd. by Thomas Daniel Young. — Baton Rouge: Louisiana State University Press, c1977. xxi, 370 p.; 22 cm. — (Louisiana paperbacks; L-94) Contains a revision of the author's The fathers, originally published in 1938, and two short stories. I. T.
PZ3.T183 Fau 1977 PS3539.A74F3x   813/.5/2   *LC* 77-22617   *ISBN* 0807103810

Tate, Allen, 1899-. • 2.12573
The fathers. — Denver: A. Swallow, [1960] 306 p. I. T.
PS3539.A74 F3x 1960   *LC* 60-3394

Tate, Allen, 1899-. 2.12574
Memoirs and opinions, 1926–1974 / Allen Tate. — 1st ed. — Chicago: Swallow Press, 1975. xi, 225 p.; 23 cm. Includes index. 1. Tate, Allen, 1899- — Biography. 2. Authors — Correspondence, reminiscences, etc. 3. Literature — History and criticism — Addresses, essays, lectures. I. T.
PS3539.A74 Z52   818/.5/209 B   *LC* 75-10757   *ISBN* 0804006628

Bishop, Ferman. • 2.12575
Allen Tate. New York: Twayne Publishers [1967] 172 p.; 21 cm. (Twayne's United States authors series, 124) 1. Tate, Allen, 1899- I. T.
PS3539.A74 Z63   818/.5/209   *LC* 67-24765

Meiners, R. K. • 2.12576
The last alternatives; a study of the works of Allen Tate [by] R. K. Meiners. — New York: Haskell House, 1973 [c1963] 217 p.; 23 cm. 1. Tate, Allen, 1899- I. T.
PS3539.A74 Z7 1973   818/.5/209   *LC* 72-4614   *ISBN* 0838315941

Squires, Radcliffe, 1917- comp. • 2.12577
Allen Tate and his work; critical evaluations. Edited with an introd. by Radcliffe Squires. Minneapolis, University of Minnesota Press [1972] 355 p. 24 cm. 1. Tate, Allen, 1899- 2. Tate, Allen, 1899- — Bibliography. I. T.
PS3539.A74 Z87   818/.5/209   *LC* 78-167297   *ISBN* 0816606277

Taylor, Peter Hillsman, 1917-. • 2.12578
[Short stories] The collected stories of Peter Taylor. New York, Farrar, Straus and Giroux [1969, c1968] vii, 535 p. 22 cm. I. T.
PS3539.A9633 A15 1969   813/.5/4   *LC* 71-87215

Taylor, Peter Hillsman, 1917-. 2.12579
In the Miro District and other stories / by Peter Taylor. — 1st ed. — New York: Knopf, 1977. 204 p.; 22 cm. I. T.
PS3539.A9633 I5 1977   813/.5/4   *LC* 76-28760   *ISBN* 0394410610

Taylor, Peter Hillsman, 1917-. • 2.12580
The widows of Thornton / Peter Taylor. — 1st ed. — New York: Harcourt, Brace, c1954. 310 p. I. T.
PS3539A9633 W5

Taylor, Peter Hillsman, 1917-. • 2.12581
A woman of means. New York, Harcourt, Brace, 1950. 160 p. illus. 21 cm. I. T.
PS 3539 A966 W87 1950   *LC* 50-7597

Teasdale, Sara, 1884-1933. • 2.12582
The collected poems of Sara Teasdale. — New York, The Macmillan company, 1937. xvi, 311 p. front. (port.) 22 cm. 'First printing.' I. T.
PS3539.E15 1937   811.5   *LC* 37-28625

Teasdale, Sara, 1884-1933. 2.12583
Mirror of the heart: poems of Sara Teasdale / edited and introduced by William Drake. — New York: Macmillan; London: Collier Macmillan, c1984. xlvi, 139 p.; 22 cm. Includes index. I. Drake, William. II. T.
PS3539.E15 A6 1984   811/.52 19   *LC* 84-7192   *ISBN* 0026168707

Drake, William. 2.12584
Sara Teasdale, woman & poet / William Drake. — 1st ed. — San Francisco: Harper & Row, c1979. xiv, 304 p., [4] leaves of plates: ill.; 24 cm. 1. Teasdale, Sara, 1884-1933 — Biography. 2. Poets, American — 20th century — Biography. I. T.
PS3539.E15 Z64 1979   811/.5/2 B   *LC* 79-1776

Sheean, Vincent, 1899-. • 2.12585
Dorothy and Red. Boston: Houghton Mifflin, 1963. xii, 363 p.: ill., ports., facsims.; 22 cm. 1. Thompson, Dorothy, 1893-1961. 2. Lewis, Sinclair, 1885-1951. I. T.
PS3539.H649 Z85   928.1   *LC* 63-21040

PS3539 Thurber

Thurber, James, 1894-1961. • 2.12586
The Thurber album; a new collection of pieces about people. — New York: Simon and Schuster, 1952. 346 p.: illus.; 22 cm. — I. T.
PS3539.H94 T46   818.5   *LC* 52-10216

Thurber, James, 1894-1961. • 2.12587
The Thurber carnival / written and illustrated by James Thurber. — New York; London: Harper & brothers, [1945] xiii, 369 p.: ill.; 23 cm. — I. T.
PS3539.H94 T5   817.5   *LC* 45-1366

Holmes, Charles Shiveley. • 2.12588
The clocks of Columbus; the literary career of James Thurber [by] Charles S. Holmes. — [1st ed.]. — New York: Atheneum, 1972. xiv, 360 p.: illus.; 25 cm. 1. Thurber, James, 1894-1961. I. T.
PS3539.H94 Z7   818/.5/209   *LC* 72-78287

Morsberger, Robert Eustis, 1929-. • 2.12589
James Thurber, by Robert E. Morsberger. New York, Twayne Publishers [1964] 224 p. 21 cm. (Twayne's United States authors series, 62) 1. Thurber, James, 1894-1961. I. T.
PS3539.H94 Z77   817.52   *LC* 64-13958

Tobias, Richard Clark, 1925-.   • 2.12590
The art of James Thurber [by] Richard C. Tobias. — Athens: Ohio University Press, [1970, c1969] 196 p.; 24 cm. 1. Thurber, James, 1894-1961. 2. Comedy I. T.
PS3539.H94 Z9 1970   818/.5/209   *LC* 68-20938   *ISBN* 0821400584

PS3539 Th–Tz

Thurman, Wallace, 1902-1934.   2.12591
The blacker the berry ... A novel of Negro life. With an introd. by Therman B. O'Daniel. — [New York]: Collier Books, [1970] xix, 231 p.; 18 cm. — (African/American library) I. T. II. Series.
PZ3.T4258 Bl9 PS3539.H957B5x   813/.5/2   *LC* 78-102975

Thurman, Wallace, 1902-1934.   2.12592
Infants of the spring: a novel / by Wallace Thurman; afterword by John A. Williams. — Carbondale: Southern Illinois University Press, [1979] c1932. 312 p.; 23 cm. — (Lost American fiction) Reprint of the ed. published by Macaulay Co., New York. I. T.
PZ3.T4258 In 1979 PS3539.H957I6x   813/.52   *LC* 78-16906
ISBN 0809308649

Tolson, Melvin Beaunorus.   2.12593
Caviar and cabbage / selected columns by Melvin B. Tolson from the Washington Tribune, 1937–1944; edited, with an introduction, by Robert M. Farnsworth. — Columbia: University of Missouri Press, 1982. x, 278 p.: port.; 22 cm. Includes index. I. Farnsworth, Robert M. II. T.
PS3539.O334 C3 1982   814/.52 19   *LC* 81-10480   *ISBN* 0826203485

Tolson, Melvin Beaunorus.   2.12594
Harlem gallery / by M.B. Tolson; with an introduction by Karl Shapiro. — New York: Twayne, [1965-. v. Poetry. 1. Afro-Americans — New York (City) — Poetry. 2. Harlem (New York, N.Y.) — Description — Poetry. I. T.
PS3539.O334 H3   *LC* 64-25063

Russell, Mariann, 1935-.   2.12595
Melvin B. Tolson's Harlem gallery: a literary analysis / Mariann Russell. — Columbia: University of Missouri Press, 1981 (c1980). 143 p.; 24 cm. Includes index. 1. Tolson, Melvin Beaunorus. Harlem gallery. 2. Afro-Americans in literature 3. Harlem (New York, N.Y.), in literature. I. T.
PS3539.O334 H337   811/.52   *LC* 80-50306   *ISBN* 0826203094

Farnsworth, Robert M.   2.12596
Melvin B. Tolson, 1898–1966: plain talk and poetic prophecy / Robert M. Farnsworth. — Columbia: University of Missouri Press, 1984. 322 p.; 25 cm. Includes index. 1. Tolson, Melvin Beaunorus. 2. Poets, American — 20th century — Biography. I. T.
PS3539.O334 Z69 1984   811/.54 19   *LC* 83-21571   *ISBN* 0826204333

Toomer, Jean, 1894-1967.   • 2.12597
Cane [by] Jean Toomer; with a foreword by Waldo Frank. New York, Boni and Liveright [c1923] xi, [1] p., 2 l., 239 p. 20 cm. I. T.
PS3539.½478 C3   *LC* 23-12749

Toomer, Jean, 1894-1967.   2.12598
The wayward and the seeking: a collection of writings by Jean Toomer / edited with an introd. by Darwin T. Turner. — Washington: Howard University Press, 1980. ix, 450 p.; 24 cm. I. Turner, Darwin T., 1931- ed. II. T.
PS3539.O478 W3 1980   818/.5207 19   *LC* 74-11026   *ISBN* 0882580140

McKay, Nellie Y.   2.12599
Jean Toomer, artist: a study of his literary life and work, 1894–1936 / Nellie Y. McKay. — Chapel Hill: University of North Carolina Press, c1984. xiv, 262 p.: ill., ports.; 24 cm. Includes index. 1. Toomer, Jean, 1894-1967. 2. Authors, American — 20th century — Biography. I. T.
PS3539.O478 Z78 1984   813/.52 B 19   *LC* 83-21570   *ISBN* 0807815837

Trilling, Lionel, 1905-1975.   2.12600
The middle of the journey. — Garden City, N.Y.: Doubleday Anchor Books, 1957. 350 p. (Anchor; A 98) I. T.
PZ3.T73 Mi5 PS3539.R56   813/.5/2

Trilling, Lionel, 1905-1975.   • 2.12601
Beyond culture; essays on literature and learning. — New York: Viking Press, [1965] xviii, 235 p.; 22 cm. I. T.
PS3539.R56 B4   809   *LC* 65-24276

Trilling, Lionel, 1905-1975.   • 2.12602
A gathering of fugitives / Lionel Trilling. — Boston: Beacon Press, 1956. viii, 167 p. — (Beacon paperback; 34) Essays. I. T.
PS3539.R56 G3   *LC* 56-14508

Trilling, Lionel, 1905-1975.   2.12603
The liberal imagination: essays on literature and society. — New York: Viking Press, 1950. xvi, 303 p.; 22 cm. I. T.
PS3539.R56 L5 1950   *LC* 50-6914

PS3543 V

Van Doren, Carl, 1885-1950.   • 2.12604
Three worlds / by Carl Van Doren. — New York: Harper, 1936. 317 p.; 23 cm. I. T. II. Title: 3 worlds.
PS3543.A555 Z5   *LC* 36-27409

Van Doren, Mark, 1894-1972.   • 2.12605
Collected and new poems, 1924–1963. [1st ed.] New York, Hill and Wang [1963] 615 p. 22 cm. I. T.
PS3543.A557 A17 1963   811.52   *LC* 63-18480

Van Doren, Mark, 1894-1972.   2.12606
Collected stories. New York, Hill and Wang [1962-68] 3 v. 22 cm. I. T.
PZ3.V28686 Co PS3543.A557 A6x   *LC* 62-15221

Van Doren, Mark, 1894-1972.   • 2.12607
Narrative poems. 1st ed. New York: Hill and Wang, [1964]. 335 p.; 22 cm. 1. American poetry — 20th century — Individual authors I. T.
PS3543.A557 N3   811.52   *LC* 64-24238

Van Doren, Mark, 1894-1972.   • 2.12608
That shining place; new poems. [1st ed.] New York, Hill and Wang [1969] ix, 81 p. 22 cm. I. T.
PS3543.A557 T45   811/.5/2   *LC* 70-75253   *ISBN* 0809092328

Van Doren, Mark, 1894-1972.   • 2.12609
Autobiography. [1st ed.] New York: Harourt, Brace, [1958] 371 p.: ill.; 22 cm. 1. Van Doren, Mark, 1894-1972 — Biography. I. T.
PS3543.A557 Z52   928.1   *LC* 58-10897   *ISBN*

Van Duyn, Mona.   2.12610
Merciful disguises: published and unpublished poems. — [1st ed.]. — New York: Atheneum, 1973. x, 245 p.; 25 cm. I. T.
PS3543.A563 M4   811/.5/4   *LC* 73-78407   *ISBN* 0689105789

Van Vechten, Carl, 1880-1964.   • 2.12611
Nigger heaven / by Carl Van Vechten. — New York; London: A. A. Knopf, 1926. 286 p.; 20 cm. I. T.
PZ3.V368Ni PS3543.A653 N5   *LC* 26-15403

Van Vogt, A. E. (Alfred Elton), 1912-.   2.12612
Slan / by A. E. Van Vogt. — 1st ed. — Sauk City, Wisconsin: Arkham House, 1946. 216 p. — (Arkham house novels of fantasy and horror; 3) Appeared serially in Astounding science-fiction in 1940. I. T.
PS3543.A6546   *LC* 47-924

Vidal, Gore, 1925-.   • 2.12613
Homage to Daniel Shays; collected essays, 1952–1972. — [1st ed.]. — New York: Random House, [1972] viii, 449 p.; 22 cm. — I. T.
PS3543.I26 A16 1972   814/.5/4   *LC* 72-6082   *ISBN* 0394482107

Vidal, Gore, 1925-.   2.12614
1876: a novel / Gore Vidal. — 1st ed. — New York: Random House, c1976. 364 p.; 25 cm. 1. United States — History — 1865-1898 — Fiction. I. T. II. Title: Eighteen seventy-six.
PS3543.I26 A6214 1976   813/.5/4   *LC* 75-34311   *ISBN* 0394497503

Vidal, Gore, 1925-.   2.12615
Burr: a novel. — [1st ed.] New York: Random House, [1973] 430 p.; 25 cm. 1. Burr, Aaron, 1756-1836 — Fiction. I. T.
PZ3.V6668Bu PS3543.I26B8   *LC* 73-3985

Vidal, Gore, 1925-.   • 2.12616
The city and the pillar / by Gore Vidal. — New York: E.P. Dutton, 1948. 314 p. I. T.
PS3543.I26 C5   *LC* 47-12503

Vidal, Gore, 1925-.   2.12617
Kalki: a novel / by Gore Vidal. — New York: Random House, c1978. 254 p.; 24 cm. — I. T.
PZ3.V6668 Kal PS3543.I26 K3x   813/.5/4   *LC* 77-90248   *ISBN* 0394420535

Vidal, Gore, 1925-. 2.12618
Lincoln: a novel / Gore Vidal. — Random House 1st ed. — New York:
Random House, c1984. 657 p.; 25 cm. 1. Lincoln, Abraham, 1809-1865 —
Fiction I. T.
PS3543.I26 L5 1984 813/.54 19 *LC* 83-43185 *ISBN* 0394528956

Vidal, Gore, 1925-. 2.12619
Myra Breckinridge / by Gore Vidal. — [1st ed.]. — Boston: Little, Brown,
1968. 264 p. Novel. I. T.
PS3543.I26 M9 *LC* 68-14745

Vidal, Gore, 1925-. 2.12620
Myron: a novel. — [1st ed.]. — New York: Random House, [1974] x, 244 p.; 22
cm. — I. T.
PZ3.V6668 Mz PS3543.I26 M92. 813/.5/4 *LC* 74-9052
ISBN 0394494776

Vidal, Gore, 1925-. • 2.12621
Romulus: a new comedy, adapted from a play of Friedrich Duerrenmatt / by
Gore Vidal. — [New York]: Dramatists Play Service, [c1962] 79 p.: ill.; 20 cm.
I. Dürrenmatt, Friedrich. Romulus der Grosse. II. T.
PS3543.I26 R65 1962 832.91 *LC* 62-53549

Vidal, Gore, 1925-. • 2.12622
A thirsty evil: seven short stories. — [1st ed.]. — New York: Zero Press, 1956.
154 p. I. T.
PS3543.I26 T45 *LC* 56-11329

Vidal, Gore, 1925-. • 2.12623
Visit to a small planet, and other television plays. — [1st ed.]. — Boston: Little,
Brown, [1956] 278 p.; 22 cm. — I. T.
PS3543.I26 V5 792 812.5* *LC* 57-5030

Vidal, Gore, 1925-. • 2.12624
Williwaw, a novel by Gore Vidal. New York, E.P. Dutton & co., 1946. 222 p. 21
cm. 'First edition.' I. T.
PS3543.I26 W5 1946 *LC* 46-4254

Dick, Bernard F. 2.12625
The apostate angel; a critical study of Gore Vidal [by] Bernard F. Dick. — [1st
ed.]. — New York: Random House, [1974] 203 p.; 22 cm. 1. Vidal, Gore, 1925-
— Criticism and interpretation. I. T.
PS3543.I26 Z65 818/.5/409 *LC* 73-20553 *ISBN* 0394481089

Kiernan, Robert F. 2.12626
Gore Vidal / Robert F. Kiernan. — New York: F. Ungar Pub. Co., c1982. xvi,
165 p.; 21 cm. — (Modern literature series.) Includes index. 1. Vidal, Gore,
1925- — Criticism and interpretation. I. T. II. Series.
PS3543.I26 Z75 1982 818/.5409 19 *LC* 81-70962 *ISBN*
0804424616

White, Ray Lewis. • 2.12627
Gore Vidal. — New York: Twayne Publishers, [1968] 157 p.; 21 cm. —
(Twayne's United States authors series, 135) 1. Vidal, Gore, 1925- I. T.
PS3543.I26 Z9 818/.5/409 *LC* 68-24294

Viereck, Peter Robert Edwin, 1916-. • 2.12628
Terror and decorum: poems, 1940–1948, by Peter Viereck. — Westport, Conn.:
Greenwood Press, [1972, c1948] xi, 110 p.; 22 cm. — I. T.
PS3543.I325 T4 1972 811/.5/4 *LC* 78-178796 *ISBN* 0837162963

PS3545 W–Wa

Wagoner, David. • 2.12629
New and selected poems. — Bloomington: Indiana University Press, [1969]
176 p.; 22 cm. — I. T.
PS3545.A345 A6 1969 811/.5/4 *LC* 69-16002

Walker, Margaret, 1915-. 2.12630
For my people / with a foreword by Stephen Vincent Benét. — New York:
Arno Press, 1968 [c1942] 58 p.; 21 cm. — (The American Negro, his history
and literature) Poems. I. T. II. Series.
PS3545.A517 F6 1968 811/.5/2 *LC* 73-4377

Walker, Margaret, 1915-. 2.12631
Jubilee. Boston, Houghton Mifflin, 1966. xii, 497 p. map (on lining papers) 22
cm. I. T.
PS3545.A517 J8 *LC* 66-11218

Ward, Mary Jane, 1905-. • 2.12632
The snake pit. — New York: Random House, c1946. 278 p.: 21 cm. — 'First
Printing' I. T.
PZ3.W2153 Sn PS3545.A695 S6 1946. Fic *LC* 46-2643

PS3545 Warren

Warren, Robert Penn, 1905-. 2.12633
Selected poems, 1923–1975 / Robert Penn Warren. — New York: Random
House, 1977. xvii, 325 p.; 25 cm. I. T.
PS3545.A748 A17 1976 811/.5/2

Warren, Robert Penn, 1905-. • 2.12634
All the king's men. With a new introd. by the author. New York, Modern
Library [1953] 464 p. 19 cm. (The Modern library of the world's best books,
170) I. T.
PS3545.A748A699 1953 *LC* 53-7891

Twentieth century interpretations of All the king's men: a 2.12635
collection of critical essays / edited by Robert H. Chambers.
Englewood Cliffs, N.J.: Prentice-Hall, c1977. vi, 161 p.; 21 cm. — (Twentieth
century interpretations) (A Spectrum book) 1. Warren, Robert Penn, 1905- All
the king's men. I. Chambers, Robert H.
PS3545.A748 A797 813/.5/2 *LC* 77-23876 *ISBN* 0130224340

Warren, Robert Penn, 1905-. • 2.12636
At heaven's gate. New York, Random House [1959, c1943] 391 p. 21 cm. I. T.
PS3545.A748A8 1959 *LC* 59-5736

Warren, Robert Penn, 1905-. • 2.12637
Band of angels. New York: Random House [1955] 375 p.; 22 cm. I. T.
PS3545.A748B3 *LC* 55-5814

Warren, Robert Penn, 1905-. 2.12638
Being here: poetry, 1977–1980 / Robert Penn Warren. — 1st ed. — New York:
Random House, c1980. 108 p.; 24 cm. — I. T.
PS3545.A748 B4 1980 811/.52 *LC* 80-11520 *ISBN* 0394513045

Warren, Robert Penn, 1905-. 2.12639
Brother to dragons: a tale in verse and voices / Robert Penn Warren. — 1st ed.,
a new version. — New York: Random House, c1979. xiv, 141 p.; 24 cm.
1. Jefferson, Thomas, 1743-1826 — Poetry. 2. Lewis, Lucy Jefferson,
1752-1811 — Poetry. 3. Lewis, Isham, d. 1815? — Poetry. 4. Lewis, Lilburn,
d. 1812 — Poetry. I. T.
PS3545.A748 B7 1979 811/.5/2 *LC* 79-10782 0394505514

Warren, Robert Penn, 1905-. • 2.12640
The cave. New York, Random House [1959] 403 p. 22 cm. I. T.
PZ3.W2549Cav PS3545.A748C3 *LC* 59-5719

Warren, Robert Penn, 1905-. • 2.12641
The circus in the attic, and other stories. [1st ed.] New York, Harcourt, Brace
[1947] 276 p. 21 cm. I. T.
PZ3.W2549 Ci PS3545.A748Cx. *LC* 48-5123

Warren, Robert Penn, 1905-. 2.12642
Meet me in the green glen. — [1st ed.]. — New York: Random House, [c1971]
376 p.; 22 cm. — I. T.
PZ3.W2549 Me PS3545.A748 M4x 813/.5/2 *LC* 70-102303
ISBN 039446141X

Warren, Robert Penn, 1905-. • 2.12643
Night rider / Robert Penn Warren. — New York: Random House, c1939.
460 p.; 21 cm. I. T.
PZ3.W2549 Ni3 PS3545.A748 N5x 813/.5/2 *LC* 76-365384

Warren, Robert Penn, 1905-. 2.12644
Now and then: poems, 1976–1978 / Robert Penn Warren. — 1st ed. — New
York: Random House, c1978. xii, 75 p.; 24 cm. I. T.
PS3545.A748 N6 811/.5/2 *LC* 78-57102 *ISBN* 0394501640

Warren, Robert Penn, 1905-. 2.12645
A place to come to: a novel / by Robert Penn Warren. — 1st ed. — New York:
Random House, c1977. 401 p.; 22 cm. — I. T.
PZ3.W2549 Pl PS3545.A748 P5x 813/.5/2 *LC* 76-50129 *ISBN*
0394410645

Warren, Robert Penn, 1905-. • 2.12646
Wilderness: a tale of the Civil War. — New York: Random House [1961] 310 p.
22 cm. 1. United States — History — Civil War, 1861-1865 — Fiction. I. T.
PS3545.A748 W5 1961 PZ3.W2549 Wi *LC* 61-6248

Warren, Robert Penn, 1905-. • 2.12647
World enough and time: a romantic novel. New York: Random House [1950]
512 p.; 22 cm. Sequel: Time's dark laughter. I. T.
PS3545.A748 W6 1950 PZ3.W2549 Wo *LC* 50-7242

Warren, Robert Penn, 1905-. 2.12648
Robert Penn Warren talking: interviews, 1950–1978 / edited by Floyd C.
Watkins and John T. Hiers. — 1st ed. — New York: Random House, c1980.

xiv, 304 p.; 22 cm. Includes index. 1. Warren, Robert Penn, 1905- Interviews.
2. Authors, American — 20th century — Interviews. I. Watkins, Floyd C.
II. Hiers, John T. III. T.
PS3545.A748 Z54   813.5/2 B   LC 79-4768   ISBN 0394510100

Bedient, Calvin.   **2.12649**
In the heart's last kingdom: Robert Penn Warren's major poetry / Calvin
Bedient. — Cambridge, Mass.: Harvard University Press, 1984. 250 p.; 24 cm.
1. Warren, Robert Penn, 1905- — Criticism and interpretation. I. T.
PS3545.A748 Z58 1984   811/.52 19   LC 84-6674   ISBN
0674445465

Bohner, Charles H.   • **2.12650**
Robert Penn Warren, by Charles H. Bohner. New York, Twayne Publishers
[1965, c1964] 175 p. 21 cm. (Twayne's United States authors series, 69)
1. Warren, Robert Penn, 1905- I. T.
PS3545.A748 Z6   818.52   LC 64-20719

Critical essays on Robert Penn Warren / [compiled by] William   **2.12651**
Bedford Clark.
Boston, Mass.: G.K. Hall, c1981. viii, 239 p.; 25 cm. — (Critical essays on
American literature.) 1. Warren, Robert Penn, 1905- — Criticism and
interpretation — Collected works. I. Clark, William Bedford. II. Series.
PS3545.A748 Z66   813/.52 19   LC 80-28716   ISBN 0816184240

Justus, James H.   **2.12652**
The achievement of Robert Penn Warren / James H. Justus. — Baton Rouge:
Louisiana State University Press, c1981. xiv, 362 p.; 24 cm. — (Southern
literary studies.) 1. Warren, Robert Penn, 1905- — Criticism and
interpretation. I. T. II. Series.
PS3545.A748 Z73   813/.52 19   LC 81-3714   ISBN 0807108758

Longley, John Lewis, ed.   • **2.12653**
Robert Penn Warren, a collection of critical essays. [New York] New York
University Press, 1965. xix, 259 p. 22 cm. 1. Warren, Robert Penn, 1905- —
Criticism and interpretation — Addresses, essays, lectures. I. T.
PS3545.A748 Z77   813.52   LC 65-13207

Robert Penn Warren, a collection of critical essays / edited by   **2.12654**
Richard Gray.
Englewood Cliffs, N. J.: Prentice-Hall, c1980. viii, 206 p.; 21 cm. (Twentieth
century views) (A Spectrum book; S-TC-149) 1. Warren, Robert, 1905- —
Criticism and interpretation — Addresses, essays, lectures. I. Gray, Richard J.
PS3545.A748 Z86 1980   813/.5/2   LC 79-23295   ISBN
0137819064

Strandberg, Victor H.   • **2.12655**
A colder fire: the poetry of Robert Penn Warren / [by] Victor H. Strandberg. —
[Lexington]: University of Kentucky Press, [1965] xii, 292 p.; 23 cm.
1. Warren, Robert Penn, 1905- I. T.
PS3545.A748 Z87   811.52   LC 65-27009

PS3545 We

Weinbaum, Stanley Grauman, 1902-1935.   **2.12656**
A Martian Odyssey and other science fiction tales; the collected short stories of
Stanley G. Weinbaum. Introd. by Sam Moskowitz. — Westport, Conn.:
Hyperion Press, [1974] 555 p.; 23 cm. — (Classics of science fiction) 1. Science
fiction, American I. T.
PZ3.W431 Mar6 PS3545.E4636   813/.5/2   LC 73-13269   ISBN
0883551233

Wellman, Manly Wade, 1905-.   **2.12657**
Who fears the devil? — Sauk City, Wis.: Arkham House, 1963. 213 p.; 20 cm.
I. T.
PS3545.E526 W46   LC 63-6225

PS3545 Welty

Welty, Eudora, 1909-.   • **2.12658**
Selected stories: containing all of A curtain of green, and other stories, and The
wide net, and other stories / with an introd. by Katherine Anne Porter. — New
York: Modern Library [1954, c1943] 289, 214 p.; 19 cm. (The Modern library of
the world's best books [290]) I. Title: A curtain of green, and other stories.
II. Title: The wide net, and other stories.
PS3545.E6 Ax   LC 54-9969

Welty, Eudora, 1909-.   • **2.12659**
The bride of the Innisfallen, and other stories / by Eudora Welty. — [1st ed.]. —
New York: Harcourt, Brace, [1955]. 207 p. I. T.
PS3545.E6 B7   Fic   LC 55-5248

Welty, Eudora, 1909-.   • **2.12660**
Delta wedding, a novel. New York: Harcourt,Brace and World, 1946. 247 p.:
plan (on lining paper) I. T.
PS3545.E6 D4 1946   LC 46-3217

Welty, Eudora, 1909-.   **2.12661**
The eye of the story: selected essays and reviews / Eudora Welty. — New York:
Random House, 1978, c1977. x, 355 p.; 22 cm. I. T.
PS3545.E6 E9   814/.5/2

Welty, Eudora, 1909-.   • **2.12662**
The golden apples. — [1st ed.]. — New York: Harcourt, Brace [1949] 244 p.; 21
cm. I. T.
PZ3.W4696Go PS3545.E6 G6   LC 49-10054

Welty, Eudora, 1909-.   • **2.12663**
Losing battles. — 1st ed. — New York: Random House, [1970] 436 p.: map.; 22
cm. — I. T.
PZ3.W4696 Lo PS3545.E6 L6x   813/.5/2   LC 74-102304

Welty, Eudora, 1909-.   **2.12664**
The optimist's daughter. — [1st ed.]. — New York: Random House, [1972]
180 p.; 22 cm. — I. T.
PS3545.E6 O6   PZ3.W4696 Op   813/.5/2   LC 76-39769   ISBN
0394480171

Welty, Eudora, 1909-.   • **2.12665**
The Ponder heart. Drawings by Joe Krush. — [1st ed.]. — New York:
Harcourt, Brace, [c1954] 158 p.: illus.; 21 cm. — I. T.
PZ3.W4696 Po   PS3545 E6Px.   LC 54-5248

Welty, Eudora, 1909-.   • **2.12666**
The robber bridegroom. New York, Harcourt, Brace [1948, c1942] 185 p. 20
cm. I. T.
PS3545.E6R6 1948   LC 48-8276 *

Welty, Eudora, 1909-.   **2.12667**
One writer's beginnings / Eudora Welty. — Cambridge, Mass.: Harvard
University Press, 1984. 104 p., [11] p. of plates: ill., ports.; 24 cm. — (William
E. Massey, Sr. lectures in the history of American civilization. 1983) Revised
versions of 3 lectures delivered at Harvard University in Apr. 1983. 1. Welty,
Eudora, 1909- — Biography — Youth — Addresses, essays, lectures.
2. Novelists, American — 20th century — Biography — Addresses, essays,
lectures. I. T. II. Series.
PS3545.E6 Z475 1984   813/.52 B 19   LC 83-18638   ISBN
0674639251

Appel, Alfred.   • **2.12668**
A season of dreams: the fiction of Eudora Welty / [by] Alfred Appel, Jr. —
Baton Rouge: Louisiana State University Press, 1965. xvi, 274 p.; 22 cm.
(Southern literary studies.) 1. Welty, Eudora, 1909- I. T. II. Series.
PS3545.E6 Z56   813.52   LC 65-20298

Devlin, Albert J.   **2.12669**
Eudora Welty's chronicle: a story of Mississippi life / by Albert J. Devlin. —
Jackson: University Press of Mississippi, c1983. xvi, 223 p.; 25 cm. 1. Welty,
Eudora, 1909- — Criticism and interpretation. 2. Mississippi in literature.
I. T.
PS3545.E6 Z64 1983   813/.52 19   LC 82-19996   ISBN 0878051767

Eudora Welty: a form of thanks / essays by Cleanth Brooks ...   **2.12670**
[et al.]; edited by Louis D. Dollarhide and Ann J. Abadie.
Jackson: University Press of Mississippi, 1979, c1978. xiii, 138 p.: port.; 22 cm.
1. Welty, Eudora, 1909- — Addresses, essays, lectures. 2. Novelists, American
— 20th century — Biography — Addresses, essays, lectures. I. Brooks,
Cleanth, 1906- II. Abadie, Ann J. III. Dollarhide, Louis D.
PS3545.E6 Z66   813/.52 19

Eudora Welty: critical essays / edited by Peggy Whitman   **2.12671**
Prenshaw.
Jackson: University Press of Mississippi, 1979. xviii, 446 p.; 24 cm. 1. Welty,
Eudora, 1909- — Criticism and interpretation — Addresses, essays, lectures.
I. Prenshaw, Peggy Whitman.
PS3545.E6 Z67   813/.5/2   LC 79-4124   ISBN 0878050930

Evans, Elizabeth, 1935-.   **2.12672**
Eudora Welty / Elizabeth Evans. — New York: F. Ungar, c1981. xiii, 172 p.; 21
cm. — (Modern literature series.) Includes index. 1. Welty, Eudora, 1909- —
Criticism and interpretation. I. T. II. Series.
PS3545.E6 Z68   813/.52 19   LC 81-2812   ISBN 0804421870

A Still moment: essays on the art of Eudora Welty / edited by John F. Desmond. • 2.12673
Metuchen, N.J.: Scarecrow Press, 1978. viii, 142 p.; 23 cm. Includes bibliographical references and index. 1. Welty, Eudora, 1909- — Criticism and interpretation — Addresses, essays, lectures. I. Desmond, John F.
PS3545.E6 Z87   813/.5/2   LC 78-3719   ISBN 0810811294

Vande Kieft, Ruth Marguerite, 1925-. • 2.12674
Eudora Welty. New York: Twayne Publishers [1962] 203 p.; 21 cm. (Twayne's United States authors series, 15) 1. Welty, Eudora, 1909- I. T.
PS3545.E6 Z9   813.52   LC 62-10272

PS3545 We–Wh

Wescott, Glenway, 1901-. • 2.12675
The pilgrim hawk; a love story. New York, Harper, 1940. 127 p. 23 cm. I. T.
PS 3545 E74 P63 1940   LC 40-35169

Wescott, Glenway, 1901-. • 2.12676
Apartment in Athens. — Westport, Conn.: Greenwood Press, [1972, c1945] 268 p.; 22 cm. — I. T.
PZ3.W512 Al6 PS3545.E827   813/.5/2   LC 76-152617   ISBN 0837160529

Wescott, Glenway, 1901-. • 2.12677
The apple of the eye / by Glenway Westcott. — New York: The Dial Press, 1924. 292 p.; 20 cm. I. T.
PS3545.E827 A66   LC 24-23494

Wescott, Glenway, 1901-. • 2.12678
The grandmothers: a family portrait / with an introduction by Fred B. Millett. — New York, Harper [1950] xvi, 388 p. 21 cm. (Harper's modern classics.) I. T. II. Series.
PZ3.W512Gr8 PS3545.E827G7 1950   LC 50-6732

Rueckert, William H. (William Howe), 1926-. • 2.12679
Glenway Wescott, by William H. Rueckert. New York, Twayne Publishers [1965] 174 p. 21 cm. (Twayne's United States authors series, 87) 1. Wescott, Glenway, 1901- I. T.
PS3545.E827 Z86   818.52   LC 65-18906

West, Jessamyn. • 2.12680
Love, death, and the ladies' drill team. — New York: Harcourt, Brace, [1955] 248 p. Short stories. I. T.
PS3545.E8315 L6   LC 55-10809

Shivers, Alfred S. • 2.12681
Jessamyn West, by Alfred S. Shivers. — New York: Twayne, [c1972] 160 p.; 21 cm. — (Twayne's United States authors series. TUSAS 192) 1. West, Jessamyn. I. T.
PS3545.E8315 Z88   813/.5/4   LC 70-147190

West, Nathanael. • 2.12682
Complete works. — New York: Farrar, Straus and Cudahy, [1957] 421 p.; 20 cm. — I. T.
PS3545.E8334 1957   813/.5/2   LC 57-6259

Comerchero, Victor. • 2.12683
Nathanael West, the ironic prophet. — [Syracuse, N.Y.]: Syracuse University Press, 1964. xii, 189 p.; 22 cm. 1. West, Nathanael, 1902-1940. I. T.
PS3545.E8334 Z6   LC 64-23342

Light, James F. • 2.12684
Nathanael West: an interpretative study, by James F. Light. — 2d ed. — Evanston [Ill.]: Northwestern University Press, 1971. xxv, 236 p.; 22 cm. 1. West, Nathanael, 1903-1940. I. T.
PS3545.E8334 Z75 1971   813/.5/2   LC 70-22930   ISBN 0810103370

Malin, Irving. • 2.12685
Nathanael West's novels. With a pref. by Harry T. Moore. Carbondale, Southern Illinois University Press [1972] viii, 141 p. 22 cm. (Crosscurrents: modern critiques) 1. West, Nathanael, 1903-1940. I. T.
PS3545.E8334 Z76   813/.5/2   LC 75-188697   ISBN 0809305771

Martin, Jay. • 2.12686
Nathanael West; the art of his life. — [1st ed.]. — New York: Farrar, Straus and Giroux, [1970] xx, 435 p.: illus., ports.; 22 cm. 1. West, Nathanael, 1903-1940. I. T.
PS3545.E8334 Z8   813/.5/2   LC 78-97610

Reid, Randall. • 2.12687
The fiction of Nathanael West; no redeemer, no promised land. — Chicago: University of Chicago Press, [1967] viii, 174 p.; 21 cm. 1. West, Nathanael, 1903-1940. I. T.
PS3545.E8334 Z85   813/.5/2   LC 67-30949

Widmer, Kingsley, 1925-. 2.12688
Nathanael West / by Kingsley Widmer. — Boston: Twayne Publishers, c1982. 146 p.; 21 cm. — (Twayne's United States authors series. TUSAS 423) Includes index. 1. West, Nathanael, 1903-1940 — Criticism and interpretation. I. T. II. Series.
PS3545.E8334 Z94 1982   813/.52 19   LC 82-11874   ISBN 0805773568

PS3545 Wharton

Wharton, Edith Newbold Jones, 1862-1937. • 2.12689
The collected short stories of Edith Wharton. Edited and with an introd. by R. W. B. Lewis. New York, Scribner [1968] 2 v. 24 cm. I. Lewis, R. W. B. (Richard Warrington Baldwin). ed. II. T.
PS3545.H16 A15 1968   813/.5/2   LC 67-24055

Wharton, Edith Newbold Jones, 1862-1937. • 2.12690
The age of innocence / introd. by R. W. B. Lewis. — New York: Scribner, [1968] xiv, 361 p.; 22 cm. Reprint of 1920 ed. I. T.
PZ3.W555 Ag23   PS3545H16 A6 1968.   LC 68-27785

Wharton, Edith Newbold Jones, 1862-1937. • 2.12691
The custom of the country; with an introd. by Blake Nevius. New York, Scribner [1956] 594 p. 22 cm. (Modern standard authors) I. T.
PS3545.H16 C8 1956   LC 56-58520

Wharton, Edith Newbold Jones, 1862-1937. • 2.12692
Ethan Frome / with a forward and a study guide by Helen T. Munn. — New York: Scribner [1960] 178 p.; 19 cm. I. T.
PZ3.W555 Et25   PS3545.H16 Ex.   LC 60-2095

Wharton, Edith Newbold Jones, 1862-1937. • 2.12693
The house of mirth; with a foreword by Marcia Davenport. New York, Scribner [1951] vii, 329 p. 22 cm. I. T.
PS3545.H16 H6x 1951   LC 51-14301

Wharton, Edith Newbold Jones, 1862-1937. • 2.12694
Hudson river bracketed. New York: Appleton-Century-Crofts, 1929. 559 p. I. T.
PS3545.H16 H8 1929   PS3162.H8 1929.   LC 29-24077

Rae, Catherine M., 1914-. 2.12695
Edith Wharton's New York quartet / Catherine M. Rae; with a foreword by R.W.B. Lewis. — Lanham, MD: University Press of America, c1984. xiv, 82 p.; 22 cm. 1. Wharton, Edith Newbold Jones, 1862-1937. Old New York. 2. New York (N.Y.) in literature. I. T.
PS3545.H16 O437 1984   813/.52 19   LC 84-11813   ISBN 0819140287

Wharton, Edith Newbold Jones, 1862-1937. • 2.12696
Old New York. — New York: Scribner, 1964, c1952. ix, 306 p.; 21 cm. I. T.
PS3545.H16 Ox   LC 64-15969

Wharton, Edith Newbold Jones, 1862-1937. • 2.12697
The reef / by Edith Wharton. — New York: Scribner [1965] xii, 367 p.; 21 cm. I. T.
PS3545.H16 R4 1965   LC 65-21879

Wharton, Edith Newbold Jones, 1862-1937. • 2.12698
A backward glance. — New York, Scribner [1964] xxvii, 385 p. illus., ports. 21 cm. 1. Authors — Correspondence, reminiscences, etc. I. T.
PS3545.H16Z5 1964   928.1   LC 64-3270

Lewis, R. W. B. (Richard Warrington Baldwin). 2.12699
Edith Wharton: a biography / R. W. B. Lewis. — 1st ed. — New York: Harper & Row, [1975] xiv, 592 p., 16 p. of plates: ill., ports. Includes index. 1. Wharton, Edith Newbold Jones, 1862-1937. I. T.
PS3545.H16 Z696   PS3545H16 Z696.   813/.5/2 B   LC 74-1833   ISBN 0060126035

Griffith, Grace Kellogg. • 2.12700
The two lives of Edith Wharton: the woman and her work / by Grace Kellogg. — New York: Appleton-Century, [c1965] xiv, 332 p.: col. port. 1. Wharton, Edith Newbold Jones, 1862-1937 — Biography. I. T. II. Title: The 2 lives of Edith Wharton.
PS3545.H16 Z6x   LC 65-5135

Wolff, Cynthia Griffin. 　　　　　　　　　　　**2.12701**
A feast of words: the triumph of Edith Wharton / Cynthia Griffin Wolff. — New York: Oxford University Press, 1977. viii, 453 p.: ports.; 24 cm. 1. Wharton, Edith Newbold Jones, 1862-1937 — Criticism and interpretation. I. T.
PS3545.H16 Z94　　　813/.5/2　　　*LC* 76-42678　　　*ISBN* 0195021177

PS3545 Wh–Wi

White, E. B. (Elwyn Brooks), 1899-. 　　　　　　　　**2.12702**
Essays of E. B. White. — 1st ed. — New York: Harper & Row, c1977. ix, 277 p.; 24 cm. I. T.
PS3545.H5187 A16 1977　　　814/.5/2　　　*LC* 77-7717　　　*ISBN* 0060145765

White, E. B. (Elwyn Brooks), 1899-. 　　　　　　　　**2.12703**
Poems and sketches of E.B. White. — New York: Harper & Row, c1981. xvi, 217 p.; 24 cm. — I. T.
PS3545.H5187 A6 1981　　　811/.52 19　　　*LC* 81-47240　　　*ISBN* 0060149000

White, E. B. (Elwyn Brooks), 1899-. 　　　　　　　• **2.12704**
One man's meat. A new and enl. ed. [By] E. B. White. New York and London, Harper & brothers [1944] viii, p., 2 l., 350 p. 20 cm. All but three of the essays are from the monthly department 'One man's meat' in Harper's magazine. cf. Note. I. T.
PS3545.H5187 O5 1944　　　817.5　　　*LC* 44-7015

White, E. B. (Elwyn Brooks), 1899-. 　　　　　　　• **2.12705**
The second tree from the corner. [1st ed.] New York: Harper [c1954] 253 p.; 22 cm. Prose and poetry. I. T.
PS3545.H5187 S4　　　817.5　　　*LC* 53-11864

White, E. B. (Elwyn Brooks), 1899-. 　　　　　　　**2.12706**
Letters of E. B. White / collected and edited by Dorothy Lobrano Guth. — 1st ed. — New York: Harper & Row, c1976. xi, 686 p., [8] leaves of plates: ill.; 24 cm. Includes index. 1. White, E. B. (Elwyn Brooks), 1899- — Correspondence. I. Guth, Dorothy Lobrano. II. T.
PS3545.H5187 Z53 1976　　　818/.5/209 B　　　*LC* 73-18660　　　*ISBN* 006014601X

Sampson, Edward C. 　　　　　　　　　　　**2.12707**
E. B. White / by Edward C. Sampson. — New York: Twayne Publishers, [1974] 190 p.; 21 cm. (Twayne's United States authors series, TUSAS 232) 1. White, E. B. (Elwyn Brooks), 1899- — Criticism and interpretation. I. T.
PS3545.H5187 Z9　　　818/.5/209　　　*LC* 73-21582　　　*ISBN* 0805707875

Wilbur, Richard, 1921-. 　　　　　　　　　• **2.12708**
The poems of Richard Wilbur. — [1st ed.]. — New York: Harcourt, Brace & World, [1963] 227 p.; 21 cm. — (A Harvest book, HB67) I. T.
PS3545.I32165 1963　　　811.52　　　*LC* 63-24265

Wilbur, Richard, 1921-. 　　　　　　　　　**2.12709**
The mind–reader: new poems / by Richard Wilbur. — New York: Harcourt Brace Jovanovich, c1976. x, 67 p.; 21 cm. I. T.
PS3545.I32165 M5　　　811/.5/2　　　*LC* 75-42312　　　*ISBN* 0151601100

Wilbur, Richard, 1921-. 　　　　　　　　　**2.12710**
Responses: prose pieces, 1953–1976 / Richard Wilbur. — Harcourt Brace Jovanovich, c1976. xii, 238 p.; 22 cm. I. T.
PS3545.I32165 R4　　　809.1　　　*LC* 76-24903　　　*ISBN* 0151769303

Wilbur, Richard, 1921-. 　　　　　　　　　**2.12711**
Walking to sleep; new poems and translations. — [1st ed.]. — New York: Harcourt, Brace & World, [1969] xiii, 79 p.; 21 cm. — I. T.
PS3545.I32165 W3　　　811/.5/2　　　*LC* 69-20054

Hill, Donald L. 　　　　　　　　　　　　• **2.12712**
Richard Wilbur / Donald L. Hill. — New York: Twayne Publishers, [1967] 192 p. (Twayne's United States authors series. TUSAS 117) 1. Wilbur, Richard, 1921- I. T. II. Series.
PS3545.I32165 Z69　　　*LC* 67-13182

Wilder, Thornton, 1897-1975. 　　　　　　　• **2.12713**
Three plays: Our town, The skin of our teeth, The matchmaker. New York, Harper [1957] 401 p. 22 cm. The matchmaker is a rewritten version of The merchant of Yonkers. I. T. II. Title: Our town. III. Title: The skin of our teeth. IV. Title: The matchmaker.
PS3545.I345 A19 1957　　　812.5　　　*LC* 57-10252

Wilder, Thornton, 1897-1975. 　　　　　　　• **2.12714**
A Thornton Wilder trio / introduction by Malcolm Cowley. — New York: Criterion Books, c1956. 309p. I. Wilder, Thornton, 1897-1975. Cabala. II. Wilder, Thornton, 1897-1975. Bridge of San Luis Rey. III. Wilder,

Thornton, 1897-1975. IV. T. V. Title: The Cabala VI. Title: The bridge of San Luis Rey VII. Title: The woman of Andros
PS3545.I345 A6 1956　　　*LC* 56-11401

Wilder, Thornton, 1897-1975. 　　　　　　　**2.12715**
The Alcestiad: or, A life in the sun: a play in three acts, with a satyr play, The drunken sisters / Thornton Wilder. — 1st trade ed. — New York: Harper & Row, c1977. xxi, 129 p.; 21 cm. (A Cass Canfield book) (Harper colophon books; cn 658) 1. Alcestis (Greek mythology) — Drama. I. Wilder, Thornton, 1897-1975. The drunken sisters. 1977. II. T.
PS3545.I345 A78 1977　　　812/.5/2　　　*LC* 77-3781　　　*ISBN* 0060146389

Wilder, Thornton, 1897-1975. 　　　　　　　• **2.12716**
The eighth day [by] Thornton Wilder. — London: Longmans, 1967. 435 p. I. T. II. Title: The 8th day.
PS3545.I345 E5x　　　813/.5/2

Wilder, Thornton, 1897-1975. 　　　　　　　• **2.12717**
Heaven's my destination. New York, London, Harper & brothers, 1935. vi p., 1 l., 304 p., 1 l. 21 cm. At head of title: Thornton Wilder. 'First edition.' I. T.
PS3545.I345 H4 1935　　　*LC* 35-323

Wilder, Thornton, 1897-1975. 　　　　　　　• **2.12718**
The ides of March. [1st ed.] New York, Harper [1948] viii, 246 p. 21 cm. 1. Caesar, Julius — Fiction. I. T.
PZ3.W6468 Id　　　PS3545.I345 I3.　　　*LC* 48-647

Wilder, Thornton, 1897-1975. 　　　　　　　**2.12719**
The journals of Thornton Wilder, 1939–1961 / selected and edited by Donald Gallup, with two scenes of an uncompleted play, 'The Emporium'; foreword by Isabel Wilder. — New Haven: Yale University Press, c1985. xxvi, 354 p.: facsim.; 24 cm. 1. Wilder, Thornton, 1897-1975 — Diaries. 2. Authors, American — 20th century — Biography. I. Gallup, Donald Clifford, 1913- II. Wilder, Thornton, 1897-1975. Emporium. Selections. 1985. III. T.
PS3545.I345 Z465 1985　　　818/.5203 B 19　　　*LC* 85-3365　　　*ISBN* 0300033753

Burbank, Rex J. 　　　　　　　　　　　**2.12720**
Thornton Wilder / by Rex Burbank. — 2d ed. — Boston: Twayne, c1978. 150 p.: port.; 21 cm. (Twayne's United States authors series; TUSAS 5) Includes index. 1. Wilder, Thornton, 1897-1975 — Criticism and interpretation. I. T.
PS3545.I345 Z57 1978　　　818.5209 19　　　*LC* 77-26237　　　*ISBN* 0805772235

Goldstein, Malcolm. 　　　　　　　　　• **2.12721**
The art of Thornton Wilder. Lincoln, University of Nebraska Press [1965] x, 179 p. 21 cm. 1. Wilder, Thornton, 1897-1975. I. T.
PS3545.I345 Z66　　　818.52　　　*LC* 65-10239

Haberman, Donald. 　　　　　　　　　　• **2.12722**
The plays of Thornton Wilder: a critical study / by Donald Haberman. — [1st ed.] Middletown, Conn.: Wesleyan University Press, [1967] xii, 162 p.; 22 cm. 1. Wilder, Thornton, 1897-1975 — Criticism and interpretation. I. T.
PS3545.I345Z68　　　812.52　　　*LC* 67-15772

PS3545 Tennessee Williams

Williams, Tennessee, 1911-. 　　　　　　　• **2.12723**
The theatre of Tennessee Williams. — New York: New Directions, 1971-72. 4 v.; 22 cm. I. T.
PS3545.I5365 A19 1971　　　812/.54 19　　　*LC* 78-159743　　　*ISBN* 0811207943

Williams, Tennessee, 1911-. 　　　　　　　**2.12724**
Stopped rocking and other screenplays / Tennessee Williams; with an introduction by Richard Gilman. — New York: New Directions Pub. Corp., 1984. xii, 384 p.; 22 cm. I. T.
PS3545.I5365 A6 1984　　　791.43/75/0973 19　　　*LC* 84-6948　　　*ISBN* 0811209016

Williams, Tennessee, 1911-. 　　　　　　　**2.12725**
Clothes for a summer hotel: a ghost play / Tennessee Williams. — New York: New Directions, 1983. 77 p.; 21 cm. 1. Fitzgerald, F. Scott (Francis Scott), 1896-1940. in fiction, drama, poetry, etc. 2. Fitzgerald, Zelda, 1900-1948. in fiction, drama, poetry, etc. I. T.
PS3545.I5365 C5 1983　　　812/.54 19　　　*LC* 83-2360　　　*ISBN* 0811208702

Williams, Tennessee, 1911-. 　　　　　　　• **2.12726**
Dragon Country, a book of plays. — [New York: New Directions, 1970] 278 p.; 22 cm. — (A New Directions book) I. T.
PS3545.I5365 D7 1970　　　812/.5/4　　　*LC* 76-79724

Williams, Tennessee, 1911-.   **2.12727**
Eight mortal ladies possessed; a book of stories. — [New York: New Directions Pub. Corp., 1974] 100 p.; 21 cm. — (A New Directions book) I. T.
PZ3.W67655 Ei3 PS3545.I5365Ex   813/.5/4   LC 73-89484   *ISBN* 0811205304

Williams, Tennessee, 1911-.   • **2.12728**
Hard candy; a book of stories. [New trade ed. New York, New Directions, 1959] 220 p. 23 cm. I. T.
PZ3.W67655Har2 PS3545.I5365H3   LC 59-16430

Williams, Tennessee, 1911-.   • **2.12729**
In the winter of cities: poems / by Tennessee Williams. — New York: New Directions Publishing Co., 1964. 129 p. –. (A New directions paperbook; NDP 154) I. T.
PS3545.I5365 I5 1964   PS3545I5365 I5 1964.   LC 64-4846   *ISBN* 0811202224

Williams, Tennessee, 1911-.   **2.12730**
A lovely Sunday for Creve Coeur / Tennessee Williams. — New York: New Directions Pub. Corp., 1980. 82 p.: ill.; 21 cm. — I. T.
PS3545.I5365 L6 1980   812/.5/4   LC 79-20589   *ISBN* 0811207560

Williams, Tennessee, 1911-.   • **2.12731**
One arm, and other stories. — [New ed.]. — [New York]: New Directions, [1954] 211 p.; 23 cm. I. T. II. Title: 1 arm.
PZ3.W67655On4   PS3545.I5365 O54 1954.   LC 57-31974

Williams, Tennessee, 1911-.   • **2.12732**
The Roman spring of Mrs. Stone / Tennessee Williams. — New York: New Directions, c1950. 148 p. — A novel. I. T.
PS3545.I5365 R6   LC 50-9067

Williams, Tennessee, 1911-.   • **2.12733**
27 wagons full of cotton, and other one–act plays. New York, New Directions, 1953. 238 p.; 22 cm. I. T.
PS3545.I5365 T9 1953   812.5   LC 53-12488

Williams, Tennessee, 1911-.   **2.12734**
[Two-character play] Out cry. [New York, Published for J. Laughlin by New Directions Pub. Corp., 1973] 72 p. 22 cm. (A New Directions book) Published in 1969 under title: The two-character play. I. T.
PS3545.I5365 T95 1973   812/.5/4   LC 73-78789   *ISBN* 0811205002 *ISBN* 0811204944

Williams, Tennessee, 1911-.   **2.12735**
Vieux carré / by Tennessee Williams. — New York: New Directions Pub. Corp., 1979. 115 p.; 21 cm. — I. T.
PS3545.I5365 V5 1979   812/.5/4   LC 78-26621   *ISBN* 0811207277

Williams, Tennessee, 1911-.   **2.12736**
Memoirs / Tennessee Williams. — 1st ed. — Garden City, N.Y.: Doubleday, 1975. xix, 264 p., [32] leaves of plates: ill.; 24 cm. Includes index. 1. Williams, Tennessee, 1911- — Biography. I. T.
PS3545.I5365 Z52   812/.5/4 B   LC 74-1523   *ISBN* 0385005733

Falk, Signi Lenea.   • **2.12737**
Tennessee Williams. — New York: Twayne Publishers, [1962, c1961] 224 p.; 21 cm. — (Twayne's United States authors series, 10) 1. Williams, Tennessee, 1911- — Criticism and interpretation. I. T.
PS3545.I5365 Z64 1962   812.54   LC 61-15670

Leavitt, Richard F.   **2.12738**
The world of Tennessee Williams / by Richard F. Leavitt; with an introd. by Tennessee Williams. — New York: Putnam, 1978 [c1977] 168 p.: ill.; 31 cm. Includes index. 1. Williams, Tennessee, 1911- 2. Dramatists, American — 20th century — Biography. I. Williams, Tennessee, 1911- II. T.
PS3545.I5365 Z735   812/.5/4 B   LC 76-28473   *ISBN* 0399117733

Tennessee Williams: a collection of critical essays / edited by Stephen S. Stanton.   **2.12739**
Englewood Cliffs, N.J.: Prentice-Hall, c1977. x, 194 p.; 21 cm. — (A Spectrum book; S-TC-131) (Twentieth century views) 1. Williams, Tennessee, 1911- — Criticism and interpretation — Addresses, essays, lectures. I. Stanton, Stephen Sadler, 1915-
PS3545.I5365 Z845   812/.5/4   LC 77-24463   *ISBN* 0139036253

PS3545 William Carlos Williams

Williams, William Carlos, 1883-1963.   • **2.12740**
Selected essays. New York: Random House, 1954. xviii, 342 p.; 22 cm. Imprint covered by label: New Directions, 1969. 1. Literature — Addresses, essays, lectures I. T.
PS3545.I544 A16 1954   814.5   LC 54-7815

Williams, William Carlos, 1883-1963.   • **2.12741**
Collected earlier poems. — [New York: [s.n.], 1951] 482 p.; 21 cm. 'A New Directions book.' I. T.
PS3545.I544 A17 1951   811.5   LC 51-8849

Williams, William Carlos, 1883-1963.   • **2.12742**
The collected later poems. — Rev. ed. — [New York]: New Directions, [1963] 276 p.; 21 cm. — I. T.
PS3545.I544 A17 1963   811.52   LC 62-19398

Williams, William Carlos, 1883-1963.   • **2.12743**
The build–up: a novel. — New York: Random House, [1952] 335 p. I. T.
PS3545.I544 B8   LC 52-5166

Williams, William Carlos, 1883-1963.   • **2.12744**
Farmers' daughters: the collected stories of William Carlos Williams / introd. by Van Wyck Brooks. Norfolk, Conn.: New Directions, c1961. xii, 374 p.; 21 cm. I. T.
PS3545I544 F3   LC 61-12776

Williams, William Carlos, 1883-1963.   • **2.12745**
In the money; White mule, part II. — Norfolk, Conn.: New Directions, [1940] 382 p. — (New Directions book.) I. Williams, William Carlos, 1883-1963. White mule, part II. II. T. III. Title: White mule, part II. IV. Series.
PS3545.I544 I5   LC 40-35170

Sankey, Benjamin.   **2.12746**
A companion to William Carlos Williams's Paterson. — Berkeley: University of California Press, 1971. ix, 235 p.: illus.; 24 cm. 1. Williams, William Carlos, 1883-1963. Paterson. I. T.
PS3545.I544 P337   811/.5/2   LC 72-121193   *ISBN* 0520017420

Williams, William Carlos, 1883-1963.   • **2.12747**
A voyage to Pagany. With an introd. by Harry Levin. — [New York: New Directions Pub. Corp., 1970] xx, 267 p.; 21 cm. — (A New Directions book) I. T.
PZ3.W6766 Vo9 PS3545.I544V6x   813/.5/2   LC 76-122108

Williams, William Carlos, 1883-1963.   • **2.12748**
White mule; a novel. — [New York: Published for J. Laughlin by New Directions Pub. Co., 1967, c1937] 291 p.; 21 cm. — I. T.
PZ3.W67667 Wh5   PS3545.I544 Wx.   LC 67-3209

Williams, William Carlos, 1883-1963.   **2.12749**
Autobiography. — New York: Random House, [1951] xiv, 401 p. 1. Williams, William Carlos, 1883-1963 — Biography. I. T.
PS3545.I544 Z5   LC 51-12522

Williams, William Carlos, 1883-1963.   **2.12750**
Interviews with William Carlos Williams: 'speaking straight ahead' / edited with an introduction by Linda Welshimer Wagner. — New York: New Directions, 1976. xix, 108 p.; 21 cm. — (A New Directions book) 1. Williams, William Carlos, 1883-1963 — Interviews. I. Wagner, Linda Welshimer. II. T.
PS3545.I544 Z526 1976   818/.5/209 B   LC 76-14797   *ISBN* 0811206203

Koch, Vivienne.   • **2.12751**
William Carlos Williams. — Norfolk, Conn., New Directions [1950] x, 278 p. port. 19 cm. —(The Makers of modern literature) 1. Williams, William Carlos, 1883-1963. I. T. II. Series.
PS3545.I544Z6   810.81   LC 50-697

Miller, J. Hillis (Joseph Hillis), 1928- ed.   • **2.12752**
William Carlos Williams; a collection of critical essays, edited by J. Hillis Miller. Englewood Cliffs, N.J., Prentice-Hall [1966] viii, 182 p. 21 cm. (Twentieth century views) (A Spectrum book.) 1. Williams, William Carlos, 1883-1963. I. T.
PS3545.I544 Z65   818.5209   LC 66-23440

Ostrom, Alan B., 1925-.   • **2.12753**
The poetic world of William Carlos Williams [by] Alan Ostrom. With a pref. by Harry T. Moore. — Carbondale: Southern Illinois University Press, [1966] xiii, 178 p.; 22 cm. — (Crosscurrents: modern critiques) Revision of thesis, Columbia University. 1. Williams, William Carlos, 1883-1963. I. T.
PS3545.I544 Z8   811.52   LC 65-16536

Paul, Sherman.   • **2.12754**
The music of survival; a biography of a poem by William Carlos Williams. — Urbana: University of Illinois Press, 1968. xi, 141 p.; 22 cm. 'The desert music [by William Carlos Williams]:' p. 3-14. 1. Williams, William Carlos, 1883-1963. The desert music. I. Williams, William Carlos, 1883-1963. The desert music. 1968. II. T.
PS3545.I544 Z83   811/.5/2   LC 68-18207   *ISBN* 0252725727

Wagner, Linda Welshimer. • 2.12755
Poems of William Carlos Williams, a critical study. [1st ed.]. — Middletown, Conn.: Wesleyan University Press, 1964. 169 p.; 23 cm. 1. Williams, William Carlos, 1883-1963. I. T.
PS3545.I544 Z93   811.52   LC 64-22371

Whittemore, Reed, 1919-. 2.12756
William Carlos Williams, poet from Jersey / Reed Whittemore. — Boston: Houghton-Mifflin, 1975. xii, 404 p., [8] leaves of plates: ill.; 24 cm. Includes index. 1. Williams, William Carlos, 1883-1963 — Biography. I. T.
PS3545.I544 Z95   811/.5/2   LC 75-20274   ISBN 0395207355

PS3545 Wi

Williamson, Jack, 1908-. 2.12757
Darker than you think / Jack Williamson. — New York: Garland Pub., 1975, c1948. 282 p.; 18 cm. (The Garland library of science fiction) Reprint of the 1969 ed. published by Berkley Pub. Corp., New York. I. T. II. Series.
PZ3.W67764 Dar6 PS3545.I557D3x   813/.5/2   LC 75-440   ISBN 0824014421

Williamson, Jack, 1908-. 2.12758
The humanoids / Jack Williamson; with a new introd. by F. M. Busby. — [s.l.]: Simon and Schuster, 1949. xvi, 239 p.: port.; 21 cm. — (The Gregg Press science fiction series) A revision of the author's And searching mind, published in Astounding science fiction. Reprint of the ed. published by Simon and Schuster, New York. I. T.
PS3545.I557 H85 1980   813/.5/2   LC 79-18576   ISBN 0839825498

Willingham, Calder, 1922-. • 2.12759
End as a man / by Calder Willingham. — New York: Vanguard Press, c1947. 350 p. I. T.
PS3545.I546 E53   PS3545I57 E53.   LC 47-1581

PS3545 Edmund Wilson

Wilson, Edmund, 1895-1972. • 2.12760
Five plays. New York, Farrar, Straus and Young, 1954. 541 p. 20 cm. I. T.
PS3545.I6245F5 1954a   812.5   LC 54-5432

Wilson, Edmund, 1895-1972. • 2.12761
I thought of Daisy. New York, Farrar, Straus and Young, 1953. 216 p. 19 cm. I. T.
PZ3.W6918It3 PS3545.I6245I2 1953   LC 53-6726

Wilson, Edmund, 1895-1972. • 2.12762
Memoirs of Hecate County. [New ed.] New York, L. C. Page [1959] 447 p. 20 cm. Short stories. I. T.
PZ3.W6918 Me2   PS3545.I6245 Mx.   LC 59-11989

Wilson, Edmund, 1895-1972. • 2.12763
Night thoughts. — New York: Farrar, Straus and Cudahy, 1961. 282 p.: ill. I. T.
PS3545.I6245 N5   LC 61-15762

Wilson, Edmund, 1895-1972. 2.12764
The forties: from notebooks and diaries of the period / Edmund Wilson; edited with an introduction by Leon Edel. — New York: Farrar, Straus, and Giroux, c1983. xxviii, 369 p., [5] leaves of plates: ill.; 20 cm. Includes index. 1. Wilson, Edmund, 1895-1972 — Diaries. 2. Authors, American — 20th century — Biography. I. Edel, Leon, 1907- II. T.
PS3545.I6245 Z465 1983   818/.5203 B 19   LC 82-21028   ISBN 0374157626

Wilson, Edmund, 1895-1972. • 2.12765
A prelude; landscapes, characters and conversations from the earlier years of my life. — New York: Farrar, Straus and Giroux, [1967] v, 278 p.: ports.; 20 cm. 1. Wilson, Edmund, 1895-1972. I. T.
PS3545.I6245 Z533   LC 67-15011

Wilson, Edmund, 1895-1972. 2.12766
The thirties: from notebooks and diaries of the period / Edmund Wilson; edited, with an introd. by Leon Edel. — New York: Farrar, Straus, and Giroux, c1980. xxxii, 753 p.; 19 cm. 1. Wilson, Edmund, 1895-1972 — Biography. 2. Authors, American — 20th century — Biography. I. Edel, Leon, 1907- II. T.
PS3545.I6245 Z535 1980   818/.5209 B   LC 79-28700   ISBN 0374275726

Wilson, Edmund, 1895-1972. 2.12767
Letters on literature and politics, 1912–1972 / Edmund Wilson; edited by Elena Wilson; introduction by Daniel Aaron; foreword by Leon Edel. — New York: Farrar, Straus and Giroux, c1977. xxxvii, 767 p.; ill.; 24 cm. 1. Wilson, Edmund, 1895-1972 — Correspondence. 2. Authors, American — 20th century — Correspondence. I. T.
PS3545.I6245 Z54 1977   818/.5/209   LC 76-58460   ISBN 0374185085

Castronovo, David. 2.12768
Edmund Wilson / David Castronovo. — New York: F. Ungar Pub. Co., c1984. xii, 205 p.; 21 cm. (Literature and life series.) Includes index. 1. Wilson, Edmund, 1895-1972 — Criticism and interpretation. I. T. II. Series.
PS3545.I6245 Z586 1984   818/.5209 19   LC 83-27341   ISBN 0804421161

Douglas, George H., 1934-. 2.12769
Edmund Wilson's America / George H. Douglas. — Lexington, Ky.: University Press of Kentucky, c1983. ix, 254 p., [8] p. of plates: ill.; 24 cm. Includes index. 1. Wilson, Edmund, 1895-1972 — Knowledge — United States. 2. Criticism — United States — History — 20th century. 3. United States — Civilization I. T.
PS3545.I6245 Z595 1983   818/.5209 19   LC 83-19696   ISBN 0813114942

Frank, Charles P. • 2.12770
Edmund Wilson, by Charles P. Frank. New York, Twayne Publishers [1970] 213 p. 21 cm. (Twayne's United States authors series, 152) 1. Wilson, Edmund, 1895-1972. I. T.
PS3545.I6245 Z65   818/.5/209   LC 75-79216

Paul, Sherman. • 2.12771
Edmund Wilson: a study of literary vocation in our time / Sherman Paul. —. Urbana: University of Illinois Press, 1965. 237 p.; 24 cm. 'Bibliographical note:' p. [222]-224. 1. Wilson, Edmund, 1895-1972. I. T.
PS3545.I6245Z8   818.5209   LC 65-15111

PS3545 Wi

Wilson, Sloan, 1920-. • 2.12772
The man in the gray flannel suit. — [New York]: Simon and Schuster, 1955. 304 p.; 22 cm. — I. T.
PZ3.W69755 Man   PS3545.I629 M3.   LC 54-9811

Winters, Yvor, 1900-1968. • 2.12773
Collected poems / by Yvor Winters. — Rev. ed. — [Denver]: A. Swallow 1960. — 146 p., 20 cm. I. T.
PS3545.I765A17 1960   811.52   LC 60-3291

PS3545 Wolfe

Wolfe, Thomas, 1900-1938. • 2.12774
From death to morning / by Thomas Wolfe. New York: C. Scribner's sons, 1935. 5 p. l., 304 p.; 20 cm. I. T.
PS3545.O337 F7   PZ3.W8314 Fr   LC 35-25839

Wolfe, Thomas, 1900-1938. • 2.12775
The hills beyond, with a note on Thomas Wolfe by Edward C. Aswell. New York, London, Harper & brothers [c1941] vi p., 1 l., 386 p., 1 l. 21 cm. 'First edition.' I. Aswell, Edward Campbell, 1900-1958. II. T.
PS3545.O337 H54 1941   LC 41-21548

Wolfe, Thomas, 1900-1938. • 2.12776
Look homeward, angel; a story of the buried life. New York Scribner 1947. 662p. I. T.
PS3545 O337 L6 1947

Wolfe, Thomas, 1900-1938. • 2.12777
Of time and the river: a legend of man's hunger in his youth / by Thomas Wolfe. — New York: C. Scribner's sons, 1935. 7 p. l., 3-912 p. 22 cm. 'First printing, February, 1935 ... third printing, March, 1935.' 'This novel is the second in a series of six ... The title of the whole work, when complete, will be the same as that of the present book, 'Of time and the river.' [The first in the series was published under title: Look homeward, angel]'—Publisher's note. I. T.
PS3545.O337 O4 1935   LC 35-27095

Wolfe, Thomas, 1900-1938. 2.12778
A stone, a leaf, a door: poems / by Thomas Wolfe; selected and arranged in verse by John S. Barnes; with a foreword by Louis Untermeyer. — New York: Scribner, c1971. ix, 166 p. (Scribner library of contemporary classics.) Orig. pub. in 1945. I. T.
PS3545.O337 S6   811.52   ISBN 0684124742

Wolfe, Thomas, 1900-1938. • 2.12779
The web and the rock. New York, London, Harper & brothers, 1939. vii p., 695, [1] p. 20 cm. 'First edition.' I. T.
PS3545.O337 W4 1939   LC 39-27574

Wolfe, Thomas, 1900-1938. 2.12780
Welcome to our city: a play in ten scenes / by Thomas Wolfe; edited with an introduction by Richard S. Kennedy. — Baton Rouge: Louisiana State University Press, c1983. xii, 132 p.; 23 cm. — (Southern literary studies.) I. Kennedy, Richard S. II. T. III. Series.
PS3545.O337 W49 1983   813/.52 19   *LC* 82-20838   *ISBN* 080711085X

Wolfe, Thomas, 1900-1938. • 2.12781
You can't go home again. New York; London: Harper [c1940] viii, 743, [1] p.; 22 cm. 'First edition.' I. T.
PS3545.O337 Y6 1940   *LC* 40-27633

Biography. Criticism

Wolfe, Thomas, 1900-1938. 2.12782
My other loneliness: letters of Thomas Wolfe and Aline Bernstein / edited by Suzanne Stutman. — Chapel Hill: University of North Carolina Press, c1983. xxv, 390 p.: ill.; 24 cm. Includes index. 1. Wolfe, Thomas, 1900-1938 — Correspondence. 2. Bernstein, Aline, 1881-1955 — Correspondence. 3. Novelists, American — 20th century — Correspondence. 4. Set designers — United States — Correspondence. I. Bernstein, Aline, 1881-1955. II. Stutman, Suzanne. III. T.
PS3545.O337 Z483 1983   813/.52 B 19   *LC* 82-20102   *ISBN* 0807815438

Wolfe, Thomas, 1900-1938. 2.12783
Beyond love and loyalty: the letters of Thomas Wolfe and Elizabeth Nowell; together with 'No more rivers': a story / by Thomas Wolfe; edited by Richard S. Kennedy. — Chapel Hill: University of North Carolina Press, c1983. xxii, 164 p.: port.; 24 cm. 1. Wolfe, Thomas, 1900-1938 — Correspondence. 2. Nowell, Elizabeth — Correspondence. 3. Novelists, American — 20th century — Correspondence. 4. Literary agents — United States — Correspondence. I. Nowell, Elizabeth. II. Wolfe, Thomas, 1900-1938. No more rivers. 1983. III. Kennedy, Richard S. IV. T.
PS3545.O337 Z49 1983   813/.52 B 19   *LC* 82-15939   *ISBN* 0807815454

Wolfe, Thomas, 1900-1938. 2.12784
The notebooks of Thomas Wolfe. Edited by Richard S. Kennedy and Paschal Reeves. — Chapel Hill: University of North Carolina Press, [1970] 2 v.: facsims. (on lining papers); 24 cm. 1. Wolfe, Thomas, 1900-1938. I. Kennedy, Richard S. ed. II. Reeves, Paschal, 1917- ed. III. T.
PS3545.O337 Z5   818/.5/2   *LC* 70-80917

Wolfe, Thomas, 1900-1938. • 2.12785
The story of a novel. — New York: Scribner, 1936. 4, 93 p.; 20 cm. 1. Wolfe, Thomas, 1900-1938. 2. Fiction — Technique I. T.
PS3545.O337 Z53 1936   *LC* 36-27278

Wolfe, Thomas, 1900-1938. • 2.12786
Letters. Collected and edited, with an introd. and explanatory text, by Elizabeth Nowell. New York, Scribner [1956] xviii, 797 p. port. 25 cm. Bibliographical footnotes. I. T.
PS3545.O337Z54   928.1   *LC* 56-9880

Wolfe, Thomas, 1900-1938. • 2.12787
Thomas Wolfe's letters to his mother, Julia Elizabeth Wolfe / edited with an introd. by John Skally Terry. — New York: Scribner's, 1943. xxxv, 368 p., [1] l. of plates: port., facsims. (on lining papers) 24 cm. 1. Wolfe, Thomas, 1900-1938. I. Wolfe, Julia Elizabeth (Westall), 1860-1945. II. Terry, John Skally, 1894- III. T.
PS3545.O337 Z55   PS3545.O337 Z496.   *LC* 43-6520

Thomas Wolfe, three decades of criticism / edited with an • 2.12788
introduction by Leslie A. Field.
New York: New York University Press, 1968. xxv, 304 p. 1. Wolfe, Thomas, 1900-1938. I. Field, Leslie A.
PS3545.O337 Z65   813   *LC* 68-13024

Evans, Elizabeth, 1935-. 2.12789
Thomas Wolfe / Elizabeth Evans. — New York: F. Ungar, c1984. xi, 190 p.; 21 cm. — (Literature and life series.) Includes index. 1. Wolfe, Thomas, 1900-1938. 2. Novelists, American — 20th century — Biography. I. T. II. Series.
PS3545.O337 Z68 1984   813/.52 B 19   *LC* 82-40275   *ISBN* 0804421889

Johnson, Pamela Hansford, 1912-. • 2.12790
The art of Thomas Wolfe. — New York: Scribner, [1963] 170 p. 1. Wolfe, Thomas, 1900-1938. I. Johnson, Pamela Hansford, 1912- Hungry Gulliver. II. T. III. Title: Hungry Gulliver.
PS3545.O337 Z72 1963   *LC* 63-24189

Holman, C. Hugh (Clarence Hugh), 1914-. 2.12791
The loneliness at the core: studies in Thomas Wolfe / C. Hugh Holman. — Baton Rouge: Louisiana State University Press, [1975] xx, 184 p.; 24 cm. — (Southern literary studies.) 1. Wolfe, Thomas, 1900-1938 — Addresses, essays, lectures. I. T. II. Series.
PS3545.O337 Z728   813/.5/2   *LC* 74-77325   *ISBN* 0807100854

Kennedy, Richard S. • 2.12792
The window of memory: the literary career of Thomas Wolfe. — Chapel Hill: University of North Carolina Press, [1962] 461 p.; 24 cm. 1. Wolfe, Thomas, 1900-1938. I. T.
PS3545.O337 Z737   818.52   *LC* 62-16110

Nowell, Elizabeth. • 2.12793
Thomas Wolfe, a biography. — [1st ed.]. — Garden City, N.Y.: Doubleday, 1960. 456 p.: illus.; 24 cm. 1. Wolfe, Thomas, 1900-1938 — Biography. I. T.
PS3545.O337 Z74   928.1   *LC* 60-8689

Muller, Herbert Joseph, 1905-. • 2.12794
Thomas Wolfe / by Herbert J. Muller. — Norfolk, Conn.: New Directions Books, [c1947]. 196 p.: port.; 19 cm. (The makers of modern literature) 1. Wolfe, Thomas, 1900-1938. I. T. II. Series.
PS3545.O337 Z8 1971

Rubin, Louis Decimus, 1923-. 2.12795
Thomas Wolfe; a collection of critical essays, edited by Louis D. Rubin, Jr. — Englewood Cliffs, N.J.: Prentice-Hall, [1973] viii, 182 p.; 22 cm. — (Twentieth century views) (A Spectrum book) 1. Wolfe, Thomas, 1900-1938. I. T.
PS3545.O337 Z848   813/.5/2   *LC* 73-7522   *ISBN* 013961656X

Rubin, Louis Decimus, 1923-. • 2.12796
Thomas Wolfe; the weather of his youth. — Baton Rouge, Louisiana State University Press [1955] 183 p. illus. 23 cm. 1. Wolfe, Thomas, 1900-1938. I. T.
PS3545.O337Z85   813.5   *LC* 55-7364

Turnbull, Andrew, 1921-. • 2.12797
Thomas Wolfe. — New York: Scribner, [1968, c1967] x, 374 p.: illus., ports.; 24 cm. 1. Wolfe, Thomas, 1900-1938. I. T.
PS3545.O337 Z865   813/.5/2   *LC* 68-10727

Watkins, Floyd C. • 2.12798
Thomas Wolfe's characters: portraits from life. — [1st ed.]. — Norman: University of Oklahoma Press, [1957] 194 p.: illus.; 22 cm. 1. Wolfe, Thomas, 1900-1938. I. T.
PS3545.O337 Z94   813.5   *LC* 57-7335

PS3545 Wo–Wr

Woollcott, Alexander, 1887-1943. • 2.12799
The portable Woollcott / selected by Joseph Hennessey; with an introd. by John Mason Brown. — Westport, Conn.: Greenwood Press, [1972, c1946] xxviii, 735 p.; 22 cm. Original ed. issued in series: The Viking portable library. I. T.
PS3545.O77 A6 1972   818/.5/209   *LC* 78-163543   *ISBN* 0837162009

Wouk, Herman, 1915-. 2.12800
War and remembrance: a novel / by Herman Wouk. — 1st trade ed. — Boston: Little, Brown, c1978. 1042 p.; 24 cm. Sequel to The winds of war. 1. World War, 1939-1945 — Fiction. I. T.
PZ3.W923 War PS3545.O98   813/.5/4   *LC* 78-17746   *ISBN* 0316955019

Wouk, Herman, 1915-. 2.12801
The winds of war, a novel. — [1st ed.]. — Boston: Little, Brown, [1971] 885 p.: plan.; 24 cm. Sequel: War and remembrance. 1. World War, 1939-1945 — Fiction. I. T.
PZ3.W923 Wi PS3545.O98   813/.5/4   *LC* 72-161857

Wouk, Herman, 1915-. • 2.12802
The Caine mutiny, a novel of World War II. Garden City, N. Y., Doubleday [1951] xii, 498 p. 22 cm. No maps on lining-papers. 1. World War, 1939-1945 — Fiction. I. T.
PZ3.W923Cai PS3545.O98C299   *LC* 51-9977

Beichman, Arnold. 2.12803
Herman Wouk, the novelist as social historian / Arnold Beichman. — New Brunswick, U.S.A.: Transaction Books, c1984. 100 p.; 24 cm. Includes index. 1. Wouk, Herman, 1915- — Political and social views. 2. Social history in literature. I. T.
PS3545.O98 Z55 1984   813/.54 19   *LC* 84-74   *ISBN* 087855498X

Wright, James Arlington, 1927-. • 2.12804
Collected poems, by James Wright. — [1st ed.]. — Middletown, Conn.: Wesleyan University Press, [1971] xiii, 215 p.; 24 cm. — I. T.
PS3545.R58 A6 1971   811/.5/4   *LC* 70-142727   *ISBN* 0819540315

Wright, James Arlington, 1927-.   **2.12805**
To a blossoming pear tree / James Wright. New York: Farrar, Straus and Giroux, [1977] p. cm. I. T.
PS3545.R58 T6   811/.5/4   *LC* 77-13577   *ISBN* 0374277982

Wright, James Arlington, 1927-.   **2.12806**
Two citizens [by] James Wright. — [1st ed.]. — New York: Farrar, Straus and Giroux, [1973] 59 p.; 22 cm. Poems. I. T.
PS3545.R58 T9   811/.5/4   *LC* 72-89887

PS3545 Richard Wright

Wright, Richard, 1908-1960.   **2.12807**
Richard Wright reader / edited by Ellen Wright and Michel Fabre; notes by Michel Fabre. — 1st ed. — New York: Harper & Row, c1978. xxiv, 886 p.: ill.; 20 cm. I. T.
PS3545.R815 A6 1978   813/.5/2   *LC* 77-76690   *ISBN* 0060147377

Wright, Richard, 1908-1960.   **2.12808**
Eight men. — Cleveland: World Pub. 1960. 250 p. Short stories. I. T.
PS3545.R815 E35   *LC* 61-5636

Wright, Richard, 1908-1960.   • **2.12809**
Lawd today. — New York: Walker, [1963] 189 p. I. T.
PS3545.R815 L38   *LC* 63-11769

Wright, Richard, 1908-1960.   **2.12810**
The long dream: a novel. — Chatham, N.J.: Chatham Bookseller, [1969, c1958] 384 p.; 23 cm. — I. T.
PZ3.W9352 Lo5 PS3545.R815 L6x   813/.5/2   *LC* 74-96383

Wright, Richard, 1908-1960.   • **2.12811**
Native son. With an introd.: How 'Bigger' was born, by the author. — New York: Harper & Row, [1969, c1940] xxxiv, 392 p.; 22 cm. — I. T.
PZ3.W9352 Nat23 PS3545.R815 N32x   813/.5/2   *LC* 79-86654

Baker, Houston A. comp.   **2.12812**
Twentieth century interpretations of Native son; a collection of critical essays. Edited by Houston A. Baker, Jr. — Englewood Cliffs, N.J.: Prentice-Hall, [1972] iii, 124 p.; 21 cm. — (Twentieth century interpretations) (A Spectrum book) 1. Wright, Richard, 1908-1960. Native son. I. T.
PS3545.R815 N33   813/.5/2   *LC* 72-8136   *ISBN* 0136099823

Wright, Richard, 1908-1960.   • **2.12813**
The outsider. [1st ed.]. — New York: Harper, [1953] 405 p.; 22 cm. — I. T.
PZ3.W9352 Ou   PS3545.R815 O87.   *LC* 53-5383

Wright, Richard, 1908-1960.   • **2.12814**
Uncle Tom's children. — New York: Harper & Row, [1969, c1938] 215 p.; 22 cm. I. T.
PZ3.W9352 Un5 PS3545.R815 U7x   813/.5/2   *LC* 76-86656

Wright, Richard, 1908-1960.   **2.12815**
American hunger / Richard Wright; afterword by Michel Fabre. — 1st ed. — New York: Harper & Row, c1977. 146 p. Autobiographical. Continues Black boy. 1. Wright, Richard, 1908-1960. 2. Authors, American — 20th century — Biography. I. T.
PS3545.R815 Z498 1977   PS3545R815 Z498 1977.   813/.5/2 B
LC 76-47248   *ISBN* 0060147687

Wright, Richard, 1908-1960.   • **2.12816**
Black boy; a record of childhood and youth. New York, Harper & Row [1966] 288 p. 19 cm. (A Perennial classic) Continued by American hunger. I. T.
PS3545.R815 Z5 1966   818.5203   *LC* 66-3155

Fabre, Michel.   **2.12817**
The unfinished quest of Richard Wright. Translated from the French by Isabel Barzun. — New York: Morrow, 1973. xx, 652 p.: illus.; 24 cm. 1. Wright, Richard, 1908-1960 — Biography. I. T.
PS3545.R815 Z6513   813/.5/2 B   *LC* 73-4227   *ISBN* 0688001637

Fishburn, Katherine, 1944-.   **2.12818**
Richard Wright's hero: the faces of a rebel–victim / by Katherine Fishburn. Metuchen, N.J.: Scarecrow Press, 1977. viii, 225 p.; 23 cm. Includes index. 1. Wright, Richard, 1908-1960 — Characters — Heroes. I. T.
PS3545.R815 Z66   813/.5/2   *LC* 76-51787   *ISBN* 0810810131

Gayle, Addison, 1932-.   **2.12819**
Richard Wright: ordeal of a native son / Addison Gayle. — 1st ed. — Garden City, N.Y.: Anchor Press/Doubleday, 1980. xvi, 342 p.; 24 cm. Includes index. 1. Wright, Richard, 1908-1960 — Biography. 2. Novelists, American — 20th century — Biography. I. T.
PS3545.R815 Z664   813/.52 B 19   *LC* 77-12854   *ISBN* 0385088779

Kinnamon, Keneth.   **2.12820**
The emergence of Richard Wright; a study in literature and society. — Urbana: University of Illinois Press, 1973 (c1972) 200 p.; 24 cm. 1. Wright, Richard, 1908-1960. I. T.
PS3545.R815 Z67   813/.5/2 B   *LC* 72-78023   *ISBN* 0252002016

Margolies, Edward.   • **2.12821**
The art of Richard Wright. With a pref. by Harry T. Moore. — Carbondale: Southern Illinois University Press, [1969] vi, 180 p.; 24 cm. — (Crosscurrents, modern critiques) 1. Wright, Richard, 1908-1960. I. T.
PS3545.R815 Z76   818/.5/208   *LC* 69-11506

Richard Wright, a collection of critical essays / edited by   **2.12822**
Richard Macksey and Frank E. Moorer.
Englewood Cliffs, N.J.: Prentice-Hall, c1984. x, 240 p.; 22 cm. — (Twentieth century views.) Includes index. 1. Wright, Richard, 1908-1960 — Criticism and interpretation — Addresses, essays, lectures. I. Macksey, Richard, 1931- II. Moorer, Frank E. III. Series.
PS3545.R815 Z815 1984   813/.52 19   *LC* 83-19285   *ISBN* 0137809247

Richard Wright: the critical reception / edited with an introd.   **2.12823**
by John M. Reilly.
[New York]: B. Franklin, c1978. xlvii, 400 p.; 24 cm. — (The American critical tradition; 6) 1. Wright, Richard, 1908-1960 — Criticism and interpretation — Addresses, essays, lectures. I. Reilly, John M.
PS3545.R815 Z82   813/.5/2   *LC* 78-5476   *ISBN* 0891021108

PS3545 Wy–Z

Wylie, Elinor, 1885-1928.   • **2.12824**
The venetian glass nephew. New York: Doran, 1925. 182 p. I. T.
PS3545.Y45 1925   811.5   *LC* 25-17616

Wylie, Elinor, 1885-1928.   • **2.12825**
Collected poems of Elinor Wylie. — New York: A. A. Knopf, 1932. xviii p., 2 l., 3-318, [1] p.: 2 port., double facsim.; 23 cm. 'First edition.' Foreword signed: William Rose Benét. I. Benét, William Rose, 1886-1950. ed. II. T.
PS3545.Y45 1932   811.5   *LC* 32-26577

Wylie, Elinor, 1885-1928.   • **2.12826**
Collected prose of Elinor Wylie. — 1st ed. — New York: Knopf, 1933. 879 p.; 23 cm. I. T.
PS3545.Y45 A16 1933   *LC* 33-27444

Wylie, Elinor, 1885-1928.   • **2.12827**
Mr. Hodge & Mr. Hazard / Elinor Wylie. — New Yok: Knopf, 1928. xi, 256 p.; 20 cm. I. T.
PZ3.W975 Mr   PS3545.Y45 M5.   *LC* 28-8711

Wylie, Elinor, 1885-1928.   • **2.12828**
The orphan angel / by Elinor Wylie. — New York: Knopf, 1926. 337 p.; 20 cm. I. T.
PZ3.W975 Or   PS3545.Y45 O7.   *LC* 26-20062

Hoyt, Nancy, 1902-.   • **2.12829**
Elinor Wylie, the portrait of an unknown lady / by Nancy Hoyt. — 1st ed. — Indianapolis; New York: Bobbs-Merrill, c1935. 203 p.: ill., facsim. ports. 1. Wylie, Elinor, 1885-1928. 2. Authors, American — 20th century — Biography. I. T.
PS3545.Y45 Z7   *LC* 35-4386

Young, Stark, 1881-1963.   • **2.12830**
So red the rose / Stark Young; with an introd. by Donald Davidson. — New York: Scribner, [1953] 431 p.; 20 cm. — (Modern standard authors) 1. United States — History — Civil War, 1861-1865 — Fiction. I. T.
PS3547.O65x PZ3.Y887So 3   813/.5/2   *LC* 53-11471

Zukofsky, Louis, 1904-1978.   **2.12831**
Prepositions: the collected critical essays of Louis Zukofsky. — Expanded ed. — Berkeley: University of California Press, c1981. x, 174 p.; 24 cm. Includes index. I. T.
PS3549.U47 A16 1981   814/.52 19   *LC* 80-23259   *ISBN* 0520043618

Zukofsky, Louis, 1904-1978.   **2.12832**
'A' / Louis Zukofsky. — Berkeley: University of California Press, c1978. 826 p.: music; 22 cm. 'A' 24 (L. Z. masque) contains excerpts from Handel's harpsichord suites 'to be performed against 4 simultaneously spoken monologues (p. 564-806) I. Handel, George Frideric, 1685-1759. Suites, harpsichord. Selections. II. T.
PS3549.U47 A68   811/.5/2   *LC* 76-7773   *ISBN* 0520032233

Ahearn, Barry. 2.12833
Zukofsky's 'A': an introduction / Barry Ahearn. — Berkeley: University of California Press, c1983. xv, 254 p.; 22 cm. 1. Zukofsky, Louis, 1904-1978. 'A'. I. T.
PS3549.U47 A6833 1983 811/.52 19 *LC* 81-13000 *ISBN* 0520043782

Zukofsky, Louis, 1904-1978. 2.12834
'A' 22 & 23 / Louis Zukofsky. — New York: Grossman, 1975. 60 p.; 18 cm. — I. T.
PS3549.U47 A734 811/.5/2 *LC* 75-17777 *ISBN* 0670005983

Zukofsky, Louis, 1904-1978. 2.12835
Arise, arise. — New York: Grossman, 1973 [c1962] 53 p.; 19 cm. Play. I. T.
PS3549.U47 A85 1973 812/.5/2 *LC* 72-90918 *ISBN* 0670132594

PS3551–3576 20th Century (1951–

PS3551 A

McCann, Garth. 2.12836
Edward Abbey / by Garth McCann. — Boise, Idaho: Boise State University, c1977. 47 p.; 21 cm. — (Boise State University Western writers series; no. 29) 1. Abbey, Edward, 1927- — Criticism and interpretation. I. T.
PS3551.B2 Z8 813/.5/4 *LC* 77-76321 *ISBN* 0884300536

Albee, Edward, 1928-. • 2.12837
All over; a play. — [1st ed.]. — New York: Atheneum, 1971. 111 p.; 22 cm. — I. T.
PS3551.L25 A5x 812/.5/4 *LC* 71-162965

Albee, Edward, 1928-. • 2.12838
The American dream, a play. — New York: Coward-McCann, [1961] 93 p.; 21 cm. — (Coward-McCann contemporary drama, CM-6) I. T.
PS3551.L25 A6x 812.54 *LC* 61-15067

Albee, Edward, 1928-. • 2.12839
A delicate balance; a play. [1st ed.] New York, Atheneum, 1966. 170 p. I. T.
PS3551.L25B3x *LC* 66-28773

Albee, Edward, 1928-. • 2.12840
The play, The ballad of the sad café / Carson McCullers' novella adapted to the stage by Edward Albee. — [1st ed.] Boston: Houghton Mifflin, 1963. 150 p.; 21 cm. I. McCullers, Carson, 1917-1967. Ballad of the sad café. 1963. II. T. III. Title: Ballad of the sad café.
PS3551.L25 B3x 812.54 *LC* 63-23325

Albee, Edward, 1928-. • 2.12841
Box and Quotations from Chairman Mao Tse-tung: two inter–related plays. — [1st ed.]. — New York: Atheneum, 1969. xi, 74 p.; 22 cm. 1. Mao, Tse-tung, 1893-1976. in fiction, drama, poetry, etc. I. T. II. Title: Box. III. Title: Quotations from Chairman Mao Tse-tung.
PS3551.L25 B6 812/.5/4 *LC* 69-15501

Albee, Edward, 1928-. 2.12842
Counting the ways and Listening: two plays / Edward Albee. 1st ed. — New York: Atheneum, 1977. 152 p.; 22 cm. I. T.
PS3551.L25 C6 812/.5/4 *LC* 76-52438 *ISBN* 0689107854

Albee, Edward, 1928-. 2.12843
The lady from Dubuque: a play / Edward Albee. — 1st ed. — New York: Atheneum, 1980. 161 p.; 22 cm. — I. T.
PS3551.L25 L3 1980 812/.54 19 *LC* 78-3192 *ISBN* 0689109253

Albee, Edward, 1928-. • 2.12844
Malcolm; [play] / adapted by Edward Albee from the novel by James Purdy. — 1st ed. — New York: Atheneum, 1966. 138 p.: ill., ports.; 22 cm. I. Purdy, James. Malcolm. II. T.
PS3551.L25 M3 1966 812/.5/4 *LC* 66-16352

Albee, Edward, 1928-. • 2.12845
Tiny Alice: a play. — New York: Atheneum, 1965. 190 p.; 22 cm. — I. T.
PS3551.L25T5x 812.54 *LC* 65-15904

Albee, Edward, 1928-. • 2.12846
Who's afraid of Virginia Woolf? A play. — [1st ed.]. — New York: Antheneum, 1962. 242 p.; 21 cm. — I. T.
PS3551.L25 W5x 812.54 *LC* 62-17691

Albee, Edward, 1928-. • 2.12847
The zoo story: The death of Bessie Smith; The sandbox; three plays / introduced by the author. — New York: Coward-McCann, [1960] 158 p.; 21 cm. I. T. II. Title: The death of Bessie. III. Title: The sandbox.
PS3551.L25 Z2x 812.54 *LC* 60-12478

Bigsby, C. W. E. comp. 2.12848
Edward Albee: a collection of critical essays / edited by C. W. E. Bigsby. — Englewood Cliffs, N.J.: Prentice-Hall, [1975] xii, 180 p.; 21 cm. (Twentieth century views) (A Spectrum book, S-TC-125) 1. Albee, Edward, 1928- — Criticism and interpretation — Addresses, essays, lectures. I. T.
PS3551.L25 Z583 812/.5/4 *LC* 74-30464 *ISBN* 013021311X

Paolucci, Anne. • 2.12849
From tension to tonic: the plays of Edward Albee. With a pref. by Harry T. Moore. — Carbondale: Southern Illinois University Press, [1972] xiv, 143 p.; 22 cm. — (Crosscurrents/modern critiques) 1. Albee, Edward, 1928- I. T.
PS3551.L25 Z8 812/.5/4 *LC* 75-179594 *ISBN* 0809305518

Anderson, Poul, 1926-. 2.12850
The broken sword. With an introd. by Lin Carter. . — New York: Ballantine Books, [1971, c1954] xvi, 207 p.; 18 cm. — (Adult fantasy) I. T.
PZ4.A549 Bt6 PS3551.N378 S9x 813/.5/4 *LC* 74-20329 *ISBN* 034502107X

Anderson, Poul, 1926-. 2.12851
Tau zero. — [1st ed.]. — Garden City, N.Y.: Doubleday, 1970. 208 p.; 22 cm. 'A short version of this novel appeared in Galaxy science fiction for June and August 1967 under title: To outlive eternity.' I. T.
PZ4.A549 Tau PS3551.N378 T3x 813/.5/4 *LC* 78-97645

Apple, Max. 2.12852
The oranging of America, and other stories / Max Apple. New York: Grossman Publishers, 1976. vii, 152 p.; 21 cm. I. T.
PZ4.A6476 Or PS3551.P56O7x 813/.5/4 *LC* 76-23436 *ISBN* 0670528013

Asimov, Isaac, 1920-. 2.12853
The caves of steel / by Isaac Asimov. — Garden City,N. Y.: Doubleday, 1954. -. 206 p.; 22 cm. — (Panther science fiction) I. T.
PS3551.S5 C39 *LC* 54-5418

Asimov, Isaac, 1920-. 2.12854
The gods themselves. — [1st ed.]. — Garden City, N.Y.: Doubleday, 1972. 288 p.; 22 cm. — I. T.
PS3551.S5 G6 PZ3.A8316 Go 813/.5/4 *LC* 72-180055

Asimov, Isaac, 1920-. 2.12855
I, robot / by Isaac Asimov. — [s.l.]: Gnome, 1950. 218 p. I. T.
PS3551 S56 I3 Fic

PS3552 B–Bara

Baldwin, James, 1924-. • 2.12856
Another country. — New York: Dial Press, 1962. 436 p.; 22 cm. I. T.
PS3552.A45 A6x *LC* 61-7367

Baldwin, James, 1924-. • 2.12857
Blues for Mister Charlie: a play. — New York: Dial Press, 1964. xv, 121 p.; 25 cm. I. T.
PS3552.A45 B5 *LC* 64-15223

Baldwin, James, 1924-. • 2.12858
Giovanni's room: a novel. — New York: Dial Press, 1956. 248 p.; 21 cm. I. T.
PS3552.A45 G5x *LC* 56-12125

Baldwin, James, 1924-. • 2.12859
Going to meet the man. — New York: Dial Press, 1965. 249 p.; 22 cm. I. T.
PS3552.A45 G65x *LC* 65-15331

Baldwin, James, 1924-. • 2.12860
Go tell it on the mountain. — New York: Knopf, 1953. 303 p.; 21 cm. I. T.
PS3552.A45 G6x *LC* 52-12199

Baldwin, James, 1924-. 2.12861
The price of the ticket: collected nonfiction, 1948–1985 / James Baldwin. — London: M. Joseph, 1985. xx, 690 p.; 24 cm. I. T.
PS3552.A45 P7 1985b 814/.54 19 *LC* 86-170185 *ISBN* 0718126408

Baldwin, James, 1924-. • 2.12862
Tell me how long the train's been gone: a novel — New York: Dial Press, 1968. 484 p.; 22 cm. I. T.
PS3552.A45 T4 *LC* 68-18639

Eckman, Fern Marja. • 2.12863
The furious passage of James Baldwin. — New York: M. Evans; distributed in association with Lippincott, Philadelphia, [c1966] 254 p.; 22 cm. 1. Baldwin, James, 1924- I. T.
PS3552.A45 Z5x   813.54   *LC* 66-11165

Kinnamon, Keneth, comp. 2.12864
James Baldwin: a collection of critical essays. — Englewood Cliffs, N.J.: Prentice-Hall, [1974] xii, 169 p.; 21 cm. — (Twentieth century views) (A Spectrum book) 1. Baldwin, James, 1924- — Criticism and interpretation. I. T.
PS3552.A45 Z76   818/.5/409   *LC* 74-6175   *ISBN* 0130555665

Bambara, Toni Cade. 2.12865
Gorilla, my love. — [1st ed.]. — New York: Random House, [1972] ix, 177 p.; 23 cm. — I. T.
PZ4.B2116 Go PS3552.A473   813/.5/4   *LC* 72-4091   *ISBN* 0394482018

Jones, LeRoi. • 2.12866
Tales. New York: Grove Press, [1967] 182 p.; 21 cm. I. T.
PS3552.A583 Ax   *LC* 67-27881

Jones, LeRoi. • 2.12867
Black magic: Sabotage, Target study, Black art; collected poetry, 1961-1967. — Indianapolis: Bobbs-Merrill, [1969] 225 p.; 22 cm. I. Sabotage II. Target study. III. Black art IV. T.
PS3552.A583 B5x   *LC* 69-13096

Baraka, Imamu Amiri, 1934-. • 2.12868
Dutchman and The slave, two plays. — New York: Morrow, 1964. 88 p.; 22 cm. Published under the author's earlier name: LeRoi Jones. I. Baraka, Imamu Amiri, 1934- The Slave. 1964. II. T. III. Title: The slave.
PS3519.O4545 D8   PS3552.A583 D8.   812.54   *LC* 64-22207

Baraka, Imamu Amiri, 1934-. 2.12869
Preface to a twenty volume suicide note: [poems] / by Le Roi Jones [i.e. I.A. Baraka]. — New York: Totem Press in association with Corinth Books, [1961] 47 p.; 21 cm. Published under the author's earlier name: LeRoi Jones. I. T.
PS3552.A583 P7   811.54   *LC* 61-14982

Jones, LeRoi. • 2.12870
The system of Dante's Hell: [a novel] — New York: Grove Press, [1965] 154 p.; 22 cm. I. T.
PS3552.A583 S9x   *LC* 65-23858

Benston, Kimberly W. 2.12871
Baraka: the renegade and the mask / Kimberly W. Benston. — New Haven: Yale University Press, 1976. xxi, 290 p.; 22 cm. — ([Yale College series; 14]) Includes index. 1. Baraka, Imamu Amiri, 1934- — Criticism and interpretation. I. T. II. Series.
PS3552.A583 Z4x   818/.5/409   *LC* 75-43302   *ISBN* 0300019580

Harris, William J., 1942-. 2.12872
The poetry and poetics of Amiri Baraka: the jazz aesthetic / William J. Harris. — Columbia: Universiy of Missouri Press, 1985. 174 p. Includes index. 1. Baraka, Imamu Amiri, 1934- Criticism and interpretation. 2. Jazz music in literature. 3. Music and literature I. T.
PS3552.A583 Z68 1985   811/.54 19   *LC* 85-1000   *ISBN* 082620483X

Hudson, Theodore R. 2.12873
From LeRoi Jones to Amiri Baraka: the literary works / [by] Theodore R. Hudson. — Durham, N.C.: Duke University Press, 1973. xiii, 222 p.; 25 cm. 1. Baraka, Imamu Amiri, 1934- I. T.
PS3552.A583 Z687 1973   818/.5/409   *LC* 72-97096   *ISBN* 0822302969

Imamu Amiri Baraka (Leroi Jones): a collection of critical 2.12874
essays / edited by Kimberly W. Benston.
Englewood Cliffs, N.J.: Prentice-Hall, c1978. xi, 195 p.; 21 cm. — (Twentieth century views) (A Spectrum book) 1. Baraka, Imamu Amiri, 1934- — Criticism and interpretation. I. Benston, Kimberly W.
PS3552.A583 Z7   818/.5/409   *LC* 78-8269   *ISBN* 0134513029

Sollors, Werner. 2.12875
Amiri Baraka/LeRoi Jones: the quest for a 'populist modernism' / Werner Sollors. — New York: Columbia University Press, 1978. xii, 338 p., [4] leaves of plates: ill.; 24 cm. Includes index. 1. Baraka, Imamu Amiri, 1934- Criticism and interpretation. I. T.
PS3552.A583 Z88   818/.5/409   *LC* 78-7499   *ISBN* 0231042264

PS3552 Bart–Baz

Barth, John. 2.12876
Chimera / by John Barth. — [1st ed.]. — New York: Random House, [1972] 308 p.; 22 cm. — I. T.
PS3552.A75 C5x   813/.5/4   *LC* 72-3389   *ISBN* 0394491399

Barth, John. • 2.12877
The floating opera. — [Rev.]. — Garden City, N.Y.: Doubleday, 1967. 252 p.; 24 cm. — I. T.
PS3552.A75 F5x   *LC* 67-12864

Barth, John. • 2.12878
Giles goat–boy; or, The revised new syllabus. — Garden City, N.Y.: Doubleday, 1966. xxxi, 710 p.; 24 cm. — I. T.
PZ4.B284 Gi 1966   PS3552.A75 Gx.   813/.5/4   *LC* 66-15666

Barth, John. 2.12879
Letters: a novel / John Barth. — New York: Putnam, c1979. xv, 772 p.; 24 cm. 'An old time epistolary novel by seven fictitious drolls & dreamers, each of which imagines himself actual.' I. T.
PS3552.A75 L4 1979   813/.5/4   *LC* 79-13503   *ISBN* 039912425X

Barth, John. • 2.12880
Lost in the funhouse: fiction for print, tape, live voice. — [1st ed.]. — Garden City, N.Y.: Doubleday, 1968. x, 201 p.; 24 cm. I. T.
PS3552.A75 L6 1968   PZ4.B284 Lo   *LC* 68-22615

Barth, John. 2.12881
Sabbatical: a romance / John Barth. — New York: Putnam, c1982. 366 p.; 24 cm. I. T.
PS3552.A75 S2 1982   813/.54 19   *LC* 81-22660   *ISBN* 0399127178

Barth, John. • 2.12882
The sot–weed factor. — [Rev. ed.]. — Garden City, N.Y.: Doubleday, 1967. x, 756 p.; 24 cm. — I. T.
PZ4.B284 So2   PS3552.A75Sx.   *LC* 67-10411

Critical essays on John Barth / [edited by] Joseph J. Waldmeir. 2.12883
Boston, Mass.: G.K. Hall, c1980. xi, 247 p.; 24 cm. — (Critical essays on American literature.) 1. Barth, John — Criticism and interpretation — Addresses, essays, lectures. I. Waldmeir, Joseph J. II. Series.
PS3552.A75 Z59 1980   813/.54 19   *LC* 80-21427   *ISBN* 081618254X

Glaser-Wöhrer, Evelyn. 2.12884
An analysis of John Barth's Weltanschauung: his view of life and literature / Evelyn Glaser-Wöhrer. — Salzburg: Univ. Salzburg, Inst. f. Engl. Sprache u. Literatur, 1978 (c1977). 282 p.; 23 cm. — (Salzburger Studien zur Anglistik und Amerikanistik; Bd. 5) Originally presented as the author's thesis, Salzburg. 1. Barth, John — Criticism and interpretation. I. T. II. Series.
PS3552.A75 Z64   813/.5/4   *LC* 78-317242

Harris, Charles B. 2.12885
Passionate virtuosity: the fiction of John Barth / Charles B. Harris. — Urbana: University of Illinois Press, c1983. xi, 217 p.; 24 cm. Includes index. 1. Barth, John — Criticism and interpretation. I. T.
PS3552.A75 Z68 1983   813/.54 19   *LC* 83-4976   *ISBN* 025201037X

Tharpe, Jac. 2.12886
John Barth; the comic sublimity of paradox. With a pref. by Harry T. Moore. — Carbondale: Southern Illinois University Press, [1974] xi, 133 p.; 22 cm. — (Crosscurrents/modern critiques) 1. Barth, John — Criticism and interpretation. I. T.
PS3552.A75 Z9   813/.5/4   *LC* 74-12263   *ISBN* 0809307022

Barthelme, Donald. 2.12887
Amateurs / Donald Barthelme. New York: Farrar, Straus and Giroux, c1976. viii, 183 p.; 21 cm. I. T.
PZ4.B285 Am PS3552.A76 A6x   813/.5/4   *LC* 76-40032   *ISBN* 0374103798

Barthelme, Donald. • 2.12888
City life. — New York: Farrar, Straus & Giroux, [1970] 168 p.: illus., ports.; 23 cm. I. T.
PZ4.B285 Ci PS3552.A76 C5x   813/.5/4   *LC* 74-113775

Barthelme, Donald. • 2.12889
Come back, Dr. Caligari / Donald Barthelme. — 1st ed. — Boston: Little, Brown, 1964. 183 p.; 21 cm. Short stories I. T.
PS3552.A76 C6x   *LC* 64-12099

Barthelme, Donald.   **2.12890**
Great days / Donald Barthelme. — New York: Farrar, Straus, Giroux, c1979. 172 p.; 21 cm. — I. T.
PZ4.B285 Gr 1979 PS3552.A76 G7x   813/.5/4   *LC* 78-10706
   ISBN 0374166285

Barthelme, Donald.   **2.12891**
Guilty pleasures. — New York: Farrar, Straus and Giroux, [1974] 165 p.: illus.; 23 cm. — I. T.
PZ4.B285 Gu PS3552.A76 G8x   813/.5/4   *LC* 74-13193   *ISBN* 0374167370

Barthelme, Donald.   • **2.12892**
Sadness. — New York: Farrar, Straus and Giroux, [1972] 183 p.: illus.; 23 cm. Short stories, chiefly reprinted from the New Yorker. I. T.
PZ4.B285 Sad PS3552.A76 S3x   813/.5/4   *LC* 72-84774   *ISBN* 0374253331

Barthelme, Donald.   **2.12893**
Snow White / Donald Barthelme. — 1st ed. — New York: Atheneum, 1967. 180 p. I. T.
PS3552.A76 S6x   *LC* 67-14324

Barthelme, Donald.   • **2.12894**
Unspeakable practices, unnatural acts. — New York: Farrar, Straus and Giroux, [1968] 170 p.; 21 cm. I. T.
PS3552.A76 U6x   *LC* 68-14918

Couturier, Maurice, 1939-.   **2.12895**
Donald Barthelme / Maurice Couturier and Régis Durand. — London; New York: Methuen, 1982. 80 p.; 20 cm. — (Contemporary writers.) 1. Barthelme, Donald — Criticism and interpretation. I. Durand, Régis. II. T. III. Series.
PS3552.A76 Z64 1982   813/.54 19   *LC* 82-12488   *ISBN* 0416318703

Gordon, Lois G.   **2.12896**
Donald Barthelme / by Lois Gordon. — Boston: Twayne Publishers, 1981. 225 p.: port.; 21 cm. — (Twayne's United States authors series. TUSAS 416) Includes index. 1. Barthelme, Donald — Criticism and interpretation. I. T. II. Series.
PS3552.A76 Z68   813/.54 19   *LC* 81-4240   *ISBN* 0805773479

Molesworth, Charles, 1941-.   **2.12897**
Donald Barthelme's fiction: the ironist saved from drowning / Charles Molesworth. — Columbia: University of Missouri Press, c1982. 89 p.; 21 cm. — (Literary frontiers edition.) 1. Barthelme, Donald — Criticism and interpretation. I. T. II. Series.
PS3552.A76 Z77 1982   813/.54 19   *LC* 81-69833   *ISBN* 0826203388

PS3552 Be–Bo

Beagle, Peter S.   **2.12898**
The fantasy worlds of Peter Beagle / Peter Beagle. — New York: Viking Press, 1978. 430 p.: ill.; 22 cm. 1. Fantastic fiction, American I. T.
PZ4.B3657 Fan 1978 PS3552.E13 F3x   813/.5/4   *LC* 78-14545
   ISBN 0670307254

Beattie, Ann.   **2.12899**
Chilly scenes of winter / Ann Beattie. — 1st ed. — Garden City, N.Y.: Doubleday, 1976. 280 p.; 22 cm. I. T.
PZ4.B3715 Ch PS3552.E177 C5x   813/.5/4   *LC* 75-44519   *ISBN* 0385116586

Beattie, Ann.   **2.12900**
Secrets and surprises: short stories / by Ann Beattie. — 1st ed. — New York: Random House, c1978. 307 p. I. T.
PZ4.B3715 Se PS3552.E177   PS3552E319 S4.   813/.5/4   *LC* 78-57098   *ISBN* 0394503147

Bell, Marvin.   **2.12901**
Stars which see, stars which do not see: poems / by Marvin Bell. 1st ed. — New York: Atheneum, 1977. 54 p.; 22 cm. I. T.
PS3552.E52 S7   811/.5/4   *LC* 76-39922   *ISBN* 068910779X

Bennett, Hal.   **2.12902**
Insanity runs in our family / Hal Bennett. — 1st ed. — Garden City, N.Y.: Doubleday, 1977. x, 299 p.; 22 cm. I. T.
PZ4.B4696 In PS3552.E546 I6x   813/.5/4   *LC* 76-48600   *ISBN* 0385066643

Berger, Thomas, 1924-.   **2.12903**
Arthur Rex: a legendary novel / Thomas Berger. — New York: Delacorte Press/Seymour Lawrence, c1978. ix, 499 p.; 24 cm. 1. Arthurian romances I. T.
PS3552.E719 A7   813/.54 19   *LC* 78-7241   *ISBN* 0440003628

Berger, Thomas, 1924-.   • **2.12904**
Little big man / by Thomas Berger. — New York: Dial, 1964. xxii, 437 p. I. T.
PZ4.B497 Li PS3552.E719 L5x   813/.5/4   *LC* 64-20284

Berger, Thomas, 1924-.   **2.12905**
Sneaky people: a novel / by Thomas Berger. — New York: Simon and Schuster, [1975] 315 p.; 22 cm. I. T.
PZ4.B497 Sn PS3552.E719 S6x   813/.5/4   *LC* 74-22320   *ISBN* 0671218972

Bester, Alfred.   **2.12906**
The demolished man / by Alfred Bester. — [1st ed.]. — Chicago: Shasta Publishers, [1953] 250 p.; 21 cm. I. T.
PZ4.B56De   PS3552.E77 D46.   813/.5/4   *LC* 53-7290

Betts, Doris.   **2.12907**
Beasts of the southern wild and other stories. — [1st ed.]. — New York: Harper & Row, [1973] 192 p.; 21 cm. — I. T.
PZ4.B565 Be PS3552.E84 B4x   813/.5/4   *LC* 73-4138   *ISBN* 0060103213

Betts, Doris.   **2.12908**
The river to Pickle Beach. — [1st ed.]. — New York: Harper & Row, [1972] 390 p.; 22 cm. — I. T.
PZ4.B565 Ri PS3552.E84 R5x   813/.5/4   *LC* 77-138779   *ISBN* 0061203653

Blackburn, Paul.   **2.12909**
The journals / Paul Blackburn; edited by Robert Kelly. — Los Angeles: Black Sparrow Press, 1975. 155 p.; 23 cm. I. T.
PS3552.L342 J68 1975   811/.5/4   *LC* 75-25714   *ISBN* 0876852401

Bly, Robert.   • **2.12910**
Silence in the snowy fields; poems. — [1st ed.]. — Middletown, Conn.: Wesleyan University Press, [1962] 60 p.; 21 cm. — I. T.
PS3552.L9 S5x   811.54   *LC* 62-18340

Nelson, Howard, 1947-.   **2.12911**
Robert Bly, an introduction to the poetry / Howard Nelson. — New York: Columbia University Press, 1984. xl, 261 p.; 21 cm. — (Columbia introductions to twentieth-century American poetry.) Includes index. 1. Bly, Robert — Criticism and interpretation. I. T. II. Series.
PS3552.L9 Z77 1984   811/.54 19   *LC* 83-14481   *ISBN* 023105310X

Bowles, Paul, 1910-.   **2.12912**
Collected stories, 1939–1976 / Paul Bowles; introd. by Gore Vidal. — Santa Barbara, CA: Black Sparrow Press, 1979. 417 p.; 24 cm. I. T.
PZ3.B6826 Co 1979 PS3552.O874Ax   813/.5/4   *LC* 79-4569
   ISBN 0876853971

Bowles, Paul, 1910-.   • **2.12913**
Let it come down. — New York: Random House, [1952] 311 p. I. T.
PS3552.O874L4x   *LC* 52-5141

Bowles, Paul, 1910-.   • **2.12914**
Without stopping: an autobiography / by Paul Bowles. — New York: Putnam, [1972] 379 p.: ill.; 23 cm. 1. Bowles, Paul, 1910- I. T.
PS3552.O874 Z5   818/.5/409 B   *LC* 72-175258

Boyle, T. Coraghessan.   **2.12915**
Descent of man: stories / by T. Coraghessan Boyle. — 1st ed. — Boston: Little, Brown, c1979. 219 p.; 22 cm. 'An Atlantic Monthly Press book.' I. T.
PZ4.B792885 De PS3552.O932 D4x   813/.5/4   *LC* 78-23812
   ISBN 0316104698

PS3552 Br–Bu

Bradley, David, 1950-.   **2.12916**
The Chaneysville incident: a novel / David Bradley. — 1st ed. — New York: Harper & Row, c1981. x, 432 p. 1. Underground railroad — Fiction. I. T.
PS3552.R226 C5 1981   PS3552R226 C5 1981.   813/.54 19   *LC* 80-8225   *ISBN* 0060104910

Bradley, David, 1950-.   **2.12917**
South Street / David Bradley. — New York: Grossman Publishers, 1975. 340 p.; 25 cm. I. T.
PZ4.B7996 So PS3552.R226 S6x   813/.5/4   *LC* 75-14343   *ISBN* 0670659355

Bradley, Marion Zimmer. 2.12918
The mists of Avalon / Marion Zimmer Bradley. — 1st ed. — New York: Knopf, 1982. xi, 876 p.; 25 cm. 1. Arthurian romances 2. Great Britain — History — Anglo-Saxon period, 449-1066 — Fiction. I. T.
PS3552.R228 M5 1982   813/.54 19   *LC* 82-47810   *ISBN* 0394524063

Bradshaw, Gillian, 1956-. 2.12919
Hawk of May / Gillian Bradshaw. — New York: Simon and Schuster, c1980. 313 p.; 22 cm. 1. Gawain (Legendary character) — Romances. I. T.
PZ4.B8112 Haw PS3552.R235 H3x   813/.54   *LC* 79-27135   *ISBN* 0671250930

Brennan, Maeve. 2.12920
Christmas Eve: 13 stories. — New York: Scribner, [1974] 244 p.; 24 cm. I. T.
PZ4.B8372 Ch PS3552.R38 C5x   813/.5/4   *LC* 73-1117   *ISBN* 0684136430

Brock, Van K. 2.12921
The hard essential landscape: poems / by Van K. Brock. — Orlando: University Presses of Florida, 1980 (c1979). viii, 92 p., [1] leaf of plates: port.; 23 cm. — (University of Central Florida contemporary poetry series) 'A University of Central Florida book.' I. T.
PS3552.R614 H3   811/.5/4   *LC* 79-21071   *ISBN* 0813006597

Broughton, T. Alan (Thomas Alan), 1936-. 2.12922
A family gathering / T. Alan Broughton. — 1st ed. — New York: Dutton, c1977. 184 p.; 22 cm. 'A Henry Robbins book.' I. T.
PZ4.B874538 Fam PS3552.R68138 F2x   813/.5/4   *LC* 76-45454

Broughton, T. Alan (Thomas Alan), 1936-. 2.12923
Far from home: poems / by T. Alan Broughton. — Pittsburgh: Carnegie-Mellon University Press, c1979. 82 p.; 22 cm. I. T.
PS3552.R68138 F37   *LC* 78-74989   *ISBN* 0915604264

Broumas, Olga, 1949-. 2.12924
Beginning with O / Olga Broumas; foreword by Stanley Kunitz. — New Haven [Conn.]: Yale University Press, 1977. 74 p.; 21 cm. — (Yale series of younger poets; v. 72) I. T. II. Series.
PS3552.R6819 B4   811/.5/4   *LC* 76-49697   *ISBN* 0300021062

Brown, Rosellen. 2.12925
Tender mercies / Rosellen Brown. — 1st ed. — New York: Knopf: distributed by Random House, 1978. 259 p.; 22 cm. — I. T.
PZ4.B87992 Te 1978 PS3552.R7 T4x   813/.5/4   *LC* 78-1315   *ISBN* 0394427416

Brown, Wesley, 1945-. 2.12926
Tragic magic: a novel / by Wesley Brown. — 1st ed. — New York: Random House, c1978. 169 p. I. T.
PZ4.B881182 Tr PS3552.R7382 T7x   813/.5/4   *LC* 78-57136   *ISBN* 0394502248

Budrys, Algis, 1931-. 2.12927
Rogue moon / Algis Budrys. — New York: Avon, 1978, c1960. 188 p.; 18 cm. I. T.
PS3552.U349 R6x   813/.5/4   *LC* 78-55738   *ISBN* 0380389509 pbl

Bullins, Ed. • 2.12928
Five plays: Goin' a Buffalo; In the wine time; A son, come home; The electronic nigger; Clara's ole man. — Indianapolis: Bobbs-Merrill, [1969,c1968] 282 p.: ill.; 22 cm. I. T.
PS3552.U45 A19 1969   *LC* 69-13087

Bullins, Ed. 2.12929
Four dynamite plays. — New York: W. Morrow, 1972 [c1971] 179 p.; 22 cm. I. T.
PS3552.U45 A19 1972   812/.5/4   *LC* 72-166348

Bullins, Ed. • 2.12930
The hungered one: early writings. — New York: Morrow, 1971. 149 p.; 22 cm. I. T.
PS3552.U45 Hx   *LC* 72-142390

Bullins, Ed. 2.12931
The theme is Blackness: 'The corner' and other plays. — New York: Morrow, 1973 [c1972] 183 p.; 21 cm. — I. T.
PS3552.U45 T5   812/.5/4   *LC* 72-10199   *ISBN* 0688000126

Bunting, Josiah. 2.12932
The lionheads: a novel. — New York: G. Braziller, [1972] ix, 213 p.; 22 cm. I. T.
PZ4.B9383 Li PS3552.U48 L5x   813/.5/4   *LC* 78-188356   *ISBN* 0807606324

Burroughs, William S., 1914-. 2.12933
Exterminator! A novel, by William S. Burroughs. — New York: Viking Press, [1973] 168 p.; 22 cm. 'A Richard Seaver book.' I. T.
PZ4.B972 Ex PS3552.U75 E9x   813/.5/4   *LC* 72-9736   *ISBN* 0670302813

Burroughs, William S., 1914-. 2.12934
[Junkie] Junky = originally published as Junkie under the pen–name of William Lee / William S. Burroughs; with an introd. by Allen Ginsberg. — 1st complete and unexpurgated ed. — New York: Penguin Books, 1977. xvi, 158 p.; 18 cm. I. T.
PZ4.B972 Ju3 PS3552.U75 J8x   813/.5/4 B   *LC* 76-48144   *ISBN* 0140043519

Burroughs, William S., 1914-. • 2.12935
Naked lunch. New York: Grove Press, [1962, c1959] 255 p.; 21 cm. I. T.
PZ4.B972Nak2 PS3552.U75N3 1962   *LC* 60-11097

Skerl, Jennie. 2.12936
William S. Burroughs / by Jennie Skerl. — Boston: Twayne Publishers, c1985. 127 p.: port.; 23 cm. (Twayne's United States authors series. TUSAS 438) Includes index. 1. Burroughs, William S., 1914- — Criticism and interpretation. I. T. II. Series.
PS3552.U75 Z85 1985   813/.54 19   *LC* 84-27899   *ISBN* 0805774386

Busch, Frederick, 1941-. 2.12937
Domestic particulars: a family chronicle / Frederick Busch. New York: New Directions Pub. Corp., 1976. 200 p.; 21 cm. (A New Directions book) I. T.
PZ4.B9767 Do PS3552.U814 D6x   813/.5/4   *LC* 76-8904   *ISBN* 081120605X

Busch, Frederick, 1941-. 2.12938
Hardwater country: stories / Frederick Busch. — 1st ed. — New York: Knopf, 1979. 209 p.; 22 cm. I. T.
PS3552.U814 H3 1979   813/.54 19   *LC* 78-23745   *ISBN* 0394505603

Busch, Frederick, 1941-. 2.12939
The mutual friend / Frederick Busch. — 1st ed. — New York: Harper & Row, c1978. 222 p.; 22 cm. 1. Dickens, Charles, 1812-1870. in fiction, drama, poetry, etc. 2. Dolby, George, d. 1900 — Fiction. I. T.
PZ4.B9767 Mu 1978 PS3552.U814 M8x   813/.5/4   *LC* 77-11793   *ISBN* 0060105275

PS3553 C

Cage, John. 2.12940
X: writings '79–'82 / John Cage. — 1st ed. — Middletown, Conn.: Wesleyan University Press; Scranton, Pa.: Distributed by Harper & Row, c1983. x, 187 p., [12] p. of plates: col. ill.; 23 cm. I. T.
PS3553.A32 X2 1983   818/.5407 19   *LC* 83-18275   *ISBN* 0819550906

Cage, John. • 2.12941
A year from Monday; new lectures and writings. [1st ed.] Middletown, Conn., Wesleyan University Press [1967] x, 167 p. 25 cm. I. T.
PS3553.A32Y4   818/.5/409   *LC* 67-24105

Calisher, Hortense. 2.12942
The collected stories of Hortense Calisher. — New York: Arbor House Pub. Co., c1975. xii, 502 p.; 24 cm. Distributed by Dutton, New York. I. T.
PZ4.C154 C03 PS3553.A4 Ax   813/.5/4   *LC* 75-11148   *ISBN* 0877951152

Calisher, Hortense, 1911-. • 2.12943
Extreme magic, a novella and other stories. — 1st ed. — Boston: Little, Brown, 1964. 260 p. I. T.
PS3553.A4 E9x   *LC* 64-15045

Calisher, Hortense, 1911-. • 2.12944
False entry: a novel / Hortense Calisher. — Boston: Little, Brown, c1961. 484 p. I. T.
PS3553.A4 F3x   [Fic]   *LC* 58-7861

Calisher, Hortense. 2.12945
The New Yorkers. — [1st ed.]. — Boston: Little, Brown, [1969] 559 p.; 24 cm. — I. T.
PZ4.C154 Ne PS3553.A4 N4x   813/.5/4   *LC* 69-15066

Calisher, Hortense, 1911-. • 2.12946
The railway police: and, The last trolley ride / Hortense Calisher. — Boston: Little, Brown, 1966. 248 p.; 21 cm. I. Calisher, Hortense, 1911- Last trolley ride. II. T. III. Title: The last trolley ride.
PS3553.A4 R3x   *LC* 66-16561

Campbell, John Wood, 1910-1971.   **2.12947**
Who goes there? Seven tales of science–fiction. [1st ed.] Chicago: Shasta Pub., 1951. 230p. I. T.
PS3553 A47 W5

Cantor, Jay.   **2.12948**
The death of Che Guevara: a novel / by Jay Cantor. — 1st ed. — New York: Knopf, 1983. 577 p.; 25 cm. 1. Guevara, Ernesto, 1928-1967 — Fiction. I. T.
PS3553.A5475 D4 1983   813/.54 19   LC 83-17487   ISBN 0394517679

Carver, Raymond.   **2.12949**
Will you please be quiet, please?: The stories of Raymond Carver / Raymond Carver. — New York: McGraw-Hill, c1976. 249 p.; 21 cm. I. T.
PZ4.C3336 Wi PS3553.A7894 W5x   813/.5/4   LC 75-23333
ISBN 0070101930

Casey, Michael, 1947-.   **2.12950**
Obscenities. — New Haven: Yale University Press, 1972. xii, 68 p.; 21 cm. — (Yale series of younger poets. v. 67) Poems. I. T. II. Series.
PS3553.A7934 O2   811/.5/4   LC 78-179470   ISBN 0300015461

Chasin, Helen.   **2.12951**
Casting stones / Helen Chasin. — 1st ed. — Boston: Little, Brown, [1975] viii, 47 p.; 21 cm. Poems. I. T.
PS3553.H34 C3   811/.5/4   LC 75-5550   ISBN 0316138223

Connell, Evan S., 1924-.   • **2.12952**
Mrs. Bridge / by Evan S. Connell, Jr. — New York: Viking Press, 1959. 254 p.; 21 cm. 'Portions of the text appeared in the Paris review under the title The beau monde of Mrs. Bridge and in Contact under the title Mademoiselle from Kansas City.' I. T.
PZ4.C753 Mi   PS3553O5 M55.   LC 59-5650

Connell, Evan S., 1924-.   • **2.12953**
Mr. Bridge [by] Evan S. Connell, Jr. — [1st ed.]. — New York: Knopf, [1969] 369 p.; 22 cm. A novel. I. T.
PZ4.C753 Mg PS3553.O5 M56x   813/.5/4   LC 69-11478

Coover, Robert.   **2.12954**
The public burning / Robert Coover. — New York: Viking Press, 1977. x, 534 p.; 24 cm. 'A Richard Seaver book.' 1. Rosenberg, Julius, 1918-1953 — Fiction. 2. Rosenberg, Ethel, 1916-1953 — Fiction. I. T.
PZ4.C78 Pu PS3553.O633 P8x   813/.5/4   LC 77-4923   ISBN 067058200X

Coover, Robert.   • **2.12955**
A theological position: plays. — [1st ed.]. — New York: Dutton, 1972. 172 p.; 22 cm. I. T.
PS3553.O633 T5   812/.5/4   LC 77-158593   ISBN 0525216006;
ISBN 0525045406

Andersen, Richard, 1946-.   **2.12956**
Robert Coover / by Richard Andersen. — Boston: Twayne Publishers, 1981. 156 p.: port.; 21 cm. — (Twayne's United States authors series; TUSAS 400) Includes index. 1. Coover, Robert — Criticism and interpretation. I. T.
PS3553.O633 Z53   813/.54 19   LC 80-26365   ISBN 0805773304

Corn, Alfred, 1943-.   **2.12957**
A call in the midst of the crowd: poems / by Alfred Corn. — New York: Viking Press, 1978. xii, 107 p.; 21 cm. — I. T.
PS3553.O655 C29 1978b   811/.5/4   LC 77-25485   ISBN 0670199796

Corn, Alfred, 1943-.   **2.12958**
Notes from a child of paradise / Alfred Corn. — New York: Viking Press, 1984. 107 p.; 24 cm. I. T.
PS3553.O655 N6 1984   811/.54 19   LC 83-40205   ISBN 0670517070

Crews, Harry, 1935-.   **2.12959**
A feast of snakes / Harry Crews. — 1st ed. — New York: Atheneum, 1976. 177 p.; 22 cm. I. T.
PZ4.C9175 Fe PS3553.R46 F4x   813/.5/4   LC 76-8206   ISBN 0689107293

Crews, Harry, 1935-.   **2.12960**
Florida frenzy / Harry Crews. — Gainesville: University Presses of Florida, c1982. 138 p.; 23 cm. 'A University of Florida book.' 1. Florida — Literary collections. I. T.
PS3553.R46 F5 1982   813/.54 19   LC 82-1997   ISBN 0813007267

A Grit's triumph: essays on the works of Harry Crews / edited   **2.12961**
by David K. Jeffrey.
Port Washington, N.Y.: Associated Faculty Press, 1983. 163 p.; 24 cm. (National university publications) 1. Crews, Harry, 1935- — Criticism and interpretation — Addresses, essays, lectures. I. Jeffrey, David K., 1942-
PS3553.R46 Z68 1983   813/.54 19   LC 83-11849   ISBN 0804693277

Cristofer, Michael.   **2.12962**
The shadow box / Michael Cristofer. — 1st ed. — New York: Drama Book Specialists, c1977. 102 p.; 22 cm. — I. T.
PS3553.R533 S5   812/.5/4   LC 77-21670   ISBN 091048290X

Crowley, John.   **2.12963**
Little, big / John Crowley. — 1st ed. — Toronto; New York: Bantam Books, c1981. 538 p.; 23 cm. — I. T.
PS3553.R597 L5   813/.54 19   LC 81-2483   ISBN 0553012665

Curley, Daniel.   **2.12964**
Love in the winter: stories / by Daniel Curley. — Urbana: University of Illinois Press, c1976. 118 p.; 21 cm. (Illinois short fiction) (An Illini book) I. T.
PZ4.C974 Lo PS3553.U65 L6x   813/.5/4   LC 76-7541   ISBN 0252005511

PS3554 D–Di

Dacey, Philip.   **2.12965**
Gerard Manley Hopkins meets Walt Whitman in heaven and other poems / Philip Dacey; wood engravings by Michael McCurdy. — 1st ed. — Great Barrington: Penmaen Press, c1982. 94 p.: ill.; 24 cm. 1. Hopkins, Gerard Manley, 1844-1889. in fiction, drama, poetry, etc. I. T.
PS3554.A23 G4 1982   811/.54 19   LC 84-149708   ISBN 0915778432

Davidson, Avram.   **2.12966**
The enquiries of Doctor Eszterhazy / by Avram Davidson. — [S.l.]: Warner, 1975. 1 v. I. T.
PS3554.A924 E6x   ISBN 0446769819

Del Vecchio, John M., 1948-.   **2.12967**
The 13th valley, a novel / by John M. Del Vecchio. — 1st ed. — New York: Bantam Books, 1982. 606 p.: maps; 24 cm. 1. Vietnamese Conflict, 1961-1975 — Fiction. I. T. II. Title: Thirteenth valley.
PS3554.E4327 A613 1982   813/.54 19   LC 81-70920   ISBN 0553050222

Delany, Samuel R.   **2.12968**
Babel–17 / Samuel R. Delany; with a new introduction by Robert Scholes. Boston: Gregg Press, 1976, c1966. x, 158 p.; 21 cm. (The Gregg Press science fiction series) Reprint of the 1969 ed. published by Sphere Books, London. I. T.
PS3554.E437 B3x   813/.5/4   LC 76-10741   ISBN 0839823282

Delany, Samuel R.   **2.12969**
Dhalgren / Samuel R. Delany; with a new introd. by Jean Mark Gawron. — Boston: Gregg Press, 1977, c1974. xliii, 879 p.; 22 cm. — (The Gregg Press science fiction series) Reprint of the ed. published by Bantam Books, New York. I. T.
PZ4.D338 Dh 1977 PS3554.E437   813/.5/4   LC 77-13712   ISBN 0839823967

Delany, Samuel R.   **2.12970**
The Einstein intersection / by Samuel R. Delany. New York: Garland Pub., 1975, c1967. 155 p.; 19 cm. (The Garland library of science fiction) Reprint of the ed. published by Ace Books, New York. I. T. II. Series.
PS3554.E437 E3x   813/.5/4   LC 75-402   ISBN 0824014073

Delany, Samuel R.   **2.12971**
Neveryóna, or, The tale of signs and cities / Samuel R. Delany. — 1st ed. — Toronto; New York: Bantam Books, 1983. ix, 385 p.; 21 cm. 'Some informal remarks toward the modular calculus, part four.' I. T. II. Title: Neveryóna.
PS3554.E437 N4 1983   813/.54 19   LC 82-90321   ISBN 055301434X

Delany, Samuel R.   **2.12972**
Tales of nevèryon / Samuel R. Delany. — [New York]: Bantam Books, 1979. 264 p. — (Bantam science fiction) I. T.
PS3554.E437 T3x   ISBN 0553123335

Dick, Philip K.   **2.12973**
The man in the high castle / Philip K. Dick, with a new introd. by Joseph Milicia. — Boston: Gregg Press, 1979, c1962. xxxiv, 239 p.; 21 cm. — (Gregg Press science fiction series) Reprint of the ed. published by Putnam, New York. I. T.
PZ4.D547 Man 1979 PS3554.I3 M3x   813/.5/4   LC 78-32091
ISBN 0839824769

Dick, Philip K.   2.12974
The three stigmata of Palmer Eldritch / Philip K. Dick. — Boston: Gregg
Press, 1979, c1965. xx, 278 p.; 21 cm. — (The Gregg science fiction series)
Reprint of the 1965 ed. published by Doubleday, New York, in series:
Doubleday science fiction; with a new introd. by Paul Williams. I. T.
PZ4.D547 Th 1979 PS3554.I3 T5x   813/.5/4   LC 79-18572   ISBN
0839824793

Dickey, James, 1923-.   • 2.12975
Poems, 1957–1967. — Middletown, Conn.: Wesleyan University Press, 1967.
xv, 299 p.; 24 cm. I. T.
PS3554.I32 A6 1967   PS3507.I268 A6 1967.   811.54   LC 67-15230

Dickey, James.   2.12976
The central motion: poems, 1968–1979 / James Dickey. — 1st ed. —
Middletown, Conn.: Wesleyan University Press; Scranton, Pa.: Distributed by
Harper & Row, c1983. x, 148 p.; 24 cm. — (Wesleyan poetry.) I. T. II. Series.
PS3554.I32 A6 1983   811/.54 19   LC 83-21734   ISBN 0819550914

Dickey, James.   • 2.12977
Deliverance. — Boston: Houghton Mifflin, 1970. 278 p.; 22 cm. — I. T.
PZ4.D5514 De PS3554.I32 D4x   813/.5/4   LC 71-100100

Dickey, James.   • 2.12978
Helmets, poems. — [1st ed.]. — Middletown, Conn.: Wesleyan University Press
[1964] 93 p. 21 cm. I. T.
PS3554.I32 H4x   811.54   LC 64-13610

Dickey, William.   • 2.12979
Interpreter's house / William Dickey. — [Columbus]: Ohio State University
Press, 1963. 94 p. Poems. I. T.
PS3554.I32Ix   811.54   LC 63-20466

Bowers, Neal, 1948-.   2.12980
James Dickey, the poet as pitchman / Neal Bowers. — Columbia: University of
Missouri Press, 1985. 86 p.; 21 cm. (Literary frontiers edition.) 1. Dickey,
James. 2. Dickey, James — Biography — Careers. 3. Authors, American —
20th century — Biography. 4. Copy writers — United States — Biography.
I. T. II. Series.
PS3554.I32 Z57 1985   811/.54 19   LC 84-21956   ISBN
0826204597

Calhoun, Richard James.   2.12981
James Dickey / by Richard J. Calhoun and Robert W. Hill. — Boston: Twayne
Publishers, c1983. 156 p., [1] p. of plates: port.; 23 cm. — (Twayne's United
States authors series. TUSAS 451) Includes index. 1. Dickey, James —
Criticism and interpretation. I. Hill, Robert W., 1941- II. T. III. Series.
PS3554.I32 Z59 1983   811/.54 19   LC 83-4380   ISBN 0805773916

The Imagination as glory: the poetry of James Dickey / edited   2.12982
and with an introduction by Bruce Weigl and T.R. Hummer.
Urbana: University of Illinois Press, c1984. 198 p.; 24 cm. 1. Dickey, James —
Criticism and interpretation — Addresses, essays, lectures. I. Weigl, Bruce,
1949- II. Hummer, T. R.
PS3554.I32 Z72 1984   811/.54 19   LC 83-5108   ISBN 0252011015

Didion, Joan.   2.12983
A book of common prayer / Joan Didion. New York: Simon and Schuster,
c1977. 272 p.; 22 cm. I. T.
PZ4.D56 Bo PS3554.I33   813/.5/4   LC 76-50067   ISBN
0671224913

Didion, Joan.   • 2.12984
Play it as it lays: a novel. — New York: Farrar, Straus & Giroux, [1970] 214 p.;
22 cm. — I. T.
PZ4.D56 Pl PS3554.I33 P5x   813/.5/4   LC 79-113779

Didion, Joan.   • 2.12985
Run River / Joan Didion. — New York: I. Obolensky, c1963. 264 p.; 22 cm.
I. T.
PS3554.I33 R8x   LC 62-18792

Joan Didion: essays & conversations / edited by Ellen G.   2.12986
Friedman.
Princeton, N.J.: Ontario Review Press; New York, NY: Distributed by Persea
Books, c1984. 190 p.; 24 cm. — (Ontario Review Press critical series.)
1. Didion, Joan — Criticism and interpretation — Addresses, essays, lectures.
I. Didion, Joan. II. Friedman, Ellen G., 1944- III. Series.
PS3554.I33 Z72 1984   813/.54 19   LC 84-5263   ISBN 086538035X

Disch, Thomas M.   2.12987
334 / Thomas M. Disch; with a new introd. by M. John Harrison. Boston:
Gregg Press, 1976, c1974. xiii, 269 p.; 22 cm. (The Gregg Press science fiction
series) Reprint of the ed. published by Avon, New York. I. T.
PZ4.D615 Th6 PS3554.I8 T5x   813/.5/4   LC 76-9057   ISBN
0839823312

PS3554 Do–Dz

Doctorow, E. L., 1931-.   2.12988
The book of Daniel; a novel, by E. L. Doctorow. — [1st ed.]. — New York:
Random House, [1971] 303 p.; 22 cm. — I. T.
PZ4.D6413 Bo PS3554.O3 B6x   813/.5/4   LC 78-140700   ISBN
0394462718

Doctorow, E. L., 1931-.   2.12989
Lives of the poets: six stories and a novella / by E.L. Doctorow. — 1st ed. —
New York: Random House, c1984. 145 p.; 24 cm. I. T.
PS3554.O3 L5 1984   813/.54 19   LC 84-42513   ISBN 0394525302

Doctorow, E. L., 1931-.   2.12990
Ragtime / by E. L. Doctorow. — 1st ed. — New York: Random House, [1975]
270 p.; 24 cm. I. T.
PZ4.D6413 Rag PS3554.O3 R3x   813/.5/4   LC 75-9613   ISBN
0394469011

E.L. Doctorow, essays and conversations / edited by Richard   2.12991
Trenner.
Princeton, N.J.: Ontario Review Press; New York: Distributed by Persea
Books, c1983. vii, 216 p.: ports.; 24 cm. — (Ontario Review Press critical
series.) 1. Doctorow, E. L., 1931- — Criticism and interpretation — Addresses,
essays, lectures. 2. Doctorow, E. L., 1931- — Interviews. I. Doctorow, E. L.,
1931- II. Trenner, Richard. III. Title: EL Doctorow, essays & conversations.
IV. Series.
PS3554.O3 Z63 1983   813/.54 19   LC 82-12569   ISBN
0865380236

Levine, Paul.   2.12992
E.L. Doctorow / Paul Levine. — London; New York: Methuen, 1985. 96 p.; 20
cm. (Contemporary writers.) 1. Doctorow, E. L., 1931- — Criticism and
interpretation. I. T. II. Series.
PS3554.O3 Z78 1985   813/.54 19   LC 85-4938   ISBN 0416348408

Donaldson, Stephen.   2.12993
The chronicles of Thomas Covenant, the Unbeliever / [by] Stephen Donaldson.
— New York: Holt, Rinehart and Winston, 1977. 3 v. 1. Fiction in English.
I. T. II. Title: Lord Foul's bane. III. Title: The Illearth War. IV. Title: The
Power that Preserves.
PS3554.O469 C5x   823/.9/1   ISBN 0006152392 pa

Duberman, Martin B.   2.12994
Visions of Kerouac: a play / by Martin Duberman. — 1st ed. — Boston: Little,
Brown, c1977. 142 p.; 21 cm. Play. 1. Kerouac, Jack, 1922-1969. in fiction,
drama, poetry, etc. I. T.
PS3554.U25 V5   812/.5/4   LC 77-23878   ISBN 0316194018. ISBN
0316194026 pbk

Dugan, Alan.   2.12995
[Works. 1983] New and collected poems, 1961–1983 / Alan Dugan. — 1st ed.
— New York, N.Y.: Ecco Press, 1983. 309 p.; 22 cm. — (American poetry
series. v. 29) I. T. II. Series.
PS3554.U33 1983   811/.54 19   LC 83-14014   ISBN 0880010304

Dugan, Alan.   2.12996
[Works. 1969] Collected poems. New Haven, Yale University Press, 1969. xii,
200 p. 22 cm. I. T.
PS3554.U33 A6 1969   811/.5/4   LC 76-89903   ISBN 0300011180

Dugan, Alan.   • 2.12997
Poems 3. — New Haven: Yale University Press, 1967. 61 p.; 21 cm. — I. T.
PS3554.U33 P6   811/.5/4   LC 67-24496

Dugan, Alan.   2.12998
Poems 4. — [1st ed.]. — Boston: Little, Brown, [1974] xiii, 58 p.; 21 cm. 'An
Atlantic Monthly Press book.' I. T.
PS3554.U33 P62   811/.5/4   LC 73-19676   ISBN 0316194700

PS3555 E

Elder, Lonne.   • 2.12999
Ceremonies in dark old men [by] Lonne Elder, III. — New York: Farrar, Straus
and Giroux, [1969] 179 p.; 21 cm. — I. T.
PS3555.L3 C4   812/.5/4   LC 70-87212

Ellin, Stanley, 1916-.   2.13000
The eighth circle. [New York: Random House, 1958] 210 p. 21 cm. (A Random
House mystery) I. T.
PS3555.L56 E5x   LC 58-9876

Ellison, Harlan.   2.13001
Deathbird stories: a Pantheon of modern gods / Harlan Ellison. — 1st ed. — New York: Harper & Row, [1975] xv, 334 p.; 22 cm. 1. Fantastic fiction, American 2. Science fiction, American I. T.
PZ4.E4695 De3 PS3555.L62   813/.5/4   *LC* 73-18663   *ISBN* 0060111763

Ellison, Harlan.   2.13002
Strange wine: fifteen new stories from the nightside of the world / Harlan Ellison. — 1st ed. — New York: Harper & Row, c1978. 262 p.; 22 cm. 1. Fantastic fiction, American I. T.
PZ4.E4695 St PS3555.L62 S8x   813/.5/4   *LC* 77-89060   *ISBN* 0060111135

Ellison, Ralph.   2.13003
Going to the territory / Ralph Ellison. — 1st ed. — New York: Random House, c1986. 338 p.; 22 cm. I. T.
PS3555.L625 G6 1986   818/.5409 19   *LC* 85-28117   *ISBN* 0394540506

Ellison, Ralph.   • 2.13004
Invisible man. New York, Random House [1952] 429 p. 22 cm. I. T.
PS3555.L625 I5 1952   *LC* 52-5159

Reilly, John M. comp.   2.13005
Twentieth century interpretations of Invisible man; a collection of critical essays. Edited by John M. Reilly. — Englewood Cliffs, N.J.: Prentice-Hall, [1970] vi, 120 p.; 21 cm. — (Twentieth century interpretations) A Spectrum book. 1. Ellison, Ralph. Invisible man. I. T. II. Title: Invisible man.
PS3555.L625 I537   813/.5/4   *LC* 70-126822   *ISBN* 0135054958

Hersey, John, 1914- comp.   2.13006
Ralph Ellison: a collection of critical essays / edited by John Hersey. — Englewood Cliffs, N.J.: Prentice-Hall, [1974] 180 p.; 21 cm. (Twentieth century views) (A Spectrum book) 1. Ellison, Ralph. I. T.
PS3555.L625 Z6x   818/.5/409   *LC* 73-16224   *ISBN* 0132743574

O'Meally, Robert G., 1948-.   2.13007
The craft of Ralph Ellison / Robert G. O'Meally. — Cambridge, Mass.: Harvard University Press, 1980. ix, 212 p.; 25 cm. Includes index. 1. Ellison, Ralph — Criticism and interpretation. I. T.
PS3555.L625 Z8   818/.5409   *LC* 80-12680   *ISBN* 0674175484

Erdrich, Louise.   2.13008
Love medicine: a novel / by Louise Erdrich. — 1st ed. — New York: Holt, Rinehart, and Winston, c1984. viii, 275 p.; 22 cm. 1. Indians of North America — North Dakota — Fiction. I. T.
PS3555.R42 L6 1984   813/.54 19   *LC* 84-3774   *ISBN* 0030706114

PS3556 F

Fair, Ronald L.   2.13009
We can't breathe [by] Ronald Fair. — [1st ed.]. — New York: Harper & Row, [c1972] 216 p.; 22 cm. — I. T.
PZ4.F1634 We PS3556.A36   813/.5/4   *LC* 72-156560   *ISBN* 0060112166

Farmer, Philip José.   2.13010
The lovers / Philip José Farmer. — 1st Ballantine Books hardcover ed. — New York: Ballantine Books, 1979. 219 p.; 22 cm. 'A Del Ray book.' I. T.
PZ4.F234 Lr PS3556.A72 L6x   813/.5/4   *LC* 78-19723   *ISBN* 0345280326

Feiffer, Jules.   • 2.13011
Little murders. — New York: Random House, [1968] 111 p.: illus.; 21 cm. — I. T.
PS3556.E42 L5   812/.5/4   *LC* 67-25077

Ferro, Robert.   2.13012
The family of Max Desir / Robert Ferro. — 1st ed. — New York: Dutton, c1983. 217 p.; 22 cm. I. T.
PS3556.E76 F3 1983   813/.54 19   *LC* 83-1433   *ISBN* 0525241973

Fetler, Andrew.   2.13013
To Byzantium: stories / by Andrew Fetler. — Urbana: University of Illinois Press, c1976. 112 p.; 20 cm. (Illinois short fiction) I. T.
PZ4.F42 To PS3556.F472 T6x   813/.5/4   *LC* 76-13854   *ISBN* 025200583X

Fiedler, Leslie A.   • 2.13014
The collected essays of Leslie Fiedler. — New York: Stein and Day, [1971] 2 v.; 22 cm. — I. T.
PS3556.I34 A16 1971   814/.5/4   *LC* 76-122420   *ISBN* 0812813332

Forché, Carolyn.   2.13015
Gathering the tribes / Carolyn Forché; foreword by Stanley Kunitz. — New Haven: Yale University Press, 1976. xv, 58 p.; 21 cm. (Yale series of younger poets. v. 71) I. T. II. Series.
PS3556.O68 G3   811/.5/4   *LC* 75-32672   *ISBN* 0300019831

Ford, Jesse Hill.   • 2.13016
The liberation of Lord Byron Jones. — [1st ed.]. — Boston: Little, Brown, [1965] 364 p.; 24 cm. (Atlantic Monthly Press book.) I. T. II. Series.
PZ4.F6983 Li   PS3556.O735 L5.   *LC* 65-17854

Friedman, Bruce Jay, 1930-.   2.13017
About Harry Towns. — [1st ed.]. — New York: Knopf, 1974. 180 p.; 22 cm. — I. T.
PZ4.F8988 Ab PS3556.R5   813/.5/4   *LC* 73-20762   *ISBN* 039448178X

Friedman, Bruce Jay. ed.   2.13018
Black humor. — New York,: Bantam Books, c1965. xi, 174 p.; 18 cm. I. T.
PS3556.R5 B5x   *LC* 65-22485

Friedman, Bruce Jay, 1930-.   • 2.13019
A mother's kisses: a novel. — New York: Simon and Schuster, 1964. 286 p.; 22 cm. — I. T.
PS3556.R5 M6x   *LC* 64-17495

Friedman, Bruce Jay, 1930-.   • 2.13020
Stern: a novel / Bruce Jay Friedman. — New York: Simon and Schuster, c1962. 191 p.; 21 cm. I. T.
PS3556.R5 S7x   [Fic]   *LC* 62-16385

Schulz, Max F.   2.13021
Bruce Jay Friedman, by Max F. Schulz. — New York: Twayne Publishers, [1974] 164 p.; 21 cm. — (Twayne's United States authors series, TUSAS 219) 1. Friedman, Bruce Jay, 1930- I. T.
PS3556.R5 Z9   813/.5/4   *LC* 72-9347   *ISBN* 0805702903

PS3557 G–Ge

Gaddis, William, 1922-.   • 2.13022
The recognitions: a novel. — [1st ed.]. — New York: Harcourt, Brace, [1955] 956 p.; 23 cm. — I. T.
PS3557.A28 R4x   *LC* 55-5247

In recognition of William Gaddis / edited with an introduction   2.13023
by John Kuehl and Steven Moore.
1st ed. — Syracuse, N.Y.: Syracuse University Press, 1984. xiii, 209 p.; 24 cm. 1. Gaddis, William, 1922- — Criticism and interpretation — Addresses, essays, lectures. I. Kuehl, John Richard, 1928- II. Moore, Steven, 1951-
PS3557.A28 Z74 1984   813/.54 19   *LC* 84-159   *ISBN* 0815623062

Gaines, Ernest J., 1933-.   2.13024
The autobiography of Miss Jane Pittman [by] Ernest J. Gaines. — New York: Dial Press, 1971. x, 245 p.: illus.; 24 cm. Novel. I. T.
PZ4.G1422 Au PS3557.A355 Ax   813/.5/4   *LC* 77-144380

Gaines, Ernest J., 1933-.   2.13025
Bloodline / by Ernest J. Gaines. — New York: Norton, 1976, c1968. 249 p.; 20 cm. — (Norton library; N798) I. T.
PZ4.G1422 Bl7 PS3557.A355 Bx   813/.5/4   *LC* 75-42393   *ISBN* 0393007987

Gaines, Ernest J., 1933-.   2.13026
A gathering of old men / Ernest J. Gaines. — New York: Knopf, 1983. p. cm. 213 p. I. T.
PS3557.A355 G3   PS3557A35 G3 1983.   813/.54 19   *LC* 82-49000   *ISBN* 0394514688

Gardner, John, 1933-.   2.13027
The art of living, and other stories / John Gardner; woodcuts by Mary Azarian. — 1st ed. — New York: Knopf: distributed by Random House, 1981. 309 p.: ill.; 22 cm. I. T.
PS3557.A712 A89 1981   813/.54 19   *LC* 80-20988   *ISBN* 0394516745

Gardner, John, 1933-.   2.13028
Grendel [by] John Gardner. Illustrated by Emil Antonucci. — [1st ed.]. — New York: Knopf, 1971. 174 p.: illus.; 22 cm. — I. T.
PZ4.G23117 Gr PS3557.A712 G7x   813/.5/4   *LC* 70-154911   *ISBN* 0394471431

Gardner, John, 1933-.　　　　　　　　　**2.13029**
Jason and Medeia / [by] John Gardner. — [1st ed.] New York: Knopf
[distributed by Random House], 1973. 354 p.: ill.; 25 cm. $7.95 1. Jason —
Romances. 2. Medea (Greek mythology) — Romances. I. T.
PS3557.A712 J3　　　811/.5/4　　　*LC* 72-11021　　　*ISBN* 0394483170

Gardner, John, 1933-.　　　　　　　　　**2.13030**
Nickel mountain; a pastoral novel [by] John Gardner. With etchings by
Thomas O'Donohue. — [1st ed.]. — New York: Knopf; [distributed by
Random House], 1973. 312 p.: illus.; 22 cm. — I. T.
PZ4.G23117 Ni PS3557.A712 N5x　　813/.5/4　　*LC* 73-7293　　*ISBN*
0394488830

Gardner, John, 1933-.　　　　　　　　　**2.13031**
October light / John Gardner; illustrated by Elaine Raphael and Don
Bolognese. 1st ed. — New York: Knopf: distributed by Random House, 1976.
433 p.: ill.; 22 cm. I. T.
PZ4.G23117 Oc PS3557.A712 O3x　　813/.5/4　　*LC* 76-13718　　*ISBN*
0394499123

Gardner, John, 1933-.　　　　　　　　　• **2.13032**
The sunlight dialogues [by] John Gardner. Illus. by John Napper. [1st ed.] New
York, Knopf; [distributed by Random House] 1972. xvi, 673 p. illus. 25 cm.
I. T.
PZ4.G23117 Su PS3557.A712 S8x　　813/.5/4　　*LC* 72-2226　　*ISBN*
039447144X

Cowart, David, 1947-.　　　　　　　　　**2.13033**
Arches & light: the fiction of John Gardner / David Cowart. — Carbondale:
Southern Illinois University Press, c1983. xii, 227 p.; 22 cm. Includes index.
1. Gardner, John, 1933- — Criticism and interpretation. I. T. II. Title: Arches
and light.
PS3557.A712 Z62 1983　　813/.54 19　　*LC* 83-335　　*ISBN*
0809311275

Morris, Gregory L.　　　　　　　　　**2.13034**
A world of order and light: the fiction of John Gardner / Gregory L. Morris. —
Athens: University of Georgia Press, c1984. 259 p.; 24 cm. Includes index.
1. Gardner, John, 1933- — Criticism and interpretation. 2. Philosophy in
literature I. T.
PS3557.A712 Z78 1984　　813/.54 19　　*LC* 83-9195　　*ISBN*
0820306967

Thor's hammer: essays on John Gardner / edited by Jeff　　**2.13035**
Henderson ... [et al.].
[Conway, Ark.]: University of Central Arkansas Press, 1985. iii, 197 p.: ill.; 23
cm. 1. Gardner, John, 1933- — Criticism and interpretation — Addresses,
essays, lectures. I. Henderson, Jeff, 1943-
PS3557.A712 Z89 1985　　813/.54 19　　*LC* 85-16373　　*ISBN*
0961514302

Garrett, George P., 1929-.　　　　　　　• **2.13036**
Death of the fox / [by] George Garrett. [1st ed.] Garden City, N.Y.: Doubleday,
1971. 739 p.; 24 cm. 1. Raleigh, Walter, Sir, 1552?-1618. in fiction, drama,
poetry, etc. I. T.
PZ4.G238 De PS3557.A72 D4x　　813/.5/4　　*LC* 79-139022

Garrett, George P., 1929-.　　　　　　　• **2.13037**
King of the mountain / George Garrett. — New York: Scribner, [1958, c1957]
184 p.; 21 cm. Short stories. I. T.
PS3557.A72 K5x

Garrett, George P., 1929-.　　　　　　　**2.13038**
The magic striptease [by] George Garrett. — [1st ed.]. — Garden City, N.Y.:
Doubleday, 1973. 272 p.; 22 cm. I. T.
PZ4.G238 Mag4 PS3557.A72 M3x　　813/.5/4　　*LC* 73-79668　　*ISBN*
0385050348

Garrett, George P., 1929-.　　　　　　　• **2.13039**
Which ones are the enemy? / George Garrett. — 1st ed. — Boston, Little,
Brown, 1961. 211 p. 21 cm. I. T.
PS3557.A72W5x 1961　　*LC* 61-5748

Garrett, Randall.　　　　　　　　　**2.13040**
Lord Darcy: a 3-in-1 volume / by Randall Garrett. — Book club ed. — Garden
City, N.Y.: Nelson Doubleday, [1983?] 600 p.; 22 cm. I. T. II. Title: Murder
and magic. III. Title: Too many magicians. IV. Title: Lord Darcy investigates.
PS3557.A7238 L6x

Gass, William H., 1924-.　　　　　　　• **2.13041**
In the heart of the heart of the country, and other stories [by] William H. Gass.
— [1st ed.]. — New York: Harper & Row, [1968] ix, 206 p.; 22 cm. I. T.
PZ4.G255 In　　PS3557.A77 I6.　　*LC* 68-11820

Gass, William H., 1924-.　　　　　　　• **2.13042**
Omensetter's luck: a novel / by William H. Gass. — New York: New American
Library, 1966. 304 p. 22 cm. I. T.
PS 3557 A84 O55 1966　　*LC* 66-13373

Geiogamah, Hanay, 1945-.　　　　　　　**2.13043**
New Native American drama: three plays / by Hanay Geiogamah; introd. by
Jeffrey Huntsman. — 1st ed. — Norman: University of Oklahoma Press, c1980.
xxiv, 133 p.: ill.; 22 cm. 1. Indians of North America — Drama I. T.
PS3557.E357 N4　　812/.54　　*LC* 79-4733　　*ISBN* 0806115866

PS3557 Gi–Gz

Gilbert, Sandra M.　　　　　　　　　**2.13044**
In the fourth world: poems / by Sandra M. Gilbert; with an introd. by Richard
Eberhart. — University: University of Alabama Press, c1979. ix, 69 p.; 22 cm.
— I. T.
PS3557.I34227 I5　　811/.5/4　　*LC* 78-11144　　*ISBN* 0817385274

Giovanni, Nikki.　　　　　　　　　**2.13045**
My house; poems. — New York: Morrow, 1972. xviii, 69 p.: illus.; 22 cm. —
I. T.
PS3557.I55 M9　　811/.5/4　　*LC* 72-116　　*ISBN* 0688000255

Giovanni, Nikki.　　　　　　　　　• **2.13046**
Gemini: an extended autobiographical statement on my first twenty–five years
of being a Black poet. — Indianapolis: Bobbs-Merrill, [1972, c1971] xii, 149 p.:
group port.; 22 cm. — I. T.
PS3557.I55 Z5 1972　　811/.5/4 B　　*LC* 75-161244

Glück, Louise, 1943-.　　　　　　　　**2.13047**
The house on marshland / Louise Glück. — New York: Ecco Press, 1975. 42 p.;
23 cm. (The American poetry series; v. 5) Poems. I. T.
PS3557.L8 H6　　811/.5/4　　*LC* 74-21764　　*ISBN* 0912946180

Godwin, Gail.　　　　　　　　　**2.13048**
Dream children: stories / by Gail Godwin. — 1st ed. — New York: Knopf,
1976. 242 p.; 22 cm. I. T.
PZ4.G576 Dr PS3557.O315　　813/.5/4　　*LC* 75-26722　　*ISBN*
0394478940

Gold, Herbert, 1924-.　　　　　　　　• **2.13049**
Fathers; a novel in the form of a memoir. — New York: Random House, [1967,
c1966] 308 p.; 22 cm. — I. T.
PS3557.O34 F3x　　*LC* 66-12012

Gold, Herbert, 1924-.　　　　　　　　• **2.13050**
Love & like / Herbert Gold. — New York: Dial Press, 1960. 307 p.; 21 cm.
Short stories. I. T.
PS3557.O34 L6x　　[Fic]　　*LC* 60-8397

Gold, Herbert, 1924-.　　　　　　　　• **2.13051**
The man who was not with it. 1st ed. Boston: Little, Brown, 1956. 314 p.; 21 cm.
I. T.
PS3557.O34 M3x　　*LC* 56-5623

Gold, Herbert, 1924-.　　　　　　　　• **2.13052**
My last two thousand years. — [1st ed.]. — New York, Random House [1972]
246 p. 22 cm. Autobiographical. 1. Gold, Herbert, 1924- I. T.
PS3557.O34 Z5　　813/.5/4　　*LC* 72-4087　　*ISBN* 0394470982

Gordone, Charles.　　　　　　　　　• **2.13053**
No place to be somebody; a black black comedy in three acts. Introd. by Joseph
Papp. — Indianapolis: Bobbs-Merrill, [1969] ix, 115 p.: illus.; 22 cm. — I. T.
PS3557.O72 N6　　812/.5/4　　*LC* 76-91390

Grau, Shirley Ann.　　　　　　　　　• **2.13054**
The black prince, and other stories. — [1st ed.]. — New York: Knopf, 1955
[c1954] 293 p.; 20 cm. — I. T.
PZ4.G775 Bl　　PS3557.R283 B5x.　　*LC* 55-5037

Grau, Shirley Ann.　　　　　　　　　**2.13055**
The condor passes. — [1st ed.]. — New York: Knopf, 1971. 421 p.; 22 cm. —
I. T.
PZ4.G775 Co　　PS3557.R283 C6x.　　813/.5/4　　*LC* 71-159831
　　ISBN 0394472497

Grau, Shirley Ann.　　　　　　　　　**2.13056**
Evidence of love / Shirley Ann Grau. 1st trade ed. — New York: Knopf:
distributed by Random House, 1977. 227 p.; 22 cm. I. T.
PZ4.G775 Ev3 PS3557.R283E8x　　813/.5/4　　*LC* 76-47920　　*ISBN*
0394411153

Grau, Shirley Ann.   • 2.13057
The hard blue sky. — [1st ed.]. — New York: Knopf, 1958. 466 p.; 22 cm. —
I. T.
PZ4.G775 Har   PS3557.R283 H3x.   LC 58-7562

Grau, Shirley Ann.   • 2.13058
The house on Coliseum Street / Shirley Ann Grau. — 1st ed. — New York:
Knopf, 1961. 242 p. I. T.
PZ4G775 Ho   PS3557R283 H6x.   LC 61-8532

Grau, Shirley Ann.   • 2.13059
The keepers of the house / Shirley Ann Grau. —[1st ed.]. — New York: Knopf,
1964. 309 p.; 22 cm. — I. T.
PZ4.G775 Ke   PS3557.R283 K4x.   LC 64-12306

Schlueter, Paul, 1933-.   2.13060
Shirley Ann Grau / by Paul Schlueter. — Boston: Twayne Publishers, 1981.
158 p.: port.; 21 cm. — (Twayne's United States authors series; TUSAS 382)
Includes index. 1. Grau, Shirley Ann — Criticism and interpretation. I. T.
PS3557.R283 Z86   813/.54 19   LC 80-29122   ISBN 0805773169

Greene, Harlan.   2.13061
Why we never danced the Charleston / Harlan Greene. — 1st ed. — New York:
St. Martin's/Marek, c1984. 151 p.; 22 cm. I. T.
PS3557.R3799 W5 1984   813/.54 19   LC 83-24680   ISBN
0312878818

Griffin, Susan.   2.13062
Woman and nature: the roaring inside her / by Susan Griffin. — 1st ed. — New
York: Harper & Row, c1978. 1 v. I. T.
PS3557.R48913 W6   811/.5/4   LC 77-3752   ISBN 0060115114

PS3558 H–He

Hacker, Marilyn, 1942-.   2.13063
Presentation piece. — New York: Viking Press, [1974] 115 p.; 23 cm. Poems.
I. T.
PS3558.A28 P7   811/.5/4   LC 73-12054   ISBN 067057399X

Hacker, Marilyn, 1942-.   2.13064
Separations / Marilyn Hacker. — 1st ed. — New York: Knopf: distributed by
Random House, 1976. viii, 109 p.; 21 cm. Poems. I. T.
PS3558.A28 S4   811/.5/4   LC 75-36789   ISBN 0394400704

Hanley, William, 1931-.   • 2.13065
Slow dance on the killing ground: a play. — New York: Random House, [1964]
135 p.; 22 cm. I. T.
PS 3558 A612 S63 1964   LC 65-11289

Harper, Michael S., 1938-.   2.13066
Dear John, dear Coltrane; poems by Michael S. Harper. [Pittsburgh] University
of Pittsburgh Press [1970] 88 p. 21 cm. (Pitt poetry series) I. T.
PS3558.A6248 D4   811/.5/4   LC 72-101194   ISBN 0822931966

Hass, Robert.   2.13067
Field guide. — New Haven: Yale University Press, 1973. xvii, 73 p.; 22 cm. —
(Yale series of younger poets. v. 68) I. T. II. Series.
PS3558.A725 F5   811/.5/4   LC 72-91296   ISBN 0300016506

Hass, Robert.   2.13068
Praise / Robert Hass. — New York: Ecco Press, 1979. 68 p.; 22 cm. — (The
American poetry series; v. 17) I. T.
PS3558.A725 P7   811/.5/4   LC 78-16016   ISBN 091294661X

Hawkes, John, 1925-.   • 2.13069
The blood oranges. — [New York]: New Directions, [1971] 271 p.; 22 cm. —
I. T.
PZ3.H3132 Bl PS3558.A82B5x   813/.5/4   LC 74-152516

Hawkes, John, 1925-.   2.13070
Death, sleep & the traveler. — [New York: New Directions Pub. Corp., 1974]
179 p.; 21 cm. — (A New directions book.) I. T.
PZ3.H3132 De   PS3558.A82 D4x.   813/.5/4   LC 73-89481
ISBN 0811205223

Hawkes, John, 1925-.   2.13071
Travesty / John Hawkes. — New York: New Directions Pub. Corp., 1976.
128 p.; 21 cm. I. T.
PZ3.H3132 Tr PS3558.A82T7x   813/.5/4   LC 75-26764   ISBN
0811205975

Berry, Eliot, 1949-.   2.13072
A poetry of force and darkness: the fiction of John Hawkes / by Eliot Berry. —
1st ed. — San Bernardino, Calif.: R. Reginald, the Borgo Press, 1979. 64 p.; 21

cm. (The Milford series. Popular writers today; v. 22 0163-2469) 1. Hawkes,
John, 1925- — Criticism and interpretation. I. T. II. Series.
PS3558.A82 Z56   813/.5/4   LC 79-282   ISBN 0893701327

Busch, Frederick, 1941-.   2.13073
Hawkes: a guide to his fictions. — [1st ed.]. — [Syracuse, N.Y.]: Syracuse
University Press, 1973. xxii, 192 p.; 23 cm. 1. Hawkes, John, 1925- I. T.
PS3558.A82 Z6   813/.5/4   LC 72-7765   ISBN 0815600895

Greiner, Donald J.   2.13074
Comic terror: the novels of John Hawkes [by] Donald J. Greiner. —
[Memphis]: Memphis State University Press, [1973] xix, 260 p.; 22 cm.
1. Hawkes, John, 1925- — Criticism and interpretation. 2. Comic, The I. T.
PS3558.A82 Z7   813/.5/4   LC 73-81555   ISBN 087870017X

O'Donnell, Patrick, 1948-.   2.13075
John Hawkes / by Patrick O'Donnell. — Boston: Twayne Publishers, c1982.
168 p.; 21 cm. — (Twayne's United States authors series. TUSAS 418) Includes
index. 1. Hawkes, John, 1925- — Criticism and interpretation. I. T. II. Series.
PS3558.A82 Z86 1982   813/.54 19   LC 81-7002   ISBN
0805773517

Hebert, Ernest.   2.13076
The dogs of March / Ernest Hebert. — New York: Viking Press, 1979. 255 p.;
23 cm. — I. T.
PZ4.H4444 Do 1979 PS3558.E277   813/.5/4   LC 78-26869   ISBN
0670277460

Hecht, Anthony, 1923-.   2.13077
Millions of strange shadows: [poems] / by Anthony Hecht. 1st ed. — New
York: Atheneum, 1977. 75 p.; 25 cm. I. T.
PS3558.E28 M5 1977   811/.5/4   LC 76-48223   ISBN 0689107846

Hecht, Anthony, 1923-.   • 2.13078
A summoning of stones. New York: Macmillan, 1954. 64 p. 22 cm. I. T.
PS3558.E28 S95 1954   LC 54-8533

Hecht, Anthony, 1923-.   2.13079
The Venetian vespers: poems / by Anthony Hecht. — 1st ed. — New York:
Atheneum, 1979. 91 p.; 25 cm. — I. T.
PS3558.E28 V4   811/.54   LC 79-52419   ISBN 0689110154

Heller, Joseph, 1923?-.   • 2.13080
Catch–22, a novel. — New York: Simon and Schuster, 1961. 443 p.; 22 cm.
1. World War, 1939-1945 — Fiction. I. T.
PS3558.E476 C3x   LC 61-12846

Heller, Joseph.   2.13081
Good as Gold / Joseph Heller. — New York: Simon and Schuster, c1979.
447 p. I. T.
PS3558.E476 G6x   PS3515E325 G66.   813/.5/4   LC 78-23894
ISBN 0671229230

Heller, Joseph.   2.13082
Something happened / Joseph Heller. — [1st ed.]. — New York: Knopf;
[distributed by Random House], 1974. -. 569 p.; 22 cm. — I. T.
PS3558.E476 S6x   PS3515 E325 S6.   813/.5/4   LC 74-8550
ISBN 0394465687

Critical essays on Joseph Heller / [edited by] James Nagel.   2.13083
Boston, Mass.: G.K. Hall, c1984. viii, 253 p.; 25 cm. (Critical essays on
American literature.) 1. Heller, Joseph — Criticism and interpretation —
Collected works. I. Nagel, James. II. Series.
PS3558.E476 Z62 1984   813/.54 19   LC 84-4656   ISBN
0816186855

Herbert, Frank.   2.13084
Dune. [1st ed.]. — Philadelphia: Chilton Books, [1965] xxvi, 412 p.: illus.; 24
cm. Sequel: Dune messiah. I. T.
PZ4.H5356 Dt PS3558.E63   LC 65-22547

PS3558 Hi–Hz

Higgins, George V., 1939-.   2.13085
A city on a hill / George V. Higgins. — 1st ed. — New York: Knopf:
distributed by Random House, 1975. 256 p.; 22 cm. I. T.
PZ4.H6365 Ci3 PS3558.I356   813/.5/4   LC 74-21308   ISBN
0394495403

Highsmith, Patricia, 1921-.   2.13086
Deep water. New York: Harper, 1957. 213 p. I. T.
PS3558.I366 D44   LC 57-8209

Hillerman, Tony.   **2.13087**
The blessing way. — [1st ed.]. — New York: Harper & Row, [1970] 201 p.; 22 cm. — I. T.
PZ4.H65 Bl PS3558.I45   813/.5/4   LC 73-96009

Hoch, Edward D., 1930-.   **2.13088**
Leopold's way: detective stories / by Edward D. Hoch; edited by Francis M. Nevins, Jr. & Martin H. Greenberg; introduction by Francis M. Nevins, Jr. — Carbondale: Southern Illinois University Press, c1985. xix, 339 p.; 22 cm. (Mystery makers.) 1. Detective and mystery stories, American I. Nevins, Francis M. II. Greenberg, Martin Harry. III. T. IV. Series.
PS3558.O337 L4 1985   813/.54 19   LC 84-27554   ISBN 0809312336

Holmes, John Clellon, 1926-.   **2.13089**
Go / John Clellon Holmes. Mamaroneck, N.Y.: P. P. Appel, 1977, c1952. xv, 311 p.; 22 cm. I. T.
PZ4.H753 Go7 PS3558.O3594   813/.5/4   LC 76-39701   ISBN 0911858342

Holthaus, Gary H., 1932-.   **2.13090**
Circling back / Gary H. Holthaus. — 1st ed. — Salt Lake City: Peregrine Smith Books, 1984. xvi, 186 p.: map; 22 cm. Map on lining papers. 1. West (U.S.) — History — Poetry. I. T.
PS3558.O43 C56 1984   813/.54 19   LC 83-20136   ISBN 0879051604

Horovitz, Israel.   • **2.13091**
The Indian wants the Bronx; a play. — [New York]: Dramatists Play Service, [1968] 39 p.; illus.; 20 cm. — I. T.
PS3558.O69 I5   812/.5/4   LC 68-7419

Howard, Richard, 1929-.   **2.13092**
Fellow feelings: poems / by Richard Howard. — 1st ed. — New York: Atheneum, 1976. 77 p.; 24 cm. — I. T.
PS3558.O8826 F4 1976   811/.54   LC 75-34063   ISBN 0689107056

Howard, Richard, 1929-.   **2.13093**
Two–part inventions: poems / by Richard Howard. — 1st ed. — New York: Atheneum, 1974. 87 p.; 24 cm. — I. T.
PS3558.O8826 T9 1974   811/.54   LC 74-77847   ISBN 068910619X

Howard, Richard, 1929-.   • **2.13094**
Untitled subjects; poems. — [1st ed.]. — New York: Atheneum, 1969. 88 p.; 24 cm. — I. T.
PS3558.O8826 U5   811/.54 19   LC 78-86548

PS3559 I

Innaurato, Albert, 1948-.   **2.13095**
Gemini; The transfiguration of Benno Blimpie: two plays / by Albert Innaurato. — Clifton, N.J.: J. T. White, c1978. 144 p.; 21 cm. I. Innaurato, Albert, 1948- Transfiguration of Benno Blimpie. 1978. II. T.
PS3559.N46 A19 1978   812/.54 19   LC 77-28515   ISBN 0883710234

Irving, John, 1942-.   **2.13096**
3 by Irving / John Irving. — 1st ed. — New York: Random House, c1980. xv, 718 p.; 24 cm. I. T.
PZ4.I714 Th PS3559.R8   813/.5/4   LC 79-5536   ISBN 0394509838

PS3560 J

Johnson, Charles Richard, 1948-.   **2.13097**
Faith and the good thing. — New York: Viking Press, [1974] 196 p.; 22 cm. — I. T.
PZ4.J6686 Fai PS3560.O3733   813/.5/4   LC 74-11   ISBN 0670305693

Johnson, Charles Richard, 1948-.   **2.13098**
Oxherding tale / Charles Johnson. — Bloomington: Indiana University Press, c1982. 176 p.; 24 cm. I. T.
PS3560.O3735 O96 1982   813/.54 19   LC 81-48629   ISBN 0253166071

Jones, Gayl.   **2.13099**
White rat: short stories / by Gayl Jones. — 1st ed. — New York: Random House, c1977. 178 p.; 22 cm. I. T.
PZ4.J7553 Wh PS3560.O483   813/.5/4   LC 77-6020   ISBN 0394499395

Jones, James, 1921-1977.   • **2.13100**
From here to eternity. New York: Scribner, 1951. 861 p.; 22 cm. I. T.
PS3560.O49 F7 1951   LC 51-9228

Jones, James, 1921-1977.   • **2.13101**
The pistol / James Jones. — New York: Scribner, [1959 c1958] 158 p.; 22 cm. 1. World War, 1939-1945 — Fiction I. T.
PS3560.O49 P57   PZ4.J77 Pi.   PS3519.O5 P5.   LC 59-5785

Jones, James, 1921-1977.   • **2.13102**
Some came running. New York Scribner [1957] 1266p. I. T.
PS3560 O49 S6   LC 57-8932

Jones, James, 1921-1977.   • **2.13103**
The thin red line / by James Jones. — New York: Scribner, [1962] 495 p.: map., music; 22cm. 1. World War, 1939-1945 — Fiction I. T.
PS3560.O49 T5x   LC 62-12099

Garrett, George P., 1929-.   **2.13104**
James Jones / by George Garrett. — 1st ed. — San Diego: Harcourt Brace Jovanovich, c1984. xxi, 218 p.: ill. 25 cm. — (HBJ album biographies.) Includes index. 1. Jones, James, 1921-1977. 2. Novelists, American — 20th century — Biography. I. T. II. Series.
PS3560.O49 Z66 1984   813/.54 B 19   LC 83-18665   ISBN 0151460493

Giles, James Richard, 1937-.   **2.13105**
James Jones / by James R. Giles. — Boston, MA: G. K. Hall, 1981. 228 p.: port.: 21 cm. — (Twayne's United States authors series; TUSAS 366) Includes index. 1. Jones, James, 1921-1977 — Criticism and interpretation. I. T.
P53560.O49 Z68   813/.54 19   LC 80-23295   ISBN 0805772936

Jordan, June, 1936-.   **2.13106**
Things that I do in the dark: selected poetry / by June Jordan. — 1st ed. — New York: Random House, c1977. xvii, 203 p.; 21 cm. — I. T.
PS3560.O73 A6 1977   811/.54 19   LC 76-53498   ISBN 039440937X

Jordan, June, 1936-.   **2.13107**
Living room: new poems / by June Jordan. — New York: Thunder's Mouth Press: Distributed by Persea Books, c1985. 134 p.; 22 cm. I. T.
PS3560.O73 L5 1985   811/.54 19   LC 84-24030   ISBN 093841027X

PS3561 K

Kenny, Maurice.   **2.13108**
Between two rivers: selected poems, 1956–84. — Fredonia, N.Y.: White Pine Press, 1987. 1 v. I. T.
PS3561.E5 B4x   ISBN 0934834733

Kesey, Ken.   **2.13109**
One flew over the cuckoo's nest / [by] Ken Kesey; text and criticism edited by John Clark Pratt. — New York: Viking Press, [1973] xviii, 560 p.; 21 cm. — (The Viking critical library) 1. Kesey, Ken. One flew over the cuckoo's nest. I. Pratt, John Clark. ed. II. T.
PZ4.K42 On5 PS3561.E667 O6x   813/.5/4   LC 72-78993   ISBN 0670526053

Kesey, Ken.   • **2.13110**
Sometimes a great notion: a novel / Ken Kesey. — New York: Viking Press, 1964. 628 p.; 22 cm. I. T.
PZ4.K42So PS3561.E667S6   [Fic]   LC 64-12227

Leeds, Barry H.   **2.13111**
Ken Kesey / Barry H. Leeds. — New York: F. Ungar Pub. Co., c1981. xii, 134 p.; 21 cm. — (Modern literature series.) Includes index. 1. Kesey, Ken — Criticism and interpretation. I. T. II. Series.
PS3561.E667 Z75   813/.54 19   LC 81-40466   ISBN 0804424977

Porter, M. Gilbert.   **2.13112**
The art of grit: Ken Kesey's fiction / M. Gilbert Porter. — Columbia: University of Missouri Press, 1982. 102 p.; 21 cm. — (Literary frontiers edition.) 1. Kesey, Ken — Criticism and interpretation. I. T. II. Series.
PS3561.E667 Z83 1982   813/.54 19   LC 81-69835   ISBN 082620368X

Tanner, Stephen L.   **2.13113**
Ken Kesey / by Stephen L. Tanner. — Boston: Twayne Publishers, c1983. 159 p., [1] leaf of plate: port.; 21 cm. — (Twayne's United States authors series. TUSAS 444) Includes index. 1. Kesey, Ken — Criticism and interpretation. I. T. II. Series.
PS3561.E667 Z88 1983   813/.54 19   LC 82-18717   ISBN 0805773835

Keyes, Daniel.   **2.13114**
Flowers for Algernon, by Daniel Keyes. — [1st ed.]. — New York: Harcourt, Brace & World, [1966] 274 p.; 21 cm. — I. T.
PS3561.E769 F6x   *LC* 66-12366

King, Stephen, 1947-.   **2.13115**
Salem's Lot / Stephen King. 1st ed. — Garden City, N.Y.: Doubleday, 1975. 439 p.; 22 cm. I. T.
PZ4.K5227 Sal PS3561.I483   813/.5/4   *LC* 73-22804   *ISBN* 0385007515

Kim, Richard E., 1932-.   • **2.13116**
The martyred, a novel. New York: G. Braziller, 1964. 316 p.; 21 cm. I. T.
PS3561.I52 M3   *LC* 64-10785

Klass, Philip, 1920-.   **2.13117**
The Wooden Star / William Tenn (pseud.). — New York: Ballantine Books, 1981. 251 p. — (Ballantine science fiction) I. T.
PS3561.L25 W6

Kopit, Arthur L.   • **2.13118**
Oh, Dad, poor Dad, Mama's hung you in the closet and I'm feelin' so sad: a pseudoclassical tragifarce in a bastard French tradition. — [1st ed.]. — New York: Hill and Wang, [1960] 89 p.; 21 cm. — (A Spotlight dramabook, SD2) I. T.
PS3561.O646 O35 1960   812/.54   *LC* 60-13996

Kosinski, Jerzy N., 1933-.   **2.13119**
Blind date / Jerzy Kosinski. — Boston: Houghton Mifflin, 1977. 236 p.; 24 cm. — I. T.
PZ4.K858 Bl PS3561.O8 B5x   813/.5/4   *LC* 77-21968   *ISBN* 0395257816

Kosinski, Jerzy N., 1933-.   **2.13120**
Cockpit: a novel / Jerzy Kosinski. — Boston: Houghton Mifflin, 1975. 248 p.; 24 cm. I. T.
PZ4.K858 Co PS3561.O8 C6x   813/.5/4   *LC* 75-4619   *ISBN* 0395206715

Kosinski, Jerzy N., 1933-.   **2.13121**
The devil tree, by Jerzy Kosinski. — [1st ed.]. — New York: Harcourt Brace Jovanovich, [1973] 208 p.; 21 cm. — I. T.
PZ4.K858 De PS3561.O8 D4x   813/.5/4   *LC* 72-88804   *ISBN* 0151253285

Kosinski, Jerzy N., 1933-.   • **2.13122**
The painted bird. Boston: Houghton Mifflin, 1965. 272 p.; 22 cm. I. T.
PS3561.O8 P3x   *LC* 65-16949

Kosinski, Jerzy N., 1933-.   • **2.13123**
Steps [by] Jerzy Kosinski. — New York. Random House, [1968] 147 p.; 22 cm. — I. T.
PZ4.K858 St PS3561.O8 S8x   813/.5/4   *LC* 68-28544

Lavers, Norman.   **2.13124**
Jerzy Kosinski / by Norman Lavers. — Boston: Twayne, c1982. 176 p.: port.; 21 cm. — (Twayne's United States authors series. TUSAS 419) Includes index. 1. Kosinski, Jerzy N., 1933- — Criticism and interpretation. I. T. II. Series.
PS3561.O8 Z75 1982   813/.54 19   *LC* 81-7045   *ISBN* 0805773525

Kotzwinkle, William.   **2.13125**
Doctor Rat / William Kotzwinkle. — 1st ed. — New York: Knopf: distributed by Random House, 1976. 243 p.; 22 cm. I. T.
PZ4.K872 Do PS3561.O85   813/.5/4   *LC* 75-36803   *ISBN* 0394400801

Kurtz, Katherine.   **2.13126**
The chronicles of the Deryni / by Katherine Kurtz. — [S.l.]: Doubleday, 1973. 3 v. I. T. II. Title: Deryni Rising. III. Title: Deryni Checkmate IV. Title: High Deryni
PS3561.U69 C5x

PS3562 L

Lafferty, R. A.   **2.13127**
Past master / R. A. Lafferty. — New York: Garland Pub., 1975, c1968. p. cm. (The Garland library of science fiction) Reprint of the ed. published by Ace Books, New York. I. T. II. Series.
PZ4.L1627 Pas6 PS3562.A28   813/.5/4   *LC* 75-416   *ISBN* 0824014219

Lardner, Ring, 1915-.   **2.13128**
The Lardners: my family remembered / Ring Lardner, Jr. 1st ed. — New York: Harper & Row, c1976. viii, 371 p.: ill.; 24 cm. Includes index. 1. Lardner, Ring, 1915- — Biography. 2. Lardner family I. T.
PS3562.A72 Z515   818/.5/209 B   *LC* 74-15837   *ISBN* 0060125179

Lathen, Emma, pseud.   **2.13129**
Banking on death / by Emma Lathen. — New York: Macmillan, 1961. 166 p. — (Cock Robin mystery) Holograph dedication to Lord Russell by the author. I. T. II. Series.
PS3562.A755 B3   *LC* 61-14708

Le Guin, Ursula K., 1929-.   **2.13130**
The dispossessed; an ambiguous Utopia [by] Ursula K. Le Guin. — [1st ed.]. — New York: Harper & Row, [1974] 341 p.; 22 cm. — I. T.
PZ4.L518 Di PS3562.E42   813/.5/4   *LC* 73-18667   *ISBN* 0060125632

Le Guin, Ursula K., 1929-.   **2.13131**
The left hand of darkness / by Ursula K. Le Guin. — 1st ed. — New York: Harper & Row, [1980] c1969. x, 213 p.; 22 cm. Originally published by Walker, New York. I. T.
PZ4.L518 Le 1980 PS3562.E42   813/.54   *LC* 79-2652   *ISBN* 0060125748

Le Guin, Ursula K., 1929-.   **2.13132**
The wind's twelve quarters: short stories / by Ursula K. Le Guin. — 1st ed. — New York: Harper & Row, [1975] 303 p.; 22 cm. I. T.
PZ4.L518 Wi PS3562.E42   813/.5/4   *LC* 75-6372   *ISBN* 0060125624

Levertov, Denise, 1923-.   **2.13133**
Collected earlier poems, 1940–1960 / Denise Levertov. — New York: New Directions Pub. Corp., 1979. x, 133 p.; 20 cm. Includes index. I. T.
PS3562.E8876 A17 1979   811/.5/4   *LC* 78-26199   *ISBN* 081120717X

Levertov, Denise, 1923-.   **2.13134**
[Poems. Selections] Poems, 1960–1967 / Denise Levertov. — New York: New Directions, 1983. 247 p.; 22 cm. Includes index. I. T.
PS3562.E8876 A6 1983   811/.54 19   *LC* 83-2263   *ISBN* 0811208583

Levertov, Denise, 1923-.   **2.13135**
[Poems. Selections] Poems 1968–1972 / Denise Levertov. — New York: New Directions Pub. Corp., 1987. 259 p.; 21 cm. Includes index. I. T.
PS3562.E8876 A6 1987   811/.54 19   *LC* 86-5389   *ISBN* 0811210049

Levine, Philip, 1928-.   **2.13136**
Ashes: poems new & old / by Philip Levine. — 1st Atheneum ed. — New York: Atheneum, 1979. 66 p.; 24 cm. I. T.
PS3562.E9 A9 1979   811/.5/4   *LC* 78-20596   *ISBN* 068910975X

Levine, Philip, 1928-.   **2.13137**
The names of the lost: poems / by Philip Levine. New York: Atheneum, 1976. 69 p.; 24 cm. I. T.
PS3562.E9 N3   811/.5/4   *LC* 76-11868   *ISBN* 068910748X

Levine, Philip, 1928-.   **2.13138**
1933; poems. — [1st ed.]. — New York: Atheneum, 1974. 68 p.; 24 cm. — I. T.
PS3562.E9 N5   811/.5/4   *LC* 73-88297   *ISBN* 068910586X

Levine, Philip, 1928-.   **2.13139**
7 years from somewhere: poems / by Philip Levine. — 1st ed. — New York: Atheneum, 1979. 70 p.; 24 cm. — I. T.
PS3562.E9 S4 1979   811/.5/4   *LC* 78-20595   *ISBN* 0689109741

Lorde, Audre.   **2.13140**
The black unicorn: poems / by Audre Lorde. — 1st ed. — New York: Norton, c1978. xi, 122 p.; 22 cm. I. T.
PS3562.O75 B55 1978   811/.5/4   *LC* 78-17569   *ISBN* 0393045080

Lorde, Audre.   **2.13141**
Coal / Audre Lorde. — 1st ed. — New York: Norton, c1976. 70 p.; 22 cm. Poems. I. T.
PS3562.O75 C6   811/.5/4   *LC* 76-4971   *ISBN* 0393044394

PS3563 M–Mac

McCaffrey, Anne.   **2.13142**
Dragonflight. — New York: Walker, [1969, c1968] x, 309 p.; 22 cm. — I. T.
PZ4.M1195 Dr PS3563.A255   813/.5/4   *LC* 69-14239

Macdonald, Dwight. 2.13143
Discriminations: essays & afterthoughts / Dwight Macdonald; new introduction by Norman Mailer. — New York, N.Y.: Da Capo Press, c1985. xvii, 466 p.; 22 cm. (A Da Capo paperback) Reprint. Originally published: New York: Grossman Publishers, 1974. I. T.
PS3563.A2765 D5 1985   814/.54 19   *LC* 85-11706   *ISBN* 030680252X

MacDonald, John D. (John Dann), 1916-1986. 2.13144
The deep blue good-by / John D. MacDonald. — Philadelphia: Lippincott, 1975, c1964. 200 p.; 23 cm. (His The Travis McGee series) I. T.
PZ3.M14439 Dh4 PS3563.A28   813/.5/4   *LC* 75-1092   *ISBN* 0397010907

McGuane, Thomas. 2.13145
An outside chance: essays on sport / Thomas McGuane. — 1st ed. — New York: Farrar, Straus, and Giroux, 1980. 243 p.; 22 cm. 1. McGuane, Thomas — Biography. 2. Sports stories 3. Authors, American — 20th century — Biography. I. T.
PS3563.A3114 Z472 1980   796   *LC* 80-36796   *ISBN* 0374104727

McKenna, Richard. 2.13146
Casey Agonistes, and other science fiction and fantasy stories. Introd. by Damon Knight. — [1st ed.]. — New York: Harper & Row, [1973] x, 150 p.; 22 cm. I. T.
PZ4.M1558 Cas PS3563.A3155 C3x   813/.5/4   *LC* 69-15281   *ISBN* 0060129115

McKillip, Patricia A. 2.13147
Riddle of stars / Patricia A. McKillip. — Garden City, N.Y.: Nelson Doubleday Inc., c1979. 604 p.; 22 cm. Trilogy in one volume I. T. II. Title: The riddle-master of Hed. III. Title: Heir of sea and fire. IV. Title: Harpist in the wind.
PS3563.A316 R5x

Peavy, Charles D. 2.13148
Larry McMurtry / Charles D. Peavy. — Boston: Twayne Publishers, c1977. 144 p.; 21 cm. — (Twayne's United States authors series; TUSAS 291) Includes index. 1. McMurtry, Larry. I. T.
PS3563.A319 Z8   813/.5/4   *LC* 77-11191   *ISBN* 0805771948

McNally, Terrence. • 2.13149
Sweet Eros, Next, and other plays / foreword by Philip Burton. — New York: Vintage Books, [1969] vi, 138 p.: ill.; 21 cm. — (A Vintage giant) I. T.
PS3563.A323 A6 1969   812/.5/4   *LC* 73-85626

McNally, Terrence. 2.13150
The Ritz and other plays / Terrence McNally. New York: Dodd, Mead, c1976. viii, 436 p.; 22 cm. I. T.
PS3563.A323 R5   812/.5/4   *LC* 76-17603   *ISBN* 0396073158

McPherson, James Alan, 1943-. 2.13151
Elbow room: stories / by James Alan McPherson. — 1st ed. — Boston: Little, Brown, c1977. ix, 241 p.; 22 cm. 'An Atlantic Monthly Press book.' I. T.
PZ4.M1732 El PS3563.A325   813/.5/4   *LC* 77-7268   *ISBN* 0316563285

McPherson, James Alan, 1943-. 2.13152
Hue and cry; short stories. — [1st ed.]. — Boston: Little, Brown, [1969] 275 p.; 21 cm. 'An Atlantic Monthly Press book.' I. T.
PZ4.M1732 Hu PS3563.A325   813/.5/4   *LC* 69-16969

PS3563 Mal–Me

Malamud, Bernard, 1914-. • 2.13153
A Malamud reader. — New York: Farrar, Straus and Giroux, [1967] xiv, 528 p.; 22 cm. I. T.
PS3563.A4 A6x   *LC* 67-28799

Malamud, Bernard. • 2.13154
The assistant; a novel. New York, Farrar, Straus and Cudahy [1957] 246 p. 22 cm. I. T.
PS3563.A4A79   *LC* 57-7397

Malamud, Bernard. 2.13155
Dubin's lives / Bernard Malamud. — New York: Farrar Straus Giroux, c1979. 361 p.; 24 cm. — I. T.
PZ4.M237 Du 1979 PS3563.A4 D8x   813/.5/4   *LC* 78-23897   *ISBN* 0374144141

Malamud, Bernard. • 2.13156
The fixer. New York: Farrar, Straus and Giroux, [1966] 335 p.; 22 cm. I. T.
PZ4.M237Fi PS3563.A4F5   *LC* 66-20164

Malamud, Bernard, 1914-. • 2.13157
Idiots first. — New York: Farrar, Straus, [1963] 212 p.; 21 cm. Short stories and a scene from a play. I. T.
PS3563.A4 I4x   *LC* 63-19562

Malamud, Bernard, 1914-. • 2.13158
The magic barrel. — New York: Farrar, Straus & Cudahy, [1958] 214 p.; 22 cm. Short stories. I. T.
PS3563.A4 M3x   *LC* 58-6841

Malamud, Bernard. • 2.13159
The natural. [1st ed.] New York: Harcourt, Brace, [1952] 237 p.; 21 cm. I. T.
PS3563.A4 N3 1952   813/.54 19   *LC* 52-9853

Malamud, Bernard. • 2.13160
A new life. New York: Farrar, Straus and Cudahy, [1960] 367 p.; 22 cm. I. T.
PS3563.A4 N4 1961   *LC* 61-11416

Malamud, Bernard. • 2.13161
Pictures of Fidelman: an exhibition. — New York: Farrar, Straus, Giroux, [1969] 208 p.; 22 cm. Fiction. I. T.
PS3563.A4 P5   813/.5/4   *LC* 69-15408

Malamud, Bernard. • 2.13162
The tenants. New York, Farrar, Straus and Giroux [1971] 230 p. 22 cm. 'First printing, 1971.' I. T.
PS3563.A4 T4   PZ4.M237 Te   813/.5/4   *LC* 71-165400   *ISBN* 0374272905

Field, Leslie A. comp. • 2.13163
Bernard Malamud and the critics. Edited with an introd. by Leslie A. Field and Joyce W. Field. — New York: New York University Press, 1970. xxvi, 353 p.; 24 cm. 1. Malamud, Bernard. I. Field, Joyce W., joint comp. II. T.
PS3563.A4 Z65   813/.5/4   *LC* 70-133016   *ISBN* 081472552X

Richman, Sidney. • 2.13164
Bernard Malamud. — New York: Twayne Publishers, [1967, c1966] 160 p.; 21 cm. — (Twayne's United States authors series, 109) 1. Malamud, Bernard. I. T.
PS3563.A4 Z87   813.54   *LC* 66-24147

Malzberg, Barry N. 2.13165
Herovit's world, by Barry N. Malzberg. — [1st ed.]. — New York: Random House, [1973] 209 p.; 22 cm. — I. T.
PZ4.M2615 He PS3563.A434   813/.5/4   *LC* 72-11447   *ISBN* 0394481410

Mamet, David. 2.13166
American buffalo: a play / by David Mamet. — New York: Grove Press, 1977, c1976. 106 p.; 21 cm. — (An Evergreen book) I. T.
PS3563.A4345 A8 1977   812/.5/4   *LC* 77-78079   *ISBN* 0802140998

Mamet, David. 2.13167
Reunion; Dark pony: two plays / by David Mamet. — 1st Evergreen ed. — New York: Grove Press: distributed by Random House, 1979. 53 p.; 21 cm. — (An Evergreen book; E-728) I. Mamet, David. Dark pony. 1979. II. T.
PS3563.A4345 R4   812/.5/4   *LC* 79-2319   *ISBN* 0394174593

Mamet, David. 2.13168
[Sexual perversity in Chicago] Sexual perversity in Chicago and The duck variations: two plays / by David Mamet. — 1st ed. — New York: Grove Press: distributed by Random House, 1978. 125 p.; 21 cm. I. Mamet, David. Duck variations. 1978. II. Duck variations. III. T.
PS3563.A4345 S4 1978   812/.5/4   *LC* 77-91885   *ISBN* 0394501616

Marshall, Paule, 1929-. 2.13169
The chosen place, the timeless people / Paule Marshall. — 1st Vintage Books ed. — New York: Vintage Books, 1984, c1969. 472 p.; 21 cm. — (Vintage contemporaries) I. T.
PS3563.A7223 C5 1984   813/.54 19   *LC* 84-40073   *ISBN* 0394726332

Martin, George R. R. 2.13170
The Armageddon rag / George R. R. Martin. — New York: Poseidon Press, c1983. 333 p.; 24 cm. I. T.
PS3563.A7239 A7 1983   813/.54 19   *LC* 83-13597   *ISBN* 0671475266

Matheson, Richard, 1926-. 2.13171
Bid time return / Richard Matheson. — New York: Viking Press, 1975. 278 p.; 22 cm. I. T.
PZ4.M429 Bi3 PS3563.A8355   813/.5/4   *LC* 74-4550   *ISBN* 0670162329

PS3563 Mi–Mz

Miller, Jason. 2.13172
That championship season. — [1st ed.]. — New York: Atheneum, 1972. xiii, 133 p.: illus.; 22 cm. — I. T.
PS3563.I412 T5 1972   812/.5/4   *LC* 72-87905

Minot, Stephen. 2.13173
Crossings: stories. — Urbana: University of Illinois Press, [1975] 166 p.; 21 cm. — (Illinois short fiction) I. T.
PZ4.M665 Cr PS3563.I475   813/.5/4   *LC* 74-14915   *ISBN* 0252005309

Mojtabai, A. G., 1937-. 2.13174
A stopping place / A. G. Mojtabai. — New York: Simon and Schuster, c1979. 349 p.; 23 cm. — I. T.
PZ4.M715 St PS3563.O374   813/.5/4   *LC* 79-18796   *ISBN* 0671230832

Momaday, N. Scott, 1934-. 2.13175
The gourd dancer: [poems] / N. Scott Momaday; drawings by the author. 1st ed. — New York: Harper & Row, c1976. 64 p.; 21 cm. I. T.
PS3563.O47 G6 1976   811/.5/4   *LC* 75-30338   *ISBN* 0060129824

Momaday, Natachee Scott. 2.13176
House made of dawn, by N. Scott Momaday. [1st ed.] New York, Harper & Row [1968] 212 p. 21 cm. I. T.
PS3563.O47H6x   *LC* 67-28820

Momaday, N. Scott, 1934-. 2.13177
The names: a memoir / by N. Scott Momaday. 1st ed. — New York: Harper & Row, c1976. 170 p.: ill.; 23 cm. 1. Momaday, N. Scott, 1934- — Biography — Youth. 2. Authors, American — 20th century — Biography. I. T.
PS3563.O47 Z52   813/.5/4 B   *LC* 75-138749   *ISBN* 0060129816

Schubnell, Matthias, 1953-. 2.13178
N. Scott Momaday, the cultural and literary background / by Matthias Schubnell. — 1st ed. — Norman: University of Oklahoma Press, c1985. viii, 336 p., [1] leaf of plates: port.; 22 cm. Includes index. 1. Momaday, N. Scott, 1934- 2. Authors, American — 20th century — Biography. 3. Kiowa Indians in literature. 4. Indians in literature I. T.
PS3563.O47 Z87 1985   818/.5409 19   *LC* 85-40479   *ISBN* 0806119519

Monaco, Richard. • 2.13179
Parsival: or, A knight's tale / Richard Monaco; illustrated by David McCall Johnston. — New York: Macmillan, 1977. 343 p.: ill.; 21 cm. Sequel: The Grail War. 1. Perceval (Legendary character) — Romances. I. T.
PZ4.M734 Par PS3563.O515   813/.5/4   *LC* 77-22150   *ISBN* 0025855409

Moore, C. L. (Catherine Lucile), 1911-. 2.13180
The best of C. L. Moore / edited and with an introd. by Lester del Rey. Garden City, N.Y.: Nelson Doubleday, c1975. 309 p.; 22 cm. 1. Science fiction, American I. T.
PZ4.M82 Be PS3563.O59   813/.5/4   *LC* 76-150242

Moore, C. L. 2.13181
Jirel of Joiry / C. L. Moore. New York: Ace, 1982. 212 p.; 18 cm. Originally published as: Black God's shadow. I. Moore, C. L. Black God's shadow. II. III. Title: Black God's shadow.
PS3563.O59 J5x   *ISBN* 0441385702

Morris, Willie. 2.13182
The last of the Southern girls / by Willie Morris. — [1st ed.]. — New York: Knopf, 1973. 287 p.; 22 cm. — I. T.
PZ4.M8795 Las PS3563.O8745   813/.5/4   *LC* 72-11040   *ISBN* 0394461010

Morrison, Toni. 2.13183
The bluest eye: a novel. — [1st ed.]. — New York: Holt, Rinehart and Winston, [1970] 164 p.; 22 cm. — I. T.
PZ4.M883 Bl PS3563.O8749 B5x   813/.5/4   *LC* 79-117270   *ISBN* 0030850746

Morrison, Toni. 2.13184
Song of Solomon / by Toni Morrison. — New York: Knopf, 1977. 337 p. I. T.
PZ4.M883 So PS3563.O8749 S6x   813/.5/4   *LC* 77-874   *ISBN* 0394497848

Morrison, Toni. 2.13185
Sula. — [1st ed.]. — New York: Knopf; [distributed by Random House], 1974 [c1973] 174 p.; 22 cm. — I. T.
PZ4.M883 Su PS3563.O8749 S8x   813/.5/4   *LC* 73-7278   *ISBN* 0394480449

Motley, Willard, 1909-1965. • 2.13186
Knock on any door. — New York; London: D. Appleton-Century company, inc., [1947] 5 p.l., 3-503, [1] p.; 22 cm. — I. T.
PZ3.M8573 Kn PS3563.O888 K5x   *LC* 47-3104

Motley, Willard, 1909-1965. • 2.13187
Let no man write my epitaph. — New York: Random House, [1958] 467 p.; 22 cm. — I. T.
PZ3.M8573 Le PS3563.O888 L4x   *LC* 58-7667

Murray, Albert. 2.13188
Train whistle guitar. — New York: McGraw-Hill, [1974] 183 p.; 22 cm. I. T.
PZ4.M97917 Tr PS3563.U764   813/.5/4   *LC* 73-20086   *ISBN* 0070440875

PS3564 N

Naylor, Gloria. 2.13189
Linden Hills / Gloria Naylor. — New York: Ticknor & Fields, 1985. 304 p. I. T.
PS3564.A895 L5 1985   813/.54 19   *LC* 84-16222   *ISBN* 0899193579

Naylor, Gloria. 2.13190
The women of Brewster Place / Gloria Naylor. — New York: Viking Press, 1982. 192 p.; 23 cm. I. T.
PS3564.A895 W6 1982   PS3564A895 W6 1982.   813/.54 19   *LC* 81-69969   *ISBN* 0670778559

Nichols, John Treadwell, 1940-. 2.13191
The Milagro beanfield war / by John Nichols; illus. by Rini Templeton. — [1st ed.] New York: Holt, Rinehart and Winston [1974] 445 p.: ill.; 24 cm. I. T.
PS3564.I274 M5 PS3564.I274   813/.54 19   *LC* 74-4409   *ISBN* 0030122511

Niven, Larry. 2.13192
The magic goes away / Larry Niven; [cover art by Boris, interior black and white drawings by Esteban Maroto]. — New York: Ace Books, 1978. 213 p.: ill.; 23 cm. — I. T.
PZ4.N734 Mag PS3564.I9M3x   813/.54   *LC* 79-124188   *ISBN* 0441515444

Niven, Larry. 2.13193
Tales of Known Space: the universe of Larry Niven. — New York: Ballantine Books, 1975. 240 p.; 18 cm. — (Ballantine science fiction) I. T.
PS3564.I9 T3x   813.54   *ISBN* 0345245636 Pbk

PS3565 O–O'B

Oates, Joyce Carol, 1938-. 2.13194
All the good people I've left behind / Joyce Carol Oates. — Santa Barbara: Black Sparrow Press, 1979, c1978. 227 p.; 23 cm. I. T.
PZ4.O122 Al 1979 PS3565.A8 A5x   813/.5/4   *LC* 78-22110   *ISBN* 0876853947

Oates, Joyce Carol, 1938-. 2.13195
Childwold / Joyce Carol Oates. — New York: Vanguard Press, c1976. 295 p.; 22 cm. I. T.
PS3565.A8 C5x   813/.5/4   *LC* 76-42086   *ISBN* 0814907776

Oates, Joyce Carol, 1938-. 2.13196
Crossing the border: fifteen tales / Joyce Carol Oates. — New York: Vanguard, 1976. viii, 256 p.; 22 cm. I. T.
PS3565.A8 C7x

Oates, Joyce Carol, 1938-. • 2.13197
A garden of earthly delights. New York, Vanguard Press [1967] 440 p. 22 cm. I. T.
PZ4.O122Gar PS3565.A8 G3x   *LC* 67-19288

Oates, Joyce Carol, 1938-. 2.13198
The hungry ghosts: seven allusive comedies. — Los Angeles: Black Sparrow Press, 1974. 200 p.; 23 cm. I. T.
PS3565.A8 H8x   813/.5/4   *LC* 74-2272   *ISBN* 0876852045

Oates, Joyce Carol, 1938-. 2.13199
Night-side: eighteen tales / Joyce Carol Oates. — New York: Vanguard Press, c1977. xii, 370 p.; 22 cm. — I. T.
PZ4.O122 Ni PS3565.A8 N5x   813/.5/4   *LC* 77-77416   *ISBN* 0814907938

Oates, Joyce Carol, 1938-. 2.13200
Son of the morning: a novel / Joyce Carol Oates. — New York: Vanguard Press, c1978. 382 p.; 22 cm. — I. T.
PZ4.O122 So 1978 PS3565.A8 S6x 813/.5/4 LC 78-56428 ISBN 0814907938

Oates, Joyce Carol, 1938-. • 2.13201
Them. — New York: Vanguard Press, [1969] 508 p.; 23 cm. — I. T.
PZ4.O122 Th PS3565.A8 T5x 813/.5/4 LC 74-89660 ISBN 0814906680

Oates, Joyce Carol, 1938-. 2.13202
The triumph of the spider monkey / Joyce Carol Oates. Santa Barbara: Black Sparrow Press, 1976. 89 p.: port.; 23 cm. I. T.
PZ4.O122 Tr PS3565.A8 T7x 813/.5/4 LC 76-50134 ISBN 0876852916

Oates, Joyce Carol, 1938-. • 2.13203
The wheel of love: and other stories. — New York: Vanguard Press, [1970] 440 p.; 23 cm. I. T.
PZ4.O122 Wh PS3565.A8 W5x 813/.5/4 LC 79-134661 ISBN 0814906761

O'Brien, Tim. 2.13204
Going after Cacciato: a novel / by Tim O'Brien. — New York: Delacorte Press/ S. Lawrence, c1978. 338 p.; 24 cm. 1. Vietnamese Conflict, 1961-1975 — Fiction. I. T.
PZ4.O1362 Go PS3565.B75 813/.5/4 LC 77-11723 ISBN 0440029481

PS3565 O'C–Oz

O'Connor, Edwin. • 2.13205
The edge of sadness. Boston, Little, Brown [1961] 460 p. 22 cm. I. T.
PZ4.O18Ed PS3565.C55E3 LC 61-5738

O'Connor, Edwin. • 2.13206
The last hurrah. Boston, Little, Brown [c1956] 427 p. 21 cm. I. T.
PZ4.O18Las PS3565.C55L3 LC 55-11224

Rank, Hugh. 2.13207
Edwin O'Connor. New York, Twayne Publishers [1974] 197 p. port. 21 cm. (Twayne's United States authors series, TUSAS 242) 1. O'Connor, Edwin. I. T.
PS3565.C55 Z85 813/.5/4 LC 73-17301 ISBN 0805705554

O'Connor, Flannery, 1925-1964. • 2.13208
The complete stories. — New York: Farrar, Straus and Giroux, [1971] xvii, 555 p.; 23 cm. — I. T.
PS3565.C57 Ax 813/.5/4 LC 72-171492 ISBN 0374127522

O'Connor, Flannery, 1925-1964. • 2.13209
The violent bear it away / Flannery O'Connor. — [New ed.]. — New York: Farrar, Straus & Giroux, c1960. 243 p.; 21 cm. — (Noonday; N-303) I. T. II. Series.
PS3565.C57 V5x ISBN 0374505241

O'Connor, Flannery, 1925-1964. • 2.13210
Wise blood. — New York: Farrar, Straus and Cudahy, [c1962] 232 p. I. T.
PS3565.C57 W5x LC 62-5776

O'Connor, Flannery. 2.13211
The habit of being: letters of Flannery O'Connor / edited and with an introd. by Sally Fitzgerald. — New York: Farrar, Straus, and Giroux, c1979. xviii, 617 p. Includes index. 1. O'Connor, Flannery — Correspondence. 2. Novelists, American — 20th century — Correspondence. I. Fitzgerald, Sally. II. T.
PS3565.C57 Z48 1978 PS3529C553 Z48 1979. 813/.5/4 B LC 78-11559 ISBN 0374167699

Asals, Frederick. 2.13212
Flannery O'Connor, the imagination of extremity / Frederick Asals. — Athens, Ga.: University of Georgia Press, c1982. 268 p.; ill.; 25 cm. Includes index. 1. O'Connor, Flannery — Criticism and interpretation. I. T.
PS3565.C57 Z52 1982 813./54 19 LC 81-10513 ISBN 0820305928

Browning, Preston M. 2.13213
Flannery O'Connor / [by] Preston M. Browning, Jr.; with a pref. by Harry T. Moore. — Carbondale: Southern Illinois University Press, [1974] x, 143 p.; 22 cm. — (Crosscurrents/modern critiques) 1. O'Connor, Flannery. I. T.
PS3565.C57 Z6 813/.5/4 LC 74-8849 ISBN 0809306727

Coles, Robert. 2.13214
Flannery O'Connor's South / Robert Coles. — Baton Rouge: Louisiana State University Press, c1980, 1981 printing. xxx, 166 p.; 24 cm. — (The Walter Lynwood Fleming lectures in southern history) 1. O'Connor, Flannery — Homes and haunts — Southern States. 2. Southern States — Intellectual life — 1865- I. T.
PS3565.C57 Z63 813/.5/4 LC 79-23057 ISBN 0807106550

Critical essays on Flannery O'Connor / [edited by] Melvin J. 2.13215
Friedman and Beverly Lyon Clark.
Boston, Mass.: G.K. Hall, c1985. ix, 227 p.; 25 cm. (Critical essays on American literature.) 1. O'Connor, Flannery — Criticism and interpretation — Addresses, essays, lectures. I. Friedman, Melvin J. II. Clark, Beverly Lyon. III. Series.
PS3565.C57 Z64 1985 813/.54 19 LC 84-27949 ISBN 0816186936

Drake, Robert, 1930-. • 2.13216
Flannery O'Connor; a critical essay. — [Grand Rapids]: Eerdmans, [1966] 48 p.; 22 cm. — (Contemporary writers in Christian perspective) 1. O'Connor, Flannery — Criticism and interpretation. I. T.
PS3565.C57 Z65 813.54 LC 66-22944

Driskell, Leon V., 1932-. 2.13217
The eternal crossroads; the art of Flannery O'Connor [by] Leon V. Driskell & Joan T. Brittain. — [Lexington]: University Press of Kentucky, [1971] xiv, 175 p.; 24 cm. 1. O'Connor, Flannery. I. Brittain, Joan T., 1928- joint author. II. T.
PS3565.C57 Z66 813/.5/4 LC 70-132828 ISBN 0813112397

Eggenschwiler, David, 1936-. 2.13218
The Christian humanism of Flannery O'Connor. — Detroit: Wayne State University Press, 1972. 148 p.; 24 cm. 1. O'Connor, Flannery. 2. Humanism, Religious I. T.
PS3565.C57 Z665 211/.6 LC 79-179560 ISBN 0814314635

Feeley, Kathleen. 2.13219
Flannery O'Connor: voice of the peacock. — New Brunswick, N.J.: Rutgers University Press, [1972] xii, 198 p.; 22 cm. 1. O'Connor, Flannery. I. T.
PS3565.C57 Z667 813/.5/4 LC 76-163958 ISBN 0813507057

Friedman, Melvin J. ed. • 2.13220
The added dimension: the art and mind of Flannery O'Connor / edited by Melvin J. Friedman and Lewis A. Lawson. — [1st ed.] New York: Fordham University Press [1966] xvii, 309 p.: port.; 24 cm. 1. O'Connor, Flannery — Criticism and interpretation — Addresses, essays, lectures. I. Lawson, Lewis A. joint ed. II. T. III. Title: The art and mind of Flannery O'Connor.
PS3565.C57 Z67 818.5409 LC 66-11070

Grimshaw, James A. 2.13221
The Flannery O'Connor companion / James A. Grimshaw, Jr. — Westport, Conn.: Greenwood Press, 1981. xx, 133 p.: ill.; 25 cm. Includes index. 1. O'Connor, Flannery — Criticism and interpretation. I. T.
PS3565.C57 Z68 813/.54 19 LC 80-26828 ISBN 0313210861

Muller, Gilbert H., 1941-. 2.13222
Nightmares and visions: Flannery O'Connor and the Catholic grotesque [by] Gilbert H. Muller. — Athens: University of Georgia Press, [1972] viii, 125 p.; 22 cm. 1. O'Connor, Flannery. 2. Grotesque in literature I. T.
PS3565.C57 Z79 813/.5/4 LC 75-184777 ISBN 0820302848

Shloss, Carol. 2.13223
Flannery O'Connor's dark comedies: the limits of inference / Carol Shloss. — Baton Rouge: Louisiana State University Press, c1980. 159 p.; 23 cm. — (Southern literary studies) Includes index. 1. O'Connor, Flannery — Criticism and interpretation. I. T. II. Series.
PS3565.C57 Z86 813/.54 LC 80-10609 ISBN 0807106747

Stephens, Martha. 2.13224
The question of Flannery O'Connor. — Baton Rouge: Louisiana State University Press, [1973] ix, 205 p.; 23 cm. — (Southern literary studies.) 1. O'Connor, Flannery — Criticism and interpretation. I. T. II. Series.
PS3565.C57 Z87 813/.5/4 LC 73-77656 ISBN 0807100005

O'Connor, Philip F. 2.13225
A season for unnatural causes: stories / by Philip F. O'Connor. — Urbana: University of Illinois Press, [1975] 116 p.; 21 cm. (Illinois short fiction) I. T.
PZ4.O194 Se PS3565.C64 813/.5/4 LC 75-2289 ISBN 025200518X

O'Hehir, Diana, 1929-. 2.13226
The power to change geography / Diana Ó Hehir. — Princeton, N.J.: Princeton University Press, c1979. 63 p.; 23 cm. (Princeton series of contemporary poets) Poems. I. T.
PS3565.H4 P6 811/.5/4 LC 78-13323 ISBN 0691063850. ISBN 0691013543 pbk

Oriard, Michael, 1948-.   **2.13227**
Dreaming of heroes: American sports fiction, 1868–1980 / Michael Oriard. —
Chicago: Nelson-Hall, c1982. viii, 382 p.; 22 cm. Includes index. 1. Sports
stories I. T.
PS3565.R53 D7 1982   813/.009/355 19   *LC* 81-16877   *ISBN*
0882295888

Ortiz, Simon J., 1941-.   **2.13228**
From Sand Creek: rising in this heart which is our America / by Simon J. Ortiz.
— New York, N.Y.: Thunder's Mouth Press, c1981. 93 p.; 24 cm. — I. T.
PS3565.R77 F7 1981   811/.54 19   *LC* 81-8795   *ISBN* 0938410032

Ortiz, Simon J., 1941-.   **2.13229**
Going for the rain: poems / by Simon J. Ortiz. 1st ed. — New York: Harper &
Row, c1976. xiv, 112 p.; 22 cm. Poems. I. T.
PS3565.R77 G6   811/.5/4   *LC* 76-8707   *ISBN* 0064515117

Osborn, Carolyn, 1934-.   **2.13230**
A horse of another color / stories by Carolyn Osborn. — Urbana: University of
Illinois Press, c1977. 130 p.; 21 cm. — (Illinois short fiction) I. T.
PZ4.O7678 Ho PS3565.S348 H6x   813/.5/4   *LC* 77-21724   *ISBN*
0252006712

Ozick, Cynthia.   **2.13231**
The cannibal galaxy / Cynthia Ozick. — 1st ed. — New York: Knopf, 1983.
161 p.; 22 cm. I. T.
PS3565.Z5 C3 1983   813/.54 19   *LC* 82-48719   *ISBN* 039452943X

PS3566 P–Pi

Packer, Nancy Huddleston.   **2.13232**
Small moments: stories / by Nancy Huddleston Packer. — Urbana: University
of Illinois Press, c1976. 155 p.; 21 cm. (Illinois short fiction) I. T.
PZ4.P1185 Sm PS3566.A318 S6x   813/.5/4   *LC* 76-7601   *ISBN*
0252006151

Paley, Grace.   **2.13233**
Enormous changes at the last minute: stories. — New York: Farrar, Straus,
Giroux, [1974] 198 p.; 22 cm. I. T.
PZ4.P158 En PS3566.A46 E6x   813/.5/4   *LC* 73-87691   *ISBN*
0374148511

Paley, Grace.   **• 2.13234**
The little disturbances of man. New York: Viking Press, [1968] 189 p.; 21 cm.
Short stories. I. T.
PS3566.A46 L5

Pangborn, Edgar.   **2.13235**
Davy. — New York: St. Martin's Press, 1964. 308 p. I. T.
PS3566.A56 D3x

Pangborn, Edgar.   **2.13236**
The trial of Callista Blake / by Edgar Pangborn. — New York: St. Martin's
Press [1962, c1961] 304 p. A novel. I. T.
PS3566.A56 T7x   813.54   *LC* 61-13391

Patrick, Robert, 1937-.   **2.13237**
Cheep theatricks! / introd.: Lanford Wilson. — New York: Winter House,
[1972] 358 p.: ill.; 22 cm. — (The Winter repertory, 5) I. T.
PS3566.A786 C5   812/.5/4   *LC* 75-186999   *ISBN* 0878060286

Paxson, Diana L.   **2.13238**
Brisingamen / Diana L. Paxson. New York: Berkley, 1984. Paperback.
1. Fantastic fiction I. T.
PS3566.A9 B7x   *ISBN* 0425072983

Percy, Walker, 1916-.   **2.13239**
Conversations with Walker Percy / edited by Lewis A. Lawson and Victor A.
Kramer. — Jackson: University Press of Mississippi, c1985. xiv, 325 p.: port.;
24 cm. (Literary conversations series.) Includes index. 1. Percy, Walker, 1916-
— Interviews. 2. Novelists, American — 20th century — Interviews.
I. Lawson, Lewis A. II. Kramer, Victor A. III. T. IV. Series.
PS3566.E6912 C6 1985   813/.54 19   *LC* 84-40715   *ISBN*
0878052518

Percy, Walker, 1916-.   **2.13240**
Lancelot / Walker Percy. New York: Farrar, Straus and Giroux, 1977. 257 p.;
22 cm. I. T.
PZ4.P43115 Lan PS3566.E6912 L3x   813/.5/4   *LC* 76-57197
     ISBN 0374183139

Percy, Walker, 1916-.   **• 2.13241**
The last gentleman. — New York: Farrar, Straus and Giroux, [1966] 409 p.; 22
cm. I. T.
PS3566.E6912 L4x   *LC* 66-18861

Percy, Walker, 1916-.   **• 2.13242**
Love in the ruins; the adventures of a bad Catholic at a time near the end of the
world. — New York: Farrar, Straus & Giroux, [1971] 403 p.; 22 cm. — I. T.
PZ4.P43115 Lo PS3566.E6912 L6x   813/.5/4   *LC* 71-143301
     ISBN 0374193029

Percy, Walker, 1916-.   **• 2.13243**
The moviegoer. — [1st ed.] New York: Knopf, 1961. 241 p.; 21 cm. I. T.
PS3566.E6912 M6x   *LC* 61-7754

The Art of Walker Percy: stratagems for being / edited by   **2.13244**
Panthea Reid Broughton.
Baton Rouge: Louisiana State University Press, c1979. xix, 311 p.; 23 cm. —
(Southern literary studies.) 1. Percy, Walker, 1916- — Criticism and
interpretation — Addresses, essays, lectures. I. Broughton, Panthea Reid.
II. Series.
PS3566.E6912 Z53   813/.5/4   *LC* 78-27494   *ISBN* 0807105600

Coles, Robert.   **2.13245**
Walker Percy, an American search / by Robert Coles. — 1st ed. — Boston:
Little, Brown, 1979 (c1978). xx, 250 p.; 24 cm. 'An Atlantic-Monthly Press
book.' Includes index. 1. Percy, Walker, 1916- 2. Christianity and
existentialism in literature. 3. Authors, American — 20th century —
Biography. I. T.
PS3566.E6912 Z6   813/.5/4 B   *LC* 78-13629   *ISBN* 0316151602

Luschei, Martin.   **2.13246**
The sovereign wayfarer; Walker Percy's diagnosis of the malaise. — Baton
Rouge: Louisiana State University Press, [1972] viii, 261 p.; 24 cm. —
(Southern literary studies.) 1. Percy, Walker, 1916- I. T. II. Series.
PS3566.E6912 Z75   813/.5/4   *LC* 72-79333   *ISBN* 0807102393

Tharpe, Jac.   **2.13247**
Walker Percy / by Jac Tharpe. — Boston: Twayne Publishers, c1983. 141 p.,
[1] p. of plates: port.; 23 cm. — (Twayne's United States authors series. TUSAS
449) Includes index. 1. Percy, Walker, 1916- — Criticism and interpretation.
I. T. II. Series.
PS3566.E6912 Z86 1983   813/.54 19   *LC* 83-4309   *ISBN*
0805773894

Walker Percy, art and ethics / edited by Jac Tharpe.   **2.13248**
Jackson: University Press of Mississippi, c1980. viii, 160 p.; 24 cm. 1. Percy,
Walker, 1916- — Criticism and interpretation — Addresses, essays, lectures.
I. Tharpe, Jac.
PS3566.E6912 Z95   813/.54   *LC* 80-12227   *ISBN* 0878051198

Petesch, Natalie L. M., 1924-.   **2.13249**
After the first death there is no other [by] Natalie L. M. Petesch. — Iowa City:
University of Iowa Press, [1974] 197 p.; 21 cm. I. T.
PZ4.P4877 Af PS3566.E772 A5x   813/.5/4   *LC* 74-8851   *ISBN*
0877450501

Piercy, Marge.   **2.13250**
Woman on the edge of time / by Marge Piercy. — 1st ed. — New York: Knopf,
1976. 369 p.; 22 cm. I. T.
PZ4.P618 Wo PS3566.I4   813/.5/4   *LC* 75-36810   *ISBN*
0394499867

Piercy, Marge.   **• 2.13251**
Going down fast. — New York: Trident Press, [1969] 349 p.; 22 cm. — I. T.
PZ4.P618 Go PS3566.I4 G6x   813/.5/4   *LC* 78-79675   *ISBN*
0671270400

Pinsky, Robert.   **2.13252**
An explanation of America / Robert Pinsky. — Princeton, N.Y.: Princeton
University Press, c1979. 65 p.; 23 cm. — (Princeton series of contemporary
poets) I. T.
PS3566.I54 E9   811/.5/4   *LC* 79-84010   *ISBN* 0691064075

Pinsky, Robert.   **2.13253**
History of my heart / Robert Pinsky. — 1st ed. — New York: Ecco Press, 1984.
51 p.; 25 cm. I. T.
PS3566.I54 H5 1984   811/.54 19   *LC* 83-16374   *ISBN* 0880010371

PS3566 Plath

Plath, Sylvia.   **2.13254**
[Poems] The collected poems / Sylvia Plath; edited by Ted Hughes. — 1st U.S.
ed. — New York: Harper & Row, c1981. 351 p.; 24 cm. (Harper colophon
books; CN900) Includes index. I. Hughes, Ted, 1930- II. T.
PS3566.L27 A17 1981   811/.54 19   *LC* 75-25057   *ISBN*
0060133694

Plath, Sylvia, 1932-1963. • 2.13255
Ariel. — [1st ed.]. — New York: Harper & Row, [1966] xi, 85 p. Poems. I. T.
PS3566.L27 A7x   LC 66-15738

Plath, Sylvia. • 2.13256
The bell jar. Biographical note by Lois Ames. Drawings by Sylvia Plath. — [1st U.S. ed.]. — New York: Harper & Row, [1971] 296 p.: illus.; 22 cm. — I. T.
PZ4.P717 Be6 PS3566.L27 B4x   813/.5/4   LC 76-149743   ISBN 0060133562

Plath, Sylvia. • 2.13257
The colossus & other poems. — [1st American ed.]. — New York: Knopf, 1962. 83 p.; 22 cm. — I. T.
PS3566.L27 C6 1962   811.54   LC 62-8685

Plath, Sylvia. • 2.13258
Winter trees. — London: Faber and Faber, 1971. 3-55 p.; 23 cm. Poems. I. T.
PS3566.L27 W5 1971   811/.5/4   LC 72-873905   ISBN 0571097391

Plath, Sylvia. 2.13259
Winter trees. — [1st U.S. ed.]. — New York: Harper & Row, [1972] 64 p.; 22 cm. Poems. I. T.
PS3566.L27 W5 1972   811/.5/4

Plath, Sylvia. 2.13260
The journals of Sylvia Plath / foreword by Ted Hughes; Ted Hughes, consulting editor; and Frances McCullough, editor. — New York: Dial Press, c1982. xiii, 370 p., [8] p. of plates: ill.; 24 cm. Includes index. 1. Plath, Sylvia — Diaries. 2. Poets, American — 20th century — Biography. I. Hughes, Ted, 1930- II. McCullough, Frances Monson, 1939- III. T.
PS3566.L27 Z469 1982   811/.54 B 19   LC 81-19435   0385272237

Plath, Sylvia. 2.13261
Letters home: correspondence, 1950–1963 / by Sylvia Plath; selected and edited with commentary by Aurelia Schober Plath. 1st ed. — New York: Harper & Row, c1975. 502 p.: ill.; 24 cm. Includes index. 1. Plath, Sylvia — Correspondence. 2. Plath, Aurelia Schober. 3. Authors, American — 20th century — Correspondence. I. Plath, Aurelia Schober. II. T.
PS3566.L27 Z53 1975   811/.5/4 B   LC 74-1849   ISBN 0060133724

Broe, Mary Lynn. 2.13262
Protean poetic: the poetry of Sylvia Plath / Mary Lynn Broe. — Columbia: University of Missouri Press, 1980. xii, 226 p.: ill.; 23 cm. Includes index. 1. Plath, Sylvia — Criticism and interpretation. I. T.
PS3566.L27 Z585   811/.5/4   LC 79-3334   ISBN 0826202918

Holbrook, David. 2.13263
Sylvia Plath: poetry and existence / by David Holbrook. — London: Athlone Press; [Atlantic Highlands] N.J.: distributed by Humanities Press, 1976. 308 p.; 23 cm. 'Sylvia Plath': p. [298]-299. 1. Plath, Sylvia — Criticism and interpretation. 2. Plath, Sylvia — Biography — Psychology. I. T.
PS3566.L27 Z7   811/.5/4   LC 77-357252   ISBN 0485111438

Kroll, Judith, 1943-. 2.13264
Chapters in a mythology: the poetry of Sylvia Plath / Judith Kroll. 1st ed. — New York: Harper & Row, c1976. xvi, 303 p.: ill.; 22 cm. Includes index. 1. Plath, Sylvia — Criticism and interpretation. I. T.
PS3566.L27 Z75 1976   811/.5/4   LC 75-6344   ISBN 0060124571

Dickie, Margaret, 1935-. 2.13265
Sylvia Plath and Ted Hughes / Margaret Dickie Uroff. — Urbana: University of Illinois Press, c1979. x, 235 p.; 24 cm. Includes index. 1. Plath, Sylvia — Criticism and interpretation. 2. Hughes, Ted, 1930- — Criticism and interpretation. I. T.
PS3566.L27 Z94   821/.9/1409   LC 79-74   ISBN 0252007344

PS3566 Pl–Pr

Plumly, Stanley. 2.13266
Out–of–the–body travel / Stanley Plumly. New York: Ecco Press, 1977, c1976. 48 p.; 22 cm. (The American poetry series; v. 10) I. T.
PS3566.L78 O9 1977   811/.5/4   LC 76-46174   ISBN 0912946350

Pohl, Frederik. 2.13267
The space merchants, by Frederik Pohl and C. M. Kornbluth. — New York: Ballantine, 1953. 216 p. 'A condensed version ... appeared in Galaxy magazine under the title the Gravy planet.' I. Kornbluth, C. M. (Cyril M.), 1924-1958. II. T.
PZ4.P748 Sp4 PS3566.O36   PS3566.O36 S62 1953.   813/.5/4   LC 53-6886   ISBN 0345296974

Powers, J. F. (James Farl), 1917-. • 2.13268
The presence of grace. — Freeport, N.Y.: Books for Libraries Press, [1969] 191 p.; 21 cm. — (Short story index reprint series.) Short stories. I. T. II. Series.
PZ3.P8743 Pp4 PS3566.O84   813/.5/4   LC 77-85694   ISBN 0836930371

Powers, J. F. (James Farl), 1917-. 2.13269
Look how the fish live / J. F. Powers. — 1st ed. — New York: Knopf, 1975. 190 p.; 22 cm. I. T.
PZ3.P8743 Lo PS3566.O84   PS3566.O84 L6.   813/.5/4   LC 75-8237   ISBN 0394496086

Powers, J. F. (James Farl), 1917-. • 2.13270
Morte d'Urban. — [1st ed.]. — Garden City, N.Y.: Doubleday, 1962. 336 p.; 22 cm. I. T.
PS3566.O84 M6x   LC 62-15893

Powers, J. F. (James Farl), 1917-. • 2.13271
Prince of Darkness: and other stories. — [1st ed.] Garden City, N.Y.: Doubleday, 1947. 277p. I. T.
PS3566 O84 P75 1947   LC 47-5299

Price, Reynolds, 1933-. • 2.13272
A long and happy life / Reynolds Price. — New York: Atheneum, 1962 [c1961] 195 p.; 21 cm. — I. T.
PZ4.P9472 Lo2   PS3566R47 L59.   LC 61-12790

Price, Reynolds, 1933-. 2.13273
Early dark: a play / Reynolds Price. — 1st ed. — New York: Atheneum, 1977. xii, 140 p.; 22 cm. — I. T.
PS3566.R54 E3 1977   812/.5/4   LC 77-3189   ISBN 0689107994

Price, Reynolds, 1933-. • 2.13274
A generous man. — New York: Atheneum, 1966. 275 p.; 20 cm. I. T.
PS3566.R54 G4x   LC 66-16357

Price, Reynolds, 1933-. • 2.13275
Permanent errors / Reynolds Price. — [1st ed.]. — New York: Atheneum, 1970. viii, 253 p.; 21 cm. — I. T.
PZ4.P9472 Pe PS3566.R54 P4x   813/.5/4   LC 70-124974

Rooke, Constance, 1942-. 2.13276
Reynolds Price / by Constance Rooke. — Boston: Twayne, c1983. 158 p.: port.; 22 cm. — (Twayne's United States authors series. TUSAS 450) Includes index. 1. Price, Reynolds, 1933- — Criticism and interpretation. I. T. II. Series.
PS3566.R54 Z86 1983   813/.54 19   LC 83-12720   ISBN 0805773908

PS3566 Pynchon

Pynchon, Thomas. • 2.13277
The crying of lot 49. [1st ed.] Philadelphia: Lippincott [1966] 183 p.; 21 cm. 'A portion of this novel was first published in Esquire magazine under the title: The world (this one), the flesh (Mrs. Oedipa Maas), and the testament of Pierce Inverarity. Another portion has appeared in Cavalier.' I. T.
PS3566.Y55C7   LC 66-12340

Pynchon, Thomas. 2.13278
Gravity's rainbow. New York, Viking Press [1973] 760 p. 23 cm. I. T.
PZ4.P997 Gr PS3566.Y55 G731x   813/.5/4   LC 72-83804   ISBN 0670348325 ISBN 0670003743

Approaches to Gravity's rainbow / edited by Charles Clerc. 2.13279
Columbus: Ohio State University Press, c1983. 307 p.; 24 cm. 1. Pynchon, Thomas. Gravity's rainbow. I. Clerc, Charles, 1926-
PS3566.Y55 G732 1983   813/.54 19   LC 82-6500   ISBN 081420337X

Siegel, Mark Richard. 2.13280
Pynchon: creative paranoia in Gravity's rainbow / Mark Richard Siegel. — Port Washington, N.Y.: Kennikat Press, 1978. viii, 136 p.; 23 cm. — (National university publications) (Literary criticism series) Includes index. 1. Pynchon, Thomas. Gravity's rainbow. 2. Paranoia in literature. I. T.
PS3566.Y55 G738   813/.5/4   LC 78-8512   ISBN 0804692130

Pynchon, Thomas. 2.13281
Slow learner: early stories / Thomas Pynchon. — 1st ed. — Boston: Little, Brown, c1984. 193 p.; 25 cm. Stories originally published in various magazines between 1959 and 1964. I. T.
PS3566.Y55 S5 1984   813/.54 19   LC 84-934   ISBN 0316724424

Pynchon, Thomas. • 2.13282
V., a novel. Philadelphia: Lippincott, 1963. 492 p. I. T.
PS3566.Y55 V2x   LC 63-8634

Cowart, David, 1947-.   2.13283
Thomas Pynchon: the art of allusion / by David Cowart. — Carbondale: Southern Illinois University Press, c1980. 154 p.; 22 cm. — (Crosscurrents/ modern critiques/new series) Includes index. 1. Pynchon, Thomas — Criticism and interpretation. 2. Arts in literature I. T.
PS3566.Y55 Z6   813/.5/4 19   LC 79-20157   ISBN 0809309440

Hite, Molly, 1947-.   2.13284
Ideas of order in the novels of Thomas Pynchon / Molly Hite. — Columbus: Ohio State University Press, c1983. x, 183 p.; 24 cm. Includes index. 1. Pynchon, Thomas — Criticism and interpretation. 2. Order (Philosophy) in literature. I. T.
PS3566.Y55 Z66 1983   813/.54 19   LC 83-4258   ISBN 0814203507

Mindful pleasures: essays on Thomas Pynchon / edited by   2.13285
George Levine and David Leverenz.
1st ed. — Boston: Little, Brown, 1976. ix, 272 p.; 21 cm. 1. Pynchon, Thomas — Criticism and interpretation — Addresses, essays, lectures. I. Levine, George Lewis. II. Leverenz, David.
PS3566.Y55 Z72   813/.5/4   LC 76-21279   ISBN 0316522309

Pynchon: a collection of critical essays / edited by Edward   2.13286
Mendelson.
Englewood Cliffs, N.J.: Prentice-Hall, c1978. viii, 225 p.; 21 cm. — (Twentieth century views) (A Spectrum book) 1. Pynchon, Thomas — Criticism and interpretation. I. Mendelson, Edward.
PS3566.Y55 Z8   813/.5/4   LC 77-12699   ISBN 0137447140

Schaub, Thomas H., 1947-.   2.13287
Pynchon, the voice of ambiguity / Thomas H. Schaub. — Urbana: University of Illinois Press, c1981. x, 165 p.; 24 cm. Includes index. 1. Pynchon, Thomas — Criticism and interpretation. I. T.
PS3566.Y55 Z87   813/.54   LC 80-11944   ISBN 0252008162

Tanner, Tony.   2.13288
Thomas Pynchon / Tony Tanner. — London; New York: Methuen, 1982. 95 p.; 20 cm. — (Contemporary writers.) 1. Pynchon, Thomas — Criticism and interpretation. I. T. II. Series.
PS3566.Y55 Z9 1982   813/.54 19   LC 81-22534   ISBN 0416316700

PS3568 R

Rabe, David.   2.13289
[Basic training of Pavlo Hummel] The basic training of Pavlo Hummel, and Sticks and bones: two plays. — New York: Viking Press, [1973] xxv, 226 p.: ill.; 21 cm. I. Rabe, David. Sticks and bones. 1973. II. T.
PS3568.A23 B3   812/.5/4   LC 72-75746   ISBN 0670148814 ISBN 0670003670

Rabe, David.   2.13290
Streamers / David Rabe. — 1st ed. — New York: Knopf: distributed by Random House, 1977. 109 p., [2] leaves of plates: ill.; 22 cm. I. T.
PS3568.A23 S85 1977   812/.5/4   LC 76-44000   ISBN 039441120X

Rafferty, S. S.   2.13291
Cork of the colonies: the first American detective / S.S. Rafferty. — New York: International Polygonics; Chicago, IL: Distributed by Academy Chicago, c1984. 311 p.; 18 cm. (Library of crime classics) Expanded ed. of: Fatal flourishes. 1979. 1. Detective and mystery stories, American I. Rafferty, S. S. Fatal flourishes II. T.
PS3568.A38 C6 1984   813/.54 19   LC 84-80232   ISBN 0930330110

Reamy, Tom.   2.13292
Blind voices / by Tom Reamy. — New York: Berkley Pub. Corp.: distributed by Putnam, c1978. 254 p.; 22 cm. — I. T.
PZ4.R28755 Bl PS3568.E25 B5x   813/.5/4   LC 78-3817   ISBN 0399122400

Reed, Ishmael, 1938-.   2.13293
Conjure; selected poems, 1963–1970. — [Amherst] University of Massachusetts Press [1972] xii, 83 p. 24 cm. I. T.
PS3568.E365 C6   811/.5/4   LC 72-77568

Reed, Ishmael, 1938-.   2.13294
Flight to Canada / Ishmael Reed. — 1st ed. — New York: Random House, c1976. 179 p.; 22 cm. 1. United States — History — Civil War, 1861-1865 — Fiction. I. T.
PZ4.R323 Fl PS3568.E365 F5x   813/.5/4   LC 76-15598   ISBN 0394487540

Reed, Ishmael, 1938-.   2.13295
Mumbo jumbo. — [1st ed.]. — Garden City, N.Y.: Doubleday, 1972. 223 p.: illus.; 22 cm. I. T.
PZ4.R323 Mu PS3568.E365 M8x   813/.5/4   LC 73-171314

Robinson, Kim Stanley.   2.13296
The wild shore / Kim Stanley Robinson. New York: Berkley Pub. Group, c1984. [384] p. (New Ace science fiction specials.) Ace Science Fiction books. 1. Science fiction I. T.
PS3568.O29 W5x   ISBN 0441888704

Rose, Wendy.   2.13297
Lost copper: poems / by Wendy Rose; illustrated by the author; with an introduction by N. Scott Momaday. — Banning, Calif. (Morongo Indian Reservation, Banning 92220): Malki Museum Press, 1980. xv, 127 p., [1] p. of plates: ill.; 24 cm. — I. T.
PS3568.O7644 L6   811/.54 19   LC 80-81849

Roth, Philip.   2.13298
The ghost writer / Philip Roth. — New York: Farrar, Straus and Giroux, c1979. 179 p. I. T.
PZ4.R8454 Gh PS3568.O855   PS3568O89 G5.   PS3568.O855 G5x.   813/.5/4   LC 79-13146   ISBN 0374161895

Roth, Philip.   • 2.13299
Goodbye, Columbus, and five short stories. Boston, Houghton Mifflin, 1959. 298 p. 21 cm. I. T.
PS3568.O855 G6x   LC 59-7579

Roth, Philip, 1933-.   2.13300
The great American novel. — [1st ed.]. — New York: Holt, Rinehart and Winston, [1973] 382 p.; 24 cm. I. T.
PS3568.O855 G7x   813/.5/4   LC 72-91577   ISBN 0030045169

Roth, Philip.   • 2.13301
Letting go. New York, Random House [1962] 630 p. 22 cm. I. T.
PS3568.O855L4 1962   LC 62-8472

Roth, Philip.   2.13302
My life as a man. — [1st ed.]. — New York: Holt, Rinehart and Winston, [1974] 330 p.; 24 cm. — I. T.
PZ4.R8454 My PS3568.O855 M9x   813/.5/4   LC 73-20847   ISBN 0030126460

Roth, Philip.   • 2.13303
Portnoy's complaint. New York: Random House [1969] 274 p.; 22 cm. I. T.
PS3568.O855 P67   813/.5/4   LC 69-16414

Roth, Philip.   2.13304
The professor of desire / Philip Roth. — New York: Farrar, Straus and Giroux, c1977. 263 p.; 22 cm. I. T.
PZ4.R8454 Pr PS3568.O855 P7x   813/.5/4   LC 77-24032   ISBN 0374237565

Jones, Judith P.   2.13305
Philip Roth / Judith Paterson Jones, Guinevera A. Nance. — New York: Ungar, c1981. x, 181 p.; 21 cm. — (Modern literature series.) Includes index. 1. Roth, Philip — Criticism and interpretation. I. Nance, Guinevera A. II. T. III. Series.
PS3568.O855 Z73   813/.54 19   LC 80-53701   ISBN 0804424381

Lee, Hermione.   2.13306
Philip Roth / Hermione Lee. — London; New York: Methuen, 1982. 95 p.; 20 cm. — (Contemporary writers.) 1. Roth, Philip — Criticism and interpretation. I. T. II. Series.
PS3568.O855 Z76 1982   813/.54 19   LC 82-8223   ISBN 0416329802

Rodgers, Bernard F., 1947-.   2.13307
Philip Roth / by Bernard F. Rodgers, Jr. — Boston: Twayne Publishers, 1978. 192 p.: ports. — (Twayne's United States authors series; TUSAS 318) Includes index. 1. Roth, Philip — Criticism and interpretation. I. T.
PS3568.O855 Z88   PS3568O89 Z85.   813/.5/4   LC 78-17105   ISBN 0805772499

Russ, Joanna, 1937-.   2.13308
The female man / Joanna Russ; with a new introd. by Marilyn Hacker. — Boston: Gregg Press, 1977. xxvii, 214 p. — (The Gregg Press science fiction series III) Reprint of the 1975 ed. published by Bantam Books, New York. I. T.
PZ4.R9548 Fe4 PS3568.U763   PS3568U773 F4 1977.   813/.5/4   LC 77-23498   ISBN 0839823517

PS3569 S–Sp

Salamanca, J. R.   2.13309
Embarkation [by] J. R. Salamanca. — [1st ed.]. — New York: Knopf; [distributed by Random House], 1973. 273 p.; 22 cm. — I. T.
PZ4.S158 Em PS3569.A458 E6x   813/.5/4   LC 73-7292   ISBN 0394460286

Salamanca, J. R.   2.13310
Southern light: a novel / by J.R. Salamanca. — 1st ed. — New York: Knopf: Distributed by Random House, 1984. 675 p. I. T.
PS3569.A458 S6 1986   813/.54 19   LC 85-19825   ISBN 0394482522

Sanchez, Sonia, 1935-.   2.13311
Love poems. — New York: Third Press, [1973] 101 p.: ill.; 20 cm. 1. Love poetry, American I. T.
PS3569.A468 L6   811/.5/4   LC 73-83168   ISBN 089388104X

Schisgal, Murray, 1929-.   • 2.13312
Luv. With an introd. by Walter Kerr, and an interview with the author by Ira Peck. New York, Coward-McCann [1965] xvii, 98 p. 21 cm. (The Coward-McCann contemporary drama series; CM-10) I. T. II. Series.
PS3569.C5 L8   812.54   LC 64-17978

Selby, Hubert.   • 2.13313
Last exit to Brooklyn, by Hubert Selby, Jr. New York, Grove Press [1964] 304 p. 21 cm. I. T.
PZ4.S463Las PS3569.E547L3   LC 63-16999

Sennett, Richard, 1943-.   2.13314
An evening of Brahms / Richard Sennett. — 1st ed. — New York: Knopf, 1984. 221 p. I. T.
PS3569.E62 E9 1984   813/.54 19   LC 83-49091   ISBN 0394513002

Sennett, Richard, 1943-.   2.13315
The frog who dared to croak / Richard Sennett. — 1st ed. — New York: Farrar, Straus & Giroux, 1982. 182 p. I. T.
PS3569.E62 F7 1982   PS3569E62 F7 1982.   813/.54 19   LC 82-1508   ISBN 0374158843

Shange, Ntozake.   2.13316
For colored girls who have considered suicide, when the rainbow is enuf: a choreopoem / Ntozake Shange. — New York: MacMillan, c1977. xvi, 64 p.; 25 cm. — I. T.
PS3569.H3324 F6 1977   811/.5/4   LC 77-3034   ISBN 0026098407

Shepard, Sam, 1943-.   2.13317
[Plays. Selections] Seven plays / Sam Shepard; introduction by Richard Gilman. — Toronto; New York: Bantam Books, 1981. xxv, 337 p.; 18 cm. Tongues and Savage/Love written in collaboration with Joseph Chaikin. I. Chaikin, Joseph, 1935- II. T.
PS3569.H394 A6 1981   812/.54 19   LC 83-100533   ISBN 0553142577

Shepard, Sam, 1943-.   2.13318
Angel City & other plays / Sam Shepard; introd. by Jack Gelber. New York: Urizen Books, [c1976] 245 p.; 23 cm. I. T.
PS3569.H394 A8   812/.5/4   LC 76-21289   ISBN 0916354180

Shepard, Sam, 1943-.   2.13319
Buried child, & Seduced, & Suicide in Bᵇ: [plays] / Sam Shepard. — New York: Urizen Books, c1979. 155 p.; 22 cm. I. T.
PS3569.H394 B8   812/.54   LC 79-66031   ISBN 0893960101

Mottram, Ron.   2.13320
Inner landscapes: the theater of Sam Shepard / Ron Mottram. — Columbia: University of Missouri Press, 1985 (c1984). ix, 172 p.; 21 cm. (Literary frontiers edition.) Includes index. 1. Shepard, Sam, 1943- 2. Dramatists, American — 20th century — Biography. I. T. II. Series.
PS3569.H394 Z77 1984   812/.54 19   LC 84-50795   ISBN 082620452X

Silko, Leslie, 1948-.   2.13321
Ceremony / Leslie Marmon Silko. New York: Viking Press, 1977. 262 p.; 22 cm. 'A Richard Seaver book.' I. T.
PZ4.S57195 Ce PS3569.I44   813/.5/4   LC 76-46936   ISBN 0670209864

Silko, Leslie, 1948-.   2.13322
Storyteller / Leslie Marmon Silko. — 1st ed. — New York: Seaver Books: distributed by Grove Press, 1981. 278 p.: ill.; 18 x 24 cm. I. T.
PS3569.I44 S8   813/.54 19   LC 80-20251   ISBN 0394515897

Silverberg, Robert.   2.13323
Dying inside. — New York: Scribner, [1972] 245 p.; 22 cm. — I. T.
PZ4.S573 Dy PS3569.I472 D9x   813/.5/4   LC 72-1231   ISBN 0684130831

Silverberg, Robert.   2.13324
A time of changes. — Garden City, N.Y.: N. Doubleday, [1971] 183 p.; 22 cm. 'First serialized in Galaxy magazine.' I. T.
PZ4.S573 Tk PS3569.I472 T5x   813/.5/4   LC 75-26203

Simpson, Eileen B.   2.13325
Poets in their youth: a memoir / Eileen Simpson. — 1st ed. — New York: Random House, c1982. 272 p.: ports.; 25 cm. 1. Simpson, Eileen B — Friends and associates. 2. Berryman, John, 1914-1972 — Biography. 3. Poets, American — 20th century — Biography. 4. Authors, American — 20th century — Biography. I. T.
PS3569.I489 Z473 1982   811/.54/09 B 19   LC 81-48295   ISBN 0394523172

Snyder, Gary.   2.13326
Axe handles: poems / by Gary Snyder. — San Francisco: North Point Press, 1983. 114 p.; 21 cm. I. T.
PS3569.N88 A97 1983   811/.54 19   LC 83-61398   ISBN 0865471193

Snyder, Gary.   2.13327
The old ways: six essays / Gary Snyder. — San Francisco: City Lights Books, c1977. 96 p.; 18 cm. I. T.
PS3569.N88 O4   814/.5/4   LC 76-58871   ISBN 0872860914

Snyder, Gary.   2.13328
Turtle Island. — [New York: New Directions, 1974] 114 p.; 21 cm. — (A New Directions book) Poems. I. T.
PS3569.N88 T8   811/.5/4   LC 74-8542   ISBN 0811205452

Molesworth, Charles, 1941-.   2.13329
Gary Snyder's vision: poetry and the real work / Charles Molesworth. — Columbia: University of Missouri Press, 1983. [8], 128 p.; 21 cm. — (Literary frontiers edition.) 'Books by Gary Snyder'—Prelim. p. [8] 1. Snyder, Gary — Criticism and interpretation. I. T. II. Series.
PS3569.N88 Z78 1983   811/.54 19   LC 83-6993   ISBN 0826204147

Sontag, Susan, 1933-.   • 2.13330
The benefactor: a novel / Susan Sontag. — New York: Farrar, Straus, [1963] 273 p. I. T.
PS3569.O6 B4 1965   LC 63-16473

Spicer, Jack.   2.13331
The collected books of Jack Spicer / edited & with a commentary by Robin Blaser. — Los Angeles: Black Sparrow Press, 1975. 382 p.: ports.; 23 cm. Poems. I. Blaser, Robin. II. T.
PS3569.P47 A6 1975   811/.5/4   LC 75-9864   ISBN 0876852428

Spinrad, Norman.   2.13332
Bug Jack Barron / Norman Spinrad; with a new introd. by Robert Louit. — Boston: Gregg Press, 1981, c1969. p. cm. — (The Gregg Press science fiction series) Reprint of the ed. published by Walker, New York. I. T.
PS3569.P55 B8 1981   813/.54 19   LC 80-28939   ISBN 0839826176

PS3569 St–Sz

Stern, Richard G., 1928-.   2.13333
Natural shocks / Richard Stern. — New York: Coward, McCann & Geoghegan, c1978. 260 p.; 22 cm. — I. T.
PZ4.S83943 Nat PS3569.T39 N3x   813/.5/4   LC 77-22952   ISBN 0698108655

Stewart, John, 1933-.   2.13334
Curving road: stories / by John Stewart. — Urbana: University of Illinois Press, [1975] 128 p.; 21 cm. (Illinois short fiction) I. T.
PZ4.S8518 Cu PS3569.T465 C8x   813   LC 75-2286   ISBN 0252005171

Stone, Robert.   2.13335
Dog soldiers, a novel. — Boston: Houghton Mifflin, 1974. 342 p.; 24 cm. — I. T.
PZ4.S8789 Do PS3569.T6418 D6x   813/.5/4   LC 74-11441   ISBN 0395184819

Straub, Peter.   2.13336
Ghost story / Peter Straub. — 1st ed. — New York: Coward, McCann & Geoghegan, Inc., c1979. 483 p.; 24 cm. — I. T.
PZ4.S9125 Gh PS3569.T6914 G5x   813/.5/4   LC 78-27120   ISBN 0698109597

Sturgeon, Theodore. 2.13337
More than human, by Theodore Sturgeon. — New York: Farrar, Straus and Young, [1953] 233 p.; 21 cm. — I. T.
PZ3.S93562 Mo PS3569.T875 M6x   LC 53-11211

Styron, William, 1925-. • 2.13338
The confessions of Nat Turner. — New York: Random House [1967] xvi, 428 p.; 22 cm. 'First printing.' 1. Turner, Nat, 1800?-1831 — Fiction. 2. Southampton Insurrection, 1831 — Fiction. I. T.
PS3569.T9 C6 1967   813/.54 19   LC 67-12732

Clarke, John Henrik, 1915-. 2.13339
William Styron's Nat Turner; ten black writers respond, edited by John Henrik Clarke. — Boston: Beacon Press, [1968] x, 120 p.: illus.; 21 cm. Appendix (p. [98]-117): The text of The confessions of Nat Turner. 1. Styron, William, 1925- The confessions of Nat Turner. I. Turner, Nat, 1800?-1831. The confessions of Nat Turner. II. T.
PS3569.T9 C633   813/.5/4   LC 68-27519

Styron, William, 1925-. 2.13340
In the clap shack. — New York: Random House, [1973] 96 p.: illus.; 22 cm. A play. I. T.
PS3569.T9 I5   812/.5/4   LC 72-11412   ISBN 0394460936

Styron, William, 1925-. • 2.13341
Lie down in darkness, a novel. Indianapolis, Bobbs-Merrill [1951] 400 p. 25 cm. I. T.
PZ4.S938Li PS3569.T9L5   LC 51-12286

Styron, William, 1925-. • 2.13342
The long march. New York: Random House [1968?, c1952] 120 p. 20 cm. I. T.
PS3569.T9L6 1968   LC 68-2195

Styron, William, 1925-. • 2.13343
Set this house on fire. New York, Random House [1960] 507 p. 22 cm. I. T.
PZ4.S938Se PS3569.T9S4   LC 60-5568

Styron, William, 1925-. 2.13344
Sophie's choice / William Styron. — 1st trade ed. — New York: Random House, c1979. 515 p.; 25 cm. 'A limited edition of this book has been privately printed'—Verso of t.p. I. T.
PS3569.T9 S67   813/.5/4   LC 78-21835   ISBN 0394461096

The Achievement of William Styron / edited by Robert K. 2.13345
Morris & Irving Malin.
Athens: University of Georgia Press, c1975. 280 p.; 24 cm. 1. Styron, William, 1925- — Criticism and interpretation — Addresses, essays, lectures. 2. Styron, William, 1925- — Bibliography. I. Morris, Robert K. II. Malin, Irving.
PS3569.T9 Z56   813/.5/4   LC 74-75942   ISBN 0820303518

Crane, John Kenny, 1942-. 2.13346
The root of all evil: the thematic unity of William Styron's fiction / by John Kenny Crane. — 1st ed. — Columbia, S.C.: University of South Carolina Press, c1984. ix, 168 p.; 24 cm. 1. Styron, William, 1925- — Criticism and interpretation. 2. Evil in literature I. T.
PS3569.T9 Z625 1984   813/.54 19   LC 84-20820   ISBN 0872494470

Critical essays on William Styron / Arthur D. Casciato and 2.13347
James L.W. West III.
Boston, Mass.: G.K. Hall, c1982. ix, 318 p.; 25 cm. — (Critical essays on American literature.) 1. Styron, William, 1925- — Criticism and interpretation — Addresses, essays, lectures. I. Casciato, Arthur D. II. West, James L. W. III. Series.
PS3569.T9 Z63 1982   813/.54 19   LC 81-24002   ISBN 0816182612

Ratner, Marc L. 2.13348
William Styron, by Marc L. Ratner. — New York: Twayne Publishers, 1973 (c1972) 170 p.; 22 cm. — (Twayne's United States authors series, TUSAS 196) 1. Styron, William, 1925- I. T.
PS3569.T9 Z87   813/.5/4   LC 70-169632

Sukenick, Ronald. 2.13349
98.6: a novel / by Ronald Sukenick. — 1st ed. — New York: Fiction Collective: distributed by G. Braziller, [1975] 188 p.; 23 cm. I. T.
PZ4.S944 Ni PS3569.U33 N5x   813/.5/4   LC 74-24913   ISBN 0914590081

Swados, Harvey. 2.13350
Celebration: a novel / by Harvey Swados. — New York: Simon and Schuster, [1975] 348 p.; 22 cm. I. T.
PZ4.S969 Ce3 PS3569.W2 C4x   813/.5/4   LC 74-23733   ISBN 0671219510

Swados, Harvey. • 2.13351
Nights in the gardens of Brooklyn. Freeport, N.Y., Books for Libraries Press [1970, c1960] 248 p. 21 cm. (Short story index reprint series) I. T.
PS3569.W2N5 1970   813/.5/4   LC 71-128751   ISBN 836936426

Switzer, Margaret, 1949-. 2.13352
Existential folktales / Margaret Switzer. — Berkeley, Calif.: Cayuse Press, c1985. 157 p.; 22 cm. 1. Tales — Fiction. I. T.
PS3569.W59 E95 1985   813/.54 19   LC 85-70818   ISBN 0933529007

PS3570 T

Terry, Megan. • 2.13353
Viet rock, Comings and goings, Keep tightly closed in a cool dry place, The gloaming, oh my darling: four plays / by Megan Terry; with an introd. by Richard Schechner. — New York, Simon and Schuster 1967. 282 p.: music; 20 cm. 'Music for Viet rock and Comings and goings, by Marianne de Pury' (for voice and piano): p. [249]-282. I. De Pury, Marianne. II. Terry, Megan. Comings and goins. III. Terry, Megan. Keep tightly closed in a cool dry place. IV. Terry, Megan. Gloaming, oh my darling. V. T. VI. Title: Comings and goings. VII. Title: Keep tightly closed in a cool dry place. VIII. Title: The gloaming, oh my darling.
PS3539.E67 A6 1967   LC 67-17889

Theroux, Paul. 2.13354
The consul's file / Paul Theroux. — Boston: Houghton Mifflin, 1977. 209 p.; 22 cm. I. T.
PZ4.T394 Co PS3570.H4 C6x   813/.5/4   LC 77-6431   ISBN 0395253993

Theroux, Paul. 2.13355
The family arsenal / Paul Theroux. — Boston: Houghton Mifflin, 1976. 309 p.; 22 cm. I. T.
PZ4.T394 Fam PS3570.H4 F3x   813/.5/4   LC 76-10212   ISBN 0395244005

Theroux, Paul. 2.13356
Saint Jack; a novel. — Boston: Houghton Mifflin, 1973. 247 p.; 22 cm. — I. T.
PZ4.T394 Sai PS3570.H4 S2x   813/.5/4   LC 72-12400   ISBN 0395171180

Theroux, Paul. 2.13357
Sinning with Annie: and other stories. — Boston: Houghton Mifflin, 1972. viii, 210 p.; 22 cm. I. T.
PZ4.T394 Si PS3570.H4 S5x   813/.5/4   LC 72-2283   ISBN 0395139961

Tiptree, James. 2.13358
Up the walls of the world / James Tiptree, Jr. — New York: Berkley Pub. Corp.: distributed by Putnam, c1978. 319 p.; 23 cm. — I. T.
PZ4.T597 Up PS3570.I66 U8x   813/.5/4   LC 77-24470   ISBN 0399120831

Toole, John Kennedy, 1937-1969. 2.13359
A confederacy of dunces / John Kennedy Toole; foreword by Walker Percy. — Baton Rouge: Louisiana State University Press, 1980. vii, 338 p.; 24 cm. — I. T.
PS3570.O54 C66 1980   813/.5/4   LC 79-20190   ISBN 0807106577

Tran, Van Dinh, 1923-. 2.13360
Blue dragon, white tiger: a Tet story / by Tran Van Dinh. — Philadelphia: TriAm Press, 1983. xi, 334 p.; 24 cm. 1. Vietnamese Conflict, 1961-1975 — Fiction. I. T.
PS3570.R3349 B5 1983   813/.54 19   LC 83-233996   ISBN 0914075004

Traver, Robert, 1903-. 2.13361
Anatomy of a murder [by] Robert Traver. — New York: St. Martin's Press, [c1958] 437 p.; 22 cm. — I. T.
PS3570.R339 A83   813/.54 19   LC 57-13115

Tyler, Anne. 2.13362
Searching for Caleb / Anne Tyler. 1st ed. — New York: Knopf, 1976, c1975. 309 p.; 22 cm. I. T.
PZ4.T979 Se PS3570.Y45 S4x   813/.5/4   LC 75-8251   ISBN 0394498488

PS3571 Updike

Updike, John. 2.13363
Tossing and turning: poems / John Updike. 1st ed. — New York: Knopf, 1977. xi, 90 p.; 21 cm. I. T.
PS3571.P4 A17 1977   811/.5/4   LC 76-44002   ISBN 0394410904

Updike, John. • 2.13364
Bech: a book. — [1st ed.] New York: Knopf, 1970. vi, 206 p.; 21 cm. 'Five of these [seven] stories first appeared in the New Yorker.' I. T.
PZ4.U64Be PS3571.P4B4   813/.5/4   LC 79-110813

Updike, John. • 2.13365
The centaur. [1st ed.] New York, Knopf, 1963. 302 p. 22 cm. I. T.
PS3571.P4C4 1963   LC 63-7873

Updike, John. 2.13366
The coup / John Updike. — 1st ed. — New York: Knopf, 1978. 298 p.; 22 cm. I. T.
PS3571.P4 C58   813/.5/4   LC 78-55399   ISBN 039450268X

Updike, John. • 2.13367
Couples. [1st ed.] New York, Knopf, 1968. 458 p. 22 cm. I. T.
PS3571.P4 C6   LC 68-12996

Updike, John. 2.13368
Hugging the shore: essays and criticism / John Updike. — 1st ed. — New York: Knopf, 1983. xx, 919 p.; 22 cm. Includes index. I. T.
PS3571.P4 H8 1983   814/.54 19   LC 83-47957   ISBN 0394531795

Updike, John. 2.13369
Marry me: a romance / John Updike. — 1st ed. — New York: Knopf, 1976. 303 p. I. T.
PS3571.P4 M4   813/.5/4   LC 76-13722   ISBN 039440856X

Updike, John. 2.13370
A month of Sundays / John Updike. — 1st ed. — New York: Knopf: distributed by Random House, 1975. 228 p.; 22 cm. I. T.
PS3571.P4 M6 1975   813/.5/4   LC 74-21327   ISBN 0394495519.
ISBN 0394497325 limited ed

Updike, John, 1932-. • 2.13371
The music school; short stories. — [1st ed.]. — New York: A. A. Knopf, 1966. 259 p.; 24 cm. — I. T.
PS3571.P4 M85x   LC 66-19404

Updike, John, 1932-. • 2.13372
Museums and women, and other stories / John Updike. — [1st ed.]. — New York: Knopf, 1972. x, 282 p.: ill.; 21 cm. — 'Of the first edition ... three hundred and fifty copes have been printed on special paper and specially bound. Each copy is signed by the author and numbered.' I. T.
PS3571.P4 M8x   813/.5/4   LC 72-2247   ISBN 0394481844

Updike, John. 2.13373
Picked–up pieces / John Updike. — 1st ed. — New York: Knopf: distributed by Random House, 1975. xx, 519, xxiii p.; 22 cm. Essays. Includes index. I. T.
PS3571.P4 P48   813/.5/4   LC 75-8252   ISBN 0394498496

Updike, John, 1932-. • 2.13374
Pigeon feathers, and other stories. — [1st ed.]. — New York: Knopf, 1962. 278 p.; 21 cm. — I. T.
PS3571.P4 P5x   LC 61-17831

Updike, John. • 2.13375
The poorhouse fair. [1st ed.] New York, Knopf, 1959 [c1958] 185 p. 21 cm. I. T.
PS3571.P4 P65 1959   813/.54 19   LC 59-5431

Updike, John. 2.13376
Rabbit is rich / John Updike. — 1st ed. — New York: Knopf: Distributed by Random House, 1981. 467 p.; 21 cm. I. T.
PS3571.P4 R25 1981   813/.54 19   LC 81-1287   ISBN 0394520874

Updike, John. • 2.13377
Rabbit redux. [1st ed.] New York, Knopf, 1971. 406 p. 22 cm. I. T.
PS3571.P4R27   813/.5/4   LC 70-154927   ISBN 0394474392

Updike, John. • 2.13378
Rabbit, run. [1st ed.] New York: Knopf, 1960. 307 p.; 21 cm. I. T.
PS3571.P4 R3x   LC 60-12552

Updike, John. 2.13379
The witches of Eastwick / John Updike. — 1st trade ed. — New York: Knopf: Distributed by Random House, 1984. 307 p.; 22 cm. I. T.
PS3571.P4 W5 1984   813/.54 19   LC 83-49048   ISBN 0394537602

Biography. Criticism

Critical essays on John Updike / [compiled by] William R. Macnaughton. 2.13380
Boston: G.K. Hall, c1982. viii, 308 p.; 25 cm. — (Critical essays on American literature.) 1. Updike, John — Criticism and interpretation — Addresses, essays, lectures. I. Macnaughton, William R., 1939- II. Series.
PS3571.P4 Z62 1982   813/.54 19   LC 81-13482

Greiner, Donald J. 2.13381
John Updike's novels / Donald J. Greiner. — Athens, Ohio: Ohio University Press, c1984. xvi, 223 p.; 24 cm. 1. Updike, John — Criticism and interpretation. I. T.
PS3571.P4 Z683 1984   813/.54 19   LC 84-7213   ISBN 0821407805

Greiner, Donald J. 2.13382
The other John Updike: poems, short stories, prose, play / Donald J. Greiner. — Athens: Ohio University Press, c1981. xxi, 297 p.; 24 cm. 1. Updike, John — Criticism and interpretation. I. T.
PS3571.P4 Z684   813/.54 19   LC 80-22377   ISBN 0821405853

Hamilton, Alice. • 2.13383
The elements of John Updike [by] Alice and Kenneth Hamilton. — [Grand Rapids, Mich.]: Eerdmans, [1970] 267 p.; 24 cm. 1. Updike, John, 1932- I. Hamilton, Kenneth. II. T.
PS3571.P4 Z69   PS3541.P47 Z69.   813/.5/4   LC 70-88075

John Updike: a collection of critical essays / edited by David Thorburn and Howard Eiland. 2.13384
Englewood Cliffs, N.J.: Prentice-Hall, c1979. ix, 222 p.; 21 cm. (Twentieth century views) (A Spectrum book) Includes index. 1. Updike, John — Criticism and interpretation — Addresses, essays, lectures. I. Thorburn, David. II. Eiland, Howard.
PS3571.P4 Z74   813/.5/4   LC 79-1481   ISBN 0139376070

Markle, Joyce B. 2.13385
Fighters and lovers; theme in the novels of John Updike [by] Joyce B. Markle. — New York: New York University Press, 1973. 205 p.; 24 cm. 1. Updike, John — Criticism and interpretation. I. T.
PS3571.P4 Z78   813/.5/4   LC 72-96469   ISBN 0814753612

Uphaus, Suzanne Henning, 1942-. 2.13386
John Updike / Suzanne Henning Uphaus. — New York: Ungar, c1980. x, 149 p.; 21 cm. — (Modern literature monographs) Includes index. 1. Updike, John — Criticism and interpretation. I. T.
PS3571.P4 Z93   813/.54   LC 79-48076   ISBN 0804429340

PS3572 V

Van Itallie, Jean Claude, 1935-. 2.13387
America hurrah and other plays / Jean–Claude van Itallie. — 1st ed. — New York: Grove Press: distributed by Random House, 1978. 261 p. in various pagings; 21 cm. I. T.
PS3572.A45 A19 1978   812/.5/4   LC 77-91355   ISBN 0802141617

Varley, John, 1947-. 2.13388
The Ophiuchi hotline / by John Varley. New York: Dial Press/James Wade, 1977. 237 p.; 24 cm. (Quantum science fiction) I. T. II. Series.
PZ4.V299 Op PS3572.A724   813/.5/4   LC 77-1903   ISBN 0803761201

Vonnegut, Kurt. 2.13389
Breakfast of champions: or, Goodbye blue Monday! / by Kurt Vonnegut, Jr.; with drawings by the author. — [New York]: Delacorte Press, [1973] 295 p.: ill.; 22 cm. — I. T.
PZ4.V948 Br PS3572.O5 B7x   813/.5/4   LC 72-13086

Vonnegut, Kurt. • 2.13390
Cat's cradle. — [1st ed.]. — New York: Holt, Rinehart and Winston, 1963. 233 p. I. T.
PS3572.O5 C3x   LC 63-10930

Vonnegut, Kurt. • 2.13391
God bless you, Mr. Rosewater, or, Pearls before swine. — [1st ed.]. — New York: Holt, Rinehart and Winston, [1965] 217 p.; 22 cm. — I. T. II. Title: Pearls before swine.
PZ4.V948 Go   PS3572.O5 G6x.   LC 65-16434

Vonnegut, Kurt. 2.13392
Happy birthday, Wanda June; a play. — New York: Delacorte Press, [1971] xiv, 199 p.: illus.; 22 cm. 'A Seymour Lawrence book.' I. T.
PS3572.O5 H3   812/.5/4   LC 75-156384

Vonnegut, Kurt. • **2.13393**
Mother night [by] Kurt Vonnegut, Jr. — 1st ed. — New York: Harper & Row, 1966. xii, 202 p.; 22 cm. I. T.
PZ4.V948 Mo4 PS3572.O5 M6x   813/.5/4   LC 66-13931

Vonnegut, Kurt. **2.13394**
Palm Sunday: an autobiographical collage / Kurt Vonnegut. — New York: Delacorte Press, c1981. xviii, 330 p.; 22 cm. — I. T.
PS3572.O5 P3   813/.54 19   LC 80-27322   ISBN 0440065933

Vonnegut, Kurt. • **2.13395**
Player piano. [New ed.] New York Holt, Rinehart and Winston [1966] 295p. I. T.
PS3572.O5 P5x 1966

Vonnegut, Kurt. **2.13396**
Slapstick: or, Lonesome no more!: a novel / by Kurt Vonnegut. — [New York]: Delacorte Press/S. Lawrence, c1976. 243 p.: ill.; 22 cm. I. T.
PS3572.O5 S58 1976   813/.5/4   LC 76-15605   ISBN 044008046X

Vonnegut, Kurt. • **2.13397**
The sirens of Titan / [by] Kurt Vonnegut, Jr. — Boston: Houghton Mifflin, 1961, c1959. 319 p.; 22 cm. I. T.
PZ4.V948 Si6 PS3572.O5 S5x   813/.5/4   LC 70-154039   ISBN

Vonnegut, Kurt. • **2.13398**
Slaughterhouse–five; or, The children's crusade, a duty–dance with death. [New York] Delacorte Press [1969] 186 p. 22 cm. 'A Seymour Lawrence book.' I. T. II. Title: Children's crusade.
PZ4.V948 Sl PS3572.O5 S6x   813/.5/4   LC 69-11929

Giannone, Richard. **2.13399**
Vonnegut: a preface to his novels / Richard Giannone. Port Washington, N.Y.: Kennikat Press, 1977. 136 p.; 23 cm. (Literary criticism series) (National university publications) Includes index. 1. Vonnegut, Kurt — Criticism and interpretation. I. T.
PS3572.O5 Z68   813/.5/4   LC 76-54943   ISBN 0804691673

Klinkowitz, Jerome. **2.13400**
Kurt Vonnegut / Jerome Klinkowitz. — London; New York: Methuen, c1982. 96 p.; 20 cm. — (Contemporary writers.) 1. Vonnegut, Kurt — Criticism and interpretation. I. T. II. Series.
PS3572.O5 Z74 1982   813/.54 19   LC 81-22558   ISBN 0416334806

Klinkowitz, Jerome. **2.13401**
The Vonnegut statement. Edited by Jerome Klinkowitz & John Somer. — [New York]: Delacorte Press, [1973] xvii, 286 p.; 21 cm. 1. Vonnegut, Kurt. I. Somer, John L. joint author. II. T.
PS3572.O5 Z75   813/.5/4   LC 72-5161

Schatt, Stanley. **2.13402**
Kurt Vonnegut, Jr. / by Stanley Schatt. Boston: Twayne Publishers, c1976. 174 p.: port.; 21 cm. (Twayne's United States authors series; TUSAS 276) Includes index. 1. Vonnegut, Kurt — Criticism and interpretation. I. T.
PS3572.O5 Z85   813/.5/4   LC 76-41754   ISBN 080577176X

Vonnegut in America: an introduction to the life and work of **2.13403**
Kurt Vonnegut / original essays edited by Jerome Klinkowitz and Donald L. Lawler.
New York: Delacorte Press/S. Lawrence, c1977. xv, 304 p.: ill.; 21 cm. Includes index. 1. Vonnegut, Kurt — Criticism and interpretation — Addresses, essays, lectures. I. Klinkowitz, Jerome. II. Lawler, Donald L.
PS3572.O5 Z9   813/.5/4   LC 77-9939   ISBN 0440093430

PS3573 W–Wh

Wakoski, Diane. • **2.13404**
The motorcycle betrayal poems. — New York: Simon and Schuster, [1971] 160 p.; 22 cm. — I. T.
PS3573.A42 M6   811/.5/4   LC 74-156164   ISBN 0671210114

Wakoski, Diane. • **2.13405**
Smudging. — Los Angeles: Black Sparrow Press, 1972. 153 p.: port.; 23 cm. Poems. I. Black Sparrow Press, Los Angeles. II. T.
PS3573.A42 S6   811/.5/4   LC 72-186536   ISBN 0876851316

Walker, Alice, 1944-. **2.13406**
The color purple: a novel / by Alice Walker. — 1st ed. — New York: Harcourt Brace Jovanovich, c1982. 245 p.; 22 cm. — I. T.
PS3573.A425 C6 1982   813/.54 19   LC 81-48242   ISBN 0151191530

Walker, Alice, 1944-. **2.13407**
In love & trouble; stories of Black women. — [1st ed.]. — New York: Harcourt Brace Jovanovich, [1973] 138 p.; 22 cm. 1. Afro-American women — Fiction. I. T.
PZ4.W176 In PS3573.A425 I6x   813/.5/4   LC 73-7607   ISBN 0151444056

Walker, Alice, 1944-. **2.13408**
Meridian / by Alice Walker. — 1st ed. — New York: Harcourt Brace Jovanovich, c1976. 228 p.; 22 cm. I. T.
PZ4.W176 Me PS3573.A425 M4x   813/.5/4   LC 76-941   ISBN 0151592659

Walker, Alice, 1944-. **2.13409**
Revolutionary petunias & other poems. — [1st ed.]. — New York: Harcourt Brace Jovanovich, [1973] 70 p.; 21 cm. — I. T.
PS3573.A425 R4   811/.5/4   LC 72-88796   ISBN 0151770905

Walker, Alice, 1944-. **2.13410**
In search of our mothers' gardens: womanist prose / by Alice Walker. — 1st ed. — San Diego: Harcourt Brace Jovanovich, c1983. xviii, 397 p.; 22 cm. 1. Walker, Alice, 1944- — Addresses, essays, lectures. 2. Authors, American — 20th century — Biography — Addresses, essays, lectures. 3. Feminism — Addresses, essays, lectures. 4. Afro-American women — Addresses, essays, lectures. I. T.
PS3573.A425 Z467 1983   818/.5409 19   LC 83-8584   ISBN 0151445257

Wallant, Edward Lewis, 1926-1962. • **2.13411**
The pawnbroker / Edward Lewis Wallant. — 1st ed. — New York: Harcourt, Brace & World, c1961. 279 p. 22 cm. I. T.
PS 3573 A45 P3 1961   PS3545A55 P3 1961.   LC 61-11910

Wallant, Edward Lewis, 1926-1962. • **2.13412**
The tenants of Moonbloom. — New York, Harcourt, Brace & World [1963] 245 p. 21 cm. I. T.
PZ4.W195Te2 PS3573.A45T4x   LC 63-13501

Walton, Evangeline. **2.13413**
The children of Llyr. Introd. by Lin Carter. — New York: Ballantine Books, [1971] xiii, 221 p.; 18 cm. — (Adult fantasy) I. Branwen ferch Llŷr. II. T.
PZ3.W1752 Ch PS3573.A6x   813/.5/2   LC 77-28096   ISBN 0345023323

Waugh, Hillary. **2.13414**
Last seen wearing ... / by Hillary Waugh; with introd. by George N. Nove; bibliography by Francis M. Nevins; ill. by Jamie Simon. — [San Diego]: University Extension, University of California, San Diego, c1978. 282 p.: ill., port. — (The Mystery library; 11) 1. Detective and mystery stories I. T. II. Series.
PS3573.A9 L38 1978   LC 78-69777   ISBN 089163049X

Weaver, Gordon. **2.13415**
Such waltzing was not easy: stories / by Gordon Weaver. — Urbana: University of Illinois Press, [1975] 132 p.; 21 cm. (Illinois short fiction) I. T.
PZ4.W3628 Su PS3573.E17 S8x   813/.5/4   LC 75-2288   ISBN 0252004760

Webb, Charles Richard, 1939-. • **2.13416**
The graduate / by Charles Webb. — [New York]: New American Library, [c1963] 238 p. I. T.
PS3573.E195 G7x 1963   Fic   LC 63-21804

Webb, James H. **2.13417**
Fields of fire: a novel / by James Webb, Jr. — Englewood Cliffs, N.J.: Prentice-Hall, c1978. 344 p.: map; 24 cm. 1. Vietnamese Conflict, 1961-1975 — Fiction. I. T.
PZ4.W3662 Fi PS3573.E1955 F5x   813/.5/4   LC 78-4046   ISBN 0133142868

Welch, James, 1940-. **2.13418**
The death of Jim Loney / James Welch. — 1st ed. — New York: Harper & Row, c1979. 179 p.; 22 cm. — I. T.
PZ4.W439 De PS3573.E44   813/.5/4   LC 79-1713   ISBN 0060145889

Welch, James, 1940 . **2.13419**
Fools crow: a novel / by James Welch. — New York, NY: Viking, 1986. 391 p.; 24 cm. Ill. on lining papers. 1. Siksika Indians — Fiction. 2. Indians of North America — Montana — Fiction. I. T.
PS3573.E44 F66 1986   813/.54 19   LC 85-41091   ISBN 0670811211

Welch, James, 1940-. 2.13420
Riding the Earthboy 40: poems / by James Welch. — 1st ed. — New York: Harper & Row, [1975] c1976. vii, 71 p.; 22 cm. I. T.
PS3573.E44 R5 1976   811/.5/4   LC 75-7890   ISBN 0064519910

Welch, James, 1940-. 2.13421
Winter in the blood. — [1st ed.]. — New York: Harper & Row, [1974] 176 p.; 22 cm. — I. T.
PZ4.W439 Wi PS3573.E44   PS3573 E4525 W5.   813/.5/4   LC 74-5985   ISBN 0064519902

Wharton, William. 2.13422
Birdy / by William Wharton. — 1st ed. — New York: Knopf, 1979. 309 p.; 22 cm. — I. T.
PZ4.W5377 Bi 1979 PS3573.H32 B5x   813/.5/4   LC 77-28023   ISBN 0394425693

White, Edmund, 1940-. 2.13423
Nocturnes for the King of Naples / Edmund White. — New York: St. Martin's Press, c1978. 148 p.; 21 cm. — I. T.
PZ4.W5829 No PS3573.H463 N6x   813/.5/4   LC 78-4384   ISBN 0312576536

Whiteman, Roberta Hill. 2.13424
Star quilt: poems / by Roberta Hill Whiteman; foreword by Carolyn Forché; illustrations by Ernest Whiteman. — Minneapolis: Holy Cow! Press, 1984. ix, 79 p.; ill.; 24 cm. I. T.
PS3573.H4875 S7 1984   811/.54 19   LC 83-80591   ISBN 0930100166

PS3573 Wi–Wz

Wideman, John Edgar. 2.13425
The lynchers. — [1st ed.]. — New York: Harcourt Brace Jovanovich, [1973] 264 p.; 21 cm. I. T.
PZ4.W638 Ly PS3573.I26 L9x   813/.5/4   LC 72-91841   ISBN 0151548005

Wilhelm, Kate. 2.13426
Where late the sweet birds sang / Kate Wilhelm. — 1st ed. — New York: Harper & Row, c1976. 251 p.; 22 cm. I. T.
PZ4.W678 Wh PS3573.I434 W5x   813/.5/4   LC 75-6379   ISBN 0060146540

Williams, John Alfred, 1925-. 2.13427
Captain Blackman: a novel / [by] John A. Williams. — [1st ed.]. — Garden City, N.Y.: Doubleday, 1972. 336 p.; 22 cm. I. T.
PZ4.W72624 Cap PS3573.I4495 C3x   813/.5/4   LC 75-171328

Williams, John Alfred, 1925-. 2.13428
!Click song / John A. Williams. — Boston: Houghton Mifflin, 1982. 430 p.; 24 cm. — I. T.
PS3573.I4495 C5 1982   813/.54 19   LC 81-13166   ISBN 0395318416

Muller, Gilbert H., 1941-. 2.13429
John A. Williams / by Gilbert H. Muller. — Boston: Twayne Publishers, c1984. 172 p.: port.; 23 cm. — (Twayne's United States authors series. TUSAS 472) Includes index. 1. Williams, John Alfred, 1925- — Criticism and interpretation. 2. Afro-Americans in literature I. T. II. Series.
PS3573.I4495 Z8 1984   813/.54 19   LC 83-26541   ISBN 0805774130

Williams, Sherley Anne, 1944-. 2.13430
The peacock poems / by Shirley [i.e. Sherley] Williams. — 1st ed. — Middletown, Conn.: Wesleyan University Press, [1975] 87 p.; 21 cm. (The Wesleyan poetry program; v. 79) I. T.
PS3573.I45546 P4   PS3573I4545 P4.   811/.5/4   LC 75-12531   ISBN 0819520799

Williams, Sherley Anne, 1944-. 2.13431
Dessa Rose / Sherley Anne Williams. — 1st ed. — New York: W. Morrow, c1986. 236 p.; 22 cm. I. T.
PS3573.I45546 D47 1986   813/.54 19   LC 85-29781   ISBN 0688051138

Williams, Thomas, 1926-. 2.13432
The hair of Harold Roux. — [1st ed.]. — New York: Random House, [1974] 373 p.; 25 cm. — I. T.
PZ4.W7275 Hai PS3573.I456 H2x   813/.5/4   LC 73-20583   ISBN 0394489888

Wilson, Lanford, 1937-. 2.13433
5th of July: a play / by Lanford Wilson. — 1st Hill & Wang ed. — New York: Hill and Wang, 1979, c1978. 128 p.: ill.; 20 cm. — (A Mermaid dramabook) I. T.
PS3573.I458 F5 1979   812/.5/4   LC 78-26477   ISBN 0809044552

Wilson, Lanford, 1937-. 2.13434
The Hot l Baltimore: a play. — [1st ed.]. — New York: Hill and Wang, [1973] xii, 145 p.; 21 cm. — (A Mermaid dramabook) I. T. II. Title: The Hotel Baltimore.
PS3573.I458 H65 1973   812/.5/4   LC 73-80217   ISBN 0809055449

Wilson, Lanford, 1937-. 2.13435
The mound builders: a play / by Lanford Wilson. 1st ed. — New York: Hill and Wang, 1976. 148 p.; 21 cm. (A Mermaid dramabook) I. T.
PS3573.I458 M6   812/.5/4   LC 76-18235   ISBN 0809071045

Woiwode, Larry. 2.13436
Beyond the bedroom wall: a family album / Larry Woiwode. — 1st ed. — New York: Farrar, Straus, Giroux, [1975] 619 p.; 24 cm. I. T.
PZ4.W852 Be PS3573.O4 B4x   813/.5/4   LC 75-6922

Wolfe, Gene. 2.13437
The shadow of the torturer / Gene Wolfe. — New York: Simon and Schuster, c1980. 303 p.; 22 cm. — (His The book of the new Sun; v. 1) I. T.
PS3573.O52 S5x   813/.5/4 19   LC 79-22371   ISBN 0671253255

Wolfe, Tom. 2.13438
Mauve gloves & madmen, clutter & vine, and other stories, sketches, and essays / [Tom Wolfe]. — New York: Farrar, Straus and Giroux, c1976. 243 p.: ill.; 22 cm. I. T.
PS3573.O526 M3   813/.5/2   LC 76-43968   ISBN 0374204241

Wright, Jay. 2.13439
The double invention of Komo / by Jay Wright. — Austin: University of Texas Press, c1980. 115 p.; 24 cm. (The University of Texas Press poetry series; 5) 1. Bambara (African people) — Poetry. I. T.
PS3573.R5364 D6   811/.5/4 19   LC 79-23580   ISBN 0292715269

Wright, Jay. 2.13440
Explications/interpretations / Jay Wright. — Lexington: University of Kentucky, 1984. 83 p.: ill.; 22 cm. (Callaloo poetry series. v. 3) I. T. II. Series.
PS3573.R5364 E9 1984   811/.54 19   LC 84-215110   ISBN 0912759011

PS3575–3576 Y–Z

Yarbro, Chelsea Quinn. 2.13441
Ariosto: Ariosto furioso, a romance for an alternate Renaissance / Chelsea Quinn Yarbro. — New York: Pocket Books, 1980. 361 p.; 18 cm. 1. Science fiction I. T.
PS3575.A7 A7x

Young, Al, 1939-. 2.13442
Snakes; a novel. — [1st ed.]. — New York: Holt, Rinehart and Winston, [1970] 149 p.; 22 cm. — I. T.
PZ4.Y67 Sn PS3575.O683   813/.5/4   LC 77-105434   ISBN 0030845351

Young, Al, 1939-. 2.13443
Dancing; poems. — [1st ed.]. — New York: Corinth Books, 1969. 63 p.; 21 cm. — I. T.
PS3575.O683 D3   811/.5/4   LC 71-98907

Young, Al, 1939-. 2.13444
Sitting pretty: a novel / by Al Young. — New York: Holt, Rinehart and Winston, c1976. 254 p.; 22 cm. I. T.
PZ4.Y67 Si PS3575.O683 S5x   813/.5/4   LC 75-21461   ISBN 0030152666

Young Bear, Ray A. 2.13445
Winter of the salamander: the keeper of importance / Ray Young Bear. — 1st ed. — San Francisco: Harper & Row, c1980. xi, 208 p.; 22 cm. — I. T.
PS3575.O865 W5 1980   811/.5/4   LC 79-4719   ISBN 0064527506

Zelazny, Roger. 2.13446
Jack of shadows. — New York: Walker, [1971] 207 p.; 22 cm. — I. T.
PZ4.Z456 Jac PS3576.E43 J3x   813/.5/4   LC 70-142849   ISBN 0802755356

Zindel, Paul.   • 2.13447
The effect of gamma rays on man–in–the–moon marigolds; a drama in two acts.
Drawings by Dong Kingman. — New York: Harper & Row, [1971] 108 p.:
illus.; 22 cm. — I. T.
PS3576.I518 E3 1971b   812/.5/4   LC 79-135772   *ISBN*
0060268298

PT1-951 HISTORY. CRITICISM

Garland, Henry B. (Henry Burnand) **2.13448**
The Oxford companion to German literature / by Henry and Mary Garland. — 2nd ed. — Oxford [Oxfordshire]; New York: Oxford University Press, 1986, c1976. p. cm. 1. German literature — Dictionaries. 2. German literature — Bio-bibliography. I. Garland, Mary. II. T.
PT41.G3 1986   830/.3 19   *LC* 85-25962   *ISBN* 0198661398

Kritisches Lexikon zur deutschsprachigen Gegenwartsliteratur / **2.13449**
hrsg. von Heinz Ludwig Arnold.
München: Edition Text & Kritik, 1978-. v. — (Edition Text & [i.e. und] Kritik) Loose-leaf for updating. At head of title: KLG. 1. Authors, German — Dictionaries 2. German literature — 20th century — Dictionaries I. Series.
PT41 K7   *ISBN* 3883770094

Reallexikon der deutschen Literaturgeschichte. Begründet von **2.13450**
Paul Merker und Wolfgang Stammler. 2. Aufl. Neu bearb. und
unter redaktioneller Mitarbeit von Klaus Kanzog, sowie
Mitwirkung zahlreicher Fachgelehrter. Hrsg. von Werner
Kohlschmidt und Wolfgang Mohr.
2. Aufl. Berlin W. de Gruyter 1958-. v. 'Bd. 4 hrsg. von Klaus Kanzog und Achim Masser. Redaktion: Dorothea Kanzog.' 1. German literature — Dictionaries 2. German literature — History and criticism 3. German literature — History and criticism — Bibliography I. Merker, Paul, 1881-, ed. II. Stammler, Wolfgang, 1886-, ed.
PT41 R4 1958

Holub, Robert C. **2.13451**
Reception theory: a critical introduction / Robert C. Holub. — London; New York: Methuen, 1984. xiv, 189 p.; 21 cm. — (New accents) Includes index. 1. Criticism — Germany (West) — History. 2. Reader-response criticism — Germany (West) 3. Literature — History and criticism I. T.
PT80.H64 1984   801/.95/0943 19   *LC* 83-13385   *ISBN* 0416335802

Boesch, Bruno, 1911-. **2.13452**
[Deutsche Literaturgeschichte in Grundzügen. English] German literature: a critical survey; edited by Bruno Boesch. Translated [from the German] by Ronald Taylor. London, Methuen [1971] 375 p. 24 cm. Distributed in USA by Barnes & Noble. Translation of Deutsche Literaturgeschichte in Grundzügen. 1. German literature — History and criticism. I. T.
PT85.B6313   830.9   *LC* 77-882930   *ISBN* 0416149405

Boor, Helmut de, 1891-. • **2.13453**
Geschichte der deutschen Literatur: von den Anfängen bis zur Gegenwart / von Helmut de Boor und Richard Newald. — 4. verb. Aufl. München: C. Beck, 1960-. v.; 23 cm. (Handbücher für das germanistische Studium) Edition varies. 1. German literature — History and criticism. I. Newald, Richard, 1894-1954 II. Rupprich, Hans, 1898- III. T. IV. Series.
PT 85 B72 1960

Burger, Heinz Otto, 1903-. • **2.13454**
Annalen der deutschen Literatur; eine Gemeinschaftsarbeit zahlreicher Fachgelehrter, hrsg. von Heinz Otto Burger. 2., überarb. Aufl. Stuttgart J.B. Metzler 1971. 838p. 1. German literature — History and criticism I. T.
PT85 B8 1971

Martini, Fritz, 1909-. **2.13455**
Deutsche Literaturgeschichte: von den Anfängen bis zur Gegenwart / von Fritz Martini. — 18., neu bearbeitete Aufl. — Stuttgart: A. Kröner, c1984. vii, 741 p.; 18 cm. (Kröners Taschenausgabe; Bd. 196) Includes indexes. 1. German literature — History and criticism. I. T.
PT85.M3 1984   830/.9 19   *LC* 84-186373   *ISBN* 3520196182

Robertson, John George, 1867-1933. • **2.13456**
A history of German literature, by J. G. Robertson. — 6th ed. by Dorothy Reich with the assistance of W. I. Lucas [and others]. — Edinburgh: Blackwood, 1970. xxvii, 817 p.; 23 cm. 1. German literature — History and criticism. I. Reich, Dorothy, ed. II. T.
PT91.R7 1970   830.9   *LC* 74-552609   *ISBN* 085158103X

Rose, Ernst, 1899-. • **2.13457**
A history of German literature / by Ernst Rose. — New York: New York University Press, 1960. xiii, 353 p. 1. German literature — History and criticism. 2. German literature — Translations into English — Bibliography. 3. English literature — Translations from German — Bibliography. I. T.
PT91.R75   *LC* 60-9405

Schmitt, Fritz, 1904-. • **2.13458**
Deutsche Literaturgeschichte in Tabellen / bearb. von Fritz Schmitt; unter Mitarbeit von Gerhard Fricke. — Bonn: Athenäum Verlag, 1949-1952. 3 v.: graphs; 25 cm. Illustrative matter in pocket. 1. German literature — Outlines, syllabi, etc. 2. German literature — Chronology. I. Fricke, Gerhard, 1901- II. T.
PT103.S4 1949   PT103.S39.   830.9   *LC* a 50-5527

PT175-405 Literary History, by Period

Ehrismann, Gustav, 1855-. • **2.13459**
Geschichte der deutschen literatur bis zum ausgang des mittelalters, von dr. Gustav Ehrismann. München, Beck, 1918-35. 2 v. in 4. 27 cm. (Handbuch des deutschen unterrichts an höheren schulen ... 6. bd., 1.-2. t.) 1. German literature — Old High German — History and criticism. 2. German literature — Middle High German — History and criticism. I. T.
PT175.E3x PF3071.M4 6bd., t.1-2   830.902   *LC* 22-6575

Salmon, Paul. **2.13460**
Literature in medieval Germany / by Paul Salmon. — New York: Barnes & Noble, 1967. xxi, 284 p.; 21 cm. — (Introductions to German literature; v. 1) 1. German literature — Old High German, 750-1050 — History and criticism. 2. German literature — Middle High German, 1050-1500 — History and criticism. I. T.
PT175.S3x   830.9

Walshe, Maurice O'C. (Maurice O'Connell) • **2.13461**
Medieval German literature: a survey / by M. O'C. Walshe. — Cambridge, Mass.: Harvard University Press, 1962. xiv, 421 p.: map. 1. German literature — Old High German, 750-1050 — History and criticism. 2. German literature — Middle High German, 1050-1500 — History and criticism. I. T.
PT175.W27   *LC* 62-52525/L

Murdoch, Brian, 1944-. **2.13462**
Old High German literature / by Brian O. Murdoch. — Boston: Twayne Publishers, c1983. 161 p.: ill.; 23 cm. — (Twayne's world authors series. TWAS 688) Includes index. 1. German literature — Old High German, 750-1050 — History and criticism. I. T. II. Series.
PT183.M85 1983   830/.9/001 19   *LC* 82-25478   *ISBN* 0805765352

Pascal, Roy, 1904-. • **2.13463**
German literature in the sixteenth and seventeenth centuries: renaissance, reformation, baroque; with a chapter on German painting by Hannah Priebsch Closs. — London: Cressent P., 1968. xix, 274 p.; 21 cm. — (Introductions to German literature, v. 2) 1. German literature — Early modern, 1500-1700 — History and criticism. 2. German literature — Early modern, 1500-1700 — Bio-bibliography. I. Closs, Hannah Priebsch. joint author. II. T.
PT238.P3   830.9/004   *LC* 70-427774

Taylor, Archer, 1890-1973. • **2.13464**
The literary history of Meistergesang, by Archer Taylor ... New York, Modern language association of America, 1937. x, 134 p. (The Modern Language Association of America. General series) 1. German poetry — History and criticism 2. Meistersingers I. T. II. Series.
PT245.T3

Bernstein, Eckhard. **2.13465**
German humanism / by Eckhard Bernstein. — Boston, Mass.: Twayne Publishers, c1983. 171 p.; 23 cm. — (Twayne's world authors series. TWAS 690) Includes index. 1. German literature — Early modern, 1500-1700 — History and criticism. 2. Humanism in literature 3. Humanism I. T. II. Series.
PT251.B46 1983   830/.9/003 19   *LC* 82-23324   *ISBN* 0805765379

PT285–321 18TH–19TH CENTURIES (1700–1860/70

Korff, Hermann August, 1882-. 2.13466
Geist der Goethezeit: Versuch einer ideellen Entwicklung der klassisch-romantischen Literaturgeschichte. — Leipzig: J.J. Weber, 1925-53. 4 v.; 25 cm. I. T.
PT285.K6

Lange, Victor, 1908-. 2.13467
The classical age of German literature, 1740–1815 / Victor Lange. — New York, N.Y.: Holmes & Meier, 1982. x, 275 p.; 22 cm. Includes index. 1. German literature — 18th century — History and criticism 2. Classicism I. T.
PT311.L26 1982   830/.9/006 19   *LC* 82-15734   *ISBN* 0841908540

Hatfield, Henry Caraway, 1912-. • 2.13468
Aesthetic paganism in German literature, from Winckelmann to the death of Goethe. — Cambridge, Harvard University Press, 1964. xi, 283 p. 22 cm. Bibliographical references included in 'Notes' (p. [239]-278) 1. German literature — 18th cent. — Hist. & crit. 2. German literature — 19th cent. — Hist. & crit. 3. Literature, Comparative — German and Greek. 4. Literature, Comparative — Greek and German. I. T.
PT313.H3   *LC* 64-13423

Loewenthal, Erich, 1895?-1944. • 2.13469
Sturm und Drang: kritische Schriften / Plan und Auswahl von Erich Loewenthal. — 3. Aufl. — Heidelberg: L. Schneider, 1972. 911 p. 1. Sturm und Drang movement I. T.
PT317.L6   830.9

Pascal, Roy, 1904-. • 2.13470
The German Sturm und Drang / by Roy Pascal. — [1st ed.], reprinted with minor corrections. — Manchester: Manchester University Press, 1967. xvi, 347 p. [4] leaves of plates: ill., ports. 1. Sturm und Drang movement I. T.
PT317.P38 1967   *LC* 68-102695   *ISBN* 0719001943

PT341–395 19TH CENTURY

Mann, Thomas, 1875-1955. • 2.13471
Last essays. Translated from the German by Richard and Clara Winston and Tania and James Stern. [1st ed.] New York, Knopf, 1959 [c1958] 211 p. port. 22 cm. 1. Schiller, Friedrich, 1759-1805. 2. German literature — 19th century — Addresses, essays, lectures. I. T.
PT343.M28   830.4   *LC* 59-5436

Seidlin, Oskar, 1911-. • 2.13472
Essays in German and comparative literature. Chapel Hill University of North Carolina Press 1961. 254p. (University of North Carolina studies in comparative literature. no. 30) 1. German literature — History and criticism I. T. II. Series.
PT343 S45

Bernd, Clifford A. 2.13473
German poetic realism / by Clifford Albrecht Bernd. — Boston: Twayne Publishers, 1981. 150 p.: ill.; 21 cm. — (Twayne's world authors series; TWAS 605: Germany) Includes index. 1. German literature — 19th century — History and criticism 2. Realism in literature I. T.
PT345.B46   831/.8/0912 19   *LC* 80-23509   *ISBN* 080576447X

Huch, Ricarda Octavia, 1864-1947. • 2.13474
Die Romantik: Ausbreitung, Blütezeit und Verfall / Ricarda Huch. — Tübingen: R. Wunderlich, 1951. 674 p. 1. Romanticism — Germany 2. German literature — 19th century — History and criticism 3. German literature — 18th century — History and criticism I. T.
PT361 H8 1951   *LC* 54-27450

Field, George Wallis, 1914-. 2.13475
The nineteenth century, 1830–1890 / G. Wallis Field. — London: E. Benn; New York: Barnes & Noble Books, 1975. xv, 214 p.; 23 cm. — (A Literary history of Germany) Includes index. 1. German literature — 19th century — History and criticism I. T. II. Series.
PT391.F5x   830/.9/007   *LC* 75-313622   *ISBN* 0510323081

Martini, Fritz, 1909-. 2.13476
Deutsche Literatur im bürgerlichen Realismus, 1848–1898 / Fritz Martini. — 4., mit neuem Vorwort und erw. Nachwort versehene Aufl. — Stuttgart: Metzler, 1981. xxi, 992, 31 p.; 23 cm. 1. German literature — 19th century — History and criticism 2. Realism in literature I. T.
PT391.M3 1981   830/.9/12 19   *LC* 81-104360   *ISBN* 3476004635

Lange, Victor, 1908-. • 2.13477
Modern German literature, 1870–1940. — Port Washington, N.Y.: Kennikat Press, [1967, c1945] xi, 223 p.; 22 cm. 1. German literature — 19th century — History and criticism 2. German literature — 20th century — History and criticism. I. T.
PT395.L3 1967   830.9/008   *LC* 67-27616

PT401–405 20TH CENTURY

Jens, Walter, 1923-. • 2.13478
Deutsche Literatur der Gegenwart; Themen, Stile, Tendenzen. [4., vom Autor durchgesehene Aufl.]. — München, R. Piper 1962, [c1961] 156, [1] p. 21 cm. 'Verweise' (bibliographical): p. 153-[157] 1. German literature — 20th cent. — Hist. & crit. I. T.
PT401.J38 1962   *LC* 63-25655

Taylor, Ronald, 1924-. 2.13479
Literature and society in Germany, 1918–1945 / Ronald Taylor. — Brighton, Sussex: Harvester Press; Totowa, N.J.: Barnes & Noble, 1980. xiii, 363 p.; 24 cm. — (Harvester studies in contemporary literature and culture. 3) Includes index. 1. German literature — 20th century — History and criticism. 2. Literature and society — Germany. I. T. II. Series.
PT401.T36 1980   830/.9/358 19   *LC* 82-189886   *ISBN* 0389200360

Ritchie, J. M. (James MacPherson), 1927-. 2.13480
German literature under National Socialism / J.M. Ritchie. — London: C. Helm; Totowa, N.J.: Barnes & Noble, 1983. 325 p.; 23 cm. Includes index. 1. German literature — 20th century — History and criticism. 2. National socialism and literature I. T.
PT403.R54 1983   830/.9/00912 19   *LC* 83-10557   *ISBN* 0389204188

Demetz, Peter, 1922-. • 2.13481
Postwar German literature; a critical introduction. — New York: Pegasus, [1970] 264 p.; 22 cm. Rev. and enl. German ed. published in 1973 under title: Die süsse Anarchie. 1. German literature — 20th century — History and criticism. I. T.
PT405.D4   830/.9/00914   *LC* 73-114169

Mandel, Siegfried. 2.13482
Group 47: the reflected intellect. With a pref. by Harry T. Moore. Carbondale, Southern Illinois University Press [1973] xii, 232 p. 22 cm. (Crosscurrents/modern critiques) 1. Gruppe 47 (Germany) I. T.
PT405.M33   830/.9/00914   *LC* 73-8698   *ISBN* 0809306417

PT500–951 Literary History, by Form

PT500–597 POETRY

Gray, Ronald D. 2.13483
German poetry: a guide to free appreciation / Ronald Gray. — Cambridge; New York: Cambridge University Press, 1976. xxxiv, 133 p.; 23 cm. Rev. ed. of An introduction to German poetry, published in 1965. Includes index. 1. German poetry — History and criticism. 2. German poetry 3. Poetry — History and criticism I. T.
PT501.G7 1976   PT501 G7 1976.   831/.008   *LC* 76-355210   *ISBN* 0521209315

Wiese, Benno von, 1903-. • 2.13484
Die deutsche Lyrik; Form und Geschichte. Düsseldorf: Pädagogischer Verlag Schwann, [1959] 2 v. 23 cm. 1. German poetry — History and criticism. I. T.
PT501.W5 1959   *LC* 62-40865

Gedichte und Interpretationen / herausgegeben von Volker Meid. 2.13485
Stuttgart: P. Reclam, 1982-. v.: ill.; 16 cm. — (Universal-Bibliothek; Nr. 7890 [etc.]) Editor varies. 1. German poetry — History and criticism. 2. German poctry I. Meid, Werner Volker, 1940-
PT 521 G29 1982   *ISBN* 3150078903

Browning, Robert Marcellus, 1911-. • 2.13486
German baroque poetry, 1618–1723 [by] Robert M. Browning. — University Park: Pennsylvania State University Press, [1971] x, 292 p.; 23 cm. — (Penn

State series in German literature.) 1. Baroque literature 2. German poetry — Early modern, 1500-1700 — History and criticism. I. T. II. Series.
PT529.B7   831/.04   *LC* 77-136959   *ISBN* 0271011467

Browning, Robert Marcellus, 1911-.   **2.13487**
German poetry in the Age of the Enlightenment: from Brockes to Klopstock / Robert M. Browning. — University Park: Pennsylvania State University Press, c1978. xi, 336 p.; 23 cm. — (Penn State series in German literature.) Includes index. 1. German poetry — 18th century — History and criticism. 2. Enlightenment 3. Germany — Intellectual life I. T. II. Series.
PT535.B7   PT535 B7.   831/.04   *LC* 77-26832   *ISBN* 0271005416

Allen, Roy F., 1937-.   **2.13488**
German expressionist poetry / Roy F. Allen. — Boston: Twayne Publishers, 1979. 158 p.; 21 cm. — (Twayne's world authors series; TWAS 543: Germany) Includes index. 1. German poetry — 20th century — History and criticism. 2. Expressionism I. T.
PT553.A4   831/.9/1209   *LC* 79-493   *ISBN* 0805763864

Closs, August, 1898-.   • **2.13489**
The genius of the German lyric; an historical survey of its formal and metaphysical values. [2d ed.] Philadelphia Dufour Editions 1962. 387p. 1. German poetry — History and criticism I. T.
PT571 C6 1962

PT605–701 Drama

Wiese, Benno von, 1903- ed.   • **2.13490**
Das deutsche Drama vom Barock bis zur Gegenwart; Interpretationen. — Düsseldorf, A. Bagel [1958] 2 v. 22 cm. Includes bibliographical references. 1. German drama — Hist. & crit. I. T.
PT615.W5 1968   *LC* 62-48227

Aikin, Judith Popovich, 1946-.   **2.13491**
German baroque drama / by Judith Popovich Aikin. — Boston: Twayne, c1982. 186 p., [1] p. of plates: port.; 21 cm. — (Twayne's world authors series. TWAS 634) Includes index. 1. German drama — Early modern, 1500-1700 — History and criticism. I. T. II. Series.
PT636.A35 1982   832/.4/09 19   *LC* 82-9270   *ISBN* 0805764771

Bennett, Benjamin, 1939-.   **2.13492**
Modern drama and German classicism: renaissance from Lessing to Brecht / Benjamin Bennett. — Ithaca, N.Y.: Cornell University Press, 1980, c1979. 359 p.; 24 cm. 1. German drama — 18th century — History and criticism. 2. German drama — History and criticism. 3. European drama — History and criticism. I. T.
PT636.B4   832/.6/09   *LC* 79-14644   *ISBN* 0801411890

Kistler, Mark Oliver, 1918-.   • **2.13493**
Drama of the storm and stress, by Mark O. Kistler. New York, Twayne Publishers [c1969] 170 p. 21 cm. (Twayne's world authors series, TWAS 83. German literature) 1. German drama — 18th century — History and criticism. 2. Sturm und Drang movement I. T.
PT643.K5   832/.6/09   *LC* 70-99550

Innes, C. D.   **2.13494**
Modern German drama: a study in form / C. D. Innes. — Cambridge [Eng.]; New York: Cambridge University Press, 1979. 297 p.: ill.; 24 cm. Includes index. 1. German drama — 20th century — History and criticism. I. T.
PT666.I5   832/.9/1409   *LC* 78-26597   *ISBN* 0521225760

Ritchie, J. M. (James MacPherson), 1927-.   **2.13495**
German expressionist drama / by J. M. Ritchie. — Boston: Twayne Publishers, c1976 [1977] 198 p.: ill. — (Twayne's world authors series; TWAS 421: Germany) Includes index. 1. German drama — 20th century — History and criticism. 2. Expressionism I. T.
PT668.R5 1977   PT668 R5 1977.   832/.8/091   *LC* 76-46324   *ISBN* 0805762612

Wiese, Benno von, 1903-.   **2.13496**
Die deutsche Tragödie von Lessing bis Hebbel / Benno von Wiese. — 8. Aufl. — Hamburg: Hoffmann und Campe Verlag, 1973. xvii, 712 p.; 22 cm. 1. German drama (Tragedy) I. T.
PT671.W5 1973   *ISBN* 345509046X

PT711–871 Fiction

Emmel, Hildegard, 1907-.   **2.13497**
[Geschichte des deutschen Romans. English] History of the German novel / Hildegard Emmel. — English-language ed. / prepared by Ellen Summerfield. — Detroit: Wayne State University Press, 1984. xv, 389 p.; 24 cm. Abridged translation with revisions of: Geschichte des deutschen Romans. 'German novels in English translation'—p. 369-380. Includes index. 1. German fiction — History and criticism. I. Summerfield, Ellen, 1949- II. T.
PT741.E5413 1984   833/.009 19   *LC* 84-15164   *ISBN* 0814317707

Pascal, Roy, 1904-.   • **2.13498**
The German novel; studies. [Toronto] University of Toronto Press [1956] 344 p. 22 cm. 1. German fiction — History and criticism. I. T.
PT741.P3 1956   833.09   *LC* 57-3904

Wiese, Benno von, 1903- ed.   • **2.13499**
Der deutsche Roman vom Barock bis zur Gegenwart; Struktur und Geschichte. — Düsseldorf: Pädag. Vlg. Schwann, [1963] 2 v. 22 cm. Includes bibliographical references. 1. German fiction — Hist. & crit. I. T.
PT745.W5   *LC* 63-25654

Swales, Martin.   **2.13500**
The German Bildungsroman from Wieland to Hesse / Martin Swales. — Princeton, N.J.: Princeton University Press, c1978. xi, 171 p.; 23 cm. — (Princeton essays in literature) 1. German fiction — History and criticism — Addresses, essays, lectures. 2. Bildungsroman I. T.
PT747.E6 S9   833/.09   *LC* 77-85568   *ISBN* 0691063591

Bennett, Edwin Keppel.   • **2.13501**
A history of the German Novelle, by E. K. Bennett. [2d ed.] rev. and continued by H. M. Waidson. Cambridge [Eng.] University Press [1961] 315p. First ed. published in 1934 under title: A history of the German Novelle from Goethe to Thomas Mann. 1. Short stories, German — History and criticism. 2. German fiction — History and criticism. I. Waidson, H. M. II. T. III. Title: German Novelle.
PT747.S6 B4 1961   *LC* 61-66451

Wagener, Hans, 1940-.   **2.13502**
The German baroque novel. — New York: Twayne Publishers, [1973] 183 p.; 21 cm. — (Twayne's world authors series, TWAS 299. Germany) 1. German fiction — Early modern, 1500-1700 — History and criticism. I. T.
PT756.W3   833/.03   *LC* 77-187628

Blackall, Eric A. (Eric Albert)   **2.13503**
The novels of the German romantics / by Eric A. Blackall. — Ithaca: Cornell University Press, 1983. 315 p.: ports.; 24 cm. Includes index. 1. German fiction — 18th century — History and criticism. 2. German fiction — 19th century — History and criticism. 3. Romanticism — Germany. I. T.
PT759.B55 1983   833/.6/09145 19   *LC* 82-22104   *ISBN* 0801415233

Silz, Walter, 1894-.   • **2.13504**
Realism and reality: studies in the German novelle of poetic realism / by Walter Silz. — Chapel Hill: University of North Carolina Press, 1954. 168 p.; 24 cm. — (Studies in the Germanic languages and literatures (Chapel Hill, N.C.); no. 11) 1. German fiction — 19th century — History and criticism 2. Realism in literature I. T. II. Series.
PT763.S55   833.609   *LC* 54-11440

Swales, Martin.   **2.13505**
The German Novelle / by Martin Swales. — Princeton, N.J.: Princeton University Press, c1977. xi, 229 p. Includes index. 1. German fiction — 19th century — History and criticism. 2. Short stories, German — History and criticism. I. T.
PT763.S86   PT763 S86.   833/.02   *LC* 76-45913   *ISBN* 0691063311

The Contemporary novel in German; a symposium. Edited, with   • **2.13506**
an introd., by Robert R. Heitner.
Austin, Published for the Dept. of Germanic Languages of the University of Texas by the University of Texas Press [1967] 141 p. 24 cm. 'Lectures at the seventh annual symposium held at the University of Texas, on November 29 and 30, and December 1, 1965, under the sponsorship of the Department of Germanic Languages.' 1. German fiction — 20th century — History and criticism — Addresses, essays, lectures. I. Heitner, Robert R. ed. II. Texas. University. Dept. of Germanic Languages.
PT772.C6   833/.9/109   *LC* 67-25327

Ryan, Judith, 1943-.   **2.13507**
The uncompleted past: postwar German novels and the Third Reich / Judith Ryan. — Detroit: Wayne State University Press, 1983. 183 p.; 24 cm. 1. German fiction — 20th century — History and criticism. 2. National socialism in literature I. T.
PT772.R9 1983   833/.914/09358 19   *LC* 83-6744   *ISBN* 0814317286

Ziolkowski, Theodore.   • **2.13508**
Dimensions of the modern novel; German texts and European contexts. — Princeton, N.J.: Princeton University Press, 1969. xi, 378 p.; 23 cm. 1. German fiction — 20th century — History and criticism. I. T.
PT772.Z5   833/.9/1209   LC 68-8970

PT881–951 Folk Literature. Legends

**Kinder– und Hausmärchen gesammelt durch die Brüder Grimm: 2.13509
vollständige Ausgabe auf der Grundlage der dritten Auflage,
1837 / herausgegeben von Heinz Rölleke.**
1. Aufl. — Frankfurt am Main: Deutscher Klassiker Verlag, 1985. 1302 p.; 19 cm. (Bibliothek deutscher Klassiker. 5) I. Grimm, Jacob, 1785-1863. II. Series.
PT921.G7x 1985   LC 86-873086   ISBN 3618606605

Kinder- und Hausmärchen. English.   **2.13510**
The complete fairy tales of the Brothers Grimm / translated and with an introduction by Jack Zipes; illustrations by John B. Gruelle. — Toronto; New York, N.Y.: Bantam, 1987. xxxiv, 733 p.: ill.; 24 cm. Translation of: Kinder- und Hausmärchen. 1. Fairy tales — Germany I. Grimm, Jacob, 1785-1863. II. Grimm, Wilhelm, 1786-1859. III. Zipes, Jack David. IV. Gruelle, Johnny, 1880?-1938. ill. V. T.
PT921.K5613 1987   398.2/1/0943 19   LC 86-47728   ISBN 0553051849

PT923 Faust Legend

Faust, d. ca. 1540.   **2.13511**
Doctor Fausti Weheklag. Die Volksbücher von D. Johann Faust und Christoph Wagner. Nach den Erstdrucken neu bearb. und eingeleitet von Helmut Wiemken. Bremen, C. Schünemann [1961] lxxiii, 310 p. illus. 18 cm. (Sammlung Dietrich, Bd. 186) I. Wiemken, Helmut, ed. II. T.
PT923.Ax

Historia von Doctor Johann Fausten. English.   • **2.13512**
The historie of the damnable life and deserved death of Doctor John Faustus. Modernized, edited, and introduced by William Rose. Foreword to the American ed. by William Karl Pfeiler. — Notre Dame, Ind.: University of Notre Dame Press, 1963. xv, 210 p.: illus.; 21 cm. 'First paperback edition. First published as a volume in the Broadway translations series (1925), in London by George Routledge & Sons, ltd., and in New York by E. P. Dutton.' The 1925 ed. included also text of The second report of Doctor John Faustus. The English Faust-book, given here in modernized spelling, was first published in 1592 as a translation of Historia von Doctor Johann Fausten. Includes facsim. of original 1592 t. p. 1. Faust — Legends. I. Rose, William, 1894-1961, ed. II. T.
PT923.E5 1963   809.92   LC 63-693

Faust, d. ca. 1540.   • **2.13513**
History of Doctor Johann Faustus / recovered from the German by H. G. Haile. — Urbana: University of Illinois Press, 1965. 136 p. I. Haile, Harry Gerald, 1931-. II. T.
PT923.E5 1965   833.4   LC 65-19570

PT941.E8–.E9 Eulenspiegel

Eulenspiegel. English.   **2.13514**
A pleasant vintage of Till Eulenspiegel, born in the country of Brunswick; how he spent his life, 95 of his tales. Translated from the edition of 1515, with introd. and critical appendix, by Paul Oppenheimer. — [1st ed.]. — Middletown, Conn.: Wesleyan University Press, 1972. xxv, 293 p.: illus.; 24 cm. Translation of Ein kurtzweilig Lesen von Dyl Vlenspiegel geborē vss dem Land zu Brunsswick, from Schröder's facsim. (1911) of the 1515 ed. I. Oppenheimer, Paul, ed. II. T.
PT941.E8 E5 1972   LC 73-184361   ISBN 0819540439

PT1100–1374 Collections of German Literature

PT1151–1241 Poetry

The Oxford book of German verse: from the 12th to the 20th   • **2.13515
century.**
3rd ed. / edited by E. L. Stahl. — Oxford, [Eng.]: Clarendon Press, 1967. xxi, 541 p.; 18 cm. German, with preface and notes in English. 1. German poetry I. Stahl, E. L. (Ernest Ludwig), 1902-
PT1155.O8 1967   LC 68-85765

Flores, Angel, 1900-.   • **2.13516**
An anthology of German poetry from Hölderlin to Rilke in English translation / edited by Angel Flores. — Gloucester, Mass.: P. Smith, 1965, c1960. xxii, 458 p.; 21 cm. 1. German poetry — Translations into English. 2. English poetry — Translations from German. I. T.
PT1160.E5 F55 1965   LC 60-5926

German poetry, 1910–1975: an anthology / translated and edited   **2.13517
by Michael Hamburger.**
New York: Urizen Books, [1976] xxxiii, 559 p. 1. German poetry — 20th century — Translations into English. 2. English poetry — 20th century — Translations from German. 3. German poetry — 20th century I. Hamburger, Michael.
PT1160.E5 H3 1976   PT1160E5 H3 1976.   831/.9/108   LC 76-21303   ISBN 0916354083

Fischer-Dieskau, Dietrich, 1925- comp.   **2.13518**
[Texte deutscher Lieder. English & German] The Fischer-Dieskau book of lieder: the original texts of over seven hundred and fifty songs / chosen and introduced by Dietrich Fischer-Dieskau; with English translations by George Bird and Richard Stokes. — 1st American ed. — New York: Knopf, 1977, c1976. 435 p.; 25 cm. First published under title: Texte deutscher Lieder. English and German. Includes indexes. 1. Songs — Texts 2. Ballads, German — Texts. I. T. II. Title: Book of lieder.
PT1160.E6 F5 1977   784/.3/00943   LC 76-47955   ISBN 0394494350

Schoolfield, George C. ed.   • **2.13519**
The German lyric of the baroque in English translation, by George C. Schoolfield. — New York: AMS Press, 1966 [c1961] 380 p.; 24 cm. Poems in English and German, with English commentary. Original ed. issued as no. 29 of the University of North Carolina studies in the Germanic languages and literatures. 1. German poetry — Early modern, 1500-1700 2. German poetry — Early modern, 1500-1700 — Translations into English. 3. English poetry — Translations from German. I. T.
PT1165.S3 1966   LC 72-184970

Prawer, Siegbert Salomon, 1925- comp.   • **2.13520**
Seventeen modern German poets, edited by Siegbert Prawer. — London: Oxford University Press, 1971. 203 p.; 19 cm. — (Clarendon German series) German text, English introd. and notes. 1. German poetry — 20th century I. T.
PT1174.P7   831/.9/108   LC 75-27732   ISBN 019832474X

PT1251–1299 Drama

Modern German drama / edited by Edgar Lohner and Hunter   • **2.13521
G. Hannum.**
Boston: Houghton Mifflin, 1966. 471 p. Texts in German; commentaries in English. 1. German drama — 19th century 2. German drama — 20th century I. Lohner, Edgar. II. Hannum, Hunter G.
PT1268.L6   PT1268.M6.   LC 66-3026

PT1301–1374 Prose

Das Oxforder Buch deutscher Prosa von Luther bis Rilke.   • **2.13522**
Hrsg. von H.G. Fiedler.
Oxford Universitäts-Verlag 1943. 684p. 1. German prose literature I. Fiedler, Hermann Georg, 1862-1945. ed.
PT1305 O8

Hofmannsthal, Hugo Hofmann, Elder von, 1874-1929, comp.   • **2.13523**
Deutsche Erzahler / H. H. Elder von Hofmannsthal. — Wiesbaden: Insel-Verlag, 1964. 995 p. 1. Short stories, German I. T.
PT1324.H6

Lange, Victor, 1908- ed.   • **2.13524**
Great German short novels and stories. Edited, with an introd., by Victor Lange. New York, Modern Library [1952] 486 p. 19 cm. (The Modern library of the world's best books) A revision of the work with the same title, edited by B. A. Cerf. 1. Short stories, German 2. German fiction — Translations into English. 3. English fiction — Translations into German. I. Cerf, Bennett, 1898-1971. ed. Great German short novels and stories. II. T.
PT1327.L3   833.081   *LC* 52-9773

Otten, Karl, 1889-1963.   • **2.13525**
Ahnung und Aufbruch; expressionistische Prosa. [Darmstadt] H. Luchterhand [1957] 567 p. 23 cm. 1. German fiction — 20th century 2. Expressionism I. T.
PT1338.O8x   *LC* a 58-4981

PT1375–1695 MIDDLE HIGH GERMAN LITERATURE (1050–1450/15

German medieval tales / edited by Francis G. Gentry; foreword   **2.13526**
by Thomas Berger.
New York: Continuum, 1983. xviii, 212 p.; 22 cm. (German library. v. 4) 1. German literature — Middle High German, 1050-1500 — Translations into English. 2. English literature — Translations from German. 3. Tales — Germany — Translations into English. 4. Tales — Translations from German. I. Gentry, Francis G. II. Series.
PT1384.G47 1983   830/.8/002 19   *LC* 82-22050   *ISBN* 0826402720

Kraus, Carl von, 1868-1952. ed.   • **2.13527**
Des Minnesangs Frühling. Nach Karl Lachmann, Moriz Haupt und Friedrich Vogt. — 35. Aufl. Neu bearb. 35. Aufl. Textausg. mit Verzeichnis der Strophenanfänge. — Leipzig, S. Hirzel, 1944. xviii, 541 p.; 21 cm. I. Lachmann, Karl Konrad Friedrich Wilhelm, 1793-1851, ed. Des Minnesangs Frühling II. T.
PT1421.K7

Brant, Sebastian, 1458-1521.   • **2.13528**
The ship of fools, by Sebastian Brant. Translated into rhyming couplets, with introduction and commentary, by Edwin H. Zeydel, with reproductions of the original woodcuts. New York Columbia University Press 1944. 399p. (Records of civilization, sources and studies.) I. T. II. Series.
PT1509 N213 1944

Gottfried, von Strassburg, 13th cent.   • **2.13529**
Tristan und Isold / Gottfried von Strassburg; hrsg. von Friedrich Ranke. — Berlin: Weidmann, 1949. 246 p. Translated from Middle High German. 1. Tristan — Romances. I. Ranke, Friedrich. II. T.
PT1525.A2 M32   831/.2 19

Jackson, W. T. H. (William Thomas Hobdell), 1915-.   **2.13530**
The anatomy of love; the Tristan of Gottfried von Strassburg [by] W. T. H. Jackson. New York, Columbia University Press, 1971. ix, 280 p. 23 cm. 1. Gottfried, von Strassburg, 13th cent. Tristan 2. Tristan — Romances — History and criticism. I. T.
PT1526.J3   831/.2   *LC* 70-154859   *ISBN* 0231035047

Hartmann, von Aue, 12th cent.   **2.13531**
[Erec. English] Erec / by Hartmann von Aue; translated, with an introduction, by J.W. Thomas. — Lincoln: University of Nebraska Press, c1982. vii, 146 p.; 23 cm. I. Thomas, J. W. (John Wesley), 1916- II. T.
PT1534.E8 1982   831/.2 19   *LC* 81-7471   *ISBN* 0803244088

Hartmann, von Aue, 12th cent.   • **2.13532**
[Gregorius. English] Gregorius; a medieval Oedipus legend. Translated in rhyming couplets with introd. and notes by Edwin H. Zeydel with the collaboration of Bayard Quincy Morgan. New York, AMS Press, 1966 [c1955] 143 p. 24 cm. Original ed. issued as no. 14 of University of North Carolina studies in the Germanic languages and literatures. I. T.
PT1534.G73 E5 1966   *LC* 73-181903

Hartmann, von Aue, 12th cent.   **2.13533**
[Iwein. English] Iwein / by Hartmann von Aue; translated, with an introd., by J. W. Thomas. — Lincoln: University of Nebraska Press, c1979. ix, 149 p.; 23 cm. I. T.
PT1534.I3 1979   831/.2 19   *LC* 79-1139   *ISBN* 0803244045

Nibelungenlied.   **2.13534**
Das Nibelungenlied, nach der Ausg. von Karl Bartsch; hrsg. von Helmut de Boor. 18. neu bearb. Aufl. — Wiesbaden, F. A. Brockhaus, 1956. lix, 389 p. fold. map. 19 cm. — (Deutsche Klassiker des Mittelalters. [3. Bd.]) Bibliography: p. liii—lvi. I. Bartsch, Karl, 1832-1888. ed. II. Boor, Helmut de, 1891- ed. III. T. IV. Series.
PT1575.B2 1956   *LC* 56-34952

Nibelungenlied.   • **2.13535**
The Nibelungenlied, a new translation by A. T. Hatto. Baltimore, Penguin Books [1965, c1964] 403 p. 18 cm. (The Penguin classics, L137) I. Hatto, A. T. (Arthur Thomas) tr. II. T.
PT1579.A3H3 1965   831.2   *LC* 65-2343

McConnell, Winder.   **2.13536**
The Nibelungenlied / by Winder McConnell. — Boston: Twayne, c1984. xxiv, 141 p.: ill.; 23 cm. — (Twayne's world authors series; TWAS 712. German literature) Includes index. 1. Nibelungenlied. I. T.
PT1589.M37 1984   831/.2 19   *LC* 83-27111   *ISBN* 080576559X

Walther, von der Vogelweide, 12th cent.   **2.13537**
Herr Walther von der Vogelweide / ausgewählt, übertragen und eingeleitet von Eugen Thurnher. — Graz: Stiasny Verlag [c1959] 128 p.; 20 cm. — (Das Österreichische Wort) Middle High German text and modern German translation on facing pages. I. Thurnher, Eugen. II. T.
PT1620.A2 T5x

Walther, von der Vogelweide, 12th cent.   • **2.13538**
Songs and sayings./ Englished by Frank Betts. Oxford: Blackwell, 1917. 54 p. I. T.
PT1670.E5 B4

Wolfram, von Eschenbach, 12th cent.   **2.13539**
Parzival / von Wolfram von Eschenbach; in Prosa übertragen von Wilhelm Stapel. — 75. Tsd. — München: A. Langen, G. Müller, 1975, c1950. 443 p.; 21 cm. 1. Edition Perceval — Romances. I. Stapel, Wilhelm, 1882-1954, tr. II. T.
PT1682.P6 S8 1975   *LC* 76-458748   *ISBN* 3784412122

Wolfram, von Eschenbach, 12th cent.   • **2.13540**
Parzival / Wolfram von Eschenbach;Translated by Helen M. Mustard & Charles E. Passage. — New York; Vintage Books [1961] lvi, 443 p.; 19 cm. (A vintage book, V-188) 1. Edition Perceval — Romances I. Mustard, Helen Meredith, 1906- tr. II. Passage, Charles E. tr. III. T.
PT1682.P8F55   831.2   *LC* 61-6849

Passage, Charles E.   **2.13541**
The Middle High German poem of Willehalm / by Wolfram of Eschenbach; translated into English prose by Charles E. Passage. — New York: F. Ungar Pub. Co., c1977. xii, 404 p.; 22 cm. Includes index. I. Wolfram, von Eschenbach, 12th cent. Willehalm. II. T. III. Title: Willehalm.
PT1682.W6 E56   831/.2   *LC* 76-15647   *ISBN* 0804421838

Weigand, Hermann John, 1892-.   • **2.13542**
Wolfram's Parzival; five essays with an introduction, by Hermann J. Weigand. Edited by Ursula Hoffmann. Ithaca [N.Y.] Cornell University Press [1969] vi, 204 p. 22 cm. 1. Wolfram, von Eschenbach, 12th cent. Parzival. I. T.
PT1688.W43   831/.2   *LC* 76-81597   *ISBN* 0801405211

PT1701–2688 GERMAN LITERATURE: INDIVIDUAL AUTHORS

PT1701–1797 1500–1700

Grimmelshausen, Hans Jakob Christoph von, 1625-1676. • 2.13543
Der abenteuerliche Simplicissimus. [Von] Grimmelshausen. [Nach den ersten Drucken des 'Simplicissimus Teutsch' und der 'Continuatio' von 1669 hrsg. und mit einem Nachwort versehen von Alfred Kelletat. Sonderausg. Neudruck] München, Winkler [1967] 681 p. 1. Thirty Years' War, 1618-1648 — Fiction. I. Kelletat, Alfred. II. T. III. Title: Continuatio des abenteuerlichen Simplicissimi.
PT1731.A6   833.5   *LC* 68-141201

Grimmelshausen, Hans Jakob Christoph von, 1625-1676. 2.13544
[Simplicissimus. English] An unabridged translation of Simplicius simplicissimus / by Johann Jacob Christoffel von Grimmelshausen; with an introduction and notes by Monte Adair. — Lanham, MD: University Press of America, c1986. xxii, 585 p.; 22 cm. Translation of: Simplicissimus. I. T. II. Title: Simplicius simplicissimus.
PT1731.A7 E5 1986   833/.5 19   *LC* 86-5646   *ISBN* 0819153486

Grimmelshausen, Hans Jakob Christoph von, 1625-1676. • 2.13545
Courage, the adventuress & The false messiah / by Hans Jacob Christoffel von Grimmelshausen; translation and introd. by Hans Speier. — Princeton, N.J.: Princeton University Press, 1964. 291 p.: ill.; 22 cm. Translation of Die landstörzerin Courasche, 1670 and Das wunderbarliche Vogelsnest, pt. 2, 1675. 1. Thirty Years' War, 1618-1648 — Fiction. I. Grimmelshausen, Hans Jakob Christoph von, 1625-1676. The false messiah. II. T. III. Title: The false messiah.
PT1731.C7 E5 1964   *LC* 63-23415

Weydt, Günther, 1906-. 2.13546
Nachahmung und Schöpfung im Barock: Studien um Grimmelshausen / Günther Weydt. — Bern: Francke, c1968. 472 p.: ill. (some col.); 24 cm. 1. Grimmelshausen, Hans Jakob Christoph von, 1625-1676. I. T.
PT1732.W37   *LC* 79-374228

Gryphius, Andreas, 1616-1664. • 2.13547
Werke in einem Band / Gryphius; ausgewählt und eingeleitet von Marian Szyrocki. — 2. Aufl. — Berlin: Aufbau-Verlag, 1966. xxvi, 317 p. — (Bibliothek deutscher Klassiker) I. Szyrocki, Marian. II. T.
PT1734.A1   *LC* 79-377542

PT1799–2592 18th–19th Centuries (1700–1860/1870)

PT1799–1832 A–B

Arnim, Ludwig Achim, Freiherr von, 1781-1831. • 2.13548
Sämtliche Romane und Erzählungen / Achim von Arnim; [auf Grund der Erstdrucke herausgegeben von Walther Migge]. — München: C. Hanser, [1962]-65. 3 v. I. Migge, Walther. II. T.
PT1809.A15M5 1962   *LC* 67-108230

Hoermann, Roland. 2.13549
Achim von Arnim / by Roland Hoermann. — Boston: Twayne, c1984. 164 p.; 23 cm. — (Twayne's world authors series; TWAS 722. German literature) Includes index. 1. Arnim, Ludwig Achim, Freiherr von, 1781-1831 — Criticism and interpretation. I. T.
PT1809.Z5 H63 1984   838/.609 19   *LC* 83-26550   *ISBN* 0805765697

Gotthelf, Jeremias, 1797-1854. 2.13550
[Werke in vierzehn Bänden.] — Zürich: Schweizer Verlagshaus, [197-] 14 v. I. T.
PT1819.B6 Ax   *ISBN* 3726302646

Waidson, H. M. • 2.13551
Jeremias Gotthelf: an introduction to the Swiss novelist / by H. M. Waidson. — Oxford: Blackwell, 1953. xi, 231 p., [3] leaves of plates: ill.; 23 cm. (Modern language studies) 1. Gotthelf, Jeremias, 1797-1854 — Criticism and interpretation. I. T.
PT1819.B6 Z95 1953   833/.7

Brentano, Clemens Maria, 1778-1842. • 2.13552
Werke / Clemens Brentano. — München: C. Hanser, [1963-68] 4 v.: ill. Vol. 1. edited by Wolfgang Frühwald, Bernhard Gajek und Friedhelm Kemp. I. Kemp, Friedhelm, 1914- II. T.
PT1825.A1 1963   838.6   *LC* 68-86578

Fetzer, John F. 2.13553
Clemens Brentano / by John F. Fetzer. — Boston: Twayne Publishers, 1981. 179 p.: port.; 21 cm. — (Twayne's world authors series; TWAS 615. Germany) Includes index. 1. Brentano, Clemens Maria, 1778-1842 — Criticism and interpretation. I. T.
PT1825.Z5 F39   838/.609 19   *LC* 81-2314   *ISBN* 0805764577

Büchner, Georg, 1813-1837. • 2.13554
Sämtliche Werke und Briefe: historisch–kritische Ausgabe mit Kommentar / hrsg. von Werner R. Lehmann. — [Hamburg]: Wegner, [1967?-. v.: ill. I. Lehmann, Werner R. II. T.
PT1828.B6 1967   *LC* 68-72235

Büchner, Georg, 1813-1837. • 2.13555
[Selected works. English] Complete plays and prose. Translated with an introd. by Carl Richard Mueller. [1st ed.] New York, Hill and Wang [1963] 177 p. 19 cm. (A Mermaid dramabook) I. T.
PT1828.B6 A26   832.6   *LC* 63-8191

Benn, Maurice B., 1914-. 2.13556
The drama of revolt: a critical study of Georg Büchner / Maurice B. Benn. — Cambridge; New York: Cambridge University Press, 1976. viii, 321 p., [2] leaves of plates: ill.; 23 cm. — (Anglica Germanica.) Includes index. 1. Büchner, Georg, 1813-1837 — Criticism and interpretation. I. T. II. Series.
PT1828.B6 B37   832/.7 19   *LC* 75-3974   *ISBN* 0521208289

Hauser, Ronald. 2.13557
Georg Büchner. — New York: Twayne publishers, [1974] 161 p.; 21 cm. — (Twayne's world authors series, TWAS 300. Germany) 1. Büchner, Georg, 1813-1837. I. T.
PT1828.B6 H3   831/.7   *LC* 73-17183   *ISBN* 0805721835

Richards, David Gleyre, 1935-. 2.13558
Georg Büchner and the birth of the modern drama / David G. Richards. 1st ed. — Albany: State University of New York Press, 1977. xii, 289 p.; 24 cm. Includes index. 1. Büchner, Georg, 1813-1837 — Criticism and interpretation. I. T.
PT1828.B6 R5   831/.7   *LC* 76-902   *ISBN* 0873953320

PT1833–1889 C–G

Chamisso, Adelbert von, 1781-1838. 2.13559
Werke in zwei Bänden / Adelbert von Chamisso; herausgegeben von Werner Feudel und Christel Laufer. — München: Hanser, 1982. 2 v.; 19 cm. I. Feudel, Werner. II. Laufer, Christel. III. T.
PT1834.A1 1982x

Droste-Hülshoff, Annette von, 1797-1848. • 2.13560
Sämtliche Werke. [Hrsg., in zeitlicher Folge geordnet und mit Nachwort und Erläuterungen versehen von Clemens Heselhaus. München C. Hanser [1966] 1180p. I. Heselhaus, Clemens, ed. II. T.
PT1848 A1 1966

Eichendorff, Joseph, Freiherr von, 1788-1857. • 2.13561
Neue Gesamtausgabe der Werke und Schriften in vier Bänden / Joseph Freiherr von Eichendorff; [herausgegeben von Gerhard Baumann]. — Stuttgart: J.G. Cotta, 1958-1978. 4 v. Vols. 1-2, 3. Aufl. I. T.
PT1856 A1 1978   *ISBN* 3768199061

Schwarz, Egon, 1922-. 2.13562
Joseph von Eichendorff. New York, Twayne [1972] 184 p. 21 cm. (Twayne's world authors series, TWAS 163. Germany) 1. Eichendorff, Joseph, Freiherr von, 1788-1857. I. T.
PT1856.Z5 S37   838/.7/09   *LC* 76-120485

Fontane, Theodor, 1819-1898. 2.13563
[Works. 1976] Werke, Schriften und Briefe / Theodor Fontane; [hrsg. von Walter Keitel u. Helmuth Nürnberger]. — München: Hanser, 1976- <c1984 >. <v. 1, pt. 7; v. 4, pt. 1-4; in 5 >; 20 cm. Abt. 1 rev. and enl. ed. of the author's Sämtliche Werke, Abt. 1, published in 1966 by Hanser. I. Keitel, Walter. II. Nürnberger, Helmuth. III. T.
PT1863.A1 1976   *LC* 78-341980   *ISBN* 3446122052

Fontane, Theodor, 1819-1898. 2.13564
[Selections. English. 1982] Short novels and other writings / Theodor Fontane; edited by Peter Demetz; foreword by Peter Gay. — New York: Continuum, 1982. xvi, 336 p.; 21 cm. — (German library. v. 48) I. Demetz, Peter, 1922- II. T. III. Series.
PT1863.A15 1982   833/.8 19   LC 81-17505   ISBN 0826402607

Fontane, Theodor, 1819-1898. 2.13565
[Adultera. English] The woman taken in adultery and The Poggenpuhl family / Theodor Fontane; translated with notes by Gabriele Annan; with an introd. by Erich Heller. — Chicago: University of Chicago Press, 1979. xxviii, 231 p.; 23 cm. Translation of L'Adultera and Die Poggenpuhls. I. Fontane, Theodor, 1819-1898. Poggenpuhls. English. 1979. II. T.
PZ3.F7347 Wo 1979 PT1863.A4x   833/.8   LC 78-31371   ISBN 0226256804

Fontane, Theodor, 1819-1898. • 2.13566
Effi Briest. Translated, with an introd., by Douglas Parmée. — [Harmondsworth, Mddx.] Penguin Books [1967] 266 p. 18 cm. — (The Penguin classics) I. T.
PT1863.E3x   LC 67-7236

Garland, Henry Burnand. 2.13567
The Berlin novels of Theodor Fontane / Henry Garland. — Oxford: Clarendon Press; New York: Oxford University Press, 1980. viii, 296 p.; 22 cm. Includes index. 1. Fontane, Theodor, 1819-1898 — Criticism and interpretation. I. T.
PT1863.Z7 G34   833/.8   LC 79-41386   ISBN 0198157657

PT1891–2239 Goethe

Goethe, Johann Wolfgang von, 1749-1832. 2.13568
Werke / hrsg. von Erich Trunz. — 11. Aufl. — München: Beck, 1978. 14 v.; 19 cm. 'Hamburger Ausgabe'. I. Trunz, Erich. II. T.
PT1891.C78x

Jantz, Harold Stein, 1907-. 2.13569
The forum of Faust: the work of art and its intrinsic structures / Harold Jantz. — Baltimore: Johns Hopkins University Press, c1978. xxi, 201 p. 1. Goethe, Johann Wolfgang von, 1749-1832. Faust I. T.
PT1925.J345   PT1925 J345.   832/.6   LC 78-1447   ISBN 0801820804

Peacock, Ronald, 1907-. • 2.13570
Goethe's major plays. Manchester University Press 1959. 236p. 1. Goethe, Johann Wolfgang von, 1749-1832 — Criticism and interpretation I. T.
PT1964 P43

Blackall, Eric A. (Eric Albert) 2.13571
Goethe and the novel / Eric A. Blackall. — Ithaca: Cornell University Press, 1976. 340 p.; 24 cm. Includes index. 1. Goethe, Johann Wolfgang von, 1749-1832 — Criticism and interpretation. I. T.
PT1984.B5   831/.6   LC 75-38426   ISBN 0801409780

Goethe, Johann Wolfgang von, 1749-1832. 2.13572
Goethes Briefe: Textkritisch durehgesehen und mit Anmerkungen versehen / von Karl Robert Mandelkow. — 2. Aufl. — München: Beck, 1976-. v.; 19 cm. 'Hamburger Ausgabe'. I. Mandelkow, Karl Robert. II. T.
PT2005.A1 1962   LC 65-30112 rev

Briefe an Goethe: textkritisch durchaesehen und Anmerkungen 2.13573
versehen / von Karl Robert Mandelkow.
2. Aufl. — München: Beck, 1982. 2 v.; 19 cm. 'Hamburger Ausgabe'. Letters in English, French, German. I. Mandelkow, Karl Robert. II. Goethe, Johann Wolfgang von, 1749-1832.
PT2005.A1 1982x

Goethe, Johann Wolfgang von, 1749-1832. 2.13574
[Works. English & German. 1983] Goethe edition. — [Cambridge, Mass.]: Suhrkamp/Insel Publishers Boston, c1983- <c1986 >. v. <1-3 >; 24 cm. English and German. Vol. 2- <3 > has also title on added t.p.: Goethe's collected works. I. T. II. Title: Goethe's collected works.
PT2026.A1 C83 1983   831/.6 19   LC 84-228090   ISBN 3518030531

Goethe, Johann Wolfgang von, 1749-1832. • 2.13575
Goethe, the lyrist: 100 poems in new translations facing the originals, with a biographical introduction by Edwin H. Zeydel; with an appendix on musical settings to the poems. — 2nd ed. revised. — Chapel Hill: University of North Carolina Press, 1955. xvii, 182 p.; 23 cm. — (University of North Carolina studies in the Germanic languages and literatures. no. 16) I. Zeydel, Edwin Hermann, 1893- II. T. III. Series.
PD25.N6 no. 16   PT2026.A3 Z4 1955.   831.69   LC 55-63007

Goethe, Johann Wolfgang von, 1749-1832. • 2.13576
Goethe's autobiography, Poetry and truth from my own life; tr. by R. O. Moon. [Bicentennial ed. Washington] Public Affairs Press [1949] xvi, 700 p. 23 cm. I. Moon, R. O. (Robert Oswald), 1865-1953. ed. and tr. II. T.
PT2027.A8M6 1949   928.3   LC 49-9277

Goethe, Johann Wolfgang von, 1749-1832. • 2.13577
[Gespräche mit Goethe. Eckermann. English] Conversations with Goethe [by] Johann Peter Eckermann; translated [from the German] by John Oxenford and [abridged and] edited by J. K. Moorehead. [1st ed. of this abridgement, reprinted], introduction by Roy Pascal. London, Dent; New York, Dutton, 1971. xxiv, 448 p. 19 cm. (Everyman's library, no. 851) Translation of Gespräche mit Goethe. Includes index. I. Eckermann, Johann Peter, 1792-1854. Gespräche mit Goethe. II. Oxenford, John, 1812-1877. tr. III. T.
PT2027.C5 O8 1971   831/.6   LC 73-168675   ISBN 046000851X

Goethe, Johann Wolfgang von, 1749-1832. • 2.13578
The sufferings of young Werther / Johann Wolfgang von Goethe; translated by Bayard Quincy Morgan. — New York: F. Ungar, c1957. xii, 160 p.; 18 cm. — (College translations) I. Goethe, Johann Wolfgang von, 1749-1832. Die Leiden des jungen Werthers. English. II. T. III. Series.
PT2027.W3 M6   LC 57-7359   ISBN 0804461902

Goethe, Johann Wolfgang von, 1749-1832. • 2.13579
Wilhelm Meister, apprenticeship and travels / [Johann Wolfgang von Goethe]; translated from the German by R. O. Moon. — London: G. T. Foulis, 1947. 2 v. I. T.
PT2027.W5 M6   LC abb49-6876

PT2044–2239 Biography. Criticism

Dieckmann, Liselotte. 2.13580
Johann Wolfgang Goethe. — New York: Twayne Publishers, [1974] 202 p.; 21 cm. — (Twayne's world authors series, TWAS 292. Germany) 1. Goethe, Johann Wolfgang von, 1749-1832. I. T.
PT2049.D5   831/.6   LC 73-20264   ISBN 0805723781

Fairley, Barker. • 2.13581
A study of Goethe / by Barker Fairley. — Oxford: Clarendon Press, 1947 (Oxford: Charles Batey at the University Press) vii, [1], 280 p.; 21.9 x 13.6 cm. 'This book is the outcome of writing its predecessor, Goethe as revealed in his poetry (1932)'. 1. Goethe, Johann Wolfgang von, 1749-1832. 2. Authors, German — 18th century — Biography. I. T.
PT2049.F33   832.62   LC 48-13433

Staiger, Emil, 1908-. • 2.13582
Goethe / Emil Staiger. — [Zürich]: Atlantis Verlag, 1952-1959. 3v.; 23 cm. 1. Goethe, Johann Wolfgang von, 1749-1832. I. T.
PT2051 S67

Hatfield, Henry Caraway, 1912-. • 2.13583
Goethe; a critical introduction. [Norfolk, Conn., J. Laughlin, 1963] ix, 238 p. illus., ports., facsim. 19 cm. (A New Directions paperbook original, no. 136) 1. Goethe, Johann Wolfgang von, 1749-1832 — Criticism and interpretation. I. T.
PT2177.H37   832.6   LC 63-13643

Viëtor, Karl, 1892-. • 2.13584
Goethe: Dichtung, Wissenschaft, Weltbild / Karl Viëtor. — Bern: A. Francke, 1949. 600 p.: port. Includes index. 'Biographischer Abriss und Chronologie der Werke': p. [573]-578. 1. Goethe, Johann Wolfgang von, 1749-1832. I. T.
PT2177 V45   PT2177 V45.   928.3   LC 49-7261

Viëtor, Karl, 1892-1951. • 2.13585
[Goethe; Dichtung, Wissenschaft, Weltbild. 1.T. English] Goethe, the poet. Translated from the German by Moses Hadas. New York, Russell & Russell [1970, c1949] x, 341 p. 25 cm. Translation of the first part of Goethe; Dichtung, Wissenschaft, Weltbild. 1. Goethe, Johann Wolfgang von, 1749-1832. I. T.
PT2177.V5 1970   831/.6   LC 72-81482

PT2250–2298 G–H

Grabbe, Christian Dietrich, 1801-1836. • 2.13586
Gesammelte Werke. [Eingeleitet und hrsg. von Fritz Siefert. Gütersloh] S. Mohn, 1964. 476 p.; 20 cm. I. Siefert, Fritz, ed. II. T.
PT2253.G3 A6 1964   LC 65-79561

Grabbe, Christian Dietrich, 1801-1836. • 2.13587
Jest, satire, irony and deeper significance: A comedy in three acts / Christian Dietrich Grabbe; translated, with an introduction, by Maurice Edwards. — New York: F. Ungar, c1966. xxxv, 69 p.; 22 cm. I. Grabbe, Christian Dietrich, 1801-1836. Scherz, Satire, Ironie und tiefere Bedeutung. English. 1966. II. Edwards, Maurice. III. T.
PT2253.G3 A7313   LC 66-19473

Cowen, Roy C., 1930-.   2.13588
Christian Dietrich Grabbe, by Roy C. Cowen. — New York, Twayne [1972] 176 p. 21 cm. — (Twayne's world authors series, TWAS 206: Germany) 1. Grabbe, Christian Dietrich, 1801-1836. I. T.
PT2253.G3 C6   832/.6   LC 76-169639

Grillparzer, Franz, 1791-1872.   2.13589
Sämtliche Werke: ausgewählte Briefe, Gespräche, Berichte / [Hrsg. von Peter Frank und Karl Pörnbacher]. — München: C. Hanser, 1969-1970. 4 v.; 19 cm. v.3-4 1st ed., 1960-64. I. Frank, Peter, Apr. 7, 1924- II. Pörnbacher, Karl. III. T.
PT2256.A1 1969

Grillparzer, Franz, 1791-1872.   2.13590
[Works. 1986] Werke in sechs Bänden / Franz Grillparzer; herausgegeben von Helmut Bachmaier. 1. Aufl. Frankfurt am Main: Deutscher Klassiker Verlag, 1986-. v. ; 19 cm. — (Bibliothek deutscher Klassiker; 14) I. Bachmaier, Helmut. II. T.
PT2256.A2 B323 1986   ISBN 3618606206

Thompson, Bruce.   2.13591
Franz Grillparzer / by Bruce Thompson. — Boston: Twayne Publishers, 1981. 165 p.: port.; 21 cm. — (Twayne's world authors series. Germany. TWAS 637) Includes index. 1. Grillparzer, Franz, 1791-1872. 2. Authors, Austrian — 19th century — Biography. I. T. II. Series.
PT2265.T5   832/.6 B 19   LC 81-4409   ISBN 080576481X

Yates, W. E.   2.13592
Grillparzer: a critical introduction, by W. E. Yates. — Cambridge [Eng.] University Press, 1972. x, 276 p. 23 cm. — (Companion studies) 1. Grillparzer, Franz, 1791-1872. I. T.
PT2265.Y34   832/.6   LC 77-158550   ISBN 0521082412

Novalis, 1772-1801.   2.13593
Schriften. Die Werke Friedrich von Hardenbergs, hrsg. von Paul Kluckhohn und Richard Sameul. — 3 Aufl. — Stuttgart W. Kohlhammer 1977-. v.; 23 cm. — I. Kluckhohn, Paul, 1886-1957, ed. II. Samuel, R. H. (Richard H.), 1900- jt. ed. III. T.
PT2291 A1 1977x

Novalis, 1772-1801.   • 2.13594
Henry von Ofterdingen: a novel / Novalis; translated from the German by Palmer Hilty. — New York: Ungar, 1964. 169 p. Translation of Heinrich von Ofterdingen. I. Hardenberg, Friedrich, Freiher von, 1772-1801. II. T.
PT2291.H3x   LC 64-15297   ISBN 0804466149

Novalis, 1772-1801.   2.13595
[Hymnen an die Nacht. English & German] Hymns to the night / Novalis; translated by Dick Higgins. — Rev. ed. — New Paltz, N.Y.: McPherson, 1984. 55 p.; 23 cm. Translation of: Hymnen an die Nacht. English and German. I. Higgins, Dick, 1938- II. T.
PT2291.H6 E55 1984   831/.6 19   LC 84-4402   ISBN 0914232673

Neubauer, John, 1933-.   2.13596
Novalis / John Neubauer. — Boston: Twayne Publishers, 1980. 185 p.: ill.; 21 cm. — (Twayne's world authors series; TWAS 556: Germany) Includes index. 1. Novalis, 1772-1801 — Criticism and interpretation. I. T.
PT2291.Z5 N44   831/.6   LC 79-14958   ISBN 0805763988

Hauff, Wilhelm, 1802-1827.   • 2.13597
Werke. Hrsg. von Bernhard Zeller. [Frankfurt a.M. Insel-Verlag] [1969] I. Zeller, Bernhard. ed. II. T.
PT2293 A1 1969   LC 78-422058

Hebbel, Friedrich, 1813-1863.   2.13598
Werke / Friedrich Hebbel; [Hrsg. von Gerhard Fricke u.a.]. — München: Carl Hanser Verlag, 1963-1967. 5 v.; 19 cm. I. Fricke, Gerhard, 1901- II. T.
PT2295.A1 1963

Hebbel, Friedrich, 1813-1863.   2.13599
Three plays. Translated and with an introd. by Marion W. Sonnenfeld. — Lewisburg [Pa.]: Bucknell University Press, [1974] 271 p.: illus.; 25 cm. I. Sonnenfeld, Marion. tr. II. T.
PT2295.A2 E58 1974   832/.7   LC 72-3531   ISBN 0838712398

Purdie, Edna, 1894-.   • 2.13600
Friedrich Hebbel: a study of his life and work. — [London]: Oxford University Press, [1969] 276 p.; 23 cm. First published in 1932. 1. Hebbel, Friedrich, 1813-1863. I. T.
PT2296.P8 1969   832/.7   LC 74-428330   ISBN 0198153902

Garland, Mary.   2.13601
Hebbel's prose tragedies: an investigation of the aesthetic aspect of Hebbel's dramatic language. Cambridge [Eng.] University Press, 1973. ix, 334 p. 23 cm. (Anglica Germanica.) 1. Hebbel, Friedrich, 1813-1863. I. T. II. Series.
PT2296.Z5 G3   832/.7   LC 72-88621   ISBN 0521200903

Hebel, Johann Peter, 1760-1826.   • 2.13602
Poetische Werke / Johann Peter Hebel; [hrsg. von Emil Strauss]. — Berlin: Tempel-Verlag, [1968] 543 p. — (Tempel-Klassiker) I. Strauss, Emil, 1866-1960 II. Hebel, Johann Peter, 1760-1826. Schatzkästlein des Rheinländischen Hausfreundes. 1968 III. T.
PT2298H3 A2 1968   PT2298H3 A2 1968.   LC 78-380988

PT2301–2354 Heine. Herder

Heine, Heinrich, 1797-1856.   2.13603
[Works. 1973] Historisch–kritische Gesamtausgabe der Werke. Hrsg. von Manfred Windfuhr. [Hamburg] Hoffmann und Campe 1973-<1986 >. <v. 1, pts. 1-2; v. 2; v. 4; v. 6; v. 7, pts. 1-2; v. 8, pts. 1-2; v. 11; v. 12, pts. 1-2; v. 15; in 13 > plates. 23 cm. 'Düsseldorfer Ausgabe.' French and German. I. Windfuhr, Manfred. ed. II. T.
PT2301.A1 1973b   831/.6 19   LC 73-327285   ISBN 3455030068

Heine, Heinrich, 1797-1856.   2.13604
[Selections. English. 1982] Poetry and prose / Heinrich Heine; edited by Jost Hermand and Robert C. Holub; foreword by Alfred Kazin. — New York: Continuum, 1982. xix, 299 p.; 22 cm. (German library. v. 32) Includes index. I. Hermand, Jost. II. Holub, Robert C. III. T. IV. Series.
PT2316.A3 H4 1982   831/.7 19   LC 82-7981   ISBN 0826402550

Heine, Heinrich, 1797-1856.   • 2.13605
Lyric poems and ballads / Heinrich Heine; translated by Ernst Feise. [Pittsburgh] University of Pittsburgh Press [1961] xxvi, 195 p.,; 23 cm. (Pitt paperback, 44) Added t.p. in German. English and German. Includes index. Added t.p. in German: Lyrische Gedichte und Balladen. I. Feise, Ernst, 1884- II. T.
PT2316.A4 F4 1961   831.7   LC 61-9402

Rose, William, 1894-.   • 2.13606
The early love poetry of Heinrich Heine; an inquiry into poetic inspiration. Oxford Clarendon Press 1962. 89p. 1. Heine, Heinrich, 1797-1856. I. T.
PT2328 R55

Sammons, Jeffrey L.   2.13607
Heinrich Heine: a modern biography / by Jeffrey L. Sammons. — Princeton, N.J.: Princeton University Press, c1979. xvii, 425 p., [8] leaves of plates: ill.; 25 cm. Includes indexes. 1. Heine, Heinrich, 1797-1856 — Biography. 2. Authors, German — 19th century — Biography. I. T.
PT2328.S2   831/.7 B   LC 79-84015   ISBN 0691063214

Fairley, Barker.   • 2.13608
Heinrich Heine: an interpretation / by Barker Fairley. — Oxford: Clarendon Press, 1954. 176 p.; 19 cm. 1. Heine, Heinrich. I. T.
PT2340.F3   LC a 55-4629

Spencer, Hanna.   2.13609
Heinrich Heine / by Hanna Spencer. — Boston: Twayne Publishers, c1982. 173 p., [1] p. of plates: port.; 21 cm. — (Twayne's world authors series. TWAS 669) Includes index. 1. Heine, Heinrich, 1797-1856 — Criticism and interpretation. I. T. II. Series.
PT2340.S64 1982   831/.7 19   LC 82-9310   ISBN 0805765166

Herder, Johann Gottfried, 1744-1803.   2.13610
[Works. 1985] Werke in zehn Bänden / Johann Gottfried Herder; herausgegeben von Martin Bollacher ... [et al.]. — 1. Aufl. — Frankfurt am Main: Deutscher Klassiker Verlag, 1985-. v. <1 >; 19 cm. (Bibliothek deutscher Klassiker; 1-) Includes index. I. Bollacher, Martin. II. T. III. Title: Werke in 10 Bänden.
PT2351.A1 1985   838/.609 19   LC 86-133179   ISBN 3618607105

Mayo, Robert S., 1939-.   2.13611
Herder and the beginnings of comparative literature, by Robert S. Mayo. Chapel Hill, University of North Carolina Press, 1969. 153 p. 23 cm. (University of North Carolina. Studies in comparative literature no. 48) 1. Herder, Johann Gottfried, 1744-1803. 2. Literature, Comparative I. T.
PT2354.M3   809   LC 70-630217

PT2355–2361 Hölderlin. Hoffman

Hölderlin, Friedrich, 1770-1843.   2.13612
[Works. 1975] Sämtliche Werke: Frankfurter Ausg.: [histor. –krit. Ausg.] / Friedrich Hölderlin; [hrsg. von D. E. Sattler]. — Frankfurt (M.): Verlag Roter Stern, 1975-<1985 >. v. <1-6, 9-11, 12-13, 14 >: ill.; 31 cm. Vol. 4/5 lacks collective title. Errata slip laid in v. 9. 'Spiegelfolie' ([1] leaf) laid in v. 10. I. Sattler, D. E. (Dietrich E.), 1939 II. T.
PT2359.H2 1975   LC 76-454793   ISBN 3878770790

Hölderlin, Friedrich, 1770-1843.   • 2.13613
[Gedichte. English and German] Poems and fragments. Translated by Michael Hamburger. Bi-lingual ed. with a pref., introd., and notes. Ann Arbor,

University of Michigan [1967] xviii, 624 p. 26 cm. Translation of Hölderlin: sämliche Werke. I. Hamburger, Michael. tr. II. T.
PT2359.H2 A6 1967   831/.6   *LC* 66-11083

Unger, Richard, 1939-.   **2.13614**
Friedrich Hölderlin / by Richard Unger. — Boston: Twayne Publishers, c1984. 155 p.; 23 cm. — (Twayne's world authors series; TWAS 738. German literature) Includes index. 1. Hölderlin, Friedrich, 1770-1843 — Criticism and interpretation. I. T.
PT2359.H2 U44 1984   831/.6 19   *LC* 83-26582   *ISBN* 0805765859

Hoffmann, E. T. A. (Ernst Theodor Amadeus), 1776-1822.   **2.13615**
[Works. 1985] Sämtliche Werke in sechs Bänden / E.T.A. Hoffmann; herausgegeben von Wulf Segebrecht und Hartmut Steinecke, unter Mitarbeit von Gerhard Allroggen und Ursula Segebrecht. — 1. Aufl. — Frankfurt am Main: Deutscher Klassiker Verlag, <c1985- >. v. <3 >: ill.; 19 cm. (Bibliothek deutscher Klassiker; <7 >) I. Segebrecht, Wulf. II. T. III. Title: Sämtliche Werke in 6 Bänden.
PT2360.A1 1985   833/.6 19   *LC* 86-133012   *ISBN* 3618608705

Hoffmann, E. T. A. (Ernst Theodor Amadeus), 1776-1822.   • **2.13616**
[Selected works. English] Selected writings of E. T. A. Hoffmann. Edited and translated by Leonard J. Kent and Elizabeth C. Knight. Illustrated by Jacob Landau. Chicago, University of Chicago Press [1969] 2 v. col. illus. 25 cm. I. Kent, Leonard J., 1927- ed. II. Knight, Elizabeth C., ed. III. T.
PZ3.H677 Se PT2360.Ax 1969   833/.6   *LC* 73-88790   *ISBN* 0226347883

Hoffmann, E. T. A. (Ernst Theodor Amadeus), 1776-1822.   **2.13617**
[Selected works. English] Three Märchen of E. T. A. Hoffmann. Translated and with an introd. by Charles E. Passage. [1st ed.] Columbia, University of South Carolina Press [1971] xxvii, 402 p. illus. 23 cm. I. T.
PZ3.H677 Th PT2360.Ax 1971   833/.6   *LC* 76-120580   *ISBN* 0872491889

Daemmrich, Horst S., 1930-.   **2.13618**
The shattered self; E. T. A. Hoffmann's tragic vision [by] Horst S. Daemmrich. Detroit, Wayne State University, 1973. 141 p. 24 cm. 1. Hoffmann, E. T. A. (Ernst Theodor Amadeus), 1776-1822. I. T.
PT2361.Z5 D28 1973   833/.6   *LC* 73-1490   *ISBN* 0814314937

PT2374–2382 Keller. Kleist. Klopstock

Keller, Gottfried, 1819-1890.   **2.13619**
Sämtliche Werke und ausgewählte Briefe / Gottfried Keller, hrsg. von Clemens Heselhaus. 4.Auflage. — München: C. Hanser; 1978-79. 3 v.; 20 cm. I. T.
PT2374.A1 1978x   *ISBN* 3446107614

Keller, Gottfried, 1819-1890.   **2.13620**
[Short stories. English. Selections] Stories / Gottfried Keller; edited by Frank G. Ryder; foreword by Max Frisch. — New York: Continuum, 1982. viii, 368 p.; 22 cm. — (German library. v. 44) I. Ryder, Frank Glessner, 1916- II. T. III. Series.
PT2374.A2 1982   833/.8 19   *LC* 81-22067   *ISBN* 0826402569

Ermatinger, Emil, 1873-1953.   • **2.13621**
Gottfried Kellers Leben, mit Benutzung von Jakob Baechtolds Biographie. 8., neu bearb. Aufl. — Zürich, Artemis-Verlag [1950] 639 p. illus., ports., facsims. 21 cm. Previously published as v. 1 of the author's Gottfried Kellers Leben, Briefe und Tagebücher. Bibliographical references included in 'Anmerkungen' (p. 603-617) 1. Keller, Gottfried, 1819-1890. I. Baechtold, Jakob, 1848-1897. II. T.
PT2374.Z4E7 1950   928.3   *LC* 50-29044

Kleist, Heinrich von, 1777-1811.   • **2.13622**
Samtliche Werke und Briefe / Hrsg. von Helmut Sembdner. — 2., verm. und auf Grund der Erstdrucke und Handschriften vollig revidierte Aufl. — Munchen: C. Hanser, 1961. 2 v. (1076 p.); 20 cm. I. Sembdner, Helmut. ed. II. T.
PT2378.A1 1961   *LC* 64-9125

Kleist, Heinrich von, 1777-1811.   **2.13623**
[Plays. English. Selections] Plays / Heinrich von Kleist; edited by Walter Hinderer; foreword by E.L. Doctorow. — New York: Continuum, 1982. xvii, 341 p.; 22 cm. — (German library. v. 25) I. Hinderer, Walter, 1934- II. T. III. Series.
PT2378.A2 E5 1982   832/.6 19   *LC* 81-22060   *ISBN* 0826402534

Kleist, Heinrich von, 1777-1811.   • **2.13624**
The Marquise of O, and other stories / Heinrich von Kleist; translated and with an introduction by Martin Greenberg; preface by Thomas Mann. — New York: Criterion Books, [1960] 318 p.; 22 cm. — I. T.
PT2378.A2 E5x   *LC* 60-14139

Helbling, Robert E.   **2.13625**
The major works of Heinrich von Kleist / by Robert E. Helbling. — New York: New Directions, 1975. ix, 275 p.; 21 cm. (A New Directions book) Includes index. 1. Kleist, Heinrich von, 1777-1811 — Criticism and interpretation. I. T.
PT2379.Z5 H4 1975   PT2379Z5 H4 1975.   838/.6/09   *LC* 74-26509   *ISBN* 0811205630

Silz, Walter, 1894-.   • **2.13626**
Heinrich von Kleist; studies in his works and literary character. Philadelphia University of Pennsylvania Press [1962, c[1961] 313p. 1. Kleist, Heinrich von, 1777-1811. I. T.
PT2379 Z5 S5

Klopstock, Friedrich Gottlieb, 1724-1803.   • **2.13627**
Ausgewählte Werke. [Hrsg. von Karl August Schleiden. Nachwort von Friedrich Georg Jünger] München C. Hanser [1962] 1378p. 1. Schleiden, Karl August, ed. I. T.
PT2381 A3 1962   *LC* 65-8159

PT2393–2426 Lenau. Lessing

Lenau, Nicolaus, 1802-1850.   • **2.13628**
Sämtliche Werke und Briefe in zwei Bänden / Nikolaus Lenau. — Berlin: Insel Verlag, 1971. 2 v.: port. — I. T.
PT2393.A1 1971   *LC* 78-860274

Schmidt, Hugo, 1929-.   • **2.13629**
Nikolaus Lenau. — New York: Twayne Publishers, [1971] 172 p.; 21 cm. — (Twayne's world authors series, TWAS 135 German literature) 1. Lenau, Nicolaus, 1802-1850. I. T.
PT2393.Z5 S3   831/.7   *LC* 68-17227

Lessing, Gotthold Ephraim, 1729-1781.   **2.13630**
[Works. 1985] Werke und Briefe in zwölf Bänden / Gotthold Ephraim Lessing; herausgegeben von Wilfried Barner zusammen mit Klaus Bohnen ... [et al.]. — 1. Aufl. — Frankfurt am Main: Deutscher Klassiker Verlag, <1985-c1987 >. <6; 11, pt. 1; in 2 >; 19 cm. — (Bibliothek deutscher Klassiker; <6, 17 >) I. Barner, Wilfried. II. T. III. Title: Werke und Briefe in 12 Bänden.
PT2396.A1 1985   832/.6 19   *LC* 86-132841   *ISBN* 3618611005

Lessing, Gotthold Ephraim, 1729-1781.   **2.13631**
Gesammelte Werke / [Hrsg. von Wolfgang Stammler]. — München: C. Hanser, [1959] 2 v.; 19 cm. I. Stammler, Wolfgang, 1886-, ed. II. T.
PT2396.A1x   *LC* 60-2534

Brown, Francis Andrew, 1915-.   **2.13632**
Gotthold Ephraim Lessing, by F. Andrew Brown. — New York: Twayne Publishers, [1971] 205 p.; 21 cm. — (Twayne's world authors series, TWAS 113: Germany) 1. Lessing, Gotthold Ephraim, 1729-1781. I. T.
PT2406.B7   838/.6/09   *LC* 75-110709

Garland, Henry Burnand.   • **2.13633**
Lessing, the founder of modern German literature. [2d ed.] London, Macmillan; New York, St. Martin's Press, 1962 [i.e. 1963] 202 p. 21 cm. 1. Lessing, Gotthold Ephraim, 1729-1781. I. T.
PT2406.G3 1963   832.6   *LC* 62-19577

Mann, Otto, 1898-.   • **2.13634**
Lessing: Sein und Leistung. 2. Aufl. [Berlin]. — De Gruyter [1965, c1961] 404, [1] p. 18 cm. Bibliography of Lessings works: p. 385-[400] Bibliography: p. 401-[405] 1. Lessing, Gotthold Ephraim, 1729-1781. I. T.
PT2406.M35 1965   *LC* 68-79235

PT2432–2454 M–R

Meyer, Conrad Ferdinand, 1825-1898.   **2.13635**
Werke in zwei Bänden / [herausgegeben von Hermann Engelhard]. — Stuttgart: Phaidon, [1982] 2 v. I. Engelhard, Hermann. II. T.
PT2432 A1 1982x

Meyer, Conrad Ferdinand, 1825-1898.   **2.13636**
[Selected works. English. 1975] The complete narrative prose of Conrad Ferdinand Meyer / translated from the German by George F. Folkers, David B. Dickens, Marion W. Sonnenfeld; with an introd. by George F. Folkers. — Lewisburg: Bucknell University Press, c1976. 2 v.; 25 cm. I. T.
PZ3.M574 Co3 PT2432.Ax   833/.7   *LC* 76-168824   *ISBN* 0838715478

Burkhard, Marianne.   **2.13637**
Conrad Ferdinand Meyer / by Marianne Burkhard. — Boston: Twayne Publishers, c1978. 157 p. port. — (Twayne's world authors series; TWAS 480:

Germany) Includes index. 1. Meyer, Conrad Ferdinand, 1825-1898 —
Criticism and interpretation. I. T.
PT2432.Z9 B84 1978   PT2432Z9 B84 1978.   831/.7   LC 77-28441
ISBN 080576321X

Mörike, Eduard Friedrich, 1804-1875.   • **2.13638**
Poems, by Eduard Mörike, tr. by Norah K. Cruickshank and Gilbert F.
Cunningham, with introduction by Jethro Bithell. London, Methuen & co., ltd.
[1959] 120 p. German text and notes on the poems, p. [81]-120. I. T.
PT2434A23   831.79

Mörike, Eduard Friedrich, 1804-1875.   **2.13639**
Sämtliche Werke / Eduard Mörike; mit einem Nachwort von Benno von Wiese
sowie Anmerkungen, Zeittafel und Bibliographie von Helga Unger. —
München: Winkler, 1967-. v.; 20 cm. I. Wiese, Benno von, 1903- II. Unger,
Helga. III. T.
PT2434.A6 1967   LC 70-384488

Raabe, Wilhelm, 1831-1910.   **2.13640**
Gesammelte Werke: Romane und Erzählungen / Wilhelm Raabe. — München:
Nymphenburger Verlagshandlung, 1980-. v. I. T.
PT2451 A1 1980   ISBN 3485003956

Raabe, Wilhelm Karl, 1831-1910.   **2.13641**
Novels / Wilhelm Raabe; edited by Volkmar Sander; foreword by Joel Agee. —
New York: Continuum, 1983. xvii, 318 p.; 21 cm. — (German library. v. 45)
I. Sander, Volkmar. II. T. III. Series.
PT2451.A2 1983   833/.8 19   LC 82-22097   ISBN 082640281X

Daemmrich, Horst S., 1930-.   **2.13642**
Wilhelm Raabe / by Horst S. Daemmrich. — Boston: Twayne, 1981. 171 p.:
port.; 21 cm. — (Twayne's world authors series; TWAS 594: Germany)
Includes index. 1. Raabe, Wilhelm Karl, 1831-1910 — Criticism and
interpretation. I. T.
PT2451.Z5 D3   833/.8 19   LC 80-20982   ISBN 0805764364

Fairley, Barker, 1887-.   • **2.13643**
Wilhelm Raabe: an introduction to his novels / by Barker Fairley. — Oxford:
Clarendon Press, 1961. 275 p. 1. Raabe, Wilhelm Karl, 1831-1910. I. T.
PT2451.Z5 F3   LC 61-1138

Jean Paul, 1763-1825.   • **2.13644**
Werke [von] Jean Paul. [Hrsg. von Norbert Miller. Nachwort von Walter
Höllerer] München: C. Hanser, [1959-63; v.1, 1960] 6 v.; 20 cm. Vol. 2 edited by
Gustav Lohmann. I. Miller, Norbert. II. T.
PT2454.A1x   838.6   LC 65-7146

Berger, Dorothea, 1907-.   **2.13645**
Jean Paul Friedrich Richter, by Dorothea Berger. New York, Twayne
Publishers [c1972] 176 p. 21 cm. (Twayne's world authors series, TWAS 192.
Germany) 1. Jean Paul, 1763-1825. I. T.
PT2456.Z4 B39   838/.6/09   LC 72-147188

PT2465–2499 Schiller

Schiller, Friedrich, 1759-1805.   **2.13646**
Sämtliche Werke. [Auf Grund der Originaldrucke, hrsg. von Gerhard Fricke
und Herbert G. Göpfert. — 6. Aufl. — München, C. Hanser 1980. 5 v.
I. Fricke, Gerhard, 1901- ed. II. Göpfert, Herbert Georg. ed. III. T.
PT2465.B60 1965   PT2465.B80x.

Schiller, Friedrich, 1759-1805.   • **2.13647**
The bride of Messina: or, The enemy brothers: a tragedy with choruses. William
Tell; Demetrius: or, The blood wedding in Moscow: a fragment / Friedrich von
Schiller; translated by Charles E. Passage. — New York: F. Ungar, c1962. xi,
109, 129, 61 p.; 21 cm. I. Schiller, Friedrich, 1759-1805. Braut von Messina.
English. II. Passage, Charles E. III. Schiller, Friedrich, 1759-1805. Wilhelm
Tell. English IV. Schiller, Friedrich, 1759-1805. Demetrius. English. V. T.
VI. Title: Wilhelm Tell. VII. Title: Demetrius.
PT2473.A4 P3 1962   LC 62-17091

Schiller, Friedrich, 1759-1805.   **2.13648**
[Kabale und Liebe. English] Plays / Friedrich Schiller; edited by Walter
Hinderer; foreword by Gordon A. Craig. — New York: Continuum, 1983. xvii,
346 p.; 22 cm. — (German library. v. 15) Translation of: Kabale und Liebe and
Don Carlos. I. Schiller, Friedrich, 1759-1805. Don Carlos. Italian. 1983.
II. Hinderer, Walter, 1934- III. T. IV. Series.
PT2473.K3 II5 1983   832/.6 19   LC 83-7741   ISBN 0826402747

Schiller, Friedrich, 1759-1805.   • **2.13649**
Mary Stuart. The Maid of Orleans. Two historical plays, translated by Charles
E. Passage. New York, F. Ungar Pub. Co. [1961] xix, 135, xi, 124 p. 21 cm.
1. Mary, Queen of Scots, 1542-1587 — Drama. 2. Joan, of Arc, Saint,

1412-1431 — Drama. I. Schiller, Friedrich, 1759-1805. The Maid of Orleans.
II. T. III. Title: The Maid of Orleans.
PT2473.M3 P3 1961   832.6   LC 60-13991

Garland, Henry Burnand.   • **2.13650**
Schiller / by H.B. Garland. — London: Harrap, 1949. viii, 280 p.: ill., facsims.,
map. 1. Schiller, Friedrich, 1759-1805. I. T.
PT2482.G3   LC 50-2381

Wiese, Benno von, 1903-.   **2.13651**
Friedrich Schiller / Benno von Wiese. — 4., durchgesehene Aufl. — Stuttgart:
Metzler, 1978. xxi, 866 p.; 24 cm. 1. Schiller, Friedrich, 1759-1805. I. T.
PT2482.Z8 W45 1978   ISBN 3476001784

Passage, Charles E.   **2.13652**
Friedrich Schiller / Charles E. Passage. — New York: F. Ungar Pub. Co.,
[1975] 205 p.: ill.; 21 cm. (World dramatists) Includes index. 1. Schiller,
Friedrich, 1759-1805 — Criticism and interpretation. I. T.
PT2492.P3   831/.6   LC 74-76129   ISBN 0804427348

Simons, John D.   **2.13653**
Friedrich Schiller / by John D. Simons. — Boston: Twayne Publishers, 1981.
163 p.: port.; 21 cm. — (Twayne's world authors series; TWAS 603. Germany)
Includes index. 1. Schiller, Friedrich, 1759-1805 — Criticism and
interpretation. I. T.
PT2492.S54   831/.6 19   LC 81-4908   ISBN 0805764453

Stahl, Ernest Ludwig.   **2.13654**
Friedrich Schiller's drama: theory and practice. — Oxford: Clarendon Press,
1954. vi, 172 p.; 23 cm. 1. Schiller, Friedrich, 1759-1805. I. T.
PT2494.S8   LC 55-1959

PT2503–2592 S–Z

Schlegel, Friedrich von, 1772-1829.   • **2.13655**
Dialogue on poetry and literary aphorisms. Translated, introduced, and
annotated by Ernst Behler & Roman Struc. — [University Park: Pennsylvania
State University Press, 1968] vi, 167 p.; 22 cm. The Dialogue on poetry
(1799-1800) was translated from the periodical Athenaeum, Bd. 3, p. 58-128,
169-187. The literary aphorisms (1797-1800) were translated from Lyceum der
schönen Künste, Bd. 1. teil 2, and the Athenaeum, Bd. 1, p. 3-146, and Bd. 3, p.
4-33. I. Behler, Ernst, 1928- ed. II. Struc, Roman, ed. III. T.
PT2503.S6 Z3 1968   808.1   LC 67-27115

Stifter, Adalbert, 1805-1868.   **2.13656**
[Works 1978] Werke und Briefe: historisch–kritische Gesamtausgabe /
Adalbert Stifter; hrsg. von Alfred Doppler u. Wolfgang Frühwald; [die Ausg.
wurde begr. von Hermann Kunisch]. — Stuttgart; Berlin; Köln; Mainz:
Kohlhammer, 1978-< 1986 >. < v. 1, pt. 1-6; v. 2, pt. 1-2; v. 5, pt. 1-3; in 10 >;
23 cm. I. Doppler, Alfred, 1921- II. Frühwald, Wolfgang. III. Kunisch,
Hermann, 1901- IV. T.
PT2525.A1 1978   LC 79-383289   ISBN 3170042327

Stifter, Adalbert, 1805-1868.   **2.13657**
Sämtliche Werke in fünf Einzelbänden. — München: Winkler, 1978-1979. 5 v.;
20 cm. I. T.
PT2525.A1 1978x

Gump, Margaret.   **2.13658**
Adalbert Stifter. — New York: Twayne Publishers, [1974] 172 p.; 21 cm. —
(Twayne's world authors series, TWAS 274. Austria) 1. Stifter, Adalbert,
1805-1868. I. T.
PT2525.Z4 G8   833/.7   LC 73-2367   ISBN 0805728643

Swales, Martin.   **2.13659**
Adalbert Stifter: a critical study / Martin and Erika Swales. — Cambridge
[Cambridgeshire]; New York: Cambridge University Press, 1984. xii, 251 p.; 22
cm. (Anglica Germanica.) Includes index. 1. Stifter, Adalbert, 1805-1868 —
Criticism and interpretation. I. Swales, Erika, 1937- II. T. III. Series.
PT2525.Z5 S92 1984   833/.7 19   LC 83-20914   ISBN 052125972X

Storm, Theodor, 1817-1888.   **2.13660**
Werke. Gesamtausg. in drei Bänden. [Hrsg. und eingeleitet von Hermann
Engelhard. Stuttgart, J. G. Cotta'sche Buchhandlung Nachf., 1958] 3 v.
I. Engelhard, Hermann, ed. II. T.
PT2528.A1x

Alt, Arthur Tilo, 1931-.   **2.13661**
Theodor Storm, by A. Tilo Alt. — New York: Twayne Publishers, [1973]
157 p.; 22 cm. — (Twayne's world authors series, TWAS 252. Germany)
1. Storm, Theodor, 1817-1888. I. T.
PT2528.Z5 A4   833/.8   LC 72-2793

Bernd, Clifford A.   • **2.13662**
Theodor Storm's craft of fiction; the torment of a narrator. 2d augm. ed. Chapel Hill University of North Carolina Press 1966. 140p. (University of North Carolina studies in the Germanic languages and literatures. no. 55) 1. Storm, Theodor, 1817-1888. I. T. II. Title: Craft of fiction III. Title: Aquis submersus IV. Title: In St. Jürgen V. Series.
PT2528 Z6 B47 1966

Tieck, Ludwig, 1773-1853.   • **2.13663**
Werke, in vier Bänden / Nach dem Text der Schriften von 1828–1854, unter Berücksichtigung der Erstdrucke; hrsg. sowie mit Nachworten und Anmerkungen versehen von Marianne Thalmann. — München: Winkler-Verlag, 1963-66. 4 v. Title from verso of t.p. Each volume has also special t.p. I. Thalmann, Marianne, 1888- II. T.
PT2536.A1 1963   838.6   *LC* 66-36399 rev

Tieck, Ludwig, 1773-1853.   **2.13664**
Der gestiefelte Kater. Puss–in–Boots [by] Ludwig Tieck. Edited and translated by Gerald Gillespie. Austin, University of Texas Press [1974] xi, 137 p. 21 cm. (Edinburgh bilingual library, 8) English and German. I. Gillespie, Gerald Ernest Paul, 1933- ed. II. T. III. Title: Puss-in-Boots. IV. Series.
PT2537.G8 1974   832/.7   *LC* 73-20869   *ISBN* 029272702X

Uhland, Ludwig, 1787-1862.   **2.13665**
Dichtungen, Briefe, Reden; eine Auswahl. Hrsg. von Walter P.H. Scheffler. Stuttgart J.F. Steinkopf [1963] 502 p.; 21 cm. I. Scheffler, Walter P. H. II. T.
PT2543 A33 1963

Arendt, Hannah.   **2.13666**
Rahel Varnhagen, the life of a Jewish woman. Translated by Richard and Clara Winston. Rev. ed. New York, Harcourt Brace Jovanovich [1974] xx, 236 p. port. 21 cm. Published in 1957 under title: Rahel Varnhagen, the life of a Jewess. 1. Varnhagen, Rahel, 1771-1833. 2. Jews — Germany I. T.
PT2546.V22 A913 1974   838/.6/08 B   *LC* 74-6478   *ISBN* 0151758506 *ISBN* 0156761009

Wieland, Christoph Martin, 1733-1813.   • **2.13667**
Werke. [Hrsg. von Fritz Martini und Hans Werner Seiffert.] München, Hanser [1964-68] 5 v. I. T.
PT2562.A1 1964   838.6   *LC* 68-81185

McCarthy, John A. (John Aloysius), 1942-.   **2.13668**
Christoph Martin Wieland / by John A. McCarthy. — Boston: Twayne Publishers, 1979. 192 p.: port.; 21 cm. (Twayne's world authors series; TWAS 528: Germany) Includes index. 1. Wieland, Christoph Martin, 1733-1813. 2. Authors, German — 18th century — Biography. I. T.
PT2569.M3   838/.6/09 B   *LC* 78-14338   *ISBN* 0805763694

Sengle, Friedrich.   • **2.13669**
Wieland / Friedrich Sengle. — [1. Aufl.]. — Stuttgart: J. B. Metzler, 1949. 610 p.: ill. 1. Wieland, Christoph Martin, 1733-1813. I. T.
PT2569.S4   *LC* A 50-4819

PT2600–2653 19th–20th Centuries (1860/1870–1960)

PT2601–2603 A–B

Aichiniger, Ilse, 1921-.   **2.13670**
Die grössere Hoffnung: roman / Ilse Aichinger. — Frankfurt am Main: Fisher, 1974. 187 p. I. T.
PT2601.I26 G7 1974   *ISBN* 3436018317

Aichinger, Ilse, 1921-.   **2.13671**
Nachricht vom Tag: Erzählungen / Ilse Aichinger. — Frankfurt am Main: Fischer-Bücherei, 1970. 190 p., 18 cm. — (Fischer-Bücherei; 1140) I. T.
PT2601.I26 N3   *LC* 71-571495   *ISBN* 3436012947

Aichinger, Ilse.   **2.13672**
Verschenkter Rat: Gedichte / Ilse Aichinger. — [1.-2. Tsd.]. — Frankfurt am Main: S. Fischer, 1978. 99 p.; 20 cm. — I. T.
PT2601.I26 V47   831/.9/14   *LC* 79-360584   *ISBN* 3100005090

Bachmann, Ingeborg.   • **2.13673**
Anrufung des Grossen Bären: Gedichte / Ingeborg Bachmann. — 8. ed. — München: R. Piper, 1983. 78 p. — (Serie Piper; Band 307) I. T.
PT2603.A147Ax   *ISBN* 3492006078

Bachmann, Ingeborg, 1926-1973.   **2.13674**
Die gestundete Zeit: Gedichte / Ingeborg Bachmann. — 6. Aufl. — München: R. Piper, 1974. 65 p.; 22 cm. I. T.
PT2603.A147 G4 1974b   *ISBN* 3492010474

Barlach, Ernst, 1870-1938.   • **2.13675**
Das dichterische Werk / Ernst Barlach. — München: R. Piper, 1956-59. 3 v.; 22 cm. I. Lazarowicz, K. II. Dross, F. III. T. IV. Title: Die Dramen V. Title: Die Prosa I VI. Title: Die Prosa II
PT2603.A53 1956   *LC* a 57-3982

Beer-Hofmann, Richard, 1866-1945.   **2.13676**
Gesammelte Werke. [Frankfurt am Main] S. Fischer 1963. 896;4p. I. T.
PT2603 E27 1963

Elstun, Esther N., 1935-.   **2.13677**
Richard Beer–Hofmann, his life and work / Esther N. Elstun. — University Park: Pennsylvania State University Press, c1983. ix, 214 p.; 24 cm. — (Penn State series in German literature.) Includes index. 1. Beer-Hofmann, Richard, 1866-1945. 2. Authors, Austrian — 20th century — Biography. I. T. II. Series.
PT2603.E27 Z63 1983   838/.91209 B 19   *LC* 82-14990   *ISBN* 0271003359

Benn, Gottfried, 1886-1956.   • **2.13678**
Gesammelte Werke / Hrsg. von Dieter Wellershoff. — [Wiesbaden]: Limes Verglag, [1958-61, v.1, 1959]. 4 v.; 19 cm. I. Wellershoff, Dieter. ed. II. T.
PT2603.E46 1958

Ritchie, James McPherson, 1927-.   **2.13679**
Gottfried Benn: the unreconstructed expressionist, by J. M. Ritchie. — London: Wolff, 1972. 126 p.; 20 cm. — (Modern German authors; texts and contexts, v. 6) 1. Benn, Gottfried, 1886-1956. I. T. II. Series.
PT2603.E46 Z774   831/.9/12   *LC* 73-152970   *ISBN* 0854960465

Keith-Smith, Brian, 1934-.   **2.13680**
Johannes Bobrowski; with four illustrations by Fritz Möser. — London: Wolff, 1970. 119 p.: 4 illus.; 19 cm. — (Modern German authors: texts and contexts, v. 4) Selections of poetry and prose translated from the German. 1. Bobrowski, Johannes, 1917-1965. I. Bobrowski, Johannes, 1917-1965. II. T. III. Series.
PT2603.O13 Z7   838/.9/1409   *LC* 76-20446   *ISBN* 0854960449

PT2603 Böll

Böll, Heinrich, 1917-.   **2.13681**
[Selections. English] Missing persons and other essays / Heinrich Böll; translated from the German by Leila Vennewitz. — New York: McGraw-Hill, c1977. viii, 281 p.; 22 cm. I. T.
PT2603.O394 A28   834/.9/14   *LC* 77-9351   *ISBN* 0070064245

Böll, Heinrich, 1917-.   • **2.13682**
Erzählungen, Hörspiele, Aufsätze. Köln, Kiepenheuer & Witsch [1962, c1961] 445 p. 21 cm. I. T.
PT2603.O394 A6 1962   *LC* 62-6857

Böll, Heinrich, 1917-.   • **2.13683**
The clown / by Heinrich Böll; translated from the German by Leila Vennewitz. — New York: McGraw-Hill, 1965. 247 p.; 21 cm. I. Böll, Heinrich, 1917- Ansichten eines Clowns, English. II. Vennewitz, Leila. III. T.
PT2603.O394 A7x   *LC* 64-7935   *ISBN* 0070064202

Böll, Heinrich, 1917-.   • **2.13684**
18 stories [by] Heinrich Böll. Translated from the German by Leila Vennewitz. — [1st ed.]. — New York: McGraw-Hill, [1966] 243 p.; 21 cm. — I. T.
PT2603.O394 Ax   *LC* 66-23273

Böll, Heinrich, 1917-.   • **2.13685**
[1947 i.e. Neunzehnhundertsiebenundvierzig] bis 1951. Selections. English] Children are civilians too. Translated from the German by Leila Vennewitz. [1st ed.] New York, McGraw-Hill [c1970] x, 189 p. 21 cm. 'These stories originally formed part of a volume entitled 1947 bis 1951.' I. T.
PZ4.B6713 Ch PT2603.O394 Ax   833/.9/14   *LC* 79-86086

Böll, Heinrich, 1917-.   • **2.13686**
Billard um Halbzehn. [2. Aufl.] Köln, Kiepenheuer & Witsch [1959] 304 p. 21 cm. I. T.
PT2603.O394 B5 1959   *LC* 60-34522

Böll, Heinrich.   • **2.13687**
Billiards at half–past nine / Heinrich Böll; translated from the German. — NewYork: McGraw-Hill, 1962. 280p. Translation of Billard um Halbzehn. I. T.
PT2603.O394 B5x   *LC* 62-15141   *ISBN* 0070064016

PT2603 Brecht

Böll, Heinrich, 1917-.   • 2.13688
Das Brot der frühen Jahre: Erzählung / Heinrich Böll. — Köln: Kiepenheuer & Witsch, [1980], c1955. 141 p.; 21 cm. I. T.
PT2603.O394 B7 1980x   *LC* 85-672869   *ISBN* 3462014161

Böll, Heinrich, 1917-.   2.13689
[Brot der frühen Jahre. English] The bread of those early years / Heinrich Böll; translated from the German by Leila Vennewitz. — New York: McGraw-Hill, c1976. 134 p.; 21 cm. Translation of Das Brot der frühen Jahre. I. T.
PZ4.B6713 Br PT2603.O394 B7x   833/.9/14   *LC* 76-17547   *ISBN* 007006427X

Böll, Heinrich, 1917-.   2.13690
Gruppenbild mit Dame. Roman. [2 Aufl.] [Köln] Kiepenheuer & Witsch [1971] 400p. I. T.
PT2603 O394 G7 1971

Böll, Heinrich, 1917-.   2.13691
[Gruppenbild mit Dame. English] Group portrait with lady. Translated from the German by Leila Vennewitz. New York, McGraw-Hill [1973] 405 p. 24 cm. Translation of Gruppenbild mit Dame. I. T.
PZ4.B6713 Gr PT2603.O394 G7x   833/.9/14   *LC* 72-8835   *ISBN* 0070064237

Böll, Heinrich, 1917-.   2.13692
Die verlorene Ehre der Katharina Blum: oder, Wie Gewalt entstehen und wohin sie führen kann: Erzählung / Heinrich Böll. — Köln: Kiepenheuer & Witsch, 1974. 188 p. I. T.
PT2603.O394 V4   PT2603 O394 V4.   *LC* 74-351123   *ISBN* 3462010336

Böll, Heinrich, 1917-.   2.13693
[Verlorene Ehre der Katharina Blum English] The lost honor of Katharina Blum: how violence develops and where it can lead / Heinrich Böll; translated from the German by Leila Vennewitz. — New York: McGraw-Hill, [1975] 140 p.; 22 cm. Translation of Die verlorene Ehre der Katharina Blum. I. T.
PZ4.B6713 Lo PT2603.O394 V4x   833/.9/14   *LC* 74-28138   *ISBN* 0070064253

Böll, Heinrich, 1917-.   • 2.13694
Wo warst du, Adam? und Erzählungen. [Neuausg.] [Köln] Middelhauve [1967] 3 v.; 20 cm. I. T.
PT2603 O394 W6 1967   *LC* 68-85579

Böll, Heinrich, 1917-.   • 2.13695
[Wo warst du Adam? English] Adam, and, The train: two novels. Translated from the German by Leila Vennewitz. [1st ed.] New York, McGraw-Hill [1970] 268 p. 22 cm. Translation of Wo warst du Adam? And Der Zug war pünktlich. Caption titles: And where were you, Adam? The train was on time. 1. World War, 1939-1945 — Fiction. I. T. II. T. III. Title: Train.
PZ4.B6713 Act PT2603.O394 W6x   833/.9/14   *LC* 71-127920

Böll, Heinrich, 1917-.   2.13696
[Was soll aus dem Jungen bloss werden? English] What's to become of the boy?, or, Something to do with books / Heinrich Böll; translated by Leila Vennewitz. — 1st American ed. — New York: A.A. Knopf, 1984. 82 p.: port.; 20 cm. Translation of: Was soll aus dem Jungen bloss werden? 1. Böll, Heinrich, 1917- — Biography — Youth. 2. Authors, German — 20th century — Biography. I. T. II. Title: Something to do with books.
PT2603.O394 Z47613 1984   833/.914 B 19   *LC* 83-49087   *ISBN* 0394530160

Conard, Robert C., 1933-.   2.13697
Heinrich Böll / Robert C. Conard. — Boston: Twayne, 1981. 228 p.: port.; 21 cm. — (Twayne's world authors series; TWAS 622. Germany) Includes index. 1. Böll, Heinrich, 1917- 2. Authors, German — 20th century — Biography. I. T.
PT2603.O394 Z596   833/.914 B 19   *LC* 81-2419   *ISBN* 080576464X

PT2603 Borchert

Borchert, Wolfgang, 1921-1947.   • 2.13698
Das Gesamtwerk. Mit einem biographischen Nachwort von Bernhard Meyer-Marwitz. — Hamburg, Rowohlt [1949, c1948] 419 p.: port.; 21 cm. I. T.
PT2603.O725 1949   *LC* 49-28633 *

Borchert, Wolfgang, 1921-1947.   2.13699
[Traurigen Geranien und andere Geschichten aus dem Nachlass. English] The sad geraniums, and other stories / Wolfgang Borchert; translated by Keith Hamnett. — New York: Ecco Press, 1973. viii, 87 p.: 21 cm. Translation of Die traurigen Geranien und andere Geschichten aus dem Nachlass. I. T.
PZ3.B64755 Sad3 PT2603.O725 T7x   833/.9/14   *LC* 73-11251   *ISBN* 0912946105

Brecht, Bertolt, 1898-1956.   2.13700
Gesammelte Werke: (In 20 Bänden. Hrsg. in Zusammenarbeit mit Elisabeth Hauptmann). — [Frankfurt a.M.]: Suhrkamp, [1967]. 20 v.; 18 cm. (Werkausgabe Edition Suhrkamp) I. T.
PT2603.R397 1967   *LC* 68-76600

Brecht, Bertolt, 1898-1956.   2.13701
Gesammelte Werke: [Supplementbände] / Bertolt Brecht; [hrsg. von Herta Ramthun]. — Werkausg. — Frankfurt am Main: Suhrkamp, 1982-. v.; 18 cm. — (Edition Suhrkamp) Includes bibliographical references and indexes. I. Ramthun, Herta. II. T. III. Title: Gedichte aus dem Nachlass.
PT2603 R397 1967 Suppl   *ISBN* 3518009443

Brecht, Bertolt, 1898-1956.   2.13702
[Short stories. English. Selections] Short stories, 1921-1946 / Bertolt Brecht; edited by John Willett and Ralph Manheim; translated by Yvonne Kapp, Hugh Rorrison, and Antony Tatlow. — London; New York: Methuen, 1983. xiii, 242 p.; 23 cm. — (Plays, poetry, and prose / Bertolt Brecht) 'Original work entitled Geschichten being Volume 11 of Gesammelte Werke of Bertolt Brecht'-T.p. verso. Includes index. I. Willett, John. II. Manheim, Ralph, 1907- III.
PT2603.R397 A2 1983   833/.912 19   *LC* 82-14095   *ISBN* 041337050X

Brecht, Bertolt, 1898-1956.   • 2.13703
[Plays. English. 1971] Collected plays. Edited by Ralph Manheim and John Willett. [1st American ed.] New York, Pantheon Books [1971- c1970-. v. 22 cm. (His Plays, poetry, and prose) Translations from the German. Vols. 7- published by Random House. I. T.
PT2603.R397 A29 1971b   832/.9/12   *LC* 75-26518   *ISBN* 0394406648

Brecht, Bertolt, 1898-1956.   2.13704
[Poems. English. 1979] Poems, 1913-1956 / Bertolt Brecht; edited by John Willett and Ralph Manheim, with the co-operation of Erich Fried. — 2d ed. — New York: Methuen, 1980. xxvii, 627 p.; 23 cm. I. Willett, John. II. Manheim, Ralph, 1907- III. Fried, Erich. IV. T.
PT2603.R397 A29 1979   831/.9/12   *LC* 79-9222   *ISBN* 0416000819

Brecht, Bertolt, 1898-1956.   2.13705
[Tagebücher 1920-1922. English] Diaries 1920-1922 / Bertolt Brecht; edited by Herta Ramthun; translated and annotated with an introductory essay by John Willett. — New York: St. Martin's Press, c1979. xxiii, 182 p., [4] leaves of plates: ill.; 22 cm. Translation of Tagebücher 1920-1922. Includes index. 1. Brecht, Bertolt, 1898-1956 — Diaries. 2. Authors, German — 20th century — Biography. I. Ramthun, Herta. II. Willett, John. III. T.
PT2603.R397 Z52513 1979   838/.9/1203   *LC* 78-21345   *ISBN* 0312077033

Demetz, Peter, 1922- ed.   • 2.13706
Brecht; a collection of critical essays. — Englewood Cliffs, N.J.: Prentice-Hall, [1962] 186 p.; 21 cm. — (Twentieth century views) (A Spectrum book, S-TC-11.) 1. Brecht, Bertolt, 1898-1956. I. T.
PT2603.R397 Z587   838.912   *LC* 62-13723

Fuegi, John.   2.13707
The essential Brecht / by John Fuegi. — Los Angeles, Hennessey & Ingalls, 1972. 343 p. ill.; 24 cm. — (University of Southern California studies in comparative literature; v. 4) 1. Brecht, Bertolt, 1898-1956. I. T.
PT2603.R397 Z6193   832/.9/12   *LC* 79-188986   *ISBN* 0912158174

Hayman, Ronald, 1932-.   2.13708
Bertolt Brecht: the plays / by Ronald Hayman. — London: Heinemann; Totowa, N.J.: Barnes & Noble, 1984. xxvi, 102 p.; 19 cm. (Contemporary playwrights.) 1. Brecht, Bertolt, 1898-1956 — Criticism and interpretation. I. T. II. Series.
PT2603.R397 Z6667 1984   832/.912 19   *LC* 84-9261   *ISBN* 0389204927

Hayman, Ronald, 1932-.   2.13709
Brecht: a biography / Ronald Hayman. — New York: Oxford University Press, 1983. xxiv, 423 p., [8] p. of plates; 25 cm. Includes index. 1. Brecht, Bertolt, 1898-1956 — Biography. 2. Authors, German — 20th century — Biography. I. T.
PT2603.R397 Z6668 1983   832/.912 B 19   *LC* 83-11405   *ISBN* 0195204344

Hill, Claude.   2.13710
Bertolt Brecht. — New York: Twayne Publishers, [1975] 208 p.: port.; 21 cm. — (Twayne's world authors series, TWAS 331. Germany) 1. Brecht, Bertolt, 1898-1956. I. T.
PT2603.R397 Z677   PT2603R397 Z677.   832/.9/12   *LC* 74-14610   *ISBN* 0805721797

Lyon, James K.   **2.13711**
Bertolt Brecht in America / James K. Lyon. — Princeton, N.J.: Princeton University Press, c1980. xiv, 408 p., [8] leaves of plates: ill.; 24 cm. 1. Brecht, Bertolt, 1898-1956 — Biography — Exile — United States. 2. Brecht, Bertolt, 1898-1956 — Appreciation — United States. 3. Authors, German — 20th century — Biography. I. T.
PT2603.R397 Z74593   832/.912 B 19   *LC* 80-7543   *ISBN* 0691064431

PT2603–2605 Broch. Busch

Broch, Hermann, 1886-1951.   **2.13712**
Gesammelte Werke. [Zürich, Rhein-Verlag, 1952-1957; v.1, 1953] 8 v. ports., facsims. 21 cm. Half-title. Each vol. has special t.p. I. T.
PT2603.R657 A1 1952x

Broch, Hermann, 1886-1951.   • **2.13713**
The sleepwalkers, a trilogy / tr. by Willa and Edwin Muir. New York: Pantheon Books, [1964]. 648 p. I. Muir, Willa, 1890- II. T.
PT2603.R657 S3x   *LC* 64-6364

Busch, Wilhelm, 1832-1908.   • **2.13714**
Das Gesamtwerk des Zeichners und Dichters. [Hrsg. und eingeleitet von Hugo Werner] Olten, Fackelverlag [1959-. v. I. Werner, Hugo. II. T.
PT2603.U8 1959a   838.8   *LC* 61-43540

Busch, Wilhelm, 1832-1908.   **2.13715**
[Selected works. English] The genius of Wilhelm Busch: comedy of frustration: an English anthology / edited and translated by Walter Arndt. — Berkeley: University of California Press, c1982. 253 p.: ill.; 26 cm. Includes index. I. Arndt, Walter W., 1916- II. T.
PT2603.U8 A22   831/.8 19   *LC* 79-63545   *ISBN* 0520038975

Lotze, Dieter P.   **2.13716**
Wilhelm Busch / by Dieter P. Lotze. — Boston: Twayne Publishers, 1979. 171 p., [6] leaves of plates: ill.; 21 cm. — (Twayne's world authors series; TWAS 525: Germany) Includes index. 1. Busch, Wilhelm, 1832-1908 — Criticism and interpretation. I. T.
PT2603.U8 Z725   831/.8   *LC* 78-14843   *ISBN* 0805763651

PT2605 C

Canetti, Elias, 1905-.   **2.13717**
Die Blendung: Roman / Elias Canetti. 44.-50. Tsd. — München: C. Hanser, 1981. 515 p.; 18 cm. I. T.
PT2605.A58 B55 1976

Canetti, Elias, 1905-.   **2.13718**
[Gewissen der Worte. English] The conscience of words / by Elias Canetti; translated from the German by Joachim Neugroschel. — New York: Seabury Press, 1979. ix, 246 p.; 24 cm. — (A Continuum book) Translation of Das Gewissen der Worte. I. T.
PT2605.A58 G4513 1979   834/.9/12   *LC* 78-15377   *ISBN* 0816493340

Canetti, Elias, 1905-.   **2.13719**
[Fackel im Ohr. English] The torch in my ear / Elias Canetti; translated from the German by Joachim Neugroschel. — New York: Farrar Straus Giroux, c1982. 371 p.; 24 cm. Translation of: Die Fackel im Ohr. 1. Canetti, Elias, 1905- — Biography. 2. Authors, German — 20th century — Biography. I. T.
PT2605.A58 Z46513 1982   833/.912 B 19   *LC* 82-7460   *ISBN* 0374278474

Canetti, Elias, 1905-.   **2.13720**
Die Fackel im Ohr: Lebensgeschichte 1921–1931 / Elias Canetti. — München; Wien: Hanser, 1980. 407 p.; 21 cm. 1. Canetti, Elias, 1905- — Biography. 2. Authors, German — 20th century — Biography. I. T.
PT2605.A58 Z513   833/.912 B 19   *LC* 80-514183   *ISBN* 3446131388

Canetti, Elias, 1905-.   **2.13721**
Die gerettete Zunge: Geschichte einer Jugend / Elias Canetti. — 2. Aufl. — München: C. Hanser, c1977. 374 p.; 21 cm. 1. Canetti, Elias, 1905- — Biography — Youth. 2. Authors, Austrian — 20th century — Biography. I. T.
PT2605.A58 Z515 1977   *LC* 77-481886   *ISBN* 3446123350

Canetti, Elias, 1905-.   **2.13722**
[Gerettete Zunge. English] The tongue set free: remembrance of a European childhood / Elias Canetti; translated from the German by Joachim Neugroschel. — New York: Seabury Press, 1979. viii, 268 p.; 24 cm. — (A Continuum book) Translation of Die gerettete Zunge. 1. Canetti, Elias, 1905-

— Biography — Youth. 2. Authors, Austrian — 20th century — Biography. I. T.
PT2605.A58 Z51513   833/.9/12 B   *LC* 79-18234   *ISBN* 0816491038

Carossa, Hans, 1878-1956.   • **2.13723**
Sämtliche Werke. [Frankfurt am Main] Insel-Verlag, 1962-. v. 18 cm. I. T.
PT2605.A65 1962   *LC* 64-37292

Celan, Paul.   **2.13724**
[Works. 1983] Gesammelte Werke in fünf Bänden / Paul Celan; [herausgegeben von Beda Allemann und Stefan Reichert unter Mitwirkung von Rudolf Bücher]. — 1. Aufl. — Frankfurt am Main: Suhrkamp, 1983. 5 v.; 21 cm. I. Allemann, Beda. II. Reichert, Stefan. III. Bücher, Rolf. IV. T. V. Title: Gesammelte Werke in 5 Bänden.
PT2605.E4 A1114 1983   831/.914 19   *LC* 84-105910   *ISBN* 3518045008

Celan, Paul.   **2.13725**
Collected prose / Paul Celan; translated from the German by Rosemarie Waldrop. — Manchester: Carcanet, 1986. 67 p.; 23 cm. Translation of: Gesammelte Werke. Vol.3. I. T.
PT2605.E4 A16 1986   838/.91408 19   *ISBN* 085635645X

Celan, Paul.   **2.13726**
Paul Celan: poems / Paul Celan; selected, translated and introduced by Michael Hamburger. — A bilingual ed. — New York: Persea Books, c1980. 307 p. English and German texts. I. Hamburger, Michael. II. T.
PT2605.F4 A6 1980   831/.914   *LC* 79-9117   *ISBN* 0892550600

PT2607–2609 D–E

Dehmel, Richard, 1863-1920.   • **2.13727**
[Works. 1972] Gesammelte Werke. — Berlin: S. Fischer, 1913. 3 v. port. 23 cm. I. T.
PT2607.E32 1972   831/.8   *LC* 14-460

Ditzen, Rudolph, 1893-1947.   • **2.13728**
Kleiner Mann, was nun?: roman / Hans Fallada. — Hamburg: Rowohlt, 1950. 246 p.; 19 cm. — (Rororo; 480) I. T.
PT2607.I6 K4   *ISBN* 3499100010

Döblin, Alfred, 1878-1957.   **2.13729**
Berlin Alexanderplatz: die Geschichte von Franz Biberkopf / Alfred Döblin; [hrsg. von Walter Muschg]. — Olten: Walter, 1977, c1961. 527 p.; 21 cm. — (His Jubiläums-Sonderausgabe zum hundertsten Geburtstag des Dichters) I. Muschg, Walter, 1898-1965. II. T.
PT2607.O35 B5 1977   833/.9/12   *LC* 78-371086   *ISBN* 3530166456

Kort, Wolfgang, 1939-.   **2.13730**
Alfred Döblin. — New York: Twayne Publishers, [1974] 165 p.: illus.; 21 cm. — (Twayne's world authors series, TWAS 290. Germany) 1. Döblin, Alfred, 1878-1957. I. T.
PT2607.O35 Z718   PT2607 O35 Z718.   838/.9/1209   *LC* 73-16222   *ISBN* 0805722661

Dürrenmatt, Friedrich.   • **2.13731**
Komödien / Friedrich Dürrenmatt. — Zürich: Verlag der Arche, [1957-1964, c1963]. 2 v.; 20 cm. Vol. 2 has title: Komödien II. und Frühe Stücke. I. T.
PT2607.U493 A19 1957   *LC* 59-3750

Dürrenmatt, Friedrich, 1921-.   • **2.13732**
Gesammelte Hörspiele. [Neue Aufl.] Zürich: Im Verlag der Arche, [1964, c1954-61] 317 p.; 20 cm. I. T.
PT2607.U493 A19 1964   *LC* 66-1921

Dürrenmatt, Friedrich.   • **2.13733**
Four plays: Romulus the Great. The marriage of Mr. Mississippi. An angel comes to Babylon. The physicist / by Friedrich Durrenmatt;[Translated from the German by Gerhard Nellhaus and others]. — New York: Grove Press, [1965]. –. 349 p.; 21 cm. — I. T.
PT2607.U493 A24   832.914   *LC* 65-14201

Dürrenmatt, Friedrich.   • **2.13734**
[Besuch der alten Dame. English] The visit; a tragi–comedy. Translated from the German by Patrick Bowles. New York, Grove Press [1962] 109 p. 21 cm. (Evergreen original, E-344) Translation of Der Besuch der alten Dame. I. T.
PT2607.U493 B43 1962   832.914   *LC* 62-16341

Tiusanen, Timo.   2.13735
Dürrenmatt: a study in plays, prose, theory / by Timo Tiusanen. — Princeton, N.J.: Princeton University Press, c1977. xiii, 486 p., [4] leaves of plates: ill. Includes index. 1. Dürrenmatt, Friedrich — Criticism and interpretation. I. T. PT2607.U493 Z89   PT2607U493 Z89.   832/.9/14   *LC* 76-45915
    ISBN 069106332X

Enzensberger, Hans Magnus.   2.13736
[Essays. English. Selections] Critical essays / Hans Magnus Enzensberger; edited by Reinhold Grimm and Bruce Armstrong; foreword by John Simon. — New York: Continuum, 1982. xvi, 250 p.; 22 cm. — (German library. v. 98) I. Grimm, Reinhold. II. Armstrong, Bruce. III. T. IV. Series. PT2609.N9 A24 1982   834/.914 19   *LC* 81-19612   *ISBN* 0826402585

Enzensberger, Hans Magnus.   2.13737
Blindenschrift. [Frankfurt/M] Suhrkamp 1965. 96p. I. T. PT2609 N9 B4

Enzensberger, Hans Magnus.   2.13738
Landessprache. Gedichte. — (Frankfurt a.M.): Suhrkamp, (1969). 97 p.; 18 cm. — (Edition Suhrkamp, 304) I. T. PT2609.N9 L3   *LC* 76-397499

PT2611–2613 F–G

Feuchtwanger, Lion, 1884-1958.   2.13739
Der falsche Nero: Roman / Lion Feuchtwanger. — 1. Aufl. — Leipzig: P. Reclam, 1984, c1963. 349 p.; 18 cm. (Belletristik.) (Reclams Universal-Bibliothek; Bd. 1038) 1. Nero, Emperor of Rome, 37-68 — Fiction. I. T. II. Series. PT2611.E85 F34 1984   833/.912 19   *LC* 84-254042

Frisch, Max, 1911-.   • 2.13740
Stucke. — Frankfurt a. M.: Suhrkamp, 1969, c1962. 2 v.; 21 cm. I. T. PT2611.R814 A19 1969   *LC* 77-441491

Frisch, Max, 1911-.   2.13741
Homo faber: ein Bericht / Max Frisch. — 3. Aufl. — Frankfurt a. M.: Suhrkamp, 1977, c1957. 202 p.; 18 cm. — (Suhrkamp Taschenbuch; 354) I. T. PT2611.R814 H6x 1977   *LC* 84-672254   *ISBN* 3518068547

Frisch, Max, 1911-.   2.13742
Der Mensch erscheint im Holozän: e. Erzählung / Max Frisch. — 1. Aufl. — Frankfurt am Main: Suhrkamp, 1979. 142 p.: ill.; 20 cm. — I. T. PT2611.R814 M44   *LC* 79-392262   *ISBN* 3518028502

Frisch, Max, 1911-.   2.13743
[Mensch erscheint im Holozän. English] Man in the Holocene: a story / Max Frisch; translated from the German by Geoffrey Skelton. — New York: Harcourt Brace Jovanovich, c1980. 113 p.: ill.; 21 cm. Translation of Der Mensch erscheint im Holozän. 'A Helen and Kurt Wolff book.' I. T. PZ3.F9186 Man PT2611.R814 M44x   833/.912 19   *LC* 79-3351
    ISBN 0151569312

Frisch, Max, 1911-.   • 2.13744
Stiller, Roman. [Frankfurt a.M.] Suhrkamp Verlag, [1965,c1954]. 576 p. 19 cm. I. T. PT2611.R814 S7 1965   *LC* 55-16371

Frisch, Max, 1911-.   • 2.13745
Three plays / Max Frisch; translated by Michael Bullock. — London: Methuen, 1962. 254 p.; 21 cm. I. T. PT2611.R814 T43   832.914   *LC* 65-1187

Frisch, Max, 1911-.   2.13746
[Montauk. English] Montauk / Max Frisch; translated by Geoffrey Skelton. — 1st ed. — New York: Harcourt Brace Jovanovich, c1976. 143 p.; 22 cm. 'A Helen and Kurt Wolff book.' 1. Frisch, Max, 1911- — Biography. 2. Authors, Swiss — Biography. I. T. PT2611.R814 Z513 1976   838/.9/1209 B   *LC* 76-70   *ISBN* 0151621004

Frisch, Max, 1911-.   2.13747
Montauk: eine Erzählung / Max Frisch. — 1. Aufl., 1.-50. Tsd. — Frankfurt (am Main): Suhrkamp, 1975. 206 p.; 19 cm. 1. Frisch, Max, 1911- — Biography. I. T. PT2611.R814 Z519 1975   838/.9/1209 B   *LC* 76-453438   *ISBN* 3518028715

Butler, Michael.   2.13748
The novels of Max Frisch / by Michael Butler. London: O. Wolff, c1976. 175 p.; 23 cm. Includes index. 1. Frisch, Max, 1911- — Criticism and interpretation. I. T. PT2611.R814 Z634 1976   PT2611R814 Z634 1976.   838/.9/1209
    LC 76-54703   *ISBN* 0854960597

Butler, Michael.   2.13749
The plays of Max Frisch / Michael Butler. — New York: St. Martin's Press, 1985. ix, 182 p.; 23 cm. Includes index. 1. Frisch, Max, 1911- — Criticism and interpretation. I. T. PT2611.R814 Z635 1985   838/.91209 19   *LC* 84-17906   *ISBN* 0312616805

George, Stefan Anton, 1868-1933.   • 2.13750
Werke. [2. Aufl.] Düsseldorf, H. Küpper, 1968. 2 v. 21 cm. "Der vorgelegte Text folgt dem der Gesamtausgabe der Werke, endgültige Fassung, 18 Bände, Berlin, Georg Bondi 1927-1934." I. T. PT2613.E47 1968

George, Stefan Anton, 1868-1933.   2.13751
[Selected works. English. 1974] The works of Stefan George, rendered into English by Olga Marx and Ernst Morwitz. 2d rev. and enl. ed. Chapel Hill, University of North Carolina Press, 1974. xxvi, 427 p. 24 cm. (University of North Carolina studies in the Germanic languages and literatures, no. 78) 'The present ... edition has been edited ... by Dietrich von Bothmer from the manuscripts and notes of the translators. Besides many changes in the poems, it contains additional translations intended to give a representative survey of Stefan George's earliest poems (which appeared in The primer), of his dramatic sketches (volume XVII of his Collected works), and of his prose writings (Days and deeds).' I. Marx, Olga, 1894- tr. II. Morwitz, Ernst, 1887-1971, tr. III. T. PT2613.E47 A25 1974   831/.8   *LC* 73-16133   *ISBN* 0807880787

PT2613 Grass

Grass, Günter, 1927-.   2.13752
Aus dem Tagebuch einer Schnecke / Günter Grass. — 3. Aufl. — Neuwied: Luchterhand, 1972. 368 p. I. T. PT2613.R338 A88 1972   *LC* 72-352779

Grass, Günter, 1927-.   2.13753
[Aus dem Tagebuch einer Schnecke. English] From the diary of a snail. Translated by Ralph Manheim. [1st ed.] New York, Harcourt Brace Jovanovich [1973] 310 p. front. 21 cm. 'A Helen and Kurt Wolff book.' Translation of Aus dem Tagebuch einer Schnecke. I. T. PZ4.G774 Fr PT2613.R338A88x   833/.9/14   *LC* 73-6680   *ISBN* 0151338000

Grass, Günter, 1927-.   • 2.13754
Die Blechtrommel; Roman. [Darmstadt] H. Luchterhand [1959] 736 p. 21 cm. I. T. PT2613.R338 B55   *LC* 60-34508

Grass, Günter, 1927-.   • 2.13755
[Blechtrommel English] The tin drum. Translated from the German by Ralph Manheim. [New York] Pantheon Books [1963, c1962] 591 p. 22 cm. I. T. PT2613.R338 B5x   *LC* 62-14256

Grass, Günter, 1927-.   2.13756
Der Butt: Roman / Günter Grass. — Darmstadt; Neuwied: Luchterhand, 1977. 693 p.; 21 cm. I. T. PT2613.R338 B8   833/.914 19   *LC* 77-564682   *ISBN* 3472860693

Grass, Günter, 1927-.   2.13757
[Butt. English] The flounder / Günter Grass; translated by Ralph Manheim. — 1st ed. — New York: Harcourt Brace Jovanovich, c1978. xi, 547 p.; 27 cm. 'A Helen and Kurt Wolff book.' Translation of Der Butt. I. T. PZ4.G774 Fl PT2613.R338 B8x   833/.914 19   *LC* 78-53891   *ISBN* 0151314861

Grass, Günter, 1927-.   2.13758
Hundejahre: roman / Günter Grass. — Neuwied und Darmstadt: Luchterhand, 1974. 473 p. (Sammlug Luchterhand; 149) I. T. PT2613.R338 H9 1974   *ISBN* 3472611499

Grass, Günter, 1927-.   • 2.13759
[Hundejahre. English] Dog years. Translated by Ralph Manheim. [1st ed.] New York, Harcourt, Brace & World [1965] 570 p. 22 cm. 'A Helen and Kurt Wolff book.' I. T. PT2613.R338 H9x   *LC* 65-14715

Grass, Günter, 1927-.   • 2.13760
Katz und Maus. Eine Novelle. [8. Aufl.] [Neuwied] Luchterhand [1967] 178p. I. T. PT2613 R338 K38 1967   *LC* 70-373231

Grass, Günter, 1927-.   • **2.13761**
[Katz und Maus. English] Cat and mouse. Translated by Ralph Manheim. [1st ed.] New York, Harcourt, Brace & World [1963] 189 p. 21 cm. I. T.
PT2613.R338 K38x   LC 63-13499

Grass, Günter, 1927-.   **2.13762**
Örtlich betäubt; Roman. — [Neuwied] Luchterhand [1969] 358 p. 21 cm. I. T.
PT2613.R338O3   LC 71-421508

Grass, Günter, 1927-.   **2.13763**
[Örtlich betäubt. English] Local anaesthetic. Translated by Ralph Manheim. [1st ed.] New York, Harcourt, Brace & World [1970] 284 p. 22 cm. 'A Helen and Kurt Wolff book.' Translation of Örtlich betäubt. I. T.
PZ4.G774 Lo PT2613.R338O3x   833/.9/14   LC 78-100501

Grass, Günter, 1927-.   **2.13764**
[Treffen in Telgte. English] The meeting at Telgte / Günter Grass; translated by Ralph Manheim; afterword by Leonard Forster. — New York: Harcourt Brace Jovanovich, c1981. 147 p.; 21 cm. Translation of Das Treffen in Telgte. 'A Helen and Kurt Wolff book.' I. T.
PT2613.R338 T713   833/.914 19   LC 80-8749   ISBN 0151585881

Hollington, Michael.   **2.13765**
Günter Grass, the writer in a pluralist society / Michael Hollington. — London; Boston: M. Boyars, 1980. 186 p.; 22 cm. — (Critical appraisals series.) Includes index. 1. Grass, Günter, 1927- — Political and social views. I. T. II. Series.
PT2613.R338 Z67   838/.91409 19   LC 79-42857   ISBN 0714526789

Reddick, John.   **2.13766**
The 'Danzig trilogy' of Günter Grass; a study of The tin drum, Cat and mouse, and Dog years. — [1st American ed.]. — New York: Harcourt Brace Jovanovich, [1975, c1974] xiii, 289 p., [1] p.; 23 cm. 'A Helen and Kurt Wolff book.' 1. Grass, Günter, 1927- — Criticism and interpretation. I. T.
PT2613.R338 Z78 1975   833/.9/14   LC 74-11027   ISBN 0151238154

PT2616–2617 Hauptmann. Hesse

Hauptmann, Gerhart, 1862-1946.   • **2.13767**
Sämtliche Werke. Hrsg. von Hans–Egon Hass. [Berlin] Propyläen Verlag, 1962-   [v.1, 1966] v. 20 cm. "Centenar-Ausgabe: zum hundertsten Geburtstag des Dichters, 13. November 1962." Vol.10-   : Edited by Martin Machatzke and Wolfgang Bungies. I. Hass, Hans-Egon, 1916-1969, ed. II. T.
PT2616.A1

Maurer, Warren R.   **2.13768**
Gerhart Hauptmann / by Warren R. Maurer. — Boston, Mass.: Twayne Publishers, c1982. 159 p., [1] p. of plates: port.; 21 cm. — (Twayne's world authors series. TWAS 670) Includes index. 1. Hauptmann, Gerhart, 1862-1946 — Criticism and interpretation. I. T. II. Series.
PT2616.Z9 M36 1982   832/.8 19   LC 82-9358   ISBN 0805765174

Hesse, Hermann, 1877-1962.   • **2.13769**
Gesammelte Schriften. — Frankfurt a.M.: Suhrkamp Verlag, 1957. 7 v.; 21 cm. Each volume also has special t.p.; v. 1-6: Gesammelte Dichtungen; v.7: Betrachtungen und Briefe. I. T.
PT2617.E85 A1 1957x

Hesse, Hermann, 1877-1962.   • **2.13770**
[Poems. English] Poems. Selected and translated by James Wright. [1st ed.] New York, Farrar, Straus and Giroux [1970] 79 p. 22 cm. 'German text selected from Die Gedichte (in Gesammelte Schriften).' German and English. I. Wright, James Arlington, 1927- comp. II. T.
PT2617.E85 A28   831/.9/12   LC 78-109558

Hesse, Hermann, 1877-1962.   • **2.13771**
[Demian. English] Demian, the story of Emil Sinclair's youth. Introd. by Thomas Mann. Translated from the German by Michael Roloff and Michael Lebeck. [1st ed.] New York, Harper & Row [1965] xii, 171 p. 22 cm. I. T.
PT2617.E85 D4x   LC 64-18078

Hesse, Hermann, 1877-1962.   **2.13772**
[Glasperlenspiel. English] The glass bead game (Magister Ludi). Translated from the German by Richard and Clara Winston. With a foreword by Theodore Ziolkowski. [1st ed.] New York, Holt, Rinehart and Winston [1969] xix, 558 p. 22 cm. Translation of Das Glasperlenspiel. I. T.
PZ3.H4525 Gl PT2617.E85 G53x   833/.9/12   LC 78-80343   ISBN 0030818516

Hesse, Hermann, 1877-1962.   • **2.13773**
[Klingsors letzter Sommer. English] Klingsor's last summer. Translated by Richard and Clara Winston. [1st ed.] New York, Farrar, Straus and Giroux [1970] 217 p. 22 cm. I. T.
PZ3.H4525 Kl PT2617.E85 K5x   833/.9/12   LC 77-122825   ISBN 0374181667

Hesse, Hermann, 1877-1962.   • **2.13774**
[Narziss und Goldmund. English] Narcissus and Goldmund. Translated by Ursule Molinaro. New York, Farrar, Straus and Giroux [1968] 315 p. 22 cm. I. T.
PT2617.E85 N3x   LC 68-17291

Hesse, Hermann, 1877-1962.   • **2.13775**
[Peter Camenzind. English] Peter Camenzind. Translated by Michael Roloff. New York, Farrar, Straus and Giroux [1969] 201 p. 22 cm. I. T.
PZ3.H4525 Pe5 PT2617.E85 P4x   LC 74-87213

Hesse, Hermann, 1877-1962.   • **2.13776**
[Siddhartha. English] Siddhartha; translated by Hilda Rosner. [New York, New Directions, 1954] 153 p. 19 cm. I. T.
PT2617.E85 S52   833.91   LC 51-13669

Hesse, Hermann, 1877-1962.   • **2.13777**
[Steppenwolf. English] Steppenwolf. Translated from the German by Basil Creighton. Rev. by Walter Sorell. New York, Modern Library [1963] 246 p. 19 cm. (The Modern library of the world's best books) I. T.
PT2617.E85 S7x   LC 63-12171

Hesse, Hermann, 1877-1962.   **2.13778**
[Correspondence. English. 1975] The Hesse–Mann letters: the correspondence of Hermann Hesse and Thomas Mann, 1910–1955 / edited by Anni Carlsson and Volker Michels; translated from the German by Ralph Manheim; annotations by Wolfgang Sauerlander; foreword by Theodore Ziolkowski. — 1st ed. — New York: Harper & Row, [1975] xxii, 196 p.: ill.; 24 cm. Translation of Briefwechsel Hermann Hesse-Thomas Mann. Includes index. 1. Hesse, Hermann, 1877-1962 — Correspondence. 2. Mann, Thomas, 1875-1955 — Correspondence. 3. Authors, German — 20th century — Correspondence. I. Mann, Thomas, 1875-1955. II. Carlsson, Anni. III. Michels, Volker. IV. T.
PT2617.E85 Z54513   838/.9/1209 B   LC 74-1818   ISBN 0060106425

Mileck, Joseph, 1922-.   **2.13779**
Hermann Hesse: life and art / Joseph Mileck. — Berkeley: University of California Press, c1978. xiii, 397 p.: ill.; 25 cm. Includes indexes. 1. Hesse, Hermann, 1877-1962. 2. Authors, German — 20th century — Biography. I. T.
PT2617.E85 Z833   838/.9/1209 B   LC 76-48020   ISBN 0520033515

Otten, Anna, comp.   **2.13780**
Hesse companion / edited by Anna Otten. — 1st American ed. — Albuquerque: University of New Mexico Press, c1977. 324 p.; 21 cm. 1. Hesse, Hermann, 1877-1962 — Criticism and interpretation — Addresses, essays, lectures. I. T.
PT2617.E85 Z85 1977   PT2617E85 Z85 1977.   833/.9/12   LC 76-57539   ISBN 0826304400

Ziolkowski, Theodore.   • **2.13781**
The novels of Hermann Hesse; a study in theme and structure. — Princeton, N.J.: Princeton University Press, 1965. xii, 375 p.; 21 cm. 1. Hesse, Hermann, 1877-1962. I. T.
PT2617.E85 Z99   833.912   LC 65-10844

PT2617.O–2619 Ho–J

Hofmannsthal, Hugo von, 1874-1929.   **2.13782**
[Works] Sämtliche Werke: krit. Ausg. / Hugo von Hofmannsthal; veranst. vom Freien Dt. Hochstift; hrsg. von Heinz Otto Burger ... [et al.]. — Frankfurt am Main: S. Fischer, 1975-< 78 >. v. < 1, 10, 12, 14, 26, 28-29 >: 25 cm. Each vol. has special editor or editors. I. Burger, Heinz Otto, 1903- II. Freies Deutsches Hochstift. III. T.
PT2617.O47 1975   LC 76-467819   ISBN 3107515141

Hofmannsthal, Hugo von, 1874-1929.   • **2.13783**
Dramen / hrsg. von Herbert Steiner. — Frankfurt am Main: S. Fischer, 1953-58. 4 v.; 21 cm. — (His Gesammelte Werke in Einzelausgaben.) I. Steiner, Herbert, 1892- ed. II. T. III. Series.
PT2617.O47 A19 1953   LC 63-6561

Bangerter, Lowell A., 1941-.   **2.13784**
Hugo von Hofmannsthal / Lowell A. Bangerter. — New York: F. Ungar Pub. Co., c1977. viii, 134 p.; 21 cm. Includes index. 1. Hofmannsthal, Hugo von, 1874-1929 — Criticism and interpretation. I. T.
PT2617.O47 Z7324   831/.9/12   LC 76-20408   ISBN 0804420289

Coghlan, Brian.   **• 2.13785**
Hofmannsthal's festival dramas: Jedermann, Das Salzburger grosse Welttheater, Der Turm / by Brian Coghlan. — Cambridge: Cambridge University Press, 1964. xxi, 396 p.; 23 cm. 1. Hofmannsthal, Hugo von, 1874-1929. I. T.
PT2617.O47 Z7354   LC 64-21537

Holz, Arno, 1863-1929.   **• 2.13786**
Werke / Arno Holz; hrsg. von Wilhelm Emrich und Anita Holz. — Neuwied am Rhein: Luchterhand, [1962-64] 7 v. I. Emrich, Wilhelm. II. Holz, Anita. III. T.
PT2617.O72 1961   838.8   LC 65-43534

Jünger, Ernst, 1895-.   **• 2.13787**
Werke. Stuttgart, E. Klett [1960-1965]. 10 v. Vol. 1 published in 1961. I. T.
PT1619.U43 1960   838.912   LC 62-58432

PT2621.A26 Kafka

Kafka, Franz, 1883-1924.   **• 2.13788**
Gesammelte Schriften / herausgegeben von Max Brod. — New York: Schocken Books, 1947-. v. ; 20 cm. Half-title; each volume has also special t.-p. I. Brod, Max, 1884-1968. ed. II. T.
PT2621.A26 1947   LC 47-24370

Kafka, Franz, 1883-1924.   **• 2.13789**
[Selections.] The complete stories. Edited by Nahum N. Glatzer. New York, Schocken Books [1971] vii, 486 p. 24 cm. I. Glatzer, Nahum Norbert, 1903- ed. II. T.
PZ3.K11 Co PT2621.A26 Ax   833/.9/12   LC 75-161559   ISBN 0805234195

Kafka, Franz, 1883-1924.   **2.13790**
Parables and paradoxes, in German and English. — New York: Schocken Books, [1961, c1958] 190 p.; 21 cm. — (Schocken paperbacks, SB12) I. T.
PT2621.A26 P27 1961   838.912   LC 61-14917

Kafka, Franz, 1883-1924.   **• 2.13791**
[Prozess. English] The trial. Translated from the German by Willa and Edwin Muir. Rev., and with additional material translated by E. M. Butler. With excerpts from Kafka's Diaries. Drawings by Franz Kafka. Definitive ed. New York, Schocken Books [1968, c1956] 282 p. illus. 21 cm. Translation of Der Prozess. I. T.
PZ3.K11 Tr23 PT2621.A26 P7x   833/.9/12   LC 68-59195

Kafka, Franz, 1883-1924.   **• 2.13792**
[Schloss. English] The castle. Translated from the German by Willa and Edwin Muir, with additional materials translated by Eithne Wilkins and Ernst Kaiser. With an homage by Thomas Mann. Definitive ed. New York, Modern Library [1969, c1954] xvi, 481 p. 19 cm. (Modern library books, 388) Translation of Das Schloss. I. T.
PZ3.K11 Cas12 PT2621.A26 S3x   833/.9/12   LC 72-3630

Kafka, Franz, 1883-1924.   **2.13793**
I am a memory come alive: autobiographical writing / by Franz Kafka. Edited by Nahum N. Glatzer. — New York: Schocken Books, [1974]. -. xvi, 264 p.; 21 cm. — 1. Kafka, Franz, 1883-1924 — Biography. I. Glatzer, Nahum Norbert, 1903- ed. II. T.
PT2621.A26 Z5   PT2621 A26 Z5 1974.   833/.9/12 B   LC 74-8781   ISBN 0805235566

Kafka, Franz, 1883-1924.   **2.13794**
[Briefe, 1902-1924. English] Letters to friends, family, and editors / Franz Kafka; translated by Richard and Clara Winston. — New York: Schocken Books, 1977. vi, 509 p.; 24 cm. Translation of Briefe, 1902-1924. 1. Kafka, Franz, 1883-1924 — Correspondence. 2. Authors, Austrian — 20th century — Correspondence. I. T.
PT2621.A26 Z5313 1977   833/.9/12 B   LC 77-3136   ISBN 0805236627

Kafka, Franz, 1883-1924.   **2.13795**
[Briefe an Felice und andere Korrespondenz aus der Verlobungszeit. English] Letters to Felice. Edited by Erich Heller and Jürgen Born. Translated by James Stern and Elisabeth Duckworth. [1st English ed.] New York, Schocken Books [1973] xxv, 592 p. port. 24 cm. Translation of Briefe an Felice und andere Korrespondenz aus der Verlobungszeit. 1. Kafka, Franz, 1883-1924 — Correspondence. 2. Bauer, Felice, 1887-1960. 3. Authors, Austrian — 20th century — Correspondence. I. Bauer, Felice, 1887-1960. II. T.
PT2621.A26 Z53813 1973   833/.912 B 19   LC 72-88262

Kafka, Franz, 1883-1924.   **2.13796**
[Briefe an Ottla und die Familie. English] Letters to Ottla and the family / Franz Kafka; translated from the German by Richard and Clara Winston; edited by N.N. Glatzer. — New York: Schocken Books, 1982. xi, 130 p., [14] leaves of plates: ill.; 24 cm. Translation of: Briefe an Ottla und die Familie. 1. Kafka, Franz, 1883-1924 — Correspondence. 2. David, Ottilie, b. 1892. 3. Authors, Austrian — 20th century — Correspondence. I. David, Ottilie, b. 1892. II. Glatzer, Nahum Norbert, 1903- III. T.
PT2621.A26 Z53913 1982   833/.912 19   LC 81-40409   ISBN 0805237720

Kuna, Franz, 1933-.   **2.13797**
Franz Kafka: literature as corrective punishment / [by] Franz Kuna. — Bloomington: Indiana University Press, [1974]. -. 196 p.; 23 cm. — 1. Kafka, Franz, 1883-1924. I. T.
PT2621.A26 Z7666 1974   833/.9/12   LC 74-4813   ISBN 0253331684

Pawel, Ernst.   **2.13798**
The nightmare of reason: a life of Franz Kafka / by Ernst Pawel. — New York: Farrar, Straus, Giroux, c1984. xiv, 466 p., [16] p. of plates: ill., ports.; 25 cm. Includes index. 1. Kafka, Franz, 1883-1924 — Biography. 2. Authors, Austrian — 20th century — Biography. I. T.
PT2621.A26 Z8155 1984   833/.912 B 19   LC 83-25376   ISBN 0374222363

Politzer, Heinrich, 1910-.   **• 2.13799**
Franz Kafka; parable and paradox, by Heinz Politzer. [Rev. and expanded ed.] Ithaca, N.Y., Cornell University Press [1966] xxvii, 398 p. facsim. 22 cm. (Cornell paperbacks, CP-22) 1. Kafka, Franz, 1883-1924. I. T.
PT2621.A26 Z817 1966   838.91209   LC 66-4480

Sokel, Walter Herbert, 1917-.   **• 2.13800**
Franz Kafka, by Walter H. Sokel. — New York: Columbia University Press, 1966. 48 p.; 21 cm. — (Columbia essays on modern writers no. 19) 1. Kafka, Franz, 1883-1924. I. T. II. Series.
PT2621.A26 Z868   838.91209   LC 66-26005

PT2621.A3–2625 K–M

Kaiser, Georg, 1878-1945.   **2.13801**
Stücke, Erzählungen, Aufsätze, Gedichte / Georg Kaiser; herausgegeben von Walther Huder. — Köln: Kiepenheuer & Witsch, 1966. 853 p. I. Huder, Walther. II. T.
PT2621.A33 A6 1966   LC 67-70993

Kaiser, Georg, 1878-1945.   **• 2.13802**
Gas I: a play in five acts / Georg Kaiser; introduction by Victor Lange; translated by Herman Scheffauer. — New York: F. Ungar, 1963. 96 p.; 19 cm. Volume 2 of a trilogy, the first of which is The coral, and the third of which is Gas II. Translated by Herman Scheffauer. I. T.
PT2621.A33 G33 1957   LC 63-22147   ISBN 0804463433

Kaiser, Georg, 1878-1945.   **• 2.13803**
Gas II: a play in three acts / Georg Kaiser; introduction by Victor Lange. — New York: Ungar, 1963. xv, 44 p. 3d vol.of the author's trilogy,the 1st of which is Coral,and the 2d of which is Gas I. Translated from German by Winifred Katzin. I. T.
PT2621.A33 G3323   832.912   LC 63-14962

Kaiser, Georg, 1878-1945.   **• 2.13804**
The coral: a play in five acts / Georg Kaiser;introd. by Victor Lange; [translated by Winifred Katzin]. — New York: Ungar, c1963. xv, 94 p. — (Ungar paperbacks; 2133) The 1st vol. of the author's trilogy, the 2d of which is Gas I, and the 3d of which is Gas II. I. T.
PT2621.A33 K853   PT2621A33 K6713 1963.   LC 63-12906

Schürer, Ernst.   **• 2.13805**
Georg Kaiser. — New York: Twayne Publishers, [c1971] 262 p.; 21 cm. — (Twayne's world authors series, TWAS 196. Germany) 1. Kaiser, Georg, 1878-1945. I. T.
PT2621.A33 Z86   832/.9/12   LC 70-161824

Kraus, Karl, 1874-1936.   **2.13806**
[Selections. English. 1977] No compromise: selected writings of Karl Kraus / edited, and with an introduction, by Frederick Ungar; [translators, Sheema Z. Buehne ... et al.]. — New York: Ungar, c1977. ix, 260 p.; 22 cm. I. T.
PT2621.R27 A235 1977   838/.9/1209   LC 76-15653   ISBN 0804424853

Zohn, Harry.   **2.13807**
Karl Kraus. — New York, Twayne Publishers [1971] 178 p. 21 cm. — (Twayne's world authors series, TWAS 116: Austria) 1. Kraus, Karl, 1874-1936. I. T.
PT2621.R27 Z95   838/.9/1209   LC 71-120020

Kunert, Günter, 1929-. 2.13808
Camera obscura / Günter Kunert. — München; Wien: Hanser, 1978. 136 p.; 19 cm. I. T.
PT2621.U665 C35 1978   838/.9/1407   *LC* 78-389278   *ISBN* 3446125973

Le Fort, Gertrud, Freün von, 1876-. • 2.13809
Erzählende Schriften. — München, Ehrenwirth [1956] 3 v. 20 cm. I. T.
PT2623.E26A15 1956   *LC* A 57-4004

Lenz, Siegfried, 1926-. 2.13810
Gesammelte Erzählungen / Siegfried Lenz; mit einem nachwort von Colin Russ. — Hamburg: Hoffmann u. Campe, c1970, 1973 printing. 632 p. I. T.
PT2623.E583 A6 1970   *LC* 74-525063   *ISBN* 3455042155

Lenz, Siegfried, 1926-. 2.13811
Deutschstunde: Roman / Siegfried Lenz. — Hamburg: Hoffmann und Campe, 1974, c1968. 559 p. I. T.
PT2623.E583 D4   *LC* 68-138700   *ISBN* 3455042074

Lenz, Siegfried, 1926-. • 2.13812
[Deutschstunde. English] The German lesson. Translated by Ernst Kaiser and Eithne Wilkins. New York, Hill and Wang [1972, c1971] 470 p. 22 cm. Translation of Deutschstunde. I. T.
PZ4.L575 Ge3 PT2623.E583 D4x   833/.9/14   *LC* 77-163567   *ISBN* 0809049074

Lenz, Siegfried, 1926-. 2.13813
Heimatmuseum: Roman / Siegfried Leng. — 3. Aufl. — Hamburg: Hoffmann und Campe, 1978. 654 p.; 21 cm. — I. T.
PT2623.E583 H4   PT2623E583 H4.   833/.9/14   *LC* 79-340256   *ISBN* 3455042228

Lenz, Siegfried, 1926-. 2.13814
[Heimatmuseum. English] The heritage / Siegfried Lenz; translated from the German by Krishna Winston. — New York: Hill and Wang, c1981. 458 p.; 22 cm. Translation of Heimatmuseum. I. T.
PT2623.E583 H413 1981   833/.914 19   *LC* 80-84608   *ISBN* 0809054663

Lenz, Siegfried, 1926-. 2.13815
Das Vorbild: Roman / Siegfried Lenz.–. Hamburg: Hoffmann und Campe 1973. 526p. I. T.
PT2623 E583 V6   *LC* 73-354233

Murdoch, Brian, 1944-. 2.13816
Siegfried Lenz / by Brian Murdoch and Malcolm Read. — London: Oswald Wolff, c1978. 157 p.; 20 cm. — (Modern German authors: New series; v.6) 1. Lenz, Siegfried, 1926- I. Read, Malcolm. II. T. III. Series.
PT2623.E583 Z815   *ISBN* 0854960686

Mann, Heinrich, 1871-1950. • 2.13817
Die Jugend des Königs Henri Quatre: Roman / Heinrich Mann. — Berlin: Aufbau Verlag, 1956, 1964. 425, 4, 7 p.; 20 cm. — (Rowohlt) 1. Henry IV, King of France, 1553-1610 — Fiction. I. T.
PT2625.A43 H4   *ISBN* 3499106892

Mann, Heinrich, 1871-1950. • 2.13818
Der Untertan. Roman. (Redaktion: Sigrid Anger) Berlin, Weimar, Aufbau-Verlag, 1965. 442 p. 20 cm. (His Gesammelte Werke, Bd.7) I. T.
PT2625.A43 U5 1965

Hamilton, Nigel. 2.13819
The brothers Mann: the lives of Heinrich and Thomas Mann, 1871–1950 and 1875–1955 / Nigel Hamilton. — New Haven: Yale University Press, 1979, c1978. 422 p.; 24 cm. 1. Mann, Thomas, 1875-1955 — Biography. 2. Mann, Heinrich, 1871-1950 — Biography. 3. Novelists, German — 20th century — Biography. I. T.
PT2625.A43 Z647 1979   833/.03 B   *LC* 78-15114   *ISBN* 0300023480

PT2625.A44 Thomas Mann

Mann, Thomas, 1875-1955. • 2.13820
Gesammelte Werke. [Frankfurt am Main] S. Fischer [1960-c1974] 14 v. I. T.
PT2625 A44 1960   *LC* 61-22211

Mann, Thomas, 1875-1955. • 2.13821
Essays of three decades, translated from the German by H. T. Lowe–Porter. [1st American ed.] New York, A. A. Knopf, 1947. vii, 472, [4] p. port. 22 cm. I. Lowe-Porter, H. T. (Helen Tracy), 1876-1963. tr. II. T.
PT2625.A44 A23   834.91   *LC* 47-4148

Mann, Thomas, 1875-1955. • 2.13822
Stories of a lifetime. London, Secker & Warburg [1961] 2 v. I. T.
PT2625.A44 A2x

Mann, Thomas, 1875-1955. • 2.13823
Stories of three decades / Thomas Mann; translated from the German by H.T. Lowe–Porter. — New York: A.A. Knopf, 1936. ix, 567 p. I. T.
PT2625.A44 Ax   *LC* 46-43883

Mann, Thomas, 1875-1955. • 2.13824
Confessions of Felix Krull, confidence man: the early years / Thomas Mann; translated from the German by Denver Lindley. — New York: A. A. Knopf, 1955. 384 p. Translation of the author's Bekenntnisse des Hochstaplers Felix Krull: Der Memoiren erster Teil. I. T.
PT2625.A44 B42   *LC* 55-9263

Mann, Thomas, 1875-1955. 2.13825
[Betrachtungen eines Unpolitischen. English] Reflections of a nonpolitical man / Thomas Mann; translated, with an introduction, by Walter D. Morris. — New York: F. Ungar, c1983. xvii, 435 p.; 26 cm. Translation of: Betrachtungen eines Unpolitischen. 1. Mann, Thomas, 1875-1955 — Political and social views. 2. World War, 1914-1918 — Influence. 3. Germany — Politics and government — 1918-1933 I. T.
PT2625.A44 B513 1983   833/.912 19   *LC* 82-40249   *ISBN* 080442585X

Mann, Thomas, 1875-1955. • 2.13826
The black swan / by Thomas Mann; translated from the German by Willard R. Trask. — New York: Knopf, 1954. 141 p.; 20 cm. Translation of Die Betrogene. Typography and binding design by W.A. Dwiggins. I. Mann, Thomas, 1875-1955. Die Betrogene. English. 1954. II. T.
PT2625.A44 B533   *LC* 54-7197

Mann, Thomas, 1875-1955. • 2.13827
Buddenbrooks / by Thomas Mann; translated from the German by H.T. Lowe–Porter. — New York: Vintage Books, 1961, c1952. 595 p.; 19 cm. I. Lowe-Porter, H. T. (Helen Tracy), 1876-1963. II. T.
PT2625.A44 B71   *LC* 61-1435

Mann, Thomas, 1875-1955. • 2.13828
[Doktor Faustus English] Doctor Faustus; the life of the German composer, Adrian Leverkühn, as told by a friend. Tr. from the German by H. T. Lowe–Porter. [1st American ed.] New York, A. A. Knopf, 1948. vi, 510 p. 22 cm. I. Lowe-Porter, H. T. (Helen Tracy), 1876-1963. tr. II. T.
PT2625.A44 D63   PZ3.M3184 Do   833.91   *LC* 48-8940

Mann, Thomas, 1875-1955. • 2.13829
[Erwählte. English] The Holy Sinner; translated from the German by H. T. Lowe–Porter. [1st ed.] New York, Knopf, 1951. 336 p. 20 cm. Translation of Der Erwählte. I. T.
PT2625.A44 E75   833.91   *LC* 51-11092

Mann, Thomas, 1875-1955. • 2.13830
Joseph and his brothers, tr. from the German by H. T. Lowe–Porter. With a new introd. by the author. New York, A. A. Knopf [c1948] xxi, 1207 p. 23 cm. Each part also pub. separately. 1. Joseph (Son of Jacob) — Fiction. I. Lowe-Porter, H. T. (Helen Tracy), 1876-1963. tr. II. T.
PT2625.A44Jx   *LC* 48-7040

Mann, Thomas, 1875-1955. • 2.13831
The beloved returns = Lotte in Weimar / Thomas Mann; translated from the German by H.T. Lowe–Porter. — New York: Knopf, 1940. 453 p.; 20 cm. Originally published as Lotte in Weimar. 1. Kestner, Charlotte Buff, Frau, 1753-1828 — Fiction. I. Mann, Thomas, 1875-1955. Lotte in Weimar. English. 1940. II. Lowe-Porter, H. T. (Helen Tracy), 1876-1963. III. Lotte in Weimar. English. IV. T. V. Title: Lotte in Weimar.
PT2625.A44 L62 1940   *LC* 40-27614

Mann, Thomas, 1875-1955. • 2.13832
[Zauberberg English] The magic mountain. Der Zauberberg. Translated from the German by H.T. Lowe–Porter. New York, Knopf, 1953. ix, 729 p. 22 cm. Includes the author's 'The making of the magic mountain,' which first appeared in the Atlantic monthly, January 1953. I. T.
PT2625.A44 Z3x   833.91   *LC* 53-8166

Mann, Thomas, 1875-1955. 2.13833
[Tagebücher. English. Selections] Diaries, 1918–1939 / Thomas Mann; selection and foreword by Hermann Kesten; translated from the German by Richard and Clara Winston. — New York: H.N. Abrams, 1982. vii, 471 p., [32] p. of plates: ports.; 28 cm. Abridged translation of his Tagebücher, 1918-1921, 1933-1934, 1935-1936, 1937-1939, originally published by S. Fischer, 1977-1980. 1. Mann, Thomas, 1875-1955 — Diaries. 2. Novelists, German — 20th century — Biography. I. Kesten, Hermann, 1900- II. T.
PT2625.A44 Z46613 1982   838/.91203 B 19   *LC* 81-22889   *ISBN* 0810913046

Mann, Thomas, 1875-1955. • **2.13834**
Briefe / Thomas Mann; [herausgegeben von Erika Mann] — [Frankfurt am Main]: S. Fischer, 1961-1965. 3 v. 1. Authors — Correspondence, reminiscences, etc. I. Mann, Erika, 1905-1969. II. T.
PT2625A44 Z523 1961   LC 63-55817

Mann, Thomas, 1875-1955. **2.13835**
[Correspondence. English. 1975] Mythology and humanism: the correspondence of Thomas Mann and Karl Kerényi / translated from the German by Alexander Gelley. — Ithaca, N.Y.: Cornell University Press, 1975. xv, 231 p.; 22 cm. Translation of Thomas Mann—Karl Kerényi: Gespräch in Briefen. 1. Mann, Thomas, 1875-1955 — Correspondence. 2. Kerényi, Karl, 1897-1973 — Correspondence. I. Kerényi, Karl, 1897-1973. II. T.
PT2625.A44 Z53713   833/.9/12 B   LC 73-20796   ISBN 0801408318

Bürgin, Hans. **2.13836**
Thomas Mann, a chronicle of his life [by] Hans Bürgin and Hans–Otto Mayer. English translation by Eugene Dobson. — University: University of Alabama Press, [1969] xi, 290 p.: facsims., ports.; 23 cm. 1. Mann, Thomas, 1875-1955. I. Mayer, Hans Otto, 1903- joint author. II. T.
PT2625.A44 Z54373   833/.9/12 B   LC 68-10989   ISBN 0817380612

De Mendelssohn, Peter, 1908-. **2.13837**
Der Zauberer: das Leben des deutschen Schriftstellers Thomas Mann / Peter de Mendelssohn. — Frankfurt am Main: S. Fischer, 1975-. v.   : port.; 23 cm. 1. Mann, Thomas, 1875-1955 — Biography. I. T.
PT2625.A44 Z5446   LC 75-512313   ISBN 3100494024

Reed, T. J. (Terence James), 1937-. **2.13838**
Thomas Mann; the uses of tradition [by] T. J. Reed. Oxford, Clarendon Press, 1974. ix, 433 p. illus. 22 cm. 1. Mann, Thomas, 1875-1955. I. T.
PT2625.A44 Z7668   833/.9/12   LC 74-182432   ISBN 0198157428

Weigand, Hermann John, 1892-. • **2.13839**
The Magic mountain: a study of Thomas Mann's novel, Der Zauberberg / by Hermann J. Weigand. — Chapel Hill: University of North Carolina Press, 1964. xi, 183 p.; 24 cm. — (University of North Carolina studies in the Germanic languages and literatures; no. 49) 1. Mann, Thomas, 1875-1955. Der Zauberberg I. T. II. Title: A Study of Thomas Mann's novel, Der Zauberberg
PD25.N6 no. 49   PT2625.A44 Z92.   LC 64-65030

PT2625.O–2635 Mo–R

Morgenstern, Christian, 1871-1914. • **2.13840**
Gesammelte Werke: in einem Band / Christian Morgenstern. — München: R.Piper, 1966. 615 p.; 21 cm. I. T.
PT2625.O64 1966   ISBN 3492014089

Hofacker, Erich, 1898-. **2.13841**
Christian Morgenstern / by Erich P. Hofacker. — Boston: Twayne, 1978. 149 p.: port. (Twayne's world authors series; TWAS 508) Includes index. 1. Morgenstern, Christian, 1871-1914. 2. Poets, German — 19th century — Biography. I. T.
PT2625.O64 Z74   PT2625O64 Z74.   831/.9/12   LC 78-18791   ISBN 080576349X

Musil, Robert, 1880-1942. • **2.13842**
Der Mann ohne Eigenschaften. [8. Aufl.] (Hamburg) Rowohlt [1967]. 1632 p. 21 cm. (His Gesammelte Werke in Einzelausgaben) I. T.
PT2625.U8 M3 1967   LC 68-142693

Musil, Robert, 1880-1942. • **2.13843**
The Man without qualities / translated from the German and with a foreword by Eithne Wilkins and Ernst Kaiser. — London: Secker and Warburg, 1953-. v. 23 cm. Also published by Capricorn Books, New York. I. T.
PT2625.U8 M33   833.91   LC 53-31034

Musil, Robert, 1880-1942. **2.13844**
Die Verwirrungen des Zöglings Törless. [Reinbeck bei Hamburg] Rowohlt [1960] 147 p. 19 cm. I. T.
PT2625.U8 V4 1960   LC 61-31175

Musil, Robert, 1880-1942. • **2.13845**
Young Törless / Robert Musil; translated from the German by Eithne Wilkins and Ernst Kaiser. — London: Secker & Warburg, 1955. v, 217 p.; 21 cm. Translation of: Die Verwirrungen des Zöglings Törless. I. T.
PT2625.U8 V413 1982   833/.912 19

Luft, David S. **2.13846**
Robert Musil and the crisis of European culture, 1880–1942 / David S. Luft. — Berkeley: University of California Press, c1980. xii, 323 p.: port.; 24 cm.

Includes index. 1. Musil, Robert, 1880-1942 — Criticism and interpretation. 2. Europe — Intellectual life I. T.
PT2625.U8 Z795   833/.912   LC 78-66008   ISBN 0520038525

Remarque, Erich Maria, 1898-1970. • **2.13847**
Im Westen nichts Neues; [Roman]. Der Weg zurück; [Roman. Köln, Kiepenheuer & Witsch, 1964] 424 p. 21 cm. Half title. 1. World War, 1914-1918 — Fiction. I. Remarque, Erich Maria, 1898-1970. Der Weg zurück. II. T. III. Title: Der Weg zurück.
PT2635.E68 I6 1964

Remarque, Erich Maria, 1898-1970. • **2.13848**
[Im Westen nichts Neues. English] All quiet on the western front; translated from the German by A. W. Wheen. Boston, Little, Brown, and company, 1929. 4 p., l., 3-291 p. 20 cm. 1. World War, 1914-1918 — Fiction. I. Wheen, Arthur Wesley, 1897- tr. II. T.
PT2635.E68 I6x   LC 29-12059

Barker, Christine R. **2.13849**
Erich Maria Remarque / by Christine R. Barker and R. W. Last. — London: Oswald Wolff; New York: Barnes & Noble Books, c1979. 174 p.; 23 cm. Includes index. 1. Remarque, Erich Maria, 1898-1970. 2. Novelists, German — 20th century — Biography. I. Last, Rex William. joint author. II. T.
PT2635.E68 Z563   833/.9/12   LC 79-10837   ISBN 0854960600

PT2635.I65 Rilke

Rilke, Rainer Maria, 1875-1926. • **2.13850**
Sämtliche Werke / [Hrsg. vom Rilke–Archiv in Verbindung mit Ruth Sieber–Rilke, besorgt durch Ernst Zinn]. — [Wiesbaden]: Insel-Verlag, 1955-1966. 6 v. I. Sieber, Ruth Rilke, 1901- II. Rilke-Archiv (Weimar, Germany) III. T.
PT2635.I65 1955   LC a 56-2928

Rilke, Rainer Maria, 1875-1926. • **2.13851**
[Poems. English] Poems, 1906 to 1926. Translated with an introd. by J. B. Leishman. [Norfolk, Conn., J. Laughlin, 1957] 402 p. 23 cm. 'A complete translation of Gedichte 1906 bis 1926, published ... in 1953, together with a translation of all the additional German poetry in the second volume (1957) of the new edition of Rilke's Sämtliche Werke.' I. T.
PT2635.I65 A2495 1957   831.91   LC 57-10694

Rilke, Rainer Maria, 1875-1926. **2.13852**
Die Aufzeichnungen des Malte Laurids Brigge / Rainer Maria Rilke. — 57.-61. Tausend. — Frankfurt am Main: Suhrkamp Verlag, 1982, c1910. 233 p.; 19 cm. — (Bibliothek Suhrkamp. Bd. 343.) I. T. II. Series.
PT2635.I65 A8 1982   ISBN 3518013432

Rilke, Rainer Maria, 1875-1926. **2.13853**
[Aufzeichnungen des Malte Laurids Brigge. English] The notebooks of Malte Laurids Brigge / Rainer Maria Rilke; translated by Stephen Mitchell. — 1st ed. — New York: Random House, c1983. 277 p.; 20 cm. Translation of: Die Aufzeichnungen des Malte Laurids Brigge. I. Mitchell, Stephen. II. T.
PT2635.I65 A83 1982   833/.912 19   LC 83-3432   ISBN 039453011X

Leppmann, Wolfgang. **2.13854**
[Rilke. English] Rilke: a life / Wolfgang Leppmann; translated from the German in collaboration with the author by Russell M. Stockman; verse translations by Richard Exner. — 1st U.S. ed. — New York: Fromm International Pub. Corp., c1984. ix, 421 p., [8] p. of plates; 25 cm. Translation of: Rilke. Includes index. 1. Rilke, Rainer Maria, 1875-1926 — Biography. 2. Authors, Austrian — 20th century — Biography. I. T.
PT2635.I65 Z782313 1984   831/.912 B 19   LC 84-6062   ISBN 0880640146

PT2635.O8–2642 R–T

Roth, Joseph, 1894-1939. **2.13855**
[Radetzkymarsch. English] The Radetzky march. Translated by Eva Tucker, based on an earlier translation by Geoffrey Dunlop. Woodstock, N.Y., Overlook Press [1974] 318 p. 23 cm. I. T.
PZ3.R7428 Rad6 PT2635.O84 R3x   833/.9/12   LC 72-97581   ISBN 0879510153

Roth, Joseph, 1894-1939. **2.13856**
Radetzkymarsch: Roman / Joseph Roth. — Köln: Kiepenheuer & Witsch, c1978 (1979 printing) 382 p.; 21 cm. I. T.
PT2635.O84 R3x 1979   LC 84-672154   ISBN 3462013327

Sachs, Nelly. • **2.13857**
[Sachs, Nelly. Eli. English. 1967] O the chimneys; selected poems, including the verse play, Eli. Translated from the German by Michael Hamburger [and others] New York, Farrar, Straus and Giroux [1967] xxi, 387 p. 23 cm. German

and English. Selected from Fahrt ins Staublose, Zeichen im Sand, and Späte Gedichte. I. Sachs, Nelly. Eli. (Eng. 1967) II. Hamburger, Michael. tr. III. T.
PT2637.A4184 A6 1967　　831/.9/14　　*LC* 67-27518

Sachs, Nelly.　　　　　　　　　　　　　　　　　　　　　**• 2.13858**
The seeker, and other poems. Translated from the German by Ruth and Matthew Mead [and] Michael Hamburger. — New York: Farrar, Straus and Giroux, [1970] xi, 399 p.; 23 cm. German and English. 'Selected from Fahrt ins Staublose ... Späte Gedichte ... and Die Suchende.' I. Mead, Ruth. tr. II. Mead, Matthew, 1924- tr. III. Hamburger, Michael. tr. IV. T.
PT2637.A4184 A6 1970　　831/.9/14　　*LC* 79-137750　　*ISBN* 0374257809

Schnitzler, Arthur, 1862-1931.　　　　　　　　　　　**2.13859**
Gesammelte Werke. — [Frankfurt am Main]: S. Fischer, 1961-. v. 1. German literature — Collected works. I. T.
PT2638.N5 1961

Schnitzler, Arthur, 1862-1931.　　　　　　　　　　　**2.13860**
[Selections. English. 1982] Plays and stories / edited by Egon Schwarz; foreword by Stanley Elkin. — New York: Continuum, 1982. xviii, 279 p.; 22 cm. — (German library. v. 55) I. Schwarz, Egon, 1922- II. T. III. Series.
PT2638.N5 A2 1982　　833/.8 19　　*LC* 82-18263　　*ISBN* 0826402704

Schnitzler, Arthur, 1862-1931.　　　　　　　　　　　**2.13861**
[Jugend in Wien. English] My youth in Vienna. Foreword by Frederic Morton. Translated by Catherine Hutter. [1st ed.] New York, Holt, Rinehart and Winston [1970] xiv, 304 p. illus., ports. 24 cm. Translation of Jugend in Wien. 1. Schnitzler, Arthur, 1862-1931. I. T.
PT2638.N5 Z8113　　832/.9/12 B　　*LC* 70-117273　　*ISBN* 0030831482

Urbach, Reinhard, 1939-.　　　　　　　　　　　　　**2.13862**
Arthur Schnitzler. Translated [from the German] by Donald Daviau. — New York: Ungar, [1973] vi, 202 p.: illus.; 20 cm. — (World dramatists) 1. Schnitzler, Arthur, 1862-1931. I. T.
PT2638.N5 Z913　　832/.9/12　　*LC* 73-178165　　*ISBN* 0804429367

Strittmatter, Erwin, 1912-.　　　　　　　　　　　　**2.13863**
Der Laden: Roman / Erwin Strittmatter. — 1. Aufl. — Berlin: Aufbau-Verlag, 1983. 535 p.; 20 cm. I. T.
PT 2639 T82 L15 1983

Trakl, Georg, 1887-1914.　　　　　　　　　　　　　**• 2.13864**
Dichtungen und Briefe. Salzburg, O. Müller, 1969. 2 v. facsims. (part fold.), port. 26 cm. "Verzeichnis der Abkürzungen": leaf inserted in v.2. "Historisch-kritische Ausgabe. Herausgegeben von Walther Killy und Hans Szklenar." I. Szklenar, Hans. II. Killy, Walther. III. T.
PT2642.R22 1969

Trakl, Georg, 1887-1914.　　　　　　　　　　　　　**• 2.13865**
Selected poems; edited by Christopher Middleton, translated [from the German] by Robert Grenier [and others]. — London: Cape, 1968. 125 p.; 19 cm. — (Cape editions, 23) Parallel German text and English translation. I. T.
PT2642.R22 A17 1968　　831/.9/12　　*LC* 74-367248　　*ISBN* 0224615114

Tucholsky, Kurt, 1890-1935.　　　　　　　　　　　　**• 2.13866**
[Works. 1960] Gesammelte Werke / Kurt Tucholsky; hrsg. v. Mary Gerold-Tucholsky, Fritz J. Raddatz. — Reinbek bei Hamburg: Rowohlt, 1960-1962. 4 v.; 21 cm. I. Gerold-Tucholsky, Mary. joint ed II. Raddatz, Fritz Joachim. joint ed. III. T.
PT2642.U4 1960　　*LC* 61-5151

PT2647-2653 W-Z

Wedekind, Frank, 1864-1918.　　　　　　　　　　　**• 2.13867**
Prosa, Dramen, Verse / Frank Wedekind. — 2. Aufl. — Munchen: A. Langen, G. Muller, 1960. 969 p. I. T.
PT2647.E26A6 1960

Best, Alan D.　　　　　　　　　　　　　　　　　　**2.13868**
Frank Wedekind / by Alan Best. — London: Wolff, 1975. 125 p.: ill.; 20 cm. — (Modern German authors; new ser., v. 4) 1. Wedekind, Frank, 1864-1918. I. T. II. Series.
PT2647.E26 Z57　　PT2647E26 Z57.　　832/.8　　*LC* 76-357909　　*ISBN* 0854960546

Werfel, Franz, 1890-1945.　　　　　　　　　　　　　**• 2.13869**
Die Dramen. [Hrsg. von Adolf D. Klarmann. — Frankfurt am Main] S. Fischer, 1959. 2 v. 21 cm. — (His Gesammelte Werke) I. T. II. Series.
PT2647.E77 Ax　　*LC* A 60-1436

Werfel, Franz, 1890-1945.　　　　　　　　　　　　　**2.13870**
The song of Bernadette, translated by Ludwig Lewisohn. New York, The Viking press, 1942. 575 p. 21 cm. At head of title: Franz Werfel. 1. Bernadette of Lourdes, Saint — Fiction. I. Lewisohn, Ludwig, 1882-1955. tr. II. T.
PZ3.W493So PT2647.E77S6　　833.91　　*LC* 42-10430

Steiman, Lionel B. (Lionel Bradley), 1941-.　　　　**2.13871**
Franz Werfel, the faith of an exile: from Prague to Beverly Hills / Lionel B. Steiman. — Waterloo, Ont., Canada: W. Laurier University Press; Atlantic Highlands, N.J.: Distributed in the U.S.A. by Humanities Press, c1985. xi, 244 p.: ill.; 24 cm. Includes index. 1. Werfel, Franz, 1890-1945. 2. Werfel, Franz, 1890-1945 — Religion. 3. Authors, German — 20th century — Biography. I. T.
PT2647.E77 Z814 1985　　833/.912 B 19　　*LC* 85-226915　　*ISBN* 0889201684

Zuckmayer, Carl, 1896-1977.　　　　　　　　　　　**2.13872**
Meisterdramen. Mit einem Nachwort von Gerhard F. Hering. — (Frankfurt a. M.) G. B. Fischer (1966) 590 p. 21 cm. I. T.
PT2653.U33A19 1966　　*LC* 66-76795

Mews, Siegfried.　　　　　　　　　　　　　　　　**2.13873**
Carl Zuckmayer / by Siegfried Mews. — Boston: Twayne, 1981. 181 p.; 21 cm. — (Twayne's world authors series. Germany. TWAS 610) Includes index. 1. Zuckmayer, Carl, 1896-1977 — Criticism and interpretation. I. T. II. Series.
PT2653.U33 Z77　　832/.912 19　　*LC* 81-4859　　*ISBN* 0805764526

Zweig, Arnold, 1887-1968.　　　　　　　　　　　　**2.13874**
Der Streit um den Sergeanten Grischa: Roman / Arnold Zweig. — Frankfurt: Fischer Taschenbuch Verlag, 1972. 383 p. 1. World War, 1914-1918 — Fiction. I. T.
PT2653.W4 S7　　*ISBN* 3436015458(pbk)

Zweig, Arnold, 1887-1968.　　　　　　　　　　　　**2.13875**
[Streit um den Sergeanten Grischa. English] The case of Sergeant Grischa / by Arnold Zweig. — New York, NY: Penguin Books, 1986. vi, 449 p.; 20 cm. (Penguin modern classics) Translation of: Streit um den Sergeanten Grischa. Reprint. Originally published: New York: Viking Press, 1928. 1. World War, 1914-1918 — Fiction. I. T.
PT2653.W4 S713 1986　　833/.912 19　　*LC* 86-742　　*ISBN* 0140070575

Salamon, George.　　　　　　　　　　　　　　　　**2.13876**
Arnold Zweig / by George Salamon. — Boston: Twayne Publishers, c1975. 200 p.: port.; 21 cm. (Twayne's world authors series; TWAS 361) Includes index. 1. Zweig, Arnold, 1887-1968. I. T.
PT2653.W4 Z84　　PT2653W4 Z84.　　833/.9/12　　*LC* 75-12736
　　ISBN 0805762124

Zweig, Stefan, 1881-1942.　　　　　　　　　　　　**2.13877**
Die Welt von Gestern: Erinnerungen eines Europäers / Stefan Zweig. — 2. Aufl. — Hamburg: S. Fischer, 1982, c1944. 494 p.; 19 cm. — (Gesammelte Werke in Einzelbänden) 1. Zweig, Stefan, 1881-1942. I. T.
PT2653.W42 Z48 1982

Zweig, Stefan, 1881-1942.　　　　　　　　　　　　**2.13878**
The world of yesterday, an autobiography by Stefan Zweig. New York, The Viking press, 1943. xiv p., 2 l., 455 p. illus. (facsim.) ports. 22 cm. 'A bibliography of the original works of Stefan Zweig': p. 443-445. I. T.
PT2653.W42Z5　　928.3　　*LC* 43-5821

Prater, Donald A., 1918-.　　　　　　　　　　　　**2.13879**
European of yesterday: a biography of Stefan Zweig [by] D. A. Prater. — Oxford, Clarendon Press, 1972. xix, 390, [8] p. illus., facsims., ports. 23 cm. 1. Zweig, Stefan, 1881-1942. I. T.
PT2653.W42 Z67　　838/.9/1209 B　　*LC* 72-183844　　*ISBN* 019815707X

PT2660–2688 20th Century (1961–

PT2661–2669 A–I

Bernhard, Thomas.　　　　　　　　　　　　　　　**2.13880**
Die Erzählungen / Thomas Bernhard. — 1. Aufl. — Frankfurt am Main: Suhrkamp, 1979. 607 p.; 21 cm. — I. T.
PT2662.E7 E79　　833/.914 19　　*LC* 80-499572　　*ISBN* 3518021427

Bernhard, Thomas.   **2.13881**
[Memoirs. English] Gathering evidence: a memoir / Thomas Bernhard; translated from the German by David McLintock. — New York: Knopf, 1985. viii, 340 p.; 24 cm. Contains translations of the 5 works which comprise the author's memoirs. 1. Bernhard, Thomas — Biography — Youth. 2. Authors, Austrian — 20th century — Biography. I. T.
PT2662.E7 Z46413 1985   838/.91409 B 19   *LC* 85-40393   *ISBN* 0394547071

Braun, Volker, 1939-.   **2.13882**
Im Querschnitt Volker Braun: Gedichte, Prosa, Stücke, Aufsätze / [hrsg. von Holger J. Schubert; mit einem Vorwort von Dieter Schlenstedt]. — Halle: Mitteldeutscher Verlag, c1978. 345 p., [8] leaves of plates: ill.; 21 cm. I. Schubert, Holger J. II. T.
PT2662.R34 A6 1978   *LC* 80-460980

Braun, Volker, 1939-.   **2.13883**
Das ungezwungne Leben Kasts; drei Berichte. [1. Aufl. Frankfurt am Main] Suhrkamp [1972] 149 p. 20 cm. I. T.
PT2662.R34 U5 1972b   *LC* 74-335486   *ISBN* 351802261X

De Bruyn, Günter, 1926-.   **2.13884**
Buridans Esel: Roman. — Halle, Mitteldeutscher Verlag [1968] 246 p. 20 cm. I. T.
PT2662.R88 B8   *LC* 71-504897

Handke, Peter.   **2.13885**
Die Angst des Tormanns beim Elfmeter: Erzählung / Peter Handke. — Frankfurt am Main: Suhrkamp, c1970. 124 p.; 20 cm. I. T.
PT2668.A5 A8   *LC* 72-478957

Handke, Peter.   **2.13886**
[Angst des Tormanns beim Elfmeter. English] The goalie's anxiety at the penalty kick, Translated by Michael Roloff. New York, Farrar, Straus and Giroux [1972] 133 p. 22 cm. Translation of Die Angst des Tormanns beim Elfmeter. I. T.
PZ4.H2363 Go PT2668.A5 A8x   833/.9/14   *LC* 70-188957   *ISBN* 0374163766

Handke, Peter.   **2.13887**
Das Gewicht der Welt: ein Journal (Nov. 1975–März 1977) / Peter Handke. — 1. Aufl. — Salzburg: Residenz Verl., c1977. 324 p.; 19 cm. — I. T.
PT2668.A5 G4   *LC* 78-344874   *ISBN* 3701701776

Handke, Peter.   **2.13888**
[Gewicht der Welt. English] The weight of the world / Peter Handke; translated by Ralph Manheim. — 1st ed. — New York: Farrar, Straus, and Giroux, 1984. 243 p.; 22 cm. Translation of: Das Gewicht der Welt. I. T.
PT2668.A5 G413 1984   838/.91403 19   *LC* 84-4196   *ISBN* 0374287457

Handke, Peter.   **2.13889**
[Kurze Brief zum langen Abschied. English] Short letter, long farewell. Translated by Ralph Manheim. New York, Farrar, Straus and Giroux [1974] 167 p. 21 cm. Translation of Der kurze Brief zum langen Abschied. I. T.
PZ4.H2363 Sh 1974 PT2668.A5 K8x   833/.9/14   *LC* 73-87695   *ISBN* 0374263183

Handke, Peter.   **2.13890**
Slow homecoming / Peter Handke; translated by Ralph Manheim. — 1st ed. — New York: Farrar, Straus, and Giroux, 1985. 278 p. Translation of: Langsame Heimkehr, Die Lehre der Sainte-Victoire, and Kindergeschichte. I. T.
PT2668.A5 L313x 1985   833/.914 19   *LC* 84-28597   *ISBN* 0374266352

Handke, Peter.   **2.13891**
Langsame Heimkehr: Erzählung / Peter Handke. — 1. Aufl. — Frankfurt am Main: Suhrkamp, 1979. 199 p.; 20 cm. I. T.
PT2668.A5 L3x 1979   *LC* 86-672114   *ISBN* 3518030213

Handke, Peter.   **2.13892**
Die linkshändige Frau: Erzählung / Peter Handke. — 7. Aufl. — Frankfurt am Main: Suhrkamp, 1979, c1976. 130 p.; 20 cm. — I. T.
PT2668.A5 L5 1979   833/.914 19   *LC* 81-161890   *ISBN* 3518030221

Handke, Peter.   **2.13893**
[Linkshändige Frau. English] The left–handed woman / Peter Handke; translated by Ralph Manheim. — 1st ed. — New York: Farrar, Straus, and Giroux, 1978. 87 p.; 21 cm. Translation of Die linkshändige Frau. I. T.
PZ4.H2363 Le PT2668.A5 L5x   833/.9/14   *LC* 78-5568   *ISBN* 0374184976

Handke, Peter.   **2.13894**
Die Stunde der wahren Empfindung / Peter Handke. — 1. Aufl. — Frankfurt am Main: Suhrkamp, 1975. 166 p.; 20 cm. I. T.
PT2668.A5 S85   *LC* 75-508138   *ISBN* 3518030299

Handke, Peter.   **2.13895**
[Stunde der wahren Empfindung. English] A moment of true feeling / Peter Handke; translated by Ralph Manheim. — 1st ed. — New York: Farrar, Straus and Giroux, 1977. 133 p.; 21 cm. Translation of Die Stunde der wahren Empfindung. I. T.
PZ4.H2363 Mo 1977 PT2668.A5 S8x   833/.9/14   *LC* 77-6616   *ISBN* 0374172919

Klinkowitz, Jerome.   **2.13896**
Peter Handke and the postmodern transformation: the goalie's journey home / Jerome Klinkowitz and James Knowlton. — Columbia: University of Missouri Press, 1983. vii, 133 p.; 21 cm. — (Literary frontiers edition.) 1. Handke, Peter — Criticism and interpretation. I. Knowlton, James, 1943- II. T. III. Series.
PT2668.A5 Z75 1983   838/.91409 19   *LC* 83-6867   *ISBN* 0826204201

Schlueter, June.   **2.13897**
The plays and novels of Peter Handke / June Schlueter. — Pittsburgh: University of Pittsburgh Press, c1981. xiii, 213 p.; 24 cm. — (Critical essays in modern literature.) Includes index. 1. Handke, Peter — Criticism and interpretation. I. T. II. Series.
PT2668.A5 Z877 1981   838/.91409 19   *LC* 81-50242   *ISBN* 0822934434

Hochhuth, Rolf.   • **2.13898**
[Stellvertreter. English] The deputy. Translated by Richard and Clara Winston. Pref. by Albert Schweitzer. New York, Grove Press [1964] 352 p. 21 cm. A play. Includes the author's 'Sidelights on history' (p. 287-352) 1. Pius XII, Pope, 1876-1958 — Drama. I. T.
PT2668.O3 S813   832.914   *LC* 64-13776

PT2670–2688 J–Z

Johnson, Uwe, 1934-.   **2.13899**
Jahrestage: aus dem Leben von Gesine Cresspahl / Uwe Johnson. — Frankfurt am Main: Suhrkamp, 1983. 4 v. I. T.
PT2670.O36 J3   Fic   *LC* 70-538803   *ISBN* 3518033301

Johnson, Uwe, 1934-.   **2.13900**
Anniversaries: from the life of Gesine Cresspahl / Uwe Johnson; translated by Leila Vennewitz. — 1st ed. — New York: Harcourt Brace Jovanovich, [1975] 504 p.; 24 cm. 'A Helen and Kurt Wolff book.' Translation based on v. 1 and part of v. 2 of Jahrestage. I. T.
PT2670.O36 J3213 1975   833/.9/14   *LC* 74-20942   *ISBN* 0151075603

Johnson, Uwe, 1934-.   • **2.13901**
Mutmassungen über Jakob; Roman. [Frankfurt/M.] Suhrkamp Verlag [c1959] 307 p. 20 cm. I. T.
PT2670.O36 M8   *LC* 60-33607

Johnson, Uwe, 1934-.   **2.13902**
Speculations about Jakob / Uwe Johnson; translated by Ursule Molinaro. — New York: Harcourt Brace Jovanovich, c1963. 240 p.; 21 cm. — (A Harvest Book; HB236) (A Helen and Kurt Wolff Book) I. Johnson, Uwe, 1934- Mutmassungen über Jakob. English. II. Molinaro, Ursule. III. T.
PT2670.O36 M8x   *ISBN* 0156847191

Boulby, Mark.   **2.13903**
Uwe Johnson. — New York: Ungar, [1974] vii, 136 p.; 21 cm. — (Modern literature monographs) 1. Johnson, Uwe, 1934- — Criticism and interpretation. I. T.
PT2670.O36 Z65   833/.9/14   *LC* 73-82315   *ISBN* 0804420629

Morgner, Irmtraud.   **2.13904**
Die Hexe im Landhaus: Gespräch in Solothurn / Irmtraud Morgner; mit einem Beitrag von Erica Pedretti; [herausgegeben von Patrizia N. Franchini, Suzanne Kappeler, Silvio Temperli in Zusammenarbeit mit Franz Zeno Küttel]. — 1. Aufl. — Zürich: Rauhreif, 1984. 124 p.: 2 ports.; 21 cm. 1. Morgner, Irmtraud — Interviews. 2. Authors, German — 20th century — Interviews. I. Pedretti, Erica. II. Franchini, Patrizia Noémi, 1953- III. T.
PT2673.O64 Z467 1984   833/.914 B 19   *LC* 85-139512   *ISBN* 390776403X

Müller, Heiner, 1929-.   **2.13905**
Shakespeare Factory 1 / Heiner Müller. — Berlin: Rotbuch Verlag, c1985. 253 p.; 21 cm. — (Rotbuch; 290) (Texte / Heiner Müller; 8) I. Shakespeare, William, 1564-1616. II. T. III. Title: Shakespeare Factory eins.
PT2673.U29 S44 1985 PT2673.U3 S5.   *ISBN* 3880222908

Müller, Heiner, 1929-. 2.13906
Hamletmachine and other texts for the stage / Heiner Müller; edited and translated by Carl Weber. — 1st ed. — New York: Performing Arts Journal Publications, c1984. 140 p.: ill., port. (PAJ playscript series) Plays. I. Weber, Carl II. T.
PT2673.U292 H3   *LC* 83-61193   *ISBN* 0933826443

Plenzdorf, Ulrich, 1934-. 2.13907
[Neuen Leiden des jungen W. English] The new sufferings of young W.: a novel / Ulrich Plenzdorf; translated by Kenneth P. Wilcox. — New York: F. Ungar Pub. Co., c1979. xii, 84 p.; 22 cm. Translation of Die neuen Leiden des jungen W. I. T.
PZ4.P7255 Ne PT2676.L39   833/.9/14   *LC* 78-20928   *ISBN* 0804427356

Plenzdorf, Ulrich, 1934-. 2.13908
Legende vom Glück ohne Ende / Ulrich Plenzdorf. — 1. Aufl. — [Frankfurt/Main]: Suhrkamp, 1981, c1979. 318 p.; 18 cm. — (Suhrkamp-Taschenbuch; 722) I. T.
PT2676.L39 L37 1981   833/.914 19   *LC* 83-114031   *ISBN* 351837222X

Strauss, Botho, 1944-. 2.13909
Die Widmung: eine Erzählung / Botho Strauss. — München: Hanser, c1977. 144 p.; 20 cm. — I. T.
PT2681.T6898 W5   *LC* 77-571419   *ISBN* 3446124152

Strauss, Botho, 1944-. 2.13910
[Widmung. English] Devotion / Botho Strauss; translated by Sophie Wilkins. — New York: Farrar, Straus and Giroux, c1979. 120 p.; 21 cm. Translation of Die Widmung. I. T.
PZ4.S9132 De 1979 PT2681.T6898W513x   833/.9/14   *LC* 79-9887   *ISBN* 0374138524

Walser, Martin, 1927-. 2.13911
Brandung: Roman / Martin Walser. — 1. Aufl. — Frankfurt am Main: Suhrkamp, 1985. 318 p.; 21 cm. I. T.
PT2685.A48 B7 1985   883/.914 19   *LC* 86-672328   *ISBN* 3518035703

Walser, Martin, 1927-. 2.13912
Das Einhorn. Roman. — (Frankfurt) Suhrkamp (1966) 488 p. 21 cm. I. T.
PT2685.A48E4   *LC* 66-76118

Walser, Martin, 1927-. 2.13913
[Einhorn. English] The Unicorn; translated by Barrie Ellis–Jones. London, Calder and Boyars, 1971. 283 p. 21 cm. Translation of Das Einhorn. I. T.
PZ4.W222 Un PT2685.A48 E4x   833/.9/14   *LC* 71-889805   *ISBN* 0714508179 *ISBN* 0714508861

Walser, Martin, 1927-. 2.13914
Ein fliehendes Pferd: Novelle / Martin Walser. — 1.-25. Tsd. — Frankfurt am Main: Suhrkamp, 1978. 150 p.; 20 cm. — I. T.
PT2685.A48 F48   *LC* 78-366616   *ISBN* 3518042696

Walser, Martin, 1927-. 2.13915
[Fliehendes Pferd. English] Runaway horse: a novel / by Martin Walser; translated by Leila Vennewitz. — New York: Holt, Rinehart, Winston, 1980. 109 p.; 22 cm. Translation of Ein fliehendes Pferd. I. T.
PZ4.W222 Ru PT2685.A48 F48x   833/.9/14   *LC* 79-22749   *ISBN* 003046501X

Walser, Martin, 1927-. 2.13916
Das Schwanenhaus: Roman / Martin Walser. — 1. Aufl. — Frankfurt a.M.: Suhrkamp, 1980. 232 p. I. T.
PT2685.A48 S35   PT2647A639 S35.   *ISBN* 3518046403

Walser, Martin, 1927-. 2.13917
[Schwanenhaus. English] The Swan Villa: a novel / by Martin Walser; translated from the German by Leila Vennewitz. — 1st American ed. — New York: Holt, Rinehart and Winston, 1982. 247 p.; 22 cm. Translation of: Das Schwanenhaus. I. T.
PT2685.A48 S35x   833/.914 19   *LC* 81-13410   *ISBN* 0030593727

Walser, Martin, 1927-. 2.13918
Seelenarbeit: Roman / Martin Walser. — 1. Aufl. — Frankfurt am Main: Suhrkamp, 1979. 294 p.; 21 cm. — I. T.
PT2685.A48 S4   833/.9/14   *LC* 79-376187   *ISBN* 3518046306

Walser, Martin, 1927-. 2.13919
[Seelenarbeit. English] The inner man: a novel / by Martin Walser; translated from the German by Leila Vennewitz. — 1st American ed. — New York: Holt, Rinehart and Winston, 1985, c1984. 276 p.; 22 cm. Translation of: Seelenarbeit. I. T.
PT2685.A48 S413 1985   833/.914 19   *LC* 84-672   *ISBN* 0030593735

Weiss, Peter, 1916-. • 2.13920
Dramen / Peter Weiss. — Frankfurt am Main: Suhrkamp, 1968. 2 v. I. T.
PT2685.E5 A19 1968   *LC* 78-366241

Hilton, Ian. 2.13921
Peter Weiss: a search for affinities. — London: Wolff, 1970. 126 p., plate.: port.; 20 cm. — (Modern German authors: texts and contexts, v. 3) 1. Weiss, Peter, 1916- I. T. II. Series.
PT2685.E5 Z7   832/.9/14   *LC* 70-18818   *ISBN* 0854960430

Wolf, Christa. 2.13922
Kassandra: Erzählung / Christa Wolf. — 2. Aufl. — Darmstadt: Luchterhand, 1983. 156 p. I. T.
PT2685O3 K3 1983   *ISBN* 3472865741

Wolf, Christa. 2.13923
[Kassandra. English] Cassandra: a novel and four essays / by Christa Wolf; translated from the German by Jan van Heurck. — New York: Farrar, Straus, Giroux, c1984. 305 p.; 22 cm. Translation of: Kassandra and Voraussetzungen einer Erzählung. I. Wolf, Christa. Voraussetzungen einer Erzählung. English. II. T.
PT2685.O36 K313 1984   838/.91409 19   *LC* 84-8056   *ISBN* 0374119562

Wolf, Christa. 2.13924
Voraussetzungen einer Erzählung, Kassandra: Frankfurter Poetik–Vorlesungen / Christa Wolf. — 2. Aufl. — Darmstadt: Luchterhand, c1983. 160 p.; 18 cm. (Sammlung Luchterhand; 456) 1. Wolf, Christa Kassandra — Addresses, essays, lectures. I. T.
PT2685.O36 K338 1983   838/.91409 19   *LC* 83-172398   *ISBN* 3472614560

Wolf, Christa. 2.13925
Kindheitsmuster: Roman / Christa Wolf. — 2. Aufl. — Darmstadt; Neuwied: Luchterhand, 1977. 480 p.; 21 cm. — I. T.
PT2685.O36 K5 1977   *LC* 78-346954   *ISBN* 3472864222

Wolf, Christa. 2.13926
[Kindheitsmuster. English] Patterns of childhood: (formerly A model childhood) / Christa Wolf; translated by Ursule Molinaro and Hedwig Rappolt. — New York: Farrar, Straus, and Giroux, 1984, c1980. 407 p.; 21 cm. Translation of: Kindheitsmuster. I. T.
PT2685.O36 K513 1984   833/.914 19   *LC* 84-4135   *ISBN* 0374518440

Wolf, Christa. 2.13927
[Lesen und Schreiben. English] The reader and the writer: essays, sketches, memories / by Christa Wolf; translated by Joan Becker. — New York: Signet, 1978, c1977. 222 p.; 19 cm. Translation of Lesen und Schreiben. I. T.
PT2685.O36 L413   834/.9/14   *LC* 77-905   *ISBN* 0717804879 pbk

Wolf, Christa. 2.13928
Nachdenken über Christa T. / Christa Wolf. — 17. Aufl. — Darmstadt: Luchterhand, 1981. 180 p. — (Sammlung Luchterhand; 31) I. T.
PT2685.O36 N3 1981

Wolf, Christa. 2.13929
[Nachdenken über Christa T. English] The quest for Christa T. Translated by Christopher Middleton. New York, Farrar, Straus & Giroux [1971, c1970] 185 p. 21 cm. Translation of Nachdenken über Christa T. I. T.
PZ4.W8532 Qe PT2685.O36 N3x   833/.9/14   *LC* 78-133199   *ISBN* 0374239886

PT3700–3746 Germany (Democratic Republic)

(Individual authors interfiled, PT2601-2688)

Huebener, Theodore, 1895-. • 2.13930
The literature of East Germany. New York, F. Ungar [1970] ix, 134 p. 22 cm. 1. German literature — Germany (East) — History and criticism. I. T.
PT3705.H8   830.9/0091   *LC* 75-114610   *ISBN* 0804424012

Flores, John. • 2.13931
Poetry in East Germany; adjustments, visions, and provocations, 1945–1970. New Haven, Yale University Press, 1971. xiv, 354 p. 25 cm. (Yale Germanic studies, 5) 1. German poetry — Germany (East) — History and criticism. I. T. II. Series.
PT3719.F5   831/.9/1409   *LC* 77-115368   *ISBN* 0300013396

Huettich, H. G., 1946-.   **2.13932**
Theater in the planned society: contemporary drama in the German
Democratic Republic in its historical, political, and cultural context / by H. G.
Huettich. — Chapel Hill: University of North Carolina Press, 1978. xv, 174 p.;
24 cm. (University of North Carolina studies in the Germanic languages and
literatures; no. 88) Includes index. 1. German drama — Germany, East —
History and criticism. 2. Communism and literature 3. Literature and state —
Germany, East. I. T.
PT3721.H8   832/.9/1409   *LC* 76-20606   *ISBN* 0807880884

Hamburger, Michael. comp.   **2.13933**
East German poetry; an anthology. Edited by Michael Hamburger. [1st ed.]
New York, Dutton, 1973. xxii, 213 p. 23 cm. German and English. 1. German
poetry — Germany (East) — 20th century — Translations into English.
2. German poetry — 20th century — Translations into English. 3. English
poetry — Translations from German. I. T.
PT3734.H3 1973   831/.9/1408   *LC* 73-158584   *ISBN* 052509668X
ISBN 0525033106

East German short stories: an introductory anthology /   **2.13934**
translated and introduced by Peter E. and Evelyn S. Firchow.
[Boston]: Twayne Publishers, 1979. 251 p.; 21 cm. 1. German fiction —
Germany (East) — Translations into English. 2. English fiction — 20th
century — Translations from German. 3. Short stories, German — Germany
(East) — Translation into English. 4. Short stories, English — Translations
from German. I. Firchow, Peter Edgerly, 1937- II. Firchow, Evelyn
Scherabon.
PT3740.E18   833/.01   *LC* 78-21686   *ISBN* 0805781595

PT3810–3828 Austrian Literature

(Individual authors interfiled, PT2601-2688)

Modern Austrian writing: literature and society after 1945 /   **2.13935**
edited by Alan Best and Hans Wolfschütz.
London: Oswald Wolff; Totowa, N.J.: Barnes & Noble, c1980. viii, 307 p.; 23
cm. 1. German literature — Austrian authors — History and criticism.
2. German literature — 20th century — History and criticism. I. Best, Alan
D. II. Wolfschütz, Hans.
PT3818.M6 1980   830/.9/9436 19   *LC* 80-508065   *ISBN*
0389200387

Williams, Cedric E.   **2.13936**
The broken eagle; the politics of Austrian literature from empire to Anschluss
[by] C. E. Williams. — New York: Barnes & Noble, [1974] xxii, 281 p.: illus.; 23
cm. 1. German literature — Austrian authors — History and criticism.
2. German literature — 20th century — History and criticism. 3. Politics and
literature — Austria. I. T.
PT3818.W5 1974   830/.9/9436   *LC* 74-180506   *ISBN* 0064977137

Austrian poetry today = Österreichische Lyrik heute / edited   **2.13937**
& translated by Milne Holton & Herbert Kuhner.
New York: Schocken Books, 1985. xiv, 274 p.; 24 cm. English and German.
1. German poetry — Austrian authors — Translations into English.
2. Austrian poetry (German) — Translations into English. 3. German poetry
— 20th century — Translations into English. 4. English poetry — Translations
from German. 5. German poetry — Austrian authors 6. Austrian poetry
(German) 7. German poetry — 20th century I. Holton, Milne. II. Kuhner,
Herbert, 1935- III. Title: Österreichische Lyrik heute.
PT3824.Z5 A8 1985   831/.914/08 19   *LC* 83-20221   *ISBN*
0805239030

An anthology of Austrian drama / edited with a historical   **2.13938**
introduction by Douglas A. Russell.
Rutherford [N.J.]: Fairleigh Dickinson University Press, c1982. 442 p.; 21 cm.
1. German drama — Austrian authors — Translations into English.
2. English drama — Translations from German. I. Russell, Douglas A.
PT3826.D8 A5 1982   832/.008   *LC* 76-19836   *ISBN* 0838620035

PT3860–3879 Swiss Literature in German

(Individual authors interfiled, PT2601-2688)

Günter, Werner, 1898-.   • **2.13939**
Dichter der neueren Schweiz / Werner Günther. — Bern: Francke, c1963-. v.;
21 cm. 1. Swiss literature (German) — History and criticism I. T.
PT3868 G8   *LC* 67-101690

PT5001–5980 DUTCH LITERATURE

Meijer, Reinder P.   **2.13940**
Literature of the low countries: a short history of Dutch literature in the Netherlands and Belgium / by Reinder P. Meijer. — New ed. — Cheltenham: Stanley Thornes (Publishers), 1978. ix, 402 p.; 24 cm. Includes index. 1. Dutch literature — History and criticism. 2. Flemish literature — History and criticism. I. T.
PT5061.M4 1978b   839.3/1/09   *LC* 79-308787   *ISBN* 0859500942

Weevers, Theodor, 1904-.   **2.13941**
Poetry of the Netherlands in its European context, 1170–1930. Illustrated with poems in original and translation. [London] University of London, Athlone Press 1960. 376p. 1. Dutch poetry — History and criticism 2. Dutch poetry — Translations into English 3. English poetry — Translations from Dutch 4. Literature, Comparative I. T.
PT5201 W4

PT5400–5547 Collections

Colledge, Edmund. comp.   **2.13942**
Reynard the Fox and other mediaeval Netherlands secular literature. [Karel ende Elegast, Walewein, Lancelot and Nu Noch]. Translated by E. Colledge [Van den Vos Reinaerde]. Translated by Prof. Adriaan J. Barnouw. Edited and introduced by E. Colledge. Leiden A.W. Sijthoff 1967. 196p. (Bibliotheca Neerlandica) 1. Dutch literature — Translations into English 2. English literature — Translations from Dutch 3. Dutch literature — Early to 1500 — History and criticism I. T.
PT5411 C6

Elckerlijc. English.   **2.13943**
The Mirror of salvation; a moral play of Everyman C. 1490. Translated from the Dutch by Adriaan J. Barnouw. — The Hague: Nijhoff, 1971. xvi, 46 p.; 22 cm. — (Bibliotheca Neerlandica extra muros, 2) I. Barnouw, Adriaan Jacob, 1877-1968. tr. II. T.
PT5443.E4 E5 1971   839.3/1/22   *LC* 72-180999   *ISBN* 9024750954

Colledge, Edmund. comp.   **2.13944**
Mediaeval Netherlands religious literature. Translated and introduced by E. Colledge. Leyden Sythoff 1965. 226p. (Bibliotheca Neerlandica) 1. Religious literature, Dutch — Translations into English 2. Dutch literature — Early to 1500 — Translations into English I. T.
PT5445 E5 C6

Dutch interior: postwar poetry of the Netherlands and Flanders   **2.13945**
/ edited by James S. Holmes and William Jay Smith; with an introduction by Cees Buddingh'.
New York: Columbia University Press, 1984. xxxix, 324 p.; 24 cm. Includes indexes. 1. Dutch poetry — 20th century — Translations into English. 2. Flemish poetry — 20th century — Translations into English. 3. English poetry — Translations from Dutch. I. Holmes, James S. II. Smith, William Jay, 1918-
PT5475.E5 D87 1984   839.3/1164/08 19   *LC* 83-27322   *ISBN* 0231057466

Krispyn, Egbert. comp.   **2.13946**
Modern stories from Holland and Flanders; an anthology. New York, Twayne Publishers [1973] xii, 283 p. 22 cm. (The Library of Netherlandic literature, v. 2) 1. Short stories, English — Translations from Dutch. 2. Short stories, Dutch — Translations into English. I. T.
PT5530.E5 B7x   833.3/1/01   *LC* 72-3913

PT5555–5886 Individual Authors, by Period

Bredero, G. A. (Gerbrand Adriaenszoon), 1585-1618.   **2.13947**
[Spaanschen Brabander. English] The Spanish Brabanter: a seventeenth-century Dutch social satire in five acts / G.A. Bredero; translated by H. David Brumble III. — Binghamton, N.Y.: Center for Medieval & Early Renaissance Studies, 1982. 137 p.: ill.; 23 cm. — (Medieval & Renaissance texts & studies. v. 11) Translation of: Spaanschen Brabander. I. Brumble, H. David. II. T. III. Series.
PT5610.S613 1982   839.3/123 19   *LC* 81-19004   *ISBN* 0866980180

Coenen, Frans, 1866-1936.   ● **2.13948**
The house on the canal / Frans Coenen. Alienation / J. van Oudshoorn. — Leyden: Sythoff, 1965. 220 p. — (Bibliotheca Neerlandica; 7) The house on the canal is a translation of Onpersoonlijke herinneringen; Alienation is a translation of Willem Mertens' levensspiegel. I. Oudshoorn, J. van, 1876-1951. Alienation II. T. III. Series.
PT5822C55 O613   *LC* 65-26681

Couperus, Louis, 1863-1923.   **2.13949**
[Van oude menschen, de dingen die voorbijgaan. English] Old people and the things that pass / trans. from the Dutch by Alexander Teikeira de Mattos. — Leyden: Sythoff, 1963. 265 p. (Bibliothéca Neerlandica) Translation of: Van oude menschen, de dingen die voorbijgaan. I. T.
PT5825 V3x   *LC* 63-22273

Multatuli.   **2.13950**
[Max Havelaar. English] Max Havelaar, or, The coffee auctions of the Dutch Trading Company / Multatuli; with an introduction by D.H. Lawrence; translated by Roy Edwards; afterword by E.M. Beekman. — Amherst: University of Massachusetts Press, 1982. 394 p.; 21 cm. — (Library of the Indies.) Translation of: Max Havelaar, of, De koffieveilingen der Nederlandsche handelmaatschappij. I. T. II. Series.
PT5829.M3 E3 1982   839.3/18509 19   *LC* 82-2043   *ISBN* 0870233599

Eeden, Frederik van, 1860-1932.   **2.13951**
The deeps of deliverance. Translated from the Netherlandic by Margaret Robinson. — New York: Twayne Publishers, [1975, c1974] 292 p.; 21 cm. — (The Library of Netherlandic literature, v. 5) Translation of Van de koele meren des doods. I. T.
PZ3.E278 D10 PT5831.V313x   839.3/1/35   *LC* 74-8923   *ISBN* 0805734198

Mulisch, Harry, 1927-.   **2.13952**
The stone bridal bed / by Harry Mulisch; translated by Adrienne Dixon. — London: Abelard-Schuman, 1962. 159 p. I. T.
PT5860.M85 S8x   *LC* 63-7049

Blaman, Anna, 1905-1960.   **2.13953**
[Op leven en dood. English] A matter of life and death [by] Anna Blaman. Translated from the Dutch by Adrienne Dixon. New York, Twayne Publishers [1974] 235 p. 22 cm. (The Library of Netherlandic literature, v. 3) Translation of Op leven en dood. I. T.
PZ4.V985 Mat3 PT5878.V85 O6x   839.3/1/362   *LC* 73-3955   *ISBN* 0805734414

Nooteboom, Cees, 1933-.   **2.13954**
[Rituelen. English] Rituals: a novel / by Cees Nooteboom; translated by Adrienne Dixon. — Baton Rouge: Louisiana State University Press, c1983. vi, 145 p.; 23 cm. Translation of: Rituelen. I. T.
PT5881.24.O55 R613 1983   839.3/1364 19   *LC* 82-17278   *ISBN* 0807110817

PT5901–5980 Dutch Literature in Indonesia

Nieuwenhuys, Robert, 1908-.   **2.13955**
[Oost-Indische Spiegel. English] Mirror of the Indies: a history of Dutch colonial literature / Rob Nieuwenhuys; translated by Frans van Rosevelt; edited by E.M. Beekman. — Amherst: University of Massachusetts Press, 1982. xxix, 336 p.; 24 cm. — (Library of the Indies.) Translation of: Oost-Indische Spiegel. 1. Dutch literature — Indonesia — History and criticism. 2. Indonesia in literature. I. Beekman, E. M., 1939- II. T. III. Series.
PT5911.N513 1982   839.3/1/099598 19   *LC* 82-4755   *ISBN* 0870233688

Memory and agony: Dutch stories from Indonesia / collected   **2.13956**
and introduced by Rob Nieuwehuys; translated by Adrienne
Dixon.
Boston: Twayne Publishers, c1979. xxvii, 260 p.; 21 cm. (The Library of Netherlandic literature; v. 12) Includes index. 1. Short stories, Dutch — Indonesia — Translations into English. 2. Short stories, English — Translations from Dutch. 3. Indonesia — Fiction. I. Nieuwenhuys, Robert, 1908-
PT5926.M46 1979   839.3/1/301   *LC* 79-13872   *ISBN* 0805781668

PT6000–6471 Flemish Literature, 1830–

Boon, Louis Paul.   **2.13957**
[Kapellekensbaan. English] Chapel Road. Translated from the Flemish by Adrienne Dixon. New York, Twayne Publishers [1972] 338 p. 22 cm. (The Library of Netherlandic literature, v. 1) Translation of De Kapellekensbaan. I. T.
PZ4.B7242 Ch PT6407.B57 K3x   839.3/2/362   *LC* 72-153455

Gijsen, Marnix, 1899-.   **2.13958**
[Klaaglied om Agnes. English] Lament for Agnes / Marnix Gijsen [i.e. J. A. Goris]; translated from the Netherlandic by W. James–Gerth. — Boston: Twayne Publishers, [1975] 97 p.; 22 cm. — (The Library of Netherlandic literature; v. 6) Translation of Klaaglied om Agnes. I. T.
PZ3.G676 Lam PT6430.G67 K5x   839.3/2/362   *LC* 74-34320   *ISBN* 0805781501

Ostaijen, Paul van, 1896-1928.   **2.13959**
Feasts of fear and agony / Paul van Ostaijen; translated by Hidde van Ameyden van Duym. — New York: New Directions Pub. Corp., 1976. 76 p.; 21 cm. (A New Directions book) I. T.
PT6442.O8 A22 1976   839.3/2/162   *LC* 75-26869   *ISBN* 0811206009. *ISBN* 0811206017 pbk

Elsschot, Willem, 1882-1960.   **2.13960**
Three novels: Soft soap; The leg; Will-o'–the wisp / Willem Elsschot; [translated by A. Brotherton]. — Leyden: Sijtjoff, 1965. 252 p. — (Bibliotheca Neerlandica; 12) Translations of Lijmen; Het been; Het dwaallicht. I. T. II. Title: Soft soap. III. Title: The leg. IV. Title: Will-o'-the-wisp. V. Series.
PT6442.R5 T48   PT6442R5 A23.   *LC* 65-24360

Insingel, Mark.   **2.13961**
A course of time / by Mark Insingel; translated by Adrienne Dixon. — New York: Red Dust, 1977. 126 p. Translation of Een tijdsverloop. I. T.
PT6466.19.N7 T513   839.31364   *LC* 76-56575   *ISBN* 0873760298

PT6500–6592 Afrikaans Literature

Cope, Jack, 1913-.   **2.13962**
The adversary within: dissident writers in Afrikaans / Jack Cope. — Cape Town: D. Philip; Atlantic Highlands, N.J.: Humanities Press, c1982. xi, 208 p.; 22 cm. Includes index. 1. Afrikaans literature — 20th century — History and criticism. 2. Authors, Afrikaans — 20th century — Political and social views. 3. Social problems in literature I. T.
PT6510.C65 1982   839.3/6/09 19   *LC* 83-148079   *ISBN* 0391026976

Breytenbach, Breyten.   **2.13963**
The true confessions of an albino terrorist / Breyten Breytenbach. — New York: Farrar, Straus, Giroux, [1985], c1983. 396 p.; 23 cm. Includes index. 1. Breytenbach, Breyten — Biography — Imprisonment. 2. Authors, Afrikaans — 20th century — Biography. 3. Civil rights movements — South Africa. 4. Political prisoners — South Africa — Biography. 5. South Africa — Race relations I. T.
PT6592.12.R4 Z475 1985   839.3/615 B 19   *LC* 84-25966   *ISBN* 0374279357

Brink, André Philippus, 1935-.   **2.13964**
[Kennis van die aand. English] Looking on darkness: a novel / by André P. Brink. — New York: Morrow, 1975, c1974. 399 p.; 24 cm. Translation of Kennis van die aand. I. T.
PZ4.B8583 Lo3 PT6592.12.R5   839.3/6/35   *LC* 75-4515   *ISBN* 0688029249

PT7001–7099 Scandinavian Literatures: General

Greenway, John L.   **2.13965**
The golden horns: mythic imagination and the Nordic past / John L. Greenway. Athens: University of Georgia Press, c1977. 226 p.; 24 cm. Includes index. 1. Scandinavian literature — History and criticism. 2. Mythology in literature I. T.
PT7048.G7   839/.5/0937   *LC* 74-30676   *ISBN* 0820303844

Bredsdorff, Elias.   • **2.13966**
An introduction to Scandinavian literature, from the earliest time to our day, by Elias Bredsdorff, Brita Mortensen [and] Ronald Popperwell. — Westport, Conn.: Greenwood Press, [1970] 245 p.; 23 cm. 1. Scandinavian literature — History and criticism. I. Mortensen, Brita M. E., joint author. II. Popperwell, Ronald G. joint author. III. T.
PT7063.B7 1970   839/.5/09   *LC* 78-98748   *ISBN* 0837128498

The Hero in Scandinavian literature: from Peer Gynt to the   **2.13967**
Present / edited by John M. Weinstock and Robert T.
Rovinsky.
Austin: University of Texas Press, [1975] 226 p.; 23 cm. Proceedings of a Scandinavian symposium, the 14th annual symposium sponsored by the Dept. of Germanic Languages, and held in Austin, May 1972. 1. Scandinavian literature — Addresses, essays, lectures. 2. Heroes in literature — Addresses, essays, lectures. I. Weinstock, John M., 1936- II. Rovinsky, Robert T., 1940- III. Texas. University at Austin. Dept. of Germanic Languages.
PT7067.H4   PT7067 H4.   839/.5   *LC* 74-26815   *ISBN* 0292730012

Rossel, Sven Hakon.   **2.13968**
[Skandinavische Literatur, 1870-1970. English] A history of Scandinavian literature, 1870–1980 / Sven H. Rossel; translated by Anne C. Ulmer in association with the University of Minnesota Press. — Minneapolis: The Press, c1982. x, 492 p.; 24 cm. — (Nordic series. v. 5) Updated translation of: Skandinavische Literatur, 1870-1970. Includes index. 1. Scandinavian literature — 20th century — History and criticism. 2. Scandinavian literature — 19th century — History and criticism. I. T. II. Series.
PT7078.R6713 1982   839/.5 19   *LC* 81-14654   *ISBN* 0816609063

Marker, Frederick J.   **2.13969**
The Scandinavian theatre: a short history / Frederick J. Marker and Lise–Lone Marker. — Totowa, N.J.: Rowman and Littlefield, 1975. xiii, 303 p.: ill.; 22 cm. (Drama and theatre studies) Includes index. 1. Scandinavian drama — History and criticism. 2. Theater — Scandinavia — History. I. Marker, Lise-Lone, 1934- joint author. II. T.
PT7082.M3   792/.0948   *LC* 75-29017   *ISBN* 0874717760

An anthology of Scandinavian literature, from the Viking period   • **2.13970**
to the twentieth century / selected and edited by Hallberg
Hallmundsson.
1st Collier Books ed. — New York: Collier Books, 1965. xix, 362 p.; 21 cm. 1. Scandinavian literature — Translations into English. 2. English literature — Translations from Scandinavian. I. Hallmundsson, Hallberg.
PT7092.E5 H3   PT7092.E5 A59.   839.508   *LC* 65-23076

Scandinavian plays of the twentieth century.   • 2.13971
Princeton University Press for the American-Scandinavian foundation, New York 1944-. v. 21 cm. 1. Scandinavian drama — Translations into English 2. English drama — Translations from Scandinavian I. Gustafson, Alrik, 1903- II. American-Scandinavian Foundation.
PT7094 S4   LC 44-40224

PT7101–7338 OLD ICELANDIC. OLD NORWEGIAN

Hermannsson, Halldór, 1878-.   2.13972
Bibliography of the Eddas / by Holldór Hermannsson. — Ithaca, N.Y.: Cornell University Library, 1920. 95 p. — (Islandica: an annual relating to Iceland and the Fiske Icelandic collection in Cornell University Library; v.13) 1. Eddas — Bibliography. I. T.
PT7103.I7 v.13   LC 21-7490

Hannesson, Jóhann S.   • 2.13973
Bibliography of the Eddas: a supplement to Bibliography of the Eddas (Islandica XIII) / by Halldór Hermannsson. — Ithaca, N. Y.: Cornell University Press, 1955. xiii, 110 p.; 24 cm. (Islandica; an annual relating to Iceland and the Fiske Icelandic Collection in Cornell University Library, v. 37) 1. Eddas — Bibliography. I. Hermannsson, Halldór, 1878- Bibliography of the Eddas. II. T.
PT7103.I7 v. 37   LC 56-2095

Turville-Petre, Gabriel.   • 2.13974
Origins of Icelandic literature / by G. Turville–Petre. — Oxford: Clarendon Press, 1953. vii, 260 p., [3] leaves of plates; facsims., map: 23 cm. 1. Old Norse literature — History and criticism. I. T.
PT7154.T87   LC 53-4361//r65   ISBN 0198111142

Old Norse–Icelandic literature: a critical guide / edited by   2.13975
Carol J. Clover and John Lindow.
Ithaca: Cornell University Press, 1985. 387 p. — (Islandica. 45) 1. Old Norse literature — History and criticism — Addresses, essays, lectures. 2. Icelandic literature — History and criticism — Addresses, essays, lectures. I. Clover, Carol J., 1940- II. Lindow, John. III. Series.
PT7161.O4 1985   839/.6/09 19   LC 85-47697   ISBN 0801417554

Hallberg, Peter.   2.13976
[Fornisländska poesien. English] Old Icelandic poetry: Eddic lay and skaldic verse / Peter Hallberg; translated with a foreword by Paul Schach and Sonja Lindgrenson. — Lincoln: University of Nebraska Press, [1975] xii, 219 p.; 21 cm. Translation of Den fornisländska poesien. Includes index. 1. Old Norse poetry — History and criticism. I. T.
PT7170.H313   839/.6/1009   LC 74-27186   ISBN 0803208553

Turville-Petre, Gabriel.   2.13977
Scaldic poetry / by E. O. G. Turville–Petre. — Oxford: Clarendon Press, 1976. lxxx, 102 p.; 23 cm. 1. Scalds and scaldic poetry 2. Icelandic and Old Norse poetry — History and criticism. I. T.
PT7172.T83   PT7172 T83.   839/.6/1009   LC 76-369573   ISBN 0198125178

Hallberg, Peter.   • 2.13978
The Icelandic saga / Peter Hallberg; translated with introduction and notes by Paul Schach. — Lincoln: University of Nebraska Press, 1962. xxii, 179 p.: ill. Translation of: Den isländska sagan. 1. Sagas — History and criticism. 2. Icelandic and Old Norse literature — History and criticism. I. T.
PT7181.H313   LC 62-7873

Andersson, Theodore Murdock, 1934-.   • 2.13979
The Icelandic family saga; an analytic reading [by] Theodore M. Andersson. — Cambridge: Harvard University Press, 1967. x, 315 p.; 22 cm. — (Harvard studies in comparative literature. 28) 'Includes synopsis and outlines of ... twenty-four sagas.' 1. Sagas I. T. II. Series.
PT7183.A45   839/.61   LC 66-21329

Edda: a collection of essays / edited by Robert J. Glendinning   2.13980
and Haraldur Bessason.
[Manitoba]: University of Manitoba Press, c1983. 332 p.; 24 cm. — (The University of Manitoba Icelandic studies, 0709-2997; 4) 1. Eddas — Addresses, essays, lectures. I. Glendinning, Robert James, 1931- II. Bessason, Haraldur, 1931-
PT7235.E32 1983   839/.6/09 19   LC 83-191783   ISBN 0887551173

Pálsson, Hermann, 1921- comp.   • 2.13981
Gautrek's saga, and other medieval tales; translated [from the Icelandic] with an introduction, by Hermann Pálsson and Paul Edwards. — London: University of London P.; New York: New York University P., 1968. 156 p.: map.; 23 cm. 1. Sagas 2. Old Norse literature — Translations into English. 3. English literature — Translations from Old Norse. I. Edwards, Paul Geoffrey, 1926- joint comp. II. T.
PT7262.E5 P3   LC 68-16829   ISBN 034009396X

Egils saga Skallagrímssonar. English.   2.13982
Egil's saga / translated with an introduction by Hermann Pálsson and Paul Edwards. — Harmondsworth; New York: Penguin, 1976. 254 p.: geneal. tables, maps; 18 cm. — (The Penguin classics) 'Probably written about 1230 by Snorri Sturluson.' 1. Egill Skallagrímsson, ca. 910-ca. 990. I. Pálsson, Hermann, 1921- II. Edwards, Paul Geoffrey, 1926- III. Snorri Sturluson, 1179?-1241. IV. T.
PT7269.E3 E57 1976   839/.6/1   LC 77-361577   ISBN 0140443215

Grettis saga.   2.13983
Grettir's saga / translated by Denton Fox and Hermann Pálsson. — Toronto: University of Toronto Press, [1974] xiii, 199 p.: ill.; 24 cm. Includes index. I. Fox, Denton. tr. II. Pálsson, Hermann, 1921- tr. III. Pálsson, Hermann. IV. T.
PT7269.G7 E53   839/.6/3   LC 72-90746   ISBN 0802019250

Allen, Richard F.   2.13984
Fire and iron: critical approaches to Njáls saga / [by] Richard F. Allen. — [Pittsburg]: University of Pittsburgh Press, [1971] xvi, 254 p. 1. Njáls saga. I. T.
PT7269.N5 A4   LC 71-134493   ISBN 0822932199

Einar Ólafur Sveinsson, 1899-.   • 2.13985
Njáls saga: a literary masterpiece, by Einar Ól. Sveinsson. Edited and translated by Paul Schach. With an introd. by E. O. G. Turville–Petre. — Lincoln: University of Nebraska Press, [1971] xvii, 210 p.; 22 cm. Based on the author's Á Njálsbuð, bók um mikið listaverk. 1. Njáls saga. I. Schach, Paul. ed. II. T.
PT7269.N5 E313   839/.6/3   LC 70-128914   ISBN 0803207891

Lönnroth, Lars.   2.13986
Njáls saga: a critical introduction / Lars Lönnroth. — Berkeley: University of California Press, c1976. xi, 275 p., [1] leaf of plates: ill.; 25 cm. 1. Njála. I. T.
PT7269.N5 L6   PT7269N5 L6.   839/.6/3   LC 73-94437   ISBN B20898

Snorri Sturluson, 1178-1241.   • 2.13987
Heimskringla: the Norse king sagas / by Snorre Sturlason; translated by Samuel Laing. — London: Dent, 1930. xxviii, 441 p. — (Everyman's library; 847) Translated from the Icelandic. Introduction and notes by John Beveridge. 1. Norway — History 2. Scandinavia — History 3. Iceland — History I. Beveridge, John, 1857- II. T. III. Title: The Norse king sagas.
PT7277.E5 L3 1930   LC a 30-973

Snorri Sturluson, 1179?-1241.   • 2.13988
King Harald's saga; Harald Hardradi of Norway. From Snorri Sturluson's Heimskringla. Translated with an introd. by Magnus Magnusson and Hermann Pálsson. Baltimore, Penguin Books [c1966] 180p. geneal. table, maps. (Penguin classics, L183) Translated from the Icelandic. 1. Harold III, Hardrada, King of Norway, 1015-1066. I. T.
PT7278.5.H32 E55 1966a   LC 67-2064

Orkneyinga saga. English.   2.13989
Orkneyinga saga: the history of the Earls of Orkney / translated from the Icelandic and introduced by Hermann Pálsson and Paul Edwards. — London: Hogarth Press, 1978. 223 p., [2] leaves of plates: ill.; 23 cm. Includes indexes. 1. Orkney — History. I. Pálsson, Hermann, 1921- II. Edwards, Paul Geoffrey, 1926- III. T.
PT7281.O7 E5 1978   839/.6/3   LC 78-318053   ISBN 0701204311

The Saga of the Völsungs, together with excerpts from the   2.13990
Nornagestsþáttr and three chapters from the Prose Edda /
translated and annotated by George K. Anderson.
Newark: University of Delaware Press, c1982. 266 p.; 22 cm. Includes index. I. Volsunga saga. English. II. Norna-Gests saga. English. III. Edda Snorra Sturlusonar. English.
PT7287.V7 E52   839/.63 19   LC 81-14833   ISBN 0874131723

Völsunga saga.   • 2.13991
The saga of the Volsungs, The saga of Ragnar Lodbrok, together with The lay of Kraka, translated from the Old Norse by Margaret Schlauch. New York, The American-Scandinavian Foundation, W.W. Norton & Company, inc. [c1930] xxxix p., 1 l., 43-270 p. 20 cm. (Scandinavian classics. [vol. xxxv]) 'First edition.' 1. Icelandic and Old Norse literature — Translations into English. 2. English literature — Translations from Icelandic and Old Norse. I. Schlauch, Margaret. II. Ragnars saga Loðbrókar ok sona hans.

III. Krákumál. IV. T. V. Title: Saga of Ragnar Lodbrok. VI. Title: Kraka, The lay of.
PT7287.V7 E57   839.6   *LC* 30-28090

Edda Snorra Sturlusonar. Prologue.   **2.13992**
Edda: prologue and Gylfaginning / Snorri Sturluson; edited by Anthony Faulkes. — Oxford: Clarendon Press; New York: Oxford University Press, 1982. xxxiv, 177 p., [1] leaf of plates: facsim.; 23 cm. Includes index.
1. Mythology, Norse 2. Scalds and scaldic poetry I. Faulkes, Anthony. II. Gylfaginning. 1982. III. T.
PT7313.E5 F38 1982   839/.63   *LC* 79-41803   *ISBN* 0198111754

PT7351–7550 MODERN ICELANDIC

Einarsson, Stefán, 1897-.   **• 2.13993**
History of Icelandic prose writers, 1800–1940. Ithaca Cornell University Press 1948. 269p. (Islandica;an annual relating to Iceland and the Fiske Icelandic Collection in Cornell University Library, v. 32-33) 1. Icelandic prose literature — History and criticism I. T. II. Series.
PT7412 E55   *LC* 48-7713

Beck, Richard, 1897- ed.   **2.13994**
Icelandic poems and stories; translations from modern Icelandic literature. — Princeton, Princeton university press, [c1943]. vii, 315 p.; 22 cm. 1. Icelandic poetry — Selections. 2. Icelandic fiction — Selections. 3. Authors, Icelandic I. T.
PT7459.B4 1968   839/.69/08003   *LC* a43-1234

Agnar Thórðarson, 1917-.   **2.13995**
[Ef sverd thitt er stutt. English] The sword. Translated from the Icelandic with introd. and notes by Paul Schach. New York, Twayne Publishers [1970] xx, 277 p. 22 cm. (Library of Scandinavian literature, v. 7) Translation of Ef sverd thitt er stutt. I. T. II. Series.
PZ4.A27 Sw3 PT7511.A4   839/.69/34

Laxness, Halldór, 1902-.   **2.13996**
[Heimsljós. English] World light (Heimsljós) [by] Halldor Laxness. Translated from the Icelandic by Magnus Magnusson. Madison, University of Wisconsin Press, 1969. xvii, 521 p. 24 cm. (The Nordic translation series) I. T.
PZ3.L449 Wo PT7511.L3   839.69/3/4   *LC* 69-16109   *ISBN* 0299051919

Laxness, Halldór, 1902-.   **2.13997**
A quire of seven / by Halldor Laxness; translated from the Icelandic by Alan Boucher. — Reykjavík: Iceland Review, 1974. 95 p. — (Iceland Review library) I. T.
PT7511.L3 Q813

Hallberg, Peter.   **2.13998**
Halldór Laxness. Translated by Rory McTurk. New York, Twayne Publishers [1971] 220 p. 21 cm. (Twayne's world authors series, TWAS89: Iceland) 1. Laxness, Halldór, 1902- I. T.
PT7511.L3 Z713   839/.69/34   *LC* 75-79208

PT7601–8260 DANISH

PT7601–8046 Literary History. Collections

Borum, Poul.   **2.13999**
Danish literature: a short critical survey / by Poul Borum. — Copenhagen: Det Danske Selskab, 1979. 141 p.: ill.; 20 cm. — (Danes of the present and past.) Includes index. 1. Danish literature — History and criticism. I. T. II. Series.
PT7671.B67   839.8/1/09 19   *LC* 80-501886   *ISBN* 8774290304

Olrik, Axel, 1864-1917. ed.   **• 2.14000**
[Danske folkeviser i udvalg. English] A book of Danish ballads, selected and with an introduction by Axel Olrik. Translated by E. M. Smith–Dampier. Freeport, N.Y., Books for Libraries Press [1968, c1939] x, 337 p. 22 cm. (Granger index reprint series) Translation of Danske folkeviser i udvalg. 1. Ballads, Danish — Denmark — Texts. 2. English poetry — Translations

from Danish. 3. Danish poetry — Translations into English. I. Smith-Dampier, E. M., tr. II. T.
PT7919.O5513 1968   839.8/1/1008   *LC* 68-57063

Jansen, Frederik Julius Billeskov, 1907- comp.   **• 2.14001**
Anthology of Danish literature. Edited by F. J. Billeskov Jansen and P. M. Mitchell. — Bilingual ed. — Carbondale: Southern Illinois University Press, [1972] ix, 606 p.; 25 cm. Danish and English. English version with corrections and additions, of the bilingual Danish-French ed. published in 1964. 1. Danish literature 2. Danish literature — Translations into English. 3. English literature — Translations from Danish. I. Mitchell, P. M. (Phillip Marshall), 1916- II. T.
PT7951.J3 1972   839.8/1/08   *LC* 72-132475   *ISBN* 0809304872

Contemporary Danish poetry: an anthology / edited by Line   **2.14002**
Jensen ... [et al.]; introd. by Torben Brostrøm.
Copenhagen, Denmark: Gyldendal; Boston: Twayne Publishers, 1977. 343 p.; 22 cm. — (The Library of Scandinavian literature; v. 31) 1. Danish poetry — 20th century. I. Jensen, Line. II. Series.
PT7978.C6   839.8/1/17408   *LC* 77-2567   *ISBN* 0805781579

Seventeen Danish poets: a bilingual anthology of contemporary   **2.14003**
Danish poetry / edited by Niels Ingwersen.
Lincoln, NE (P.O. Box 82213, Lincoln 68501): Windflower Press, c1981. 164 p.; 22 cm. — (Numbers two and three of the Blue Hotel, volume 1) 1. Danish poetry — 20th century — Translations into English. 2. English poetry — Translations from Danish. 3. Danish poetry — 20th century. I. Ingwersen, Niels.
PT7983.E5 I5 1981   839.8/1174/08 19   *LC* 81-184264

Contemporary Danish prose; an anthology. [Introd. by F.J.   **• 2.14004**
Billeskov Jansen. Supervision of translation, and notes, by Elias Bredsdorff]
Copenhagen Gyldendal 1958. 375p. 1. Short stories, Danish — Translations into English 2. Short stories, English — Translations from Danish I. Jansen, Frederik Julius Billeskov, 1907- II. Bredsdorff, Elias.
PT8024 E5 C6

The Royal guest, and other classical Danish narrative /   **2.14005**
translated and edited by P. M. Mitchell and Kenneth H. Ober.
Chicago: University of Chicago Press, 1977. vi, 242 p.; 21 cm. 1. Short stories, Danish — Translations into English. 2. Short stories, English — Translations from Danish. I. Mitchell, P. M. (Phillip Marshall), 1916- II. Ober, Kenneth H.
PT8024.E5 R6x   839.8/1301/08 19   *LC* 77-78070   *ISBN* 0226532135

PT8050–8176 Individual Authors

Holberg, Ludvig, baron.   **• 2.14006**
The journey of Niels Klim to the world underground / introd. and edited by James I. McNelis. — Lincoln: Univ. of Neb. press, [c1960, 1742]. xxxi, 236 p. I. McNelis, James Ignatius, ed. II. T.
PT8085.N54 1960   839.817   *LC* 60-11897

Billeskov Jansen, F. J. (Frederik Julius), 1907-.   **2.14007**
Ludvig Holberg, by F. J. Billeskov Jansen. New York, Twayne Publishers [1974] 135 p. port. 21 cm. (Twayne's world authors series, TWAS 321) 1. Holberg, Ludvig, baron, 1684-1754. 2. Authors, Danish — 18th century — History. I. T.
PT8087.B48   839.8/1/8409   *LC* 74-2171   *ISBN* 0805724311

Andersen, H. C. (Hans Christian), 1805-1875.   **2.14008**
[Tales. English. Selections] Tales and stories / by Hans Christian Andersen; translated with an introduction, by Patricia L. Conroy and Sven H. Rossel. — Seattle: University of Washington Press, c1980. xxxvi, 279 p.: ill.; 24 cm. I. Conroy, Patricia L. II. Rossel, Sven Hakon. III. T.
PT8116.E5 1980   839.8/136   *LC* 80-50867   *ISBN* 0295957697

Bredsdorff, Elias.   **2.14009**
Hans Christian Andersen: the story of his life and work, 1805–75 / Elias Bredsdorff. — New York: Scribner, c1975. 376 p.: ill.; 25 cm. Includes index. 1. Andersen, H. C. (Hans Christian), 1805-1875. I. T.
PT8119.B6532 1975   839.8/1/36 B   *LC* 75-23827   *ISBN* 0684144573

Grønbech, Bo.   **2.14010**
Hans Christian Andersen / by Bo Grønbech. — Boston: Twayne Publishers, 1980. 171 p.: port.; 21 cm. — (Twayne's world authors series; TWAS 612:

Denmark) Includes index. 1. Andersen, H. C. (Hans Christian), 1805-1875. 2. Authors, Danish — 19th century — Biography. I. T.
PT8120.G74   839.8/136   *LC* 80-13621   *ISBN* 0805764542

Bang, Herman, 1857-1912.   **2.14011**
[Tine. English] Tina / Herman Bang; translated from the Danish by Paul Christophersen; with a foreword by Walter Allen; illustrated by Svend Otto S. — London; Dover, N.H., USA: Athlone Press, 1984. xiv, 185 p.; 21 cm. Translation of: Tine. 1. Schleswig-Holstein War, 1864 — Fiction. I. T.
PT8123.B3 T513 1984   839.8/136 19   *LC* 84-12286   *ISBN* 048511254X

Jacobsen, J. P. (Jens Peter), 1847-1885.   **2.14012**
[Fru Marie Grubbe. English] Marie Grubbe, a lady of the seventeenth century / J. P. Jacobsen; translated from the Danish by Hanna Astrup Larsen; rev. and with an introd. by Robert Raphael. — 2d ed. — [New York]: Twayne Publishers, c1975. xviii, 261 p.; 22 cm. (The Library of Scandinavian literature; v. 30) I. T.
PZ3.J157 Mar17 PT8140   PT8140 M213 1975.   839.8/1/36   *LC* 75-330359   *ISBN* 0890670536

Jacobsen, J. P. (Jens Peter), 1847-1885.   • **2.14013**
Niels Lyhne [by] J. P. Jacobsen. Translated from the Danish by Hanna Astrup Larsen. Introd. by Börge Gedsö Madsen. New York, Twayne Publishers [1967] 244 p. 22 cm. (The Library of Scandinavian literature v. 2) I. T.
PT8140.N5 E54 1967   *LC* 66-28157

Jensen, Niels Lyhne.   **2.14014**
Jens Peter Jacobsen / by Niels Lyhne Jensen. — Boston: Twayne Publishers, 1980. 187 p.: port.; 21 cm. — (Twayne's world authors series; TWAS 573: Denmark) Includes index. 1. Jacobsen, J. P. (Jens Peter), 1847-1885 — Criticism and interpretation. I. T.
PT8140.Z5 J4   839.8/136   *LC* 80-11521   *ISBN* 0805764151

Kierkegaard, Søren, 1813-1855.   **2.14015**
[Literair anmeldelse. English] Two ages: the age of revolution and the present age: a literary review / by Søren Kierkegaard; edited and translated with introd. and notes by Howard V. Hong, and Edna H. Hong. — Princeton, N.J.: Princeton University Press, c1978. xii, 187 p.; 22 cm. (Kierkegaard's writings; 14) Translation of En literair anmeldelse. Includes index. 1. Gyllembourg, Thomasine, 1773-1856. To tidsaldre. I. Hong, Howard Vincent, 1912- II. Hong, Edna Hatlestad, 1913- III. T.
PT8142.A1x 1962   839.8/1/36   *LC* 77-71986   *ISBN* 0691072264

Kierkegaard, Søren, 1813-1855.   • **2.14016**
[Enten-eller. English] Either/or. Translated by David F. Swenson and Lillian Marvin Swenson, with revisions and a foreword by Howard A. Johnson. Garden City, N.Y., Doubleday, 1959. 2 v. 19 cm. (Anchor books, A181 a-b) Vol. 2 translated by Walter Lowrie with revisions and a foreword by Howard A. Johnson. I. T.
PT8142.Z5 A34   198/.9 19   *LC* 59-9782

Blixen, Karen (Dinesen) baronesse.   • **2.14017**
Anecdotes of destiny [by] Isak Dinesen [pseud.] New York, Random House [1958] 244 p. I. T.
PT8175.B545 Ax   839.8137   *LC* 58-13594

Blixen, Karen Dinesen, baronesse, 1885-1962.   • **2.14018**
Ehrengard [by] Isak Dinesen [pseud] New York, Random House, [1963] 111 p. 22 cm. I. T.
PT8175.B545 Ex   *LC* 63-11618

Dinesen, Isak, 1885-1962.   • **2.14019**
Seven Gothic tales, by Isak Dinesen [pseud.] with an introduction by Dorothy Canfield. — New York, The Modern library [1939] x p. 2 l., 420 p. 19 cm. — (Half-title: The modern library of the world's best books) 'First Modern library edition.' I. Fisher, Dorothea Frances (Canfield), Mrs. 1879- II. T.
PT8175.B545 S4x   *LC* 39-27353

Dinesen, Isak, 1885-1962.   **2.14020**
Letters from Africa, 1914–1931 / Isak Dinesen [i.e. K. Blixen]; edited for the Rungstedlund Foundation by Frans Lasson; translated by Anne Born. — Chicago: University of Chicago Press, 1981. xli, 474 p., [28] leaves of plates: ill.; 24 cm. 'Originally published in two volumes as Breve fra Afrika 1914-24 and Breve fra Afrika 1925-31.' 1. Dinesen, Isak, 1885-1962 — Correspondence. 2. Authors, Danish — 20th century — Correspondence. I. Lasson, Frans. II. T.
PT8175.B545 Z5313 1981   839.8/1372 B 19   *LC* 80-25856   *ISBN* 0226153096

Thurman, Judith, 1946-.   **2.14021**
Isak Dinesen: the life of a storyteller / Judith Thurman. — 1st ed. — New York, N.Y.: St Martin's Press, c1982. xvi, 495 p.: ports.; 25 cm. 1. Dinesen,

Isak, 1885-1962 — Biography. 2. Authors, Danish — 20th century — Biography. I. T.
PT8175.B545 Z89 1982   839.8/1372 B 19   *LC* 82-5573   *ISBN* 0312437374

Branner, H. C. (Hans Christian), 1903-1966.   • **2.14022**
Two minutes of silence; selected short stories. Translated from the Danish by Vera Lindholm Vance, with an introd. by Richard B. Vowles. Madison, University of Wisconsin Press, 1966. 211 p. 23 cm. (The Nordic translation series) I. Vance, Vera Lindholm. II. T.
PT8175.B743 T613 1966   *LC* 66-22865

Hansen, Martin Alfred, 1909-1955.   **2.14023**
[Løgneren. English] The liar. Translated from the Danish by John Jepson Egglishaw. New York, Twayne Publishers [1969] 207 p. map. 22 cm. (The Library of Scandinavian literature, v. 5) Translation of Løgneren. I. T. II. Series.
PZ3.H19866 Li5 PT8175.H33 L6x   839.81/3/72   *LC* 73-99540

Hansen, Martin Alfred, 1909-1955.   **2.14024**
[Lykkelige Kristoffer. English] Lucky Kristoffer [by] Martin A. Hansen. Translated from the Danish by John Jepson Egglishaw. Introd. by Niels Ingwersen. New York, Twayne Publishers [1974] 377 p. 22 cm. (The Library of Scandinavian literature, v. 25) Translation of Lykkelige Kristoffer. I. T. II. Series.
PZ3.H19866 Lu5 PT8175.H33 L9x   839.8/1/372   *LC* 73-9298   *ISBN* 0805733396

Ingwersen, Faith.   **2.14025**
Martin A. Hansen / by Faith and Niels Ingwersen. — Boston: Twayne Publishers, c1976. 197 p. cm. — (Twayne's world authors series; TWAS 419: Denmark) Includes index. 1. Hansen, Martin Alfred, 1909-1955 — Criticism and interpretation. I. Ingwersen, Niels. joint author. II. T.
PT8175.H33 Z7 PT8175H33 Z7.   839.8/1/372 B   *LC* 76-21278   *ISBN* 0805762590

Kristensen, Tom, 1893-1974.   • **2.14026**
[Hærværk. English] Havoc. Hærværk. Translated from the Danish by Carl Malmberg. With an introd. by Børge Gedsø Madsen. Madison, University of Wisconsin Press, 1968 [c1930] xvii, 427 p. 25 cm. (Nordic translation series) I. T.
PT8175.K78 H3x   *LC* 68-14037

Andersen Nexø, Martin, 1869-1954.   • **2.14027**
Ditte / by Martin Andersen Nexö. — New York: P. Smith, [1931], c1922. vi, 333, 385, 268 p. I. T.
PZ3 N49 Ditt   PT8175N4 D5 1931.   *LC* 31-28473

Andersen Nexø, Martin, 1869-1954.   • **2.14028**
Pelle the conqueror / by Martin Anderson Nexö; translated from the Danish by Jesse Muir and Bernard Miall. — New York: P. Smith, 1930. 2 v. in 1 (v, 562, 587 p.); 21 cm. Translation of Pelle erobreren. I. T.
PT8175.N4 P413

Ingwersen, Faith.   **2.14029**
Quests for a promised land: the works of Martin Andersen Nexø / Faith Ingwersen and Niels Ingwersen. — Westport, Conn.: Greenwood Press, c1984. xvi, 156 p.; 22 cm. (Contributions to the study of world literature. 0738-9345; no. 8) Includes index. 1. Andersen Nexø, Martin, 1869-1954 — Criticism and interpretation. I. Ingwersen, Niels. II. T. III. Series.
PT8175.N4 Z778 1984   839.8/1372 19   *LC* 84-8916   *ISBN* 0313244693

PT8301–9155 Norwegian

PT8301–8733 Literary History. Collections

Beyer, Harald, 1891-.   • **2.14030**
A history of Norwegian literature / by Harald Beyer; translated and edited by Einar Haugen. — New York: New York Univ. press, 1956. 370 p.: ill. 1. Norwegian literature — History and criticism. I. T.
PT8360.B42   839.8209   *LC* 56-6801   1320

McFarlane, James Walter.   • **2.14031**
Ibsen and the temper of Norwegian literature / James Walter McFarlane. — London; New York: Oxford University Press, 1960. 208 p.; 23 cm. Includes

index. 1. Norwegian literature — History and criticism. 2. Authors, Norwegian I. T.
PT8363.M3   *LC* 60-2068

20 contemporary Norwegian poets: a bilingual anthology / Terje   **2.14032**
Johanssen (ed.).
New York: St. Martin's Press, 1984. 232 p.; 25 cm. English and Norwegian.
1. Norwegian poetry — 20th century — Translations into English. 2. English poetry — Translations from Norwegian. 3. Norwegian poetry — 20th century I. Johanssen, Terje, 1942- II. Title: Twenty contemporary Norwegian poets.
PT8683.E5 J64 1984   839.8/2174/08 19   *LC* 83-16002   *ISBN*
031282422X

Slaves of love and other Norwegian short stories / selected and   **2.14033**
edited by James McFarlane; translated by James McFarlane
and Janet Garton.
Oxford [Oxfordshire]; New York: Oxford University Press, 1982. xii, 265 p.; 23 cm. 1. Short stories, Norwegian — Translations into English. 2. Short stories, English — Translations from Norwegian. I. McFarlane, James Walter.
PT8721.S54 1982   839.8/2301/08 19   *LC* 82-2269   *ISBN*
0192126016

PT8750–8951 Individual Authors, by Period

PT8851–8900 Ibsen

Ibsen, Henrik, 1828-1906.   ● **2.14034**
[Works. English] The Oxford Ibsen. Translated and edited by James Walter McFarlane. London, New York, Oxford University Press, 1960-1977. 8 v. 23 cm. Spine title: Ibsen. Vol. 6 has title: Ibsen. Vol. 1, 1970; v. 2, 1962; v. 3, 1972; v. 4, 1963; v. 5, 1961; v. 6, 1960; v. 7, 1966; v. 8, 1977. I. McFarlane, James Walter. II. T.
PT8852.E5 M3   839.8/2/26   *LC* 60-4863

Ibsen, Henrik, 1828-1906.   **2.14035**
[Selected works. English. 1978] The complete major prose plays / Henrik Ibsen; translated and introduced by Rolf Fjelde. — 1st ed. — New York: Farrar, Straus & Giroux, 1978. vi, 1143 p.; 21 cm. I. Fjelde, Rolf. II. T.
PT8854.F5 1978   839.8/2/26   *LC* 77-28349   *ISBN* 0374174148

Koht, Halvdan, 1873-1965.   ● **2.14036**
[Henrik Ibsen, eit diktarliv. English] Life of Ibsen. Translated and edited by Einar Haugen and A. E. Santaniello. New York, B. Blom, 1971. 507 p. geneal. table, port. 26 cm. Translation of Henrik Ibsen, eit diktarliv. 1. Ibsen, Henrik, 1828-1906. I. T.
PT8890.K62 1971   839.8/2/26 B   *LC* 69-16322

Meyer, Hans Georg.   **2.14037**
[Henrik Ibsen. English] Henrik Ibsen. Translated by Helen Sebba. New York, Ungar [1972] v, 201 p. illus. 21 cm. (World dramatists) 1. Ibsen, Henrik, 1828-1906. I. T.
PT8890.M4413   839.8/2/26   *LC* 72-163145   *ISBN* 0804426163

Meyer, Michael Leverson.   ● **2.14038**
[Henrik Ibsen] Ibsen, a biography [by] Michael Meyer. [1st ed.] Garden City, N. Y. Doubleday, 1971. xvii, 865 p. illus., facsims., ports. 25 cm. First published in London under title: Henrik Ibsen. 1. Ibsen, Henrik, 1828-1906. I. T.
PT8890.M47   839.8/2/26 B   *LC* 78-150906

Beyer, Edvard, 1920-.   **2.14039**
[Henrik Ibsen. English] Ibsen, the man and his work / by Edvard Beyer; translated by Marie Wells. — New York: Taplinger Pub. Co., [1980] c1978. 223 p.: ill.; 22 cm. Translation of Henrik Ibsen. 1. Ibsen, Henrik, 1828-1906 — Criticism and interpretation. I. T.
PT8895.B4413 1980   839.8/2/26   *LC* 79-1917   *ISBN* 0800840550

Shaw, Bernard, 1856-1950.   **2.14040**
Shaw and Ibsen: Bernard Shaw's The quintessence of Ibsenism, and related writings / edited with an introductory essay by J. L. Wisenthal. — Toronto; Buffalo: University of Toronto Press, c1979. viii, 268 p.; 24 cm. 1. Ibsen, Henrik, 1828-1906 — Criticism and interpretation — Addresses, essays, lectures. I. Wisenthal, J. L. II. Shaw, Bernard, 1856-1950. The quintessence of Ibsenism. 1979. III. T.
PT8895.S53 1979   839.8/2/26   *LC* 79-14858   *ISBN* 0802054544

Northam, John, 1922-.   ● **2.14041**
Ibsen's dramatic method. A study of the prose dramas, by John Northam. — [2. ed.]. — Oslo: Universitetsforlaget, 1971. 232 p.; 22 cm. — (Scandia books, 12) 1. Ibsen, Henrik, 1828-1906 — Technique. I. T.
PT8897.D7 N6 1971   839.82/2/6   *LC* 72-192938

PT8901–8951 20th Century, A–Z

Bojer, Johan, 1872-1959.   ● **2.14042**
The emigrants, by Johan Bojer; translated from the Norwegian by A. G. Jayne. New York, London, The Century Co. [c1925] 3 p. l., 3-351 p. 21 cm. I. Jayne, Arthur Garland, 1882- II. T.
PT8950.B6 V513   *LC* 25-26996

Hamsun, Knut, 1859-1952.   **2.14043**
[Landstrykere. English] Wayfarers / Knut Hamsun; translated from the Norwegian by James McFarlane. — New York: Farrar, Straus Giroux, 1980. 459 p.; 20 cm. Translation of Landstrykere. I. T.
PZ3.H1903 Way 1980 PT8950.H3 L3x   839.8/236   *LC* 79-27034
    ISBN 0374286728

Hamsun, Knut, 1859-1952.   ● **2.14044**
[Markens grøde] Growth of the soil, tr. from the Norwegian of Knut Hamsun by W. W. Worster. New York, A. A. Knopf, 1921. 2 v. front. (port.) 20 cm. 'Original title 'Markens grøde."—Note on verso of t.-p. 'Knut Hamsun, by W. W. Worster': v. 2, p. 257-276. I. Worster, William John Alexander, 1882-1929, tr. II. T.
PT8950.H3 M3x   *LC* 21-3287

Hamsun, Knut, 1859-1952.   ● **2.14045**
[Mysterier. English] Mysteries. Newly translated from the Norwegian by Gerry Bothmer. New York, Farrar, Straus and Giroux [1971] 340 p. 21 cm. I. T.
PZ3.H1903 My6 PT8950.H3 M9x   839.8/2/36   *LC* 74-115753
    ISBN 0374217645

Hamsun, Knut, 1859-1952.   ● **2.14046**
Pan: from Lieutenant Thomas Glahn's papers / Knut Hamsun; translated from the Norwegian by James W. McFarlane. — New York: Noonday Press, 1975, c1956. 192 p. I. T.
PT8950.H3 P33 1975   *ISBN* 0374500169 pa

Hamsun, Knut, 1859-1952.   ● **2.14047**
[Sult. English] Hunger. Newly translated from the Norwegian by Robert Bly. With introductions by Robert Bly and Isaac Bashevis Singer. New York, Farrar, Straus and Giroux [1967] xxii, 231 p. 21 cm. Translation of Sult. I. T.
PT8950.H3 S8x   *LC* 67-21525

Hamsun, Knut, 1859-1952.   **2.14048**
[Under høststjernen. English] The wanderer / Knut Hamsun; translated by Oliver and Gunnvor Stallybrass. — New York: Farrar, Straus and Giroux, 1975. 281 p.; 21 cm. Translation of Under høststjernen and En vandrer spiller med sordin. I. Hamsun, Knut, 1859-1952. En vandrer spiller med sordin. English. 1975. II. T.
PZ3.H1903 Vy3 PT8950.H3 U6x   839.8/2/36   *LC* 75-5915   *ISBN* 0374286361

Næss, Harald.   **2.14049**
Knut Hamsun / by Harald Næss. — Boston: Twayne Publishers, c1984. 194 p.: port.; 23 cm. — (Twayne's world authors series. TWAS 715) Includes index. 1. Hamsun, Knut, 1859-1952 — Criticism and interpretation. I. T. II. Series.
PT8950.H3 Z745 1984   839.8/236 19   *LC* 83-18343   *ISBN* 080576562X

Sandemose, Aksel, 1899-1965.   ● **2.14050**
The werewolf. Translated from the Norwegian by Gustaf Lannestock. With an introduction by Harald S. Næss. Madison, University of Wisconsin Press, 1966. xvii, 374 p. 24 cm. (The Nordic translation series) Translation of Varulven. I. T.
PT8950.S23 Vx   *LC* 65-24188

Birn, Randi.   **2.14051**
Aksel Sandemose: exile in search of a home / Randi Birn. — Westport, Conn.: Greenwood Press, 1984. xv, 150 p.; 25 cm. — (Contributions to the study of world literature. 0738-9345; no. 2) Includes index. 1. Sandemose, Aksel, 1899-1965 — Biography. 2. Authors, Norwegian — 20th century — Biography. I. T. II. Series.
PT8950.S23 Z58 1984   839.8/2372 19   *LC* 83-13034   *ISBN* 0313241635

Undset, Sigrid.   ● **2.14052**
Four stories / Sigrid Unset; translated from the Norwegian by Naomi Walford. — 1st American ed. — New York: Knopf, 1959. 245 p.; 20 cm. I. T.
PT8950.U5 Ax   839.82372   *LC* 59-7982

Undset, Sigrid, 1882-1949.   **2.14053**
Kristin Lavransdatter: The bridal wreath, The mistress of Husaby, The cross. — New York, Knopf [1935, c1927] 1069 p. illus. 20 cm. The bridal wreath translated by Charles Archer and J. S. Scott. The mistress of Husaby and The cross tr. by Charles Archer. One-volume ed. completely reset and published in present format 1935. I. T.
PZ3.U568Kr7 PT8950.U5K713 1935   *LC* 47-38836

PT9131–9150 Norwegian Literature in America

PT9150 Rolvaag

Rølvaag, O. E. (Ole Edvart), 1876-1931.   • **2.14054**
Giants in the earth; a saga of the prairie. New York Harper 1927. 465p. I. T.
PT9150 R55 I313 1927

Rølvaag, O. E. (Ole Edvart), 1876-1931.   • **2.14055**
Their fathers' God; a novel. Translated from the Norwegian by Trygve M. Ager. — New York: Harper, 1931. vi, 338 p.; 22 cm. Translation of Den signede dag. I. T.
PZ3.R6275 Th10 PT9150.R55 L3x   839.8/2/372   *LC* 31-29967

Rølvaag, O. E. (Ole Edvart), 1876-1931.   • **2.14056**
Peder Victorious, a novel by O.E. Rölvaag ... translated from the Norwegian, English text by Nora O. Solum ... and the author. New York Harper 1929. 4;350p. I. Solum, Nora Olava, tr. II. T.
PT9150 R55 P413

Rølvaag, O. E. (Ole Edvart), 1876-1931.   • **2.14057**
The boat of longing: a novel / translated from the Norwegian Længselens baat by Nora O. Solum. — New York: Harper, 1933. 304 p.; 22 cm. I. T.
PZ3.R6275 Bo5 PT9150.R55 S5x   839.8/2/36   *LC* 33-1840

Rølvaag, O. E. (Ole Edvart), 1876-1931.   • **2.14058**
Pure gold / by O. E. Rölvaag; English text by Sivert Erdahl and the author. — New York; London: Harper & Brothers, 1930. 346 p.; 20 cm. I. T.
PT9150.R55 T6x   *LC* 30-4299/r41

Rølvaag Symposium, St. Olaf College, Northfield, Minn., 1974.   **2.14059**
Ole Rølvaag, artist and cultural leader: papers presented at the Rølvaag Symposium held at St. Olaf College, October 28–29, 1974 / edited by Gerald Thorson. — Northfield, Minn.: St. Olaf College Press, 1975. iv, 74 p.; 24 cm. 1. Rølvaag, Ole Edvart, 1876-1931 — Congresses. I. Thorson, Gerald. II. T.
PT9150.R55 Z8 1974

Reigstad, Paul.   • **2.14060**
Rölvaag: his life and art. — Lincoln: University of Nebraska Press, [1972] xi, 160 p.: illus.; 23 cm. 1. Rølvaag, Ole Edvart, 1876-1931. I. T.
PT9150.R55 Z84   839.8/2/372 B   *LC* 70-175804   *ISBN* 0803208030

PT9201–9999 Swedish

PT9201–9639 Literary History. Collections

Gustafson, Alrik, 1903-.   • **2.14061**
A history of Swedish literature. Minneapolis, Published for the American-Scandinavian Foundation by the University of Minnesota Press [1961] xv, 708 p. illus., ports., facsims. 25 cm. 'A bibliographical guide': p. 567-644. 'A list of translations into English': p. 645-660. 1. Swedish literature — History and criticism. I. T.
PT9263.G8 1961   839.709   *LC* 61-7722

Bly, Robert. comp.   **2.14062**
Friends, you drank some darkness: three Swedish poets, Harry Martinson, Gunnar Ekelöf, and Tomas Tranströmer / chosen and translated by Robert Bly. — Boston: Beacon Press, [1975] xi, 267 p.: ports.; 21 cm. Poems in English and Swedish; commentary in English. 'Seventies press books.' 1. Swedish poetry — 20th century I. Martinson, Harry, 1904- II. Ekelöf, Gunnar, 1907-1968. III. Tranströemer, Tomas, 1931- IV. T.
PT9583.B62   PT9583 B62.   839.7/1/708   *LC* 73-6244   *ISBN* 0807063908

Contemporary Swedish poetry / translated by John Matthias   **2.14063**
and Göran Printz–Påhlson.
Chicago: Swallow Press, c1980. 135 p.; 25 cm. 1. Swedish poetry — 20th century — Translations into English. 2. English poetry — Translations from Swedish. I. Matthias, John, 1941- II. Printz-Påhlson, Göran, 1931-
PT9590.E5 C6   839.7/174/08 19   *LC* 79-9655   *ISBN* 0804008116

PT9650–9876 Individual Authors, by Period

Lagerlof, Selma Ottiliana Lovisa, 1858-1940.   • **2.14064**
The story of Gosta Berling. — Stockholm: Fritzes K. Hovbokhandel, 1962. 393 p. — I. T.
PT9767.G6 1962

Lagerlöf, Selma, 1858-1940.   • **2.14065**
[Jerusalem. English] Jerusalem. Translated from the Swedish by Jessie Bröchner. Westport, Conn., Greenwood Press [1970] viii, 396 p. 23 cm. Reprint of the 1903 ed. I. Bröchner, Jessie, tr. II. T.
PZ3.L136 J10 PT9767 J4x   839.7/3/72   *LC* 76-98777   *ISBN* 0837131200

PT9800–9816 Strindberg

Strindberg, August, 1849-1912.   • **2.14066**
The Vasa trilogy: Master Olof, Gustav Vasa, Erik XIV. Translations and introductions by Walter Johnson. — Seattle, University of Washington Press, 1959. ix, 341 p. illus., geneal. table. 22 cm. — (The historical plays of August Strindberg) 1. Gustaf I Vasa, King of Sweden, 1496-1560 — Drama. 2. Erik XIV, King of Sweden, 1533-1577. I. T.
PT9804.J6   839.726   *LC* 59-6636

Strindberg, August, 1849-1912.   • **2.14067**
[Selected works. English] Inferno, Alone, and other writings. In new translations. Edited and introduced by Evert Sprinchorn. [1st ed.] Garden City, N.Y., Anchor Books, 1968. 429 p. 18 cm. I. Sprinchorn, Evert. ed. II. T.
PT9804.S6   *LC* 67-22458

Strindberg, August, 1849-1912.   **2.14068**
[Plays. English. Selections] Apologia and two folk plays / by August Strindberg; translations and introductions by Walter Johnson. — Seattle, Wash.: University of Washington Press, c1981. 225 p., [2] leaves of plates: ill.; 23 cm. — (His The Washington Strindberg) I. T.
PT9811.A3 J56 1981   839.7/26 19   *LC* 80-51072   *ISBN* 0295957603

Strindberg, August, 1849-1912.   **2.14069**
Plays from the cynical life / by August Strindberg; translations and introductions by Walter Johnson. — Seattle: University of Washington Press, c1983. 147 p., [4] p. of plates: ill.; 22 cm. — (The Washington Strindberg) I. T.
PT9811.A3 J6 1983   839.7/26 19   *LC* 82-13581   *ISBN* 0295959800

Strindberg, August, 1849-1912.   • **2.14070**
[Plays. English. Selections] Eight expressionist plays. Translated and with prefaces to the pilgrimage plays by Arvid Paulson. Introd. and with a pref. to the Ghost Sonata by John Gassner. New York, New York University Press [1972] x, 499 p. 24 cm. I. T.
PT9811.A3 P29 1972   839.7/2/6   *LC* 72-183237   *ISBN* 0814765564

Strindberg, August, 1849-1912.   • **2.14071**
[Selected works. English. 1969] Strindberg's one–act plays. Translated from the Swedish by Arvid Paulson. Introd. by Barry Jacobs. New York, Washington Square Press [1969] xxxii, 368 p. 18 cm. I. Paulson, Arvid. tr. II. T.
PT9811.A3 P33   839.7/2/6   *LC* 79-4286   *ISBN* 0671474901

Strindberg, August, 1849-1912.   **2.14072**
[Dödsdansen. English] The dance of death / August Strindberg; translated by Arvid Paulson; with an introd. by Daniel Seltzer, and performance notes by Arvid Paulson. — New York: Norton, c1976. xvi, 7-125 p.; 20 cm. Translation of Dödsdansen. I. T.
PT9812.D6 E56 1976   839.7/2/6   *LC* 76-362974   *ISBN* 0393044378

Strindberg, August, 1849-1912.   **2.14073**
[Till Damaskus. English] Plays of confession and therapy / by August Strindberg; translations and introductions by Walter Johnson. — Seattle: University of Washington Press, c1979. 252 p., [2] leaves of plates: ill.; 22 cm. — (The Washington Strindberg) I. Johnson, Walter Gilbert, 1905- II. T.
PT9812.T5 E5 1979   839.7/2/6   LC 78-20962   ISBN 0295955678

Strindberg, August, 1849-1912.   **2.14074**
[Giftas. English] Getting married. Translated from the Swedish, edited, and introduced by Mary Sandbach. New York, Viking Press [1973, c1972] 384 p. 22 cm. Translation of Giftas. I. T.
PZ3.S9179 Gd3 PT9813.G5   839.7/3/6   LC 72-11063   ISBN 0670337609

Strindberg, August, 1849-1912.   ● **2.14075**
Natives of Hemsö. Translated from the Swedish by Arvid Paulson.Introd.by Richard B.Vowles. New York: P.S.Eriksson, [1966, 1965] 202p. I. Paulson, Arvid. tr. II. T.
PT9813.H4 A36 1965   LC 65-15780

Strindberg, August, 1849-1912.   ● **2.14076**
The son of a servant: the story of the evolution of a human being, 1849–67; newly translated [from the Swedish] with an introduction and notes, by Evert Sprinchorn. — Garden City, N.Y.: Anchor Books, 1966. xxi, 243 p.; 19 cm. Translation of Tjänstekvinnans son. I. T.
PT9813.T6x   LC 66-11748

Strindberg, August, 1849-1912.   ● **2.14077**
[Plaidoyer d'un fou. English] A madman's defense; Le plaidoyer d'un fou. Translation based on Ellie Schleussner's version, The confession of a fool. Rev. and edited by Evert Sprinchorn. [1st ed.] Garden City, N.Y., Anchor Books, 1967. xxvi, 293 p. 18 cm. 'A4926.' Translation of Le plaidoyer d'un fou. I. T.
PT9814.P513 1967x   LC 67-10387

Brandell, Gunnar.   **2.14078**
Strindberg in inferno. Translated by Barry Jacobs. — Cambridge, Mass.: Harvard University Press, 1974. xviii, 336 p.; 24 cm. Revised translation of Strindbergs infernokris published in 1950. Based on the author's akademisk avhandling, Stockholms högskola, 1950. 1. Strindberg, August, 1849-1912. I. T.
PT9815.B7213 1974   839.7/2/6   LC 73-90851   ISBN 0674843258

Lagercrantz, Olof Gustaf Hugo, 1911-.   **2.14079**
[August Strindberg. English] August Strindberg / Olof Lagercrantz; translated by Anselm Hollo. — New York: Farrar, Straus, Giroux, c1984. 398 p.: ill., ports.; 26 cm. Translation of: August Strindberg. Includes index. 1. Strindberg, August, 1849-1912 — Biography. 2. Authors, Swedish — 19th century — Biography. I. T.
PT9815.L313 1984   839.7/26 B 19   LC 84-42803   ISBN 0374106851

Johannesson, Eric O.   ● **2.14080**
The novels of August Strindberg; a study in theme and structure, by Eric O. Johannesson. — Berkeley: University of California Press, 1968. xviii, 317 p.; 24 cm. 1. Strindberg, August, 1849-1912. I. T.
PT9816.J55   839.7/3/6   LC 68-29156

Lamm, Martin, 1880-1950.   ● **2.14081**
[August Strindberg. English] August Strindberg. Translated and edited by Harry G. Carlson. New York, B. Blom, 1971. xxi, 561 p. 26 cm. Translated from the 1948 rev. ed. 1. Strindberg, August, 1849-1912.
PT9816.L27213   839.7/2/6 B   LC 69-16323

Sprinchorn, Evert.   **2.14082**
Strindberg as dramatist / Evert Sprinchorn. — New Haven: Yale University Press, c1982. xi, 332 p., [12] p. of plates: ill.; 24 cm. 1. Strindberg, August, 1849-1912 — Criticism and interpretation. I. T.
PT9816.S64 1982   839.7/26 19   LC 81-23992   ISBN 0300027311

PT9875–9876 20TH CENTURY, A–Z

Bergman, Ingmar, 1918-.   ● **2.14083**
Four screenplays; translated from the Swedish by Lars Malmstrom and David Kushner. — New York: Simon and Schuster, 1960. 329 p.: illus.; 24 cm. — I. T.
PT9875.B533 A25   791.437   LC 60-14283

Fridegård, Jan, 1897-1968.   **2.14084**
[Jag Lars Hård. English] I, Lars Hård / Jan Fridegård; translated, with an introduction and notes, by Robert E. Bjork. — Lincoln: University of Nebraska Press, c1983. xvi, 105 p.; 23 cm. Translation of: Jag Lars Hård. I. Bjork, Robert E., 1949- II. T.
PT9875.F788 J313 1983   839.7/372 19   LC 83-1098   ISBN 0803219636

Isaksson, Hans, 1942-.   **2.14085**
Lars Gyllensten / Hans Isaksson; translated from the Swedish by Katy Lissbrant. — Boston: Twayne Publishers, c1978. 194 p. — (Twayne's world authors series; TWAS 473) Includes index. 1. Gyllensten, Lars Johan Wictor, 1921- 2. Authors, Swedish — 20th century — Biography. I. T.
PT9875.G95 Z74 1978   PT9875G95 Z74 1978.   839.7/3/74   LC 77-15551   ISBN 0805763147

Johnson, Eyvind, 1900-.   ● **2.14086**
Return to Ithaca, the Odyssey retold as a modern novel; with a pref. by Mark Van Doren. London, New York, Thames and Hudson [1952] x, 474 p. 22 cm. 'Originally published in Swedish as Strändernas svall, and rendered into English by M.A. Michael.' 1. Homer — Parodies, travesties, etc. I. T.
PT9875.J6 S813   839.736 839.737*   LC 52-13394

Lagerkvist, Pär, 1891-1974.   ● **2.14087**
The death of Ahasuerus. Translated from the Swedish by Naomi Walford. Drawings by Emil Antonucci. New York, Random House, 1962. 118 p. ill. 22 cm. Translation of Ahasverus Död. I. T. II. Title: Ahasverus död.
PT9875.L2A73x   LC 61-12177

Lagerkvist, Pär, 1891-1974.   ● **2.14088**
Barabbas; translated by Alan Blair, with a pref. by Lucien Maury and a letter by André Gide. — New York, Random House [1951] 180 p. 21 cm. 1. Barabbas — Fiction. I. T.
PT9875.L2 B3x   839.736   LC 51-13110

Lagerkvist, Pär, 1891-1974.   ● **2.14089**
The dwarf / by Pär Lagerkvist; translated from the Swedish by Alexandra Dick. — London: Chatto & Windus, 1953. 175 p.; 21 cm. Translation of Dvärgen. I. T.
PT9875.L2 Dx

Lagerkvist, Pär, 1891-1974.   ● **2.14090**
The Holy Land / by Pär Lagerkvist. Translated from the Swedish by Naomi Walford. Illustrated by Emil Antonucci. 1st American ed. New York: Random House, 1966. 85 p. illus. 21 cm. I. T.
PT9875.L2 H38x   Fic   LC 66-12001

Lagerkvist, Pär, 1891-1974.   **2.14091**
The marriage feast [by] Pär Lagerkvist. New York, Hill and Wang [1973] 222 p. 22 cm. The stories have been translated by Alan Blair, with the exception of On the scales of Osiris, which was translated by Carl Eric Lindin. I. T.
PZ3.L1354 Mar5 PT9875.L2 M3x   839.7/3/72   LC 73-75187   ISBN 0809067862 ISBN 080901372X

Lagerkvist, Pär, 1891-1974.   ● **2.14092**
Modern theatre; seven plays and an essay [by] Pär Lagerkvist. Translated, with an introd., by Thomas R. Buckman. Lincoln, University of Nebraska Press [1966] xxiv, 305 p. 21 cm. 1. Swedish literature — Translations into English. 2. English literature — Translations from Swedish. I. T.
PT9875.L2M6   839.7272   LC 64-11582

Lagerkvist, Pär, 1891-1974.   ● **2.14093**
Pilgrim at sea. Translated from the Swedish by Naomi Walford. Drawings by Emil Antonucci. New York, Random House [1964] 116 p. illus. 21 cm. I. T.
PT9875.L2 P54x   LC 64-10533

Lagerkvist, Pär, 1891-1974.   ● **2.14094**
The sibyl. Translated by Naomi Walford. New York, Random House, 1958. 154 p. I. T.
PT9875.L2 S913   ISBN 0394702409

Martinson, Harry, 1904-.   **2.14095**
Aniara: a review of man in time and space / Harry Martinson; adapted from the Swedish by Hugh MacDiamid and Elspeth Harley Schubert; introduction by Tord Hall. — New York: Alfred A. Knopf, 1963. 132 p. I. T.
PT9875M35 A643 1963   PT9875M35 A66 1963.

Moberg, Vilhelm, 1898-1973.   ● **2.14096**
Unto a good land, a novel; translated from the Swedish by Gustaf Lannestock. New York, Simon and Schuster [1954] 309 p. 22 cm. Translation of Invandrarna. Second part of a triology; the first part has title: The emigrants. I. T.
PT9875.M5 I6x   839.736   LC 54-9057

Moberg, Vilhelm.   ● **2.14097**
The last letter home: a novel / translated from the Swedish by Gustaf Lannestock. — New York: Simon and Schuster, 1961. 383 p. Parts 3 and 4 of

the author's cycle, the first of which is The emigrants and the second, Unto a good land. I. T.
PT9875.M5 Nx   839.7   Fic   *LC* 61-5843

Moberg, Vilhelm, 1898-1973.   • **2.14098**
The emigrants: a novel / by Vilhelm Moberg; translated from the Swedish by Gustaf Lannestock. — New York: Simon & Schuster, 1951. xv, 366 p. Translation of Utvandrarna. I. T.
PT9875.M5U8x 1951 A   839/.7/36   *LC* 51-11040

Sundman, Per Olof, 1922-.   • **2.14099**
[Ingenjör Andrées luftfärd. English] The flight of the Eagle. Translated from the Swedish by Mary Sandbach. [1st American ed.] New York, Pantheon Books [1970] 382 p. illus., map (on lining papers), ports. 22 cm. Translation of Ingenjör Andrées luftfärd. 1. Andrée, Salomon August, 1854-1897 — Fiction. I. T.
PZ4.S957 Fl3 PT9876.29.U5 I5x   839.7/3/74   *LC* 69-20190

PZ1 SHORT STORIES
(Collections from several literatures)

Maugham, W. Somerset (William Somerset), 1874-1965. comp.   • **2.14100**
Tellers of tales; 100 short stories from the United States, England, France, Russia and Germany, selected and with an introduction by W. Somerset Maugham. New York, Doubleday, Doran & company, inc., 1939. xxxix p., 1 l., 1526 p. 24 cm. 'First edition.' 1. Short stories I. T.
PZ1M431 Te   *LC* 39-20438

PZ8.3 NURSERY RHYMES

Mother Goose.   **2.14101**
The annotated Mother Goose, nursery rhymes old and new, arr. and explained by William S. Baring–Gould & Ceil Baring–Gould. Illustrated by Walter Crane [and others] With chapter decorations by E. M. Simon. — New York: Crown, 1982. 350 p.: illus.; 28 cm. I. Baring-Gould, William Stuart, 1913- II. Baring-Gould, Ceil. III. T.
PZ8.3.M85 Bar   398.8   *LC* 62-21606   *ISBN* 0517546290

Opie, Iona Archibald. ed.   • **2.14102**
The Oxford dictionary of nursery rhymes, edited by Iona and Peter Opie. — Oxford: Clarendon Press, 1951. xxvii, 467 p.: illus.; 24 cm. 1. Nursery rhymes I. Opie, Peter. joint ed. II. T.
PZ8.3.O6 Ox   *LC* 51-14126